The Bill James Handbook 2005

Baseball Info Solutions

www.baseballinfosolutions.com

Published by ACTA Sports

A Division of ACTA Publications

Cover by Tom A. Wright

Cover Photos by Scott Jordan Levy

First Edition: November 2004

Published by:
ACTA Sports, a division of ACTA Publications
4848 N. Clark Street, Chicago, IL 60640
(800) 397-2282
www.actasports.com www.actapublications.com

ISBN 0-87946-274-4

Printed in the United States of America

Dedication

To my family, for all your love and support. Mom and dad, I owe so much of who I am to you.

To my beautiful wife, Kelly, for putting up with all the things that drive you crazy. To our son, Avery, for enabling me to relive my childhood. And to our little princess Paige, the sunshine of my life.

And to Leia for being man's best friend.

- Damon Lichtenwalner

Acknowledgments

And now for something completely different—let's go backwards this year:

Thanks to our friends with a connection to the baseball industry: Greg Ambrosius, Jeff Barton, Jim Callis, Frank Cooney, Doug Dennis, Jeff Erickson, Steve Goldstein, Steve Greenberg, Jason Grey, John Hunt, Peter Kreutzer, Josh Lewin, Gene McCaffrey, Rob Neyer, Mat Olkin, Mike Phillips, Hal Richman, Peter Schoenke, Jon Sciambi, Ron Shandler, Sam Walker, Mark Watson, Rick Wolf, Trace Wood and Todd Zola.

Thanks to our network of helpers all over the United States: Bryce Babcock, Kevin Barge, Darin Brown, Marla Clancy, Dennis Crowley, Brian DewBerry-Jones, David Dick, Joe Dimino, Mariusz Robert Dudek, Vinay Kumar, Randy Lillard, Donald Masi, Al Melchior, John Menna, Red Merchant, Gus Papadopoulos, Daryl Ravani, Bob Routier, Kenn Ruby, Wayne Sit, Karen Thomas, John Wagner and Ted Ward.

Thanks to our local helper crew: Ray Benedetto, James Blas, Cory Brodhead, Mike Brodhead, Ryan Brodhead, Dedan Brozino, John Corpora, Kevin Drake, Mike Fagan, Pete Febbraro, Brian Frazier, Greg Gambler, Kyle Geist, James Hamill, David Houck, Wes Koser, Chippy Lichtenwalner, Jesse Lichtenwalner, John Millets, Bob Moser, Joe Munley, Jeff Niece, John Newcomer, Gino Pavan, Joe Raniszewski, Chris Ruddick, Anthony Stamile, Andrew Tavares, Dustin Webb, Mike Welsh and Dan Zettlemoyer.

Thanks to Durward Hamil, whose voluntary 11th hour editing help always makes the Handbook better.

Thanks to Jon Vrecsics, who far exceeded the bounds of what we'd consider an excellent contributor. Be assured your help above and beyond the call of duty was much appreciated.

Thanks to Greg Pierce, Andrew Yankech and the rest of the ACTA staff.

Thanks to Sig Mejdal, a NASA mathematician and baseball researcher, who brings a unique combination of skills to the group. For the first time that we know of, a comprehensive and statistically sound analysis of player injuries and, more importantly, player injury projections have been completed.

Thanks to Mike Canter, who despite a new full-time employment endeavor this year, still found time to help make the book-production baton-pass a smooth one.

Thanks to Teddy Cleborne and Dan Tucker for your efforts during your time at BIS.

Thanks to the full-time staff, some of whom are willingly suffering through their first "book crunch" as I type: Andy Bausher (special congrats on the addition of Hannah Grace to the Bausher family), Nate Birtwell, Ryan Galla, Damon Lichtenwalner (special congrats on the addition of Paige Olivia to the Lichtenwalner family), Matt Lorenzo, David Pinto, Pat Quinn, Todd Radcliffe and Gary Read.

Thanks to the owners of the company, veteran statistical warrior John Dewan and his wife Sue.

And finally, thanks to—drum roll, please—with the obligatory "last but certainly not least"—Bill James, who continues to innovate and support other innovators at a time when he could easily sit back and spend the rest of his life simply admiring what he's already accomplished.

To quote an outdated, non-innovative phrase—"for all you do, this Bud's for you."

Steve Moyer
President
Baseball Info Solutions

Table of Contents

Introduction

There was a humorous review of the phone book once. It basically said that there were a lot of characters but no plot. Just as you were introduced to one person, the author moved on to the next. No one was developed, just a name and a number.

This is a book about names and numbers, but unlike the white pages, our characters are fleshed out. The numbers tell the story. In these pages you'll see the saga of a flawed hero trying to reach an historic milestone. You'll discover youngsters flaming out, and veterans regaining lost glory. There are new characters with numbers that hint at future glory; others you'll never see again. The actors come to life as your baseball knowledge takes the statistics from page to imagination.

The Bill James Handbook arrives November 1st so you can enjoy it all winter. Take it out for a few minutes every night and read the stories. Read the classic tales of Randy Johnson and Barry Bonds. Peruse the adventures of Ichiro and A-Rod. Thrill to the meteoric rises of Johan Santana and Albert Pujols. Use the numbers to get into the minds of the managers and the gloves of the fielders.

With the third edition of the Bill James Handbook, we continue to add new features. Look for Bill James' new Team Efficiency Summary, Hitter Projections and Injury Projections. Of course, all the Bill James stats you love are here. Win shares, runs created, manager studies all return for 2005. We love to hear feedback from our readers as well. Mail us at info@baseballinfosolutions.com and let us know what you would like to see in future editions.

- David Pinto

2004 Team Statistics

2004 American League Standings

Overall

EAST

Team	W-L	Pct	GB	D1	LD1	LLd
New York Yankees	101-61	.623	0.0	144	10/3	10.5
Boston Red Sox*	98-64	.605	3.0	43	5/31	3.0
Baltimore Orioles	78-84	.481	23.0	21	5/19	1.0
Tampa Bay Devil Rays	70-91	.435	30.5	10	4/16	1.0
Toronto Blue Jays	67-94	.416	33.5	0	-	0.0

CENTRAL

Team	W-L	Pct	GB	D1	LD1	LLd
Minnesota Twins	92-70	.568	0.0	155	10/3	13.5
Chicago White Sox	83-79	.512	9.0	46	7/26	2.5
Cleveland Indians	80-82	.494	12.0	0	-	0.0
Detroit Tigers	72-90	.444	20.0	13	4/17	2.0
Kansas City Royals	58-104	.358	34.0	1	4/5	0.0

WEST

Team	W-L	Pct	GB	D1	LD1	LLd
Anaheim Angels	92-70	.568	0.0	53	10/3	3.5
Oakland Athletics	91-71	.562	1.0	97	9/30	4.0
Texas Rangers	89-73	.549	3.0	68	8/22	4.5
Seattle Mariners	63-99	.389	29.0	0	-	0.0

* Clinched Wild Card Birth on 9/28. Division Clinch Dates: Minnesota 9/20, New York 9/30, Anaheim 10/2.
D1 = Number of days a team had at least a share of first place of their division; LD1 = Last date the team had at least a share of first place; LLd = The largest number of games that a team led their division

East Division

Tm	AT Home	AT Road	VERSUS East	Cent	West	NL	LHS	RHS	COND Day	Night	Grass	Turf	GAME 1-Rn	5+Rn	XInn	MONTHLY Apr	May	June	July	Aug	Sep	ALL-STAR Pre	Post
NYY	57-24	44-37	49-27	20-12	22-14	10-8	36-12	65-49	28-20	73-41	89-51	12-10	24-16	27-28	5-4	11-10	18-8	19-7	16-12	16-12	19-9	55-31	46-30
Bos	55-26	43-38	48-28	19-13	22-14	9-9	32-24	66-40	24-21	74-43	85-55	13-9	16-18	36-20	6-6	15-6	16-14	11-14	14-12	21-7	18-10	48-38	50-26
Bal	38-43	40-41	37-39	21-15	15-17	5-13	22-29	56-55	28-29	50-55	63-77	15-7	15-22	34-25	6-7	12-9	12-14	8-19	14-14	13-15	18-10	37-48	41-36
TB	41-39	29-52	26-49	19-17	10-22	15-3	25-21	45-70	20-29	50-62	23-43	47-48	17-19	18-26	6-7	6-13	11-17	20-6	11-17	10-18	9-18	42-45	28-46
Tor	40-41	27-53	29-46	13-19	17-19	8-10	20-29	47-65	24-31	43-63	22-43	45-51	17-22	19-26	4-7	7-15	15-14	12-15	11-14	9-20	11-15	39-49	28-45

Central Division

Tm	AT Home	AT Road	VERSUS East	Cent	West	NL	LHS	RHS	COND Day	Night	Grass	Turf	GAME 1-Rn	5+Rn	XInn	MONTHLY Apr	May	June	July	Aug	Sep	ALL-STAR Pre	Post
Min	49-32	43-38	19-17	46-30	16-16	11-7	30-23	62-47	27-25	65-45	37-35	55-35	24-16	22-22	12-6	15-7	12-16	14-12	17-10	15-13	17-11	47-40	45-30
CWS	46-35	37-44	16-16	40-36	19-17	8-10	21-35	62-44	31-21	52-58	74-65	9-14	28-18	25-17	6-7	13-8	16-12	12-13	11-16	12-17	17-12	46-38	37-41
Cle	44-37	36-45	17-15	36-40	19-17	10-8	24-34	56-48	23-22	57-60	76-70	4-12	26-20	22-23	11-13	9-13	13-13	15-16	15-12	14-15	12-14	42-45	38-37
Det	38-43	34-47	12-20	36-40	15-21	9-9	24-38	48-52	24-33	48-57	62-84	10-6	12-27	23-22	6-9	12-11	11-16	14-12	13-15	11-17	10-17	42-45	30-45
KC	33-47	25-57	12-24	32-44	8-24	6-12	22-25	36-79	17-44	41-60	54-90	4-14	14-19	19-37	4-7	7-14	10-17	12-15	7-20	10-19	11-17	31-54	27-50

West Division

Tm	AT Home	AT Road	VERSUS East	Cent	West	NL	LHS	RHS	COND Day	Night	Grass	Turf	GAME 1-Rn	5+Rn	XInn	MONTHLY Apr	May	June	July	Aug	Sep	ALL-STAR Pre	Post
Ana	45-36	47-34	25-18	28-15	32-26	7-11	34-17	58-53	26-19	66-51	84-63	8-7	19-21	29-21	4-6	13-10	17-10	11-16	15-12	19-8	15-13	47-40	45-30
Oak	52-29	39-42	23-20	27-16	31-27	10-8	29-18	62-53	36-24	55-47	82-67	9-4	33-19	22-22	12-7	11-12	15-11	17-10	15-12	20-8	12-16	47-39	44-32
Tex	51-30	38-43	25-18	23-20	31-27	10-8	29-24	60-49	25-26	64-47	86-67	3-6	24-19	27-19	5-4	13-9	14-13	17-9	13-14	16-12	14-15	49-37	40-36
Sea	38-44	25-55	13-30	19-24	22-36	9-9	19-31	44-68	20-29	43-70	60-89	3-10	20-30	12-22	11-6	8-15	11-16	12-14	8-19	12-16	11-17	32-54	31-45

Team vs. Team Breakdown

	EAST NYY	Bos	Bal	TB	Tor	CENTRAL Min	CWS	Cle	Det	KC	WEST Ana	Oak	Tex	Sea
New York Yankees	-	8	14	15	12	4	4	4	3	5	4	7	5	6
Boston Red Sox	11	-	9	14	14	2	4	3	6	4	5	8	4	5
Baltimore Orioles	5	10	-	11	11	4	2	3	6	6	3	0	5	7
Tampa Bay Devil Rays	4	5	8	-	9	5	2	3	3	6	1	2	2	5
Toronto Blue Jays	7	5	8	9	-	2	4	2	2	3	5	3	2	7
Minnesota Twins	2	4	5	4	4	-	10	12	12	12	4	2	5	5
Chicago White Sox	3	2	4	4	3	9	-	10	8	13	4	2	6	7
Cleveland Indians	2	4	3	3	5	7	9	-	9	11	5	6	1	5
Detroit Tigers	4	1	0	3	4	7	11	10	-	8	2	4	4	5
Kansas City Royals	1	2	3	3	3	7	6	8	11	-	0	2	4	2
Anaheim Angels	5	5	6	6	4	5	5	4	7	7	-	10	9	13
Oakland Athletics	2	1	7	7	6	5	7	3	5	7	9	-	11	11
Texas Rangers	4	5	2	7	7	2	3	8	5	5	10	9	-	12
Seattle Mariners	3	4	2	2	2	4	2	4	4	5	7	8	7	-

2004 National League Standings

Overall

EAST Team	W-L	Pct	GB	D1	LD1	LLd
Atlanta Braves	96-66	.593	0.0	80	10/3	11.0
Philadelphia Phillies	86-76	.531	10.0	45	7/22	3.0
Florida Marlins	83-79	.512	13.0	82	6/30	3.5
New York Mets	71-91	.438	25.0	2	4/7	0.0
Montreal Expos	67-95	.414	29.0	1	4/7	0.0

CENTRAL Team	W-L	Pct	GB	D1	LD1	LLd
St Louis Cardinals	105-57	.648	0.0	116	10/3	18.0
Houston Astros*	92-70	.568	13.0	33	5/27	3.0
Chicago Cubs	89-73	.549	16.0	21	5/27	1.0
Cincinnati Reds	76-86	.469	29.0	39	6/12	2.5
Pittsburgh Pirates	72-89	.447	32.5	3	4/8	0.0
Milwaukee Brewers	67-94	.416	37.5	4	4/8	0.5

WEST Team	W-L	Pct	GB	D1	LD1	LLd
Los Angeles Dodgers	93-69	.574	0.0	133	10/3	7.5
San Francisco Giants	91-71	.562	2.0	25	7/15	3.0
San Diego Padres	87-75	.537	6.0	38	7/7	2.0
Colorado Rockies	68-94	.420	25.0	1	4/7	0.0
Arizona Diamondbacks	51-111	.315	42.0	2	4/8	0.0

* Clinched Wild Card Birth on 10/3. Division Clinch Dates: St Louis 9/18, Atlanta 9/24, Los Angeles 10/2.
D1 = Number of days a team had at least a share of first place of their division; LD1 = Last date the team had at least a share of first place; LLd = The largest number of games that a team led their division

East Division

Tm	Home	Road	East	Cent	West	AL	LHS	RHS	Day	Night	Grass	Turf	1-Rn	5+Rn	XInn	Apr	May	June	July	Aug	Sep	Pre	Post
Atl	49-32	47-34	51-25	18-18	19-13	8-10	34-19	62-47	28-19	68-47	89-64	7-2	27-17	32-15	7-8	11-10	14-15	12-15	20-6	20-8	17-11	45-42	51-24
Phi	42-39	44-37	39-37	18-18	20-12	9-9	23-23	63-53	29-27	57-49	79-71	7-5	23-20	24-17	10-8	10-11	17-11	13-14	13-15	12-16	19-8	46-41	40-35
Fla	42-38	41-41	43-33	15-21	18-14	7-11	25-20	58-59	31-18	52-61	76-74	7-5	20-17	21-22	5-10	15-8	15-13	11-16	11-15	16-10	14-15	45-43	38-36
NYM	38-43	33-48	29-47	15-21	17-15	10-8	17-27	54-64	25-30	46-61	65-84	6-7	23-24	19-19	11-6	9-14	15-12	13-13	12-15	11-17	10-18	44-43	27-48
Mon	35-45	32-50	28-48	17-19	15-17	7-11	21-28	46-67	17-26	50-69	31-48	36-47	16-30	17-31	5-8	5-19	11-15	10-16	15-13	15-13	9-18	31-56	36-39

Central Division

Tm	Home	Road	East	Cent	West	AL	LHS	RHS	Day	Night	Grass	Turf	1-Rn	5+Rn	XInn	Apr	May	June	July	Aug	Sep	Pre	Post
StL	53-28	52-29	19-11	54-36	21-9	11-1	26-13	79-44	36-21	69-36	104-55	1-2	29-20	32-13	9-4	12-11	15-12	19-9	20-5	21-7	16-12	54-33	51-24
Hou	48-33	44-37	16-14	55-35	14-16	7-5	19-17	73-53	33-19	59-51	91-68	1-2	24-18	32-20	3-7	13-9	14-14	13-14	12-15	17-11	20-7	44-44	48-26
ChC	45-37	44-36	16-14	50-40	15-15	8-4	25-15	64-58	49-38	40-35	87-72	2-1	19-30	29-15	10-9	13-9	14-14	15-12	14-13	16-12	16-11	47-40	42-33
Cin	40-41	36-45	18-12	38-52	15-15	5-7	23-24	53-62	27-30	49-56	74-85	2-1	25-20	11-35	12-7	12-10	18-11	12-14	9-18	11-16	13-15	47-41	29-45
Pit	39-41	33-48	17-13	37-52	16-14	2-10	14-21	58-68	23-30	49-59	71-86	1-3	20-26	17-24	8-7	10-11	13-13	9-19	17-10	12-17	9-18	39-47	33-42
Mil	36-45	31-49	11-19	35-54	13-17	8-4	11-21	56-73	24-32	43-62	63-92	4-2	18-20	12-25	5-12	12-11	13-13	15-10	10-19	6-21	10-18	45-41	22-53

West Division

Tm	Home	Road	East	Cent	West	AL	LHS	RHS	Day	Night	Grass	Turf	1-Rn	5+Rn	XInn	Apr	May	June	July	Aug	Sep	Pre	Post
LA	49-32	44-37	14-18	22-14	47-29	10-8	23-22	70-47	23-22	70-47	90-65	3-4	32-16	23-17	11-3	14-8	13-14	12-14	21-7	17-11	15-13	48-38	45-31
SF	47-35	44-36	19-13	20-16	41-35	11-7	32-18	59-53	28-25	63-46	88-69	3-2	18-25	22-20	8-10	10-14	16-10	18-10	13-15	16-12	16-9	49-40	42-31
SD	42-39	45-36	18-14	19-17	41-34	8-10	29-23	58-52	22-17	65-58	84-74	2-1	25-15	28-18	7-4	15-9	13-14	13-13	16-10	13-14	15-13	47-41	40-34
Col	38-43	30-51	11-21	10-26	39-36	8-10	26-21	42-73	24-35	44-59	67-88	1-5	16-24	22-26	3-11	9-12	10-19	9-17	18-9	9-18	13-15	36-51	32-43
Ari	29-52	22-59	9-23	15-21	21-55	6-12	13-41	38-70	12-30	39-81	49-107	2-4	15-31	8-37	6-8	9-13	9-20	10-17	5-23	8-18	8-19	31-58	20-53

Team vs. Team Breakdown

	Atl	Phi	Fla	NYM	Mon	StL	Hou	ChC	Cin	Pit	Mil	LA	SF	SD	Col	Ari
Atlanta Braves	-	10	14	12	15	2	3	3	2	4	4	4	4	3	4	4
Philadelphia Phillies	9	-	7	11	12	3	0	3	3	3	6	5	2	5	3	5
Florida Marlins	5	12	-	15	11	2	3	3	2	1	4	3	2	4	5	4
New York Mets	7	8	4	-	10	1	4	2	3	1	4	3	4	1	5	4
Montreal Expos	4	7	8	9	-	3	4	3	2	4	1	3	1	1	4	6
St Louis Cardinals	4	3	4	5	3	-	8	11	14	12	9	4	3	4	5	5
Houston Astros	3	6	3	2	2	10	-	9	11	12	13	1	2	2	5	4
Chicago Cubs	3	3	3	4	3	8	10	-	9	13	10	2	2	4	5	2
Cincinnati Reds	4	3	4	3	4	5	6	8	-	9	10	4	3	2	3	3
Pittsburgh Pirates	2	3	5	5	2	5	5	5	10	-	12	0	5	3	4	4
Milwaukee Brewers	2	0	2	2	5	8	6	7	8	6	-	3	1	2	4	3
Los Angeles Dodgers	3	1	3	3	4	2	5	4	2	6	3	-	10	10	11	16
San Francisco Giants	3	4	5	2	5	3	4	4	3	1	5	9	-	7	11	14
San Diego Padres	3	1	2	6	6	2	4	2	4	3	4	9	12	-	8	12
Colorado Rockies	2	5	1	1	2	1	1	1	3	2	2	8	8	10	-	13
Arizona Diamondbacks	2	1	3	3	0	1	2	4	3	2	3	3	5	7	6	-

American League Batting

Tm	G	AB	H	2B	3B	HR	(Hm	Rd)	TB	R	RBI	TBB	IBB	SO	HBP	SH	SF	ShO	SB	CS	SB%	GDP	LOB	Avg	OBP	Slg
Bos	162	5720	1613	373	25	222	(111	111)	2702	949	912	659	39	1189	69	12	55	3	68	30	.69	122	1257	.282	.360	.472
NYY	162	5527	1483	281	20	242	(126	116)	2530	897	863	670	40	982	80	37	50	7	84	33	.72	157	1190	.268	.353	.458
CWS	162	5534	1481	284	19	242	(145	97)	2529	865	823	499	25	1030	63	58	42	8	78	51	.60	118	1031	.268	.333	.457
Tex	162	5615	1492	323	34	227	(116	111)	2564	860	825	500	41	1099	61	23	57	9	69	36	.66	91	1098	.266	.329	.457
Cle	162	5676	1565	345	29	184	(70	114)	2520	858	820	606	41	1009	78	47	42	6	94	55	.63	141	1197	.276	.351	.444
Bal	162	5736	1614	319	18	169	(82	87)	2476	842	803	528	34	949	57	46	62	12	101	41	.71	126	1216	.281	.345	.432
Ana	162	5675	1603	272	37	162	(77	85)	2435	836	783	450	43	942	73	56	41	10	143	46	.76	122	1133	.282	.341	.429
Det	162	5623	1531	284	54	201	(87	114)	2526	827	800	518	32	1144	50	50	43	5	86	50	.63	110	1116	.272	.337	.449
Oak	162	5728	1545	336	15	189	(100	89)	2478	793	752	608	40	1061	55	25	43	3	47	22	.68	141	1274	.270	.343	.433
Min	162	5623	1494	310	24	191	(89	102)	2425	780	735	513	42	982	64	46	40	4	116	46	.72	130	1110	.266	.332	.431
KC	162	5538	1432	261	29	150	(56	94)	2201	720	675	461	28	1057	76	40	38	13	67	48	.58	131	1099	.259	.322	.397
Tor	161	5531	1438	290	34	145	(80	65)	2231	719	680	513	34	1083	71	20	42	12	58	31	.65	137	1164	.260	.328	.403
TB	161	5483	1416	278	46	145	(74	71)	2221	714	685	469	33	944	55	35	56	13	132	42	.76	98	1096	.258	.320	.405
Sea	162	5722	1544	276	20	136	(71	65)	2268	698	658	492	49	1058	54	46	48	12	110	42	.72	132	1241	.270	.331	.396
AL	1133	78731	21251	4232	404	2605	(1284	1321)	34106	11358	10814	7486	512	14529	906	541	659	117	1253	573	.69	1756	16222	.270	.338	.433

American League Pitching

Tm	G	CG	Rel	IP	BFP	H	R	ER	HR	SH	SF	HB	TBB	IBB	SO	WP	Bk	W	L	Pct.	ShO	Sv-Op	Hld	OAvg	OOBP	OSlg	ERA
Min	162	4	435	1476.0	6269	1523	715	661	167	46	35	54	431	27	1123	45	1	92	70	.568	9	48-68	48	.267	.323	.406	4.03
Ana	162	2	343	1454.1	6246	1476	734	692	170	35	47	44	502	27	1164	61	7	92	70	.568	11	50-67	54	.263	.326	.415	4.28
Oak	162	10	414	1471.1	6313	1466	742	682	164	54	43	68	544	49	1034	39	5	91	71	.562	8	35-63	71	.262	.332	.409	4.17
Bos	162	4	435	1451.1	6222	1430	768	674	159	37	46	92	447	28	1132	39	1	98	64	.605	12	36-49	53	.255	.318	.408	4.18
Tex	162	5	468	1439.2	6345	1536	794	724	182	51	48	81	547	29	979	34	11	89	73	.549	9	52-66	76	.274	.344	.432	4.53
NYY	162	1	436	1443.2	6240	1532	808	752	182	28	57	60	445	32	1058	57	4	101	61	.623	5	59-76	70	.271	.328	.432	4.69
Tor	161	6	431	1421.0	6281	1505	823	775	181	42	56	58	608	47	956	60	11	67	94	.416	11	37-53	47	.273	.348	.434	4.91
Sea	162	7	414	1459.1	6389	1498	823	772	212	43	48	72	575	32	1036	45	7	63	99	.389	7	28-49	42	.265	.338	.441	4.76
Bal	162	8	452	1455.1	6459	1488	830	760	159	36	40	62	687	43	1090	68	9	78	84	.481	10	27-47	54	.264	.348	.404	4.70
CWS	162	8	399	1432.1	6189	1505	831	782	224	39	46	48	527	36	1013	43	3	83	79	.512	8	34-46	57	.272	.338	.453	4.91
TB	161	3	401	1417.0	6261	1459	842	757	192	30	52	93	580	35	923	55	7	71	91	.435	5	35-45	46	.265	.342	.438	4.81
Det	162	7	432	1439.2	6296	1542	844	788	190	52	43	54	530	33	995	71	6	72	90	.444	9	35-63	58	.275	.340	.441	4.93
Cle	162	8	479	1466.2	6450	1553	857	784	201	39	43	62	579	47	1115	43	6	80	82	.494	8	32-60	55	.271	.342	.445	4.81
KC	162	6	409	1420.1	6320	1638	905	813	208	38	57	56	518	49	887	60	10	58	104	.358	3	25-47	48	.290	.352	.476	5.15
AL	1133	79	5950	20248.0	88280	21151	11316	10432	2591	570	661	904	7520	514	14505	720	88	1134	1132	.500	115	533-799	779	.269	.337	.431	4.64

American League Fielding

Team	G	Inn	PO	Ast	OFAst	E	(Throw	Field)	TC	DP	GDP	SB	CS	SB%	CPkof	PPkof	PB	UER	UERA	FPct
Oakland	162	1471.1	4414	1806	26	91	41	50	6311	172	146	74	49	.60	1	6	14	60	0.37	.986
Anaheim	162	1454.1	4363	1508	33	90	33	57	5961	126	96	87	44	.66	6	7	11	42	0.26	.985
Toronto	161	1421.0	4263	1629	34	91	48	43	5983	149	120	91	41	.69	2	1	11	45	0.29	.985
Chicago	162	1432.1	4297	1668	36	100	42	58	6065	166	137	90	48	.65	2	5	14	49	0.31	.984
Minnesota	162	1476.0	4428	1656	21	102	52	50	6186	160	132	73	44	.62	0	4	6	52	0.32	.984
New York	162	1443.2	4331	1566	26	99	45	54	5996	148	118	90	32	.74	1	3	13	56	0.35	.983
Cleveland	162	1466.2	4400	1671	32	106	32	74	6177	152	117	117	40	.75	0	4	15	72	0.44	.983
Seattle	162	1459.1	4378	1469	30	103	51	52	5950	140	116	64	38	.63	1	4	11	51	0.31	.983
Baltimore	162	1455.1	4366	1680	24	110	60	50	6156	163	136	82	39	.68	1	4	15	69	0.43	.982
Boston	162	1451.1	4354	1647	20	118	53	65	6119	130	106	123	31	.80	2	6	21	92	0.57	.981
Texas	162	1439.2	4319	1602	24	117	49	68	6038	152	131	71	39	.65	0	8	16	67	0.42	.981
Tampa Bay	161	1417.0	4251	1526	29	119	57	62	5896	140	124	67	32	.68	1	7	8	83	0.53	.980
Kansas City	162	1420.1	4261	1631	35	131	65	66	6023	170	142	84	35	.71	1	4	17	90	0.57	.978
Detroit	162	1439.2	4319	1708	34	144	69	75	6171	160	145	71	41	.63	1	2	10	56	0.35	.977
American League	1133	20248.0	60744	22767	404	1521	697	824	85032	2128	1766	1184	553	.68	19	65	182	884	0.39	.982

National League Batting

Tm	G	AB	H	2B	3B	HR	(Hm	Rd)	TB	R	RBI	TBB	IBB	SO	HBP	SH	SF	ShO	SB	CS	SB%	GDP	LOB	Avg	OBP	Slg
StL	162	5555	1544	319	24	214	(93	121)	2553	855	817	548	64	1085	51	73	70	4	111	47	.70	120	1156	.278	.344	.460
SF	162	5546	1500	314	33	183	(88	95)	2429	850	805	705	153	874	72	92	51	4	43	23	.65	140	1289	.270	.357	.438
Phi	162	5643	1505	303	23	215	(113	102)	2499	840	802	645	58	1133	58	64	46	4	100	27	.79	122	1236	.267	.345	.443
Col	162	5577	1531	331	34	202	(111	91)	2536	833	795	568	51	1181	54	97	37	6	44	33	.57	133	1167	.275	.345	.455
Hou	162	5468	1458	294	36	187	(96	91)	2385	803	756	590	54	999	61	98	52	3	89	30	.75	128	1175	.267	.342	.436
Atl	162	5570	1503	304	37	178	(92	86)	2415	803	767	587	51	1158	59	75	48	7	86	32	.73	124	1230	.270	.343	.434
ChC	162	5628	1508	308	29	235	(137	98)	2579	789	755	489	46	1080	38	78	48	12	66	28	.70	120	1121	.268	.328	.458
SD	162	5573	1521	304	32	139	(57	82)	2306	768	722	566	45	910	56	52	66	3	52	25	.68	129	1235	.273	.342	.414
LA	162	5542	1450	226	30	203	(100	103)	2345	761	731	536	45	1092	62	69	35	12	102	41	.71	120	1152	.262	.332	.423
Cin	162	5518	1380	287	28	194	(92	102)	2305	750	713	599	38	1335	81	55	25	10	77	25	.75	123	1176	.250	.331	.418
Fla	162	5486	1447	275	32	148	(71	77)	2230	718	677	499	37	968	58	77	40	8	96	43	.69	138	1127	.264	.329	.406
NYM	162	5532	1376	289	20	185	(85	100)	2260	684	658	512	54	1159	61	69	34	12	107	23	.82	127	1142	.249	.317	.409
Pit	161	5483	1428	267	39	142	(78	64)	2199	680	648	415	33	1066	95	79	42	8	63	40	.61	117	1123	.260	.321	.401
Mon	162	5474	1361	276	27	151	(69	82)	2144	635	605	496	51	925	35	100	33	16	109	38	.74	117	1123	.249	.313	.392
Mil	161	5483	1358	295	32	135	(66	69)	2122	634	601	540	49	1312	68	56	40	16	138	40	.78	120	1199	.248	.321	.387
Ari	162	5544	1401	295	38	135	(78	57)	2177	615	582	441	38	1022	35	56	37	9	53	32	.62	136	1108	.253	.310	.393
NL	1295	88622	23271	4687	494	2846	(1426	1420)	37484	12018	11434	8736	867	17299	944	1190	704	134	1336	527	.72	2014	18759	.263	.333	.423

National League Pitching

Tm	G	CG	Rel	IP	BFP	H	R	ER	HR	SH	SF	HB	TBB	IBB	SO	WP	Bk	W	L	Pct.	ShO	Sv-Op	Hld	OAvg	OOBP	OSlg	ERA
StL	162	4	469	1453.2	6104	1378	659	605	169	76	37	67	440	24	1041	42	4	105	57	.648	12	57-73	89	.251	.313	.403	3.75
ChC	162	3	460	1465.1	6262	1363	665	621	169	78	44	76	545	33	1346	50	9	89	73	.549	6	42-66	68	.247	.321	.395	3.81
Atl	162	4	483	1450.0	6218	1475	668	603	154	69	42	27	523	50	1025	36	6	96	66	.593	13	48-68	71	.265	.329	.400	3.74
LA	162	2	459	1453.1	6155	1386	684	647	178	88	39	54	521	47	1066	43	2	93	69	.574	6	51-60	57	.254	.323	.408	4.01
Hou	162	3	493	1443.0	6201	1416	698	650	174	74	35	68	525	61	1282	45	3	92	70	.568	13	47-70	74	.258	.328	.417	4.05
Fla	162	6	404	1439.0	6110	1395	700	655	166	55	36	51	513	61	1116	35	3	83	79	.512	14	53-75	54	.256	.324	.412	4.10
SD	162	3	437	1441.0	6135	1460	705	645	184	73	41	48	422	39	1079	27	2	87	75	.537	8	44-64	76	.263	.318	.431	4.03
NYM	162	2	474	1449.0	6333	1452	731	658	156	77	44	49	592	70	977	30	8	71	91	.438	6	31-52	70	.261	.335	.405	4.09
Pit	161	3	464	1428.0	6197	1451	744	680	149	80	48	63	576	64	1079	45	3	72	89	.447	8	46-69	76	.267	.342	.416	4.29
Mil	161	6	423	1442.0	6204	1440	757	679	164	58	52	51	476	27	1098	59	5	67	94	.416	10	42-64	59	.259	.320	.417	4.24
Mon	162	11	462	1447.0	6307	1477	769	696	191	54	36	79	582	76	1032	43	2	67	95	.414	11	31-49	59	.266	.342	.431	4.33
SF	162	8	521	1457.0	6321	1481	770	695	161	74	37	47	548	35	1020	52	2	91	71	.562	8	46-74	87	.265	.332	.423	4.29
Phi	162	4	476	1462.2	6308	1488	781	724	214	74	38	66	502	60	1070	40	3	86	76	.531	5	43-68	82	.264	.330	.448	4.45
Ari	162	5	471	1436.0	6418	1480	899	794	197	74	47	75	668	79	1153	71	8	51	111	.315	6	33-55	55	.266	.350	.439	4.98
Cin	162	5	497	1443.2	6451	1595	907	832	236	75	54	54	572	55	992	73	3	76	86	.469	8	47-77	80	.280	.348	.481	5.19
Col	162	3	473	1435.1	6535	1634	923	883	198	82	56	71	697	84	947	66	6	68	94	.420	2	36-70	67	.290	.372	.471	5.54
NL	1295	71	7466	23146.0	100259	23371	12060	11095	2860	1161	702	946	8702	865	17323	757	69	1294	1296	.500	136	697-1054	1124	.263	.333	.425	4.31

National League Fielding

Team	G	Inn	PO	Ast	OFAst	E	(Throw	Field)	TC	DP	GDP	SB	CS	SB%	CPkof	PPkof	PB	UER	UERA	FPct
Los Angeles	162	1453.1	4360	1665	21	73	37	36	6098	145	129	96	40	.71	3	1	15	37	0.23	.988
Philadelphia	162	1462.2	4388	1626	34	81	34	47	6095	142	121	103	26	.80	1	0	7	55	0.34	.987
Chicago	162	1465.1	4396	1575	24	86	38	48	6057	126	104	108	39	.73	1	1	9	42	0.26	.986
Colorado	162	1435.1	4306	1819	29	89	50	39	6214	161	138	111	32	.78	0	11	15	40	0.25	.986
Florida	162	1439.0	4317	1598	23	86	35	51	6001	154	122	118	38	.76	1	5	11	45	0.28	.986
St Louis	162	1453.2	4361	1831	24	98	37	61	6290	154	129	53	29	.65	2	4	9	54	0.33	.984
Montreal	162	1447.0	4341	1696	41	99	43	56	6136	171	134	58	41	.59	4	5	7	73	0.45	.984
San Francisco	162	1457.0	4371	1734	25	101	38	63	6206	154	129	72	24	.75	0	4	11	67	0.41	.984
Houston	162	1443.0	4329	1614	28	101	43	58	6044	136	117	101	39	.72	2	1	4	48	0.30	.983
Pittsburgh	161	1428.0	4284	1689	20	103	42	61	6076	189	159	72	38	.65	0	2	2	60	0.38	.983
San Diego	162	1441.0	4323	1599	26	108	44	64	6030	146	126	69	25	.73	0	3	9	60	0.37	.982
Atlanta	162	1450.0	4350	1787	40	116	50	66	6253	172	150	91	29	.76	2	3	10	64	0.40	.981
Cincinnati	162	1443.2	4331	1641	34	113	54	59	6085	123	100	67	29	.70	1	1	17	71	0.44	.981
Milwaukee	161	1442.0	4326	1594	22	117	42	75	6037	132	109	89	29	.75	1	7	7	74	0.46	.981
New York	162	1449.0	4347	1741	28	137	57	80	6225	145	121	100	39	.72	0	1	12	71	0.44	.978
Arizona	162	1436.0	4308	1712	26	139	65	74	6159	144	116	97	50	.66	1	2	18	104	0.65	.977
National League	1295	23146.0	69438	26921	445	1647	709	938	98006	2394	2004	1405	547	.72	19	51	163	965	0.38	.983

Team Efficiency Summary

Bill James

The new chart this year, the Team Efficiency Summary, starts, in a way, with the 2003 Boston Red Sox. The Red Sox in 2003—and actually, for several years before 2003—were an inefficient team, in terms of producing a good group outcome from their discrete individual achievements. The number of runs we scored, as a team, was not what it should have been, given the number of hits and walks and homers that our hitters accumulated. The number of runs we allowed was higher than it ought to have been, given the number of hits and walks and home runs allowed by our pitchers. Things didn't add up well for us—as, in fact, they haven't added up well for us for several years.

The Red Sox have a sophisticated front office and a sophisticated media—well, a complex media including sophisticated elements—and so this systematic inefficiency has come to be well known in the Boston area. We were talking about it one day, and Theo Epstein asked me, "What do you make of this? It can't be bad luck, year after year. Why haven't we scored as many runs as we should have scored? Why haven't we won quite as many games as we should have won?"

My instinctive reaction was that this was normal "slippage" from that which we focused on. Suppose that you had a team that decided that the team with the best athletes usually wins, which certainly must be true to some extent, and suppose that this team then focused on putting the best available athletes on the field. There are some teams that do this. What would happen is, that team would certainly have a low ratio of wins to athletic ability at the end of the season, since they would be stronger in terms of athletic ability than in any other area of the game.

Or suppose that you had a team that believed that pitching was everything, and focused entirely on pitching. That team, at the end of the year, would have stronger pitching than anything else—thus, their ratio of wins to pitching strength would be unusually low. Normal slippage. Whatever you focus on, you're going to be stronger in that area than you are overall. Perhaps this is just our normal slippage from the criteria that we use to make player decisions.

Except that there are two serious problems with this answer. First, we don't make decisions on individual player stats; in fact, we are very careful not to. We pay attention to scouting reports, work habits, leadership, video—all that stuff. We are careful every day not to put too much reliance on player performance records, since, after all, those only describe the player's past, not his future.

And second, the Red Sox have scored fewer runs than would be predicted by the runs created formula every year since 1987. The present Red Sox management team was assembled during and after the 2002 season, mostly after.

My second instinctive reaction to this problem was that this discussion was likely to wander all over the map and waste time. Do you remember those high school/college bull sessions that start out with a question like "Do you believe in ghosts?" This drifts into a general discussion of the paranormal, so that, beginning with ghosts, you find yourself in the middle of a meandering discussion which involves reincarnation, mind reading, witchcraft, whether or not some people have some ability to foresee future events, psychic crime-solving, dreams, teleportation, karma, angels, altered states of consciousness, the afterlife, the soul, and the movies *Poltergeist* and *Ghost Busters*. Eventually, some greasy-haired slacker from the third floor will bring up alien abductions, at which point it is time to hit the books.

These subjects are not really related, one to another, but what you are talking about is the unknown. It has no very specific dimensions or borders. The discussion bounces from one area to another because no one knows exactly where one ends and the next begins.

Discussing "team inefficiency" has the same problem. What you are really talking about is "the unknown"—the undocumented and unmeasured components of team success. If you're not careful, within minutes of bringing up the subject you will find yourself with a dog's breakfast of essentially unrelated topics—bad baserunning, failing to advance runners, strikeouts, striking out vs. failing to execute on offense, clutch hitting, baserunning speed/slowness versus baserunning judgment versus baserunning aggressiveness, lineup construction, productive outs, hitting behind the runner, sacrifice bunts, the role of random bad luck, the merits of the runs created formula vs. some other offensive measurement, one-run records, and whether or not it is important to be able to play "small ball" in post-season play. Eventually, some TV broadcaster will begin talking about "team character", at which point it is time to hit the mute button before you throw something at the television.

I am not saying that these are not serious topics. They are very serious topics. But it is also:

a) a subject which has huge potential to waste time, and

b) a tempting target for casual associations which have no basis in logic or evidence.

It is so easy for somebody to say "Well, the reason the Oakland A's don't win in the post season is because they don't execute on offense." It's hogwash, but by the time you prove that it is hogwash you've wasted three weeks of your life, and the discussion has moved on and nobody is paying any attention anyway.

But there is a problem with this answer, as well, which is this. My view of the baseball world is that there are a mountain of unknowns. My job is to chip away at the mountain of unknowns, to take a few things which previously were "unknown" and change them to "known". That's really all I do for a living—do battle against baseball's unknowns. I can't afford to turn down the challenge represented by a set of unknowns, merely because I'm afraid it is going to waste a few weeks of my life and nobody will care what I find anyway. I have to step up and try to figure something out.

Part of the systematic shortfall of the Red Sox can be traced to the Runs Created formula not working as well as it should. The basis of the Runs Created formula that we have used here was developed in the 1980s or early 1990s. Over time, the game of baseball changes in ways that affect the accuracy of the formula. That runs created formula, although it works very well for seasons prior to 1990, gives a little bit too much credit to power hitting, and thus tends to over project runs scored for most major league teams since 1990. Thus, the first thing we need to do, in order to understand this problem better, is to fix the Runs Created formula.

The Runs Created formula has three basic parts—an "A" factor, a "B" factor, and "C" factor. Runs Created are A times B, divided by C.

The "A" factor represents runners on base. This factor was, and remains, Hits, plus Walks, plus Hit Batsmen, minus Runners Caught Stealing, minus GIDP (Grounded Into Double Play). That hasn't changed.

The "C" factor represents opportunities. This factor was, and remains, At Bats, plus Walks, plus Hit Batsmen, plus Sacrifice Hits, plus Sacrifice Flies. This hasn't changed.

The "B" factor represents everything the team does to advance baserunners, and this element of the formula I have now changed to better accommodate the modern power-hitting offenses. In the simplest versions of the runs created formula, the "B" factor is simply Total Bases. In the version of the formula used last year, the "B" factor was Total Bases, plus .24 times (Walks plus Hit Batsmen, Minus Intentional Walks), plus .62 times Stolen Bases, plus .5 times (Sacrifice Hits plus Sacrifice Flies), minus .03 times Strikeouts.

The biggest problem with this is that this assumes that a home run does four times as much to advance a runner as a single does, which it really doesn't. Within historically normal ranges of team performance you'd never notice the difference, but with the very large number of home runs hit in the majors since 1993, the formula has begun to lose accuracy. So I replaced the "B" factor with the following:

Singles times 1.125,
Plus Doubles times 1.69,
Plus Triples times 3.02,
Plus Home Runs times 3.73,
Plus .29 times (Walks plus Hit Batsmen, Minus Intentional Walks),
Plus .492 times (Sacrifice Hits plus Sacrifice Walks plus Stolen Bases),
Minus .04 times Strikeouts.

The first four factors add up to "adjusted Total Bases"…I think that some other people have come up with similar concepts in their own systems. Historically, Total Bases and Adjusted Total Bases for most teams are almost exactly the same. In 1986, for example, only two major league teams (the White Sox and Cardinals) had even a one percent discrepancy between adjusted and actual Total Bases. But in recent years this is less true. In 2003 twelve major league teams had at least a one percent discrepancy between adjusted and actual total bases. Thus, it becomes necessary to tweak the formula.

This formula is eight percent more accurate than the previous formula, for all teams for whom the complete data set is available (all teams since 1955). It is more accurate for the years 1955-1992; it is significantly more accurate since 1992.

The Red Sox have scored fewer runs than expected, in part, because their Adjusted Total Bases have been consistently lower than their actual total bases. In part, but only in part. Using the previous Runs Created formula, the Red Sox offense has under achieved for seventeen straight seasons and by a total of 516 runs. Using the new formula, the Red Sox have under achieved in fourteen of those seventeen seasons, and by a total of 317 runs. Thus, the new formula helps a little to reduce the size of what we don't understand.

A second allegation has been that the Red Sox have been inefficient in terms of preventing runners from scoring, in a similar way—that the runs we allow are higher than they ought to be, given the hits and walks and home runs allowed by our pitchers.

I've never had a formula for "Expected Runs Allowed", or "Runs Created Against", or whatever you would call it. I have produced some similar things, like Component ERA, but I have never exactly faced the question of how many runs a team should allow, given their other pitching and defensive statistics.

So I have now developed a formula that does that…I am calling it Expected Runs Allowed, or ExRA for short. The Expected Runs Allowed formula, again, is an "A times B, divided by C" type of formula, similar to the Runs Created formulas, only composed of elements from the pitching and fielding records instead of from the hitting record.

The A element is:
>   Hits,
>   Plus Walks,
>   Plus Hit Batsmen,
>   Plus (.7 times Errors)
>   Minus Double Plays.

The B element is:
>   Home Runs times 4,
>   Plus other hits (H - HR) times 1.048,
>   Plus Errors,
>   Plus .7 times (Passed Balls + Balks + Wild Pitches)\
>   Plus .32 times (Walks + Hit Batsmen - Intentional Walks)

The C element is simply Batters Facing pitcher.

It's a similar formula to Runs Created…when you have a different set of facts to work with you naturally wind up with different weights, but it's essentially the same.   For all major league teams from 1955 to the present, the average error of this formula is 18.1356 runs.

The worst this formula has ever done for any team was for the unfortunate 1978 Red Sox.   The Red Sox that year should have allowed 725 runs by this formula, but actually allowed only 657.   The 2003 Red Sox, however, were on the top-five list, going the other way; they should have allowed only 746 runs, but actually allowed 809.   Which just goes to show: formulas like this are stupid and don't work.

No, seriously, the two teams are quite similar in terms of hits, walks and home runs allowed—but 152 runs apart in runs allowed. This is unusual. There are 417 teams since 1955 which came within ten runs of allowing the number they expected, and there are 746 teams which are within twenty runs. There are only 204 teams which are off by more than thirty runs, and only 33 teams which are off by more than fifty runs. These formulas USUALLY work, but there is a certain latitude.

As of 2003, the Red Sox are also working on a string of thirteen consecutive seasons in which they have allowed more runs than projected by this formula every year except once, when they tied the formula (921-921, 1996). This is very difficult to explain. Creating a formula like this is a necessary step in converting this inefficiency from an unknown into a known element of the game. Once we have the formula, we can ask "What are the characteristics of the 'efficient' teams? What are the characteristics of the 'inefficient' teams? How do we convert ourselves from an inefficient team into an efficient team?" In our spare time, we trap poltergeists in file cabinets.

Anyway, there is a third element of "inefficiency" which is a part of this discussion, which is win efficiency. If a team scores 859 runs and allows 665 runs, as the Boston Red Sox did in 2002, they can be expected to win about 101 games; the formula for this is so well known that I'm not even going to bother to explain it. The 2002 Red Sox actually won only 93 games, an inefficient result.

We haven't done great in this measure of efficiency, either; in fact, we haven't won more games than expected, by this measure, since 1996, although we have broken even a couple of times. As a Red Sox employee, I spent a goodly amount of time worrying about this. But as a writer, it occurs to me that this is also probably a subject of some general interest—whether a team is or is not efficient in the production of wins from other statistical parameters—and so we decided, in this book, to introduce a "Team Efficiency Summary".

The Team Efficiency Summary consists of twelve columns. Those columns are:

1) Runs Created
2) Actual Runs Scored
3) Hitting Efficiency

4) Expected Runs Allowed
5) Actual Runs Allowed
6) Pitching Efficiency

7) Expected Wins from Runs Scored and Runs Allowed
8) Actual Wins
9) Run Efficiency

10) Expected Wins from Run Elements
 (I will also call this "Efficient Wins")
11) Actual Wins
12) Overall Efficiency

"Hitting Efficiency" is Runs Created, divided by Actual Runs Scored, times 100. An average team will have an efficiency of 100.

"Pitching Efficiency" is Actual Runs Allowed, divided by Expected Runs Allowed, times 100. I am calling it "Pitching Efficiency" rather than "Defensive Efficiency" because the term "Defensive Efficiency" is already in common use with a different meaning.

"Run Efficiency", of course, is Wins, Divided by Expected Wins from the Pythagorean method.

Expected Wins from Runs Elements (Efficient Wins) is just Pythagorean Wins, except using Runs Created instead of Runs Scored and Expected Runs Allowed instead of Runs Allowed. Overall Efficiency is Actual Wins divided by Expected Wins from Run Elements, times 100.

I am spending a lot of time, for reasons outlined above, studying charts of "efficient" and "inefficient" teams, trying to figure out what distinguishes one from another. You probably would not enjoy a book-length dissertation on this subject, but I thought, as a way of further introducing the concept, maybe you'd like to see what some of the most efficient and least efficient historical teams are. Let's do a quick summary:

The 1950s

The most efficient team of the 1950s was the 1959 Chicago White Sox, commonly known as the Go-Go Sox. The White Sox led the majors in stolen bases with 113, were last in the majors in home runs with 97. Based on their other stats they should have won only 82 games, but they actually won 94, plus a couple (not enough) in the World Series. Their shortstop and second basemen were first and second in the MVP voting, while their top starting pitcher was third. All three players (Luis Aparicio, Nellie Fox and Early Wynn) are now in the Hall of Fame.

The least efficient team of the 1950s was the Pittsburgh Pirates of 1950 (Ralph Kiner era), who should have won about 71 games, but finished 57-96.

The 1960s

The most efficient team of the 1960s was the 1963 Los Angeles Dodgers, who won the World Championship.

The 1963 Dodgers were more like that 1959 White Sox than any other team of the 1960s. Their top starting pitcher, Koufax, was the MVP, while their shortstop (Maury Wills) was

> a) the previous season's MVP, and
> b) the best available skills match for Luis Aparicio.

Their second baseman, Junior Gilliam, was also comparable to Nellie Fox, and was also prominent in the MVP vote in 1963. The Dodgers should have finished about 83-79 based on their individual stats, but went 99-63, and swept the Yankees in October. The 1963 Dodgers, with 16 more wins than expected, were in fact the most efficient team since 1950.

The fact that the 1959 White Sox were the most efficient team of the 1950s and a very similar team was the most efficient team of the 1960s is a singular coincidence, and this invites us to race ahead of ourselves and draw the conclusion that baserunning and middle-infield defense are the keys to efficiency. I certainly take seriously the possibility that baserunning is underrated in some very subtle way.

But a more cautious analysis might lead to a completely different conclusion. There have been, in the last fifty years, many home-run-hitting teams and some bad defensive teams which were very efficient. There have been many singles-and-defense teams which were terribly inefficient. The 1959 White Sox were able to work magic with that team—but the 1960 White Sox, who had almost all of the same players and almost all of the same tendencies, were an inefficient team (slightly. They were -1). The 1963 Dodgers repeated the Go-Go Sox—but the 1964 Dodgers, with most of the same players, were an inefficient team (-4). Over the last 50 years the 100 most efficient teams averaged 91 stolen bases and 71 sacrifice bunts. The 100 least efficient teams averaged 93 stolen bases and 66 sac bunts. The "efficient" teams averaged 131 homers, 35 triples, 121 GIDP. The "inefficient" teams averaged 140 homers, 38 triples, 124 GIDP.

Many teams have been built on speed and defense. We need to avoid jumping to conclusions because a couple of them have had good years.

Anyway, the least efficient team of the 1960s was the 1965 Red Sox, who lost 100 games with individual stats that should have put them fairly close to .500. Worst defensive team I ever saw…

The 1970s

The most efficient team of the 1970s was the 1972 New York Mets, who went 83-73 with stats that would have suggested 70-86. This got them nowhere, as they were still not in serious contention. The '73 team, which rode very little talent into the World Series, was also an efficient team, but not to the same degree; they were +5.

Two of the most efficient teams of the 1970s were the 1971 Braves (+11) and the aforementioned 1978 Red Sox (also +11). Those teams were of a very different cut—power-hitting teams with little or no speed.

The most inefficient team of the 1970s was the 1975 Dodgers, who should have won 100 games (100-62), but actually won only 88.

The 1980s

The most efficient teams of the 1980s were:

Year	Team	Lg	Should Have Finished	But Actually Finished	Difference
1988	A's	AL	93-69	104-58	+11
1989	Astros	NL	75-87	86-76	+11
1987	Twins	AL	75-87	85-77	+10
1988	Cardinals	NL	85-77	95-67	+10
1984	Mets	NL	80-82	90-72	+10

The least efficient teams of the 1980s were:

Year	Team	Lg	Should Have Finished	But Actually Finished	Difference
1984	Astros	NL	91-71	80-82	-11
1985	Red Sox	AL	92-70	81-81	-11
1982	Dodgers	NL	100-62	88-74	-12
1984	Phillies	NL	94-68	81-81	-13
1980	Cardinals	NL	90-72	74-88	-16

The 1980 Cardinals, a team I remember well, were widely perceived as a team that didn't play up to their ability. The shortstop, Garry Templeton, had been tabbed a young superstar, and was having some emotional difficulty carrying that load or, as it were, shrugging it off. The manager, Ken Boyer, was fired. Whitey Herzog came in, explained to the owner (Gussie Busch) that he couldn't do anything with this team unless he had the authority to make player moves, got the authority to make player moves, went to the winter meetings and dealt wildly over the next two seasons, sending stars like Templeton, Ted Simmons and Keith Hernandez scattering like dust. It's interesting to note that the statistical method developed twenty years later has the same view of that particular team that the press and public did at the time—that this was a team of historic underachievers.

Since 1990

Since 1990 (but not including 2004) the ten most efficient teams in baseball have been:

Year	Team	Lg	Should Have Finished	But Actually Finished	Difference
1992	Angels	AL	59-103	72-90	+13
1991	A's	AL	74- 88	84-78	+10
1992	A's	AL	87- 75	96-66	+9
1997	Giants	NL	81- 81	90-72	+9
1993	Rockies	NL	59-103	67-95	+8
1996	Astros	NL	74- 88	82-80	+8
2003	Royals	AL	75- 87	83-79	+8
1990	White Sox	AL	86- 76	94-68	+8
2003	Reds	NL	61-101	69-93	+8
1998	Cubs	NL	82- 81	90-73	+8

The 1992 California Angels' team leader in home runs, Gary Gaetti, had 12. Only one player on the team drove in even 50 runs, that being Junior Felix, who drove in 72. Four of their nine regulars hit .226 or less. They were last in the league in batting average (as a team), last in on-base percentage, and last in slugging average, with the fairly remarkable team slugging average of .338.

Their pitching wasn't great, either; they were eighth in the league in ERA (3.84), eighth of fourteen teams. In fielding percentage, they were 11th. They should have lost 100 games, but, by combining their elements remarkably well, they managed to lose only 90.

The least efficient teams since 1990 have been:

Year	Team	Lg	Should Have Finished	But Actually Finished	Difference
1992	Mariners	AL	75-87	64- 98	-11
1991	Reds	NL	85-77	74- 88	-11
1999	Orioles	AL	89-73	78- 84	-11
1992	Phillies	NL	82-80	70- 92	-12
2002	Red Sox	AL	105-57	93- 69	-12
1993	Mets	NL	71-91	59-103	-12
2002	Cubs	NL	80-82	67- 95	-13
1994	Padres	NL	60-57	47- 70	-13
1995	Orioles	AL	85-59	71- 73	-14
2001	Rockies	NL	89-73	73- 89	-16

18

The 2001 Rockies were in fact the most inefficient team since 1950, edging out the 1980 Cardinals.

Most of you reading this article have probably had the thought that much of what causes "inefficiency" or "efficiency" in this way is actually just luck—therefore, that you could probably make money by betting on the teams which were highly efficient one year to decline the next year, and vice versa. Yes, that's true; there is a lot of luck here, and "efficiency" does have a relatively low rate of persistance. Relatively low, but not zero; there is some persistance in the trait. This, after all, is what set me off investigating the phenomenon—the Red Sox persistant inefficiency.

There are a lot of things that could contribute to that, including baserunning, subtle defensive skills, bullpens, witchcraft, alien abduction, and selling Babe Ruth. I may be able to figure out some of it; I may not. I may be able to tell you what I have figured out next year; I may not. I thought it might be worthwhile to organize the data and take a look, and so we have.

2004 American League Team Efficiency Summary

	RC	Runs	Hit Eff	Exp RA	RA	Pit Eff	Exp Wins	Wins	Runs Eff	Eff Wins	Wins	Overall Eff
New York Yankees	885	897	101	767	808	95	89	101	113	92	101	109
Texas Rangers	834	860	103	824	794	104	87	89	102	82	89	109
Minnesota Twins	793	780	98	727	715	102	88	92	105	88	92	104
Chicago White Sox	819	865	106	818	831	98	84	83	99	81	83	102
Anaheim Angels	835	836	100	740	734	101	91	92	101	91	92	101
Tampa Bay Devil Rays	718	714	99	818	842	97	68	70	103	71	70	99
Oakland Athletics	843	793	94	728	742	98	86	91	105	93	91	98
Kansas City Royals	699	720	103	908	905	100	63	58	92	60	58	96
Cleveland Indians	870	858	99	841	857	98	81	80	99	84	80	95
Toronto Blue Jays	725	719	99	816	823	99	70	67	96	71	67	94
Boston Red Sox	969	949	98	707	768	92	98	98	100	106	98	93
Baltimore Orioles	858	842	98	809	830	97	82	78	95	86	78	91
Detroit Tigers	839	827	99	840	844	100	79	72	91	81	72	89
Seattle Mariners	753	698	93	826	823	100	68	63	93	74	63	86

2004 National League Team Efficiency Summary

	RC	Runs	Hit Eff	Exp RA	RA	Pit Eff	Exp Wins	Wins	Runs Eff	Eff Wins	Wins	Overall Eff
Cincinnati Reds	761	750	99	921	907	102	66	76	116	66	76	116
Atlanta Braves	828	803	97	719	668	108	96	96	100	92	96	104
Los Angeles Dodgers	776	761	98	686	684	100	90	93	104	91	93	102
St Louis Cardinals	873	855	98	659	659	100	102	105	103	103	105	102
Houston Astros	820	803	98	722	698	103	92	92	100	91	92	101
Montreal Expos	670	635	95	787	769	102	66	67	102	68	67	98
San Francisco Giants	868	850	98	742	770	96	89	91	102	94	91	97
San Diego Padres	796	768	96	711	705	101	88	87	99	90	87	97
Florida Marlins	728	718	99	682	700	97	83	83	100	86	83	96
Philadelphia Phillies	874	840	96	772	781	99	87	86	99	91	86	94
New York Mets	710	684	96	755	731	103	76	71	94	76	71	93
Chicago Cubs	826	789	96	689	665	104	95	89	94	96	89	93
Colorado Rockies	852	833	98	940	923	102	73	68	94	73	68	93
Pittsburgh Pirates	701	680	97	727	744	98	74	72	98	78	72	92
Arizona Diamondbacks	652	615	94	866	899	96	52	51	99	59	51	87
Milwaukee Brewers	687	634	92	719	757	95	67	67	100	77	67	87

Career Register

Beyond the obvious:

Age is seasonal age as of June 30, 2005.

For pitchers BFP is batters facing pitcher; TBB is total walks (both intentional and unintentional); Op is save opportunities; Hld is holds.

The Career Register includes Runs Created (RC) for batters and Component ERA (ERC) for pitchers. RC is a method of measuring every facet of a hitter's strengths and weaknesses, and combining those factors into one production number. It was invented by Bill James many years ago and he has revised the formula several times. ERC estimates what a pitcher's ERA should have been based upon his raw pitching statistics, such as Hits, Home Runs, and Walks Allowed, etc. It gives a good indication of whether or not a pitcher "deserved" his ERA, whether he was saved or deserted by pitchers that followed him, etc. ERC was also invented by Bill James. You can find complete definitions and formulas for each in the Baseball Glossary.

Players who have appeared in fewer than three major league seasons have full minor league statistics included. Other 2004 major leaguers who spent time in the minors last year have just their 2004 minor league totals included (indicated by an asterisk).

When a player led the league in a particular category, his register total will be in boldface.

David Aardsma

Pitches: R **Bats:** R **Pos:** RP-11 **Ht:** 6'5" **Wt:** 200 **Born:** 12/27/1981 **Age:** 23

		HOW MUCH HE PITCHED						WHAT HE GAVE UP											THE RESULTS					
Year Team	Lg	G	GS	CG	GF	IP	BFP	H	R	ER	HR	SH	SF	HB	TBB	IBB	SO	WP	Bk	W	L	Pct	ShO	Sv-Op	Hld	ERC	ERA
2003 San Jose	A+	18	0	0	12	18.1	74	14	4	4	2	1	0	0	7	0	28	0	0	1	1	.500	0	8--	-	2.85	1.96
2004 Fresno	AAA	44	0	0	29	55.1	245	46	21	19	2	0	0	4	29	3	53	1	0	6	4	.600	0	11--	-	3.27	3.09
2004 San Francisco	NL	11	0	0	5	10.2	61	20	8	8	1	0	1	2	10	0	5	0	0	1	0	1.000	0	0-1	1	13.38	6.75

Paul Abbott

Pitches: R **Bats:** R **Pos:** SP-19; RP-1 **Ht:** 6'3" **Wt:** 204 **Born:** 9/15/1967 **Age:** 37

		HOW MUCH HE PITCHED						WHAT HE GAVE UP											THE RESULTS					
Year Team	Lg	G	GS	CG	GF	IP	BFP	H	R	ER	HR	SH	SF	HB	TBB	IBB	SO	WP	Bk	W	L	Pct	ShO	Sv-Op	Hld	ERC	ERA
2004 Scrtn/WlksBr*	AAA	5	5	1	0	26.1	119	26	18	18	4	0	1	2	17	0	19	1	0	1	2	.333	0	0--	-	5.83	6.15
1990 Minnesota	AL	7	7	0	0	34.2	162	37	24	23	0	1	1	1	28	0	25	1	0	0	5	.000	0	0-0	-	5.53	5.97
1991 Minnesota	AL	15	3	0	1	47.1	210	38	27	25	5	7	3	0	36	1	43	5	0	3	1	.750	0	0-0	-	4.42	4.75
1992 Minnesota	AL	6	0	0	5	11.0	50	12	4	4	1	0	1	1	5	0	13	1	0	0	-		0	0-0	-	5.10	3.27
1993 Cleveland	AL	5	5	0	0	18.1	84	19	15	13	5	0	0	0	11	1	7	1	0	0	1	.000	0	0-0	-	6.28	6.38
1998 Seattle	AL	4	4	0	0	24.2	105	24	11	11	2	0	1	0	10	0	22	3	0	3	1	.750	0	0-0	-	3.85	4.01
1999 Seattle	AL	25	7	0	8	72.2	298	50	31	25	9	3	4	0	32	3	68	2	0	6	2	.750	0	0-2	3	2.65	3.10
2000 Seattle	AL	35	27	0	2	179.0	766	164	89	84	23	1	4	5	80	4	100	3	0	9	7	.563	0	0-0	4	4.09	4.22
2001 Seattle	AL	28	27	1	0	163.0	710	145	79	77	21	3	5	7	87	5	118	11	0	17	4	.810	0	0-0	-	4.33	4.25
2002 Seattle	AL	7	5	0	1	26.1	137	40	36	35	5	1	1	1	20	0	22	2	0	1	3	.250	0	0-0	-	9.89	11.96
2003 Kansas City	AL	10	8	0	0	47.2	214	47	29	28	8	2	1	2	26	2	32	2	1	1	2	.333	0	0-0	-	5.17	5.29
2004 TB-Phi		20	19	0	0	96.0	451	106	76	69	22	1	1	4	58	1	46	6	0	3	11	.214	0	0-0	-	6.64	6.47
2004 Tampa Bay	AL	10	9	0	0	47.0	222	49	39	35	8	0	1	3	27	0	25	3	0	2	5	.286	0	0-0	-	5.65	6.70
2004 Philadelphia	NL	10	10	0	0	49.0	229	57	37	34	14	1	0	1	31	1	21	3	0	1	6	.143	0	0-0	-	7.67	6.24
11 ML YEARS		162	112	1	17	720.2	3187	682	421	394	101	19	22	21	393	17	496	37	1	43	37	.538	0	0-2	7	4.73	4.92

Bobby Abreu

Bats: L **Throws:** R **Pos:** RF-159; PH-2 **Ht:** 6'0" **Wt:** 195 **Born:** 3/11/1974 **Age:** 31

		BATTING																BASERUNNING				AVERAGES		
Year Team	Lg	G	AB	H	2B	3B	HR	(Hm | Rd)	TB	R	RBI	RC	TBB	IBB	SO	HBP	SH	SF	SB	CS	SB%	GDP	Avg	OBP	Slg
1996 Houston	NL	15	22	5	1	0	0	(0 | 0)	6	1	1	1	2	0	3	0	0	0	0	0	-	1	.227	.292	.273
1997 Houston	NL	59	188	47	10	2	3	(3 | 0)	70	22	26	25	21	0	48	1	0	0	7	2	.78	0	.250	.329	.372
1998 Philadelphia	NL	151	497	155	29	6	17	(10 | 7)	247	68	74	101	84	14	133	0	4	4	19	10	.66	6	.312	.409	.497
1999 Philadelphia	NL	152	546	183	35	11	20	(13 | 7)	300	118	93	131	109	8	113	3	0	4	27	9	.75	13	.335	.446	.549
2000 Philadelphia	NL	154	576	182	42	10	25	(14 | 11)	319	103	79	130	100	9	116	1	0	3	28	8	.78	12	.316	.416	.554
2001 Philadelphia	NL	162	588	170	48	4	31	(13 | 18)	319	118	110	125	106	11	137	1	0	9	36	14	.72	13	.289	.393	.543
2002 Philadelphia	NL	157	572	176	50	6	20	(8 | 12)	298	102	85	112	104	9	117	3	0	6	31	12	.72	11	.308	.413	.521
2003 Philadelphia	NL	158	577	173	35	1	20	(11 | 9)	270	99	101	120	109	13	126	2	0	7	22	9	.71	13	.300	.409	.468
2004 Philadelphia	NL	159	574	173	47	1	30	(13 | 17)	312	118	105	139	127	10	116	5	0	7	40	5	.89	5	.301	.428	.544
9 ML YEARS		1167	4140	1264	297	41	166	(85 | 81)	2141	749	674	884	762	74	909	16	4	40	210	69	.75	74	.305	.412	.517

Jose Acevedo

Pitches: R **Bats:** R **Pos:** SP-27; RP-12 **Ht:** 6'0" **Wt:** 185 **Born:** 12/18/1977 **Age:** 27

		HOW MUCH HE PITCHED						WHAT HE GAVE UP											THE RESULTS					
Year Team	Lg	G	GS	CG	GF	IP	BFP	H	R	ER	HR	SH	SF	HB	TBB	IBB	SO	WP	Bk	W	L	Pct	ShO	Sv-Op	Hld	ERC	ERA
2001 Cincinnati	NL	18	18	0	0	96.0	417	101	61	58	17	6	3	3	34	2	68	4	0	5	7	.417	0	0-0	0	4.84	5.44
2002 Cincinnati	NL	6	5	0	0	23.2	112	28	21	19	8	2	0	2	12	0	14	1	0	4	2	.667	0	0-0	0	7.81	7.23
2003 Cincinnati	NL	5	4	1	1	27.0	103	17	8	8	3	1	2	1	6	1	23	1	0	2	0	1.000	0	0-0	0	1.75	2.67
2004 Cincinnati	NL	39	27	0	3	157.2	704	188	108	104	30	3	7	5	45	8	117	3	1	5	12	.294	0	0-0	2	5.36	5.94
4 ML YEARS		68	54	1	4	304.1	1336	334	198	189	58	12	12	11	97	11	222	9	1	16	21	.432	0	0-0	2	5.01	5.59

Mike Adams

Pitches: R **Bats:** R **Pos:** RP-46 **Ht:** 6'5" **Wt:** 190 **Born:** 7/29/1978 **Age:** 26

		HOW MUCH HE PITCHED						WHAT HE GAVE UP											THE RESULTS					
Year Team	Lg	G	GS	CG	GF	IP	BFP	H	R	ER	HR	SH	SF	HB	TBB	IBB	SO	WP	Bk	W	L	Pct	ShO	Sv-Op	Hld	ERC	ERA
2001 Ogden	R+	23	0	0	21	32.0	129	26	10	10	4	1	1	3	6	1	44	0	0	2	2	.500	0	12--	-	2.74	2.81
2002 Beloit	A	11	0	0	8	15.1	60	13	6	6	1	1	0	0	2	0	21	0	0	0	0	-	0	5--	-	2.09	3.52
2002 High Desert	A+	10	0	0	7	14.0	59	9	6	6	2	0	0	0	7	0	23	2	0	2	1	.667	0	5--	-	2.73	3.86
2002 Huntsville	AA	13	0	0	7	18.2	81	14	11	11	3	1	0	1	12	0	17	1	0	1	0	1.000	0	1--	-	4.30	5.30
2003 Huntsville	AA	45	2	0	34	74.1	318	58	30	26	6	4	0	2	33	1	83	3	2	3	7	.300	0	14--	-	2.93	3.15
2004 Indianapolis	AAA	10	2	0	1	31.0	116	23	10	9	3	1	0	2	4	0	37	0	0	2	0	1.000	0	0--	-	2.08	2.61
2004 Milwaukee	NL	46	0	0	13	53.0	225	50	21	20	5	5	2	2	14	2	39	2	0	2	3	.400	0	0-5	12	3.22	3.40

Russ Adams

Bats: L **Throws:** R **Pos:** SS-21; PH-4 **Ht:** 6'1" **Wt:** 180 **Born:** 8/30/1980 **Age:** 24

		BATTING																BASERUNNING				AVERAGES		
Year Team	Lg	G	AB	H	2B	3B	HR	(Hm | Rd)	TB	R	RBI	RC	TBB	IBB	SO	HBP	SH	SF	SB	CS	SB%	GDP	Avg	OBP	Slg
2002 Auburn	A-	30	113	40	7	3	0	(- | -)	53	25	16	28	24	0	11	1	1	2	13	1	.93	1	.354	.464	.469
2002 Dunedin	A+	37	147	34	4	2	1	(- | -)	45	23	12	16	18	0	17	2	1	1	5	2	.71	1	.231	.321	.306
2003 Dunedin	A+	68	258	72	9	5	3	(- | -)	100	50	16	42	38	1	27	6	5	3	9	2	.82	5	.279	.380	.388
2003 New Haven	AA	65	271	75	10	4	4	(- | -)	105	42	26	39	30	1	37	0	4	0	8	1	.89	5	.277	.349	.387
2004 Syracuse	AAA	122	483	139	37	3	5	(- | -)	197	58	54	70	45	1	62	5	2	5	6	2	.75	9	.288	.351	.408
2004 Toronto	AL	22	72	22	2	1	4	(1 | 3)	38	10	10	11	5	0	5	1	0	0	1	0	1.00	3	.306	.359	.528

Terry Adams

Pitches: R **Bats:** R **Pos:** RP-61   **Ht:** 6'3" **Wt:** 215 **Born:** 3/6/1973 **Age:** 32

Year Team	Lg	G	GS	CG	GF	IP	BFP	H	R	ER	HR	SH	SF	HB	TBB	IBB	SO	WP	Bk	W	L	Pct	ShO	Sv-Op	Hld	ERC	ERA
1995 Chicago	NL	18	0	0	7	18.0	86	22	15	13	0	0	0	0	10	1	15	1	0	1	1	.500	0	1-1	0	4.95	6.50
1996 Chicago	NL	69	0	0	22	101.0	423	84	36	33	6	7	3	1	49	6	78	5	1	3	6	.333	0	4-8	11	3.20	2.94
1997 Chicago	NL	74	0	0	39	74.0	341	91	43	38	3	1	2	1	40	6	64	6	0	2	9	.182	0	18-22	11	5.49	4.62
1998 Chicago	NL	63	0	0	15	72.2	330	72	39	35	7	3	3	1	41	3	73	4	3	7	7	.500	0	1-7	13	4.55	4.33
1999 Chicago	NL	52	0	0	38	65.0	277	60	33	29	9	1	3	0	28	2	57	6	0	6	3	.667	0	13-18	3	4.00	4.02
2000 Los Angeles	NL	66	0	0	18	84.1	369	80	42	33	6	3	0	0	39	0	56	5	0	6	9	.400	0	2-7	15	3.77	3.52
2001 Los Angeles	NL	43	22	0	10	166.1	708	172	84	80	9	6	0	3	54	1	141	7	2	12	8	.600	0	0-1	4	3.74	4.33
2002 Philadelphia	NL	46	19	0	10	136.2	590	132	76	66	9	10	2	3	58	5	96	8	0	7	9	.438	0	0-1	12	3.77	4.35
2003 Philadelphia	NL	66	0	0	16	68.0	284	68	22	20	1	3	2	2	23	4	51	4	0	1	4	.200	0	0-0	16	3.35	2.65
2004 Tor-Bos	AL	61	0	0	21	70.0	316	84	39	37	10	3	5	2	28	3	56	8	0	6	4	.600	0	3-6	3	5.63	4.76
2004 Toronto	AL	42	0	0	20	43.0	197	49	20	19	4	3	2	1	22	2	35	6	0	4	4	.500	0	3-6	2	5.27	3.98
2004 Boston	AL	19	0	0	1	27.0	119	35	19	18	6	0	3	1	6	1	21	2	0	2	0	1.000	0	0-0	1	6.16	6.00
10 ML YEARS		558	41	0	196	856.0	3724	865	429	384	60	37	20	13	370	31	687	54	6	51	60	.459	0	42-71	88	4.06	4.04

Jon Adkins

Pitches: R **Bats:** L **Pos:** RP-50   **Ht:** 6'0" **Wt:** 200 **Born:** 8/30/1977 **Age:** 27

Year Team	Lg	G	GS	CG	GF	IP	BFP	H	R	ER	HR	SH	SF	HB	TBB	IBB	SO	WP	Bk	W	L	Pct	ShO	Sv-Op	Hld	ERC	ERA
1999 Modesto	A+	26	15	0	2	102.0	460	113	65	54	6	4	6	9	30	1	93	8	0	9	5	.643	0	1--	-	4.17	4.76
2000 Athletics	R	4	2	0	1	15.0	68	15	6	5	1	4	0	1	3	0	17	0	0	1	1	.500	0	0--	-	3.03	3.00
2000 Sacramento	AAA	1	1	0	0	4.0	19	6	4	4	2	0	0	0	1	0	2	0	0	0	1	.000	0	0--	-	9.51	9.00
2000 Modesto	A+	9	7	1	0	49.2	203	41	17	10	1	1	2	1	17	0	38	2	0	5	2	.714	0	0--	-	2.51	1.81
2001 Midland	AA	24	24	1	0	137.1	590	147	71	68	9	5	2	9	36	1	74	0	0	8	8	.500	1	0--	-	3.94	4.46
2001 Sacramento	AAA	3	2	0	0	12.2	60	17	9	6	1	1	0	0	8	0	7	0	0	1	0	1.000	0	0--	-	7.11	4.26
2002 Sacramento	AAA	20	20	0	0	97.0	457	139	74	65	9	3	4	6	33	0	76	2	0	7	6	.538	0	0--	-	6.63	6.03
2002 Modesto	A+	1	1	0	0	6.2	32	11	7	6	0	1	0	1	1	0	4	1	0	0	1	.000	0	0--	-	6.79	8.10
2002 Charlotte	AAA	8	7	1	1	46.1	196	47	20	19	4	0	1	2	12	0	31	1	0	4	2	.667	0	0--	-	3.68	3.69
2003 Charlotte	AAA	26	19	1	2	122.2	518	119	65	54	11	2	7	7	34	1	59	2	1	7	8	.467	1	1--	-	3.57	3.96
2003 Chicago	AL	4	0	0	2	9.1	42	8	5	5	1	1	1	1	7	0	3	0	0	0	0	-	0	0-0	0	5.27	4.82
2004 Chicago	AL	50	0	0	19	62.0	271	75	35	32	13	3	1	1	20	3	44	1	0	2	3	.400	0	0-0	5	5.90	4.65
2 ML YEARS		54	0	0	21	71.1	313	83	40	37	14	4	2	2	27	3	47	1	0	2	3	.400	0	0-0	5	5.83	4.67

Jeremy Affeldt

Pitches: L **Bats:** L **Pos:** RP-30; SP-8   **Ht:** 6'4" **Wt:** 215 **Born:** 6/6/1979 **Age:** 26

Year Team	Lg	G	GS	CG	GF	IP	BFP	H	R	ER	HR	SH	SF	HB	TBB	IBB	SO	WP	Bk	W	L	Pct	ShO	Sv-Op	Hld	ERC	ERA
2004 Omaha*	AAA	4	0	0	4	4.0	14	2	0	0	0	0	0	0	0	0	5	0	0	0	0	-	0	3--	-	0.54	0.00
2002 Kansas City	AL	34	7	0	4	77.2	353	85	41	40	8	2	1	3	37	4	67	5	2	3	4	.429	0	0-1	1	4.97	4.64
2003 Kansas City	AL	36	18	0	5	126.0	533	126	58	55	12	2	5	5	38	1	98	2	1	7	6	.538	0	4-4	3	3.82	3.93
2004 Kansas City	AL	38	8	0	26	76.1	344	91	49	42	6	4	4	3	32	2	49	4	3	3	4	.429	0	13-17	0	5.26	4.95
3 ML YEARS		108	33	0	35	280.0	1230	302	148	137	26	8	10	11	107	7	214	11	6	13	14	.481	0	17-22	4	4.52	4.40

Chris Aguila

Bats: R **Throws:** R **Pos:** RF-14; PH-8; LF-6; PR-4   **Ht:** 5'11" **Wt:** 180 **Born:** 2/23/1979 **Age:** 26

Year Team	Lg	G	AB	H	2B	3B	HR	(Hm	Rd)	TB	R	RBI	RC	TBB	IBB	SO	HBP	SH	SF	SB	CS	SB%	GDP	Avg	OBP	Slg
1997 Marlins	R	46	157	34	7	0	1	(-	-)	44	12	17	14	21	0	49	1	2	2	2	1	.67	3	.217	.309	.280
1998 Marlins	R	51	171	46	12	3	4	(-	-)	76	29	29	25	19	1	49	2	1	0	6	2	.75	4	.269	.349	.444
1999 Kane County	A	122	430	105	21	7	15	(-	-)	185	74	78	58	40	2	127	9	3	2	14	4	.78	9	.244	.320	.430
2000 Brevard Cnty	A+	136	518	125	27	3	9	(-	-)	185	68	56	50	37	1	105	1	3	3	8	8	.50	11	.241	.292	.357
2001 Brevard Cnty	A+	73	272	75	15	3	10	(-	-)	126	44	34	39	21	1	54	2	0	4	8	4	.67	7	.276	.328	.463
2001 Portland	AA	64	241	62	16	1	4	(-	-)	92	25	29	26	18	1	50	3	3	4	5	7	.42	4	.257	.312	.382
2002 Portland	AA	130	429	126	28	4	6	(-	-)	180	62	46	66	48	0	101	4	5	2	14	8	.64	8	.294	.369	.420
2003 Marlins	R	1	4	3	0	0	1	(-	-)	6	1	2	2	0	0	1	0	0	0	0	0	-	0	.750	.750	1.500
2003 Carolina	AA	93	337	108	21	3	11	(-	-)	168	58	55	63	36	5	67	2	2	5	6	2	.75	6	.320	.384	.499
2004 Albuquerque	AAA	97	330	103	23	2	11	(-	-)	163	61	56	60	37	0	82	2	2	5	8	3	.73	8	.312	.380	.494
2004 Florida	NL	29	45	10	2	1	3	(1	2)	23	10	5	3	2	0	12	0	1	0	0	0	-	0	.222	.255	.511

Kurt Ainsworth

Pitches: R **Bats:** R **Pos:** SP-7   **Ht:** 6'3" **Wt:** 192 **Born:** 9/9/1978 **Age:** 26

Year Team	Lg	G	GS	CG	GF	IP	BFP	H	R	ER	HR	SH	SF	HB	TBB	IBB	SO	WP	Bk	W	L	Pct	ShO	Sv-Op	Hld	ERC	ERA
2004 Aberdeen*	A-	2	2	0	0	6.2	26	2	1	1	0	1	0	0	3	0	8	1	0	0	1	.000	0	0--	-	0.76	1.35
2004 Ottawa*	AAA	1	1	0	0	4.0	18	7	4	4	1	0	0	1	1	0	6	0	0	0	0	-	0	0--	-	12.24	9.00
2001 San Francisco	NL	2	0	0	2	2.0	12	3	3	3	1	0	0	1	2	0	3	0	0	0	0	-	0	0-0	0	16.26	13.50
2002 San Francisco	NL	6	4	0	2	25.2	108	22	7	6	1	2	0	1	12	0	15	1	0	1	2	.333	0	0-0	0	3.34	2.10
2003 SF-Bal		14	11	0	2	68.1	298	72	34	31	8	2	2	1	27	0	52	2	0	5	5	.500	0	0-0	0	4.55	4.08
2004 Baltimore	AL	7	7	0	0	30.2	151	39	34	33	6	2	2	5	20	0	24	4	0	0	1	.000	0	0-0	0	8.42	9.68
2003 San Francisco	NL	11	11	0	0	66.0	283	66	31	28	7	2	2	1	26	0	48	2	0	5	4	.556	0	0-0	0	4.19	3.82
2003 Baltimore	AL	3	0	0	2	2.1	15	6	3	3	1	0	0	0	1	0	4	0	0	0	1	.000	0	0-0	0	16.91	11.57
4 ML YEARS		29	22	0	4	126.2	569	136	78	73	16	6	4	8	61	0	90	7	0	6	8	.429	0	0-0	0	5.32	5.19

Manny Alexander

Bats: R Throws: R Pos: 2B-11; SS-7; PR-4; 3B-3   Ht: 5'10" Wt: 180 Born: 3/20/1971 Age: 34

Year Team	Lg	G	AB	H	2B	3B	HR	(Hm	Rd)	TB	R	RBI	RC	TBB	IBB	SO	HBP	SH	SF	SB	CS	SB%	GDP	Avg	OBP	Slg
2004 Oklahoma*	AAA	93	361	104	29	4	10	(-	-)	171	65	49	55	27	0	45	1	1	2	8	4	.67	6	.288	.338	.474
1992 Baltimore	AL	4	5	1	0	0	0	(0	0)	1	1	0	0	0	0	3	0	0	0	0	0	-	0	.200	.200	.200
1993 Baltimore	AL	3	0	0	0	0	0	(0	0)	0	1	0	0	0	0	0	0	0	0	0	0	-	0	-	-	-
1995 Baltimore	AL	94	242	57	9	1	3	(2	1)	77	35	23	24	20	0	30	2	4	0	11	4	.73	2	.236	.299	.318
1996 Baltimore	AL	54	68	7	0	0	0	(0	0)	7	6	4	0	3	0	27	0	2	0	3	3	.50	2	.103	.141	.103
1997 NYM-ChC	NL	87	248	66	12	4	3	(0	3)	95	37	22	30	17	3	54	3	3	1	13	1	.93	6	.266	.320	.383
1998 Chicago	NL	108	264	60	10	1	5	(1	4)	87	34	25	23	18	1	66	1	5	1	4	1	.80	6	.227	.278	.330
1999 Chicago	NL	90	177	48	11	2	0	(0	0)	63	17	15	20	10	0	38	0	1	1	4	0	1.00	1	.271	.309	.356
2000 Boston	AL	101	194	41	4	3	4	(1	3)	63	30	19	16	13	0	41	0	2	0	2	0	1.00	0	.211	.261	.325
2004 Texas	AL	21	21	5	2	0	0	(0	0)	7	3	3	3	1	0	7	0	0	0	0	0	-	0	.238	.273	.333
1997 New York	NL	54	149	37	9	3	2	(0	2)	58	26	15	18	9	1	38	1	1	1	11	0	1.00	3	.248	.294	.389
1997 Chicago	NL	33	99	29	3	1	1	(0	1)	37	11	7	12	8	2	16	2	2	0	2	1	.67	3	.293	.358	.374
9 ML YEARS		562	1219	285	48	11	15	(4	11)	400	164	111	116	82	4	266	6	17	3	37	9	.80	17	.234	.285	.328

Jason Alfaro

Bats: R Throws: R Pos: PH-4; SS-3   Ht: 5'10" Wt: 185 Born: 11/29/1977 Age: 27

Year Team	Lg	G	AB	H	2B	3B	HR	(Hm	Rd)	TB	R	RBI	RC	TBB	IBB	SO	HBP	SH	SF	SB	CS	SB%	GDP	Avg	OBP	Slg
1997 Astros	R	34	102	27	5	0	2	(-	-)	38	8	13	13	8	0	14	1	2	0	6	0	1.00	2	.265	.324	.373
1998 Astros	R	47	178	43	8	0	1	(-	-)	54	20	18	13	11	0	24	0	2	0	5	5	.50	5	.242	.286	.303
1999 Michigan	A	118	473	128	25	4	5	(-	-)	176	74	50	51	23	0	62	1	5	7	5	5	.50	10	.271	.302	.372
2000 Kissimmee	A+	117	460	115	20	1	7	(-	-)	158	58	41	40	25	1	63	1	5	5	2	6	.25	15	.250	.287	.343
2001 Round Rock	AA	87	284	69	16	2	2	(-	-)	95	26	29	20	7	1	40	2	3	2	2	1	.67	13	.243	.264	.335
2002 Round Rock	AA	124	455	143	36	2	16	(-	-)	231	71	74	84	50	6	75	11	0	3	11	9	.55	13	.314	.393	.508
2003 Round Rock	AA	22	81	12	3	0	0	(-	-)	15	6	9	0	5	0	20	0	0	0	1	0	1.00	1	.148	.198	.185
2003 New Orleans	AAA	105	361	107	20	4	9	(-	-)	162	45	49	53	30	1	53	3	4	2	2	3	.40	14	.296	.354	.449
2004 New Orleans	AAA	126	465	151	32	0	13	(-	-)	222	62	67	74	26	1	58	4	3	3	3	6	.33	11	.325	.363	.477
2004 Houston	NL	7	11	2	0	0	0	(0	0)	2	1	0	0	0	0	5	0	1	0	0	0	-	1	.182	.182	.182

Antonio Alfonseca

Pitches: R Bats: R Pos: RP-79   Ht: 6'5" Wt: 250 Born: 4/16/1972 Age: 33

Year Team	Lg	G	GS	CG	GF	IP	BFP	H	R	ER	HR	SH	SF	HB	TBB	IBB	SO	WP	Bk	W	L	Pct	ShO	Sv-Op	Hld	ERC	ERA
1997 Florida	NL	17	0	0	2	25.2	123	36	16	14	3	1	0	1	10	3	19	1	0	1	3	.250	0	0-2	0	6.41	4.91
1998 Florida	NL	58	0	0	27	70.2	316	75	32	32	10	7	6	3	33	9	46	1	0	4	6	.400	0	8-14	9	4.96	4.08
1999 Florida	NL	73	0	0	49	77.2	325	79	28	28	4	3	1	4	29	6	46	1	0	4	5	.444	0	21-25	5	3.96	3.24
2000 Florida	NL	68	0	0	62	70.0	311	82	35	33	7	3	1	1	24	3	47	0	2	5	6	.455	0	45-49	0	4.79	4.24
2001 Florida	NL	58	0	0	52	61.2	268	68	24	21	6	5	1	5	15	3	40	2	0	4	4	.500	0	28-34	0	4.24	3.06
2002 Chicago	NL	66	0	0	55	74.1	330	73	34	33	5	4	3	3	36	3	61	1	0	2	5	.286	0	19-28	0	4.12	4.00
2003 Chicago	NL	60	0	0	17	66.1	296	76	43	43	7	4	1	2	27	3	51	0	0	3	1	.750	0	0-4	9	5.05	5.83
2004 Atlanta	NL	79	0	0	11	73.2	313	71	24	21	5	6	1	0	28	5	45	5	0	3	4	.600	0	0-1	13	3.47	2.57
8 ML YEARS		479	0	0	275	520.0	2282	560	236	225	47	33	14	19	202	35	355	11	2	29	34	.460	0	121-157	36	4.44	3.89

Edgardo Alfonzo

Bats: R Throws: R Pos: 3B-128; PH-9; 2B-5   Ht: 5'11" Wt: 187 Born: 11/8/1973 Age: 31

Year Team	Lg	G	AB	H	2B	3B	HR	(Hm	Rd)	TB	R	RBI	RC	TBB	IBB	SO	HBP	SH	SF	SB	CS	SB%	GDP	Avg	OBP	Slg
1995 New York	NL	101	335	93	13	5	4	(0	4)	128	26	41	37	12	1	37	1	4	4	1	1	.50	7	.278	.301	.382
1996 New York	NL	123	368	96	15	2	4	(2	2)	127	36	40	38	25	2	56	0	9	5	2	0	1.00	8	.261	.304	.345
1997 New York	NL	151	518	163	27	2	10	(4	6)	224	84	72	91	63	0	56	5	8	5	11	6	.65	4	.315	.391	.432
1998 New York	NL	144	557	155	28	2	17	(8	9)	238	94	78	85	65	1	75	3	2	3	8	3	.73	11	.278	.355	.427
1999 New York	NL	158	628	191	41	1	27	(11	16)	315	123	108	121	85	2	85	3	1	9	9	2	.82	14	.304	.385	.502
2000 New York	NL	150	544	176	40	2	25	(13	12)	295	109	94	122	95	1	70	5	0	6	3	2	.60	12	.324	.425	.542
2001 New York	NL	124	457	111	22	0	17	(6	11)	184	64	49	62	51	0	62	5	1	5	5	0	1.00	7	.243	.322	.403
2002 New York	NL	135	490	151	26	1	16	(8	8)	225	78	56	90	62	8	55	7	0	3	6	0	1.00	5	.308	.391	.459
2003 San Francisco	NL	142	514	133	25	2	13	(6	7)	201	56	81	76	58	4	41	4	3	7	5	2	.71	14	.259	.334	.391
2004 San Francisco	NL	139	519	150	26	1	11	(8	3)	211	66	77	75	46	2	40	5	2	4	1	1	.50	16	.289	.350	.407
10 ML YEARS		1367	4930	1419	263	17	144	(66	78)	2148	736	696	797	562	21	579	38	30	51	51	17	.75	98	.288	.362	.436

Chad Allen

Bats: R Throws: R Pos: LF-12; DH-5; PH-5; RF-1   Ht: 6'1" Wt: 195 Born: 2/6/1975 Age: 30

Year Team	Lg	G	AB	H	2B	3B	HR	(Hm	Rd)	TB	R	RBI	RC	TBB	IBB	SO	HBP	SH	SF	SB	CS	SB%	GDP	Avg	OBP	Slg
2004 Oklahoma*	AAA	93	386	138	28	3	7	(-	-)	193	75	70	77	31	2	72	5	0	5	18	2	.90	9	.358	.407	.500
1999 Minnesota	AL	137	481	133	21	3	10	(4	6)	190	69	46	61	37	1	89	2	1	2	14	7	.67	10	.277	.330	.395
2000 Minnesota	AL	15	50	15	3	0	0	(0	0)	18	2	7	6	3	0	14	1	0	1	0	2	.00	1	.300	.345	.360
2001 Minnesota	AL	57	175	46	13	2	4	(1	3)	75	20	20	23	19	1	37	0	0	1	1	2	.33	7	.263	.333	.429
2002 Cleveland	AL	5	10	1	1	0	0	(0	0)	2	0	0	0	0	0	2	0	1	0	0	0	-	1	.100	.100	.200
2003 Florida	NL	12	24	5	1	1	0	(0	0)	8	2	0	0	0	0	5	1	0	0	0	0	-	1	.208	.240	.333
2004 Texas	AL	20	58	14	4	1	0	(0	0)	20	4	6	2	2	0	13	0	2	1	0	1	.00	1	.241	.262	.345
6 ML YEARS		246	798	214	43	7	14	(5	9)	313	97	79	92	61	2	160	4	4	5	15	12	.56	21	.268	.321	.392

Armando Almanza

Pitches: L **Bats:** L **Pos:** RP-13 **Ht:** 6'3" **Wt:** 240 **Born:** 10/26/1972 **Age:** 32

Year Team	Lg	G	GS	CG	GF	IP	BFP	H	R	ER	HR	SH	SF	HB	TBB	IBB	SO	WP	Bk	W	L	Pct	ShO	Sv-Op	Hld	ERC	ERA
2004 Greenville*	AA	5	2	0	0	6.2	31	12	6	6	0	0	0	0	3	0	5	1	0	0	3	.000	0	0- -	-	9.29	8.10
2004 Richmond*	AAA	20	0	0	4	25.1	116	26	13	10	1	0	0	0	15	0	20	2	0	1	1	.500	0	1- -	-	4.45	3.55
1999 Florida	NL	14	0	0	2	15.2	64	8	4	3	1	1	1	1	9	1	20	0	1	0	1	.000	0	0-0	3	2.09	1.72
2000 Florida	NL	67	0	0	8	46.1	216	38	27	25	3	2	2	2	43	6	46	1	0	4	2	.667	0	0-4	13	4.79	4.86
2001 Florida	NL	52	0	0	8	41.0	178	34	24	22	8	1	3	0	26	1	45	2	0	2	2	.500	0	0-2	12	4.73	4.83
2002 Florida	NL	51	0	0	10	45.2	191	36	22	22	8	3	3	0	23	1	57	2	1	3	2	.600	0	2-4	12	3.83	4.34
2003 Florida	NL	51	0	0	15	50.1	230	59	37	34	10	1	3	2	25	2	49	2	1	5	4	.444	0	0-2	6	6.42	6.08
2004 Atlanta	NL	13	0	0	5	11.2	54	9	8	8	3	0	1	1	7	2	13	0	1	1	1	.500	0	0-0	4	4.48	6.17
6 ML YEARS		248	0	0	48	210.2	933	184	122	114	33	8	13	6	133	13	230	7	4	14	13	.519	0	2-12	46	4.72	4.87

Carlos Almanzar

Pitches: R **Bats:** R **Pos:** RP-67 **Ht:** 6'2" **Wt:** 200 **Born:** 11/6/1973 **Age:** 31

Year Team	Lg	G	GS	CG	GF	IP	BFP	H	R	ER	HR	SH	SF	HB	TBB	IBB	SO	WP	Bk	W	L	Pct	ShO	Sv-Op	Hld	ERC	ERA
1997 Toronto	AL	4	0	0	2	3.1	12	1	1	1	1	0	0	0	1	0	4	0	0	0	1	.000	0	0-0	0	1.39	2.70
1998 Toronto	AL	25	0	0	8	28.2	129	34	18	17	4	1	0	1	8	2	20	0	0	2	2	.500	0	0-3	1	4.85	5.34
1999 San Diego	NL	28	0	0	11	37.1	173	48	32	31	6	2	1	3	15	2	30	2	0	0	0	-	0	0-0	0	6.54	7.47
2000 San Diego	NL	62	0	0	11	69.2	308	73	35	34	12	2	3	4	25	2	56	2	0	4	5	.444	0	0-3	8	4.83	4.39
2001 New York	AL	10	0	0	7	10.2	46	14	4	4	2	1	1	0	2	1	6	0	0	1	0	1.000	0	0-2	5	5.63	3.38
2002 Cincinnati	NL	8	1	0	4	11.2	45	6	4	3	0	0	2	0	5	1	7	1	0	0	1	.000	0	0-0	0	1.26	2.31
2004 Texas	AL	67	0	0	18	72.2	298	66	32	30	8	2	3	4	19	4	44	1	0	7	3	.700	0	0-2	20	3.28	3.72
7 ML YEARS		204	1	0	61	234.0	1011	242	126	120	33	8	10	12	75	12	167	6	0	13	13	.500	0	0-10	29	4.36	4.62

Roberto Alomar

Bats: B **Throws:** R **Pos:** 2B-41; PH-10; DH-6; PR-1 **Ht:** 6'0" **Wt:** 185 **Born:** 2/5/1968 **Age:** 37

Year Team	Lg	G	AB	H	2B	3B	HR	(Hm	Rd)	TB	R	RBI	RC	TBB	IBB	SO	HBP	SH	SF	SB	CS	SB%	GDP	Avg	OBP	Slg
2004 Tucson*	AAA	2	5	2	0	0	0	(-	-)	2	2	0	1	1	0	2	0	0	0	0	0	-	0	.400	.500	.400
1988 San Diego	NL	143	545	145	24	6	9	(5	4)	208	84	41	68	47	5	83	3	16	0	24	6	.80	15	.266	.328	.382
1989 San Diego	NL	158	623	184	27	1	7	(3	4)	234	82	56	85	53	4	76	1	17	8	42	17	.71	10	.295	.347	.376
1990 San Diego	NL	147	586	168	27	5	6	(4	2)	223	80	60	76	48	1	72	2	5	5	24	7	.77	16	.287	.340	.381
1991 Toronto	AL	161	637	188	41	11	9	(6	3)	278	88	69	106	57	3	86	4	16	5	53	11	.83	5	.295	.354	.436
1992 Toronto	AL	152	571	177	27	8	8	(5	3)	244	105	76	109	87	5	52	5	6	2	49	9	.84	8	.310	.405	.427
1993 Toronto	AL	153	589	192	35	6	17	(8	9)	290	109	93	121	80	5	67	5	4	5	55	15	.79	13	.326	.408	.492
1994 Toronto	AL	107	392	120	25	4	8	(4	4)	177	78	38	67	51	2	41	2	7	3	19	8	.70	14	.306	.386	.452
1995 Toronto	AL	130	517	155	24	7	13	(7	6)	232	71	66	84	47	3	45	0	6	7	30	3	.91	16	.300	.354	.449
1996 Baltimore	AL	153	588	193	43	4	22	(14	8)	310	132	94	126	90	10	65	1	8	12	17	6	.74	14	.328	.411	.527
1997 Baltimore	AL	112	412	137	23	2	14	(10	4)	206	64	60	78	40	2	43	3	7	7	9	3	.75	10	.333	.390	.500
1998 Baltimore	AL	147	588	166	36	1	14	(7	7)	246	86	56	87	59	3	70	2	3	5	18	5	.78	11	.282	.347	.418
1999 Cleveland	AL	159	563	182	40	3	24	(12	12)	300	138	120	131	99	3	96	7	12	13	37	6	.86	13	.323	.422	.533
2000 Cleveland	AL	155	610	189	40	2	19	(8	11)	290	111	89	111	64	4	82	6	11	6	39	4	.91	19	.310	.378	.475
2001 Cleveland	AL	157	575	193	34	12	20	(7	13)	311	113	100	130	80	5	71	4	9	9	30	6	.83	9	.336	.415	.541
2002 New York	NL	149	590	157	24	4	11	(4	7)	222	73	53	75	57	4	83	1	6	1	16	4	.80	12	.266	.331	.376
2003 NYM-CWS		140	516	133	28	2	5	(3	2)	180	76	39	65	59	3	77	3	12	8	12	2	.86	17	.258	.333	.349
2004 Ari-CWS		56	171	45	6	2	4	(4	0)	67	18	24	24	14	0	31	1	3	1	0	2	.00	4	.263	.321	.392
2003 New York	NL	73	263	69	17	1	2	(1	1)	94	34	22	36	29	2	40	2	4	4	6	0	1.00	8	.262	.336	.357
2003 Chicago	AL	67	253	64	11	1	3	(2	1)	86	42	17	29	30	1	37	1	8	4	6	2	.75	9	.253	.330	.340
2004 Arizona	NL	38	110	34	5	2	3	(3	0)	52	14	16	18	12	0	18	1	2	0	0	2	.00	2	.309	.382	.473
2004 Chicago	AL	18	61	11	1	0	1	(1	0)	15	4	8	6	2	0	13	0	1	1	0	0	-	2	.180	.203	.246
17 ML YEARS		2379	9073	2724	504	80	210	(111	99)	4018	1508	1134	1543	1032	62	1140	50	148	97	474	114	.81	206	.300	.371	.443

Sandy Alomar Jr.

Bats: R **Throws:** R **Pos:** C-49; DH-1; PH-1 **Ht:** 6'5" **Wt:** 235 **Born:** 6/18/1966 **Age:** 39

Year Team	Lg	G	AB	H	2B	3B	HR	(Hm	Rd)	TB	R	RBI	RC	TBB	IBB	SO	HBP	SH	SF	SB	CS	SB%	GDP	Avg	OBP	Slg
1988 San Diego	NL	1	1	0	0	0	0	(0	0)	0	0	0	0	0	0	1	0	0	0	0	0	-	0	.000	.000	.000
1989 San Diego	NL	7	19	4	1	0	1	(1	0)	8	1	6	2	3	1	3	0	0	0	0	0	-	1	.211	.318	.421
1990 Cleveland	AL	132	445	129	26	2	9	(5	4)	186	60	66	60	25	2	46	2	5	6	4	1	.80	10	.290	.326	.418
1991 Cleveland	AL	51	184	40	9	0	0	(0	0)	49	10	7	10	8	1	24	4	2	1	0	4	.00	4	.217	.264	.266
1992 Cleveland	AL	89	299	75	16	0	2	(1	1)	97	22	26	26	13	3	32	5	3	0	3	3	.50	7	.251	.293	.324
1993 Cleveland	AL	64	215	58	7	1	6	(3	3)	85	24	32	28	11	0	28	6	1	4	3	1	.75	3	.270	.318	.395
1994 Cleveland	AL	80	292	84	15	1	14	(4	10)	143	44	43	48	25	2	31	2	0	1	8	4	.67	7	.288	.347	.490
1995 Cleveland	AL	66	203	61	6	0	10	(4	6)	97	32	35	30	7	0	26	3	4	1	3	1	.75	8	.300	.332	.478
1996 Cleveland	AL	127	418	110	23	0	11	(3	8)	166	53	50	44	19	0	42	3	2	2	1	0	1.00	20	.263	.299	.397
1997 Cleveland	AL	125	451	146	37	0	21	(9	12)	246	63	83	78	19	2	48	3	6	1	0	2	.00	16	.324	.354	.545
1998 Cleveland	AL	117	409	96	26	2	6	(3	3)	144	45	44	33	18	0	45	3	5	3	0	3	.00	15	.235	.270	.352
1999 Cleveland	AL	37	137	42	13	0	6	(4	2)	73	19	25	23	4	0	23	0	1	2	0	1	.00	1	.307	.322	.533
2000 Cleveland	AL	97	356	103	16	2	7	(5	2)	144	44	42	45	16	1	41	4	4	4	2	2	.50	9	.289	.324	.404
2001 Chicago	AL	70	220	54	8	1	4	(1	3)	76	17	21	20	12	1	17	2	3	2	1	2	.33	6	.245	.288	.345
2002 CWS-Col		89	283	79	14	1	7	(5	2)	116	29	37	30	9	0	33	1	1	2	0	0	-	11	.279	.302	.410
2003 Chicago	AL	75	194	52	12	0	5	(3	2)	79	22	26	21	4	0	17	0	5	1	0	0	-	4	.268	.281	.407
2004 Chicago	AL	50	146	35	4	0	2	(1	1)	45	15	14	12	11	2	13	2	3	2	0	0	-	4	.240	.298	.308
2002 Chicago	AL	51	167	48	10	1	7	(5	2)	81	21	25	22	5	0	14	1	1	2	0	0	-	5	.287	.309	.485
2002 Colorado	NL	38	116	31	4	0	0	(0	0)	35	8	12	8	4	0	19	0	0	0	0	0	-	6	.267	.292	.302
17 ML YEARS		1277	4272	1168	233	10	111	(52	59)	1754	500	557	510	204	15	470	40	45	32	25	24	.51	126	.273	.310	.411

Moises Alou

Bats: R **Throws:** R **Pos:** LF-154; DH-1; PH-1   **Ht:** 6'3" **Wt:** 220 **Born:** 7/3/1966 **Age:** 38

								BATTING											BASERUNNING				AVERAGES		
Year Team	Lg	G	AB	H	2B	3B	HR	(Hm | Rd)	TB	R	RBI	RC	TBB	IBB	SO	HBP	SH	SF	SB	CS	SB%	GDP	Avg	OBP	Slg
1990 Pit-Mon	NL	16	20	4	0	1	0	(0 | 0)	6	4	0	1	0	0	3	0	1	0	0	0	-	1	.200	.200	.300
1992 Montreal	NL	115	341	96	28	2	9	(6 | 3)	155	53	56	53	25	0	46	1	5	5	16	2	.89	5	.282	.328	.455
1993 Montreal	NL	136	482	138	29	6	18	(10 | 8)	233	70	85	79	38	9	53	5	3	7	17	6	.74	9	.286	.340	.483
1994 Montreal	NL	107	422	143	31	5	22	(9 | 13)	250	81	78	92	42	10	63	2	0	5	7	6	.54	7	.339	.397	.592
1995 Montreal	NL	93	344	94	22	0	14	(4 | 10)	158	48	58	52	29	6	56	9	0	4	4	3	.57	9	.273	.342	.459
1996 Montreal	NL	143	540	152	28	2	21	(14 | 7)	247	87	96	81	49	7	83	2	0	7	9	4	.69	15	.281	.339	.457
1997 Florida	NL	150	538	157	29	5	23	(12 | 11)	265	88	115	97	70	9	85	4	0	7	9	5	.64	13	.292	.373	.493
1998 Houston	NL	159	584	182	34	5	38	(19 | 19)	340	104	124	130	84	11	87	5	0	6	11	3	.79	14	.312	.399	.582
2000 Houston	NL	126	454	161	28	2	30	(17 | 13)	283	82	114	104	52	4	45	2	0	9	3	3	.50	21	.355	.416	.623
2001 Houston	NL	136	513	170	31	1	27	(15 | 12)	284	79	108	104	57	14	57	3	0	8	5	1	.83	18	.331	.396	.554
2002 Chicago	NL	132	484	133	21	1	15	(7 | 8)	203	50	61	59	47	4	61	0	0	3	8	0	1.00	15	.275	.337	.419
2003 Chicago	NL	151	565	158	35	1	22	(14 | 8)	261	83	91	94	63	7	67	7	0	3	3	1	.75	16	.280	.357	.462
2004 Chicago	NL	155	601	176	36	3	39	**(29** | 10)	335	106	106	114	68	2	80	0	0	6	3	0	1.00	12	.293	.361	.557
1990 Pittsburgh	NL	2	5	1	0	0	0	(0 | 0)	1	0	0	0	0	0	0	0	0	0	0	0	-	1	.200	.200	.200
1990 Montreal	NL	14	15	3	0	1	0	(0 | 0)	5	4	0	1	0	0	3	0	1	0	0	0	-	0	.200	.200	.333
13 ML YEARS		1619	5888	1764	354	34	278	(156 | 122)	3020	935	1092	1060	624	83	786	40	9	70	95	34	.74	155	.300	.367	.513

Abe Alvarez

Pitches: L **Bats:** L **Pos:** SP-1   **Ht:** 6'2" **Wt:** 190 **Born:** 10/17/1982 **Age:** 22

		HOW MUCH HE PITCHED						WHAT HE GAVE UP											THE RESULTS						
Year Team	Lg	G	GS	CG	GF	IP	BFP	H	R	ER	HR	SH	SF	HB	TBB	IBB	SO	WP	Bk	W	L	Pct	ShO	Sv-Op	Hld	ERC	ERA
2003 Lowell	A-	9	9	0	0	19.0	68	9	2	0	0	0	1	0	2	1	19	0	0	0	0	-	0	0--	-	0.61	0.00
2004 Portland	AA	26	26	0	0	135.1	562	133	65	55	13	4	3	5	32	0	108	2	0	10	9	.526	0	0--	-	3.48	3.66
2004 Boston	AL	1	1	0	0	5.0	25	8	5	5	2	0	0	0	5	0	2	0	0	0	1	.000	0	0-0	0	15.00	9.00

Tony Alvarez

Bats: R **Throws:** R **Pos:** RF-9; PH-9; CF-4; LF-3; PR-2   **Ht:** 6'1" **Wt:** 200 **Born:** 5/10/1979 **Age:** 26

								BATTING											BASERUNNING				AVERAGES		
Year Team	Lg	G	AB	H	2B	3B	HR	(Hm	Rd)	TB	R	RBI	RC	TBB	IBB	SO	HBP	SH	SF	SB	CS	SB%	GDP	Avg	OBP	Slg
1998 Pirates	R	50	190	47	13	1	4	(-	-)	74	27	29	24	13	1	24	3	1	5	19	1	.95	4	.247	.299	.389
1999 Williamsport	A-	58	196	63	14	1	7	(-	-)	100	44	45	45	21	1	36	16	1	6	38	9	.81	2	.321	.418	.510
2000 Hickory	A	118	442	126	25	4	15	(-	-)	204	75	77	72	39	2	93	15	0	8	52	21	.71	8	.285	.357	.462
2001 Lynchburg	A+	25	93	32	4	0	2	(-	-)	42	10	11	16	7	0	11	0	0	0	7	3	.70	2	.344	.390	.452
2001 Altoona	AA	67	254	81	16	1	6	(-	-)	117	34	25	38	9	0	30	7	2	0	17	11	.61	6	.319	.359	.461
2002 Altoona	AA	125	507	161	37	1	15	(-	-)	245	79	59	83	27	1	71	9	2	3	29	18	.62	6	.318	.361	.483
2003 Nashville	AAA	106	349	104	27	3	9	(-	-)	164	50	53	57	28	1	69	9	1	5	22	9	.71	8	.298	.361	.470
2004 Nashville	AAA	99	335	97	12	1	14	(-	-)	153	59	48	54	35	0	63	6	0	2	19	12	.61	6	.290	.365	.457
2002 Pittsburgh	NL	14	26	8	2	0	1	(0	1)	13	6	2	4	3	0	5	0	1	0	1	0	1.00	0	.308	.379	.500
2004 Pittsburgh	NL	24	38	8	2	0	1	(1	0)	13	5	8	5	4	0	7	1	0	2	0	0	-	1	.211	.289	.342
2 ML YEARS		38	64	16	4	0	2	(1	1)	26	11	10	9	7	0	12	1	1	2	1	0	1.00	1	.250	.324	.406

Wilson Alvarez

Pitches: L **Bats:** L **Pos:** RP-25; SP-15   **Ht:** 6'1" **Wt:** 245 **Born:** 3/24/1970 **Age:** 35

		HOW MUCH HE PITCHED						WHAT HE GAVE UP											THE RESULTS						
Year Team	Lg	G	GS	CG	GF	IP	BFP	H	R	ER	HR	SH	SF	HB	TBB	IBB	SO	WP	Bk	W	L	Pct	ShO	Sv-Op	Hld	ERC	ERA
1989 Texas	AL	1	1	0	0	0.0	5	3	3	3	2	0	0	0	2	0	0	0	0	0	1	.000	0	0-0	0	-	-
1991 Chicago	AL	10	9	2	0	56.1	237	47	26	22	9	3	1	0	29	0	32	2	0	3	2	.600	1	0-0	0	4.09	3.51
1992 Chicago	AL	34	9	0	4	100.1	455	103	64	58	12	3	4	4	65	2	66	2	0	5	3	.625	0	1-1	3	5.61	5.20
1993 Chicago	AL	31	31	1	0	207.2	877	168	78	68	14	**13**	6	7	**122**	8	155	2	1	15	8	.652	1	0-0	0	3.69	2.95
1994 Chicago	AL	24	24	2	0	161.2	682	147	72	62	16	6	3	0	62	1	108	3	0	12	8	.600	1	0-0	0	3.49	3.45
1995 Chicago	AL	29	29	3	0	175.0	769	171	96	84	21	6	5	2	93	4	118	1	2	8	11	.421	0	0-0	0	4.66	4.32
1996 Chicago	AL	35	35	0	0	217.1	946	216	106	102	21	5	2	4	97	3	181	2	0	15	10	.600	0	0-0	0	4.26	4.22
1997 CWS-SF		33	33	2	0	212.0	896	180	97	82	18	10	6	4	91	4	179	5	1	13	11	.542	1	0-0	0	3.30	3.48
1998 Tampa Bay	AL	25	25	0	0	142.2	624	130	78	75	18	1	2	6	68	0	107	4	0	6	14	.300	0	0-0	0	4.30	4.73
1999 Tampa Bay	AL	28	28	1	0	160.0	703	159	92	75	22	3	3	6	79	1	128	3	0	9	9	.500	0	0-0	0	4.87	4.22
2002 Tampa Bay	AL	23	10	0	3	75.0	338	80	47	44	13	2	3	4	36	3	56	2	0	2	3	.400	0	1-1	2	5.48	5.28
2003 Los Angeles	AL	21	12	1	2	95.0	377	80	27	25	5	2	1	5	23	1	82	1	0	6	2	.750	0	1-1	1	2.61	2.37
2004 Los Angeles	NL	40	15	0	6	120.2	499	109	56	54	12	11	5	5	31	2	102	1	0	7	6	.538	0	1-2	2	3.13	4.03
1997 Chicago	AL	22	22	2	0	145.2	613	126	61	49	9	6	5	3	55	1	110	4	0	9	8	.529	1	0-0	0	3.05	3.03
1997 San Francisco	NL	11	11	0	0	66.1	283	54	36	33	9	4	1	1	36	3	69	1	1	4	3	.571	0	0-0	0	3.86	4.48
13 ML YEARS		334	261	12	15	1723.2	7408	1593	842	754	183	65	41	50	798	29	1314	28	4	101	88	.534	5	4-5	8	4.06	3.94

Alfredo Amezaga

Bats: B **Throws:** R **Pos:** SS-32; 3B-27; 2B-16; PR-6; PH-5   **Ht:** 5'10" **Wt:** 165 **Born:** 1/16/1978 **Age:** 27

								BATTING											BASERUNNING				AVERAGES		
Year Team	Lg	G	AB	H	2B	3B	HR	(Hm	Rd)	TB	R	RBI	RC	TBB	IBB	SO	HBP	SH	SF	SB	CS	SB%	GDP	Avg	OBP	Slg
2004 Salt Lake*	AAA	32	135	35	5	2	2	(-	-)	50	15	14	18	13	1	18	1	1	0	7	0	1.00	1	.259	.329	.370
2002 Anaheim	AL	12	13	7	2	0	0	(0	0)	9	3	2	6	0	0	1	0	0	0	1	0	1.00	1	.538	.538	.692
2003 Anaheim	AL	37	105	22	3	2	2	(0	2)	35	15	7	7	9	0	23	1	5	0	2	2	.50	2	.210	.278	.333
2004 Anaheim	AL	73	93	15	2	0	2	(0	2)	23	12	11	5	3	0	24	3	6	0	3	2	.60	2	.161	.212	.247
3 ML YEARS		122	211	44	7	2	4	(0	4)	67	30	20	18	12	0	48	4	11	0	6	4	.60	5	.209	.264	.318

Brian Anderson

Pitches: L **Bats:** R **Pos:** SP-26; RP-9 **Ht:** 6'1" **Wt:** 183 **Born:** 4/26/1972 **Age:** 33

			HOW MUCH HE PITCHED						WHAT HE GAVE UP										THE RESULTS						
Year Team	Lg	G	GS	CG	GF	IP	BFP	H	R	ER	HR	SH	SF	HB	TBB	IBB	SO	WP	Bk	W	L	Pct	ShO	Sv-Op	Hld	ERC	ERA
1993 California	AL	4	1	0	3	11.1	45	11	5	5	1	0	0	0	2	0	4	0	0	0	0	-	0	0-0	0	3.08	3.97
1994 California	AL	18	18	0	0	101.2	441	120	63	59	13	3	6	5	27	0	47	5	5	7	5	.583	0	0-0	0	5.05	5.22
1995 California	AL	18	17	1	0	99.2	433	110	66	65	24	5	5	3	30	2	45	1	3	6	8	.429	0	0-0	0	5.37	5.87
1996 Cleveland	AL	10	9	0	0	51.1	215	58	29	28	9	2	3	0	14	1	21	2	0	3	1	.750	0	0-0	1	4.96	4.91
1997 Cleveland	AL	8	8	0	0	48.0	199	55	28	25	7	0	5	0	11	0	22	1	0	4	2	.667	0	0-0	0	4.71	4.69
1998 Arizona	NL	32	32	2	0	208.0	845	221	100	100	39	8	3	4	24	2	95	3	6	12	13	.480	1	0-0	0	3.99	4.33
1999 Arizona	NL	31	19	2	4	130.0	549	144	69	66	18	4	0	1	28	3	75	0	2	8	2	.800	1	1-2	1	4.23	4.57
2000 Arizona	NL	33	32	2	0	213.1	876	226	101	96	38	6	6	3	39	7	104	1	4	11	7	.611	0	0-0	0	4.15	4.05
2001 Arizona	NL	29	22	1	1	133.1	571	156	93	77	25	7	4	1	30	2	55	2	1	4	9	.308	0	0-1	0	5.00	5.20
2002 Arizona	NL	35	24	0	1	156.0	659	174	86	83	23	6	8	1	32	3	81	2	5	6	11	.353	0	0-0	1	4.28	4.79
2003 Cle-KC	AL	32	31	2	0	197.2	821	212	110	83	27	4	12	4	43	3	87	3	1	14	11	.560	1	0-0	0	4.14	3.78
2004 Kansas City	AL	35	26	2	2	166.0	745	217	123	104	33	5	7	1	53	4	70	2	0	6	12	.333	1	0-0	2	6.36	5.64
2003 Cleveland	AL	25	24	0	0	148.0	623	162	88	61	21	3	10	4	32	3	72	2	1	9	10	.474	1	0-0	0	4.29	3.71
2003 Kansas City	AL	7	7	2	0	49.2	198	50	22	22	6	1	2	0	11	0	15	1	0	5	1	.833	1	0-0	0	3.72	3.99
12 ML YEARS		285	239	12	11	1516.1	6399	1704	873	791	257	50	59	23	333	27	706	22	27	81	81	.500	4	1-3	5	4.63	4.69

Garret Anderson

Bats: L **Throws:** L **Pos:** CF-94; DH-19; PH-2 **Ht:** 6'3" **Wt:** 228 **Born:** 6/30/1972 **Age:** 33

					BATTING															BASERUNNING				AVERAGES		
Year Team	Lg	G	AB	H	2B	3B	HR	(Hm	Rd)	TB	R	RBI	RC	TBB	IBB	SO	HBP	SH	SF	SB	CS	SB%	GDP	Avg	OBP	Slg
2004 R Cucamnga*	A+	3	9	4	0	0	1	(-	-)	7	1	1	3	1	0	1	0	0	0	0	0	-	0	.444	.500	.778
1994 California	AL	5	13	5	0	0	0	(0	0)	5	0	1	2	0	0	2	0	0	0	0	0	-	0	.385	.385	.385
1995 California	AL	106	374	120	19	1	16	(7	9)	189	50	69	63	19	4	65	1	2	4	6	2	.75	8	.321	.352	.505
1996 California	AL	150	607	173	33	2	12	(7	5)	246	79	72	68	27	5	84	0	5	3	7	9	.44	22	.285	.314	.405
1997 Anaheim	AL	154	624	189	36	3	8	(5	3)	255	76	92	80	30	6	70	2	1	5	10	4	.71	20	.303	.334	.409
1998 Anaheim	AL	156	622	183	41	7	15	(4	11)	283	62	79	88	29	8	80	1	3	3	8	3	.73	13	.294	.325	.455
1999 Anaheim	AL	157	620	188	36	2	21	(10	11)	291	88	80	92	34	8	81	0	0	6	3	4	.43	15	.303	.336	.469
2000 Anaheim	AL	159	647	185	40	3	35	(20	15)	336	92	117	95	24	5	87	0	1	9	7	6	.54	21	.286	.307	.519
2001 Anaheim	AL	161	672	194	39	2	28	(13	15)	321	83	123	97	27	4	100	0	0	5	13	6	.68	12	.289	.314	.478
2002 Anaheim	AL	158	638	195	56	3	29	(13	16)	344	93	123	108	30	11	80	0	0	10	6	4	.60	11	.306	.332	.539
2003 Anaheim	AL	159	638	201	49	4	29	(12	17)	345	80	116	114	31	10	83	0	0	4	6	3	.67	15	.315	.345	.541
2004 Anaheim	AL	112	442	133	20	1	14	(4	10)	197	57	75	70	29	6	75	1	0	3	2	1	.67	3	.301	.343	.446
11 ML YEARS		1477	5897	1766	369	28	207	(95	112)	2812	760	947	877	280	67	807	5	12	52	68	42	.62	140	.299	.329	.477

Jason Anderson

Pitches: R **Bats:** L **Pos:** RP-1 **Ht:** 6'0" **Wt:** 170 **Born:** 6/9/1979 **Age:** 26

				HOW MUCH HE PITCHED						WHAT HE GAVE UP										THE RESULTS						
Year Team	Lg	G	GS	CG	GF	IP	BFP	H	R	ER	HR	SH	SF	HB	TBB	IBB	SO	WP	Bk	W	L	Pct	ShO	Sv-Op	Hld	ERC	ERA
2000 Staten Island	A-	15	15	0	0	80.0	342	84	41	36	1	2	2	5	25	0	73	5	4	6	5	.545	0	0- -	-	3.68	4.05
2001 Greensboro	A	23	19	1	3	124.0	530	127	68	52	9	3	8	3	40	1	101	8	0	7	9	.438	0	1- -	-	3.80	3.77
2001 Staten Island	A-	7	7	0	0	48.0	184	32	9	9	2	0	0	4	12	0	56	1	1	5	1	.833	0	0- -	-	1.87	1.69
2002 Tampa	A+	12	3	0	3	24.1	102	27	13	11	2	1	2	0	3	0	22	2	1	4	2	.667	0	1- -	-	3.43	4.07
2002 Norwich	AA	16	0	0	10	19.1	72	14	2	2	1	1	0	0	5	1	21	3	0	1	1	.500	0	2- -	-	1.94	0.93
2002 Columbus	AAA	26	0	0	25	34.1	138	26	13	12	3	2	1	1	11	0	28	0	1	5	1	.833	0	7- -	-	2.55	3.15
2003 Columbus	AAA	6	0	0	6	7.2	29	3	0	0	0	1	0	0	2	0	13	0	0	0	0	-	0	3- -	-	0.68	0.00
2003 Norfolk	AAA	10	5	0	4	23.1	91	18	8	7	3	0	0	0	7	0	9	1	1	1	3	.250	0	4- -	-	2.76	2.70
2004 Buffalo	AAA	9	0	0	4	16.1	65	15	5	5	1	1	0	2	2	1	11	0	0	2	1	.667	0	1- -	-	2.80	2.76
2004 Columbus	AAA	36	0	0	20	44.2	197	48	24	23	4	0	0	3	12	0	38	2	0	1	3	.250	0	1- -	-	4.07	4.63
2003 NYY-NYM		28	0	0	14	31.1	147	33	19	17	5	0	4	3	19	5	16	3	0	1	0	1.000	0	0-0	0	5.74	4.88
2004 Cleveland	AL	1	0	0	0	1.0	8	1	5	5	1	0	0	0	4	1	1	0	0	0	0	-	0	0-0	0	28.92	45.00
2003 New York	AL	22	0	0	12	20.2	100	23	13	11	3	0	2	2	14	4	9	3	0	1	0	1.000	0	0-0	0	6.19	4.79
2003 New York	NL	6	0	0	2	10.2	47	10	6	6	2	0	2	1	5	1	7	0	0	0	0	-	0	0-0	0	4.86	5.06
2 ML YEARS		29	0	0	14	32.1	155	34	24	22	6	0	4	3	23	6	17	3	0	1	0	1.000	0	0-0	0	6.32	6.12

Jimmy Anderson

Pitches: L **Bats:** L **Pos:** RP-12 **Ht:** 6'1" **Wt:** 218 **Born:** 1/22/1976 **Age:** 29

				HOW MUCH HE PITCHED						WHAT HE GAVE UP										THE RESULTS						
Year Team	Lg	G	GS	CG	GF	IP	BFP	H	R	ER	HR	SH	SF	HB	TBB	IBB	SO	WP	Bk	W	L	Pct	ShO	Sv-Op	Hld	ERC	ERA
2004 Iowa*	AAA	16	15	0	0	94.2	411	108	54	45	7	6	6	2	35	1	42	2	0	6	5	.545	0	0- -	-	4.74	4.28
2004 Pawtucket*	AAA	1	0	0	0	1.2	11	1	1	1	0	0	0	0	1	0	1	0	0	0	0	-	0	0- -	-	2.03	5.40
1999 Pittsburgh	NL	13	4	0	2	29.1	127	25	15	13	2	2	1	1	16	2	13	4	0	2	1	.667	0	0-0	0	3.62	3.99
2000 Pittsburgh	NL	27	26	1	0	144.0	648	169	94	84	13	5	3	7	58	2	73	6	0	5	11	.313	0	0-0	0	5.21	5.25
2001 Pittsburgh	NL	34	34	1	0	206.1	922	232	123	117	15	11	9	11	83	14	89	6	1	9	17	.346	0	0-0	0	4.69	5.10
2002 Pittsburgh	NL	28	25	1	1	140.2	636	167	91	85	20	5	4	5	63	5	47	4	0	8	13	.381	0	0-0	0	5.84	5.44
2003 Cincinnati	NL	8	7	0	1	38.2	184	60	39	38	8	0	3	0	14	1	13	0	0	1	5	.167	0	0-0	0	8.22	8.84
2004 ChC-Bos		12	0	0	4	15.2	70	19	9	9	0	0	0	2	6	0	6	2	0	0	0	-	0	1-1	0	5.14	5.17
2004 Chicago	NL	7	0	0	2	9.2	42	9	5	5	0	0	0	2	3	0	3	1	0	0	0	-	0	1-1	0	3.43	4.66
2004 Boston	AL	5	0	0	2	6.0	28	10	4	4	0	0	0	0	3	0	3	1	0	0	0	-	0	0-0	0	8.39	6.00
6 ML YEARS		122	96	3	8	574.2	2587	672	371	346	58	23	20	26	240	24	241	22	1	25	47	.347	0	1-1	0	5.28	5.42

Marlon Anderson

Bats: L **Throws:** R **Pos:** PH-54; 2B-37; LF-28; RF-11; PR-3; 1B-2; DH-1 **Ht:** 5'11" **Wt:** 200 **Born:** 1/6/1974 **Age:** 31

					BATTING															BASERUNNING				AVERAGES		
Year Team	Lg	G	AB	H	2B	3B	HR	(Hm	Rd)	TB	R	RBI	RC	TBB	IBB	SO	HBP	SH	SF	SB	CS	SB%	GDP	Avg	OBP	Slg
1998 Philadelphia	NL	17	43	14	3	0	1	(1	0)	20	4	4	7	1	0	6	0	0	0	2	0	1.00	0	.326	.333	.465
1999 Philadelphia	NL	129	452	114	26	4	5	(4	1)	163	48	54	49	24	1	61	2	4	2	13	2	.87	6	.252	.292	.361
2000 Philadelphia	NL	41	162	37	8	1	1	(1	0)	50	10	15	12	12	0	22	0	0	0	2	2	.50	5	.228	.282	.309

			BATTING																	BASERUNNING				AVERAGES		
Year Team	Lg	G	AB	H	2B	3B	HR	(Hm	Rd)	TB	R	RBI	RC	TBB	IBB	SO	HBP	SH	SF	SB	CS	SB%	GDP	Avg	OBP	Slg
2001 Philadelphia	NL	147	522	153	30	2	11	(7	4)	220	69	61	72	35	5	74	2	10	5	8	5	.62	12	.293	.337	.421
2002 Philadelphia	NL	145	539	139	30	6	8	(4	4)	205	64	48	53	42	14	71	5	2	4	5	1	.83	16	.258	.315	.380
2003 Tampa Bay	AL	145	482	130	27	3	6	(2	4)	181	59	67	70	41	5	60	3	4	5	19	3	.86	6	.270	.328	.376
2004 St Louis	NL	113	253	60	12	0	8	(2	6)	96	31	28	23	12	1	38	1	0	5	6	2	.75	5	.237	.269	.379
7 ML YEARS		737	2453	647	136	16	40	(21	19)	935	285	277	286	167	26	332	13	20	22	55	15	.79	50	.264	.311	.381

Rick Ankiel

Pitches: L Bats: L Pos: RP-5   **Ht: 6'1" Wt: 210 Born: 7/19/1979 Age: 25**

		HOW MUCH HE PITCHED						WHAT HE GAVE UP												THE RESULTS						
Year Team	Lg	G	GS	CG	GF	IP	BFP	H	R	ER	HR	SH	SF	HB	TBB	IBB	SO	WP	Bk	W	L	Pct	ShO	Sv-Op	Hld	ERC	ERA
2004 Palm Beach*	A+	3	3	0	0	8.2	32	5	4	2	0	0	2	0	0	0	11	0	0	0	1	.000	0	0- -	-	0.68	2.08
2004 Tennessee*	AA	2	2	0	0	9.0	32	3	1	0	0	0	0	0	2	0	7	0	0	1	0	1.000	0	0- -	-	0.52	0.00
2004 Memphis*	AAA	1	1	0	0	6.0	20	1	1	0	0	0	0	1	0	0	5	0	0	1	0	1.000	0	0- -	-	0.19	0.00
1999 St Louis	NL	9	5	0	0	33.0	137	26	12	12	2	1	0	1	14	0	39	2	0	0	1	.000	0	1-1	0	2.89	3.27
2000 St Louis	NL	31	30	0	0	175.0	735	137	80	68	21	8	6	6	90	2	194	12	2	11	7	.611	0	0- -	1	3.63	3.50
2001 St Louis	NL	6	6	0	0	24.0	124	25	21	19	7	2	3	3	25	0	27	5	0	1	2	.333	0	0- -	0	9.17	7.13
2004 St Louis	NL	5	0	0	0	10.0	43	10	6	6	2	1	0	2	1	0	9	1	0	1	0	1.000	0	0-0	2	4.27	5.40
4 ML YEARS		51	41	0	0	242.0	1039	198	119	105	32	12	9	12	130	2	269	20	2	13	10	.565	0	1-1	3	4.04	3.90

Kevin Appier

Pitches: R Bats: R Pos: SP-2   **Ht: 6'2" Wt: 200 Born: 12/6/1967 Age: 37**

		HOW MUCH HE PITCHED						WHAT HE GAVE UP												THE RESULTS						
Year Team	Lg	G	GS	CG	GF	IP	BFP	H	R	ER	HR	SH	SF	HB	TBB	IBB	SO	WP	Bk	W	L	Pct	ShO	Sv-Op	Hld	ERC	ERA
2004 Wichita*	AA	4	4	0	0	14.2	67	19	9	8	1	2	0	0	4	0	3	2	0	0	0	-	0	0- -	-	4.90	4.91
2004 Omaha*	AAA	1	1	0	0	4.0	20	7	3	3	1	0	1	0	2	0	2	0	0	0	0	-	0	0- -	-	10.96	6.75
1989 Kansas City	AL	6	5	0	0	21.2	106	34	22	22	3	0	3	0	12	1	10	0	0	1	4	.200	0	0-0	0	8.72	9.14
1990 Kansas City	AL	32	24	3	1	185.2	784	179	67	57	13	5	9	6	54	2	127	6	1	12	8	.600	3	0-0	0	3.34	2.76
1991 Kansas City	AL	34	31	6	1	207.2	881	205	97	79	13	8	6	2	61	3	158	7	1	13	10	.565	3	0-0	1	3.32	3.42
1992 Kansas City	AL	30	30	3	0	208.1	852	167	59	57	10	8	3	2	68	5	150	4	0	15	8	.652	0	0-0	0	2.41	2.46
1993 Kansas City	AL	34	34	5	0	238.2	953	183	74	68	8	3	5	1	81	3	186	5	0	18	8	.692	1	0-0	0	**2.25**	**2.56**
1994 Kansas City	AL	23	23	1	0	155.0	653	137	68	66	11	**9**	7	4	63	7	145	11	1	7	6	.538	0	0-0	0	3.31	3.83
1995 Kansas City	AL	31	31	4	0	201.1	832	163	90	87	14	3	3	8	80	1	185	5	0	15	10	.600	1	0-0	0	3.01	3.89
1996 Kansas City	AL	32	32	5	0	211.1	874	192	87	85	17	7	4	5	75	2	207	10	1	14	11	.560	1	0-0	0	3.41	3.62
1997 Kansas City	AL	34	34	4	0	235.2	972	215	96	89	24	4	4	7	74	2	196	**14**	1	9	13	.409	1	0-0	0	3.37	3.40
1998 Kansas City	AL	3	3	0	0	15.0	69	21	13	13	3	0	1	1	5	1	9	1	0	1	2	.333	0	0-0	0	7.33	7.80
1999 KC-Oak	AL	34	34	1	0	209.0	926	230	131	120	27	7	5	7	84	4	131	10	1	16	14	.533	0	0-0	0	4.99	5.17
2000 Oakland	AL	31	31	0	0	195.1	884	200	109	98	23	5	6	9	**102**	10	129	6	0	15	11	.577	1	0-0	0	4.89	4.52
2001 New York	NL	33	33	1	0	206.2	856	181	89	82	22	6	7	15	64	4	172	12	0	11	10	.524	1	0-0	0	3.38	3.57
2002 Anaheim	AL	32	32	0	0	188.1	795	191	89	82	23	1	8	7	64	2	132	7	0	14	12	.538	0	0-0	0	4.29	3.92
2003 Ana-KC	AL	23	23	0	0	111.2	499	120	69	67	21	1	1	8	43	4	55	6	1	8	9	.471	0	0-0	0	5.29	5.40
2004 Kansas City	AL	2	2	0	0	4.0	22	7	8	6	0	0	0	0	3	0	2	2	0	1	0	1.000	0	0-0	0	9.15	13.50
1999 Kansas City	AL	22	22	1	0	140.1	613	153	81	76	18	5	3	6	51	3	78	5	0	9	9	.500	0	0-0	0	4.83	4.87
1999 Oakland	AL	12	12	0	0	68.2	313	77	50	44	9	2	2	1	33	1	53	5	1	7	5	.583	0	0-0	0	5.32	5.77
2003 Anaheim	AL	19	19	0	0	92.2	422	105	60	58	17	0	1	8	36	4	50	4	1	7	7	.500	0	0-0	0	5.65	5.63
2003 Kansas City	AL	4	4	0	0	19.0	77	15	9	9	4	1	0	0	7	0	5	2	0	1	2	.333	0	0-0	0	3.56	4.26
16 ML YEARS		414	402	34	2	2595.1	10958	2425	1168	1078	232	67	72	79	933	51	1994	106	7	169	137	.552	12	0-0	1	3.59	3.74

Greg Aquino

Pitches: R Bats: R Pos: RP-34   **Ht: 6'1" Wt: 188 Born: 1/11/1978 Age: 27**

		HOW MUCH HE PITCHED						WHAT HE GAVE UP												THE RESULTS						
Year Team	Lg	G	GS	CG	GF	IP	BFP	H	R	ER	HR	SH	SF	HB	TBB	IBB	SO	WP	Bk	W	L	Pct	ShO	Sv-Op	Hld	ERC	ERA
1999 Diamndbcks	R	13	2	0	4	19.0	89	17	11	8	0	0	1	2	13	0	20	2	0	1	2	.333	0	0- -	-	4.10	3.79
2000 South Bend	A	29	18	0	5	119.0	538	119	67	59	9	4	2	6	56	0	93	9	2	5	7	.417	0	0- -	-	4.26	4.46
2001 Lancaster	A+	25	4	0	6	42.0	211	59	40	38	7	3	1	2	24	0	39	6	0	2	5	.286	0	0- -	-	7.86	8.14
2001 Yakima	A-	8	8	0	0	46.1	194	39	18	17	2	1	0	2	14	1	39	10	0	4	2	.667	0	0- -	-	2.57	3.30
2002 Yakima	A-	6	6	0	0	35.0	141	26	9	8	0	1	1	0	17	0	34	3	0	1	1	.500	0	0- -	-	2.46	2.06
2002 Lancaster	A+	8	8	0	0	49.0	209	50	20	20	3	1	0	3	18	0	50	3	0	4	1	.800	0	0- -	-	4.12	3.67
2003 El Paso	AA	20	20	0	0	106.2	458	115	43	41	5	3	0	4	38	1	91	7	3	7	3	.700	0	0- -	-	4.17	3.46
2004 Tucson	AAA	21	2	0	7	29.2	141	33	25	21	2	0	0	1	18	0	19	2	0	1	3	.250	0	1- - -	-	5.30	6.37
2004 Arizona	NL	34	0	0	26	35.1	147	24	15	12	4	2	2	2	17	2	26	4	0	0	2	.000	0	16-19	1	2.87	3.06

Danny Ardoin

Bats: R Throws: R Pos: C-6   **Ht: 6'0" Wt: 218 Born: 7/8/1974 Age: 30**

			BATTING																	BASERUNNING				AVERAGES		
Year Team	Lg	G	AB	H	2B	3B	HR	(Hm	Rd)	TB	R	RBI	RC	TBB	IBB	SO	HBP	SH	SF	SB	CS	SB%	GDP	Avg	OBP	Slg
1995 Sth Oregon	A-	58	175	41	9	1	2	(-	-)	58	28	23	25	31	0	50	9	5	4	2	1	.67	2	.234	.370	.331
1996 Modesto	A+	91	317	83	13	3	6	(-	-)	120	55	34	45	47	0	81	9	3	2	5	7	.42	9	.262	.371	.379
1997 Huntsville	AA	57	208	48	10	1	4	(-	-)	72	26	23	19	17	0	38	3	0	2	2	3	.40	7	.231	.296	.346
1997 Visalia	A+	43	145	34	7	1	3	(-	-)	52	16	19	18	21	0	39	4	1	0	0	1	.00	3	.234	.347	.359
1998 Huntsville	AA	109	363	90	21	0	16	(-	-)	159	67	62	58	62	0	87	7	6	1	8	4	.67	10	.248	.367	.438
1999 Vancouver	AAA	109	336	85	13	2	8	(-	-)	126	53	46	47	50	0	78	9	9	1	3	5	.50	12	.253	.364	.375
2000 Modesto	A+	4	10	3	1	0	0	(-	-)	4	1	2	1	0	0	4	1	0	0	0	0	-	0	.300	.364	.400
2000 Sacramento	AAA	67	234	65	16	1	6	(-	-)	101	42	34	40	34	3	72	8	3	2	6	0	1.00	5	.278	.385	.432
2000 Salt Lake	AAA	3	9	2	0	0	0	(-	-)	2	1	0	1	3	0	4	0	0	0	0	0	-	0	.222	.417	.222
2001 Edmonton	AAA	88	302	77	18	1	5	(-	-)	112	37	37	30	22	1	81	1	2	4	2	6	.25	8	.255	.304	.371
2002 Omaha	AAA	25	77	16	3	0	3	(-	-)	28	10	10	9	11	0	25	0	0	3	1	0	1.00	0	.208	.297	.364
2002 Oklahoma	AAA	33	106	24	5	0	2	(-	-)	35	10	11	10	10	1	31	2	2	1	0	0	-	5	.226	.303	.330
2002 Tulsa	AA	8	21	3	0	0	0	(-	-)	3	1	0	1	4	0	9	0	0	0	0	0	-	0	.143	.280	.143
2003 Oklahoma	AAA	74	239	58	11	2	7	(-	-)	94	35	35	26	21	0	58	3	1	1	0	2	.00	9	.243	.311	.393
2004 Oklahoma	AAA	68	237	73	12	0	10	(-	-)	115	50	44	48	41	0	66	8	2	3	1	1	.50	9	.308	.422	.485

				BATTING																		BASERUNNING				AVERAGES		
Year Team	Lg	G	AB	H	2B	3B	HR	(Hm	Rd)	TB	R	RBI	RC	TBB	IBB	SO	HBP	SH	SF		SB	CS	SB%	GDP	Avg	OBP	Slg
2000 Minnesota	AL	15	32	4	1	0	1	(0	1)	8	4	5	2	8	0	10	0	0	0		0	0	-	0	.125	.300	.250
2004 Texas	AL	6	8	1	0	0	0	(0	0)	1	1	1	1	3	0	2	0	0	0		0	0	-	0	.125	.364	.125
2 ML YEARS		21	40	5	1	0	1	(0	0)	9	5	6	3	11	0	12	0	0	0		0	0	-	0	.125	.314	.225

Tony Armas Jr.

Pitches: R **Bats:** R **Pos:** SP-16 — **Ht:** 6'4" **Wt:** 215 **Born:** 4/29/1978 **Age:** 27

		HOW MUCH HE PITCHED						WHAT HE GAVE UP											THE RESULTS						
Year Team	Lg	G	GS	CG	GF	IP	BFP	H	R	ER	HR	SH	SF	HB	TBB	IBB	SO	WP	Bk	W	L	Pct	ShO	Sv-Op	Hld	ERC	ERA
2004 Brevard Cnty*	A+	3	3	0	0	9.1	38	5	7	7	1	2	0	1	7	0	7	1	0	0	1	.000	0	0--	-	3.57	6.75
2004 Edmonton*	AAA	2	2	0	0	10.0	42	11	4	2	0	1	0	0	1	0	8	0	0	0	0	-	0	0--	-	2.74	1.80
1999 Montreal	NL	1	1	0	0	6.0	28	8	4	1	0	0	1	0	2	1	2	2	0	1	0	1.000	0	0-0	-	4.53	1.50
2000 Montreal	NL	17	17	0	0	95.0	403	74	49	46	10	7	3	3	50	2	59	3	0	7	9	.438	0	0-0	-	3.49	4.36
2001 Montreal	NL	34	34	0	0	196.2	851	180	101	88	18	15	6	10	91	6	176	9	1	9	14	.391	0	0-0	-	3.95	4.03
2002 Montreal	NL	29	29	0	0	164.1	705	149	87	81	22	6	2	7	78	12	131	14	2	12	12	.500	0	0-0	-	4.19	4.44
2003 Montreal	NL	5	5	0	0	31.0	124	25	9	9	4	2	2	1	8	0	23	0	0	2	1	.667	0	0-0	-	2.84	2.61
2004 Montreal	NL	16	16	0	0	72.0	320	66	41	39	13	2	2	4	45	6	54	0	0	2	4	.333	0	0-0	-	5.26	4.88
6 ML YEARS		102	102	0	0	565.0	2431	502	291	264	67	32	16	25	274	27	445	28	3	32	41	.438	0	0-0	-	4.04	4.21

Bronson Arroyo

Pitches: R **Bats:** R **Pos:** SP-29; RP-3 — **Ht:** 6'5" **Wt:** 194 **Born:** 2/24/1977 **Age:** 28

		HOW MUCH HE PITCHED						WHAT HE GAVE UP											THE RESULTS						
Year Team	Lg	G	GS	CG	GF	IP	BFP	H	R	ER	HR	SH	SF	HB	TBB	IBB	SO	WP	Bk	W	L	Pct	ShO	Sv-Op	Hld	ERC	ERA
2000 Pittsburgh	NL	20	12	0	1	71.2	338	88	61	51	10	5	2	4	36	6	50	3	1	2	6	.250	0	0-0	0	6.18	6.40
2001 Pittsburgh	NL	24	13	1	1	88.1	390	99	54	50	12	4	6	4	34	6	39	4	1	5	7	.417	0	0-0	0	5.09	5.09
2002 Pittsburgh	NL	9	4	0	1	27.0	123	30	14	12	1	1	1	0	15	3	22	0	0	2	1	.667	0	0-0	1	4.64	4.00
2003 Boston	AL	6	0	0	2	17.1	66	10	5	4	0	0	0	1	4	2	14	0	0	0	0	-	0	1-1	0	1.14	2.08
2004 Boston	AL	32	29	0	0	178.2	764	171	99	80	17	5	4	20	47	3	142	5	0	10	9	.526	0	0-0	0	3.65	4.03
5 ML YEARS		91	58	1	5	383.0	1681	398	233	197	40	15	13	29	136	20	267	12	2	19	23	.452	0	1-1	3	4.35	4.63

Miguel Asencio

Pitches: R **Bats:** R **Pos:** SP — **Ht:** 6'2" **Wt:** 160 **Born:** 9/29/1980 **Age:** 24

		HOW MUCH HE PITCHED						WHAT HE GAVE UP											THE RESULTS						
Year Team	Lg	G	GS	CG	GF	IP	BFP	H	R	ER	HR	SH	SF	HB	TBB	IBB	SO	WP	Bk	W	L	Pct	ShO	Sv-Op	Hld	ERC	ERA
1999 Phillies	R	9	5	0	3	28.2	137	35	24	19	1	0	4	2	16	0	14	1	0	1	4	.200	0	0--	-	5.71	5.97
2000 Clearwater	A+	5	5	0	0	33.0	132	22	10	10	2	0	0	0	17	0	24	1	1	2	1	.667	0	0--	-	2.58	2.73
2000 Batavia	A-	7	7	1	0	39.2	165	32	23	22	3	1	1	3	17	0	28	2	0	2	2	.500	0	0--	-	3.32	4.99
2001 Clearwater	A+	28	21	2	1	155.1	649	124	62	49	7	3	6	2	70	1	123	9	2	12	5	.706	1	0--	-	2.86	2.84
2003 Wichita	AA	1	1	0	0	4.0	14	1	0	0	0	0	0	0	1	0	3	0	0	0	0	-	0	0--	-	0.40	0.00
2002 Kansas City	AL	31	21	0	7	123.1	557	136	73	70	17	2	6	3	64	2	58	7	0	4	7	.364	0	0-0	0	5.55	5.11
2003 Kansas City	AL	8	8	1	0	48.1	215	54	29	28	4	3	5	3	21	0	27	1	0	2	1	.667	0	0-0	0	5.08	5.21
2 ML YEARS		39	29	1	7	171.2	772	190	102	98	21	5	11	6	85	2	85	8	0	6	8	.429	0	0-0	0	5.42	5.14

Andy Ashby

Pitches: R **Bats:** R **Pos:** RP-2 — **Ht:** 6'1" **Wt:** 202 **Born:** 7/11/1967 **Age:** 37

		HOW MUCH HE PITCHED						WHAT HE GAVE UP											THE RESULTS						
Year Team	Lg	G	GS	CG	GF	IP	BFP	H	R	ER	HR	SH	SF	HB	TBB	IBB	SO	WP	Bk	W	L	Pct	ShO	Sv-Op	Hld	ERC	ERA
1991 Philadelphia	NL	8	8	0	0	42.0	186	41	28	28	5	1	3	4	19	0	26	6	0	1	5	.167	0	0-0	-	4.54	6.00
1992 Philadelphia	NL	10	8	0	0	37.0	171	42	31	31	6	2	2	1	21	0	24	2	0	1	3	.250	0	0-0	-	6.17	7.54
1993 Col-SD	NL	32	21	0	3	123.0	577	168	100	93	19	6	7	4	56	5	77	6	3	3	10	.231	0	1-1	0	7.10	6.80
1994 San Diego	NL	24	24	4	0	164.1	682	145	75	62	16	11	3	3	43	12	121	6	1	6	11	.353	0	0-0	-	2.82	3.40
1995 San Diego	NL	31	31	2	0	192.2	800	180	79	63	17	10	4	11	62	3	150	7	0	12	10	.545	2	0-0	0	3.60	2.94
1996 San Diego	NL	24	24	1	0	150.2	612	147	60	54	17	6	2	3	34	1	85	3	0	9	5	.643	0	0-0	-	3.50	3.23
1997 San Diego	NL	30	30	2	0	200.2	851	207	108	92	17	13	6	5	49	2	144	3	0	9	11	.450	1	0-0	-	3.59	4.13
1998 San Diego	NL	33	33	5	0	226.2	939	223	90	84	23	8	5	7	58	8	151	7	0	17	9	.654	1	0-0	-	3.55	3.34
1999 San Diego	NL	31	31	4	0	206.0	862	204	95	87	26	10	1	7	54	4	132	6	0	14	10	.583	3	0-0	-	3.78	3.80
2000 Phi-Atl	NL	31	31	3	0	199.1	867	216	124	109	29	18	10	6	61	9	106	6	1	12	13	.480	0	0-0	-	4.52	4.92
2001 Los Angeles	NL	2	2	0	0	11.2	49	14	5	5	2	0	0	0	1	0	7	0	0	2	0	1.000	0	0-0	-	4.42	3.86
2002 Los Angeles	NL	30	30	0	0	181.2	771	179	85	79	20	7	6	8	65	3	107	2	0	9	13	.409	0	0-0	-	4.10	3.91
2003 Los Angeles	NL	21	12	0	5	73.0	318	90	42	42	8	7	2	3	17	2	41	5	0	3	10	.231	0	0-0	-	4.99	5.18
2004 San Diego	NL	2	0	0	2	2.0	7	1	0	0	0	0	0	0	0	0	2	0	0	0	0	-	0	0-0	0	0.54	0.00
1993 Colorado	NL	20	9	0	3	54.0	277	89	54	51	5	3	3	3	32	4	33	2	3	0	4	.000	0	1-1	-	9.06	8.50
1993 San Diego	NL	12	12	0	0	69.0	300	79	46	42	14	3	4	1	24	1	44	4	0	3	6	.333	0	0-0	-	5.58	5.48
2000 Philadelphia	NL	16	16	1	0	101.1	455	113	75	64	17	11	9	5	38	5	51	4	0	4	7	.364	0	0-0	-	5.20	5.68
2000 Atlanta	NL	15	15	2	0	98.0	412	103	49	45	12	7	1	1	23	4	55	2	1	8	6	.571	0	0-0	-	3.84	4.13
14 ML YEARS		309	285	21	10	1810.2	7692	1857	922	829	205	99	51	61	540	49	1173	58	4	98	110	.471	7	1-1	0	4.02	4.12

Pedro Astacio

Pitches: R **Bats:** R **Pos:** RP-4; SP-1 — **Ht:** 6'2" **Wt:** 210 **Born:** 11/28/1969 **Age:** 35

		HOW MUCH HE PITCHED						WHAT HE GAVE UP											THE RESULTS						
Year Team	Lg	G	GS	CG	GF	IP	BFP	H	R	ER	HR	SH	SF	HB	TBB	IBB	SO	WP	Bk	W	L	Pct	ShO	Sv-Op	Hld	ERC	ERA
2004 Red Sox*	R	2	1	0	0	4.2	19	4	3	0	0	0	0	0	0	0	6	0	0	1	0	1.000	0	0--	-	1.36	0.00
2004 Portland*	AA	1	1	0	0	4.0	16	3	0	0	0	0	0	1	1	0	4	1	0	0	0	-	0	0--	-	2.58	0.00
2004 Pawtucket*	AAA	2	2	0	0	9.1	35	9	4	3	1	1	0	1	1	0	7	0	0	0	1	.000	0	0--	-	3.57	2.89
1992 Los Angeles	NL	11	11	4	0	82.0	341	80	23	18	1	3	2	2	20	4	43	1	0	5	5	.500	4	0-0	-	2.78	1.98
1993 Los Angeles	NL	31	31	3	0	186.1	777	165	80	74	14	7	8	5	68	5	122	8	9	14	9	.609	2	0-0	-	3.24	3.57
1994 Los Angeles	NL	23	23	3	0	149.0	625	142	77	71	18	6	5	4	47	4	108	4	0	6	8	.429	1	0-0	-	3.71	4.29
1995 Los Angeles	NL	48	11	1	7	104.0	436	103	54	49	12	5	3	4	29	5	80	5	0	7	8	.467	1	0-1	3	3.76	4.24
1996 Los Angeles	NL	35	32	0	0	211.2	885	207	86	81	18	11	5	9	67	9	130	6	2	9	8	.529	0	0-0	0	3.69	3.44

Year Team	Lg	G	GS	CG	GF	IP	BFP	H	R	ER	HR	SH	SF	HB	TBB	IBB	SO	WP	Bk	W	L	Pct	ShO	Sv-Op	Hld	ERC	ERA
1997 LA-Col	NL	33	31	2	2	202.1	862	200	98	93	24	9	7	9	61	0	166	6	3	12	10	.545	1	0-0	0	3.92	4.14
1998 Colorado	NL	35	34	0	0	209.1	938	245	160	145	39	12	3	17	74	0	170	2	0	13	14	.481	0	0-0	0	5.91	6.23
1999 Colorado	NL	34	34	7	0	232.0	1008	258	140	130	38	6	10	11	75	6	210	5	0	17	11	.607	0	0-0	0	5.08	5.04
2000 Colorado	NL	32	32	3	0	196.1	875	217	119	115	32	7	4	15	77	5	193	8	0	12	9	.571	0	0-0	0	5.42	5.27
2001 Col-Hou	NL	26	26	4	0	169.2	733	181	101	96	22	6	5	13	54	3	144	2	0	8	14	.364	1	0-0	0	4.68	5.09
2002 New York	NL	31	31	3	0	191.2	828	192	106	102	32	8	7	16	63	5	152	1	2	12	11	.522	1	0-0	0	4.57	4.79
2003 New York	NL	7	7	0	0	36.2	174	47	30	30	8	1	1	3	18	1	20	4	0	3	2	.600	0	0-0	0	7.42	7.36
2004 Boston	AL	5	1	0	1	8.2	43	13	10	10	2	0	0	0	5	0	6	1	0	0	0	-	0	0-0	0	9.09	10.38
1997 Los Angeles	NL	26	24	2	2	153.2	654	151	75	70	15	9	5	4	47	0	115	4	3	7	9	.438	1	0-0	0	3.67	4.10
1997 Colorado	NL	7	7	0	0	48.2	208	49	23	23	9	0	2	5	14	0	51	2	0	5	1	.833	0	0-0	0	4.72	4.25
2001 Colorado	NL	22	22	4	0	141.0	617	151	91	86	21	5	4	10	50	3	125	2	0	6	13	.316	1	0-0	0	4.94	5.49
2001 Houston	NL	4	4	0	0	28.2	116	30	10	10	1	1	1	3	4	0	19	0	0	2	1	.667	0	0-0	0	3.43	3.14
13 ML YEARS		351	304	30	10	1979.2	8525	2050	1083	1014	260	81	60	108	658	47	1544	53	16	118	109	.520	11	0-1	2	4.44	4.61

Scott Atchison

Pitches: R **Bats:** R **Pos:** RP-25   **Ht:** 6'2" **Wt:** 180 **Born:** 3/29/1976 **Age:** 29

Year Team	Lg	G	GS	CG	GF	IP	BFP	H	R	ER	HR	SH	SF	HB	TBB	IBB	SO	WP	Bk	W	L	Pct	ShO	Sv-Op	Hld	ERC	ERA
1999 Wisconsin	A	15	13	0	0	81.2	326	67	34	31	4	2	2	3	25	1	85	4	1	4	5	.444	0	0- -	-	2.64	3.42
2000 Tacoma	AAA	5	5	0	0	26.0	103	22	11	11	3	0	0	0	6	0	18	0	1	1	1	.500	0	0- -	-	2.76	3.81
2000 Lancaster	A+	19	19	1	0	97.2	436	117	58	40	10	2	4	4	21	0	77	2	0	5	5	.500	0	0- -	-	4.52	3.69
2001 San Antonio	AA	24	24	1	0	136.0	596	171	84	64	11	8	5	12	28	0	83	6	0	9	10	.474	0	0- -	-	5.07	4.24
2002 Tacoma	AAA	27	21	0	3	124.1	528	123	68	64	13	3	5	9	31	0	112	1	0	5	10	.333	0	2- -	-	3.72	4.63
2003 Tacoma	AAA	39	7	0	10	108.2	474	114	57	52	8	7	2	3	37	2	83	2	0	6	9	.400	0	1- -	-	3.96	4.31
2004 Tacoma	AAA	40	1	0	16	69.1	304	71	35	32	8	2	2	2	26	2	76	5	0	5	3	.625	0	7- -	-	4.23	4.15
2004 Seattle	AL	25	0	0	8	30.2	133	29	12	12	4	2	1	0	14	2	36	2	0	2	3	.400	0	0-0	2	4.08	3.52

Garrett Atkins

Bats: R **Throws:** R **Pos:** PH-7; 3B-4; 1B-3; LF-3   **Ht:** 6'3" **Wt:** 210 **Born:** 12/12/1979 **Age:** 25

Year Team	Lg	G	AB	H	2B	3B	HR	(Hm	Rd)	TB	R	RBI	RC	TBB	IBB	SO	HBP	SH	SF	SB	CS	SB%	GDP	Avg	OBP	Slg
2000 Portland	A-	69	251	76	12	0	7	(-	-)	109	34	47	48	45	1	48	2	0	1	2	0	1.00	3	.303	.411	.434
2001 Salem	A+	135	465	151	43	5	5	(-	-)	219	70	67	92	74	10	98	8	2	6	6	4	.60	8	.325	.421	.471
2002 Carolina	AA	128	510	138	27	3	12	(-	-)	207	71	61	71	59	2	77	2	0	6	6	6	.50	12	.271	.345	.406
2003 Co Springs	AAA	118	439	140	30	1	13	(-	-)	211	80	67	77	45	2	52	3	0	5	2	4	.33	9	.319	.382	.481
2004 Co Springs	AAA	122	445	163	43	3	15	(-	-)	257	88	94	100	57	4	45	4	0	10	0	0	-	20	.366	.434	.578
2003 Colorado	NL	25	69	11	2	0	0	(0	0)	13	6	4	2	3	0	14	1	0	0	0	0	-	0	.159	.205	.188
2004 Colorado	NL	15	28	10	2	0	1	(1	0)	15	3	8	8	4	0	3	0	0	1	0	0	-	1	.357	.424	.536
2 ML YEARS		40	97	21	4	0	1	(1	0)	28	9	12	10	7	0	17	1	0	1	0	0	-	1	.216	.274	.289

Rich Aurilia

Bats: R **Throws:** R **Pos:** SS-79; 3B-29; PH-11; 2B-7; 1B-1   **Ht:** 6'1" **Wt:** 185 **Born:** 9/2/1971 **Age:** 33

Year Team	Lg	G	AB	H	2B	3B	HR	(Hm	Rd)	TB	R	RBI	RC	TBB	IBB	SO	HBP	SH	SF	SB	CS	SB%	GDP	Avg	OBP	Slg
1995 San Francisco	NL	9	19	9	3	0	2	(0	2)	18	4	4	7	1	0	2	0	1	0	1	0	1.00	1	.474	.476	.947
1996 San Francisco	NL	105	318	76	7	1	3	(1	2)	94	27	26	29	25	2	52	1	6	2	4	1	.80	1	.239	.295	.296
1997 San Francisco	NL	46	102	28	8	0	5	(1	4)	51	16	19	16	8	0	15	0	1	2	1	1	.50	3	.275	.321	.500
1998 San Francisco	NL	122	413	110	27	2	9	(5	4)	168	54	49	54	31	3	62	2	5	2	3	3	.50	3	.266	.319	.407
1999 San Francisco	NL	152	558	157	23	1	22	(9	13)	248	68	80	79	43	3	71	5	3	5	2	3	.40	16	.281	.336	.444
2000 San Francisco	NL	141	509	138	24	2	20	(12	8)	226	67	79	74	54	2	90	0	4	4	1	2	.33	15	.271	.339	.444
2001 San Francisco	NL	156	636	206	37	5	37	(15	22)	364	114	97	124	47	2	83	0	3	3	1	3	.25	14	.324	.369	.572
2002 San Francisco	NL	133	538	138	35	2	15	(4	11)	222	76	61	60	37	0	90	4	3	7	1	2	.33	15	.257	.305	.413
2003 San Francisco	NL	129	505	140	26	1	13	(6	7)	207	65	58	56	36	0	82	1	0	3	2	2	.50	18	.277	.325	.410
2004 Sea-SD		124	399	98	21	2	6	(3	3)	141	49	44	39	37	1	71	4	7	3	1	0	1.00	13	.246	.314	.353
2004 Seattle	AL	73	261	63	13	0	4	(2	2)	88	27	28	25	22	1	43	2	6	1	1	0	1.00	14	.241	.304	.337
2004 San Diego	NL	51	138	35	8	2	2	(1	1)	53	22	16	14	15	0	28	2	1	2	0	0	-	2	.254	.331	.384
10 ML YEARS		1117	3997	1100	211	16	132	(56	76)	1739	540	517	538	319	13	618	17	33	32	17	17	.50	99	.275	.329	.435

Brad Ausmus

Bats: R **Throws:** R **Pos:** C-128; PH-3   **Ht:** 5'11" **Wt:** 200 **Born:** 4/14/1969 **Age:** 36

Year Team	Lg	G	AB	H	2B	3B	HR	(Hm	Rd)	TB	R	RBI	RC	TBB	IBB	SO	HBP	SH	SF	SB	CS	SB%	GDP	Avg	OBP	Slg
1993 San Diego	NL	49	160	41	8	1	5	(4	1)	66	18	12	19	6	0	28	0	0	0	2	0	1.00	2	.256	.283	.413
1994 San Diego	NL	101	327	82	12	1	7	(6	1)	117	45	24	36	30	12	63	1	6	2	5	1	.83	8	.251	.314	.358
1995 San Diego	NL	103	328	96	16	4	5	(2	3)	135	44	34	49	31	3	56	2	4	4	16	5	.76	6	.293	.353	.412
1996 SD-Det		125	375	83	16	0	5	(2	3)	114	46	35	32	39	1	72	5	6	2	4	8	.33	8	.221	.302	.304
1997 Houston	NL	130	425	113	25	1	4	(1	3)	152	45	44	51	38	4	78	3	6	6	14	6	.70	8	.266	.326	.358
1998 Houston	NL	128	412	111	10	4	6	(2	4)	147	62	45	51	53	11	60	3	3	1	10	3	.77	18	.269	.356	.357
1999 Detroit	AL	127	458	126	25	6	9	(5	4)	190	62	54	69	51	0	71	14	3	1	12	9	.57	11	.275	.365	.415
2000 Detroit	AL	150	523	139	25	3	7	(3	4)	191	75	51	68	69	0	79	6	4	2	11	5	.69	19	.266	.357	.365
2001 Houston	NL	128	422	98	23	4	5	(4	1)	144	45	34	38	30	6	64	1	6	2	4	1	.80	13	.232	.284	.341
2002 Houston	NL	130	447	115	19	3	6	(4	2)	158	57	50	44	38	3	71	6	2	3	2	3	.40	30	.257	.322	.353
2003 Houston	NL	143	450	103	12	2	4	(1	3)	131	43	47	44	46	1	66	4	4	5	5	3	.63	8	.229	.303	.291
2004 Houston	NL	129	403	100	14	1	5	(2	3)	131	38	31	34	33	11	56	2	7	3	2	2	.50	13	.248	.306	.325
1996 San Diego	NL	50	149	27	4	0	1	(0	1)	34	16	13	6	13	0	27	3	1	0	1	4	.20	4	.181	.247	.228
1996 Detroit	AL	75	226	56	12	0	4	(2	2)	80	30	22	26	26	1	45	2	5	2	3	4	.43	4	.248	.328	.354
12 ML YEARS		1443	4730	1207	205	30	68	(36	32)	1676	580	461	535	464	52	764	47	51	31	87	46	.65	144	.255	.326	.354

Luis Ayala

Pitches: R **Bats:** R **Pos:** RP-81   **Ht:** 6'2" **Wt:** 170 **Born:** 1/2/1978 **Age:** 27

Year Team	Lg	G	GS	CG	GF	IP	BFP	H	R	ER	HR	SH	SF	HB	TBB	IBB	SO	WP	Bk	W	L	Pct	ShO	Sv-Op	Hld	ERC	ERA
1997 Saltillo	AAA	37	2	0	0	62.1	269	76	37	32	3	1	7	3	21	4	30	2	1	7	5	.583	0	0- -	-	4.99	4.62
1998 Saltillo	AAA	47	4	0	0	83.1	381	105	52	52	2	10	1	4	45	13	29	3	0	7	8	.467	0	7- -	-	5.65	5.62
1999 Saltillo	AAA	61	0	0	0	79.0	287	54	17	15	1	3	0	3	22	5	28	3	0	7	3	.700	0	41- -	-	1.76	1.71
2000 Saltillo	AAA	55	0	0	52	65.1	269	69	22	20	4	4	0	3	13	1	38	1	0	5	3	.625	0	25- -	-	3.59	2.76
2001 Salem	A+	33	0	0	33	40.0	164	34	11	9	2	3	2	0	11	0	34	0	0	1	2	.333	0	21- -	-	2.47	2.03
2001 Saltillo	AAA	13	0	0	12	13.1	61	19	10	6	0	1	0	2	5	0	10	2	1	0	1	.000	0	7- -	-	6.67	4.05
2002 Saltillo	AAA	49	0	0	43	53.2	225	43	16	10	2	2	0	7	15	0	43	0	0	3	5	.375	0	23- -	-	2.60	1.68
2002 Ottawa	AAA	6	0	0	3	7.2	32	7	3	3	1	0	0	0	4	0	6	0	0	0	0	-	0	0- -	-	4.48	3.52
2003 Expos	R	2	2	0	0	3.2	15	2	0	0	0	0	0	0	2	0	2	0	0	0	0	-	0	0- -	-	1.65	0.00
2003 Montreal	NL	65	0	0	24	71.0	288	65	27	23	8	3	1	5	13	3	46	1	0	10	3	.769	0	5-8	19	3.11	2.92
2004 Montreal	NL	81	0	0	28	90.1	367	92	30	27	6	2	2	5	15	2	63	3	1	6	12	.333	0	2-7	21	3.32	2.69
2 ML YEARS		146	0	0	52	161.1	655	157	57	50	14	5	3	10	28	5	109	4	1	16	15	.516	0	7-15	40	3.23	2.79

Brandon Backe

Pitches: R **Bats:** R **Pos:** RP-24; SP-9   **Ht:** 6'0" **Wt:** 190 **Born:** 4/5/1978 **Age:** 27

Year Team	Lg	G	GS	CG	GF	IP	BFP	H	R	ER	HR	SH	SF	HB	TBB	IBB	SO	WP	Bk	W	L	Pct	ShO	Sv-Op	Hld	ERC	ERA
2004 New Orleans*	AAA	19	9	0	3	64.1	267	57	26	20	7	5	0	1	26	1	74	2	0	6	5	.545	0	0- -	-	3.64	2.80
2002 Tampa Bay	AL	9	0	0	4	13.0	61	15	10	10	3	0	0	2	7	0	6	0	0	0	0	-	0	0-0	0	7.37	6.92
2003 Tampa Bay	AL	28	0	0	8	44.2	192	40	28	27	6	2	1	2	25	1	36	3	0	1	1	.500	0	0-0	5	4.64	5.44
2004 Houston	NL	33	9	0	8	67.0	293	75	33	32	10	5	1	1	27	4	54	1	0	5	3	.625	0	0-0	3	5.18	4.30
3 ML YEARS		70	9	0	20	124.2	546	130	71	69	19	7	2	5	59	5	96	4	0	6	4	.600	0	0-0	8	5.20	4.98

Mike Bacsik

Pitches: L **Bats:** L **Pos:** SP-3   **Ht:** 6'3" **Wt:** 190 **Born:** 11/11/1977 **Age:** 27

Year Team	Lg	G	GS	CG	GF	IP	BFP	H	R	ER	HR	SH	SF	HB	TBB	IBB	SO	WP	Bk	W	L	Pct	ShO	Sv-Op	Hld	ERC	ERA
2004 Oklahoma*	AAA	34	9	0	3	95.0	426	106	64	48	16	5	1	1	23	1	50	0	0	8	6	.571	0	0- -	-	4.37	4.55
2001 Cleveland	AL	3	0	0	0	9.0	45	13	10	9	0	0	1	0	3	1	4	0	0	0	0	-	0	0-0	0	5.56	9.00
2002 New York	NL	11	9	1	1	55.2	247	63	29	27	8	5	1	4	19	3	30	0	0	3	2	.600	0	0-0	0	5.13	4.37
2003 New York	NL	5	3	0	1	17.2	85	28	21	20	5	0	1	0	8	0	12	0	0	1	2	.333	0	0-0	0	9.79	10.19
2004 Texas	AL	3	3	0	0	15.2	63	16	8	8	2	0	0	2	1	0	6	0	0	1	1	.500	0	0-0	0	3.67	4.60
4 ML YEARS		22	15	1	2	98.0	440	120	68	64	15	5	3	7	31	4	52	0	0	5	5	.500	0	0-0	0	5.70	5.88

Cha Seung Baek

Pitches: R **Bats:** R **Pos:** SP-5; RP-2   **Ht:** 6'4" **Wt:** 190 **Born:** 5/29/1980 **Age:** 25

Year Team	Lg	G	GS	CG	GF	IP	BFP	H	R	ER	HR	SH	SF	HB	TBB	IBB	SO	WP	Bk	W	L	Pct	ShO	Sv-Op	Hld	ERC	ERA
1999 Mariners	R	8	4	0	1	27.0	112	30	13	11	2	2	0	0	6	0	25	2	3	3	0	1.000	0	0- -	-	3.91	3.67
2000 Wisconsin	A	24	24	0	0	127.2	547	137	71	56	13	6	2	5	36	0	99	6	0	8	5	.615	0	0- -	-	4.21	3.95
2001 Sn Brnardino	A+	5	4	0	0	21.0	81	17	10	8	2	0	1	2	2	0	16	0	0	1	0	1.000	0	0- -	-	2.34	3.43
2003 San Antonio	AA	9	9	0	0	56.0	229	49	18	16	2	2	0	4	17	1	46	0	0	3	3	.500	0	0- -	-	2.92	2.57
2004 Mariners	R	2	2	0	0	7.0	25	3	2	1	0	0	0	0	1	0	5	1	0	0	0	-	0	0- -	-	0.60	1.29
2004 Tacoma	AAA	14	14	0	0	72.2	323	85	41	34	7	4	5	2	24	0	56	2	0	5	4	.556	0	0- -	-	4.83	4.21
2004 Seattle	AL	7	5	0	2	31.0	139	35	23	19	5	0	0	2	11	1	20	2	0	2	4	.333	0	0-0	0	5.26	5.52

Carlos Baerga

Bats: B **Throws:** R **Pos:** PH-70; 1B-6; DH-2   **Ht:** 5'11" **Wt:** 215 **Born:** 11/4/1968 **Age:** 36

Year Team	Lg	G	AB	H	2B	3B	HR	(Hm	Rd)	TB	R	RBI	RC	TBB	IBB	SO	HBP	SH	SF	SB	CS	SB%	GDP	Avg	OBP	Slg
2004 Tucson*	AAA	1	4	1	1	0	0	(-	-)	2	1	0	0	0	0	0	0	0	0	0	0	-	0	.250	.250	.500
1990 Cleveland	AL	108	312	81	17	2	7	(3	4)	123	46	47	36	16	2	57	4	1	5	0	2	.00	4	.260	.300	.394
1991 Cleveland	AL	158	593	171	28	2	11	(2	9)	236	80	69	81	48	5	74	6	4	3	3	2	.60	12	.288	.346	.398
1992 Cleveland	AL	161	657	205	32	1	20	(9	11)	299	92	105	103	35	10	76	13	2	9	10	2	.83	15	.312	.354	.455
1993 Cleveland	AL	154	624	200	28	6	21	(8	13)	303	105	114	104	34	7	68	6	3	13	15	4	.79	17	.321	.355	.486
1994 Cleveland	AL	103	442	139	32	2	19	(8	11)	232	81	80	74	10	1	45	6	3	8	8	2	.80	10	.314	.333	.525
1995 Cleveland	AL	135	557	175	28	2	15	(7	8)	252	87	90	87	35	6	31	3	0	5	11	2	.85	15	.314	.355	.452
1996 Cle-NYM		126	507	129	28	0	12	(5	7)	193	59	66	51	21	0	27	9	2	5	1	1	.50	23	.254	.293	.381
1997 New York	NL	133	467	131	25	1	9	(4	5)	185	53	52	53	20	1	54	3	0	4	2	6	.25	13	.281	.311	.396
1998 New York	NL	147	511	136	27	1	7	(3	4)	186	46	53	51	24	6	55	6	3	7	0	1	.00	21	.266	.303	.364
1999 SD-Cle		55	137	33	1	0	3	(2	1)	43	10	10	13	10	1	24	2	2	1	2	1	.67	5	.241	.300	.314
2002 Boston	AL	73	182	52	11	0	2	(1	1)	69	17	19	18	7	1	20	2	1	2	6	0	1.00	6	.286	.316	.379
2003 Arizona	NL	105	207	71	13	0	4	(4	0)	96	31	39	38	18	1	20	2	1	3	1	1	.50	6	.343	.396	.464
2004 Arizona	NL	79	85	20	2	0	2	(0	2)	28	6	11	10	6	0	12	3	0	0	0	0	-	7	.235	.309	.329
1996 Cleveland	AL	100	424	113	25	0	10	(5	5)	168	54	55	47	16	0	25	7	2	4	1	1	.50	15	.267	.302	.396
1996 New York	NL	26	83	16	3	0	2	(0	2)	25	5	11	4	5	0	2	2	0	1	0	0	-	8	.193	.253	.301
1999 San Diego	NL	33	80	20	1	0	2	(1	1)	27	6	5	9	6	0	14	2	1	0	1	0	1.00	5	.250	.318	.338
1999 Cleveland	AL	22	57	13	0	0	1	(1	0)	16	4	5	3	4	1	10	0	1	1	1	1	.50	3	.228	.274	.281
13 ML YEARS		1537	5281	1543	272	17	132	(56	76)	2245	713	755	718	284	41	563	65	25	66	59	24	.71	154	.292	.332	.425

Danys Baez

Pitches: R **Bats:** R **Pos:** RP-62   **Ht:** 6'3" **Wt:** 225 **Born:** 9/10/1977 **Age:** 27

Year Team	Lg	G	GS	CG	GF	IP	BFP	H	R	ER	HR	SH	SF	HB	TBB	IBB	SO	WP	Bk	W	L	Pct	ShO	Sv-Op	Hld	ERC	ERA
2001 Cleveland	AL	43	0	0	8	50.1	202	34	22	14	5	0	1	3	20	4	52	3	0	5	3	.625	0	0-1	14	2.51	2.50
2002 Cleveland	AL	39	26	1	9	165.1	726	160	84	81	14	2	8	9	82	5	130	6	1	10	11	.476	0	6-8	0	4.35	4.41
2003 Cleveland	AL	73	0	0	46	75.2	318	65	36	32	9	6	1	4	23	0	66	5	0	2	9	.182	0	25-35	5	3.22	3.81
2004 Tampa Bay	AL	62	0	0	59	68.0	295	60	31	27	6	5	1	7	29	4	52	3	1	4	4	.500	0	30-33	1	3.73	3.57
4 ML YEARS		217	26	1	122	359.1	1541	319	173	154	34	13	11	23	154	13	300	17	2	21	27	.438	0	61-77	20	3.72	3.86

Jeff Bagwell

Bats: R **Throws:** R **Pos:** 1B-152; DH-2; PH-2   **Ht:** 6'0" **Wt:** 215 **Born:** 5/27/1968 **Age:** 37

Year Team	Lg	G	AB	H	2B	3B	HR	(Hm	Rd)	TB	R	RBI	RC	TBB	IBB	SO	HBP	SH	SF	SB	CS	SB%	GDP	Avg	OBP	Slg
1991 Houston	NL	156	554	163	26	4	15	(6	9)	242	79	82	95	75	5	116	13	1	7	7	4	.64	12	.294	.387	.437
1992 Houston	NL	162	586	160	34	6	18	(8	10)	260	87	96	96	84	13	97	12	2	13	10	6	.63	17	.273	.368	.444
1993 Houston	NL	142	535	171	37	4	20	(9	11)	276	76	88	102	62	6	73	3	0	9	13	4	.76	20	.320	.388	.516
1994 Houston	NL	110	400	147	32	2	39	(23	16)	300	104	116	121	65	14	65	4	0	10	15	4	.79	12	.368	.451	.750
1995 Houston	NL	114	448	130	29	0	21	(10	11)	222	88	87	89	79	12	102	6	0	6	12	5	.71	9	.290	.399	.496
1996 Houston	NL	162	568	179	48	2	31	(16	15)	324	111	120	144	135	20	114	10	0	6	21	7	.75	15	.315	.451	.570
1997 Houston	NL	162	566	162	40	2	43	(22	21)	335	109	135	142	127	27	122	16	0	8	31	10	.76	10	.286	.425	.592
1998 Houston	NL	147	540	164	33	1	34	(20	14)	301	124	111	125	109	8	90	7	0	5	19	7	.73	14	.304	.424	.557
1999 Houston	NL	162	562	171	35	0	42	(12	30)	332	143	126	148	149	16	127	11	0	7	30	11	.73	18	.304	.454	.591
2000 Houston	NL	159	590	183	37	1	47	(28	19)	363	152	132	144	107	11	116	15	0	7	9	6	.60	19	.310	.424	.615
2001 Houston	NL	161	600	173	43	4	39	(21	18)	341	126	130	130	106	5	135	6	0	5	11	3	.79	20	.288	.397	.568
2002 Houston	NL	158	571	166	33	2	31	(16	15)	296	94	98	108	101	8	130	10	0	9	7	3	.70	16	.291	.401	.518
2003 Houston	NL	160	605	168	28	2	39	(22	17)	317	109	100	116	88	3	119	6	0	3	11	4	.73	25	.278	.373	.524
2004 Houston	NL	156	572	152	29	2	27	(18	9)	266	104	89	106	96	6	131	8	0	3	6	4	.60	12	.266	.377	.465
14 ML YEARS		2111	7697	2289	484	32	446	(231	215)	4175	1506	1510	1666	1383	154	1537	127	3	98	202	78	.72	219	.297	.408	.542

Jeff Bajenaru

Pitches: R **Bats:** R **Pos:** RP-9   **Ht:** 6'1" **Wt:** 190 **Born:** 3/21/1978 **Age:** 27

Year Team	Lg	G	GS	CG	GF	IP	BFP	H	R	ER	HR	SH	SF	HB	TBB	IBB	SO	WP	Bk	W	L	Pct	ShO	Sv-Op	Hld	ERC	ERA
2000 Bristol	R+	12	0	0	11	14.1	61	10	6	6	2	0	0	0	5	0	31	2	0	1	1	.500	0	5--	-	2.35	3.77
2000 Winstn-Salm	A+	10	0	0	7	12.1	52	7	6	6	1	0	3	2	5	0	15	4	0	2	0	1.000	0	2--	-	2.23	4.38
2001 Winstn-Salm	A+	35	0	0	0	40.1	21	32	16	15	3	0	0	1	21	2	51	3	1	2	4	.333	0	10--	-	30.58	3.35
2001 Birmingham	AA	2	0	0	28	4.1	174	4	0	0	0	4	0	0	3	0	5	1	0	0	0	-	0	0--	-	0.39	0.00
2003 Birmingham	AA	50	0	0	27	64.2	271	53	29	23	2	2	5	0	28	3	62	8	0	4	2	.667	0	14--	-	2.69	3.20
2004 Birmingham	AA	32	0	0	25	33.2	132	19	9	5	3	0	0	0	11	0	51	0	0	2	0	1.000	0	12--	-	1.58	1.34
2004 Charlotte	AAA	16	0	0	15	20.0	76	12	6	4	2	0	0	1	3	0	16	1	0	1	2	.333	0	10--	-	1.46	1.80
2004 Chicago	AL	9	0	0	4	8.1	44	15	10	10	0	1	0	0	6	1	8	0	0	0	1	.000	0	0-0	0	9.52	10.80

Paul Bako

Bats: L **Throws:** R **Pos:** C-47; PH-3   **Ht:** 6'2" **Wt:** 205 **Born:** 6/20/1972 **Age:** 33

Year Team	Lg	G	AB	H	2B	3B	HR	(Hm	Rd)	TB	R	RBI	RC	TBB	IBB	SO	HBP	SH	SF	SB	CS	SB%	GDP	Avg	OBP	Slg
1998 Detroit	AL	96	305	83	12	1	3	(2	1)	106	23	30	34	23	4	82	0	1	4	1	1	.50	3	.272	.319	.348
1999 Houston	NL	73	215	55	14	1	2	(2	0)	77	16	17	26	26	3	57	0	3	3	1	1	.50	4	.256	.332	.358
2000 Hou-Fla-Atl	NL	81	221	50	10	1	2	(2	0)	68	18	20	20	27	10	64	1	1	1	0	0	-	6	.226	.312	.308
2001 Atlanta	NL	61	137	29	10	1	2	(0	2)	47	19	15	15	20	2	34	0	0	0	1	0	1.00	3	.212	.312	.343
2002 Milwaukee	NL	87	234	55	8	1	4	(2	2)	77	24	20	20	20	3	46	0	3	0	0	2	.00	4	.235	.295	.329
2003 Chicago	NL	70	188	43	13	3	0	(0	0)	62	19	17	21	22	3	47	1	1	1	0	1	.00	2	.229	.311	.330
2004 Chicago	NL	49	138	28	8	0	1	(1	0)	39	13	10	11	15	3	29	2	1	1	1	0	1.00	4	.203	.288	.283
2000 Houston	NL	1	2	0	0	0	0	(0	0)	0	0	0	0	0	0	1	0	0	0	0	0	-	0	.000	.000	.000
2000 Florida	NL	56	161	39	6	1	0	(0	0)	47	10	14	16	22	7	48	1	1	1	0	0	-	4	.242	.335	.292
2000 Atlanta	NL	24	58	11	4	0	2	(2	0)	21	8	6	4	5	3	15	0	0	0	0	0	-	2	.190	.254	.362
7 ML YEARS		517	1438	343	75	8	14	(9	5)	476	132	129	147	153	28	359	4	10	10	4	5	.44	26	.239	.312	.331

Rocco Baldelli

Bats: R **Throws:** R **Pos:** CF-124; DH-13; PR-2; PH-1   **Ht:** 6'4" **Wt:** 187 **Born:** 9/25/1981 **Age:** 23

Year Team	Lg	G	AB	H	2B	3B	HR	(Hm	Rd)	TB	R	RBI	RC	TBB	IBB	SO	HBP	SH	SF	SB	CS	SB%	GDP	Avg	OBP	Slg
2000 Princeton	R+	60	232	50	9	2	3	(-	-)	72	33	25	19	12	0	56	5	2	0	11	3	.79	5	.216	.269	.310
2001 Chrlstn - SC	A	113	406	101	23	6	8	(-	-)	160	58	55	48	23	0	89	11	5	6	25	9	.74	7	.249	.303	.394
2002 Bakersfield	A+	77	312	104	19	1	14	(-	-)	167	63	51	62	18	2	63	7	4	1	21	6	.78	2	.333	.382	.535
2002 Orlando	AA	17	70	26	3	1	2	(-	-)	37	10	13	15	5	0	11	2	0	3	3	2	.60	1	.371	.413	.529
2002 Durham	AAA	23	96	28	6	1	3	(-	-)	45	13	7	10	0	0	23	0	2	0	2	5	.29	1	.292	.292	.469
2003 Tampa Bay	AL	156	637	184	32	8	11	(2	9)	265	89	78	77	30	4	128	6	3	7	27	10	.73	10	.289	.326	.416
2004 Tampa Bay	AL	136	518	145	27	3	16	(6	10)	226	79	74	70	30	2	88	8	3	6	17	4	.81	12	.280	.326	.436
2 ML YEARS		292	1155	329	59	11	27	(8	19)	491	168	152	147	60	6	216	16	6	12	44	14	.76	22	.285	.326	.425

James Baldwin

Pitches: R **Bats:** R **Pos:** SP-2   **Ht:** 6'3" **Wt:** 235 **Born:** 7/15/1971 **Age:** 33

Year Team	Lg	G	GS	CG	GF	IP	BFP	H	R	ER	HR	SH	SF	HB	TBB	IBB	SO	WP	Bk	W	L	Pct	ShO	Sv-Op	Hld	ERC	ERA
2004 Norfolk*	AAA	5	5	0	0	31.0	131	34	11	10	3	3	0	2	5	0	24	0	0	3	2	.600	0	0--	-	3.91	2.90
2004 Toledo*	AAA	18	16	3	2	115.2	457	110	52	48	12	7	2	3	20	3	61	0	0	5	7	.417	0	1--	-	3.14	3.73
1995 Chicago	AL	6	4	0	0	14.2	81	32	22	21	6	0	0	0	9	1	10	1	0	0	1	.000	0	0-0	0	16.49	12.89

(Pitching — continued)

Year Team	Lg	G	GS	CG	GF	IP	BFP	H	R	ER	HR	SH	SF	HB	TBB	IBB	SO	WP	Bk	W	L	Pct	ShO	Sv-Op	Hld	ERC	ERA
1996 Chicago	AL	28	28	0	0	169.0	719	168	88	83	24	2	2	4	57	3	127	12	1	11	6	.647	0	0-0	0	4.17	4.42
1997 Chicago	AL	32	32	1	0	200.0	879	205	128	117	19	3	6	5	83	3	140	14	3	12	15	.444	0	0-0	0	4.28	5.27
1998 Chicago	AL	37	24	1	3	159.0	712	176	103	94	18	3	5	10	60	2	108	5	1	13	6	.684	0	0-1	0	4.89	5.32
1999 Chicago	AL	35	33	1	1	199.1	886	219	103	113	34	4	7	7	81	1	123	11	1	12	13	.480	0	0-0	0	5.33	5.10
2000 Chicago	AL	29	28	2	0	178.0	758	185	96	92	34	6	5	8	59	3	116	4	1	14	7	.667	1	0-0	0	4.91	4.65
2001 CWS-LA	AL	29	28	2	0	175.0	764	191	95	86	25	7	7	7	63	1	95	7	0	10	11	.476	1	0-0	0	4.94	4.42
2002 Seattle	AL	30	23	0	4	150.0	662	179	95	88	26	4	2	7	49	2	88	1	0	7	10	.412	0	0-0	0	5.70	5.28
2003 Minnesota	AL	10	0	0	3	15.0	69	21	10	9	6	0	2	0	4	1	7	0	0	0	1	.000	0	1-2	1	8.09	5.40
2004 New York	NL	2	2	0	0	6.0	36	13	10	10	3	1	0	1	5	1	1	0	0	0	2	.000	0	0-0	0	18.95	15.00
2001 Chicago	AL	17	16	2	0	95.2	431	109	56	49	15	3	5	4	38	0	42	4	0	7	5	.583	1	0-0	0	5.44	4.61
2001 Los Angeles	NL	12	12	0	0	79.1	333	82	39	37	10	4	2	3	25	1	53	3	0	3	6	.333	0	0-0	0	4.35	4.20
10 ML YEARS		238	202	7	11	1266.0	5566	1389	766	713	195	30	36	49	470	18	815	55	7	79	72	.523	2	1-3	1	5.07	5.07

Grant Balfour

Pitches: R Bats: R Pos: RP-36 **Ht: 6'2" Wt: 185 Born: 12/30/1977 Age: 27**

Year Team	Lg	G	GS	CG	GF	IP	BFP	H	R	ER	HR	SH	SF	HB	TBB	IBB	SO	WP	Bk	W	L	Pct	ShO	Sv-Op	Hld	ERC	ERA
2001 Minnesota	AL	2	0	0	0	2.2	14	3	0	4	2	0	0	0	3	0	2	0	0	0	0	-	0	0-0	0	13.78	13.50
2003 Minnesota	AL	17	1	0	6	26.0	115	23	12	12	4	2	1	0	14	2	30	0	0	1	0	1.000	0	0-1	1	4.14	4.15
2004 Minnesota	AL	36	0	0	14	39.1	172	35	19	19	4	2	0	2	21	1	42	3	0	4	1	.800	0	0-1	4	4.16	4.35
3 ML YEARS		55	1	0	20	68.0	301	61	31	35	10	4	1	2	38	3	74	3	0	5	1	.833	0	0-2	5	4.47	4.63

Rod Barajas

Bats: R Throws: R Pos: C-105; 1B-2; PR-2; PH-1 **Ht: 6'2" Wt: 229 Born: 9/5/1975 Age: 29**

Year Team	Lg	G	AB	H	2B	3B	HR	(Hm	Rd)	TB	R	RBI	RC	TBB	IBB	SO	HBP	SH	SF	SB	CS	SB%	GDP	Avg	OBP	Slg
1999 Arizona	NL	5	16	4	1	0	1	(1	0)	8	3	3	2	1	0	1	0	1	0	0	0	-	0	.250	.294	.500
2000 Arizona	NL	5	13	3	0	0	1	(1	0)	6	1	3	1	0	0	4	0	0	0	0	0	-	0	.231	.231	.462
2001 Arizona	NL	51	106	17	3	0	3	(2	1)	29	9	9	4	4	0	26	0	0	0	0	0	-	0	.160	.191	.274
2002 Arizona	NL	70	154	36	10	0	3	(1	2)	55	12	23	15	10	4	25	3	2	3	1	0	1.00	4	.234	.288	.357
2003 Arizona	NL	80	220	48	15	0	3	(3	0)	72	19	28	19	14	7	43	1	1	3	0	0	-	6	.218	.265	.327
2004 Texas	AL	108	358	89	26	1	15	(8	7)	162	50	58	43	13	0	63	3	8	7	0	1	.00	3	.249	.276	.453
6 ML YEARS		319	867	197	55	1	26	(16	10)	332	94	124	84	42	11	162	7	12	13	1	1	.50	13	.227	.265	.383

Josh Bard

Bats: B Throws: R Pos: C-7 **Ht: 6'3" Wt: 215 Born: 3/20/1978 Age: 27**

Year Team*	Lg	G	AB	H	2B	3B	HR	(Hm	Rd)	TB	R	RBI	RC	TBB	IBB	SO	HBP	SH	SF	SB	CS	SB%	GDP	Avg	OBP	Slg
2004 Akron*	AA	10	30	5	1	0	0	(-	-)	6	5	5	1	7	1	5	0	1	0	0	0	-	2	.167	.324	.200
2004 Buffalo*	AAA	40	156	41	10	0	4	(-	-)	63	25	18	17	11	1	23	0	1	1	0	0	-	7	.263	.310	.404
2002 Cleveland	AL	24	90	20	5	0	3	(2	1)	34	9	12	7	4	0	13	0	1	0	0	0	-	6	.222	.255	.378
2003 Cleveland	AL	91	303	74	13	1	8	(5	3)	113	25	36	34	22	1	53	0	1	3	0	2	.00	9	.244	.293	.373
2004 Cleveland	AL	7	19	8	2	0	1	(1	0)	13	5	4	6	3	0	10	0	0	0	0	0	-	0	.421	.478	.684
3 ML YEARS		122	412	102	20	1	12	(8	4)	160	39	52	47	29	1	66	0	2	4	0	2	.00	15	.248	.264	.388

Clint Barmes

Bats: R Throws: R Pos: 2B-9; SS-9; PH-1; PR-1 **Ht: 6'0" Wt: 175 Born: 3/6/1979 Age: 26**

Year Team	Lg	G	AB	H	2B	3B	HR	(Hm	Rd)	TB	R	RBI	RC	TBB	IBB	SO	HBP	SH	SF	SB	CS	SB%	GDP	Avg	OBP	Slg
2000 Asheville	A	19	81	14	4	0	0	(-	-)	18	11	4	4	10	0	13	1	2	1	4	1	.80	3	.173	.269	.222
2000 Portland	A-	45	181	51	6	4	2	(-	-)	71	37	16	26	18	0	28	5	0	1	12	9	.57	1	.282	.361	.392
2001 Asheville	A	74	285	74	14	1	5	(-	-)	105	40	24	33	17	0	37	7	3	3	21	7	.75	6	.260	.314	.368
2001 Salem	A+	38	121	30	3	3	0	(-	-)	39	17	9	14	15	0	20	4	2	0	4	1	.80	5	.248	.350	.322
2002 Carolina	AA	103	438	119	23	2	15	(-	-)	191	62	60	62	31	3	72	9	2	5	15	11	.58	3	.272	.329	.436
2003 Co Springs	AAA	136	493	136	35	1	7	(-	-)	194	63	54	59	22	2	63	9	4	5	12	7	.63	6	.276	.316	.394
2004 Co Springs	AAA	125	533	175	42	2	16	(-	-)	269	104	51	98	28	1	61	15	9	4	20	8	.71	5	.328	.376	.505
2003 Colorado	NL	12	25	8	2	0	0	(0	0)	10	2	2	3	0	0	10	2	0	1	0	0	-	0	.320	.357	.400
2004 Colorado	NL	20	71	20	3	1	2	(0	2)	31	14	10	12	3	0	10	1	2	0	0	1	.00	2	.282	.320	.437
2 ML YEARS		32	96	28	5	1	2	(0	2)	41	16	12	15	3	0	20	3	2	1	0	1	.00	2	.292	.330	.427

Michael Barrett

Bats: R Throws: R Pos: C-130; PH-11 **Ht: 6'2" Wt: 200 Born: 10/22/1976 Age: 28**

Year Team	Lg	G	AB	H	2B	3B	HR	(Hm	Rd)	TB	R	RBI	RC	TBB	IBB	SO	HBP	SH	SF	SB	CS	SB%	GDP	Avg	OBP	Slg
1998 Montreal	NL	8	23	7	2	0	1	(0	1)	12	3	2	5	3	0	6	1	0	0	0	0	-	0	.304	.407	.522
1999 Montreal	NL	126	433	127	32	3	8	(5	3)	189	53	52	59	32	4	39	3	0	1	0	2	.00	18	.293	.345	.436
2000 Montreal	NL	89	271	58	15	1	1	(0	1)	78	28	22	19	23	5	35	1	1	1	0	1	.00	7	.214	.277	.288
2001 Montreal	NL	132	472	118	33	2	6	(3	3)	173	42	38	46	25	2	54	2	4	3	2	1	.67	14	.250	.289	.367
2002 Montreal	NL	117	376	99	20	1	12	(4	8)	157	41	49	49	40	7	65	1	6	5	6	3	.67	14	.263	.332	.418
2003 Montreal	NL	70	226	47	9	2	10	(5	5)	90	33	30	25	21	7	37	2	2	1	0	0	-	6	.208	.280	.398
2004 Chicago	NL	134	456	131	32	6	16	(9	7)	223	55	65	67	33	4	64	5	4	8	1	4	.20	13	.287	.337	.489
7 ML YEARS		676	2257	587	143	15	54	(26	28)	922	255	258	270	177	29	300	15	17	19	9	11	.45	72	.260	.316	.409

Jason Bartlett

Bats: R Throws: R Pos: SS-5; PR-4; 2B-1; DH-1; PH-1   Ht: 6'0" Wt: 180 Born: 10/30/1979 Age: 25

								BATTING											BASERUNNING				AVERAGES		
Year Team	Lg	G	AB	H	2B	3B	HR	(Hm	Rd)	TB	R	RBI	RC	TBB	IBB	SO	HBP	SH	SF	SB	CS	SB%	GDP	Avg	OBP	Slg
2001 Eugene	A-	68	267	80	12	4	3	(-	-)	109	49	37	42	28	0	47	4	2	3	12	4	.75	6	.300	.371	.408
2002 Lk Elsinore	A+	75	308	77	14	4	1	(-	-)	102	57	33	37	32	0	53	5	1	2	24	5	.83	7	.250	.329	.331
2002 Fort Myers	A+	39	145	38	7	0	2	(-	-)	51	24	9	20	17	0	24	2	1	3	11	2	.85	1	.262	.341	.352
2003 New Britain	AA	139	548	162	31	8	8	(-	-)	233	96	48	90	58	3	67	20	4	6	41	24	.63	7	.296	.380	.425
2004 Twins	R	5	14	5	1	0	0	(-	-)	6	1	1	2	0	0	3	1	0	0	0	0	-	0	.357	.400	.429
2004 Rochester	AAA	67	269	89	15	7	3	(-	-)	127	54	29	55	33	1	37	7	2	2	7	3	.70	1	.331	.415	.472
2004 Minnesota	AL	8	12	1	0	0	0	(0	0)	1	2	1	1	1	0	1	0	1	0	2	0	1.00	0	.083	.154	.083

Cliff Bartosh

Pitches: L Bats: L Pos: RP-34   Ht: 6'2" Wt: 180 Born: 9/5/1979 Age: 25

		HOW MUCH HE PITCHED						WHAT HE GAVE UP											THE RESULTS						
Year Team	Lg	G	GS	CG	GF	IP	BFP	H	R	ER	HR	SH	SF	HB	TBB	IBB	SO	WP	Bk	W	L	Pct	ShO	Sv-Op	Hld	ERC	ERA
1998 Padres	R	13	5	0	0	44.0	190	43	23	17	2	1	2	4	16	0	43	4	0	3	2	.600	0	0- -	-	3.79	3.48
1999 Fort Wayne	A	24	20	1	1	129.2	567	146	76	64	14	0	4	10	49	0	100	7	2	5	12	.294	1	0- -	-	4.67	4.44
2000 Fort Wayne	A	50	4	0	18	77.0	335	50	40	26	6	2	3	5	44	3	94	8	2	8	4	.667	0	1- -	-	2.77	3.04
2001 Lk Elsinore	A+	38	0	0	25	45.2	194	42	17	8	2	2	1	2	12	5	66	7	2	6	2	.750	0	10- -	-	2.67	1.58
2001 Mobile	AA	20	0	0	9	22.2	103	20	12	10	5	2	1	1	13	1	20	2	0	1	2	.333	0	2- -	-	4.92	3.97
2002 Mobile	AA	62	0	0	42	70.2	298	54	28	25	4	4	4	2	32	5	70	5	0	2	4	.333	0	25- -	-	2.69	3.18
2003 Portland	AAA	64	0	0	29	71.1	299	67	36	34	4	4	1	3	22	1	51	4	0	2	5	.286	0	10- -	-	3.25	4.29
2004 Buffalo	AAA	28	0	0	16	35.1	144	26	11	11	3	0	0	4	8	2	46	2	0	0	3	.000	0	3- -	-	2.26	2.80
2004 Cleveland	AL	34	0	0	2	19.1	91	22	10	10	4	0	0	0	11	0	25	0	1	1	0	1.000	0	0-2	3	6.28	4.66

Miguel Batista

Pitches: R Bats: R Pos: SP-31; RP-7   Ht: 6'2" Wt: 195 Born: 2/19/1971 Age: 34

		HOW MUCH HE PITCHED						WHAT HE GAVE UP											THE RESULTS						
Year Team	Lg	G	GS	CG	GF	IP	BFP	H	R	ER	HR	SH	SF	HB	TBB	IBB	SO	WP	Bk	W	L	Pct	ShO	Sv-Op	Hld	ERC	ERA
1992 Pittsburgh	NL	1	0	0	1	2.0	13	4	2	2	1	0	0	0	3	0	1	0	0	0	0	-	0	0-0	0	20.26	9.00
1996 Florida	NL	9	0	0	4	11.1	49	9	8	7	0	3	0	0	7	2	6	1	0	0	0	-	0	0-0	0	2.77	5.56
1997 Chicago	NL	11	6	0	2	36.1	168	36	24	23	4	4	4	1	24	2	27	2	0	0	5	.000	0	0-0	0	5.09	5.70
1998 Montreal	NL	56	13	0	12	135.0	598	141	66	57	12	7	5	6	65	7	92	6	1	3	5	.375	0	0-0	3	4.70	3.80
1999 Montreal	NL	39	17	2	3	134.2	606	146	88	73	10	8	11	7	58	2	95	6	0	8	7	.533	1	1-1	0	4.62	4.88
2000 Mon-KC		18	9	0	2	65.1	310	85	68	62	19	1	2	2	37	2	37	4	0	2	7	.222	0	0-2	0	8.37	8.54
2001 Arizona	NL	48	18	0	6	139.1	581	113	57	52	13	9	3	10	60	2	90	6	0	11	8	.579	0	0-0	4	3.43	3.36
2002 Arizona	NL	36	29	1	2	184.2	790	172	99	88	12	5	8	6	70	3	112	9	2	8	9	.471	0	0-0	2	3.45	4.29
2003 Arizona	NL	36	29	2	5	193.1	822	197	85	76	13	10	6	8	60	3	142	7	0	10	9	.526	1	0-0	0	3.77	3.54
2004 Toronto	AL	38	31	2	7	198.2	867	206	115	106	22	7	6	3	96	1	104	12	0	10	13	.435	1	5-5	0	4.84	4.80
2000 Montreal	NL	4	0	0	0	8.1	49	19	14	13	2	1	1	2	3	0	7	0	0	0	1	.000	0	0-2	0	14.73	14.04
2000 Kansas City	AL	14	9	0	2	57.0	261	66	54	49	17	0	1	0	34	2	30	4	0	2	6	.250	0	0-0	0	7.50	7.74
10 ML YEARS		292	152	7	44	1100.2	4804	1109	612	546	106	54	45	43	480	24	706	53	3	52	63	.452	3	6-8	9	4.38	4.46

Tony Batista

Bats: R Throws: R Pos: 3B-155; PH-5   Ht: 6'0" Wt: 205 Born: 12/9/1973 Age: 31

								BATTING											BASERUNNING				AVERAGES		
Year Team	Lg	G	AB	H	2B	3B	HR	(Hm	Rd)	TB	R	RBI	RC	TBB	IBB	SO	HBP	SH	SF	SB	CS	SB%	GDP	Avg	OBP	Slg
1996 Oakland	AL	74	238	71	10	2	6	(1	5)	103	38	25	37	19	0	49	1	0	2	7	3	.70	2	.298	.350	.433
1997 Oakland	AL	68	188	38	10	1	4	(0	4)	62	22	18	14	14	0	31	2	3	0	2	2	.50	8	.202	.265	.330
1998 Arizona	NL	106	293	80	16	1	18	(9	9)	152	46	41	46	18	0	52	3	0	4	1	1	.50	7	.273	.318	.519
1999 Ari-Tor		142	519	144	30	1	31	(10	21)	269	77	100	87	38	4	96	6	3	7	4	0	1.00	12	.277	.330	.518
2000 Toronto	AL	154	620	163	32	2	41	(25	16)	322	96	114	94	35	1	121	6	0	3	5	4	.56	15	.263	.307	.519
2001 Tor-Bal	AL	156	579	138	27	6	25	(14	11)	252	70	87	70	32	1	113	4	0	7	5	2	.71	9	.238	.280	.435
2002 Baltimore	AL	161	615	150	36	1	31	(14	17)	281	90	87	79	50	9	107	11	0	6	4	4	.56	13	.244	.309	.457
2003 Baltimore	AL	161	631	148	20	1	26	(10	16)	248	76	99	66	28	4	102	5	0	6	4	3	.57	20	.235	.270	.393
2004 Montreal	NL	157	606	146	30	2	32	(13	19)	276	76	110	68	26	4	78	4	4	10	14	6	.70	14	.241	.272	.455
1999 Arizona	NL	44	144	37	5	0	5	(1	4)	57	16	21	21	16	3	17	2	0	2	2	0	1.00	1	.257	.335	.396
1999 Toronto	AL	98	375	107	25	1	26	(9	17)	212	61	79	66	22	1	79	4	3	5	2	0	1.00	11	.285	.328	.565
2001 Toronto	AL	72	271	56	11	1	13	(9	4)	108	29	45	27	13	1	66	4	0	3	0	1	.00	2	.207	.251	.399
2001 Baltimore	AL	84	308	82	16	5	12	(5	7)	144	41	42	43	19	0	47	0	0	4	5	1	.83	7	.266	.305	.468
9 ML YEARS		1179	4289	1078	211	17	214	(96	118)	1965	591	681	561	260	23	749	42	10	45	47	25	.65	100	.251	.298	.458

Rick Bauer

Pitches: R Bats: R Pos: RP-21; SP-2   Ht: 6'6" Wt: 212 Born: 1/10/1977 Age: 28

		HOW MUCH HE PITCHED						WHAT HE GAVE UP											THE RESULTS						
Year Team	Lg	G	GS	CG	GF	IP	BFP	H	R	ER	HR	SH	SF	HB	TBB	IBB	SO	WP	Bk	W	L	Pct	ShO	Sv-Op	Hld	ERC	ERA
2004 Bowie*	AA	1	1	0	0	3.0	11	2	0	0	0	0	0	0	0	0	1	0	0	0	0	-	0	0- -	-	0.91	0.00
2004 Ottawa*	AAA	11	11	0	0	63.0	266	69	28	28	3	4	3	4	19	0	42	1	2	3	5	.375	0	0- -	-	4.25	4.00
2001 Baltimore	AL	6	6	0	0	33.0	143	35	22	17	7	0	1	1	9	0	16	0	0	0	5	.000	0	0-0	0	4.74	4.64
2002 Baltimore	AL	56	1	0	15	83.2	358	84	41	37	12	2	2	4	36	4	45	4	0	6	7	.462	0	1-5	12	4.78	3.98
2003 Baltimore	AL	35	0	0	10	61.1	259	58	36	31	5	1	3	4	24	3	43	6	0	0	0	-	0	0-1	3	3.87	4.55
2004 Baltimore	AL	23	2	0	7	53.2	230	49	31	28	4	0	0	4	20	0	37	1	0	2	1	.667	0	0-1	0	3.59	4.70
4 ML YEARS		120	9	0	32	231.2	990	226	130	113	28	3	6	13	89	7	141	11	0	8	13	.381	0	1-7	15	4.25	4.39

Danny Bautista

Bats: R Throws: R Pos: RF-134; PH-3; CF-2; DH-1   Ht: 5'11" Wt: 204 Born: 5/24/1972 Age: 33

Year Team	Lg	G	AB	H	2B	3B	HR	(Hm	Rd)	TB	R	RBI	RC	TBB	IBB	SO	HBP	SH	SF	SB	CS	SB%	GDP	Avg	OBP	Slg
1993 Detroit	AL	17	61	19	3	0	1	(0	1)	25	6	9	8	1	0	10	0	0	1	3	1	.75	1	.311	.317	.410
1994 Detroit	AL	31	99	23	4	1	4	(1	3)	41	12	15	9	3	0	18	0	0	0	1	2	.33	3	.232	.255	.414
1995 Detroit	AL	89	271	55	9	0	4	(3	4)	85	28	27	18	12	0	68	0	6	0	4	1	.80	6	.203	.237	.314
1996 Det-Atl		42	84	19	2	0	2	(1	1)	27	13	9	8	11	0	20	1	0	0	1	2	.33	4	.226	.323	.321
1997 Atlanta	NL	64	103	25	3	2	3	(1	2)	41	14	9	11	5	1	24	1	2	1	2	0	1.00	3	.243	.282	.398
1998 Atlanta	NL	82	144	36	11	0	3	(2	1)	56	17	17	15	7	0	21	0	3	2	1	0	1.00	4	.250	.281	.389
1999 Florida	NL	70	205	59	10	1	5	(2	3)	86	32	24	25	4	0	30	1	0	1	3	0	1.00	5	.288	.303	.420
2000 Fla-Ari	NL	131	351	100	20	7	11	(5	6)	167	54	59	54	25	4	50	3	4	5	6	2	.75	11	.285	.333	.476
2001 Arizona	NL	100	222	67	11	2	5	(0	5)	97	26	26	31	14	1	31	1	2	0	3	2	.60	7	.302	.346	.437
2002 Arizona	NL	40	154	50	5	2	6	(4	2)	77	22	23	26	11	2	21	0	0	1	4	2	.67	4	.325	.367	.500
2003 Arizona	NL	88	284	78	16	3	4	(2	2)	112	29	36	34	21	2	50	4	2	3	3	2	.60	7	.275	.330	.394
2004 Arizona	NL	141	539	154	27	1	11	(4	7)	216	64	65	67	35	2	66	4	1	3	6	2	.75	19	.286	.332	.401
1996 Detroit	AL	25	64	16	2	0	2	(1	1)	24	12	8	8	9	0	15	0	0	0	1	2	.33	1	.250	.342	.375
1996 Atlanta	NL	17	20	3	0	0	0	(0	0)	3	1	1	0	2	0	5	1	0	0	0	0	-	3	.150	.261	.150
2000 Florida	NL	44	89	17	4	0	4	(1	3)	33	9	12	8	5	0	20	0	0	0	1	0	1.00	1	.191	.234	.371
2000 Arizona	NL	87	262	83	16	7	7	(4	3)	134	45	47	46	20	4	30	3	4	5	5	2	.71	10	.317	.366	.511
12 ML YEARS		895	2517	685	121	19	62	(25	37)	1030	317	319	306	149	12	409	15	20	17	37	16	.70	74	.272	.315	.409

Denny Bautista

Pitches: R Bats: R Pos: SP-5; RP-2   Ht: 6'5" Wt: 170 Born: 8/23/1980 Age: 24

Year Team	Lg	G	GS	CG	GF	IP	BFP	H	R	ER	HR	SH	SF	HB	TBB	IBB	SO	WP	Bk	W	L	Pct	ShO	Sv-Op	Hld	ERC	ERA
2000 Marlins	R	11	11	2	0	60.0	260	49	24	17	1	1	0	8	17	1	58	3	1	6	2	.750	0	0- -		2.45	2.55
2000 Utica	A-	1	1	0	0	5.0	21	4	3	2	0	0	0	1	2	0	5	0	0	0	0	-	0	0- -		3.13	3.60
2001 Kane County	A	8	7	0	0	39.1	172	43	21	19	2	2	1	2	14	0	20	4	2	3	1	.750	0	0- -		4.30	4.35
2001 Utica	A-	7	7	0	0	39.0	156	25	16	9	0	0	2	4	6	0	31	3	0	3	1	.750	0	0- -		1.30	2.08
2002 Jupiter	A+	19	15	0	1	88.1	379	80	52	49	6	3	2	4	40	0	79	15	3	4	6	.400	0	0- -		3.73	4.99
2003 Jupiter	A+	14	14	0	0	84.0	353	68	32	30	2	1	2	5	35	0	77	7	1	8	4	.667	0	0- -		2.82	3.21
2003 Carolina	AA	11	11	0	0	53.1	239	45	33	22	5	3	1	1	35	0	61	8	0	4	5	.444	0	0- -		4.17	3.71
2004 Bowie	AA	14	13	0	0	62.2	280	58	37	33	5	4	2	1	33	1	72	5	0	3	5	.375	0	0- -		3.95	4.74
2004 Wichita	AA	12	12	2	0	81.2	341	68	32	23	3	4	3	4	32	0	73	10	1	4	3	.571	0	0- -		2.92	2.53
2004 Bal-KC	AL	7	5	0	0	29.2	142	44	28	28	3	0	1	3	13	1	19	3	2	0	4	.000	0	0-0		7.76	8.49
2004 Baltimore	AL	2	0	0	0	2.0	15	6	8	8	1	0	1	1	2	0	1	1	0	0	0	-	0	0-0		28.67	36.00
2004 Kansas City	AL	5	5	0	0	27.2	127	38	20	20	2	0	0	2	11	1	18	2	2	0	4	.000	0	0-0		6.50	6.51

Jose Bautista

Bats: R Throws: R Pos: RF-19; 3B-17; PH-17; PR-14; LF-5; CF-3; DH-2   Ht: 6'0" Wt: 192 Born: 10/19/1980 Age: 24

Year Team	Lg	G	AB	H	2B	3B	HR	(Hm	Rd)	TB	R	RBI	RC	TBB	IBB	SO	HBP	SH	SF	SB	CS	SB%	GDP	Avg	OBP	Slg
2001 Williamsport	A-	62	220	63	10	3	5	(-	-)	94	43	30	35	21	0	41	6	0	0	8	1	.89	5	.286	.364	.427
2002 Hickory	A	129	438	132	26	3	14	(-	-)	206	72	57	82	67	3	104	8	5	2	3	2	.60	12	.301	.402	.470
2003 Pirates	R	7	23	8	1	0	1	(-	-)	12	5	3	5	4	1	7	0	0	1	0	0	-	0	.348	.429	.522
2003 Lynchburg	A+	51	165	40	14	2	4	(-	-)	70	28	20	24	27	0	48	3	0	1	1	5	.17	1	.242	.359	.424
2004 Bal-TB-KC-Pit		64	88	18	3	0	0	(0	0)	21	6	2	2	7	0	40	0	1	0	0	1	.00	1	.205	.263	.239
2004 Baltimore	AL	16	11	3	0	0	0	(0	0)	3	3	0	1	1	0	3	0	0	0	0	0	-	0	.273	.333	.273
2004 Tampa Bay	AL	12	12	2	0	0	0	(0	0)	2	1	1	0	3	0	7	0	0	0	0	1	.00	0	.167	.333	.167
2004 Kansas City	AL	13	25	5	1	0	0	(0	0)	6	1	1	0	1	0	12	0	0	0	0	0	-	0	.200	.231	.240
2004 Pittsburgh	NL	23	40	8	2	0	0	(0	0)	10	1	0	1	2	0	18	0	1	0	0	0	-	1	.200	.238	.250

Jason Bay

Bats: R Throws: R Pos: LF-117; PH-6; CF-5   Ht: 6'2" Wt: 200 Born: 9/20/1978 Age: 26

Year Team	Lg	G	AB	H	2B	3B	HR	(Hm	Rd)	TB	R	RBI	RC	TBB	IBB	SO	HBP	SH	SF	SB	CS	SB%	GDP	Avg	OBP	Slg
2000 Vermont	A-	35	135	41	5	0	2	(-	-)	52	17	12	20	11	0	25	1	0	1	17	4	.81	2	.304	.358	.385
2001 Jupiter	A+	38	123	24	4	1	1	(-	-)	33	12	10	10	18	1	26	2	1	1	10	3	.77	4	.195	.306	.268
2001 Clinton	A	87	318	115	20	4	13	(-	-)	182	67	61	80	48	0	62	4	1	2	15	2	.88	4	.362	.449	.572
2002 St. Lucie	A+	69	261	71	12	2	9	(-	-)	114	48	54	45	34	3	54	5	2	3	22	2	.92	4	.272	.363	.437
2002 Binghamton	AA	34	107	31	4	2	4	(-	-)	51	17	19	21	15	0	23	3	0	3	13	3	.81	2	.290	.383	.477
2002 Mobile	AA	23	81	25	5	2	4	(-	-)	46	16	12	18	13	1	22	1	0	0	4	2	.67	0	.309	.411	.568
2003 Portland	AAA	91	307	93	11	1	20	(-	-)	166	64	59	71	55	1	71	5	0	6	23	4	.85	3	.303	.410	.541
2004 Nashville	AAA	4	10	4	2	1	0	(-	-)	9	3	3	3	3	0	5	0	0	0	0	0	-	0	.400	.538	.900
2003 SD-Pit	NL	30	87	25	7	1	4	(2	2)	46	15	14	19	19	0	29	1	0	0	3	1	.75	0	.287	.421	.529
2004 Pittsburgh	NL	120	411	116	24	4	26	(15	11)	226	61	82	75	41	2	129	10	5	5	4	6	.40	9	.282	.358	.550
2003 San Diego	NL	3	8	2	1	0	0	(0	0)	6	2	2	2	1	0	1	0	0	0	0	0	-	0	.250	.400	.750
2003 Pittsburgh	NL	27	79	23	6	1	3	(2	1)	40	13	12	17	18	0	28	0	0	0	3	1	.75	0	.291	.423	.506
2 ML YEARS		150	498	141	31	5	30	(17	13)	272	76	96	94	60	2	158	11	5	5	7	7	.50	9	.283	.369	.546

Rod Beck

Pitches: R Bats: R Pos: RP-26   Ht: 6'1" Wt: 235 Born: 8/3/1968 Age: 36

Year Team	Lg	G	GS	CG	GF	IP	BFP	H	R	ER	HR	SH	SF	HB	TBB	IBB	SO	WP	Bk	W	L	Pct	ShO	Sv-Op	Hld	ERC	ERA
1991 San Francisco	NL	31	0	0	10	52.1	214	53	22	22	4	4	2	1	13	2	38	0	0	1	1	.500	0	1-1	1	3.52	3.78
1992 San Francisco	NL	65	0	0	42	92.0	352	62	20	18	4	6	2	2	15	2	87	5	2	3	3	.500	0	17-23	4	1.44	1.76
1993 San Francisco	NL	76	0	0	71	79.1	309	57	20	19	11	6	3	3	13	4	86	4	0	3	1	.750	0	48-52	0	2.05	2.16
1994 San Francisco	NL	48	0	0	47	48.2	207	49	17	15	10	3	3	0	13	2	39	0	0	2	4	.333	0	28-28	0	4.17	2.77
1995 San Francisco	NL	60	0	0	52	58.2	255	60	31	29	7	4	3	2	21	3	42	2	0	5	6	.455	0	33-43	0	4.20	4.45
1996 San Francisco	NL	63	0	0	58	62.0	248	56	23	23	9	0	2	1	10	2	48	1	0	0	9	.000	0	35-42	0	2.95	3.34

HOW MUCH HE PITCHED / WHAT HE GAVE UP / THE RESULTS

Year Team	Lg	G	GS	CG	GF	IP	BFP	H	R	ER	HR	SH	SF	HB	TBB	IBB	SO	WP	Bk	W	L	Pct	ShO	Sv-Op	Hld	ERC	ERA
1997 San Francisco	NL	73	0	0	66	70.0	281	67	31	27	7	1	0	2	8	2	53	1	0	7	4	.636	0	37-45	1	2.84	3.47
1998 Chicago	NL	81	0	0	70	80.1	349	86	33	27	11	2	5	2	20	4	81	2	0	3	4	.429	0	51-58	1	4.05	3.02
1999 ChC-Bos	AL	43	0	0	27	44.0	196	50	29	29	5	2	2	1	18	3	25	1	0	2	5	.286	0	10-15	3	4.99	5.93
2000 Boston	AL	34	0	0	8	40.2	169	34	15	14	2	2	0	2	12	1	35	1	0	3	0	1.000	0	0-3	7	2.59	3.10
2001 Boston	AL	68	0	0	28	80.2	342	77	42	35	15	3	2	3	28	6	63	5	1	6	4	.600	0	6-11	15	4.25	3.90
2003 San Diego	NL	36	0	0	30	35.1	140	25	7	7	4	1	0	1	11	2	32	0	0	3	2	.600	0	20-20	1	2.35	1.78
2004 San Diego	NL	26	0	0	10	24.0	108	27	18	17	8	0	2	0	9	0	15	1	0	2	0	.000	0	0-0	5	6.28	6.38
1999 Chicago	NL	31	0	0	19	30.0	141	41	26	26	5	2	2	0	13	3	13	1	0	2	4	.333	0	7-11	0	6.75	7.80
1999 Boston	AL	12	0	0	8	14.0	55	9	3	3	0	0	0	1	5	0	12	0	0	0	1	.000	0	3-4	2	1.79	1.93
13 ML YEARS		704	0	0	519	768.0	3170	703	308	282	97	34	26	20	191	33	644	23	3	38	45	.458	0	286-341	38	3.23	3.30

Josh Beckett

Pitches: R Bats: R Pos: SP-26   **Ht: 6'5" Wt: 216 Born: 5/15/1980 Age: 25**

Year Team	Lg	G	GS	CG	GF	IP	BFP	H	R	ER	HR	SH	SF	HB	TBB	IBB	SO	WP	Bk	W	L	Pct	ShO	Sv-Op	Hld	ERC	ERA
2001 Florida	NL	4	4	0	0	24.0	99	14	9	4	3	0	0	1	11	0	24	1	0	2	2	.500	0	0-0	0	2.36	1.50
2002 Florida	NL	23	21	0	0	107.2	454	93	56	49	13	5	3	1	44	2	113	5	0	6	7	.462	0	0-0	0	3.50	4.10
2003 Florida	NL	24	23	0	1	142.0	601	132	54	48	9	5	1	2	56	4	152	6	1	9	8	.529	0	0-0	0	3.44	3.04
2004 Florida	NL	26	26	1	0	156.2	654	137	72	66	16	9	3	6	54	3	152	5	0	9	9	.500	1	0-0	0	3.32	3.79
4 ML YEARS		77	74	1	1	430.1	1808	376	191	167	41	19	7	10	165	9	441	17	1	26	26	.500	1	0-0	0	3.35	3.49

Erik Bedard

Pitches: L Bats: L Pos: SP-26; RP-1   **Ht: 6'1" Wt: 186 Born: 3/6/1979 Age: 26**

Year Team	Lg	G	GS	CG	GF	IP	BFP	H	R	ER	HR	SH	SF	HB	TBB	IBB	SO	WP	Bk	W	L	Pct	ShO	Sv-Op	Hld	ERC	ERA
1999 Orioles	R	8	6	0	1	29.0	117	20	7	6	1	0	0	0	13	0	41	3	0	2	1	.667	0	0--	-	2.25	1.86
2000 Delmarva	A	29	22	1	2	111.0	466	98	48	44	2	1	0	10	35	0	131	14	0	9	4	.692	1	2--	-	2.91	3.57
2001 Frederick	A+	17	17	0	0	96.1	382	68	27	23	4	3	1	9	26	0	130	3	0	9	2	.818	0	0--	-	2.09	2.15
2001 Orioles	R	2	2	0	0	6.0	25	4	2	2	0	0	0	0	3	0	7	0	0	1	0	1.000	0	0--	-	3.36	3.00
2002 Bowie	AA	13	12	0	1	68.2	282	43	18	15	0	2	3	3	30	0	66	6	0	6	3	.667	0	0--	-	1.79	1.97
2003 Orioles	R	3	3	0	0	8.0	28	4	1	1	0	0	0	0	2	0	11	1	0	0	0	-	0	0--	-	1.01	1.13
2003 Aberdeen	A-	2	2	0	0	7.2	31	7	2	2	0	0	0	0	1	0	13	1	0	0	0	-	0	0--	-	1.98	2.35
2004 Ottawa	AAA	2	2	0	0	5.0	26	8	4	4	1	0	1	0	3	0	3	0	0	0	1	.000	0	0--	-	9.38	7.20
2002 Baltimore	AL	2	0	0	0	0.2	4	2	1	1	0	0	0	0	0	0	1	0	0	0	0	-	0	0-0	0	14.52	13.50
2004 Baltimore	AL	27	26	0	0	137.1	633	149	83	70	13	0	4	7	71	1	121	7	2	6	10	.375	0	0-0	0	5.11	4.59
2 ML YEARS		29	26	0	0	138.0	637	151	84	71	13	0	4	7	71	1	122	7	2	6	10	.375	0	0-0	0	5.15	4.63

Joe Beimel

Pitches: L Bats: L Pos: RP-3   **Ht: 6'3" Wt: 215 Born: 4/19/1977 Age: 28**

Year Team	Lg	G	GS	CG	GF	IP	BFP	H	R	ER	HR	SH	SF	HB	TBB	IBB	SO	WP	Bk	W	L	Pct	ShO	Sv-Op	Hld	ERC	ERA
2004 Rochester*	AAA	49	1	0	15	62.0	292	83	54	48	12	3	2	2	24	1	44	3	0	2	4	.333	0	2--	-	6.81	6.97
2001 Pittsburgh	NL	42	15	0	9	115.1	511	131	72	67	12	3	1	6	49	4	58	3	0	7	11	.389	0	0-0	0	5.24	5.23
2002 Pittsburgh	NL	53	8	0	8	85.1	391	88	49	44	9	7	3	4	45	12	53	2	0	2	5	.286	0	0-1	5	4.65	4.64
2003 Pittsburgh	NL	69	0	0	11	62.1	275	69	35	35	7	3	5	4	33	6	42	0	1	1	3	.250	0	0-5	12	5.65	5.05
2004 Minnesota	AL	3	0	0	0	1.2	15	8	8	8	1	0	0	0	2	0	2	0	0	0	0	-	0	0-0	0	44.44	43.20
4 ML YEARS		167	23	0	28	264.2	1192	296	164	154	29	13	9	14	129	22	155	5	1	10	19	.345	0	0-6	17	5.32	5.24

David Bell

Bats: R Throws: R Pos: 3B-143; PH-1   **Ht: 5'10" Wt: 195 Born: 9/14/1972 Age: 32**

Year Team	Lg	G	AB	H	2B	3B	HR	(Hm	Rd)	TB	R	RBI	RC	TBB	IBB	SO	HBP	SH	SF	SB	CS	SB%	GDP	Avg	OBP	Slg
1995 Cle-StL		41	146	36	7	2	2	(1	1)	53	13	19	14	4	0	25	2	0	1	1	2	.33	0	.247	.275	.363
1996 St Louis	NL	62	145	31	6	0	1	(1	0)	40	12	9	9	10	2	22	1	0	1	1	1	.50	3	.214	.268	.276
1997 St Louis	NL	66	142	30	7	2	1	(1	0)	44	9	12	11	10	2	28	0	2	1	1	0	1.00	3	.211	.261	.310
1998 StL-Cle-Sea		132	429	117	30	2	10	(2	8)	181	48	49	53	27	4	65	2	1	5	0	4	.00	11	.273	.315	.422
1999 Seattle	AL	157	597	160	31	2	21	(11	10)	258	92	78	87	58	0	90	2	3	7	7	4	.64	7	.268	.331	.432
2000 Seattle	AL	133	454	112	24	2	11	(4	7)	173	57	47	54	42	0	66	6	6	4	2	3	.40	11	.247	.316	.381
2001 Seattle	AL	135	470	122	28	0	15	(7	8)	195	62	64	58	28	1	59	3	5	4	2	1	.67	8	.260	.303	.415
2002 San Francisco	NL	154	552	144	29	2	20	(7	13)	237	82	73	79	54	2	80	9	6	7	1	2	.33	18	.261	.333	.429
2003 Philadelphia	NL	85	297	58	14	0	4	(1	3)	84	32	37	27	41	1	40	4	0	6	0	0	-	7	.195	.296	.283
2004 Philadelphia	NL	143	533	155	33	1	18	(10	8)	244	67	77	87	57	4	75	6	2	5	1	1	.50	14	.291	.363	.458
1995 Cleveland	AL	2	2	0	0	0	0	(0	0)	0	0	0	0	0	0	0	0	0	0	0	0	-	0	.000	.000	.000
1995 St Louis	NL	39	144	36	7	2	2	(1	1)	53	13	19	14	4	0	25	2	0	1	1	2	.33	0	.250	.278	.368
1998 St Louis	NL	4	9	2	1	0	0	(0	0)	3	0	0	1	0	0	3	0	0	0	0	0	-	0	.222	.222	.333
1998 Cleveland	AL	107	340	89	21	2	10	(2	8)	144	37	41	41	22	4	54	2	1	5	0	4	.00	8	.262	.306	.424
1998 Seattle	AL	21	80	26	8	0	0	(0	0)	34	11	8	11	5	0	8	0	0	0	0	0	-	0	.325	.365	.425
10 ML YEARS		1108	3765	965	209	13	103	(45	58)	1509	474	465	479	331	16	550	35	25	41	16	18	.47	81	.256	.319	.401

Heath Bell

Pitches: R Bats: R Pos: RP-17   **Ht: 6'2" Wt: 244 Born: 9/29/1977 Age: 27**

Year Team	Lg	G	GS	CG	GF	IP	BFP	H	R	ER	HR	SH	SF	HB	TBB	IBB	SO	WP	Bk	W	L	Pct	ShO	Sv-Op	Hld	ERC	ERA
1998 Kingsport	R+	22	0	0	11	46.0	189	40	15	13	5	1	2	2	11	0	61	4	0	1	0	1.000	0	8--	-	2.96	2.54
1999 Capital City	A	55	0	0	48	62.1	251	47	23	18	3	2	0	0	17	0	68	3	1	1	7	.125	0	25--	-	1.99	2.60
2000 St. Lucie	A+	48	0	0	37	60.0	241	43	19	17	4	2	2	2	21	2	75	1	0	5	1	.833	0	23--	-	2.30	2.55
2001 Binghamton	AA	43	0	0	22	61.1	285	82	44	41	13	1	4	5	19	3	55	4	0	3	1	.750	0	4--	-	6.81	6.02

Year Team	Lg	G	GS	CG	GF	IP	BFP	H	R	ER	HR	SH	SF	HB	TBB	IBB	SO	WP	Bk	W	L	Pct	ShO	Sv-Op	Hld	ERC	ERA
2002 Binghamton	AA	24	0	0	16	38.0	139	22	6	5	0	1	1	0	6	0	49	3	0	1	0	1.000	0	6--	-	1.00	1.18
2002 Norfolk	AAA	22	0	0	14	31.2	142	38	15	15	2	5	1	1	9	1	28	1	0	3	4	.429	0	5--	-	4.47	4.26
2003 Norfolk	AAA	40	0	0	25	49.2	206	54	26	26	4	4	1	2	8	0	54	4	0	2	3	.400	0	3--	-	3.70	4.71
2004 Binghamton	AA	1	0	0	0	2.0	8	2	0	0	0	0	0	0	0	0	0	0	0	0	0	-	0	---	-	1.95	0.00
2004 Norfolk	AAA	45	0	0	30	55.2	237	42	21	20	4	1	0	4	24	2	68	6	1	3	1	.750	0	16--	-	2.84	3.23
2004 New York	NL	17	0	0	2	24.1	94	22	9	9	5	1	0	0	6	0	27	0	0	0	2	.000	0	0-1	1	3.86	3.33

Rob Bell

Pitches: R **Bats:** R **Pos:** SP-19; RP-5 **Ht:** 6'5" **Wt:** 225 **Born:** 1/17/1977 **Age:** 28

Year Team	Lg	G	GS	CG	GF	IP	BFP	H	R	ER	HR	SH	SF	HB	TBB	IBB	SO	WP	Bk	W	L	Pct	ShO	Sv-Op	Hld	ERC	ERA
2004 Durham*	AAA	7	7	0	0	37.1	142	28	7	7	3	1	0	0	8	0	35	1	0	5	0	1.000	0	0--	-	2.07	1.69
2000 Cincinnati	NL	26	26	1	0	140.1	618	130	84	78	32	8	2	1	73	6	112	11	0	7	8	.467	0	0-0	0	4.98	5.00
2001 Cin-Tex		27	27	0	0	149.2	670	176	115	111	32	3	9	7	64	1	97	9	0	5	10	.333	0	0-0	0	6.40	6.67
2002 Texas	AL	17	15	0	0	94.0	425	113	69	65	16	1	6	1	35	0	70	7	0	4	3	.571	0	0-0	0	5.67	6.22
2003 Tampa Bay	AL	19	18	0	0	101.0	441	103	64	62	15	2	2	5	39	1	44	0	0	4	5	.556	0	0-0	0	4.66	5.52
2004 Tampa Bay	AL	24	19	1	3	123.0	529	121	71	61	16	2	2	5	41	0	57	10	0	8	8	.500	0	0-0	0	4.06	4.46
2001 Cincinnati	NL	9	9	0	0	44.1	188	46	28	27	9	0	1	3	17	1	33	1	0	0	5	.000	0	0-0	0	5.43	5.48
2001 Texas	AL	18	18	0	0	105.1	482	130	87	84	23	3	8	4	47	0	64	8	0	5	5	.500	0	0-0	0	6.82	7.18
5 ML YEARS		113	105	2	3	608.0	2683	643	403	377	111	16	21	19	252	8	380	37	0	29	33	.468	0	0-0	0	5.17	5.58

Mark Bellhorn

Bats: B **Throws:** R **Pos:** 2B-124; 3B-16; PH-2; SS-1; DH-1; PR-1 **Ht:** 6'1" **Wt:** 205 **Born:** 8/23/1974 **Age:** 30

Year Team	Lg	G	AB	H	2B	3B	HR	(Hm	Rd)	TB	R	RBI	RC	TBB	IBB	SO	HBP	SH	SF	SB	CS	SB%	GDP	Avg	OBP	Slg
2004 Pawtucket*	AAA	2	6	1	1	0	0	(-	-)	2	1	0	0	0	0	2	0	0	0	0	0	-	0	.167	.167	.333
1997 Oakland	AL	68	224	51	9	1	6	(3	3)	80	33	19	29	32	0	70	1	0	5	7	1	.88	1	.228	.324	.357
1998 Oakland	AL	11	12	1	1	0	0	(0	0)	2	1	1	1	3	0	4	1	0	0	2	0	1.00	0	.083	.313	.167
2000 Oakland	AL	9	13	2	0	0	0	(0	0)	2	2	0	1	2	0	6	0	0	0	0	0	-	0	.154	.267	.154
2001 Oakland	AL	38	74	10	1	2	1	(1	0)	18	11	4	3	7	0	37	0	1	0	0	0	-	1	.135	.210	.243
2002 Chicago	NL	146	445	115	24	4	27	(15	12)	228	86	56	79	76	3	144	6	2	7	5		.58	6	.258	.374	.512
2003 ChC-Col	NL	99	249	55	10	1	2	(1	1)	73	27	26	26	50	1	78	3	1	4	5	6	.45	3	.221	.353	.293
2004 Boston	AL	138	523	138	37	3	17	(11	6)	232	93	82	95	88	1	177	5	1	3	6	1	.86	8	.264	.373	.444
2003 Chicago	NL	51	139	29	7	1	2	(1	1)	44	15	22	17	29	1	46	1	0	4	3		.50	2	.209	.341	.317
2003 Colorado	NL	48	110	26	3	0	0	(0	0)	29	12	4	9	21	0	32	2	1	0	2	3	.40	1	.236	.368	.264
7 ML YEARS		509	1540	372	82	11	53	(31	22)	635	253	188	234	258	5	516	15	10	7	27	13	.68	19	.242	.354	.412

Ronnie Belliard

Bats: R **Throws:** R **Pos:** 2B-151; PH-3; DH-1 **Ht:** 5'8" **Wt:** 197 **Born:** 4/7/1975 **Age:** 30

Year Team	Lg	G	AB	H	2B	3B	HR	(Hm	Rd)	TB	R	RBI	RC	TBB	IBB	SO	HBP	SH	SF	SB	CS	SB%	GDP	Avg	OBP	Slg
1998 Milwaukee	NL	8	5	1	0	0	0	(0	0)	1	1	0	0	0	0	0	0	0	0	0	0	-	0	.200	.200	.200
1999 Milwaukee	NL	124	457	135	29	4	8	(5	3)	196	60	58	72	64	0	59	0	6	4	4	5	.44	16	.295	.379	.429
2000 Milwaukee	NL	152	571	150	30	9	8	(4	4)	222	83	54	81	82	4	84	3	4	7	7	5	.58	12	.263	.354	.389
2001 Milwaukee	NL	101	364	96	30	3	11	(7	4)	165	69	36	56	33	2	65	5	4	2	5	2	.71	5	.264	.335	.453
2002 Milwaukee	NL	104	289	61	13	0	3	(0	3)	83	30	26	15	18	0	46	1	6	3	2	3	.40	7	.211	.257	.287
2003 Colorado	NL	116	447	124	31	2	8	(6	2)	183	73	50	71	49	0	71	2	6	2	7	2	.78	7	.277	.351	.409
2004 Cleveland	AL	152	599	169	48	1	12	(4	8)	255	78	70	87	60	5	98	2	0	3	3	2	.60	18	.282	.348	.426
7 ML YEARS		757	2732	736	181	19	50	(26	24)	1105	394	294	382	308	11	423	13	26	19	28	19	.60	66	.269	.344	.404

Carlos Beltran

Bats: B **Throws:** R **Pos:** CF-158; PH-2 **Ht:** 6'1" **Wt:** 190 **Born:** 4/24/1977 **Age:** 28

Year Team	Lg	G	AB	H	2B	3B	HR	(Hm	Rd)	TB	R	RBI	RC	TBB	IBB	SO	HBP	SH	SF	SB	CS	SB%	GDP	Avg	OBP	Slg
1998 Kansas City	AL	14	58	16	5	3	0	(0	0)	27	12	7	9	3	0	12	1	0	1	3	0	1.00	1	.276	.317	.466
1999 Kansas City	AL	156	663	194	27	7	22	(12	10)	301	112	108	100	46	2	123	4	0	10	27	8	.77	17	.293	.337	.454
2000 Kansas City	AL	98	372	92	15	4	7	(4	3)	136	49	44	43	35	2	69	0	2	4	13	0	1.00	12	.247	.309	.366
2001 Kansas City	AL	155	617	189	32	12	24	(7	17)	317	106	101	118	52	2	120	5	1	5	31	1	.97	7	.306	.362	.514
2002 Kansas City	AL	162	637	174	44	7	29	(19	10)	319	114	105	117	71	1	135	4	3	7	35	7	.83	12	.273	.346	.501
2003 Kansas City	AL	141	521	160	14	10	26	(10	16)	272	102	100	117	72	4	81	2	0	7	41	4	.91	8	.307	.389	.522
2004 KC-Hou		159	599	160	36	9	38	(15	23)	328	121	104	124	92	10	101	7	3	7	42	3	.93	8	.267	.367	.548
2004 Kansas City	AL	69	266	74	19	2	15	(8	7)	142	51	51	57	37	7	44	2	1	3	14	3	.82	4	.278	.367	.534
2004 Houston	NL	90	333	86	17	7	23	(7	16)	186	70	53	67	55	3	57	5	2	4	28	0	1.00	4	.258	.368	.559
7 ML YEARS		885	3467	985	173	52	146	(67	79)	1700	616	569	628	371	21	641	23	9	41	192	23	.89	66	.284	.353	.490

Francis Beltran

Pitches: R **Bats:** R **Pos:** RP-45 **Ht:** 6'5" **Wt:** 220 **Born:** 11/29/1979 **Age:** 25

Year Team	Lg	G	GS	CG	GF	IP	BFP	H	R	ER	HR	SH	SF	HB	TBB	IBB	SO	WP	Bk	W	L	Pct	ShO	Hld	ERC	ERA
1997 Cubs	R	16	0	0	5	23.2	111	27	18	9	1	1	1	3	8	0	17	3	2	0	1	.000	0	1--	-	4.49	3.42
1998 Cubs	R	12	5	0	3	35.2	165	49	23	22	1	4	2	2	14	1	26	1	1	1	1	.500	0	0--	-	5.96	5.55
1999 Cubs	R	7	0	0	6	10.2	38	5	3	0	0	0	1	1	1	0	8	0	0	1	0	.000	0	2--	-	0.78	0.00
1999 Eugene	A-	16	0	0	7	28.0	142	41	32	26	2	0	1	3	14	0	28	6	0	0	2	.000	0	0--	-	7.34	8.36
2000 Lansing	A	16	0	0	11	17.2	97	24	22	19	0	0	3	4	19	0	16	4	0	1	1	.500	0	0--	-	9.24	9.68
2000 Eugene	A-	25	0	0	13	43.2	180	28	16	13	1	1	1	1	20	2	52	6	0	2	2	.500	0	8--	-	1.93	2.68
2001 Daytona	A+	21	18	0	0	95.1	424	93	62	53	10	1	4	9	40	1	72	4	0	6	9	.400	0	0--	-	4.35	5.00
2002 W Tennessee	AA	39	0	0	35	41.2	171	28	14	12	2	3	1	2	19	2	43	3	2	2	2	.500	0	23--	-	2.34	2.59
2003 Iowa	AAA	31	2	0	23	48.2	206	46	17	16	2	0	0	1	19	3	33	0	0	6	2	.750	0	4--	-	3.34	2.96

Year Team	Lg	G	GS	CG	GF	IP	BFP	H	R	ER	HR	SH	SF	HB	TBB	IBB	SO	WP	Bk	W	L	Pct	ShO	Sv-Op	Hld	ERC	ERA
2004 Edmonton	AAA	5	0	0	5	5.0	21	4	1	1	0	0	0	0	2	0	6	0	0	0	0	-	0	3--	-	2.31	1.80
2004 Iowa	AAA	6	0	0	6	6.1	25	5	2	2	1	0	0	0	1	0	6	0	0	0	0	-	0	4--	-	2.37	2.84
2002 Chicago	NL	11	0	0	4	12.0	65	14	11	10	2	3	1	0	16	1	11	2	0	0	0	-	0	0-0	0	9.45	7.50
2004 ChC-Mon	NL	45	0	0	13	49.1	221	47	31	30	11	4	2	2	27	1	48	2	0	2	2	.500	0	1-1	5	5.40	5.47
2004 Chicago	NL	34	0	0	10	35.0	152	27	19	18	8	3	1	0	22	0	40	1	0	2	2	.500	0	0-0	5	4.58	4.63
2004 Montreal	NL	11	0	0	3	14.1	69	20	12	12	3	1	1	2	5	1	8	1	0	0	0	-	0	1-1	0	7.56	7.53
2 ML YEARS		56	0	0	17	61.1	286	61	42	40	13	7	3	2	43	2	59	4	0	2	2	.500	0	1-1	5	6.18	5.87

Rigo Beltran

Pitches: R Bats: L Pos: RP-2   Ht: 6'6" Wt: 235 Born: 12/31/2004 Age: 0

Year Team	Lg	G	GS	CG	GF	IP	BFP	H	R	ER	HR	SH	SF	HB	TBB	IBB	SO	WP	Bk	W	L	Pct	ShO	Sv-Op	Hld	ERC	ERA
2004 Edmonton*	AAA	26	8	0	9	65.1	271	65	27	26	5	3	6	0	17	1	54	0	1	3	2	.600	0	3--	-	3.35	3.58
1997 St Louis	NL	35	4	0	16	54.1	224	47	25	21	4	3	6	3	17	0	50	1	0	1	2	.333	0	1-1	2	2.72	3.48
1998 New York	NL	7	0	0	0	8.0	33	6	3	3	1	0	1	0	4	0	5	0	0	0	0	-	0	0-0	0	3.32	3.38
1999 NYM-Col	NL	33	0	0	12	42.0	195	50	23	21	7	3	0	1	19	3	50	7	0	1	1	.500	0	0-0	1	5.78	4.50
2000 Colorado	NL	1	1	0	0	1.1	13	6	6	6	2	0	0	0	3	0	1	0	0	0	0	-	0	0-0	0	61.44	40.50
2004 Montreal	NL	2	0	0	0	0.2	3	1	1	1	0	0	0	0	0	0	0	0	0	0	0	-	0	0-0	0	4.47	13.50
1999 Colorado	NL	12	0	0	2	11.0	61	20	9	9	2	1	0	1	7	1	15	1	0	0	0	-	0	0-0	1	11.14	7.36
1999 New York	NL	21	0	0	10	31.0	134	30	14	12	5	2	0	0	12	2	35	6	0	1	1	.500	0	0-0	0	4.11	3.48
5 ML YEARS		78	5	0	28	106.1	468	110	58	52	13	9	4	1	43	3	106	8	0	2	3	.400	0	1-1	3	4.39	4.40

Adrian Beltre

Bats: R Throws: R Pos: 3B-155; SS-1; PH-1   Ht: 5'11" Wt: 170 Born: 4/7/1979 Age: 26

Year Team	Lg	G	AB	H	2B	3B	HR	(Hm	Rd)	TB	R	RBI	RC	TBB	IBB	SO	HBP	SH	SF	SB	CS	SB%	GDP	Avg	OBP	Slg
1998 Los Angeles	NL	77	195	42	9	0	7	(5	2)	72	18	22	20	14	0	37	3	2	0	3	1	.75	4	.215	.278	.369
1999 Los Angeles	NL	152	538	148	27	5	15	(6	9)	230	84	67	84	61	12	105	6	4	5	18	7	.72	4	.275	.352	.428
2000 Los Angeles	NL	138	510	148	30	2	20	(7	13)	242	71	85	85	56	2	80	2	3	4	12	5	.71	13	.290	.360	.475
2001 Los Angeles	NL	126	475	126	22	4	13	(4	9)	195	59	60	60	28	1	82	5	2	5	13	4	.76	9	.265	.310	.411
2002 Los Angeles	NL	159	587	151	26	5	21	(7	14)	250	70	75	74	37	4	96	4	1	6	7	5	.58	17	.257	.303	.426
2003 Los Angeles	NL	158	559	134	30	2	23	(13	10)	237	50	80	66	37	4	103	5	1	6	2	2	.50	13	.240	.290	.424
2004 Los Angeles	NL	156	598	200	32	0	48	(23	25)	376	104	121	120	53	9	87	2	0	4	7	2	.78	15	.334	.388	.629
7 ML YEARS		966	3462	949	176	18	147	(65	82)	1602	456	510	509	286	32	590	27	13	30	62	26	.70	75	.274	.332	.463

Armando Benitez

Pitches: R Bats: R Pos: RP-64   Ht: 6'4" Wt: 229 Born: 11/3/1972 Age: 32

Year Team	Lg	G	GS	CG	GF	IP	BFP	H	R	ER	HR	SH	SF	HB	TBB	IBB	SO	WP	Bk	W	L	Pct	ShO	Sv-Op	Hld	ERC	ERA
1994 Baltimore	AL	3	0	0	1	10.0	42	8	1	1	0	0	0	1	4	0	14	0	0	0	0	-	0	0-0	0	2.71	0.90
1995 Baltimore	AL	44	0	0	18	47.2	221	37	33	30	8	2	3	5	37	2	56	3	1	1	5	.167	0	2-5	6	5.06	5.66
1996 Baltimore	AL	18	0	0	8	14.1	56	7	6	6	2	0	1	0	6	0	20	1	0	0	1	1.000	0	4-5	1	1.78	3.77
1997 Baltimore	AL	71	0	0	26	73.1	307	49	22	20	7	2	4	1	43	5	106	1	0	4	5	.444	0	9-10	20	2.92	2.45
1998 Baltimore	AL	71	0	0	54	68.1	289	48	29	29	10	3	2	4	39	2	87	0	0	5	6	.455	0	22-26	3	3.63	3.82
1999 New York	NL	77	0	0	42	78.0	312	40	17	16	4	0	0	0	41	4	128	2	0	4	3	.571	0	22-28	17	1.69	1.85
2000 New York	NL	76	0	0	68	76.0	304	39	24	22	10	2	1	0	38	2	106	0	0	4	4	.500	0	41-46	0	2.08	2.61
2001 New York	NL	73	0	0	64	76.1	320	59	32	32	12	2	1	1	40	6	93	5	0	6	4	.600	0	43-46	0	3.67	3.77
2002 New York	NL	62	0	0	52	67.1	275	46	20	17	8	3	2	3	25	0	79	1	0	0	1	1.000	0	33-37	0	2.55	2.27
2003 NYM-NYY-Sea		69	0	0	49	73.0	312	59	27	24	6	0	1	0	41	3	75	3	1	4	4	.500	0	21-29	5	3.46	2.96
2004 Florida	NL	64	0	0	59	69.2	262	36	11	10	6	3	1	0	21	4	62	0	0	2	2	.500	0	47-51	0	1.36	1.29
2003 New York	NL	45	0	0	40	49.1	209	41	18	17	5	0	1	0	24	1	50	3	1	3	3	.500	0	21-28	0	3.46	3.10
2003 New York	AL	9	0	0	2	9.1	39	8	4	2	0	0	0	0	6	1	10	0	0	1	1	.500	0	0-0	4	3.50	1.93
2003 Seattle	AL	15	0	0	7	14.1	64	10	5	5	1	0	0	0	11	1	15	0	0	0	0	-	0	0-1	1	3.40	3.14
11 ML YEARS		628	0	0	441	654.0	2700	428	222	207	73	17	16	15	335	28	826	16	2	32	33	.492	0	244-283	52	2.76	2.85

Gary Bennett

Bats: R Throws: R Pos: C-75; PR-1   Ht: 6'0" Wt: 208 Born: 4/17/1972 Age: 33

Year Team	Lg	G	AB	H	2B	3B	HR	(Hm	Rd)	TB	R	RBI	RC	TBB	IBB	SO	HBP	SH	SF	SB	CS	SB%	GDP	Avg	OBP	Slg
1995 Philadelphia	NL	1	1	0	0	0	0	(0	0)	0	0	0	0	0	0	1	0	0	0	0	0	-	0	.000	.000	.000
1996 Philadelphia	NL	6	16	4	0	0	0	(0	0)	4	0	1	1	2	1	6	0	0	0	0	0	-	0	.250	.333	.250
1998 Philadelphia	NL	9	31	9	0	0	0	(0	0)	9	4	3	4	5	0	5	0	0	0	0	0	-	1	.290	.378	.290
1999 Philadelphia	NL	36	88	24	4	0	1	(0	1)	31	7	21	7	4	0	11	0	0	2	0	0	-	2	.273	.298	.352
2000 Philadelphia	NL	31	74	18	5	0	2	(0	2)	29	8	5	5	13	0	15	2	0	0	0	0	-	0	.243	.371	.392
2001 Phi-NYM-Col	NL	46	131	32	6	1	2	(2	0)	46	15	10	15	12	4	24	1	2	2	0	0	-	1	.244	.308	.351
2002 Colorado	NL	90	291	77	10	2	4	(2	2)	103	26	26	29	15	2	45	6	2	0	1	3	.25	10	.265	.314	.354
2003 San Diego	NL	96	307	73	15	0	2	(1	1)	94	26	42	33	24	3	48	2	3	2	3	0	1.00	8	.238	.296	.306
2004 Milwaukee	NL	75	219	49	14	0	3	(3	0)	72	18	20	15	22	3	32	2	0	1	1	0	1.00	0	.224	.297	.329
2001 Philadelphia	NL	26	75	16	3	1	1	(1	0)	24	8	6	7	9	1	19	0	1	1	0	0	-	1	.213	.294	.320
2001 New York	NL	1	1	1	0	0	0	(0	0)	1	0	1	0	0	0	0	0	0	0	0	0	-	0	1.000	1.000	1.000
2001 Colorado	NL	19	55	15	3	0	1	(1	0)	21	7	4	7	3	3	5	1	1	1	0	0	-	0	.273	.317	.382
9 ML YEARS		390	1158	286	54	3	14	(8	6)	388	104	128	116	97	13	187	13	7	10	5	3	.63	36	.247	.310	.335

Jeff Bennett

Pitches: R **Bats:** R **Pos:** RP-60   **Ht:** 6'3" **Wt:** 200 **Born:** 6/10/1980 **Age:** 25

Year Team	Lg	G	GS	CG	GF	IP	BFP	H	R	ER	HR	SH	SF	HB	TBB	IBB	SO	WP	Bk	W	L	Pct	ShO	Sv-Op	Hld	ERC	ERA
1998 Pirates	R	13	11	0	0	46.2	212	50	29	24	4	0	2	7	13	0	18	2	0	2	4	.333	0	0- -	-	4.33	4.63
1999 Pirates	R	8	8	0	0	44.2	191	53	27	21	1	2	1	0	9	0	28	2	3	3	4	.429	0	0- -	-	3.80	4.23
1999 Hickory	A	8	6	0	2	35.0	161	48	25	23	5	2	0	1	9	0	16	2	0	2	2	.500	0	0- -	-	6.06	5.91
2000 Hickory	A	27	27	1	0	171.2	761	189	116	84	14	5	7	16	47	1	126	11	2	10	13	.435	0	0- -	-	4.30	4.40
2001 Lynchburg	A+	25	25	2	0	166.0	691	171	78	63	14	6	2	13	30	1	98	2	0	11	10	.524	1	0- -	-	3.62	3.42
2001 Altoona	AA	1	1	0	0	7.0	34	9	3	3	0	0	0	2	2	0	6	0	0	0	1	.000	0	0- -	-	5.48	3.86
2002 Lynchburg	A+	24	20	0	1	124.1	535	137	64	50	7	2	5	8	30	0	90	2	0	10	6	.625	0	0- -	-	3.97	3.62
2003 Altoona	AA	33	2	0	1	59.2	249	45	22	18	2	0	1	1	23	3	62	0	0	4	4	.500	0	1- -	-	2.24	2.72
2003 Nashville	AAA	9	5	0	1	23.1	111	26	21	17	4	2	2	1	12	0	16	1	0	1	3	.250	0	0- -	-	5.69	6.56
2004 Milwaukee	NL	60	0	0	20	71.1	316	78	43	38	12	2	5	2	26	2	45	6	0	1	5	.167	0	0-1	8	4.98	4.79

Joaquin Benoit

Pitches: R **Bats:** R **Pos:** SP-15; RP-13   **Ht:** 6'3" **Wt:** 205 **Born:** 7/26/1977 **Age:** 27

Year Team	Lg	G	GS	CG	GF	IP	BFP	H	R	ER	HR	SH	SF	HB	TBB	IBB	SO	WP	Bk	W	L	Pct	ShO	Sv-Op	Hld	ERC	ERA
2004 Frisco*	AA	1	1	0	0	2.0	6	0	0	0	0	0	0	0	0	0	6	0	0	0	0	-	0	0- -	-	0.00	0.00
2001 Texas	AL	1	1	0	0	5.0	26	8	6	6	3	0	1	0	3	0	4	0	0	0	0	-	0	0-0	0	13.11	10.80
2002 Texas	AL	17	13	0	2	84.2	405	91	51	50	6	4	3	5	58	2	59	7	0	4	5	.444	0	1-1	0	5.52	5.31
2003 Texas	AL	25	17	0	1	105.0	462	99	67	64	23	1	4	3	51	0	87	3	1	8	5	.615	0	0-0	0	5.03	5.49
2004 Texas	AL	28	15	0	2	103.0	456	113	67	65	19	2	10	8	31	0	95	3	0	3	5	.375	0	0-0	0	5.10	5.68
4 ML YEARS		71	46	0	5	297.2	1349	311	191	185	51	7	18	16	143	2	245	13	1	15	15	.500	0	1-1	0	5.34	5.59

Kris Benson

Pitches: R **Bats:** R **Pos:** SP-31   **Ht:** 6'4" **Wt:** 200 **Born:** 11/7/1974 **Age:** 30

Year Team	Lg	G	GS	CG	GF	IP	BFP	H	R	ER	HR	SH	SF	HB	TBB	IBB	SO	WP	Bk	W	L	Pct	ShO	Sv-Op	Hld	ERC	ERA
1999 Pittsburgh	NL	31	31	2	0	196.2	840	184	105	89	16	6	7	6	83	5	139	2	1	11	14	.440	0	0-0	0	3.78	4.07
2000 Pittsburgh	NL	32	32	2	0	217.2	936	206	104	93	24	7	6	10	86	5	184	5	0	10	12	.455	1	0-0	0	3.97	3.85
2002 Pittsburgh	NL	25	25	0	0	130.1	575	152	76	68	18	5	3	3	50	8	79	3	1	9	6	.600	0	0-0	0	5.32	4.70
2003 Pittsburgh	NL	18	18	0	0	105.0	475	127	67	58	14	3	4	1	36	4	68	7	0	5	9	.357	0	0-0	0	5.20	4.97
2004 Pit-NYM	NL	31	31	1	0	200.1	854	202	106	96	15	8	6	10	61	8	134	5	0	12	12	.500	1	0-0	0	3.71	4.31
2004 Pittsburgh	NL	20	20	0	0	132.1	564	137	69	62	7	7	4	6	44	5	83	2	0	8	8	.500	0	0-0	0	3.84	4.22
2004 New York	NL	11	11	1	0	68.0	290	65	37	34	8	1	2	4	17	3	51	3	0	4	4	.500	1	0-0	0	3.45	4.50
5 ML YEARS		137	137	5	0	850.0	3680	871	458	404	87	29	26	30	316	30	604	22	2	47	53	.470	2	0-0	0	4.21	4.28

Chad Bentz

Pitches: L **Bats:** R **Pos:** RP-36   **Ht:** 6'2" **Wt:** 215 **Born:** 5/5/1980 **Age:** 25

Year Team	Lg	G	GS	CG	GF	IP	BFP	H	R	ER	HR	SH	SF	HB	TBB	IBB	SO	WP	Bk	W	L	Pct	ShO	Sv-Op	Hld	ERC	ERA
2001 Vermont	A-	8	8	0	0	36.2	163	39	23	20	2	2	2	0	11	0	38	4	0	1	3	.250	0	0- -	-	3.55	4.91
2002 Brevard Cnty	A+	23	0	0	16	29.2	136	30	14	12	1	3	1	2	14	2	34	2	0	1	0	1.000	0	5- -	-	3.93	3.64
2003 Harrisburg	AA	52	0	0	28	84.2	350	72	31	24	4	8	4	0	39	2	56	7	0	1	4	.200	0	16- -	-	3.18	2.55
2004 Harrisburg	AA	5	1	0	2	7.1	32	5	7	7	2	0	1	0	8	0	2	0	0	0	1	.000	0	1- -	-	7.77	8.59
2004 Edmonton	AAA	5	0	0	2	5.0	23	5	2	2	1	0	0	0	3	0	2	0	0	0	0	-	0	0- -	-	5.52	3.60
2004 Montreal	NL	36	0	0	5	27.2	126	23	19	18	5	0	0	2	23	3	18	1	0	0	3	.000	0	0-0	5	5.66	5.86

Dave Berg

Bats: R **Throws:** R **Pos:** LF-31; PH-10; 1B-7; DH-5; 2B-4; 3B-3; PR-3; RF-1   **Ht:** 5'11" **Wt:** 196 **Born:** 9/3/1970 **Age:** 34

Year Team	Lg	G	AB	H	2B	3B	HR	(Hm	Rd)	TB	R	RBI	RC	TBB	IBB	SO	HBP	SH	SF	SB	CS	SB%	GDP	Avg	OBP	Slg
1998 Florida	NL	81	182	57	11	0	2	(1	1)	74	18	21	32	26	1	46	0	4	3	3	0	1.00	5	.313	.393	.407
1999 Florida	NL	109	304	87	18	1	3	(1	2)	116	42	25	39	27	0	59	2	3	0	2	2	.50	7	.286	.348	.382
2000 Florida	NL	82	210	53	14	1	1	(1	0)	72	23	21	26	25	0	46	5	1	4	3	0	1.00	5	.252	.340	.343
2001 Florida	NL	82	215	52	12	1	4	(2	2)	78	26	16	22	14	0	39	2	2	2	0	1	.00	3	.242	.292	.363
2002 Toronto	AL	109	374	101	26	2	4	(3	1)	143	42	39	47	26	1	57	5	4	5	0	2	.00	6	.270	.322	.382
2003 Toronto	AL	61	161	41	6	1	4	(2	2)	61	26	18	13	11	0	34	0	1	1	0	1	.00	7	.255	.301	.379
2004 Toronto	AL	58	154	39	4	0	3	(3	0)	52	13	23	16	4	0	27	2	0	2	0	1	.00	4	.253	.278	.338
7 ML YEARS		582	1600	430	91	6	21	(13	8)	596	190	163	195	133	2	308	16	15	17	8	7	.53	33	.269	.328	.373

Brandon Berger

Bats: R **Throws:** R **Pos:** LF-10; RF-1   **Ht:** 5'11" **Wt:** 205 **Born:** 2/21/1975 **Age:** 30

Year Team	Lg	G	AB	H	2B	3B	HR	(Hm	Rd)	TB	R	RBI	RC	TBB	IBB	SO	HBP	SH	SF	SB	CS	SB%	GDP	Avg	OBP	Slg
2004 Wichita*	AA	70	267	75	18	2	12	(-	-)	133	42	50	46	34	1	40	2	0	5	3	2	.60	6	.281	.360	.498
2004 Omaha*	AAA	39	146	34	9	0	14	(-	-)	85	25	37	25	19	0	22	2	0	5	1	1	.50	5	.233	.327	.582
2001 Kansas City	AL	6	16	5	1	1	2	(1	1)	14	4	2	5	2	0	2	0	0	0	0	0	-	0	.313	.389	.875
2002 Kansas City	AL	51	134	27	5	1	6	(5	1)	52	16	17	16	8	2	32	2	0	1	1	0	1.00	3	.201	.255	.388
2003 Kansas City	AL	13	32	7	0	0	0	(0	0)	7	3	3	4	5	0	4	0	1	0	0	0	-	0	.219	.324	.219
2004 Kansas City	AL	11	35	7	2	0	0	(0	0)	9	5	2	1	0	0	7	0	0	0	1	1	.50	1	.200	.200	.257
4 ML YEARS		81	217	46	8	2	8	(6	2)	82	28	24	26	15	2	45	2	2	1	2	1	.67	3	.212	.268	.378

Peter Bergeron

Bats: L **Throws:** R **Pos:** CF-11   **Ht:** 6'0" **Wt:** 190 **Born:** 11/9/1977 **Age:** 27

Year Team	Lg	G	AB	H	2B	3B	HR	(Hm	Rd)	TB	R	RBI	RC	TBB	IBB	SO	HBP	SH	SF	SB	CS	SB%	GDP	Avg	OBP	Slg
2004 Brevard Cnty*	A+	4	17	3	0	1	0	(-	-)	5	3	0	0	0	0	2	0	0	0	3	0	1.00	2	.176	.176	.294
2004 Indianapolis*	AAA	82	317	86	9	8	3	(-	-)	120	46	22	39	20	1	39	1	7	1	12	7	.63	2	.271	.316	.379
2004 Edmonton*	AAA	11	41	21	4	1	1	(-	-)	30	8	5	13	3	0	1	0	0	0	2	0	1.00	0	.512	.545	.732
1999 Montreal	NL	16	45	11	2	0	0	(0	0)	13	12	1	6	9	0	5	0	1	0	0	0	-	0	.244	.370	.289
2000 Montreal	NL	148	518	127	25	7	5	(3	2)	181	80	31	58	58	0	100	0	14	2	11	13	.46	4	.245	.320	.349
2001 Montreal	NL	102	375	79	11	4	3	(1	2)	107	53	16	28	28	2	87	5	8	0	10	7	.59	5	.211	.275	.285
2002 Montreal	NL	31	123	23	3	2	0	(0	0)	30	24	7	14	22	0	44	0	3	0	10	3	.77	0	.187	.310	.244
2004 Montreal	NL	11	42	9	0	0	0	(0	0)	9	2	1	2	2	0	16	0	1	0	0	1	.00	0	.214	.250	.214
5 ML YEARS		308	1103	249	41	13	8	(4	4)	340	171	56	108	119	2	252	5	27	2	31	24	.56	9	.226	.303	.308

Dusty Bergman

Pitches: L **Bats:** L **Pos:** RP-1   **Ht:** 6'5" **Wt:** 200 **Born:** 2/1/1978 **Age:** 27

Year Team	Lg	G	GS	CG	GF	IP	BFP	H	R	ER	HR	SH	SF	HB	TBB	IBB	SO	WP	Bk	W	L	Pct	ShO	Sv-Op	Hld	ERC	ERA
1999 Boise	A-	15	15	0	0	74.1	340	102	58	54	12	1	1	1	18	2	46	6	0	5	5	.500	0	0--	-	6.02	6.54
2000 Cedar Rpds	A	28	25	6	0	163.2	727	174	102	71	12	9	2	5	60	0	108	10	0	4	15	.211	1	0--	-	4.14	3.90
2000 Lk Elsinore	A+	1	1	0	0	4.0	18	3	4	1	0	0	0	0	1	0	3	0	0	0	1	.000	0	0--	-	1.47	2.25
2001 Arkansas	AA	27	25	1	0	153.1	704	196	100	87	10	4	8	14	53	0	83	15	2	7	13	.350	0	0--	-	5.60	5.11
2002 Arkansas	AA	35	0	0	12	56.0	224	48	21	15	3	2	1	0	8	0	38	5	0	5	0	1.000	0	3--	-	2.07	2.41
2002 Salt Lake	AAA	21	0	0	6	29.1	129	34	25	21	7	0	1	2	9	0	26	1	0	1	1	.500	0	1--	-	5.99	6.44
2003 Arkansas	AA	50	10	0	13	109.1	472	116	54	46	7	5	6	3	33	3	82	3	0	6	5	.545	0	0--	-	3.82	3.79
2003 Salt Lake	AAA	1	0	0	0	1.1	10	5	5	3	0	1	1	0	1	0	0	0	0	0	1	.000	0	--	-	24.33	20.25
2004 Salt Lake	AAA	45	0	0	16	72.2	313	82	35	23	2	0	1	2	13	0	54	1	0	1	2	.333	0	1--	-	3.47	2.85
2004 Anaheim	AL	1	0	0	1	2.0	11	4	3	3	0	0	1	0	1	0	1	1	0	0	0	-	0	0-0	0	9.72	13.50

Lance Berkman

Bats: B **Throws:** L **Pos:** RF-90; LF-70; 1B-4; CF-2; PH-1   **Ht:** 6'1" **Wt:** 220 **Born:** 2/10/1976 **Age:** 29

Year Team	Lg	G	AB	H	2B	3B	HR	(Hm	Rd)	TB	R	RBI	RC	TBB	IBB	SO	HBP	SH	SF	SB	CS	SB%	GDP	Avg	OBP	Slg
1999 Houston	NL	34	93	22	2	0	4	(2	2)	36	10	15	12	12	0	21	0	0	1	5	1	.83	2	.237	.321	.387
2000 Houston	NL	114	353	105	28	1	21	(10	11)	198	76	67	76	56	1	73	1	0	7	6	2	.75	6	.297	.388	.561
2001 Houston	NL	156	577	191	**55**	5	34	(13	21)	358	110	126	144	92	5	121	13	0	6	7	9	.44	8	.331	.430	.620
2002 Houston	NL	158	578	169	35	2	42	(20	22)	334	106	**128**	130	107	20	118	4	0	3	8	4	.67	10	.292	.405	.578
2003 Houston	NL	153	538	155	35	6	25	(11	14)	277	110	93	115	107	13	108	9	1	3	5	3	.63	10	.288	.412	.515
2004 Houston	NL	160	544	172	40	3	30	(8	22)	308	104	106	126	127	14	101	10	0	6	9	7	.56	11	.316	.450	.566
6 ML YEARS		775	2683	814	195	17	156	(64	92)	1511	516	535	603	501	53	542	37	1	26	40	26	.61	47	.303	.416	.563

Adam Bernero

Pitches: R **Bats:** R **Pos:** RP-14; SP-2   **Ht:** 6'4" **Wt:** 205 **Born:** 11/28/1976 **Age:** 28

Year Team	Lg	G	GS	CG	GF	IP	BFP	H	R	ER	HR	SH	SF	HB	TBB	IBB	SO	WP	Bk	W	L	Pct	ShO	Sv-Op	Hld	ERC	ERA
2004 Tulsa*	AA	1	1	0	0	6.0	21	2	0	0	0	0	0	0	1	1	3	0	0	1	0	1.000	0	0--	-	0.60	0.00
2004 Co Springs*	AAA	9	8	0	0	48.1	204	57	23	17	0	3	4	1	10	0	48	0	0	3	2	.600	0	0--	-	3.77	3.17
2000 Detroit	AL	12	4	0	4	34.1	141	33	18	16	3	2	3	1	13	1	20	1	0	0	1	.000	0	0-0	1	3.94	4.19
2001 Detroit	AL	5	0	0	4	12.1	56	13	13	10	4	0	1	1	4	0	8	1	0	0	0	-	0	0-0	0	5.79	7.30
2002 Detroit	AL	28	11	0	5	101.2	459	128	74	70	17	3	5	6	31	1	69	5	1	4	7	.364	0	0-0	0	5.95	6.20
2003 Det-Col	NL	49	17	0	5	133.1	589	137	90	87	19	5	8	8	54	1	80	3	0	1	14	.067	0	0-2	5	4.77	5.87
2004 Colorado	NL	16	2	0	4	32.1	147	36	20	20	7	0	3	0	17	2	21	0	0	1	1	.500	0	0-1	1	6.03	5.57
2003 Detroit	AL	18	17	0	0	100.2	447	104	68	68	14	3	6	7	41	0	54	1	0	1	12	.077	0	0-0	0	4.83	6.08
2003 Colorado	NL	31	0	0	5	32.2	142	33	22	19	5	2	2	1	13	1	26	2	0	0	2	.000	0	0-2	5	4.58	5.23
5 ML YEARS		110	34	0	22	314.0	1392	347	215	203	50	10	20	16	119	5	198	10	1	6	23	.207	0	0-3	7	5.22	5.82

Angel Berroa

Bats: R **Throws:** R **Pos:** SS-133; PR-2   **Ht:** 6'0" **Wt:** 175 **Born:** 1/27/1978 **Age:** 27

Year Team	Lg	G	AB	H	2B	3B	HR	(Hm	Rd)	TB	R	RBI	RC	TBB	IBB	SO	HBP	SH	SF	SB	CS	SB%	GDP	Avg	OBP	Slg
2004 Wichita*	AA	11	51	16	1	0	3	(-	-)	26	8	10	8	2	0	8	0	0	0	3	2	.60	0	.314	.340	.510
2001 Kansas City	AL	15	53	16	2	0	0	(0	0)	18	8	4	6	3	0	10	0	0	0	2	0	1.00	0	.302	.339	.340
2002 Kansas City	AL	20	75	17	7	1	0	(0	0)	26	8	5	8	7	1	10	1	0	0	3	0	1.00	1	.227	.301	.347
2003 Kansas City	AL	158	567	163	28	7	17	(6	11)	256	92	73	82	29	3	100	18	13	8	21	5	.81	13	.287	.338	.451
2004 Kansas City	AL	134	512	134	27	6	8	(3	5)	197	72	43	61	23	0	87	12	5	2	14	8	.64	10	.262	.308	.385
4 ML YEARS		327	1207	330	64	14	25	(9	16)	497	180	125	157	62	4	207	31	18	10	40	13	.75	26	.273	.323	.412

Rafael Betancourt

Pitches: R **Bats:** R **Pos:** RP-68   **Ht:** 6'2" **Wt:** 176 **Born:** 4/29/1975 **Age:** 30

Year Team	Lg	G	GS	CG	GF	IP	BFP	H	R	ER	HR	SH	SF	HB	TBB	IBB	SO	WP	Bk	W	L	Pct	ShO	Sv-Op	Hld	ERC	ERA
1997 Michigan	A	27	0	0	0	32.1	125	26	9	7	2	1	0	0	2	0	52	3	1	0	3	.000	0	11--	-	1.64	1.95
1998 Red Sox	R	11	0	0	5	10.0	22	6	5	4	1	0	1	0	1	0	4	1	1	0	2	.000	0	0--	-	5.00	7.20
1998 Sarasota	A+	20	0	0	4	28.0	111	22	12	11	2	1	0	0	6	0	33	0	0	3	1	.750	0	2--	-	2.10	3.54
1998 Trenton	AA	7	0	0	3	9.1	42	9	7	7	0	1	0	0	3	0	9	0	0	0	0	-	0	0--	-	2.67	6.75
1999 Sarasota	A+	6	0	0	5	7.0	25	5	0	0	0	0	0	0	1	0	6	0	0	0	0	-	0	4--	-	1.42	0.00
1999 Trenton	AA	39	0	0	30	54.2	218	50	24	22	7	4	2	0	10	0	57	0	1	6	2	.750	0	13--	-	3.00	3.62
2001 Trenton	AA	16	0	0	10	24.0	100	28	16	15	0	0	0	2	3	0	27	1	0	0	1	.000	0	4--	-	3.66	5.63
2003 Akron	AA	31	0	0	20	45.1	183	33	10	7	0	1	0	0	13	2	75	1	0	0	0	-	0	16--	-	1.61	1.39

Year	Team	Lg	G	GS	CG	GF	IP	BFP	H	R	ER	HR	SH	SF	HB	TBB	IBB	SO	WP	Bk	W	L	Pct	ShO	Sv-Op	Hld	ERC	ERA
2003	Buffalo	AAA	4	0	0	2	6.2	27	6	3	3	1	0	0	0	2	0	6	1	0	0	0	-	0	1- -	-	3.55	4.05
2004	Akron	AA	1	0	0	0	1.0	4	0	0	0	0	0	0	0	1	0	2	0	0	0	0	-	0	0- -	-	0.95	0.00
2003	Cleveland	AL	33	0	0	13	38.0	154	27	11	9	5	1	1	1	13	2	36	1	0	2	2	.500	0	1-3	4	2.54	2.13
2004	Cleveland	AL	68	0	0	21	66.2	286	71	32	29	7	1	2	0	18	6	76	5	1	5	6	.455	0	4-11	12	3.77	3.92
	2 ML YEARS		101	0	0	34	104.2	440	98	43	38	12	2	3	1	31	8	112	6	1	7	8	.467	0	5-14	16	3.31	3.27

Wilson Betemit

Bats: B **Throws:** R **Pos:** SS-11; 3B-7; PH-4; PR-2 **Ht:** 6'3" **Wt:** 190 **Born:** 7/28/1980 **Age:** 24

					BATTING																	BASERUNNING				AVERAGES		
Year	Team	Lg	G	AB	H	2B	3B	HR	(Hm	Rd)	TB	R	RBI	RC	TBB	IBB	SO	HBP	SH	SF	SB	CS	SB%	GDP	Avg	OBP	Slg
1997	Braves	R	32	113	24	6	1	0	(-	-)	32	12	15	7	9	0	32	0	0	0	0	0	-	3	.212	.270	.283
1998	Braves	R	51	173	38	8	4	5	(-	-)	69	23	16	20	20	0	49	0	0	0	6	5	.55	1	.220	.301	.399
1999	Danville	A+	67	259	82	18	2	5	(-	-)	119	39	53	44	27	1	63	1	1	3	6	3	.67	4	.317	.379	.459
1999	Danville	R+	67	259	83	18	2	5	(-	-)	120	39	53	45	27	1	63	1	1	3	6	3	.67	4	.320	.383	.463
2000	Jamestown	A-	69	269	89	15	2	5	(-	-)	123	54	37	48	30	2	37	1	3	5	3	4	.43	4	.331	.393	.457
2001	Myrtle Beach	A+	84	318	88	29	1	7	(-	-)	140	38	43	41	23	1	71	1	0	4	8	5	.62	8	.277	.324	.440
2001	Greenville	AA	47	183	65	14	0	5	(-	-)	94	22	19	35	12	0	36	1	1	2	6	2	.75	4	.355	.394	.514
2002	Richmond	AAA	93	343	84	17	1	8	(-	-)	127	43	34	39	34	0	82	1	3	3	1	0	1.00	7	.245	.312	.370
2002	Braves	R	7	19	5	4	0	0	(-	-)	9	2	2	3	5	0	2	0	0	0	1	0	1.00	0	.263	.417	.474
2003	Richmond	AAA	127	478	125	23	13	8	(-	-)	198	55	65	61	38	2	115	0	3	2	8	5	.62	8	.262	.315	.414
2004	Richmond	AAA	105	356	99	24	2	13	(-	-)	166	48	59	48	32	3	99	0	1	2	3	3	.50	18	.278	.336	.466
2001	Atlanta	NL	8	3	0	0	0	0	(0	0)	0	1	0	0	2	0	3	0	0	0	1	0	1.00	0	.000	.000	.000
2004	Atlanta	NL	22	47	8	0	0	0	(0	0)	8	2	3	0	4	0	16	0	0	1	0	1	.00	0	.170	.231	.170
	2 ML YEARS		30	50	8	0	0	0	(0	0)	8	3	3	0	6	0	19	0	0	1	1	1	.50	0	.160	.246	.160

Rocky Biddle

Pitches: R **Bats:** R **Pos:** RP-38; SP-9 **Ht:** 6'3" **Wt:** 230 **Born:** 5/21/1976 **Age:** 29

					HOW MUCH HE PITCHED				WHAT HE GAVE UP											THE RESULTS							
Year	Team	Lg	G	GS	CG	GF	IP	BFP	H	R	ER	HR	SH	SF	HB	TBB	IBB	SO	WP	Bk	W	L	Pct	ShO	Sv-Op	Hld	ERC	ERA
2000	Chicago	AL	4	4	0	0	22.2	105	31	25	21	5	0	2	0	8	0	7	2	0	1	2	.333	0	0-0	0	7.01	8.34
2001	Chicago	AL	30	21	0	1	128.2	571	137	87	77	16	4	3	8	52	3	85	6	0	7	8	.467	0	0-3	1	4.85	5.39
2002	Chicago	AL	44	7	0	9	77.2	339	72	42	35	13	0	1	5	39	4	64	5	0	3	4	.429	0	1-3	4	4.78	4.06
2003	Montreal	NL	73	0	0	58	71.2	327	71	43	37	10	4	1	6	40	5	54	8	0	5	8	.385	0	34-41	5	5.13	4.65
2004	Montreal	NL	47	9	0	19	78.0	364	98	69	60	15	3	3	8	31	3	51	5	0	4	8	.333	0	11-15	1	6.66	6.92
	5 ML YEARS		198	41	0	87	378.2	1706	409	266	230	59	11	10	27	170	15	261	26	0	20	30	.400	0	46-62	10	5.37	5.47

Nick Bierbrodt

Pitches: L **Bats:** L **Pos:** SP-4 **Ht:** 6'5" **Wt:** 214 **Born:** 5/16/1978 **Age:** 27

					HOW MUCH HE PITCHED				WHAT HE GAVE UP											THE RESULTS							
Year	Team	Lg	G	GS	CG	GF	IP	BFP	H	R	ER	HR	SH	SF	HB	TBB	IBB	SO	WP	Bk	W	L	Pct	ShO	Sv-Op	Hld	ERC	ERA
2004	Frisco*	AA	5	5	0	0	25.0	116	29	14	13	1	0	0	3	11	2	21	2	0	1	2	.333	0	0- -	-	4.99	4.68
2004	Oklahoma*	AAA	5	5	0	0	24.2	120	26	21	20	5	2	1	2	22	0	26	0	0	1	3	.250	0	0- -	-	7.76	7.30
2001	Ari-TB	AL	16	16	0	0	84.1	389	100	59	52	17	0	2	4	39	1	73	3	0	5	6	.455	0	0-0	0	6.37	5.55
2003	TB-Cle	AL	18	5	0	4	43.1	222	64	47	44	9	2	5	5	27	3	29	4	1	0	2	.000	0	0-0	0	9.29	9.14
2004	Texas	AL	4	4	0	0	17.0	81	14	11	11	4	2	1	2	19	0	10	2	0	1	1	.500	0	0-0	0	7.94	5.82
2001	Arizona	NL	5	5	0	0	23.0	108	29	21	21	6	0	1	0	12	0	17	0	0	2	2	.500	0	0-0	0	7.43	8.22
2001	Tampa Bay	AL	11	11	0	0	61.1	281	71	38	31	11	0	1	4	27	1	56	3	0	3	4	.429	0	0-0	0	5.99	4.55
2003	Tampa Bay	AL	13	5	0	1	35.1	189	59	41	38	9	2	3	5	23	3	20	4	1	0	2	.000	0	0-0	0	11.39	9.68
2003	Cleveland	AL	5	0	0	3	8.0	33	5	6	6	0	0	2	0	4	0	9	0	0	0	0	-	0	0-0	0	1.84	6.75
	3 ML YEARS		38	25	0	4	144.2	692	178	117	107	30	4	8	11	85	4	112	9	1	6	9	.400	0	0-0	0	7.41	6.66

Larry Bigbie

Bats: L **Throws:** R **Pos:** LF-114; CF-30; PR-5; PH-3; DH-2 **Ht:** 6'4" **Wt:** 190 **Born:** 11/4/1977 **Age:** 27

					BATTING																	BASERUNNING				AVERAGES		
Year	Team	Lg	G	AB	H	2B	3B	HR	(Hm	Rd)	TB	R	RBI	RC	TBB	IBB	SO	HBP	SH	SF	SB	CS	SB%	GDP	Avg	OBP	Slg
2004	Frederick*	A+	1	5	2	0	0	2	(-	-)	8	2	2	2	0	0	1	0	0	0	0	0	-	0	.400	.400	1.600
2001	Baltimore	AL	47	131	30	6	0	2	(0	2)	42	15	11	14	17	1	42	0	1	0	4	1	.80	2	.229	.318	.321
2002	Baltimore	AL	16	34	6	1	0	0	(0	0)	7	1	3	1	1	0	11	0	0	1	1	0	1.00	1	.176	.194	.206
2003	Baltimore	AL	83	287	87	15	1	9	(4	5)	131	43	31	47	29	3	60	0	0	1	7	1	.88	2	.303	.365	.456
2004	Baltimore	AL	139	478	134	23	1	15	(8	7)	204	76	68	65	45	0	113	1	3	4	8	3	.73	7	.280	.341	.427
	4 ML YEARS		285	930	257	45	2	26	(12	14)	384	135	113	127	92	4	226	1	5	7	20	5	.80	12	.276	.340	.413

Craig Biggio

Bats: R **Throws:** R **Pos:** LF-83; CF-66; PH-6; DH-1 **Ht:** 5'11" **Wt:** 185 **Born:** 12/14/1965 **Age:** 39

					BATTING																	BASERUNNING				AVERAGES		
Year	Team	Lg	G	AB	H	2B	3B	HR	(Hm	Rd)	TB	R	RBI	RC	TBB	IBB	SO	HBP	SH	SF	SB	CS	SB%	GDP	Avg	OBP	Slg
1988	Houston	NL	50	123	26	6	1	3	(1	2)	43	14	5	11	7	2	29	0	1	0	6	1	.86	1	.211	.254	.350
1989	Houston	NL	134	443	114	21	2	13	(6	7)	178	64	60	64	49	8	64	6	6	5	21	3	.88	7	.257	.336	.402
1990	Houston	NL	150	555	153	24	2	4	(2	2)	193	53	42	68	53	1	79	3	9	1	25	11	.69	11	.276	.342	.348
1991	Houston	NL	149	546	161	23	4	4	(0	4)	204	79	46	79	53	3	71	2	5	3	19	6	.76	2	.295	.358	.374
1992	Houston	NL	162	613	170	32	3	6	(3	3)	226	96	39	95	94	9	95	7	5	2	38	15	.72	5	.277	.378	.369
1993	Houston	NL	155	610	175	41	5	21	(8	13)	289	98	64	105	77	7	93	10	4	5	15	17	.47	10	.287	.373	.474
1994	Houston	NL	114	437	139	44	5	6	(4	2)	211	88	56	94	62	1	58	8	2	2	39	4	.91	5	.318	.411	.483
1995	Houston	NL	141	553	167	30	2	22	(6	16)	267	123	77	116	80	1	85	22	11	7	33	8	.80	6	.302	.406	.483
1996	Houston	NL	162	605	174	24	4	15	(9	6)	251	113	75	105	75	0	72	27	8	8	25	7	.78	10	.288	.386	.415
1997	Houston	NL	162	619	191	37	8	22	(7	15)	310	146	81	139	84	6	107	34	0	7	47	10	.82	0	.309	.415	.501
1998	Houston	NL	160	646	210	51	2	20	(10	10)	325	123	88	135	64	6	113	23	1	4	50	8	.86	10	.325	.403	.503
1999	Houston	NL	160	639	188	56	0	16	(10	6)	292	123	73	117	88	9	107	11	5	5	28	14	.67	5	.294	.386	.457

Year Team	Lg	G	AB	H	2B	3B	HR	(Hm	Rd)	TB	R	RBI	RC	TBB	IBB	SO	HBP	SH	SF	SB	CS	SB%	GDP	Avg	OBP	Slg
2000 Houston	NL	101	377	101	13	5	8	(2	6)	148	67	35	63	61	3	73	16	7	5	12	2	.86	10	.268	.388	.393
2001 Houston	NL	155	617	180	35	3	20	(10	10)	281	118	70	109	66	4	100	28	0	6	7	4	.64	11	.292	.382	.455
2002 Houston	NL	145	577	146	36	3	15	(7	8)	233	96	58	71	50	2	111	17	9	2	16	2	.89	15	.253	.330	.404
2003 Houston	NL	153	628	166	44	2	15	(6	9)	259	102	62	97	57	3	116	27	3	2	8	4	.67	4	.264	.350	.412
2004 Houston	NL	156	633	178	47	0	24	(13	11)	297	100	63	87	40	0	94	15	9	3	7	2	.78	8	.281	.337	.469
17 ML YEARS		2409	9221	2639	564	51	234	(102	132)	4007	1603	994	1555	1060	65	1467	256	85	68	396	118	.77	120	.286	.373	.435

Travis Blackley

Pitches: L **Bats:** L **Pos:** SP-6   **Ht:** 6'3" **Wt:** 190 **Born:** 11/4/1982 **Age:** 22

		HOW MUCH HE PITCHED						WHAT HE GAVE UP											THE RESULTS						
Year Team	Lg	G	GS	CG	GF	IP	BFP	H	R	ER	HR	SH	SF	HB	TBB	IBB	SO	WP	Bk	W	L	Pct	ShO	Sv-Op	Hld	ERC	ERA
2001 Everett	A-	14	14	0	0	78.2	319	60	34	29	7	2	2	1	29	0	90	3	0	6	1	.857	0	0--	-	2.70	3.32
2002 Sn Brnardino	A+	21	20	1	1	121.1	505	102	52	47	11	4	0	7	44	0	152	11	2	5	9	.357	0	0--	-	3.25	3.49
2003 San Antonio	AA	27	27	0	0	162.1	658	125	55	47	11	5	4	6	62	0	144	9	2	17	3	.850	0	0--	-	2.77	2.61
2004 Tacoma	AAA	19	18	2	0	110.1	455	100	49	47	14	6	1	3	47	0	80	9	3	8	6	.571	2	0--	-	4.12	3.83
2004 Seattle	AL	6	6	0	0	26.0	134	35	31	29	9	1	1	1	22	0	16	3	1	1	3	.250	0	0-0	0	10.52	10.04

Casey Blake

Bats: R **Throws:** R **Pos:** 3B-152; 1B-8   **Ht:** 6'2" **Wt:** 205 **Born:** 8/23/1973 **Age:** 31

		BATTING																	BASERUNNING				AVERAGES		
Year Team	Lg	G	AB	H	2B	3B	HR	(Hm	Rd)	TB	R	RBI	RC	TBB	IBB	SO	HBP	SH	SF	SB	CS	SB%	GDP	Avg	OBP	Slg
1999 Toronto	AL	14	39	10	2	0	1	(0	1)	15	6	1	4	2	0	7	0	0	0	0	0	-	1	.256	.293	.385
2000 Minnesota	AL	7	16	3	2	0	0	(0	0)	5	1	1	2	3	0	7	1	0	1	0	0	-	1	.188	.333	.313
2001 Min-Bal	AL	19	37	9	1	0	1	(0	1)	13	3	4	5	4	1	12	0	0	0	3	0	1.00	0	.243	.317	.351
2002 Minnesota	AL	9	20	4	1	0	0	(0	0)	5	2	1	1	2	0	7	0	0	0	0	0	-	0	.200	.273	.250
2003 Cleveland	AL	152	557	143	35	0	17	(2	15)	229	80	67	68	38	1	109	10	8	8	7	9	.44	11	.257	.312	.411
2004 Cleveland	AL	152	587	159	36	3	28	(13	15)	285	93	88	88	68	2	139	9	1	3	5	8	.38	19	.271	.354	.486
2001 Minnesota	AL	13	22	7	1	0	0	(0	0)	8	1	2	4	3	1	8	0	0	0	1	0	1.00	0	.318	.400	.364
2001 Baltimore	AL	6	15	2	0	0	1	(0	1)	5	2	2	1	1	0	4	0	0	0	2	0	1.00	0	.133	.188	.333
6 ML YEARS		353	1256	328	77	3	47	(15	32)	552	185	162	168	117	4	281	20	9	12	15	17	.47	32	.261	.331	.439

Hank Blalock

Bats: L **Throws:** R **Pos:** 3B-159; PH-4   **Ht:** 6'1" **Wt:** 195 **Born:** 11/28/1980 **Age:** 24

		BATTING																	BASERUNNING				AVERAGES		
Year Team	Lg	G	AB	H	2B	3B	HR	(Hm	Rd)	TB	R	RBI	RC	TBB	IBB	SO	HBP	SH	SF	SB	CS	SB%	GDP	Avg	OBP	Slg
2002 Texas	AL	49	147	31	8	0	3	(2	1)	48	16	17	15	20	1	43	1	2	2	0	0	-	2	.211	.306	.327
2003 Texas	AL	143	567	170	33	3	29	(18	11)	296	89	90	90	44	1	97	1	0	3	2	3	.40	17	.300	.350	.522
2004 Texas	AL	159	624	172	38	3	32	(16	16)	312	107	110	119	75	7	149	6	0	8	2	2	.50	13	.276	.355	.500
3 ML YEARS		351	1338	373	79	6	64	(36	28)	656	212	217	224	139	9	289	8	2	13	4	5	.44	32	.279	.347	.490

Andres Blanco

Bats: B **Throws:** R **Pos:** SS-19   **Ht:** 5'10" **Wt:** 150 **Born:** 4/11/1984 **Age:** 21

		BATTING																	BASERUNNING				AVERAGES		
Year Team	Lg	G	AB	H	2B	3B	HR	(Hm	Rd)	TB	R	RBI	RC	TBB	IBB	SO	HBP	SH	SF	SB	CS	SB%	GDP	Avg	OBP	Slg
2002 Royals	R	52	193	48	8	0	0	(-	-)	56	27	14	20	15	0	29	4	6	1	16	4	.80	2	.249	.315	.290
2002 Wilmington	A+	5	13	4	1	0	0	(-	-)	5	2	0	1	1	0	4	0	2	0	0	0	-	0	.308	.357	.385
2003 Wilmington	A+	113	394	96	11	3	0	(-	-)	113	61	25	41	44	1	50	8	21	2	13	7	.65	9	.244	.330	.287
2004 Wichita	AA	93	324	80	10	2	0	(-	-)	94	34	21	25	18	2	44	7	8	2	7	6	.54	14	.247	.299	.290
2004 Kansas City	AL	19	60	19	2	2	0	(0	0)	25	9	5	12	5	0	6	1	1	0	1	2	.33	0	.317	.379	.417

Henry Blanco

Bats: R **Throws:** R **Pos:** C-114; PR-3   **Ht:** 5'11" **Wt:** 220 **Born:** 8/29/1971 **Age:** 33

		BATTING																	BASERUNNING				AVERAGES		
Year Team	Lg	G	AB	H	2B	3B	HR	(Hm	Rd)	TB	R	RBI	RC	TBB	IBB	SO	HBP	SH	SF	SB	CS	SB%	GDP	Avg	OBP	Slg
1997 Los Angeles	NL	3	5	2	0	0	1	(0	1)	5	1	1	2	0	0	1	0	0	0	0	0	-	0	.400	.400	1.000
1999 Colorado	NL	88	263	61	12	3	6	(3	3)	97	30	28	32	34	1	38	1	3	2	1	1	.50	4	.232	.320	.369
2000 Milwaukee	NL	93	284	67	24	0	7	(3	4)	112	29	31	33	36	6	60	0	4	0	3	0	.00	9	.236	.318	.394
2001 Milwaukee	NL	104	314	66	18	3	6	(4	2)	108	33	31	30	34	6	72	2	5	2	3	1	.75	10	.210	.290	.344
2002 Atlanta	NL	81	221	45	9	1	6	(4	2)	74	17	22	15	20	5	51	1	2	5	0	2	.00	5	.204	.267	.335
2003 Atlanta	NL	55	151	30	8	0	1	(0	1)	41	11	13	13	10	2	21	1	3	1	0	0	-	3	.199	.252	.272
2004 Minnesota	AL	114	315	65	19	1	10	(4	6)	116	36	37	25	21	0	56	3	11	3	0	3	.00	8	.206	.260	.368
7 ML YEARS		538	1553	336	90	8	37	(18	19)	553	157	163	150	155	20	299	8	24	17	4	10	.29	39	.216	.288	.356

Joe Blanton

Pitches: R **Bats:** R **Pos:** RP-3   **Ht:** 6'3" **Wt:** 225 **Born:** 12/11/1980 **Age:** 24

		HOW MUCH HE PITCHED						WHAT HE GAVE UP											THE RESULTS						
Year Team	Lg	G	GS	CG	GF	IP	BFP	H	R	ER	HR	SH	SF	HB	TBB	IBB	SO	WP	Bk	W	L	Pct	ShO	Sv-Op	Hld	ERC	ERA
2002 Vancouver	A-	4	2	0	0	14.1	53	11	5	5	0	0	0	0	2	0	15	0	0	1	1	.500	0	0--	-	1.55	3.14
2002 Modesto	A+	2	1	0	0	6.0	33	8	6	5	1	0	0	0	6	0	6	0	1	0	1	.000	0	0--	-	8.82	7.50
2003 Kane County	A	21	21	2	0	133.0	531	110	47	38	6	2	3	5	19	0	144	1	0	8	7	.533	2	0--	-	2.02	2.57
2003 Midland	AA	7	5	1	2	35.2	129	21	6	5	1	1	0	0	7	0	30	0	0	3	1	.750	0	1--	-	1.22	1.26
2004 Sacramento	AAA	28	26	1	0	176.1	756	199	101	82	13	5	14	6	34	2	143	6	0	11	8	.579	0	0--	-	3.88	4.19
2004 Oakland	AL	3	0	0	1	8.0	30	6	5	5	1	0	0	0	2	0	6	0	0	0	0	-	0	0-0	0	2.52	5.63

Willie Bloomquist

Bats: R **Throws:** R **Pos:** 3B-31; PR-26; SS-20; 1B-19; LF-8; DH-6; PH-3; 2B-1; CF-1   **Ht:** 5'11" **Wt:** 180 **Born:** 11/27/1977 **Age:** 27

Year Team	Lg	G	AB	H	2B	3B	HR	(Hm	Rd)	TB	R	RBI	RC	TBB	IBB	SO	HBP	SH	SF	SB	CS	SB%	GDP	Avg	OBP	Slg
2004 Tacoma*	AAA	3	12	5	0	0	1	(-	-)	8	2	3	3	0	0	2	0	0	0	1	0	1.00	0	.417	.417	.667
2002 Seattle	AL	12	33	15	4	0	0	(0	0)	19	11	7	10	5	0	2	0	0	0	3	1	.75	0	.455	.526	.576
2003 Seattle	AL	89	196	49	7	2	1	(1	0)	63	30	14	18	19	1	39	1	2	2	4	1	.80	6	.250	.317	.321
2004 Seattle	AL	93	188	46	10	0	2	(0	2)	62	27	18	18	10	0	48	0	3	0	13	2	.87	2	.245	.283	.330
3 ML YEARS		194	417	110	21	2	3	(1	2)	144	68	39	46	34	1	89	1	5	2	20	4	.83	8	.264	.319	.345

Geoff Blum

Bats: B **Throws:** R **Pos:** 3B-59; 2B-52; PH-8; LF-7; 1B-2; DH-2; SS-1; PR-1   **Ht:** 6'3" **Wt:** 200 **Born:** 4/26/1973 **Age:** 32

Year Team	Lg	G	AB	H	2B	3B	HR	(Hm	Rd)	TB	R	RBI	RC	TBB	IBB	SO	HBP	SH	SF	SB	CS	SB%	GDP	Avg	OBP	Slg
1999 Montreal	NL	45	133	32	7	2	8	(0	8)	67	21	18	22	17	3	25	0	3	0	1	0	1.00	3	.241	.327	.504
2000 Montreal	NL	124	343	97	20	2	11	(5	6)	154	40	45	50	26	2	60	3	3	4	1	4	.20	4	.283	.335	.449
2001 Montreal	NL	148	453	107	25	0	9	(6	3)	159	57	50	49	43	8	94	10	3	5	9	5	.64	12	.236	.313	.351
2002 Houston	NL	130	368	104	20	4	10	(6	4)	162	45	52	62	49	5	70	1	1	2	2	0	1.00	8	.283	.367	.440
2003 Houston	NL	123	420	110	19	0	10	(6	4)	159	51	52	40	20	1	50	2	2	5	0	0	-	15	.262	.295	.379
2004 Tampa Bay	AL	112	339	73	21	0	8	(2	6)	118	38	35	29	24	1	58	0	4	2	2	3	.40	4	.215	.266	.348
6 ML YEARS		682	2056	523	112	8	56	(25	31)	819	252	252	252	179	20	357	16	16	18	15	12	.56	46	.254	.316	.398

Hiram Bocachica

Bats: R **Throws:** R **Pos:** CF-32; RF-12; PR-8; DH-2; PH-2; LF-1   **Ht:** 5'11" **Wt:** 165 **Born:** 3/4/1976 **Age:** 29

Year Team	Lg	G	AB	H	2B	3B	HR	(Hm	Rd)	TB	R	RBI	RC	TBB	IBB	SO	HBP	SH	SF	SB	CS	SB%	GDP	Avg	OBP	Slg
2004 Tacoma*	AAA	40	136	39	5	1	10	(-	-)	76	22	25	30	17	2	36	8	4	2	12	3	.80	2	.287	.393	.559
2000 Los Angeles	NL	8	10	3	0	0	0	(0	0)	3	2	0	1	0	0	2	0	0	0	0	0	-	0	.300	.300	.300
2001 Los Angeles	NL	75	133	31	11	1	2	(2	0)	50	15	9	15	9	0	33	1	0	0	4	1	.80	1	.233	.287	.376
2002 LA-Det		83	168	37	7	0	8	(2	6)	68	26	17	13	10	0	41	0	1	0	3	3	.50	3	.220	.264	.405
2003 Detroit	AL	6	22	1	1	0	0	(0	0)	2	1	0	0	0	0	7	0	0	0	0	0	-	0	.045	.045	.091
2004 Seattle	AL	50	90	22	5	0	3	(3	0)	36	9	6	9	12	0	27	1	3	1	5	4	.56	1	.244	.337	.400
2002 Los Angeles	NL	49	65	14	3	0	4	(1	3)	29	12	9	6	5	0	19	0	0	0	1	1	.50	1	.215	.271	.446
2002 Detroit	AL	34	103	23	4	0	4	(1	3)	39	14	8	7	5	0	22	0	1	0	2	2	.50	2	.223	.259	.379
5 ML YEARS		222	423	94	24	1	13	(7	6)	159	53	32	38	31	0	110	2	4	1	12	8	.60	5	.222	.278	.376

Brian Boehringer

Pitches: R **Bats:** B **Pos:** RP-21   **Ht:** 6'2" **Wt:** 190 **Born:** 1/8/1970 **Age:** 35

Year Team	Lg	G	GS	CG	GF	IP	BFP	H	R	ER	HR	SH	SF	HB	TBB	IBB	SO	WP	Bk	W	L	Pct	ShO	Sv-Op	Hld	ERC	ERA
1995 New York	AL	7	3	0	0	17.2	99	24	27	27	5	0	1	1	22	1	10	3	0	0	3	.000	0	0-1	0	11.86	13.75
1996 New York	AL	15	3	0	1	46.1	205	46	28	28	6	3	3	1	21	2	37	1	0	2	4	.333	0	0-1	4	4.42	5.44
1997 New York	AL	34	0	0	11	48.0	210	39	16	14	4	3	2	0	32	6	53	2	0	3	2	.600	0	0-3	5	3.74	2.63
1998 San Diego	NL	56	1	0	18	76.1	347	75	38	37	10	5	1	4	45	4	67	1	0	5	2	.714	0	0-1	7	5.06	4.36
1999 San Diego	NL	33	11	0	4	94.1	409	97	38	34	10	6	4	1	35	4	64	2	0	6	5	.545	0	0-2	3	4.12	3.24
2000 San Diego	NL	7	3	0	1	15.2	74	18	15	10	4	0	1	0	10	0	9	0	0	0	3	.000	0	0-1	0	7.15	5.74
2001 NYY-SF		51	0	0	17	69.0	311	67	35	28	7	2	4	5	29	5	60	0	0	0	4	.000	0	2-2	3	4.02	3.65
2002 Pittsburgh	NL	70	0	0	20	79.2	328	65	30	30	5	6	3	2	33	6	65	1	0	4	4	.500	0	1-6	28	2.92	3.39
2003 Pittsburgh	NL	62	0	0	18	62.1	277	64	39	38	11	3	2	3	30	3	47	0	1	5	4	.556	0	0-3	15	5.06	5.49
2004 Pittsburgh	NL	21	0	0	4	25.1	115	27	14	13	2	1	3	1	17	3	20	0	0	1	1	.500	0	0-2	1	5.48	4.62
2001 New York	AL	22	0	0	8	34.2	155	35	15	12	3	1	2	3	12	0	33	0	0	0	1	.000	0	1-1	1	4.03	3.12
2001 San Francisco	NL	29	0	0	9	34.1	156	32	20	16	4	1	2	2	17	5	27	0	0	0	3	.000	0	1-1	2	4.01	4.19
10 ML YEARS		356	21	0	98	534.2	2375	522	280	259	64	29	24	18	274	34	432	10	1	26	32	.448	0	3-22	66	4.54	4.36

Jeremy Bonderman

Pitches: R **Bats:** R **Pos:** SP-32; RP-1   **Ht:** 6'2" **Wt:** 210 **Born:** 10/28/1982 **Age:** 22

Year Team	Lg	G	GS	CG	GF	IP	BFP	H	R	ER	HR	SH	SF	HB	TBB	IBB	SO	WP	Bk	W	L	Pct	ShO	Sv-Op	Hld	ERC	ERA
2002 Modesto	A+	25	25	1	0	144.2	627	129	77	58	15	6	7	5	55	1	160	9	3	9	8	.529	0	0--	-	3.45	3.61
2002 Lakeland	A+	2	2	1	0	12.0	49	11	8	8	3	1	0	2	4	0	10	1	0	0	1	.000	0	0--	-	5.42	6.00
2003 Detroit	AL	33	28	0	0	162.0	727	193	118	100	23	3	6	4	58	2	108	12	2	6	19	.240	0	0-0	0	5.39	5.56
2004 Detroit	AL	33	32	2	0	184.0	793	168	101	100	24	10	5	10	73	5	168	7	0	11	13	.458	2	0-0	0	3.93	4.89
2 ML YEARS		66	60	2	0	346.0	1520	361	219	200	47	13	11	14	131	7	276	19	2	17	32	.347	2	0-0	0	4.59	5.20

Barry Bonds

Bats: L **Throws:** L **Pos:** LF-132; PH-8; DH-7   **Ht:** 6'2" **Wt:** 228 **Born:** 7/24/1964 **Age:** 40

Year Team	Lg	G	AB	H	2B	3B	HR	(Hm	Rd)	TB	R	RBI	RC	TBB	IBB	SO	HBP	SH	SF	SB	CS	SB%	GDP	Avg	OBP	Slg
1986 Pittsburgh	NL	113	413	92	26	3	16	(9	7)	172	72	48	64	65	2	102	2	2	2	36	7	.84	4	.223	.330	.416
1987 Pittsburgh	NL	150	551	144	34	9	25	(12	13)	271	99	59	92	54	3	88	3	0	3	32	10	.76	4	.261	.329	.492
1988 Pittsburgh	NL	144	538	152	30	5	24	(14	10)	264	97	58	89	72	14	82	2	0	2	17	11	.61	3	.283	.368	.491
1989 Pittsburgh	NL	159	580	144	34	6	19	(7	12)	247	96	58	91	93	22	93	1	1	4	32	10	.76	9	.248	.351	.426
1990 Pittsburgh	NL	151	519	156	32	3	33	(14	19)	293	104	114	121	93	15	83	3	0	6	52	13	.80	8	.301	.406	.565
1991 Pittsburgh	NL	153	510	149	28	5	25	(12	13)	262	95	116	113	107	25	73	4	0	13	43	13	.77	8	.292	.410	.514
1992 Pittsburgh	NL	140	473	147	36	5	34	(15	19)	295	109	103	134	127	32	69	5	0	7	39	8	.83	9	.311	.456	.624
1993 San Francisco	NL	159	539	181	38	4	46	(21	25)	365	129	123	155	126	43	79	2	0	7	29	12	.71	11	.336	.458	.677
1994 San Francisco	NL	112	391	122	18	1	37	(15	22)	253	89	81	105	74	18	43	6	0	3	29	9	.76	3	.312	.426	.647
1995 San Francisco	NL	144	506	149	30	7	33	(16	17)	292	109	104	125	120	22	83	5	0	4	31	10	.76	12	.294	.431	.577
1996 San Francisco	NL	158	517	159	27	3	42	(23	19)	318	122	129	148	151	30	76	1	0	6	40	7	.85	11	.308	.461	.615

43

Year Team	Lg	G	AB	H	2B	3B	HR	(Hm	Rd)	TB	R	RBI	RC	TBB	IBB	SO	HBP	SH	SF	SB	CS	SB%	GDP	Avg	OBP	Slg
1997 San Francisco	NL	159	532	155	26	5	40	(24	16)	311	123	101	140	**145**	34	87	8	0	5	37	8	.82	13	.291	.446	.585
1998 San Francisco	NL	156	552	167	44	7	37	(21	16)	336	120	122	141	130	**29**	92	8	1	6	28	12	.70	15	.303	.438	.609
1999 San Francisco	NL	102	355	93	20	2	34	(16	18)	219	91	83	85	73	9	62	3	0	3	15	2	.88	6	.262	.389	.617
2000 San Francisco	NL	143	480	147	28	4	49	(25	24)	330	129	106	139	**117**	22	77	3	0	7	11	3	.79	6	.306	.440	.688
2001 San Francisco	NL	153	476	156	32	2	73	**(37**	**36)**	411	129	137	**191**	**177**	35	93	9	0	2	13	3	.81	5	.328	**.515**	**.863**
2002 San Francisco	NL	143	403	149	31	2	46	(19	**27)**	322	117	110	160	**198**	68	47	9	0	2	9	2	.82	4	**.370**	**.582**	.799
2003 San Francisco	NL	130	390	133	22	1	45	(23	**22)**	292	111	90	129	**148**	61	58	10	0	2	7	0	1.00	1	.341	**.529**	.749
2004 San Francisco	NL	147	373	135	27	3	45	(26	19)	303	129	101	171	**232**	**120**	41	9	0	3	6	1	.86	5	.362	**.609**	.812
19 ML YEARS		2716	9098	2730	563	77	703	(349	354)	5556	2070	1843	2401	2302	604	1428	93	4	87	506	141	.78	143	.300	.443	.611

Jung Bong

Pitches: L Bats: L Pos: SP-3   **Ht:** 6'3" **Wt:** 175 **Born:** 7/15/1980 **Age:** 24

Year Team	Lg	G	GS	CG	GF	IP	BFP	H	R	ER	HR	SH	SF	HB	TBB	IBB	SO	WP	Bk	W	L	Pct	ShO	Sv-Op	Hld	ERC	ERA
2004 Reds*	R	2	2	0	0	3.0	15	3	5	4	0	0	0	0	2	0	3	1	0	0	-	-	0	0- -	-	3.91	12.00
2004 Louisville*	AAA	19	19	0	0	94.1	413	118	66	61	13	5	3	2	31	0	65	7	0	8	8	.500	0	0- -	-	5.79	5.82
2002 Atlanta	NL	1	1	0	0	6.0	27	8	5	5	0	0	0	0	2	0	4	0	0	1	0	1.000	0	0-0	0	5.03	7.50
2003 Atlanta	NL	44	0	0	14	57.0	247	56	32	32	8	3	1	2	31	6	47	6	1	6	2	.750	0	1-3	2	4.97	5.05
2004 Cincinnati	NL	3	3	0	0	15.1	75	17	13	8	3	2	0	0	10	0	11	1	0	1	1	.500	0	0-0	0	6.18	4.70
3 ML YEARS		48	4	0	14	78.1	349	81	50	45	11	5	1	2	43	6	62	7	1	7	4	.636	0	1-3	2	5.21	5.17

Aaron Boone

Bats: R Throws: R Pos: 3B   **Ht:** 6'2" **Wt:** 200 **Born:** 3/9/1973 **Age:** 32

Year Team	Lg	G	AB	H	2B	3B	HR	(Hm	Rd)	TB	R	RBI	RC	TBB	IBB	SO	HBP	SH	SF	SB	CS	SB%	GDP	Avg	OBP	Slg
1997 Cincinnati	NL	16	49	12	1	0	0	(0	0)	13	5	5	3	2	0	5	0	1	0	1	0	1.00	1	.245	.275	.265
1998 Cincinnati	NL	58	181	51	13	2	2	(2	0)	74	24	28	27	15	1	36	5	3	2	6	1	.86	3	.282	.350	.409
1999 Cincinnati	NL	139	472	132	26	5	14	(7	7)	210	56	72	70	30	2	79	8	5	5	17	6	.74	6	.280	.330	.445
2000 Cincinnati	NL	84	291	83	18	0	12	(5	7)	137	44	43	50	24	1	52	10	2	4	6	1	.86	5	.285	.356	.471
2001 Cincinnati	NL	103	381	112	26	2	14	(10	4)	184	54	62	63	29	1	71	8	3	6	6	3	.67	9	.294	.351	.483
2002 Cincinnati	NL	162	606	146	38	2	26	(14	12)	266	83	87	83	56	4	111	10	9	4	32	8	.80	9	.241	.314	.439
2003 Cin-NYY		160	592	158	32	3	24	(13	11)	268	92	96	89	46	2	104	8	6	2	23	3	.88	13	.267	.327	.453
2003 Cincinnati	NL	106	403	110	19	3	18	(10	8)	189	61	65	65	35	2	74	5	3	0	15	3	.83	6	.273	.339	.469
2003 New York	AL	54	189	48	13	0	6	(3	3)	79	31	31	24	11	0	30	3	3	2	8	0	1.00	7	.254	.302	.418
7 ML YEARS		722	2572	694	154	14	92	(51	41)	1152	358	393	385	202	11	458	49	29	23	91	22	.81	46	.270	.332	.448

Bret Boone

Bats: R Throws: R Pos: 2B-148   **Ht:** 5'10" **Wt:** 190 **Born:** 4/6/1969 **Age:** 36

Year Team	Lg	G	AB	H	2B	3B	HR	(Hm	Rd)	TB	R	RBI	RC	TBB	IBB	SO	HBP	SH	SF	SB	CS	SB%	GDP	Avg	OBP	Slg
1992 Seattle	AL	33	129	25	4	0	4	(2	2)	41	15	15	7	4	0	34	1	1	0	1	1	.50	4	.194	.224	.318
1993 Seattle	AL	76	271	68	12	2	12	(7	5)	120	31	38	35	17	1	52	4	6	4	2	3	.40	6	.251	.301	.443
1994 Cincinnati	NL	108	381	122	25	2	12	(5	7)	187	59	68	65	24	1	74	8	5	6	3	4	.43	10	.320	.368	.491
1995 Cincinnati	NL	138	513	137	34	2	15	(6	9)	220	63	68	70	41	0	84	6	5	5	5	1	.83	14	.267	.326	.429
1996 Cincinnati	NL	142	520	121	21	3	12	(7	5)	184	56	69	50	31	0	100	3	5	9	3	2	.60	9	.233	.275	.354
1997 Cincinnati	NL	139	443	99	25	1	7	(4	3)	147	40	46	42	45	4	101	4	4	5	5	5	.50	11	.223	.298	.332
1998 Cincinnati	NL	157	583	155	38	1	24	(13	11)	267	76	95	80	48	3	104	4	9	4	6	4	.60	23	.266	.324	.458
1999 Atlanta	NL	152	608	153	38	1	20	(9	11)	253	102	63	77	47	0	112	5	9	2	14	9	.61	11	.252	.310	.416
2000 San Diego	NL	127	463	116	18	2	19	(8	11)	195	61	74	63	50	7	97	5	0	7	8	4	.67	11	.251	.326	.421
2001 Seattle	AL	158	623	206	37	3	37	(19	18)	360	118	**141**	126	40	5	110	9	5	13	5	5	.50	11	.331	.372	.578
2002 Seattle	AL	155	608	169	34	3	24	(13	11)	281	88	107	95	53	4	102	6	2	4	12	5	.71	11	.278	.339	.462
2003 Seattle	AL	159	622	183	35	5	35	(16	19)	333	111	117	111	68	3	125	7	1	7	16	3	.84	11	.294	.366	.535
2004 Seattle	AL	148	593	149	30	0	24	(12	12)	251	74	83	66	56	2	135	3	2	4	10	5	.67	18	.251	.317	.423
13 ML YEARS		1692	6357	1703	351	25	245	(121	124)	2839	894	984	887	524	30	1230	65	54	72	90	51	.64	156	.268	.327	.447

Joe Borchard

Bats: B Throws: R Pos: RF-54; PH-6; DH-3; CF-2; PR-1   **Ht:** 6'5" **Wt:** 220 **Born:** 11/25/1978 **Age:** 26

Year Team	Lg	G	AB	H	2B	3B	HR	(Hm	Rd)	TB	R	RBI	RC	TBB	IBB	SO	HBP	SH	SF	SB	CS	SB%	GDP	Avg	OBP	Slg
2004 Charlotte*	AAA	82	301	80	21	0	16	(-	-)	149	44	48	46	30	1	68	2	0	3	4	3	.57	8	.266	.333	.495
2002 Chicago	AL	16	36	8	0	0	2	(0	2)	14	5	5	5	1	0	14	0	0	0	0	0	-	0	.222	.243	.389
2003 Chicago	AL	16	49	9	1	0	1	(0	1)	13	5	5	2	5	0	18	0	0	3	0	1	.00	0	.184	.246	.265
2004 Chicago	AL	63	201	35	4	1	9	(6	3)	68	26	20	13	19	1	57	1	1	0	1	0	1.00	4	.174	.249	.338
3 ML YEARS		95	286	52	5	1	12	(6	6)	95	36	30	20	25	1	89	1	1	3	1	1	.50	4	.182	.248	.332

Pat Borders

Bats: R Throws: R Pos: C-38; PR-1   **Ht:** 6'2" **Wt:** 200 **Born:** 5/14/1963 **Age:** 42

Year Team	Lg	G	AB	H	2B	3B	HR	(Hm	Rd)	TB	R	RBI	RC	TBB	IBB	SO	HBP	SH	SF	SB	CS	SB%	GDP	Avg	OBP	Slg
2004 Tacoma*	AAA	36	137	35	5	1	5	(-	-)	57	16	13	14	3	1	28	3	0	0	0	1	.00	4	.255	.287	.416
1988 Toronto	AL	56	154	42	6	3	5	(2	3)	69	15	21	18	3	0	24	0	2	1	0	0	-	5	.273	.285	.448
1989 Toronto	AL	94	241	62	11	1	3	(1	2)	84	22	29	22	11	2	45	1	1	2	2	1	.67	7	.257	.290	.349
1990 Toronto	AL	125	346	99	24	2	15	(10	5)	172	36	49	48	18	2	57	0	1	3	0	1	.00	17	.286	.319	.497
1991 Toronto	AL	105	291	71	17	0	5	(2	3)	103	22	36	26	11	1	45	1	6	3	0	0	-	8	.244	.271	.354
1992 Toronto	AL	138	480	116	26	2	13	(7	6)	185	47	53	52	33	3	75	2	1	5	1	1	.50	13	.242	.290	.385
1993 Toronto	AL	138	488	124	30	0	9	(6	3)	181	38	55	46	20	2	66	2	7	3	2	2	.50	18	.254	.285	.371
1994 Toronto	AL	85	295	73	13	1	3	(3	0)	97	24	26	25	15	0	50	0	1	0	1	1	.50	7	.247	.284	.329
1995 KC-Hou		63	178	37	8	1	4	(1	3)	59	15	13	14	9	2	29	0	0	0	0	0	-	3	.208	.246	.331

BATTING

Year Team	Lg	G	AB	H	2B	3B	HR	(Hm	Rd)	TB	R	RBI	RC	TBB	IBB	SO	HBP	SH	SF	SB	CS	SB%	GDP	Avg	OBP	Slg
1996 StL-Cal-CWS		76	220	61	7	0	5	(3	2)	83	15	18	23	9	0	43	0	5	0	0	2	.00	4	.277	.306	.377
1997 Cleveland	AL	55	159	47	7	1	4	(0	4)	68	17	15	21	9	0	27	2	0	0	0	2	.00	5	.296	.341	.428
1998 Cleveland	AL	54	160	38	6	0	0	(0	0)	44	12	6	11	10	0	40	2	2	1	0	2	.00	3	.238	.289	.275
1999 Cle-Tor	AL	12	34	9	0	1	1	(1	0)	14	3	6	4	1	0	5	0	0	0	0	1	.00	0	.265	.286	.412
2001 Seattle	AL	5	6	3	0	0	0	(0	0)	3	1	0	1	0	0	1	0	1	0	0	0	-	0	.500	.500	.500
2002 Seattle	AL	4	4	2	1	0	0	(0	0)	3	0	1	1	0	0	1	0	0	0	0	0	-	0	.500	.500	.750
2003 Seattle	AL	12	14	2	1	0	0	(0	0)	3	1	1	1	1	0	5	0	0	0	0	0	-	0	.143	.200	.214
2004 Sea-Min	AL	38	95	22	6	0	1	(0	1)	31	9	10	7	1	0	22	1	2	0	3	1	.75	2	.232	.247	.326
1995 Kansas City	AL	52	143	33	8	1	4	(1	3)	55	14	13	14	7	1	22	0	0	0	0	0	-	1	.231	.267	.385
1995 Houston	NL	11	35	4	0	0	0	(0	0)	4	1	0	0	2	1	7	0	0	0	0	0	-	2	.114	.162	.114
1996 St Louis	NL	26	69	22	3	0	0	(0	0)	25	3	4	7	1	0	14	0	1	0	0	1	.00	1	.319	.329	.362
1996 California	AL	19	57	13	3	0	2	(2	0)	22	6	8	5	3	0	11	0	1	0	0	1	.00	1	.228	.267	.386
1996 Chicago	AL	31	94	26	1	0	3	(1	2)	36	6	6	11	5	0	18	0	3	0	0	0	-	2	.277	.313	.383
1999 Cleveland	AL	6	20	6	0	1	0	(0	0)	8	2	3	2	0	0	3	0	0	0	0	1	.00	0	.300	.300	.400
1999 Toronto	AL	6	14	3	0	0	1	(1	0)	6	1	3	2	1	0	2	0	0	0	0	0	-	0	.214	.267	.429
2004 Seattle	AL	19	53	10	2	0	1	(0	1)	15	6	5	1	1	0	12	0	1	0	1	1	.50	2	.189	.204	.283
2004 Minnesota	AL	19	42	12	4	0	0	(0	0)	16	3	5	6	0	0	10	1	1	0	2	0	1.00	0	.286	.302	.381
16 ML YEARS		1060	3165	808	163	12	68	(36	32)	1199	277	339	320	151	12	535	11	29	18	9	14	.39	90	.255	.290	.379

Dave Borkowski

Pitches: R **Bats:** R **Pos:** RP-9; SP-8 **Ht:** 6'1" **Wt:** 220 **Born:** 2/7/1977 **Age:** 28

Year Team	Lg	G	GS	CG	GF	IP	BFP	H	R	ER	HR	SH	SF	HB	TBB	IBB	SO	WP	Bk	W	L	Pct	ShO	Sv-Op	Hld	ERC	ERA
2004 Ottawa*	AAA	16	16	0	0	85.1	369	99	53	46	6	2	4	6	26	0	56	1	0	6	9	.400	0	0--	-	4.80	4.85
1999 Detroit	AL	17	12	0	2	76.2	351	86	58	52	10	1	2	4	40	0	50	3	0	2	6	.250	0	0-	0	5.75	6.10
2000 Detroit	AL	2	1	0	0	5.1	34	11	13	13	2	0	1	0	7	1	1	0	0	0	1	.000	0	0-	0	17.78	21.94
2001 Detroit	AL	15	0	0	7	29.2	135	30	21	21	5	0	2	3	15	3	30	0	0	2	0	.000	0	0-	0	5.28	6.37
2004 Baltimore	AL	17	8	0	2	56.0	247	65	37	32	6	2	2	3	15	1	45	2	1	3	4	.429	0	0-1	1	4.67	5.14
4 ML YEARS		51	21	0	11	167.2	767	192	129	118	23	3	7	10	77	5	126	5	1	5	13	.278	0	0-1	1	5.62	6.33

Toby Borland

Pitches: R **Bats:** R **Pos:** RP-18 **Ht:** 6'6" **Wt:** 210 **Born:** 5/29/1969 **Age:** 36

Year Team	Lg	G	GS	CG	GF	IP	BFP	H	R	ER	HR	SH	SF	HB	TBB	IBB	SO	WP	Bk	W	L	Pct	ShO	Sv-Op	Hld	ERC	ERA
2004 Albuquerque*	AAA	34	0	0	28	39.1	155	24	10	10	2	2	0	2	12	2	38	1	0	4	2	.667	0	11--	-	1.62	2.29
1994 Philadelphia	NL	24	0	0	7	34.1	144	31	10	9	1	1	4	1	14	3	26	4	0	1	0	1.000	0	1-1	0	3.50	2.36
1995 Philadelphia	NL	50	0	0	18	74.0	339	81	37	31	3	3	2	5	37	7	59	12	0	1	3	.250	0	6-9	11	4.62	3.77
1996 Philadelphia	NL	69	0	0	11	90.2	399	83	51	41	9	4	1	3	43	3	76	10	0	7	3	.700	0	0-2	10	3.89	4.07
1997 NYM-Bos		16	0	0	5	16.2	89	17	14	14	2	0	0	3	21	0	8	3	0	0	1	.000	0	1-2	1	8.72	7.56
1998 Philadelphia	NL	6	0	0	3	9.0	39	8	5	5	1	1	0	0	5	0	9	2	0	0	0	-	0	0-0	0	4.17	5.00
2001 Anaheim	AL	2	0	0	1	3.1	19	8	5	4	1	1	0	0	1	0	0	0	0	0	1	.000	0	0-1	0	14.71	10.80
2002 Florida	NL	15	0	0	3	13.2	62	14	8	8	3	0	2	3	5	0	11	2	0	1	0	1.000	0	0-0	1	5.85	5.27
2003 Florida	NL	7	0	0	1	9.2	40	3	3	2	0	0	1	0	8	1	4	0	0	0	0	-	0	0-0	0	1.40	1.86
2004 Florida	NL	18	0	0	5	18.1	86	18	11	11	3	2	1	0	12	5	18	0	0	1	1	.500	0	0-1	3	4.81	5.40
1997 New York	NL	13	0	0	5	13.1	65	11	9	9	1	0	0	1	14	0	7	3	0	0	1	.000	0	1-2	1	5.68	6.08
1997 Boston	AL	3	0	0	0	3.1	24	6	5	5	1	0	0	2	7	0	1	0	0	0	0	-	0	0-0	0	23.38	13.50
9 ML YEARS		207	0	0	54	269.2	1217	263	144	125	23	12	7	18	146	19	211	33	0	11	9	.550	0	8-16	26	4.49	4.17

Joe Borowski

Pitches: R **Bats:** R **Pos:** RP-22 **Ht:** 6'2" **Wt:** 240 **Born:** 5/4/1971 **Age:** 34

Year Team	Lg	G	GS	CG	GF	IP	BFP	H	R	ER	HR	SH	SF	HB	TBB	IBB	SO	WP	Bk	W	L	Pct	ShO	Sv-Op	Hld	ERC	ERA
2004 Iowa*	AAA	7	3	0	0	7.2	36	9	8	7	1	0	0	0	4	0	2	0	0	0	3	.000	0	0--	-	5.69	8.22
1995 Baltimore	AL	6	0	0	3	7.1	30	5	1	1	0	0	0	0	4	0	3	0	0	0	0	-	0	0-0	0	2.32	1.23
1996 Atlanta	NL	22	0	0	8	26.0	121	33	15	14	4	5	0	1	13	4	15	1	0	2	4	.333	0	0-0	1	6.46	4.85
1997 Atl-NYY		21	0	0	9	26.0	123	29	13	12	2	1	0	0	20	5	8	0	0	2	3	.400	0	0-0	0	5.74	4.15
1998 New York	AL	8	0	0	6	9.2	42	11	7	7	0	0	0	0	4	0	7	0	0	1	0	1.000	0	0-0	0	4.27	6.52
2001 Chicago	NL	1	1	0	0	1.2	13	6	6	6	1	0	0	0	3	0	1	0	0	0	1	.000	0	0-0	0	39.91	32.40
2002 Chicago	NL	73	0	0	25	95.2	391	84	31	29	10	5	3	1	29	6	97	1	0	4	4	.500	0	2-6	12	3.05	2.73
2003 Chicago	NL	68	0	0	59	68.1	280	53	23	20	5	4	0	1	19	1	66	0	0	2	2	.500	0	33-37	1	2.26	2.63
2004 Chicago	NL	22	0	0	19	21.1	106	27	19	19	3	1	1	0	15	2	17	0	0	2	4	.333	0	9-11	0	6.92	8.02
1997 Atlanta	NL	20	0	0	8	24.0	111	27	11	10	2	1	0	0	16	4	6	0	0	2	2	.500	0	0-0	0	5.51	3.75
1997 New York	AL	1	0	0	1	2.0	12	2	2	2	0	0	0	0	4	1	2	0	0	0	1	.000	0	0-0	0	8.25	9.00
8 ML YEARS		221	1	0	129	256.0	1106	248	115	108	25	17	4	3	107	18	214	2	0	13	18	.419	0	44-54	16	3.87	3.80

Ricky Bottalico

Pitches: R **Bats:** L **Pos:** RP-60 **Ht:** 6'1" **Wt:** 215 **Born:** 8/26/1969 **Age:** 35

Year Team	Lg	G	GS	CG	GF	IP	BFP	H	R	ER	HR	SH	SF	HB	TBB	IBB	SO	WP	Bk	W	L	Pct	ShO	Sv-Op	Hld	ERC	ERA
2004 Norfolk*	AAA	5	0	0	2	7.1	32	7	1	0	0	0	0	0	4	0	8	1	0	0	0	-	0	0--	-	3.68	0.00
1994 Philadelphia	NL	3	0	0	3	3.0	13	3	0	0	0	0	0	0	1	0	3	0	0	0	0	-	0	0-0	0	3.05	0.00
1995 Philadelphia	NL	62	0	0	20	87.2	360	50	25	24	7	3	1	4	42	3	87	1	0	5	3	.625	0	1-5	20	2.17	2.46
1996 Philadelphia	NL	61	0	0	56	67.2	269	47	24	24	6	4	2	2	23	2	74	3	0	4	5	.444	0	34-38	0	2.29	3.19
1997 Philadelphia	NL	69	0	0	61	74.0	324	68	31	30	7	1	2	2	42	4	89	3	0	2	5	.286	0	34-41	0	4.29	3.65
1998 Philadelphia	NL	39	0	0	28	43.1	206	54	31	31	7	1	2	1	25	5	27	2	0	1	5	.167	0	6-7	3	6.63	6.44
1999 St Louis	NL	68	0	0	40	73.1	347	83	45	40	8	3	0	3	49	1	66	6	0	3	7	.300	0	20-28	8	6.16	4.91
2000 Kansas City	AL	62	0	0	50	72.2	319	65	40	39	12	3	1	2	41	3	56	5	1	9	6	.600	0	16-23	1	4.65	4.83
2001 Philadelphia	NL	66	0	0	18	67.0	281	58	31	29	11	7	4	4	25	2	57	5	0	3	4	.429	0	3-7	22	3.88	3.90
2002 Philadelphia	NL	30	0	0	6	27.1	128	33	16	14	3	2	1	2	13	2	24	2	0	0	1	.000	0	0-1	15	5.80	4.61

Year Team	Lg	HOW MUCH HE PITCHED						WHAT HE GAVE UP												THE RESULTS							
		G	GS	CG	GF	IP	BFP	H	R	ER	HR	SH	SF	HB	TBB	IBB	SO	WP	Bk	W	L	Pct	ShO	Sv-Op	Hld	ERC	ERA
2003 Arizona	NL	2	0	0	0	1.2	10	3	1	1	0	0	0	0	2	1	2	0	0	1	0	1.000	0	0-0	1	10.00	5.40
2004 New York	NL	60	0	0	8	69.1	296	54	30	26	3	3	4	4	34	7	61	3	0	3	2	.600	0	0-4	12	2.87	3.38
11 ML YEARS		522	0	0	290	587.0	2543	518	274	258	64	27	17	24	297	30	546	30	1	31	40	.437	0	114-154	82	3.98	3.96

Rob Bowen

Bats: B **Throws:** R **Pos:** C-15; DH-1; PH-1; PR-1 **Ht:** 6'3" **Wt:** 225 **Born:** 2/24/1981 **Age:** 24

Year Team	Lg	BATTING								TB	R	RBI	RC	TBB	IBB	SO	HBP	SH	SF	BASERUNNING				AVERAGES		
		G	AB	H	2B	3B	HR	(Hm	Rd)											SB	CS	SB%	GDP	Avg	OBP	Slg
1999 Twins	R	29	77	20	4	0	0	(-	-)	24	10	11	12	20	0	15	0	1	3	2	2	.50	0	.260	.400	.312
2000 Elizabethton	R+	21	73	21	3	0	4	(-	-)	36	17	19	14	11	0	18	0	0	0	0	0	-	0	.288	.381	.493
2001 Quad City	A	106	385	98	18	2	16	(-	-)	168	47	70	51	37	2	112	2	2	3	4	0	1.00	11	.255	.321	.436
2002 Fort Myers	A+	100	342	63	12	1	10	(-	-)	107	52	49	27	38	0	69	5	2	5	1	0	1.00	12	.184	.272	.313
2002 Quad City	A	5	21	4	1	0	0	(-	-)	5	1	0	1	2	0	4	0	0	0	0	0	-	0	.190	.261	.238
2003 New Britain	AA	42	134	41	13	0	1	(-	-)	57	17	16	22	13	0	24	2	1	0	0	0	-	0	.306	.376	.425
2003 Rochester	AAA	30	105	27	7	0	6	(-	-)	52	14	17	15	11	1	25	1	0	0	0	0	-	3	.257	.333	.495
2004 New Britain	AA	77	249	49	10	0	9	(-	-)	86	28	24	25	31	1	76	3	1	1	3	0	1.00	3	.197	.292	.345
2003 Minnesota	AL	7	10	1	0	0	0	(0	0)	1	0	1	0	0	0	4	0	0	1	0	0	-	1	.100	.091	.100
2004 Minnesota	AL	17	27	3	0	0	1	(0	1)	6	1	2	2	4	0	10	0	1	0	0	0	-	1	.111	.226	.222
2 ML YEARS		24	37	4	0	0	1	(0	1)	7	1	3	2	4	0	14	0	1	1	0	0	-	2	.108	.190	.189

Jason Boyd

Pitches: R **Bats:** R **Pos:** RP-12 **Ht:** 6'3" **Wt:** 173 **Born:** 2/23/1973 **Age:** 32

Year Team	Lg	HOW MUCH HE PITCHED						WHAT HE GAVE UP												THE RESULTS							
		G	GS	CG	GF	IP	BFP	H	R	ER	HR	SH	SF	HB	TBB	IBB	SO	WP	Bk	W	L	Pct	ShO	Sv-Op	Hld	ERC	ERA
2004 Nashville*	AAA	11	0	0	5	16.1	76	23	7	7	2	0	0	1	3	1	11	2	0	1	3	.250	0	0- -	-	5.75	3.86
1999 Pittsburgh	NL	4	0	0	0	5.1	24	5	2	2	0	0	1	1	2	0	4	1	0	0	0	-	0	0-0	0	3.53	3.38
2000 Philadelphia	NL	30	0	0	11	34.1	161	39	28	25	2	3	0	1	24	4	32	1	0	0	1	.000	0	0-1	2	5.71	6.55
2002 San Diego	NL	23	0	0	6	28.1	131	33	29	25	6	3	3	0	15	1	18	3	0	1	0	1.000	0	0-3	4	6.35	7.94
2003 Cleveland	AL	44	0	0	13	52.1	221	38	25	25	4	0	2	3	26	1	31	2	0	3	1	.750	0	0-1	8	2.98	4.30
2004 Pittsburgh	NL	12	0	0	4	13.0	64	13	9	8	4	3	0	3	8	1	12	0	0	1	0	1.000	0	0-0	0	7.20	5.54
5 ML YEARS		113	0	0	34	133.1	601	128	93	85	16	9	6	8	75	7	97	7	0	5	2	.714	0	0-5	14	4.76	5.74

Chad Bradford

Pitches: R **Bats:** R **Pos:** RP-68 **Ht:** 6'5" **Wt:** 203 **Born:** 9/14/1974 **Age:** 30

Year Team	Lg	HOW MUCH HE PITCHED						WHAT HE GAVE UP												THE RESULTS							
		G	GS	CG	GF	IP	BFP	H	R	ER	HR	SH	SF	HB	TBB	IBB	SO	WP	Bk	W	L	Pct	ShO	Sv-Op	Hld	ERC	ERA
2004 Sacramento*	AAA	2	0	0	0	2.0	7	1	0	0	0	0	0	0	0	0	3	0	0	0	0	-	0	0- -	-	0.54	0.00
1998 Chicago	AL	29	0	0	8	30.2	125	27	16	11	0	0	0	0	7	0	11	1	1	2	1	.667	0	1-3	9	2.16	3.23
1999 Chicago	AL	3	0	0	0	3.2	24	9	8	8	1	0	0	0	5	0	1	0	0	0	0	-	0	0-0	0	21.34	19.64
2000 Chicago	AL	12	0	0	5	13.2	52	13	4	3	0	0	0	1	1	1	9	0	0	0	1	1.000	0	0-0	2	2.01	1.98
2001 Oakland	AL	35	0	0	19	36.2	154	41	12	11	6	1	0	1	6	0	34	0	0	2	1	.667	0	1-4	4	4.36	2.70
2002 Oakland	AL	75	0	0	14	75.1	311	73	29	26	2	2	2	5	14	5	56	0	1	4	2	.667	0	2-5	24	2.77	3.11
2003 Oakland	AL	72	0	0	12	77.0	322	67	28	26	7	1	0	7	30	9	62	0	1	7	4	.636	0	2-5	23	3.50	3.04
2004 Oakland	AL	68	0	0	16	59.0	251	51	32	29	5	3	1	5	24	9	34	0	0	5	7	.417	0	1-4	14	3.35	4.42
7 ML YEARS		294	0	0	74	296.0	1239	281	129	114	21	7	3	18	87	24	206	2	3	21	15	.583	0	7-21	76	3.33	3.47

Milton Bradley

Bats: B **Throws:** R **Pos:** CF-93; RF-31; LF-17; PH-4 **Ht:** 6'0" **Wt:** 190 **Born:** 4/15/1978 **Age:** 27

Year Team	Lg	BATTING								TB	R	RBI	RC	TBB	IBB	SO	HBP	SH	SF	BASERUNNING				AVERAGES		
		G	AB	H	2B	3B	HR	(Hm	Rd)											SB	CS	SB%	GDP	Avg	OBP	Slg
2000 Montreal	NL	42	154	34	8	1	2	(1	1)	50	20	15	14	14	0	32	1	1	1	2	1	.67	3	.221	.288	.325
2001 Mon-Cle	NL	77	238	53	17	3	1	(0	1)	79	22	19	21	21	0	65	1	2	0	8	5	.62	7	.223	.288	.332
2002 Cleveland	AL	98	325	81	18	3	9	(4	5)	132	48	38	40	32	2	58	0	1	0	6	3	.67	12	.249	.317	.406
2003 Cleveland	AL	101	377	101	24	2	10	(4	6)	189	61	56	77	64	8	73	5	0	5	17	7	.71	10	.321	.421	.501
2004 Los Angeles	NL	141	516	138	24	0	19	(8	11)	219	72	67	70	71	3	123	6	3	1	15	11	.58	12	.267	.362	.424
2001 Montreal	NL	67	220	49	16	3	1	(0	1)	74	19	19	20	19	0	62	1	2	0	7	4	.64	6	.223	.288	.336
2001 Cleveland	AL	10	18	4	1	0	0	(0	0)	5	3	0	1	2	0	3	0	0	0	1	1	.50	1	.222	.300	.278
5 ML YEARS		459	1610	427	101	9	41	(17	24)	669	223	195	222	202	13	351	13	7	7	48	27	.64	44	.265	.350	.416

Darren Bragg

Bats: L **Throws:** R **Pos:** PH-23; CF-14; RF-11; LF-2 **Ht:** 5'9" **Wt:** 180 **Born:** 9/7/1969 **Age:** 35

Year Team	Lg	BATTING								TB	R	RBI	RC	TBB	IBB	SO	HBP	SH	SF	BASERUNNING				AVERAGES		
		G	AB	H	2B	3B	HR	(Hm	Rd)											SB	CS	SB%	GDP	Avg	OBP	Slg
2004 Louisville*	AAA	13	46	11	1	0	2	(-	-)	18	4	4	5	5	0	13	0	0	0	1	0	1.00	2	.239	.314	.391
2004 Columbus*	AAA	70	273	77	21	3	8	(-	-)	128	41	29	46	37	0	45	0	4	1	7	2	.78	6	.282	.367	.469
1994 Seattle	AL	8	19	3	1	0	0	(0	0)	4	4	2	1	3	1	5	0	0	0	0	0	-	0	.158	.238	.211
1995 Seattle	AL	52	145	34	5	1	3	(1	2)	50	20	12	19	18	1	37	4	1	2	9	0	1.00	3	.234	.331	.345
1996 Sea-Bos	AL	127	417	109	26	2	10	(3	7)	169	74	47	66	69	6	74	4	2	7	14	9	.61	5	.261	.366	.405
1997 Boston	AL	153	513	132	35	2	9	(3	6)	198	65	57	65	61	5	102	3	5	4	10	6	.63	16	.257	.337	.386
1998 Boston	AL	129	409	114	29	3	8	(3	5)	173	51	57	58	42	0	99	6	4	4	5	3	.63	16	.279	.351	.423
1999 St Louis	NL	93	273	71	12	1	6	(4	2)	103	38	26	41	44	1	67	3	5	0	3	0	1.00	5	.260	.369	.377
2000 Colorado	NL	71	149	33	7	1	3	(3	0)	51	16	21	16	17	1	41	0	0	3	4	1	.80	3	.221	.296	.342
2001 NYM-NYY		23	61	16	7	0	0	(0	0)	23	5	5	8	4	0	24	1	1	0	3	2	.60	0	.262	.318	.377
2002 Atlanta	NL	109	212	57	15	2	3	(2	1)	85	34	15	27	24	0	52	2	1	1	5	2	.71	4	.269	.347	.401
2003 Atlanta	NL	104	162	39	5	1	0	(0	0)	46	21	9	14	13	1	38	2	4	0	2	1	.67	1	.241	.305	.284
2004 SD-Cin	NL	47	101	19	3	1	4	(2	2)	36	13	9	8	10	1	31	0	1	0	1	0	1.00	2	.188	.261	.356
1996 Seattle	AL	69	195	53	12	1	7	(4	3)	88	36	25	35	33	4	35	2	1	0	8	5	.62	0	.272	.376	.451
1996 Boston	AL	58	222	56	14	1	3	(3	0)	81	38	22	31	36	2	39	2	1	3	6	4	.60	3	.252	.357	.365

(continued)

Year Team	Lg	G	AB	H	2B	3B	HR	(Hm Rd)	TB	R	RBI	RC	TBB	IBB	SO	HBP	SH	SF	SB	CS	SB%	GDP	Avg	OBP	Slg
2001 New York	NL	18	57	15	6	0	0	(0 0)	21	4	5	7	4	0	23	1	1	0	3	2	.60	0	.263	.323	.368
2001 New York	AL	5	4	1	1	0	0	(0 0)	2	1	0	1	0	0	1	0	0	0	0	0	-	0	.250	.250	.500
2004 San Diego	NL	9	7	1	0	0	0	(0 0)	1	2	0	1	2	0	2	0	0	0	0	0	-	0	.143	.333	.143
2004 Cincinnati	NL	38	94	18	3	1	4	(2 2)	35	11	9	7	8	1	29	0	1	0	1	0	1.00	2	.191	.255	.372
11 ML YEARS		916	2461	627	145	14	46	(25 21)	938	341	260	323	304	17	570	25	24	21	56	24	.70	54	.255	.340	.381

Russell Branyan

Bats: L **Throws:** R **Pos:** 3B-44; PH-8; 1B-2   **Ht:** 6'3" **Wt:** 195 **Born:** 12/19/1975 **Age:** 29

Year Team	Lg	G	AB	H	2B	3B	HR	(Hm Rd)	TB	R	RBI	RC	TBB	IBB	SO	HBP	SH	SF	SB	CS	SB%	GDP	Avg	OBP	Slg
2004 Richmond*	AAA	11	28	5	0	0	1	(- -)	8	5	4	5	13	2	11	1	0	0	1	0	1.00	0	.179	.452	.286
2004 Buffalo*	AAA	82	313	90	16	2	25	(- -)	185	58	75	65	42	4	102	5	0	6	5	2	.71	5	.288	.374	.591
1998 Cleveland	AL	1	4	0	0	0	0	(0 0)	0	0	0	0	0	0	2	0	0	0	0	0	-	0	.000	.000	.000
1999 Cleveland	AL	11	38	8	2	0	1	(0 1)	13	4	6	4	3	0	19	1	0	0	0	0	-	0	.211	.286	.342
2000 Cleveland	AL	67	193	46	7	2	16	(13 3)	105	32	38	34	22	1	76	4	0	1	0	0	-	2	.238	.327	.544
2001 Cleveland	AL	113	315	73	16	2	20	(11 9)	153	48	54	50	38	1	132	3	0	5	1	1	.50	2	.232	.316	.486
2002 Cle-Cin		134	378	86	13	1	24	(5 19)	173	50	56	49	51	3	151	2	0	4	4	3	.57	5	.228	.320	.458
2003 Cincinnati	NL	74	176	38	12	0	9	(7 2)	77	22	26	23	27	0	69	1	0	1	0	0	-	1	.216	.322	.438
2004 Milwaukee	NL	51	158	37	11	1	11	(8 3)	83	21	27	23	20	0	68	2	0	2	1	0	1.00	1	.234	.324	.525
2002 Cleveland	AL	50	161	33	4	0	8	(1 7)	61	16	17	14	17	0	65	0	0	2	1	2	.33	3	.205	.278	.379
2002 Cincinnati	NL	84	217	53	9	1	16	(4 12)	112	34	39	35	34	3	86	2	0	2	3	1	.75	2	.244	.349	.516
7 ML YEARS		451	1262	288	61	6	81	(44 37)	604	177	207	183	161	5	517	13	0	13	6	4	.60	11	.228	.319	.479

Craig Brazell

Bats: L **Throws:** R **Pos:** PH-18; 1B-7   **Ht:** 6'3" **Wt:** 211 **Born:** 5/10/1980 **Age:** 25

Year Team	Lg	G	AB	H	2B	3B	HR	(Hm Rd)	TB	R	RBI	RC	TBB	IBB	SO	HBP	SH	SF	SB	CS	SB%	GDP	Avg	OBP	Slg
1998 Mets	R	13	47	14	3	1	1	(- -)	22	6	6	7	2	0	13	1	0	0	0	0	-	0	.298	.340	.468
1999 Kingsport	R+	59	221	85	16	1	6	(- -)	121	27	39	45	7	4	34	8	2	1	6	5	.55	5	.385	.422	.548
2000 Capital City	A	112	406	98	28	0	8	(- -)	150	35	57	39	15	1	82	9	1	8	3	3	.50	6	.241	.279	.369
2001 Capital City	A	83	331	102	25	5	19	(- -)	194	51	72	61	15	3	74	5	0	5	0	3	.00	3	.308	.343	.586
2002 St. Lucie	A+	100	402	107	25	3	16	(- -)	186	38	82	52	13	3	78	6	0	10	2	1	.67	7	.266	.292	.463
2002 Binghamton	AA	35	130	40	8	0	6	(- -)	66	14	19	20	1	0	28	6	0	0	2	0	.00	2	.308	.343	.508
2003 Binghamton	AA	111	432	126	23	2	17	(- -)	204	58	76	66	23	4	97	6	0	7	2	1	.67	4	.292	.331	.472
2003 Norfolk	AAA	12	46	12	3	0	0	(- -)	15	4	1	4	1	1	8	1	0	0	1	0	1.00	0	.261	.292	.326
2004 Norfolk	AAA	121	475	126	22	2	23	(- -)	221	66	67	63	21	5	99	3	5	1	1	2	.33	5	.265	.300	.465
2004 New York	NL	24	34	9	2	0	1	(1 0)	14	3	3	2	1	0	7	0	0	0	0	0	-	1	.265	.286	.412

Dewon Brazelton

Pitches: R **Bats:** R **Pos:** SP-21; RP-1   **Ht:** 6'4" **Wt:** 205 **Born:** 6/16/1980 **Age:** 25

Year Team	Lg	G	GS	CG	GF	IP	BFP	H	R	ER	HR	SH	SF	HB	TBB	IBB	SO	WP	Bk	W	L	Pct	ShO	Sv-Op	Hld	ERC	ERA
2004 Durham*	AAA	10	10	0	0	49.2	221	61	35	26	0	1	3	1	15	0	38	2	0	4	4	.500	0	0--		4.31	4.71
2002 Tampa Bay	AL	2	2	0	0	13.0	51	12	7	7	3	0	0	2	6	0	5	0	0	0	1	.000	0	0-0		6.29	4.85
2003 Tampa Bay	AL	10	10	0	0	48.1	225	57	40	37	9	2	2	3	23	1	24	1	0	1	6	.143	0	0-0		6.29	6.89
2004 Tampa Bay	AL	22	21	0	0	120.2	535	121	71	64	12	0	6	11	53	2	64	2	1	6	8	.429	0	0-0		4.58	4.77
3 ML YEARS		34	33	0	0	182.0	811	190	127	108	24	2	8	16	82	3	93	3	1	7	15	.318	0	0-0		5.13	5.34

Yhency Brazoban

Pitches: R **Bats:** R **Pos:** RP-31   **Ht:** 6'1" **Wt:** 170 **Born:** 6/11/1980 **Age:** 25

Year Team	Lg	G	GS	CG	GF	IP	BFP	H	R	ER	HR	SH	SF	HB	TBB	IBB	SO	WP	Bk	W	L	Pct	ShO	Sv-Op	Hld	ERC	ERA
2002 Yankees	R	6	0	0	0	6.0	27	3	3	3	0	0	0	1	4	0	11	2	0	0	0	-	0	0--		2.17	4.50
2003 Yankees	R	3	0	0	0	3.0	15	5	3	2	0	1	0	0	1	1	5	0	0	0	0	-	0	0--		6.14	6.00
2003 Tampa	A+	24	0	0	22	28.2	124	27	13	9	0	0	1	1	12	2	34	2	0	2	0	.000	0	15--		3.12	2.83
2003 Trenton	AA	20	0	0	16	27.2	127	33	25	24	5	3	3	2	14	1	19	4	0	2	2	.500	0	3--		6.65	7.81
2004 Jacksonville	AA	37	0	0	33	51.0	214	38	18	15	4	1	1	1	22	1	61	1	0	4	4	.500	0	13--		2.69	2.65
2004 Las Vegas	AAA	10	0	0	7	12.1	52	14	3	3	1	0	0	0	1	0	17	0	0	2	0	1.000	0	1--		3.36	2.19
2004 Los Angeles	NL	31	0	0	10	32.2	133	25	9	9	2	4	0	0	15	2	27	1	0	6	2	.750	0	0-0	5	2.76	2.48

Juan Brito

Bats: R **Throws:** R **Pos:** C-54   **Ht:** 5'11" **Wt:** 205 **Born:** 11/7/1979 **Age:** 25

Year Team	Lg	G	AB	H	2B	3B	HR	(Hm Rd)	TB	R	RBI	RC	TBB	IBB	SO	HBP	SH	SF	SB	CS	SB%	GDP	Avg	OBP	Slg
1997 Royals	R	25	70	22	4	0	3	(- -)	35	14	15	12	5	1	5	1	1	0	0	0	-	1	.314	.368	.500
1998 Lansing	A	63	212	52	7	0	0	(- -)	59	16	22	18	17	0	41	2	1	2	2	2	.50	6	.245	.305	.278
1999 Wilmington	A+	14	46	13	1	0	0	(- -)	14	3	1	4	1	0	11	0	0	0	0	0	-	1	.283	.298	.304
1999 Chrlstn - WV	A+	61	208	50	6	0	0	(- -)	56	14	19	13	11	0	37	1	3	0	1	2	.33	8	.240	.282	.269
1999 Omaha	AAA	2	7	2	2	0	0	(- -)	4	1	0	0	0	0	2	0	0	0	0	0	-	0	.286	.286	.571
1999 Wichita	AA	4	11	1	0	0	0	(- -)	1	0	0	0	2	0	3	0	0	0	0	0	-	2	.091	.231	.091
2000 Wichita	AA	34	105	27	2	0	0	(- -)	29	9	10	10	11	2	15	1	0	2	2	1	.67	4	.257	.328	.276
2000 Wilmington	A+	22	54	12	4	0	0	(- -)	16	4	9	5	8	0	7	1	0	1	1	0	1.00	4	.222	.317	.296
2000 Omaha	AAA	17	49	14	1	0	1	(- -)	18	8	2	6	3	0	10	0	1	0	1	1	.50	1	.286	.327	.367
2001 Wichita	AA	70	236	63	10	0	4	(- -)	85	22	28	31	17	0	29	0	7	1	3	3	.50	9	.267	.315	.360
2002 Omaha	AAA	3	9	2	1	0	0	(- -)	3	1	1	0	1	0	1	0	0	0	0	0	-	0	.222	.300	.333
2002 Wichita	AA	89	302	77	11	0	7	(- -)	109	40	38	31	21	1	46	1	5	3	1	1	.50	5	.255	.303	.361
2003 Omaha	AAA	36	122	29	2	0	2	(- -)	37	14	12	7	3	0	25	1	4	0	0	2	.00	4	.238	.262	.303
2004 Tucson	AAA	34	102	32	5	2	3	(- -)	50	22	16	16	6	0	25	1	3	0	1	0	1.00	3	.314	.358	.490

Year Team	Lg	G	AB	H	2B	3B	HR	(Hm Rd)	TB	R	RBI	RC	TBB	IBB	SO	HBP	SH	SF	SB	CS	SB%	GDP	Avg	OBP	Slg
2002 Kansas City	AL	9	23	7	2	0	0	(0 0)	9	1	1	0	0	0	3	0	0	0	0	0	-	2	.304	.304	.391
2004 Arizona	NL	54	171	35	7	0	3	(3 0)	51	17	12	7	9	1	41	1	1	2	1	0	1.00	6	.205	.246	.298
2 ML YEARS		63	194	42	9	0	3	(3 0)	60	18	13	7	9	1	44	1	1	2	1	0	1.00	8	.216	.252	.309

Doug Brocail

Pitches: R Bats: L Pos: RP-43 **Ht: 6'5" Wt: 235 Born: 5/16/1967 Age: 38**

Year Team	Lg	G	GS	CG	GF	IP	BFP	H	R	ER	HR	SH	SF	HB	TBB	IBB	SO	WP	Bk	W	L	Pct	ShO	Sv-Op	Hld	ERC	ERA
2004 Frisco*	AA	1	1	0	0	4.1	14	2	1	1	0	0	0	0	0	0	6	0	0	0	0	-	0	0--	-	1.04	2.08
2004 Oklahoma*	AAA	12	0	0	2	19.1	79	20	9	9	1	0	0	2	2	0	19	1	0	2	0	1.000	0	0--	-	3.26	4.19
1992 San Diego	NL	3	3	0	0	14.0	64	17	10	10	2	2	0	0	5	0	15	0	0	0	0	-	0	0-0	0	5.33	6.43
1993 San Diego	NL	24	24	0	0	128.1	571	143	75	65	16	10	8	4	42	4	70	4	1	4	13	.235	0	0-0	0	4.60	4.56
1994 San Diego	NL	12	0	0	4	17.0	78	21	13	11	1	1	1	2	5	3	11	1	1	0	0	-	0	0-1	0	4.79	5.82
1995 Houston	NL	36	7	0	12	77.1	339	87	40	36	10	1	1	4	22	2	39	1	1	4	6	.600	0	1-1	0	4.68	4.19
1996 Houston	NL	23	4	0	4	53.0	231	58	31	27	7	3	2	2	23	1	34	0	0	1	5	.167	0	0-0	1	5.26	4.58
1997 Detroit	AL	61	4	0	20	78.0	332	74	31	28	10	1	3	3	36	4	60	6	0	3	4	.429	0	2-9	16	4.42	3.23
1998 Detroit	AL	60	0	0	24	62.2	247	47	23	19	2	2	3	1	18	3	55	6	0	5	2	.714	0	0-1	11	1.99	2.73
1999 Detroit	AL	70	0	0	22	82.0	326	60	23	23	7	4	2	4	25	1	78	4	1	4	4	.500	0	2-4	23	2.43	2.52
2000 Detroit	AL	49	0	0	10	50.2	221	57	25	23	5	3	3	1	14	2	41	1	1	5	4	.556	0	0-5	19	4.25	4.09
2004 Texas	AL	43	0	0	14	52.1	232	54	29	24	2	4	2	5	20	1	43	2	1	4	1	.800	0	1-1	4	4.05	4.13
10 ML YEARS		381	42	0	110	615.1	2641	618	300	266	62	31	25	26	210	21	446	25	6	32	37	.464	0	6-22	74	3.99	3.89

Frank Brooks

Pitches: L Bats: L Pos: RP-10; SP-1 **Ht: 6'1" Wt: 200 Born: 9/6/1978 Age: 26**

Year Team	Lg	G	GS	CG	GF	IP	BFP	H	R	ER	HR	SH	SF	HB	TBB	IBB	SO	WP	Bk	W	L	Pct	ShO	Sv-Op	Hld	ERC	ERA
1999 Batavia	A-	16	12	1	2	77.1	312	64	26	25	2	0	1	2	33	0	58	2	6	7	3	.700	1	0--	-	2.98	2.91
2000 Piedmont	A	29	27	3	1	177.2	734	152	78	68	17	7	8	14	60	0	138	8	1	14	8	.636	2	0--	-	3.38	3.44
2001 Clearwater	A+	37	15	0	5	112.2	504	113	70	59	18	1	5	9	58	2	92	9	0	5	10	.333	0	1--	-	5.33	4.71
2002 Clearwater	A+	35	0	0	24	39.0	178	34	18	15	2	2	2	1	27	3	33	2	1	3	5	.375	0	7--	-	4.01	3.46
2002 Reading	AA	17	1	0	9	29.0	122	29	11	10	1	1	1	0	12	0	23	0	0	1	1	.500	0	2--	-	3.77	3.10
2003 Altoona	AA	1	0	0	1	2.1	10	3	2	2	1	2	3	0	0	0	4	0	0	0	0	-	0	0--	-	6.14	7.71
2003 Reading	AA	34	0	0	19	58.2	224	40	16	15	5	2	3	0	13	1	71	2	0	3	4	.429	0	9--	-	1.75	2.30
2003 Nashville	AAA	16	0	0	4	28.1	113	22	9	8	2	1	0	0	11	2	22	1	0	2	0	1.000	0	0--	-	2.64	2.54
2004 Nashville	AAA	42	8	0	6	83.1	345	81	42	38	13	5	4	0	22	0	55	0	0	6	3	.667	0	2--	-	3.78	4.10
2004 Pittsburgh	NL	11	1	0	3	17.1	73	13	10	9	5	0	0	0	9	2	18	0	1	0	1	.000	0	0-0	0	4.24	4.67

Ben Broussard

Bats: L Throws: L Pos: 1B-133; PH-16; PR-2 **Ht: 6'2" Wt: 220 Born: 9/24/1976 Age: 28**

Year Team	Lg	G	AB	H	2B	3B	HR	(Hm Rd)	TB	R	RBI	RC	TBB	IBB	SO	HBP	SH	SF	SB	CS	SB%	GDP	Avg	OBP	Slg
2002 Cleveland	AL	39	112	27	4	0	4	(2 2)	43	10	9	9	7	1	25	1	0	0	0	0	-	3	.241	.292	.384
2003 Cleveland	AL	116	386	96	21	3	16	(7 9)	171	53	55	53	32	2	75	5	3	3	5	2	.71	6	.249	.312	.443
2004 Cleveland	AL	139	418	115	28	5	17	(9 8)	204	57	82	79	52	3	95	12	1	2	4	2	.67	7	.275	.370	.488
3 ML YEARS		294	916	238	53	8	37	(18 19)	418	120	146	141	91	6	195	18	4	5	9	4	.69	16	.260	.337	.456

Jim Brower

Pitches: R Bats: R Pos: RP-89 **Ht: 6'3" Wt: 215 Born: 12/29/1972 Age: 32**

Year Team	Lg	G	GS	CG	GF	IP	BFP	H	R	ER	HR	SH	SF	HB	TBB	IBB	SO	WP	Bk	W	L	Pct	ShO	Sv-Op	Hld	ERC	ERA
1999 Cleveland	AL	9	2	0	1	25.2	113	27	13	13	8	1	1	1	10	1	18	0	0	3	1	.750	0	0-0	0	5.96	4.56
2000 Cleveland	AL	17	11	0	1	62.0	293	80	45	43	11	1	0	2	31	1	32	3	0	2	3	.400	0	0-0	0	6.95	6.24
2001 Cincinnati	NL	46	10	0	13	129.1	559	119	65	57	17	9	3	5	60	5	94	5	1	7	10	.412	0	1-2	2	4.21	3.97
2002 Cin-Mon	NL	52	0	0	23	80.1	344	77	40	39	7	2	1	4	32	2	57	1	0	3	2	.600	0	0-1	6	3.94	4.37
2003 San Francisco	NL	51	5	0	13	100.0	412	90	48	44	8	5	4	1	39	2	65	4	0	8	5	.615	0	2-3	2	3.45	3.96
2004 San Francisco	NL	89	0	0	21	93.0	401	90	42	34	6	11	2	4	36	2	63	10	0	7	7	.500	0	1-5	24	3.72	3.29
2002 Cincinnati	NL	22	0	0	11	39.1	158	38	18	17	2	1	1	0	10	1	24	0	0	2	0	1.000	0	0-0	0	3.08	3.89
2002 Montreal	NL	30	0	0	12	41.0	186	39	22	22	5	1	0	4	22	1	33	1	0	1	2	.333	0	0-1	6	4.79	4.83
6 ML YEARS		264	28	0	72	490.1	2122	483	253	230	57	29	11	17	208	13	329	23	1	30	28	.517	0	4-11	34	4.32	4.22

Adrian Brown

Bats: B Throws: R Pos: LF-4; RF-1 **Ht: 6'0" Wt: 200 Born: 2/7/1974 Age: 31**

Year Team	Lg	G	AB	H	2B	3B	HR	(Hm Rd)	TB	R	RBI	RC	TBB	IBB	SO	HBP	SH	SF	SB	CS	SB%	GDP	Avg	OBP	Slg
2004 Omaha*	AAA	114	444	118	17	7	7	(- -)	170	69	51	65	57	1	74	0	5	3	28	4	.88	7	.266	.347	.383
1997 Pittsburgh	NL	48	147	28	6	0	1	(0 1)	37	17	10	10	13	0	18	4	2	1	8	4	.67	3	.190	.273	.252
1998 Pittsburgh	NL	41	152	43	4	1	0	(0 0)	49	20	5	16	9	0	18	0	4	0	4	0	1.00	3	.283	.323	.322
1999 Pittsburgh	NL	116	226	61	5	2	4	(2 2)	82	34	17	31	33	2	39	1	6	1	5	3	.63	5	.270	.364	.363
2000 Pittsburgh	NL	104	308	97	18	3	4	(2 2)	133	64	28	53	29	1	34	0	2	1	13	1	.93	1	.315	.373	.432
2001 Pittsburgh	NL	8	31	6	0	0	1	(0 1)	9	3	2	2	3	0	3	0	0	0	2	1	.67	1	.194	.265	.290
2002 Pittsburgh	NL	91	208	45	10	2	1	(0 1)	62	20	21	16	19	0	34	1	3	1	10	6	.63	5	.216	.284	.298
2003 Boston	AL	9	15	3	0	0	0	(0 0)	3	2	1	1	1	0	4	0	0	0	2	0	1.00	0	.200	.250	.200
2004 Kansas City	AL	5	11	3	0	0	0	(0 0)	3	0	0	1	0	0	2	0	0	0	0	0	-	0	.273	.273	.273
8 ML YEARS		422	1098	286	43	8	11	(4 7)	378	160	84	130	107	3	152	6	17	4	44	15	.75	18	.260	.328	.344

Dee Brown

Bats: L **Throws:** R **Pos:** LF-53; PH-6; DH-1   **Ht:** 6'0" **Wt:** 225 **Born:** 3/27/1978 **Age:** 27

Year Team	Lg	G	AB	H	2B	3B	HR	(Hm	Rd)	TB	R	RBI	RC	TBB	IBB	SO	HBP	SH	SF	SB	CS	SB%	GDP	Avg	OBP	Slg
2004 Wichita*	AA	61	241	73	19	2	12	(-	-)	132	42	50	43	24	8	38	2	0	3	1	4	.20	4	.303	.367	.548
2004 Omaha*	AAA	10	40	5	0	0	2	(-	-)	11	2	5	0	0	0	12	0	0	0	0	0	-	3	.125	.125	.275
1998 Kansas City	AL	5	3	0	0	0	0	(0	0)	0	2	0	0	0	0	1	0	0	0	0	0	-	0	.000	.000	.000
1999 Kansas City	AL	12	25	2	0	0	0	(0	0)	2	1	0	0	2	0	7	0	0	0	0	0	-	0	.080	.148	.080
2000 Kansas City	AL	15	25	4	1	0	0	(0	0)	5	4	4	1	3	0	9	0	0	0	0	0	-	0	.160	.250	.200
2001 Kansas City	AL	106	380	93	19	0	7	(4	3)	133	39	40	34	22	4	81	1	1	2	5	3	.63	12	.245	.286	.350
2002 Kansas City	AL	16	51	12	3	1	1	(0	1)	20	5	7	4	4	0	20	0	0	0	0	0	-	0	.235	.291	.392
2003 Kansas City	AL	50	132	30	7	0	2	(1	1)	43	16	14	15	8	1	37	2	0	1	1	1	.50	0	.227	.280	.326
2004 Kansas City	AL	59	195	49	7	0	4	(2	2)	68	19	24	21	11	0	50	1	1	1	2	2	.50	1	.251	.293	.349
7 ML YEARS		263	811	190	37	1	14	(7	7)	271	86	89	75	50	5	205	4	2	4	8	6	.57	13	.234	.281	.334

Jamie Brown

Pitches: R **Bats:** R **Pos:** RP-4   **Ht:** 6'2" **Wt:** 205 **Born:** 3/31/1977 **Age:** 28

Year Team	Lg	G	GS	CG	GF	IP	BFP	H	R	ER	HR	SH	SF	HB	TBB	IBB	SO	WP	Bk	W	L	Pct	ShO	Sv-Op	Hld	ERC	ERA
1997 Watertown	A-	13	13	1	0	73.0	303	66	35	25	6	1	2	4	15	0	57	1	1	10	2	.833	0	0- -	-	2.86	3.08
1998 Kinston	A+	27	27	2	0	172.2	717	162	91	73	12	10	3	11	44	1	148	4	2	11	9	.550	0	0- -	-	3.23	3.81
1998 Akron	AA	1	1	0	0	7.0	28	5	2	2	1	0	0	1	1	0	5	0	0	1	0	1.000	0	0- -	-	2.38	2.57
1999 Akron	AA	23	23	1	0	138.0	586	140	72	70	11	7	10	13	39	1	98	2	3	5	9	.357	0	0- -	-	3.97	4.57
1999 Buffalo	AAA	1	0	0	0	5.0	23	8	4	3	0	1	0	1	0	2	0	0	1	0	1.000	0	0- -	-	6.13	5.40
2000 Akron	AA	17	17	1	0	96.2	416	95	49	47	12	4	1	6	26	0	57	1	0	7	6	.538	0	0- -	-	3.80	4.38
2001 Akron	AA	4	4	0	0	19.2	88	22	11	11	2	0	0	2	7	0	12	0	0	1	1	.500	0	0- -	-	5.00	5.03
2002 Akron	AA	18	17	0	0	103.2	422	98	41	32	5	2	2	8	17	0	72	1	1	9	5	.643	0	0- -	-	2.87	2.78
2003 Pawtucket	AAA	13	10	0	0	61.1	246	45	26	24	4	3	1	5	17	1	26	0	0	4	4	.500	0	0- -	-	2.31	3.52
2003 Pawtucket	AAA	18	3	0	6	51.2	202	40	17	13	1	3	1	2	5	1	39	2	0	4	1	.800	0	1- -	-	1.53	2.26
2004 Pawtucket	AAA	23	20	2	2	127.0	530	128	76	68	21	5	11	6	17	0	92	2	0	4	6	.400	1	0- -	-	3.62	4.82
2004 Boston	AL	4	0	0	3	7.2	41	15	7	5	1	0	1	0	4	0	6	0	0	0	0	-	0	0-0	0	11.10	5.87

Kevin Brown

Pitches: R **Bats:** R **Pos:** SP-22   **Ht:** 6'4" **Wt:** 200 **Born:** 3/14/1965 **Age:** 40

Year Team	Lg	G	GS	CG	GF	IP	BFP	H	R	ER	HR	SH	SF	HB	TBB	IBB	SO	WP	Bk	W	L	Pct	ShO	Sv-Op	Hld	ERC	ERA
2004 Staten Island*	A-	1	1	0	0	6.0	26	6	4	2	0	0	0	0	1	0	6	0	0	0	1	.000	0	0- -	-	2.37	3.00
2004 Trenton*	AA	1	1	0	0	2.0	13	7	5	3	0	0	0	0	0	0	0	0	0	0	1	.000	0	0- -	-	18.39	13.50
1986 Texas	AL	1	1	0	0	5.0	19	6	2	2	0	0	0	0	0	0	4	0	0	1	0	1.000	0	0-0	0	3.25	3.60
1988 Texas	AL	4	4	1	0	23.1	110	33	15	11	2	1	0	1	8	0	12	1	0	1	1	.500	0	0-0	0	6.33	4.24
1989 Texas	AL	28	28	7	0	191.0	798	167	81	71	10	3	6	4	70	2	104	7	2	12	9	.571	0	0-0	0	3.02	3.35
1990 Texas	AL	26	26	6	0	180.0	757	175	84	72	13	2	7	3	60	3	88	9	2	12	10	.545	2	0-0	0	3.54	3.60
1991 Texas	AL	33	33	0	0	210.2	934	233	116	103	17	6	4	13	90	5	96	12	3	9	12	.429	0	0-0	0	4.92	4.40
1992 Texas	AL	35	35	11	0	265.2	1108	262	117	98	11	7	8	10	76	2	173	8	2	21	11	.656	1	0-0	0	3.34	3.32
1993 Texas	AL	34	34	12	0	233.0	1001	228	105	93	14	5	3	15	74	5	142	8	1	15	12	.556	3	0-0	0	3.55	3.59
1994 Texas	AL	26	25	3	1	170.0	760	218	109	91	18	2	7	6	50	3	123	7	0	7	9	.438	0	0-0	0	5.49	4.82
1995 Baltimore	AL	26	26	3	0	172.1	706	155	73	69	10	5	2	9	48	1	117	3	0	10	9	.526	1	0-0	0	3.03	3.60
1996 Florida	NL	32	32	5	0	233.0	906	187	60	49	8	4	4	16	33	2	159	6	1	17	11	.607	3	0-0	0	2.00	1.89
1997 Florida	NL	33	33	6	0	237.1	976	214	77	71	10	5	1	14	66	7	205	7	1	16	8	.667	2	0-0	0	2.92	2.69
1998 San Diego	NL	36	35	7	0	257.0	1032	225	77	68	8	13	3	10	49	4	257	10	0	18	7	.720	3	0-0	0	2.35	2.38
1999 Los Angeles	NL	35	35	5	0	252.1	1018	210	99	84	19	7	1	7	59	1	221	4	1	18	9	.667	1	0-0	0	2.51	3.00
2000 Los Angeles	NL	33	33	5	0	230.0	921	181	76	66	21	13	4	9	47	1	216	4	0	13	6	.684	1	0-0	0	2.30	2.58
2001 Los Angeles	NL	20	19	1	0	115.2	465	94	41	34	8	5	0	2	38	2	104	3	1	10	4	.714	0	0-0	0	2.71	2.65
2002 Los Angeles	NL	17	10	0	0	63.2	277	68	36	34	9	2	0	5	23	1	58	2	0	3	4	.429	0	0-0	0	4.98	4.81
2003 Los Angeles	NL	32	32	0	0	211.0	856	184	67	56	11	12	2	5	56	2	185	5	1	14	9	.609	0	0-0	0	2.88	2.39
2004 New York	AL	22	22	0	0	132.0	551	132	65	60	14	0	9	3	35	0	83	6	0	10	6	.625	0	0-0	0	3.71	4.09
18 ML YEARS		473	463	72	1	3183.0	13195	2972	1300	1132	203	92	61	132	882	41	2347	102	15	207	137	.602	17	0-0	2	3.16	3.20

Brian Bruney

Pitches: R **Bats:** R **Pos:** RP-30   **Ht:** 6'3" **Wt:** 226 **Born:** 2/17/1982 **Age:** 23

Year Team	Lg	G	GS	CG	GF	IP	BFP	H	R	ER	HR	SH	SF	HB	TBB	IBB	SO	WP	Bk	W	L	Pct	ShO	Sv-Op	Hld	ERC	ERA
2000 Diamndbcks	R	20	2	0	11	25.0	131	21	23	18	2	0	1	6	29	0	24	5	1	4	1	.800	0	2- -	-	6.82	6.48
2001 South Bend	A	26	0	0	20	32.2	142	24	19	15	1	2	1	3	19	2	40	3	2	1	4	.200	0	8- -	-	3.05	4.13
2001 Yakima	A-	15	0	0	11	21.0	102	19	14	12	2	3	2	2	11	0	28	7	0	1	2	.333	0	2- -	-	3.93	5.14
2002 South Bend	A	37	0	0	28	48.1	203	37	15	9	1	5	3	2	17	4	54	2	1	4	3	.571	0	10- -	-	2.12	1.68
2002 El Paso	AA	10	0	0	4	12.1	47	11	5	4	1	0	1	1	4	1	14	1	0	0	2	.000	0	4- -	-	3.66	2.92
2003 El Paso	AA	28	0	0	25	31.1	140	29	17	9	1	1	1	1	13	2	28	0	1	0	2	.000	0	14- -	-	3.11	2.59
2003 Tucson	AAA	32	0	0	29	32.0	139	24	12	10	0	0	3	2	18	0	32	2	0	3	1	.750	0	12- -	-	2.82	2.81
2004 Tucson	AAA	31	0	0	14	38.0	156	18	8	6	1	0	0	2	20	1	42	1	1	2	0	1.000	0	5- -	-	1.56	1.42
2004 Arizona	NL	30	0	0	14	31.1	135	20	16	15	2	1	0	1	27	5	34	2	0	3	4	.429	0	0-1	3	3.54	4.31

Eric Bruntlett

Bats: R **Throws:** R **Pos:** SS-33; 2B-5; PH-5; PR-5; LF-1; CF-1   **Ht:** 6'0" **Wt:** 200 **Born:** 3/29/1978 **Age:** 27

Year Team	Lg	G	AB	H	2B	3B	HR	(Hm	Rd)	TB	R	RBI	RC	TBB	IBB	SO	HBP	SH	SF	SB	CS	SB%	GDP	Avg	OBP	Slg
2000 Martinsville	R+	50	172	47	11	4	1	(-	-)	69	40	21	34	30	0	22	11	1	0	14	1	.93	1	.273	.413	.401
2001 Round Rock	AA	123	503	134	23	3	3	(-	-)	172	84	40	64	50	1	76	8	5	3	23	7	.77	7	.266	.340	.342
2001 New Orleans	AAA	5	16	2	0	0	0	(-	-)	2	3	1	0	2	0	1	0	0	0	0	0	-	1	.125	.222	.125
2002 Round Rock	AA	116	464	123	21	2	2	(-	-)	154	81	48	58	56	0	61	10	4	8	35	12	.74	17	.265	.351	.332
2002 New Orleans	AAA	18	68	14	3	0	0	(-	-)	17	9	1	4	10	0	10	0	1	0	1	1	.50	3	.206	.308	.250

Year Team	Lg	G	AB	H	2B	3B	HR	(Hm Rd)	TB	R	RBI	RC	TBB	IBB	SO	HBP	SH	SF	SB	CS	SB%	GDP	Avg	OBP	Slg
2003 New Orleans	AAA	84	324	84	10	0	2	(- -)	100	48	27	38	35	0	51	3	3	5	9	4	.69	3	.259	.332	.309
2004 New Orleans	AAA	86	332	83	12	4	6	(- -)	121	50	37	41	35	1	72	7	2	4	14	4	.78	10	.250	.331	.364
2003 Houston	NL	31	54	14	3	0	1	(1 0)	20	3	4	5	0	0	10	0	1	1	0	0	-		.259	.255	.370
2004 Houston	NL	45	52	13	2	0	4	(3 1)	27	14	8	9	7	0	13	0	0	2	4	0	1.00	0	.250	.328	.519
2 ML YEARS		76	106	27	5	0	5	(4 1)	47	17	12	14	7	0	23	0	1	3	4	0	1.00	1	.255	.293	.443

Brian Buchanan

Bats: R **Throws:** R **Pos:** PH-19; LF-15; 1B-4; RF-3; PR-1   **Ht:** 6'4" **Wt:** 230 **Born:** 7/21/1973 **Age:** 31

Year Team	Lg	G	AB	H	2B	3B	HR	(Hm Rd)	TB	R	RBI	RC	TBB	IBB	SO	HBP	SH	SF	SB	CS	SB%	GDP	Avg	OBP	Slg
2004 Lk Elsinore*	A+	4	10	3	2	0	0	(- -)	5	1	1	2	1	0	3	1	0	0	0	0	-	0	.300	.417	.500
2004 Portland*	AAA	12	42	15	8	0	2	(- -)	29	9	12	12	9	0	7	1	0	0	0	0	-	1	.357	.481	.690
2000 Minnesota	AL	30	82	19	3	0	1	(1 0)	25	10	8	6	8	0	22	1	0	2	0	2	.00	3	.232	.301	.305
2001 Minnesota	AL	69	197	54	12	0	10	(7 3)	96	28	32	33	19	0	58	2	0	1	1	1	.50	2	.274	.342	.487
2002 Min-SD		92	227	61	10	1	11	(7 4)	106	31	28	28	15	0	59	3	0	0	2	2	.50	6	.269	.322	.467
2003 San Diego	NL	115	198	52	10	2	8	(3 5)	90	29	29	27	24	1	51	3	0	3	6	2	.75	8	.263	.346	.455
2004 SD-NYM	NL	40	63	12	2	0	2	(2 0)	20	7	6	2	7	2	20	1	0	1	0	0	-	2	.190	.278	.317
2002 Minnesota	AL	44	135	34	5	1	5	(3 2)	56	19	15	11	6	0	33	2	0	0	2	1	.67	4	.252	.294	.415
2002 San Diego	NL	48	92	27	5	0	6	(4 2)	50	12	13	17	9	0	26	1	0	0	0	1	.00	2	.293	.363	.543
2004 San Diego	NL	38	60	12	2	0	2	(2 0)	20	7	6	2	6	2	19	1	0	1	0	0	-	2	.200	.279	.333
2004 New York	NL	2	3	0	0	0	0	(0 0)	0	0	0	0	1	0	1	0	0	0	0	0	-	0	.000	.250	.000
5 ML YEARS		346	767	198	37	3	32	(20 12)	337	105	103	96	73	3	210	10	0	7	9	7	.56	21	.258	.328	.439

John Buck

Bats: R **Throws:** R **Pos:** C-68; DH-3   **Ht:** 6'3" **Wt:** 210 **Born:** 7/7/1980 **Age:** 24

Year Team	Lg	G	AB	H	2B	3B	HR	(Hm Rd)	TB	R	RBI	RC	TBB	IBB	SO	HBP	SH	SF	SB	CS	SB%	GDP	Avg	OBP	Slg
1998 Astros	R	36	126	36	9	0	3	(- -)	54	24	15	19	13	0	22	2	1	0	2	2	.50	0	.286	.362	.429
1999 Auburn	A-	63	233	57	17	0	3	(- -)	83	36	29	27	25	1	48	5	1	2	7	1	.88	7	.245	.328	.356
1999 Michigan	A	4	10	1	1	0	0	(- -)	2	1	0	0	2	0	3	0	0	0	0	0	-	0	.100	.250	.200
2000 Michigan	A	109	390	110	33	0	10	(- -)	173	57	71	63	55	6	81	5	0	5	2	4	.33	8	.282	.374	.444
2001 Lexington	A	122	443	122	24	1	22	(- -)	214	72	73	69	37	0	84	12	2	4	4	9	.31	8	.275	.345	.483
2002 Round Rock	AA	120	448	118	29	3	12	(- -)	189	48	89	56	31	1	93	6	0	9	2	3	.40	11	.263	.314	.422
2003 New Orleans	AAA	78	274	70	18	2	2	(- -)	98	32	39	26	14	0	53	4	1	0	1	0	1.00	11	.255	.301	.358
2004 New Orleans	AAA	65	227	68	11	0	12	(- -)	115	31	35	37	21	2	39	4	1	1	0	1	.00	13	.300	.368	.507
2004 Kansas City	AL	71	238	56	9	0	12	(6 6)	101	36	30	26	15	0	79	0	4	1	1	1	.50	6	.235	.280	.424

Mark Buehrle

Pitches: L **Bats:** L **Pos:** SP-35   **Ht:** 6'2" **Wt:** 200 **Born:** 3/23/1979 **Age:** 26

Year Team	Lg	G	GS	CG	GF	IP	BFP	H	R	ER	HR	SH	SF	HB	TBB	IBB	SO	WP	Bk	W	L	Pct	ShO	Sv-Op	Hld	ERC	ERA
2000 Chicago	AL	28	3	0	6	51.1	225	55	27	24	5	1	0	3	19	1	37	0	0	4	1	.800	0	0-2	3	4.56	4.21
2001 Chicago	AL	32	32	4	0	221.1	885	188	89	81	24	9	4	8	48	2	126	1	5	16	8	.667	2	0-0	0	2.79	3.29
2002 Chicago	AL	34	34	5	0	239.0	984	236	102	95	25	9	3	3	61	7	134	6	1	19	12	.613	2	0-0	0	3.53	3.58
2003 Chicago	AL	35	35	2	0	230.1	978	250	124	106	22	7	7	5	61	2	119	1	0	14	14	.500	0	0-0	0	4.10	4.14
2004 Chicago	AL	35	35	4	0	245.1	1016	257	119	106	33	4	6	8	51	2	165	0	0	16	10	.615	1	0-0	0	4.00	3.89
5 ML YEARS		164	139	15	6	987.1	4088	986	461	412	109	30	20	27	240	14	581	8	6	69	45	.605	5	0-2	3	3.66	3.76

Ryan Bukvich

Pitches: R **Bats:** R **Pos:** RP-9   **Ht:** 6'3" **Wt:** 237 **Born:** 5/13/1978 **Age:** 27

Year Team	Lg	G	GS	CG	GF	IP	BFP	H	R	ER	HR	SH	SF	HB	TBB	IBB	SO	WP	Bk	W	L	Pct	ShO	Sv-Op	Hld	ERC	ERA
2004 Omaha*	AAA	38	0	0	24	47.1	211	33	25	23	4	0	2	6	30	0	60	5	0	3	4	.429	0	7- -	-	3.59	4.37
2002 Kansas City	AL	26	0	0	2	25.0	121	26	19	17	2	4	3	1	19	3	20	1	0	1	0	1.000	0	0-1	5	5.39	6.12
2003 Kansas City	AL	9	0	0	6	10.1	52	12	11	11	2	1	1	0	9	0	8	1	0	1	0	1.000	0	0-0	1	7.65	9.58
2004 Kansas City	AL	9	0	0	6	7.1	30	4	3	3	0	1	0	0	7	0	7	0	0	0	0	-	0	1-1	1	3.21	3.68
3 ML YEARS		44	0	0	14	42.2	203	42	33	31	4	6	4	1	35	3	35	2	0	2	0	1.000	0	1-2	6	5.53	6.54

Kirk Bullinger

Pitches: R **Bats:** R **Pos:** RP-27   **Ht:** 6'2" **Wt:** 170 **Born:** 10/28/1969 **Age:** 35

Year Team	Lg	G	GS	CG	GF	IP	BFP	H	R	ER	HR	SH	SF	HB	TBB	IBB	SO	WP	Bk	W	L	Pct	ShO	Sv-Op	Hld	ERC	ERA
2004 New Orleans*	AAA	28	0	0	25	30.0	129	24	10	10	3	2	0	2	9	2	14	1	0	3	1	.750	0	14- -	-	2.63	3.00
1998 Montreal	NL	8	0	0	0	7.0	35	14	0	7	1	0	0	0	0	0	2	0	0	1	0	1.000	0	0-0	0	8.74	9.00
1999 Boston	AL	4	0	0	0	2.0	9	2	0	1	0	0	0	0	2	0	0	0	0	0	0	-	0	0-0	0	6.15	4.50
2000 Philadelphia	NL	3	0	0	0	3.1	14	4	0	2	0	0	0	0	0	0	4	0	0	0	0	-	0	0-0	0	2.89	5.40
2003 Houston	NL	7	0	0	3	8.0	33	7	6	6	2	0	0	0	1	0	5	0	0	0	0	-	0	0-0	1	3.06	6.75
2004 Houston	NL	27	0	0	7	30.2	140	36	22	21	5	2	1	1	10	2	11	0	0	1	0	1.000	0	1-2	1	5.10	6.16
5 ML YEARS		49	0	0	10	51.0	231	63	28	37	8	2	1	1	13	2	22	0	0	2	0	1.000	0	1-2	2	5.12	6.53

Nate Bump

Pitches: R **Bats:** R **Pos:** RP-48; SP-2   **Ht:** 6'2" **Wt:** 185 **Born:** 7/24/1976 **Age:** 28

			HOW MUCH HE PITCHED					WHAT HE GAVE UP										THE RESULTS						
Year Team	Lg	G	GS	CG	GF	IP	BFP	H	R	ER	HR	SH	SF	HB	TBB	IBB	SO	WP	Bk	W	L	Pct	ShO	Sv-Op	Hld	ERC	ERA
1998 Salem-Keizer	A-	2	2	0	0	8.0	31	5	0	0	0	0	0	2	3	0	8	1	0	0		-	0	0- -		2.48	0.00
1998 San Jose	A+	11	11	0	0	61.2	240	37	13	12	2	1	1	2	24	0	61	2	0	6	1	.857	0	0- -		1.77	1.75
1999 Shreveport	AA	17	17	1	0	92.1	394	85	40	34	9	6	0	5	32	0	59	2	0	4	10	.286	1	0- -		3.59	3.31
1999 Portland	AA	8	8	0	0	43.0	203	57	38	29	3	1	2	5	12	0	33	1	0	2	6	.250	0	0- -		5.58	6.07
2000 Portland	AA	26	26	3	0	149.2	663	169	85	76	16	5	4	15	49	1	98	5	0	8	9	.471	1	0- -		5.00	4.57
2001 Portland	AA	11	8	0	2	54.2	228	55	41	32	10	2	1	3	10	0	41	0	0	4	5	.444	0	0- -		4.01	5.27
2002 Portland	AA	20	20	3	0	127.2	525	110	56	48	5	3	1	8	29	0	81	2	1	7	6	.538	0	0- -		2.52	3.38
2003 Albuquerque	AAA	15	15	0	0	85.1	368	89	48	42	4	3	1	7	24	1	52	1	0	6	5	.545	0	0- -		3.77	4.43
2004 Albuquerque	AAA	3	2	0	1	13.0	43	7	2	2	0	0	0	0	1	0	12	0	0	0	0		0	0- -		0.81	1.38
2003 Florida	NL	32	0	0	8	36.1	166	34	21	19	3	1	1	7	20	0	17	0	0	4	0	1.000	0	0-0	6	4.94	4.71
2004 Florida	NL	50	2	0	13	73.2	329	86	46	41	7	2	2	3	32	8	44	2	0	2	4	.333	0	1-4	5	5.20	5.01
2 ML YEARS		82	2	0	21	110.0	495	120	67	60	10	3	3	10	52	8	61	2	0	6	4	.600	0	1-4	11	5.12	4.91

Dave Burba

Pitches: R **Bats:** R **Pos:** RP-51   **Ht:** 6'4" **Wt:** 240 **Born:** 7/7/1966 **Age:** 38

			HOW MUCH HE PITCHED					WHAT HE GAVE UP										THE RESULTS						
Year Team	Lg	G	GS	CG	GF	IP	BFP	H	R	ER	HR	SH	SF	HB	TBB	IBB	SO	WP	Bk	W	L	Pct	ShO	Sv-Op	Hld	ERC	ERA
1990 Seattle	AL	6	0	0	2	8.0	35	8	6	4	0	2	0	1	2	0	4	0	0	0	0		0	0-0	0	3.19	4.50
1991 Seattle	AL	22	2	0	11	36.2	153	34	16	15	6	0	0	0	14	3	16	1	0	2	2	.500	0	1-1	0	3.97	3.68
1992 San Francisco	NL	23	11	0	4	70.2	318	80	43	39	4	2	4	2	31	2	47	1	1	2	7	.222	0	0-0	0	4.71	4.97
1993 San Francisco	NL	54	5	0	9	95.1	408	95	49	45	14	6	3	3	37	5	88	4	0	10	3	.769	0	0-0	10	4.44	4.25
1994 San Francisco	NL	57	0	0	13	74.0	322	59	39	36	5	3	1	6	45	3	84	3	0	3	6	.333	0	0-3	11	3.80	4.38
1995 SF-Cin	NL	52	9	1	7	106.2	451	90	50	47	9	4	1	0	51	3	96	5	0	10	4	.714	1	0-1	5	3.38	3.97
1996 Cincinnati	NL	34	33	0	0	195.0	849	179	96	83	18	5	12	2	97	9	148	9	1	11	13	.458	0	0-0	0	3.89	3.83
1997 Cincinnati	NL	30	27	2	1	160.0	706	157	88	84	22	6	3	9	73	10	131	6	0	11	10	.524	0	0-0	0	4.57	4.73
1998 Cleveland	AL	32	31	0	0	203.2	870	210	100	93	30	3	10	7	69	4	132	6	0	15	10	.600	0	0-0	0	4.50	4.11
1999 Cleveland	AL	34	34	1	0	220.0	940	211	113	104	30	2	3	8	96	3	174	13	0	15	9	.625	0	0-0	0	4.45	4.25
2000 Cleveland	AL	32	32	0	0	191.1	848	199	99	95	19	5	5	2	91	2	180	7	0	16	6	.727	0	0-0	0	4.62	4.47
2001 Cleveland	AL	32	27	1	4	150.2	684	188	112	104	16	5	7	3	54	2	118	6	0	10	10	.500	0	0-0	0	5.43	6.21
2002 Tex-Cle	AL	35	21	1	2	145.1	645	155	91	84	16	2	3	9	57	3	95	9	1	5	5	.500	0	0-2	1	4.69	5.20
2003 Milwaukee	NL	17	2	0	2	43.1	193	42	19	17	5	2	0	4	19	2	35	2	0	1	1	.500	0	0-0	4	4.40	3.53
2004 Mil-SF	NL	51	0	0	16	77.0	326	70	40	36	7	4	3	2	26	2	50	3	1	4	1	.800	0	2-5	4	3.30	4.21
1995 San Francisco	NL	37	0	0	7	43.1	191	38	26	24	5	3	1	0	25	2	46	2	0	4	2	.667	0	0-1	5	4.07	4.98
1995 Cincinnati	NL	15	9	1	0	63.1	260	52	24	23	4	1	0	0	26	1	50	3	0	6	2	.750	1	0-0	0	2.93	3.27
2002 Texas	AL	23	18	1	2	111.1	499	125	71	67	13	2	2	7	40	3	70	9	1	4	5	.444	0	0-1	0	4.90	5.42
2002 Cleveland	AL	12	3	0	0	34.0	146	30	20	17	3	0	1	2	17	0	25	0	0	1	0	1.000	0	0-1	1	4.01	4.50
2004 Milwaukee	NL	45	0	0	15	70.2	299	63	36	32	6	4	3	2	24	2	47	2	1	3	1	.750	0	2-4	3	3.17	4.08
2004 San Francisco	NL	6	0	0	1	6.1	27	7	4	4	1	0	0	0	2	0	3	1	0	1	0	1.000	0	0-1	1	4.83	5.68
15 ML YEARS		511	234	6	71	1777.2	7748	1777	961	886	201	51	55	58	762	53	1398	75	4	115	87	.569	1	3-12	31	4.37	4.49

Chris Burke

Bats: R **Throws:** R **Pos:** PH-10; 2B-7; PR-2   **Ht:** 5'11" **Wt:** 180 **Born:** 3/11/1980 **Age:** 25

			BATTING																	BASERUNNING				AVERAGES		
Year Team	Lg	G	AB	H	2B	3B	HR	(Hm	Rd)	TB	R	RBI	RC	TBB	IBB	SO	HBP	SH	SF	SB	CS	SB%	GDP	Avg	OBP	Slg
2001 Michigan	A	56	233	70	11	6	3	(-	-)	102	47	17	40	26	2	31	3	2	1	21	8	.72	3	.300	.376	.438
2002 Round Rock	AA	136	481	127	19	8	3	(-	-)	171	66	37	56	39	3	61	10	5	3	16	15	.52	8	.264	.330	.356
2003 Round Rock	AA	137	549	165	23	8	3	(-	-)	213	88	41	89	57	1	57	14	11	2	34	10	.77	8	.301	.379	.388
2004 New Orleans	AAA	123	483	152	33	6	16	(-	-)	245	93	52	96	55	2	76	13	4	5	37	14	.73	7	.315	.396	.507
2004 Houston	NL	17	17	1	0	0	0	(0	0)	1	2	0	0	3	0	3	0	0	0	0	0	-	0	.059	.200	.059

Jamie Burke

Bats: R **Throws:** R **Pos:** C-45; PH-6; 1B-2; 3B-2; RF-2; DH-2; PR-1   **Ht:** 6'0" **Wt:** 195 **Born:** 9/24/1971 **Age:** 33

			BATTING																	BASERUNNING				AVERAGES		
Year Team	Lg	G	AB	H	2B	3B	HR	(Hm	Rd)	TB	R	RBI	RC	TBB	IBB	SO	HBP	SH	SF	SB	CS	SB%	GDP	Avg	OBP	Slg
2004 Charlotte*	AAA	37	134	31	6	0	2	(-	-)	43	12	12	11	9	0	15	2	3	2	0	0	-	5	.231	.286	.321
2001 Anaheim	AL	9	5	1	0	0	0	(0	0)	1	1	0	0	0	0	2	0	0	0	0	0	-	0	.200	.200	.200
2003 Chicago	AL	6	8	3	0	0	0	(0	0)	3	0	2	2	0	0	0	0	0	0	0	0	-	0	.375	.375	.375
2004 Chicago	AL	57	120	40	9	0	0	(0	0)	49	22	15	21	10	0	13	1	1	1	0	0	-	3	.333	.386	.408
3 ML YEARS		72	133	44	9	0	0	(0	0)	53	23	17	23	10	0	15	1	1	1	0	0	-	3	.331	.379	.398

Ellis Burks

Bats: R **Throws:** R **Pos:** DH-8; PH-3   **Ht:** 6'2" **Wt:** 205 **Born:** 9/11/1964 **Age:** 40

			BATTING																	BASERUNNING				AVERAGES		
Year Team	Lg	G	AB	H	2B	3B	HR	(Hm	Rd)	TB	R	RBI	RC	TBB	IBB	SO	HBP	SH	SF	SB	CS	SB%	GDP	Avg	OBP	Slg
2004 Pawtucket*	AAA	1	2	0	0	0	0	(-	-)	0	1	0	0	0	0	0	1	0	0	0	0	-	0	.000	.333	.000
1987 Boston	AL	133	558	152	30	2	20	(11	9)	246	94	59	84	41	0	98	2	4	1	27	6	.82	1	.272	.324	.441
1988 Boston	AL	144	540	159	37	5	18	(8	10)	260	93	92	97	62	1	89	3	4	6	25	9	.74	8	.294	.367	.481
1989 Boston	AL	97	399	121	19	6	12	(6	6)	188	73	61	69	36	2	52	5	2	4	21	5	.81	8	.303	.365	.471
1990 Boston	AL	152	588	174	33	8	21	(10	11)	286	89	89	91	48	4	82	1	2	2	9	11	.45	18	.296	.349	.486
1991 Boston	AL	130	474	119	33	3	14	(8	6)	200	56	56	60	39	2	81	6	2	3	6	11	.35	7	.251	.314	.422
1992 Boston	AL	66	235	60	8	3	8	(4	4)	98	35	30	32	25	2	48	1	0	2	5	2	.71	5	.255	.327	.417
1993 Chicago	AL	146	499	137	24	4	17	(7	10)	220	75	74	76	60	2	97	4	3	8	6	9	.40	11	.275	.352	.441
1994 Colorado	NL	42	149	48	8	3	13	(7	6)	101	33	24	36	16	3	39	0	0	1	3	1	.75	3	.322	.388	.678
1995 Colorado	NL	103	278	74	10	6	14	(8	6)	138	41	49	49	39	0	72	2	1	1	7	3	.70	7	.266	.359	.496
1996 Colorado	NL	156	613	211	45	8	40	(23	17)	392	142	128	147	61	2	114	6	3	2	32	6	.84	19	.344	.408	.639
1997 Colorado	NL	119	424	123	19	2	32	(17	15)	242	91	82	82	47	0	75	3	1	2	7	2	.78	17	.290	.363	.571
1998 Col-SF	NL	142	504	147	28	6	21	(10	11)	250	76	76	89	58	1	111	4	5	6	11	8	.58	12	.292	.365	.496

51

Year Team	Lg	G	AB	H	2B	3B	HR	(Hm	Rd)	TB	R	RBI	RC	TBB	IBB	SO	HBP	SH	SF	SB	CS	SB%	GDP	Avg	OBP	Slg
1999 San Francisco	NL	120	390	110	19	0	31	(16	15)	222	73	96	84	69	2	86	6	0	4	7	5	.58	11	.282	.394	.569
2000 San Francisco	NL	122	393	135	21	5	24	(15	9)	238	74	96	94	56	5	49	1	0	8	5	1	.83	10	.344	.419	.606
2001 Cleveland	AL	124	439	123	29	1	28	(15	13)	238	83	74	85	62	2	85	5	0	9	5	1	.83	16	.280	.369	.542
2002 Cleveland	AL	138	518	156	28	0	32	(16	16)	280	92	91	104	44	3	108	6	1	1	2	3	.40	13	.301	.362	.541
2003 Cleveland	AL	55	198	52	11	1	6	(2	4)	83	27	28	32	27	2	46	3	0	0	1	1	.50	4	.263	.360	.419
2004 Boston	AL	11	33	6	0	0	1	(0	1)	9	6	1	2	3	0	8	1	0	0	2	0	1.00	1	.182	.270	.273
1998 Colorado	NL	100	357	102	22	5	16	(8	8)	182	54	54	60	39	0	80	2	2	5	3	7	.30	10	.286	.355	.510
1998 San Francisco	NL	42	147	45	6	1	5	(2	3)	68	22	22	29	19	1	31	3	4	4	8	1	.89	2	.306	.387	.463
18 ML YEARS		2000	7232	2107	402	63	352	(183	169)	3691	1253	1206	1313	793	33	1340	60	29	62	181	84	.68	171	.291	.363	.510

A.J. Burnett

Pitches: R Bats: R Pos: SP-19; RP-1 **Ht: 6'4" Wt: 229 Born: 1/3/1977 Age: 28**

Year Team	Lg	G	GS	CG	GF	IP	BFP	H	R	ER	HR	SH	SF	HB	TBB	IBB	SO	WP	Bk	W	L	Pct	ShO	Sv-Op	Hld	ERC	ERA
2004 Jupiter*	A+	1	1	0	0	4.0	16	2	1	0	0	0	0	0	2	0	4	2	0	0	0	-	0	0--	-	1.41	0.00
2004 Albuquerque*	AAA	1	1	0	0	3.1	19	7	4	4	1	0	0	1	2	0	6	1	0	0	0	-	0	0--	-	16.41	10.80
1999 Florida	NL	7	7	0	0	41.1	182	37	23	16	3	1	3	0	25	2	33	0	0	4	2	.667	0	0-0	0	4.00	3.48
2000 Florida	NL	13	13	0	0	82.2	364	80	46	44	8	6	3	2	44	3	57	2	0	3	7	.300	0	0-0	0	4.45	4.79
2001 Florida	NL	27	27	2	0	173.1	733	164	82	78	20	6	8	7	83	3	128	7	1	11	12	.478	1	0-0	0	3.76	4.05
2002 Florida	NL	31	29	7	0	204.1	844	153	84	75	12	9	4	9	90	5	203	14	0	12	9	.571	5	0-1	0	2.77	3.30
2003 Florida	NL	4	4	0	0	23.0	106	18	13	12	2	2	1	2	18	2	21	2	0	0	2	.000	0	0-0	0	4.36	4.70
2004 Florida	NL	20	19	1	0	120.0	490	102	50	49	9	3	3	4	38	0	113	7	0	7	6	.538	0	0-0	0	2.95	3.68
6 ML YEARS		102	99	10	0	644.2	2719	535	298	274	54	27	22	24	298	15	555	32	1	37	38	.493	6	0-1	0	3.41	3.83

Sean Burnett

Pitches: L Bats: L Pos: SP-13 **Ht: 5'11" Wt: 190 Born: 9/17/1982 Age: 22**

Year Team	Lg	G	GS	CG	GF	IP	BFP	H	R	ER	HR	SH	SF	HB	TBB	IBB	SO	WP	Bk	W	L	Pct	ShO	Sv-Op	Hld	ERC	ERA
2000 Pirates	R	8	6	0	1	31.0	128	31	17	14	0	0	1	0	3	0	24	2	1	2	1	.667	0	0--	-	2.24	4.06
2001 Hickory	A	26	26	1	0	161.0	667	164	63	47	11	6	5	4	33	0	134	7	1	11	8	.579	0	0--	-	3.33	2.63
2002 Lynchburg	A+	26	26	1	0	155.1	605	118	46	31	4	5	1	1	33	0	96	3	1	13	4	.765	0	0--	-	1.78	1.80
2003 Altoona	AA	27	27	2	0	159.2	649	158	60	57	2	8	9	7	29	1	86	10	0	14	6	.700	1	0--	-	2.83	3.21
2004 Nashville	AAA	10	10	0	0	47.0	205	58	29	28	5	2	3	2	17	2	25	1	0	1	5	.167	0	0--	-	5.66	5.36
2004 Pittsburgh	NL	13	13	1	0	71.2	318	86	41	40	9	2	1	1	28	2	30	2	0	5	5	.500	1	0-0	0	5.49	5.02

Jeromy Burnitz

Bats: L Throws: R Pos: RF-79; CF-69; LF-21; PH-9; DH-3 **Ht: 6'0" Wt: 213 Born: 4/15/1969 Age: 36**

Year Team	Lg	G	AB	H	2B	3B	HR	(Hm	Rd)	TB	R	RBI	RC	TBB	IBB	SO	HBP	SH	SF	SB	CS	SB%	GDP	Avg	OBP	Slg
1993 New York	NL	86	263	64	10	6	13	(6	7)	125	49	38	42	38	4	66	1	2	2	3	6	.33	2	.243	.339	.475
1994 New York	NL	45	143	34	4	0	3	(2	1)	47	26	15	17	23	0	45	1	1	0	1	1	.50	2	.238	.347	.329
1995 Cleveland	AL	9	7	4	1	0	0	(0	0)	5	4	0	2	0	0	0	0	0	0	0	0	-	0	.571	.571	.714
1996 Cle-Mil	AL	94	200	53	14	0	9	(5	4)	94	38	40	37	33	2	47	4	0	2	4	1	.80	4	.265	.377	.470
1997 Milwaukee	AL	153	494	139	37	8	27	(18	9)	273	85	85	100	75	8	111	5	3	0	20	13	.61	8	.281	.382	.553
1998 Milwaukee	NL	161	609	160	28	1	38	(17	21)	304	92	125	102	70	7	158	4	1	7	7	4	.64	9	.263	.339	.499
1999 Milwaukee	NL	130	467	126	33	2	33	(12	21)	262	87	103	104	91	7	124	16	0	6	7	3	.70	11	.270	.402	.561
2000 Milwaukee	NL	161	564	131	29	2	31	(12	19)	257	91	98	94	99	10	121	14	0	9	6	4	.60	12	.232	.356	.456
2001 Milwaukee	NL	154	562	141	32	4	34	(16	18)	283	104	100	97	80	9	150	5	0	4	0	4	.00	8	.251	.347	.504
2002 New York	NL	154	479	103	15	0	19	(12	7)	175	65	54	47	58	5	135	10	1	2	10	7	.59	11	.215	.311	.365
2003 NYM-LA	NL	126	464	111	22	0	31	(10	21)	226	63	77	61	35	9	112	5	0	1	5	4	.56	5	.239	.299	.487
2004 Colorado	NL	150	540	153	30	4	37	(24	13)	302	94	110	99	58	7	124	5	0	3	5	6	.45	7	.283	.356	.559
1996 Cleveland	AL	71	128	36	10	0	7	(4	3)	67	30	26	27	25	1	31	2	0	0	2	1	.67	3	.281	.406	.523
1996 Milwaukee	AL	23	72	17	4	0	2	(1	1)	27	8	14	10	8	1	16	2	0	2	2	0	1.00	1	.236	.321	.375
2003 New York	NL	65	234	64	18	0	18	(4	14)	136	38	45	41	21	6	55	4	0	0	1	4	.20	1	.274	.344	.581
2003 Los Angeles	NL	61	230	47	4	0	13	(6	7)	90	25	32	20	14	3	57	1	0	1	4	0	1.00	1	.204	.252	.391
12 ML YEARS		1423	4792	1219	255	27	275	(134	141)	2353	798	845	802	660	68	1193	70	8	36	68	53	.56	79	.254	.351	.491

Pat Burrell

Bats: R Throws: R Pos: LF-123; PH-5 **Ht: 6'4" Wt: 222 Born: 10/10/1976 Age: 28**

Year Team	Lg	G	AB	H	2B	3B	HR	(Hm	Rd)	TB	R	RBI	RC	TBB	IBB	SO	HBP	SH	SF	SB	CS	SB%	GDP	Avg	OBP	Slg
2004 Reading*	AA	4	15	3	0	0	2	(-	-)	9	2	4	2	3	0	7	0	0	0	0	0	-	0	.200	.333	.600
2000 Philadelphia	NL	111	408	106	27	1	18	(7	11)	189	57	79	69	63	2	139	1	0	2	0	0	-	0	.260	.359	.463
2001 Philadelphia	NL	155	539	139	29	2	27	(10	17)	253	70	89	86	70	7	162	5	0	4	2	1	.67	12	.258	.346	.469
2002 Philadelphia	NL	157	586	165	39	2	37	(18	19)	319	96	116	104	89	9	153	3	0	6	1	0	1.00	16	.282	.376	.544
2003 Philadelphia	NL	146	522	109	31	4	21	(9	12)	211	57	64	57	72	2	142	4	0	1	0	0	-	18	.209	.309	.404
2004 Philadelphia	NL	127	448	115	17	0	24	(14	10)	204	66	84	72	78	7	130	2	0	6	2	0	1.00	10	.257	.365	.455
5 ML YEARS		696	2503	634	143	9	127	(58	69)	1176	346	432	388	372	27	726	15	0	19	5	1	.83	61	.253	.351	.470

Sean Burroughs

Bats: L Throws: R Pos: 3B-125; PH-6; PR-1 **Ht: 6'2" Wt: 200 Born: 9/12/1980 Age: 24**

Year Team	Lg	G	AB	H	2B	3B	HR	(Hm	Rd)	TB	R	RBI	RC	TBB	IBB	SO	HBP	SH	SF	SB	CS	SB%	GDP	Avg	OBP	Slg
2002 San Diego	NL	63	192	52	5	1	0	(0	1)	59	18	11	15	12	1	30	1	1	0	2	0	1.00	6	.271	.317	.323
2003 San Diego	NL	146	517	148	27	6	7	(2	5)	208	62	58	68	44	4	75	11	2	4	7	2	.78	13	.286	.352	.402
2004 San Diego	NL	130	523	156	23	3	2	(0	2)	191	76	47	70	31	4	52	9	1	0	5	4	.56	6	.298	.348	.365
3 ML YEARS		339	1232	356	55	10	10	(2	8)	461	156	116	153	87	9	157	21	4	4	14	6	.70	25	.289	.345	.374

Dave Bush

Pitches: R Bats: R Pos: SP-16   Ht: 6'2" Wt: 212 Born: 11/9/1979 Age: 25

		HOW MUCH HE PITCHED						WHAT HE GAVE UP										THE RESULTS						
Year Team	Lg	G	GS	CG	GF	IP	BFP	H	R	ER	HR	SH	SF	HB	TBB	IBB	SO	WP	Bk	W	L	Pct	ShO	Sv-Op	Hld	ERC	ERA
2002 Auburn	A-	18	0	0	17	22.1	91	13	9	7	1	0	0	2	7	2	39	0	0	1	1	.500	0	10--	-	1.53	2.82
2002 Dunedin	A+	7	0	0	1	13.1	49	10	3	3	1	1	0	1	2	0	9	1	1	0	1	.000	0	0--	-	2.18	2.03
2003 Dunedin	A+	14	14	0	0	77.0	310	64	29	24	6	3	3	7	9	0	75	4	0	7	3	.700	0	0--	-	2.31	2.81
2003 New Haven	AA	14	14	1	0	81.0	333	73	26	25	4	3	2	4	19	1	73	2	0	7	3	.700	0	0--	-	2.76	2.78
2004 Syracuse	AAA	16	16	2	0	99.2	426	108	52	45	7	7	5	6	20	1	88	4	1	6	6	.500	1	0--	-	3.75	4.06
2004 Toronto	AL	16	16	1	0	97.2	412	95	47	40	11	4	4	6	25	2	64	3	0	5	4	.556	1	0-0	0	3.65	3.69

Homer Bush

Bats: R Throws: R Pos: PR-6; 2B-4; DH-1   Ht: 5'10" Wt: 185 Born: 11/12/1972 Age: 32

		BATTING																	BASERUNNING				AVERAGES		
Year Team	Lg	G	AB	H	2B	3B	HR	(Hm	Rd)	TB	R	RBI	RC	TBB	IBB	SO	HBP	SH	SF	SB	CS	SB%	GDP	Avg	OBP	Slg
2004 Columbus*	AAA	63	234	68	15	0	2	(-	-)	89	35	18	28	11	0	41	2	9	1	3	3	.50	4	.291	.327	.380
1997 New York	AL	10	11	4	0	0	0	(0	0)	4	2	3	1	0	0	0	0	0	0	0	0	-	0	.364	.364	.364
1998 New York	AL	45	71	27	3	0	1	(1	0)	33	17	5	13	5	0	19	0	2	0	6	3	.67	1	.380	.421	.465
1999 Toronto	AL	128	485	155	26	4	5	(2	3)	204	69	55	73	21	0	82	6	8	3	32	8	.80	9	.320	.353	.421
2000 Toronto	AL	76	297	64	8	0	1	(1	0)	75	38	18	17	18	0	60	5	4	1	9	4	.69	10	.215	.271	.253
2001 Toronto	AL	78	271	83	11	1	3	(2	1)	105	32	27	37	8	1	50	6	2	4	13	4	.76	2	.306	.336	.387
2002 Tor-Fla		63	132	30	2	0	1	(1	0)	35	16	7	6	5	0	25	2	2	0	4	1	.80	2	.227	.266	.265
2004 New York	AL	9	7	0	0	0	0	(0	0)	0	2	0	0	0	0	2	1	0	0	1	0	1.00	1	.000	.125	.000
2002 Toronto	AL	23	78	18	2	0	1	(1	0)	23	9	2	4	2	0	12	2	1	0	2	0	1.00	2	.231	.268	.295
2002 Florida	NL	40	54	12	0	0	0	(0	0)	12	7	5	2	3	0	13	0	1	0	2	1	.67	0	.222	.263	.222
7 ML YEARS		409	1274	363	50	5	11	(7	4)	456	176	115	147	57	1	238	20	18	8	65	20	.76	25	.285	.324	.358

Mike Bynum

Pitches: L Bats: L Pos: RP-2   Ht: 6'4" Wt: 200 Born: 3/20/1978 Age: 27

		HOW MUCH HE PITCHED						WHAT HE GAVE UP										THE RESULTS						
Year Team	Lg	G	GS	CG	GF	IP	BFP	H	R	ER	HR	SH	SF	HB	TBB	IBB	SO	WP	Bk	W	L	Pct	ShO	Sv-Op	Hld	ERC	ERA
2004 Portland*	AAA	62	0	0	33	79.0	356	72	33	28	6	2	1	4	44	8	75	2	1	6	6	.500	0	6--	-	3.95	3.19
2002 San Diego	NL	14	3	0	3	27.1	130	33	16	16	3	3	2	3	15	2	17	2	0	1	0	1.000	0	0-0	0	6.31	5.27
2003 San Diego	NL	13	5	0	3	36.0	165	44	35	35	14	1	0	1	15	0	35	0	0	1	4	.200	0	0-0	0	7.83	8.75
2004 San Diego	NL	2	0	0	0	0.2	6	1	4	4	0	0	0	0	3	0	0	0	0	0	1	.000	0	0-0	0	24.61	54.00
3 ML YEARS		29	8	0	6	64.0	301	78	55	55	17	4	2	4	33	2	52	2	0	2	5	.286	0	0-0	0	7.41	7.73

Marlon Byrd

Bats: R Throws: R Pos: CF-92; PH-12; PR-3   Ht: 6'0" Wt: 225 Born: 8/30/1977 Age: 27

		BATTING																	BASERUNNING				AVERAGES		
Year Team	Lg	G	AB	H	2B	3B	HR	(Hm	Rd)	TB	R	RBI	RC	TBB	IBB	SO	HBP	SH	SF	SB	CS	SB%	GDP	Avg	OBP	Slg
2004 Scrtn/WlksBr*	AAA	37	152	40	11	1	2	(-	-)	59	13	17	17	10	1	18	4	0	1	2	3	.40	5	.263	.323	.388
2002 Philadelphia	NL	10	35	8	2	0	1	(1	0)	13	2	1	0	1	0	8	0	0	0	0	2	.00	0	.229	.250	.371
2003 Philadelphia	NL	135	495	150	28	4	7	(3	4)	207	86	45	72	44	3	94	7	4	3	11	1	.92	8	.303	.366	.418
2004 Philadelphia	NL	106	346	79	13	2	5	(3	2)	111	48	33	35	22	1	68	7	2	1	2	2	.50	10	.228	.287	.321
3 ML YEARS		251	876	237	43	6	13	(7	6)	331	136	79	107	67	4	170	14	6	4	13	5	.72	18	.271	.331	.378

Paul Byrd

Pitches: R Bats: R Pos: SP-19   Ht: 6'1" Wt: 185 Born: 12/3/1970 Age: 34

		HOW MUCH HE PITCHED						WHAT HE GAVE UP										THE RESULTS						
Year Team	Lg	G	GS	CG	GF	IP	BFP	H	R	ER	HR	SH	SF	HB	TBB	IBB	SO	WP	Bk	W	L	Pct	ShO	Sv-Op	Hld	ERC	ERA
2004 Greenville*	AA	3	3	0	0	12.2	56	13	10	10	2	0	0	2	5	0	8	0	0	1	1	.500	0	0--	-	5.36	7.11
2004 Richmond*	AAA	1	1	0	0	4.2	20	3	4	4	0	0	0	0	2	0	5	0	0	0	1	.000	0	0--	-	1.62	7.71
1995 New York	NL	17	0	0	6	22.0	91	18	6	5	1	0	2	1	7	1	26	1	2	2	0	1.000	0	0-0	3	2.53	2.05
1996 New York	NL	38	0	0	14	46.2	204	48	22	22	7	1	1	0	21	4	31	3	0	1	2	.333	0	0-2	3	4.67	4.24
1997 Atlanta	NL	31	4	0	9	53.0	236	47	34	31	6	2	2	4	28	4	37	3	1	4	4	.500	0	0-0	1	4.15	5.26
1998 Atl-Phi		9	8	2	0	57.0	233	45	19	17	6	2	1	0	18	1	39	2	0	5	2	.714	1	0-0	0	2.62	2.68
1999 Philadelphia	NL	32	32	1	0	199.2	872	205	119	102	34	5	6	17	70	2	106	11	3	15	11	.577	0	0-0	0	4.87	4.60
2000 Philadelphia	NL	17	15	0	0	83.0	371	89	67	60	17	3	1	3	35	2	53	1	0	2	9	.182	0	0-0	0	5.42	6.51
2001 Phi-KC		19	16	1	1	103.1	444	120	54	51	12	4	6	2	26	1	52	2	0	6	7	.462	0	0-0	0	4.62	4.44
2002 Kansas City	AL	33	33	7	0	228.1	935	224	111	99	36	2	13	7	38	1	129	3	1	17	11	.607	2	0-0	0	3.55	3.90
2004 Atlanta	NL	19	19	0	0	114.1	482	123	57	50	18	3	3	2	19	0	79	1	0	8	7	.533	0	0-0	0	3.98	3.94
1998 Atlanta	NL	1	0	0	0	2.0	11	4	3	3	0	0	0	0	1	0	1	0	0	0	0	-	0	0-0	0	9.72	13.50
1998 Philadelphia	NL	8	8	2	0	55.0	222	41	16	14	6	2	1	0	17	1	38	2	0	5	2	.714	1	0-0	0	2.41	2.29
2001 Philadelphia	NL	3	1	0	1	10.0	45	10	9	9	1	2	2	1	4	0	3	1	0	0	1	.000	0	0-0	0	4.36	8.10
2001 Kansas City	AL	16	15	1	0	93.1	399	110	45	42	11	2	4	1	22	1	49	1	0	6	6	.500	0	0-0	0	4.65	4.05
9 ML YEARS		215	127	11	30	907.1	3868	919	489	437	137	22	35	36	262	16	552	27	7	60	53	.531	3	0-2	9	4.18	4.33

Eric Byrnes

Bats: R Throws: R Pos: LF-110; CF-33; RF-20; PR-3; PH-2   Ht: 6'2" Wt: 210 Born: 2/16/1976 Age: 29

		BATTING																	BASERUNNING				AVERAGES		
Year Team	Lg	G	AB	H	2B	3B	HR	(Hm	Rd)	TB	R	RBI	RC	TBB	IBB	SO	HBP	SH	SF	SB	CS	SB%	GDP	Avg	OBP	Slg
2000 Oakland	AL	10	10	3	0	0	0	(0	0)	3	5	0	1	0	0	1	1	0	0	2	1	.67	0	.300	.364	.300
2001 Oakland	AL	19	38	9	1	0	3	(2	1)	19	9	5	7	4	0	6	1	0	0	1	0	1.00	0	.237	.326	.500
2002 Oakland	AL	90	94	23	4	2	3	(2	1)	40	24	11	10	4	0	17	3	1	2	3	0	1.00	3	.245	.291	.426
2003 Oakland	AL	121	414	109	27	9	12	(7	5)	190	64	51	68	42	4	71	2	0	3	10	2	.83	3	.263	.333	.459
2004 Oakland	AL	143	569	161	39	3	20	(10	10)	266	91	73	87	46	0	111	12	0	5	17	1	.94	11	.283	.347	.467
5 ML YEARS		383	1125	305	71	14	38	(21	17)	518	193	140	173	96	4	206	19	1	9	33	4	.89	17	.271	.336	.460

Daniel Cabrera

Pitches: R Bats: R Pos: SP-27; RP-1   Ht: 6'5" Wt: 230 Born: 5/28/1981 Age: 24

Year Team	Lg	G	GS	CG	GF	IP	BFP	H	R	ER	HR	SH	SF	HB	TBB	IBB	SO	WP	Bk	W	L	Pct	ShO	Sv-Op	Hld	ERC	ERA
2001 Orioles	R	12	7	0	0	40.2	188	31	29	25	1	0	0	5	39	2	36	2	0	2	3	.400	0	0- -	-	4.79	5.53
2002 Bluefield	R+	12	12	0	0	60.1	253	52	25	22	0	1	1	4	25	0	69	2	2	5	2	.714	0	0- -	-	2.99	3.28
2003 Delmarva	A	26	26	1	0	125.1	556	105	74	59	6	2	6	3	78	0	120	5	3	5	9	.357	0	0- -	-	3.70	4.24
2004 Bowie	AA	5	5	0	0	27.1	108	11	10	8	1	2	1	2	12	0	35	1	0	0	1	.000	0	0- -	-	1.29	2.63
2004 Baltimore	AL	28	27	1	1	147.2	662	145	85	82	14	4	7	2	89	2	76	12	0	12	8	.600	1	1-1	0	4.79	5.00

Fernando Cabrera

Pitches: R Bats: R Pos: RP-4   Ht: 6'4" Wt: 170 Born: 11/16/1981 Age: 23

Year Team	Lg	G	GS	CG	GF	IP	BFP	H	R	ER	HR	SH	SF	HB	TBB	IBB	SO	WP	Bk	W	L	Pct	ShO	Sv-Op	Hld	ERC	ERA
2000 Burlington	R+	13	13	0	0	68.1	282	64	42	35	4	2	2	4	20	0	50	14	0	3	7	.300	0	0- -	-	3.33	4.61
2001 Columbus	A	20	20	0	0	94.2	410	89	49	38	7	2	1	2	37	1	96	10	0	5	6	.455	0	0- -	-	3.53	3.61
2002 Kinston	A+	21	21	0	0	110.0	450	83	48	43	7	3	3	2	40	2	107	3	1	6	8	.429	0	0- -	-	2.44	3.52
2002 Akron	AA	7	4	0	1	27.0	118	26	16	16	1	0	0	3	12	0	29	0	0	1	2	.333	0	1- -	-	4.06	5.33
2003 Akron	AA	36	15	0	14	109.0	456	96	41	36	8	6	3	2	40	0	115	3	1	9	4	.692	0	5- -	-	3.20	2.97
2004 Buffalo	AAA	44	0	0	17	75.0	328	57	37	32	9	0	1	3	43	3	92	5	0	4	3	.571	0	5- -	-	3.58	3.84
2004 Cleveland	AL	4	0	0	2	5.1	20	3	3	2	0	0	1	0	1	0	6	0	0	0	0	-	0	0-0	0	0.99	3.38

Jolbert Cabrera

Bats: R Throws: R Pos: 3B-36; 1B-23; LF-21; 2B-18; SS-14; PR-7; PH-6; DH-3; CF-1; RF-1   Ht: 6'1" Wt: 190 Born: 12/8/1972 Age: 32

Year Team	Lg	G	AB	H	2B	3B	HR	(Hm	Rd)	TB	R	RBI	RC	TBB	IBB	SO	HBP	SH	SF	SB	CS	SB%	GDP	Avg	OBP	Slg
1998 Cleveland	AL	1	2	0	0	0	0	(0	0)	0	0	0	0	0	0	1	0	0	0	0	0	-	0	.000	.000	.000
1999 Cleveland	AL	30	37	7	1	0	0	(0	0)	8	6	0	2	1	0	8	1	0	0	3	0	1.00	1	.189	.231	.216
2000 Cleveland	AL	100	175	44	3	1	2	(2	0)	55	27	15	16	8	0	15	2	1	1	6	4	.60	1	.251	.290	.314
2001 Cleveland	AL	141	287	75	16	3	1	(1	0)	100	50	38	32	16	0	41	6	1	2	10	4	.71	4	.261	.312	.348
2002 Cle-LA		48	84	12	2	0	0	(0	0)	14	8	8	3	7	0	15	1	1	1	1	1	.50	3	.143	.215	.167
2003 Los Angeles	NL	128	347	98	32	2	6	(4	2)	152	43	37	41	17	3	62	10	3	3	6	4	.60	10	.282	.332	.438
2004 Seattle	AL	113	359	97	19	2	6	(2	4)	138	38	47	44	16	1	70	8	3	5	10	3	.77	13	.270	.312	.384
2002 Cleveland	AL	38	72	8	1	0	0	(0	0)	9	5	7	1	5	0	13	1	0	1	1	1	.50	3	.111	.177	.125
2002 Los Angeles	NL	10	12	4	1	0	0	(0	0)	5	3	1	2	2	0	2	0	1	0	0	0	-	0	.333	.429	.417
7 ML YEARS		561	1291	333	73	8	15	(9	6)	467	172	145	138	65	4	212	28	9	12	36	16	.69	32	.258	.305	.362

Miguel Cabrera

Bats: R Throws: R Pos: RF-100; LF-59; DH-1; PH-1   Ht: 6'2" Wt: 185 Born: 4/18/1983 Age: 22

Year Team	Lg	G	AB	H	2B	3B	HR	(Hm	Rd)	TB	R	RBI	RC	TBB	IBB	SO	HBP	SH	SF	SB	CS	SB%	GDP	Avg	OBP	Slg
2000 Marlins	R	57	219	57	10	2	2	(-	-)	77	38	22	27	23	0	46	6	0	2	1	0	1.00	6	.260	.344	.352
2000 Utica	A-	8	32	8	2	0	0	(-	-)	10	3	6	3	2	0	6	0	0	0	0	0	-	0	.250	.294	.313
2001 Kane County	A	110	422	134	19	4	7	(-	-)	182	61	66	68	37	2	76	2	1	3	3	0	1.00	10	.318	.373	.431
2002 Jupiter	A+	124	489	134	43	1	9	(-	-)	206	77	75	64	38	2	85	9	1	8	10	1	.91	19	.274	.333	.421
2003 Carolina	AA	69	266	97	29	3	10	(-	-)	162	46	59	61	31	7	49	2	0	4	9	4	.69	8	.365	.429	.609
2003 Florida	NL	87	314	84	21	3	12	(7	5)	147	39	62	51	25	3	84	2	4	1	0	2	.00	12	.268	.325	.468
2004 Florida	NL	160	603	177	31	1	33	(14	19)	309	101	112	92	68	5	148	6	0	8	5	2	.71	20	.294	.366	.512
2 ML YEARS		247	917	261	52	4	45	(21	24)	456	140	174	143	93	8	232	8	4	9	5	4	.56	32	.285	.352	.497

Orlando Cabrera

Bats: R Throws: R Pos: SS-159; PH-2   Ht: 5'10" Wt: 185 Born: 11/2/1974 Age: 30

Year Team	Lg	G	AB	H	2B	3B	HR	(Hm	Rd)	TB	R	RBI	RC	TBB	IBB	SO	HBP	SH	SF	SB	CS	SB%	GDP	Avg	OBP	Slg
1997 Montreal	NL	16	18	4	0	0	0	(0	0)	4	4	2	0	1	0	3	0	1	0	1	2	.33	1	.222	.263	.222
1998 Montreal	NL	79	261	73	16	5	3	(2	1)	108	44	22	34	18	1	27	0	5	1	6	2	.75	6	.280	.325	.414
1999 Montreal	NL	104	382	97	23	5	8	(6	2)	154	48	39	42	18	4	38	3	4	0	2	2	.50	9	.254	.293	.403
2000 Montreal	NL	125	422	100	25	1	13	(7	6)	166	47	55	43	25	3	28	1	3	3	4	4	.50	12	.237	.279	.393
2001 Montreal	NL	162	626	173	41	6	14	(7	7)	268	64	96	85	43	5	54	4	4	7	19	7	.73	15	.276	.324	.428
2002 Montreal	NL	153	563	148	43	1	7	(3	4)	214	64	56	61	48	4	53	2	9	4	25	7	.78	16	.263	.321	.380
2003 Montreal	NL	162	626	186	47	2	17	(8	9)	288	95	80	92	52	3	64	1	3	9	24	2	.92	18	.297	.347	.460
2004 Mon-Bos		161	618	163	38	3	10	(2	8)	237	74	62	62	39	0	54	3	3	10	16	4	.80	16	.264	.306	.383
2004 Montreal	NL	103	390	96	19	2	4	(1	3)	131	41	31	38	28	0	31	2	2	3	12	3	.80	13	.246	.298	.336
2004 Boston	AL	58	228	67	19	1	6	(1	5)	106	33	31	30	11	0	23	1	1	7	4	1	.80	3	.294	.320	.465
8 ML YEARS		962	3516	944	233	23	72	(35	37)	1439	440	412	425	244	20	321	14	32	34	97	30	.76	93	.268	.316	.409

Miguel Cairo

Bats: R Throws: R Pos: 2B-113; 3B-8; SS-3; PH-2; 1B-1; PR-1   Ht: 6'1" Wt: 200 Born: 5/4/1974 Age: 31

Year Team	Lg	G	AB	H	2B	3B	HR	(Hm	Rd)	TB	R	RBI	RC	TBB	IBB	SO	HBP	SH	SF	SB	CS	SB%	GDP	Avg	OBP	Slg
1996 Toronto	AL	9	27	6	2	0	0	(0	0)	8	5	1	2	2	0	9	1	0	0	0	0	-	1	.222	.300	.296
1997 Chicago	NL	16	29	7	1	0	0	(0	0)	8	7	1	3	2	0	3	1	0	0	0	0	-	0	.241	.313	.276
1998 Tampa Bay	AL	150	515	138	26	5	5	(3	2)	189	49	46	58	24	0	44	6	11	2	19	8	.70	9	.268	.307	.367
1999 Tampa Bay	AL	120	465	137	15	5	3	(1	2)	171	61	36	57	24	0	46	7	7	5	22	7	.76	13	.295	.335	.368
2000 Tampa Bay	AL	119	375	98	18	2	1	(0	1)	123	49	34	42	29	0	34	2	6	5	28	7	.80	7	.261	.314	.328
2001 ChC-StL	NL	93	156	46	8	1	3	(2	1)	65	25	16	23	18	1	23	0	7	1	2	1	.67	4	.295	.366	.417
2002 St Louis	NL	108	184	46	9	2	2	(1	1)	65	28	23	18	13	2	36	3	6	2	1	1	.50	5	.250	.307	.353
2003 St Louis	NL	92	261	64	15	2	5	(2	3)	98	41	32	25	13	1	30	6	3	7	4	1	.80	6	.245	.289	.375
2004 New York	AL	122	360	105	17	5	6	(4	2)	150	48	42	50	18	1	49	14	12	4	11	3	.79	7	.292	.346	.417

Year Team		Lg	G	AB	H	2B	3B	HR	(Hm	Rd)	TB	R	RBI	RC	TBB	IBB	SO	HBP	SH	SF	SB	CS	SB%	GDP	Avg	OBP	Slg
									BATTING													**BASERUNNING**				**AVERAGES**		
2001 Chicago		NL	66	123	35	3	1	2	(1	1)	46	20	9	17	16	1	21	0	0	7	2	1	.67	3	.285	.364	.374
2001 St Louis		NL	27	33	11	5	0	1	(1	0)	19	5	7	6	2	0	2	0	0	0	0	0	-	1	.333	.371	.576
9 ML YEARS			829	2372	647	111	22	25	(13	12)	877	313	231	278	143	5	274	40	52	26	87	28	.76	52	.273	.322	.370

Kiko Calero

Pitches: R **Bats:** R **Pos:** RP-41   **Ht:** 6'1" **Wt:** 185 **Born:** 1/9/1975 **Age:** 30

Year Team		Lg	G	GS	CG	GF	IP	BFP	H	R	ER	HR	SH	SF	HB	TBB	IBB	SO	WP	Bk	W	L	Pct	ShO	Sv-Op	Hld	ERC	ERA
				HOW MUCH HE PITCHED								**WHAT HE GAVE UP**											**THE RESULTS**					
1996 Spokane	A-	17	11	0	3	75.0	318	77	34	21	5	6	6	3	18	0	61	2	2	4	2	.667	0	1- -	-	3.51	2.52
1997 Wichita	AA	23	22	2	0	127.2	541	120	78	63	15	4	6	4	44	0	100	2	2	11	9	.550	0	0- -	-	3.76	4.44
1998 Lansing	A	4	4	0	0	16.2	76	19	7	7	1	0	0	2	7	0	10	1	1	1	0	1.000	0	0- -	-	5.15	3.78
1998 Wilmington	A+	17	17	0	0	97.2	409	74	33	31	7	1	3	7	51	1	90	6	0	7	3	.700	0	0- -	-	3.36	2.86
1998 Wichita	AA	3	3	0	0	14.0	72	23	16	15	2	1	0	1	6	0	5	0	0	1	0	1.000	0	0- -	-	8.68	9.64
1999 Wichita	AA	26	23	1	1	129.1	579	143	67	59	14	2	2	6	57	3	92	7	2	9	3	.750	1	1- -	-	5.07	4.11
2000 Wichita	AA	28	25	0	0	153.2	648	141	74	62	16	7	3	10	66	2	130	7	1	10	7	.588	0	0- -	-	4.11	3.63
2001 Wichita	AA	27	19	0	1	124.1	531	110	57	46	10	3	6	7	51	1	94	7	1	14	5	.737	0	0- -	-	3.54	3.33
2002 Wichita	AA	5	2	0	0	16.0	64	10	5	4	2	0	1	0	5	0	15	1	0	1	0	1.000	0	0- -	-	1.93	2.25
2002 Omaha	AAA	20	18	0	0	125.2	510	112	52	48	11	5	7	4	35	1	109	6	1	7	7	.500	0	0- -	-	3.11	3.44
2004 Memphis	AAA	12	3	0	1	25.1	104	20	8	7	3	0	3	1	11	2	33	2	0	0	0	-	0	1- -	-	3.30	2.49
2003 St Louis	NL	26	1	0	7	38.1	162	29	12	12	5	1	3	1	20	2	51	3	1	1	1	.500	0	1-4	1	3.44	2.82
2004 St Louis	NL	41	0	0	4	45.1	168	27	14	14	5	4	0	1	10	1	47	1	0	3	1	.750	0	2-3	12	1.62	2.78
2 ML YEARS		67	1	0	11	83.2	330	56	26	26	10	5	3	2	30	3	98	4	1	4	2	.667	0	3-7	13	2.40	2.80

Carmen Cali

Pitches: L **Bats:** L **Pos:** RP-10   **Ht:** 5'10" **Wt:** 185 **Born:** 11/4/1978 **Age:** 26

Year Team		Lg	G	GS	CG	GF	IP	BFP	H	R	ER	HR	SH	SF	HB	TBB	IBB	SO	WP	Bk	W	L	Pct	ShO	Sv-Op	Hld	ERC	ERA
				HOW MUCH HE PITCHED								**WHAT HE GAVE UP**											**THE RESULTS**					
2000 New Jersey	A-	14	14	0	0	70.0	301	68	45	38	3	2	3	5	30	0	55	11	0	2	7	.222	0	0- -	-	3.97	4.89
2001 Peoria	A	39	0	0	15	48.0	229	53	40	32	4	6	0	1	29	0	47	9	1	7	3	.700	0	1- -	-	5.27	6.00
2001 Potomac	A+	12	0	0	4	12.1	52	12	4	3	1	2	0	1	6	1	9	3	0	1	0	1.000	0	0- -	-	4.56	2.19
2002 Potomac	A+	29	0	0	6	35.0	154	31	18	16	1	2	0	6	21	2	24	2	0	2	2	.500	0	0- -	-	4.39	4.11
2002 Peoria	A	24	0	0	5	35.1	156	36	17	7	0	2	1	0	14	0	27	1	0	1	1	.500	0	2- -	-	3.36	1.78
2003 Palm Beach	A+	62	0	0	23	70.1	321	72	49	39	2	7	4	6	32	6	70	2	0	2	1	.667	0	3- -	-	3.97	4.99
2004 Tennessee	AA	38	0	0	23	46.1	205	43	19	15	3	0	1	3	19	3	47	2	0	1	2	.333	0	14- -	-	3.50	2.91
2004 Memphis	AAA	17	0	0	7	20.0	81	17	6	6	4	0	0	0	8	0	20	2	0	1	1	.500	0	3- -	-	3.06	2.70
2004 St Louis	NL	10	0	0	2	7.1	40	13	7	7	1	0	1	0	6	1	8	1	0	0	0	-	0	0-0	0	10.96	8.59

Mickey Callaway

Pitches: R **Bats:** R **Pos:** SP-3; RP-1   **Ht:** 6'2" **Wt:** 200 **Born:** 5/13/1975 **Age:** 30

Year Team		Lg	G	GS	CG	GF	IP	BFP	H	R	ER	HR	SH	SF	HB	TBB	IBB	SO	WP	Bk	W	L	Pct	ShO	Sv-Op	Hld	ERC	ERA
				HOW MUCH HE PITCHED								**WHAT HE GAVE UP**											**THE RESULTS**					
2004 Frisco*	AA	2	2	0	0	12.0	39	3	0	0	0	0	0	0	4	0	9	0	0	2	0	1.000	0	0- -	-	0.56	0.00
1999 Tampa Bay	AL	5	4	0	0	19.1	99	30	20	16	2	0	1	0	14	1	11	1	0	1	2	.333	0	0-0	-	8.89	7.45
2001 Tampa Bay	AL	2	0	0	2	5.0	20	3	4	4	2	0	0	0	2	0	2	0	0	0	0	-	0	0-0	0	3.65	7.20
2002 Anaheim	AL	6	6	0	0	34.1	147	31	20	16	4	1	0	3	11	0	23	2	0	2	1	.667	0	0-0	-	3.63	4.19
2003 Ana-Tex	AL	23	7	0	8	60.2	284	84	50	45	7	2	5	2	24	1	41	2	0	1	7	.125	0	0-0	-	6.62	6.68
2004 Texas	AL	4	3	0	1	11.1	58	18	10	10	2	0	1	1	7	0	9	0	1	1	0	1.000	0	0-0	-	9.93	7.94
2003 Anaheim	AL	17	4	0	8	38.1	184	57	32	29	7	0	2	1	16	1	22	0	0	1	4	.200	0	0-0	-	7.91	6.81
2003 Texas	AL	6	3	0	0	22.1	100	27	18	16	0	2	3	1	8	0	19	2	0	0	3	.000	0	0-0	-	4.55	6.45
5 ML YEARS		40	20	0	11	130.2	608	166	104	91	17	3	7	6	58	2	86	5	1	4	11	.267	0	0-0	-	6.26	6.27

Ron Calloway

Bats: L **Throws:** L **Pos:** PH-28; RF-15; LF-6   **Ht:** 6'1" **Wt:** 210 **Born:** 9/4/1976 **Age:** 28

Year Team		Lg	G	AB	H	2B	3B	HR	(Hm	Rd)	TB	R	RBI	RC	TBB	IBB	SO	HBP	SH	SF	SB	CS	SB%	GDP	Avg	OBP	Slg
								BATTING													**BASERUNNING**				**AVERAGES**		
1997 Lethbridge	R+	43	148	37	5	0	0	(-	-)	42	23	9	12	14	0	29	3	0	2	5	8	.38	4	.250	.323	.284
1997 South Bend	A	9	25	7	1	0	0	(-	-)	8	3	1	2	2	0	8	0	0	0	1	0	1.00	1	.280	.333	.320
1998 High Desert	A+	44	156	44	8	2	3	(-	-)	65	30	27	20	12	0	38	2	2	2	2	4	.33	3	.282	.337	.417
1998 South Bend	A	69	251	66	12	2	3	(-	-)	91	29	33	31	25	1	50	2	1	3	7	5	.58	3	.263	.331	.363
1999 High Desert	A+	60	196	62	14	1	3	(-	-)	87	41	23	37	30	0	34	2	2	0	22	7	.76	5	.316	.412	.444
1999 El Paso	AA	11	32	7	0	0	0	(-	-)	7	4	1	3	7	0	7	0	0	0	1	2	.33	0	.219	.359	.219
1999 Jupiter	A+	54	211	57	8	4	3	(-	-)	82	30	25	23	15	0	45	2	4	0	5	6	.45	9	.270	.325	.389
2000 Jupiter	A+	135	530	147	24	6	6	(-	-)	201	78	65	71	55	3	89	4	1	6	34	14	.71	13	.277	.346	.379
2001 Harrisburg	AA	74	279	92	22	4	9	(-	-)	149	48	47	56	24	2	46	3	5	3	25	7	.78	2	.330	.385	.534
2001 Ottawa	AAA	61	239	63	12	0	10	(-	-)	105	27	35	33	16	2	64	6	2	2	11	1	.92	6	.264	.323	.439
2002 Ottawa	AAA	128	447	118	21	5	14	(-	-)	191	72	60	58	44	3	89	6	4	5	16	12	.57	18	.264	.335	.427
2004 Edmonton	AAA	59	223	63	17	1	5	(-	-)	97	36	46	36	34	1	39	4	0	1	13	5	.72	10	.283	.385	.435
2003 Montreal	NL	126	340	81	17	1	9	(5	4)	127	36	52	39	20	1	80	2	4	3	9	2	.82	13	.238	.282	.374
2004 Montreal	NL	46	84	14	2	0	1	(1	0)	19	4	10	3	5	0	22	0	1	1	2	0	1.00	3	.167	.211	.226
2 ML YEARS		172	424	95	19	1	10	(6	4)	146	40	62	42	25	1	102	2	5	4	11	2	.85	16	.224	.268	.344

Mike Cameron

Bats: R **Throws:** R **Pos:** CF-136; PR-3; PH-2   **Ht:** 6'2" **Wt:** 195 **Born:** 1/8/1973 **Age:** 32

Year Team		Lg	G	AB	H	2B	3B	HR	(Hm	Rd)	TB	R	RBI	RC	TBB	IBB	SO	HBP	SH	SF	SB	CS	SB%	GDP	Avg	OBP	Slg
								BATTING													**BASERUNNING**				**AVERAGES**		
1995 Chicago	AL	28	38	7	2	0	1	(0	1)	12	4	2	3	3	0	15	0	3	0	0	0	-	0	.184	.244	.316
1996 Chicago	AL	11	11	1	0	0	0	(0	0)	1	1	0	0	1	0	3	0	0	0	0	1	.00	0	.091	.167	.091
1997 Chicago	AL	116	379	98	18	3	14	(10	4)	164	63	55	63	55	1	105	5	2	5	23	2	**.92**	8	.259	.356	.433

Year Team	Lg	G	AB	H	2B	3B	HR	(Hm	Rd)	TB	R	RBI	RC	TBB	IBB	SO	HBP	SH	SF	SB	CS	SB%	GDP	Avg	OBP	Slg
1998 Chicago	AL	141	396	83	16	5	8	(5	3)	133	53	43	39	37	0	101	6	1	3	27	11	.71	6	.210	.285	.336
1999 Cincinnati	NL	146	542	139	34	9	21	(12	9)	254	93	66	96	80	2	145	6	5	3	38	12	.76	4	.256	.357	.469
2000 Seattle	AL	155	543	145	28	4	19	(5	14)	238	96	78	91	78	0	133	9	7	6	24	7	.77	10	.267	.365	.438
2001 Seattle	AL	150	540	144	30	5	25	(7	18)	259	99	110	96	69	3	155	10	1	13	34	5	.87	13	.267	.353	.480
2002 Seattle	AL	158	545	130	26	5	25	(7	18)	241	84	80	78	79	3	176	5	4	5	31	8	.79	8	.239	.340	.442
2003 Seattle	AL	147	534	135	31	5	18	(11	7)	230	74	76	80	70	1	137	5	1	2	17	7	.71	13	.253	.344	.431
2004 New York	NL	140	493	114	30	1	30	(11	19)	236	76	76	70	57	2	143	8	1	3	22	6	.79	5	.231	.319	.479
10 ML YEARS		1192	4021	996	215	37	161	(68	93)	1768	643	586	616	529	12	1113	56	25	40	216	59	.79	67	.248	.340	.440

Shawn Camp

Pitches: R Bats: R Pos: RP-42   Ht: 6'1" Wt: 200 Born: 11/18/1975 Age: 29

Year Team	Lg	G	GS	CG	GF	IP	BFP	H	R	ER	HR	SH	SF	HB	TBB	IBB	SO	WP	Bk	W	L	Pct	ShO	Sv-Op	Hld	ERC	ERA
1997 Idaho Falls	R+	30	0	0	24	32.2	150	41	22	20	3	1	2		14	0	41	4	0	2	1	.667	0	12--	-	5.94	5.51
1998 Clinton	A	47	0	0	39	55.0	240	48	19	16	0	3	3	7	20	4	62	6	1	3	5	.375	0	13--	-	2.84	2.62
1999 R Cucamnga	A+	53	0	0	28	66.0	285	68	37	29	4	4	4	1	25	3	78	7	1	1	5	.167	0	6--	-	3.87	3.95
2000 R Cucamnga	A+	14	0	0	13	18.2	72	10	3	3	0	0	0	2	5	0	18	2	0	1	0	1.000	0	6--	-	1.29	1.45
2000 Mobile	AA	45	0	0	11	59.1	252	47	23	16	4	2	2	1	30	2	53	4	0	3	3	.500	0	1--	-	3.13	2.43
2001 Mobile	AA	35	1	0	0	48.2	204	46	24	24	2	5	2	6	15	1	55	2	0	6	2	.750	0	0--	-	3.54	4.44
2001 Portland	AAA	4	1	0	1	7.0	22	2	0	0	0	0	0	0	1	0	6	0	0	1	0	1.000	0	0--	-	0.37	0.00
2001 Altoona	AA	8	3	0	1	23.1	103	25	14	11	3	0	2	3	8	1	19	1	1	4	0	1.000	0	0--	-	4.95	4.24
2001 Nashville	AAA	11	0	0	1	17.0	67	11	4	4	1	0	1	0	8	1	15	0	0	0	0	-	0	0--	-	2.24	2.12
2002 Nashville	AAA	39	0	0	15	58.1	234	50	22	21	5	3	1	6	15	3	59	0	1	4	1	.800	0	2--	-	3.10	3.24
2003 Altoona	AA	18	0	0	3	29.0	127	26	14	14	2	2	0	4	11	0	35	2	0	0	2	.000	0	0--	-	3.68	4.34
2003 Nashville	AAA	33	1	0	9	43.1	193	50	26	24	2	2	1	2	15	2	36	4	0	1	1	.500	0	0--	-	4.42	4.98
2004 Omaha	AAA	15	0	0	7	22.0	99	26	14	13	2	0	0	1	6	0	21	1	0	1	1	.500	0	1--	-	4.60	5.32
2004 Kansas City	AL	42	0	0	12	66.2	286	74	37	29	10	2	3	5	16	1	51	2	1	2	2	.500	0	2-3	5	4.74	3.92

Jorge Cantu

Bats: R Throws: R Pos: 2B-33; 3B-11; DH-4; PR-2; SS-1; PH-1   Ht: 6'1" Wt: 184 Born: 1/30/1982 Age: 23

Year Team	Lg	G	AB	H	2B	3B	HR	(Hm	Rd)	TB	R	RBI	RC	TBB	IBB	SO	HBP	SH	SF	SB	CS	SB%	GDP	Avg	OBP	Slg
1999 Hudson Val	A-	72	281	73	17	2	1	(-	-)	97	33	33	28	20	0	59	2	4	1	3	4	.43	8	.260	.313	.345
2000 Chrlstn - SC	A	46	186	56	13	2	2	(-	-)	79	25	24	26	10	1	39	3	2	1	3	3	.50	3	.301	.345	.425
2000 St. Petersburg	A+	36	130	38	5	2	1	(-	-)	50	18	14	15	3	0	13	1	3	0	4	2	.67	3	.292	.313	.385
2001 Orlando	AA	130	512	131	26	3	4	(-	-)	175	58	45	45	17	0	93	8	5	7	4	9	.31	13	.256	.287	.342
2002 Orlando	AA	131	512	124	31	1	3	(-	-)	166	50	43	40	23	2	74	4	1	5	2	6	.25	13	.242	.278	.324
2003 Orlando	AA	43	158	34	10	0	3	(-	-)	53	15	17	11	9	0	27	1	3	2	0	3	.00	3	.215	.259	.335
2003 Durham	AAA	60	200	59	16	1	4	(-	-)	89	26	30	27	8	1	21	2	1	6	2	1	.67	5	.295	.319	.445
2004 Durham	AAA	95	368	111	33	1	22	(-	-)	212	57	80	63	16	2	64	4	1	3	3	0	1.00	11	.302	.335	.576
2004 Tampa Bay	AL	50	173	52	20	1	2	(0	2)	80	25	17	22	9	0	44	2	0	1	0	0	-	5	.301	.341	.462

Jose Capellan

Pitches: R Bats: R Pos: SP-2; RP-1   Ht: 6'4" Wt: 235 Born: 1/13/1981 Age: 24

Year Team	Lg	G	GS	CG	GF	IP	BFP	H	R	ER	HR	SH	SF	HB	TBB	IBB	SO	WP	Bk	W	L	Pct	ShO	Sv-Op	Hld	ERC	ERA
2001 Danville	A+	3	3	0	0	16.1	66	12	7	3	1	0	0	2	4	0	25	1	1	0	0	-	0	0--	-	0.59	0.45
2003 Braves	R	5	5	0	0	17.0	75	18	7	5	0	1	0	1	8	0	17	0	0	1	0	1.000	0	0--	-	4.23	2.65
2003 Rome	A	14	12	1	0	47.1	194	43	23	20	2	3	2	0	19	0	32	2	1	1	2	.333	0	0--	-	3.30	3.80
2004 Myrtle Beach	A+	8	8	1	0	46.1	179	27	11	10	0	2	3	2	11	0	62	0	0	5	1	.833	1	0--	-	1.22	1.94
2004 Greenville	AA	9	8	0	1	50.1	205	53	15	14	1	2	1	0	19	0	53	1	1	5	1	.833	0	0--	-	3.98	2.50
2004 Richmond	AAA	7	7	0	0	43.0	172	33	13	12	0	3	1	0	15	1	37	3	0	4	2	.667	0	0--	-	2.05	2.51
2004 Atlanta	NL	3	2	0	0	8.0	42	14	10	10	2	1	1	0	5	0	4	0	0	0	1	.000	0	0-0	0	11.31	11.25

Chris Capuano

Pitches: L Bats: L Pos: SP-17   Ht: 6'2" Wt: 219 Born: 8/19/1978 Age: 26

Year Team	Lg	G	GS	CG	GF	IP	BFP	H	R	ER	HR	SH	SF	HB	TBB	IBB	SO	WP	Bk	W	L	Pct	ShO	Sv-Op	Hld	ERC	ERA
2000 South Bend	A	18	18	0	0	101.2	408	68	35	25	2	4	1	5	45	0	105	2	2	10	4	.714	0	0--	-	2.23	2.21
2001 El Paso	AA	28	28	2	0	159.1	733	184	109	94	13	4	8	11	75	0	167	9	2	10	11	.476	2	0--	-	5.38	5.31
2002 Tucson	AAA	6	6	0	0	36.1	146	30	12	11	1	1	2	0	11	0	29	1	0	4	1	.800	0	0--	-	2.37	2.72
2003 Tucson	AAA	23	23	0	0	142.2	602	133	66	53	9	11	4	11	43	2	108	6	1	9	5	.643	0	0--	-	3.35	3.34
2004 Beloit	A	1	1	0	0	2.2	12	3	1	1	1	0	0	0	1	0	4	0	0	0	0	-	0	0--	-	6.59	3.38
2004 High Desert	A+	1	1	0	0	2.0	15	6	6	6	1	0	0	0	3	0	2	0	0	0	1	.000	0	0--	-	28.67	27.00
2004 Indianapolis	AAA	2	2	0	0	8.2	39	10	9	8	1	1	1	1	5	0	9	2	0	0	1	.000	0	0--	-	6.67	8.31
2003 Arizona	NL	9	5	0	2	33.0	139	27	19	17	3	4	1	6	11	1	23	3	0	2	4	.333	0	0-0	-	3.45	4.64
2004 Milwaukee	NL	17	17	0	0	88.1	385	91	55	49	18	4	1	5	37	1	80	3	1	6	8	.429	0	0-0	0	5.37	4.99
2 ML YEARS		26	22	0	2	121.1	524	118	74	66	21	8	2	11	48	2	103	6	1	8	12	.400	0	0-0	0	4.83	4.90

Chris Carpenter

Pitches: R Bats: R Pos: SP-28   Ht: 6'6" Wt: 215 Born: 4/27/1975 Age: 30

Year Team	Lg	G	GS	CG	GF	IP	BFP	H	R	ER	HR	SH	SF	HB	TBB	IBB	SO	WP	Bk	W	L	Pct	ShO	Sv-Op	Hld	ERC	ERA
1997 Toronto	AL	14	13	1	1	81.1	374	108	55	46	7	1	2	2	37	0	55	7	1	3	7	.300	1	0-0	0	6.38	5.09
1998 Toronto	AL	33	24	1	4	175.0	742	177	97	85	18	4	5	5	61	1	136	5	1	12	7	.632	0	0-0	0	4.12	4.37
1999 Toronto	AL	24	24	4	0	150.0	663	177	81	73	16	4	6	3	48	1	106	9	1	9	8	.529	1	0-0	0	4.90	4.38
2000 Toronto	AL	34	27	2	1	175.1	795	204	130	122	30	3	1	5	83	3	113	3	0	10	12	.455	0	0-0	0	6.04	6.26
2001 Toronto	AL	34	34	3	0	215.2	930	229	112	98	29	3	1	16	75	5	157	5	0	11	11	.500	2	0-0	0	4.82	4.09

Year Team	Lg	G	GS	CG	GF	IP	BFP	H	R	ER	HR	SH	SF	HB	TBB	IBB	SO	WP	Bk	W	L	Pct	ShO	Sv-Op	Hld	ERC	ERA
2002 Toronto	AL	13	13	1	0	73.1	327	89	45	43	11	1	4	4	27	0	45	3	0	4	5	.444	0	0-0	0	5.91	5.28
2004 St Louis	NL	28	28	1	0	182.0	746	169	75	70	24	6	3	8	38	2	152	4	0	15	5	.750	0	0-0	0	3.32	3.46
7 ML YEARS		180	163	13	6	1052.2	4577	1153	595	537	135	22	22	43	369	10	764	36	2	64	55	.538	5	0-0	0	4.83	4.59

Giovanni Carrara

Pitches: R **Bats:** R **Pos:** RP-42   **Ht:** 6'2" **Wt:** 235 **Born:** 3/4/1968 **Age:** 37

Year Team	Lg	G	GS	CG	GF	IP	BFP	H	R	ER	HR	SH	SF	HB	TBB	IBB	SO	WP	Bk	W	L	Pct	ShO	Sv-Op	Hld	ERC	ERA
2004 Iowa*	AAA	20	0	0	4	28.1	120	29	12	12	3	1	1	3	8	1	23	0	0	1	2	.333	0	1- -	-	4.24	3.81
2004 Las Vegas*	AAA	11	0	0	5	14.1	62	11	4	4	1	0	0	0	8	2	15	1	0	0	1	.000	0	2- -	-	2.92	2.51
1995 Toronto	AL	12	7	1	2	48.2	229	64	46	39	10	1	2	1	25	1	27	1	0	2	4	.333	0	0-0	0	7.43	7.21
1996 Tor-Cin		19	5	0	4	38.0	188	54	36	34	11	1	0	2	25	3	23	1	0	1	1	.500	0	0-1	0	9.71	8.05
1997 Cincinnati	NL	2	2	0	0	10.1	49	14	9	9	4	1	0	0	6	1	5	0	0	0	1	.000	0	0-0	0	9.47	7.84
2000 Colorado	NL	8	0	0	2	13.1	72	21	19	19	5	0	1	1	11	2	15	0	0	0	1	.000	0	0-1	0	12.21	12.83
2001 Los Angeles	NL	47	3	0	2	85.1	348	73	30	30	12	6	1	1	24	3	70	0	0	6	1	.857	0	0-3	9	3.10	3.16
2002 Los Angeles	NL	63	1	0	13	90.2	387	83	34	33	14	6	2	6	32	4	56	1	0	6	3	.667	0	1-6	14	3.97	3.28
2003 Seattle	AL	23	0	0	7	29.0	137	40	22	22	6	1	0	2	14	0	13	0	0	2	0	1.000	0	0-0	4	8.10	6.83
2004 Los Angeles	NL	42	0	0	15	53.2	227	46	15	13	1	4	0	1	20	3	48	1	0	5	2	.714	0	2-3	6	2.60	2.18
1996 Toronto	AL	11	0	0	3	15.0	76	23	19	19	5	0	0	0	12	2	10	1	0	0	1	.000	0	0-1	0	11.46	11.40
1996 Cincinnati	NL	8	5	0	1	23.0	112	31	17	15	6	1	0	2	13	1	13	0	0	1	0	1.000	0	0-0	0	8.62	5.87
8 ML YEARS		216	18	1	45	369.0	1637	395	211	199	63	20	6	14	157	17	257	4	0	22	13	.629	0	3-14	33	5.19	4.85

D.J. Carrasco

Pitches: R **Bats:** R **Pos:** RP-30   **Ht:** 6'2" **Wt:** 190 **Born:** 4/12/1977 **Age:** 28

Year Team	Lg	G	GS	CG	GF	IP	BFP	H	R	ER	HR	SH	SF	HB	TBB	IBB	SO	WP	Bk	W	L	Pct	ShO	Sv-Op	Hld	ERC	ERA
1998 Watertown	A-	13	1	0	6	31.2	145	36	23	19	3	1	0	2	14	0	38	1	0	1	1	.500	0	2- -	-	5.20	5.40
1999 Williamsport	A-	18	4	0	6	51.2	212	43	20	17	2	1	3	3	23	0	49	7	4	4	2	.667	0	0- -	-	3.27	2.96
1999 Lynchburg	A+	2	0	0	0	5.2	29	9	8	4	0	1	0	0	3	0	4	0	0	1	0	.000	0	0- -	-	7.15	6.35
2000 Hickory	A	27	0	0	25	40.1	176	35	10	6	0	1	0	7	20	1	40	2	0	5	4	.556	0	6- -	-	3.66	1.34
2000 Lynchburg	A+	8	0	0	6	10.1	45	16	5	4	1	1	0	0	8	0	10	1	0	0	1	.000	0	2- -	-	10.96	3.48
2000 Altoona	AA	9	0	0	3	14.0	68	16	14	13	0	0	0	1	13	0	10	1	0	1	1	.500	0	0- -	-	6.73	8.36
2001 Lynchburg	A+	22	0	0	11	36.0	141	18	7	6	1	0	1	2	14	1	40	1	2	4	0	1.000	0	7- -	-	1.29	1.50
2001 Altoona	AA	27	1	0	11	37.0	169	34	22	17	2	2	0	0	25	2	35	2	0	2	2	.500	0	1- -	-	4.17	4.14
2002 Lynchburg	A+	55	0	0	44	72.2	286	52	18	13	1	4	4	6	18	1	83	2	0	4	4	.500	0	29- -	-	1.86	1.61
2004 Omaha	AAA	32	1	0	16	56.1	247	60	22	20	2	0	0	4	18	0	50	1	0	2	1	.667	0	3- -	-	3.21	3.20
2003 Kansas City	AL	50	2	0	21	80.1	355	82	44	43	8	1	4	7	40	4	57	6	0	6	5	.545	0	2-5	6	4.94	4.82
2004 Kansas City	AL	30	0	0	11	35.1	163	41	22	19	5	1	1	3	15	3	22	2	0	2	2	.500	0	0-3	4	5.56	4.84
2 ML YEARS		80	2	0	32	115.2	518	123	66	62	13	2	5	10	55	7	79	8	0	8	7	.533	0	2-8	10	5.13	4.82

Jamey Carroll

Bats: R **Throws:** R **Pos:** 2B-51; PH-34; 3B-13; SS-10; PR-3; LF-2   **Ht:** 5'10" **Wt:** 175 **Born:** 2/18/1975 **Age:** 30

Year Team	Lg	G	AB	H	2B	3B	HR	(Hm	Rd)	TB	R	RBI	RC	TBB	IBB	SO	HBP	SH	SF	SB	CS	SB%	GDP	Avg	OBP	Slg
2002 Montreal	NL	16	71	22	5	3	1	(1	0)	36	16	6	12	4	0	12	0	4	0	1	0	1.00	1	.310	.347	.507
2003 Montreal	NL	105	227	59	10	1	1	(1	0)	74	31	10	18	19	0	39	3	9	2	5	2	.71	10	.260	.323	.326
2004 Montreal	NL	102	218	63	14	2	0	(0	0)	81	36	16	28	32	1	21	1	2	3	5	1	.83	3	.289	.378	.372
3 ML YEARS		223	516	144	29	6	2	(2	0)	191	83	32	58	55	1	72	4	15	5	11	3	.79	14	.279	.350	.370

Lance Carter

Pitches: R **Bats:** R **Pos:** RP-56   **Ht:** 6'1" **Wt:** 190 **Born:** 12/18/1974 **Age:** 30

Year Team	Lg	G	GS	CG	GF	IP	BFP	H	R	ER	HR	SH	SF	HB	TBB	IBB	SO	WP	Bk	W	L	Pct	ShO	Sv-Op	Hld	ERC	ERA
1999 Kansas City	AL	6	0	0	3	5.1	21	3	3	3	2	0	0	0	3	0	3	0	0	0	1	.000	0	0-0	0	4.22	5.06
2002 Tampa Bay	AL	8	0	0	7	20.1	79	15	3	3	2	0	0	0	5	1	14	0	0	2	0	1.000	0	2-2	0	2.12	1.33
2003 Tampa Bay	AL	62	0	0	55	79.0	328	72	39	38	12	1	6	4	19	6	47	0	0	7	5	.583	0	26-33	2	3.38	4.33
2004 Tampa Bay	AL	56	0	0	27	80.1	336	77	32	31	12	1	5	1	23	2	36	1	0	3	3	.500	0	0-1	7	3.74	3.47
4 ML YEARS		132	0	0	92	185.0	764	167	77	75	28	2	11	5	50	9	100	1	0	12	9	.571	0	28-36	9	3.41	3.65

Sean Casey

Bats: L **Throws:** R **Pos:** 1B-145; PH-2; DH-1   **Ht:** 6'4" **Wt:** 225 **Born:** 7/2/1974 **Age:** 30

Year Team	Lg	G	AB	H	2B	3B	HR	(Hm	Rd)	TB	R	RBI	RC	TBB	IBB	SO	HBP	SH	SF	SB	CS	SB%	GDP	Avg	OBP	Slg
1997 Cleveland	AL	6	10	2	0	0	0	(0	0)	2	1	1	1	1	0	2	1	0	0	0	0	-	0	.200	.333	.200
1998 Cincinnati	NL	96	302	82	21	1	7	(3	4)	126	44	52	45	43	3	45	3	0	3	1	1	.50	11	.272	.365	.417
1999 Cincinnati	NL	151	594	197	42	3	25	(11	14)	320	103	99	119	61	13	88	9	0	5	0	2	.00	15	.332	.399	.539
2000 Cincinnati	NL	133	480	151	33	2	20	(9	11)	248	69	85	91	52	4	80	7	0	6	1	0	1.00	16	.315	.385	.517
2001 Cincinnati	NL	145	533	165	40	0	13	(5	8)	244	69	89	86	43	8	63	9	0	3	3	1	.75	16	.310	.369	.458
2002 Cincinnati	NL	120	425	111	25	0	6	(3	3)	154	56	42	45	43	6	47	5	0	3	2	1	.67	11	.261	.334	.362
2003 Cincinnati	NL	147	573	167	19	3	14	(8	6)	234	71	80	84	51	4	58	2	0	3	4	0	1.00	19	.291	.350	.408
2004 Cincinnati	NL	146	571	185	44	2	24	(9	15)	305	101	99	104	46	5	36	10	0	6	2	0	1.00	16	.324	.381	.534
8 ML YEARS		944	3488	1060	224	11	109	(48	61)	1633	514	547	575	340	43	419	46	0	29	13	5	.72	104	.304	.370	.468

Kevin Cash

Bats: R **Throws:** R **Pos:** C-60; PH-1   **Ht:** 6'0" **Wt:** 185 **Born:** 12/6/1977 **Age:** 27

							BATTING												BASERUNNING				AVERAGES		
Year Team	Lg	G	AB	H	2B	3B	HR	(Hm | Rd)	TB	R	RBI	RC	TBB	IBB	SO	HBP	SH	SF	SB	CS	SB%	GDP	Avg	OBP	Slg
2002 Toronto	AL	7	14	2	0	0	0	(0 | 0)	2	1	0	0	1	0	4	0	0	0	0	0	-	1	.143	.200	.143
2003 Toronto	AL	34	106	15	3	0	1	(1 | 0)	21	10	8	0	4	0	22	1	5	1	0	0	-	6	.142	.179	.198
2004 Toronto	AL	60	181	35	9	0	4	(2 | 2)	56	18	21	11	10	0	59	4	0	2	0	0	-	3	.193	.249	.309
3 ML YEARS		101	301	52	12	0	5	(3 | 2)	79	29	29	11	15	0	85	5	5	3	0	0	-	10	.173	.222	.262

Vinny Castilla

Bats: R **Throws:** R **Pos:** 3B-148; PH-1   **Ht:** 6'1" **Wt:** 205 **Born:** 7/4/1967 **Age:** 37

							BATTING												BASERUNNING				AVERAGES		
Year Team	Lg	G	AB	H	2B	3B	HR	(Hm | Rd)	TB	R	RBI	RC	TBB	IBB	SO	HBP	SH	SF	SB	CS	SB%	GDP	Avg	OBP	Slg
1991 Atlanta	NL	12	5	1	0	0	0	(0 | 0)	1	1	0	0	0	0	2	0	1	0	0	0	-	0	.200	.200	.200
1992 Atlanta	NL	9	16	4	1	0	0	(0 | 0)	5	1	1	2	1	1	4	1	0	0	0	0	-	0	.250	.333	.313
1993 Colorado	NL	105	337	86	9	7	9	(5 | 4)	136	36	30	34	13	4	45	2	0	5	2	5	.29	10	.255	.283	.404
1994 Colorado	NL	52	130	43	11	1	3	(1 | 2)	65	16	18	22	7	1	23	0	1	3	2	1	.67	3	.331	.357	.500
1995 Colorado	NL	139	527	163	34	2	32	(23 | 9)	297	82	90	94	30	2	87	4	4	6	2	8	.20	15	.309	.347	.564
1996 Colorado	NL	160	629	191	34	0	40	(27 | 13)	345	97	113	110	35	7	88	5	0	4	7	2	.78	20	.304	.343	.548
1997 Colorado	NL	159	612	186	25	2	40	(21 | 19)	335	94	113	110	44	9	108	8	0	4	2	4	.33	17	.304	.356	.547
1998 Colorado	NL	162	645	206	28	4	46	(26 | 20)	380	108	144	122	40	7	89	6	0	6	5	9	.36	24	.319	.362	.589
1999 Colorado	NL	158	615	169	24	1	33	(20 | 13)	294	83	102	93	53	7	75	1	0	5	2	3	.40	15	.275	.331	.478
2000 Tampa Bay	AL	85	331	73	9	1	6	(2 | 4)	102	22	42	22	14	3	41	3	0	6	1	2	.33	9	.221	.254	.308
2001 TB-Hou		146	538	140	34	1	25	(12 | 13)	251	69	91	70	35	3	108	4	0	4	1	4	.20	22	.260	.308	.467
2002 Atlanta	NL	143	543	126	23	2	12	(5 | 7)	189	56	61	36	22	4	69	7	0	6	4	1	.80	22	.232	.268	.348
2003 Atlanta	NL	147	542	150	28	3	22	(6 | 16)	250	65	76	70	26	3	86	3	1	6	1	2	.33	22	.277	.310	.461
2004 Colorado	NL	148	583	158	43	3	35	(14 | 21)	312	93	131	88	51	6	113	6	0	8	0	0	-	22	.271	.332	.535
2001 Tampa Bay	AL	24	93	20	6	0	2	(2 | 0)	32	7	9	7	3	0	22	1	0	0	0	0	-	3	.215	.247	.344
2001 Houston	NL	122	445	120	28	1	23	(10 | 13)	219	62	82	63	32	3	86	3	0	4	1	4	.20	19	.270	.320	.492
14 ML YEARS		1625	6053	1696	303	27	303	(162 | 141)	2962	823	1012	873	371	57	938	50	7	63	29	41	.41	201	.280	.324	.489

Alberto Castillo

Bats: R **Throws:** R **Pos:** C-29   **Ht:** 6'0" **Wt:** 200 **Born:** 2/10/1970 **Age:** 35

							BATTING												BASERUNNING				AVERAGES		
Year Team	Lg	G	AB	H	2B	3B	HR	(Hm | Rd)	TB	R	RBI	RC	TBB	IBB	SO	HBP	SH	SF	SB	CS	SB%	GDP	Avg	OBP	Slg
2004 Omaha*	AAA	48	161	41	9	0	1	(- | -)	53	15	15	18	20	0	20	3	2	0	0	0	-	8	.255	.348	.329
1995 New York	NL	13	29	3	0	0	0	(0 | 0)	3	2	0	0	3	0	9	1	0	0	1	0	1.00	0	.103	.212	.103
1996 New York	NL	6	11	4	0	0	0	(0 | 0)	4	1	0	1	0	0	4	0	0	0	0	0	-	0	.364	.364	.364
1997 New York	NL	35	59	12	1	0	0	(0 | 0)	13	3	7	3	9	0	16	0	2	1	0	1	.00	3	.203	.304	.220
1998 New York	NL	38	83	17	4	0	2	(0 | 2)	27	13	7	7	9	0	17	1	6	0	0	2	.00	1	.205	.290	.325
1999 St Louis	NL	93	255	67	8	0	4	(2 | 2)	87	21	31	29	24	1	48	2	5	4	0	0	-	6	.263	.326	.341
2000 Toronto	AL	66	185	39	7	0	1	(1 | 0)	49	14	16	14	21	0	36	0	2	3	0	0	-	3	.211	.287	.265
2001 Toronto	AL	66	131	26	4	0	1	(0 | 1)	33	9	4	7	7	0	30	3	5	0	1	1	.50	2	.198	.255	.252
2002 New York	AL	15	37	5	1	1	0	(0 | 0)	8	3	4	1	1	0	12	0	3	0	0	0	-	2	.135	.158	.216
2003 San Francisco	NL	11	15	3	1	0	1	(1 | 0)	7	2	4	2	0	0	5	0	0	0	0	0	-	0	.200	.200	.467
2004 Kansas City	AL	29	89	24	6	0	1	(0 | 1)	33	12	11	10	14	0	10	0	1	1	0	2	.00	1	.270	.365	.371
10 ML YEARS		372	894	200	32	1	10	(4 | 6)	264	80	84	74	88	1	187	7	24	9	2	6	.25	18	.224	.296	.295

Frank Castillo

Pitches: R **Bats:** R **Pos:** RP-2   **Ht:** 6'1" **Wt:** 198 **Born:** 4/1/1969 **Age:** 36

		HOW MUCH HE PITCHED						WHAT HE GAVE UP											THE RESULTS						
Year Team	Lg	G	GS	CG	GF	IP	BFP	H	R	ER	HR	SH	SF	HB	TBB	IBB	SO	WP	Bk	W	L	Pct	ShO	Sv-Op	Hld	ERC	ERA
2004 Pawtucket*	AAA	27	25	0	0	168.1	693	169	87	82	28	11	5	5	34	0	123	3	1	10	9	.526	0	0- -	-	3.92	4.38
1991 Chicago	NL	18	18	4	0	111.2	467	107	56	54	5	6	3	0	33	2	73	5	1	6	7	.462	0	0-0	0	3.04	4.35
1992 Chicago	NL	33	33	0	0	205.1	856	179	91	79	19	11	5	6	63	6	135	11	0	10	11	.476	0	0-0	0	3.02	3.46
1993 Chicago	NL	29	25	2	0	141.1	614	162	83	76	20	10	3	9	39	4	84	5	3	5	8	.385	0	0-0	0	4.98	4.84
1994 Chicago	NL	4	4	1	0	23.0	96	25	13	11	3	1	0	0	5	0	19	0	0	2	1	.667	0	0-0	0	4.09	4.30
1995 Chicago	NL	29	29	2	0	188.0	795	179	75	67	22	11	3	6	52	4	135	3	1	11	10	.524	2	0-0	0	3.49	3.21
1996 Chicago	NL	33	33	1	0	182.1	789	209	112	107	28	4	5	8	46	4	139	2	1	7	16	.304	1	0-0	0	4.87	5.28
1997 ChC-Col		34	33	0	0	184.1	830	220	121	111	25	17	2	8	69	4	126	3	0	12	12	.500	0	0-0	0	5.51	5.42
1998 Detroit	AL	27	19	0	4	116.0	531	150	91	88	17	2	6	5	44	0	81	0	0	3	9	.250	0	1-1	0	6.32	6.83
2000 Toronto	AL	25	24	0	1	138.0	576	112	58	55	18	5	2	5	56	0	104	0	0	10	5	.667	0	0-0	0	3.42	3.59
2001 Boston	AL	26	26	0	0	136.2	580	138	72	64	14	3	6	5	35	2	89	3	1	10	9	.526	0	0-0	0	3.68	4.21
2002 Boston	AL	36	23	0	2	163.1	711	174	101	92	19	1	11	7	58	6	112	1	2	6	15	.286	0	1-2	0	4.51	5.07
2004 Boston	AL	2	0	0	2	1.0	4	1	0	0	0	0	0	0	1	0	0	0	0	0	0	-	0	0-0	0	6.99	0.00
1997 Chicago	NL	20	19	0	0	98.0	446	113	64	59	9	11	0	4	44	1	67	1	0	6	9	.400	0	0-0	0	5.23	5.42
1997 Colorado	NL	14	14	0	0	86.1	384	107	57	52	16	6	2	4	25	3	59	2	0	6	3	.667	0	0-0	0	5.83	5.42
12 ML YEARS		296	267	10	9	1591.0	6849	1656	873	804	190	71	46	59	501	32	1097	33	9	82	103	.443	3	2-3	0	4.22	4.55

Jose Castillo

Bats: R **Throws:** R **Pos:** 2B-123; PH-4; SS-2; PR-1   **Ht:** 6'1" **Wt:** 200 **Born:** 3/19/1981 **Age:** 24

							BATTING												BASERUNNING				AVERAGES		
Year Team	Lg	G	AB	H	2B	3B	HR	(Hm | Rd)	TB	R	RBI	RC	TBB	IBB	SO	HBP	SH	SF	SB	CS	SB%	GDP	Avg	OBP	Slg
1999 Pirates	R	47	173	46	9	0	4	(- | -)	67	27	30	22	11	1	23	3	3	3	8	0	1.00	4	.266	.316	.387
2000 Hickory	A	125	529	158	32	8	16	(- | -)	254	95	72	82	29	0	107	10	7	2	16	12	.57	10	.299	.346	.480
2001 Lynchburg	A+	125	485	119	20	7	7	(- | -)	174	57	49	48	21	2	94	9	4	2	23	10	.70	9	.245	.288	.359
2002 Lynchburg	A+	134	503	151	25	2	16	(- | -)	228	82	81	80	49	1	95	11	1	8	27	14	.66	18	.300	.370	.453
2003 Altoona	AA	126	498	143	24	6	5	(- | -)	194	68	66	63	40	1	81	3	0	8	19	10	.66	18	.287	.339	.390
2004 Pittsburgh	NL	129	383	98	15	2	8	(3 | 5)	141	44	39	40	23	5	92	1	5	2	3	2	.60	12	.256	.298	.368

Luis Castillo

Bats: B Throws: R Pos: 2B-148; PH-2; PR-1 Ht: 5'11" Wt: 190 Born: 9/12/1975 Age: 29

Year Team	Lg	G	AB	H	2B	3B	HR	(Hm	Rd)	TB	R	RBI	RC	TBB	IBB	SO	HBP	SH	SF	SB	CS	SB%	GDP	Avg	OBP	Slg
1996 Florida	NL	41	164	43	2	1	1	(0	1)	50	26	8	19	14	0	46	0	2	0	17	4	.81	0	.262	.320	.305
1997 Florida	NL	75	263	63	8	0	0	(0	0)	71	27	8	21	27	0	53	0	1	0	16	10	.62	6	.240	.310	.270
1998 Florida	NL	44	153	31	3	2	1	(0	1)	41	21	10	14	22	0	33	1	1	0	3	0	1.00	1	.203	.307	.268
1999 Florida	NL	128	487	147	23	4	0	(0	0)	178	76	28	78	67	0	85	0	6	3	50	17	.75	3	.302	.384	.366
2000 Florida	NL	136	539	180	17	3	2	(1	1)	209	101	17	95	78	0	86	0	9	0	62	22	.74	11	.334	.418	.388
2001 Florida	NL	134	537	141	16	10	2	(1	1)	183	76	45	67	67	0	90	1	4	3	33	16	.67	6	.263	.344	.341
2002 Florida	NL	146	606	185	18	5	2	(0	2)	219	86	39	84	55	4	76	2	4	1	48	15	.76	7	.305	.364	.361
2003 Florida	NL	152	595	187	19	6	6	(2	4)	236	99	39	87	63	0	60	2	15	1	21	19	.53	7	.314	.381	.397
2004 Florida	NL	150	564	164	12	7	2	(1	1)	196	91	47	84	75	2	68	1	5	4	21	4	.84	15	.291	.373	.348
9 ML YEARS		1006	3908	1141	118	38	16	(5	11)	1383	603	241	549	468	6	597	7	47	12	271	107	.72	56	.292	.368	.354

Juan Castro

Bats: R Throws: R Pos: 3B-78; SS-31; PH-13; 2B-12; 1B-4; PR-3 Ht: 5'11" Wt: 195 Born: 6/20/1972 Age: 33

Year Team	Lg	G	AB	H	2B	3B	HR	(Hm	Rd)	TB	R	RBI	RC	TBB	IBB	SO	HBP	SH	SF	SB	CS	SB%	GDP	Avg	OBP	Slg
2004 Louisville*	AAA	5	18	3	1	0	0	(-	-)	4	1	3	0	1	0	2	0	0	1	0	0	-	0	.167	.200	.222
1995 Los Angeles	NL	11	4	1	0	0	0	(0	0)	1	0	0	1	1	0	1	0	0	0	0	0	-	0	.250	.400	.250
1996 Los Angeles	NL	70	132	26	5	3	0	(0	0)	37	16	5	8	10	0	27	0	4	0	1	0	1.00	3	.197	.254	.280
1997 Los Angeles	NL	40	75	11	3	1	0	(0	0)	16	3	4	2	7	1	20	0	2	0	0	0	-	0	.147	.220	.213
1998 Los Angeles	NL	89	220	43	7	0	2	(0	2)	56	25	14	12	15	0	37	0	9	2	0	0	-	5	.195	.245	.255
1999 Los Angeles	NL	2	1	0	0	0	0	(0	0)	0	0	0	0	0	0	1	0	0	0	0	0	-	0	.000	.000	.000
2000 Cincinnati	NL	82	224	54	12	2	4	(1	3)	82	20	23	20	14	1	33	0	4	2	0	2	.00	9	.241	.283	.366
2001 Cincinnati	NL	96	242	54	10	0	3	(0	3)	73	27	13	16	13	2	50	0	4	2	0	0	-	9	.223	.261	.302
2002 Cincinnati	NL	54	82	18	3	0	2	(0	2)	27	5	11	11	7	0	18	0	1	1	0	0	-	0	.220	.278	.329
2003 Cincinnati	NL	113	320	81	14	1	9	(4	5)	124	28	33	36	18	1	58	0	7	3	2	3	.40	7	.253	.290	.388
2004 Cincinnati	NL	111	299	73	21	2	5	(3	2)	113	36	26	26	14	1	51	0	2	1	1	0	1.00	11	.244	.277	.378
10 ML YEARS		668	1599	361	75	9	25	(8	17)	529	160	129	132	99	6	296	0	33	11	4	5	.44	46	.226	.269	.331

Ramon A Castro

Bats: R Throws: R Pos: 3B-6; PH-2; PR-2; SS-1; DH-1 Ht: 6'0" Wt: 195 Born: 10/23/1979 Age: 25

Year Team	Lg	G	AB	H	2B	3B	HR	(Hm	Rd)	TB	R	RBI	RC	TBB	IBB	SO	HBP	SH	SF	SB	CS	SB%	GDP	Avg	OBP	Slg
1997 Eugene	A-	71	226	45	8	3	1	(-	-)	62	20	23	19	24	0	56	6	4	3	7	1	.88	5	.199	.290	.274
1998 Eugene	A-	74	296	77	10	1	3	(-	-)	98	33	33	35	22	0	49	5	5	2	8	1	.89	1	.260	.320	.331
1999 Macon	A	105	350	91	12	4	3	(-	-)	120	32	33	39	24	0	55	2	7	2	13	5	.72	4	.260	.310	.343
2000 Myrtle Beach	A+	108	385	97	20	3	5	(-	-)	138	52	44	52	44	0	76	12	3	1	13	5	.72	4	.252	.346	.358
2001 Greenville	AA	76	261	80	19	5	6	(-	-)	127	35	31	45	25	0	56	9	7	3	5	8	.38	5	.307	.383	.487
2001 Richmond	AAA	36	135	30	8	2	1	(-	-)	45	14	15	9	7	0	30	1	3	0	1	2	.33	5	.222	.266	.333
2002 Richmond	AAA	39	121	28	7	1	6	(-	-)	55	22	14	18	14	0	22	6	1	0	4	3	.57	1	.231	.340	.455
2002 Greenville	AA	56	210	68	17	2	5	(-	-)	104	47	22	47	39	2	44	9	1	2	14	8	.64	3	.324	.446	.495
2002 Braves	R	9	32	8	0	0	1	(-	-)	11	3	4	4	3	0	6	1	1	0	2	0	1.00	1	.250	.333	.344
2003 Greenville	AA	66	204	59	9	1	5	(-	-)	85	33	20	33	27	0	39	2	3	1	4	5	.44	1	.289	.376	.417
2003 Richmond	AAA	33	84	13	2	0	0	(-	-)	15	11	8	3	10	0	22	0	1	1	0	0	-	2	.155	.242	.179
2004 Midland	AA	28	93	23	2	3	0	(-	-)	31	16	12	12	12	0	18	4	1	3	3	2	.60	1	.247	.348	.333
2004 Sacramento	AAA	40	123	28	8	2	1	(-	-)	43	15	16	13	15	0	20	2	2	2	2	2	.50	4	.228	.317	.350
2004 Oakland	AL	9	15	2	1	0	0	(0	0)	3	2	3	0	1	1	3	0	0	0	0	0	-	1	.133	.188	.200

Ramon Castro

Bats: R Throws: R Pos: C-31; PH-1; PR-1 Ht: 6'3" Wt: 235 Born: 3/1/1976 Age: 29

Year Team	Lg	G	AB	H	2B	3B	HR	(Hm	Rd)	TB	R	RBI	RC	TBB	IBB	SO	HBP	SH	SF	SB	CS	SB%	GDP	Avg	OBP	Slg
1999 Florida	NL	24	67	12	4	0	2	(0	2)	22	4	4	6	10	3	14	0	0	1	0	0	-	1	.179	.282	.328
2000 Florida	NL	50	138	33	4	0	2	(0	2)	43	10	14	14	16	7	36	1	0	2	0	0	-	1	.239	.318	.312
2001 Florida	NL	7	11	2	0	0	0	(0	0)	2	0	1	0	1	0	1	0	0	0	0	0	-	0	.182	.250	.182
2002 Florida	NL	54	101	24	4	0	6	(4	2)	46	11	18	14	14	3	24	0	1	3	0	0	-	4	.238	.322	.455
2003 Florida	NL	40	53	15	2	0	5	(4	1)	32	6	8	8	4	0	11	0	0	0	0	0	-	0	.283	.333	.604
2004 Florida	NL	32	96	13	3	0	3	(0	3)	25	9	8	4	11	2	30	1	0	0	0	0	-	1	.135	.231	.260
6 ML YEARS		207	466	99	17	0	18	(8	10)	170	40	53	46	56	15	116	2	1	6	0	0	-	7	.212	.296	.365

Frank Catalanotto

Bats: L Throws: R Pos: LF-41; DH-28; PH-13 Ht: 5'11" Wt: 195 Born: 4/27/1974 Age: 31

Year Team	Lg	G	AB	H	2B	3B	HR	(Hm	Rd)	TB	R	RBI	RC	TBB	IBB	SO	HBP	SH	SF	SB	CS	SB%	GDP	Avg	OBP	Slg
1997 Detroit	AL	13	26	8	2	0	0	(0	0)	10	2	3	4	3	0	7	0	0	0	0	0	-	0	.308	.379	.385
1998 Detroit	AL	89	213	60	13	2	6	(3	3)	95	23	25	30	12	1	39	4	0	5	3	2	.60	4	.282	.325	.446
1999 Detroit	AL	100	286	79	19	0	11	(6	5)	131	41	35	42	15	1	49	9	0	5	3	4	.43	5	.276	.327	.458
2000 Texas	AL	103	282	82	13	2	10	(6	4)	129	55	42	49	33	0	36	6	3	1	6	2	.75	5	.291	.375	.457
2001 Texas	AL	133	463	153	31	5	11	(4	7)	227	77	54	88	39	3	55	8	1	1	15	5	.75	5	.330	.391	.490
2002 Texas	AL	68	212	57	16	6	3	(2	1)	94	42	23	39	25	0	27	8	3	2	9	5	.64	3	.269	.364	.443
2003 Toronto	AL	133	489	146	34	6	13	(7	6)	231	83	59	84	35	1	62	6	2	3	2	2	.50	9	.299	.351	.472
2004 Toronto	AL	75	249	73	19	1	1	(1	0)	97	27	26	34	17	1	33	4	1	3	1	0	1.00	7	.293	.344	.390
8 ML YEARS		714	2220	658	147	22	55	(29	26)	1014	350	267	370	179	7	308	45	10	21	39	20	.66	38	.296	.358	.457

Roger Cedeno

Bats: B **Throws:** R **Pos:** PH-47; RF-35; LF-23; PR-2; DH-1   **Ht:** 6'1" **Wt:** 205 **Born:** 8/16/1974 **Age:** 30

								BATTING												BASERUNNING				AVERAGES		
Year Team	Lg	G	AB	H	2B	3B	HR	(Hm	Rd)	TB	R	RBI	RC	TBB	IBB	SO	HBP	SH	SF	SB	CS	SB%	GDP	Avg	OBP	Slg
2004 Memphis*	AAA	7	23	5	0	0	0	(-	-)	5	3	1	1	2	0	6	0	0	0	0	0	-	0	.217	.280	.217
1995 Los Angeles	NL	40	42	10	2	0	0	(0	0)	12	4	3	3	3	0	10	0	0	1	1	0	1.00	1	.238	.283	.286
1996 Los Angeles	NL	86	211	52	11	1	2	(0	2)	71	26	18	26	24	0	47	1	2	0	5	1	.83	0	.246	.326	.336
1997 Los Angeles	NL	80	194	53	10	2	3	(3	0)	76	31	17	31	25	2	44	3	3	2	9	1	.90	1	.273	.362	.392
1998 Los Angeles	NL	105	240	58	11	1	2	(2	0)	77	33	17	27	27	2	57	0	3	1	8	2	.80	1	.242	.317	.321
1999 New York	NL	155	453	142	23	4	4	(4	0)	185	90	36	82	60	3	100	3	7	2	66	17	.80	5	.313	.396	.408
2000 Houston	NL	74	259	73	2	5	6	(3	3)	103	54	26	42	43	0	47	0	2	1	25	11	.69	6	.282	.383	.398
2001 Detroit	AL	131	523	153	14	11	6	(3	3)	207	79	48	76	36	1	83	2	6	5	55	15	.79	5	.293	.337	.396
2002 New York	NL	149	511	133	19	2	7	(2	5)	177	65	41	60	42	1	92	2	5	2	25	4	.86	10	.260	.318	.346
2003 New York	NL	148	484	129	25	4	7	(5	2)	183	70	37	52	38	3	86	1	2	2	14	9	.61	8	.267	.320	.378
2004 St Louis	NL	95	200	53	9	2	3	(0	3)	75	22	23	29	19	2	41	0	3	1	5	1	.83	5	.265	.327	.375
10 ML YEARS		**1063**	**3117**	**856**	**126**	**32**	**40**	**(22**	**18)**	**1166**	**474**	**266**	**428**	**317**	**14**	**607**	**12**	**33**	**17**	**213**	**61**	**.78**	**42**	**.275**	**.342**	**.374**

Matt Cepicky

Bats: L **Throws:** R **Pos:** PH-19; LF-9; RF-2; DH-2   **Ht:** 6'2" **Wt:** 215 **Born:** 11/10/1977 **Age:** 27

								BATTING												BASERUNNING				AVERAGES		
Year Team	Lg	G	AB	H	2B	3B	HR	(Hm	Rd)	TB	R	RBI	RC	TBB	IBB	SO	HBP	SH	SF	SB	CS	SB%	GDP	Avg	OBP	Slg
2004 Edmonton*	AAA	82	312	83	15	3	15	(-	-)	149	51	67	43	18	2	75	0	0	4	2	1	.67	4	.266	.302	.478
2002 Montreal	NL	32	74	16	3	0	3	(2	1)	28	7	15	8	4	1	21	0	0	0	0	0	-	0	.216	.256	.378
2003 Montreal	NL	5	8	2	1	0	0	(0	0)	3	0	0	0	0	0	2	0	0	0	0	0	-	0	.250	.250	.375
2004 Montreal	NL	32	60	13	4	0	1	(1	0)	20	4	3	2	1	0	18	0	0	0	1	0	1.00	1	.217	.230	.333
3 ML YEARS		**69**	**142**	**31**	**8**	**0**	**4**	**(3**	**1)**	**51**	**11**	**18**	**10**	**5**	**1**	**41**	**0**	**0**	**0**	**1**	**0**	**1.00**	**1**	**.218**	**.245**	**.359**

Jaime Cerda

Pitches: L **Bats:** L **Pos:** RP-53   **Ht:** 6'0" **Wt:** 175 **Born:** 10/26/1978 **Age:** 26

		HOW MUCH HE PITCHED						WHAT HE GAVE UP											THE RESULTS						
Year Team	Lg	G	GS	CG	GF	IP	BFP	H	R	ER	HR	SH	SF	HB	TBB	IBB	SO	WP	Bk	W	L	Pct	ShO	Sv-Op	Hld	ERC	ERA
2004 Omaha*	AAA	4	0	0	1	6.0	27	8	2	2	0	1	0	0	3	0	2	1	0	0	0	-	0	0--	-	5.93	3.00
2002 New York	NL	32	0	0	7	25.2	114	22	7	7	0	0	3	1	14	0	21	0	1	0	0	-	0	0-0	4	3.19	2.45
2003 New York	NL	27	0	0	9	32.1	144	32	21	21	4	2	2	0	20	1	19	3	1	1	1	.500	0	0-1	2	5.08	5.85
2004 Kansas City	AL	53	0	0	16	45.2	206	41	21	16	1	2	3	3	30	3	33	4	0	1	4	.200	0	2-3	12	4.04	3.15
3 ML YEARS		**112**	**0**	**0**	**32**	**103.2**	**464**	**95**	**49**	**44**	**5**	**4**	**8**	**4**	**64**	**4**	**73**	**7**	**2**	**2**	**5**	**.286**	**0**	**2-4**	**18**	**4.14**	**3.82**

Gustavo Chacin

Pitches: L **Bats:** L **Pos:** SP-2   **Ht:** 5'11" **Wt:** 193 **Born:** 12/4/1980 **Age:** 24

		HOW MUCH HE PITCHED						WHAT HE GAVE UP											THE RESULTS						
Year Team	Lg	G	GS	CG	GF	IP	BFP	H	R	ER	HR	SH	SF	HB	TBB	IBB	SO	WP	Bk	W	L	Pct	ShO	Sv-Op	Hld	ERC	ERA
1999 Medicine Hat	R+	15	9	0	2	64.0	280	68	33	22	6	4	4	7	23	0	50	4	3	4	3	.571	0	1--	-	4.73	3.09
2000 Dunedin	A+	25	21	0	1	127.2	584	138	69	57	14	1	2	3	64	0	77	9	0	9	5	.643	0	0--	-	5.03	4.02
2000 Tennessee	AA	2	2	0	0	5.0	31	10	7	7	1	0	0	1	6	0	5	0	1	0	2	.000	0	0--	-	16.75	12.60
2001 Tennessee	AA	25	23	1	0	140.1	588	138	66	62	17	2	3	7	39	0	86	5	0	11	8	.579	1	0--	-	3.88	3.98
2002 Tennessee	AA	35	13	1	8	116.2	542	131	73	62	12	6	5	8	59	0	68	4	1	6	5	.545	0	1--	-	5.30	4.66
2003 New Haven	AA	46	2	0	9	69.1	314	78	39	32	1	3	4	2	29	1	55	7	3	3	4	.429	0	2--	-	4.23	4.15
2004 New Hamp	AA	25	25	0	0	141.2	577	113	53	45	15	4	1	5	49	0	109	3	0	16	2	.889	0	0--	-	2.99	2.86
2004 Syracuse	AAA	2	2	0	0	11.2	53	16	4	3	0	1	1	0	3	0	14	0	0	2	0	1.000	0	0--	-	4.85	2.31
2004 Toronto	AL	2	2	0	0	14.0	52	8	4	4	0	0	0	1	3	0	6	0	0	1	1	.500	0	0-0	-	1.24	2.57

Shawn Chacon

Pitches: R **Bats:** R **Pos:** RP-66   **Ht:** 6'3" **Wt:** 212 **Born:** 12/23/1977 **Age:** 27

		HOW MUCH HE PITCHED						WHAT HE GAVE UP											THE RESULTS						
Year Team	Lg	G	GS	CG	GF	IP	BFP	H	R	ER	HR	SH	SF	HB	TBB	IBB	SO	WP	Bk	W	L	Pct	ShO	Sv-Op	Hld	ERC	ERA
2001 Colorado	NL	27	27	0	0	160.0	711	157	96	90	26	6	3	10	87	10	134	6	0	6	10	.375	0	0-0	0	5.22	5.06
2002 Colorado	NL	21	21	0	0	119.1	537	122	84	76	25	5	2	7	60	3	67	0	1	5	11	.313	0	0-0	0	5.63	5.73
2003 Colorado	NL	22	23	0	0	137.0	596	124	73	70	12	10	5	12	58	4	93	8	0	11	8	.579	0	0-0	0	3.82	4.60
2004 Colorado	NL	66	0	0	60	63.1	316	71	52	50	12	7	0	5	52	7	52	9	0	1	9	.100	0	35-44	0	7.30	7.11
4 ML YEARS		**137**	**71**	**0**	**60**	**479.2**	**2160**	**474**	**305**	**286**	**75**	**28**	**10**	**34**	**257**	**24**	**346**	**23**	**1**	**23**	**38**	**.377**	**0**	**35-44**	**0**	**5.17**	**5.37**

Endy Chavez

Bats: L **Throws:** L **Pos:** CF-127; PH-5; PR-1   **Ht:** 6'0" **Wt:** 165 **Born:** 2/7/1978 **Age:** 27

								BATTING												BASERUNNING				AVERAGES		
Year Team	Lg	G	AB	H	2B	3B	HR	(Hm	Rd)	TB	R	RBI	RC	TBB	IBB	SO	HBP	SH	SF	SB	CS	SB%	GDP	Avg	OBP	Slg
2004 Edmonton*	AAA	14	61	21	3	2	0	(-	-)	28	9	7	12	7	0	7	0	0	1	5	2	.71	0	.344	.406	.459
2001 Kansas City	AL	29	77	16	2	0	0	(0	0)	18	4	5	2	3	0	8	0	0	0	2	2	.00	3	.208	.238	.234
2002 Montreal	NL	36	125	37	8	5	1	(0	1)	58	20	9	14	5	0	16	0	7	1	3	5	.38	0	.296	.321	.464
2003 Montreal	NL	141	483	121	25	5	5	(4	1)	171	66	47	56	31	3	59	0	9	3	18	7	.72	7	.251	.294	.354
2004 Montreal	NL	132	502	139	20	6	5	(4	1)	186	65	34	56	30	0	40	1	12	2	32	7	.82	6	.277	.318	.371
4 ML YEARS		**338**	**1187**	**313**	**55**	**16**	**11**	**(8**	**3)**	**433**	**155**	**95**	**128**	**69**	**3**	**123**	**1**	**28**	**6**	**53**	**21**	**.72**	**16**	**.264**	**.303**	**.365**

Eric Chavez

Bats: L **Throws:** R **Pos:** 3B-125; LF-1   **Ht:** 6'1" **Wt:** 206 **Born:** 12/7/1977 **Age:** 27

Year Team	Lg	G	AB	H	2B	3B	HR	(Hm	Rd)	TB	R	RBI	RC	TBB	IBB	SO	HBP	SH	SF	SB	CS	SB%	GDP	Avg	OBP	Slg
2004 Sacramento*	AAA	3	13	4	1	0	0	(-	-)	5	2	0	1	1	1	2	0	0	0	0	0	-	0	.308	.357	.385
1998 Oakland	AL	16	45	14	4	1	0	(0	0)	20	6	6	7	3	1	5	0	0	0	1	1	.50	1	.311	.354	.444
1999 Oakland	AL	115	356	88	21	2	13	(8	5)	152	47	50	50	46	4	56	0	0	0	1	1	.50	7	.247	.333	.427
2000 Oakland	AL	153	501	139	23	4	26	(15	11)	248	89	86	86	62	8	94	1	0	5	2	2	.50	9	.277	.355	.495
2001 Oakland	AL	151	552	159	43	0	32	(14	18)	298	91	114	99	41	9	99	4	0	7	8	2	.80	7	.288	.338	.540
2002 Oakland	AL	153	585	161	31	3	34	(17	17)	300	87	109	103	65	13	119	1	0	2	8	3	.73	8	.275	.348	.513
2003 Oakland	AL	156	588	166	39	5	29	(12	17)	302	94	101	97	62	10	89	1	0	3	8	3	.73	14	.282	.350	.514
2004 Oakland	AL	125	475	131	20	0	29	(15	14)	238	87	77	84	95	10	99	3	0	4	6	3	.67	21	.276	.397	.501
7 ML YEARS		869	3102	858	181	15	163	(81	82)	1558	501	543	526	374	55	561	10	0	21	34	15	.69	67	.277	.354	.502

Raul Chavez

Bats: R **Throws:** R **Pos:** C-61; PH-3   **Ht:** 5'11" **Wt:** 210 **Born:** 3/18/1973 **Age:** 32

Year Team	Lg	G	AB	H	2B	3B	HR	(Hm	Rd)	TB	R	RBI	RC	TBB	IBB	SO	HBP	SH	SF	SB	CS	SB%	GDP	Avg	OBP	Slg
1996 Montreal	NL	4	5	1	0	0	0	(0	0)	1	1	0	0	1	0	1	0	0	0	1	0	1.00	1	.200	.333	.200
1997 Montreal	NL	13	26	7	0	0	0	(0	0)	7	0	2	2	0	0	5	0	0	1	1	0	1.00	0	.269	.259	.269
1998 Seattle	AL	1	1	0	0	0	0	(0	0)	0	0	0	0	0	0	0	0	0	0	0	0	-	0	.000	.000	.000
2000 Houston	NL	14	43	11	2	0	1	(0	1)	16	3	5	3	3	2	6	0	0	1	0	0	-	5	.256	.298	.372
2002 Houston	NL	2	4	1	1	0	0	(0	0)	2	1	0	1	1	0	0	0	0	0	0	0	-	0	.250	.500	.500
2003 Houston	NL	19	37	10	1	1	1	(0	1)	16	5	4	4	1	0	6	0	0	0	0	0	-	3	.270	.289	.432
2004 Houston	NL	64	162	34	8	0	0	(0	0)	42	9	23	10	10	3	38	1	4	0	0	1	.00	9	.210	.256	.259
7 ML YEARS		117	278	64	12	1	2	(0	2)	84	19	34	20	16	5	56	1	4	2	2	1	.67	18	.230	.273	.302

Bruce Chen

Pitches: L **Bats:** L **Pos:** SP-7; RP-1   **Ht:** 6'2" **Wt:** 210 **Born:** 6/19/1977 **Age:** 28

Year Team	Lg	G	GS	CG	GF	IP	BFP	H	R	ER	HR	SH	SF	HB	TBB	IBB	SO	WP	Bk	W	L	Pct	ShO	Sv-Op	Hld	ERC	ERA
2004 Syracuse*	AAA	3	3	0	0	10.1	54	17	12	10	4	1	1	0	5	1	8	0	0	0	1	.000	0	0- -	-	11.15	8.71
2004 Ottawa*	AAA	22	17	1	0	95.0	394	85	41	34	12	7	1	1	30	1	108	1	2	4	3	.571	1	0- -	-	3.37	3.22
1998 Atlanta	NL	4	4	0	0	20.1	91	23	9	9	3	1	0	1	9	1	17	0	0	2	0	1.000	0	0-0	0	5.55	3.98
1999 Atlanta	NL	16	7	0	3	51.0	214	38	32	31	11	1	1	2	27	3	45	0	0	2	2	.500	0	0-0	0	4.07	5.47
2000 Atl-Phi	NL	37	15	0	4	134.0	559	116	54	49	18	8	3	2	46	4	112	4	1	7	4	.636	0	0-0	0	3.35	3.29
2001 Phi-NYM	NL	27	27	0	0	146.0	634	146	90	79	29	4	7	1	59	4	126	5	0	7	7	.500	0	0-0	0	4.75	4.87
2002 NYM-Mon-Cin	NL	55	6	0	9	77.2	360	85	53	48	16	2	3	2	43	5	80	4	0	2	5	.286	0	0-0	4	5.99	5.56
2003 Hou-Bos	NL	16	2	0	4	24.1	110	26	16	15	6	3	3	2	10	1	20	0	0	0	1	.000	0	0-0	1	5.81	5.55
2004 Baltimore	AL	8	7	1	0	47.2	196	39	19	16	7	2	1	0	16	0	32	0	0	2	1	.667	0	0-0	0	3.13	3.02
2000 Atlanta	NL	22	0	0	4	39.2	176	35	15	11	4	3	2	1	19	2	32	0	1	4	0	1.000	0	0-0	0	3.62	2.50
2000 Philadelphia	NL	15	15	0	0	94.1	383	81	39	38	14	5	1	1	27	2	80	4	0	3	4	.429	0	0-0	0	3.22	3.63
2001 Philadelphia	NL	16	16	0	0	86.1	381	90	53	48	19	2	4	1	31	4	79	2	0	4	5	.444	0	0-0	0	4.87	5.00
2001 New York	NL	11	11	0	0	59.2	253	56	37	31	10	2	3	0	28	0	47	3	0	3	2	.600	0	0-0	0	4.58	4.68
2002 New York	NL	1	0	0	0	0.2	3	1	0	0	0	0	0	0	0	0	0	0	0	0	0	-	0	0-0	0	4.47	0.00
2002 Montreal	NL	15	5	0	4	37.1	179	47	29	29	9	0	0	1	23	3	43	3	0	2	3	.400	0	0-0	0	7.69	6.99
2002 Cincinnati	NL	39	1	0	5	39.2	178	37	24	19	7	2	3	1	20	2	37	1	0	0	2	.000	0	0-0	4	4.55	4.31
2003 Houston	NL	11	0	0	2	12.0	60	14	8	8	2	3	2	2	8	1	8	0	0	0	0	-	0	0-0	1	7.11	6.00
2003 Boston	AL	5	2	0	2	12.1	50	12	8	7	4	0	1	0	2	0	12	0	0	0	1	.000	0	0-0	0	4.40	5.11
7 ML YEARS		163	68	1	20	501.0	2164	473	273	247	90	21	18	10	210	18	432	13	1	22	20	.524	0	0-0	5	4.39	4.44

Chin-Feng Chen

Bats: R **Throws:** R **Pos:** PH-4; LF-3; PR-1   **Ht:** 6'1" **Wt:** 189 **Born:** 10/28/1977 **Age:** 27

Year Team	Lg	G	AB	H	2B	3B	HR	(Hm	Rd)	TB	R	RBI	RC	TBB	IBB	SO	HBP	SH	SF	SB	CS	SB%	GDP	Avg	OBP	Slg
2004 Las Vegas*	AAA	81	308	89	19	6	20	(-	-)	180	59	65	62	35	1	78	2	0	6	6	2	.75	4	.289	.359	.584
2002 Los Angeles	NL	3	5	0	0	0	0	(0	0)	0	1	0	0	1	0	3	0	0	0	0	0	-	0	.000	.167	.000
2003 Los Angeles	NL	1	1	0	0	0	0	(0	0)	0	0	0	0	0	0	0	0	0	0	0	0	-	0	.000	.000	.000
2004 Los Angeles	NL	8	8	0	0	0	0	(0	0)	0	1	0	0	2	0	3	0	0	0	0	0	-	1	.000	.200	.000
3 ML YEARS		12	14	0	0	0	0	(0	0)	0	2	0	0	3	0	6	0	0	0	0	0	-	1	.000	.176	.000

Randy Choate

Pitches: L **Bats:** L **Pos:** RP-74   **Ht:** 6'1" **Wt:** 180 **Born:** 9/5/1975 **Age:** 29

Year Team	Lg	G	GS	CG	GF	IP	BFP	H	R	ER	HR	SH	SF	HB	TBB	IBB	SO	WP	Bk	W	L	Pct	ShO	Sv-Op	Hld	ERC	ERA
2004 Tucson*	AAA	15	0	0	4	12.2	57	10	8	8	1	0	0	1	8	1	7	0	0	0	0	-	0	1- -	-	3.73	5.68
2000 New York	AL	22	0	0	6	17.0	75	14	10	9	3	0	1	1	8	0	12	1	0	0	1	.000	0	0-0	2	3.99	4.76
2001 New York	AL	37	0	0	13	48.1	207	34	21	18	0	2	1	9	27	2	35	3	0	3	1	.750	0	0-0	3	3.03	3.35
2002 New York	AL	18	0	0	11	22.1	101	18	18	15	1	0	0	3	15	0	17	4	0	0	0	-	0	0-0	0	4.13	6.04
2003 New York	AL	5	0	0	2	3.2	16	7	3	3	0	0	0	0	1	0	0	0	0	0	0	-	0	0-0	0	9.72	7.36
2004 Arizona	NL	74	0	0	17	50.2	232	52	26	26	1	0	4	5	28	11	49	1	1	2	4	.333	0	0-2	11	4.18	4.62
5 ML YEARS		156	0	0	49	142.0	631	125	78	71	5	2	6	18	79	13	113	9	1	5	6	.455	0	0-2	16	3.87	4.50

Hee Seop Choi

Bats: L **Throws:** L **Pos:** 1B-112; PH-15   **Ht:** 6'5" **Wt:** 235 **Born:** 3/16/1979 **Age:** 26

Year Team	Lg	G	AB	H	2B	3B	HR	(Hm	Rd)	TB	R	RBI	RC	TBB	IBB	SO	HBP	SH	SF	SB	CS	SB%	GDP	Avg	OBP	Slg
2002 Chicago	NL	24	50	9	1	0	2	(1	1)	16	6	4	2	7	0	15	0	0	0	0	0	-	2	.180	.281	.320
2003 Chicago	NL	80	202	44	17	0	8	(5	3)	85	31	28	28	37	1	71	4	2	0	1	1	.50	2	.218	.350	.421
2004 Fla-LA	NL	126	343	86	21	1	15	(8	7)	154	53	46	58	63	6	96	4	2	4	1	0	1.00	5	.251	.370	.449
2004 Florida	NL	95	281	76	16	1	15	(8	7)	139	48	40	54	52	4	78	3	2	2	1	0	1.00	3	.270	.388	.495
2004 Los Angeles	NL	31	62	10	5	0	0	(0	0)	15	5	6	4	11	2	18	1	0	2	0	0	-	2	.161	.289	.242
3 ML YEARS		230	595	139	39	1	25	(14	11)	255	90	78	88	107	7	182	8	4	4	2	1	.67	9	.234	.356	.429

Jason Christiansen

Pitches: L **Bats:** R **Pos:** RP-60   **Ht:** 6'5" **Wt:** 241 **Born:** 9/21/1969 **Age:** 35

		HOW MUCH HE PITCHED						WHAT HE GAVE UP										THE RESULTS						
Year Team	Lg	G	GS	CG	GF	IP	BFP	H	R	ER	HR	SH	SF	HB	TBB	IBB	SO	WP	Bk	W	L	Pct	ShO	Sv-Op	Hld	ERC	ERA
1995 Pittsburgh	NL	63	0	0	13	56.1	255	49	28	26	5	6	3	3	34	9	53	4	1	1	3	.250	0	0-4	12	3.89	4.15
1996 Pittsburgh	NL	33	0	0	9	44.1	205	56	34	33	7	2	3	1	19	2	38	4	1	3	3	.500	0	0-2	2	6.19	6.70
1997 Pittsburgh	NL	39	0	0	9	33.2	154	37	11	11	2	0	0	2	17	3	37	4	0	3	0	1.000	0	0-2	8	4.80	2.94
1998 Pittsburgh	NL	60	0	0	19	64.2	269	51	22	18	2	5	1	0	27	7	71	3	0	3	3	.500	0	6-10	15	2.39	2.51
1999 Pittsburgh	NL	39	0	0	17	37.2	158	26	17	17	2	2	1	2	22	4	35	0	0	2	3	.400	0	3-5	7	2.85	4.06
2000 Pit-StL	NL	65	0	0	19	48.0	210	41	29	27	3	4	1	2	27	5	53	3	0	3	8	.273	0	1-4	22	3.60	5.06
2001 StL-SF	NL	55	0	0	11	36.1	149	29	13	13	5	1	3	1	15	1	31	4	0	2	1	.667	0	3-4	11	3.41	3.22
2002 San Francisco	NL	6	0	0	2	5.0	21	6	3	3	1	0	0	0	2	0	1	0	0	1	0	1.000	0	0-0	6	6.48	5.40
2003 San Francisco	NL	40	0	0	7	26.0	115	25	15	15	3	0	0	1	11	0	22	2	0	0	0	-	0	0-1	7	4.11	5.19
2004 San Francisco	NL	60	0	0	11	36.0	167	34	20	18	3	0	2	3	26	1	22	3	0	4	3	.571	0	3-6	8	5.19	4.50
2000 Pittsburgh	NL	44	0	0	17	38.0	164	28	22	21	2	3	1	0	25	4	41	3	0	2	8	.200	0	1-3	13	3.11	4.97
2000 St Louis	NL	21	0	0	2	10.0	46	13	7	6	1	1	0	2	2	1	12	0	0	1	0	1.000	0	0-1	9	5.64	5.40
2001 St Louis	NL	30	0	0	8	19.1	83	15	10	10	4	0	1	1	10	1	19	0	0	1	1	.500	0	3-3	4	4.12	4.66
2001 San Francisco	NL	25	0	0	3	17.0	66	14	3	3	1	1	2	0	5	0	12	4	0	1	0	1.000	0	0-1	7	2.62	1.59
10 ML YEARS		460	0	0	117	388.0	1703	354	192	181	33	20	14	15	200	32	363	27	2	21	25	.457	0	16-38	92	3.92	4.20

Vinnie Chulk

Pitches: R **Bats:** R **Pos:** RP-47   **Ht:** 6'2" **Wt:** 185 **Born:** 12/19/1978 **Age:** 26

		HOW MUCH HE PITCHED						WHAT HE GAVE UP										THE RESULTS						
Year Team	Lg	G	GS	CG	GF	IP	BFP	H	R	ER	HR	SH	SF	HB	TBB	IBB	SO	WP	Bk	W	L	Pct	ShO	Sv-Op	Hld	ERC	ERA
2000 Medicine Hat	R+	14	13	0	0	68.2	295	75	36	29	5	0	2	2	20	0	51	3	0	2	4	.333	0	0- -	-	4.11	3.80
2001 Dunedin	A+	16	1	0	4	34.2	157	38	16	12	2	2	2	0	13	1	50	4	0	1	2	.333	0	1- -	-	4.00	3.12
2001 Tennessee	AA	24	1	0	7	43.0	169	34	15	15	5	5	4	2	8	1	43	1	0	2	5	.286	0	2- -	-	2.45	3.14
2001 Syracuse	AAA	5	0	0	2	6.0	25	5	1	0	1	0	0	0	4	0	3	3	0	1	0	1.000	0	0- -	-	4.98	0.00
2002 Tennessee	AA	25	24	0	1	152.0	626	133	55	50	12	3	2	5	53	0	108	6	0	13	5	.722	0	1- -	-	3.24	2.96
2002 Syracuse	AAA	2	1	0	1	4.2	27	6	6	3	0	0	0	0	6	0	2	2	0	0	1	.000	0	0- -	-	8.06	5.79
2003 Syracuse	AAA	23	21	1	1	119.1	524	118	70	56	14	6	6	5	46	0	90	5	0	8	10	.444	0	0- -	-	4.17	4.22
2004 Syracuse	AAA	18	0	0	11	28.2	129	27	13	9	5	0	2	1	11	2	26	0	0	4	2	.667	0	3- -	-	3.99	2.83
2003 Toronto	AL	3	0	0	2	5.1	25	6	3	3	0	0	0	0	3	0	2	0	0	0	0	-	0	0-1	0	4.53	5.06
2004 Toronto	AL	47	0	0	10	56.0	248	59	30	29	6	1	1	1	27	1	44	2	0	1	3	.250	0	2-5	13	4.83	4.66
2 ML YEARS		50	0	0	12	61.1	273	65	33	32	6	1	1	1	30	1	46	2	0	1	3	.250	0	2-6	13	4.81	4.70

Ryan Church

Bats: L **Throws:** L **Pos:** PH-14; LF-12; RF-6; CF-2; PR-1   **Ht:** 6'1" **Wt:** 190 **Born:** 10/14/1978 **Age:** 26

Year Team	Lg	G	AB	H	2B	3B	HR	(Hm	Rd)	TB	R	RBI	RC	TBB	IBB	SO	HBP	SH	SF	SB	CS	SB%	GDP	Avg	OBP	Slg
2000 Mahning VI	A-	73	272	81	16	5	10	(-	-)	137	51	65	54	38	3	49	8	0	3	11	4	.73	4	.298	.396	.504
2001 Columbus	A	101	363	104	23	3	17	(-	-)	184	64	76	68	54	0	79	6	0	3	4	6	.40	6	.287	.385	.507
2001 Kinston	A+	24	83	20	7	0	5	(-	-)	42	16	15	16	18	2	23	1	0	1	1	0	1.00	1	.241	.379	.506
2002 Kinston	A+	53	181	59	12	1	10	(-	-)	103	30	30	41	31	6	51	4	0	1	4	4	.50	3	.326	.433	.569
2002 Akron	AA	71	291	86	17	4	12	(-	-)	147	39	51	44	12	2	58	2	0	3	1	0	1.00	8	.296	.325	.505
2003 Akron	AA	99	371	97	17	3	13	(-	-)	159	47	52	46	32	1	64	4	0	2	4	3	.57	17	.261	.325	.429
2004 Edmonton	AAA	98	347	119	29	8	17	(-	-)	215	74	78	85	51	7	62	4	1	5	0	1	.00	4	.343	.428	.620
2004 Montreal	NL	30	63	11	1	0	1	(0	1)	15	6	6	2	7	1	16	0	1	0	0	0	-	3	.175	.257	.238

Alex Cintron

Bats: B **Throws:** R **Pos:** SS-133; 2B-19; PH-7; 3B-1   **Ht:** 6'2" **Wt:** 185 **Born:** 12/17/1978 **Age:** 26

Year Team	Lg	G	AB	H	2B	3B	HR	(Hm	Rd)	TB	R	RBI	RC	TBB	IBB	SO	HBP	SH	SF	SB	CS	SB%	GDP	Avg	OBP	Slg
2001 Arizona	NL	8	7	2	0	1	0	(0	0)	4	0	0	1	0	0	0	0	0	0	0	0	-	0	.286	.286	.571
2002 Arizona	NL	38	75	16	0	0	0	(0	0)	22	11	4	5	12	2	13	0	3	0	0	0	-	2	.213	.322	.293
2003 Arizona	NL	117	448	142	26	6	13	(6	7)	219	70	51	70	29	0	33	2	5	3	2	3	.40	7	.317	.359	.489
2004 Arizona	NL	154	564	148	31	7	4	(1	3)	205	56	49	59	31	2	59	2	12	4	3	3	.50	11	.262	.301	.363
4 ML YEARS		317	1094	308	63	14	17	(7	10)	450	137	104	135	72	4	105	4	20	7	5	6	.45	20	.282	.326	.411

Jeff Cirillo

Bats: R **Throws:** R **Pos:** 3B-11; PH-11; 1B-10; 2B-4; PR-2; LF-1   **Ht:** 6'1" **Wt:** 190 **Born:** 9/23/1969 **Age:** 35

Year Team	Lg	G	AB	H	2B	3B	HR	(Hm	Rd)	TB	R	RBI	RC	TBB	IBB	SO	HBP	SH	SF	SB	CS	SB%	GDP	Avg	OBP	Slg
2004 Portland*	AAA	7	23	8	3	0	0	(-	-)	11	3	2	5	5	0	1	0	1	0	1	0	1.00	1	.348	.464	.478
1994 Milwaukee	AL	39	126	30	9	0	3	(1	2)	48	17	12	14	11	0	16	2	0	0	1	0	1.00	5	.238	.309	.381
1995 Milwaukee	AL	125	328	91	19	4	9	(6	3)	145	57	39	55	47	0	42	4	1	4	7	2	.78	8	.277	.371	.442
1996 Milwaukee	AL	158	566	184	46	5	15	(6	9)	285	101	83	105	58	0	69	7	6	6	4	9	.31	14	.325	.391	.504
1997 Milwaukee	AL	154	580	167	46	2	10	(6	4)	247	74	82	91	60	0	74	14	4	3	4	3	.57	13	.288	.367	.426

Year Team	Lg	G	AB	H	2B	3B	HR	(Hm	Rd)	TB	R	RBI	RC	TBB	IBB	SO	HBP	SH	SF	SB	CS	SB%	GDP	Avg	OBP	Slg
1998 Milwaukee	NL	156	604	194	31	1	14	(6	8)	269	97	68	103	79	3	88	4	5	2	10	4	.71	26	.321	.402	.445
1999 Milwaukee	NL	157	607	198	35	1	15	(6	9)	280	98	88	111	75	4	83	5	3	7	7	4	.64	15	.326	.401	.461
2000 Colorado	NL	157	598	195	53	2	11	(9	2)	285	111	115	108	67	4	72	6	1	12	3	4	.43	19	.326	.392	.477
2001 Colorado	NL	138	528	165	26	4	17	(9	8)	253	72	83	89	43	6	63	5	1	9	12	2	.86	15	.313	.364	.473
2002 Seattle	AL	146	485	121	20	0	6	(2	4)	159	51	54	52	31	0	67	9	13	9	8	4	.67	12	.249	.301	.328
2003 Seattle	AL	87	258	53	11	0	2	(1	1)	70	24	23	23	24	1	32	5	4	2	1	1	.50	6	.205	.284	.271
2004 San Diego	NL	33	75	16	3	0	1	(0	1)	22	12	7	6	5	0	14	0	0	1	0	0	-	0	.213	.259	.293
11 ML YEARS		1350	4755	1414	299	19	103	(52	51)	2060	714	654	757	500	18	620	61	38	55	56	34	.62	132	.297	.368	.433

Brady Clark
Bats: R Throws: R Pos: RF-123; PH-25; CF-9; PR-8; LF-3   Ht: 6'2" Wt: 195 Born: 4/18/1973 Age: 32

Year Team	Lg	G	AB	H	2B	3B	HR	(Hm	Rd)	TB	R	RBI	RC	TBB	IBB	SO	HBP	SH	SF	SB	CS	SB%	GDP	Avg	OBP	Slg
2000 Cincinnati	NL	11	11	3	1	0	0	(0	0)	4	1	2	1	0	0	2	0	0	0	0	0	-	0	.273	.273	.364
2001 Cincinnati	NL	89	129	34	3	0	6	(4	2)	55	22	18	21	22	1	16	1	4	1	4	1	.80	6	.264	.373	.426
2002 Cin-NYM	NL	61	78	15	4	0	0	(0	0)	19	9	10	7	7	2	11	1	1	0	1	2	.33	2	.192	.267	.244
2003 Milwaukee	NL	128	315	86	21	1	6	(5	1)	127	33	40	40	21	0	40	9	2	7	13	2	.87	12	.273	.330	.403
2004 Milwaukee	NL	138	353	99	18	1	7	(1	6)	140	41	46	56	53	2	48	9	1	3	15	8	.65	9	.280	.385	.397
2002 Cincinnati	NL	51	66	10	3	0	0	(0	0)	13	6	9	5	6	2	9	1	1	0	1	2	.33	2	.152	.233	.197
2002 New York	NL	10	12	5	1	0	0	(0	0)	6	3	1	2	1	0	2	0	0	0	0	0	-	0	.417	.462	.500
5 ML YEARS		427	886	237	47	2	19	(10	9)	345	106	116	125	103	5	117	20	8	11	33	13	.72	29	.267	.353	.389

Howie Clark
Bats: L Throws: R Pos: 1B-11; RF-11; LF-9; PH-6; DH-4; PR-2; 2B-1; 3B-1   Ht: 5'11" Wt: 180 Born: 2/13/1974 Age: 31

Year Team	Lg	G	AB	H	2B	3B	HR	(Hm	Rd)	TB	R	RBI	RC	TBB	IBB	SO	HBP	SH	SF	SB	CS	SB%	GDP	Avg	OBP	Slg
2004 Syracuse*	AAA	72	256	80	14	2	6	(-	-)	116	43	32	50	40	2	18	3	3	3	1	0	1.00	3	.313	.407	.453
2002 Baltimore	AL	14	53	16	5	0	0	(0	0)	21	3	4	3	3	0	6	2	0	0	0	0	-	5	.302	.362	.396
2003 Toronto	AL	38	70	25	3	1	0	(0	0)	30	9	7	13	3	0	6	2	2	0	0	1	.00	3	.357	.400	.429
2004 Toronto	AL	40	115	25	6	0	3	(3	0)	40	17	12	11	13	0	15	0	3	2	0	0	-	2	.217	.292	.348
3 ML YEARS		92	238	66	14	1	3	(3	0)	91	29	23	27	19	0	27	4	5	2	0	1	.00	10	.277	.338	.382

Jermaine Clark
Bats: L Throws: R Pos: RF-6; PH-5; 2B-2; LF-1; CF-1; PR-1   Ht: 5'10" Wt: 175 Born: 9/29/1976 Age: 28

Year Team	Lg	G	AB	H	2B	3B	HR	(Hm	Rd)	TB	R	RBI	RC	TBB	IBB	SO	HBP	SH	SF	SB	CS	SB%	GDP	Avg	OBP	Slg
2004 Louisville*	AAA	115	398	113	15	5	10	(-	-)	168	77	52	71	63	0	54	7	4	6	24	9	.73	4	.284	.386	.422
2001 Detroit	AL	3	0	0	0	0	0	(0	0)	0	1	0	0	0	0	0	0	0	0	0	0	-	0	-	-	-
2003 Tex-SD		25	48	8	2	0	0	(0	0)	10	2	7	5	6	0	5	0	1	2	2	2	.50	1	.167	.250	.208
2004 Cincinnati	NL	14	30	4	1	0	0	(0	0)	5	4	2	2	1	0	8	2	0	1	1	0	1.00	0	.133	.212	.167
2003 Texas	AL	24	46	8	2	0	0	(0	0)	10	2	6	5	6	0	4	0	1	1	2	1	.67	1	.174	.264	.217
2003 San Diego	NL	1	2	0	0	0	0	(0	0)	0	0	1	0	0	0	1	0	0	1	0	1	.00	0	.000	.000	.000
3 ML YEARS		42	78	12	3	0	0	(0	0)	15	7	9	7	7	0	13	2	2	2	3	2	.60	1	.154	.236	.192

Tony Clark
Bats: B Throws: R Pos: 1B-99; PH-10; DH-1; PR-1   Ht: 6'7" Wt: 245 Born: 6/15/1972 Age: 33

Year Team	Lg	G	AB	H	2B	3B	HR	(Hm	Rd)	TB	R	RBI	RC	TBB	IBB	SO	HBP	SH	SF	SB	CS	SB%	GDP	Avg	OBP	Slg
1995 Detroit	AL	27	101	24	5	1	3	(0	3)	40	10	11	11	8	0	30	0	0	0	0	0	-	2	.238	.294	.396
1996 Detroit	AL	100	376	94	14	0	27	(17	10)	189	56	72	55	29	1	127	0	0	6	0	1	.00	7	.250	.299	.503
1997 Detroit	AL	159	580	160	28	3	32	(18	14)	290	105	117	107	93	13	144	3	0	5	1	3	.25	11	.276	.376	.500
1998 Detroit	AL	157	602	175	37	0	34	(18	16)	314	84	103	107	63	5	128	3	0	3	3	3	.50	16	.291	.358	.522
1999 Detroit	AL	143	536	150	29	0	31	(12	19)	272	74	99	94	64	7	133	6	0	3	2	1	.67	14	.280	.361	.507
2000 Detroit	AL	60	208	57	14	0	13	(6	7)	110	32	37	35	24	2	51	0	0	0	0	0	-	10	.274	.349	.529
2001 Detroit	AL	126	428	123	29	3	16	(7	9)	206	67	75	74	62	10	108	1	0	6	0	1	.00	14	.287	.374	.481
2002 Boston	AL	90	275	57	12	1	3	(1	2)	80	25	29	19	21	0	57	1	0	1	0	0	-	11	.207	.265	.291
2003 New York	NL	125	254	59	13	0	16	(9	7)	120	29	43	29	24	2	73	1	0	1	0	0	-	8	.232	.300	.472
2004 New York	AL	106	253	56	12	0	16	(5	11)	116	37	49	37	26	3	92	2	0	2	0	0	-	6	.221	.297	.458
10 ML YEARS		1093	3613	955	193	8	191	(93	98)	1737	519	635	568	414	43	943	17	0	29	6	9	.40	99	.264	.340	.481

Brandon Claussen
Pitches: L Bats: R Pos: SP-14   Ht: 6'2" Wt: 175 Born: 5/1/1979 Age: 26

Year Team	Lg	G	GS	CG	GF	IP	BFP	H	R	ER	HR	SH	SF	HB	TBB	IBB	SO	WP	Bk	W	L	Pct	ShO	Sv-Op	Hld	ERC	ERA
1999 Yankees	R	2	2	0	0	11.1	42	7	4	4	2	0	0	0	2	0	16	0	0	0	1	.000	0	0--	-	1.79	3.18
1999 Staten Island	A-	12	12	1	0	72.0	295	70	30	27	4	3	0	3	12	2	89	4	4	6	4	.600	0	0--	-	2.87	3.38
1999 Greensboro	A	1	1	1	0	6.0	29	8	7	7	1	0	0	0	2	0	5	1	1	0	1	.000	0	0--	-	5.90	10.50
2000 Greensboro	A	17	17	1	0	97.2	416	91	49	44	9	4	4	1	44	0	98	3	0	8	5	.615	0	0--	-	3.92	4.05
2000 Tampa	A+	9	9	1	0	52.1	220	49	24	18	1	1	0	2	17	0	44	2	1	2	5	.286	1	0--	-	3.04	3.10
2001 Tampa	A+	8	8	0	0	56.0	227	47	21	17	2	2	2	0	13	0	69	1	2	5	2	.714	0	0--	-	2.19	2.73
2001 Norwich	AA	21	21	1	0	131.0	554	101	43	31	6	7	6	5	55	0	151	5	3	9	2	.818	1	0--	-	2.66	2.13
2002 Columbus	AAA	15	15	0	0	93.1	408	85	47	34	4	7	3	1	46	3	73	2	0	2	8	.200	0	0--	-	3.48	3.28
2003 Columbus	AAA	11	11	1	0	68.2	275	53	28	21	4	1	6	1	18	0	39	0	2	2	1	.667	0	0--	-	2.17	2.75
2003 Louisville	AAA	3	3	0	0	15.2	65	17	13	13	1	0	1	0	6	0	16	0	0	1	0	1.000	0	0--	-	5.47	7.47
2003 Tampa	A+	4	4	0	0	22.0	86	16	5	4	0	0	2	0	3	0	26	0	1	2	0	1.000	0	0--	-	1.33	1.64
2004 Louisville	AAA	18	18	0	0	100.1	437	98	56	52	10	3	6	5	47	0	111	1	1	8	6	.571	0	0--	-	4.46	4.66

Year Team	Lg	G	GS	CG	GF	IP	BFP	H	R	ER	HR	SH	SF	HB	TBB	IBB	SO	WP	Bk	W	L	Pct	ShO	Sv-Op	Hld	ERC	ERA
2003 New York	AL	1	1	0	0	6.1	28	8	2	1	1	0	0	0	1	0	5	0	0	1	0	1.000	0	0-0	0	4.89	1.42
2004 Cincinnati	NL	14	14	0	0	66.0	313	80	50	45	9	5	3	2	35	2	45	3	0	2	8	.200	0	0-0	0	6.11	6.14
2 ML YEARS		15	15	0	0	72.1	341	88	52	46	10	5	3	2	36	2	50	3	0	3	8	.273	0	0-0	0	6.01	5.72

Royce Clayton

Bats: R **Throws:** R **Pos:** SS-144; PH-3; PR-1 **Ht:** 6'0" **Wt:** 185 **Born:** 1/2/1970 **Age:** 35

													BATTING								BASERUNNING				AVERAGES		
Year Team	Lg	G	AB	H	2B	3B	HR	(Hm	Rd)	TB	R	RBI	RC	TBB	IBB	SO	HBP	SH	SF	SB	CS	SB%	GDP	Avg	OBP	Slg
1991 San Francisco	NL	9	26	3	1	0	0	(0	0)	4	0	2	0	1	0	6	0	0	0	0	0	-	1	.115	.148	.154
1992 San Francisco	NL	98	321	72	7	4	4	(3	1)	99	31	24	25	26	3	63	0	3	2	8	4	.67	11	.224	.281	.308
1993 San Francisco	NL	153	549	155	21	5	6	(5	1)	204	54	70	64	38	2	91	5	8	7	11	10	.52	16	.282	.331	.372
1994 San Francisco	NL	108	385	91	14	6	3	(1	2)	126	38	30	40	30	2	74	3	3	2	23	3	.88	7	.236	.295	.327
1995 San Francisco	NL	138	509	124	29	3	5	(2	3)	174	56	58	53	38	1	109	3	4	3	24	9	.73	7	.244	.298	.342
1996 St Louis	NL	129	491	136	20	4	6	(6	0)	182	64	35	56	33	4	89	1	2	4	33	15	.69	13	.277	.321	.371
1997 St Louis	NL	154	576	153	39	5	9	(5	4)	229	75	61	67	33	4	109	3	2	5	30	10	.75	19	.266	.306	.398
1998 StL-Tex		142	541	136	31	2	9	(2	7)	198	89	53	62	53	1	83	3	6	5	24	11	.69	16	.251	.319	.366
1999 Texas	AL	133	465	134	21	5	14	(6	8)	207	69	52	71	39	1	100	4	9	3	8	6	.57	6	.288	.346	.445
2000 Texas	AL	148	513	124	21	5	14	(9	5)	197	70	54	54	42	1	92	3	12	3	11	7	.61	21	.242	.301	.384
2001 Chicago	AL	135	433	114	21	4	9	(6	3)	170	62	60	50	33	2	72	3	9	7	10	7	.59	16	.263	.315	.393
2002 Chicago	AL	112	342	86	14	2	7	(4	3)	125	51	35	37	20	0	67	3	7	4	5	1	.83	7	.251	.295	.365
2003 Milwaukee	NL	146	483	110	16	1	11	(5	6)	161	49	39	37	49	10	92	3	4	4	5	2	.71	25	.228	.301	.333
2004 Colorado	NL	146	574	160	36	4	8	(6	2)	228	95	54	75	48	0	125	4	4	24	10	5	.67	13	.279	.338	.397
1998 St Louis	NL	90	355	83	19	1	4	(1	3)	116	59	29	37	40	1	51	2	3	2	19	6	.76	10	.234	.313	.327
1998 Texas	AL	52	186	53	12	1	5	(1	4)	82	30	24	25	13	0	32	1	3	3	5	5	.50	6	.285	.330	.441
14 ML YEARS		1751	6208	1598	291	50	105	(60	45)	2304	803	627	691	483	31	1172	38	93	51	202	90	.69	178	.257	.313	.371

Roger Clemens

Pitches: R **Bats:** R **Pos:** SP-33 **Ht:** 6'4" **Wt:** 235 **Born:** 8/4/1962 **Age:** 42

		HOW MUCH HE PITCHED						WHAT HE GAVE UP												THE RESULTS							
Year Team	Lg	G	GS	CG	GF	IP	BFP	H	R	ER	HR	SH	SF	HB	TBB	IBB	SO	WP	Bk	W	L	Pct	ShO	Sv-Op	Hld	ERC	ERA
1984 Boston	AL	21	20	5	0	133.1	575	146	67	64	13	2	3	2	29	3	126	4	0	9	4	.692	1	0-0	0	3.81	4.32
1985 Boston	AL	15	15	3	0	98.1	407	83	38	36	5	1	2	3	37	0	74	1	3	7	5	.583	1	0-0	0	2.96	3.29
1986 Boston	AL	33	33	10	0	254.0	997	179	77	70	21	4	6	4	67	0	238	11	3	24	4	.857	1	0-0	0	2.03	2.48
1987 Boston	AL	36	36	18	0	281.2	1157	248	100	93	19	6	4	9	83	4	256	4	0	20	9	.690	7	0-0	0	2.94	2.97
1988 Boston	AL	35	35	14	0	264.0	1063	217	93	86	17	6	3	6	62	4	291	4	7	18	12	.600	8	0-0	0	2.36	2.93
1989 Boston	AL	35	35	8	0	253.1	1044	215	101	88	20	9	5	8	93	5	230	7	0	17	11	.607	3	0-0	0	3.13	3.13
1990 Boston	AL	31	31	7	0	228.1	920	193	59	49	7	7	5	7	54	3	209	8	0	21	6	.778	4	0-0	0	2.33	1.93
1991 Boston	AL	35	35	13	0	271.1	1077	219	93	79	15	6	8	5	65	12	241	6	0	18	10	.643	4	0-0	0	2.23	2.62
1992 Boston	AL	32	32	11	0	246.2	989	203	80	66	11	5	5	9	62	5	208	3	0	18	11	.621	5	0-0	0	2.38	2.41
1993 Boston	AL	29	29	2	0	191.2	808	175	99	95	17	5	7	11	67	4	160	3	1	11	14	.440	1	0-0	0	3.53	4.46
1994 Boston	AL	24	24	3	0	170.2	692	124	62	54	15	2	5	4	71	1	168	4	0	9	7	.563	1	0-0	0	2.72	2.85
1995 Boston	AL	23	23	0	0	140.0	623	141	70	65	15	2	3	14	60	0	132	9	0	10	5	.667	0	0-0	0	4.67	4.18
1996 Boston	AL	34	34	6	0	242.2	1032	216	106	98	19	4	7	4	106	2	257	8	1	10	13	.435	2	0-0	0	3.52	3.63
1997 Toronto	AL	34	34	9	0	264.0	1044	204	65	60	9	5	2	12	68	1	292	4	0	21	7	.750	3	0-0	0	2.17	2.05
1998 Toronto	AL	33	33	5	0	234.2	961	169	78	69	11	8	2	7	88	0	271	6	0	20	6	.769	3	0-0	0	2.27	2.65
1999 New York	AL	30	30	1	0	187.2	822	185	101	96	20	10	5	9	90	0	163	8	0	14	10	.583	1	0-0	0	4.59	4.60
2000 New York	AL	32	32	1	0	204.1	878	184	96	84	26	1	2	10	84	0	188	2	1	13	8	.619	0	0-0	0	3.93	3.70
2001 New York	AL	33	33	0	0	220.1	918	205	94	86	19	4	4	5	72	1	213	14	0	20	3	.870	0	0-0	0	3.43	3.51
2002 New York	AL	29	29	0	0	180.0	768	172	94	87	18	5	5	7	63	6	192	14	0	13	6	.684	0	0-0	0	3.72	4.35
2003 New York	AL	33	33	1	0	211.2	878	199	99	92	24	3	6	5	58	1	190	5	0	17	9	.654	1	0-0	0	3.44	3.91
2004 Houston	NL	33	33	0	0	214.1	878	169	76	71	15	8	7	6	79	5	218	5	0	18	4	.818	0	0-0	0	2.72	2.98
21 ML YEARS		640	639	117	0	4493.0	18531	3846	1748	1588	336	103	96	147	1458	57	4317	130	19	328	164	.667	46	0-0	0	2.97	3.18

Matt Clement

Pitches: R **Bats:** R **Pos:** SP-30 **Ht:** 6'3" **Wt:** 213 **Born:** 8/12/1974 **Age:** 30

		HOW MUCH HE PITCHED						WHAT HE GAVE UP												THE RESULTS							
Year Team	Lg	G	GS	CG	GF	IP	BFP	H	R	ER	HR	SH	SF	HB	TBB	IBB	SO	WP	Bk	W	L	Pct	ShO	Sv-Op	Hld	ERC	ERA
1998 San Diego	NL	4	2	0	0	13.2	62	15	8	7	0	2	0	0	7	1	13	2	0	1	0	1.000	0	0-0	0	4.14	4.61
1999 San Diego	NL	31	31	0	0	180.2	803	190	106	90	18	7	6	9	86	2	135	11	0	10	12	.455	0	0-0	0	4.89	4.48
2000 San Diego	NL	34	34	0	0	205.0	940	194	131	117	22	12	5	16	125	4	170	23	0	13	17	.433	0	0-0	0	4.87	5.14
2001 Florida	NL	31	31	0	0	169.1	760	172	102	95	15	14	3	15	85	2	134	15	0	9	10	.474	0	0-0	0	4.84	5.05
2002 Chicago	NL	32	32	3	0	205.0	858	162	84	82	18	11	4	6	85	7	215	7	0	12	11	.522	2	0-0	0	2.96	3.60
2003 Chicago	NL	32	32	2	0	201.2	851	169	100	92	22	10	2	14	79	2	171	13	0	14	12	.538	1	0-0	0	3.47	4.11
2004 Chicago	NL	30	30	0	0	181.0	775	155	79	74	23	5	4	12	77	4	190	14	1	9	13	.409	0	0-0	0	3.78	3.68
7 ML YEARS		194	192	5	0	1156.1	5049	1057	610	557	118	61	24	72	544	22	1028	85	1	69	75	.479	3	0-0	0	4.09	4.34

J.D. Closser

Bats: B **Throws:** R **Pos:** C-32; PH-6 **Ht:** 5'10" **Wt:** 176 **Born:** 1/15/1980 **Age:** 25

													BATTING								BASERUNNING				AVERAGES		
Year Team	Lg	G	AB	H	2B	3B	HR	(Hm	Rd)	TB	R	RBI	RC	TBB	IBB	SO	HBP	SH	SF	SB	CS	SB%	GDP	Avg	OBP	Slg
1998 Diamndbcks	R	45	150	47	13	2	4	(-	-)	76	26	21	34	37	2	36	2	0	1	3	2	.60	3	.313	.453	.507
1998 South Bend	A	4	14	3	1	0	0	(-	-)	4	3	2	1	2	0	7	0	1	0	0	0	-	0	.214	.313	.286
1999 South Bend	A	52	174	42	8	0	3	(-	-)	59	29	27	24	34	0	37	1	0	3	0	1	.00	3	.241	.363	.339
1999 Missoula	R+	76	275	89	22	0	10	(-	-)	141	73	54	66	71	2	57	2	1	6	9	3	.75	8	.324	.458	.513
2000 South Bend	A	101	331	74	19	1	8	(-	-)	119	54	37	44	60	4	61	3	1	1	6	2	.75	7	.224	.347	.360
2001 Lancaster	A+	128	468	136	26	6	21	(-	-)	237	85	87	85	65	4	106	2	1	4	6	7	.46	9	.291	.377	.506
2002 Carolina	AA	95	315	89	27	1	13	(-	-)	157	43	62	55	44	4	69	0	0	1	9	3	.75	7	.283	.369	.498
2003 Tulsa	AA	118	410	116	28	5	13	(-	-)	193	62	54	66	47	3	79	3	0	3	3	2	.60	10	.283	.359	.471
2004 Co Springs	AAA	83	298	89	19	1	7	(-	-)	131	53	54	52	41	0	47	2	4	3	2	0	.00	3	.299	.384	.440
2004 Colorado	NL	36	113	36	6	0	1	(0	1)	45	5	10	15	6	0	22	2	3	0	0	1	-	3	.319	.364	.398

Greg Colbrunn

Bats: R **Throws:** R **Pos:** PH-16; 1B-2; DH-2   **Ht:** 6'0" **Wt:** 212 **Born:** 7/26/1969 **Age:** 35

Year Team	Lg	G	AB	H	2B	3B	HR	(Hm	Rd)	TB	R	RBI	RC	TBB	IBB	SO	HBP	SH	SF	SB	CS	SB%	GDP	Avg	OBP	Slg
2004 Tucson*	AAA	3	10	3	1	0	1	(-	-)	7	1	5	1	0	0	2	0	0	0	0	0	-	0	.300	.300	.700
1992 Montreal	NL	52	168	45	8	0	2	(1	1)	59	12	18	18	6	1	34	2	0	4	3	2	.60	1	.268	.294	.351
1993 Montreal	NL	70	153	39	9	0	4	(2	2)	60	15	23	17	6	1	33	1	1	3	4	2	.67	1	.255	.282	.392
1994 Florida	NL	47	155	47	10	0	6	(3	3)	75	17	31	25	9	0	27	2	0	2	1	1	.50	3	.303	.345	.484
1995 Florida	NL	138	528	146	22	1	23	(12	11)	239	70	89	71	22	4	69	6	0	4	11	3	.79	15	.277	.311	.453
1996 Florida	NL	141	511	146	26	2	16	(7	9)	224	60	69	68	25	1	76	14	0	5	4	5	.44	22	.286	.333	.438
1997 Min-Atl		98	271	76	17	0	7	(3	4)	114	27	35	32	10	1	49	2	1	2	1	2	.33	8	.280	.309	.421
1998 Col-Atl	NL	90	166	51	11	2	3	(1	2)	75	18	23	26	10	0	34	4	0	0	4	3	.57	1	.307	.361	.452
1999 Arizona	NL	67	135	44	5	3	5	(2	3)	70	20	24	26	12	0	23	4	0	2	1	1	.50	3	.326	.392	.519
2000 Arizona	NL	116	329	103	22	1	15	(6	9)	172	48	57	66	43	2	45	10	0	3	0	1	.00	13	.313	.405	.523
2001 Arizona	NL	59	97	28	8	0	4	(4	0)	48	12	18	16	9	0	14	4	0	0	0	0	-	5	.289	.373	.495
2002 Arizona	NL	72	171	57	16	2	10	(3	7)	107	30	27	33	13	1	19	0	0	1	0	0	-	5	.333	.378	.626
2003 Seattle	AL	22	58	16	1	1	3	(1	2)	28	7	7	6	4	0	16	0	0	0	0	1	.00	3	.276	.323	.483
2004 Arizona	NL	20	27	3	0	0	0	(0	0)	3	1	1	1	1	0	5	0	0	0	0	0	-	0	.111	.143	.111
1997 Minnesota	AL	70	217	61	14	0	5	(2	3)	90	24	26	25	8	1	38	1	0	2	1	2	.33	7	.281	.307	.415
1997 Atlanta	NL	28	54	15	3	0	2	(1	1)	24	3	9	7	2	0	11	1	1	0	0	0	-	1	.278	.316	.444
1998 Colorado	NL	62	122	38	8	2	2	(1	1)	56	12	13	19	8	0	23	1	0	0	3	3	.50	1	.311	.359	.459
1998 Atlanta	NL	28	44	13	3	0	1	(0	1)	19	6	10	7	2	0	11	3	0	0	1	0	1.00	0	.295	.367	.432
13 ML YEARS		992	2769	801	155	12	98	(45	53)	1274	337	422	405	170	11	444	49	2	26	29	21	.58	80	.289	.338	.460

Lou Collier

Bats: R **Throws:** R **Pos:** PH-22; LF-8; PR-3; 3B-1   **Ht:** 5'10" **Wt:** 191 **Born:** 8/21/1973 **Age:** 31

Year Team	Lg	G	AB	H	2B	3B	HR	(Hm	Rd)	TB	R	RBI	RC	TBB	IBB	SO	HBP	SH	SF	SB	CS	SB%	GDP	Avg	OBP	Slg
2004 Scrtn/WlksBr*	AAA	101	387	126	26	3	14	(-	-)	200	62	66	73	34	1	82	4	0	3	14	3	.82	8	.326	.383	.517
1997 Pittsburgh	NL	18	37	5	0	0	0	(0	0)	5	3	3	0	1	0	11	0	0	1	1	0	1.00	1	.135	.158	.135
1998 Pittsburgh	NL	110	334	82	13	6	2	(1	1)	113	30	34	35	31	6	70	6	3	5	2	2	.50	8	.246	.316	.338
1999 Milwaukee	NL	74	135	35	9	0	2	(2	0)	50	18	21	17	14	0	32	0	1	2	3	2	.60	2	.259	.325	.370
2000 Milwaukee	NL	14	32	7	1	0	1	(0	1)	11	9	2	4	6	0	4	0	0	1	0	0	-	1	.219	.333	.344
2001 Milwaukee	NL	50	127	32	8	1	2	(1	1)	48	19	14	19	17	0	30	1	1	2	5	1	.83	0	.252	.340	.378
2002 Montreal	NL	13	11	1	1	0	0	(0	0)	2	3	0	0	1	1	3	1	1	0	0	0	-	0	.091	.231	.182
2003 Boston	AL	4	1	0	0	0	0	(0	0)	0	0	0	0	0	0	0	0	0	0	0	0	-	0	.000	.000	.000
2004 Philadelphia	NL	32	36	10	1	0	1	(1	0)	14	7	4	6	5	0	10	1	0	0	1	0	1.00	0	.278	.381	.389
8 ML YEARS		315	713	172	33	7	8	(5	3)	243	89	78	81	75	7	160	9	6	10	12	6	.67	14	.241	.317	.341

Jesus Colome

Pitches: R **Bats:** R **Pos:** RP-33   **Ht:** 6'4" **Wt:** 205 **Born:** 12/23/1977 **Age:** 27

Year Team	Lg	G	GS	CG	GF	IP	BFP	H	R	ER	HR	SH	SF	HB	TBB	IBB	SO	WP	Bk	W	L	Pct	ShO	Sv-Op	Hld	ERC	ERA
2004 Durham*	AAA	18	0	0	7	30.2	134	27	12	12	0	2	0	1	16	0	17	3	0	2	1	.667	0	2- -	-	3.26	3.52
2001 Tampa Bay	AL	30	0	0	9	48.2	209	37	24	22	8	2	2	2	25	4	31	2	0	2	3	.400	0	0-0	6	3.62	3.33
2002 Tampa Bay	AL	32	0	0	15	41.1	205	56	41	38	6	4	1	2	33	5	33	5	0	2	7	.222	0	0-5	3	8.53	8.27
2003 Tampa Bay	AL	54	0	0	24	74.0	334	69	37	37	9	2	4	3	46	5	69	7	0	3	7	.300	0	2-8	11	4.76	4.50
2004 Tampa Bay	AL	33	0	0	9	41.1	169	28	16	15	4	5	0	1	18	1	40	1	1	2	2	.500	0	3-4	8	2.54	3.27
4 ML YEARS		149	0	0	57	205.1	917	190	116	108	27	13	7	8	122	15	173	15	1	9	19	.321	0	5-17	28	4.68	4.73

Bartolo Colon

Pitches: R **Bats:** R **Pos:** SP-34   **Ht:** 6'0" **Wt:** 235 **Born:** 5/24/1973 **Age:** 32

Year Team	Lg	G	GS	CG	GF	IP	BFP	H	R	ER	HR	SH	SF	HB	TBB	IBB	SO	WP	Bk	W	L	Pct	ShO	Sv-Op	Hld	ERC	ERA
1997 Cleveland	AL	19	17	1	0	94.0	427	107	66	59	12	4	1	3	45	1	66	5	0	4	7	.364	0	0-0	0	5.53	5.65
1998 Cleveland	AL	31	31	6	0	204.0	883	205	91	84	15	10	2	3	79	5	158	4	0	14	9	.609	2	0-0	0	3.87	3.71
1999 Cleveland	AL	32	32	1	0	205.0	858	185	97	90	24	5	4	7	76	5	161	4	0	18	5	.783	1	0-0	0	3.68	3.95
2000 Cleveland	AL	30	30	2	0	188.0	807	163	86	81	21	2	3	4	98	4	212	4	0	15	8	.652	1	0-0	0	3.97	3.88
2001 Cleveland	AL	34	34	1	0	222.1	947	220	106	101	26	8	4	2	90	2	201	4	1	14	12	.538	0	0-0	0	4.24	4.09
2002 Cle-Mon		33	33	8	0	233.1	966	219	85	76	20	19	6	2	70	5	149	4	0	20	8	.714	3	0-0	0	3.29	2.93
2003 Chicago	AL	34	34	9	0	242.0	984	223	107	104	30	5	8	5	67	3	173	8	3	15	13	.536	0	0-0	0	3.47	3.87
2004 Anaheim	AL	34	34	0	0	208.1	897	215	122	116	38	5	8	3	71	1	158	1	0	18	12	.600	0	0-0	0	4.64	5.01
2002 Cleveland	AL	16	16	4	0	116.1	467	104	37	33	11	6	3	2	31	1	75	3	0	10	4	.714	2	0-0	0	3.09	2.55
2002 Montreal	NL	17	17	4	0	117.0	499	115	48	43	9	13	3	0	39	4	74	1	0	10	4	.714	1	0-0	0	3.48	3.31
8 ML YEARS		247	245	28	0	1597.0	6769	1537	760	711	186	58	36	29	596	26	1278	34	4	118	74	.615	7	0-0	0	3.95	4.01

Roman Colon

Pitches: R **Bats:** R **Pos:** RP-18   **Ht:** 6'6" **Wt:** 225 **Born:** 8/13/1979 **Age:** 25

Year Team	Lg	G	GS	CG	GF	IP	BFP	H	R	ER	HR	SH	SF	HB	TBB	IBB	SO	WP	Bk	W	L	Pct	ShO	Sv-Op	Hld	ERC	ERA
1997 Braves	R	14	12	0	1	63.0	289	68	47	30	2	4	3	2	28	0	44	3	0	3	4	.429	0	0- -	-	4.17	4.29
1998 Danville	A+	13	13	0	0	73.1	336	92	59	47	7	1	0	2	28	0	53	11	0	1	7	.125	0	0- -	-	5.53	5.77
1999 Jamestown	A-	15	15	1	0	77.1	329	77	48	39	4	1	3	2	25	0	61	7	2	7	5	.583	0	0- -	-	3.52	4.54
2001 Macon	A	23	21	0	1	128.0	543	136	69	51	9	5	7	3	26	0	91	16	4	7	7	.500	0	0- -	-	3.50	3.59
2002 Myrtle Beach	A+	26	26	1	0	163.0	683	170	81	64	8	4	8	2	38	1	94	3	0	9	8	.529	0	0- -	-	3.37	3.53
2003 Greenville	AA	39	12	1	8	107.0	448	104	48	40	9	9	3	4	33	3	58	3	0	11	3	.786	0	2- -	-	3.30	3.36
2004 Greenville	AA	3	0	0	2	3.0	11	1	1	0	0	0	0	0	1	0	5	0	0	1	0	1.000	0	0- -	-	0.69	0.00
2004 Richmond	AAA	51	0	0	11	74.0	318	72	33	30	4	1	1	3	22	1	64	1	0	4	1	.800	0	0- -	-	3.28	3.65
2004 Atlanta	NL	18	0	0	7	19.0	82	18	9	7	0	1	2	0	8	1	15	0	0	2	1	.667	0	0-1	1	3.05	3.32

Steve Colyer

Pitches: L **Bats:** L **Pos:** RP-41   **Ht:** 6'4" **Wt:** 205 **Born:** 2/22/1979 **Age:** 26

Year Team	Lg	G	GS	CG	GF	IP	BFP	H	R	ER	HR	SH	SF	HB	TBB	IBB	SO	WP	Bk	W	L	Pct	ShO	Sv-Op	Hld	ERC	ERA
1998 Yakima	A-	15	12	0	2	65.1	302	72	46	36	2	1	1	4	36	0	75	5	0	2	2	.500	0	0- -	-	4.94	4.96
1999 Sn Brnardino	A+	27	25	1	0	145.2	644	145	82	76	12	3	7	8	86	0	131	8	3	7	9	.438	0	0- -	-	5.03	4.70
2000 Vero Beach	A+	26	18	1	2	95.1	442	97	74	61	9	2	7	7	68	0	80	6	0	5	7	.417	0	0- -	-	5.77	5.76
2001 Vero Beach	A+	24	24	0	0	120.1	524	101	62	53	16	4	4	7	77	0	118	3	1	4	8	.333	0	0- -	-	4.69	3.96
2002 Jacksonville	AA	59	0	0	46	62.2	284	50	29	24	6	4	3	2	40	3	68	4	0	5	4	.556	0	21- -	-	3.74	3.45
2003 Las Vegas	AAA	44	0	0	44	47.2	206	44	18	17	1	1	1	1	22	0	50	1	0	2	3	.400	0	23- -	-	3.40	3.21
2004 Toledo	AAA	25	0	0	6	25.2	128	26	13	12	2	0	0	0	25	1	23	3	0	2	1	.667	0	0- -	-	6.06	4.21
2003 Los Angeles	NL	13	0	0	3	19.2	84	22	6	6	0	1	0	1	9	0	16	1	0	0	0	-	0	0-0	0	4.44	2.75
2004 Detroit	AL	41	0	0	9	32.0	147	33	24	23	8	0	0	1	24	1	31	3	0	1	0	1.000	0	0-0	4	7.19	6.47
2 ML YEARS		54	0	0	12	51.2	231	55	30	29	8	1	0	1	33	1	47	4	0	1	0	1.000	0	0-0	4	6.11	5.05

Jeff Conine

Bats: R **Throws:** R **Pos:** LF-83; 1B-57; PH-2   **Ht:** 6'1" **Wt:** 220 **Born:** 6/27/1966 **Age:** 39

Year Team	Lg	G	AB	H	2B	3B	HR	(Hm	Rd)	TB	R	RBI	RC	TBB	IBB	SO	HBP	SH	SF	SB	CS	SB%	GDP	Avg	OBP	Slg
1990 Kansas City	AL	9	20	5	2	0	0	(0	0)	7	3	2	2	2	0	5	0	0	0	0	0	-	1	.250	.318	.350
1992 Kansas City	AL	28	91	23	5	2	0	(0	0)	32	10	9	10	8	1	23	0	0	0	0	0	-	1	.253	.313	.352
1993 Florida	NL	162	595	174	24	3	12	(5	7)	240	75	79	83	52	2	135	5	0	6	2	2	.50	14	.292	.351	.403
1994 Florida	NL	115	451	144	27	6	18	(8	10)	237	60	82	84	40	4	92	1	0	4	1	2	.33	8	.319	.373	.525
1995 Florida	NL	133	483	146	26	2	25	(13	12)	251	72	105	93	66	5	94	1	0	12	2	0	1.00	13	.302	.379	.520
1996 Florida	NL	157	597	175	32	2	26	(15	11)	289	84	95	99	62	1	121	4	0	7	1	4	.20	11	.293	.360	.484
1997 Florida	NL	151	405	98	13	1	17	(7	10)	164	46	61	55	57	3	89	2	0	2	2	0	1.00	11	.242	.337	.405
1998 Kansas City	AL	93	309	79	26	0	8	(4	4)	129	30	43	40	26	1	68	2	0	6	3	0	1.00	8	.256	.312	.417
1999 Baltimore	AL	139	444	129	31	1	13	(7	6)	201	54	75	64	30	0	40	3	1	7	0	3	.00	12	.291	.335	.453
2000 Baltimore	AL	119	409	116	20	2	13	(6	7)	179	53	46	58	36	1	53	2	0	4	4	3	.57	14	.284	.341	.438
2001 Baltimore	AL	139	524	163	23	2	14	(5	9)	232	75	97	89	64	6	75	5	0	8	12	8	.60	12	.311	.386	.443
2002 Baltimore	AL	116	451	123	26	4	15	(12	3)	202	44	63	61	25	6	66	2	0	10	8	0	1.00	10	.273	.307	.448
2003 Bal-Fla		149	577	163	36	3	20	(11	9)	265	88	95	84	50	5	70	5	1	13	5	0	1.00	16	.282	.338	.459
2004 Florida	NL	140	521	146	35	1	14	(9	5)	225	55	83	78	48	3	78	2	2	6	5	5	.50	15	.280	.340	.432
2003 Baltimore	AL	124	493	143	33	3	15	(8	7)	227	75	80	73	37	5	60	5	0	12	5	0	1.00	14	.290	.338	.460
2003 Florida	NL	25	84	20	3	0	5	(3	2)	38	13	15	11	13	0	10	0	1	1	0	0	-	2	.238	.337	.452
14 ML YEARS		1650	5877	1684	326	29	195	(102	93)	2653	749	935	900	566	38	1009	34	4	85	45	27	.63	152	.287	.348	.451

Jason Conti

Bats: L **Throws:** R **Pos:** CF-20; LF-1; PH-1; PR-1   **Ht:** 5'11" **Wt:** 175 **Born:** 1/27/1975 **Age:** 30

Year Team	Lg	G	AB	H	2B	3B	HR	(Hm	Rd)	TB	R	RBI	RC	TBB	IBB	SO	HBP	SH	SF	SB	CS	SB%	GDP	Avg	OBP	Slg
2004 Oklahoma*	AAA	104	421	138	26	5	8	(-	-)	198	63	61	74	33	1	84	5	3	3	5	1	.83	8	.328	.381	.470
2000 Arizona	NL	47	91	21	4	3	1	(1	0)	34	11	15	10	7	2	30	1	0	0	3	0	1.00	2	.231	.293	.374
2001 Arizona	NL	5	4	1	0	0	0	(0	0)	1	1	0	1	1	0	2	0	0	0	0	0	-	0	.250	.400	.250
2002 Tampa Bay	AL	78	222	57	15	2	3	(2	1)	85	26	21	25	18	1	55	1	4	0	4	2	.67	5	.257	.315	.383
2003 Milwaukee	NL	30	48	11	2	0	2	(1	1)	19	3	7	5	2	0	18	0	1	1	0	1	.00	1	.229	.255	.396
2004 Texas	AL	22	55	10	3	0	0	(0	0)	13	6	4	4	5	0	19	0	0	0	0	2	.00	0	.182	.250	.236
5 ML YEARS		182	420	100	24	5	6	(4	2)	152	47	47	45	33	3	124	2	5	1	7	5	.58	8	.238	.296	.362

Jose Contreras

Pitches: R **Bats:** R **Pos:** SP-31   **Ht:** 6'4" **Wt:** 230 **Born:** 12/12/1971 **Age:** 33

Year Team	Lg	G	GS	CG	GF	IP	BFP	H	R	ER	HR	SH	SF	HB	TBB	IBB	SO	WP	Bk	W	L	Pct	ShO	Sv-Op	Hld	ERC	ERA
2003 Staten Island	A-	1	1	0	0	7.0	25	2	0	0	0	0	0	0	0	0	15	0	0	0	0	-	0	0- -	-	0.19	0.00
2003 Tampa	A+	1	1	0	0	4.0	18	4	2	2	0	0	0	1	3	0	5	1	0	0	0	-	0	0- -	-	6.15	4.50
2003 Trenton	AA	1	1	0	0	1.2	8	1	0	0	0	0	0	0	2	0	3	0	0	0	0	-	0	0- -	-	3.97	0.00
2003 Columbus	AAA	3	3	0	0	15.0	56	10	2	2	1	0	0	1	2	0	18	0	0	2	0	1.000	0	0- -	-	1.60	1.20
2004 Columbus	AAA	2	2	0	0	13.2	58	11	5	5	2	0	0	2	5	0	19	4	0	2	0	1.000	0	0- -	-	3.75	3.29
2003 New York	AL	18	9	0	2	71.0	293	52	27	26	4	0	1	5	30	1	72	2	0	7	2	.778	0	0-1	1	2.71	3.30
2004 NYY-CWS	AL	31	31	0	0	170.1	758	166	114	104	31	3	6	8	84	1	150	17	0	13	9	.591	0	0-0	0	5.05	5.50
2004 New York	AL	18	18	0	0	95.2	425	93	66	60	22	1	4	6	42	1	82	10	0	8	5	.615	0	0-0	0	5.18	5.64
2004 Chicago	AL	13	13	0	0	74.2	333	73	48	44	9	2	2	2	42	0	68	7	0	5	4	.556	0	0-0	0	4.87	5.30
2 ML YEARS		49	40	0	2	241.1	1051	218	141	130	35	3	7	13	114	2	222	19	0	20	11	.645	0	0-1	1	4.32	4.85

Aaron Cook

Pitches: R **Bats:** R **Pos:** SP-16   **Ht:** 6'3" **Wt:** 175 **Born:** 2/8/1979 **Age:** 26

Year Team	Lg	G	GS	CG	GF	IP	BFP	H	R	ER	HR	SH	SF	HB	TBB	IBB	SO	WP	Bk	W	L	Pct	ShO	Sv-Op	Hld	ERC	ERA
2004 Co Springs*	AAA	7	7	1	0	46.0	177	34	15	14	1	1	0	3	8	0	25	5	0	3	1	.750	1	0- -	-	1.76	2.74
2002 Colorado	NL	9	5	0	1	35.2	154	41	18	18	4	0	0	2	13	0	14	0	0	2	1	.667	0	0-0	1	5.31	4.54
2003 Colorado	NL	43	16	1	4	124.0	579	160	89	83	8	4	6	8	57	7	43	10	0	6	4	.600	0	0-0	1	5.95	6.02
2004 Colorado	NL	16	16	1	0	96.2	433	112	47	46	7	5	1	7	39	5	40	6	1	6	4	.600	0	0-0	0	5.05	4.28
3 ML YEARS		68	37	2	5	256.1	1166	313	154	147	19	9	7	17	109	12	97	16	1	12	11	.522	0	0-0	2	5.52	5.16

Brian Cooper

Pitches: R **Bats:** R **Pos:** RP-3; SP-2   **Ht:** 6'1" **Wt:** 185 **Born:** 8/19/1974 **Age:** 30

Year Team	Lg	G	GS	CG	GF	IP	BFP	H	R	ER	HR	SH	SF	HB	TBB	IBB	SO	WP	Bk	W	L	Pct	ShO	Sv-Op	Hld	ERC	ERA
2004 Fresno*	AAA	4	4	0	0	21.2	89	19	9	5	3	3	2	0	6	0	15	1	0	0	0	-	0	0- -	-	3.16	2.08
1999 Anaheim	AL	5	5	0	0	27.2	124	23	15	15	3	0	1	4	18	0	15	0	0	1	1	.500	0	0-0	0	4.79	4.88
2000 Anaheim	AL	15	15	1	0	87.0	396	105	66	57	18	4	4	2	35	1	36	1	0	4	8	.333	1	0-0	0	6.17	5.90
2001 Anaheim	AL	7	1	0	5	13.2	55	10	5	4	2	0	1	0	4	0	7	0	0	0	0	.000	0	0-0	0	2.51	2.63
2002 Toronto	AL	2	2	0	0	8.1	41	14	13	13	5	1	1	0	4	0	3	1	0	0	1	.000	0	0-0	0	13.71	14.04
2004 San Francisco	NL	5	2	0	0	13.1	61	15	13	13	4	2	1	1	5	1	7	1	0	0	2	.000	0	0-0	0	6.25	8.78
5 ML YEARS		34	25	1	5	150.0	677	167	112	102	32	7	8	7	66	2	68	3	0	5	13	.278	1	0-0	0	5.92	6.12

Alex Cora

Bats: L **Throws:** R **Pos:** 2B-138; PH-5; PR-1   **Ht:** 6'0" **Wt:** 180 **Born:** 10/18/1975 **Age:** 29

Year Team	Lg	G	AB	H	2B	3B	HR	(Hm	Rd)	TB	R	RBI	RC	TBB	IBB	SO	HBP	SH	SF	SB	CS	SB%	GDP	Avg	OBP	Slg
1998 Los Angeles	NL	29	33	4	0	1	0	(0	0)	6	1	0	1	2	0	8	1	2	0	0	0	-	0	.121	.194	.182
1999 Los Angeles	NL	11	30	5	1	0	0	(0	0)	6	2	3	0	4	1	0	0	0	1	.167	.194	.200
2000 Los Angeles	NL	109	353	84	18	6	4	(2	2)	126	39	32	38	26	4	53	7	6	2	4	1	.80	6	.238	.302	.357
2001 Los Angeles	NL	134	405	88	18	3	4	(2	2)	124	38	29	30	31	6	58	8	3	2	0	2	.00	16	.217	.285	.306
2002 Los Angeles	NL	115	258	75	14	4	5	(4	1)	112	37	28	46	26	4	38	7	2	0	7	2	.78	3	.291	.371	.434
2003 Los Angeles	NL	148	477	119	24	3	4	(3	1)	161	39	34	46	16	3	59	10	9	2	4	2	.67	5	.249	.287	.338
2004 Los Angeles	NL	138	405	107	9	4	10	(4	6)	154	47	47	63	47	10	41	18	12	2	3	4	.43	9	.264	.364	.380
7 ML YEARS		684	1961	482	84	21	27	(15	12)	689	203	173	224	148	27	261	52	34	8	18	11	.62	40	.246	.314	.351

Roy Corcoran

Pitches: R **Bats:** R **Pos:** RP-5   **Ht:** 5'10" **Wt:** 170 **Born:** 5/11/1980 **Age:** 25

Year Team	Lg	G	GS	CG	GF	IP	BFP	H	R	ER	HR	SH	SF	HB	TBB	IBB	SO	WP	Bk	W	L	Pct	ShO	Sv-Op	Hld	ERC	ERA
2001 Expos	R	13	0	0	9	17.1	69	12	4	3	2	0	0	2	2	0	21	0	0	2	0	1.000	0	2- -	-	1.91	1.56
2001 Jupiter	A+	1	0	0	0	2.0	8	0	0	0	0	0	0	0	2	0	0	0	0	0	0	-	0	0- -	-	0.95	0.00
2002 Clinton	A	48	1	0	31	80.0	356	82	51	37	5	5	1	2	24	1	106	9	2	3	4	.429	0	11- -	-	3.46	4.16
2003 Brevard Cnty	A+	28	0	0	25	33.0	131	19	8	7	1	6	1	2	11	1	35	0	0	5	3	.625	0	12- -	-	1.52	1.91
2003 Harrisburg	AA	14	0	0	11	23.2	96	14	4	1	0	1	0	4	7	1	26	0	0	1	1	.500	0	3- -	-	1.58	0.38
2003 Edmonton	AAA	2	0	0	1	2.0	6	0	0	0	0	0	0	0	0	0	1	0	0	0	0	-	0	0- -	-	0.00	0.00
2004 Edmonton	AAA	30	0	0	17	44.1	198	39	16	15	0	1	0	2	24	1	35	1	0	5	1	.833	0	5- -	-	3.28	3.05
2003 Montreal	NL	5	0	0	2	7.1	31	7	2	1	0	0	0	0	3	0	2	1	0	0	0	-	0	0-0	0	3.20	1.23
2004 Montreal	NL	5	0	0	3	5.1	28	7	4	4	0	0	0	0	5	0	4	0	0	0	0	-	0	0-0	0	7.12	6.75
2 ML YEARS		10	0	0	5	12.2	59	14	6	5	0	0	0	0	8	0	6	1	0	0	0	-	0	0-0	0	4.77	3.55

Chad Cordero

Pitches: R **Bats:** R **Pos:** RP-69   **Ht:** 6'0" **Wt:** 195 **Born:** 5/18/1982 **Age:** 23

Year Team	Lg	G	GS	CG	GF	IP	BFP	H	R	ER	HR	SH	SF	HB	TBB	IBB	SO	WP	Bk	W	L	Pct	ShO	Sv-Op	Hld	ERC	ERA
2003 Brevard Cnty	A+	19	0	0	13	26.1	103	17	8	6	1	4	2	1	10	0	17	0	0	1	1	.500	0	6- -	-	2.00	2.05
2003 Montreal	NL	12	0	0	4	11.0	40	4	2	2	1	1	0	0	3	1	12	1	0	1	0	1.000	0	0-0	6	1.68	1.64
2004 Montreal	NL	69	0	0	40	82.2	357	68	28	27	8	2	4	1	43	4	83	5	0	7	3	.700	0	14-18	8	3.47	2.94
2 ML YEARS		81	0	0	44	93.2	397	72	30	29	9	3	4	1	46	5	95	6	0	8	3	.727	0	15-19	9	3.07	2.79

Francisco Cordero

Pitches: R **Bats:** R **Pos:** RP-67   **Ht:** 6'2" **Wt:** 200 **Born:** 5/11/1975 **Age:** 30

Year Team	Lg	G	GS	CG	GF	IP	BFP	H	R	ER	HR	SH	SF	HB	TBB	IBB	SO	WP	Bk	W	L	Pct	ShO	Sv-Op	Hld	ERC	ERA
1999 Detroit	AL	20	0	0	4	19.0	91	19	7	7	2	2	4	0	18	2	19	1	0	2	2	.500	0	0-0	6	6.19	3.32
2000 Texas	AL	56	0	0	13	77.1	365	87	51	46	11	2	6	4	48	3	49	7	0	1	2	.333	0	0-3	4	6.15	5.35
2001 Texas	AL	3	0	0	2	2.1	12	3	1	1	0	0	0	0	2	1	1	1	0	0	1	.000	0	0-0	1	5.73	3.86
2002 Texas	AL	39	0	0	25	45.1	177	33	12	9	2	0	0	2	13	1	41	1	0	2	0	1.000	0	10-12	1	2.11	1.79
2003 Texas	AL	73	0	0	36	82.2	352	70	33	27	4	3	4	2	38	6	90	0	0	5	8	.385	0	15-25	18	3.08	2.94
2004 Texas	AL	67	0	0	63	71.2	304	60	19	17	1	5	1	1	32	2	79	3	2	3	4	.429	0	49-54	0	2.78	2.13
6 ML YEARS		258	0	0	143	298.1	1301	272	123	107	20	12	15	9	151	15	279	13	2	13	17	.433	0	74-94	30	3.79	3.23

Wil Cordero

Bats: R **Throws:** R **Pos:** 1B-13; PH-11; LF-3   **Ht:** 6'2" **Wt:** 200 **Born:** 10/3/1971 **Age:** 33

Year Team	Lg	G	AB	H	2B	3B	HR	(Hm	Rd)	TB	R	RBI	RC	TBB	IBB	SO	HBP	SH	SF	SB	CS	SB%	GDP	Avg	OBP	Slg
2004 Jupiter*	A+	3	8	4	0	0	2	(-	-)	10	3	5	4	1	0	1	0	0	0	0	0	-	0	.500	.556	1.250
1992 Montreal	NL	45	126	38	4	1	2	(1	1)	50	17	8	17	9	0	31	1	1	0	0	0	-	3	.302	.353	.397
1993 Montreal	NL	138	475	118	32	2	10	(8	2)	184	56	58	55	34	8	60	7	4	1	12	3	.80	12	.248	.308	.387
1994 Montreal	NL	110	415	122	30	3	15	(5	10)	203	65	63	74	41	3	62	6	2	3	16	3	.84	8	.294	.363	.489
1995 Montreal	NL	131	514	147	35	2	10	(2	8)	216	64	49	72	36	4	88	9	1	4	9	5	.64	11	.286	.341	.420
1996 Boston	AL	59	198	57	14	0	3	(2	1)	80	29	37	24	11	4	31	2	1	1	2	1	.67	8	.288	.330	.404
1997 Boston	AL	140	570	166	26	3	18	(11	7)	246	82	72	75	31	7	122	4	0	4	1	3	.25	11	.291	.320	.432
1998 Chicago	AL	96	341	91	18	2	13	(5	8)	152	58	49	47	22	0	66	3	1	4	2	1	.67	7	.267	.314	.446
1999 Cleveland	AL	54	194	58	15	0	8	(3	5)	97	35	32	34	15	0	37	6	0	2	0	0	1.00	7	.299	.364	.500
2000 Pit-Cle		127	496	137	35	5	16	(8	8)	230	64	68	70	32	1	76	7	0	1	1	2	.33	18	.276	.328	.464
2001 Cleveland	AL	89	268	67	11	1	4	(2	2)	92	30	21	28	22	2	50	4	2	3	0	0	-	7	.250	.313	.343
2002 Cle-Mon		72	161	43	9	0	6	(2	4)	70	22	30	28	17	0	29	2	0	4	2	0	1.00	4	.267	.337	.435
2003 Montreal	NL	130	436	121	27	0	16	(8	8)	196	57	71	68	49	5	90	4	0	3	1	1	.50	11	.278	.354	.450
2004 Florida	NL	27	66	13	3	0	1	(0	1)	19	6	6	3	3	0	19	2	0	1	0	0	1.00	2	.197	.250	.288

Year Team	Lg	G	AB	H	2B	3B	HR	(Hm	Rd)	TB	R	RBI	RC	TBB	IBB	SO	HBP	SH	SF	SB	CS	SB%	GDP	Avg	OBP	Slg
2000 Pittsburgh	NL	89	348	98	24	3	16	(8	8)	176	46	51	55	25	1	58	4	0	1	1	2	.33	11	.282	.336	.506
2000 Cleveland	AL	38	148	39	11	2	0	(0	0)	54	18	17	15	7	0	18	3	0	0	0	0	-	7	.264	.310	.365
2002 Cleveland	AL	6	18	4	0	0	0	(0	0)	4	1	1	1	0	0	3	0	0	0	0	0	-	1	.222	.222	.222
2002 Montreal	NL	66	143	39	9	0	6	(2	4)	66	21	29	27	17	0	26	2	0	4	2	0	1.00	3	.273	.349	.462
13 ML YEARS		1218	4260	1172	259	19	122	(57	65)	1835	585	564	595	322	34	761	57	12	31	49	19	.72	110	.275	.332	.431

Marty Cordova

Bats: R **Throws:** R **Pos:** DH   **Ht:** 6'0" **Wt:** 206 **Born:** 7/10/1969 **Age:** 35

Year Team	Lg	G	AB	H	2B	3B	HR	(Hm	Rd)	TB	R	RBI	RC	TBB	IBB	SO	HBP	SH	SF	SB	CS	SB%	GDP	Avg	OBP	Slg
1995 Minnesota	AL	137	512	142	27	4	24	(16	8)	249	81	84	88	52	1	111	10	0	5	20	7	.74	10	.277	.352	.486
1996 Minnesota	AL	145	569	176	46	1	16	(10	6)	272	97	111	97	53	4	96	8	0	9	11	5	.69	18	.309	.371	.478
1997 Minnesota	AL	103	378	93	18	4	15	(4	11)	164	44	51	47	30	2	92	3	0	2	5	3	.63	13	.246	.305	.434
1998 Minnesota	AL	119	438	111	20	2	10	(6	4)	165	52	69	52	50	3	103	5	0	6	3	6	.33	14	.253	.333	.377
1999 Minnesota	AL	124	425	121	28	3	14	(9	5)	197	62	70	68	48	2	96	9	0	6	13	4	.76	22	.285	.365	.464
2000 Toronto	AL	62	200	49	7	0	4	(3	1)	68	23	18	21	18	0	35	3	0	0	3	2	.60	6	.245	.317	.340
2001 Cleveland	AL	122	409	123	20	2	20	(9	11)	207	61	69	68	23	0	81	8	0	2	0	3	.00	9	.301	.348	.506
2002 Baltimore	AL	131	458	116	25	2	18	(11	7)	199	55	64	63	47	3	111	3	2	3	1	6	.14	17	.253	.325	.434
2003 Baltimore	AL	9	30	7	1	0	1	(1	0)	11	5	4	7	8	1	5	1	0	0	1	0	1.00	1	.233	.410	.367
9 ML YEARS		952	3419	938	192	18	122	(69	53)	1532	480	540	511	329	16	730	50	2	33	57	36	.61	110	.274	.344	.448

Mark Corey

Pitches: R **Bats:** R **Pos:** RP-31   **Ht:** 6'3" **Wt:** 210 **Born:** 11/16/1974 **Age:** 30

Year Team	Lg	G	GS	CG	GF	IP	BFP	H	R	ER	HR	SH	SF	HB	TBB	IBB	SO	WP	Bk	W	L	Pct	ShO	Sv-Op	Hld	ERC	ERA
2004 Nashville*	AAA	34	0	0	25	38.2	171	40	21	19	4	1	0	2	15	1	39	2	0	1	4	.200	0	16--	-	4.36	4.42
2001 New York	NL	2	0	0	0	1.2	13	5	3	3	0	0	0	0	3	1	3	0	0	0	0	-	0	0-0	0	21.72	16.20
2002 NYM-Col	NL	26	0	0	8	22.0	114	32	23	21	9	1	0	3	16	2	21	1	0	0	0	-	0	0-0	1	11.75	8.59
2003 Pittsburgh	NL	22	0	0	10	30.1	131	29	19	18	2	1	3	1	11	1	27	2	0	1	2	.333	0	0-0	4	3.47	5.34
2004 Pittsburgh	NL	31	0	0	13	35.2	164	39	20	18	3	0	1	2	19	3	28	4	0	1	2	.333	0	0-1	2	5.07	4.54
2002 New York	NL	12	0	0	5	10.0	48	10	7	5	2	0	0	1	8	1	9	1	0	0	3	.000	0	0-0	0	6.76	4.50
2002 Colorado	NL	14	0	0	3	12.0	66	22	16	16	7	1	0	2	8	1	12	0	0	0	0	-	0	0-0	1	16.43	12.00
4 ML YEARS		81	0	0	31	89.2	422	105	65	60	14	2	4	6	49	7	79	7	0	2	7	.222	0	0-1	7	6.23	6.02

Lance Cormier

Pitches: R **Bats:** R **Pos:** RP-12; SP-5   **Ht:** 6'1" **Wt:** 192 **Born:** 8/19/1980 **Age:** 24

Year Team	Lg	G	GS	CG	GF	IP	BFP	H	R	ER	HR	SH	SF	HB	TBB	IBB	SO	WP	Bk	W	L	Pct	ShO	Sv-Op	Hld	ERC	ERA
2002 Yakima	A-	1	0	0	0	1.0	8	4	4	3	0	0	0	0	0	3	0	0	0	-	0	0--	-	19.55	27.00
2002 South Bend	A	11	3	0	4	27.2	116	29	9	9	1	1	1	0	2	0	17	2	2	3	0	1.000	0	1--	-	2.57	2.93
2003 Lancaster	A+	15	15	0	0	94.1	390	102	55	40	6	5	3	2	16	1	59	4	1	6	5	.545	0	0--	-	3.49	3.82
2003 El Paso	AA	9	8	0	0	41.1	201	59	33	28	3	3	1	0	22	0	26	4	0	2	3	.400	0	0--	-	6.95	6.10
2003 Tucson	AAA	5	4	0	0	27.2	108	26	10	8	1	3	0	0	5	0	11	1	0	1	1	.500	0	0--	-	2.64	2.60
2004 El Paso	AA	10	8	0	0	63.0	259	66	19	16	3	8	2	2	17	0	58	3	1	2	3	.400	0	0--	-	3.74	2.29
2004 Tucson	AAA	8	8	2	0	50.1	212	50	17	15	0	1	1	2	17	1	37	3	0	3	3	.500	1	0--	-	3.28	2.68
2004 Arizona	NL	17	5	0	3	45.1	218	62	42	41	13	2	3	2	25	2	24	2	1	1	4	.200	0	0-0	2	8.76	8.14

Rheal Cormier

Pitches: L **Bats:** L **Pos:** RP-84   **Ht:** 5'10" **Wt:** 187 **Born:** 4/23/1967 **Age:** 38

Year Team	Lg	G	GS	CG	GF	IP	BFP	H	R	ER	HR	SH	SF	HB	TBB	IBB	SO	WP	Bk	W	L	Pct	ShO	Sv-Op	Hld	ERC	ERA
1991 St Louis	NL	11	10	2	1	67.2	281	74	35	31	5	1	3	2	8	1	38	2	1	4	5	.444	0	0-0	0	3.41	4.12
1992 St Louis	NL	31	30	3	1	186.0	772	194	83	76	15	11	3	5	33	2	117	4	2	10	10	.500	0	0-0	0	3.42	3.68
1993 St Louis	NL	38	21	1	4	145.1	619	163	80	70	18	10	4	4	27	3	75	6	0	7	6	.538	0	0-0	0	4.13	4.33
1994 St Louis	NL	7	7	0	0	39.2	169	40	24	24	6	1	2	3	7	0	26	2	0	3	2	.600	0	0-0	0	3.80	5.45
1995 Boston	AL	48	12	0	3	115.0	488	131	60	52	12	6	2	3	31	2	69	4	0	7	5	.583	0	0-2	9	4.54	4.07
1996 Montreal	NL	33	27	1	1	159.2	674	165	80	74	16	4	3	0	41	3	100	8	0	7	10	.412	1	0-0	0	3.93	4.17
1997 Montreal	NL	1	1	0	0	1.1	9	4	5	5	1	0	0	0	1	0	0	0	0	0	1	.000	0	0-0	0	27.46	33.75
1999 Boston	AL	60	0	0	7	63.1	275	61	34	26	4	1	3	5	18	2	39	1	0	2	0	1.000	0	0-3	15	3.33	3.69
2000 Boston	AL	64	0	0	12	68.1	293	74	40	35	7	5	2	0	17	2	43	1	0	3	3	.500	0	0-2	9	3.86	4.61
2001 Philadelphia	NL	60	0	0	16	51.1	222	49	26	24	5	3	0	4	17	4	37	1	0	5	6	.455	0	1-6	12	3.67	4.21
2002 Philadelphia	NL	54	0	0	7	60.0	268	61	38	35	6	0	2	4	32	6	49	4	0	5	6	.455	0	0-0	0	4.85	5.25
2003 Philadelphia	NL	65	0	0	21	84.2	327	54	18	16	4	4	0	1	25	2	67	0	0	8	0	1.000	0	1-4	14	1.63	1.70
2004 Philadelphia	NL	84	0	0	8	81.0	330	70	32	32	7	3	1	5	26	6	46	1	0	4	5	.444	0	0-7	28	3.16	3.56
13 ML YEARS		556	108	7	81	1123.1	4727	1140	555	500	106	49	30	45	283	33	706	34	4	65	59	.524	1	2-27	96	3.66	4.01

Nate Cornejo

Pitches: R **Bats:** R **Pos:** SP-5   **Ht:** 6'5" **Wt:** 240 **Born:** 9/24/1979 **Age:** 25

Year Team	Lg	G	GS	CG	GF	IP	BFP	H	R	ER	HR	SH	SF	HB	TBB	IBB	SO	WP	Bk	W	L	Pct	ShO	Sv-Op	Hld	ERC	ERA
2004 Toledo*	AAA	4	3	0	0	8.2	38	11	4	4	2	0	1	0	2	0	8	0	0	0	0	-	0	0--	-	5.94	4.15
2001 Detroit	AL	10	10	0	0	42.2	217	63	38	35	10	2	0	3	28	4	22	1	0	4	4	.500	0	0-0	0	9.48	7.38
2002 Detroit	AL	9	9	1	0	50.0	230	63	33	28	6	1	1	2	18	0	23	2	0	1	5	.167	0	0-0	0	5.69	5.04
2003 Detroit	AL	32	32	2	0	194.2	842	236	111	101	18	7	6	3	58	8	46	1	0	6	17	.261	0	0-0	0	4.94	4.67
2004 Detroit	AL	5	5	0	0	25.2	125	42	25	24	4	1	0	1	11	1	12	1	1	1	3	.250	0	0-0	0	8.96	8.42
4 ML YEARS		56	56	3	0	313.0	1414	404	207	188	38	11	7	9	115	13	103	5	1	12	29	.293	0	0-0	0	5.95	5.41

Kevin Correia

Pitches: R **Bats:** R **Pos:** RP-11; SP-1   **Ht:** 6'3" **Wt:** 200 **Born:** 8/24/1980 **Age:** 24

		HOW MUCH HE PITCHED						WHAT HE GAVE UP											THE RESULTS							
Year Team	Lg	G	GS	CG	GF	IP	BFP	H	R	ER	HR	SH	SF	HB	TBB	IBB	SO	WP	Bk	W	L	Pct	ShO	Sv-Op	Hld	ERC	ERA
2002 Salem-Keizer	A-	10	8	0	1	37.2	163	37	20	19	1	1	1	3	14	0	31	1	0	2	2	.500	0	0--	-	3.66	4.54
2003 Norwich	AA	16	14	0	0	86.1	363	80	38	35	3	4	3	4	30	0	73	4	1	6	6	.500	0	0--	-	3.23	3.65
2003 Fresno	AAA	3	3	0	0	19.0	74	16	8	6	3	0	0	0	2	0	23	2	0	1	0	1.000	0	0--	-	2.47	2.84
2004 Fresno	AAA	29	16	0	0	105.1	462	118	61	53	12	8	5	3	35	3	70	2	0	3	7	.300	0	0--	-	4.65	4.53
2003 San Francisco	NL	10	7	0	1	39.1	173	41	16	16	6	1	1	4	18	1	28	2	0	3	1	.750	0	0-0	0	5.46	3.66
2004 San Francisco	NL	12	1	0	5	19.0	92	25	20	17	3	3	3	1	10	0	14	0	0	0	1	.000	0	0-0	0	7.12	8.05
2 ML YEARS		22	8	0	6	58.1	265	66	36	33	9	4	4	5	28	1	42	2	0	3	2	.600	0	0-0	0	5.99	5.09

Humberto Cota

Bats: R **Throws:** R **Pos:** C-24; PH-12; PR-1   **Ht:** 6'0" **Wt:** 205 **Born:** 2/7/1979 **Age:** 26

		BATTING																BASERUNNING				AVERAGES		
Year Team	Lg	G	AB	H	2B	3B	HR	(Hm | Rd)	TB	R	RBI	RC	TBB	IBB	SO	HBP	SH	SF	SB	CS	SB%	GDP	Avg	OBP	Slg
2004 Nashville*	AAA	8	27	7	0	0	1	(0 | -)	10	4	2	2	3	0	7	0	0	0	0	0	-	3	.259	.333	.370
2001 Pittsburgh	NL	7	9	2	0	0	0	(0 | 0)	2	0	1	0	0	0	5	0	0	0	0	0	-	0	.222	.222	.222
2002 Pittsburgh	NL	7	17	5	1	0	0	(0 | 0)	6	2	0	1	1	1	4	0	0	0	0	0	-	0	.294	.333	.353
2003 Pittsburgh	NL	10	16	4	1	0	0	(0 | 0)	5	1	1	0	1	0	5	0	0	0	0	0	-	0	.250	.294	.313
2004 Pittsburgh	NL	36	66	15	1	1	5	(3 | 2)	33	10	8	7	3	1	20	1	0	0	0	0	-	1	.227	.271	.500
4 ML YEARS		60	108	26	3	1	5	(3 | 2)	46	13	10	8	5	2	34	1	0	0	0	0	-	1	.241	.281	.426

Neal Cotts

Pitches: L **Bats:** L **Pos:** RP-55; SP-1   **Ht:** 6'2" **Wt:** 200 **Born:** 3/25/1980 **Age:** 25

		HOW MUCH HE PITCHED						WHAT HE GAVE UP											THE RESULTS							
Year Team	Lg	G	GS	CG	GF	IP	BFP	H	R	ER	HR	SH	SF	HB	TBB	IBB	SO	WP	Bk	W	L	Pct	ShO	Sv-Op	Hld	ERC	ERA
2001 Vancouver	A-	9	7	0	0	35.0	145	28	14	12	2	0	1	1	13	0	44	4	1	1	0	1.000	0	0--	-	2.72	3.09
2001 Visalia	A+	7	7	0	0	31.0	139	27	14	8	0	0	1	1	15	0	34	0	0	3	2	.600	0	0--	-	3.22	2.32
2002 Modesto	A+	28	28	0	0	137.2	611	123	72	63	5	1	3	5	87	0	178	7	2	12	6	.667	0	0--	-	4.07	4.12
2003 Birmingham	AA	21	21	0	0	108.1	440	67	32	26	2	2	2	3	56	1	133	0	0	9	7	.563	0	0--	-	2.11	2.16
2003 Chicago	AL	4	4	0	0	13.1	69	15	12	12	1	1	0	0	17	0	10	0	0	1	1	.500	0	0-0	0	8.43	8.10
2004 Chicago	AL	56	1	0	12	65.1	281	61	45	41	13	0	1	3	30	2	58	8	0	4	4	.500	0	0-2	4	4.84	5.65
2 ML YEARS		60	5	0	12	78.2	350	76	57	53	14	1	1	3	47	2	68	8	0	5	5	.500	0	0-2	4	5.45	6.06

Craig Counsell

Bats: L **Throws:** R **Pos:** SS-129; PH-9; PR-2; 3B-1   **Ht:** 6'0" **Wt:** 175 **Born:** 8/21/1970 **Age:** 34

		BATTING																BASERUNNING				AVERAGES		
Year Team	Lg	G	AB	H	2B	3B	HR	(Hm | Rd)	TB	R	RBI	RC	TBB	IBB	SO	HBP	SH	SF	SB	CS	SB%	GDP	Avg	OBP	Slg
1995 Colorado	NL	3	1	0	0	0	0	(0 | 0)	0	0	0	0	1	0	0	0	0	0	0	0	-	0	.000	.500	.000
1997 Col-Fla	NL	52	164	49	9	2	1	(1 | 0)	65	20	16	24	18	2	17	3	3	1	1	1	.50	5	.299	.376	.396
1998 Florida	NL	107	335	84	19	5	4	(2 | 2)	125	43	40	48	51	7	47	4	8	1	3	0	1.00	5	.251	.355	.373
1999 Fla-LA	NL	87	174	38	7	0	0	(0 | 0)	45	24	11	12	14	0	24	0	5	2	1	0	1.00	2	.218	.274	.259
2000 Arizona	NL	67	152	48	8	1	2	(0 | 2)	64	23	11	25	20	0	18	2	1	1	3	3	.50	4	.316	.400	.421
2001 Arizona	NL	141	458	126	22	3	4	(4 | 0)	166	76	38	61	61	3	76	2	6	6	8	8	.43	9	.275	.359	.362
2002 Arizona	NL	112	436	123	22	1	2	(0 | 2)	153	63	51	65	45	3	52	1	4	3	7	5	.58	10	.282	.348	.351
2003 Arizona	NL	89	303	71	6	3	3	(3 | 0)	92	40	21	29	41	0	32	2	3	2	11	4	.73	4	.234	.328	.304
2004 Milwaukee	NL	140	473	114	19	5	2	(1 | 1)	149	59	23	48	59	9	88	5	5	3	17	4	.81	5	.241	.330	.315
1997 Colorado	NL	1	0	0	0	0	0	(0 | 0)	0	0	0	0	0	0	0	0	0	0	0	0	-	0	-	-	-
1997 Florida	NL	51	164	49	9	2	1	(1 | 0)	65	20	16	24	18	2	17	3	3	1	1	1	.50	5	.299	.376	.396
1999 Florida	NL	37	66	10	1	0	0	(0 | 0)	11	4	2	1	5	0	10	0	2	0	0	0	-	1	.152	.211	.167
1999 Los Angeles	NL	50	108	28	6	0	0	(0 | 0)	34	20	9	11	9	0	14	0	3	2	1	0	1.00	1	.259	.311	.315
9 ML YEARS		798	2496	653	112	20	18	(11 | 7)	859	348	211	312	310	24	354	19	35	19	49	25	.66	44	.262	.345	.344

Jesse Crain

Pitches: R **Bats:** R **Pos:** RP-22   **Ht:** 6'1" **Wt:** 205 **Born:** 7/5/1981 **Age:** 23

		HOW MUCH HE PITCHED						WHAT HE GAVE UP											THE RESULTS							
Year Team	Lg	G	GS	CG	GF	IP	BFP	H	R	ER	HR	SH	SF	HB	TBB	IBB	SO	WP	Bk	W	L	Pct	ShO	Sv-Op	Hld	ERC	ERA
2002 Quad City	A	9	0	0	6	12.0	45	6	3	2	0	1	0	1	4	0	11	0	0	1	1	.500	0	1--	-	1.31	1.50
2002 Elizabethton	R+	9	0	0	6	15.2	61	4	2	1	0	2	1	1	7	3	18	0	0	2	1	.667	0	2--	-	0.62	0.57
2003 Fort Myers	A+	10	0	0	3	19.0	70	10	6	6	0	0	0	1	5	0	25	0	0	2	1	.667	0	0--	-	1.06	2.84
2003 New Britain	AA	22	0	0	15	39.0	143	13	4	3	0	1	0	1	10	1	56	2	1	1	1	.500	0	9--	-	0.58	0.69
2003 Rochester	AAA	23	0	0	20	26.0	113	24	10	9	0	3	1	1	10	1	33	2	0	3	1	.750	0	10--	-	2.91	3.12
2004 Rochester	AAA	41	0	0	33	50.2	204	38	20	14	5	1	0	1	17	2	64	1	0	3	2	.600	0	19--	-	2.54	2.49
2004 Minnesota	AL	22	0	0	3	27.0	109	17	6	6	2	1	0	1	12	1	14	1	0	3	0	1.000	0	0-1	2	2.25	2.00

Carl Crawford

Bats: L **Throws:** L **Pos:** LF-123; CF-30; DH-5; PH-4; PR-1   **Ht:** 6'2" **Wt:** 219 **Born:** 8/5/1981 **Age:** 23

		BATTING																BASERUNNING				AVERAGES		
Year Team	Lg	G	AB	H	2B	3B	HR	(Hm | Rd)	TB	R	RBI	RC	TBB	IBB	SO	HBP	SH	SF	SB	CS	SB%	GDP	Avg	OBP	Slg
2002 Tampa Bay	AL	63	259	67	11	6	2	(1 | 1)	96	23	30	34	9	0	41	3	6	1	9	5	.64	0	.259	.290	.371
2003 Tampa Bay	AL	151	630	177	18	9	5	(5 | 0)	228	80	54	80	26	4	102	1	1	4	55	10	.85	5	.281	.309	.362
2004 Tampa Bay	AL	152	626	185	26	19	11	(6 | 5)	282	104	55	96	35	2	81	1	4	6	59	15	.80	2	.296	.331	.450
3 ML YEARS		366	1515	429	55	34	18	(12 | 6)	606	207	139	210	70	6	224	5	11	10	123	30	.80	7	.283	.315	.400

Joe Crede

Bats: R **Throws:** R **Pos:** 3B-144 **Ht:** 6'2" **Wt:** 195 **Born:** 4/26/1978 **Age:** 27

Year Team	Lg	G	AB	H	2B	3B	HR	(Hm Rd)	TB	R	RBI	RC	TBB	IBB	SO	HBP	SH	SF	SB	CS	SB%	GDP	Avg	OBP	Slg
2000 Chicago	AL	7	14	5	1	0	0	(0 0)	6	2	3	2	0	0	3	0	0	1	0	0	-	0	.357	.333	.429
2001 Chicago	AL	17	50	11	1	1	0	(0 0)	14	1	7	4	3	0	11	1	0	1	1	0	1.00	1	.220	.273	.280
2002 Chicago	AL	53	200	57	10	0	12	(7 5)	103	28	35	31	8	0	40	0	0	1	0	2	.00	1	.285	.311	.515
2003 Chicago	AL	151	536	140	31	2	19	(11 8)	232	68	75	69	32	1	75	6	2	4	1	1	.50	10	.261	.308	.433
2004 Chicago	AL	144	490	117	25	0	21	(12 9)	205	67	69	58	34	0	81	10	4	5	1	2	.33	13	.239	.299	.418
5 ML YEARS		372	1290	330	68	3	52	(30 22)	560	166	189	164	77	1	210	17	6	12	3	5	.38	25	.256	.304	.434

Cesar Crespo

Bats: B **Throws:** R **Pos:** SS-27; 2B-11; LF-10; PR-8; CF-7; PH-3; RF-2 **Ht:** 5'11" **Wt:** 170 **Born:** 5/23/1979 **Age:** 26

Year Team	Lg	G	AB	H	2B	3B	HR	(Hm Rd)	TB	R	RBI	RC	TBB	IBB	SO	HBP	SH	SF	SB	CS	SB%	GDP	Avg	OBP	Slg
2004 Pawtucket*	AAA	55	221	60	13	3	4	(- -)	91	30	19	31	21	0	53	0	2	1	10	2	.83	2	.271	.333	.412
2001 San Diego	NL	55	153	32	6	0	4	(0 4)	50	27	12	17	25	0	50	0	1	0	6	2	.75	2	.209	.320	.327
2002 San Diego	NL	25	29	5	2	0	0	(0 0)	7	5	0	0	3	0	6	0	1	0	3	2	.60	0	.172	.250	.241
2004 Boston	AL	52	79	13	2	1	0	(0 0)	17	6	2	0	0	0	20	0	0	0	2	0	1.00	1	.165	.165	.215
3 ML YEARS		132	261	50	10	1	4	(0 4)	74	38	14	17	28	0	76	0	2	0	11	4	.73	3	.192	.270	.284

Jack Cressend

Pitches: R **Bats:** R **Pos:** RP-11 **Ht:** 6'1" **Wt:** 185 **Born:** 5/13/1975 **Age:** 30

Year Team	Lg	G	GS	CG	GF	IP	BFP	H	R	ER	HR	SH	SF	HB	TBB	IBB	SO	WP	Bk	W	L	Pct	ShO	Sv-Op	Hld	ERC	ERA
2004 Buffalo*	AAA	24	4	0	3	52.2	238	73	30	30	7	1	2	0	10	0	41	1	1	10	1	.909	0	1--		5.65	5.13
2000 Minnesota	AL	11	0		4	13.2	61	20	8	8	0	0	0	6	0	6	0	0	0	0	-		0-0		6.65	5.27
2001 Minnesota	AL	44	0	0	9	56.1	232	50	24	23	6	2	2	1	16	0	40	2	0	3	2	.600	0	0-2	5	3.13	3.67
2002 Minnesota	AL	23	0	0	4	32.0	154	40	25	21	6	1	2	1	19	4	22	1	0	0	1	.000	0	0-0	6	6.92	5.91
2003 Cleveland	AL	33	0	0	8	43.0	174	40	12	12	1	4	0	2	9	1	28	1	0	2	1	.667	0	0-1	5	2.67	2.51
2004 Cleveland	AL	11	0	0	1	15.2	78	22	11	11	4	1	1	0	10	2	8	0	0	0	1	.000	0	0-0	2	8.59	6.32
5 ML YEARS		122	0	0	26	160.2	699	172	80	75	17	8	5	4	60	7	104	4	0	5	5	.500	0	0-3	12	4.46	4.20

Coco Crisp

Bats: B **Throws:** R **Pos:** CF-94; LF-37; DH-6; PH-6; PR-5 **Ht:** 6'0" **Wt:** 185 **Born:** 11/1/1979 **Age:** 25

Year Team	Lg	G	AB	H	2B	3B	HR	(Hm Rd)	TB	R	RBI	RC	TBB	IBB	SO	HBP	SH	SF	SB	CS	SB%	GDP	Avg	OBP	Slg
2002 Cleveland	AL	32	127	33	9	2	1	(1 0)	49	16	9	19	11	0	19	0	3	2	4	1	.80	4	.260	.314	.386
2003 Cleveland	AL	99	414	110	15	6	3	(3 0)	146	55	27	48	23	1	51	0	7	3	15	9	.63	4	.266	.302	.353
2004 Cleveland	AL	139	491	146	24	2	15	(8 7)	219	78	71	73	36	4	69	0	9	2	20	13	.61	8	.297	.344	.446
3 ML YEARS		270	1032	289	48	10	19	(12 7)	414	149	107	140	70	5	139	0	19	7	39	23	.63	12	.280	.324	.401

Bobby Crosby

Bats: R **Throws:** R **Pos:** SS-152 **Ht:** 6'3" **Wt:** 195 **Born:** 1/12/1980 **Age:** 25

Year Team	Lg	G	AB	H	2B	3B	HR	(Hm Rd)	TB	R	RBI	RC	TBB	IBB	SO	HBP	SH	SF	SB	CS	SB%	GDP	Avg	OBP	Slg
2001 Modesto	A+	11	38	15	5	0	1	(- -)	23	7	3	8	3	0	8	0	0	0	0	0	-	1	.395	.439	.605
2002 Modesto	A+	73	280	86	17	2	2	(- -)	113	47	38	47	33	0	43	7	2	1	5	0	1.00	5	.307	.393	.404
2002 Midland	AA	59	228	64	16	0	7	(- -)	101	31	31	31	19	1	41	0	3	1	9	2	.82	9	.281	.335	.443
2003 Sacramento	AAA	127	465	143	32	6	22	(- -)	253	86	90	95	63	2	110	7	4	4	24	4	.86	16	.308	.395	.544
2003 Oakland	AL	11	12	0	0	0	0	(0 0)	0	1	0	0	1	0	5	1	0	0	0	0	-	0	.000	.143	.000
2004 Oakland	AL	151	545	130	34	1	22	(11 11)	232	70	64	60	58	0	141	9	5	6	7	3	.70	19	.239	.319	.426
2 ML YEARS		162	557	130	34	1	22	(11 11)	232	71	64	60	59	0	146	10	5	6	7	3	.70	19	.233	.315	.417

Bubba Crosby

Bats: L **Throws:** L **Pos:** RF-25; PR-15; CF-12; LF-11; PH-6; DH-2 **Ht:** 5'11" **Wt:** 185 **Born:** 8/11/1976 **Age:** 28

Year Team	Lg	G	AB	H	2B	3B	HR	(Hm Rd)	TB	R	RBI	RC	TBB	IBB	SO	HBP	SH	SF	SB	CS	SB%	GDP	Avg	OBP	Slg
1998 Sn Brnardino	A+	56	199	43	9	2	0	(- -)	56	25	14	14	17	0	38	4	4	3	3	5	.38	3	.216	.274	.281
1999 Sn Brnardino	A+	96	371	110	21	3	1	(- -)	140	53	37	56	42	3	71	6	4	1	19	8	.70	6	.296	.376	.377
2000 Vero Beach	A+	73	274	73	13	8	8	(- -)	126	50	51	43	31	3	41	7	3	1	27	10	.73	9	.266	.355	.460
2000 Sn Brnardino	A+	3	12	3	0	0	0	(- -)	3	2	2	0	0	0	4	0	0	0	1	0	1.00	0	.250	.250	.250
2001 Las Vegas	AAA	13	42	9	2	1	0	(- -)	13	5	5	2	1	0	8	0	0	0	1	1	.50	0	.214	.233	.310
2001 Jacksonville	AA	107	384	116	22	5	6	(- -)	166	68	47	64	37	2	60	8	7	7	22	6	.79	7	.302	.369	.432
2002 Las Vegas	AAA	73	279	73	12	1	9	(- -)	114	26	36	36	19	1	47	2	3	1	3	1	.75	3	.262	.312	.409
2002 Jacksonville	AA	38	150	39	6	2	2	(- -)	55	14	20	18	11	0	23	2	1	1	7	3	.70	2	.260	.317	.367
2003 Columbus	AAA	16	63	19	2	1	2	(- -)	29	9	8	11	6	0	12	1	0	1	3	0	1.00	0	.302	.368	.460
2003 Las Vegas	AAA	76	277	100	24	8	12	(- -)	176	57	57	67	25	0	47	3	1	7	8	0	1.00	6	.361	.410	.635
2004 Columbus	AAA	33	116	32	5	2	1	(- -)	44	18	15	17	14	0	26	4	1	3	3	3	.50	2	.276	.365	.379
2003 Los Angeles	NL	9	12	1	0	0	0	(0 0)	1	0	1	0	0	0	3	0	0	0	0	0	-	0	.083	.083	.083
2004 New York	AL	55	53	8	2	0	2	(2 0)	16	8	7	7	2	0	13	1	2	0	2	0	1.00	0	.151	.196	.302
2 ML YEARS		64	65	9	2	0	2	(2 0)	17	8	8	7	2	0	16	1	2	0	2	0	1.00	0	.138	.176	.262

Jim Crowell

Pitches: L **Bats:** R **Pos:** RP-4   **Ht:** 6'4" **Wt:** 225 **Born:** 5/14/1974 **Age:** 31

		HOW MUCH HE PITCHED						WHAT HE GAVE UP												THE RESULTS							
Year Team	Lg	G	GS	CG	GF	IP	BFP	H	R	ER	HR	SH	SF	HB	TBB	IBB	SO	WP	Bk	W	L	Pct	ShO	Sv-Op	Hld	ERC	ERA
1995 Watertown	A-	12	9	0	0	56.2	241	50	22	18	1	0	2	1	27	1	48	2	1	5	2	.714	0	0- -	-	3.21	2.86
1996 Columbus	A	28	28	3	0	165.1	710	163	89	76	16	9	5	9	69	0	104	12	0	7	10	.412	0	0- -	-	4.33	4.14
1997 Kinston	A+	17	17	0	0	114.0	461	96	41	30	4	3	2	8	26	0	94	3	0	9	4	.692	0	0- -	-	2.47	2.37
1997 Akron	AA	3	3	0	0	18.0	80	13	12	9	2	1	1	1	11	0	7	1	0	1	0	1.000	0	0- -	-	3.52	4.50
1997 Chattanooga	AA	3	3	0	0	19.0	75	19	6	6	2	1	1	0	5	0	14	0	0	1	.667	0	0- -	-	3.82	2.84
1997 Indianapolis	AAA	3	3	1	0	19.2	85	19	7	6	1	0	2	0	8	0	6	2	0	1	1	.500	1	0- -	-	3.53	2.75
1998 Chrlstn - WV	A	5	5	0	0	15.0	83	28	23	22	1	0	2	2	9	0	9	1	0	0	4	.000	0	0- -	-	10.68	13.20
1998 Chattanooga	AA	5	5	0	0	24.1	129	38	27	23	2	0	3	0	17	0	10	2	2	0	4	.000	0	0- -	-	8.40	8.51
1998 Indianapolis	AAA	1	1	0	0	4.0	19	7	3	3	0	0	0	0	0	0	2	0	0	0	0	-	0	0- -	-	5.92	6.75
2002 Scrtn/WlksBr	AAA	4	4	0	0	25.0	102	20	7	7	2	2	0	1	11	0	19	1	0	2	0	1.000	0	0- -	-	3.27	2.52
2003 Scrtn/WlksBr	AAA	54	0	0	34	54.2	251	63	31	25	5	5	2	2	23	5	42	0	1	0	8	.000	0	9- -	-	4.85	4.12
2004 Scrtn/WlksBr	AAA	46	0	0	37	63.2	266	61	22	17	6	1	0	1	14	4	44	0	1	7	3	.700	0	16- -	-	3.03	2.40
1997 Cincinnati	NL	2	1	0	1	6.1		12	7	7	2				5	0	3	0	0	0	1	.000	0	0-	-		9.95
2004 Philadelphia	NL	4	0	0	0	3.0	18	6	2	1	0	0	0	0	0	0	1	0	0	0	0	-	0	0-0	0	6.14	3.00
2 ML YEARS		6	1	0	1	9.1	18	18	9	8	2	0	0	0	5	0	4	0	0	0	1	.000	0	0-0	0	33.68	7.71

Eric Crozier

Bats: L **Throws:** L **Pos:** DH-7; 1B-5; PH-3   **Ht:** 6'4" **Wt:** 200 **Born:** 8/11/1978 **Age:** 26

		BATTING																		BASERUNNING				AVERAGES		
Year Team	Lg	G	AB	H	2B	3B	HR	(Hm	Rd)	TB	R	RBI	RC	TBB	IBB	SO	HBP	SH	SF	SB	CS	SB%	GDP	Avg	OBP	Slg
2000 Mahning VI	A-	52	179	38	9	0	4	(-	-)	59	31	24	20	30	0	61	0	1	1	4	2	.67	3	.212	.324	.330
2001 Columbus	A	67	221	52	9	2	4	(-	-)	77	41	19	28	37	1	84	1	2	1	5	3	.63	3	.235	.346	.348
2002 Kinston	A+	72	258	84	16	2	9	(-	-)	131	40	55	55	42	2	57	4	0	3	4	3	.57	4	.326	.423	.508
2002 Akron	AA	43	142	42	8	1	1	(-	-)	55	19	13	24	21	0	50	3	3	0	1	0	1.00	6	.296	.398	.387
2003 Akron	AA	108	347	85	10	3	19	(-	-)	158	52	52	55	51	3	92	3	0	3	5	3	.63	3	.245	.344	.455
2004 Syracuse	AAA	25	94	26	8	0	1	(-	-)	37	12	16	14	16	1	27	2	1	0	3	2	.60	2	.277	.393	.394
2004 Buffalo	AAA	84	296	88	21	0	20	(-	-)	169	55	53	58	36	0	67	1	1	0	5	1	.83	8	.297	.375	.571
2004 Toronto	AL	14	33	5	2	0	2	(1	1)	13	5	4	4	6	0	19	0	0	0	0	0	-	0	.152	.282	.394

Francisco Cruceta

Pitches: R **Bats:** R **Pos:** SP-2   **Ht:** 6'2" **Wt:** 180 **Born:** 7/4/1981 **Age:** 23

		HOW MUCH HE PITCHED						WHAT HE GAVE UP												THE RESULTS							
Year Team	Lg	G	GS	CG	GF	IP	BFP	H	R	ER	HR	SH	SF	HB	TBB	IBB	SO	WP	Bk	W	L	Pct	ShO	Sv-Op	Hld	ERC	ERA
2002 Sth Georgia	A	20	20	3	0	112.2	466	98	42	35	7	0	2	4	34	0	111	10	0	8	5	.615	2	0- -	-	2.89	2.80
2002 Kinston	A+	7	7	0	0	39.2	169	31	13	11	2	0	1	0	25	1	37	1	1	2	0	1.000	0	0- -	-	3.42	2.50
2003 Akron	AA	27	25	6	1	163.1	684	141	70	56	7	3	6	2	66	0	134	3	4	13	9	.591	0	0- -	-	3.02	3.09
2004 Akron	AA	15	15	1	0	88.2	381	89	58	52	11	2	3	2	33	0	45	5	1	4	8	.333	0	0- -	-	4.26	5.28
2004 Buffalo	AAA	14	14	1	0	83.0	341	78	35	30	6	2	2	0	36	0	62	9	1	6	5	.545	0	0- -	-	3.86	3.25
2004 Cleveland	AL	2	2	0	0	7.2	39	10	9	8	1	0	1	1	4	0	9	1	0	0	1	.000	0	0-0	0	6.85	9.39

Deivi Cruz

Bats: R **Throws:** R **Pos:** SS-103; PH-24; 2B-2; 3B-1; PR-1   **Ht:** 6'0" **Wt:** 184 **Born:** 11/6/1972 **Age:** 32

		BATTING																		BASERUNNING				AVERAGES		
Year Team	Lg	G	AB	H	2B	3B	HR	(Hm	Rd)	TB	R	RBI	RC	TBB	IBB	SO	HBP	SH	SF	SB	CS	SB%	GDP	Avg	OBP	Slg
2004 Fresno*	AAA	12	42	13	3	0	1	(-	-)	19	5	6	6	3	0	2	0	0	1	0	0	-	1	.310	.348	.452
1997 Detroit	AL	147	436	105	26	4	2	(0	2)	137	35	40	31	14	0	55	0	14	3	3	6	.33	9	.241	.263	.314
1998 Detroit	AL	135	454	118	22	3	5	(5	0)	161	52	45	42	13	0	55	3	5	2	3	4	.43	11	.260	.284	.355
1999 Detroit	AL	155	518	147	35	0	13	(9	4)	221	64	58	64	12	0	57	4	14	5	1	4	.20	10	.284	.302	.427
2000 Detroit	AL	156	583	176	46	5	10	(1	9)	262	68	82	74	13	2	43	4	8	7	1	4	.20	25	.302	.318	.449
2001 Detroit	AL	110	414	106	28	1	7	(2	5)	157	39	52	42	17	0	46	4	1	2	4	1	.80	13	.256	.291	.379
2002 San Diego	NL	151	514	135	28	2	7	(3	4)	188	49	47	40	22	2	58	3	3	5	2	3	.40	20	.263	.294	.366
2003 Baltimore	AL	152	548	137	24	2	14	(7	7)	207	61	65	55	13	1	49	2	7	2	1	2	.33	13	.250	.269	.378
2004 San Francisco	NL	127	397	116	30	2	7	(2	5)	171	46	55	54	17	6	32	3	8	6	1	3	.25	12	.292	.322	.431
8 ML YEARS		1133	3864	1040	239	15	65	(29	36)	1504	414	444	402	121	11	395	23	60	32	16	27	.37	113	.269	.293	.389

Jacob Cruz

Bats: L **Throws:** L **Pos:** PH-67; RF-26; 1B-6; LF-4; DH-2; PR-1   **Ht:** 6'0" **Wt:** 210 **Born:** 1/28/1973 **Age:** 32

		BATTING																		BASERUNNING				AVERAGES		
Year Team	Lg	G	AB	H	2B	3B	HR	(Hm	Rd)	TB	R	RBI	RC	TBB	IBB	SO	HBP	SH	SF	SB	CS	SB%	GDP	Avg	OBP	Slg
2004 Louisville*	AAA	17	54	17	4	0	3	(-	-)	30	12	7	11	10	1	10	0	0	1	0	0	-	0	.315	.415	.556
1996 San Francisco	NL	33	77	18	3	0	3	(3	0)	30	10	10	10	12	0	24	2	1	0	0	1	.00	2	.234	.352	.390
1997 San Francisco	NL	16	25	4	1	0	0	(0	0)	5	3	3	1	3	0	4	0	0	1	0	0	-	3	.160	.241	.200
1998 SF-Cle		4	4	0	0	0	0	(0	0)	0	0	0	0	0	0	3	0	0	0	0	0	-	0	.000	.000	.000
1999 Cleveland	AL	32	88	29	5	1	3	(3	0)	45	14	17	14	5	0	13	1	1	1	0	2	.00	4	.330	.368	.511
2000 Cleveland	AL	11	29	7	3	0	0	(0	0)	10	3	5	5	4	1	4	1	0	1	1	0	1.00	4	.241	.361	.345
2001 Cle-Col		72	144	31	5	0	4	(2	2)	48	19	18	13	15	0	50	4	1	2	0	4	.00	4	.215	.303	.333
2002 Detroit	AL	35	88	24	3	1	2	(0	2)	35	12	6	11	13	0	20	3	1	2	3	1	.75	2	.273	.377	.398
2004 Cincinnati	NL	96	147	33	8	0	3	(2	1)	50	22	28	20	16	2	43	4	0	0	0	0	-	5	.224	.317	.340
1998 San Francisco	NL	3	3	0	0	0	0	(0	0)	0	0	0	0	0	0	2	0	0	0	0	0	-	0	.000	.000	.000
1998 Cleveland	AL	1	1	0	0	0	0	(0	0)	0	0	0	0	0	0	1	0	0	0	0	0	-	0	.000	.000	.000
2001 Cleveland	AL	28	68	15	4	0	3	(2	1)	28	12	11	7	5	0	23	3	0	2	0	2	.00	3	.221	.303	.412
2001 Colorado	NL	44	76	16	1	0	1	(0	1)	20	7	7	6	10	0	27	1	1	0	0	2	.00	1	.211	.303	.263
8 ML YEARS		299	602	146	28	2	15	(10	5)	223	83	87	74	69	2	161	15	4	7	4	8	.33	20	.243	.332	.370

Jose Cruz

Bats: B **Throws:** R **Pos:** RF-151; PH-3; CF-1; PR-1 — **Ht:** 6'0" **Wt:** 210 **Born:** 4/19/1974 **Age:** 31

Year Team	Lg	G	AB	H	2B	3B	HR	(Hm	Rd)	TB	R	RBI	RC	TBB	IBB	SO	HBP	SH	SF	SB	CS	SB%	GDP	Avg	OBP	Slg
1997 Sea-Tor	AL	104	395	98	19	1	26	(11	15)	197	59	68	63	41	2	117	0	1	5	7	2	.78	5	.248	.315	.499
1998 Toronto	AL	105	352	89	14	3	11	(4	7)	142	55	42	55	57	3	99	0	1	0	11	4	.73	0	.253	.354	.403
1999 Toronto	AL	106	349	84	19	3	14	(8	6)	151	63	45	57	64	5	91	0	1	0	14	4	.78	6	.241	.358	.433
2000 Toronto	AL	**162**	603	146	32	5	31	(15	16)	281	91	76	91	71	3	129	2	2	3	15	5	.75	11	.242	.323	.466
2001 Toronto	AL	146	577	158	38	4	34	(15	19)	306	92	88	101	45	4	138	1	2	2	32	5	.86	8	.274	.326	.530
2002 Toronto	AL	124	466	114	26	5	18	(11	7)	204	64	70	71	51	1	106	0	1	4	7	1	.88	8	.245	.317	.438
2003 San Francisco	NL	158	539	135	26	1	20	(9	11)	223	90	68	71	102	6	121	0	2	7	5	8	.38	14	.250	.366	.414
2004 Tampa Bay	AL	153	545	132	25	8	21	(13	8)	236	76	78	79	76	8	117	2	5	8	11	6	.65	6	.242	.333	.433
1997 Seattle	AL	49	183	49	12	1	12	(7	5)	99	28	34	31	13	0	45	0	1	1	1	0	1.00	3	.268	.315	.541
1997 Toronto	AL	55	212	49	7	0	14	(4	10)	98	31	34	32	28	2	72	0	0	4	6	2	.75	2	.231	.316	.462
8 ML YEARS		1058	3826	956	199	30	175	(86	89)	1740	590	535	588	507	32	918	5	14	33	102	35	.74	58	.250	.336	.455

Juan Cruz

Pitches: R **Bats:** R **Pos:** RP-50 — **Ht:** 6'2" **Wt:** 165 **Born:** 10/15/1978 **Age:** 26

Year Team	Lg	G	GS	CG	GF	IP	BFP	H	R	ER	HR	SH	SF	HB	TBB	IBB	SO	WP	Bk	W	L	Pct	ShO	Sv-Op	Hld	ERC	ERA
2001 Chicago	NL	8	8	0	0	44.2	185	40	16	16	4	2	0	2	17	1	39	0	0	3	1	.750	0	0-0	0	3.59	3.22
2002 Chicago	NL	45	9	0	14	97.1	431	84	56	43	11	7	8	8	59	4	81	1	0	3	11	.214	0	1-4	3	4.49	3.98
2003 Chicago	NL	25	6	0	3	61.0	284	66	44	41	7	7	2	7	28	0	65	4	0	2	7	.222	0	0-1	1	5.23	6.05
2004 Atlanta	NL	50	0	0	22	72.0	300	59	24	22	7	4	1	2	30	1	70	1	0	6	2	.750	0	0-0	2	3.25	2.75
4 ML YEARS		128	23	0	39	275.0	1200	249	140	122	29	20	11	19	134	6	255	6	0	14	21	.400	0	1-5	6	4.17	3.99

Darwin Cubillan

Pitches: R **Bats:** R **Pos:** RP-7 — **Ht:** 6'2" **Wt:** 170 **Born:** 11/15/1972 **Age:** 32

Year Team	Lg	G	GS	CG	GF	IP	BFP	H	R	ER	HR	SH	SF	HB	TBB	IBB	SO	WP	Bk	W	L	Pct	ShO	Sv-Op	Hld	ERC	ERA
2004 Ottawa*	AAA	51	0	0	42	51.0	222	52	26	26	7	0	0	2	17	1	53	1	0	3	4	.429	0	24--	-	4.25	4.59
2000 Tor-Tex	AL	20	0	0	6	33.1	172	52	36	35	9	0	3	1	25	0	27	1	0	1	0	1.000	0	0-0	0	11.03	9.45
2001 Montreal	NL	29	0	0	11	26.1	121	31	13	12	1	1	3	0	12	1	19	1	0	0	0	-	0	0-0	1	4.69	4.10
2004 Baltimore	AL	7	0	0	0	10.0	50	13	7	6	3	0	0	0	7	0	8	1	0	0	0	-	0	0-1	0	8.72	5.40
2000 Toronto	AL	7	0	0	1	15.2	75	20	14	14	5	0	0	1	11	0	14	0	0	1	0	1.000	0	0-0	0	9.56	8.04
2000 Texas	AL	13	0	0	5	17.2	97	32	22	21	4	0	3	0	14	0	13	1	0	0	0	-	0	0-0	0	12.33	10.70
3 ML YEARS		56	0	0	17	69.2	343	96	56	53	13	1	6	1	44	1	54	3	0	1	0	1.000	0	0-1	1	8.13	6.85

Mike Cuddyer

Bats: R **Throws:** R **Pos:** 2B-48; 3B-43; PH-12; 1B-10; RF-8; LF-7; DH-4; PR-3 — **Ht:** 6'2" **Wt:** 190 **Born:** 3/27/1979 **Age:** 26

Year Team	Lg	G	AB	H	2B	3B	HR	(Hm	Rd)	TB	R	RBI	RC	TBB	IBB	SO	HBP	SH	SF	SB	CS	SB%	GDP	Avg	OBP	Slg
2001 Minnesota	AL	8	18	4	2	0	0	(0	0)	6	1	1	2	2	0	6	0	0	0	1	0	1.00	1	.222	.300	.333
2002 Minnesota	AL	41	112	29	7	0	4	(2	2)	48	12	13	14	8	0	30	1	1	1	2	0	1.00	3	.259	.311	.429
2003 Minnesota	AL	35	102	25	1	3	4	(1	3)	44	14	8	10	12	0	19	0	0	0	1	1	.50	6	.245	.325	.431
2004 Minnesota	AL	115	339	89	22	1	12	(8	4)	149	49	45	50	37	2	74	3	2	1	5	5	.50	8	.263	.339	.440
4 ML YEARS		199	571	147	32	4	20	(11	9)	247	76	67	76	59	2	129	4	3	2	9	6	.60	18	.257	.330	.433

Midre Cummings

Bats: L **Throws:** R **Pos:** DH-12; PH-10; LF-2 — **Ht:** 6'0" **Wt:** 195 **Born:** 10/14/1971 **Age:** 33

Year Team	Lg	G	AB	H	2B	3B	HR	(Hm	Rd)	TB	R	RBI	RC	TBB	IBB	SO	HBP	SH	SF	SB	CS	SB%	GDP	Avg	OBP	Slg
2004 Durham*	AAA	119	414	118	26	3	27	(-	-)	231	83	89	93	86	12	107	3	0	4	13	2	.87	6	.285	.408	.558
1993 Pittsburgh	NL	13	36	4	1	0	0	(0	0)	5	5	3	0	4	0	9	0	0	0	0	0	-	1	.111	.195	.139
1994 Pittsburgh	NL	24	86	21	4	0	1	(1	0)	28	11	12	8	4	0	18	1	0	1	0	0	-	0	.244	.283	.326
1995 Pittsburgh	NL	59	152	37	7	1	2	(1	1)	52	13	15	16	13	3	30	0	0	0	1	0	1.00	0	.243	.303	.342
1996 Pittsburgh	NL	24	85	19	3	1	3	(2	1)	33	11	7	7	0	0	16	0	1	1	0	0	-	0	.224	.221	.388
1997 Pit-Phi	NL	115	314	83	22	6	4	(3	1)	129	35	31	42	31	0	56	1	2	2	2	3	.40	3	.264	.330	.411
1998 Boston	AL	67	120	34	8	0	5	(4	1)	57	20	15	21	17	0	19	2	1	0	3	3	.50	2	.283	.381	.475
1999 Minnesota	AL	16	38	10	0	0	1	(1	0)	13	1	9	4	3	0	7	0	0	1	2	0	1.00	0	.263	.310	.342
2000 Min-Bos	AL	98	206	57	10	0	4	(2	2)	79	29	24	25	17	1	28	3	1	0	0	0	-	0	.277	.341	.383
2001 Arizona	NL	20	20	6	1	0	0	(0	0)	7	1	1	1	0	0	4	0	0	0	0	0	-	2	.300	.286	.350
2004 Tampa Bay	AL	22	54	15	4	0	2	(2	0)	25	10	7	12	5	0	12	2	0	0	1	0	1.00	0	.278	.361	.463
1997 Pittsburgh	NL	52	106	20	6	2	3	(2	1)	39	11	8	9	8	0	26	1	1	0	0	0	-	0	.189	.252	.368
1997 Philadelphia	NL	63	208	63	16	4	1	(1	0)	90	24	23	33	23	0	30	0	1	2	2	3	.40	2	.303	.369	.433
2000 Boston	AL	21	25	7	0	0	0	(0	0)	7	1	2	3	6	0	3	0	0	0	0	0	-	0	.280	.419	.280
2000 Minnesota	AL	77	181	50	10	0	4	(2	2)	72	28	22	22	11	1	25	3	1	0	0	0	-	4	.276	.328	.398
10 ML YEARS		458	1111	286	60	8	22	(16	6)	428	136	124	136	94	4	199	9	5	7	9	6	.60	14	.257	.319	.385

Will Cunnane

Pitches: R **Bats:** R **Pos:** RP-9 — **Ht:** 6'1" **Wt:** 205 **Born:** 4/24/1974 **Age:** 31

Year Team	Lg	G	GS	CG	GF	IP	BFP	H	R	ER	HR	SH	SF	HB	TBB	IBB	SO	WP	Bk	W	L	Pct	ShO	Sv-Op	Hld	ERC	ERA
2004 Richmond*	AAA	35	2	0	14	43.0	200	52	27	25	4	0	0	0	22	1	42	1	0	1	7	.125	0	2--	-	5.61	5.23
1997 San Diego	NL	54	8	0	16	91.1	430	114	69	59	11	1	1	5	49	3	79	3	0	6	3	.667	0	0-2	4	6.48	5.81
1998 San Diego	NL	3	0	0	1	3.0	14	4	2	2	1	0	0	0	1	1	1	0	0	0	0	-	0	0-0	0	6.84	6.00
1999 San Diego	NL	24	0	0	2	31.0	130	34	19	18	8	2	0	0	12	3	22	3	0	2	1	.667	0	0-0	5	5.87	5.23
2000 San Diego	NL	27	3	0	4	38.1	169	35	21	18	2	1	1	1	21	0	34	1	0	1	1	.500	0	0-0	1	3.90	4.23
2001 Milwaukee	NL	31	1	0	6	51.2	238	66	34	31	6	7	1	2	22	6	37	0	0	0	3	.000	0	0-0	1	5.93	5.40

Year Team	Lg	G	GS	CG	GF	IP	BFP	H	R	ER	HR	SH	SF	HB	TBB	IBB	SO	WP	Bk	W	L	Pct	ShO	Sv-Op	Hld	ERC	ERA
2002 Chicago	NL	16	0	0	2	26.1	115	27	16	16	5	1	0	1	13	1	30	1	0	1	1	.500	0	0-1	1	5.49	5.47
2003 Atlanta	NL	20	0	0	8	20.0	80	14	6	6	2	0	0	0	6	2	20	1	0	2	2	.500	0	3-3	5	2.00	2.70
2004 Atlanta	NL	9	0	0	5	12.1	59	18	10	10	3	0	2	1	4	1	11	0	0	1	1	.500	0	0-1	0	7.88	7.30
8 ML YEARS		184	12	0	44	274.0	1235	312	177	160	38	12	5	10	128	17	234	9	0	13	12	.520	0	3-7	17	5.53	5.26

Jack Cust

Bats: L Throws: R Pos: PH-1   **Ht: 6'1" Wt: 205 Born: 1/16/1979 Age: 26**

Year Team	Lg	G	AB	H	2B	3B	HR	(Hm	Rd)	TB	R	RBI	RC	TBB	IBB	SO	HBP	SH	SF	SB	CS	SB%	GDP	Avg	OBP	Slg
2004 Ottawa*	AAA	102	344	81	15	1	17	(-	-)	149	55	55	55	65	3	127	2	0	2	4	0	1.00	7	.235	.358	.433
2001 Arizona	NL	3	2	1	0	0	0	(0	0)	1	0	0	1	1	0	0	0	0	0	0	0	-	0	.500	.667	.500
2002 Colorado	NL	35	65	11	2	0	1	(0	1)	16	8	8	6	12	0	32	0	0	1	0	1	.00	3	.169	.295	.246
2003 Baltimore	AL	27	73	19	7	0	4	(2	2)	38	7	11	17	10	0	25	1	0	0	0	0	-	0	.260	.357	.521
2004 Baltimore	AL	1	1	0	0	0	0	(0	0)	0	0	0	0	0	0	1	0	0	0	0	0	-	0	.000	.000	.000
4 ML YEARS		66	141	31	9	0	5	(2	3)	55	15	19	24	23	0	58	1	0	1	0	1	.00	3	.220	.331	.390

Omar Daal

Pitches: L Bats: L Pos: SP   **Ht: 6'3" Wt: 204 Born: 3/1/1972 Age: 33**

Year Team	Lg	G	GS	CG	GF	IP	BFP	H	R	ER	HR	SH	SF	HB	TBB	IBB	SO	WP	Bk	W	L	Pct	ShO	Sv-Op	Hld	ERC	ERA
1993 Los Angeles	NL	47	0	0	12	35.1	155	36	20	20	5	2	2	0	21	3	19	1	2	2	3	.400	0	0-1	7	5.29	5.09
1994 Los Angeles	NL	24	0	0	5	13.2	55	12	5	5	1	1	0	0	5	0	9	1	1	0	0	-	0	0-0	3	3.24	3.29
1995 Los Angeles	NL	28	0	0	8	20.0	100	29	16	16	1	1	1	1	15	4	11	0	1	4	0	1.000	0	0-1	4	7.85	7.20
1996 Montreal	NL	64	6	0	9	87.1	366	74	40	39	10	2	2	1	37	3	82	1	1	4	5	.444	0	0-4	9	3.44	4.02
1997 Mon-Tor	NL	42	3	0	6	57.1	270	82	48	45	7	7	1	2	21	3	44	2	0	2	3	.400	0	1-3	3	6.76	7.06
1998 Arizona	NL	33	23	3	4	162.2	664	146	60	52	12	9	6	3	51	3	132	0	1	8	12	.400	1	0-0	1	3.12	2.88
1999 Arizona	NL	32	32	2	0	214.2	895	188	92	87	21	4	7	7	79	3	148	3	2	16	9	.640	1	0-0	0	3.39	3.65
2000 Ari-Phi	NL	32	28	0	1	167.0	775	208	128	114	26	6	9	6	72	11	96	0	2	4	19	.174	0	0-0	0	6.17	6.14
2001 Philadelphia	NL	32	32	0	0	185.2	801	199	100	92	26	7	5	5	56	3	107	0	3	13	7	.650	0	0-0	0	4.45	4.46
2002 Los Angeles	NL	39	23	0	3	161.1	668	142	73	70	20	11	4	4	54	3	105	0	0	11	9	.550	0	0-0	1	3.42	3.90
2003 Baltimore	AL	19	17	0	1	93.2	434	134	69	66	11	8	3	2	30	1	53	2	0	4	11	.267	0	0-0	0	6.57	6.34
1997 Montreal	NL	33	0	0	6	30.1	150	48	35	33	4	5	1	2	15	3	16	1	0	1	2	.333	0	1-3	3	8.60	9.79
1997 Toronto	AL	9	3	0	0	27.0	120	34	13	12	3	2	0	0	6	0	28	1	0	1	1	.500	0	0-0	0	4.85	4.00
2000 Arizona	NL	20	16	0	1	96.0	460	127	88	77	17	3	5	7	42	11	45	0	1	2	10	.167	0	0-0	0	6.78	7.22
2000 Philadelphia	NL	12	12	0	0	71.0	315	81	40	37	9	3	1	2	30	0	51	0	1	2	9	.182	0	0-0	0	5.37	4.69
11 ML YEARS		392	164	5	41	1198.2	5183	1250	651	606	140	58	37	34	441	37	806	10	13	68	78	.466	2	1-9	29	4.40	4.55

Casey Daigle

Pitches: R Bats: R Pos: SP-10   **Ht: 6'5" Wt: 217 Born: 4/4/1981 Age: 24**

Year Team	Lg	G	GS	CG	GF	IP	BFP	H	R	ER	HR	SH	SF	HB	TBB	IBB	SO	WP	Bk	W	L	Pct	ShO	Sv-Op	Hld	ERC	ERA
2000 Missoula	R+	15	15	0	0	82.2	390	88	57	45	4	2	0	9	54	0	56	10	3	3	5	.375	0	0--	-	5.48	4.90
2001 South Bend	A	28	27	2	0	164.0	727	180	100	75	11	3	9	14	55	0	85	16	4	10	10	.500	1	0--	-	4.45	4.12
2002 Lancaster	A+	21	21	0	0	122.0	137	137	82	69	19	7	8	9	42	0	85	7	2	4	10	.286	0	0--	-	22.52	5.09
2002 El Paso	AA	7	7	2	0	44.1	182	46	19	16	5	2	1	3	9	0	29	2	0	3	2	.600	0	0--	-	3.99	3.25
2003 El Paso	AA	29	27	1	0	176.1	793	219	108	90	9	7	8	6	51	1	115	14	0	11	11	.500	0	0--	-	4.73	4.59
2004 Tucson	AAA	18	15	0	0	100.2	474	154	85	77	21	4	4	5	24	0	51	3	0	4	9	.308	0	0--	-	7.71	6.88
2004 Arizona	NL	10	10	0	0	49.0	230	63	41	39	9	3	1	2	27	3	17	1	1	2	3	.400	0	0-0	0	7.30	7.16

Brian Dallimore

Bats: R Throws: R Pos: 2B-9; PH-8; 3B-6; PR-1   **Ht: 6'1" Wt: 180 Born: 11/15/1973 Age: 31**

Year Team	Lg	G	AB	H	2B	3B	HR	(Hm	Rd)	TB	R	RBI	RC	TBB	IBB	SO	HBP	SH	SF	SB	CS	SB%	GDP	Avg	OBP	Slg
1996 Auburn	A-	74	290	77	17	3	5	(-	-)	115	50	30	37	18	0	38	10	0	4	7	5	.58	5	.266	.326	.397
1997 Quad City	A	130	492	128	23	3	6	(-	-)	175	80	48	59	38	0	76	20	6	5	24	8	.75	19	.260	.335	.356
1997 Kissimmee	A+	1	3	0	0	0	0	(-	-)	0	0	0	0	0	0	2	0	0	0	0	0	-	0	.000	.000	.000
1998 Kissimmee	A+	62	240	61	11	1	0	(-	-)	74	34	19	23	19	0	42	5	4	1	7	5	.58	6	.254	.321	.308
1999 Kissimmee	A+	19	74	20	2	0	0	(-	-)	22	12	3	8	4	0	10	3	1	1	2	1	.67	1	.270	.329	.297
1999 Jackson	AA	70	251	67	13	1	5	(-	-)	97	38	19	31	16	0	44	10	2	1	13	3	.81	12	.267	.335	.386
2000 Round Rock	AA	5	11	2	1	0	1	(-	-)	6	1	3	1	1	0	3	0	0	0	0	0	-	0	.182	.250	.545
2000 El Paso	AA	107	356	99	16	1	4	(-	-)	129	50	53	43	25	3	55	6	3	5	17	3	.85	13	.278	.332	.362
2001 El Paso	AA	127	517	169	38	6	8	(-	-)	243	74	67	86	30	1	56	13	12	1	11	13	.46	9	.327	.378	.470
2002 Tucson	AAA	122	419	123	26	2	6	(-	-)	171	62	50	59	28	0	72	9	7	6	13	4	.76	10	.294	.346	.408
2003 Fresno	AAA	91	330	116	16	2	4	(-	-)	148	53	46	66	37	0	37	10	8	5	6	4	.60	6	.352	.427	.448
2004 Fresno	AAA	111	432	140	21	4	8	(-	-)	193	72	65	77	40	3	53	15	4	6	9	2	.82	13	.324	.390	.447
2004 San Francisco	NL	20	43	12	2	0	1	(1	0)	17	8	7	6	4	0	7	1	0	1	0	1	.00	0	.279	.347	.395

Jeff D'Amico

Pitches: R Bats: R Pos: SP-7   **Ht: 6'7" Wt: 250 Born: 12/27/1975 Age: 29**

Year Team	Lg	G	GS	CG	GF	IP	BFP	H	R	ER	HR	SH	SF	HB	TBB	IBB	SO	WP	Bk	W	L	Pct	ShO	Sv-Op	Hld	ERC	ERA
2004 Lake County*	A	2	1	0	0	2.0	7	1	0	0	0	0	0	0	0	0	1	0	0	0	0	-	0	0--	-	0.54	0.00
2004 Buffalo*	AAA	3	3	0	0	10.1	53	18	12	12	3	0	1	0	3	0	6	2	0	0	0	-	0	0--	-	9.49	10.45
1996 Milwaukee	AL	17	17	0	0	86.0	367	88	53	52	21	3	3	0	31	0	53	1	0	6	6	.500	0	0-0	0	5.11	5.44
1997 Milwaukee	AL	23	23	1	0	135.2	585	139	81	71	25	4	4	8	43	2	94	3	1	9	7	.563	1	0-0	0	4.69	4.71
1999 Milwaukee	NL	1	0	0	1	1.0	4	1	0	0	0	0	0	0	0	1	0	0	0	0	0	-	0	0-0	0	1.95	0.00
2000 Milwaukee	NL	23	23	1	0	162.1	667	143	55	48	14	10	3	6	46	5	101	5	0	12	7	.632	0	0-0	0	3.01	2.66
2001 Milwaukee	NL	10	10	0	0	47.1	216	60	42	32	11	2	1	1	16	4	32	2	0	2	4	.333	0	0-0	0	6.30	6.08

Year Team	Lg	G	GS	CG	GF	IP	BFP	H	R	ER	HR	SH	SF	HB	TBB	IBB	SO	WP	Bk	W	L	Pct	ShO	Sv-Op	Hld	ERC	ERA
2002 New York	NL	29	22	1	1	145.2	621	152	84	80	20	8	4	3	37	8	101	0	0	6	10	.375	1	0-0	0	3.96	4.94
2003 Pittsburgh	NL	29	29	2	0	175.1	765	204	104	93	23	11	5	7	42	6	100	6	0	9	16	.360	1	0-0	0	4.67	4.77
2004 Cleveland	AL	7	7	0	0	30.2	144	45	29	26	6	0	2	1	6	0	16	0	0	1	2	.333	0	0-0	0	6.74	7.63
8 ML YEARS		139	131	5	2	784.0	3369	832	448	402	120	38	22	26	221	25	498	17	2	45	52	.464	4	0-0	0	4.39	4.61

Johnny Damon

Bats: L Throws: L Pos: CF-148; PH-3; DH-1; PR-1   Ht: 6'2" Wt: 190 Born: 11/5/1973 Age: 31

							BATTING												BASERUNNING				AVERAGES		
Year Team	Lg	G	AB	H	2B	3B	HR	(Hm	Rd)	TB	R	RBI	RC	TBB	IBB	SO	HBP	SH	SF	SB	CS	SB%	GDP	Avg	OBP	Slg
1995 Kansas City	AL	47	188	53	11	5	3	(1	2)	83	32	23	29	12	0	22	1	2	3	7	0	1.00	2	.282	.324	.441
1996 Kansas City	AL	145	517	140	22	5	6	(3	3)	190	61	50	64	31	3	64	3	10	5	25	5	.83	4	.271	.313	.368
1997 Kansas City	AL	146	472	130	12	8	8	(3	5)	182	70	48	63	42	2	70	3	6	1	16	10	.62	3	.275	.338	.386
1998 Kansas City	AL	161	642	178	30	10	18	(11	7)	282	104	66	98	58	4	84	4	3	3	26	12	.68	4	.277	.339	.439
1999 Kansas City	AL	145	583	179	39	9	14	(5	9)	278	101	77	108	67	5	50	3	3	4	36	6	.86	13	.307	.379	.477
2000 Kansas City	AL	159	655	214	42	10	16	(10	6)	324	136	88	129	65	4	60	1	8	12	46	9	.84	7	.327	.382	.495
2001 Oakland	AL	155	644	165	34	4	9	(2	7)	234	108	49	79	61	1	70	5	5	4	27	12	.69	7	.256	.324	.363
2002 Boston	AL	154	623	178	34	11	14	(5	9)	276	118	63	101	65	5	70	6	3	5	31	6	.84	4	.286	.356	.443
2003 Boston	AL	145	608	166	32	6	12	(5	7)	246	103	67	92	68	4	74	2	6	6	30	6	.83	5	.273	.345	.405
2004 Boston	AL	150	621	189	35	6	20	(9	11)	296	123	94	115	76	1	71	2	0	3	19	8	.70	8	.304	.380	.477
10 ML YEARS		1407	5553	1592	291	74	120	(54	66)	2391	956	625	878	545	29	635	30	46	46	263	74	.78	57	.287	.351	.431

Vic Darensbourg

Pitches: L Bats: L Pos: RP-7   Ht: 5'8" Wt: 170 Born: 11/13/1970 Age: 34

							HOW MUCH HE PITCHED						WHAT HE GAVE UP						THE RESULTS						
Year Team	Lg	G	GS	CG	GF	IP	BFP	H	R	ER	HR	SH	SF	HB	TBB	IBB	SO	WP	Bk	W	L	Pct	ShO	Sv-Op	Hld	ERC	ERA
2004 Norfolk*	AAA	18	0	0	7	22.2	93	13	9	8	1	0	0	0	12	2	21	0	1	1	1	.500	0	0--	-	1.85	3.18
2004 Charlotte*	AAA	24	0	0	5	30.2	132	25	10	9	1	1	0	5	9	2	33	0	0	3	3	.500	0	0--	-	2.66	2.64
1998 Florida	NL	59	0	0	10	71.0	287	52	5	29	5	3	3	0	30	6	74	4	0	0	7	.000	0	1-2	13	2.47	3.68
1999 Florida	NL	56	0	0	5	34.2	180	50	36	34	3	5	2	5	21	1	16	1	3	0	1	.000	0	0-1	10	7.90	8.83
2000 Florida	NL	56	0	0	17	62.0	274	61	32	28	7	3	6	2	28	1	59	1	0	5	3	.625	0	0-1	3	4.33	4.06
2001 Florida	NL	58	0	0	19	48.2	202	52	24	23	4	1	2	1	10	6	33	0	0	2	2	.333	0	1-3	11	3.52	4.25
2002 Florida	NL	42	0	0	13	48.1	233	61	34	33	10	2	3	2	26	4	33	0	0	1	2	.333	0	0-0	3	6.98	6.14
2003 Col-Mon	NL	9	0	0	3	9.0	46	17	9	8	2	1	0	0	4	0	4	0	0	0	0	-	0	0-0	9	9.00	8.00
2004 CWS-NYM		7	0	0	4	7.0	32	11	5	5	1	1	2	0	3	0	1	0	0	0	1	.000	0	0-0	6	8.67	6.43
2003 Colorado	NL	3	0	0	2	2.1	12	4	1	0	0	0	0	0	0	0	0	0	0	0	0	-	0	0-0	5	5.18	0.00
2003 Montreal	NL	6	0	0	1	6.2	34	13	8	8	2	1	0	0	4	0	4	0	0	0	1	.000	0	0-0	4	10.54	10.80
2004 Chicago	AL	2	0	0	2	1.1	4	1	0	0	0	0	1	0	1	0	0	0	0	0	0	-	0	0-0	5	5.10	0.00
2004 New York	NL	5	0	0	2	5.2	28	10	5	5	1	1	2	0	2	0	1	0	0	0	1	.000	0	0-0	0	9.47	7.94
7 ML YEARS		287	0	0	71	280.2	1254	304	145	160	32	16	18	10	119	18	220	6	3	7	16	.304	0	2-7	40	4.75	5.13

Brian Daubach

Bats: L Throws: R Pos: 1B-14; PH-9; LF-6; RF-1; PR-1   Ht: 6'1" Wt: 233 Born: 2/11/1972 Age: 33

							BATTING												BASERUNNING				AVERAGES		
Year Team	Lg	G	AB	H	2B	3B	HR	(Hm	Rd)	TB	R	RBI	RC	TBB	IBB	SO	HBP	SH	SF	SB	CS	SB%	GDP	Avg	OBP	Slg
2004 Pawtucket*	AAA	93	336	91	23	0	21	(-	-)	177	63	81	71	71	7	93	3	0	2	0	1	.00	1	.271	.400	.527
1998 Florida	NL	10	15	3	1	0	0	(0	0)	4	0	3	1	1	0	5	1	0	0	0	0	-	0	.200	.294	.267
1999 Boston	AL	110	381	112	33	3	21	(11	10)	214	61	73	74	36	0	92	3	0	0	0	1	.00	5	.294	.360	.562
2000 Boston	AL	142	495	123	32	2	21	(10	11)	222	55	76	70	44	2	130	6	0	4	1	1	.50	8	.248	.315	.448
2001 Boston	AL	122	407	107	28	3	22	(11	11)	207	54	71	71	53	7	108	5	1	6	1	0	1.00	10	.263	.350	.509
2002 Boston	AL	137	444	118	24	2	20	(11	9)	206	62	78	76	51	4	126	7	0	4	2	1	.67	10	.266	.348	.464
2003 Chicago	AL	95	183	42	11	0	6	(4	2)	71	26	21	25	34	1	54	1	0	1	1	0	1.00	3	.230	.352	.388
2004 Boston	AL	30	75	17	8	0	2	(1	1)	31	9	8	11	10	0	21	1	0	0	0	0	-	1	.227	.326	.413
7 ML YEARS		646	2000	522	137	10	92	(48	44)	955	267	330	328	229	14	536	24	1	15	5	3	.63	35	.261	.342	.478

Jeff DaVanon

Bats: B Throws: R Pos: CF-39; RF-29; LF-24; DH-19; PH-18; PR-2   Ht: 6'0" Wt: 185 Born: 12/8/1973 Age: 31

							BATTING												BASERUNNING				AVERAGES		
Year Team	Lg	G	AB	H	2B	3B	HR	(Hm	Rd)	TB	R	RBI	RC	TBB	IBB	SO	HBP	SH	SF	SB	CS	SB%	GDP	Avg	OBP	Slg
2004 Salt Lake*	AAA	3	8	5	0	0	1	(-	-)	8	4	1	4	2	0	0	0	0	0	1	1	.50	0	.625	.700	1.000
1999 Anaheim	AL	7	20	4	0	1	1	(1	0)	9	4	4	2	2	0	7	0	0	0	0	1	.00	0	.200	.273	.450
2001 Anaheim	AL	40	88	17	2	1	5	(3	2)	36	7	9	9	11	0	29	0	0	1	1	3	.25	1	.193	.280	.409
2002 Anaheim	AL	16	30	5	3	0	1	(1	0)	11	3	4	4	2	0	6	0	1	0	1	0	1.00	0	.167	.219	.367
2003 Anaheim	AL	123	330	93	16	1	12	(3	9)	147	56	43	56	42	0	59	1	4	5	17	5	.77	6	.282	.360	.445
2004 Anaheim	AL	108	285	79	11	4	7	(4	3)	119	41	34	47	46	2	54	0	1	5	18	3	.86	2	.277	.372	.418
5 ML YEARS		294	753	198	32	7	26	(11	15)	322	111	94	118	103	2	155	1	6	11	37	12	.76	9	.263	.348	.428

Ben Davis

Bats: B Throws: R Pos: C-67; PH-1; PR-1   Ht: 6'4" Wt: 214 Born: 3/10/1977 Age: 28

							BATTING												BASERUNNING				AVERAGES		
Year Team	Lg	G	AB	H	2B	3B	HR	(Hm	Rd)	TB	R	RBI	RC	TBB	IBB	SO	HBP	SH	SF	SB	CS	SB%	GDP	Avg	OBP	Slg
2004 Tacoma*	AAA	39	141	35	9	0	4	(-	-)	56	18	15	16	15	0	29	0	0	1	1	0	1.00	6	.248	.321	.397
1998 San Diego	NL	1	1	0	0	0	0	(0	0)	0	0	0	0	0	0	0	0	0	0	0	0	-	0	.000	.000	.000
1999 San Diego	NL	76	266	65	14	1	5	(1	4)	96	29	30	27	25	3	70	0	0	2	2	1	.67	9	.244	.307	.361
2000 San Diego	NL	43	130	29	6	0	3	(1	2)	44	12	14	13	14	1	35	0	3	1	1	1	.50	2	.223	.297	.338
2001 San Diego	NL	138	448	107	20	0	11	(3	8)	160	56	57	54	66	5	112	4	1	7	4	4	.50	13	.239	.337	.357
2002 Seattle	AL	80	228	59	10	1	7	(1	6)	92	24	43	32	18	1	58	2	1	4	1	1	.50	6	.259	.313	.404
2003 Seattle	AL	80	246	58	18	0	6	(2	4)	94	25	42	28	18	2	61	0	1	4	0	0	-	9	.236	.284	.382
2004 Sea-CWS	AL	68	193	40	9	0	6	(3	3)	67	22	18	15	12	0	49	1	1	1	1	1	.50	5	.207	.256	.347

Year Team	Lg	G	AB	H	2B	3B	HR	(Hm	Rd)	TB	R	RBI	RC	TBB	IBB	SO	HBP	SH	SF	SB	CS	SB%	GDP	Avg	OBP	Slg
2004 Seattle	AL	14	33	3	0	0	0	(0	0)	3	1	2	0	3	0	9	0	0	1	0	0	-	3	.091	.162	.091
2004 Chicago	AL	54	160	37	9	0	6	(3	3)	64	21	16	15	9	0	40	1	1	0	1	1	.50	2	.231	.276	.400
7 ML YEARS		486	1512	358	77	2	38	(11	27)	553	168	204	169	153	12	385	7	7	19	9	8	.53	40	.237	.306	.366

Doug Davis

Pitches: L Bats: R Pos: SP-34   Ht: 6'4" Wt: 190 Born: 9/21/1975 Age: 29

Year Team	Lg	G	GS	CG	GF	IP	BFP	H	R	ER	HR	SH	SF	HB	TBB	IBB	SO	WP	Bk	W	L	Pct	ShO	Sv-Op	Hld	ERC	ERA
1999 Texas	AL	2	0	0	0	2.2	20	12	10	10	3	0	0	0	0	0	3	0	0	0	0	-	0	0-0	0	41.42	33.75
2000 Texas	AL	30	13	1	4	98.2	450	109	61	59	14	6	4	3	58	3	66	5	1	7	6	.538	0	0-3	2	5.93	5.38
2001 Texas	AL	30	30	1	0	186.0	828	220	103	92	14	4	6	3	69	1	115	7	2	11	10	.524	0	0-0	0	4.90	4.45
2002 Texas	AL	10	10	1	0	59.2	262	67	36	33	7	3	3	3	22	0	28	2	2	3	5	.375	1	0-0	0	5.05	4.98
2003 Tex-Tor-Mil		21	20	1	0	109.1	491	123	55	49	16	6	2	1	51	1	62	7	0	7	8	.467	0	0-0	0	5.46	4.03
2004 Milwaukee	NL	34	34	0	0	207.1	880	192	84	78	14	11	5	7	79	3	166	4	1	12	12	.500	0	0-0	0	3.49	3.39
2003 Texas	AL	1	1	0	0	3.0	17	4	4	4	2	0	0	0	4	0	2	0	0	0	0	-	0	0-0	0	15.81	12.00
2003 Toronto	AL	12	11	0	0	54.0	250	70	33	30	6	3	0	1	26	1	25	6	0	4	6	.400	0	0-0	0	6.39	5.00
2003 Milwaukee	NL	8	8	1	0	52.1	224	49	18	15	8	3	2	0	21	0	35	1	0	3	2	.600	0	0-0	0	4.06	2.58
6 ML YEARS		127	107	4	4	663.2	2931	723	349	321	68	30	20	17	279	8	440	25	6	40	41	.494	1	0-3	2	4.79	4.35

J.J. Davis

Bats: R Throws: R Pos: RF-12; PH-7; LF-5; PR-3   Ht: 6'5" Wt: 250 Born: 10/25/1978 Age: 26

Year Team	Lg	G	AB	H	2B	3B	HR	(Hm	Rd)	TB	R	RBI	RC	TBB	IBB	SO	HBP	SH	SF	SB	CS	SB%	GDP	Avg	OBP	Slg
2004 Nashville*	AAA	27	84	21	6	1	8	(-	-)	53	11	17	14	3	1	28	0	0	2	3	0	1.00	0	.250	.270	.631
2002 Pittsburgh	NL	9	10	1	0	0	0	(0	0)	1	1	0	0	0	0	4	1	0	0	0	0	-	1	.100	.182	.100
2003 Pittsburgh	NL	19	35	7	0	0	1	(1	0)	10	1	4	2	3	0	13	0	0	1	0	1	.00	0	.200	.263	.286
2004 Pittsburgh	NL	25	35	5	1	0	0	(0	0)	6	4	3	2	4	0	10	0	0	1	2	0	1.00	0	.143	.225	.171
3 ML YEARS		53	80	13	1	0	1	(1	0)	17	6	7	4	7	0	27	1	0	1	2	1	.67	1	.163	.236	.213

Jason Davis

Pitches: R Bats: R Pos: SP-19; RP-7   Ht: 6'6" Wt: 195 Born: 5/8/1980 Age: 25

Year Team	Lg	G	GS	CG	GF	IP	BFP	H	R	ER	HR	SH	SF	HB	TBB	IBB	SO	WP	Bk	W	L	Pct	ShO	Sv-Op	Hld	ERC	ERA
2004 Buffalo*	AAA	9	9	0	0	54.0	226	53	26	18	4	1	2	2	18	1	39	7	1	3	2	.600	0	0- -	-	3.73	3.00
2002 Cleveland	AL	3	2	0	0	14.2	60	12	3	3	1	1	0	0	4	0	11	0	1	1	0	1.000	0	0-0	0	2.40	1.84
2003 Cleveland	AL	27	27	1	0	165.1	696	172	101	86	25	7	3	8	47	4	85	9	2	8	11	.421	0	0-0	0	4.44	4.68
2004 Cleveland	AL	26	19	0	2	114.1	540	148	81	70	13	7	2	4	51	1	72	7	1	2	7	.222	0	0-0	1	6.17	5.51
3 ML YEARS		56	48	1	2	294.1	1296	332	185	159	39	15	5	12	102	5	168	16	4	11	18	.379	0	0-0	1	4.99	4.86

Joe Dawley

Pitches: R Bats: R Pos: SP-2   Ht: 6'4" Wt: 205 Born: 9/19/1971 Age: 33

Year Team	Lg	G	GS	CG	GF	IP	BFP	H	R	ER	HR	SH	SF	HB	TBB	IBB	SO	WP	Bk	W	L	Pct	ShO	Sv-Op	Hld	ERC	ERA
2004 Buffalo*	AAA	1	1	0	0	5.2	23	4	3	0	0	0	1	0	1	0	7	0	0	0	0	-	0	0- -	-	1.30	0.00
2004 Omaha*	AAA	9	3	0	0	31.0	129	26	14	11	1	2	1	2	8	0	29	1	0	1	2	.333	0	0- -	-	2.44	3.19
2002 Atlanta	NL	1	0	0	1	0.1	7	0	0	0	0	0	0	0	0	0	1	0	0	0	0	-	0	0-0	0	0.00	0.00
2003 Atlanta	NL	5	0	0	4	7.0	41	15	14	14	3	0	0	1	3	0	8	1	0	0	0	-	0	0-0	0	15.12	18.00
2004 Cleveland	AL	2	2	0	0	8.1	37	7	5	5	1	0	0	0	7	0	8	0	0	0	0	-	0	0-0	0	5.24	5.40
3 ML YEARS		8	2	0	5	15.2	79	22	19	19	4	0	0	1	10	0	17	1	0	0	0	-	0	0-0	0	9.16	10.91

Zach Day

Pitches: R Bats: R Pos: SP-19   Ht: 6'4" Wt: 185 Born: 6/15/1978 Age: 27

Year Team	Lg	G	GS	CG	GF	IP	BFP	H	R	ER	HR	SH	SF	HB	TBB	IBB	SO	WP	Bk	W	L	Pct	ShO	Sv-Op	Hld	ERC	ERA
2002 Montreal	NL	19	2	0	5	37.1	153	28	18	15	3	1	1	1	15	2	25	1	0	4	1	.800	0	1-2	2	2.66	3.62
2003 Montreal	NL	23	23	1	0	131.1	580	132	64	61	8	2	5	10	59	3	61	13	0	9	8	.529	1	0-0	0	4.28	4.18
2004 Montreal	NL	19	19	1	0	116.2	496	117	53	51	13	4	1	4	45	7	61	5	0	5	10	.333	1	0-0	0	4.24	3.93
3 ML YEARS		61	44	2	5	285.1	1229	277	135	127	24	7	7	15	119	12	147	19	0	18	19	.486	2	1-2	2	4.04	4.01

Jorge de la Rosa

Pitches: L Bats: L Pos: SP-5   Ht: 6'1" Wt: 190 Born: 4/5/1981 Age: 24

Year Team	Lg	G	GS	CG	GF	IP	BFP	H	R	ER	HR	SH	SF	HB	TBB	IBB	SO	WP	Bk	W	L	Pct	ShO	Sv-Op	Hld	ERC	ERA
1998 Diamndbcks	R	13	0	0	2	14.0	59	8	7	7	3	0	0	1	8	0	21	2	0	1	0	1.000	0	1- -	-		4.50
1999 Diamndbcks	R	8	0	0	6	14.0	56	12	5	5	1	0	0	0	3	0	17	2	1	0	0	-	0	2- -	-	2.46	3.21
1999 High Desert	A+	2	0	0	2	3.0	12	1	0	0	0	0	0	0	2	0	3	0	0	0	0	-	0	0- -	-	1.26	0.00
1999 Missoula	R+	13	0	0	6	12.2	75	22	17	13	2	0	0	0	9	0	14	4	0	0	1	.000	0	2- -	-	8.19	7.98
2001 Sarasota	A+	12	0	0	10	29.2	114	13	7	4	0	0	0	0	12	0	27	0	0	1	0	1.000	0	1- -	-	1.06	1.21
2001 Trenton	AA	29	0	0	4	37.0	187	56	35	24	4	1	1	4	20	1	27	6	0	1	3	.250	0	0- -	-	8.31	5.84
2002 Sarasota	A+	23	23	1	0	120.2	515	105	53	49	10	1	2	6	52	1	95	5	1	7	7	.500	1	0- -	-	3.54	3.65
2002 Trenton	AA	4	4	0	0	18.0	82	17	12	11	0	0	0	2	9	0	15	3	0	1	2	.333	0	0- -	-	3.73	5.50
2003 Portland	AA	22	20	0	1	99.2	413	87	39	31	6	2	2	5	36	0	102	8	1	6	3	.667	0	1- -	-	3.21	2.80
2003 Pawtucket	AAA	5	5	0	0	24.0	110	27	14	10	1	0	1	0	12	0	17	2	1	2	3	.333	0	0- -	-	4.34	3.75
2004 Indianapolis	AAA	20	20	0	0	85.2	368	80	45	43	9	4	4	8	36	1	86	5	2	5	6	.455	0	0- -	-	4.23	4.52
2004 Milwaukee	NL	5	5	0	0	22.2	113	29	20	16	1	1	3	1	14	0	5	3	0	0	3	.000	0	0-0	0	6.12	6.35

Valerio de los Santos

Pitches: L **Bats:** L **Pos:** RP-17   **Ht:** 6'2" **Wt:** 206 **Born:** 10/6/1972 **Age:** 32

Year Team	Lg	G	GS	CG	GF	IP	BFP	H	R	ER	HR	SH	SF	HB	TBB	IBB	SO	WP	Bk	W	L	Pct	ShO	Sv-Op	Hld	ERC	ERA
1998 Milwaukee	NL	13	0	0	3	21.2	75	11	7	7	4	0	0	0	2	0	18	1	0	0	0	-	0	0-0	0	1.25	2.91
1999 Milwaukee	NL	7	0	0	3	8.1	43	12	6	6	1	0	0	1	7	0	5	1	0	0	1	.000	0	0-0	0	9.65	6.48
2000 Milwaukee	NL	66	2	0	15	73.2	320	72	43	42	15	2	1	1	33	7	70	3	1	2	3	.400	0	0-1	9	4.79	5.13
2001 Milwaukee	NL	1	0	0	0	1.0	5	1	1	1	0	0	0	0	1	0	1	0	0	0	0	-	0	0-0	0	5.48	9.00
2002 Milwaukee	NL	51	0	0	12	57.2	237	42	21	20	4	3	7	2	26	3	38	1	0	2	3	.400	0	0-0	7	2.70	3.12
2003 Mil-Phi	NL	51	0	0	6	52.0	228	45	31	26	8	7	4	5	25	0	39	2	0	4	3	.571	0	1-4	11	4.37	4.50
2004 Toronto	AL	17	0	0	1	11.2	56	11	8	8	0	1	0	1	10	2	10	3	0	0	0	-	0	0-1	0	4.29	6.17
2003 Milwaukee	NL	45	0	0	5	48.0	205	38	24	22	8	6	4	4	22	0	35	1	0	3	3	.500	0	1-4	11	3.92	4.13
2003 Philadelphia	NL	6	0	0	1	4.0	23	7	7	4	0	1	0	1	3	0	4	1	0	1	0	1.000	0	0-0	0	10.26	9.00
7 ML YEARS		206	2	0	40	226.0	964	194	117	110	32	13	13	9	104	12	181	11	1	8	10	.444	0	1-6	27	3.90	4.38

Mike DeJean

Pitches: R **Bats:** R **Pos:** RP-54   **Ht:** 6'4" **Wt:** 219 **Born:** 9/28/1970 **Age:** 34

Year Team	Lg	G	GS	CG	GF	IP	BFP	H	R	ER	HR	SH	SF	HB	TBB	IBB	SO	WP	Bk	W	L	Pct	ShO	Sv-Op	Hld	ERC	ERA
1997 Colorado	NL	55	0	0	15	67.2	295	74	34	30	4	3	1	3	24	2	38	2	0	5	2	.714	0	2-4	13	4.29	3.99
1998 Colorado	NL	59	1	0	9	74.1	307	78	29	25	4	4	4	1	24	1	27	3	0	3	1	.750	0	2-3	11	3.92	3.03
1999 Colorado	NL	56	0	0	17	61.0	288	83	61	57	13	3	3	2	32	8	31	3	0	2	4	.333	0	0-4	9	7.77	8.41
2000 Colorado	NL	54	0	0	15	53.1	235	54	31	29	9	3	1	0	30	6	34	5	0	4	4	.500	0	0-4	7	5.22	4.89
2001 Milwaukee	NL	75	0	0	19	84.1	371	75	31	26	4	1	4	9	39	7	68	8	0	4	2	.667	0	2-4	8	3.56	2.77
2002 Milwaukee	NL	68	0	0	60	75.0	326	66	28	26	7	4	2	2	39	8	65	7	0	1	5	.167	0	27-30	0	3.74	3.12
2003 Mil-StL	NL	76	0	0	45	82.2	365	86	46	43	13	1	3	2	39	7	71	3	0	5	8	.385	0	19-27	10	5.00	4.68
2004 Bal-NYM		54	0	0	20	61.0	288	70	34	31	2	4	2	8	33	8	60	4	0	0	5	.000	0	0-0	3	5.21	4.57
2003 Milwaukee	NL	58	0	0	40	64.2	286	69	38	35	12	0	3	1	27	7	58	3	0	4	7	.364	0	18-26	5	5.02	4.87
2003 St Louis	NL	18	0	0	5	18.0	79	17	8	8	1	1	0	1	12	0	13	0	0	1	1	.500	0	1-1	5	4.89	4.00
2004 Baltimore	AL	37	0	0	12	39.2	197	49	29	27	2	2	2	6	28	6	36	2	0	0	5	.000	0	0-0	1	6.64	6.13
2004 New York	NL	17	0	0	8	21.1	91	21	5	4	0	2	0	2	5	2	24	2	0	0	0	-	0	0-0	2	2.85	1.69
8 ML YEARS		497	1	0	200	559.1	2475	586	294	267	56	23	20	27	260	47	394	35	0	24	29	.453	0	52-76	61	4.69	4.30

David DeJesus

Bats: L **Throws:** L **Pos:** CF-85; RF-6; LF-4; PH-1; PR-1   **Ht:** 5'11" **Wt:** 170 **Born:** 12/20/1979 **Age:** 25

Year Team	Lg	G	AB	H	2B	3B	HR	(Hm	Rd)	TB	R	RBI	RC	TBB	IBB	SO	HBP	SH	SF	SB	CS	SB%	GDP	Avg	OBP	Slg
2002 Wilmington	A+	87	334	99	22	6	4	(-	-)	145	69	41	61	48	2	42	13	10	5	15	6	.71	8	.296	.400	.434
2002 Wichita	AA	25	79	20	5	2	2	(-	-)	35	7	15	12	8	0	10	5	1	3	3	1	.75	3	.253	.347	.443
2003 Wichita	AA	17	71	24	4	0	2	(-	-)	34	14	10	13	9	0	8	2	0	1	1	3	.25	3	.338	.422	.479
2003 Omaha	AAA	59	215	64	16	3	5	(-	-)	101	49	23	40	34	2	30	9	5	2	8	4	.67	9	.298	.412	.470
2004 Omaha	AAA	50	197	62	14	4	6	(-	-)	102	38	16	37	21	0	30	7	1	0	7	6	.54	5	.315	.400	.518
2003 Kansas City	AL	12	7	2	0	1	0	(0	0)	4	0	0	2	1	0	2	1	1	0	0	0	-	0	.286	.444	.571
2004 Kansas City	AL	96	363	104	15	3	7	(2	5)	146	58	39	53	33	0	53	9	8	0	8	11	.42	7	.287	.360	.402
2 ML YEARS		108	370	106	15	4	7	(2	5)	150	58	39	55	34	0	55	10	9	0	8	11	.42	7	.286	.362	.405

Carlos Delgado

Bats: L **Throws:** R **Pos:** 1B-120; DH-8   **Ht:** 6'3" **Wt:** 230 **Born:** 6/25/1972 **Age:** 33

Year Team	Lg	G	AB	H	2B	3B	HR	(Hm	Rd)	TB	R	RBI	RC	TBB	IBB	SO	HBP	SH	SF	SB	CS	SB%	GDP	Avg	OBP	Slg
2004 Dunedin*	A+	2	8	2	0	0	1	(-	-)	5	1	2	0	0	0	0	0	0	0	0	0	-	1	.250	.250	.625
2004 Syracuse*	AAA	2	9	5	0	0	1	(-	-)	10	2	4	3	0	0	0	0	0	0	0	0	-	0	.556	.556	1.111
1993 Toronto	AL	2	1	0	0	0	0	(0	0)	0	0	0	0	1	0	0	0	0	0	0	0	-	0	.000	.500	.000
1994 Toronto	AL	43	130	28	2	0	9	(5	4)	57	17	24	20	25	4	46	3	0	1	1	1	.50	5	.215	.352	.438
1995 Toronto	AL	37	91	15	3	0	3	(2	1)	27	7	11	5	6	0	26	0	0	2	0	0	-	1	.165	.212	.297
1996 Toronto	AL	138	488	132	28	2	25	(12	13)	239	68	92	83	58	2	139	9	0	8	0	0	-	13	.270	.353	.490
1997 Toronto	AL	153	519	136	42	3	30	(17	13)	274	79	91	94	64	9	133	8	0	4	0	3	.00	6	.262	.350	.528
1998 Toronto	AL	142	530	155	43	1	38	(20	18)	314	94	115	117	73	13	139	11	0	6	3	0	1.00	6	.292	.385	.592
1999 Toronto	AL	152	573	156	39	0	44	(17	27)	327	113	134	121	86	7	141	15	0	7	1	1	.50	11	.272	.377	.571
2000 Toronto	AL	162	569	196	57	1	41	(30	11)	378	115	137	164	123	18	104	15	0	4	0	1	.00	12	.344	.470	.664
2001 Toronto	AL	162	574	160	31	1	39	(13	26)	310	102	102	126	111	22	136	16	0	3	3	0	1.00	4	.279	.408	.540
2002 Toronto	AL	143	505	140	34	2	33	(17	16)	277	103	108	117	102	18	126	13	0	8	1	0	1.00	8	.277	.406	.549
2003 Toronto	AL	161	570	172	38	1	42	(24	18)	338	117	145	146	109	23	137	19	0	7	0	0	-	9	.302	.426	.593
2004 Toronto	AL	128	458	123	26	0	32	(18	14)	245	74	99	88	69	12	115	13	0	11	0	1	.00	11	.269	.372	.535
12 ML YEARS		1423	5008	1413	343	11	336	(175	161)	2786	889	1058	1081	827	128	1242	122	0	61	9	7	.56	93	.282	.392	.556

Wilson Delgado

Bats: B **Throws:** R **Pos:** SS-39; PH-4   **Ht:** 5'11" **Wt:** 165 **Born:** 7/15/1972 **Age:** 32

Year Team	Lg	G	AB	H	2B	3B	HR	(Hm	Rd)	TB	R	RBI	RC	TBB	IBB	SO	HBP	SH	SF	SB	CS	SB%	GDP	Avg	OBP	Slg
2004 Norfolk*	AAA	108	352	92	18	5	3	(-	-)	129	40	23	38	27	1	73	2	7	1	6	1	.14	7	.261	.317	.366
1996 San Francisco	NL	6	22	8	0	0	0	(0	0)	8	3	2	4	1	0	5	2	0	0	1	0	1.00	0	.364	.440	.364
1997 San Francisco	NL	8	7	1	1	0	0	(0	0)	2	1	1	0	0	0	2	0	1	0	0	0	-	0	.143	.143	.286
1998 San Francisco	NL	10	12	2	1	0	0	(0	0)	3	1	1	1	1	0	3	0	0	0	0	0	-	0	.167	.231	.250
1999 San Francisco	NL	35	71	18	2	1	0	(0	0)	22	7	3	7	5	0	9	1	1	0	1	0	1.00	2	.254	.312	.310
2000 NYY-KC	AL	64	128	33	2	0	1	(0	1)	38	21	11	12	11	0	26	0	0	2	2	1	.67	2	.258	.312	.297
2001 Kansas City	AL	14	25	3	0	0	0	(0	0)	3	1	1	0	3	0	10	0	0	0	0	0	-	1	.120	.214	.120
2002 St Louis	NL	12	20	4	2	0	2	(2	0)	12	2	5	2	0	0	6	0	1	0	0	0	-	0	.200	.200	.600
2003 StL-Ana	NL	62	127	29	3	0	0	(0	0)	32	12	7	8	10	1	18	1	0	1	0	0	-	5	.228	.293	.252
2004 New York	NL	42	130	38	4	1	2	(2	0)	50	11	13	20	15	3	29	0	2	0	1	0	1.00	3	.292	.366	.385
2000 New York	AL	31	45	11	1	0	1	(0	1)	15	6	4	5	5	0	9	0	0	1	1	0	1.00	1	.244	.314	.333

		BATTING																		BASERUNNING				AVERAGES		
Year Team	Lg	G	AB	H	2B	3B	HR	(Hm	Rd)	TB	R	RBI	RC	TBB	IBB	SO	HBP	SH	SF	SB	CS	SB%	GDP	Avg	OBP	Slg
2000 Kansas City	AL	33	83	22	1	0	0	(0	0)	23	15	7	7	6	0	17	0	0	1	1	1	.50	1	.265	.311	.277
2003 St Louis	NL	43	77	13	3	0	0	(0	0)	16	8	3	1	3	0	10	1	0	1	0	0	-	4	.169	.207	.208
2003 Anaheim	AL	19	50	16	0	0	0	(0	0)	16	4	4	7	8	0	8	0	0	0	0	0	-	1	.320	.414	.320
9 ML YEARS		253	542	136	15	2	5	(4	1)	170	59	43	54	47	3	108	4	5	3	5	1	.83	11	.251	.314	.314

David Dellucci

Bats: L **Throws:** L **Pos:** LF-84; PH-11; DH-9; CF-7; RF-6   **Ht:** 5'11" **Wt:** 198 **Born:** 10/31/1973 **Age:** 31

		BATTING																		BASERUNNING				AVERAGES		
Year Team	Lg	G	AB	H	2B	3B	HR	(Hm	Rd)	TB	R	RBI	RC	TBB	IBB	SO	HBP	SH	SF	SB	CS	SB%	GDP	Avg	OBP	Slg
1997 Baltimore	AL	17	27	6	1	0	1	(0	1)	10	3	3	3	4	1	7	1	0	0	0	0	-	2	.222	.344	.370
1998 Arizona	NL	124	416	108	19	12	5	(1	4)	166	43	51	51	33	2	103	3	0	1	3	5	.38	6	.260	.318	.399
1999 Arizona	NL	63	109	43	7	1	1	(0	1)	55	27	15	24	11	0	24	3	0	0	2	0	1.00	3	.394	.463	.505
2000 Arizona	NL	34	50	15	3	0	0	(0	0)	18	2	2	6	4	0	9	0	0	0	0	2	.00	1	.300	.352	.360
2001 Arizona	NL	115	217	60	10	2	10	(5	5)	104	28	40	36	22	4	52	2	0	0	2	1	.67	2	.276	.349	.479
2002 Arizona	NL	97	229	56	11	2	7	(2	5)	92	34	29	26	28	5	55	1	0	3	2	4	.33	7	.245	.326	.402
2003 Ari-NYY		91	216	49	12	3	3	(3	0)	76	26	23	23	23	1	58	5	2	2	12	0	1.00	6	.227	.313	.352
2004 Texas	AL	107	331	80	13	1	17	(9	8)	146	59	61	56	47	3	88	5	1	3	9	4	.69	4	.242	.342	.441
2003 Arizona	NL	70	165	40	11	3	2	(2	0)	63	18	19	21	19	1	45	3	1	2	9	0	1.00	4	.242	.328	.382
2003 New York	AL	21	51	9	1	0	1	(1	0)	13	8	4	2	4	0	13	2	1	0	3	0	1.00	2	.176	.263	.255
8 ML YEARS		648	1595	417	76	21	44	(20	24)	667	222	224	225	172	16	396	20	3	9	30	16	.65	31	.261	.339	.418

Ryan Dempster

Pitches: R **Bats:** R **Pos:** RP-23   **Ht:** 6'3" **Wt:** 215 **Born:** 5/3/1977 **Age:** 28

		HOW MUCH HE PITCHED						WHAT HE GAVE UP											THE RESULTS						
Year Team	Lg	G	GS	CG	GF	IP	BFP	H	R	ER	HR	SH	SF	HB	TBB	IBB	SO	WP	Bk	W	L	Pct	ShO	Sv-Op	Hld	ERC	ERA
2004 Lansing*	A	5	5	0	0	18.1	76	20	5	4	0	0	0	1	2	0	21	1	0	0	0	-	0	0--	-	3.01	1.96
2004 Iowa*	AAA	6	4	0	0	21.0	85	19	9	9	1	0	0	2	10	0	20	2	0	1	1	.500	0	0--	-	4.19	3.86
1998 Florida	NL	14	11	0	1	54.2	272	72	47	43	6	5	6	9	38	1	35	5	0	1	5	.167	0	0-1	0	8.14	7.08
1999 Florida	NL	25	25	0	0	147.0	666	146	77	77	21	3	6	6	93	2	126	8	0	7	8	.467	0	0-0	0	5.49	4.71
2000 Florida	NL	33	33	2	0	226.1	974	210	102	92	30	4	5	5	97	7	209	4	0	14	10	.583	1	0-0	0	4.04	3.66
2001 Florida	NL	34	34	2	0	211.1	954	218	123	116	21	15	7	10	112	5	171	5	0	15	12	.556	1	0-0	0	4.91	4.94
2002 Fla-Cin	NL	33	33	4	0	209.0	915	228	127	125	28	9	6	10	93	2	153	2	0	10	13	.435	0	0-0	0	5.35	5.38
2003 Cincinnati	NL	22	20	0	1	115.2	545	134	89	84	14	9	4	5	70	4	84	3	0	3	7	.300	0	0-0	0	6.11	6.54
2004 Chicago	NL	23	0	0	8	20.2	93	16	9	9	1	1	0	2	13	0	18	1	0	1	1	.500	0	2-2	3	3.61	3.92
2002 Florida	NL	18	18	3	0	120.1	521	126	66	64	12	7	3	7	55	1	87	0	0	5	8	.385	0	0-0	0	4.95	4.79
2002 Cincinnati	NL	15	15	1	0	88.2	394	102	61	61	16	2	3	3	38	1	66	2	0	5	5	.500	0	0-0	0	5.90	6.19
7 ML YEARS		184	156	8	10	984.2	4419	1024	574	546	121	46	34	47	516	21	796	28	0	51	56	.477	2	2-3	3	5.16	4.99

Kyle Denney

Pitches: R **Bats:** R **Pos:** SP-4   **Ht:** 6'2" **Wt:** 190 **Born:** 7/27/1977 **Age:** 27

		HOW MUCH HE PITCHED						WHAT HE GAVE UP											THE RESULTS						
Year Team	Lg	G	GS	CG	GF	IP	BFP	H	R	ER	HR	SH	SF	HB	TBB	IBB	SO	WP	Bk	W	L	Pct	ShO	Sv-Op	Hld	ERC	ERA
1999 Burlington	R+	12	3	0	4	34.0	143	26	14	13	7	4	1	2	15	0	37	2	3	4	4	.429	0	1--	-	3.87	3.44
1999 Mahning VI	A-	1	1	0	0	5.0	16	5	1	1	1	0	0	0	0	0	5	0	0	1	0	1.000	0	0--	-	3.96	1.80
2000 Columbus	A	28	24	0	1	138.2	584	135	55	47	12	4	1	4	46	0	131	5	0	8	6	.571	0	0--	-	3.72	3.05
2001 Kinston	A+	11	10	0	0	57.0	219	32	14	13	2	1	1	3	13	1	80	0	0	5	3	.625	0	0--	-	1.27	2.05
2002 Kinston	A+	15	14	0	1	85.0	363	76	37	34	5	2	4	2	41	2	68	3	1	7	6	.538	0	0--	-	3.61	3.60
2002 Akron	AA	6	5	0	0	34.2	135	23	7	6	2	1	0	3	5	0	32	2	0	3	1	.750	0	0--	-	1.57	1.56
2003 Akron	AA	18	18	1	0	104.0	433	97	34	28	7	2	5	4	24	0	87	1	1	7	3	.700	0	0--	-	2.97	2.42
2003 Buffalo	AAA	6	6	0	0	30.2	139	35	18	18	4	1	0	1	10	2	26	0	0	2	1	.667	0	0--	-	4.68	5.28
2004 Buffalo	AAA	24	24	1	0	134.2	576	134	74	66	17	4	9	8	39	1	113	1	1	10	5	.667	1	0--	-	4.00	4.41
2004 Cleveland	AL	4	4	0	0	16.0	86	32	17	17	3	1	1	0	8	0	13	1	0	1	2	.333	0	0-0	0	11.88	9.56

Jorge DePaula

Pitches: R **Bats:** R **Pos:** RP-2; SP-1   **Ht:** 6'1" **Wt:** 160 **Born:** 11/10/1978 **Age:** 26

		HOW MUCH HE PITCHED						WHAT HE GAVE UP											THE RESULTS						
Year Team	Lg	G	GS	CG	GF	IP	BFP	H	R	ER	HR	SH	SF	HB	TBB	IBB	SO	WP	Bk	W	L	Pct	ShO	Sv-Op	Hld	ERC	ERA
1999 Portland	AA	16	16	0	0	85.1	392	97	67	57	8	5	4	5	43	0	77	7	1	6	6	.500	0	0--	-	5.48	6.01
2000 Asheville	A	28	27	1	0	155.0	691	151	90	81	16	0	0	13	62	0	187	7	2	8	13	.381	1	0--	-	4.18	4.70
2001 Asheville	A	3	3	0	0	16.2	76	19	13	7	3	0	0	3	2	0	26	1	0	1	1	.500	0	0--	-	4.79	3.78
2001 Greensboro	A	8	8	0	0	55.2	221	35	19	17	2	1	0	4	21	0	67	2	3	6	1	.857	0	0--	-	1.98	2.75
2001 Tampa	A+	16	13	0	1	83.0	365	65	43	33	3	1	2	3	53	2	77	3	1	9	5	.643	0	0--	-	3.40	3.58
2002 Norwich	AA	27	26	6	0	175.0	710	141	74	67	11	7	6	5	52	0	152	6	3	14	6	.700	1	0--	-	2.54	3.45
2003 New York	AL	4	1	0	3	11.1	38	3	1	1	1	0	0	1	1	0	7	0	0	0	0	-	0	0-0	0	0.54	0.79
2004 New York	AL	3	1	0	0	9.0	38	9	6	5	2	0	2	0	4	0	2	0	0	1	0	1.000	0	0-0	0	5.32	5.00
2 ML YEARS		7	2	0	3	20.1	76	12	7	6	3	0	2	1	5	0	9	0	0	1	0	1.000	0	0-0	0	1.97	2.66

Mark DeRosa

Bats: R **Throws:** R **Pos:** 3B-72; PH-32; SS-11; 2B-5; PR-5; LF-3   **Ht:** 6'1" **Wt:** 205 **Born:** 2/26/1975 **Age:** 30

		BATTING																		BASERUNNING				AVERAGES		
Year Team	Lg	G	AB	H	2B	3B	HR	(Hm	Rd)	TB	R	RBI	RC	TBB	IBB	SO	HBP	SH	SF	SB	CS	SB%	GDP	Avg	OBP	Slg
1998 Atlanta	NL	5	3	1	0	0	0	(0	0)	1	2	0	0	0	0	1	0	0	0	0	0	-	0	.333	.333	.333
1999 Atlanta	NL	7	8	0	0	0	0	(0	0)	0	0	0	0	0	0	2	0	0	0	0	0	-	0	.000	.000	.000
2000 Atlanta	NL	22	13	4	1	0	0	(0	0)	5	9	3	2	2	0	1	0	0	0	0	0	-	0	.308	.400	.385
2001 Atlanta	NL	66	164	47	8	0	3	(3	0)	64	27	20	22	12	6	19	5	1	2	2	1	.67	3	.287	.350	.390
2002 Atlanta	NL	72	212	63	9	2	5	(3	2)	91	24	23	27	12	3	24	3	2	3	2	3	.40	5	.297	.339	.429

Year Team	Lg	G	AB	H	2B	3B	HR	(Hm	Rd)	TB	R	RBI	RC	TBB	IBB	SO	HBP	SH	SF	SB	CS	SB%	GDP	Avg	OBP	Slg
								BATTING												BASERUNNING				AVERAGES		
2003 Atlanta	NL	103	266	70	14	0	6	(3	3)	102	40	22	28	16	0	49	5	0	1	1	0	1.00	6	.263	.316	.383
2004 Atlanta	NL	118	309	74	16	0	3	(0	3)	99	33	31	24	23	3	53	3	4	6	1	3	.25	6	.239	.293	.320
7 ML YEARS		393	975	259	48	2	17	(9	8)	362	135	99	103	65	12	149	16	7	12	6	7	.46	20	.266	.318	.371

Elmer Dessens

Pitches: R **Bats:** R **Pos:** RP-40; SP-10   **Ht:** 6'0" **Wt:** 187 **Born:** 1/13/1972 **Age:** 33

Year Team	Lg	G	GS	CG	GF	IP	BFP	H	R	ER	HR	SH	SF	HB	TBB	IBB	SO	WP	Bk	W	L	Pct	ShO	Sv-Op	Hld	ERC	ERA
		HOW MUCH HE PITCHED						WHAT HE GAVE UP												THE RESULTS							
1996 Pittsburgh	NL	15	3	0	1	25.0	112	40	23	23	2	3	1	0	4	0	13	0	0	0	2	.000	0	0-0	3	6.77	8.28
1997 Pittsburgh	NL	3	0	0	1	3.1	13	2	0	0	0	0	0	1	0	0	2	0	0	0	0	-	0	0-0	0	1.31	0.00
1998 Pittsburgh	NL	43	5	0	8	74.2	332	90	50	47	10	4	3	0	25	2	43	1	0	2	6	.250	0	0-1	6	5.19	5.67
2000 Cincinnati	NL	40	16	1	6	147.1	640	170	73	70	10	12	7	3	43	7	85	4	0	11	5	.688	0	1-1	1	4.31	4.28
2001 Cincinnati	NL	34	34	1	0	205.0	862	221	103	102	32	7	7	1	56	1	128	4	1	10	14	.417	1	0-0	0	4.49	4.48
2002 Cincinnati	NL	30	30	0	0	178.0	737	173	70	60	24	7	1	7	49	8	93	3	1	8	8	.467	0	0-0	0	3.82	3.03
2003 Arizona	NL	34	30	0	1	175.2	781	212	107	99	22	9	3	4	57	6	113	3	2	8	8	.500	0	0-0	0	5.19	5.07
2004 Ari-LA	NL	50	10	0	9	105.0	468	123	61	52	15	4	3	1	31	4	73	2	0	2	6	.250	0	2-5	4	4.83	4.46
2004 Arizona	NL	38	9	0	7	85.1	386	107	54	45	11	4	3	1	23	4	55	2	0	1	6	.143	0	2-4	4	5.08	4.75
2004 Los Angeles	NL	12	1	0	2	19.2	82	16	7	7	4	0	0	0	8	0	18	0	0	1	0	1.000	0	0-1	0	3.74	3.20
8 ML YEARS		249	128	2	26	914.0	3945	1031	487	453	115	46	25	17	265	28	550	17	4	40	49	.449	1	3-7	14	4.60	4.46

Doug DeVore

Bats: L **Throws:** L **Pos:** LF-18; PH-18; RF-15; PR-3; CF-1   **Ht:** 6'4" **Wt:** 217 **Born:** 12/14/1977 **Age:** 27

Year Team	Lg	G	AB	H	2B	3B	HR	(Hm	Rd)	TB	R	RBI	RC	TBB	IBB	SO	HBP	SH	SF	SB	CS	SB%	GDP	Avg	OBP	Slg
								BATTING												BASERUNNING				AVERAGES		
1999 Missoula	R+	32	115	27	4	4	3	(-	-)	48	22	22	17	14	0	36	4	0	2	2	0	1.00	6	.235	.333	.417
2000 South Bend	A	127	452	132	27	4	15	(-	-)	212	64	60	73	47	5	101	2	2	4	9	6	.60	9	.292	.358	.469
2001 El Paso	AA	128	476	140	32	11	15	(-	-)	239	67	74	83	46	7	118	4	1	4	11	3	.79	7	.294	.358	.502
2002 Tucson	AAA	125	436	114	20	6	14	(-	-)	188	57	59	56	27	2	103	5	1	2	9	6	.60	7	.261	.311	.431
2003 Tucson	AAA	134	462	135	29	7	14	(-	-)	220	74	75	73	44	5	95	3	1	1	5	7	.42	11	.292	.357	.476
2004 Tucson	AAA	61	234	63	13	0	14	(-	-)	118	32	43	36	21	1	67	0	0	1	3	2	.60	3	.269	.328	.504
2004 Arizona	NL	50	107	24	3	2	3	(3	0)	40	5	13	11	7	0	31	0	0	0	1	1	.50	1	.224	.272	.374

Einar Diaz

Bats: R **Throws:** R **Pos:** C-44; PH-10; 3B-1; PR-1   **Ht:** 5'10" **Wt:** 190 **Born:** 12/28/1972 **Age:** 32

Year Team	Lg	G	AB	H	2B	3B	HR	(Hm	Rd)	TB	R	RBI	RC	TBB	IBB	SO	HBP	SH	SF	SB	CS	SB%	GDP	Avg	OBP	Slg
								BATTING												BASERUNNING				AVERAGES		
1996 Cleveland	AL	4	1	0	0	0	0	(0	0)	0	0	0	0	0	0	0	0	0	0	0	0	-	0	.000	.000	.000
1997 Cleveland	AL	5	7	1	1	0	0	(0	0)	2	1	1	0	0	0	2	0	0	0	0	0	-	0	.143	.143	.286
1998 Cleveland	AL	17	48	11	1	0	2	(1	1)	18	8	9	5	3	0	2	2	0	3	0	0	-	1	.229	.286	.375
1999 Cleveland	AL	119	392	110	21	1	3	(2	1)	142	43	32	46	23	0	41	5	6	1	11	4	.73	10	.281	.328	.362
2000 Cleveland	AL	75	250	68	14	2	4	(2	2)	98	29	25	30	11	0	29	8	6	0	4	2	.67	7	.272	.323	.392
2001 Cleveland	AL	134	437	121	34	1	4	(0	4)	169	54	56	53	17	0	44	16	8	0	1	2	.33	11	.277	.328	.387
2002 Cleveland	AL	102	320	66	19	0	2	(1	1)	91	34	16	14	17	1	27	6	6	2	0	1	.00	13	.206	.258	.284
2003 Texas	AL	101	334	86	14	1	4	(2	2)	114	30	35	31	9	0	32	10	4	4	3	1	.75	12	.257	.294	.341
2004 Montreal	NL	55	139	31	6	1	1	(1	0)	42	9	11	9	11	3	10	4	2	3	2	0	1.00	6	.223	.293	.302
9 ML YEARS		612	1928	494	110	6	20	(9	11)	676	208	185	188	91	4	187	51	32	13	21	10	.68	61	.256	.305	.351

Felix Diaz

Pitches: R **Bats:** R **Pos:** RP-11; SP-7   **Ht:** 6'1" **Wt:** 180 **Born:** 7/27/1980 **Age:** 24

Year Team	Lg	G	GS	CG	GF	IP	BFP	H	R	ER	HR	SH	SF	HB	TBB	IBB	SO	WP	Bk	W	L	Pct	ShO	Sv-Op	Hld	ERC	ERA
		HOW MUCH HE PITCHED						WHAT HE GAVE UP												THE RESULTS							
2000 Giants	R	11	11	0	0	62.2	270	56	35	29	0	4	4	5	16	0	58	3	3	3	4	.429	0	0- -	-	2.48	4.16
2000 Salem-Keizer	A-	3	0	0	2	3.1	19	6	6	3	2	2	0	1	1	0	2	0	0	0	1	.000	0	0- -	-	13.89	8.10
2001 Hagerstown	A	15	12	0	0	51.2	222	49	27	21	4	0	2	4	16	0	56	3	0	1	4	.200	0	0- -	-	3.54	3.66
2002 Birmingham	AA	7	6	0	0	31.0	129	25	14	12	4	0	0	0	8	0	30	0	0	4	0	1.000	0	0- -	-	2.57	3.48
2002 Shreveport	AA	12	12	1	0	60.0	255	54	22	18	1	2	1	4	23	0	48	4	2	3	5	.375	0	0- -	-	3.15	2.70
2003 Brevard Cnty	A+	1	0	0	1	1.0	5	1	0	0	0	0	0	0	1	0	0	0	0	0	0	-	0	0- -	-	5.48	0.00
2003 Charlotte	AAA	27	18	1	3	115.2	497	122	59	51	12	3	5	4	33	3	83	5	2	5	7	.417	0	0- -	-	4.04	3.97
2004 Charlotte	AAA	19	17	0	0	115.0	436	95	41	38	14	8	3	2	24	0	96	0	1	10	2	.833	0	0- -	-	2.80	2.97
2004 Chicago	AL	18	7	0	3	49.1	226	62	38	37	13	2	3	3	16	1	33	0	0	2	5	.286	0	0-0	0	6.70	6.75

Matt Diaz

Bats: R **Throws:** R **Pos:** DH-4; LF-3; PH-3; RF-1   **Ht:** 6'1" **Wt:** 206 **Born:** 3/3/1978 **Age:** 27

Year Team	Lg	G	AB	H	2B	3B	HR	(Hm	Rd)	TB	R	RBI	RC	TBB	IBB	SO	HBP	SH	SF	SB	CS	SB%	GDP	Avg	OBP	Slg
								BATTING												BASERUNNING				AVERAGES		
1999 Hudson Val	A-	54	208	51	15	2	1	(-	-)	73	22	20	19	6	0	43	6	2	2	6	2	.75	5	.245	.284	.351
2000 St. Petersburg	A+	106	392	106	21	3	6	(-	-)	151	37	53	39	11	0	54	11	1	5	2	3	.40	21	.270	.305	.385
2001 Bakersfield	A+	131	524	172	40	2	17	(-	-)	267	79	81	93	24	3	73	14	4	5	11	5	.69	11	.328	.370	.510
2002 Orlando	AA	122	449	123	28	1	10	(-	-)	183	71	50	61	34	1	72	10	3	3	31	9	.78	11	.274	.337	.408
2003 Orlando	AA	60	227	87	21	0	5	(-	-)	123	32	41	49	19	6	24	8	1	3	9	5	.64	7	.383	.444	.542
2003 Durham	AAA	67	253	83	18	3	8	(-	-)	131	35	45	46	16	3	45	8	0	3	6	2	.75	8	.328	.382	.518
2004 Durham	AAA	134	503	167	47	5	21	(-	-)	287	81	93	99	26	0	96	13	1	5	15	4	.79	10	.332	.377	.571
2003 Tampa Bay	AL	4	9	1	0	0	0	(0	0)	1	2	0	0	1	0	3	0	0	0	0	0	-	0	.111	.200	.111
2004 Tampa Bay	AL	10	21	4	1	1	1	(1	0)	10	3	3	2	1	0	6	2	0	0	0	0	-	0	.190	.292	.476
2 ML YEARS		14	30	5	1	1	1	(1	0)	11	5	3	2	2	0	9	2	0	0	0	0	-	0	.167	.265	.367

Victor Diaz

Bats: R Throws: R Pos: RF-14; PH-2   Ht: 6'0" Wt: 200 Born: 12/10/1981 Age: 23

						BATTING												BASERUNNING				AVERAGES		
Year Team	Lg	G	AB	H	2B	3B	HR	(Hm | Rd)	TB	R	RBI	RC	TBB	IBB	SO	HBP	SH	SF	SB	CS	SB%	GDP	Avg	OBP	Slg
2001 Dodgers	R	53	195	69	22	2	3	(- | -)	104	36	31	40	16	1	23	6	1	3	6	3	.67	3	.354	.414	.533
2002 Sth Georgia	A	91	349	122	26	2	10	(- | -)	182	64	58	72	27	6	69	10	0	5	20	6	.77	4	.350	.407	.521
2002 Jacksonville	AA	42	152	32	7	0	4	(- | -)	51	22	24	11	7	0	42	3	0	1	7	5	.58	3	.211	.258	.336
2003 Jacksonville	AA	85	316	92	20	2	10	(- | -)	146	42	54	46	27	1	60	6	1	5	8	10	.44	10	.291	.353	.462
2003 Binghamton	AA	45	175	62	11	0	6	(- | -)	91	29	23	32	8	0	32	1	1	2	7	5	.58	3	.354	.382	.520
2004 Norfolk	AAA	141	528	154	31	1	24	(- | -)	259	81	94	80	31	1	133	5	5	9	6	7	.46	12	.292	.332	.491
2004 New York	NL	15	51	15	3	0	3	(1 | 2)	27	8	8	6	1	0	15	1	0	0	0	0	-	3	.294	.321	.529

R.A. Dickey

Pitches: R Bats: R Pos: SP-15; RP-10   Ht: 6'3" Wt: 205 Born: 10/29/1974 Age: 30

			HOW MUCH HE PITCHED						WHAT HE GAVE UP											THE RESULTS						
Year Team	Lg	G	GS	CG	GF	IP	BFP	H	R	ER	HR	SH	SF	HB	TBB	IBB	SO	WP	Bk	W	L	Pct	ShO	Sv-Op	Hld	ERC	ERA
2004 Frisco*	AA	4	4	0	0	13.2	58	16	5	3	0	0	1	0	1	0	9	0	0	1	1	.500	0	0--	-	3.00	1.98
2001 Texas	AL	4	0	0	0	12.0	53	13	9	9	3	0	0	0	7	1	4	1	0	0	1	.000	0	0-0	0	6.57	6.75
2003 Texas	AL	38	13	1	6	116.2	513	135	68	66	16	4	3	5	38	5	94	5	2	9	8	.529	1	1-1	3	5.09	5.09
2004 Texas	AL	25	15	0	2	104.1	480	136	77	65	17	3	3	4	33	1	57	5	1	6	7	.462	0	1-1	0	6.08	5.61
3 ML YEARS		67	28	1	9	233.0	1046	284	154	140	36	7	6	9	78	7	155	11	3	15	16	.484	1	2-2	3	5.60	5.41

Mike DiFelice

Bats: R Throws: R Pos: C-16; DH-1; PH-1; PR-1   Ht: 6'2" Wt: 205 Born: 5/28/1969 Age: 36

						BATTING												BASERUNNING				AVERAGES		
Year Team	Lg	G	AB	H	2B	3B	HR	(Hm	Rd)	TB	R	RBI	RC	TBB	IBB	SO	HBP	SH	SF	SB	CS	SB%	GDP	Avg	OBP	Slg
2004 Toledo*	AAA	64	237	64	14	0	5	(-	-)	93	20	36	27	14	0	37	1	0	2	1	0	1.00	7	.270	.311	.392
1996 St Louis	NL	4	7	2	1	0	0	(0	0)	3	0	2	1	0	0	1	0	0	0	0	0	-	0	.286	.286	.429
1997 St Louis	NL	93	260	62	10	1	4	(1	3)	86	16	30	23	19	0	61	3	6	1	1	1	.50	11	.238	.297	.331
1998 Tampa Bay	AL	84	248	57	12	3	3	(1	2)	84	17	23	19	15	0	56	1	3	2	0	0	-	12	.230	.274	.339
1999 Tampa Bay	AL	51	179	55	11	0	6	(5	1)	84	21	27	29	8	0	23	3	0	1	0	0	-	1	.307	.346	.469
2000 Tampa Bay	AL	60	204	49	13	1	6	(4	2)	82	23	19	21	12	0	40	0	5	2	0	0	-	8	.240	.280	.402
2001 TB-Ari		60	170	32	5	1	2	(0	2)	45	14	10	10	8	0	49	4	3	2	1	1	.50	3	.188	.239	.265
2002 St Louis	NL	70	174	40	11	0	4	(3	1)	63	17	19	17	17	3	42	1	2	3	0	0	-	4	.230	.297	.362
2003 Kansas City	AL	62	189	48	16	1	3	(1	2)	75	29	25	26	9	0	30	4	1	2	1	0	1.00	6	.254	.299	.397
2004 Det-ChC		17	25	3	0	1	0	(0	0)	5	3	2	1	3	0	4	0	0	0	0	0	-	3	.120	.214	.200
2001 Tampa Bay	AL	48	149	31	5	1	2	(0	2)	44	13	9	10	8	0	39	3	2	2	1	1	.50	3	.208	.259	.295
2001 Arizona	NL	12	21	1	0	0	0	(0	0)	1	1	1	0	0	0	10	1	1	0	0	0	-	0	.048	.091	.048
2004 Detroit	AL	13	22	3	0	1	0	(0	0)	5	3	2	1	3	0	3	0	0	0	0	0	-	3	.136	.240	.227
2004 Chicago	NL	4	3	0	0	0	0	(0	0)	0	0	0	0	0	0	1	0	0	0	0	0	-	0	.000	.000	.000
9 ML YEARS		501	1456	348	79	8	28	(15	13)	527	140	157	147	91	3	306	16	20	13	3	2	.60	48	.239	.289	.362

Lenny Dinardo

Pitches: L Bats: L Pos: RP-22   Ht: 6'4" Wt: 195 Born: 9/19/1979 Age: 25

			HOW MUCH HE PITCHED						WHAT HE GAVE UP										THE RESULTS						
Year Team	Lg	G	GS	CG	GF	IP	BFP	H	R	ER	HR	SH	SF	HB	TBB	IBB	SO	WP	W	L	Pct	ShO	Sv-Op	Hld	ERC	ERA
2001 Brooklyn	A-	9	5	0	0	36.0	148	26	10	8	0	0	0	1	17	0	40	4	1	2	.333	0	0--	-	2.35	2.00
2002 Capital City	A	24	19	0	1	101.1	466	106	60	49	3	5	5	13	56	1	103	11	5	5	.500	0	1--	-	4.90	4.35
2003 St. Lucie	A+	19	13	1	2	85.0	325	64	27	19	1	3	1	3	14	0	93	5	3	8	.273	0	1--	-	1.65	2.01
2003 Binghamton	AA	7	7	1	0	40.0	169	35	19	16	3	1	3	4	13	0	36	0	1	3	.250	0	0--	-	3.31	3.60
2004 Red Sox	R	2	1	0	0	3.0	11	3	0	0	0	0	0	0	0	0	5	0	0	0	-	0	0--	-	2.18	0.00
2004 Sarasota	A+	1	1	0	0	3.0	11	2	0	0	0	0	0	0	0	0	2	0	0	0	-	0	0--	-	0.91	0.00
2004 Portland	AA	3	0	0	0	5.2	26	8	6	6	1	0	0	0	1	0	4	1	1	0	1.000	0	0--	-	6.00	9.53
2004 Pawtucket	AAA	1	1	0	0	3.0	12	3	0	0	0	0	0	0	0	0	4	0	0	0	-	0	0--	-	1.95	0.00
2004 Boston	AL	22	0	0	6	27.2	130	34	17	13	1	1	1	2	12	1	21	1	0	0	-	0	0-0	0	5.17	4.23

Craig Dingman

Pitches: R Bats: R Pos: RP-24   Ht: 6'4" Wt: 215 Born: 3/12/1974 Age: 31

			HOW MUCH HE PITCHED						WHAT HE GAVE UP										THE RESULTS						
Year Team	Lg	G	GS	CG	GF	IP	BFP	H	R	ER	HR	SH	SF	HB	TBB	IBB	SO	WP	Bk	W	L	Pct	ShO	Sv-Op	Hld	ERC	ERA
2002 Louisville	AAA	22	0	0	7	26.0	109	20	12	12	3	1	0	2	13	0	26	2	0	0	1	.000	0	0--	-	3.67	4.15
2002 Columbus	AAA	2	0	0	0	1.1	12	6	6	2	0	0	0	0	1	1	2	0	0	0	0	-	0	0--	-	25.83	13.50
2003 W Tennesse	AA	4	0	0	1	6.0	28	6	4	4	2	1	0	0	5	1	5	0	0	0	1	.000	0	0--	-	7.59	6.00
2003 Iowa	AAA	11	0	0	5	18.0	74	14	4	4	0	0	1	0	7	1	12	1	0	1	0	1.000	0	0--	-	2.14	2.00
2004 Toledo	AAA	21	0	0	7	25.2	115	26	14	13	5	0	1	1	11	2	31	0	0	1	2	.333	0	0--	-	4.87	4.56
2004 Detroit	AL	24	0	0	5	29.1	141	33	22	22	3	1	2	4	22	3	16	1	0	2	2	.500	0	0-2	0	6.77	6.75

Greg Dobbs

Bats: L Throws: R Pos: 3B-14; PH-5; DH-1   Ht: 6'1" Wt: 205 Born: 7/2/1978 Age: 26

						BATTING												BASERUNNING				AVERAGES		
Year Team	Lg	G	AB	H	2B	3B	HR	(Hm	Rd)	TB	R	RBI	RC	TBB	IBB	SO	HBP	SH	SF	SB	CS	SB%	GDP	Avg	OBP	Slg
2001 Everett	A-	65	249	80	17	2	6	(-	-)	119	37	41	47	30	3	39	2	1	2	5	3	.63	2	.321	.396	.478
2001 Sn Brnardino	A+	3	13	5	1	0	1	(-	-)	9	2	3	3	0	0	4	0	0	1	0	0	-	0	.385	.357	.692
2002 Wisconsin	A	86	320	88	16	2	10	(-	-)	138	43	48	47	31	4	50	1	0	3	13	3	.81	6	.275	.338	.431
2002 San Antonio	AA	27	96	35	2	0	5	(-	-)	52	13	15	20	9	2	17	1	2	0	1	2	.33	2	.365	.425	.542
2003 San Antonio	AA	2	6	2	2	0	0	(-	-)	4	0	0	1	0	0	1	0	0	0	0	0	-	0	.333	.333	.667
2004 San Antonio	AA	51	203	66	14	4	5	(-	-)	103	25	34	35	11	2	23	5	0	1	5	4	.56	5	.325	.373	.507
2004 Tacoma	AAA	67	255	69	9	8	3	(-	-)	106	28	31	26	5	2	36	1	0	1	4	3	.57	10	.271	.286	.416
2004 Seattle	AL	18	53	12	1	0	1	(1	0)	16	4	9	5	1	0	14	1	0	1	0	0	-	0	.226	.250	.302

Scott Dohmann

Pitches: R **Bats:** R **Pos:** RP-41   **Ht:** 6'1" **Wt:** 180 **Born:** 2/13/1978 **Age:** 27

				HOW MUCH HE PITCHED			WHAT HE GAVE UP											THE RESULTS						
Year Team	Lg	G	GS	CG	GF	IP	BFP	H	R	ER	HR	SH	SF	HB	TBB	IBB	SO	WP	Bk	W	L	Pct	ShO	Sv-Op	Hld	ERC	ERA
2000 Portland	A-	5	4	0	0	23.0	85	14	3	2	0	0	0	1	5	0	23	0	0	2	1	.667	0	0- -	-	1.31	0.78
2000 Asheville	A	7	7	0	0	32.2	149	43	24	22	3	0	3	3	8	0	36	3	1	1	5	.167	0	0- -	-	5.58	6.06
2001 Asheville	A	28	28	3	0	173.0	717	165	88	83	27	5	3	18	33	5	154	3	0	11	13	.458	1	0- -	-	3.77	4.32
2002 Salem	A+	28	28	0	0	170.1	720	141	85	80	22	6	6	15	53	0	131	8	0	13	5	.722	0	0- -	-	3.55	4.23
2003 Tulsa	AA	50	4	0	17	93.2	403	94	47	43	11	4	2	5	29	2	102	6	0	9	4	.692	0	4- -	-	4.01	4.13
2004 Co Springs	AAA	18	0	0	6	22.0	94	22	5	4	1	1	0	0	7	1	31	2	0	1	0	1.000	0	2- -	-	3.27	1.64
2004 Colorado	NL	41	0	0	13	46.0	198	41	22	21	8	2	3	0	19	0	49	3	0	0	3	.000	0	0-4	4	3.94	4.11

Juan Dominguez

Pitches: R **Bats:** R **Pos:** SP-4   **Ht:** 6'2" **Wt:** 180 **Born:** 5/18/1980 **Age:** 25

				HOW MUCH HE PITCHED			WHAT HE GAVE UP											THE RESULTS						
Year Team	Lg	G	GS	CG	GF	IP	BFP	H	R	ER	HR	SH	SF	HB	TBB	IBB	SO	WP	Bk	W	L	Pct	ShO	Sv-Op	Hld	ERC	ERA
2001 Rangers	R	11	9	1	0	58.1	243	56	29	26	4	0	2	5	12	0	55	0	1	4	2	.667	1	0- -	-	3.23	4.01
2001 Charlotte	A+	2	0	0	0	1.2	19	4	2	2	1	0	1	0	1	0	5	0	0	1	0	1.000	0	0- -	-	10.06	10.80
2003 Stockton	A+	16	9	0	1	63.1	266	55	27	20	3	0	1	6	16	0	72	3	1	4	0	1.000	0	1- -	-	2.78	2.84
2003 Frisco	AA	9	9	0	0	55.1	220	35	17	16	2	0	1	1	21	0	54	1	0	5	0	1.000	0	0- -	-	1.81	2.60
2003 Oklahoma	AAA	3	3	0	0	18.0	71	15	7	7	1	2	0	0	3	0	14	1	0	1	0	1.000	0	0- -	-	2.09	3.50
2004 Frisco	AA	3	2	0	0	8.1	30	4	1	1	0	0	0	0	1	0	11	0	0	0	0	-	0	0- -	-	0.68	1.08
2004 Oklahoma	AAA	9	9	1	0	54.2	206	41	20	19	3	0	1	2	19	0	41	1	0	5	1	.833	0	0- -	-	2.66	3.13
2003 Texas	AL	6	3	0	1	16.1	73	16	14	13	5	1	1	0	12	0	13	1	0	0	2	.000	0	0-0	0	7.22	7.16
2004 Texas	AL	4	4	0	0	23.0	98	25	11	10	2	1	1	2	5	0	14	0	2	1	2	.333	0	0-0	0	4.13	3.91
2 ML YEARS		10	7	0	1	39.1	171	41	25	23	7	2	2	2	17	0	27	1	2	1	4	.200	0	0-0	0	5.34	5.26

Andy Dominique

Bats: R **Throws:** R **Pos:** 1B-5; PH-3; C-1   **Ht:** 6'0" **Wt:** 220 **Born:** 10/30/1975 **Age:** 29

							BATTING														BASERUNNING				AVERAGES		
Year Team	Lg	G	AB	H	2B	3B	HR	(Hm	Rd)	TB	R	RBI	RC	TBB	IBB	SO	HBP	SH	SF	SB	CS	SB%	GDP	Avg	OBP	Slg
1997 Batavia	A-	72	277	77	17	0	14	(-	-)	136	52	48	47	26	0	60	10	0	5	4	1	.80	6	.278	.355	.491
1998 Piedmont	A	133	514	145	38	0	24	(-	-)	255	82	102	90	61	4	97	12	0	4	0	2	.00	9	.282	.369	.496
1999 Clearwater	A+	130	487	124	29	5	14	(-	-)	205	77	92	73	69	4	84	10	3	8	3	3	.50	13	.255	.354	.421
2000 Reading	AA	104	327	78	27	0	13	(-	-)	144	46	50	44	35	0	56	8	3	4	0	1	.00	9	.239	.324	.440
2001 Reading	AA	76	261	73	16	0	12	(-	-)	125	43	49	45	37	2	45	1	0	2	3	1	.75	6	.280	.369	.479
2001 Scrtn/WlksBr	AAA	40	135	23	6	0	3	(-	-)	38	16	18	7	12	0	34	1	1	0	0	0	-	4	.170	.243	.281
2002 Clearwater	A+	8	34	14	5	0	0	(-	-)	19	5	2	7	1	0	4	1	0	0	0	0	-	0	.412	.444	.559
2002 Trenton	AA	103	361	98	21	1	8	(-	-)	145	40	51	51	36	1	60	9	0	6	2	1	.67	9	.271	.347	.402
2003 Portland	AA	32	97	35	7	0	3	(-	-)	51	18	21	23	16	0	15	3	0	0	1	0	-	1	.361	.454	.526
2003 Pawtucket	AAA	79	289	88	18	0	13	(-	-)	145	42	57	49	22	0	45	7	1	3	2	1	.67	10	.304	.364	.502
2004 Pawtucket	AAA	111	419	112	28	0	15	(-	-)	185	54	69	65	55	1	87	8	0	4	0	2	.00	11	.267	.360	.442
2004 Boston	AL	7	11	2	0	0	0	(0	0)	2	0	1	0	0	0	3	0	0	0	0	0	-	0	.182	.182	.182

Brendan Donnelly

Pitches: R **Bats:** R **Pos:** RP-40   **Ht:** 6'3" **Wt:** 200 **Born:** 7/4/1971 **Age:** 33

				HOW MUCH HE PITCHED			WHAT HE GAVE UP											THE RESULTS						
Year Team	Lg	G	GS	CG	GF	IP	BFP	H	R	ER	HR	SH	SF	HB	TBB	IBB	SO	WP	Bk	W	L	Pct	ShO	Sv-Op	Hld	ERC	ERA
2004 R Cucamnga*	A+	2	0	0	1	3.0	13	3	0	0	0	0	0	0	1	0	5	1	0	0	0	-	0	0- -	-	3.05	0.00
2004 Salt Lake*	AAA	3	0	0	1	2.1	11	2	2	2	0	0	0	0	2	0	6	0	0	0	0	-	0	0- -	-	4.14	7.71
2002 Anaheim	AL	46	0	0	11	49.2	199	32	13	12	2	3	1	2	19	3	54	1	0	1	1	.500	0	1-3	13	1.89	2.17
2003 Anaheim	AL	63	0	0	15	74.0	307	55	14	13	2	3	1	4	24	1	79	1	0	2	2	.500	0	3-5	29	2.12	1.58
2004 Anaheim	AL	40	0	0	10	42.0	172	34	14	14	5	2	2	1	15	0	56	0	0	5	2	.714	0	0-0	5	3.12	3.00
3 ML YEARS		149	0	0	36	165.2	678	121	41	39	9	8	4	7	58	4	189	2	0	8	5	.615	0	4-8	47	2.29	2.12

Octavio Dotel

Pitches: R **Bats:** R **Pos:** RP-77   **Ht:** 6'0" **Wt:** 200 **Born:** 11/25/1973 **Age:** 31

				HOW MUCH HE PITCHED			WHAT HE GAVE UP											THE RESULTS						
Year Team	Lg	G	GS	CG	GF	IP	BFP	H	R	ER	HR	SH	SF	HB	TBB	IBB	SO	WP	Bk	W	L	Pct	ShO	Sv-Op	Hld	ERC	ERA
1999 New York	NL	19	14	0	1	85.1	368	69	52	51	12	3	5	6	49	1	85	3	2	8	3	.727	0	0-0	0	4.30	5.38
2000 Houston	NL	50	16	0	25	125.0	563	127	80	75	26	7	8	7	61	3	142	6	0	3	7	.300	0	16-23	0	5.47	5.40
2001 Houston	NL	61	4	0	20	105.0	438	79	35	31	5	2	2	2	47	2	145	4	0	7	5	.583	0	2-4	14	2.62	2.66
2002 Houston	NL	83	0	0	22	97.1	376	58	21	20	7	3	7	4	27	2	118	2	0	6	4	.600	0	6-10	31	1.61	1.85
2003 Houston	NL	76	0	0	13	87.0	346	53	25	24	9	2	1	3	31	2	97	2	0	6	4	.600	0	4-6	33	2.02	2.48
2004 Hou-Oak	NL	77	0	0	70	85.1	356	68	38	35	13	4	2	4	33	7	122	4	1	6	6	.500	0	36-45	0	3.31	3.69
2004 Houston	NL	32	0	0	29	34.2	146	27	15	12	4	2	1	1	15	4	50	3	1	0	4	.000	0	14-17	0	3.01	3.12
2004 Oakland	AL	45	0	0	41	50.2	210	41	23	23	9	2	1	3	18	3	72	1	0	6	2	.750	0	22-28	0	3.52	4.09
6 ML YEARS		366	34	0	151	585.0	2447	454	251	236	72	21	25	26	248	17	709	21	3	36	29	.554	0	64-88	78	3.22	3.63

Sean Douglass

Pitches: R **Bats:** R **Pos:** RP-11; SP-3   **Ht:** 6'6" **Wt:** 198 **Born:** 4/28/1979 **Age:** 26

				HOW MUCH HE PITCHED			WHAT HE GAVE UP											THE RESULTS						
Year Team	Lg	G	GS	CG	GF	IP	BFP	H	R	ER	HR	SH	SF	HB	TBB	IBB	SO	WP	Bk	W	L	Pct	ShO	Sv-Op	Hld	ERC	ERA
2004 Syracuse*	AAA	18	18	1	0	89.0	382	92	53	47	7	8	4	3	37	0	74	6	0	5	6	.455	0	0- -	-	4.41	4.75
2001 Baltimore	AL	4	4	0	0	20.1	94	21	12	12	3	0	1	1	11	0	17	1	1	2	1	.667	0	0-0	0	5.27	5.31
2002 Baltimore	AL	15	8	0	2	53.1	245	58	41	36	10	2	1	2	35	2	44	3	0	0	5	.000	0	0-0	0	6.56	6.08
2003 Baltimore	AL	3	0	0	0	8.0	44	14	12	12	2	0	0	1	6	0	3	0	0	0	0	-	0	0-0	0	12.56	13.50
2004 Toronto	AL	14	3	0	4	38.2	179	37	27	27	6	0	2	2	28	4	36	2	0	0	2	.000	0	0-0	0	5.59	6.28
4 ML YEARS		36	15	0	6	120.1	562	130	92	87	21	2	4	6	80	6	100	6	1	2	8	.200	0	0-0	0	6.38	6.51

Scott Downs

Pitches: L **Bats:** L **Pos:** SP-12   **Ht:** 6'2" **Wt:** 190 **Born:** 3/17/1976 **Age:** 29

		HOW MUCH HE PITCHED						WHAT HE GAVE UP										THE RESULTS						
Year Team	Lg	G	GS	CG	GF	IP	BFP	H	R	ER	HR	SH	SF	HB	TBB	IBB	SO	WP	Bk	W	L	Pct	ShO	Sv-Op	Hld	ERC	ERA
2004 Edmonton*	AAA	22	22	2	0	135.1	559	143	57	53	16	10	3	3	26	0	67	1	1	10	6	.625	2	0--	-	3.84	3.52
2000 ChC-Mon	NL	19	19	0	0	97.0	442	122	0	57	13	0	0	0	40	0	63	0	0	4	3	.571	0	0-0	0	5.92	5.29
2003 Montreal	NL	1	1	0	0	3.0	17	5	5	5	2	0	0	0	3	2	4	0	1	0	1	.000	0	0-0	0	15.01	15.00
2004 Montreal	NL	12	12	1	0	63.0	284	79	47	36	9	2	1	3	23	2	38	2	0	3	6	.333	1	0-0	0	5.97	5.14
2000 Chicago	NL	18	18	0	0	94.0	426	117	0	54	13	0	0	0	37	0	63	0	0	4	3	.571	0	0-0	0	5.78	5.17
2000 Montreal	NL	1	1	0	0	3.0	16	5	0	3	0	0	0	0	3	0	0	0	0	0	0	-	0	0-0	0	10.34	9.00
3 ML YEARS		32	32	1	0	163.0	743	206	52	98	24	2	1	3	66	4	105	2	1	7	10	.412	1	0-0	0	6.08	5.41

Kelly Dransfeldt

Bats: R **Throws:** R **Pos:** SS-8; PH-5; 3B-3; PR-2; DH-1   **Ht:** 6'2" **Wt:** 195 **Born:** 4/16/1975 **Age:** 30

		BATTING																		BASERUNNING				AVERAGES		
Year Team	Lg	G	AB	H	2B	3B	HR	(Hm	Rd)	TB	R	RBI	RC	TBB	IBB	SO	HBP	SH	SF	SB	CS	SB%	GDP	Avg	OBP	Slg
2004 Charlotte*	AAA	88	305	76	18	1	5	(-	-)	111	34	30	30	15	0	63	3	5	4	5	2	.71	8	.249	.287	.364
1999 Texas	AL	16	53	10	1	0	1	(1	0)	14	3	5	2	3	0	12	0	1	0	0	0	-	2	.189	.232	.264
2000 Texas	AL	16	26	3	2	0	0	(0	0)	5	2	2	0	1	0	14	0	0	0	0	0	-	0	.115	.148	.192
2001 Texas	AL	4	3	0	0	0	0	(0	0)	0	0	0	0	0	0	0	0	0	0	0	0	-	0	.000	.000	.000
2004 Chicago	AL	15	30	10	0	0	0	(0	0)	10	5	4	6	0	0	6	0	0	0	0	0	-	0	.333	.333	.333
4 ML YEARS		51	112	23	3	0	1	(1	0)	29	10	11	8	4	0	32	0	1	0	0	0	-	2	.205	.233	.259

Darren Dreifort

Pitches: R **Bats:** R **Pos:** RP-60   **Ht:** 6'2" **Wt:** 211 **Born:** 5/3/1972 **Age:** 33

		HOW MUCH HE PITCHED						WHAT HE GAVE UP										THE RESULTS						
Year Team	Lg	G	GS	CG	GF	IP	BFP	H	R	ER	HR	SH	SF	HB	TBB	IBB	SO	WP	Bk	W	L	Pct	ShO	Sv-Op	Hld	ERC	ERA
1994 Los Angeles	NL	27	0	0	15	29.0	148	45	21	20	0	3	0	4	15	3	22	1	0	0	5	.000	0	6-9	3	7.39	6.21
1996 Los Angeles	NL	19	0	0	5	23.2	106	23	13	13	2	3	1	0	12	4	24	2	1	1	4	.200	0	0-2	1	3.84	4.94
1997 Los Angeles	NL	48	0	0	15	63.0	265	45	21	20	3	5	2	1	34	2	63	3	1	5	2	.714	0	4-7	9	2.72	2.86
1998 Los Angeles	NL	32	26	1	0	180.0	752	171	84	80	12	11	6	10	57	2	168	9	0	8	12	.400	1	0-0	0	3.50	4.00
1999 Los Angeles	NL	30	29	1	0	178.2	773	177	105	95	20	8	2	7	76	2	140	9	4	13	13	.500	1	0-0	0	4.39	4.79
2000 Los Angeles	NL	32	32	1	0	192.2	842	175	105	89	31	9	0	12	87	1	164	17	3	12	9	.571	1	0-0	0	4.40	4.16
2001 Los Angeles	NL	16	16	0	0	94.2	416	89	62	54	11	7	1	6	47	0	91	10	0	4	7	.364	0	0-0	0	4.50	5.13
2003 Los Angeles	NL	10	10	0	0	60.1	261	58	29	27	6	3	1	0	25	0	67	3	1	4	4	.500	0	0-0	0	3.87	4.03
2004 Los Angeles	NL	60	0	0	9	50.2	227	43	25	25	5	4	2	0	36	2	63	5	0	1	4	.200	0	1-4	15	4.34	4.44
9 ML YEARS		274	113	3	44	872.2	3790	826	465	423	90	53	15	40	389	16	802	59	10	48	60	.444	3	11-22	28	4.13	4.36

Ryan Drese

Pitches: R **Bats:** R **Pos:** SP-33; RP-1   **Ht:** 6'3" **Wt:** 220 **Born:** 4/5/1976 **Age:** 29

		HOW MUCH HE PITCHED						WHAT HE GAVE UP										THE RESULTS						
Year Team	Lg	G	GS	CG	GF	IP	BFP	H	R	ER	HR	SH	SF	HB	TBB	IBB	SO	WP	Bk	W	L	Pct	ShO	Sv-Op	Hld	ERC	ERA
2004 Oklahoma*	AAA	1	1	0	0	5.0	20	6	1	1	1	0	0	0	1	0	3	0	0	1	0	1.000	0	0--	-	4.38	1.80
2001 Cleveland	AL	9	4	0	2	36.2	149	32	15	14	2	1	0	1	15	2	24	0	0	1	2	.333	0	0-0	0	3.27	3.44
2002 Cleveland	AL	26	26	1	0	137.1	635	176	104	100	15	3	9	6	62	1	102	11	0	10	9	.526	0	0-0	0	6.26	6.55
2003 Texas	AL	11	8	0	0	46.0	223	61	42	35	8	0	5	0	24	1	26	2	0	4	4	.333	0	0-0	1	7.60	6.85
2004 Texas	AL	34	33	2	1	207.2	897	233	104	97	16	6	5	11	58	6	98	1	0	14	10	.583	0	0-0	0	4.32	4.20
4 ML YEARS		80	71	3	3	427.2	1904	502	265	246	41	10	14	23	159	10	250	14	0	27	25	.519	0	0-0	1	5.16	5.18

J.D. Drew

Bats: L **Throws:** R **Pos:** RF-138; CF-8; DH-1; PH-1; PR-1   **Ht:** 6'1" **Wt:** 195 **Born:** 11/20/1975 **Age:** 29

		BATTING																		BASERUNNING				AVERAGES		
Year Team	Lg	G	AB	H	2B	3B	HR	(Hm	Rd)	TB	R	RBI	RC	TBB	IBB	SO	HBP	SH	SF	SB	CS	SB%	GDP	Avg	OBP	Slg
1998 St Louis	NL	14	36	15	3	1	5	(4	1)	35	9	13	12	4	0	10	0	0	1	0	0	-	4	.417	.463	.972
1999 St Louis	NL	104	368	89	16	6	13	(5	8)	156	72	39	58	50	0	77	6	3	3	19	3	.86	4	.242	.340	.424
2000 St Louis	NL	135	407	120	17	2	18	(11	7)	195	73	57	80	67	4	99	6	5	1	17	9	.65	3	.295	.401	.479
2001 St Louis	NL	109	375	121	18	5	27	(15	12)	230	80	73	92	57	4	75	4	3	4	13	3	.81	6	.323	.414	.613
2002 St Louis	NL	135	424	107	19	1	18	(9	9)	182	61	56	65	57	4	104	8	3	4	8	2	.80	4	.252	.349	.429
2003 St Louis	NL	100	287	83	13	3	15	(7	8)	147	60	42	58	36	0	48	3	2	0	2	2	.50	6	.289	.374	.512
2004 Atlanta	NL	145	518	158	28	8	31	(14	17)	295	118	93	122	118	2	116	5	1	3	12	3	.80	7	.305	.436	.569
7 ML YEARS		742	2415	693	114	26	127	(65	62)	1240	473	373	487	389	14	529	32	17	16	71	22	.76	34	.287	.391	.513

Tim Drew

Pitches: R **Bats:** R **Pos:** RP-11   **Ht:** 6'1" **Wt:** 195 **Born:** 8/31/1978 **Age:** 26

		HOW MUCH HE PITCHED						WHAT HE GAVE UP										THE RESULTS						
Year Team	Lg	G	GS	CG	GF	IP	BFP	H	R	ER	HR	SH	SF	HB	TBB	IBB	SO	WP	Bk	W	L	Pct	ShO	Sv-Op	Hld	ERC	ERA
2004 Richmond*	AAA	19	13	0	2	81.2	346	92	35	30	5	3	3	6	24	1	44	3	0	4	5	.444	0	1--	1	3.31	3.31
2000 Cleveland	AL	3	3	0	0	9.0	51	17	12	10	1	0	2	1	8	0	5	0	0	1	0	1.000	0	0-0	0	12.94	10.00
2001 Cleveland	AL	8	6	0	0	35.0	173	51	39	31	9	1	2	4	16	0	15	5	0	0	2	.000	0	0-0	0	8.95	7.97
2002 Montreal	NL	7	1	0	3	16.0	64	12	8	5	1	1	1	0	2	0	10	0	0	1	0	1.000	0	2-3	1	1.57	2.81
2003 Montreal	NL	6	1	0	3	8.2	46	12	12	12	3	1	2	0	8	1	3	3	0	0	2	.000	0	0-0	0	10.57	12.46
2004 Atlanta	NL	11	0	0	7	16.0	73	21	11	8	2	1	0	1	5	0	7	0	0	0	0	-	0	0-0	0	6.04	4.50
5 ML YEARS		35	11	0	13	84.2	407	113	82	66	16	4	7	6	39	1	40	8	0	2	4	.333	0	2-3	1	7.28	7.02

81

Travis Driskill

Pitches: R Bats: R Pos: RP-5   Ht: 6'0" Wt: 225 Born: 8/1/1971 Age: 33

Year Team	Lg	G	GS	CG	GF	IP	BFP	H	R	ER	HR	SH	SF	HB	TBB	IBB	SO	WP	Bk	W	L	Pct	ShO	Sv-Op	Hld	ERC	ERA
2004 Co Springs*	AAA	28	13	0	4	111.2	491	141	70	67	18	8	4	5	24	0	81	10	0	5	5	.500	0	2- -	-	5.52	5.40
2002 Baltimore	AL	29	19	0	6	132.2	589	150	78	73	21	2	2	8	48	1	78	6	0	8	8	.500	0	0-0	0	5.36	4.95
2003 Baltimore	AL	20	0	0	6	48.0	215	62	35	32	8	3	2	1	9	2	33	3	0	3	5	.375	0	1-1	0	5.30	6.00
2004 Colorado	NL	5	0	0	1	8.1	39	13	6	6	0	0	0	0	3	0	6	0	0	0	0	-	0	0-1	0	6.62	6.48
3 ML YEARS		54	19	0	13	189.0	843	225	119	111	29	5	4	9	60	3	117	9	0	11	13	.458	0	1-2	0	5.40	5.29

Jason Dubois

Bats: R Throws: R Pos: PH-16; RF-4; 1B-1; LF-1   Ht: 6'5" Wt: 220 Born: 3/26/1979 Age: 26

Year Team	Lg	G	AB	H	2B	3B	HR	(Hm	Rd)	TB	R	RBI	RC	TBB	IBB	SO	HBP	SH	SF	SB	CS	SB%	GDP	Avg	OBP	Slg
2001 Lansing	A	118	443	131	28	9	24	(-	-)	249	76	92	88	46	2	120	14	2	3	1	2	.33	8	.296	.377	.562
2002 Daytona	A+	99	361	116	25	1	20	(-	-)	203	64	85	82	57	0	95	9	0	4	6	2	.75	7	.321	.422	.562
2003 W Tennesse	AA	130	443	119	31	4	15	(-	-)	203	57	73	72	57	3	118	15	0	6	2	4	.33	12	.269	.367	.458
2004 Iowa	AAA	109	386	122	26	1	31	(-	-)	243	76	99	85	41	2	97	7	0	3	2	0	1.00	10	.316	.389	.630
2004 Chicago	NL	20	23	5	0	1	1	(1	0)	10	2	5	4	1	0	7	0	0	1	0	0	-	0	.217	.240	.435

Eric DuBose

Pitches: L Bats: L Pos: SP-14   Ht: 6'3" Wt: 231 Born: 5/15/1976 Age: 29

Year Team	Lg	G	GS	CG	GF	IP	BFP	H	R	ER	HR	SH	SF	HB	TBB	IBB	SO	WP	Bk	W	L	Pct	ShO	Sv-Op	Hld	ERC	ERA
2002 Baltimore	AL	4	0	0	2	6.0	25	7	2	2	1	0	0	1	1	0	4	0	0	0	0	-	0	0-0	0	5.59	3.00
2003 Baltimore	AL	17	10	1	3	73.2	305	60	33	31	6	2	3	5	25	2	44	0	1	3	6	.333	0	0-1	1	2.95	3.79
2004 Baltimore	AL	14	14	0	0	74.2	338	76	55	53	12	1	1	3	44	0	48	5	1	4	6	.400	0	0-0	0	5.60	6.39
3 ML YEARS		35	24	1	5	154.1	668	143	90	86	19	3	4	9	70	2	96	5	2	7	12	.368	0	0-1	1	4.27	5.02

Justin Duchscherer

Pitches: R Bats: R Pos: RP-53   Ht: 6'3" Wt: 190 Born: 11/19/1977 Age: 27

Year Team	Lg	G	GS	CG	GF	IP	BFP	H	R	ER	HR	SH	SF	HB	TBB	IBB	SO	WP	Bk	W	L	Pct	ShO	Sv-Op	Hld	ERC	ERA
2001 Texas	AL	5	2	0	0	14.2	76	24	0	20	5	0	0	0	4	0	11	0	0	1	1	.500	0	0-0	0	8.77	12.27
2003 Oakland	AL	4	3	0	0	16.1	71	17	7	6	1	1	0	2	3	0	15	0	0	1	1	.500	0	0-0	0	3.58	3.31
2004 Oakland	AL	53	0	0	18	96.1	398	85	37	35	13	7	1	5	32	6	59	1	1	7	6	.538	0	0-2	6	3.57	3.27
3 ML YEARS		62	5	0	18	127.1	545	126	44	61	19	8	1	7	39	6	85	1	1	9	8	.529	0	0-2	6	4.11	4.31

Brandon Duckworth

Pitches: R Bats: R Pos: RP-13; SP-6   Ht: 6'2" Wt: 185 Born: 1/23/1976 Age: 29

Year Team	Lg	G	GS	CG	GF	IP	BFP	H	R	ER	HR	SH	SF	HB	TBB	IBB	SO	WP	Bk	W	L	Pct	ShO	Sv-Op	Hld	ERC	ERA
2004 New Orleans*	AAA	14	13	0	0	70.0	314	81	44	43	10	5	4	4	28	1	63	3	0	5	5	.500	0	0- -	-	5.56	5.53
2001 Philadelphia	NL	11	11	0	0	69.0	289	57	29	27	2	7	3	6	29	5	40	2	0	3	2	.600	0	0-0	0	2.98	3.52
2002 Philadelphia	NL	30	29	0	0	163.0	725	167	103	98	26	7	3	7	69	5	167	10	0	8	9	.471	0	0-0	0	4.80	5.41
2003 Philadelphia	NL	24	18	0	2	93.0	424	98	58	51	12	9	1	10	44	3	68	5	0	4	7	.364	0	0-0	0	5.25	4.94
2004 Houston	NL	19	6	0	6	39.1	180	55	30	30	11	3	1	0	13	3	23	3	0	1	2	.333	0	0-0	0	7.56	6.86
4 ML YEARS		84	64	0	8	364.1	1618	377	220	206	51	26	8	23	155	16	298	20	0	16	20	.444	0	0-0	0	4.83	5.09

Jeff Duncan

Bats: L Throws: L Pos: PH-8; PR-3; LF-2; CF-2   Ht: 6'2" Wt: 188 Born: 12/9/1978 Age: 26

Year Team	Lg	G	AB	H	2B	3B	HR	(Hm	Rd)	TB	R	RBI	RC	TBB	IBB	SO	HBP	SH	SF	SB	CS	SB%	GDP	Avg	OBP	Slg
2000 Pittsfield	A-	53	186	45	3	5	2	(-	-)	64	39	13	30	34	0	46	4	4	0	20	3	.87	1	.242	.371	.344
2001 Capital City	A	88	318	69	16	8	3	(-	-)	110	49	23	43	46	0	97	3	4	2	41	3	.93	1	.217	.320	.346
2002 St. Lucie	A+	29	102	35	5	0	2	(-	-)	46	20	10	24	24	1	15	1	1	0	10	1	.91	4	.343	.472	.451
2002 Capital City	A	40	150	59	13	3	4	(-	-)	90	33	17	40	18	1	34	3	1	0	15	3	.83	1	.393	.468	.600
2003 Binghamton	AA	76	278	80	11	5	4	(-	-)	113	49	23	47	36	2	59	5	8	3	24	10	.71	0	.288	.376	.406
2003 Norfolk	AAA	4	15	4	1	0	2	(-	-)	11	2	4	3	1	0	7	0	1	0	1	0	1.00	0	.267	.313	.733
2004 Binghamton	AA	38	133	34	6	1	0	(-	-)	42	19	9	18	21	0	38	3	1	1	10	2	.83	1	.256	.367	.316
2004 Norfolk	AAA	55	203	52	12	1	2	(-	-)	72	26	14	25	23	0	52	0	7	1	11	5	.69	1	.256	.330	.355
2003 New York	NL	56	139	27	0	2	1	(1	0)	34	13	10	14	17	3	41	2	8	0	4	2	.67	1	.194	.291	.245
2004 New York	NL	13	15	1	0	0	0	(0	0)	1	2	1	1	1	0	5	0	1	0	3	0	1.00	0	.067	.125	.067
2 ML YEARS		69	154	28	0	2	1	(1	0)	35	15	11	15	18	3	46	2	9	0	7	2	.78	1	.182	.276	.227

Adam Dunn

Bats: L Throws: R Pos: LF-156; 1B-10; PH-2; DH-1   Ht: 6'6" Wt: 240 Born: 11/9/1979 Age: 25

Year Team	Lg	G	AB	H	2B	3B	HR	(Hm	Rd)	TB	R	RBI	RC	TBB	IBB	SO	HBP	SH	SF	SB	CS	SB%	GDP	Avg	OBP	Slg
2001 Cincinnati	NL	66	244	64	18	1	19	(8	11)	141	54	43	51	38	2	74	4	0	0	4	2	.67	4	.262	.371	.578
2002 Cincinnati	NL	158	535	133	28	2	26	(13	13)	243	84	71	96	128	13	170	9	1	3	19	9	.68	8	.249	.400	.454
2003 Cincinnati	NL	116	381	82	12	1	27	(16	11)	177	70	57	61	74	8	126	10	0	4	8	2	.80	4	.215	.354	.465
2004 Cincinnati	NL	161	568	151	34	0	46	(25	21)	323	105	102	108	108	11	**195**	5	0	0	6	1	.86	8	.266	.388	.569
4 ML YEARS		501	1728	430	92	4	118	(62	56)	884	313	273	316	348	34	565	28	1	7	37	14	.73	24	.249	.382	.512

Scott Dunn

Pitches: R **Bats:** R **Pos:** RP-3   **Ht:** 6'3" **Wt:** 200 **Born:** 5/23/1978 **Age:** 27

Year Team	Lg	G	GS	CG	GF	IP	BFP	H	R	ER	HR	SH	SF	HB	TBB	IBB	SO	WP	Bk	W	L	Pct	ShO	Sv-Op	Hld	ERC	ERA
1999 Billings	R+	9	8	0	0	39.2	178	36	24	19	3	0	1	3	24	0	36	3	2	1	3	.250	0	0- -	-	4.47	4.31
2000 Clinton	A	26	26	2	0	147.2	638	123	78	65	9	2	3	4	89	1	159	20	0	11	3	.786	1	0- -	-	3.79	3.96
2001 Mudville	A+	10	10	1	0	59.2	248	45	17	14	2	0	0	1	31	0	73	4	0	5	3	.625	1	0- -	-	2.86	2.11
2001 Chattanooga	AA	17	17	0	0	98.1	450	96	51	45	10	8	2	2	71	0	87	8	0	7	2	.778	0	0- -	-	5.37	4.12
2002 Chattanooga	AA	37	12	0	11	110.1	470	99	57	48	10	4	3	5	54	3	114	6	0	5	7	.417	0	1- -	-	4.00	3.92
2003 Arkansas	AA	3	0	0	2	5.0	16	2	0	0	0	0	0	0	0	0	7	1	0	1	0	1.000	0	0- -	-	0.38	0.00
2003 Birmingham	AA	8	0	0	5	10.2	43	8	2	2	0	1	0	0	5	2	14	0	0	3	1	.750	0	1- -	-	2.15	1.69
2003 Chattanooga	AA	31	0	0	17	40.1	166	31	21	17	3	2	1	0	16	2	54	6	0	3	2	.600	0	8- -	-	2.59	3.79
2003 Salt Lake	AAA	6	0	0	0	7.2	43	9	10	10	1	0	0	0	10	0	11	1	0	0	0	-	0	0- -	-	8.83	11.74
2004 Salt Lake	AAA	46	6	0	9	89.2	393	72	36	32	6	1	3	3	56	0	84	4	0	10	4	.714	0	1- -	-	3.73	3.21
2004 Anaheim	AL	3	0	0	1	3.0	17	7	3	3	0	0	0	0	1	0	2	1	0	0	0	-	0	0-0	0	11.27	9.00

Erubiel Durazo

Bats: L **Throws:** L **Pos:** DH-132; PH-13; 1B-4   **Ht:** 6'3" **Wt:** 240 **Born:** 1/23/1974 **Age:** 31

Year Team	Lg	G	AB	H	2B	3B	HR	(Hm	Rd)	TB	R	RBI	RC	TBB	IBB	SO	HBP	SH	SF	SB	CS	SB%	GDP	Avg	OBP	Slg
1999 Arizona	NL	52	155	51	4	2	11	(4	7)	92	31	30	38	26	1	43	1	0	3	1	1	.50	1	.329	.422	.594
2000 Arizona	NL	67	196	52	11	0	8	(3	5)	87	35	33	34	34	2	43	1	0	2	1	0	1.00	3	.265	.373	.444
2001 Arizona	NL	92	175	47	11	0	12	(4	8)	94	34	38	36	28	1	49	2	0	2	0	0	-	1	.269	.372	.537
2002 Arizona	NL	76	222	58	12	2	16	(11	5)	122	46	48	46	49	2	60	2	0	3	0	1	.00	1	.261	.395	.550
2003 Oakland	AL	154	537	139	29	0	21	(10	11)	231	92	77	92	100	12	105	2	0	6	1	1	.50	11	.259	.374	.430
2004 Oakland	AL	142	511	164	35	1	22	(12	10)	267	80	88	101	56	9	104	9	0	2	3	2	.60	7	.321	.396	.523
6 ML YEARS		583	1796	511	102	5	90	(44	46)	893	318	314	347	293	27	404	17	0	18	6	5	.55	24	.285	.387	.497

Chad Durbin

Pitches: R **Bats:** R **Pos:** RP-16; SP-8   **Ht:** 6'2" **Wt:** 200 **Born:** 12/3/1977 **Age:** 27

Year Team	Lg	G	GS	CG	GF	IP	BFP	H	R	ER	HR	SH	SF	HB	TBB	IBB	SO	WP	Bk	W	L	Pct	ShO	Sv-Op	Hld	ERC	ERA
2004 Buffalo*	AAA	9	9	0	0	52.0	216	55	22	20	7	2	1	0	16	0	40	1	0	3	3	.500	0	0- -	-	4.42	3.46
1999 Kansas City	AL	1	0	0	0	2.1	9	1	0	0	0	0	0	0	1	0	3	1	0	0	0	-	0	0-0	0	1.08	0.00
2000 Kansas City	AL	16	16	0	0	72.1	349	91	71	66	14	6	1	3	43	1	37	7	0	2	5	.286	0	0-0	0	7.05	8.21
2001 Kansas City	AL	29	29	2	0	179.0	777	201	109	98	26	2	7	11	58	0	95	6	0	9	16	.360	0	0-0	0	5.15	4.93
2002 Kansas City	AL	2	2	0	0	8.1	43	13	11	11	3	0	0	1	4	0	5	0	0	1	0	1.000	0	0-0	0	10.58	11.88
2003 Cleveland	AL	3	1	0	0	8.2	45	18	12	7	2	0	0	0	3	0	8	2	0	1	0	1.000	0	0-0	0	12.37	7.27
2004 Cle-Ari		24	8	1	5	60.2	291	72	50	47	11	2	2	5	35	3	48	5	0	6	7	.462	0	0-0	1	6.75	6.97
2004 Cleveland	AL	17	8	1	5	51.1	239	63	40	38	10	0	2	4	24	3	38	3	0	5	6	.455	0	0-0	0	6.70	6.66
2004 Arizona	NL	7	0	0	0	9.1	52	9	10	9	1	2	0	1	11	0	10	2	0	1	1	.500	0	0-0	1	6.92	8.68
6 ML YEARS		75	56	3	5	331.1	1514	396	253	229	56	5	12	17	144	4	196	21	0	17	30	.362	0	0-0	1	6.11	6.22

J.D. Durbin

Pitches: R **Bats:** R **Pos:** RP-3; SP-1   **Ht:** 6'0" **Wt:** 200 **Born:** 2/24/1982 **Age:** 23

Year Team	Lg	G	GS	CG	GF	IP	BFP	H	R	ER	HR	SH	SF	HB	TBB	IBB	SO	WP	Bk	W	L	Pct	ShO	Sv-Op	Hld	ERC	ERA
2000 Twins	R	2	0	0	0	2.0	9	2	2	0	0	0	0	0	0	0	4	0	0	0	0	-	0	0- -	-	1.68	0.00
2001 Elizabethton	R+	8	7	0	0	33.2	145	23	13	7	2	1	1	4	17	0	39	5	1	3	2	.600	0	0- -	-	2.87	1.87
2002 Quad City	A	27	27	0	0	161.0	666	144	66	57	14	3	4	5	51	1	163	6	1	13	4	.765	0	0- -	-	3.23	3.19
2003 Fort Myers	A+	14	14	0	0	87.1	355	73	35	30	3	1	3	3	22	0	69	3	1	9	2	.818	0	0- -	-	2.37	3.09
2003 New Britain	AA	14	14	2	0	94.2	401	102	39	33	10	0	0	4	29	0	70	1	0	6	3	.667	0	0- -	-	4.46	3.14
2004 New Britain	AA	13	13	0	0	64.1	274	62	21	18	4	3	0	4	22	0	53	1	0	4	1	.800	0	0- -	-	3.64	2.52
2004 Rochester	AAA	7	7	0	0	35.2	168	49	27	18	4	0	0	1	16	0	38	1	0	3	2	.600	0	0- -	-	6.78	4.54
2004 Minnesota	AL	4	1	0	2	7.1	38	12	6	6	0	0	1	0	6	0	6	1	0	0	1	.000	0	0-0	0	9.19	7.36

Ray Durham

Bats: B **Throws:** R **Pos:** 2B-118; PH-5   **Ht:** 5'8" **Wt:** 180 **Born:** 11/30/1971 **Age:** 33

Year Team	Lg	G	AB	H	2B	3B	HR	(Hm	Rd)	TB	R	RBI	RC	TBB	IBB	SO	HBP	SH	SF	SB	CS	SB%	GDP	Avg	OBP	Slg
2004 San Jose*	A+	1	3	1	0	0	0	(-	-)	1	0	0	0	0	0	0	0	0	0	0	0	-	0	.333	.333	.333
2004 Fresno*	AAA	5	14	8	0	1	1	(-	-)	13	4	5	6	2	1	2	1	0	0	0	1	.00	0	.571	.647	.929
1995 Chicago	AL	125	471	121	27	6	7	(1	6)	181	68	51	57	31	2	83	6	5	4	18	5	.78	8	.257	.309	.384
1996 Chicago	AL	156	557	153	33	5	10	(3	7)	226	79	65	87	58	4	95	10	7	7	30	4	.88	6	.275	.350	.406
1997 Chicago	AL	155	634	172	27	5	11	(3	8)	242	106	53	83	61	0	96	6	2	8	33	16	.67	14	.271	.337	.382
1998 Chicago	AL	158	635	181	35	8	19	(10	9)	289	126	67	110	73	3	105	6	6	3	36	9	.80	5	.285	.363	.455
1999 Chicago	AL	153	612	181	30	8	13	(7	6)	266	109	60	103	73	1	105	4	3	2	34	11	.76	9	.296	.373	.435
2000 Chicago	AL	151	614	172	35	9	17	(5	12)	276	121	75	100	75	0	105	7	5	8	25	13	.66	13	.280	.361	.450
2001 Chicago	AL	152	611	163	42	10	20	(9	11)	285	104	65	97	64	3	110	4	6	6	23	10	.70	10	.267	.337	.466
2002 CWS-Oak	AL	150	564	163	34	6	15	(11	4)	254	114	70	96	73	1	93	7	10	5	26	7	.79	15	.289	.374	.450
2003 San Francisco	NL	110	410	117	30	5	8	(3	5)	181	61	33	56	50	2	82	3	4	2	7	7	.50	4	.285	.366	.441
2004 San Francisco	NL	120	471	133	28	8	17	(8	9)	228	95	65	82	57	3	60	6	4	4	10	4	.71	6	.282	.364	.484
2002 Chicago	AL	96	345	103	20	2	9	(6	3)	154	71	48	61	49	0	59	5	8	4	20	5	.80	13	.299	.390	.446
2002 Oakland	AL	54	219	60	14	4	6	(5	1)	100	43	22	35	24	1	34	2	2	1	6	2	.75	2	.274	.350	.457
10 ML YEARS		1430	5579	1556	321	70	137	(60	77)	2428	983	604	871	615	19	934	59	52	49	242	86	.74	90	.279	.354	.435

Trent Durrington

Bats: R **Throws:** R **Pos:** PH-30; 3B-11; PR-9; 2B-6; DH-1   **Ht:** 5'10" **Wt:** 188 **Born:** 8/27/1975 **Age:** 29

Year Team	Lg	G	AB	H	2B	3B	HR	(Hm	Rd)	TB	R	RBI	RC	TBB	IBB	SO	HBP	SH	SF	SB	CS	SB%	GDP	Avg	OBP	Slg
2004 Indianapolis*	AAA	51	162	36	1	0	1	(-	-)	40	19	9	12	16	0	34	2	6	1	17	5	.77	6	.222	.298	.247
1999 Anaheim	AL	43	122	22	2	0	0	(0	0)	24	14	2	6	9	0	28	0	5	0	4	3	.57	1	.180	.237	.197
2000 Anaheim	AL	4	3	0	0	0	0	(0	0)	0	0	0	0	0	0	0	0	0	0	0	0	-	1	.000	.000	.000
2003 Anaheim	AL	12	14	2	0	0	0	(0	0)	2	5	1	0	3	0	0	0	0	0	1	1	.50	0	.143	.294	.143
2004 Milwaukee	NL	53	82	19	2	3	2	(2	0)	33	13	4	8	4	0	23	0	1	0	4	0	1.00	1	.232	.267	.402
4 ML YEARS		112	221	43	4	3	2	(2	0)	59	32	7	14	16	0	51	0	6	0	9	4	.69	3	.195	.249	.267

Jermaine Dye

Bats: R **Throws:** R **Pos:** RF-135; DH-2; PH-2   **Ht:** 6'5" **Wt:** 220 **Born:** 1/28/1974 **Age:** 31

Year Team	Lg	G	AB	H	2B	3B	HR	(Hm	Rd)	TB	R	RBI	RC	TBB	IBB	SO	HBP	SH	SF	SB	CS	SB%	GDP	Avg	OBP	Slg
1996 Atlanta	NL	98	292	82	16	0	12	(4	8)	134	32	37	36	8	0	67	3	0	3	1	4	.20	11	.281	.304	.459
1997 Kansas City	AL	75	263	62	14	0	7	(3	4)	97	26	22	26	17	0	51	1	1	1	2	1	.67	6	.236	.284	.369
1998 Kansas City	AL	60	214	50	5	1	5	(3	2)	72	24	23	17	11	2	46	1	0	4	2	2	.50	8	.234	.270	.336
1999 Kansas City	AL	158	608	179	44	8	27	(15	12)	320	96	119	106	58	4	119	1	0	6	2	3	.40	17	.294	.354	.526
2000 Kansas City	AL	157	601	193	41	2	33	(15	18)	337	107	118	125	69	6	99	3	0	6	0	1	.00	12	.321	.390	.561
2001 KC-Oak	AL	158	599	169	31	1	26	(16	10)	280	91	106	99	57	6	112	7	1	11	9	1	.90	8	.282	.346	.467
2002 Oakland	AL	131	488	123	27	1	24	(13	11)	224	74	86	70	52	2	108	10	0	5	2	0	1.00	15	.252	.333	.459
2003 Oakland	AL	65	221	38	6	0	4	(3	1)	56	28	20	10	25	2	42	3	0	4	1	0	1.00	11	.172	.261	.253
2004 Oakland	AL	137	532	141	29	4	23	(12	11)	247	87	80	69	49	4	128	4	0	5	4	2	.67	16	.265	.329	.464
2001 Kansas City	AL	97	367	100	14	0	13	(8	5)	153	50	47	54	30	3	68	6	1	6	7	1	.88	2	.272	.333	.417
2001 Oakland	AL	61	232	69	17	1	13	(8	5)	127	41	59	45	27	3	44	1	0	5	2	0	1.00	6	.297	.366	.547
9 ML YEARS		1039	3818	1037	213	17	161	(84	77)	1767	565	611	558	346	26	772	33	2	45	23	14	.62	104	.272	.334	.463

Damion Easley

Bats: R **Throws:** R **Pos:** PH-35; 2B-25; 1B-18; SS-15; 3B-6; RF-5; DH-3; PR-2   **Ht:** 5'11" **Wt:** 187 **Born:** 11/11/1969 **Age:** 35

Year Team	Lg	G	AB	H	2B	3B	HR	(Hm	Rd)	TB	R	RBI	RC	TBB	IBB	SO	HBP	SH	SF	SB	CS	SB%	GDP	Avg	OBP	Slg
1992 California	AL	47	151	39	5	0	1	(1	0)	47	14	12	14	8	0	26	3	2	1	9	5	.64	2	.258	.307	.311
1993 California	AL	73	230	72	13	2	2	(0	2)	95	33	22	37	28	2	35	3	1	2	6	6	.50	5	.313	.392	.413
1994 California	AL	88	316	68	16	1	6	(4	2)	104	41	30	28	29	0	48	4	4	2	4	5	.44	8	.215	.288	.329
1995 California	AL	114	357	77	14	2	4	(1	3)	107	35	35	30	32	1	47	6	6	4	5	2	.71	11	.216	.288	.300
1996 Cal-Det	AL	49	112	30	2	0	4	(1	3)	44	14	17	16	10	0	25	1	5	1	3	1	.75	0	.268	.331	.393
1997 Detroit	AL	151	527	139	37	3	22	(12	10)	248	97	72	88	68	3	102	16	4	5	28	13	.68	18	.264	.362	.471
1998 Detroit	AL	153	594	161	38	2	27	(19	8)	284	84	100	94	39	2	112	16	0	2	15	5	.75	8	.271	.332	.478
1999 Detroit	AL	151	549	146	30	1	20	(12	8)	238	83	65	82	51	2	124	19	2	6	11	3	.79	15	.266	.346	.434
2000 Detroit	AL	126	464	120	27	2	14	(5	9)	193	76	58	69	55	1	79	11	4	1	13	4	.76	11	.259	.350	.416
2001 Detroit	AL	154	585	146	27	7	11	(4	7)	220	77	65	72	52	3	90	13	4	4	10	5	.67	10	.250	.323	.376
2002 Detroit	AL	85	304	68	14	1	8	(4	4)	108	29	30	29	27	3	43	11	1	3	1	3	.25	4	.224	.307	.355
2003 Tampa Bay	AL	36	107	20	3	1	1	(0	1)	28	8	7	3	2	0	18	0	1	0	0	0	-	3	.187	.202	.262
2004 Florida	NL	98	223	53	20	1	9	(5	4)	102	26	43	34	24	1	36	8	0	2	4	1	.80	6	.238	.331	.457
1996 California	AL	28	45	7	1	0	2	(1	1)	14	4	7	4	6	0	12	0	3	0	0	0	-	0	.156	.255	.311
1996 Detroit	AL	21	67	23	1	0	2	(0	2)	30	10	10	12	4	0	13	1	2	1	3	1	.75	0	.343	.384	.448
13 ML YEARS		1325	4519	1139	246	23	129	(68	61)	1818	617	556	596	425	18	785	111	34	33	109	53	.67	101	.252	.329	.402

Adam Eaton

Pitches: R **Bats:** R **Pos:** SP-33   **Ht:** 6'2" **Wt:** 190 **Born:** 11/23/1977 **Age:** 27

Year Team	Lg	G	GS	CG	GF	IP	BFP	H	R	ER	HR	SH	SF	HB	TBB	IBB	SO	WP	Bk	W	L	Pct	ShO	Sv-Op	Hld	ERC	ERA
2000 San Diego	NL	22	22	0	0	135.0	583	134	63	62	14	1	3	2	61	3	90	3	0	7	4	.636	0	0-0	0	4.34	4.13
2001 San Diego	NL	17	17	2	0	116.2	499	108	61	56	20	3	2	5	40	3	109	3	0	8	5	.615	0	0-0	0	4.01	4.32
2002 San Diego	NL	6	6	0	0	33.1	142	28	20	20	5	2	2	2	17	0	25	2	0	1	1	.500	0	0-0	0	4.28	5.40
2003 San Diego	NL	31	31	1	0	183.0	789	173	91	83	20	5	5	7	68	6	146	7	1	9	12	.429	0	0-0	0	3.78	4.08
2004 San Diego	NL	33	33	0	0	199.1	848	204	113	102	28	12	7	10	52	3	153	5	0	11	14	.440	0	0-0	0	4.10	4.61
5 ML YEARS		109	109	3	0	667.1	2861	647	348	323	87	23	19	26	238	15	523	20	1	36	36	.500	0	0-0	0	4.05	4.36

David Eckstein

Bats: R **Throws:** R **Pos:** SS-140; PH-3; DH-1   **Ht:** 5'8" **Wt:** 170 **Born:** 1/20/1975 **Age:** 30

Year Team	Lg	G	AB	H	2B	3B	HR	(Hm	Rd)	TB	R	RBI	RC	TBB	IBB	SO	HBP	SH	SF	SB	CS	SB%	GDP	Avg	OBP	Slg
2001 Anaheim	AL	153	582	166	26	2	4	(3	1)	208	82	41	80	43	0	60	21	16	2	29	4	.88	11	.285	.355	.357
2002 Anaheim	AL	152	608	178	22	6	8	(3	5)	236	107	63	93	45	0	44	27	14	8	21	13	.62	7	.293	.363	.388
2003 Anaheim	AL	120	452	114	22	1	3	(1	2)	147	59	31	53	36	0	45	15	10	4	16	5	.76	9	.252	.325	.325
2004 Anaheim	AL	142	566	156	24	1	2	(2	0)	188	92	35	60	42	1	49	13	14	2	16	5	.76	11	.276	.339	.332
4 ML YEARS		567	2208	614	94	10	17	(9	8)	779	340	170	286	166	1	198	76	54	16	82	27	.75	38	.278	.347	.353

Jim Edmonds

Bats: L **Throws:** L **Pos:** CF-146; PH-6; 1B-1; DH-1   **Ht:** 6'1" **Wt:** 212 **Born:** 6/27/1970 **Age:** 35

Year Team	Lg	G	AB	H	2B	3B	HR	(Hm	Rd)	TB	R	RBI	RC	TBB	IBB	SO	HBP	SH	SF	SB	CS	SB%	GDP	Avg	OBP	Slg
1993 California	AL	18	61	15	4	1	0	(0	0)	21	5	4	4	2	1	16	0	0	0	0	2	.00	1	.246	.270	.344
1994 California	AL	94	289	79	13	1	5	(3	2)	109	35	37	38	30	3	72	1	1	1	4	2	.67	3	.273	.343	.377
1995 California	AL	141	558	162	30	4	33	(16	17)	299	120	107	100	51	4	130	5	1	5	1	4	.20	10	.290	.352	.536
1996 California	AL	114	431	131	28	3	27	(17	10)	246	73	66	88	46	2	101	4	0	2	4	0	1.00	8	.304	.375	.571
1997 Anaheim	AL	133	502	146	27	0	26	(14	12)	251	82	80	90	60	5	80	4	0	5	5	7	.42	8	.291	.368	.500

Year Team	Lg	G	AB	H	2B	3B	HR	(Hm	Rd)	TB	R	RBI	RC	TBB	IBB	SO	HBP	SH	SF	SB	CS	SB%	GDP	Avg	OBP	Slg
1998 Anaheim	AL	154	599	184	42	1	25	(9	16)	303	115	91	104	57	7	114	1	1	1	7	5	.58	16	.307	.368	.506
1999 Anaheim	AL	55	204	51	17	2	5	(3	2)	87	34	23	30	28	0	45	0	0	1	5	4	.56	3	.250	.339	.426
2000 St Louis	NL	152	525	155	25	0	42	(22	20)	306	129	108	126	103	3	167	6	1	8	10	3	.77	5	.295	.411	.583
2001 St Louis	NL	150	500	152	38	1	30	(16	14)	282	95	110	113	93	12	136	4	1	10	5	5	.50	8	.304	.410	.564
2002 St Louis	NL	144	476	148	31	2	28	(17	11)	267	96	83	101	86	14	134	8	0	6	4	3	.57	9	.311	.420	.561
2003 St Louis	NL	137	447	123	32	2	39	(17	**22**)	276	89	89	87	77	6	127	4	1	2	1	3	.25	11	.275	.385	.617
2004 St Louis	NL	153	498	150	38	3	42	(24	18)	320	102	111	115	101	12	150	5	0	8	8	3	.73	4	.301	.418	.643
12 ML YEARS		1445	5090	1496	325	20	302	(158	144)	2767	975	909	996	734	69	1272	42	6	49	54	41	.57	86	.294	.384	.544

Joey Eischen

Pitches: L Bats: L Pos: RP-21   Ht: 6'0" Wt: 210 Born: 5/25/1970 Age: 35

Year Team	Lg	G	GS	CG	GF	IP	BFP	H	R	ER	HR	SH	SF	HB	TBB	IBB	SO	WP	Bk	W	L	Pct	ShO	Sv-Op	Hld	ERC	ERA
2004 Expos*	R	1	1	0	0	1.0	3	0	0	0	0	0	0	0	0	0	2	0	0	0	0	-	0	0--	-	0.00	0.00
2004 Brevard Cnty*	A+	4	4	0	0	6.0	24	5	4	0	0	0	0	0	1	0	7	0	0	0	0	-	0	0--	-	1.74	0.00
1994 Montreal	NL	1	0	0	0	0.2	7	4	4	4	0	0	0	1	0	0	1	0	0	0	0	-	0	0-0	0	47.92	54.00
1995 Los Angeles	NL	17	0	0	8	20.1	95	19	9	7	1	0	0	2	11	1	15	1	0	0	0	-	0	0-0	1	3.97	3.10
1996 LA-Det		52	0	0	14	68.1	308	75	36	32	7	3	2	4	34	7	51	4	0	1	2	.333	0	0-2	2	5.15	4.21
1997 Cincinnati	NL	1	0	0	0	1.1	7	2	2	1	0	0	0	0	1	0	2	1	0	0	0	-	0	0-0	0	7.52	6.75
2001 Montreal	NL	24	0	0	7	29.2	131	29	17	16	4	1	0	1	16	1	19	1	0	0	1	.000	0	0-2	4	4.89	4.85
2002 Montreal	NL	59	0	0	18	53.2	217	43	11	8	1	3	2	2	18	5	51	6	1	6	1	.857	0	2-3	11	2.31	1.34
2003 Montreal	NL	70	0	0	15	53.0	221	57	27	18	7	3	0	3	13	1	40	3	0	2	2	.500	0	1-4	15	4.44	3.06
2004 Montreal	NL	21	0	0	3	18.1	80	16	10	8	2	1	1	1	8	2	17	0	0	2	1	.000	0	0-1	2	3.53	3.93
1996 Los Angeles	NL	28	0	0	11	43.1	198	48	25	23	4	3	1	4	20	4	36	1	0	1	1	.500	0	0-0	1	5.07	4.78
1996 Detroit	AL	24	0	0	3	25.0	110	27	11	9	3	0	1	0	14	3	15	3	0	1	1	.500	0	0-2	1	5.30	3.24
8 ML YEARS		245	0	0	65	245.1	1066	245	116	94	22	11	5	14	101	17	196	16	1	9	7	.563	0	3-12	33	4.18	3.45

Scott Elarton

Pitches: R Bats: R Pos: SP-29   Ht: 6'8" Wt: 240 Born: 2/23/1976 Age: 29

Year Team	Lg	G	GS	CG	GF	IP	BFP	H	R	ER	HR	SH	SF	HB	TBB	IBB	SO	WP	Bk	W	L	Pct	ShO	Sv-Op	Hld	ERC	ERA
2004 Buffalo*	AAA	3	3	1	0	20.0	82	19	7	7	1	1	0	1	5	0	10	0	0	1	1	.500	1	0--	-	3.15	3.15
1998 Houston	NL	28	2	0	7	57.0	227	40	21	21	5	1	1	1	20	0	56	1	0	2	1	.667	0	2-3	2	2.35	3.32
1999 Houston	NL	42	15	0	8	124.0	524	111	55	48	8	7	4	4	43	0	121	3	0	9	5	.643	0	1-4	5	3.16	3.48
2000 Houston	NL	30	30	2	0	192.2	855	198	117	103	29	5	7	6	84	1	131	8	0	17	7	.708	0	0-0	0	4.82	4.81
2001 Hou-Col	NL	24	24	0	0	132.2	595	146	105	104	34	7	2	6	59	2	87	5	0	4	10	.286	0	0-0	0	6.21	7.06
2003 Colorado	NL	11	10	0	0	51.2	253	73	46	36	13	3	4	4	20	3	20	3	0	4	4	.500	0	0-0	0	7.79	6.27
2004 Col-Cle		29	29	1	0	158.2	697	164	107	104	33	5	7	4	62	3	103	8	0	3	11	.214	1	0-0	0	5.04	5.90
2001 Houston	NL	20	20	0	0	109.2	499	126	88	87	26	7	2	6	49	1	76	5	0	4	8	.333	0	0-0	0	6.42	7.14
2001 Colorado	NL	4	4	0	0	23.0	96	20	17	17	8	0	0	0	10	1	11	0	0	0	2	.000	0	0-0	0	5.18	6.65
2004 Colorado	NL	8	8	0	0	41.1	199	57	45	45	8	2	3	0	20	1	23	5	0	0	6	.000	0	0-0	0	7.35	9.80
2004 Cleveland	AL	21	21	1	0	117.1	498	107	62	59	25	3	4	4	42	2	80	3	0	3	5	.375	1	0-0	0	4.28	4.53
6 ML YEARS		164	110	3	15	716.2	3151	732	451	416	122	28	25	25	288	9	518	28	0	39	38	.506	1	3-7	7	4.80	5.22

Cal Eldred

Pitches: R Bats: R Pos: RP-52   Ht: 6'4" Wt: 235 Born: 11/24/1967 Age: 37

Year Team	Lg	G	GS	CG	GF	IP	BFP	H	R	ER	HR	SH	SF	HB	TBB	IBB	SO	WP	Bk	W	L	Pct	ShO	Sv-Op	Hld	ERC	ERA
1991 Milwaukee	AL	3	3	0	0	16.0	73	20	9	8	2	0	0	0	6	0	10	0	0	2	0	1.000	0	0-0	0	5.57	4.50
1992 Milwaukee	AL	14	14	2	0	100.1	394	76	21	20	4	1	0	2	23	0	62	3	0	11	2	.846	1	0-0	0	1.94	1.79
1993 Milwaukee	AL	36	36	8	0	258.0	1087	232	120	115	32	5	12	10	91	5	180	2	0	16	16	.500	1	0-0	0	3.62	4.01
1994 Milwaukee	AL	25	25	6	0	179.0	769	158	96	93	23	5	7	4	84	0	98	2	0	11	11	.500	0	0-0	0	3.97	4.68
1995 Milwaukee	AL	4	4	0	0	23.2	104	24	10	9	4	1	0	1	10	0	18	1	1	1	1	.500	0	0-0	0	4.91	3.42
1996 Milwaukee	AL	15	15	0	0	84.2	363	82	43	42	8	0	4	4	38	0	50	1	0	4	4	.500	0	0-0	0	4.33	4.46
1997 Milwaukee	AL	34	34	1	0	202.0	885	207	118	112	31	4	6	9	89	0	122	5	0	13	15	.464	1	0-0	0	5.00	4.99
1998 Milwaukee	NL	23	23	0	0	133.0	602	157	82	71	14	5	3	4	61	3	86	6	0	4	8	.333	0	0-0	0	5.54	4.80
1999 Milwaukee	NL	20	15	0	2	82.0	392	101	75	71	19	2	3	1	46	0	60	8	1	2	8	.200	0	0-0	0	7.13	7.79
2000 Chicago	AL	20	20	2	0	112.0	492	103	61	57	12	3	2	5	59	0	97	4	0	10	2	.833	1	0-0	0	4.36	4.58
2001 Chicago	AL	2	2	0	0	6.0	34	12	9	9	1	0	0	3	3	1	6	0	0	0	1	.000	0	0-0	0	14.25	13.50
2003 St Louis	NL	62	0	0	18	67.1	293	62	32	28	9	5	3	4	31	4	67	4	0	7	4	.636	0	8-14	11	4.25	3.74
2004 St Louis	NL	52	0	0	10	67.0	282	71	31	28	11	5	2	1	17	1	54	3	0	4	2	.667	0	1-3	9	4.34	3.76
13 ML YEARS		310	191	19	30	1331.0	5770	1305	707	663	170	36	42	48	558	14	910	39	2	85	74	.535	4	9-17	20	4.38	4.48

Mark Ellis

Bats: R Throws: R Pos: 2B   Ht: 5'11" Wt: 180 Born: 6/6/1977 Age: 28

Year Team	Lg	G	AB	H	2B	3B	HR	(Hm	Rd)	TB	R	RBI	RC	TBB	IBB	SO	HBP	SH	SF	SB	CS	SB%	GDP	Avg	OBP	Slg
1999 Spokane	A-	71	281	92	14	0	7	(-	-)	127	67	47	59	47	3	40	3	5	4	21	7	.75	1	.327	.424	.452
2000 Wilmington	A+	132	484	146	27	4	6	(-	-)	199	83	62	87	78	0	72	7	4	3	25	7	.78	11	.302	.404	.411
2000 Wichita	AA	7	22	7	1	0	0	(-	-)	8	4	4	4	5	0	5	0	0	0	1	0	1.00	0	.318	.444	.364
2001 Sacramento	AAA	132	472	129	38	4	10	(-	-)	197	71	53	68	54	4	78	5	5	5	21	7	.75	13	.273	.351	.417
2002 Sacramento	AAA	21	84	25	10	1	0	(-	-)	37	14	5	14	6	0	13	4	0	0	4	0	1.00	1	.298	.372	.440
2002 Oakland	AL	98	345	94	16	4	6	(6	0)	136	58	35	55	44	1	54	4	8	3	6	2	.67	3	.272	.359	.394
2003 Oakland	AL	154	553	137	31	5	9	(7	2)	205	78	52	69	48	4	94	7	9	5	6	2	.75	7	.248	.313	.371
2 ML YEARS		252	898	231	47	9	15	(13	2)	341	136	87	124	92	5	148	11	17	8	10	4	.71	10	.257	.331	.380

Jason Ellison

Bats: R **Throws:** R **Pos:** PR-9; CF-4; PH-1   **Ht:** 5'10" **Wt:** 180 **Born:** 4/4/1978 **Age:** 27

									BATTING												BASERUNNING				AVERAGES		
Year Team	Lg	G	AB	H	2B	3B	HR	(Hm	Rd)	TB	R	RBI	RC	TBB	IBB	SO	HBP	SH	SF		SB	CS	SB%	GDP	Avg	OBP	Slg
2000 Salem-Keizer	A-	74	300	90	15	2	0	(-	-)	109	67	28	45	29	0	45	7	4	1		13	7	.65	1	.300	.374	.363
2001 Hagerstown	A	130	494	144	38	3	8	(-	-)	212	95	55	84	71	3	68	10	13	5		19	15	.56	6	.291	.388	.429
2002 San Jose	A+	81	322	87	13	0	5	(-	-)	115	40	40	35	25	2	37	2	4	2		9	9	.50	10	.270	.325	.357
2002 Fresno	AAA	49	196	61	8	1	3	(-	-)	80	31	8	33	21	0	28	4	0	0		16	3	.84	4	.311	.389	.408
2003 Fresno	AAA	119	461	136	22	4	6	(-	-)	184	74	39	66	39	1	52	6	6	3		21	13	.62	7	.295	.356	.399
2004 Fresno	AAA	125	505	159	32	7	9	(-	-)	232	90	40	83	40	0	66	3	3	1		27	12	.69	8	.315	.368	.459
2003 San Francisco	NL	7	10	1	0	0	0	(0	0)	1	1	0	0	0	0	1	0	0	0		0	0	-	0	.100	.100	.100
2004 San Francisco	NL	13	4	2	0	0	1	(0	1)	5	4	3	3	0	0	1	0	0	0		2	0	1.00	0	.500	.500	1.250
2 ML YEARS		20	14	3	0	0	1	(0	1)	6	5	3	3	0	0	2	0	0	0		2	0	1.00	0	.214	.214	.429

Alan Embree

Pitches: L **Bats:** L **Pos:** RP-71   **Ht:** 6'2" **Wt:** 190 **Born:** 1/23/1970 **Age:** 35

		HOW MUCH HE PITCHED						WHAT HE GAVE UP											THE RESULTS						
Year Team	Lg	G	GS	CG	GF	IP	BFP	H	R	ER	HR	SH	SF	HB	TBB	IBB	SO	WP	Bk	W	L	Pct	ShO	Sv-Op	Hld	ERC	ERA
1992 Cleveland	AL	4	4	0	0	18.0	81	19	14	14	3	0	2	1	8	0	12	1	1	0	2	.000	0	0-0	0	5.25	7.00
1995 Cleveland	AL	23	0	0	8	24.2	111	23	16	14	2	2	0	0	16	0	23	1	0	3	2	.600	0	1-1	6	4.51	5.11
1996 Cleveland	AL	24	0	0	2	31.0	141	30	26	22	10	1	3	0	21	3	33	3	0	1	1	.500	0	0-0	1	6.58	6.39
1997 Atlanta	NL	66	0	0	15	46.0	190	36	13	13	1	4	1	2	20	2	45	3	1	3	1	.750	0	0-0	16	2.66	2.54
1998 Atl-Ari	NL	55	0	0	16	53.2	237	56	32	25	7	4	1	1	23	0	43	3	0	4	2	.667	0	1-3	12	4.71	4.19
1999 San Francisco	NL	68	0	0	13	58.2	244	42	22	22	6	3	2	3	26	2	53	3	0	3	2	.600	0	0-3	22	2.86	3.38
2000 San Francisco	NL	63	0	0	21	60.0	263	62	34	33	4	4	5	3	25	2	49	1	0	3	5	.375	0	2-5	9	4.24	4.95
2001 SF-CWS		61	0	0	17	54.0	245	65	47	44	14	0	6	3	17	2	59	3	0	1	4	.200	0	0-3	9	6.20	7.33
2002 SD-Bos		68	0	0	20	62.0	251	47	19	14	6	1	2	1	20	3	81	1	0	4	6	.400	0	2-7	18	2.48	2.03
2003 Boston	AL	65	0	0	15	55.0	221	49	26	26	5	0	2	0	16	3	45	0	0	4	1	.800	0	1-2	14	3.01	4.25
2004 Boston	AL	71	0	0	11	52.1	217	49	28	24	7	2	2	1	11	1	37	0	0	2	2	.500	0	0-1	20	3.21	4.13
1998 Atlanta	NL	20	0	0	5	18.2	87	23	14	9	2	1	1	0	10	0	19	0	0	1	0	1.000	0	0-1	6	6.06	4.34
1998 Arizona	NL	35	0	0	11	35.0	150	33	18	16	5	3	0	1	13	0	24	3	0	3	2	.600	0	1-2	6	4.03	4.11
2001 San Francisco	NL	22	0	0	7	20.0	106	34	26	25	7	0	3	2	10	2	25	1	0	0	2	.000	0	0-1	0	11.29	11.25
2001 Chicago	AL	39	0	0	10	34.0	139	31	21	19	7	0	3	1	7	0	34	2	0	1	2	.333	0	0-2	9	3.61	5.03
2002 San Diego	NL	36	0	0	13	28.2	118	23	7	3	2	0	0	0	9	2	38	1	0	3	4	.429	0	0-2	10	2.38	0.94
2002 Boston	AL	32	0	0	7	33.1	133	24	12	11	4	1	2	1	11	1	43	0	0	1	2	.333	0	2-5	8	2.56	2.97
11 ML YEARS		568	4	0	138	515.1	2201	478	277	251	65	21	28	15	203	18	480	19	2	28	28	.500	0	7-25	127	3.88	4.38

Juan Encarnacion

Bats: R **Throws:** R **Pos:** RF-125; LF-9; PH-2   **Ht:** 6'3" **Wt:** 215 **Born:** 3/8/1976 **Age:** 29

									BATTING												BASERUNNING				AVERAGES		
Year Team	Lg	G	AB	H	2B	3B	HR	(Hm	Rd)	TB	R	RBI	RC	TBB	IBB	SO	HBP	SH	SF		SB	CS	SB%	GDP	Avg	OBP	Slg
1997 Detroit	AL	11	33	7	1	1	1	(1	0)	13	3	5	4	3	0	12	2	0	0		5	1	.75	1	.212	.316	.394
1998 Detroit	AL	40	164	54	9	4	7	(4	3)	92	30	21	31	7	0	31	1	0	3		7	4	.64	2	.329	.354	.561
1999 Detroit	AL	132	509	130	30	6	19	(6	13)	229	62	74	64	14	1	113	9	4	2		33	12	.73	12	.255	.287	.450
2000 Detroit	AL	141	547	158	25	6	14	(4	10)	237	75	72	76	29	1	90	7	3	4		16	4	.80	15	.289	.330	.433
2001 Detroit	AL	120	417	101	19	7	12	(4	8)	170	52	52	48	25	1	93	6	5	4		9	5	.64	9	.242	.292	.408
2002 Cin-Fla	NL	152	584	158	22	5	24	(8	16)	262	77	85	74	46	0	113	4	3	7		21	9	.70	18	.271	.324	.449
2003 Florida	NL	156	601	162	37	6	19	(9	10)	268	80	94	76	37	0	82	4	5	6		19	8	.70	17	.270	.313	.446
2004 LA-Fla	NL	135	484	114	30	2	16	(8	8)	196	63	62	60	38	2	86	7	1	2		5	4	.56	10	.236	.299	.405
2002 Cincinnati	NL	83	321	89	11	2	16	(6	10)	152	43	51	42	26	0	63	1	3	3		9	4	.69	7	.277	.330	.474
2002 Florida	NL	69	263	69	11	3	8	(2	6)	110	34	34	32	20	0	50	3	0	4		12	5	.71	11	.262	.317	.418
2004 Los Angeles	NL	86	324	76	18	1	13	(6	7)	135	42	43	38	21	0	53	4	0	1		3	3	.50	8	.235	.289	.417
2004 Florida	NL	49	160	38	12	1	3	(2	1)	61	21	19	22	17	2	33	3	1	1		2	1	.67	2	.238	.320	.381
8 ML YEARS		887	3339	884	173	37	112	(44	68)	1467	442	465	433	199	5	620	40	21	28		113	47	.71	84	.265	.311	.439

John Ennis

Pitches: R **Bats:** R **Pos:** RP-12   **Ht:** 6'5" **Wt:** 220 **Born:** 10/17/1979 **Age:** 25

		HOW MUCH HE PITCHED						WHAT HE GAVE UP											THE RESULTS						
Year Team	Lg	G	GS	CG	GF	IP	BFP	H	R	ER	HR	SH	SF	HB	TBB	IBB	SO	WP	Bk	W	L	Pct	ShO	Sv-Op	Hld	ERC	ERA
1998 Braves	R	8	2	0	2	25.1	113	30	16	13	0	1	2	0	6	1	18	1	0	0	3	.000	0	0--	-	3.91	4.62
1999 Danville	R+	13	13	0	0	65.2	296	71	46	37	7	3	2	9	21	0	60	3	2	4	3	.571	0	0--	-	4.73	5.07
2000 Macon	A	18	16	0	0	98.2	403	77	37	28	5	2	1	6	25	0	105	3	0	7	4	.636	0	0--	-	2.27	2.55
2001 Myrtle Beach	A+	25	25	1	0	138.1	569	111	63	55	12	4	5	7	45	0	144	2	3	6	8	.429	0	0--	-	2.84	3.58
2002 Greenville	AA	26	26	0	0	148.2	625	131	79	69	7	11	5	7	62	0	103	6	0	9	9	.500	0	0--	-	3.35	4.18
2003 Richmond	AAA	28	15	0	4	100.1	461	121	70	62	11	14	6	7	37	1	76	3	2	2	11	.154	0	0--	-	5.41	5.56
2003 Toledo	AAA	3	3	0	0	15.2	72	22	9	9	0	2	1	2	5	0	7	1	0	1	0	1.000	0	0--	-	6.03	5.17
2003 Greenville	AA	1	1	0	0	3.2	16	4	1	1	1	0	0	0	2	0	3	0	0	0	0	-	0	0--	-	6.83	2.45
2004 Toledo	AAA	38	13	0	16	102.2	438	100	49	41	10	2	2	4	36	3	77	4	1	9	5	.643	0	10--	-	3.83	3.59
2002 Atlanta	NL	1	1	0	0	4.0	18	5	2	2	0	1	1	0	3	0	1	0	0	0	0	-	0	0-0	0	6.70	4.50
2004 Detroit	AL	12	0	0	5	16.0	75	20	16	15	3	0	1	0	5	0	13	1	1	0	0	-	0	1-2	0	5.53	8.44
2 ML YEARS		13	1	0	5	20.0	93	25	18	17	3	1	2	0	8	0	14	1	1	0	0	-	0	1-2	0	5.78	7.65

Morgan Ensberg

Bats: R **Throws:** R **Pos:** 3B-118; PH-19; SS-1; PR-1   **Ht:** 6'2" **Wt:** 210 **Born:** 8/26/1975 **Age:** 29

									BATTING												BASERUNNING				AVERAGES		
Year Team	Lg	G	AB	H	2B	3B	HR	(Hm	Rd)	TB	R	RBI	RC	TBB	IBB	SO	HBP	SH	SF		SB	CS	SB%	GDP	Avg	OBP	Slg
2000 Houston	NL	4	7	2	0	0	0	(0	0)	2	0	0	1	0	0	1	0	0	0		0	0	-	0	.286	.286	.286
2002 Houston	NL	49	132	32	7	2	3	(2	1)	52	14	19	13	18	0	25	3	0	0		2	0	1.00	8	.242	.346	.394
2003 Houston	NL	127	385	112	15	1	25	(16	9)	204	69	60	71	48	1	60	6	1	1		2	0	1.00	5	.291	.377	.530
2004 Houston	NL	131	411	113	20	3	10	(9	1)	169	51	66	57	36	1	46	0	5	4		6	4	.60	17	.275	.330	.411
4 ML YEARS		311	935	259	42	6	38	(27	11)	427	134	145	142	102	2	132	9	6	5		15	6	.71	35	.277	.352	.457

Matt Erickson

Bats: L **Throws:** R **Pos:** PH-2; 2B-1; SS-1   **Ht:** 5'11" **Wt:** 190 **Born:** 7/30/1975 **Age:** 29

									BATTING											BASERUNNING				AVERAGES		
Year Team	Lg	G	AB	H	2B	3B	HR	(Hm	Rd)	TB	R	RBI	RC	TBB	IBB	SO	HBP	SH	SF	SB	CS	SB%	GDP	Avg	OBP	Slg
1997 Utica	A-	69	238	78	10	0	5	(-	-)	103	44	44	52	48	3	36	11	2	4	9	3	.75	7	.328	.455	.433
1998 Kane County	A	124	441	143	32	2	4	(-	-)	191	83	64	90	72	1	62	18	7	3	17	7	.71	8	.324	.436	.433
1999 Portland	AA	107	361	97	20	2	0	(-	-)	121	38	35	47	51	0	65	3	5	5	2	3	.40	9	.269	.360	.335
2000 Portland	AA	100	335	101	23	4	2	(-	-)	138	56	41	61	59	3	62	9	1	3	8	3	.73	9	.301	.416	.412
2001 Calgary	AAA	115	413	128	21	1	2	(-	-)	157	66	29	62	39	0	69	12	8	0	11	4	.73	13	.310	.386	.380
2002 Calgary	AAA	108	379	109	30	2	1	(-	-)	146	63	27	52	31	1	63	11	6	0	15	4	.79	11	.288	.359	.385
2003 Albuquerque	AAA	98	298	102	22	4	2	(-	-)	138	43	35	61	43	2	42	10	4	0	14	9	.61	7	.342	.442	.463
2004 Indianapolis	AAA	122	402	109	27	1	2	(-	-)	144	57	34	54	45	0	68	11	11	1	12	10	.55	5	.271	.359	.358
2004 Milwaukee	NL	4	6	1	0	0	0	(0	0)	1	0	0	0	0	0	1	0	0	0	0	0	-	0	.167	.167	.167

Scott Erickson

Pitches: R **Bats:** R **Pos:** SP-6   **Ht:** 6'4" **Wt:** 230 **Born:** 2/2/1968 **Age:** 37

			HOW MUCH HE PITCHED						WHAT HE GAVE UP											THE RESULTS							
Year Team	Lg	G	GS	CG	GF	IP	BFP	H	R	ER	HR	SH	SF	HB	TBB	IBB	SO	WP	Bk	W	L	Pct	ShO	Sv-Op	Hld	ERC	ERA
2004 St. Lucie*	A+	2	2	0	0	7.0	27	6	0	0	0	0	0	0	0	0	5	0	0	1	0	1.000	0	0--	-	1.44	0.00
2004 Norfolk*	AAA	8	8	0	0	52.0	217	56	30	26	5	1	2	4	12	0	30	0	0	3	3	.500	0	0--	-	4.25	4.50
2004 Oklahoma*	AAA	2	2	0	0	11.0	59	17	13	12	1	0	1	2	9	0	11	1	0	0	1	.000	0	0--	-	10.15	9.82
1990 Minnesota	AL	19	17	1	1	113.0	485	108	49	36	9	5	2	5	51	4	53	3	0	8	4	.667	0	0-0	0	4.07	2.87
1991 Minnesota	AL	32	32	5	0	204.0	851	189	80	72	13	5	7	6	71	3	108	4	0	20	8	.714	3	0-0	0	3.36	3.18
1992 Minnesota	AL	32	32	5	0	212.0	888	197	86	80	18	9	7	8	83	3	101	6	1	13	12	.520	3	0-0	0	3.75	3.40
1993 Minnesota	AL	34	34	1	0	218.2	976	266	138	126	17	10	13	10	71	1	116	5	0	8	19	.296	0	0-0	0	5.05	5.19
1994 Minnesota	AL	23	23	2	0	144.0	654	173	95	87	15	3	4	9	59	0	104	10	0	8	11	.421	1	0-0	0	5.61	5.44
1995 Min-Bal	AL	32	31	7	1	196.1	836	213	108	105	18	3	3	5	67	0	106	3	2	13	10	.565	2	0-0	0	4.48	4.81
1996 Baltimore	AL	34	34	6	0	222.1	968	262	137	124	21	5	5	11	66	4	100	1	0	13	12	.520	0	0-0	0	4.90	5.02
1997 Baltimore	AL	34	33	3	0	221.2	922	218	100	91	16	3	4	5	61	5	131	11	0	16	7	.696	2	0-0	0	3.40	3.69
1998 Baltimore	AL	36	36	11	0	251.1	1102	284	125	112	23	7	2	13	69	4	186	4	0	16	13	.552	2	0-0	0	4.40	4.01
1999 Baltimore	AL	34	34	6	0	230.1	995	244	127	123	27	7	6	11	99	4	106	10	0	15	12	.556	3	0-0	0	4.97	4.81
2000 Baltimore	AL	16	16	1	0	92.2	446	127	81	81	14	3	5	5	48	0	41	3	0	5	8	.385	0	0-0	0	7.50	7.87
2002 Baltimore	AL	29	28	3	0	160.2	719	192	109	99	20	3	7	8	68	2	74	5	0	5	12	.294	1	0-0	0	5.80	5.55
2004 NYM-Tex		6	6	0	0	27.0	136	38	22	20	3	0	3	0	20	0	9	2	0	1	4	.200	0	0-0	0	8.11	6.67
1995 Minnesota	AL	15	15	0	0	87.2	390	102	61	58	11	2	1	4	32	0	45	1	0	4	6	.400	0	0-0	0	5.29	5.95
1995 Baltimore	AL	17	16	7	1	108.2	446	111	47	47	7	1	2	1	35	0	61	2	2	9	4	.692	2	0-0	0	3.84	3.89
2004 New York	NL	2	2	0	0	8.0	42	15	9	7	1	0	0	0	4	0	3	1	0	0	1	.000	0	0-0	0	10.35	7.88
2004 Texas	AL	4	4	0	0	19.0	94	23	13	13	2	0	3	0	16	0	6	1	0	1	3	.250	0	0-0	0	7.21	6.16
13 ML YEARS		361	356	51	2	2294.0	9978	2511	1257	1156	214	63	68	96	833	30	1235	67	3	141	132	.516	17	0-0	0	4.62	4.54

Darin Erstad

Bats: L **Throws:** L **Pos:** 1B-125; PR-1   **Ht:** 6'2" **Wt:** 220 **Born:** 6/4/1974 **Age:** 31

									BATTING											BASERUNNING				AVERAGES		
Year Team	Lg	G	AB	H	2B	3B	HR	(Hm	Rd)	TB	R	RBI	RC	TBB	IBB	SO	HBP	SH	SF	SB	CS	SB%	GDP	Avg	OBP	Slg
2004 Salt Lake*	AAA	4	16	2	0	0	0	(-	-)	2	2	3	0	1	0	1	0	0	0	0	0	-	0	.125	.176	.125
1996 California	AL	57	208	59	5	1	4	(1	3)	78	34	20	26	17	1	29	0	1	3	3	3	.50	3	.284	.333	.375
1997 Anaheim	AL	139	539	161	34	4	16	(8	8)	251	99	77	92	51	4	86	4	5	6	23	8	.74	5	.299	.360	.466
1998 Anaheim	AL	133	537	159	39	4	19	(9	10)	261	84	82	94	43	7	77	6	1	3	20	6	.77	2	.296	.353	.486
1999 Anaheim	AL	142	585	148	22	5	13	(7	6)	219	84	53	64	47	3	101	1	2	3	13	7	.65	16	.253	.308	.374
2000 Anaheim	AL	157	676	240	39	6	25	(11	14)	366	121	100	145	64	9	82	1	2	4	28	8	.78	8	.355	.409	.541
2001 Anaheim	AL	157	631	163	35	1	9	(3	6)	227	89	63	79	62	7	113	10	1	7	24	10	.71	8	.258	.331	.360
2002 Anaheim	AL	150	625	177	28	4	10	(2	8)	243	99	73	74	27	4	67	2	5	4	23	3	.88	9	.283	.313	.389
2003 Anaheim	AL	67	258	65	7	1	4	(1	3)	86	35	17	22	18	1	40	4	2	2	9	1	.90	8	.252	.309	.333
2004 Anaheim	AL	125	495	146	29	1	7	(3	4)	198	79	69	76	37	1	74	4	3	4	16	1	.94	9	.295	.346	.400
9 ML YEARS		1127	4554	1318	238	26	107	(45	62)	1929	724	554	672	366	37	669	32	22	36	159	47	.77	68	.289	.344	.424

Felix Escalona

Bats: R **Throws:** R **Pos:** SS-4; 3B-1; PH-1   **Ht:** 6'0" **Wt:** 196 **Born:** 3/12/1979 **Age:** 26

									BATTING											BASERUNNING				AVERAGES		
Year Team	Lg	G	AB	H	2B	3B	HR	(Hm	Rd)	TB	R	RBI	RC	TBB	IBB	SO	HBP	SH	SF	SB	CS	SB%	GDP	Avg	OBP	Slg
2004 Columbus*	AAA	130	448	138	32	1	7	(-	-)	193	79	59	67	31	0	56	17	11	6	2	4	.33	20	.308	.371	.431
2002 Tampa Bay	AL	59	157	34	8	2	0	(0	0)	46	17	9	12	3	0	44	7	3	1	7	2	.78	2	.217	.262	.293
2003 Tampa Bay	AL	10	27	5	2	0	0	(0	0)	7	2	2	3	2	0	6	0	0	0	1	0	1.00	0	.185	.241	.259
2004 New York	AL	5	8	0	0	0	0	(0	0)	0	1	0	0	0	0	2	1	0	0	0	0	-	0	.000	.111	.000
3 ML YEARS		74	192	39	10	2	0	(0	0)	53	20	11	15	5	0	52	8	3	1	8	2	.80	2	.203	.252	.276

Alex Escobar

Bats: R **Throws:** R **Pos:** CF-21; RF-16; LF-8; DH-3; PH-1   **Ht:** 6'1" **Wt:** 180 **Born:** 9/6/1978 **Age:** 26

									BATTING											BASERUNNING				AVERAGES		
Year Team	Lg	G	AB	H	2B	3B	HR	(Hm	Rd)	TB	R	RBI	RC	TBB	IBB	SO	HBP	SH	SF	SB	CS	SB%	GDP	Avg	OBP	Slg
2004 Buffalo*	AAA	16	63	18	5	0	4	(-	-)	35	10	10	11	4	0	15	2	0	0	1	1	.00	0	.286	.348	.556
2001 New York	NL	18	50	10	1	0	3	(3	0)	20	3	8	5	3	0	19	0	0	0	1	0	1.00	1	.200	.245	.400
2003 Cleveland	AL	28	99	27	2	0	5	(4	1)	44	16	14	9	7	1	33	1	0	1	1	0	1.00	0	.273	.324	.444
2004 Cleveland	AL	46	152	32	8	2	1	(0	1)	47	20	12	17	23	0	42	1	3	0	1	1	.50	1	.211	.318	.309
3 ML YEARS		92	301	69	11	2	9	(7	2)	111	39	34	31	33	1	94	2	3	1	3	1	.75	2	.229	.309	.369

Kelvim Escobar

Pitches: R **Bats:** R **Pos:** SP-33   **Ht:** 6'1" **Wt:** 210 **Born:** 4/11/1976 **Age:** 29

Year Team	Lg	G	GS	CG	GF	IP	BFP	H	R	ER	HR	SH	SF	HB	TBB	IBB	SO	WP	Bk	W	L	Pct	ShO	Sv-Op	Hld	ERC	ERA
1997 Toronto	AL	27	0	0	23	31.0	139	28	12	10	1	2	0	0	19	2	36	0	0	3	2	.600	0	14-17	1	3.68	2.90
1998 Toronto	AL	22	10	0	2	79.2	342	72	37	33	5	0	3	0	35	0	72	0	0	7	3	.700	0	0-1	5	3.41	3.73
1999 Toronto	AL	33	30	1	2	174.0	795	203	118	110	19	2	8	10	81	2	129	6	1	14	11	.560	0	0-0	1	5.62	5.69
2000 Toronto	AL	43	24	3	8	180.0	794	186	118	107	26	5	4	3	85	3	142	4	0	10	15	.400	1	2-3	3	4.94	5.35
2001 Toronto	AL	59	11	1	15	126.0	517	93	51	49	8	2	5	3	52	5	121	2	0	6	8	.429	1	0-0	13	2.54	3.50
2002 Toronto	AL	76	0	0	68	78.0	355	75	39	37	10	1	0	5	44	6	85	4	0	5	7	.417	0	38-46	0	4.77	4.27
2003 Toronto	AL	41	26	1	12	180.1	797	189	94	86	15	5	5	9	78	3	159	9	0	13	9	.591	1	4-5	0	4.53	4.29
2004 Anaheim	AL	33	33	0	0	208.1	878	192	91	91	21	3	6	7	76	2	191	9	0	11	12	.478	0	0-0	0	3.65	3.93
8 ML YEARS		334	134	6	130	1057.1	4617	1038	560	523	105	20	31	37	470	23	935	34	1	69	67	.507	3	58-72	22	4.25	4.45

Bobby Estalella

Bats: R **Throws:** R **Pos:** C-9; PH-3; DH-2   **Ht:** 6'1" **Wt:** 213 **Born:** 8/23/1974 **Age:** 30

Year Team	Lg	G	AB	H	2B	3B	HR	(Hm	Rd)	TB	R	RBI	RC	TBB	IBB	SO	HBP	SH	SF	SB	CS	SB%	GDP	Avg	OBP	Slg
2004 Syracuse*	AAA	6	24	6	0	0	2	(-	-)	12	3	3	3	1	0	6	0	0	0	0	0	-	0	.250	.280	.500
1996 Philadelphia	NL	7	17	6	0	0	2	(0	2)	12	5	4	4	1	0	6	0	0	0	1	0	1.00	0	.353	.389	.706
1997 Philadelphia	NL	13	29	10	1	0	4	(1	3)	23	9	9	9	7	0	7	0	0	0	0	0	-	2	.345	.472	.793
1998 Philadelphia	NL	47	165	31	6	1	8	(3	5)	63	16	20	15	13	0	49	1	0	3	0	0	-	4	.188	.247	.382
1999 Philadelphia	NL	9	18	3	0	0	0	(0	0)	3	2	1	1	4	0	7	0	0	0	0	1	.00	0	.167	.318	.167
2000 San Francisco	NL	106	299	70	22	3	14	(6	8)	140	45	53	52	57	9	92	2	0	3	3	0	1.00	4	.234	.357	.468
2001 SF-NYY		32	97	19	5	1	3	(2	1)	35	12	10	10	12	2	30	2	0	0	0	0	-	2	.196	.297	.361
2002 Colorado	NL	38	112	23	8	0	8	(6	2)	55	17	25	17	14	0	33	0	0	4	0	1	.00	1	.205	.285	.491
2003 Colorado	NL	46	140	28	7	0	7	(2	5)	56	17	21	17	19	0	55	1	2	3	2	0	1.00	4	.200	.294	.400
2004 Ari-Tor		12	27	5	0	0	2	(1	1)	11	3	4	3	3	0	11	1	0	0	0	0	-	1	.185	.290	.407
2001 San Francisco	NL	29	93	19	5	1	3	(2	1)	35	11	10	10	11	2	28	1	0	0	0	0	-	2	.204	.295	.376
2001 New York	AL	3	4	0	0	0	0	(0	0)	0	1	0	0	1	0	2	1	0	0	0	0	-	0	.000	.333	.000
2004 Arizona	NL	7	14	2	0	0	2	(1	1)	8	2	4	2	0	0	6	0	0	0	0	0	-	0	.143	.143	.571
2004 Toronto	AL	5	13	3	0	0	0	(0	0)	3	1	0	1	3	0	5	1	0	0	0	0	-	1	.231	.412	.231
9 ML YEARS		310	904	195	49	5	48	(21	27)	398	126	147	128	130	11	290	7	2	13	6	2	.75	18	.216	.315	.440

Shawn Estes

Pitches: L **Bats:** R **Pos:** SP-34   **Ht:** 6'2" **Wt:** 200 **Born:** 2/18/1973 **Age:** 32

Year Team	Lg	G	GS	CG	GF	IP	BFP	H	R	ER	HR	SH	SF	HB	TBB	IBB	SO	WP	Bk	W	L	Pct	ShO	Sv-Op	Hld	ERC	ERA
1995 San Francisco	NL	3	3	0	0	17.1	76	16	14	13	2	0	0	1	5	0	14	4	0	0	3	.000	0	0-0	0	3.37	6.75
1996 San Francisco	NL	11	11	0	0	70.0	305	63	30	28	3	5	0	2	39	3	60	4	0	3	5	.375	0	0-0	0	3.78	3.60
1997 San Francisco	NL	32	32	3	0	201.0	849	162	80	71	12	13	2	8	100	2	181	10	2	19	5	.792	2	0-0	0	3.28	3.18
1998 San Francisco	NL	25	25	1	0	149.1	661	150	89	84	14	15	4	5	80	6	136	6	1	7	12	.368	1	0-0	0	4.71	5.06
1999 San Francisco	NL	32	32	1	0	203.0	914	209	121	111	21	14	3	5	112	2	159	15	1	11	11	.500	1	0-0	0	4.96	4.92
2000 San Francisco	NL	30	30	4	0	190.1	829	194	99	90	11	7	6	3	108	1	136	11	0	15	6	.714	2	0-0	0	4.75	4.26
2001 San Francisco	NL	27	27	0	0	159.0	693	151	78	71	11	5	9	5	77	7	109	10	2	9	8	.529	0	0-0	0	3.96	4.02
2002 NYM-Cin	NL	29	29	1	0	160.2	713	171	94	91	13	7	6	9	83	9	109	3	1	5	12	.294	1	0-0	0	5.00	5.10
2003 Chicago	NL	29	28	1	0	152.1	699	182	113	97	20	11	7	1	83	1	103	6	0	8	11	.421	1	0-0	0	6.15	5.73
2004 Colorado	NL	34	34	1	0	202.0	904	223	133	131	30	13	8	11	105	5	117	4	2	15	8	.652	0	0-0	0	5.86	5.84
2002 New York	NL	23	23	1	0	132.2	580	133	70	67	12	7	4	5	66	9	92	2	1	4	9	.308	1	0-0	0	4.51	4.55
2002 Cincinnati	NL	6	6	0	0	28.0	133	38	24	24	1	0	2	4	17	0	17	1	0	1	3	.250	0	0-0	0	7.52	7.71
10 ML YEARS		252	251	12	0	1505.0	6643	1521	851	787	137	90	45	50	792	36	1124	73	9	92	81	.532	8	0-0	0	4.73	4.71

Johnny Estrada

Bats: B **Throws:** R **Pos:** C-133; PH-12   **Ht:** 5'11" **Wt:** 209 **Born:** 6/27/1976 **Age:** 29

Year Team	Lg	G	AB	H	2B	3B	HR	(Hm	Rd)	TB	R	RBI	RC	TBB	IBB	SO	HBP	SH	SF	SB	CS	SB%	GDP	Avg	OBP	Slg
2001 Philadelphia	NL	89	298	68	15	0	8	(7	1)	107	26	37	25	16	6	32	4	2	4	0	0	-	15	.228	.273	.359
2002 Philadelphia	NL	10	17	2	1	0	0	(0	0)	3	0	2	0	2	1	2	0	0	0	0	0	-	0	.118	.211	.176
2003 Atlanta	NL	16	36	11	0	0	0	(0	0)	11	2	2	2	0	0	3	0	0	0	0	0	-	1	.306	.359	.306
2004 Atlanta	NL	134	462	145	36	0	9	(4	5)	208	56	76	78	39	7	66	11	1	4	0	0	-	18	.314	.378	.450
4 ML YEARS		249	813	226	52	0	17	(11	6)	329	84	117	105	57	14	103	18	3	8	0	0	-	34	.278	.336	.405

Leo Estrella

Pitches: R **Bats:** R **Pos:** RP-2   **Ht:** 6'1" **Wt:** 185 **Born:** 2/20/1975 **Age:** 30

Year Team	Lg	G	GS	CG	GF	IP	BFP	H	R	ER	HR	SH	SF	HB	TBB	IBB	SO	WP	Bk	W	L	Pct	ShO	Sv-Op	Hld	ERC	ERA
2004 Fresno*	AAA	38	5	0	8	77.2	383	125	71	66	15	2	1	3	33	0	34	6	0	0	8	.000	0	0- -	-	9.01	7.65
2000 Toronto	AL	2	0	0	0	4.2	21	9	3	3	1	0	0	0	0	0	3	0	0	0	0	-	0	0-0	0	9.77	5.79
2003 Milwaukee	NL	58	0	0	18	66.0	290	75	32	32	10	4	3	3	21	5	25	2	1	7	3	.700	0	3-8	9	4.97	4.36
2004 San Francisco	NL	2	0	0	0	1.1	13	8	4	4	0	0	1	0	1	0	0	0	0	0	0	-	0	0-0	0	43.81	27.00
3 ML YEARS		62	0	0	18	72.0	324	92	36	39	11	4	4	3	22	5	28	2	1	7	3	.700	0	3-8	9	5.80	4.88

Adam Everett

Bats: R **Throws:** R **Pos:** SS-99; PH-4; PR-2   **Ht:** 6'0" **Wt:** 156 **Born:** 2/2/1977 **Age:** 28

Year Team	Lg	G	AB	H	2B	3B	HR	(Hm	Rd)	TB	R	RBI	RC	TBB	IBB	SO	HBP	SH	SF	SB	CS	SB%	GDP	Avg	OBP	Slg
2001 Houston	NL	9	3	0	0	0	0	(0	0)	0	1	0	0	0	0	1	0	0	0	1	0	1.00	0	.000	.000	.000
2002 Houston	NL	40	88	17	3	0	0	(0	0)	20	11	4	6	12	1	19	1	2	0	3	0	1.00	1	.193	.297	.227

Year Team	Lg	G	AB	H	2B	3B	HR	(Hm	Rd)	TB	R	RBI	RC	TBB	IBB	SO	HBP	SH	SF	SB	CS	SB%	GDP	Avg	OBP	Slg
				BATTING																BASERUNNING				AVERAGES		
2003 Houston	NL	128	387	99	18	3	8	(5	3)	147	51	51	50	28	6	66	9	11	1	8	1	.89	7	.256	.320	.380
2004 Houston	NL	104	384	105	15	2	8	(5	3)	148	66	31	51	17	0	56	9	22	3	13	2	.87	4	.273	.317	.385
4 ML YEARS		281	862	221	36	5	16	(10	6)	315	129	86	107	57	7	142	19	35	4	25	3	.89	12	.256	.315	.365

Carl Everett

Bats: B **Throws:** R **Pos:** DH-44; LF-20; RF-14; PH-4   **Ht:** 6'0" **Wt:** 215 **Born:** 6/3/1971 **Age:** 34

Year Team	Lg	G	AB	H	2B	3B	HR	(Hm	Rd)	TB	R	RBI	RC	TBB	IBB	SO	HBP	SH	SF	SB	CS	SB%	GDP	Avg	OBP	Slg
				BATTING																BASERUNNING				AVERAGES		
2004 Brevard Cnty*	A+	5	15	6	1	0	0	(-	-)	7	2	3	3	2	0	3	0	0	1	0	0	-	0	.400	.444	.467
1993 Florida	NL	11	19	2	0	0	0	(0	0)	2	0	0	0	1	0	9	0	0	0	1	0	1.00	0	.105	.150	.105
1994 Florida	NL	16	51	11	1	0	2	(2	0)	18	7	6	5	3	0	15	0	0	0	4	0	1.00	0	.216	.259	.353
1995 New York	NL	79	289	75	13	1	12	(9	3)	126	48	54	41	39	2	67	2	1	0	2	5	.29	11	.260	.352	.436
1996 New York	NL	101	192	46	8	1	1	(1	0)	59	29	16	21	21	2	53	4	1	1	6	0	1.00	4	.240	.326	.307
1997 New York	NL	142	443	110	28	3	14	(11	3)	186	58	57	58	32	3	102	7	3	2	19	9	.65	3	.248	.308	.420
1998 Houston	NL	133	467	138	34	4	15	(5	10)	225	72	76	76	44	2	102	3	3	2	14	12	.54	11	.296	.359	.482
1999 Houston	NL	123	464	151	33	3	25	(11	14)	265	86	108	105	50	5	94	11	2	8	27	7	.79	5	.325	.398	.571
2000 Boston	AL	137	496	149	32	4	34	(17	17)	291	82	108	106	52	5	113	8	0	5	11	4	.73	4	.300	.373	.587
2001 Boston	AL	102	409	105	24	4	14	(6	8)	179	61	58	59	27	3	104	13	0	0	9	2	.82	3	.257	.323	.438
2002 Texas	AL	105	374	100	16	0	16	(11	5)	164	47	62	60	33	4	77	6	1	4	2	3	.40	7	.267	.333	.439
2003 Tex-CWS	AL	147	526	151	27	3	28	(15	13)	268	93	92	102	53	6	84	15	4	4	8	4	.67	7	.287	.366	.510
2004 Mon-CWS	AL	82	281	73	17	1	7	(3	4)	113	29	35	37	16	3	45	10	0	3	1	0	1.00	11	.260	.319	.402
2003 Texas	AL	74	270	74	13	3	18	(10	8)	147	53	51	57	31	2	48	5	4	3	4	1	.80	2	.274	.356	.544
2003 Chicago	AL	73	256	77	14	0	10	(5	5)	121	40	41	45	22	4	36	10	0	1	4	3	.57	5	.301	.377	.473
2004 Montreal	NL	39	127	32	10	0	2	(1	1)	48	8	14	13	8	2	19	5	0	1	0	0	-	8	.252	.319	.378
2004 Chicago	AL	43	154	41	7	1	5	(2	3)	65	21	21	24	8	1	26	5	0	2	1	0	1.00	3	.266	.320	.422
12 ML YEARS		1178	4011	1111	233	24	168	(91	77)	1896	612	672	670	371	35	865	79	15	29	102	46	.69	66	.277	.348	.473

Scott Eyre

Pitches: L **Bats:** L **Pos:** RP-83   **Ht:** 6'1" **Wt:** 210 **Born:** 5/30/1972 **Age:** 33

Year Team	Lg	G	GS	CG	GF	IP	BFP	H	R	ER	HR	SH	SF	HB	TBB	IBB	SO	WP	Bk	W	L	Pct	ShO	Sv-Op	Hld	ERC	ERA
			HOW MUCH HE PITCHED								WHAT HE GAVE UP											THE RESULTS				
2004 Fresno*	AAA	3	0	0	3	3.0	14	3	0	0	0	0	0	0	2	0	1	0	0	0	0	-	0	0--	-	4.23	0.00
1997 Chicago	AL	11	11	0	0	60.2	267	62	36	34	11	1	2	1	31	1	36	2	0	4	4	.500	0	0-0	0	5.37	5.04
1998 Chicago	AL	33	17	0	10	107.0	491	114	78	64	24	2	3	2	64	0	73	7	0	3	8	.273	0	0-0	0	6.31	5.38
1999 Chicago	AL	21	0	0	0	25.0	129	38	22	21	6	0	1	1	15	2	17	1	0	1	1	.500	0	0-0	1	9.23	7.56
2000 Chicago	AL	13	1	0	3	19.0	93	29	15	14	3	0	2	1	12	0	16	0	0	1	1	.500	0	0-0	0	9.49	6.63
2001 Toronto	AL	17	0	0	5	15.2	66	15	6	6	1	0	1	1	7	2	16	2	0	1	2	.333	0	2-3	3	3.96	3.45
2002 Tor-SF		70	3	0	6	74.2	333	80	41	37	4	2	4	0	36	8	58	5	0	2	4	.333	0	0-1	18	4.26	4.46
2003 San Francisco	NL	74	0	0	10	57.0	256	60	23	21	4	2	3	1	26	0	35	6	0	2	1	.667	0	1-3	20	4.37	3.32
2004 San Francisco	NL	83	0	0	12	52.2	229	43	26	24	8	3	3	0	27	3	49	3	0	2	2	.500	0	1-5	33	3.67	4.10
2002 Toronto	AL	49	3	0	3	63.1	283	69	37	35	4	2	4	0	29	7	51	4	0	2	4	.333	0	0-1	12	4.32	4.97
2002 San Francisco	NL	21	0	0	3	11.1	50	11	4	2	0	0	0	0	7	1	7	1	0	0	0	-	0	0-0	6	3.91	1.59
8 ML YEARS		322	32	0	54	411.2	1864	441	247	221	61	10	19	7	218	16	300	26	0	16	23	.410	0	4-12	65	5.37	4.83

Brian Falkenborg

Pitches: R **Bats:** R **Pos:** RP-6   **Ht:** 6'6" **Wt:** 190 **Born:** 1/18/1978 **Age:** 27

Year Team	Lg	G	GS	CG	GF	IP	BFP	H	R	ER	HR	SH	SF	HB	TBB	IBB	SO	WP	Bk	W	L	Pct	ShO	Sv-Op	Hld	ERC	ERA
			HOW MUCH HE PITCHED								WHAT HE GAVE UP											THE RESULTS				
1996 Orioles	R	8	6	0	1	28.0	116	21	13	8	1	0	0	1	8	0	36	2	1	0	3	.000	0	0--	-	2.01	2.57
1996 High Desert	A+	1	0	0	0	1.0	3	1	0	0	0	0	0	0	0	0	1	0	0	0	0	-	0	0--	-	2.79	0.00
1997 Delmarva	A	25	25	0	0	127.0	547	122	73	63	6	3	2	13	46	2	107	17	0	7	9	.438	0	0--	-	3.73	4.46
1997 Bowie	AA	1	1	0	0	1.2	11	3	3	3	0	0	0	0	3	0	0	0	0	0	1	.000	0	0--	-	14.26	16.20
1998 Frederick	A+	15	14	1	0	78.0	338	83	42	39	6	3	2	4	18	0	70	8	0	5	5	.500	1	0--	-	3.73	4.50
1999 Bowie	AA	16	16	0	0	83.1	361	77	40	35	11	2	0	5	36	0	77	1	0	3	6	.333	0	0--	-	4.24	3.78
1999 Orioles	R	3	2	0	0	9.0	37	6	2	2	0	0	0	0	3	0	11	1	0	1	0	1.000	0	0--	-	1.53	2.00
2001 San Antonio	AA	12	12	2	0	66.0	296	80	47	40	9	2	3	5	24	0	56	5	0	5	6	.455	1	0--	-	5.85	5.45
2001 Tacoma	AAA	8	8	0	0	48.1	206	50	25	24	6	1	2	2	18	0	27	1	0	2	4	.333	0	0--	-	4.61	4.47
2002 Tacoma	AAA	9	9	0	0	49.1	207	51	22	15	3	0	2	1	13	0	42	0	0	4	4	.500	0	0--	-	3.57	2.74
2003 Tacoma	AAA	17	14	0	0	79.2	331	66	28	26	7	1	3	2	26	0	62	2	0	4	2	.667	0	0--	-	2.86	2.94
2004 Las Vegas	AAA	18	16	0	2	89.0	394	104	66	61	17	5	6	4	25	0	87	3	0	4	6	.400	0	1--	-	5.38	6.17
1999 Baltimore	AL	2	0	0	1	3.0	12	2	0	0	0	0	0	0	2	0	1	0	0	0	0	-	0	0-0	0	-	0.00
2004 Los Angeles	NL	6	0	0	0	14.1	73	19	14	12	2	2	0	3	9	0	11	1	0	1	0	1.000	0	0-0	0	8.19	7.53
2 ML YEARS		8	0	0	1	17.1	73	21	14	12	2	2	0	3	11	0	12	1	0	1	0	1.000	0	0-0	0	8.45	6.23

Kyle Farnsworth

Pitches: R **Bats:** R **Pos:** RP-72   **Ht:** 6'4" **Wt:** 235 **Born:** 4/14/1976 **Age:** 29

Year Team	Lg	G	GS	CG	GF	IP	BFP	H	R	ER	HR	SH	SF	HB	TBB	IBB	SO	WP	Bk	W	L	Pct	ShO	Sv-Op	Hld	ERC	ERA
			HOW MUCH HE PITCHED								WHAT HE GAVE UP											THE RESULTS				
1999 Chicago	NL	27	21	1	1	130.0	579	140	80	73	28	6	2	3	52	1	70	7	1	5	9	.357	0	0-0	0	5.39	5.05
2000 Chicago	NL	46	5	0	8	77.0	371	90	58	55	14	4	4	0	48	4	74	3	0	2	9	.182	0	1-6	6	6.72	6.43
2001 Chicago	NL	76	0	0	24	82.0	339	65	26	25	8	2	2	1	29	2	107	2	2	4	6	.400	0	2-3	24	2.76	2.74
2002 Chicago	NL	45	0	0	17	46.2	213	53	47	38	9	2	5	1	24	7	46	1	0	4	6	.400	0	1-7	6	5.89	7.33
2003 Chicago	NL	77	0	0	13	76.1	312	53	31	28	6	4	1	0	36	1	92	6	0	3	2	.600	0	0-3	19	2.58	3.30
2004 Chicago	NL	72	0	0	25	66.2	298	67	39	35	10	5	0	2	33	1	78	1	0	4	5	.444	0	0-4	18	4.91	4.73
6 ML YEARS		343	26	1	88	478.2	2112	468	281	254	75	23	14	11	224	20	467	20	3	22	37	.373	1	4-23	73	4.61	4.78

Jeff Fassero

Pitches: L Bats: L Pos: RP-29; SP-12   Ht: 6'1" Wt: 200 Born: 1/5/1963 Age: 42

Year Team	Lg	G	GS	CG	GF	IP	BFP	H	R	ER	HR	SH	SF	HB	TBB	IBB	SO	WP	Bk	W	L	Pct	ShO	Sv-Op	Hld	ERC	ERA
1991 Montreal	NL	51	0	0	30	55.1	223	39	17	15	1	6	0	1	17	1	42	4	0	2	5	.286	0	8-11	7	1.75	2.44
1992 Montreal	NL	70	0	0	22	85.2	368	81	35	27	1	5	2	2	34	6	63	7	1	8	7	.533	0	1-7	12	3.10	2.84
1993 Montreal	NL	56	15	1	10	149.2	616	119	50	38	7	7	4	0	54	0	140	5	0	12	5	.706	0	1-3	6	2.48	2.29
1994 Montreal	NL	21	21	1	0	138.2	569	119	54	46	13	7	2	1	40	4	119	6	0	8	6	.571	0	0-0	0	2.82	2.99
1995 Montreal	NL	30	30	1	0	189.0	833	207	102	91	15	19	7	2	74	3	164	7	1	13	14	.481	0	0-0	0	4.43	4.33
1996 Montreal	NL	34	34	5	0	231.2	967	217	95	85	20	16	5	3	55	3	222	5	2	15	11	.577	1	0-0	0	3.00	3.30
1997 Seattle	AL	35	35	2	0	234.1	1010	226	108	94	21	7	10	3	84	6	189	13	2	16	9	.640	1	0-0	0	3.60	3.61
1998 Seattle	AL	32	32	7	0	224.2	954	223	115	99	33	8	8	10	66	2	176	12	0	13	12	.520	0	0-0	0	4.10	3.97
1999 Sea-Tex	AL	37	27	0	2	156.1	751	208	135	125	35	2	7	4	83	3	114	9	0	5	14	.263	0	0-0	2	7.69	7.20
2000 Boston	AL	38	5	0	3	130.0	577	153	72	69	16	7	2	1	50	2	97	2	0	8	8	.500	0	0-0	5	5.25	4.78
2001 Chicago	NL	82	0	0	30	73.2	308	66	31	28	6	1	2	1	23	5	79	3	0	4	4	.500	0	12-17	25	2.97	3.42
2002 ChC-StL	NL	73	0	0	18	69.0	315	81	43	41	9	7	1	3	27	5	56	2	1	8	6	.571	0	0-3	13	5.25	5.35
2003 St Louis	NL	62	6	0	15	77.2	354	93	51	49	17	3	1	2	34	4	55	2	0	1	7	.125	0	3-6	11	6.34	5.68
2004 Col-Ari	NL	41	12	0	2	112.0	508	136	73	68	9	5	7	4	44	5	60	4	1	3	8	.273	0	0-0	2	5.20	5.46
1999 Seattle	AL	30	24	0	1	139.0	669	188	123	114	34	1	6	4	73	3	101	7	0	4	14	.222	0	0-0	2	8.02	7.38
1999 Texas	AL	7	3	0	1	17.1	82	20	12	11	1	1	1	0	10	0	13	2	0	1	0	1.000	0	0-0	0	5.21	5.71
2002 Chicago	NL	57	0	0	17	51.0	240	65	37	35	5	6	1	3	22	5	44	2	1	5	6	.455	0	0-1	6	5.79	6.18
2002 St Louis	NL	16	0	0	1	18.0	75	16	6	6	4	1	0	0	5	0	12	0	0	3	0	1.000	0	0-2	7	3.70	3.00
2004 Colorado	NL	40	12	0	2	111.0	505	136	73	68	9	5	7	4	44	5	59	4	1	3	8	.273	0	0-0	2	5.29	5.51
2004 Arizona	NL	1	0	0	0	1.0	3	0	0	0	0	0	0	0	0	0	1	0	0	0	0	-	0	0-0	0	0.00	0.00
14 ML YEARS		662	235	17	133	1927.2	8353	1968	981	875	203	100	58	37	685	49	1576	81	8	116	116	.500	2	25-47	83	4.06	4.09

Pedro Feliciano

Pitches: L Bats: L Pos: RP-22   Ht: 5'10" Wt: 185 Born: 8/25/1976 Age: 28

Year Team	Lg	G	GS	CG	GF	IP	BFP	H	R	ER	HR	SH	SF	HB	TBB	IBB	SO	WP	Bk	W	L	Pct	ShO	Sv-Op	Hld	ERC	ERA
2004 Norfolk*	AAA	32	0	0	9	35.2	158	35	25	21	4	1	0	4	15	1	25	3	0	4	3	.571	0	2- -	-	4.52	5.30
2002 New York	NL	6	0	0	3	6.0	26	9	5	5	0	0	0	0	1	0	4	0	0	0	0	-	0	0-0	0	5.56	7.50
2003 New York	NL	23	0	0	8	48.1	218	52	21	18	5	0	1	3	21	3	43	3	1	0	0	-	0	0-0	0	4.77	3.35
2004 New York	NL	22	0	0	3	18.1	82	14	12	11	2	1	1	1	12	0	14	1	0	1	1	.500	0	0-0	2	3.93	5.40
3 ML YEARS		51	0	0	14	72.2	326	75	38	34	7	1	2	4	34	3	61	4	1	1	1	.500	0	0-0	2	4.61	4.21

Pedro Feliz

Bats: R Throws: R Pos: 1B-70; 3B-51; PH-25; SS-19; LF-2; RF-2   Ht: 6'1" Wt: 205 Born: 4/27/1977 Age: 28

Year Team	Lg	G	AB	H	2B	3B	HR	(Hm	Rd)	TB	R	RBI	RC	TBB	IBB	SO	HBP	SH	SF	SB	CS	SB%	GDP	Avg	OBP	Slg
2000 San Francisco	NL	8	7	2	0	0	0	(0	0)	2	1	0	1	0	0	1	0	0	0	0	0	-	0	.286	.286	.286
2001 San Francisco	NL	94	220	50	9	1	7	(3	4)	82	23	22	20	10	2	50	2	3	3	2	1	.67	5	.227	.264	.373
2002 San Francisco	NL	67	146	37	4	1	2	(1	1)	49	14	13	12	6	1	27	0	0	-	2	0	-	2	.253	.281	.336
2003 San Francisco	NL	95	235	58	9	3	16	(6	10)	121	31	48	34	10	0	53	1	1	2	2	2	.50	7	.247	.278	.515
2004 San Francisco	NL	144	503	139	33	3	22	(11	11)	244	72	84	56	23	1	85	0	0	5	5	2	.71	16	.276	.305	.485
5 ML YEARS		408	1111	286	55	8	47	(21	26)	498	141	167	123	49	4	216	3	4	11	9	5	.64	30	.257	.288	.448

Jared Fernandez

Pitches: R Bats: R Pos: SP-1; RP-1   Ht: 6'2" Wt: 225 Born: 2/2/1972 Age: 33

Year Team	Lg	G	GS	CG	GF	IP	BFP	H	R	ER	HR	SH	SF	HB	TBB	IBB	SO	WP	Bk	W	L	Pct	ShO	Sv-Op	Hld	ERC	ERA
2004 New Orleans*	AAA	35	28	3	3	196.1	822	208	120	104	27	9	7	5	46	2	98	7	0	7	11	.389	0	0- -	-	4.14	4.77
2001 Cincinnati	NL	5	2	0	2	12.1	57	13	9	6	1	0	0	2	6	0	5	1	0	0	1	.000	0	0-0	0	5.21	4.38
2002 Cincinnati	NL	14	8	0	2	50.2	232	59	31	25	5	1	2	3	24	1	36	3	0	1	3	.250	0	0-0	0	5.54	4.44
2003 Houston	NL	12	6	0	3	38.1	161	37	17	17	2	3	1	2	12	2	19	3	0	3	3	.500	0	0-0	0	3.38	3.99
2004 Houston	NL	2	1	0	0	1.0	14	6	6	6	0	0	1	0	5	0	0	0	0	0	0	-	0	0-0	0	66.63	54.00
4 ML YEARS		33	17	0	7	102.1	464	115	63	54	8	4	4	7	47	3	60	7	0	4	7	.364	0	0-0	0	5.10	4.75

Mike Fetters

Pitches: R Bats: R Pos: RP-23   Ht: 6'4" Wt: 239 Born: 12/19/1964 Age: 40

Year Team	Lg	G	GS	CG	GF	IP	BFP	H	R	ER	HR	SH	SF	HB	TBB	IBB	SO	WP	Bk	W	L	Pct	ShO	Sv-Op	Hld	ERC	ERA
2004 Tucson*	AAA	7	0	0	2	8.0	36	11	5	4	0	0	0	0	1	0	10	1	0	0	0	-	0	1- -	-	4.26	4.50
1989 California	AL	1	0	0	0	3.1	16	5	4	3	1	0	0	0	1	0	4	2	0	0	0	-	0	0-0	0	8.14	8.10
1990 California	AL	26	2	0	10	67.2	291	77	33	31	9	1	0	2	20	0	35	3	0	1	1	.500	0	1-1	1	4.88	4.12
1991 California	AL	19	4	0	8	44.2	206	53	29	24	4	1	0	3	28	2	24	4	0	2	5	.286	0	0-1	0	6.44	4.84
1992 Milwaukee	AL	50	0	0	11	62.2	243	38	15	13	3	5	2	7	24	2	43	4	1	5	1	.833	0	2-5	8	2.13	1.87
1993 Milwaukee	AL	45	0	0	14	59.1	246	59	29	22	4	5	5	2	22	4	23	0	0	3	3	.500	0	0-0	8	3.89	3.34
1994 Milwaukee	AL	42	0	0	31	46.0	202	41	16	13	0	2	3	1	27	5	31	3	1	1	4	.200	0	17-20	3	3.36	2.54
1995 Milwaukee	AL	40	0	0	34	34.2	163	40	16	13	3	2	1	0	20	4	33	5	0	0	3	.000	0	22-27	2	5.27	3.38
1996 Milwaukee	AL	61	0	0	55	61.1	268	65	28	23	4	0	4	1	26	4	53	5	0	3	3	.500	0	32-38	1	4.24	3.38
1997 Milwaukee	AL	51	0	0	20	70.1	298	62	30	27	4	6	4	1	33	3	62	2	1	1	5	.167	0	6-11	11	3.41	3.45
1998 Oak-Ana	AL	60	0	0	28	58.2	264	62	34	28	5	4	2	1	25	2	43	6	0	2	8	.200	0	5-9	11	4.29	4.30
1999 Baltimore	AL	27	0	0	10	31.0	151	35	23	20	5	1	0	2	22	2	22	1	1	1	0	1.000	0	0-3	2	6.66	5.81
2000 Los Angeles	NL	51	0	0	20	50.0	201	35	18	18	7	3	0	2	25	2	40	3	0	6	2	.750	0	5-7	11	3.34	3.24
2001 LA-Pit	NL	54	0	0	21	47.1	223	49	32	29	7	1	3	4	26	1	37	7	0	3	2	.600	0	9-12	14	5.37	5.51
2002 Pit-Ari	NL	65	0	0	22	55.0	252	55	31	25	4	0	2	3	37	6	53	8	0	3	3	.500	0	0-2	16	4.75	4.09
2003 Minnesota	AL	5	0	0	2	6.0	22	2	0	0	0	0	0	0	1	0	1	0	0	0	0	-	0	0-0	0	0.69	0.00
2004 Arizona	NL	23	0	0	6	18.2	94	23	22	18	2	0	2	1	14	2	14	4	0	0	1	.000	0	1-1	1	6.82	8.68
1998 Oakland	AL	48	0	0	22	47.1	214	48	26	21	3	4	2	1	21	2	34	3	0	1	6	.143	0	5-8	10	3.93	3.99
1998 Anaheim	AL	12	0	0	6	11.1	50	14	8	7	2	0	0	0	4	0	9	3	0	1	2	.333	0	0-1	1	5.95	5.56

Year Team	Lg	G	GS	CG	GF	IP	BFP	H	R	ER	HR	SH	SF	HB	TBB	IBB	SO	WP	Bk	W	L	Pct	ShO	Sv-Op	Hld	ERC	ERA
2001 Los Angeles	NL	34	0	0	7	29.2	139	33	23	20	6	1	3	1	13	0	26	6	0	2	1	.667	0	1-3	14	5.53	6.07
2001 Pittsburgh	NL	20	0	0	14	17.2	84	16	9	9	1	0	0	3	13	1	11	1	0	1	1	.500	0	8-9	0	5.01	4.58
2002 Pittsburgh	NL	32	0	0	13	30.1	134	25	13	11	3	0	1	1	18	1	29	2	0	1	0	1.000	0	0-1	11	3.86	3.26
2002 Arizona	NL	33	0	0	9	24.2	118	28	18	14	1	0	1	2	19	5	24	6	0	2	3	.400	0	0-1	5	5.91	5.11
16 ML YEARS		620	6	0	292	716.2	3140	699	360	307	62	31	28	31	351	39	518	57	4	31	41	.431	0	100-137	89	4.30	3.86

Robert Fick

Bats: L **Throws:** R **Pos:** DH-33; PH-29; LF-13; 1B-11; RF-8; C-3   **Ht:** 6'1" **Wt:** 200 **Born:** 3/15/1974 **Age:** 31

Year Team	Lg	G	AB	H	2B	3B	HR	(Hm	Rd)	TB	R	RBI	RC	TBB	IBB	SO	HBP	SH	SF	SB	CS	SB%	GDP	Avg	OBP	Slg
2004 Portland*	AAA	12	50	19	4	0	2	(-	-)	29	8	6	10	2	0	11	0	0	0	1	0	1.00	0	.380	.404	.580
1998 Detroit	AL	7	22	8	1	0	3	(0	3)	18	6	7	6	2	0	7	0	0	0	1	0	1.00	1	.364	.417	.818
1999 Detroit	AL	15	41	9	0	0	3	(1	2)	18	6	10	6	7	0	6	0	0	1	1	0	1.00	1	.220	.327	.439
2000 Detroit	AL	66	163	41	7	2	3	(0	3)	61	18	22	21	22	2	39	1	0	2	2	1	.67	4	.252	.340	.374
2001 Detroit	AL	124	401	109	21	2	19	(8	11)	191	62	61	62	39	3	62	4	0	4	0	3	.00	10	.272	.339	.476
2002 Detroit	AL	148	556	150	36	2	17	(12	5)	241	66	63	70	46	4	90	7	0	5	0	1	.00	17	.270	.331	.433
2003 Atlanta	NL	126	409	110	26	1	11	(4	7)	171	52	80	68	42	4	47	2	0	7	1	0	1.00	9	.269	.335	.418
2004 TB-SD		89	226	45	5	2	6	(3	3)	72	14	26	22	22	2	36	3	0	2	0	0	-	2	.199	.277	.319
2004 Tampa Bay	AL	76	214	43	5	2	6	(3	3)	70	12	26	21	20	2	32	2	0	2	0	0	-	2	.201	.273	.327
2004 San Diego	NL	13	12	2	0	0	0	(0	0)	2	2	0	1	2	0	4	1	0	0	0	0	-	0	.167	.333	.167
7 ML YEARS		575	1818	472	96	9	62	(28	34)	772	224	269	255	180	15	287	17	0	21	5	5	.50	44	.260	.329	.425

Nate Field

Pitches: R **Bats:** R **Pos:** RP-43   **Ht:** 6'2" **Wt:** 200 **Born:** 12/11/1975 **Age:** 29

Year Team	Lg	G	GS	CG	GF	IP	BFP	H	R	ER	HR	SH	SF	HB	TBB	IBB	SO	WP	Bk	W	L	Pct	ShO	Sv-Op	Hld	ERC	ERA
2002 Kansas City	AL	5	0	0	0	5.0	26	8	5	5	2	1	0	0	3	1	3	2	0	0	0	-	0	0-0	0	10.82	9.00
2003 Kansas City	AL	19	0	0	7	21.2	97	19	10	10	3	0	1	1	14	1	19	0	0	1	1	.500	0	0-0	2	4.74	4.15
2004 Kansas City	AL	43	0	0	23	44.1	191	40	25	21	5	1	2	2	19	2	30	2	0	2	3	.400	0	3-5	2	3.82	4.26
3 ML YEARS		67	0	0	30	71.0	314	67	40	36	10	2	3	3	36	4	52	4	0	3	4	.429	0	3-5	4	4.53	4.56

Chone Figgins

Bats: B **Throws:** R **Pos:** 3B-92; CF-55; 2B-20; SS-13; RF-2; PR-2; LF-1; PH-1   **Ht:** 5'9" **Wt:** 155 **Born:** 1/22/1978 **Age:** 27

Year Team	Lg	G	AB	H	2B	3B	HR	(Hm	Rd)	TB	R	RBI	RC	TBB	IBB	SO	HBP	SH	SF	SB	CS	SB%	GDP	Avg	OBP	Slg
2002 Anaheim	AL	15	12	2	1	0	0	(0	0)	3	6	1	0	0	0	5	0	0	0	2	1	.67	1	.167	.167	.250
2003 Anaheim	AL	71	240	71	9	4	0	(0	0)	88	34	27	39	20	0	38	0	6	4	13	7	.65	1	.296	.345	.367
2004 Anaheim	AL	148	577	171	22	17	5	(3	2)	242	83	60	93	49	0	94	0	10	2	34	13	.72	6	.296	.350	.419
3 ML YEARS		234	829	244	32	21	5	(3	2)	333	123	88	132	69	0	137	0	16	6	49	21	.70	8	.294	.346	.402

Nelson Figueroa

Pitches: R **Bats:** R **Pos:** RP-7; SP-3   **Ht:** 6'1" **Wt:** 155 **Born:** 5/18/1974 **Age:** 31

Year Team	Lg	G	GS	CG	GF	IP	BFP	H	R	ER	HR	SH	SF	HB	TBB	IBB	SO	WP	Bk	W	L	Pct	ShO	Sv-Op	Hld	ERC	ERA
2004 Nashville*	AAA	25	23	3	1	152.1	648	168	79	71	20	6	3	4	36	1	129	2	0	12	8	.600	1	0--	-	4.34	4.19
2000 Arizona	NL	3	3	0	0	15.2	68	17	13	13	4	1	2	0	5	0	7	2	0	0	1	.000	0	0-0	0	5.31	7.47
2001 Philadelphia	NL	19	13	0	1	89.0	393	95	40	39	8	4	0	7	37	3	61	2	0	4	5	.444	0	0-0	0	4.76	3.94
2002 Milwaukee	NL	30	11	0	4	93.0	412	96	59	52	18	11	5	4	37	6	51	5	0	1	7	.125	0	0-0	1	4.94	5.03
2003 Pittsburgh	NL	12	3	0	1	35.1	146	28	13	13	8	2	2	2	13	2	23	2	0	2	1	.667	0	0-0	0	3.80	3.31
2004 Pittsburgh	NL	10	3	0	0	28.1	121	32	18	18	4	4	0	0	11	1	10	3	0	0	3	.000	0	0-0	0	5.21	5.72
5 ML YEARS		74	33	0	6	261.1	1140	268	143	135	42	22	9	13	103	12	152	14	0	7	17	.292	0	0-0	1	4.78	4.65

Jeremy Fikac

Pitches: R **Bats:** R **Pos:** RP-19   **Ht:** 6'2" **Wt:** 185 **Born:** 4/8/1975 **Age:** 30

Year Team	Lg	G	GS	CG	GF	IP	BFP	H	R	ER	HR	SH	SF	HB	TBB	IBB	SO	WP	Bk	W	L	Pct	ShO	Sv-Op	Hld	ERC	ERA
2004 Edmonton*	AAA	28	0	0	10	40.1	189	44	30	27	9	0	0	2	21	1	33	3	0	5	5	.500	0	1--	-	6.04	6.02
2001 San Diego	NL	23	0	0	5	26.1	99	15	6	4	2	2	0	1	5	1	19	0	0	2	0	1.000	0	0-2	6	1.33	1.37
2002 San Diego	NL	65	0	0	15	69.0	318	74	50	42	13	2	2	3	34	8	66	6	1	4	7	.364	0	0-6	12	5.39	5.48
2003 Oakland	AL	14	0	0	1	16.0	71	14	8	8	4	0	0	3	11	1	9	0	0	0	1	.000	0	0-0	2	6.69	4.50
2004 Montreal	NL	19	0	0	6	25.0	112	26	16	15	5	3	1	0	13	4	22	1	0	1	2	.333	0	0-0	2	5.24	5.40
4 ML YEARS		121	0	0	27	136.1	600	129	80	69	24	7	3	7	63	14	116	7	1	7	10	.412	0	0-8	22	4.57	4.56

Bob File

Pitches: R **Bats:** R **Pos:** RP-24   **Ht:** 6'4" **Wt:** 215 **Born:** 1/28/1977 **Age:** 28

Year Team	Lg	G	GS	CG	GF	IP	BFP	H	R	ER	HR	SH	SF	HB	TBB	IBB	SO	WP	Bk	W	L	Pct	ShO	Sv-Op	Hld	ERC	ERA
2004 Syracuse*	AAA	24	0	0	17	35.0	145	31	11	10	2	0	0	2	7	0	11	2	0	3	3	.500	0	7--	-	2.60	2.57
2001 Toronto	AL	60	0	0	18	74.1	299	57	28	27	6	3	1	7	29	8	38	2	0	5	3	.625	0	0-2	6	2.98	3.27
2002 Toronto	AL	5	0	0	3	3.1	20	8	7	7	0	1	0	0	2	0	2	0	0	0	1	.000	0	0-0	1	13.02	18.90
2004 Toronto	AL	24	0	0	6	33.2	154	45	19	18	4	0	4	2	12	2	15	1	0	1	0	1.000	0	0-0	2	6.28	4.81
3 ML YEARS		89	0	0	27	111.1	473	110	54	52	10	4	5	9	43	10	55	3	0	6	4	.600	0	0-2	9	4.17	4.20

Steve Finley

Bats: L **Throws:** L **Pos:** CF-157; PH-3; DH-1   **Ht:** 6'2" **Wt:** 195 **Born:** 3/12/1965 **Age:** 40

							BATTING											BASERUNNING				AVERAGES		
Year Team	Lg	G	AB	H	2B	3B	HR	(Hm | Rd)	TB	R	RBI	RC	TBB	IBB	SO	HBP	SH	SF	SB	CS	SB%	GDP	Avg	OBP	Slg
1989 Baltimore	AL	81	217	54	5	2	2	(0 | 2)	69	35	25	23	15	1	30	1	6	2	17	3	.85	3	.249	.298	.318
1990 Baltimore	AL	142	464	119	16	4	3	(1 | 2)	152	46	37	47	32	3	53	2	10	5	22	9	.71	8	.256	.304	.328
1991 Houston	NL	159	596	170	28	10	8	(0 | 8)	242	84	54	80	42	5	65	2	10	6	34	18	.65	8	.285	.331	.406
1992 Houston	NL	162	607	177	29	13	5	(5 | 0)	247	84	55	93	58	6	63	3	16	2	44	9	.83	10	.292	.355	.407
1993 Houston	NL	142	545	145	15	13	8	(1 | 7)	210	69	44	64	28	1	65	3	6	3	19	6	.76	8	.266	.304	.385
1994 Houston	NL	94	373	103	16	5	11	(4 | 7)	162	64	33	54	28	0	52	2	13	1	13	7	.65	3	.276	.329	.434
1995 San Diego	NL	139	562	167	23	8	10	(4 | 6)	236	104	44	90	59	5	62	3	4	2	36	12	.75	8	.297	.366	.420
1996 San Diego	NL	161	655	195	45	9	30	(15 | 15)	348	126	95	117	56	5	87	4	1	5	22	8	.73	20	.298	.354	.531
1997 San Diego	NL	143	560	146	26	5	28	(5 | 23)	266	101	92	84	43	2	92	3	2	7	15	3	.83	10	.261	.313	.475
1998 San Diego	NL	159	619	154	40	6	14	(8 | 6)	248	92	67	76	45	0	103	3	3	4	12	3	.80	9	.249	.301	.401
1999 Arizona	NL	156	590	156	32	10	34	(17 | 17)	310	100	103	105	63	7	94	3	2	5	8	4	.67	4	.264	.336	.525
2000 Arizona	NL	152	539	151	27	5	35	(17 | 18)	293	100	96	104	65	7	87	8	2	9	12	6	.67	9	.280	.361	.544
2001 Arizona	NL	140	495	136	27	4	14	(6 | 8)	213	66	73	71	47	9	67	1	2	3	11	7	.61	8	.275	.337	.430
2002 Arizona	NL	150	505	145	24	4	25	(14 | 11)	252	82	89	94	65	7	73	3	1	3	16	4	.80	10	.287	.370	.499
2003 Arizona	NL	147	516	148	24	10	22	(10 | 12)	258	82	70	85	57	4	94	6	0	3	15	8	.65	6	.287	.363	.500
2004 Ari-LA	NL	162	628	170	28	1	36	(23 | 13)	308	92	94	86	61	1	82	1	9	7	9	7	.56	14	.271	.333	.490
2004 Arizona	NL	104	404	111	16	1	23	(14 | 9)	198	61	48	52	40	1	52	1	6	5	8	4	.67	9	.275	.338	.490
2004 Los Angeles	NL	58	224	59	12	0	13	(9 | 4)	110	31	46	34	21	0	30	0	3	2	1	3	.25	5	.263	.324	.491
16 ML YEARS		2289	8471	2336	405	109	285	(132 | 153)	3814	1327	1071	1273	764	63	1169	48	87	67	305	114	.73	138	.276	.337	.450

John Flaherty

Bats: R **Throws:** R **Pos:** C-46; PR-2; PH-1   **Ht:** 6'1" **Wt:** 196 **Born:** 10/21/1967 **Age:** 37

							BATTING											BASERUNNING				AVERAGES		
Year Team	Lg	G	AB	H	2B	3B	HR	(Hm	Rd)	TB	R	RBI	RC	TBB	IBB	SO	HBP	SH	SF	SB	CS	SB%	GDP	Avg	OBP	Slg
1992 Boston	AL	35	66	13	2	0	0	(0	0)	15	3	2	3	3	0	7	0	1	1	0	0	-	0	.197	.229	.227
1993 Boston	AL	13	25	3	2	0	0	(0	0)	5	3	2	1	2	0	6	1	1	0	0	0	-	0	.120	.214	.200
1994 Detroit	AL	34	40	6	1	0	0	(0	0)	7	2	4	0	1	0	11	0	2	1	0	1	.00	1	.150	.167	.175
1995 Detroit	AL	112	354	86	22	1	11	(6	5)	143	39	40	39	18	0	47	3	8	2	0	0	-	8	.243	.284	.404
1996 Det-SD	AL	119	416	118	24	0	13	(8	5)	181	40	64	53	17	2	61	3	4	4	3	3	.50	13	.284	.314	.435
1997 San Diego	NL	129	439	120	21	1	9	(4	5)	170	38	46	52	33	7	62	0	2	2	4	4	.50	11	.273	.323	.387
1998 Tampa Bay	AL	91	304	63	11	0	3	(1	2)	83	21	24	17	22	0	46	1	4	3	0	5	.00	9	.207	.261	.273
1999 Tampa Bay	AL	117	446	124	19	0	14	(3	11)	185	53	71	54	19	0	64	6	1	10	0	2	.00	14	.278	.310	.415
2000 Tampa Bay	AL	109	394	103	15	0	10	(7	3)	148	36	39	41	20	2	57	0	2	2	0	0	-	11	.261	.296	.376
2001 Tampa Bay	AL	78	248	59	17	1	4	(3	1)	90	20	29	22	10	1	33	1	5	1	1	0	1.00	6	.238	.269	.363
2002 Tampa Bay	AL	76	281	73	20	0	4	(4	0)	105	27	33	32	15	0	50	1	2	4	2	2	.50	6	.260	.296	.374
2003 New York	AL	40	105	28	8	0	4	(0	4)	48	16	14	12	4	1	19	1	5	1	0	0	-	4	.267	.297	.457
2004 New York	AL	47	127	32	9	0	6	(6	0)	59	11	16	13	5	2	25	1	2	0	0	2	.00	5	.252	.286	.465
1996 Detroit	AL	47	152	38	12	0	4	(2	2)	62	18	23	17	8	1	25	1	3	1	1	0	1.00	5	.250	.290	.408
1996 San Diego	NL	72	264	80	12	0	9	(6	3)	119	22	41	36	9	1	36	2	1	3	2	3	.40	8	.303	.327	.451
13 ML YEARS		1000	3245	828	171	3	78	(42	36)	1239	309	384	339	169	15	488	18	39	31	10	19	.34	93	.255	.293	.382

Jose Flores

Bats: R **Throws:** R **Pos:** PR-6; PH-2; 2B-1; 3B-1   **Ht:** 5'11" **Wt:** 180 **Born:** 6/28/1973 **Age:** 32

							BATTING											BASERUNNING				AVERAGES		
Year Team	Lg	G	AB	H	2B	3B	HR	(Hm	Rd)	TB	R	RBI	RC	TBB	IBB	SO	HBP	SH	SF	SB	CS	SB%	GDP	Avg	OBP	Slg
1994 Batavia	A-	68	229	58	7	3	0	(-	-)	71	41	16	33	41	0	31	6	2	2	23	8	.74	3	.253	.378	.310
1995 Clearwater	A+	49	185	41	4	3	1	(-	-)	54	25	19	16	15	0	27	4	7	1	12	5	.71	4	.222	.293	.292
1995 Piedmont	A	61	186	49	7	0	0	(-	-)	56	22	19	20	24	0	29	3	5	4	11	8	.58	6	.263	.350	.301
1996 Scrtn/WlksBr	AAA	26	70	18	1	0	0	(-	-)	19	10	3	8	12	0	10	2	1	1	0	1	.00	2	.257	.376	.271
1996 Clearwater	A+	84	281	64	6	5	1	(-	-)	83	39	39	30	34	0	42	3	5	1	15	2	.88	6	.228	.317	.295
1997 Scrtn/WlksBr	AAA	71	204	51	14	1	1	(-	-)	70	32	18	26	28	1	51	2	5	2	3	1	.75	2	.250	.343	.343
1998 Scrtn/WlksBr	AAA	98	345	104	18	2	6	(-	-)	144	53	34	58	49	1	45	2	7	2	12	6	.67	7	.301	.389	.417
1999 Scrtn/WlksBr	AAA	64	228	56	6	2	0	(-	-)	66	35	14	31	37	1	43	7	4	0	13	3	.81	1	.246	.368	.289
1999 Tacoma	AAA	42	143	44	6	1	3	(-	-)	61	33	15	32	37	1	23	5	2	2	4	3	.57	2	.308	.460	.427
2000 New Haven	AA	12	38	7	3	0	0	(-	-)	10	5	1	4	7	0	5	2	1	0	0	0	-	0	.184	.340	.263
2000 Tacoma	AAA	91	328	93	14	4	3	(-	-)	124	53	30	54	53	0	44	5	1	3	19	7	.73	6	.284	.388	.378
2001 Co Springs	AAA	100	316	93	21	5	2	(-	-)	130	61	36	56	48	1	57	3	4	1	8	2	.80	1	.294	.391	.411
2002 Sacramento	AAA	95	363	111	19	1	2	(-	-)	138	64	38	60	56	1	53	3	7	6	16	4	.80	11	.306	.397	.380
2003 Sacramento	AAA	107	370	101	12	2	2	(-	-)	123	72	38	53	62	1	48	3	5	5	2	2	.50	16	.273	.377	.332
2004 Las Vegas	AAA	99	319	100	20	1	7	(-	-)	143	64	51	61	49	1	30	4	1	4	6	2	.75	6	.313	.407	.448
2002 Oakland	AL	7	3	0	0	0	0	(0	0)	0	2	0	0	1	0	0	1	0	0	1	1	.50	0	.000	.400	.000
2004 Los Angeles	NL	9	4	1	0	0	0	(0	0)	1	0	0	0	1	0	2	0	0	0	0	0	-	0	.250	.400	.250
2 ML YEARS		16	7	1	0	0	0	(0	0)	1	2	0	0	2	0	2	1	0	0	1	1	.50	0	.143	.400	.143

Randy Flores

Pitches: L **Bats:** L **Pos:** RP-8; SP-1   **Ht:** 6'0" **Wt:** 180 **Born:** 7/31/1975 **Age:** 29

		HOW MUCH HE PITCHED						WHAT HE GAVE UP											THE RESULTS						
Year Team	Lg	G	GS	CG	GF	IP	BFP	H	R	ER	HR	SH	SF	HB	TBB	IBB	SO	WP	Bk	W	L	Pct	ShO	Sv-Op	Hld	ERC	ERA
1997 Oneonta	A-	13	13	2	0	74.2	308	64	32	27	3	0	1	4	23	1	70	5	1	4	4	.500	1	0- -	-	2.77	3.25
1998 Tampa	A+	5	5	0	0	23.2	115	28	23	17	2	2	2	1	16	2	15	0	4	1	2	.333	0	0- -	-	6.07	6.46
1998 Greensboro	A	21	20	2	0	130.2	535	119	48	38	6	2	3	7	33	0	139	2	4	12	7	.632	1	0- -	-	2.92	2.62
1999 Tampa	A+	21	20	1	1	135.0	555	118	56	43	4	4	4	7	38	0	99	5	0	11	4	.733	1	0- -	-	2.71	2.87
1999 Norwich	AA	4	4	0	0	25.0	120	32	20	18	0	2	0	1	11	1	19	1	1	0	1	.000	0	0- -	-	4.97	6.48
2000 Norwich	AA	31	20	3	3	141.0	601	138	64	46	8	4	2	5	59	1	97	8	1	10	9	.526	0	1- -	-	3.92	2.94
2000 Columbus	AAA	4	4	0	0	23.1	117	43	21	19	3	0	0	0	7	0	16	1	1	2	2	.333	0	0- -	-	9.21	7.33
2001 Columbus	AAA	3	0	0	1	5.2	23	5	4	3	2	0	0	0	2	0	4	1	0	0	1	.000	0	0- -	-	5.04	4.76
2001 Norwich	AA	25	25	3	0	158.2	677	156	64	49	15	5	3	1	63	0	115	3	3	14	6	.700	2	0- -	-	3.90	2.78
2002 Oklahoma	AAA	15	0	0	6	20.1	89	22	13	13	1	1	0	1	5	1	16	1	0	1	1	.500	0	1- -	-	3.59	5.75
2002 Co Springs	AAA	7	7	0	0	35.2	156	36	15	13	1	0	2	2	18	0	27	0	0	2	2	.500	0	0- -	-	4.32	3.28

Year Team	Lg	G	GS	CG	GF	IP	BFP	H	R	ER	HR	SH	SF	HB	TBB	IBB	SO	WP	Bk	W	L	Pct	ShO	Sv-Op	Hld	ERC	ERA
2003 Co Springs	AAA	28	24	0	1	142.2	651	156	89	79	16	8	4	10	67	4	116	8	1	10	8	.556	0	0- -	-	5.18	4.98
2004 Memphis	AAA	36	15	1	4	122.2	512	115	60	52	10	8	4	3	46	1	99	1	0	5	7	.417	1	2- -	-	3.66	3.82
2002 Tex-Col		28	2	0	9	29.0	140	40	26	24	7	2	2	3	16	3	14	4	0	0	2	.000	0	1-2	2	8.69	7.45
2004 St Louis	NL	9	1	0	3	14.0	57	13	3	3	0	1	1	3	3	1	7	0	0	1	0	1.000	0	0-0	0	3.15	1.93
2002 Texas	AL	20	0	0	5	12.0	52	11	7	6	2	1	2	0	8	2	7	3	0	0	0	-	0	1-2	2	5.07	4.50
2002 Colorado	NL	8	2	0	4	17.0	88	29	19	18	5	1	0	3	8	1	7	1	0	0	2	.000	0	0-0	0	11.52	9.53
2 ML YEARS		37	3	0	12	43.0	197	53	29	27	7	3	3	6	19	4	21	4	0	1	2	.333	0	1-2	2	6.74	5.65

Cliff Floyd

Bats: L Throws: R Pos: LF-108; PH-5; DH-1   Ht: 6'4" Wt: 260 Born: 12/5/1972 Age: 32

Year Team	Lg	G	AB	H	2B	3B	HR	(Hm	Rd)	TB	R	RBI	RC	TBB	IBB	SO	HBP	SH	SF	SB	CS	SB%	GDP	Avg	OBP	Slg
2004 St. Lucie*	A+	1	4	2	0	0	0	(-	-)	2	2	1	0	0	0	2	0	0	0	0	0	-	0	.500	.500	.500
1993 Montreal	NL	10	31	7	0	0	1	(0	1)	10	3	2	2	0	0	9	0	0	0	0	0	-	0	.226	.226	.323
1994 Montreal	NL	100	334	94	19	4	4	(2	2)	133	43	41	46	24	0	63	3	2	3	10	3	.77	3	.281	.332	.398
1995 Montreal	NL	29	69	9	1	0	1	(1	0)	13	6	8	2	7	0	22	1	0	0	3	0	1.00	1	.130	.221	.188
1996 Montreal	NL	117	227	55	15	4	6	(3	3)	96	29	26	35	30	1	52	5	1	3	7	1	.88	3	.242	.340	.423
1997 Florida	NL	61	137	32	9	1	6	(2	4)	61	23	19	23	24	0	33	2	1	1	6	2	.75	3	.234	.354	.445
1998 Florida	NL	153	588	166	45	3	22	(10	12)	283	85	90	92	47	7	112	3	0	3	27	14	.66	10	.282	.337	.481
1999 Florida	NL	69	251	76	19	1	11	(4	7)	130	37	49	45	30	5	47	2	0	2	5	6	.45	8	.303	.379	.518
2000 Florida	NL	121	420	126	30	0	22	(13	9)	222	75	91	88	50	5	82	8	0	9	24	3	.89	4	.300	.378	.529
2001 Florida	NL	149	555	176	44	4	31	(16	15)	321	123	103	121	59	19	101	10	0	5	18	3	.86	9	.317	.390	.578
2002 Fla-Mon-Bos		146	520	150	43	0	28	(13	15)	277	86	79	92	76	19	106	10	0	3	15	5	.75	6	.288	.388	.533
2003 New York	NL	108	365	106	25	2	18	(10	8)	189	57	68	69	51	2	66	3	0	6	3	0	1.00	10	.290	.376	.518
2004 New York	NL	113	396	103	26	0	18	(7	11)	183	55	63	63	47	6	103	11	0	3	11	4	.73	8	.260	.352	.462
2002 Florida	NL	84	296	85	20	0	18	(7	11)	159	49	57	64	58	18	68	7	0	1	10	5	.67	1	.287	.414	.537
2002 Montreal	NL	15	53	11	2	0	3	(3	0)	22	7	4	2	3	1	10	1	0	0	1	0	1.00	0	.208	.263	.415
2002 Boston	AL	47	171	54	21	0	7	(3	4)	96	30	18	26	15	0	28	2	0	2	4	0	1.00	6	.316	.374	.561
12 ML YEARS		1176	3893	1100	276	19	168	(81	87)	1918	622	639	678	445	64	796	58	4	38	129	41	.76	65	.283	.362	.493

Gavin Floyd

Pitches: R Bats: R Pos: SP-4; RP-2   Ht: 6'4" Wt: 212 Born: 1/27/1983 Age: 22

Year Team	Lg	G	GS	CG	GF	IP	BFP	H	R	ER	HR	SH	SF	HB	TBB	IBB	SO	WP	Bk	W	L	Pct	ShO	Sv-Op	Hld	ERC	ERA
2002 Lakewood	A	27	27	3	0	166.0	671	119	59	51	13	4	1	8	64	0	140	14	0	11	10	.524	0	0- -	-	2.60	2.77
2003 Clearwater	A+	24	20	1	0	138.0	577	128	61	46	9	4	3	7	45	0	115	6	0	7	8	.467	1	0- -	-	3.39	3.00
2004 Reading	AA	20	20	2	0	119.0	496	93	39	34	5	6	5	9	46	1	94	1	2	6	6	.500	1	0- -	-	2.74	2.57
2004 Scrtn/WlksBr	AAA	5	5	0	0	30.2	139	39	20	17	4	2	1	3	9	0	18	3	0	1	3	.250	0	0- -	-	5.91	4.99
2004 Philadelphia	NL	6	4	0	0	28.1	126	25	11	11	1	1	0	5	16	0	24	1	1	2	0	1.000	0	0-0	0	4.33	3.49

Josh Fogg

Pitches: R Bats: R Pos: SP-32   Ht: 6'0" Wt: 202 Born: 12/13/1976 Age: 28

Year Team	Lg	G	GS	CG	GF	IP	BFP	H	R	ER	HR	SH	SF	HB	TBB	IBB	SO	WP	Bk	W	L	Pct	ShO	Sv-Op	Hld	ERC	ERA
2001 Chicago	AL	11	0	0	4	13.1	53	10	3	3	0	0	1	1	3	1	17	0	0	0	0	-	0	0-0	2	1.73	2.03
2002 Pittsburgh	NL	33	33	0	0	194.1	832	199	102	94	28	6	3	8	69	12	113	2	0	12	12	.500	0	0-0	0	4.46	4.35
2003 Pittsburgh	NL	26	26	1	0	142.0	625	166	90	83	22	6	4	9	40	0	71	2	0	10	9	.526	0	0-0	0	5.25	5.26
2004 Pittsburgh	NL	32	32	0	0	178.1	770	193	98	92	17	9	6	8	66	8	82	4	1	11	10	.524	0	0-0	0	4.59	4.64
4 ML YEARS		102	91	1	4	528.0	2280	568	293	272	67	21	14	26	178	21	283	8	1	33	31	.516	0	0-0	2	4.64	4.64

Jesse Foppert

Pitches: R Bats: R Pos: RP-1   Ht: 6'6" Wt: 210 Born: 7/10/1980 Age: 24

Year Team	Lg	G	GS	CG	GF	IP	BFP	H	R	ER	HR	SH	SF	HB	TBB	IBB	SO	WP	Bk	W	L	Pct	ShO	Sv-Op	Hld	ERC	ERA
2001 Salem-Keizer	A-	14	14	0	0	70.0	264	35	18	15	7	0	3	5	23	0	88	4	3	8	1	.889	0	0- -	-	1.65	1.93
2002 Shreveport	AA	11	11	1	0	61.1	249	44	22	19	3	3	1	3	21	0	74	3	0	3	3	.500	0	0- -	-	2.24	2.79
2002 Fresno	AAA	14	14	0	0	79.0	337	71	37	35	12	3	5	3	35	0	109	7	1	3	6	.333	0	0- -	-	4.23	3.99
2003 San Jose	A+	1	1	0	0	3.0	14	5	3	3	0	0	1	0	0	0	3	0	0	0	0	-	0	0- -	-	5.42	9.00
2003 Fresno	AAA	1	1	0	0	5.0	19	3	1	1	0	0	0	1	0	0	9	3	0	0	0	-	0	0- -	-	1.11	1.80
2004 Giants	R	1	1	0	0	1.0	6	3	1	1	0	0	0	0	0	0	2	0	0	0	0	-	0	0- -	-	14.52	9.00
2004 San Jose	A+	4	4	0	0	9.1	33	4	2	2	1	1	1	1	4	0	11	0	0	0	0	-	0	0- -	-	1.99	1.93
2004 Fresno	AAA	4	4	0	0	14.2	66	14	11	9	2	3	1	0	9	0	13	3	0	0	0	-	0	0- -	-	4.91	5.52
2003 San Francisco	NL	23	21	0	0	111.0	500	103	69	62	16	5	9	3	69	4	101	12	0	8	9	.471	0	0-0	0	4.89	5.03
2004 San Francisco	NL	1	0	0	0	1.0	4	1	0	0	0	0	0	0	0	0	2	0	0	0	0	-	0	0-0	0	1.95	0.00
2 ML YEARS		24	21	0	0	112.0	504	104	69	62	16	5	9	3	69	4	103	12	0	8	9	.471	0	0-0	0	4.87	4.98

Ben Ford

Pitches: R Bats: R Pos: RP-19   Ht: 6'7" Wt: 230 Born: 8/15/1975 Age: 29

Year Team	Lg	G	GS	CG	GF	IP	BFP	H	R	ER	HR	SH	SF	HB	TBB	IBB	SO	WP	Bk	W	L	Pct	ShO	Sv-Op	Hld	ERC	ERA
2004 Indianapolis*	AAA	32	1	0	23	42.2	199	52	25	23	2	0	0	1	21	2	36	3	0	2	2	.500	0	9- -	-	5.26	4.85
1998 Arizona	NL	8	0	0	2	10.0	49	13	12	11	2	0	0	2	3	0	5	1	0	0	0	-	0	0-0	0	6.78	9.90
2000 New York	AL	4	2	0	0	11.0	52	14	11	11	1	0	0	3	7	0	5	0	0	0	1	.000	0	0-0	0	8.38	9.00
2004 Milwaukee	NL	19	0	0	5	24.0	107	25	17	17	4	1	1	2	10	0	13	0	0	1	1	.500	0	0-3	2	5.20	6.38
3 ML YEARS		31	2	0	7	45.0	208	52	40	39	7	1	1	7	20	0	23	1	0	1	2	.333	0	0-3	2	6.30	7.80

Lew Ford

Bats: R **Throws:** R **Pos:** LF-81; CF-46; DH-26; RF-10; PH-3   **Ht:** 6'0" **Wt:** 190 **Born:** 8/12/1976 **Age:** 28

						BATTING														BASERUNNING				AVERAGES		
Year Team	Lg	G	AB	H	2B	3B	HR	(Hm	Rd)	TB	R	RBI	RC	TBB	IBB	SO	HBP	SH	SF	SB	CS	SB%	GDP	Avg	OBP	Slg
1999 Lowell	A-	62	250	70	17	4	7	(-	-)	116	48	34	39	19	1	35	5	0	3	15	2	.88	6	.280	.339	.464
2000 Augusta	A	126	514	162	35	11	9	(-	-)	246	122	74	100	52	3	83	12	3	2	52	4	.93	12	.315	.390	.479
2001 Fort Myers	A+	67	265	79	15	2	2	(-	-)	104	42	24	41	21	3	30	12	1	2	19	9	.68	3	.298	.373	.392
2001 New Britain	AA	62	252	55	9	3	7	(-	-)	91	30	25	25	20	0	35	6	1	2	5	5	.50	4	.218	.289	.361
2002 New Britain	AA	93	373	116	27	2	15	(-	-)	192	81	51	76	49	0	47	8	4	1	17	5	.77	5	.311	.401	.515
2002 Edmonton	AAA	47	193	64	11	2	5	(-	-)	94	40	24	37	13	0	21	6	1	1	11	1	.92	2	.332	.390	.487
2003 Rochester	AAA	53	211	64	18	2	3	(-	-)	95	33	31	32	10	1	28	8	0	1	4	5	.44	1	.303	.357	.450
2004 Rochester	AAA	1	5	1	0	0	0	(-	-)	1	0	0	0	0	0	1	0	0	0	0	0	-	0	.200	.200	.200
2003 Minnesota	AL	34	73	24	7	1	3	(2	1)	42	16	15	16	8	0	9	1	1	0	2	0	1.00	1	.329	.402	.575
2004 Minnesota	AL	154	569	170	31	4	15	(6	9)	254	89	72	101	67	3	75	13	2	7	20	2	.91	15	.299	.381	.446
2 ML YEARS		188	642	194	38	5	18	(8	10)	296	105	87	117	75	3	84	14	3	7	22	2	.92	16	.302	.383	.461

Brook Fordyce

Bats: R **Throws:** R **Pos:** C-51; PH-3; DH-1; PR-1   **Ht:** 6'0" **Wt:** 190 **Born:** 5/7/1970 **Age:** 35

						BATTING														BASERUNNING				AVERAGES		
Year Team	Lg	G	AB	H	2B	3B	HR	(Hm	Rd)	TB	R	RBI	RC	TBB	IBB	SO	HBP	SH	SF	SB	CS	SB%	GDP	Avg	OBP	Slg
1995 New York	NL	4	2	1	1	0	0	(0	0)	2	1	0	1	1	0	0	0	0	0	0	0	-	0	.500	.667	1.000
1996 Cincinnati	NL	4	7	2	1	0	0	(0	0)	3	0	1	2	3	0	1	0	0	0	0	0	-	0	.286	.500	.429
1997 Cincinnati	NL	47	96	20	5	0	1	(1	0)	28	7	8	8	8	1	15	0	0	1	2	0	1.00	0	.208	.267	.292
1998 Cincinnati	NL	57	146	37	9	0	3	(3	0)	55	8	14	16	11	3	28	0	1	0	0	1	.00	2	.253	.306	.377
1999 Chicago	AL	105	333	99	25	1	9	(5	4)	153	36	49	52	21	0	48	3	3	2	2	0	1.00	5	.297	.343	.459
2000 CWS-Bal	AL	93	302	91	18	1	14	(8	6)	153	41	49	51	17	0	50	4	2	5	0	0	-	4	.301	.341	.507
2001 Baltimore	AL	95	292	61	18	0	5	(0	5)	94	30	19	23	21	1	56	3	3	1	1	2	.33	7	.209	.268	.322
2002 Baltimore	AL	56	130	30	8	0	1	(1	0)	41	7	8	11	9	0	19	4	3	0	1	0	1.00	5	.231	.301	.315
2003 Baltimore	AL	108	348	95	12	2	6	(3	3)	129	28	31	31	19	1	44	1	6	2	2	3	.40	10	.273	.311	.371
2004 Tampa Bay	AL	54	151	31	6	0	2	(2	0)	43	14	9	7	9	0	34	2	1	0	0	0	-	3	.205	.259	.285
2000 Chicago	AL	40	125	34	7	1	5	(3	2)	58	18	21	18	6	0	23	2	2	1	0	0	-	1	.272	.313	.464
2000 Baltimore	AL	53	177	57	11	0	9	(5	4)	95	23	28	33	11	0	27	2	0	4	0	0	-	3	.322	.361	.537
10 ML YEARS		623	1807	467	103	4	41	(23	18)	701	172	188	202	119	6	295	17	19	11	8	6	.57	36	.258	.309	.388

Bartolome Fortunato

Pitches: R **Bats:** R **Pos:** RP-18   **Ht:** 6'1" **Wt:** 197 **Born:** 8/24/1974 **Age:** 30

		HOW MUCH HE PITCHED						WHAT HE GAVE UP										THE RESULTS						
Year Team	Lg	G	GS	CG	GF	IP	BFP	H	R	ER	HR	SH	SF	HB	TBB	IBB	SO	WP	Bk	W	L	Pct	ShO	Sv-Op	Hld	ERC	ERA
2000 Princeton	R+	17	5	0	2	46.2	223	56	31	24	4	2	1	4	19	0	51	8	0	3	4	.429	0	1--	-	5.26	4.63
2001 Hudson Val	A-	16	9	0	2	59.2	266	70	35	34	3	1	0	2	29	0	53	11	0	2	5	.286	0	0--	-	5.33	5.13
2002 Bakersfield	A+	25	5	0	0	60.2	263	58	31	27	3	4	2	1	25	0	85	3	2	2	4	.333	0	0--	-	3.55	4.01
2002 Orlando	AA	10	2	0	0	25.2	103	16	7	6	2	1	1	1	11	1	34	1	0	3	0	1.000	0	0--	-	2.20	2.10
2002 Durham	AAA	2	0	0	0	4.1	21	6	3	2	1	0	1	0	2	0	0	0	0	1	0	1.000	0	0--	-	7.56	4.15
2003 Orlando	AA	35	1	0	8	53.0	227	48	25	18	4	5	2	2	20	1	63	1	0	4	2	.667	0	1--	-	3.37	3.06
2003 Durham	AAA	5	4	0	1	21.2	91	15	11	8	3	1	1	0	11	0	20	1	0	1	2	.333	0	0--	-	3.03	3.32
2004 Norfolk	AAA	6	0	0	1	5.1	24	4	2	2	0	0	1	1	3	0	5	0	0	0	0	-	0	0--	-	3.21	3.38
2004 Durham	AAA	34	0	0	24	44.2	182	28	14	12	4	0	0	0	21	1	54	2	1	4	3	.571	0	9--	-	2.27	2.42
2004 TB-NYM		18	0	0	6	26.0	112	24	11	11	3	0	0	0	15	0	25	2	0	1	0	1.000	0	1-2	2	4.57	3.81
2004 Tampa Bay	AL	3	0	0	1	7.1	30	10	3	3	1	0	0	0	2	0	5	1	0	0	0	-	0	0-0	0	6.67	3.68
2004 New York	NL	15	0	0	5	18.2	82	14	8	8	2	0	0	0	13	0	20	1	0	1	0	1.000	0	1-2	2	3.85	3.86

Casey Fossum

Pitches: L **Bats:** L **Pos:** SP-27   **Ht:** 6'1" **Wt:** 165 **Born:** 1/6/1978 **Age:** 27

		HOW MUCH HE PITCHED						WHAT HE GAVE UP										THE RESULTS						
Year Team	Lg	G	GS	CG	GF	IP	BFP	H	R	ER	HR	SH	SF	HB	TBB	IBB	SO	WP	Bk	W	L	Pct	ShO	Sv-Op	Hld	ERC	ERA
2004 El Paso*	AA	2	2	0	0	4.1	19	5	1	1	0	0	0	0	3	0	5	0	0	0	0	-	0	0--	-	2.74	2.08
2004 Tucson*	AAA	3	3	0	0	15.0	59	11	2	1	0	0	2	0	3	0	16	2	0	2	0	1.000	0	0--	-	1.49	0.60
2001 Boston	AL	13	7	0	3	44.1	197	44	26	24	4	0	1	6	20	1	26	1	1	3	2	.600	0	0-0	0	4.70	4.87
2002 Boston	AL	43	12	0	13	106.2	461	113	56	41	12	2	4	4	30	0	101	3	0	5	4	.556	0	1-1	3	4.14	3.46
2003 Boston	AL	19	14	0	2	79.0	346	82	55	48	9	1	3	4	34	0	63	4	0	6	5	.545	0	1-1	0	4.77	5.47
2004 Arizona	NL	27	27	0	0	142.0	652	171	111	105	31	8	4	10	63	5	117	4	2	4	15	.211	0	0-0	0	6.67	6.65
4 ML YEARS		102	60	0	18	372.0	1656	410	248	218	56	11	12	24	147	6	307	12	3	18	26	.409	0	2-2	3	5.27	5.27

Keith Foulke

Pitches: R **Bats:** R **Pos:** RP-72   **Ht:** 6'0" **Wt:** 210 **Born:** 10/19/1972 **Age:** 32

		HOW MUCH HE PITCHED						WHAT HE GAVE UP										THE RESULTS						
Year Team	Lg	G	GS	CG	GF	IP	BFP	H	R	ER	HR	SH	SF	HB	TBB	IBB	SO	WP	Bk	W	L	Pct	ShO	Sv-Op	Hld	ERC	ERA
1997 SF-CWS		27	8	0	5	73.1	326	88	52	52	13	3	1	4	23	2	54	1	0	4	5	.444	0	3-6	5	5.68	6.38
1998 Chicago	AL	54	0	0	18	65.1	267	51	31	30	9	2	2	4	20	3	57	3	1	3	2	.600	0	1-2	13	2.95	4.13
1999 Chicago	AL	67	0	0	31	105.1	411	72	28	26	11	3	0	3	21	4	123	1	0	3	3	.500	0	9-13	22	1.80	2.22
2000 Chicago	AL	72	0	0	58	88.0	350	66	31	29	9	5	2	2	22	2	91	1	0	3	1	.750	0	34-39	3	2.28	2.97
2001 Chicago	AL	72	0	0	69	81.0	322	57	21	21	3	4	1	8	22	1	75	1	0	4	9	.308	0	42-45	0	2.06	2.33
2002 Chicago	AL	65	0	0	35	77.2	306	65	26	25	7	7	2	2	13	2	58	1	0	4	4	.333	0	11-14	8	2.38	2.90
2003 Oakland	AL	72	0	0	67	86.2	338	57	21	20	10	1	1	7	20	2	88	0	1	9	1	.900	0	43-48	0	2.07	2.08
2004 Boston	AL	72	0	0	61	83.0	333	63	22	20	8	2	4	6	15	5	79	3	0	5	3	.625	0	32-39	0	2.14	2.17
1997 San Francisco	NL	11	8	0	0	44.2	209	60	41	41	9	2	1	0	18	1	33	1	0	1	5	.167	0	0-1	0	7.41	8.26
1997 Chicago	AL	16	0	0	5	28.2	117	28	11	11	4	1	1	0	5	1	21	0	0	3	0	1.000	0	3-5	5	3.27	3.45
8 ML YEARS		501	8	0	344	660.1	2653	519	232	223	70	22	11	36	156	21	625	11	2	33	28	.541	0	175-206	51	2.53	3.04

Andy Fox

Bats: L **Throws:** R **Pos:** PH-24; 2B-6; PR-6; 3B-5; SS-5; 1B-1; LF-1; RF-1; DH-1   **Ht:** 6'4" **Wt:** 202 **Born:** 1/12/1971 **Age:** 34

							BATTING													BASERUNNING				AVERAGES		
Year Team	Lg	G	AB	H	2B	3B	HR	(Hm	Rd)	TB	R	RBI	RC	TBB	IBB	SO	HBP	SH	SF	SB	CS	SB%	GDP	Avg	OBP	Slg
2004 Oklahoma*	AAA	34	125	38	10	0	1	(-	-)	51	22	13	20	14	1	25	4	0	0	1	2	.33	0	.304	.392	.408
1996 New York	AL	113	189	37	4	0	3	(1	2)	50	26	13	15	20	0	28	1	9	0	11	3	.79	2	.196	.276	.265
1997 New York	AL	22	31	7	1	0	0	(0	0)	8	13	1	3	7	0	9	0	2	0	2	1	.67	1	.226	.368	.258
1998 Arizona	NL	139	502	139	21	6	9	(5	4)	199	67	44	74	43	0	97	18	0	1	14	7	.67	2	.277	.355	.396
1999 Arizona	NL	99	274	70	12	2	6	(4	2)	104	34	33	38	33	10	61	9	1	3	4	1	.80	4	.255	.351	.380
2000 Ari-Fla	NL	100	250	58	8	2	4	(2	2)	82	29	20	25	22	4	53	3	0	0	10	4	.71	2	.232	.302	.328
2001 Florida	NL	54	81	15	0	1	3	(3	0)	26	8	7	9	15	1	17	2	0	0	1	0	1.00	2	.185	.327	.321
2002 Florida	NL	133	435	109	14	5	4	(3	1)	145	55	41	58	49	6	94	10	5	3	31	7	.82	9	.251	.338	.333
2003 Florida	NL	70	108	21	5	1	0	(0	0)	28	12	8	8	7	0	29	4	1	0	1	2	.33	2	.194	.269	.259
2004 Mon-Tex	NL	46	55	5	0	0	1	(0	1)	8	4	1	0	1	0	19	0	0	0	0	0	-	1	.091	.107	.145
2000 Arizona	NL	31	86	18	4	0	1	(1	0)	25	10	10	5	4	1	16	0	0	0	2	1	.67	1	.209	.244	.291
2000 Florida	NL	69	164	40	4	2	3	(1	2)	57	19	10	20	18	3	37	3	0	0	8	3	.73	1	.244	.330	.348
2004 Montreal	NL	34	43	4	0	0	1	(0	1)	7	2	1	0	0	0	16	0	0	0	0	0	-	1	.093	.093	.163
2004 Texas	AL	12	12	1	0	0	0	(0	0)	1	2	0	0	1	0	3	0	0	0	0	0	-	0	.083	.154	.083
9 ML YEARS		776	1925	461	65	17	30	(18	12)	650	248	168	230	197	21	407	47	18	7	74	25	.75	25	.239	.324	.338

Chad Fox

Pitches: R **Bats:** R **Pos:** RP-12   **Ht:** 6'3" **Wt:** 206 **Born:** 9/3/1970 **Age:** 34

		HOW MUCH HE PITCHED						WHAT HE GAVE UP										THE RESULTS						
Year Team	Lg	G	GS	CG	GF	IP	BFP	H	R	ER	HR	SH	SF	HB	TBB	IBB	SO	WP	Bk	W	L	Pct	ShO	Sv-Op	Hld	ERC	ERA
1997 Atlanta	NL	30	0	0	8	27.1	120	24	12	10	4	0	0	0	16	0	28	4	0	0	1	.000	0	0-1	7	4.44	3.29
1998 Milwaukee	NL	49	0	0	12	57.0	242	56	27	25	4	6	0	1	20	0	64	5	0	1	4	.200	0	0-2	20	3.66	3.95
1999 Milwaukee	NL	6	0	0	2	6.2	36	11	8	8	1	0	0	1	4	0	12	1	1	0	0	-	0	0-0	1	9.96	10.80
2001 Milwaukee	NL	65	0	0	9	66.2	287	44	16	14	6	2	1	5	36	7	80	5	1	5	2	.714	0	2-4	20	2.75	1.89
2002 Milwaukee	NL	3	0	0	1	4.2	25	6	3	3	0	1	0	0	5	1	3	0	0	1	0	1.000	0	0-0	1	7.03	5.79
2003 Bos-Fla	NL	38	0	0	13	43.1	198	35	16	15	3	5	5	1	31	4	46	6	0	3	3	.500	0	3-5	7	3.80	3.12
2004 Florida	NL	12	0	0	1	10.2	49	9	8	8	1	0	0	1	8	0	17	1	0	1	0	1.000	0	0-2	5	4.88	6.75
2003 Boston	AL	17	0	0	10	18.0	93	19	10	9	2	2	1	1	17	2	19	1	0	1	2	.333	0	3-5	6	6.42	4.50
2003 Florida	AL	21	0	0	3	25.1	105	16	6	6	1	3	4	0	14	2	27	5	0	2	1	.667	0	0-0	7	2.18	2.13
7 ML YEARS		203	0	0	45	216.1	957	185	90	83	19	14	6	9	120	12	250	22	2	10	11	.476	0	5-14	60	3.79	3.45

Jeff Francis

Pitches: L **Bats:** L **Pos:** SP-7   **Ht:** 6'5" **Wt:** 200 **Born:** 1/8/1981 **Age:** 24

		HOW MUCH HE PITCHED						WHAT HE GAVE UP										THE RESULTS						
Year Team	Lg	G	GS	CG	GF	IP	BFP	H	R	ER	HR	SH	SF	HB	TBB	IBB	SO	WP	Bk	W	L	Pct	ShO	Sv-Op	Hld	ERC	ERA
2002 Tri-City	A-	4	3	0	0	10.2	40	5	0	0	0	0	0	1	4	0	16	0	0	0	0	-	0	0--	-	1.33	0.00
2002 Asheville	A	4	4	0	0	20.0	16	16	6	4	2	2	0	2	4	0	23	0	0	0	0	-	0	0--	-	15.60	1.80
2003 Visalia	A+	27	27	2	0	160.2	648	135	66	62	8	4	5	5	45	1	153	6	0	12	9	.571	2	0--	-	2.60	3.47
2004 Tulsa	AA	17	17	1	0	113.2	435	73	26	25	9	4	1	5	22	0	147	2	0	13	1	.929	1	0--	-	1.62	1.98
2004 Co Springs	AAA	7	7	0	0	41.0	165	35	16	13	3	0	1	4	7	0	49	2	0	3	2	.600	0	0--	-	2.66	2.85
2004 Colorado	NL	7	7	0	0	36.2	164	42	22	21	8	2	1	1	13	1	32	2	0	3	2	.600	0	0-0	0	5.62	5.15

Frank Francisco

Pitches: R **Bats:** R **Pos:** RP-45   **Ht:** 6'2" **Wt:** 180 **Born:** 9/11/1979 **Age:** 25

		HOW MUCH HE PITCHED						WHAT HE GAVE UP										THE RESULTS						
Year Team	Lg	G	GS	CG	GF	IP	BFP	H	R	ER	HR	SH	SF	HB	TBB	IBB	SO	WP	Bk	W	L	Pct	ShO	Sv-Op	Hld	ERC	ERA
2002 Sarasota	A+	16	16	0	0	53.0	217	33	16	15	1	3	5	4	27	0	58	4	0	1	5	.167	0	0--	-	2.28	2.55
2002 Winstn-Salm	A+	6	6	0	0	25.2	120	31	23	23	3	1	0	1	18	0	25	4	2	0	4	.000	0	0--	-	7.12	8.06
2002 Trenton	AA	9	0	0	1	16.0	77	10	13	10	0	1	0	2	16	1	18	3	0	2	2	.500	0	0--	-	3.67	5.63
2003 Winstn-Salm	A+	16	16	1	0	78.1	332	59	40	31	7	1	4	6	36	0	67	4	1	7	3	.700	1	0--	-	3.16	3.56
2003 Frisco	AA	7	6	0	0	35.1	167	43	33	33	5	0	4	4	18	1	22	0	0	2	3	.400	0	0--	-	6.58	8.41
2004 Frisco	AA	15	0	0	14	17.2	72	7	6	5	1	0	0	2	10	1	30	4	1	1	3	.250	0	6--	-	1.66	2.55
2004 Texas	AL	45	0	0	7	51.1	216	36	19	19	4	2	1	3	28	2	60	4	1	5	1	.833	0	0-3	10	3.04	3.33

John Franco

Pitches: L **Bats:** L **Pos:** RP-52   **Ht:** 5'10" **Wt:** 185 **Born:** 9/17/1960 **Age:** 44

		HOW MUCH HE PITCHED						WHAT HE GAVE UP										THE RESULTS						
Year Team	Lg	G	GS	CG	GF	IP	BFP	H	R	ER	HR	SH	SF	HB	TBB	IBB	SO	WP	Bk	W	L	Pct	ShO	Sv-Op	Hld	ERC	ERA
1984 Cincinnati	NL	54	0	0	30	79.1	335	74	28	23	3	4	4	2	36	4	55	2	0	6	2	.750	0	4-9	1	3.58	2.61
1985 Cincinnati	NL	67	0	0	33	99.0	407	83	27	24	5	11	1	1	40	8	61	4	0	12	3	.800	0	12-15	1	2.86	2.18
1986 Cincinnati	NL	74	0	0	52	101.0	429	90	40	33	7	8	3	2	44	12	84	4	2	6	6	.500	0	29-38	1	3.30	2.94
1987 Cincinnati	NL	68	0	0	60	82.0	344	76	26	23	6	5	2	0	27	6	61	1	0	8	5	.615	0	32-41	0	3.10	2.52
1988 Cincinnati	NL	70	0	0	61	86.0	336	60	18	15	3	5	1	0	27	3	46	1	2	6	6	.500	0	39-42	0	1.82	1.57
1989 Cincinnati	NL	60	0	0	50	80.2	345	77	35	28	3	7	3	0	36	8	60	3	2	4	8	.333	0	32-39	0	3.42	3.12
1990 New York	NL	55	0	0	48	67.2	287	66	22	19	4	3	1	0	21	2	56	7	2	5	3	.625	0	33-39	0	3.24	2.53
1991 New York	NL	52	0	0	48	55.1	247	61	27	18	2	3	0	1	18	4	45	6	0	5	9	.357	0	30-35	0	3.73	2.93
1992 New York	NL	31	0	0	30	33.0	128	24	6	6	1	0	2	0	11	2	20	0	0	6	2	.750	0	15-17	0	2.00	1.64
1993 New York	NL	35	0	0	30	36.1	172	46	24	21	6	4	1	1	19	3	29	5	0	4	3	.571	0	10-17	0	6.62	5.20
1994 New York	NL	47	0	0	43	50.0	216	47	20	15	2	1	1	0	19	0	42	1	0	1	4	.200	0	30-36	0	3.27	2.70
1995 New York	NL	48	0	0	41	51.2	213	48	17	14	4	4	1	0	17	2	41	0	0	5	3	.625	0	29-36	0	3.26	2.44
1996 New York	NL	51	0	0	44	54.0	235	54	15	11	2	6	0	0	21	0	48	2	0	4	3	.571	0	28-36	0	3.53	1.83
1997 New York	NL	59	0	0	53	60.0	244	49	18	17	3	5	1	1	20	2	53	6	0	5	3	.625	0	36-42	0	2.57	2.55
1998 New York	NL	61	0	0	54	64.2	289	66	28	26	4	4	5	4	29	7	59	2	0	0	8	.000	0	38-46	0	4.11	3.62
1999 New York	NL	46	0	0	34	40.2	182	40	14	13	1	3	1	2	19	1	41	0	0	0	2	.000	0	19-21	1	3.77	2.88
2000 New York	NL	62	0	0	14	55.2	239	46	24	21	6	3	0	2	26	6	56	2	0	5	4	.556	0	4-4	20	3.36	3.40
2001 New York	NL	58	0	0	16	53.1	232	55	25	24	8	4	0	0	19	2	50	1	0	6	2	.750	0	2-7	17	4.50	4.05

		HOW MUCH HE PITCHED		WHAT HE GAVE UP			THE RESULTS		
Year Team	Lg	G GS CG GF	IP BFP	H R ER HR SH SF HB	TBB IBB SO WP Bk	W L Pct ShO	Sv-Op	Hld	ERC ERA
2003 New York	NL	38 0 0 13	34.1 148	35 11 10 5 1 1 1	13 2 16 2 0	0 3 .000 0	2-3	4	4.48 2.62
2004 New York	NL	52 0 0 16	46.0 207	46 28 27 6 2 2 1	24 2 36 2 0	2 7 .222 0	0-1	11	4.74 5.28
20 ML YEARS		1088 0 0 770	1230.2 5235	1143 453 388 81 82 31 21	486 76 959 54 9	90 86 .511 0	424-524	66	3.40 2.84

Julio Franco

Bats: R **Throws:** R **Pos:** 1B-84; PH-50; DH-1   **Ht:** 6'1" **Wt:** 188 **Born:** 8/23/1958 **Age:** 46

		BATTING														BASERUNNING				AVERAGES		
Year Team	Lg	G	AB	H	2B	3B	HR	(Hm Rd)	TB	R	RBI	RC	TBB	IBB	SO	HBP	SH	SF	SB	CS	SB% GDP	Avg OBP Slg
1982 Philadelphia	NL	16	29	8	1	0	0	(0 0)	9	3	3	2	2	1	4	0	1	0	0	2	.00 1	.276 .323 .310
1983 Cleveland	AL	149	560	153	24	8	8	(6 2)	217	68	80	62	27	1	50	2	3	6	32	12	.73 21	.273 .306 .388
1984 Cleveland	AL	160	658	188	22	5	3	(1 2)	229	82	79	72	43	1	68	6	1	10	19	10	.66 23	.286 .331 .348
1985 Cleveland	AL	160	636	183	33	4	6	(3 3)	242	97	90	78	54	2	74	4	0	9	13	9	.59 26	.288 .343 .381
1986 Cleveland	AL	149	599	183	30	5	10	(4 6)	253	80	74	76	32	1	66	0	0	5	10	7	.59 28	.306 .338 .422
1987 Cleveland	AL	128	495	158	24	3	8	(5 3)	212	86	52	81	57	2	56	3	0	5	32	9	.78 23	.319 .389 .428
1988 Cleveland	AL	152	613	186	23	6	10	(3 7)	251	88	54	89	56	4	72	2	1	4	25	11	.69 17	.303 .361 .409
1989 Texas	AL	150	548	173	31	5	13	(9 4)	253	80	92	93	66	11	69	1	0	6	21	3	.88 27	.316 .386 .462
1990 Texas	AL	157	582	172	27	1	11	(4 7)	234	96	69	94	82	3	83	2	2	2	31	10	.76 12	.296 .383 .402
1991 Texas	AL	146	589	201	27	3	15	(7 8)	279	108	78	113	65	8	78	3	0	2	36	9	.80 13	.341 .408 .474
1992 Texas	AL	35	107	25	7	0	2	(2 0)	38	19	8	12	15	2	17	0	1	0	1	1	.50 3	.234 .328 .355
1993 Texas	AL	144	532	154	31	3	14	(6 8)	233	85	84	83	62	4	95	1	5	7	9	3	.75 16	.289 .360 .438
1994 Chicago	AL	112	433	138	19	2	20	(10 10)	221	72	98	87	62	4	75	5	0	5	8	1	.89 14	.319 .406 .510
1996 Cleveland	AL	112	432	139	20	1	14	(7 7)	203	72	76	79	61	2	82	3	0	3	8	8	.50 14	.322 .407 .470
1997 Cle-Mil	AL	120	430	116	16	1	7	(5 2)	155	68	44	58	69	4	116	1	1	4	15	6	.71 17	.270 .369 .360
1999 Tampa Bay	AL	1	1	0	0	0	0	(0 0)	0	0	0	0	0	0	1	0	0	0	0	0	- 0	.000 .000 .000
2001 Atlanta	NL	25	90	27	4	0	3	(2 1)	40	13	11	14	10	1	20	1	0	0	0	0	- 3	.300 .376 .444
2002 Atlanta	NL	125	338	96	13	1	6	(3 3)	129	51	30	39	39	3	75	1	2	3	5	1	.83 13	.284 .357 .382
2003 Atlanta	NL	103	197	58	12	2	5	(1 4)	89	28	31	31	25	5	43	0	0	1	0	1	.00 8	.294 .372 .452
2004 Atlanta	NL	125	320	99	18	3	6	(5 1)	141	37	57	57	36	4	68	1	1	3	4	2	.67 10	.309 .378 .441
1997 Cleveland	AL	78	289	82	13	1	3	(2 1)	106	46	25	37	38	2	75	0	1	0	8	5	.62 13	.284 .367 .367
1997 Milwaukee	AL	42	141	34	3	0	4	(3 1)	49	22	19	21	31	2	41	1	0	4	7	1	.88 4	.241 .373 .348
20 ML YEARS		2269	8189	2457	382	53	161	(83 78)	3428	1233	1110	1220	863	63	1212	36	18	75	269	105	.72 289	.300 .366 .419

Ryan Franklin

Pitches: R **Bats:** R **Pos:** SP-32   **Ht:** 6'3" **Wt:** 165 **Born:** 3/5/1973 **Age:** 32

		HOW MUCH HE PITCHED		WHAT HE GAVE UP			THE RESULTS		
Year Team	Lg	G GS CG GF	IP BFP	H R ER HR SH SF HB	TBB IBB SO WP Bk	W L Pct ShO	Sv-Op	Hld	ERC ERA
1999 Seattle	AL	6 0 0 2	11.1 51	10 6 6 2 0 0 1	8 1 6 0 0	0 0 - 0	0-0	1	5.52 4.76
2001 Seattle	AL	38 0 0 14	78.1 335	76 32 31 13 1 2 4	24 4 60 2 0	5 1 .833 0	0-1	5	4.08 3.56
2002 Seattle	AL	41 12 0 10	118.2 495	117 62 53 14 5 5 5	22 1 65 0 0	7 5 .583 0	0-1	3	3.40 4.02
2003 Seattle	AL	32 32 2 0	212.0 877	199 93 84 34 8 5 9	61 3 99 1 2	11 13 .458 1	0-0	0	3.90 3.57
2004 Seattle	AL	32 32 2 0	200.1 870	224 116 109 33 2 11 10	61 1 104 0 3	4 16 .200 1	0-0	0	5.08 4.90
5 ML YEARS		149 76 4 26	620.2 2628	626 309 283 96 16 23 29	176 10 334 3 5	27 35 .435 2	0-2	9	4.22 4.10

Wayne Franklin

Pitches: L **Bats:** L **Pos:** RP-41; SP-2   **Ht:** 6'2" **Wt:** 205 **Born:** 3/9/1974 **Age:** 31

		HOW MUCH HE PITCHED		WHAT HE GAVE UP			THE RESULTS		
Year Team	Lg	G GS CG GF	IP BFP	H R ER HR SH SF HB	TBB IBB SO WP Bk	W L Pct ShO	Sv-Op	Hld	ERC ERA
2004 Fresno*	AAA	3 3 0 0	9.1 40	6 4 4 0 1 2 1	4 0 11 0 0	0 2 .000 0	0- -	-	1.96 3.86
2000 Houston	NL	25 0 0 4	21.1 103	24 14 13 2 0 2 4	12 1 21 0 1	0 0 - 0	0-0	8	6.01 5.48
2001 Houston	NL	11 0 0 3	12.0 60	17 9 9 4 0 0 0	9 0 9 0 0	0 0 - 0	0-0	1	10.43 6.75
2002 Milwaukee	NL	4 4 0 0	24.0 103	16 8 7 1 1 0 0	17 1 17 0 0	2 1 .667 0	0-0	0	2.96 2.63
2003 Milwaukee	NL	36 34 1 1	194.2 870	201 129 119 36 12 3 10	94 2 116 3 4	10 13 .435 1	0-0	0	5.43 5.50
2004 San Francisco	NL	43 2 0 8	50.2 227	55 37 36 11 4 2 3	22 2 40 0 0	2 1 .667 0	0-1	5	5.77 6.39
5 ML YEARS		119 40 1 16	302.2 1363	313 197 184 54 17 7 17	154 6 203 3 5	14 15 .483 1	0-1	14	5.50 5.47

Jason Frasor

Pitches: R **Bats:** R **Pos:** RP-63   **Ht:** 5'10" **Wt:** 170 **Born:** 8/9/1977 **Age:** 27

		HOW MUCH HE PITCHED		WHAT HE GAVE UP			THE RESULTS		
Year Team	Lg	G GS CG GF	IP BFP	H R ER HR SH SF HB	TBB IBB SO WP Bk	W L Pct ShO	Sv-Op	Hld	ERC ERA
1999 W Michigan	A	4 4 0 0	24.0 9	17 10 7 2 0 0 2	9 0 33 0 3	2 1 .667 1	0- -	-	34.48 2.63
1999 Oneonta	A-	12 11 0 0	58.2 22	36 16 11 3 0 1 1	22 0 69 3 2	3 3 .500 0	0- -	-	24.30 1.69
2000 W Michigan	A	14 14 0 0	71.1 300	55 32 26 2 0 2 4	29 0 65 5 1	5 3 .625 0	0- -	-	2.58 3.28
2002 Lakeland	A+	24 24 0 0	117.0 494	112 54 46 10 2 2 8	46 1 87 2 2	5 6 .455 0	0- -	-	4.07 3.54
2003 Vero Beach	A+	15 0 0 9	24.1 94	16 7 5 0 1 1 0	4 0 36 0 1	1 0 1.000 0	6- -	-	1.19 1.85
2003 Jacksonville	AA	35 0 0 32	36.2 154	33 14 12 2 2 0 1	14 0 50 1 0	1 0 1.000 0	17- -	-	3.28 2.95
2004 Syracuse	AAA	3 0 0 2	4.0 18	1 1 1 0 0 0 0	5 0 6 0 0	0 0 - 0	0- -	-	2.38 2.25
2004 Toronto	AL	63 0 0 37	68.1 299	64 31 31 4 3 3 2	36 3 54 4 2	4 6 .400 0	17-19	8	3.97 4.08

Kevin Frederick

Pitches: R **Bats:** L **Pos:** RP-22   **Ht:** 6'1" **Wt:** 208 **Born:** 11/4/1976 **Age:** 28

		HOW MUCH HE PITCHED		WHAT HE GAVE UP			THE RESULTS		
Year Team	Lg	G GS CG GF	IP BFP	H R ER HR SH SF HB	TBB IBB SO WP Bk	W L Pct ShO	Sv-Op	Hld	ERC ERA
1998 Elizabethton	R+	17 0 0 10	29.2 130	28 21 14 4 1 0 0	10 1 46 4 0	1 4 .200 0	1- -	-	3.53 4.25
1999 Twins	R	2 0 0 0	2.1 14	6 5 4 0 0 1 0	1 0 3 0 0	0 0 - 0	0- -	-	13.44 15.43
2000 Quad City	A	27 0 0 11	46.0 193	34 17 12 1 3 1 4	23 4 51 4 0	5 0 1.000 0	4- -	-	2.74 2.35
2000 Fort Myers	A+	19 0 0 7	30.0 123	20 11 9 0 1 1 1	14 1 37 4 2	2 1 .667 0	3- -	-	2.02 2.70
2001 Fort Myers	A+	9 0 0 4	18.0 65	9 2 2 1 0 0 0	3 1 19 0 0	2 0 1.000 0	1- -	-	0.94 1.00
2001 New Britain	AA	44 0 0 18	82.2 331	56 17 15 5 6 2 8	28 7 109 4 0	6 2 .750 0	7- -	-	2.19 1.63

Year Team	Lg	G	GS	CG	GF	IP	BFP	H	R	ER	HR	SH	SF	HB	TBB	IBB	SO	WP	Bk	W	L	Pct	ShO	Sv-Op	Hld	ERC	ERA
2002 Edmonton	AAA	46	2	0	38	55.0	246	63	31	28	8	1	4	2	21	1	47	4	0	3	6	.333	0	22--	-	5.29	4.58
2003 New Haven	AA	25	0	0	18	29.1	135	32	16	11	3	1	2	0	14	2	27	6	0	2	2	.500	0	7--	-	4.65	3.38
2003 Syracuse	AAA	24	0	0	14	25.2	129	40	28	23	5	2	2	1	12	3	20	2	0	1	3	.250	0	2--	-	8.44	8.06
2004 New Hamp	AA	18	0	0	7	21.1	86	15	7	3	1	0	0	1	5	0	26	1	0	2	0	1.000	0	1--	-	1.76	1.27
2004 Syracuse	AAA	20	0	0	15	27.1	109	18	6	3	2	0	0	0	9	0	26	0	0	3	2	.600	0	5--	-	1.89	0.99
2002 Minnesota	AL	8	0	0	3	11.2	56	13	13	13	3	0	0	0	10	0	5	2	0	0	0	-	0	0-0	0	8.14	10.03
2004 Toronto	AL	22	0	0	4	28.2	133	32	21	21	4	0	3	1	16	1	22	0	0	0	2	.000	0	0-1	3	5.74	6.59
2 ML YEARS		30	0	0	7	40.1	189	45	34	34	7	0	3	1	26	1	27	2	0	0	2	.000	0	0-1	3	6.40	7.59

Ryan Freel

Bats: R **Throws:** R **Pos:** 3B-56; RF-46; CF-42; 2B-15; LF-12; PR-4; PH-3   **Ht:** 5'10" **Wt:** 178 **Born:** 3/8/1976 **Age:** 29

Year Team	Lg	G	AB	H	2B	3B	HR	(Hm	Rd)	TB	R	RBI	RC	TBB	IBB	SO	HBP	SH	SF	SB	CS	SB%	GDP	Avg	OBP	Slg
2001 Toronto	AL	9	22	6	1	0	0	(0	0)	7	1	3	3	1	0	4	1	0	0	2	1	.67	0	.273	.333	.318
2003 Cincinnati	NL	43	137	39	6	1	4	(0	4)	59	23	12	17	9	1	13	4	2	1	9	4	.69	2	.285	.344	.431
2004 Cincinnati	NL	143	505	140	21	8	3	(1	2)	186	74	28	73	67	0	88	12	8	0	37	10	.79	7	.277	.375	.368
3 ML YEARS		195	664	185	28	9	7	(1	6)	252	98	43	93	77	1	105	17	10	1	48	15	.76	9	.279	.368	.380

Choo Freeman

Bats: R **Throws:** R **Pos:** CF-41; PR-6; PH-5   **Ht:** 6'2" **Wt:** 200 **Born:** 10/20/1979 **Age:** 25

Year Team	Lg	G	AB	H	2B	3B	HR	(Hm	Rd)	TB	R	RBI	RC	TBB	IBB	SO	HBP	SH	SF	SB	CS	SB%	GDP	Avg	OBP	Slg
1998 Rockies	R	40	147	47	3	6	1	(-	-)	65	35	24	29	15	0	25	4	0	3	14	1	.93	2	.320	.391	.442
1999 Asheville	A	131	485	133	22	4	14	(-	-)	205	82	66	71	39	1	132	7	1	2	16	4	.80	3	.274	.336	.423
2000 Salem	A+	127	429	114	18	7	5	(-	-)	161	73	54	53	37	0	104	4	1	5	16	8	.67	7	.266	.326	.375
2001 Salem	A+	132	517	124	16	5	8	(-	-)	174	63	42	52	31	1	108	9	8	5	19	7	.73	8	.240	.292	.337
2002 Carolina	AA	124	430	125	18	6	12	(-	-)	191	81	64	74	64	1	101	15	4	1	15	13	.54	15	.291	.400	.444
2003 Co Springs	AAA	103	327	83	9	4	7	(-	-)	121	44	36	36	23	1	71	7	4	2	8	8	.20	7	.254	.315	.370
2004 Co Springs	AAA	103	360	107	21	7	10	(-	-)	172	58	50	57	26	2	84	6	3	5	7	3	.70	11	.297	.350	.478
2004 Colorado	NL	45	90	17	3	2	1	(0	1)	27	15	11	7	14	1	21	0	1	0	1	1	.50	5	.189	.298	.300

Brian Fuentes

Pitches: L **Bats:** L **Pos:** RP-47   **Ht:** 6'4" **Wt:** 220 **Born:** 8/9/1975 **Age:** 29

Year Team	Lg	G	GS	CG	GF	IP	BFP	H	R	ER	HR	SH	SF	HB	TBB	IBB	SO	WP	Bk	W	L	Pct	ShO	Sv-Op	Hld	ERC	ERA
2004 Co Springs*	AAA	5	5	0	0	5.0	19	1	0	0	0	0	0	0	3	0	6	0	0	0	0	-	0	0--	-	0.79	0.00
2001 Seattle	AL	10	0	0	3	11.2	47	6	6	6	2	0	1	3	8	0	10	1	0	1	1	.500	0	0-1	1	4.39	4.63
2002 Colorado	NL	31	0	0	9	26.2	118	25	14	14	4	0	2	3	13	0	38	1	0	2	0	1.000	0	0-0	0	4.91	4.73
2003 Colorado	NL	75	0	0	23	75.1	320	64	24	23	7	0	3	6	34	2	82	2	1	3	3	.500	0	4-6	19	3.71	2.75
2004 Colorado	NL	47	0	0	12	44.2	201	46	30	28	5	7	0	4	19	6	48	3	0	2	4	.333	0	0-1	13	4.50	5.64
4 ML YEARS		163	0	0	47	158.1	686	141	74	71	18	7	6	16	74	8	178	7	1	8	8	.500	0	4-8	33	4.18	4.04

Brad Fullmer

Bats: L **Throws:** R **Pos:** DH-65; PH-10; 1B-4   **Ht:** 6'0" **Wt:** 220 **Born:** 1/17/1975 **Age:** 30

Year Team	Lg	G	AB	H	2B	3B	HR	(Hm	Rd)	TB	R	RBI	RC	TBB	IBB	SO	HBP	SH	SF	SB	CS	SB%	GDP	Avg	OBP	Slg
1997 Montreal	NL	19	40	12	2	0	3	(1	2)	23	4	8	8	2	1	7	1	0	0	0	0	-	0	.300	.349	.575
1998 Montreal	NL	140	505	138	44	2	13	(3	10)	225	58	73	70	39	4	70	2	0	1	6	6	.50	12	.273	.327	.446
1999 Montreal	NL	100	347	96	34	2	9	(4	5)	161	38	47	47	22	6	35	2	0	3	2	3	.40	14	.277	.321	.464
2000 Toronto	AL	133	482	142	29	1	32	(16	16)	269	76	104	86	30	3	68	6	0	6	3	1	.75	14	.295	.340	.558
2001 Toronto	AL	146	522	143	31	2	18	(8	10)	232	71	83	73	38	8	88	6	0	7	5	2	.71	13	.274	.326	.444
2002 Anaheim	AL	130	429	124	35	6	19	(9	10)	228	75	59	71	32	6	44	15	0	3	10	3	.77	7	.289	.357	.531
2003 Anaheim	AL	63	206	63	9	2	9	(3	6)	103	32	35	40	26	4	31	2	0	1	5	4	.56	4	.306	.387	.500
2004 Texas	AL	76	258	60	19	1	11	(4	7)	114	41	33	29	27	1	30	3	0	2	1	2	.33	7	.233	.310	.442
8 ML YEARS		807	2789	778	203	16	114	(48	66)	1355	395	442	424	216	33	373	37	0	23	32	21	.60	71	.279	.336	.486

Aaron Fultz

Pitches: L **Bats:** L **Pos:** RP-55   **Ht:** 6'0" **Wt:** 200 **Born:** 9/4/1973 **Age:** 31

Year Team	Lg	G	GS	CG	GF	IP	BFP	H	R	ER	HR	SH	SF	HB	TBB	IBB	SO	WP	Bk	W	L	Pct	ShO	Sv-Op	Hld	ERC	ERA
2004 Rochester*	AAA	7	0	0	1	8.1	36	6	1	1	0	0	0	0	5	0	5	0	0	0	0	-	0	0--	-	2.58	0.00
2000 San Francisco	NL	58	0	0	18	69.1	299	67	38	36	8	7	6	3	28	0	62	0	2	5	2	.714	0	1-3	5	4.19	4.67
2001 San Francisco	NL	66	0	0	17	71.0	300	70	40	36	9	3	4	1	21	3	67	1	0	3	1	.750	0	1-2	12	3.75	4.56
2002 San Francisco	NL	43	0	0	12	41.1	185	47	22	22	4	2	1	3	19	3	31	1	0	2	2	.500	0	0-1	4	5.36	4.79
2003 Texas	AL	64	0	0	10	67.1	297	75	43	39	9	4	2	2	27	7	53	1	1	1	3	.250	0	0-0	19	4.97	5.21
2004 Minnesota	AL	55	0	0	16	50.0	216	50	28	28	5	1	4	1	23	2	37	3	0	3	3	.500	0	1-4	5	4.40	5.04
5 ML YEARS		286	0	0	73	299.0	1297	309	171	161	35	17	17	10	118	15	250	6	3	14	11	.560	0	3-10	47	4.45	4.85

Rafael Furcal

Bats: B **Throws:** R **Pos:** SS-131; PH-10; PR-2; 2B-1   **Ht:** 5'10" **Wt:** 165 **Born:** 10/24/1977 **Age:** 27

Year Team	Lg	G	AB	H	2B	3B	HR	(Hm	Rd)	TB	R	RBI	RC	TBB	IBB	SO	HBP	SH	SF	SB	CS	SB%	GDP	Avg	OBP	Slg
2000 Atlanta	NL	131	455	134	20	4	4	(1	3)	174	87	37	78	73	0	80	3	9	2	40	14	.74	2	.295	.394	.382
2001 Atlanta	NL	79	324	89	19	4	4	(3	1)	120	39	30	41	24	1	56	1	4	6	22	6	.79	5	.275	.321	.370
2002 Atlanta	NL	154	636	175	31	8	8	(4	4)	246	95	47	80	43	0	114	3	9	2	27	15	.64	8	.275	.323	.387

			BATTING															BASERUNNING				AVERAGES		
Year Team	Lg	G	AB	H	2B	3B	HR	(Hm | Rd)	TB	R	RBI	RC	TBB	IBB	SO	HBP	SH	SF	SB	CS	SB%	GDP	Avg	OBP	Slg
2003 Atlanta	NL	156	664	194	35	**10**	15	(4 | 11)	294	130	61	107	60	2	76	3	3	4	25	2	**.93**	1	.292	.352	.443
2004 Atlanta	NL	143	563	157	24	5	14	(5 | 9)	233	103	59	81	58	4	71	1	5	5	29	6	.83	9	.279	.344	.414
5 ML YEARS		663	2642	749	129	27	45	(17 | 28)	1067	454	234	387	258	7	397	11	30	19	143	43	.77	25	.283	.347	.404

Eric Gagne

Pitches: R **Bats:** R **Pos:** RP-70   **Ht:** 6'2" **Wt:** 195 **Born:** 1/7/1976 **Age:** 29

		HOW MUCH HE PITCHED						WHAT HE GAVE UP										THE RESULTS							
Year Team	Lg	G	GS	CG	GF	IP	BFP	H	R	ER	HR	SH	SF	HB	TBB	IBB	SO	WP	Bk	W	L	Pct	ShO	Sv-Op	Hld	ERC	ERA
1999 Los Angeles	NL	5	5	0	0	30.0	119	18	8	7	3	1	0	0	15	0	30	1	0	1	1	.500	0	0-0	0	2.42	2.10
2000 Los Angeles	NL	20	19	0	0	101.1	464	106	62	58	20	5	3	3	60	1	79	4	0	4	6	.400	0	0-0	0	5.97	5.15
2001 Los Angeles	NL	33	24	0	3	151.2	649	144	90	80	24	6	8	16	46	1	130	3	1	6	7	.462	0	0-0	0	4.22	4.75
2002 Los Angeles	NL	77	0	0	68	82.1	314	55	18	18	6	3	2	2	16	4	114	1	0	4	1	.800	0	52-56	1	1.60	1.97
2003 Los Angeles	NL	77	0	0	67	82.1	306	37	12	11	2	4	0	3	20	2	137	0	0	2	3	.400	0	**55-55**	0	0.93	1.20
2004 Los Angeles	NL	70	0	0	59	82.1	326	53	24	20	5	4	2	5	22	3	114	2	0	7	3	.700	0	45-47	0	1.72	2.19
6 ML YEARS		282	48	0	197	530.0	2178	413	214	194	60	23	15	29	179	11	604	13	1	24	21	.533	0	152-158	1	2.92	3.29

Andres Galarraga

Bats: R **Throws:** R **Pos:** PH-5; DH-4; 1B-1   **Ht:** 6'3" **Wt:** 250 **Born:** 6/18/1961 **Age:** 44

			BATTING															BASERUNNING				AVERAGES		
Year Team	Lg	G	AB	H	2B	3B	HR	(Hm	Rd)	TB	R	RBI	RC	TBB	IBB	SO	HBP	SH	SF	SB	CS	SB%	GDP	Avg	OBP	Slg
2004 Salt Lake*	AAA	25	102	31	3	0	4	(-	-)	46	10	19	13	6	1	24	1	0	2	0	0	-	8	.304	.342	.451
1985 Montreal	NL	24	75	14	1	0	2	(0	2)	21	9	4	4	3	0	18	1	0	0	1	2	.33	1	.187	.228	.280
1986 Montreal	NL	105	321	87	13	0	10	(4	6)	130	39	42	42	30	5	79	3	1	1	6	5	.55	8	.271	.338	.405
1987 Montreal	NL	147	551	168	40	3	13	(7	6)	253	72	90	86	41	13	127	10	0	4	7	10	.41	11	.305	.361	.459
1988 Montreal	NL	157	609	**184**	**42**	8	29	(14	15)	**329**	99	92	110	39	9	**153**	10	0	3	13	4	.76	12	.302	.352	.540
1989 Montreal	NL	152	572	147	30	1	23	(13	10)	248	76	85	79	48	10	**158**	**13**	0	3	12	5	.71	12	.257	.327	.434
1990 Montreal	NL	155	579	148	29	0	20	(6	14)	237	65	87	70	40	8	169	4	0	5	10	1	.91	14	.256	.306	.409
1991 Montreal	NL	107	375	82	13	2	9	(3	6)	126	34	33	30	23	5	86	2	0	0	5	6	.45	6	.219	.268	.336
1992 St Louis	NL	95	325	79	14	2	10	(4	6)	127	38	39	33	11	0	69	8	0	3	5	4	.56	8	.243	.282	.391
1993 Colorado	NL	120	470	174	35	4	22	(13	9)	283	71	98	102	24	12	73	6	0	6	2	4	.33	9	**.370**	.403	.602
1994 Colorado	NL	103	417	133	21	0	31	(16	15)	247	77	85	82	19	8	93	8	0	5	8	3	.73	10	.319	.356	.592
1995 Colorado	NL	143	554	155	29	3	31	(18	13)	283	89	106	90	32	6	**146**	13	0	5	12	2	.86	14	.280	.331	.511
1996 Colorado	NL	159	626	190	39	3	**47**	(**32**	15)	376	119	**150**	130	40	3	157	17	0	8	18	8	.69	6	.304	.357	.601
1997 Colorado	NL	154	600	191	31	3	41	(21	20)	351	120	140	126	54	2	141	17	0	3	15	8	.65	16	.318	.389	.585
1998 Atlanta	NL	153	555	169	27	1	44	(16	28)	330	103	121	124	63	11	146	25	0	5	7	6	.54	8	.305	.397	.595
2000 Atlanta	NL	141	494	149	25	1	28	(14	14)	260	67	100	88	36	5	126	17	0	1	3	5	.38	15	.302	.369	.526
2001 Tex-SF		121	399	102	28	1	17	(8	9)	183	50	69	56	31	2	117	12	0	3	1	3	.25	12	.256	.326	.459
2002 Montreal	NL	104	292	76	12	0	9	(7	2)	115	30	40	36	30	6	81	9	0	3	2	2	.50	8	.260	.344	.394
2003 San Francisco	NL	110	272	82	15	0	12	(6	6)	133	36	42	42	19	1	61	2	0	0	1	3	.25	9	.301	.352	.489
2004 Anaheim	AL	7	10	3	0	0	1	(0	1)	6	1	2	1	0	0	3	1	0	0	0	0	-	1	.300	.364	.600
2001 Texas	AL	72	243	57	16	0	10	(5	5)	103	33	34	30	18	1	68	9	0	1	1	0	1.00	9	.235	.310	.424
2001 San Francisco	NL	49	156	45	12	1	7	(3	4)	80	17	35	26	13	1	49	3	0	2	0	3	.00	3	.288	.351	.513
19 ML YEARS		2257	8096	2333	444	32	399	(202	197)	4038	1195	1425	1331	583	106	2003	178	1	58	128	81	.61	179	.288	.347	.499

Mike Gallo

Pitches: L **Bats:** L **Pos:** RP-69   **Ht:** 6'0" **Wt:** 175 **Born:** 4/2/1977 **Age:** 28

		HOW MUCH HE PITCHED						WHAT HE GAVE UP										THE RESULTS							
Year Team	Lg	G	GS	CG	GF	IP	BFP	H	R	ER	HR	SH	SF	HB	TBB	IBB	SO	WP	Bk	W	L	Pct	ShO	Sv-Op	Hld	ERC	ERA
1999 Auburn	A-	3	3	0	0	14.2	63	13	4	2	0	0	0	0	7	0	11	0	0	1	0	1.000	0	0- -	-	3.03	1.23
1999 Michigan	A	12	12	0	0	60.0	268	76	47	39	6	1	2	1	23	0	32	1	0	2	3	.400	0	0- -	-	5.76	5.85
2000 Michigan	A	24	13	0	3	90.2	406	104	58	49	6	5	6	3	27	1	56	4	1	8	3	.727	0	0- -	-	4.26	4.86
2001 Michigan	A	44	0	0	17	84.1	360	83	38	36	4	1	2	8	19	1	67	3	1	9	2	.818	0	4- -	-	3.26	3.84
2002 Lexington	A	42	2	0	25	88.1	359	69	29	18	6	3	2	1	26	4	93	2	0	4	4	.500	0	8- -	-	2.29	1.83
2002 Round Rock	AA	1	0	0	0	1.1	5	1	1	1	0	0	0	0	0	0	0	0	0	0	0	-	0	0- -	-	4.25	6.75
2003 Round Rock	AA	17	0	0	8	19.2	78	17	3	3	1	2	1	0	6	2	22	0	0	1	1	.500	0	2- -	-	2.63	1.37
2003 New Orleans	AAA	16	0	0	3	17.1	64	13	4	4	0	0	0	1	3	0	11	0	0	3	0	1.000	0	0- -	-	1.75	2.08
2004 New Orleans	AAA	3	0	0	1	4.0	13	0	0	0	0	0	0	0	2	0	4	0	0	0	0	-	0	1- -	-	0.29	0.00
2003 Houston	NL	32	0	0	6	30.0	121	28	10	10	3	2	3	1	10	2	16	0	0	1	0	1.000	0	0-1	6	3.66	3.00
2004 Houston	NL	69	0	0	5	49.1	223	55	27	26	12	2	1	6	20	7	34	3	0	2	0	1.000	0	0-1	4	6.16	4.74
2 ML YEARS		101	0	0	11	79.1	344	83	37	36	15	4	4	7	30	9	50	3	0	3	0	1.000	0	0-2	10	5.18	4.08

Danny Garcia

Bats: R **Throws:** R **Pos:** 2B-45; PH-14   **Ht:** 6'1" **Wt:** 174 **Born:** 4/12/1980 **Age:** 25

			BATTING															BASERUNNING				AVERAGES		
Year Team	Lg	G	AB	H	2B	3B	HR	(Hm	Rd)	TB	R	RBI	RC	TBB	IBB	SO	HBP	SH	SF	SB	CS	SB%	GDP	Avg	OBP	Slg
2001 Brooklyn	A-	15	56	18	2	0	1	(-	-)	23	10	6	9	4	0	10	2	0	0	3	2	.60	0	.321	.387	.411
2001 Capital City	A	30	103	31	12	1	2	(-	-)	51	25	16	22	15	0	18	6	4	3	7	3	.70	0	.301	.409	.495
2002 St. Lucie	A+	122	432	118	34	5	4	(-	-)	174	69	52	70	53	0	77	15	6	4	13	6	.68	0	.273	.369	.403
2003 Binghamton	AA	32	117	39	12	1	3	(-	-)	62	22	22	22	10	0	20	3	1	3	2	2	.50	2	.333	.391	.530
2003 Norfolk	AAA	101	388	102	23	3	4	(-	-)	143	45	54	48	22	1	60	9	2	6	11	1	.92	6	.263	.313	.369
2004 Norfolk	AAA	63	242	63	14	1	2	(-	-)	85	28	19	27	15	0	35	7	5	0	9	5	.64	5	.260	.322	.351
2003 New York	NL	19	56	12	2	0	2	(1	1)	20	5	6	4	2	0	11	3	1	1	0	0	-	1	.214	.274	.357
2004 New York	NL	58	138	32	7	1	3	(1	2)	50	23	17	22	22	2	34	9	4	1	3	0	1.00	2	.232	.371	.362
2 ML YEARS		77	194	44	9	1	5	(2	3)	70	28	23	26	24	2	45	12	5	2	3	0	1.00	3	.227	.345	.361

Freddy Garcia

Pitches: R **Bats:** R **Pos:** SP-31   **Ht:** 6'4" **Wt:** 235 **Born:** 6/10/1976 **Age:** 29

Year Team	Lg	G	GS	CG	GF	IP	BFP	H	R	ER	HR	SH	SF	HB	TBB	IBB	SO	WP	Bk	W	L	Pct	ShO	Sv-Op	Hld	ERC	ERA
1999 Seattle	AL	33	33	2	0	201.1	888	205	96	91	18	3	6	10	90	4	170	12	3	17	8	.680	1	0-0	0	4.46	4.07
2000 Seattle	AL	21	20	0	0	124.1	538	112	62	54	16	6	1	2	64	4	79	4	2	9	5	.643	0	0-0	0	4.20	3.91
2001 Seattle	AL	34	34	4	0	238.2	971	199	88	81	16	8	5	5	69	6	163	3	1	18	6	.750	3	0-0	0	2.61	3.05
2002 Seattle	AL	34	34	1	0	223.2	955	227	110	109	30	4	8	6	63	3	181	8	1	16	10	.615	0	0-0	0	3.98	4.39
2003 Seattle	AL	33	33	1	0	201.1	862	196	109	101	31	2	8	11	71	2	144	11	0	12	14	.462	0	0-0	0	4.33	4.51
2004 Sea-CWS	AL	31	31	1	0	210.0	878	192	92	89	22	8	3	7	64	3	184	8	0	13	11	.542	0	0-0	0	3.37	3.81
2004 Seattle	AL	15	15	1	0	107.0	446	96	39	38	8	4	1	2	32	1	82	5	0	4	7	.364	0	0-0	0	3.00	3.20
2004 Chicago	AL	16	16	0	0	103.0	432	96	53	51	14	4	2	5	32	2	102	3	0	9	4	.692	0	0-0	0	3.77	4.46
6 ML YEARS		186	185	9	0	1199.1	5092	1131	557	525	133	31	31	41	421	22	921	46	7	85	54	.612	4	0-0	0	3.75	3.94

Jairo Garcia

Pitches: R **Bats:** R **Pos:** RP-4   **Ht:** 6'0" **Wt:** 164 **Born:** 3/7/1983 **Age:** 22

Year Team	Lg	G	GS	CG	GF	IP	BFP	H	R	ER	HR	SH	SF	HB	TBB	IBB	SO	WP	Bk	W	L	Pct	ShO	Sv-Op	Hld	ERC	ERA
2001 Athletics	R	12	7	0	3	47.1	184	37	19	15	2	2	0	2	6	0	50	5	0	4	2	.667	0	0- -	-	1.80	2.85
2002 Athletics	R	13	8	0	1	59.0	242	56	24	16	5	5	3	3	17	0	66	4	1	2	1	.667	0	1- -	-	3.56	2.44
2002 Vancouver	A-	3	3	0	0	12.1	59	15	11	10	1	0	1	1	7	0	16	1	1	0	3	.000	0	0- -	-	6.18	7.30
2003 Kane County	A	14	9	0	1	42.1	183	40	14	12	0	1	0	3	19	0	28	5	0	0	1	.000	0	0- -	-	3.55	2.55
2004 Kane County	A	25	0	0	24	30.0	117	16	2	1	0	0	0	4	6	2	49	3	0	1	0	1.000	0	16- -	-	1.12	0.30
2004 Midland	AA	13	0	0	9	18.0	80	10	3	3	0	0	0	1	15	0	32	2	0	2	0	1.000	0	2- -	-	2.71	1.50
2004 Sacramento	AAA	11	0	0	10	13.2	60	10	6	6	1	0	0	0	9	1	21	0	0	1	2	.333	0	1- -	-	3.21	3.95
2004 Oakland	AL	4	0	0	2	5.2	32	5	8	8	3	0	0	1	9	0	5	0	0	0	0	-	0	0-0	0	13.22	12.71

Jesse Garcia

Bats: R **Throws:** R **Pos:** SS-25; PH-14; 2B-11; PR-9; 3B-3   **Ht:** 5'10" **Wt:** 171 **Born:** 9/24/1973 **Age:** 31

Year Team	Lg	G	AB	H	2B	3B	HR	(Hm	Rd)	TB	R	RBI	RC	TBB	IBB	SO	HBP	SH	SF	SB	CS	SB%	GDP	Avg	OBP	Slg
2004 Richmond*	AAA	20	78	17	2	0	0	(-	-)	19	6	2	3	4	0	13	1	0	0	0	2	.00	3	.218	.253	.244
1999 Baltimore	AL	17	29	6	0	0	2	(1	1)	12	6	2	3	2	0	3	0	3	0	0	0	-	0	.207	.258	.414
2000 Baltimore	AL	14	17	1	0	0	0	(0	0)	1	2	0	0	2	0	2	0	1	0	0	0	-	0	.059	.158	.059
2001 Atlanta	NL	22	5	1	0	0	0	(0	0)	1	3	0	0	0	0	1	0	1	0	6	2	.75	0	.200	.200	.200
2002 Atlanta	NL	39	61	12	1	0	0	(0	0)	13	6	5	4	0	0	14	0	0	0	0	1	.00	1	.197	.197	.213
2003 Atlanta	NL	13	10	4	0	1	0	(0	0)	6	6	2	3	0	0	1	0	0	0	0	1	.00	0	.400	.400	.600
2004 Atlanta	NL	50	115	29	4	1	1	(1	0)	38	14	10	10	1	0	16	1	1	0	1	2	.33	2	.252	.265	.330
6 ML YEARS		155	237	53	5	2	3	(2	1)	71	37	19	20	5	0	37	1	5	0	7	6	.54	4	.224	.243	.300

Karim Garcia

Bats: L **Throws:** L **Pos:** RF-59; PH-17; CF-15; PR-2; 1B-1   **Ht:** 6'0" **Wt:** 195 **Born:** 10/29/1975 **Age:** 29

Year Team	Lg	G	AB	H	2B	3B	HR	(Hm	Rd)	TB	R	RBI	RC	TBB	IBB	SO	HBP	SH	SF	SB	CS	SB%	GDP	Avg	OBP	Slg
2004 Binghamton*	AA	3	12	1	1	0	0	(-	-)	2	1	3	0	1	0	2	0	0	1	0	0	-	0	.083	.143	.167
1995 Los Angeles	NL	13	20	4	0	0	0	(0	0)	4	1	0	0	0	0	4	0	0	0	0	0	-	0	.200	.200	.200
1996 Los Angeles	NL	1	1	0	0	0	0	(0	0)	0	0	0	0	0	0	1	0	0	0	0	0	-	0	.000	.000	.000
1997 Los Angeles	NL	15	39	5	0	0	1	(0	1)	8	5	8	2	6	1	14	0	0	1	0	0	-	0	.128	.239	.205
1998 Arizona	NL	113	333	74	10	8	9	(4	5)	127	39	43	31	18	1	78	0	0	3	5	4	.56	6	.222	.260	.381
1999 Detroit	AL	96	288	69	10	3	14	(4	10)	127	38	32	36	20	1	67	0	0	1	2	4	.33	2	.240	.288	.441
2000 Det-Bal	AL	16	33	3	0	0	0	(0	0)	3	1	0	0	0	0	10	0	0	0	0	0	-	1	.091	.091	.091
2001 Cleveland	AL	20	45	14	3	0	5	(1	4)	32	8	9	11	3	0	13	1	0	1	0	0	-	1	.311	.360	.711
2002 NYY-Cle	AL	53	202	60	8	0	16	(7	9)	116	30	52	35	6	0	41	0	0	2	0	3	.00	6	.297	.314	.574
2003 Cle-NYY	AL	76	244	64	6	0	11	(4	7)	103	25	35	30	14	2	52	1	0	3	0	2	.00	3	.262	.302	.422
2004 NYM-Bal	AL	85	258	59	7	2	10	(4	6)	100	33	33	24	14	1	50	0	0	7	3	0	1.00	7	.229	.265	.388
2000 Detroit	AL	8	17	3	0	0	0	(0	0)	3	1	0	0	0	0	4	0	0	0	0	0	-	1	.176	.176	.176
2000 Baltimore	AL	8	16	0	0	0	0	(0	0)	0	0	0	0	0	0	6	0	0	0	0	0	-	0	.000	.000	.000
2002 New York	AL	2	5	1	0	0	0	(0	0)	1	1	0	0	0	0	1	0	0	0	0	0	-	0	.200	.200	.200
2002 Cleveland	AL	51	197	59	8	0	16	(7	9)	115	29	52	35	6	0	40	0	0	2	0	3	.00	6	.299	.317	.584
2003 Cleveland	AL	24	93	18	1	0	5	(1	4)	34	8	14	7	5	1	20	1	0	2	0	0	-	4	.194	.238	.366
2003 New York	AL	52	151	46	5	0	6	(3	3)	69	17	21	23	9	1	32	0	0	1	0	2	.00	4	.305	.342	.457
2004 New York	NL	62	192	45	7	2	7	(3	4)	77	24	22	18	10	0	35	0	0	6	3	0	1.00	6	.234	.272	.401
2004 Baltimore	AL	23	66	14	0	0	3	(1	2)	23	9	11	6	4	1	15	0	0	3	0	0	-	1	.212	.247	.348
10 ML YEARS		488	1463	352	44	13	66	(24	42)	620	180	212	169	81	6	330	2	0	14	10	13	.43	31	.241	.279	.424

Rosman Garcia

Pitches: R **Bats:** R **Pos:** RP-4   **Ht:** 6'2" **Wt:** 160 **Born:** 1/3/1979 **Age:** 26

Year Team	Lg	G	GS	CG	GF	IP	BFP	H	R	ER	HR	SH	SF	HB	TBB	IBB	SO	WP	Bk	W	L	Pct	ShO	Sv-Op	Hld	ERC	ERA
1998 Yankees	R	12	8	0	2	57.1	226	39	15	13	2	0	2	1	19	0	77	3	4	4	2	.667	0	0- -	-	1.88	2.04
1999 Greensboro	A	9	9	0	0	42.1	204	60	33	30	4	0	1	2	20	0	31	12	3	2	3	.400	0	0- -	-	7.05	6.38
1999 Staten Island	A-	18	10	0	1	69.2	310	86	40	33	3	3	3	4	14	2	40	4	1	2	6	.250	0	1- -	-	4.31	4.26
2000 Greensboro	A	23	15	1	1	104.1	454	115	67	53	12	3	1	4	35	0	73	5	1	6	6	.500	0	0- -	-	4.70	4.57
2000 Tampa	A+	4	3	0	1	18.0	77	18	13	11	0	3	2	2	4	0	6	0	1	0	2	.000	0	1- -	-	3.48	5.50
2001 Tampa	A+	26	7	0	4	59.2	263	56	30	23	2	4	2	5	22	6	42	4	0	2	6	.250	0	1- -	-	3.21	3.47
2001 Norwich	AA	1	1	0	0	6.0	28	5	4	0	0	0	0	1	2	0	6	2	0	1	0	1.000	0	0- -	-	2.55	0.00
2002 Tulsa	AA	53	0	0	28	74.2	326	75	34	25	1	10	3	3	32	9	38	3	2	8	5	.615	0	2- -	-	3.54	3.01
2003 Oklahoma	AAA	17	2	0	13	28.1	109	20	7	6	1	1	0	0	6	0	21	0	0	1	2	.333	0	10- -	-	1.60	1.91
2004 Oklahoma	AAA	41	0	0	10	71.2	348	87	41	37	6	0	0	3	36	3	49	5	0	4	6	.400	0	2- -	-	5.44	4.65

Year	Team	Lg	G	GS	CG	GF	IP	BFP	H	R	ER	HR	SH	SF	HB	TBB	IBB	SO	WP	Bk	W	L	Pct	ShO	Sv-Op	Hld	ERC	ERA
2003	Texas	AL	46	0	0	7	46.1	224	63	33	31	4	1	1	2	23	0	25	1	1	1	2	.333	0	0-2	7	6.62	6.02
2004	Texas	AL	4	0	0	1	6.2	35	9	5	4	1	0	1	0	5	0	5	0	0	0	0	-	0	0-0	0	7.70	5.40
	2 ML YEARS		50	0	0	8	53.0	259	72	38	35	5	1	2	2	28	0	30	1	1	1	2	.333	0	0-2	7	6.76	5.94

Nomar Garciaparra

Bats: R **Throws:** R **Pos:** SS-79; PH-2; DH-1   **Ht:** 6'0" **Wt:** 190 **Born:** 7/23/1973 **Age:** 31

							BATTING														BASERUNNING				AVERAGES		
Year	Team	Lg	G	AB	H	2B	3B	HR	(Hm	Rd)	TB	R	RBI	RC	TBB	IBB	SO	HBP	SH	SF	SB	CS	SB%	GDP	Avg	OBP	Slg
2004	Pawtucket*	AAA	6	21	5	1	0	1	(-	-)	9	1	3	2	1	0	3	0	0	0	0	0	-	0	.238	.273	.429
1996	Boston	AL	24	87	21	2	3	4	(3	1)	41	11	16	13	4	0	14	0	1	1	5	0	1.00	0	.241	.272	.471
1997	Boston	AL	153	684	209	44	11	30	(11	19)	365	122	98	122	35	2	92	6	2	7	22	9	.71	9	.306	.342	.534
1998	Boston	AL	143	604	195	37	8	35	(17	18)	353	111	122	117	33	1	62	8	0	7	12	6	.67	20	.323	.362	.584
1999	Boston	AL	135	532	190	42	4	27	(14	13)	321	103	104	125	51	7	39	8	0	4	14	3	.82	11	.357	.418	.603
2000	Boston	AL	140	529	197	51	3	21	(7	14)	317	104	96	127	61	20	50	2	0	7	5	2	.71	8	.372	.434	.599
2001	Boston	AL	21	83	24	3	0	4	(3	1)	39	13	8	13	7	0	9	1	0	0	0	1	.00	1	.289	.352	.470
2002	Boston	AL	156	635	197	56	5	24	(10	14)	335	101	120	113	41	4	63	6	0	11	5	2	.71	17	.310	.352	.528
2003	Boston	AL	156	658	198	37	13	28	(18	10)	345	120	105	114	39	1	61	11	1	10	19	5	.79	10	.301	.345	.524
2004	Bos-ChC		81	321	99	21	3	9	(6	3)	153	52	41	53	24	2	30	6	1	2	4	1	.80	10	.308	.365	.477
2004	Boston	AL	38	156	50	7	3	5	(3	2)	78	24	21	26	8	2	16	4	0	1	2	0	1.00	4	.321	.367	.500
2004	Chicago	NL	43	165	49	14	0	4	(3	1)	75	28	20	27	16	0	14	2	1	1	2	1	.67	6	.297	.364	.455
	9 ML YEARS		1009	4133	1330	293	50	182	(89	93)	2269	737	710	797	295	37	420	48	5	49	86	29	.75	86	.322	.370	.549

Jon Garland

Pitches: R **Bats:** R **Pos:** SP-33; RP-1   **Ht:** 6'6" **Wt:** 205 **Born:** 9/27/1979 **Age:** 25

							HOW MUCH HE PITCHED		WHAT HE GAVE UP												THE RESULTS					
Year	Team	Lg	G	GS	CG	GF	IP	BFP	H	R	ER	HR	SH	SF	HB	TBB	IBB	SO	WP	Bk	W	L	Pct	ShO	Sv-Op	Hld	ERC	ERA
2000	Chicago	AL	15	13	0	1	69.2	324	82	55	50	10	0	2	1	40	0	42	4	0	4	8	.333	0	0-0	1	6.26	6.46
2001	Chicago	AL	35	16	0	8	117.0	510	123	59	48	16	2	5	4	55	2	61	3	0	6	7	.462	0	1-1	2	5.16	3.69
2002	Chicago	AL	33	33	1	0	192.2	827	188	109	98	23	3	4	9	83	1	112	5	0	12	12	.500	1	0-0	0	4.46	4.58
2003	Chicago	AL	32	32	0	0	191.2	813	188	103	96	28	4	4	8	74	1	108	8	0	12	13	.480	0	0-0	0	4.38	4.51
2004	Chicago	AL	34	33	1	0	217.0	923	223	125	118	34	9	5	4	76	2	113	3	0	12	11	.522	0	0-0	0	4.56	4.89
	5 ML YEARS		149	127	2	9	788.0	3397	804	451	410	111	18	24	22	328	6	436	23	0	46	51	.474	1	1-1	3	4.72	4.68

Joey Gathright

Bats: L **Throws:** R **Pos:** CF-11; LF-4; PH-2; RF-1; DH-1; PR-1   **Ht:** 5'10" **Wt:** 170 **Born:** 4/27/1981 **Age:** 24

							BATTING														BASERUNNING				AVERAGES		
Year	Team	Lg	G	AB	H	2B	3B	HR	(Hm	Rd)	TB	R	RBI	RC	TBB	IBB	SO	HBP	SH	SF	SB	CS	SB%	GDP	Avg	OBP	Slg
2002	Chrlstn - SC	A	59	208	55	1	0	0	(-	-)	56	30	14	26	21	1	36	10	5	0	22	7	.76	1	.264	.360	.269
2003	Bakersfield	A+	89	340	110	6	3	0	(-	-)	122	65	23	61	41	0	54	6	2	0	57	13	.81	3	.324	.406	.359
2003	Orlando	AA	22	85	32	1	0	0	(-	-)	33	12	5	16	5	0	15	2	0	1	12	3	.80	0	.376	.419	.388
2004	Montgomery	AA	32	126	43	5	1	0	(-	-)	50	23	8	20	11	0	30	1	0	0	10	6	.63	1	.341	.399	.397
2004	Durham	AAA	60	236	77	9	1	0	(-	-)	88	34	8	35	19	0	46	3	2	0	33	13	.72	5	.326	.384	.373
2004	Tampa Bay	AL	19	52	13	0	0	0	(0	0)	13	11	1	4	2	0	14	3	0	0	6	1	.86	2	.250	.316	.250

Chad Gaudin

Pitches: R **Bats:** R **Pos:** RP-22; SP-4   **Ht:** 5'11" **Wt:** 165 **Born:** 3/24/1983 **Age:** 22

							HOW MUCH HE PITCHED		WHAT HE GAVE UP												THE RESULTS					
Year	Team	Lg	G	GS	CG	GF	IP	BFP	H	R	ER	HR	SH	SF	HB	TBB	IBB	SO	WP	Bk	W	L	Pct	ShO	Sv-Op	Hld	ERC	ERA
2002	Chrlstn - SC	A	26	17	0	5	119.1	491	106	43	30	5	3	5	11	37	0	106	4	3	6	4	.400	0	1- -	-	3.17	2.26
2003	Bakersfield	A+	14	14	1	0	80.1	323	63	23	19	2	3	1	1	23	0	70	0	2	5	3	.625	0	0- -	-	2.12	2.13
2003	Orlando	AA	3	3	1	0	19.0	64	8	1	1	0	0	0	0	3	0	23	0	0	2	0	1.000	1	0- -	-	0.65	0.47
2004	Durham	AAA	17	7	0	7	47.2	205	48	26	25	8	2	1	2	17	0	52	0	1	1	3	.250	0	2- -	-	4.61	4.72
2003	Tampa Bay	AL	15	3	0	5	40.0	173	37	18	16	4	0	2	1	16	0	23	1	0	2	0	1.000	0	0-0	0	3.70	3.60
2004	Tampa Bay	AL	26	4	0	5	42.2	201	59	27	23	4	2	4	4	16	4	30	0	0	1	2	.333	0	0-1	5	6.46	4.85
	2 ML YEARS		41	7	0	10	82.2	374	96	45	39	8	2	6	5	32	4	53	1	0	3	2	.600	0	0-1	5	5.06	4.25

Geoff Geary

Pitches: R **Bats:** R **Pos:** RP-33   **Ht:** 6'0" **Wt:** 175 **Born:** 8/26/1976 **Age:** 28

							HOW MUCH HE PITCHED		WHAT HE GAVE UP												THE RESULTS					
Year	Team	Lg	G	GS	CG	GF	IP	BFP	H	R	ER	HR	SH	SF	HB	TBB	IBB	SO	WP	Bk	W	L	Pct	ShO	Sv-Op	Hld	ERC	ERA
1998	Batavia	A-	16	16	1	0	95.1	368	78	20	17	6	3	0	0	14	0	101	3	0	9	1	.900	1	0- -	-	2.03	1.60
1999	Clearwater	A+	24	19	2	0	139.0	611	175	77	61	11	6	4	5	31	1	77	6	3	10	5	.667	0	0- -	-	4.85	3.95
2000	Reading	AA	22	22	1	0	129.1	553	141	66	59	15	2	4	7	22	0	112	1	2	7	6	.538	0	0- -	-	3.94	4.11
2001	Scrtn/WlksBr	AAA	7	3	0	0	22.0	101	35	17	17	2	1	0	1	6	1	21	0	1	0	3	.000	0	0- -	-	7.49	6.95
2001	Reading	AA	29	13	0	10	112.1	449	101	48	45	14	7	5	3	21	3	88	4	3	9	7	.563	0	2- -	-	2.98	3.61
2002	Scrtn/WlksBr	AAA	38	8	0	6	101.0	427	108	46	34	9	0	1	4	32	1	82	1	0	4	2	.667	0	1- -	-	4.31	3.03
2003	Scrtn/WlksBr	AAA	46	3	0	18	87.2	343	73	26	21	3	2	5	4	13	1	80	1	0	9	4	.692	0	5- -	-	2.08	2.16
2004	Scrtn/WlksBr	AAA	21	0	0	20	23.1	104	20	7	6	1	2	0	1	13	3	23	1	0	1	2	.333	0	10- -	-	3.34	2.31
2003	Philadelphia	NL	5	0	0	2	6.0	28	8	3	3	0	1	0	0	3	0	3	0	0	0	0	-	0	0-0	0	5.70	4.50
2004	Philadelphia	NL	33	0	0	16	44.2	200	52	29	27	8	1	2	3	16	3	30	2	1	1	0	1.000	0	0-0	0	5.63	5.44
	2 ML YEARS		38	0	0	18	50.2	228	60	32	30	8	2	2	3	19	3	33	2	1	1	0	1.000	0	0-0	0	5.65	5.33

Chris George

Pitches: L **Bats:** L **Pos:** SP-7; RP-3   **Ht:** 6'2" **Wt:** 200 **Born:** 9/16/1979 **Age:** 25

Year Team	Lg	G	GS	CG	GF	IP	BFP	H	R	ER	HR	SH	SF	HB	TBB	IBB	SO	WP	Bk	W	L	Pct	ShO	Sv-Op	Hld	ERC	ERA
2004 Omaha*	AAA	20	19	2	0	105.1	435	97	45	40	7	6	5	2	40	0	74	4	1	8	6	.571	1	0- -	-	3.51	3.42
2001 Kansas City	AL	13	13	1	0	74.0	313	83	48	46	14	3	4	0	18	0	32	3	2	4	8	.333	0	0-0	0	4.82	5.59
2002 Kansas City	AL	6	6	0	0	27.1	124	37	17	17	2	0	1	1	8	0	13	1	0	0	4	.000	0	0-0	0	5.70	5.60
2003 Kansas City	AL	18	18	0	0	93.2	441	120	75	74	22	2	4	3	44	2	39	5	3	9	6	.600	0	0-0	0	7.19	7.11
2004 Kansas City	AL	10	7	0	1	42.1	207	60	39	34	1	0	1	0	25	1	15	0	0	1	2	.333	0	0-0	0	6.68	7.23
4 ML YEARS		47	44	1	1	237.1	1085	300	179	171	39	5	10	4	95	3	99	9	5	14	20	.412	0	0-0	0	6.19	6.48

Esteban German

Bats: R **Throws:** R **Pos:** 3B-15; 2B-10; PH-5; PR-4   **Ht:** 5'9" **Wt:** 165 **Born:** 1/26/1978 **Age:** 27

Year Team	Lg	G	AB	H	2B	3B	HR	(Hm	Rd)	TB	R	RBI	RC	TBB	IBB	SO	HBP	SH	SF	SB	CS	SB%	GDP	Avg	OBP	Slg
2004 Sacramento*	AAA	55	231	76	8	4	2	(-	-)	98	33	29	40	19	1	28	3	1	5	18	2	.90	6	.329	.380	.424
2002 Oakland	AL	9	35	7	0	0	0	(0	0)	7	4	0	2	4	0	11	1	0	0	1	0	1.00	0	.200	.300	.200
2003 Oakland	AL	5	4	1	0	0	0	(0	0)	1	0	1	1	0	0	1	0	0	0	0	0	-	1	.250	.250	.250
2004 Oakland	AL	31	60	15	1	1	0	(0	0)	18	9	7	8	4	0	13	0	1	0	0	1	.00	1	.250	.297	.300
3 ML YEARS		45	99	23	1	1	0	(0	0)	26	13	8	11	8	0	25	1	1	0	1	1	.50	2	.232	.296	.263

Franklyn German

Pitches: R **Bats:** R **Pos:** RP-16   **Ht:** 6'4" **Wt:** 265 **Born:** 1/20/1980 **Age:** 25

Year Team	Lg	G	GS	CG	GF	IP	BFP	H	R	ER	HR	SH	SF	HB	TBB	IBB	SO	WP	Bk	W	L	Pct	ShO	Sv-Op	Hld	ERC	ERA
2004 Toledo*	AAA	49	0	0	44	49.0	220	46	25	25	6	1	0	2	25	2	60	1	0	3	5	.375	0	27- -	-	4.32	4.59
2002 Detroit	AL	7	0	0	1	6.2	25	3	0	0	0	2	0	1	2	1	6	0	0	1	0	1.000	0	1-1	-	1.09	0.00
2003 Detroit	AL	45	0	0	15	44.2	222	47	32	30	5	2	1	2	45	3	41	8	0	2	4	.333	0	5-7	4	7.06	6.04
2004 Detroit	AL	16	0	0	5	14.2	73	17	15	12	4	1	0	0	11	1	8	2	0	1	0	1.000	0	0-1	1	7.53	7.36
3 ML YEARS		68	0	0	21	66.0	320	67	47	42	9	5	1	3	58	5	55	10	0	4	4	.500	0	6-9	6	6.43	5.73

Justin Germano

Pitches: R **Bats:** R **Pos:** SP-5; RP-2   **Ht:** 6'1" **Wt:** 190 **Born:** 8/6/1982 **Age:** 22

Year Team	Lg	G	GS	CG	GF	IP	BFP	H	R	ER	HR	SH	SF	HB	TBB	IBB	SO	WP	Bk	W	L	Pct	ShO	Sv-Op	Hld	ERC	ERA
2000 Padres	R	17	8	0	4	66.2	277	65	36	34	4	3	1	3	9	0	67	5	1	5	5	.500	0	1- -	-	2.78	4.59
2001 Fort Wayne	A	13	13	0	0	65.0	293	80	47	36	7	2	3	7	16	1	55	6	0	2	6	.250	0	0- -	-	5.22	4.98
2001 Eugene	A-	13	13	2	0	80.0	333	77	35	31	5	1	3	4	11	0	74	1	0	6	5	.545	0	0- -	-	2.75	3.49
2002 Fort Wayne	A	24	24	1	0	155.2	645	166	63	56	14	2	3	1	19	2	119	4	2	12	5	.706	0	0- -	-	3.27	3.18
2002 Lk Elsinore	A+	3	3	0	0	19.0	75	12	3	2	1	0	0	9	5	0	18	1	0	2	0	1.000	0	0- -	-	3.33	0.95
2003 Lk Elsinore	A+	19	19	1	0	110.2	482	127	61	52	4	3	2	9	25	1	78	2	0	9	5	.643	0	0- -	-	4.06	4.23
2003 Mobile	AA	9	9	1	0	58.0	246	60	34	28	6	3	1	5	13	3	44	0	0	2	5	.286	0	0- -	-	3.87	4.34
2004 Mobile	AA	5	5	0	0	32.1	129	31	11	9	3	1	0	1	7	0	20	0	0	2	1	.667	0	0- -	-	3.35	2.51
2004 Portland	AAA	20	20	2	0	122.2	496	113	48	46	12	5	6	5	25	0	98	3	0	9	5	.643	2	0- -	-	3.09	3.38
2004 San Diego	NL	7	5	0	0	21.1	109	31	24	21	2	3	1	0	14	0	16	0	0	1	2	.333	0	0-0	0	7.69	8.86

Jody Gerut

Bats: L **Throws:** L **Pos:** RF-118; CF-12; PH-7; LF-2; DH-1; PR-1   **Ht:** 6'0" **Wt:** 190 **Born:** 9/18/1977 **Age:** 27

Year Team	Lg	G	AB	H	2B	3B	HR	(Hm	Rd)	TB	R	RBI	RC	TBB	IBB	SO	HBP	SH	SF	SB	CS	SB%	GDP	Avg	OBP	Slg
1999 Salem	A+	133	499	144	33	11	11	(-	-)	232	80	63	83	61	4	65	3	1	3	25	12	.68	10	.289	.367	.465
2000 Carolina	AA	109	362	103	32	3	3	(-	-)	150	48	57	64	76	2	54	2	1	7	18	11	.62	9	.285	.405	.414
2002 Buffalo	AAA	55	183	59	7	2	1	(-	-)	73	31	21	29	23	0	20	1	0	3	5	.38	6	.322	.401	.399
2002 Akron	AA	65	256	72	15	2	9	(-	-)	118	44	39	41	34	3	30	1	0	0	17	8	.68	7	.281	.368	.461
2003 Buffalo	AAA	17	65	18	5	0	5	(-	-)	38	13	19	14	11	0	11	0	0	1	4	0	1.00	1	.277	.377	.585
2003 Cleveland	AL	127	480	134	33	2	22	(13	9)	237	66	75	73	35	4	70	7	1	2	4	5	.44	13	.279	.336	.494
2004 Cleveland	AL	134	481	121	31	5	11	(3	8)	195	72	51	60	54	4	59	7	3	3	13	6	.68	9	.252	.334	.405
2 ML YEARS		261	961	255	64	7	33	(16	17)	432	138	126	133	89	8	129	14	4	5	17	11	.61	22	.265	.335	.450

Byron Gettis

Bats: R **Throws:** R **Pos:** LF-11; RF-10; PR-2   **Ht:** 6'0" **Wt:** 240 **Born:** 3/13/1980 **Age:** 25

Year Team	Lg	G	AB	H	2B	3B	HR	(Hm	Rd)	TB	R	RBI	RC	TBB	IBB	SO	HBP	SH	SF	SB	CS	SB%	GDP	Avg	OBP	Slg
1998 Royals	R	27	88	19	2	0	0	(-	-)	21	11	4	4	4	0	20	0	1	1	0	0	-	2	.216	.247	.239
1999 Royals	R	28	95	30	6	2	5	(-	-)	55	20	21	22	17	0	21	3	0	3	3	2	.60	2	.316	.424	.579
1999 Chrlstn - WV	A	43	149	44	7	2	2	(-	-)	61	19	13	23	10	0	36	6	4	1	10	3	.77	3	.295	.361	.409
2000 Chrlstn - WV	A	94	344	74	18	3	5	(-	-)	113	43	50	33	31	0	95	11	2	4	11	7	.61	5	.215	.297	.328
2000 Wilmington	A+	30	97	15	2	0	0	(-	-)	17	13	10	4	13	0	33	2	2	1	2	1	.67	1	.155	.265	.175
2001 Burlington	A	37	140	44	9	2	5	(-	-)	72	26	26	26	14	1	25	4	1	3	4	3	.57	3	.314	.385	.514
2001 Wilmington	A+	82	303	76	21	2	6	(-	-)	119	34	51	36	20	0	70	12	3	1	4	5	.44	7	.251	.321	.393
2002 Wilmington	A+	120	449	127	33	2	8	(-	-)	188	76	70	69	48	3	103	13	10	6	10	5	.67	8	.283	.364	.419
2003 Wichita	AA	140	510	154	31	4	16	(-	-)	241	80	103	89	55	5	110	13	2	11	15	11	.58	11	.302	.377	.473
2004 Wichita	AA	17	58	21	4	1	2	(-	-)	33	6	11	13	8	1	12	1	0	0	1	0	1.00	1	.362	.448	.569
2004 Omaha	AAA	51	179	46	7	0	4	(-	-)	65	23	19	26	33	0	61	0	0	4	4	1	.80	4	.257	.366	.363
2004 Kansas City	AL	21	39	7	1	1	0	(0	0)	10	7	1	3	8	1	14	1	0	0	0	1	.00	0	.179	.327	.256

Jason Giambi

Bats: L Throws: R Pos: 1B-47; DH-28; PH-5 Ht: 6'3" Wt: 235 Born: 1/8/1971 Age: 34

Year Team	Lg	G	AB	H	2B	3B	HR	(Hm	Rd)	TB	R	RBI	RC	TBB	IBB	SO	HBP	SH	SF	SB	CS	SB%	GDP	Avg	OBP	Slg
2004 Tampa*	A+	2	6	1	0	0	0	(-	-)	1	0	0	0	1	1	1	0	0	0	0	0	-	0	.167	.286	.167
1995 Oakland	AL	54	176	45	7	0	6	(3	3)	70	27	25	27	28	0	31	3	1	2	2	1	.67	4	.256	.364	.398
1996 Oakland	AL	140	536	156	40	1	20	(6	14)	258	84	79	88	51	3	95	5	1	5	0	1	.00	15	.291	.355	.481
1997 Oakland	AL	142	519	152	41	2	20	(14	6)	257	66	81	91	55	3	89	6	0	8	0	1	.00	11	.293	.362	.495
1998 Oakland	AL	153	562	166	28	0	27	(12	15)	275	92	110	103	81	7	102	5	0	9	2	2	.50	16	.295	.384	.489
1999 Oakland	AL	158	575	181	36	1	33	(17	16)	318	115	123	132	105	6	106	7	0	8	1	1	.50	11	.315	.422	.553
2000 Oakland	AL	152	510	170	29	1	43	(23	20)	330	108	137	152	137	6	96	9	0	8	2	0	1.00	9	.333	.476	.647
2001 Oakland	AL	154	520	178	47	2	38	(27	11)	343	109	120	153	129	24	83	13	0	9	2	0	1.00	17	.342	.477	.660
2002 New York	AL	155	560	176	34	1	41	(19	22)	335	120	122	139	109	4	112	15	0	5	2	2	.50	18	.314	.435	.598
2003 New York	AL	156	535	134	25	0	41	(12	29)	282	97	107	120	129	9	140	21	0	5	2	1	.67	9	.250	.412	.527
2004 New York	AL	80	264	55	9	0	12	(5	7)	100	33	40	42	47	1	62	8	0	3	0	1	.00	7	.208	.342	.379
10 ML YEARS		1344	4757	1413	296	8	281	(138	143)	2568	851	944	1047	871	63	916	92	2	62	13	10	.57	115	.297	.411	.540

Jeremy Giambi

Bats: L Throws: L Pos: DH Ht: 5'11" Wt: 216 Born: 9/30/1974 Age: 30

Year Team	Lg	G	AB	H	2B	3B	HR	(Hm	Rd)	TB	R	RBI	RC	TBB	IBB	SO	HBP	SH	SF	SB	CS	SB%	GDP	Avg	OBP	Slg
2004 Dodgers*	R	6	15	4	1	0	1	(-	-)	8	2	3	4	5	0	4	1	0	0	0	0	-	0	.267	.476	.533
2004 Las Vegas*	AAA	11	23	3	0	0	1	(-	-)	6	3	1	1	3	0	8	0	0	0	0	0	-	0	.130	.231	.261
1998 Kansas City	AL	18	58	13	4	0	2	(0	2)	23	6	8	7	11	0	9	0	0	1	0	1	.00	3	.224	.343	.397
1999 Kansas City	AL	90	288	82	13	1	3	(2	1)	106	34	34	41	40	5	67	3	1	4	0	0	-	7	.285	.373	.368
2000 Oakland	AL	104	260	66	10	2	10	(3	7)	110	42	50	37	32	2	61	3	3	4	0	0	-	7	.254	.338	.423
2001 Oak-Phi		124	371	105	26	0	12	(5	7)	167	64	57	64	63	1	83	4	3	2	0	1	.00	13	.283	.391	.450
2002 Oak-Phi		124	313	81	17	0	20	(12	8)	158	58	45	58	79	2	94	4	1	0	0	1	.00	5	.259	.414	.505
2003 Boston	AL	50	127	25	5	0	5	(2	3)	45	15	15	14	26	0	42	2	1	0	1	0	1.00	3	.197	.342	.354
2002 Oakland	AL	42	157	43	7	0	8	(6	2)	74	26	17	24	27	0	40	3	0	0	0	0	-	4	.274	.390	.471
2002 Philadelphia	NL	82	156	38	10	0	12	(6	6)	84	32	28	34	52	2	54	1	1	0	0	1	.00	1	.244	.435	.538
6 ML YEARS		510	1417	372	75	3	52	(24	28)	609	219	209	221	251	10	356	16	9	11	1	3	.25	38	.263	.377	.430

Jay Gibbons

Bats: L Throws: L Pos: RF-66; DH-16; 1B-14; PH-4 Ht: 6'0" Wt: 200 Born: 3/2/1977 Age: 28

Year Team	Lg	G	AB	H	2B	3B	HR	(Hm	Rd)	TB	R	RBI	RC	TBB	IBB	SO	HBP	SH	SF	SB	CS	SB%	GDP	Avg	OBP	Slg
2004 Frederick*	A+	3	11	2	1	0	1	(-	-)	6	2	5	1	2	0	2	0	0	0	0	0	-	0	.182	.308	.545
2004 Bowie*	AA	5	15	1	0	0	0	(-	-)	1	3	1	0	2	0	2	0	0	1	0	0	-	1	.067	.167	.067
2001 Baltimore	AL	73	225	53	10	0	15	(9	6)	108	27	36	31	17	0	39	4	0	0	0	1	.00	7	.236	.301	.480
2002 Baltimore	AL	136	490	121	29	1	28	(17	11)	236	71	69	71	45	3	66	2	0	4	1	3	.25	9	.247	.311	.482
2003 Baltimore	AL	160	625	173	39	2	23	(12	11)	285	80	100	94	49	11	89	3	0	5	0	1	.00	12	.277	.330	.456
2004 Baltimore	AL	97	346	85	14	1	10	(4	6)	131	36	47	38	29	0	64	1	1	3	1	1	.50	11	.246	.303	.379
4 ML YEARS		466	1686	432	92	4	76	(42	34)	760	214	252	234	140	14	258	10	1	12	2	6	.25	39	.256	.315	.451

Geronimo Gil

Bats: R Throws: R Pos: C-11; PH-1 Ht: 6'2" Wt: 195 Born: 8/7/1975 Age: 29

Year Team	Lg	G	AB	H	2B	3B	HR	(Hm	Rd)	TB	R	RBI	RC	TBB	IBB	SO	HBP	SH	SF	SB	CS	SB%	GDP	Avg	OBP	Slg
2004 Ottawa*	AAA	106	375	97	24	0	6	(-	-)	139	55	34	43	32	1	67	6	5	0	2	1	.67	12	.259	.327	.371
2001 Baltimore	AL	17	58	17	2	0	0	(0	0)	19	3	6	7	5	0	7	2	1	0	0	0	-	1	.293	.369	.328
2002 Baltimore	AL	125	422	98	19	0	12	(5	7)	153	33	45	33	21	1	88	1	5	1	2	2	.50	17	.232	.270	.363
2003 Baltimore	AL	54	169	40	4	0	3	(2	1)	53	22	16	18	12	0	34	3	2	0	0	0	-	2	.237	.299	.314
2004 Baltimore	AL	12	32	9	2	0	0	(0	0)	11	1	4	5	3	1	5	0	0	0	0	0	-	0	.281	.343	.344
4 ML YEARS		208	681	164	27	0	15	(7	8)	236	59	71	63	41	2	134	6	8	1	2	2	.50	20	.241	.289	.347

Jerry Gil

Bats: R Throws: R Pos: SS-28; PH-1; PR-1 Ht: 6'3" Wt: 183 Born: 10/14/1982 Age: 22

Year Team	Lg	G	AB	H	2B	3B	HR	(Hm	Rd)	TB	R	RBI	RC	TBB	IBB	SO	HBP	SH	SF	SB	CS	SB%	GDP	Avg	OBP	Slg
2000 Missoula	R+	58	227	51	10	2	0	(-	-)	65	24	20	15	11	1	63	2	0	1	7	3	.70	5	.225	.266	.286
2001 South Bend	A	105	363	78	14	5	2	(-	-)	108	40	31	20	8	0	103	4	8	0	19	7	.73	12	.215	.240	.298
2002 Lancaster	A+	10	37	8	0	0	1	(-	-)	11	4	4	2	1	0	1	0	0	0	1	1	.50	0	.216	.237	.297
2002 Yakima	A-	65	224	56	11	2	2	(-	-)	77	21	28	21	6	0	47	2	2	2	14	1	.93	6	.250	.274	.344
2003 South Bend	A	116	429	111	16	6	4	(-	-)	151	52	58	40	10	0	90	2	10	6	19	10	.66	7	.259	.275	.352
2004 Tucson	AAA	114	421	117	31	8	11	(-	-)	197	53	58	58	12	1	94	2	5	3	12	1	.92	4	.278	.299	.468
2004 Arizona	NL	29	86	15	2	1	0	(0	0)	19	3	8	4	0	0	33	1	0	1	2	0	1.00	2	.174	.182	.221

Brian Giles

Bats: L Throws: L Pos: RF-159; PH-1 Ht: 5'10" Wt: 202 Born: 1/20/1971 Age: 34

Year Team	Lg	G	AB	H	2B	3B	HR	(Hm	Rd)	TB	R	RBI	RC	TBB	IBB	SO	HBP	SH	SF	SB	CS	SB%	GDP	Avg	OBP	Slg
1995 Cleveland	AL	6	9	5	0	0	1	(0	1)	8	6	3	3	0	0	1	0	0	0	0	0	-	0	.556	.556	.889
1996 Cleveland	AL	51	121	43	14	1	5	(2	3)	74	26	27	29	19	4	13	0	0	3	3	0	1.00	6	.355	.434	.612
1997 Cleveland	AL	130	377	101	15	3	17	(7	10)	173	62	61	66	63	2	50	1	3	7	13	3	.81	10	.268	.368	.459
1998 Cleveland	AL	112	350	94	19	0	16	(10	6)	161	56	66	66	73	8	75	3	1	3	10	5	.67	9	.269	.396	.460
1999 Pittsburgh	NL	141	521	164	33	3	39	(24	15)	320	109	115	127	95	7	80	3	0	8	6	2	.75	14	.315	.418	.614
2000 Pittsburgh	NL	156	559	176	37	7	35	(16	19)	332	111	123	139	114	13	69	7	0	8	6	0	1.00	15	.315	.432	.594
2001 Pittsburgh	NL	160	576	178	37	7	37	(18	19)	340	116	95	131	90	14	67	4	0	4	13	6	.68	10	.309	.404	.590

Year Team	Lg	G	AB	H	2B	3B	HR	(Hm	Rd)	TB	R	RBI	RC	TBB	IBB	SO	HBP	SH	SF	SB	CS	SB%	GDP	Avg	OBP	Slg
2002 Pittsburgh	NL	153	497	148	37	5	38	(15	23)	309	95	103	128	135	24	74	7	0	5	15	6	.71	10	.298	.450	.622
2003 Pit-SD	NL	134	492	147	34	6	20	(12	8)	253	93	88	102	105	12	58	8	0	4	4	3	.57	12	.299	.427	.514
2004 San Diego	NL	159	609	173	33	7	23	(10	13)	289	97	94	102	89	6	80	4	0	9	10	3	.77	12	.284	.374	.475
2003 Pittsburgh	NL	105	388	116	30	4	16	(10	6)	202	70	70	79	85	11	48	6	0	2	0	3	.00	8	.299	.430	.521
2003 San Diego	NL	29	104	31	4	2	4	(2	2)	51	23	18	23	20	1	10	2	0	2	4	0	1.00	4	.298	.414	.490
10 ML YEARS		1202	4111	1229	259	39	231	(114	117)	2259	771	775	893	783	90	567	37	4	51	80	28	.74	96	.299	.411	.550

Marcus Giles

Bats: R **Throws:** R **Pos:** 2B-97; PH-7; PR-1 **Ht:** 5'8" **Wt:** 180 **Born:** 5/18/1978 **Age:** 27

Year Team	Lg	G	AB	H	2B	3B	HR	(Hm	Rd)	TB	R	RBI	RC	TBB	IBB	SO	HBP	SH	SF	SB	CS	SB%	GDP	Avg	OBP	Slg
2004 Rome*	A	1	2	0	0	0	0	(-	-)	0	0	0	0	2	0	0	0	0	0	0	0	-	0	.000	.500	.000
2004 Myrtle Beach*	A+	4	13	1	1	0	0	(-	-)	2	1	2	0	1	0	4	0	0	1	0	0	-	0	.077	.133	.154
2001 Atlanta	NL	68	244	64	10	2	9	(5	4)	105	36	31	33	28	0	37	0	1	0	2	5	.29	8	.262	.338	.430
2002 Atlanta	NL	68	213	49	10	1	8	(4	4)	85	27	23	22	25	3	41	2	1	1	1	1	.50	5	.230	.315	.399
2003 Atlanta	NL	145	551	174	49	2	21	(9	12)	290	101	69	101	59	2	80	11	10	4	14	4	.78	7	.316	.390	.526
2004 Atlanta	NL	102	379	118	22	2	8	(6	2)	168	61	48	66	36	0	70	9	3	7	17	4	.81	6	.311	.378	.443
4 ML YEARS		383	1387	405	91	7	46	(24	22)	648	225	171	222	148	5	228	22	15	12	34	14	.71	26	.292	.366	.467

Keith Ginter

Bats: R **Throws:** R **Pos:** 2B-54; 3B-47; PH-10; RF-2; DH-2 **Ht:** 5'10" **Wt:** 190 **Born:** 5/5/1976 **Age:** 29

Year Team	Lg	G	AB	H	2B	3B	HR	(Hm	Rd)	TB	R	RBI	RC	TBB	IBB	SO	HBP	SH	SF	SB	CS	SB%	GDP	Avg	OBP	Slg
2004 Indianapolis*	AAA	4	14	3	2	0	1	(-	-)	8	3	3	1	1	0	4	0	0	0	0	0	-	0	.214	.267	.571
2000 Houston	NL	5	8	2	0	0	1	(1	0)	5	3	3	2	1	0	3	0	0	1	0	0	-	0	.250	.300	.625
2001 Houston	NL	1	1	0	0	0	0	(0	0)	0	0	0	0	0	0	0	0	0	0	0	0	-	0	.000	.000	.000
2002 Hou-Mil	NL	28	81	19	9	0	1	(1	0)	31	7	8	13	17	0	15	1	0	0	0	0	-	0	.235	.374	.383
2003 Milwaukee	NL	127	358	92	15	2	14	(9	5)	153	51	44	52	37	1	87	17	0	3	1	1	.50	8	.257	.352	.427
2004 Milwaukee	NL	113	386	101	23	2	19	(9	10)	185	47	60	57	37	2	100	6	4	4	8	1	.89	9	.262	.333	.479
2002 Houston	NL	7	5	1	1	0	0	(0	0)	2	1	0	1	2	0	1	0	0	0	0	0	-	0	.200	.500	.400
2002 Milwaukee	NL	21	76	18	8	0	1	(1	0)	29	6	8	12	15	0	14	1	0	0	0	0	-	0	.237	.363	.382
5 ML YEARS		274	834	214	47	4	35	(20	15)	374	108	115	124	92	3	205	24	4	8	9	2	.82	17	.257	.344	.448

Matt Ginter

Pitches: R **Bats:** R **Pos:** SP-14; RP-1 **Ht:** 6'1" **Wt:** 220 **Born:** 12/24/1977 **Age:** 27

Year Team	Lg	G	GS	CG	GF	IP	BFP	H	R	ER	HR	SH	SF	HB	TBB	IBB	SO	WP	Bk	W	L	Pct	ShO	Sv-Op	Hld	ERC	ERA
2004 Norfolk*	AAA	11	11	0	0	64.0	255	55	26	21	4	5	2	1	8	1	49	1	2	1	5	.167	0	0- -	-	2.11	2.95
2000 Chicago	AL	7	0	0	3	9.1	52	18	14	14	5	0	1	0	7	0	6	1	0	1	0	1.000	0	0-1	0	16.24	13.50
2001 Chicago	AL	20	0	0	7	39.2	167	34	23	23	2	0	3	7	14	2	24	2	0	1	0	1.000	0	0-0	0	3.44	5.22
2002 Chicago	AL	33	0	0	15	54.1	236	59	34	27	6	0	2	1	21	0	37	2	0	1	1	1.000	0	1-1	0	4.72	4.47
2003 Chicago	AL	3	0	0	0	3.1	15	2	5	5	1	1	0	2	1	0	0	0	0	0	0	-	0	0-0	0	5.16	13.50
2004 New York	NL	15	14	0	0	69.1	313	82	41	35	8	3	1	5	20	5	38	1	0	1	3	.250	0	0-0	0	4.87	4.54
5 ML YEARS		78	14	0	25	176.0	783	195	117	104	22	4	7	15	63	7	105	6	0	4	3	.571	0	1-2	0	4.99	5.32

Charles Gipson

Bats: R **Throws:** R **Pos:** SS-2; CF-2; LF-1; DH-1; PH-1 **Ht:** 6'1" **Wt:** 195 **Born:** 12/16/1972 **Age:** 32

Year Team	Lg	G	AB	H	2B	3B	HR	(Hm	Rd)	TB	R	RBI	RC	TBB	IBB	SO	HBP	SH	SF	SB	CS	SB%	GDP	Avg	OBP	Slg
2004 Durham*	AAA	96	297	88	14	3	2	(-	-)	114	50	27	45	35	0	57	7	6	2	8	8	.50	5	.296	.381	.384
1998 Seattle	AL	44	51	12	1	0	0	(0	0)	13	11	2	4	5	1	9	1	0	0	2	1	.67	1	.235	.316	.255
1999 Seattle	AL	55	80	18	5	2	0	(0	0)	27	16	9	6	6	0	13	1	2	0	3	4	.43	2	.225	.287	.338
2000 Seattle	AL	59	29	9	1	1	0	(0	0)	12	7	3	4	4	0	9	0	0	0	2	3	.40	1	.310	.394	.414
2001 Seattle	AL	94	64	14	2	2	0	(0	0)	20	16	5	5	4	0	20	2	1	1	1	1	.50	2	.219	.282	.313
2002 Seattle	AL	79	72	17	5	2	0	(0	0)	26	22	8	7	9	0	14	1	2	0	4	0	1.00	3	.236	.329	.361
2003 New York	AL	18	10	2	0	0	0	(0	0)	2	3	2	1	1	0	2	0	1	0	2	1	.67	0	.200	.273	.200
2004 Tampa Bay	AL	5	4	2	0	0	0	(0	0)	2	1	0	2	0	0	1	0	1	0	1	0	1.00	0	.500	.500	.500
7 ML YEARS		354	310	74	14	7	0	(0	0)	102	76	29	29	29	1	68	5	7	1	15	10	.60	8	.239	.313	.329

Chris Gissell

Pitches: R **Bats:** R **Pos:** RP-4; SP-1 **Ht:** 6'5" **Wt:** 210 **Born:** 1/4/1978 **Age:** 27

Year Team	Lg	G	GS	CG	GF	IP	BFP	H	R	ER	HR	SH	SF	HB	TBB	IBB	SO	WP	Bk	W	L	Pct	ShO	Sv-Op	Hld	ERC	ERA
1996 Cubs	R	11	10	0	0	61.1	246	54	23	16	1	0	1	4	8	0	64	1	3	4	2	.667	0	0- -	-	2.18	2.35
1997 Rockford	A	26	24	3	1	143.2	646	155	89	71	7	5	4	11	62	1	105	11	3	6	11	.353	1	0- -	-	4.54	4.45
1998 Daytona	A+	22	21	1	0	136.0	597	149	80	63	12	3	5	11	38	1	123	7	0	7	6	.538	0	0- -	-	4.33	4.17
1998 Rockford	A	5	5	0	0	33.2	138	27	8	3	0	1	1	1	15	0	23	1	0	3	0	1.000	0	0- -	-	2.70	0.80
1998 W Tennessee	AA	1	1	0	0	4.0	21	5	7	6	2	0	0	0	4	2	4	0	0	0	1	.000	0	- -	-	10.62	13.50
1999 W Tennessee	AA	20	18	0	0	97.2	470	121	76	65	10	4	6	10	62	3	57	9	2	3	8	.273	0	0- -	-	6.94	5.99
2000 W Tennessee	AA	16	16	0	0	93.0	395	80	39	32	6	3	2	6	41	1	65	2	0	7	5	.583	0	0- -	-	3.48	3.10
2001 W Tennessee	AA	28	27	0	0	159.2	695	159	91	80	13	5	8	9	63	0	136	7	0	5	11	.313	0	0- -	-	4.12	4.51
2002 Iowa	AAA	28	27	2	0	154.1	699	177	108	105	19	6	6	15	61	3	133	1	1	8	12	.400	1	0- -	-	5.46	6.12
2003 Co Springs	AAA	38	10	0	6	109.0	467	96	53	43	8	7	1	11	35	0	82	4	0	8	4	.667	0	1- -	-	3.26	3.55
2004 Co Springs	AAA	24	8	0	2	90.2	366	80	41	37	11	3	3	5	17	0	74	1	2	14	2	.875	0	0- -	-	3.00	3.67
2004 Colorado	NL	5	1	0	2	8.2	48	20	14	14	4	1	0	0	3	0	11	1	0	0	1	.000	0	0-0	0	16.25	14.54

Doug Glanville

Bats: R Throws: R Pos: CF-57; PH-18; LF-13; PR-13   Ht: 6'2" Wt: 174 Born: 8/25/1970 Age: 34

								BATTING												BASERUNNING				AVERAGES		
Year Team	Lg	G	AB	H	2B	3B	HR	(Hm	Rd)	TB	R	RBI	RC	TBB	IBB	SO	HBP	SH	SF	SB	CS	SB%	GDP	Avg	OBP	Slg
1996 Chicago	NL	49	83	20	5	1	1	(1	0)	30	10	10	9	3	0	11	0	2	1	2	0	1.00	0	.241	.264	.361
1997 Chicago	NL	146	474	142	22	5	4	(2	2)	186	79	35	60	24	0	46	1	9	2	19	11	.63	9	.300	.333	.392
1998 Philadelphia	NL	158	**678**	189	28	7	8	(3	5)	255	106	49	86	42	1	89	6	5	4	23	6	.79	7	.279	.325	.376
1999 Philadelphia	NL	150	628	204	38	6	11	(5	6)	287	101	73	112	48	1	82	6	5	5	34	2	.94	9	.325	.376	.457
2000 Philadelphia	NL	154	637	175	27	6	8	(3	5)	238	89	52	75	31	1	76	2	12	7	31	8	.79	11	.275	.307	.374
2001 Philadelphia	NL	153	634	166	24	3	14	(6	8)	238	74	55	70	19	1	91	4	10	7	28	6	.82	7	.262	.285	.375
2002 Philadelphia	NL	138	422	105	16	3	6	(3	3)	145	49	29	35	25	4	57	2	8	3	19	2	.90	5	.249	.292	.344
2003 Tex-ChC		80	246	65	5	0	5	(3	2)	85	24	16	19	8	1	29	0	3	1	4	1	.80	2	.264	.286	.346
2004 Philadelphia	NL	87	162	34	1	1	2	(1	1)	43	21	14	12	8	1	21	0	3	2	8	0	1.00	5	.210	.244	.265
2003 Texas	AL	52	195	53	5	0	4	(2	2)	70	22	14	16	6	1	25	0	2	0	4	0	1.00	2	.272	.294	.359
2003 Chicago	NL	28	51	12	0	0	1	(1	0)	15	2	2	3	2	0	4	0	1	1	0	1	.00	0	.235	.259	.294
9 ML YEARS		1115	3964	1100	166	32	59	(27	32)	1507	553	333	478	208	10	502	21	57	32	168	36	.82	55	.277	.315	.380

Troy Glaus

Bats: R Throws: R Pos: DH-39; 3B-19   Ht: 6'5" Wt: 245 Born: 8/3/1976 Age: 28

								BATTING												BASERUNNING				AVERAGES		
Year Team	Lg	G	AB	H	2B	3B	HR	(Hm	Rd)	TB	R	RBI	RC	TBB	IBB	SO	HBP	SH	SF	SB	CS	SB%	GDP	Avg	OBP	Slg
2004 R Cucamnga*	A+	5	15	3	0	0	2	(-	-)	9	4	4	4	6	0	5	0	0	0	0	0	-	0	.200	.429	.600
1998 Anaheim	AL	48	165	36	9	0	1	(0	1)	48	19	23	13	15	0	51	0	0	2	1	0	1.00	3	.218	.280	.291
1999 Anaheim	AL	154	551	132	29	0	29	(12	17)	248	85	79	84	71	1	143	6	0	3	5	1	.83	9	.240	.331	.450
2000 Anaheim	AL	159	563	160	37	1	**47**	(24	23)	340	120	102	129	112	6	163	2	0	1	14	11	.56	14	.284	.404	.604
2001 Anaheim	AL	161	588	147	38	2	41	(22	19)	312	100	108	114	107	7	158	6	0	7	10	3	.77	16	.250	.367	.531
2002 Anaheim	AL	156	569	142	24	1	30	(13	17)	258	99	111	100	88	4	144	6	0	8	10	3	.77	12	.250	.352	.453
2003 Anaheim	AL	91	319	79	17	2	16	(9	7)	148	53	50	48	46	4	73	1	0	1	7	2	.78	8	.248	.343	.464
2004 Anaheim	AL	58	207	52	11	1	18	(9	9)	119	47	42	41	31	3	52	3	0	1	2	3	.40	6	.251	.355	.575
7 ML YEARS		827	2962	748	165	7	182	(89	93)	1473	523	515	529	470	25	784	24	0	23	49	23	.68	68	.253	.357	.497

Tom Glavine

Pitches: L Bats: L Pos: SP-33   Ht: 6'0" Wt: 185 Born: 3/25/1966 Age: 39

		HOW MUCH HE PITCHED						WHAT HE GAVE UP												THE RESULTS						
Year Team	Lg	G	GS	CG	GF	IP	BFP	H	R	ER	HR	SH	SF	HB	TBB	IBB	SO	WP	Bk	W	L	Pct	ShO	Sv-Op	Hld	ERC	ERA
1987 Atlanta	NL	9	9	0	0	50.1	238	55	34	31	5	2	3	3	33	4	20	1	1	2	4	.333	0	0-0	0	5.70	5.54
1988 Atlanta	NL	34	34	1	0	195.1	844	201	111	99	12	17	11	8	63	7	84	2	2	7	**17**	.292	0	0-0	0	3.74	4.56
1989 Atlanta	NL	29	29	6	0	186.0	766	172	88	76	20	11	4	2	40	3	90	2	0	14	8	.636	4	0-0	0	2.99	3.68
1990 Atlanta	NL	33	33	1	0	214.1	929	232	111	102	18	**21**	2	1	78	10	129	8	1	10	12	.455	0	0-0	0	4.24	4.28
1991 Atlanta	NL	34	34	**9**	0	246.2	989	201	83	70	17	7	6	2	69	6	192	10	2	**20**	11	.645	1	0-0	0	2.47	2.55
1992 Atlanta	NL	33	33	7	0	225.0	919	197	81	69	6	2	6	2	70	7	129	5	0	**20**	8	.714	**5**	0-0	0	2.61	2.76
1993 Atlanta	NL	36	**36**	4	0	239.1	1014	236	91	85	16	10	2	2	90	7	120	4	0	**22**	6	.786	2	0-0	0	3.70	3.20
1994 Atlanta	NL	25	25	2	0	165.1	731	173	76	73	10	9	5	4	70	10	140	8	1	13	9	.591	0	0-0	0	4.02	3.97
1995 Atlanta	NL	29	29	3	0	198.2	822	182	76	68	9	7	5	5	66	0	127	3	0	16	7	.696	1	0-0	0	3.14	3.08
1996 Atlanta	NL	36	**36**	1	0	235.1	994	222	91	78	14	15	2	0	85	7	181	4	0	15	10	.600	0	0-0	0	3.29	2.98
1997 Atlanta	NL	33	33	5	0	240.0	970	197	86	79	20	11	6	4	79	9	152	3	0	14	7	.667	2	0-0	0	2.80	2.96
1998 Atlanta	NL	33	33	4	0	229.1	934	202	67	63	13	6	2	2	74	2	157	3	0	**20**	6	.769	3	0-0	0	2.93	2.47
1999 Atlanta	NL	35	**35**	2	0	234.0	1023	**259**	115	107	18	**22**	10	4	83	14	138	2	0	14	11	.560	0	0-0	0	4.31	4.12
2000 Atlanta	NL	35	**35**	4	0	241.0	992	222	101	91	24	9	5	4	65	6	152	0	0	**21**	9	.700	2	0-0	0	3.19	3.40
2001 Atlanta	NL	35	**35**	1	0	219.1	929	213	92	87	24	18	5	4	97	10	116	2	0	16	7	.696	1	0-0	0	4.21	3.57
2002 Atlanta	NL	36	**36**	2	0	224.2	936	210	85	74	21	12	6	8	78	8	127	2	0	18	11	.621	1	0-0	0	3.61	2.96
2003 New York	NL	32	32	0	0	183.1	790	205	94	92	21	7	4	2	66	7	82	2	0	9	14	.391	0	0-0	0	4.77	4.52
2004 New York	NL	33	33	1	0	212.1	904	204	94	85	20	13	**10**	0	70	10	109	0	0	11	14	.440	1	0-0	0	3.43	3.60
18 ML YEARS		570	570	53	0	3740.1	15724	3583	1576	1429	288	186	98	52	1276	127	2245	61	7	262	171	.605	23	0-0		3.48	3.44

Ross Gload

Bats: L Throws: L Pos: 1B-42; PH-30; RF-22; LF-17; PR-13; DH-12; CF-1   Ht: 6'0" Wt: 185 Born: 4/5/1976 Age: 29

								BATTING												BASERUNNING				AVERAGES		
Year Team	Lg	G	AB	H	2B	3B	HR	(Hm	Rd)	TB	R	RBI	RC	TBB	IBB	SO	HBP	SH	SF	SB	CS	SB%	GDP	Avg	OBP	Slg
2000 Chicago	NL	18	31	6	0	1	1	(0	1)	11	4	3	3	3	0	10	0	0	1	0	0	-	0	.194	.257	.355
2002 Colorado	NL	26	31	8	1	0	1	(1	0)	12	4	4	3	3	0	7	0	0	0	0	0	-	0	.258	.324	.387
2004 Chicago	AL	110	234	75	16	0	7	(3	4)	112	28	44	41	20	1	37	2	1	3	0	3	.00	11	.321	.375	.479
3 ML YEARS		154	296	89	17	1	9	(4	5)	135	36	51	47	26	1	54	2	1	4	0	3	.00	12	.301	.357	.456

Gary Glover

Pitches: R Bats: R Pos: SP-3; RP-1   Ht: 6'5" Wt: 205 Born: 12/3/1976 Age: 28

		HOW MUCH HE PITCHED						WHAT HE GAVE UP												THE RESULTS						
Year Team	Lg	G	GS	CG	GF	IP	BFP	H	R	ER	HR	SH	SF	HB	TBB	IBB	SO	WP	Bk	W	L	Pct	ShO	Sv-Op	Hld	ERC	ERA
2004 Indianapolis*	AAA	8	6	0	0	40.2	172	47	19	18	1	3	4	1	11	0	18	2	0	3	3	.500	0	0--	-	4.12	3.98
2004 Rochester*	AAA	5	4	0	0	16.0	73	27	15	15	6	0	1	0	5	0	8	0	0	0	1	.000	0	0--	-	11.18	8.44
2004 Iowa*	AAA	20	1	0	5	30.2	151	43	29	27	8	0	1	3	14	0	18	1	1	3	2	.600	0	0--	-	8.43	7.92
1999 Toronto	AL	1	0	0	1	1.0	3	0	0	0	0	0	0	0	1	0	0	0	0	0	0	-	0	0-0	0	1.26	0.00
2001 Chicago	AL	46	11	0	10	100.1	429	98	61	55	16	2	2	4	32	3	63	4	0	5	5	.500	0	0-1	7	4.12	4.93
2002 Chicago	AL	41	22	0	0	138.1	604	136	86	80	21	6	2	7	52	1	70	6	0	7	8	.467	0	1-1	2	4.39	5.20
2003 CWS-Ana	AL	42	0	0	15	62.2	279	77	33	33	6	0	5	3	22	3	37	2	0	1	0	1.000	0	0-0	5	5.37	4.74
2004 Milwaukee	NL	4	3	0	0	18.0	82	18	9	7	2	2	2	2	8	1	8	1	0	2	1	.667	0	0-0	0	4.57	3.50
2003 Chicago	AL	24	0	0	8	35.2	160	43	18	18	3	0	3	2	14	2	23	1	0	1	0	1.000	0	0-0	1	5.32	4.54
2003 Anaheim	AL	18	0	0	7	27.0	119	34	15	15	3	0	2	1	8	1	14	1	0	1	0	1.000	0	0-0	4	5.44	5.00
5 ML YEARS		134	36	0	36	320.1	1397	329	189	175	45	10	11	16	115	8	178	13	0	16	14	.533	0	1-2	10	4.49	4.92

Ryan Glynn

Pitches: R **Bats:** R **Pos:** RP-4; SP-2 **Ht:** 6'3" **Wt:** 200 **Born:** 11/1/1974 **Age:** 30

			HOW MUCH HE PITCHED						WHAT HE GAVE UP									THE RESULTS							
Year Team	Lg	G	GS	CG	GF	IP	BFP	H	R	ER	HR	SH	SF	HB	TBB	IBB	SO	WP	Bk	W	L	Pct	ShO	Sv-Op	Hld	ERC	ERA
2004 Richmond*	AAA	11	0	0	3	17.2	96	26	11	11	0	0	1	3	14	0	19	2	0	1	1	.500	0	0- -	-	8.24	5.60
2004 Syracuse*	AAA	16	16	1	0	92.2	385	82	38	35	7	11	4	1	34	0	75	3	0	7	2	.778	1	0- -	-	3.23	3.40
1999 Texas	AL	13	10	0	2	54.2	262	71	46	44	10	0	1	1	35	0	39	3	1	2	4	.333	0	0-0	0	7.77	7.24
2000 Texas	AL	16	16	0	0	88.2	412	107	65	55	15	3	0	3	41	2	33	3	0	5	7	.417	0	0-0	0	6.12	5.58
2001 Texas	AL	12	9	0	3	46.0	219	59	38	36	7	0	2	0	26	1	15	5	0	1	5	.167	0	0-0	0	6.81	7.04
2004 Toronto	AL	6	2	0	0	20.0	89	19	9	9	4	1	1	3	8	1	14	0	0	1	0	1.000	0	0-0	0	4.99	4.05
4 ML YEARS		47	37	0	5	209.1	982	256	158	144	36	4	4	7	110	4	101	11	1	9	16	.360	0	0-0	0	6.58	6.19

Jimmy Gobble

Pitches: L **Bats:** L **Pos:** SP-24; RP-1 **Ht:** 6'3" **Wt:** 190 **Born:** 7/19/1981 **Age:** 23

			HOW MUCH HE PITCHED						WHAT HE GAVE UP									THE RESULTS							
Year Team	Lg	G	GS	CG	GF	IP	BFP	H	R	ER	HR	SH	SF	HB	TBB	IBB	SO	WP	Bk	W	L	Pct	ShO	Sv-Op	Hld	ERC	ERA
1999 Royals	R	4	1	0	0	6.2	32	6	3	2	0	0	0	0	5	0	8	1	1	0	0	-	0	0- -	-	3.85	2.70
2000 Chrlstn - WV	A	25	25	3	0	145.0	604	144	75	59	10	1	2	4	34	0	115	1	1	12	10	.545	2	0- -	-	3.30	3.66
2001 Wilmington	A	27	27	0	0	162.1	649	134	58	46	8	9	4	9	33	3	154	7	0	10	6	.625	0	0- -	-	2.31	2.55
2002 Wichita	AA	13	13	0	0	69.1	291	71	29	26	3	2	2	2	19	2	52	5	0	5	7	.417	0	0- -	-	3.43	3.38
2003 Wichita	AA	22	22	2	0	132.2	559	128	57	47	11	5	5	5	40	1	100	5	0	12	8	.600	1	0- -	-	3.52	3.19
2004 Omaha	AAA	4	4	0	0	19.2	90	25	20	10	5	0	0	0	7	0	15	0	0	3	1	.750	0	0- -	-	6.61	4.58
2003 Kansas City	AL	9	9	0	0	52.2	230	56	32	27	8	1	3	4	15	0	31	1	0	4	5	.444	0	0-0	0	4.61	4.61
2004 Kansas City	AL	25	24	1	0	148.0	638	157	94	88	24	4	7	3	43	0	49	4	0	9	8	.529	0	0-0	0	4.47	5.35
2 ML YEARS		34	33	1	0	200.2	868	213	126	115	32	5	10	7	58	0	80	5	0	13	13	.500	0	0-0	0	4.50	5.16

Jonny Gomes

Bats: R **Throws:** R **Pos:** DH-4; PH-1 **Ht:** 6'1" **Wt:** 205 **Born:** 11/22/1980 **Age:** 24

					BATTING														BASERUNNING				AVERAGES		
Year Team	Lg	G	AB	H	2B	3B	HR	(Hm	Rd)	TB	R	RBI	RC	TBB	IBB	SO	HBP	SH	SF	SB	CS	SB%	GDP	Avg	OBP	Slg
2001 Princeton	R+	62	206	60	11	2	16	(-	-)	123	58	44	55	33	0	73	26	1	4	15	4	.79	1	.291	.442	.597
2002 Bakersfield	A+	134	446	124	24	9	30	(-	-)	256	102	72	111	94	6	173	31	0	1	15	3	.83	4	.278	.432	.574
2003 Orlando	AA	120	442	110	28	3	17	(-	-)	195	68	56	71	53	1	148	16	0	4	23	2	.92	5	.249	.348	.441
2003 Durham	AAA	5	19	6	2	1	0	(-	-)	10	2	1	4	2	0	5	2	0	0	0	0	-	0	.316	.435	.526
2004 Durham	AAA	114	390	100	27	1	26	(-	-)	207	73	78	74	51	0	136	22	0	7	8	5	.62	6	.256	.368	.531
2003 Tampa Bay	AL	8	15	2	1	0	0	(0	0)	3	1	0	0	1	0	6	1	0	0	0	0	-	0	.133	.188	.200
2004 Tampa Bay	AL	5	14	1	0	0	0	(0	0)	1	0	1	0	1	0	6	0	0	0	0	0	-	0	.071	.133	.071
2 ML YEARS		13	29	3	1	0	0	(0	0)	4	1	1	0	1	0	12	1	0	0	0	0	-	0	.103	.161	.138

Alexis Gomez

Bats: L **Throws:** L **Pos:** LF-6; RF-5; CF-2; PR-2 **Ht:** 6'2" **Wt:** 180 **Born:** 8/6/1980 **Age:** 24

					BATTING														BASERUNNING				AVERAGES		
Year Team	Lg	G	AB	H	2B	3B	HR	(Hm	Rd)	TB	R	RBI	RC	TBB	IBB	SO	HBP	SH	SF	SB	CS	SB%	GDP	Avg	OBP	Slg
1999 Royals	R	56	214	59	12	1	5	(-	-)	88	44	31	35	32	0	48	1	1	1	13	5	.72	1	.276	.371	.411
2000 Wilmington	A+	121	461	117	13	4	1	(-	-)	141	63	33	48	45	1	121	2	7	1	21	10	.68	8	.254	.322	.306
2001 Wilmington	A+	48	169	51	8	2	1	(-	-)	66	29	9	22	11	2	43	1	2	0	7	3	.70	4	.302	.348	.391
2001 Wichita	AA	83	342	96	15	6	4	(-	-)	135	55	34	46	27	1	70	4	1	4	16	10	.62	4	.281	.337	.395
2002 Wichita	AA	114	461	136	21	8	14	(-	-)	215	72	75	72	45	5	84	3	2	4	36	24	.60	9	.295	.359	.466
2003 Omaha	AAA	121	456	123	23	8	8	(-	-)	186	49	58	53	26	1	91	1	2	4	4	5	.44	12	.270	.308	.408
2004 Omaha	AAA	109	383	96	17	8	7	(-	-)	150	45	34	38	19	0	96	1	4	4	8	6	.57	12	.251	.285	.392
2002 Kansas City	AL	5	10	2	0	0	0	(0	0)	2	0	0	0	0	0	2	0	0	0	0	0	-	0	.200	.200	.200
2004 Kansas City	AL	13	29	8	1	0	0	(0	0)	9	1	4	3	2	0	8	0	0	1	0	0	-	1	.276	.323	.310
2 ML YEARS		18	39	10	1	0	0	(0	0)	11	1	4	3	2	0	10	0	0	1	0	0	-	1	.256	.293	.282

Chris Gomez

Bats: R **Throws:** R **Pos:** SS-77; 1B-19; PH-8; 3B-5; DH-4; PR-4; 2B-3 **Ht:** 6'1" **Wt:** 185 **Born:** 6/16/1971 **Age:** 34

					BATTING														BASERUNNING				AVERAGES		
Year Team	Lg	G	AB	H	2B	3B	HR	(Hm	Rd)	TB	R	RBI	RC	TBB	IBB	SO	HBP	SH	SF	SB	CS	SB%	GDP	Avg	OBP	Slg
1993 Detroit	AL	46	128	32	7	1	0	(0	0)	41	11	11	12	9	0	17	1	3	0	2	2	.50	2	.250	.304	.320
1994 Detroit	AL	84	296	76	19	0	8	(5	3)	119	32	53	39	33	0	64	3	3	1	5	3	.63	8	.257	.336	.402
1995 Detroit	AL	123	431	96	20	2	11	(5	6)	153	49	50	43	41	0	96	3	3	4	4	1	.80	13	.223	.292	.355
1996 Det-SD		137	456	117	21	1	4	(2	2)	152	53	45	52	57	1	84	7	6	2	3	3	.50	16	.257	.347	.333
1997 San Diego	NL	150	522	132	19	2	5	(2	3)	170	62	54	52	53	1	114	5	3	5	8	8	.50	16	.253	.326	.326
1998 San Diego	NL	145	449	120	32	3	4	(3	1)	170	55	39	58	51	7	87	5	7	3	1	3	.25	11	.267	.346	.379
1999 San Diego	NL	76	234	59	8	1	1	(1	0)	72	20	15	23	27	3	49	1	2	1	1	2	.33	6	.252	.331	.308
2000 San Diego	NL	33	54	12	0	0	0	(0	0)	12	4	3	4	7	0	5	0	1	1	0	0	-	1	.222	.306	.222
2001 SD-TB		98	301	78	19	0	8	(5	3)	121	37	43	36	17	0	38	2	6	5	4	0	1.00	6	.259	.298	.402
2002 Tampa Bay	AL	130	461	122	31	3	10	(2	8)	189	51	46	51	21	0	58	7	6	3	1	3	.25	8	.265	.305	.410
2003 Minnesota	AL	58	175	44	9	3	1	(0	1)	62	14	15	15	7	1	13	0	2	1	2	1	.67	10	.251	.279	.354
2004 Toronto	AL	109	341	96	11	1	3	(1	2)	118	41	37	48	28	0	41	2	3	3	3	2	.60	4	.282	.337	.346
1996 Detroit	AL	48	128	31	5	0	1	(1	0)	39	21	16	13	18	0	20	1	3	0	1	1	.50	5	.242	.340	.305
1996 San Diego	NL	89	328	86	16	1	3	(1	2)	113	32	29	39	39	1	64	6	3	2	2	2	.50	11	.262	.349	.345
2001 San Diego	NL	40	112	21	3	0	0	(0	0)	24	6	7	4	9	0	14	0	2	2	1	0	1.00	5	.188	.244	.214
2001 Tampa Bay	AL	58	189	57	16	0	8	(5	3)	97	31	36	32	8	0	24	2	4	3	3	0	1.00	1	.302	.332	.513
12 ML YEARS		1189	3848	984	196	17	55	(26	29)	1379	429	411	433	351	13	666	36	45	27	31	28	.53	104	.256	.322	.358

Adrian Gonzalez

Bats: L **Throws:** L **Pos:** 1B-11; PH-5; DH-1   **Ht:** 6'2" **Wt:** 220 **Born:** 5/8/1982 **Age:** 23

Year Team	Lg	G	AB	H	2B	3B	HR	(Hm	Rd)	TB	R	RBI	RC	TBB	IBB	SO	HBP	SH	SF	SB	CS	SB%	GDP	Avg	OBP	Slg
2000 Marlins	R	53	193	57	10	1	0	(-	-)	69	24	30	30	32	3	35	2	0	2	0	0	-	6	.295	.397	.358
2000 Utica	A-	8	29	9	3	0	0	(-	-)	12	7	3	6	7	0	6	0	0	0	0	0	-	0	.310	.444	.414
2001 Kane County	A	127	516	161	37	1	17	(-	-)	251	86	103	89	57	6	83	5	0	6	5	5	.50	17	.312	.382	.486
2002 Portland	AA	138	508	135	34	1	17	(-	-)	222	70	96	73	54	6	112	8	0	3	6	3	.67	13	.266	.344	.437
2003 Frisco	AA	45	173	49	6	2	3	(-	-)	68	16	17	21	11	2	27	1	0	2	0	0	-	6	.283	.326	.393
2003 Carolina	AA	36	137	42	9	1	1	(-	-)	56	15	16	19	14	0	25	0	0	1	1	1	.50	6	.307	.368	.409
2003 Albuquerque	AAA	39	139	30	5	1	1	(-	-)	40	17	18	10	14	0	25	0	0	1	1	0	1.00	6	.216	.286	.288
2004 Oklahoma	AAA	123	457	139	28	3	12	(-	-)	209	61	88	71	39	1	73	6	2	4	1	1	.50	17	.304	.364	.457
2004 Texas	AL	16	42	10	3	0	1	(1	0)	16	7	7	7	2	0	6	0	0	0	0	0	-	0	.238	.273	.381

Alex Gonzalez

Bats: R **Throws:** R **Pos:** SS-158; PH-1   **Ht:** 6'0" **Wt:** 200 **Born:** 2/15/1977 **Age:** 28

Year Team	Lg	G	AB	H	2B	3B	HR	(Hm	Rd)	TB	R	RBI	RC	TBB	IBB	SO	HBP	SH	SF	SB	CS	SB%	GDP	Avg	OBP	Slg
1998 Florida	NL	25	86	13	2	0	3	(1	2)	24	11	7	5	9	0	30	1	2	0	0	0	-	2	.151	.240	.279
1999 Florida	NL	136	560	155	28	4	14	(7	7)	241	81	59	69	15	0	113	12	1	3	5	5	.38	13	.277	.308	.430
2000 Florida	NL	109	385	77	17	4	7	(5	2)	123	35	42	26	13	0	77	2	5	2	7	1	.88	7	.200	.229	.319
2001 Florida	NL	145	515	129	36	1	9	(5	4)	194	57	48	56	30	6	107	10	3	3	2	2	.50	13	.250	.303	.377
2002 Florida	NL	42	151	34	7	1	2	(1	1)	49	15	18	14	12	1	32	4	3	2	3	1	.75	2	.225	.296	.325
2003 Florida	NL	150	528	135	33	6	18	(7	11)	234	52	77	67	33	13	106	13	3	5	0	4	.00	8	.256	.313	.443
2004 Florida	NL	159	561	130	30	3	23	(13	10)	235	67	79	58	27	9	126	4	3	4	3	1	.75	16	.232	.270	.419
7 ML YEARS		766	2786	673	153	23	76	(39	37)	1100	318	330	295	139	29	591	46	20	19	18	14	.56	61	.242	.287	.395

Alex S Gonzalez

Bats: R **Throws:** R **Pos:** SS-81; PH-4; PR-1   **Ht:** 6'0" **Wt:** 200 **Born:** 4/8/1973 **Age:** 32

Year Team	Lg	G	AB	H	2B	3B	HR	(Hm	Rd)	TB	R	RBI	RC	TBB	IBB	SO	HBP	SH	SF	SB	CS	SB%	GDP	Avg	OBP	Slg
2004 Iowa*	AAA	8	24	8	3	0	0	(-	-)	11	7	0	4	4	0	7	0	0	0	1	0	1.00	1	.333	.429	.458
1994 Toronto	AL	15	53	8	3	1	0	(0	0)	13	7	1	2	4	0	17	1	1	0	3	1	.75	2	.151	.224	.245
1995 Toronto	AL	111	367	89	19	4	10	(8	2)	146	51	42	47	44	1	114	1	9	4	4	4	.50	7	.243	.322	.398
1996 Toronto	AL	147	527	124	30	5	14	(3	11)	206	64	64	61	45	0	127	5	7	3	16	6	.73	12	.235	.300	.391
1997 Toronto	AL	126	426	102	23	2	12	(4	8)	165	46	35	50	34	1	94	5	11	2	15	6	.71	9	.239	.302	.387
1998 Toronto	AL	158	568	136	28	1	13	(7	6)	205	70	51	56	28	1	121	6	13	3	21	6	.78	13	.239	.281	.361
1999 Toronto	AL	38	154	45	13	0	2	(1	1)	64	22	12	23	16	0	23	3	0	0	4	2	.67	4	.292	.370	.416
2000 Toronto	AL	141	527	133	31	2	15	(5	10)	213	68	69	64	43	0	113	4	**16**	1	4	4	.50	14	.252	.313	.404
2001 Toronto	AL	154	636	161	25	5	17	(9	8)	247	79	76	72	43	0	149	7	7	10	18	11	.62	16	.253	.303	.388
2002 Chicago	NL	142	513	127	27	5	18	(13	5)	218	58	61	59	46	7	136	3	4	2	5	3	.63	11	.248	.312	.425
2003 Chicago	NL	152	536	122	37	0	20	(11	9)	219	71	59	57	47	1	123	6	8	4	3	3	.50	17	.228	.295	.409
2004 ChC-Mon-SD	NL	83	285	64	18	1	7	(2	5)	105	36	27	23	14	0	64	1	4	0	2	2	.50	7	.225	.263	.368
2004 Chicago	NL	37	129	28	10	0	3	(0	3)	47	15	8	6	4	0	26	0	2	0	1	1	.50	6	.217	.241	.364
2004 Montreal	NL	35	133	32	7	0	4	(2	2)	51	19	16	14	8	0	32	1	2	0	1	1	.50	1	.241	.289	.383
2004 San Diego	NL	11	23	4	1	1	0	(0	0)	7	2	3	3	2	0	6	0	0	0	0	0	-	0	.174	.240	.304
11 ML YEARS		1267	4592	1111	254	26	128	(63	65)	1801	572	497	514	364	11	1081	42	80	29	95	47	.67	112	.242	.302	.392

Dicky Gonzalez

Pitches: R **Bats:** R **Pos:** RP-4   **Ht:** 5'11" **Wt:** 170 **Born:** 12/21/1978 **Age:** 26

Year Team	Lg	G	GS	CG	GF	IP	BFP	H	R	ER	HR	SH	SF	HB	TBB	IBB	SO	WP	Bk	W	L	Pct	ShO	Sv-Op	Hld	ERC	ERA
1996 Mets	R	11	8	2	1	47.1	195	50	19	14	1	2	0	2	3	0	51	1	0	4	2	.667	1	0--	-	2.72	2.66
1996 Kingsport	R+	1	1	0	0	5.0	20	4	2	1	0	1	0	0	0	0	7	1	0	1	0	1.000	0	0--	-	1.21	1.80
1997 Capital City	A	10	7	1	2	47.1	204	50	28	26	8	2	1	1	15	0	49	2	0	1	4	.200	0	0--	-	4.63	4.94
1997 Kingsport	R+	12	12	1	0	66.0	282	70	38	32	7	4	2	4	10	0	76	0	0	3	6	.333	0	0--	-	3.63	4.36
1998 Capital City	A	18	18	1	0	111.1	449	104	57	41	9	5	1	9	14	1	107	5	1	10	3	.769	0	0--	-	2.88	3.31
1998 St. Lucie	A+	8	8	0	0	46.2	193	46	22	16	8	1	0	1	13	0	23	1	0	2	1	.667	0	0--	-	4.16	3.09
1999 St. Lucie	A+	25	25	3	0	168.2	673	156	66	53	11	4	0	6	30	1	143	4	1	14	9	.609	0	0--	-	2.80	2.83
1999 Norfolk	AAA	1	1	0	0	6.2	23	5	2	2	0	0	0	0	1	0	3	0	0	1	0	1.000	0	0--	-	1.62	2.70
2000 Binghamton	AA	26	25	2	0	147.2	609	130	75	63	14	4	2	11	36	0	138	6	0	13	5	.722	1	0--	-	3.08	3.84
2001 Norfolk	AAA	17	16	2	0	96.0	392	96	35	33	10	4	6	4	20	1	70	2	0	6	5	.545	2	0--	-	3.59	3.09
2002 Norfolk	AAA	1	1	0	0	5.0	23	6	2	2	1	0	0	0	2	0	7	0	0	0	0	-	0	0--	-	5.87	3.60
2002 Ottawa	AAA	22	22	0	0	119.2	521	137	59	50	10	3	5	4	33	2	72	3	1	8	5	.615	0	0--	-	4.39	3.76
2003 Pawtucket	AAA	27	25	1	2	151.2	654	180	77	68	13	3	3	9	29	1	104	3	0	8	8	.500	0	0--	-	4.45	4.04
2004 Durham	AAA	6	6	0	0	30.0	119	28	16	16	3	0	1	1	7	0	30	0	0	1	2	.333	0	0--	-	3.35	4.80
2001 New York	NL	16	7	0	2	57.0	261	72	33	32	4	2	6	1	17	3	31	5	0	3	2	.600	0	0-0	-	4.81	5.05
2004 Tampa Bay	AL	4	0	0	1	7.1	32	9	5	5	1	0	1	0	2	0	7	2	0	0	0	-	0	0-0	-	5.18	6.14
2 ML YEARS		20	7	0	3	64.1	293	81	38	37	5	2	7	1	19	3	38	7	0	3	2	.600	0	0-0	-	4.85	5.18

Edgar Gonzalez

Pitches: R **Bats:** R **Pos:** SP-10   **Ht:** 6'0" **Wt:** 215 **Born:** 2/23/1983 **Age:** 22

Year Team	Lg	G	GS	CG	GF	IP	BFP	H	R	ER	HR	SH	SF	HB	TBB	IBB	SO	WP	Bk	W	L	Pct	ShO	Sv-Op	Hld	ERC	ERA
2002 South Bend	A	23	23	4	0	151.1	625	141	66	49	4	4	7	7	34	0	110	10	1	11	8	.579	2	0--	-	2.73	2.91
2002 Lancaster	A+	4	4	0	0	23.0	97	24	7	2	1	0	1	2	3	0	21	0	0	3	0	1.000	0	0--	-	3.19	0.78
2003 El Paso	AA	6	6	0	0	36.0	155	40	18	14	1	1	0	1	11	0	30	3	0	2	2	.500	0	0--	-	3.96	3.50
2003 Tucson	AAA	20	19	1	1	129.2	542	126	65	54	4	6	5	8	28	0	69	5	1	8	7	.533	0	0--	-	2.98	3.75
2004 Tucson	AAA	15	15	1	0	94.0	395	99	52	51	15	9	3	6	25	0	66	4	0	5	5	.500	1	0--	-	4.63	4.88

Year Team	Lg	G	GS	CG	GF	IP	BFP	H	R	ER	HR	SH	SF	HB	TBB	IBB	SO	WP	Bk	W	L	Pct	ShO	Sv-Op	Hld	ERC	ERA
2003 Arizona	NL	9	2	0	1	18.1	85	28	10	10	3	1	1	0	7	2	14	2	0	2	1	.667	0	0-1	0	7.81	4.91
2004 Arizona	NL	10	10	0	0	46.1	228	72	49	48	15	5	1	5	18	4	31	3	1	0	9	.000	0	0-0	0	9.78	9.32
2 ML YEARS		19	12	0	1	64.2	313	100	59	58	18	6	2	5	25	6	45	5	1	2	10	.167	0	0-1	0	9.22	8.07

Jeremi Gonzalez

Pitches: R **Bats:** R **Pos:** SP-8; RP-3   **Ht:** 6'0" **Wt:** 220 **Born:** 1/8/1975 **Age:** 30

Year Team	Lg	G	GS	CG	GF	IP	BFP	H	R	ER	HR	SH	SF	HB	TBB	IBB	SO	WP	Bk	W	L	Pct	ShO	Sv-Op	Hld	ERC	ERA
2004 Durham*	AAA	18	8	0	4	56.2	231	50	27	25	7	1	1	1	18	0	44	4	0	4	2	.667	0	1- --	-	3.41	3.97
1997 Chicago	NL	23	23	1	0	144.0	613	126	73	68	16	4	5	2	69	5	93	1	1	11	9	.550	1	0-0	0	3.79	4.25
1998 Chicago	NL	20	20	1	0	110.0	493	124	72	65	13	5	2	3	41	5	70	2	3	7	7	.500	1	0-0	0	4.80	5.32
2003 Tampa Bay	AL	25	25	2	0	156.1	668	131	71	68	18	3	9	12	69	1	97	3	2	6	11	.353	0	0-0	0	3.74	3.91
2004 Tampa Bay	AL	11	8	0	1	50.1	235	72	42	39	9	1	3	3	20	0	22	4	0	0	5	.000	0	0-0	0	7.77	6.97
4 ML YEARS		79	76	4	1	460.2	2009	453	258	240	56	13	19	20	199	11	282	10	6	24	32	.429	2	0-0	4	4.40	4.69

Juan Gonzalez

Bats: R **Throws:** R **Pos:** RF-29; DH-4   **Ht:** 6'3" **Wt:** 220 **Born:** 10/16/1969 **Age:** 35

Year Team	Lg	G	AB	H	2B	3B	HR	(Hm	Rd)	TB	R	RBI	RC	TBB	IBB	SO	HBP	SH	SF	SB	CS	SB%	GDP	Avg	OBP	Slg
1989 Texas	AL	24	60	9	3	0	1	(1	0)	15	6	7	2	6	0	17	0	2	0	0	0	--	4	.150	.227	.250
1990 Texas	AL	25	90	26	7	1	4	(3	1)	47	11	12	14	2	0	18	2	0	1	0	1	.00	2	.289	.316	.522
1991 Texas	AL	142	545	144	34	1	27	(7	20)	261	78	102	81	42	7	118	5	0	3	4	4	.50	10	.264	.321	.479
1992 Texas	AL	155	584	152	24	2	43	(19	24)	309	77	109	90	35	1	143	5	0	0	0	1	.00	16	.260	.304	.529
1993 Texas	AL	140	536	166	33	1	46	(24	22)	339	105	118	116	37	7	99	13	0	1	4	1	.80	12	.310	.368	.632
1994 Texas	AL	107	422	116	18	4	19	(6	13)	199	57	85	60	30	10	66	7	0	4	6	4	.60	18	.275	.330	.472
1995 Texas	AL	90	352	104	20	2	27	(15	12)	209	57	82	61	17	3	66	0	0	5	0	0	--	15	.295	.324	.594
1996 Texas	AL	134	541	170	33	2	47	(23	24)	348	89	144	119	45	12	82	3	0	3	2	0	1.00	10	.314	.368	.643
1997 Texas	AL	133	533	158	24	3	42	(18	24)	314	87	131	100	33	7	107	3	0	10	0	0	--	12	.296	.335	.589
1998 Texas	AL	154	606	193	50	2	45	(21	24)	382	110	157	128	46	9	126	6	0	11	2	1	.67	20	.318	.366	.630
1999 Texas	AL	144	562	183	36	1	39	(14	25)	338	114	128	121	51	7	105	4	0	12	3	3	.50	10	.326	.378	.601
2000 Detroit	AL	115	461	133	30	2	22	(8	14)	233	69	67	73	32	3	84	2	0	1	1	2	.33	13	.289	.337	.505
2001 Cleveland	AL	140	532	173	34	1	35	(22	13)	314	97	140	108	41	5	94	6	0	16	1	0	1.00	18	.325	.370	.590
2002 Texas	AL	70	277	78	21	1	8	(4	4)	125	38	35	38	17	1	56	1	0	1	2	0	1.00	11	.282	.324	.451
2003 Texas	AL	82	327	96	17	1	24	(11	13)	187	49	70	54	14	1	73	4	0	1	1	1	.50	10	.294	.329	.572
2004 Kansas City	AL	33	127	35	4	1	5	(1	4)	56	17	17	18	9	1	19	1	0	1	0	1	.00	3	.276	.326	.441
16 ML YEARS		1688	6555	1936	388	25	434	(197	237)	3676	1061	1404	1183	457	74	1273	62	2	78	26	19	.58	184	.295	.343	.561

Luis Gonzalez

Bats: L **Throws:** R **Pos:** LF-103; DH-1; PH-1   **Ht:** 6'2" **Wt:** 195 **Born:** 9/3/1967 **Age:** 37

Year Team	Lg	G	AB	H	2B	3B	HR	(Hm	Rd)	TB	R	RBI	RC	TBB	IBB	SO	HBP	SH	SF	SB	CS	SB%	GDP	Avg	OBP	Slg
1990 Houston	NL	12	21	4	2	0	0	(0	0)	6	1	0	2	2	1	5	0	0	0	0	0	--	0	.190	.261	.286
1991 Houston	NL	137	473	120	28	9	13	(4	9)	205	51	69	64	40	4	101	8	1	4	10	7	.59	5	.254	.320	.433
1992 Houston	NL	122	387	94	19	3	10	(4	6)	149	40	55	41	24	3	52	2	1	2	7	7	.50	6	.243	.289	.385
1993 Houston	NL	154	540	162	34	3	15	(8	7)	247	82	72	90	47	7	83	10	3	10	20	9	.69	9	.300	.361	.457
1994 Houston	NL	112	392	107	29	4	8	(3	5)	168	57	67	57	49	6	57	3	0	6	15	13	.54	10	.273	.353	.429
1995 Hou-ChC	NL	133	471	130	29	8	13	(6	7)	214	69	69	72	57	8	63	6	1	6	6	8	.43	16	.276	.357	.454
1996 Chicago	NL	146	483	131	30	4	15	(6	9)	214	70	79	75	61	8	49	4	1	6	9	6	.60	13	.271	.354	.443
1997 Houston	NL	152	550	142	31	2	10	(4	6)	207	78	68	73	71	7	67	5	0	5	10	7	.59	12	.258	.345	.376
1998 Detroit	AL	154	547	146	35	5	23	(15	8)	260	84	71	89	57	7	62	8	0	8	12	7	.63	8	.267	.340	.475
1999 Arizona	NL	153	614	206	45	4	26	(10	16)	337	112	111	129	66	6	63	7	1	5	9	5	.64	13	.336	.403	.549
2000 Arizona	NL	162	618	192	47	2	31	(14	17)	336	106	114	128	76	6	85	12	2	12	2	4	.33	12	.311	.392	.544
2001 Arizona	NL	162	609	198	36	7	57	(26	31)	419	128	142	164	100	24	83	14	0	5	1	1	.50	14	.325	.429	.688
2002 Arizona	NL	148	524	151	19	3	28	(11	17)	260	90	103	114	97	8	76	5	0	7	9	2	.82	12	.288	.400	.496
2003 Arizona	NL	156	579	176	46	4	26	(6	20)	308	92	104	113	94	17	67	3	0	3	5	3	.63	19	.304	.402	.532
2004 Arizona	NL	105	379	98	28	5	17	(10	7)	187	69	48	62	68	11	58	2	0	2	2	2	.50	9	.259	.373	.493
1995 Houston	NL	56	209	54	10	4	6	(1	5)	90	35	35	26	18	3	30	3	1	3	1	3	.25	8	.258	.322	.431
1995 Houston	NL	77	262	76	19	4	7	(5	2)	124	34	34	46	39	5	33	3	0	3	5	5	.50	8	.290	.384	.473
15 ML YEARS		2008	7187	2057	458	63	292	(127	165)	3517	1129	1172	1273	911	123	971	89	10	81	117	81	.59	163	.286	.370	.489

Luis A Gonzalez

Bats: R **Throws:** R **Pos:** 2B-40; PH-22; LF-20; 3B-18; RF-11; SS-10; PR-2; DH-1   **Ht:** 5'11" **Wt:** 170 **Born:** 6/26/1979 **Age:** 26

Year Team	Lg	G	AB	H	2B	3B	HR	(Hm	Rd)	TB	R	RBI	RC	TBB	IBB	SO	HBP	SH	SF	SB	CS	SB%	GDP	Avg	OBP	Slg
1998 Columbus	A	101	320	87	14	1	3	(-	-)	112	48	32	41	28	0	63	8	10	1	10	3	.77	5	.272	.345	.350
1999 Columbus	A	83	299	88	18	2	7	(-	-)	131	41	50	46	26	0	40	5	4	5	6	5	.55	5	.294	.355	.438
1999 Kinston	A+	1	1	0	0	0	0	(-	-)	0	0	0	0	0	0	0	0	0	0	0	0	--	0	.000	.000	.000
2000 Kinston	A+	79	284	70	11	0	2	(-	-)	87	32	33	27	21	0	54	6	12	2	6	6	.50	6	.246	.310	.306
2001 Kinston	A+	52	183	59	14	0	5	(-	-)	88	31	19	33	14	0	36	8	1	2	3	5	.38	1	.322	.391	.481
2001 Akron	AA	52	199	60	12	2	5	(-	-)	91	41	17	28	7	0	26	2	0	2	2	3	.40	3	.302	.329	.457
2002 Akron	AA	73	263	70	10	3	6	(-	-)	104	42	24	32	12	0	37	5	5	6	4	0	1.00	6	.266	.304	.395
2002 Buffalo	AAA	6	19	2	0	0	0	(-	-)	2	0	1	0	1	0	4	1	0	0	0	0	--	1	.105	.190	.105
2003 Akron	AA	116	431	137	22	4	7	(-	-)	188	72	62	72	46	2	41	6	2	8	1	0	1.00	17	.318	.385	.436
2004 Colorado	NL	102	322	94	17	2	12	(4	8)	151	42	40	45	15	1	67	4	9	1	1	5	.17	5	.292	.330	.469

Mike Gonzalez

Pitches: L **Bats:** R **Pos:** RP-47   **Ht:** 6'2" **Wt:** 213 **Born:** 5/23/1978 **Age:** 27

			HOW MUCH HE PITCHED						WHAT HE GAVE UP													THE RESULTS							
Year Team	Lg	G	GS	CG	GF	IP	BFP	H	R	ER	HR	SH	SF	HB	TBB	IBB	SO	WP	Bk	W	L	Pct	ShO	Sv-Op	Hld	ERC	ERA
1997 Pirates	R	7	3	0	0	29.0	115	21	9	8	0	1	0	1	8	0	33	3	3	2	0	1.000	0	0--	-	1.75	2.48
1997 Augusta	A	4	3	0	1	19.1	76	11	5	4	1	1	0	0	8	0	22	3	0	1	1	.500	0	0--	-	1.68	1.86
1998 Lynchburg	A+	7	7	0	0	28.1	131	40	21	21	5	0	1	3	13	0	22	1	0	0	3	.000	0	0--	-	8.38	6.67
1998 Augusta	A	11	9	0	0	50.2	221	43	24	16	2	1	1	7	26	0	72	3	4	4	2	.667	0	0--	-	3.80	2.84
1999 Lynchburg	A+	20	20	0	0	112.0	478	98	55	50	10	2	1	4	63	0	119	10	0	10	4	.714	0	0--	-	4.19	4.02
1999 Altoona	AA	7	5	0	0	26.2	133	34	25	24	4	2	1	2	19	0	31	3	3	2	3	.400	0	0--	-	7.75	8.10
2000 Pirates	R	2	1	0	1	6.0	35	8	6	3	1	0	0	1	4	0	7	3	0	1	0	1.000	0	0--	-	7.34	4.50
2000 Lynchburg	A+	12	10	0	1	56.0	256	57	34	29	6	5	2	3	34	0	53	1	0	4	3	.571	0	0--	-	5.28	4.66
2001 Lynchburg	A+	14	2	0	7	30.2	127	28	14	10	3	3	1	0	7	1	32	5	1	2	2	.500	0	0--	-	2.83	2.93
2001 Altoona	AA	14	14	1	0	87.1	367	81	38	36	5	6	2	0	36	0	66	2	1	5	4	.556	1	0--	-	3.48	3.71
2002 Altoona	AA	16	16	0	0	85.1	367	77	38	36	4	0	0	4	47	2	82	7	1	8	4	.667	0	0--	-	3.97	3.80
2002 Pirates	R	2	2	0	0	13.1	47	5	1	0	0	0	0	0	3	0	14	0	0	2	0	1.000	0	0--	-	0.63	0.00
2003 Lynchburg	A+	5	0	0	0	7.0	32	7	9	4	0	1	0	0	5	0	9	0	0	0	1	.000	0	0--	-	4.56	5.14
2003 Altoona	AA	5	0	0	2	7.1	28	4	1	1	1	0	0	0	2	0	10	0	0	0	0	-	0	1--	-	1.58	1.23
2003 Nashville	AAA	7	0	0	2	10.0	45	9	5	5	0	0	0	2	4	1	10	0	0	0	0	-	0	2--	-	3.30	4.50
2003 Pawtucket	AAA	2	0	0	1	1.2	8	2	0	0	0	0	0	0	1	0	2	0	0	0	0	-	0	1--	-	5.10	0.00
2004 Nashville	AAA	14	0	0	3	20.0	73	12	2	2	0	0	0	0	7	0	35	2	0	2	0	1.000	0	2--	-	1.52	0.90
2003 Pittsburgh	NL	16	0	0	2	8.1	38	7	7	7	4	1	1	0	6	0	6	1	0	0	1	.000	0	0-0	3	7.18	7.56
2004 Pittsburgh	NL	47	0	0	12	43.1	169	32	7	6	2	3	0	1	6	0	55	4	0	3	1	.750	0	1-4	13	1.60	1.25
2 ML YEARS		63	0	0	14	51.2	207	39	14	13	6	4	1	1	12	0	61	5	0	3	2	.600	0	1-4	16	2.31	2.26

Raul Gonzalez

Bats: R **Throws:** R **Pos:** PH-4; RF-3; LF-1   **Ht:** 5'9" **Wt:** 190 **Born:** 12/27/1973 **Age:** 31

							BATTING													BASERUNNING				AVERAGES		
Year Team*	Lg	G	AB	H	2B	3B	HR	(Hm	Rd)	TB	R	RBI	RC	TBB	IBB	SO	HBP	SH	SF	SB	CS	SB%	GDP	Avg	OBP	Slg
2004 Norfolk*	AAA	18	65	17	6	1	1	(-	-)	28	5	6	8	6	0	9	1	1	0	1	2	.33	2	.262	.333	.431
2004 Buffalo*	AAA	56	232	72	13	1	9	(-	-)	114	36	40	34	13	0	19	0	1	1	5	5	.50	11	.310	.346	.491
2000 Chicago	NL	3	2	0	0	0	0	(0	0)	0	0	0	0	0	0	2	0	0	0	0	0	-	0	.000	.000	.000
2001 Cincinnati	NL	11	14	3	0	0	0	(0	0)	3	0	0	1	1	0	3	0	0	0	0	0	-	0	.214	.267	.214
2002 Cin-NYM	NL	40	104	27	3	0	3	(1	2)	39	13	12	13	6	0	22	0	0	1	4	2	.67	5	.260	.297	.375
2003 New York	NL	107	217	50	12	2	2	(1	1)	72	28	21	26	27	1	34	1	0	1	3	0	1.00	8	.230	.317	.332
2004 Cleveland	AL	7	11	1	0	0	0	(0	0)	1	0	0	0	0	0	4	0	0	0	0	0	-	0	.091	.091	.091
2002 Cincinnati	NL	10	23	6	1	0	0	(0	0)	7	4	1	2	2	0	5	0	0	0	2	0	1.00	1	.261	.320	.304
2002 New York	NL	30	81	21	2	0	3	(1	2)	32	9	11	11	4	0	17	0	0	1	2	2	.50	2	.259	.291	.395
5 ML YEARS		168	348	81	15	2	5	(2	3)	115	41	33	40	34	1	65	1	0	2	7	2	.78	11	.233	.301	.330

Andy Good

Pitches: R **Bats:** R **Pos:** RP-15; SP-2   **Ht:** 6'1" **Wt:** 209 **Born:** 9/19/1979 **Age:** 25

					HOW MUCH HE PITCHED					WHAT HE GAVE UP											THE RESULTS					
Year Team	Lg	G	GS	CG	GF	IP	BFP	H	R	ER	HR	SH	SF	HB	TBB	IBB	SO	WP	Bk	W	L	Pct	ShO	Sv-Op	Hld	ERC	ERA
1998 Diamndbcks	R	9	8	0	0	33.2	152	46	25	16	1	0	1	2	7	0	25	3	0	1	3	.250	0	0--	-	5.13	4.28
1998 South Bend	A	2	0	0	1	6.0	28	7	4	2	0	0	0	2	1	0	6	0	1	0	1	.000	0	0--	-	4.53	3.00
1999 South Bend	A	27	27	0	0	153.2	662	160	80	70	9	3	9	9	42	0	146	7	0	11	10	.524	0	0--	-	3.72	4.10
2001 Lancaster	A+	19	18	0	0	101.1	454	108	63	54	12	6	4	13	27	0	104	5	0	8	6	.571	0	0--	-	4.43	4.80
2001 El Paso	AA	10	9	0	0	56.2	270	79	44	37	2	1	2	3	20	0	46	3	0	2	3	.400	0	0--	-	5.80	5.88
2002 El Paso	AA	28	27	2	0	178.0	730	179	89	70	21	5	6	7	26	0	127	3	0	13	6	.684	1	0--	-	3.09	3.54
2003 Tucson	AAA	11	11	0	0	63.0	276	78	36	35	12	1	0	2	13	0	45	1	0	4	4	.500	0	0--	-	5.45	5.00
2004 El Paso	AA	4	4	0	0	9.2	39	7	2	1	0	0	0	0	3	0	9	0	0	0	0	-	0	0--	-	1.71	0.93
2004 Tucson	AAA	5	3	0	0	23.2	98	25	12	8	4	0	0	1	4	0	17	2	0	3	2	.600	0	0--	-	4.15	3.04
2003 Arizona	NL	16	10	0	0	66.1	289	74	42	39	15	3	4	3	16	2	42	3	0	4	2	.667	0	0-0	1	5.06	5.29
2004 Arizona	NL	17	2	0	3	40.2	177	43	25	24	8	1	2	3	13	0	26	2	0	1	2	.333	0	0-0	0	5.09	5.31
2 ML YEARS		33	12	0	3	107.0	466	117	67	63	23	4	6	6	29	2	68	5	0	5	4	.556	0	0-0	1	5.07	5.30

Tom Goodwin

Bats: L **Throws:** R **Pos:** PH-55; LF-14; CF-8; RF-7; PR-3   **Ht:** 6'1" **Wt:** 175 **Born:** 7/27/1968 **Age:** 36

							BATTING													BASERUNNING				AVERAGES		
Year Team	Lg	G	AB	H	2B	3B	HR	(Hm	Rd)	TB	R	RBI	RC	TBB	IBB	SO	HBP	SH	SF	SB	CS	SB%	GDP	Avg	OBP	Slg
1991 Los Angeles	NL	16	7	1	0	0	0	(0	0)	1	3	0	0	0	0	0	0	0	0	1	1	.50	0	.143	.143	.143
1992 Los Angeles	NL	57	73	17	1	1	0	(0	0)	20	15	3	6	6	0	10	0	0	0	7	3	.70	0	.233	.291	.274
1993 Los Angeles	NL	30	17	5	1	0	0	(0	0)	6	6	1	1	1	0	4	0	0	0	1	2	.33	1	.294	.333	.353
1994 Kansas City	AL	2	2	0	0	0	0	(0	0)	0	0	0	0	0	0	1	0	0	0	0	0	-	0	.000	.000	.000
1995 Kansas City	AL	133	480	138	16	3	4	(2	2)	172	72	28	64	38	0	72	5	14	0	50	18	.74	7	.288	.346	.358
1996 Kansas City	AL	143	524	148	14	4	1	(0	1)	173	80	35	65	39	0	79	2	21	1	66	22	.75	3	.282	.334	.330
1997 KC-Tex	AL	150	574	149	26	6	2	(0	2)	193	90	39	65	44	1	88	3	11	3	50	16	.76	7	.260	.314	.336
1998 Texas	AL	154	520	151	13	3	2	(2	0)	176	102	33	74	73	0	90	2	10	3	38	20	.66	2	.290	.378	.338
1999 Texas	AL	109	405	105	12	6	3	(1	2)	138	63	33	49	40	0	61	0	7	3	39	11	.78	7	.259	.324	.341
2000 Col-LA	NL	147	528	139	11	9	6	(4	2)	186	94	58	74	68	2	117	1	5	4	55	10	.85	7	.263	.346	.352
2001 Los Angeles	NL	105	286	66	8	5	4	(1	3)	96	51	22	29	23	0	58	0	1	2	22	8	.73	3	.231	.286	.336
2002 San Francisco	NL	78	154	40	5	2	1	(0	1)	52	23	17	21	14	0	25	0	3	0	16	2	.89	3	.260	.321	.338
2003 Chicago	NL	87	171	49	10	0	1	(0	1)	62	26	12	19	11	0	33	0	1	1	19	5	.79	3	.287	.328	.363
2004 Chicago	NL	77	105	21	8	0	0	(0	0)	29	11	3	5	8	0	22	0	0	1	5	0	1.00	1	.200	.254	.276
1997 Kansas City	AL	97	367	100	13	4	2	(0	2)	127	51	22	42	19	0	51	2	11	1	34	10	.77	5	.272	.311	.346
1997 Texas	AL	53	207	49	13	2	0	(0	0)	66	39	17	23	25	1	37	1	0	2	16	6	.73	2	.237	.319	.319
2000 Colorado	NL	91	317	86	8	8	5	(4	1)	125	65	47	54	50	2	76	1	5	4	39	7	.85	3	.271	.368	.394
2000 Los Angeles	NL	56	211	53	3	1	1	(0	1)	61	29	11	20	18	0	41	0	0	0	16	3	.84	4	.251	.310	.289
14 ML YEARS		1288	3846	1029	125	39	24	(10	14)	1304	636	284	472	365	3	660	13	73	18	369	118	.76	44	.268	.332	.339

Tom Gordon

Pitches: R **Bats:** R **Pos:** RP-80   **Ht:** 5'10" **Wt:** 190 **Born:** 11/18/1967 **Age:** 37

Year Team	Lg	G	GS	CG	GF	IP	BFP	H	R	ER	HR	SH	SF	HB	TBB	IBB	SO	WP	Bk	W	L	Pct	ShO	Sv-Op	Hld	ERC	ERA
1988 Kansas City	AL	5	2	0	0	15.2	67	16	9	9	1	0	0	0	7	0	18	0	0	0	2	.000	0	0-0	2	4.22	5.17
1989 Kansas City	AL	49	16	1	16	163.0	677	122	67	66	10	4	4	1	86	4	153	12	0	17	9	.654	1	1-7	3	2.97	3.64
1990 Kansas City	AL	32	32	6	0	195.1	858	192	99	81	17	8	2	3	99	1	175	11	0	12	11	.522	1	0-0	0	4.37	3.73
1991 Kansas City	AL	45	14	1	11	158.0	684	129	76	68	16	5	3	4	87	6	167	5	0	9	14	.391	0	1-4	4	3.67	3.87
1992 Kansas City	AL	40	11	0	13	117.2	516	116	67	60	9	2	6	4	55	4	98	5	2	6	10	.375	0	0-2	0	4.17	4.59
1993 Kansas City	AL	48	14	2	18	155.2	651	125	65	62	11	6	6	1	77	5	143	17	0	12	6	.667	0	1-6	2	3.18	3.58
1994 Kansas City	AL	24	24	0	0	155.1	675	136	79	75	15	3	8	3	87	3	126	12	1	11	7	.611	0	0-0	0	4.04	4.35
1995 Kansas City	AL	31	31	2	0	189.0	843	204	110	93	12	7	11	4	89	4	119	9	0	12	12	.500	0	0-0	0	4.59	4.43
1996 Boston	AL	34	34	4	0	215.2	998	249	143	134	28	2	11	4	105	5	171	6	1	12	9	.571	1	0-0	0	5.50	5.59
1997 Boston	AL	42	25	2	16	182.2	774	155	85	76	10	3	4	3	78	1	159	5	0	6	10	.375	1	11-13	0	3.08	3.74
1998 Boston	AL	73	0	0	69	79.1	317	55	24	24	2	2	2	0	25	1	78	9	0	7	4	.636	0	46-47	0	1.72	2.72
1999 Boston	AL	21	0	0	15	17.2	82	17	11	11	2	0	0	1	12	2	24	0	0	0	2	.000	0	11-13	1	5.04	5.60
2001 Chicago	NL	47	0	0	40	45.1	187	32	18	17	4	0	0	1	16	1	67	2	0	1	2	.333	0	27-31	0	2.27	3.38
2002 ChC-Hou	NL	34	0	0	10	42.2	181	42	19	16	3	3	0	1	16	3	48	0	0	1	3	.250	0	0-0	6	3.71	3.38
2003 Chicago	AL	66	0	0	35	74.0	310	57	29	26	4	4	3	4	31	3	91	5	0	7	6	.538	0	12-17	7	2.74	3.16
2004 New York	AL	80	0	0	15	89.2	342	56	23	22	5	5	2	1	23	5	96	3	0	9	4	.692	0	4-10	36	1.50	2.21
2002 Chicago	NL	19	0	0	7	23.2	104	27	12	9	1	0	1	0	10	1	31	0	0	1	1	.500	0	0-0	2	4.75	3.42
2002 Houston	NL	15	0	0	3	19.0	77	15	7	7	2	2	0	0	6	2	17	0	0	0	2	.000	0	0-0	4	2.53	3.32
16 ML YEARS		671	203	18	258	1896.2	8162	1703	924	840	149	54	62	35	893	48	1733	101	4	122	111	.524	4	114-150	61	3.66	3.99

Mike Gosling

Pitches: L **Bats:** L **Pos:** SP-4; RP-2   **Ht:** 6'2" **Wt:** 210 **Born:** 9/23/1980 **Age:** 24

Year Team	Lg	G	GS	CG	GF	IP	BFP	H	R	ER	HR	SH	SF	HB	TBB	IBB	SO	WP	Bk	W	L	Pct	ShO	Sv-Op	Hld	ERC	ERA
2002 El Paso	AA	27	27	2	0	166.2	705	149	66	58	7	8	6	4	62	4	115	9	1	14	5	.737	2	0--	-	3.03	3.13
2003 Tucson	AAA	26	26	0	0	136.1	645	190	106	85	13	5	5	3	56	0	89	13	0	9	12	.429	0	0--	-	6.50	5.61
2004 Tucson	AAA	24	21	0	0	128.1	581	160	101	83	16	5	8	3	53	0	67	12	0	9	5	.643	0	0--	-	5.94	5.82
2004 Arizona	NL	6	4	0	0	25.1	112	26	13	13	5	2	0	2	13	1	14	2	0	1	1	.500	0	0-0	0	5.83	4.62

Ruben Gotay

Bats: B **Throws:** R **Pos:** 2B-42; PH-1; PR-1   **Ht:** 5'11" **Wt:** 160 **Born:** 12/25/1982 **Age:** 22

Year Team	Lg	G	AB	H	2B	3B	HR	(Hm	Rd)	TB	R	RBI	RC	TBB	IBB	SO	HBP	SH	SF	SB	CS	SB%	GDP	Avg	OBP	Slg
2001 Royals	R	52	184	58	15	1	3	(-	-)	84	29	19	35	26	1	22	9	2	1	5	6	.45	2	.315	.423	.457
2002 Burlington	A	133	509	145	42	9	9	(-	-)	232	87	83	90	73	1	110	8	4	9	5	4	.56	5	.285	.377	.456
2003 Wilmington	A+	134	502	131	31	2	9	(-	-)	193	68	72	71	60	1	97	7	4	9	8	1	.89	7	.261	.343	.384
2004 Wichita	AA	106	404	117	22	6	9	(-	-)	178	71	68	66	51	0	60	6	9	5	9	10	.47	9	.290	.373	.441
2004 Kansas City	AL	44	152	41	7	3	1	(1	0)	57	17	16	17	9	0	36	2	1	2	0	1	.00	4	.270	.315	.375

John Grabow

Pitches: L **Bats:** L **Pos:** RP-68   **Ht:** 6'3" **Wt:** 185 **Born:** 11/4/1978 **Age:** 26

Year Team	Lg	G	GS	CG	GF	IP	BFP	H	R	ER	HR	SH	SF	HB	TBB	IBB	SO	WP	Bk	W	L	Pct	ShO	Sv-Op	Hld	ERC	ERA
1997 Pirates	R	11	8	0	0	45.1	204	57	32	23	0	1	2	0	14	0	28	3	0	2	7	.222	0	0--	-	4.38	4.57
1998 Augusta	A	17	16	0	0	71.2	329	84	59	46	7	1	5	3	34	0	67	9	0	6	3	.667	0	0--	-	5.52	5.78
1999 Hickory	A	26	26	0	0	156.1	654	152	82	66	16	3	3	5	32	0	164	3	0	9	10	.474	0	0--	-	3.26	3.80
2000 Altoona	AA	24	24	1	0	145.1	637	145	81	70	10	1	6	5	65	0	109	8	1	8	7	.533	0	0--	-	4.16	4.33
2001 Pirates	R	6	6	0	0	12.0	50	11	6	5	1	0	0	1	4	0	9	2	0	1	0	1.000	0	0--	-	3.65	3.75
2001 Lynchburg	A+	7	7	0	0	36.2	174	42	30	26	3	3	0	2	26	0	35	2	0	1	3	.250	0	0--	-	6.34	6.38
2001 Altoona	AA	10	10	0	0	50.2	214	30	23	19	1	2	0	2	39	0	42	5	3	2	5	.286	0	0--	-	2.91	3.38
2002 Altoona	AA	28	27	1	1	146.1	653	181	94	89	10	6	6	6	47	0	97	9	5	8	13	.381	1	0--	-	5.09	5.47
2003 Altoona	AA	24	9	0	5	83.0	341	87	34	31	9	6	5	1	19	2	73	3	1	6	1	.857	0	1--	-	3.84	3.36
2003 Nashville	AAA	17	0	0	4	24.2	112	31	17	13	0	1	0	0	7	2	26	0	0	0	2	.000	0	0--	-	4.07	4.74
2003 Pittsburgh	NL	5	0	0	0	5.0	22	6	3	2	0	0	0	0	0	0	9	0	0	0	0	-	0	0-0	0	2.73	3.60
2004 Pittsburgh	NL	68	0	0	10	61.2	285	81	39	35	8	6	1	0	28	7	64	5	0	2	5	.286	0	1-7	11	6.24	5.11
2 ML YEARS		73	0	0	11	66.2	307	87	42	37	8	6	1	0	28	7	73	5	0	2	5	.286	0	1-7	11	5.94	5.00

Jason Grabowski

Bats: L **Throws:** R **Pos:** PH-81; LF-30; 1B-3; RF-3; DH-3   **Ht:** 6'3" **Wt:** 200 **Born:** 5/24/1976 **Age:** 29

Year Team	Lg	G	AB	H	2B	3B	HR	(Hm	Rd)	TB	R	RBI	RC	TBB	IBB	SO	HBP	SH	SF	SB	CS	SB%	GDP	Avg	OBP	Slg
2002 Oakland	AL	4	8	3	1	1	0	(0	0)	6	3	1	3	3	0	1	0	0	0	0	0	-	0	.375	.545	.750
2003 Oakland	AL	8	8	0	0	0	0	(0	0)	0	0	0	0	1	0	5	0	0	0	0	0	-	0	.000	.111	.000
2004 Los Angeles	NL	113	173	38	7	0	7	(3	4)	66	18	20	21	19	0	50	0	0	0	0	0	-	4	.220	.297	.382
3 ML YEARS		125	189	41	8	1	7	(3	4)	72	21	21	24	23	0	56	0	0	0	0	0	-	4	.217	.302	.381

Franklyn Gracesqui

Pitches: L **Bats:** B **Pos:** RP-7   **Ht:** 6'5" **Wt:** 210 **Born:** 8/20/1979 **Age:** 25

Year Team	Lg	G	GS	CG	GF	IP	BFP	H	R	ER	HR	SH	SF	HB	TBB	IBB	SO	WP	Bk	W	L	Pct	ShO	Sv-Op	Hld	ERC	ERA
1998 St. Catharines	A-	11	0	0	9	16.1	81	16	12	12	2	0	0	3	12	0	19	5	2	1	0	1.000	0	0--	-	6.61	6.61
1999 St. Catharines	A-	15	10	0	1	46.1	220	44	30	26	4	0	2	3	41	0	45	6	2	2	3	.400	0	1--	-	5.93	5.05
2000 Medicine Hat	R+	8	4	0	0	24.0	105	15	11	7	1	1	0	2	21	0	20	5	0	0	1	.000	0	0--	-	3.79	2.63
2000 Hagerstown	A	3	1	0	1	7.1	33	4	4	4	1	0	0	0	9	0	6	0	0	0	1	.000	0	0--	-	5.95	4.91
2001 Chrlstn - WV	A	35	2	0	11	65.1	286	60	40	23	1	2	2	2	34	0	66	9	1	2	8	.200	0	1--	-	3.58	3.17

Year Team	Lg	G	GS	CG	GF	IP	BFP	H	R	ER	HR	SH	SF	HB	TBB	IBB	SO	WP	Bk	W	L	Pct	ShO	Sv-Op	Hld	ERC	ERA
2001 Dunedin	A+	4	0	0	0	5.2	24	2	0	0	0	0	0	0	8	0	6	0	0	1	0	1.000	0	0- -	-	3.88	0.00
2002 Tennessee	AA	41	0	0	14	42.2	198	40	26	22	3	0	4	5	34	0	48	4	0	4	2	.667	0	1- -	-	5.66	4.64
2002 Dunedin	A+	10	0	0	3	21.2	91	15	8	6	1	1	1	0	11	0	25	1	0	2	1	.667	0	1- -	-	2.45	2.49
2003 Carolina	AA	44	0	0	14	58.0	259	44	19	16	0	2	3	2	43	1	75	11	1	3	3	.500	0	5- -	-	3.37	2.48
2004 Marlins	R	2	2	0	0	2.2	13	1	1	0	0	0	0	0	4	0	4	0	0	1	0	1.000	0	0- -	-	3.80	0.00
2004 Albuquerque	AAA	19	0	0	5	22.0	94	10	9	8	2	0	0	1	19	0	16	1	0	1	0	1.000	0	1- -	-	3.00	3.27
2004 Florida	NL	7	0	0	5	4.0	23	6	5	5	0	0	0	2	3	0	1	0	0	0	1	.000	0	1-1	0	9.66	11.25

Tony Graffanino

Bats: R **Throws:** R **Pos:** 2B-75; PH-1; PR-1　　　　**Ht:** 6'1" **Wt:** 190 **Born:** 6/6/1972 **Age:** 33

							BATTING												BASERUNNING				AVERAGES		
Year Team	Lg	G	AB	H	2B	3B	HR	(Hm | Rd)	TB	R	RBI	RC	TBB	IBB	SO	HBP	SH	SF	SB	CS	SB%	GDP	Avg	OBP	Slg
2004 Omaha*	AAA	4	14	3	0	0	1	(- | -)	6	2	2	2	3	0	5	0	0	0	0	0	-	0	.214	.353	.429
1996 Atlanta	NL	22	46	8	1	1	0	(0 | 0)	11	7	2	3	4	0	13	1	0	1	0	0	-	0	.174	.250	.239
1997 Atlanta	NL	104	186	48	9	1	8	(5 | 3)	83	33	20	29	26	1	46	1	3	5	6	4	.60	3	.258	.344	.446
1998 Atlanta	NL	105	289	61	14	1	5	(3 | 2)	92	32	22	22	24	0	68	2	1	1	1	4	.20	7	.211	.275	.318
1999 Tampa Bay	AL	39	130	41	9	4	2	(0 | 2)	64	20	19	23	9	0	22	1	2	0	3	2	.60	1	.315	.364	.492
2000 TB-CWS	AL	70	168	46	6	1	2	(1 | 1)	60	33	17	23	22	0	27	2	1	1	7	4	.64	2	.274	.363	.357
2001 Chicago	AL	74	145	44	9	0	2	(1 | 1)	59	23	15	22	16	0	29	1	4	3	4	1	.80	4	.303	.370	.407
2002 Chicago	AL	70	229	60	12	4	6	(4 | 2)	98	35	31	35	22	1	38	2	4	2	2	1	.67	2	.262	.329	.428
2003 Chicago	AL	90	250	65	15	3	7	(4 | 3)	107	51	23	36	24	1	37	3	3	1	8	0	1.00	1	.260	.331	.428
2004 Kansas City	AL	75	278	73	11	0	3	(0 | 3)	93	37	26	35	27	0	38	3	4	2	10	2	.83	5	.263	.332	.335
2000 Tampa Bay	AL	13	20	6	1	0	0	(0 | 0)	7	8	1	2	1	0	2	1	0	0	0	0	-	1	.300	.364	.350
2000 Chicago	AL	57	148	40	5	1	2	(1 | 1)	53	25	16	21	21	0	25	1	1	1	7	4	.64	1	.270	.363	.358
9 ML YEARS		649	1721	446	86	15	35	(18 | 17)	667	271	175	228	174	3	318	16	22	16	41	18	.69	25	.259	.330	.388

Alex Graman

Pitches: L **Bats:** L **Pos:** SP-2; RP-1　　　　**Ht:** 6'4" **Wt:** 210 **Born:** 11/17/1977 **Age:** 27

						HOW MUCH HE PITCHED			WHAT HE GAVE UP											THE RESULTS						
Year Team	Lg	G	GS	CG	GF	IP	BFP	H	R	ER	HR	SH	SF	HB	TBB	IBB	SO	WP	Bk	W	L	Pct	ShO	Sv-Op	Hld	ERC	ERA
1999 Staten Island	A-	14	14	0	0	81.1	324	74	30	27	7	3	1	1	16	0	85	1	1	6	3	.667	0	0- -	-	2.84	2.99
2000 Tampa	A+	28	28	3	0	143.0	598	120	64	58	6	5	2	3	58	1	111	9	1	8	9	.471	1	0- -	-	2.91	3.65
2000 Norwich	AA	1	1	0	0	5.1	25	6	7	7	3	0	0	1	4	0	3	0	0	0	1	.000	0	0- -	-	11.94	11.81
2001 Norwich	AA	28	28	1	0	166.1	723	174	83	65	10	3	6	2	60	0	138	6	0	12	9	.571	0	0- -	-	3.92	3.52
2002 Norwich	AA	8	8	2	0	50.0	208	46	19	16	2	3	0	0	13	0	31	4	2	5	2	.714	0	0- -	-	2.68	2.88
2002 Columbus	AAA	20	20	1	0	124.0	545	141	74	64	11	5	3	3	37	3	98	10	2	6	9	.400	0	0- -	-	4.38	4.65
2003 Columbus	AAA	26	26	0	0	142.2	612	135	77	71	14	8	0	1	63	0	110	5	1	9	10	.474	1	0- -	-	3.97	4.48
2004 Columbus	AAA	24	22	1	0	131.0	550	115	56	49	12	10	5	3	53	0	129	7	0	11	6	.647	1	0- -	-	3.48	3.37
2004 New York	AL	3	2	0	1	5.0	31	14	11	11	1	0	1	0	2	0	4	0	0	0	0	-	0	0-0	0	17.28	19.80

Curtis Granderson

Bats: L **Throws:** R **Pos:** CF-8; PH-1; PR-1　　　　**Ht:** 6'1" **Wt:** 185 **Born:** 3/16/1981 **Age:** 24

							BATTING												BASERUNNING				AVERAGES		
Year Team	Lg	G	AB	H	2B	3B	HR	(Hm	Rd)	TB	R	RBI	RC	TBB	IBB	SO	HBP	SH	SF	SB	CS	SB%	GDP	Avg	OBP	Slg
2002 Oneonta	A-	52	212	73	15	4	3	(-	-)	105	45	34	44	20	0	35	7	0	1	9	2	.82	1	.344	.417	.495
2003 Lakeland	A+	127	476	136	29	10	11	(-	-)	218	71	51	80	49	2	91	12	5	3	10	7	.59	5	.286	.365	.458
2004 Erie	AA	123	462	140	19	8	21	(-	-)	238	89	93	98	80	3	95	4	3	4	14	8	.64	3	.303	.407	.515
2004 Detroit	AL	9	25	6	1	1	0	(0	0)	9	2	0	2	3	0	8	0	0	0	0	0	-	1	.240	.321	.360

Danny Graves

Pitches: R **Bats:** R **Pos:** RP-68　　　　**Ht:** 6'0" **Wt:** 185 **Born:** 8/7/1973 **Age:** 31

						HOW MUCH HE PITCHED			WHAT HE GAVE UP											THE RESULTS						
Year Team	Lg	G	GS	CG	GF	IP	BFP	H	R	ER	HR	SH	SF	HB	TBB	IBB	SO	WP	Bk	W	L	Pct	ShO	Sv-Op	Hld	ERC	ERA
1996 Cleveland	AL	15	0	0	5	29.2	129	28	18	15	2	0	1	0	10	0	22	1	0	2	0	1.000	0	0-1	0	3.37	4.55
1997 Cle-Cin		15	0	0	3	26.0	134	41	22	16	2	3	2	0	20	1	11	1	0	0	0	-	0	0-0	1	9.10	5.54
1998 Cincinnati	NL	62	0	0	35	81.1	340	76	31	30	6	2	5	2	28	4	44	4	0	2	1	.667	0	8-8	6	3.38	3.32
1999 Cincinnati	NL	75	0	0	56	111.0	454	90	42	38	10	5	2	2	49	4	69	3	0	8	7	.533	0	27-36	0	3.25	3.08
2000 Cincinnati	NL	66	0	0	57	91.1	388	81	31	26	8	6	4	3	42	7	53	3	1	10	5	.667	0	30-35	0	3.64	2.56
2001 Cincinnati	NL	66	0	0	54	80.1	337	83	41	37	7	3	2	4	18	6	49	2	1	6	5	.545	0	32-39	0	3.59	4.15
2002 Cincinnati	NL	68	4	0	54	98.2	412	99	37	35	7	3	6	3	25	9	58	5	0	7	3	.700	0	32-39	0	3.33	3.19
2003 Cincinnati	NL	30	26	2	3	169.0	741	204	108	100	30	6	3	7	41	6	60	2	0	4	15	.211	1	2-2	0	5.32	5.33
2004 Cincinnati	NL	68	0	0	59	68.1	290	77	39	30	12	0	2	2	13	6	40	2	0	1	6	.143	0	41-50	0	4.47	3.95
1997 Cleveland	AL	5	0	0	2	11.1	56	15	8	6	2	0	1	0	9	0	4	0	0	0	0	-	0	0-0	0	8.52	4.76
1997 Cincinnati	NL	10	0	0	1	14.2	78	26	14	10	0	3	1	0	11	1	7	1	0	0	0	-	0	0-0	1	9.52	6.14
9 ML YEARS		465	30	2	326	755.2	3225	780	369	327	84	28	27	23	246	43	406	23	2	40	42	.488	1	172-210	7	4.10	3.89

Andy Green

Bats: R **Throws:** R **Pos:** 3B-18; 2B-14; PH-11; LF-9; PR-3　　　　**Ht:** 5'9" **Wt:** 180 **Born:** 7/7/1977 **Age:** 27

							BATTING												BASERUNNING				AVERAGES		
Year Team	Lg	G	AB	H	2B	3B	HR	(Hm	Rd)	TB	R	RBI	RC	TBB	IBB	SO	HBP	SH	SF	SB	CS	SB%	GDP	Avg	OBP	Slg
2000 South Bend	A	3	9	0	0	0	0	(-	-)	0	1	0	0	0	0	1	2	0	0	0	0	-	0	.000	.182	.000
2000 Missoula	R+	23	83	19	2	1	0	(-	-)	23	10	16	9	12	0	9	2	1	5	8	3	.73	1	.229	.324	.277
2001 South Bend	A	128	477	143	18	6	5	(-	-)	188	76	59	81	59	1	50	7	11	8	51	15	.77	7	.300	.379	.394
2002 Tucson	AAA	27	99	22	8	0	1	(-	-)	33	13	13	9	9	0	17	1	0	2	1	1	.67	2	.222	.294	.333
2002 Lancaster	A+	102	401	124	36	4	6	(-	-)	186	74	50	74	60	0	59	5	6	5	15	10	.60	7	.309	.401	.464
2003 El Paso	AA	126	490	148	38	2	2	(-	-)	196	70	51	74	38	1	51	13	11	3	17	9	.65	6	.302	.366	.400
2004 Tucson	AAA	77	309	101	31	3	9	(-	-)	165	56	45	63	34	1	45	3	7	4	10	4	.71	3	.327	.394	.534
2004 Arizona	NL	46	109	22	2	1	1	(1	0)	29	13	4	7	5	0	17	1	3	1	1	1	.50	2	.202	.241	.266

Nick Green

Bats: R **Throws:** R **Pos:** 2B-75; PR-13; PH-9; 3B-5; RF-1   **Ht:** 6'0" **Wt:** 178 **Born:** 9/10/1978 **Age:** 26

								BATTING											BASERUNNING				AVERAGES		
Year Team	Lg	G	AB	H	2B	3B	HR	(Hm Rd)	TB	R	RBI	RC	TBB	IBB	SO	HBP	SH	SF	SB	CS	SB%	GDP	Avg	OBP	Slg
1999 Jamestown	A-	73	273	81	15	0	11	(- -)	129	52	41	47	26	0	66	4	0	3	14	4	.78	4	.297	.363	.473
1999 Macon	A	3	10	2	0	0	1	(- -)	5	1	3	1	0	0	4	0	0	0	1	0	1.00	0	.200	.200	.500
2000 Macon	A	91	229	83	19	4	11	(- -)	143	47	43	55	22	0	75	5	1	6	10	4	.71	4	.362	.420	.624
2000 Myrtle Beach	A+	27	91	22	6	0	1	(- -)	31	13	6	11	10	0	23	3	1	0	3	2	.60	0	.242	.337	.341
2001 Myrtle Beach	A+	80	297	79	18	1	10	(- -)	129	49	42	47	32	0	70	7	1	3	9	2	.82	5	.266	.348	.434
2001 Richmond	AAA	2	5	1	0	0	0	(- -)	1	0	1	0	0	0	3	0	0	0	0	0	-	0	.200	.200	.200
2002 Greenville	AA	94	355	85	16	2	15	(- -)	150	49	50	45	36	3	92	8	0	3	2	5	.29	9	.239	.321	.423
2003 Richmond	AAA	124	399	99	26	1	11	(- -)	160	40	51	46	26	1	79	7	2	4	7	5	.58	7	.248	.303	.401
2004 Richmond	AAA	22	77	29	4	1	0	(- -)	35	8	11	14	6	0	9	4	1	1	0	3	.00	3	.377	.443	.455
2004 Atlanta	NL	95	264	72	15	3	3	(3 0)	102	40	26	36	12	1	63	4	8	2	1	2	.33	0	.273	.312	.386

Shawn Green

Bats: L **Throws:** L **Pos:** 1B-111; RF-52; DH-3; PH-1   **Ht:** 6'4" **Wt:** 200 **Born:** 11/10/1972 **Age:** 32

								BATTING											BASERUNNING				AVERAGES		
Year Team	Lg	G	AB	H	2B	3B	HR	(Hm Rd)	TB	R	RBI	RC	TBB	IBB	SO	HBP	SH	SF	SB	CS	SB%	GDP	Avg	OBP	Slg
1993 Toronto	AL	3	6	0	0	0	0	(0 0)	0	0	0	0	0	0	1	0	0	0	0	0	-	0	.000	.000	.000
1994 Toronto	AL	14	33	3	1	0	0	(0 0)	4	1	1	0	1	0	8	0	0	0	1	0	1.00	1	.091	.118	.121
1995 Toronto	AL	121	379	109	31	4	15	(5 10)	193	52	54	61	20	3	68	3	0	3	1	2	.33	4	.288	.326	.509
1996 Toronto	AL	132	422	118	32	3	11	(7 4)	189	52	45	64	33	3	75	8	0	2	5	1	.83	9	.280	.342	.448
1997 Toronto	AL	135	429	123	22	4	16	(10 6)	201	57	53	70	36	4	99	1	1	4	14	3	.82	4	.287	.340	.469
1998 Toronto	AL	158	630	175	33	4	35	(21 14)	321	106	100	108	50	2	142	5	1	3	35	12	.74	6	.278	.334	.510
1999 Toronto	AL	153	614	190	45	0	42	(20 22)	361	134	123	132	66	4	117	11	0	5	20	7	.74	13	.309	.384	.588
2000 Los Angeles	NL	162	610	164	44	4	24	(15 9)	288	98	99	107	90	9	121	8	0	6	24	5	.83	18	.269	.367	.472
2001 Los Angeles	NL	161	619	184	31	4	49	(19 30)	370	121	125	134	72	10	107	5	0	5	20	4	.83	10	.297	.372	.598
2002 Los Angeles	NL	158	582	166	31	1	42	(18 24)	325	110	114	106	93	22	112	5	0	5	8	5	.62	26	.285	.385	.558
2003 Los Angeles	NL	160	611	171	49	2	19	(10 9)	281	84	85	92	68	2	112	6	0	6	6	2	.75	18	.280	.355	.460
2004 Los Angeles	NL	157	590	157	28	1	28	(16 12)	271	92	86	76	71	6	114	6	0	3	5	2	.71	17	.266	.352	.459
12 ML YEARS		1514	5525	1560	347	27	281	(141 140)	2804	907	885	950	600	65	1076	60	2	41	139	43	.76	126	.282	.357	.508

Khalil Greene

Bats: R **Throws:** R **Pos:** SS-136; PR-3   **Ht:** 5'11" **Wt:** 210 **Born:** 10/21/1979 **Age:** 25

								BATTING											BASERUNNING				AVERAGES		
Year Team	Lg	G	AB	H	2B	3B	HR	(Hm Rd)	TB	R	RBI	RC	TBB	IBB	SO	HBP	SH	SF	SB	CS	SB%	GDP	Avg	OBP	Slg
2002 Eugene	A-	10	37	10	1	0	0	(- -)	11	5	6	5	5	1	6	3	0	0	0	0	-	1	.270	.400	.297
2002 Lk Elsinore	A+	46	183	58	9	1	9	(- -)	96	33	32	32	12	0	33	4	0	2	0	0	-	7	.317	.368	.525
2003 Mobile	AA	59	229	63	17	2	3	(- -)	93	20	20	27	16	0	55	2	0	1	2	3	.40	7	.275	.327	.406
2003 Portland	AAA	76	319	92	19	0	10	(- -)	141	42	47	49	20	1	52	11	0	5	5	4	.56	3	.288	.346	.442
2003 San Diego	NL	20	65	14	4	1	2	(0 2)	26	8	6	4	4	0	19	1	0	0	0	1	.00	3	.215	.271	.400
2004 San Diego	NL	139	484	132	31	4	15	(3 12)	216	67	65	73	53	10	94	8	1	8	4	2	.67	9	.273	.349	.446
2 ML YEARS		159	549	146	35	5	17	(3 14)	242	75	71	77	57	10	113	9	1	8	4	3	.57	12	.266	.340	.441

Todd Greene

Bats: R **Throws:** R **Pos:** C-53; PH-22   **Ht:** 5'10" **Wt:** 208 **Born:** 5/8/1971 **Age:** 34

								BATTING											BASERUNNING				AVERAGES		
Year Team	Lg	G	AB	H	2B	3B	HR	(Hm Rd)	TB	R	RBI	RC	TBB	IBB	SO	HBP	SH	SF	SB	CS	SB%	GDP	Avg	OBP	Slg
2004 Co Springs*	AAA	4	12	4	1	0	1	(- -)	8	2	4	2	1	0	3	0	0	0	0	0	-	0	.333	.385	.667
1996 California	AL	29	79	15	1	0	2	(1 1)	22	9	9	4	4	0	11	1	0	0	2	0	1.00	4	.190	.238	.278
1997 Anaheim	AL	34	124	36	6	0	9	(5 4)	69	24	24	22	7	1	25	0	0	0	2	0	1.00	1	.290	.328	.556
1998 Anaheim	AL	29	71	18	4	0	1	(0 1)	25	3	7	7	2	0	20	0	0	0	0	0	-	0	.254	.274	.352
1999 Anaheim	AL	97	321	78	20	0	14	(7 7)	140	36	42	35	12	0	63	3	0	2	1	4	.20	8	.243	.275	.436
2000 Toronto	AL	34	85	20	2	0	5	(2 3)	37	11	10	9	5	0	18	0	0	0	0	0	-	4	.235	.278	.435
2001 New York	AL	35	96	20	4	0	1	(1 0)	27	9	11	5	3	0	21	1	0	0	0	0	-	3	.208	.240	.281
2002 Texas	AL	42	112	30	5	0	10	(6 4)	65	15	19	11	2	0	23	1	1	2	0	0	-	4	.268	.282	.580
2003 Texas	AL	62	205	47	10	1	10	(4 6)	89	25	20	14	2	0	47	2	0	1	0	0	-	2	.229	.243	.434
2004 Colorado	NL	75	195	55	14	0	10	(6 4)	99	23	35	27	13	4	38	0	0	1	0	0	-	9	.282	.325	.508
9 ML YEARS		437	1288	319	66	1	62	(32 30)	573	155	177	134	50	5	266	8	1	6	5	4	.56	35	.248	.279	.445

Kevin Gregg

Pitches: R **Bats:** R **Pos:** RP-55   **Ht:** 6'6" **Wt:** 220 **Born:** 6/20/1978 **Age:** 27

		HOW MUCH HE PITCHED						WHAT HE GAVE UP												THE RESULTS						
Year Team	Lg	G	GS	CG	GF	IP	BFP	H	R	ER	HR	SH	SF	HB	TBB	IBB	SO	WP	Bk	W	L	Pct	ShO	Sv-Op	Hld	ERC	ERA
1996 Athletics	R	11	9	0	0	40.2	169	30	14	14	1	1	1	2	21	0	48	11	0	3	3	.500	0	0--	-	2.83	3.10
1997 Visalia	A+	25	24	0	0	115.1	534	116	81	73	8	2	3	5	74	0	136	28	0	6	8	.429	0	0--	-	4.95	5.70
1998 Modesto	A+	30	24	0	0	144.0	640	139	72	61	7	9	2	6	76	2	141	7	0	8	7	.533	0	1--	-	4.13	3.81
1999 Visalia	A+	13	11	1	2	64.0	271	60	34	27	3	1	2	4	23	0	48	7	1	4	4	.500	1	1--	-	3.48	3.80
1999 Midland	AA	16	16	2	0	91.1	380	75	45	38	7	0	2	6	31	1	66	6	0	4	7	.364	0	0--	-	2.96	3.74
1999 Vancouver	AAA	1	1	0	0	5.0	21	6	2	2	0	0	0	0	2	0	4	2	0	1	0	1.000	0	0--	-	4.80	3.60
2000 Midland	AA	28	27	0	0	140.2	655	171	120	100	18	5	6	8	73	0	97	6	0	5	14	.263	0	0--	-	6.34	6.40
2001 Midland	AA	44	1	0	10	81.1	366	88	48	41	5	1	0	4	40	4	72	8	1	5	5	.500	0	1--	-	4.74	4.54
2002 Midland	AA	11	4	0	0	37.2	162	31	20	18	3	0	1	3	18	0	45	3	0	3	3	.500	0	0--	-	3.56	4.30
2002 Sacramento	AAA	16	8	0	2	58.2	280	82	56	49	7	0	4	6	23	0	45	3	1	2	5	.286	0	0--	-	7.04	7.52
2002 Visalia	A+	3	3	0	0	17.1	69	8	5	4	0	2	1	1	9	0	11	2	0	2	1	.667	0	0--	-	1.48	2.08
2003 Arkansas	AA	15	11	2	0	66.1	279	60	29	26	2	2	5	4	19	0	60	2	0	4	3	.571	0	0--	-	2.86	3.53
2003 Salt Lake	AAA	15	15	0	0	91.2	378	90	47	40	10	0	1	8	35	0	75	4	0	7	4	.636	0	0--	-	3.64	4.03
2003 Anaheim	AL	5	3	0	0	24.2	97	16	9	9	3	0	0	1	8	0	14	0	0	2	0	1.000	0	0-0	-	2.74	3.28
2004 Anaheim	AL	55	0	0	23	87.2	377	86	43	41	6	4	5	3	28	3	84	13	1	5	2	.714	0	1-2	3	3.47	4.21
2 ML YEARS		60	3	0	23	112.1	474	104	52	50	9	4	5	4	36	3	98	13	1	7	2	.778	0	1-2	3	3.31	4.01

Zack Greinke

Pitches: R Bats: R Pos: SP-24

Ht: 6'2" **Wt:** 200 **Born:** 10/21/1983 **Age:** 21

Year Team	Lg	G	GS	CG	GF	IP	BFP	H	R	ER	HR	SH	SF	HB	TBB	IBB	SO	WP	Bk	W	L	Pct	ShO	Sv-Op	Hld	ERC	ERA
2002 Royals	R	3	3	0	0	4.2	20	3	1	1	0	0	0	0	3	0	4	1	0	0	0	-	0	0- -	-		1.93
2002 Spokane	A-	2	2	0	0	4.2	23	9	4	4	0	0	0	0	0	0	5	1	0	0	0	-	0	0- -	-	7.03	7.71
2002 Wilmington	A+	1	0	0	0	2.0	6	1	0	0	0	0	0	0	0	0	0	0	0	0	0	-	0	0- -	-	0.63	0.00
2003 Wilmington	A+	14	14	3	0	87.0	330	56	16	11	5	1	0	2	13	0	78	1	0	11	1	.917	1	0- -	-	1.39	1.14
2003 Wichita	AA	9	9	0	0	53.0	214	58	20	19	5	0	3	3	5	2	34	0	0	4	3	.571	0	0- -	-	3.65	3.23
2004 Omaha	AAA	6	6	0	0	28.2	119	25	8	8	2	3	1	2	6	0	23	2	1	1	1	.500	0	0- -	-	2.69	2.51
2004 Kansas City	AL	24	24	0	0	145.0	599	143	64	64	26	3	2	8	26	3	100	1	1	8	11	.421	0	0-0	0	3.85	3.97

Seth Greisinger

Pitches: R Bats: R Pos: SP-9; RP-3

Ht: 6'3" **Wt:** 200 **Born:** 7/29/1975 **Age:** 29

Year Team	Lg	G	GS	CG	GF	IP	BFP	H	R	ER	HR	SH	SF	HB	TBB	IBB	SO	WP	Bk	W	L	Pct	ShO	Sv-Op	Hld	ERC	ERA
2004 Rochester*	AAA	13	13	0	0	74.1	320	94	44	41	10	5	6	5	19	0	44	1	3	5	5	.500	0	0- -	-	5.82	4.96
1998 Detroit	AL	21	21	0	0	130.0	562	142	79	74	17	2	5	4	48	2	66	3	0	6	9	.400	0	0-0	0	4.89	5.12
2002 Detroit	AL	8	8	0	0	37.2	168	46	26	26	4	1	1	1	13	2	14	0	0	2	2	.500	0	0-0	0	5.23	6.21
2004 Minnesota	AL	12	9	0	1	51.0	233	68	40	35	12	1	2	2	15	1	36	1	0	2	5	.286	0	0-0	0	6.79	6.18
3 ML YEARS		41	38	0	1	218.2	963	256	145	135	33	4	8	7	76	5	116	4	0	10	16	.385	0	0-0	0	5.38	5.56

Ben Grieve

Bats: L Throws: R Pos: RF-68; PH-54; LF-1; DH-1

Ht: 6'4" **Wt:** 216 **Born:** 5/4/1976 **Age:** 29

Year Team	Lg	G	AB	H	2B	3B	HR	(Hm	Rd)	TB	R	RBI	RC	TBB	IBB	SO	HBP	SH	SF	SB	CS	SB%	GDP	Avg	OBP	Slg
1997 Oakland	AL	24	93	29	6	0	3	(3	0)	44	12	24	18	13	1	25	1	1	0	0	0	-	1	.312	.402	.473
1998 Oakland	AL	155	583	168	41	2	18	(5	13)	267	94	89	101	85	3	123	9	0	1	2	2	.50	18	.288	.386	.458
1999 Oakland	AL	148	486	129	21	0	28	(13	15)	234	80	86	81	63	2	108	8	0	1	4	0	1.00	17	.265	.358	.481
2000 Oakland	AL	158	594	166	40	1	27	(13	14)	289	92	104	95	73	2	130	3	0	5	3	0	1.00	32	.279	.359	.487
2001 Tampa Bay	AL	154	542	143	30	2	11	(5	6)	210	72	72	82	87	2	159	8	0	2	7	1	.88	13	.264	.372	.387
2002 Tampa Bay	AL	136	482	121	30	0	19	(7	12)	208	62	64	68	69	5	121	8	0	2	8	2	.80	15	.251	.353	.432
2003 Tampa Bay	AL	55	165	38	7	0	4	(2	2)	57	28	17	19	32	1	41	6	0	2	0	0	-	3	.230	.371	.345
2004 Mil-ChC	NL	123	250	65	17	0	8	(3	5)	106	30	35	39	39	5	70	2	0	3	0	0	-	4	.260	.361	.424
2004 Milwaukee	NL	108	234	61	15	0	7	(3	4)	97	28	29	36	39	5	65	0	0	1	0	0	-	4	.261	.364	.415
2004 Chicago	NL	15	16	4	2	0	1	(0	1)	9	2	6	3	0	0	5	2	0	1	0	0	-	0	.250	.316	.563
8 ML YEARS		953	3195	859	192	5	118	(51	67)	1415	470	491	503	461	21	777	45	1	16	24	5	.83	103	.269	.367	.443

Ken Griffey Jr.

Bats: L Throws: L Pos: CF-76; PH-5; RF-1; DH-1

Ht: 6'3" **Wt:** 205 **Born:** 11/21/1969 **Age:** 35

Year Team	Lg	G	AB	H	2B	3B	HR	(Hm	Rd)	TB	R	RBI	RC	TBB	IBB	SO	HBP	SH	SF	SB	CS	SB%	GDP	Avg	OBP	Slg
1989 Seattle	AL	127	455	120	23	0	16	(10	6)	191	61	61	64	44	8	83	2	1	4	16	7	.70	4	.264	.329	.420
1990 Seattle	AL	155	597	179	28	7	22	(8	14)	287	91	80	101	63	12	81	2	0	4	16	11	.59	12	.300	.366	.481
1991 Seattle	AL	154	548	179	42	1	22	(16	6)	289	76	100	112	71	21	82	1	4	9	18	6	.75	10	.327	.399	.527
1992 Seattle	AL	142	565	174	39	4	27	(16	11)	302	83	103	102	44	15	67	5	0	3	10	5	.67	15	.308	.361	.535
1993 Seattle	AL	156	582	180	38	3	45	(21	24)	359	113	109	137	96	25	91	6	0	7	17	9	.65	14	.309	.408	.617
1994 Seattle	AL	111	433	140	24	4	40	(18	22)	292	94	90	107	56	19	73	2	0	2	11	3	.79	9	.323	.402	.674
1995 Seattle	AL	72	260	67	7	0	17	(13	4)	125	52	42	49	52	6	53	0	0	2	4	2	.67	4	.258	.379	.481
1996 Seattle	AL	140	545	165	26	2	49	(26	23)	342	125	140	131	78	13	104	7	1	7	16	1	.94	7	.303	.392	.628
1997 Seattle	AL	157	608	185	34	3	56	(27	29)	393	125	147	142	76	23	121	8	0	12	15	4	.79	12	.304	.382	.646
1998 Seattle	AL	161	633	180	33	3	56	(30	26)	387	120	146	136	76	11	121	7	0	4	20	5	.80	14	.284	.365	.611
1999 Seattle	AL	160	606	173	26	3	48	(27	21)	349	123	134	132	91	17	108	7	0	2	24	7	.77	8	.285	.384	.576
2000 Cincinnati	NL	145	520	141	22	3	40	(22	18)	289	100	118	111	94	17	117	9	0	8	6	4	.60	7	.271	.387	.556
2001 Cincinnati	NL	111	364	104	20	2	22	(12	10)	194	57	65	69	44	6	72	4	1	4	2	0	1.00	8	.286	.365	.533
2002 Cincinnati	NL	70	197	52	8	0	8	(4	4)	84	17	23	27	28	6	39	3	0	4	1	2	.33	6	.264	.358	.426
2003 Cincinnati	NL	53	166	41	12	1	13	(5	8)	94	34	26	26	27	5	44	6	1	1	1	0	1.00	3	.247	.370	.566
2004 Cincinnati	NL	83	300	76	18	0	20	(11	9)	154	49	60	56	44	3	67	2	0	2	1	0	1.00	8	.253	.351	.513
16 ML YEARS		1997	7379	2156	400	36	501	(266	235)	4131	1320	1444	1502	984	207	1323	71	8	75	178	66	.73	141	.292	.377	.560

Jeremy Griffiths

Pitches: R Bats: R Pos: SP-1

Ht: 6'6" **Wt:** 240 **Born:** 3/22/1978 **Age:** 27

Year Team	Lg	G	GS	CG	GF	IP	BFP	H	R	ER	HR	SH	SF	HB	TBB	IBB	SO	WP	Bk	W	L	Pct	ShO	Sv-Op	Hld	ERC	ERA
1999 Kingsport	R+	14	14	1	0	76.1	321	68	40	28	6	1	3	1	36	1	74	5	1	3	5	.375	0	0- -	-	3.71	3.30
2000 Capital City	A	26	26	0	0	128.2	548	120	78	62	12	1	4	8	39	0	138	8	0	7	12	.368	0	0- -	-	3.48	4.34
2001 St. Lucie	A+	23	20	2	0	132.0	551	126	63	55	9	9	3	5	35	1	95	11	3	7	8	.467	0	0- -	-	3.23	3.75
2001 Binghamton	AA	2	2	1	0	13.0	51	8	3	1	0	1	0	0	4	0	12	1	0	2	0	1.000	0	0- -	-	1.37	0.69
2002 Binghamton	AA	27	26	2	0	152.2	652	157	75	66	12	5	4	11	54	0	126	5	0	8	6	.571	0	0- -	-	4.28	3.89
2003 Norfolk	AAA	21	19	1	1	115.0	459	94	43	35	6	1	4	9	26	0	78	5	0	7	6	.538	0	1- -	-	2.50	2.74
2004 Norfolk	AAA	13	13	0	0	70.0	288	63	30	27	6	5	5	5	29	1	31	5	1	5	2	.714	0	0- -	-	3.92	3.47
2004 New Orleans	AAA	15	14	0	0	80.0	349	95	55	52	9	6	9	3	26	1	58	5	0	3	6	.333	0	0- -	-	5.19	5.85
2003 New York	NL	9	6	0	1	41.0	199	57	34	32	5	4	0	2	19	2	25	1	0	1	4	.200	0	0-0	0	6.88	7.02
2004 Houston	NL	1	1	0	0	4.1	20	4	5	5	1	0	0	0	3	0	5	0	0	0	0	-	0	0-0	0	5.68	10.38
2 ML YEARS		10	7	0	1	45.1	219	61	39	37	6	4	0	2	22	2	30	1	0	1	4	.200	0	0-0	0	6.77	7.35

Jason Grilli

Pitches: R **Bats:** R **Pos:** SP-8 **Ht:** 6'5" **Wt:** 210 **Born:** 11/11/1976 **Age:** 28

				HOW MUCH HE PITCHED						WHAT HE GAVE UP											THE RESULTS						
Year Team	Lg	G	GS	CG	GF	IP	BFP	H	R	ER	HR	SH	SF	HB	TBB	IBB	SO	WP	Bk	W	L	Pct	ShO	Sv-Op	Hld	ERC	ERA
2004 Charlotte*	AAA	25	25	2	0	152.2	665	163	95	82	22	5	6	11	58	0	101	9	4	9	9	.500	1	0- -	-	5.08	4.83
2000 Florida	NL	1	1	0	0	6.2	35	11	4	4	0	2	0	2	2	0	3	0	0	0	1	1.000	0	0-0	0	7.84	5.40
2001 Florida	NL	6	5	0	1	26.2	115	30	18	18	6	1	0	2	11	0	17	0	0	2	2	.500	0	0-0	0	6.44	6.08
2004 Chicago	AL	8	8	1	0	45.0	203	52	38	37	11	2	1	3	20	0	26	2	0	2	3	.400	0	0-0	0	6.67	7.40
3 ML YEARS		15	14	1	1	78.1	353	93	60	59	17	5	1	7	33	0	46	2	0	5	5	.500	0	0-0	0	6.70	6.78

Jason Grimsley

Pitches: R **Bats:** R **Pos:** RP-73 **Ht:** 6'3" **Wt:** 205 **Born:** 8/7/1967 **Age:** 37

				HOW MUCH HE PITCHED						WHAT HE GAVE UP											THE RESULTS						
Year Team	Lg	G	GS	CG	GF	IP	BFP	H	R	ER	HR	SH	SF	HB	TBB	IBB	SO	WP	Bk	W	L	Pct	ShO	Sv-Op	Hld	ERC	ERA
1989 Philadelphia	NL	4	4	0	0	18.1	91	19	13	12	2	1	0	0	19	1	7	2	0	1	3	.250	0	0-0	0	6.86	5.89
1990 Philadelphia	NL	11	11	0	0	57.1	255	47	21	21	1	2	1	2	43	0	41	6	1	3	2	.600	0	0-0	0	3.98	3.30
1991 Philadelphia	NL	12	12	0	0	61.0	272	54	34	33	4	3	2	3	41	3	42	14	0	1	7	.125	0	0-0	0	4.39	4.87
1993 Cleveland	AL	10	6	0	1	42.1	194	52	26	25	3	1	0	1	20	1	27	2	0	3	4	.429	0	0-0	1	5.57	5.31
1994 Cleveland	AL	14	13	1	0	82.2	368	91	47	42	7	4	2	6	34	1	59	6	1	5	2	.714	0	0-0	0	4.89	4.57
1995 Cleveland	AL	15	2	0	2	34.0	165	37	24	23	4	1	2	2	32	1	25	7	0	0	0	-	0	1-1	0	7.37	6.09
1996 California	AL	35	20	2	4	130.1	620	150	110	99	14	4	5	13	74	5	82	11	0	5	7	.417	1	0-0	0	5.98	6.84
1999 New York	AL	55	0	0	25	75.0	336	66	39	30	7	3	3	4	40	5	49	8	0	7	2	.778	0	1-4	8	3.87	3.60
2000 New York	AL	63	4	0	18	96.1	428	100	58	54	10	2	6	5	42	1	53	16	0	3	2	.600	0	1-4	4	4.63	5.04
2001 Kansas City	AL	73	0	0	24	80.1	327	71	32	27	8	2	1	2	28	5	61	4	0	1	5	.167	0	0-7	26	3.34	3.02
2002 Kansas City	AL	70	0	0	26	71.1	310	64	32	31	4	1	0	1	37	8	59	8	0	4	7	.364	0	1-3	13	3.51	3.91
2003 Kansas City	AL	76	0	0	5	75.0	346	88	47	43	6	6	5	5	36	5	58	4	0	2	6	.250	0	0-7	28	5.40	5.16
2004 KC-Bal	AL	73	0	0	7	63.0	285	61	36	27	4	3	1	3	35	6	30	6	0	5	7	.417	0	0-9	17	4.20	3.86
2004 Kansas City	AL	32	0	0	4	26.2	118	24	11	10	1	1	0	1	15	3	18	4	0	3	3	.500	0	0-3	5	3.62	3.38
2004 Baltimore	AL	41	0	0	3	36.1	167	37	25	17	3	2	1	2	20	3	21	2	0	2	4	.333	0	0-6	12	4.63	4.21
13 ML YEARS		511	72	3	112	887.0	3997	900	519	467	74	33	28	47	481	42	602	94	2	40	54	.426	1	4-35	97	4.73	4.74

Marquis Grissom

Bats: R **Throws:** R **Pos:** CF-141; PH-5 **Ht:** 5'11" **Wt:** 188 **Born:** 4/17/1967 **Age:** 38

					BATTING															BASERUNNING				AVERAGES		
Year Team	Lg	G	AB	H	2B	3B	HR	(Hm	Rd)	TB	R	RBI	RC	TBB	IBB	SO	HBP	SH	SF	SB	CS	SB%	GDP	Avg	OBP	Slg
1989 Montreal	NL	26	74	19	2	0	1	(0	1)	24	16	2	10	12	0	21	0	1	0	1	0	1.00	1	.257	.360	.324
1990 Montreal	NL	98	288	74	14	2	1	(2	1)	101	42	29	37	27	2	40	0	4	1	22	2	.92	3	.257	.320	.351
1991 Montreal	NL	148	558	149	23	9	6	(3	3)	208	73	39	71	34	0	89	1	4	0	76	17	.82	8	.267	.310	.373
1992 Montreal	NL	159	653	180	39	6	14	(8	6)	273	99	66	96	42	6	81	5	3	4	78	13	.86	12	.276	.322	.418
1993 Montreal	NL	157	630	188	27	2	19	(9	10)	276	104	95	103	52	6	76	3	0	8	53	10	.84	9	.298	.351	.438
1994 Montreal	NL	110	475	137	25	4	11	(4	7)	203	96	45	73	41	4	66	1	0	4	36	6	.86	10	.288	.344	.427
1995 Atlanta	NL	139	551	142	23	3	12	(5	7)	207	80	42	68	47	4	61	3	1	4	29	9	.76	8	.258	.317	.376
1996 Atlanta	NL	158	671	207	32	10	23	(11	12)	328	106	74	111	41	6	73	3	4	4	28	11	.72	12	.308	.349	.489
1997 Cleveland	AL	144	558	146	27	6	12	(5	7)	221	74	66	69	43	1	89	6	6	9	22	13	.63	12	.262	.317	.396
1998 Milwaukee	NL	142	542	147	28	1	10	(2	8)	207	57	60	59	24	2	78	2	2	2	13	8	.62	12	.271	.304	.382
1999 Milwaukee	NL	154	603	161	27	1	20	(9	11)	250	92	83	81	49	4	109	1	0	4	24	6	.80	12	.267	.320	.415
2000 Milwaukee	NL	146	595	145	18	2	14	(4	10)	209	67	62	59	39	2	99	0	2	4	20	10	.67	9	.244	.288	.351
2001 Los Angeles	NL	135	448	99	17	1	21	(9	12)	181	56	60	41	16	0	107	2	0	2	7	5	.58	12	.221	.250	.404
2002 Los Angeles	NL	111	343	95	21	4	17	(10	7)	175	57	60	54	22	2	68	2	0	4	5	1	.83	6	.277	.321	.510
2003 San Francisco	NL	149	587	176	33	3	20	(10	10)	275	82	79	88	20	0	82	2	3	6	11	3	.79	14	.300	.322	.468
2004 San Francisco	NL	145	562	157	26	2	22	(11	11)	253	78	90	73	37	5	83	1	2	4	3	1	.75	21	.279	.323	.450
16 ML YEARS		2121	8138	2222	382	56	225	(102	123)	3391	1179	952	1093	546	44	1222	31	36	61	428	115	.79	161	.273	.319	.417

Buddy Groom

Pitches: L **Bats:** L **Pos:** RP-60 **Ht:** 6'2" **Wt:** 207 **Born:** 7/10/1965 **Age:** 39

				HOW MUCH HE PITCHED						WHAT HE GAVE UP											THE RESULTS						
Year Team	Lg	G	GS	CG	GF	IP	BFP	H	R	ER	HR	SH	SF	HB	TBB	IBB	SO	WP	Bk	W	L	Pct	ShO	Sv-Op	Hld	ERC	ERA
1992 Detroit	AL	12	7	0	3	38.2	177	48	28	25	4	3	2	0	22	4	15	0	1	0	5	.000	0	1-2	0	6.20	5.82
1993 Detroit	AL	19	3	0	8	36.2	170	48	25	25	4	2	4	2	13	5	15	2	1	0	2	.000	0	0-0	1	5.72	6.14
1994 Detroit	AL	40	0	0	10	32.0	139	31	14	14	4	0	3	2	13	2	27	0	0	1	1	.000	0	1-1	11	4.25	3.94
1995 Det-Fla		37	4	0	11	55.2	274	81	47	46	8	2	2	2	32	4	35	3	0	2	5	.286	0	1-3	0	8.05	7.44
1996 Oakland	AL	72	1	0	16	77.1	341	85	37	33	8	2	0	3	34	3	57	5	0	5	0	1.000	0	2-4	10	5.00	3.84
1997 Oakland	AL	78	0	0	7	64.2	285	75	38	37	9	0	4	0	24	1	45	3	0	2	2	.500	0	3-5	12	5.18	5.15
1998 Oakland	AL	75	0	0	13	57.1	251	62	30	27	4	1	3	1	20	1	36	1	0	3	1	.750	0	0-6	16	4.12	4.24
1999 Oakland	AL	76	0	0	6	46.0	196	48	29	26	1	2	0	1	18	5	32	2	1	3	2	.600	0	0-3	27	3.71	5.09
2000 Baltimore	AL	70	0	0	14	59.1	260	63	37	32	5	5	5	0	21	2	44	1	0	6	3	.667	0	4-11	27	4.01	4.85
2001 Baltimore	AL	70	0	0	35	66.0	265	64	28	26	4	0	1	1	9	0	54	2	0	1	4	.200	0	11-13	16	2.75	3.55
2002 Baltimore	AL	70	0	0	17	62.0	239	44	11	11	4	0	1	2	12	3	48	0	0	3	2	.600	0	2-4	19	1.73	1.60
2003 Baltimore	AL	60	0	0	20	45.1	207	58	27	27	7	1	1	3	14	2	34	1	0	1	3	.250	0	1-3	16	5.93	5.36
2004 Baltimore	AL	60	0	0	22	52.2	236	67	30	28	6	0	2	1	16	1	32	0	1	4	1	.800	0	0-2	8	5.43	4.78
1995 Detroit	AL	23	4	0	6	40.2	203	55	35	34	6	2	2	2	26	4	23	3	0	1	3	.250	0	1-3	0	7.54	7.52
1995 Florida	NL	14	0	0	5	15.0	71	26	12	12	2	0	0	0	6	0	12	0	0	1	2	.333	0	0-0	0	9.52	7.20
13 ML YEARS		739	15	0	182	693.2	3040	774	381	357	68	18	28	18	248	33	474	20	4	30	31	.492	0	26-57	163	4.59	4.63

Gabe Gross

Bats: L **Throws:** R **Pos:** LF-38; DH-6; PH-6 **Ht:** 6'3" **Wt:** 209 **Born:** 10/21/1979 **Age:** 25

					BATTING															BASERUNNING				AVERAGES		
Year Team	Lg	G	AB	H	2B	3B	HR	(Hm	Rd)	TB	R	RBI	RC	TBB	IBB	SO	HBP	SH	SF	SB	CS	SB%	GDP	Avg	OBP	Slg
2001 Dunedin	A+	35	126	38	9	2	4	(-	-)	63	23	15	27	26	1	29	2	0	1	4	2	.67	2	.302	.426	.500
2001 Tennessee	AA	11	41	10	1	0	3	(-	-)	20	8	11	7	6	1	12	3	0	1	0	1	.00	1	.244	.373	.488
2002 Tennessee	AA	112	403	96	17	5	10	(-	-)	153	57	54	54	53	4	71	5	2	2	8	2	.80	4	.238	.333	.380

113

Year Team	Lg	G	AB	H	2B	3B	HR	(Hm Rd)	TB	R	RBI	RC	TBB	IBB	SO	HBP	SH	SF	SB	CS	SB%	GDP	Avg	OBP	Slg
2003 New Haven	AA	84	310	99	23	3	7	(- -)	149	52	51	62	52	1	53	5	2	2	3	2	.60	9	.319	.423	.481
2003 Syracuse	AAA	53	182	48	16	2	5	(- -)	83	22	23	31	31	3	56	3	0	0	1	1	.50	2	.264	.380	.456
2004 Syracuse	AAA	103	377	111	29	2	9	(- -)	171	52	54	63	53	2	81	1	0	2	4	5	.44	8	.294	.381	.454
2004 Toronto	AL	44	129	27	4	0	3	(2 1)	40	18	16	15	19	0	31	0	0	0	2	2	.50	1	.209	.311	.310

Mark Grudzielanek

Bats: R Throws: R Pos: 2B-76; PH-11   Ht: 6'1" Wt: 185 Born: 6/30/1970 Age: 35

Year Team	Lg	G	AB	H	2B	3B	HR	(Hm Rd)	TB	R	RBI	RC	TBB	IBB	SO	HBP	SH	SF	SB	CS	SB%	GDP	Avg	OBP	Slg
2004 Iowa*	AAA	8	28	7	3	0	2	(- -)	16	6	4	3	0	0	4	0	0	0	0	0	-	1	.250	.250	.571
1995 Montreal	NL	78	269	66	12	2	1	(1 0)	85	27	20	24	14	4	47	7	3	0	8	3	.73	7	.245	.300	.316
1996 Montreal	NL	153	657	201	34	4	6	(5 1)	261	99	49	90	26	3	83	9	1	3	33	7	.83	10	.306	.340	.397
1997 Montreal	NL	156	649	177	54	3	4	(1 3)	249	76	51	75	23	0	76	10	3	3	25	9	.74	13	.273	.307	.384
1998 Mon-LA	NL	156	589	160	21	1	10	(5 5)	213	62	62	64	26	2	73	11	8	7	18	5	.78	18	.272	.311	.362
1999 Los Angeles	NL	123	488	159	23	5	7	(4 3)	213	72	46	76	31	1	65	10	2	3	6	6	.50	13	.326	.376	.436
2000 Los Angeles	NL	148	617	172	35	6	7	(4 3)	240	101	49	80	45	0	81	9	2	3	12	3	.80	16	.279	.335	.389
2001 Los Angeles	NL	133	539	146	21	3	13	(8 5)	212	83	55	66	28	0	83	11	3	5	4	4	.50	9	.271	.317	.393
2002 Los Angeles	NL	150	536	145	23	0	9	(5 4)	195	56	50	53	22	4	89	3	1	4	4	1	.80	17	.271	.301	.364
2003 Chicago	NL	121	481	151	38	1	3	(2 1)	200	73	38	71	30	0	64	11	7	2	6	2	.75	12	.314	.366	.416
2004 Chicago	NL	81	257	79	12	1	6	(3 3)	111	32	23	35	15	0	32	1	4	1	1	1	.50	7	.307	.347	.432
1998 Montreal	NL	105	396	109	15	1	8	(3 5)	150	51	41	47	21	1	50	9	5	5	11	5	.69	11	.275	.323	.379
1998 Los Angeles	NL	51	193	51	6	0	2	(2 0)	63	11	21	17	5	1	23	2	3	3	7	0	1.00	1	.264	.286	.326
10 ML YEARS		1299	5082	1456	273	26	66	(38 28)	1979	681	443	634	260	14	693	82	34	31	117	41	.74	122	.287	.330	.389

Kevin Gryboski

Pitches: R Bats: R Pos: RP-69   Ht: 6'5" Wt: 235 Born: 11/15/1973 Age: 31

Year Team	Lg	G	GS	CG	GF	IP	BFP	H	R	ER	HR	SH	SF	HB	TBB	IBB	SO	WP	Bk	W	L	Pct	ShO	Sv-Op	Hld	ERC	ERA
2002 Atlanta	NL	57	0	0	10	51.2	238	50	20	20	6	1	0	5	37	5	33	2	0	2	1	.667	0	0-2	11	5.58	3.48
2003 Atlanta	NL	64	0	0	9	44.1	190	44	22	19	3	4	0	2	23	6	32	2	0	6	4	.600	0	0-4	12	4.39	3.86
2004 Atlanta	NL	69	0	0	10	50.2	217	54	22	16	2	1	0	0	23	4	24	5	0	3	2	.600	0	2-4	16	4.22	2.84
3 ML YEARS		190	0	0	29	146.2	645	148	64	55	11	6	0	7	83	15	89	9	0	11	7	.611	0	2-10	39	4.74	3.38

Eddie Guardado

Pitches: L Bats: R Pos: RP-41   Ht: 6'0" Wt: 194 Born: 10/2/1970 Age: 34

Year Team	Lg	G	GS	CG	GF	IP	BFP	H	R	ER	HR	SH	SF	HB	TBB	IBB	SO	WP	Bk	W	L	Pct	ShO	Sv-Op	Hld	ERC	ERA
1993 Minnesota	AL	19	16	0	2	94.2	426	123	68	64	13	1	3	1	36	2	46	0	0	3	8	.273	0	0-0	0	6.18	6.18
1994 Minnesota	AL	4	4	0	0	17.0	81	26	16	16	3	1	2	0	4	0	8	0	0	0	2	.000	0	0-0	0	7.01	8.47
1995 Minnesota	AL	51	5	0	10	91.1	410	99	54	52	13	6	5	0	45	2	71	5	1	4	9	.308	0	2-5	5	5.20	5.12
1996 Minnesota	AL	83	0	0	17	73.2	313	61	45	43	12	6	4	3	33	4	74	3	0	6	5	.545	0	4-7	18	3.81	5.25
1997 Minnesota	AL	69	0	0	20	46.0	201	45	23	20	7	2	1	2	17	2	54	2	0	0	4	.000	0	1-1	13	4.23	3.91
1998 Minnesota	AL	79	0	0	12	65.2	286	66	34	33	10	3	6	0	28	6	53	2	0	3	1	.750	0	0-4	16	4.42	4.52
1999 Minnesota	AL	63	0	0	13	48.0	197	37	25	25	6	2	1	2	25	4	50	0	0	2	5	.286	0	2-4	15	3.63	4.69
2000 Minnesota	AL	70	0	0	36	61.2	262	55	27	27	14	3	2	1	25	3	52	1	1	7	4	.636	0	9-11	8	4.34	3.94
2001 Minnesota	AL	67	0	0	26	66.2	270	47	27	26	5	5	3	1	23	4	67	4	0	7	1	.875	0	12-14	14	2.13	3.51
2002 Minnesota	AL	68	0	0	62	67.2	270	53	22	22	9	2	2	1	18	2	70	0	0	1	3	.250	0	45-51	0	2.66	2.93
2003 Minnesota	AL	66	0	0	60	65.1	261	50	22	21	7	3	2	0	14	2	60	0	0	5	5	.375	0	41-45	0	2.13	2.89
2004 Seattle	AL	41	0	0	35	45.1	176	31	14	14	8	0	1	1	14	0	45	0	0	2	2	.500	0	18-25	0	2.69	2.78
12 ML YEARS		680	25	0	293	743.0	3153	693	377	364	107	34	32	12	282	31	650	22	2	38	49	.437	0	134-167	89	3.92	4.41

Vladimir Guerrero

Bats: R Throws: R Pos: RF-144; DH-13   Ht: 6'3" Wt: 210 Born: 2/9/1976 Age: 29

Year Team	Lg	G	AB	H	2B	3B	HR	(Hm Rd)	TB	R	RBI	RC	TBB	IBB	SO	HBP	SH	SF	SB	CS	SB%	GDP	Avg	OBP	Slg
1996 Montreal	NL	9	27	5	0	0	1	(0 1)	8	2	1	1	0	0	3	0	0	0	0	0	-	1	.185	.185	.296
1997 Montreal	NL	90	325	98	22	2	11	(5 6)	157	44	40	51	19	2	39	7	0	3	3	4	.43	11	.302	.350	.483
1998 Montreal	NL	159	623	202	37	7	38	(19 19)	367	108	109	124	42	13	95	7	0	5	11	9	.55	15	.324	.371	.589
1999 Montreal	NL	160	610	193	37	5	42	(23 19)	366	102	131	127	55	14	62	7	0	2	14	7	.67	18	.316	.378	.600
2000 Montreal	NL	154	571	197	28	11	44	(25 19)	379	101	123	137	58	23	74	8	0	4	9	10	.47	15	.345	.410	.664
2001 Montreal	NL	159	599	184	45	4	34	(21 13)	339	107	108	116	60	24	88	9	0	3	37	16	.70	24	.307	.377	.566
2002 Montreal	NL	161	614	206	37	2	39	(20 19)	364	106	111	123	84	32	70	6	0	5	40	20	.67	20	.336	.417	.593
2003 Montreal	NL	112	394	130	20	3	25	(15 10)	231	71	79	83	63	21	53	6	0	4	9	5	.64	18	.330	.426	.586
2004 Anaheim	AL	156	612	206	39	2	39	(19 20)	366	124	126	122	52	14	74	8	0	8	15	3	.83	18	.337	.391	.598
9 ML YEARS		1160	4375	1421	265	36	273	(147 126)	2577	765	828	884	433	143	558	58	0	34	138	74	.65	140	.325	.390	.589

Wilton Guerrero

Bats: B Throws: R Pos: 2B-8; PR-6; SS-3; 1B-2; 3B-2; CF-2; LF-1; PH-1   Ht: 6'0" Wt: 175 Born: 10/24/1974 Age: 30

Year Team	Lg	G	AB	H	2B	3B	HR	(Hm Rd)	TB	R	RBI	RC	TBB	IBB	SO	HBP	SH	SF	SB	CS	SB%	GDP	Avg	OBP	Slg
2004 Omaha*	AAA	72	282	92	14	4	3	(- -)	123	30	40	39	8	0	33	2	10	0	12	8	.60	10	.326	.349	.436
1996 Los Angeles	NL	5	2	0	0	0	0	(0 0)	0	1	0	0	0	0	2	0	0	0	0	0	-	0	.000	.000	.000
1997 Los Angeles	NL	111	357	104	10	9	4	(2 2)	144	39	32	41	8	1	52	0	13	2	6	5	.55	7	.291	.305	.403
1998 LA-Mon	NL	116	402	114	14	9	2	(0 2)	152	50	27	47	14	0	63	1	6	3	8	2	.80	4	.284	.307	.378
1999 Montreal	NL	132	315	92	15	7	2	(0 2)	127	42	31	40	13	0	38	2	10	0	7	6	.54	4	.292	.324	.403
2000 Montreal	NL	127	288	77	7	2	2	(2 0)	94	30	23	30	19	0	41	0	6	1	8	1	.89	6	.267	.312	.326
2001 Cincinnati	NL	60	142	48	5	1	1	(1 0)	58	16	8	20	3	0	17	0	2	0	5	2	.71	1	.338	.352	.408
2002 Cin-Mon	NL	103	140	31	2	1	0	(0 0)	35	12	5	9	7	1	32	0	9	0	7	1	.88	2	.221	.259	.250

Year Team	Lg	G	AB	H	2B	3B	HR	(Hm	Rd)	TB	R	RBI	RC	TBB	IBB	SO	HBP	SH	SF	SB	CS	SB%	GDP	Avg	OBP	Slg
2004 Kansas City	AL	24	32	7	0	1	0	(0	0)	9	7	1	1	0	0	4	0	0	0	1	0	1.00	1	.219	.219	.281
1998 Los Angeles	NL	64	180	51	4	3	0	(0	0)	61	21	7	18	4	0	33	1	3	2	5	2	.71	3	.283	.299	.339
1998 Montreal	NL	52	222	63	10	6	2	(0	2)	91	29	20	29	10	0	30	0	3	1	3	0	1.00	1	.284	.313	.410
2002 Cincinnati	NL	59	78	19	1	1	0	(0	0)	22	9	4	8	6	0	13	0	5	0	2	1	.67	1	.244	.298	.282
2002 Montreal	NL	44	62	12	1	0	0	(0	0)	13	3	1	1	1	1	19	0	4	0	5	0	1.00	1	.194	.206	.210
8 ML YEARS		678	1678	473	53	30	11	(5	6)	619	197	127	188	64	2	249	3	46	6	42	17	.71	25	.282	.308	.369

Matt Guerrier

Pitches: R **Bats:** R **Pos:** RP-7; SP-2 **Ht:** 6'3" **Wt:** 185 **Born:** 8/2/1978 **Age:** 26

| | | HOW MUCH HE PITCHED | | | | | | WHAT HE GAVE UP | | | | | | | | | | THE RESULTS | | | | | | |
Year Team	Lg	G	GS	CG	GF	IP	BFP	H	R	ER	HR	SH	SF	HB	TBB	IBB	SO	WP	Bk	W	L	Pct	ShO	Sv-Op	Hld	ERC	ERA
1999 Bristol	R+	21	0	0	19	25.2	109	18	9	2	1	0	2	1	14	2	37	1	1	5	0	1.000	0	10--	-	2.61	0.70
1999 Winstn-Salm	A+	4	0	0	4	3.1	15	3	2	2	0	0	0	1	0	0	5	2	0	0	0	-	0	2--	-	2.26	5.40
2000 Winstn-Salm	A+	30	0	0	28	34.2	147	25	13	5	0	2	1	3	12	0	35	2	0	0	3	.000	0	19--	-	2.01	1.30
2000 Birmingham	AA	23	0	0	19	23.1	95	17	9	7	1	0	0	1	12	1	19	3	0	3	1	.750	0	7--	-	2.87	2.70
2001 Birmingham	AA	15	15	1	0	98.2	402	85	42	34	8	5	0	5	32	1	75	5	0	11	3	.786	1	0--	-	3.17	3.10
2001 Charlotte	AAA	12	12	3	0	81.1	328	75	33	32	7	4	2	4	18	0	43	2	0	7	1	.875	0	0--	-	3.14	3.54
2002 Nashville	AAA	27	26	2	0	157.0	676	154	88	80	20	7	4	10	47	3	130	7	0	7	12	.368	1	0--	-	3.93	4.59
2003 Nashville	AAA	20	19	0	1	105.1	442	108	56	53	15	4	3	4	18	1	78	5	0	4	6	.400	0	0--	-	3.69	4.53
2004 Rochester	AAA	24	23	0	1	144.0	579	135	65	51	15	8	9	5	25	0	97	2	0	5	10	.333	0	0--	-	3.08	3.19
2004 Minnesota	AL	9	2	0	5	19.0	84	22	13	12	5	2	0	1	6	0	11	0	0	0	1	.000	0	0-0	0	6.10	5.68

Aaron Guiel

Bats: L **Throws:** R **Pos:** LF-38; PH-3; DH-2; RF-1 **Ht:** 5'10" **Wt:** 190 **Born:** 10/5/1972 **Age:** 32

| | | BATTING | | | | | | | | | | | | | | | | | | BASERUNNING | | | | AVERAGES | | |
Year Team	Lg	G	AB	H	2B	3B	HR	(Hm	Rd)	TB	R	RBI	RC	TBB	IBB	SO	HBP	SH	SF	SB	CS	SB%	GDP	Avg	OBP	Slg
2004 Royals*	R	4	17	8	1	0	2	(-	-)	15	3	5	6	0	0	2	1	0	0	0	0	-	0	.471	.500	.882
2004 Wichita*	AA	6	20	5	0	0	0	(-	-)	5	7	0	5	8	0	6	3	0	0	2	0	1.00	0	.250	.516	.250
2004 Omaha*	AAA	30	116	36	6	0	10	(-	-)	72	29	30	29	21	1	33	6	0	1	0	2	.00	1	.310	.438	.621
2002 Kansas City	AL	70	240	56	13	0	4	(4	0)	81	30	38	33	19	1	61	4	2	4	1	5	.17	3	.233	.296	.338
2003 Kansas City	AL	99	354	98	30	0	15	(4	11)	173	63	52	59	27	0	63	13	2	5	5	3	.38	3	.277	.346	.489
2004 Kansas City	AL	42	135	21	4	0	5	(2	3)	40	15	13	8	17	0	42	3	1	1	1	1	.50	3	.156	.263	.296
3 ML YEARS		211	729	175	47	0	24	(10	14)	294	108	103	100	63	1	166	20	5	10	5	11	.31	9	.240	.314	.403

Carlos Guillen

Bats: B **Throws:** R **Pos:** SS-135; PH-3 **Ht:** 6'1" **Wt:** 202 **Born:** 9/30/1975 **Age:** 29

| | | BATTING | | | | | | | | | | | | | | | | | | BASERUNNING | | | | AVERAGES | | |
Year Team	Lg	G	AB	H	2B	3B	HR	(Hm	Rd)	TB	R	RBI	RC	TBB	IBB	SO	HBP	SH	SF	SB	CS	SB%	GDP	Avg	OBP	Slg
1998 Seattle	AL	10	39	13	1	1	0	(0	0)	16	9	5	7	3	0	9	0	0	0	2	0	1.00	0	.333	.381	.410
1999 Seattle	AL	5	19	3	0	0	1	(1	0)	6	2	3	1	1	0	6	0	1	0	0	0	-	1	.158	.200	.316
2000 Seattle	AL	90	288	74	15	2	7	(3	4)	114	45	42	36	28	0	53	2	7	3	1	3	.25	6	.257	.324	.396
2001 Seattle	AL	140	456	118	21	4	5	(2	3)	162	72	53	56	53	0	89	1	7	6	4	1	.80	9	.259	.333	.355
2002 Seattle	AL	134	475	124	24	6	9	(4	5)	187	73	56	58	46	4	91	1	3	3	4	5	.44	8	.261	.326	.394
2003 Seattle	AL	109	388	107	19	3	7	(4	3)	153	63	52	53	52	2	64	1	5	5	4	4	.50	12	.276	.359	.394
2004 Detroit	AL	136	522	166	37	10	20	(7	13)	283	97	97	99	52	3	87	2	3	4	12	5	.71	11	.318	.379	.542
7 ML YEARS		624	2187	605	117	26	49	(21	28)	921	361	308	310	235	9	399	7	26	21	27	18	.60	47	.277	.346	.421

Jose Guillen

Bats: R **Throws:** R **Pos:** LF-136; DH-10; RF-4; PH-2 **Ht:** 5'11" **Wt:** 195 **Born:** 5/17/1976 **Age:** 29

| | | BATTING | | | | | | | | | | | | | | | | | | BASERUNNING | | | | AVERAGES | | |
Year Team	Lg	G	AB	H	2B	3B	HR	(Hm	Rd)	TB	R	RBI	RC	TBB	IBB	SO	HBP	SH	SF	SB	CS	SB%	GDP	Avg	OBP	Slg
1997 Pittsburgh	NL	143	498	133	20	5	14	(5	9)	205	58	70	56	17	0	88	8	0	3	1	2	.33	16	.267	.300	.412
1998 Pittsburgh	NL	153	573	153	38	2	14	(10	4)	237	60	84	68	21	0	100	6	1	4	3	5	.38	7	.267	.298	.414
1999 Pit-TB		87	288	73	16	0	3	(1	2)	98	42	31	28	20	2	57	7	1	2	1	0	1.00	16	.253	.315	.340
2000 Tampa Bay	AL	105	316	80	16	5	10	(5	5)	136	40	41	43	18	1	65	13	2	0	3	1	.75	6	.253	.320	.430
2001 Tampa Bay	AL	41	135	37	5	0	3	(0	3)	51	14	11	15	6	2	26	3	0	1	2	3	.40	2	.274	.317	.378
2002 Ari-Cin	NL	85	240	57	7	0	8	(5	3)	88	25	31	16	14	1	43	3	1	1	4	5	.44	13	.238	.287	.367
2003 Cin-Oak		136	485	151	28	2	31	(14	17)	276	77	86	86	24	2	95	14	8	3	1	3	.25	16	.311	.359	.569
2004 Anaheim	AL	148	565	166	28	3	27	(13	14)	281	88	104	98	37	5	92	15	0	3	5	4	.56	14	.294	.352	.497
1999 Pittsburgh	AL	40	120	32	6	0	1	(0	1)	41	18	18	12	10	1	21	0	1	1	1	0	1.00	7	.267	.321	.342
1999 Tampa Bay	AL	47	168	41	10	0	2	(1	1)	57	24	13	16	10	1	36	7	0	1	0	0	-	9	.244	.312	.339
2002 Arizona	NL	54	131	30	4	0	4	(3	1)	46	13	15	7	7	1	25	2	0	1	3	4	.43	7	.229	.277	.351
2002 Cincinnati	NL	31	109	27	3	0	4	(2	2)	42	12	16	9	7	0	18	1	1	0	1	1	.50	6	.248	.299	.385
2003 Cincinnati	NL	91	315	106	21	1	23	(10	13)	198	52	63	64	17	1	63	9	6	2	1	3	.25	8	.337	.385	.629
2003 Oakland	AL	45	170	45	7	1	8	(4	4)	78	25	23	22	7	1	32	5	2	1	0	0	-	8	.265	.311	.459
8 ML YEARS		898	3100	850	158	17	110	(53	57)	1372	404	458	410	157	13	566	69	13	17	20	23	.47	90	.274	.322	.443

Jeremy Guthrie

Pitches: R **Bats:** R **Pos:** RP-6 **Ht:** 6'1" **Wt:** 200 **Born:** 4/8/1979 **Age:** 26

| | | HOW MUCH HE PITCHED | | | | | | WHAT HE GAVE UP | | | | | | | | | | THE RESULTS | | | | | | |
Year Team	Lg	G	GS	CG	GF	IP	BFP	H	R	ER	HR	SH	SF	HB	TBB	IBB	SO	WP	Bk	W	L	Pct	ShO	Sv-Op	Hld	ERC	ERA
2003 Akron	AA	10	9	2	0	62.2	243	44	11	10	0	3	2	0	14	0	35	2	1	6	2	.750	0	0--	-	1.47	1.44
2003 Buffalo	AAA	18	18	1	0	96.2	444	129	75	70	15	3	1	7	30	1	62	3	1	4	9	.308	0	0--	-	6.43	6.52
2004 Akron	AA	23	21	1	1	130.1	587	145	76	61	16	6	5	16	42	0	94	5	0	8	8	.500	0	0--	-	5.02	4.21
2004 Buffalo	AAA	4	4	0	0	19.1	99	23	19	17	0	0	1	4	18	0	10	2	1	1	2	.333	0	0--	-	7.48	7.91
2004 Cleveland	AL	6	0	0	2	11.2	49	9	6	6	1	0	0	1	6	0	7	1	0	0	0	-	0	0-0	0	3.58	4.63

Ricky Gutierrez

Bats: R **Throws:** R **Pos:** 2B-32; PH-8; SS-6; PR-3; 3B-2   **Ht:** 6'1" **Wt:** 190 **Born:** 5/23/1970 **Age:** 35

Year Team	Lg	G	AB	H	2B	3B	HR	(Hm	Rd)	TB	R	RBI	RC	TBB	IBB	SO	HBP	SH	SF	SB	CS	SB%	GDP	Avg	OBP	Slg
2004 Daytona*	A+	4	13	1	0	0	0	(-	-)	1	1	3	0	1	0	3	2	0	1	0	0	-	1	.077	.235	.077
2004 Iowa*	AAA	21	68	25	5	0	0	(-	-)	30	5	10	12	6	0	10	0	0	0	0	1	.00	1	.368	.419	.441
1993 San Diego	NL	133	438	110	10	5	5	(5	0)	145	76	26	50	50	2	97	5	1	1	4	3	.57	7	.251	.334	.331
1994 San Diego	NL	90	275	66	11	2	1	(1	0)	84	27	28	25	32	1	54	2	2	3	2	6	.25	8	.240	.321	.305
1995 Houston	NL	52	156	43	6	0	0	(0	0)	49	22	12	16	10	3	33	1	1	1	5	0	1.00	4	.276	.321	.314
1996 Houston	NL	89	218	62	8	1	1	(1	0)	75	28	15	29	23	3	42	3	4	1	6	1	.86	4	.284	.359	.344
1997 Houston	NL	102	303	79	14	4	3	(0	3)	110	33	34	30	21	2	50	3	0	0	5	2	.71	17	.261	.315	.363
1998 Houston	NL	141	491	128	24	3	2	(1	1)	164	55	46	54	54	5	84	6	3	7	13	7	.65	20	.261	.337	.334
1999 Houston	NL	85	268	70	7	5	1	(0	1)	90	33	25	31	37	4	45	2	3	1	2	5	.29	9	.261	.354	.336
2000 Chicago	NL	125	449	124	19	2	11	(7	4)	180	73	56	72	66	0	58	7	16	4	8	2	.80	10	.276	.375	.401
2001 Chicago	NL	147	528	153	23	3	10	(7	3)	212	76	66	74	40	0	56	10	17	11	4	3	.57	13	.290	.345	.402
2002 Cleveland	AL	94	353	97	13	0	4	(2	2)	122	38	38	41	20	0	48	7	3	1	0	1	.00	14	.275	.325	.346
2003 Cleveland	AL	16	50	13	3	0	0	(0	0)	16	2	3	3	3	0	5	1	1	1	0	0	-	1	.260	.309	.320
2004 NYM-Bos		45	103	22	3	0	0	(0	0)	25	8	8	5	8	0	14	1	0	0	1	0	1.00	5	.214	.277	.243
2004 New York	NL	24	63	11	2	0	0	(0	0)	13	2	5	3	6	0	8	1	0	0	0	0	-	3	.175	.257	.206
2004 Boston	AL	21	40	11	1	0	0	(0	0)	12	6	3	2	2	0	6	0	0	0	1	0	1.00	2	.275	.310	.300
12 ML YEARS		1119	3632	967	141	25	38	(25	13)	1272	471	357	430	364	20	586	48	51	31	50	30	.63	112	.266	.338	.350

Cristian Guzman

Bats: B **Throws:** R **Pos:** SS-145; PR-1   **Ht:** 6'0" **Wt:** 195 **Born:** 3/21/1978 **Age:** 27

Year Team	Lg	G	AB	H	2B	3B	HR	(Hm	Rd)	TB	R	RBI	RC	TBB	IBB	SO	HBP	SH	SF	SB	CS	SB%	GDP	Avg	OBP	Slg
1999 Minnesota	AL	131	420	95	12	3	1	(1	0)	116	47	26	29	22	0	90	3	7	4	9	7	.56	5	.226	.267	.276
2000 Minnesota	AL	156	631	156	25	20	8	(3	5)	245	89	54	76	46	1	101	2	7	4	28	10	.74	5	.247	.299	.388
2001 Minnesota	AL	118	493	149	28	14	10	(7	3)	235	80	51	79	21	0	78	5	8	0	25	8	.76	6	.302	.337	.477
2002 Minnesota	AL	148	623	170	31	6	9	(6	3)	240	80	59	63	17	2	79	2	8	6	12	13	.48	12	.273	.292	.385
2003 Minnesota	AL	143	534	143	15	14	3	(1	2)	195	78	53	62	30	0	79	5	12	4	18	9	.67	4	.268	.311	.365
2004 Minnesota	AL	145	576	158	31	4	8	(5	3)	221	84	46	65	30	4	64	1	13	4	10	5	.67	15	.274	.309	.384
6 ML YEARS		841	3277	871	142	61	39	(23	16)	1252	458	289	374	166	7	491	18	55	22	102	52	.66	47	.266	.303	.382

Freddy Guzman

Bats: B **Throws:** R **Pos:** CF-17; PR-2; PH-1   **Ht:** 5'10" **Wt:** 165 **Born:** 1/20/1981 **Age:** 24

Year Team	Lg	G	AB	H	2B	3B	HR	(Hm	Rd)	TB	R	RBI	RC	TBB	IBB	SO	HBP	SH	SF	SB	CS	SB%	GDP	Avg	OBP	Slg
2001 Idaho Falls	R+	12	46	16	4	1	0	(-	-)	22	11	5	9	2	0	10	1	1	0	5	0	1.00	0	.348	.388	.478
2002 Lk Elsinore	A+	21	81	21	3	0	1	(-	-)	27	13	6	10	8	0	12	0	0	0	14	4	.78	0	.259	.326	.333
2002 Fort Wayne	A	47	190	53	7	5	0	(-	-)	70	35	18	29	18	0	37	0	2	0	39	7	.85	0	.279	.341	.368
2002 Eugene	A-	21	80	18	2	1	0	(-	-)	22	14	8	9	7	0	15	2	1	3	16	1	.94	0	.225	.293	.275
2003 Lk Elsinore	A+	70	281	80	12	3	2	(-	-)	104	64	22	47	40	1	60	2	1	2	49	10	.83	1	.285	.375	.370
2003 Mobile	AA	46	177	48	5	2	1	(-	-)	60	30	11	28	26	2	34	1	1	0	38	7	.84	0	.271	.368	.339
2003 Portland	AAA	2	10	3	0	0	0	(-	-)	3	1	0	1	0	0	1	0	0	0	3	0	1.00	0	.300	.300	.300
2004 Mobile	AA	35	138	39	5	2	1	(-	-)	51	21	7	20	16	1	28	1	1	1	17	5	.77	2	.283	.359	.370
2004 Portland	AAA	66	264	77	12	4	1	(-	-)	100	48	19	45	30	1	46	1	4	1	48	5	.91	1	.292	.365	.379
2004 San Diego	NL	20	76	16	3	0	0	(0	0)	19	8	5	4	3	0	13	1	0	0	5	2	.71	0	.211	.250	.250

Travis Hafner

Bats: L **Throws:** R **Pos:** DH-126; 1B-11; PH-9   **Ht:** 6'3" **Wt:** 240 **Born:** 6/3/1977 **Age:** 28

Year Team	Lg	G	AB	H	2B	3B	HR	(Hm	Rd)	TB	R	RBI	RC	TBB	IBB	SO	HBP	SH	SF	SB	CS	SB%	GDP	Avg	OBP	Slg
2002 Texas	AL	23	62	15	4	1	1	(0	1)	24	6	6	7	8	1	15	0	0	0	0	1	.00	0	.242	.329	.387
2003 Cleveland	AL	91	291	74	19	3	14	(7	7)	141	35	40	42	22	2	81	10	0	1	2	1	.67	7	.254	.327	.485
2004 Cleveland	AL	140	482	150	41	3	28	(7	21)	281	96	109	103	68	7	111	17	0	6	3	2	.60	11	.311	.410	.583
3 ML YEARS		254	835	239	64	7	43	(14	29)	446	137	155	152	98	10	207	27	0	7	5	4	.56	18	.286	.376	.534

Scott Hairston

Bats: R **Throws:** R **Pos:** 2B-84; PH-14; LF-2; RF-2; PR-2   **Ht:** 6'0" **Wt:** 188 **Born:** 5/25/1980 **Age:** 25

Year Team	Lg	G	AB	H	2B	3B	HR	(Hm	Rd)	TB	R	RBI	RC	TBB	IBB	SO	HBP	SH	SF	SB	CS	SB%	GDP	Avg	OBP	Slg
2001 Missoula	R+	74	291	101	16	6	14	(-	-)	171	81	65	69	38	2	50	7	0	2	2	2	.50	5	.347	.424	.588
2002 South Bend	A	109	394	131	35	4	16	(-	-)	222	79	72	89	58	3	74	10	1	5	9	3	.75	11	.332	.426	.563
2002 Lancaster	A+	18	79	32	11	1	6	(-	-)	63	20	26	21	6	0	16	0	0	1	1	0	1.00	4	.405	.442	.797
2003 El Paso	AA	88	337	93	21	7	10	(-	-)	158	53	47	51	30	1	80	6	0	1	6	2	.75	10	.276	.345	.469
2003 Tucson	AAA	1	0	0	0	0	0	(-	-)	0	0	1	0	0	0	0	0	0	0	0	0	-	0	-	.000	-
2004 Tucson	AAA	28	115	36	8	3	5	(-	-)	65	29	20	22	11	0	21	1	0	1	0	3	.00	1	.313	.375	.565
2004 Arizona	NL	101	339	84	15	6	13	(6	7)	150	39	29	32	21	0	88	1	2	1	3	3	.50	4	.248	.293	.442

Jerry Hairston Jr.

Bats: R **Throws:** R **Pos:** RF-27; DH-21; CF-15; 2B-12; LF-10; PR-3; PH-2; 3B-1   **Ht:** 5'10" **Wt:** 175 **Born:** 5/29/1976 **Age:** 29

Year Team	Lg	G	AB	H	2B	3B	HR	(Hm	Rd)	TB	R	RBI	RC	TBB	IBB	SO	HBP	SH	SF	SB	CS	SB%	GDP	Avg	OBP	Slg
1998 Baltimore	AL	6	7	0	0	0	0	(0	0)	0	2	0	0	0	0	1	0	0	0	0	0	-	0	.000	.000	.000
1999 Baltimore	AL	50	175	47	12	1	4	(1	3)	73	26	17	24	11	0	24	3	4	0	9	4	.69	2	.269	.323	.417
2000 Baltimore	AL	49	180	46	5	0	5	(2	3)	66	27	19	22	21	0	22	6	5	0	8	5	.62	8	.256	.353	.367
2001 Baltimore	AL	159	532	124	25	5	8	(5	3)	183	63	47	57	44	0	73	13	9	4	29	11	.73	12	.233	.305	.344
2002 Baltimore	AL	122	426	114	25	3	5	(2	3)	160	55	32	55	34	0	55	7	8	4	21	6	.78	5	.268	.329	.376

		BATTING																	BASERUNNING				AVERAGES		
Year Team	Lg	G	AB	H	2B	3B	HR	(Hm Rd)	TB	R	RBI	RC	TBB	IBB	SO	HBP	SH	SF	SB	CS	SB%	GDP	Avg	OBP	Slg
2003 Baltimore	AL	58	218	59	12	2	2	(1 1)	81	25	21	32	23	0	25	6	10	2	14	5	.74	8	.271	.353	.372
2004 Baltimore	AL	86	287	87	19	1	2	(0 2)	114	43	24	45	29	1	29	8	6	4	13	8	.62	3	.303	.378	.397
7 ML YEARS		530	1825	477	98	12	26	(11 15)	677	241	160	235	162	1	229	43	42	14	94	39	.71	38	.261	.334	.371

John Halama

Pitches: L **Bats:** L **Pos:** RP-20; SP-14 **Ht:** 6'5" **Wt:** 210 **Born:** 2/22/1972 **Age:** 33

		HOW MUCH HE PITCHED						WHAT HE GAVE UP											THE RESULTS							
Year Team	Lg	G	GS	CG	GF	IP	BFP	H	R	ER	HR	SH	SF	HB	TBB	IBB	SO	WP	Bk	W	L	Pct	ShO	Sv-Op	Hld	ERC	ERA
1998 Houston	NL	6	6	0	0	32.1	147	37	21	21	0	3	4	2	13	0	21	2	1	1	1	.500	0	0-0	0	4.34	5.85
1999 Seattle	AL	38	24	1	7	179.0	763	193	88	84	20	5	9	7	56	3	105	4	0	11	10	.524	1	0-0	1	4.47	4.22
2000 Seattle	AL	30	30	1	0	166.2	736	206	108	94	19	4	6	2	56	0	87	4	1	14	9	.609	1	0-0	0	5.42	5.08
2001 Seattle	AL	31	17	0	6	110.1	485	132	69	58	18	3	4	6	26	0	50	2	0	10	7	.588	0	0-0	1	5.21	4.73
2002 Seattle	AL	31	10	0	12	101.0	438	112	45	40	9	3	2	1	33	5	70	2	1	6	5	.545	0	0-0	4	4.29	3.56
2003 Oakland	AL	35	13	0	4	108.2	484	117	68	51	18	7	3	2	36	2	51	3	3	5	5	.375	0	0-0	3	4.61	4.22
2004 Tampa Bay	AL	34	14	0	7	118.2	513	134	68	62	17	1	3	10	27	3	59	1	1	7	6	.538	0	0-0	0	4.76	4.70
7 ML YEARS		205	114	2	36	816.2	3566	931	467	410	101	26	31	30	247	13	443	18	7	52	43	.547	2	0-0	5	4.80	4.52

Bill Hall

Bats: R **Throws:** R **Pos:** 2B-50; SS-37; PH-30; 3B-11 **Ht:** 6'0" **Wt:** 175 **Born:** 12/28/1979 **Age:** 25

		BATTING																	BASERUNNING				AVERAGES		
Year Team	Lg	G	AB	H	2B	3B	HR	(Hm Rd)	TB	R	RBI	RC	TBB	IBB	SO	HBP	SH	SF	SB	CS	SB%	GDP	Avg	OBP	Slg
2002 Milwaukee	NL	19	36	7	1	1	1	(0 1)	13	5	5	3	3	0	13	0	0	1	0	1	.00	1	.194	.256	.361
2003 Milwaukee	NL	52	142	37	9	2	5	(2 3)	65	23	20	18	7	0	28	1	4	1	1	2	.33	5	.261	.298	.458
2004 Milwaukee	NL	126	390	93	20	3	9	(5 4)	146	43	53	42	20	1	119	1	2	2	12	6	.67	4	.238	.276	.374
3 ML YEARS		197	568	137	30	6	15	(7 8)	224	69	78	63	30	1	160	2	6	3	13	9	.59	10	.241	.280	.394

Toby Hall

Bats: R **Throws:** R **Pos:** C-119 **Ht:** 6'3" **Wt:** 240 **Born:** 10/21/1975 **Age:** 29

		BATTING																	BASERUNNING				AVERAGES		
Year Team	Lg	G	AB	H	2B	3B	HR	(Hm Rd)	TB	R	RBI	RC	TBB	IBB	SO	HBP	SH	SF	SB	CS	SB%	GDP	Avg	OBP	Slg
2000 Tampa Bay	AL	4	12	2	0	0	1	(0 1)	5	1	1	1	1	0	0	0	0	0	0	0	-	0	.167	.231	.417
2001 Tampa Bay	AL	49	188	56	16	0	4	(1 3)	84	28	30	25	4	0	16	3	0	1	2	2	.50	5	.298	.321	.447
2002 Tampa Bay	AL	85	330	85	19	1	6	(2 4)	124	37	42	39	17	3	27	1	2	3	0	1	.00	14	.258	.293	.376
2003 Tampa Bay	AL	130	463	117	23	0	12	(4 8)	176	50	47	45	23	4	40	7	0	5	0	1	.00	14	.253	.295	.380
2004 Tampa Bay	AL	119	404	103	21	0	8	(6 2)	148	35	60	42	24	1	41	5	1	7	0	2	.00	20	.255	.300	.366
5 ML YEARS		387	1397	363	79	1	31	(13 18)	537	151	180	152	69	8	124	16	3	16	2	6	.25	53	.260	.299	.384

Roy Halladay

Pitches: R **Bats:** R **Pos:** SP-21 **Ht:** 6'6" **Wt:** 230 **Born:** 5/14/1977 **Age:** 28

		HOW MUCH HE PITCHED						WHAT HE GAVE UP											THE RESULTS							
Year Team	Lg	G	GS	CG	GF	IP	BFP	H	R	ER	HR	SH	SF	HB	TBB	IBB	SO	WP	Bk	W	L	Pct	ShO	Sv-Op	Hld	ERC	ERA
1998 Toronto	AL	2	2	1	0	14.0	53	9	4	3	2	0	0	0	2	0	13	0	0	1	0	1.000	0	0-0	0	1.61	1.93
1999 Toronto	AL	36	18	1	6	149.1	668	156	76	65	19	3	4	4	79	1	82	6	0	8	7	.533	1	1-1	2	5.19	3.92
2000 Toronto	AL	19	13	0	4	67.2	349	107	80	80	14	2	3	2	42	0	44	6	1	4	7	.364	0	0-0	0	9.70	10.64
2001 Toronto	AL	17	16	1	0	105.1	432	97	41	37	3	3	1	1	25	0	96	4	1	5	3	.625	1	0-0	0	2.61	3.16
2002 Toronto	AL	34	34	2	0	239.1	993	223	93	78	10	9	2	7	62	6	168	4	1	19	7	.731	1	0-0	0	2.85	2.93
2003 Toronto	AL	36	36	9	0	266.0	1071	253	111	96	26	3	2	9	32	1	204	6	1	22	7	.759	2	0-0	0	2.86	3.25
2004 Toronto	AL	21	21	1	0	133.0	561	140	66	62	13	4	3	1	39	1	95	2	2	8	8	.500	1	0-0	0	4.00	4.20
7 ML YEARS		165	140	15	6	974.2	4127	985	478	421	87	24	15	24	281	9	702	28	6	67	39	.632	6	1-1	2	3.71	3.89

Brad Halsey

Pitches: L **Bats:** L **Pos:** SP-7; RP-1 **Ht:** 6'1" **Wt:** 180 **Born:** 2/14/1981 **Age:** 24

		HOW MUCH HE PITCHED						WHAT HE GAVE UP											THE RESULTS							
Year Team	Lg	G	GS	CG	GF	IP	BFP	H	R	ER	HR	SH	SF	HB	TBB	IBB	SO	WP	Bk	W	L	Pct	ShO	Sv-Op	Hld	ERC	ERA
2002 Staten Island	A-	11	10	0	0	56.0	223	39	15	12	0	1	1	4	17	0	53	0	0	6	1	.857	0	0- -	-	1.83	1.93
2003 Tampa	A+	14	13	0	0	84.0	354	96	36	32	3	3	2	1	14	0	56	4	0	10	4	.714	0	0- -	-	3.57	3.43
2003 Trenton	AA	15	15	0	0	91.1	410	123	51	50	4	4	0	5	22	0	78	3	0	7	5	.583	0	0- -	-	5.29	4.93
2004 Columbus	AAA	24	23	3	0	144.0	589	128	46	42	8	3	3	7	37	0	109	2	1	11	4	.733	2	0- -	-	2.86	2.63
2004 New York	AL	8	7	0	0	32.0	153	41	26	23	4	1	2	2	14	0	25	0	0	1	3	.250	0	0-0	0	6.20	6.47

Shane Halter

Bats: R **Throws:** R **Pos:** 3B-33; 2B-6; 1B-4; SS-3; DH-3; PH-3; PR-1 **Ht:** 6'0" **Wt:** 180 **Born:** 11/8/1969 **Age:** 35

		BATTING																	BASERUNNING				AVERAGES		
Year Team	Lg	G	AB	H	2B	3B	HR	(Hm Rd)	TB	R	RBI	RC	TBB	IBB	SO	HBP	SH	SF	SB	CS	SB%	GDP	Avg	OBP	Slg
2004 R Cucamnga*	A+	5	19	4	1	0	0	(- -)	5	4	1	1	2	0	4	1	0	0	2	0	1.00	1	.211	.318	.263
2004 Salt Lake*	AAA	35	131	36	7	1	6	(- -)	63	18	18	19	15	0	21	0	0	0	2	3	.40	5	.275	.349	.481
1997 Kansas City	AL	74	123	34	5	1	2	(1 1)	47	16	10	16	10	0	28	2	4	0	4	3	.57	1	.276	.341	.382
1998 Kansas City	AL	86	204	45	12	0	2	(0 2)	63	17	13	15	12	0	38	1	7	2	2	5	.29	3	.221	.265	.309
1999 New York	NL	7	0	0	0	0	0	(0 0)	0	0	0	0	0	0	0	0	0	0	0	0	-	0	-	-	-
2000 Detroit	AL	105	238	62	12	2	3	(0 3)	87	26	27	26	14	0	49	1	10	2	5	2	.71	5	.261	.302	.366
2001 Detroit	AL	136	450	128	32	7	12	(4 8)	210	53	65	69	37	2	100	7	7	6	3	3	.50	14	.284	.344	.467
2002 Detroit	AL	122	410	98	22	6	10	(4 6)	162	46	39	44	39	1	92	4	1	4	0	4	.00	12	.239	.309	.395
2003 Detroit	AL	114	360	78	5	2	12	(6 6)	123	33	30	25	27	0	77	0	3	3	2	3	.40	11	.217	.269	.342
2004 Anaheim	AL	46	114	23	5	0	4	(2 2)	40	10	13	11	7	0	30	0	0	0	1	1	.50	3	.202	.248	.351
8 ML YEARS		690	1899	468	93	18	45	(17 28)	732	201	197	206	146	3	414	15	32	17	17	21	.45	49	.246	.303	.385

Robby Hammock

Bats: R **Throws:** R **Pos:** C-45; LF-12; PH-4; 3B-1   **Ht:** 5'10" **Wt:** 187 **Born:** 5/13/1977 **Age:** 28

								BATTING											BASERUNNING				AVERAGES		
Year Team	Lg	G	AB	H	2B	3B	HR	(Hm | Rd)	TB	R	RBI	RC	TBB	IBB	SO	HBP	SH	SF	SB	CS	SB%	GDP	Avg	OBP	Slg
1998 Lethbridge	R+	62	227	65	14	2	10	(- | -)	113	46	56	40	28	1	34	2	0	2	5	4	.56	3	.286	.367	.498
1999 High Desert	A+	114	379	26	20	7	9	(- | -)	87	80	72	3	47	2	63	2	0	6	3	6	.33	8	.069	.173	.230
2000 High Desert	A+	40	136	48	15	1	3	(- | -)	74	25	23	31	27	1	24	1	0	3	3	3	.50	5	.353	.455	.544
2000 El Paso	AA	45	140	35	5	1	1	(- | -)	45	22	15	14	11	1	25	1	0	2	1	2	.33	1	.250	.305	.321
2001 El Paso	AA	26	74	12	5	0	0	(- | -)	17	6	4	2	7	0	18	0	1	0	2	2	.50	1	.162	.235	.230
2001 South Bend	A	34	125	31	3	2	2	(- | -)	44	16	14	13	14	0	21	0	1	0	5	6	.45	2	.248	.324	.352
2001 Lancaster	A+	45	190	59	11	3	4	(- | -)	88	33	36	32	16	1	42	7	0	4	3	2	.60	6	.311	.378	.463
2002 El Paso	AA	122	441	128	28	4	11	(- | -)	197	68	73	68	43	0	68	8	1	8	5	4	.56	14	.290	.358	.447
2003 Tucson	AAA	33	116	31	6	2	2	(- | -)	47	14	17	15	11	0	24	0	0	4	1	0	1.00	2	.267	.321	.405
2004 Lancaster	A+	2	9	6	2	0	0	(- | -)	8	2	3	4	1	0	1	0	0	0	0	0	-	0	.667	.700	.889
2004 Tucson	AAA	8	21	6	1	0	0	(- | -)	7	1	4	3	2	0	1	0	0	1	2	0	1.00	0	.286	.333	.333
2003 Arizona	NL	65	195	55	10	2	8	(5 | 3)	93	30	28	28	17	3	44	2	0	2	3	2	.60	5	.282	.343	.477
2004 Arizona	NL	62	195	47	16	2	4	(1 | 3)	79	22	18	14	13	6	39	0	1	1	3	3	.50	9	.241	.287	.405
2 ML YEARS		127	390	102	26	4	12	(6 | 6)	172	52	46	42	30	9	83	2	1	3	6	5	.55	14	.262	.315	.441

Chris Hammond

Pitches: L **Bats:** L **Pos:** RP-41   **Ht:** 6'1" **Wt:** 195 **Born:** 1/21/1966 **Age:** 39

		HOW MUCH HE PITCHED						WHAT HE GAVE UP											THE RESULTS						
Year Team	Lg	G	GS	CG	GF	IP	BFP	H	R	ER	HR	SH	SF	HB	TBB	IBB	SO	WP	Bk	W	L	Pct	ShO	Sv-Op	Hld	ERC	ERA
2004 Sacramento*	AAA	3	3	0	0	4.0	18	6	0	0	0	0	0	0	0	0	5	0	0	0	0	-	0	0- -	-	4.47	0.00
1990 Cincinnati	NL	3	3	0	0	11.1	56	13	9	8	2	1	0	0	12	1	4	1	3	0	2	.000	0	0-0	0	8.50	6.35
1991 Cincinnati	NL	20	18	0	0	99.2	425	92	51	45	4	6	1	2	48	3	50	3	0	7	7	.500	0	0-0	0	3.63	4.06
1992 Cincinnati	NL	28	26	0	1	147.1	627	149	75	69	13	5	3	3	55	6	79	6	0	7	10	.412	0	0-0	0	4.02	4.21
1993 Florida	NL	32	32	1	0	191.0	826	207	106	99	18	10	2	1	66	2	108	10	5	11	12	.478	0	0-0	0	4.31	4.66
1994 Florida	NL	13	13	1	0	73.1	312	79	30	25	5	5	2	1	23	1	40	3	0	4	4	.500	1	0-0	0	4.03	3.07
1995 Florida	NL	25	24	3	0	161.0	683	157	73	68	17	7	7	9	47	2	126	3	1	9	6	.600	2	0-0	0	3.75	3.80
1996 Florida	NL	38	9	0	5	81.0	368	104	65	59	14	3	4	4	27	3	50	1	0	5	8	.385	0	0-0	5	6.21	6.56
1997 Boston	AL	29	8	0	6	65.1	293	81	45	43	5	0	3	2	27	4	48	2	0	3	4	.429	0	1-2	4	5.47	5.92
1998 Florida	NL	3	3	0	0	13.2	67	20	11	10	3	2	0	1	8	0	8	0	0	0	2	.000	0	0-0	0	9.33	6.59
2002 Atlanta	NL	63	0	0	6	76.0	311	53	15	8	1	5	2	1	31	9	63	1	0	7	2	.778	0	0-2	17	1.85	0.95
2003 New York	NL	62	0	0	16	63.0	262	65	23	20	5	5	3	2	11	0	45	1	0	3	2	.600	0	1-4	17	3.36	2.86
2004 Oakland	AL	41	0	0	9	53.2	224	56	21	16	4	3	3	3	13	1	34	0	0	4	1	.800	0	1-3	3	3.79	2.68
12 ML YEARS		357	136	5	43	1036.1	4454	1076	524	470	91	52	30	29	368	32	655	31	9	60	60	.500	3	3-11	46	4.12	4.08

Jeffrey Hammonds

Bats: R **Throws:** R **Pos:** RF-19; PH-13; LF-7; CF-1   **Ht:** 6'0" **Wt:** 200 **Born:** 3/5/1971 **Age:** 34

								BATTING											BASERUNNING				AVERAGES		
Year Team	Lg	G	AB	H	2B	3B	HR	(Hm	Rd)	TB	R	RBI	RC	TBB	IBB	SO	HBP	SH	SF	SB	CS	SB%	GDP	Avg	OBP	Slg
1993 Baltimore	AL	33	105	32	8	0	3	(2	1)	49	10	19	15	2	1	16	0	1	2	4	0	1.00	3	.305	.312	.467
1994 Baltimore	AL	68	250	74	18	2	8	(6	2)	120	45	31	42	17	1	39	2	0	5	5	0	1.00	3	.296	.339	.480
1995 Baltimore	AL	57	178	43	9	1	4	(2	2)	66	18	23	18	9	0	30	1	1	2	4	2	.67	3	.242	.279	.371
1996 Baltimore	AL	71	248	56	10	1	9	(3	6)	95	38	27	27	23	1	53	4	6	1	3	3	.50	7	.226	.301	.383
1997 Baltimore	AL	118	397	105	19	3	21	(9	12)	193	71	55	64	32	1	73	3	0	2	15	1	.94	6	.264	.323	.486
1998 Bal-Cin		89	257	72	16	2	6	(1	5)	110	50	39	45	39	1	56	3	3	4	8	3	.73	2	.280	.376	.428
1999 Cincinnati	NL	123	262	73	13	0	17	(5	12)	137	43	41	45	27	0	64	1	2	1	3	6	.33	4	.279	.347	.523
2000 Colorado	NL	122	454	152	24	2	20	(14	6)	240	94	106	90	44	4	83	5	2	6	14	7	.67	11	.335	.395	.529
2001 Milwaukee	NL	49	174	43	11	1	6	(3	3)	74	20	21	23	14	1	42	4	0	2	5	3	.63	2	.247	.314	.425
2002 Milwaukee	NL	128	448	115	26	5	9	(2	7)	178	47	41	53	52	0	86	2	1	7	4	5	.44	13	.257	.332	.397
2003 Mil-SF	NL	46	132	32	12	0	4	(3	1)	56	22	13	15	16	0	28	1	0	0	1	0	1.00	3	.242	.329	.424
2004 San Francisco	NL	40	95	20	5	0	3	(2	1)	34	14	6	9	15	0	22	3	0	0	1	0	1.00	5	.211	.336	.358
1998 Baltimore	AL	63	171	46	12	1	6	(1	5)	78	36	28	31	26	1	38	3	0	3	7	2	.78	2	.269	.369	.456
1998 Cincinnati	NL	26	86	26	4	1	0	(0	0)	32	14	11	14	13	0	18	0	3	1	1	1	.50	0	.302	.390	.372
2003 Milwaukee	NL	10	38	6	2	0	1	(1	0)	11	2	3	3	3	0	7	0	0	0	0	0	-	2	.158	.220	.289
2003 San Francisco	NL	36	94	26	10	0	3	(2	1)	45	20	10	15	13	0	21	1	0	0	1	0	1.00	1	.277	.370	.479
12 ML YEARS		944	3000	817	171	17	110	(52	58)	1352	472	422	446	290	10	592	29	16	32	67	30	.69	59	.272	.339	.451

Mike Hampton

Pitches: L **Bats:** R **Pos:** SP-29   **Ht:** 5'10" **Wt:** 180 **Born:** 9/9/1972 **Age:** 32

		HOW MUCH HE PITCHED						WHAT HE GAVE UP											THE RESULTS						
Year Team	Lg	G	GS	CG	GF	IP	BFP	H	R	ER	HR	SH	SF	HB	TBB	IBB	SO	WP	Bk	W	L	Pct	ShO	Sv-Op	Hld	ERC	ERA
1993 Seattle	AL	13	3	0	4	17.0	95	28	20	18	3	1	1	0	17	3	8	1	1	1	3	.250	0	1-1	0	11.09	9.53
1994 Houston	NL	44	0	0	7	41.1	181	46	19	17	4	0	0	2	16	1	24	5	1	2	1	.667	0	0-1	10	4.88	3.70
1995 Houston	NL	24	24	0	0	150.2	641	141	73	56	13	11	5	4	49	3	115	3	1	9	8	.529	0	0-0	0	3.37	3.35
1996 Houston	NL	27	27	2	0	160.1	691	175	79	64	12	10	3	3	49	1	101	7	2	10	10	.500	1	0-0	0	4.11	3.59
1997 Houston	NL	34	34	7	0	223.0	941	217	105	95	16	11	7	2	77	2	139	6	1	15	10	.600	2	0-0	0	3.56	3.83
1998 Houston	NL	32	32	1	0	211.2	917	227	92	79	18	7	7	5	81	1	137	4	2	11	7	.611	1	0-0	0	4.45	3.36
1999 Houston	NL	34	34	3	0	239.0	979	206	86	77	12	10	9	5	101	2	177	9	0	22	4	.846	2	0-0	0	3.25	2.90
2000 New York	NL	33	33	3	0	217.2	920	194	89	76	10	11	5	8	99	5	151	10	0	15	10	.600	1	0-0	0	3.44	3.14
2001 Colorado	NL	32	32	2	0	203.0	904	236	138	122	31	8	6	8	85	7	122	6	0	14	13	.519	1	0-0	0	5.69	5.41
2002 Colorado	NL	30	30	0	0	178.2	838	228	135	122	24	2	9	7	91	4	74	9	2	7	15	.318	0	0-0	0	6.61	6.15
2003 Atlanta	NL	31	31	1	0	190.0	823	186	91	81	14	10	5	1	78	4	110	10	1	14	8	.636	0	0-0	0	3.77	3.84
2004 Atlanta	NL	29	29	1	0	172.1	760	198	86	82	15	8	3	1	65	3	87	3	2	13	9	.591	0	0-0	0	4.76	4.28
12 ML YEARS		363	309	20	9	2004.2	8699	2082	1013	889	172	89	60	46	808	36	1245	73	13	133	98	.576	8	1-2	12	4.29	3.99

Josh Hancock

Pitches: R **Bats:** R **Pos:** SP-11; RP-5   **Ht:** 6'3" **Wt:** 217 **Born:** 4/11/1978 **Age:** 27

Year Team	Lg	G	GS	CG	GF	IP	BFP	H	R	ER	HR	SH	SF	HB	TBB	IBB	SO	WP	Bk	W	L	Pct	ShO	Sv-Op	Hld	ERC	ERA
2004 Scrtn/WlksBr*	AAA	18	18	1	0	107.2	443	106	52	48	10	12	8	1	21	1	65	2	0	8	7	.533	0	0--	-	3.17	4.01
2002 Boston	AL	3	1	0	2	7.1	28	5	3	3	1	1	0	0	2	0	6	0	0	0	1	.000	0	0-0	0	2.25	3.68
2003 Philadelphia	NL	2	0	0	0	3.0	11	2	1	1	0	0	0	0	0	0	4	0	0	0	0	-	0	0-0	0	0.91	3.00
2004 Phi-Cin	NL	16	11	0	2	63.2	293	73	43	36	17	3	2	1	28	2	36	5	0	5	2	.714	0	0-0	0	6.24	5.09
2004 Philadelphia	NL	4	2	0	0	9.0	42	13	9	9	3	0	0	0	3	0	5	0	0	0	1	.000	0	0-0	0	8.40	9.00
2004 Cincinnati	NL	12	9	0	2	54.2	251	60	34	27	14	3	2	1	25	2	31	5	0	5	1	.833	0	0-0	0	5.91	4.45
3 ML YEARS		21	12	0	4	74.0	332	80	47	40	18	4	2	1	30	2	46	5	0	5	3	.625	0	0-0	0	5.52	4.86

Dave Hansen

Bats: L **Throws:** R **Pos:** PH-64; 1B-14; 3B-8; DH-8   **Ht:** 6'0" **Wt:** 195 **Born:** 11/24/1968 **Age:** 36

Year Team	Lg	G	AB	H	2B	3B	HR	(Hm	Rd)	TB	R	RBI	RC	TBB	IBB	SO	HBP	SH	SF	SB	CS	SB%	GDP	Avg	OBP	Slg
1990 Los Angeles	NL	5	7	1	0	0	0	(0	0)	1	0	1	0	0	0	3	0	0	0	0	0	-	0	.143	.143	.143
1991 Los Angeles	NL	53	56	15	4	0	1	(0	1)	22	3	5	6	2	0	12	0	0	0	1	0	1.00	2	.268	.293	.393
1992 Los Angeles	NL	132	341	73	11	0	6	(1	5)	102	30	22	27	34	3	49	1	0	2	0	2	.00	9	.214	.286	.299
1993 Los Angeles	NL	84	105	38	3	0	4	(2	2)	53	13	30	25	21	3	13	0	0	1	0	1	.00	0	.362	.465	.505
1994 Los Angeles	NL	40	44	15	3	0	0	(0	0)	18	3	5	8	5	0	5	0	0	0	0	0	-	0	.341	.408	.409
1995 Los Angeles	NL	100	181	52	10	0	1	(0	1)	65	19	14	26	28	4	28	1	0	1	0	0	-	4	.287	.384	.359
1996 Los Angeles	NL	80	104	23	1	0	0	(0	0)	24	7	6	6	11	1	22	0	0	1	0	0	-	4	.221	.293	.231
1997 Chicago	NL	90	151	47	8	2	3	(1	2)	68	19	21	31	31	1	32	1	2	1	1	2	.33	1	.311	.429	.450
1999 Los Angeles	NL	100	107	27	8	1	2	(2	0)	43	14	17	19	26	0	20	2	0	1	0	0	-	2	.252	.404	.402
2000 Los Angeles	NL	102	121	35	6	2	8	(4	4)	69	18	26	27	26	0	32	0	0	0	1	0	.00	3	.289	.415	.570
2001 Los Angeles	NL	92	140	33	10	0	2	(1	1)	49	13	20	20	32	5	29	0	0	3	0	1	.00	3	.236	.371	.350
2002 Los Angeles	NL	96	120	35	6	0	2	(0	2)	47	15	17	17	14	3	22	0	0	1	1	0	1.00	4	.292	.363	.392
2003 San Diego	NL	110	135	33	4	1	2	(2	0)	45	13	15	18	23	3	25	1	0	0	1	0	1.00	4	.244	.358	.333
2004 Sea-SD		86	106	26	5	0	2	(2	0)	37	15	12	14	21	3	21	0	0	1	0	0	-	6	.245	.367	.349
2004 Seattle	AL	57	78	22	5	0	2	(2	0)	33	14	12	14	18	3	16	0	0	1	0	0	-	3	.282	.412	.423
2004 San Diego	NL	29	28	4	0	0	0	(0	0)	4	1	0	0	3	0	5	0	0	0	0	0	-	3	.143	.226	.143
14 ML YEARS		1170	1718	453	79	6	33	(15	18)	643	182	211	244	274	26	313	6	2	12	4	7	.36	39	.264	.365	.374

Aaron Harang

Pitches: R **Bats:** R **Pos:** SP-28   **Ht:** 6'7" **Wt:** 240 **Born:** 5/9/1978 **Age:** 27

Year Team	Lg	G	GS	CG	GF	IP	BFP	H	R	ER	HR	SH	SF	HB	TBB	IBB	SO	WP	Bk	W	L	Pct	ShO	Sv-Op	Hld	ERC	ERA
2004 Louisville*	AAA	1	1	0	0	3.0	22	9	8	4	1	0	0	1	3	0	3	0	0	0	1	.000	0	0--	-	25.56	12.00
2002 Oakland	AL	16	15	0	0	78.1	354	84	44	42	7	3	4	3	45	2	64	1	0	5	4	.556	0	0-0	0	4.76	4.83
2003 Oak-Cin		16	15	0	1	76.1	327	89	47	45	11	5	1	1	19	0	42	3	1	5	6	.455	0	0-0	0	4.84	5.31
2004 Cincinnati	NL	28	28	1	0	161.0	711	177	90	87	26	13	6	5	53	5	125	7	0	10	9	.526	1	0-0	0	4.81	4.86
2003 Oakland	AL	7	6	0	1	30.1	136	41	19	18	5	2	1	0	9	0	16	0	1	1	3	.250	0	0-0	0	6.32	5.34
2003 Cincinnati	NL	9	9	0	0	46.0	191	48	28	27	6	3	0	1	10	0	26	3	0	4	3	.571	0	0-0	0	3.94	5.28
3 ML YEARS		60	58	1	1	315.2	1392	344	181	174	44	21	11	9	117	7	231	11	1	20	19	.513	1	0-0	0	4.82	4.96

Rich Harden

Pitches: R **Bats:** L **Pos:** SP-31   **Ht:** 6'1" **Wt:** 180 **Born:** 11/30/1981 **Age:** 23

Year Team	Lg	G	GS	CG	GF	IP	BFP	H	R	ER	HR	SH	SF	HB	TBB	IBB	SO	WP	Bk	W	L	Pct	ShO	Sv-Op	Hld	ERC	ERA
2001 Vancouver	A-	18	14	0	3	74.1	309	47	29	24	3	3	1	4	38	0	100	8	1	2	4	.333	0	0--	-	2.35	3.39
2002 Visalia	A+	12	12	1	0	67.2	271	49	27	22	4	0	2	1	24	0	85	3	1	3	5	.571	0	0--	-	2.29	2.93
2002 Midland	AA	16	16	1	0	85.1	365	67	33	28	2	1	0	3	52	1	102	1	1	8	3	.727	0	0--	-	3.32	2.95
2003 Midland	AA	2	2	0	0	13.0	39	0	0	0	0	0	0	0	0	0	17	0	0	2	0	1.000	0	0--	-	0.00	0.00
2003 Sacramento	AAA	16	14	0	0	88.2	357	72	34	31	6	1	1	1	35	0	91	5	0	9	4	.692	0	0--	-	2.98	3.15
2004 Sacramento	AAA	1	1	0	0	5.0	24	6	3	3	0	1	0	0	3	0	6	0	0	0	0	-	0	0--	-	5.10	5.40
2003 Oakland	AL	15	13	0	0	74.2	324	72	38	37	5	2	3	1	40	1	67	6	0	5	4	.556	0	0-0	0	4.28	4.46
2004 Oakland	AL	31	31	0	0	189.2	803	171	90	84	16	5	6	3	81	6	167	4	1	11	7	.611	0	0-0	0	3.57	3.99
2 ML YEARS		46	44	0	0	264.1	1127	243	128	121	21	7	9	4	121	7	234	10	1	16	11	.593	0	0-0	0	3.76	4.12

Danny Haren

Pitches: R **Bats:** R **Pos:** RP-9; SP-5   **Ht:** 6'5" **Wt:** 220 **Born:** 9/17/1980 **Age:** 24

Year Team	Lg	G	GS	CG	GF	IP	BFP	H	R	ER	HR	SH	SF	HB	TBB	IBB	SO	WP	Bk	W	L	Pct	ShO	Sv-Op	Hld	ERC	ERA
2001 New Jersey	A-	12	8	0	1	52.1	210	47	22	18	6	0	0	5	8	0	57	1	0	3	3	.500	0	1--	-	3.10	3.10
2002 Peoria	A	14	14	1	0	101.2	399	89	32	22	6	4	4	2	12	0	89	4	2	7	3	.700	0	0--	-	2.23	1.95
2002 Potomac	A+	14	14	1	0	92.0	383	90	43	37	8	3	1	3	19	2	82	2	1	3	6	.333	0	0--	-	3.20	3.62
2003 Tennessee	AA	8	8	0	0	55.0	209	36	8	5	2	3	0	1	6	0	49	1	0	6	0	1.000	0	0--	-	1.24	0.82
2003 Memphis	AAA	8	8	0	0	45.2	197	50	25	25	6	1	0	4	8	1	35	1	1	2	1	.667	0	0--	-	4.24	4.93
2004 Memphis	AAA	21	21	0	0	128.0	540	136	60	59	19	7	3	3	33	1	150	2	0	11	4	.733	0	0--	-	4.32	4.15
2003 St Louis	NL	14	14	0	0	72.2	320	84	44	41	9	4	2	5	22	0	43	3	0	3	7	.300	0	0-0	0	5.07	5.08
2004 St Louis	NL	14	5	0	2	46.0	195	45	23	23	4	4	2	2	17	2	32	1	0	3	3	.500	0	0-0	0	3.91	4.50
2 ML YEARS		28	19	0	2	118.2	515	129	67	64	13	8	4	7	39	2	75	4	0	6	10	.375	0	0-0	0	4.61	4.85

Tim Harikkala

Pitches: R Bats: R Pos: RP-55   Ht: 6'2" Wt: 185 Born: 7/15/1971 Age: 33

Year Team	Lg	HOW MUCH HE PITCHED						WHAT HE GAVE UP											THE RESULTS						
		G	GS	CG	GF	IP	BFP	H	R	ER	HR	SH	SF	HB	TBB	IBB	SO	WP	Bk	W	L	Pct	ShO	Sv-Op	Hld	ERC	ERA
2004 Co Springs*	AAA	4	0	0	4	4.0	21	5	2	2	0	0	0	0	2	1	5	1	0	0	0	-	0	3- -	-	4.05	4.50
1995 Seattle	AL	1	0	0	1	3.1	18	7	6	6	1	0	0	0	1	0	1	0	0	0	0	-	0	0-0	0	12.43	16.20
1996 Seattle	AL	1	1	0	0	4.1	20	4	6	6	1	1	0	1	2	0	1	0	0	0	1	.000	0	0-0	0	5.68	12.46
1999 Boston	AL	7	0	0	2	13.0	58	15	9	9	0	2	0	1	6	1	7	1	0	1	1	.500	0	0-0	0	4.72	6.23
2004 Colorado	NL	55	0	0	11	62.2	262	55	34	33	10	2	2	1	23	5	30	0	1	6	6	.500	0	0-7	15	3.62	4.74
4 ML YEARS		64	1	0	14	83.1	358	81	55	54	12	5	2	3	32	6	39	1	1	7	8	.467	0	0-7	15	4.20	5.83

Travis Harper

Pitches: R Bats: R Pos: RP-52   Ht: 6'4" Wt: 192 Born: 5/21/1976 Age: 29

Year Team	Lg	HOW MUCH HE PITCHED						WHAT HE GAVE UP											THE RESULTS						
		G	GS	CG	GF	IP	BFP	H	R	ER	HR	SH	SF	HB	TBB	IBB	SO	WP	Bk	W	L	Pct	ShO	Sv-Op	Hld	ERC	ERA
2004 Durham*	AAA	2	1	0	0	7.2	34	10	3	3	1	0	0	0	0	0	5	0	0	1	0	1.000	0	0- -	-	4.14	3.52
2000 Tampa Bay	AL	6	5	1	0	32.0	141	30	17	17	5	1	1	1	15	0	14	1	0	1	2	.333	1	0-0	0	4.46	4.78
2001 Tampa Bay	AL	2	2	0	0	7.0	36	15	11	6	5	0	0	0	3	0	2	1	0	0	2	.000	0	0-0	0	19.14	7.71
2002 Tampa Bay	AL	37	7	0	16	85.2	394	101	54	52	14	5	4	9	27	3	60	2	0	5	9	.357	0	1-2	3	5.49	5.46
2003 Tampa Bay	AL	61	0	0	14	93.0	388	86	45	39	9	7	3	6	31	8	64	6	0	4	8	.333	0	1-6	15	3.56	3.77
2004 Tampa Bay	AL	52	0	0	11	78.2	330	69	37	34	8	3	2	7	23	3	59	3	0	6	2	.750	0	0-1	9	3.27	3.89
5 ML YEARS		158	14	1	41	296.1	1289	301	164	148	41	16	10	23	99	14	199	13	0	16	23	.410	1	2-9	27	4.39	4.49

Brendan Harris

Bats: R Throws: R Pos: 2B-11; 3B-7; PH-7   Ht: 6'1" Wt: 200 Born: 8/26/1980 Age: 24

Year Team	Lg	BATTING																	BASERUNNING				AVERAGES		
		G	AB	H	2B	3B	HR	(Hm	Rd)	TB	R	RBI	RC	TBB	IBB	SO	HBP	SH	SF	SB	CS	SB%	GDP	Avg	OBP	Slg
2001 Lansing	A	32	113	31	5	1	4	(-	-)	50	25	22	19	17	0	26	2	1	3	5	1	.83	4	.274	.370	.442
2002 Daytona	A+	110	425	140	35	6	13	(-	-)	226	82	54	85	43	4	57	4	1	2	16	4	.80	7	.329	.395	.532
2002 W Tennessee	AA	13	53	17	4	1	2	(-	-)	29	8	11	9	2	0	5	0	0	1	1	1	.50	1	.321	.345	.547
2003 W Tennessee	AA	120	435	122	34	7	5	(-	-)	185	56	52	66	51	1	72	8	5	3	6	7	.46	10	.280	.364	.425
2004 Iowa	AAA	69	254	79	21	1	11	(-	-)	135	48	35	42	16	1	40	1	3	0	1	2	.00	8	.311	.353	.531
2004 Edmonton	AAA	33	123	35	6	0	6	(-	-)	59	20	24	19	10	2	21	3	1	3	0	1	.00	3	.285	.345	.480
2004 ChC-Mon	NL	23	59	10	3	0	1	(0	1)	16	4	3	2	3	0	12	1	0	0	0	0	-	0	.169	.222	.271
2004 Chicago	NL	3	9	2	1	0	0	(0	0)	3	0	1	1	1	0	1	0	0	0	0	0	-	0	.222	.300	.333
2004 Montreal	NL	20	50	8	2	0	1	(0	1)	13	4	2	1	2	0	11	1	0	0	0	0	-	0	.160	.208	.260

Lenny Harris

Bats: L Throws: R Pos: PH-64; LF-8; RF-6; 3B-3; DH-2   Ht: 5'10" Wt: 220 Born: 10/28/1964 Age: 40

Year Team	Lg	BATTING																	BASERUNNING				AVERAGES		
		G	AB	H	2B	3B	HR	(Hm	Rd)	TB	R	RBI	RC	TBB	IBB	SO	HBP	SH	SF	SB	CS	SB%	GDP	Avg	OBP	Slg
1988 Cincinnati	NL	16	43	16	1	0	0	(0	0)	17	7	8	8	5	0	4	0	1	2	4	1	.80	0	.372	.420	.395
1989 Cin-LA	NL	115	335	79	10	1	3	(1	2)	100	36	26	23	20	0	33	2	1	0	14	9	.61	14	.236	.283	.299
1990 Los Angeles	NL	137	431	131	16	4	2	(0	2)	161	61	29	55	29	2	31	1	3	1	15	10	.60	8	.304	.348	.374
1991 Los Angeles	NL	145	429	123	16	1	3	(1	2)	150	59	38	52	37	5	32	5	12	2	12	3	.80	16	.287	.349	.350
1992 Los Angeles	NL	135	347	94	11	0	0	(0	0)	105	28	30	33	24	3	24	1	6	2	19	7	.73	10	.271	.318	.303
1993 Los Angeles	NL	107	160	38	6	1	2	(0	2)	52	20	11	15	15	4	15	0	1	0	3	1	.75	4	.238	.303	.325
1994 Cincinnati	NL	66	100	31	3	1	0	(0	0)	36	13	14	13	5	0	13	0	0	1	7	2	.78	0	.310	.340	.360
1995 Cincinnati	NL	101	197	41	8	3	2	(0	2)	61	32	16	15	14	0	20	0	3	1	10	1	.91	6	.208	.259	.310
1996 Cincinnati	NL	125	302	86	17	2	5	(2	3)	122	33	32	41	21	1	31	1	6	3	14	6	.70	3	.285	.330	.404
1997 Cincinnati	NL	120	238	65	13	1	3	(2	1)	89	32	28	27	18	1	18	2	3	2	4	3	.57	10	.273	.327	.374
1998 Cin-NYM	NL	132	290	75	15	0	6	(2	4)	108	30	27	29	17	3	21	2	4	4	6	5	.55	13	.259	.300	.372
1999 Col-Ari	NL	110	187	58	13	0	1	(1	0)	74	17	20	23	6	0	7	0	0	1	2	1	.67	7	.310	.330	.396
2000 Ari-NYM	NL	112	223	58	7	4	4	(2	2)	85	31	26	28	20	2	22	0	2	3	13	1	.93	7	.260	.317	.381
2001 New York	NL	110	135	30	5	1	0	(0	0)	37	12	9	9	8	0	9	0	0	0	3	2	.60	3	.222	.266	.274
2002 Milwaukee	NL	122	197	60	8	2	3	(2	1)	81	23	17	26	14	1	17	2	1	1	4	1	.80	4	.305	.351	.411
2003 ChC-Fla	NL	88	145	28	3	0	1	(0	1)	34	14	8	9	16	3	21	0	1	1	1	0	1.00	2	.193	.272	.234
2004 Florida	NL	79	95	20	5	0	1	(1	0)	28	7	17	4	3	0	8	0	0	1	0	0	-	1	.211	.232	.295
1989 Cincinnati	NL	61	188	42	4	0	2	(0	2)	52	17	11	11	9	0	20	1	1	0	10	6	.63	5	.223	.263	.277
1989 Los Angeles	NL	54	147	37	6	1	1	(1	0)	48	19	15	12	11	0	13	1	0	0	4	3	.57	9	.252	.308	.327
1998 Cincinnati	NL	57	122	36	8	0	0	(0	0)	44	12	10	12	8	2	9	1	0	2	1	3	.25	8	.295	.338	.361
1998 New York	NL	75	168	39	7	0	6	(2	4)	64	18	17	17	9	1	12	1	4	2	5	2	.71	5	.232	.272	.381
1999 Colorado	NL	91	158	47	12	0	0	(0	0)	59	15	13	17	6	0	6	0	0	1	1	1	.50	7	.297	.323	.373
1999 Arizona	NL	19	29	11	1	0	1	(1	0)	15	2	7	6	0	0	1	0	0	0	1	0	1.00	0	.379	.367	.517
2000 Arizona	NL	36	85	16	1	1	1	(1	0)	22	9	13	9	3	1	5	0	0	3	5	0	1.00	3	.188	.209	.259
2000 New York	NL	76	138	42	6	3	3	(1	2)	63	22	13	24	17	1	17	0	2	0	8	1	.89	4	.304	.381	.457
2003 Chicago	NL	75	131	24	3	0	1	(0	1)	30	11	7	7	13	3	20	0	1	1	1	0	1.00	1	.183	.255	.229
2003 Florida	NL	13	14	4	0	0	0	(0	0)	4	3	1	2	3	0	1	0	0	0	0	0	-	1	.286	.412	.286
17 ML YEARS		1820	3854	1033	157	21	36	(14	22)	1340	455	356	410	272	25	326	16	44	25	131	53	.71	108	.268	.317	.348

Willie Harris

Bats: L Throws: R Pos: 2B-92; CF-29; PH-19; PR-3; LF-1; DH-1   Ht: 5'9" Wt: 175 Born: 6/22/1978 Age: 27

Year Team	Lg	BATTING																	BASERUNNING				AVERAGES		
		G	AB	H	2B	3B	HR	(Hm	Rd)	TB	R	RBI	RC	TBB	IBB	SO	HBP	SH	SF	SB	CS	SB%	GDP	Avg	OBP	Slg
2001 Baltimore	AL	9	24	3	1	0	0	(0	0)	4	3	0	0	0	0	7	0	1	0	0	0	-	0	.125	.125	.167
2002 Chicago	AL	49	163	38	4	0	2	(2	0)	48	14	12	15	9	0	21	0	3	2	8	0	1.00	3	.233	.270	.294
2003 Chicago	AL	79	137	28	3	1	0	(0	0)	33	19	5	11	10	0	28	0	3	0	12	2	.86	1	.204	.259	.241
2004 Chicago	AL	129	409	107	15	2	2	(2	0)	132	68	27	53	51	0	79	1	7	3	19	7	.73	4	.262	.343	.323
4 ML YEARS		266	733	176	23	3	4	(4	0)	217	104	44	79	70	0	135	1	14	5	39	9	.81	8	.240	.305	.296

Bo Hart

Bats: R **Throws:** R **Pos:** PH-6; 2B-4; SS-1   **Ht:** 5'11" **Wt:** 175 **Born:** 9/27/1976 **Age:** 28

Year Team	Lg	G	AB	H	2B	3B	HR	(Hm	Rd)	TB	R	RBI	RC	TBB	IBB	SO	HBP	SH	SF	SB	CS	SB%	GDP	Avg	OBP	Slg
1999 New Jersey	A-	50	163	30	3	3	3	(-	-)	48	23	15	14	10	0	38	12	3	0	4	2	.67	1	.184	.281	.294
2000 Potomac	A+	75	273	70	25	4	0	(-	-)	103	42	20	36	23	0	42	13	4	1	9	6	.60	2	.256	.342	.377
2001 Potomac	A+	81	279	85	23	3	5	(-	-)	129	48	34	47	17	1	69	15	4	1	16	7	.70	3	.305	.375	.462
2002 New Haven	AA	104	405	101	17	6	4	(-	-)	142	61	39	51	43	1	82	12	1	2	14	7	.67	6	.249	.338	.351
2003 Memphis	AAA	67	266	79	14	2	7	(-	-)	118	30	31	39	15	1	55	0	0	3	4	2	.67	2	.297	.331	.444
2004 Memphis	AAA	116	445	133	25	7	8	(-	-)	196	81	45	67	25	0	66	13	6	4	8	7	.53	9	.299	.351	.440
2003 St Louis	NL	77	296	82	13	5	4	(1	3)	117	46	28	38	12	0	64	6	6	1	3	1	.75	3	.277	.317	.395
2004 St Louis	NL	11	13	2	0	0	0	(0	0)	2	0	2	0	1	0	3	0	0	0	0	0	-	0	.154	.214	.154
2 ML YEARS		88	309	84	13	5	4	(1	3)	119	46	30	38	13	0	67	6	6	1	3	1	.75	3	.272	.313	.385

Corey Hart

Bats: R **Throws:** R **Pos:** PH-1   **Ht:** 6'6" **Wt:** 200 **Born:** 3/24/1982 **Age:** 23

Year Team	Lg	G	AB	H	2B	3B	HR	(Hm	Rd)	TB	R	RBI	RC	TBB	IBB	SO	HBP	SH	SF	SB	CS	SB%	GDP	Avg	OBP	Slg
2000 Ogden	R+	57	216	62	9	1	2	(-	-)	79	32	30	27	13	0	27	2	1	1	6	0	1.00	6	.287	.332	.366
2001 Ogden	R+	69	262	89	18	1	11	(-	-)	142	53	62	56	26	1	47	2	0	6	14	1	.93	4	.340	.395	.542
2002 High Desert	A+	100	393	113	26	10	22	(-	-)	225	76	84	75	37	2	101	5	1	1	24	11	.69	3	.288	.356	.573
2002 Huntsville	AA	28	94	25	3	0	2	(-	-)	34	16	15	12	7	0	16	4	0	1	3	2	.60	1	.266	.340	.362
2003 Wichita	AA	93	334	92	9	0	4	(-	-)	113	40	47	47	49	4	69	2	3	3	12	4	.75	5	.275	.369	.338
2003 Huntsville	AA	130	493	149	40	1	13	(-	-)	230	70	94	76	28	5	101	5	0	9	25	8	.76	7	.302	.340	.467
2004 Wichita	AA	75	240	55	13	0	1	(-	-)	71	37	29	26	42	0	52	3	1	5	6	6	.00	4	.229	.345	.296
2004 Indianapolis	AAA	121	441	124	29	8	15	(-	-)	214	68	67	71	41	3	92	3	0	6	17	7	.71	7	.281	.342	.485
2004 Omaha	AAA	21	65	17	3	0	1	(-	-)	23	8	2	6	3	0	15	0	2	0	0	0	-	2	.262	.294	.354
2004 Milwaukee	NL	1	1	0	0	0	0	(0	0)	0	0	0	0	0	0	1	0	0	0	0	0	-	0	.000	.000	.000

Ken Harvey

Bats: R **Throws:** R **Pos:** 1B-73; DH-41; LF-4; PH-2   **Ht:** 6'2" **Wt:** 240 **Born:** 3/1/1978 **Age:** 27

Year Team	Lg	G	AB	H	2B	3B	HR	(Hm	Rd)	TB	R	RBI	RC	TBB	IBB	SO	HBP	SH	SF	SB	CS	SB%	GDP	Avg	OBP	Slg
2001 Kansas City	AL	4	12	3	1	0	0	(-	-)	4	1	2	0	0	0	4	0	0	0	0	1	.00	1	.250	.250	.333
2003 Kansas City	AL	135	485	129	30	0	13	(5	8)	198	50	64	58	29	4	94	5	3	2	2	3	.40	15	.266	.313	.408
2004 Kansas City	AL	120	456	131	20	1	13	(6	7)	192	47	55	59	28	2	89	8	0	2	1	1	.50	14	.287	.338	.421
3 ML YEARS		259	953	263	51	1	26	(11	15)	394	98	121	117	57	6	187	13	3	4	3	5	.38	30	.276	.324	.413

Chad Harville

Pitches: R **Bats:** R **Pos:** RP-59   **Ht:** 5'9" **Wt:** 185 **Born:** 9/16/1976 **Age:** 28

Year Team	Lg	G	GS	CG	GF	IP	BFP	H	R	ER	HR	SH	SF	HB	TBB	IBB	SO	WP	Bk	W	L	Pct	ShO	Sv-Op	Hld	ERC	ERA
2004 Round Rock*	AA	2	2	0	0	3.0	11	0	0	0	0	0	0	0	2	0	2	1	0	0	0	-	0	0- -	-	0.46	0.00
1999 Oakland	AL	15	0	0	0	14.1	69	18	0	11	2	0	0	0	10	0	15	0	0	0	2	.000	0	0-0	0	7.23	6.91
2001 Oakland	AL	3	0	0	0	3.0	11	2	0	0	0	0	0	0	0	0	2	0	0	0	0	-	0	0-0	0	0.91	0.00
2003 Oakland	AL	21	0	0	5	21.2	103	25	15	14	3	0	1	1	17	1	18	3	0	1	0	1.000	0	1-1	0	7.20	5.82
2004 Oak-Hou		59	0	0	15	55.2	249	56	36	29	8	2	0	2	27	2	46	5	0	3	2	.600	0	0-4	4	4.81	4.69
2004 Oakland	AL	3	0	0	1	2.2	11	2	1	1	0	0	0	0	1	0	0	0	0	0	0	-	0	0-0	1	2.01	3.38
2004 Houston	NL	56	0	0	14	53.0	238	54	35	28	8	2	0	2	26	2	46	5	0	3	2	.600	0	0-4	3	4.96	4.75
4 ML YEARS		98	0	0	20	94.2	432	101	51	54	13	2	1	3	54	3	81	8	0	4	4	.500	0	1-5	4	5.52	5.13

Shigetoshi Hasegawa

Pitches: R **Bats:** R **Pos:** RP-68   **Ht:** 5'11" **Wt:** 178 **Born:** 8/1/1968 **Age:** 36

Year Team	Lg	G	GS	CG	GF	IP	BFP	H	R	ER	HR	SH	SF	HB	TBB	IBB	SO	WP	Bk	W	L	Pct	ShO	Sv-Op	Hld	ERC	ERA
1997 Anaheim	AL	50	7	0	17	116.2	497	118	60	51	14	5	5	3	46	6	83	2	1	3	7	.300	0	0-1	3	4.37	3.93
1998 Anaheim	AL	61	0	0	20	97.1	401	86	37	34	14	4	6	2	32	2	73	5	2	8	3	.727	0	5-7	10	3.54	3.14
1999 Anaheim	AL	64	1	0	26	77.0	333	80	45	42	14	3	4	2	34	2	44	4	0	4	6	.400	0	2-5	6	5.25	4.91
2000 Anaheim	AL	66	0	0	26	95.2	415	100	43	38	11	2	3	2	38	6	59	2	1	10	6	.625	0	9-18	19	4.44	3.57
2001 Anaheim	AL	46	0	0	10	55.2	235	52	28	25	5	1	2	2	20	5	41	2	0	5	6	.455	0	0-6	12	3.50	4.04
2002 Seattle	AL	53	0	0	20	70.1	288	60	26	25	4	3	1	2	30	8	39	0	1	8	3	.727	0	1-5	8	3.13	3.20
2003 Seattle	AL	63	0	0	36	73.0	282	62	12	12	5	1	0	0	18	3	32	0	0	2	4	.333	0	16-17	12	2.58	1.48
2004 Seattle	AL	68	0	0	19	68.0	300	67	42	39	5	5	4	2	31	4	46	1	1	4	6	.400	0	0-5	12	4.00	5.16
8 ML YEARS		471	8	0	174	653.2	2751	625	293	266	72	24	25	15	249	36	417	16	6	44	41	.518	0	33-64	82	3.90	3.66

Scott Hatteberg

Bats: L **Throws:** R **Pos:** 1B-149; PH-6; DH-2   **Ht:** 6'1" **Wt:** 210 **Born:** 12/14/1969 **Age:** 35

Year Team	Lg	G	AB	H	2B	3B	HR	(Hm	Rd)	TB	R	RBI	RC	TBB	IBB	SO	HBP	SH	SF	SB	CS	SB%	GDP	Avg	OBP	Slg
1995 Boston	AL	2	2	1	0	0	0	(0	0)	1	1	0	0	0	0	0	0	0	0	0	0	-	1	.500	.500	.500
1996 Boston	AL	10	11	2	1	0	0	(0	0)	3	3	0	1	3	0	2	0	0	0	0	0	-	0	.182	.357	.273
1997 Boston	AL	114	350	97	23	1	10	(5	5)	152	46	44	52	40	2	70	2	2	1	0	1	.00	11	.277	.354	.434
1998 Boston	AL	112	359	99	23	1	12	(4	8)	160	46	43	56	43	3	58	5	0	3	0	0	-	11	.276	.359	.446
1999 Boston	AL	30	80	22	5	0	1	(1	0)	30	12	11	14	18	0	14	1	0	1	0	0	-	4	.275	.410	.375
2000 Boston	AL	92	230	61	15	0	8	(2	6)	100	21	36	36	38	3	39	0	1	2	0	1	.00	8	.265	.367	.435
2001 Boston	AL	94	278	68	19	0	3	(2	1)	96	34	25	32	33	0	26	4	0	1	1	1	.50	7	.245	.332	.345
2002 Oakland	AL	136	492	138	22	4	15	(8	7)	213	58	61	77	68	1	56	6	1	1	0	0	-	8	.280	.374	.433

121

Year Team	Lg	G	AB	H	2B	3B	HR	(Hm	Rd)	TB	R	RBI	RC	TBB	IBB	SO	HBP	SH	SF	SB	CS	SB%	GDP	Avg	OBP	Slg
2003 Oakland	AL	147	541	137	34	0	12	(6	6)	207	63	61	80	66	0	53	9	3	3	0	1	.00	14	.253	.342	.383
2004 Oakland	AL	152	550	156	30	0	15	(8	7)	231	87	82	90	72	5	48	5	3	8	0	0	-	10	.284	.367	.420
10 ML YEARS		889	2893	781	172	6	76	(36	40)	1193	371	363	438	381	14	366	32	10	20	1	4	.20	74	.270	.359	.412

LaTroy Hawkins

Pitches: R **Bats:** R **Pos:** RP-77   **Ht:** 6'5" **Wt:** 204 **Born:** 12/21/1972 **Age:** 32

		HOW MUCH HE PITCHED						WHAT HE GAVE UP										THE RESULTS						
Year Team	Lg	G	GS	CG	GF	IP	BFP	H	R	ER	HR	SH	SF	TBB	IBB	SO	WP	Bk	W	L	Pct	ShO	Sv-Op	Hld	ERC	ERA
1995 Minnesota	AL	6	6	1	0	27.0	131	39	29	26	3	0	3	12	0	9	1	1	2	3	.400	0	0-0	0	7.14	8.67
1996 Minnesota	AL	7	6	0	1	26.1	124	42	24	24	8	1	1	9	0	24	1	1	1	1	.500	0	0-0	0	9.49	8.20
1997 Minnesota	AL	20	20	0	0	103.1	478	134	71	67	19	2	2	47	0	58	6	3	6	12	.333	0	0-0	0	7.01	5.84
1998 Minnesota	AL	33	33	0	0	190.1	840	227	126	111	27	4	10	5	61	1	105	10	2	7	14	.333	0	0-0	0	5.31	5.25
1999 Minnesota	AL	33	33	1	0	174.1	803	238	136	129	29	1	5	1	60	2	103	9	0	10	14	.417	0	0-0	0	6.55	6.66
2000 Minnesota	AL	66	0	0	38	87.2	370	85	34	33	7	4	1	1	32	1	59	6	0	2	5	.286	0	14-14	1	3.70	3.39
2001 Minnesota	AL	62	0	0	51	51.1	248	59	34	34	3	1	4	1	39	3	36	7	0	1	5	.167	0	28-37	1	6.02	5.96
2002 Minnesota	AL	65	0	0	15	80.1	310	63	23	19	5	2	3	0	15	1	63	5	0	6	0	1.000	0	0-3	13	1.99	2.13
2003 Minnesota	AL	74	0	0	12	77.1	310	69	20	16	4	4	1	1	15	1	75	5	0	9	3	.750	0	2-8	28	2.48	1.86
2004 Chicago	NL	77	0	0	50	82.0	333	72	27	24	10	6	2	2	14	5	69	2	0	5	4	.556	0	25-34	4	2.66	2.63
10 ML YEARS		443	98	2	167	900.0	3947	1028	524	483	115	25	32	16	304	14	601	52	7	49	61	.445	0	69-96	53	4.91	4.83

Brad Hawpe

Bats: L **Throws:** L **Pos:** RF-32; PH-10; LF-2   **Ht:** 6'3" **Wt:** 200 **Born:** 6/22/1979 **Age:** 26

		BATTING																		BASERUNNING				AVERAGES		
Year Team	Lg	G	AB	H	2B	3B	HR	(Hm	Rd)	TB	R	RBI	RC	TBB	IBB	SO	HBP	SH	SF	SB	CS	SB%	GDP	Avg	OBP	Slg
2000 Portland	A-	62	205	59	19	2	7	(-	-)	103	38	29	43	40	2	57	2	0	7	2	0	1.00	1	.288	.398	.502
2001 Asheville	A	111	393	105	22	3	22	(-	-)	199	78	72	71	59	3	113	6	0	10	7	4	.64	8	.267	.363	.506
2002 Salem	A+	122	450	156	38	2	22	(-	-)	264	87	97	109	81	23	84	2	0	2	1	1	.50	7	.347	.447	.587
2003 Tulsa	AA	93	346	96	27	0	17	(-	-)	174	52	68	54	31	2	84	1	0	1	1	3	.25	5	.277	.338	.503
2004 Co Springs	AAA	92	345	111	19	1	31	(-	-)	225	62	86	76	36	1	91	1	3	3	3	2	.60	10	.322	.384	.652
2004 Colorado	NL	42	105	26	3	2	3	(1	2)	42	12	9	11	11	3	34	1	0	1	1	1	.50	4	.248	.322	.400

Jimmy Haynes

Pitches: R **Bats:** R **Pos:** SP-4; RP-1   **Ht:** 6'4" **Wt:** 219 **Born:** 9/5/1972 **Age:** 32

		HOW MUCH HE PITCHED						WHAT HE GAVE UP										THE RESULTS						
Year Team	Lg	G	GS	CG	GF	IP	BFP	H	R	ER	HR	SH	SF	HB	TBB	IBB	SO	WP	Bk	W	L	Pct	ShO	Sv-Op	Hld	ERC	ERA
2004 Toledo*	AAA	5	3	0	0	13.1	65	19	13	13	0	0	0	0	6	0	9	0	0	0	1	.000	0	0- -	-	5.82	8.78
1995 Baltimore	AL	4	3	0	0	24.0	94	11	6	6	2	1	0	0	12	1	22	0	0	2	1	.667	0	0-0	0	1.61	2.25
1996 Baltimore	AL	26	11	0	8	89.0	435	122	84	82	14	4	5	2	58	1	65	5	0	3	6	.333	0	1-1	0	8.05	8.29
1997 Oakland	AL	13	13	0	0	73.1	329	74	38	36	7	1	4	2	40	1	65	4	1	3	6	.333	0	0-0	0	4.75	4.42
1998 Oakland	AL	33	33	1	0	194.1	875	229	124	110	25	5	9	5	88	4	134	11	0	11	9	.550	1	0-0	0	5.69	5.09
1999 Oakland	AL	30	25	0	2	142.0	652	158	112	100	21	4	5	2	80	3	93	7	2	7	12	.368	0	0-0	0	5.79	6.34
2000 Milwaukee	NL	33	33	0	0	199.1	897	228	128	118	21	10	6	7	100	7	88	7	0	12	13	.480	0	0-0	0	5.54	5.33
2001 Milwaukee	NL	31	29	0	0	172.2	756	182	98	93	20	14	7	4	78	17	112	8	0	8	17	.320	0	0-0	0	4.69	4.85
2002 Cincinnati	NL	34	34	0	0	196.2	852	210	97	90	21	7	6	3	81	4	126	6	0	15	10	.600	0	0-0	0	4.66	4.12
2003 Cincinnati	NL	18	18	1	0	94.1	448	118	74	66	14	7	2	3	57	3	49	2	0	2	12	.143	0	0-0	0	6.94	6.30
2004 Cincinnati	NL	5	4	0	1	15.0	79	26	17	16	3	2	0	2	7	0	8	1	0	0	3	.000	0	0	0	10.45	9.60
10 ML YEARS		227	203	2	11	1200.2	5417	1358	778	717	148	55	44	30	601	41	762	51	3	63	89	.414	1	1-1	0	5.52	5.37

Aaron Heilman

Pitches: R **Bats:** R **Pos:** SP-5   **Ht:** 6'5" **Wt:** 220 **Born:** 11/12/1978 **Age:** 26

		HOW MUCH HE PITCHED						WHAT HE GAVE UP										THE RESULTS						
Year Team	Lg	G	GS	CG	GF	IP	BFP	H	R	ER	HR	SH	SF	HB	TBB	IBB	SO	WP	Bk	W	L	Pct	ShO	Sv-Op	Hld	ERC	ERA
2001 St. Lucie	A+	7	7	0	0	38.1	153	26	11	10	0	1	1	1	13	0	39	1	0	0	1	.000	0	0- -	-	1.70	2.35
2002 Binghamton	AA	17	17	0	0	96.2	397	85	43	41	7	2	2	6	28	2	97	5	0	4	4	.500	0	0- -	-	3.07	3.82
2002 Norfolk	AAA	10	7	0	2	49.1	196	42	18	18	3	3	1	1	16	1	35	0	0	2	3	.400	0	0- -	-	2.91	3.28
2003 Norfolk	AAA	16	16	0	0	94.1	399	99	37	34	5	3	1	2	32	0	71	1	0	6	4	.600	0	0- -	-	3.95	3.24
2004 Norfolk	AAA	26	26	1	0	151.2	668	156	88	73	15	8	4	10	66	0	123	5	0	7	10	.412	0	0- -	-	4.66	4.33
2003 New York	NL	14	13	0	0	65.1	315	79	53	49	13	5	3	3	41	2	51	5	0	2	7	.222	0	0-0	0	7.16	6.75
2004 New York	NL	5	5	0	0	28.0	119	27	17	17	4	1	0	0	13	0	22	0	0	1	3	.250	0	0-0	0	4.54	5.46
2 ML YEARS		19	18	0	0	93.1	434	106	70	66	17	6	3	3	54	2	73	5	0	3	10	.231	0	0-0	0	6.35	6.36

Wes Helms

Bats: R **Throws:** R **Pos:** 3B-67; PH-16; 1B-10   **Ht:** 6'4" **Wt:** 230 **Born:** 5/12/1976 **Age:** 29

		BATTING																		BASERUNNING				AVERAGES		
Year Team	Lg	G	AB	H	2B	3B	HR	(Hm	Rd)	TB	R	RBI	RC	TBB	IBB	SO	HBP	SH	SF	SB	CS	SB%	GDP	Avg	OBP	Slg
2004 Indianapolis*	AAA	6	19	6	1	0	0	(-	-)	7	4	1	3	3	0	4	0	0	0	0	0	-	0	.316	.409	.368
1998 Atlanta	NL	7	13	4	1	0	1	(0	1)	8	2	2	2	0	0	4	0	0	0	0	0	-	0	.308	.308	.615
2000 Atlanta	NL	6	5	1	0	0	0	(0	0)	1	0	0	0	0	0	2	0	0	0	0	0	-	0	.200	.200	.200
2001 Atlanta	NL	100	216	48	10	3	10	(6	4)	94	28	36	27	21	2	56	1	0	1	1	1	.50	3	.222	.293	.435
2002 Atlanta	NL	85	210	51	16	0	6	(4	2)	85	20	22	15	11	2	57	3	1	6	1	1	.50	5	.243	.283	.405
2003 Milwaukee	NL	134	476	124	21	0	23	(16	7)	214	56	67	66	43	3	131	10	0	7	0	1	.00	10	.261	.330	.450
2004 Milwaukee	NL	92	274	72	13	1	4	(3	1)	99	24	28	28	24	1	60	5	1	2	0	1	.00	10	.263	.331	.361
6 ML YEARS		424	1194	300	61	4	44	(29	15)	501	130	155	138	99	8	310	19	2	16	2	4	.33	28	.251	.315	.420

Todd Helton

Bats: L **Throws:** L **Pos:** 1B-153; PH-3   **Ht:** 6'2" **Wt:** 204 **Born:** 8/20/1973 **Age:** 31

								BATTING												BASERUNNING				AVERAGES		
Year Team	Lg	G	AB	H	2B	3B	HR	(Hm Rd)	TB	R	RBI	RC	TBB	IBB	SO	HBP	SH	SF	SB	CS	SB%	GDP	Avg	OBP	Slg
1997 Colorado	NL	35	93	26	2	1	5	(3 2)	45	13	11	15	8	0	11	0	0	0	0	1	.00	1	.280	.337	.484
1998 Colorado	NL	152	530	167	37	1	25	(13 12)	281	78	97	101	53	5	54	6	1	5	3	3	.50	15	.315	.380	.530
1999 Colorado	NL	159	578	185	39	5	35	(23 12)	339	114	113	124	68	6	77	6	0	4	7	6	.54	14	.320	.395	.587
2000 Colorado	NL	160	580	216	59	2	42	(27 15)	405	138	147	169	103	22	61	4	0	10	5	3	.63	12	.372	.463	.698
2001 Colorado	NL	159	587	197	54	2	49	(27 22)	402	132	146	157	98	15	104	5	1	5	7	5	.58	14	.336	.432	.685
2002 Colorado	NL	156	553	182	39	4	30	(18 12)	319	107	109	127	99	21	91	5	0	10	5	1	.83	10	.329	.429	.577
2003 Colorado	NL	160	583	209	49	5	33	(23 10)	367	135	117	160	111	21	72	2	0	7	0	4	.00	19	.358	.458	.630
2004 Colorado	NL	154	547	190	49	2	32	(21 11)	339	115	96	143	127	19	72	3	0	6	3	0	1.00	12	.347	.469	.620
8 ML YEARS		1135	4051	1372	328	22	251	(155 96)	2497	832	836	996	667	109	542	31	2	47	30	23	.57	97	.339	.432	.616

Ben Hendrickson

Pitches: R **Bats:** R **Pos:** SP-9; RP-1   **Ht:** 6'4" **Wt:** 190 **Born:** 2/4/1981 **Age:** 24

				HOW MUCH HE PITCHED				WHAT HE GAVE UP											THE RESULTS						
Year Team	Lg	G	GS	CG	GF	IP	BFP	H	R	ER	HR	SH	SF	HB	TBB	IBB	SO	WP	Bk	W	L	Pct	ShO	Sv-Op	Hld	ERC	ERA
2000 Ogden	R+	13	7	0	2	50.2	237	50	37	32	7	1	2	1	29	0	48	12	0	4	3	.571	0	1--	-	4.82	5.68
2001 Beloit	A	25	25	1	0	133.1	576	122	58	42	3	1	1	6	72	0	133	9	1	8	9	.471	0	0--	-	3.83	2.84
2002 High Desert	A+	14	14	0	0	81.1	338	61	31	23	3	1	2	2	41	0	70	3	0	5	5	.500	0	0--	-	2.83	2.55
2002 Huntsville	AA	13	13	0	0	69.2	295	57	31	23	2	8	2	3	35	0	50	2	1	4	2	.667	0	0--	-	3.18	2.97
2003 Huntsville	AA	17	16	0	0	78.1	327	82	35	30	6	3	1	0	28	0	56	3	0	7	6	.538	0	0--	-	4.15	3.45
2004 Indianapolis	AAA	21	21	2	0	125.0	492	114	32	28	6	6	3	1	26	0	93	6	1	11	3	.786	2	0--	-	2.68	2.02
2004 Milwaukee	NL	10	9	0	1	46.1	215	58	33	32	6	2	2	4	20	1	29	1	0	1	8	.111	0	0-0	0	6.28	6.22

Mark Hendrickson

Pitches: L **Bats:** L **Pos:** SP-30; RP-2   **Ht:** 6'9" **Wt:** 230 **Born:** 6/23/1974 **Age:** 31

				HOW MUCH HE PITCHED				WHAT HE GAVE UP											THE RESULTS						
Year Team	Lg	G	GS	CG	GF	IP	BFP	H	R	ER	HR	SH	SF	HB	TBB	IBB	SO	WP	Bk	W	L	Pct	ShO	Sv-Op	Hld	ERC	ERA
2002 Toronto	AL	16	4	0	0	36.2	142	25	11	10	1	2	2	2	12	3	21	0	0	3	0	1.000	0	0-1	1	1.90	2.45
2003 Toronto	AL	30	30	1	0	158.1	703	207	111	97	24	1	8	0	40	3	76	4	0	9	9	.500	1	0-0	0	5.64	5.51
2004 Tampa Bay	AL	32	30	2	1	183.1	803	211	113	98	21	4	5	7	46	5	87	5	2	10	15	.400	0	0-0	0	4.51	4.81
3 ML YEARS		78	64	3	1	378.1	1648	443	235	205	46	7	15	9	98	11	184	9	2	22	24	.478	1	0-1	1	4.69	4.88

Brad Hennessey

Pitches: R **Bats:** R **Pos:** SP-7   **Ht:** 6'2" **Wt:** 185 **Born:** 2/7/1980 **Age:** 25

				HOW MUCH HE PITCHED				WHAT HE GAVE UP											THE RESULTS						
Year Team	Lg	G	GS	CG	GF	IP	BFP	H	R	ER	HR	SH	SF	HB	TBB	IBB	SO	WP	Bk	W	L	Pct	ShO	Sv-Op	Hld	ERC	ERA
2001 Salem-Keizer	A-	9	9	0	0	34.0	132	28	9	9	1	0	0	4	11	0	22	2	0	1	0	1.000	0	0--	-	2.86	2.38
2003 Hagerstown	A	15	15	1	0	79.1	346	81	49	37	6	3	4	5	27	0	44	4	0	3	9	.250	0	0--	-	4.00	4.20
2004 Norwich	AA	18	18	0	0	101.0	425	106	42	40	8	7	4	3	34	0	55	0	0	5	5	.500	0	0--	-	4.20	3.56
2004 Fresno	AAA	5	5	0	0	35.2	141	26	8	8	2	2	0	0	15	0	16	1	0	4	1	.800	0	0--	-	2.55	2.02
2004 San Francisco	NL	7	7	0	0	34.1	163	42	24	19	2	4	1	0	15	1	25	1	0	2	2	.500	0	0-0	0	4.91	4.98

Matt Hensley

Pitches: R **Bats:** R **Pos:** RP-16   **Ht:** 6'2" **Wt:** 220 **Born:** 8/18/1978 **Age:** 26

				HOW MUCH HE PITCHED				WHAT HE GAVE UP											THE RESULTS						
Year Team	Lg	G	GS	CG	GF	IP	BFP	H	R	ER	HR	SH	SF	HB	TBB	IBB	SO	WP	Bk	W	L	Pct	ShO	Sv-Op	Hld	ERC	ERA
2000 Butte	R+	8	5	0	0	28.0	132	29	21	8	0	0	0	2	10	0	22	3	3	1	2	.333	0	0--	-	3.34	2.57
2000 Cedar Rpds	A	5	5	1	0	30.1	129	33	16	14	1	0	2	2	10	0	26	1	2	2	2	.500	0	0--	-	4.20	4.15
2000 Lk Elsinore	A+	1	0	0	0	4	1	1	0	0	0	0	0	0	0	0	2	0	0	0	0		0	0--	-	1.95	0.00
2001 Cedar Rpds	A	11	11	1	0	71.2	321	80	42	29	10	0	2	4	19	0	63	6	3	5	3	.625	0	0--	-	4.54	3.64
2001 R Cucamnga	A+	14	12	0	0	68.1	319	85	57	45	4	2	7	8	24	0	58	4	1	2	7	.222	0	0--	-	5.36	5.93
2002 R Cucamnga	A+	12	2	0	0	31.2	145	42	21	19	3	0	1	1	11	0	27	3	1	1	1	.500	0	0--	-	5.89	5.40
2002 Salt Lake	AAA	19	18	1	1	117.2	511	132	76	65	16	3	2	8	39	0	106	5	2	7	5	.583	0	0--	-	5.14	4.97
2003 Salt Lake	AAA	27	27	1	0	158.1	710	194	105	86	16	4	5	11	49	0	85	4	1	8	12	.400	0	0--	-	5.32	4.89
2004 Salt Lake	AAA	30	0	0	23	43.0	170	29	16	14	6	0	0	2	12	0	49	0	0	1	3	.250	0	5--	-	2.35	2.93
2004 Anaheim	AL	16	0	0	13	27.2	120	32	15	15	5	1	1	2	7	1	30	0	0	0	2	.000	0	0-0	0	5.27	4.88

Pat Hentgen

Pitches: R **Bats:** R **Pos:** SP-16; RP-2   **Ht:** 6'2" **Wt:** 195 **Born:** 11/13/1968 **Age:** 36

				HOW MUCH HE PITCHED				WHAT HE GAVE UP											THE RESULTS						
Year Team	Lg	G	GS	CG	GF	IP	BFP	H	R	ER	HR	SH	SF	HB	TBB	IBB	SO	WP	Bk	W	L	Pct	ShO	Sv-Op	Hld	ERC	ERA
1991 Toronto	AL	3	1	0	1	7.1	30	5	2	2	1	1	0	2	3	0	3	1	0	0	0		0	0-0	0	3.87	2.45
1992 Toronto	AL	28	2	0	10	50.1	229	49	30	30	7	2	2	0	32	5	39	2	1	5	2	.714	0	0-1	1	4.94	5.36
1993 Toronto	AL	34	32	3	0	216.1	926	215	103	93	27	6	5	7	74	0	122	11	1	19	9	.679	0	0-0	0	4.11	3.87
1994 Toronto	AL	24	24	6	0	174.2	728	158	74	66	21	6	3	3	59	1	147	5	1	13	8	.619	3	0-0	0	3.52	3.40
1995 Toronto	AL	30	30	2	0	200.2	913	236	129	114	24	2	1	5	90	6	135	7	2	10	14	.417	0	0-0	0	5.49	5.11
1996 Toronto	AL	35	35	10	0	265.2	1100	238	105	95	20	5	8	5	94	3	177	8	0	20	10	.667	3	0-0	0	3.26	3.22
1997 Toronto	AL	35	35	9	0	264.0	1085	253	116	108	31	9	3	7	71	2	160	6	2	15	10	.600	3	0-0	0	3.61	3.68
1998 Toronto	AL	29	29	0	0	177.2	795	208	100	102	28	5	7	5	69	1	94	7	1	12	11	.522	0	0-0	0	5.58	5.17
1999 Toronto	AL	34	34	1	0	199.0	869	225	115	106	32	3	11	3	65	1	118	8	1	11	12	.478	0	0-0	0	5.04	4.79
2000 St Louis	NL	33	33	1	0	194.1	846	202	107	102	24	13	8	3	89	4	118	4	0	15	12	.556	1	0-0	0	4.81	4.72
2001 Baltimore	AL	9	9	1	0	62.1	252	51	25	24	7	1	1	0	19	3	33	1	0	2	3	.400	0	0-0	0	2.77	3.47
2002 Baltimore	AL	4	4	0	0	22.0	103	31	20	19	6	0	1	0	10	0	11	1	0	0	4	.000	0	0-0	0	8.38	7.77
2003 Baltimore	AL	28	22	1	2	160.2	676	150	74	73	25	3	2	5	58	1	100	4	1	7	8	.467	0	1-1	0	4.09	4.09
2004 Toronto	AL	18	16	0	2	80.1	373	90	67	62	16	1	8	4	42	2	33	1	0	2	9	.182	0	0-0	0	6.15	6.95
14 ML YEARS		344	306	34	15	2075.1	8925	2111	1076	996	269	57	60	49	775	29	1290	66	10	131	112	.539	10	1-2	1	4.37	4.32

Felix Heredia

Pitches: L **Bats:** L **Pos:** RP-47   **Ht:** 6'0" **Wt:** 190 **Born:** 6/18/1975 **Age:** 30

Year Team	Lg	G	GS	CG	GF	IP	BFP	H	R	ER	HR	SH	SF	HB	TBB	IBB	SO	WP	Bk	W	L	Pct	ShO	Sv-Op	Hld	ERC	ERA
2004 Tampa*	A+	2	2	0	0	5.0	21	4	1	1	0	0	0	0	3	0	3	0	0	0	0	-	0	0- -	-	3.13	1.80
2004 Trenton*	AA	3	1	0	1	5.0	23	7	6	3	0	0	0	1	0	0	8	0	0	0	1	.000	0	0- -	-	4.69	5.40
2004 Columbus*	AAA	3	0	0	0	3.2	14	2	0	0	0	0	0	0	1	0	5	0	0	0	0	-	0	0- -	-	1.10	0.00
1996 Florida	NL	21	0	0	5	16.2	78	21	8	8	1	0	1	0	10	1	10	2	0	1	1	.500	0	0-0	2	6.08	4.32
1997 Florida	NL	56	0	0	10	56.2	259	53	30	27	3	2	2	5	30	1	54	2	0	5	3	.625	0	0-1	7	4.06	4.29
1998 Fla-ChC	NL	71	2	0	18	58.2	268	57	33	33	2	1	2	1	38	3	54	6	1	3	3	.500	0	2-5	17	4.31	5.06
1999 Chicago	NL	69	0	0	15	52.0	237	56	35	28	7	1	4	1	25	2	50	2	0	3	1	.750	0	1-7	12	5.01	4.85
2000 Chicago	NL	74	0	0	24	58.2	250	46	31	31	6	4	2	2	33	4	52	5	0	7	3	.700	0	2-5	12	3.59	4.76
2001 Chicago	NL	48	0	0	9	35.0	165	45	27	24	6	1	3	2	16	1	28	3	0	2	2	.500	0	0-3	8	6.75	6.17
2002 Toronto	AL	53	0	0	15	52.1	232	51	29	21	5	3	2	2	26	3	31	5	0	1	2	.333	0	0-2	7	4.31	3.61
2003 Cin-NYY	NL	69	0	0	22	87.0	365	74	32	26	10	4	2	2	33	7	45	5	0	5	3	.625	0	1-5	8	3.23	2.69
2004 New York	AL	47	0	0	9	38.2	182	44	28	27	5	1	1	2	20	0	25	1	0	1	1	.500	0	0-1	5	5.66	6.28
1998 Florida	NL	41	2	0	12	41.0	194	38	25	25	1	1	2	1	32	2	38	5	1	0	3	.000	0	2-3	9	4.44	5.49
1998 Chicago	NL	30	0	0	6	17.2	74	19	8	8	1	0	0	0	6	1	16	1	0	3	0	1.000	0	0-2	8	3.99	4.08
2003 Cincinnati	NL	57	0	0	18	72.0	303	61	27	24	9	4	2	2	28	5	41	5	0	5	2	.714	0	1-4	7	3.35	3.00
2003 New York	AL	12	0	0	4	15.0	62	13	5	2	1	0	0	0	5	2	4	0	0	0	1	.000	0	0-1	1	2.69	1.20
9 ML YEARS		**508**	**2**	**0**	**127**	**455.2**	**2036**	**447**	**253**	**225**	**45**	**17**	**19**	**17**	**231**	**22**	**349**	**31**	**1**	**28**	**19**	**.596**	**0**	**6-29**	**78**	**4.40**	**4.44**

Matt Herges

Pitches: R **Bats:** L **Pos:** RP-70   **Ht:** 6'0" **Wt:** 200 **Born:** 4/1/1970 **Age:** 35

Year Team	Lg	G	GS	CG	GF	IP	BFP	H	R	ER	HR	SH	SF	HB	TBB	IBB	SO	WP	Bk	W	L	Pct	ShO	Sv-Op	Hld	ERC	ERA
1999 Los Angeles	NL	17	0	0	9	24.1	104	24	13	11	5	1	0	1	8	0	18	0	0	0	2	.000	0	0-2	1	4.61	4.07
2000 Los Angeles	NL	59	4	0	17	110.2	461	100	43	39	7	9	4	6	40	5	75	4	0	11	3	.786	0	1-3	4	3.35	3.17
2001 Los Angeles	NL	75	0	0	22	99.1	435	97	39	38	8	4	3	8	46	12	76	2	0	9	8	.529	0	1-8	15	4.20	3.44
2002 Montreal	NL	62	0	0	25	64.2	298	80	33	29	10	6	2	2	26	8	50	3	0	2	5	.286	0	6-14	9	5.74	4.04
2003 SD-SF	NL	67	0	0	24	79.0	332	68	27	23	3	2	6	3	29	2	68	1	1	3	2	.600	0	3-6	9	2.87	2.62
2004 San Francisco	NL	70	0	0	43	65.1	301	90	44	38	8	7	4	3	21	4	39	2	0	4	5	.444	0	23-31	5	6.29	5.23
2003 San Diego	NL	40	0	0	21	44.0	192	40	16	14	2	1	5	2	20	2	40	1	0	2	2	.500	0	3-5	4	3.45	2.86
2003 San Francisco	NL	27	0	0	3	35.0	140	28	11	9	1	1	1	1	9	0	28	0	1	1	0	1.000	0	0-1	5	2.18	2.31
6 ML YEARS		**350**	**4**	**0**	**140**	**443.1**	**1931**	**459**	**199**	**178**	**41**	**29**	**19**	**23**	**170**	**31**	**326**	**12**	**1**	**29**	**25**	**.537**	**0**	**34-64**	**43**	**4.26**	**3.61**

Chad Hermansen

Bats: R **Throws:** R **Pos:** LF-4; PH-1   **Ht:** 6'2" **Wt:** 192 **Born:** 9/10/1977 **Age:** 27

Year Team	Lg	G	AB	H	2B	3B	HR	(Hm	Rd)	TB	R	RBI	RC	TBB	IBB	SO	HBP	SH	SF	SB	CS	SB%	GDP	Avg	OBP	Slg
2004 Syracuse*	AAA	42	146	35	9	1	6	(-	-)	64	18	18	20	16	0	52	0	0	4	0	0	-	1	.240	.307	.438
1999 Pittsburgh	NL	19	60	14	3	0	1	(0	1)	20	5	1	7	7	1	19	1	1	0	2	2	.50	0	.233	.324	.333
2000 Pittsburgh	NL	33	108	20	4	1	2	(2	0)	32	12	8	6	6	0	37	0	2	1	0	0	-	3	.185	.226	.296
2001 Pittsburgh	NL	22	55	9	1	0	2	(1	1)	16	5	5	2	1	0	18	0	0	0	0	1	.00	0	.164	.179	.291
2002 Pit-ChC	NL	100	237	49	14	1	8	(4	4)	89	25	18	19	22	0	82	1	4	1	7	5	.58	1	.207	.276	.376
2003 Los Angeles	NL	11	25	4	1	0	0	(0	0)	5	2	2	1	2	0	9	0	0	0	0	0	-	0	.160	.222	.200
2004 Toronto	AL	4	7	0	0	0	0	(0	0)	0	0	0	0	0	0	3	0	0	0	0	0	-	0	.000	.000	.000
2002 Pittsburgh	NL	65	194	40	11	1	7	(4	3)	74	22	15	16	17	0	68	1	3	1	7	5	.58	1	.206	.272	.381
2002 Chicago	NL	35	43	9	3	0	1	(0	1)	15	3	3	3	5	0	14	0	1	0	0	0	-	0	.209	.292	.349
6 ML YEARS		**189**	**492**	**96**	**23**	**2**	**13**	**(7**	**6)**	**162**	**49**	**34**	**35**	**38**	**1**	**168**	**2**	**7**	**2**	**9**	**8**	**.53**	**4**	**.195**	**.255**	**.329**

Dustin Hermanson

Pitches: R **Bats:** R **Pos:** RP-29; SP-18   **Ht:** 6'2" **Wt:** 200 **Born:** 12/21/1972 **Age:** 32

Year Team	Lg	G	GS	CG	GF	IP	BFP	H	R	ER	HR	SH	SF	HB	TBB	IBB	SO	WP	Bk	W	L	Pct	ShO	Sv-Op	Hld	ERC	ERA
1995 San Diego	NL	26	0	0	6	31.2	151	35	26	24	8	3	0	1	22	1	19	3	0	3	1	.750	0	0-0	1	7.19	6.82
1996 San Diego	NL	8	0	0	4	13.2	62	18	15	13	3	2	3	0	4	0	11	0	1	1	0	1.000	0	0-0	0	6.37	8.56
1997 Montreal	NL	32	28	1	0	158.1	656	134	68	65	15	10	6	1	66	2	136	4	1	8	8	.500	1	0-0	0	3.32	3.69
1998 Montreal	NL	32	30	1	0	187.0	768	163	80	65	21	9	3	3	56	3	154	4	3	14	11	.560	0	0-0	1	3.12	3.13
1999 Montreal	NL	34	34	0	0	216.1	928	225	110	101	20	16	7	7	69	4	145	4	1	9	14	.391	0	0-0	0	4.03	4.20
2000 Montreal	NL	38	30	2	7	198.0	876	226	128	105	26	10	9	4	75	5	94	5	0	12	14	.462	1	4-7	1	5.10	4.77
2001 St Louis	NL	33	33	0	0	192.1	830	195	106	95	34	7	2	8	73	3	123	6	0	14	13	.519	0	0-0	0	4.80	4.45
2002 Boston	AL	12	1	0	4	22.0	107	35	19	19	3	0	1	0	7	0	13	2	0	1	1	.500	0	0-1	2	7.52	7.77
2003 StL-SF	NL	32	6	0	12	68.2	291	70	32	31	9	4	2	3	24	4	39	3	0	3	3	.500	0	1-6	1	4.38	4.06
2004 San Francisco	NL	47	18	0	26	131.0	565	132	71	66	15	5	7	3	46	5	102	4	0	6	9	.400	0	17-20	1	4.03	4.53
2003 St Louis	NL	23	0	0	10	29.2	129	35	18	18	4	2	1	1	14	2	12	1	0	1	2	.333	0	1-6	1	6.04	5.46
2003 San Francisco	NL	9	6	0	2	39.0	162	35	14	13	5	2	1	2	10	2	27	2	0	2	1	.667	0	0-0	0	3.25	3.00
10 ML YEARS		**294**	**180**	**4**	**59**	**1219.0**	**5234**	**1233**	**655**	**584**	**154**	**66**	**40**	**30**	**442**	**27**	**836**	**35**	**6**	**71**	**74**	**.490**	**2**	**22-34**	**7**	**4.26**	**4.31**

Adrian Hernandez

Pitches: R **Bats:** R **Pos:** RP-5; SP-1   **Ht:** 6'2" **Wt:** 185 **Born:** 3/25/1975 **Age:** 30

Year Team	Lg	G	GS	CG	GF	IP	BFP	H	R	ER	HR	SH	SF	HB	TBB	IBB	SO	WP	Bk	W	L	Pct	ShO	Sv-Op	Hld	ERC	ERA
2004 Indianapolis*	AAA	20	15	0	0	94.1	415	111	61	60	9	9	6	9	39	2	83	2	4	0	8	.000	0	0- -	-	5.72	5.72
2001 New York	AL	6	3	0	1	22.0	91	15	10	9	7	0	0	2	10	1	10	4	0	0	3	.000	0	0-0	0	4.30	3.68
2002 New York	AL	2	1	0	0	6.0	34	10	8	8	2	0	0	0	6	0	9	1	0	0	1	.000	0	0-0	0	13.15	12.00
2004 Milwaukee	NL	6	1	0	2	16.0	84	20	18	15	1	1	1	0	14	0	14	3	0	0	2	.000	0	0-1	0	6.87	8.44
3 ML YEARS		**14**	**5**	**0**	**3**	**44.0**	**209**	**45**	**36**	**32**	**10**	**1**	**1**	**2**	**30**	**1**	**33**	**8**	**0**	**0**	**6**	**.000**	**0**	**0-1**	**0**	**6.38**	**6.55**

Carlos Hernandez

Pitches: L **Bats:** B **Pos:** SP-9   **Ht:** 5'10" **Wt:** 185 **Born:** 4/22/1980 **Age:** 25

Year Team	Lg	G	GS	CG	GF	IP	BFP	H	R	ER	HR	SH	SF	HB	TBB	IBB	SO	WP	Bk	W	L	Pct	ShO	Sv-Op	Hld	ERC	ERA
2004 New Orleans*	AAA	23	23	0	0	127.2	528	115	54	51	9	11	8	5	46	1	81	3	0	9	4	.692	0	0- -	-	3.39	3.60
2001 Houston	NL	3	3	0	0	17.2	70	11	2	2	1	1	0	0	7	0	17	2	0	1	0	1.000	0	0-0	0	1.88	1.02
2002 Houston	NL	23	21	0	0	111.0	495	112	56	54	11	2	0	3	61	5	93	1	2	7	5	.583	0	0-0	0	4.77	4.38
2004 Houston	NL	9	9	0	0	42.0	200	50	31	30	11	4	3	5	23	0	26	1	0	1	3	.250	0	0-0	0	7.66	6.43
3 ML YEARS		35	33	0	0	170.2	765	173	89	86	23	7	3	8	91	5	136	4	2	9	8	.529	0	0-0	0	5.10	4.54

Jose Hernandez

Bats: R **Throws:** R **Pos:** 2B-50; PH-21; SS-13; 3B-12; LF-9; 1B-8; PR-3   **Ht:** 6'1" **Wt:** 188 **Born:** 7/14/1969 **Age:** 35

Year Team	Lg	G	AB	H	2B	3B	HR	(Hm	Rd)	TB	R	RBI	RC	TBB	IBB	SO	HBP	SH	SF	SB	CS	SB%	GDP	Avg	OBP	Slg
1991 Texas	AL	45	98	18	2	1	0	(0	0)	22	8	4	2	3	0	31	0	6	0	0	1	.00	2	.184	.208	.224
1992 Cleveland	AL	3	4	0	0	0	0	(0	0)	0	0	0	0	0	0	2	0	0	0	0	0	.00	0	.000	.000	.000
1994 Chicago	NL	56	132	32	2	3	1	(0	1)	43	18	9	11	8	0	29	1	5	0	2	2	.50	4	.242	.291	.326
1995 Chicago	NL	93	245	60	11	4	13	(6	7)	118	37	40	31	13	3	69	0	8	2	1	0	1.00	8	.245	.281	.482
1996 Chicago	NL	131	331	80	14	1	10	(4	6)	126	52	41	35	24	4	97	1	5	2	4	0	1.00	10	.242	.293	.381
1997 Chicago	NL	121	183	50	8	5	7	(4	3)	89	33	26	26	14	2	42	0	1	1	2	5	.29	5	.273	.323	.486
1998 Chicago	NL	149	488	124	23	7	23	(11	12)	230	76	75	67	40	3	140	1	2	2	4	6	.40	12	.254	.311	.471
1999 ChC-Atl	NL	147	508	135	20	2	19	(6	13)	216	79	62	73	52	6	145	5	2	1	11	3	.79	10	.266	.339	.425
2000 Milwaukee	NL	124	446	109	22	1	11	(8	3)	166	51	59	48	41	3	125	6	0	3	3	7	.30	12	.244	.315	.372
2001 Milwaukee	NL	152	542	135	26	2	25	(9	16)	240	67	78	69	39	8	185	2	5	4	5	4	.56	9	.249	.300	.443
2002 Milwaukee	NL	152	525	151	24	2	24	(13	11)	251	72	73	76	52	5	188	4	0	1	3	5	.38	19	.288	.356	.478
2003 Col-ChC-Pit	NL	150	519	117	18	3	13	(7	6)	180	58	57	41	46	0	177	1	0	5	2	1	.67	16	.225	.287	.347
2004 Los Angeles	NL	95	211	61	12	1	13	(5	8)	114	32	29	33	26	6	61	1	0	0	3	1	.75	3	.289	.370	.540
1999 Chicago	NL	99	342	93	12	2	15	(5	10)	154	57	43	55	40	3	101	5	1	0	7	2	.78	5	.272	.357	.450
1999 Atlanta	NL	48	166	42	8	0	4	(1	3)	62	22	19	18	12	3	44	0	1	1	4	1	.80	5	.253	.302	.373
2003 Colorado	NL	69	257	61	6	1	8	(4	4)	93	33	27	23	27	0	95	0	0	2	1	1	.50	6	.237	.308	.362
2003 ChC	NL	23	69	13	3	1	2	(1	1)	24	6	9	4	3	0	26	0	0	0	0	0	-	1	.188	.222	.348
2003 Pittsburgh	NL	58	193	43	9	1	3	(2	1)	63	19	21	14	16	0	56	1	0	3	1	0	1.00	6	.223	.282	.326
13 ML YEARS		1418	4232	1072	182	32	159	(73	86)	1795	583	553	512	358	40	1291	22	34	21	40	35	.53	110	.253	.313	.424

Livan Hernandez

Pitches: R **Bats:** R **Pos:** SP-35   **Ht:** 6'2" **Wt:** 240 **Born:** 2/20/1975 **Age:** 30

Year Team	Lg	G	GS	CG	GF	IP	BFP	H	R	ER	HR	SH	SF	HB	TBB	IBB	SO	WP	Bk	W	L	Pct	ShO	Sv-Op	Hld	ERC	ERA
1996 Florida	NL	1	0	0	0	3.0	13	3	0	0	0	0	0	0	2	0	2	0	0	0	0	-	0	0-0	0	4.60	0.00
1997 Florida	NL	17	17	0	0	96.1	405	81	39	34	5	4	7	3	38	1	72	0	0	9	3	.750	0	0-0	0	2.96	3.18
1998 Florida	NL	33	33	9	0	234.1	1040	265	133	123	37	8	5	6	104	8	162	4	3	10	12	.455	0	0-0	0	5.58	4.72
1999 Fla-SF	NL	30	30	2	0	199.2	886	227	110	103	23	7	6	2	76	5	144	2	2	8	12	.400	0	0-0	0	4.88	4.64
2000 San Francisco	NL	33	33	5	0	240.0	1030	254	114	100	22	12	9	4	73	3	165	3	0	17	11	.607	2	0-0	0	4.01	3.75
2001 San Francisco	NL	34	34	2	0	226.2	1008	266	143	132	24	12	12	3	85	7	138	7	0	13	15	.464	0	0-0	0	5.03	5.24
2002 San Francisco	NL	33	33	5	0	216.0	921	233	113	105	19	14	4	8	71	5	134	1	1	12	16	.429	3	0-0	0	4.26	4.38
2003 Montreal	NL	33	33	8	0	233.1	967	225	92	83	27	6	4	10	57	3	178	6	1	15	10	.600	1	0-0	0	3.55	3.20
2004 Montreal	NL	35	35	9	0	255.0	1053	234	105	102	26	11	4	10	83	9	186	1	0	11	15	.423	2	0-0	0	3.52	3.60
1999 Florida	NL	20	20	2	0	136.0	612	161	78	72	17	3	4	2	55	3	97	2	1	5	9	.357	0	0-0	0	5.37	4.76
1999 San Francisco	NL	10	10	0	0	63.2	274	66	32	31	6	4	2	0	21	2	47	0	1	3	3	.500	0	0-0	0	3.88	4.38
9 ML YEARS		249	248	40	0	1704.1	7323	1788	849	782	183	74	55	42	589	41	1181	24	7	95	94	.503	7	0-0	0	4.28	4.13

Orlando Hernandez

Pitches: R **Bats:** R **Pos:** SP-15   **Ht:** 6'2" **Wt:** 220 **Born:** 10/11/1969 **Age:** 35

Year Team	Lg	G	GS	CG	GF	IP	BFP	H	R	ER	HR	SH	SF	HB	TBB	IBB	SO	WP	Bk	W	L	Pct	ShO	Sv-Op	Hld	ERC	ERA
2004 Tampa*	A+	3	3	0	0	12.0	44	3	4	2	0	0	0	1	7	0	11	0	0	1	0	1.000	0	0- -	-	1.10	1.50
2004 Columbus*	AAA	3	3	0	0	17.2	72	17	11	11	3	0	0	0	3	0	16	0	0	2	1	.667	0	0- -	-	3.40	5.60
1998 New York	AL	21	21	3	0	141.0	574	113	53	49	11	3	5	6	52	1	131	5	2	12	4	.750	1	0-0	0	2.96	3.13
1999 New York	AL	33	33	2	0	214.1	910	187	108	98	24	3	11	8	87	2	157	4	0	17	9	.654	1	0-0	0	3.60	4.12
2000 New York	AL	29	29	3	0	195.2	820	186	104	98	34	4	5	6	51	2	141	1	0	12	13	.480	0	0-0	0	3.82	4.51
2001 New York	AL	17	16	0	0	94.2	414	90	51	51	19	2	2	5	42	1	77	0	0	4	7	.364	0	0-0	0	4.87	4.85
2002 New York	AL	24	22	0	1	146.0	606	131	63	59	17	1	5	8	36	2	113	8	0	8	5	.615	0	1-1	1	3.20	3.64
2004 New York	AL	15	15	0	0	84.2	359	73	31	31	9	0	1	5	36	0	84	3	0	8	2	.800	0	0-0	0	3.71	3.30
6 ML YEARS		139	136	8	1	876.1	3683	780	410	386	114	13	29	38	304	8	703	21	2	61	40	.604	2	1-1	1	3.62	3.96

Ramon Hernandez

Bats: R **Throws:** R **Pos:** C-108; PH-4   **Ht:** 6'0" **Wt:** 210 **Born:** 5/20/1976 **Age:** 29

Year Team	Lg	G	AB	H	2B	3B	HR	(Hm	Rd)	TB	R	RBI	RC	TBB	IBB	SO	HBP	SH	SF	SB	CS	SB%	GDP	Avg	OBP	Slg
2004 Portland*	AAA	7	19	6	1	0	0	(-	-)	7	2	6	2	2	0	3	0	0	0	0	0	-	1	.316	.381	.368
1999 Oakland	AL	40	136	38	7	0	3	(4	4)	54	13	21	20	18	0	11	1	1	2	1	0	1.00	5	.279	.363	.397
2000 Oakland	AL	143	419	101	19	0	14	(7	7)	162	52	62	49	38	1	64	7	10	5	1	0	1.00	14	.241	.311	.387
2001 Oakland	AL	136	453	115	25	0	15	(5	10)	185	55	60	58	37	3	68	6	9	4	1	1	.50	10	.254	.316	.408
2002 Oakland	AL	136	403	94	20	0	7	(3	4)	135	51	42	41	43	1	64	5	3	3	0	0	-	14	.233	.313	.335
2003 Oakland	AL	140	483	132	24	1	21	(9	12)	221	70	78	69	33	2	79	12	2	6	0	0	-	14	.273	.331	.458
2004 San Diego	NL	111	384	106	23	0	18	(10	8)	183	45	63	50	35	0	45	5	4	4	1	1	1.00	16	.276	.341	.477
6 ML YEARS		706	2278	586	118	1	78	(35	43)	940	286	326	287	204	7	331	36	29	24	4	1	.80	70	.257	.325	.413

Roberto Hernandez

Pitches: R **Bats:** R **Pos:** RP-63   **Ht:** 6'4" **Wt:** 250 **Born:** 11/11/1964 **Age:** 40

Year Team	Lg	G	GS	CG	GF	IP	BFP	H	R	ER	HR	SH	SF	HB	TBB	IBB	SO	WP	Bk	W	L	Pct	ShO	Sv-Op	Hld	ERC	ERA
1991 Chicago	AL	9	3	0	1	15.0	69	18	15	13	1	0	0	0	7	0	6	1	0	1	0	1.000	0	0-0	0	5.19	7.80
1992 Chicago	AL	43	0	0	27	71.0	277	45	15	13	4	0	3	4	20	1	68	2	0	7	3	.700	0	12-16	6	1.74	1.65
1993 Chicago	AL	70	0	0	67	78.2	314	66	21	20	6	2	2	0	20	1	71	2	0	3	4	.429	0	38-44	0	2.54	2.29
1994 Chicago	AL	45	0	0	43	47.2	206	44	29	26	5	0	1	1	19	1	50	1	0	4	4	.500	0	14-20	0	3.66	4.91
1995 Chicago	AL	60	0	0	57	59.2	272	63	30	26	9	4	0	3	28	4	84	1	0	3	7	.300	0	32-42	0	5.04	3.92
1996 Chicago	AL	72	0	0	61	84.2	355	65	21	18	2	2	2	0	38	5	85	6	0	6	5	.545	0	38-46	0	2.40	1.91
1997 CWS-SF		74	0	0	50	80.2	340	67	24	22	7	2	1	1	38	5	82	3	0	10	3	.769	0	31-39	9	3.30	2.45
1998 Tampa Bay	AL	67	0	0	58	71.1	310	55	33	32	5	4	0	5	41	4	55	1	0	2	6	.250	0	26-35	0	3.43	4.04
1999 Tampa Bay	AL	72	0	0	66	73.1	321	68	27	25	1	2	3	4	33	1	69	3	0	2	3	.400	0	43-47	0	3.40	3.07
2000 Tampa Bay	AL	68	0	0	58	73.1	315	76	33	26	9	7	3	3	23	1	61	2	1	4	7	.364	0	32-40	1	4.24	3.19
2001 Kansas City	AL	63	0	0	55	67.2	287	69	34	31	7	1	0	1	26	3	46	6	0	5	6	.455	0	28-34	0	4.23	4.12
2002 Kansas City	AL	53	0	0	42	52.0	227	62	29	25	6	4	1	3	12	2	39	3	0	1	3	.250	0	26-33	0	4.79	4.33
2003 Atlanta	NL	66	0	0	12	60.0	282	61	36	29	10	4	0	3	43	7	45	0	0	5	3	.625	0	0-4	19	5.95	4.35
2004 Philadelphia	NL	63	0	0	11	56.2	260	66	33	30	9	7	1	1	29	3	44	3	0	3	5	.375	0	0-4	9	5.94	4.76
1997 Chicago	AL	46	0	0	43	48.0	203	38	15	13	5	1	1	1	24	4	47	2	0	5	1	.833	0	27-31	0	3.30	2.44
1997 San Francisco	NL	28	0	0	7	32.2	137	29	9	9	2	1	0	0	14	1	35	1	0	5	2	.714	0	4-8	9	3.29	2.48
14 ML YEARS		825	3	0	608	891.2	3835	825	386	336	81	39	17	29	377	38	805	34	1	56	59	.487	0	320-404	44	3.73	3.39

Runelvys Hernandez

Pitches: R **Bats:** R **Pos:** SP   **Ht:** 6'1" **Wt:** 205 **Born:** 4/27/1978 **Age:** 27

Year Team	Lg	G	GS	CG	GF	IP	BFP	H	R	ER	HR	SH	SF	HB	TBB	IBB	SO	WP	Bk	W	L	Pct	ShO	Sv-Op	Hld	ERC	ERA
2001 Burlington	A	17	17	0	0	100.2	426	94	46	38	5	2	2	3	29	0	100	6	3	7	5	.583	0	0- -	-	3.01	3.40
2002 Wilmington	A+	2	2	0	0	12.0	46	12	6	5	0	1	0	0	1	0	9	0	0	1	1	.500	0	0- -	-	2.40	3.75
2002 Wichita	AA	16	14	2	1	106.1	422	96	38	32	3	5	4	3	24	1	86	5	1	8	3	.727	0	0- -	-	2.63	2.71
2003 Wichita	AA	2	2	0	0	9.1	40	9	4	4	0	0	0	0	5	0	5	0	0	2	0	1.000	0	0- -	-	3.78	3.86
2003 Omaha	AAA	1	1	0	0	5.0	20	3	1	1	0	0	0	1	2	0	5	0	0	1	0	1.000	0	0- -	-	2.16	1.80
2002 Kansas City	AL	12	12	0	0	74.1	316	79	36	36	8	1	3	1	22	0	45	2	0	4	4	.500	0	0-0	0	4.16	4.36
2003 Kansas City	AL	16	16	0	0	91.2	397	87	51	47	9	1	4	6	37	0	48	2	1	7	5	.583	0	0-0	0	4.05	4.61
2 ML YEARS		28	28	0	0	166.0	713	166	87	83	17	2	7	7	59	0	93	4	1	11	9	.550	0	0-0	0	4.10	4.50

Mike Hessman

Bats: R **Throws:** R **Pos:** 1B-16; PH-9; 3B-7; LF-3; PR-2   **Ht:** 6'5" **Wt:** 215 **Born:** 3/5/1978 **Age:** 27

Year Team	Lg	G	AB	H	2B	3B	HR	(Hm	Rd)	TB	R	RBI	RC	TBB	IBB	SO	HBP	SH	SF	SB	CS	SB%	GDP	Avg	OBP	Slg
1996 Braves	R	53	190	41	10	1	1	(-	-)	56	13	15	15	12	1	41	4	4	0	1	1	.50	0	.216	.277	.295
1997 Macon	A	122	459	108	25	0	21	(-	-)	196	69	74	57	41	0	167	6	0	2	0	2	.00	6	.235	.305	.427
1998 Danville	A+	118	445	89	21	0	20	(-	-)	170	47	63	40	30	0	172	6	0	2	3	3	.50	6	.200	.259	.382
1999 Myrtle Beach	A+	103	365	90	25	0	23	(-	-)	184	62	54	61	47	3	135	11	0	3	0	3	.00	3	.247	.347	.504
2000 Greenville	AA	127	437	80	23	1	19	(-	-)	162	52	50	37	37	0	178	8	0	2	3	1	.75	9	.183	.258	.371
2001 Greenville	AA	129	478	110	23	2	26	(-	-)	215	66	80	61	39	2	124	7	0	0	2	4	.33	5	.230	.298	.450
2002 Richmond	AAA	134	484	127	28	1	26	(-	-)	235	67	77	69	34	2	107	10	0	4	1	5	.17	13	.262	.321	.486
2003 Danville	R+	5	15	1	0	0	0	(-	-)	1	1	2	0	2	0	2	1	0	2	0	0	-	0	.067	.200	.067
2003 Richmond	AAA	96	359	89	15	3	16	(-	-)	158	47	52	46	24	0	87	4	0	8	3	1	.75	6	.248	.296	.440
2004 Richmond	AAA	78	265	76	14	1	19	(-	-)	149	48	54	52	28	3	65	7	0	4	4	0	1.00	6	.287	.365	.562
2003 Atlanta	NL	19	21	6	2	0	2	(1	1)	14	2	3	5	5	1	6	0	0	0	0	0	-	2	.286	.423	.667
2004 Atlanta	NL	29	69	9	3	0	2	(2	0)	18	8	5	1	1	0	24	1	0	0	0	0	-	0	.130	.155	.261
2 ML YEARS		48	90	15	5	0	4	(3	1)	32	10	8	6	6	1	30	1	0	0	0	0	-	2	.167	.227	.356

Richard Hidalgo

Bats: R **Throws:** R **Pos:** RF-139; LF-5; PH-3   **Ht:** 6'3" **Wt:** 220 **Born:** 7/2/1975 **Age:** 29

Year Team	Lg	G	AB	H	2B	3B	HR	(Hm	Rd)	TB	R	RBI	RC	TBB	IBB	SO	HBP	SH	SF	SB	CS	SB%	GDP	Avg	OBP	Slg
1997 Houston	NL	19	62	19	5	0	2	(0	2)	30	8	6	11	4	0	18	1	0	0	1	0	1.00	0	.306	.358	.484
1998 Houston	NL	74	211	64	15	0	7	(3	4)	100	31	35	34	17	0	37	2	0	4	3	3	.50	5	.303	.355	.474
1999 Houston	NL	108	383	87	25	2	15	(5	10)	161	49	56	55	56	2	73	4	0	5	8	5	.62	5	.227	.328	.420
2000 Houston	NL	153	558	175	42	3	44	(16	28)	355	118	122	130	56	3	110	21	0	9	13	6	.68	13	.314	.391	.636
2001 Houston	NL	146	512	141	29	3	19	(13	6)	233	70	80	81	54	3	107	16	0	11	3	5	.38	15	.275	.356	.455
2002 Houston	NL	114	388	91	17	4	15	(4	11)	161	54	48	42	43	1	85	6	0	2	6	2	.75	13	.235	.319	.415
2003 Houston	NL	141	514	159	43	4	28	(11	17)	294	91	88	87	58	8	104	8	0	5	9	7	.56	10	.309	.385	.572
2004 Hou-NYM	NL	144	523	125	26	3	25	(13	12)	232	67	82	59	44	7	129	5	0	6	4	4	.50	19	.239	.301	.444
2004 Houston	NL	58	199	51	15	2	4	(2	2)	82	21	30	22	17	4	53	0	0	4	1	2	.33	7	.256	.309	.412
2004 New York	NL	86	324	74	11	1	21	(11	10)	150	46	52	37	27	3	76	5	0	2	3	2	.60	12	.228	.296	.463
8 ML YEARS		899	3151	861	202	19	155	(65	90)	1566	488	517	499	332	24	663	63	0	42	47	32	.59	80	.273	.350	.497

Joe Hietpas

Bats: R **Throws:** R **Pos:** C-1   **Ht:** 6'3" **Wt:** 220 **Born:** 5/1/1979 **Age:** 26

Year Team	Lg	G	AB	H	2B	3B	HR	(Hm	Rd)	TB	R	RBI	RC	TBB	IBB	SO	HBP	SH	SF	SB	CS	SB%	GDP	Avg	OBP	Slg
2001 Kingsport	R+	11	27	5	1	0	0	(-	-)	6	3	1	2	6	0	11	1	0	0	0	0	-	0	.185	.353	.222
2001 Binghamton	AA	2	3	0	0	0	0	(-	-)	0	0	0	0	0	0	1	0	0	0	0	0	-	0	.000	.000	.000
2002 Capital City	A	33	105	26	8	0	1	(-	-)	37	9	16	12	14	0	23	0	1	0	0	2	.00	1	.248	.336	.352
2002 Brooklyn	A-	32	117	30	5	0	1	(-	-)	38	11	13	11	8	1	31	2	0	1	0	1	.00	6	.256	.313	.325
2003 St. Lucie	A+	63	195	31	8	1	1	(-	-)	44	12	19	6	14	0	60	2	1	3	3	1	.75	6	.159	.220	.226
2003 Binghamton	AA	5	10	1	1	0	0	(-	-)	2	1	0	0	0	0	2	0	0	0	0	0	-	0	.100	.100	.200

Year Team	Lg	G	AB	H	2B	3B	HR	(Hm	Rd)	TB	R	RBI	RC	TBB	IBB	SO	HBP	SH	SF	SB	CS	SB%	GDP	Avg	OBP	Slg
								BATTING												BASERUNNING				AVERAGES		
2004 St. Lucie	A+	55	191	48	15	1	2	(-	-)	71	23	27	23	18	0	51	4	3	0	1	1	.50	3	.251	.329	.372
2004 Binghamton	AA	43	139	32	10	0	3	(-	-)	51	13	19	15	19	0	41	3	1	0	0	2	.00	6	.230	.335	.367
2004 New York	NL	1	0	0	0	0	0	(0	0)	0	0	0	0	0	0	0	0	0	0	0	0	-	0	-	-	-

Bobby Higginson

Bats: L **Throws:** R **Pos:** RF-115; DH-9; PH-6; PR-2   **Ht:** 5'11" **Wt:** 202 **Born:** 8/18/1970 **Age:** 34

Year Team	Lg	G	AB	H	2B	3B	HR	(Hm	Rd)	TB	R	RBI	RC	TBB	IBB	SO	HBP	SH	SF	SB	CS	SB%	GDP	Avg	OBP	Slg
1995 Detroit	AL	131	410	92	17	5	14	(10	4)	161	61	43	56	62	3	107	5	2	7	6	4	.60	5	.224	.329	.393
1996 Detroit	AL	130	440	141	35	0	26	(15	11)	254	75	81	99	65	7	66	1	3	6	6	3	.67	7	.320	.404	.577
1997 Detroit	AL	146	546	163	30	5	27	(16	11)	284	94	101	105	70	2	85	3	0	4	12	7	.63	10	.299	.379	.520
1998 Detroit	AL	157	612	174	37	4	25	(10	15)	294	92	85	100	63	2	101	6	0	4	3	3	.50	16	.284	.355	.480
1999 Detroit	AL	107	377	90	18	0	12	(8	4)	144	51	46	54	64	2	66	2	0	2	4	6	.40	2	.239	.351	.382
2000 Detroit	AL	154	597	179	44	4	30	(12	18)	321	104	102	121	74	6	99	2	2	3	15	3	.83	5	.300	.377	.538
2001 Detroit	AL	147	541	150	28	6	17	(7	10)	241	84	71	91	80	3	65	2	1	9	20	12	.63	8	.277	.367	.445
2002 Detroit	AL	119	444	125	24	3	10	(6	4)	185	50	63	72	41	3	45	6	1	7	12	5	.71	8	.282	.345	.417
2003 Detroit	AL	130	469	110	13	4	14	(6	8)	173	61	52	54	59	3	73	3	1	6	8	8	.50	12	.235	.320	.369
2004 Detroit	AL	131	448	110	24	2	12	(4	8)	174	63	64	71	70	5	84	7	2	4	5	2	.71	10	.246	.353	.388
10 ML YEARS		1352	4884	1334	270	33	187	(94	93)	2231	735	708	823	648	36	791	37	12	52	91	53	.63	83	.273	.359	.457

Bobby Hill

Bats: B **Throws:** R **Pos:** PH-70; 2B-40; 3B-25   **Ht:** 5'10" **Wt:** 190 **Born:** 4/3/1978 **Age:** 27

Year Team	Lg	G	AB	H	2B	3B	HR	(Hm	Rd)	TB	R	RBI	RC	TBB	IBB	SO	HBP	SH	SF	SB	CS	SB%	GDP	Avg	OBP	Slg
2002 Chicago	NL	59	190	48	7	2	4	(1	3)	71	26	20	24	17	4	42	4	4	0	6	1	.86	0	.253	.327	.374
2003 ChC-Pit	NL	6	7	2	0	0	0	(0	0)	2	1	0	2	2	0	2	0	0	0	0	0	-	1	.286	.444	.286
2004 Pittsburgh	NL	126	233	62	7	2	2	(1	1)	79	28	27	25	20	2	39	12	1	1	0	3	.00	12	.266	.353	.339
2003 Chicago	NL	5	4	1	0	0	0	(0	0)	1	0	0	1	1	0	2	0	0	0	0	0	-	1	.250	.400	.250
2003 Pittsburgh	NL	1	3	1	0	0	0	(0	0)	1	1	0	1	1	0	0	0	0	0	0	0	-	0	.333	.500	.333
3 ML YEARS		191	430	112	14	4	6	(2	4)	152	55	47	51	39	6	83	16	5	1	6	4	.60	13	.260	.344	.353

Koyie Hill

Bats: B **Throws:** R **Pos:** C-11; PH-2   **Ht:** 6'0" **Wt:** 190 **Born:** 3/9/1979 **Age:** 26

Year Team	Lg	G	AB	H	2B	3B	HR	(Hm	Rd)	TB	R	RBI	RC	TBB	IBB	SO	HBP	SH	SF	SB	CS	SB%	GDP	Avg	OBP	Slg
2000 Yakima	A-	64	251	65	13	1	2	(-	-)	86	26	29	25	25	2	47	0	5	2	0	7	.00	7	.259	.324	.343
2001 Wilmington	A+	134	498	150	20	2	8	(-	-)	198	65	79	75	49	14	82	7	2	6	21	12	.64	7	.301	.368	.398
2002 Jacksonville	AA	130	468	127	25	1	11	(-	-)	187	67	64	70	76	11	88	0	1	7	5	3	.63	14	.271	.368	.400
2003 Jacksonville	AA	25	101	23	7	0	0	(-	-)	30	9	7	6	6	2	19	0	0	0	2	1	.67	3	.228	.271	.297
2003 Las Vegas	AAA	85	312	98	18	0	3	(-	-)	125	48	36	43	15	3	39	1	1	2	5	0	1.00	1	.314	.345	.401
2004 Las Vegas	AAA	91	350	100	26	0	13	(-	-)	165	57	54	52	28	3	69	2	0	3	0	1	.00	9	.286	.339	.471
2003 Los Angeles	NL	3	3	1	1	0	0	(0	0)	2	0	0	0	0	0	2	0	0	0	0	0	-	0	.333	.333	.667
2004 Arizona	NL	13	36	9	1	0	1	(1	0)	13	3	6	5	2	1	6	0	0	0	1	0	1.00	1	.250	.289	.361
2 ML YEARS		16	39	10	2	0	1	(1	0)	15	3	6	5	2	1	8	0	0	0	1	0	1.00	1	.256	.293	.385

Shawn Hill

Pitches: R **Bats:** R **Pos:** SP-3   **Ht:** 6'2" **Wt:** 185 **Born:** 4/28/1981 **Age:** 24

Year Team	Lg	G	GS	CG	GF	IP	BFP	H	R	ER	HR	SH	SF	HB	TBB	IBB	SO	WP	Bk	W	L	Pct	ShO	Sv-Op	Hld	ERC	ERA
						HOW MUCH HE PITCHED					WHAT HE GAVE UP											THE RESULTS					
2000 Expos	R	7	7	0	0	24.1	117	25	17	13	0	1	1	6	10	0	20	3	1	1	3	.250	0	0--	-	4.22	4.81
2001 Vermont	A-	7	7	0	0	35.2	144	22	12	9	0	1	0	7	8	0	23	2	0	2	2	.500	0	0--	-	1.60	2.27
2002 Clinton	A	25	25	0	0	146.2	149	75	56	7	3	6	11	35	2	99	11	1	12	7	.632	0	0--	-	16.16	3.44
2003 Brevard Cnty	A+	22	21	2	0	126.2	525	118	47	36	3	6	7	10	26	0	66	1	0	9	4	.692	1	0--	-	2.76	2.56
2003 Harrisburg	AA	4	4	0	0	20.1	96	23	12	8	0	0	1	1	11	1	12	0	0	3	1	.750	0	0--	-	4.63	3.54
2004 Harrisburg	AA	17	17	2	0	87.2	357	90	39	33	4	4	0	5	20	0	53	2	1	5	7	.417	0	0--	-	3.55	3.39
2004 Montreal	NL	3	3	0	0	9.0	51	17	16	16	1	0	2	1	7	0	10	0	0	1	2	.333	0	0-0	0	12.14	16.00

Shea Hillenbrand

Bats: R **Throws:** R **Pos:** 1B-130; 3B-17; PH-2   **Ht:** 6'1" **Wt:** 211 **Born:** 7/27/1975 **Age:** 29

Year Team	Lg	G	AB	H	2B	3B	HR	(Hm	Rd)	TB	R	RBI	RC	TBB	IBB	SO	HBP	SH	SF	SB	CS	SB%	GDP	Avg	OBP	Slg
2001 Boston	AL	139	468	123	20	2	12	(5	7)	183	52	49	49	13	3	61	7	1	4	3	4	.43	12	.263	.291	.391
2002 Boston	AL	156	634	186	43	4	18	(5	13)	291	94	83	88	25	4	95	12	0	5	4	2	.67	18	.293	.330	.459
2003 Bos-Ari		134	515	144	35	1	20	(11	9)	241	60	97	66	24	4	70	6	0	9	1	0	1.00	13	.280	.314	.468
2004 Arizona	NL	148	562	174	36	3	15	(9	6)	261	68	80	82	24	2	49	12	0	6	2	0	1.00	17	.310	.348	.464
2003 Boston	AL	49	185	56	17	0	3	(0	3)	82	20	38	27	7	1	26	4	0	4	1	0	1.00	4	.303	.335	.443
2003 Arizona	NL	85	330	88	18	1	17	(11	6)	159	40	59	39	17	3	44	2	0	5	0	0	-	13	.267	.302	.482
4 ML YEARS		577	2179	627	134	10	65	(30	35)	976	274	309	285	86	13	275	37	1	24	10	6	.63	69	.288	.322	.448

A.J. Hinch

Bats: R **Throws:** R **Pos:** C-4   **Ht:** 6'1" **Wt:** 205 **Born:** 5/15/1974 **Age:** 31

Year Team	Lg	G	AB	H	2B	3B	HR	(Hm	Rd)	TB	R	RBI	RC	TBB	IBB	SO	HBP	SH	SF	SB	CS	SB%	GDP	Avg	OBP	Slg
2004 Scrtn/WlksBr*	AAA	77	265	61	9	1	2	(-	-)	78	21	32	26	24	0	48	8	1	3	0	0	-	5	.230	.310	.294
1998 Oakland	AL	120	337	78	10	0	9	(4	5)	115	34	35	36	30	0	89	4	13	7	3	0	1.00	6	.231	.296	.341
1999 Oakland	AL	76	205	44	4	1	7	(3	4)	71	26	24	18	11	0	41	2	9	1	6	2	.75	4	.215	.260	.346
2000 Oakland	AL	6	8	2	0	0	0	(0	0)	2	1	0	1	1	0	1	0	0	0	0	0	-	0	.250	.333	.250
2001 Kansas City	AL	45	121	19	3	0	6	(4	2)	40	10	15	7	8	1	26	3	1	1	1	1	.50	5	.157	.226	.331
2002 Kansas City	AL	72	197	49	7	1	7	(6	1)	79	25	27	27	18	0	35	3	2	0	3	3	.50	2	.249	.321	.401
2003 Detroit	AL	27	74	15	3	1	3	(1	2)	29	7	11	7	3	0	18	2	1	2	0	0	-	3	.203	.247	.392
2004 Philadelphia	NL	4	11	2	1	0	0	(0	0)	3	1	0	0	0	0	4	0	0	0	0	0	-	0	.182	.182	.273
7 ML YEARS		350	953	209	28	3	32	(18	14)	339	104	112	96	71	1	214	14	26	11	13	6	.68	20	.219	.280	.356

Eric Hinske

Bats: L **Throws:** R **Pos:** 3B-153; PH-5; DH-1; PR-1   **Ht:** 6'2" **Wt:** 225 **Born:** 8/5/1977 **Age:** 27

Year Team	Lg	G	AB	H	2B	3B	HR	(Hm	Rd)	TB	R	RBI	RC	TBB	IBB	SO	HBP	SH	SF	SB	CS	SB%	GDP	Avg	OBP	Slg
2002 Toronto	AL	151	566	158	38	2	24	(15	9)	272	99	84	103	77	5	138	2	0	5	13	1	.93	12	.279	.365	.481
2003 Toronto	AL	124	449	109	45	3	12	(4	8)	196	74	63	66	59	1	104	1	0	5	12	2	.86	11	.243	.329	.437
2004 Toronto	AL	155	570	140	23	3	15	(6	9)	214	66	69	60	54	2	109	4	0	6	12	8	.60	14	.246	.312	.375
3 ML YEARS		430	1585	407	106	8	51	(25	26)	682	239	216	229	190	8	351	7	0	16	37	11	.77	37	.257	.336	.430

Sterling Hitchcock

Pitches: L **Bats:** L **Pos:** SP-4   **Ht:** 6'0" **Wt:** 205 **Born:** 4/29/1971 **Age:** 34

Year Team	Lg	G	GS	CG	GF	IP	BFP	H	R	ER	HR	SH	SF	HB	TBB	IBB	SO	WP	Bk	W	L	Pct	ShO	Sv-Op	Hld	ERC	ERA
2004 Lk Elsinore*	A+	2	2	0	0	9.0	35	8	1	1	0	0	1	0	0	0	13	1	0	1	0	1.000	0	0--	-	1.53	1.00
2004 Portland*	AAA	3	3	0	0	11.1	51	17	9	8	1	2	0	0	1	0	6	0	0	1	1	.500	0	0--	-	5.60	6.35
1992 New York	AL	3	3	0	0	13.0	68	23	12	12	2	0	0	1	6	0	6	0	0	0	2	.000	0	0-0	0	9.98	8.31
1993 New York	AL	6	6	0	0	31.0	135	32	18	16	4	0	2	1	14	1	26	3	2	1	2	.333	0	0-0	0	4.83	4.65
1994 New York	AL	23	5	1	4	49.1	218	48	24	23	3	1	7	0	29	1	37	5	0	4	1	.800	0	2-2	3	4.38	4.20
1995 New York	AL	27	27	4	0	168.1	719	155	91	88	22	5	9	5	68	1	121	5	2	11	10	.524	1	0-0	0	3.97	4.70
1996 Seattle	AL	35	35	0	0	196.2	885	245	131	117	27	3	8	7	73	4	132	4	1	13	9	.591	0	0-0	0	5.86	5.35
1997 San Diego	NL	32	28	1	1	161.0	693	172	102	93	24	7	4	4	55	2	106	6	2	10	11	.476	0	0-0	0	4.71	5.20
1998 San Diego	NL	39	27	2	3	176.1	743	169	83	77	29	9	3	9	48	2	158	11	1	9	7	.563	1	1-2	3	3.95	3.93
1999 San Diego	NL	33	33	1	0	205.2	892	202	99	94	29	9	6	5	76	6	194	15	2	12	14	.462	0	0-0	0	4.14	4.11
2000 San Diego	NL	11	11	0	0	65.2	292	69	38	36	12	2	1	5	26	1	61	4	0	1	6	.143	0	0-0	0	5.22	4.93
2001 SD-NYY		13	12	1	0	70.1	323	89	46	44	6	2	4	3	21	0	43	3	1	6	5	.545	0	0-0	0	5.15	5.63
2002 New York	AL	20	2	0	11	39.1	193	57	29	24	4	1	1	1	15	3	31	1	0	2	2	.333	0	0-0	0	6.43	5.49
2003 NYY-StL		35	7	0	8	87.2	383	91	50	46	14	4	3	1	32	4	68	3	0	6	4	.600	0	0-0	2	4.49	4.72
2004 San Diego	NL	4	4	0	0	21.1	91	22	15	15	5	0	0	0	8	0	14	1	0	0	3	.000	0	0-0	0	5.18	6.33
2001 San Diego	NL	3	3	0	0	19.0	85	22	9	7	1	1	0	1	3	0	15	1	0	2	1	.667	0	0-0	0	3.68	3.32
2001 New York	AL	10	9	1	0	51.1	238	67	37	37	5	1	4	2	18	0	28	2	1	4	4	.500	0	0-0	0	5.74	6.49
2003 New York	AL	27	1	0	8	49.2	221	57	33	30	6	1	2	0	18	3	36	1	0	1	3	.250	0	0-0	2	4.77	5.44
2003 St Louis	NL	8	6	0	0	38.0	162	34	17	16	8	3	1	1	14	1	32	2	0	5	1	.833	0	0-0	0	4.12	3.79
13 ML YEARS		281	200	10	27	1285.2	5635	1374	738	685	181	43	48	42	471	25	997	61	11	74	76	.493	2	3-4	8	4.71	4.80

Denny Hocking

Bats: B **Throws:** R **Pos:** LF-20; SS-13; PH-10; 2B-8; CF-8; RF-4; 3B-2; PR-2   **Ht:** 5'10" **Wt:** 183 **Born:** 4/2/1970 **Age:** 35

Year Team	Lg	G	AB	H	2B	3B	HR	(Hm	Rd)	TB	R	RBI	RC	TBB	IBB	SO	HBP	SH	SF	SB	CS	SB%	GDP	Avg	OBP	Slg
2004 Iowa*	AAA	39	104	30	12	0	3	(-	-)	51	20	22	16	11	0	20	1	0	1	0	2	.00	1	.288	.359	.490
1993 Minnesota	AL	15	36	5	1	0	0	(0	0)	6	7	0	1	6	0	8	0	0	0	1	0	1.00	1	.139	.262	.167
1994 Minnesota	AL	11	31	10	3	0	0	(0	0)	13	3	2	4	0	0	4	0	0	0	2	0	1.00	1	.323	.323	.419
1995 Minnesota	AL	9	25	5	0	2	0	(0	0)	9	4	3	2	2	1	2	0	1	0	1	0	1.00	1	.200	.259	.360
1996 Minnesota	AL	49	127	25	6	0	1	(0	1)	34	16	10	6	8	0	24	0	1	1	3	3	.50	3	.197	.243	.268
1997 Minnesota	AL	115	253	65	12	4	2	(0	2)	91	28	25	26	18	0	51	1	5	1	3	5	.38	6	.257	.308	.360
1998 Minnesota	AL	110	198	40	6	1	3	(1	2)	57	32	15	14	16	1	44	0	3	2	2	1	.67	2	.202	.259	.288
1999 Minnesota	AL	136	386	103	18	2	7	(2	5)	146	47	41	43	22	1	54	3	4	6	11	7	.61	10	.267	.307	.378
2000 Minnesota	AL	134	373	111	24	4	4	(1	3)	155	52	47	61	48	1	77	0	7	5	7	5	.58	2	.298	.373	.416
2001 Minnesota	AL	112	327	82	16	2	3	(1	2)	111	34	25	35	29	1	67	2	4	1	6	1	.86	7	.251	.315	.339
2002 Minnesota	AL	102	260	65	13	0	2	(1	1)	84	28	25	26	24	0	44	1	4	5	0	2	.00	3	.250	.310	.323
2003 Minnesota	AL	83	188	45	10	2	3	(0	3)	68	22	22	19	15	0	37	0	3	3	0	1	.00	3	.239	.291	.362
2004 Colorado	NL	55	94	19	2	0	0	(0	0)	21	7	4	5	7	0	20	0	5	0	0	1	.00	3	.202	.257	.223
12 ML YEARS		931	2298	575	111	17	25	(6	19)	795	280	219	242	195	5	432	7	37	24	36	26	.58	42	.250	.308	.346

Trevor Hoffman

Pitches: R **Bats:** R **Pos:** RP-55   **Ht:** 6'0" **Wt:** 205 **Born:** 10/13/1967 **Age:** 37

Year Team	Lg	G	GS	CG	GF	IP	BFP	H	R	ER	HR	SH	SF	HB	TBB	IBB	SO	WP	Bk	W	L	Pct	ShO	Sv-Op	Hld	ERC	ERA
1993 Fla-SD	NL	67	0	0	26	90.0	391	80	43	39	10	4	5	1	39	13	79	5	0	4	6	.400	0	5-8	15	3.40	3.90
1994 San Diego	NL	47	0	0	41	56.0	225	39	16	16	4	1	2	0	20	6	68	3	0	4	4	.500	0	20-23	1	2.02	2.57
1995 San Diego	NL	55	0	0	51	53.1	218	48	25	23	10	0	0	0	14	3	52	1	0	7	4	.636	0	31-38	0	3.48	3.88
1996 San Diego	NL	70	0	0	62	88.0	348	50	23	22	6	2	2	2	31	5	111	2	0	9	5	.643	0	42-49	0	1.58	2.25
1997 San Diego	NL	70	0	0	59	81.1	322	59	25	24	9	2	1	0	24	4	111	7	0	6	4	.600	0	37-44	0	2.27	2.66
1998 San Diego	NL	66	0	0	61	73.0	274	41	12	12	2	3	0	1	21	2	86	8	0	4	2	.667	0	53-54	0	1.32	1.48
1999 San Diego	NL	64	0	0	54	67.1	263	48	23	16	5	1	3	0	15	2	73	4	0	2	3	.400	0	40-43	0	1.78	2.14
2000 San Diego	NL	70	0	0	59	72.1	292	61	29	24	7	3	5	0	11	4	85	4	0	4	7	.364	0	43-50	0	2.18	2.99
2001 San Diego	NL	62	0	0	55	60.1	248	48	25	23	10	2	2	1	21	2	63	3	0	3	4	.429	0	43-46	0	3.20	3.43
2002 San Diego	NL	61	0	0	52	59.1	245	52	20	18	2	2	2	1	18	2	69	3	0	2	5	.286	0	38-41	0	2.63	2.73

Year Team	Lg	G	GS	CG	GF	IP	BFP	H	R	ER	HR	SH	SF	HB	TBB	IBB	SO	WP	Bk	W	L	Pct	ShO	Sv-Op	Hld	ERC	ERA
		HOW MUCH HE PITCHED						**WHAT HE GAVE UP**												**THE RESULTS**							
2003 San Diego	NL	9	0	0	7	9.0	36	7	2	2	1	0	0	0	3	0	11	0	0	0	0	-	0	0-0	0	2.76	2.00
2004 San Diego	NL	55	0	0	51	54.2	209	42	14	14	5	2	0	0	8	1	53	2	0	3	3	.500	0	41-45	0	1.92	2.30
1993 Florida	NL	28	0	0	13	35.2	152	24	13	13	5	2	1	0	19	7	26	3	0	2	2	.500	0	2-3	8	2.71	3.28
1993 San Diego	NL	39	0	0	13	54.1	239	56	30	26	5	2	4	1	20	6	53	2	0	2	4	.333	0	3-5	7	3.88	4.31
12 ML YEARS		696	0	0	578	764.2	3070	575	257	233	71	22	22	6	225	44	861	42	0	48	47	.505	0	393-441	16	2.28	2.74

Todd Hollandsworth

Bats: L **Throws:** L **Pos:** RF-32; PH-18; LF-4; 1B-3; DH-3 **Ht:** 6'2" **Wt:** 207 **Born:** 4/20/1973 **Age:** 32

Year Team	Lg	G	AB	H	2B	3B	HR	(Hm	Rd)	TB	R	RBI	RC	TBB	IBB	SO	HBP	SH	SF	SB	CS	SB%	GDP	Avg	OBP	Slg
		BATTING																		**BASERUNNING**				**AVERAGES**		
1995 Los Angeles	NL	41	103	24	2	0	5	(3	2)	41	16	13	13	10	2	29	1	0	1	2	1	.67	1	.233	.304	.398
1996 Los Angeles	NL	149	478	139	26	4	12	(2	10)	209	64	59	76	41	1	93	2	3	2	21	6	.78	2	.291	.348	.437
1997 Los Angeles	NL	106	296	73	20	2	4	(1	3)	109	39	31	28	17	2	60	0	2	2	5	5	.50	8	.247	.286	.368
1998 Los Angeles	NL	55	175	47	6	4	3	(1	2)	70	23	20	21	9	0	42	1	2	0	4	3	.57	2	.269	.308	.400
1999 Los Angeles	NL	92	261	74	12	2	9	(5	4)	117	39	32	41	24	1	61	1	0	1	5	2	.71	2	.284	.345	.448
2000 LA-Col	NL	137	428	115	20	0	19	(13	6)	192	81	47	63	41	3	99	1	0	1	18	7	.72	8	.269	.333	.449
2001 Colorado	NL	33	117	43	15	1	6	(3	3)	78	21	19	30	8	2	20	0	0	0	5	0	1.00	1	.368	.408	.667
2002 Col-Tex		134	430	122	27	1	16	(11	5)	199	55	67	67	40	4	98	1	3	3	8	8	.50	8	.284	.344	.463
2003 Florida	NL	93	228	58	23	3	3	(1	2)	96	32	20	26	22	4	55	0	2	2	2	3	.40	2	.254	.317	.421
2004 Chicago	NL	57	148	47	6	2	8	(3	5)	81	28	22	27	17	3	26	1	1	0	1	1	.50	2	.318	.392	.547
2000 Los Angeles	NL	81	261	61	12	0	8	(6	2)	97	42	24	31	30	2	61	1	0	1	11	4	.73	4	.234	.314	.372
2000 Colorado	NL	56	167	54	8	0	11	(7	4)	95	39	23	32	11	1	38	0	0	0	7	3	.70	4	.323	.365	.569
2002 Colorado	NL	95	298	88	21	1	11	(9	2)	144	39	48	45	26	4	71	1	1	2	7	8	.47	8	.295	.352	.483
2002 Texas	AL	39	132	34	6	0	5	(2	3)	55	16	19	22	14	0	27	0	2	1	1	0	1.00	0	.258	.327	.417
10 ML YEARS		897	2664	742	157	19	85	(43	42)	1192	398	330	392	229	22	583	8	13	12	71	36	.66	36	.279	.336	.447

Matt Holliday

Bats: R **Throws:** R **Pos:** LF-115; PH-10 **Ht:** 6'4" **Wt:** 235 **Born:** 1/15/1980 **Age:** 25

Year Team	Lg	G	AB	H	2B	3B	HR	(Hm	Rd)	TB	R	RBI	RC	TBB	IBB	SO	HBP	SH	SF	SB	CS	SB%	GDP	Avg	OBP	Slg
		BATTING																		**BASERUNNING**				**AVERAGES**		
1998 Rockies	R	32	117	40	4	1	7	(-	-)	61	20	23	26	15	2	21	2	0	4	2	1	.67	0	.342	.413	.521
1999 Asheville	A	121	444	117	28	0	16	(-	-)	193	76	64	68	53	0	116	9	0	5	10	3	.77	8	.264	.350	.435
2000 Salem	A+	123	460	126	28	2	7	(-	-)	179	64	72	59	43	1	74	2	0	5	11	5	.69	12	.274	.335	.389
2001 Salem	A+	72	255	121	16	1	11	(-	-)	172	36	52	79	33	3	42	3	0	5	11	3	.79	10	.475	.530	.675
2002 Carolina	AA	130	463	128	19	2	10	(-	-)	181	79	64	72	67	2	102	7	1	1	16	2	.89	14	.276	.375	.391
2003 Tulsa	AA	135	522	132	28	5	12	(-	-)	206	65	72	63	43	4	74	6	0	7	15	9	.63	9	.253	.313	.395
2004 Co Springs	AAA	6	22	8	5	0	2	(-	-)	19	8	4	7	5	0	6	0	0	0	2	0	1.00	1	.364	.481	.864
2004 Colorado	NL	121	400	116	31	3	14	(10	4)	195	65	57	61	31	0	86	6	1	1	3	3	.50	10	.290	.349	.488

Damon Hollins

Bats: R **Throws:** L **Pos:** LF-6; PH-2; RF-1 **Ht:** 5'11" **Wt:** 180 **Born:** 6/12/1974 **Age:** 31

Year Team	Lg	G	AB	H	2B	3B	HR	(Hm	Rd)	TB	R	RBI	RC	TBB	IBB	SO	HBP	SH	SF	SB	CS	SB%	GDP	Avg	OBP	Slg
		BATTING																		**BASERUNNING**				**AVERAGES**		
1992 Braves	R	49	179	41	12	1	1	(-	-)	58	35	15	23	30	0	22	2	2	0	15	2	.88	3	.229	.346	.324
1993 Danville	A+	62	240	77	15	2	7	(-	-)	117	37	51	42	19	0	30	1	0	3	10	2	.83	5	.321	.369	.488
1994 Durham	A+	131	485	131	28	4	23	(-	-)	228	76	88	73	45	0	115	4	2	3	12	7	.63	9	.270	.335	.470
1995 Greenville	AA	129	466	115	26	2	18	(-	-)	199	64	77	60	44	6	120	4	0	6	6	6	.50	7	.247	.313	.427
1996 Richmond	AAA	42	146	29	9	0	0	(-	-)	38	16	8	9	16	1	37	0	1	0	2	3	.40	2	.199	.278	.260
1997 Richmond	AAA	134	498	132	31	3	20	(-	-)	229	73	63	69	45	4	84	3	6	1	7	2	.78	18	.265	.329	.460
1998 Richmond	AAA	119	436	115	26	3	13	(-	-)	186	61	48	58	45	2	85	0	1	4	10	2	.83	16	.264	.330	.427
1999 Indianapolis	AAA	106	328	86	19	0	9	(-	-)	132	58	43	41	31	1	44	1	1	0	11	2	.85	13	.262	.328	.402
2000 Indianapolis	AAA	87	287	82	16	3	2	(-	-)	110	33	32	37	21	0	35	1	0	2	5	3	.63	5	.286	.334	.383
2001 Edmonton	AAA	69	232	64	8	2	6	(-	-)	94	29	30	30	22	0	44	2	2	1	3	3	.50	8	.276	.342	.405
2001 Richmond	AAA	43	160	42	10	2	5	(-	-)	71	27	24	19	14	2	34	0	0	2	2	2	.50	7	.263	.318	.444
2002 Richmond	AAA	128	498	139	34	1	12	(-	-)	211	66	59	66	35	1	77	1	4	3	10	2	.83	13	.279	.326	.424
2003 Richmond	AAA	91	307	84	23	4	11	(-	-)	148	39	45	44	22	0	62	2	2	2	7	2	.78	10	.274	.324	.482
2004 Richmond	AAA	109	356	107	26	2	20	(-	-)	197	50	67	61	24	2	57	0	2	4	5	3	.63	10	.301	.341	.553
2004 Atlanta	NL	7	22	8	2	0	0	(0	0)	10	3	5	2	0	0	4	0	1	0	0	0	-	0	.364	.364	.455

Joe Horgan

Pitches: L **Bats:** L **Pos:** RP-47 **Ht:** 6'1" **Wt:** 200 **Born:** 6/7/1977 **Age:** 28

Year Team	Lg	G	GS	CG	GF	IP	BFP	H	R	ER	HR	SH	SF	HB	TBB	IBB	SO	WP	Bk	W	L	Pct	ShO	Sv-Op	Hld	ERC	ERA
		HOW MUCH HE PITCHED						**WHAT HE GAVE UP**												**THE RESULTS**							
1996 Burlington	R+	23	0	0	18	34.1	157	37	25	16	1	0	0	4	9	0	48	4	0	1	2	.333	0	7- -	-	3.70	4.19
1997 Watertown	A-	15	4	0	2	38.1	179	48	31	26	4	2	2	1	18	1	31	4	1	0	1	.000	0	0- -	-	5.90	6.10
1997 Kinston	A+	4	2	0	0	17.1	83	23	15	14	1	1	1	1	9	0	9	0	0	1	2	.333	0	0- -	-	6.40	7.27
1998 Columbus	A	22	1	0	9	34.0	134	19	9	9	3	0	0	0	21	0	27	7	0	2	1	.667	0	0- -	-	2.63	2.38
1999 Bakersfield	A+	25	19	1	0	117.1	520	129	76	68	18	2	2	10	43	0	101	5	2	6	10	.375	0	0- -	-	5.29	5.22
2000 San Jose	A+	27	27	1	0	166.1	739	190	104	85	15	5	6	14	66	0	92	14	0	14	10	.583	0	0- -	-	5.25	4.60
2000 Shreveport	AA	1	0	0	1	5.1	22	2	2	2	0	0	0	0	2	1	3	0	0	0	0	-	0	0- -	-	0.71	3.38
2001 Shreveport	AA	31	14	0	3	103.2	438	97	51	42	10	6	7	4	27	1	61	2	0	3	5	.375	0	1- -	-	3.23	3.65
2001 Fresno	AAA	3	1	0	0	7.2	36	11	5	5	1	0	0	0	3	0	5	0	0	0	0	-	0	0- -	-	6.93	5.87
2002 Fresno	AAA	27	4	0	8	57.2	258	65	38	38	8	4	2	4	21	0	37	5	0	2	2	.500	0	0- -	-	5.22	5.93
2002 Shreveport	AA	10	10	1	0	56.0	257	69	35	27	5	4	4	3	20	1	35	0	0	4	3	.571	0	0- -	-	5.29	4.34
2003 Fresno	AAA	55	0	0	23	74.2	333	80	51	47	9	4	4	5	30	1	65	7	1	7	7	.500	0	3- -	-	4.87	5.67
2004 Memphis	AAA	10	0	0	6	9.2	45	14	7	7	3	1	1	0	3	0	8	1	0	1	0	1.000	0	0- -	-	8.11	6.52
2004 Edmonton	AAA	13	0	0	4	17.0	70	15	6	6	2	0	0	2	4	0	11	1	0	1	0	1.000	0	0- -	-	3.41	3.18
2004 Montreal	NL	47	0	0	12	40.0	178	35	18	14	5	1	0	3	22	3	30	0	0	4	1	.800	0	2-3	12	4.27	3.15

J.R. House

Bats: R **Throws:** R **Pos:** C-3; PH-2 **Ht:** 5'10" **Wt:** 202 **Born:** 11/11/1979 **Age:** 25

Year Team	Lg	G	AB	H	2B	3B	HR	(Hm	Rd)	TB	R	RBI	RC	TBB	IBB	SO	HBP	SH	SF	SB	CS	SB%	GDP	Avg	OBP	Slg
1999 Pirates	R	33	113	37	9	3	5	(-	-)	67	13	23	25	11	0	23	2	0	1	1	0	1.00	1	.327	.394	.593
1999 Williamsport	A-	26	100	30	6	0	1	(-	-)	39	11	13	13	9	0	21	0	0	0	0	1	.00	2	.300	.358	.390
1999 Hickory	A	4	11	3	0	0	0	(-	-)	3	1	0	0	0	0	3	0	0	0	0	0	-	0	.273	.273	.273
2000 Hickory	A	110	420	146	29	1	23	(-	-)	246	78	90	94	46	2	91	6	0	6	1	2	.33	7	.348	.414	.586
2001 Altoona	AA	112	426	110	25	1	11	(-	-)	170	51	56	52	37	2	103	5	0	2	1	1	.50	12	.258	.323	.399
2002 Pirates	R	5	16	5	2	0	1	(-	-)	10	3	2	3	3	0	1	0	0	0	0	0	-	0	.313	.421	.625
2002 Altoona	AA	30	91	24	6	0	2	(-	-)	36	9	11	12	13	0	21	0	0	2	0	0	-	4	.264	.349	.396
2003 Pirates	R	20	65	26	9	0	4	(-	-)	47	16	23	20	12	1	5	1	0	4	0	0	-	0	.400	.476	.723
2003 Altoona	AA	20	63	21	6	0	2	(-	-)	33	12	11	10	5	0	11	0	0	0	0	0	-	4	.333	.382	.524
2004 Nashville	AAA	92	309	89	21	1	15	(-	-)	157	38	49	50	23	1	72	4	0	1	1	1	.50	6	.288	.344	.508
2003 Pittsburgh	NL	1	1	1	0	0	0	(0	0)	1	0	0	1	0	0	0	0	0	0	0	0	-	0	1.000	1.000	1.000
2004 Pittsburgh	NL	5	9	1	1	0	0	(0	0)	2	1	0	0	0	0	2	0	0	0	0	0	-	1	.111	.111	.222
2 ML YEARS		6	10	2	1	0	0	(0	0)	3	1	0	1	0	0	2	0	0	0	0	0	-	1	.200	.200	.300

Ben Howard

Pitches: R **Bats:** R **Pos:** RP-31 **Ht:** 6'2" **Wt:** 190 **Born:** 1/15/1979 **Age:** 26

Year Team	Lg	G	GS	CG	GF	IP	BFP	H	R	ER	HR	SH	SF	HB	TBB	IBB	SO	WP	Bk	W	L	Pct	ShO	Sv-Op	Hld	ERC	ERA
2004 Albuquerque*	AAA	23	0	0	4	34.1	151	29	16	14	3	0	0	0	22	2	28	4	0	3	0	1.000	0	1--	-	3.95	3.67
2002 San Diego	NL	3	2	0	0	10.2	58	13	11	11	4	0	1	0	14	1	10	0	0	0	1	.000	0	0-0	0	11.84	9.28
2003 San Diego	NL	6	6	0	0	34.2	148	31	17	14	10	1	0	0	15	1	24	1	0	1	3	.250	0	0-0	0	4.84	3.63
2004 Florida	NL	31	0	0	7	37.2	167	37	23	23	6	1	2	1	21	3	33	3	0	1	1	.500	0	0-0	3	5.06	5.50
3 ML YEARS		40	8	0	7	83.0	373	81	51	48	20	2	3	1	50	5	67	4	0	2	5	.286	0	0-0	3	5.78	5.20

Ryan Howard

Bats: L **Throws:** L **Pos:** PH-11; 1B-8 **Ht:** 6'4" **Wt:** 230 **Born:** 11/19/1979 **Age:** 25

Year Team	Lg	G	AB	H	2B	3B	HR	(Hm	Rd)	TB	R	RBI	RC	TBB	IBB	SO	HBP	SH	SF	SB	CS	SB%	GDP	Avg	OBP	Slg
2001 Batavia	A-	48	169	46	7	3	6	(-	-)	77	26	35	31	30	5	55	2	0	2	0	0	-	1	.272	.384	.456
2002 Lakewood	A	135	493	138	20	6	19	(-	-)	227	56	87	82	66	13	145	5	1	5	5	4	.56	9	.280	.367	.460
2003 Clearwater	A+	130	490	149	32	1	23	(-	-)	252	67	82	88	50	9	151	8	0	5	0	0	-	12	.304	.374	.514
2004 Reading	AA	102	374	111	18	1	37	(-	-)	242	73	102	86	46	6	129	10	0	3	1	2	.33	6	.297	.386	.647
2004 Scrtn/WlksBr	AAA	29	111	30	10	0	9	(-	-)	67	21	29	21	14	1	37	2	0	0	0	0	-	4	.270	.362	.604
2004 Philadelphia	NL	19	39	11	5	0	2	(1	1)	22	5	5	7	2	0	13	1	0	0	0	0	-	2	.282	.333	.564

Bob Howry

Pitches: R **Bats:** L **Pos:** RP-37 **Ht:** 6'5" **Wt:** 220 **Born:** 8/4/1973 **Age:** 31

Year Team	Lg	G	GS	CG	GF	IP	BFP	H	R	ER	HR	SH	SF	HB	TBB	IBB	SO	WP	Bk	W	L	Pct	ShO	Sv-Op	Hld	ERC	ERA
2004 Buffalo*	AAA	18	0	0	5	26.0	108	22	15	15	3	0	0	2	6	0	24	0	0	1	1	.500	0	0--	-	2.94	5.19
1998 Chicago	AL	44	0	0	15	54.1	217	37	20	19	7	2	3	2	19	2	51	2	0	0	3	.000	0	9-11	19	2.50	3.15
1999 Chicago	AL	69	0	0	54	67.2	298	58	34	27	8	3	1	3	38	3	80	3	1	5	3	.625	0	28-34	1	4.11	3.59
2000 Chicago	AL	65	0	0	29	71.0	289	54	26	25	6	2	4	4	29	2	60	2	0	4	4	.333	0	7-12	14	2.96	3.17
2001 Chicago	AL	69	0	0	23	78.2	346	85	45	41	11	4	3	4	30	9	64	6	0	4	5	.444	0	5-11	21	4.78	4.69
2002 CWS-Bos	AL	67	0	0	26	68.2	292	67	37	32	9	4	6	5	21	4	45	2	0	3	5	.375	0	0-1	15	4.00	4.19
2003 Boston	AL	4	0	0	3	4.1	27	11	6	6	1	0	1	0	3	1	4	0	0	0	0	-	0	0-1	0	16.51	12.46
2004 Cleveland	AL	37	0	0	6	42.2	178	37	14	13	5	1	1	2	12	0	39	0	0	4	2	.667	0	0-2	8	3.15	2.74
2002 Chicago	AL	47	0	0	17	50.2	209	45	22	22	7	1	4	3	17	2	31	1	0	2	2	.500	0	0-0	10	3.72	3.91
2002 Boston	AL	20	0	0	9	18.0	83	22	15	10	2	3	2	2	4	2	14	1	0	1	3	.250	0	0-1	5	4.79	5.00
7 ML YEARS		355	0	0	156	387.1	1647	349	178	163	47	16	19	20	152	21	343	15	1	18	22	.450	0	49-72	78	3.77	3.79

Ken Huckaby

Bats: R **Throws:** R **Pos:** C-24; PH-1; PR-1 **Ht:** 6'1" **Wt:** 205 **Born:** 1/27/1971 **Age:** 34

Year Team	Lg	G	AB	H	2B	3B	HR	(Hm	Rd)	TB	R	RBI	RC	TBB	IBB	SO	HBP	SH	SF	SB	CS	SB%	GDP	Avg	OBP	Slg
2004 Oklahoma*	AAA	35	127	35	8	1	2	(-	-)	51	18	20	14	9	0	18	0	2	3	0	0	-	6	.276	.317	.402
2001 Arizona	NL	1	1	0	0	0	0	(0	0)	0	0	0	0	0	0	1	0	0	0	0	0	-	0	.000	.000	.000
2002 Toronto	AL	88	273	67	6	1	3	(1	2)	84	29	22	19	9	1	44	0	1	0	0	0	-	10	.245	.270	.308
2003 Toronto	AL	5	11	2	1	0	0	(0	0)	3	1	2	1	0	0	2	0	0	0	0	0	-	0	.182	.182	.273
2004 Tex-Bal	AL	24	50	7	3	0	0	(0	0)	10	4	0	0	5	0	12	0	0	1	0	0	-	1	.140	.218	.200
2004 Texas	AL	16	38	5	2	0	0	(0	0)	7	3	0	0	5	0	12	0	0	1	0	0	-	1	.132	.233	.184
2004 Baltimore	AL	8	12	2	1	0	0	(0	0)	3	1	0	0	0	0	0	0	0	0	0	0	-	0	.167	.167	.250
4 ML YEARS		118	335	76	10	1	3	(1	2)	97	34	24	20	14	1	59	0	1	0	0	0	-	11	.227	.258	.290

Luke Hudson

Pitches: R **Bats:** R **Pos:** SP-9 **Ht:** 6'3" **Wt:** 195 **Born:** 5/2/1977 **Age:** 28

Year Team	Lg	G	GS	CG	GF	IP	BFP	H	R	ER	HR	SH	SF	HB	TBB	IBB	SO	WP	Bk	W	L	Pct	ShO	Sv-Op	Hld	ERC	ERA
1998 Portland	A-	15	15	0	0	79.2	361	68	46	42	8	4	1	5	51	0	82	8	3	6	6	.333	0	0--	-	4.30	4.74
1999 Asheville	A	21	20	1	1	88.0	372	89	47	42	10	2	2	8	24	0	96	3	3	6	5	.545	0	0--	-	4.16	4.30
2000 Salem	A+	19	19	2	0	110.0	462	101	47	40	9	3	4	10	34	0	80	5	1	5	8	.385	2	0--	-	3.53	3.27
2001 Carolina	AA	29	28	1	0	165.0	729	159	90	77	19	5	4	15	68	0	145	18	1	7	12	.368	0	0--	-	4.34	4.20
2002 Louisville	AAA	30	17	0	6	117.2	518	102	64	59	6	4	4	16	57	1	129	10	1	5	9	.357	0	3--	-	3.80	4.51
2004 Chattanooga	AA	16	16	0	0	86.2	341	71	35	32	9	4	3	8	25	1	91	9	0	7	7	.500	0	0--	-	3.22	3.32
2004 Louisville	AAA	3	3	0	0	19.0	74	15	8	6	2	0	1	0	5	0	17	0	0	2	1	.667	0	0--	-	2.57	2.84

Year Team	Lg	G	GS	CG	GF	IP	BFP	H	R	ER	HR	SH	SF	HB	TBB	IBB	SO	WP	Bk	W	L	Pct	ShO	Sv-Op	Hld	ERC	ERA
2002 Cincinnati	NL	3	0	0	0	6.0	28	5	5	3	1	0	0	0	6	0	7	2	0	0	0	-	0	0-0	1	6.15	4.50
2004 Cincinnati	NL	9	9	0	0	48.1	204	36	16	13	3	2	2	2	25	1	38	5	0	4	2	.667	0	0-0	0	3.01	2.42
2 ML YEARS		12	9	0	0	54.1	232	41	21	16	4	2	2	2	31	1	45	7	0	4	2	.667	0	0-0	1	3.32	2.65

Orlando Hudson

Bats: B **Throws:** R **Pos:** 2B-133; PH-4   **Ht:** 6'0" **Wt:** 185 **Born:** 12/12/1977 **Age:** 27

								BATTING													BASERUNNING				AVERAGES		
Year Team	Lg	G	AB	H	2B	3B	HR	(Hm	Rd)	TB	R	RBI	RC	TBB	IBB	SO	HBP	SH	SF	SB	CS	SB%	GDP	Avg	OBP	Slg
2002 Toronto	AL	54	192	53	10	5	4	(2	2)	85	20	23	30	11	0	27	2	0	2	0	1	.00	6	.276	.319	.443
2003 Toronto	AL	142	474	127	21	6	9	(5	4)	187	54	57	64	39	1	87	5	0	3	5	4	.56	13	.268	.328	.395
2004 Toronto	AL	135	489	132	32	7	12	(5	7)	214	73	58	71	51	0	98	4	3	4	7	3	.70	12	.270	.341	.438
3 ML YEARS		331	1155	312	63	18	25	(12	13)	486	147	138	165	101	1	212	11	3	9	12	8	.60	31	.270	.332	.421

Tim Hudson

Pitches: R **Bats:** R **Pos:** SP-27   **Ht:** 6'1" **Wt:** 164 **Born:** 7/14/1975 **Age:** 29

								HOW MUCH HE PITCHED			WHAT HE GAVE UP								THE RESULTS							
Year Team	Lg	G	GS	CG	GF	IP	BFP	H	R	ER	HR	SH	SF	HB	TBB	IBB	SO	WP	Bk	W	L	Pct	ShO	Sv-Op	Hld	ERC	ERA
2004 Sacramento*	AAA	1	1	0	0	3.0	15	2	2	2	0	0	0	1	2	0	3	2	0	0	0	-	0	0- -		3.35	6.00
1999 Oakland	AL	21	21	1	0	136.1	580	121	56	49	8	1	2	4	62	2	132	6	0	11	2	.846	0	0-0	0	3.50	3.23
2000 Oakland	AL	32	32	2	0	202.1	847	169	100	93	24	5	7	7	82	5	169	7	0	20	6	.769	2	0-0	0	3.43	4.14
2001 Oakland	AL	35	35	3	0	235.0	980	216	100	88	20	12	8	6	71	5	181	9	1	18	9	.667	0	0-0	0	3.22	3.37
2002 Oakland	AL	34	34	4	0	238.1	983	237	87	79	19	6	5	8	62	9	152	7	1	15	9	.625	2	0-0	0	3.51	2.98
2003 Oakland	AL	34	34	3	0	240.0	967	197	84	72	15	11	2	10	61	9	162	6	0	16	7	.696	2	0-0	0	2.47	2.70
2004 Oakland	AL	27	27	3	0	188.2	793	194	82	74	8	7	4	12	44	3	103	4	1	12	6	.667	2	0-0	0	3.44	3.53
6 ML YEARS		183	183	16	0	1240.2	5150	1134	509	455	94	42	28	47	382	33	899	39	3	92	39	.702	8	0-0	0	3.22	3.30

Aubrey Huff

Bats: L **Throws:** R **Pos:** 3B-87; 1B-38; DH-34; LF-8; PH-2; RF-1   **Ht:** 6'4" **Wt:** 231 **Born:** 12/20/1976 **Age:** 28

								BATTING													BASERUNNING				AVERAGES		
Year Team	Lg	G	AB	H	2B	3B	HR	(Hm	Rd)	TB	R	RBI	RC	TBB	IBB	SO	HBP	SH	SF	SB	CS	SB%	GDP	Avg	OBP	Slg
2000 Tampa Bay	AL	39	122	35	7	0	4	(3	1)	54	12	14	15	5	1	18	1	0	1	0	0	-	6	.287	.318	.443
2001 Tampa Bay	AL	111	411	102	25	1	8	(5	3)	153	42	45	37	23	2	72	0	0	0	1	3	.25	18	.248	.288	.372
2002 Tampa Bay	AL	113	454	142	25	0	23	(17	6)	236	67	59	66	37	7	55	1	0	2	4	1	.80	17	.313	.364	.520
2003 Tampa Bay	AL	162	636	198	47	3	34	(15	19)	353	91	107	112	53	17	80	8	0	9	2	3	.40	19	.311	.367	.555
2004 Tampa Bay	AL	157	600	178	27	2	29	(16	13)	296	92	104	96	56	6	74	6	0	5	5	1	.83	10	.297	.360	.493
5 ML YEARS		582	2223	655	131	6	98	(56	42)	1092	304	329	326	174	33	299	16	0	17	12	8	.60	70	.295	.348	.491

Travis Hughes

Pitches: R **Bats:** R **Pos:** RP-2   **Ht:** 6'5" **Wt:** 240 **Born:** 5/25/1978 **Age:** 27

								HOW MUCH HE PITCHED			WHAT HE GAVE UP								THE RESULTS							
Year Team	Lg	G	GS	CG	GF	IP	BFP	H	R	ER	HR	SH	SF	HB	TBB	IBB	SO	WP	Bk	W	L	Pct	ShO	Sv-Op	Hld	ERC	ERA
1998 Pulaski	R+	22	3	0	17	41.2	188	30	25	18	2	0	4	4	25	1	48	8	3	2	6	.250	0	2- -		3.11	3.89
1999 Savannah	A	30	23	1	5	157.0	646	127	60	49	9	3	3	11	54	0	150	9	2	11	7	.611	0	2- -		2.85	2.81
2000 Charlotte	A+	39	14	19	19	126.1	553	122	76	62	9	6	1	12	54	3	96	11	0	9	9	.500	0	9- -		4.13	4.42
2001 Tulsa	AA	47	5	0	29	87.1	393	91	52	45	8	3	4	4	45	2	86	2	1	5	7	.417	0	8- -		4.86	4.64
2002 Tulsa	AA	26	26	1	0	143.1	637	139	68	56	11	1	2	7	82	0	137	3	0	9	7	.563	1	0- -		4.65	3.52
2003 Frisco	AA	24	10	1	3	74.0	330	81	47	41	6	2	5	5	26	1	58	0	0	4	8	.333	1	0- -		4.47	4.99
2003 Oklahoma	AAA	11	11	0	0	57.2	278	79	41	35	4	3	3	5	27	0	36	1	0	1	3	.250	0	0- -		6.66	5.46
2004 Frisco	AA	40	0	0	19	62.2	282	63	34	26	4	0	1	1	33	5	66	6	1	3	6	.333	0	7- -		4.20	3.73
2004 Oklahoma	AAA	13	0	0	2	25.2	107	21	15	15	2	0	0	0	9	0	24	2	0	1	2	.333	0	0- -		2.72	5.26
2004 Texas	AL	2	0	0	1	1.1	10	4	2	2	0	0	0	0	2	0	4	0	0	0	0	-	0	0-0	0	22.07	13.50

Justin Huisman

Pitches: R **Bats:** R **Pos:** RP-14   **Ht:** 6'1" **Wt:** 195 **Born:** 4/16/1979 **Age:** 26

								HOW MUCH HE PITCHED			WHAT HE GAVE UP								THE RESULTS							
Year Team	Lg	G	GS	CG	GF	IP	BFP	H	R	ER	HR	SH	SF	HB	TBB	IBB	SO	WP	Bk	W	L	Pct	ShO	Sv-Op	Hld	ERC	ERA
2000 Portland	A-	16	3	0	6	43.2	180	31	16	9	1	2	2	1	17	1	32	0	0	3	6	.333	0	1- -		2.05	1.85
2001 Asheville	A	55	0	0	51	58.1	230	35	20	11	1	1	2	3	14	2	53	4	0	0	3	.000	0	30- -		1.31	1.70
2002 Salem	A+	41	0	0	37	51.2	212	47	11	9	0	5	1	4	14	3	24	1	0	3	4	.429	0	20- -		2.69	1.57
2002 Carolina	AA	18	0	0	10	24.1	116	30	22	18	4	0	0	1	12	3	10	2	0	0	3	.000	0	2- -		6.14	6.66
2003 Tulsa	AA	57	0	0	52	61.2	250	55	22	12	1	4	0	4	7	1	46	2	1	7	2	.778	0	26- -		2.12	1.75
2004 Omaha	AAA	32	0	0	21	42.1	197	49	23	17	3	0	0	1	18	2	37	2	0	4	2	.667	0	6- -		4.69	3.61
2004 Kansas City	AL	14	0	0	4	25.0	116	36	20	19	3	0	0	1	8	3	13	0	0	0	0	-	0	1-1	1	6.55	6.84

Tim Hummel

Bats: R **Throws:** R **Pos:** 3B-32; PH-18; 1B-13; PR-3; 2B-1; SS-1   **Ht:** 6'2" **Wt:** 195 **Born:** 11/18/1978 **Age:** 26

								BATTING													BASERUNNING				AVERAGES		
Year Team	Lg	G	AB	H	2B	3B	HR	(Hm	Rd)	TB	R	RBI	RC	TBB	IBB	SO	HBP	SH	SF	SB	CS	SB%	GDP	Avg	OBP	Slg
2000 Burlington	A	33	144	47	9	1	1	(-	-)	61	22	21	27	21	0	20	1	0	2	8	3	.73	2	.326	.411	.424
2000 Winstn-Salm	A+	27	98	32	7	0	1	(-	-)	42	15	9	17	13	1	12	2	0	9	1	1	.50	4	.327	.385	.429
2001 Birmingham	AA	134	524	152	33	6	7	(-	-)	218	83	63	83	62	2	69	5	8	10	14	3	.82	12	.290	.364	.416
2002 Charlotte	AAA	142	523	136	33	0	4	(-	-)	181	55	41	64	51	0	95	10	10	9	6	5	.55	7	.260	.332	.346
2003 Charlotte	AAA	128	476	135	25	3	15	(-	-)	211	72	80	73	46	2	83	5	10	4	9	3	.75	10	.284	.350	.443
2004 Louisville	AAA	42	152	44	13	0	2	(-	-)	63	18	20	31	12	1	27	2	0	2	2	0	1.00	4	.289	.345	.414

Year Team	Lg	G	AB	H	2B	3B	HR	(Hm Rd)	TB	R	RBI	RC	TBB	IBB	SO	HBP	SH	SF	SB	CS	SB%	GDP	Avg	OBP	Slg
2003 Cincinnati	NL	26	84	19	5	0	2	(0 2)	30	9	10	9	8	0	13	0	1	1	0	0	-	1	.226	.290	.357
2004 Cincinnati	NL	56	110	24	4	0	1	(1 0)	31	10	7	8	8	2	17	2	4	1	1	0	1.00	2	.218	.281	.282
2 ML YEARS		82	194	43	9	0	3	(1 2)	61	19	17	17	16	2	30	2	5	2	1	0	1.00	3	.222	.285	.314

Todd Hundley

Bats: B Throws: R Pos: PH   Ht: 5'11" Wt: 200 Born: 5/27/1969 Age: 36

Year Team	Lg	G	AB	H	2B	3B	HR	(Hm Rd)	TB	R	RBI	RC	TBB	IBB	SO	HBP	SH	SF	SB	CS	SB%	GDP	Avg	OBP	Slg
1990 New York	NL	36	67	14	6	0	0	(0 0)	20	8	2	5	6	0	18	0	1	0	0	0	-	1	.209	.274	.299
1991 New York	NL	21	60	8	0	1	1	(1 0)	13	5	7	1	6	0	14	1	1	1	0	0	-	3	.133	.221	.217
1992 New York	NL	123	358	75	17	0	7	(2 5)	113	32	32	27	19	4	76	4	7	2	3	0	1.00	8	.209	.256	.316
1993 New York	NL	130	417	95	17	2	11	(5 6)	149	40	53	37	23	7	62	2	2	4	1	1	.50	10	.228	.269	.357
1994 New York	NL	91	291	69	10	1	16	(8 8)	129	45	42	39	25	4	73	3	3	1	2	1	.67	3	.237	.303	.443
1995 New York	NL	90	275	77	11	0	15	(6 9)	133	39	51	52	42	5	64	5	1	3	1	0	1.00	4	.280	.382	.484
1996 New York	NL	153	540	140	32	1	41	(20 21)	297	85	112	102	79	15	146	3	0	2	1	3	.25	9	.259	.356	.550
1997 New York	NL	132	417	114	21	2	30	(14 16)	229	78	86	87	83	16	116	3	0	5	2	3	.40	10	.273	.394	.549
1998 New York	NL	53	124	20	4	0	3	(1 2)	33	8	12	9	16	0	55	1	0	1	1	1	.50	0	.161	.261	.266
1999 Los Angeles	NL	114	376	78	14	0	24	(10 14)	164	49	55	50	44	3	113	4	1	3	3	0	1.00	5	.207	.295	.436
2000 Los Angeles	NL	90	299	85	16	0	24	(10 14)	173	49	70	63	45	6	69	2	1	6	0	1	.00	5	.284	.375	.579
2001 Chicago	NL	79	246	46	10	0	12	(4 8)	92	23	31	23	25	0	89	3	0	2	0	0	-	7	.187	.268	.374
2002 Chicago	NL	92	266	56	8	0	16	(8 8)	112	32	35	28	32	3	80	3	1	1	0	0	-	6	.211	.301	.421
2003 Los Angeles	NL	21	33	6	1	0	2	(1 1)	13	2	11	7	8	0	13	0	0	0	1	0	.00	0	.182	.341	.394
14 ML YEARS		1225	3769	883	167	7	202	(90 112)	1670	495	599	530	453	63	988	34	18	31	14	11	.56	71	.234	.320	.443

Torii Hunter

Bats: R Throws: R Pos: CF-126; DH-10; PH-2; PR-1   Ht: 6'2" Wt: 205 Born: 7/18/1975 Age: 29

Year Team	Lg	G	AB	H	2B	3B	HR	(Hm Rd)	TB	R	RBI	RC	TBB	IBB	SO	HBP	SH	SF	SB	CS	SB%	GDP	Avg	OBP	Slg
1997 Minnesota	AL	1	0	0	0	0	0	(0 0)	0	0	0	0	0	0	0	0	0	0	0	0	-	0	-	-	-
1998 Minnesota	AL	6	17	4	1	0	0	(0 0)	5	0	2	1	2	0	6	0	0	0	0	1	.00	1	.235	.316	.294
1999 Minnesota	AL	135	384	98	17	2	9	(2 7)	146	52	35	44	26	1	72	6	1	5	10	6	.63	9	.255	.309	.380
2000 Minnesota	AL	99	336	94	14	7	5	(4 1)	137	44	44	39	18	2	68	2	0	2	4	3	.57	13	.280	.318	.408
2001 Minnesota	AL	148	564	147	32	5	27	(13 14)	270	82	92	79	29	0	125	8	1	1	9	6	.60	12	.261	.306	.479
2002 Minnesota	AL	148	561	162	37	4	29	(13 16)	294	89	94	85	35	3	118	5	0	3	23	8	.74	17	.289	.334	.524
2003 Minnesota	AL	154	581	145	31	4	26	(12 14)	262	83	102	76	50	7	106	5	0	6	6	7	.46	15	.250	.312	.451
2004 Minnesota	AL	138	520	141	37	0	23	(9 14)	247	79	81	69	40	4	101	7	0	2	21	7	.75	23	.271	.330	.475
8 ML YEARS		829	2963	791	169	22	119	(53 66)	1361	429	450	393	200	17	596	33	2	19	73	38	.66	90	.267	.319	.459

Adam Hyzdu

Bats: R Throws: R Pos: LF-11; RF-4; PR-4; PH-3; DH-2   Ht: 6'2" Wt: 205 Born: 12/6/1971 Age: 33

Year Team	Lg	G	AB	H	2B	3B	HR	(Hm Rd)	TB	R	RBI	RC	TBB	IBB	SO	HBP	SH	SF	SB	CS	SB%	GDP	Avg	OBP	Slg
2004 Pawtucket*	AAA	129	465	140	33	2	29	(- -)	264	92	79	103	84	1	106	7	1	4	8	4	.67	12	.301	.413	.568
2000 Pittsburgh	NL	12	18	7	2	0	1	(0 1)	12	2	4	4	0	0	4	0	0	0	0	0	-	0	.389	.389	.667
2001 Pittsburgh	NL	51	72	15	1	0	5	(0 5)	31	7	9	8	4	0	18	1	0	0	0	1	.00	1	.208	.260	.431
2002 Pittsburgh	NL	59	155	36	6	0	11	(6 5)	75	24	34	27	21	0	44	1	0	2	0	0	-	1	.232	.324	.484
2003 Pittsburgh	NL	51	63	13	5	0	1	(0 1)	21	16	8	6	10	0	21	1	0	1	0	0	-	2	.206	.320	.333
2004 Boston	AL	17	10	3	2	0	1	(0 1)	8	3	2	2	1	0	2	0	0	0	0	0	-	0	.300	.364	.800
5 ML YEARS		190	318	74	16	0	19	(6 13)	147	52	57	47	36	0	89	3	0	3	0	1	.00	4	.233	.314	.462

Raul Ibanez

Bats: L Throws: R Pos: LF-110; 1B-10; PH-4; RF-3; DH-2   Ht: 6'2" Wt: 200 Born: 6/2/1972 Age: 33

Year Team	Lg	G	AB	H	2B	3B	HR	(Hm Rd)	TB	R	RBI	RC	TBB	IBB	SO	HBP	SH	SF	SB	CS	SB%	GDP	Avg	OBP	Slg
2004 Tacoma*	AAA	4	17	4	1	0	0	(- -)	5	2	1	1	0	0	6	0	0	0	0	0	-	0	.235	.235	.294
1996 Seattle	AL	4	5	0	0	0	0	(0 0)	0	0	0	0	0	0	1	1	0	0	0	0	-	0	.000	.167	.000
1997 Seattle	AL	11	26	4	1	1	1	(1 0)	9	3	4	1	0	0	6	0	0	0	0	0	-	0	.154	.154	.346
1998 Seattle	AL	37	98	25	7	1	2	(1 1)	40	12	12	10	5	0	22	0	0	4	0	0	-	4	.255	.291	.408
1999 Seattle	AL	87	209	54	7	0	9	(3 6)	88	23	27	28	17	1	32	0	0	1	5	1	.83	4	.258	.313	.421
2000 Seattle	AL	92	140	32	8	0	2	(2 0)	46	21	15	15	14	1	25	1	0	1	2	0	1.00	1	.229	.301	.329
2001 Kansas City	AL	104	279	78	11	5	13	(5 8)	138	44	54	46	32	2	51	0	0	1	0	2	.00	6	.280	.353	.495
2002 Kansas City	AL	137	497	146	37	6	24	(14 10)	267	70	103	89	40	5	76	2	1	4	5	3	.63	11	.294	.346	.537
2003 Kansas City	AL	157	608	179	33	5	18	(8 10)	276	95	90	91	49	5	81	3	1	10	8	4	.67	10	.294	.345	.454
2004 Seattle	AL	123	481	146	31	1	16	(9 7)	227	67	62	67	36	5	72	3	0	4	1	2	.33	10	.304	.353	.472
9 ML YEARS		752	2343	664	134	19	85	(43 42)	1091	335	367	347	193	19	366	10	2	21	21	12	.64	46	.283	.338	.466

Omar Infante

Bats: R Throws: R Pos: 2B-105; SS-23; 3B-10; CF-5; PH-4; PR-2   Ht: 5'9" Wt: 150 Born: 12/26/1981 Age: 23

Year Team	Lg	G	AB	H	2B	3B	HR	(Hm Rd)	TB	R	RBI	RC	TBB	IBB	SO	HBP	SH	SF	SB	CS	SB%	GDP	Avg	OBP	Slg
2002 Detroit	AL	18	72	24	3	0	1	(0 1)	30	4	6	12	3	0	10	0	0	0	1	0	.00	0	.333	.360	.417
2003 Detroit	AL	69	221	49	6	1	0	(0 0)	57	24	8	16	18	0	37	0	3	2	6	3	.67	1	.222	.278	.258
2004 Detroit	AL	142	503	133	27	9	16	(7 9)	226	69	55	69	40	3	112	1	7	5	13	7	.65	4	.264	.317	.449
3 ML YEARS		229	796	206	36	10	17	(7 10)	313	97	69	97	61	3	159	1	10	7	19	11	.63	5	.259	.310	.393

Brandon Inge

Bats: R **Throws:** R **Pos:** 3B-73; C-39; CF-19; PR-9; LF-7; PH-4; RF-2   **Ht:** 5'11" **Wt:** 189 **Born:** 5/19/1977 **Age:** 28

							BATTING												BASERUNNING				AVERAGES		
Year Team	Lg	G	AB	H	2B	3B	HR	(Hm | Rd)	TB	R	RBI	RC	TBB	IBB	SO	HBP	SH	SF	SB	CS	SB%	GDP	Avg	OBP	Slg
2001 Detroit	AL	79	189	34	11	0	0	(0 | 0)	45	13	15	6	9	0	41	0	2	2	1	4	.20	2	.180	.215	.238
2002 Detroit	AL	95	321	65	15	3	7	(3 | 4)	107	27	24	24	24	0	101	4	1	1	1	3	.25	7	.202	.266	.333
2003 Detroit	AL	104	330	67	15	3	8	(4 | 4)	112	32	30	23	24	0	79	5	4	3	4	4	.50	9	.203	.265	.339
2004 Detroit	AL	131	408	117	15	7	13	(9 | 4)	185	43	64	63	32	0	72	4	8	6	5	4	.56	4	.287	.340	.453
4 ML YEARS		409	1248	283	56	13	28	(16 | 12)	449	115	133	116	89	0	293	13	15	12	11	15	.42	22	.227	.283	.360

Kazuhisa Ishii

Pitches: L **Bats:** L **Pos:** SP-31   **Ht:** 6'0" **Wt:** 190 **Born:** 9/9/1973 **Age:** 31

		HOW MUCH HE PITCHED						WHAT HE GAVE UP											THE RESULTS						
Year Team	Lg	G	GS	CG	GF	IP	BFP	H	R	ER	HR	SH	SF	HB	TBB	IBB	SO	WP	Bk	W	L	Pct	ShO	Sv-Op	Hld	ERC	ERA
2002 Los Angeles	NL	28	28	0	0	154.0	692	137	82	73	20	6	5	4	106	3	143	7	0	14	10	.583	0	0-0	0	4.90	4.27
2003 Los Angeles	NL	27	27	0	0	147.0	656	129	72	63	16	6	2	6	101	4	140	10	2	9	7	.563	0	0-0	0	4.75	3.86
2004 Los Angeles	NL	31	31	2	0	172.0	749	155	97	90	21	10	7	4	98	2	99	3	0	13	8	.619	2	0-0	0	4.47	4.71
3 ML YEARS		86	86	2	0	473.0	2097	421	251	226	57	22	14	14	305	9	382	20	2	36	25	.590	2	0-0	0	4.70	4.30

Jason Isringhausen

Pitches: R **Bats:** R **Pos:** RP-74   **Ht:** 6'3" **Wt:** 230 **Born:** 9/7/1972 **Age:** 32

		HOW MUCH HE PITCHED						WHAT HE GAVE UP											THE RESULTS						
Year Team	Lg	G	GS	CG	GF	IP	BFP	H	R	ER	HR	SH	SF	HB	TBB	IBB	SO	WP	Bk	W	L	Pct	ShO	Sv-Op	Hld	ERC	ERA
1995 New York	NL	14	14	1	0	93.0	385	88	29	29	6	3	3	2	31	2	55	4	1	9	2	.818	0	0-0	0	3.40	2.81
1996 New York	NL	27	27	2	0	171.2	766	190	103	91	13	7	9	8	73	5	114	14	0	6	14	.300	1	0-0	0	4.75	4.77
1997 New York	NL	6	6	0	0	29.2	145	40	27	25	3	1	2	1	22	0	25	3	0	2	2	.500	0	0-0	0	7.99	7.58
1999 NYM-Oak		33	5	0	20	64.2	286	64	35	34	9	0	1	2	34	4	51	5	0	1	4	.200	0	9-9	0	4.86	4.73
2000 Oakland	AL	66	0	0	57	69.0	304	67	34	29	6	2	1	3	32	5	57	5	1	6	4	.600	0	33-40	0	4.09	3.78
2001 Oakland	AL	65	0	0	54	71.1	293	54	24	21	5	3	1	0	23	5	74	2	0	4	3	.571	0	34-43	0	2.18	2.65
2002 St Louis	NL	60	0	0	51	65.1	257	46	22	18	0	4	3	1	18	1	68	0	0	3	2	.600	0	32-37	1	1.61	2.48
2003 St Louis	NL	40	0	0	31	42.0	174	31	14	11	2	1	0	0	18	1	41	6	0	0	1	.000	0	22-25	1	2.40	2.36
2004 St Louis	NL	74	0	0	66	75.1	308	55	27	24	5	6	1	2	23	4	71	1	0	4	2	.667	0	47-54	0	2.09	2.87
1999 New York	NL	13	5	0	2	39.1	179	43	29	28	7	0	1	1	22	2	31	3	0	1	3	.250	0	1-1	0	5.93	6.41
1999 Oakland	AL	20	0	0	18	25.1	107	21	6	6	2	0	0	1	12	2	20	2	0	0	1	.000	0	8-8	0	3.33	2.13
9 ML YEARS		385	52	3	279	682.0	2918	635	315	282	49	27	21	19	274	27	556	40	2	35	34	.507	1	177-208	1	3.54	3.72

Cesar Izturis

Bats: B **Throws:** R **Pos:** SS-159   **Ht:** 5'9" **Wt:** 175 **Born:** 2/10/1980 **Age:** 25

							BATTING												BASERUNNING				AVERAGES		
Year Team	Lg	G	AB	H	2B	3B	HR	(Hm	Rd)	TB	R	RBI	RC	TBB	IBB	SO	HBP	SH	SF	SB	CS	SB%	GDP	Avg	OBP	Slg
2001 Toronto	AL	46	134	36	6	2	2	(1	1)	52	19	9	16	2	0	15	0	4	0	8	1	.89	0	.269	.279	.388
2002 Los Angeles	NL	135	439	102	24	2	1	(0	1)	133	43	31	26	14	1	39	0	10	5	7	7	.50	12	.232	.253	.303
2003 Los Angeles	NL	158	558	140	21	6	1	(0	1)	176	47	40	42	25	8	70	0	7	3	10	5	.67	9	.251	.282	.315
2004 Los Angeles	NL	159	670	193	32	9	4	(1	3)	255	90	62	95	43	2	70	0	12	3	25	9	.74	6	.288	.330	.381
4 ML YEARS		498	1801	471	83	19	8	(2	6)	616	199	142	179	84	11	194	0	33	11	50	22	.69	27	.262	.293	.342

Maicer Izturis

Bats: B **Throws:** R **Pos:** SS-23; 2B-10; PH-1   **Ht:** 5'8" **Wt:** 155 **Born:** 9/12/1980 **Age:** 24

							BATTING												BASERUNNING				AVERAGES		
Year Team	Lg	G	AB	H	2B	3B	HR	(Hm	Rd)	TB	R	RBI	RC	TBB	IBB	SO	HBP	SH	SF	SB	CS	SB%	GDP	Avg	OBP	Slg
1998 Burlington	R+	55	217	63	8	2	2	(-	-)	81	33	33	28	17	0	32	0	2	0	16	6	.73	4	.290	.342	.373
1999 Columbus	A	57	220	66	5	3	4	(-	-)	89	46	23	35	20	0	28	1	1	3	14	2	.88	2	.300	.357	.405
2000 Columbus	A	10	29	8	1	0	0	(-	-)	9	4	1	3	3	0	3	0	0	0	0	0	-	1	.276	.344	.310
2001 Kinston	A+	114	433	104	16	6	1	(-	-)	135	47	39	43	31	1	81	8	10	4	32	9	.78	8	.240	.300	.312
2002 Kinston	A+	58	233	61	13	1	1	(-	-)	79	28	30	29	24	0	26	1	3	1	24	6	.80	2	.262	.332	.339
2002 Akron	AA	67	253	70	12	7	0	(-	-)	96	34	32	30	17	0	28	3	5	3	8	4	.67	10	.277	.326	.379
2003 Akron	AA	54	218	61	11	5	1	(-	-)	85	31	20	31	24	1	23	1	6	2	14	6	.70	4	.280	.351	.390
2003 Buffalo	AAA	85	301	79	16	4	2	(-	-)	109	43	29	32	24	0	28	1	9	2	14	6	.70	14	.262	.317	.362
2004 Edmonton	AAA	99	376	127	19	2	3	(-	-)	159	65	36	69	57	1	30	4	4	2	14	12	.54	12	.338	.428	.423
2004 Montreal	NL	32	107	22	5	2	1	(1	0)	34	10	4	8	10	1	20	2	2	0	4	0	1.00	1	.206	.286	.318

Damian Jackson

Bats: R **Throws:** R **Pos:** PH-11; 2B-6; RF-3; PR-2; SS-1; LF-1; CF-1; DH-1   **Ht:** 5'11" **Wt:** 185 **Born:** 8/16/1973 **Age:** 31

							BATTING												BASERUNNING				AVERAGES		
Year Team	Lg	G	AB	H	2B	3B	HR	(Hm	Rd)	TB	R	RBI	RC	TBB	IBB	SO	HBP	SH	SF	SB	CS	SB%	GDP	Avg	OBP	Slg
2004 Iowa*	AAA	27	93	25	6	3	3	(-	-)	46	17	12	16	11	1	20	0	1	0	3	1	.75	0	.269	.346	.495
2004 Omaha*	AAA	48	169	52	13	1	8	(-	-)	91	46	27	39	30	1	36	6	2	2	12	2	.86	3	.308	.425	.538
1996 Cleveland	AL	5	10	3	2	0	0	(0	0)	5	2	1	2	1	0	4	0	0	0	0	0	-	0	.300	.364	.500
1997 Cle-Cin		20	36	7	2	1	1	(0	1)	14	8	2	4	4	1	8	1	1	0	2	1	.67	0	.194	.293	.389
1998 Cincinnati	NL	13	38	12	5	0	0	(0	0)	17	4	7	7	6	0	4	0	0	1	2	0	1.00	1	.316	.400	.447
1999 San Diego	NL	133	388	87	20	2	9	(6	3)	138	56	39	50	53	3	105	3	0	3	34	10	.77	2	.224	.320	.356
2000 San Diego	NL	138	470	120	27	6	6	(5	1)	177	68	37	66	62	2	108	3	4	2	28	6	.82	7	.255	.345	.377
2001 San Diego	NL	122	440	106	21	6	4	(1	3)	151	67	38	51	44	2	128	6	2	2	23	6	.79	6	.241	.316	.343
2002 Detroit	AL	81	245	63	20	1	1	(0	1)	88	31	25	32	21	0	36	3	2	3	12	3	.80	3	.257	.320	.359
2003 Boston	AL	109	161	42	7	0	1	(0	1)	52	34	13	12	8	0	28	0	2	1	16	8	.67	4	.261	.294	.323
2004 ChC-KC		21	30	3	2	0	1	(1	0)	8	2	3	1	4	2	12	0	0	0	0	0	-	0	.100	.206	.267
1997 Cleveland	AL	8	9	1	0	0	0	(0	0)	1	0	0	0	1	0	1	1	0	0	1	0	1.00	0	.111	.200	.111
1997 Cincinnati	NL	12	27	6	2	1	1	(0	1)	13	6	2	4	4	1	7	0	1	0	1	1	.50	0	.222	.323	.481

			BATTING																BASERUNNING				AVERAGES		
Year Team	Lg	G	AB	H	2B	3B	HR	(Hm Rd)	TB	R	RBI	RC	TBB	IBB	SO	HBP	SH	SF	SB	CS	SB%	GDP	Avg	OBP	Slg
2004 Chicago	NL	7	15	1	0	0	1	(1 0)	4	1	1	0	3	2	6	0	0	0	0	0	-	0	.067	.222	.267
2004 Kansas City	AL	14	15	2	2	0	0	(0 0)	4	1	2	1	1	0	6	0	0	0	0	0	-	0	.133	.188	.267
9 ML YEARS		642	1818	443	106	16	23	(13 10)	650	272	165	225	203	10	433	16	11	13	117	34	.77	23	.244	.323	.358

Edwin Jackson

Pitches: R Bats: R Pos: SP-5; RP-3   Ht: 6'3" Wt: 190 Born: 9/9/1983 Age: 21

		HOW MUCH HE PITCHED						WHAT HE GAVE UP												THE RESULTS						
Year Team	Lg	G	GS	CG	GF	IP	BFP	H	R	ER	HR	SH	SF	HB	TBB	IBB	SO	WP	Bk	W	L	Pct	ShO	Sv-Op	Hld	ERC	ERA
2001 Dodgers	R	12	2	0	1	22.0	106	14	12	6	1	3	0	3	19	0	23	2	0	2	1	.667	0	0- -	-	3.66	2.45
2002 Sth Georgia	A	19	19	0	0	104.2	428	79	34	23	2	2	2	6	33	0	85	3	1	5	2	.714	0	0- -	-	2.17	1.98
2003 Jacksonville	AA	27	27	0	0	148.1	619	121	68	61	9	4	3	8	53	0	157	9	1	7	7	.500	0	0- -	-	2.85	3.70
2004 Las Vegas	AAA	19	19	0	0	90.2	410	90	65	59	4	9	6	8	55	1	70	10	0	6	4	.600	0	0- -	-	4.81	5.86
2003 Los Angeles	NL	4	3	0	0	22.0	91	17	6	6	2	1	1	1	11	1	19	3	0	2	1	.667	0	0-0	-	3.36	2.45
2004 Los Angeles	NL	8	5	0	1	24.2	113	31	20	20	7	1	0	0	11	1	16	0	0	2	1	.667	0	0-0	-	7.21	7.30
2 ML YEARS		12	8	0	1	46.2	204	48	26	26	9	2	1	1	22	2	35	3	0	4	2	.667	0	0-0	0	5.30	5.01

Mike Jackson

Pitches: R Bats: R Pos: RP-45   Ht: 6'2" Wt: 215 Born: 12/22/1964 Age: 40

		HOW MUCH HE PITCHED						WHAT HE GAVE UP												THE RESULTS						
Year Team	Lg	G	GS	CG	GF	IP	BFP	H	R	ER	HR	SH	SF	HB	TBB	IBB	SO	WP	Bk	W	L	Pct	ShO	Sv-Op	Hld	ERC	ERA
1986 Philadelphia	NL	9	0	0	4	13.1	54	12	5	5	2	0	0	2	4	1	3	0	0	0	0	-	0	0-1	0	4.19	3.38
1987 Philadelphia	NL	55	7	0	8	109.1	468	88	55	51	16	3	4	3	56	6	93	6	8	3	10	.231	0	1-2	6	3.76	4.20
1988 Seattle	AL	62	0	0	29	99.1	412	74	37	29	10	3	10	2	43	10	76	6	6	6	5	.545	0	4-11	10	2.76	2.63
1989 Seattle	AL	65	0	0	27	99.1	431	81	43	35	8	6	2	6	54	6	94	1	2	4	6	.400	0	7-10	9	3.60	3.17
1990 Seattle	AL	63	0	0	28	77.1	338	64	42	39	8	8	5	2	44	12	69	9	2	5	7	.417	0	3-12	13	3.61	4.54
1991 Seattle	AL	72	0	0	35	88.2	363	64	35	32	5	4	0	6	34	11	74	3	0	7	7	.500	0	14-22	9	2.35	3.25
1992 San Francisco	NL	67	0	0	24	82.0	346	76	35	34	7	5	2	4	33	10	80	1	0	6	6	.500	0	2-3	9	3.64	3.73
1993 San Francisco	NL	81	0	0	17	77.1	317	58	28	26	7	4	2	3	24	6	70	2	2	6	6	.500	0	1-6	34	2.36	3.03
1994 San Francisco	NL	36	0	0	12	42.1	158	23	8	7	4	4	1	2	11	0	51	0	0	3	2	.600	0	4-6	9	1.55	1.49
1995 Cincinnati	NL	40	0	0	10	49.0	200	38	13	13	5	1	1	1	19	1	41	1	1	6	1	.857	0	2-4	9	2.92	2.39
1996 Seattle	AL	73	0	0	23	72.0	302	61	32	29	11	0	1	6	24	3	70	2	0	1	1	.500	0	6-8	15	3.59	3.63
1997 Cleveland	AL	71	0	0	38	75.0	313	59	33	27	3	3	3	4	29	5	74	2	0	2	5	.286	0	15-17	14	2.58	3.24
1998 Cleveland	AL	69	0	0	57	64.0	239	43	11	11	4	1	0	4	13	0	55	1	3	1	1	.500	0	40-45	1	1.82	1.55
1999 Cleveland	AL	72	0	0	65	68.2	291	60	32	31	11	2	2	2	26	1	55	0	1	3	4	.429	0	39-43	0	3.76	4.06
2001 Houston	NL	67	0	0	16	69.0	292	68	36	36	14	4	2	2	22	3	46	2	0	5	3	.625	0	4-9	19	4.45	4.70
2002 Minnesota	AL	58	0	0	17	55.0	232	59	20	20	5	4	3	4	13	3	29	2	0	2	3	.400	0	0-2	20	4.05	3.27
2004 Chicago	AL	45	0	0	12	46.2	210	55	27	26	7	2	3	3	15	2	26	1	2	2	0	1.000	0	0-0	3	5.31	5.01
17 ML YEARS		1005	7	0	422	1188.1	4966	983	492	451	127	54	41	56	464	80	1006	39	27	62	67	.481	0	142-201	180	3.23	3.42

Bucky Jacobsen

Bats: R Throws: R Pos: 1B-21; DH-20; PH-2   Ht: 6'4" Wt: 220 Born: 8/30/1975 Age: 29

			BATTING																BASERUNNING				AVERAGES		
Year Team	Lg	G	AB	H	2B	3B	HR	(Hm Rd)	TB	R	RBI	RC	TBB	IBB	SO	HBP	SH	SF	SB	CS	SB%	GDP	Avg	OBP	Slg
1997 Ogden	R+	67	238	78	17	2	8	(- -)	123	57	52	51	41	0	44	3	0	4	6	6	.50	4	.328	.427	.517
1998 Beloit	A	135	499	146	31	1	27	(- -)	260	96	100	101	83	3	133	8	0	4	5	2	.71	10	.293	.399	.521
1999 Huntsville	AA	47	150	29	6	1	3	(- -)	46	20	19	14	20	0	32	3	0	5	4	1	.80	4	.193	.292	.307
1999 Stockton	A+	46	156	39	8	0	5	(- -)	62	22	22	21	21	1	40	4	0	1	3	3	.50	4	.250	.352	.397
2000 Huntsville	AA	81	268	74	14	0	18	(- -)	142	44	50	54	51	2	69	4	0	4	4	2	.67	8	.276	.394	.530
2001 Indianapolis	AAA	86	300	74	18	1	12	(- -)	130	42	53	36	26	1	78	4	1	3	0	0	-	13	.247	.312	.433
2001 Huntsville	AA	27	93	41	9	0	10	(- -)	80	21	28	32	15	2	14	1	0	1	1	2	.33	3	.441	.518	.860
2002 Huntsville	AA	61	198	50	9	2	11	(- -)	96	31	39	30	22	1	41	4	1	2	2	2	.50	6	.253	.336	.485
2002 New Haven	AA	34	102	30	11	0	4	(- -)	53	13	21	18	9	0	25	2	0	1	0	0	-	0	.294	.360	.520
2003 Tennessee	AA	131	447	133	24	1	31	(- -)	252	84	84	93	56	8	91	13	0	5	3	1	.75	7	.298	.388	.564
2004 Tacoma	AAA	81	292	91	22	1	26	(- -)	193	59	86	73	50	3	88	8	0	3	1	1	.50	8	.312	.422	.661
2004 Seattle	AL	42	160	44	9	0	9	(7 2)	80	17	28	22	14	0	47	1	0	1	0	0	-	3	.275	.335	.500

Kevin Jarvis

Pitches: R Bats: L Pos: RP-10   Ht: 6'2" Wt: 200 Born: 8/1/1969 Age: 35

		HOW MUCH HE PITCHED						WHAT HE GAVE UP												THE RESULTS						
Year Team	Lg	G	GS	CG	GF	IP	BFP	H	R	ER	HR	SH	SF	HB	TBB	IBB	SO	WP	Bk	W	L	Pct	ShO	Sv-Op	Hld	ERC	ERA
2004 Nashville*	AAA	11	11	1	0	65.2	288	93	31	30	3	4	3	2	12	1	46	0	0	2	5	.286	0	0- -	-	5.47	4.11
2004 Co Springs*	AAA	6	6	1	0	37.1	165	44	34	24	12	2	2	1	10	0	25	0	0	0	4	.000	0	0- -	-	6.24	5.79
1994 Cincinnati	NL	6	3	0	0	17.2	79	22	14	14	4	1	0	0	5	0	10	1	0	1	1	.500	0	0-0	-	5.91	7.13
1995 Cincinnati	NL	19	11	1	2	79.0	354	91	56	50	13	2	5	3	32	2	33	2	0	3	4	.429	1	0-0	-	5.60	5.70
1996 Cincinnati	NL	24	20	2	2	120.1	552	152	93	80	17	6	2	2	43	5	63	3	0	8	9	.471	1	0-0	-	5.68	5.98
1997 Cin-Min-Det		32	5	0	13	68.0	329	99	62	58	17	2	1	1	29	0	48	4	0	0	4	.000	0	1-1	-	8.21	7.68
1999 Oakland	AL	4	1	0	0	14.0	75	28	19	18	6	0	1	1	6	0	11	0	0	1	0	1.000	0		0	14.40	11.57
2000 Colorado	NL	24	19	0	0	115.0	505	138	83	76	26	6	2	4	33	3	60	2	0	3	4	.429	0	0-0	-	5.86	5.95
2001 San Diego	NL	32	32	1	0	193.1	809	189	107	103	37	7	4	5	49	4	133	1	0	12	11	.522	1	0-0	-	4.05	4.79
2002 San Diego	NL	7	7	0	0	35.0	146	36	19	17	5	0	1	1	10	1	24	2	0	2	4	.333	0	0-0	-	4.24	4.37
2003 San Diego	NL	16	16	0	0	92.0	413	113	65	60	15	2	5	2	32	5	49	2	0	4	8	.333	0	0-0	-	5.68	5.87
2004 Sea-Col		10	0	0	2	15.0	78	24	18	18	5	1	0	0	9	2	7	2	0	1	0	1.000	0	0-0	-	11.60	10.80
1997 Cincinnati	NL	9	0	0	3	13.1	70	21	16	15	4	1	0	1	7	0	12	2	0	0	0	-	0	1-1	-	9.98	10.13
1997 Minnesota	AL	6	2	0	1	13.0	70	23	18	18	4	0	0	0	8	0	9	2	0	1	0	.000	0		-	11.69	12.46
1997 Detroit	AL	17	3	0	9	41.2	189	55	28	25	9	1	1	0	14	0	27	0	0	0	3	.000	0	0-0	-	6.64	5.40
2004 Seattle	AL	8	0	0	1	13.0	63	20	12	12	4	0	0	0	5	0	7	2	0	1	0	1.000	0	0-0	-	9.03	8.31
2004 Colorado	NL	2	0	0	0	2.0	15	6	6	6	1	1	0	0	4	2	0	0	0	0	0	-	0	0-0	0	30.23	27.00
10 ML YEARS		174	114	4	19	749.1	3340	894	536	494	145	27	21	19	248	22	438	19	0	34	46	.425	3	1-1	-	5.66	5.93

Geoff Jenkins

Bats: L Throws: R Pos: LF-156; PH-1   Ht: 6'1" Wt: 213 Born: 7/21/1974 Age: 30

Year Team	Lg	G	AB	H	2B	3B	HR	(Hm	Rd)	TB	R	RBI	RC	TBB	IBB	SO	HBP	SH	SF	SB	CS	SB%	GDP	Avg	OBP	Slg
1998 Milwaukee	NL	84	262	60	12	1	9	(4	5)	101	33	28	26	20	4	61	2	0	1	1	3	.25	7	.229	.288	.385
1999 Milwaukee	NL	135	447	140	43	3	21	(10	11)	252	70	82	88	35	7	87	7	3	1	5	1	.83	10	.313	.371	.564
2000 Milwaukee	NL	135	512	155	36	4	34	(15	19)	301	100	94	104	33	6	135	15	0	4	11	1	.92	9	.303	.360	.588
2001 Milwaukee	NL	105	397	105	21	1	20	(11	9)	188	60	63	60	36	7	120	8	0	5	4	2	.67	11	.264	.334	.474
2002 Milwaukee	NL	67	243	59	17	1	10	(4	6)	108	35	29	28	22	1	60	6	0	1	1	2	.33	8	.243	.320	.444
2003 Milwaukee	NL	124	487	144	30	2	28	(16	12)	262	81	95	90	58	10	120	6	0	3	0	0	-	12	.296	.375	.538
2004 Milwaukee	NL	157	617	163	36	6	27	(13	14)	292	88	93	76	46	10	152	12	0	6	3	1	.75	19	.264	.325	.473
7 ML YEARS		807	2965	826	195	18	149	(73	76)	1504	467	484	472	250	45	735	56	3	21	25	10	.71	76	.279	.344	.507

Jason Jennings

Pitches: R Bats: L Pos: SP-33   Ht: 6'2" Wt: 242 Born: 7/17/1978 Age: 26

Year Team	Lg	G	GS	CG	GF	IP	BFP	H	R	ER	HR	SH	SF	HB	TBB	IBB	SO	WP	Bk	W	L	Pct	ShO	Sv-Op	Hld	ERC	ERA
2001 Colorado	NL	7	7	1	0	39.1	174	42	21	20	2	1	1	1	19	0	26	1	0	4	1	.800	1	0-0	0	4.58	4.58
2002 Colorado	NL	32	32	0	0	185.1	808	201	102	93	26	9	3	8	70	2	127	10	0	16	8	.667	0	0-0	0	4.98	4.52
2003 Colorado	NL	32	32	1	0	181.1	820	212	115	103	20	11	6	5	88	7	119	6	0	12	13	.480	0	0-0	0	5.60	5.11
2004 Colorado	NL	33	33	0	0	201.0	925	241	125	123	27	9	3	7	101	14	133	6	1	11	12	.478	0	0-0	0	5.99	5.51
4 ML YEARS		104	104	2	0	607.0	2727	696	363	339	75	30	13	21	278	23	405	23	1	43	34	.558	1	0-0	0	5.47	5.03

Derek Jeter

Bats: R Throws: R Pos: SS-154   Ht: 6'3" Wt: 195 Born: 6/26/1974 Age: 31

Year Team	Lg	G	AB	H	2B	3B	HR	(Hm	Rd)	TB	R	RBI	RC	TBB	IBB	SO	HBP	SH	SF	SB	CS	SB%	GDP	Avg	OBP	Slg
1995 New York	AL	15	48	12	4	1	0	(0	0)	18	5	7	5	3	0	11	0	0	0	0	0	-	0	.250	.294	.375
1996 New York	AL	157	582	183	25	6	10	(3	7)	250	104	78	92	48	1	102	9	6	9	14	7	.67	13	.314	.370	.430
1997 New York	AL	159	654	190	31	7	10	(5	5)	265	116	70	99	74	0	125	10	8	2	23	12	.66	14	.291	.370	.405
1998 New York	AL	149	626	203	25	8	19	(9	10)	301	127	84	115	57	1	119	5	3	3	30	6	.83	13	.324	.384	.481
1999 New York	AL	158	627	219	37	9	24	(15	9)	346	134	102	146	91	5	116	12	3	6	19	8	.70	12	.349	.438	.552
2000 New York	AL	148	593	201	31	4	15	(8	7)	285	119	73	118	68	4	99	12	3	3	22	4	.85	14	.339	.416	.481
2001 New York	AL	150	614	191	35	3	21	(13	8)	295	110	74	112	56	3	99	10	5	1	27	3	.90	13	.311	.377	.480
2002 New York	AL	157	644	191	26	0	18	(8	10)	271	124	75	108	73	2	114	7	3	3	32	3	.91	14	.297	.373	.421
2003 New York	AL	119	482	156	25	3	10	(7	3)	217	87	52	86	43	2	88	13	3	1	11	5	.69	10	.324	.393	.450
2004 New York	AL	154	643	188	44	1	23	(11	12)	303	111	78	100	46	1	99	14	16	2	23	4	.85	19	.292	.352	.471
10 ML YEARS		1366	5513	1734	283	42	150	(79	71)	2551	1037	693	981	559	19	972	92	50	30	201	52	.79	122	.315	.385	.463

D'Angelo Jimenez

Bats: B Throws: R Pos: 2B-146; SS-5; PH-4   Ht: 6'0" Wt: 194 Born: 12/21/1977 Age: 27

Year Team	Lg	G	AB	H	2B	3B	HR	(Hm	Rd)	TB	R	RBI	RC	TBB	IBB	SO	HBP	SH	SF	SB	CS	SB%	GDP	Avg	OBP	Slg
1999 New York	AL	7	20	8	2	0	0	(0	0)	10	3	4	5	3	0	4	0	0	0	0	0	-	0	.400	.478	.500
2001 San Diego	NL	86	308	85	19	0	3	(2	1)	113	45	33	39	39	4	68	0	0	2	2	3	.40	9	.276	.355	.367
2002 SD-CWS		114	429	108	15	7	4	(3	1)	149	61	44	54	50	1	73	1	0	2	6	3	.67	11	.252	.330	.347
2003 CWS-Cin		146	561	153	24	7	14	(6	8)	233	69	57	78	66	1	89	2	6	4	11	7	.61	7	.273	.349	.415
2004 Cincinnati	NL	152	563	152	28	3	12	(6	6)	222	76	67	87	82	1	99	2	3	2	13	7	.65	15	.270	.364	.394
2002 San Diego	NL	87	321	77	11	4	3	(2	1)	105	39	33	34	34	1	63	0	0	2	4	2	.67	10	.240	.311	.327
2002 Chicago	AL	27	108	31	4	3	1	(1	0)	44	22	11	20	16	0	10	1	0	0	2	1	.67	1	.287	.384	.407
2003 Chicago	AL	73	271	69	11	5	7	(3	4)	111	35	26	35	32	1	46	0	4	1	4	3	.57	3	.255	.332	.410
2003 Cincinnati	NL	73	290	84	13	2	7	(3	4)	122	34	31	43	34	0	43	2	2	3	7	4	.64	4	.290	.365	.421
5 ML YEARS		505	1881	506	88	17	33	(17	16)	727	254	205	263	240	7	333	5	9	10	32	20	.62	42	.269	.352	.386

Jose Jimenez

Pitches: R Bats: R Pos: RP-31   Ht: 6'3" Wt: 228 Born: 7/7/1973 Age: 31

Year Team	Lg	G	GS	CG	GF	IP	BFP	H	R	ER	HR	SH	SF	HB	TBB	IBB	SO	WP	Bk	W	L	Pct	ShO	Sv-Op	Hld	ERC	ERA
2004 Buffalo*	AAA	2	0	0	0	3.0	13	3	0	0	0	0	0	0	1	0	3	0	0	0	0	-	0	0- -		3.05	0.00
1998 St Louis	NL	4	3	0	0	21.1	94	22	8	7	0	1	1	0	8	0	12	0	0	3	0	1.000	0	0-0	0	3.35	2.95
1999 St Louis	NL	29	28	2	0	163.0	727	173	114	106	16	10	6	11	71	2	113	10	1	5	14	.263	2	0-1	0	4.81	5.85
2000 Colorado	NL	72	0	0	55	70.2	301	63	27	25	4	4	2	3	28	6	44	5	0	5	2	.714	0	24-30	2	3.18	3.18
2001 Colorado	NL	56	0	0	49	55.0	237	56	27	25	6	2	1	0	22	4	37	3	0	6	1	.857	0	17-22	0	4.14	4.09
2002 Colorado	NL	74	0	0	69	73.1	307	76	34	29	7	4	2	3	11	4	47	0	0	2	10	.167	0	41-47	1	3.31	3.56
2003 Colorado	NL	63	7	0	40	101.2	471	137	62	59	7	4	3	6	32	5	45	4	0	2	10	.167	0	20-23	2	5.64	5.22
2004 Cleveland	AL	31	0	0	18	36.1	170	45	37	34	6	0	0	4	14	2	21	0	0	1	7	.125	0	8-11	1	6.22	8.42
7 ML YEARS		329	38	2	231	521.1	2307	572	309	285	46	25	15	27	186	23	319	22	1	24	44	.353	2	110-134	5	4.48	4.92

Charles Johnson

Bats: R Throws: R Pos: C-91; PH-19   Ht: 6'3" Wt: 250 Born: 7/20/1971 Age: 33

Year Team	Lg	G	AB	H	2B	3B	HR	(Hm	Rd)	TB	R	RBI	RC	TBB	IBB	SO	HBP	SH	SF	SB	CS	SB%	GDP	Avg	OBP	Slg
1994 Florida	NL	4	11	5	1	0	1	(1	0)	9	5	4	3	1	0	4	0	0	1	0	0	-	1	.455	.462	.818
1995 Florida	NL	97	315	79	15	1	11	(3	8)	129	40	39	44	46	2	71	4	4	2	0	2	.00	11	.251	.351	.410
1996 Florida	NL	120	386	84	13	1	13	(9	4)	138	34	37	35	40	6	91	2	2	4	1	0	1.00	20	.218	.292	.358
1997 Florida	NL	124	416	104	26	1	19	(7	12)	189	43	63	63	60	6	109	3	3	2	0	2	.00	13	.250	.347	.454
1998 Fla-LA	NL	133	459	100	18	0	19	(14	5)	175	44	58	48	45	1	129	1	0	1	0	2	.00	12	.218	.289	.381
1999 Baltimore	AL	135	426	107	19	1	16	(8	8)	176	54	54	59	55	2	107	4	4	3	0	0	-	13	.251	.340	.413
2000 Bal-CWS	AL	128	421	128	24	0	31	(19	12)	245	76	91	89	52	0	106	1	1	3	2	0	1.00	8	.304	.379	.582

BATTING																			BASERUNNING				AVERAGES		
Year Team	Lg	G	AB	H	2B	3B	HR	(Hm Rd)	TB	R	RBI	RC	TBB	IBB	SO	HBP	SH	SF	SB	CS	SB%	GDP	Avg	OBP	Slg
2001 Florida	NL	128	451	117	32	0	18	(5 13)	203	51	75	64	38	2	133	4	0	3	0	0	-	8	.259	.321	.450
2002 Florida	NL	83	244	53	19	0	6	(2 4)	90	18	36	22	31	7	61	0	1	4	0	0	-	10	.217	.301	.369
2003 Colorado	NL	108	356	82	20	0	20	(12 8)	162	49	61	46	49	2	84	1	1	1	1	3	.25	8	.230	.320	.455
2004 Colorado	NL	109	305	72	20	0	13	(7 6)	131	42	47	46	49	1	91	5	2	1	2	1	.67	6	.236	.350	.430
1998 Florida	NL	31	113	25	5	0	7	(5 2)	51	13	23	16	16	0	30	0	0		0	1	.00	3	.221	.315	.451
1998 Los Angeles	NL	102	346	75	13	0	12	(9 3)	124	31	35	32	29	1	99	1	0	0	0	1	.00	9	.217	.279	.358
2000 Baltimore	AL	84	286	84	16	0	21	(12 9)	163	52	55	56	32	0	69	0	1	1	2	0	1.00	8	.294	.364	.570
2000 Chicago	AL	44	135	44	8	0	10	(7 3)	82	24	36	33	20	0	37	1	0	2	0	1	.00	4	.326	.411	.607
11 ML YEARS		1169	3790	931	207	4	167	(87 80)	1647	460	565	519	466	29	986	25	18	31	6	10	.38	110	.246	.330	.435

Jason Johnson

Pitches: R **Bats:** R **Pos:** SP-33   **Ht:** 6'6" **Wt:** 235 **Born:** 10/27/1973 **Age:** 31

HOW MUCH HE PITCHED								WHAT HE GAVE UP											THE RESULTS							
Year Team	Lg	G	GS	CG	GF	IP	BFP	H	R	ER	HR	SH	SF	HB	TBB	IBB	SO	WP	Bk	W	L	Pct	ShO	Sv-Op	Hld	ERC	ERA
1997 Pittsburgh	NL	3	0	0	0	6.0	27	10	4	4	2	0	1	0	1	0	3	0	0	0	0	-	0	0-0	0	9.59	6.00
1998 Tampa Bay	AL	13	13	0	0	60.0	274	74	38	38	9	1	1	3	27	0	36	2	0	2	5	.286	0	0-0	0	6.35	5.70
1999 Baltimore	AL	22	21	0	0	115.1	515	120	74	70	16	2	4	3	55	0	71	5	1	8	7	.533	0	0-0	0	4.99	5.46
2000 Baltimore	AL	25	13	0	3	107.2	501	119	95	84	21	3	5	4	61	2	79	3	0	1	10	.091	0	0-0	2	6.18	7.02
2001 Baltimore	AL	32	32	2	0	196.0	856	194	109	99	28	6	6	13	77	3	114	9	0	10	12	.455	0	0-0	0	4.53	4.59
2002 Baltimore	AL	22	22	1	0	131.1	561	141	68	67	19	0	3	6	41	2	97	4	0	5	14	.263	0	0-0	0	4.70	4.59
2003 Baltimore	AL	32	32	0	0	189.2	858	216	100	88	22	3	1	10	80	8	118	7	0	10	10	.500	0	0-0	0	5.21	4.18
2004 Detroit	AL	33	33	2	0	196.2	859	222	121	112	22	1	10	5	60	3	125	7	1	8	15	.348	1	0-0	0	4.58	5.13
8 ML YEARS		182	166	5	3	1002.2	4451	1096	609	552	139	16	31	44	402	18	643	37	2	44	73	.376	1	0-0	2	5.05	4.95

Mark L Johnson

Bats: L **Throws:** R **Pos:** C-5; PH-2   **Ht:** 6'0" **Wt:** 185 **Born:** 9/12/1975 **Age:** 29

BATTING																			BASERUNNING				AVERAGES		
Year Team	Lg	G	AB	H	2B	3B	HR	(Hm Rd)	TB	R	RBI	RC	TBB	IBB	SO	HBP	SH	SF	SB	CS	SB%	GDP	Avg	OBP	Slg
2004 Indianapolis*	AAA	88	278	72	18	0	5	(- -)	105	39	38	40	43	1	41	1	2	2	3	2	.60	4	.259	.358	.378
2004 Las Vegas*	AAA	37	19	3	0	0	0	(- -)	3	0	0	0	1	0	9	0	4	0	0	0	-	0	.158	.200	.158
1998 Chicago	AL	7	23	2	0	2	0	(0 0)	6	2	1	1	1	0	8	0	0	0	0	0	-	0	.087	.125	.261
1999 Chicago	AL	73	207	47	11	0	4	(2 2)	70	27	16	27	36	0	58	2	1	2	3	1	.75	2	.227	.344	.338
2000 Chicago	AL	75	213	48	11	0	3	(2 1)	68	29	23	23	27	0	40	1	10	0	3	2	.60	3	.225	.315	.319
2001 Chicago	AL	61	173	43	6	1	5	(2 3)	66	21	18	23	23	1	31	2	10	3	2	1	.67	5	.249	.338	.382
2002 Chicago	AL	86	263	55	8	1	4	(1 3)	77	31	18	24	30	1	52	3	6	0	0	0	-	4	.209	.297	.293
2003 Oakland	AL	13	27	3	1	0	0	(0 0)	4	3	3	0	3	0	4	1	1	1	0	0	-	0	.111	.219	.148
2004 Milwaukee	NL	7	11	1	0	0	0	(0 0)	1	1	2	1	3	1	2	0	0	1	0	0	-	0	.091	.267	.091
7 ML YEARS		322	917	199	37	4	16	(7 9)	292	114	81	98	123	3	195	9	28	7	8	4	.67	14	.217	.313	.318

Nick Johnson

Bats: L **Throws:** L **Pos:** 1B-73; PH-2   **Ht:** 6'3" **Wt:** 224 **Born:** 9/19/1978 **Age:** 26

BATTING																			BASERUNNING				AVERAGES		
Year Team	Lg	G	AB	H	2B	3B	HR	(Hm Rd)	TB	R	RBI	RC	TBB	IBB	SO	HBP	SH	SF	SB	CS	SB%	GDP	Avg	OBP	Slg
2004 Brevard Cnty*	A+	6	21	4	0	0	1	(- -)	7	3	5	2	4	1	6	0	0	0	0	0	-	1	.190	.320	.333
2004 Edmonton*	AAA	3	9	2	1	0	0	(- -)	3	2	0	1	4	0	3	0	0	0	0	0	-	1	.222	.462	.333
2001 New York	AL	23	67	13	2	0	2	(1 1)	21	6	8	6	7	0	15	4	0	0	0	0	-	3	.194	.308	.313
2002 New York	AL	129	378	92	15	0	15	(7 8)	152	56	58	59	48	5	98	12	3	0	1	3	.25	11	.243	.347	.402
2003 New York	AL	96	324	92	19	0	14	(8 6)	153	60	47	65	70	4	57	8	3	1	5	2	.71	9	.284	.422	.472
2004 Montreal	NL	73	251	63	16	0	7	(4 3)	100	35	33	36	40	2	58	3	0	1	6	3	.67	5	.251	.359	.398
4 ML YEARS		321	1020	260	52	0	38	(20 18)	426	157	146	166	165	11	228	27	6	2	12	8	.60	28	.255	.372	.418

Randy Johnson

Pitches: L **Bats:** R **Pos:** SP-35   **Ht:** 6'10" **Wt:** 232 **Born:** 9/10/1963 **Age:** 41

HOW MUCH HE PITCHED								WHAT HE GAVE UP											THE RESULTS							
Year Team	Lg	G	GS	CG	GF	IP	BFP	H	R	ER	HR	SH	SF	HB	TBB	IBB	SO	WP	Bk	W	L	Pct	ShO	Sv-Op	Hld	ERC	ERA
1988 Montreal	NL	4	4	1	0	26.0	109	23	8	7	3	0	0	0	7	0	25	3	0	3	0	1.000	0	0-0	0	2.96	2.42
1989 Mon-Sea		29	28	2	1	160.2	715	147	100	86	13	10	13	3	96	2	130	7	7	7	13	.350	0	0-0	0	4.26	4.82
1990 Seattle	AL	33	33	5	0	219.2	944	174	103	89	26	7	6	5	120	2	194	4	2	14	11	.560	2	0-0	0	3.68	3.65
1991 Seattle	AL	33	33	2	0	201.1	889	151	96	89	15	9	8	12	152	0	228	12	2	13	10	.565	1	0-0	0	4.15	3.98
1992 Seattle	AL	31	31	6	0	210.1	922	154	104	88	13	3	8	18	144	1	241	13	1	12	14	.462	2	0-0	0	3.75	3.77
1993 Seattle	AL	35	34	10	1	255.1	1043	185	97	92	22	8	7	16	99	1	308	8	2	19	8	.704	3	1-1	0	2.73	3.24
1994 Seattle	AL	23	23	9	0	172.0	694	132	65	61	14	3	1	6	72	2	204	5	0	13	6	.684	4	0-0	0	2.99	3.19
1995 Seattle	AL	30	30	6	0	214.1	866	159	65	59	12	2	1	6	65	1	294	5	2	18	2	.900	3	0-0	0	2.18	2.48
1996 Seattle	AL	14	8	0	2	61.1	256	48	27	25	8	1	0	2	25	0	85	3	1	5	0	1.000	0	1-2	0	3.24	3.67
1997 Seattle	AL	30	29	5	0	213.0	850	147	60	54	20	4	1	10	77	2	291	4	0	20	4	.833	2	0-0	0	2.47	2.28
1998 Sea-Hou		34	34	10	0	244.1	1014	203	102	89	23	5	2	14	86	1	329	7	2	19	11	.633	6	0-0	0	3.16	3.28
1999 Arizona	NL	35	35	12	0	271.2	1079	207	86	75	30	4	3	9	70	3	364	4	2	17	9	.654	2	0-0	0	2.49	2.48
2000 Arizona	NL	35	35	8	0	248.2	1001	202	89	73	23	14	5	6	76	1	347	5	2	19	7	.731	3	0-0	0	2.80	2.64
2001 Arizona	NL	35	34	3	1	249.2	994	181	74	69	19	10	5	18	71	2	372	8	1	21	6	.778	2	0-0	0	2.35	2.49
2002 Arizona	NL	35	35	8	0	260.0	1035	197	78	67	26	4	2	13	71	1	334	3	2	24	5	.828	4	0-0	0	2.54	2.32
2003 Arizona	NL	18	18	1	0	114.0	489	125	61	54	16	4	3	8	27	3	125	1	1	6	8	.429	1	0-0	0	4.52	4.26
2004 Arizona	NL	35	35	4	0	245.2	964	177	88	71	18	7	5	10	44	1	290	3	1	16	14	.533	2	0-0	0	1.82	2.60
1989 Montreal	NL	7	6	0	1	29.2	143	29	25	22	2	3	4	0	26	1	26	2	2	0	4	.000	0	0-0	0	5.42	6.67
1989 Seattle	AL	22	22	2	0	131.0	572	118	75	64	11	7	9	3	70	1	104	5	5	7	9	.438	0	0-0	0	4.01	4.40
1998 Seattle	AL	23	23	6	0	160.0	685	146	90	77	19	5	1	11	60	0	213	7	2	9	10	.474	2	0-0	0	3.88	4.33
1998 Houston	NL	11	11	4	0	84.1	329	57	12	12	4	0	1	3	26	1	116	0	0	10	1	.909	4	0-0	0	1.93	1.28
17 ML YEARS		489	479	92	5	3368.0	13864	2612	1303	1148	301	95	70	156	1302	23	4161	95	28	246	128	.658	37	2-3	0	2.94	3.07

Reed Johnson

Bats: R **Throws:** R **Pos:** LF-57; RF-53; CF-33; PH-9; DH-4; PR-1   **Ht:** 5'10" **Wt:** 180 **Born:** 12/8/1976 **Age:** 28

Year Team	Lg	G	AB	H	2B	3B	HR	(Hm	Rd)	TB	R	RBI	RC	TBB	IBB	SO	HBP	SH	SF	SB	CS	SB%	GDP	Avg	OBP	Slg
1999 St. Ctharines	A-	60	191	46	8	2	2	(-	-)	64	24	23	21	24	1	31	2	4	4	5	5	.50	4	.241	.326	.335
2000 Hagerstown	A	95	324	94	24	5	8	(-	-)	152	66	70	67	62	1	49	14	2	3	14	2	.88	9	.290	.422	.469
2000 Dunedin	A+	36	133	42	9	2	4	(-	-)	67	26	28	28	14	0	27	11	1	3	3	2	.60	1	.316	.416	.504
2001 Tennessee	AA	136	554	174	29	4	13	(-	-)	250	104	74	97	45	2	79	18	5	2	42	12	.78	11	.314	.383	.451
2002 Dunedin	A+	8	33	9	3	0	0	(-	-)	12	7	6	4	3	0	3	2	0	0	1	0	.00	0	.273	.368	.364
2002 Syracuse	AAA	44	159	37	8	3	2	(-	-)	57	27	10	18	12	0	23	8	3	1	1	4	.20	1	.233	.317	.358
2003 Syracuse	AAA	26	101	33	4	1	2	(-	-)	45	14	16	17	3	0	13	5	0	2	3	1	.75	2	.327	.369	.446
2003 Toronto	AL	114	412	121	21	2	10	(6	4)	176	79	52	64	20	1	67	20	1	4	5	3	.63	10	.294	.353	.427
2004 Toronto	AL	141	537	145	25	2	10	(8	2)	204	68	61	65	28	2	98	12	3	2	6	3	.67	17	.270	.320	.380
2 ML YEARS		255	949	266	46	4	20	(14	6)	380	147	113	129	48	3	165	32	4	6	11	6	.65	27	.280	.334	.400

Mike Johnston

Pitches: L **Bats:** L **Pos:** RP-24   **Ht:** 6'2" **Wt:** 215 **Born:** 3/30/1979 **Age:** 26

		HOW MUCH HE PITCHED						WHAT HE GAVE UP										THE RESULTS						
Year Team	Lg	G	GS	CG	GF	IP	BFP	H	R	ER	HR	SH	SF	HB	TBB	IBB	SO	WP	Bk	W	L	Pct	ShO	Sv-Op	Hld	ERC	ERA
1998 Pirates	R	13	3	0	3	29.2	127	28	17	11	1	2	2	0	10	0	17	5	1	1	2	.333	0	0- -	-	3.01	3.34
1998 Erie	AA	2	0	0	2	2.0	11	4	4	1	0	0	0	0	1	0	2	0	0	0	0	-	0	0- -	-	9.72	4.50
1999 Williamsport	A-	14	2	0	3	42.1	193	46	26	20	5	0	0	3	18	0	30	3	1	3	2	.600	0	2- -	-	5.00	4.25
2000 Hickory	A	26	0	0	7	50.2	245	66	42	35	2	2	2	5	30	0	52	0	2	4	2	.667	0	2- -	-	6.63	6.22
2001 Hickory	A	16	16	0	0	93.1	404	88	47	35	5	0	4	5	42	1	80	7	1	4	5	.444	0	0- -	-	3.83	3.38
2001 Lynchburg	A+	11	10	1	0	62.0	276	66	27	23	2	4	2	3	24	0	44	4	2	4	4	.500	0	0- -	-	4.02	3.34
2002 Lynchburg	A+	15	10	1	0	57.0	253	50	29	23	2	1	2	7	26	0	50	8	0	4	2	.667	0	0- -	-	3.54	3.63
2003 Altoona	AA	46	0	0	19	72.1	285	49	17	17	4	5	2	5	27	3	65	7	1	6	2	.750	0	7- -	-	2.30	2.12
2004 Nashville	AAA	19	0	0	1	15.0	79	19	14	14	3	0	0	2	13	1	6	0	0	0	0	-	0	0- -	-	8.84	8.40
2004 Pittsburgh	NL	24	0	0	5	22.2	110	29	16	11	2	1	0	2	15	1	18	0	0	0	3	.000	0	0-1	4	7.12	4.37

Andruw Jones

Bats: R **Throws:** R **Pos:** CF-154; PH-1   **Ht:** 6'1" **Wt:** 210 **Born:** 4/23/1977 **Age:** 28

Year Team	Lg	G	AB	H	2B	3B	HR	(Hm	Rd)	TB	R	RBI	RC	TBB	IBB	SO	HBP	SH	SF	SB	CS	SB%	GDP	Avg	OBP	Slg
1996 Atlanta	NL	31	106	23	7	1	5	(3	2)	47	11	13	13	7	0	29	0	0	0	3	0	1.00	1	.217	.265	.443
1997 Atlanta	NL	153	399	92	18	1	18	(5	13)	166	60	70	54	56	2	107	4	5	3	20	11	.65	11	.231	.329	.416
1998 Atlanta	NL	159	582	158	33	8	31	(16	15)	300	89	90	97	40	8	129	4	1	4	27	4	.87	10	.271	.321	.515
1999 Atlanta	NL	162	592	163	35	5	26	(10	16)	286	97	84	103	76	11	103	9	0	2	24	12	.67	12	.275	.365	.483
2000 Atlanta	NL	161	656	199	36	6	36	(15	21)	355	122	104	127	59	0	100	9	0	5	21	6	.78	12	.303	.366	.541
2001 Atlanta	NL	161	625	157	25	2	34	(16	18)	288	104	104	90	56	3	142	3	0	9	11	4	.73	10	.251	.312	.461
2002 Atlanta	NL	154	560	148	34	0	35	(18	17)	287	91	94	94	83	4	135	10	0	6	8	3	.73	14	.264	.366	.513
2003 Atlanta	NL	156	595	165	28	2	36	(16	20)	305	101	116	92	53	2	125	5	0	6	4	3	.57	18	.277	.338	.513
2004 Atlanta	NL	154	570	149	34	4	29	(13	16)	278	85	91	75	71	9	147	3	0	2	6	6	.50	24	.261	.345	.488
9 ML YEARS		1291	4685	1254	250	29	250	(112	138)	2312	760	766	745	501	39	1017	47	6	37	124	49	.72	112	.268	.342	.493

Bobby M Jones

Pitches: L **Bats:** R **Pos:** RP-3   **Ht:** 6'0" **Wt:** 178 **Born:** 4/11/1972 **Age:** 33

		HOW MUCH HE PITCHED						WHAT HE GAVE UP										THE RESULTS						
Year Team	Lg	G	GS	CG	GF	IP	BFP	H	R	ER	HR	SH	SF	HB	TBB	IBB	SO	WP	Bk	W	L	Pct	ShO	Sv-Op	Hld	ERC	ERA
1997 Colorado	NL	4	4	0	0	19.1	96	30	18	18	2	2	3	0	12	0	5	0	0	1	1	.500	0	0-0	0	8.63	8.38
1998 Colorado	NL	35	20	1	1	141.1	630	153	87	82	12	9	6	6	66	0	109	4	1	7	8	.467	0	0-0	1	4.91	5.22
1999 Colorado	NL	30	20	0	1	112.1	546	132	91	79	24	7	4	6	77	0	74	4	0	6	10	.375	0	0-0	0	7.41	6.33
2000 New York	NL	11	1	0	4	21.2	99	18	11	10	2	0	1	3	14	1	20	0	0	1	0	1.000	0	0-0	0	4.43	4.15
2002 NYM-SD	NL	16	2	0	1	26.2	126	30	18	17	4	2	1	1	18	2	18	0	0	0	0	-	0	0-0	1	6.37	5.74
2004 Boston	AL	3	0	0	1	3.1	20	3	2	2	1	1	0	0	8	1	3	0	0	0	1	.000	0	0-0	0	13.87	5.40
2002 New York	NL	12	0	0	1	17.0	81	20	11	10	3	2	0	1	11	2	11	0	0	0	0	-	0	0-0	1	6.82	5.29
2002 San Diego	NL	4	2	0	0	9.2	45	10	7	7	1	0	1	0	7	0	7	0	0	0	0	-	0	0-0	0	5.61	6.52
6 ML YEARS		99	47	1	8	324.2	1517	366	227	208	45	21	15	16	195	4	229	8	1	14	21	.400	0	0-0	2	6.13	5.77

Chipper Jones

Bats: B **Throws:** R **Pos:** 3B-96; LF-30; DH-7; PH-7   **Ht:** 6'4" **Wt:** 210 **Born:** 4/24/1972 **Age:** 33

Year Team	Lg	G	AB	H	2B	3B	HR	(Hm	Rd)	TB	R	RBI	RC	TBB	IBB	SO	HBP	SH	SF	SB	CS	SB%	GDP	Avg	OBP	Slg
2004 Rome*	A	1	4	0	0	0	0	(-	-)	0	0	0	0	0	0	0	0	0	0	0	0	-	0	.000	.000	.000
1993 Atlanta	NL	8	3	2	1	0	0	(0	0)	3	2	0	2	1	0	1	0	0	0	0	0	-	0	.667	.750	1.000
1995 Atlanta	NL	140	524	139	22	3	23	(15	8)	236	87	86	84	73	1	99	0	1	4	8	4	.67	10	.265	.353	.450
1996 Atlanta	NL	157	598	185	32	5	30	(18	12)	317	114	110	123	87	0	88	0	1	7	14	1	.93	14	.309	.393	.530
1997 Atlanta	NL	157	597	176	41	3	21	(7	14)	286	100	111	104	76	8	88	0	0	6	20	5	.80	19	.295	.371	.479
1998 Atlanta	NL	160	601	188	29	5	34	(17	17)	329	123	107	129	96	1	93	1	1	8	16	6	.73	17	.313	.404	.547
1999 Atlanta	NL	157	567	181	41	1	45	(25	20)	359	116	110	150	126	18	94	2	0	6	25	3	.89	20	.319	.441	.633
2000 Atlanta	NL	156	579	180	38	1	36	(18	18)	328	118	111	128	95	10	64	2	0	10	14	7	.67	14	.311	.404	.566
2001 Atlanta	NL	159	572	189	33	5	38	(19	19)	346	113	102	136	98	20	82	2	0	5	9	10	.47	13	.330	.427	.605
2002 Atlanta	NL	158	548	179	35	1	26	(17	9)	294	90	100	119	107	23	89	2	0	5	8	2	.80	18	.327	.435	.536
2003 Atlanta	NL	153	555	169	33	2	27	(16	11)	287	103	106	110	94	13	83	1	0	6	2	2	.50	10	.305	.402	.517
2004 Atlanta	NL	137	472	117	20	1	30	(19	11)	229	69	96	83	84	8	96	4	0	7	2	0	1.00	15	.248	.362	.485
11 ML YEARS		1542	5616	1705	325	27	310	(171	139)	3014	1035	1039	1168	937	102	877	14	3	64	118	40	.75	150	.304	.401	.537

Jacque Jones

Bats: L **Throws:** L **Pos:** RF-141; PH-7; DH-3; CF-2   **Ht:** 5'10" **Wt:** 176 **Born:** 4/25/1975 **Age:** 30

Year Team	Lg	G	AB	H	2B	3B	HR	(Hm	Rd)	TB	R	RBI	RC	TBB	IBB	SO	HBP	SH	SF	SB	CS	SB%	GDP	Avg	OBP	Slg
1999 Minnesota	AL	95	322	93	24	2	9	(5	4)	148	54	44	46	17	1	63	4	1	3	3	4	.43	7	.289	.329	.460
2000 Minnesota	AL	154	523	149	26	5	19	(11	8)	242	66	76	70	24	4	111	0	1	0	7	5	.58	17	.285	.319	.463
2001 Minnesota	AL	149	475	131	25	0	14	(5	9)	198	57	49	63	39	2	92	3	2	0	12	9	.57	10	.276	.335	.417
2002 Minnesota	AL	149	577	173	37	2	27	(6	21)	295	96	85	100	37	2	129	2	4	6	6	7	.46	8	.300	.341	.511
2003 Minnesota	AL	136	517	157	33	1	16	(7	9)	240	76	69	73	21	2	105	4	1	5	13	1	.93	10	.304	.333	.464
2004 Minnesota	AL	151	555	141	22	1	24	(9	15)	237	69	80	73	40	2	117	10	2	1	13	10	.57	12	.254	.315	.427
6 ML YEARS		834	2969	844	167	11	109	(43	66)	1360	418	403	425	180	13	617	23	11	15	54	36	.60	64	.284	.329	.458

Todd Jones

Pitches: R **Bats:** B **Pos:** RP-78   **Ht:** 6'3" **Wt:** 230 **Born:** 4/24/1968 **Age:** 37

Year Team	Lg	G	GS	CG	GF	IP	BFP	H	R	ER	HR	SH	SF	HB	TBB	IBB	SO	WP	Bk	W	L	Pct	ShO	Sv-Op	Hld	ERC	ERA
1993 Houston	NL	27	0	0	8	37.1	150	28	14	13	4	2	1	1	15	2	25	1	1	1	2	.333	0	2-3	6	2.90	3.13
1994 Houston	NL	48	0	0	20	72.2	288	52	23	22	3	3	1	1	26	4	63	1	0	5	2	.714	0	5-9	8	2.10	2.72
1995 Houston	NL	68	0	0	40	99.2	442	89	38	34	8	5	4	6	52	17	96	5	0	6	5	.545	0	15-20	8	3.70	3.07
1996 Houston	NL	51	0	0	37	57.1	263	61	30	28	5	2	1	5	32	6	44	3	0	6	3	.667	0	17-23	1	5.16	4.40
1997 Detroit	AL	68	0	0	51	70.0	301	60	29	24	3	1	4	1	35	2	70	7	0	5	4	.556	0	31-36	5	3.27	3.09
1998 Detroit	AL	65	0	0	53	63.1	279	58	38	35	7	2	6	2	36	4	57	5	0	1	4	.200	0	28-32	0	4.37	4.97
1999 Detroit	AL	65	0	0	62	66.1	287	64	30	28	7	3	1	1	35	1	64	2	0	4	4	.500	0	30-35	0	4.55	3.80
2000 Detroit	AL	67	0	0	60	64.0	271	67	28	25	6	1	1	1	25	1	67	2	0	2	4	.333	0	42-46	0	4.43	3.52
2001 Det-Min	AL	69	0	0	36	68.0	314	87	39	32	9	3	3	0	29	1	54	3	0	5	5	.500	0	13-21	10	6.03	4.24
2002 Colorado	NL	79	0	0	20	82.1	352	84	43	43	10	6	3	3	28	3	73	1	0	1	4	.200	0	1-3	30	4.22	4.70
2003 Col-Bos	NL	59	1	0	14	68.2	326	93	58	54	10	3	3	1	31	2	59	0	0	3	5	.375	0	0-5	4	6.73	7.08
2004 Cin-Phi	NL	78	0	0	16	82.1	358	84	39	38	7	5	6	6	33	5	59	2	0	11	5	.688	0	2-8	17	4.32	4.15
2001 Detroit	AL	45	0	0	28	48.2	225	60	31	25	6	2	3	0	22	1	39	3	0	4	5	.444	0	11-17	3	5.74	4.62
2001 Minnesota	AL	24	0	0	8	19.1	89	27	8	7	3	1	0	0	7	0	15	0	0	1	0	1.000	0	2-4	7	6.80	3.26
2003 Colorado	NL	33	1	0	7	39.1	193	61	39	36	8	3	2	1	18	0	28	0	0	1	4	.200	0	0-5	3	8.77	8.24
2003 Boston	AL	26	0	0	7	29.1	133	32	19	18	2	0	1	0	13	2	31	0	0	2	1	.667	0	0-0	1	4.30	5.52
2004 Cincinnati	NL	51	0	0	10	57.0	235	49	25	24	4	2	5	1	25	2	37	2	0	8	2	.800	0	1-6	22	3.37	3.79
2004 Philadelphia	NL	27	0	0	6	25.1	123	35	14	14	3	3	1	5	8	3	22	0	0	3	3	.500	0	1-2	5	6.65	4.97
12 ML YEARS		744	1	0	417	832.0	3631	827	409	376	79	36	34	28	377	48	731	32	1	50	47	.515	0	186-241	99	4.27	4.07

Brian Jordan

Bats: R **Throws:** R **Pos:** RF-44; DH-17; PH-3; LF-1   **Ht:** 6'1" **Wt:** 205 **Born:** 3/29/1967 **Age:** 38

Year Team*	Lg	G	AB	H	2B	3B	HR	(Hm	Rd)	TB	R	RBI	RC	TBB	IBB	SO	HBP	SH	SF	SB	CS	SB%	GDP	Avg	OBP	Slg
2004 Frisco*	AA	6	19	3	1	0	0	(-	-)	4	1	0	0	0	0	6	0	0	0	0	0	-	0	.158	.158	.211
2004 Oklahoma*	AAA	7	26	10	2	0	0	(-	-)	12	3	8	6	3	1	3	1	0	0	1	0	1.00	0	.385	.467	.462
1992 St Louis	NL	55	193	40	9	4	5	(3	2)	72	17	22	16	10	1	48	1	0	0	7	2	.78	6	.207	.250	.373
1993 St Louis	NL	67	223	69	10	6	10	(4	6)	121	33	44	39	12	0	35	4	0	3	6	6	.50	6	.309	.351	.543
1994 St Louis	NL	53	178	46	8	2	5	(4	1)	73	14	15	22	16	0	40	1	0	2	4	3	.57	6	.258	.320	.410
1995 St Louis	NL	131	490	145	20	4	22	(14	8)	239	83	81	80	22	4	79	11	0	2	24	9	.73	5	.296	.339	.488
1996 St Louis	NL	140	513	159	36	1	17	(3	14)	248	82	104	88	29	4	84	7	2	9	22	5	.81	6	.310	.349	.483
1997 St Louis	NL	47	145	34	5	0	0	(0	0)	39	17	10	13	10	1	21	6	0	0	6	1	.86	4	.234	.311	.269
1998 St Louis	NL	150	564	178	34	7	25	(9	16)	301	100	91	104	40	1	66	9	0	4	17	5	.77	18	.316	.368	.534
1999 Atlanta	NL	153	576	163	28	4	23	(11	12)	268	100	115	92	51	2	81	9	0	9	13	8	.62	9	.283	.346	.465
2000 Atlanta	NL	133	489	129	26	0	17	(7	10)	206	71	77	66	38	1	80	5	0	5	10	2	.83	12	.264	.320	.421
2001 Atlanta	NL	148	560	165	32	3	25	(14	11)	278	82	97	87	31	3	88	6	0	8	3	2	.60	18	.295	.334	.496
2002 Los Angeles	NL	128	471	134	27	3	18	(7	11)	221	65	80	72	34	3	86	6	0	4	2	2	.50	10	.285	.338	.469
2003 Los Angeles	NL	66	224	67	9	0	6	(3	3)	94	28	28	34	23	3	30	4	0	2	1	1	.50	3	.299	.372	.420
2004 Texas	AL	61	212	47	13	1	5	(4	1)	77	27	23	14	16	2	35	1	0	4	2	2	.50	7	.222	.275	.363
13 ML YEARS		1332	4838	1376	257	35	178	(83	95)	2237	719	787	727	332	25	773	70	2	52	117	48	.71	110	.284	.336	.462

Jorge Julio

Pitches: R **Bats:** R **Pos:** RP-65   **Ht:** 6'1" **Wt:** 190 **Born:** 3/3/1979 **Age:** 26

Year Team	Lg	G	GS	CG	GF	IP	BFP	H	R	ER	HR	SH	SF	HB	TBB	IBB	SO	WP	Bk	W	L	Pct	ShO	Sv-Op	Hld	ERC	ERA
2001 Baltimore	AL	18	0	0	8	21.1	99	25	13	9	2	2	0	1	9	0	22	1	0	1	1	.500	0	0-1	3	5.17	3.80
2002 Baltimore	AL	67	0	0	61	68.0	289	55	22	15	5	1	1	2	27	3	55	8	0	5	6	.455	0	25-31	1	2.83	1.99
2003 Baltimore	AL	64	0	0	51	61.2	273	60	36	30	10	2	1	2	34	4	52	0	0	0	7	.000	0	36-44	2	5.05	4.38
2004 Baltimore	AL	65	0	0	50	69.0	306	59	35	35	11	2	3	3	39	4	70	7	0	2	5	.286	0	22-26	2	4.35	4.57
4 ML YEARS		214	0	0	170	220.0	967	199	106	89	28	7	5	8	109	11	199	16	0	8	19	.296	0	83-102	8	4.12	3.64

Eric Junge

Pitches: R **Bats:** R **Pos:** RP   **Ht:** 6'5" **Wt:** 215 **Born:** 1/5/1977 **Age:** 28

Year Team	Lg	G	GS	CG	GF	IP	BFP	H	R	ER	HR	SH	SF	HB	TBB	IBB	SO	WP	Bk	W	L	Pct	ShO	Sv-Op	Hld	ERC	ERA
1999 Yakima	A-	15	15	0	0	82.0	363	98	60	53	10	3	6	0	31	0	55	3	0	5	7	.417	0	0- -	-	5.34	5.82
2000 Sn Brnardino	A+	29	24	0	2	158.0	666	159	69	59	8	3	5	9	53	0	116	8	2	8	1	.889	0	1- -	-	3.82	3.36
2001 Jacksonville	AA	27	27	1	0	164.0	686	143	72	63	19	11	3	13	56	2	116	6	0	10	11	.476	1	0- -	-	3.57	3.46
2002 Scrtn/WlksBr	AAA	29	29	1	0	180.2	766	170	77	71	16	8	4	5	67	1	126	10	0	12	6	.667	0	0- -	-	3.67	3.54
2003 Scrtn/WlksBr	AAA	10	8	0	0	47.0	196	38	20	16	2	1	3	3	16	1	42	1	0	1	0	1.000	0	0- -	-	2.64	3.06
2004 Phillies	R	2	2	0	0	3.2	22	6	4	3	0	0	0	1	4	0	4	0	0	0	1	.000	0	0- -	-	11.10	7.36
2004 Clearwater	A+	5	5	0	0	14.0	62	15	12	10	1	0	1	3	5	0	14	1	0	1	1	.000	0	0- -	-	5.09	6.43
2004 Scrtn/WlksBr	AAA	9	5	0	3	26.1	130	42	29	29	1	0	0	1	16	1	17	1	0	0	4	.000	0	0- -	-	8.49	9.91

Year Team	Lg	HOW MUCH HE PITCHED						WHAT HE GAVE UP											THE RESULTS						
		G	GS	CG	GF	IP	BFP	H	R	ER	HR	SH	SF	HB	TBB	IBB	SO	WP	Bk	W	L	Pct	ShO	Sv-Op	Hld	ERC	ERA
2002 Philadelphia	NL	4	1	0	2	12.2	57	14	3	2	0	2	0	0	5	0	11	0	0	2	0	1.000	0	0-0	0	3.81	1.42
2003 Philadelphia	NL	6	0	0	1	7.2	28	5	3	3	1	0	0	0	1	0	5	0	0	0	0	-	0	0-0	0	1.62	3.52
2 ML YEARS		10	1	0	3	20.1	85	19	6	5	1	2	0	0	6	0	16	0	0	2	0	1.000	0	0-0	0	2.96	2.21

Gabe Kapler

Bats: R **Throws:** R **Pos:** RF-101; PR-19; LF-18; CF-17; PH-7; DH-2   **Ht:** 6'2" **Wt:** 208 **Born:** 8/31/1975 **Age:** 29

Year Team	Lg	BATTING																			BASERUNNING				AVERAGES		
		G	AB	H	2B	3B	HR	(Hm	Rd)	TB	R	RBI	RC	TBB	IBB	SO	HBP	SH	SF		SB	CS	SB%	GDP	Avg	OBP	Slg
1998 Detroit	AL	7	25	5	0	1	0	(0	0)	7	3	0	2	1	0	4	0	0	0		2	0	1.00	0	.200	.231	.280
1999 Detroit	AL	130	416	102	22	4	18	(12	6)	186	60	49	59	42	0	74	2	4	4		11	5	.69	7	.245	.315	.447
2000 Texas	AL	116	444	134	32	1	14	(11	3)	210	59	66	72	42	2	70	3	2	3		8	4	.67	12	.302	.360	.473
2001 Texas	AL	134	483	129	29	1	17	(11	6)	211	77	72	77	61	2	70	3	2	7		23	6	.79	10	.267	.348	.437
2002 Tex-Col		112	315	88	16	4	2	(1	1)	118	37	34	44	16	0	53	1	7	3		11	4	.73	5	.279	.313	.375
2003 Col-Bos		107	225	61	13	1	4	(2	2)	88	39	27	28	22	1	41	0	0	0		6	2	.75	8	.271	.336	.391
2004 Boston	AL	136	290	79	14	1	6	(3	3)	113	51	33	32	15	0	49	2	1	2		5	4	.56	5	.272	.311	.390
2002 Texas	AL	72	196	51	12	1	0	(0	0)	65	25	17	20	8	0	30	0	7	3		5	2	.71	3	.260	.285	.332
2002 Colorado	NL	40	119	37	4	3	2	(1	1)	53	12	17	24	8	0	23	1	0	0		6	2	.75	2	.311	.359	.445
2003 Colorado	NL	39	67	15	2	0	0	(0	0)	17	10	4	5	8	1	18	0	0	0		2	0	1.00	3	.224	.307	.254
2003 Boston	AL	68	158	46	11	1	4	(2	2)	71	29	23	23	14	0	23	0	0	0		4	2	.67	5	.291	.349	.449
7 ML YEARS		742	2198	598	126	13	61	(40	21)	933	326	281	314	199	5	348	8	16	19		66	25	.73	47	.272	.332	.424

Eric Karros

Bats: R **Throws:** R **Pos:** 1B-22; PH-11; DH-10   **Ht:** 6'4" **Wt:** 226 **Born:** 11/4/1967 **Age:** 37

Year Team	Lg	BATTING																			BASERUNNING				AVERAGES		
		G	AB	H	2B	3B	HR	(Hm	Rd)	TB	R	RBI	RC	TBB	IBB	SO	HBP	SH	SF		SB	CS	SB%	GDP	Avg	OBP	Slg
1991 Los Angeles	NL	14	14	1	1	0	0	(0	0)	2	0	1	0	1	0	6	0	0	0		0	0	-	0	.071	.133	.143
1992 Los Angeles	NL	149	545	140	30	1	20	(6	14)	232	63	88	66	37	3	103	2	0	5		2	4	.33	15	.257	.304	.426
1993 Los Angeles	NL	158	619	153	27	2	23	(13	10)	253	74	80	68	34	1	82	2	0	3		0	1	.00	17	.247	.287	.409
1994 Los Angeles	NL	111	406	108	21	1	14	(5	9)	173	51	46	52	29	1	53	2	0	11		2	0	1.00	13	.266	.310	.426
1995 Los Angeles	NL	143	551	164	29	3	32	(19	13)	295	83	105	103	61	4	115	4	0	4		4	4	.50	14	.298	.369	.535
1996 Los Angeles	NL	154	608	158	29	1	34	(16	18)	291	84	111	86	53	2	121	1	0	8		8	0	1.00	27	.260	.316	.479
1997 Los Angeles	NL	**162**	628	167	28	0	31	(13	18)	288	86	104	95	61	2	116	2	0	9		15	7	.68	10	.266	.329	.459
1998 Los Angeles	NL	139	507	150	20	1	23	(9	14)	241	59	87	86	47	1	93	3	0	7		7	2	.78	7	.296	.355	.475
1999 Los Angeles	NL	153	578	176	40	0	34	(17	17)	318	74	112	107	53	0	119	2	0	6		8	5	.62	18	.304	.362	.550
2000 Los Angeles	NL	155	584	146	29	0	31	(16	15)	268	84	106	84	63	2	122	4	0	12		4	3	.57	18	.250	.321	.459
2001 Los Angeles	NL	121	438	103	22	0	15	(7	8)	170	42	63	49	41	2	101	3	0	3		3	1	.75	15	.235	.303	.388
2002 Los Angeles	NL	142	524	142	26	1	13	(9	4)	209	52	73	73	37	1	74	6	0	6		4	2	.67	11	.271	.323	.399
2003 Chicago	NL	114	336	96	16	1	12	(7	5)	150	37	40	44	28	1	46	0	0	1		1	1	.50	14	.286	.340	.446
2004 Oakland	AL	40	103	20	6	0	2	(1	1)	32	8	11	7	7	1	16	0	0	1		1	0	1.00	3	.194	.243	.311
14 ML YEARS		1755	6441	1724	324	11	284	(138	146)	2922	797	1027	920	552	21	1167	31	0	76		59	30	.66	181	.268	.325	.454

Steve Karsay

Pitches: R **Bats:** R **Pos:** RP-7   **Ht:** 6'3" **Wt:** 215 **Born:** 3/24/1972 **Age:** 33

Year Team	Lg	HOW MUCH HE PITCHED						WHAT HE GAVE UP												THE RESULTS						
		G	GS	CG	GF	IP	BFP	H	R	ER	HR	SH	SF	HB	TBB	IBB	SO	WP	Bk	W	L	Pct	ShO	Sv-Op	Hld	ERC	ERA
2004 Staten Island*	A-	3	0	0	0	3.0	9	0	0	0	0	0	0	0	0	0	2	0	0	0	0	-	0	0- -		0.00	0.00
2004 Trenton*	AA	4	0	0	1	6.0	28	6	5	5	0	0	0	0	4	0	7	1	0	1	0	1.000	0	0- -		4.23	7.50
2004 Columbus*	AAA	11	0	0	1	11.1	53	12	10	7	0	0	0	1	6	0	8	0	0	0	0	-	0	0- -		4.37	5.56
1993 Oakland	AL	8	8	0	0	49.0	210	49	23	22	4	0	2	2	16	1	33	1	0	3	3	.500	0	0-0	0	3.78	4.04
1994 Oakland	AL	4	4	1	0	28.0	115	26	8	8	1	2	1	1	8	0	15	0	0	1	1	.500	0	0-0	0	3.01	2.57
1997 Oakland	AL	24	24	0	0	132.2	609	166	92	85	20	2	5	9	47	3	92	7	0	3	12	.200	0	0-0	0	5.97	5.77
1998 Cleveland	AL	11	1	0	4	24.1	111	31	16	16	3	1	2	2	6	1	13	2	0	0	0	.000	0	0-0	2	5.40	5.92
1999 Cleveland	AL	50	3	0	13	78.2	324	71	29	26	6	2	3	2	30	3	68	5	0	10	2	.833	0	1-3	9	3.45	2.97
2000 Cleveland	AL	72	0	0	46	76.2	329	79	33	32	5	2	2	3	25	4	66	0	0	5	9	.357	0	20-29	11	3.79	3.76
2001 Cle-Atl		74	0	0	29	88.0	356	73	27	23	5	6	4	1	25	10	83	3	0	5	5	.375	0	8-12	12	3.36	2.35
2002 New York	AL	78	0	0	38	88.1	379	87	33	32	7	7	3	2	30	14	65	3	0	6	4	.600	0	12-16	14	3.42	3.26
2004 New York	AL	7	0	0	6	6.2	27	5	3	2	2	0	2	0	2	0	4	1	0	0	0	-	0	0-0	0	3.50	2.70
2001 Cleveland	AL	31	0	0	8	43.1	166	29	6	6	1	3	1	0	8	2	44	2	0	1	0	1.000	0	1-1	8	3.31	1.25
2001 Atlanta	NL	43	0	0	21	44.2	190	44	21	17	4	3	3	1	17	8	39	1	0	3	4	.429	0	7-11	4	3.68	3.43
9 ML YEARS		328	40	1	136	572.1	2460	587	264	246	53	22	24	22	189	36	439	22	0	31	38	.449	0	41-60	48	3.94	3.87

Matt Kata

Bats: B **Throws:** R **Pos:** 2B-38; 3B-3; PH-1; PR-1   **Ht:** 6'1" **Wt:** 185 **Born:** 3/14/1978 **Age:** 27

Year Team	Lg	BATTING																			BASERUNNING				AVERAGES		
		G	AB	H	2B	3B	HR	(Hm	Rd)	TB	R	RBI	RC	TBB	IBB	SO	HBP	SH	SF		SB	CS	SB%	GDP	Avg	OBP	Slg
1999 South Bend	A	78	318	83	14	5	3	(-	-)	116	40	33	38	28	0	46	4	1	1		5	6	.45	5	.261	.328	.365
2000 South Bend	A	133	521	133	22	9	6	(-	-)	191	82	59	66	52	2	58	6	3	5		38	12	.76	10	.255	.327	.367
2001 Lancaster	A+	119	494	146	19	6	10	(-	-)	207	80	54	77	41	3	79	5	4	1		30	8	.79	4	.296	.355	.419
2001 El Paso	AA	4	16	7	2	0	0	(-	-)	9	4	4	3	2	0	2	0	0	0		0	1	.00	0	.438	.500	.563
2002 El Paso	AA	136	598	172	33	9	11	(-	-)	256	95	57	87	37	4	79	4	4	5		12	7	.63	6	.298	.341	.443
2003 Tucson	AAA	48	201	58	13	5	3	(-	-)	90	31	25	28	9	1	29	3	0	1		2	3	.40	1	.289	.327	.448
2003 Arizona	NL	78	288	74	16	5	7	(3	4)	121	42	29	40	25	0	53	1	5	3		3	2	.60	4	.257	.315	.420
2004 Arizona	NL	42	162	40	9	2	2	(1	1)	59	17	13	19	13	2	29	0	1	1		4	1	.80	1	.247	.301	.364
2 ML YEARS		120	450	114	25	7	9	(4	5)	180	59	42	59	38	2	82	1	6	4		7	3	.70	5	.253	.310	.400

Scott Kazmir

Pitches: L **Bats:** L **Pos:** SP-7; RP-1   **Ht:** 6'0" **Wt:** 170 **Born:** 1/24/1984 **Age:** 21

Year Team	Lg	G	GS	CG	GF	IP	BFP	H	R	ER	HR	SH	SF	HB	TBB	IBB	SO	WP	Bk	W	L	Pct	ShO	Sv-Op	Hld	ERC	ERA
2002 Brooklyn	A-	5	5	0	0	18.0	65	5	2	1	0	0	0	2	7	0	34	0	0	0	1	.000	0	0--	-	0.86	0.50
2003 Capital City	A	18	18	0	0	76.1	304	50	26	20	6	3	0	3	28	0	105	12	1	4	4	.500	0	0--	-	2.20	2.36
2003 St. Lucie	A+	7	7	0	0	33.0	141	29	15	12	0	1	1	2	16	0	40	2	0	1	2	.333	0	0--	-	3.30	3.27
2004 St. Lucie	A+	11	11	0	0	50.0	211	49	20	19	3	5	5	0	22	0	51	5	0	1	2	.333	0	0--	-	3.95	3.42
2004 Montgomery	AA	4	4	0	0	25.0	96	14	7	4	0	3	2	1	11	0	24	1	0	1	2	.333	0	0--	-	1.63	1.44
2004 Binghamton	AA	4	4	0	0	26.0	100	16	6	5	0	3	2	3	9	0	29	1	0	2	1	.667	0	0--	-	1.82	1.73
2004 Tampa Bay	AL	8	7	0	0	33.1	152	33	22	21	4	0	0	2	21	0	41	3	0	2	3	.400	0	0-0	0	5.36	5.67

Austin Kearns

Bats: R **Throws:** R **Pos:** RF-60; PH-4; CF-1; PR-1   **Ht:** 6'3" **Wt:** 220 **Born:** 5/20/1980 **Age:** 25

Year Team	Lg	G	AB	H	2B	3B	HR	(Hm	Rd)	TB	R	RBI	RC	TBB	IBB	SO	HBP	SH	SF	SB	CS	SB%	GDP	Avg	OBP	Slg
2004 Louisville*	AAA	25	83	28	7	1	2	(-	-)	43	19	15	20	19	1	16	2	0	0	3	1	.75	3	.337	.471	.518
2002 Cincinnati	NL	107	372	117	24	3	13	(7	6)	186	66	56	70	54	3	81	6	0	3	6	3	.67	11	.315	.407	.500
2003 Cincinnati	NL	82	292	77	11	0	15	(8	7)	133	39	58	52	41	1	68	5	0	0	5	2	.71	7	.264	.364	.455
2004 Cincinnati	NL	64	217	50	10	2	9	(3	6)	91	28	32	26	28	0	71	1	0	0	2	1	.67	8	.230	.321	.419
3 ML YEARS		253	881	244	45	5	37	(18	19)	410	133	146	148	123	4	220	12	0	3	13	6	.68	26	.277	.372	.465

Dave Kelton

Bats: R **Throws:** R **Pos:** PH-6; LF-2; RF-1; PR-1   **Ht:** 6'3" **Wt:** 205 **Born:** 12/17/1979 **Age:** 25

Year Team	Lg	G	AB	H	2B	3B	HR	(Hm	Rd)	TB	R	RBI	RC	TBB	IBB	SO	HBP	SH	SF	SB	CS	SB%	GDP	Avg	OBP	Slg
1998 Cubs	R	50	181	48	7	5	6	(-	-)	83	39	29	31	23	0	58	2	0	1	16	3	.84	2	.265	.353	.459
1999 Lansing	A	124	509	137	17	4	13	(-	-)	201	75	68	64	39	1	121	2	0	3	22	9	.71	11	.269	.322	.395
2000 Daytona	A+	132	523	140	30	7	18	(-	-)	238	75	84	71	38	4	120	2	1	5	7	8	.47	9	.268	.317	.455
2001 W Tennessee	AA	58	224	70	9	4	12	(-	-)	123	33	45	44	24	0	55	1	0	2	1	3	.25	1	.313	.378	.549
2002 W Tennessee	AA	129	498	130	28	6	20	(-	-)	230	68	79	73	52	2	129	2	0	3	12	6	.67	10	.261	.332	.462
2003 Iowa	AAA	121	442	119	24	3	16	(-	-)	197	62	67	66	46	1	115	2	1	4	8	2	.80	7	.269	.338	.446
2004 Iowa	AAA	121	420	103	26	1	19	(-	-)	188	57	68	54	33	1	92	4	0	5	7	2	.78	10	.245	.303	.448
2003 Chicago	NL	10	12	2	1	0	0	(0	0)	3	1	1	1	0	0	5	0	0	0	0	0	-	1	.167	.167	.250
2004 Chicago	NL	8	10	1	1	0	0	(0	0)	2	1	0	0	0	0	3	0	0	0	0	0	-	0	.100	.100	.200
2 ML YEARS		18	22	3	2	0	0	(0	0)	5	2	1	1	0	0	8	0	0	0	0	0	-	1	.136	.136	.227

Jason Kendall

Bats: R **Throws:** R **Pos:** C-146; PH-2   **Ht:** 6'0" **Wt:** 195 **Born:** 6/26/1974 **Age:** 31

Year Team	Lg	G	AB	H	2B	3B	HR	(Hm	Rd)	TB	R	RBI	RC	TBB	IBB	SO	HBP	SH	SF	SB	CS	SB%	GDP	Avg	OBP	Slg
1996 Pittsburgh	NL	130	414	124	23	5	3	(2	1)	166	54	42	63	35	11	30	15	3	4	5	2	.71	7	.300	.372	.401
1997 Pittsburgh	NL	144	486	143	36	4	8	(5	3)	211	71	49	86	49	2	53	31	1	5	18	6	.75	11	.294	.391	.434
1998 Pittsburgh	NL	149	535	175	36	3	12	(6	6)	253	95	75	110	51	3	51	31	2	8	26	5	.84	6	.327	.411	.473
1999 Pittsburgh	NL	78	280	93	20	3	8	(5	3)	143	61	41	63	38	3	32	12	0	4	22	3	.88	8	.332	.428	.511
2000 Pittsburgh	NL	152	579	185	33	6	14	(7	7)	272	112	58	112	79	3	79	15	1	4	22	12	.65	13	.320	.412	.470
2001 Pittsburgh	NL	157	606	161	22	2	10	(3	7)	217	84	53	68	44	4	48	20	0	2	13	14	.48	18	.266	.335	.358
2002 Pittsburgh	NL	145	545	154	25	3	3	(1	2)	194	59	44	66	49	1	29	9	0	2	15	8	.65	11	.283	.350	.356
2003 Pittsburgh	NL	150	587	191	29	3	6	(3	3)	244	84	58	97	49	3	40	25	1	3	8	7	.53	9	.325	.399	.416
2004 Pittsburgh	NL	147	574	183	32	0	3	(2	1)	224	86	51	95	60	2	41	19	1	4	11	8	.58	12	.319	.399	.390
9 ML YEARS		1252	4606	1409	256	29	67	(34	33)	1924	706	471	760	454	32	403	177	9	36	140	65	.68	95	.306	.387	.418

Adam Kennedy

Bats: L **Throws:** R **Pos:** 2B-145; PH-1; PR-1   **Ht:** 6'1" **Wt:** 192 **Born:** 1/10/1976 **Age:** 29

Year Team	Lg	G	AB	H	2B	3B	HR	(Hm	Rd)	TB	R	RBI	RC	TBB	IBB	SO	HBP	SH	SF	SB	CS	SB%	GDP	Avg	OBP	Slg
1999 St Louis	NL	33	102	26	10	1	1	(1	0)	41	12	16	12	3	0	8	2	1	2	0	1	.00	1	.255	.284	.402
2000 Anaheim	AL	156	598	159	33	11	9	(7	2)	241	82	72	72	28	5	73	3	8	4	22	8	.73	10	.266	.300	.403
2001 Anaheim	AL	137	478	129	25	3	6	(4	2)	178	48	40	57	27	3	71	11	7	9	12	7	.63	7	.270	.318	.372
2002 Anaheim	AL	144	474	148	32	6	7	(6	1)	213	65	52	70	19	1	80	7	5	4	17	4	.81	5	.312	.345	.449
2003 Anaheim	AL	143	449	121	17	1	13	(8	5)	179	71	49	61	45	4	73	9	2	5	22	9	.71	7	.269	.344	.399
2004 Anaheim	AL	144	468	130	20	5	10	(5	5)	190	70	48	60	41	7	92	13	9	2	15	5	.75	10	.278	.351	.406
6 ML YEARS		757	2569	713	137	27	46	(31	15)	1042	348	277	332	163	20	397	45	32	26	88	34	.72	40	.278	.329	.406

Joe Kennedy

Pitches: L **Bats:** R **Pos:** SP-27   **Ht:** 6'4" **Wt:** 237 **Born:** 5/24/1979 **Age:** 26

Year Team	Lg	G	GS	CG	GF	IP	BFP	H	R	ER	HR	SH	SF	HB	TBB	IBB	SO	WP	Bk	W	L	Pct	ShO	Sv-Op	Hld	ERC	ERA
2004 Co Springs*	AAA	3	2	0	0	12.2	56	17	11	10	1	1	0	0	2	0	12	0	0	1	1	.500	0	0--	-	4.88	7.11
2001 Tampa Bay	AL	20	20	0	0	117.2	498	122	63	58	16	2	5	3	34	0	78	5	1	7	8	.467	0	0-0	0	4.23	4.44
2002 Tampa Bay	AL	30	30	5	0	196.2	840	204	114	99	23	2	9	16	55	0	109	4	0	8	11	.421	1	0-0	0	4.29	4.53
2003 Tampa Bay	AL	32	22	1	7	133.2	619	167	101	91	19	1	8	11	47	1	77	3	1	3	12	.200	1	1-2	1	5.92	6.13
2004 Colorado	NL	27	27	1	0	162.1	705	163	68	66	17	9	6	8	67	12	117	5	0	9	7	.563	0	0-0	0	4.29	3.66
4 ML YEARS		109	99	7	7	610.1	2662	656	346	314	75	14	28	38	203	13	381	17	2	27	38	.415	2	1-2	1	4.63	4.63

Logan Kensing

Pitches: R **Bats:** R **Pos:** SP-3; RP-2　　　　**Ht:** 6'1" **Wt:** 185 **Born:** 7/3/1982 **Age:** 22

				HOW MUCH HE PITCHED						WHAT HE GAVE UP								THE RESULTS							
Year Team	Lg	G	GS	CG	GF	IP	BFP	H	R	ER	HR	SH	SF	HB	TBB	IBB	SO	WP	Bk	W	L	Pct	ShO	Sv-Op	Hld	ERC	ERA
2003 Jamestown	A-	8	6	0	0	33.0	155	48	23	21	1	0	2	3	6	0	20	2	0	2	4	.333	0	0- -	-	5.57	5.73
2003 Greensboro	A	4	4	0	0	20.0	82	18	10	10	2	1	1	1	5	0	11	0	0	2	0	.000	0	0- -	-	3.17	4.50
2004 Jupiter	A+	23	23	1	0	127.2	525	120	53	42	5	7	8	8	35	1	100	8	1	6	7	.462	0	0- -	-	3.16	2.96
2004 Florida	NL	5	3	0	2	13.2	66	19	15	15	5	0	1	1	9	0	7	2	0	0	3	.000	0	0-0	0	10.74	9.88

Jeff Kent

Bats: R **Throws:** R **Pos:** 2B-139; PH-4; DH-2　　　　**Ht:** 6'1" **Wt:** 220 **Born:** 3/7/1968 **Age:** 37

							BATTING														BASERUNNING				AVERAGES		
Year Team	Lg	G	AB	H	2B	3B	HR	(Hm	Rd)	TB	R	RBI	RC	TBB	IBB	SO	HBP	SH	SF		SB	CS	SB%	GDP	Avg	OBP	Slg
1992 Tor-NYM		102	305	73	21	2	11	(4	7)	131	52	50	40	27	0	76	7	0	4		2	3	.40	5	.239	.312	.430
1993 New York	NL	140	496	134	24	0	21	(9	12)	221	65	80	68	30	2	88	8	6	4		4	4	.50	11	.270	.320	.446
1994 New York	NL	107	415	121	24	5	14	(10	4)	197	53	68	64	23	3	84	10	1	3		1	4	.20	7	.292	.341	.475
1995 New York	NL	125	472	131	22	3	20	(11	9)	219	65	65	69	29	3	89	8	1	4		3	3	.50	9	.278	.327	.464
1996 NYM-Cle		128	437	124	27	1	12	(4	8)	189	61	55	61	31	1	78	2	1	6		6	4	.60	8	.284	.330	.432
1997 San Francisco	NL	155	580	145	38	2	29	(13	16)	274	90	121	86	48	6	133	13	0	10		11	3	.79	14	.250	.316	.472
1998 San Francisco	NL	137	526	156	37	3	31	(17	14)	292	94	128	100	48	9	110	9	1	10		9	4	.69	16	.297	.359	.555
1999 San Francisco	NL	138	511	148	40	2	23	(11	12)	261	86	101	93	61	3	112	5	0	8		13	6	.68	12	.290	.366	.511
2000 San Francisco	NL	159	587	196	41	7	33	(14	19)	350	114	125	138	90	6	107	9	0	9		12	9	.57	17	.334	.424	.596
2001 San Francisco	NL	159	607	181	49	6	22	(8	14)	308	84	106	112	65	4	96	11	0	13		7	6	.54	11	.298	.369	.507
2002 San Francisco	NL	152	623	195	42	2	37	(11	26)	352	102	108	105	52	3	101	4	0	3		5	1	.83	20	.313	.368	.565
2003 Houston	NL	130	505	150	39	1	22	(9	13)	257	77	93	92	39	2	85	5	0	3		6	2	.75	13	.297	.351	.509
2004 Houston	NL	145	540	156	34	8	27	(14	13)	287	96	107	87	49	3	96	6	0	11		7	3	.70	23	.289	.348	.531
1992 Toronto	AL	65	192	46	13	1	8	(2	6)	85	36	35	28	20	0	47	6	0	4		2	1	.67	3	.240	.324	.443
1992 New York	NL	37	113	27	8	1	3	(2	1)	46	16	15	12	7	0	29	1	0	0		0	2	.00	2	.239	.289	.407
1996 New York	NL	89	335	97	20	1	9	(2	7)	146	45	39	46	21	1	56	1	1	3		4	3	.57	7	.290	.331	.436
1996 Cleveland	AL	39	102	27	7	0	3	(2	1)	43	16	16	15	10	0	22	1	0	3		2	1	.67	1	.265	.328	.422
13 ML YEARS		1777	6604	1910	438	42	302	(135	167)	3338	1039	1207	1115	592	40	1255	97	10	88		86	52	.62	166	.289	.352	.505

Jeff Keppinger

Bats: R **Throws:** R **Pos:** 2B-32; PH-3　　　　**Ht:** 6'1" **Wt:** 181 **Born:** 4/21/1980 **Age:** 25

							BATTING														BASERUNNING				AVERAGES		
Year Team	Lg	G	AB	H	2B	3B	HR	(Hm	Rd)	TB	R	RBI	RC	TBB	IBB	SO	HBP	SH	SF		SB	CS	SB%	GDP	Avg	OBP	Slg
2002 Hickory	A	126	478	132	23	4	10	(-	-)	193	75	73	67	47	0	33	6	2	7		6	2	.75	13	.276	.344	.404
2003 Lynchburg	A+	92	342	111	21	2	3	(-	-)	145	55	51	51	23	0	28	1	3	4		3	2	.60	10	.325	.365	.424
2004 Altoona	AA	82	323	108	17	2	1	(-	-)	132	45	33	49	27	1	17	0	2	2		10	6	.63	13	.334	.384	.409
2004 Binghamton	AA	14	47	17	3	1	0	(-	-)	22	14	5	9	6	1	2	0	0	1		2	1	.67	2	.362	.426	.468
2004 Norfolk	AAA	6	19	6	1	0	0	(-	-)	7	1	2	3	4	0	2	1	0	0		0	0	-	2	.316	.458	.368
2004 New York	NL	33	116	33	2	0	3	(3	0)	44	9	9	11	6	0	7	0	0	1		2	1	.67	6	.284	.317	.379

Jason Kershner

Pitches: L **Bats:** L **Pos:** RP-22; SP-2　　　　**Ht:** 6'2" **Wt:** 165 **Born:** 12/19/1976 **Age:** 28

				HOW MUCH HE PITCHED						WHAT HE GAVE UP								THE RESULTS							
Year Team	Lg	G	GS	CG	GF	IP	BFP	H	R	ER	HR	SH	SF	HB	TBB	IBB	SO	WP	Bk	W	L	Pct	ShO	Sv-Op	Hld	ERC	ERA
2004 Syracuse*	AAA	28	0	0	11	36.1	167	45	23	21	6	0	0	3	10	2	31	1	0	3	2	.600	0	4- -	-	5.56	5.20
2002 SD-Tor		25	0	0	4	24.0	107	20	16	13	3	0	0	2	14	1	18	3	0	1	0	1.000	0	1-2	1	4.24	4.88
2003 Toronto	AL	40	0	0	8	54.0	220	43	21	19	5	2	3	2	15	2	32	2	0	3	3	.500	0	0-1	7	2.56	3.17
2004 Toronto	AL	24	2	0	2	22.1	103	30	16	15	3	0	0	0	8	0	15	3	1	0	1	.000	0	0-0	2	6.18	6.04
2002 San Diego	NL	15	0	0	2	18.2	81	15	14	12	2	0	0	2	10	0	11	0	0	0	0	-	0	0-0	4	4.00	5.79
2002 Toronto	AL	10	0	0	2	5.1	26	5	2	1	1	0	0	0	4	1	7	3	0	0	0	-	0	1-2	1	5.11	1.69
3 ML YEARS		89	2	0	14	100.1	430	93	53	47	11	2	3	4	37	3	65	8	1	3	5	.375	0	1-3	10	3.69	4.22

Masao Kida

Pitches: R **Bats:** R **Pos:** RP-10　　　　**Ht:** 6'3" **Wt:** 210 **Born:** 9/12/1968 **Age:** 36

				HOW MUCH HE PITCHED						WHAT HE GAVE UP								THE RESULTS							
Year Team	Lg	G	GS	CG	GF	IP	BFP	H	R	ER	HR	SH	SF	HB	TBB	IBB	SO	WP	Bk	W	L	Pct	ShO	Sv-Op	Hld	ERC	ERA
2004 Dodgers*	R	2	2	0	0	4.0	14	2	0	0	0	0	0	0	0	0	0	0	0	0	0	-	0	0- -	-	0.54	0.00
2004 Las Vegas*	AAA	9	5	0	0	37.2	162	40	25	25	10	2	2	1	16	0	32	6	0	3	1	.750	0	0- -	-	6.05	5.97
1999 Detroit	AL	49	0	0	0	64.2	292	73	0	45	6	0	0	0	30	0	50	0	0	1	0	1.000	0	1-0	0	4.99	6.26
2000 Detroit	AL	2	0	0	0	2.2	13	5	0	3	1	0	0	0	0	0	0	0	0	0	0	-	0	0-0	0	9.86	10.13
2003 Los Angeles	NL	3	2	0	1	12.0	53	15	5	4	0	0	0	0	3	0	8	3	0	0	1	.000	0	0-0	0	4.14	3.00
2004 LA-Sea		10	0	0	1	14.1	66	19	9	9	1	0	0	2	6	0	10	0	0	0	0	-	0	0-0	0	6.67	5.65
2004 Los Angeles	NL	3	0	0	1	4.2	19	4	0	0	0	0	0	1	1	0	5	0	0	0	0	-	0	0-0	0	2.84	0.00
2004 Seattle	AL	7	0	0	0	9.2	47	15	9	9	1	0	0	1	5	0	5	0	0	0	0	-	0	0-0	0	8.82	8.38
4 ML YEARS		64	2	0	2	93.2	424	112	14	61	8	0	0	2	39	0	68	3	0	1	1	.500	0	1-0	0	5.25	5.86

Bobby Kielty

Bats: B **Throws:** R **Pos:** LF-51; RF-21; PH-14; DH-10　　　　**Ht:** 6'1" **Wt:** 215 **Born:** 8/5/1976 **Age:** 28

							BATTING														BASERUNNING				AVERAGES		
Year Team	Lg	G	AB	H	2B	3B	HR	(Hm	Rd)	TB	R	RBI	RC	TBB	IBB	SO	HBP	SH	SF		SB	CS	SB%	GDP	Avg	OBP	Slg
2001 Minnesota	AL	37	104	26	8	0	2	(1	1)	40	8	14	13	8	2	25	1	0	5		3	0	1.00	2	.250	.297	.385
2002 Minnesota	AL	112	289	84	14	3	12	(8	4)	140	49	46	59	52	4	66	5	0	2		4	1	.80	4	.291	.405	.484
2003 Min-Tor	AL	137	427	104	26	1	13	(6	7)	171	71	57	68	71	6	92	7	0	4		8	3	.73	11	.244	.358	.400
2004 Oakland	AL	83	238	51	14	1	7	(6	1)	88	29	31	29	35	0	47	3	1	1		1	0	1.00	5	.214	.321	.370

							BATTING													BASERUNNING				AVERAGES		
Year Team	Lg	G	AB	H	2B	3B	HR	(Hm	Rd)	TB	R	RBI	RC	TBB	IBB	SO	HBP	SH	SF	SB	CS	SB%	GDP	Avg	OBP	Slg
2003 Minnesota	AL	75	238	60	13	0	9	(4	5)	100	40	32	41	42	2	56	3	0	1	6	2	.75	5	.252	.370	.420
2003 Toronto	AL	62	189	44	13	1	4	(2	2)	71	31	25	27	29	4	36	4	0	3	2	1	.67	6	.233	.342	.376
4 ML YEARS		369	1058	265	62	5	34	(21	13)	439	157	148	169	166	12	230	16	1	12	16	4	.80	22	.250	.357	.415

Brooks Kieschnick

Bats: L **Throws:** R **Pos:** RP-32; PH-48   **Ht:** 6'4" **Wt:** 230 **Born:** 6/6/1972 **Age:** 33

							BATTING													BASERUNNING				AVERAGES		
Year Team	Lg	G	AB	H	2B	3B	HR	(Hm	Rd)	TB	R	RBI	RC	TBB	IBB	SO	HBP	SH	SF	SB	CS	SB%	GDP	Avg	OBP	Slg
1996 Chicago	NL	25	29	10	2	0	1	(0	1)	15	6	6	6	3	0	8	0	0	0	0	0	-	0	.345	.406	.517
1997 Chicago	NL	39	90	18	2	0	4	(3	1)	32	9	12	9	12	0	21	0	0	0	1	0	1.00	2	.200	.294	.356
2000 Cincinnati	NL	14	12	0	0	0	0	(0	0)	0	0	0	0	1	0	5	0	0	0	0	0	-	0	.000	.077	.000
2001 Colorado	NL	35	42	10	2	1	3	(1	2)	23	5	9	6	3	0	13	0	0	0	0	0	-	1	.238	.289	.548
2003 Milwaukee	NL	70	70	21	1	0	7	(2	5)	43	12	12	10	6	0	13	0	0	0	0	0	-	0	.300	.355	.614
2004 Milwaukee	NL	77	63	17	3	0	1	(1	0)	23	2	7	7	5	1	16	0	0	0	0	0	-	3	.270	.324	.365
6 ML YEARS		260	306	76	10	1	16	(7	9)	136	34	46	38	30	1	76	0	0	0	1	0	1.00	8	.248	.315	.444

		HOW MUCH HE PITCHED						WHAT HE GAVE UP												THE RESULTS						
Year Team	Lg	G	GS	CG	GF	IP	BFP	H	R	ER	HR	SH	SF	HB	TBB	IBB	SO	WP	Bk	W	L	Pct	ShO	Sv-Op	Hld	ERC	ERA
2004 Indianapolis*	AAA	2	2	0	0	2.0	7	1	0	0	0	0	0	0	0	0	1	0	0	0	0	-	0	0- -	-	0.54	0.00
2003 Milwaukee	NL	42	0	0	15	53.0	242	66	32	31	7	5	2	6	13	4	39	2	0	1	1	.500	0	0-0	2	5.07	5.26
2004 Milwaukee	NL	32	0	0	9	43.0	183	44	19	18	6	2	0	0	13	3	28	1	0	1	1	.500	0	0-1	5	3.96	3.77
2 ML YEARS		74	0	0	24	96.0	425	110	51	49	11	4	0	6	26	7	67	3	0	2	2	.500	0	0-1	7	4.57	4.59

Byung-Hyun Kim

Pitches: R **Bats:** R **Pos:** RP-4; SP-3   **Ht:** 5'11" **Wt:** 177 **Born:** 1/19/1979 **Age:** 26

		HOW MUCH HE PITCHED						WHAT HE GAVE UP												THE RESULTS						
Year Team	Lg	G	GS	CG	GF	IP	BFP	H	R	ER	HR	SH	SF	HB	TBB	IBB	SO	WP	Bk	W	L	Pct	ShO	Sv-Op	Hld	ERC	ERA
2004 Sarasota*	A+	1	1	0	0	2.0	5	0	0	0	0	0	1	0	0	0	2	0	0	0	0	-	0	0- -	-	0.00	0.00
2004 Pawtucket*	AAA	22	19	0	0	60.2	262	71	43	36	6	2	2	6	12	0	39	0	1	2	6	.250	0	0- -	3	4.68	5.34
1999 Arizona	NL	25	0	0	10	27.1	121	20	15	14	2	1	0	5	20	2	31	4	1	1	2	.333	0	1-4	3	4.35	4.61
2000 Arizona	NL	61	1	0	30	70.2	320	52	39	35	9	2	3	9	46	5	111	3	2	6	6	.500	0	14-20	5	4.04	4.46
2001 Arizona	NL	78	0	0	44	98.0	392	58	32	32	10	5	0	8	44	3	113	5	1	5	6	.455	0	19-23	11	2.45	2.94
2002 Arizona	NL	72	0	0	66	84.0	343	64	20	19	5	1	2	6	26	2	92	2	0	8	3	.727	0	36-42	2	2.45	2.04
2003 Ari-Bos		56	12	0	35	122.1	517	104	55	45	12	6	2	12	33	3	102	1	0	9	10	.474	0	16-19	1	3.02	3.31
2004 Boston	AL	7	3	0	2	17.1	77	17	15	12	1	0	2	2	7	1	6	1	0	2	1	.667	0	0-0	0	3.98	6.23
2003 Arizona	NL	7	7	0	0	43.0	181	34	17	17	6	3	0	4	15	0	33	0	0	1	5	.167	0	0-0	0	3.32	3.56
2003 Boston	AL	49	5	0	35	79.1	336	70	38	28	6	3	2	8	18	3	69	1	0	8	5	.615	0	16-19	1	2.87	3.18
6 ML YEARS		299	16	0	187	419.2	1770	315	176	157	39	15	9	42	176	16	455	16	4	31	28	.525	0	86-108	20	3.06	3.37

Sunny Kim

Pitches: R **Bats:** R **Pos:** RP-26; SP-17   **Ht:** 6'2" **Wt:** 188 **Born:** 9/4/1977 **Age:** 27

		HOW MUCH HE PITCHED						WHAT HE GAVE UP												THE RESULTS						
Year Team	Lg	G	GS	CG	GF	IP	BFP	H	R	ER	HR	SH	SF	HB	TBB	IBB	SO	WP	Bk	W	L	Pct	ShO	Sv-Op	Hld	ERC	ERA
2001 Boston	AL	20	2	0	7	41.2	201	54	27	27	1	3	0	4	21	5	27	5	0	0	2	.000	0	0-0	1	5.72	5.83
2002 Bos-Mon		19	5	0	7	49.1	208	52	26	26	5	0	2	2	14	2	29	2	0	3	0	1.000	0	0-0	2	4.10	4.74
2003 Montreal	NL	4	3	0	1	14.0	72	24	13	13	6	0	1	4	8	0	5	0	0	0	1	.000	0	0-0	0	14.93	8.36
2004 Montreal	NL	43	17	0	3	135.2	603	145	80	69	17	5	3	13	55	10	87	6	0	4	6	.400	0	0-0	2	4.97	4.58
2002 Boston	AL	15	2	0	7	29.0	128	34	24	24	5	0	2	1	7	0	18	2	0	2	0	1.000	0	0-0	2	5.01	7.45
2002 Montreal	NL	4	3	0	0	20.1	80	18	2	2	0	0	0	1	7	2	11	0	0	1	0	1.000	0	0-0	0	2.82	0.89
4 ML YEARS		86	27	0	18	240.2	1084	275	146	135	29	8	6	23	98	17	148	13	0	7	9	.438	0	0-0	5	5.40	5.05

Ray King

Pitches: L **Bats:** L **Pos:** RP-86   **Ht:** 6'1" **Wt:** 242 **Born:** 1/15/1974 **Age:** 31

		HOW MUCH HE PITCHED						WHAT HE GAVE UP												THE RESULTS						
Year Team	Lg	G	GS	CG	GF	IP	BFP	H	R	ER	HR	SH	SF	HB	TBB	IBB	SO	WP	Bk	W	L	Pct	ShO	Sv-Op	Hld	ERC	ERA
1999 Chicago	NL	10	0	0	0	10.2	50	11	8	7	2	1	0	1	10	0	5	1	0	0	0	-	0	0-0	2	8.10	5.91
2000 Milwaukee	NL	36	0	0	8	28.2	111	18	7	4	1	0	1	0	10	1	19	1	0	3	2	.600	0	0-1	5	1.64	1.26
2001 Milwaukee	NL	82	0	0	19	55.0	234	49	22	22	5	3	2	1	25	7	49	2	0	0	4	.000	0	1-4	18	3.51	3.60
2002 Milwaukee	NL	76	0	0	15	65.0	273	61	24	22	5	5	2	3	24	6	50	0	1	3	2	.600	0	0-1	15	3.55	3.05
2003 Atlanta	NL	80	0	0	9	59.0	247	46	30	23	3	1	2	1	27	2	43	4	0	3	4	.429	0	0-1	18	2.79	3.51
2004 St Louis	NL	86	0	0	9	62.0	248	43	19	18	1	2	1	3	24	4	40	2	0	5	2	.714	0	0-1	31	2.13	2.61
6 ML YEARS		370	0	0	60	280.1	1163	228	110	96	17	12	8	9	120	16	206	10	1	14	14	.500	0	1-8	89	2.98	3.08

Matt Kinney

Pitches: R **Bats:** R **Pos:** RP-37; SP-6   **Ht:** 6'5" **Wt:** 220 **Born:** 12/16/1976 **Age:** 28

		HOW MUCH HE PITCHED						WHAT HE GAVE UP												THE RESULTS						
Year Team	Lg	G	GS	CG	GF	IP	BFP	H	R	ER	HR	SH	SF	HB	TBB	IBB	SO	WP	Bk	W	L	Pct	ShO	Sv-Op	Hld	ERC	ERA
2000 Minnesota	AL	8	8	0	0	42.1	186	41	26	24	7	0	4	0	25	1	24	4	0	2	2	.500	0	0-0	0	5.20	5.10
2002 Minnesota	AL	14	12	0	1	66.0	305	78	39	34	13	3	4	1	33	0	45	5	0	2	7	.222	0	0-0	0	6.35	4.64
2003 Milwaukee	NL	33	31	1	1	190.2	847	201	121	110	27	10	11	6	80	4	152	10	2	10	13	.435	0	0-0	0	4.82	5.19
2004 Mil-KC		43	6	0	14	78.2	370	104	55	53	11	2	4	4	30	2	73	7	0	3	5	.375	0	0-0	3	6.31	6.06
2004 Milwaukee	NL	32	6	0	10	62.1	286	77	41	40	8	2	3	2	23	1	52	5	0	3	4	.429	0	0-0	3	5.57	5.78
2004 Kansas City	AL	11	0	0	4	16.1	84	27	14	13	3	0	1	2	7	1	21	2	0	0	1	.000	0	0-0	0	9.35	7.16
4 ML YEARS		98	57	1	16	377.2	1708	424	241	221	58	15	23	11	168	7	294	26	2	17	27	.386	0	0-0	3	5.43	5.27

Ryan Klesko

Bats: L **Throws:** L **Pos:** LF-104; 1B-18; PH-7; DH-3 **Ht:** 6'3" **Wt:** 220 **Born:** 6/12/1971 **Age:** 34

Year Team	Lg	G	AB	H	2B	3B	HR	(Hm	Rd)	TB	R	RBI	RC	TBB	IBB	SO	HBP	SH	SF	SB	CS	SB%	GDP	Avg	OBP	Slg
1992 Atlanta	NL	13	14	0	0	0	0	(0	0)	0	0	1	0	0	0	5	1	0	0	0	0	-	0	.000	.067	.000
1993 Atlanta	NL	22	17	6	1	0	2	(2	0)	13	3	5	5	3	1	4	0	0	0	0	0	-	0	.353	.450	.765
1994 Atlanta	NL	92	245	68	13	3	17	(7	10)	138	42	47	45	26	3	48	1	0	4	1	0	1.00	8	.278	.344	.563
1995 Atlanta	NL	107	329	102	25	2	23	(15	8)	200	48	70	73	47	10	72	2	0	3	5	4	.56	8	.310	.396	.608
1996 Atlanta	NL	153	528	149	21	4	34	(20	14)	280	90	93	99	68	10	129	2	0	4	6	3	.67	10	.282	.364	.530
1997 Atlanta	NL	143	467	122	23	6	24	(10	14)	229	67	84	73	48	5	130	4	1	2	4	4	.50	12	.261	.334	.490
1998 Atlanta	NL	129	427	117	29	1	18	(8	10)	202	69	70	72	56	5	66	3	0	4	5	3	.63	9	.274	.359	.473
1999 Atlanta	NL	133	404	120	28	2	21	(12	9)	215	55	80	80	53	8	69	2	0	7	5	2	.71	6	.297	.376	.532
2000 San Diego	NL	145	494	140	33	2	26	(9	17)	255	88	92	101	91	9	81	1	0	4	23	7	.77	10	.283	.393	.516
2001 San Diego	NL	146	538	154	34	6	30	(15	15)	290	105	113	111	88	7	89	3	0	9	23	4	.85	16	.286	.384	.539
2002 San Diego	NL	146	540	162	39	1	29	(11	18)	290	90	95	111	76	11	86	4	1	4	6	2	.75	7	.300	.388	.537
2003 San Diego	NL	121	397	100	18	0	21	(8	13)	181	47	67	59	65	5	83	3	0	9	2	5	.29	11	.252	.354	.456
2004 San Diego	NL	127	402	117	32	2	9	(3	6)	180	58	66	76	73	6	67	1	1	3	3	2	.60	8	.291	.399	.448
13 ML YEARS		1477	4802	1357	296	29	254	(120	134)	2473	762	883	905	694	80	929	27	3	53	83	36	.70	105	.283	.373	.515

Steve Kline

Pitches: L **Bats:** B **Pos:** RP-67 **Ht:** 6'1" **Wt:** 215 **Born:** 8/22/1972 **Age:** 32

		HOW MUCH HE PITCHED						WHAT HE GAVE UP											THE RESULTS						
Year Team	Lg	G	GS	CG	GF	IP	BFP	H	R	ER	HR	SH	SF	HB	TBB	IBB	SO	WP	Bk	W	L	Pct	ShO	Sv-Op	Hld	ERC	ERA
1997 Cle-Mon		46	1	0	7	52.2	248	73	37	35	10	4	2	2	23	4	37	4	1	4	4	.500	0	0-3	5	7.39	5.98
1998 Montreal	NL	78	0	0	18	71.2	319	62	25	22	4	1	2	3	41	7	76	5	0	3	6	.333	0	1-2	18	3.60	2.76
1999 Montreal	NL	82	0	0	18	69.2	297	56	32	29	8	3	1	3	33	6	69	2	0	7	4	.636	0	0-2	16	3.40	3.75
2000 Montreal	NL	83	0	0	42	82.1	349	88	36	32	8	2	1	3	27	2	64	4	0	1	5	.167	0	14-18	12	4.37	3.50
2001 St Louis	NL	89	0	0	26	75.0	303	53	16	15	3	4	5	4	29	7	54	1	0	3	3	.500	0	9-10	17	2.20	1.80
2002 St Louis	NL	66	0	0	17	58.1	241	54	23	22	3	2	2	1	21	2	41	1	0	2	1	.667	0	6-8	21	3.28	3.39
2003 St Louis	NL	78	0	0	22	63.2	275	56	29	27	5	3	2	3	30	5	31	2	0	5	5	.500	0	3-7	18	3.58	3.82
2004 St Louis	NL	67	0	0	22	50.1	202	37	12	10	3	3	1	4	17	4	35	1	0	2	2	.500	0	3-4	15	2.43	1.79
1997 Cleveland	AL	20	1	0	0	26.1	130	42	19	17	6	1	0	1	13	1	17	3	1	3	1	.750	0	0-2	4	9.58	5.81
1997 Montreal	NL	26	0	0	7	26.1	118	31	18	18	4	3	2	1	10	3	20	1	0	1	3	.250	0	0-1	1	5.39	6.15
8 ML YEARS		589	1	0	172	523.2	2234	479	210	192	44	22	16	23	221	37	407	20	1	27	30	.474	0	36-54	122	3.66	3.30

Justin Knoedler

Bats: R **Throws:** R **Pos:** C-1 **Ht:** 6'2" **Wt:** 210 **Born:** 7/17/1980 **Age:** 24

Year Team	Lg	G	AB	H	2B	3B	HR	(Hm	Rd)	TB	R	RBI	RC	TBB	IBB	SO	HBP	SH	SF	SB	CS	SB%	GDP	Avg	OBP	Slg
2002 Hagerstown	A	86	280	72	16	2	5	(-	-)	107	32	33	37	37	0	56	4	2	3	6	5	.55	8	.257	.349	.382
2003 San Jose	A+	101	354	91	25	2	10	(-	-)	150	48	43	49	35	0	78	3	2	4	13	3	.81	5	.257	.326	.424
2004 Norwich	AA	115	409	112	28	3	9	(-	-)	173	64	47	57	32	0	98	8	0	5	5	3	.63	7	.274	.335	.423
2004 San Francisco	NL	1	1	0	0	0	0	(0	0)	0	0	0	0	0	0	0	0	0	0	0	0	-	0	.000	.000	.000

Jon Knott

Bats: R **Throws:** R **Pos:** PH-6; LF-5 **Ht:** 6'3" **Wt:** 220 **Born:** 8/4/1978 **Age:** 26

Year Team	Lg	G	AB	H	2B	3B	HR	(Hm	Rd)	TB	R	RBI	RC	TBB	IBB	SO	HBP	SH	SF	SB	CS	SB%	GDP	Avg	OBP	Slg
2002 Fort Wayne	A	37	126	42	12	3	3	(-	-)	69	19	18	27	17	1	33	1	0	2	2	1	.67	1	.333	.411	.548
2002 Lk Elsinore	A+	93	367	125	33	8	6	(-	-)	192	55	73	75	46	2	68	3	0	4	5	4	.56	7	.341	.414	.523
2003 Mobile	AA	127	432	109	32	0	27	(-	-)	222	83	82	88	82	1	117	17	0	6	5	3	.63	1	.252	.387	.514
2003 Portland	AAA	7	26	9	1	0	1	(-	-)	13	5	5	5	4	0	3	0	0	0	0	0	-	1	.346	.433	.500
2004 Portland	AAA	113	435	126	22	3	26	(-	-)	232	79	85	83	58	0	110	7	0	8	5	3	.63	12	.290	.376	.533
2004 San Diego	NL	9	14	3	2	0	0	(0	0)	5	1	1	1	1	0	5	0	0	0	0	0	-	0	.214	.267	.357

Gary Knotts

Pitches: R **Bats:** R **Pos:** SP-19; RP-17 **Ht:** 6'4" **Wt:** 200 **Born:** 2/12/1977 **Age:** 28

		HOW MUCH HE PITCHED						WHAT HE GAVE UP											THE RESULTS						
Year Team	Lg	G	GS	CG	GF	IP	BFP	H	R	ER	HR	SH	SF	HB	TBB	IBB	SO	WP	Bk	W	L	Pct	ShO	Sv-Op	Hld	ERC	ERA
2001 Florida	NL	2	1	0	0	6.0	28	7	4	4	1	0	0	2	1	0	9	0	0	0	1	.000	0	0-0	0	5.84	6.00
2002 Florida	NL	28	0	0	7	30.2	127	21	15	15	6	0	1	1	16	0	21	1	0	3	1	.750	0	0-1	5	3.62	4.40
2003 Detroit	AL	20	18	0	0	95.1	442	111	70	64	14	1	4	4	47	0	51	4	0	3	8	.273	0	0-0	0	5.90	6.04
2004 Detroit	AL	36	19	0	6	135.1	599	142	83	79	20	4	2	4	58	3	81	11	0	7	6	.538	0	2-2	4	4.89	5.25
4 ML YEARS		86	38	0	13	267.1	1196	281	172	162	41	5	7	11	122	3	162	16	0	13	16	.448	0	2-3	7	5.11	5.45

Billy Koch

Pitches: R **Bats:** R **Pos:** RP-47 **Ht:** 6'3" **Wt:** 215 **Born:** 12/14/1974 **Age:** 30

		HOW MUCH HE PITCHED						WHAT HE GAVE UP											THE RESULTS						
Year Team	Lg	G	GS	CG	GF	IP	BFP	H	R	ER	HR	SH	SF	HB	TBB	IBB	SO	WP	Bk	W	L	Pct	ShO	Sv-Op	Hld	ERC	ERA
1999 Toronto	AL	56	0	0	48	63.2	272	55	26	24	5	4	1	3	30	5	57	0	0	0	5	.000	0	31-35	1	3.53	3.39
2000 Toronto	AL	68	0	0	62	78.2	326	78	28	23	6	4	0	2	18	4	60	1	0	9	3	.750	0	33-38	0	3.25	2.63
2001 Toronto	AL	69	0	0	56	69.1	308	69	39	37	7	5	4	6	33	7	55	5	0	2	5	.286	0	36-44	0	4.54	4.80
2002 Oakland	AL	84	0	0	79	93.2	398	73	38	34	7	6	1	4	46	6	93	5	0	11	4	.733	0	44-50	5	3.10	3.27
2003 Chicago	AL	55	0	0	45	53.0	244	59	36	34	10	2	3	1	28	1	42	3	0	5	5	.500	0	11-15	1	5.93	5.77
2004 CWS-Fla	AL	47	0	0	35	49.0	229	45	25	24	6	1	3	2	36	4	50	5	0	2	3	.400	0	8-11	4	5.03	4.41
2004 Chicago	AL	24	0	0	19	23.1	114	24	15	14	3	0	2	2	16	4	25	4	0	1	1	.500	0	8-11	1	5.41	5.40
2004 Florida	NL	23	0	0	16	25.2	115	21	10	10	3	1	1	0	20	0	25	1	0	1	2	.333	0	0-0	3	4.69	3.51
6 ML YEARS		379	0	0	325	407.1	1777	379	192	176	41	22	12	18	191	27	357	19	0	29	25	.537	0	163-193	5	4.01	3.89

Danny Kolb

Pitches: R **Bats:** R **Pos:** RP-64   **Ht:** 6'4" **Wt:** 215 **Born:** 3/29/1975 **Age:** 30

Year Team	Lg	G	GS	CG	GF	IP	BFP	H	R	ER	HR	SH	SF	HB	TBB	IBB	SO	WP	Bk	W	L	Pct	ShO	Sv-Op	Hld	ERC	ERA
1999 Texas	AL	16	0	0	6	31.0	139	33	18	16	2	0	0	1	15	0	15	2	0	2	1	.667	0	0-0	0	4.63	4.65
2000 Texas	AL	1	0	0	0	0.2	9	5	5	5	0	1	0	0	2	0	0	0	0	0	0	-	0	0-0	0	69.84	67.50
2001 Texas	AL	17	0	0	1	15.1	70	15	8	8	2	1	1	0	10	1	15	3	0	0	0	-	0	0-0	7	5.03	4.70
2002 Texas	AL	34	0	0	14	32.0	145	27	17	15	1	1	2	1	22	2	20	6	0	3	6	.333	0	1-4	2	3.74	4.22
2003 Milwaukee	NL	37	0	0	25	41.1	175	34	10	9	2	1	0	1	19	3	39	1	0	1	2	.333	0	21-23	4	2.96	1.96
2004 Milwaukee	NL	64	0	0	48	57.1	236	50	22	19	3	3	1	3	15	1	21	2	0	0	4	.000	0	39-44	1	2.73	2.98
6 ML YEARS		169	0	0	94	177.2	774	164	80	72	10	6	5	6	83	7	110	14	0	6	13	.316	0	61-71	14	3.64	3.65

Paul Konerko

Bats: R **Throws:** R **Pos:** 1B-139; DH-16; PH-1   **Ht:** 6'2" **Wt:** 215 **Born:** 3/5/1976 **Age:** 29

Year Team	Lg	G	AB	H	2B	3B	HR	(Hm	Rd)	TB	R	RBI	RC	TBB	IBB	SO	HBP	SH	SF	SB	CS	SB%	GDP	Avg	OBP	Slg
1997 Los Angeles	NL	6	7	1	0	0	0	(0	0)	1	0	0	0	1	0	2	0	0	0	0	0	-	1	.143	.250	.143
1998 LA-Cin	NL	75	217	47	4	0	7	(2	5)	72	21	29	17	16	0	40	3	0	3	0	1	.00	10	.217	.276	.332
1999 Chicago	AL	142	513	151	31	4	24	(16	8)	262	71	81	86	45	0	68	2	1	3	1	0	1.00	19	.294	.352	.511
2000 Chicago	AL	143	524	156	31	1	21	(10	11)	252	84	97	86	47	0	72	10	0	5	1	0	1.00	22	.298	.363	.481
2001 Chicago	AL	156	582	164	35	0	32	(19	13)	295	92	99	99	54	6	89	9	0	5	1	0	1.00	17	.282	.349	.507
2002 Chicago	AL	151	570	173	30	0	27	(13	14)	284	81	104	96	44	2	72	9	0	7	0	0	-	17	.304	.359	.498
2003 Chicago	AL	137	444	104	19	0	18	(9	9)	177	49	65	42	43	7	50	4	0	4	0	0	-	28	.234	.305	.399
2004 Chicago	AL	155	563	156	22	0	41	(29	12)	301	84	117	106	69	5	107	6	0	5	1	0	1.00	23	.277	.359	.535
1998 Los Angeles	NL	49	144	31	1	0	4	(2	2)	44	14	16	10	10	0	30	2	0	2	0	1	.00	5	.215	.272	.306
1998 Cincinnati	NL	26	73	16	3	0	3	(0	3)	28	7	13	7	6	0	10	1	0	1	0	0	-	5	.219	.284	.384
8 ML YEARS		965	3420	952	172	5	170	(98	72)	1644	482	592	532	319	20	500	43	1	32	4	1	.80	137	.278	.345	.481

Mike Koplove

Pitches: R **Bats:** R **Pos:** RP-76   **Ht:** 6'0" **Wt:** 170 **Born:** 8/30/1976 **Age:** 28

Year Team	Lg	G	GS	CG	GF	IP	BFP	H	R	ER	HR	SH	SF	HB	TBB	IBB	SO	WP	Bk	W	L	Pct	ShO	Sv-Op	Hld	ERC	ERA
2001 Arizona	NL	9	0	0	1	10.0	50	8	7	4	1	1	0	2	9	1	14	1	0	0	1	.000	0	0-0	1	5.25	3.60
2002 Arizona	NL	55	0	0	15	61.2	249	47	24	23	2	4	1	0	23	4	46	1	0	6	1	.857	0	0-0	10	2.23	3.36
2003 Arizona	NL	31	0	0	5	37.2	157	31	11	9	3	2	2	5	10	1	27	1	0	3	0	1.000	0	0-1	5	2.93	2.15
2004 Arizona	NL	76	0	0	24	86.2	371	86	42	39	7	8	1	5	37	10	55	4	0	4	4	.500	0	2-8	19	4.14	4.05
4 ML YEARS		171	0	0	45	196.0	827	172	84	75	13	15	4	12	79	16	142	7	0	13	6	.684	0	2-9	35	3.32	3.44

Corey Koskie

Bats: L **Throws:** R **Pos:** 3B-115; PH-4; DH-1   **Ht:** 6'3" **Wt:** 217 **Born:** 6/28/1973 **Age:** 32

Year Team	Lg	G	AB	H	2B	3B	HR	(Hm	Rd)	TB	R	RBI	RC	TBB	IBB	SO	HBP	SH	SF	SB	CS	SB%	GDP	Avg	OBP	Slg
1998 Minnesota	AL	11	29	4	0	0	1	(1	0)	7	2	2	1	2	0	10	0	0	0	0	0	-	0	.138	.194	.241
1999 Minnesota	AL	117	342	106	21	0	11	(4	7)	160	42	58	61	40	4	72	5	2	3	4	4	.50	6	.310	.387	.468
2000 Minnesota	AL	146	474	142	32	4	9	(1	8)	209	79	65	84	77	7	104	4	1	3	5	4	.56	11	.300	.400	.441
2001 Minnesota	AL	153	562	155	37	2	26	(11	15)	274	100	103	99	68	9	118	12	0	7	27	6	.82	16	.276	.362	.488
2002 Minnesota	AL	140	490	131	37	3	15	(6	9)	219	71	69	72	72	4	127	9	0	5	10	11	.48	14	.267	.368	.447
2003 Minnesota	AL	131	469	137	29	2	14	(8	6)	212	76	69	84	77	5	113	7	0	9	11	5	.69	5	.292	.393	.452
2004 Minnesota	AL	118	422	106	24	2	25	(16	9)	209	68	71	67	49	10	103	12	0	5	9	3	.75	6	.251	.342	.495
7 ML YEARS		816	2788	781	180	13	101	(47	54)	1290	438	437	468	385	39	647	49	3	32	66	33	.67	58	.280	.373	.463

Casey Kotchman

Bats: L **Throws:** L **Pos:** 1B-34; PH-5; DH-1   **Ht:** 6'3" **Wt:** 210 **Born:** 2/22/1983 **Age:** 22

Year Team	Lg	G	AB	H	2B	3B	HR	(Hm	Rd)	TB	R	RBI	RC	TBB	IBB	SO	HBP	SH	SF	SB	CS	SB%	GDP	Avg	OBP	Slg
2001 Angels	R	4	15	9	1	0	1	(-	-)	13	5	5	6	3	1	2	0	0	1	0	0	-	0	.600	.632	.867
2001 Provo	R+	7	22	11	3	0	0	(-	-)	14	6	7	6	2	0	0	0	0	0	0	0	-	0	.500	.542	.636
2002 Cedar Rpds	A	81	288	81	30	1	5	(-	-)	128	42	50	50	48	2	37	6	1	4	2	1	.67	7	.281	.390	.444
2003 Angels	R	7	27	9	1	0	2	(-	-)	16	5	6	5	2	1	3	0	0	0	0	0	-	1	.333	.379	.593
2003 R Cucamnga	A+	57	206	72	12	0	8	(-	-)	108	42	28	47	30	5	16	6	0	3	2	0	1.00	4	.350	.441	.524
2004 Arkansas	AA	28	114	42	11	0	3	(-	-)	62	19	18	24	10	0	7	5	0	1	0	0	-	6	.368	.438	.544
2004 Salt Lake	AAA	49	199	74	22	0	5	(-	-)	111	32	38	41	14	0	25	5	0	2	0	0	-	2	.372	.423	.558
2004 Anaheim	AL	38	116	26	6	0	0	(0	0)	32	7	15	14	7	3	11	4	0	1	3	0	1.00	3	.224	.289	.276

Mark Kotsay

Bats: L **Throws:** L **Pos:** CF-146; PH-6; DH-1; PR-1   **Ht:** 6'0" **Wt:** 201 **Born:** 12/2/1975 **Age:** 29

Year Team	Lg	G	AB	H	2B	3B	HR	(Hm	Rd)	TB	R	RBI	RC	TBB	IBB	SO	HBP	SH	SF	SB	CS	SB%	GDP	Avg	OBP	Slg
1997 Florida	NL	14	52	10	1	1	0	(0	0)	13	5	4	3	4	0	7	0	1	0	3	0	1.00	1	.192	.250	.250
1998 Florida	NL	154	578	161	25	7	11	(5	6)	233	72	68	70	34	2	61	1	7	3	10	5	.67	17	.279	.318	.403
1999 Florida	NL	148	495	134	23	9	8	(5	3)	199	57	50	58	29	5	50	0	2	9	7	6	.54	11	.271	.306	.402
2000 Florida	NL	152	530	158	31	5	12	(5	7)	235	87	57	78	42	2	46	0	2	4	19	9	.68	17	.298	.347	.443
2001 San Diego	NL	119	406	118	29	1	10	(3	7)	179	67	58	65	48	1	58	2	1	3	13	5	.72	11	.291	.366	.441
2002 San Diego	NL	153	578	169	27	7	17	(11	6)	261	82	61	92	59	0	89	3	2	4	11	9	.55	10	.292	.359	.452
2003 San Diego	NL	128	482	128	28	4	7	(1	6)	185	64	38	59	56	3	82	1	1	1	6	3	.67	8	.266	.343	.384
2004 Oakland	AL	148	606	190	37	3	15	(9	6)	278	78	63	94	55	5	70	2	5	5	8	5	.62	6	.314	.370	.459
8 ML YEARS		1016	3727	1068	201	37	80	(39	41)	1583	512	399	519	327	18	463	9	21	29	77	42	.65	81	.287	.343	.425

Josh Kroeger

Bats: L **Throws:** L **Pos:** LF-11; RF-8; PR-3; CF-2; PH-2   **Ht:** 6'2" **Wt:** 200 **Born:** 8/31/1982 **Age:** 22

Year Team	Lg	G	AB	H	2B	3B	HR	(Hm	Rd)	TB	R	RBI	RC	TBB	IBB	SO	HBP	SH	SF	SB	CS	SB%	GDP	Avg	OBP	Slg
2000 Diamndbcks	R	54	222	66	9	3	4	(-	-)	93	40	28	33	21	1	41	1	0	1	5	4	.56	3	.297	.359	.419
2001 South Bend	A	79	292	80	15	1	3	(-	-)	106	36	37	32	18	0	49	4	0	1	4	4	.50	10	.274	.324	.363
2002 Lancaster	A+	133	497	117	20	7	7	(-	-)	172	63	58	43	23	1	136	4	3	2	2	4	.33	10	.235	.274	.346
2003 Lancaster	A+	78	305	104	30	6	5	(-	-)	161	50	55	59	35	4	58	2	0	3	6	6	.50	9	.341	.409	.528
2003 El Paso	AA	54	208	57	9	2	3	(-	-)	79	26	22	21	10	2	54	3	2	1	3	5	.38	7	.274	.315	.380
2004 El Paso	AA	65	245	81	28	4	9	(-	-)	144	44	46	50	21	3	48	5	0	1	2	1	.67	7	.331	.393	.588
2004 Tucson	AAA	59	208	69	23	0	10	(-	-)	122	30	41	39	15	1	47	2	0	4	2	1	.67	8	.332	.376	.587
2004 Arizona	NL	22	54	9	3	0	0	(0	0)	12	5	2	1	1	0	21	0	0	0	0	1	.00	2	.167	.182	.222

Marc Kroon

Pitches: R **Bats:** R **Pos:** RP-6   **Ht:** 6'2" **Wt:** 190 **Born:** 4/2/1973 **Age:** 32

	HOW MUCH HE PITCHED						WHAT HE GAVE UP											THE RESULTS							
Year Team	Lg	G	GS	CG	GF	IP	BFP	H	R	ER	HR	SH	SF	HB	TBB	IBB	SO	WP	Bk	W	L	Pct	ShO	Sv-Op	Hld	ERC	ERA
2004 Co Springs*	AAA	50	0	0	44	49.2	220	44	23	15	3	0	0	1	26	0	72	9	0	2	3	.400	0	20- -	-	3.63	2.72
1995 San Diego	NL	2	0	0	1	1.2	7	1	2	2	0	0	0	0	2	0	2	0	0	0	1	.000	0	0-0	1	4.62	10.80
1997 San Diego	NL	12	0	0	2	11.1	56	14	9	9	2	0	0	1	5	0	12	1	0	0	1	.000	0	0-0	1	6.21	7.15
1998 SD-Cin	NL	6	0	0	4	7.2	38	7	8	8	0	0	0	1	9	0	6	2	1	0	0	-	0	0-0	2	6.49	9.39
2004 Colorado	NL	6	0	0	1	6.0	32	7	4	4	1	1	1	0	10	0	3	1	0	0	0	-	0	0-0	0	12.08	6.00
1998 Cincinnati	NL	4	0	0	2	5.1	30	7	8	8	0	0	0	1	8	0	4	2	1	0	0	-	0	0-0	0	11.01	13.50
1998 San Diego	NL	2	0	0	2	2.1	8	0	0	0	0	0	0	0	1	0	2	0	0	0	0	-	0	0-0	1	0.20	0.00
4 ML YEARS		26	0	0	8	26.2	133	29	23	23	3	1	1	2	26	0	23	4	1	0	2	.000	0	0-0	1	7.45	7.76

Dave Krynzel

Bats: L **Throws:** L **Pos:** RF-8; PH-6; CF-2; PR-1   **Ht:** 6'1" **Wt:** 180 **Born:** 11/7/1981 **Age:** 23

Year Team	Lg	G	AB	H	2B	3B	HR	(Hm	Rd)	TB	R	RBI	RC	TBB	IBB	SO	HBP	SH	SF	SB	CS	SB%	GDP	Avg	OBP	Slg
2000 Ogden	R+	34	131	47	8	3	1	(-	-)	64	25	29	29	16	3	23	5	1	2	8	4	.67	0	.359	.442	.489
2001 Beloit	A	35	141	43	1	1	1	(-	-)	49	22	19	19	9	2	28	4	0	0	11	5	.69	1	.305	.364	.348
2001 High Desert	A+	89	383	106	19	5	5	(-	-)	150	65	33	50	27	1	122	4	3	2	34	17	.67	6	.277	.329	.392
2002 High Desert	A+	97	365	98	13	12	11	(-	-)	168	76	45	68	64	3	100	11	1	3	29	17	.63	2	.268	.391	.460
2002 Huntsville	AA	31	129	31	2	3	2	(-	-)	45	13	13	12	4	0	30	1	0	0	13	5	.72	0	.240	.269	.349
2003 Huntsville	AA	124	457	122	13	11	2	(-	-)	163	72	34	64	60	4	119	6	5	3	43	21	.67	3	.267	.357	.357
2004 Brewers	R	5	16	8	1	1	0	(-	-)	11	8	0	6	3	0	2	1	0	0	2	0	1.00	0	.500	.600	.688
2004 Indianapolis	AAA	69	257	71	10	4	6	(-	-)	107	36	27	36	20	1	65	3	8	3	10	8	.56	0	.276	.332	.416
2004 Milwaukee	NL	16	41	9	1	0	0	(0	0)	10	6	3	4	3	0	15	3	0	0	0	0	-	0	.220	.319	.244

Jason Kubel

Bats: L **Throws:** R **Pos:** DH-9; RF-8; PH-7; LF-2   **Ht:** 5'11" **Wt:** 200 **Born:** 5/25/1982 **Age:** 23

Year Team	Lg	G	AB	H	2B	3B	HR	(Hm	Rd)	TB	R	RBI	RC	TBB	IBB	SO	HBP	SH	SF	SB	CS	SB%	GDP	Avg	OBP	Slg
2000 Twins	R	23	78	22	3	2	0	(-	-)	29	17	13	11	10	0	9	1	1	1	0	0	-	1	.282	.367	.372
2001 Twins	R	37	124	41	10	4	1	(-	-)	62	14	30	25	19	3	14	2	0	2	3	2	.60	3	.331	.422	.500
2002 Quad City	A	115	424	136	26	4	17	(-	-)	221	60	69	77	41	2	48	1	2	3	3	5	.38	11	.321	.380	.521
2003 Fort Myers	A+	116	420	125	20	4	5	(-	-)	168	56	82	61	48	8	54	1	0	13	4	6	.40	11	.298	.361	.400
2004 New Britain	AA	37	138	52	14	4	6	(-	-)	92	25	29	36	19	1	19	1	0	1	0	2	.00	3	.377	.453	.667
2004 Rochester	AAA	90	350	120	28	4	16	(-	-)	196	71	71	76	34	2	40	1	1	4	16	3	.84	2	.343	.398	.560
2004 Minnesota	AL	23	60	18	2	0	2	(0	2)	26	10	7	13	6	0	9	0	0	1	1	1	.50	0	.300	.358	.433

John Labandeira

Bats: R **Throws:** R **Pos:** SS-3; PH-3; 2B-2   **Ht:** 5'7" **Wt:** 180 **Born:** 2/25/1979 **Age:** 26

Year Team	Lg	G	AB	H	2B	3B	HR	(Hm	Rd)	TB	R	RBI	RC	TBB	IBB	SO	HBP	SH	SF	SB	CS	SB%	GDP	Avg	OBP	Slg
2001 Vermont	A-	1	3	1	0	0	0	(-	-)	1	2	0	0	0	0	0	0	0	0	0	0	-	0	.333	.333	.333
2002 Clinton	A	129	493	141	27	3	8	(-	-)	198	60	67	68	45	1	73	10	3	12	15	12	.56	16	.286	.350	.402
2003 Brevard Cnty	A+	62	238	77	13	4	0	(-	-)	98	41	25	37	24	0	35	1	2	1	6	5	.55	6	.324	.386	.412
2003 Harrisburg	AA	60	238	57	18	2	2	(-	-)	85	25	26	23	20	0	38	1	4	3	0	2	.00	7	.239	.298	.357
2004 Harrisburg	AA	134	514	139	22	4	9	(-	-)	196	72	33	73	53	1	92	16	6	0	9	5	.64	10	.270	.357	.381
2004 Montreal	NL	7	14	0	0	0	0	(0	0)	0	0	0	0	0	0	4	0	0	0	0	0	-	1	.000	.000	.000

John Lackey

Pitches: R **Bats:** R **Pos:** SP-32; RP-1   **Ht:** 6'6" **Wt:** 205 **Born:** 10/23/1978 **Age:** 26

	HOW MUCH HE PITCHED						WHAT HE GAVE UP											THE RESULTS							
Year Team	Lg	G	GS	CG	GF	IP	BFP	H	R	ER	HR	SH	SF	HB	TBB	IBB	SO	WP	Bk	W	L	Pct	ShO	Sv-Op	Hld	ERC	ERA
2002 Anaheim	AL	18	18	1	0	108.1	465	113	52	44	10	0	4	4	33	0	69	7	2	9	4	.692	0	0-0	0	4.03	3.66
2003 Anaheim	AL	33	33	2	0	204.0	885	223	117	105	31	2	6	10	66	4	151	11	1	10	16	.385	2	0-0	0	4.88	4.63
2004 Anaheim	AL	33	32	1	0	198.1	855	215	108	103	22	9	4	8	60	4	144	11	1	14	13	.519	1	0-0	0	4.39	4.67
3 ML YEARS		84	83	4	0	510.2	2205	551	277	252	63	11	14	22	159	8	364	29	4	33	33	.500	3	0-0	0	4.51	4.44

Gerald Laird

Bats: R **Throws:** R **Pos:** C-49   **Ht:** 6'2" **Wt:** 195 **Born:** 11/3/1979 **Age:** 25

Year Team	Lg	G	AB	H	2B	3B	HR	(Hm	Rd)	TB	R	RBI	RC	TBB	IBB	SO	HBP	SH	SF	SB	CS	SB%	GDP	Avg	OBP	Slg
1999 Sth Oregon	A-	60	228	65	7	2	2	(-	-)	82	45	39	32	28	0	43	2	2	5	10	5	.67	4	.285	.361	.360
2000 Visalia	A+	33	103	25	3	0	0	(-	-)	28	14	13	10	14	0	27	1	0	2	7	2	.78	3	.243	.333	.272
2000 Athletics	R	14	50	15	2	1	0	(-	-)	19	10	9	7	6	0	7	1	0	1	2	0	1.00	1	.300	.379	.380
2001 Modesto	A+	119	443	113	13	5	5	(-	-)	151	71	46	53	48	1	101	10	4	6	10	9	.53	9	.255	.337	.341
2002 Tulsa	AA	123	442	122	21	4	11	(-	-)	184	70	67	61	45	1	95	5	1	10	8	6	.57	14	.276	.343	.416
2003 Oklahoma	AAA	99	338	88	20	5	9	(-	-)	145	50	42	49	37	4	61	7	1	2	9	3	.75	7	.260	.344	.429
2004 Oklahoma	AAA	6	22	4	2	0	0	(-	-)	6	2	2	1	2	0	8	0	0	0	1	0	1.00	1	.182	.250	.273
2003 Texas	AL	19	44	12	2	1	1	(0	1)	19	9	4	5	5	0	11	1	0	0	0	0	-	2	.273	.360	.432
2004 Texas	AL	49	147	33	6	0	1	(1	0)	42	20	16	11	12	0	35	2	4	3	0	1	.00	5	.224	.287	.286
2 ML YEARS		68	191	45	8	1	2	(1	1)	61	29	20	16	17	0	46	3	4	3	0	1	.00	7	.236	.304	.319

Tim Laker

Bats: R **Throws:** R **Pos:** C-41; PR-2; PH-1   **Ht:** 6'3" **Wt:** 225 **Born:** 11/27/1969 **Age:** 35

Year Team	Lg	G	AB	H	2B	3B	HR	(Hm	Rd)	TB	R	RBI	RC	TBB	IBB	SO	HBP	SH	SF	SB	CS	SB%	GDP	Avg	OBP	Slg
1992 Montreal	NL	28	46	10	3	0	0	(0	0)	13	8	4	2	2	0	14	0	0	0	1	1	.50	1	.217	.250	.283
1993 Montreal	NL	43	86	17	2	1	0	(0	0)	21	3	7	4	2	0	16	1	3	0	2	0	1.00	1	.198	.222	.244
1995 Montreal	NL	64	141	33	8	1	3	(1	2)	52	17	20	14	14	4	38	1	1	1	0	1	.00	5	.234	.306	.369
1997 Baltimore	AL	7	14	0	0	0	0	(0	0)	0	0	1	0	2	0	9	0	1	1	0	0	-	0	.000	.118	.000
1998 TB-Pit		17	29	10	1	0	1	(0	1)	14	3	2	5	2	0	4	0	0	1	0	1	.00	1	.345	.375	.483
1999 Pittsburgh	NL	6	9	3	0	0	0	(0	0)	3	0	0	1	0	0	2	0	0	0	0	0	-	0	.333	.333	.333
2001 Cleveland	AL	16	33	6	0	0	1	(0	1)	9	5	5	3	6	0	8	0	1	0	0	0	-	1	.182	.308	.273
2003 Cleveland	AL	52	162	39	11	0	3	(1	2)	59	17	21	18	9	1	38	0	5	0	2	2	.50	4	.241	.281	.364
2004 Cleveland	AL	44	117	25	2	0	3	(0	3)	36	12	17	10	7	1	28	1	2	1	0	0	-	5	.214	.262	.308
1998 Tampa Bay	AL	3	5	1	0	0	0	(0	0)	1	1	0	0	1	0	1	0	0	0	0	1	.00	0	.200	.333	.200
1998 Pittsburgh	NL	14	24	9	1	0	1	(0	1)	13	2	2	5	1	0	3	0	0	1	0	0	-	1	.375	.385	.542
9 ML YEARS		277	637	143	27	2	11	(2	9)	207	65	77	57	44	6	157	3	13	5	5	5	.50	19	.224	.276	.325

Mike Lamb

Bats: L **Throws:** R **Pos:** 3B-57; PH-42; 1B-10; 2B-7; DH-1   **Ht:** 6'1" **Wt:** 195 **Born:** 8/9/1975 **Age:** 29

Year Team	Lg	G	AB	H	2B	3B	HR	(Hm	Rd)	TB	R	RBI	RC	TBB	IBB	SO	HBP	SH	SF	SB	CS	SB%	GDP	Avg	OBP	Slg
2000 Texas	AL	138	493	137	25	2	6	(4	2)	184	65	47	59	34	6	60	4	5	2	0	2	.00	10	.278	.328	.373
2001 Texas	AL	76	284	87	18	0	4	(1	3)	117	42	35	40	14	1	27	5	1	2	2	1	.67	6	.306	.348	.412
2002 Texas	AL	115	314	89	13	0	9	(7	2)	129	54	33	46	33	5	48	3	2	3	0	0	-	7	.283	.354	.411
2003 Texas	AL	28	38	5	0	0	0	(0	0)	5	3	2	0	2	0	7	1	0	1	1	0	1.00	1	.132	.190	.132
2004 Houston	NL	112	278	80	14	3	14	(8	6)	142	38	58	51	31	3	63	0	0	3	1	1	.50	4	.288	.356	.511
5 ML YEARS		469	1407	398	70	5	33	(20	13)	577	202	175	196	114	15	205	13	8	11	4	4	.50	28	.283	.340	.410

Jason Lane

Bats: R **Throws:** L **Pos:** PH-41; LF-35; RF-24; CF-17; 1B-3; PR-1   **Ht:** 6'2" **Wt:** 215 **Born:** 12/22/1976 **Age:** 28

Year Team	Lg	G	AB	H	2B	3B	HR	(Hm	Rd)	TB	R	RBI	RC	TBB	IBB	SO	HBP	SH	SF	SB	CS	SB%	GDP	Avg	OBP	Slg
2002 Houston	NL	44	69	20	3	1	4	(2	2)	37	12	10	11	10	1	12	0	0	1	1	1	.50	0	.290	.375	.536
2003 Houston	NL	18	27	8	2	0	4	(4	0)	22	5	10	6	0	0	2	0	0	0	0	0	-	0	.296	.296	.815
2004 Houston	NL	107	136	37	10	2	4	(4	0)	63	21	19	23	16	0	33	1	1	2	1	0	1.00	2	.272	.348	.463
3 ML YEARS		169	232	65	15	3	12	(10	2)	122	38	39	40	26	1	47	1	1	3	2	1	.67	2	.280	.351	.526

Ray Lankford

Bats: L **Throws:** L **Pos:** LF-66; PH-30; PR-7; CF-4   **Ht:** 5'11" **Wt:** 200 **Born:** 6/5/1967 **Age:** 38

Year Team	Lg	G	AB	H	2B	3B	HR	(Hm	Rd)	TB	R	RBI	RC	TBB	IBB	SO	HBP	SH	SF	SB	CS	SB%	GDP	Avg	OBP	Slg
2004 Memphis*	AAA	9	33	7	0	0	3	(-	-)	16	5	5	4	3	0	10	1	1	0	0	0	-	1	.212	.297	.485
1990 St Louis	NL	39	126	36	10	1	3	(2	1)	57	12	12	21	13	0	27	0	0	0	8	2	.80	1	.286	.353	.452
1991 St Louis	NL	151	566	142	23	15	9	(4	5)	222	83	69	68	41	1	114	1	4	9	44	20	.69	4	.251	.301	.393
1992 St Louis	NL	153	598	175	40	6	20	(13	7)	287	87	86	106	72	6	147	5	2	5	42	24	.64	5	.293	.371	.480
1993 St Louis	NL	127	407	97	17	3	7	(6	1)	141	64	45	55	81	7	111	3	1	3	14	14	.50	5	.238	.366	.346
1994 St Louis	NL	109	416	111	25	5	19	(8	11)	203	89	57	74	58	3	113	4	0	4	11	10	.52	0	.267	.359	.488
1995 St Louis	NL	132	483	134	35	2	25	(16	9)	248	81	82	89	63	6	110	2	0	5	24	8	.75	10	.277	.360	.513
1996 St Louis	NL	149	545	150	36	8	21	(8	13)	265	100	86	100	79	10	133	3	1	7	35	7	.83	12	.275	.366	.486
1997 St Louis	NL	133	465	137	36	3	31	(10	21)	272	94	98	108	95	10	125	0	0	5	21	11	.66	9	.295	.411	.585
1998 St Louis	NL	154	533	156	37	1	31	(20	11)	288	94	105	115	86	5	151	3	0	4	26	5	.84	4	.293	.391	.540
1999 St Louis	NL	122	422	129	32	1	15	(8	7)	208	77	63	79	44	3	110	3	0	2	14	4	.78	6	.306	.380	.493
2000 St Louis	NL	128	392	99	16	3	26	(18	8)	199	73	65	73	70	1	148	4	0	6	5	6	.45	5	.253	.367	.508
2001 StL-SD	NL	131	389	98	28	4	19	(10	9)	191	58	58	69	62	9	145	4	1	3	10	2	.83	6	.252	.358	.491
2002 San Diego	NL	81	205	46	7	1	6	(3	3)	73	20	26	25	30	3	61	2	1	2	2	2	.50	3	.224	.326	.356
2004 St Louis	NL	92	200	51	14	1	6	(2	4)	85	36	22	24	29	4	55	2	0	4	2	2	.50	5	.255	.349	.425
2001 St Louis	NL	91	264	62	18	3	15	(7	8)	131	38	39	45	44	8	105	2	1	3	4	2	.67	4	.235	.345	.496
2001 San Diego	NL	40	125	36	10	1	4	(3	1)	60	20	19	24	18	1	40	2	0	0	6	0	1.00	2	.288	.386	.480
14 ML YEARS		1701	5747	1561	356	54	238	(128	110)	2739	968	874	1006	828	68	1550	36	10	53	258	117	.69	76	.272	.364	.477

Barry Larkin

Bats: R **Throws:** R **Pos:** SS-85; PH-28   **Ht:** 6'0" **Wt:** 185 **Born:** 4/28/1964 **Age:** 41

							BATTING												BASERUNNING				AVERAGES		
Year Team	Lg	G	AB	H	2B	3B	HR	(Hm | Rd)	TB	R	RBI	RC	TBB	IBB	SO	HBP	SH	SF	SB	CS	SB%	GDP	Avg	OBP	Slg
1986 Cincinnati	NL	41	159	45	4	3	3	(3 | 0)	64	27	19	22	9	1	21	0	0	1	8	0	1.00	2	.283	.320	.403
1987 Cincinnati	NL	125	439	107	16	2	12	(6 | 6)	163	64	43	52	36	3	52	5	5	3	21	6	.78	8	.244	.306	.371
1988 Cincinnati	NL	151	588	174	32	5	12	(9 | 3)	252	91	56	94	41	3	24	8	10	5	40	7	.85	7	.296	.347	.429
1989 Cincinnati	NL	97	325	111	14	4	4	(1 | 3)	145	47	36	53	20	5	23	2	2	8	10	5	.67	7	.342	.375	.446
1990 Cincinnati	NL	158	614	185	25	6	7	(4 | 3)	243	85	67	90	49	3	49	7	7	4	30	5	.86	14	.301	.358	.396
1991 Cincinnati	NL	123	464	140	27	4	20	(16 | 4)	235	88	69	90	55	1	64	3	3	2	24	6	.80	7	.302	.378	.506
1992 Cincinnati	NL	140	533	162	32	6	12	(8 | 4)	242	76	78	92	63	8	58	4	2	7	15	4	.79	13	.304	.377	.454
1993 Cincinnati	NL	100	384	121	20	3	8	(4 | 4)	171	57	51	68	51	6	33	1	1	3	14	1	.93	13	.315	.394	.445
1994 Cincinnati	NL	110	427	119	23	5	9	(3 | 6)	179	78	52	79	64	3	58	0	5	5	26	2	.93	6	.279	.369	.419
1995 Cincinnati	NL	131	496	158	29	6	15	(8 | 7)	244	98	66	104	61	2	49	3	3	4	51	5	.91	6	.319	.394	.492
1996 Cincinnati	NL	152	517	154	32	4	33	(14 | 19)	293	117	89	118	96	3	52	7	0	7	36	10	.78	20	.298	.410	.567
1997 Cincinnati	NL	73	224	71	17	3	4	(0 | 4)	106	34	20	50	47	6	24	3	1	1	14	3	.82	3	.317	.440	.473
1998 Cincinnati	NL	145	538	166	34	10	17	(8 | 9)	271	93	72	109	79	5	69	2	4	3	26	3	.90	12	.309	.397	.504
1999 Cincinnati	NL	161	583	171	30	4	12	(7 | 5)	245	108	75	102	93	5	57	2	5	4	30	8	.79	12	.293	.390	.420
2000 Cincinnati	NL	102	396	124	26	5	11	(6 | 5)	193	71	41	73	48	0	31	1	2	0	14	6	.70	10	.313	.389	.487
2001 Cincinnati	NL	45	156	40	12	0	2	(1 | 1)	58	29	17	23	27	2	25	2	0	0	3	2	.60	2	.256	.373	.372
2002 Cincinnati	NL	145	507	124	37	2	7	(4 | 3)	186	72	47	52	44	9	57	3	6	7	13	4	.76	13	.245	.305	.367
2003 Cincinnati	NL	70	241	68	16	1	2	(2 | 0)	92	39	18	33	22	0	32	1	1	0	2	0	1.00	7	.282	.345	.382
2004 Cincinnati	NL	111	346	100	15	3	8	(5 | 3)	145	55	44	45	34	1	39	1	2	3	2	0	1.00	16	.289	.352	.419
19 ML YEARS		2180	7937	2340	441	76	198	(109 | 89)	3527	1329	960	1343	939	66	817	55	59	67	379	77	.83	178	.295	.371	.444

Adam LaRoche

Bats: L **Throws:** L **Pos:** 1B-98; PH-18   **Ht:** 6'3" **Wt:** 180 **Born:** 11/6/1979 **Age:** 25

							BATTING												BASERUNNING				AVERAGES		
Year Team	Lg	G	AB	H	2B	3B	HR	(Hm | Rd)	TB	R	RBI	RC	TBB	IBB	SO	HBP	SH	SF	SB	CS	SB%	GDP	Avg	OBP	Slg
2000 Danville	R+	56	201	62	13	3	7	(- | -)	102	38	45	39	24	2	46	2	1	4	4	1	.80	2	.308	.381	.507
2001 Myrtle Beach	A+	126	471	118	31	0	7	(- | -)	170	49	47	47	30	3	108	9	0	4	10	8	.56	13	.251	.305	.361
2002 Myrtle Beach	A+	69	250	84	17	0	9	(- | -)	128	30	53	50	27	4	37	4	2	2	0	2	.00	3	.336	.406	.512
2002 Greenville	AA	45	173	50	9	0	4	(- | -)	71	17	19	24	19	2	38	1	0	0	1	1	.50	6	.289	.363	.410
2003 Greenville	AA	61	219	62	12	1	12	(- | -)	112	42	37	40	34	3	53	3	0	4	1	2	.33	6	.283	.381	.511
2003 Richmond	AAA	72	264	78	21	0	8	(- | -)	123	33	35	42	27	3	58	3	0	6	1	2	.33	6	.295	.360	.466
2004 Richmond	AAA	4	11	2	0	0	1	(- | -)	5	1	2	0	1	0	0	0	0	0	0	0	-	2	.182	.250	.455
2004 Atlanta	NL	110	324	90	27	1	13	(7 | 6)	158	45	45	45	27	1	78	1	2	2	0	0	-	10	.278	.333	.488

Brandon Larson

Bats: R **Throws:** R **Pos:** 3B-35; PH-6   **Ht:** 6'0" **Wt:** 210 **Born:** 5/24/1976 **Age:** 29

							BATTING												BASERUNNING				AVERAGES		
Year Team	Lg	G	AB	H	2B	3B	HR	(Hm | Rd)	TB	R	RBI	RC	TBB	IBB	SO	HBP	SH	SF	SB	CS	SB%	GDP	Avg	OBP	Slg
2004 Chattanooga*	AA	2	7	2	1	0	1	(- | -)	6	1	1	1	0	0	4	0	0	0	0	0	-	0	.286	.286	.857
2004 Louisville*	AAA	32	117	33	5	0	9	(- | -)	65	14	25	18	5	1	39	1	0	1	0	0	-	4	.282	.315	.556
2001 Cincinnati	NL	14	33	4	2	0	0	(0 | 0)	6	2	1	2	0	0	10	0	0	0	0	0	-	1	.121	.171	.182
2002 Cincinnati	NL	23	51	14	2	0	4	(4 | 0)	28	8	13	9	6	1	10	1	0	0	1	0	1.00	6	.275	.362	.549
2003 Cincinnati	NL	32	89	9	1	0	1	(0 | 1)	13	6	9	2	13	0	31	0	0	2	2	2	.50	2	.101	.212	.146
2004 Cincinnati	NL	40	118	25	6	0	3	(1 | 2)	40	13	14	11	14	0	35	2	0	1	1	0	1.00	2	.212	.304	.339
4 ML YEARS		109	291	52	11	0	8	(5 | 3)	87	29	37	22	35	1	86	3	0	3	4	2	.67	6	.179	.271	.299

Jason LaRue

Bats: R **Throws:** R **Pos:** C-111; PH-3; RF-1; DH-1; PR-1   **Ht:** 5'11" **Wt:** 200 **Born:** 3/19/1974 **Age:** 31

							BATTING												BASERUNNING				AVERAGES		
Year Team	Lg	G	AB	H	2B	3B	HR	(Hm | Rd)	TB	R	RBI	RC	TBB	IBB	SO	HBP	SH	SF	SB	CS	SB%	GDP	Avg	OBP	Slg
2004 Louisville*	AAA	3	10	1	0	0	1	(- | -)	4	3	4	1	1	0	3	1	0	2	0	0	-	0	.100	.214	.400
1999 Cincinnati	NL	36	90	19	7	0	3	(1 | 2)	35	12	10	10	11	1	32	2	0	0	4	1	.80	4	.211	.311	.389
2000 Cincinnati	NL	31	98	23	3	0	5	(1 | 4)	41	12	12	12	5	2	19	4	0	0	0	0	-	1	.235	.299	.418
2001 Cincinnati	NL	121	364	86	21	2	12	(3 | 9)	147	39	43	42	27	4	106	9	1	2	3	3	.50	11	.236	.303	.404
2002 Cincinnati	NL	113	353	88	17	1	12	(5 | 7)	143	42	52	44	27	6	117	13	2	2	1	2	.33	13	.249	.324	.405
2003 Cincinnati	NL	118	379	87	23	1	16	(12 | 4)	160	52	50	47	33	4	111	20	1	4	3	3	.50	9	.230	.321	.422
2004 Cincinnati	NL	114	390	98	24	2	14	(3 | 11)	168	46	55	53	26	5	108	24	2	3	0	2	.00	6	.251	.334	.431
6 ML YEARS		533	1674	401	95	6	62	(25 | 37)	694	203	222	208	129	22	493	72	6	11	11	11	.50	44	.240	.319	.415

Brian Lawrence

Pitches: R **Bats:** R **Pos:** SP-34   **Ht:** 6'0" **Wt:** 195 **Born:** 5/14/1976 **Age:** 29

		HOW MUCH HE PITCHED					WHAT HE GAVE UP											THE RESULTS							
Year Team	Lg	G	GS	CG	GF	IP	BFP	H	R	ER	HR	SH	SF	HB	TBB	IBB	SO	WP	Bk	W	L	Pct	ShO	Sv-Op	Hld	ERC	ERA
2001 San Diego	NL	27	15	1	5	114.2	484	107	53	44	10	4	3	5	34	5	84	1	0	5	5	.500	0	0-0	0	3.30	3.45
2002 San Diego	NL	35	31	2	0	210.0	894	230	97	86	16	8	4	11	52	6	149	2	1	12	12	.500	2	0-0	1	4.45	3.69
2003 San Diego	NL	33	33	1	0	210.2	884	206	106	98	27	11	6	11	57	8	116	4	0	10	15	.400	0	0-0	0	3.81	4.19
2004 San Diego	NL	34	34	2	0	203.0	870	226	101	93	26	11	9	7	55	7	121	2	0	15	14	.517	1	0-0	0	4.53	4.12
4 ML YEARS		129	113	6	5	738.1	3132	769	357	321	79	34	22	34	198	26	470	9	1	42	46	.477	3	0-0	1	3.99	3.91

Matt Lawton

Bats: L **Throws:** R **Pos:** LF-125; RF-19; PH-5; DH-3   **Ht:** 5'10" **Wt:** 186 **Born:** 11/3/1971 **Age:** 33

							BATTING												BASERUNNING				AVERAGES		
Year Team	Lg	G	AB	H	2B	3B	HR	(Hm Rd)	TB	R	RBI	RC	TBB	IBB	SO	HBP	SH	SF	SB	CS	SB%	GDP	Avg	OBP	Slg
1995 Minnesota	AL	21	60	19	4	1	1	(1 0)	28	11	12	11	7	0	11	3	0	0	1	1	.50	1	.317	.414	.467
1996 Minnesota	AL	79	252	65	7	1	6	(1 5)	92	34	42	31	28	1	28	4	0	2	4	4	.50	6	.258	.339	.365
1997 Minnesota	AL	142	460	114	29	3	14	(8 6)	191	74	60	73	76	3	81	10	1	1	7	4	.64	7	.248	.366	.415
1998 Minnesota	AL	152	557	155	36	6	21	(11 10)	266	91	77	105	86	6	64	15	0	4	16	8	.67	10	.278	.387	.478
1999 Minnesota	AL	118	406	105	18	0	7	(2 5)	144	58	54	57	57	7	42	6	0	7	26	4	.87	11	.259	.353	.355
2000 Minnesota	AL	156	561	171	44	2	13	(8 5)	258	84	88	109	91	8	63	7	0	5	23	7	.77	10	.305	.405	.460
2001 Min-NYM		151	559	155	36	1	13	(5 8)	232	95	64	92	85	6	80	11	0	2	29	8	.78	16	.277	.382	.415
2002 Cleveland	AL	114	416	98	19	2	15	(8 7)	166	71	57	59	59	0	34	8	1	0	8	9	.47	13	.236	.342	.399
2003 Cleveland	AL	99	374	93	19	0	15	(6 9)	157	57	53	57	47	0	47	7	0	1	10	3	.77	8	.249	.343	.420
2004 Cleveland	AL	150	591	164	25	0	20	(10 10)	249	109	70	85	74	3	84	11	0	4	23	9	.72	21	.277	.366	.421
2001 Minnesota	AL	103	376	110	25	0	10	(4 6)	165	71	51	66	63	6	46	3	0	2	19	6	.76	14	.293	.396	.439
2001 New York	NL	48	183	45	11	1	3	(1 2)	67	24	13	26	22	0	34	8	0	0	10	2	.83	2	.246	.352	.366
10 ML YEARS		1182	4236	1139	237	16	125	(60 65)	1783	684	577	679	610	34	534	82	2	26	147	57	.72	103	.269	.370	.421

Brandon League

Pitches: R **Bats:** R **Pos:** RP-3   **Ht:** 6'3" **Wt:** 192 **Born:** 3/16/1983 **Age:** 22

			HOW MUCH HE PITCHED						WHAT HE GAVE UP										THE RESULTS						
Year Team	Lg	G	GS	CG	GF	IP	BFP	H	R	ER	HR	SH	SF	HB	TBB	IBB	SO	WP	Bk	W	L	Pct	ShO	Sv-Op	Hld	ERC	ERA
2001 Medicine Hat	R+	9	9	0	0	38.2	165	36	23	20	3	1	2	4	11	1	38	2	0	2	2	.500	0	0- -		3.42	4.66
2002 Auburn	A-	16	19	0	0	85.2	357	80	42	30	2	2	1	8	23	0	72	6	0	7	2	.778	0	0- -		3.09	3.15
2003 Chrlstn - WV	A	12	12	0	0	70.2	277	58	15	15	1	0	1	4	18	0	61	3	0	2	3	.400	0	0- -		2.37	1.91
2003 Dunedin	A+	13	12	0	0	66.1	296	76	40	35	3	5	1	6	20	0	34	8	1	4	3	.571	0	0- -		4.43	4.75
2004 New Hamp	AA	41	10	0	6	104.0	441	92	44	39	3	2	1	8	41	1	90	8	0	6	4	.600	0	2- -		3.23	3.38
2004 Toronto	AL	3	0	0	0	4.2	18	3	0	0	0	0	0	0	1	0	2	0	0	1	0	1.000	0	0-0	1	1.26	0.00

Matt LeCroy

Bats: R **Throws:** R **Pos:** DH-30; C-26; 1B-23; PH-19   **Ht:** 6'2" **Wt:** 225 **Born:** 12/13/1975 **Age:** 29

							BATTING												BASERUNNING				AVERAGES		
Year Team	Lg	G	AB	H	2B	3B	HR	(Hm Rd)	TB	R	RBI	RC	TBB	IBB	SO	HBP	SH	SF	SB	CS	SB%	GDP	Avg	OBP	Slg
2000 Minnesota	AL	56	167	29	10	0	5	(2 3)	54	18	17	12	17	2	38	2	1	3	0	0	-	6	.174	.254	.323
2001 Minnesota	AL	15	40	17	5	0	3	(0 3)	31	6	12	11	0	0	8	1	0	1	0	1	.00	0	.425	.429	.775
2002 Minnesota	AL	63	181	47	11	1	7	(2 5)	81	19	27	24	13	1	38	0	0	2	0	2	.00	5	.260	.306	.448
2003 Minnesota	AL	107	345	99	19	0	17	(9 8)	169	39	64	60	25	1	82	4	0	0	0	1	.00	8	.287	.342	.490
2004 Minnesota	AL	88	264	71	14	0	9	(5 4)	112	25	39	32	16	0	60	5	0	2	0	0	-	7	.269	.321	.424
5 ML YEARS		329	997	263	59	1	41	(18 23)	447	107	159	139	71	4	226	12	1	8	0	4	.00	26	.264	.318	.448

Ricky Ledee

Bats: L **Throws:** L **Pos:** PH-67; CF-16; RF-12; LF-10; DH-2; PR-1   **Ht:** 6'1" **Wt:** 190 **Born:** 11/22/1973 **Age:** 31

							BATTING												BASERUNNING				AVERAGES		
Year Team	Lg	G	AB	H	2B	3B	HR	(Hm Rd)	TB	R	RBI	RC	TBB	IBB	SO	HBP	SH	SF	SB	CS	SB%	GDP	Avg	OBP	Slg
1998 New York	AL	42	79	19	5	2	1	(0 1)	31	13	12	9	7	0	29	0	0	1	3	1	.75	1	.241	.299	.392
1999 New York	AL	88	250	69	13	5	9	(4 5)	119	45	40	41	28	5	73	0	0	2	4	3	.57	2	.276	.346	.476
2000 NYY-Cle-Tex	AL	137	467	110	19	5	13	(6 7)	178	59	77	56	59	4	98	2	0	3	13	6	.68	17	.236	.322	.381
2001 Texas	AL	78	242	56	21	1	2	(1 1)	85	33	36	26	23	0	58	3	1	3	3	3	.50	3	.231	.303	.351
2002 Philadelphia	NL	96	203	46	13	1	8	(4 4)	85	33	23	24	35	0	50	1	1	1	1	2	.33	3	.227	.342	.419
2003 Philadelphia	NL	121	255	63	15	2	13	(6 7)	121	37	46	36	34	5	59	0	1	1	0	0	-	4	.247	.334	.475
2004 Phi-SF	NL	104	176	41	9	0	7	(3 4)	71	25	30	24	27	2	47	1	0	1	3	0	1.00	6	.233	.337	.403
2000 New York	AL	62	191	46	11	1	7	(2 5)	80	23	31	26	26	2	39	1	0	2	7	3	.70	7	.241	.332	.419
2000 Cleveland	AL	17	63	14	2	1	2	(2 0)	24	13	8	7	8	0	9	0	0	0	0	0	-	3	.222	.310	.381
2000 Texas	AL	58	213	50	6	3	4	(2 2)	74	23	38	23	25	2	50	1	0	1	6	3	.67	7	.235	.317	.347
2004 Philadelphia	NL	73	123	35	7	0	7	(3 4)	63	19	26	23	22	2	27	0	0	0	2	0	1.00	5	.285	.393	.512
2004 San Francisco	NL	31	53	6	2	0	0	(0 0)	8	6	4	1	5	0	20	1	0	1	1	0	1.00	1	.113	.200	.151
7 ML YEARS		666	1672	404	95	16	53	(24 29)	690	245	264	216	213	16	414	7	3	12	27	15	.64	36	.242	.328	.413

Wil Ledezma

Pitches: L **Bats:** L **Pos:** SP-8; RP-7   **Ht:** 6'3" **Wt:** 150 **Born:** 1/21/1981 **Age:** 24

			HOW MUCH HE PITCHED						WHAT HE GAVE UP										THE RESULTS						
Year Team	Lg	G	GS	CG	GF	IP	BFP	H	R	ER	HR	SH	SF	HB	TBB	IBB	SO	WP	Bk	W	L	Pct	ShO	Sv-Op	Hld	ERC	ERA
1999 Red Sox	R	13	6	0	2	57.1	242	51	24	21	2	1	1	1	20	0	52	3	1	5	1	.833	0	1- -		2.88	3.30
2000 Augusta	A	14	14	0	0	52.2	240	51	33	30	3	1	1	2	36	0	60	5	0	2	4	.333	0	0- -		4.86	5.13
2002 Red Sox	R	1	0	0	0	3.0	13	4	2	2	0	0	0	0	0	0	3	0	0	0	0	-	0	0- -		3.56	6.00
2002 Augusta	A	5	5	0	0	23.2	101	23	10	10	0	0	0	1	8	0	38	2	0	2	2	.500	0	0- -		3.14	3.80
2004 Erie	AA	17	16	2	0	111.2	448	95	36	30	8	4	2	4	24	0	98	1	0	10	3	.769	1	0- -		2.57	2.42
2003 Detroit	AL	34	8	0	13	84.0	373	99	55	54	12	1	4	3	35	3	49	2	0	3	7	.300	0	0-1	1	5.72	5.79
2004 Detroit	AL	15	8	0	1	53.1	225	55	28	26	3	0	3	2	18	0	29	3	1	4	3	.571	0	0-1	0	3.94	4.39
2 ML YEARS		49	16	0	14	137.1	598	154	83	80	15	1	7	5	53	3	78	5	1	7	10	.412	0	0-2	1	5.00	5.24

Carlos Lee

Bats: R **Throws:** R **Pos:** LF-148; DH-5   **Ht:** 6'2" **Wt:** 235 **Born:** 6/20/1976 **Age:** 29

							BATTING												BASERUNNING				AVERAGES		
Year Team	Lg	G	AB	H	2B	3B	HR	(Hm Rd)	TB	R	RBI	RC	TBB	IBB	SO	HBP	SH	SF	SB	CS	SB%	GDP	Avg	OBP	Slg
1999 Chicago	AL	127	492	144	32	2	16	(10 6)	228	66	84	68	13	0	72	4	1	7	4	2	.67	11	.293	.312	.463
2000 Chicago	AL	152	572	172	29	2	24	(12 12)	277	107	92	91	38	1	94	3	1	5	13	4	.76	17	.301	.345	.484
2001 Chicago	AL	150	558	150	33	3	24	(12 12)	261	75	84	81	38	2	85	6	1	2	17	7	.71	15	.269	.321	.468
2002 Chicago	AL	140	492	130	26	3	26	(14 12)	238	82	80	86	75	4	73	2	0	7	1	4	.20	5	.264	.359	.484

(continued)

Year Team	Lg	G	AB	H	2B	3B	HR	(Hm	Rd)	TB	R	RBI	RC	TBB	IBB	SO	HBP	SH	SF	SB	CS	SB%	GDP	Avg	OBP	Slg
2003 Chicago	AL	158	623	181	35	1	31	(18	13)	311	100	113	105	37	2	91	4	0	7	18	4	.82	20	.291	.331	.499
2004 Chicago	AL	153	591	180	37	3	31	(17	14)	310	103	99	112	54	3	86	7	0	6	11	5	.69	10	.305	.366	.525
6 ML YEARS		880	3328	957	192	10	152	(83	69)	1625	533	552	543	255	12	501	26	3	34	64	26	.71	78	.288	.340	.488

Cliff Lee

Pitches: L **Bats:** L **Pos:** SP-33   **Ht:** 6'3" **Wt:** 190 **Born:** 8/30/1978 **Age:** 26

Year Team	Lg	G	GS	CG	GF	IP	BFP	H	R	ER	HR	SH	SF	HB	TBB	IBB	SO	WP	Bk	W	L	Pct	ShO	Sv-Op	Hld	ERC	ERA
2002 Cleveland	AL	2	2	0	0	10.1	44	6	2	2	0	1	0	0	8	1	6	0	1	0	1	.000	0	0-0	0	2.38	1.74
2003 Cleveland	AL	9	9	0	0	52.1	210	41	28	21	7	1	1	2	20	1	44	3	0	3	3	.500	0	0-0	0	3.29	3.61
2004 Cleveland	AL	33	33	0	0	179.0	802	188	113	108	30	2	6	13	81	1	161	6	0	14	8	.636	0	0-0	0	5.31	5.43
3 ML YEARS		44	44	0	0	241.2	1056	235	143	131	37	4	7	13	109	3	211	9	1	17	12	.586	0	0-0	0	4.72	4.88

Dave Lee

Pitches: R **Bats:** R **Pos:** RP-4   **Ht:** 6'1" **Wt:** 202 **Born:** 3/12/1973 **Age:** 32

Year Team	Lg	G	GS	CG	GF	IP	BFP	H	R	ER	HR	SH	SF	HB	TBB	IBB	SO	WP	Bk	W	L	Pct	ShO	Sv-Op	Hld	ERC	ERA
2004 Buffalo*	AAA	51	0	0	37	66.1	302	63	37	36	6	1	0	5	35	3	55	2	0	2	4	.333	0	9--	-	4.33	4.88
1999 Colorado	NL	36	0	0	0	49.0	212	43	0	20	4	0	0	0	29	0	38	0	0	3	2	.600	0	0-0	0	4.06	3.67
2000 Colorado	NL	7	0	0	0	5.2	35	10	0	7	3	0	0	0	6	0	6	0	0	0	0	-	0	1-0	0	15.31	11.12
2001 San Diego	NL	41	0	0	0	48.2	222	52	0	20	6	0	0	0	27	0	42	0	0	1	0	1.000	0	0-0	0	5.22	3.70
2003 Cleveland	AL	8	0	0	2	7.2	34	4	4	4	1	0	0	0	6	1	7	1	0	1	0	1.000	0	0-0	1	2.79	4.70
2004 Cleveland	AL	4	0	0	2	4.1	27	8	7	5	0	0	0	0	4	0	4	1	0	0	0	-	0	0-0	0	9.76	10.38
5 ML YEARS		96	0	0	4	115.1	530	117	11	56	14	0	0	0	72	1	97	2	0	5	2	.714	0	1-0	1	5.13	4.37

Derrek Lee

Bats: R **Throws:** R **Pos:** 1B-161; PH-1   **Ht:** 6'5" **Wt:** 248 **Born:** 9/6/1975 **Age:** 29

Year Team	Lg	G	AB	H	2B	3B	HR	(Hm	Rd)	TB	R	RBI	RC	TBB	IBB	SO	HBP	SH	SF	SB	CS	SB%	GDP	Avg	OBP	Slg
1997 San Diego	NL	22	54	14	3	0	1	(0	1)	20	9	4	8	9	0	24	0	0	0	0	0	-	1	.259	.365	.370
1998 Florida	NL	141	454	106	29	1	17	(4	13)	188	62	74	59	47	1	120	10	0	2	5	2	.71	12	.233	.318	.414
1999 Florida	NL	70	218	45	9	1	5	(0	5)	71	21	20	18	17	1	70	0	0	1	2	1	.67	3	.206	.263	.326
2000 Florida	NL	158	477	134	18	3	28	(9	19)	242	70	70	84	63	6	123	4	0	2	0	3	.00	14	.281	.368	.507
2001 Florida	NL	158	561	158	37	4	21	(8	13)	266	83	75	88	50	1	126	8	0	6	4	2	.67	18	.282	.346	.474
2002 Florida	NL	162	581	157	35	7	27	(9	18)	287	95	86	96	98	8	164	5	0	4	19	9	.68	14	.270	.378	.494
2003 Florida	NL	155	539	146	31	2	31	(11	20)	274	91	92	99	88	7	131	10	0	6	21	8	.72	9	.271	.379	.508
2004 Chicago	NL	161	605	168	39	1	32	(18	14)	305	90	98	101	68	4	128	8	2	5	12	5	.71	14	.278	.356	.504
8 ML YEARS		1027	3489	928	201	19	162	(59	103)	1653	521	519	553	440	28	886	45	2	26	63	30	.68	85	.266	.353	.474

Travis Lee

Bats: L **Throws:** L **Pos:** 1B-6; PH-1   **Ht:** 6'3" **Wt:** 210 **Born:** 5/26/1975 **Age:** 30

Year Team	Lg	G	AB	H	2B	3B	HR	(Hm	Rd)	TB	R	RBI	RC	TBB	IBB	SO	HBP	SH	SF	SB	CS	SB%	GDP	Avg	OBP	Slg
2004 Tampa*	A+	4	16	4	1	0	0	(-	-)	5	2	3	1	1	0	4	0	0	0	0	0	-	1	.250	.294	.313
1998 Arizona	NL	146	562	151	20	2	22	(12	10)	241	71	72	83	67	5	123	0	0	1	8	1	.89	13	.269	.346	.429
1999 Arizona	NL	120	375	89	16	2	9	(7	2)	136	57	50	49	58	4	50	0	0	3	17	3	.85	10	.237	.337	.363
2000 Ari-Phi	NL	128	404	95	24	1	9	(2	7)	148	53	54	53	65	1	79	2	0	2	8	1	.89	12	.235	.342	.366
2001 Philadelphia	NL	157	555	143	34	2	20	(11	9)	241	75	90	81	71	5	109	4	1	9	3	4	.43	15	.258	.341	.434
2002 Philadelphia	NL	153	536	142	26	2	13	(8	5)	211	55	70	65	54	10	104	0	0	2	5	3	.63	12	.265	.331	.394
2003 Tampa Bay	AL	145	542	149	37	3	19	(9	10)	249	75	70	77	64	4	97	0	1	6	6	2	.75	13	.275	.348	.459
2004 New York	AL	7	19	2	1	0	0	(0	0)	3	1	2	0	1	1	3	0	0	0	0	0	-	2	.105	.150	.158
2000 Arizona	NL	72	224	52	13	0	8	(1	7)	89	34	40	27	25	1	46	0	0	1	5	1	.83	6	.232	.308	.397
2000 Philadelphia	NL	56	180	43	11	1	1	(1	0)	59	19	14	26	40	0	33	2	0	1	3	0	1.00	6	.239	.381	.328
7 ML YEARS		856	2993	771	158	12	92	(49	43)	1229	387	408	408	380	30	565	6	2	23	47	14	.77	77	.258	.340	.411

Justin Lehr

Pitches: R **Bats:** R **Pos:** RP-27   **Ht:** 6'1" **Wt:** 200 **Born:** 8/3/1977 **Age:** 27

Year Team	Lg	G	GS	CG	GF	IP	BFP	H	R	ER	HR	SH	SF	HB	TBB	IBB	SO	WP	Bk	W	L	Pct	ShO	Sv-Op	Hld	ERC	ERA
1999 Sth Oregon	A-	14	4	0	7	42.1	207	62	36	28	3	5	1	2	17	3	40	9	0	2	6	.250	0	0--	-	6.56	5.95
2000 Sacramento	AAA	1	1	0	0	4.0	21	7	5	5	1	0	0	0	3	0	3	0	0	0	0	-	0	0--	-	12.23	11.25
2000 Modesto	A+	29	25	0	1	175.0	709	161	71	62	10	8	4	5	46	1	138	15	5	13	6	.684	0	0--	-	3.01	3.19
2001 Midland	AA	29	27	0	2	155.1	709	206	107	94	20	6	2	11	43	1	103	4	2	11	12	.478	0	0--	-	6.00	5.45
2002 Midland	AA	58	0	0	21	80.0	348	88	39	36	7	7	4	3	31	10	59	3	0	8	3	.727	0	4--	-	4.52	4.05
2003 Sacramento	AAA	53	0	0	16	75.0	320	74	34	31	3	3	0	4	27	3	64	5	0	3	2	.600	0	4--	-	3.60	3.72
2004 Sacramento	AAA	32	0	0	28	37.1	159	37	14	11	1	0	1	1	10	0	40	6	0	4	2	.667	0	13--	-	3.07	2.65
2004 Oakland	AL	27	0	0	11	32.2	144	35	19	19	3	1	2	2	14	2	16	2	0	1	1	.500	0	0-1	5	4.73	5.23

Jon Leicester

Pitches: R **Bats:** R **Pos:** RP-32   **Ht:** 6'3" **Wt:** 230 **Born:** 2/7/1979 **Age:** 26

Year Team	Lg	G	GS	CG	GF	IP	BFP	H	R	ER	HR	SH	SF	HB	TBB	IBB	SO	WP	Bk	W	L	Pct	ShO	Sv-Op	Hld	ERC	ERA
2000 Eugene	A-	17	7	0	1	49.2	224	47	36	30	4	6	4	2	22	1	31	2	0	1	5	.167	0	0--	-	3.76	5.44
2001 Lansing	A	28	27	1	1	153.0	693	182	117	90	16	2	4	16	58	0	109	12	1	9	10	.474	0	0--	-	5.61	5.29
2002 Daytona	A+	20	14	0	0	81.2	371	77	43	36	2	2	2	8	48	1	57	8	1	2	3	.400	0	0--	-	4.25	3.97

Al Leiter

Pitches: L **Bats:** L **Pos:** SP-30

Ht: 6'3" **Wt:** 220 **Born:** 10/23/1965 **Age:** 39

Year Team	Lg	G	GS	CG	GF	IP	BFP	H	R	ER	HR	SH	SF	HB	TBB	IBB	SO	WP	Bk	W	L	Pct	ShO	Sv-Op	Hld	ERC	ERA
1987 New York	AL	4	4	0	0	22.2	104	24	16	16	2	1	0	0	15	0	28	4	0	2	2	.500	0	0-0	0	5.41	6.35
1988 New York	AL	14	14	0	0	57.1	251	49	27	25	7	1	0	5	33	0	60	1	4	4	4	.500	0	0-0	0	4.51	3.92
1989 NYY-Tor	AL	5	5	0	0	33.1	154	32	23	21	2	1	1	2	23	0	26	2	1	1	2	.333	0	0-0	0	4.90	5.67
1990 Toronto	AL	4	0	0	2	6.1	22	1	0	0	0	0	0	0	2	0	5	0	0	0	0	-	0	0-0	0	0.33	0.00
1991 Toronto	AL	3	0	0	1	1.2	13	3	5	5	0	1	0	0	5	0	1	0	0	0	0	-	0	0-0	0	19.88	27.00
1992 Toronto	AL	1	0	0	0	1.0	7	1	1	1	0	0	0	0	2	0	0	0	0	0	0	-	0	0-0	0	8.07	9.00
1993 Toronto	AL	34	12	1	4	105.0	454	93	52	48	8	3	3	4	56	2	66	2	2	9	6	.600	1	2-3	3	3.94	4.11
1994 Toronto	AL	20	20	1	0	111.2	516	125	68	63	6	3	8	2	65	3	100	7	5	6	7	.462	0	0-0	0	5.14	5.08
1995 Toronto	AL	28	28	2	0	183.0	805	162	80	74	15	6	4	6	108	1	153	14	0	11	11	.500	1	0-0	0	4.18	3.64
1996 Florida	NL	33	33	2	0	215.1	896	153	74	70	14	7	3	11	119	3	200	5	0	16	12	.571	1	0-0	0	3.09	2.93
1997 Florida	NL	27	27	0	0	151.1	668	133	78	73	13	10	3	12	91	4	132	2	0	11	9	.550	0	0-0	0	4.39	4.34
1998 New York	NL	28	28	4	0	193.0	789	151	55	53	8	6	2	11	71	2	174	4	1	17	6	.739	2	0-0	0	2.65	2.47
1999 New York	NL	32	32	1	0	213.0	923	209	107	100	19	13	10	9	93	8	162	4	1	13	12	.520	1	0-0	0	4.17	4.23
2000 New York	NL	31	31	2	0	208.0	874	176	84	74	19	10	6	11	76	1	200	4	1	16	8	.667	1	0-0	0	3.23	3.20
2001 New York	NL	29	29	0	0	187.1	772	178	81	69	18	9	6	4	46	3	142	5	2	11	11	.500	0	0-0	0	3.26	3.31
2002 New York	NL	33	33	2	0	204.1	868	194	99	79	23	12	2	8	69	5	172	1	1	13	13	.500	2	0-0	0	3.75	3.48
2003 New York	NL	30	30	1	0	180.2	798	176	83	80	15	11	6	9	94	11	139	5	1	15	9	.625	1	0-0	0	4.40	3.99
2004 New York	NL	30	30	0	0	173.2	750	138	65	62	16	8	2	11	97	8	117	1	1	10	8	.556	0	0-0	0	3.68	3.21
1989 New York	AL	4	4	0	0	26.2	123	23	20	18	1	1	1	2	21	0	22	1	1	1	2	.333	0	0-0	0	4.62	6.08
1989 Toronto	AL	1	1	0	0	6.2	31	9	3	3	1	0	0	0	2	0	4	1	0	0	0	-	0	0-0	0	5.96	4.05
18 ML YEARS		386	356	16	7	2248.2	9664	1998	998	913	185	102	56	105	1065	51	1877	61	20	155	120	.564	10	2-3	3	3.78	3.65

Jose Leon

Bats: R **Throws:** R **Pos:** 1B-16; PH-7; 3B-6; DH-5; PR-4

Ht: 6'0" **Wt:** 175 **Born:** 12/8/1976 **Age:** 28

Year Team	Lg	G	AB	H	2B	3B	HR	(Hm	Rd)	TB	R	RBI	RC	TBB	IBB	SO	HBP	SH	SF	SB	CS	SB%	GDP	Avg	OBP	Slg
2004 Ottawa*	AAA	83	283	91	21	2	17	(-	-)	167	45	55	56	24	2	68	7	0	5	1	1	.50	11	.322	.382	.590
2002 Baltimore	AL	36	89	22	2	0	3	(1	2)	33	8	10	10	3	0	20	1	0	0	1	0	1.00	2	.247	.280	.371
2003 Baltimore	AL	21	54	13	1	0	0	(0	0)	14	6	0	2	3	0	18	2	0	0	0	0	-	1	.241	.305	.259
2004 Baltimore	AL	31	66	12	2	0	2	(2	0)	20	4	8	1	2	0	19	0	0	1	0	0	-	6	.182	.203	.303
3 ML YEARS		88	209	47	5	0	5	(3	2)	67	18	18	13	8	0	57	3	0	1	1	0	1.00	9	.225	.262	.321

Justin Leone

Bats: R **Throws:** R **Pos:** 3B-28; SS-2; PH-2

Ht: 6'1" **Wt:** 190 **Born:** 7/9/1977 **Age:** 27

Year Team	Lg	G	AB	H	2B	3B	HR	(Hm	Rd)	TB	R	RBI	RC	TBB	IBB	SO	HBP	SH	SF	SB	CS	SB%	GDP	Avg	OBP	Slg
1999 Everett	A-	62	205	54	14	2	6	(-	-)	90	34	35	32	32	0	49	2	1	5	5	3	.63	5	.263	.361	.439
2000 Wisconsin	A	115	374	100	32	3	18	(-	-)	192	77	63	80	79	1	107	11	2	3	9	2	.82	3	.267	.407	.513
2001 Sn Brnardino	A+	130	485	113	27	4	22	(-	-)	214	70	69	66	57	2	158	5	6	3	4	3	.57	8	.233	.318	.441
2002 Sn Brnardino	A+	98	358	89	20	5	18	(-	-)	173	64	58	61	57	1	98	5	0	2	6	0	1.00	9	.249	.358	.483
2003 San Antonio	AA	135	455	131	38	7	21	(-	-)	246	103	92	98	92	10	104	3	0	8	20	6	.77	7	.288	.405	.541
2004 Tacoma	AAA	68	253	68	10	5	21	(-	-)	151	56	51	47	26	0	82	4	1	2	5	6	.45	4	.269	.344	.597
2004 Seattle	AL	31	102	22	5	0	6	(2	4)	45	15	13	14	9	0	32	3	1	0	1	0	1.00	0	.216	.298	.441

Curtis Leskanic

Pitches: R **Bats:** R **Pos:** RP-51

Ht: 6'0" **Wt:** 196 **Born:** 4/2/1968 **Age:** 37

Year Team	Lg	G	GS	CG	GF	IP	BFP	H	R	ER	HR	SH	SF	HB	TBB	IBB	SO	WP	Bk	W	L	Pct	ShO	Sv-Op	Hld	ERC	ERA
1993 Colorado	NL	18	8	0	1	57.0	260	59	40	34	7	5	4	2	27	1	30	8	2	1	5	.167	0	0-0	0	4.71	5.37
1994 Colorado	NL	8	3	0	2	22.1	98	27	14	14	2	2	0	0	10	0	17	2	0	1	1	.500	0	0-0	0	5.62	5.64
1995 Colorado	NL	76	0	0	27	98.0	406	83	38	37	7	3	2	0	33	1	107	6	1	6	3	.667	0	10-16	19	2.79	3.40
1996 Colorado	NL	70	0	0	32	73.2	334	82	51	51	12	3	3	2	38	1	76	6	2	7	5	.583	0	6-10	9	5.81	6.23
1997 Colorado	NL	55	0	0	23	58.1	248	59	36	36	8	2	4	0	24	0	53	4	0	4	4	.500	0	2-4	6	4.55	5.55
1998 Colorado	NL	66	0	0	20	75.2	332	75	37	37	9	0	0	1	40	2	55	3	1	6	4	.600	0	2-5	12	4.74	4.40
1999 Colorado	NL	63	0	0	5	85.0	382	87	54	48	7	5	3	5	49	4	77	5	0	8	8	.500	0	0-3	8	5.00	5.08
2000 Milwaukee	NL	73	0	0	39	77.1	333	58	23	22	7	1	4	3	51	5	75	5	0	9	3	.750	0	12-13	11	3.72	2.56
2001 Milwaukee	NL	70	0	0	58	69.1	297	63	30	28	11	3	0	2	31	5	64	2	0	2	6	.250	0	17-24	2	4.18	3.63
2003 Mil-KC		53	0	0	14	52.2	217	38	15	13	2	0	1	1	29	1	50	3	0	5	0	1.000	0	2-3	11	2.84	2.22
2004 KC-Bos	AL	51	0	0	23	43.1	204	47	27	25	8	3	2	1	30	3	37	2	0	3	5	.375	0	4-8	6	6.41	5.19
2003 Milwaukee	NL	26	0	0	5	26.2	116	22	8	8	1	0	0	1	18	0	28	2	0	4	0	1.000	0	0-0	4	3.93	2.70
2003 Kansas City	AL	27	0	0	9	26.0	101	16	7	5	1	0	1	0	11	1	22	1	0	1	0	1.000	0	2-3	7	1.84	1.73
2004 Kansas City	AL	19	0	0	7	15.2	85	23	16	14	5	0	0	0	14	0	15	2	0	0	3	.000	0	2-5	4	10.88	8.04
2004 Boston	AL	32	0	0	16	27.2	119	24	11	11	3	3	2	1	16	3	22	0	0	3	2	.600	0	2-3	2	4.14	3.58
11 ML YEARS		603	11	0	244	712.2	3111	678	365	345	80	27	23	17	362	23	641	46	6	50	34	.595	0	55-86	84	4.38	4.36

Al Levine

Pitches: R **Bats:** L **Pos:** RP-65   **Ht:** 6'3" **Wt:** 190 **Born:** 5/22/1968 **Age:** 37

Year Team	Lg		HOW MUCH HE PITCHED							WHAT HE GAVE UP												THE RESULTS						
		G	GS	CG	GF	IP	BFP	H	R	ER	HR	SH	SF	HB	TBB	IBB	SO	WP	Bk	W	L	Pct	ShO	Sv-Op	Hld	ERC	ERA
1996 Chicago	AL	16	0	0	5	18.1	85	22	14	11	1	0	1	1	7	1	12	0	0	0	1	.000	0	0-1	0	4.80	5.40
1997 Chicago	AL	25	0	0	6	27.1	133	35	22	21	4	1	2	2	16	1	22	2	0	2	2	.500	0	0-1	3	7.10	6.91
1998 Texas	AL	30	0	0	11	58.0	251	68	30	29	6	1	3	0	16	1	19	5	0	0	1	.000	0	0-0	0	4.58	4.50
1999 Anaheim	AL	50	1	0	12	85.0	349	76	40	32	13	2	7	3	29	2	37	3	0	1	1	.500	0	0-1	3	3.81	3.39
2000 Anaheim	AL	51	5	0	12	95.1	426	98	46	41	10	3	3	2	49	5	42	1	0	3	4	.429	0	2-2	5	4.71	3.87
2001 Anaheim	AL	64	1	0	21	75.2	316	71	25	20	7	5	5	2	28	4	40	6	0	8	10	.444	0	2-6	17	3.66	2.38
2002 Anaheim	AL	52	0	0	21	63.2	286	61	35	30	8	2	7	2	34	3	40	2	0	4	4	.500	0	5-7	10	4.53	4.24
2003 TB-KC	AL	54	0	0	21	71.0	303	67	29	22	9	4	0	3	29	1	30	2	0	3	6	.333	0	1-4	10	4.17	2.79
2004 Detroit	AL	65	0	0	14	70.2	310	83	37	36	10	2	2	1	24	1	32	3	0	3	4	.429	0	0-1	16	5.23	4.58
2003 Tampa Bay	AL	36	0	0	14	49.2	208	45	23	16	7	3	0	2	18	0	25	2	0	3	5	.375	0	0-2	8	3.89	2.90
2003 Kansas City	AL	18	0	0	7	21.1	95	22	6	6	2	1	0	1	11	1	5	0	0	0	1	.000	0	1-2	2	4.82	2.53
9 ML YEARS		407	7	0	123	565.0	2459	581	276	242	68	20	30	16	232	19	274	24	0	24	33	.421	0	10-23	64	4.51	3.85

Colby Lewis

Pitches: R **Bats:** R **Pos:** SP-3   **Ht:** 6'4" **Wt:** 215 **Born:** 8/2/1979 **Age:** 25

Year Team	Lg		HOW MUCH HE PITCHED							WHAT HE GAVE UP												THE RESULTS						
		G	GS	CG	GF	IP	BFP	H	R	ER	HR	SH	SF	HB	TBB	IBB	SO	WP	Bk	W	L	Pct	ShO	Sv-Op	Hld	ERC	ERA
2002 Texas	AL	15	4	0	4	34.1	168	42	26	24	4	2	0	2	26	2	28	3	1	1	3	.250	0	0-2	1	7.22	6.29
2003 Texas	AL	26	26	0	0	127.0	594	163	104	103	23	2	2	5	70	1	88	5	0	10	9	.526	0	0-0	0	7.38	7.30
2004 Texas	AL	3	3	0	0	15.1	71	13	7	7	1	0	0	1	13	0	11	0	0	1	1	.500	0	0-0	0	4.98	4.11
3 ML YEARS		44	33	0	4	176.2	833	218	137	134	28	4	2	8	109	3	127	8	1	12	13	.480	0	0-2	1	7.14	6.83

Brad Lidge

Pitches: R **Bats:** R **Pos:** RP-80   **Ht:** 6'5" **Wt:** 200 **Born:** 12/23/1976 **Age:** 28

Year Team	Lg		HOW MUCH HE PITCHED							WHAT HE GAVE UP												THE RESULTS						
		G	GS	CG	GF	IP	BFP	H	R	ER	HR	SH	SF	HB	TBB	IBB	SO	WP	Bk	W	L	Pct	ShO	Sv-Op	Hld	ERC	ERA
2002 Houston	NL	6	1	0	2	8.2	48	12	6	6	0	1	0	2	9	1	12	0	0	1	0	1.000	0	0-0	0	8.90	6.23
2003 Houston	NL	78	0	0	9	85.0	349	60	36	34	6	2	3	6	42	7	97	4	1	6	3	.667	0	1-6	28	2.82	3.60
2004 Houston	NL	80	0	0	44	94.2	369	57	21	20	8	3	2	6	30	5	157	3	1	6	5	.545	0	29-33	17	1.85	1.90
3 ML YEARS		164	1	0	55	188.1	766	129	63	60	14	6	5	13	81	13	266	7	2	13	8	.619	0	30-39	45	2.55	2.87

Cory Lidle

Pitches: R **Bats:** R **Pos:** SP-34   **Ht:** 5'11" **Wt:** 192 **Born:** 3/22/1972 **Age:** 33

Year Team	Lg		HOW MUCH HE PITCHED							WHAT HE GAVE UP												THE RESULTS						
		G	GS	CG	GF	IP	BFP	H	R	ER	HR	SH	SF	HB	TBB	IBB	SO	WP	Bk	W	L	Pct	ShO	Sv-Op	Hld	ERC	ERA
1997 New York	NL	54	2	0	20	81.2	345	86	38	32	7	4	4	3	20	4	54	2	0	7	2	.778	0	2-3	9	3.75	3.53
1999 Tampa Bay	AL	5	1	0	1	5.0	24	8	4	4	0	0	0	0	2	0	4	0	0	1	0	1.000	0	0-0	0	6.98	7.20
2000 Tampa Bay	AL	31	11	0	5	96.2	424	114	61	54	13	3	1	3	29	3	62	6	0	4	6	.400	0	0-0	2	5.06	5.03
2001 Oakland	AL	29	29	1	0	188.0	762	170	84	75	23	2	1	10	47	7	118	5	0	13	6	.684	0	0-0	0	3.35	3.59
2002 Oakland	AL	31	30	2	0	192.0	796	191	90	83	17	5	6	6	39	3	111	6	1	8	10	.444	2	0-0	1	3.31	3.89
2003 Toronto	AL	31	31	2	0	192.2	840	216	133	123	24	5	5	5	60	3	112	9	0	12	15	.444	0	0-0	0	4.67	5.75
2004 Cin-Phi	NL	34	34	5	0	211.1	911	224	123	115	27	14	6	10	61	5	126	8	0	12	12	.500	3	0-0	0	4.31	4.90
2004 Cincinnati	NL	24	24	3	0	149.0	656	170	95	88	24	12	4	5	44	4	93	6	0	7	10	.412	1	0-0	0	4.96	5.32
2004 Philadelphia	NL	10	10	2	0	62.1	255	54	28	27	3	2	2	5	17	1	33	0	0	5	2	.714	2	0-0	0	2.86	3.90
7 ML YEARS		215	138	10	26	967.1	4102	1009	533	486	111	33	23	37	258	25	587	36	1	57	51	.528	5	2-3	11	4.02	4.52

Jon Lieber

Pitches: R **Bats:** L **Pos:** SP-27   **Ht:** 6'2" **Wt:** 230 **Born:** 4/2/1970 **Age:** 35

Year Team	Lg		HOW MUCH HE PITCHED							WHAT HE GAVE UP												THE RESULTS						
		G	GS	CG	GF	IP	BFP	H	R	ER	HR	SH	SF	HB	TBB	IBB	SO	WP	Bk	W	L	Pct	ShO	Sv-Op	Hld	ERC	ERA
2004 Tampa*	A+	1	1	0	0	7.0	22	2	0	0	0	0	0	0	0	0	4	0	0	1	0	1.000	0	0-	-	0.20	0.00
1994 Pittsburgh	NL	17	17	1	0	108.2	460	116	62	45	12	3	3	1	25	3	71	2	3	6	7	.462	0	0-0	0	3.83	3.73
1995 Pittsburgh	NL	21	12	0	3	72.2	327	103	56	51	7	5	6	4	14	0	45	3	0	4	7	.364	0	0-1	3	5.96	6.32
1996 Pittsburgh	NL	51	15	0	6	142.0	600	156	70	63	19	7	2	3	28	2	94	0	0	9	5	.643	0	1-4	9	4.12	3.99
1997 Pittsburgh	NL	33	32	1	0	188.1	799	193	102	94	23	6	7	1	51	8	160	3	1	11	14	.440	0	0-0	0	3.78	4.49
1998 Pittsburgh	NL	29	28	2	1	171.0	731	182	93	78	23	7	4	3	40	4	138	0	3	8	14	.364	0	1-1	0	4.00	4.11
1999 Chicago	NL	31	31	3	0	203.1	875	226	107	92	28	7	11	1	46	6	186	2	2	10	11	.476	1	0-0	0	4.19	4.07
2000 Chicago	NL	35	35	6	0	251.0	1047	248	130	123	36	9	7	10	54	3	192	2	2	12	11	.522	1	0-0	0	3.70	4.41
2001 Chicago	NL	34	34	5	0	232.1	958	226	104	98	25	13	9	7	41	4	148	4	1	20	6	.769	1	0-0	0	3.19	3.80
2002 Chicago	NL	21	21	3	0	141.0	582	153	64	58	15	10	6	1	12	2	87	0	0	6	8	.429	0	0-0	0	3.33	3.70
2004 New York	AL	27	27	0	0	176.2	749	216	95	85	20	3	7	2	18	2	102	7	0	14	8	.636	0	0-0	0	4.26	4.33
10 ML YEARS		299	252	21	10	1687.0	7128	1819	883	787	208	70	62	33	329	34	1223	23	12	100	91	.524	3	2-6	12	3.89	4.20

Mike Lieberthal

Bats: R **Throws:** R **Pos:** C-130; PH-5   **Ht:** 6'0" **Wt:** 190 **Born:** 1/18/1972 **Age:** 33

Year Team	Lg		BATTING																				BASERUNNING				AVERAGES		
		G	AB	H	2B	3B	HR	(Hm	Rd)	TB	R	RBI	RC	TBB	IBB	SO	HBP	SH	SF	SB	CS	SB%	GDP	Avg	OBP	Slg
1994 Philadelphia	NL	24	79	21	3	1	1	(1	0)	29	6	5	8	3	0	5	1	1	0	0	0	-	4	.266	.301	.367
1995 Philadelphia	NL	16	47	12	2	0	0	(0	0)	14	1	4	5	5	0	5	0	2	0	0	0	-	4	.255	.327	.298
1996 Philadelphia	NL	50	166	42	8	0	7	(4	3)	71	21	23	21	10	0	30	2	0	4	0	0	-	4	.253	.297	.428
1997 Philadelphia	NL	134	455	112	27	1	20	(11	9)	201	59	77	62	44	1	76	4	0	7	3	4	.43	10	.246	.314	.442
1998 Philadelphia	NL	86	313	80	15	3	8	(5	3)	125	39	45	39	17	1	44	7	0	5	2	1	.67	5	.256	.304	.399
1999 Philadelphia	NL	145	510	153	33	1	31	(10	21)	281	84	96	96	44	7	86	11	1	8	0	0	-	15	.300	.363	.551
2000 Philadelphia	NL	108	389	108	30	0	15	(8	7)	183	55	71	62	40	3	53	6	0	3	2	0	1.00	6	.278	.352	.470
2001 Philadelphia	NL	34	121	28	8	0	2	(0	2)	42	21	11	13	12	2	21	3	0	0	0	0	-	2	.231	.316	.347

Year Team	Lg	G	AB	H	2B	3B	HR	(Hm Rd)	TB	R	RBI	RC	TBB	IBB	SO	HBP	SH	SF	SB	CS	SB%	GDP	Avg	OBP	Slg
2002 Philadelphia	NL	130	476	133	29	2	15	(7 8)	211	46	52	56	38	2	58	14	0	2	0	1	.00	16	.279	.349	.443
2003 Philadelphia	NL	131	508	159	30	1	13	(6 7)	230	68	81	81	38	2	59	12	0	3	0	0	-	14	.313	.373	.453
2004 Philadelphia	NL	131	476	129	31	1	17	(8 9)	213	58	61	49	37	2	69	11	1	4	1	1	.50	19	.271	.335	.447
11 ML YEARS		989	3540	977	216	10	129	(60 69)	1600	458	526	492	288	20	506	71	5	36	8	7	.53	101	.276	.340	.452

Jeff Liefer

Bats: L **Throws:** R **Pos:** PH-9; RF-3; DH-3; PR-1 **Ht:** 6'3" **Wt:** 210 **Born:** 8/17/1974 **Age:** 30

Year Team	Lg	G	AB	H	2B	3B	HR	(Hm Rd)	TB	R	RBI	RC	TBB	IBB	SO	HBP	SH	SF	SB	CS	SB%	GDP	Avg	OBP	Slg
2004 Indianapolis*	AAA	106	368	104	25	1	20	(- -)	191	60	83	65	47	6	62	4	0	6	1	0	1.00	12	.283	.365	.519
1999 Chicago	AL	45	113	28	7	1	0	(0 0)	37	8	14	11	8	0	28	0	0	1	2	0	1.00	3	.248	.295	.327
2000 Chicago	AL	5	11	2	0	0	0	(0 0)	2	0	0	0	0	0	4	0	0	0	0	0	-	0	.182	.182	.182
2001 Chicago	AL	83	254	65	13	0	18	(10 8)	132	36	39	40	20	1	69	2	1	2	0	1	.00	6	.256	.313	.520
2002 Chicago	AL	76	204	47	8	0	7	(4 3)	76	28	26	24	19	2	60	0	0	1	0	0	-	3	.230	.295	.373
2003 Mon-TB		44	113	20	4	0	4	(0 4)	36	10	21	13	6	1	39	0	0	1	0	1	.00	2	.177	.217	.319
2004 Milwaukee	NL	16	28	6	2	0	1	(0 1)	11	2	5	2	2	0	8	0	0	1	0	0	-	2	.214	.258	.393
2003 Montreal		35	88	17	3	0	3	(0 3)	29	6	18	11	3	0	26	0	0	1	0	1	.00	2	.193	.217	.330
2003 Tampa Bay	AL	9	25	3	1	0	1	(0 1)	7	4	3	2	3	1	13	0	0	0	0	0	-	0	.120	.214	.280
6 ML YEARS		269	723	168	34	1	30	(14 16)	294	84	105	90	55	4	208	2	1	6	2	2	.50	16	.232	.286	.407

Kerry Ligtenberg

Pitches: R **Bats:** R **Pos:** RP-57 **Ht:** 6'2" **Wt:** 215 **Born:** 5/11/1971 **Age:** 34

Year Team	Lg	G	GS	CG	GF	IP	BFP	H	R	ER	HR	SH	SF	HB	TBB	IBB	SO	WP	Bk	W	L	Pct	ShO	Sv-Op	Hld	ERC	ERA
1997 Atlanta	NL	15	0	0	9	15.0	61	12	5	5	4	0	0	0	4	2	19	0	0	1	0	1.000	0	1-1	0	3.26	3.00
1998 Atlanta	NL	75	0	0	56	73.0	290	51	24	22	6	1	1	0	24	1	79	3	0	3	2	.600	0	30-34	11	2.13	2.71
2000 Atlanta	NL	59	0	0	19	52.1	217	43	21	21	7	2	1	0	24	5	51	0	0	2	3	.400	0	12-14	12	3.46	3.61
2001 Atlanta	NL	53	0	0	24	59.2	254	50	22	20	4	1	2	0	30	8	56	3	0	3	3	.500	0	1-2	0	3.14	3.02
2002 Atlanta	NL	52	0	0	25	66.2	281	52	23	22	6	3	1	0	33	3	51	1	1	3	4	.429	0	0-0	2	3.10	2.97
2003 Baltimore	AL	68	0	0	21	59.1	247	60	23	22	9	2	1	2	14	3	47	0	0	4	2	.667	0	1-4	14	3.93	3.34
2004 Toronto	AL	57	0	0	20	55.0	263	73	40	39	6	3	0	2	25	7	49	5	0	1	6	.143	0	3-5	4	6.12	6.38
7 ML YEARS		379	0	0	174	381.0	1613	341	158	151	42	12	6	4	154	29	352	12	1	17	20	.459	0	48-60	43	3.50	3.57

Ted Lilly

Pitches: L **Bats:** L **Pos:** SP-32 **Ht:** 6'0" **Wt:** 185 **Born:** 1/4/1976 **Age:** 29

Year Team	Lg	G	GS	CG	GF	IP	BFP	H	R	ER	HR	SH	SF	HB	TBB	IBB	SO	WP	Bk	W	L	Pct	ShO	Sv-Op	Hld	ERC	ERA
1999 Montreal	NL	9	3	0	1	23.2	110	30	20	20	7	0	1	3	9	0	28	1	0	0	1	.000	0	0-0	0	7.76	7.61
2000 New York	AL	7	0	0	1	8.0	39	8	6	5	1	0	0	0	5	0	11	1	1	0	0	-	0	0-0	0	4.76	5.63
2001 New York	AL	26	21	0	2	120.2	537	126	81	72	20	2	5	7	51	1	112	9	2	5	6	.455	0	0-0	0	5.10	5.37
2002 NYY-Oak	AL	22	16	2	1	100.0	413	80	43	41	15	0	3	6	31	3	77	6	1	5	7	.417	1	0-0	0	3.14	3.69
2003 Oakland	AL	32	31	0	0	178.1	773	179	92	86	24	3	4	5	58	3	147	5	4	12	10	.545	0	0-0	0	4.06	4.34
2004 Toronto	AL	32	32	2	0	197.1	845	171	92	89	26	3	3	6	89	2	168	6	4	12	10	.545	0	0-0	0	3.84	4.06
2002 New York	AL	16	11	2	1	76.2	314	57	31	29	10	0	3	5	24	3	59	6	0	3	6	.333	1	0-0	0	2.74	3.40
2002 Oakland	AL	6	5	0	0	23.1	99	23	12	12	5	0	0	1	7	0	18	0	1	2	1	.667	0	0-0	0	4.56	4.63
6 ML YEARS		128	103	4	5	628.0	2717	594	334	313	93	8	16	27	243	9	543	28	12	34	34	.500	2	0-0	0	4.17	4.49

Jose Lima

Pitches: R **Bats:** R **Pos:** SP-24; RP-12 **Ht:** 6'2" **Wt:** 205 **Born:** 9/30/1972 **Age:** 32

Year Team	Lg	G	GS	CG	GF	IP	BFP	H	R	ER	HR	SH	SF	HB	TBB	IBB	SO	WP	Bk	W	L	Pct	ShO	Sv-Op	Hld	ERC	ERA
1994 Detroit	AL	3	1	0	1	6.2	34	11	10	10	2	0	0	0	3	1	7	1	0	0	1	.000	0	0-0	0	9.61	13.50
1995 Detroit	AL	15	15	0	0	73.2	320	85	52	50	10	2	1	4	18	4	37	5	0	3	9	.250	0	0-0	0	4.73	6.11
1996 Detroit	AL	39	4	0	15	72.2	329	87	48	46	13	5	3	5	22	4	59	3	0	5	6	.455	0	3-7	6	5.53	5.70
1997 Houston	NL	52	1	0	15	75.0	321	79	45	44	9	6	3	5	16	2	63	2	0	1	6	.143	0	2-2	3	3.96	5.28
1998 Houston	NL	33	33	3	0	233.1	950	229	100	96	34	11	5	7	32	1	169	4	0	16	8	.667	1	0-0	0	3.36	3.70
1999 Houston	NL	35	35	3	0	246.1	1024	256	108	98	30	5	7	2	44	2	187	8	0	21	10	.677	0	0-0	0	3.58	3.58
2000 Houston	NL	33	33	0	0	196.1	895	251	152	145	48	12	12	2	68	3	124	0	0	7	16	.304	0	0-0	0	6.59	6.65
2001 Hou-Det		32	27	2	3	165.2	719	197	114	102	35	5	9	9	38	3	84	4	0	6	12	.333	0	0-0	0	5.53	5.54
2002 Detroit	AL	20	12	0	3	68.1	304	86	60	59	12	1	6	2	21	0	33	2	0	4	6	.400	0	0-0	0	5.97	7.77
2003 Kansas City	AL	14	14	0	0	73.1	321	80	40	40	7	1	3	5	26	0	32	2	2	8	3	.727	0	0-0	0	4.69	4.91
2004 Los Angeles	NL	36	24	0	3	170.1	702	178	81	77	33	9	1	1	34	6	93	3	0	13	5	.722	0	0-0	1	4.18	4.77
2001 Houston	NL	14	9	0	3	53.0	249	77	48	43	12	4	4	5	16	1	41	3	0	1	2	.333	0	0-0	0	7.90	7.30
2001 Detroit	AL	18	18	2	0	112.2	470	120	66	59	23	1	5	4	22	2	43	1	0	5	10	.333	0	0-0	0	4.49	4.71
11 ML YEARS		312	199	8	40	1381.2	5919	1539	810	767	233	57	50	42	322	26	888	37	2	84	82	.506	1	5-9	10	4.63	5.00

Mike Lincoln

Pitches: R **Bats:** R **Pos:** RP-13 **Ht:** 6'2" **Wt:** 203 **Born:** 4/10/1975 **Age:** 30

Year Team	Lg	G	GS	CG	GF	IP	BFP	H	R	ER	HR	SH	SF	HB	TBB	IBB	SO	WP	Bk	W	L	Pct	ShO	Sv-Op	Hld	ERC	ERA
1999 Minnesota	AL	18	15	0	0	76.1	353	102	59	58	11	2	6	1	26	0	27	4	0	3	10	.231	0	0-0	1	6.16	6.84
2000 Minnesota	AL	8	4	0	1	20.2	109	36	25	25	10	0	4	2	13	0	15	1	0	0	3	.000	0	0-0	0	14.32	10.89
2001 Pittsburgh	NL	31	0	0	5	40.1	168	34	16	12	3	1	1	4	11	0	24	2	0	2	1	.667	0	0-2	7	2.94	2.68
2002 Pittsburgh	NL	55	0	0	9	72.1	309	80	28	25	7	2	4	0	27	8	50	2	0	0	3	.000	0	0-3	11	4.49	3.11
2003 Pittsburgh	NL	36	0	0	14	36.1	153	38	22	21	5	1	1	1	13	0	28	1	0	3	4	.429	0	5-8	5	4.70	5.20
2004 St Louis	NL	13	0	0	1	17.1	71	10	12	10	1	1	2	1	6	0	14	0	0	3	2	.600	0	0-2	1	1.63	5.19
6 ML YEARS		161	19	0	30	263.1	1163	300	162	151	37	7	14	9	96	8	158	10	0	13	24	.351	0	5-15	25	5.15	5.16

Todd Linden

Bats: B **Throws:** R **Pos:** LF-7; PH-6; RF-4; PR-1 **Ht:** 6'3" **Wt:** 210 **Born:** 6/30/1980 **Age:** 25

Year Team	Lg	G	AB	H	2B	3B	HR	(Hm	Rd)	TB	R	RBI	RC	TBB	IBB	SO	HBP	SH	SF	SB	CS	SB%	GDP	Avg	OBP	Slg
2002 Shreveport	AA	111	392	123	26	2	12	(-	-)	189	64	52	77	61	7	101	12	1	3	9	5	.64	12	.314	.419	.482
2002 Fresno	AAA	29	100	25	2	1	3	(-	-)	38	18	10	16	20	0	35	1	0	0	2	0	1.00	2	.250	.380	.380
2003 Fresno	AAA	125	471	131	24	3	11	(-	-)	194	75	56	70	40	2	105	17	4	0	14	4	.78	9	.278	.356	.412
2004 Fresno	AAA	130	489	127	28	2	23	(-	-)	228	93	75	77	63	3	149	7	3	5	8	6	.57	9	.260	.349	.466
2003 San Francisco	NL	18	38	8	1	0	1	(0	1)	12	2	6	5	1	0	8	0	0	0	0	0	-	2	.211	.231	.316
2004 San Francisco	NL	16	32	5	1	0	0	(0	0)	6	6	1	1	5	0	7	1	2	0	0	0	-	0	.156	.289	.188
2 ML YEARS		34	70	13	2	0	1	(0	1)	18	8	7	6	6	0	15	1	2	0	0	0	-	2	.186	.260	.257

Scott Linebrink

Pitches: R **Bats:** R **Pos:** RP-73 **Ht:** 6'2" **Wt:** 200 **Born:** 8/4/1976 **Age:** 28

Year Team	Lg	G	GS	CG	GF	IP	BFP	H	R	ER	HR	SH	SF	HB	TBB	IBB	SO	WP	Bk	W	L	Pct	ShO	Sv-Op	Hld	ERC	ERA
2000 SF-Hou	NL	11	0	0	4	12.0	63	18	8	8	4	0	0	3	8	0	6	0	0	0	0	-	0	0-0	0	11.88	6.00
2001 Houston	NL	9	0	0	2	10.1	44	6	4	3	0	1	1	2	6	0	9	1	0	0	0	-	0	0-0	0	2.54	2.61
2002 Houston	NL	22	0	0	4	24.1	119	31	21	19	2	0	2	1	13	4	24	0	0	0	0	-	0	0-0	1	5.75	7.03
2003 Hou-SD	NL	52	6	0	8	92.1	397	93	37	34	9	4	6	6	36	4	68	11	0	3	2	.600	0	0-0	6	4.32	3.31
2004 San Diego	NL	73	0	0	7	84.0	326	61	22	20	8	2	3	3	26	2	83	3	0	7	3	.700	0	0-5	28	2.48	2.14
2000 San Francisco	NL	3	0	0	1	2.1	16	7	3	3	1	0	0	0	2	0	0	0	0	0	0	-	0	0-0	0	24.13	11.57
2000 Houston	NL	8	0	0	3	9.2	47	11	5	5	3	0	0	3	6	0	6	0	0	0	0	-	0	0-0	0	9.21	4.66
2003 Houston	NL	9	6	0	2	31.2	140	38	15	15	4	2	1	3	14	1	17	5	0	1	1	.500	0	0-0	0	6.27	4.26
2003 San Diego	NL	43	0	0	6	60.2	257	55	22	19	5	2	5	3	22	3	51	6	0	2	1	.667	0	0-0	6	3.41	2.82
5 ML YEARS		167	6	0	25	223.0	949	209	92	84	23	7	12	15	89	10	190	15	0	10	5	.667	0	0-5	35	4.00	3.39

Pedro Liriano

Pitches: R **Bats:** R **Pos:** RP-11 **Ht:** 6'2" **Wt:** 170 **Born:** 10/23/1980 **Age:** 24

Year Team	Lg	G	GS	CG	GF	IP	BFP	H	R	ER	HR	SH	SF	HB	TBB	IBB	SO	WP	Bk	W	L	Pct	ShO	Sv-Op	Hld	ERC	ERA
2001 Provo	R+	15	14	0	1	77.2	342	80	39	24	3	1	3	5	31	0	76	4	3	11	2	.846	0	0--	-	4.03	2.78
2002 R Cucamnga	A+	28	28	1	0	167.1	699	129	86	67	14	6	1	10	74	1	174	5	0	10	14	.417	1	0--	-	3.12	3.60
2003 Huntsville	AA	27	26	0	0	142.2	621	138	77	60	12	7	5	7	62	2	116	9	1	9	13	.409	0	0--	-	4.09	3.79
2004 Indianapolis	AAA	29	21	1	2	126.1	555	149	81	73	21	4	4	5	50	1	97	7	3	3	10	.231	0	1--	-	5.93	5.20
2004 Milwaukee	NL	11	0	0	1	15.2	67	15	10	7	3	0	0	1	3	0	10	1	0	0	0	-	0	0-0	1	3.73	4.02

Mark Little

Bats: R **Throws:** R **Pos:** CF-5; LF-4; RF-4; PH-2 **Ht:** 6'0" **Wt:** 195 **Born:** 7/11/1972 **Age:** 32

Year Team	Lg	G	AB	H	2B	3B	HR	(Hm	Rd)	TB	R	RBI	RC	TBB	IBB	SO	HBP	SH	SF	SB	CS	SB%	GDP	Avg	OBP	Slg
2004 Buffalo*	AAA	68	239	75	17	4	11	(-	-)	133	37	39	42	9	0	40	7	1	6	4	6	.40	3	.314	.349	.556
1998 St-Louis	NL	7	12	1	0	0	0	(0	0)	1	0	0	0	2	0	5	0	1	0	1	0	1.00	0	.083	.214	.083
2001 Colorado	NL	51	85	29	6	0	3	(3	0)	44	18	13	16	1	1	20	4	0	0	5	2	.71	0	.341	.378	.518
2002 Col-NYM-Ari	NL	79	130	27	5	3	0	(0	0)	38	28	7	16	15	0	34	8	1	0	2	2	.50	1	.208	.327	.292
2004 Cleveland	AL	11	20	4	0	0	0	(0	0)	4	0	2	1	0	0	7	2	0	1	0	0	-	0	.200	.261	.200
2002 Colorado	NL	61	105	21	5	2	0	(0	0)	30	20	5	11	13	0	28	4	1	0	2	1	.67	1	.200	.311	.286
2002 New York	NL	3	3	0	0	0	0	(0	0)	0	0	0	0	0	0	1	0	0	0	0	1	.00	0	.000	.000	.000
2002 Arizona	NL	15	22	6	0	1	0	(0	0)	8	8	2	5	2	0	5	4	0	0	0	0	-	0	.273	.429	.364
4 ML YEARS		148	247	61	11	3	3	(3	0)	87	46	22	33	18	1	66	14	2	1	8	4	.67	1	.247	.332	.352

Paul Lo Duca

Bats: R **Throws:** R **Pos:** C-130; LF-9; PH-7; 1B-3 **Ht:** 5'10" **Wt:** 185 **Born:** 4/12/1972 **Age:** 33

Year Team	Lg	G	AB	H	2B	3B	HR	(Hm	Rd)	TB	R	RBI	RC	TBB	IBB	SO	HBP	SH	SF	SB	CS	SB%	GDP	Avg	OBP	Slg
1998 Los Angeles	NL	6	14	4	1	0	0	(0	0)	5	2	1	1	0	0	1	0	0	0	0	0	-	0	.286	.286	.357
1999 Los Angeles	NL	36	95	22	1	0	3	(1	2)	32	11	11	9	10	4	9	2	1	2	1	2	.33	3	.232	.312	.337
2000 Los Angeles	NL	34	65	16	2	0	2	(0	2)	24	6	8	6	6	0	8	2	2	2	0	2	.00	2	.246	.301	.369
2001 Los Angeles	NL	125	460	147	28	0	25	(11	14)	250	71	90	89	39	2	30	6	5	9	2	4	.33	11	.320	.374	.543
2002 Los Angeles	NL	149	580	163	38	1	10	(5	5)	233	74	64	73	34	2	31	10	4	4	3	1	.75	20	.281	.330	.402
2003 Los Angeles	NL	147	568	155	34	2	7	(4	3)	214	64	52	67	44	6	54	10	7	1	0	2	.00	21	.273	.335	.377
2004 LA-Fla	NL	143	535	153	29	2	13	(8	5)	225	68	80	78	36	0	49	9	8	6	4	5	.44	21	.286	.338	.421
2004 Los Angeles	NL	91	349	105	18	1	10	(6	4)	155	41	49	51	22	0	27	6	2	2	2	4	.33	15	.301	.351	.444
2004 Florida	NL	52	186	48	11	1	3	(2	1)	70	27	31	27	14	0	22	3	6	4	2	1	.67	6	.258	.314	.376
7 ML YEARS		640	2317	660	133	5	60	(29	31)	983	296	306	323	169	14	182	37	27	24	10	16	.38	78	.285	.340	.424

Esteban Loaiza

Pitches: R **Bats:** R **Pos:** SP-27; RP-4 **Ht:** 6'3" **Wt:** 205 **Born:** 12/31/1971 **Age:** 33

Year Team	Lg	G	GS	CG	GF	IP	BFP	H	R	ER	HR	SH	SF	HB	TBB	IBB	SO	WP	Bk	W	L	Pct	ShO	Sv-Op	Hld	ERC	ERA
1995 Pittsburgh	NL	32	31	1	0	172.2	762	205	115	99	21	10	9	5	55	3	85	6	1	8	9	.471	0	0-0	0	5.10	5.16
1996 Pittsburgh	NL	10	10	1	0	52.2	236	65	32	29	11	3	1	2	19	2	32	0	0	2	3	.400	1	0-0	0	6.30	4.96
1997 Pittsburgh	NL	33	32	1	0	196.1	851	214	99	90	17	10	7	12	56	9	122	2	3	11	11	.500	0	0-0	0	4.20	4.13
1998 Pit-Tex		35	28	1	3	171.0	751	199	107	98	28	7	12	5	52	4	108	4	2	9	11	.450	0	0-1	0	5.19	5.16
1999 Texas	AL	30	15	0	4	120.1	517	128	65	61	10	7	4	0	40	2	77	2	0	9	5	.643	0	0-0	0	4.03	4.56
2000 Tex-Tor	AL	34	31	1	2	199.1	871	228	112	101	29	4	5	13	57	1	137	1	0	10	13	.435	1	1-1	0	5.07	4.56
2001 Toronto	AL	36	30	1	1	190.0	837	239	113	106	27	6	4	9	40	1	110	1	1	11	11	.500	0	0-0	0	5.30	5.02
2002 Toronto	AL	25	25	3	0	151.1	670	192	102	96	18	1	6	4	38	3	87	1	0	9	10	.474	1	0-0	0	5.26	5.71
2003 Chicago	AL	34	34	1	0	226.1	922	196	75	73	17	7	6	10	56	2	207	3	1	21	9	.700	0	0-0	0	2.79	2.90

(continued)

Year Team	Lg	G	GS	CG	GF	IP	BFP	H	R	ER	HR	SH	SF	HB	TBB	IBB	SO	WP	Bk	W	L	Pct	ShO	Sv-Op	Hld	ERC	ERA
2004 CWS-NYY	AL	31	27	2	1	183.0	818	217	124	116	32	1	10	3	71	5	117	4	0	10	7	.588	1	0-0	0	5.72	5.70
1998 Pittsburgh	NL	21	14	0	3	91.2	394	96	50	46	13	5	7	3	30	1	53	1	2	6	5	.545	0	0-1	0	4.48	4.52
1998 Texas	AL	14	14	1	0	79.1	357	103	57	52	15	2	5	2	22	3	55	3	0	3	6	.333	0	0-0	0	6.04	5.90
2000 Texas	AL	20	17	0	2	107.1	480	133	67	64	21	2	4	3	31	1	75	1	0	5	6	.455	0	1-1	0	5.81	5.37
2000 Toronto	AL	14	14	1	0	92.0	391	95	45	37	8	2	1	10	26	0	62	0	0	5	7	.417	1	0-0	0	4.22	3.62
2004 Chicago	AL	21	21	2	0	140.2	604	156	81	76	23	1	5	1	45	3	83	2	0	9	5	.643	1	0-0	0	4.89	4.86
2004 New York	AL	10	6	0	1	42.1	214	61	43	40	9	0	5	2	26	2	34	2	0	1	2	.333	0	0-0	0	8.70	8.50
10 ML YEARS		300	263	12	11	1663.0	7235	1883	944	869	210	56	64	63	484	32	1082	24	8	100	89	.529	5	1-2	0	4.72	4.70

Kameron Loe

Pitches: R Bats: R Pos: SP-1; RP-1   **Ht: 6'8" Wt: 225 Born: 9/10/1981 Age: 23**

Year Team	Lg	G	GS	CG	GF	IP	BFP	H	R	ER	HR	SH	SF	HB	TBB	IBB	SO	WP	Bk	W	L	Pct	ShO	Sv-Op	Hld	ERC	ERA
2002 Pulaski	R+	14	11	0	2	58.1	263	64	34	29	3	3	1	6	17	0	55	6	1	4	4	.500	0	1--	-	4.12	4.47
2003 Clinton	A	23	11	0	5	97.0	388	78	34	21	3	5	1	4	19	0	94	1	0	4	3	.571	0	2--	-	2.03	1.95
2003 Stockton	A+	9	4	0	2	37.2	152	26	7	4	1	0	1	3	6	0	31	3	0	3	0	1.000	0	1--	-	1.51	0.96
2004 Frisco	AA	19	19	0	0	112.2	478	122	42	39	5	6	4	6	29	3	97	5	1	7	7	.500	0	0--	-	3.81	3.12
2004 Oklahoma	AAA	8	8	0	0	52.1	206	52	20	19	6	1	0	2	13	0	42	2	0	5	2	.714	0	0--	-	3.98	3.27
2004 Texas	AL	2	1	0	0	6.2	29	6	5	4	0	0	0	1	6	0	3	0	0	0	0	-	0	0-0	0	5.87	5.40

Kenny Lofton

Bats: L Throws: L Pos: CF-65; RF-10; PH-9; DH-4; PR-1   **Ht: 6'0" Wt: 180 Born: 5/31/1967 Age: 38**

Year Team	Lg	G	AB	H	2B	3B	HR	(Hm Rd)	TB	R	RBI	RC	TBB	IBB	SO	HBP	SH	SF	SB	CS	SB%	GDP	Avg	OBP	Slg
2004 Tampa*	A+	4	4	1	0	0	0	(- -)	1	1	0	0	0	0	5	0	0	0	0	0	-	0	.250	.250	.250
2004 Trenton*	AA	4	14	3	1	0	0	(- -)	4	0	2	1	1	0	3	0	0	0	0	0	-	0	.214	.267	.286
1991 Houston	NL	20	74	15	1	0	0	(0 0)	16	9	0	4	5	0	19	0	0	0	2	1	.67	0	.203	.253	.216
1992 Cleveland	AL	148	576	164	15	8	5	(3 2)	210	96	42	68	68	3	54	2	4	1	66	12	.85	7	.285	.362	.365
1993 Cleveland	AL	148	569	185	28	8	1	(1 0)	232	116	42	107	81	6	83	1	2	4	70	14	.83	8	.325	.408	.408
1994 Cleveland	AL	112	459	160	32	9	12	(10 2)	246	105	57	105	52	5	56	2	4	6	60	12	.83	5	.349	.412	.536
1995 Cleveland	AL	118	481	149	22	13	7	(5 2)	218	93	53	83	40	6	49	1	4	3	54	15	.78	6	.310	.362	.453
1996 Cleveland	AL	154	662	210	35	4	14	(7 7)	295	132	67	118	61	3	82	0	7	6	75	17	.82	7	.317	.372	.446
1997 Atlanta	NL	122	493	164	20	6	5	(3 2)	211	90	48	84	64	5	83	2	2	3	27	20	.57	10	.333	.409	.428
1998 Cleveland	AL	154	600	169	31	6	12	(6 6)	248	101	64	103	87	1	80	2	3	6	54	10	.84	7	.282	.371	.413
1999 Cleveland	AL	120	465	140	28	6	7	(1 6)	201	110	39	89	79	2	84	6	5	5	25	6	.81	6	.301	.405	.432
2000 Cleveland	AL	137	543	151	23	5	15	(10 5)	229	107	73	79	79	3	72	4	6	8	30	7	.81	11	.278	.369	.422
2001 Cleveland	AL	133	517	135	21	4	14	(9 5)	206	91	66	67	47	1	69	2	5	5	16	8	.67	8	.261	.322	.398
2002 CWS-SF		139	532	139	30	9	11	(3 8)	220	98	51	83	72	0	73	1	5	1	29	11	.73	1	.261	.350	.414
2003 Pit-ChC	NL	140	547	162	32	8	12	(5 7)	246	97	46	79	46	3	51	4	7	6	30	9	.77	6	.296	.352	.450
2004 New York	AL	83	276	76	10	7	3	(2 1)	109	51	18	36	31	1	27	1	1	4	7	3	.70	4	.275	.346	.395
2002 Chicago	AL	93	352	91	20	6	8	(3 5)	147	68	42	57	49	0	51	0	4	1	22	8	.73	0	.259	.348	.418
2002 San Francisco	NL	46	180	48	10	3	3	(0 3)	73	30	9	26	23	0	22	1	1	0	7	3	.70	1	.267	.353	.406
2003 Pittsburgh	NL	84	339	94	19	4	9	(4 5)	148	58	26	42	28	1	29	2	2	3	18	5	.78	2	.277	.333	.437
2003 Chicago	NL	56	208	68	13	4	3	(1 2)	98	39	20	37	18	2	22	2	5	3	12	4	.75	4	.327	.381	.471
14 ML YEARS		1728	6794	2019	328	93	118	(65 53)	2887	1296	666	1137	812	39	882	28	55	58	545	145	.79	86	.297	.372	.425

Nook Logan

Bats: B Throws: R Pos: CF-46; PR-3   **Ht: 6'2" Wt: 180 Born: 11/28/1979 Age: 25**

Year Team	Lg	G	AB	H	2B	3B	HR	(Hm Rd)	TB	R	RBI	RC	TBB	IBB	SO	HBP	SH	SF	SB	CS	SB%	GDP	Avg	OBP	Slg
2000 Tigers	R	43	136	38	2	2	0	(- -)	44	29	14	25	31	0	36	1	1	2	20	3	.87	1	.279	.412	.324
2000 Lakeland	A+	11	42	14	1	0	0	(- -)	15	4	3	5	2	0	13	0	1	0	2	1	.67	0	.333	.364	.357
2001 W Michigan	A	128	522	137	19	8	1	(- -)	175	82	27	66	53	2	129	2	3	4	67	19	.78	4	.262	.330	.335
2002 Lakeland	A+	124	506	136	14	7	2	(- -)	170	75	26	62	40	0	111	0	6	2	55	16	.77	2	.269	.321	.336
2003 Erie	AA	136	514	129	14	7	4	(- -)	171	71	38	59	51	3	103	1	12	6	37	13	.74	5	.251	.316	.333
2004 Toledo	AAA	105	427	112	14	9	2	(- -)	150	67	27	49	23	0	95	3	7	2	38	11	.78	3	.262	.303	.351
2004 Detroit	AL	47	133	37	5	2	0	(0 0)	46	12	10	15	13	0	24	0	5	1	8	2	.80	1	.278	.340	.346

Kyle Lohse

Pitches: R Bats: R Pos: SP-34; RP-1   **Ht: 6'2" Wt: 190 Born: 10/4/1978 Age: 26**

Year Team	Lg	G	GS	CG	GF	IP	BFP	H	R	ER	HR	SH	SF	HB	TBB	IBB	SO	WP	Bk	W	L	Pct	ShO	Sv-Op	Hld	ERC	ERA
2001 Minnesota	AL	19	16	0	2	90.1	402	102	60	57	16	1	5	8	29	0	64	5	0	4	7	.364	0	0-0	0	5.43	5.68
2002 Minnesota	AL	32	31	1	0	180.2	783	181	92	85	26	3	3	9	70	2	124	8	0	13	8	.619	1	0-1	0	4.55	4.23
2003 Minnesota	AL	33	33	2	0	201.0	850	211	107	103	28	8	5	5	45	1	130	10	1	14	11	.560	1	0-0	0	4.00	4.61
2004 Minnesota	AL	35	34	1	1	194.0	883	240	128	115	28	5	7	7	76	5	111	6	0	9	13	.409	1	0-0	0	5.89	5.34
4 ML YEARS		119	114	4	3	666.0	2918	734	387	360	98	17	20	29	220	8	429	29	1	40	39	.506	3	0-1	0	4.88	4.86

Terrence Long

Bats: L Throws: L Pos: LF-61; PH-58; CF-28; RF-9; DH-1   **Ht: 6'1" Wt: 202 Born: 2/29/1976 Age: 29**

Year Team	Lg	G	AB	H	2B	3B	HR	(Hm Rd)	TB	R	RBI	RC	TBB	IBB	SO	HBP	SH	SF	SB	CS	SB%	GDP	Avg	OBP	Slg
1999 New York	NL	3	3	0	0	0	0	(0 0)	0	0	0	0	0	0	2	0	0	0	0	0	-	1	.000	.000	.000
2000 Oakland	AL	138	584	168	34	4	18	(9 9)	264	104	80	85	43	1	77	1	0	3	5	0	1.00	18	.288	.336	.452
2001 Oakland	AL	162	629	178	37	4	12	(6 6)	259	90	85	84	52	8	103	0	0	6	9	3	.75	17	.283	.335	.412
2002 Oakland	AL	162	587	141	32	4	16	(9 7)	229	71	67	61	48	6	96	2	0	3	3	6	.33	17	.240	.298	.390

		BATTING																	BASERUNNING				AVERAGES		
Year Team	Lg	G	AB	H	2B	3B	HR	(Hm	Rd)	TB	R	RBI	RC	TBB	IBB	SO	HBP	SH	SF	SB	CS	SB%	GDP	Avg	OBP	Slg
2003 Oakland	AL	140	486	119	22	2	14	(8	6)	187	64	61	61	31	4	67	3	0	2	4	1	.80	9	.245	.293	.385
2004 San Diego	NL	136	288	85	19	4	3	(1	2)	121	31	28	30	19	4	51	1	0	5	3	2	.60	13	.295	.335	.420
6 ML YEARS		741	2577	691	144	18	63	(33	30)	1060	360	321	321	193	23	396	7	0	19	24	12	.67	75	.268	.319	.411

Braden Looper

Pitches: R **Bats:** R **Pos:** RP-71   **Ht:** 6'3" **Wt:** 220 **Born:** 10/28/1974 **Age:** 30

		HOW MUCH HE PITCHED						WHAT HE GAVE UP											THE RESULTS						
Year Team	Lg	G	GS	CG	GF	IP	BFP	H	R	ER	HR	SH	SF	HB	TBB	IBB	SO	WP	Bk	W	L	Pct	ShO	Sv-Op	Hld	ERC	ERA
1998 St Louis	NL	4	0	0	3	3.1	16	5	4	2	1	0	1	0	1	0	4	1	0	0	1	.000	0	0-2	0	8.14	5.40
1999 Florida	NL	72	0	0	22	83.0	370	96	43	35	7	5	5	1	31	5	50	2	2	3	3	.500	0	0-4	8	4.67	3.80
2000 Florida	NL	73	0	0	23	67.1	311	71	41	33	3	3	2	5	36	6	29	5	0	5	1	.833	0	2-5	18	4.55	4.41
2001 Florida	NL	71	0	0	21	71.0	295	63	28	28	8	0	3	2	30	3	52	0	0	3	3	.500	0	3-6	16	3.77	3.55
2002 Florida	NL	78	0	0	40	86.0	349	73	31	30	8	3	0	1	28	3	55	1	0	2	5	.286	0	13-16	16	2.98	3.14
2003 Florida	NL	74	0	0	64	80.2	347	82	34	33	4	3	3	1	29	1	56	2	0	6	4	.600	0	28-34	0	3.67	3.68
2004 New York	NL	71	0	0	60	83.1	346	86	28	25	5	2	2	3	16	3	60	1	0	2	5	.286	0	29-34	0	3.28	2.70
7 ML YEARS		443	0	0	233	474.2	2034	476	209	186	36	16	16	13	171	21	306	12	2	21	22	.488	0	75-101	58	3.81	3.53

Aquilino Lopez

Pitches: R **Bats:** R **Pos:** RP-18   **Ht:** 6'3" **Wt:** 165 **Born:** 4/21/1975 **Age:** 30

		HOW MUCH HE PITCHED						WHAT HE GAVE UP											THE RESULTS						
Year Team	Lg	G	GS	CG	GF	IP	BFP	H	R	ER	HR	SH	SF	HB	TBB	IBB	SO	WP	Bk	W	L	Pct	ShO	Sv-Op	Hld	ERC	ERA
1999 Everett	A-	15	15	1	0	87.2	365	76	44	37	8	1	2	2	30	2	93	2	0	7	6	.538	0	0- -	-	3.12	3.80
2000 Wisconsin	A	39	5	1	29	68.0	268	47	16	14	1	0	1	4	20	4	67	3	0	6	1	.857	1	17- -	-	1.76	1.85
2001 San Antonio	AA	42	0	0	13	62.2	265	48	24	21	4	2	2	6	25	2	79	5	0	4	3	.571	0	2- -	-	2.85	3.02
2002 Tacoma	AAA	34	11	0	10	109.1	438	89	33	29	6	3	4	2	27	2	103	4	4	4	4	.500	0	5- -	-	2.30	2.39
2004 Syracuse	AAA	32	0	0	17	42.2	198	58	36	34	8	0	0	2	10	0	32	4	0	1	6	.143	0	5- -	-	6.23	7.17
2003 Toronto	AL	72	0	0	34	73.2	315	58	31	28	5	2	2	5	34	5	64	2	1	1	3	.250	0	14-16	16	3.05	3.42
2004 Toronto	AL	18	0	0	6	21.0	95	21	15	14	5	0	1	2	13	3	13	0	0	1	1	.500	0	0-0	3	6.32	6.00
2 ML YEARS		90	0	0	40	94.2	410	79	46	42	10	2	3	7	47	8	77	2	1	2	4	.333	0	14-16	19	3.71	3.99

Felipe Lopez

Bats: B **Throws:** R **Pos:** SS-51; 3B-24; PR-4; 2B-2; PH-2   **Ht:** 6'0" **Wt:** 185 **Born:** 5/12/1980 **Age:** 25

		BATTING																		BASERUNNING				AVERAGES		
Year Team	Lg	G	AB	H	2B	3B	HR	(Hm	Rd)	TB	R	RBI	RC	TBB	IBB	SO	HBP	SH	SF	SB	CS	SB%	GDP	Avg	OBP	Slg
2004 Louisville*	AAA	75	293	80	11	3	9	(-	-)	124	50	44	41	25	0	71	2	1	5	2	3	.40	2	.273	.329	.423
2001 Toronto	AL	49	177	46	5	4	5	(3	2)	74	21	23	22	12	1	39	0	1	2	4	3	.57	2	.260	.304	.418
2002 Toronto	AL	85	282	64	15	3	8	(5	3)	109	35	34	32	23	1	90	1	2	1	5	4	.56	4	.227	.287	.387
2003 Cincinnati	NL	59	197	42	7	2	2	(0	2)	59	28	13	21	28	1	59	1	2	1	8	5	.62	2	.213	.313	.299
2004 Cincinnati	NL	79	264	64	18	2	7	(3	4)	107	35	31	34	25	0	81	1	2	1	1	1	.50	1	.242	.314	.405
4 ML YEARS		272	920	216	45	11	22	(11	11)	349	119	101	109	88	3	269	5	7	5	18	13	.58	9	.235	.304	.379

Javier Lopez

Pitches: L **Bats:** L **Pos:** RP-64   **Ht:** 6'4" **Wt:** 200 **Born:** 7/11/1977 **Age:** 27

		HOW MUCH HE PITCHED						WHAT HE GAVE UP											THE RESULTS						
Year Team	Lg	G	GS	CG	GF	IP	BFP	H	R	ER	HR	SH	SF	HB	TBB	IBB	SO	WP	Bk	W	L	Pct	ShO	Sv-Op	Hld	ERC	ERA
1998 South Bend	A	16	9	0	1	44.0	218	60	36	32	2	2	3	0	30	0	31	7	0	4	4	.333	0	0- -	-	6.93	6.55
1999 South Bend	A	20	20	0	0	99.0	458	122	74	66	9	1	4	3	43	0	70	9	0	4	6	.400	0	0- -	-	5.58	6.00
2000 High Desert	A+	30	21	0	4	136.1	602	152	87	79	14	4	7	6	57	0	98	8	2	4	8	.333	0	2- -	-	5.08	5.22
2001 Lancaster	A+	17	0	0	10	24.0	103	30	9	7	2	2	0	0	5	0	18	1	1	1	3	.250	0	1- -	-	4.69	2.63
2001 El Paso	AA	22	1	0	4	40.0	191	64	39	33	6	2	1	0	14	2	21	1	0	1	0	1.000	0	0- -	-	7.97	7.43
2002 El Paso	AA	61	0	0	25	46.1	186	34	16	14	3	2	1	0	16	1	47	1	0	2	2	.500	0	6- -	-	2.44	2.72
2002 Vero Beach	A+	1	0	0	0	0.1	7	2	4	2	0	0	0	0	3	0	0	0	0	0	0	-	0	0- -	-	74.92	54.00
2004 Co Springs	AAA	8	0	0	2	9.0	39	10	4	4	2	0	0	0	2	0	9	0	0	0	1	.000	0	0- -	-	4.72	4.00
2003 Colorado	NL	75	0	0	11	58.1	242	58	25	24	5	1	0	4	12	2	40	1	3	4	1	.800	0	1-2	15	3.44	3.70
2004 Colorado	NL	64	0	0	10	40.2	187	45	34	34	1	1	0	3	26	4	20	3	0	1	2	.333	0	0-1	12	5.28	7.52
2 ML YEARS		139	0	0	21	99.0	429	103	59	58	6	2	0	7	38	6	60	4	3	5	3	.625	0	1-3	27	4.19	5.27

Javy Lopez

Bats: R **Throws:** R **Pos:** C-132; DH-21; PH-4   **Ht:** 6'3" **Wt:** 225 **Born:** 11/5/1970 **Age:** 34

		BATTING																		BASERUNNING				AVERAGES		
Year Team	Lg	G	AB	H	2B	3B	HR	(Hm	Rd)	TB	R	RBI	RC	TBB	IBB	SO	HBP	SH	SF	SB	CS	SB%	GDP	Avg	OBP	Slg
1992 Atlanta	NL	9	16	6	2	0	0	(0	0)	8	3	2	3	0	0	1	0	0	0	0	0	-	0	.375	.375	.500
1993 Atlanta	NL	8	16	6	1	1	1	(0	1)	12	1	2	4	0	0	2	1	0	0	0	0	-	0	.375	.412	.750
1994 Atlanta	NL	80	277	68	9	0	13	(4	9)	116	27	35	31	17	0	61	5	2	2	0	2	.00	12	.245	.299	.419
1995 Atlanta	NL	100	333	105	11	4	14	(8	6)	166	37	51	51	14	0	57	2	0	3	0	1	.00	13	.315	.344	.498
1996 Atlanta	NL	138	489	138	19	1	23	(10	13)	228	56	69	66	28	5	84	3	1	5	1	6	.14	17	.282	.322	.466
1997 Atlanta	NL	123	414	122	28	1	23	(11	12)	221	52	68	76	40	10	82	5	1	4	1	1	.50	9	.295	.361	.534
1998 Atlanta	NL	133	489	139	21	1	34	(18	16)	264	73	106	79	30	1	85	6	1	8	5	3	.63	22	.284	.328	.540
1999 Atlanta	NL	65	246	78	18	1	11	(1	10)	131	34	45	45	20	2	41	3	0	0	0	3	.00	6	.317	.375	.533
2000 Atlanta	NL	134	481	138	21	1	24	(12	12)	233	60	89	72	35	3	80	4	0	5	0	0	-	20	.287	.337	.484
2001 Atlanta	NL	128	438	117	16	1	17	(10	7)	186	45	66	58	28	3	82	10	1	5	1	0	1.00	18	.267	.322	.425
2002 Atlanta	NL	109	347	81	15	0	11	(1	10)	129	31	52	40	26	8	63	8	0	4	0	1	.00	15	.233	.299	.372
2003 Atlanta	NL	129	457	150	29	3	43	(26	17)	314	89	109	102	33	5	90	4	0	1	0	1	.00	10	.328	.378	.687
2004 Baltimore	AL	150	579	183	33	3	23	(14	9)	291	83	86	90	47	4	97	6	0	6	0	0	-	16	.316	.370	.502
13 ML YEARS		1306	4582	1331	223	17	237	(115	122)	2299	591	780	717	318	41	825	57	6	43	8	18	.31	152	.290	.341	.502

Jose Lopez

Bats: R **Throws:** R **Pos:** SS-57; 3B-1; PR-1   **Ht:** 6'2" **Wt:** 170 **Born:** 11/24/1983 **Age:** 21

Year Team	Lg	G	AB	H	2B	3B	HR	(Hm	Rd)	TB	R	RBI	RC	TBB	IBB	SO	HBP	SH	SF	SB	CS	SB%	GDP	Avg	OBP	Slg
2001 Everett	A-	70	289	74	15	0	2	(-	-)	95	42	20	30	13	0	44	10	1	2	13	6	.68	3	.256	.309	.329
2002 Sn Brnardino	A+	123	522	169	39	5	8	(-	-)	242	82	60	84	27	2	45	5	4	4	31	13	.70	8	.324	.360	.464
2003 San Antonio	AA	132	538	139	35	2	13	(-	-)	217	82	69	63	27	3	56	10	7	6	18	8	.69	12	.258	.303	.403
2004 Mariners	R	4	12	2	1	0	0	(-	-)	3	3	1	0	2	0	1	0	0	1	1	0	1.00	1	.167	.267	.250
2004 Tacoma	AAA	74	275	81	19	0	13	(-	-)	139	40	39	47	16	0	30	6	2	4	5	2	.71	2	.295	.342	.505
2004 Seattle	AL	57	207	48	13	0	5	(4	1)	76	28	22	20	8	0	31	1	1	1	0	1	.00	1	.232	.263	.367

Luis Lopez

Bats: R **Throws:** R **Pos:** 1B-8; PH-4   **Ht:** 6'0" **Wt:** 205 **Born:** 10/5/1973 **Age:** 31

Year Team	Lg	G	AB	H	2B	3B	HR	(Hm	Rd)	TB	R	RBI	RC	TBB	IBB	SO	HBP	SH	SF	SB	CS	SB%	GDP	Avg	OBP	Slg
1995 Ogden	R+	46	182	65	15	0	7	(-	-)	101	36	39	38	16	0	20	2	3	2	1	1	.50	5	.357	.411	.555
1996 St. Ctharines	A-	74	260	74	17	2	7	(-	-)	116	36	40	42	27	1	31	7	4	3	2	3	.40	4	.285	.364	.446
1997 Hagerstown	A	136	503	180	47	4	11	(-	-)	268	96	99	106	60	4	45	8	0	6	5	8	.38	14	.358	.430	.533
1998 Syracuse	AAA	11	41	9	0	0	1	(-	-)	12	6	3	3	6	0	6	0	0	1	0	0	-	2	.220	.313	.293
1998 Knoxville	AA	119	450	141	27	1	15	(-	-)	215	70	85	80	58	3	55	3	0	8	2	2	.00	18	.313	.389	.478
1999 Syracuse	AAA	136	531	171	35	2	4	(-	-)	222	76	69	78	40	2	58	1	2	8	1	0	1.00	22	.322	.366	.418
2000 Syracuse	AAA	130	491	161	27	1	7	(-	-)	211	64	79	83	48	1	33	2	0	8	3	1	.75	10	.328	.384	.430
2002 Sacramento	AAA	131	516	146	28	0	9	(-	-)	201	66	72	72	64	1	63	1	0	4	2	3	.40	17	.283	.361	.390
2003 Sacramento	AAA	131	498	122	28	0	18	(-	-)	204	67	72	57	40	1	68	4	0	6	0	1	.00	17	.245	.303	.410
2004 Richmond	AAA	68	231	77	18	0	9	(-	-)	122	37	51	46	30	1	27	3	0	2	0	0	-	11	.333	.414	.528
2004 Edmonton	AAA	23	68	14	1	0	1	(-	-)	18	9	9	5	9	0	11	0	0	1	0	0	-	2	.206	.295	.265
2001 Toronto	AL	41	119	29	4	0	3	(2	1)	42	10	10	8	8	1	16	0	1	0	0	0	-	10	.244	.291	.353
2004 Montreal	NL	11	26	4	0	0	0	(-	-)	4	0	0	0	0	0	9	1	0	0	0	0	-	1	.154	.185	.154
2 ML YEARS		52	145	33	4	0	3	(2	1)	46	10	10	8	8	1	25	1	1	0	0	0	-	11	.228	.273	.317

Luis M Lopez

Bats: B **Throws:** R **Pos:** PH-17; SS-14; 3B-11; DH-8; 1B-6; 2B-6; PR-5   **Ht:** 5'11" **Wt:** 175 **Born:** 9/4/1970 **Age:** 34

Year Team	Lg	G	AB	H	2B	3B	HR	(Hm	Rd)	TB	R	RBI	RC	TBB	IBB	SO	HBP	SH	SF	SB	CS	SB%	GDP	Avg	OBP	Slg
1993 San Diego	NL	17	43	5	1	0	0	(0	0)	6	1	1	0	0	0	8	0	0	1	0	0	-	0	.116	.114	.140
1994 San Diego	NL	77	235	65	16	1	2	(2	0)	89	29	20	27	15	2	39	3	2	2	3	2	.60	7	.277	.325	.379
1996 San Diego	NL	63	139	25	3	0	2	(1	1)	34	10	11	5	9	1	35	1	1	1	0	0	-	7	.180	.233	.245
1997 New York	NL	78	178	48	12	1	1	(1	0)	65	19	19	21	12	2	42	4	2	0	2	4	.33	2	.270	.330	.365
1998 New York	NL	117	266	67	13	2	2	(1	1)	90	37	22	26	20	3	60	4	3	2	2	2	.50	10	.252	.312	.338
1999 New York	NL	68	104	22	4	0	2	(1	1)	32	11	13	10	12	0	33	3	1	1	1	1	.50	1	.212	.308	.308
2000 Milwaukee	NL	78	201	53	14	0	6	(3	3)	85	24	27	26	9	1	35	5	8	2	1	2	.33	2	.264	.309	.423
2001 Milwaukee	NL	92	222	60	8	3	4	(2	2)	86	22	18	27	14	2	44	5	5	1	0	1	.00	6	.270	.326	.387
2002 Mil-Bal		58	117	23	6	0	2	(1	1)	35	11	10	7	5	0	21	0	0	0	1	0	1.00	3	.197	.230	.299
2004 Baltimore	AL	56	88	16	5	0	1	(0	1)	24	7	8	3	3	0	20	1	2	3	0	0	-	1	.182	.211	.273
2002 Milwaukee	NL	6	8	0	0	0	0	(0	0)	0	1	1	0	2	0	1	0	0	0	0	0	-	0	.000	.200	.000
2002 Baltimore	AL	52	109	23	6	0	2	(1	1)	35	10	9	7	3	0	20	0	0	0	1	0	1.00	3	.211	.232	.321
10 ML YEARS		704	1593	384	82	7	22	(12	10)	546	171	149	152	99	11	337	26	24	13	10	12	.45	39	.241	.294	.343

Mendy Lopez

Bats: R **Throws:** R **Pos:** 2B-6; 3B-4; SS-4; 1B-2; LF-2; RF-2; PH-2; PR-1   **Ht:** 6'2" **Wt:** 200 **Born:** 10/15/1974 **Age:** 30

Year Team	Lg	G	AB	H	2B	3B	HR	(Hm	Rd)	TB	R	RBI	RC	TBB	IBB	SO	HBP	SH	SF	SB	CS	SB%	GDP	Avg	OBP	Slg
2004 Omaha*	AAA	31	123	36	6	1	13	(-	-)	83	20	26	23	9	0	31	0	1	0	1	2	.33	6	.293	.341	.675
1998 Kansas City	AL	74	206	50	10	2	1	(1	0)	67	18	15	18	12	0	40	1	5	1	5	2	.71	6	.243	.286	.325
1999 Kansas City	AL	7	20	8	0	1	0	(0	0)	10	2	3	4	0	0	5	1	0	0	0	0	-	0	.400	.429	.500
2000 Florida	NL	4	3	0	0	0	0	(0	0)	0	0	0	0	1	0	1	0	0	0	0	0	-	0	.000	.250	.000
2001 Hou-Pit	NL	32	58	14	3	1	1	(0	1)	22	8	7	8	6	1	20	1	0	0	0	0	-	0	.241	.318	.379
2002 Pittsburgh	NL	3	3	0	0	0	0	(0	0)	0	0	0	0	0	0	3	0	0	0	0	0	-	0	.000	.000	.000
2003 Kansas City	AL	52	94	26	5	1	3	(3	0)	42	13	11	12	4	0	28	0	2	0	2	0	1.00	3	.277	.306	.447
2004 Kansas City	AL	18	38	4	0	0	1	(1	0)	7	4	4	1	4	0	9	1	1	0	0	0	-	0	.105	.209	.184
2001 Houston	NL	10	15	4	0	0	1	(0	1)	7	3	3	3	2	0	4	1	0	0	0	0	-	0	.267	.389	.467
2001 Pittsburgh	NL	22	43	10	3	1	0	(0	0)	15	5	4	5	4	1	16	0	0	0	0	0	-	0	.233	.292	.349
7 ML YEARS		190	422	102	18	5	6	(5	1)	148	45	40	43	27	1	106	4	8	2	7	2	.78	12	.242	.292	.351

Mickey Lopez

Bats: B **Throws:** R **Pos:** 2B-3; PH-3; PR-2; DH-1   **Ht:** 5'9" **Wt:** 170 **Born:** 11/17/1973 **Age:** 31

Year Team	Lg	G	AB	H	2B	3B	HR	(Hm	Rd)	TB	R	RBI	RC	TBB	IBB	SO	HBP	SH	SF	SB	CS	SB%	GDP	Avg	OBP	Slg
1995 Helena	R+	57	225	73	19	2	1	(-	-)	99	66	41	45	38	3	20	5	2	4	12	8	.60	1	.324	.426	.440
1996 Stockton	A+	64	217	61	10	1	0	(-	-)	73	30	25	30	23	0	36	4	9	1	6	4	.60	0	.281	.359	.336
1996 Beloit	A	61	236	64	10	2	0	(-	-)	78	35	14	27	28	0	36	1	10	0	12	8	.60	8	.271	.351	.331
1997 El Paso	AA	134	483	145	21	10	3	(-	-)	195	79	58	74	48	2	60	5	9	5	20	10	.67	10	.300	.366	.404
1998 El Paso	AA	120	459	127	24	9	2	(-	-)	175	81	64	59	46	1	61	2	4	5	12	10	.55	11	.277	.342	.381
1998 Louisville	AAA	3	4	1	0	0	0	(-	-)	1	1	0	0	2	1	0	0	0	0	0	0	-	0	.250	.500	.250
1999 Huntsville	AA	83	315	94	16	5	5	(-	-)	135	58	40	58	46	2	46	5	3	4	31	4	.89	9	.298	.392	.429
1999 Louisville	AAA	49	181	58	17	2	5	(-	-)	94	43	31	41	37	0	25	2	2	1	11	7	.61	1	.320	.439	.519
2000 Indianapolis	AAA	67	208	54	14	1	2	(-	-)	76	38	22	31	37	0	26	4	1	4	14	7	.67	5	.260	.375	.365
2000 Huntsville	AA	53	212	71	22	4	4	(-	-)	113	42	26	44	30	0	32	0	6	1	16	7	.70	5	.335	.416	.533
2001 El Paso	AA	107	382	104	18	6	11	(-	-)	167	71	47	68	63	2	58	7	6	2	21	6	.78	6	.272	.383	.437
2002 W Tennessee	AA	17	62	17	2	0	0	(-	-)	19	11	7	7	5	0	9	1	0	3	5	2	.71	0	.274	.324	.306
2002 Iowa	AAA	107	338	89	25	1	5	(-	-)	131	48	39	46	39	0	45	4	3	7	8	5	.62	5	.263	.340	.388

Year Team	Lg	G	AB	H	2B	3B	HR	(Hm	Rd)	TB	R	RBI	RC	TBB	IBB	SO	HBP	SH	SF	SB	CS	SB%	GDP	Avg	OBP	Slg
						BATTING														**BASERUNNING**				**AVERAGES**		
2003 Tacoma	AAA	129	455	125	23	4	7	(-	-)	177	68	41	61	47	2	50	6	5	6	20	12	.63	12	.275	.346	.389
2004 Tacoma	AAA	109	391	112	20	5	10	(-	-)	172	70	41	63	45	2	59	7	6	2	13	10	.57	6	.286	.369	.440
2004 Seattle	AL	6	4	1	0	0	0	(0	0)	1	1	0	1	1	0	0	1	0	0	0	0	-	0	.250	.500	.250

Rodrigo Lopez

Pitches: R **Bats:** R **Pos:** SP-23; RP-14   **Ht:** 6'1" **Wt:** 180 **Born:** 12/14/1975 **Age:** 29

Year Team	Lg	G	GS	CG	GF	IP	BFP	H	R	ER	HR	SH	SF	HB	TBB	IBB	SO	WP	Bk	W	L	Pct	ShO	Sv-Op	Hld	ERC	ERA
		HOW MUCH HE PITCHED						**WHAT HE GAVE UP**												**THE RESULTS**							
2000 San Diego	NL	6	6	0	1	24.2	120	40	24	24	5	0	1	0	13	0	17	0	0	0	3	.000	0	0-0	0	9.78	8.76
2002 Baltimore	AL	33	28	1	0	196.2	809	172	83	78	23	2	4	5	62	4	136	2	1	15	9	.625	0	0-0	0	3.27	3.57
2003 Baltimore	AL	26	26	3	0	147.0	663	188	101	95	24	3	7	10	43	6	103	2	1	7	10	.412	1	0-0	0	6.00	5.82
2004 Baltimore	AL	37	23	1	3	170.2	714	164	71	68	21	5	2	2	54	2	121	4	1	14	9	.609	1	0-1	4	3.74	3.59
4 ML YEARS		102	83	5	3	539.0	2306	564	279	265	73	10	14	17	172	12	377	8	3	36	31	.537	2	0-1	4	4.39	4.42

Mark Loretta

Bats: R **Throws:** R **Pos:** 2B-154   **Ht:** 6'0" **Wt:** 186 **Born:** 8/14/1971 **Age:** 33

Year Team	Lg	G	AB	H	2B	3B	HR	(Hm	Rd)	TB	R	RBI	RC	TBB	IBB	SO	HBP	SH	SF	SB	CS	SB%	GDP	Avg	OBP	Slg
						BATTING														**BASERUNNING**				**AVERAGES**		
1995 Milwaukee	AL	19	50	13	3	0	1	(0	1)	19	13	3	6	4	0	7	1	1	0	1	1	.50	1	.260	.327	.380
1996 Milwaukee	AL	73	154	43	3	0	1	(0	1)	49	20	13	16	14	0	15	0	2	0	2	1	.67	7	.279	.339	.318
1997 Milwaukee	AL	132	418	120	17	5	5	(2	3)	162	56	47	56	47	2	60	2	5	10	5	5	.50	15	.287	.354	.388
1998 Milwaukee	NL	140	434	137	29	0	6	(3	3)	184	55	54	68	42	1	47	7	4	4	9	6	.60	14	.316	.382	.424
1999 Milwaukee	NL	153	587	170	34	5	5	(2	3)	229	93	67	82	52	1	59	10	9	6	4	1	.80	14	.290	.354	.390
2000 Milwaukee	NL	91	352	99	21	1	7	(3	4)	143	49	40	48	37	2	38	1	8	1	0	3	.00	9	.281	.350	.406
2001 Milwaukee	NL	102	384	111	14	2	2	(0	2)	135	40	29	48	28	0	46	7	7	3	1	2	.33	6	.289	.346	.352
2002 Mil-Hou	NL	107	283	86	18	0	4	(2	2)	116	33	27	50	32	1	37	5	6	3	1	1	.50	7	.304	.381	.410
2003 San Diego	NL	154	589	185	28	4	13	(10	3)	260	74	72	93	54	2	62	3	3	4	5	4	.56	17	.314	.372	.441
2004 San Diego	NL	154	620	208	47	2	16	(11	5)	307	108	76	112	58	3	45	9	4	16	5	3	.63	10	.335	.391	.495
2002 Milwaukee	NL	86	217	58	14	0	2	(1	1)	78	23	19	33	23	1	32	5	6	1	0	0	-	6	.267	.350	.359
2002 Houston	NL	21	66	28	4	0	2	(1	1)	38	10	8	17	9	0	5	0	0	2	1	1	.50	1	.424	.481	.576
10 ML YEARS		1125	3871	1172	214	19	60	(33	27)	1604	541	428	579	368	12	416	45	49	47	33	27	.55	100	.303	.366	.414

Derek Lowe

Pitches: R **Bats:** R **Pos:** SP-33   **Ht:** 6'6" **Wt:** 214 **Born:** 6/1/1973 **Age:** 32

Year Team	Lg	G	GS	CG	GF	IP	BFP	H	R	ER	HR	SH	SF	HB	TBB	IBB	SO	WP	Bk	W	L	Pct	ShO	Sv-Op	Hld	ERC	ERA
		HOW MUCH HE PITCHED						**WHAT HE GAVE UP**												**THE RESULTS**							
1997 Sea-Bos	AL	20	9	0	1	69.0	298	74	49	47	11	4	2	4	23	3	52	2	0	2	6	.250	0	0-2	1	4.88	6.13
1998 Boston	AL	63	10	0	8	123.0	527	126	65	55	5	4	5	4	42	5	77	8	0	3	9	.250	0	4-9	12	3.64	4.02
1999 Boston	AL	74	0	0	32	109.1	436	84	35	32	7	1	2	4	25	1	80	1	0	6	3	.667	0	15-20	22	2.14	2.63
2000 Boston	AL	74	0	0	64	91.1	379	90	27	26	6	4	1	2	22	5	79	1	1	4	4	.500	0	42-47	3	3.17	2.56
2001 Boston	AL	67	3	0	50	91.2	404	103	39	36	7	5	1	5	29	9	82	4	0	5	10	.333	0	24-30	4	4.31	3.53
2002 Boston	AL	32	32	1	0	219.2	854	166	65	63	12	5	2	12	48	0	127	5	0	21	8	.724	1	0-0	0	2.13	2.58
2003 Boston	AL	33	33	1	0	203.1	886	216	113	101	17	3	5	11	72	4	110	3	0	17	7	.708	0	0-0	0	4.32	4.47
2004 Boston	AL	33	33	0	0	182.2	839	224	138	110	15	8	4	8	71	2	105	3	0	14	12	.538	0	0-0	0	5.31	5.42
1997 Seattle	AL	12	9	0	1	53.0	234	59	43	41	11	2	1	2	20	2	39	2	0	2	4	.333	0	0-0	0	5.55	6.96
1997 Boston	AL	8	0	0	0	16.0	64	15	6	6	0	2	1	2	3	1	13	0	0	0	2	.000	0	0-2	1	2.78	3.38
8 ML YEARS		396	120	2	155	1090.0	4623	1083	531	470	80	34	22	50	332	29	712	27	1	72	59	.550	1	85-108	39	3.63	3.88

Mike Lowell

Bats: R **Throws:** R **Pos:** 3B-154; DH-3; PH-2   **Ht:** 6'3" **Wt:** 217 **Born:** 2/24/1974 **Age:** 31

Year Team	Lg	G	AB	H	2B	3B	HR	(Hm	Rd)	TB	R	RBI	RC	TBB	IBB	SO	HBP	SH	SF	SB	CS	SB%	GDP	Avg	OBP	Slg
						BATTING														**BASERUNNING**				**AVERAGES**		
1998 New York	AL	8	15	4	0	0	0	(0	0)	4	1	0	1	0	0	1	0	0	0	0	0	-	0	.267	.267	.267
1999 Florida	NL	97	308	78	15	0	12	(7	5)	129	32	47	40	26	1	69	5	0	5	0	0	-	8	.253	.317	.419
2000 Florida	NL	140	508	137	38	0	22	(11	11)	241	73	91	86	54	4	75	9	0	11	4	0	1.00	4	.270	.344	.474
2001 Florida	NL	146	551	156	37	0	18	(12	6)	247	65	100	84	43	3	79	10	0	10	1	2	.33	9	.283	.340	.448
2002 Florida	NL	160	597	165	44	0	24	(13	11)	281	88	92	84	65	5	92	4	0	11	3	5	.57	16	.276	.346	.471
2003 Florida	NL	130	492	136	27	1	32	(14	18)	261	76	105	88	56	6	78	3	0	6	3	1	.75	14	.276	.350	.530
2004 Florida	NL	158	598	175	44	1	27	(14	13)	302	87	85	96	64	8	77	6	0	3	5	1	.83	17	.293	.365	.505
7 ML YEARS		839	3069	851	205	2	135	(71	64)	1465	422	520	479	308	27	471	37	0	46	17	7	.71	68	.277	.346	.477

Noah Lowry

Pitches: L **Bats:** L **Pos:** SP-14; RP-2   **Ht:** 6'2" **Wt:** 190 **Born:** 10/10/1980 **Age:** 24

Year Team	Lg	G	GS	CG	GF	IP	BFP	H	R	ER	HR	SH	SF	HB	TBB	IBB	SO	WP	Bk	W	L	Pct	ShO	Sv-Op	Hld	ERC	ERA
		HOW MUCH HE PITCHED						**WHAT HE GAVE UP**												**THE RESULTS**							
2001 Salem-Keizer	A-	8	7	0	0	25.0	109	26	15	10	2	0	2	1	8	0	28	2	0	1	1	.500	0	0- -	-	3.94	3.60
2002 San Jose	A+	15	12	0	0	58.2	229	38	21	14	4	1	1	3	20	0	62	1	0	6	5	.545	0	0- -	-	2.10	2.15
2003 Norwich	AA	23	23	2	0	118.1	509	127	66	62	7	7	5	4	47	0	97	3	2	9	6	.600	0	0- -	-	4.43	4.72
2003 Fresno	AAA	4	4	0	0	19.0	74	15	5	5	0	2	0	0	6	0	13	0	0	1	0	1.000	0	0- -	-	2.14	2.37
2004 Fresno	AAA	17	17	1	0	89.1	386	98	53	41	9	9	4	0	28	0	73	4	1	7	5	.583	1	0- -	-	4.28	4.13
2003 San Francisco	NL	4	0	0	3	6.1	24	1	0	0	0	0	0	1	2	0	5	0	0	0	0	-	0	0-0	0	0.00	0.00
2004 San Francisco	NL	16	14	2	0	92.0	383	91	41	39	10	2	1	0	28	1	72	2	0	6	0	1.000	1	0-0	0	3.73	3.82
2 ML YEARS		20	14	2	3	98.1	407	92	41	39	10	2	1	1	30	1	77	2	0	6	0	1.000	1	0-0	0	3.42	3.57

Ryan Ludwick

Bats: R **Throws:** L **Pos:** RF-15   **Ht:** 6'3" **Wt:** 203 **Born:** 7/13/1978 **Age:** 26

								BATTING												BASERUNNING				AVERAGES		
Year Team	Lg	G	AB	H	2B	3B	HR	(Hm	Rd)	TB	R	RBI	RC	TBB	IBB	SO	HBP	SH	SF	SB	CS	SB%	GDP	Avg	OBP	Slg
2004 Akron*	AA	8	26	7	2	0	1	(-	-)	12	4	5	3	1	0	5	0	0	1	0	0	-	0	.269	.286	.462
2004 Buffalo*	AAA	44	166	45	15	0	8	(-	-)	84	25	30	27	16	0	52	4	0	2	0	0	-	4	.271	.346	.506
2002 Texas	AL	23	81	19	6	0	1	(1	0)	28	10	9	6	7	0	24	0	0	0	2	1	.67	4	.235	.295	.346
2003 Tex-Cle	AL	47	162	40	8	1	7	(2	5)	71	17	26	28	12	1	48	0	1	0	2	0	1.00	1	.247	.299	.438
2004 Cleveland	AL	15	50	11	2	0	2	(0	2)	19	3	4	4	2	0	14	2	0	0	0	0	-	0	.220	.278	.380
2003 Texas	AL	8	26	4	1	0	0	(0	0)	5	3	0	1	4	0	9	0	0	0	0	0	-	0	.154	.267	.192
2003 Cleveland	AL	39	136	36	7	1	7	(2	5)	66	14	26	27	8	1	39	0	1	0	2	0	1.00	1	.265	.306	.485
3 ML YEARS		85	293	70	16	1	10	(3	7)	118	30	39	38	21	1	86	2	1	0	4	1	.80	5	.239	.294	.403

Julio Lugo

Bats: R **Throws:** R **Pos:** SS-143; 2B-8; DH-5; PH-2   **Ht:** 6'1" **Wt:** 170 **Born:** 11/16/1975 **Age:** 29

								BATTING												BASERUNNING				AVERAGES		
Year Team	Lg	G	AB	H	2B	3B	HR	(Hm	Rd)	TB	R	RBI	RC	TBB	IBB	SO	HBP	SH	SF	SB	CS	SB%	GDP	Avg	OBP	Slg
2000 Houston	NL	116	420	119	22	5	10	(6	4)	181	78	40	62	37	0	93	4	3	1	22	9	.71	9	.283	.346	.431
2001 Houston	NL	140	513	135	20	3	10	(6	4)	191	93	37	63	46	0	116	5	15	7	12	11	.52	7	.263	.326	.372
2002 Houston	NL	88	322	84	15	1	8	(6	2)	125	45	35	43	28	3	74	2	4	2	9	3	.75	6	.261	.322	.388
2003 Hou-TB		139	498	135	16	4	15	(5	10)	204	64	55	68	44	1	100	4	7	3	12	4	.75	7	.271	.333	.410
2004 Tampa Bay	AL	157	581	160	41	4	7	(3	4)	230	83	75	86	54	0	106	5	7	8	21	5	.81	8	.275	.338	.396
2003 Houston	NL	22	65	16	3	0	0	(0	0)	19	6	2	7	9	1	12	0	0	0	2	1	.67	2	.246	.338	.292
2003 Tampa Bay	AL	117	433	119	13	4	15	(5	10)	185	58	53	61	35	0	88	4	7	3	10	3	.77	5	.275	.333	.427
5 ML YEARS		640	2334	633	114	17	50	(26	24)	931	363	242	322	209	4	489	20	36	21	76	32	.70	37	.271	.334	.399

Hector Luna

Bats: R **Throws:** R **Pos:** PH-28; SS-24; 2B-19; 3B-16; LF-8; CF-2; PR-2   **Ht:** 6'1" **Wt:** 170 **Born:** 2/1/1980 **Age:** 25

								BATTING												BASERUNNING				AVERAGES		
Year Team	Lg	G	AB	H	2B	3B	HR	(Hm	Rd)	TB	R	RBI	RC	TBB	IBB	SO	HBP	SH	SF	SB	CS	SB%	GDP	Avg	OBP	Slg
2000 Burlington	A	55	201	41	2	0	0	(-	-)	43	25	15	15	27	1	36	5	1	1	19	5	.79	9	.204	.312	.214
2000 Burlington	R+	55	201	41	5	0	1	(-	-)	49	25	15	18	27	0	35	3	0	1	19	4	.83	4	.204	.306	.244
2000 Mahning VI	A-	5	19	6	2	0	0	(-	-)	8	2	4	2	1	0	3	0	1	0	0	0	-	0	.316	.350	.421
2001 Columbus	A	66	241	64	8	3	3	(-	-)	87	36	23	33	23	0	48	5	3	2	15	4	.79	2	.266	.339	.361
2002 Kinston	A+	128	468	129	15	6	11	(-	-)	189	67	51	65	39	0	73	3	6	2	32	11	.74	7	.276	.334	.404
2003 Akron	AA	127	462	137	19	2	2	(-	-)	166	87	38	66	48	1	64	5	5	2	17	5	.77	10	.297	.368	.359
2004 St Louis	NL	83	173	43	7	2	3	(1	2)	63	25	22	20	13	0	37	2	1	3	6	3	.67	2	.249	.304	.364

Brandon Lyon

Pitches: R **Bats:** R **Pos:** RP   **Ht:** 6'1" **Wt:** 185 **Born:** 8/10/1979 **Age:** 25

		HOW MUCH HE PITCHED						WHAT HE GAVE UP										THE RESULTS							
Year Team	Lg	G	GS	CG	GF	IP	BFP	H	R	ER	HR	SH	SF	HB	TBB	IBB	SO	WP	Bk	W	L	Pct	ShO	Sv-Op	Hld	ERC	ERA
2004 Tucson*	AAA	6	3	0	1	8.1	45	15	14	14	3			0	4	0	4	0		2	3	.400	0	0- -	-	11.44	15.12
2001 Toronto	AL	11	11	0	0	63.0	261	63	31	30	6	2	6	1	15	0	35	0	1	5	4	.556	0	0-0	0	3.50	4.29
2002 Toronto	AL	15	10	0	0	62.0	279	78	47	45	14	3	2	2	19	2	30	2	0	1	4	.200	0	0-1	0	6.24	6.53
2003 Boston	AL	49	0	0	31	59.0	273	73	33	27	6	1	4	2	19	5	50	0	0	4	6	.400	0	9-12	2	4.96	4.12
3 ML YEARS		75	21	0	31	184.0	813	214	111	102	26	6	12	5	53	7	115	2	1	10	14	.417	0	9-13	2	4.86	4.99

John Mabry

Bats: L **Throws:** R **Pos:** LF-39; RF-25; 3B-20; 1B-14; PH-10; CF-1   **Ht:** 6'4" **Wt:** 210 **Born:** 10/17/1970 **Age:** 34

								BATTING												BASERUNNING				AVERAGES		
Year Team	Lg	G	AB	H	2B	3B	HR	(Hm	Rd)	TB	R	RBI	RC	TBB	IBB	SO	HBP	SH	SF	SB	CS	SB%	GDP	Avg	OBP	Slg
2004 Memphis*	AAA	39	136	46	7	0	12	(-	-)	89	27	35	33	17	2	29	2	0	5	0	0	-	3	.338	.406	.654
1994 St Louis	NL	6	23	7	3	0	0	(0	0)	10	2	3	4	2	0	4	0	0	0	0	0	-	0	.304	.360	.435
1995 St Louis	NL	129	388	119	21	1	5	(2	3)	157	35	41	53	24	5	45	2	0	4	0	3	.00	6	.307	.347	.405
1996 St Louis	NL	151	543	161	30	2	13	(3	10)	234	63	74	74	37	11	84	3	3	5	3	2	.60	21	.297	.342	.431
1997 St Louis	NL	116	388	110	19	0	5	(5	0)	144	40	36	49	39	9	77	3	2	2	0	1	.00	11	.284	.352	.371
1998 St Louis	NL	142	377	94	22	0	9	(4	5)	143	41	46	42	30	6	76	1	3	2	0	2	.00	6	.249	.305	.379
1999 Seattle	AL	87	262	64	14	0	9	(5	4)	105	34	33	30	20	1	60	0	2	1	2	1	.67	6	.244	.297	.401
2000 Sea-SD		95	226	53	13	0	8	(3	5)	90	35	32	25	15	0	69	2	0	1	0	1	.00	4	.235	.287	.398
2001 StL-Fla	NL	87	154	32	7	0	6	(2	4)	57	14	20	16	13	1	46	5	0	2	1	0	1.00	6	.208	.287	.370
2002 Phi-Oak		110	214	59	13	1	11	(8	3)	107	28	43	34	15	2	42	1	0	4	1	1	.50	7	.276	.321	.500
2003 Seattle	AL	64	104	22	6	0	3	(1	2)	37	12	16	11	15	2	21	3	0	0	0	0	-	3	.212	.328	.356
2004 St Louis	NL	87	240	71	11	0	13	(7	6)	121	32	40	37	26	5	63	1	5	3	0	1	.00	6	.296	.363	.504
2000 Seattle	AL	47	103	25	5	0	1	(0	1)	33	18	7	11	10	0	31	2	0	0	0	1	.00	1	.243	.322	.320
2000 San Diego	NL	48	123	28	8	0	7	(3	4)	57	17	25	14	5	0	38	0	0	1	0	0	-	3	.228	.256	.463
2001 St Louis	NL	5	7	0	0	0	0	(0	0)	0	0	0	0	0	0	2	0	0	0	0	0	-	0	.000	.000	.000
2001 Florida	NL	82	147	32	7	0	6	(2	4)	57	14	20	16	13	1	44	5	0	2	1	0	1.00	6	.218	.299	.388
2002 Philadelphia	NL	21	21	6	0	0	0	(0	0)	6	1	3	3	1	1	5	0	0	0	0	0	-	0	.286	.304	.286
2002 Oakland	AL	89	193	53	13	1	11	(8	3)	101	27	40	31	14	1	37	1	0	3	1	1	.50	7	.275	.322	.523
11 ML YEARS		1074	2919	792	159	4	82	(40	42)	1205	336	384	375	236	42	587	21	15	24	7	12	.37	76	.271	.328	.413

Mike MacDougal

Pitches: R **Bats:** B **Pos:** RP-13   **Ht:** 6'4" **Wt:** 195 **Born:** 3/5/1977 **Age:** 28

		HOW MUCH HE PITCHED						WHAT HE GAVE UP										THE RESULTS							
Year Team	Lg	G	GS	CG	GF	IP	BFP	H	R	ER	HR	SH	SF	HB	TBB	IBB	SO	WP	Bk	W	L	Pct	ShO	Sv-Op	Hld	ERC	ERA
2004 Wichita*	AA	17	2	0	5	18.1	83	14	7	3	0	0	0	0	14	0	13	2	0	1	0	1.000	0	1- -	-	3.33	1.47
2004 Omaha*	AAA	14	0	0	6	14.1	66	12	9	9	1	0	0	0	11	0	8	2	0	0	1	.000	0	2- -	-	4.26	5.65
2001 Kansas City	AL	3	3	0	0	15.1	67	18	10	8	2	0	0	1	4	0	7	3	0	1	1	.500	0	0-0	0	5.04	4.70

158

Year Team	Lg	G	GS	CG	GF	IP	BFP	H	R	ER	HR	SH	SF	HB	TBB	IBB	SO	WP	Bk	W	L	Pct	ShO	Sv-Op	Hld	ERC	ERA
2002 Kansas City	AL	6	0	0	1	9.0	38	5	5	5	0	0	0	0	7	1	10	1	0	0	1	.000	0	0-0	0	2.26	5.00
2003 Kansas City	AL	68	0	0	61	64.0	285	64	36	29	4	3	2	8	32	0	57	6	0	3	5	.375	0	27-35	1	4.76	4.08
2004 Kansas City	AL	13	0	0	8	11.1	61	16	8	7	2	0	0	1	9	0	14	2	0	1	1	.500	0	1-3	0	9.04	5.56
4 ML YEARS		90	3	0	70	99.2	451	103	59	49	8	3	2	10	52	1	88	12	0	5	8	.385	0	28-38	1	5.01	4.42

Andy Machado

Bats: B Throws: R Pos: SS-17   Ht: 5'11" Wt: 165 Born: 1/25/1981 Age: 24

					BATTING														BASERUNNING				AVERAGES		
Year Team	Lg	G	AB	H	2B	3B	HR	(Hm	Rd)	TB	R	RBI	RC	TBB	IBB	SO	HBP	SH	SF	SB	CS	SB%	GDP	Avg	OBP	Slg
1999 Phillies	R	68	143	37	6	3	2	(-	-)	55	26	12	19	15	2	38	2	7	1	6	3	.67	1	.259	.335	.385
1999 Clearwater	A+	1	2	0	0	0	0	(-	-)	0	0	0	0	0	0	1	0	0	0	0	0	-	0	.000	.000	.000
1999 Piedmont	A	20	60	14	4	2	0	(-	-)	22	7	7	7	7	0	20	1	1	0	2	1	.67	0	.233	.324	.367
2000 Clearwater	A+	117	417	102	19	7	1	(-	-)	138	55	35	46	54	0	103	0	5	2	32	18	.64	7	.245	.330	.331
2000 Reading	AA	3	11	4	1	0	1	(-	-)	8	2	2	2	0	0	4	0	0	0	0	0	-	0	.364	.364	.727
2001 Clearwater	A+	82	272	71	5	8	5	(-	-)	107	49	36	39	31	2	66	4	10	3	23	9	.72	3	.261	.342	.393
2001 Reading	AA	31	101	15	2	0	1	(-	-)	20	13	8	4	12	0	25	0	3	1	5	2	.71	1	.149	.237	.198
2002 Reading	AA	126	450	113	24	3	12	(-	-)	179	71	77	69	72	4	118	2	18	5	40	11	.78	5	.251	.353	.398
2003 Reading	AA	123	423	83	19	4	5	(-	-)	125	80	20	58	108	0	120	1	8	1	49	15	.77	2	.196	.360	.296
2004 Louisville	AAA	31	109	25	5	2	0	(-	-)	34	14	12	10	10	0	26	1	1	2	3	2	.60	1	.229	.295	.312
2004 Clearwater	A+	7	22	5	0	0	0	(-	-)	5	0	1	2	4	0	2	0	0	0	0	0	-	0	.227	.346	.227
2004 Scrtn/WlksBr	AAA	78	295	67	12	5	6	(-	-)	107	51	26	40	50	0	73	1	11	4	11	6	.65	1	.227	.337	.363
2003 Philadelphia	NL	1	0	0	0	0	0	(0	0)	0	0	0	0	0	0	0	0	0	0	1	0	1.00	0	-	-	-
2004 Cincinnati	NL	17	56	15	5	1	0	(0	0)	22	6	4	8	10	2	26	0	0	0	3	1	.75	0	.268	.379	.393
2 ML YEARS		18	56	15	5	1	0	(0	0)	22	6	4	8	10	2	26	0	0	0	4	1	.80	0	.268	.379	.393

Robert Machado

Bats: R Throws: R Pos: C-35; PH-4   Ht: 6'1" Wt: 210 Born: 6/3/1973 Age: 32

					BATTING														BASERUNNING				AVERAGES		
Year Team	Lg	G	AB	H	2B	3B	HR	(Hm	Rd)	TB	R	RBI	RC	TBB	IBB	SO	HBP	SH	SF	SB	CS	SB%	GDP	Avg	OBP	Slg
2004 Ottawa*	AAA	34	126	40	12	0	3	(-	-)	61	22	20	19	10	1	20	0	0	0	0	1	.00	5	.317	.368	.484
1996 Chicago	AL	4	6	4	1	0	0	(0	0)	5	1	2	2	0	0	0	0	0	0	0	0	-	0	.667	.667	.833
1997 Chicago	AL	10	15	3	0	1	0	(0	0)	5	1	2	1	1	0	6	0	1	0	0	0	-	0	.200	.250	.333
1998 Chicago	AL	34	111	23	6	0	3	(2	1)	38	14	15	9	7	0	22	0	3	0	0	0	-	3	.207	.254	.342
1999 Montreal	NL	17	22	4	1	0	0	(0	0)	5	3	0	1	2	0	6	0	0	0	0	0	-	0	.182	.250	.227
2000 Seattle	AL	8	14	3	0	0	1	(1	0)	6	2	1	2	1	0	4	0	0	0	0	0	-	0	.214	.267	.429
2001 Chicago	NL	52	135	30	10	0	2	(1	1)	46	13	13	11	7	3	26	1	3	0	0	0	-	4	.222	.266	.341
2002 ChC-Mil	NL	73	211	55	14	1	3	(1	2)	80	19	22	22	17	4	41	1	2	2	0	0	-	7	.261	.316	.379
2003 Baltimore	AL	18	49	13	1	0	1	(1	0)	17	8	3	5	6	0	12	0	0	0	0	0	-	2	.265	.345	.347
2004 Baltimore	AL	37	73	11	3	0	1	(0	1)	17	5	3	1	4	0	18	0	0	0	0	0	-	2	.151	.195	.233
2002 Chicago	NL	22	58	16	4	0	1	(0	1)	23	5	5	7	5	0	11	0	1	0	0	0	-	2	.276	.333	.397
2002 Milwaukee	NL	51	153	39	10	1	2	(1	1)	57	14	17	15	12	4	30	1	1	2	0	0	-	5	.255	.310	.373
9 ML YEARS		253	636	146	36	2	11	(7	4)	219	66	61	54	45	7	135	2	9	2	0	0	-	17	.230	.282	.344

Jose Macias

Bats: B Throws: R Pos: PH-51; 3B-18; 2B-16; RF-13; LF-8; CF-7; PR-3   Ht: 5'10" Wt: 189 Born: 1/25/1972 Age: 33

					BATTING														BASERUNNING				AVERAGES		
Year Team	Lg	G	AB	H	2B	3B	HR	(Hm	Rd)	TB	R	RBI	RC	TBB	IBB	SO	HBP	SH	SF	SB	CS	SB%	GDP	Avg	OBP	Slg
1999 Detroit	AL	5	4	1	0	0	1	(1	0)	4	2	2	1	0	0	1	0	0	0	0	0	-	0	.250	.250	1.000
2000 Detroit	AL	73	173	44	3	5	2	(2	0)	63	25	24	21	18	0	24	1	4	0	2	0	1.00	3	.254	.328	.364
2001 Detroit	AL	137	488	131	24	6	8	(7	1)	191	62	51	62	32	0	54	3	8	3	21	6	.78	7	.268	.316	.391
2002 Det-Mon	AL	123	338	84	21	1	7	(4	3)	128	43	39	40	21	0	57	2	4	0	8	8	.50	6	.249	.293	.379
2003 Montreal	NL	111	272	65	15	2	4	(3	1)	96	31	22	23	11	1	45	2	2	1	4	3	.57	5	.239	.273	.353
2004 Chicago	NL	98	194	52	6	3	3	(2	1)	73	23	22	22	5	0	38	2	2	1	4	1	.80	2	.268	.292	.376
2002 Detroit	AL	33	107	25	4	0	0	(0	0)	29	10	6	7	8	0	13	1	4	1	3	2	.60	4	.234	.291	.271
2002 Montreal	NL	90	231	59	17	1	7	(4	3)	99	33	33	33	13	0	44	1	4	3	5	6	.45	2	.255	.294	.429
6 ML YEARS		547	1469	377	69	17	25	(19	6)	555	186	160	169	87	1	219	10	24	9	39	18	.68	23	.257	.301	.378

Rob Mackowiak

Bats: L Throws: R Pos: RF-79; 3B-55; LF-25; PH-24; CF-19; 1B-1; PR-1   Ht: 5'10" Wt: 190 Born: 6/20/1976 Age: 29

					BATTING														BASERUNNING				AVERAGES		
Year Team	Lg	G	AB	H	2B	3B	HR	(Hm	Rd)	TB	R	RBI	RC	TBB	IBB	SO	HBP	SH	SF	SB	CS	SB%	GDP	Avg	OBP	Slg
2001 Pittsburgh	NL	83	214	57	15	2	4	(3	1)	88	30	21	28	15	5	52	3	2	3	4	3	.57	3	.266	.319	.411
2002 Pittsburgh	NL	136	385	94	22	0	16	(9	7)	164	57	48	57	42	5	120	7	3	2	9	3	.75	0	.244	.328	.426
2003 Pittsburgh	NL	77	174	47	4	4	6	(1	5)	77	20	19	27	15	2	53	4	0	0	6	0	1.00	1	.270	.342	.443
2004 Pittsburgh	NL	155	491	121	22	6	17	(11	6)	206	65	75	73	50	2	114	6	1	7	13	4	.76	3	.246	.319	.420
4 ML YEARS		451	1264	319	63	12	43	(24	19)	535	172	163	185	122	14	339	20	6	12	32	10	.76	7	.252	.325	.423

Greg Maddux

Pitches: R Bats: R Pos: SP-33   Ht: 6'0" Wt: 185 Born: 4/14/1966 Age: 39

		HOW MUCH HE PITCHED						WHAT HE GAVE UP											THE RESULTS							
Year Team	Lg	G	GS	CG	GF	IP	BFP	H	R	ER	HR	SH	SF	HB	TBB	IBB	SO	WP	Bk	W	L	Pct	ShO	Sv-Op	Hld	ERC	ERA
1986 Chicago	NL	6	5	1	1	31.0	144	44	20	19	3	1	0	1	11	2	20	2	0	2	4	.333	0	0-0	0	6.45	5.52
1987 Chicago	NL	30	27	1	2	155.2	701	181	111	97	17	7	1	4	74	13	101	4	7	6	14	.300	1	0-0	0	5.42	5.61
1988 Chicago	NL	34	34	9	0	249.0	1047	230	97	88	13	11	2	9	81	16	140	1	3	18	8	.692	3	0-0	0	3.09	3.18
1989 Chicago	NL	35	35	7	0	238.1	1002	222	90	78	13	18	6	6	82	13	135	5	3	19	12	.613	1	0-0	0	3.20	2.95
1990 Chicago	NL	35	35	8	0	237.0	1011	242	116	91	11	18	5	4	71	10	144	3	3	15	15	.500	2	0-0	0	3.41	3.46
1991 Chicago	NL	37	37	7	0	263.0	1070	232	113	98	18	16	3	6	66	9	198	6	3	15	11	.577	2	0-0	0	2.73	3.35
1992 Chicago	NL	35	35	9	0	268.0	1061	201	68	65	7	15	3	14	70	7	199	5	0	20	11	.645	4	0-0	0	2.01	2.18

Year Team	Lg	G	GS	CG	GF	IP	BFP	H	R	ER	HR	SH	SF	HB	TBB	IBB	SO	WP	Bk	W	L	Pct	ShO	Sv-Op	Hld	ERC	ERA
1993 Atlanta	NL	36	36	8	0	267.0	1064	228	85	70	14	15	7	6	52	7	197	5	1	20	10	.667	1	0-0	0	2.32	2.36
1994 Atlanta	NL	25	25	10	0	202.0	774	150	44	35	4	6	5	6	31	3	156	3	1	16	6	.727	3	0-0	0	1.59	1.56
1995 Atlanta	NL	28	28	10	0	209.2	785	147	39	38	8	9	1	4	23	3	181	1	0	19	2	.905	3	0-0	0	1.41	1.63
1996 Atlanta	NL	35	35	5	0	245.0	978	225	85	74	11	8	5	3	28	11	172	4	0	15	11	.577	1	0-0	0	2.22	2.72
1997 Atlanta	NL	33	33	5	0	232.2	893	200	58	57	9	11	7	6	20	6	177	0	0	19	4	.826	2	0-0	0	1.95	2.20
1998 Atlanta	NL	34	34	9	0	251.0	987	201	75	62	13	15	5	7	45	10	204	4	0	18	9	.667	5	0-0	0	2.01	2.22
1999 Atlanta	NL	33	33	4	0	219.1	940	258	103	87	16	15	5	4	37	8	136	1	0	19	9	.679	0	0-0	0	3.95	3.57
2000 Atlanta	NL	35	35	6	0	249.1	1012	225	91	83	19	8	5	10	42	12	190	1	2	19	9	.679	3	0-0	0	2.60	3.00
2001 Atlanta	NL	34	34	3	0	233.0	927	220	86	79	20	12	11	7	27	10	173	2	0	17	11	.607	3	0-0	0	2.70	3.05
2002 Atlanta	NL	34	34	0	0	199.1	820	194	67	58	14	13	4	4	45	7	118	1	0	16	6	.727	0	0-0	0	3.11	2.62
2003 Atlanta	NL	36	36	1	0	218.1	901	225	110	96	24	10	9	8	33	7	124	3	0	16	11	.593	0	0-0	0	3.44	3.96
2004 Chicago	NL	33	33	2	0	212.2	872	218	103	95	35	12	8	9	33	4	151	2	0	16	11	.593	1	0-0	0	3.86	4.02
19 ML YEARS		608	604	105	3	4181.1	16989	3843	1563	1370	269	220	92	118	871	158	2916	55	26	305	174	.637	35	0-0	0	2.76	2.95

Bobby Madritsch

Pitches: L **Bats:** L **Pos:** SP-11; RP-4   **Ht:** 6'2" **Wt:** 190 **Born:** 2/28/1976 **Age:** 29

Year Team	Lg	G	GS	CG	GF	IP	BFP	H	R	ER	HR	SH	SF	HB	TBB	IBB	SO	WP	Bk	W	L	Pct	ShO	Sv-Op	Hld	ERC	ERA
1998 Billings	R+	14	13	0	0	80.1	341	72	30	25	3	3	2	1	35	1	87	2	1	7	3	.700	0	0--	-	3.25	2.80
2000 Reds	R	6	4	0	0	22.1	90	15	5	5	0	1	0	2	9	0	27	0	0	1	1	.500	0	0--	-	2.11	2.01
2000 Dayton	A	2	2	0	0	10.0	44	8	1	1	0	0	1	0	7	0	7	1	0	0	0	-	0	0--	-	3.38	0.90
2003 San Antonio	AA	27	27	2	0	158.2	668	133	75	64	11	6	5	2	67	0	154	5	2	13	7	.650	1	0--	-	3.11	3.63
2004 Tacoma	AAA	12	12	0	0	62.1	272	61	33	26	3	2	1	4	26	0	53	3	0	5	2	.714	0	0--	-	3.90	3.75
2004 Seattle	AL	15	11	1	4	88.0	359	74	33	32	3	3	0	4	33	2	60	2	1	6	3	.667	0	0-0	0	2.91	3.27

Ryan Madson

Pitches: R **Bats:** L **Pos:** RP-51; SP-1   **Ht:** 6'6" **Wt:** 180 **Born:** 8/28/1980 **Age:** 24

Year Team	Lg	G	GS	CG	GF	IP	BFP	H	R	ER	HR	SH	SF	HB	TBB	IBB	SO	WP	Bk	W	L	Pct	ShO	Sv-Op	Hld	ERC	ERA
1998 Martinsville	R+	12	10	0	0	54.0	237	57	38	29	5	0	2	0	20	0	52	9	1	3	5	.375	0	0--	-	4.34	4.83
1999 Batavia	A-	15	15	0	0	87.2	383	80	51	46	5	2	4	10	43	0	75	10	0	5	5	.500	0	0--	-	4.12	4.72
2000 Piedmont	A	21	21	2	0	135.2	564	113	50	39	5	3	0	13	45	0	123	5	1	5	3	.625	1	0--	-	2.88	2.59
2001 Clearwater	A+	22	21	1	0	117.2	530	137	68	51	4	0	5	5	49	1	101	5	1	9	4	.692	0	0--	-	4.75	3.90
2002 Reading	AA	26	26	2	0	171.1	699	150	68	61	11	9	6	12	53	0	132	5	0	16	4	.800	0	0--	-	3.17	3.20
2003 Clearwater	A+	2	2	0	0	8.0	36	11	5	5	0	0	0	0	2	0	9	0	0	0	0	-	0	0--	-	4.89	5.63
2003 Scrtn/WlksBr	AAA	26	26	0	0	157.0	658	157	70	61	9	2	5	10	42	2	138	6	0	12	8	.600	0	0--	-	3.54	3.50
2004 Reading	AA	2	1	0	0	2.0	11	3	2	1	1	0	0	0	2	0	1	0	0	0	0	-	0	0--	-	13.58	4.50
2003 Philadelphia	NL	1	0	0	0	2.0		0	0	0	0	0	0	0	0	0	0	0	0	0	0	-	0	0-0	0	0.00	0.00
2004 Philadelphia	NL	52	1	0	14	77.0	312	68	23	20	6	1	1	5	19	4	55	7	0	9	3	.750	0	1-2	7	2.95	2.94
2 ML YEARS		53	1	0	14	79.0	318	68	23	20	6	1	1	5	19	4	55	7	0	9	3	.750	0	1-2	7	2.80	2.28

Chris Magruder

Bats: B **Throws:** R **Pos:** PH-35; RF-16; LF-10; PR-2   **Ht:** 5'11" **Wt:** 200 **Born:** 4/26/1977 **Age:** 28

Year Team	Lg	G	AB	H	2B	3B	HR	(Hm	Rd)	TB	R	RBI	RC	TBB	IBB	SO	HBP	SH	SF	SB	CS	SB%	GDP	Avg	OBP	Slg
2004 Indianapolis*	AAA	79	305	83	17	4	6	(-	-)	126	37	39	42	21	4	55	10	1	2	7	4	.64	4	.272	.337	.413
2001 Texas	AL	17	29	5	0	0	0	(0	0)	5	3	1	0	1	0	5	1	0	0	0	0	-	0	.172	.226	.172
2002 Cleveland	AL	87	258	56	15	1	6	(3	3)	91	34	29	20	15	2	55	1	2	2	2	0	1.00	7	.217	.261	.353
2003 Cleveland	AL	9	26	9	2	1	1	(1	0)	16	3	3	6	3	0	6	1	0	0	0	1	.00	0	.346	.433	.615
2004 Milwaukee	NL	56	89	21	6	1	2	(1	1)	35	11	10	8	8	2	21	2	1	1	0	1	.00	3	.236	.310	.393
4 ML YEARS		169	402	91	23	3	9	(5	4)	147	51	43	34	27	4	87	5	3	3	2	2	.50	11	.226	.281	.366

Ron Mahay

Pitches: L **Bats:** L **Pos:** RP-60   **Ht:** 6'2" **Wt:** 190 **Born:** 6/28/1971 **Age:** 34

Year Team	Lg	G	GS	CG	GF	IP	BFP	H	R	ER	HR	SH	SF	HB	TBB	IBB	SO	WP	Bk	W	L	Pct	ShO	Sv-Op	Hld	ERC	ERA
1997 Boston	AL	28	0	0	7	25.0	105	19	7	7	3	1	0	0	11	0	22	3	0	3	0	1.000	0	0-2	6	3.01	2.52
1998 Boston	AL	29	0	0	6	26.0	120	26	16	10	2	0	4	2	15	1	14	3	0	1	1	.500	0	1-2	7	4.76	3.46
1999 Oakland	AL	6	1	0	2	19.1	68	8	4	4	2	0	0	0	3	0	15	0	0	2	0	1.000	0	1-1	0	0.88	1.86
2000 Oak-Fla		23	2	0	7	41.1	199	57	35	33	10	1	2	0	25	1	32	4	0	1	1	.500	0	0-0	4	8.55	7.19
2001 Chicago	NL	17	0	0	4	20.2	86	14	6	6	4	0	0	0	15	1	24	1	0	0	0	-	0	0-0	2	4.32	2.61
2002 Chicago	NL	11	0	0	1	14.2	65	13	14	14	6	0	0	0	8	0	14	0	0	2	0	1.000	0	0-0	4	6.11	8.59
2003 Texas	AL	35	0	0	5	45.1	189	33	19	16	3	0	0	0	20	7	38	4	0	3	3	.500	0	0-3	9	2.31	3.18
2004 Texas	AL	60	0	0	12	67.0	290	60	23	19	5	4	0	2	29	5	54	2	0	3	0	1.000	0	0-2	14	3.39	2.55
2000 Oakland	AL	5	2	0	1	16.0	82	26	18	16	4	1	0	0	9	0	5	2	0	1	0	1.000	0	0-0	2	9.97	9.00
2000 Florida	NL	18	0	0	6	25.1	117	31	17	17	6	0	1	0	16	1	27	2	0	1	0	1.000	0	0-0	2	7.67	6.04
8 ML YEARS		209	3	0	44	259.1	1122	230	124	109	35	6	6	4	126	15	213	17	0	15	5	.750	0	2-10	40	3.97	3.78

John Maine

Pitches: R **Bats:** R **Pos:** SP-1   **Ht:** 6'4" **Wt:** 193 **Born:** 5/8/1981 **Age:** 24

Year Team	Lg	G	GS	CG	GF	IP	BFP	H	R	ER	HR	SH	SF	HB	TBB	IBB	SO	WP	Bk	W	L	Pct	ShO	Sv-Op	Hld	ERC	ERA
2002 Aberdeen	A-	4	2	0	1	11.0	42	6	2	2	0	0	0	0	3	0	21	2	0	1	1	.500	0	0--	-	1.17	1.74
2002 Delmarva	A	6	5	0	0	33.0	128	21	8	5	0	3	1	2	4	0	39	2	1	1	1	.500	0	0--	-	1.16	1.36
2003 Delmarva	A	14	14	1	0	76.1	283	43	16	13	1	2	0	2	18	0	108	1	1	7	3	.700	0	0--	-	1.21	1.53
2003 Frederick	A+	12	12	1	0	70.1	276	48	27	24	1	1	0	1	20	0	77	0	0	6	1	.857	1	0--	-	1.92	3.07

Year Team	Lg	G	GS	CG	GF	IP	BFP	H	R	ER	HR	SH	SF	HB	TBB	IBB	SO	WP	Bk	W	L	Pct	ShO	Sv-Op	Hld	ERC	ERA
2004 Bowie	AA	5	5	0	0	28.0	109	16	8	7	1	0	1	1	7	0	34	0	0	4	0	1.000	0	0- -	-	1.32	2.25
2004 Ottawa	AAA	22	22	0	0	119.2	512	123	59	52	12	12	5	5	52	0	105	2	1	5	7	.417	0	0- -	-	4.69	3.91
2004 Baltimore	AL	1	1	0	0	3.2	19	7	4	4	1	0	0	0	3	0	1	1	0	0	1	.000	0	0-0	0	14.87	9.82

Gary Majewski

Pitches: R **Bats:** R **Pos:** RP-16   **Ht:** 6'1" **Wt:** 215 **Born:** 2/26/1980 **Age:** 25

Year Team	Lg	G	GS	CG	GF	IP	BFP	H	R	ER	HR	SH	SF	HB	TBB	IBB	SO	WP	Bk	W	L	Pct	ShO	Sv-Op	Hld	ERC	ERA
1999 Bristol	R+	13	13	1	0	76.2	325	67	34	26	4	4	1	7	37	0	91	1	0	7	1	.875	1	0- -	-	3.82	3.05
1999 Burlington	R+	3	0	0	0	3.1	28	11	14	14	3	1	0	2	4	0	1	0	0	0	0	-	0	0- -	-	37.10	37.80
2000 Burlington	R+	22	22	3	0	134.2	546	83	53	46	8	3	6	12	68	0	137	2	0	6	7	.462	3	0- -	-	2.57	3.07
2000 Winstn-Salm	A+	6	6	0	0	37.0	163	32	21	21	1	2	2	8	17	0	24	2	0	2	4	.333	0	0- -	-	3.88	5.11
2001 Vero Beach	A+	23	13	0	5	75.0	351	103	57	52	9	3	4	5	36	0	41	3	1	4	5	.444	0	1- -	-	7.32	6.24
2001 Winstn-Salm	A+	9	6	1	3	43.0	176	42	15	14	3	2	0	6	10	0	31	1	0	4	2	.667	0	0- -	-	3.80	2.93
2002 Birmingham	AA	57	1	0	26	74.2	317	61	31	22	3	2	2	3	34	2	75	1	1	5	3	.625	0	3- -	-	2.98	2.65
2003 Charlotte	AAA	42	1	0	13	72.2	307	62	33	32	3	3	1	5	29	2	72	3	0	6	4	.600	0	4- -	-	3.10	3.96
2004 Charlotte	AAA	35	0	0	31	42.1	175	30	16	15	2	1	0	3	16	0	41	1	0	3	3	.500	0	14- -	-	2.36	3.19
2004 Edmonton	AAA	14	0	0	10	15.1	72	18	8	7	0	0	0	0	8	1	17	1	0	1	2	.333	0	1- -	-	4.53	4.11
2004 Montreal	NL	16	0	0	7	21.0	95	28	15	9	2	1	1	2	5	1	12	0	0	0	1	.000	0	1-2	0	5.68	3.86

Val Majewski

Bats: L **Throws:** L **Pos:** CF-3; PH-3; DH-2; PR-2; RF-1   **Ht:** 6'2" **Wt:** 200 **Born:** 6/19/1981 **Age:** 24

Year Team	Lg	G	AB	H	2B	3B	HR	(Hm	Rd)	TB	R	RBI	RC	TBB	IBB	SO	HBP	SH	SF	SB	CS	SB%	GDP	Avg	OBP	Slg
2002 Aberdeen	A-	31	110	33	7	4	1	(-	-)	51	22	15	18	13	0	14	1	0	1	8	4	.67	3	.300	.376	.464
2002 Delmarva	A	7	17	2	0	1	0	(-	-)	5	2	3	0	1	0	1	0	0	0	0	0	-	1	.118	.158	.294
2003 Orioles	R	1	3	1	0	0	0	(-	-)	1	0	0	0	1	0	0	0	0	0	0	0	-	0	.333	.500	.333
2003 Aberdeen	A-	4	16	6	2	2	0	(-	-)	12	2	3	4	1	0	2	0	0	0	1	0	1.00	0	.375	.412	.750
2003 Delmarva	A	56	208	63	15	8	7	(-	-)	115	38	48	44	28	2	20	1	0	3	10	1	.91	3	.303	.383	.553
2003 Frederick	A+	41	159	46	18	1	5	(-	-)	81	15	20	24	7	0	23	1	0	1	0	0	-	2	.289	.321	.509
2004 Bowie	AA	112	433	133	24	5	15	(-	-)	212	71	80	75	33	3	68	5	0	5	14	4	.78	7	.307	.359	.490
2004 Baltimore	AL	9	13	2	1	0	0	(0	0)	3	3	1	0	0	0	1	0	0	0	0	0	-	0	.154	.154	.231

Mark Malaska

Pitches: L **Bats:** L **Pos:** RP-19   **Ht:** 6'3" **Wt:** 191 **Born:** 1/17/1978 **Age:** 27

Year Team	Lg	G	GS	CG	GF	IP	BFP	H	R	ER	HR	SH	SF	HB	TBB	IBB	SO	WP	Bk	W	L	Pct	ShO	Sv-Op	Hld	ERC	ERA
2000 Chrlstn - SC	A	2	0	0	0	2.0	8	3	2	2	1	0	0	0	0	0	3	0	0	0	0	-	0	0- -	-	9.22	9.00
2000 Hudson Val	A-	10	5	0	0	40.1	176	44	27	22	1	0	0	1	14	2	36	8	0	0	2	.000	0	0- -	-	3.84	4.91
2001 Chrlstn - SC	A	25	25	1	0	157.0	659	153	71	51	11	5	2	2	35	0	152	13	1	7	12	.368	0	0- -	-	3.05	2.92
2001 Bakersfield	A+	3	3	0	0	17.2	70	14	8	8	1	1	0	0	5	0	13	1	0	2	1	.667	0	0- -	-	2.33	4.08
2002 Bakersfield	A+	15	15	2	0	91.1	393	98	48	30	5	1	1	7	12	0	94	3	0	7	4	.636	2	0- -	-	3.32	2.96
2002 Orlando	AA	12	11	1	1	70.2	314	82	37	29	4	2	1	2	28	2	49	4	0	4	5	.444	0	1- -	-	4.76	3.69
2003 Orlando	AA	19	0	0	5	25.0	96	21	6	6	2	2	1	0	4	1	22	0	0	1	1	.500	0	1- -	-	2.25	2.16
2003 Durham	AAA	15	0	0	5	23.0	99	24	12	11	1	0	0	3	8	0	22	5	0	1	1	.500	0	0- -	-	3.91	4.30
2004 Pawtucket	AAA	33	0	0	8	36.1	163	42	17	17	7	0	0	3	11	2	31	1	0	1	1	.500	0	1- -	-	5.46	4.21
2003 Tampa Bay	AL	22	0	0	3	16.0	70	13	7	5	0	1	0	1	12	3	17	0	0	2	1	.667	0	0-3	7	3.64	2.81
2004 Boston	AL	19	0	0	8	20.0	93	21	11	10	2	1	0	1	12	1	12	0	0	1	1	.500	0	0-0	1	5.21	4.50
2 ML YEARS		41	0	0	11	36.0	163	34	18	15	2	2	0	2	24	4	29	0	0	3	2	.600	0	0-3	8	4.52	3.75

Matt Mantei

Pitches: R **Bats:** R **Pos:** RP-12   **Ht:** 6'1" **Wt:** 200 **Born:** 7/7/1973 **Age:** 31

Year Team	Lg	G	GS	CG	GF	IP	BFP	H	R	ER	HR	SH	SF	HB	TBB	IBB	SO	WP	Bk	W	L	Pct	ShO	Sv-Op	Hld	ERC	ERA
1995 Florida	NL	12	0	0	3	13.1	64	12	8	7	1	1	1	0	13	0	15	1	0	0	1	.000	0	0-0	0	5.54	4.73
1996 Florida	NL	14	0	0	1	18.1	89	13	13	13	2	1	0	1	21	1	25	2	0	1	0	1.000	0	0-1	0	5.46	6.38
1998 Florida	NL	42	0	0	23	54.2	224	38	19	18	1	3	4	7	23	3	63	0	0	3	4	.429	0	9-12	2	2.44	2.96
1999 Fla-Ari	NL	65	0	0	60	65.1	284	44	21	20	5	1	1	5	44	1	99	2	0	1	3	.250	0	32-37	0	3.42	2.76
2000 Arizona	NL	47	0	0	38	45.1	200	31	24	23	4	2	0	2	35	1	53	5	0	1	1	.500	0	17-20	0	3.80	4.57
2001 Arizona	NL	8	0	0	7	7.0	31	6	2	2	2	0	0	0	4	0	12	2	0	0	0	-	0	2-2	5	5.18	2.57
2002 Arizona	NL	31	0	0	6	26.2	122	28	15	14	3	0	1	0	12	0	26	1	0	2	2	.500	0	0-1	2	4.64	4.73
2003 Arizona	NL	50	0	0	44	55.0	220	37	17	16	6	4	2	2	18	1	68	1	0	5	4	.556	0	29-32	0	2.26	2.62
2004 Arizona	NL	12	0	0	9	10.2	55	17	15	14	5	0	1	0	6	1	13	0	0	0	3	.000	0	4-7	0	11.44	11.81
1999 Florida	NL	35	0	0	32	36.1	157	24	11	11	4	0	1	2	25	1	50	0	0	1	2	.333	0	10-12	0	3.55	2.72
1999 Arizona	NL	30	0	0	28	29.0	127	20	10	9	1	1	0	3	19	0	49	2	0	0	1	.000	0	22-25	0	3.25	2.79
9 ML YEARS		281	0	0	191	296.1	1289	226	134	127	29	12	9	18	176	8	374	14	0	13	18	.419	0	93-112	5	3.67	3.86

Josias Manzanillo

Pitches: R **Bats:** R **Pos:** RP-26   **Ht:** 6'0" **Wt:** 205 **Born:** 10/16/1967 **Age:** 37

Year Team	Lg	G	GS	CG	GF	IP	BFP	H	R	ER	HR	SH	SF	HB	TBB	IBB	SO	WP	Bk	W	L	Pct	ShO	Sv-Op	Hld	ERC	ERA
2004 Albuquerque*	AAA	11	0	0	9	12.0	52	15	8	7	3	0	0	0	1	0	9	0	0	0	1	.000	0	5- -	-	5.13	5.25
1991 Boston	AL	1	0	0	1	1.0	8	2	2	2	0	0	0	0	0	0	0	0	0	0	0	-	0	0-0	0	21.46	18.00
1993 Mil-NYM		16	1	0	6	29.0	140	30	27	22	2	3	3	2	19	3	21	1	0	1	1	.500	0	1-2	0	4.92	6.83
1994 New York	NL	37	0	0	14	47.1	186	34	15	14	4	0	0	3	13	2	48	2	0	3	2	.600	0	2-5	11	2.28	2.66
1995 NYM-NYY		23	0	0	8	33.1	157	37	19	18	4	2	1	2	15	4	25	6	0	1	2	.333	0	0-0	0	4.97	4.86
1997 Seattle	AL	16	0	0	4	18.1	88	19	13	11	3	0	2	0	17	1	18	2	0	0	1	.000	0	0-1	1	6.97	5.40
1999 New York	NL	12	0	0	1	18.2	80	19	12	12	5	1	1	2	4	1	25	0	0	0	0	-	0	0-0	1	4.90	5.79

Year Team	Lg	G	GS	CG	GF	IP	BFP	H	R	ER	HR	SH	SF	HB	TBB	IBB	SO	WP	Bk	W	L	Pct	ShO	Sv-Op	Hld	ERC	ERA
2000 Pittsburgh	NL	43	0	0	11	58.2	246	50	23	22	6	4	2	0	32	4	39	1	0	2	2	.500	0	0-2	5	3.85	3.38
2001 Pittsburgh	NL	71	0	0	25	79.2	329	60	32	30	4	5	8	5	26	3	80	4	0	3	2	.600	0	2-7	9	2.33	3.39
2002 Pittsburgh	NL	13	0	0	5	13.0	61	20	11	11	5	0	0	1	5	0	4	0	0	0	0	-	0	0-1	0	10.63	7.62
2003 Cincinnati	NL	9	0	0	1	10.2	59	21	20	15	7	1	0	0	4	0	12	0	0	0	2	.000	0	0-1	0	14.74	12.66
2004 Florida	NL	26	0	0	7	32.1	151	38	24	22	6	2	1	3	15	2	27	0	0	3	3	.500	0	1-4	5	6.26	6.12
1993 Milwaukee	AL	10	1	0	4	17.0	86	22	20	18	1	2	2	2	10	3	10	1	0	1	1	.500	0	1-2	0	6.15	9.53
1993 New York	AL	6	0	0	2	12.0	54	8	7	4	1	1	1	0	9	0	11	0	0	0	0		0	0-0	0	3.32	3.00
1995 New York	NL	12	0	0	4	16.0	73	18	15	14	3	0	1	0	6	2	14	5	0	1	2	.333	0	0-0	0	4.93	7.88
1995 New York	AL	11	0	0	4	17.1	81	19	4	4	1	2	0	2	9	2	11	1	0	0	0		0	0-0	0	4.96	2.08
11 ML YEARS		267	1	0	83	342.0	1502	330	198	179	46	18	18	18	153	20	300	16	0	13	15	.464	0	6-23	29	4.40	4.71

Mike Maroth

Pitches: L Bats: L Pos: SP-33   Ht: 6'0" Wt: 180 Born: 8/17/1977 Age: 27

Year Team	Lg	G	GS	CG	GF	IP	BFP	H	R	ER	HR	SH	SF	HB	TBB	IBB	SO	WP	Bk	W	L	Pct	ShO	Sv-Op	Hld	ERC	ERA
2002 Detroit	AL	21	21	0	0	128.2	538	136	68	64	7	5	3	2	36	1	58	4	0	6	10	.375	0	0-0	0	3.73	4.48
2003 Detroit	AL	33	33	1	0	193.1	847	231	131	123	34	9	8	8	50	2	87	7	0	9	21	.300	0	0-0	0	5.36	5.73
2004 Detroit	AL	33	33	2	0	217.0	928	244	112	104	25	11	4	7	59	1	108	10	1	11	13	.458	1	0-0	0	4.57	4.31
3 ML YEARS		87	87	3	0	539.0	2313	611	311	291	66	25	15	17	145	4	253	21	1	26	44	.371	1	0-0	0	4.64	4.86

Jason Marquis

Pitches: R Bats: L Pos: SP-32   Ht: 6'1" Wt: 210 Born: 8/21/1978 Age: 26

Year Team	Lg	G	GS	CG	GF	IP	BFP	H	R	ER	HR	SH	SF	HB	TBB	IBB	SO	WP	Bk	W	L	Pct	ShO	Sv-Op	Hld	ERC	ERA
2000 Atlanta	NL	15	0	0	7	23.1	103	23	16	13	4	1	1	1	12	1	17	1	0	1	0	1.000	0	0-1	1	5.13	5.01
2001 Atlanta	NL	38	16	0	9	129.1	556	113	62	50	14	6	5	4	59	4	98	1	2	5	6	.455	0	0-2	2	3.70	3.48
2002 Atlanta	NL	22	22	0	0	114.1	507	127	66	64	19	4	3	3	49	3	84	4	0	8	9	.471	0	0-0	0	5.43	5.04
2003 Atlanta	NL	21	2	0	10	40.2	182	43	27	25	3	0	3	2	18	2	19	2	0	0	0	-	0	1-1	0	4.45	5.53
2004 St Louis	NL	32	32	0	0	201.1	874	215	90	83	26	5	6	10	70	1	138	6	0	15	7	.682	0	0-0	0	4.69	3.71
5 ML YEARS		128	72	0	26	509.0	2222	521	261	235	66	16	18	20	208	11	356	14	2	29	22	.569	0	1-4	3	4.59	4.16

Eli Marrero

Bats: R Throws: R Pos: LF-47; RF-25; PH-19; CF-4; PR-1   Ht: 6'1" Wt: 180 Born: 11/17/1973 Age: 31

Year Team	Lg	G	AB	H	2B	3B	HR	(Hm	Rd)	TB	R	RBI	RC	TBB	IBB	SO	HBP	SH	SF	SB	CS	SB%	GDP	Avg	OBP	Slg
2004 Greenville*	AA	3	12	5	1	0	2	(-	-)	12	3	5	4	2	0	6	0	0	0	0	0	-	1	.417	.500	1.000
2004 Richmond*	AAA	6	24	5	2	0	0	(-	-)	7	1	3	1	1	0	3	0	0	0	0	0	-	0	.208	.240	.292
1997 St Louis	NL	17	45	11	2	0	2	(0	2)	19	4	7	6	2	1	13	0	0	1	4	0	1.00	1	.244	.271	.422
1998 St Louis	NL	83	254	62	18	1	4	(2	2)	94	28	20	30	28	5	42	0	1	1	6	2	.75	5	.244	.318	.370
1999 St Louis	NL	114	317	61	13	1	6	(3	3)	94	32	34	18	18	4	56	1	4	3	11	2	.85	14	.192	.236	.297
2000 St Louis	NL	53	102	23	3	1	5	(2	3)	43	21	17	14	9	0	16	3	0	2	5	0	1.00	3	.225	.302	.422
2001 St Louis	NL	86	203	54	11	3	6	(2	4)	89	37	23	27	15	2	36	0	3	3	6	3	.67	4	.266	.312	.438
2002 St Louis	NL	131	397	104	19	1	18	(9	9)	179	63	66	59	40	11	72	0	5	4	14	2	.88	5	.262	.327	.451
2003 St Louis	NL	41	107	24	4	2	2	(1	1)	38	10	20	15	7	0	18	0	0	2	0	1	.00	0	.224	.267	.355
2004 Atlanta	NL	90	250	80	18	1	10	(6	4)	130	37	40	50	23	1	50	1	2	4	4	1	.80	4	.320	.374	.520
8 ML YEARS		615	1675	419	88	10	53	(25	28)	686	232	227	219	142	24	303	5	15	20	50	11	.82	36	.250	.307	.410

Sam Marsonek

Pitches: R Bats: R Pos: RP-1   Ht: 6'6" Wt: 225 Born: 7/10/1978 Age: 26

Year Team	Lg	G	GS	CG	GF	IP	BFP	H	R	ER	HR	SH	SF	HB	TBB	IBB	SO	WP	Bk	W	L	Pct	ShO	Sv-Op	Hld	ERC	ERA
1997 Charlotte	A+	2	2	0	0	8.1	41	14	10	7	3	0	0	1	2	0	7	3	0	0	2	.000	0	0--	-	10.48	7.56
1997 Pulaski	R+	12	11	0	0	71.2	331	90	57	40	4	2	3	3	20	0	65	13	3	7	3	.700	0	0--	-	4.72	5.02
1998 Savannah	A	2	2	0	0	7.0	36	7	7	3	0	0	1	3	3	0	4	1	0	0	0	-	0	0--	-	4.63	3.86
1998 Rangers	R	2	2	0	0	4.2	18	2	1	0	0	0	0	1	0	0	2	0	0	0	0	-	0	0--	-	0.67	0.00
1999 Charlotte	A+	15	15	2	0	91.0	420	111	69	56	8	4	4	14	27	0	61	4	1	3	9	.250	0	0--	-	5.40	5.54
2000 Greensboro	A	18	18	1	0	114.1	510	114	64	54	8	1	3	23	51	0	78	15	2	6	7	.462	0	0--	-	4.90	4.25
2001 Tampa	A+	24	23	5	0	138.1	590	128	67	54	6	5	2	21	39	2	120	12	1	8	8	.500	2	0--	-	3.38	3.51
2002 Norwich	AA	19	13	1	3	100.2	454	111	68	56	6	4	1	12	34	1	75	6	1	5	8	.385	0	0--	-	4.51	5.01
2003 Columbus	AAA	54	2	0	34	83.2	370	84	52	45	9	2	3	8	31	0	57	3	0	4	4	.500	0	18--	-	4.36	4.84
2004 Yankees	R	2	1	0	1	3.0	11	2	1	1	1	0	0	0	0	0	3	0	0	0	0	-	0	1--	-	1.99	3.00
2004 Tampa	A+	3	0	0	1	4.0	15	3	0	0	0	0	0	0	0	0	3	0	0	0	0	-	0	0--	-	1.13	0.00
2004 Columbus	AAA	35	0	0	30	40.0	170	36	20	14	5	1	0	3	12	2	28	3	0	1	5	.167	0	17--	-	3.47	3.15
2004 New York	AL	1	0	0	1	1.1	6	2	0	0	0	0	0	0	0	0	0	0	0	0	0	-	0	0-0	0	4.47	0.00

Damaso Marte

Pitches: L Bats: L Pos: RP-74   Ht: 6'2" Wt: 200 Born: 2/14/1975 Age: 30

Year Team	Lg	G	GS	CG	GF	IP	BFP	H	R	ER	HR	SH	SF	HB	TBB	IBB	SO	WP	Bk	W	L	Pct	ShO	Sv-Op	Hld	ERC	ERA
1999 Seattle	AL	5	0	0	2	8.2	47	16	9	9	3	0	0	0	6	0	3	0	0	0	1	.000	0	0-0	0	13.32	9.35
2001 Pittsburgh	NL	23	0	0	4	36.1	154	34	21	19	5	1	2	3	12	3	39	1	0	0	1	.000	0	0-0	0	3.93	4.71
2002 Chicago	AL	68	0	0	22	60.1	240	44	19	19	5	1	1	4	18	2	72	3	1	1	1	.500	0	10-12	14	2.42	2.83
2003 Chicago	AL	71	0	0	25	79.2	314	50	16	14	3	3	3	3	34	6	87	1	0	4	2	.667	0	11-18	14	1.96	1.58
2004 Chicago	AL	74	0	0	26	73.2	303	56	28	28	10	2	3	6	34	4	68	3	0	6	5	.545	0	6-12	21	3.39	3.42
5 ML YEARS		241	0	0	77	258.2	1058	200	93	89	26	7	12	13	104	15	269	8	1	11	10	.524	0	27-42	49	3.03	3.10

Tom Martin

Pitches: L Bats: L Pos: RP-76

Ht: 6'1" Wt: 206 Born: 5/21/1970 Age: 35

		HOW MUCH HE PITCHED					WHAT HE GAVE UP											THE RESULTS							
Year Team	Lg	G	GS	CG	GF	IP	BFP	H	R	ER	HR	SH	SF	HB	TBB	IBB	SO	WP	Bk	W	L	Pct	ShO	Sv-Op	Hld	ERC	ERA
1997 Houston	NL	55	0	0	18	56.0	236	52	13	13	2	6	1	1	23	2	36	3	0	5	3	.625	0	2-3	7	3.34	2.09
1998 Cleveland	AL	14	0	0	1	14.2	85	29	21	21	3	1	1	0	12	0	9	2	0	1	1	.500	0	0-0	3	13.19	12.89
1999 Cleveland	AL	6	0	0	0	9.1	44	13	9	9	2	0	1	0	3	1	8	0	0	0	1	.000	0	0-0	0	6.64	8.68
2000 Cleveland	AL	31	0	0	7	33.1	143	32	16	15	3	0	1	0	15	2	21	1	0	1	0	1.000	0	0-0	0	4.05	4.05
2001 New York	NL	14	0	0	2	17.0	85	23	22	19	4	1	1	1	10	2	12	0	0	1	0	1.000	0	0-0	1	8.02	10.06
2002 Tampa Bay	AL	2	0	0	2	1.2	11	5	3	3	0	0	0	0	1	0	1	0	0	0	0	-	0			17.54	16.20
2003 Los Angeles	NL	80	0	0	13	51.0	210	36	21	20	6	0	2	2	24	4	51	1	0	1	2	.333	0	0-1	28	2.94	3.53
2004 LA-Atl	NL	76	0	0	11	45.1	204	49	20	20	7	5	4	3	19	3	30	1	0	0	2	.000	0	1-4	12	5.14	3.97
2004 Los Angeles	NL	47	0	0	9	28.1	132	32	13	13	3	3	2	3	14	1	18	1	0	0	1	.000	0	1-1	5	5.58	4.13
2004 Atlanta	NL	29	0	0	2	17.0	72	17	7	7	4	2	2	0	5	2	12	0	0	0	1	.000	0	0-3	7	4.36	3.71
8 ML YEARS		278	0	0	54	228.1	1018	239	125	120	27	13	11	8	107	14	168	8	0	9	9	.500	0	3-8	51	4.78	4.73

Anastacio Martinez

Pitches: R Bats: R Pos: RP-11

Ht: 6'2" Wt: 180 Born: 11/3/1978 Age: 26

		HOW MUCH HE PITCHED					WHAT HE GAVE UP											THE RESULTS							
Year Team	Lg	G	GS	CG	GF	IP	BFP	H	R	ER	HR	SH	SF	HB	TBB	IBB	SO	WP	Bk	W	L	Pct	ShO	Sv-Op	Hld	ERC	ERA
1998 Red Sox	R	12	10	0	0	51.0	212	45	28	18	2	1	2	3	12	0	50	4	0	2	3	.400	0	0--	-	2.61	3.18
1999 Augusta	A	10	10	0	0	40.0	188	44	37	28	7	0	0	4	18	0	36	1	3	2	4	.333	0	0--	-	5.37	6.30
1999 Lowell	A-	11	11	0	0	51.1	234	61	36	21	4	0	1	4	18	0	43	9	2	0	3	.000	0	0--	-	5.05	3.68
2000 Red Sox	R	2	1	0	0	6.2	38	15	9	7	0	0	1	0	3	0	1	0	0	0	1	.000	0	0--	-	11.23	9.45
2000 Augusta	A	23	23	0	0	120.1	526	130	69	62	8	4	4	2	50	0	107	12	1	9	6	.600	0	0--	-	4.46	4.64
2001 Sarasota	A+	25	24	1	0	145.0	606	130	69	54	12	4	1	9	39	0	123	6	0	9	12	.429	0	0--	-	3.11	3.35
2002 Trenton	AA	27	27	0	0	139.0	637	152	98	82	12	4	2	6	75	0	127	15	1	5	12	.294	0	0--	-	5.23	5.31
2003 Altoona	AA	3	0	0	3	4.0	16	6	1	1	1	0	0	0	1	0	1	1	0	0	0	-	0	0--	-	8.99	2.25
2003 Portland	AA	34	0	0	32	40.0	179	31	13	10	3	1	4	4	24	0	37	5	0	3	1	.750	0	14--	-	3.71	2.25
2003 Pawtucket	AAA	8	0	0	2	14.0	56	12	3	3	2	0	0	0	3	0	15	0	0	2	1	.667	0	0--	-	2.88	1.93
2004 Pawtucket	AAA	38	0	0	12	67.1	308	73	37	28	5	0	2	3	31	2	57	9	0	3	3	.500	0	1--	-	4.63	3.74
2004 Boston	AL	11	0	0	7	10.2	52	13	10	10	2	0	0	1	6	0	5	0	0	2	1	.667	0	0-0	0	7.01	8.44

Edgar Martinez

Bats: R Throws: R Pos: DH-122; PH-23; 3B-1

Ht: 5'11" Wt: 210 Born: 1/2/1963 Age: 42

		BATTING																		BASERUNNING				AVERAGES		
Year Team	Lg	G	AB	H	2B	3B	HR	(Hm	Rd)	TB	R	RBI	RC	TBB	IBB	SO	HBP	SH	SF	SB	CS	SB%	GDP	Avg	OBP	Slg
2004 Portland*	AA	53	141	23	3	0	1	(-	-)	29	9	10	3	3	0	20	5	4	1	0	0	-	3	.163	.207	.206
1987 Seattle	AL	13	43	16	5	2	0	(0	0)	25	6	5	10	2	0	5	1	0	0	0	0	-	0	.372	.413	.581
1988 Seattle	AL	14	32	9	4	0	0	(0	0)	13	0	5	5	4	0	7	0	1	1	0	0	-	0	.281	.351	.406
1989 Seattle	AL	65	171	41	5	0	2	(0	2)	52	20	20	17	17	1	26	3	2	3	2	1	.67	3	.240	.314	.304
1990 Seattle	AL	144	487	147	27	2	11	(3	8)	211	71	49	83	74	3	62	5	1	3	1	4	.20	13	.302	.397	.433
1991 Seattle	AL	150	544	167	35	1	14	(8	6)	246	98	52	97	84	9	72	8	2	4	0	3	.00	19	.307	.405	.452
1992 Seattle	AL	135	528	181	46	3	18	(11	7)	287	100	73	110	54	2	61	4	1	5	14	4	.78	15	.343	.404	.544
1993 Seattle	AL	42	135	32	7	0	4	(1	3)	51	20	13	20	28	1	19	0	1	1	0	0		4	.237	.366	.378
1994 Seattle	AL	89	326	93	23	1	13	(4	9)	157	47	51	63	53	3	42	3	2	3	6	2	.75	2	.285	.387	.482
1995 Seattle	AL	145	511	182	52	0	29	(16	13)	321	121	113	144	116	19	87	8	0	4	4	3	.57	11	.356	.479	.628
1996 Seattle	AL	139	499	163	52	2	26	(14	12)	297	121	103	132	123	12	84	8	0	4	3	3	.50	15	.327	.464	.595
1997 Seattle	AL	155	542	179	35	1	28	(12	16)	300	104	108	130	119	11	86	11	0	6	2	4	.33	21	.330	.456	.554
1998 Seattle	AL	154	556	179	46	1	29	(17	12)	314	86	102	130	106	4	96	3	0	7	1	1	.50	13	.322	.429	.565
1999 Seattle	AL	142	502	169	35	1	24	(12	12)	278	86	86	121	97	6	99	6	0	3	7	2	.78	12	.337	.447	.554
2000 Seattle	AL	153	556	180	31	0	37	(19	18)	322	100	145	130	96	8	95	5	0	8	3	0	1.00	13	.324	.423	.579
2001 Seattle	AL	132	470	144	40	1	23	(10	13)	255	80	116	108	93	9	90	9	0	9	1	1	.80	11	.306	.423	.543
2002 Seattle	AL	97	328	91	23	0	15	(9	6)	159	42	59	60	67	8	69	6	0	6	1	1	.50	6	.277	.403	.485
2003 Seattle	AL	145	497	146	25	0	24	(16	8)	243	72	98	100	92	7	95	7	0	7	0	1	.00	17	.294	.406	.489
2004 Seattle	AL	141	486	128	23	0	12	(5	7)	187	45	63	61	58	10	107	2	0	3	1	0	1.00	15	.263	.342	.385
18 ML YEARS		2055	7213	2247	514	15	309	(149	160)	3718	1219	1261	1522	1283	113	1202	89	10	77	49	30	.62	190	.312	.418	.515

Pedro Martinez

Pitches: R Bats: R Pos: SP-33

Ht: 5'11" Wt: 180 Born: 10/25/1971 Age: 33

		HOW MUCH HE PITCHED					WHAT HE GAVE UP											THE RESULTS							
Year Team	Lg	G	GS	CG	GF	IP	BFP	H	R	ER	HR	SH	SF	HB	TBB	IBB	SO	WP	Bk	W	L	Pct	ShO	Sv-Op	Hld	ERC	ERA
1992 Los Angeles	NL	2	1	0	1	8.0	31	6	2	2	0	0	0	0	1	0	8	0	0	0	1	.000	0	0-0	0	1.38	2.25
1993 Los Angeles	NL	65	2	0	20	107.0	444	76	34	31	5	0	5	4	57	4	119	3	1	10	5	.667	0	2-3	14	2.79	2.61
1994 Montreal	NL	24	23	1	1	144.2	584	115	58	55	11	2	3	11	45	3	142	6	0	11	5	.688	1	1-1	0	2.81	3.42
1995 Montreal	NL	30	30	2	0	194.2	784	158	79	76	21	7	3	11	66	1	174	5	2	14	10	.583	2	0-0	0	3.19	3.51
1996 Montreal	NL	33	33	4	0	216.2	901	189	100	89	19	9	6	3	70	3	222	6	0	13	10	.565	1	0-0	0	3.02	3.70
1997 Montreal	NL	31	31	13	0	241.1	947	158	65	51	16	9	1	9	67	5	305	3	1	17	8	.680	4	0-0	0	1.79	1.90
1998 Boston	AL	33	33	3	0	233.2	951	188	82	75	26	4	7	8	67	3	251	9	0	19	7	.731	2	0-0	0	2.78	2.89
1999 Boston	AL	31	29	5	1	213.1	835	160	56	49	9	3	6	9	37	1	313	6	0	23	4	.852	1	0-0	0	1.79	2.07
2000 Boston	AL	29	29	7	0	217.0	817	128	44	42	17	2	1	14	32	0	284	1	0	18	6	.750	4	0-0	0	1.39	1.74
2001 Boston	AL	18	18	1	0	116.2	456	84	33	31	5	2	0	6	25	0	163	4	0	7	3	.700	0	0-0	5	1.84	2.39
2002 Boston	AL	30	30	2	0	199.1	787	144	62	50	13	2	4	15	40	1	239	3	0	20	4	.833	2	0-0	0	1.98	2.26
2003 Boston	AL	29	29	3	0	186.2	749	147	52	46	7	4	4	9	47	0	206	0	0	14	4	.778	0	0-0	0	2.22	2.22
2004 Boston	AL	33	33	1	0	217.0	903	193	99	94	26	5	9	16	61	0	227	2	0	16	9	.640	1	0-0	0	3.44	3.90
13 ML YEARS		388	321	42	23	2296.0	9189	1746	766	691	175	49	49	115	615	21	2653	53	4	182	76	.705	16	3-4	14	2.37	2.71

Ramon Martinez

Bats: R **Throws:** R **Pos:** SS-73; 3B-24; PH-12; 2B-6; PR-3   **Ht:** 6'1" **Wt:** 183 **Born:** 10/10/1972 **Age:** 32

Year Team	Lg	G	AB	H	2B	3B	HR	(Hm	Rd)	TB	R	RBI	RC	TBB	IBB	SO	HBP	SH	SF	SB	CS	SB%	GDP	Avg	OBP	Slg
1998 San Francisco	NL	19	19	6	1	0	0	(0	0)	7	4	0	4	4	0	2	0	1	0	0	0	-	0	.316	.435	.368
1999 San Francisco	NL	61	144	38	6	0	5	(3	2)	59	21	19	19	14	0	17	0	6	1	1	2	.33	2	.264	.327	.410
2000 San Francisco	NL	88	189	57	13	2	6	(4	2)	92	30	25	31	15	1	22	1	4	1	3	2	.60	6	.302	.354	.487
2001 San Francisco	NL	128	391	99	18	3	5	(1	4)	138	48	37	44	38	6	52	5	6	6	1	2	.33	11	.253	.323	.353
2002 San Francisco	NL	72	181	49	10	2	4	(4	0)	75	26	25	32	14	2	26	4	0	1	2	0	1.00	1	.271	.335	.414
2003 Chicago	NL	108	293	83	16	1	3	(3	0)	110	30	34	34	24	1	50	2	6	8	0	1	.00	8	.283	.333	.375
2004 Chicago	NL	102	260	64	15	1	3	(1	2)	90	22	30	28	26	3	40	1	7	4	0	1	1.00	5	.246	.313	.346
7 ML YEARS		578	1477	396	79	9	26	(16	10)	571	181	170	192	135	13	209	13	30	21	8	7	.53	33	.268	.330	.387

Sandy Martinez

Bats: L **Throws:** R **Pos:** C-4; PH-1   **Ht:** 6'2" **Wt:** 215 **Born:** 10/8/1970 **Age:** 34

Year Team	Lg	G	AB	H	2B	3B	HR	(Hm	Rd)	TB	R	RBI	RC	TBB	IBB	SO	HBP	SH	SF	SB	CS	SB%	GDP	Avg	OBP	Slg
2004 Buffalo*	AAA	62	197	54	8	1	17	(-	-)	115	29	47	32	12	2	44	0	4	0	2	0	1.00	7	.274	.316	.584
1995 Toronto	AL	62	191	46	12	0	2	(1	1)	64	12	25	16	7	0	45	1	0	1	0	0	-	0	.241	.270	.335
1996 Toronto	AL	76	229	52	9	3	3	(2	1)	76	17	18	21	16	0	58	4	1	1	0	0	-	4	.227	.288	.332
1997 Toronto	AL	3	2	0	0	0	0	(0	0)	0	1	0	0	1	0	1	0	0	0	0	0	-	0	.000	.333	.000
1998 Chicago	NL	45	87	23	9	1	0	(0	0)	34	7	7	12	13	0	21	1	0	1	1	0	1.00	3	.264	.363	.391
1999 Chicago	NL	17	30	5	0	0	1	(0	1)	8	1	1	0	0	0	11	0	0	0	0	0	-	0	.167	.167	.267
2000 Florida	NL	10	18	4	2	0	0	(0	0)	6	1	0	1	0	0	8	0	0	0	0	0	-	0	.222	.222	.333
2001 Montreal	NL	1	1	0	0	0	0	(0	0)	0	0	0	0	0	0	0	0	0	0	0	0	-	1	.000	.000	.000
2004 Cle-Bos	AL	4	6	0	0	0	0	(0	0)	0	0	0	0	0	0	3	0	0	0	0	0	-	0	.000	.000	.000
2004 Cleveland	AL	1	2	0	0	0	0	(0	0)	0	0	0	0	0	0	1	0	0	0	0	0	-	0	.000	.000	.000
2004 Boston	AL	3	4	0	0	0	0	(0	0)	0	0	0	0	0	0	2	0	0	0	0	0	-	0	.000	.000	.000
8 ML YEARS		218	564	130	32	4	6	(3	3)	188	39	51	50	37	0	147	6	1	3	1	0	1.00	9	.230	.284	.333

Tino Martinez

Bats: L **Throws:** R **Pos:** 1B-114; DH-19; PH-8   **Ht:** 6'2" **Wt:** 210 **Born:** 12/7/1967 **Age:** 37

Year Team	Lg	G	AB	H	2B	3B	HR	(Hm	Rd)	TB	R	RBI	RC	TBB	IBB	SO	HBP	SH	SF	SB	CS	SB%	GDP	Avg	OBP	Slg
1990 Seattle	AL	24	68	15	4	0	0	(0	0)	19	4	5	7	9	0	9	0	0	1	0	0	-	0	.221	.308	.279
1991 Seattle	AL	36	112	23	2	0	4	(3	1)	37	11	9	10	11	0	24	0	0	2	0	0	-	2	.205	.272	.330
1992 Seattle	AL	136	460	118	19	2	16	(10	6)	189	53	66	54	42	9	77	2	1	8	2	1	.67	24	.257	.316	.411
1993 Seattle	AL	109	408	108	25	1	17	(9	8)	186	48	60	62	45	9	56	5	3	3	0	3	.00	7	.265	.343	.456
1994 Seattle	AL	97	329	86	21	0	20	(8	12)	167	42	61	51	29	2	52	1	4	3	1	2	.33	9	.261	.320	.508
1995 Seattle	AL	141	519	152	35	3	31	(14	17)	286	92	111	102	62	15	91	4	2	6	0	0	-	10	.293	.369	.551
1996 New York	AL	155	595	174	28	0	25	(9	16)	277	82	117	97	68	4	85	2	1	5	2	1	.67	18	.292	.364	.466
1997 New York	AL	158	594	176	31	2	44	(18	26)	343	96	141	122	75	14	75	3	0	13	3	1	.75	15	.296	.371	.577
1998 New York	AL	142	531	149	33	1	28	(12	16)	268	92	123	92	61	3	83	6	0	10	2	1	.67	18	.281	.355	.505
1999 New York	AL	159	589	155	27	2	28	(7	21)	270	95	105	90	69	7	86	3	0	4	3	4	.43	14	.263	.341	.458
2000 New York	AL	155	569	147	37	4	16	(12	4)	240	69	91	76	52	9	74	8	0	3	4	1	.80	16	.258	.328	.422
2001 New York	AL	154	589	165	24	2	34	(22	12)	295	89	113	93	42	2	89	2	0	2	1	2	.33	12	.280	.329	.501
2002 St Louis	NL	150	511	134	25	1	21	(12	9)	224	63	75	70	58	9	71	2	1	4	3	2	.60	12	.262	.337	.438
2003 St Louis	NL	138	476	130	25	2	15	(6	9)	204	66	69	64	53	7	71	9	2	7	1	1	.50	14	.273	.352	.461
2004 Tampa Bay	AL	138	458	120	20	1	23	(9	14)	211	63	76	77	66	9	72	9	0	5	3	1	.75	10	.262	.362	.461
15 ML YEARS		1892	6808	1852	356	21	322	(151	171)	3216	965	1222	1067	742	99	1015	56	14	76	25	20	.56	181	.272	.345	.472

Victor Martinez

Bats: B **Throws:** R **Pos:** C-132; PH-9; DH-7   **Ht:** 6'2" **Wt:** 170 **Born:** 12/23/1978 **Age:** 26

Year Team	Lg	G	AB	H	2B	3B	HR	(Hm	Rd)	TB	R	RBI	RC	TBB	IBB	SO	HBP	SH	SF	SB	CS	SB%	GDP	Avg	OBP	Slg
2002 Cleveland	AL	12	32	9	1	0	1	(1	0)	13	2	5	5	3	0	2	0	0	1	0	0	-	1	.281	.333	.406
2003 Cleveland	AL	49	159	46	4	0	1	(0	1)	53	15	16	17	13	0	21	1	0	1	1	1	.50	8	.289	.345	.333
2004 Cleveland	AL	141	520	147	38	1	23	(8	15)	256	77	108	89	60	11	69	5	0	6	0	1	.00	16	.283	.359	.492
3 ML YEARS		202	711	202	43	1	25	(9	16)	322	94	129	111	76	11	92	6	0	8	1	2	.33	25	.284	.355	.453

Henry Mateo

Bats: B **Throws:** R **Pos:** PH-28; 2B-9; PR-4; LF-1   **Ht:** 5'11" **Wt:** 170 **Born:** 10/14/1976 **Age:** 28

Year Team	Lg	G	AB	H	2B	3B	HR	(Hm	Rd)	TB	R	RBI	RC	TBB	IBB	SO	HBP	SH	SF	SB	CS	SB%	GDP	Avg	OBP	Slg
2004 Expos*	R	5	14	4	2	0	0	(-	-)	6	7	2	5	6	0	2	2	0	0	4	0	1.00	0	.286	.545	.429
2004 Edmonton*	AAA	30	119	36	8	3	0	(-	-)	50	23	9	17	8	0	16	2	0	1	10	1	.91	5	.303	.354	.420
2001 Montreal	NL	5	9	3	1	0	0	(0	0)	4	1	0	1	0	0	1	0	0	0	0	0	-	0	.333	.333	.444
2002 Montreal	NL	22	23	4	0	1	0	(0	0)	6	1	0	1	2	1	6	0	0	0	2	0	1.00	0	.174	.240	.261
2003 Montreal	NL	100	154	37	3	1	0	(0	0)	42	29	7	16	11	0	38	3	1	0	11	1	.92	0	.240	.304	.273
2004 Montreal	NL	40	44	12	2	0	0	(0	0)	14	3	0	1	1	0	9	0	1	0	2	3	.40	1	.273	.289	.318
4 ML YEARS		167	230	56	6	2	0	(0	0)	66	34	7	19	14	1	54	3	2	0	15	4	.79	1	.243	.296	.287

Julio Mateo

Pitches: R **Bats:** R **Pos:** RP-45   **Ht:** 6'0" **Wt:** 177 **Born:** 8/2/1977 **Age:** 27

			HOW MUCH HE PITCHED						WHAT HE GAVE UP										THE RESULTS						
Year Team	Lg	G	GS	CG	GF	IP	BFP	H	R	ER	HR	SH	SF	HB	TBB	IBB	SO	WP	Bk	W	L	Pct	ShO	Sv-Op	Hld	ERC	ERA
2002 Seattle	AL	12	0	0	7	21.0	94	20	10	10	2	0	0	1	12	0	15	1	0	0	0	-	0	0-0	2	4.63	4.29

			HOW MUCH HE PITCHED					WHAT HE GAVE UP											THE RESULTS							
Year Team		Lg	G	GS	CG	GF	IP	BFP	H	R	ER	HR	SH	SF	HB	TBB	IBB	SO	WP	Bk	W	L	Pct	ShO	Sv-Op	Hld	ERC	ERA
2003 Seattle		AL	50	0	0	17	85.2	338	69	32	30	14	2	4	5	13	1	71	1	1	4	0	1.000	0	1-1	2	2.71	3.15
2004 Seattle		AL	45	0	0	9	57.2	248	56	30	30	11	0	4	5	16	3	43	2	0	1	2	.333	0	1-4	6	4.26	4.68
3 ML YEARS			107	0	0	33	164.1	680	145	72	70	27	2	8	11	41	4	129	4	1	5	2	.714	0	2-5	10	3.48	3.83

Ruben Mateo

Bats: R **Throws:** R **Pos:** RF-19; LF-13; PH-11; CF-10; DH-1; PR-1   **Ht:** 6'0" **Wt:** 185 **Born:** 2/10/1978 **Age:** 27

							BATTING											BASERUNNING				AVERAGES		
Year Team		Lg	G	AB	H	2B	3B	HR	(Hm | Rd)	TB	R	RBI	RC	TBB	IBB	SO	HBP	SH	SF	SB	CS	SB%	GDP	Avg	OBP	Slg
1999 Texas	AL	32	122	29	9	1	5	(2 | 3)	55	16	18	15	4	0	28	1	0	0	3	0	1.00	2	.238	.268	.451
2000 Texas	AL	52	206	60	11	0	7	(3 | 4)	92	32	19	31	10	1	34	5	1	0	6	0	1.00	5	.291	.339	.447
2001 Texas	AL	40	129	32	5	2	1	(0 | 1)	44	18	13	14	9	0	28	6	1	2	1	0	1.00	4	.248	.322	.341
2002 Cincinnati	NL	46	86	22	6	0	2	(2 | 0)	34	11	7	7	6	0	20	2	0	0	0	0	-	1	.256	.319	.395
2003 Cincinnati	NL	74	207	50	9	0	3	(2 | 1)	68	16	18	21	12	1	53	3	0	2	0	0	-	4	.242	.290	.329
2004 Pit-KC		51	126	26	4	3	3	(1 | 2)	45	13	14	13	8	1	26	3	0	0	1	1	.50	3	.206	.270	.357
2004 Pittsburgh	NL	19	33	8	0	0	3	(1 | 2)	17	4	7	7	5	1	6	1	0	0	0	0	-	1	.242	.359	.515
2004 Kansas City	AL	32	93	18	4	3	0	(0 | 0)	28	9	7	6	3	0	20	2	0	0	1	1	.50	2	.194	.235	.301
6 ML YEARS		295	876	219	44	6	21	(10 | 11)	338	106	89	101	49	3	189	20	2	4	11	1	.92	19	.250	.303	.386

Mike Matheny

Bats: R **Throws:** R **Pos:** C-122; PH-2; 1B-1   **Ht:** 6'3" **Wt:** 205 **Born:** 9/22/1970 **Age:** 34

							BATTING											BASERUNNING				AVERAGES		
Year Team		Lg	G	AB	H	2B	3B	HR	(Hm | Rd)	TB	R	RBI	RC	TBB	IBB	SO	HBP	SH	SF	SB	CS	SB%	GDP	Avg	OBP	Slg
1994 Milwaukee	AL	28	53	12	3	0	1	(1 | 0)	18	3	2	5	3	0	13	2	1	0	0	1	.00	1	.226	.293	.340
1995 Milwaukee	AL	80	166	41	9	1	0	(0 | 0)	52	13	21	16	12	0	28	2	1	0	2	1	.67	3	.247	.306	.313
1996 Milwaukee	AL	106	313	64	15	2	8	(5 | 3)	107	31	46	23	14	0	80	3	7	4	3	2	.60	9	.204	.243	.342
1997 Milwaukee	AL	123	320	78	16	1	4	(2 | 2)	108	29	32	30	17	0	68	7	9	3	0	1	.00	6	.244	.294	.338
1998 Milwaukee	NL	108	320	76	13	0	6	(4 | 2)	107	24	27	28	11	0	63	7	3	0	1	0	1.00	6	.238	.278	.334
1999 Toronto	AL	57	163	35	6	0	3	(1 | 2)	50	16	17	13	12	0	37	1	2	1	0	0	-	3	.215	.271	.307
2000 St Louis	NL	128	417	109	22	1	6	(2 | 4)	151	43	47	46	32	8	96	4	7	4	0	0	-	11	.261	.317	.362
2001 St Louis	NL	121	381	83	12	0	7	(4 | 3)	116	40	42	29	28	5	76	4	8	3	0	1	.00	11	.218	.276	.304
2002 St Louis	NL	110	315	77	12	1	3	(1 | 2)	100	31	35	36	32	6	49	2	8	6	1	3	.25	3	.244	.313	.317
2003 St Louis	NL	141	441	111	18	2	8	(4 | 4)	157	43	47	52	44	16	81	2	8	3	1	1	.50	11	.252	.320	.356
2004 St Louis	NL	122	385	95	22	1	5	(4 | 1)	134	28	50	32	23	7	83	3	5	3	0	2	.00	12	.247	.292	.348
11 ML YEARS		1124	3274	781	148	9	51	(28 | 23)	1100	301	366	310	228	42	674	37	59	27	8	12	.40	79	.239	.293	.336

Luis Matos

Bats: R **Throws:** R **Pos:** CF-89; PR-1   **Ht:** 6'0" **Wt:** 179 **Born:** 10/30/1978 **Age:** 26

							BATTING											BASERUNNING				AVERAGES		
Year Team		Lg	G	AB	H	2B	3B	HR	(Hm | Rd)	TB	R	RBI	RC	TBB	IBB	SO	HBP	SH	SF	SB	CS	SB%	GDP	Avg	OBP	Slg
2000 Baltimore	AL	72	182	41	6	3	1	(1 | 0)	56	21	17	15	12	0	30	3	2	1	13	4	.76	1	.225	.281	.308
2001 Baltimore	AL	31	98	21	7	0	4	(1 | 3)	40	16	12	14	11	0	30	1	2	0	7	0	1.00	1	.214	.300	.408
2002 Baltimore	AL	17	31	4	1	0	0	(0 | 0)	5	0	1	0	1	0	6	0	1	0	1	0	1.00	1	.129	.156	.161
2003 Baltimore	AL	109	439	133	23	3	13	(6 | 7)	201	70	45	66	28	0	90	7	10	2	15	7	.68	9	.303	.353	.458
2004 Baltimore	AL	89	330	74	18	0	6	(2 | 4)	110	36	28	27	19	2	60	5	3	2	12	4	.75	7	.224	.275	.333
5 ML YEARS		318	1080	273	55	6	24	(10 | 14)	412	143	103	122	71	2	216	16	18	6	48	15	.76	25	.253	.307	.381

Hideki Matsui

Bats: L **Throws:** R **Pos:** LF-162; CF-3   **Ht:** 6'2" **Wt:** 210 **Born:** 6/12/1974 **Age:** 31

							BATTING											BASERUNNING				AVERAGES		
Year Team		Lg	G	AB	H	2B	3B	HR	(Hm | Rd)	TB	R	RBI	RC	TBB	IBB	SO	HBP	SH	SF	SB	CS	SB%	GDP	Avg	OBP	Slg
1993 Yomiuri	Jap	57	184	41	9	0	11	(- | -)	83	27	27	24	17	0	50	2	0	0	1	0	1.00	1	.223	.296	.451
1994 Yomiuri	Jap	130	503	148	23	4	20	(- | -)	239	70	66	86	57	1	101	4	1	4	6	3	.67	12	.294	.368	.475
1995 Yomiuri	Jap	131	501	142	31	1	22	(- | -)	241	76	80	83	62	1	93	2	2	2	9	7	.56	12	.283	.363	.481
1996 Yomiuri	Jap	130	487	153	34	1	38	(- | -)	303	97	99	114	71	1	98	4	0	7	7	2	.78	5	.314	.401	.622
1997 Yomiuri	Jap	135	484	144	18	0	37	(- | -)	273	93	103	114	100	10	84	6	0	6	9	3	.75	5	.298	.419	.564
1998 Yomiuri	Jap	135	487	142	24	3	34	(- | -)	274	103	100	113	104	2	101	8	0	4	3	5	.38	7	.292	.421	.563
1999 Yomiuri	Jap	135	471	143	24	2	42	(- | -)	297	100	95	117	93	0	99	2	0	6	0	4	.00	3	.304	.416	.631
2000 Yomiuri	Jap	135	474	150	32	1	42	(- | -)	310	116	108	129	106	5	108	2	0	7	5	2	.71	1	.316	.438	.654
2001 Yomiuri	Jap	140	481	160	23	3	36	(- | -)	297	107	104	132	120	6	96	3	0	7	3	3	.50	9	.333	.463	.617
2002 Yomiuri	Jap	140	500	167	27	1	50	(- | -)	346	112	107	145	114	17	104	6	0	3	3	4	.43	4	.334	.461	.692
2003 New York	AL	163	623	179	42	1	16	(9 | 7)	271	82	106	96	63	5	86	3	0	6	2	2	.50	25	.287	.353	.435
2004 New York	AL	162	584	174	34	2	31	(18 | 13)	305	109	108	117	88	2	103	3	0	5	3	0	1.00	11	.298	.390	.522
2 ML YEARS		325	1207	353	76	3	47	(27 | 20)	576	191	214	213	151	7	189	6	0	11	5	2	.71	36	.292	.371	.477

Kazuo Matsui

Bats: B **Throws:** R **Pos:** SS-111; 2B-3; PH-2; PR-1   **Ht:** 5'10" **Wt:** 183 **Born:** 10/23/1975 **Age:** 29

							BATTING											BASERUNNING				AVERAGES		
Year Team		Lg	G	AB	H	2B	3B	HR	(Hm | Rd)	TB	R	RBI	RC	TBB	IBB	SO	HBP	SH	SF	SB	CS	SB%	GDP	Avg	OBP	Slg
1995 Seibu	Jap	69	204	45	9	1	2	(- | -)	62	25	15	18	7	-	26	0	7	1	21	1	.95	4	.221	.245	.304
1996 Seibu	Jap	130	473	134	22	5	1	(- | -)	169	51	29	59	14	-	93	3	26	2	50	9	.85	2	.283	.307	.357
1997 Seibu	Jap	135	576	178	23	13	7	(- | -)	248	91	63	98	44	-	89	5	18	2	62	15	.81	4	.309	.362	.431
1998 Seibu	Jap	135	575	179	38	5	9	(- | -)	254	92	58	99	55	-	89	1	6	4	43	14	.75	10	.311	.370	.442
1999 Seibu	Jap	135	539	178	24	4	15	(- | -)	260	87	67	106	56	-	75	0	8	6	32	7	.82	7	.330	.389	.482
2000 Seibu	Jap	135	550	177	40	11	23	(- | -)	308	99	90	117	46	-	60	2	6	7	26	3	.90	8	.322	.372	.560
2001 Seibu	Jap	140	552	170	28	2	24	(- | -)	274	94	76	106	46	-	83	6	4	5	26	0	1.00	13	.308	.365	.496
2002 Seibu	Jap	140	582	193	46	6	36	(- | -)	359	119	87	136	53	-	112	4	9	3	33	11	.75	3	.332	.389	.617
2003 Seibu	Jap	140	587	179	36	4	33	(- | -)	322	104	84	115	55	-	124	4	3	6	13	10	.57	4	.305	.365	.549
2004 New York	NL	114	460	125	32	2	7	(4 | 3)	182	65	44	63	40	4	97	2	5	2	14	3	.82	3	.272	.331	.396

Daisuke Matsuzaka

Pitches: R **Bats:** R **Pos:** SP　　　　　　　　　　**Ht:** 6'0" **Wt:** 187 **Born:** 9/13/1980 **Age:** 24

Year Team	Lg	G	GS	CG	GF	IP	BFP	H	R	ER	HR	SH	SF	HB	TBB	IBB	SO	WP	Bk	W	L	Pct	ShO	Sv-Op	Hld	ERC	ERA
1999 Seibu	Jap	25	18	6	1	180.0	743	124	55	52	14	-	-	8	87	-	151	5	-	16	5	.762	2	0--	-	2.65	2.60
2000 Seibu	Jap	27	18	6	2	167.2	727	132	85	74	12	-	-	4	95	-	144	2	-	14	7	.667	2	1--	-	3.27	3.97
2001 Seibu	Jap	33	20	12	1	240.1	1004	184	104	96	27	-	-	8	117	-	214	9	-	15	15	.500	2	0--	-	3.26	3.60
2002 Seibu	Jap	14	9	2	0	73.1	302	60	30	30	13	-	-	7	15	-	78	2	-	6	2	.750	0	0--	-	3.08	3.68
2003 Seibu	Jap	29	19	8	1	194.0	801	165	71	61	13	-	-	9	63	-	215	4	-	16	7	.696	2	0--	-	2.88	2.83
2004 Seibu	Jap	23	23	10	0	143.1	605	127	50	47	7	-	-	6	42	-	127	5	-	10	6	.625	0	0--	-	2.75	2.95

Mike Matthews

Pitches: L **Bats:** L **Pos:** RP-35　　　　　　　　　　**Ht:** 6'2" **Wt:** 175 **Born:** 10/24/1973 **Age:** 31

Year Team	Lg	G	GS	CG	GF	IP	BFP	H	R	ER	HR	SH	SF	HB	TBB	IBB	SO	WP	Bk	W	L	Pct	ShO	Sv-Op	Hld	ERC	ERA
2004 Louisville*	AAA	15	0	0	3	17.2	69	12	3	3	1	0	0	0	5	0	16	3	0	1	0	1.000	0	1--	-	1.78	1.53
2000 St Louis	NL	14	0	0	4	9.1	54	15	12	12	2	0	0	1	10	2	8	0	0	0	0	-	0	0-0	2	11.83	11.57
2001 St Louis	NL	51	10	0	7	89.0	368	74	32	32	11	4	1	4	33	4	72	4	1	3	4	.429	0	1-3	5	3.34	3.24
2002 StL-Mil	NL	47	0	0	10	45.2	205	43	23	20	5	2	4	2	29	3	34	5	1	2	1	.667	0	0-2	4	4.84	3.94
2003 San Diego	NL	77	0	0	20	64.2	282	65	34	32	4	3	5	4	29	5	44	4	0	6	4	.600	0	0-3	16	4.18	4.45
2004 Cincinnati	NL	35	0	0	6	30.0	137	31	22	21	7	1	1	2	16	1	15	4	1	2	1	.667	0	0-0	5	6.01	6.30
2002 St Louis	NL	43	0	0	10	41.2	184	40	21	18	5	2	4	2	22	2	32	5	0	2	1	.667	0	0-2	4	4.64	3.89
2002 Milwaukee	NL	4	0	0	0	4.0	21	3	2	2	0	0	0	0	7	1	2	0	1	0	0	-	0	0-0	0	6.63	4.50
5 ML YEARS		224	10	0	47	238.2	1046	228	123	117	29	10	11	13	117	15	173	17	3	13	10	.565	0	1-8	30	4.47	4.41

Gary Matthews Jr.

Bats: B **Throws:** R **Pos:** RF-66; CF-30; LF-3; PH-2; PR-2　　　　**Ht:** 6'3" **Wt:** 210 **Born:** 8/25/1974 **Age:** 30

Year Team	Lg	G	AB	H	2B	3B	HR	(Hm	Rd)	TB	R	RBI	RC	TBB	IBB	SO	HBP	SH	SF	SB	CS	SB%	GDP	Avg	OBP	Slg
2004 Oklahoma*	AAA	38	145	47	9	4	9	(-	-)	91	33	36	35	23	1	29	0	0	3	4	1	.80	2	.324	.409	.628
1999 San Diego	NL	23	36	8	0	0	0	(0	0)	8	4	7	4	9	0	9	0	0	0	2	0	1.00	1	.222	.378	.222
2000 Chicago	NL	80	158	30	1	2	4	(2	2)	47	24	14	13	15	1	28	1	1	0	3	0	1.00	3	.190	.264	.297
2001 ChC-Pit	NL	152	405	92	15	2	14	(4	10)	153	63	44	51	60	2	100	1	5	1	8	5	.62	8	.227	.328	.378
2002 NYM-Bal		111	345	95	25	3	7	(6	1)	147	54	38	55	43	1	69	1	5	4	15	5	.75	4	.275	.354	.426
2003 Bal-SD		144	468	116	31	2	6	(3	3)	169	71	42	51	43	0	95	2	0	0	12	8	.60	8	.248	.314	.361
2004 Texas	AL	87	280	77	17	1	11	(7	4)	129	37	36	48	33	5	64	1	0	3	5	1	.83	1	.275	.350	.461
2001 Chicago	NL	106	258	56	9	1	9	(2	7)	94	41	30	31	38	2	55	1	5	0	5	3	.63	4	.217	.320	.364
2001 Pittsburgh	NL	46	147	36	6	1	5	(2	3)	59	22	14	20	22	0	45	0	0	1	3	2	.60	4	.245	.341	.401
2002 New York	NL	2	1	0	0	0	0	(0	0)	0	0	0	0	0	0	0	0	0	0	0	0	-	0	.000	.000	.000
2002 Baltimore	AL	109	344	95	25	3	7	(6	1)	147	54	38	55	43	1	69	1	5	4	15	5	.75	4	.276	.355	.427
2003 Baltimore	AL	41	162	33	12	1	2	(2	0)	53	21	20	15	9	0	29	1	0	0	0	3	.00	4	.204	.250	.327
2003 San Diego	NL	103	306	83	19	1	4	(1	3)	116	50	22	36	34	0	66	1	0	0	12	5	.71	4	.271	.346	.379
6 ML YEARS		597	1692	418	89	10	42	(22	20)	653	253	181	222	203	9	365	6	11	8	45	19	.70	24	.247	.328	.386

Joe Mauer

Bats: L **Throws:** R **Pos:** C-32; PH-5; DH-1　　　　　　**Ht:** 6'4" **Wt:** 220 **Born:** 4/19/1983 **Age:** 22

Year Team	Lg	G	AB	H	2B	3B	HR	(Hm	Rd)	TB	R	RBI	RC	TBB	IBB	SO	HBP	SH	SF	SB	CS	SB%	GDP	Avg	OBP	Slg
2001 Elizabethton	R+	32	110	44	6	2	0	(-	-)	54	14	14	26	19	0	10	1	0	0	4	0	1.00	5	.400	.492	.491
2002 Quad City	A	110	411	124	23	1	4	(-	-)	161	58	62	64	61	4	42	2	0	2	0	0	-	16	.302	.393	.392
2003 Fort Myers	A+	62	233	78	13	1	1	(-	-)	96	25	44	37	24	3	24	1	0	3	3	0	1.00	11	.335	.395	.412
2003 New Britain	AA	73	276	94	17	1	4	(-	-)	125	48	41	48	25	4	25	5	0	4	0	0	-	10	.341	.400	.453
2004 Fort Myers	A+	2	6	4	0	0	0	(-	-)	4	0	2	2	2	1	2	0	0	0	0	0	-	0	.667	.750	.667
2004 Rochester	AAA	5	19	6	3	0	0	(-	-)	9	1	2	2	1	0	4	0	0	1	0	0	-	1	.316	.333	.474
2004 Minnesota	AL	35	107	33	8	1	6	(4	2)	61	18	17	21	11	0	14	1	0	3	1	0	1.00	1	.308	.369	.570

Dave Maurer

Pitches: L **Bats:** R **Pos:** RP-3　　　　　　　　　　**Ht:** 6'2" **Wt:** 205 **Born:** 2/23/1975 **Age:** 30

Year Team	Lg	G	GS	CG	GF	IP	BFP	H	R	ER	HR	SH	SF	HB	TBB	IBB	SO	WP	Bk	W	L	Pct	ShO	Sv-Op	Hld	ERC	ERA
2004 Syracuse*	AAA	43	4	0	9	65.2	278	58	27	26	7	1	1	5	26	0	64	3	0	0	0	-	0	2--	3	3.79	3.56
2000 San Diego	NL	14	0	0	1	14.2	64	15	8	6	2	0	0	2	5	1	13	1	0	1	0	1.000	0	0-1	2	4.71	3.68
2001 San Diego	NL	3	0	0	1	5.0	27	6	6	6	1	0	0	0	4	0	4	1	0	0	0	-	0	0-0	0	10.33	10.80
2002 Cleveland	AL	2	0	0	2	1.1	7	3	2	2	1	0	0	0	0	0	0	0	0	0	0	.000	0	0-0	0	16.20	13.50
2004 Toronto	AL	3	0	0	0	1.1	15	8	8	8	1	0	0	0	5	0	1	0	0	0	0	-	0	0-0	0	58.57	54.00
4 ML YEARS		22	0	0	4	22.1	113	32	24	22	5	0	0	2	14	1	18	2	0	1	1	.500	0	0-1	2	9.09	8.87

Darrell May

Pitches: L **Bats:** L **Pos:** SP-31　　　　　　　　　　**Ht:** 6'2" **Wt:** 184 **Born:** 6/13/1972 **Age:** 33

Year Team	Lg	G	GS	CG	GF	IP	BFP	H	R	ER	HR	SH	SF	HB	TBB	IBB	SO	WP	Bk	W	L	Pct	ShO	Sv-Op	Hld	ERC	ERA
1995 Atlanta	NL	2	0	0	1	4.0	21	10	5	5	0	0	1	0	0	0	1	0	0	0	0	-	0	0-0	0	11.41	11.25
1996 Pit-Cal		10	2	0	2	11.1	60	18	13	12	6	0	2	1	6	0	6	0	0	0	1	.000	0	0-0	1	12.24	9.53
1997 Anaheim	AL	29	2	0	7	51.2	234	56	31	30	6	3	4	0	25	2	42	2	0	2	1	.667	0	0-1	2	4.87	5.23
2002 Kansas City	AL	30	21	2	3	131.1	579	144	83	78	28	3	5	1	50	3	95	2	0	4	10	.286	1	0-1	0	5.35	5.35
2003 Kansas City	AL	35	32	2	1	210.0	868	197	98	88	31	5	6	2	53	1	115	5	0	10	8	.556	1	0-0	0	3.50	3.77
2004 Kansas City	AL	31	31	3	0	186.0	832	234	130	116	38	1	9	2	55	4	120	2	0	9	**19**	.321	1	0-0	0	5.94	5.61

		HOW MUCH HE PITCHED					WHAT HE GAVE UP										THE RESULTS					
Year Team	Lg	G	GS	CG	GF	IP	BFP	H	R	ER	HR	SH	SF	HB	TBB	IBB	SO	WP	Bk	W	L	Pct	ShO
1996 Pittsburgh	NL	5	2	0	0	8.2	47	15	10	9	5	0	0	1	4	0	5	0	0	0	1	.000	0
1996 California	AL	5	0	0	2	2.2	13	3	3	3	1	0	2	0	1	0	1	0	0	0	0		0
6 ML YEARS		137	88	7	14	594.1	2594	659	360	329	109	12	27	6	189	10	379	11	0	25	39	.391	3

(Sv-Op / Hld / ERC / ERA continued: 1996 Pittsburgh 0-0 1 13.48 9.35; 1996 California 0-0 0 8.41 10.13; 6 ML YEARS 0-3 3 4.95 4.98)

Brent Mayne

Bats: L **Throws:** R **Pos:** C-76; PH-9; 1B-1 **Ht:** 6'1" **Wt:** 190 **Born:** 4/19/1968 **Age:** 37

		BATTING																			BASERUNNING				AVERAGES		
Year Team	Lg	G	AB	H	2B	3B	HR	(Hm	Rd)	TB	R	RBI	RC	TBB	IBB	SO	HBP	SH	SF	SB	CS	SB%	GDP	Avg	OBP	Slg
2004 Tucson*	AAA	5	11	1	0	0	0	(-	-)	1	1	0	0	1	0	4	0	0	0	0	0	-	0	.091	.167	.091
1990 Kansas City	AL	5	13	3	0	0	0	(0	0)	3	2	1	1	3	0	3	0	0	0	0	1	.00	0	.231	.375	.231
1991 Kansas City	AL	85	231	58	8	0	3	(2	1)	75	22	31	22	23	4	42	0	2	3	2	4	.33	6	.251	.315	.325
1992 Kansas City	AL	82	213	48	10	0	0	(0	0)	58	16	18	12	11	0	26	0	2	3	0	4	.00	5	.225	.260	.272
1993 Kansas City	AL	71	205	52	9	1	2	(0	2)	69	22	22	20	18	7	31	1	3	0	3	2	.60	6	.254	.317	.337
1994 Kansas City	AL	46	144	37	5	1	2	(1	1)	50	19	20	16	14	1	27	0	0	0	1	0	1.00	0	.257	.323	.347
1995 Kansas City	AL	110	307	77	18	1	1	(1	0)	100	23	27	27	25	1	41	3	11	1	0	0		16	.251	.313	.326
1996 New York	NL	70	99	26	6	0	1	(0	1)	35	9	6	11	12	1	22	0	2	0	0	1	.00	4	.263	.342	.354
1997 Oakland	AL	85	256	74	12	0	6	(4	2)	104	29	22	35	18	1	33	4	2	2	1	0	1.00	6	.289	.343	.406
1998 San Francisco	NL	94	275	75	15	0	3	(0	3)	99	26	32	36	37	3	47	1	2	2	2	1	.67	8	.273	.359	.360
1999 San Francisco	NL	117	322	97	32	0	2	(1	1)	135	39	39	50	43	5	65	5	1	3	2	2	.50	16	.301	.389	.419
2000 Colorado	NL	117	335	101	21	0	6	(3	3)	140	36	64	52	47	13	48	1	4	8	1	3	.25	12	.301	.381	.418
2001 Col-KC		100	326	93	11	1	2	(1	1)	112	28	40	35	26	5	41	1	0	6	1	2	.33	12	.285	.334	.344
2002 Kansas City	AL	101	326	77	8	2	4	(2	2)	101	35	30	33	34	1	54	2	4	4	4	4	.50	8	.236	.309	.310
2003 Kansas City	AL	113	372	91	17	1	6	(1	5)	128	39	36	41	32	5	59	3	4	3	0	2	.00	10	.245	.307	.344
2004 Ari-LA	NL	83	190	42	6	1	0	(0	0)	50	14	15	13	27	8	41	0	4	3	1	0	1.00	7	.221	.314	.263
2001 Colorado	NL	49	160	53	7	0	0	(0	0)	60	15	20	23	16	3	24	0	0	3	0	0	-	4	.331	.385	.375
2001 Kansas City	AL	51	166	40	4	1	2	(1	1)	52	13	20	12	10	2	17	1	0	3	1	2	.33	8	.241	.283	.313
2004 Arizona	NL	36	94	24	6	1	0	(0	0)	32	9	10	9	13	4	17	0	3	1	1	0	1.00	5	.255	.343	.340
2004 Los Angeles	NL	47	96	18	0	0	0	(0	0)	18	5	5	4	14	4	24	0	1	2	0	0	-	2	.188	.286	.188
15 ML YEARS		1279	3614	951	178	8	38	(16	22)	1259	359	403	404	370	55	580	21	41	38	18	27	.40	119	.263	.332	.348

Joe Mays

Pitches: R **Bats:** B **Pos:** SP **Ht:** 6'1" **Wt:** 185 **Born:** 12/10/1975 **Age:** 29

		HOW MUCH HE PITCHED						WHAT HE GAVE UP											THE RESULTS							
Year Team	Lg	G	GS	CG	GF	IP	BFP	H	R	ER	HR	SH	SF	HB	TBB	IBB	SO	WP	Bk	W	L	Pct	ShO	Sv-Op	Hld	ERC	ERA
1999 Minnesota	AL	49	20	2	8	171.0	746	179	92	83	24	7	6	2	67	2	115	6	0	6	11	.353	1	0-0	2	4.62	4.37
2000 Minnesota	AL	31	28	2	1	160.1	723	193	105	99	20	3	5	2	67	1	102	11	0	7	15	.318	1	0-0	0	5.59	5.56
2001 Minnesota	AL	34	34	4	0	233.2	957	205	87	82	25	8	8	5	64	2	123	11	0	17	13	.567	2	0-0	0	3.05	3.16
2002 Minnesota	AL	17	17	1	0	95.1	418	113	60	57	14	2	2	2	25	0	38	6	0	4	8	.333	1	0-0	0	4.99	5.38
2003 Minnesota	AL	31	21	0	4	130.0	576	159	92	91	21	3	3	4	39	2	50	3	0	8	8	.500	0	0-1	1	5.55	6.30
5 ML YEARS		162	120	9	13	790.1	3420	849	436	412	104	23	24	15	262	7	428	37	0	42	55	.433	5	0-1	3	4.51	4.69

Dave McCarty

Bats: R **Throws:** L **Pos:** 1B-67; PH-23; LF-10; RF-7; PR-5; DH-3 **Ht:** 6'5" **Wt:** 215 **Born:** 11/23/1969 **Age:** 35

		BATTING																			BASERUNNING				AVERAGES		
Year Team	Lg	G	AB	H	2B	3B	HR	(Hm	Rd)	TB	R	RBI	RC	TBB	IBB	SO	HBP	SH	SF	SB	CS	SB%	GDP	Avg	OBP	Slg
2004 Lowell*	A-	1	3	2	1	0	0	(-	-)	3	1	1	1	1	0	0	0	0	0	0	0	-	0	.667	.750	1.000
2004 Pawtucket*	AAA	3	7	2	0	0	0	(-	-)	2	2	1	2	4	0	2	1	0	0	0	0	-	0	.286	.583	.286
1993 Minnesota	AL	98	350	75	15	2	2	(2	0)	100	36	21	18	19	0	80	1	1	0	2	6	.25	13	.214	.257	.286
1994 Minnesota	AL	44	131	34	8	2	1	(1	0)	49	21	12	15	7	1	32	5	0	0	2	1	.67	3	.260	.322	.374
1995 Min-SF		37	75	17	4	1	0	(0	0)	23	11	6	6	6	0	22	1	0	1	1	1	.50	1	.227	.289	.307
1996 San Francisco	NL	91	175	38	3	0	6	(5	1)	59	16	24	17	18	0	43	2	0	2	2	1	.67	5	.217	.294	.337
1998 Seattle	AL	8	18	5	0	0	1	(1	0)	8	1	2	4	5	0	4	0	0	0	1	0	1.00	0	.278	.435	.444
2000 Kansas City	AL	103	270	75	14	2	12	(6	6)	129	34	53	41	22	1	68	0	0	3	0	0	-	6	.278	.329	.478
2001 Kansas City	AL	98	200	50	10	0	7	(5	2)	81	26	26	26	24	1	45	1	1	4	0	0	-	8	.250	.328	.405
2002 KC-TB		25	66	9	1	0	2	(0	2)	16	5	4	2	6	0	19	2	0	0	0	0	-	0	.136	.230	.242
2003 Oak-Bos		24	53	18	5	0	1	(1	0)	26	6	8	10	3	0	14	0	0	1	0	0	-	0	.340	.368	.491
2004 Boston	AL	91	151	39	8	1	4	(2	2)	61	24	17	17	14	0	40	2	0	1	1	0	1.00	5	.258	.327	.404
1995 Minnesota	AL	25	55	12	3	1	0	(0	0)	17	10	4	4	4	0	18	1	0	1	1	0	1.00	1	.218	.279	.309
1995 San Francisco	NL	12	20	5	1	0	0	(0	0)	6	1	2	2	2	0	4	0	0	0	0	1	1.00	0	.250	.318	.300
2002 Kansas City	AL	13	32	3	1	0	1	(0	1)	7	3	2	2	2	0	10	0	0	0	0	0	-	1	.094	.147	.219
2002 Tampa Bay	AL	12	34	6	0	0	1	(0	1)	9	2	2	2	4	0	9	2	0	0	0	0	-	0	.176	.300	.265
2003 Oakland	AL	8	26	7	2	0	0	(0	0)	9	2	2	2	1	0	7	0	0	1	0	0	-	0	.269	.286	.346
2003 Boston	AL	16	27	11	3	0	1	(1	0)	17	4	6	8	2	0	7	0	0	0	0	0	-	0	.407	.448	.630
10 ML YEARS		619	1489	360	68	8	36	(23	13)	552	180	173	156	124	3	367	14	2	12	9	9	.50	42	.242	.304	.371

Seth McClung

Pitches: R **Bats:** R **Pos:** RP **Ht:** 6'6" **Wt:** 235 **Born:** 2/7/1981 **Age:** 24

		HOW MUCH HE PITCHED						WHAT HE GAVE UP											THE RESULTS							
Year Team	Lg	G	GS	CG	GF	IP	BFP	H	R	ER	HR	SH	SF	HB	TBB	IBB	SO	WP	Bk	W	L	Pct	ShO	Sv-Op	Hld	ERC	ERA
1999 Princeton	R+	13	10	0	0	45.2	244	53	47	39	3	0	1	9	48	0	46	20	0	2	4	.333	0	0- -	-	7.69	7.69
2000 Hudson Val	A-	8	8	0	0	43.2	186	37	18	9	0	1	2	3	17	0	38	6	1	2	2	.500	0	0- -	-	2.76	1.85
2000 Chrlstn - SC	A	6	6	0	0	31.0	145	30	14	11	0	1	0	3	19	0	26	8	0	2	1	.667	0	0- -	-	4.21	3.19
2001 Chrlstn - SC	A	28	28	2	0	164.1	683	142	72	51	6	4	1	11	53	1	165	3	2	10	11	.476	1	0- -	-	2.88	2.79
2002 Bakersfield	A+	7	7	0	0	37.0	158	35	16	12	1	1	0	2	11	0	48	0	1	3	2	.600	0	0- -	-	3.05	2.92
2002 Orlando	AA	20	19	0	1	114.0	533	138	74	68	12	2	7	9	53	0	64	7	1	5	7	.417	0	0- -	-	5.90	5.37
2004 Chrlstn - SC	A	3	3	0	0	9.1	39	7	0	0	0	2	0	0	4	0	10	0	0	0	0	-	0	0- -	-	1.31	0.00
2004 Montgomery	AA	3	3	0	0	13.1	55	10	7	3	1	1	1	0	4	0	8	0	0	1	1	.500	0	0- -	-	3.36	4.73
2004 Durham	AAA	11	0	0	2	13.2	58	10	5	5	0	0	0	0	7	0	12	2	0	2	1	.667	0	0- -	-	2.35	3.29
2003 Tampa Bay	AL	12	5	0	2	38.2	167	33	23	23	6	1	1	3	25	1	25	2	0	4	1	.800	0	0-0	1	5.11	5.35

Sam McConnell

Pitches: L **Bats:** L **Pos:** RP-10   **Ht:** 6'5" **Wt:** 228 **Born:** 12/31/1975 **Age:** 29

					HOW MUCH HE PITCHED			WHAT HE GAVE UP											THE RESULTS						
Year Team	Lg	G	GS	CG	GF	IP	BFP	H	R	ER	HR	SH	SF	HB	TBB	IBB	SO	WP	Bk	W	L	Pct	ShO	Sv-Op	Hld	ERC	ERA
1997 Erie	A-	17	10	0	0	58.2	261	56	38	33	7	1	3	3	24	0	45	6	0	2	2	.500	0	0--		4.06	5.06
1998 Augusta	A	8	8	1	0	45.0	183	36	22	16	2	1	0	1	13	1	35	1	1	4	3	.571	0	0--		2.30	3.20
1998 Lynchburg	A+	19	19	3	0	121.0	483	118	48	39	4	2	1	1	20	0	80	2	0	8	5	.615	1	0--		2.72	2.90
1998 Carolina	AA	2	1	0	0	12.0	53	15	7	6	2	1	1	0	3	0	5	0	0	1	0	.000	0	0--		5.38	4.50
1999 Altoona	AA	13	12	1	0	62.1	299	82	52	46	3	6	3	2	33	1	40	1	1	1	7	.125	0	0--		6.10	6.64
1999 Lynchburg	A+	15	15	4	0	101.2	402	84	41	36	8	3	5	5	27	1	70	6	0	7	3	.700	2	0--		2.78	3.19
2000 Altoona	AA	20	13	3	0	106.0	422	83	24	19	3	2	2	2	26	0	61	1	1	9	2	.818	1	0--		2.02	1.61
2000 Nashville	AAA	8	8	0	0	49.0	216	58	36	35	8	1	2	4	16	0	22	1	0	1	4	.200	0	0--		5.78	6.43
2001 Nashville	AAA	26	23	1	1	134.1	600	159	103	90	20	3	7	3	41	2	98	7	1	7	10	.412	0	0--		5.11	6.03
2002 Reading	AA	29	7	0	8	69.0	293	78	31	28	7	1	2	2	19	3	43	1	0	2	4	.333	0	3--		4.48	3.65
2002 Scrtn/WlksBr	AAA	7	7	0	0	35.2	159	41	17	14	6	1	1	0	16	0	23	0	0	0	3	.000	0	0--		5.72	3.53
2003 Greenville	AA	16	0	0	4	15.1	65	18	7	7	0	0	1	0	4	0	8	0	2	1	0	1.000	0	0--		3.88	4.11
2003 Richmond	AAA	22	13	0	1	93.1	383	94	31	28	5	6	3	2	17	2	64	1	2	8	4	.667	0	0--		3.05	2.70
2004 Richmond	AAA	22	18	1	3	103.2	430	102	51	45	8	4	6	5	28	0	56	1	0	7	7	.500	0	0--		3.58	3.91
2004 Atlanta	NL	10	0	0	1	9.1	44	11	4	4	0	1	0	1	4	1	4	0	0	1	0	1.000	0	0-0		4.53	3.86

Quinton McCracken

Bats: B **Throws:** R **Pos:** LF-31; PH-19; PR-11; RF-10; CF-7; DH-5   **Ht:** 5'7" **Wt:** 173 **Born:** 3/16/1970 **Age:** 35

								BATTING											BASERUNNING				AVERAGES		
Year Team	Lg	G	AB	H	2B	3B	HR	(Hm	Rd)	TB	R	RBI	RC	TBB	IBB	SO	HBP	SH	SF	SB	CS	SB%	GDP	Avg	OBP	Slg
2004 Tucson*	AAA	15	58	19	5	1	1	(-	-)	29	7	8	9	3	0	5	0	0	0	2	2	.50	1	.328	.361	.500
1995 Colorado	NL	3	1	0	0	0	0	(0	0)	0	0	0	0	0	0	1	0	0	0	0	0	-	0	.000	.000	.000
1996 Colorado	NL	124	283	82	13	6	3	(2	1)	116	50	40	43	32	4	62	1	12	1	17	6	.74	5	.290	.363	.410
1997 Colorado	NL	147	325	95	11	1	3	(1	2)	117	69	36	47	42	0	62	1	6	1	28	11	.72	6	.292	.374	.360
1998 Tampa Bay	AL	155	614	179	38	7	7	(5	2)	252	77	59	83	41	1	107	3	9	8	19	10	.66	12	.292	.335	.410
1999 Tampa Bay	AL	40	148	37	6	1	1	(1	0)	48	20	18	13	14	0	23	1	1	1	6	5	.55	7	.250	.317	.324
2000 Tampa Bay	AL	15	31	4	0	0	0	(0	0)	4	5	2	0	6	0	4	0	0	0	0	1	.00	3	.129	.270	.129
2001 Minnesota	AL	24	64	14	2	2	0	(0	0)	20	7	3	5	5	0	13	0	1	0	0	1	.00	2	.219	.275	.313
2002 Arizona	NL	123	349	108	27	8	3	(1	2)	160	60	40	62	32	0	68	2	13	4	5	4	.56	3	.309	.367	.458
2003 Arizona	NL	115	203	46	5	2	0	(0	0)	55	17	18	16	15	2	34	0	5	3	5	1	.83	4	.227	.276	.271
2004 Sea-Ari		74	176	48	11	1	2	(2	0)	67	26	13	20	15	0	27	0	3	1	3	5	.38	3	.273	.328	.381
2004 Seattle	AL	19	20	3	0	0	0	(0	0)	3	6	0	0	2	0	4	0	1	0	1	1	.50	1	.150	.227	.150
2004 Arizona	NL	55	156	45	11	1	2	(2	0)	64	20	13	20	13	0	23	0	2	1	2	4	.33	2	.288	.341	.410
10 ML YEARS		820	2194	613	113	28	19	(12	7)	839	331	229	289	202	7	401	8	50	19	83	44	.65	45	.279	.340	.382

Darnell McDonald

Bats: R **Throws:** R **Pos:** RF-8; CF-4; PR-3; PH-2; LF-1   **Ht:** 5'11" **Wt:** 210 **Born:** 11/17/1978 **Age:** 26

								BATTING											BASERUNNING				AVERAGES		
Year Team	Lg	G	AB	H	2B	3B	HR	(Hm	Rd)	TB	R	RBI	RC	TBB	IBB	SO	HBP	SH	SF	SB	CS	SB%	GDP	Avg	OBP	Slg
1998 Delmarva	A	134	528	138	24	5	6	(-	-)	190	87	44	61	33	0	117	5	4	5	35	11	.76	5	.261	.308	.360
1998 Frederick	A+	4	18	4	2	0	1	(-	-)	9	3	2	2	3	0	6	0	0	0	2	0	1.00	1	.222	.333	.500
1999 Frederick	A+	130	507	135	23	5	6	(-	-)	186	81	73	68	61	0	92	5	7	7	26	9	.74	13	.266	.347	.367
2000 Bowie	AA	116	459	111	13	6	6	(-	-)	152	59	43	45	29	0	87	4	6	4	11	4	.73	7	.242	.290	.331
2001 Bowie	AA	30	117	33	7	1	3	(-	-)	51	16	21	16	9	0	28	1	0	1	3	3	.50	1	.282	.336	.436
2001 Rochester	AAA	104	391	93	19	2	2	(-	-)	122	37	35	33	29	0	75	1	2	2	13	9	.59	8	.238	.291	.312
2002 Bowie	AA	37	144	42	9	1	4	(-	-)	65	21	15	26	22	0	27	2	0	0	9	3	.75	1	.292	.393	.451
2002 Rochester	AAA	91	332	96	21	6	6	(-	-)	147	43	35	51	32	0	78	2	1	2	11	3	.79	8	.289	.353	.443
2003 Ottawa	AAA	40	152	45	7	1	0	(-	-)	54	19	20	20	18	0	27	1	1	0	5	7	.42	3	.296	.374	.355
2004 Ottawa	AAA	107	410	96	32	1	7	(-	-)	151	44	44	40	34	0	100	3	2	5	12	6	.67	12	.234	.294	.368
2004 Baltimore	AL	17	32	5	1	0	0	(0	0)	6	3	1	2	2	0	6	0	0	0	1	0	1.00	0	.156	.206	.188

John McDonald

Bats: R **Throws:** R **Pos:** SS-30; PR-19; 2B-12; 3B-9; DH-7; PH-7   **Ht:** 5'11" **Wt:** 175 **Born:** 9/24/1974 **Age:** 30

								BATTING											BASERUNNING				AVERAGES		
Year Team	Lg	G	AB	H	2B	3B	HR	(Hm	Rd)	TB	R	RBI	RC	TBB	IBB	SO	HBP	SH	SF	SB	CS	SB%	GDP	Avg	OBP	Slg
1999 Cleveland	AL	18	21	7	0	0	0	(0	0)	7	2	0	1	0	0	3	0	0	0	0	1	.00	2	.333	.333	.333
2000 Cleveland	AL	9	9	4	0	0	0	(0	0)	4	0	0	2	0	0	1	0	0	0	0	0	-	0	.444	.444	.444
2001 Cleveland	AL	17	22	2	1	0	0	(0	0)	3	1	0	1	0	0	7	1	1	0	0	0	-	0	.091	.167	.136
2002 Cleveland	AL	93	264	66	11	3	1	(0	1)	86	35	12	24	10	0	50	5	7	2	3	0	1.00	4	.250	.288	.326
2003 Cleveland	AL	82	214	46	9	1	1	(0	1)	60	21	14	18	11	0	31	2	4	2	3	3	.50	4	.215	.258	.280
2004 Cleveland	AL	66	93	19	5	1	2	(0	2)	32	17	7	6	4	0	11	0	3	0	0	0	-	1	.204	.237	.344
6 ML YEARS		285	623	144	26	5	4	(0	4)	192	76	33	51	26	0	103	8	15	4	6	4	.60	11	.231	.269	.308

Joe McEwing

Bats: R **Throws:** R **Pos:** 2B-35; SS-13; PR-13; 1B-11; PH-11; LF-8; CF-6; 3B-1; RF-1   **Ht:** 5'11" **Wt:** 170 **Born:** 10/19/1972 **Age:** 32

								BATTING											BASERUNNING				AVERAGES		
Year Team	Lg	G	AB	H	2B	3B	HR	(Hm	Rd)	TB	R	RBI	RC	TBB	IBB	SO	HBP	SH	SF	SB	CS	SB%	GDP	Avg	OBP	Slg
1998 St Louis	NL	10	20	4	1	0	0	(0	0)	5	5	1	1	1	0	3	1	1	0	0	1	.00	0	.200	.273	.250
1999 St Louis	NL	152	513	141	28	4	9	(5	4)	204	65	44	70	41	8	87	6	9	5	7	4	.64	3	.275	.333	.398
2000 New York	NL	87	153	34	14	1	2	(1	1)	56	20	19	14	5	0	29	1	8	2	3	1	.75	2	.222	.248	.366
2001 New York	NL	116	283	80	17	3	8	(3	5)	127	41	30	44	17	0	57	10	6	3	8	5	.62	2	.283	.342	.449
2002 New York	NL	105	196	39	8	1	3	(2	1)	58	22	26	14	9	0	50	3	3	3	4	4	.50	0	.199	.242	.296
2003 New York	NL	119	278	67	11	0	1	(0	1)	81	31	16	26	25	4	57	3	6	1	3	0	1.00	6	.241	.309	.291
2004 New York	NL	75	138	35	3	1	1	(1	0)	43	17	16	17	9	4	32	0	6	1	4	1	.80	0	.254	.297	.312
7 ML YEARS		664	1581	400	82	10	24	(12	12)	574	201	152	186	107	16	315	24	39	15	29	16	.64	13	.253	.307	.363

Fred McGriff

Bats: L **Throws:** L **Pos:** DH-14; PH-9; 1B-6   **Ht:** 6'3" **Wt:** 225 **Born:** 10/31/1963 **Age:** 41

Year Team	Lg	G	AB	H	2B	3B	HR	(Hm	Rd)	TB	R	RBI	RC	TBB	IBB	SO	HBP	SH	SF	SB	CS	SB%	GDP	Avg	OBP	Slg
2004 Durham*	AAA	7	21	5	0	0	1	(-	-)	8	4	4	3	5	0	6	0	0	0	0	0	-	0	.238	.385	.381
1986 Toronto	AL	3	5	1	0	0	0	(0	0)	1	1	0	0	0	0	2	0	0	0	0	0	-	0	.200	.200	.200
1987 Toronto	AL	107	295	73	16	0	20	(7	13)	149	58	43	57	60	4	104	1	0	0	3	2	.60	3	.247	.376	.505
1988 Toronto	AL	154	536	151	35	4	34	(18	16)	296	100	82	107	79	3	149	4	0	4	6	1	.86	15	.282	.376	.552
1989 Toronto	AL	161	551	148	27	3	36	(18	18)	289	98	92	115	119	12	132	4	1	5	7	4	.64	14	.269	.399	.525
1990 Toronto	AL	153	557	167	21	1	35	(14	21)	295	91	88	117	94	12	108	2	1	4	5	3	.63	7	.300	.400	.530
1991 San Diego	NL	153	528	147	19	1	31	(18	13)	261	84	106	102	105	26	135	2	0	7	4	1	.80	14	.278	.396	.494
1992 San Diego	NL	152	531	152	30	4	35	(21	14)	295	79	104	110	96	23	108	1	0	4	8	6	.57	14	.286	.394	.556
1993 SD-Atl	NL	151	557	162	29	2	37	(15	22)	306	111	101	110	76	6	106	2	0	5	5	3	.63	14	.291	.375	.549
1994 Atlanta	NL	113	424	135	25	1	34	(13	21)	264	81	94	96	50	8	76	1	0	3	7	3	.70	8	.318	.389	.623
1995 Atlanta	NL	144	528	148	27	1	27	(15	12)	258	85	93	87	65	6	99	5	0	6	3	6	.33	19	.280	.361	.489
1996 Atlanta	NL	159	617	182	37	1	28	(17	11)	305	81	107	105	68	12	116	2	0	4	7	3	.70	20	.295	.365	.494
1997 Atlanta	NL	152	564	156	25	1	22	(8	14)	249	77	97	85	68	4	112	4	0	5	5	0	1.00	22	.277	.356	.441
1998 Tampa Bay	AL	151	564	160	33	0	19	(14	5)	250	73	81	93	79	9	118	2	0	4	7	2	.78	14	.284	.371	.443
1999 Tampa Bay	AL	144	529	164	30	1	32	(18	14)	292	75	104	114	86	11	107	1	0	4	1	0	1.00	12	.310	.405	.552
2000 Tampa Bay	AL	158	566	157	18	0	27	(10	17)	256	82	106	95	91	10	120	0	0	7	2	0	1.00	16	.277	.373	.452
2001 TB-ChC		146	513	157	25	2	31	(11	14)	279	67	102	101	66	13	106	3	0	4	1	2	.33	13	.306	.386	.544
2002 Chicago	NL	146	523	143	27	2	30	(11	19)	264	67	103	87	63	6	99	4	0	5	1	2	.33	13	.273	.353	.505
2003 Los Angeles	NL	86	297	74	14	0	13	(7	6)	127	32	40	42	31	4	66	1	0	0	0	0	-	7	.249	.322	.428
2004 Tampa Bay	AL	27	72	13	3	0	2	(0	2)	22	7	7	7	9	2	19	0	0	0	0	0	-	0	.181	.272	.306
1993 San Diego	NL	83	302	83	11	1	18	(7	11)	150	52	46	52	42	4	55	1	0	4	4	3	.57	9	.275	.361	.497
1993 Atlanta	NL	68	255	79	18	1	19	(8	11)	156	59	55	58	34	2	51	1	0	1	1	0	1.00	5	.310	.392	.612
2001 Tampa Bay	AL	97	343	109	18	0	19	(10	9)	184	40	61	67	40	9	69	0	0	2	1	1	.50	7	.318	.387	.536
2001 Chicago	NL	49	170	48	7	2	12	(7	5)	95	27	41	34	26	4	37	3	0	2	0	1	.00	6	.282	.383	.559
19 ML YEARS		2460	8757	2490	441	24	493	(241	252)	4458	1349	1550	1630	1305	171	1882	39	2	71	72	38	.65	226	.284	.377	.509

Cody McKay

Bats: L **Throws:** R **Pos:** C-18; PH-16; 3B-7; 1B-1; PR-1   **Ht:** 6'0" **Wt:** 208 **Born:** 1/11/1974 **Age:** 31

Year Team	Lg	G	AB	H	2B	3B	HR	(Hm	Rd)	TB	R	RBI	RC	TBB	IBB	SO	HBP	SH	SF	SB	CS	SB%	GDP	Avg	OBP	Slg
1996 Sth Oregon	A-	69	254	68	13	0	3	(-	-)	90	33	30	30	25	0	42	6	1	3	0	5	.00	7	.268	.344	.354
1997 Modesto	A+	125	390	97	20	1	7	(-	-)	140	47	50	52	46	2	69	16	3	4	2	4	.67	9	.249	.349	.359
1998 Modesto	A+	107	402	114	25	1	6	(-	-)	159	59	58	59	40	1	62	17	3	3	2	4	.33	12	.284	.370	.396
1998 Huntsville	AA	9	21	6	0	0	1	(-	-)	9	5	1	5	6	0	5	2	0	0	0	0	-	0	.286	.483	.429
1998 Edmonton	AAA	19	57	13	3	0	0	(-	-)	16	6	5	6	7	0	5	3	2	0	1	0	1.00	0	.228	.343	.281
1999 Midland	AA	94	333	98	21	1	6	(-	-)	139	59	43	51	38	5	40	8	1	5	1	2	.33	11	.294	.375	.417
2000 Midland	AA	115	427	136	35	2	5	(-	-)	190	70	89	78	67	6	54	10	0	10	1	5	.17	15	.319	.414	.445
2000 Sacramento	AAA	16	58	13	4	0	1	(-	-)	20	8	7	6	5	1	14	1	0	0	0	0	-	0	.224	.297	.345
2001 Sacramento	AAA	99	350	92	19	0	6	(-	-)	129	36	41	40	27	1	64	5	2	1	1	0	1.00	12	.263	.324	.369
2002 Sacramento	AAA	108	378	109	16	1	13	(-	-)	166	55	57	57	21	0	59	10	4	6	2	1	.67	4	.288	.337	.439
2003 Indianapolis	AAA	109	371	86	15	1	6	(-	-)	121	32	43	33	26	2	50	9	1	6	2	2	.50	13	.232	.294	.326
2004 Memphis	AAA	27	90	25	4	1	3	(-	-)	40	9	15	13	4	1	15	3	2	2	0	0	-	1	.278	.323	.444
2002 Oakland	AL	2	3	2	0	0	0	(0	0)	2	0	2	1	0	0	1	0	0	0	0	0	-	0	.667	.500	.667
2004 St Louis	NL	35	74	17	2	0	0	(0	0)	19	7	6	5	2	0	14	2	1	0	0	0	-	3	.230	.269	.257
2 ML YEARS		37	77	19	2	0	0	(0	0)	21	7	8	6	2	0	15	2	1	0	0	0	-	3	.247	.280	.273

Marty McLeary

Pitches: R **Bats:** R **Pos:** RP-3   **Ht:** 6'5" **Wt:** 230 **Born:** 10/26/1974 **Age:** 30

Year Team	Lg	G	GS	CG	GF	IP	BFP	H	R	ER	HR	SH	SF	HB	TBB	IBB	SO	WP	Bk	W	L	Pct	ShO	Sv-Op	Hld	ERC	ERA
1997 Lowell	A-	13	13	0	0	62.1	275	53	38	26	2	3	3	5	36	1	43	6	2	3	6	.333	0	0--	-	3.71	3.75
1998 Michigan	A	37	7	0	11	88.2	396	99	58	41	4	1	3	5	35	2	54	5	1	5	7	.417	0	0--	-	4.49	4.16
1999 Sarasota	A+	8	0	0	0	12.2	73	29	20	17	1	2	1	1	7	0	11	2	0	1	0	1.000	0	0--	-	13.60	12.08
1999 Augusta	A	35	9	0	16	80.2	338	73	34	28	8	3	2	4	25	1	90	5	2	5	6	.455	0	3--	-	3.37	3.12
2000 Trenton	AA	43	8	0	22	96.2	449	114	66	49	5	2	6	2	53	3	63	8	1	2	9	.182	0	5--	-	5.35	4.56
2001 Trenton	AA	35	0	0	14	54.2	252	58	30	21	2	4	1	5	30	5	42	2	0	9	6	.600	0	0--	-	4.69	3.46
2001 Pawtucket	AAA	18	0	0	7	30.0	127	28	13	10	4	2	1	1	15	1	20	1	0	1	2	.333	0	0--	-	4.58	3.00
2002 Trenton	AA	11	0	0	7	16.2	76	20	12	9	0	1	2	1	8	2	10	2	0	2	0	.000	0	0--	-	4.85	4.86
2002 Pawtucket	AAA	18	1	0	6	35.2	168	44	30	29	6	1	1	2	23	0	19	6	0	1	1	.500	0	0--	-	7.50	7.32
2003 Carolina	AA	11	2	0	1	30.0	124	22	8	6	1	0	0	3	15	0	22	3	0	1	1	.500	0	0--	-	3.03	1.80
2003 Albuquerque	AAA	20	1	0	4	33.1	160	40	22	16	3	1	2	3	18	1	17	3	0	1	1	.500	0	0--	-	5.95	4.32
2004 Portland	AAA	44	7	0	23	84.1	357	65	30	28	4	3	0	5	42	1	81	5	1	5	4	.556	0	13--	-	3.06	2.99
2004 San Diego	NL	3	0	0	2	3.2	20	7	6	6	2	1	1	0	2	0	4	0	0	0	0	-	0	0-0	0	14.71	14.73

Mark McLemore

Bats: B **Throws:** R **Pos:** 2B-47; 3B-28; PH-8; LF-1   **Ht:** 5'11" **Wt:** 207 **Born:** 10/4/1964 **Age:** 40

Year Team	Lg	G	AB	H	2B	3B	HR	(Hm	Rd)	TB	R	RBI	RC	TBB	IBB	SO	HBP	SH	SF	SB	CS	SB%	GDP	Avg	OBP	Slg
2004 Sacramento*	AAA	6	19	10	1	0	0	(-	-)	11	2	5	7	5	0	2	0	0	0	0	0	-	0	.526	.625	.579
1986 California	AL	5	4	0	0	0	0	(0	0)	0	0	0	0	1	0	2	0	0	1	0	1	.00	0	.000	.200	.000
1987 California	AL	138	433	102	13	3	3	(0	3)	130	61	41	44	48	0	72	0	15	3	25	8	.76	7	.236	.310	.300
1988 California	AL	77	233	56	11	2	2	(1	1)	77	38	16	24	25	0	28	0	5	2	13	7	.65	6	.240	.312	.330
1989 California	AL	32	103	25	3	1	0	(0	0)	30	12	14	9	7	0	19	1	3	1	6	1	.86	5	.243	.295	.291
1990 Cal-Cle	AL	28	60	9	2	0	0	(0	0)	11	6	2	1	4	0	15	0	1	0	1	1	.00	1	.150	.203	.183
1991 Houston	NL	21	61	9	1	0	0	(0	0)	10	6	2	1	6	0	13	0	0	1	0	1	.00	1	.148	.221	.164
1992 Baltimore	AL	101	228	56	7	2	0	(0	0)	67	40	27	20	21	1	26	0	6	1	11	5	.69	6	.246	.308	.294
1993 Baltimore	AL	148	581	165	27	5	4	(2	2)	214	81	72	72	64	4	92	1	11	6	21	15	.58	21	.284	.353	.368
1994 Baltimore	AL	104	343	88	11	1	3	(2	1)	110	44	29	44	51	3	50	1	4	1	20	5	.80	7	.257	.354	.321
1995 Texas	AL	129	467	122	20	5	5	(3	2)	167	73	41	59	59	6	71	3	10	3	21	11	.66	10	.261	.346	.358

Year Team	Lg	G	AB	H	2B	3B	HR	(Hm	Rd)	TB	R	RBI	RC	TBB	IBB	SO	HBP	SH	SF	SB	CS	SB%	GDP	Avg	OBP	Slg
						BATTING														**BASERUNNING**				**AVERAGES**		
1996 Texas	AL	147	517	150	23	4	5	(3	2)	196	84	46	81	87	5	69	0	2	5	27	10	.73	16	.290	.389	.379
1997 Texas	AL	89	349	91	17	2	1	(0	1)	115	47	25	41	40	1	54	2	6	2	7	5	.58	5	.261	.338	.330
1998 Texas	AL	126	461	114	15	1	5	(4	1)	146	79	53	60	89	1	64	2	12	3	12	4	.75	15	.247	.369	.317
1999 Texas	AL	144	566	155	20	7	6	(2	4)	207	105	45	81	83	2	79	0	9	6	16	8	.67	8	.274	.363	.366
2000 Seattle	AL	138	481	118	23	1	3	(2	1)	152	72	46	59	81	2	78	1	11	4	30	14	.68	12	.245	.353	.316
2001 Seattle	AL	125	409	117	16	9	5	(2	3)	166	78	57	73	69	0	84	0	3	6	39	7	.85	6	.286	.384	.406
2002 Seattle	AL	104	337	91	17	2	7	(4	3)	133	54	41	60	61	1	63	1	4	4	18	10	.64	3	.270	.380	.395
2003 Seattle	AL	99	309	72	15	2	2	(1	1)	97	34	37	36	38	0	71	2	0	3	5	5	.50	4	.233	.318	.314
2004 Oakland	AL	77	250	62	14	0	2	(0	2)	82	29	21	29	41	3	33	1	2	1	0	2	.00	4	.248	.355	.328
1990 California	AL	20	48	7	2	0	0	(0	0)	9	4	2	1	4	0	9	0	1	0	1	0	1.00	1	.146	.212	.188
1990 Cleveland	AL	8	12	2	0	0	0	(0	0)	2	2	0	0	0	0	6	0	0	0	0	0	-	0	.167	.167	.167
19 ML YEARS		1832	6192	1602	255	47	53	(29	24)	2110	943	615	794	875	29	983	15	105	52	272	119	.70	134	.259	.349	.341

Billy McMillon

Bats: L **Throws:** L **Pos:** PH-32; LF-20; DH-5; 1B-3; RF-1   **Ht:** 5'11" **Wt:** 195 **Born:** 11/17/1971 **Age:** 33

Year Team	Lg	G	AB	H	2B	3B	HR	(Hm	Rd)	TB	R	RBI	RC	TBB	IBB	SO	HBP	SH	SF	SB	CS	SB%	GDP	Avg	OBP	Slg
						BATTING														**BASERUNNING**				**AVERAGES**		
2004 Sacramento*	AAA	10	32	14	4	0	3	(-	-)	27	7	10	12	7	0	3	1	0	0	0	0	-	0	.438	.550	.844
1996 Florida	NL	28	51	11	0	0	0	(0	0)	11	4	4	3	5	1	14	0	0	0	0	0	-	1	.216	.286	.216
1997 Phi-Fla	NL	37	90	23	5	1	2	(0	2)	36	10	14	11	6	0	24	0	0	3	2	1	.67	1	.256	.293	.400
2000 Detroit	AL	46	123	37	7	1	4	(1	3)	58	20	24	24	19	0	19	1	2	4	1	0	1.00	2	.301	.388	.472
2001 Det-Oak	AL	40	92	20	8	1	1	(1	0)	33	7	14	10	7	0	25	2	0	1	1	0	1.00	1	.217	.284	.359
2003 Oakland	AL	66	153	41	11	0	6	(2	4)	70	15	26	25	19	1	36	2	0	1	0	0	-	3	.268	.354	.458
2004 Oakland	AL	52	92	17	4	0	3	(1	2)	30	10	11	6	8	0	22	1	0	1	0	1	.00	2	.185	.255	.326
1997 Philadelphia	NL	24	72	21	4	1	2	(0	2)	33	10	13	11	6	0	17	0	0	3	2	1	.67	1	.292	.333	.458
1997 Florida	NL	13	18	2	1	0	0	(0	0)	3	0	1	0	0	0	7	0	0	0	0	0	-	0	.111	.111	.167
2001 Detroit	AL	20	34	3	1	0	1	(1	0)	7	1	4	0	2	0	12	1	0	0	0	0	-	1	.088	.162	.206
2001 Oakland	AL	20	58	17	7	1	0	(0	0)	26	6	10	10	5	0	13	1	0	1	1	0	1.00	0	.293	.354	.448
6 ML YEARS		269	601	149	35	3	16	(5	11)	238	66	93	79	64	2	140	6	2	10	4	2	.67	10	.248	.322	.396

Dallas McPherson

Bats: L **Throws:** R **Pos:** 3B-14; PH-2; PR-2   **Ht:** 6'4" **Wt:** 230 **Born:** 7/23/1980 **Age:** 24

Year Team	Lg	G	AB	H	2B	3B	HR	(Hm	Rd)	TB	R	RBI	RC	TBB	IBB	SO	HBP	SH	SF	SB	CS	SB%	GDP	Avg	OBP	Slg
						BATTING														**BASERUNNING**				**AVERAGES**		
2001 Provo	R+	31	124	49	11	0	5	(-	-)	75	30	29	30	12	0	22	0	0	0	1	0	1.00	2	.395	.449	.605
2002 Cedar Rpds	A	132	499	138	24	3	15	(-	-)	213	71	88	86	78	3	128	7	0	2	30	6	.83	9	.277	.381	.427
2003 R Cucamnga	A+	77	292	90	21	6	18	(-	-)	177	65	59	66	41	2	79	6	0	0	12	6	.67	4	.308	.404	.606
2003 Arkansas	AA	28	102	32	9	1	5	(-	-)	58	22	27	22	19	4	25	1	0	0	4	0	1.00	4	.314	.426	.569
2004 Arkansas	AA	68	262	84	17	6	20	(-	-)	173	53	69	63	34	5	74	4	0	2	6	5	.55	2	.321	.404	.660
2004 Salt Lake	AAA	67	259	81	19	8	20	(-	-)	176	54	57	57	23	4	95	1	0	1	6	3	.67	5	.313	.370	.680
2004 Anaheim	AL	16	40	9	1	0	3	(2	1)	19	5	6	5	3	0	17	0	0	0	1	0	1.00	0	.225	.279	.475

Brian Meadows

Pitches: R **Bats:** R **Pos:** RP-68   **Ht:** 6'4" **Wt:** 220 **Born:** 11/21/1975 **Age:** 29

Year Team	Lg	G	GS	CG	GF	IP	BFP	H	R	ER	HR	SH	SF	HB	TBB	IBB	SO	WP	Bk	W	L	Pct	ShO	Sv-Op	Hld	ERC	ERA
		HOW MUCH HE PITCHED						**WHAT HE GAVE UP**												**THE RESULTS**							
1998 Florida	NL	31	31	1	0	174.1	772	222	106	101	20	14	4	3	46	3	88	5	1	11	13	.458	0	0-0	0	5.29	5.21
1999 Florida	NL	31	31	0	0	178.1	795	214	117	111	31	16	8	5	57	5	72	4	1	11	15	.423	0	0-0	0	5.51	5.60
2000 SD-KC		33	32	2	0	196.1	869	234	119	112	32	7	5	8	64	6	79	3	0	13	10	.565	0	0-0	0	5.52	5.13
2001 Kansas City	AL	10	10	0	0	50.1	224	73	41	39	12	1	2	1	12	2	21	1	0	1	6	.143	0	0-0	0	7.47	6.97
2002 Pittsburgh	NL	11	11	0	0	62.2	259	62	29	27	7	2	0	1	14	8	31	2	0	1	6	.143	0	0-0	0	3.29	3.88
2003 Pittsburgh	NL	34	7	0	11	76.1	329	91	45	40	8	2	1	1	11	2	38	4	0	2	1	.667	0	1-1	5	4.12	4.72
2004 Pittsburgh	NL	68	0	0	15	78.0	323	76	40	31	7	6	5	0	19	7	46	5	0	2	4	.333	0	1-2	13	3.13	3.58
2000 San Diego	NL	22	22	0	0	124.2	565	150	80	74	24	7	2	8	50	6	53	3	0	7	8	.467	0	0-0	0	6.23	5.34
2000 Kansas City	AL	11	10	2	0	71.2	304	84	39	38	8	0	3	0	14	0	26	0	0	6	2	.750	0	0-0	0	4.35	4.77
7 ML YEARS		218	122	3	26	816.1	3571	972	497	461	117	48	25	19	223	33	375	24	2	41	55	.427	0	2-3	18	5.02	5.08

Gil Meche

Pitches: R **Bats:** R **Pos:** SP-23   **Ht:** 6'3" **Wt:** 200 **Born:** 9/8/1978 **Age:** 26

Year Team	Lg	G	GS	CG	GF	IP	BFP	H	R	ER	HR	SH	SF	HB	TBB	IBB	SO	WP	Bk	W	L	Pct	ShO	Sv-Op	Hld	ERC	ERA
		HOW MUCH HE PITCHED						**WHAT HE GAVE UP**												**THE RESULTS**							
2004 Tacoma*	AAA	10	10	0	0	57.0	251	55	37	32	8	0	4	1	27	1	45	4	0	1	3	.250	0	0- -	1	4.46	5.05
1999 Seattle	AL	16	15	0	0	85.2	375	73	48	45	9	5	3	2	57	1	47	1	0	8	4	.667	0	0-0	0	4.47	4.73
2000 Seattle	AL	15	15	1	0	85.2	363	75	37	36	7	5	4	1	40	0	60	2	0	4	4	.500	1	0-0	0	3.60	3.78
2003 Seattle	AL	32	32	1	0	186.1	785	187	97	95	30	3	5	3	63	2	130	7	0	15	13	.536	0	0-0	0	4.39	4.59
2004 Seattle	AL	23	23	1	0	127.2	565	139	73	71	21	1	3	5	47	0	99	4	0	7	7	.500	1	0-0	0	5.06	5.01
4 ML YEARS		86	85	3	0	485.1	2088	474	255	247	67	14	15	11	207	3	336	14	0	34	28	.548	2	0-0	0	4.44	4.58

Jim Mecir

Pitches: R **Bats:** B **Pos:** RP-65   **Ht:** 6'1" **Wt:** 230 **Born:** 5/16/1970 **Age:** 35

Year Team	Lg	G	GS	CG	GF	IP	BFP	H	R	ER	HR	SH	SF	HB	TBB	IBB	SO	WP	Bk	W	L	Pct	ShO	Sv-Op	Hld	ERC	ERA
		HOW MUCH HE PITCHED						**WHAT HE GAVE UP**												**THE RESULTS**							
1995 Seattle	AL	2	0	0	1	4.2	21	5	1	0	0	0	0	0	2	0	3	0	0	0	0	-	0	0-0	0	3.75	0.00
1996 New York	AL	26	0	0	10	40.1	185	42	24	23	6	5	4	0	23	4	38	6	0	1	1	.500	0	0-0	0	5.10	5.13
1997 New York	AL	25	0	0	11	33.2	142	36	23	22	5	0	1	2	10	1	25	1	0	0	4	.000	0	0-1	1	4.73	5.88
1998 Tampa Bay	AL	68	0	0	23	84.0	343	68	30	29	6	3	2	3	33	5	77	2	0	7	2	.778	0	0-3	14	2.95	3.11
1999 Tampa Bay	AL	17	0	0	3	20.2	91	15	7	6	0	0	2	1	14	0	15	0	0	1	0	1.000	0	0-2	5	3.05	2.61
2000 TB-Oak	AL	63	0	0	17	85.0	352	70	31	28	4	1	2	2	36	2	70	2	0	10	3	.769	0	5-13	21	2.95	2.96

Year Team	Lg	G	GS	CG	GF	IP	BFP	H	R	ER	HR	SH	SF	HB	TBB	IBB	SO	WP	Bk	W	L	Pct	ShO	Sv-Op	Hld	ERC	ERA
2001 Oakland	AL	54	0	0	14	63.0	264	54	25	24	4	3	0	1	26	7	61	2	0	2	8	.200	0	3-8	17	3.00	3.43
2002 Oakland	AL	61	0	0	10	67.2	304	68	36	32	5	4	4	4	29	4	53	4	1	6	4	.600	0	1-6	20	4.05	4.26
2003 Oakland	AL	41	0	0	7	37.0	165	40	25	23	4	3	2	1	16	1	25	1	0	2	3	.400	0	1-2	12	4.77	5.59
2004 Oakland	AL	65	0	0	17	47.2	212	45	21	19	5	1	0	4	19	2	49	1	0	0	5	.000	0	2-7	21	3.94	3.59
2000 Tampa Bay	AL	38	0	0	10	49.2	199	35	17	17	2	1	1	1	22	0	33	0	0	7	2	.778	0	1-4	11	2.44	3.08
2000 Oakland	AL	25	0	0	7	35.1	153	35	14	11	2	0	1	1	14	2	37	2	0	3	1	.750	0	4-9	10	3.71	2.80
10 ML YEARS		422	0	0	113	483.2	2079	443	223	206	39	20	17	18	208	26	416	19	1	28	31	.475	0	12-42	112	3.64	3.83

Adam Melhuse

Bats: B **Throws:** R **Pos:** C-65; PH-6; 3B-3; 1B-1   **Ht:** 6'2" **Wt:** 200 **Born:** 3/27/1972 **Age:** 33

							BATTING												BASERUNNING				AVERAGES		
Year Team	Lg	G	AB	H	2B	3B	HR	(Hm	Rd)	TB	R	RBI	RC	TBB	IBB	SO	HBP	SH	SF	SB	CS	SB%	GDP	Avg	OBP	Slg
2000 LA-Col	NL	24	24	4	0	1	0	(0	0)	6	3	4	2	3	0	6	0	0	0	0	0	-	1	.167	.259	.250
2001 Colorado	NL	40	71	13	2	0	1	(0	1)	18	5	8	4	6	0	18	0	0	2	1	0	1.00	1	.183	.241	.254
2003 Oakland	AL	40	77	23	7	0	5	(2	3)	45	13	14	15	9	0	19	0	0	0	0	0	-	2	.299	.372	.584
2004 Oakland	AL	69	214	55	11	0	11	(3	8)	99	23	31	21	16	1	47	0	1	0	0	1	.00	4	.257	.309	.463
2000 Los Angeles	NL	1	1	0	0	0	0	(0	0)	0	0	0	0	0	0	1	0	0	0	0	0	-	0	.000	.000	.000
2000 Colorado	NL	23	23	4	0	1	0	(0	0)	6	3	4	2	3	0	5	0	0	0	0	0	-	1	.174	.269	.261
4 ML YEARS		173	386	95	20	1	17	(5	12)	168	44	57	42	34	1	90	0	1	2	1	1	.50	10	.246	.306	.435

Kevin Mench

Bats: R **Throws:** R **Pos:** RF-62; LF-53; DH-14; PH-7; CF-5   **Ht:** 6'0" **Wt:** 215 **Born:** 1/7/1978 **Age:** 27

							BATTING												BASERUNNING				AVERAGES		
Year Team	Lg	G	AB	H	2B	3B	HR	(Hm	Rd)	TB	R	RBI	RC	TBB	IBB	SO	HBP	SH	SF	SB	CS	SB%	GDP	Avg	OBP	Slg
2004 Frisco*	AA	4	16	5	0	0	1	(-	-)	8	3	1	2	1	0	0	0	0	0	0	0	-	0	.313	.353	.500
2002 Texas	AL	110	366	95	20	2	15	(8	7)	164	52	60	59	31	0	83	8	2	5	1	1	.50	4	.260	.327	.448
2003 Texas	AL	38	125	40	12	0	2	(1	1)	58	15	11	23	10	0	17	3	0	1	1	1	.50	2	.320	.381	.464
2004 Texas	AL	125	438	122	30	3	26	(14	12)	236	69	71	72	33	2	63	6	0	4	0	0	-	6	.279	.335	.539
3 ML YEARS		273	929	257	62	5	43	(23	20)	458	136	142	154	74	2	163	17	2	10	2	2	.50	12	.277	.338	.493

Ramiro Mendoza

Pitches: R **Bats:** R **Pos:** RP-27   **Ht:** 6'2" **Wt:** 195 **Born:** 6/15/1972 **Age:** 33

Year Team	Lg	G	GS	CG	GF	IP	BFP	H	R	ER	HR	SH	SF	HB	TBB	IBB	SO	WP	Bk	W	L	Pct	ShO	Sv-Op	Hld	ERC	ERA
2004 Sarasota*	A+	2	2	0	0	4.0	18	6	2	2	0	0	0	0	0	0	3	0	0	0	1	.000	0	0--	-	4.47	4.50
2004 Pawtucket*	AAA	6	0	0	1	8.2	39	13	5	4	2	0	0	0	0	0	3	0	0	0	1	.000	0	0--	-	6.16	4.15
1996 New York	AL	12	11	0	0	53.0	249	80	43	40	5	1	1	4	10	1	34	2	1	4	5	.444	0	0-0	0	6.42	6.79
1997 New York	AL	39	15	0	9	133.2	578	157	67	63	15	3	5	5	28	2	82	2	1	8	6	.571	0	2-4	4	4.52	4.24
1998 New York	AL	41	14	1	6	130.1	548	131	50	47	9	6	7	9	30	6	56	3	0	10	2	.833	1	1-4	5	3.44	3.25
1999 New York	AL	53	6	0	15	123.2	536	141	68	59	13	6	4	3	27	3	80	2	0	9	9	.500	0	3-6	4	4.19	4.29
2000 New York	AL	14	9	1	0	65.2	281	66	32	31	9	1	2	4	20	1	30	0	0	7	4	.636	1	0-1	0	4.21	4.25
2001 New York	AL	56	2	0	11	100.2	401	89	44	42	9	4	3	2	23	3	70	2	0	8	4	.667	0	6-8	13	2.84	3.75
2002 New York	AL	62	0	0	14	91.2	394	102	43	35	8	1	4	2	16	2	61	1	0	8	4	.667	0	4-8	12	3.70	3.44
2003 Boston	AL	37	5	0	8	66.2	311	98	51	50	10	1	4	5	20	4	36	1	0	3	5	.375	0	0-1	3	7.22	6.75
2004 Boston	AL	27	0	0	12	30.2	119	25	12	12	3	0	0	1	7	1	13	1	1	2	1	.667	0	0-0	3	2.63	3.52
9 ML YEARS		341	62	2	75	796.0	3417	889	410	379	81	23	30	35	181	23	462	14	3	59	40	.596	2	16-32	44	4.19	4.29

Frank Menechino

Bats: R **Throws:** R **Pos:** 2B-42; DH-19; SS-14; PH-9; 3B-7; PR-1   **Ht:** 5'8" **Wt:** 198 **Born:** 1/7/1971 **Age:** 34

							BATTING												BASERUNNING				AVERAGES		
Year Team	Lg	G	AB	H	2B	3B	HR	(Hm	Rd)	TB	R	RBI	RC	TBB	IBB	SO	HBP	SH	SF	SB	CS	SB%	GDP	Avg	OBP	Slg
2004 Midland*	AA	4	13	4	0	0	0	(-	-)	4	1	0	2	2	0	1	0	0	0	0	0	-	0	.308	.400	.308
2004 Sacramento*	AAA	4	15	4	0	0	0	(-	-)	4	2	1	1	1	0	0	1	0	0	0	0	-	0	.267	.353	.267
1999 Oakland	AL	9	9	2	0	0	0	(0	0)	2	0	0	0	0	0	4	0	0	0	0	0	-	0	.222	.222	.222
2000 Oakland	AL	66	145	37	9	1	6	(3	3)	66	31	26	22	20	0	45	1	1	2	1	4	.20	1	.255	.345	.455
2001 Oakland	AL	139	471	114	22	2	12	(4	8)	176	82	60	69	79	0	97	19	3	6	2	3	.40	13	.242	.369	.374
2002 Oakland	AL	38	132	27	7	0	3	(2	1)	43	22	15	14	20	0	32	1	0	1	0	0	-	4	.205	.312	.326
2003 Oakland	AL	43	83	16	0	0	2	(1	1)	22	10	9	11	19	1	16	4	2	1	0	0	-	2	.193	.364	.265
2004 Oak-Tor	AL	85	269	74	13	4	9	(6	3)	122	40	26	44	37	1	52	4	1	0	0	2	.00	4	.275	.371	.454
2004 Oakland	AL	13	33	3	0	0	0	(0	0)	3	0	1	0	1	0	8	1	0	0	0	0	-	2	.091	.143	.091
2004 Toronto	AL	72	236	71	13	4	9	(6	3)	119	40	25	44	36	1	44	3	1	0	0	2	.00	2	.301	.400	.504
6 ML YEARS		380	1109	270	51	7	32	(16	16)	431	185	136	160	175	2	246	29	7	10	3	9	.25	24	.243	.358	.389

Kent Mercker

Pitches: L **Bats:** L **Pos:** RP-71   **Ht:** 6'2" **Wt:** 195 **Born:** 2/1/1968 **Age:** 37

Year Team	Lg	G	GS	CG	GF	IP	BFP	H	R	ER	HR	SH	SF	HB	TBB	IBB	SO	WP	Bk	W	L	Pct	ShO	Sv-Op	Hld	ERC	ERA
1989 Atlanta	NL	2	1	0	1	4.1	26	6	6	6	0	0	0	0	6	0	4	0	0	0	0		0	0-0	0	13.19	12.46
1990 Atlanta	NL	36	0	0	28	48.1	211	43	22	17	6	1	2	2	24	3	39	2	0	4	7	.364	0	7-10	4	4.04	3.17
1991 Atlanta	NL	50	4	0	28	73.1	306	56	23	21	5	2	2	1	35	3	62	4	1	5	3	.625	0	6-8	3	2.88	2.58
1992 Atlanta	NL	53	0	0	18	68.1	289	51	27	26	4	4	1	3	35	1	49	6	0	3	2	.600	0	6-9	6	2.99	3.42
1993 Atlanta	NL	43	6	0	9	66.0	283	52	24	21	2	0	0	2	36	3	59	5	1	3	1	.750	0	0-3	4	3.02	2.86
1994 Atlanta	NL	20	17	2	0	112.1	461	90	46	43	16	4	3	0	45	3	111	4	1	9	4	.692	1	0-0	0	3.27	3.45
1995 Atlanta	NL	29	26	0	1	143.0	622	140	73	66	16	8	7	3	61	2	102	6	2	7	8	.467	0	0-0	0	4.19	4.15
1996 Bal-Cle	AL	24	12	0	2	69.2	329	83	60	54	13	3	6	3	38	2	29	3	1	4	6	.400	0	0-0	2	6.56	6.98
1997 Cincinnati	NL	28	25	0	0	144.2	616	135	65	63	16	8	4	2	62	6	75	2	1	8	11	.421	0	0-0	0	3.91	3.92
1998 St Louis	NL	30	29	0	1	161.2	716	199	99	91	11	10	9	3	53	4	72	6	4	11	11	.500	0	0-0	0	4.96	5.07
1999 StL-Bos	NL	30	23	0	2	129.1	589	148	85	69	16	8	4	3	64	3	81	3	1	8	5	.615	0	0-0	0	5.54	4.80

Year Team	Lg	G	GS	CG	GF	IP	BFP	H	R	ER	HR	SH	SF	HB	TBB	IBB	SO	WP	Bk	W	L	Pct	ShO	Sv-Op	Hld	ERC	ERA
					HOW MUCH HE PITCHED				WHAT HE GAVE UP													THE RESULTS					
2000 Anaheim	AL	21	7	0	2	48.1	225	57	35	35	12	3	1	2	29	3	30	2	0	1	3	.250	0	0-0	1	7.35	6.52
2002 Colorado	NL	58	0	0	8	44.0	208	55	33	30	12	0	0	2	22	2	37	1	0	3	1	.750	0	0-3	9	7.45	6.14
2003 Cin-Atl	NL	67	0	0	15	55.1	242	46	16	12	6	6	1	0	32	4	48	4	1	0	2	.000	0	1-5	11	3.72	1.95
2004 Chicago	NL	71	0	0	7	53.0	223	39	15	15	4	0	3	3	27	2	51	4	1	3	1	.750	0	0-3	16	3.07	2.55
1996 Baltimore	AL	14	12	0	0	58.0	283	73	56	50	12	3	4	3	35	1	22	3	1	3	6	.333	0	0-0	0	7.45	7.76
1996 Cleveland	AL	10	0	0	2	11.2	46	10	4	4	1	0	2	0	3	1	7	0	0	1	0	1.000	0	0-0	2	2.65	3.09
1999 St Louis	NL	25	18	0	2	103.2	476	125	73	59	16	8	3	2	51	3	64	3	1	6	5	.545	0	0-0	0	6.15	5.12
1999 Boston	AL	5	5	0	0	25.2	113	23	12	10	0	0	1	1	13	0	17	0	0	2	0	1.000	0	0-0	0	3.29	3.51
2003 Cincinnati	NL	49	0	0	8	38.1	169	31	13	10	5	6	0	0	25	2	41	2	1	0	2	.000	0	0-3	10	4.09	2.35
2003 Atlanta	NL	18	0	0	7	17.0	73	15	3	2	1	0	1	0	7	2	7	2	0	0	-		0	1-2	1	2.95	1.06
15 ML YEARS		562	150	2	122	1221.2	5346	1202	629	569	139	57	43	29	569	41	849	52	14	69	65	.515	1	20-41	52	4.39	4.19

Lou Merloni

Bats: R **Throws:** R **Pos:** 1B-42; 3B-10; PH-10; 2B-7; LF-4; DH-3; PR-3   **Ht:** 5'10" **Wt:** 201 **Born:** 4/6/1971 **Age:** 34

| | | | | | | | | | BATTING | | | | | | | | | | | | BASERUNNING | | | | AVERAGES | | |
Year Team	Lg	G	AB	H	2B	3B	HR	(Hm	Rd)	TB	R	RBI	RC	TBB	IBB	SO	HBP	SH	SF	SB	CS	SB%	GDP	Avg	OBP	Slg
2004 Mahning VI*	A-	2	8	2	0	0	1	(-	-)	5	1	4	1	0	0	3	0	0	0	0	0	-	0	.250	.250	.625
1998 Boston	AL	39	96	27	6	0	1	(1	0)	36	10	15	13	7	1	20	2	1	0	1	0	1.00	1	.281	.343	.375
1999 Boston	AL	43	126	32	7	0	1	(0	1)	42	18	13	12	8	0	16	2	3	1	0	0	-	6	.254	.307	.333
2000 Boston	AL	40	128	41	11	2	0	(0	0)	56	10	18	17	4	1	22	1	4	2	1	0	1.00	8	.320	.341	.438
2001 Boston	AL	52	146	39	10	0	3	(0	3)	58	21	13	16	6	0	31	3	2	2	2	1	.67	6	.267	.306	.397
2002 Boston	AL	84	194	48	12	2	4	(1	3)	76	28	18	26	20	0	35	5	2	1	1	2	.33	4	.247	.332	.392
2003 SD-Bos		80	181	48	8	2	1	(1	0)	63	24	18	22	26	2	41	1	2	3	2	3	.40	3	.265	.355	.348
2004 Cleveland	AL	71	190	55	12	1	4	(1	3)	81	25	28	28	14	1	41	3	4	3	1	2	.33	8	.289	.343	.426
2003 San Diego	NL	65	151	41	7	2	1	(1	0)	55	20	17	19	22	2	33	1	2	3	2	3	.40	3	.272	.362	.364
2003 Boston	AL	15	30	7	1	0	0	(0	0)	8	4	1	3	4	0	8	0	0	0	0	0	-	0	.233	.324	.267
7 ML YEARS		409	1061	290	66	7	14	(4	10)	412	136	123	134	85	5	206	17	18	12	8	8	.50	36	.273	.334	.388

Jose Mesa

Pitches: R **Bats:** R **Pos:** RP-70   **Ht:** 6'3" **Wt:** 225 **Born:** 5/22/1966 **Age:** 39

| | | | | | HOW MUCH HE PITCHED | | | | WHAT HE GAVE UP | | | | | | | | | | | | THE RESULTS | | | | | |
Year Team	Lg	G	GS	CG	GF	IP	BFP	H	R	ER	HR	SH	SF	HB	TBB	IBB	SO	WP	Bk	W	L	Pct	ShO	Sv-Op	Hld	ERC	ERA
1987 Baltimore	AL	6	5	0	0	31.1	143	38	23	21	7	0	0	0	15	0	17	4	0	1	3	.250	0	0-0	1	6.67	6.03
1990 Baltimore	AL	7	7	0	0	46.2	202	37	20	20	2	2	2	1	27	2	24	1	1	3	2	.600	0	0-0	0	3.21	3.86
1991 Baltimore	AL	23	23	2	0	123.2	566	151	86	82	11	5	4	3	62	2	64	3	0	6	11	.353	1	0-0	0	5.85	5.97
1992 Bal-Cle	AL	28	27	1	1	160.2	700	169	86	82	14	2	5	4	70	1	62	2	0	7	12	.368	1	0-0	0	4.57	4.59
1993 Cleveland	AL	34	33	3	0	208.2	897	232	122	114	21	9	9	7	62	2	118	8	2	10	12	.455	0	0-0	0	4.48	4.92
1994 Cleveland	AL	51	0	0	22	73.0	315	71	33	31	3	3	4	3	26	7	63	3	0	7	5	.583	0	2-8	3	3.31	3.82
1995 Cleveland	AL	62	0	0	57	64.0	250	49	9	8	3	4	2	0	17	2	58	5	0	3	0	1.000	0	46-48	0	2.06	1.13
1996 Cleveland	AL	69	0	0	60	72.1	304	69	32	30	6	2	2	3	28	4	64	4	0	2	7	.222	0	39-44	0	3.81	3.73
1997 Cleveland	AL	66	0	0	38	82.1	356	83	28	22	7	2	2	3	28	3	69	1	0	4	4	.500	0	16-21	9	3.83	2.40
1998 Cle-SF		76	0	0	36	84.2	383	91	50	43	8	6	2	4	38	5	63	10	0	8	7	.533	0	1-4	13	4.68	4.57
1999 Seattle	AL	68	0	0	68	68.2	325	84	42	38	11	2	4	4	40	4	42	7	0	3	6	.333	0	33-38	1	6.83	4.98
2000 Seattle	AL	66	0	0	29	80.2	372	89	48	48	11	2	6	5	41	0	84	3	0	4	6	.400	0	1-3	11	5.60	5.36
2001 Philadelphia	NL	71	0	0	59	69.1	291	65	26	18	4	2	3	2	20	2	59	2	1	3	3	.500	0	42-46	1	3.07	2.34
2002 Philadelphia	NL	74	0	0	64	75.2	331	65	26	25	5	6	1	4	39	7	64	9	0	4	6	.400	0	45-54	0	3.51	2.97
2003 Philadelphia	NL	61	0	0	47	58.0	273	71	44	42	7	1	0	1	31	2	45	3	0	5	7	.417	0	24-28	2	6.07	6.52
2004 Pittsburgh	NL	70	0	0	65	69.1	295	78	26	25	6	4	2	1	20	3	37	1	0	5	2	.714	0	43-48	0	4.31	3.25
1992 Baltimore	AL	13	12	0	1	67.2	300	77	41	39	9	0	3	2	27	1	22	2	0	3	8	.273	0	0-0	0	5.25	5.19
1992 Cleveland	AL	15	15	1	0	93.0	400	92	45	43	5	2	2	2	43	0	40	0	0	4	4	.500	1	0-0	0	4.09	4.16
1998 Cleveland	AL	44	0	0	18	54.0	244	61	36	31	7	2	2	4	20	3	35	2	0	3	4	.429	0	1-3	7	5.07	5.17
1998 San Francisco	NL	32	0	0	18	30.2	139	30	14	12	1	4	0	0	18	2	28	8	0	5	3	.625	0	0-1	6	3.99	3.52
16 ML YEARS		832	95	6	538	1369.0	6003	1442	701	649	126	52	48	45	564	46	933	66	4	75	93	.446	2	292-340	46	4.46	4.27

Dan Meyer

Pitches: L **Bats:** R **Pos:** RP-2   **Ht:** 6'3" **Wt:** 210 **Born:** 7/3/1981 **Age:** 23

| | | | | | HOW MUCH HE PITCHED | | | | WHAT HE GAVE UP | | | | | | | | | | | | THE RESULTS | | | | | |
Year Team	Lg	G	GS	CG	GF	IP	BFP	H	R	ER	HR	SH	SF	HB	TBB	IBB	SO	WP	Bk	W	L	Pct	ShO	Sv-Op	Hld	ERC	ERA
2002 Danville	A+	13	13	1	0	65.2	262	47	22	20	4	2	0	5	18	0	77	4	0	3	3	.500	0	0- -	-	2.19	2.74
2003 Rome	A	15	15	0	0	81.2	330	76	35	26	6	2	1	6	15	1	95	7	0	4	4	.500	0	0- -	-	3.03	2.87
2003 Myrtle Beach	A+	13	13	0	0	78.1	315	69	29	25	7	1	2	3	17	1	63	1	0	3	6	.333	0	0- -	-	2.84	2.87
2004 Greenville	AA	14	13	0	0	65.0	253	50	17	16	1	4	1	4	12	0	86	2	0	6	3	.667	0	0- -	-	1.87	2.22
2004 Richmond	AAA	12	11	0	1	61.1	263	62	23	19	6	6	1	1	25	1	60	2	1	3	3	.500	0	0- -	-	4.25	2.79
2004 Atlanta	NL	2	0	0	1	2.0	8	2	0	0	0	0	0	0	1	1	1	0	0	0	0	-	0	0-0	0	3.21	0.00

Danny Miceli

Pitches: R **Bats:** R **Pos:** RP-74   **Ht:** 6'0" **Wt:** 216 **Born:** 9/9/1970 **Age:** 34

| | | | | | HOW MUCH HE PITCHED | | | | WHAT HE GAVE UP | | | | | | | | | | | | THE RESULTS | | | | | |
Year Team	Lg	G	GS	CG	GF	IP	BFP	H	R	ER	HR	SH	SF	HB	TBB	IBB	SO	WP	Bk	W	L	Pct	ShO	Sv-Op	Hld	ERC	ERA
1993 Pittsburgh	NL	9	0	0	1	5.1	25	6	3	3	0	0	0	0	3	0	4	0	1	0	0	-	0	0-0	0	4.53	5.06
1994 Pittsburgh	NL	28	0	0	9	27.1	121	28	19	18	5	1	2	2	11	2	27	2	0	2	1	.667	0	2-3	4	4.98	5.93
1995 Pittsburgh	NL	58	0	0	51	58.0	264	61	30	30	7	2	4	4	28	5	56	4	0	4	4	.500	0	21-27	2	4.93	4.66
1996 Pittsburgh	NL	44	9	0	17	85.2	398	99	65	55	15	3	7	3	45	5	66	9	0	2	10	.167	0	1-1	4	6.09	5.78
1997 Detroit	AL	71	0	0	24	82.2	357	77	49	46	13	5	3	1	38	4	79	3	0	3	2	.600	0	3-8	11	4.30	5.01
1998 San Diego	NL	67	0	0	18	72.2	302	64	28	26	6	3	2	1	27	4	70	5	1	10	5	.667	0	2-8	20	3.20	3.22
1999 San Diego	NL	66	0	0	28	68.2	296	67	39	34	7	4	2	2	36	5	59	2	0	5	4	.444	0	2-4	9	4.57	4.46
2000 Florida	NL	45	0	0	9	48.2	207	45	23	23	4	1	1	1	18	2	40	3	0	6	4	.600	0	0-3	11	3.42	4.25
2001 Fla-Col	NL	51	0	0	15	45.0	199	47	29	24	7	2	2	0	16	2	48	4	0	2	5	.286	0	1-4	8	4.34	4.80
2002 Texas	AL	9	0	0	5	8.1	42	13	8	8	1	0	0	0	3	0	5	0	1	0	2	.000	0	0-1	0	7.11	8.64
2003 Col-Cle-NYY-Hou		57	0	0	16	70.1	293	59	27	25	13	3	0	2	25	3	58	4	1	2	4	.333	0	1-2	5	3.61	3.20

Year Team	Lg	G	GS	CG	GF	IP	BFP	H	R	ER	HR	SH	SF	HB	TBB	IBB	SO	WP	Bk	W	L	Pct	ShO	Sv-Op	Hld	ERC	ERA
2004 Houston	NL	74	0	0	15	77.2	336	74	34	31	10	5	3	2	27	12	83	4	0	6	6	.500	0	2-8	24	3.58	3.59
2001 Florida	NL	29	0	0	9	24.2	114	29	21	19	5	1	1	0	11	2	31	3	0	5		.000	0	0-3	8	5.80	6.93
2001 Colorado	NL	22	0	0	6	20.1	85	18	8	5	2	1	1	0	5	0	17	1	0	2	0	1.000	0	1-1	0	2.77	2.21
2003 Colorado	NL	14	0	0	1	20.2	95	24	13	13	7	1	0	1	9	1	18	1	0	0	2	.000	0	0-0	1	7.07	5.66
2003 Cleveland	AL	13	0	0	4	15.0	61	9	4	2	1	0	0	0	6	1	19	1	0	1	1	.500	0	0-1	0	1.70	1.20
2003 New York	AL	7	0	0	3	4.2	21	4	3	3	2	0	0	0	3	0	1	0	0	0	0	-	0	1-1	1	6.53	5.79
2003 Houston	NL	23	0	0	8	30.0	116	22	7	7	3	2	0	1	7	1	20	2	1	1	1	.500	0	0-0	3	2.22	2.10
12 ML YEARS		579	9	0	208	650.1	2840	640	354	323	88	29	26	18	277	44	595	40	4	41	48	.461	0	35-69	98	4.32	4.47

Jason Michaels

Bats: R **Throws:** R **Pos:** CF-44; PH-40; LF-39; RF-12; DH-1   **Ht:** 6'0" **Wt:** 204 **Born:** 5/4/1976 **Age:** 29

| | | | | | | | BATTING | | | | | | | | | | | BASERUNNING | | | | AVERAGES | | |
Year Team	Lg	G	AB	H	2B	3B	HR	(Hm	Rd)	TB	R	RBI	RC	TBB	IBB	SO	HBP	SH	SF	SB	CS	SB%	GDP	Avg	OBP	Slg
2001 Philadelphia	NL	6	6	1	0	0	0	(0	0)	1	0	1	0	0	0	2	0	0	0	0	0	-	0	.167	.167	.167
2002 Philadelphia	NL	81	105	28	10	3	2	(0	2)	50	16	11	14	13	1	33	1	0	2	1	1	.50	1	.267	.347	.476
2003 Philadelphia	NL	76	109	36	11	0	5	(1	4)	62	20	17	19	15	1	22	1	0	0	0	0	-	3	.330	.416	.569
2004 Philadelphia	NL	115	299	82	12	0	10	(5	5)	124	44	40	47	42	1	80	2	0	3	2	2	.50	3	.274	.364	.415
4 ML YEARS		278	519	147	33	3	17	(6	11)	237	80	69	80	70	3	137	4	0	5	3	3	.50	7	.283	.370	.457

Doug Mientkiewicz

Bats: L **Throws:** R **Pos:** 1B-125; PH-3; PR-2; 2B-1   **Ht:** 6'2" **Wt:** 200 **Born:** 6/19/1974 **Age:** 31

| | | | | | | | BATTING | | | | | | | | | | | BASERUNNING | | | | AVERAGES | | |
Year Team	Lg	G	AB	H	2B	3B	HR	(Hm	Rd)	TB	R	RBI	RC	TBB	IBB	SO	HBP	SH	SF	SB	CS	SB%	GDP	Avg	OBP	Slg
1998 Minnesota	AL	8	25	5	1	0	0	(0	0)	6	1	2	2	4	0	3	0	0	0	1	1	.50	0	.200	.310	.240
1999 Minnesota	AL	118	327	75	21	3	2	(0	2)	108	34	32	34	43	3	51	4	3	2	1	1	.50	13	.229	.324	.330
2000 Minnesota	AL	3	14	6	0	0	0	(0	0)	6	0	4	2	0	0	0	0	0	0	1	0	-	1	.429	.400	.429
2001 Minnesota	AL	151	543	166	39	1	15	(11	4)	252	77	74	96	67	6	92	9	0	7	2	6	.25	10	.306	.387	.464
2002 Minnesota	AL	143	467	122	29	1	10	(6	4)	183	60	64	76	74	8	69	6	0	7	1	2	.33	7	.261	.365	.392
2003 Minnesota	AL	142	487	146	38	1	11	(6	5)	219	67	65	89	74	4	55	5	2	6	4	1	.80	9	.300	.393	.450
2004 Min-Bos	AL	127	391	93	24	1	6	(1	5)	137	47	35	46	48	2	56	4	2	2	2	3	.40	12	.238	.326	.350
2004 Minnesota	AL	78	284	70	18	0	5	(1	4)	103	34	25	34	38	2	38	3	2	1	2	2	.50	9	.246	.340	.363
2004 Boston	AL	49	107	23	6	1	1	(0	1)	34	13	10	12	10	0	18	1	0	1	0	1	.00	3	.215	.286	.318
7 ML YEARS		692	2254	613	152	7	44	(24	20)	911	286	276	345	310	23	326	28	7	25	11	14	.44	52	.272	.363	.404

Aaron Miles

Bats: B **Throws:** R **Pos:** 2B-128; PH-12; PR-1   **Ht:** 5'8" **Wt:** 170 **Born:** 12/15/1976 **Age:** 28

| | | | | | | | BATTING | | | | | | | | | | | BASERUNNING | | | | AVERAGES | | |
Year Team	Lg	G	AB	H	2B	3B	HR	(Hm	Rd)	TB	R	RBI	RC	TBB	IBB	SO	HBP	SH	SF	SB	CS	SB%	GDP	Avg	OBP	Slg
1995 Astros	R	47	171	44	9	3	0	(-	-)	59	32	18	18	14	0	14	0	4	1	9	6	.60	3	.257	.312	.345
1996 Astros	R	55	214	63	3	2	0	(-	-)	70	48	15	28	20	0	18	1	5	0	14	7	.67	3	.294	.357	.327
1997 Quad City	A	97	370	97	13	2	1	(-	-)	117	55	35	38	30	0	45	2	7	4	18	11	.62	8	.262	.318	.316
1998 Quad City	A	108	369	90	22	6	2	(-	-)	130	42	37	36	25	3	52	1	7	1	28	13	.68	6	.244	.293	.352
1999 Michigan	A	112	470	149	28	8	10	(-	-)	223	72	71	75	28	3	33	2	6	7	17	12	.59	8	.317	.353	.474
2000 Kissimmee	A+	75	295	86	20	1	2	(-	-)	114	40	36	39	28	0	29	0	2	1	11	6	.65	7	.292	.352	.386
2001 Birmingham	AA	84	343	89	16	3	8	(-	-)	135	53	42	39	26	0	35	2	3	3	3	5	.38	10	.259	.313	.394
2002 Birmingham	AA	138	531	171	39	1	9	(-	-)	239	67	68	87	40	4	45	2	11	5	25	16	.61	4	.322	.369	.450
2003 Charlotte	AAA	133	546	166	34	5	11	(-	-)	243	80	50	82	40	2	52	1	5	3	8	9	.47	9	.304	.351	.445
2004 Co Springs	AAA	12	54	18	3	0	0	(-	-)	21	8	8	7	2	0	4	0	0	2	2	2	.50	1	.333	.345	.389
2003 Chicago	AL	8	12	4	3	0	0	(0	0)	7	3	2	3	0	0	0	0	0	0	0	0	-	0	.333	.333	.583
2004 Colorado	NL	134	522	153	15	3	6	(4	2)	192	75	47	70	29	0	53	2	7	6	12	7	.63	12	.293	.329	.368
2 ML YEARS		142	534	157	18	3	6	(4	2)	199	78	49	73	29	0	53	2	7	6	12	7	.63	12	.294	.329	.373

Kevin Millar

Bats: R **Throws:** R **Pos:** 1B-69; RF-55; LF-20; DH-8; PH-7   **Ht:** 6'0" **Wt:** 210 **Born:** 9/24/1971 **Age:** 33

| | | | | | | | BATTING | | | | | | | | | | | BASERUNNING | | | | AVERAGES | | |
Year Team	Lg	G	AB	H	2B	3B	HR	(Hm	Rd)	TB	R	RBI	RC	TBB	IBB	SO	HBP	SH	SF	SB	CS	SB%	GDP	Avg	OBP	Slg
1998 Florida	NL	2	2	1	0	0	0	(0	0)	1	0	1	0	1	0	0	0	0	0	0	0	-	0	.500	.667	.500
1999 Florida	NL	105	351	100	17	4	9	(3	6)	152	48	67	57	40	2	64	7	1	8	1	0	1.00	6	.285	.362	.433
2000 Florida	NL	123	259	67	14	3	14	(6	8)	129	36	42	47	36	0	47	8	0	2	0	0	-	5	.259	.364	.498
2001 Florida	NL	144	449	141	39	5	20	(13	7)	250	62	85	89	39	2	70	5	0	2	0	0	-	8	.314	.374	.557
2002 Florida	NL	126	438	134	41	0	16	(11	5)	223	58	57	63	40	0	74	5	0	6	0	2	.00	15	.306	.366	.509
2003 Boston	AL	148	544	150	30	1	25	(10	15)	257	83	96	87	60	5	108	5	0	9	3	2	.60	14	.276	.348	.472
2004 Boston	AL	150	508	151	36	0	18	(12	6)	241	74	74	90	57	0	91	17	0	6	1	1	.50	16	.297	.383	.474
7 ML YEARS		798	2551	744	177	13	102	(55	47)	1253	362	421	434	273	9	454	47	1	33	5	5	.50	65	.292	.366	.491

Corky Miller

Bats: R **Throws:** R **Pos:** C-12; PH-1   **Ht:** 6'1" **Wt:** 225 **Born:** 3/18/1976 **Age:** 29

| | | | | | | | BATTING | | | | | | | | | | | BASERUNNING | | | | AVERAGES | | |
Year Team	Lg	G	AB	H	2B	3B	HR	(Hm	Rd)	TB	R	RBI	RC	TBB	IBB	SO	HBP	SH	SF	SB	CS	SB%	GDP	Avg	OBP	Slg
2004 Louisville*	AAA	74	227	50	14	0	6	(-	-)	82	31	37	27	25	0	44	9	1	5	0	0	-	4	.220	.316	.361
2001 Cincinnati	NL	17	49	9	2	0	3	(1	2)	20	5	7	6	4	0	16	2	0	2	1	0	1.00	1	.184	.263	.408
2002 Cincinnati	NL	39	114	29	10	0	3	(2	1)	48	9	15	15	9	2	20	4	1	1	0	0	-	5	.254	.328	.421
2003 Cincinnati	NL	14	30	8	0	0	0	(0	0)	8	4	1	5	5	0	7	2	0	1	0	0	-	0	.267	.395	.267
2004 Cincinnati	NL	13	39	1	0	0	0	(0	0)	1	2	3	0	6	0	12	3	0	1	0	0	-	3	.026	.204	.026
4 ML YEARS		83	232	47	12	0	6	(3	3)	77	20	26	26	24	2	55	11	1	5	1	0	1.00	12	.203	.301	.332

Damian Miller

Bats: R **Throws:** R **Pos:** C-109; PH-1   **Ht:** 6'2" **Wt:** 218 **Born:** 10/13/1969 **Age:** 35

								BATTING													BASERUNNING				AVERAGES		
Year Team	Lg	G	AB	H	2B	3B	HR	(Hm Rd)	TB	R	RBI	RC	TBB	IBB	SO	HBP	SH	SF	SB	CS	SB%	GDP	Avg	OBP	Slg
1997 Minnesota	AL	25	66	18	1	0	2	(1 1)	25	5	13	7	2	0	12	0	0	3	0	0	-	2	.273	.282	.379
1998 Arizona	NL	57	168	48	14	2	3	(2 1)	75	17	14	25	11	2	43	2	2	0	1	0	1.00	2	.286	.337	.446
1999 Arizona	NL	86	296	80	19	0	11	(3 8)	132	35	47	40	19	3	78	2	0	3	0	0	-	6	.270	.316	.446
2000 Arizona	NL	100	324	89	24	0	10	(6 4)	143	43	44	49	36	4	74	1	1	2	2	2	.50	6	.275	.347	.441
2001 Arizona	NL	123	380	103	19	0	13	(9 4)	161	45	47	52	35	9	80	4	4	2	0	1	.00	9	.271	.337	.424
2002 Arizona	NL	101	297	74	22	0	11	(4 7)	129	40	42	35	38	5	88	3	2	0	0	0	-	14	.249	.340	.434
2003 Chicago	NL	114	352	82	19	1	9	(6 3)	130	34	36	36	39	6	91	1	7	1	1	0	1.00	15	.233	.310	.369
2004 Oakland	AL	110	397	108	25	0	9	(5 4)	160	39	58	54	39	0	87	2	2	2	0	1	.00	19	.272	.339	.403
8 ML YEARS		716	2280	602	143	3	68	(36 32)	955	258	301	298	219	29	553	15	18	13	4	4	.50	73	.264	.331	.419

Justin Miller

Pitches: R **Bats:** R **Pos:** SP-15; RP-4   **Ht:** 6'2" **Wt:** 195 **Born:** 8/27/1977 **Age:** 27

		HOW MUCH HE PITCHED						WHAT HE GAVE UP												THE RESULTS							
Year Team	Lg	G	GS	CG	GF	IP	BFP	H	R	ER	HR	SH	SF	HB	TBB	IBB	SO	WP	Bk	W	L	Pct	ShO	Sv-Op	Hld	ERC	ERA
1997 Portland	A-	14	11	0	1	67.1	288	68	26	16	3	2	2	4	20	0	54	6	0	4	2	.667	0	0--	-	3.57	2.14
1998 Asheville	A	27	27	3	0	163.1	705	177	89	67	14	4	3	15	40	0	142	5	0	13	8	.619	1	0--	-	4.20	3.69
1999 Salem	A+	8	8	0	0	37.0	159	35	18	17	3	0	0	5	11	0	35	5	0	1	2	.333	0	0--	-	3.76	4.14
2000 Midland	AA	18	18	0	0	87.0	371	74	49	44	8	2	0	6	41	1	82	9	1	5	4	.556	0	0--	-	3.76	4.55
2000 Sacramento	AAA	9	9	0	0	54.2	217	42	18	15	3	0	1	3	13	0	34	2	0	4	1	.800	0	0--	-	2.22	2.47
2001 Sacramento	AAA	29	28	1	0	165.0	718	174	94	87	26	4	4	16	64	1	134	11	0	7	10	.412	0	0--	-	5.27	4.75
2002 Syracuse	AAA	8	8	0	0	44.2	183	34	11	8	0	1	2	0	16	0	29	1	0	3	2	.600	0	0--	-	2.02	1.61
2003 Dunedin	A+	1	1	0	0	6.0	22	3	3	3	0	1	0	1	2	0	5	0	0	1	0	1.000	0	0--	-	1.54	4.50
2004 Syracuse	AAA	3	3	0	0	16.2	70	16	6	4	2	0	0	0	4	0	21	1	0	1	0	.500	0	0--	-	2.16	2.16
2002 Toronto	AL	25	18	0	2	102.1	469	103	70	63	12	1	6	11	66	2	68	6	0	9	5	.643	0	0-0	1	5.73	5.54
2004 Toronto	AL	19	15	0	0	81.2	375	101	58	55	14	2	6	5	42	3	47	3	1	3	4	.429	0	0-0	0	6.91	6.06
2 ML YEARS		44	33	0	2	184.0	844	204	128	118	26	3	12	16	108	5	115	9	1	12	9	.571	0	0-0	1	6.25	5.77

Matt Miller

Pitches: R **Bats:** R **Pos:** RP-57   **Ht:** 6'3" **Wt:** 215 **Born:** 11/23/1971 **Age:** 33

		HOW MUCH HE PITCHED						WHAT HE GAVE UP												THE RESULTS							
Year Team	Lg	G	GS	CG	GF	IP	BFP	H	R	ER	HR	SH	SF	HB	TBB	IBB	SO	WP	Bk	W	L	Pct	ShO	Sv-Op	Hld	ERC	ERA
1998 Savannah	A	17	0	0	10	35.1	137	25	9	9	0	2	0	2	10	0	46	2	0	3	1	.750	0	3--	-	1.82	2.29
1999 Charlotte	A+	22	0	0	20	29.2	132	25	9	9	0	0	1	1	13	1	39	2	0	1	2	.333	0	8--	-	2.60	2.73
1999 Tulsa	AA	34	0	0	25	56.0	235	42	24	21	2	4	5	1	28	2	83	5	0	6	4	.600	0	7--	-	2.69	3.38
2000 Rangers	R	1	0	0	0	2.0	9	2	1	1	0	0	0	1	0	0	4	0	0	0	0	-	0	0--	-	3.63	4.50
2000 Tulsa	AA	3	0	0	0	3.2	22	7	7	6	0	0	1	0	4	0	4	1	0	0	0	-	0	0--	-	11.78	14.73
2000 Oklahoma	AAA	39	0	0	25	60.1	276	61	29	24	6	4	4	3	34	4	69	4	0	3	3	.500	0	4--	-	4.80	3.58
2001 Portland	AAA	44	0	0	31	44.2	192	48	22	18	1	3	0	2	14	2	43	5	0	1	7	.125	0	17--	-	3.18	3.63
2002 Sacramento	AAA	54	0	0	39	71.0	322	81	42	34	5	4	2	5	28	8	63	3	0	3	7	.300	0	6--	-	4.68	4.31
2003 Co Springs	AAA	61	0	0	13	63.1	260	46	17	15	0	5	1	6	23	1	83	2	1	5	0	1.000	0	3--	-	2.19	2.13
2004 Buffalo	AAA	13	0	0	9	14.0	59	10	4	3	0	0	1	1	6	1	17	0	0	2	2	.333	0	2--	-	2.13	1.93
2003 Colorado	NL	4	0	0	2	4.1	18	5	1	1	0	0	0	0	2	0	5	0	0	0	0	-	0	0-0	0	4.86	2.08
2004 Cleveland	AL	57	0	0	13	55.1	226	42	22	19	1	2	1	6	23	8	55	1	1	4	1	.800	0	1-2	7	2.56	3.09
2 ML YEARS		61	0	0	15	59.2	244	47	23	20	1	2	1	6	25	8	60	1	1	4	1	.800	0	1-2	7	2.71	3.02

Trever Miller

Pitches: L **Bats:** R **Pos:** RP-60   **Ht:** 6'4" **Wt:** 195 **Born:** 5/29/1973 **Age:** 32

		HOW MUCH HE PITCHED						WHAT HE GAVE UP												THE RESULTS							
Year Team	Lg	G	GS	CG	GF	IP	BFP	H	R	ER	HR	SH	SF	HB	TBB	IBB	SO	WP	Bk	W	L	Pct	ShO	Sv-Op	Hld	ERC	ERA
1996 Detroit	AL	5	4	0	0	16.2	88	28	17	17	3	2	2	2	9	0	8	0	0	0	4	.000	0	0-0	0	10.15	9.18
1998 Houston	NL	37	1	0	15	53.1	235	57	21	18	4	0	0	1	20	1	30	1	0	2	0	1.000	0	1-2	1	4.18	3.04
1999 Houston	NL	47	0	0	11	49.2	232	58	29	28	6	2	2	5	29	1	37	4	0	3	2	.600	0	1-1	4	6.48	5.07
2000 Phi-LA	NL	16	0	0	2	16.1	90	27	22	19	3	1	1	2	12	1	11	1	0	0	0	-	0	0-0	0	10.68	10.47
2003 Toronto	AL	79	0	0	18	52.2	234	46	30	24	7	1	0	5	28	3	44	2	0	2	2	.500	0	4-5	16	4.36	4.61
2004 Tampa Bay	AL	60	0	0	15	49.0	208	48	21	17	3	3	0	3	15	4	43	2	0	1	1	.500	0	1-3	9	3.45	3.12
2000 Philadelphia	NL	14	0	0	2	14.0	72	19	16	13	3	1	1	1	9	1	10	1	0	0	0	-	0	0-0	0	8.14	8.36
2000 Los Angeles	NL	2	0	0	0	2.1	18	8	6	6	0	0	0	1	3	0	1	0	0	0	0	-	0	0-0	0	28.18	23.14
6 ML YEARS		244	5	0	61	237.2	1087	264	140	126	26	9	5	18	113	10	173	10	0	8	9	.471	0	7-11	30	5.30	4.77

Wade Miller

Pitches: R **Bats:** R **Pos:** SP-15   **Ht:** 6'2" **Wt:** 210 **Born:** 9/13/1976 **Age:** 28

		HOW MUCH HE PITCHED						WHAT HE GAVE UP												THE RESULTS							
Year Team	Lg	G	GS	CG	GF	IP	BFP	H	R	ER	HR	SH	SF	HB	TBB	IBB	SO	WP	Bk	W	L	Pct	ShO	Sv-Op	Hld	ERC	ERA
1999 Houston	NL	5	1	0	2	10.1	52	17	11	11	4	0	0	0	5	0	8	0	0	0	0	1.000	0	0-0	0	11.07	9.58
2000 Houston	NL	16	16	2	0	105.0	453	104	66	60	14	3	1	3	42	1	89	1	0	6	6	.500	0	0-0	0	4.37	5.14
2001 Houston	NL	32	32	1	0	212.0	873	183	91	80	31	7	5	4	76	3	183	8	0	16	8	.667	0	0-0	0	3.57	3.40
2002 Houston	NL	26	26	1	0	164.2	688	151	63	60	14	8	5	6	62	9	144	4	0	15	4	.789	1	0-0	0	3.54	3.28
2003 Houston	NL	33	33	1	0	187.1	797	168	96	86	17	8	7	10	77	1	161	4	0	14	13	.519	0	0-0	0	3.70	4.13
2004 Houston	NL	15	15	0	0	88.2	383	76	35	33	11	5	1	0	44	0	74	1	0	7	7	.500	1	0-0	0	3.78	3.35
6 ML YEARS		127	123	5	2	768.0	3246	699	362	330	91	31	19	23	306	14	659	18	0	58	39	.598	1	0-0	0	3.82	3.87

Kevin Millwood

Pitches: R Bats: R Pos: SP-25 | **Ht: 6'4" Wt: 220 Born: 12/24/1974 Age: 30**

		HOW MUCH HE PITCHED						WHAT HE GAVE UP												THE RESULTS							
Year Team	Lg	G	GS	CG	GF	IP	BFP	H	R	ER	HR	SH	SF	HB	TBB	IBB	SO	WP	Bk	W	L	Pct	ShO	Sv-Op	Hld	ERC	ERA
1997 Atlanta	NL	12	8	0	2	51.1	227	55	26	23	1	3	5	2	21	1	42	1	0	5	3	.625	0	0-0	0	4.03	4.03
1998 Atlanta	NL	31	29	3	1	174.1	748	175	86	79	18	8	3	3	56	3	163	6	1	17	8	.680	1	0-0	1	3.81	4.08
1999 Atlanta	NL	33	33	2	0	228.0	906	168	80	68	24	9	3	4	59	2	205	5	0	18	7	.720	0	0-0	0	**2.26**	2.68
2000 Atlanta	NL	36	35	0	0	212.2	903	213	115	110	26	8	5	3	62	2	168	4	0	10	13	.435	0	0-0	0	3.83	4.66
2001 Atlanta	NL	21	21	0	0	121.0	515	121	66	58	20	7	2	1	40	6	84	5	1	7	7	.500	0	0-0	0	4.20	4.31
2002 Atlanta	NL	35	34	1	0	217.0	895	186	83	78	16	9	4	8	65	7	178	4	0	18	8	.692	1	0-0	0	2.85	3.24
2003 Philadelphia	NL	35	35	5	0	222.0	930	210	103	99	19	12	5	4	68	6	169	2	0	14	12	.538	3	0-0	0	3.35	4.01
2004 Philadelphia	NL	25	25	0	0	141.0	628	155	81	76	14	11	2	7	51	5	125	4	0	9	6	.600	0	0-0	0	4.57	4.85
8 ML YEARS		228	220	11	3	1367.1	5752	1283	640	591	138	67	29	32	422	32	1134	31	2	98	64	.605	5	0-0	1	3.43	3.89

Eric Milton

Pitches: L Bats: L Pos: SP-34 | **Ht: 6'3" Wt: 220 Born: 8/4/1975 Age: 29**

		HOW MUCH HE PITCHED						WHAT HE GAVE UP												THE RESULTS							
Year Team	Lg	G	GS	CG	GF	IP	BFP	H	R	ER	HR	SH	SF	HB	TBB	IBB	SO	WP	Bk	W	L	Pct	ShO	Sv-Op	Hld	ERC	ERA
1998 Minnesota	AL	32	32	1	0	172.1	772	195	113	108	25	2	6	2	70	0	107	1	0	8	14	.364	0	0-0	0	5.21	5.64
1999 Minnesota	AL	34	34	4	0	206.1	858	190	111	103	28	3	6	3	63	2	163	2	0	7	11	.389	2	0-0	0	3.56	4.49
2000 Minnesota	AL	33	33	0	0	200.0	849	205	123	108	35	4	6	7	44	0	160	5	0	13	10	.565	0	0-0	0	4.09	4.86
2001 Minnesota	AL	35	34	2	0	220.2	944	222	109	106	35	8	6	5	61	0	157	2	0	15	7	.682	1	0-0	0	4.05	4.32
2002 Minnesota	AL	29	29	2	0	171.0	707	173	96	92	24	0	4	3	30	0	121	4	0	13	9	.591	1	0-0	0	3.59	4.84
2003 Minnesota	AL	3	3	0	0	17.0	66	15	5	5	2	0	1	0	1	0	7	0	0	1	0	1.000	0	0-0	0	2.29	2.65
2004 Philadelphia	NL	34	34	0	0	201.0	862	196	110	106	**43**	11	6	1	75	6	161	3	0	14	6	.700	0	0-0	0	4.57	4.75
7 ML YEARS		200	199	9	0	1188.1	5058	1196	667	628	192	28	35	21	344	8	876	17	0	71	57	.555	4	0-0	0	4.13	4.76

Damon Minor

Bats: L Throws: L Pos: 1B-16; PH-8; DH-1 | **Ht: 6'7" Wt: 230 Born: 1/5/1974 Age: 31**

		BATTING																		BASERUNNING				AVERAGES		
Year Team	Lg	G	AB	H	2B	3B	HR	(Hm	Rd)	TB	R	RBI	RC	TBB	IBB	SO	HBP	SH	SF	SB	CS	SB%	GDP	Avg	OBP	Slg
2004 Fresno*	AAA	97	338	102	23	3	17	(-	-)	182	48	56	69	50	2	78	6	0	2	0	0	-	7	.302	.399	.538
2000 San Francisco	NL	10	9	4	0	0	3	(2	1)	13	3	6	5	2	0	1	0	0	0	0	0	-	0	.444	.545	1.444
2001 San Francisco	NL	19	45	7	1	0	0	(0	0)	8	3	3	1	3	1	8	0	0	0	0	0	-	1	.156	.208	.178
2002 San Francisco	NL	83	173	41	6	0	10	(3	7)	77	21	24	18	24	6	34	2	0	2	0	0	-	1	.237	.333	.445
2004 San Francisco	NL	24	58	14	2	0	0	(0	0)	16	8	6	9	12	0	18	4	0	0	0	0	-	2	.241	.405	.276
4 ML YEARS		136	285	66	9	0	13	(5	8)	114	35	39	33	41	7	61	6	0	2	0	0	-	11	.232	.338	.400

Doug Mirabelli

Bats: R Throws: R Pos: C-53; DH-4; PH-4; PR-1 | **Ht: 6'1" Wt: 227 Born: 10/18/1970 Age: 34**

		BATTING																		BASERUNNING				AVERAGES		
Year Team	Lg	G	AB	H	2B	3B	HR	(Hm	Rd)	TB	R	RBI	RC	TBB	IBB	SO	HBP	SH	SF	SB	CS	SB%	GDP	Avg	OBP	Slg
1996 San Francisco	NL	9	18	4	1	0	0	(0	0)	5	2	1	2	3	0	4	0	0	0	0	0	-	0	.222	.333	.278
1997 San Francisco	NL	6	7	1	0	0	0	(0	0)	1	0	0	0	1	0	3	0	0	0	0	0	-	0	.143	.250	.143
1998 San Francisco	NL	10	17	4	2	0	1	(1	0)	9	2	4	3	2	0	6	0	0	0	0	0	-	0	.235	.316	.529
1999 San Francisco	NL	33	87	22	6	0	1	(1	0)	31	10	18	10	9	1	25	1	0	1	0	0	-	1	.253	.327	.356
2000 San Francisco	NL	82	230	53	10	2	6	(2	4)	85	23	28	30	36	2	57	2	3	2	1	0	1.00	6	.230	.337	.370
2001 Tex-Bos	AL	77	190	43	10	0	11	(5	6)	86	20	29	29	27	2	57	4	1	2	0	0	-	3	.226	.332	.453
2002 Boston	AL	57	151	34	7	0	7	(5	2)	62	17	25	19	17	0	33	3	0	2	0	0	-	6	.225	.312	.411
2003 Boston	AL	62	163	42	13	0	6	(3	3)	73	23	18	15	11	0	36	1	0	1	0	0	-	3	.258	.307	.448
2004 Boston	AL	59	160	45	12	0	9	(3	6)	84	27	32	32	19	0	46	3	0	0	0	0	-	5	.281	.368	.525
2001 Texas	AL	23	49	5	2	0	2	(1	1)	13	4	3	3	10	0	21	0	0	0	0	0	-	3	.102	.254	.265
2001 Boston	AL	54	141	38	8	0	9	(4	5)	73	16	26	26	17	2	36	4	1	2	0	0	-	2	.270	.360	.518
9 ML YEARS		395	1023	248	61	2	41	(20	21)	436	124	147	140	125	5	267	14	4	8	1	0	1.00	24	.242	.331	.426

Sergio Mitre

Pitches: R Bats: R Pos: SP-9; RP-3 | **Ht: 6'4" Wt: 210 Born: 2/16/1981 Age: 24**

		HOW MUCH HE PITCHED						WHAT HE GAVE UP												THE RESULTS							
Year Team	Lg	G	GS	CG	GF	IP	BFP	H	R	ER	HR	SH	SF	HB	TBB	IBB	SO	WP	Bk	W	L	Pct	ShO	Sv-Op	Hld	ERC	ERA
2001 Boise	A-	15	15	1	0	91.0	371	85	37	31	2	0	0	3	18	1	71	3	3	8	4	.667	1	0--	-	2.58	3.07
2002 Lansing	A	27	27	2	0	168.2	685	166	72	53	7	6	6	10	27	1	96	10	0	8	10	.444	0	0--	-	2.96	2.83
2003 W Tennesse	AA	25	24	0	0	145.2	639	162	75	54	6	9	3	12	41	0	128	6	0	7	9	.438	0	0--	-	4.12	3.34
2004 Iowa	AAA	18	15	1	1	102.2	424	97	38	34	9	8	0	6	39	1	95	7	1	6	3	.667	1	1--	-	3.99	2.98
2003 Chicago	NL	3	2	0	1	8.2	43	15	8	8	1	0	1	0	4	1	3	0	0	0	1	.000	0	0-0	0	9.02	8.31
2004 Chicago	NL	12	9	0	2	51.2	244	71	38	38	6	3	0	4	20	1	37	5	1	2	4	.333	0	0-0	0	6.69	6.62
2 ML YEARS		15	11	0	3	60.1	287	86	46	46	7	3	1	4	24	2	40	5	1	2	5	.286	0	0-0	0	7.01	6.86

Chad Moeller

Bats: R Throws: R Pos: C-100; PH-1 | **Ht: 6'3" Wt: 210 Born: 2/18/1975 Age: 30**

		BATTING																		BASERUNNING				AVERAGES		
Year Team	Lg	G	AB	H	2B	3B	HR	(Hm	Rd)	TB	R	RBI	RC	TBB	IBB	SO	HBP	SH	SF	SB	CS	SB%	GDP	Avg	OBP	Slg
2000 Minnesota	AL	48	128	27	3	1	1	(1	0)	35	13	9	8	9	0	33	0	1	1	1	0	1.00	4	.211	.261	.273
2001 Arizona	NL	25	56	13	0	1	1	(1	0)	18	8	2	5	6	1	12	0	0	0	0	0	-	2	.232	.306	.321
2002 Arizona	NL	37	105	30	11	1	2	(2	0)	49	10	16	17	17	3	23	0	1	0	0	1	.00	6	.286	.385	.467
2003 Arizona	NL	78	239	64	17	1	7	(4	3)	104	29	29	28	23	11	59	2	3	2	1	2	.33	7	.268	.335	.435
2004 Milwaukee	NL	101	317	66	13	1	5	(3	2)	96	25	27	14	21	1	74	4	6	1	0	1	.00	12	.208	.265	.303
5 ML YEARS		289	845	200	44	5	16	(9	7)	302	85	83	72	76	16	201	6	12	4	2	4	.33	31	.237	.303	.357

Dustan Mohr

Bats: R **Throws:** R **Pos:** RF-55; LF-43; PH-25; CF-6; PR-5; DH-2   **Ht:** 6'0" **Wt:** 210 **Born:** 6/19/1976 **Age:** 29

						BATTING													BASERUNNING				AVERAGES		
Year Team	Lg	G	AB	H	2B	3B	HR	(Hm | Rd)	TB	R	RBI	RC	TBB	IBB	SO	HBP	SH	SF	SB	CS	SB%	GDP	Avg	OBP	Slg
2001 Minnesota	AL	20	51	12	2	0	0	(0 | 0)	14	6	4	4	5	0	17	0	0	1	1	1	.50	0	.235	.298	.275
2002 Minnesota	AL	120	383	103	23	2	12	(3 | 9)	166	55	45	51	31	3	86	1	2	0	6	3	.67	5	.269	.325	.433
2003 Minnesota	AL	121	348	87	22	0	10	(4 | 6)	139	50	36	37	33	0	106	1	2	3	5	2	.71	10	.250	.314	.399
2004 San Francisco	NL	117	263	72	20	1	7	(3 | 4)	115	52	28	43	46	3	64	8	4	3	0	3	.00	5	.274	.394	.437
4 ML YEARS		378	1045	274	67	3	29	(10 | 19)	434	163	113	135	115	6	273	10	8	7	12	9	.57	20	.262	.339	.415

Ben Molina

Bats: R **Throws:** R **Pos:** C-90; PH-6; DH-5   **Ht:** 5'11" **Wt:** 210 **Born:** 7/20/1974 **Age:** 30

						BATTING													BASERUNNING				AVERAGES		
Year Team	Lg	G	AB	H	2B	3B	HR	(Hm	Rd)	TB	R	RBI	RC	TBB	IBB	SO	HBP	SH	SF	SB	CS	SB%	GDP	Avg	OBP	Slg
1998 Anaheim	AL	2	1	0	0	0	0	(0	0)	0	0	0	0	0	0	0	0	0	0	0	0	-	0	.000	.000	.000
1999 Anaheim	AL	31	101	26	5	0	1	(0	1)	34	8	10	9	6	0	6	2	0	0	0	1	.00	5	.257	.312	.337
2000 Anaheim	AL	130	473	133	20	2	14	(11	3)	199	59	71	60	23	0	33	6	4	7	1	0	1.00	17	.281	.318	.421
2001 Anaheim	AL	96	325	85	11	0	6	(6	0)	114	31	40	34	16	3	51	8	2	4	0	1	.00	8	.262	.309	.351
2002 Anaheim	AL	122	428	105	18	0	5	(2	3)	138	34	47	33	15	3	34	4	6	6	0	0	-	15	.245	.274	.322
2003 Anaheim	AL	119	409	115	24	0	14	(7	7)	181	37	71	57	13	2	31	2	2	4	1	1	.50	17	.281	.304	.443
2004 Anaheim	AL	97	337	93	13	0	10	(5	5)	136	36	54	45	18	1	35	2	2	4	0	1	.00	17	.276	.313	.404
7 ML YEARS		597	2074	557	91	2	50	(31	19)	802	205	293	238	91	9	190	24	16	25	2	4	.33	79	.269	.304	.387

Jose Molina

Bats: R **Throws:** R **Pos:** C-70; 1B-2; PR-2; DH-1   **Ht:** 6'1" **Wt:** 215 **Born:** 6/3/1975 **Age:** 30

						BATTING													BASERUNNING				AVERAGES		
Year Team	Lg	G	AB	H	2B	3B	HR	(Hm	Rd)	TB	R	RBI	RC	TBB	IBB	SO	HBP	SH	SF	SB	CS	SB%	GDP	Avg	OBP	Slg
1999 Chicago	NL	10	19	5	1	0	0	(0	0)	6	3	1	2	2	1	4	0	0	0	0	0	-	0	.263	.333	.316
2001 Anaheim	AL	15	37	10	3	0	2	(0	2)	19	8	4	6	3	0	8	0	2	0	0	0	-	2	.270	.325	.514
2002 Anaheim	AL	29	70	19	3	0	0	(0	0)	22	5	5	4	5	0	15	0	4	2	0	2	.00	2	.271	.312	.314
2003 Anaheim	AL	53	114	21	4	0	0	(0	0)	25	12	6	5	1	0	26	3	4	1	0	0	-	1	.184	.210	.219
2004 Anaheim	AL	73	203	53	10	2	3	(1	2)	76	26	25	19	10	0	52	0	5	0	4	1	.80	7	.261	.296	.374
5 ML YEARS		180	443	108	21	2	5	(1	4)	148	54	41	36	21	1	105	3	15	3	4	3	.57	12	.244	.281	.334

Yadier Molina

Bats: R **Throws:** R **Pos:** C-51; PH-1   **Ht:** 5'11" **Wt:** 225 **Born:** 7/13/1982 **Age:** 22

						BATTING													BASERUNNING				AVERAGES		
Year Team	Lg	G	AB	H	2B	3B	HR	(Hm	Rd)	TB	R	RBI	RC	TBB	IBB	SO	HBP	SH	SF	SB	CS	SB%	GDP	Avg	OBP	Slg
2001 Johnson City	R+	44	158	41	11	0	4	(-	-)	64	18	18	19	12	1	23	3	0	2	1	1	.50	4	.259	.320	.405
2002 Peoria	A	112	393	110	20	7	7	(-	-)	165	39	50	49	21	0	36	10	4	2	2	7	.22	14	.280	.331	.420
2003 Tennessee	AA	104	364	100	13	1	2	(-	-)	121	32	51	40	25	2	45	5	0	3	0	1	.00	11	.275	.327	.332
2004 Memphis	AAA	37	129	39	6	0	1	(-	-)	48	19	14	20	17	0	14	2	0	2	0	0	-	2	.302	.387	.372
2004 St Louis	NL	51	135	36	6	0	2	(1	1)	48	12	15	15	13	3	20	0	2	1	0	1	.00	4	.267	.329	.356

Raul Mondesi

Bats: R **Throws:** R **Pos:** LF-14; RF-12; CF-7; DH-1   **Ht:** 5'11" **Wt:** 230 **Born:** 3/12/1971 **Age:** 34

						BATTING													BASERUNNING				AVERAGES		
Year Team	Lg	G	AB	H	2B	3B	HR	(Hm	Rd)	TB	R	RBI	RC	TBB	IBB	SO	HBP	SH	SF	SB	CS	SB%	GDP	Avg	OBP	Slg
2004 R Cucamnga*	A+	2	8	1	0	0	0	(-	-)	1	2	0	0	1	0	2	0	0	0	0	0	-	1	.125	.222	.125
2004 Salt Lake*	AAA	2	6	2	0	0	1	(-	-)	5	1	2	1	1	0	2	0	0	0	0	0	-	0	.333	.429	.833
1993 Los Angeles	NL	42	86	25	3	1	4	(2	2)	42	13	10	14	4	0	16	0	1	0	4	1	.80	1	.291	.322	.488
1994 Los Angeles	NL	112	434	133	27	8	16	(10	6)	224	63	56	69	16	5	78	2	0	2	11	8	.58	9	.306	.333	.516
1995 Los Angeles	NL	139	536	153	23	6	26	(13	13)	266	91	88	89	33	4	96	4	0	7	27	4	.87	7	.285	.328	.496
1996 Los Angeles	NL	157	634	188	40	7	24	(11	13)	314	98	88	102	32	9	122	5	0	2	14	7	.67	6	.297	.334	.495
1997 Los Angeles	NL	159	616	191	42	5	30	(16	14)	333	95	87	114	44	7	105	6	1	3	32	15	.68	11	.310	.360	.541
1998 Los Angeles	NL	148	580	162	26	5	30	(13	17)	288	85	90	88	30	4	112	3	0	4	16	10	.62	8	.279	.316	.497
1999 Los Angeles	NL	159	601	152	29	5	33	(18	15)	290	98	99	102	71	6	134	3	0	5	36	9	.80	3	.253	.332	.483
2000 Toronto	AL	96	388	105	22	2	24	(10	14)	203	78	67	67	32	0	73	3	0	3	22	6	.79	8	.271	.329	.523
2001 Toronto	AL	149	572	144	26	4	27	(10	17)	259	88	84	89	73	3	128	6	0	2	30	11	.73	13	.252	.342	.453
2002 Tor-NYY	AL	146	569	132	34	1	26	(16	10)	246	90	88	73	59	3	103	5	0	4	15	6	.71	11	.232	.308	.432
2003 NYY-Ari	NL	143	523	142	31	4	24	(14	10)	253	83	71	65	56	6	97	3	0	4	22	11	.67	9	.272	.343	.484
2004 Pit-Ana		34	133	32	9	0	3	(2	1)	50	10	15	16	13	0	31	1	0	0	0	3	.00	2	.241	.313	.376
2002 Toronto	AL	75	299	67	16	1	15	(10	5)	130	51	45	37	31	1	57	3	0	2	9	2	.82	8	.224	.301	.435
2002 New York	AL	71	270	65	18	0	11	(6	5)	116	39	43	36	28	2	46	2	0	2	6	4	.60	3	.241	.315	.430
2003 New York	AL	98	361	93	23	3	16	(9	7)	170	56	49	42	38	6	66	2	0	2	17	7	.71	6	.258	.330	.471
2003 Arizona	NL	45	162	49	8	1	8	(5	3)	83	27	22	23	18	0	31	1	0	2	5	4	.56	3	.302	.372	.512
2004 Pittsburgh	NL	26	99	28	8	0	2	(1	1)	42	8	14	16	11	0	27	0	0	0	0	2	.00	1	.283	.355	.424
2004 Anaheim	AL	8	34	4	1	0	1	(1	0)	8	2	1	0	2	0	4	1	0	0	0	1	.00	1	.118	.189	.235
12 ML YEARS		1484	5672	1559	312	48	267	(135	132)	2768	892	843	888	463	47	1095	41	2	36	229	91	.72	88	.275	.332	.488

Craig Monroe

Bats: R **Throws:** R **Pos:** LF-65; RF-51; CF-27; PH-5; DH-3; PR-2   **Ht:** 6'1" **Wt:** 195 **Born:** 2/27/1977 **Age:** 28

						BATTING													BASERUNNING				AVERAGES		
Year Team	Lg	G	AB	H	2B	3B	HR	(Hm	Rd)	TB	R	RBI	RC	TBB	IBB	SO	HBP	SH	SF	SB	CS	SB%	GDP	Avg	OBP	Slg
2004 Toledo*	AAA	6	25	8	4	0	2	(-	-)	18	4	6	5	0	0	6	0	0	1	0	0	-	0	.320	.308	.720
2001 Texas	AL	27	52	11	1	0	2	(1	1)	18	8	5	6	6	0	18	0	0	0	2	0	1.00	1	.212	.293	.346
2002 Detroit	AL	13	25	3	1	0	1	(0	1)	7	3	1	0	0	0	5	1	0	0	0	2	.00	1	.120	.154	.280

Year Team	Lg	G	AB	H	2B	3B	HR	(Hm	Rd)	TB	R	RBI	RC	TBB	IBB	SO	HBP	SH	SF	SB	CS	SB%	GDP	Avg	OBP	Slg
2003 Detroit	AL	128	425	102	18	1	23	(10	13)	191	51	70	61	27	2	89	2	1	3	4	2	.67	10	.240	.287	.449
2004 Detroit	AL	128	447	131	27	3	18	(9	9)	218	65	72	66	29	1	79	2	0	3	3	4	.43	8	.293	.337	.488
4 ML YEARS		296	949	247	47	4	44	(20	24)	434	127	148	133	62	3	191	5	1	6	9	8	.53	20	.260	.307	.457

Melvin Mora

Bats: R **Throws:** R **Pos:** 3B-138; PH-2; SS-1; DH-1   **Ht:** 5'10" **Wt:** 180 **Born:** 2/2/1972 **Age:** 33

Year Team	Lg	G	AB	H	2B	3B	HR	(Hm	Rd)	TB	R	RBI	RC	TBB	IBB	SO	HBP	SH	SF	SB	CS	SB%	GDP	Avg	OBP	Slg
1999 New York	NL	66	31	5	0	0	0	(0	0)	5	6	1	2	4	0	7	1	3	0	2	1	.67	0	.161	.278	.161
2000 NYM-Bal		132	414	114	22	5	8	(5	3)	170	60	47	56	35	3	80	6	4	5	12	11	.52	5	.275	.337	.411
2001 Baltimore	AL	128	436	109	28	0	7	(6	1)	158	49	48	55	41	2	91	14	5	7	11	4	.73	6	.250	.329	.362
2002 Baltimore	AL	149	557	130	30	4	19	(8	11)	225	86	64	78	70	2	108	20	1	4	16	10	.62	7	.233	.338	.404
2003 Baltimore	AL	96	344	109	17	1	15	(8	7)	173	68	48	67	49	0	71	12	6	2	6	3	.67	3	.317	.418	.503
2004 Baltimore	AL	140	550	187	41	0	27	(15	12)	309	111	104	115	66	0	95	11	6	3	11	6	.65	10	.340	.419	.562
2000 New York	NL	79	215	56	13	2	6	(4	2)	91	35	30	29	18	3	48	2	2	5	7	3	.70	3	.260	.317	.423
2000 Baltimore	AL	53	199	58	9	3	2	(1	1)	79	25	17	27	17	0	32	4	2	0	5	8	.38	2	.291	.359	.397
6 ML YEARS		711	2332	654	138	10	76	(42	34)	1040	380	312	373	265	7	452	64	25	21	58	35	.62	31	.280	.367	.446

Mike Mordecai

Bats: R **Throws:** R **Pos:** PH-45; 3B-19; PR-7; 2B-4; SS-3; C-1   **Ht:** 5'10" **Wt:** 185 **Born:** 12/13/1967 **Age:** 37

Year Team	Lg	G	AB	H	2B	3B	HR	(Hm	Rd)	TB	R	RBI	RC	TBB	IBB	SO	HBP	SH	SF	SB	CS	SB%	GDP	Avg	OBP	Slg
1994 Atlanta	NL	4	4	1	0	0	1	(1	0)	4	1	3	1	1	0	0	0	0	0	0	0	-	0	.250	.400	1.000
1995 Atlanta	NL	69	75	21	6	0	3	(1	2)	36	10	11	13	9	0	16	0	2	1	0	0	-	0	.280	.353	.480
1996 Atlanta	NL	66	108	26	5	0	2	(0	2)	37	12	8	11	9	1	24	0	4	1	1	0	1.00	1	.241	.297	.343
1997 Atlanta	NL	61	81	14	2	1	0	(0	0)	18	8	3	2	6	0	16	0	1	1	0	1	.00	4	.173	.227	.222
1998 Montreal	NL	73	119	24	4	2	3	(1	2)	41	12	10	10	9	0	20	0	2	0	1	0	1.00	2	.202	.258	.345
1999 Montreal	NL	109	226	53	10	2	5	(4	1)	82	29	25	24	20	0	31	1	1	2	5	5	.29	1	.235	.297	.363
2000 Montreal	NL	86	169	48	16	0	4	(2	2)	76	20	16	25	12	0	34	1	1	0	2	2	.50	1	.284	.335	.450
2001 Montreal	NL	96	254	71	17	2	3	(1	2)	101	28	32	32	19	1	53	1	1	2	2	2	.50	6	.280	.330	.398
2002 Mon-Fla	NL	93	151	37	8	0	0	(0	0)	45	19	11	15	13	4	27	2	10	0	2	2	.50	3	.245	.313	.298
2003 Florida	NL	65	89	19	4	0	2	(1	1)	29	11	8	6	8	3	21	0	3	1	3	0	1.00	0	.213	.276	.326
2004 Florida	NL	69	84	19	3	0	1	(0	1)	25	7	5	9	6	0	18	0	0	0	1	1	.00	1	.226	.278	.298
2002 Montreal	NL	55	74	15	4	0	0	(0	0)	19	9	4	6	8	3	14	1	7	0	1	1	.50	2	.203	.289	.257
2002 Florida	NL	38	77	22	4	0	0	(0	0)	26	10	7	9	5	1	13	1	3	0	1	1	.50	1	.286	.337	.338
11 ML YEARS		791	1360	333	75	7	24	(11	13)	494	157	132	148	112	9	260	5	25	8	13	13	.50	19	.245	.303	.363

Orber Moreno

Pitches: R **Bats:** R **Pos:** RP-33   **Ht:** 6'3" **Wt:** 200 **Born:** 4/27/1977 **Age:** 28

		HOW MUCH HE PITCHED						WHAT HE GAVE UP											THE RESULTS						
Year Team	Lg	G	GS	CG	GF	IP	BFP	H	R	ER	HR	SH	SF	HB	TBB	IBB	SO	WP	Bk	W	L	Pct	ShO	Sv-Op	Hld	ERC	ERA
2004 Mets*	R	1	1	0	0	0.2	7	4	3	3	0	0	0	0	1	0	1	0	0	0	1	.000	0	0- -		47.92	40.50
2004 St. Lucie*	A+	1	0	0	0	1.0	7	4	3	3	0	0	0	0	0	0	2	1	0	0	0	-	0	0- -		22.42	27.00
1999 Kansas City	AL	7	0	0	0	8.0	34	4	0	5	1	0	0	0	6	0	7	0	0	0	0	-	0	0-1	0	2.84	5.63
2003 New York	NL	7	0	0	4	8.0	36	10	7	7	1	1	0	0	3	0	5	0	0	0	0	-	0	0-0	0	5.65	7.88
2004 New York	NL	33	0	0	8	34.2	146	29	17	13	0	1	0	3	11	0	29	2	1	3	1	.750	0	1-3	3	2.52	3.38
3 ML YEARS		47	0	0	12	50.2	216	43	24	25	2	2	0	3	20	0	41	2	1	3	1	.750	0	1-4	3	3.01	4.44

Justin Morneau

Bats: L **Throws:** R **Pos:** 1B-61; DH-11; PH-2   **Ht:** 6'4" **Wt:** 225 **Born:** 5/15/1981 **Age:** 24

Year Team	Lg	G	AB	H	2B	3B	HR	(Hm	Rd)	TB	R	RBI	RC	TBB	IBB	SO	HBP	SH	SF	SB	CS	SB%	GDP	Avg	OBP	Slg
1999 Twins	R	17	53	16	5	0	0	(-	-)	21	3	9	6	2	0	6	1	1	1	0	1	.00	2	.302	.333	.396
2000 Twins	R	52	194	78	21	0	10	(-	-)	129	47	58	53	30	7	18	0	0	2	3	1	.75	5	.402	.478	.665
2000 Elizabethton	R+	6	23	5	0	0	1	(-	-)	8	4	3	2	1	0	6	0	0	0	0	0	-	0	.217	.250	.348
2001 Quad City	A	64	236	84	17	2	12	(-	-)	141	50	53	55	26	1	38	3	0	4	0	0	-	4	.356	.420	.597
2001 Fort Myers	A+	53	197	58	10	3	4	(-	-)	86	25	40	35	24	1	41	8	0	5	0	0	-	4	.294	.385	.437
2001 New Britain	AA	10	38	6	1	0	0	(-	-)	7	3	4	0	3	0	8	0	0	1	0	0	-	1	.158	.214	.184
2002 New Britain	AA	126	494	147	31	4	16	(-	-)	234	72	80	82	42	5	88	6	0	6	7	0	1.00	8	.298	.356	.474
2003 New Britain	AA	20	79	26	3	1	6	(-	-)	49	14	13	17	7	2	14	0	0	0	0	0	-	1	.329	.384	.620
2003 Rochester	AAA	71	265	71	11	1	16	(-	-)	132	39	42	44	28	3	56	4	0	2	0	2	.00	2	.268	.344	.498
2004 Rochester	AAA	72	288	88	23	0	22	(-	-)	177	51	63	60	32	4	47	3	0	3	1	1	.50	7	.306	.377	.615
2003 Minnesota	AL	40	106	24	4	0	4	(1	3)	40	14	16	11	9	1	30	0	0	0	0	0	-	4	.226	.287	.377
2004 Minnesota	AL	74	280	76	17	0	19	(9	10)	150	39	58	48	28	8	54	2	0	2	0	0	-	4	.271	.340	.536
2 ML YEARS		114	386	100	21	0	23	(10	13)	190	53	74	59	37	9	84	2	0	2	0	0	-	8	.259	.326	.492

Matt Morris

Pitches: R **Bats:** R **Pos:** SP-32   **Ht:** 6'5" **Wt:** 210 **Born:** 8/9/1974 **Age:** 30

		HOW MUCH HE PITCHED						WHAT HE GAVE UP											THE RESULTS						
Year Team	Lg	G	GS	CG	GF	IP	BFP	H	R	ER	HR	SH	SF	HB	TBB	IBB	SO	WP	Bk	W	L	Pct	ShO	Sv-Op	Hld	ERC	ERA
1997 St Louis	NL	33	33	3	0	217.0	900	208	88	77	12	11	7	7	69	2	149	5	3	12	9	.571	1	0-0	0	3.41	3.19
1998 St Louis	NL	17	17	2	0	113.2	468	101	37	32	8	6	1	3	42	6	79	3	0	7	5	.583	1	0-0	0	3.25	2.53
2000 St Louis	NL	31	0	0	12	53.0	226	53	22	21	3	3	1	2	17	1	34	0	0	3	3	.500	0	4-7	7	3.58	3.57
2001 St Louis	NL	34	34	2	0	216.1	909	218	86	76	13	14	5	13	54	3	185	5	1	22	8	.733	1	0-0	0	3.50	3.16
2002 St Louis	NL	32	32	1	0	210.1	890	210	86	80	16	7	8	6	64	3	171	3	0	17	9	.654	1	0-0	0	3.63	3.42
2003 St Louis	NL	27	27	5	0	172.1	703	164	76	72	20	5	3	4	39	1	120	3	0	11	8	.579	3	0-0	0	3.37	3.76
2004 St Louis	NL	32	32	3	0	202.0	850	205	116	106	35	13	5	6	56	3	131	3	1	15	10	.600	2	0-0	0	4.30	4.72
7 ML YEARS		206	175	16	12	1184.2	4946	1159	511	464	107	59	30	41	341	19	869	22	5	87	52	.626	8	4-7	7	3.60	3.53

Damian Moss

Pitches: L **Bats:** R **Pos:** RP-3; SP-2   **Ht:** 6'0" **Wt:** 187 **Born:** 11/24/1976 **Age:** 28

Year Team	Lg	G	GS	CG	GF	IP	BFP	H	R	ER	HR	SH	SF	HB	TBB	IBB	SO	WP	Bk	W	L	Pct	ShO	Sv-Op	Hld	ERC	ERA
2004 Louisville*	AAA	4	3	0	0	18.2	96	29	23	22	4	1	1	1	15	0	12	1	1	0	3	.000	0	0- -	-	10.99	10.61
2004 Durham*	AAA	20	17	0	2	89.0	421	109	68	58	7	5	3	2	65	0	67	10	1	5	9	.357	0	0- -	-	6.90	5.87
2001 Atlanta	NL	5	1	0	2	9.0	41	3	3	3	1	1	0	0	9	0	8	1	0	0	0	-	0	0-0	0	2.61	3.00
2002 Atlanta	NL	33	29	0	2	179.0	743	140	80	68	20	12	3	6	89	5	111	13	2	12	6	.667	0	0-0	0	3.51	3.42
2003 SF-Bal		31	29	0	0	165.2	762	184	102	95	24	5	6	11	92	5	79	12	3	10	12	.455	0	0-0	0	5.97	5.16
2004 Tampa Bay	AL	5	2	0	2	8.0	43	13	15	15	2	0	0	1	5	0	6	1	0	0	1	.000	0	0-0	0	10.76	16.88
2003 San Francisco	NL	21	20	0	0	115.0	518	121	62	60	12	3	4	5	63	3	57	11	3	9	7	.563	0	0-0	0	5.18	4.70
2003 Baltimore		10	9	0	0	50.2	244	63	40	35	12	2	2	6	29	2	22	1	0	1	5	.167	0	0-0	0	7.87	6.22
4 ML YEARS		74	61	0	6	361.2	1589	340	200	181	47	18	9	18	195	10	204	27	5	22	19	.537	0	0-0	0	4.71	4.50

Guillermo Mota

Pitches: R **Bats:** R **Pos:** RP-78   **Ht:** 6'4" **Wt:** 205 **Born:** 7/25/1973 **Age:** 31

Year Team	Lg	G	GS	CG	GF	IP	BFP	H	R	ER	HR	SH	SF	HB	TBB	IBB	SO	WP	Bk	W	L	Pct	ShO	Sv-Op	Hld	ERC	ERA
1999 Montreal	NL	51	0	0	18	55.1	243	54	24	18	5	3	3	2	25	3	27	1	1	2	4	.333	0	0-1	3	4.10	2.93
2000 Montreal	NL	29	0	0	7	30.0	126	27	21	20	3	1	1	2	12	0	24	1	1	1	1	.500	0	0-0	5	3.86	6.00
2001 Montreal	NL	53	0	0	12	49.2	212	51	30	29	9	3	2	1	18	1	31	1	0	1	3	.250	0	0-3	12	4.77	5.26
2002 Los Angeles	NL	43	0	0	11	60.2	256	45	30	28	4	3	1	2	27	6	49	3	0	1	3	.250	0	0-1	4	2.57	4.15
2003 Los Angeles	NL	76	0	0	18	105.0	410	78	23	23	7	3	1	1	26	4	99	0	0	6	3	.667	0	1-3	13	2.01	1.97
2004 LA-Fla	NL	78	0	0	18	96.2	393	75	33	33	8	5	3	4	37	6	85	5	0	8	5	.529	0	4-8	30	2.82	3.07
2004 Los Angeles	NL	52	0	0	11	63.0	259	51	15	15	4	4	2	2	27	5	52	5	0	8	4	.667	0	1-1	17	2.98	2.14
2004 Florida	NL	26	0	0	7	33.2	134	24	18	18	4	1	1	2	10	1	33	0	0	1	4	.200	0	3-7	13	2.51	4.81
6 ML YEARS		330	0	0	84	397.1	1640	330	161	151	36	18	11	12	145	20	315	11	2	20	22	.476	0	5-16	67	3.03	3.42

Chad Mottola

Bats: R **Throws:** R **Pos:** LF-3; RF-2; PH-1   **Ht:** 6'3" **Wt:** 220 **Born:** 10/15/1971 **Age:** 33

Year Team	Lg	G	AB	H	2B	3B	HR	(Hm	Rd)	TB	R	RBI	RC	TBB	IBB	SO	HBP	SH	SF	SB	CS	SB%	GDP	Avg	OBP	Slg
2004 Ottawa*	AAA	117	457	121	22	0	22	(-	-)	209	60	69	61	22	0	90	9	0	5	8	5	1.00	13	.265	.308	.457
1996 Cincinnati	NL	35	79	17	3	0	3	(1	2)	29	10	6	7	6	1	16	0	0	0	2	2	.50	0	.215	.271	.367
2000 Toronto	AL	3	9	2	0	0	0	(0	0)	2	1	2	0	0	0	4	1	0	0	0	0	-	0	.222	.300	.222
2001 Florida	NL	5	7	0	0	0	0	(0	0)	0	1	1	0	2	0	2	0	0	1	0	0	-	0	.000	.200	.000
2004 Baltimore	AL	6	14	2	1	0	1	(0	1)	6	2	3	2	2	0	3	0	0	0	0	0	-	1	.143	.250	.429
4 ML YEARS		49	109	21	4	0	4	(1	3)	37	14	12	9	10	1	25	1	0	1	2	2	.50	1	.193	.264	.339

Jamie Moyer

Pitches: L **Bats:** L **Pos:** SP-33; RP-1   **Ht:** 6'0" **Wt:** 175 **Born:** 11/18/1962 **Age:** 42

Year Team	Lg	G	GS	CG	GF	IP	BFP	H	R	ER	HR	SH	SF	HB	TBB	IBB	SO	WP	Bk	W	L	Pct	ShO	Sv-Op	Hld	ERC	ERA
1986 Chicago	NL	16	16	1	0	87.1	395	107	52	49	10	3	3	3	42	1	45	3	3	7	4	.636	1	0-0	0	6.13	5.05
1987 Chicago	NL	35	33	1	1	201.0	899	210	127	114	28	14	7	5	97	9	147	11	2	12	15	.444	0	0-0	0	4.96	5.10
1988 Chicago	NL	34	30	3	1	202.0	855	212	84	78	20	14	4	4	55	7	121	4	0	9	15	.375	1	0-2	0	3.89	3.48
1989 Texas	AL	15	15	1	0	76.0	337	84	51	41	10	1	4	2	33	0	44	1	0	4	9	.308	0	0-0	0	5.20	4.86
1990 Texas	AL	33	10	1	6	102.1	447	115	59	53	6	1	7	4	39	4	58	1	0	2	6	.250	0	0-0	1	4.57	4.66
1991 St Louis	NL	8	7	0	1	31.1	142	38	21	20	5	4	2	1	16	0	20	2	1	0	5	.000	0	0-0	0	6.58	5.74
1993 Baltimore	AL	25	25	3	0	152.0	630	154	63	58	11	3	1	6	38	2	90	1	1	12	9	.571	1	0-0	0	3.58	3.43
1994 Baltimore	AL	23	23	0	0	149.0	631	158	81	79	23	5	2	2	38	3	87	1	0	5	7	.417	0	0-0	0	4.24	4.77
1995 Baltimore	AL	27	18	0	3	115.2	483	117	70	67	18	5	3	3	30	0	65	0	0	8	6	.571	0	0-0	0	4.11	5.21
1996 Bos-Sea	AL	34	21	0	1	160.2	703	177	86	71	23	7	6	2	46	5	79	3	1	13	3	.813	0	0-0	1	4.42	3.98
1997 Seattle	AL	30	30	2	0	188.2	787	187	82	81	21	6	1	7	43	2	113	3	0	17	5	.773	0	0-0	0	3.56	3.86
1998 Seattle	AL	34	34	4	0	234.1	974	234	99	92	23	4	3	10	42	2	158	3	1	15	9	.625	3	0-0	0	3.34	3.53
1999 Seattle	AL	32	32	4	0	228.0	945	235	108	98	23	6	2	9	48	1	137	3	0	14	8	.636	0	0-0	0	3.71	3.87
2000 Seattle	AL	26	26	0	0	154.0	678	173	103	94	22	3	3	3	53	2	98	4	1	13	10	.565	0	0-0	0	4.91	5.49
2001 Seattle	AL	33	33	1	0	209.2	851	187	84	80	24	5	11	10	44	4	119	1	0	20	6	.769	0	0-0	0	3.03	3.43
2002 Seattle	AL	34	34	4	0	230.2	931	187	89	85	28	5	7	9	50	4	147	3	0	13	8	.619	2	0-0	0	2.89	3.32
2003 Seattle	AL	33	33	1	0	215.0	897	199	83	78	19	7	6	8	66	3	129	0	0	21	7	.750	0	0-0	0	3.37	3.27
2004 Seattle	AL	34	33	1	1	202.0	888	217	127	117	44	9	6	11	63	3	125	1	0	7	13	.350	0	0-0	0	5.13	5.21
1996 Boston	AL	23	10	0	1	90.0	405	110	50	45	14	4	3	1	27	2	50	2	1	7	1	.875	0	0-0	1	5.37	4.50
1996 Seattle	AL	11	11	0	0	70.2	298	66	36	26	9	3	3	1	19	3	29	1	0	6	2	.750	0	0-0	0	3.31	3.31
18 ML YEARS		506	453	27	14	2939.2	12473	3002	1469	1355	358	102	78	99	843	52	1782	45	10	192	145	.570	8	0-2	2	4.02	4.15

Bill Mueller

Bats: B **Throws:** R **Pos:** 3B-96; 2B-14; PH-1   **Ht:** 5'10" **Wt:** 180 **Born:** 3/17/1971 **Age:** 34

Year Team	Lg	G	AB	H	2B	3B	HR	(Hm	Rd)	TB	R	RBI	RC	TBB	IBB	SO	HBP	SH	SF	SB	CS	SB%	GDP	Avg	OBP	Slg
2004 Pawtucket*	AAA	4	13	4	2	0	0	(-	-)	6	1	2	2	2	0	0	0	0	0	0	0	-	0	.308	.400	.462
1996 San Francisco	NL	55	200	66	15	1	0	(0	0)	83	31	19	35	24	0	26	1	1	2	1	1	.50	4	.330	.401	.415
1997 San Francisco	NL	128	390	114	26	3	7	(5	2)	167	51	44	62	48	1	71	3	6	6	4	3	.57	10	.292	.369	.428
1998 San Francisco	NL	145	534	157	27	0	9	(1	8)	211	93	59	83	79	1	83	1	3	5	3	3	.50	12	.294	.383	.395
1999 San Francisco	NL	116	414	120	24	0	2	(1	1)	150	61	36	62	65	1	52	3	8	2	4	2	.67	11	.290	.388	.362
2000 San Francisco	NL	153	560	150	29	4	10	(3	7)	217	97	55	72	52	0	62	6	7	6	4	2	.67	16	.268	.333	.388
2001 Chicago	NL	70	210	62	12	1	6	(4	2)	94	38	23	39	37	3	19	3	4	3	1	1	.50	4	.295	.403	.448
2002 ChC-SF	NL	111	366	96	19	4	7	(4	3)	144	51	38	56	52	2	42	0	4	5	0	0	-	9	.262	.350	.393
2003 Boston	AL	146	524	171	45	5	19	(6	13)	283	85	85	102	59	2	77	7	4	6	1	4	.20	11	.326	.398	.540
2004 Boston	AL	110	399	113	27	1	12	(9	3)	178	75	57	61	51	1	56	4	0	6	2	2	.50	8	.283	.365	.446

			BATTING																		BASERUNNING					AVERAGES		
Year Team	Lg	G	AB	H	2B	3B	HR	(Hm	Rd)	TB	R	RBI	RC	TBB	IBB	SO	HBP	SH	SF	SB	CS	SB%	GDP	Avg	OBP	Slg
2002 Chicago	NL	103	353	94	19	4	7	(4	3)	142	51	37	56	51	2	41	0	4	5	0	0	-	8	.266	.355	.402
2002 San Francisco	NL	8	13	2	0	0	0	(0	0)	2	0	1	0	1	0	1	0	0	0	0	0	-	1	.154	.214	.154
9 ML YEARS		1034	3597	1049	224	19	72	(32	40)	1527	582	416	572	467	11	488	28	37	41	19	17	.53	82	.292	.374	.425

Mark Mulder

Pitches: L **Bats:** L **Pos:** SP-33   **Ht:** 6'6" **Wt:** 215 **Born:** 8/5/1977 **Age:** 27

		HOW MUCH HE PITCHED						WHAT HE GAVE UP										THE RESULTS						
Year Team	Lg	G	GS	CG	GF	IP	BFP	H	R	ER	HR	SH	SF	HB	TBB	IBB	SO	WP	Bk	W	L	Pct	ShO	Sv-Op	Hld	ERC	ERA
2000 Oakland	AL	27	27	0	0	154.0	705	191	106	93	22	3	8	4	69	3	88	6	0	9	10	.474	0	0-0	0	6.14	5.44
2001 Oakland	AL	34	34	6	0	229.1	927	214	92	88	16	8	3	5	51	4	153	4	0	21	8	.724	4	0-0	0	2.95	3.45
2002 Oakland	AL	30	30	2	0	207.1	862	182	88	80	21	6	4	11	55	3	159	7	1	19	7	.731	1	0-0	0	3.06	3.47
2003 Oakland	AL	26	26	9	0	186.2	747	180	66	65	15	7	2	2	40	2	128	7	0	15	9	.625	2	0-0	0	3.17	3.13
2004 Oakland	AL	33	33	5	0	225.2	952	223	119	111	25	7	6	12	83	1	140	10	0	17	8	.680	1	0-0	0	4.27	4.43
5 ML YEARS		150	150	22	0	1003.0	4193	990	471	437	99	31	23	34	298	13	668	34	1	81	42	.659	8	0-0	0	3.76	3.92

Terry Mulholland

Pitches: L **Bats:** R **Pos:** RP-24; SP-15   **Ht:** 6'3" **Wt:** 220 **Born:** 3/9/1963 **Age:** 42

		HOW MUCH HE PITCHED						WHAT HE GAVE UP										THE RESULTS						
Year Team	Lg	G	GS	CG	GF	IP	BFP	H	R	ER	HR	SH	SF	HB	TBB	IBB	SO	WP	Bk	W	L	Pct	ShO	Sv-Op	Hld	ERC	ERA
1986 San Francisco	NL	15	10	0	1	54.2	245	51	33	30	3	5	1	1	35	2	27	6	0	1	7	.125	0	0-0	0	4.31	4.94
1988 San Francisco	NL	9	6	2	1	46.0	191	50	20	19	3	5	0	1	7	0	18	1	0	2	1	.667	1	0-0	1	3.46	3.72
1989 SF-Phi	NL	25	18	2	4	115.1	513	137	66	63	8	7	1	4	36	3	66	3	0	4	7	.364	1	0-0	1	4.64	4.92
1990 Philadelphia	NL	33	26	6	2	180.2	746	172	78	67	15	7	12	4	42	7	75	7	2	9	10	.474	1	0-1	0	3.04	3.34
1991 Philadelphia	NL	34	34	8	0	232.0	956	231	100	93	15	11	6	3	49	2	142	3	0	16	13	.552	3	0-0	0	3.15	3.61
1992 Philadelphia	NL	32	32	12	0	229.0	937	227	101	97	14	10	7	3	46	3	125	3	0	13	11	.542	2	0-0	0	3.07	3.81
1993 Philadelphia	NL	29	28	7	0	191.0	786	177	80	69	20	5	4	3	40	2	116	5	0	12	9	.571	2	0-0	0	2.99	3.25
1994 New York	AL	24	19	2	4	120.2	542	150	94	87	24	3	4	3	37	1	72	5	0	6	7	.462	0	0-0	0	5.92	6.49
1995 San Francisco	NL	29	24	2	2	149.0	666	190	112	96	25	11	6	4	38	1	65	4	0	5	13	.278	0	0-0	0	5.67	5.80
1996 Phi-Sea		33	33	3	0	202.2	871	232	112	105	22	11	8	5	49	4	86	6	0	13	11	.542	0	0-0	0	4.41	4.66
1997 ChC-SF	NL	40	27	1	5	186.2	794	190	100	88	24	17	4	11	51	3	99	3	0	6	13	.316	0	0-0	1	4.09	4.24
1998 Chicago	NL	70	6	0	14	112.0	476	100	49	36	7	5	3	4	39	7	72	4	0	6	5	.545	0	3-5	19	3.04	2.89
1999 ChC-Atl	NL	42	24	0	7	170.1	736	201	95	83	21	9	4	1	45	6	83	3	0	10	8	.556	0	1-1	4	4.73	4.39
2000 Atlanta	NL	54	20	1	14	156.2	702	198	96	89	24	10	5	4	41	7	78	3	0	9	9	.500	0	1-3	2	5.43	5.11
2001 Pit-LA	NL	41	4	0	8	65.2	285	78	35	34	12	1	1	2	17	1	42	1	0	1	1	.500	0	0-0	7	5.34	4.66
2002 LA-Cle		37	3	0	17	79.0	358	101	56	50	15	2	6	6	21	3	38	1	0	3	2	.600	0	0-0	2	6.08	5.70
2003 Cleveland	AL	45	3	0	14	99.0	444	117	60	54	17	0	6	6	37	6	42	1	0	3	4	.429	0	0-2	2	5.76	4.91
2004 Minnesota	AL	39	15	0	9	123.1	549	163	76	71	17	7	5	5	33	3	60	2	0	5	9	.357	0	0-0	1	5.94	5.18
1989 San Francisco	NL	5	1	0	2	11.0	51	15	5	5	0	0	0	0	4	0	6	0	0	0	0	-	0	0-0	1	5.23	4.09
1989 Philadelphia	NL	20	17	2	2	104.1	462	122	61	58	8	7	1	4	32	3	60	3	0	4	7	.364	1	0-0	0	4.58	5.00
1996 Philadelphia	NL	21	21	3	0	133.1	571	157	74	69	17	6	5	3	21	1	52	5	0	8	7	.533	0	0-0	0	4.36	4.66
1996 Seattle	AL	12	12	0	0	69.1	300	75	38	36	5	5	3	2	28	3	34	1	0	5	4	.556	0	0-0	0	4.49	4.67
1997 Chicago	NL	25	25	1	0	157.0	668	162	79	71	20	13	3	9	45	2	74	2	0	6	12	.333	0	0-0	0	4.24	4.07
1997 San Francisco	NL	15	2	0	5	29.2	126	28	21	17	4	4	1	2	6	1	25	1	0	0	1	.000	0	0-0	1	3.34	5.16
1999 Chicago	NL	26	16	0	4	110.0	485	137	71	63	16	6	3	1	32	4	44	2	0	6	6	.500	0	0-0	1	5.42	5.15
1999 Atlanta	NL	16	8	0	3	60.1	251	64	24	20	5	3	1	0	13	2	39	1	0	4	2	.667	0	1-1	3	3.55	2.98
2001 Pittsburgh	NL	22	1	0	3	36.1	150	38	15	15	5	1	1	1	10	1	17	1	0	0	0	-	0	0-0	3	4.32	3.72
2001 Los Angeles	NL	19	3	0	5	29.1	135	40	20	19	7	0	0	1	7	0	25	0	0	1	1	.500	0	0-0	4	6.67	5.83
2002 Los Angeles	NL	21	0	0	12	32.0	148	45	29	26	10	0	2	2	7	0	17	1	0	0	0	-	0	0-0	3	7.62	7.31
2002 Cleveland	AL	16	3	0	5	47.0	210	56	27	24	5	2	4	4	14	3	21	0	0	3	2	.600	0	0-0	2	5.05	4.60
18 ML YEARS		631	332	46	102	2513.2	10797	2765	1363	1231	286	126	83	68	663	61	1306	61	2	124	140	.470	10	5-12	41	4.27	4.41

Arnie Munoz

Pitches: L **Bats:** L **Pos:** RP-10; SP-1   **Ht:** 5'9" **Wt:** 170 **Born:** 6/21/1982 **Age:** 23

		HOW MUCH HE PITCHED						WHAT HE GAVE UP										THE RESULTS						
Year Team	Lg	G	GS	CG	GF	IP	BFP	H	R	ER	HR	SH	SF	HB	TBB	IBB	SO	WP	Bk	W	L	Pct	ShO	Sv-Op	Hld	ERC	ERA
1999 White Sox	R	14	0	0	7	12.0	61	13	10	7	1	0	0	2	8	0	12	1	1	0	2	.000	0	1--	-	5.82	5.25
2000 Burlington	A	22	0	0	8	38.1	185	45	34	29	2	1	0	6	25	0	44	7	5	2	3	.400	0	0--	-	6.43	6.81
2001 Kannapolis	A-	60	0	0	30	79.2	310	41	24	22	2	2	4	7	42	2	115	8	4	6	3	.667	0	12--	-	1.97	2.49
2002 Birmingham	AA	51	0	0	18	72.1	306	62	29	21	6	5	3	1	29	0	78	5	2	6	0	1.000	0	6--	-	3.21	2.61
2003 Charlotte	AAA	49	0	0	17	55.0	238	52	35	29	7	3	0	3	27	2	63	7	1	4	3	.571	0	6--	-	4.56	4.75
2004 Birmingham	AA	13	13	0	0	74.2	293	52	24	17	1	2	3	4	22	3	68	3	2	7	2	.778	0	0--	-	1.80	2.05
2004 Charlotte	AAA	13	13	0	0	69.2	316	81	48	44	11	3	2	2	29	0	60	6	2	6	6	.250	0	0--	-	5.61	5.68
2004 Chicago	AL	11	1	0	3	14.1	75	20	16	16	4	1	2	1	12	1	11	2	0	0	1	.000	0	0-0	0	10.17	10.05

Pete Munro

Pitches: R **Bats:** R **Pos:** SP-19; RP-2   **Ht:** 6'2" **Wt:** 200 **Born:** 6/14/1975 **Age:** 30

		HOW MUCH HE PITCHED						WHAT HE GAVE UP										THE RESULTS						
Year Team	Lg	G	GS	CG	GF	IP	BFP	H	R	ER	HR	SH	SF	HB	TBB	IBB	SO	WP	Bk	W	L	Pct	ShO	Sv-Op	Hld	ERC	ERA
2004 Rochester*	AAA	10	10	0	0	51.0	214	51	30	22	6	3	3	1	11	0	34	1	0	6	3	.667	0	0--	-	3.51	3.88
1999 Toronto	AL	31	2	0	9	55.1	250	70	38	37	6	1	4	2	23	0	38	3	0	0	2	.000	0	0-1	4	6.04	6.02
2000 Toronto	AL	9	3	0	2	25.2	127	38	22	17	1	1	0	3	16	0	16	1	0	1	1	.500	0	0-0	1	8.18	5.96
2002 Houston	NL	19	14	0	0	80.2	347	89	37	32	5	7	0	3	23	3	45	2	0	5	5	.500	0	0-0	1	4.04	3.57
2003 Houston	NL	40	2	0	8	54.0	249	63	30	28	7	3	1	5	26	2	27	1	0	3	4	.429	0	0-1	3	5.97	4.67
2004 Houston	NL	21	19	0	1	99.2	446	120	59	57	12	9	4	10	26	2	63	2	0	4	7	.364	0	0-0	1	5.20	5.15
5 ML YEARS		120	40	0	20	315.1	1419	380	186	171	31	21	9	23	114	7	189	9	0	13	19	.406	0	0-2	8	5.40	4.88

Eric Munson

Bats: L **Throws:** R **Pos:** 3B-94; PH-17; DH-7; C-1   **Ht:** 6'3" **Wt:** 228 **Born:** 10/3/1977 **Age:** 27

Year Team	Lg	G	AB	H	2B	3B	HR	(Hm	Rd)	TB	R	RBI	RC	TBB	IBB	SO	HBP	SH	SF	SB	CS	SB%	GDP	Avg	OBP	Slg
2000 Detroit	AL	3	5	0	0	0	0	(0	0)	0	0	1	0	0	0	1	0	0	0	0	0	-	0	.000	.000	.000
2001 Detroit	AL	17	66	10	3	1	1	(1	0)	18	4	6	2	3	0	21	0	0	0	0	1	.00	2	.152	.188	.273
2002 Detroit	AL	18	59	11	0	0	2	(0	2)	17	3	5	3	6	0	11	1	0	1	0	0	-	1	.186	.269	.288
2003 Detroit	AL	99	313	75	9	0	18	(7	11)	138	28	50	45	35	1	61	1	1	7	3	0	1.00	4	.240	.312	.441
2004 Detroit	AL	109	321	68	14	2	19	(13	6)	143	36	49	48	29	3	90	6	1	0	1	1	.50	1	.212	.289	.445
5 ML YEARS		246	764	164	26	3	40	(21	19)	316	71	111	98	73	4	184	8	2	8	4	2	.67	8	.215	.287	.414

Donald Murphy

Bats: R **Throws:** R **Pos:** 2B-7   **Ht:** 5'10" **Wt:** 180 **Born:** 3/10/1983 **Age:** 22

Year Team	Lg	G	AB	H	2B	3B	HR	(Hm	Rd)	TB	R	RBI	RC	TBB	IBB	SO	HBP	SH	SF	SB	CS	SB%	GDP	Avg	OBP	Slg
2002 Spokane	A-	28	109	33	10	2	0	(-	-)	47	20	15	16	6	0	17	3	0	0	0	0	-	2	.303	.356	.431
2003 Burlington	A	132	504	158	29	6	5	(-	-)	214	77	98	90	65	1	78	9	3	7	15	6	.71	8	.313	.397	.425
2004 Wilmington	A+	129	485	124	32	5	10	(-	-)	196	67	75	62	52	2	96	4	2	8	1	1	.50	16	.256	.328	.404
2004 Kansas City	AL	7	27	5	3	0	0	(0	0)	8	1	3	2	0	0	7	0	0	0	1	0	1.00	1	.185	.185	.296

Calvin Murray

Bats: R **Throws:** R **Pos:** CF-5; PR-3; RF-2; PH-2; LF-1   **Ht:** 5'11" **Wt:** 184 **Born:** 7/30/1971 **Age:** 33

Year Team	Lg	G	AB	H	2B	3B	HR	(Hm	Rd)	TB	R	RBI	RC	TBB	IBB	SO	HBP	SH	SF	SB	CS	SB%	GDP	Avg	OBP	Slg
2004 Iowa*	AAA	130	457	142	24	7	7	(-	-)	201	84	54	77	43	1	65	2	9	6	25	4	.86	10	.311	.368	.440
1999 San Francisco	NL	15	19	5	2	0	0	(0	0)	7	1	5	3	2	0	4	0	0	0	1	0	1.00	0	.263	.333	.368
2000 San Francisco	NL	108	194	47	12	1	2	(1	1)	67	35	22	27	29	0	33	3	2	1	9	3	.75	0	.242	.348	.345
2001 San Francisco	NL	106	326	80	14	2	6	(3	3)	116	54	25	36	32	0	57	3	3	0	8	8	.50	5	.245	.319	.356
2002 SF-Tex		48	89	13	5	1	0	(0	0)	20	16	1	5	7	0	17	1	2	0	4	0	1.00	0	.146	.216	.225
2004 Chicago	NL	11	5	1	0	0	0	(0	0)	1	2	1	1	1	0	0	0	0	0	0	0	-	0	.200	.333	.200
2002 San Francisco	NL	11	12	0	0	0	0	(0	0)	0	0	0	0	1	0	2	0	0	0	0	0	-	0	.000	.077	.000
2002 Texas	AL	37	77	13	5	1	0	(0	0)	20	16	1	5	6	0	15	1	2	0	4	0	1.00	0	.169	.238	.260
5 ML YEARS		288	633	146	33	4	8	(4	4)	211	108	54	72	71	0	111	7	7	1	22	11	.67	5	.231	.315	.333

Mike Mussina

Pitches: R **Bats:** L **Pos:** SP-27   **Ht:** 6'2" **Wt:** 185 **Born:** 12/8/1968 **Age:** 36

Year Team	Lg	G	GS	CG	GF	IP	BFP	H	R	ER	HR	SH	SF	HB	TBB	IBB	SO	WP	Bk	W	L	Pct	ShO	Sv-Op	Hld	ERC	ERA
2004 Columbus*	AAA	1	1	0	0	3.0	11	2	0	0	0	0	0	0	0	0	5	0	0	-	-	0--	-	0--	-	0.91	0.00
1991 Baltimore	AL	12	12	2	0	87.2	349	77	31	28	7	3	2	1	21	0	52	3	1	4	5	.444	0	0-0	0	2.80	2.87
1992 Baltimore	AL	32	32	8	0	241.0	957	212	70	68	16	13	6	2	48	2	130	6	0	18	5	.783	4	0-0	0	2.54	2.54
1993 Baltimore	AL	25	25	3	0	167.2	693	163	84	83	20	6	4	3	44	2	117	5	0	14	6	.700	2	0-0	0	3.61	4.46
1994 Baltimore	AL	24	24	3	0	176.1	712	163	63	60	19	3	9	1	42	1	99	0	0	16	5	.762	0	0-0	0	3.16	3.06
1995 Baltimore	AL	32	32	7	0	221.2	882	187	86	81	24	2	2	1	50	4	158	2	0	19	9	.679	4	0-0	0	2.66	3.29
1996 Baltimore	AL	36	36	4	0	243.1	1039	264	137	130	31	4	4	3	69	0	204	3	0	19	11	.633	1	0-0	0	4.36	4.81
1997 Baltimore	AL	33	33	4	0	224.2	905	197	87	80	27	3	2	3	54	3	218	5	0	15	8	.652	1	0-0	0	3.00	3.20
1998 Baltimore	AL	29	29	4	0	206.1	835	189	85	80	22	6	3	4	41	3	175	10	0	13	10	.565	2	0-0	0	2.96	3.49
1999 Baltimore	AL	31	31	4	0	203.1	842	207	88	79	16	9	7	1	52	0	172	2	0	18	7	.720	0	0-0	0	3.54	3.50
2000 Baltimore	AL	34	34	6	0	237.2	987	236	105	100	28	8	6	3	46	0	210	3	0	11	15	.423	1	0-0	0	3.37	3.79
2001 New York	AL	34	34	4	0	228.2	909	202	87	80	20	5	6	4	42	2	214	6	0	17	11	.607	3	0-0	0	2.65	3.15
2002 New York	AL	33	33	2	0	215.2	886	208	103	97	27	5	5	5	48	1	182	7	0	18	10	.643	2	0-0	0	3.46	4.05
2003 New York	AL	31	31	2	0	214.2	855	192	86	81	21	1	4	3	40	4	195	4	0	17	8	.680	1	0-0	0	2.75	3.40
2004 New York	AL	27	27	1	0	164.2	697	178	91	84	22	5	4	2	40	1	132	5	0	12	9	.571	0	0-0	0	4.19	4.59
14 ML YEARS		413	413	54	0	2833.1	11548	2675	1203	1131	300	73	64	36	637	23	2258	61	1	211	119	.639	21	0-0	0	3.20	3.59

Brett Myers

Pitches: R **Bats:** R **Pos:** SP-31; RP-1   **Ht:** 6'4" **Wt:** 215 **Born:** 8/17/1980 **Age:** 24

Year Team	Lg	G	GS	CG	GF	IP	BFP	H	R	ER	HR	SH	SF	HB	TBB	IBB	SO	WP	Bk	W	L	Pct	ShO	Sv-Op	Hld	ERC	ERA
2002 Philadelphia	NL	12	12	1	0	72.0	307	73	38	34	11	6	2	6	29	1	34	2	1	4	5	.444	0	0-0	0	5.04	4.25
2003 Philadelphia	NL	32	32	1	0	193.0	848	205	99	95	20	6	3	9	76	8	143	9	0	14	9	.609	1	0-0	0	4.56	4.43
2004 Philadelphia	NL	32	31	1	1	176.0	778	196	113	108	31	9	3	6	62	4	116	5	0	11	11	.500	1	0-0	0	5.17	5.52
3 ML YEARS		76	75	3	1	441.0	1933	474	250	237	62	21	8	21	167	13	293	16	1	29	25	.537	2	0-0	0	4.88	4.84

Greg Myers

Bats: L **Throws:** R **Pos:** C-4; PH-3; DH-1   **Ht:** 6'2" **Wt:** 225 **Born:** 4/14/1966 **Age:** 39

Year Team	Lg	G	AB	H	2B	3B	HR	(Hm	Rd)	TB	R	RBI	RC	TBB	IBB	SO	HBP	SH	SF	SB	CS	SB%	GDP	Avg	OBP	Slg
1987 Toronto	AL	7	9	1	0	0	0	(0	0)	1	1	0	0	0	0	3	0	0	0	0	0	-	2	.111	.111	.111
1989 Toronto	AL	17	44	5	2	0	0	(0	0)	7	0	1	0	2	0	9	0	0	0	0	1	.00	2	.114	.152	.159
1990 Toronto	AL	87	250	59	7	1	5	(3	2)	83	33	22	21	22	0	33	0	1	4	0	1	.00	12	.236	.293	.332
1991 Toronto	AL	107	309	81	22	0	8	(5	3)	127	25	36	35	21	4	45	0	0	3	0	0	-	13	.262	.306	.411
1992 Tor-Cal		30	78	18	7	0	1	(0	1)	28	4	13	7	5	0	11	0	1	2	0	0	-	2	.231	.271	.359
1993 California	AL	108	290	74	10	0	7	(4	3)	105	27	40	29	17	2	47	2	3	3	3	3	.50	8	.255	.298	.362
1994 California	AL	45	126	31	6	0	2	(1	1)	43	10	8	12	10	3	27	0	5	1	0	0	-	3	.246	.299	.341
1995 California	AL	85	273	71	12	2	9	(6	3)	114	35	38	34	17	3	49	1	1	2	0	1	.00	6	.260	.304	.418
1996 Minnesota	AL	97	329	94	22	3	6	(3	3)	140	37	47	42	19	3	52	0	0	5	0	0	-	11	.286	.320	.426
1997 Min-Atl		71	174	45	11	1	5	(3	2)	73	24	29	23	17	2	32	0	0	2	0	0	-	4	.259	.321	.420
1998 San Diego	NL	69	171	42	10	0	4	(1	3)	64	19	20	18	17	1	36	0	0	1	0	1	.00	6	.246	.312	.374

180

Year Team	Lg	G	AB	H	2B	3B	HR	(Hm	Rd)	TB	R	RBI	RC	TBB	IBB	SO	HBP	SH	SF	SB	CS	SB%	GDP	Avg	OBP	Slg
								BATTING												BASERUNNING				AVERAGES		
1999 SD-Atl	NL	84	200	53	6	0	5	(3	2)	74	19	24	26	26	4	30	0	0	1	0	0	-	6	.265	.348	.370
2000 Baltimore	AL	43	125	28	6	0	3	(1	2)	43	9	12	9	8	0	29	0	1	0	0	0	-	7	.224	.271	.344
2001 Bal-Oak	AL	58	161	36	3	0	11	(5	6)	72	24	31	22	21	1	38	0	0	0	0	0	-	5	.224	.313	.447
2002 Oakland	AL	65	144	32	5	0	6	(2	4)	55	15	21	17	26	3	36	0	0	0	0	0	-	4	.222	.341	.382
2003 Toronto	AL	121	329	101	19	0	15	(8	7)	165	51	52	51	37	2	57	0	0	3	0	3	.00	14	.307	.374	.502
2004 Toronto	AL	8	18	4	2	0	0	(0	0)	6	0	1	1	2	0	4	0	0	0	0	0	-	1	.222	.300	.333
1992 Toronto	AL	22	61	14	6	0	1	(0	1)	23	4	13	6	5	0	5	0	0	2	0	0	-	2	.230	.279	.377
1992 California	AL	8	17	4	1	0	0	(0	0)	5	0	0	1	0	0	6	0	1	0	0	0	-	0	.235	.235	.294
1997 Minnesota	AL	62	165	44	11	1	5	(3	2)	72	24	28	23	16	2	29	0	0	2	0	0	-	4	.267	.328	.436
1997 Atlanta	NL	9	9	1	0	0	0	(0	0)	1	0	1	0	1	0	3	0	0	0	0	0	-	0	.111	.200	.111
1999 San Diego	NL	50	128	37	4	0	3	(2	1)	50	9	15	17	13	2	14	0	0	0	0	0	-	5	.289	.355	.391
1999 Atlanta	NL	34	72	16	2	0	2	(1	1)	24	10	9	9	13	2	16	0	0	1	0	0	-	1	.222	.337	.333
2001 Baltimore	AL	25	74	20	2	0	4	(3	1)	34	11	18	11	8	0	17	0	0	0	0	0	-	3	.270	.341	.459
2001 Oakland	AL	33	87	16	1	0	7	(2	5)	38	13	13	11	13	1	21	0	0	0	0	0	-	2	.184	.290	.437
17 ML YEARS		1102	3030	775	150	7	87	(45	42)	1200	333	395	347	267	28	538	3	12	27	3	12	.20	104	.256	.314	.396

Mike Myers

Pitches: L **Bats:** L **Pos:** RP-75   **Ht:** 6'4" **Wt:** 212 **Born:** 6/26/1969 **Age:** 36

Year Team	Lg	G	GS	CG	GF	IP	BFP	H	R	ER	HR	SH	SF	HB	TBB	IBB	SO	WP	Bk	W	L	Pct	ShO	Sv-Op	Hld	ERC	ERA
											WHAT HE GAVE UP											THE RESULTS					
1995 Fla-Det		13	0	0	5	8.1	42	11	7	7	1	0	1	2	7	0	4	0	0	1	0	1.000	0	0-1	1	9.61	7.56
1996 Detroit	AL	83	0	0	25	64.2	298	70	41	36	6	2	1	4	34	8	69	2	0	1	5	.167	0	6-8	17	4.97	5.01
1997 Detroit	AL	88	0	0	23	53.2	246	58	36	34	12	4	3	2	25	2	50	0	0	0	4	.000	0	2-5	18	5.70	5.70
1998 Milwaukee	NL	70	0	0	14	50.0	211	44	19	15	5	4	2	6	22	1	40	2	1	2	2	.500	0	1-3	23	4.14	2.70
1999 Milwaukee	NL	71	0	0	14	41.1	179	46	24	24	7	5	0	3	13	1	35	1	0	2	1	.667	0	0-3	14	5.24	5.23
2000 Colorado	NL	78	0	0	22	45.1	177	24	10	10	2	1	0	2	24	3	41	1	0	0	1	.000	0	1-2	15	1.94	1.99
2001 Colorado	NL	73	0	0	14	40.0	169	32	17	16	2	1	1	1	24	7	36	0	0	2	3	.400	0	0-2	10	3.29	3.60
2002 Arizona	NL	69	0	0	15	37.0	171	39	18	18	2	3	1	8	17	0	31	0	0	4	3	.571	0	4-9	17	5.13	4.38
2003 Arizona	NL	64	0	0	17	36.1	172	38	23	23	4	1	0	5	21	1	21	1	0	0	1	.000	0	0-3	6	5.54	5.70
2004 Sea-Bos	AL	75	0	0	15	42.2	192	45	22	22	5	2	1	2	23	5	32	2	0	5	1	.833	0	0-0	10	5.11	4.64
1995 Florida	NL	2	0	0	2	2.0	9	1	0	0	0	0	0	0	3	0	0	0	0	0	0	-	0	0-0	0	5.03	0.00
1995 Detroit	AL	11	0	0	3	6.1	33	10	7	7	1	0	1	2	4	0	4	0	0	1	0	1.000	0	0-1	1	11.13	9.95
2004 Seattle	AL	50	0	0	10	27.2	126	29	15	15	3	2	1	2	17	4	23	1	0	4	1	.800	0	0-0	8	5.40	4.88
2004 Boston	AL	25	0	0	5	15.0	66	16	7	7	2	0	0	0	6	1	9	1	0	1	0	1.000	0	0-0	2	4.55	4.20
10 ML YEARS		684	0	0	164	419.1	1857	407	217	205	46	23	10	35	210	28	359	9	1	17	21	.447	0	14-36	131	4.63	4.40

Rodney Myers

Pitches: R **Bats:** R **Pos:** RP-1   **Ht:** 6'1" **Wt:** 215 **Born:** 6/26/1969 **Age:** 36

Year Team	Lg	G	GS	CG	GF	IP	BFP	H	R	ER	HR	SH	SF	HB	TBB	IBB	SO	WP	Bk	W	L	Pct	ShO	Sv-Op	Hld	ERC	ERA
						HOW MUCH HE PITCHED					WHAT HE GAVE UP											THE RESULTS					
2004 Kingsport*	R+	2	1	0	0	2.1	16	5	7	6	1	0	0	0	4	0	3	1	0	0	2	.000	0	0--	-	21.72	23.14
2004 Las Vegas*	AAA	24	0	0	6	38.0	169	42	22	20	3	1	0	0	11	2	25	1	0	4	1	.800	0	0--	-	3.84	4.74
1996 Chicago	NL	45	0	0	8	67.1	298	61	38	35	6	1	5	3	38	3	50	4	1	2	1	.667	0	0-0	1	4.20	4.68
1997 Chicago	NL	5	1	0	2	9.0	44	12	6	6	1	0	0	1	7	1	6	0	0	0	0	-	0	0-0	0	8.42	6.00
1998 Chicago	NL	12	0	0	3	18.0	82	26	14	14	3	0	0	0	6	0	15	1	0	0	0	-	0	0-1	0	7.19	7.00
1999 Chicago	NL	46	0	0	5	63.2	278	71	34	31	10	4	2	1	25	2	41	2	0	3	1	.750	0	0-1	8	5.22	4.38
2000 San Diego	NL	3	0	0	1	2.0	8	2	1	1	0	0	0	0	0	0	3	1	0	0	0	-	0	0-0	0	1.95	4.50
2001 San Diego	NL	37	0	0	16	47.1	211	53	31	28	6	1	4	4	20	0	29	2	0	1	2	.333	0	1-2	3	5.50	5.32
2002 San Diego	NL	14	0	0	4	21.1	101	29	20	14	1	1	0	3	10	0	11	2	0	1	1	.500	0	0-0	2	6.83	5.91
2003 Los Angeles	NL	4	0	0	3	9.0	42	10	7	6	1	0	0	1	4	0	5	0	0	0	0	-	0	0-0	0	5.30	6.00
2004 Los Angeles	NL	1	0	0	1	2.0	6	1	0	0	0	0	0	0	0	0	1	0	0	0	0	-	0	0-0	0	0.63	0.00
9 ML YEARS		167	1	0	43	239.2	1070	265	151	135	28	7	11	13	110	6	161	12	1	7	5	.583	0	1-4	14	5.29	5.07

Aaron Myette

Pitches: R **Bats:** R **Pos:** RP-5   **Ht:** 6'4" **Wt:** 210 **Born:** 9/26/1977 **Age:** 27

Year Team	Lg	G	GS	CG	GF	IP	BFP	H	R	ER	HR	SH	SF	HB	TBB	IBB	SO	WP	Bk	W	L	Pct	ShO	Sv-Op	Hld	ERC	ERA
						HOW MUCH HE PITCHED					WHAT HE GAVE UP											THE RESULTS					
2004 Louisville*	AAA	41	4	0	7	62.1	270	45	27	20	2	0	0	4	36	4	58	3	0	3	3	.500	0	19--	-	2.86	2.89
1999 Chicago	AL	4	3	0	0	15.2	80	17	11	11	2	0	0	2	14	1	11	2	0	0	2	.000	0	0-0	1	7.09	6.32
2000 Chicago	AL	2	0	0	1	2.2	12	0	0	0	0	0	0	0	4	0	1	0	0	0	0	-	0	0-0	0	1.96	0.00
2001 Texas	AL	19	15	0	1	80.2	376	94	65	64	12	3	4	11	37	0	67	2	0	4	5	.444	0	0-0	0	6.23	7.14
2002 Texas	AL	15	12	0	2	48.1	248	64	57	54	11	1	4	6	41	0	48	5	0	2	5	.286	0	0-0	0	9.83	10.06
2003 Cleveland	AL	2	0	0	1	2.2	18	7	7	7	1	0	0	1	2	0	1	0	0	0	0	-	0	0-0	0	21.83	23.63
2004 Cincinnati	NL	5	0	0	2	4.1	26	3	4	4	0	0	0	2	8	0	6	0	0	0	0	-	0	0-0	0	8.74	8.31
6 ML YEARS		47	30	0	7	154.1	760	185	144	140	26	4	8	22	106	1	134	9	0	6	12	.333	0	0-0	1	7.64	8.16

Xavier Nady

Bats: R **Throws:** R **Pos:** LF-18; PH-11; CF-4; RF-2; DH-2; PR-2   **Ht:** 6'0" **Wt:** 180 **Born:** 11/14/1978 **Age:** 26

Year Team	Lg	G	AB	H	2B	3B	HR	(Hm	Rd)	TB	R	RBI	RC	TBB	IBB	SO	HBP	SH	SF	SB	CS	SB%	GDP	Avg	OBP	Slg
								BATTING												BASERUNNING				AVERAGES		
2004 Portland*	AAA	74	291	96	19	1	22	(-	-)	183	52	70	64	22	2	42	7	0	0	3	0	1.00	8	.330	.391	.629
2000 San Diego	NL	1	1	1	0	0	0	(0	0)	1	1	0	1	0	0	0	0	0	0	0	0	-	0	1.000	1.000	1.000
2003 San Diego	NL	110	371	99	17	1	9	(5	4)	145	50	39	39	24	0	74	6	2	1	6	2	.75	14	.267	.321	.391
2004 San Diego	NL	34	77	19	4	0	3	(1	2)	32	7	9	8	5	0	13	1	1	0	0	0	-	4	.247	.301	.416
3 ML YEARS		145	449	119	21	1	12	(6	6)	178	58	48	48	29	0	87	7	3	1	6	2	.75	18	.265	.319	.396

Clint Nageotte

Pitches: R Bats: R Pos: RP-7; SP-5   Ht: 6'3" Wt: 200 Born: 10/25/1980 Age: 24

Year Team	Lg	G	GS	CG	GF	IP	BFP	H	R	ER	HR	SH	SF	HB	TBB	IBB	SO	WP	Bk	W	L	Pct	ShO	Sv-Op	Hld	ERC	ERA
2000 Mariners	R	12	7	0	1	50.0	207	29	15	12	0	0	2	3	28	0	59	2	0	4	1	.800	0	1--	-	2.04	2.16
2001 Wisconsin	A	28	26	0	0	152.1	648	141	65	53	10	10	1	11	50	1	187	6	4	11	8	.579	0	0--	-	3.41	3.13
2002 Sn Brnardino	A+	29	29	1	0	164.2	723	153	101	83	10	3	4	12	68	0	214	11	2	9	6	.600	0	0--	-	3.67	4.54
2003 San Antonio	AA	27	27	2	0	154.0	653	127	60	53	6	2	3	14	67	1	157	8	1	11	7	.611	1	0--	-	3.19	3.10
2004 Tacoma	AAA	14	14	0	0	80.2	350	78	42	40	9	3	3	5	35	0	63	8	0	6	6	.500	0	0--	-	4.39	4.46
2004 Seattle	AL	12	5	0	4	36.2	185	48	31	30	3	4	2	4	27	1	24	3	0	1	6	.143	0	0-0	0	7.59	7.36

Mike Nakamura

Pitches: R Bats: R Pos: RP-19   Ht: 5'10" Wt: 178 Born: 9/6/1976 Age: 28

Year Team	Lg	G	GS	CG	GF	IP	BFP	H	R	ER	HR	SH	SF	HB	TBB	IBB	SO	WP	Bk	W	L	Pct	ShO	Sv-Op	Hld	ERC	ERA
1998 Fort Wayne	A	29	9	0	6	80.0	347	82	41	29	8	4	3	3	29	0	70	3	2	2	5	.286	0	1--	-	4.21	3.26
1998 Fort Myers	A+	8	6	1	1	28.2	123	28	15	11	3	2	0	2	10	0	21	1	0	1	3	.250	0	0--	-	4.07	3.45
1999 Fort Myers	A+	14	0	0	6	19.2	74	9	5	4	1	2	2	0	5	0	18	1	0	2	0	1.000	0	2--	-	0.99	1.83
2000 Fort Myers	A+	32	0	0	19	41.1	162	33	9	7	0	2	1	2	11	1	46	2	0	1	0	1.000	0	12--	-	2.13	1.52
2001 New Britain	AA	48	1	0	19	86.1	357	75	20	17	3	3	1	2	24	5	109	3	0	5	1	.833	0	5--	-	2.47	1.77
2002 Edmonton	AAA	46	4	0	7	87.1	368	85	51	46	7	0	5	6	22	0	80	7	1	4	3	.571	0	2--	-	3.48	4.74
2004 Syracuse	AAA	31	1	0	9	55.0	225	42	20	19	3	3	1	2	17	2	76	2	1	3	2	.600	0	4--	-	2.27	3.11
2003 Minnesota	AL	12	0	0	7	12.2	62	20	11	11	4	0	0	1	2	0	14	0	0	0	0	-	0	1-1	1	8.35	7.82
2004 Toronto	AL	19	0	0	2	25.2	114	27	23	21	7	1	1	2	7	0	24	3	0	0	3	.000	0	0-0	2	5.23	7.36
2 ML YEARS		31	0	0	9	38.1	176	47	34	32	11	1	1	3	9	0	38	3	0	0	3	.000	0	1-1	3	6.22	7.51

Norihiro Nakamura

Bats: R Throws: R Pos: 3B   Ht: 5'11" Wt: 203 Born: 7/24/1973 Age: 31

Year Team	Lg	G	AB	H	2B	3B	HR	(Hm	Rd)	TB	R	RBI	RC	TBB	IBB	SO	HBP	SH	SF	SB	CS	SB%	GDP	Avg	OBP	Slg
1992 Kintetsu	Jap	11	27	6	1	0	2	(-	-)	13	4	5	3	0	-	8	0	0	0	0	0	-		.222	.222	.481
1993 Kintetsu	Jap	8	9	1	0	0	0	(-	-)	1	1	1	0	2	-	4	0	0	1	0	0	-		.111	.250	.111
1994 Kintetsu	Jap	101	192	54	13	1	8	(-	-)	93	23	36	32	19	-	49	0	2	2	0	0	-		.281	.343	.484
1995 Kintetsu	Jap	129	470	107	19	1	20	(-	-)	188	62	64	60	51	-	92	3	3	1	0	1	.00		.228	.307	.400
1996 Kintetsu	Jap	110	411	112	15	1	26	(-	-)	207	60	67	72	39	-	89	4	0	0	4	1	.80		.273	.341	.504
1997 Kintetsu	Jap	128	455	109	22	3	19	(-	-)	194	54	68	66	54	-	105	5	2	3	3	2	.60		.240	.325	.426
1998 Kintetsu	Jap	132	481	125	14	1	32	(-	-)	237	74	90	89	74	-	114	5	2	2	1	1	.50		.260	.363	.493
1999 Kintetsu	Jap	135	514	134	23	0	31	(-	-)	250	83	95	95	79	-	116	4	1	3	3	0	1.00		.261	.362	.486
2000 Osaka Kin	Jap	127	476	132	26	0	39	(-	-)	275	82	110	105	80	-	112	3	0	5	1	1	.50		.277	.381	.578
2001 Osaka Kin	Jap	140	525	168	25	0	46	(-	-)	331	109	132	140	104	-	106	4	0	3	3	2	.60		.320	.434	.630
2002 Osaka Kin	Jap	140	511	150	27	1	42	(-	-)	305	87	115	120	86	10	136	5	0	0	2	1	.67		.294	.400	.597
2003 Osaka Kin	Jap	117	381	90	14	1	23	(-	-)	175	54	67	66	72	4	96	1	0	2	1	1	.50		.236	.357	.459
2004 Osaka Kin	Jap	105	387	106	16	1	19	(-	-)	181	59	66	74	73	-	88	1	0	0	0	0	-	13	.274	.390	.468

Shane Nance

Pitches: L Bats: L Pos: RP-19   Ht: 5'8" Wt: 180 Born: 9/7/1977 Age: 27

Year Team	Lg	G	GS	CG	GF	IP	BFP	H	R	ER	HR	SH	SF	HB	TBB	IBB	SO	WP	Bk	W	L	Pct	ShO	Sv-Op	Hld	ERC	ERA
2004 Tucson*	AAA	46	2	0	18	45.1	223	60	38	31	5	2	1	3	22	2	48	5	1	2	4	.333	0	2--	-	6.41	6.15
2002 Milwaukee	NL	4	0	0	0	6.1	27	4	3	3	1	0	0	0	4	0	5	0	0	0	0	-	0	0-0	0	3.29	4.26
2003 Milwaukee	NL	26	0	0	6	24.1	118	34	16	13	5	1	2	1	10	1	25	1	0	0	2	.000	0	0-1	1	7.31	4.81
2004 Arizona	NL	19	0	0	2	12.1	69	19	11	8	2	0	0	3	12	4	9	1	0	1	1	.500	0	0-1	3	11.04	5.84
3 ML YEARS		49	0	0	8	43.0	214	57	30	24	8	1	2	4	26	5	39	2	0	1	3	.250	0	0-2	4	7.71	5.02

Sam Narron

Pitches: L Bats: L Pos: SP-1   Ht: 6'7" Wt: 200 Born: 7/12/1981 Age: 23

Year Team	Lg	G	GS	CG	GF	IP	BFP	H	R	ER	HR	SH	SF	HB	TBB	IBB	SO	WP	Bk	W	L	Pct	ShO	Sv-Op	Hld	ERC	ERA
2002 Pulaski	R+	14	9	0	5	69.2	279	78	34	30	10	1	3	0	8	0	50	3	0	6	1	.857	0	3--	-	4.06	3.88
2003 Stockton	A+	26	14	0	4	103.1	417	107	48	40	8	3	4	3	19	0	75	2	0	10	4	.714	0	0--	-	3.52	3.48
2004 Oklahoma	AAA	17	16	1	0	101.2	436	123	55	50	14	8	7	4	24	0	31	1	1	8	2	.800	1	0--	-	5.18	4.43
2004 Frisco	AA	13	8	0	0	53.1	223	56	23	14	6	2	1	0	10	0	27	0	2	6	0	1.000	0	0--	-	3.58	2.36
2004 Texas	AL	1	1	0	0	2.2	17	5	4	4	3	0	0	0	4	0	1	1	0	0	0	-	0	0-0	0	26.52	13.50

Joe Nathan

Pitches: R Bats: R Pos: RP-73   Ht: 6'4" Wt: 195 Born: 11/22/1974 Age: 30

Year Team	Lg	G	GS	CG	GF	IP	BFP	H	R	ER	HR	SH	SF	HB	TBB	IBB	SO	WP	Bk	W	L	Pct	ShO	Sv-Op	Hld	ERC	ERA
1999 San Francisco	NL	19	14	0	2	90.1	395	84	45	42	17	2	0	1	46	0	54	2	0	7	4	.636	0	1-1	0	4.78	4.18
2000 San Francisco	NL	20	15	0	2	93.1	426	89	63	54	12	5	5	4	63	4	61	5	0	5	2	.714	0	0-1	0	5.23	5.21
2002 San Francisco	NL	4	0	0	3	3.2	12	1	0	0	0	0	0	0	0	0	2	0	0	0	0	-	0	0-0	0	0.17	0.00
2003 San Francisco	NL	78	0	0	24	79.0	316	51	26	26	7	2	4	3	33	3	83	4	1	12	4	.750	0	0-3	20	2.34	2.96
2004 Minnesota	AL	73	0	0	63	72.1	284	48	14	13	3	2	0	2	23	3	89	5	0	1	2	.333	0	44-47	0	1.78	1.62
5 ML YEARS		194	29	0	77	338.2	1433	273	148	135	39	11	9	10	165	10	289	16	1	25	12	.676	0	45-52	20	3.53	3.59

Dioner Navarro

Bats: B **Throws:** R **Pos:** C-4; PH-1   **Ht:** 5'10" **Wt:** 189 **Born:** 2/9/1984 **Age:** 21

Year Team	Lg	G	AB	H	2B	3B	HR	(Hm	Rd)	TB	R	RBI	RC	TBB	IBB	SO	HBP	SH	SF	SB	CS	SB%	GDP	Avg	OBP	Slg
2001 Yankees	R	43	143	40	10	1	2	(-	-)	58	27	22	21	17	0	23	0	1	5	1	0	1.00	4	.280	.345	.406
2002 Greensboro	A	92	328	78	12	2	8	(-	-)	118	41	36	38	39	0	61	5	0	2	1	2	.33	9	.238	.326	.360
2002 Tampa	A+	1	2	1	0	0	0	(-	-)	1	1	0	0	0	0	0	0	0	0	0	0	-	0	.500	.500	.500
2003 Tampa	A+	52	197	59	16	4	3	(-	-)	92	28	28	33	17	0	27	4	1	2	1	0	1.00	4	.299	.364	.467
2003 Trenton	AA	58	208	71	15	0	4	(-	-)	98	28	37	36	18	1	26	1	1	5	2	3	.40	6	.341	.388	.471
2004 Trenton	AA	70	255	69	14	1	3	(-	-)	94	32	29	34	33	3	44	1	1	2	1	0	1.00	5	.271	.354	.369
2004 Columbus	AAA	40	136	34	8	2	1	(-	-)	49	18	16	16	14	0	17	1	0	4	1	0	1.00	4	.250	.316	.360
2004 New York	AL	5	7	3	0	0	0	(0	0)	3	2	1	1	0	0	0	0	0	0	0	0	-	1	.429	.429	.429

Denny Neagle

Pitches: L **Bats:** L **Pos:** SP   **Ht:** 6'3" **Wt:** 225 **Born:** 9/13/1968 **Age:** 36

Year Team	Lg	G	GS	CG	GF	IP	BFP	H	R	ER	HR	SH	SF	HB	TBB	IBB	SO	WP	Bk	W	L	Pct	ShO	Sv-Op	Hld	ERC	ERA
1991 Minnesota	AL	7	3	0	2	20.0	92	28	9	9	3	0	0	0	7	2	14	1	0	0	1	.000	0	0-0	0	6.53	4.05
1992 Pittsburgh	NL	55	6	0	8	86.1	380	81	46	43	9	4	3	2	43	8	77	3	2	4	6	.400	0	2-4	5	4.04	4.48
1993 Pittsburgh	NL	50	7	0	13	81.1	360	82	49	48	10	1	1	3	37	3	73	5	0	3	5	.375	0	1-1	6	4.57	5.31
1994 Pittsburgh	NL	24	24	2	0	137.0	587	135	80	78	18	7	6	3	49	3	122	2	0	9	10	.474	0	0-0	0	4.09	5.12
1995 Pittsburgh	NL	31	31	5	0	209.2	876	221	91	80	20	13	6	3	45	3	150	6	0	13	8	.619	1	0-0	0	3.67	3.43
1996 Pit-Atl	NL	33	33	2	0	221.1	910	226	93	86	26	10	4	3	48	2	149	3	1	16	9	.640	0	0-0	0	3.69	3.50
1997 Atlanta	NL	34	34	4	0	233.1	947	204	87	77	18	12	6	6	49	5	172	3	0	20	5	.800	4	0-0	0	2.60	2.97
1998 Atlanta	NL	32	31	5	0	210.1	861	196	91	83	25	7	3	6	60	3	165	6	1	16	11	.593	2	0-0	0	3.55	3.55
1999 Cincinnati	NL	20	19	0	0	111.2	467	95	54	53	23	3	5	4	40	3	76	4	0	9	5	.643	0	0-0	0	3.88	4.27
2000 Cin-NYY		34	33	1	0	209.0	906	210	109	105	31	8	6	5	81	4	146	7	1	15	9	.625	0	0-0	0	4.45	4.52
2001 Colorado	NL	30	30	0	0	170.2	760	192	107	102	29	8	9	7	60	3	139	2	0	9	8	.529	0	0-0	0	5.21	5.38
2002 Colorado	NL	35	28	1	0	164.1	724	170	101	96	26	5	6	10	63	5	111	4	1	8	11	.421	0	0-0	2	4.80	5.26
2003 Colorado	NL	7	7	0	0	35.1	161	47	31	31	12	1	0	1	12	0	21	1	0	2	4	.333	0	0-0	0	7.90	7.90
1996 Pittsburgh	NL	27	27	1	0	182.2	745	186	67	62	21	9	3	3	34	2	131	2	1	14	6	.700	0	0-0	0	3.55	3.05
1996 Atlanta	NL	6	6	1	0	38.2	165	40	26	24	5	1	1	0	14	0	18	1	0	2	3	.400	0	0-0	0	4.37	5.59
2000 Cincinnati	NL	18	18	0	0	117.2	506	111	48	46	15	2	1	3	50	3	88	3	0	8	2	.800	0	0-0	0	4.12	3.52
2000 New York	AL	16	15	1	0	91.1	400	99	61	59	16	6	5	2	31	1	58	4	1	7	7	.500	0	0-0	0	4.89	5.81
13 ML YEARS		392	286	20	23	1890.1	8031	1887	948	891	250	79	55	53	594	44	1415	47	6	124	92	.574	7	3-5	13	4.03	4.24

Blaine Neal

Pitches: R **Bats:** L **Pos:** RP-40   **Ht:** 6'5" **Wt:** 240 **Born:** 4/6/1978 **Age:** 27

Year Team	Lg	G	GS	CG	GF	IP	BFP	H	R	ER	HR	SH	SF	HB	TBB	IBB	SO	WP	Bk	W	L	Pct	ShO	Sv-Op	Hld	ERC	ERA
2004 Portland*	AAA	27	0	0	4	38.2	157	32	10	8	0	0	0	0	12	2	38	1	0	4	2	.667	0	1- -		2.14	1.86
2001 Florida	NL	4	0	0	0	5.1	28	7	4	4	0	0	0	0	5	0	3	1	0	0	0	-	0	0-0	0	7.12	6.75
2002 Florida	NL	32	0	0	6	33.0	144	32	12	10	1	1	0	0	14	2	33	4	0	3	0	1.000	0	0-0	2	3.35	2.73
2003 Florida	NL	18	0	0	6	21.0	108	38	20	19	2	1	5	1	9	1	10	1	0	0	0	-	0	0-0	2	9.42	8.14
2004 San Diego	NL	40	0	0	4	42.0	183	49	19	19	6	2	2	2	11	3	36	0	0	1	1	.500	0	0-2	5	4.88	4.07
4 ML YEARS		94	0	0	20	101.1	463	126	55	52	9	4	7	3	39	6	82	6	0	4	1	.800	0	0-2	7	5.33	4.62

Jeff Nelson

Pitches: R **Bats:** R **Pos:** RP-29   **Ht:** 6'8" **Wt:** 235 **Born:** 11/17/1966 **Age:** 38

Year Team	Lg	G	GS	CG	GF	IP	BFP	H	R	ER	HR	SH	SF	HB	TBB	IBB	SO	WP	Bk	W	L	Pct	ShO	Sv-Op	Hld	ERC	ERA
2004 Frisco*	AA	3	3	0	0	3.2	15	2	1	1	0	0	0	1	1	0	3	0	0	0	0	-	0	0- -	-	1.65	2.45
2004 Oklahoma*	AAA	2	2	0	0	1.2	8	3	3	3	0	0	0	0	0	0	3	0	0	0	1	.000	0	0- -	-	6.23	16.20
1992 Seattle	AL	66	0	0	27	81.0	352	71	34	31	7	9	3	6	44	12	46	2	0	1	7	.125	0	6-14	6	3.93	3.44
1993 Seattle	AL	71	0	0	13	60.0	269	57	30	29	5	2	4	8	34	10	61	2	0	5	3	.625	0	1-11	17	4.62	4.35
1994 Seattle	AL	28	0	0	7	42.1	185	35	18	13	3	1	1	8	20	4	44	2	0	0	0	-	0	0-0	2	3.77	2.76
1995 Seattle	AL	62	0	0	24	78.2	318	58	21	19	4	5	3	6	27	5	96	1	0	7	3	.700	0	2-4	14	2.39	2.17
1996 New York	AL	73	0	0	27	74.1	328	75	38	36	6	3	1	2	36	1	91	4	0	4	4	.500	0	2-4	10	4.41	4.36
1997 New York	AL	77	0	0	22	78.2	327	53	32	25	7	7	3	4	37	12	81	4	0	3	7	.300	0	2-8	22	2.48	2.86
1998 New York	AL	45	0	0	13	40.1	192	44	18	17	1	1	3	8	22	4	35	2	0	5	3	.625	0	3-6	10	5.13	3.79
1999 New York	AL	39	0	0	8	30.1	139	27	14	14	2	2	2	3	22	2	35	2	1	2	1	.667	0	1-2	10	4.76	4.15
2000 New York	AL	73	0	0	13	69.2	296	44	24	19	2	6	2	2	45	1	71	4	0	8	4	.667	0	0-4	15	2.61	2.45
2001 Seattle	AL	69	0	0	16	65.1	273	30	21	20	3	2	0	6	44	1	88	2	0	4	3	.571	0	4-5	26	2.20	2.76
2002 Seattle	AL	41	0	0	12	45.2	199	36	20	20	4	2	4	3	27	3	55	5	0	3	2	.600	0	2-4	12	3.70	3.94
2003 Sea-NYY	AL	70	0	0	28	55.1	240	51	25	23	4	4	2	4	24	3	68	3	1	4	2	.667	0	8-14	14	3.76	3.74
2004 Texas	AL	29	0	0	9	23.2	103	17	16	14	3	1	1	0	19	0	22	2	0	1	1	.500	0	1-1	9	4.35	5.32
2003 Seattle	AL	46	0	0	25	37.2	159	34	16	14	3	4	2	2	14	1	47	2	1	3	2	.600	0	7-11	6	3.48	3.35
2003 New York	AL	24	0	0	3	17.2	81	17	9	9	1	0	0	2	10	2	21	1	0	1	0	1.000	0	1-3	8	4.37	4.58
13 ML YEARS		743	0	0	219	745.1	3221	598	311	280	51	45	28	60	401	58	793	35	2	47	41	.534	0	32-77	167	3.48	3.38

Joe Nelson

Pitches: R **Bats:** R **Pos:** RP-3   **Ht:** 6'2" **Wt:** 185 **Born:** 10/25/1974 **Age:** 30

Year Team	Lg	G	GS	CG	GF	IP	BFP	H	R	ER	HR	SH	SF	HB	TBB	IBB	SO	WP	Bk	W	L	Pct	ShO	Sv-Op	Hld	ERC	ERA
1996 Eugene	A-	14	13	0	0	70.0	309	70	43	34	5	3	1	5	29	1	67	6	0	5	3	.625	0	0- -		4.15	4.37
1997 Durham	AAA	25	24	0	0	124.2	543	114	74	66	17	5	4	12	61	1	99	5	0	10	6	.625	0	0- -		4.64	4.76
1998 Greenville	AA	45	12	1	15	108.1	506	124	76	60	9	8	4	5	69	2	74	11	1	6	9	.400	1	2- -		5.97	4.98
1999 Greenville	AA	25	0	0	15	30.1	130	19	15	8	2	2	1	3	14	2	37	0	0	1	1	.500	0	8- -		2.28	2.37
1999 Richmond	AAA	12	3	0	2	33.2	150	33	18	17	2	4	1	0	14	0	37	3	0	2	3	.400	0	1- -		3.59	4.54
2000 Braves	R	4	0	0	1	4.0	18	3	1	1	0	0	0	0	3	0	7	0	0	1	0	1.000	0	1- -		3.21	2.25
2001 Richmond	AAA	29	0	0	12	39.2	152	23	6	5	1	4	0	0	14	2	40	3	0	1	2	.333	0	8- -		1.44	1.13

Year Team	Lg	G	GS	CG	GF	IP	BFP	H	R	ER	HR	SH	SF	HB	TBB	IBB	SO	WP	Bk	W	L	Pct	ShO	Sv-Op	Hld	ERC	ERA
2002 Trenton	AA	4	0	0	1	4.1	25	9	8	7	1	0	0	1	2	0	3	2	0	0	0		0	0- -	-	13.57	14.54
2004 Portland	AA	25	0	0	22	30.1	123	16	8	6	1	0	1	1	15	0	49	1	0	3	2	.600	0	13- -	-	1.70	1.78
2004 Pawtucket	AAA	16	0	0	2	21.1	102	27	14	11	1	0	0	0	9	0	31	1	0	0	0		0	0- -	-	5.53	4.64
2001 Atlanta	NL	2	0	0	0	2.0	16	7	9	8	1	0	1	1	2	0	0	0	0	0	0	-	0	0-0	0	33.03	36.00
2004 Boston	AL	3	0	0	1	2.2	17	4	5	5	0	1	0	2	3	0	5	0	0	0	0	-	0	0-0	0	12.43	16.88
2 ML YEARS		5	0	0	1	4.2	33	11	14	13	1	1	1	3	5	0	5	0	0	0	0	-	0	0-0	0	20.77	25.07

Mike Neu

Pitches: R **Bats:** B **Pos:** RP-1 **Ht:** 5'10" **Wt:** 175 **Born:** 3/9/1978 **Age:** 27

Year Team	Lg	G	GS	CG	GF	IP	BFP	H	R	ER	HR	SH	SF	HB	TBB	IBB	SO	WP	Bk	W	L	Pct	ShO	Sv-Op	Hld	ERC	ERA
1999 Rockford	A	9	0	0	2	18.0	84	17	10	9	1	0	1	2	12	1	23	4	0	0	1	.000	0	1- -	-	4.74	4.50
2000 Clinton	A	58	0	0	54	69.0	306	47	27	24	5	4	3	1	52	8	95	10	0	7	7	.500	0	24- -	-	3.27	3.13
2001 Mudville	A+	53	0	0	44	64.2	277	50	21	17	3	4	1	3	30	4	102	5	1	3	2	.600	0	21- -	-	2.75	2.37
2002 Louisville	AAA	40	0	0	34	40.1	172	35	19	18	4	2	1	0	18	0	47	1	0	2	3	.400	0	16- -	-	3.49	4.02
2002 Chattanooga	AA	21	0	0	12	27.0	113	22	4	4	0	1	1	1	9	1	38	3	0	1	0	1.000	0	7- -	-	2.24	1.33
2004 Albuquerque	AAA	35	0	0	17	38.1	192	47	33	28	2	0	0	6	24	1	28	4	0	1	2	.333	0	6- -	-	6.37	6.57
2003 Oakland	AL	32	0	0	26	42.0	194	43	18	17	2	1	0	2	26	2	20	4	0	0	0	-	0	1-1	-	4.73	3.64
2004 Florida	NL	1	0	0	0	4.0	18	5	2	2	1	0	0	0	2	0	2	0	0	0	0	-	0	0-0	0	7.44	4.50
2 ML YEARS		33	0	0	26	46.0	212	48	20	19	3	1	0	2	28	2	22	4	0	0	0	-	0	1-1	0	4.96	3.72

Phil Nevin

Bats: R **Throws:** R **Pos:** 1B-144; DH-2; PH-2; C-1 **Ht:** 6'2" **Wt:** 231 **Born:** 1/19/1971 **Age:** 34

Year Team	Lg	G	AB	H	2B	3B	HR	Hm	Rd	TB	R	RBI	RC	TBB	IBB	SO	HBP	SH	SF	SB	CS	SB%	GDP	Avg	OBP	Slg
1995 Hou-Det		47	156	28	4	1	2	(2	0)	40	13	13	10	18	1	40	4	1	0	1	0	1.00	5	.179	.281	.256
1996 Detroit	AL	38	120	35	5	0	8	(3	5)	64	15	19	21	8	0	39	1	0	1	1	0	1.00	3	.292	.338	.533
1997 Detroit	AL	93	251	59	16	1	9	(4	5)	104	32	35	31	25	1	68	1	0	1	0	1	.00	5	.235	.306	.414
1998 Anaheim	AL	75	237	54	8	1	8	(3	5)	88	27	27	25	17	0	67	5	0	2	0	0	-	6	.228	.291	.371
1999 San Diego	NL	128	383	103	27	0	24	(12	12)	202	52	85	71	51	1	82	1	1	5	1	0	1.00	7	.269	.352	.527
2000 San Diego	NL	143	538	163	34	1	31	(13	18)	292	87	107	102	59	9	121	4	0	4	2	0	1.00	17	.303	.374	.543
2001 San Diego	NL	149	546	167	31	0	41	(19	22)	321	97	126	116	71	7	147	4	0	3	4	4	.50	13	.306	.388	.588
2002 San Diego	NL	107	407	116	16	0	12	(5	7)	168	53	57	52	38	4	87	1	0	4	4	0	1.00	12	.285	.344	.413
2003 San Diego	NL	59	226	63	8	0	13	(6	7)	110	30	46	37	21	1	44	0	0	1	2	0	1.00	9	.279	.339	.487
2004 San Diego	NL	147	547	158	31	1	26	(12	14)	269	78	105	97	66	5	121	5	0	5	0	0	-	16	.289	.368	.492
1995 Houston	NL	18	60	7	1	0	0	(0	0)	8	4	1	0	7	1	13	1	1	0	1	0	1.00	2	.117	.221	.133
1995 Detroit	AL	29	96	21	3	1	2	(2	0)	32	9	12	10	11	0	27	3	0	0	0	0	-	3	.219	.318	.333
10 ML YEARS		986	3411	946	180	5	174	(79	95)	1658	484	620	562	374	29	816	26	2	26	15	5	.75	91	.277	.351	.486

David Newhan

Bats: L **Throws:** R **Pos:** DH-32; RF-24; LF-19; 3B-17; PH-4; 1B-2; PR-1 **Ht:** 5'10" **Wt:** 180 **Born:** 9/7/1973 **Age:** 31

Year Team	Lg	G	AB	H	2B	3B	HR	Hm	Rd	TB	R	RBI	RC	TBB	IBB	SO	HBP	SH	SF	SB	CS	SB%	GDP	Avg	OBP	Slg
2004 Oklahoma*	AAA	61	262	86	21	6	9	(-	-)	146	57	38	55	26	0	55	1	0	3	10	0	1.00	3	.328	.387	.557
1999	NL	32	43	6	1	0	2	(1	1)	13	7	6	1	1	0	11	0	0	0	2	1	.67	0	.140	.159	.302
2000 SD-Phi	NL	24	37	6	1	0	1	(1	0)	10	8	2	2	8	1	13	0	0	0	0	0	-	2	.162	.311	.270
2001 Philadelphia	NL	7	6	2	1	0	0	(0	0)	3	2	1	1	1	0	0	0	0	1	0	0	-	0	.333	.375	.500
2004 Baltimore	AL	95	373	116	15	7	8	(3	5)	169	66	54	70	27	0	72	4	5	3	11	1	.92	4	.311	.361	.453
2000 San Diego	NL	14	20	3	1	0	1	(1	0)	7	5	2	2	6	1	7	0	0	0	0	0	-	2	.150	.346	.350
2000 Philadelphia	NL	10	17	3	0	0	0	(0	0)	3	3	0	0	2	0	6	0	0	0	0	0	-	2	.176	.263	.176
4 ML YEARS		158	459	130	18	7	11	(5	6)	195	83	63	74	37	1	96	4	5	4	13	2	.87	6	.283	.339	.425

C.J. Nitkowski

Pitches: L **Bats:** L **Pos:** RP-41 **Ht:** 6'3" **Wt:** 205 **Born:** 3/9/1973 **Age:** 32

Year Team	Lg	G	GS	CG	GF	IP	BFP	H	R	ER	HR	SH	SF	HB	TBB	IBB	SO	WP	Bk	W	L	Pct	ShO	Sv-Op	Hld	ERC	ERA
2004 Columbus*	AAA	16	0	0	1	12.2	50	8	3	2	0	0	0	1	3	0	11	2	0	0	0		0	0- -	-	1.43	1.42
1995 Cin-Det		20	18	0	1	71.2	338	94	57	53	11	2	4	5	35	3	31	2	2	2	7	.222	0	0-1	0	7.04	6.66
1996 Detroit	AL	11	8	0	0	45.2	234	62	44	41	7	0	2	7	38	1	36	2	0	2	3	.400	0	0-0	0	9.44	8.08
1998 Houston	NL	43	0	0	11	59.2	250	49	27	25	4	4	2	6	23	2	44	3	1	3	3	.500	0	3-5	8	3.19	3.77
1999 Detroit	AL	68	7	0	7	81.2	349	63	44	39	11	1	4	6	45	3	66	4	3	4	5	.444	0	0-0	11	3.73	4.30
2000 Detroit	AL	67	11	0	7	109.2	497	124	79	64	13	3	8	4	49	3	81	3	1	4	9	.308	0	0-2	15	5.23	5.25
2001 Det-NYM	NL	61	0	0	14	51.0	241	54	30	28	7	3	1	5	34	8	42	1	0	1	3	.250	0	0-6	6	5.89	4.94
2002 Texas	AL	12	0	0	2	13.2	63	11	4	4	0	1	0	0	13	0	14	0	0	0	1	.000	0	0-0	1	4.35	2.63
2003 Texas	AL	6	0	0	0	9.2	52	17	8	8	0	1	2	0	8	1	5	0	0	0	0		0	0-0	1	9.69	7.45
2004 Atl-NYY	NL	41	0	0	14	33.0	160	40	22	21	4	1	2	6	16	0	26	5	0	2	1	.667	0	0-0	0	6.50	5.73
1995 Cincinnati	NL	9	7	0	0	32.1	154	41	25	22	4	2	1	2	15	1	18	1	2	1	3	.250	0	0-1	0	6.20	6.12
1995 Detroit	AL	11	11	0	0	39.1	184	53	32	31	7	0	3	3	20	2	13	1	0	1	4	.200	0	0-0	0	7.76	7.09
2001 Detroit	AL	56	0	0	12	45.1	220	51	30	28	7	3	1	5	31	7	38	1	0	0	3	.000	0	0-6	6	6.53	5.56
2001 New York	NL	5	0	0	2	5.2	21	3	0	0	0	0	0	0	3	1	4	0	0	1	0	1.000	0			1.52	0.00
2004 Atlanta	NL	22	0	0	10	20.0	95	22	11	10	3	1	2	2	10	0	16	3	0	1	0	1.000	0	0-0	0	5.66	4.50
2004 New York	AL	19	0	0	4	13.0	65	18	11	11	1	0	0	4	6	0	10	2	0	1	1	.500	0	0-0	0	7.83	7.62
9 ML YEARS		329	44	0	55	475.2	2184	514	315	283	57	16	25	36	261	21	345	20	7	18	32	.360	0	3-14	42	5.54	5.35

Ramon Nivar

Bats: R **Throws:** R **Pos:** CF-6; PR-1   **Ht:** 5'10" **Wt:** 170 **Born:** 2/22/1980 **Age:** 25

Year Team	Lg	G	AB	H	2B	3B	HR	(Hm	Rd)	TB	R	RBI	RC	TBB	IBB	SO	HBP	SH	SF	SB	CS	SB%	GDP	Avg	OBP	Slg
2003 Frisco	AA	79	317	110	17	4	4	(-	-)	147	53	37	54	20	0	23	2	8	2	9	9	.50	5	.347	.387	.464
2003 Oklahoma	AAA	23	89	30	2	2	2	(-	-)	42	11	12	15	5	0	5	0	1	1	6	1	.86	4	.337	.368	.472
2004 Oklahoma	AAA	113	462	122	21	0	10	(-	-)	173	62	52	45	14	1	43	4	12	2	15	15	.50	10	.264	.290	.374
2003 Texas	AL	28	90	19	1	2	0	(0	0)	24	9	7	7	4	0	10	1	2	0	4	2	.67	1	.211	.253	.267
2004 Texas	AL	7	18	4	0	0	0	(0	0)	4	3	4	1	0	0	7	0	2	1	1	1	.50	0	.222	.211	.222
2 ML YEARS		35	108	23	1	2	0	(0	0)	28	12	11	8	4	0	17	1	4	1	5	3	.63	1	.213	.246	.259

Laynce Nix

Bats: L **Throws:** L **Pos:** CF-111; PH-8; RF-3   **Ht:** 6'0" **Wt:** 190 **Born:** 10/30/1980 **Age:** 24

Year Team	Lg	G	AB	H	2B	3B	HR	(Hm	Rd)	TB	R	RBI	RC	TBB	IBB	SO	HBP	SH	SF	SB	CS	SB%	GDP	Avg	OBP	Slg
2000 Rangers	R	51	199	45	7	1	2	(-	-)	60	34	25	20	23	1	37	2	2	4	4	2	.67	1	.226	.307	.302
2001 Savannah	A	104	407	113	26	8	8	(-	-)	179	50	59	58	37	2	94	2	1	5	9	6	.60	7	.278	.337	.440
2001 Charlotte	AAA	9	37	11	3	1	0	(-	-)	16	4	2	4	1	0	13	0	0	0	0	0	-	2	.297	.316	.432
2002 Charlotte	AAA	137	512	146	27	3	21	(-	-)	242	86	110	93	72	8	105	6	0	9	17	1	.94	9	.285	.374	.473
2003 Frisco	AA	87	335	95	23	0	15	(-	-)	163	52	63	55	34	6	68	0	0	6	9	2	.82	4	.284	.344	.487
2004 Frisco	AA	7	26	7	1	0	0	(-	-)	8	2	2	1	1	0	10	0	0	0	0	1	.00	1	.269	.296	.308
2003 Texas	AL	53	184	47	10	0	8	(7	1)	81	25	30	25	9	0	53	0	1	1	3	0	1.00	1	.255	.289	.440
2004 Texas	AL	115	371	92	20	4	14	(9	5)	162	58	46	44	23	4	113	2	1	3	1	1	.50	6	.248	.293	.437
2 ML YEARS		168	555	139	30	4	22	(16	6)	243	83	76	69	32	4	166	2	2	4	4	1	.80	7	.250	.292	.438

Trot Nixon

Bats: L **Throws:** L **Pos:** RF-40; PH-11; DH-2   **Ht:** 6'2" **Wt:** 211 **Born:** 4/11/1974 **Age:** 31

Year Team	Lg	G	AB	H	2B	3B	HR	(Hm	Rd)	TB	R	RBI	RC	TBB	IBB	SO	HBP	SH	SF	SB	CS	SB%	GDP	Avg	OBP	Slg
2004 Sarasota*	A+	1	3	2	1	0	0	(-	-)	3	1	1	1	0	0	0	0	0	0	0	0	-	0	.667	.667	1.000
2004 Pawtucket*	AAA	6	21	7	1	0	0	(-	-)	8	2	2	3	2	0	3	0	0	0	0	0	-	0	.333	.391	.381
1996 Boston	AL	2	4	2	1	0	0	(0	0)	3	2	0	1	0	0	1	0	0	0	1	0	1.00	0	.500	.500	.750
1998 Boston	AL	13	27	7	1	0	0	(0	0)	8	3	0	2	1	0	3	0	0	0	0	0	-	0	.259	.286	.296
1999 Boston	AL	124	381	103	22	5	15	(3	12)	180	67	52	66	53	1	75	3	2	8	3	1	.75	7	.270	.357	.472
2000 Boston	AL	123	427	118	27	8	12	(4	8)	197	66	60	74	63	2	85	2	5	5	8	1	.89	11	.276	.368	.461
2001 Boston	AL	148	535	150	31	4	27	(14	13)	270	100	88	102	79	1	113	7	6	6	7	4	.64	8	.280	.376	.505
2002 Boston	AL	152	532	136	36	3	24	(8	16)	250	81	94	85	65	2	109	5	3	7	4	2	.67	7	.256	.338	.470
2003 Boston	AL	134	441	135	24	6	28	(10	18)	255	81	87	90	65	4	96	3	1	3	4	2	.67	3	.306	.396	.578
2004 Boston	AL	48	149	47	9	1	6	(3	3)	76	24	23	23	15	1	24	1	0	2	0	0	-	3	.315	.377	.510
8 ML YEARS		744	2496	698	151	27	112	(42	70)	1239	424	404	443	341	11	506	21	17	31	27	10	.73	39	.280	.367	.496

Hideo Nomo

Pitches: R **Bats:** R **Pos:** SP-18   **Ht:** 6'2" **Wt:** 210 **Born:** 8/31/1968 **Age:** 36

Year Team	Lg	G	GS	CG	GF	IP	BFP	H	R	ER	HR	SH	SF	HB	TBB	IBB	SO	WP	Bk	W	L	Pct	ShO	Sv-Op	Hld	ERC	ERA
2004 Las Vegas*	AAA	4	4	0	0	17.1	77	22	11	11	4	3	2	0	8	0	25	1	0	0	-	-		0- -	-	7.29	5.71
1995 Los Angeles	NL	28	28	4	0	191.1	780	124	63	54	14	11	4	5	78	2	236	19	5	13	6	.684	3	0-0	0	2.16	2.54
1996 Los Angeles	NL	33	33	3	0	228.1	932	180	93	81	23	12	6	2	85	6	234	11	3	16	11	.593	2	0-0	0	2.86	3.19
1997 Los Angeles	NL	33	33	1	0	207.1	904	193	104	98	23	7	1	9	92	2	233	10	4	14	12	.538	0	0-0	0	4.06	4.25
1998 LA-NYM	NL	29	28	3	0	157.1	687	130	88	86	19	8	5	4	94	2	167	13	4	6	12	.333	0	0-0	0	4.10	4.92
1999 Milwaukee	NL	28	28	0	0	176.1	767	173	96	89	27	5	5	3	78	2	161	10	1	12	8	.600	0	0-0	0	4.57	4.54
2000 Detroit	AL	32	31	1	0	190.0	828	191	102	100	31	6	3	3	89	1	181	16	0	8	12	.400	0	0-0	0	4.95	4.74
2001 Boston	AL	33	33	2	0	198.0	849	171	105	99	26	4	7	3	96	1	220	6	0	13	10	.565	2	0-0	0	3.90	4.50
2002 Los Angeles	NL	34	34	0	0	220.1	926	189	92	83	26	17	4	2	101	5	193	6	0	16	6	.727	0	0-0	0	3.68	3.39
2003 Los Angeles	NL	33	33	2	0	218.1	897	175	82	75	24	11	3	1	98	6	177	11	0	16	13	.552	2	0-0	0	3.30	3.09
2004 Los Angeles	NL	18	18	0	0	84.0	393	105	77	77	19	7	3	4	42	1	54	3	0	4	11	.267	0	0-0	0	7.22	8.25
1998 Los Angeles	NL	12	12	2	0	67.2	295	57	39	38	8	2	2	3	38	0	73	4	1	2	7	.222	0	0-0	0	4.13	5.05
1998 New York	NL	17	16	1	0	89.2	392	73	49	48	11	6	3	1	56	2	94	9	3	4	5	.444	0	0-0	0	4.07	4.82
10 ML YEARS		301	299	16	0	1871.1	7963	1631	902	842	232	88	41	36	853	29	1856	105	17	118	101	.539	9	0-0	0	3.81	4.05

Greg Norton

Bats: B **Throws:** R **Pos:** 3B-18; PH-15; 1B-7; LF-6; DH-5   **Ht:** 6'1" **Wt:** 200 **Born:** 7/6/1972 **Age:** 32

Year Team	Lg	G	AB	H	2B	3B	HR	(Hm	Rd)	TB	R	RBI	RC	TBB	IBB	SO	HBP	SH	SF	SB	CS	SB%	GDP	Avg	OBP	Slg
2004 Toledo*	AAA	53	184	38	6	1	4	(-	-)	58	26	16	17	24	0	48	0	0	1	1	1	.50	4	.207	.297	.315
1996 Chicago	AL	11	23	5	0	0	2	(0	2)	11	4	3	3	4	0	6	0	0	0	0	1	.00	0	.217	.333	.478
1997 Chicago	AL	18	34	9	2	2	0	(0	0)	15	5	1	5	2	0	8	0	1	0	0	0	-	0	.265	.306	.441
1998 Chicago	AL	105	299	71	17	2	9	(6	3)	119	38	36	33	26	1	77	2	1	2	3	3	.50	11	.237	.301	.398
1999 Chicago	AL	132	436	111	26	0	16	(5	11)	185	62	50	66	69	3	93	2	1	4	4	4	.50	11	.255	.358	.424
2000 Chicago	AL	71	201	49	6	1	6	(4	2)	75	25	28	27	26	0	47	0	2	0	1	0	1.00	2	.244	.333	.373
2001 Colorado	NL	117	225	60	13	2	13	(7	6)	116	30	40	36	19	2	65	0	0	2	1	0	1.00	6	.267	.321	.516
2002 Colorado	NL	113	168	37	8	1	7	(3	4)	68	19	37	22	24	0	52	0	1	2	2	3	.40	4	.220	.314	.405
2003 Colorado	NL	114	179	47	15	0	6	(2	4)	80	19	31	26	16	0	47	1	0	1	2	1	.67	4	.263	.325	.447
2004 Detroit	AL	41	86	15	1	0	2	(1	1)	22	9	2	1	12	1	21	0	1	0	0	0	-	3	.174	.276	.256
9 ML YEARS		722	1651	404	88	8	61	(28	33)	691	211	228	219	198	7	416	7	5	11	13	12	.52	41	.245	.326	.419

Phil Norton

Pitches: L **Bats:** R **Pos:** RP-69 **Ht:** 6'0" **Wt:** 210 **Born:** 2/1/1976 **Age:** 29

Year Team	Lg	G	GS	CG	GF	IP	BFP	H	R	ER	HR	SH	SF	HB	TBB	IBB	SO	WP	Bk	W	L	Pct	ShO	Sv-Op	Hld	ERC	ERA
2000 Chicago	NL	2	2	0	0	8.2	47	14	10	9	5	0	0	0	7	0	6	0	0	0	1	.000	0	0-0	0	14.18	9.35
2003 ChC-Cin	NL	21	0	0	4	18.0	68	9	6	6	0	1	0	0	9	0	7	1	0	0	0	-	0	0-0	5	1.50	3.00
2004 Cincinnati	NL	69	0	0	14	65.2	296	71	41	37	5	4	2	2	38	7	48	2	0	2	5	.286	0	0-2	9	5.09	5.07
2003 Chicago	NL	4	0	0	2	3.1	14	2	2	2	0	0	0	0	3	0	0	1	0	0	0	-	0	0-0	0	3.21	5.40
2003 Cincinnati	NL	17	0	0	2	14.2	54	7	4	4	0	1	0	0	6	0	7	0	0	0	0	-	0	0-0	5	1.24	2.45
3 ML YEARS		92	2	0	18	92.1	411	94	47	52	10	5	2	2	54	7	61	3	0	2	6	.250	0	0-2	14	5.02	5.07

Roberto Novoa

Pitches: R **Bats:** R **Pos:** RP-16 **Ht:** 6'5" **Wt:** 200 **Born:** 8/15/1979 **Age:** 25

Year Team	Lg	G	GS	CG	GF	IP	BFP	H	R	ER	HR	SH	SF	HB	TBB	IBB	SO	WP	Bk	W	L	Pct	ShO	Sv-Op	Hld	ERC	ERA
2001 Williamsport	A-	14	13	1	1	79.2	331	76	40	30	4	5	1	7	20	0	55	4	1	5	5	.500	0	0- -	-	3.30	3.39
2002 Williamsport	A-	12	12	0	0	66.2	277	62	32	27	4	3	1	6	8	0	56	5	0	8	3	.727	0	0- -	-	2.66	3.65
2002 Hickory	A	10	10	0	0	42.2	205	61	30	26	2	1	3	4	15	0	29	7	1	1	5	.167	0	0- -	-	6.33	5.48
2003 Lakeland	A+	19	15	2	1	99.0	414	93	45	41	8	1	0	5	25	0	71	2	2	4	5	.444	0	0- -	-	3.23	3.73
2004 Erie	AA	41	0	0	11	79.0	317	63	32	26	7	2	2	1	18	1	59	4	1	7	0	1.000	0	4- -	-	2.31	2.96
2004 Detroit	AL	16	0	0	2	21.0	94	25	15	13	4	1	4	2	6	0	15	1	0	1	1	.500	0	0-1	3	5.79	5.57

Abraham Nunez

Bats: B **Throws:** R **Pos:** RF-74; LF-28; PR-11; PH-10; CF-4; DH-2 **Ht:** 6'2" **Wt:** 186 **Born:** 2/5/1977 **Age:** 28

| | | | | | | | BATTING | | | | | | | | | | | BASERUNNING | | | | AVERAGES | | |
Year Team	Lg	G	AB	H	2B	3B	HR	(Hm	Rd)	TB	R	RBI	RC	TBB	IBB	SO	HBP	SH	SF	SB	CS	SB%	GDP	Avg	OBP	Slg
1997 Diamndbcks	R	54	213	65	17	4	0	(-	-)	90	52	21	34	26	0	40	2	2	1	3	3	.50	4	.305	.384	.423
1997 Lethbridge	R+	2	6	1	0	0	0	(-	-)	1	2	1	0	1	0	0	0	0	0	0	0	-	0	.167	.286	.167
1998 South Bend	A	110	364	93	14	2	9	(-	-)	138	44	47	54	67	4	81	3	3	5	12	14	.46	4	.255	.371	.379
1999 High Desert	A+	130	488	133	29	6	22	(-	-)	240	106	93	92	86	2	122	2	1	8	40	13	.75	10	.273	.378	.492
2000 Portland	AA	74	221	61	17	3	6	(-	-)	102	39	42	40	44	1	64	0	0	3	8	6	.57	3	.276	.392	.462
2000 Brevard Cnty	A+	31	103	20	4	0	1	(-	-)	27	17	9	13	28	1	34	2	0	0	11	3	.79	3	.194	.376	.262
2001 Portland	AA	136	467	112	14	9	17	(-	-)	195	75	53	71	83	3	155	3	5	2	26	19	.58	4	.240	.357	.418
2002 Calgary	AAA	129	428	107	24	5	21	(-	-)	204	68	60	68	51	3	112	1	0	4	31	6	.84	4	.250	.329	.477
2003 Jupiter	A+	8	29	8	3	0	0	(-	-)	11	6	2	4	4	0	9	0	0	0	1	0	1.00	1	.276	.364	.379
2003 Albuquerque	AAA	59	212	66	13	2	11	(-	-)	116	35	38	45	32	2	56	0	0	2	9	4	.69	1	.311	.398	.547
2002 Florida	NL	19	17	2	0	0	0	(0	0)	2	2	1	0	0	0	5	0	0	0	0	1	.00	1	.118	.118	.118
2004 Fla-KC		117	285	61	10	1	6	(0	6)	91	40	34	30	34	1	69	0	2	1	1	3	.25	7	.214	.297	.319
2004 Florida	NL	58	64	11	1	1	1	(0	1)	17	9	5	3	9	0	21	0	2	0	1	2	.33	3	.172	.274	.266
2004 Kansas City	AL	59	221	50	9	0	5	(0	5)	74	31	29	27	25	1	48	0	0	1	0	1	.00	4	.226	.304	.335
2 ML YEARS		136	302	63	10	1	6	(0	6)	93	42	35	30	34	1	74	0	2	1	1	4	.20	8	.209	.288	.308

Abraham O Nunez

Bats: B **Throws:** R **Pos:** PH-68; 2B-32; SS-13; 3B-6; DH-1; PR-1 **Ht:** 5'11" **Wt:** 185 **Born:** 3/16/1976 **Age:** 29

| | | | | | | | BATTING | | | | | | | | | | | BASERUNNING | | | | AVERAGES | | |
Year Team	Lg	G	AB	H	2B	3B	HR	(Hm	Rd)	TB	R	RBI	RC	TBB	IBB	SO	HBP	SH	SF	SB	CS	SB%	GDP	Avg	OBP	Slg
1997 Pittsburgh	NL	19	40	9	2	2	0	(0	0)	15	3	6	4	3	0	10	1	0	1	1	0	1.00	1	.225	.289	.375
1998 Pittsburgh	NL	24	52	10	2	0	1	(0	1)	15	6	2	6	12	0	14	0	3	0	4	2	.67	1	.192	.344	.288
1999 Pittsburgh	NL	90	259	57	8	0	0	(0	0)	65	25	17	22	28	0	54	1	13	0	9	1	.90	2	.220	.299	.251
2000 Pittsburgh	NL	40	91	20	1	0	1	(0	1)	24	10	8	6	8	1	14	0	0	0	0	0	-	3	.220	.283	.264
2001 Pittsburgh	NL	115	301	79	11	4	1	(0	1)	101	30	21	36	28	1	53	1	4	1	8	2	.80	0	.262	.326	.336
2002 Pittsburgh	NL	112	253	59	14	1	2	(2	0)	81	28	15	25	27	1	44	2	3	1	3	4	.43	2	.233	.311	.320
2003 Pittsburgh	NL	118	311	77	8	7	4	(2	2)	111	37	35	28	26	1	53	3	9	2	9	3	.75	8	.248	.310	.357
2004 Pittsburgh	NL	112	182	43	9	0	2	(1	1)	58	17	13	12	10	0	36	0	2	1	1	3	.25	8	.236	.275	.319
8 ML YEARS		630	1489	354	55	14	11	(5	6)	470	156	117	139	142	4	278	8	34	6	35	15	.70	25	.238	.306	.316

Franklin Nunez

Pitches: R **Bats:** R **Pos:** RP-8 **Ht:** 6'0" **Wt:** 175 **Born:** 1/18/1977 **Age:** 28

Year Team	Lg	G	GS	CG	GF	IP	BFP	H	R	ER	HR	SH	SF	HB	TBB	IBB	SO	WP	Bk	W	L	Pct	ShO	Sv-Op	Hld	ERC	ERA
1998 Martinsville	R+	6	4	0	0	25.1	109	23	10	7	0	0	2	8	0	19	2	3	2	2	.500	0	0- -	-	2.81	2.49
1999 Piedmont	A	13	13	1	0	77.0	326	69	39	29	4	4	1	6	25	0	88	2	1	4	8	.333	0	0- -	-	3.18	3.39
2000 Clearwater	A+	23	14	1	6	112.0	492	112	54	45	4	1	3	7	57	0	81	9	1	10	4	.714	0	2- -	-	4.35	3.62
2001 Reading	AA	39	14	0	10	110.0	486	107	68	54	9	3	2	6	51	3	112	9	0	8	7	.533	0	3- -	-	4.18	4.42
2002 Phillies	R	1	1	0	0	2.0	9	2	0	0	0	0	0	0	1	0	4	0	0	0	0	-	0	0- -	-	3.63	0.00
2002 Scrtn/WlksBr	AAA	4	4	0	0	17.0	69	9	6	6	2	0	0	0	12	0	16	1	0	2	1	.667	0	0- -	-	2.93	3.18
2003 Brooklyn	A-	7	0	0	3	5.1	26	5	4	3	0	0	1	1	4	0	8	1	0	0	0	-	0	0- -	-	4.88	5.06
2004 Montgomery	AA	6	0	0	0	10.2	38	4	3	1	0	0	0	0	3	0	19	1	0	1	0	1.000	0	0- -	-	0.72	0.84
2004 Durham	AAA	40	0	0	21	51.1	227	36	21	16	1	0	0	0	34	0	70	5	0	4	2	.667	0	9- -	-	2.78	2.81
2004 Tampa Bay	AL	8	0	0	0	10.2	54	11	8	7	1	1	2	3	7	0	14	2	0	0	3	.000	0	0-1	0	6.11	5.91

Vladimir Nunez

Pitches: R **Bats:** R **Pos:** RP-22 **Ht:** 6'4" **Wt:** 240 **Born:** 3/15/1975 **Age:** 30

Year Team	Lg	G	GS	CG	GF	IP	BFP	H	R	ER	HR	SH	SF	HB	TBB	IBB	SO	WP	Bk	W	L	Pct	ShO	Sv-Op	Hld	ERC	ERA
2004 Co Springs*	AAA	22	7	0	12	58.1	255	69	39	35	4	1	1	2	18	0	55	3	0	2	4	.333	0	3- -	-	4.72	5.40
1998 Arizona	NL	4	0	0	2	5.1	25	7	6	6	0	0	1	0	2	0	2	0	0	0	0	-	0	0-0	0	4.87	10.13
1999 Ari-Fla	NL	44	12	0	12	108.2	463	95	63	49	11	7	6	4	54	6	86	8	1	7	10	.412	0	1-3	4	3.88	4.06
2000 Florida	NL	17	12	0	3	68.1	322	88	63	60	12	5	5	2	34	2	45	5	0	0	6	.000	0	0- -	1	6.88	7.90

Year Team	Lg	G	GS	CG	GF	IP	BFP	H	R	ER	HR	SH	SF	HB	TBB	IBB	SO	WP	Bk	W	L	Pct	ShO	Sv-Op	Hld	ERC	ERA
2001 Florida	NL	52	3	0	13	92.0	380	79	33	28	9	2	5	5	30	5	64	1	1	4	5	.444	0	0-1	4	3.17	2.74
2002 Florida	NL	77	0	0	43	97.2	404	80	38	37	8	6	4	0	37	1	73	2	0	6	5	.545	0	20-28	11	2.88	3.41
2003 Florida	NL	14	0	0	4	10.2	63	21	21	19	7	1	2	0	7	0	10	0	0	0	3	.000	0	0-3	2	16.12	16.03
2004 Colorado	NL	22	0	0	6	25.2	114	26	22	20	6	1	5	1	14	0	22	4	0	3	3	.500	0	0-3	3	6.01	7.01
1999 Arizona	NL	27	0	0	11	34.0	146	29	15	11	2	2	3	1	20	5	28	3	0	3	2	.600	0	1-2	3	3.63	2.91
1999 Florida	NL	17	12	0	1	74.2	317	66	48	38	9	5	3	3	34	1	58	5	1	4	8	.333	0	0-1	1	3.98	4.58
7 ML YEARS		230	27	0	83	408.1	1771	396	246	219	53	22	28	12	178	14	302	20	3	20	32	.385	0	21-38	25	4.33	4.83

Wes Obermueller

Pitches: R Bats: R Pos: SP-20; RP-5   Ht: 6'2" Wt: 195 Born: 12/22/1976 Age: 28

Year Team	Lg	G	GS	CG	GF	IP	BFP	H	R	ER	HR	SH	SF	HB	TBB	IBB	SO	WP	Bk	W	L	Pct	ShO	Sv-Op	Hld	ERC	ERA
2004 Indianapolis*	AAA	4	4	1	0	26.0	111	30	16	15	3	3	1	1	7	0	17	1	0	0	3	.000	0	0- -	-	4.81	5.19
2002 Kansas City	AL	2	2	0	0	7.2	39	14	10	10	3	0	0	0	2	0	5	0	0	0	2	.000	0	0-0	0	11.04	11.74
2003 Milwaukee	NL	12	11	0	0	65.2	303	81	40	37	10	1	2	6	25	2	34	5	0	2	5	.286	0	0-0	0	6.08	5.07
2004 Milwaukee	NL	25	20	1	1	118.0	529	138	80	76	15	4	5	3	42	0	59	4	0	6	8	.429	1	0-0	0	5.14	5.80
3 ML YEARS		39	33	1	1	191.1	871	233	130	123	28	5	7	9	69	2	98	9	0	8	15	.348	1	0-0	0	5.67	5.79

Jose Offerman

Bats: B Throws: R Pos: DH-38; PH-36; 1B-7; 2B-3; PR-1   Ht: 6'0" Wt: 192 Born: 11/11/1968 Age: 36

Year Team	Lg	G	AB	H	2B	3B	HR	(Hm	Rd)	TB	R	RBI	RC	TBB	IBB	SO	HBP	SH	SF	SB	CS	SB%	GDP	Avg	OBP	Slg
1990 Los Angeles	NL	29	58	9	0	0	1	(1	0)	12	7	7	2	4	1	14	0	1	0	1	0	1.00	0	.155	.210	.207
1991 Los Angeles	NL	52	113	22	2	0	0	(0	0)	24	10	3	9	25	2	32	1	1	0	3	2	.60	5	.195	.345	.212
1992 Los Angeles	NL	149	534	139	20	8	1	(1	0)	178	67	30	60	57	4	98	0	5	2	23	16	.59	5	.260	.331	.333
1993 Los Angeles	NL	158	590	159	21	6	1	(1	0)	195	77	62	72	71	7	75	2	25	8	30	13	.70	12	.269	.346	.331
1994 Los Angeles	NL	72	243	51	8	4	1	(0	1)	70	27	25	23	38	4	38	0	6	2	2	1	.67	6	.210	.314	.288
1995 Los Angeles	NL	119	429	123	14	6	4	(2	2)	161	69	33	66	69	0	67	3	10	0	2	7	.22	5	.287	.389	.375
1996 Kansas City	AL	151	561	170	33	8	5	(1	4)	234	85	47	93	74	3	98	1	7	2	24	10	.71	9	.303	.384	.417
1997 Kansas City	AL	106	424	126	23	6	2	(2	0)	167	59	39	59	41	3	64	0	6	0	9	10	.47	5	.297	.359	.394
1998 Kansas City	AL	158	607	191	28	13	7	(4	3)	266	102	66	116	89	1	96	5	2	6	45	12	.79	7	.315	.403	.438
1999 Boston	AL	149	586	172	37	11	8	(5	3)	255	107	69	102	96	5	79	2	2	7	18	12	.60	11	.294	.391	.435
2000 Boston	AL	116	451	115	14	3	9	(3	6)	162	73	41	58	70	0	70	1	2	3	0	8	.00	9	.255	.354	.359
2001 Boston	AL	128	524	140	23	3	9	(4	5)	196	76	49	69	61	2	97	1	3	1	5	2	.71	9	.267	.342	.374
2002 Bos-Sea	AL	101	284	66	12	1	5	(2	3)	95	48	31	34	37	0	38	1	1	3	9	6	.60	12	.232	.320	.335
2004 Minnesota	AL	77	172	44	14	2	2	(0	2)	68	22	22	24	29	2	31	0	1	1	1	1	.50	1	.256	.363	.395
2002 Boston	AL	72	237	55	10	0	4	(1	3)	77	39	27	31	33	0	29	1	1	3	8	5	.62	9	.232	.325	.325
2002 Seattle	AL	29	47	11	2	1	1	(1	0)	18	9	4	3	4	0	9	0	0	0	1	1	.50	3	.234	.294	.383
14 ML YEARS		1565	5576	1527	249	71	55	(26	29)	2083	829	524	787	761	34	897	17	72	38	172	100	.63	96	.274	.361	.374

Tomo Ohka

Pitches: R Bats: R Pos: SP-15   Ht: 6'1" Wt: 180 Born: 3/18/1976 Age: 29

Year Team	Lg	G	GS	CG	GF	IP	BFP	H	R	ER	HR	SH	SF	HB	TBB	IBB	SO	WP	Bk	W	L	Pct	ShO	Sv-Op	Hld	ERC	ERA
1999 Boston	AL	8	2	0	3	13.0	65	21	12	9	2	1	0	6	6	0	8	0	0	1	2	.333	0	0-0	0	8.56	6.23
2000 Boston	AL	13	12	0	1	69.1	297	70	25	24	7	1	2	2	26	0	40	3	0	3	6	.333	0	0-0	0	4.19	3.12
2001 Bos-Mon		22	21	0	1	107.0	469	134	70	65	15	2	2	3	29	0	68	2	1	3	9	.250	0	0-0	0	5.52	5.47
2002 Montreal	NL	32	31	2	1	192.2	806	194	83	68	19	13	6	7	45	7	118	2	1	13	8	.619	0	0-0	0	3.55	3.18
2003 Montreal	NL	34	34	2	0	199.0	864	233	106	92	24	8	3	9	45	11	118	8	0	10	12	.455	0	0-0	0	4.59	4.16
2004 Montreal	NL	15	15	0	0	84.2	367	98	40	32	11	4	2	1	20	1	38	3	0	3	7	.300	0	0-0	0	4.53	3.40
2001 Boston	AL	12	11	0	0	52.1	241	69	40	36	7	1	1	2	19	0	37	1	1	2	5	.286	0	0-0	0	6.24	6.19
2001 Montreal	NL	10	10	0	1	54.2	228	65	30	29	8	1	1	1	10	0	31	1	0	1	4	.200	0	0-0	0	4.83	4.77
6 ML YEARS		124	115	4	6	665.2	2868	750	336	290	78	28	16	22	171	19	390	18	2	33	44	.429	0	0-0	0	4.44	3.92

Augie Ojeda

Bats: B Throws: R Pos: 2B-20; SS-7; PR-6; 3B-4   Ht: 5'8" Wt: 170 Born: 12/20/1974 Age: 30

Year Team	Lg	G	AB	H	2B	3B	HR	(Hm	Rd)	TB	R	RBI	RC	TBB	IBB	SO	HBP	SH	SF	SB	CS	SB%	GDP	Avg	OBP	Slg
2004 Rochester*	AAA	89	327	80	19	0	2	(-	-)	105	49	21	36	39	0	33	6	7	2	7	5	.58	10	.245	.334	.321
2000 Chicago	NL	28	77	17	3	1	2	(1	1)	28	10	8	9	10	1	9	0	1	1	0	1	.00	1	.221	.307	.364
2001 Chicago	NL	78	144	29	5	1	1	(1	0)	39	16	12	10	12	1	20	2	2	2	1	0	1.00	2	.201	.269	.271
2002 Chicago	NL	30	70	13	4	0	0	(0	0)	17	4	4	4	5	0	5	1	4	1	1	0	1.00	2	.186	.247	.243
2003 Chicago	NL	12	25	3	0	0	0	(0	0)	3	2	0	0	1	1	5	1	0	0	0	0	-	1	.120	.185	.120
2004 Minnesota	AL	30	59	20	1	0	2	(0	2)	27	16	7	11	10	0	3	0	2	1	1	1	.50	0	.339	.429	.458
5 ML YEARS		178	375	82	13	2	5	(2	3)	114	48	31	34	38	3	42	4	9	5	3	2	.60	6	.219	.294	.304

Miguel Ojeda

Bats: R Throws: R Pos: C-50; PH-17   Ht: 6'2" Wt: 190 Born: 1/29/1975 Age: 30

Year Team	Lg	G	AB	H	2B	3B	HR	(Hm	Rd)	TB	R	RBI	RC	TBB	IBB	SO	HBP	SH	SF	SB	CS	SB%	GDP	Avg	OBP	Slg
1993 Pirates	R	27	97	27	3	1	3	(-	-)	41	9	11	15	10	0	18	0	1	2	2	0	1.00	1	.278	.339	.423
1994 Welland	A-	48	142	27	6	0	2	(-	-)	39	11	8	8	5	0	30	2	2	0	1	0	1.00	0	.190	.228	.275
1998 Carolina	AA	18	58	9	2	0	1	(-	-)	14	4	4	2	3	0	12	1	2	0	0	0	-	0	.155	.210	.241
2004 Portland	AAA	5	19	5	0	0	2	(-	-)	11	4	3	3	2	0	3	0	0	0	0	0	-	0	.263	.333	.579
2003 San Diego	NL	61	141	33	6	0	4	(3	1)	51	13	22	20	18	2	26	3	0	1	1	1	.50	2	.234	.331	.362
2004 San Diego	NL	62	156	40	3	0	8	(1	7)	67	23	26	24	15	1	34	1	0	2	0	0	-	1	.256	.322	.429
2 ML YEARS		123	297	73	9	0	12	(4	8)	118	36	48	44	33	3	60	4	0	3	1	1	.50	3	.246	.326	.397

John Olerud

Bats: L **Throws:** L **Pos:** 1B-124; PH-5   **Ht:** 6'5" **Wt:** 220 **Born:** 8/5/1968 **Age:** 36

Year Team	Lg	G	AB	H	2B	3B	HR	(Hm	Rd)	TB	R	RBI	RC	TBB	IBB	SO	HBP	SH	SF	SB	CS	SB%	GDP	Avg	OBP	Slg
1989 Toronto	AL	6	8	3	0	0	0	(0	0)	3	2	0	1	0	0	1	0	0	0	0	0	-	0	.375	.375	.375
1990 Toronto	AL	111	358	95	15	1	14	(11	3)	154	43	48	57	57	6	75	1	1	4	0	2	.00	5	.265	.364	.430
1991 Toronto	AL	139	454	116	30	1	17	(7	10)	199	64	68	71	68	9	84	6	3	10	0	2	.00	12	.256	.353	.438
1992 Toronto	AL	138	458	130	28	0	16	(4	12)	206	68	66	76	70	11	61	1	1	7	1	0	1.00	15	.284	.375	.450
1993 Toronto	AL	158	551	200	**54**	2	24	(9	15)	330	109	107	**146**	114	**33**	65	7	0	7	0	2	.00	12	**.363**	**.473**	.599
1994 Toronto	AL	108	384	114	29	2	12	(6	6)	183	47	67	70	61	12	53	3	0	5	1	2	.33	11	.297	.393	.477
1995 Toronto	AL	135	492	143	32	0	8	(1	7)	199	72	54	80	84	10	54	4	0	1	0	0	-	17	.291	.398	.404
1996 Toronto	AL	125	398	109	25	0	18	(9	9)	188	59	61	72	60	6	37	10	0	1	1	0	1.00	10	.274	.382	.472
1997 New York	NL	154	524	154	34	1	22	(13	9)	256	90	102	101	85	5	67	13	0	8	0	0	-	19	.294	.400	.489
1998 New York	NL	160	557	197	36	4	22	(13	9)	307	91	93	131	96	11	73	4	1	7	2	2	.50	15	.354	.447	.551
1999 New York	NL	162	581	173	39	0	19	(11	8)	269	107	96	118	125	5	66	11	0	6	3	0	1.00	22	.298	.427	.463
2000 Seattle	AL	159	565	161	45	0	14	(8	6)	248	84	103	98	102	11	96	4	2	10	0	2	.00	17	.285	.392	.439
2001 Seattle	AL	159	572	173	32	1	21	(15	6)	270	91	95	106	94	19	70	5	1	7	3	1	.75	21	.302	.401	.472
2002 Seattle	AL	154	553	166	39	0	22	(9	13)	271	85	102	108	98	6	66	5	0	12	0	0	-	19	.300	.403	.490
2003 Seattle	AL	152	539	145	35	0	10	(8	2)	210	64	83	79	84	7	67	6	2	3	0	1	.00	20	.269	.372	.390
2004 Sea-NYY	AL	127	425	110	20	1	9	(5	4)	159	45	48	57	61	4	61	8	1	5	0	0	-	11	.259	.359	.374
2004 Seattle	AL	78	261	64	13	1	5	(2	3)	94	29	22	30	40	3	41	6	1	4	0	0	-	6	.245	.354	.360
2004 New York	AL	49	164	46	7	0	4	(3	1)	65	16	26	27	21	1	20	2	0	1	0	0	-	5	.280	.367	.396
16 ML YEARS		2147	7419	2189	493	13	248	(129	119)	3452	1121	1193	1371	1259	155	996	88	12	93	11	14	.44	226	.295	.399	.465

Darren Oliver

Pitches: L **Bats:** R **Pos:** RP-17; SP-10   **Ht:** 6'2" **Wt:** 220 **Born:** 10/6/1970 **Age:** 34

		HOW MUCH HE PITCHED						WHAT HE GAVE UP											THE RESULTS						
Year Team	Lg	G	GS	CG	GF	IP	BFP	H	R	ER	HR	SH	SF	HB	TBB	IBB	SO	WP	Bk	W	L	Pct	ShO	Sv-Op	Hld	ERC	ERA
1993 Texas	AL	2	0	0	0	3.1	14	2	1	1	1	0	0	0	1	1	4	0	0	0	0	-	0	0-0	0	2.15	2.70
1994 Texas	AL	43	0	0	10	50.0	226	40	24	19	4	6	0	6	35	4	50	2	2	4	0	1.000	0	2-3	9	4.29	3.42
1995 Texas	AL	17	7	0	2	49.0	222	47	25	23	3	5	1	1	32	1	39	4	0	4	2	.667	0	0-0	0	4.59	4.22
1996 Texas	AL	30	30	1	0	173.2	777	190	97	90	20	2	7	10	76	3	112	5	1	14	6	.700	1	0-0	0	5.10	4.66
1997 Texas	AL	32	32	3	0	201.1	887	213	111	94	29	2	5	11	82	3	104	7	0	13	12	.520	1	0-0	0	4.98	4.20
1998 Tex-StL		29	29	2	0	160.1	749	204	115	102	18	8	8	10	66	2	87	7	4	10	11	.476	0	0-0	0	6.01	5.73
1999 St Louis	NL	30	30	2	0	196.1	842	197	96	93	16	11	4	11	74	4	119	6	2	9	9	.500	1	0-0	0	4.11	4.26
2000 Texas	AL	21	21	0	0	108.0	501	151	95	89	16	5	4	4	42	3	49	4	1	2	9	.182	0	0-0	0	7.04	7.42
2001 Texas	AL	28	28	1	0	154.0	696	189	109	103	23	1	5	6	65	0	104	8	2	11	11	.500	0	0-0	0	6.14	6.02
2002 Boston	AL	14	9	1	0	58.0	258	70	30	30	7	1	3	6	27	0	32	1	0	4	5	.444	1	0-0	0	6.49	4.66
2003 Colorado	NL	33	32	1	0	180.1	786	201	108	101	21	4	5	8	61	3	88	0	0	13	11	.542	0	0-0	0	4.80	5.04
2004 Fla-Hou	NL	27	10	0	5	72.2	314	87	50	48	14	4	3	1	21	1	46	1	0	3	3	.500	0	0-0	0	5.59	5.94
1998 Texas	AL	19	19	2	0	103.1	493	140	84	75	11	3	6	10	43	1	58	6	1	6	7	.462	0	0-0	0	6.68	6.53
1998 St Louis	NL	10	10	0	0	57.0	256	64	31	27	7	5	2	0	23	1	29	1	3	4	4	.500	0	0-0	0	4.85	4.26
2004 Florida	NL	18	8	0	0	58.2	260	75	44	42	13	4	3	1	17	1	33	1	0	2	3	.400	0	0-0	0	6.30	6.44
2004 Houston	NL	9	2	0	2	14.0	54	12	6	6	1	0	0	0	4	0	13	0	0	1	0	1.000	0	0-0	0	2.89	3.86
12 ML YEARS		306	228	11	17	1407.0	6272	1591	861	793	172	49	45	74	582	25	834	45	12	87	79	.524	4	2-3	9	5.29	5.07

Miguel Olivo

Bats: R **Throws:** R **Pos:** C-95; PR-6; PH-2   **Ht:** 6'0" **Wt:** 180 **Born:** 7/15/1978 **Age:** 26

Year Team	Lg	G	AB	H	2B	3B	HR	(Hm	Rd)	TB	R	RBI	RC	TBB	IBB	SO	HBP	SH	SF	SB	CS	SB%	GDP	Avg	OBP	Slg
2004 Everett*	A-	2	6	0	0	0	0	(-	-)	0	0	0	0	0	0	2	0	0	0	0	0	-	0	.000	.000	.000
2002 Chicago	AL	6	19	4	1	0	1	(0	1)	8	2	5	4	2	0	5	0	0	0	0	0	-	1	.211	.286	.421
2003 Chicago	AL	114	317	75	19	1	6	(4	2)	114	37	27	32	19	0	80	4	4	2	6	4	.60	3	.237	.287	.360
2004 CWS-Sea	AL	96	301	70	15	4	13	(8	5)	132	46	40	33	20	2	84	3	4	1	7	6	.54	4	.233	.286	.439
2004 Chicago	AL	46	141	38	7	2	7	(4	3)	70	21	26	21	10	1	29	0	4	1	5	4	.56	2	.270	.316	.496
2004 Seattle	AL	50	160	32	8	2	6	(4	2)	62	25	14	12	10	1	55	3	0	0	2	2	.50	2	.200	.260	.388
3 ML YEARS		216	637	149	35	5	20	(12	8)	254	85	72	69	41	2	169	7	8	3	13	10	.57	8	.234	.286	.399

Ray Olmedo

Bats: B **Throws:** R **Pos:** SS-7; PH-1   **Ht:** 5'11" **Wt:** 155 **Born:** 5/31/1981 **Age:** 24

Year Team	Lg	G	AB	H	2B	3B	HR	(Hm	Rd)	TB	R	RBI	RC	TBB	IBB	SO	HBP	SH	SF	SB	CS	SB%	GDP	Avg	OBP	Slg
1999 Reds	R	54	195	46	12	1	1	(-	-)	63	30	19	17	12	0	28	1	1	2	13	7	.65	1	.236	.281	.323
2000 Dayton	A	111	369	94	19	1	4	(-	-)	127	50	41	37	30	1	70	1	14	4	17	11	.61	11	.255	.309	.344
2001 Mudville	A+	129	536	131	23	4	0	(-	-)	162	57	28	43	24	0	121	8	13	4	38	17	.69	15	.244	.285	.302
2002 Chattanooga	AA	132	478	118	21	1	3	(-	-)	150	62	30	51	53	2	86	7	14	0	15	16	.48	4	.247	.331	.314
2003 Chattanooga	AA	49	160	47	11	0	2	(-	-)	64	23	15	21	14	1	29	0	7	1	3	3	.50	3	.294	.349	.400
2003 Louisville	AAA	9	25	6	1	0	1	(-	-)	10	4	4	3	2	0	6	0	4	0	0	0	-	0	.240	.296	.400
2004 Louisville	AAA	82	294	84	13	7	2	(-	-)	117	33	26	39	23	1	40	2	8	0	2	3	.40	8	.286	.342	.398
2003 Cincinnati	NL	79	230	55	6	1	0	(0	0)	63	24	17	19	13	0	46	0	7	0	1	1	.50	4	.239	.280	.274
2004 Cincinnati	NL	8	1	0	0	0	0	(0	0)	0	0	0	0	1	0	0	0	0	0	0	0	-	0	.000	.500	.000
2 ML YEARS		87	231	55	6	1	0	(0	0)	63	24	17	19	14	0	46	0	7	0	1	1	.50	4	.238	.282	.273

Tim Olson

Bats: R **Throws:** R **Pos:** 3B-19; SS-17; PH-11; CF-2; LF-1; RF-1; PR-1   **Ht:** 6'2" **Wt:** 200 **Born:** 8/1/1978 **Age:** 26

Year Team	Lg	G	AB	H	2B	3B	HR	(Hm	Rd)	TB	R	RBI	RC	TBB	IBB	SO	HBP	SH	SF	SB	CS	SB%	GDP	Avg	OBP	Slg
2000 South Bend	A	68	261	57	14	2	2	(-	-)	81	37	26	23	15	0	49	8	0	1	15	3	.83	5	.218	.281	.310
2001 Lancaster	A+	61	239	69	12	4	6	(-	-)	107	36	32	33	14	0	49	3	2	0	13	9	.59	4	.289	.336	.448
2001 El Paso	AA	46	167	53	13	0	2	(-	-)	72	29	24	25	11	0	36	6	0	1	4	4	.50	4	.317	.378	.431
2002 El Paso	AA	126	433	118	24	2	10	(-	-)	176	61	64	55	27	1	91	19	4	7	9	11	.45	13	.273	.337	.406

188

Year Team	Lg	G	AB	H	2B	3B	HR	(Hm	Rd)	TB	R	RBI	RC	TBB	IBB	SO	HBP	SH	SF	SB	CS	SB%	GDP	Avg	OBP	Slg
2003 El Paso	AA	14	56	11	2	0	2	(-	-)	19	5	8	3	5	0	19	0	0	1	0	2	.00	1	.196	.258	.339
2003 Tucson	AAA	115	397	104	22	0	6	(-	-)	144	59	40	45	31	2	77	6	3	2	11	2	.85	14	.262	.323	.363
2004 Tucson	AAA	37	147	44	11	0	7	(-	-)	76	32	25	27	16	0	28	2	1	1	5	1	.83	2	.299	.373	.517
2004 Arizona	NL	48	97	18	7	0	2	(2	0)	31	8	5	8	16	0	18	0	1	0	1	0	1.00	4	.186	.301	.320

Magglio Ordonez

Bats: R **Throws:** R **Pos:** RF-43; DH-7; PH-2   **Ht:** 6'0" **Wt:** 210 **Born:** 1/28/1974 **Age:** 31

Year Team	Lg	G	AB	H	2B	3B	HR	(Hm	Rd)	TB	R	RBI	RC	TBB	IBB	SO	HBP	SH	SF	SB	CS	SB%	GDP	Avg	OBP	Slg
1997 Chicago	AL	21	69	22	6	0	4	(2	2)	40	12	11	12	2	0	8	0	1	0	1	2	.33	1	.319	.338	.580
1998 Chicago	AL	145	535	151	25	2	14	(8	6)	222	70	65	67	28	1	53	9	2	4	9	7	.56	19	.282	.326	.415
1999 Chicago	AL	157	624	188	34	3	30	(16	14)	318	100	117	102	47	4	64	1	0	5	13	6	.68	24	.301	.349	.510
2000 Chicago	AL	153	588	185	34	3	32	(21	11)	321	102	126	112	60	3	64	2	0	15	18	4	.82	28	.315	.371	.546
2001 Chicago	AL	160	593	181	40	1	31	(17	14)	316	97	113	117	70	7	70	5	0	3	25	7	.78	14	.305	.382	.533
2002 Chicago	AL	153	590	189	47	1	38	(24	14)	352	116	135	119	53	2	77	7	0	3	7	5	.58	21	.320	.381	.597
2003 Chicago	AL	160	606	192	46	3	29	(17	12)	331	95	99	109	57	1	73	7	0	4	9	5	.64	20	.317	.380	.546
2004 Chicago	AL	52	202	59	8	2	9	(4	5)	98	32	37	39	16	2	22	3	0	1	0	2	.00	4	.292	.351	.485
8 ML YEARS		1001	3807	1167	240	15	187	(109	78)	1998	624	703	677	333	20	431	34	3	35	82	38	.68	131	.307	.364	.525

Rey Ordonez

Bats: R **Throws:** R **Pos:** SS-22; PH-1   **Ht:** 5'9" **Wt:** 159 **Born:** 1/11/1971 **Age:** 34

Year Team	Lg	G	AB	H	2B	3B	HR	(Hm	Rd)	TB	R	RBI	RC	TBB	IBB	SO	HBP	SH	SF	SB	CS	SB%	GDP	Avg	OBP	Slg
2004 Daytona*	A+	3	8	1	1	0	0	(-	-)	2	0	1	0	0	0	1	0	0	1	0	0	-	0	.125	.111	.250
2004 Iowa*	AAA	6	24	7	2	0	0	(-	-)	9	3	3	2	1	0	1	0	0	0	0	0	-	0	.292	.320	.375
1996 New York	NL	151	502	129	12	4	1	(0	1)	152	51	30	39	22	12	53	1	4	1	1	3	.25	12	.257	.289	.303
1997 New York	NL	120	356	77	5	3	1	(1	0)	91	35	33	19	18	3	36	1	14	2	11	5	.69	10	.216	.255	.256
1998 New York	NL	153	505	124	20	2	1	(0	1)	151	46	42	37	23	7	60	1	15	4	3	6	.33	11	.246	.278	.299
1999 New York	NL	154	520	134	24	2	1	(1	0)	165	49	60	51	49	12	59	1	11	7	8	4	.67	16	.258	.319	.317
2000 New York	NL	45	133	25	5	0	0	(0	0)	30	10	9	8	17	2	16	0	4	1	0	0	-	4	.188	.278	.226
2001 New York	NL	149	461	114	24	4	3	(0	3)	155	31	44	41	34	17	43	1	7	2	3	2	.60	17	.247	.299	.336
2002 New York	NL	144	460	117	25	2	1	(0	1)	149	53	42	37	24	11	46	2	9	4	2	2	.50	19	.254	.292	.324
2003 Tampa Bay	NL	34	117	37	11	0	3	(1	2)	57	14	22	17	2	0	12	1	2	2	0	2	.00	3	.316	.328	.487
2004 Chicago	NL	23	61	10	3	0	1	(1	0)	16	2	5	4	2	0	14	0	4	0	0	0	-	1	.164	.190	.262
9 ML YEARS		973	3115	767	129	17	12	(4	8)	966	291	287	253	191	64	339	8	70	23	28	24	.54	93	.246	.289	.310

Eddie Oropesa

Pitches: L **Bats:** L **Pos:** RP-16   **Ht:** 6'3" **Wt:** 215 **Born:** 11/23/1971 **Age:** 33

Year Team	Lg	G	GS	CG	GF	IP	BFP	H	R	ER	HR	SH	SF	HB	TBB	IBB	SO	WP	Bk	W	L	Pct	ShO	Sv-Op	Hld	ERC	ERA
2004 Portland*	AAA	37	0	0	12	46.1	192	31	15	12	2	0	0	3	19	1	54	3	0	3	3	.500	0	1--	-	2.19	2.33
2001 Philadelphia	NL	30	0	0	4	19.0	87	16	10	10	1	0	0	0	17	6	15	1	0	1	0	1.000	0	0-1	6	4.20	4.74
2002 Arizona	NL	32	0	0	5	25.1	132	39	30	29	6	2	1	2	15	0	18	1	1	2	0	1.000	0	0-1	7	9.65	10.30
2003 Arizona	NL	47	0	0	9	38.2	180	38	27	25	3	3	0	2	27	2	39	3	1	3	3	.500	0	0-0	10	5.06	5.82
2004 San Diego	NL	16	0	0	4	9.0	45	6	12	11	1	0	0	0	13	3	6	1	0	2	1	.667	0	0-0	1	5.67	11.00
4 ML YEARS		125	0	0	22	92.0	444	99	79	75	11	6	1	4	72	11	78	6	2	8	4	.667	0	0-2	24	6.14	7.34

David Ortiz

Bats: L **Throws:** L **Pos:** DH-115; 1B-34; PH-5   **Ht:** 6'4" **Wt:** 230 **Born:** 11/18/1975 **Age:** 29

Year Team	Lg	G	AB	H	2B	3B	HR	(Hm	Rd)	TB	R	RBI	RC	TBB	IBB	SO	HBP	SH	SF	SB	CS	SB%	GDP	Avg	OBP	Slg
1997 Minnesota	AL	15	49	16	3	0	1	(0	1)	22	10	6	7	2	0	19	0	0	0	0	0	-	1	.327	.353	.449
1998 Minnesota	AL	86	278	77	20	0	9	(2	7)	124	47	46	46	39	3	72	5	0	4	1	0	1.00	8	.277	.371	.446
1999 Minnesota	AL	10	20	0	0	0	0	(0	0)	0	1	0	0	5	0	12	0	0	0	0	0	-	2	.000	.200	.000
2000 Minnesota	AL	130	415	117	36	1	10	(7	3)	185	59	63	66	57	2	81	0	0	6	1	0	1.00	13	.282	.364	.446
2001 Minnesota	AL	89	303	71	17	1	18	(6	12)	144	46	48	46	40	8	68	1	1	2	1	0	1.00	6	.234	.324	.475
2002 Minnesota	AL	125	412	112	32	1	20	(5	15)	206	52	75	62	43	0	87	3	0	8	1	2	.33	5	.272	.339	.500
2003 Boston	AL	128	448	129	39	2	31	(17	14)	265	79	101	80	58	8	83	1	0	2	0	0	-	9	.288	.369	.592
2004 Boston	AL	150	582	175	47	3	41	(17	24)	351	94	139	127	75	8	133	4	0	8	0	0	-	12	.301	.380	.603
8 ML YEARS		733	2507	697	194	8	130	(54	76)	1297	388	478	434	319	29	555	14	1	30	4	2	.67	56	.278	.359	.517

Ramon Ortiz

Pitches: R **Bats:** R **Pos:** RP-20; SP-14   **Ht:** 6'0" **Wt:** 170 **Born:** 3/23/1973 **Age:** 32

Year Team	Lg	G	GS	CG	GF	IP	BFP	H	R	ER	HR	SH	SF	HB	TBB	IBB	SO	WP	Bk	W	L	Pct	ShO	Sv-Op	Hld	ERC	ERA
1999 Anaheim	AL	9	9	0	0	48.1	218	50	35	35	7	0	2	2	25	0	44	2	2	2	3	.400	0	0-0	0	5.23	6.52
2000 Anaheim	AL	18	18	2	0	111.1	472	96	69	63	18	4	4	2	55	0	73	7	4	8	6	.571	0	0-0	0	4.24	5.09
2001 Anaheim	AL	32	32	2	0	208.2	916	223	114	101	25	9	6	12	76	6	135	7	0	13	11	.542	0	0-0	0	4.65	4.36
2002 Anaheim	AL	32	32	4	0	217.1	896	188	97	91	40	2	5	5	68	0	162	7	3	15	9	.625	1	0-0	0	3.64	3.77
2003 Anaheim	AL	32	32	1	0	180.0	814	209	121	104	28	3	7	12	63	0	94	4	0	16	13	.552	0	0-0	0	5.44	5.20
2004 Anaheim	AL	34	14	0	13	128.0	543	139	64	63	18	2	3	4	38	4	82	5	3	5	7	.417	0	0-0	0	4.61	4.43
6 ML YEARS		157	137	9	13	893.2	3859	905	500	457	136	20	27	37	325	10	590	32	12	59	49	.546	1	0-0	0	4.53	4.60

Russ Ortiz

Pitches: R **Bats:** R **Pos:** SP-34   **Ht:** 6'1" **Wt:** 208 **Born:** 6/5/1974 **Age:** 31

Year Team	Lg	G	GS	CG	GF	IP	BFP	H	R	ER	HR	SH	SF	HB	TBB	IBB	SO	WP	Bk	W	L	Pct	ShO	Sv-Op	Hld	ERC	ERA
1998 San Francisco	NL	22	13	0	3	88.1	394	90	51	49	11	5	4	4	46	1	75	3	0	4	4	.500	0	0-0	1	5.05	4.99
1999 San Francisco	NL	33	33	3	0	207.2	922	189	109	88	24	11	6	6	125	5	164	13	0	18	9	.667	0	0-0	0	4.56	3.81
2000 San Francisco	NL	33	32	0	0	195.2	871	192	117	109	28	10	6	7	112	1	167	8	0	14	12	.538	0	0-0	0	5.17	5.01
2001 San Francisco	NL	33	33	1	0	218.2	911	187	90	80	13	10	4	0	91	3	169	8	1	17	9	.654	1	0-0	0	3.08	3.29
2002 San Francisco	NL	33	33	2	0	214.1	911	191	89	86	15	15	6	4	94	5	137	5	0	14	10	.583	0	0-0	0	3.46	3.61
2003 Atlanta	NL	34	34	1	0	212.1	912	177	101	90	17	6	7	4	102	7	149	5	0	21	7	.750	1	0-0	0	3.32	3.81
2004 Atlanta	NL	34	34	2	0	204.2	896	197	98	94	23	10	7	3	112	7	143	4	1	15	9	.625	0	0-0	0	4.60	4.13
7 ML YEARS		222	212	9	3	1341.2	5817	1223	655	596	131	67	40	28	682	29	1004	46	2	103	60	.632	3	0-0	1	4.05	4.00

Donovan Osborne

Pitches: L **Bats:** L **Pos:** RP-7; SP-2   **Ht:** 6'2" **Wt:** 210 **Born:** 6/21/1969 **Age:** 36

Year Team	Lg	G	GS	CG	GF	IP	BFP	H	R	ER	HR	SH	SF	HB	TBB	IBB	SO	WP	Bk	W	L	Pct	ShO	Sv-Op	Hld	ERC	ERA
2004 Portland*	AAA	7	2	0	2	13.2	71	26	14	13	4	1	1	1	5	0	12	1	0	2	2	.500	0	0- -	1	11.96	8.56
1992 St Louis	NL	34	29	0	2	179.0	754	193	91	75	14	7	4	2	38	2	104	6	0	11	9	.550	0	0-0	1	3.65	3.77
1993 St Louis	NL	26	26	1	0	155.2	657	153	73	65	18	6	2	7	47	4	83	4	0	10	7	.588	0	0-0	0	3.86	3.76
1995 St Louis	NL	19	19	0	0	113.1	477	112	58	48	17	8	3	2	34	2	82	0	0	4	6	.400	0	0-0	0	4.01	3.81
1996 St Louis	NL	30	30	2	0	198.2	822	191	87	78	22	7	4	1	57	5	134	6	1	13	9	.591	1	0-0	0	3.51	3.53
1997 St Louis	NL	14	14	0	0	80.1	337	84	46	44	10	3	3	1	23	2	51	1	0	3	7	.300	0	0-0	0	4.13	4.93
1998 St Louis	NL	14	14	1	0	83.2	358	84	42	38	11	3	4	1	22	2	60	1	0	5	4	.556	1	0-0	0	3.70	4.09
1999 St Louis	NL	6	6	0	0	29.1	130	34	18	18	4	3	1	2	10	0	21	1	0	1	3	.250	0	0-0	0	5.35	5.52
2002 Chicago	NL	11	0	0	1	16.0	77	19	11	11	1	2	1	0	10	2	13	0	0	0	1	.000	0	0-0	0	5.40	6.19
2004 New York	AL	9	2	0	2	17.2	79	25	16	14	3	0	0	2	5	0	10	0	0	2	0	1.000	0	0-0	0	7.52	7.13
9 ML YEARS		163	140	4	5	873.2	3691	895	442	391	100	39	22	18	246	19	558	19	1	49	46	.516	2	0-0	1	3.91	4.03

Keith Osik

Bats: R **Throws:** R **Pos:** C-11; PH-1   **Ht:** 6'0" **Wt:** 200 **Born:** 10/22/1968 **Age:** 36

Year Team	Lg	G	AB	H	2B	3B	HR	(Hm	Rd)	TB	R	RBI	RC	TBB	IBB	SO	HBP	SH	SF	SB	CS	SB%	GDP	Avg	OBP	Slg
2004 Durham*	AAA	26	82	20	0	0	1	(-	-)	23	6	8	7	6	0	10	1	3	1	0	0	-	1	.244	.300	.280
2004 Albuquerque*	AAA	19	56	10	3	1	1	(-	-)	18	5	5	2	5	1	7	1	1	0	0	0	-	0	.179	.254	.321
1996 Pittsburgh	NL	48	140	41	14	1	1	(0	1)	60	18	14	21	14	1	22	1	1	0	1	0	1.00	3	.293	.361	.429
1997 Pittsburgh	NL	49	105	27	9	1	0	(0	0)	38	10	7	12	9	1	21	1	2	0	1	0	.00	1	.257	.322	.362
1998 Pittsburgh	NL	39	98	21	4	0	0	(0	0)	25	8	7	7	13	2	16	2	2	1	1	2	.33	4	.214	.316	.255
1999 Pittsburgh	NL	66	167	31	3	1	2	(1	1)	42	12	13	7	11	0	30	1	1	1	0	0	-	8	.186	.239	.251
2000 Pittsburgh	NL	46	123	36	6	1	4	(1	3)	56	11	22	23	14	0	11	5	1	0	3	0	1.00	2	.293	.387	.455
2001 Pittsburgh	NL	56	120	25	4	0	2	(0	2)	35	9	13	11	13	0	24	3	0	1	1	0	1.00	1	.208	.299	.292
2002 Pittsburgh	NL	55	100	16	3	0	2	(1	1)	25	6	11	4	6	0	25	1	2	2	0	0	-	2	.160	.211	.250
2003 Milwaukee	NL	80	241	60	12	0	2	(1	1)	78	22	21	20	31	0	44	3	0	0	0	1	.00	7	.249	.342	.324
2004 Baltimore	AL	11	25	2	0	0	0	(0	0)	2	0	0	0	0	0	7	0	0	0	0	0	-	1	.080	.080	.080
9 ML YEARS		450	1119	259	55	4	13	(4	9)	361	96	108	105	111	4	200	17	9	5	6	4	.60	29	.231	.309	.323

Antonio Osuna

Pitches: R **Bats:** R **Pos:** RP-31   **Ht:** 5'11" **Wt:** 205 **Born:** 4/12/1973 **Age:** 32

Year Team	Lg	G	GS	CG	GF	IP	BFP	H	R	ER	HR	SH	SF	HB	TBB	IBB	SO	WP	Bk	W	L	Pct	ShO	Sv-Op	Hld	ERC	ERA
2004 Lk Elsinore*	A+	7	2	0	0	7.1	26	2	2	2	0	0	0	0	2	0	12	0	0	0	0	-	0	0- -	0	0.47	2.45
1995 Los Angeles	NL	39	0	0	8	44.2	186	39	22	22	5	2	1	1	20	2	46	1	0	2	4	.333	0	0-2	11	3.76	4.43
1996 Los Angeles	NL	73	0	0	21	84.0	342	65	33	28	6	7	5	2	32	12	85	3	2	9	6	.600	0	4-9	16	2.53	3.00
1997 Los Angeles	NL	48	0	0	18	61.2	245	46	15	15	6	4	1	1	19	2	68	2	0	3	4	.429	0	0-0	10	2.43	2.19
1998 Los Angeles	NL	54	0	0	25	64.2	272	50	26	22	8	2	2	2	32	0	72	1	0	7	1	.875	0	6-11	12	3.50	3.06
1999 Los Angeles	NL	5	0	0	1	4.2	22	4	5	4	0	0	0	1	3	0	5	1	0	0	0	-	0	0-0	2	4.14	7.71
2000 Los Angeles	NL	46	0	0	16	67.1	293	57	30	28	7	4	3	2	35	2	70	1	2	3	6	.333	0	0-3	4	3.74	3.74
2001 Chicago	AL	4	0	0	1	4.1	23	8	10	10	3	0	1	1	2	1	6	0	0	0	0	-	0	0-1	0	16.71	20.77
2002 Chicago	AL	59	0	0	28	67.2	296	64	32	29	1	5	3	4	28	4	66	0	1	8	2	.800	0	11-14	9	3.31	3.86
2003 New York	AL	48	0	0	16	50.2	232	58	22	21	3	2	2	2	20	3	47	3	0	2	5	.286	0	0-1	9	4.51	3.73
2004 San Diego	NL	31	0	0	6	36.2	151	32	11	10	3	0	1	1	11	0	36	0	0	2	1	.667	0	0-2	2	3.00	2.45
10 ML YEARS		407	0	0	139	486.1	2062	423	206	189	42	26	19	17	202	26	501	12	5	36	29	.554	0	21-43	75	3.38	3.50

Roy Oswalt

Pitches: R **Bats:** R **Pos:** SP-35; RP-1   **Ht:** 6'0" **Wt:** 175 **Born:** 8/29/1977 **Age:** 27

Year Team	Lg	G	GS	CG	GF	IP	BFP	H	R	ER	HR	SH	SF	HB	TBB	IBB	SO	WP	Bk	W	L	Pct	ShO	Sv-Op	Hld	ERC	ERA
2001 Houston	NL	28	20	3	4	141.2	575	126	48	43	13	4	4	6	24	2	144	0	0	14	3	.824	1	0-0	0	2.68	2.73
2002 Houston	NL	35	34	0	0	233.0	956	215	86	78	17	12	7	5	62	4	208	3	0	19	9	.679	0	0-0	0	3.05	3.01
2003 Houston	NL	21	21	0	0	127.1	514	116	48	42	15	7	1	5	29	0	108	1	0	10	5	.667	0	0-0	0	3.26	2.97
2004 Houston	NL	36	35	2	0	237.0	983	233	100	92	17	11	4	11	62	5	206	5	1	20	10	.667	2	0-0	0	3.46	3.49
4 ML YEARS		120	110	5	4	739.0	3028	690	282	255	62	34	16	27	177	11	666	9	1	63	27	.700	3	0-0	0	3.14	3.11

Akinori Otsuka

Pitches: R **Bats:** R **Pos:** RP-73   **Ht:** 6'0" **Wt:** 200 **Born:** 1/13/1972 **Age:** 33

Year Team	Lg	G	GS	CG	GF	IP	BFP	H	R	ER	HR	SH	SF	HB	TBB	IBB	SO	WP	Bk	W	L	Pct	ShO	Sv-Op	Hld	ERC	ERA
2004 San Diego	NL	73	0	0	18	77.1	312	56	16	15	6	4	0	0	26	6	87	0	0	7	2	.778	0	2-7	34	2.14	1.75

Lyle Overbay

Bats: L **Throws:** L **Pos:** 1B-158; PH-4   **Ht:** 6'2" **Wt:** 215 **Born:** 1/28/1977 **Age:** 28

					BATTING																BASERUNNING				AVERAGES		
Year Team	Lg	G	AB	H	2B	3B	HR	(Hm	Rd)	TB	R	RBI	RC	TBB	IBB	SO	HBP	SH	SF	SB	CS	SB%	GDP	Avg	OBP	Slg
2001 Arizona	NL	2	2	1	0	0	0	(0	0)	1	0	0	0	0	0	1	0	0	0	0	0	-	0	.500	.500	.500
2002 Arizona	NL	10	10	1	0	0	0	(0	0)	1	0	1	0	0	0	5	0	0	0	0	0	-	0	.100	.100	.100
2003 Arizona	NL	86	254	70	20	0	4	(2	2)	102	23	28	34	35	7	67	2	0	2	1	0	1.00	8	.276	.365	.402
2004 Milwaukee	NL	159	579	174	53	1	16	(6	10)	277	83	87	94	81	9	128	2	0	6	2	1	.67	11	.301	.385	.478
4 ML YEARS		257	845	246	73	1	20	(8	12)	381	106	116	128	116	16	201	4	0	8	3	1	.75	19	.291	.376	.451

Juan Padilla

Pitches: R **Bats:** R **Pos:** RP-18   **Ht:** 6'0" **Wt:** 200 **Born:** 2/17/1977 **Age:** 28

		HOW MUCH HE PITCHED						WHAT HE GAVE UP												THE RESULTS						
Year Team	Lg	G	GS	CG	GF	IP	BFP	H	R	ER	HR	SH	SF	HB	TBB	IBB	SO	WP	Bk	W	L	Pct	ShO	Sv-Op	Hld	ERC	ERA
1998 Twins	R	17	0	0	14	25.2	100	19	4	4	1	1	0	2	1	0	27	1	0	1	1	.500	0	10- -	-	1.47	1.40
1999 Quad City	A	14	0	0	4	15.0	69	18	8	4	0	0	1	0	6	2	16	4	1	0	2	.000	0	0- -	-	4.10	2.40
1999 New Britain	AA	11	0	0	3	19.0	92	31	15	14	3	2	1	1	7	0	12	2	0	1	1	.500	0	2- -	-	8.76	6.63
1999 Fort Myers	A+	22	0	0	11	33.2	146	32	14	13	1	3	2	1	17	2	28	3	0	2	2	.500	0	0- -	-	3.76	3.48
2000 Quad City	A	32	0	0	27	33.0	133	24	7	7	0	3	0	1	9	2	40	1	0	2	2	.500	0	16- -	-	1.64	1.91
2000 New Britain	AA	23	0	0	6	33.2	144	35	15	14	1	1	0	2	11	0	24	0	0	1	0	1.000	0	0- -	-	3.79	3.74
2001 Fort Myers	A+	56	0	0	49	69.1	306	72	35	23	2	1	1	3	25	6	77	1	0	6	4	.600	0	23- -	-	3.58	2.99
2002 New Britain	AA	54	0	0	48	65.1	283	69	30	24	2	1	2	4	18	6	52	2	0	3	5	.375	0	29- -	-	3.47	3.31
2003 Rochester	AAA	57	0	0	29	91.0	386	94	40	34	7	8	3	4	17	3	68	5	0	7	4	.636	0	6- -	-	3.33	3.36
2004 Trenton	AA	3	0	0	1	4.0	19	4	4	4	1	0	0	1	3	0	4	0	0	0	0	-	0	0- -	-	8.11	9.00
2004 Columbus	AAA	45	0	0	11	58.0	228	49	20	13	1	0	0	2	6	2	52	4	1	2	1	.667	0	3- -	-	1.79	2.02
2004 NYY-Cin		18	0	0	3	25.2	124	39	22	22	7	1	0	1	12	0	17	0	0	1	0	1.000	0	0-0	0	9.43	7.71
2004 New York	AL	6	0	0	1	11.1	50	16	5	5	1	0	0	0	4	0	5	0	0	0	0	-	0	0-0	0	6.60	3.97
2004 Cincinnati	NL	12	0	0	2	14.1	74	23	17	17	6	1	0	1	8	0	12	0	0	1	0	1.000	0	0-0	0	11.76	10.67

Vicente Padilla

Pitches: R **Bats:** B **Pos:** SP-20   **Ht:** 6'2" **Wt:** 200 **Born:** 9/27/1977 **Age:** 27

		HOW MUCH HE PITCHED						WHAT HE GAVE UP												THE RESULTS						
Year Team	Lg	G	GS	CG	GF	IP	BFP	H	R	ER	HR	SH	SF	HB	TBB	IBB	SO	WP	Bk	W	L	Pct	ShO	Sv-Op	Hld	ERC	ERA
2004 Clearwater*	A+	1	1	0	0	2.0	10	3	2	2	0	0	0	0	1	0	1	0	0	0	1	.000	0	0- -	-	6.48	9.00
2004 Scrtn/WlksBr*	AAA	2	2	0	0	4.2	25	6	7	7	1	2	0	0	5	0	6	0	0	0	0	-	0	0- -	-	9.58	13.50
1999 Arizona	NL	5	0	0	2	2.2	19	7	5	5	1	1	0	0	3	0	0	0	0	0	1	.000	0	0-1	1	20.65	16.88
2000 Ari-Phi	NL	55	0	0	16	65.1	291	72	33	27	3	5	3	1	28	7	51	1	0	4	7	.364	0	2-7	15	4.22	3.72
2001 Philadelphia	NL	23	0	0	5	34.0	144	36	18	16	1	0	0	0	12	0	29	1	0	3	1	.750	0	0-3	1	3.80	4.24
2002 Philadelphia	NL	32	32	1	0	206.0	861	198	83	75	16	10	3	15	53	5	128	6	2	14	11	.560	1	0-0	0	3.43	3.28
2003 Philadelphia	NL	32	32	1	0	208.2	876	196	94	84	22	11	7	16	62	4	133	3	2	14	12	.538	1	0-0	0	3.68	3.62
2004 Philadelphia	NL	20	20	0	0	115.1	503	119	63	58	16	7	5	10	36	6	82	2	0	7	7	.500	0	0-0	0	4.42	4.53
2000 Arizona	NL	27	0	0	12	35.0	143	32	10	9	0	0	1	0	10	2	30	0	0	2	1	.667	0	0-1	7	2.48	2.31
2000 Philadelphia	NL	28	0	0	4	30.1	148	40	23	18	3	5	2	1	18	5	21	1	0	2	6	.250	0	2-6	8	6.52	5.34
6 ML YEARS		167	84	2	23	632.0	2694	628	296	265	59	34	18	42	194	22	423	13	4	42	39	.519	2	2-11	17	3.85	3.77

Orlando Palmeiro

Bats: L **Throws:** L **Pos:** PH-76; LF-20; RF-13; CF-4; PR-1   **Ht:** 5'10" **Wt:** 182 **Born:** 1/19/1969 **Age:** 36

					BATTING																BASERUNNING				AVERAGES		
Year Team	Lg	G	AB	H	2B	3B	HR	(Hm	Rd)	TB	R	RBI	RC	TBB	IBB	SO	HBP	SH	SF	SB	CS	SB%	GDP	Avg	OBP	Slg
1995 California	AL	15	20	7	0	0	0	(0	0)	7	3	1	3	1	0	1	0	0	0	0	0	-	0	.350	.381	.350
1996 California	AL	50	87	25	6	1	0	(0	0)	33	6	6	12	8	1	13	2	1	0	0	1	.00	1	.287	.361	.379
1997 Anaheim	AL	74	134	29	2	2	0	(0	0)	35	19	8	10	17	1	11	1	3	1	2	2	.50	4	.216	.307	.261
1998 Anaheim	AL	75	165	53	7	2	0	(0	0)	64	28	21	26	20	1	11	0	7	0	5	4	.56	2	.321	.395	.388
1999 Anaheim	AL	109	317	88	12	1	1	(0	1)	105	46	23	41	39	1	30	6	6	3	5	5	.50	4	.278	.364	.331
2000 Anaheim	AL	108	243	73	20	2	0	(0	0)	97	38	25	42	38	0	20	2	10	3	4	1	.80	5	.300	.395	.399
2001 Anaheim	AL	104	230	56	10	1	2	(0	2)	74	29	23	25	25	2	24	3	7	5	6	6	.50	3	.243	.319	.322
2002 Anaheim	AL	110	263	79	12	1	0	(0	0)	93	35	31	39	30	1	22	0	4	3	7	2	.78	7	.300	.368	.354
2003 St Louis	NL	141	317	86	13	1	3	(1	2)	110	37	33	37	32	3	31	2	7	6	3	3	.50	1	.271	.336	.347
2004 Houston	NL	102	133	32	5	0	3	(1	2)	46	19	12	18	18	1	19	3	2	0	2	1	.67	1	.241	.344	.346
10 ML YEARS		888	1909	528	87	11	9	(2	7)	664	260	183	253	228	11	182	19	47	21	34	25	.58	27	.277	.356	.348

Rafael Palmeiro

Bats: L **Throws:** L **Pos:** 1B-130; DH-20; PH-7   **Ht:** 6'0" **Wt:** 190 **Born:** 9/24/1964 **Age:** 40

					BATTING																BASERUNNING				AVERAGES		
Year Team	Lg	G	AB	H	2B	3B	HR	(Hm	Rd)	TB	R	RBI	RC	TBB	IBB	SO	HBP	SH	SF	SB	CS	SB%	GDP	Avg	OBP	Slg
1986 Chicago	NL	22	73	18	4	0	3	(1	2)	31	9	12	8	4	0	6	1	0	0	1	1	.50	4	.247	.295	.425
1987 Chicago	NL	84	221	61	15	1	14	(5	9)	120	32	30	39	20	1	26	1	0	2	2	2	.50	4	.276	.336	.543
1988 Chicago	NL	152	580	178	41	5	8	(0	8)	253	75	53	88	38	6	34	3	2	6	12	2	.86	11	.307	.349	.436
1989 Texas	AL	156	559	154	23	4	8	(4	4)	209	76	64	73	63	3	48	6	2	2	4	3	.57	18	.275	.354	.374
1990 Texas	AL	154	598	191	35	6	14	(9	5)	280	72	89	93	40	6	59	3	2	8	3	3	.50	24	.319	.361	.468
1991 Texas	AL	159	631	203	49	3	26	(12	14)	336	115	88	123	68	10	72	6	2	7	4	3	.57	17	.322	.389	.532
1992 Texas	AL	159	608	163	27	4	22	(8	14)	264	84	85	94	72	8	83	10	5	6	2	3	.40	10	.268	.352	.434
1993 Texas	AL	160	597	176	40	2	37	(22	15)	331	124	105	123	73	22	85	7	1	9	22	3	.88	8	.295	.371	.554
1994 Baltimore	AL	111	436	139	32	0	23	(11	12)	240	82	76	90	54	1	63	2	0	6	7	3	.70	11	.319	.392	.550
1995 Baltimore	AL	143	554	172	30	1	39	(21	18)	323	89	104	116	62	5	65	3	0	5	3	1	.75	12	.310	.380	.583
1996 Baltimore	AL	162	626	181	40	2	39	(21	18)	342	110	142	130	95	12	96	3	0	8	8	0	1.00	9	.289	.381	.546
1997 Baltimore	AL	158	614	156	24	2	38	(20	18)	298	95	110	97	67	7	109	5	0	4	5	2	.71	14	.254	.329	.485
1998 Baltimore	AL	162	619	183	36	1	43	(25	18)	350	98	121	126	79	8	91	7	0	4	11	7	.61	14	.296	.379	.565
1999 Texas	AL	158	565	183	30	1	47	(28	19)	356	96	148	139	97	14	69	3	0	9	2	4	.33	13	.324	.420	.630
2000 Texas	AL	158	565	163	29	3	39	(26	13)	315	102	120	121	103	17	77	3	0	7	2	1	.67	14	.288	.397	.558
2001 Texas	AL	160	600	164	33	0	47	(23	24)	338	98	123	128	101	8	90	7	0	6	1	1	.50	8	.273	.381	.563

BATTING																		BASERUNNING				AVERAGES		
Year Team	Lg	G	AB	H	2B	3B	HR	(Hm Rd)	TB	R	RBI	RC	TBB	IBB	SO	HBP	SH	SF	SB	CS	SB%	GDP	Avg	OBP	Slg
2002 Texas	AL	155	546	149	34	0	43	(23 20)	312	99	105	104	104	16	94	6	0	7	2	0	1.00	10	.273	.391	.571
2003 Texas	AL	154	561	146	21	2	38	(21 17)	285	92	112	106	84	9	77	5	0	4	2	0	1.00	7	.260	.359	.508
2004 Baltimore	AL	154	550	142	29	0	23	(12 11)	240	68	88	81	86	15	61	6	0	9	2	1	.67	15	.258	.359	.436
19 ML YEARS		2721	10103	2922	572	38	551	(300 251)	5223	1616	1775	1879	1310	168	1305	85	15	111	95	40	.70	223	.289	.372	.517

Chan Ho Park

Pitches: R **Bats:** R **Pos:** SP-16　　　　　　　　　　　**Ht:** 6'2" **Wt:** 204 **Born:** 6/30/1973 **Age:** 32

HOW MUCH HE PITCHED						WHAT HE GAVE UP												THE RESULTS							
Year Team	Lg	G	GS	CG	GF	IP	BFP	H	R	ER	HR	SH	SF	HB	TBB	IBB	SO	WP	Bk	W	L	Pct	ShO	Sv-Op	Hld	ERC	ERA
2004 Rangers*	R	4	4	0	0	21.0	85	15	6	4	0	1	0	2	6	0	20	0	0	1	1	.500	0	0- -	-	1.90	1.71
2004 Frisco*	AA	2	2	0	0	11.1	51	16	11	11	1	1	2	0	5	0	5	0	0	0	2	.000	0	0- -	-	7.00	8.74
2004 Oklahoma*	AAA	4	4	0	0	19.1	79	21	8	8	4	0	0	1	3	0	19	0	0	2	.000	0	0- -	-	4.67	3.72
1994 Los Angeles	NL	2	0	0	1	4.0	23	5	5	5	1	0	0	1	5	0	6	0	0	0	0	-	0	0-0	0	11.69	11.25
1995 Los Angeles	NL	2	1	0	0	4.0	16	2	2	2	1	0	0	0	2	0	7	0	0	0	0	-	0	0-0	0	2.70	4.50
1996 Los Angeles	NL	48	10	0	7	108.2	477	82	48	44	7	8	1	4	71	3	119	4	3	5	5	.500	0	0-0	0	3.50	3.64
1997 Los Angeles	NL	32	29	2	1	192.0	792	149	80	72	24	9	5	8	70	1	166	4	1	14	8	.636	0	0-0	0	3.04	3.38
1998 Los Angeles	NL	34	34	2	0	220.2	946	199	101	91	16	11	10	11	97	1	191	6	2	15	9	.625	0	0-0	0	3.69	3.71
1999 Los Angeles	NL	33	33	0	0	194.1	883	208	120	113	31	10	5	14	100	4	174	11	1	13	11	.542	0	0-0	0	5.68	5.23
2000 Los Angeles	NL	34	34	3	0	226.0	963	173	92	82	21	12	5	12	124	4	217	13	0	18	10	.643	1	0-0	0	3.51	3.27
2001 Los Angeles	NL	36	35	2	0	234.0	981	183	98	91	23	16	7	20	91	1	218	3	3	15	11	.577	1	0-0	0	3.15	3.50
2002 Texas	AL	25	25	0	0	145.2	666	154	95	93	20	4	3	17	78	2	121	9	0	9	8	.529	0	0-0	0	5.75	5.75
2003 Texas	AL	7	7	0	0	29.2	146	34	26	25	5	1	3	6	25	0	16	1	1	1	3	.250	0	0-0	0	8.56	7.58
2004 Texas	AL	16	16	0	0	95.2	428	105	63	58	22	4	4	13	33	0	63	1	1	4	7	.364	0	0-0	0	5.97	5.46
11 ML YEARS		269	224	9	9	1454.2	6321	1294	730	676	171	75	43	106	696	16	1298	52	13	94	72	.566	2	0-0	4	4.17	4.18

Jose Parra

Pitches: R **Bats:** R **Pos:** RP-13　　　　　　　　　　**Ht:** 5'11" **Wt:** 175 **Born:** 11/28/1972 **Age:** 32

HOW MUCH HE PITCHED						WHAT HE GAVE UP												THE RESULTS							
Year Team	Lg	G	GS	CG	GF	IP	BFP	H	R	ER	HR	SH	SF	HB	TBB	IBB	SO	WP	Bk	W	L	Pct	ShO	Sv-Op	Hld	ERC	ERA
2004 Binghamton*	AA	1	0	0	0	1.0	3	0	0	0	0	0	0	0	0	0	2	0	0	0	0	-	0	0- -	-	0.00	0.00
2004 Norfolk*	AAA	24	0	0	22	27.2	111	19	6	5	1	0	1	0	10	1	35	0	0	2	1	.667	0	16- -	-	1.88	1.63
1995 LA-Min		20	12	0	0	72.0	339	93	67	57	13	0	4	3	28	1	36	3	1	1	5	.167	0	0-0	0	6.41	7.13
1996 Minnesota	AL	27	5	0	7	70.0	320	88	48	47	15	1	3	3	27	0	50	4	1	5	5	.500	0	0-1	0	6.63	6.04
2000 Pittsburgh	NL	6	2	0	1	11.2	57	17	9	9	3	1	0	1	7	0	9	0	0	1	0	1.000	0	0-0	0	9.86	6.94
2002 Arizona	NL	16	0	0	3	14.0	63	13	5	5	0	1	0	1	11	2	8	1	0	0	1	.000	0	0-0	4	4.57	3.21
2004 New York	NL	13	0	0	7	14.0	61	14	6	5	2	0	0	0	6	1	14	0	0	1	0	1.000	0	0-0	1	4.36	3.21
1995 Los Angeles	NL	8	0	0	0	10.1	47	10	8	5	2	0	1	1	6	1	7	0	1	0	0	-	0	0-0	0	5.56	4.35
1995 Minnesota	AL	12	12	0	0	61.2	292	83	59	52	11	0	3	2	22	0	29	3	0	1	5	.167	0	0-0	0	6.55	7.59
5 ML YEARS		82	19	0	18	181.2	840	225	135	123	33	2	7	8	79	4	117	8	2	7	12	.368	0	0-1	5	6.40	6.09

John Parrish

Pitches: L **Bats:** L **Pos:** RP-55; SP-1　　　　　　　**Ht:** 5'11" **Wt:** 181 **Born:** 11/26/1977 **Age:** 27

HOW MUCH HE PITCHED						WHAT HE GAVE UP												THE RESULTS							
Year Team	Lg	G	GS	CG	GF	IP	BFP	H	R	ER	HR	SH	SF	HB	TBB	IBB	SO	WP	Bk	W	L	Pct	ShO	Sv-Op	Hld	ERC	ERA
2000 Baltimore	AL	8	8	0	0	36.1	167	40	0	29	6	0	0	0	35	0	28	0	0	2	4	.333	0	0-0	0	7.59	7.18
2001 Baltimore	AL	16	1	0	0	22.0	107	22	0	15	5	0	0	0	17	0	20	0	0	1	2	.333	0	0-0	0	6.34	6.14
2003 Baltimore	AL	14	0	0	2	23.2	93	17	7	5	2	0	1	1	8	2	15	2	0	0	1	.000	0	0-2	1	2.39	1.90
2004 Baltimore	AL	56	1	0	17	78.0	353	68	39	30	4	3	6	3	55	6	71	6	0	6	3	.667	0	1-1	2	4.17	3.46
4 ML YEARS		94	10	0	19	160.0	733	147	46	79	17	3	7	4	115	8	134	8	0	9	10	.474	0	1-3	3	4.91	4.44

Val Pascucci

Bats: R **Throws:** R **Pos:** RF-13; PH-13; 1B-5; LF-4　　　**Ht:** 6'6" **Wt:** 235 **Born:** 11/17/1978 **Age:** 26

BATTING																		BASERUNNING				AVERAGES		
Year Team	Lg	G	AB	H	2B	3B	HR	(Hm Rd)	TB	R	RBI	RC	TBB	IBB	SO	HBP	SH	SF	SB	CS	SB%	GDP	Avg	OBP	Slg
1999 Vermont	A-	72	259	91	26	1	7	(- -)	140	62	48	69	53	3	46	14	0	2	17	2	.89	5	.351	.482	.541
2000 Cape Fear	A	20	69	22	4	0	3	(- -)	35	17	10	16	16	0	15	0	0	1	5	0	1.00	2	.319	.442	.507
2000 Jupiter	A+	113	405	115	30	2	14	(- -)	191	70	66	76	66	0	98	11	0	5	14	6	.70	9	.284	.394	.472
2001 Harrisburg	AA	138	476	116	17	1	21	(- -)	198	79	67	65	54	1	114	11	1	6	8	8	.50	8	.244	.331	.416
2002 Harrisburg	AA	137	459	116	14	1	27	(- -)	213	73	82	86	93	3	115	13	0	7	2	0	1.00	13	.253	.388	.464
2003 Edmonton	AAA	138	459	129	29	1	15	(- -)	205	80	85	90	101	9	132	9	1	2	3	2	.60	11	.281	.419	.447
2004 Edmonton	AAA	109	392	117	32	1	25	(- -)	226	83	92	90	78	4	95	8	0	2	9	2	.82	11	.298	.423	.577
2004 Montreal	NL	32	62	11	1	0	2	(0 2)	18	6	6	5	10	1	22	1	0	1	1	0	1.00	3	.177	.297	.290

Corey Patterson

Bats: L **Throws:** R **Pos:** CF-157; PH-2　　　　　　　**Ht:** 5'9" **Wt:** 175 **Born:** 8/13/1979 **Age:** 25

BATTING																		BASERUNNING				AVERAGES		
Year Team	Lg	G	AB	H	2B	3B	HR	(Hm Rd)	TB	R	RBI	RC	TBB	IBB	SO	HBP	SH	SF	SB	CS	SB%	GDP	Avg	OBP	Slg
2000 Chicago	NL	11	42	7	1	0	2	(1 1)	14	9	2	3	3	0	14	1	1	0	1	1	.50	0	.167	.239	.333
2001 Chicago	NL	59	131	29	3	0	4	(1 3)	44	26	14	13	6	0	33	3	2	3	4	0	1.00	1	.221	.266	.336
2002 Chicago	NL	153	592	150	30	5	14	(7 7)	232	71	54	61	19	1	142	8	4	5	18	3	.86	8	.253	.284	.392
2003 Chicago	NL	83	329	98	17	7	13	(7 6)	168	49	55	55	15	2	77	1	0	2	16	5	.76	5	.298	.329	.511
2004 Chicago	NL	157	631	168	33	6	24	(14 10)	285	91	72	87	45	7	168	5	5	1	32	9	.78	7	.266	.320	.452
5 ML YEARS		463	1725	452	84	18	57	(30 27)	743	246	197	219	88	10	434	18	12	11	71	18	.80	21	.262	.303	.431

Danny Patterson

Pitches: R **Bats:** R **Pos:** RP-37   **Ht:** 6'0" **Wt:** 185 **Born:** 2/17/1971 **Age:** 34

		HOW MUCH HE PITCHED						WHAT HE GAVE UP											THE RESULTS						
Year Team	Lg	G	GS	CG	GF	IP	BFP	H	R	ER	HR	SH	SF	HB	TBB	IBB	SO	WP	Bk	W	L	Pct	ShO	Sv-Op	Hld	ERC	ERA
2004 Toledo*	AAA	3	0	0	1	4.1	18	3	2	2	0	0	0	0	2	1	3	1	1	1	0	1.000	0	0- -	-	1.70	4.15
2004 Memphis*	AAA	9	0	0	3	6.2	38	8	5	5	0	0	0	3	7	0	7	0	0	0	0	-	0	0- -	-	8.74	6.75
1996 Texas	AL	7	0	0	5	8.2	38	10	4	0	0	0	0	0	3	1	5	0	0	0	0	-	0	0-0	-	3.81	0.00
1997 Texas	AL	54	0	0	17	71.0	296	70	29	27	3	4	3	0	23	4	69	7	1	10	6	.625	0	1-8	9	3.27	3.42
1998 Texas	AL	56	0	0	21	60.2	257	64	31	30	11	1	1	2	19	2	33	3	0	2	5	.286	0	2-2	19	4.79	4.45
1999 Texas	AL	53	0	0	18	60.1	275	77	38	38	5	0	2	1	19	3	43	2	0	2	0	1.000	0	0-1	4	5.11	5.67
2000 Detroit	AL	58	0	0	12	56.2	244	69	26	25	4	3	2	2	14	2	29	1	0	5	1	.833	0	0-2	12	4.68	3.97
2001 Detroit	AL	60	0	0	16	64.2	258	64	24	22	4	5	3	4	12	5	27	2	0	4	5	.556	0	1-5	16	3.21	3.06
2002 Detroit	AL	6	0	0	1	3.0	17	5	5	5	0	0	0	1	2	0	1	0	0	0	2	.000	0	0-1	0	9.70	15.00
2003 Detroit	AL	19	0	0	9	17.2	73	15	8	8	1	2	0	1	4	0	19	0	0	0	0	-	0	3-3	1	2.51	4.08
2004 Detroit	AL	37	0	0	16	41.2	179	44	24	22	7	2	0	5	16	2	24	3	0	0	4	.000	0	2-4	3	5.47	4.75
9 ML YEARS		350	0	0	115	384.1	1637	418	189	177	35	17	11	16	112	19	250	18	1	24	22	.522	0	9-26	64	4.23	4.14

John Patterson

Pitches: R **Bats:** R **Pos:** SP-19   **Ht:** 6'5" **Wt:** 183 **Born:** 1/30/1978 **Age:** 27

		HOW MUCH HE PITCHED						WHAT HE GAVE UP											THE RESULTS						
Year Team	Lg	G	GS	CG	GF	IP	BFP	H	R	ER	HR	SH	SF	HB	TBB	IBB	SO	WP	Bk	W	L	Pct	ShO	Sv-Op	Hld	ERC	ERA
2004 Brevard Cnty*	A+	2	2	0	0	7.2	27	3	0	0	0	0	0	0	1	0	7	0	0	0	0	-	0	0- -	-	0.51	0.00
2004 Harrisburg*	AA	1	1	0	0	4.0	14	0	0	0	0	0	0	0	2	0	9	0	0	0	0	-	0	0- -	-	0.27	0.00
2002 Arizona	NL	7	5	0	1	30.2	123	27	11	11	7	0	0	1	7	0	31	2	0	2	0	1.000	0	0-0	0	3.76	3.23
2003 Arizona	NL	16	8	0	3	55.0	252	61	39	37	7	1	2	2	30	5	43	4	0	1	4	.200	0	1-1	0	5.50	6.05
2004 Montreal	NL	19	19	0	0	98.1	445	100	58	55	18	4	2	8	46	4	99	0	0	4	7	.364	0	0-0	0	5.26	5.03
3 ML YEARS		42	32	0	4	184.0	820	188	108	103	32	5	4	11	83	9	173	6	0	7	11	.389	0	1-1	0	5.09	5.04

Josh Paul

Bats: R **Throws:** R **Pos:** C-37; PR-8; PH-7; LF-4; DH-2   **Ht:** 6'1" **Wt:** 200 **Born:** 5/19/1975 **Age:** 30

		BATTING																	BASERUNNING				AVERAGES		
Year Team	Lg	G	AB	H	2B	3B	HR	(Hm	Rd)	TB	R	RBI	RC	TBB	IBB	SO	HBP	SH	SF	SB	CS	SB%	GDP	Avg	OBP	Slg
1999 Chicago	AL	6	18	4	1	0	0	(0	0)	5	2	1	1	0	0	4	0	0	0	0	0	-	0	.222	.222	.278
2000 Chicago	AL	36	71	20	3	2	1	(1	0)	30	15	8	9	5	0	17	1	2	0	1	0	1.00	3	.282	.338	.423
2001 Chicago	AL	57	139	37	11	0	3	(0	3)	57	20	18	19	13	0	25	0	1	1	6	2	.75	3	.266	.327	.410
2002 Chicago	AL	33	104	25	4	0	0	(0	0)	29	11	11	12	9	0	22	1	2	2	2	0	1.00	1	.240	.302	.279
2003 CWS-ChC		16	23	6	0	0	0	(0	0)	6	6	4	5	3	0	6	0	1	0	0	0	-	0	.261	.346	.261
2004 Anaheim	AL	46	70	17	3	0	2	(0	2)	26	11	10	9	7	0	17	0	0	3	2	1	.67	2	.243	.308	.371
2003 Chicago	AL	13	17	6	0	0	0	(0	0)	6	6	4	5	3	0	3	0	0	0	0	0	-	0	.353	.450	.353
2003 Chicago	NL	3	6	0	0	0	0	(0	0)	0	0	0	0	0	0	3	0	1	0	0	0	-	0	.000	.000	.000
6 ML YEARS		194	425	109	22	2	6	(1	5)	153	65	52	55	37	0	91	2	9	4	11	3	.79	9	.256	.316	.360

Carl Pavano

Pitches: R **Bats:** R **Pos:** SP-31   **Ht:** 6'5" **Wt:** 230 **Born:** 1/8/1976 **Age:** 29

		HOW MUCH HE PITCHED						WHAT HE GAVE UP											THE RESULTS						
Year Team	Lg	G	GS	CG	GF	IP	BFP	H	R	ER	HR	SH	SF	HB	TBB	IBB	SO	WP	Bk	W	L	Pct	ShO	Sv-Op	Hld	ERC	ERA
1998 Montreal	NL	24	23	0	0	134.2	580	130	70	63	18	5	6	8	43	1	83	1	0	6	9	.400	0	0-0	0	3.97	4.21
1999 Montreal	NL	19	18	1	0	104.0	457	117	66	65	8	5	2	4	35	1	70	1	3	6	8	.429	1	0-0	0	4.51	5.63
2000 Montreal	NL	15	15	0	0	97.0	408	89	40	33	8	4	3	8	34	1	64	1	1	8	4	.667	0	0-0	0	3.67	3.06
2001 Montreal	NL	8	8	0	0	42.2	199	59	33	30	7	2	1	2	16	1	36	0	1	1	6	.143	0	0-0	0	6.99	6.33
2002 Mon-Fla	NL	37	22	0	2	136.0	618	174	88	78	19	4	4	10	45	8	92	3	2	6	10	.375	0	0-0	3	5.99	5.16
2003 Florida	NL	33	32	2	1	201.0	846	204	99	96	19	9	10	7	49	10	133	3	2	12	13	.480	0	0-0	0	3.57	4.30
2004 Florida	NL	31	31	2	0	222.1	909	212	80	74	16	7	4	11	49	13	139	2	3	18	8	.692	2	0-0	0	3.10	3.00
2002 Montreal	NL	15	14	0	0	74.1	349	98	55	52	14	2	2	7	31	5	51	2	1	3	8	.273	0	0-0	0	7.09	6.30
2002 Florida	NL	22	8	0	2	61.2	269	76	33	26	5	2	2	3	14	3	41	1	1	3	2	.600	0	0-0	3	4.74	3.79
7 ML YEARS		167	149	5	3	937.2	4017	985	476	439	95	36	30	50	271	35	617	11	12	57	58	.496	3	0-0	3	4.10	4.21

Jay Payton

Bats: R **Throws:** R **Pos:** CF-128; PH-11; LF-9; DH-1   **Ht:** 5'10" **Wt:** 185 **Born:** 11/22/1972 **Age:** 32

		BATTING																	BASERUNNING				AVERAGES		
Year Team	Lg	G	AB	H	2B	3B	HR	(Hm	Rd)	TB	R	RBI	RC	TBB	IBB	SO	HBP	SH	SF	SB	CS	SB%	GDP	Avg	OBP	Slg
1998 New York	NL	15	22	7	1	0	0	(0	0)	8	2	0	3	1	0	4	0	0	0	0	0	-	0	.318	.348	.364
1999 New York	NL	13	8	2	1	0	0	(0	0)	3	1	1	0	0	0	2	1	0	0	1	2	.33	0	.250	.333	.375
2000 New York	NL	149	488	142	23	1	17	(9	8)	218	63	62	68	30	0	60	3	0	8	5	11	.31	9	.291	.331	.447
2001 New York	NL	104	361	92	16	1	8	(6	2)	134	44	34	37	18	1	52	5	0	2	4	3	.57	11	.255	.298	.371
2002 NYM-Col	NL	134	445	135	20	7	16	(9	7)	217	69	59	71	29	0	54	4	2	1	7	4	.64	11	.303	.351	.488
2003 Colorado	NL	157	600	181	32	5	28	(13	15)	307	93	89	95	43	3	77	7	5	3	6	4	.60	27	.302	.354	.512
2004 San Diego	NL	143	458	119	17	4	8	(0	8)	168	57	55	61	43	2	56	4	2	4	2	0	1.00	12	.260	.326	.367
2002 New York	NL	87	275	78	6	3	8	(4	4)	114	33	31	38	21	0	34	1	2	1	4	1	.80	8	.284	.336	.415
2002 Colorado	NL	47	170	57	14	4	8	(5	3)	103	36	28	33	8	0	20	3	0	0	3	3	.50	3	.335	.376	.606
7 ML YEARS		715	2382	678	110	18	77	(37	40)	1055	329	300	335	164	6	305	24	9	18	25	24	.51	70	.285	.335	.443

Josh Pearce

Pitches: R **Bats:** R **Pos:** RP-3   **Ht:** 6'3" **Wt:** 215 **Born:** 8/20/1977 **Age:** 27

		HOW MUCH HE PITCHED						WHAT HE GAVE UP											THE RESULTS						
Year Team	Lg	G	GS	CG	GF	IP	BFP	H	R	ER	HR	SH	SF	HB	TBB	IBB	SO	WP	Bk	W	L	Pct	ShO	Sv-Op	Hld	ERC	ERA
2004 Memphis*	AAA	26	0	0	13	30.1	132	34	12	12	1	2	0	2	6	1	31	1	0	3	2	.600	0	1- -	-	3.63	3.56
2002 St Louis	NL	3	3	0	0	13.0	66	20	13	11	1	3	1	1	8	0	1	0	0	0	0	-	0	0-0	-	8.51	7.62

					HOW MUCH HE PITCHED			WHAT HE GAVE UP													THE RESULTS						
Year Team	Lg	G	GS	CG	GF	IP	BFP	H	R	ER	HR	SH	SF	HB	TBB	IBB	SO	WP	Bk	W	L	Pct	ShO	Sv-Op	Hld	ERC	ERA
2003 St Louis	NL	7	0	0	2	9.0	39	11	3	3	0	0	0	1	2	0	4	1	0	0	0	-	0	0-0	1	4.45	3.00
2004 St Louis	NL	3	0	0	1	2.1	9	3	1	1	0	1	0	0	0	0	0	0	0	0	0	-	0	0-0	0	3.75	3.86
3 ML YEARS		13	3	0	3	24.1	114	34	17	15	1	4	1	2	10	0	5	1	0	0	0	-	0	0-0	1	6.48	5.55

Jake Peavy

Pitches: R **Bats:** R **Pos:** SP-27

Ht: 6'1" **Wt:** 180 **Born:** 5/31/1981 **Age:** 24

					HOW MUCH HE PITCHED			WHAT HE GAVE UP													THE RESULTS						
Year Team	Lg	G	GS	CG	GF	IP	BFP	H	R	ER	HR	SH	SF	HB	TBB	IBB	SO	WP	Bk	W	L	Pct	ShO	Sv-Op	Hld	ERC	ERA
2004 Mobile*	AA	1	1	0	0	4.2	25	4	3	3	1	0	0	0	2	0	4	0	0	0	0	-	0	0- -	-	7.34	5.79
2002 San Diego	NL	17	17	0	0	97.2	430	106	54	49	11	5	2	3	33	4	90	4	1	6	7	.462	0	0-0	0	4.41	4.52
2003 San Diego	NL	32	32	0	0	194.2	827	173	94	89	33	7	5	6	82	3	156	2	0	12	11	.522	0	0-0	0	4.13	4.11
2004 San Diego	NL	27	27	0	0	166.1	694	146	49	42	13	5	6	11	53	4	173	1	1	15	6	.714	0	0-0	0	3.18	2.27
3 ML YEARS		76	76	0	0	458.2	1951	425	197	180	57	17	13	20	168	11	419	7	2	33	24	.579	0	0-0	0	3.84	3.53

Kit Pellow

Bats: R **Throws:** R **Pos:** RF-27; PH-20; LF-11; 1B-5; C-4; 3B-4; PR-1

Ht: 6'1" **Wt:** 200 **Born:** 8/28/1973 **Age:** 31

							BATTING												BASERUNNING				AVERAGES		
Year Team	Lg	G	AB	H	2B	3B	HR	(Hm	Rd)	TB	R	RBI	RC	TBB	IBB	SO	HBP	SH	SF	SB	CS	SB%	GDP	Avg	OBP	Slg
2004 Co Springs*	AAA	13	42	15	4	0	3	(-	-)	28	10	14	10	4	1	7	1	0	1	0	0	-	0	.357	.417	.667
2002 Kansas City	AL	29	63	15	1	0	1	(0	1)	19	6	5	7	9	0	21	1	0	0	1	1	.50	2	.238	.342	.302
2003 Colorado	NL	11	18	8	3	1	1	(0	1)	16	6	4	5	0	0	4	2	0	1	0	0	-	0	.444	.476	.889
2004 Colorado	NL	59	121	29	5	1	2	(1	1)	42	15	10	11	8	1	43	4	0	0	1	0	1.00	3	.240	.308	.347
3 ML YEARS		99	202	52	9	2	4	(1	3)	77	27	19	23	17	1	68	7	0	1	2	1	.67	5	.257	.335	.381

Carlos Pena

Bats: L **Throws:** L **Pos:** 1B-135; PH-6; DH-5

Ht: 6'2" **Wt:** 210 **Born:** 5/17/1978 **Age:** 27

							BATTING												BASERUNNING				AVERAGES		
Year Team	Lg	G	AB	H	2B	3B	HR	(Hm	Rd)	TB	R	RBI	RC	TBB	IBB	SO	HBP	SH	SF	SB	CS	SB%	GDP	Avg	OBP	Slg
2001 Texas	AL	22	62	16	4	1	3	(2	1)	31	6	12	11	10	0	17	0	0	0	0	0	-	1	.258	.361	.500
2002 Oak-Det	AL	115	396	96	19	1	19	(10	9)	174	43	52	56	41	0	111	3	0	0	2	2	.50	7	.242	.316	.448
2003 Detroit	AL	131	452	112	21	6	18	(8	10)	199	51	50	51	53	1	123	6	1	4	4	5	.44	6	.248	.332	.440
2004 Detroit	AL	142	481	116	22	4	27	(10	17)	227	89	82	73	70	2	146	3	2	5	7	1	.88	11	.241	.338	.472
2002 Oakland	AL	40	124	27	4	0	7	(5	2)	52	12	16	17	15	0	38	1	0	1	0	0	-	2	.218	.305	.419
2002 Detroit	AL	75	273	69	13	4	12	(5	7)	126	31	36	39	26	0	73	2	0	1	2	2	.50	5	.253	.321	.462
4 ML YEARS		410	1392	340	64	15	67	(30	37)	635	189	196	201	174	3	397	12	3	11	13	8	.62	25	.244	.331	.456

Wily Mo Pena

Bats: R **Throws:** R **Pos:** RF-51; CF-46; PH-21; PR-2; LF-1

Ht: 6'3" **Wt:** 215 **Born:** 1/23/1982 **Age:** 23

							BATTING												BASERUNNING				AVERAGES		
Year Team	Lg	G	AB	H	2B	3B	HR	(Hm	Rd)	TB	R	RBI	RC	TBB	IBB	SO	HBP	SH	SF	SB	CS	SB%	GDP	Avg	OBP	Slg
2002 Cincinnati	NL	13	18	4	0	0	1	(1	0)	7	1	1	1	0	0	11	0	0	0	0	0	-	0	.222	.222	.389
2003 Cincinnati	NL	80	165	36	6	1	5	(1	4)	59	20	16	14	12	2	53	3	1	0	3	2	.60	2	.218	.283	.358
2004 Cincinnati	NL	110	336	87	10	1	26	(13	13)	177	45	66	54	22	1	108	6	0	0	5	2	.71	7	.259	.316	.527
3 ML YEARS		203	519	127	16	2	32	(15	17)	243	66	83	69	34	3	172	9	1	0	8	4	.67	9	.245	.302	.468

Brad Penny

Pitches: R **Bats:** R **Pos:** SP-24

Ht: 6'4" **Wt:** 247 **Born:** 5/24/1978 **Age:** 27

					HOW MUCH HE PITCHED			WHAT HE GAVE UP													THE RESULTS						
Year Team	Lg	G	GS	CG	GF	IP	BFP	H	R	ER	HR	SH	SF	HB	TBB	IBB	SO	WP	Bk	W	L	Pct	ShO	Sv-Op	Hld	ERC	ERA
2000 Florida	NL	23	22	0	0	119.2	529	120	70	64	13	6	2	5	60	4	80	4	1	8	7	.533	0	0-0	0	4.70	4.81
2001 Florida	NL	31	31	1	0	205.0	833	183	92	84	15	8	2	7	54	3	154	2	0	10	10	.500	1	0-0	0	2.96	3.69
2002 Florida	NL	24	24	1	0	129.1	574	148	76	67	18	6	4	1	50	7	93	4	0	8	7	.533	1	0-0	0	5.08	4.66
2003 Florida	NL	32	32	0	0	196.1	833	195	96	90	21	7	5	3	56	6	138	3	4	14	10	.583	0	0-0	0	3.73	4.13
2004 Fla-LA	NL	24	24	0	0	143.0	590	130	55	50	12	3	3	3	45	6	111	5	0	9	10	.474	0	0-0	0	3.20	3.15
2004 Florida	NL	21	21	0	0	131.1	545	124	50	46	10	3	3	3	39	6	105	5	0	8	8	.500	0	0-0	0	3.26	3.15
2004 Los Angeles	NL	3	3	0	0	11.2	45	6	5	4	2	0	0	0	6	0	6	0	0	1	2	.333	0	0-0	0	2.51	3.09
5 ML YEARS		134	133	2	0	793.1	3337	776	389	355	79	30	16	19	265	26	576	18	5	49	44	.527	2	0-0	0	3.78	4.03

Jhonny Peralta

Bats: R **Throws:** R **Pos:** SS-7; 3B-2

Ht: 6'1" **Wt:** 180 **Born:** 5/28/1982 **Age:** 23

							BATTING												BASERUNNING				AVERAGES		
Year Team	Lg	G	AB	H	2B	3B	HR	(Hm	Rd)	TB	R	RBI	RC	TBB	IBB	SO	HBP	SH	SF	SB	CS	SB%	GDP	Avg	OBP	Slg
2000 Columbus	A	106	349	84	13	1	3	(-	-)	108	52	34	39	59	0	102	2	1	2	7	6	.54	13	.241	.352	.309
2001 Kinston	A+	125	441	106	24	2	7	(-	-)	155	57	47	49	58	0	148	1	2	3	4	8	.33	9	.240	.328	.351
2002 Akron	AA	130	470	132	28	5	15	(-	-)	215	62	62	77	45	0	97	5	7	11	4	2	.67	11	.281	.343	.457
2003 Buffalo	AAA	63	237	61	12	1	1	(-	-)	78	25	21	22	15	0	45	3	3	0	1	3	.25	6	.257	.310	.329
2004 Buffalo	AAA	138	556	181	44	2	15	(-	-)	274	109	86	99	54	0	126	4	0	9	8	4	.67	16	.326	.384	.493
2003 Cleveland	AL	77	242	55	10	1	4	(3	1)	79	24	21	24	20	0	65	4	2	2	1	3	.25	5	.227	.295	.326
2004 Cleveland	AL	8	25	6	1	0	0	(0	0)	7	2	2	2	3	0	6	0	0	0	0	1	.00	0	.240	.321	.280
2 ML YEARS		85	267	61	11	1	4	(3	1)	86	26	23	26	23	0	71	4	2	2	1	4	.20	5	.228	.297	.322

Troy Percival

Pitches: R **Bats:** R **Pos:** RP-52   **Ht:** 6'3" **Wt:** 235 **Born:** 8/9/1969 **Age:** 35

Year Team	Lg	G	GS	CG	GF	IP	BFP	H	R	ER	HR	SH	SF	HB	TBB	IBB	SO	WP	Bk	W	L	Pct	ShO	Sv-Op	Hld	ERC	ERA
1995 California	AL	62	0	0	16	74.0	284	37	19	16	6	4	1	1	26	2	94	2	2	3	2	.600	0	3-6	29	1.44	1.95
1996 Anaheim	AL	62	0	0	52	74.0	291	38	20	19	8	2	1	2	31	4	100	2	0	0	2	.000	0	36-39	2	1.76	2.31
1997 Anaheim	AL	55	0	0	46	52.0	224	40	20	20	6	1	2	4	22	2	72	5	0	5	5	.500	0	27-31	0	3.15	3.46
1998 Anaheim	AL	67	0	0	60	66.2	287	45	31	27	5	3	2	3	37	4	87	3	0	2	7	.222	0	42-48	0	2.74	3.65
1999 Anaheim	AL	60	0	0	50	57.0	230	38	24	24	9	0	1	3	22	0	58	3	0	4	6	.400	0	31-39	0	2.83	3.79
2000 Anaheim	AL	54	0	0	45	50.0	221	42	27	25	7	3	2	2	30	4	49	1	0	5	5	.500	0	32-42	0	4.24	4.50
2001 Anaheim	AL	57	0	0	50	57.2	230	39	19	17	3	1	0	2	18	1	71	2	0	4	2	.667	0	39-42	0	1.90	2.65
2002 Anaheim	AL	58	0	0	50	56.1	226	38	12	12	5	0	1	0	25	1	68	5	0	4	1	.800	0	40-44	0	2.47	1.92
2003 Anaheim	AL	52	0	0	49	49.1	206	33	22	19	7	0	1	3	23	1	48	1	0	0	5	.000	0	33-37	0	2.99	3.47
2004 Anaheim	AL	52	0	0	48	49.2	211	43	19	16	7	0	2	3	19	3	33	2	0	2	3	.400	0	33-38	0	3.67	2.90
10 ML YEARS		579	0	0	466	586.2	2410	393	213	195	63	14	13	23	253	22	680	26	2	29	38	.433	0	316-366	31	2.57	2.99

Antonio Perez

Bats: R **Throws:** R **Pos:** PH-8; PR-3; 2B-2; SS-1   **Ht:** 5'11" **Wt:** 175 **Born:** 1/26/1980 **Age:** 25

				BATTING															BASERUNNING				AVERAGES		
Year Team	Lg	G	AB	H	2B	3B	HR	(Hm | Rd)	TB	R	RBI	RC	TBB	IBB	SO	HBP	SH	SF	SB	CS	SB%	GDP	Avg	OBP	Slg
1999 Rockford	A	119	385	111	20	3	7	(- | -)	158	69	41	60	43	0	80	13	8	3	35	24	.59	3	.288	.376	.410
2000 Lancaster	A+	98	395	109	36	6	17	(- | -)	208	90	63	75	58	1	99	8	9	4	28	16	.64	3	.276	.376	.527
2001 San Antonio	AA	5	21	3	0	0	0	(- | -)	3	3	0	0	0	0	7	0	0	0	0	0	-	0	.143	.143	.143
2002 San Antonio	AA	72	240	62	8	2	2	(- | -)	80	30	24	25	11	0	64	10	8	5	15	9	.63	3	.258	.312	.333
2002 Mariners	R	6	15	5	1	0	1	(- | -)	9	3	3	5	4	0	2	1	0	1	4	0	1.00	0	.333	.476	.600
2003 Orlando	AA	24	81	22	5	1	2	(- | -)	35	16	10	17	18	0	18	4	1	1	3	1	.75	0	.272	.423	.432
2003 Durham	AAA	34	134	38	12	2	6	(- | -)	72	27	20	23	10	0	38	3	1	1	3	1	.75	2	.284	.345	.537
2004 Las Vegas	AAA	125	476	141	24	6	22	(- | -)	243	92	88	93	61	1	87	7	3	7	22	12	.65	1	.296	.379	.511
2003 Tampa Bay	AL	48	125	31	6	1	2	(0 | 2)	45	19	12	19	18	0	34	1	2	1	4	1	.80	1	.248	.345	.360
2004 Los Angeles	NL	13	13	3	1	0	0	(0 | 0)	4	5	0	1	0	0	5	1	0	0	1	0	1.00	0	.231	.286	.308
2 ML YEARS		61	138	34	7	1	2	(0 | 2)	49	24	12	20	18	0	39	2	2	1	5	1	.83	1	.246	.340	.355

Eddie Perez

Bats: R **Throws:** R **Pos:** C-66; PH-9; PR-2; 1B-1   **Ht:** 6'1" **Wt:** 220 **Born:** 5/4/1968 **Age:** 37

				BATTING															BASERUNNING				AVERAGES		
Year Team	Lg	G	AB	H	2B	3B	HR	(Hm	Rd)	TB	R	RBI	RC	TBB	IBB	SO	HBP	SH	SF	SB	CS	SB%	GDP	Avg	OBP	Slg
1995 Atlanta	NL	7	13	4	1	0	1	(0	1)	8	1	4	2	0	0	2	0	0	0	0	0	-	0	.308	.308	.615
1996 Atlanta	NL	68	156	40	9	1	4	(2	2)	63	19	17	17	8	0	19	1	0	2	0	0	-	6	.256	.293	.404
1997 Atlanta	NL	73	191	41	5	0	6	(4	2)	64	20	18	14	10	0	35	2	1	2	0	1	.00	8	.215	.259	.335
1998 Atlanta	NL	61	149	50	12	0	6	(3	3)	80	18	32	30	15	0	28	2	1	0	1	1	.50	3	.336	.404	.537
1999 Atlanta	NL	104	309	77	17	0	7	(0	7)	115	30	30	32	17	4	40	6	4	3	0	1	.00	9	.249	.299	.372
2000 Atlanta	NL	7	22	4	1	0	0	(0	0)	5	0	3	1	0	0	2	0	0	0	0	0	-	0	.182	.182	.227
2001 Atlanta	NL	5	10	3	0	0	0	(0	0)	3	0	0	1	0	0	2	0	0	0	0	0	-	0	.300	.300	.300
2002 Cleveland	AL	42	117	25	9	0	0	(0	0)	34	6	4	4	5	0	25	1	2	0	0	0	-	6	.214	.252	.291
2003 Milwaukee	NL	107	350	95	17	1	11	(5	6)	147	26	45	38	17	3	47	0	6	2	0	1	.00	16	.271	.304	.420
2004 Atlanta	NL	74	170	39	12	0	3	(1	2)	60	14	13	12	11	1	29	3	3	1	0	0	-	5	.229	.286	.353
10 ML YEARS		548	1487	378	83	2	38	(15	23)	579	134	166	151	83	8	229	15	17	10	1	4	.20	53	.254	.298	.389

Eduardo Perez

Bats: R **Throws:** R **Pos:** 1B-5; DH-3; PH-3; LF-2; 3B-1; RF-1   **Ht:** 6'4" **Wt:** 215 **Born:** 9/11/1969 **Age:** 35

				BATTING															BASERUNNING				AVERAGES		
Year Team	Lg	G	AB	H	2B	3B	HR	(Hm	Rd)	TB	R	RBI	RC	TBB	IBB	SO	HBP	SH	SF	SB	CS	SB%	GDP	Avg	OBP	Slg
1993 California	AL	52	180	45	6	2	4	(2	2)	67	16	30	18	9	0	39	2	0	1	5	4	.56	4	.250	.292	.372
1994 California	AL	38	129	27	7	0	5	(3	2)	49	10	16	13	12	1	29	0	1	1	3	0	1.00	5	.209	.275	.380
1995 California	AL	29	71	12	4	1	1	(0	1)	21	9	7	6	12	0	9	2	0	1	0	2	.00	3	.169	.302	.296
1996 Cincinnati	NL	18	36	8	0	0	3	(3	0)	17	8	5	5	5	1	9	0	0	0	0	0	-	2	.222	.317	.472
1997 Cincinnati	NL	106	297	75	18	0	16	(7	9)	141	44	52	45	29	1	76	2	0	2	5	1	.83	6	.253	.321	.475
1998 Cincinnati	NL	84	172	41	4	0	4	(1	3)	57	20	30	19	21	2	45	2	1	2	0	1	.00	7	.238	.325	.331
1999 St Louis	NL	21	32	11	2	0	1	(0	1)	16	6	9	8	7	0	6	0	0	0	0	0	-	0	.344	.462	.500
2000 St Louis	NL	35	91	27	4	0	3	(0	3)	40	9	10	14	5	0	19	3	2	1	1	0	1.00	3	.297	.350	.440
2002 St Louis	NL	96	154	31	9	0	10	(4	6)	70	22	26	26	17	0	36	3	1	2	0	0	-	7	.201	.290	.455
2003 St Louis	NL	105	253	72	16	0	11	(5	6)	121	47	41	38	29	1	53	4	1	2	5	2	.71	7	.285	.365	.478
2004 Tampa Bay	AL	13	38	8	2	0	1	(1	0)	13	2	7	6	4	0	9	0	0	0	0	0	-	1	.211	.286	.342
11 ML YEARS		597	1453	357	72	3	59	(26	33)	612	193	233	189	150	6	330	18	6	12	19	10	.66	39	.246	.321	.421

Neifi Perez

Bats: B **Throws:** R **Pos:** SS-76; 2B-40; PH-14; PR-5; 3B-2   **Ht:** 6'0" **Wt:** 175 **Born:** 6/2/1973 **Age:** 32

				BATTING															BASERUNNING				AVERAGES		
Year Team	Lg	G	AB	H	2B	3B	HR	(Hm	Rd)	TB	R	RBI	RC	TBB	IBB	SO	HBP	SH	SF	SB	CS	SB%	GDP	Avg	OBP	Slg
2004 Iowa*	AAA	10	34	7	1	0	0	(-	-)	8	1	3	1	0	0	5	0	0	0	0	0	-	0	.206	.206	.235
1996 Colorado	NL	17	45	7	2	0	0	(0	0)	9	4	3	0	0	0	8	0	1	0	2	2	.50	2	.156	.156	.200
1997 Colorado	NL	83	313	91	13	10	5	(3	2)	139	46	31	46	21	4	43	1	5	4	4	3	.57	3	.291	.333	.444
1998 Colorado	NL	162	647	177	25	9	9	(6	3)	247	80	59	77	38	0	70	1	22	4	5	6	.45	8	.274	.313	.382
1999 Colorado	NL	157	690	193	27	11	12	(8	4)	278	108	70	87	28	0	54	1	9	4	13	5	.72	4	.280	.307	.403
2000 Colorado	NL	162	651	187	39	11	10	(7	3)	278	92	71	85	30	6	63	0	7	11	3	6	.33	9	.287	.314	.427
2001 Col-KC		136	581	162	26	9	8	(7	1)	230	83	59	69	26	1	68	1	11	4	9	6	.60	10	.279	.309	.396
2002 Kansas City	AL	145	554	131	20	4	3	(1	2)	168	65	37	37	20	2	53	0	5	6	8	9	.47	11	.236	.260	.303
2003 San Francisco	NL	120	328	84	19	4	1	(1	0)	114	27	31	29	14	3	23	0	9	2	3	2	.60	5	.256	.285	.348
2004 SF-ChC	NL	126	381	97	17	1	4	(2	2)	128	40	39	39	24	3	41	0	11	4	1	1	.50	8	.255	.296	.336
2001 Colorado	NL	87	382	114	19	8	7	(7	0)	170	65	47	53	16	1	49	0	4	1	6	2	.75	8	.298	.326	.445
2001 Kansas City	AL	49	199	48	7	1	1	(0	1)	60	18	12	16	10	0	19	1	7	3	3	4	.43	2	.241	.277	.302

Year Team	Lg	G	AB	H	2B	3B	HR	(Hm	Rd)	TB	R	RBI	RC	TBB	IBB	SO	HBP	SH	SF	SB	CS	SB%	GDP	Avg	OBP	Slg
2004 San Francisco	NL	103	319	74	12	1	2	(0	2)	94	28	33	26	21	3	35	0	9	4	0	1	.00	7	.232	.276	.295
2004 Chicago	NL	23	62	23	5	0	2	(2	0)	34	12	6	13	3	0	6	0	2	0	1	0	1.00		.371	.400	.548
9 ML YEARS		1108	4190	1129	188	59	52	(35	17)	1591	545	400	469	201	19	423	4	80	39	48	40	.55	64	.269	.301	.380

Odalis Perez

Pitches: L **Bats:** L **Pos:** SP-31　　　　　　　　　　**Ht:** 6'0" **Wt:** 150 **Born:** 6/11/1977 **Age:** 28

Year Team	Lg	G	GS	CG	GF	IP	BFP	H	R	ER	HR	SH	SF	HB	TBB	IBB	SO	WP	Bk	W	L	Pct	ShO	Sv-Op	Hld	ERC	ERA
1998 Atlanta	NL	10	0	0	0	10.2	45	10	5	5	1	0	0	0	4	0	5	0	0	0	1	.000	0	0-1	5	3.60	4.22
1999 Atlanta	NL	18	17	0	0	93.0	424	100	65	62	12	3	4	1	53	2	82	5	3	4	6	.400	0	0-0	0	5.42	6.00
2001 Atlanta	NL	24	16	0	1	95.1	418	108	55	52	7	3	3	1	39	0	71	2	3	7	8	.467	0	0-0	0	4.79	4.91
2002 Los Angeles	NL	32	32	4	0	222.1	869	182	76	74	21	13	7	4	38	5	155	2	3	15	10	.600	2	0-0	0	2.31	3.00
2003 Los Angeles	NL	30	30	0	0	185.1	772	191	98	93	28	5	3	3	46	4	141	2	1	12	12	.500	0	0-0	0	4.07	4.52
2004 Los Angeles	NL	31	31	0	0	196.1	787	180	76	71	26	16	3	3	44	4	128	2	2	7	6	.538	0	0-0	0	3.26	3.25
6 ML YEARS		145	126	4	1	803.0	3315	771	375	357	95	40	20	12	224	15	582	13	12	45	43	.511	2	0-1	5	3.58	4.00

Oliver Perez

Pitches: L **Bats:** L **Pos:** SP-30　　　　　　　　　　**Ht:** 6'3" **Wt:** 160 **Born:** 8/15/1981 **Age:** 23

Year Team	Lg	G	GS	CG	GF	IP	BFP	H	R	ER	HR	SH	SF	HB	TBB	IBB	SO	WP	Bk	W	L	Pct	ShO	Sv-Op	Hld	ERC	ERA
2002 San Diego	NL	16	15	0	0	90.0	387	71	37	35	13	5	3	5	48	1	94	3	0	4	5	.444	0	0-0	0	3.93	3.50
2003 SD-Pit	NL	24	24	0	0	126.2	579	129	80	77	22	5	2	4	77	3	141	7	1	4	10	.286	0	0-0	0	5.66	5.47
2004 Pittsburgh	NL	30	30	2	0	196.0	805	145	71	65	22	9	5	9	81	2	239	2	1	12	10	.545	1	0-0	0	2.99	2.98
2003 San Diego	NL	19	19	0	0	103.2	473	103	65	62	20	4	2	3	65	2	117	6	1	4	7	.364	0	0-0	0	5.74	5.38
2003 Pittsburgh	NL	5	5	0	0	23.0	106	26	15	15	2	1	0	1	12	1	24	1	0	0	3	.000	0	0-0	0	5.29	5.87
3 ML YEARS		70	69	2	0	412.2	1771	345	188	177	57	19	10	18	206	6	474	12	2	20	25	.444	1	0-0	0	3.97	3.86

Timo Perez

Bats: L **Throws:** L **Pos:** RF-49; PH-27; CF-25; LF-12; DH-6; PR-4　　　**Ht:** 5'9" **Wt:** 167 **Born:** 4/8/1975 **Age:** 30

Year Team	Lg	G	AB	H	2B	3B	HR	(Hm	Rd)	TB	R	RBI	RC	TBB	IBB	SO	HBP	SH	SF	SB	CS	SB%	GDP	Avg	OBP	Slg
2000 New York	NL	24	49	14	4	1	1	(0	1)	23	11	3	8	3	0	5	1	0	1	1	1	.50	0	.286	.333	.469
2001 New York	NL	85	239	59	9	1	5	(2	3)	85	26	22	23	12	0	25	2	6	1	1	6	.14	1	.247	.287	.356
2002 New York	NL	136	444	131	27	6	8	(3	5)	194	52	47	63	23	2	36	2	10	2	10	6	.63	10	.295	.331	.437
2003 New York	NL	127	346	93	21	0	4	(1	3)	126	32	42	37	18	1	29	2	7	9	5	6	.45	5	.269	.301	.364
2004 Chicago	AL	103	293	72	12	0	5	(2	3)	99	38	40	39	15	0	29	2	9	2	3	1	.75	9	.246	.285	.338
5 ML YEARS		475	1371	369	73	8	23	(8	15)	527	159	154	170	71	3	124	9	32	15	20	20	.50	25	.269	.306	.384

Tomas Perez

Bats: B **Throws:** R **Pos:** PH-29; 3B-22; 2B-17; 1B-10; SS-10; PR-1　　**Ht:** 5'11" **Wt:** 177 **Born:** 12/29/1973 **Age:** 31

Year Team	Lg	G	AB	H	2B	3B	HR	(Hm	Rd)	TB	R	RBI	RC	TBB	IBB	SO	HBP	SH	SF	SB	CS	SB%	GDP	Avg	OBP	Slg
1995 Toronto	AL	41	98	24	3	1	1	(1	0)	32	12	8	7	7	0	18	0	0	1	0	1	.00	6	.245	.292	.327
1996 Toronto	AL	91	295	74	13	4	1	(1	0)	98	24	19	28	25	0	29	1	6	1	1	2	.33	10	.251	.311	.332
1997 Toronto	AL	40	123	24	3	2	0	(0	0)	31	9	9	8	11	0	28	1	3	0	1	1	.50	2	.195	.267	.252
1998 Toronto	AL	6	9	1	0	0	0	(0	0)	1	1	0	0	1	0	3	0	1	0	0	0	-	1	.111	.200	.111
2000 Philadelphia	NL	45	140	31	7	1	1	(0	1)	43	17	13	11	11	2	30	1	1	0	1	1	.50	3	.221	.278	.307
2001 Philadelphia	NL	62	135	41	7	1	3	(2	1)	59	11	19	20	7	1	22	2	1	0	1	0	.00	2	.304	.347	.437
2002 Philadelphia	NL	92	212	53	13	1	5	(2	3)	83	22	20	20	21	6	40	1	2	1	1	0	1.00	5	.250	.319	.392
2003 Philadelphia	NL	125	298	79	18	1	5	(2	3)	114	39	33	33	23	11	54	0	4	2	0	1	.00	7	.265	.316	.383
2004 Philadelphia	NL	86	176	38	13	2	6	(4	2)	73	22	21	20	9	2	44	1	3	1	0	0	-	2	.216	.257	.415
9 ML YEARS		588	1486	365	77	13	22	(12	10)	534	157	142	143	115	22	268	6	21	6	4	7	.36	38	.246	.301	.359

Matt Perisho

Pitches: L **Bats:** L **Pos:** RP-66　　　　　　　　　　**Ht:** 6'0" **Wt:** 205 **Born:** 6/8/1975 **Age:** 30

Year Team	Lg	G	GS	CG	GF	IP	BFP	H	R	ER	HR	SH	SF	HB	TBB	IBB	SO	WP	Bk	W	L	Pct	ShO	Sv-Op	Hld	ERC	ERA
1997 Anaheim	AL	11	8	0	2	45.0	217	59	34	30	6	2	2	3	28	0	35	5	2	0	2	.000	0	0-0	0	7.56	6.00
1998 Texas	AL	2	2	0	0	5.0	30	15	17	15	2	0	0	2	8	0	2	0	0	0	2	.000	0	0-0	0	30.09	27.00
1999 Texas	AL	4	1	0	3	10.1	40	8	3	3	0	0	0	0	2	1	17	1	0	0	0	-	0	0-0	1	1.55	2.61
2000 Texas	AL	34	13	0	4	105.0	515	136	99	86	20	6	5	6	67	3	74	4	0	2	7	.222	0	0-1	0	7.79	7.37
2001 Detroit	AL	30	4	0	5	39.1	186	54	29	25	5	2	1	4	14	1	19	0	0	2	3	.400	0	0-2	4	6.71	5.72
2002 Detroit	AL	5	0	0	1	10.1	50	16	11	10	2	0	1	0	6	0	3	0	0	0	0	-	0	0-0	0	9.45	8.71
2004 Florida	NL	66	0	0	16	47.0	212	45	23	23	6	1	1	2	26	2	42	1	0	5	3	.625	0	0-2	10	4.68	4.40
7 ML YEARS		152	28	0	31	262.0	1260	333	216	192	41	11	10	17	151	7	192	11	2	9	17	.346	0	0-5	14	7.12	6.60

Herbert Perry

Bats: R **Throws:** R **Pos:** DH-21; 1B-15; PH-12; 3B-6　　　　**Ht:** 6'2" **Wt:** 225 **Born:** 9/15/1969 **Age:** 35

Year Team	Lg	G	AB	H	2B	3B	HR	(Hm	Rd)	TB	R	RBI	RC	TBB	IBB	SO	HBP	SH	SF	SB	CS	SB%	GDP	Avg	OBP	Slg
2004 Frisco*	AA	8	29	12	3	0	0	(-	-)	15	4	4	6	3	0	7	0	0	1	0	0	-	0	.414	.455	.517
1994 Cleveland	AL	4	9	1	0	0	0	(0	0)	1	1	1	1	3	1	1	1	0	1	0	0	-	0	.111	.357	.111
1995 Cleveland	AL	52	162	51	13	1	3	(3	0)	75	23	23	26	13	0	28	4	3	2	1	3	.25	5	.315	.376	.463
1996 Cleveland	AL	7	12	1	1	0	0	(0	0)	2	1	0	0	1	0	2	0	0	0	1	0	1.00	0	.083	.154	.167
1999 Tampa Bay	AL	66	209	53	10	1	6	(5	1)	83	29	32	25	16	1	42	10	0	4	0	0	-	13	.254	.331	.397

BATTING / BASERUNNING / AVERAGES

Year Team	Lg	G	AB	H	2B	3B	HR	(Hm	Rd)	TB	R	RBI	RC	TBB	IBB	SO	HBP	SH	SF	SB	CS	SB%	GDP	Avg	OBP	Slg
2000 TB-CWS	AL	116	411	124	30	1	12	(7	5)	192	71	62	64	24	1	75	9	2	4	4	1	.80	13	.302	.350	.467
2001 Chicago	AL	92	285	73	21	1	7	(5	2)	117	38	32	35	23	1	55	7	0	1	2	2	.50	11	.256	.326	.411
2002 Texas	AL	132	450	124	24	1	22	(9	13)	216	64	77	64	34	1	66	6	4	2	4	2	.67	17	.276	.333	.480
2003 Texas	AL	11	24	4	1	0	0	(0	0)	5	1	2	1	0	0	3	0	0	0	0	0	-	0	.167	.167	.208
2004 Texas	AL	49	134	30	2	1	5	(3	2)	49	13	17	14	14	0	19	3	0	2	0	0	-	0	.224	.307	.366
2000 Tampa Bay	AL	7	28	6	1	0	0	(0	0)	7	2	1	2	2	0	7	0	0	0	0	0	-	0	.214	.267	.250
2000 Chicago	AL	109	383	118	29	1	12	(7	5)	185	69	61	62	22	1	68	9	2	4	4	1	.80	13	.308	.356	.483
9 ML YEARS		529	1696	461	102	6	55	(32	23)	740	241	246	230	128	5	291	40	9	16	12	8	.60	62	.272	.335	.436

Robert Person

Pitches: R **Bats:** R **Pos:** SP   **Ht:** 6'0" **Wt:** 193 **Born:** 10/6/1969 **Age:** 35

Year Team	Lg	G	GS	CG	GF	IP	BFP	H	R	ER	HR	SH	SF	HB	TBB	IBB	SO	WP	Bk	W	L	Pct	ShO	Sv-Op	Hld	ERC	ERA
1995 New York	NL	3	1	0	0	12.0	44	5	1	1	1	0	0	0	2	0	10	0	0	1	0	1.000	0	0-0	0	0.82	0.75
1996 New York	NL	27	13	0	1	89.2	390	86	50	45	16	1	4	2	35	3	76	3	0	4	5	.444	0	0-0	1	4.32	4.52
1997 Toronto	AL	23	22	0	0	128.1	566	125	86	80	19	4	6	5	60	2	99	7	0	5	10	.333	0	0-0	4	4.65	5.61
1998 Toronto	AL	27	0	0	14	38.1	184	45	31	30	9	2	5	2	22	1	31	0	0	3	1	.750	0	6-8	0	6.94	7.04
1999 Tor-Phi		42	22	0	8	148.0	659	139	84	77	24	7	6	6	85	2	139	5	1	10	7	.588	0	2-2	1	5.04	4.68
2000 Philadelphia	NL	28	28	1	0	173.1	743	144	73	70	13	4	9	6	95	1	164	10	1	9	7	.563	1	0-0	0	3.70	3.63
2001 Philadelphia	NL	33	33	3	0	208.1	867	179	103	97	34	8	6	8	80	3	183	10	1	15	7	.682	1	0-0	0	3.84	4.19
2002 Philadelphia	NL	16	16	0	0	87.2	388	79	58	53	13	2	2	5	51	0	61	2	0	4	5	.444	0	0-0	0	4.85	5.44
2003 Boston	AL	7	0	0	3	11.2	55	11	10	10	0	0	2	2	8	0	10	2	0	0	0	-	0	1-1	0	4.30	7.71
1999 Toronto	AL	11	0	0	7	11.0	60	9	12	12	1	0	2	4	15	1	12	2	0	0	2	.000	0	2-2	1	8.06	9.82
1999 Philadelphia	NL	31	22	0	1	137.0	599	130	72	65	23	7	4	2	70	1	127	3	1	10	5	.667	0	0-0	0	4.78	4.27
9 ML YEARS		206	135	4	26	897.1	3896	813	496	463	129	28	40	35	438	12	773	39	3	51	42	.548	2	9-11	2	4.34	4.64

Adam Peterson

Pitches: R **Bats:** R **Pos:** RP-3   **Ht:** 6'3" **Wt:** 220 **Born:** 5/18/1979 **Age:** 26

Year Team	Lg	G	GS	CG	GF	IP	BFP	H	R	ER	HR	SH	SF	HB	TBB	IBB	SO	WP	Bk	W	L	Pct	ShO	Sv-Op	Hld	ERC	ERA
2002 Auburn	A-	18	0	0	10	31.1	130	29	10	8	2	2	0	1	9	1	19	1	0	2	0	1.000	0	5--	-	3.09	2.30
2003 Christn - WV	A	10	0	0	6	24.2	99	15	8	6	1	5	0	2	13	2	19	3	1	1	4	.333	0	1--	-	2.37	2.19
2003 Dunedin	A+	9	0	0	3	12.2	44	5	1	1	1	0	0	1	0	0	13	0	0	1	0	1.000	0	1--	-	0.62	0.71
2003 New Haven	AA	24	0	0	19	24.0	105	24	13	13	1	2	2	2	7	1	24	1	0	2	2	.500	0	9--	-	3.42	4.88
2004 New Hamp	AA	27	0	0	25	28.1	114	20	8	8	1	0	1	0	10	0	38	3	1	2	2	.500	0	15--	-	1.98	2.54
2004 Syracuse	AAA	19	0	0	8	21.0	119	38	30	30	6	0	0	2	16	1	19	2	0	2	2	.500	0	0--	-	12.88	12.86
2004 Toronto	AL	3	0	0	1	2.2	18	7	5	5	1	0	0	0	3	0	2	0	0	0	0	-	0	0-0	0	21.83	16.88

Andy Pettitte

Pitches: L **Bats:** L **Pos:** SP-15   **Ht:** 6'5" **Wt:** 225 **Born:** 6/15/1972 **Age:** 33

Year Team	Lg	G	GS	CG	GF	IP	BFP	H	R	ER	HR	SH	SF	HB	TBB	IBB	SO	WP	Bk	W	L	Pct	ShO	Sv-Op	Hld	ERC	ERA
2004 Round Rock*	AA	2	2	0	0	8.0	29	4	2	2	1	1	0	0	2	0	9	0	0	0	0	-	0	0--	-	1.40	2.25
1995 New York	AL	31	26	3	1	175.0	745	183	86	81	15	4	5	1	63	3	114	8	1	12	9	.571	0	0-0	0	4.13	4.17
1996 New York	AL	35	34	2	1	221.0	929	229	105	95	23	7	3	3	72	2	162	6	1	21	8	.724	0	0-0	0	4.14	3.87
1997 New York	AL	35	35	4	0	240.1	986	233	86	77	7	6	2	3	65	0	166	7	0	18	7	.720	1	0-0	0	3.05	2.88
1998 New York	AL	33	32	5	0	216.1	932	226	110	102	20	6	7	6	87	1	146	5	0	16	11	.593	0	0-0	0	4.46	4.24
1999 New York	AL	31	31	0	0	191.2	851	216	105	100	20	6	6	3	89	3	121	3	1	14	11	.560	0	0-0	0	5.22	4.70
2000 New York	AL	32	32	3	0	204.2	903	219	111	99	17	7	4	4	80	4	125	4	2	19	9	.679	1	0-0	0	4.32	4.35
2001 New York	AL	31	31	2	0	200.2	858	224	103	89	14	8	7	6	41	3	164	2	2	15	10	.600	0	0-0	0	3.82	3.99
2002 New York	AL	22	22	3	0	134.2	570	144	58	49	6	3	2	4	32	2	97	2	1	13	5	.722	1	0-0	0	3.55	3.27
2003 New York	AL	33	33	1	0	208.1	896	227	109	93	21	5	5	1	50	3	180	5	0	21	8	.724	0	0-0	0	3.89	4.02
2004 Houston	NL	15	15	0	0	83.0	346	71	37	36	8	1	0	0	31	2	79	4	0	6	4	.600	0	0-0	0	3.12	3.90
10 ML YEARS		298	291	23	2	1875.2	8016	1972	910	821	151	53	41	31	610	23	1354	44	9	155	82	.654	3	0-0	0	4.00	3.94

Josh Phelps

Bats: R **Throws:** R **Pos:** DH-80; 1B-20; PH-6   **Ht:** 6'3" **Wt:** 220 **Born:** 5/12/1978 **Age:** 27

Year Team	Lg	G	AB	H	2B	3B	HR	(Hm	Rd)	TB	R	RBI	RC	TBB	IBB	SO	HBP	SH	SF	SB	CS	SB%	GDP	Avg	OBP	Slg
2000 Toronto	AL	1	1	0	0	0	0	(0	0)	0	0	0	0	0	0	1	0	0	0	0	0	-	0	.000	.000	.000
2001 Toronto	AL	8	12	0	0	0	0	(0	0)	0	3	1	0	2	0	5	0	0	0	1	0	1.00	1	.000	.143	.000
2002 Toronto	AL	74	265	82	20	1	15	(6	9)	149	41	58	52	19	0	82	3	0	0	0	0	-	7	.309	.362	.562
2003 Toronto	AL	119	396	106	18	1	20	(11	9)	186	57	66	65	39	3	115	17	0	1	1	2	.33	12	.268	.358	.470
2004 Tor-Cle	AL	103	371	93	19	2	17	(9	8)	167	51	61	50	22	2	93	7	0	1	0	0	-	13	.251	.304	.450
2004 Toronto	AL	79	295	70	13	2	12	(7	5)	123	38	51	40	18	2	73	7	0	1	0	0	-	9	.237	.296	.417
2004 Cleveland	AL	24	76	23	6	0	5	(2	3)	44	13	10	10	4	0	20	0	0	0	0	0	-	4	.303	.338	.579
5 ML YEARS		305	1045	281	57	4	52	(26	26)	502	152	186	167	82	5	296	27	0	2	2	2	.50	33	.269	.337	.480

Tommy Phelps

Pitches: L **Bats:** L **Pos:** RP-15; SP-4   **Ht:** 6'3" **Wt:** 192 **Born:** 3/4/1974 **Age:** 31

Year Team	Lg	G	GS	CG	GF	IP	BFP	H	R	ER	HR	SH	SF	HB	TBB	IBB	SO	WP	Bk	W	L	Pct	ShO	Sv-Op	Hld	ERC	ERA
1993 Burlington	A	8	8	0	0	41.0	173	36	18	17	4	1	1	1	13	0	33	2	0	2	4	.333	0	0--	-	3.11	3.73
1993 Jamestown	A-	16	15	1	0	92.1	416	102	62	47	4	4	3	5	37	1	74	7	1	3	8	.273	0	0--	-	4.39	4.58
1994 Burlington	A	23	23	1	0	118.1	534	143	94	73	9	7	7	5	48	1	82	7	0	8	8	.500	1	0--	-	5.33	5.55
1995 W Palm Bch	A+	2	2	0	0	5.0	33	10	10	9	0	0	0	0	11	0	5	2	0	0	2	.000	0	0--	-	19.29	16.20
1995 Albany	A	24	24	1	0	135.1	597	142	76	50	6	0	4	5	45	0	119	5	1	10	9	.526	0	0--	-	3.74	3.33
1996 W Palm Bch	A+	18	18	1	0	112.0	468	105	42	36	5	4	1	2	35	0	71	8	0	10	2	.833	1	0--	-	3.10	2.89

Year Team	Lg	G	GS	CG	GF	IP	BFP	H	R	ER	HR	SH	SF	HB	TBB	IBB	SO	WP	Bk	W	L	Pct	ShO	Sv-Op	Hld	ERC	ERA
1996 Harrisburg	AA	8	8	2	0	47.1	195	43	16	13	3	2	0	1	19	2	23	0	0	2	2	.500	2	0--	-	3.46	2.47
1997 Harrisburg	AA	18	18	0	0	101.1	462	115	68	53	14	8	5	5	39	1	86	3	1	10	6	.625	0	0--	-	5.15	4.71
1998 Jupiter	A+	7	7	0	0	41.0	181	42	21	20	3	0	2	2	15	0	21	1	0	2	2	.500	0	0--	-	4.00	4.39
1998 Jupiter	A	12	10	0	0	59.2	247	57	29	24	5	4	3	0	26	0	26	2	0	5	4	.556	0	0--	-	4.02	3.62
1999 Harrisburg	AA	13	13	1	0	64.2	306	76	53	41	13	3	6	7	26	0	36	2	0	3	6	.333	0	0--	-	6.14	5.71
2000 Jacksonville	AA	38	11	0	7	102.0	435	111	59	56	17	1	0	7	26	2	62	1	0	6	6	.500	0	0--	-	4.78	4.94
2001 Toledo	AAA	29	0	0	8	59.2	271	74	30	24	4	0	1	3	19	3	53	1	0	3	2	.600	0	1--	-	4.95	3.62
2001 Erie	AA	15	2	0	5	32.2	139	33	14	13	1	3	2	3	8	2	31	2	0	1	1	.500	0	2--	-	3.31	3.58
2002 Calgary	AAA	51	0	0	10	74.1	314	76	27	26	8	4	1	2	21	3	62	3	0	4	2	.667	0	2--	-	3.85	3.15
2003 Jupiter	A+	2	1	0	0	3.0	14	5	2	2	0	0	0	0	0	0	3	0	0	0	0	-	0	0--	-	5.42	6.00
2003 Albuquerque	AAA	5	0	0	1	7.2	26	5	1	1	1	0	0	0	3	0	13	1	0	0	0	-	0	0--	-	2.95	1.17
2004 Marlins	R	1	1	0	0	1.0	3	0	0	0	0	0	0	0	0	0	1	0	0	0	0	-	0	0--	-	0.00	0.00
2004 Jupiter	A+	1	0	0	0	1.1	6	2	3	0	0	0	0	0	0	0	1	0	0	0	0	-	0	0--	-	4.47	0.00
2003 Florida	NL	27	7	0	8	63.0	276	70	32	28	3	1	2	2	23	1	43	1	0	3	2	.600	0	0-0	1	4.31	4.00
2004 Florida	NL	19	4	0	2	34.0	144	34	20	18	6	3	2	0	12	0	28	0	0	1	1	.500	0	0-0	4	4.46	4.76
2 ML YEARS		46	11	0	10	97.0	420	104	52	46	9	4	4	2	35	1	71	1	0	4	3	.571	0	0-0	5	4.37	4.27

Travis Phelps

Pitches: R **Bats:** R **Pos:** RP-4 · **Ht:** 6'2" **Wt:** 166 **Born:** 7/25/1977 **Age:** 27

Year Team	Lg	G	GS	CG	GF	IP	BFP	H	R	ER	HR	SH	SF	HB	TBB	IBB	SO	WP	Bk	W	L	Pct	ShO	Sv-Op	Hld	ERC	ERA
2004 Indianapolis*	AAA	28	14	0	3	107.0	442	114	58	52	11	5	4	3	25	1	84	2	1	2	2	.615	0	0--	-	3.92	4.37
2001 Tampa Bay	AL	49	0	0	15	62.0	268	53	30	24	6	2	4	3	24	1	54	2	1	2	2	.500	0	5-6	13	3.27	3.48
2002 Tampa Bay	AL	26	0	0	9	37.2	169	30	20	20	7	0	2	5	27	0	36	6	2	1	2	.333	0	0-0	3	5.45	4.78
2004 Milwaukee	NL	4	0	0	0	6.0	31	8	7	7	2	0	0	0	3	0	3	0	0	0	1	.000	0	0-0	0	7.69	10.50
3 ML YEARS		79	0	0	25	105.2	468	91	57	51	15	2	6	8	54	1	93	8	3	3	5	.375	0	5-6	16	4.24	4.34

Andy Phillips

Bats: R **Throws:** R **Pos:** 3B-4; DH-1; PH-1; PR-1 · **Ht:** 6'0" **Wt:** 205 **Born:** 4/6/1977 **Age:** 28

Year Team	Lg	G	AB	H	2B	3B	HR	(Hm	Rd)	TB	R	RBI	RC	TBB	IBB	SO	HBP	SH	SF	SB	CS	SB%	GDP	Avg	OBP	Slg
1999 Staten Island	A-	64	233	75	11	7	7	(-	-)	121	35	48	50	37	1	40	3	0	3	3	3	.50	4	.322	.417	.519
2000 Tampa	A+	127	478	137	33	2	13	(-	-)	213	66	58	73	46	0	98	2	0	8	2	0	1.00	9	.287	.346	.446
2000 Norwich	AA	7	28	7	2	1	0	(-	-)	11	5	3	3	3	0	11	0	1	0	1	0	1.00	1	.250	.323	.393
2001 Norwich	AA	51	183	49	9	2	6	(-	-)	80	23	25	26	21	2	54	0	0	2	1	0	1.00	6	.268	.340	.437
2001 Tampa	A+	75	288	87	17	4	11	(-	-)	145	43	50	49	25	1	55	3	1	10	3	3	.50	6	.302	.353	.503
2002 Norwich	AA	73	272	83	24	2	19	(-	-)	168	58	51	58	33	2	56	3	0	4	4	3	.57	6	.305	.381	.618
2002 Columbus	AAA	51	205	54	11	1	9	(-	-)	94	32	36	24	10	0	56	0	1	1	0	1	.00	8	.263	.296	.459
2003 Columbus	AAA	17	67	14	4	0	2	(-	-)	24	7	5	4	5	0	17	0	0	0	0	0	-	4	.209	.264	.358
2004 Trenton	AA	10	42	15	2	1	4	(-	-)	31	8	16	11	3	0	1	0	0	2	3	0	1.00	1	.357	.383	.738
2004 Columbus	AAA	115	434	138	19	6	26	(-	-)	247	83	85	87	51	5	60	2	1	5	2	1	.67	18	.318	.388	.569
2004 New York	AL	5	8	2	0	0	1	(0	1)	5	1	2	1	0	0	1	0	0	0	0	0	-	1	.250	.250	.625

Brandon Phillips

Bats: R **Throws:** R **Pos:** 2B-6 · **Ht:** 5'11" **Wt:** 185 **Born:** 6/28/1981 **Age:** 24

Year Team	Lg	G	AB	H	2B	3B	HR	(Hm	Rd)	TB	R	RBI	RC	TBB	IBB	SO	HBP	SH	SF	SB	CS	SB%	GDP	Avg	OBP	Slg
2004 Buffalo*	AAA	135	521	158	34	4	8	(-	-)	224	83	50	79	44	0	56	8	9	6	14	11	.56	12	.303	.363	.430
2002 Cleveland	AL	11	31	8	3	1	0	(0	0)	13	5	4	5	3	0	6	1	1	0	0	0	-	0	.258	.343	.419
2003 Cleveland	AL	112	370	77	18	1	6	(3	3)	115	36	33	22	14	0	77	3	5	1	4	5	.44	12	.208	.242	.311
2004 Cleveland	AL	6	22	4	2	0	0	(0	0)	6	1	1	0	2	0	5	0	0	0	0	2	.00	1	.182	.250	.273
3 ML YEARS		129	423	89	23	2	6	(3	3)	134	42	38	27	19	0	88	4	6	1	4	7	.36	13	.210	.251	.317

Jason Phillips

Bats: R **Throws:** R **Pos:** C-88; 1B-38; PH-11 · **Ht:** 6'1" **Wt:** 177 **Born:** 9/27/1976 **Age:** 28

Year Team	Lg	G	AB	H	2B	3B	HR	(Hm	Rd)	TB	R	RBI	RC	TBB	IBB	SO	HBP	SH	SF	SB	CS	SB%	GDP	Avg	OBP	Slg
2001 New York	NL	6	7	1	1	0	0	(0 | 0)	2	2	0	0	0	0	0	1	0	0	0	0	0	-	0	.143	.143	.286
2002 New York	NL	11	19	7	0	0	1	(0	1)	10	4	3	3	1	0	1	1	0	1	0	0	-	1	.368	.409	.526
2003 New York	NL	119	403	120	25	0	11	(7	4)	178	45	58	65	39	3	50	10	0	1	0	1	.00	21	.298	.373	.442
2004 New York	NL	128	362	79	18	0	7	(2	5)	118	34	34	30	35	4	42	8	2	5	0	1	.00	11	.218	.298	.326
4 ML YEARS		264	791	207	44	0	19	(9	10)	308	85	95	98	75	7	94	19	2	7	0	2	.00	33	.262	.337	.389

Paul Phillips

Bats: R **Throws:** R **Pos:** C-4 · **Ht:** 5'11" **Wt:** 185 **Born:** 4/15/1977 **Age:** 28

Year Team	Lg	G	AB	H	2B	3B	HR	(Hm	Rd)	TB	R	RBI	RC	TBB	IBB	SO	HBP	SH	SF	SB	CS	SB%	GDP	Avg	OBP	Slg
1998 Spokane	A-	59	234	72	12	2	4	(-	-)	100	55	25	39	18	0	19	4	0	1	12	1	.92	2	.308	.366	.427
1998 Wilmington	A+	2	5	2	0	0	0	(- | -)	2	0	2	0	0	0	1	0	0	0	0	0	0	-	0	.400	.333	.400
1999 Wichita	AA	108	393	105	20	2	3	(-	-)	138	58	56	41	26	0	38	2	3	3	8	9	.47	8	.267	.314	.351
2000 Wichita	AA	82	291	85	11	5	4	(-	-)	118	49	30	37	21	1	22	1	1	4	4	5	.44	11	.292	.338	.405
2003 Wilmington	A+	13	46	11	1	0	0	(-	-)	12	1	6	2	1	0	6	1	0	0	1	0	1.00	3	.239	.271	.261
2004 Omaha	AAA	86	311	97	17	1	6	(-	-)	134	40	41	45	20	0	36	3	0	1	4	3	.57	10	.312	.358	.405
2004 Kansas City	AL	4	5	1	0	0	0	(0	0)	1	2	0	0	0	0	1	1	0	0	0	0	-	0	.200	.333	.200

Mike Piazza

Bats: R **Throws:** R **Pos:** 1B-69; C-50; DH-8; PH-6 **Ht:** 6'3" **Wt:** 215 **Born:** 9/4/1968 **Age:** 36

Year Team	Lg	G	AB	H	2B	3B	HR	(Hm	Rd)	TB	R	RBI	RC	TBB	IBB	SO	HBP	SH	SF	SB	CS	SB%	GDP	Avg	OBP	Slg
2004 St. Lucie*	A+	2	6	3	1	0	0	(-	-)	4	0	2	2	1	0	0	0	0	1	0	0	-	0	.500	.500	.667
1992 Los Angeles	NL	21	69	16	3	0	1	(1	0)	22	5	7	6	4	0	12	1	0	0	0	0	-	1	.232	.284	.319
1993 Los Angeles	NL	149	547	174	24	2	35	(21	14)	307	81	112	107	46	6	86	3	0	6	3	4	.43	10	.318	.370	.561
1994 Los Angeles	NL	107	405	129	18	0	24	(13	11)	219	64	92	74	33	10	65	1	0	2	1	3	.25	11	.319	.370	.541
1995 Los Angeles	NL	112	434	150	17	0	32	(9	23)	263	82	93	96	39	10	80	1	0	1	1	0	1.00	10	.346	.400	.606
1996 Los Angeles	NL	148	547	184	16	0	36	(14	22)	308	87	105	117	81	21	93	1	0	2	0	3	.00	21	.336	.422	.563
1997 Los Angeles	NL	152	556	201	32	1	40	(22	18)	355	104	124	137	69	11	77	3	0	5	5	1	.83	19	.362	.431	.638
1998 LA-Fla-NYM	NL	151	561	184	38	1	32	(15	17)	320	88	111	116	58	14	80	2	0	5	1	0	1.00	15	.328	.390	.570
1999 New York	NL	141	534	162	25	0	40	(18	22)	307	100	124	99	51	11	70	1	0	7	2	2	.50	27	.303	.361	.575
2000 New York	NL	136	482	156	26	0	38	(17	21)	296	90	113	107	58	10	69	3	0	2	4	2	.67	15	.324	.398	.614
2001 New York	NL	141	503	151	29	0	36	(16	20)	288	81	94	100	67	19	87	2	0	1	0	2	.00	20	.300	.384	.573
2002 New York	NL	135	478	134	23	2	33	(12	21)	260	69	98	82	57	9	82	3	0	3	0	3	.00	26	.280	.359	.544
2003 New York	NL	68	234	67	13	0	11	(4	7)	113	37	34	42	35	3	40	1	0	0	0	0	-	11	.286	.377	.483
2004 New York	NL	129	455	121	21	0	20	(12	8)	202	47	54	63	68	14	78	2	0	3	0	0	-	14	.266	.362	.444
1998 Los Angeles	NL	37	149	42	5	0	9	(5	4)	74	20	30	23	11	4	27	0	0	1	0	0	-	3	.282	.329	.497
1998 Florida	NL	5	18	5	0	1	0	(0	0)	7	1	5	2	0	0	0	0	0	0	0	0	-	0	.278	.263	.389
1998 New York	NL	109	394	137	33	0	23	(10	13)	239	67	76	91	47	10	53	2	0	3	1	0	1.00	12	.348	.417	.607
13 ML YEARS		1590	5805	1829	285	6	378	(174	204)	3260	935	1161	1146	666	138	919	24	0	40	17	20	.46	200	.315	.385	.562

Calvin Pickering

Bats: L **Throws:** L **Pos:** DH-27; 1B-8 **Ht:** 6'5" **Wt:** 267 **Born:** 9/29/1976 **Age:** 28

Year Team	Lg	G	AB	H	2B	3B	HR	(Hm	Rd)	TB	R	RBI	RC	TBB	IBB	SO	HBP	SH	SF	SB	CS	SB%	GDP	Avg	OBP	Slg
2004 Omaha*	AAA	89	299	94	12	1	35	(-	-)	213	65	79	86	70	7	85	7	0	3	0	1	.00	8	.314	.451	.712
1998 Baltimore	AL	9	21	5	0	0	2	(1	1)	11	4	3	3	3	0	4	0	0	0	1	0	1.00	0	.238	.333	.524
1999 Baltimore	AL	23	40	5	1	0	1	(1	0)	9	4	5	3	11	0	16	0	0	0	0	0	-	1	.125	.314	.225
2001 Cin-Bos		21	54	15	1	0	3	(1	2)	25	4	8	7	8	0	15	0	0	0	0	0	-	4	.278	.371	.463
2004 Kansas City	AL	35	122	30	8	1	7	(4	3)	61	21	26	25	18	1	42	0	0	2	0	0	-	6	.246	.338	.500
2001 Boston	AL	17	50	14	1	0	3	(0	0)	24	4	7	7	8	0	13	0	0	0	0	0	-	4	.280	.379	.480
2001 Cincinnati	NL	4	4	1	0	0	0	(1	2)	1	0	1	0	0	0	2	0	0	0	0	0	-	0	.250	.250	.250
4 ML YEARS		88	237	55	10	1	13	(4	3)	106	33	42	38	40	1	77	0	0	2	1	0	1.00	13	.232	.341	.447

Jorge Piedra

Bats: L **Throws:** L **Pos:** CF-18; LF-14; PH-9; RF-7; PR-1 **Ht:** 6'0" **Wt:** 190 **Born:** 4/17/1979 **Age:** 26

Year Team	Lg	G	AB	H	2B	3B	HR	(Hm	Rd)	TB	R	RBI	RC	TBB	IBB	SO	HBP	SH	SF	SB	CS	SB%	GDP	Avg	OBP	Slg
1998 Great Falls	R+	72	282	108	22	7	2	(-	-)	150	72	33	66	39	3	29	1	3	0	16	7	.70	4	.383	.460	.532
1999 Sn Brnardino	A+	8	30	9	2	0	0	(-	-)	11	6	3	4	3	0	3	0	1	2	1	0	1.00	0	.300	.343	.367
1999 Vero Beach	A+	15	59	17	3	1	1	(-	-)	25	13	6	9	7	1	9	0	0	1	2	2	.50	0	.288	.358	.424
2000 Vero Beach	A+	92	360	102	11	6	6	(-	-)	143	59	52	52	29	1	57	5	3	7	21	5	.81	6	.283	.339	.397
2000 Daytona	A+	34	139	48	11	1	1	(-	-)	64	24	17	23	6	0	15	0	2	2	8	4	.67	0	.345	.367	.460
2001 W Tennessee	AA	124	441	108	26	6	8	(-	-)	170	55	54	53	37	2	80	8	2	7	12	5	.71	8	.245	.310	.385
2002 W Tennessee	AA	23	60	10	3	1	0	(-	-)	15	5	4	2	3	0	11	1	1	0	2	0	1.00	1	.167	.219	.250
2002 Salem	A+	104	392	118	37	12	13	(-	-)	218	64	64	77	37	3	55	8	3	8	10	2	.83	4	.301	.366	.556
2003 Tulsa	AA	96	357	98	17	7	18	(-	-)	183	56	53	61	31	4	50	8	0	5	5	2	.71	6	.275	.342	.513
2004 Co Springs	AAA	99	377	126	29	5	15	(-	-)	210	71	55	72	23	1	56	3	3	6	4	3	.57	7	.334	.372	.557
2004 Colorado	NL	38	91	27	8	0	3	(1	2)	44	15	10	11	5	0	19	1	1	0	0	1	.00	1	.297	.340	.484

Juan Pierre

Bats: L **Throws:** L **Pos:** CF-162 **Ht:** 6'0" **Wt:** 180 **Born:** 8/14/1977 **Age:** 27

Year Team	Lg	G	AB	H	2B	3B	HR	(Hm	Rd)	TB	R	RBI	RC	TBB	IBB	SO	HBP	SH	SF	SB	CS	SB%	GDP	Avg	OBP	Slg
2000 Colorado	NL	51	200	62	2	0	0	(0	0)	64	26	20	23	13	0	15	1	4	1	7	6	.54	2	.310	.353	.320
2001 Colorado	NL	156	617	202	26	11	2	(0	2)	256	108	55	101	41	1	29	10	14	1	46	17	.73	6	.327	.378	.415
2002 Colorado	NL	152	592	170	20	5	1	(0	1)	203	90	35	79	31	0	52	9	8	0	47	12	.80	7	.287	.332	.343
2003 Florida	NL	162	668	204	28	7	1	(1	0)	249	100	41	92	55	1	35	5	15	3	65	20	.76	9	.305	.361	.373
2004 Florida	NL	162	678	221	22	12	3	(1	2)	276	100	49	101	45	1	35	8	15	2	45	24	.65	9	.326	.374	.407
5 ML YEARS		683	2755	859	98	35	7	(2	5)	1048	424	200	396	185	3	166	33	56	7	210	79	.73	33	.312	.361	.380

A.J. Pierzynski

Bats: L **Throws:** R **Pos:** C-117; PH-14 **Ht:** 6'3" **Wt:** 220 **Born:** 12/30/1976 **Age:** 28

Year Team	Lg	G	AB	H	2B	3B	HR	(Hm	Rd)	TB	R	RBI	RC	TBB	IBB	SO	HBP	SH	SF	SB	CS	SB%	GDP	Avg	OBP	Slg
1998 Minnesota	AL	7	10	3	0	0	0	(0	0)	3	1	1	2	1	0	2	1	0	1	0	0	-	0	.300	.385	.300
1999 Minnesota	AL	9	22	6	2	0	0	(0	0)	8	3	3	3	1	0	4	1	0	0	0	0	-	0	.273	.333	.364
2000 Minnesota	AL	33	88	27	5	1	2	(1	1)	40	12	11	14	5	0	14	2	0	1	1	0	1.00	1	.307	.354	.455
2001 Minnesota	AL	114	381	110	33	2	7	(3	4)	168	51	55	50	16	4	57	4	1	3	1	7	.13	7	.289	.322	.441
2002 Minnesota	AL	130	440	132	31	6	6	(2	4)	193	54	49	60	13	1	61	11	2	3	1	2	.33	14	.300	.334	.439
2003 Minnesota	AL	137	487	152	35	3	11	(6	5)	226	63	74	80	24	12	55	15	2	5	3	1	.75	13	.312	.360	.464
2004 San Francisco	NL	131	471	128	28	2	11	(3	8)	193	45	77	58	19	4	27	15	2	3	0	1	.00	27	.272	.319	.410
7 ML YEARS		561	1899	558	134	14	37	(15	22)	831	229	270	267	79	21	220	49	7	16	6	11	.35	62	.294	.336	.438

Joel Pineiro

Pitches: R Bats: R Pos: SP-21   Ht: 6'1" Wt: 180 Born: 9/25/1978 Age: 26

Year Team	Lg	G	GS	CG	GF	IP	BFP	H	R	ER	HR	SH	SF	HB	TBB	IBB	SO	WP	Bk	W	L	Pct	ShO	Sv-Op	Hld	ERC	ERA
2000 Seattle	AL	8	1	0	5	19.1	94	25	13	12	3	0	2	0	13	0	10	0	0	1	0	1.000	0	0-0	0	7.44	5.59
2001 Seattle	AL	17	11	0	1	75.1	289	50	24	17	2	1	2	3	21	0	56	2	0	6	2	.750	0	0-0	2	1.71	2.03
2002 Seattle	AL	37	28	2	4	194.1	812	189	75	70	24	5	7	7	54	1	136	8	0	14	7	.667	1	0-0	3	3.77	3.24
2003 Seattle	AL	32	32	3	0	211.2	890	192	94	89	19	3	9	6	76	3	151	5	0	16	11	.593	2	0-0	3	3.43	3.78
2004 Seattle	AL	21	21	1	0	140.2	596	144	77	73	21	1	5	4	43	1	111	4	0	6	11	.353	0	0-0	0	4.32	4.67
5 ML YEARS		115	93	6	10	641.1	2681	600	283	261	69	10	25	20	207	5	464	19	0	43	31	.581	3	0-0	5	3.61	3.66

Scott Podsednik

Bats: L Throws: L Pos: CF-153; PH-2   Ht: 6'0" Wt: 170 Born: 3/18/1976 Age: 29

Year Team	Lg	G	AB	H	2B	3B	HR	(Hm	Rd)	TB	R	RBI	RC	TBB	IBB	SO	HBP	SH	SF	SB	CS	SB%	GDP	Avg	OBP	Slg
2001 Seattle	AL	5	6	1	0	1	0	(0	0)	3	1	3	0	0	0	1	0	0	0	0	0	-	1	.167	.167	.500
2002 Seattle	AL	14	20	4	0	0	1	(0	1)	7	2	5	3	4	0	6	0	0	1	0	0	-	1	.200	.320	.350
2003 Milwaukee	NL	154	558	175	29	8	9	(7	2)	247	100	58	101	56	2	91	4	8	2	43	10	.81	11	.314	.379	.443
2004 Milwaukee	NL	154	640	156	27	7	12	(3	9)	233	85	39	76	58	2	105	7	6	1	70	13	.84	7	.244	.313	.364
4 ML YEARS		327	1224	336	56	16	22	(10	12)	490	188	105	180	118	4	203	11	14	4	113	23	.83	20	.275	.343	.400

Placido Polanco

Bats: R Throws: R Pos: 2B-109; 3B-13; PH-8   Ht: 5'10" Wt: 168 Born: 10/10/1975 Age: 29

Year Team	Lg	G	AB	H	2B	3B	HR	(Hm	Rd)	TB	R	RBI	RC	TBB	IBB	SO	HBP	SH	SF	SB	CS	SB%	GDP	Avg	OBP	Slg
2004 Reading*	AA	1	3	2	0	0	0	(-	-)	2	0	0	1	0	0	0	0	0	0	0	0	-	0	.667	.667	.667
2004 Scrtn/WlksBr*	AAA	1	3	0	0	0	0	(-	-)	0	1	0	0	1	0	0	0	0	0	0	0	-	0	.000	.250	.000
1998 St Louis	NL	45	114	29	3	2	1	(1	0)	39	10	11	12	5	0	9	1	2	0	2	0	1.00	1	.254	.292	.342
1999 St Louis	NL	88	220	61	9	3	1	(0	1)	79	24	19	23	15	1	24	0	3	2	1	3	.25	7	.277	.321	.359
2000 St Louis	NL	118	323	102	12	3	5	(2	3)	135	50	39	44	16	0	26	1	7	3	4	4	.50	8	.316	.347	.418
2001 St Louis	NL	144	564	173	26	4	3	(1	2)	216	87	38	70	25	0	43	6	14	1	12	3	.80	22	.307	.342	.383
2002 StL-Phi	NL	147	548	158	32	2	9	(8	1)	221	75	49	64	26	1	41	8	13	0	5	3	.63	15	.288	.330	.403
2003 Philadelphia	NL	122	492	142	30	3	14	(7	7)	220	87	63	74	42	1	38	8	8	4	14	2	.88	16	.289	.352	.447
2004 Philadelphia	NL	126	503	150	21	0	17	(10	7)	222	74	55	71	27	0	39	12	7	6	7	4	.64	13	.298	.345	.441
2002 St Louis	NL	94	342	97	19	1	5	(5	0)	133	47	27	38	12	1	27	4	9	0	3	1	.75	12	.284	.316	.389
2002 Philadelphia	NL	53	206	61	13	1	4	(3	1)	88	28	22	26	14	0	14	4	4	0	2	2	.50	3	.296	.353	.427
7 ML YEARS		790	2764	815	133	17	50	(29	21)	1132	407	274	358	156	3	220	36	54	16	45	19	.70	82	.295	.339	.410

Cliff Politte

Pitches: R Bats: R Pos: RP-54   Ht: 5'11" Wt: 185 Born: 2/27/1974 Age: 31

Year Team	Lg	G	GS	CG	GF	IP	BFP	H	R	ER	HR	SH	SF	HB	TBB	IBB	SO	WP	Bk	W	L	Pct	ShO	Sv-Op	Hld	ERC	ERA
1998 St Louis	NL	8	8	0	0	37.0	172	45	32	26	6	3	1	1	18	0	22	2	1	2	3	.400	0	0-0	0	6.28	6.32
1999 Philadelphia	NL	13	0	0	0	17.2	85	19	14	14	2	1	0	0	15	0	15	2	0	1	0	1.000	0	0-0	1	6.47	7.13
2000 Philadelphia	NL	12	8	0	1	59.0	251	55	24	24	8	1	1	0	27	1	50	3	0	4	3	.571	0	0-0	0	4.20	3.66
2001 Philadelphia	NL	23	0	0	7	26.0	109	24	8	7	2	1	3	1	8	3	23	1	0	2	3	.400	0	0-0	1	3.11	2.42
2002 Phi-Tor		68	0	0	20	73.2	304	57	33	30	5	3	1	2	28	2	72	2	0	3	3	.500	0	1-4	25	2.64	3.67
2003 Toronto	AL	54	0	0	30	49.1	216	52	32	31	11	1	3	1	17	4	40	1	0	1	5	.167	0	12-18	8	4.93	5.66
2004 Chicago	AL	54	0	0	9	51.1	225	52	26	25	6	0	2	2	22	5	48	2	0	0	3	.000	0	1-1	19	4.38	4.38
2002 Philadelphia	NL	13	0	0	7	16.1	77	19	10	7	0	1	0	1	9	1	15	1	0	2	0	1.000	0	0-1	0	4.89	3.86
2002 Toronto	AL	55	0	0	13	57.1	227	38	23	23	5	2	1	1	19	1	57	1	0	1	3	.250	0	1-3	25	2.06	3.61
7 ML YEARS		232	16	0	67	314.0	1362	304	169	157	40	10	11	7	135	15	270	13	1	13	20	.394	0	14-23	54	4.21	4.50

Simon Pond

Bats: L Throws: R Pos: LF-6; DH-6; RF-3; PH-1   Ht: 6'1" Wt: 205 Born: 10/27/1976 Age: 28

Year Team	Lg	G	AB	H	2B	3B	HR	(Hm	Rd)	TB	R	RBI	RC	TBB	IBB	SO	HBP	SH	SF	SB	CS	SB%	GDP	Avg	OBP	Slg
1994 Expos	R	40	147	38	7	0	0	(-	-)	45	18	15	15	16	1	25	1	0	3	1	1	.50	4	.259	.329	.306
1995 Albany	R	23	80	17	5	0	0	(-	-)	22	4	7	4	4	0	25	1	0	0	1	0	1.00	3	.213	.259	.275
1995 Expos	R	45	133	20	6	1	0	(-	-)	28	13	12	6	22	0	34	1	0	0	2	3	.40	3	.150	.276	.211
1996 Vermont	A-	69	253	76	16	1	3	(-	-)	103	37	40	38	26	2	26	3	1	3	9	3	.75	7	.300	.368	.407
1997 Cape Fear	A	118	444	120	11	0	3	(-	-)	140	48	47	43	37	1	46	2	1	4	12	8	.60	22	.270	.326	.315
1998 Jupiter	A+	105	344	82	15	1	1	(-	-)	102	40	32	29	24	2	58	6	2	4	1	4	.20	7	.238	.296	.297
1998 Harrisburg	AA	2	3	0	0	0	0	(-	-)	0	0	0	0	0	0	1	0	0	0	0	0	-	0	.000	.250	.000
1999 Jupiter	A+	127	434	111	25	1	10	(-	-)	168	47	77	57	48	3	83	14	1	11	4	8	.33	10	.256	.341	.387
2000 Jupiter	A+	19	63	13	1	0	3	(-	-)	23	7	8	8	9	0	13	1	0	0	1	0	1.00	0	.206	.315	.365
2000 Kinston	A+	64	237	76	18	0	6	(-	-)	112	40	37	41	22	1	49	3	0	2	14	3	.82	9	.321	.383	.473
2001 Kinston	A+	25	97	33	8	1	4	(-	-)	55	13	24	17	10	0	12	1	0	2	1	1	.50	0	.340	.400	.567
2001 Akron	AA	114	388	104	29	3	11	(-	-)	172	46	46	51	30	2	70	2	2	5	2	3	.40	9	.268	.320	.443
2002 Dunedin	A+	103	401	114	25	7	13	(-	-)	192	58	88	65	46	11	73	3	1	6	2	3	.40	9	.284	.357	.479
2003 New Haven	AA	61	228	77	11	1	7	(-	-)	117	44	49	50	39	6	33	4	0	2	1	1	.50	6	.338	.440	.513
2003 Syracuse	AAA	63	248	76	21	1	5	(-	-)	114	33	36	37	16	1	42	2	0	0	1	1	.50	5	.306	.353	.460
2004 Syracuse	AAA	78	302	84	24	1	7	(-	-)	131	36	35	40	19	1	72	3	0	2	1	0	1.00	7	.278	.325	.434
2004 Toronto	AL	16	49	8	2	0	1	(0	1)	13	4	6	2	5	0	12	1	0	1	0	0	-	3	.163	.250	.265

Sidney Ponson

Pitches: R Bats: R Pos: SP-33　　　　　　　　　　　　　　**Ht: 6'1" Wt: 225 Born: 11/2/1976 Age: 28**

Year Team	Lg	G	GS	CG	GF	IP	BFP	H	R	ER	HR	SH	SF	HB	TBB	IBB	SO	WP	Bk	W	L	Pct	ShO	Sv-Op	Hld	ERC	ERA
1998 Baltimore	AL	31	20	0	5	135.0	588	157	82	79	19	3	4	3	42	2	85	4	1	8	9	.471	0	1-2	0	5.07	5.27
1999 Baltimore	AL	32	32	6	0	210.0	897	227	118	110	35	4	7	1	80	2	112	4	0	12	12	.500	0	0-0	0	5.08	4.71
2000 Baltimore	AL	32	32	6	0	222.0	953	223	125	119	30	3	3	1	83	0	152	5	0	9	13	.409	1	0-0	0	4.26	4.82
2001 Baltimore	AL	23	23	3	0	138.1	605	161	83	76	21	3	2	6	37	0	84	2	0	5	10	.333	1	0-0	0	5.04	4.94
2002 Baltimore	AL	28	28	3	0	176.0	736	172	84	80	26	2	3	2	63	1	120	3	0	7	9	.438	0	0-0	0	4.24	4.09
2003 Bal-SF		31	31	4	0	216.0	898	211	94	90	16	6	5	5	61	5	134	9	0	17	12	.586	0	0-0	0	3.41	3.75
2004 Baltimore	AL	33	33	5	0	215.2	954	265	136	127	23	6	3	8	69	3	115	8	2	11	15	.423	2	0-0	0	5.33	5.30
2003 Baltimore	AL	21	21	4	0	148.0	622	147	65	62	10	2	3	4	43	2	100	6	0	14	6	.700	0	0-0	0	3.50	3.77
2003 San Francisco	NL	10	10	0	0	68.0	276	64	29	28	6	4	2	1	18	3	34	3	0	3	6	.333	0	0-0	0	3.23	3.71
7 ML YEARS		210	199	27	5	1313.0	5631	1416	722	681	170	27	27	26	435	13	802	35	3	69	80	.463	4	1-2	0	4.58	4.67

Colin Porter

Bats: L Throws: L Pos: PH-12; RF-8; LF-6; CF-2　　　　　　　**Ht: 6'2" Wt: 210 Born: 11/23/1975 Age: 29**

Year Team	Lg	G	AB	H	2B	3B	HR	(Hm	Rd)	TB	R	RBI	RC	TBB	IBB	SO	HBP	SH	SF	SB	CS	SB%	GDP	Avg	OBP	Slg
1998 Auburn	A-	67	240	68	18	4	4	(-	-)	106	40	30	34	19	0	61	5	2	1	14	11	.56	3	.283	.347	.442
1999 Michigan	A	127	453	132	28	9	18	(-	-)	232	91	68	83	53	2	123	7	3	8	23	13	.64	4	.291	.369	.512
2000 Round Rock	AA	124	435	119	25	5	14	(-	-)	196	76	57	70	56	4	130	6	0	1	17	9	.65	6	.274	.363	.451
2001 Round Rock	AA	25	100	32	5	5	2	(-	-)	53	14	12	17	5	2	25	1	0	0	1	3	.25	0	.320	.358	.530
2001 New Orleans	AAA	101	312	74	14	1	7	(-	-)	111	48	33	36	34	2	105	3	1	4	11	6	.65	2	.237	.314	.356
2002 New Orleans	AAA	134	461	122	30	5	6	(-	-)	180	59	38	61	46	8	127	0	2	1	28	7	.80	5	.265	.331	.390
2003 New Orleans	AAA	102	356	114	23	6	11	(-	-)	182	52	50	64	22	3	80	3	2	4	22	6	.79	3	.320	.361	.511
2004 Memphis	AAA	101	330	86	20	2	10	(-	-)	140	46	34	42	25	5	75	2	1	1	13	5	.72	5	.261	.316	.424
2003 Houston	NL	24	32	6	0	0	0	(0	0)	6	5	0	0	1	0	17	0	0	0	1	0	1.00	1	.188	.212	.188
2004 St Louis	NL	23	35	11	1	0	1	(0	1)	15	3	2	3	0	0	13	0	0	0	0	0	-	2	.314	.314	.429
2 ML YEARS		47	67	17	1	0	1	(0	1)	21	8	2	3	1	0	30	0	0	0	1	0	1.00	3	.254	.265	.313

Jorge Posada

Bats: B Throws: R Pos: C-134; PH-11　　　　　　　　　　　**Ht: 6'2" Wt: 205 Born: 8/17/1971 Age: 33**

Year Team	Lg	G	AB	H	2B	3B	HR	(Hm	Rd)	TB	R	RBI	RC	TBB	IBB	SO	HBP	SH	SF	SB	CS	SB%	GDP	Avg	OBP	Slg
1995 New York	AL	1	0	0	0	0	0	(0	0)	0	0	0	0	0	0	0	0	0	0	0	0	-	0			
1996 New York	AL	8	14	1	0	0	0	(0	0)	1	1	0	0	1	0	6	0	0	0	0	0	-	1	.071	.133	.071
1997 New York	AL	60	188	47	12	0	6	(2	4)	77	29	25	29	30	2	33	3	1	2	1	2	.33	2	.250	.359	.410
1998 New York	AL	111	358	96	23	0	17	(6	11)	170	56	63	56	47	7	92	0	0	4	0	1	.00	14	.268	.350	.475
1999 New York	AL	112	379	93	19	2	12	(4	8)	152	50	57	52	53	2	91	3	0	2	1	0	1.00	9	.245	.341	.401
2000 New York	AL	151	505	145	35	1	28	(18	10)	266	92	86	110	107	10	151	8	0	4	2	2	.50	11	.287	.417	.527
2001 New York	AL	138	484	134	28	1	22	(14	8)	230	59	95	80	62	10	132	6	0	5	2	6	.25	10	.277	.363	.475
2002 New York	AL	143	511	137	40	1	20	(12	8)	239	79	99	91	81	9	143	3	0	3	1	0	1.00	23	.268	.370	.468
2003 New York	AL	142	481	135	24	0	30	(15	15)	249	83	101	98	93	6	110	10	0	4	2	4	.33	13	.281	.405	.518
2004 New York	AL	137	449	122	31	0	21	(11	10)	216	72	81	78	88	5	92	9	0	1	1	3	.25	24	.272	.400	.481
10 ML YEARS		1003	3369	910	212	5	156	(82	74)	1600	521	607	594	562	51	850	42	1	25	10	18	.36	107	.270	.379	.475

Lou Pote

Pitches: R Bats: R Pos: RP-2　　　　　　　　　　　　　　**Ht: 6'3" Wt: 208 Born: 8/21/1971 Age: 33**

Year Team	Lg	G	GS	CG	GF	IP	BFP	H	R	ER	HR	SH	SF	HB	TBB	IBB	SO	WP	Bk	W	L	Pct	ShO	Sv-Op	Hld	ERC	ERA
2004 Portland*	AAA	4	0	0	3	5.0	23	5	4	4	1	0	0	0	3	0	6	2	0	1	0	1.000	0	1--	-	5.52	7.20
2004 Sacramento*	AAA	19	0	0	7	26.2	114	23	10	10	1	0	0	0	12	1	20	3	0	1	2	.333	0	2--	-	2.99	3.38
1999 Anaheim	AL	20	0	0	10	29.1	118	23	9	7	1	1	0	0	12	1	20	1	0	1	1	.500	0	3-3	3	2.56	2.15
2000 Anaheim	AL	32	1	0	12	50.1	214	52	23	19	4	1	1	0	17	1	44	3	0	1	1	.500	0	1-1	2	3.87	3.40
2001 Anaheim	AL	44	1	0	15	86.2	380	88	41	40	11	1	3	3	32	5	66	3	0	2	0	1.000	0	2-3	0	4.21	4.15
2002 Anaheim	AL	31	0	0	13	50.1	206	33	20	18	7	2	5	3	26	2	32	3	0	0	2	.000	0	0-1	1	3.16	3.22
2004 Cleveland	AL	2	0	0	1	3.0	13	3	3	3	0	0	0	0	1	0	5	0	0	0	0	-	0	0-0	0	3.05	9.00
5 ML YEARS		129	2	0	51	219.2	931	199	96	87	23	5	9	6	88	9	167	10	0	4	4	.500	0	6-8	6	3.64	3.56

Brian Powell

Pitches: R Bats: R Pos: RP-15; SP-2　　　　　　　　　　**Ht: 6'2" Wt: 205 Born: 10/10/1973 Age: 31**

Year Team	Lg	G	GS	CG	GF	IP	BFP	H	R	ER	HR	SH	SF	HB	TBB	IBB	SO	WP	Bk	W	L	Pct	ShO	Sv-Op	Hld	ERC	ERA
2004 Scrtn/WlksBr*	AAA	8	8	2	0	44.1	165	27	11	8	2	2	0	0	6	0	29	0	0	3	1	.750	1	0--	-	1.17	1.62
1998 Detroit	AL	18	16	0	1	83.2	383	101	67	59	17	1	1	2	36	2	46	3	0	3	8	.273	0	0-0	0	6.25	6.35
2000 Houston	NL	9	5	0	1	31.1	140	34	21	20	8	2	2	1	13	0	14	0	0	2	1	.667	0	0-0	0	5.88	5.74
2001 Houston	NL	1	1	0	0	3.0	17	5	6	6	1	0	0	0	3	0	3	0	0	0	1	.000	0	0-0	0	13.15	18.00
2002 Detroit	AL	13	9	0	1	57.2	254	64	34	31	11	0	2	1	21	0	30	2	0	1	5	.167	0	0-0	0	5.39	4.84
2003 San Francisco	NL	1	1	0	0	4.2	22	8	7	7	3	0	0	1	1	0	3	0	0	0	1	.000	0	0-0	0	12.71	13.50
2004 Philadelphia	NL	17	2	0	9	39.1	166	39	23	22	5	2	5	1	16	4	24	3	0	1	2	.333	0	0-0	0	4.31	5.03
6 ML YEARS		59	34	0	12	219.2	982	251	158	145	45	5	10	5	90	6	120	8	0	7	18	.280	0	0-0	0	5.79	5.94

Jay Powell

Pitches: R **Bats:** R **Pos:** RP-23 **Ht:** 6'4" **Wt:** 225 **Born:** 1/9/1972 **Age:** 33

Year Team	Lg	G	GS	CG	GF	IP	BFP	H	R	ER	HR	SH	SF	HB	TBB	IBB	SO	WP	Bk	W	L	Pct	ShO	Sv-Op	Hld	ERC	ERA
1995 Florida	NL	9	0	0	1	8.1	38	7	2	1	0	1	0	2	6	1	4	0	0	0	0		0	0-0	2	4.44	1.08
1996 Florida	NL	67	0	0	16	71.1	321	71	41	36	5	2	1	4	36	1	52	3	0	4	3	.571	0	2-5	10	4.39	4.54
1997 Florida	NL	74	0	0	23	79.2	337	71	35	29	3	6	4	4	30	3	65	3	0	7	2	.778	0	2-4	24	3.10	3.28
1998 Fla-Hou	NL	62	0	0	35	70.1	302	58	28	26	6	3	1	3	37	9	62	1	0	7	7	.500	0	7-11	3	3.46	3.33
1999 Houston	NL	67	0	0	26	75.0	341	82	38	36	3	5	2	3	40	4	77	5	0	5	4	.556	0	4-7	16	4.75	4.32
2000 Houston	NL	29	0	0	10	27.0	127	29	18	17	1	1	0	0	19	1	16	0	0	1	1	.500	0	0-0	5	5.10	5.67
2001 Hou-Col	NL	74	0	0	20	75.0	327	75	36	27	9	5	1	2	31	3	54	0	1	5	3	.625	0	7-13	8	4.30	3.24
2002 Texas	AL	51	0	0	5	49.2	224	50	28	19	5	1	0	1	24	4	35	2	0	3	2	.600	0	0-4	12	4.28	3.44
2003 Texas	AL	51	0	0	20	58.2	279	75	58	51	7	1	6	2	34	3	40	6	0	3	0	1.000	0	0-0	2	6.72	7.82
2004 Texas	AL	23	0	0	4	24.0	103	24	11	9	3	1	1	0	11	1	17	0	0	1	1	.500	0	0-0	4	4.50	3.38
1998 Florida	NL	33	0	0	26	36.1	165	36	19	17	5	3	1	2	22	6	24	1	0	4	4	.500	0	3-6	0	5.07	4.21
1998 Houston	NL	29	0	0	9	34.0	137	22	9	9	1	0	0	1	15	3	38	0	0	3	3	.500	0	4-5	3	1.96	2.38
2001 Houston	NL	35	0	0	5	36.1	170	41	18	15	4	1	1	0	19	0	28	0	1	2	2	.500	0	0-5	5	5.23	3.72
2001 Colorado	NL	39	0	0	15	38.2	157	34	18	12	5	4	0	2	12	3	26	0	0	3	1	.750	0	7-8	3	3.45	2.79
10 ML YEARS		507	0	0	160	539.0	2399	542	295	251	42	26	16	21	268	30	422	20	1	36	23	.610	0	22-44	86	4.37	4.19

Andy Pratt

Pitches: L **Bats:** L **Pos:** RP-4 **Ht:** 5'11" **Wt:** 160 **Born:** 8/27/1979 **Age:** 25

Year Team	Lg	G	GS	CG	GF	IP	BFP	H	R	ER	HR	SH	SF	HB	TBB	IBB	SO	WP	Bk	W	L	Pct	ShO	Sv-Op	Hld	ERC	ERA
1998 Rangers	R	12	8	0	1	56.0	225	49	25	24	4	1	3	1	14	0	49	0	1	4	3	.571	0	0- -	-	2.77	3.86
1999 Savannah	A	13	13	1	0	71.2	299	66	30	23	4	4	2	4	16	0	100	4	0	4	4	.500	1	0- -	-	2.86	2.89
2000 Charlotte	A+	16	16	2	0	92.2	365	68	37	28	8	1	2	1	26	0	95	1	2	7	4	.636	1	0- -	-	2.24	2.72
2000 Tulsa	AA	11	11	0	0	52.1	255	66	48	42	7	0	2	2	33	0	42	5	1	1	6	.143	0	0- -	-	6.96	7.22
2001 Tulsa	AA	27	26	3	0	168.0	730	175	99	86	18	8	5	6	57	0	132	9	1	8	10	.444	1	0- -	-	4.24	4.61
2002 Greenville	AA	20	18	1	0	93.0	404	92	54	44	5	4	3	2	44	0	67	6	0	4	9	.308	1	0- -	-	4.09	4.26
2002 Richmond	AAA	6	6	1	0	40.2	163	35	15	14	2	2	1	0	9	0	36	3	0	4	2	.667	1	0- -	-	2.37	3.10
2003 Richmond	AAA	28	27	1	0	156.0	685	146	77	59	10	5	8	11	77	0	161	14	0	7	10	.412	0	0- -	-	4.11	3.40
2004 Huntsville	AA	1	1	0	0	5.0	18	5	1	1	1	0	0	0	0	0	6	0	0	1	0	1.000	0	0- -	-	3.45	1.80
2004 Cubs	R	4	3	0	0	8.0	34	5	6	6	0	0	0	0	4	0	10	0	0	1	0	1.000	0	0- -	-	1.77	6.75
2004 Lansing	A	5	1	0	0	9.1	47	13	10	9	2	3	2	0	4	0	6	1	0	0	1	.000	0	0- -	-	6.99	8.68
2004 W Tennesse	AA	6	5	0	0	21.1	107	24	27	22	6	1	4	0	21	0	26	5	0	0	5	.000	0	0- -	-	8.88	9.28
2004 Iowa	AAA	4	4	0	0	9.0	56	14	19	19	2	3	3	1	15	0	8	3	0	0	4	.000	0	0- -	-	15.23	19.00
2002 Atlanta	NL	1	0	0	0	1.1	9	1	1	1	0	0	0	0	4	0	1	0	0	0	0	-	0	0-0	0	12.03	6.75
2004 Chicago	NL	4	0	0	1	1.2	13	0	4	4	0	0	0	1	7	1	1	0	0	0	1	.000	0	0-0	0	12.47	21.60
2 ML YEARS		5	0	0	1	3.0	22	1	5	5	0	0	0	1	11	1	2	0	0	0	1	.000	0	0-0	0	12.34	15.00

Todd Pratt

Bats: R **Throws:** R **Pos:** C-43; PH-2 **Ht:** 6'3" **Wt:** 230 **Born:** 2/9/1967 **Age:** 38

Year Team	Lg	G	AB	H	2B	3B	HR	(Hm	Rd)	TB	R	RBI	RC	TBB	IBB	SO	HBP	SH	SF	SB	CS	SB%	GDP	Avg	OBP	Slg
1992 Philadelphia	NL	16	46	13	1	0	2	(2	0)	20	6	10	6	4	0	12	0	0	0	0	0	-	2	.283	.340	.435
1993 Philadelphia	NL	33	87	25	6	0	5	(4	1)	46	8	13	15	5	0	19	1	1	1	0	0	-	2	.287	.330	.529
1994 Philadelphia	NL	28	102	20	6	1	2	(1	1)	34	10	9	9	12	0	29	0	0	0	0	1	.00	3	.196	.281	.333
1995 Chicago	NL	25	60	8	2	0	0	(0	0)	10	3	4	1	6	1	21	0	0	1	0	0	-	1	.133	.209	.167
1997 New York	NL	39	106	30	6	0	2	(1	1)	42	12	19	16	13	0	32	2	0	0	0	1	.00	1	.283	.372	.396
1998 New York	NL	41	69	19	9	1	2	(1	1)	36	9	18	11	2	0	20	0	0	0	0	0	-	0	.275	.296	.522
1999 New York	NL	71	140	41	4	0	3	(1	2)	54	18	21	22	15	0	32	3	0	2	2	0	1.00	3	.293	.369	.386
2000 New York	NL	80	160	44	6	0	8	(2	6)	74	33	25	28	22	1	31	5	2	1	0	0	-	5	.275	.378	.463
2001 NYM-Phi	NL	80	173	32	8	0	4	(0	4)	52	18	11	18	34	3	61	3	1	1	1	0	1.00	6	.185	.327	.301
2002 Philadelphia	NL	39	106	33	8	0	3	(2	1)	53	14	16	21	24	6	28	4	0	2	2	0	1.00	3	.311	.449	.500
2003 Philadelphia	NL	43	125	34	10	1	4	(3	1)	58	16	20	25	22	0	38	6	1	1	0	0	-	3	.272	.400	.464
2004 Philadelphia	NL	45	128	33	5	0	3	(2	1)	47	16	16	18	10	0	38	1	1	1	0	0	-	5	.258	.351	.367
2001 New York	NL	45	80	13	5	0	2	(0	2)	24	6	4	7	15	1	36	2	0	1	1	0	1.00	4	.163	.306	.300
2001 Philadelphia	NL	35	93	19	3	0	2	(0	2)	28	12	7	11	19	2	25	1	1	0	0	0	-	2	.204	.345	.301
12 ML YEARS		540	1302	332	74	3	38	(19	19)	526	163	182	190	177	11	361	25	6	11	5	2	.71	32	.255	.352	.404

Curtis Pride

Bats: L **Throws:** R **Pos:** LF-15; PH-12; RF-7; PR-4; CF-2; DH-1 **Ht:** 6'0" **Wt:** 210 **Born:** 12/17/1968 **Age:** 36

Year Team	Lg	G	AB	H	2B	3B	HR	(Hm	Rd)	TB	R	RBI	RC	TBB	IBB	SO	HBP	SH	SF	SB	CS	SB%	GDP	Avg	OBP	Slg
2004 Angels*	R	4	14	3	1	0	0	(-	-)	4	1	3	1	1	1	6	0	0	1	1	0	1.00	0	.214	.250	.286
2004 Salt Lake*	AAA	19	65	28	8	1	2	(-	-)	44	13	10	18	4	0	12	1	1	1	2	0	1.00	0	.431	.465	.677
1993 Montreal	NL	10	9	4	1	1	1	(0	0)	10	3	5	5	0	0	3	0	0	1	1	0	1.00	0	.444	.444	1.111
1995 Montreal	NL	48	63	11	1	0	0	(0	0)	12	10	2	3	5	0	16	0	1	0	3	2	.60	2	.175	.235	.190
1996 Detroit	AL	95	267	80	17	5	10	(5	5)	137	52	31	52	31	4	63	0	3	0	11	6	.65	2	.300	.372	.513
1997 Det-Bos	AL	81	164	35	4	4	3	(3	0)	56	22	20	19	24	1	46	1	2	1	6	4	.60	4	.213	.316	.341
1998 Atlanta	NL	70	107	27	6	1	3	(1	2)	44	19	9	15	9	0	29	3	1	1	4	0	1.00	2	.252	.325	.411
2000 Boston	AL	9	20	5	1	0	0	(0	0)	6	4	0	2	1	0	7	0	0	0	0	0	-	0	.250	.286	.300
2001 Montreal	NL	36	76	19	3	1	1	(0	1)	27	8	9	9	9	0	22	2	0	0	3	2	.60	4	.250	.345	.355
2003 New York	AL	4	12	1	0	0	0	(1	0)	4	1	1	0	0	0	2	0	0	0	0	0	-	0	.083	.083	.333
2004 Anaheim	AL	35	40	10	3	0	0	(0	0)	13	5	3	3	0	0	11	1	1	0	1	0	1.00	1	.250	.268	.325
1997 Detroit	AL	79	162	34	4	4	2	(2	0)	52	21	19	17	24	1	45	1	2	1	6	4	.60	4	.210	.314	.321
1997 Boston	AL	2	2	1	0	0	0	(1	0)	4	1	1	2	0	0	1	0	0	0	0	0	-	0	.500	.500	2.000
9 ML YEARS		388	758	192	36	12	19	(10	8)	309	124	80	108	79	2	199	7	8	2	29	14	.67	16	.253	.329	.408

Alex Prieto

Bats: R **Throws:** R **Pos:** 2B-8; 3B-5; SS-3; PR-2; DH-1; PH-1   **Ht:** 5'11" **Wt:** 200 **Born:** 6/19/1976 **Age:** 29

							BATTING												BASERUNNING					AVERAGES		
Year Team	Lg	G	AB	H	2B	3B	HR	(Hm	Rd)	TB	R	RBI	RC	TBB	IBB	SO	HBP	SH	SF	SB	CS	SB%	GDP	Avg	OBP	Slg
1993 Royals	R	43	114	28	3	0	0	(-	-)	31	14	6	10	9	1	13	0	4	0	4	2	.67	1	.246	.301	.272
1994 Royals	R	18	60	18	5	0	2	(-	-)	29	15	17	10	2	1	5	4	1	4	1	0	1.00	0	.300	.343	.483
1995 Springfield	A	124	431	108	9	3	2	(-	-)	129	61	44	44	40	1	69	6	12	2	11	7	.61	10	.251	.322	.299
1996 Wilmington	A+	119	447	127	19	6	1	(-	-)	161	65	40	54	31	0	66	3	8	5	26	15	.63	7	.284	.331	.360
1997 Wilmington	A+	129	437	94	13	3	3	(-	-)	122	52	38	36	41	1	59	2	11	6	20	8	.71	6	.215	.282	.279
1998 Wichita	AA	113	384	101	18	7	2	(-	-)	139	61	35	42	31	0	54	2	8	0	4	6	.40	13	.263	.321	.362
1999 Wichita	AA	114	360	106	23	4	6	(-	-)	155	56	41	54	35	1	47	1	13	3	12	6	.67	10	.294	.356	.431
2000 Omaha	AAA	118	384	101	19	0	7	(-	-)	141	54	37	43	26	0	40	6	8	2	14	6	.70	12	.263	.318	.367
2001 Omaha	AAA	105	376	106	21	3	8	(-	-)	157	45	44	53	36	0	59	1	4	3	9	2	.82	12	.282	.344	.418
2002 Edmonton	AAA	80	276	73	14	1	7	(-	-)	110	38	29	33	19	1	47	2	0	1	4	4	.50	5	.264	.315	.399
2003 Rochester	AAA	69	234	62	9	1	5	(-	-)	88	27	21	25	12	1	49	0	4	2	6	3	.67	6	.265	.298	.376
2004 Rochester	AAA	84	289	72	13	0	6	(-	-)	103	39	22	33	29	0	52	1	4	4	2	3	.40	5	.249	.316	.356
2003 Minnesota	AL	8	11	1	0	0	0	(0	0)	1	1	0	0	0	0	4	0	0	0	0	0	-	0	.091	.091	.091
2004 Minnesota	AL	16	32	8	1	0	1	(0	1)	12	4	4	2	3	0	9	0	0	1	0	1	.00	1	.250	.306	.375
2 ML YEARS		24	43	9	1	0	1	(0	1)	13	5	4	2	3	0	13	0	0	1	0	1	.00	1	.209	.255	.302

Bret Prinz

Pitches: R **Bats:** R **Pos:** RP-26   **Ht:** 6'3" **Wt:** 185 **Born:** 6/15/1977 **Age:** 28

		HOW MUCH HE PITCHED						WHAT HE GAVE UP												THE RESULTS							
Year Team	Lg	G	GS	CG	GF	IP	BFP	H	R	ER	HR	SH	SF	HB	TBB	IBB	SO	WP	Bk	W	L	Pct	ShO	Sv-Op	Hld	ERC	ERA
2004 Columbus*	AAA	29	0	0	18	30.2	127	27	12	12	3	0	0	2	9	0	33	0	0	3	1	.750	0	11- -		3.27	3.52
2001 Arizona	NL	46	0	0	26	41.0	174	33	13	12	4	3	1	1	19	1	27	1	1	4	1	.800	0	9-12	6	3.27	2.63
2002 Arizona	NL	20	0	0	5	13.1	71	23	14	14	1	2	1	1	10	1	10	3	0	0	2	.000	0	0-2	5	10.34	9.45
2003 Ari-NYY		3	0	0	2	3.0	20	7	4	4	1	0	0	0	4	2	3	0	0	0	0	-	0	0-0	0	18.22	12.00
2004 New York	AL	26	0	0	10	28.1	124	28	17	16	5	0	1	1	14	0	22	2	0	1	0	1.000	0	0-0	1	5.16	5.08
2003 Arizona	NL	1	0	0	0	1.0	5	1	0	0	0	0	0	0	1	1	1	0	0	0	0	-	0	0-0	0	3.46	0.00
2003 New York	AL	2	0	0	2	2.0	15	6	4	4	1	0	0	0	3	1	2	0	0	0	0	-	0	0-0	0	27.15	18.00
4 ML YEARS		95	0	0	43	85.2	389	91	48	46	11	5	3	3	47	4	62	6	1	5	3	.625	0	9-14	12	5.31	4.83

Mark Prior

Pitches: R **Bats:** R **Pos:** SP-21   **Ht:** 6'5" **Wt:** 225 **Born:** 9/7/1980 **Age:** 24

		HOW MUCH HE PITCHED						WHAT HE GAVE UP												THE RESULTS							
Year Team	Lg	G	GS	CG	GF	IP	BFP	H	R	ER	HR	SH	SF	HB	TBB	IBB	SO	WP	Bk	W	L	Pct	ShO	Sv-Op	Hld	ERC	ERA
2004 Lansing*	A	2	2	0	0	7.1	23	2	1	1	0	1	0	0	1	0	13	0	0	0	0	-	0	0- -		0.34	1.23
2004 Iowa*	AAA	1	1	0	0	5.1	19	3	2	2	2	0	0	0	1	0	10	0	0	1	0	1.000	0	0- -		2.57	3.38
2002 Chicago	NL	19	19	1	0	116.2	486	98	45	43	14	3	4	7	38	0	147	1	0	6	6	.500	0	0-0	0	3.27	3.32
2003 Chicago	NL	30	30	3	0	211.1	863	183	67	57	15	9	2	9	50	4	245	9	0	18	6	.750	1	0-0	0	2.69	2.43
2004 Chicago	NL	21	21	0	0	118.2	510	112	53	53	14	8	4	3	48	2	139	2	1	6	4	.600	0	0-0	0	3.97	4.02
3 ML YEARS		70	70	4	0	446.2	1859	393	165	153	43	20	10	19	136	6	531	12	1	30	16	.652	1	0-0	0	3.17	3.08

Scott Proctor

Pitches: R **Bats:** R **Pos:** RP-26   **Ht:** 6'1" **Wt:** 198 **Born:** 1/2/1977 **Age:** 28

		HOW MUCH HE PITCHED						WHAT HE GAVE UP												THE RESULTS							
Year Team	Lg	G	GS	CG	GF	IP	BFP	H	R	ER	HR	SH	SF	HB	TBB	IBB	SO	WP	Bk	W	L	Pct	ShO	Sv-Op	Hld	ERC	ERA
1998 Yakima	A-	3	1	0	2	5.0	26	9	8	6	1	1	1	0	1	0	4	1	2	0	1	.000	0	2- -	-	8.48	10.80
1999 Yakima	A-	16	6	0	5	50.0	235	57	45	40	4	1	4	5	26	0	41	7	1	4	2	.667	0	0- -	-	5.56	7.20
2000 Vero Beach	A+	35	5	0	15	89.0	413	93	65	51	13	2	4	6	54	1	70	6	1	3	7	.300	0	1- -	-	5.76	5.16
2001 Vero Beach	A+	15	15	0	0	90.2	366	73	30	25	8	2	2	9	30	1	79	3	0	6	4	.600	0	0- -	-	3.16	2.48
2001 Jacksonville	AA	10	9	0	0	49.2	215	39	26	23	6	3	2	2	31	1	48	2	0	4	3	.571	0	0- -	-	4.06	4.17
2002 Jacksonville	AA	26	25	0	0	133.1	592	111	63	52	10	6	5	7	85	1	131	9	1	7	9	.438	0	0- -	-	4.05	3.51
2003 Jacksonville	AA	17	0	0	12	27.0	108	20	6	3	0	2	3	0	7	3	24	1	1	2	2	.333	0	0- -	-	1.54	1.00
2003 Las Vegas	AAA	24	0	0	8	39.1	160	35	17	16	2	4	1	0	13	3	35	0	0	4	2	.667	0	1- -	-	2.84	3.66
2003 Columbus	AAA	10	0	0	1	19.0	71	13	3	3	2	1	0	1	3	0	26	0	0	2	0	1.000	0	0- -	-	1.90	1.42
2004 Columbus	AAA	35	0	0	15	44.0	187	37	15	14	4	1	0	1	18	2	42	3	0	2	3	.400	0	4- -	-	3.15	2.86
2004 New York	AL	26	0	0	12	25.0	118	29	18	15	5	0	2	0	14	0	21	1	1	2	1	.667	0	0-0	2	6.32	5.40

Brandon Puffer

Pitches: R **Bats:** R **Pos:** RP-14   **Ht:** 6'3" **Wt:** 190 **Born:** 10/5/1975 **Age:** 29

		HOW MUCH HE PITCHED						WHAT HE GAVE UP												THE RESULTS							
Year Team	Lg	G	GS	CG	GF	IP	BFP	H	R	ER	HR	SH	SF	HB	TBB	IBB	SO	WP	Bk	W	L	Pct	ShO	Sv-Op	Hld	ERC	ERA
2004 Portland*	AAA	22	0	0	5	32.1	140	32	15	12	1	0	0	2	10	2	19	0	0	1	1	.500	0	2- -	-	3.27	3.34
2004 Pawtucket*	AAA	24	0	0	21	30.1	134	31	11	11	1	0	0	1	11	3	21	4	0	3	2	.600	0	10- -	-	3.45	3.26
2002 Houston	NL	55	0	0	19	69.0	311	67	37	34	3	5	2	5	38	8	48	2	0	3	3	.500	0	0-0	2	4.13	4.43
2003 Houston	NL	13	0	0	4	21.0	100	24	13	12	2	2	0	1	16	3	10	1	0	0	0	-	0	0-1	1	6.35	5.14
2004 San Diego	NL	14	0	0	9	18.0	89	24	13	11	3	2	0	1	11	1	12	0	0	0	1	.000	0	0-0	0	7.59	5.50
3 ML YEARS		82	0	0	32	108.0	500	115	63	57	8	9	2	7	65	12	70	3	0	3	4	.429	0	0-1	3	5.10	4.75

Albert Pujols

Bats: R **Throws:** R **Pos:** 1B-150; DH-3; PH-1   **Ht:** 6'3" **Wt:** 210 **Born:** 1/16/1980 **Age:** 25

							BATTING												BASERUNNING					AVERAGES		
Year Team	Lg	G	AB	H	2B	3B	HR	(Hm	Rd)	TB	R	RBI	RC	TBB	IBB	SO	HBP	SH	SF	SB	CS	SB%	GDP	Avg	OBP	Slg
2001 St Louis	NL	161	590	194	47	4	37	(18	19)	360	112	130	132	69	6	93	9	1	7	1	3	.25	21	.329	.403	.610
2002 St Louis	NL	157	590	185	40	2	34	(14	20)	331	118	127	121	72	13	69	9	0	4	2	4	.33	20	.314	.394	.561

		BATTING																	BASERUNNING				AVERAGES		
Year Team	Lg	G	AB	H	2B	3B	HR	(Hm Rd)	TB	R	RBI	RC	TBB	IBB	SO	HBP	SH	SF	SB	CS	SB%	GDP	Avg	OBP	Slg
2003 St Louis	NL	157	591	212	51	1	43	(21 22)	394	137	124	160	79	12	65	10	0	5	5	1	.83	13	.359	.439	.667
2004 St Louis	NL	154	592	196	51	2	46	(18 28)	389	133	123	143	84	12	52	7	0	9	5	5	.50	21	.331	.415	.657
4 ML YEARS		629	2363	787	189	9	160	(71 89)	1474	500	504	556	304	43	279	35	1	25	13	13	.50	75	.333	.413	.624

Carlos Pulido

Pitches: L **Bats:** L **Pos:** RP-6   **Ht:** 6'0" **Wt:** 200 **Born:** 8/5/1971 **Age:** 33

		HOW MUCH HE PITCHED						WHAT HE GAVE UP										THE RESULTS						
Year Team	Lg	G	GS	CG	GF	IP	BFP	H	R	ER	HR	SH	SF	HB	TBB	IBB	SO	WP	Bk	W	L	Pct	ShO	Sv-Op	Hld	ERC	ERA
2004 Rochester*	AAA	5	5	0	0	17.2	90	29	24	23	7	0	5	0	7	0	12	1	0	1	3	.250	0	0- -	-	10.32	11.72
1994 Minnesota	AL	19	14	0	0	84.1	366	87	0	56	17	0	0	0	40	0	32	0	0	3	7	.300	0	0-0	0	5.41	5.98
2003 Minnesota	AL	7	1	0	1	15.2	65	15	9	7	0	1	2	0	3	0	6	1	0	0	1	.000	0	0-0	1	2.37	4.02
2004 Minnesota	AL	6	0	0	3	11.1	55	16	13	11	2	0	2	1	4	1	9	0	0	0	0	-	0	0-0	1	7.02	8.74
3 ML YEARS		32	15	0	4	111.1	486	118	22	74	19	1	4	1	47	1	47	1	0	3	8	.273	0	0-0	2	5.09	5.98

Nick Punto

Bats: B **Throws:** R **Pos:** 2B-19; SS-11; PR-6; PH-4; 3B-2; CF-2; DH-1   **Ht:** 5'9" **Wt:** 170 **Born:** 11/8/1977 **Age:** 27

		BATTING																	BASERUNNING				AVERAGES		
Year Team	Lg	G	AB	H	2B	3B	HR	(Hm Rd)	TB	R	RBI	RC	TBB	IBB	SO	HBP	SH	SF	SB	CS	SB%	GDP	Avg	OBP	Slg
2004 Quad City*	A	4	16	7	1	0	1	(- -)	11	4	6	4	2	1	2	0	0	0	1	0	1.00	0	.438	.500	.688
2001 Philadelphia	NL	4	5	2	0	0	0	(0 0)	2	0	0	1	0	0	0	0	0	0	0	0	-	0	.400	.400	.400
2002 Philadelphia	NL	9	6	1	0	0	0	(0 0)	1	0	0	0	0	0	3	0	1	0	0	0	-	0	.167	.167	.167
2003 Philadelphia	NL	64	92	20	2	0	1	(0 1)	25	14	4	7	7	1	22	0	0	0	2	1	.67	0	.217	.273	.272
2004 Minnesota	AL	38	91	23	0	0	2	(2 0)	29	17	12	15	12	0	19	0	0	0	6	0	1.00	2	.253	.340	.319
4 ML YEARS		115	194	46	2	0	3	(2 1)	57	31	16	23	19	1	44	0	1	0	8	1	.89	2	.237	.305	.294

J.J. Putz

Pitches: R **Bats:** R **Pos:** RP-54   **Ht:** 6'5" **Wt:** 220 **Born:** 2/22/1977 **Age:** 28

		HOW MUCH HE PITCHED						WHAT HE GAVE UP										THE RESULTS						
Year Team	Lg	G	GS	CG	GF	IP	BFP	H	R	ER	HR	SH	SF	HB	TBB	IBB	SO	WP	Bk	W	L	Pct	ShO	Sv-Op	Hld	ERC	ERA
1999 Everett	A-	10	0	0	3	22.1	99	23	13	12	2	1	4	2	11	1	17	0	1	0	0	-	0	2- -	-	4.91	4.84
2000 Wisconsin	A	26	25	3	0	142.2	611	130	71	50	4	6	7	9	63	2	105	8	0	12	6	.667	2	0- -	-	3.49	3.15
2001 San Antonio	AA	27	26	0	0	148.0	642	145	80	63	11	10	6	9	59	2	135	12	0	7	9	.438	0	0- -	-	4.00	3.83
2002 San Antonio	AA	15	15	1	0	84.0	354	84	41	34	7	0	3	5	28	0	60	5	0	3	10	.231	1	0- -	-	4.02	3.64
2002 Tacoma	AAA	9	9	0	0	54.0	225	51	23	23	4	1	1	4	21	0	39	8	0	2	4	.333	0	0- -	-	3.99	3.83
2003 Tacoma	AAA	41	0	0	22	86.0	352	69	30	24	4	7	1	3	34	0	60	3	0	0	3	.000	0	11- -	-	2.83	2.51
2004 Tacoma	AAA	7	0	0	5	8.1	39	10	5	4	2	0	0	0	3	0	13	0	0	0	0	-	0	3- -	-	5.82	4.32
2003 Seattle	AL	3	0	0	0	3.2	18	4	2	2	0	0	0	0	3	0	3	0	0	0	0	-	0	0-0	0	5.31	4.91
2004 Seattle	AL	54	0	0	30	63.0	275	66	35	33	10	3	2	5	24	4	47	1	0	0	3	.000	0	9-13	3	4.97	4.71
2 ML YEARS		57	0	0	30	66.2	293	70	37	35	10	3	2	5	27	4	50	1	0	0	3	.000	0	9-13	3	5.00	4.73

Chad Qualls

Pitches: R **Bats:** R **Pos:** RP-25   **Ht:** 6'5" **Wt:** 220 **Born:** 8/17/1978 **Age:** 26

		HOW MUCH HE PITCHED						WHAT HE GAVE UP										THE RESULTS						
Year Team	Lg	G	GS	CG	GF	IP	BFP	H	R	ER	HR	SH	SF	HB	TBB	IBB	SO	WP	Bk	W	L	Pct	ShO	Sv-Op	Hld	ERC	ERA
2001 Michigan	A	26	26	3	0	162.0	673	149	77	67	2	2	6	11	31	0	125	10	2	15	6	.714	2	0- -	-	2.51	3.72
2002 Round Rock	AA	29	29	0	0	163.0	722	174	92	79	3	3	6	9	67	3	142	3	4	6	13	.316	0	0- -	-	4.08	4.36
2003 Round Rock	AA	28	28	3	0	175.1	744	174	85	75	12	6	8	10	61	0	132	8	0	8	11	.421	2	0- -	-	3.89	3.85
2004 New Orleans	AAA	32	14	1	8	106.2	483	134	69	66	8	7	8	7	30	3	72	2	0	3	6	.333	0	1- -	-	5.06	5.57
2004 Houston	NL	25	0	0	4	33.0	141	34	13	13	3	0	1	4	8	1	24	0	0	4	0	1.000	0	1-2	9	4.02	3.55

Paul Quantrill

Pitches: R **Bats:** L **Pos:** RP-86   **Ht:** 6'1" **Wt:** 195 **Born:** 11/3/1968 **Age:** 36

		HOW MUCH HE PITCHED						WHAT HE GAVE UP										THE RESULTS						
Year Team	Lg	G	GS	CG	GF	IP	BFP	H	R	ER	HR	SH	SF	HB	TBB	IBB	SO	WP	Bk	W	L	Pct	ShO	Sv-Op	Hld	ERC	ERA
1992 Boston	AL	27	0	0	10	49.1	213	55	18	12	1	4	2	1	15	5	24	1	0	2	3	.400	0	1-5	3	3.70	2.19
1993 Boston	AL	49	14	1	8	138.0	594	151	73	60	13	4	2	2	44	14	66	0	1	6	12	.333	1	1-2	3	4.16	3.91
1994 Bos-Phi		35	1	0	9	53.0	236	64	31	29	7	5	3	5	15	4	28	0	2	3	3	.500	0	1-4	3	5.34	4.92
1995 Philadelphia	NL	33	29	0	1	179.1	784	212	102	93	20	9	6	6	44	3	103	0	3	11	12	.478	0	0-0	0	4.67	4.67
1996 Toronto	AL	38	20	0	7	134.1	609	172	90	81	27	5	7	2	51	3	86	1	1	5	14	.263	0	0-2	1	6.52	5.43
1997 Toronto	AL	77	0	0	29	88.0	373	103	25	19	5	5	3	1	17	3	56	1	0	6	7	.462	0	5-10	16	3.94	1.94
1998 Toronto	AL	82	0	0	32	80.0	345	88	26	23	5	7	4	3	22	6	59	1	0	4	9	.429	0	7-14	27	3.90	2.59
1999 Toronto	AL	41	0	0	13	48.2	212	53	19	18	5	1	2	4	17	1	28	0	0	3	2	.600	0	0-4	8	4.77	3.33
2000 Toronto	AL	68	0	0	24	83.2	367	100	45	42	7	1	3	2	25	1	47	1	0	2	5	.286	0	1-3	13	4.78	4.52
2001 Toronto	AL	80	0	0	20	83.0	341	86	29	28	6	7	2	6	12	7	58	0	0	11	2	.846	0	2-9	21	3.31	3.04
2002 Los Angeles	NL	86	0	0	22	76.2	330	80	27	23	1	1	1	3	25	7	53	0	0	5	4	.556	0	1-3	33	3.42	2.70
2003 Los Angeles	NL	89	0	0	21	77.1	291	61	18	15	2	4	0	3	15	2	44	0	0	2	5	.286	0	1-5	28	2.03	1.75
2004 New York	AL	86	0	0	17	95.1	424	124	54	50	5	3	4	4	20	9	37	0	0	7	3	.700	0	1-5	22	4.68	4.72
1994 Boston	AL	17	0	0	4	23.0	101	25	10	9	4	2	2	2	5	1	15	0	0	1	1	.500	0	0-2	1	4.53	3.52
1994 Philadelphia	NL	18	1	0	5	30.0	135	39	21	20	3	3	1	3	10	3	13	0	2	2	2	.500	0	1-2	1	5.97	6.00
13 ML YEARS		791	64	1	213	1186.2	5119	1349	557	493	104	56	39	42	322	65	689	5	7	66	76	.465	1	21-66	178	4.33	3.74

Robb Quinlan

Bats: R **Throws:** R **Pos:** 3B-33; 1B-13; LF-6; PH-5; DH-4; RF-3; PR-2   **Ht:** 6'1" **Wt:** 195 **Born:** 3/17/1977 **Age:** 28

Year Team	Lg	G	AB	H	2B	3B	HR	(Hm	Rd)	TB	R	RBI	RC	TBB	IBB	SO	HBP	SH	SF	SB	CS	SB%	GDP	Avg	OBP	Slg
1999 Boise	A-	73	295	95	20	1	9	(-	-)	144	51	77	56	35	2	52	4	0	1	5	3	.63	5	.322	.400	.488
2000 Lk Elsinore	A+	127	482	153	35	5	5	(-	-)	213	79	85	87	67	1	82	2	2	9	6	4	.60	7	.317	.396	.442
2001 Arkansas	AA	129	492	145	33	7	14	(-	-)	234	82	79	81	53	9	84	6	0	7	0	4	.00	12	.295	.366	.476
2002 Salt Lake	AAA	136	528	176	31	13	20	(-	-)	293	95	112	104	41	2	93	4	0	15	8	2	.80	16	.333	.376	.555
2003 Salt Lake	AAA	95	393	122	18	4	9	(-	-)	175	55	68	60	25	2	59	1	0	2	10	3	.77	9	.310	.352	.445
2004 Salt Lake	AAA	27	108	32	9	1	2	(-	-)	49	15	17	17	14	1	14	0	0	0	1	1	.50	3	.296	.377	.454
2003 Anaheim	AL	38	94	27	4	2	0	(0	0)	35	13	4	8	6	0	16	0	1	0	1	2	.33	3	.287	.330	.372
2004 Anaheim	AL	56	160	55	14	0	5	(3	2)	84	23	23	33	14	0	26	2	0	1	3	1	.75	1	.344	.401	.525
2 ML YEARS		94	254	82	18	2	5	(3	2)	119	36	27	41	20	0	42	2	1	1	4	3	.57	4	.323	.375	.469

Humberto Quintero

Bats: R **Throws:** R **Pos:** C-21; PH-2   **Ht:** 6'1" **Wt:** 190 **Born:** 8/8/1979 **Age:** 25

Year Team	Lg	G	AB	H	2B	3B	HR	(Hm	Rd)	TB	R	RBI	RC	TBB	IBB	SO	HBP	SH	SF	SB	CS	SB%	GDP	Avg	OBP	Slg
1999 Bristol	R+	48	155	43	5	2	0	(-	-)	52	30	15	18	9	0	19	6	3	0	11	1	.92	8	.277	.341	.335
2000 Burlington	A	75	248	59	12	2	0	(-	-)	75	23	24	19	15	1	31	3	4	2	10	6	.63	8	.238	.287	.302
2000 White Sox	R	15	56	22	2	2	0	(-	-)	28	13	8	10	0	0	3	2	0	0	1	0	1.00	2	.393	.414	.500
2001 Kannapolis	A-	60	197	53	7	1	1	(-	-)	65	32	20	21	8	1	20	7	8	0	7	3	.70	5	.269	.321	.330
2001 Birmingham	AA	5	19	4	0	0	0	(-	-)	4	0	2	1	0	0	2	1	0	0	0	0	-	0	.211	.250	.211
2001 Winstn-Salm	A+	43	154	37	6	0	0	(-	-)	43	15	12	11	5	0	19	2	2	3	9	3	.75	3	.240	.268	.279
2002 Winstn-Salm	A+	52	160	31	1	1	0	(-	-)	34	15	12	6	8	0	23	4	7	2	2	3	.40	4	.194	.247	.213
2002 Birmingham	AA	4	12	6	0	0	0	(-	-)	6	1	3	3	0	0	1	1	1	0	1	0	1.00	0	.500	.538	.500
2002 Charlotte	AAA	15	41	9	1	0	0	(-	-)	10	2	5	1	3	0	8	0	0	0	0	0	-	3	.220	.273	.244
2002 Mobile	AA	37	125	30	8	0	1	(-	-)	41	11	14	9	5	0	12	3	1	0	3	0	.00	3	.240	.286	.328
2003 Mobile	AA	110	386	115	26	0	3	(-	-)	150	37	52	47	19	5	41	9	4	3	0	0	-	17	.298	.343	.389
2004 Portland	AAA	68	259	82	25	0	5	(-	-)	122	36	30	39	8	0	18	5	1	1	0	0	-	7	.317	.348	.471
2003 San Diego	NL	12	23	5	0	0	0	(0	0)	5	1	2	1	1	1	6	0	0	0	0	0	-	0	.217	.250	.217
2004 San Diego	NL	23	72	18	3	0	2	(1	1)	27	7	10	6	5	0	16	0	0	1	0	2	.00	5	.250	.295	.375
2 ML YEARS		35	95	23	3	0	2	(1	1)	32	8	12	8	6	1	22	0	0	1	0	2	.00	5	.242	.284	.337

Guillermo Quiroz

Bats: R **Throws:** R **Pos:** C-15; DH-2; PR-1   **Ht:** 6'1" **Wt:** 202 **Born:** 11/29/1981 **Age:** 23

Year Team	Lg	G	AB	H	2B	3B	HR	(Hm	Rd)	TB	R	RBI	RC	TBB	IBB	SO	HBP	SH	SF	SB	CS	SB%	GDP	Avg	OBP	Slg
1999 Medicine Hat	R+	63	208	46	7	0	9	(-	-)	80	25	28	22	18	0	55	4	2	0	0	2	.00	4	.221	.296	.385
2000 Queens	A-	55	196	44	9	0	5	(-	-)	68	27	29	22	27	0	48	4	0	1	2	3	.33	4	.224	.329	.347
2000 Hagerstown	A	43	136	22	4	0	1	(-	-)	29	14	12	7	16	0	44	4	3	0	0	1	.00	3	.162	.269	.213
2001 Chrlstn - WV	A	82	261	52	12	0	7	(-	-)	85	25	25	25	29	0	67	6	7	0	5	1	.83	5	.199	.294	.326
2002 Dunedin	A+	111	411	107	28	1	12	(-	-)	173	50	68	52	35	2	91	9	2	3	1	0	1.00	18	.260	.330	.421
2002 Syracuse	AAA	13	45	10	4	0	1	(-	-)	17	7	6	4	3	0	14	0	1	0	0	0	-	1	.222	.271	.378
2003 New Haven	AA	108	369	104	27	0	20	(-	-)	191	63	79	67	45	1	83	12	1	7	0	0	-	13	.282	.372	.518
2004 Syracuse	AAA	76	255	58	19	1	8	(-	-)	103	32	32	29	28	1	54	3	0	2	0	0	-	8	.227	.309	.404
2004 Toronto	AL	17	52	11	2	0	0	(0	0)	13	2	6	4	2	0	8	2	0	1	1	0	1.00	1	.212	.263	.250

Ryan Raburn

Bats: R **Throws:** R **Pos:** 2B-11; PH-5   **Ht:** 6'0" **Wt:** 185 **Born:** 4/17/1981 **Age:** 24

Year Team	Lg	G	AB	H	2B	3B	HR	(Hm	Rd)	TB	R	RBI	RC	TBB	IBB	SO	HBP	SH	SF	SB	CS	SB%	GDP	Avg	OBP	Slg
2001 Tigers	R	19	58	9	2	0	1	(-	-)	14	4	5	4	9	1	19	3	0	0	2	1	.67	0	.155	.300	.241
2001 Oneonta	A-	44	171	62	17	8	8	(-	-)	119	25	42	40	17	1	42	0	0	1	1	3	.25	7	.363	.418	.696
2002 Tigers	R	8	30	9	3	1	1	(-	-)	17	4	5	5	3	0	7	0	0	0	0	0	-	2	.300	.364	.567
2002 W Michigan	A	40	150	33	10	1	6	(-	-)	63	27	28	18	16	1	46	4	0	3	0	2	.00	2	.220	.306	.420
2003 W Michigan	A	16	57	20	7	0	3	(-	-)	36	14	12	13	6	0	14	2	0	0	1	1	.50	0	.351	.431	.632
2003 Lakeland	A+	95	325	72	14	3	12	(-	-)	128	52	56	44	45	0	89	10	0	2	2	1	.67	6	.222	.332	.394
2004 Lakeland	A+	3	11	3	1	0	1	(-	-)	7	1	3	2	1	0	6	0	0	0	0	0	-	0	.273	.333	.636
2004 Erie	AA	98	366	110	29	4	16	(-	-)	195	66	63	72	47	1	96	7	1	1	3	0	1.00	9	.301	.390	.533
2004 Detroit	AL	12	29	4	1	0	0	(0	0)	5	4	1	1	2	0	15	0	0	0	1	0	1.00	0	.138	.194	.172

Brad Radke

Pitches: R **Bats:** R **Pos:** SP-34   **Ht:** 6'2" **Wt:** 188 **Born:** 10/27/1972 **Age:** 32

Year Team	Lg	G	GS	CG	GF	IP	BFP	H	R	ER	HR	SH	SF	HB	TBB	IBB	SO	WP	Bk	W	L	Pct	ShO	Sv-Op	Hld	ERC	ERA
1995 Minnesota	AL	29	28	2	0	181.0	772	195	112	107	32	2	9	4	47	0	75	4	0	11	14	.440	1	0-0	0	4.58	5.32
1996 Minnesota	AL	35	35	3	0	232.0	973	231	125	115	40	5	6	4	57	2	148	1	0	11	16	.407	0	0-0	0	3.97	4.46
1997 Minnesota	AL	35	35	4	0	239.2	989	238	114	103	28	2	9	3	48	1	174	1	1	20	10	.667	1	0-0	0	3.41	3.87
1998 Minnesota	AL	32	32	5	0	213.2	904	238	109	102	23	9	3	9	43	1	146	3	1	12	14	.462	1	0-0	0	4.18	4.30
1999 Minnesota	AL	33	33	4	0	218.2	910	239	97	91	28	5	1	4	44	0	121	4	0	12	14	.462	0	0-0	0	4.07	3.75
2000 Minnesota	AL	34	34	4	0	226.2	978	261	119	112	27	7	4	5	51	1	141	5	0	12	16	.429	1	0-0	0	4.44	4.45
2001 Minnesota	AL	33	33	6	0	226.0	919	235	105	99	24	10	6	10	26	0	137	4	1	15	11	.577	2	0-0	0	3.45	3.94
2002 Minnesota	AL	21	21	2	0	118.1	490	124	64	62	12	2	5	7	20	0	62	0	0	9	5	.643	1	0-0	0	3.73	4.72
2003 Minnesota	AL	33	33	3	0	212.1	888	242	111	106	32	12	4	5	28	2	120	0	0	14	10	.583	1	0-0	0	4.24	4.49
2004 Minnesota	AL	34	34	1	0	219.2	901	229	92	85	23	5	5	6	26	1	143	2	0	11	8	.579	1	0-0	0	3.35	3.48
10 ML YEARS		319	318	34	0	2088.0	8724	2232	1048	982	269	59	56	54	390	8	1267	24	3	127	118	.518	9	0-0	0	3.93	4.23

Tim Raines Jr

Bats: B **Throws:** R **Pos:** CF-27; RF-10; PR-8; DH-4; PH-4; LF-1 **Ht:** 5'10" **Wt:** 183 **Born:** 8/31/1979 **Age:** 25

							BATTING														BASERUNNING				AVERAGES		
Year Team	Lg	G	AB	H	2B	3B	HR	(Hm	Rd)	TB	R	RBI	RC	TBB	IBB	SO	HBP	SH	SF	SB	CS	SB%	GDP	Avg	OBP	Slg
2004 Ottawa*	AAA	72	267	70	13	1	1	(-	-)	88	32	23	30	18	0	69	5	7	6	24	7	.77	4	.262	.314	.330
2001 Baltimore	AL	7	23	4	2	0	0	(0	0)	6	6	0	2	3	0	8	0	1	0	3	0	1.00	0	.174	.269	.261
2003 Baltimore	AL	20	43	6	1	1	0	(0	0)	9	4	2	2	2	0	12	1	0	0	0	0	-	2	.140	.196	.209
2004 Baltimore	AL	48	94	24	6	0	0	(0	0)	30	14	5	9	4	0	16	1	2	0	7	3	.70	2	.255	.293	.319
3 ML YEARS		75	160	34	9	1	0	(0	0)	45	24	7	13	9	0	36	2	3	0	10	3	.77	4	.213	.263	.281

Aaron Rakers

Pitches: R **Bats:** R **Pos:** RP-3 **Ht:** 6'3" **Wt:** 205 **Born:** 1/22/1977 **Age:** 28

		HOW MUCH HE PITCHED						WHAT HE GAVE UP											THE RESULTS						
Year Team	Lg	G	GS	CG	GF	IP	BFP	H	R	ER	HR	SH	SF	HB	TBB	IBB	SO	WP	Bk	W	L	Pct	ShO	Sv-Op	Hld	ERC	ERA
1999 Bluefield	R+	3	0	0	1	7.0	28	5	2	2	1	0	0	0	3	0	12	0	0	0	0	-	0	8- -	-	3.01	2.57
1999 Delmarva	A	18	0	0	16	25.1	97	9	6	4	0	0	1	0	13	0	38	1	1	4	1	.800	0	8- -	-	1.05	1.42
2000 Frederick	A+	26	0	0	19	40.2	157	23	8	7	2	0	2	2	12	1	57	1	0	1	1	.500	0	8- -	-	1.48	1.55
2000 Bowie	AA	24	0	0	18	29.0	118	20	11	9	5	1	3	1	10	0	21	0	0	3	2	.600	0	8- -	-	2.76	2.79
2001 Bowie	AA	51	0	0	39	60.1	257	53	21	16	8	1	1	2	20	1	74	4	0	4	4	.500	0	14- -	-	3.38	2.39
2002 Bowie	AA	31	0	0	29	48.0	189	39	12	11	3	5	3	1	12	2	45	1	0	5	1	.833	0	10- -	-	2.38	2.06
2003 Bowie	AA	31	0	0	21	39.1	161	27	12	12	7	2	0	2	19	1	42	1	0	5	0	1.000	0	8- -	-	3.43	2.75
2003 Ottawa	AAA	21	0	0	8	26.1	111	19	18	15	1	0	0	2	11	2	26	3	0	2	4	.333	0	1- -	-	2.38	5.13
2004 Ottawa	AAA	54	1	0	18	78.2	326	65	27	24	8	0	1	2	25	4	80	2	0	4	5	.444	0	1- -	-	2.83	2.75
2004 Baltimore	AL	3	0	0	1	4.1	19	5	2	2	0	0	0	0	1	0	3	0	0	0	0	-	0	0-0	0	3.47	4.15

Aramis Ramirez

Bats: R **Throws:** R **Pos:** 3B-144; PH-4 **Ht:** 6'1" **Wt:** 211 **Born:** 6/25/1978 **Age:** 27

							BATTING														BASERUNNING				AVERAGES		
Year Team	Lg	G	AB	H	2B	3B	HR	(Hm	Rd)	TB	R	RBI	RC	TBB	IBB	SO	HBP	SH	SF	SB	CS	SB%	GDP	Avg	OBP	Slg
1998 Pittsburgh	NL	72	251	59	9	1	6	(3	3)	88	23	24	26	18	0	72	4	1	1	0	1	.00	3	.235	.296	.351
1999 Pittsburgh	NL	18	56	10	2	1	0	(0	0)	14	2	7	4	6	0	9	0	1	1	0	0	-	0	.179	.254	.250
2000 Pittsburgh	NL	73	254	65	15	2	6	(4	2)	102	19	35	28	10	0	36	5	1	4	0	0	-	9	.256	.293	.402
2001 Pittsburgh	NL	158	603	181	40	4	34	(16	18)	323	83	112	108	40	4	100	8	0	4	5	4	.56	9	.300	.350	.536
2002 Pittsburgh	NL	142	522	122	26	0	18	(7	11)	202	51	71	49	29	3	95	8	0	11	2	0	1.00	17	.234	.279	.387
2003 Pit-ChC	NL	159	607	165	32	2	27	(10	17)	282	75	106	88	42	3	99	10	0	11	2	2	.50	21	.272	.324	.465
2004 Chicago	NL	145	547	174	32	1	36	(22	14)	316	99	103	100	49	6	62	3	0	7	0	2	.00	25	.318	.373	.578
2003 Pittsburgh	NL	96	375	105	25	1	12	(6	6)	168	44	67	49	25	3	68	7	0	8	1	1	.50	17	.280	.330	.448
2003 Chicago	NL	63	232	60	7	1	15	(4	11)	114	31	39	39	17	0	31	3	0	3	1	1	.50	4	.259	.314	.491
7 ML YEARS		767	2840	776	156	7	127	(62	65)	1327	352	458	403	194	16	473	38	3	39	9	9	.50	84	.273	.324	.467

Elizardo Ramirez

Pitches: R **Bats:** R **Pos:** RP-7 **Ht:** 6'0" **Wt:** 180 **Born:** 1/28/1983 **Age:** 22

		HOW MUCH HE PITCHED						WHAT HE GAVE UP											THE RESULTS						
Year Team	Lg	G	GS	CG	GF	IP	BFP	H	R	ER	HR	SH	SF	HB	TBB	IBB	SO	WP	Bk	W	L	Pct	ShO	Sv-Op	Hld	ERC	ERA
2002 Phillies	R	11	11	2	0	73.1	275	44	18	9	3	3	1	3	2	0	73	3	1	7	1	.875	1	0- -	-	0.97	1.10
2003 Clearwater	A+	27	25	1	0	157.1	668	181	85	66	4	4	2	4	33	0	101	4	2	13	9	.591	0	0- -	-	3.78	3.78
2004 Clearwater	A+	9	9	1	0	59.0	230	55	17	16	3	1	1	4	8	0	33	0	0	5	1	.833	0	0- -	-	2.79	2.44
2004 Reading	AA	8	8	1	0	33.2	162	51	34	25	4	2	4	1	14	1	20	1	1	2	5	.286	0	0- -	-	7.56	6.68
2004 Chattanooga	AA	5	5	1	0	31.0	129	35	11	11	6	1	1	2	4	1	23	0	0	1	0	1.000	1	0- -	-	4.66	3.19
2004 Philadelphia	NL	7	0	0	5	15.0	67	17	8	8	3	0	1	1	5	1	9	1	0	0	0	-	0	0-0	0	5.44	4.80

Erasmo Ramirez

Pitches: L **Bats:** L **Pos:** RP-34 **Ht:** 6'0" **Wt:** 180 **Born:** 4/29/1976 **Age:** 29

		HOW MUCH HE PITCHED						WHAT HE GAVE UP											THE RESULTS						
Year Team	Lg	G	GS	CG	GF	IP	BFP	H	R	ER	HR	SH	SF	HB	TBB	IBB	SO	WP	Bk	W	L	Pct	ShO	Sv-Op	Hld	ERC	ERA
1998 Bakersfield	A+	14	0	0	2	21.1	80	10	8	8	0	2	0	2	6	0	17	1	3	1	1	.500	0	3- -	-	1.11	3.38
1998 Salem-Keizer	A-	9	2	0	0	19.1	81	19	11	8	3	1	0	1	2	0	23	0	0	0	1	.000	0	0- -	-	3.26	3.72
1999 San Jose	A+	31	0	0	12	57.1	219	42	18	17	2	2	4	1	8	0	52	2	0	2	0	1.000	0	5- -	-	1.56	2.67
2000 Shreveport	AA	39	2	0	13	58.2	269	80	45	42	7	6	4	3	21	5	46	0	0	5	0	.000	0	1- -	-	6.39	6.44
2001 San Jose	A+	17	0	0	6	31.2	126	23	14	12	2	2	0	0	5	0	33	2	0	3	2	.600	0	1- -	-	1.58	3.41
2001 Shreveport	AA	22	1	0	6	33.1	132	25	10	8	1	0	0	3	5	0	39	2	0	2	0	1.000	0	1- -	-	1.83	2.16
2001 Tulsa	AA	12	0	0	6	16.1	68	17	8	8	3	0	0	0	5	0	18	0	0	2	1	.667	0	0- -	-	4.63	4.41
2002 Tulsa	AA	34	0	0	3	54.0	215	51	23	18	1	2	0	4	8	0	34	1	0	4	2	.667	0	2- -	-	2.67	3.00
2002 Oklahoma	AAA	25	0	0	7	21.0	83	15	5	3	0	0	1	1	4	1	17	1	0	4	1	.800	0	1- -	-	1.47	1.29
2003 Frisco	AA	3	0	0	2	3.0	15	4	2	2	1	0	0	0	1	0	4	1	0	1	0	1.000	0	0- -	-	6.91	6.00
2003 Oklahoma	AAA	22	0	0	11	35.1	147	36	8	6	0	4	1	0	2	0	20	0	0	2	1	.667	0	4- -	-	2.16	1.53
2004 Oklahoma	AAA	14	0	0	5	20.0	92	25	16	16	2	0	0	1	6	1	10	1	0	1	0	1.000	0	0- -	-	5.10	7.20
2003 Texas	AL	34	0	0	9	49.0	199	46	21	21	4	2	2	4	9	0	28	1	0	3	1	.750	0	0-1	2	3.17	3.86
2004 Texas	AL	34	0	0	6	35.2	148	34	19	17	5	2	1	3	7	1	21	1	0	5	3	.625	0	0-2	3	3.58	4.29
2 ML YEARS		68	0	0	15	84.2	347	80	40	38	9	4	3	7	16	1	49	2	0	8	4	.667	0	0-3	5	3.34	4.04

Horacio Ramirez

Pitches: L **Bats:** L **Pos:** SP-9; RP-1 **Ht:** 6'1" **Wt:** 170 **Born:** 11/24/1979 **Age:** 25

		HOW MUCH HE PITCHED						WHAT HE GAVE UP											THE RESULTS						
Year Team	Lg	G	GS	CG	GF	IP	BFP	H	R	ER	HR	SH	SF	HB	TBB	IBB	SO	WP	Bk	W	L	Pct	ShO	Sv-Op	Hld	ERC	ERA
1997 Braves	R	11	8	0	2	44.0	175	30	13	11	1	0	1	0	18	0	61	4	0	3	3	.500	0	0- -	-	2.02	2.25
1998 Macon	A	12	12	0	0	55.1	249	70	50	36	8	2	3	2	16	0	38	2	0	1	7	.125	0	0- -	-	5.64	5.86
1998 Eugene	A-	16	8	0	3	55.2	273	84	51	39	4	3	6	4	17	0	39	4	2	2	7	.222	0	0- -	-	6.61	6.31
1999 Macon	A	17	14	1	0	77.2	316	70	30	23	6	2	5	2	25	0	43	1	1	6	3	.667	1	0- -	-	3.28	2.67

Year Team	Lg	G	GS	CG	GF	IP	BFP	H	R	ER	HR	SH	SF	HB	TBB	IBB	SO	WP	Bk	W	L	Pct	ShO	Sv-Op	Hld	ERC	ERA
2000 Myrtle Beach	A+	27	26	3	0	148.1	609	136	57	53	14	1	1	2	42	0	125	6	4	15	8	.652	2	0- -	-	3.22	3.22
2001 Greenville	AA	3	3	0	0	14.2	66	17	8	8	2	2	0	1	8	0	17	0	0	1	1	.500	0	0- -	-	6.43	4.91
2002 Macon	A	2	1	0	0	6.0	35	11	10	4	0	1	0	1	2	0	5	0	0	0	2	.000	0	0- -	-	7.82	6.00
2002 Greenville	AA	16	16	0	0	92.0	376	85	41	31	5	1	7	0	32	0	64	3	1	9	5	.643	0	0- -	-	3.25	3.03
2004 Greenville	AA	3	2	0	0	11.2	48	15	4	4	0	2	2	0	3	0	2	1	0	2	0	1.000	0	0- -	-	4.77	3.09
2004 Richmond	AAA	2	2	0	0	9.0	42	15	8	8	1	2	2	0	1	0	3	0	0	0	0	-	0	0- -	-	6.97	8.00
2003 Atlanta	NL	29	29	1	0	182.1	781	181	91	81	21	12	3	6	72	10	100	5	1	12	4	.750	0	0-0	0	4.21	4.00
2004 Atlanta	NL	10	9	1	0	60.1	259	51	24	16	7	2	1	0	30	5	31	0	2	2	4	.333	0	0-0	0	3.55	2.39
2 ML YEARS		39	38	2	0	242.2	1040	232	115	97	28	14	4	6	102	15	131	5	3	14	8	.636	0	0-0	0	4.04	3.60

Manny Ramirez

Bats: R Throws: R Pos: LF-132; DH-18; PH-2 **Ht: 6'0" Wt: 213 Born: 5/30/1972 Age: 33**

Year Team	Lg	G	AB	H	2B	3B	HR	(Hm	Rd)	TB	R	RBI	RC	TBB	IBB	SO	HBP	SH	SF	SB	CS	SB%	GDP	Avg	OBP	Slg
1993 Cleveland	AL	22	53	9	1	0	2	(0	2)	16	5	5	2	2	0	8	0	0	0	0	0	-	3	.170	.200	.302
1994 Cleveland	AL	91	290	78	22	0	17	(9	8)	151	51	60	53	42	4	72	0	0	4	4	2	.67	6	.269	.357	.521
1995 Cleveland	AL	137	484	149	26	1	31	(12	19)	270	85	107	103	75	6	112	5	2	5	6	6	.50	13	.308	.402	.558
1996 Cleveland	AL	152	550	170	45	3	33	(19	14)	320	94	112	120	85	8	104	3	0	9	8	5	.62	18	.309	.399	.582
1997 Cleveland	AL	150	561	184	40	0	26	(14	12)	302	99	88	117	79	5	115	7	0	4	2	3	.40	19	.328	.415	.538
1998 Cleveland	AL	150	571	168	35	2	45	(25	20)	342	108	145	121	76	6	121	6	0	10	5	3	.63	18	.294	.377	.599
1999 Cleveland	AL	147	522	174	34	3	44	(21	23)	346	131	165	141	96	9	131	13	0	9	2	4	.33	12	.333	.442	.663
2000 Cleveland	AL	118	439	154	34	2	38	(22	16)	306	92	122	127	86	9	117	3	0	4	1	1	.50	9	.351	.457	.697
2001 Boston	AL	142	529	162	33	2	41	(21	20)	322	93	125	122	81	25	147	8	0	2	0	1	.00	16	.306	.405	.609
2002 Boston	AL	120	436	152	31	0	33	(18	15)	282	84	107	125	73	14	85	8	0	1	0	0	-	13	.349	.450	.647
2003 Boston	AL	154	569	185	36	1	37	(18	19)	334	117	104	128	97	28	94	8	0	5	3	1	.75	22	.325	.427	.587
2004 Boston	AL	152	568	175	44	0	43	(23	20)	348	108	130	124	82	15	124	6	0	7	2	4	.33	17	.308	.397	.613
12 ML YEARS		1535	5572	1760	381	14	390	(202	188)	3339	1067	1270	1283	874	129	1230	67	2	60	33	30	.52	159	.316	.411	.599

Joe Randa

Bats: R Throws: R Pos: 3B-119; DH-6; 1B-3; PH-2 **Ht: 5'11" Wt: 190 Born: 12/18/1969 Age: 35**

Year Team	Lg	G	AB	H	2B	3B	HR	(Hm	Rd)	TB	R	RBI	RC	TBB	IBB	SO	HBP	SH	SF	SB	CS	SB%	GDP	Avg	OBP	Slg
1995 Kansas City	AL	34	70	12	2	0	1	(1	0)	17	6	5	3	6	0	17	0	0	0	0	1	.00	2	.171	.237	.243
1996 Kansas City	AL	110	337	102	24	1	6	(2	4)	146	36	47	50	26	4	47	1	2	4	13	4	.76	10	.303	.351	.433
1997 Pittsburgh	NL	126	443	134	27	9	7	(5	2)	200	58	60	72	41	1	64	6	4	5	4	2	.67	10	.302	.366	.451
1998 Detroit	AL	138	460	117	21	2	9	(3	6)	169	56	50	54	41	1	70	7	3	3	8	7	.53	9	.254	.323	.367
1999 Kansas City	AL	156	628	197	36	8	16	(7	9)	297	92	84	103	50	4	80	3	1	7	5	4	.56	15	.314	.363	.473
2000 Kansas City	AL	158	612	186	29	4	15	(9	6)	268	88	106	88	36	3	66	6	1	10	6	3	.67	19	.304	.343	.438
2001 Kansas City	AL	151	581	147	34	2	13	(8	5)	224	59	83	67	42	2	80	6	1	6	3	2	.60	15	.253	.307	.386
2002 Kansas City	AL	151	549	155	36	5	11	(6	5)	234	63	80	77	46	1	69	9	2	11	2	1	.67	13	.282	.341	.426
2003 Kansas City	AL	131	502	146	31	1	16	(9	7)	227	80	72	79	41	0	61	7	9	7	1	0	1.00	12	.291	.348	.452
2004 Kansas City	AL	128	485	139	31	2	8	(1	7)	198	65	56	67	40	1	77	6	0	8	0	1	.00	11	.287	.343	.408
10 ML YEARS		1283	4667	1335	271	34	102	(51	51)	1980	603	643	660	369	17	631	51	23	61	42	25	.63	116	.286	.341	.424

Stephen Randolph

Pitches: L Bats: L Pos: RP-39; SP-6 **Ht: 6'3" Wt: 202 Born: 5/1/1974 Age: 31**

Year Team	Lg	G	GS	CG	GF	IP	BFP	H	R	ER	HR	SH	SF	HB	TBB	IBB	SO	WP	Bk	W	L	Pct	ShO	Sv-Op	Hld	ERC	ERA
1995 Yankees	R	8	3	0	1	24.1	94	11	7	6	1	0	0	1	16	0	34	3	1	4	0	1.000	0	0- -	-	2.11	2.22
1995 Oneonta	A-	6	6	0	0	21.2	109	19	22	18	0	0	2	1	23	0	31	5	0	0	3	.000	0	0- -	-	5.12	7.48
1996 Greensboro	A	32	17	0	7	100.1	451	64	46	42	8	4	5	5	96	1	111	13	3	4	7	.364	0	0- -	-	4.27	3.77
1997 Tampa	A+	34	13	1	6	95.1	417	74	55	41	8	7	3	3	63	5	108	4	1	4	7	.364	0	1- -	-	3.76	3.87
1998 High Desert	A+	17	17	0	0	85.1	357	71	44	34	6	3	2	3	42	0	104	0	0	4	4	.500	0	0- -	-	3.52	3.59
1998 Tucson	AAA	17	1	0	3	22.2	99	16	11	8	1	0	2	0	19	2	23	3	0	1	3	.250	0	0- -	-	3.63	3.18
1999 El Paso	AA	8	8	0	0	44.1	186	39	14	13	1	2	0	1	23	0	38	1	1	2	2	.500	0	0- -	-	3.53	2.64
1999 Tucson	AAA	11	10	1	0	41.2	204	47	37	32	7	1	2	2	32	1	26	1	0	0	7	.000	0	0- -	-	6.99	6.91
1999 Diamndbcks	R	2	2	0	0	6.0	25	5	3	3	0	0	0	0	2	0	7	0	0	0	0	-	0	0- -	-	2.26	4.50
2000 Tucson	AAA	5	3	0	1	13.1	69	13	13	13	3	1	1	0	19	0	6	0	0	0	0	-	0	0- -	-	8.32	8.78
2001 El Paso	AA	18	14	1	0	75.0	342	69	50	43	11	1	2	3	53	1	66	7	1	5	6	.455	1	0- -	-	5.35	5.16
2001 Tucson	AAA	18	0	0	7	21.1	109	24	15	15	2	1	2	2	19	1	16	2	0	2	0	1.000	0	0- -	-	6.91	6.33
2002 Tucson	AAA	28	27	1	1	163.1	704	151	70	63	15	6	7	6	81	2	129	6	0	15	7	.682	1	0- -	-	4.15	3.47
2003 Tucson	AAA	7	0	0	2	9.1	41	8	5	4	1	0	2	1	3	0	6	2	0	1	0	1.000	0	0- -	-	3.28	3.86
2003 Arizona	NL	50	0	0	9	60.0	271	50	28	27	7	5	0	2	43	3	50	3	2	8	1	.889	0	0-0	2	4.51	4.05
2004 Arizona	NL	45	6	0	5	81.2	393	73	56	50	11	2	4	1	76	2	62	3	0	2	5	.286	0	0-0	2	5.77	5.51
2 ML YEARS		95	6	0	14	141.2	664	123	84	77	18	7	4	3	119	5	112	6	2	10	6	.625	0	0-0	4	5.23	4.89

Cody Ransom

Bats: R Throws: R Pos: SS-45; PR-20; 2B-16; PH-15; 3B-1; LF-1 **Ht: 6'2" Wt: 196 Born: 2/17/1976 Age: 29**

Year Team	Lg	G	AB	H	2B	3B	HR	(Hm	Rd)	TB	R	RBI	RC	TBB	IBB	SO	HBP	SH	SF	SB	CS	SB%	GDP	Avg	OBP	Slg
2004 Fresno*	AAA	36	136	42	6	2	10	(-	-)	82	29	21	32	19	1	30	1	2	0	8	0	1.00	1	.309	.397	.603
2001 San Francisco	NL	9	7	0	0	0	0	(0	0)	0	1	0	0	0	0	5	0	0	0	0	0	-	0	.000	.000	.000
2002 San Francisco	NL	7	3	2	0	0	0	(0	0)	2	2	1	1	1	1	1	0	0	0	0	0	-	0	.667	.750	.667
2003 San Francisco	NL	20	27	6	1	0	1	(1	0)	10	7	1	1	1	0	11	0	0	0	0	0	-	0	.222	.250	.370
2004 San Francisco	NL	78	68	17	6	0	1	(0	1)	26	13	11	9	6	0	20	1	3	0	2	2	.50	2	.250	.320	.382
4 ML YEARS		114	105	25	7	0	2	(1	1)	38	23	13	11	8	1	37	1	3	0	2	2	.50	2	.238	.298	.362

Jon Rauch

Pitches: R Bats: R Pos: RP-7; SP-4   Ht: 6'10" Wt: 230 Born: 9/27/1978 Age: 26

			HOW MUCH HE PITCHED						WHAT HE GAVE UP											THE RESULTS						
Year Team	Lg	G	GS	CG	GF	IP	BFP	H	R	ER	HR	SH	SF	HB	TBB	IBB	SO	WP	Bk	W	L	Pct	ShO	Sv-Op	Hld	ERC	ERA
1999 Bristol	R+	14	9	0	3	56.2	264	65	44	28	4	1	2	3	16	1	66	6	2	4	4	.500	0	2- -		4.11	4.45
1999 Winstn-Salm	A+	1	1	0	0	6.0	26	4	3	2	1	0	0	0	3	0	7	1	0	0	0	-	0	0- -		2.91	3.00
2000 Winstn-Salm	A+	18	18	1	0	110.0	456	102	49	35	10	4	3	5	33	0	124	4	1	11	3	.786	0	0- -		3.45	2.86
2000 Birmingham	AA	8	8	2	0	56.0	220	36	18	14	4	1	0	2	16	0	63	2	0	5	1	.833	2	0- -		1.81	2.25
2001 Charlotte	AAA	6	6	0	0	28.0	121	28	20	18	8	0	0	1	7	0	27	1	0	1	3	.250	0	0- -		4.73	5.79
2002 Charlotte	AAA	19	19	1	0	109.1	451	91	60	52	14	2	1	3	42	2	97	2	0	7	8	.467	0	0- -		3.41	4.28
2003 Charlotte	AAA	24	23	1	1	124.2	517	121	60	57	16	4	6	2	35	1	94	3	0	7	1	.875	0	0- -		3.73	4.11
2004 Edmonton	AAA	3	3	0	0	18.0	72	17	9	9	3	2	2	0	2	0	13	0	0	1	1	.500	0	0- -		3.06	4.50
2004 Charlotte	AAA	14	13	0	0	72.1	286	57	27	25	9	4	2	1	25	0	61	1	1	6	3	.667	0	0- -		3.06	3.11
2002 Chicago	AL	8	6	0	1	28.2	130	28	26	21	7	0	1	2	14	2	19	1	1	2	1	.667	0	0-0	0	5.41	6.59
2004 CWS-Mon		11	4	0	1	32.0	131	30	10	10	1	2	1	0	11	2	22	2	0	4	1	.800	0	0-0	0	3.05	2.81
2004 Chicago	AL	2	2	0	0	8.2	43	16	6	6	0	1	1	0	4	0	4	1	0	1	1	.500	0	0-0	0	9.15	6.23
2004 Montreal	NL	9	2	0	1	23.1	88	14	4	4	1	1	0	0	7	2	18	1	0	3	0	1.000	0	0-0	0	1.44	1.54
2 ML YEARS		19	10	0	2	60.2	261	58	36	31	8	2	2	2	25	4	41	3	1	6	2	.750	0	0-0	0	4.14	4.60

Tim Redding

Pitches: R Bats: R Pos: SP-17; RP-10   Ht: 6'0" Wt: 195 Born: 2/12/1978 Age: 27

			HOW MUCH HE PITCHED						WHAT HE GAVE UP											THE RESULTS						
Year Team	Lg	G	GS	CG	GF	IP	BFP	H	R	ER	HR	SH	SF	HB	TBB	IBB	SO	WP	Bk	W	L	Pct	ShO	Sv-Op	Hld	ERC	ERA
2004 New Orleans*	AAA	5	5	0	0	28.1	127	30	21	19	2	1	1	2	12	0	26	3	1	1	3	.250	0	0- -		4.53	6.04
2001 Houston	NL	13	9	0	1	55.2	249	62	38	34	11	2	3	3	24	0	55	2	0	3	1	.750	0	0-0	0	5.87	5.50
2002 Houston	NL	18	14	0	1	73.1	325	78	49	44	10	4	3	0	35	3	63	5	1	3	6	.333	0	0-0	0	4.96	5.40
2003 Houston	NL	33	32	0	0	176.0	769	179	85	72	16	7	3	7	65	4	116	3	0	10	14	.417	0	0-0	0	4.07	3.68
2004 Houston	NL	27	17	0	2	100.2	465	125	73	64	15	10	3	5	43	3	56	2	0	5	7	.417	0	0-0	0	6.14	5.72
4 ML YEARS		91	72	0	4	405.2	1808	444	245	214	52	23	12	15	167	10	290	12	1	21	28	.429	0	0-0	0	4.97	4.75

Mark Redman

Pitches: L Bats: L Pos: SP-32   Ht: 6'5" Wt: 245 Born: 1/5/1974 Age: 31

			HOW MUCH HE PITCHED						WHAT HE GAVE UP											THE RESULTS						
Year Team	Lg	G	GS	CG	GF	IP	BFP	H	R	ER	HR	SH	SF	HB	TBB	IBB	SO	WP	Bk	W	L	Pct	ShO	Sv-Op	Hld	ERC	ERA
1999 Minnesota	AL	5	1	0	0	12.2	65	17	13	12	3	0	0	1	7	0	11	0	0	1	0	1.000	0	0-0	0	7.86	8.53
2000 Minnesota	AL	32	24	0	3	151.1	651	168	81	80	22	3	2	3	45	0	117	6	0	12	9	.571	0	0-0	0	4.73	4.76
2001 Min-Det	AL	11	11	0	0	58.0	261	68	32	29	7	2	0	1	23	0	33	6	0	2	6	.250	0	0-0	0	5.26	4.50
2002 Detroit	AL	30	30	3	0	203.0	858	211	107	95	15	5	8	6	51	2	109	11	1	8	15	.348	0	0-0	0	3.64	4.21
2003 Florida	NL	29	29	3	0	190.2	802	172	82	76	16	10	5	5	61	3	151	7	2	14	9	.609	0	0-0	0	3.17	3.59
2004 Oakland	AL	32	32	2	0	191.0	832	218	110	100	28	5	7	6	68	6	102	6	1	11	12	.478	0	0-0	0	5.23	4.71
2001 Minnesota	AL	9	9	0	0	49.0	219	57	26	23	6	1	0	0	19	0	29	6	0	2	4	.333	0	0-0	0	5.11	4.22
2001 Detroit	AL	2	2	0	0	9.0	42	11	6	6	1	1	0	1	4	0	4	0	0	0	2	.000	0	0-0	0	6.12	6.00
6 ML YEARS		139	127	8	3	806.2	3469	854	425	392	91	25	22	22	255	11	523	36	4	48	51	.485	0	0-0	0	4.26	4.37

Tike Redman

Bats: L Throws: L Pos: CF-147; PH-13; PR-2   Ht: 5'11" Wt: 166 Born: 3/10/1977 Age: 28

							BATTING													BASERUNNING				AVERAGES		
Year Team	Lg	G	AB	H	2B	3B	HR	(Hm	Rd)	TB	R	RBI	RC	TBB	IBB	SO	HBP	SH	SF	SB	CS	SB%	GDP	Avg	OBP	Slg
2000 Pittsburgh	NL	9	18	6	1	0	1	(0	1)	10	2	1	4	1	0	7	0	0	0	1	0	1.00	0	.333	.368	.556
2001 Pittsburgh	NL	37	125	28	4	1	1	(1	0)	37	8	4	8	4	0	25	0	0	1	3	5	.38	2	.224	.246	.296
2003 Pittsburgh	NL	56	230	76	16	5	3	(2	1)	111	36	19	41	14	0	18	2	2	0	7	3	.70	1	.330	.374	.483
2004 Pittsburgh	NL	155	546	153	19	4	8	(5	3)	204	65	51	61	23	2	52	3	4	5	18	6	.75	6	.280	.310	.374
4 ML YEARS		257	919	263	40	10	13	(8	5)	362	111	75	114	42	2	102	5	6	6	29	14	.67	9	.286	.319	.394

Mike Redmond

Bats: R Throws: R Pos: C-79; PH-3   Ht: 5'11" Wt: 208 Born: 5/5/1971 Age: 34

							BATTING													BASERUNNING				AVERAGES		
Year Team	Lg	G	AB	H	2B	3B	HR	(Hm	Rd)	TB	R	RBI	RC	TBB	IBB	SO	HBP	SH	SF	SB	CS	SB%	GDP	Avg	OBP	Slg
1998 Florida	NL	37	118	39	9	0	2	(1	1)	54	10	12	18	5	2	16	2	4	0	0	0		6	.331	.368	.458
1999 Florida	NL	84	242	73	9	0	1	(0	1)	85	22	27	33	26	2	34	5	5	0	0	0		8	.302	.381	.351
2000 Florida	NL	87	210	53	8	1	0	(0	0)	63	17	15	20	13	3	19	8	1	3	0	0		5	.252	.316	.300
2001 Florida	NL	48	141	44	4	0	4	(3	1)	60	19	14	21	13	4	13	2	1	1	0	0		6	.312	.376	.426
2002 Florida	NL	89	256	78	15	0	2	(1	1)	99	19	28	37	21	8	34	8	2	3	0	2	.00	4	.305	.372	.387
2003 Florida	NL	59	125	30	7	1	0	(0	0)	39	12	11	10	7	0	16	5	2	2	0	0		2	.240	.302	.312
2004 Florida	NL	81	246	63	15	0	2	(0	2)	84	19	25	27	14	0	28	8	3	2	1	0	1.00	10	.256	.315	.341
7 ML YEARS		485	1338	380	67	2	11	(5	6)	484	118	132	166	99	19	160	38	18	11	1	2	.33	41	.284	.348	.362

Jeremy Reed

Bats: L Throws: L Pos: CF-16; PH-3; LF-1   Ht: 6'0" Wt: 185 Born: 6/15/1981 Age: 24

							BATTING													BASERUNNING				AVERAGES		
Year Team	Lg	G	AB	H	2B	3B	HR	(Hm	Rd)	TB	R	RBI	RC	TBB	IBB	SO	HBP	SH	SF	SB	CS	SB%	GDP	Avg	OBP	Slg
2002 Kannapolis	A-	57	210	67	15	0	4	(-	-)	94	37	31	35	11	1	24	11	3	4	17	5	.77	7	.319	.377	.448
2003 Winstn-Salm	A+	65	222	74	18	1	4	(-	-)	106	37	52	49	41	3	17	1	5	5	27	6	.82	5	.333	.431	.477
2003 Birmingham	AA	66	242	99	17	3	7	(-	-)	143	51	43	59	29	5	19	2	7	1	18	13	.58	7	.409	.474	.591
2004 Charlotte	AAA	73	276	76	14	1	8	(-	-)	116	44	37	42	36	0	34	3	2	7	12	7	.63	7	.275	.357	.420
2004 Tacoma	AAA	61	233	71	10	5	5	(-	-)	106	40	36	39	23	1	22	0	2	1	13	2	.87	6	.305	.366	.455
2004 Seattle	AL	18	58	23	4	0	0	(0	0)	27	11	5	11	7	1	4	1	0	0	3	1	.75	2	.397	.470	.466

Steve Reed

Pitches: R **Bats:** R **Pos:** RP-65   **Ht:** 6'2" **Wt:** 212 **Born:** 3/11/1966 **Age:** 39

Year Team	Lg	G	GS	CG	GF	IP	BFP	H	R	ER	HR	SH	SF	HB	TBB	IBB	SO	WP	Bk	W	L	Pct	ShO	Sv-Op	Hld	ERC	ERA
1992 San Francisco	NL	18	0	0	2	15.2	63	13	5	4	2	0	0	1	3	0	11	0	0	1	0	1.000	0	0-0	1	2.80	2.30
1993 Colorado	NL	64	0	0	14	84.1	347	80	47	42	13	2	3	3	30	5	51	1	0	9	5	.643	0	3-6	9	4.19	4.48
1994 Colorado	NL	61	0	0	11	64.0	297	79	33	28	9	0	7	6	26	3	51	1	0	3	2	.600	0	3-10	14	6.09	3.94
1995 Colorado	NL	71	0	0	15	84.0	327	61	24	20	8	3	1	1	21	3	79	0	2	5	2	.714	0	3-6	11	2.11	2.14
1996 Colorado	NL	70	0	0	7	75.0	307	66	38	33	11	2	4	6	19	0	51	1	0	4	3	.571	0	0-6	22	3.52	3.96
1997 Colorado	NL	63	0	0	23	62.1	260	49	28	28	10	3	1	5	27	1	43	0	0	4	6	.400	0	6-13	10	3.78	4.04
1998 SF-Cle		70	0	0	19	80.1	322	56	29	28	8	2	0	5	27	5	73	0	0	4	3	.571	0	1-6	21	2.42	3.14
1999 Cleveland	AL	63	0	0	15	61.2	274	69	33	29	10	4	5	3	20	5	44	2	0	3	2	.600	0	0-3	8	4.91	4.23
2000 Cleveland	AL	57	0	0	16	56.0	243	58	30	27	7	4	1	1	21	4	39	2	1	2	0	1.000	0	0-1	9	4.31	4.34
2001 Cle-Atl		70	0	0	14	58.1	250	52	25	23	6	3	1	3	23	5	46	0	0	3	3	.500	0	1-2	11	3.51	3.55
2002 SD-NYM	NL	64	0	0	15	67.0	269	56	15	15	2	6	0	8	14	3	50	2	0	2	5	.286	0	1-4	17	2.48	2.01
2003 Colorado	NL	67	0	0	22	63.1	269	59	24	23	9	2	1	8	26	3	39	1	2	5	3	.625	0	0-2	14	4.61	3.27
2004 Colorado	NL	65	0	0	18	66.0	285	72	29	27	7	4	1	7	17	7	38	1	0	3	8	.273	0	0-4	15	4.36	3.68
1998 San Francisco	NL	50	0	0	14	54.2	213	30	10	9	4	2	0	4	19	5	50	0	0	2	1	.667	0	1-5	13	1.64	1.48
1998 Cleveland	AL	20	0	0	5	25.2	109	26	19	19	4	0	0	1	8	0	23	0	0	2	2	.500	0	0-1	8	4.38	6.66
2001 Cleveland	AL	31	0	0	8	27.1	116	22	11	11	3	0	0	2	10	2	21	0	0	1	1	.500	0	0-1	6	3.06	3.62
2001 Atlanta	NL	39	0	0	6	31.0	134	30	14	12	3	3	1	1	13	3	25	0	0	2	2	.500	0	1-1	5	3.92	3.48
2002 San Diego	NL	40	0	0	11	41.0	166	33	9	9	2	5	0	6	10	2	36	1	0	2	4	.333	0	1-3	11	2.65	1.98
2002 New York	NL	24	0	0	4	26.0	103	23	6	6	0	1	0	2	4	1	14	1	0	0	1	.000	0	0-1	6	2.22	2.08
13 ML YEARS		**803**	**0**	**0**	**191**	**838.0**	**3513**	**770**	**360**	**327**	**102**	**35**	**25**	**57**	**274**	**44**	**615**	**11**	**5**	**48**	**42**	**.533**	**0**	**18-63**	**162**	**3.71**	**3.51**

Pokey Reese

Bats: R **Throws:** R **Pos:** SS-71; 2B-30; PR-7   **Ht:** 5'11" **Wt:** 188 **Born:** 6/10/1973 **Age:** 32

Year Team	Lg	G	AB	H	2B	3B	HR	(Hm	Rd)	TB	R	RBI	RC	TBB	IBB	SO	HBP	SH	SF	SB	CS	SB%	GDP	Avg	OBP	Slg
1997 Cincinnati	NL	128	397	87	15	0	4	(3	1)	114	48	26	35	31	2	82	5	4	0	25	7	.78	1	.219	.284	.287
1998 Cincinnati	NL	59	133	34	2	2	1	(0	1)	43	20	16	14	14	1	28	0	2	2	3	2	.60	3	.256	.322	.323
1999 Cincinnati	NL	149	585	167	37	5	10	(5	5)	244	85	52	84	35	3	81	6	5	5	38	7	.84	9	.285	.330	.417
2000 Cincinnati	NL	135	518	132	20	6	12	(3	9)	200	76	46	69	45	5	86	6	3	5	29	3	.91	8	.255	.319	.386
2001 Cincinnati	NL	133	428	96	20	2	9	(4	5)	147	50	40	44	34	4	82	3	5	4	25	4	.86	7	.224	.284	.343
2002 Pittsburgh	NL	119	421	111	25	0	4	(3	1)	148	46	50	60	41	4	81	3	5	5	12	1	.92	4	.264	.330	.352
2003 Pittsburgh	NL	37	107	23	2	0	1	(0	1)	28	9	12	9	9	1	31	0	2	2	6	0	1.00	2	.215	.271	.262
2004 Boston	AL	96	244	54	7	2	3	(3	0)	74	32	29	20	17	1	60	0	6	1	6	2	.75	5	.221	.271	.303
8 ML YEARS		**856**	**2833**	**704**	**128**	**17**	**44**	**(21**	**23)**	**998**	**366**	**271**	**335**	**226**	**21**	**531**	**23**	**32**	**24**	**144**	**26**	**.85**	**39**	**.248**	**.307**	**.352**

Nick Regilio

Pitches: R **Bats:** R **Pos:** SP-4; RP-2   **Ht:** 6'2" **Wt:** 205 **Born:** 9/4/1978 **Age:** 26

Year Team	Lg	G	GS	CG	GF	IP	BFP	H	R	ER	HR	SH	SF	HB	TBB	IBB	SO	WP	Bk	W	L	Pct	ShO	Sv-Op	Hld	ERC	ERA
1999 Pulaski	R+	11	8	1	0	49.2	194	30	12	9	2	0	1	3	16	0	58	4	1	4	2	.667	1	0- -	-	1.68	1.63
2000 Charlotte	A+	20	20	0	0	85.2	369	94	54	43	8	3	1	7	29	0	63	10	2	4	3	.571	0	0- -	-	4.80	4.52
2001 Charlotte	A+	11	11	1	0	64.0	254	47	16	11	5	1	1	1	16	0	60	0	1	6	2	.750	1	0- -	-	2.07	1.55
2001 Tulsa	AA	10	10	0	0	52.0	236	62	34	32	2	2	1	4	20	0	40	2	0	1	3	.250	0	0- -	-	4.96	5.54
2002 Tulsa	AA	19	19	2	0	104.2	452	97	46	40	8	3	3	3	47	2	59	4	0	6	8	.429	1	0- -	-	3.77	3.44
2002 Oklahoma	AAA	1	1	0	0	5.0	29	9	6	6	1	0	1	0	5	0	4	0	0	1	0	1.000	0	0- -	-	12.73	10.80
2003 Rangers	R	2	2	0	0	5.0	19	4	2	0	0	0	0	1	1	0	7	0	0	0	0	-	0	0- -	-	2.62	0.00
2003 Frisco	AA	1	0	0	0	1.2	10	5	4	4	0	0	0	0	1	0	2	1	0	0	1	.000	0	0- -	-	19.35	21.60
2004 Oklahoma	AAA	17	17	0	0	91.2	399	98	49	48	6	2	3	3	46	0	72	4	0	6	5	.545	0	0- -	-	4.92	4.71
2004 Texas	AL	6	4	0	1	19.1	91	20	16	13	3	1	1	2	15	1	12	1	0	0	4	.000	0	0-0	0	6.75	6.05

Brian Reith

Pitches: R **Bats:** R **Pos:** RP-22   **Ht:** 6'5" **Wt:** 220 **Born:** 2/28/1978 **Age:** 27

Year Team	Lg	G	GS	CG	GF	IP	BFP	H	R	ER	HR	SH	SF	HB	TBB	IBB	SO	WP	Bk	W	L	Pct	ShO	Sv-Op	Hld	ERC	ERA
2004 Louisville*	AAA	26	1	0	4	36.1	172	51	17	15	1	1	0	2	13	0	32	3	0	2	3	.400	0	0- -	-	5.89	3.72
2001 Cincinnati	NL	9	8	0	0	40.1	192	56	0	35	13	0	0	0	16	0	22	0	0	0	7	.000	0	0-0	0	8.08	7.81
2003 Cincinnati	NL	42	1	0	15	61.1	277	61	32	28	8	3	5	1	36	6	39	1	0	2	3	.400	0	1-1	4	4.89	4.11
2004 Cincinnati	NL	22	0	0	4	26.0	128	30	21	21	5	2	0	3	19	1	24	3	0	2	2	.500	0	0-1	4	7.52	7.27
3 ML YEARS		**73**	**9**	**0**	**19**	**127.2**	**597**	**147**	**53**	**84**	**26**	**5**	**5**	**4**	**71**	**7**	**85**	**4**	**0**	**4**	**12**	**.250**	**0**	**1-2**	**8**	**6.41**	**5.92**

Chris Reitsma

Pitches: R **Bats:** R **Pos:** RP-84   **Ht:** 6'5" **Wt:** 215 **Born:** 12/31/1977 **Age:** 27

Year Team	Lg	G	GS	CG	GF	IP	BFP	H	R	ER	HR	SH	SF	HB	TBB	IBB	SO	WP	Bk	W	L	Pct	ShO	Sv-Op	Hld	ERC	ERA
2001 Cincinnati	NL	36	29	0	1	182.0	800	209	121	107	23	13	6	5	49	6	96	5	0	7	15	.318	0	0-0	1	4.59	5.29
2002 Cincinnati	NL	32	21	1	6	138.1	598	144	73	56	17	4	4	5	45	5	84	4	0	6	12	.333	1	0-0	0	4.24	3.64
2003 Cincinnati	NL	57	3	0	36	84.0	351	92	41	40	14	4	1	9	19	6	53	2	0	9	5	.643	0	12-18	3	4.33	4.29
2004 Atlanta	NL	84	0	0	12	79.2	344	89	38	36	9	2	6	3	20	3	60	1	0	6	4	.600	0	2-9	31	4.32	4.07
4 ML YEARS		**209**	**53**	**1**	**55**	**484.0**	**2093**	**534**	**273**	**239**	**63**	**23**	**19**	**13**	**133**	**20**	**293**	**12**	**0**	**28**	**36**	**.438**	**1**	**14-27**	**35**	**4.40**	**4.44**

Desi Relaford

Bats: B **Throws:** R **Pos:** 3B-42; 2B-36; LF-22; SS-12; RF-9; PH-9; CF-3　　　　　**Ht:** 5'9" **Wt:** 174 **Born:** 9/16/1973 **Age:** 31

							BATTING												BASERUNNING				AVERAGES		
Year Team	Lg	G	AB	H	2B	3B	HR	(Hm	Rd)	TB	R	RBI	RC	TBB	IBB	SO	HBP	SH	SF	SB	CS	SB%	GDP	Avg	OBP	Slg
2004 Omaha*	AAA	4	15	4	1	0	0	(-	-)	5	1	3	2	2	0	1	0	0	0	0	0	-	0	.267	.353	.333
1996 Philadelphia	NL	15	40	7	2	0	0	(0	0)	9	2	1	2	3	0	9	0	1	0	1	0	1.00	1	.175	.233	.225
1997 Philadelphia	NL	15	38	7	1	2	0	(0	0)	12	3	6	4	5	0	6	0	1	0	3	0	1.00	0	.184	.279	.316
1998 Philadelphia	NL	142	494	121	25	3	5	(4	1)	167	45	41	48	33	4	87	3	10	6	9	5	.64	9	.245	.293	.338
1999 Philadelphia	NL	65	211	51	11	2	1	(0	1)	69	31	26	22	19	2	34	6	6	0	4	3	.57	5	.242	.322	.327
2000 Phi-SD	NL	128	410	88	14	3	5	(0	5)	123	55	46	51	75	7	71	12	3	2	13	0	1.00	10	.215	.351	.300
2001 New York	NL	120	301	91	27	0	8	(4	4)	142	43	36	52	27	1	65	5	2	5	13	5	.72	4	.302	.364	.472
2002 Seattle	AL	112	329	88	13	2	6	(1	5)	123	55	43	43	33	2	51	6	1	7	10	3	.77	6	.267	.339	.374
2003 Kansas City	AL	141	500	127	27	5	8	(5	3)	188	70	59	68	40	1	70	6	8	3	20	4	.83	10	.254	.315	.376
2004 Kansas City	AL	114	380	84	14	0	6	(2	4)	116	45	34	37	34	3	56	8	4	4	5	4	.56	10	.221	.296	.305
2000 Philadelphia	NL	83	253	56	12	3	3	(0	3)	83	29	30	34	48	7	45	9	2	1	5	0	1.00	7	.221	.363	.328
2000 San Diego	NL	45	157	32	2	0	2	(0	2)	40	26	16	17	27	0	26	3	1	1	8	0	1.00	3	.204	.330	.255
9 ML YEARS		852	2703	664	134	17	39	(16	23)	949	349	292	327	269	20	449	46	36	27	78	24	.76	55	.246	.322	.351

Mike Remlinger

Pitches: L **Bats:** L **Pos:** RP-48　　　　　**Ht:** 6'1" **Wt:** 210 **Born:** 3/23/1966 **Age:** 39

		HOW MUCH HE PITCHED							WHAT HE GAVE UP										THE RESULTS						
Year Team	Lg	G	GS	CG	GF	IP	BFP	H	R	ER	HR	SH	SF	HB	TBB	IBB	SO	WP	Bk	W	L	Pct	ShO	Sv-Op	Hld	ERC	ERA
2004 Iowa*	AAA	2	0	0	0	1.2	9	3	3	3	1	0	0	1	0	0	1	0	0	0	0	0--	-	14.69	16.20
1991 San Francisco	NL	8	6	1	1	35.0	155	36	17	17	5	1	1	0	20	1	19	2	1	2	1	.667	1	0-0	5	5.30	4.37
1994 New York	NL	10	9	0	0	54.2	252	55	30	28	9	2	3	1	35	4	33	3	0	1	5	.167	0	0-0	1	5.46	4.61
1995 NYM-Cin	NL	7	0	0	4	6.2	34	9	6	5	1	1	0	0	5	0	7	0	0	1	0	1.000	0	0-1	0	7.94	6.75
1996 Cincinnati	NL	19	4	0	2	27.1	125	24	17	17	4	3	1	3	19	2	19	2	2	0	1	.000	0	0-0	1	5.23	5.60
1997 Cincinnati	NL	69	12	2	10	124.0	525	100	61	57	11	6	4	7	60	6	145	12	2	8	8	.500	0	2-2	14	3.43	4.14
1998 Cincinnati	NL	35	28	1	0	164.1	727	164	96	88	23	12	7	5	87	1	144	11	1	8	15	.348	1	0-0	0	5.04	4.82
1999 Atlanta	NL	73	0	0	14	83.2	346	66	24	22	9	2	1	1	35	5	81	5	0	10	1	.909	0	1-3	21	3.03	2.37
2000 Atlanta	NL	71	0	0	18	72.2	311	55	29	28	6	3	2	3	37	1	72	3	0	5	3	.625	0	12-16	23	3.15	3.47
2001 Atlanta	NL	74	0	0	6	75.0	313	67	25	23	9	2	0	2	23	4	93	4	0	3	3	.500	0	1-5	31	3.27	2.76
2002 Atlanta	NL	73	0	0	7	68.0	275	48	17	15	3	4	0	1	28	3	69	0	0	7	3	.700	0	0-5	30	2.24	1.99
2003 Chicago	NL	73	0	0	26	69.0	301	54	30	28	11	2	2	2	39	4	83	2	0	6	5	.545	0	0-1	17	3.88	3.65
2004 Chicago	NL	48	0	0	6	36.2	156	33	16	14	3	1	4	1	16	3	35	1	0	1	2	.333	0	2-6	13	3.53	3.44
1995 New York	NL	5	0	0	4	5.2	27	7	5	4	1	1	0	0	2	0	6	0	0	1	0	1.000	0	0-1	0	5.47	6.35
1995 Cincinnati	NL	2	0	0	0	1.0	7	2	1	1	0	0	0	0	3	0	1	0	0	0	0	-	0	0-0	0	24.60	9.00
12 ML YEARS		560	59	4	94	817.0	3520	711	368	342	94	39	25	26	404	34	800	45	6	51	48	.515	2	18-39	151	3.89	3.77

Edgar Renteria

Bats: R **Throws:** R **Pos:** SS-149; PH-1　　　　　**Ht:** 6'1" **Wt:** 180 **Born:** 8/7/1975 **Age:** 29

							BATTING												BASERUNNING				AVERAGES		
Year Team	Lg	G	AB	H	2B	3B	HR	(Hm	Rd)	TB	R	RBI	RC	TBB	IBB	SO	HBP	SH	SF	SB	CS	SB%	GDP	Avg	OBP	Slg
1996 Florida	NL	106	431	133	18	3	5	(2	3)	172	68	31	62	33	0	68	2	2	3	16	2	.89	12	.309	.358	.399
1997 Florida	NL	154	617	171	21	3	4	(3	1)	210	90	52	68	45	1	108	4	19	6	32	15	.68	17	.277	.327	.340
1998 Florida	NL	133	517	146	18	2	3	(2	1)	177	79	31	61	48	1	78	4	9	2	41	22	.65	13	.282	.347	.342
1999 St Louis	NL	154	585	161	36	2	11	(6	5)	234	92	63	81	53	0	82	2	6	7	37	8	.82	16	.275	.334	.400
2000 St Louis	NL	150	562	156	32	1	16	(4	12)	238	94	76	80	63	3	77	1	8	9	21	13	.62	19	.278	.346	.423
2001 St Louis	NL	141	493	128	19	3	10	(3	7)	183	54	57	57	39	4	73	3	8	6	17	4	.81	15	.260	.314	.371
2002 St Louis	NL	152	544	166	36	2	11	(4	7)	239	77	83	94	49	7	57	4	7	5	22	7	.76	17	.305	.364	.439
2003 St Louis	NL	157	587	194	47	1	13	(4	9)	282	96	100	103	65	12	54	1	3	7	34	7	.83	21	.330	.394	.480
2004 St Louis	NL	149	586	168	37	0	10	(7	3)	235	84	72	74	39	5	78	1	6	10	17	11	.61	14	.287	.327	.401
9 ML YEARS		1296	4922	1423	264	17	83	(35	48)	1970	734	565	680	434	33	675	22	68	55	237	89	.73	144	.289	.346	.400

Mike Restovich

Bats: R **Throws:** R **Pos:** LF-12; RF-7; PR-6; DH-5; PH-5　　　　　**Ht:** 6'4" **Wt:** 233 **Born:** 1/3/1979 **Age:** 26

							BATTING												BASERUNNING				AVERAGES		
Year Team	Lg	G	AB	H	2B	3B	HR	(Hm	Rd)	TB	R	RBI	RC	TBB	IBB	SO	HBP	SH	SF	SB	CS	SB%	GDP	Avg	OBP	Slg
2004 Rochester*	AAA	106	425	105	20	3	20	(-	-)	191	65	62	49	25	3	104	2	0	2	4	3	.57	14	.247	.291	.449
2002 Minnesota	AL	8	13	4	0	0	1	(0	1)	7	3	1	0	1	0	4	0	0	0	1	0	1.00	0	.308	.357	.538
2003 Minnesota	AL	24	53	15	3	2	0	(0	0)	22	10	4	8	10	0	12	1	0	0	0	0	-	3	.283	.406	.415
2004 Minnesota	AL	29	47	12	3	0	2	(1	1)	21	9	6	6	4	0	10	0	0	0	0	0	-	0	.255	.314	.447
3 ML YEARS		61	113	31	6	2	3	(1	2)	50	22	11	14	15	0	26	1	0	0	1	0	1.00	5	.274	.364	.442

Al Reyes

Pitches: R **Bats:** R **Pos:** RP-10; SP-2　　　　　**Ht:** 6'1" **Wt:** 206 **Born:** 4/10/1971 **Age:** 34

		HOW MUCH HE PITCHED							WHAT HE GAVE UP										THE RESULTS						
Year Team	Lg	G	GS	CG	GF	IP	BFP	H	R	ER	HR	SH	SF	HB	TBB	IBB	SO	WP	Bk	W	L	Pct	ShO	Sv-Op	Hld	ERC	ERA
2004 Durham*	AAA	21	0	0	20	23.0	97	22	6	6	0	1	0	3	6	1	22	0	0	2	1	.667	0	10--	-	3.07	2.35
2004 Memphis*	AAA	37	0	0	33	39.2	168	32	13	13	7	0	0	3	14	3	47	0	0	2	2	.500	0	23--	-	3.46	2.95
1995 Milwaukee	AL	27	0	0	13	33.1	138	19	9	9	3	1	2	3	18	2	29	0	0	1	1	.500	0	1-1	4	2.51	2.43
1996 Milwaukee	AL	5	0	0	2	5.2	27	8	5	5	1	0	0	0	2	0	2	2	0	1	0	1.000	0	0-0	0	6.79	7.94
1997 Milwaukee	AL	19	0	0	7	29.2	131	32	19	18	4	2	0	3	9	0	28	1	0	1	2	.333	0	1-1	1	4.76	5.46
1998 Milwaukee	NL	50	0	0	13	57.0	253	55	26	25	9	2	1	2	31	1	58	2	0	5	1	.833	0	0-1	10	5.01	3.95
1999 Mil-Bal	NL	53	0	0	12	65.2	287	50	33	33	9	4	3	6	41	3	67	3	0	4	3	.571	0	0-4	5	4.19	4.52
2000 Bal-LA	NL	19	0	0	6	19.2	86	15	10	10	2	1	2	0	12	1	18	0	0	1	0	1.000	0	0-1	3	3.43	4.58
2001 Los Angeles	NL	19	0	0	9	25.2	120	28	13	11	3	0	2	1	13	1	23	0	1	1	2	.667	0	1-2	0	5.07	3.86
2002 Pittsburgh	NL	15	0	0	6	17.0	67	9	5	5	1	1	1	2	7	0	21	1	0	0	0	-	0	0-1	3	1.93	2.65
2003 New York	NL	13	0	0	2	17.0	73	13	7	6	1	0	0	0	9	1	9	1	0	0	0	-	0	0-1	0	2.86	3.18
2004 St Louis	NL	12	2	0	4	12.0	41	3	1	1	0	2	0	0	2	0	11	0	0	0	0	-	0	0-0	0	0.31	0.75
1999 Milwaukee	NL	26	0	0	6	36.0	161	27	17	17	5	1	1	3	25	1	39	2	0	2	0	1.000	0	0-1	2	4.35	4.25

Year Team	Lg	G	GS	CG	GF	IP	BFP	H	R	ER	HR	SH	SF	HB	TBB	IBB	SO	WP	Bk	W	L	Pct	ShO	Sv-Op	Hld	ERC	ERA
1999 Baltimore	AL	27	0	0	6	29.2	126	23	16	16	4	3	2	3	16	2	28	1	0	2	3	.400	0	0-3	4	3.99	4.85
2000 Baltimore	AL	13	0	0	2	13.0	62	13	10	10	2	1	2	0	11	1	10	0	0	1	0	1.000	0	0-1	2	6.14	6.92
2000 Los Angeles	NL	6	0	0	4	6.2	24	2	0	0	0	0	0	0	1	0	8	0	0	0	0	-	0	0-0	1	0.35	0.00
10 ML YEARS		232	2	0	74	282.2	1223	232	128	123	33	13	11	17	144	9	266	10	1	15	8	.652	0	3-12	27	3.79	3.92

Dennys Reyes

Pitches: L **Bats:** R **Pos:** RP-28; SP-12   **Ht:** 6'3" **Wt:** 246 **Born:** 4/19/1977 **Age:** 28

Year Team	Lg	G	GS	CG	GF	IP	BFP	H	R	ER	HR	SH	SF	HB	TBB	IBB	SO	WP	Bk	W	L	Pct	ShO	Sv-Op	Hld	ERC	ERA
1997 Los Angeles	NL	14	5	0	0	47.0	207	51	21	20	4	5	1	1	18	3	36	2	1	2	3	.400	0	0-0	0	4.34	3.83
1998 LA-Cin	NL	19	10	0	4	67.1	300	62	36	34	3	7	2	1	47	5	77	6	1	3	5	.375	0	0-0	0	4.37	4.54
1999 Cincinnati	NL	65	1	0	12	61.2	277	53	30	26	5	4	3	3	39	1	72	5	1	2	2	.500	0	2-3	14	4.16	3.79
2000 Cincinnati	NL	62	0	0	15	43.2	200	43	31	22	5	3	3	1	29	0	36	6	0	2	1	.667	0	0-1	10	5.24	4.53
2001 Cincinnati	NL	35	6	0	2	53.0	246	51	35	29	5	2	2	1	35	1	52	5	0	2	6	.250	0	0-0	4	4.77	4.92
2002 Col-Tex		58	5	0	15	82.2	378	98	52	49	10	3	2	0	45	4	59	10	1	4	4	.500	0	0-0	6	5.90	5.33
2003 Pit-Ari		15	0	0	4	12.2	63	15	16	15	2	1	2	0	10	1	16	5	0	0	0	-	0	0-0	2	6.96	10.66
2004 Kansas City	AL	40	12	0	5	108.0	483	114	64	57	12	7	5	4	50	3	91	6	2	4	8	.333	0	0-1	5	4.81	4.75
1998 Los Angeles	NL	11	3	0	4	28.2	130	27	17	15	1	3	1	0	20	4	33	1	1	0	4	.000	0	0-0	0	4.16	4.71
1998 Cincinnati	NL	8	7	0	0	38.2	170	35	19	19	2	4	1	1	27	1	44	5	0	3	1	.750	0	0-0	0	4.54	4.42
2002 Colorado	NL	43	0	0	13	40.1	182	43	19	19	1	2	2	0	24	3	30	4	0	0	1	.000	0	0-0	4	4.55	4.24
2002 Texas	AL	15	5	0	2	42.1	196	55	33	30	9	1	0	0	21	1	29	6	1	4	3	.571	0	0-0	2	6.24	6.38
2003 Pittsburgh	NL	12	0	0	4	10.1	50	10	13	12	1	1	2	0	9	1	11	5	0	0	0	-	0	0-0	2	5.43	10.45
2003 Arizona	NL	3	0	0	0	2.1	13	5	3	3	1	0	0	0	1	0	5	0	0	0	0	-	0	0-0	0	14.73	11.57
8 ML YEARS		308	39	0	57	476.0	2154	487	285	252	46	32	20	11	273	18	439	45	6	19	29	.396	0	2-5	41	4.89	4.76

Jose Reyes

Bats: B **Throws:** R **Pos:** 2B-43; SS-10; PH-4   **Ht:** 6'0" **Wt:** 160 **Born:** 6/11/1983 **Age:** 22

Year Team	Lg	G	AB	H	2B	3B	HR	(Hm	Rd)	TB	R	RBI	RC	TBB	IBB	SO	HBP	SH	SF	SB	CS	SB%	GDP	Avg	OBP	Slg
2000 Kingsport	R+	49	132	33	3	3	0	(-	-)	42	22	8	18	20	0	37	3	3	1	10	4	.71	1	.250	.359	.318
2001 Capital City	A	108	407	125	22	15	5	(-	-)	192	71	48	65	18	0	71	2	5	3	30	10	.75	4	.307	.337	.472
2002 St. Lucie	A+	69	288	83	10	11	6	(-	-)	133	58	38	47	30	1	35	1	4	4	31	13	.70	5	.288	.353	.462
2002 Binghamton	AA	65	275	79	16	8	2	(-	-)	117	46	24	39	16	1	42	2	2	0	27	11	.71	2	.287	.331	.425
2003 Norfolk	AAA	42	160	43	6	4	0	(-	-)	57	28	13	22	15	0	25	1	4	1	26	5	.84	2	.269	.333	.356
2004 St. Lucie	A+	6	23	6	2	0	0	(-	-)	8	3	1	1	0	0	3	0	0	0	2	0	1.00	1	.261	.261	.348
2004 Binghamton	AA	4	18	2	0	0	0	(-	-)	2	2	3	0	2	0	4	0	0	1	3	1	.75	0	.111	.190	.111
2003 New York	NL	69	274	84	12	4	5	(1	4)	119	47	32	46	13	0	36	0	2	3	13	3	.81	1	.307	.334	.434
2004 New York	NL	53	220	56	16	2	2	(1	1)	82	33	14	25	5	0	31	0	4	0	19	2	.90	1	.255	.271	.373
2 ML YEARS		122	494	140	28	6	7	(2	5)	201	80	46	71	18	0	67	0	6	3	32	5	.86	2	.283	.307	.407

Rene Reyes

Bats: B **Throws:** R **Pos:** CF-16; PH-8; RF-4; LF-1; PR-1   **Ht:** 5'11" **Wt:** 213 **Born:** 2/21/1978 **Age:** 27

Year Team	Lg	G	AB	H	2B	3B	HR	(Hm	Rd)	TB	R	RBI	RC	TBB	IBB	SO	HBP	SH	SF	SB	CS	SB%	GDP	Avg	OBP	Slg
1998 Rockies	R	49	177	76	9	4	5	(-	-)	108	40	39	48	8	1	15	15	0	1	18	7	.72	5	.429	.493	.610
1999 Rockies	R	22	97	35	4	4	1	(-	-)	50	21	20	19	4	0	14	2	0	0	6	1	.86	2	.361	.398	.515
1999 Asheville	A	40	160	56	6	1	3	(-	-)	73	26	19	27	6	0	22	1	0	0	1	0	1.00	1	.350	.377	.456
2001 Asheville	A	128	484	156	27	2	11	(-	-)	220	71	61	84	28	2	80	12	0	4	53	12	.82	9	.322	.371	.455
2002 Carolina	AA	123	455	133	33	4	14	(-	-)	216	64	54	66	29	4	69	5	2	4	10	11	.48	10	.292	.339	.475
2003 Co Springs	AAA	98	370	127	23	3	6	(-	-)	174	60	50	61	22	0	56	2	1	3	12	8	.60	11	.343	.380	.470
2004 Co Springs	AAA	87	313	96	23	1	6	(-	-)	139	44	47	45	18	1	60	2	1	0	10	5	.67	7	.307	.348	.444
2003 Colorado	NL	53	116	30	7	1	2	(2	0)	45	13	7	9	5	0	19	0	1	1	2	1	.67	3	.259	.287	.388
2004 Colorado	NL	28	61	9	2	0	0	(0	0)	11	5	1	0	5	2	17	0	0	0	0	0	-	0	.148	.212	.180
2 ML YEARS		81	177	39	9	1	2	(2	0)	56	18	8	9	10	2	36	0	1	1	2	1	.67	3	.220	.261	.316

Shane Reynolds

Pitches: R **Bats:** R **Pos:** SP-1   **Ht:** 6'3" **Wt:** 215 **Born:** 3/26/1968 **Age:** 37

Year Team	Lg	G	GS	CG	GF	IP	BFP	H	R	ER	HR	SH	SF	HB	TBB	IBB	SO	WP	Bk	W	L	Pct	ShO	Sv-Op	Hld	ERC	ERA
2004 El Paso*	AA	2	2	0	0	4.2	23	7	3	3	0	0	0	0	2	0	3	0	0	0	1	.000	0	0- -	-	6.19	5.79
2004 Tucson*	AAA	5	5	1	0	27.1	114	30	16	16	5	1	1	2	3	0	28	2	0	2	1	.667	1	0- -	-	4.35	5.27
1992 Houston	NL	8	5	0	0	25.1	122	42	22	20	2	6	1	0	6	1	10	1	1	1	3	.250	0	0-0	0	7.07	7.11
1993 Houston	NL	5	1	0	0	11.0	49	11	4	1	0	0	0	0	6	1	10	0	0	0	0	-	0	0-0	0	3.72	0.82
1994 Houston	NL	33	14	1	5	124.0	517	128	46	42	10	4	0	6	21	3	110	3	2	8	5	.615	1	0-0	5	3.38	3.05
1995 Houston	NL	30	30	3	0	189.1	792	196	87	73	15	8	0	2	37	6	175	7	1	10	11	.476	2	0-0	0	3.31	3.47
1996 Houston	NL	35	35	4	0	239.0	981	227	103	97	20	11	7	8	44	3	204	5	1	16	10	.615	1	0-0	0	2.97	3.65
1997 Houston	NL	30	30	2	0	181.0	773	189	92	85	19	9	5	3	47	5	152	5	2	9	10	.474	0	0-0	0	3.79	4.23
1998 Houston	NL	35	35	3	0	233.1	986	257	99	91	25	5	7	2	53	2	209	5	0	19	8	.704	1	0-0	0	4.05	3.51
1999 Houston	NL	35	35	4	0	231.2	963	250	108	99	23	11	5	1	37	0	197	4	0	16	14	.533	2	0-0	0	3.58	3.85
2000 Houston	NL	22	22	0	0	131.0	588	160	86	76	20	6	8	6	45	2	93	5	0	7	8	.467	0	0-0	0	5.17	5.22
2001 Houston	NL	28	28	3	0	182.2	772	208	95	88	24	13	2	4	36	2	102	2	0	14	11	.560	0	0-0	0	4.38	4.34
2002 Houston	NL	13	13	0	0	74.0	322	80	43	40	13	2	1	1	26	2	47	1	0	3	6	.333	0	0-0	0	4.90	4.86
2003 Atlanta	NL	30	29	0	0	167.1	731	191	104	101	20	10	3	8	59	6	94	0	1	11	9	.550	0	0-0	0	5.07	5.43
2004 Arizona	NL	1	1	0	0	2.0	14	6	6	1	0	0	0	0	2	0	0	0	0	0	1	.000	0	0-0	0	19.55	4.50
13 ML YEARS		305	278	20	5	1791.2	7610	1935	895	814	191	85	39	41	419	33	1403	38	8	114	96	.543	7	0-0	5	3.97	4.09

Arthur Rhodes

Pitches: L **Bats:** L **Pos:** RP-37　　　　**Ht:** 6'2" **Wt:** 205 **Born:** 10/24/1969 **Age:** 35

		HOW MUCH HE PITCHED						WHAT HE GAVE UP										THE RESULTS						
Year Team	Lg	G	GS	CG	GF	IP	BFP	H	R	ER	HR	SH	SF	HB	TBB	IBB	SO	WP	Bk	W	L	Pct	ShO	Sv-Op	Hld	ERC	ERA
2004 Sacramento*	AAA	2	2	0	0	2.0	7	0	0	0	0	0	0	0	1	0	3	0	0	0	0	-	0	0--	-	0.27	0.00
1991 Baltimore	AL	8	8	0	0	36.0	174	47	35	32	4	1	3	0	23	0	23	2	0	0	3	.000	0	0-0	0	7.00	8.00
1992 Baltimore	AL	15	15	2	0	94.1	394	87	39	38	6	5	1	1	38	2	77	2	1	7	5	.583	1	0-0	0	3.48	3.63
1993 Baltimore	AL	17	17	0	0	85.2	387	91	62	62	16	2	3	1	49	1	49	2	0	5	6	.455	0	0-0	0	5.88	6.51
1994 Baltimore	AL	10	10	3	0	52.2	238	51	34	34	8	2	3	2	30	1	47	3	0	3	5	.375	2	0-0	0	5.03	5.81
1995 Baltimore	AL	19	9	0	3	75.1	336	68	53	52	13	4	0	0	48	1	77	3	1	2	5	.286	0	0-1	0	4.97	6.21
1996 Baltimore	AL	28	2	0	5	53.0	224	48	28	24	6	1	1	0	23	3	62	0	0	9	1	.900	0	1-1	2	3.72	4.08
1997 Baltimore	AL	53	0	0	6	95.1	378	75	32	32	9	0	4	4	26	5	102	2	0	10	3	.769	0	1-2	9	2.58	3.02
1998 Baltimore	AL	45	0	0	10	77.0	321	65	30	30	8	2	5	1	34	2	83	1	1	4	4	.500	0	4-8	10	3.47	3.51
1999 Baltimore	AL	43	0	0	11	53.0	244	43	37	32	9	2	2	0	45	6	59	4	0	3	4	.429	0	3-5	5	5.07	5.43
2000 Seattle	AL	72	0	0	9	69.1	281	51	34	33	6	1	2	0	29	3	77	4	0	5	8	.385	0	0-7	24	2.62	4.28
2001 Seattle	AL	71	0	0	16	68.0	258	46	14	13	5	1	0	1	12	0	83	3	0	8	0	1.000	0	3-7	32	1.61	1.72
2002 Seattle	AL	66	0	0	9	69.2	257	45	18	18	4	2	1	0	13	1	81	2	0	10	4	.714	0	2-7	27	1.46	2.33
2003 Seattle	AL	67	0	0	14	54.0	229	53	25	25	4	2	0	1	18	2	48	2	0	3	3	.500	0	3-6	18	3.55	4.17
2004 Oakland	AL	37	0	0	25	38.2	182	46	23	22	9	3	1	0	21	4	34	2	0	3	3	.500	0	9-14	3	6.54	5.12
14 ML YEARS		551	61	5	108	922.0	3903	816	464	447	107	28	26	11	409	31	902	32	3	72	54	.571	3	26-58	130	3.74	4.36

John Riedling

Pitches: R **Bats:** R **Pos:** RP-70　　　　**Ht:** 5'11" **Wt:** 190 **Born:** 8/29/1975 **Age:** 29

		HOW MUCH HE PITCHED						WHAT HE GAVE UP										THE RESULTS						
Year Team	Lg	G	GS	CG	GF	IP	BFP	H	R	ER	HR	SH	SF	HB	TBB	IBB	SO	WP	Bk	W	L	Pct	ShO	Sv-Op	Hld	ERC	ERA
2000 Cincinnati	NL	13	0	0	5	15.1	63	11	7	4	1	1	0	1	8	0	18	1	0	3	1	.750	0	1-2	2	3.12	2.35
2001 Cincinnati	NL	29	0	0	14	33.2	136	22	9	9	1	2	0	2	14	0	23	5	0	1	1	.500	0	1-3	5	2.13	2.41
2002 Cincinnati	NL	33	0	0	7	46.2	202	39	16	14	2	6	1	3	26	6	30	1	0	2	4	.333	0	0-0	8	3.42	2.70
2003 Cincinnati	NL	55	8	0	11	101.0	455	107	61	55	7	2	6	3	47	0	65	7	1	2	3	.400	0	1-4	6	4.50	4.90
2004 Cincinnati	NL	70	0	0	15	77.2	365	90	54	44	10	3	3	4	40	5	46	6	0	5	3	.625	0	0-7	14	5.69	5.10
5 ML YEARS		200	8	0	52	274.1	1221	269	147	126	21	14	10	13	135	11	182	20	1	13	12	.520	0	3-16	35	4.24	4.13

Adam Riggs

Bats: R **Throws:** R **Pos:** LF-8; DH-4; PH-3; 1B-1; 2B-1; PR-1　　　　**Ht:** 6'0" **Wt:** 190 **Born:** 10/4/1972 **Age:** 32

		BATTING																	BASERUNNING				AVERAGES		
Year Team	Lg	G	AB	H	2B	3B	HR	(Hm	Rd)	TB	R	RBI	RC	TBB	IBB	SO	HBP	SH	SF	SB	CS	SB%	GDP	Avg	OBP	Slg
2004 Salt Lake*	AAA	112	450	149	38	8	29	(-	-)	285	104	90	98	30	2	80	4	2	7	8	3	.73	5	.331	.373	.633
1997 Los Angeles	NL	9	20	4	1	0	0	(0	0)	5	3	1	2	4	1	3	0	0	0	1	0	1.00	1	.200	.333	.250
2001 San Diego	NL	12	36	7	1	0	0	(0	0)	8	2	1	2	2	0	8	0	0	0	1	1	.50	1	.194	.237	.222
2003 Anaheim	AL	24	61	15	4	1	3	(0	3)	30	11	5	6	9	0	9	0	0	2	3	1	.75	2	.246	.343	.492
2004 Anaheim	AL	16	36	7	3	0	0	(0	0)	10	2	3	2	1	0	10	0	0	0	1	0	1.00	2	.194	.216	.278
4 ML YEARS		61	153	33	9	1	3	(0	3)	53	18	10	12	16	1	30	0	2	0	6	2	.75	5	.216	.290	.346

Matt Riley

Pitches: L **Bats:** L **Pos:** SP-13; RP-1　　　　**Ht:** 6'1" **Wt:** 201 **Born:** 8/2/1979 **Age:** 25

		HOW MUCH HE PITCHED						WHAT HE GAVE UP										THE RESULTS						
Year Team	Lg	G	GS	CG	GF	IP	BFP	H	R	ER	HR	SH	SF	HB	TBB	IBB	SO	WP	Bk	W	L	Pct	ShO	Sv-Op	Hld	ERC	ERA
2004 Ottawa*	AAA	10	10	0	0	42.0	170	26	9	8	3	4	3	0	23	0	51	2	0	1	2	.333	0	0--	-	2.48	1.71
1999 Baltimore	AL	3	3	0	0	11.0	59	17	9	9	4	0	0	0	13	0	6	0	0	0	0	-	0	0-0	0	14.43	7.36
2003 Baltimore	AL	2	2	0	0	10.0	41	7	2	2	1	0	0	0	5	0	8	0	0	1	0	1.000	0	0-0	0	2.88	1.80
2004 Baltimore	AL	14	13	0	0	64.0	292	60	43	40	11	1	0	1	44	0	60	2	0	3	4	.429	0	0-0	0	5.46	5.63
3 ML YEARS		19	18	0	0	85.0	392	84	45	51	16	1	0	1	62	0	74	2	0	4	4	.500	0	0-0	0	6.12	5.40

Juan Rincon

Pitches: R **Bats:** R **Pos:** RP-77　　　　**Ht:** 5'11" **Wt:** 190 **Born:** 1/23/1979 **Age:** 26

		HOW MUCH HE PITCHED						WHAT HE GAVE UP										THE RESULTS						
Year Team	Lg	G	GS	CG	GF	IP	BFP	H	R	ER	HR	SH	SF	HB	TBB	IBB	SO	WP	Bk	W	L	Pct	ShO	Sv-Op	Hld	ERC	ERA
2001 Minnesota	AL	4	0	0	1	5.2	28	7	5	4	1	1	0	0	5	0	4	0	0	0	0	-	0	0-0	0	8.33	6.35
2002 Minnesota	AL	10	3	0	0	28.2	135	44	23	20	5	0	1	0	9	0	21	2	0	0	2	.000	0	0-1	0	7.62	6.28
2003 Minnesota	AL	58	0	0	20	85.2	370	74	38	35	5	2	4	5	38	7	63	7	0	5	6	.455	0	0-1	5	3.21	3.68
2004 Minnesota	AL	77	0	0	18	82.0	327	52	27	24	5	3	3	2	32	1	106	2	0	11	6	.647	0	2-6	16	2.00	2.63
4 ML YEARS		149	3	0	39	202.0	860	177	93	83	16	6	9	6	84	8	194	11	0	16	14	.533	0	2-8	21	3.35	3.70

Ricardo Rincon

Pitches: L **Bats:** L **Pos:** RP-67　　　　**Ht:** 5'9" **Wt:** 187 **Born:** 4/13/1970 **Age:** 35

		HOW MUCH HE PITCHED						WHAT HE GAVE UP										THE RESULTS						
Year Team	Lg	G	GS	CG	GF	IP	BFP	H	R	ER	HR	SH	SF	HB	TBB	IBB	SO	WP	Bk	W	L	Pct	ShO	Sv-Op	Hld	ERC	ERA
1997 Pittsburgh	NL	62	0	0	23	60.0	254	51	26	23	5	5	1	2	24	6	71	2	3	4	8	.333	0	4-6	18	3.10	3.45
1998 Pittsburgh	NL	60	0	0	27	65.0	272	50	31	21	6	1	2	0	29	2	64	2	0	0	2	.000	0	14-17	11	2.88	2.91
1999 Cleveland	AL	59	0	0	14	44.2	193	41	22	22	6	2	1	1	24	5	30	2	1	2	3	.400	0	0-2	11	4.38	4.43
2000 Cleveland	AL	35	0	0	4	20.0	90	17	7	6	1	0	0	1	13	1	20	1	0	2	0	1.000	0	0-0	10	3.89	2.70
2001 Cleveland	AL	67	0	0	19	54.0	223	44	18	17	3	2	3	0	21	5	50	1	0	2	1	.667	0	2-4	12	2.62	2.83
2002 Cle-Oak	AL	71	0	0	9	56.0	222	47	28	26	4	2	4	1	11	1	49	0	0	1	4	.200	0	1-5	27	2.36	4.18
2003 Oakland	AL	64	0	0	16	55.1	241	45	21	20	4	8	2	3	32	4	40	0	0	8	4	.667	0	0-3	13	3.62	3.25
2004 Oakland	AL	67	0	0	10	44.0	201	45	22	18	3	1	1	1	22	4	40	4	0	1	1	.500	0	0-4	18	4.16	3.68
2002 Cleveland	AL	46	0	0	6	35.2	150	36	21	19	3	2	2	1	8	1	30	0	0	1	4	.200	0	0-3	11	3.38	4.79
2002 Oakland	AL	25	0	0	3	20.1	72	11	7	7	1	0	2	0	3	0	19	0	0	0	0	-	0	1-2	16	1.06	3.10
8 ML YEARS		485	0	0	122	399.0	1696	340	175	153	32	21	14	9	176	28	364	12	4	20	23	.465	0	21-41	120	3.25	3.45

Alexis Rios

Bats: R **Throws:** R **Pos:** RF-108; CF-3; PH-1   **Ht:** 6'5" **Wt:** 194 **Born:** 2/18/1981 **Age:** 24

								BATTING												BASERUNNING				AVERAGES		
Year Team	Lg	G	AB	H	2B	3B	HR	(Hm Rd)	TB	R	RBI	RC	TBB	IBB	SO	HBP	SH	SF	SB	CS	SB%	GDP	Avg	OBP	Slg
1999 Medicine Hat	R+	67	234	63	7	3	0	(- -)	76	35	13	24	17	0	31	1	0	0	8	4	.67	6	.269	.321	.325
2000 Queens	A-	50	206	55	9	2	1	(- -)	71	22	25	21	11	2	22	4	1	2	5	5	.50	5	.267	.314	.345
2000 Hagerstown	A	22	74	17	3	1	0	(- -)	22	5	5	4	2	0	14	1	0	1	2	3	.40	0	.230	.256	.297
2001 Chrlstn - WV	A	130	480	126	20	9	2	(- -)	170	40	58	47	25	1	59	4	3	14	22	14	.61	16	.263	.296	.354
2002 Dunedin	A+	111	456	139	22	8	3	(- -)	186	60	61	60	27	0	55	3	1	5	14	8	.64	19	.305	.344	.408
2003 New Haven	AA	127	514	181	32	11	11	(- -)	268	86	82	98	39	4	85	6	1	3	11	3	.79	22	.352	.402	.521
2004 Syracuse	AAA	46	185	48	10	1	3	(- -)	69	14	23	16	9	0	30	0	0	1	2	1	.67	10	.259	.292	.373
2004 Toronto	AL	111	426	122	24	7	1	(0 1)	163	55	28	49	31	0	84	2	1	0	15	3	.83	13	.286	.338	.383

David Riske

Pitches: R **Bats:** R **Pos:** RP-72   **Ht:** 6'2" **Wt:** 175 **Born:** 10/23/1976 **Age:** 28

		HOW MUCH HE PITCHED						WHAT HE GAVE UP											THE RESULTS							
Year Team	Lg	G	GS	CG	GF	IP	BFP	H	R	ER	HR	SH	SF	HB	TBB	IBB	SO	WP	Bk	W	L	Pct	ShO	Sv-Op	Hld	ERC	ERA
1999 Cleveland	AL	12	0	0	3	14.0	68	20	15	13	2	1	1	0	6	0	16	0	0	1	1	.500	0	0-1	0	6.96	8.36
2001 Cleveland	AL	26	0	0	6	27.1	118	20	7	6	3	0	1	2	18	3	29	1	0	2	0	1.000	0	1-1	3	3.81	1.98
2002 Cleveland	AL	51	0	0	17	51.1	237	49	32	30	8	4	3	4	35	4	65	1	0	2	2	.500	0	1-1	5	5.55	5.26
2003 Cleveland	AL	68	0	0	24	74.2	294	52	21	19	9	4	1	3	20	3	82	1	0	2	2	.500	0	8-13	17	2.25	2.29
2004 Cleveland	AL	72	0	0	27	77.1	336	69	32	32	11	3	2	2	41	4	78	3	0	7	3	.700	0	5-12	9	4.32	3.72
5 ML YEARS		229	0	0	77	244.2	1053	210	107	100	33	12	8	11	120	14	270	6	0	14	8	.636	0	15-28	34	3.97	3.68

Todd Ritchie

Pitches: R **Bats:** R **Pos:** SP-2; RP-2   **Ht:** 6'3" **Wt:** 210 **Born:** 11/7/1971 **Age:** 33

		HOW MUCH HE PITCHED						WHAT HE GAVE UP											THE RESULTS							
Year Team	Lg	G	GS	CG	GF	IP	BFP	H	R	ER	HR	SH	SF	HB	TBB	IBB	SO	WP	Bk	W	L	Pct	ShO	Sv-Op	Hld	ERC	ERA
2004 Chrlstn - SC*	A	2	2	0	0	11.0	45	13	6	5	0	0	0	0	3	0	13	2	0	1	1	.500	0	0- -	-	4.15	4.09
2004 Montgomery*	AA	2	2	0	0	11.0	41	8	4	3	1	0	0	1	3	0	4	1	0	1	0	1.000	0	0- -	-	2.70	2.45
2004 Durham*	AAA	16	16	0	0	88.2	399	112	71	62	19	4	6	3	23	0	41	3	0	4	6	.400	0	0- -	-	5.97	6.29
1997 Minnesota	AL	42	0	0	19	74.2	331	87	41	38	11	0	1	2	28	0	44	11	0	2	3	.400	0	0-2	3	5.44	4.58
1998 Minnesota	AL	15	0	0	7	24.0	113	30	17	15	1	0	0	0	9	0	21	3	0	0	0	-	0	0-0	0	4.75	5.63
1999 Pittsburgh	NL	28	26	2	0	172.2	715	169	79	67	17	3	4	4	54	3	107	7	0	15	9	.625	0	0-0	1	3.76	3.49
2000 Pittsburgh	NL	31	31	1	0	187.0	804	208	111	100	26	8	5	3	51	1	124	5	1	9	8	.529	1	0-0	0	4.55	4.81
2001 Pittsburgh	NL	33	33	4	0	207.1	887	211	118	103	23	9	5	7	52	7	124	7	0	11	15	.423	2	0-0	0	3.68	4.47
2002 Chicago	AL	26	23	0	1	133.2	623	176	104	90	18	6	7	5	52	2	77	10	0	5	15	.250	0	0-0	0	6.27	6.06
2003 Milwaukee	NL	5	5	0	0	28.1	132	36	17	16	4	2	2	4	10	0	15	3	0	1	2	.333	0	0-0	0	6.40	5.08
2004 Tampa Bay	AL	4	2	0	2	8.0	42	12	9	8	4	0	0	1	6	0	4	0	0	0	2	.000	0	0-0	0	13.23	9.00
8 ML YEARS		184	120	7	29	835.2	3647	929	496	437	104	28	22	26	262	13	516	46	1	43	54	.443	3	0-2	4	4.64	4.71

Luis Rivas

Bats: R **Throws:** R **Pos:** 2B-109; PR-5   **Ht:** 5'11" **Wt:** 175 **Born:** 8/30/1979 **Age:** 25

								BATTING												BASERUNNING				AVERAGES		
Year Team	Lg	G	AB	H	2B	3B	HR	(Hm Rd)	TB	R	RBI	RC	TBB	IBB	SO	HBP	SH	SF	SB	CS	SB%	GDP	Avg	OBP	Slg
2004 Rochester*	AAA	3	14	3	0	0	0	(- -)	3	2	1	1	0	0	2	1	0	0	1	0	1.00	0	.214	.267	.214
2000 Minnesota	AL	16	58	18	4	1	0	(0 0)	24	8	6	8	2	0	4	0	2	2	2	0	1.00	1	.310	.323	.414
2001 Minnesota	AL	153	563	150	21	6	7	(3 4)	204	70	47	65	40	0	99	6	5	5	31	11	.74	15	.266	.319	.362
2002 Minnesota	AL	93	316	81	23	4	4	(2 2)	124	46	35	35	19	2	51	3	4	0	9	4	.69	12	.256	.305	.392
2003 Minnesota	AL	135	475	123	16	9	8	(4 4)	181	69	43	46	30	0	65	5	8	3	17	7	.71	20	.259	.308	.381
2004 Minnesota	AL	109	336	86	19	5	10	(4 6)	145	44	34	34	13	0	53	1	5	3	15	1	.94	8	.256	.283	.432
5 ML YEARS		506	1748	458	83	25	29	(13 16)	678	237	165	188	104	2	272	15	28	13	74	23	.76	57	.262	.307	.388

Carlos Rivera

Bats: L **Throws:** L **Pos:** 1B-7   **Ht:** 6'1" **Wt:** 245 **Born:** 6/10/1978 **Age:** 27

								BATTING												BASERUNNING				AVERAGES		
Year Team	Lg	G	AB	H	2B	3B	HR	(Hm Rd)	TB	R	RBI	RC	TBB	IBB	SO	HBP	SH	SF	SB	CS	SB%	GDP	Avg	OBP	Slg
1996 Pirates	R	48	183	52	8	3	3	(- -)	75	24	26	23	15	1	22	1	0	2	1	1	.50	8	.284	.338	.410
1997 Augusta	A	120	415	113	16	5	9	(- -)	166	52	65	52	19	2	82	10	0	6	4	1	.80	9	.272	.316	.400
1998 Lynchburg	A+	29	113	26	4	0	4	(- -)	42	11	16	8	0	0	19	1	0	1	0	1	.00	3	.230	.235	.372
1998 Augusta	A	87	316	90	17	1	5	(- -)	124	38	53	36	11	2	46	6	0	3	3	5	.38	9	.285	.318	.392
1999 Hickory	A	119	457	147	30	1	13	(- -)	218	63	86	72	15	2	45	11	0	4	2	1	.67	13	.322	.355	.477
2000 Pirates	R	6	24	7	0	0	0	(- -)	7	2	0	2	1	0	2	0	0	0	0	0	-	1	.292	.320	.292
2000 Lynchburg	A+	64	233	63	17	0	5	(- -)	95	20	47	25	6	1	34	2	0	9	0	1	.00	7	.270	.284	.408
2001 Altoona	AA	111	389	91	30	0	10	(- -)	151	44	50	33	13	2	71	1	1	4	0	2	.00	11	.234	.258	.388
2002 Altoona	AA	128	494	149	28	2	22	(- -)	247	67	84	77	27	3	75	8	0	4	1	1	.50	18	.302	.345	.500
2003 Nashville	AAA	72	262	69	18	0	9	(- -)	114	28	31	33	13	3	38	1	0	1	3	1	.75	2	.263	.300	.435
2004 Nashville	AAA	93	312	91	19	0	17	(- -)	161	46	50	48	24	4	55	3	0	0	6	7	.46	13	.292	.348	.516
2003 Pittsburgh	NL	78	95	21	5	0	3	(2 1)	35	12	10	8	8	2	28	1	1	2	0	0	-	2	.221	.283	.368
2004 Pittsburgh	NL	7	15	3	0	0	0	(0 0)	3	1	1	1	1	1	3	0	1	0	0	0	-	0	.200	.250	.200
2 ML YEARS		85	110	24	5	0	3	(2 1)	38	13	11	9	9	3	31	1	1	2	0	0	-	2	.218	.279	.345

Juan Rivera

Bats: R **Throws:** R **Pos:** RF-104; PH-21; CF-13; LF-10; PR-3   **Ht:** 6'2" **Wt:** 170 **Born:** 7/3/1978 **Age:** 26

								BATTING												BASERUNNING				AVERAGES		
Year Team	Lg	G	AB	H	2B	3B	HR	(Hm Rd)	TB	R	RBI	RC	TBB	IBB	SO	HBP	SH	SF	SB	CS	SB%	GDP	Avg	OBP	Slg
2001 New York	AL	3	4	0	0	0	0	(0 0)	0	0	0	0	0	0	0	0	0	0	0	0	-	0	.000	.000	.000
2002 New York	AL	28	83	22	5	0	1	(0 1)	30	9	6	8	6	0	10	0	1	1	1	1	.50	4	.265	.311	.361

Year Team	Lg	G	AB	H	2B	3B	HR	(Hm	Rd)	TB	R	RBI	RC	TBB	IBB	SO	HBP	SH	SF	SB	CS	SB%	GDP	Avg	OBP	Slg
2003 New York	AL	57	173	46	14	0	7	(4	3)	81	22	26	23	10	1	27	0	1	1	0	0	-	8	.266	.304	.468
2004 Montreal	NL	134	391	120	24	1	12	(6	6)	182	48	49	60	34	7	45	1	0	0	6	2	.75	11	.307	.364	.465
4 ML YEARS		222	651	188	43	1	20	(10	10)	293	79	81	91	50	8	82	1	2	2	7	3	.70	23	.289	.339	.450

Mariano Rivera

Pitches: R **Bats:** R **Pos:** RP-74   **Ht:** 6'2" **Wt:** 185 **Born:** 11/29/1969 **Age:** 35

Year Team	Lg	G	GS	CG	GF	IP	BFP	H	R	ER	HR	SH	SF	HB	TBB	IBB	SO	WP	Bk	W	L	Pct	ShO	Sv-Op	Hld	ERC	ERA
1995 New York	AL	19	10	0	2	67.0	301	71	43	41	11	0	2	2	30	0	51	0	1	5	3	.625	0	0-1	0	5.14	5.51
1996 New York	AL	61	0	0	14	107.2	425	73	25	25	1	2	1	2	34	3	130	1	0	8	3	.727	0	5-8	27	1.65	2.09
1997 New York	AL	66	0	0	56	71.2	301	65	17	15	5	3	4	0	20	6	68	2	0	6	4	.600	0	43-52	0	2.73	1.88
1998 New York	AL	54	0	0	49	61.1	246	48	13	13	3	2	3	1	17	1	36	0	0	3	0	1.000	0	36-41	0	2.21	1.91
1999 New York	AL	66	0	0	63	69.0	268	43	15	14	2	0	2	3	18	3	52	2	1	4	3	.571	0	45-49	0	1.47	1.83
2000 New York	AL	66	0	0	61	75.2	311	58	26	24	4	5	2	0	25	3	58	2	0	7	4	.636	0	36-41	0	2.20	2.85
2001 New York	AL	71	0	0	66	80.2	310	61	24	21	5	4	1	1	12	2	83	1	0	4	6	.400	0	50-57	0	1.74	2.34
2002 New York	AL	45	0	0	37	46.0	187	35	16	14	3	2	0	2	11	2	41	1	1	1	4	.200	0	28-32	2	2.08	2.74
2003 New York	AL	64	0	0	57	70.2	279	61	15	13	3	1	2	4	10	1	63	0	0	5	2	.714	0	40-46	0	2.27	1.66
2004 New York	AL	74	0	0	69	78.2	316	65	17	17	3	2	0	5	20	3	66	0	0	4	2	.667	0	53-57	0	2.45	1.94
10 ML YEARS		586	10	0	474	728.1	2944	580	211	197	40	21	17	20	197	24	648	9	3	47	31	.603	0	336-384	29	2.30	2.43

Rene Rivera

Bats: R **Throws:** R **Pos:** C-2; PH-2   **Ht:** 5'10" **Wt:** 190 **Born:** 7/31/1983 **Age:** 21

Year Team	Lg	G	AB	H	2B	3B	HR	(Hm	Rd)	TB	R	RBI	RC	TBB	IBB	SO	HBP	SH	SF	SB	CS	SB%	GDP	Avg	OBP	Slg
2001 Mariners	R	21	71	24	4	0	2	(-	-)	34	13	12	12	2	0	11	1	0	1	0	0	-	0	.338	.360	.479
2001 Everett	A-	15	45	4	1	0	2	(-	-)	11	3	3	0	1	0	19	0	1	1	0	0	-	1	.089	.106	.244
2002 Everett	A-	62	227	55	18	1	1	(-	-)	78	29	26	25	16	1	38	9	1	3	5	2	.71	3	.242	.314	.344
2003 Wisconsin	A	116	407	112	19	0	9	(-	-)	158	39	54	56	38	2	81	7	1	5	2	2	.50	6	.275	.344	.388
2004 InlandEmpire	A+	107	379	89	22	1	6	(-	-)	131	41	53	35	28	1	70	9	4	4	0	1	.00	17	.235	.300	.346
2004 Tacoma	AAA	4	15	6	1	0	1	(-	-)	10	3	1	3	0	0	3	0	0	0	0	0	-	0	.400	.400	.667
2004 Seattle	AL	2	3	0	0	0	0	(0	0)	0	0	0	0	0	0	1	0	0	0	0	0	-	0	.000	.000	.000

Joe Roa

Pitches: R **Bats:** R **Pos:** RP-48   **Ht:** 6'1" **Wt:** 194 **Born:** 10/11/1971 **Age:** 33

Year Team	Lg	G	GS	CG	GF	IP	BFP	H	R	ER	HR	SH	SF	HB	TBB	IBB	SO	WP	Bk	W	L	Pct	ShO	Sv-Op	Hld	ERC	ERA
1995 Cleveland	AL	1	1	0	0	6.0	28	9	4	4	1	1	0	0	2	0	0	0	0	0	1	.000	0	0-0	0	7.46	6.00
1996 Cleveland	AL	1	0	0	0	1.2	11	4	2	2	0	0	0	0	3	0	0	0	0	0	0	-	0	0-0	0	20.57	10.80
1997 San Francisco	NL	28	3	0	4	65.2	289	86	40	38	8	5	4	2	20	5	34	0	1	2	5	.286	0	0-0	2	5.85	5.21
2002 Philadelphia	NL	14	11	0	1	71.1	298	78	33	32	11	1	3	1	13	2	35	0	1	4	4	.500	0	0-0	0	4.14	4.04
2003 Phi-Col-SD	NL	28	4	0	9	51.1	232	69	36	35	10	3	1	2	10	0	38	1	0	1	3	.250	0	0-0	0	6.06	6.14
2004 Minnesota	NL	48	0	0	11	70.0	318	84	38	35	9	4	2	5	24	0	47	1	0	2	3	.400	0	0-1	2	5.47	4.50
2003 Philadelphia	NL	6	3	0	1	19.1	88	28	13	13	3	1	0	1	4	0	16	1	0	0	2	.000	0	0-0	0	6.67	6.05
2003 Colorado	NL	4	0	0	3	6.2	26	7	3	3	2	0	0	0	0	0	4	0	0	0	0	-	0	0-0	0	4.06	4.05
2003 San Diego	NL	18	1	0	5	25.1	118	34	20	19	5	2	1	1	6	0	18	0	0	1	1	.500	0	0-0	0	6.12	6.75
6 ML YEARS		120	19	0	25	266.0	1176	330	153	146	39	14	10	10	72	7	154	2	2	9	16	.360	0	0-1	4	5.44	4.94

Jake Robbins

Pitches: R **Bats:** R **Pos:** RP-2   **Ht:** 6'5" **Wt:** 190 **Born:** 5/23/1976 **Age:** 29

Year Team	Lg	G	GS	CG	GF	IP	BFP	H	R	ER	HR	SH	SF	HB	TBB	IBB	SO	WP	Bk	W	L	Pct	ShO	Sv-Op	Hld	ERC	ERA
1994 Yankees	R	8	3	0	0	23.0	102	21	16	13	2	1	2	1	15	0	14	2	1	0	2	.000	0	0--	-	4.73	5.09
1995 Yankees	R	14	3	0	3	37.1	159	32	26	23	2	2	1	1	18	1	17	4	0	2	3	.400	0	0--	-	3.36	5.54
1995 Oneonta	A-	1	0	0	1	1.0	3	0	0	0	0	0	0	0	0	0	1	0	0	0	0	-	0	0--	-	0.00	0.00
1996 Oneonta	A-	11	11	0	0	66.0	298	64	42	33	3	5	1	2	35	1	47	6	1	3	4	.429	0	0--	-	4.01	4.50
1996 Greensboro	A	18	12	0	2	74.0	349	80	59	53	5	4	5	7	49	0	50	10	4	1	8	.111	0	0--	-	5.74	6.45
1997 Tampa	A+	3	3	0	0	16.0	73	18	14	9	2	0	2	0	10	1	5	2	0	1	1	.500	0	0--	-	5.92	5.06
1997 Greensboro	A	20	19	0	0	101.1	462	114	81	65	6	2	3	2	55	1	72	7	0	6	4	.600	0	0--	-	5.14	5.77
1998 Tampa	A+	26	25	2	0	152.1	674	167	85	65	5	5	6	1	72	2	87	4	1	11	6	.647	2	0--	-	4.46	3.84
1999 Tampa	A+	7	7	0	0	41.2	187	44	30	22	3	1	2	2	19	2	31	5	0	3	3	.500	0	0--	-	4.48	4.75
1999 Norwich	AA	20	19	2	0	111.0	508	118	80	67	7	4	8	3	60	3	63	2	2	3	12	.200	1	0--	-	4.71	5.43
2000 Norwich	AA	48	4	0	13	71.1	326	68	45	22	4	2	3	6	40	1	53	5	0	3	5	.375	0	0--	-	4.33	2.78
2000 Columbus	AAA	1	0	0	1	1.0	7	3	1	1	0	0	0	0	1	0	0	0	0	0	0	-	0	0--	-	19.55	9.00
2001 Richmond	AAA	57	0	0	17	78.1	352	73	51	48	1	4	1	6	51	3	53	9	0	5	3	.625	0	1--	-	4.29	5.51
2002 Co Springs	AAA	11	0	0	3	12.0	70	17	18	16	3	2	1	2	13	0	15	4	0	1	2	.333	0	0--	-	11.34	12.00
2002 Richmond	AAA	47	0	0	17	56.2	270	59	36	30	3	3	2	3	43	6	37	12	0	1	4	.200	0	3--	-	5.35	4.76
2003 Akron	AA	34	0	0	16	58.1	234	44	18	14	1	5	1	2	24	0	38	8	0	6	3	.667	0	8--	-	2.49	2.16
2004 Akron	AA	12	0	0	3	24.2	100	16	10	9	4	0	0	2	7	0	21	1	0	2	1	.667	0	1--	-	2.42	3.28
2004 Buffalo	AAA	32	2	0	11	65.2	278	51	24	23	4	1	1	6	29	1	41	6	0	6	1	.857	0	4--	-	3.08	3.15
2004 Cleveland	AL	2	0	0	0	1.2	8	3	1	1	1	0	0	0	0	0	0	0	0	0	0	-	0	0-0	0	11.17	5.40

Brian Roberts

Bats: B **Throws:** R **Pos:** 2B-150; DH-6; PH-4; PR-2   **Ht:** 5'9" **Wt:** 170 **Born:** 10/9/1977 **Age:** 27

Year Team	Lg	G	AB	H	2B	3B	HR	(Hm	Rd)	TB	R	RBI	RC	TBB	IBB	SO	HBP	SH	SF	SB	CS	SB%	GDP	Avg	OBP	Slg
2001 Baltimore	AL	75	273	69	12	3	2	(0	2)	93	42	17	27	13	0	36	0	3	3	12	3	.80	3	.253	.284	.341
2002 Baltimore	AL	38	128	29	6	0	1	(1	0)	38	18	11	12	15	0	21	1	3	2	9	2	.82	3	.227	.308	.297

Year Team	Lg	G	AB	H	2B	3B	HR	(Hm	Rd)	TB	R	RBI	RC	TBB	IBB	SO	HBP	SH	SF	SB	CS	SB%	GDP	Avg	OBP	Slg
								BATTING												BASERUNNING				AVERAGES		
2003 Baltimore	AL	112	460	124	22	4	5	(3	2)	169	65	41	62	46	1	58	1	4	1	23	6	.79	9	.270	.337	.367
2004 Baltimore	AL	159	641	175	50	2	4	(0	4)	241	107	53	91	71	1	95	1	15	6	29	12	.71	3	.273	.344	.376
4 ML YEARS		384	1502	397	90	9	12	(4	8)	541	232	122	192	145	2	210	3	25	12	73	23	.76	18	.264	.328	.360

Dave Roberts

Bats: L **Throws:** L **Pos:** LF-66; CF-35; PR-15; RF-14; PH-9; DH-1   **Ht:** 5'10" **Wt:** 180 **Born:** 5/31/1972 **Age:** 33

Year Team	Lg	G	AB	H	2B	3B	HR	(Hm	Rd)	TB	R	RBI	RC	TBB	IBB	SO	HBP	SH	SF	SB	CS	SB%	GDP	Avg	OBP	Slg
2004 Vero Beach*	A+	2	8	0	0	0	0	(-	-)	0	0	0	0	0	0	0	0	0	0	0	0	.000	0	.000	.000	.000
1999 Cleveland	AL	41	143	34	4	0	2	(1	1)	44	26	12	14	9	0	16	0	3	1	11	3	.79	0	.238	.281	.308
2000 Cleveland	AL	19	10	2	0	0	0	(0	0)	2	1	0	1	2	0	2	0	1	0	1	1	.50	0	.200	.333	.200
2001 Cleveland	AL	15	12	4	1	0	0	(0	0)	5	3	2	2	1	0	2	0	0	0	0	1	.00	0	.333	.385	.417
2002 Los Angeles	NL	127	422	117	14	7	3	(0	3)	154	63	34	67	48	0	51	2	6	1	45	10	.82	1	.277	.353	.365
2003 Los Angeles	NL	107	388	97	6	5	2	(1	1)	119	56	16	43	43	1	39	4	5	0	40	14	.74	0	.250	.331	.307
2004 LA-Bos		113	319	81	14	7	4	(2	2)	121	64	35	52	38	0	48	5	3	6	38	3	.93	4	.254	.337	.379
2004 Los Angeles	NL	68	233	59	4	7	2	(1	1)	83	45	21	41	28	0	31	4	2	3	33	1	.97	2	.253	.340	.356
2004 Boston	AL	45	86	22	10	0	2	(1	1)	38	19	14	11	10	0	17	1	1	3	5	2	.71	2	.256	.330	.442
6 ML YEARS		422	1294	335	39	19	11	(4	7)	445	213	99	179	141	1	158	11	18	8	135	32	.81	5	.259	.335	.344

Grant Roberts

Pitches: R **Bats:** R **Pos:** RP-4   **Ht:** 6'3" **Wt:** 205 **Born:** 9/13/1977 **Age:** 27

Year Team	Lg	G	GS	CG	GF	IP	BFP	H	R	ER	HR	SH	SF	HB	TBB	IBB	SO	WP	Bk	W	L	Pct	ShO	Sv-Op	Hld	ERC	ERA
2000 New York	NL	4	1	0	0	7.0	38	11	10	9	0	0	2	0	4	1	6	0	0	0	0	-	0	0-0	0	6.53	11.57
2001 New York	NL	16	0	0	2	26.0	110	24	11	11	2	1	1	0	8	1	29	0	1	1	0	1.000	0	0-1	1	3.03	3.81
2002 New York	NL	34	0	0	6	45.0	192	43	12	11	3	3	2	1	16	7	31	0	0	3	1	.750	0	0-0	3	3.25	2.20
2003 New York	NL	18	0	0	5	19.0	79	19	9	8	0	1	0	1	3	1	10	0	0	0	3	.000	0	1-1	4	2.60	3.79
2004 New York	NL	4	0	0	1	4.2	29	9	9	9	2	1	1	0	6	1	1	0	0	0	0	-	0	0-0	0	17.13	17.36
5 ML YEARS		76	1	0	14	101.2	448	106	51	48	7	6	6	2	37	11	77	0	1	4	4	.500	0	1-2	5	3.77	4.25

Willis Roberts

Pitches: R **Bats:** R **Pos:** RP-9   **Ht:** 6'3" **Wt:** 175 **Born:** 6/19/1975 **Age:** 30

Year Team	Lg	G	GS	CG	GF	IP	BFP	H	R	ER	HR	SH	SF	HB	TBB	IBB	SO	WP	Bk	W	L	Pct	ShO	Sv-Op	Hld	ERC	ERA
2004 Nashville*	AAA	35	0	0	21	38.1	174	45	26	25	5	1	0	3	13	2	32	2	0	6	3	.667	0	5--	-	5.23	5.87
1999 Detroit	AL	1	0	0	0	1.1	8	3	4	2	0	0	1	1	0	0	0	0	0	0	0	-	0	0-0	0	12.64	13.50
2001 Baltimore	AL	46	18	1	20	132.0	593	142	75	72	15	5	4	11	55	1	95	3	2	9	10	.474	0	6-10	1	4.98	4.91
2002 Baltimore	AL	66	0	0	24	75.0	334	79	34	28	5	1	4	4	32	3	51	7	0	5	4	.556	0	1-3	13	4.35	3.36
2003 Baltimore	AL	26	0	0	9	39.1	174	41	26	25	7	1	0	7	16	2	26	2	0	3	1	.750	0	0-0	1	5.72	5.72
2004 Pittsburgh	NL	9	0	0	1	12.0	56	12	7	7	0	0	2	2	9	0	7	1	0	0	0	-	0	0-0	2	5.47	5.25
5 ML YEARS		148	18	1	54	259.2	1165	277	146	134	27	7	11	25	112	6	179	13	2	17	15	.531	0	7-13	17	4.97	4.64

Jeriome Robertson

Pitches: L **Bats:** L **Pos:** RP-8   **Ht:** 6'1" **Wt:** 190 **Born:** 3/30/1977 **Age:** 28

Year Team	Lg	G	GS	CG	GF	IP	BFP	H	R	ER	HR	SH	SF	HB	TBB	IBB	SO	WP	Bk	W	L	Pct	ShO	Sv-Op	Hld	ERC	ERA
2004 Buffalo*	AAA	14	12	0	0	64.1	300	91	58	52	10	2	5	3	22	1	28	4	1	4	5	.444	0	0--	-	6.99	7.27
2004 Edmonton*	AAA	7	7	0	0	33.0	143	44	21	21	6	2	2	0	10	0	22	1	0	1	3	.250	0	0--	-	6.59	5.73
2002 Houston	NL	11	1	0	1	9.2	46	13	8	7	4	5	3	0	5	3	6	2	0	0	2	.000	0	0-0	0	8.70	6.52
2003 Houston	NL	32	31	0	0	160.2	711	180	98	91	23	8	5	6	64	8	99	1	2	15	9	.625	0	0-0	0	5.19	5.10
2004 Cleveland	AL	8	0	0	2	14.0	75	22	22	19	5	0	1	2	9	2	6	1	0	1	1	.500	0	0-1	2	11.27	12.21
3 ML YEARS		51	32	0	3	184.1	832	215	128	117	32	13	9	8	78	13	111	4	2	16	12	.571	0	0-1	2	5.78	5.71

Nate Robertson

Pitches: L **Bats:** R **Pos:** SP-32; RP-2   **Ht:** 6'2" **Wt:** 215 **Born:** 9/3/1977 **Age:** 27

Year Team	Lg	G	GS	CG	GF	IP	BFP	H	R	ER	HR	SH	SF	HB	TBB	IBB	SO	WP	Bk	W	L	Pct	ShO	Sv-Op	Hld	ERC	ERA
2002 Florida	NL	6	1	0	1	8.1	46	7	11	11	3	0	0	2	4	1	3	0	0	0	1	.000	0	0-0	0	12.69	11.88
2003 Detroit	AL	8	8	0	0	44.2	203	55	27	27	6	0	0	2	23	2	33	3	0	1	2	.333	0	0-0	0	6.24	5.44
2004 Detroit	AL	34	32	1	1	196.2	852	210	116	107	30	12	4	4	66	1	155	5	1	12	10	.545	0	1-1	0	4.65	4.90
3 ML YEARS		48	41	1	2	249.2	1101	280	154	145	39	12	4	6	93	4	191	8	1	13	13	.500	0	1-1	0	5.16	5.23

Kerry Robinson

Bats: L **Throws:** L **Pos:** LF-39; PH-29; PR-14; CF-9; RF-2; DH-2   **Ht:** 6'0" **Wt:** 175 **Born:** 10/3/1973 **Age:** 31

Year Team	Lg	G	AB	H	2B	3B	HR	(Hm	Rd)	TB	R	RBI	RC	TBB	IBB	SO	HBP	SH	SF	SB	CS	SB%	GDP	Avg	OBP	Slg
2004 Portland*	AAA	42	170	52	6	3	2	(-	-)	70	31	20	31	19	0	15	3	4	1	25	1	.96	4	.306	.383	.412
1998 Tampa Bay	AL	2	3	0	0	0	0	(0	0)	0	0	0	0	0	0	1	0	0	0	0	0	-	0	.000	.000	.000
1999 Cincinnati	NL	9	1	0	0	0	0	(0	0)	0	4	0	0	0	0	1	0	0	0	0	1	.00	0	.000	.000	.000
2001 St Louis	NL	114	186	53	6	1	1	(1	0)	64	34	15	24	12	0	20	2	4	3	11	2	.85	1	.285	.330	.344
2002 St Louis	NL	124	181	47	7	4	1	(0	1)	65	27	15	20	11	3	29	0	2	1	7	4	.64	1	.260	.301	.359
2003 St Louis	NL	116	208	52	6	3	1	(1	0)	67	19	16	21	8	3	27	1	4	0	6	1	.86	3	.250	.281	.322
2004 San Diego	NL	80	92	27	4	0	0	(0	0)	31	20	5	10	5	0	8	1	1	2	11	4	.73	0	.293	.330	.337
6 ML YEARS		445	671	179	23	8	3	(2	1)	227	104	51	75	36	6	86	4	11	6	35	12	.74	5	.267	.305	.338

Fernando Rodney

Pitches: R **Bats:** R **Pos:** RP   **Ht:** 5'11" **Wt:** 170 **Born:** 3/18/1977 **Age:** 28

Year Team	Lg	G	GS	CG	GF	IP	BFP	H	R	ER	HR	SH	SF	HB	TBB	IBB	SO	WP	Bk	W	L	Pct	ShO	Sv-Op	Hld	ERC	ERA
1999 Tigers	R	22	0	0	20	30.0	129	20	8	8	1	3	2	3	21	0	39	1	1	3	3	.500	0	9--	-	3.35	2.40
1999 Lakeland	A+	4	0	0	4	6.1	25	7	1	1	0	0	0	1	1	0	5	0	0	1	0	1.000	0	2--	-	4.01	1.42
2000 W Michigan	A	22	10	0	1	82.2	353	74	34	27	2	5	0	2	35	0	56	3	0	6	4	.600	0	0--	-	3.15	2.94
2001 Lakeland	A+	16	9	0	4	55.1	235	53	26	21	2	2	0	1	19	1	44	1	1	4	2	.667	0	0--	-	3.22	3.42
2001 Tigers	R	1	1	0	0	1.0	3	0	0	0	0	0	0	0	1	0	1	0	0	0	0	-	0	0--	-	1.26	0.00
2001 Erie	AA	4	0	0	2	6.1	30	7	3	3	1	0	1	2	3	0	8	0	0	0	0	-	0	1--	-	6.86	4.26
2002 Erie	AA	21	0	0	19	20.1	77	14	4	3	0	0	0	0	5	0	18	3	0	1	0	1.000	0	11--	-	1.51	1.33
2002 Toledo	AAA	20	0	0	11	22.1	90	13	4	2	1	1	3	1	9	0	25	2	2	1	1	.500	0	4--	-	1.76	0.81
2003 Toledo	AAA	38	0	0	35	40.2	156	22	6	6	0	1	3	4	13	0	58	3	0	1	1	.500	0	23--	-	1.41	1.33
2002 Detroit	AL	20	0	0	10	18.0	89	25	15	12	2	2	1	0	10	2	10	0	1	1	3	.250	0	0-4	0	6.77	6.00
2003 Detroit	AL	27	0	0	11	29.2	143	35	20	20	2	3	3	1	17	1	33	0	0	1	3	.250	0	3-6	3	5.46	6.07
2 ML YEARS		47	0	0	21	47.2	232	60	35	32	4	5	4	1	27	3	43	0	1	2	6	.250	0	3-10	3	5.94	6.04

Alex Rodriguez

Bats: R **Throws:** R **Pos:** 3B-155; SS-2   **Ht:** 6'3" **Wt:** 210 **Born:** 7/27/1975 **Age:** 29

								BATTING											BASERUNNING				AVERAGES		
Year Team	Lg	G	AB	H	2B	3B	HR	(Hm Rd)	TB	R	RBI	RC	TBB	IBB	SO	HBP	SH	SF	SB	CS	SB%	GDP	Avg	OBP	Slg
1994 Seattle	AL	17	54	11	0	0	0	(0 0)	11	4	2	3	3	0	20	0	1	1	3	0	1.00	0	.204	.241	.204
1995 Seattle	AL	48	142	33	6	2	5	(1 4)	58	15	19	15	6	0	42	0	1	0	4	2	.67	0	.232	.264	.408
1996 Seattle	AL	146	601	215	54	1	36	(18 18)	379	141	123	144	59	1	104	4	6	7	15	4	.79	15	.358	.414	.631
1997 Seattle	AL	141	587	176	40	3	23	(16 7)	291	100	84	100	41	1	99	5	4	1	29	6	.83	14	.300	.350	.496
1998 Seattle	AL	161	686	213	35	5	42	(18 24)	384	123	124	135	45	0	121	10	3	4	46	13	.78	12	.310	.360	.560
1999 Seattle	AL	129	502	143	25	0	42	(20 22)	294	110	111	102	56	2	109	5	1	8	21	7	.75	12	.285	.357	.586
2000 Seattle	AL	148	554	175	34	2	41	(13 28)	336	134	132	138	100	5	121	7	0	11	15	4	.79	10	.316	.420	.606
2001 Texas	AL	162	632	201	34	1	52	(26 26)	393	133	135	148	75	6	131	16	0	9	18	3	.86	17	.318	.399	.622
2002 Texas	AL	162	624	187	27	2	57	(34 23)	389	125	142	152	87	12	122	10	0	4	9	4	.69	14	.300	.392	.623
2003 Texas	AL	161	607	181	30	6	47	(26 21)	364	124	118	131	87	10	126	15	0	6	17	3	.85	16	.298	.396	.600
2004 New York	AL	155	601	172	24	2	36	(17 19)	308	112	106	112	80	6	131	10	0	7	28	4	.88	18	.286	.375	.512
11 ML YEARS		1430	5590	1707	309	24	381	(189 192)	3207	1121	1096	1180	639	43	1126	82	16	58	205	50	.80	128	.305	.381	.574

Eddy Rodriguez

Pitches: R **Bats:** R **Pos:** RP-29   **Ht:** 6'1" **Wt:** 194 **Born:** 8/8/1981 **Age:** 23

Year Team	Lg	G	GS	CG	GF	IP	BFP	H	R	ER	HR	SH	SF	HB	TBB	IBB	SO	WP	Bk	W	L	Pct	ShO	Sv-Op	Hld	ERC	ERA
2000 Orioles	R	18	0	0	14	27.0	116	17	8	6	0	3	0	2	19	1	31	0	0	2	1	.667	0	6--	-	2.74	2.00
2000 Delmarva	A	4	0	0	1	5.0	21	5	1	1	1	0	0	0	2	0	3	0	0	0	0	-	0	0--	-	4.93	1.80
2001 Delmarva	A	41	0	0	6	61.0	261	58	27	23	4	0	1	2	23	0	64	4	0	5	3	.625	0	1--	-	3.59	3.39
2001 Bowie	AA	5	0	0	3	8.2	37	7	2	2	0	1	0	0	6	1	10	0	0	1	1	.500	0	2--	-	3.31	2.08
2002 Frederick	A+	38	0	0	30	48.1	196	28	14	12	3	2	4	4	20	3	58	2	0	0	0	-	0	11--	-	1.93	2.23
2002 Bowie	AA	6	0	0	4	8.0	38	6	6	5	1	0	0	1	7	0	7	1	0	0	0	-	0	1--	-	5.09	5.63
2003 Bowie	AA	56	0	0	43	73.0	309	49	26	19	3	4	2	6	35	2	66	3	0	3	4	.429	0	13--	-	2.45	2.34
2004 Ottawa	AAA	28	0	0	17	31.2	152	34	19	18	4	0	1	3	18	0	31	1	0	1	0	1.000	0	3--	-	5.56	5.12
2004 Baltimore	AL	29	0	0	10	43.1	193	36	23	23	5	1	1	5	30	5	37	2	1	1	0	1.000	0	0-0	0	4.73	4.78

Felix Rodriguez

Pitches: R **Bats:** R **Pos:** RP-76   **Ht:** 6'1" **Wt:** 198 **Born:** 9/9/1972 **Age:** 32

Year Team	Lg	G	GS	CG	GF	IP	BFP	H	R	ER	HR	SH	SF	HB	TBB	IBB	SO	WP	Bk	W	L	Pct	ShO	Sv-Op	Hld	ERC	ERA
1995 Los Angeles	NL	11	0	0	5	10.2	45	11	3	3	2	0	0	0	5	0	5	0	0	1	1	.500	0	0-1	0	5.43	2.53
1997 Cincinnati	NL	26	1	0	13	46.0	212	48	23	22	2	0	1	6	28	2	34	4	1	0	0	-	0	0-0	0	5.22	4.30
1998 Arizona	NL	43	0	0	23	44.0	207	44	31	30	5	4	3	1	29	1	36	5	2	0	2	.000	0	5-8	0	5.11	6.14
1999 San Francisco	NL	47	0	0	26	66.1	292	67	32	28	6	2	3	2	29	2	55	2	0	2	3	.400	0	0-1	3	4.25	3.80
2000 San Francisco	NL	76	0	0	19	81.2	346	65	29	24	5	2	3	3	42	2	95	3	1	4	2	.667	0	3-8	30	3.26	2.64
2001 San Francisco	NL	80	0	0	13	80.1	314	53	16	15	5	1	3	1	27	2	91	1	0	9	1	.900	0	0-3	32	1.92	1.68
2002 San Francisco	NL	71	0	0	12	69.0	288	53	33	32	5	2	3	4	29	1	58	4	0	8	6	.571	0	0-6	24	2.92	4.17
2003 San Francisco	NL	68	0	0	24	61.0	265	59	21	21	5	3	1	4	29	2	46	5	1	8	2	.800	0	2-3	19	4.33	3.10
2004 SF-Phi	NL	76	0	0	13	65.2	289	61	25	24	8	4	1	5	29	4	59	4	0	5	8	.385	0	1-4	20	4.15	3.29
2004 San Francisco	NL	53	0	0	8	44.2	199	43	18	17	7	3	1	4	19	2	31	4	0	3	5	.375	0	0-3	13	4.58	3.43
2004 Philadelphia	NL	23	0	0	5	21.0	90	18	7	7	1	1	0	1	10	2	28	0	0	2	3	.400	0	1-1	7	3.25	3.00
9 ML YEARS		498	1	0	148	524.2	2258	461	213	199	43	18	18	26	247	16	479	28	5	37	25	.597	0	11-34	128	3.70	3.41

Francisco Rodriguez

Pitches: R **Bats:** R **Pos:** RP-69   **Ht:** 6'0" **Wt:** 175 **Born:** 1/7/1982 **Age:** 23

Year Team	Lg	G	GS	CG	GF	IP	BFP	H	R	ER	HR	SH	SF	HB	TBB	IBB	SO	WP	Bk	W	L	Pct	ShO	Sv-Op	Hld	ERC	ERA
2004 Bristol*	R+	5	0	0	4	7.2	41	13	7	6	0	0	0	1	4	0	9	0	0	0	0	-	0	0--	-	8.37	7.04
2002 Anaheim	AL	5	0	0	4	5.2	21	3	0	0	0	0	0	1	2	1	13	0	0	0	0	-	0	0-0	0	1.52	0.00
2003 Anaheim	AL	59	0	0	23	86.0	334	50	30	29	12	2	4	2	35	5	95	7	0	8	3	.727	0	2-6	7	2.25	3.03
2004 Anaheim	AL	69	0	0	29	84.0	335	51	21	17	2	2	1	1	33	1	123	5	0	4	1	.800	0	12-19	27	1.64	1.82
3 ML YEARS		133	0	0	56	175.2	690	104	51	46	14	4	5	4	70	7	231	12	0	12	4	.750	0	14-25	34	1.92	2.36

Ivan Rodriguez

Bats: R Throws: R Pos: C-125; DH-8; PH-3   Ht: 5'9" Wt: 205 Born: 11/30/1971 Age: 33

Year Team	Lg	G	AB	H	2B	3B	HR	(Hm	Rd)	TB	R	RBI	RC	TBB	IBB	SO	HBP	SH	SF	SB	CS	SB%	GDP	Avg	OBP	Slg
1991 Texas	AL	88	280	74	16	0	3	(3	0)	99	24	27	23	5	0	42	0	2	1	0	1	.00	10	.264	.276	.354
1992 Texas	AL	123	420	109	16	1	8	(4	4)	151	39	37	41	24	2	73	1	7	2	0	0	-	15	.260	.300	.360
1993 Texas	AL	137	473	129	28	4	10	(7	3)	195	56	66	57	29	3	70	4	5	8	8	7	.53	16	.273	.315	.412
1994 Texas	AL	99	363	108	19	1	16	(7	9)	177	56	57	61	31	5	42	7	0	4	6	3	.67	10	.298	.360	.488
1995 Texas	AL	130	492	149	32	2	12	(5	7)	221	56	67	68	16	2	48	4	0	5	0	2	.00	11	.303	.327	.449
1996 Texas	AL	153	639	192	47	3	19	(10	9)	302	116	86	99	38	7	55	4	0	4	5	0	1.00	15	.300	.342	.473
1997 Texas	AL	150	597	187	34	4	20	(12	8)	289	98	77	98	38	7	89	8	1	4	7	3	.70	18	.313	.360	.484
1998 Texas	AL	145	579	186	40	4	21	(12	9)	297	88	91	100	32	4	88	3	0	3	9	0	1.00	18	.321	.358	.513
1999 Texas	AL	144	600	199	29	1	35	(12	23)	335	116	113	104	24	2	64	1	0	5	25	12	.68	31	.332	.356	.558
2000 Texas	AL	91	363	126	27	4	27	(16	11)	242	66	83	78	19	5	48	1	0	6	5	5	.50	17	.347	.375	.667
2001 Texas	AL	111	442	136	24	2	25	(16	9)	239	70	65	77	23	3	73	4	0	1	10	3	.77	13	.308	.347	.541
2002 Texas	AL	108	408	128	32	2	19	(15	4)	221	67	60	63	25	2	71	2	1	4	5	4	.56	13	.314	.353	.542
2003 Florida	NL	144	511	152	36	3	16	(8	8)	242	90	85	91	55	6	92	6	1	5	10	6	.63	18	.297	.369	.474
2004 Detroit	AL	135	527	176	32	2	19	(7	12)	269	72	86	98	41	6	91	3	0	4	7	4	.64	16	.334	.383	.510
14 ML YEARS		1758	6694	2051	412	33	250	(134	116)	3279	1014	1000	1058	400	54	946	48	17	56	97	50	.66	221	.306	.347	.490

Ricardo Rodriguez

Pitches: R Bats: R Pos: SP-4; RP-1   Ht: 6'3" Wt: 165 Born: 5/21/1978 Age: 27

Year Team	Lg	G	GS	CG	GF	IP	BFP	H	R	ER	HR	SH	SF	HB	TBB	IBB	SO	WP	Bk	W	L	Pct	ShO	Sv-Op	Hld	ERC	ERA
2004 Oklahoma*	AAA	6	6	1	0	37.0	156	42	23	21	5	1	4	2	12	0	18	1	0	2	2	.500	0	0--	-	5.29	5.11
2002 Cleveland	AL	7	7	0	0	41.1	183	40	27	26	5	0	0	8	18	3	24	1	0	2	2	.500	0	0-0	-	4.92	5.66
2003 Cleveland	AL	15	15	0	0	81.2	360	89	57	52	16	3	2	3	28	1	41	4	1	3	9	.250	0	0-0	-	5.14	5.73
2004 Cleveland	AL	5	4	0	0	26.2	119	28	10	6	1	0	0	0	12	0	15	1	1	3	1	.750	0	0-0	-	4.03	2.03
3 ML YEARS		27	26	0	0	149.2	662	157	94	84	22	3	2	11	58	4	80	6	2	8	12	.400	0	0-0	1	4.89	5.05

Kenny Rogers

Pitches: L Bats: L Pos: SP-35   Ht: 6'1" Wt: 217 Born: 11/10/1964 Age: 40

Year Team	Lg	G	GS	CG	GF	IP	BFP	H	R	ER	HR	SH	SF	HB	TBB	IBB	SO	WP	Bk	W	L	Pct	ShO	Sv-Op	Hld	ERC	ERA
1989 Texas	AL	73	0	0	24	73.2	314	60	28	24	2	6	3	4	42	9	63	6	0	3	4	.429	0	2-5	15	3.26	2.93
1990 Texas	AL	69	3	0	46	97.2	428	93	40	34	6	7	4	1	42	5	74	5	0	10	6	.625	0	15-23	6	3.53	3.13
1991 Texas	AL	63	9	0	20	109.2	511	121	80	66	14	9	5	6	61	7	73	3	1	10	10	.500	0	5-6	11	5.57	5.42
1992 Texas	AL	81	0	0	38	78.2	337	80	32	27	7	4	1	0	26	8	70	4	1	3	6	.333	0	6-10	18	3.63	3.09
1993 Texas	AL	35	33	5	0	208.1	885	210	108	95	18	7	5	4	71	2	140	6	5	16	10	.615	0	0-0	1	3.88	4.10
1994 Texas	AL	24	24	6	0	167.1	714	169	93	83	24	3	6	3	52	1	120	3	1	11	8	.579	2	0-0	0	4.12	4.46
1995 Texas	AL	31	31	3	0	208.0	877	192	87	78	26	3	5	2	76	1	140	8	1	17	7	.708	1	0-0	0	3.72	3.38
1996 New York	AL	30	30	2	0	179.0	786	179	97	93	16	6	3	8	83	2	92	5	0	12	8	.600	1	0-0	0	4.43	4.68
1997 New York	AL	31	22	1	4	145.0	651	161	100	91	18	2	4	7	62	1	78	2	2	6	7	.462	0	0-0	0	5.18	5.65
1998 Oakland	AL	34	34	7	0	238.2	970	215	96	84	19	4	5	7	67	0	138	5	2	16	8	.667	1	0-0	0	3.13	3.17
1999 Oak-NYM		31	31	5	0	195.1	845	206	101	91	16	7	7	13	69	1	126	4	1	10	4	.714	1	0-0	0	4.38	4.19
2000 Texas	AL	34	34	2	0	227.1	998	257	126	115	20	3	4	11	78	2	127	1	1	13	13	.500	0	0-0	0	4.72	4.55
2001 Texas	AL	20	20	0	0	120.2	552	150	88	83	18	1	6	8	49	2	74	4	1	5	7	.417	0	0-0	0	6.22	6.19
2002 Texas	AL	33	33	2	0	210.2	892	212	101	90	21	3	1	6	70	1	107	5	1	13	8	.619	1	0-0	0	3.99	3.84
2003 Minnesota	AL	33	31	0	0	195.0	851	227	108	99	22	9	3	11	50	5	116	6	4	13	8	.619	0	0-0	0	4.73	4.57
2004 Texas	AL	35	35	2	0	211.2	935	248	117	112	24	7	4	9	66	0	126	2	1	18	9	.667	1	0-0	0	4.99	4.76
1999 Oakland	AL	19	19	3	0	119.1	528	135	66	57	8	4	6	9	41	0	68	3	1	5	3	.625	0	0-0	0	4.68	4.30
1999 New York	NL	12	12	2	0	76.0	317	71	35	34	8	3	1	4	28	1	58	1	0	5	1	.833	1	0-0	0	3.91	4.03
16 ML YEARS		657	370	35	132	2666.2	11546	2780	1402	1265	271	81	66	100	964	47	1664	69	22	176	123	.589	8	28-44	50	4.31	4.27

Scott Rolen

Bats: R Throws: R Pos: 3B-142   Ht: 6'4" Wt: 226 Born: 4/4/1975 Age: 30

Year Team	Lg	G	AB	H	2B	3B	HR	(Hm	Rd)	TB	R	RBI	RC	TBB	IBB	SO	HBP	SH	SF	SB	CS	SB%	GDP	Avg	OBP	Slg
1996 Philadelphia	NL	37	130	33	7	0	4	(2	2)	52	10	18	16	13	0	27	1	0	2	0	2	.00	4	.254	.322	.400
1997 Philadelphia	NL	156	561	159	35	3	21	(11	10)	263	93	92	103	76	4	138	13	0	7	16	6	.73	6	.283	.377	.469
1998 Philadelphia	NL	160	601	174	45	4	31	(19	12)	320	120	110	124	93	6	141	11	0	6	14	7	.67	10	.290	.391	.532
1999 Philadelphia	NL	112	421	113	26	1	26	(9	17)	221	74	77	83	67	2	114	3	0	6	12	2	.86	8	.268	.368	.525
2000 Philadelphia	NL	128	483	144	32	6	26	(12	14)	266	88	89	97	51	9	99	5	0	2	8	1	.89	4	.298	.370	.551
2001 Philadelphia	NL	151	554	160	39	1	25	(12	13)	276	96	107	108	74	6	127	13	0	12	16	5	.76	6	.289	.378	.498
2002 Phi-StL	NL	155	580	154	29	8	31	(14	17)	292	89	110	98	72	4	102	12	0	3	8	4	.67	22	.266	.357	.503
2003 St Louis	NL	154	559	160	49	1	28	(12	16)	295	98	104	104	82	5	104	9	0	7	13	3	.81	19	.286	.382	.528
2004 St Louis	NL	142	500	157	32	4	34	(10	24)	299	109	124	124	72	5	92	13	1	7	4	3	.57	8	.314	.409	.598
2002 Philadelphia	NL	100	375	97	21	4	17	(8	9)	177	52	66	60	52	2	68	8	0	3	5	2	.71	12	.259	.358	.472
2002 St Louis	NL	55	205	57	8	4	14	(6	8)	115	37	44	38	20	2	34	4	0	0	3	2	.60	10	.278	.354	.561
9 ML YEARS		1195	4389	1254	296	28	226	(101	125)	2284	777	831	857	600	41	944	80	1	52	91	33	.73	87	.286	.378	.520

Jimmy Rollins

Bats: B Throws: R Pos: SS-155   Ht: 5'8" Wt: 165 Born: 11/27/1978 Age: 26

Year Team	Lg	G	AB	H	2B	3B	HR	(Hm	Rd)	TB	R	RBI	RC	TBB	IBB	SO	HBP	SH	SF	SB	CS	SB%	GDP	Avg	OBP	Slg
2000 Philadelphia	NL	14	53	17	1	1	0	(0	0)	20	5	5	8	2	0	7	0	0	0	3	0	1.00	5	.321	.345	.377
2001 Philadelphia	NL	158	656	180	29	12	14	(8	6)	275	97	54	96	48	2	108	2	9	5	46	8	.85	5	.274	.323	.419
2002 Philadelphia	NL	154	637	156	33	10	11	(3	8)	242	82	60	71	54	3	103	4	6	4	31	13	.70	14	.245	.306	.380
2003 Philadelphia	NL	156	628	165	42	6	8	(5	3)	243	85	62	76	54	4	113	0	5	2	20	12	.63	9	.263	.320	.387
2004 Philadelphia	NL	154	657	190	43	12	14	(8	6)	299	119	73	108	57	3	73	3	6	2	30	9	.77	6	.289	.348	.455
5 ML YEARS		636	2631	708	148	41	47	(24	23)	1079	388	254	359	215	12	404	9	26	13	130	42	.76	32	.269	.325	.410

Damian Rolls

Bats: R Throws: R Pos: 3B-19; LF-16; PH-8; PR-7; CF-5; RF-5; DH-3; 2B-2; 1B-1   Ht: 6'2" Wt: 215 Born: 9/15/1977 Age: 27

Year Team	Lg	G	AB	H	2B	3B	HR	(Hm	Rd)	TB	R	RBI	RC	TBB	IBB	SO	HBP	SH	SF	SB	CS	SB%	GDP	Avg	OBP	Slg
2004 Durham*	AAA	23	97	27	7	0	3	(-	-)	43	23	14	14	7	0	17	3	0	0	2	1	.75	2	.278	.346	.443
2000 Tampa Bay	AL	4	3	1	0	0	0	(0	0)	1	0	0	0	0	0	1	0	0	0	0	0	-	0	.333	.333	.333
2001 Tampa Bay	AL	81	237	62	11	1	2	(2	0)	81	33	12	23	10	0	47	0	2	0	12	4	.75	5	.262	.291	.342
2002 Tampa Bay	AL	21	89	26	6	1	0	(0	0)	34	15	6	7	3	0	16	2	1	0	2	5	.29	1	.292	.330	.382
2003 Tampa Bay	AL	107	373	95	20	0	7	(4	3)	136	43	46	43	19	1	84	7	2	3	11	3	.79	5	.255	.301	.365
2004 Tampa Bay	AL	53	117	19	5	0	0	(0	0)	24	12	9	5	10	0	36	1	2	2	2	1	.67	4	.162	.231	.205
5 ML YEARS		266	819	203	42	2	9	(6	3)	276	103	73	78	42	1	184	10	7	5	27	13	.68	15	.248	.291	.337

Jason Romano

Bats: R Throws: R Pos: PH-12; RF-6; CF-5; PR-4; 2B-1; LF-1   Ht: 6'0" Wt: 185 Born: 6/24/1979 Age: 26

Year Team	Lg	G	AB	H	2B	3B	HR	(Hm	Rd)	TB	R	RBI	RC	TBB	IBB	SO	HBP	SH	SF	SB	CS	SB%	GDP	Avg	OBP	Slg
2004 Louisville*	AAA	40	163	55	12	4	2	(-	-)	81	22	16	27	3	2	24	0	0	1	3	1	.75	0	.337	.347	.497
2002 Tex-Col		47	91	23	4	1	0	(0	0)	29	17	5	10	7	0	24	0	2	1	6	1	.86	0	.253	.303	.319
2003 Los Angeles	NL	37	36	3	0	0	0	(0	0)	3	3	0	0	1	0	8	0	0	0	2	0	1.00	2	.083	.108	.083
2004 TB-Cin		26	34	5	0	0	1	(1	0)	8	3	4	2	2	0	12	0	1	0	0	0	-	0	.147	.194	.235
2002 Texas	AL	29	54	11	4	0	0	(0	0)	15	8	4	5	4	0	13	0	1	1	2	0	1.00	0	.204	.254	.278
2002 Colorado	NL	18	37	12	0	1	0	(0	0)	14	9	1	5	3	0	11	0	1	0	4	1	.80	0	.324	.375	.378
2004 Tampa Bay	AL	4	8	1	0	0	0	(0	0)	1	0	1	0	0	0	2	0	0	0	0	0	-	0	.125	.125	.125
2004 Cincinnati	NL	22	26	4	0	0	1	(1	0)	7	3	3	2	2	0	10	0	1	0	0	0	-	0	.154	.214	.269
3 ML YEARS		110	161	31	4	1	1	(1	0)	40	23	9	12	10	0	44	0	3	1	8	1	.89	2	.193	.238	.248

J.C. Romero

Pitches: L Bats: B Pos: RP-74   Ht: 5'11" Wt: 195 Born: 6/4/1976 Age: 29

		HOW MUCH HE PITCHED						WHAT HE GAVE UP												THE RESULTS						
Year Team	Lg	G	GS	CG	GF	IP	BFP	H	R	ER	HR	SH	SF	HB	TBB	IBB	SO	WP	Bk	W	L	Pct	ShO	Sv-Op	Hld	ERC	ERA
2004 Rochester*	AAA	3	3	0	0	8.0	32	4	2	2	1	2	2	1	5	0	11	0	0	0	0	-	0	0- -	-	3.05	2.25
1999 Minnesota	AL	5	0	0	3	9.2	39	13	4	4	0	0	0	0	4	0	4	0	0	0	0	-	0	0-0	0	3.95	3.72
2000 Minnesota	AL	12	11	0	0	57.2	268	72	51	45	8	4	2	1	30	0	50	2	1	2	7	.222	0	0-0	0	6.48	7.02
2001 Minnesota	AL	14	11	0	1	65.0	286	71	48	45	10	3	2	1	24	1	39	1	0	1	4	.200	0	0-0	0	4.89	6.23
2002 Minnesota	AL	81	0	0	15	81.0	332	62	17	17	3	1	0	4	36	4	76	9	0	9	2	.818	0	1-5	33	2.74	1.89
2003 Minnesota	AL	73	0	0	17	63.0	295	66	37	35	7	4	0	6	42	7	50	9	2	2	0	1.000	0	0-4	22	5.72	5.00
2004 Minnesota	AL	74	0	0	12	74.1	319	61	32	29	4	3	1	5	38	6	69	5	0	7	4	.636	0	1-8	16	3.33	3.51
6 ML YEARS		259	22	0	48	350.2	1539	345	189	175	32	15	5	17	170	18	288	26	3	21	17	.553	0	2-17	71	4.39	4.49

Rodrigo Rosario

Pitches: R Bats: R Pos: SP   Ht: 6'2" Wt: 165 Born: 12/14/1977 Age: 27

		HOW MUCH HE PITCHED						WHAT HE GAVE UP												THE RESULTS						
Year Team	Lg	G	GS	CG	GF	IP	BFP	H	R	ER	HR	SH	SF	HB	TBB	IBB	SO	WP	Bk	W	L	Pct	ShO	Sv-Op	Hld	ERC	ERA
1998 Astros	R	13	12	0	1	67.2	286	63	36	31	6	1	2	4	30	0	65	4	1	2	2	.500	0	0- -	-	4.13	4.12
1998 Auburn	A-	2	0	0	2	2.0	9	0	0	0	0	0	0	0	3	0	2	1	0	0	0	-	0	0- -	-	1.96	0.00
1999 Martinsville	R+	14	14	0	0	78.2	345	78	46	41	9	7	3	11	32	0	86	7	0	5	5	.500	0	0- -	-	4.78	4.69
2000 Auburn	A-	14	14	0	0	75.2	330	67	36	29	3	2	1	6	32	1	67	2	0	5	6	.455	0	0- -	-	3.33	3.45
2001 Lexington	A	30	21	1	5	147.0	584	105	46	35	8	7	2	10	36	1	131	3	0	13	4	.765	0	2- -	-	2.00	2.14
2002 Round Rock	AA	26	23	0	1	130.1	561	106	56	45	5	2	4	19	59	1	94	2	0	11	6	.647	0	0- -	-	3.37	3.11
2003 New Orleans	AAA	15	15	1	0	87.0	364	71	40	39	7	4	1	7	32	0	68	3	0	5	7	.417	1	0- -	-	3.14	4.03
2003 Houston	NL	2	2	0	0	8.0	33	5	2	1	0	0	0	1	3	0	6	1	0	1	0	1.000	0	0-0	0	1.67	1.13

Mike Rose

Bats: B Throws: R Pos: C-2; PH-1; PR-1   Ht: 6'1" Wt: 185 Born: 8/25/1976 Age: 28

Year Team	Lg	G	AB	H	2B	3B	HR	(Hm	Rd)	TB	R	RBI	RC	TBB	IBB	SO	HBP	SH	SF	SB	CS	SB%	GDP	Avg	OBP	Slg
1995 Astros	R	35	89	23	2	1	1	(-	-)	30	13	9	12	11	0	18	3	0	0	2	1	.67	1	.258	.359	.337
1996 Kissimmee	A+	2	1	0	0	0	0	(-	-)	0	0	0	0	0	0	1	0	0	0	0	0	-	0	.000	.000	.000
1996 Auburn	A-	61	180	45	5	1	2	(-	-)	58	20	11	23	30	0	41	1	4	0	9	3	.75	5	.250	.360	.322
1997 Quad City	A	79	234	60	6	1	3	(-	-)	77	22	27	30	28	0	62	4	8	3	3	1	.75	1	.256	.342	.329
1998 Quad City	A	88	267	81	13	2	7	(-	-)	119	48	40	50	52	3	56	1	3	1	10	8	.56	5	.303	.417	.446
1998 Kissimmee	A+	18	62	14	4	0	3	(-	-)	27	9	9	8	8	0	14	0	1	0	1	0	1.00	2	.226	.314	.435
1999 Kissimmee	A+	95	303	84	16	2	11	(-	-)	137	61	32	56	59	0	64	3	0	2	12	6	.67	7	.277	.398	.452
1999 Jackson	AA	15	45	11	0	0	3	(-	-)	20	8	8	8	13	1	10	0	1	0	0	2	.00	1	.244	.414	.444
2000 El Paso	AA	117	352	100	22	1	10	(-	-)	154	58	62	58	68	2	70	1	1	4	8	11	.42	16	.284	.398	.438
2001 Tucson	AAA	20	55	10	1	2	0	(-	-)	15	9	8	5	12	1	16	0	1	1	0	0	-	3	.182	.324	.273
2001 El Paso	AA	62	205	53	13	1	3	(-	-)	77	28	23	29	37	1	40	0	0	1	4	1	.80	8	.259	.370	.376
2001 Trenton	AA	9	24	4	0	0	1	(-	-)	7	3	2	1	6	1	10	0	0	0	4	0	.00	0	.167	.333	.292
2002 Trenton	AA	10	29	3	1	1	0	(-	-)	6	1	0	0	5	0	7	0	0	0	0	0	-	2	.103	.235	.207
2002 Omaha	AAA	52	177	46	12	2	3	(-	-)	71	22	17	24	28	1	40	1	1	0	2	3	.40	7	.260	.364	.401
2002 Wichita	AA	14	59	18	5	0	2	(-	-)	29	13	14	9	7	0	11	0	0	0	1	0	.00	3	.305	.379	.492
2003 Sacramento	AAA	70	221	58	10	1	8	(-	-)	94	44	30	38	44	4	50	4	2	3	2	1	.67	6	.262	.390	.425
2004 Sacramento	AAA	107	349	98	20	2	6	(-	-)	140	56	49	61	76	1	80	3	1	7	0	0	-	14	.281	.407	.401
2004 Oakland	AL	2	2	0	0	0	0	(0	0)	0	1	0	0	0	0	0	0	0	0	0	0	-	0	.000	.000	.000

Dave Ross

Bats: R **Throws:** R **Pos:** C-67; PH-5   **Ht:** 6'2" **Wt:** 205 **Born:** 3/19/1977 **Age:** 28

Year Team	Lg	G	AB	H	2B	3B	HR	(Hm	Rd)	TB	R	RBI	RC	TBB	IBB	SO	HBP	SH	SF	SB	CS	SB%	GDP	Avg	OBP	Slg
2002 Los Angeles	NL	8	10	2	1	0	1	(0	1)	6	2	2	2	2	0	4	1	0	0	0	0	-	0	.200	.385	.600
2003 Los Angeles	NL	40	124	32	7	0	10	(5	5)	69	19	18	18	13	0	42	2	0	1	0	0	-	4	.258	.336	.556
2004 Los Angeles	NL	70	165	28	3	1	5	(2	3)	48	13	15	11	15	1	62	5	0	5	0	0	-	3	.170	.253	.291
3 ML YEARS		118	299	62	11	1	16	(7	9)	123	34	35	31	30	1	108	8	0	6	0	0	-	7	.207	.292	.411

Aaron Rowand

Bats: R **Throws:** R **Pos:** CF-126; RF-12; PH-10; PR-3   **Ht:** 6'1" **Wt:** 200 **Born:** 8/29/1977 **Age:** 27

Year Team	Lg	G	AB	H	2B	3B	HR	(Hm	Rd)	TB	R	RBI	RC	TBB	IBB	SO	HBP	SH	SF	SB	CS	SB%	GDP	Avg	OBP	Slg
2001 Chicago	AL	63	123	36	5	0	4	(3	1)	53	21	20	22	15	0	28	4	5	1	5	1	.83	2	.293	.385	.431
2002 Chicago	AL	126	302	78	16	2	7	(5	2)	119	41	29	37	12	1	54	6	9	2	0	1	.00	8	.258	.298	.394
2003 Chicago	AL	93	157	45	8	0	6	(5	1)	71	22	24	28	7	0	21	3	2	1	0	0	-	1	.287	.327	.452
2004 Chicago	AL	140	487	151	38	2	24	(12	12)	265	94	69	92	30	1	91	10	5	2	17	5	.77	5	.310	.361	.544
4 ML YEARS		422	1069	310	67	4	41	(25	16)	508	178	142	179	64	2	194	23	21	6	22	7	.76	16	.290	.342	.475

Kirk Rueter

Pitches: L **Bats:** L **Pos:** SP-33   **Ht:** 6'3" **Wt:** 212 **Born:** 12/1/1970 **Age:** 34

		HOW MUCH HE PITCHED						WHAT HE GAVE UP											THE RESULTS							
Year Team	Lg	G	GS	CG	GF	IP	BFP	H	R	ER	HR	SH	SF	HB	TBB	IBB	SO	WP	Bk	W	L	Pct	ShO	Sv-Op	Hld	ERC	ERA
1993 Montreal	NL	14	14	1	0	85.2	341	85	33	26	5	1	0	0	18	1	31	0	0	8	0	1.000	0	0-0	0	3.14	2.73
1994 Montreal	NL	20	20	0	0	92.1	397	106	60	53	11	6	6	2	23	1	50	2	0	7	3	.700	0	0-0	0	4.54	5.17
1995 Montreal	NL	9	9	1	0	47.1	184	38	17	17	3	4	0	1	9	0	28	0	0	5	3	.625	1	0-0	0	2.19	3.23
1996 Mon-SF	NL	20	19	0	0	102.0	430	109	50	45	12	4	1	2	27	0	46	2	0	6	8	.429	0	0-0	0	4.18	3.97
1997 San Francisco	NL	32	32	0	0	190.2	802	194	83	73	17	10	6	1	51	8	115	3	0	13	6	.684	0	0-0	0	3.54	3.45
1998 San Francisco	NL	33	33	1	0	187.2	806	193	100	91	27	5	8	7	57	3	102	6	0	16	9	.640	0	0-0	0	4.27	4.36
1999 San Francisco	NL	33	33	1	0	184.2	804	219	118	111	28	6	4	2	55	2	94	2	0	15	10	.600	0	0-0	0	5.19	5.41
2000 San Francisco	NL	32	31	0	0	184.0	799	205	92	81	23	19	9	2	62	5	71	1	0	11	9	.550	0	0-0	0	4.68	3.96
2001 San Francisco	NL	34	34	0	0	195.1	840	213	105	96	25	11	6	4	66	4	83	1	0	14	12	.538	0	0-0	0	4.65	4.42
2002 San Francisco	NL	33	33	0	0	203.2	846	204	83	73	22	6	6	1	54	7	76	3	0	14	8	.636	0	0-0	0	3.61	3.23
2003 San Francisco	NL	27	27	0	0	147.0	631	170	77	74	14	9	2	1	47	2	41	0	0	10	5	.667	0	0-0	0	4.72	4.53
2004 San Francisco	NL	33	33	0	0	190.1	840	225	108	100	21	9	4	1	66	5	56	1	0	9	12	.429	0	0-0	0	4.98	4.73
1996 Montreal	NL	16	16	0	0	78.2	338	91	44	40	12	4	1	2	22	0	30	0	0	5	6	.455	0	0-0	0	5.06	4.58
1996 San Francisco	NL	4	3	0	0	23.1	92	18	6	5	0	0	0	0	5	0	16	2	0	1	2	.333	0	0-0	0	1.66	1.93
12 ML YEARS		320	318	4	0	1810.2	7720	1961	926	840	208	90	52	24	535	38	793	21	0	128	85	.601	1	0-0	0	4.29	4.18

Glendon Rusch

Pitches: L **Bats:** L **Pos:** SP-16; RP-16   **Ht:** 6'1" **Wt:** 200 **Born:** 11/7/1974 **Age:** 30

		HOW MUCH HE PITCHED						WHAT HE GAVE UP											THE RESULTS							
Year Team	Lg	G	GS	CG	GF	IP	BFP	H	R	ER	HR	SH	SF	HB	TBB	IBB	SO	WP	Bk	W	L	Pct	ShO	Sv-Op	Hld	ERC	ERA
2004 Iowa*	AAA	4	4	0	0	19.0	73	18	6	4	0	1	1	0	1	0	16	0	0	2	0	1.000	0	0--	-	1.99	1.89
1997 Kansas City	AL	30	27	1	0	170.1	758	206	111	104	28	8	7	7	52	0	116	0	1	6	9	.400	0	0-0	0	5.56	5.50
1998 Kansas City	AL	29	24	1	2	154.2	686	191	104	101	22	1	2	4	50	0	94	1	0	6	15	.286	1	1-1	0	5.62	5.88
1999 KC-NYM		4	0	0	2	5.0	26	8	7	7	1	0	0	1	3	0	4	0	0	1	0	1.000	0	0-0	0	10.75	12.60
2000 New York	NL	31	30	2	0	190.2	802	196	91	85	18	10	7	6	44	2	157	2	0	11	11	.500	0	0-0	0	3.64	4.01
2001 New York	NL	33	33	1	0	179.0	785	216	101	92	23	11	5	7	43	2	156	3	2	8	12	.400	0	0-0	0	4.97	4.63
2002 Milwaukee	NL	34	34	4	0	210.2	913	227	118	110	30	14	5	5	76	1	140	6	0	10	16	.385	1	0-0	0	4.80	4.70
2003 Milwaukee	NL	32	19	1	1	123.1	573	171	93	88	11	5	2	4	45	3	93	3	0	1	12	.077	0	1-1	7	6.27	6.42
2004 Chicago	NL	32	16	0	5	129.2	545	127	54	50	10	8	2	4	33	1	90	1	1	6	2	.750	0	2-2	3	3.33	3.47
1999 Kansas City	AL	3	0	0	1	4.0	23	7	7	7	1	0	0	1	3	0	4	0	0	0	1	.000	0	0-0	0	12.89	15.75
1999 New York	NL	1	0	0	1	1.0	3	1	0	0	0	0	0	0	0	0	0	0	0	0	0	-	0	0-0	0	2.79	0.00
8 ML YEARS		225	183	10	10	1163.1	5088	1342	679	637	143	57	30	38	346	9	850	16	4	48	78	.381	2	4-4	10	4.84	4.93

B.J. Ryan

Pitches: L **Bats:** L **Pos:** RP-76   **Ht:** 6'6" **Wt:** 230 **Born:** 12/28/1975 **Age:** 29

		HOW MUCH HE PITCHED						WHAT HE GAVE UP											THE RESULTS							
Year Team	Lg	G	GS	CG	GF	IP	BFP	H	R	ER	HR	SH	SF	HB	TBB	IBB	SO	WP	Bk	W	L	Pct	ShO	Sv-Op	Hld	ERC	ERA
1999 Cin-Bal		14	0	0	3	20.1	82	13	7	7	0	0	1	0	13	1	29	1	0	1	0	1.000	0	0-0	0	2.42	3.10
2000 Baltimore	AL	42	0	0	9	42.2	193	36	29	28	7	1	1	0	31	1	41	2	1	2	3	.400	0	0-3	7	4.87	5.91
2001 Baltimore	AL	61	0	0	9	53.0	237	47	31	25	6	1	2	2	30	4	54	0	0	2	4	.333	0	2-4	14	4.13	4.25
2002 Baltimore	AL	67	0	0	13	57.2	252	51	31	30	7	3	0	4	33	4	56	4	0	2	1	.667	0	1-2	12	4.48	4.68
2003 Baltimore	AL	76	0	0	17	50.1	219	42	19	19	1	1	3	3	27	0	63	2	0	4	1	.800	0	0-2	19	3.33	3.40
2004 Baltimore	AL	76	0	0	19	87.0	361	64	24	22	4	3	2	1	35	9	122	0	0	4	6	.400	0	3-7	21	2.20	2.28
1999 Cincinnati	NL	1	0	0	0	2.0	9	4	1	1	0	0	0	0	1	0	1	0	0	0	0	-	0	0-0	0	12.01	4.50
1999 Baltimore	AL	13	0	0	3	18.1	73	9	6	6	0	0	1	0	12	1	28	1	0	1	0	1.000	0	0-0	0	1.73	2.95
6 ML YEARS		336	0	0	70	311.0	1344	253	141	131	25	9	9	10	169	19	365	9	1	15	15	.500	0	6-18	73	3.47	3.79

Mike Ryan

Bats: L **Throws:** R **Pos:** PH-14; DH-11; LF-10; PR-5; RF-3; CF-2   **Ht:** 6'0" **Wt:** 185 **Born:** 7/6/1977 **Age:** 27

Year Team	Lg	G	AB	H	2B	3B	HR	(Hm	Rd)	TB	R	RBI	RC	TBB	IBB	SO	HBP	SH	SF	SB	CS	SB%	GDP	Avg	OBP	Slg
2004 Rochester*	AAA	50	175	37	7	1	6	(-	-)	64	29	16	16	16	1	38	1	4	0	3	4	.43	3	.211	.281	.366
2002 Minnesota	AL	7	11	1	0	0	0	(0	0)	1	3	0	0	0	0	2	0	0	0	0	0	-	0	.091	.091	.091
2003 Minnesota	AL	27	61	24	7	0	5	(4	1)	46	13	13	15	6	0	12	0	0	1	2	1	.67	4	.393	.441	.754
2004 Minnesota	AL	36	71	17	2	1	0	(0	0)	21	9	7	5	4	1	16	0	0	0	1	1	.50	2	.239	.280	.296
3 ML YEARS		70	143	42	9	1	5	(4	1)	68	25	20	20	10	1	30	0	0	1	3	2	.60	6	.294	.338	.476

Kirk Saarloos

Pitches: R **Bats:** R **Pos:** SP-5; RP-1   **Ht:** 6'0" **Wt:** 185 **Born:** 5/23/1979 **Age:** 26

		HOW MUCH HE PITCHED						WHAT HE GAVE UP											THE RESULTS						
Year Team	Lg	G	GS	CG	GF	IP	BFP	H	R	ER	HR	SH	SF	HB	TBB	IBB	SO	WP	Bk	W	L	Pct	ShO	Sv-Op	Hld	ERC	ERA
2004 New Orleans*	AAA	2	2	0	0	7.0	40	17	15	12	4	0	1	0	1	0	6	0	0	0	2	.000	0	0--	-	16.40	15.43
2004 Sacramento*	AAA	5	5	0	0	20.1	88	19	8	8	1	1	0	1	9	0	17	0	0	2	0	1.000	0	0--	-	3.71	3.54
2002 Houston	NL	17	17	1	0	85.1	372	100	59	57	12	5	2	6	27	5	54	1	0	6	7	.462	1	0-0	0	5.35	6.01
2003 Houston	NL	36	4	0	11	49.1	218	55	31	27	4	1	1	3	17	3	43	0	0	2	1	.667	0	0-0	4	4.51	4.93
2004 Oakland	AL	6	5	0	0	24.1	112	27	13	12	4	2	1	2	12	0	10	0	0	2	1	.667	0	0-0	0	5.91	4.44
3 ML YEARS		59	26	1	12	159.0	702	182	103	96	20	8	4	11	56	8	107	1	0	10	9	.526	1	0-0	4	5.17	5.43

C.C. Sabathia

Pitches: L **Bats:** L **Pos:** SP-30   **Ht:** 6'7" **Wt:** 270 **Born:** 7/21/1980 **Age:** 24

		HOW MUCH HE PITCHED						WHAT HE GAVE UP											THE RESULTS						
Year Team	Lg	G	GS	CG	GF	IP	BFP	H	R	ER	HR	SH	SF	HB	TBB	IBB	SO	WP	Bk	W	L	Pct	ShO	Sv-Op	Hld	ERC	ERA
2001 Cleveland	AL	33	33	0	0	180.1	763	149	93	88	19	3	5	7	95	1	171	7	3	17	5	.773	0	0-0	0	3.86	4.39
2002 Cleveland	AL	33	33	2	0	210.0	891	198	109	102	17	5	10	1	88	2	149	6	3	13	11	.542	0	0-0	0	3.74	4.37
2003 Cleveland	AL	30	30	2	0	197.2	832	190	85	79	19	10	4	6	66	3	141	4	2	13	9	.591	1	0-0	0	3.70	3.60
2004 Cleveland	AL	30	30	1	0	188.0	787	176	90	86	20	3	6	7	72	3	139	1	1	11	10	.524	1	0-0	0	3.91	4.12
4 ML YEARS		126	126	5	0	776.0	3273	713	377	355	75	21	25	21	321	9	600	18	9	54	35	.607	2	0-0	0	3.80	4.12

Donnie Sadler

Bats: R **Throws:** R **Pos:** PH-6; PR-6; SS-3; LF-3; CF-3; 2B-2; 3B-2; RF-1   **Ht:** 5'6" **Wt:** 175 **Born:** 6/17/1975 **Age:** 30

		BATTING																	BASERUNNING				AVERAGES		
Year Team	Lg	G	AB	H	2B	3B	HR	(Hm	Rd)	TB	R	RBI	RC	TBB	IBB	SO	HBP	SH	SF	SB	CS	SB%	GDP	Avg	OBP	Slg
2004 Charlotte*	AAA	3	7	1	0	0	0	(-	-)	1	0	0	0	1	0	3	0	0	0	0	0	-	0	.143	.250	.143
1998 Boston	AL	58	124	28	4	4	3	(0	3)	49	21	15	15	6	0	28	3	5	1	4	0	1.00	1	.226	.276	.395
1999 Boston	AL	49	107	30	5	1	0	(0	0)	37	18	4	12	5	0	20	0	3	0	2	1	.67	1	.280	.313	.346
2000 Boston	AL	49	99	22	5	0	1	(0	1)	30	14	10	8	5	0	18	1	5	2	3	1	.75	1	.222	.262	.303
2001 Cin-KC		93	185	30	6	0	1	(0	1)	39	28	5	8	18	0	37	2	5	1	7	4	.64	3	.162	.243	.211
2002 KC-Tex		73	98	16	2	1	0	(0	0)	20	16	7	4	7	0	19	2	1	1	5	3	.63	1	.163	.231	.204
2003 Texas		77	131	26	5	2	1	(0	1)	38	27	5	10	13	0	34	2	2	2	4	3	.57	1	.198	.277	.290
2004 Arizona	NL	18	23	3	2	0	0	(0	0)	5	1	0	0	1	0	7	0	0	0	0	0	-	0	.130	.167	.217
2001 Cincinnati	NL	39	84	17	3	0	1	(0	1)	23	9	3	5	9	0	20	0	2	0	3	3	.50	3	.202	.280	.274
2001 Kansas City	AL	54	101	13	3	0	0	(0	0)	16	19	2	3	9	0	17	2	3	1	4	1	.80	0	.129	.212	.158
2002 Kansas City	AL	35	68	13	1	1	0	(0	0)	16	10	5	4	4	0	12	0	0	1	3	1	.75	0	.191	.233	.235
2002 Texas	AL	38	30	3	1	0	0	(0	0)	4	6	2	0	3	0	7	2	1	0	2	2	.50	1	.100	.229	.133
7 ML YEARS		417	767	155	29	8	6	(0	6)	218	125	46	57	55	0	163	10	21	7	25	12	.68	8	.202	.262	.284

Chris Saenz

Pitches: R **Bats:** R **Pos:** SP-1   **Ht:** 6'3" **Wt:** 200 **Born:** 8/14/1981 **Age:** 23

		HOW MUCH HE PITCHED						WHAT HE GAVE UP											THE RESULTS						
Year Team	Lg	G	GS	CG	GF	IP	BFP	H	R	ER	HR	SH	SF	HB	TBB	IBB	SO	WP	Bk	W	L	Pct	ShO	Sv-Op	Hld	ERC	ERA
2001 Ogden	R+	21	4	0	5	46.2	195	43	25	22	5	4	3	2	14	2	48	1	0	3	1	.750	0	0--	-	3.41	4.24
2002 Beloit	A	37	0	0	23	74.1	322	59	31	29	5	6	4	8	32	1	99	1	2	3	5	.375	0	8--	-	3.16	3.51
2003 High Desert	A+	26	26	1	0	128.0	559	121	80	74	20	3	2	15	56	0	136	7	0	9	9	.500	0	0--	-	4.84	5.20
2003 Huntsville	AA	1	0	0	1	6.0	23	4	2	1	0	0	0	0	3	0	6	0	0	0	0	-	0	0--	-	2.25	1.50
2004 Huntsville	AA	14	14	0	0	84.2	340	76	41	39	10	2	2	5	18	1	84	2	3	5	5	.500	0	0--	-	3.20	4.15
2004 Milwaukee	NL	1	1	0	0	6.0	24	2	0	0	0	0	0	1	3	0	7	0	0	1	0	1.000	0	0-0	0	1.26	0.00

Olmedo Saenz

Bats: R **Throws:** R **Pos:** PH-55; 1B-25; DH-4; 3B-2   **Ht:** 5'11" **Wt:** 221 **Born:** 10/8/1970 **Age:** 34

		BATTING																	BASERUNNING				AVERAGES		
Year Team	Lg	G	AB	H	2B	3B	HR	(Hm	Rd)	TB	R	RBI	RC	TBB	IBB	SO	HBP	SH	SF	SB	CS	SB%	GDP	Avg	OBP	Slg
1994 Chicago	AL	5	14	2	0	1	0	(0	0)	4	2	0	0	0	0	5	0	1	0	0	0	-	1	.143	.143	.286
1999 Oakland	AL	97	255	70	18	0	11	(8	3)	121	41	41	44	22	1	47	15	0	3	1	1	.50	6	.275	.363	.475
2000 Oakland	AL	76	214	67	12	2	9	(3	6)	110	40	33	42	25	2	40	7	0	1	1	0	1.00	6	.313	.401	.514
2001 Oakland	AL	106	305	67	21	1	9	(6	3)	117	33	32	32	19	1	64	13	1	3	0	1	.00	9	.220	.291	.384
2002 Oakland	AL	68	156	43	10	1	6	(3	3)	73	15	18	23	13	1	31	7	0	2	1	1	.50	2	.276	.354	.468
2004 Los Angeles	NL	77	111	31	1	0	8	(3	5)	56	17	22	18	12	1	33	2	0	3	0	0	-	4	.279	.352	.505
6 ML YEARS		429	1055	280	62	5	43	(23	20)	481	148	146	159	91	6	220	44	2	12	3	3	.50	28	.265	.345	.456

Tim Salmon

Bats: R **Throws:** R **Pos:** DH-39; PH-14; RF-6; LF-3   **Ht:** 6'3" **Wt:** 225 **Born:** 8/24/1968 **Age:** 36

		BATTING																	BASERUNNING				AVERAGES		
Year Team	Lg	G	AB	H	2B	3B	HR	(Hm	Rd)	TB	R	RBI	RC	TBB	IBB	SO	HBP	SH	SF	SB	CS	SB%	GDP	Avg	OBP	Slg
2004 R Cucamnga*	A+	7	23	8	1	0	2	(-	-)	17	5	6	6	4	0	6	0	0	0	0	0	-	0	.348	.444	.739
1992 California	AL	23	79	14	1	0	2	(1	1)	21	8	6	6	11	1	23	1	0	1	1	1	.50	1	.177	.283	.266
1993 California	AL	142	515	146	35	1	31	(23	8)	276	93	95	104	82	5	135	5	0	8	5	6	.45	6	.283	.382	.536
1994 California	AL	100	373	107	18	2	23	(12	11)	198	67	70	75	54	2	102	5	0	3	1	3	.25	3	.287	.382	.531
1995 California	AL	143	537	177	34	3	34	(15	19)	319	111	105	130	91	2	111	6	0	4	5	5	.50	9	.330	.429	.594
1996 California	AL	156	581	166	27	4	30	(18	12)	291	90	98	113	93	7	125	4	0	3	4	2	.67	8	.286	.386	.501
1997 Anaheim	AL	157	582	172	28	1	33	(17	16)	301	95	129	117	95	1	142	7	0	11	9	12	.43	7	.296	.394	.517
1998 Anaheim	AL	136	463	139	28	1	26	(13	13)	247	84	88	103	90	5	100	3	0	10	0	1	.00	4	.300	.410	.533
1999 Anaheim	AL	98	353	94	24	2	17	(7	10)	173	60	69	66	63	2	82	0	0	6	4	1	.80	7	.266	.372	.490
2000 Anaheim	AL	158	568	165	36	2	34	(17	17)	307	108	97	120	104	5	139	6	0	2	0	2	.00	14	.290	.404	.540
2001 Anaheim	AL	137	475	108	21	1	17	(11	6)	182	63	49	72	96	4	121	8	0	2	9	3	.75	11	.227	.365	.383
2002 Anaheim	AL	138	483	138	37	1	22	(10	12)	243	84	88	98	71	3	102	7	0	7	6	3	.67	6	.286	.380	.503

Year Team	Lg	G	AB	H	2B	3B	HR	(Hm	Rd)	TB	R	RBI	RC	TBB	IBB	SO	HBP	SH	SF	SB	CS	SB%	GDP	Avg	OBP	Slg
2003 Anaheim	AL	148	528	145	35	4	19	(10	9)	245	78	72	91	77	3	93	10	0	6	3	1	.75	12	.275	.374	.464
2004 Anaheim	AL	60	186	47	7	0	2	(1	1)	60	15	23	21	14	0	41	2	0	4	1	0	1.00	2	.253	.306	.323
13 ML YEARS		1596	5723	1618	331	22	290	(155	135)	2863	956	989	1116	941	44	1316	64	0	67	48	40	.55	90	.283	.386	.500

Alex Sanchez

Bats: L **Throws:** L **Pos:** CF-78; PR-2 **Ht:** 5'10" **Wt:** 159 **Born:** 8/26/1976 **Age:** 28

Year Team	Lg	G	AB	H	2B	3B	HR	(Hm	Rd)	TB	R	RBI	RC	TBB	IBB	SO	HBP	SH	SF	SB	CS	SB%	GDP	Avg	OBP	Slg
2004 Toledo*	AAA	2	10	0	0	0	0	(-	-)	0	0	0	0	0	0	6	0	0	0	0	0	-	0	.000	.000	.000
2001 Milwaukee	NL	30	68	14	3	2	0	(0	0)	21	7	4	6	5	0	13	0	0	0	6	2	.75	0	.206	.260	.309
2002 Milwaukee	NL	112	394	114	10	7	1	(0	1)	141	55	33	54	31	0	62	2	6	2	37	14	.73	4	.289	.343	.358
2003 Mil-Det		144	557	160	23	8	1	(0	1)	202	58	32	60	25	0	74	3	9	5	52	24	.68	5	.287	.319	.363
2004 Detroit	AL	79	332	107	9	3	2	(1	1)	128	41	26	40	7	0	50	0	12	1	19	13	.59	5	.322	.335	.386
2003 Milwaukee	NL	43	163	46	10	3	0	(0	0)	62	15	10	17	7	0	28	2	2	2	8	6	.57	1	.282	.316	.380
2003 Detroit	AL	101	394	114	13	5	1	(0	1)	140	43	22	43	18	0	46	1	7	3	44	18	.71	4	.289	.320	.355
4 ML YEARS		365	1351	395	45	20	4	(1	3)	492	161	95	160	68	0	199	5	27	8	114	53	.68	14	.292	.327	.364

Duaner Sanchez

Pitches: R **Bats:** R **Pos:** RP-67 **Ht:** 6'0" **Wt:** 190 **Born:** 10/14/1979 **Age:** 25

		HOW MUCH HE PITCHED						WHAT HE GAVE UP											THE RESULTS							
Year Team	Lg	G	GS	CG	GF	IP	BFP	H	R	ER	HR	SH	SF	HB	TBB	IBB	SO	WP	Bk	W	L	Pct	ShO	Sv-Op	Hld	ERC	ERA
2002 Ari-Pit	NL	9	0	0	5	6.0	31	6	6	6	2	0	0	0	7	0	6	0	0	0	0	-	0	0-1	1	9.19	9.00
2003 Pittsburgh	NL	6	0	0	2	6.0	34	15	11	11	2	0	1	2	1	0	3	0	0	1	0	1.000	0	0-0	0	17.96	16.50
2004 Los Angeles	NL	67	0	0	27	80.0	342	81	34	30	9	2	3	6	27	2	44	6	0	3	1	.750	0	0-1	4	4.31	3.38
2002 Arizona	NL	6	0	0	3	3.2	19	3	2	2	1	0	0	0	5	0	4	0	0	0	0	-	0	0-1	1	8.32	4.91
2002 Pittsburgh	NL	3	0	0	2	2.1	12	3	4	4	1	0	0	0	2	0	2	0	0	0	0	-	0	0-0	0	10.55	15.43
3 ML YEARS		82	0	0	34	92.0	407	102	51	47	13	2	4	8	35	2	53	6	0	4	1	.800	0	0-2	5	5.32	4.60

Freddy Sanchez

Bats: R **Throws:** R **Pos:** SS-4; 2B-3; PH-3; 3B-1; PR-1 **Ht:** 5'11" **Wt:** 185 **Born:** 12/21/1977 **Age:** 27

Year Team	Lg	G	AB	H	2B	3B	HR	(Hm	Rd)	TB	R	RBI	RC	TBB	IBB	SO	HBP	SH	SF	SB	CS	SB%	GDP	Avg	OBP	Slg
2004 Nashville*	AAA	44	125	33	7	1	1	(-	-)	45	10	11	15	11	0	17	1	2	1	4	1	.80	3	.264	.326	.360
2002 Boston	AL	12	16	3	0	0	0	(0	0)	3	3	2	1	2	0	3	0	0	0	0	0	-	0	.188	.278	.188
2003 Boston	AL	20	34	8	2	0	0	(0	0)	10	6	2	1	0	0	8	0	0	0	0	0	-	0	.235	.235	.294
2004 Pittsburgh	NL	9	19	3	0	0	0	(0	0)	3	2	2	2	0	0	3	0	1	0	0	0	-	0	.158	.158	.158
3 ML YEARS		41	69	14	2	0	0	(0	0)	16	11	6	4	2	0	14	0	1	0	0	0	-	0	.203	.225	.232

Jesus Sanchez

Pitches: L **Bats:** L **Pos:** SP-3 **Ht:** 5'11" **Wt:** 175 **Born:** 10/11/1974 **Age:** 30

		HOW MUCH HE PITCHED						WHAT HE GAVE UP											THE RESULTS							
Year Team	Lg	G	GS	CG	GF	IP	BFP	H	R	ER	HR	SH	SF	HB	TBB	IBB	SO	WP	Bk	W	L	Pct	ShO	Sv-Op	Hld	ERC	ERA
2004 Syracuse*	AAA	7	4	0	1	25.0	114	28	21	19	5	1	2	1	13	1	20	2	0	1	4	.200	0	0---	-	6.17	6.84
2004 Louisville*	AAA	22	5	0	6	60.0	254	49	22	20	6	0	0	1	28	0	51	1	0	3	2	.600	0	1---	-	3.33	3.00
1998 Florida	NL	35	29	0	1	173.0	765	178	98	86	18	12	4	4	91	2	137	8	5	7	9	.438	0	0-1	0	4.91	4.47
1999 Florida	NL	59	10	0	8	76.1	362	84	53	51	16	2	7	4	60	11	62	5	2	5	7	.417	0	0-2	11	7.28	6.01
2000 Florida	NL	32	32	2	0	182.0	805	197	118	108	32	9	12	4	76	4	123	4	0	9	12	.429	2	0-0	0	5.24	5.34
2001 Florida	NL	16	9	0	3	62.2	274	61	33	33	7	2	1	2	31	2	46	0	0	2	4	.333	0	0-0	5	4.49	4.74
2002 Chicago	NL	8	0	0	2	8.1	15	15	12	12	4	0	2	1	10	1	6	3	0	0	0	-	0	0-0	0	17.13	12.96
2003 Colorado	NL	9	0	0	4	8.0	38	11	8	8	1	0	0	0	4	2	2	1	0	0	0	-	0	0-0	5	6.48	9.00
2004 Cincinnati	NL	3	3	0	0	14.1	68	18	12	12	4	0	0	0	9	0	8	0	0	0	2	.000	0	0-0	0	8.15	7.53
7 ML YEARS		162	83	2	18	524.2	2363	564	334	310	82	25	26	15	281	22	384	21	7	23	34	.404	2	0-3	12	5.58	5.32

Rey Sanchez

Bats: R **Throws:** R **Pos:** 2B-87; SS-4; PH-4 **Ht:** 5'9" **Wt:** 175 **Born:** 10/5/1967 **Age:** 37

Year Team	Lg	G	AB	H	2B	3B	HR	(Hm	Rd)	TB	R	RBI	RC	TBB	IBB	SO	HBP	SH	SF	SB	CS	SB%	GDP	Avg	OBP	Slg
1991 Chicago	NL	13	23	6	0	0	0	(0	0)	6	1	2	3	4	0	3	0	0	0	0	0	-	0	.261	.370	.261
1992 Chicago	NL	74	255	64	14	3	1	(1	0)	87	24	19	23	10	1	17	3	5	2	2	1	.67	7	.251	.285	.341
1993 Chicago	NL	105	344	97	11	2	0	(0	0)	112	35	28	34	15	7	22	3	9	2	1	1	.50	8	.282	.316	.326
1994 Chicago	NL	96	291	83	13	1	0	(0	0)	98	26	24	32	20	4	29	7	4	1	2	5	.29	9	.285	.345	.337
1995 Chicago	NL	114	428	119	22	2	3	(0	3)	154	57	27	44	14	2	48	1	8	2	6	4	.60	9	.278	.301	.360
1996 Chicago	NL	95	289	61	9	0	1	(1	0)	73	28	12	19	22	6	42	3	8	2	7	1	.88	6	.211	.272	.253
1997 ChC-NYY		135	343	94	21	0	2	(1	1)	121	35	27	34	16	2	47	1	9	1	4	6	.40	8	.274	.307	.353
1998 San Francisco	NL	109	316	90	14	2	2	(0	2)	114	44	30	35	16	0	47	4	1	2	0	0	-	11	.285	.325	.361
1999 Kansas City	AL	134	479	141	18	6	2	(1	1)	177	66	56	56	22	2	48	4	10	3	11	5	.69	14	.294	.329	.370
2000 Kansas City	AL	143	509	139	18	2	1	(1	0)	164	68	38	49	28	0	55	4	11	3	7	3	.70	17	.273	.314	.322
2001 KC-Atl		149	544	153	18	6	0	(0	0)	183	56	37	52	15	1	49	2	13	5	11	1	.92	20	.281	.300	.336
2002 Boston	AL	107	357	102	12	3	1	(1	0)	123	46	38	42	17	1	31	2	5	1	2	2	.50	9	.286	.318	.345
2003 NYM-Sea		102	344	86	8	2	0	(0	0)	98	33	23	25	16	3	39	2	4	3	2	1	.67	10	.250	.285	.285
2004 Tampa Bay	AL	91	285	70	14	3	2	(2	0)	96	23	26	28	12	0	28	3	4	3	0	1	.00	6	.246	.281	.337
1997 Chicago	NL	97	205	51	9	0	1	(1	0)	63	14	12	16	11	2	26	0	4	0	1	1	.50	7	.249	.287	.307
1997 New York	AL	38	138	43	12	0	1	(0	1)	58	21	15	18	5	0	21	1	5	1	3	5	.38	1	.312	.338	.420
2001 Kansas City	AL	100	390	118	14	5	0	(0	0)	142	46	28	45	11	0	34	2	9	4	9	1	.90	11	.303	.322	.364
2001 Atlanta	NL	49	154	35	4	1	0	(0	0)	41	10	9	7	4	1	15	0	4	1	2	0	1.00	9	.227	.245	.266
2003 New York	NL	56	174	36	3	1	0	(0	0)	41	11	12	7	8	2	18	0	1	1	1	1	.50	7	.207	.240	.236
2003 Seattle	AL	46	170	50	5	1	0	(0	0)	57	22	11	18	8	1	21	2	4	2	1	0	1.00	3	.294	.330	.335
14 ML YEARS		1467	4807	1305	192	32	15	(8	7)	1606	542	387	476	227	29	505	39	91	34	55	31	.64	134	.271	.308	.334

Reggie Sanders

Bats: R Throws: R Pos: RF-81; LF-38; PH-18; DH-1; PR-1   Ht: 6'1" Wt: 205 Born: 12/1/1967 Age: 37

							BATTING												BASERUNNING				AVERAGES		
Year Team	Lg	G	AB	H	2B	3B	HR	(Hm | Rd)	TB	R	RBI	RC	TBB	IBB	SO	HBP	SH	SF	SB	CS	SB%	GDP	Avg	OBP	Slg
1991 Cincinnati	NL	9	40	8	0	0	1	(0 | 1)	11	6	3	1	0	0	9	0	0	0	1	1	.50	1	.200	.200	.275
1992 Cincinnati	NL	116	385	104	26	6	12	(6 | 6)	178	62	36	64	48	2	98	4	0	1	16	7	.70	6	.270	.356	.462
1993 Cincinnati	NL	138	496	136	16	4	20	(8 | 12)	220	90	83	76	51	7	118	5	3	8	27	10	.73	10	.274	.343	.444
1994 Cincinnati	NL	107	400	105	20	8	17	(10 | 7)	192	66	62	65	41	1	114	2	1	3	21	9	.70	2	.263	.332	.480
1995 Cincinnati	NL	133	484	148	36	6	28	(9 | 19)	280	91	99	109	69	4	122	8	0	6	36	12	.75	9	.306	.397	.579
1996 Cincinnati	NL	81	287	72	17	1	14	(7 | 7)	133	49	33	47	44	4	86	2	0	1	24	8	.75	8	.251	.353	.463
1997 Cincinnati	NL	86	312	79	19	2	19	(11 | 8)	159	52	56	53	42	3	93	3	1	0	13	7	.65	9	.253	.347	.510
1998 Cincinnati	NL	135	481	129	18	6	14	(7 | 7)	201	83	59	69	51	2	137	7	4	2	20	9	.69	10	.268	.346	.418
1999 San Diego	NL	133	478	136	24	7	26	(11 | 15)	252	92	72	94	65	1	108	6	0	1	36	13	.73	10	.285	.376	.527
2000 Atlanta	NL	103	340	79	23	1	11	(4 | 7)	137	43	37	42	32	2	78	2	3	0	21	4	.84	9	.232	.302	.403
2001 Arizona	NL	126	441	116	21	3	33	(19 | 14)	242	84	90	80	46	7	126	5	1	3	14	10	.58	2	.263	.337	.549
2002 San Francisco	NL	140	505	126	23	6	23	(12 | 11)	230	75	85	65	47	3	121	12	0	7	18	6	.75	10	.250	.324	.455
2003 Pittsburgh	NL	130	453	129	27	4	31	(17 | 14)	257	74	87	78	38	4	110	5	0	2	15	5	.75	10	.285	.345	.567
2004 St Louis	NL	135	446	116	27	3	22	(8 | 14)	215	64	67	65	33	5	118	4	1	3	21	5	.81	5	.260	.315	.482
14 ML YEARS		1572	5548	1483	297	57	271	(129 | 142)	2707	931	869	908	607	45	1438	65	14	37	283	106	.73	101	.267	.344	.488

Johan Santana

Pitches: L Bats: L Pos: SP-34   Ht: 6'0" Wt: 195 Born: 3/13/1979 Age: 26

		HOW MUCH HE PITCHED						WHAT HE GAVE UP										THE RESULTS							
Year Team	Lg	G	GS	CG	GF	IP	BFP	H	R	ER	HR	SH	SF	HB	TBB	IBB	SO	WP	Bk	W	L	Pct	ShO	Sv-Op	Hld	ERC	ERA
2000 Minnesota	AL	30	5	0	9	86.0	398	102	64	62	11	1	3	2	54	0	64	5	2	2	3	.400	0	0-0	0	6.59	6.49
2001 Minnesota	AL	15	4	0	5	43.2	195	50	25	23	6	2	3	3	16	0	28	3	0	1	0	1.000	0	0-0	0	5.36	4.74
2002 Minnesota	AL	27	14	0	2	108.1	452	84	41	36	7	3	3	1	49	0	137	15	2	8	6	.571	0	1-1	3	2.86	2.99
2003 Minnesota	AL	45	18	0	7	158.1	643	127	56	54	17	2	4	3	47	1	169	6	2	12	3	.800	0	0-0	5	2.74	3.07
2004 Minnesota	AL	34	34	1	0	228.0	881	156	70	66	24	3	3	9	54	0	265	7	0	20	6	.769	1	0-0	0	2.07	2.61
5 ML YEARS		151	75	1	23	624.1	2569	519	256	241	65	11	16	18	220	1	663	36	6	43	18	.705	1	1-1	8	3.14	3.47

Benito Santiago

Bats: R Throws: R Pos: C-49   Ht: 6'1" Wt: 200 Born: 3/9/1965 Age: 40

							BATTING												BASERUNNING				AVERAGES		
Year Team	Lg	G	AB	H	2B	3B	HR	(Hm	Rd)	TB	R	RBI	RC	TBB	IBB	SO	HBP	SH	SF	SB	CS	SB%	GDP	Avg	OBP	Slg
1986 San Diego	NL	17	62	18	2	0	3	(2	1)	29	10	6	9	2	0	12	0	0	1	0	1	.00	0	.290	.308	.468
1987 San Diego	NL	146	546	164	33	2	18	(11	7)	255	64	79	77	16	2	112	5	1	4	21	12	.64	12	.300	.324	.467
1988 San Diego	NL	139	492	122	22	2	10	(3	7)	178	49	46	45	24	2	82	1	5	5	15	7	.68	18	.248	.282	.362
1989 San Diego	NL	129	462	109	16	3	16	(8	8)	179	50	62	47	26	6	89	1	3	2	11	6	.65	9	.236	.277	.387
1990 San Diego	NL	100	344	93	8	5	11	(5	6)	144	42	53	47	27	2	55	3	1	7	5	5	.50	4	.270	.323	.419
1991 San Diego	NL	152	580	155	22	3	17	(6	11)	234	60	87	61	23	5	114	4	0	7	8	10	.44	21	.267	.296	.403
1992 San Diego	NL	106	386	97	21	0	10	(8	2)	148	37	42	37	21	1	52	0	0	4	2	5	.29	14	.251	.287	.383
1993 Florida	NL	139	469	108	19	6	13	(6	7)	178	49	50	50	37	2	88	5	0	4	10	7	.59	9	.230	.291	.380
1994 Florida	NL	101	337	92	14	2	11	(4	7)	143	35	41	43	25	1	57	1	2	4	1	2	.33	11	.273	.322	.424
1995 Cincinnati	NL	81	266	76	20	0	11	(7	4)	129	40	44	43	24	1	48	4	0	2	2	2	.50	7	.286	.351	.485
1996 Philadelphia	NL	136	481	127	21	2	30	(8	22)	242	71	85	79	49	7	104	1	0	2	2	0	1.00	8	.264	.332	.503
1997 Toronto	AL	97	341	83	10	0	13	(7	6)	132	31	42	35	17	1	80	2	1	5	1	0	1.00	10	.243	.279	.387
1998 Toronto	AL	15	29	9	5	0	0	(0	0)	14	3	4	4	1	0	6	0	0	0	0	0	-	1	.310	.333	.483
1999 Chicago	NL	109	350	87	18	3	7	(2	5)	132	28	36	39	32	6	71	2	0	2	1	1	.50	12	.249	.313	.377
2000 Cincinnati	NL	89	252	66	11	1	8	(7	1)	103	22	45	30	19	8	45	1	0	5	2	2	.50	7	.262	.310	.409
2001 San Francisco	NL	133	477	125	25	4	6	(3	3)	176	39	45	46	23	0	78	2	7	6	5	4	.56	19	.262	.295	.369
2002 San Francisco	NL	126	478	133	24	5	16	(6	10)	215	56	74	57	27	8	73	2	3	7	4	2	.67	19	.278	.315	.450
2003 San Francisco	NL	108	401	112	21	2	11	(2	9)	170	53	56	50	29	0	69	2	0	2	0	1	.00	13	.279	.329	.424
2004 Kansas City	AL	49	175	48	10	0	6	(3	3)	76	15	23	19	8	0	32	2	3	1	1	2	.33	9	.274	.312	.434
19 ML YEARS		1972	6928	1824	322	40	217	(98	119)	2877	754	920	818	430	52	1267	38	26	70	91	69	.57	203	.263	.307	.415

Ramon Santiago

Bats: B Throws: R Pos: SS-16; PR-4; DH-1   Ht: 5'11" Wt: 150 Born: 8/31/1979 Age: 25

							BATTING												BASERUNNING				AVERAGES		
Year Team	Lg	G	AB	H	2B	3B	HR	(Hm	Rd)	TB	R	RBI	RC	TBB	IBB	SO	HBP	SH	SF	SB	CS	SB%	GDP	Avg	OBP	Slg
2004 Tacoma*	AAA	71	243	47	7	2	1	(-	-)	61	35	24	19	24	1	31	10	12	4	9	6	.60	3	.193	.288	.251
2002 Detroit	AL	65	222	54	5	5	4	(3	1)	81	33	20	23	13	0	48	8	4	2	8	5	.62	2	.243	.306	.365
2003 Detroit	AL	141	444	100	18	1	2	(1	1)	126	41	29	38	33	0	66	10	18	1	10	4	.71	9	.225	.292	.284
2004 Seattle	AL	19	39	7	1	0	0	(0	0)	8	8	2	1	3	0	3	1	2	0	0	0	-	1	.179	.256	.205
3 ML YEARS		225	705	161	24	6	6	(4	2)	215	82	51	62	49	0	117	19	24	4	18	9	.67	12	.228	.295	.305

Victor Santos

Pitches: R Bats: R Pos: SP-28; RP-3   Ht: 6'3" Wt: 195 Born: 10/2/1976 Age: 28

		HOW MUCH HE PITCHED						WHAT HE GAVE UP										THE RESULTS							
Year Team	Lg	G	GS	CG	GF	IP	BFP	H	R	ER	HR	SH	SF	HB	TBB	IBB	SO	WP	Bk	W	L	Pct	ShO	Sv-Op	Hld	ERC	ERA
2004 Indianapolis*	AAA	3	3	0	0	10.1	45	12	4	4	1	1	0	0	4	0	11	0	0	0	0	-	0	0- -	-	5.04	3.48
2001 Detroit	AL	33	7	0	6	76.1	335	62	33	28	9	1	3	3	49	4	52	0	0	2	2	.500	0	0-0	2	4.18	3.30
2002 Colorado	NL	24	2	0	6	26.0	140	41	30	30	3	3	1	0	23	3	25	2	0	0	4	.000	0	0-0	1	9.37	10.38
2003 Texas	AL	8	4	0	2	25.2	117	29	21	20	5	1	1	1	16	1	15	0	0	0	2	.000	0	0-0	0	6.82	7.01
2004 Milwaukee	NL	31	28	0	2	154.0	684	169	95	85	18	6	7	7	57	5	115	2	1	11	12	.478	0	0-0	0	4.73	4.97
4 ML YEARS		96	41	0	16	282.0	1276	301	179	163	35	11	12	11	144	13	207	4	1	13	20	.394	0	0-0	3	5.16	5.20

Scott Sauerbeck

Pitches: L **Bats:** R **Pos:** RP   **Ht:** 6'3" **Wt:** 197 **Born:** 11/9/1971 **Age:** 33

Year Team	Lg	G	GS	CG	GF	IP	BFP	H	R	ER	HR	SH	SF	HB	TBB	IBB	SO	WP	Bk	W	L	Pct	ShO	Sv-Op	Hld	ERC	ERA
1999 Pittsburgh	NL	65	0	0	16	67.2	287	53	19	15	6	4	0	4	38	5	55	3	0	4	1	.800	0	2-5	10	3.60	2.00
2000 Pittsburgh	NL	75	0	0	13	75.2	349	76	36	34	4	3	3	1	61	8	83	9	2	5	4	.556	0	1-4	13	5.31	4.04
2001 Pittsburgh	NL	70	0	0	14	62.2	281	61	41	39	4	2	0	2	40	6	79	3	0	2	2	.500	0	2-4	19	4.60	5.60
2002 Pittsburgh	NL	78	0	0	21	62.2	255	50	18	16	4	0	0	1	27	4	70	2	1	5	4	.556	0	0-0	28	2.91	2.30
2003 Pit-Bos		79	0	0	13	56.2	261	47	34	30	6	2	1	5	43	5	50	1	0	3	5	.375	0	0-5	18	4.71	4.76
2003 Pittsburgh	NL	53	0	0	11	40.0	174	30	20	18	5	2	0	1	25	2	32	0	0	3	4	.429	0	0-4	16	3.72	4.05
2003 Boston	AL	26	0	0	2	16.2	87	17	14	12	1	0	1	4	18	3	18	1	0	0	1	.000	0	0-1	2	7.20	6.48
5 ML YEARS		367	0	0	77	325.1	1433	287	148	134	24	11	4	13	209	28	337	18	3	19	16	.543	0	5-18	88	4.23	3.71

Curt Schilling

Pitches: R **Bats:** R **Pos:** SP-32   **Ht:** 6'4" **Wt:** 231 **Born:** 11/14/1966 **Age:** 38

Year Team	Lg	G	GS	CG	GF	IP	BFP	H	R	ER	HR	SH	SF	HB	TBB	IBB	SO	WP	Bk	W	L	Pct	ShO	Sv-Op	Hld	ERC	ERA
1988 Baltimore	AL	4	4	0	0	14.2	76	22	19	16	3	0	3	1	10	1	4	2	0	0	3	.000	0	0-0	0	9.43	9.82
1989 Baltimore	AL	5	1	0	0	8.2	38	10	6	6	2	0	0	0	3	0	6	1	0	0	1	.000	0	0-0	0	5.74	6.23
1990 Baltimore	AL	35	0	0	16	46.0	191	38	13	13	1	2	4	0	19	0	32	0	0	1	2	.333	0	3-9	5	2.68	2.54
1991 Houston	NL	56	0	0	34	75.2	336	79	35	32	2	5	1	0	39	7	71	4	1	3	5	.375	0	8-11	5	4.08	3.81
1992 Philadelphia	NL	42	26	10	10	226.1	895	165	67	59	11	7	8	1	59	4	147	4	0	14	11	.560	4	2-3	0	1.86	2.35
1993 Philadelphia	NL	34	34	7	0	235.1	982	234	114	105	23	9	7	4	57	6	186	9	3	16	7	.696	2	0-0	0	3.44	4.02
1994 Philadelphia	NL	13	13	1	0	82.1	360	87	42	41	10	6	1	3	28	3	58	3	1	2	8	.200	0	0-0	0	4.36	4.48
1995 Philadelphia	NL	17	17	1	0	116.0	473	96	52	46	12	5	2	3	26	2	114	0	1	7	5	.583	0	0-0	0	2.55	3.57
1996 Philadelphia	NL	26	26	8	0	183.1	732	149	69	65	16	6	4	3	50	5	182	5	0	9	10	.474	2	0-0	0	2.59	3.19
1997 Philadelphia	NL	35	35	7	0	254.1	1009	208	96	84	25	8	8	5	58	3	319	5	1	17	11	.607	2	0-0	0	2.55	2.97
1998 Philadelphia	NL	35	35	15	0	268.2	1089	236	101	97	23	14	7	6	61	3	300	12	0	15	14	.517	2	0-0	0	2.75	3.25
1999 Philadelphia	NL	24	24	8	0	180.1	735	159	74	71	25	11	3	5	44	0	152	4	0	15	6	.714	1	0-0	0	3.20	3.54
2000 Phi-Ari	NL	29	29	8	0	210.1	862	204	90	89	27	11	4	1	45	4	168	4	0	11	12	.478	2	0-0	0	3.38	3.81
2001 Arizona	NL	35	35	6	0	256.2	1021	237	86	85	37	8	5	1	39	0	293	4	0	22	6	.786	1	0-0	0	3.03	2.98
2002 Arizona	NL	36	35	5	0	259.1	1017	218	95	93	29	4	3	3	33	1	316	6	0	23	7	.767	1	0-0	0	2.33	3.23
2003 Arizona	NL	24	24	3	0	168.0	673	144	58	55	17	11	1	3	32	2	194	4	0	8	9	.471	2	0-0	0	2.59	2.95
2004 Boston	AL	32	32	3	0	226.2	910	206	84	82	23	3	6	5	35	0	203	3	0	21	6	.778	0	0-0	0	2.75	3.26
2000 Philadelphia	NL	16	16	4	0	112.2	474	110	49	49	17	5	1	1	32	4	96	4	0	6	6	.500	1	0-0	0	3.79	3.91
2000 Arizona	NL	13	13	4	0	97.2	388	94	41	40	10	6	3	0	13	0	72	0	0	5	6	.455	1	0-0	0	2.91	3.69
17 ML YEARS		482	370	82	60	2812.2	11399	2492	1101	1039	286	110	67	44	638	41	2745	70	7	184	123	.599	19	13-23	10	2.86	3.32

Jason Schmidt

Pitches: R **Bats:** R **Pos:** SP-32   **Ht:** 6'5" **Wt:** 205 **Born:** 1/29/1973 **Age:** 32

Year Team	Lg	G	GS	CG	GF	IP	BFP	H	R	ER	HR	SH	SF	HB	TBB	IBB	SO	WP	Bk	W	L	Pct	ShO	Sv-Op	Hld	ERC	ERA
2004 San Jose*	A+	1	1	0	0	5.0	18	2	0	0	0	0	0	1	0	7	1	0	0	1	.000	0	0- -		0.63	0.00
1995 Atlanta	NL	9	2	0	1	25.0	119	27	17	16	2	2	4	1	18	3	19	1	0	2	2	.500	0	0-1	0	5.56	5.76
1996 Atl-Pit	NL	19	17	1	0	96.1	445	108	67	61	10	4	9	2	53	0	74	8	1	5	6	.455	0	0-0	0	5.46	5.70
1997 Pittsburgh	NL	32	32	2	0	187.2	825	193	106	96	16	10	3	9	76	2	136	8	0	10	9	.526	0	0-0	0	4.31	4.60
1998 Pittsburgh	NL	33	33	0	0	214.1	916	228	106	97	24	10	3	4	71	3	158	15	1	11	14	.440	0	0-0	0	4.35	4.07
1999 Pittsburgh	NL	33	33	2	0	212.2	937	219	110	99	24	7	7	3	85	4	148	6	4	13	11	.542	0	0-0	0	4.30	4.19
2000 Pittsburgh	NL	11	11	0	0	63.1	295	71	43	38	6	1	2	1	41	2	51	1	0	2	5	.286	0	0-0	0	5.77	5.40
2001 Pit-SF	NL	25	25	1	0	150.1	641	138	75	68	13	5	3	7	61	3	142	8	1	13	7	.650	0	0-0	0	3.72	4.07
2002 San Francisco	NL	29	29	2	0	185.1	769	148	78	71	15	11	5	2	73	1	196	12	0	13	8	.619	2	0-0	0	2.87	3.45
2003 San Francisco	NL	29	29	5	0	207.2	819	152	56	54	14	6	3	5	46	1	208	7	1	17	5	.773	3	0-0	0	1.93	2.34
2004 San Francisco	NL	32	32	4	0	225.0	907	165	84	80	18	7	3	3	77	3	251	7	1	18	7	.720	3	0-0	0	2.37	3.20
1996 Atlanta	NL	13	11	0	0	58.2	274	69	48	44	8	3	6	0	32	0	48	5	1	3	4	.429	0	0-0	0	5.92	6.75
1996 Pittsburgh	NL	6	6	1	0	37.2	171	39	19	17	2	1	3	2	21	0	26	3	0	2	2	.500	0	0-0	0	4.75	4.06
2001 Pittsburgh	NL	14	14	1	0	84.0	357	81	46	43	11	3	2	7	28	2	77	3	1	6	6	.500	0	0-0	0	4.17	4.61
2001 San Francisco	NL	11	11	0	0	66.1	284	57	29	25	2	2	1	0	33	1	65	5	0	7	1	.875	0	0-0	0	3.16	3.39
10 ML YEARS		252	243	17	1	1567.2	6673	1449	742	680	142	63	42	37	601	22	1383	73	9	104	74	.584	8	0-1	0	3.59	3.90

Brian Schneider

Bats: L **Throws:** R **Pos:** C-133; PH-5   **Ht:** 6'1" **Wt:** 200 **Born:** 11/26/1976 **Age:** 28

Year Team	Lg	G	AB	H	2B	3B	HR	(Hm	Rd)	TB	R	RBI	RC	TBB	IBB	SO	HBP	SH	SF	SB	CS	SB%	GDP	Avg	OBP	Slg
2000 Montreal	NL	45	115	27	6	0	0	(0	0)	33	6	11	8	7	2	24	0	0	1	0	1	.00	1	.235	.276	.287
2001 Montreal	NL	27	41	13	3	0	1	(1	0)	19	4	6	8	6	1	3	0	0	1	0	0	-	0	.317	.396	.463
2002 Montreal	NL	73	207	57	19	2	5	(3	2)	95	21	29	29	21	8	41	0	2	2	1	2	.33	7	.275	.339	.459
2003 Montreal	NL	108	335	77	26	1	9	(9	0)	132	34	46	36	37	8	75	2	1	2	0	2	.00	12	.230	.309	.394
2004 Montreal	NL	135	436	112	20	3	12	(5	7)	174	40	49	52	42	10	63	3	5	2	0	1	.00	9	.257	.325	.399
5 ML YEARS		388	1134	286	74	6	27	(18	9)	453	105	141	133	113	29	206	5	8	8	1	6	.14	29	.252	.321	.399

Scott Schoeneweis

Pitches: L **Bats:** L **Pos:** SP-19; RP-1   **Ht:** 6'0" **Wt:** 185 **Born:** 10/2/1973 **Age:** 31

Year Team	Lg	G	GS	CG	GF	IP	BFP	H	R	ER	HR	SH	SF	HB	TBB	IBB	SO	WP	Bk	W	L	Pct	ShO	Sv-Op	Hld	ERC	ERA
1999 Anaheim	AL	31	0	0	6	39.1	175	47	27	24	4	0	1	6	14	1	22	1	0	1	1	.500	0	0-0	3	4.99	5.49
2000 Anaheim	AL	27	27	1	0	170.0	742	183	112	103	21	2	5	6	67	2	78	4	3	7	10	.412	1	0-0	0	4.84	5.45
2001 Anaheim	AL	32	32	1	0	205.1	910	227	122	116	21	3	8	14	77	2	104	4	1	10	11	.476	0	0-0	0	4.87	5.08
2002 Anaheim	AL	54	15	0	11	118.0	510	119	68	64	17	1	5	5	49	4	65	1	1	9	8	.529	0	1-4	11	4.68	4.88
2003 Ana-CWS	AL	59	0	0	19	64.2	276	63	35	30	3	2	1	4	19	5	56	3	0	3	2	.600	0	0-2	4	3.25	4.18
2004 Chicago	AL	20	19	0	0	112.2	500	129	74	70	17	3	2	3	49	0	69	3	0	6	9	.400	0	0-0	0	5.65	5.59

Year Team	Lg	G	GS	CG	GF	IP	BFP	H	R	ER	HR	SH	SF	HB	TBB	IBB	SO	WP	Bk	W	L	Pct	ShO	Sv-Op	Hld	ERC	ERA
																						THE RESULTS					
										WHAT HE GAVE UP																	
2003 Anaheim	AL	39	0	0	12	38.2	163	37	19	17	2	1	1	3	10	3	29	1	0	1	1	.500	0	0-1	4	3.14	3.96
2003 Chicago	AL	20	0	0	7	26.0	113	26	16	13	1	1	0	1	9	2	27	2	0	2	1	.667	0	0-1	0	3.41	4.50
6 ML YEARS		223	93	2	29	710.0	3113	768	438	407	83	11	22	32	275	14	394	16	5	36	41	.468	1	1-6	18	4.80	5.16

Marco Scutaro

Bats: R **Throws:** R **Pos:** 2B-124; SS-16; PH-12; 3B-1   **Ht:** 5'10" **Wt:** 170 **Born:** 10/30/1975 **Age:** 29

Year Team	Lg	G	AB	H	2B	3B	HR	(Hm	Rd)	TB	R	RBI	RC	TBB	IBB	SO	HBP	SH	SF	SB	CS	SB%	GDP	Avg	OBP	Slg
2002 New York	NL	27	36	8	0	1	1	(1	0)	13	2	6	2	0	0	11	0	1	1	0	1	.00	1	.222	.216	.361
2003 New York	NL	48	75	16	4	0	2	(0	2)	26	10	6	10	13	2	14	1	1	1	2	0	1.00	1	.213	.333	.347
2004 Oakland	AL	137	455	124	32	1	7	(6	1)	179	50	43	48	16	1	58	0	5	1	0	0	-	9	.273	.297	.393
3 ML YEARS		212	566	148	36	2	10	(7	3)	218	62	55	60	29	3	83	1	7	3	2	1	.67	11	.261	.297	.385

Rudy Seanez

Pitches: R **Bats:** R **Pos:** RP-39   **Ht:** 5'11" **Wt:** 205 **Born:** 10/20/1968 **Age:** 36

Year Team	Lg	G	GS	CG	GF	IP	BFP	H	R	ER	HR	SH	SF	HB	TBB	IBB	SO	WP	Bk	W	L	Pct	ShO	Sv-Op	Hld	ERC	ERA
2004 Omaha*	AAA	24	0	0	11	34.1	136	19	8	6	3	0	0	2	12	0	41	3	0	2	1	.667	0	3- -	-	1.75	1.57
1989 Cleveland	AL	5	0	0	2	5.0	20	1	2	2	0	0	2	0	4	1	7	1	1	0	0	-	0	0-0	0	0.94	3.60
1990 Cleveland	AL	24	0	0	12	27.1	127	22	17	17	2	0	1	1	25	1	24	5	0	2	1	.667	0	0-0	3	4.85	5.60
1991 Cleveland	AL	5	0	0	0	5.0	33	10	12	9	2	0	0	0	7	0	7	2	0	0	0	-	0	0-1	0	17.96	16.20
1993 San Diego	NL	3	0	0	3	3.1	20	8	6	5	1	1	0	0	2	0	1	0	0	0	0	-	0	0-0	0	16.31	13.50
1994 Los Angeles	NL	17	0	0	6	23.2	104	24	7	7	2	4	2	1	9	1	18	3	0	1	1	.500	0	0-1	1	4.01	2.66
1995 Los Angeles	NL	37	0	0	12	34.2	159	39	27	26	5	3	0	1	18	3	29	0	0	1	3	.250	0	3-4	6	5.57	6.75
1998 Atlanta	NL	34	0	0	8	36.0	148	25	13	11	2	1	2	1	16	0	50	2	0	4	1	.800	0	2-4	8	2.44	2.75
1999 Atlanta	NL	56	0	0	13	53.2	225	47	21	20	3	0	2	1	21	1	41	3	0	6	1	.857	0	3-8	18	3.12	3.35
2000 Atlanta	NL	23	0	0	8	21.0	89	15	11	10	3	1	0	1	9	1	20	0	0	2	4	.333	0	2-3	6	2.95	4.29
2001 SD-Atl	NL	38	0	0	8	36.0	150	23	12	11	4	0	1	1	19	0	41	4	0	0	2	.000	0	1-3	9	2.78	2.75
2002 Texas	AL	33	0	0	4	33.0	150	28	25	21	5	3	1	0	24	1	40	6	0	1	3	.250	0	0-4	10	4.77	5.73
2003 Boston	AL	9	0	0	4	8.2	44	11	7	6	2	0	1	0	6	1	9	3	0	0	1	.000	0	0-1	0	7.45	6.23
2004 KC-Fla		39	0	0	15	46.0	193	39	17	17	3	0	3	0	19	3	46	4	0	3	2	.600	0	0-2	4	2.96	3.33
2001 San Diego	NL	26	0	0	8	24.0	102	15	8	7	3	0	1	1	15	0	24	1	0	0	2	.000	0	1-3	5	3.21	2.63
2001 Atlanta	NL	12	0	0	0	12.0	48	8	4	4	1	0	0	0	4	0	17	3	0	0	0	-	0	0-0	4	1.99	3.00
2004 Kansas City	AL	16	0	0	7	23.0	100	21	10	10	0	0	0	3	11	2	21	3	0	0	1	.000	0	0-1	1	3.01	3.91
2004 Florida	NL	23	0	0	8	23.0	93	18	7	7	3	0	0	0	8	1	25	1	0	3	1	.750	0	0-1	3	2.87	2.74
13 ML YEARS		323	0	0	95	333.1	1462	292	177	162	34	13	15	7	179	13	333	33	1	20	19	.513	0	11-31	65	3.91	4.37

Bobby Seay

Pitches: L **Bats:** L **Pos:** RP-21   **Ht:** 6'2" **Wt:** 235 **Born:** 6/20/1978 **Age:** 27

Year Team	Lg	G	GS	CG	GF	IP	BFP	H	R	ER	HR	SH	SF	HB	TBB	IBB	SO	WP	Bk	W	L	Pct	ShO	Sv-Op	Hld	ERC	ERA
2004 Durham*	AAA	29	0	0	11	36.2	144	26	9	7	3	0	0	1	9	0	35	4	0	2	1	.667	0	1- -	-	2.02	1.72
2001 Tampa Bay	AL	12	0	0	0	13.0	58	13	0	9	3	0	0	0	5	0	12	0	0	1	1	.500	0	0-0	0	4.74	6.23
2003 Tampa Bay	AL	12	0	0	2	9.0	39	7	3	3	0	0	2	0	6	0	5	0	0	0	0	-	0	0-1	0	3.17	3.00
2004 Tampa Bay	AL	21	0	0	6	22.2	95	21	6	6	2	0	0	2	5	1	17	1	0	0	0	-	0	0-0	0	3.15	2.38
3 ML YEARS		45	0	0	8	44.2	192	41	9	18	5	0	2	2	16	1	34	1	0	1	1	.500	0	0-1	0	3.62	3.63

David Segui

Bats: B **Throws:** L **Pos:** DH-15; PH-3; 1B-2   **Ht:** 6'1" **Wt:** 202 **Born:** 7/19/1966 **Age:** 38

Year Team	Lg	G	AB	H	2B	3B	HR	(Hm	Rd)	TB	R	RBI	RC	TBB	IBB	SO	HBP	SH	SF	SB	CS	SB%	GDP	Avg	OBP	Slg
2004 Frederick*	A+	3	10	1	0	0	1	(-	-)	4	1	2	0	1	0	2	0	0	1	0	0	-	0	.100	.167	.400
2004 Bowie*	AA	3	11	4	1	0	0	(-	-)	5	2	1	1	0	0	3	1	0	0	0	0	-	1	.364	.417	.455
1990 Baltimore	AL	40	123	30	7	0	2	(1	1)	43	14	15	10	11	2	15	1	1	0	0	0	-	12	.244	.311	.350
1991 Baltimore	AL	86	212	59	7	0	2	(1	1)	72	15	22	21	12	2	19	0	3	1	1	1	.50	7	.278	.316	.340
1992 Baltimore	AL	115	189	44	9	0	1	(1	0)	56	21	17	17	20	3	23	0	2	0	1	0	1.00	4	.233	.306	.296
1993 Baltimore	AL	146	450	123	27	0	10	(6	4)	180	54	60	62	58	4	53	0	3	8	2	1	.67	18	.273	.351	.400
1994 New York	NL	92	336	81	17	1	10	(5	5)	130	46	43	40	33	6	43	1	1	3	0	0	-	6	.241	.308	.387
1995 NYM-Mon	NL	130	456	141	25	4	12	(6	6)	210	68	68	73	40	5	47	3	8	3	2	7	.22	10	.309	.367	.461
1996 Montreal	NL	115	416	119	30	1	11	(6	5)	184	69	58	69	60	4	54	0	0	1	4	4	.50	8	.286	.375	.442
1997 Montreal	NL	125	459	141	22	3	21	(10	11)	232	75	68	86	57	12	66	1	0	6	1	0	1.00	6	.307	.380	.505
1998 Seattle	AL	143	522	159	36	1	19	(10	9)	254	79	84	89	49	4	80	0	0	9	3	1	.75	12	.305	.359	.487
1999 Sea-Tor	AL	121	440	131	27	3	14	(5	9)	206	57	52	70	40	4	60	1	1	4	1	2	.33	10	.298	.355	.468
2000 Tex-Cle	AL	150	574	192	42	1	19	(8	11)	293	93	103	105	53	2	84	1	0	6	0	1	.00	20	.334	.388	.510
2001 Baltimore	AL	82	292	88	18	1	10	(5	5)	138	48	46	57	49	5	61	4	0	2	1	1	.50	4	.301	.406	.473
2002 Baltimore	AL	26	95	25	4	0	2	(1	1)	35	10	16	15	11	0	22	0	0	1	0	0	-	0	.263	.336	.368
2003 Baltimore	AL	67	224	59	10	1	5	(2	3)	86	26	25	29	26	2	47	1	0	1	1	0	1.00	8	.263	.341	.384
2004 Baltimore	AL	18	59	20	3	0	1	(0	1)	26	8	7	9	5	1	13	1	0	0	0	0	-	3	.339	.400	.441
1995 New York	NL	33	73	24	3	1	2	(2	0)	35	9	11	14	12	1	9	1	4	2	1	3	.25	2	.329	.420	.479
1995 Montreal	NL	97	383	117	22	3	10	(4	6)	175	59	57	59	28	4	38	2	4	1	1	4	.20	8	.305	.355	.457
1999 Seattle	AL	90	345	101	22	3	9	(4	5)	156	43	39	52	32	4	43	1	1	3	1	2	.33	9	.293	.352	.452
1999 Toronto	AL	31	95	30	5	0	5	(1	4)	50	14	13	18	8	0	17	0	0	1	0	0	-	1	.316	.365	.526
2000 Texas	AL	93	351	118	29	1	11	(4	7)	182	52	57	66	34	1	51	0	0	1	0	0	1.00	12	.336	.391	.519
2000 Cleveland	AL	57	223	74	13	0	8	(4	4)	111	41	46	39	19	1	33	1	0	2	0	1	.00	8	.332	.384	.498
15 ML YEARS		1456	4847	1412	284	16	139	(67	72)	2145	683	684	752	524	56	687	14	19	45	17	19	.47	131	.291	.359	.443

Phil Seibel

Pitches: L **Bats:** L **Pos:** RP-2   **Ht:** 6'1" **Wt:** 195 **Born:** 1/28/1979 **Age:** 26

Year Team	Lg	G	GS	CG	GF	IP	BFP	H	R	ER	HR	SH	SF	HB	TBB	IBB	SO	WP	Bk	W	L	Pct	ShO	Sv-Op	Hld	ERC	ERA
2001 Jupiter	A+	29	21	0	1	134.1	572	144	70	59	12	5	6	6	28	0	88	5	1	10	7	.588	0	0- -	-	3.80	3.95
2002 Binghamton	AA	28	25	2	1	149.2	630	147	78	66	17	8	5	10	49	2	114	6	0	10	8	.556	0	0- -	-	4.11	3.97
2003 Binghamton	AA	17	17	0	0	82.2	358	79	48	33	6	3	8	3	32	0	71	3	0	5	5	.500	0	0- -	-	3.69	3.59
2003 Norfolk	AAA	11	5	0	0	34.1	158	38	25	23	5	1	1	4	17	0	25	0	2	2	3	.400	0	0- -	-	5.94	6.03
2004 Red Sox	R	3	3	0	0	4.0	15	2	1	1	1	0	0	0	1	0	6	0	0	0	0	-	0	0- -	-	1.80	2.25
2004 Portland	AA	3	1	0	0	6.0	28	8	5	5	3	0	0	1	2	0	6	1	0	0	1	.000	0	0- -	-	10.01	7.50
2004 Pawtucket	AAA	8	7	0	0	44.2	176	42	16	15	7	1	2	1	12	0	31	0	0	1	2	.333	0	0- -	-	3.93	3.02
2004 Boston	AL	2	0	0	0	3.2	18	0	0	0	0	0	0	1	5	0	1	0	0	0	0	-	0	0-0	0	2.19	0.00

Aaron Sele

Pitches: R **Bats:** R **Pos:** SP-24; RP-4   **Ht:** 6'5" **Wt:** 220 **Born:** 6/25/1970 **Age:** 35

Year Team	Lg	G	GS	CG	GF	IP	BFP	H	R	ER	HR	SH	SF	HB	TBB	IBB	SO	WP	Bk	W	L	Pct	ShO	Sv-Op	Hld	ERC	ERA
1993 Boston	AL	18	18	0	0	111.2	484	100	42	34	5	2	5	7	48	2	93	5	0	7	2	.778	0	0-0	-	3.40	2.74
1994 Boston	AL	22	22	2	0	143.1	615	140	68	61	13	4	5	9	60	2	105	4	0	8	7	.533	0	0-0	-	4.26	3.83
1995 Boston	AL	6	6	0	0	32.1	146	32	14	11	3	1	1	3	14	0	21	3	0	3	1	.750	0	0-0	-	4.35	3.06
1996 Boston	AL	29	29	1	0	157.1	722	192	110	93	14	6	7	8	67	2	137	2	0	7	11	.389	0	0-0	-	5.56	5.32
1997 Boston	AL	33	33	1	0	177.1	810	196	115	106	25	5	7	15	80	4	122	7	0	13	12	.520	0	0-0	-	5.47	5.38
1998 Texas	AL	33	33	3	0	212.2	954	239	116	100	14	5	7	13	84	6	167	4	0	19	11	.633	2	0-0	-	4.69	4.23
1999 Texas	AL	33	33	2	0	205.0	920	244	115	109	21	1	3	12	70	3	186	4	0	18	9	.667	2	0-0	-	5.17	4.79
2000 Seattle	AL	34	34	2	0	211.2	908	221	110	106	17	5	8	5	74	7	137	5	0	17	10	.630	2	0-0	-	4.06	4.51
2001 Seattle	AL	34	33	2	0	215.0	899	216	93	86	25	5	9	7	51	2	114	1	0	15	5	.750	1	0-0	-	3.70	3.60
2002 Anaheim	AL	26	26	1	0	160.0	706	190	92	87	21	5	10	7	49	2	82	5	0	8	9	.471	1	0-0	-	5.20	4.89
2003 Anaheim	AL	25	25	0	0	121.2	552	135	82	78	17	2	5	12	58	1	53	5	0	7	11	.389	0	0-0	-	5.78	5.77
2004 Anaheim	AL	28	24	0	1	132.0	593	163	84	74	16	3	8	5	51	2	51	4	2	9	4	.692	0	0-0	-	5.77	5.05
12 ML YEARS		321	316	14	1	1880.0	8309	2068	1041	945	191	44	75	103	706	33	1268	49	2	131	92	.587	8	0-0	-	4.76	4.52

Jae Seo

Pitches: R **Bats:** R **Pos:** SP-21; RP-3   **Ht:** 6'1" **Wt:** 215 **Born:** 5/24/1977 **Age:** 28

Year Team	Lg	G	GS	CG	GF	IP	BFP	H	R	ER	HR	SH	SF	HB	TBB	IBB	SO	WP	Bk	W	L	Pct	ShO	Sv-Op	Hld	ERC	ERA
2004 Norfolk*	AAA	4	4	0	0	22.1	87	22	7	7	1	0	0	2	8	0	20	0	1	0	2	.000	0	0- -	-	4.27	2.82
2002 New York	NL	1	0	0	1	1.0	3	0	0	0	0	0	0	0	1	0	0	0	0	0	0	-	0	0-0	0	0.00	0.00
2003 New York	NL	32	31	0	0	188.1	806	193	94	80	18	8	4	6	46	11	110	2	0	9	12	.429	0	0-0	-	3.54	3.82
2004 New York	NL	24	21	0	1	117.2	512	133	67	64	17	12	3	2	50	7	54	0	1	5	10	.333	0	0-0	-	5.39	4.90
3 ML YEARS		57	52	0	2	307.0	1321	326	161	144	35	20	7	8	96	18	165	2	1	14	22	.389	0	0-0	-	4.19	4.22

Jimmy Serrano

Pitches: R **Bats:** R **Pos:** SP-5; RP-5   **Ht:** 5'10" **Wt:** 170 **Born:** 5/9/1976 **Age:** 29

Year Team	Lg	G	GS	CG	GF	IP	BFP	H	R	ER	HR	SH	SF	HB	TBB	IBB	SO	WP	Bk	W	L	Pct	ShO	Sv-Op	Hld	ERC	ERA
1998 Vermont	A-	7	0	0	7	7.2	28	3	1	1	0	0	0	0	1	0	12	1	0	0	0	-	0	5- -	-	0.49	1.17
1998 Cape Fear	A	15	0	0	8	24.2	116	22	11	10	2	1	2	1	15	0	29	5	0	2	0	1.000	0	3- -	-	4.03	3.65
1999 Jupiter	A+	44	1	0	24	93.0	365	59	25	22	4	2	5	7	27	4	118	8	0	8	5	.615	0	8- -	-	1.72	2.13
2000 Harrisburg	AA	55	0	0	34	75.0	335	64	39	35	6	6	5	7	43	2	80	6	0	4	5	.444	0	16- -	-	4.06	4.20
2001 Harrisburg	AA	47	0	0	42	54.0	216	30	20	13	4	2	3	0	24	4	73	0	0	6	3	.667	0	20- -	-	1.71	2.17
2001 Ottawa	AAA	9	0	0	5	8.0	42	11	5	4	0	0	0	1	6	0	11	1	0	1	0	1.000	0	0- -	-	7.25	4.50
2002 Norfolk	AAA	53	0	0	20	74.0	342	88	40	33	3	2	4	4	31	5	76	1	0	8	6	.571	0	3- -	-	4.79	4.01
2003 Norfolk	AAA	27	0	0	9	49.0	193	38	13	13	2	3	0	1	19	3	47	2	0	1	2	.333	0	0- -	-	2.58	2.39
2003 Omaha	AAA	19	0	0	6	28.0	118	25	12	10	2	0	4	1	11	0	28	1	0	3	2	.600	0	3- -	-	3.42	3.21
2004 Wichita	AA	11	11	1	0	64.1	247	42	18	14	6	1	4	2	18	0	74	2	0	3	1	.750	1	0- -	-	2.00	1.96
2004 Omaha	AAA	16	1	0	5	32.1	156	32	23	18	4	1	2	4	21	0	41	2	0	1	1	.500	0	0- -	-	5.49	5.01
2004 Kansas City	AL	10	5	0	2	32.2	141	35	17	17	5	0	3	1	12	0	25	2	0	1	2	.333	0	0-0	-	4.94	4.68

Scott Service

Pitches: R **Bats:** R **Pos:** RP-21   **Ht:** 6'6" **Wt:** 240 **Born:** 2/26/1967 **Age:** 38

Year Team	Lg	G	GS	CG	GF	IP	BFP	H	R	ER	HR	SH	SF	HB	TBB	IBB	SO	WP	Bk	W	L	Pct	ShO	Sv-Op	Hld	ERC	ERA
2004 Tucson*	AAA	24	0	0	22	25.0	108	28	9	9	2	1	0	0	6	0	28	1	0	5	0	1.000	0	9- -	-	3.92	3.24
1988 Philadelphia	NL	5	0	0	1	5.1	23	7	1	1	0	0	0	1	1	0	6	0	0	0	0	-	0	0-0	-	5.34	1.69
1992 Montreal	NL	5	0	0	0	7.0	41	15	11	11	1	0	0	0	5	0	11	0	0	0	0	-	0	0-0	1	13.24	14.14
1993 Col-Cin	NL	29	0	0	7	46.0	197	44	24	22	6	2	4	2	16	4	43	0	0	2	2	.500	0	2-2	3	3.85	4.30
1994 Cincinnati	NL	6	0	0	2	7.1	35	8	9	6	2	2	0	0	3	0	5	0	0	1	2	.333	0	0-0	-	5.42	7.36
1995 San Francisco	NL	28	0	0	6	31.0	129	18	11	11	4	3	2	2	20	4	30	3	0	3	1	.750	0	0-0	7	3.04	3.19
1996 Cincinnati	NL	34	1	0	5	48.0	213	51	21	21	7	4	1	6	18	4	46	5	0	1	0	1.000	0	0-0	5	5.07	3.94
1997 Cin-KC		16	0	0	3	22.1	95	28	16	16	2	2	1	0	6	0	22	2	0	0	3	.000	0	0-1	3	5.14	6.45
1998 Kansas City	AL	73	0	0	26	82.2	353	70	35	32	7	2	5	9	34	4	95	10	1	6	4	.600	0	4-8	18	3.52	3.48
1999 Kansas City	AL	68	0	0	29	75.1	352	87	51	51	13	4	7	3	42	8	68	3	0	5	5	.500	0	8-15	8	6.14	6.09
2000 Oakland	AL	20	0	0	6	36.2	172	45	31	26	5	1	2	1	19	1	35	0	0	1	2	.333	0	1-1	1	6.22	6.38
2003 Ari-Tor		33	0	0	11	34.1	146	38	18	18	4	1	2	0	8	1	35	1	0	0	2	.000	0	1-2	3	4.08	4.72
2004 Arizona	NL	21	0	0	5	20.1	97	24	17	16	5	0	1	2	10	2	17	1	0	1	1	.500	0	0-2	1	6.77	7.08
1993 Colorado	NL	3	0	0	0	4.2	24	8	5	5	1	0	2	1	1	0	3	0	0	0	0	-	0	0-0	0	9.48	9.64
1993 Cincinnati	NL	26	0	0	7	41.1	173	36	19	17	5	2	2	1	15	4	40	0	0	2	2	.500	0	2-2	3	3.31	3.70
1997 Cincinnati	NL	4	0	0	2	5.1	26	11	7	7	1	1	0	0	1	0	3	2	0	0	0	-	0	0-0	1	11.35	11.81
1997 Kansas City	AL	12	0	0	1	17.0	69	17	9	9	1	1	1	0	5	0	19	0	0	0	3	.000	0	0-1	2	3.53	4.76

Year Team	Lg	G	GS	CG	GF	IP	BFP	H	R	ER	HR	SH	SF	HB	TBB	IBB	SO	WP	Bk	W	L	Pct	ShO	Sv-Op	Hld	ERC	ERA
2003 Arizona	NL	18	0	0	7	18.1	77	21	10	10	1	1	1	0	2	1	18	1	0	0	2	.000	0	1-1	0	3.32	4.91
2003 Toronto	AL	15	0	0	4	16.0	69	17	8	8	3	0	1	0	6	0	17	0	0	0	0	-	0	0-1	3	5.00	4.50
12 ML YEARS		338	1	0	101	416.1	1853	435	245	231	56	21	25	26	182	28	413	25	1	20	22	.476	0	16-31	48	4.87	4.99

Richie Sexson

Bats: R **Throws:** R **Pos:** 1B-23   **Ht:** 6'8" **Wt:** 227 **Born:** 12/29/1974 **Age:** 30

Year Team	Lg	G	AB	H	2B	3B	HR	(Hm	Rd)	TB	R	RBI	RC	TBB	IBB	SO	HBP	SH	SF	SB	CS	SB%	GDP	Avg	OBP	Slg
1997 Cleveland	AL	5	11	3	0	0	0	(0	0)	3	1	0	0	0	0	2	0	0	0	0	0	-	2	.273	.273	.273
1998 Cleveland	AL	49	174	54	14	1	11	(9	2)	103	28	35	33	6	0	42	3	0	0	1	1	.50	3	.310	.344	.592
1999 Cleveland	AL	134	479	122	17	7	31	(18	13)	246	72	116	70	34	0	117	4	0	8	3	3	.50	19	.255	.305	.514
2000 Cle-Mil		148	537	146	30	1	30	(15	15)	268	89	91	91	59	2	159	7	0	4	2	0	1.00	11	.272	.349	.499
2001 Milwaukee	NL	158	598	162	24	3	45	(28	17)	327	94	125	103	60	5	178	6	0	3	2	4	.33	20	.271	.342	.547
2002 Milwaukee	NL	157	570	159	37	2	29	(13	16)	287	86	102	98	70	7	136	8	0	4	0	0	-	17	.279	.363	.504
2003 Milwaukee	NL	162	606	165	28	2	45	(23	22)	332	97	124	116	98	7	151	9	0	5	2	3	.40	18	.272	.379	.548
2004 Arizona	NL	23	90	21	4	0	9	(6	3)	52	20	23	18	14	0	21	0	0	0	0	0	-	2	.233	.337	.578
2000 Cleveland	AL	91	324	83	16	1	16	(8	8)	149	45	44	45	25	0	96	4	0	3	1	0	1.00	8	.256	.315	.460
2000 Milwaukee	NL	57	213	63	14	0	14	(7	7)	119	44	47	46	34	2	63	3	0	1	1	0	1.00	3	.296	.398	.559
8 ML YEARS		836	3065	832	154	16	200	(112	88)	1618	487	616	529	341	21	806	37	0	24	10	11	.48	92	.271	.349	.528

Ben Sheets

Pitches: R **Bats:** R **Pos:** SP-34   **Ht:** 6'1" **Wt:** 203 **Born:** 7/18/1978 **Age:** 26

Year Team	Lg	G	GS	CG	GF	IP	BFP	H	R	ER	HR	SH	SF	HB	TBB	IBB	SO	WP	Bk	W	L	Pct	ShO	Sv-Op	Hld	ERC	ERA
2001 Milwaukee	NL	25	25	1	0	151.1	653	166	89	80	23	8	5	5	48	6	94	3	0	11	10	.524	1	0-0	0	4.78	4.76
2002 Milwaukee	NL	34	34	1	0	216.2	934	237	105	100	21	10	0	10	70	10	170	9	0	11	16	.407	0	0-0	0	4.45	4.15
2003 Milwaukee	NL	34	34	1	0	220.2	931	232	122	109	29	11	6	6	43	2	157	7	0	11	13	.458	0	0-0	0	3.83	4.45
2004 Milwaukee	NL	34	34	5	0	237.0	937	201	85	71	25	6	4	4	32	1	264	8	1	12	14	.462	0	0-0	0	2.37	2.70
4 ML YEARS		127	127	8	0	825.2	3455	836	401	360	98	35	15	25	193	19	685	27	1	45	53	.459	1	0-0	0	3.71	3.92

Gary Sheffield

Bats: R **Throws:** R **Pos:** RF-136; DH-18; 3B-2   **Ht:** 6'0" **Wt:** 205 **Born:** 11/18/1968 **Age:** 36

Year Team	Lg	G	AB	H	2B	3B	HR	(Hm	Rd)	TB	R	RBI	RC	TBB	IBB	SO	HBP	SH	SF	SB	CS	SB%	GDP	Avg	OBP	Slg
1988 Milwaukee	AL	24	80	19	1	0	4	(1	3)	32	12	12	8	7	0	7	0	1	1	3	1	.75	5	.238	.295	.400
1989 Milwaukee	AL	95	368	91	18	0	5	(2	3)	124	34	32	38	27	0	33	4	3	3	10	6	.63	4	.247	.303	.337
1990 Milwaukee	AL	125	487	143	30	1	10	(3	7)	205	67	67	73	44	1	41	3	4	9	25	10	.71	11	.294	.350	.421
1991 Milwaukee	AL	50	175	34	12	2	2	(2	0)	56	25	22	15	19	1	15	3	1	5	5	5	.50	3	.194	.277	.320
1992 San Diego	NL	146	557	184	34	3	33	(23	10)	323	87	100	113	48	5	40	6	0	7	5	6	.45	19	.330	.385	.580
1993 SD-Fla	NL	140	494	145	20	5	20	(10	10)	235	67	73	84	47	6	64	9	0	7	17	5	.77	11	.294	.361	.476
1994 Florida	NL	87	322	89	16	1	27	(15	12)	188	61	78	68	51	11	50	6	0	5	12	6	.67	10	.276	.380	.584
1995 Florida	NL	63	213	69	8	0	16	(4	12)	125	46	46	60	55	8	45	4	0	2	19	4	.83	3	.324	.467	.587
1996 Florida	NL	161	519	163	33	1	42	(19	23)	324	118	120	144	142	16	66	10	0	6	16	9	.64	16	.314	.465	.624
1997 Florida	NL	135	444	111	22	1	21	(13	8)	198	86	71	92	121	11	79	15	0	2	11	7	.61	7	.250	.424	.446
1998 Fla-LA	NL	130	437	132	27	2	22	(11	11)	229	73	85	102	95	12	46	8	0	9	22	7	.76	7	.302	.428	.524
1999 Los Angeles	NL	152	549	165	20	0	34	(15	19)	287	103	101	118	101	4	64	4	0	9	11	5	.69	10	.301	.407	.523
2000 Los Angeles	NL	141	501	163	24	3	43	(23	20)	322	105	109	131	101	7	71	4	0	6	4	6	.40	13	.325	.438	.643
2001 Los Angeles	NL	143	515	160	28	2	36	(16	20)	300	98	100	120	94	13	67	4	0	5	10	4	.71	12	.311	.417	.583
2002 Atlanta	NL	135	492	151	26	0	25	(10	15)	252	82	84	102	72	2	53	11	0	4	12	2	.86	16	.307	.404	.512
2003 Atlanta	NL	155	576	190	37	2	39	(21	19)	348	126	132	134	86	6	55	8	0	8	18	4	.82	16	.330	.419	.604
2004 New York	NL	154	573	166	30	1	36	(19	17)	306	117	121	123	92	7	83	11	0	8	5	6	.45	16	.290	.393	.534
1993 San Diego	NL	68	258	76	12	2	10	(6	4)	122	34	36	40	18	0	30	3	0	3	5	1	.83	9	.295	.344	.473
1993 Florida	NL	72	236	69	8	3	10	(4	6)	113	33	37	44	29	6	34	6	0	4	12	4	.75	2	.292	.378	.479
1998 Florida	NL	40	136	37	11	1	6	(6	0)	68	21	28	27	26	1	16	2	0	2	4	2	.67	3	.272	.392	.500
1998 Los Angeles	NL	90	301	95	16	1	16	(5	11)	161	52	57	75	69	11	30	6	0	7	18	5	.78	4	.316	.444	.535
17 ML YEARS		2036	7302	2175	386	24	415	(206	209)	3854	1307	1353	1525	1202	113	879	110	9	96	205	93	.69	179	.298	.400	.528

Chris Shelton

Bats: R **Throws:** R **Pos:** DH-10; 1B-8; PH-7; C-6; RF-1   **Ht:** 6'0" **Wt:** 220 **Born:** 6/26/1980 **Age:** 25

Year Team	Lg	G	AB	H	2B	3B	HR	(Hm	Rd)	TB	R	RBI	RC	TBB	IBB	SO	HBP	SH	SF	SB	CS	SB%	GDP	Avg	OBP	Slg
2001 Williamsport	A-	50	174	53	11	0	2	(-	-)	70	22	33	33	33	1	31	2	1	3	4	1	.80	1	.305	.415	.402
2002 Hickory	A	93	332	113	27	2	17	(-	-)	195	72	65	79	47	2	74	5	0	0	0	0	-	3	.340	.425	.587
2003 Lynchburg	A+	95	315	113	24	1	21	(-	-)	202	71	69	88	68	8	67	5	0	1	1	4	.20	5	.359	.478	.641
2003 Altoona	AA	35	122	34	10	1	0	(-	-)	46	17	14	15	8	0	23	2	0	1	0	1	.00	1	.279	.331	.377
2004 Toledo	AAA	18	62	21	2	0	0	(-	-)	23	5	7	11	10	0	13	0	0	0	0	0	-	1	.339	.425	.371
2004 Detroit	AL	27	46	9	1	0	1	(1	0)	13	6	3	4	9	0	14	0	0	1	0	0	-	2	.196	.321	.283

George Sherrill

Pitches: L **Bats:** L **Pos:** RP-21   **Ht:** 6'0" **Wt:** 210 **Born:** 4/19/1977 **Age:** 28

Year Team	Lg	G	GS	CG	GF	IP	BFP	H	R	ER	HR	SH	SF	HB	TBB	IBB	SO	WP	Bk	W	L	Pct	ShO	Sv-Op	Hld	ERC	ERA
2003 San Antonio	AA	16	0	0	6	27.1	111	19	2	1	1	2	1	0	12	1	31	0	0	3	0	1.000	0	0- -	-	2.18	0.33
2004 Tacoma	AAA	36	0	0	25	50.1	201	42	13	13	4	0	0	0	9	1	62	0	0	4	2	.667	0	13- -	-	2.21	2.32
2004 Seattle	AL	21	0	0	4	23.2	104	24	12	10	3	0	1	1	9	1	16	4	1	2	1	.667	0	0-0	3	4.31	3.80

Scot Shields

Pitches: R **Bats:** R **Pos:** RP-60   **Ht:** 6'1" **Wt:** 175 **Born:** 7/22/1975 **Age:** 29

		HOW MUCH HE PITCHED						WHAT HE GAVE UP												THE RESULTS						
Year Team	Lg	G	GS	CG	GF	IP	BFP	H	R	ER	HR	SH	SF	HB	TBB	IBB	SO	WP	Bk	W	L	Pct	ShO	Sv-Op	Hld	ERC	ERA
2001 Anaheim	AL	8	0	0	6	11.0	48	8	1	0	0	0	0	1	7	0	7	2	0	0	0	-	0	0-0	0	3.10	0.00
2002 Anaheim	AL	29	1	0	13	49.0	188	31	13	12	4	1	0	1	21	1	30	1	0	5	3	.625	0	0-0	3	2.35	2.20
2003 Anaheim	AL	44	13	0	5	148.1	609	138	56	47	12	3	4	5	38	6	111	4	0	5	6	.455	0	1-1	3	3.12	2.85
2004 Anaheim	AL	60	0	0	12	105.1	454	97	42	39	6	2	2	3	40	5	109	4	0	8	2	.800	0	4-7	17	3.24	3.33
4 ML YEARS		141	14	0	36	313.2	1299	274	112	98	22	6	6	10	106	12	257	13	0	18	11	.621	0	5-8	23	3.04	2.81

Brian Shouse

Pitches: L **Bats:** L **Pos:** RP-53   **Ht:** 5'11" **Wt:** 180 **Born:** 9/26/1968 **Age:** 36

		HOW MUCH HE PITCHED						WHAT HE GAVE UP												THE RESULTS						
Year Team	Lg	G	GS	CG	GF	IP	BFP	H	R	ER	HR	SH	SF	HB	TBB	IBB	SO	WP	Bk	W	L	Pct	ShO	Sv-Op	Hld	ERC	ERA
2004 Oklahoma*	AAA	9	0	0	1	7.1	43	12	5	5	1	0	0	2	4	1	3	0	0	0	0	-	0	0- -		9.02	6.14
1993 Pittsburgh	NL	6	0	0	1	4.0	22	7	4	4	1	0	1	0	2	0	3	1	0	0	0	-	0	0-0	0	9.92	9.00
1998 Boston	AL	7	0	0	4	8.0	36	9	5	5	2	0	1	0	4	0	5	0	0	0	1	.000	0	0-0	1	6.42	5.63
2002 Kansas City	AL	23	0	0	7	14.2	71	15	10	10	3	1	1	2	9	1	11	2	0	0	0	-	0	0-0	2	6.11	6.14
2003 Texas	AL	62	0	0	14	61.0	253	62	24	21	1	3	0	4	14	6	40	2	0	0	1	.000	0	1-1	10	3.10	3.10
2004 Texas	AL	53	0	0	14	44.1	184	36	12	11	3	2	2	1	18	3	34	0	0	2	0	1.000	0	0-0	12	2.87	2.23
5 ML YEARS		151	0	0	40	132.0	566	129	55	51	10	6	4	7	47	10	93	5	0	2	2	.500	0	1-1	25	3.70	3.48

Ruben Sierra

Bats: B **Throws:** R **Pos:** DH-56; PH-31; RF-22; LF-8   **Ht:** 6'1" **Wt:** 215 **Born:** 10/6/1965 **Age:** 39

		BATTING																			BASERUNNING				AVERAGES		
Year Team	Lg	G	AB	H	2B	3B	HR	(Hm	Rd)	TB	R	RBI	RC	TBB	IBB	SO	HBP	SH	SF	SB	CS	SB%	GDP	Avg	OBP	Slg
1986 Texas	AL	113	382	101	13	10	16	(8	8)	182	50	55	52	22	3	65	1	1	5	7	8	.47	8	.264	.302	.476
1987 Texas	AL	158	643	169	35	4	30	(15	15)	302	97	109	86	39	4	114	2	0	12	16	11	.59	18	.263	.302	.470
1988 Texas	AL	156	615	156	32	2	23	(15	8)	261	77	91	78	44	10	91	1	0	8	18	4	.82	15	.254	.301	.424
1989 Texas	AL	162	634	194	35	14	29	(21	8)	344	101	119	118	43	2	82	2	0	10	8	2	.80	7	.306	.347	.543
1990 Texas	AL	159	608	170	37	2	16	(10	6)	259	70	96	84	49	13	86	1	0	8	9	0	1.00	15	.280	.330	.426
1991 Texas	AL	161	661	203	44	5	25	(12	13)	332	110	116	114	56	7	91	0	0	8	16	4	.80	17	.307	.357	.502
1992 Tex-Oak	AL	151	601	167	34	7	17	(10	7)	266	83	87	86	45	12	68	0	0	10	14	4	.78	11	.278	.323	.443
1993 Oakland	AL	158	630	147	23	5	22	(9	13)	246	77	101	70	52	16	97	0	0	10	25	5	.83	17	.233	.288	.390
1994 Oakland	AL	110	426	114	21	1	23	(11	12)	206	71	92	58	23	4	64	0	0	11	8	5	.62	15	.268	.298	.484
1995 Oak-NYY	AL	126	479	126	32	0	19	(8	11)	215	73	86	69	46	4	76	0	0	8	4	5	.56	8	.263	.323	.449
1996 NYY-Det	AL	142	518	128	26	2	12	(4	8)	194	61	72	62	60	12	83	0	0	9	4	4	.50	12	.247	.320	.375
1997 Cin-Tor	AL	39	138	32	5	3	3	(3	0)	52	10	12	14	9	2	34	0	0	1	0	0	-	1	.232	.277	.377
1998 Chicago	AL	27	74	16	4	1	4	(0	4)	34	7	11	8	3	0	11	0	0	0	2	0	1.00	0	.216	.247	.459
2000 Texas	AL	20	60	14	0	0	1	(0	1)	17	5	7	5	4	0	9	0	0	0	1	0	1.00	1	.233	.281	.283
2001 Texas	AL	94	344	100	22	1	23	(13	10)	193	55	67	58	19	0	52	0	0	6	2	0	1.00	13	.291	.322	.561
2002 Seattle	AL	122	419	113	23	0	13	(6	7)	175	47	60	47	31	5	66	0	0	2	4	0	1.00	17	.270	.319	.418
2003 Tex-NYY	AL	106	307	83	17	1	9	(7	2)	129	33	43	35	27	3	47	0	0	2	2	1	.67	9	.270	.327	.420
2004 New York	AL	107	307	75	12	1	17	(8	9)	140	40	65	46	25	4	55	0	0	6	1	0	1.00	5	.244	.296	.456
1992 Texas	AL	124	500	139	30	6	14	(8	6)	223	66	70	70	31	6	59	0	0	8	12	4	.75	9	.278	.315	.446
1992 Oakland	AL	27	101	28	4	1	3	(2	1)	43	17	17	16	14	6	9	0	0	2	2	0	1.00	2	.277	.359	.426
1995 Oakland	AL	70	264	70	17	0	12	(3	9)	123	40	42	40	24	2	42	0	0	3	4	4	.50	2	.265	.323	.466
1995 New York	AL	56	215	56	15	0	7	(5	2)	92	33	44	29	22	2	34	0	0	5	1	0	1.00	6	.260	.322	.428
1996 New York	AL	96	360	93	17	1	11	(4	7)	145	39	52	46	40	11	58	0	0	7	1	3	.25	10	.258	.327	.403
1996 Detroit	AL	46	158	35	9	1	1	(0	1)	49	22	20	16	20	1	25	0	0	2	3	1	.75	2	.222	.306	.310
1997 Cincinnati	NL	25	90	22	5	1	2	(2	0)	35	6	7	10	6	1	21	0	0	0	0	0	-	0	.244	.292	.389
1997 Toronto	AL	14	48	10	0	2	1	(1	0)	17	4	5	4	3	1	13	0	0	1	0	0	-	1	.208	.250	.354
2003 Texas	AL	43	133	35	9	0	3	(2	1)	53	14	12	15	14	1	27	0	0	0	1	1	.50	2	.263	.333	.398
2003 New York	AL	63	174	48	8	1	6	(5	1)	76	19	31	20	13	2	20	0	0	2	1	0	1.00	7	.276	.323	.437
18 ML YEARS		2111	7846	2108	415	59	302	(160	142)	3547	1067	1289	1090	597	101	1191	7	1	117	142	52	.73	191	.269	.317	.452

Carlos Silva

Pitches: R **Bats:** R **Pos:** SP-33   **Ht:** 6'4" **Wt:** 225 **Born:** 4/23/1979 **Age:** 26

		HOW MUCH HE PITCHED						WHAT HE GAVE UP												THE RESULTS						
Year Team	Lg	G	GS	CG	GF	IP	BFP	H	R	ER	HR	SH	SF	HB	TBB	IBB	SO	WP	Bk	W	L	Pct	ShO	Sv-Op	Hld	ERC	ERA
2002 Philadelphia	NL	68	0	0	21	84.0	350	88	34	30	4	9	3	4	22	6	41	3	0	5	0	1.000	0	1-5	8	3.60	3.21
2003 Philadelphia	NL	62	1	0	15	87.1	380	92	43	43	7	6	1	8	37	5	48	12	1	3	1	.750	0	1-3	4	4.73	4.43
2004 Minnesota	AL	33	33	1	0	203.0	869	255	100	95	23	6	0	5	35	2	76	5	1	14	8	.636	1	0-0	0	4.89	4.21
3 ML YEARS		163	34	1	36	374.1	1599	435	177	168	34	21	4	17	94	13	165	20	2	22	9	.710	1	2-8	12	4.56	4.04

Randall Simon

Bats: L **Throws:** L **Pos:** 1B-47; PH-17; DH-10   **Ht:** 6'0" **Wt:** 230 **Born:** 5/26/1975 **Age:** 30

		BATTING																			BASERUNNING				AVERAGES		
Year Team	Lg	G	AB	H	2B	3B	HR	(Hm	Rd)	TB	R	RBI	RC	TBB	IBB	SO	HBP	SH	SF	SB	CS	SB%	GDP	Avg	OBP	Slg
2004 Nashville*	AAA	17	64	17	4	0	1	(-	-)	24	5	6	5	2	1	8	1	0	1	0	1	0	1.00	4	.266	.294	.375
1997 Atlanta	NL	13	14	6	1	0	0	(0	0)	7	2	1	3	1	0	2	0	0	0	0	0	-	1	.429	.467	.500
1998 Atlanta	NL	7	16	3	0	0	0	(0	0)	3	2	4	0	0	0	1	0	0	0	0	0	-	0	.188	.176	.188
1999 Atlanta	NL	90	218	69	16	0	5	(2	3)	100	26	25	33	17	6	25	1	0	1	2	2	.50	10	.317	.367	.459
2001 Detroit	AL	81	256	78	14	2	6	(1	5)	114	28	37	36	15	2	28	0	1	2	0	1	.00	9	.305	.341	.445
2002 Detroit	AL	130	482	145	17	1	19	(13	6)	221	51	82	69	13	5	30	4	0	7	0	1	.00	13	.301	.320	.459
2003 Pit-ChC	NL	124	410	113	17	0	16	(4	12)	178	47	72	61	16	2	37	4	0	1	0	0	-	7	.276	.309	.434
2004 Pit-TB	NL	69	192	36	6	0	3	(0	3)	51	16	14	10	18	5	19	3	0	0	0	0	-	8	.188	.266	.266
2003 Pittsburgh	NL	91	307	84	14	0	10	(4	6)	128	34	51	40	12	1	30	2	0	0	0	0	-	6	.274	.305	.417
2003 Chicago	NL	33	103	29	3	0	6	(0	6)	50	13	21	21	4	1	7	2	0	1	0	0	-	1	.282	.318	.485

			BATTING															BASERUNNING				AVERAGES		
Year Team	Lg	G	AB	H	2B	3B	HR	(Hm	Rd)	TB	R	RBI	RC	TBB	IBB	SO	HBP	SH	SF	SB	CS	SB%	GDP	Avg	OBP	Slg
2004 Pittsburgh	NL	61	175	34	6	0	3	(0	3)	49	14	14	10	15	5	17	2	0	1	0	0	-	8	.194	.264	.280
2004 Tampa Bay	AL	8	17	2	0	0	0	(0	0)	2	2	0	0	3	0	2	1	0	0	0	0	-	0	.118	.286	.118
7 ML YEARS		514	1588	450	71	3	49	(20	29)	674	172	235	212	80	20	142	12	1	13	2	4	.33	48	.283	.320	.424

Jason Simontacchi

Pitches: R **Bats:** R **Pos:** RP-13 **Ht:** 6'2" **Wt:** 185 **Born:** 11/13/1973 **Age:** 31

		HOW MUCH HE PITCHED						WHAT HE GAVE UP											THE RESULTS						
Year Team	Lg	G	GS	CG	GF	IP	BFP	H	R	ER	HR	SH	SF	HB	TBB	IBB	SO	WP	Bk	W	L	Pct	ShO	Sv-Op	Hld	ERC	ERA
2004 Memphis*	AAA	33	8	0	9	81.0	356	101	44	39	8	6	6	4	12	2	55	5	0	7	4	.636	0	2- -	-	4.56	4.33
2002 St Louis	NL	24	24	0	0	143.1	600	134	68	64	18	6	4	6	54	4	72	1	0	11	5	.688	0	0-0	0	4.01	4.02
2003 St Louis	NL	46	16	1	7	126.1	563	153	82	78	21	2	4	5	41	0	74	4	0	9	5	.643	0	1-3	7	5.68	5.56
2004 St Louis	NL	13	0	0	6	15.1	67	17	10	9	5	2	1	1	7	0	3	0	0	0	0	-	0	0-0	0	7.26	5.28
3 ML YEARS		83	40	1	13	285.0	1230	304	160	151	44	10	9	12	102	4	149	5	0	20	10	.667	0	1-3	7	4.90	4.77

Allan Simpson

Pitches: R **Bats:** R **Pos:** RP-32 **Ht:** 6'4" **Wt:** 185 **Born:** 8/26/1977 **Age:** 27

		HOW MUCH HE PITCHED						WHAT HE GAVE UP											THE RESULTS						
Year Team	Lg	G	GS	CG	GF	IP	BFP	H	R	ER	HR	SH	SF	HB	TBB	IBB	SO	WP	Bk	W	L	Pct	ShO	Sv-Op	Hld	ERC	ERA
1997 Everett	A-	16	0	0	6	26.1	127	26	23	20	1	1	1	2	24	1	26	3	0	0	3	.000	0	0- -	-	5.80	6.84
1998 Wisconsin	A	19	19	0	0	93.1	420	89	52	46	5	4	2	7	61	0	86	5	2	3	5	.375	0	0- -	-	4.84	4.44
1998 Mariners	R	3	0	0	1	9.1	37	8	2	1	1	0	0	0	3	0	12	0	0	1	0	1.000	0	1- -	-	3.18	0.96
1999 Wisconsin	A	24	13	1	3	90.1	402	83	56	44	4	4	8	3	48	0	88	4	1	2	9	.182	0	0- -	-	3.79	4.38
1999 Lancaster	A+	9	0	0	0	21.1	96	17	16	15	4	0	2	2	14	0	25	2	1	0	0	-	0	0- -	-	4.91	6.33
2000 Lancaster	A+	46	0	0	20	52.0	217	34	17	12	1	0	2	2	27	1	67	2	0	3	2	.600	0	6- -	-	2.26	2.08
2001 Sn Brnardino	A+	16	0	0	5	30.0	121	19	7	6	1	1	1	0	12	1	40	2	0	1	0	1.000	0	9- -	-	1.73	1.80
2001 San Antonio	AA	22	0	0	16	38.2	157	25	8	8	1	1	3	2	15	1	37	2	0	1	1	.667	0	9- -	-	1.89	1.86
2002 San Antonio	AA	56	0	0	28	82.1	346	53	33	28	4	4	4	6	50	5	99	5	0	10	5	.667	0	7- -	-	2.80	3.06
2003 Tacoma	AAA	43	0	0	23	62.2	291	60	30	29	7	3	1	6	42	1	69	2	0	2	5	.286	0	1- -	-	5.33	4.16
2004 Co Springs	AAA	27	0	0	19	35.1	154	30	14	11	1	1	0	7	10	0	43	4	1	2	1	.667	0	4- -	-	2.97	2.80
2004 Colorado	NL	32	0	0	9	39.0	183	44	26	22	4	3	4	4	20	0	46	3	0	2	1	.667	0	0-1	1	5.64	5.08

Grady Sizemore

Bats: L **Throws:** L **Pos:** CF-42; PH-1; PR-1 **Ht:** 6'2" **Wt:** 200 **Born:** 8/2/1982 **Age:** 22

				BATTING															BASERUNNING				AVERAGES		
Year Team	Lg	G	AB	H	2B	3B	HR	(Hm	Rd)	TB	R	RBI	RC	TBB	IBB	SO	HBP	SH	SF	SB	CS	SB%	GDP	Avg	OBP	Slg
2000 Expos	R	55	205	60	8	3	1	(-	-)	77	31	14	34	23	0	24	6	2	0	16	2	.89	1	.293	.380	.376
2001 Clinton	A	123	451	121	16	4	2	(-	-)	151	64	61	68	81	4	92	4	0	5	32	11	.74	7	.268	.381	.335
2002 Brevard Cnty	A+	75	256	66	15	4	0	(-	-)	89	37	26	31	36	3	41	2	0	2	9	9	.50	6	.258	.351	.348
2002 Kinston	A+	47	172	59	9	3	3	(-	-)	83	31	20	38	33	2	30	1	1	0	14	7	.67	1	.343	.451	.483
2003 Akron	AA	128	496	151	26	11	13	(-	-)	238	96	78	88	46	1	73	11	1	5	10	9	.53	5	.304	.373	.480
2004 Buffalo	AAA	101	418	120	23	8	8	(-	-)	183	73	51	66	42	0	72	8	1	4	15	10	.60	6	.287	.360	.438
2004 Cleveland	AL	43	138	34	6	2	4	(2	2)	56	15	24	21	14	0	34	5	0	2	2	0	1.00	0	.246	.333	.406

Terrmel Sledge

Bats: L **Throws:** L **Pos:** LF-79; RF-43; PH-17; 1B-10; CF-4 **Ht:** 6'0" **Wt:** 185 **Born:** 3/18/1977 **Age:** 28

				BATTING															BASERUNNING				AVERAGES		
Year Team	Lg	G	AB	H	2B	3B	HR	(Hm	Rd)	TB	R	RBI	RC	TBB	IBB	SO	HBP	SH	SF	SB	CS	SB%	GDP	Avg	OBP	Slg
1999 Everett	A-	62	233	74	8	3	5	(-	-)	103	43	32	43	27	0	35	9	2	2	9	8	.53	2	.318	.406	.442
2000 Wisconsin	A	7	23	5	2	2	0	(-	-)	11	5	3	3	3	0	3	1	0	0	1	0	1.00	1	.217	.333	.478
2000 Lancaster	A+	103	384	130	22	7	11	(-	-)	199	90	75	96	72	3	49	17	1	5	35	11	.76	4	.339	.458	.518
2001 Harrisburg	AA	129	448	124	22	6	9	(-	-)	185	66	48	72	51	0	72	9	3	5	30	8	.79	5	.277	.359	.413
2002 Harrisburg	AA	102	396	119	18	6	8	(-	-)	173	74	43	72	55	2	70	12	4	1	11	8	.58	4	.301	.401	.437
2002 Ottawa	AAA	24	80	21	5	2	1	(-	-)	33	12	11	11	11	0	15	1	0	0	1	1	.50	2	.263	.359	.413
2003 Edmonton	AAA	131	497	161	26	9	22	(-	-)	271	95	92	104	61	3	93	5	0	9	13	5	.72	10	.324	.397	.545
2004 Montreal	NL	133	398	107	20	6	15	(6	9)	184	45	62	66	40	4	66	1	6	1	3	3	.50	2	.269	.336	.462

Aaron Small

Pitches: R **Bats:** R **Pos:** RP-7 **Ht:** 6'5" **Wt:** 237 **Born:** 11/23/1971 **Age:** 33

		HOW MUCH HE PITCHED						WHAT HE GAVE UP											THE RESULTS						
Year Team	Lg	G	GS	CG	GF	IP	BFP	H	R	ER	HR	SH	SF	HB	TBB	IBB	SO	WP	Bk	W	L	Pct	ShO	Sv-Op	Hld	ERC	ERA
2004 Albuquerque*	AAA	27	24	2	1	154.2	671	199	95	87	18	5	4	3	29	2	109	5	0	9	9	.500	0	0- -	-	5.11	5.06
1994 Toronto	AL	1	0	0	1	2.0	13	5	2	2	1	0	1	0	2	0	0	0	0	0	0	-	0	0-0	0	21.61	9.00
1995 Florida	NL	7	0	0	1	6.1	32	7	2	1	1	0	0	0	6	0	5	0	0	1	0	1.000	0	0-0	0	7.30	1.42
1996 Oakland	AL	12	3	0	4	28.2	144	37	28	26	3	0	1	1	22	1	17	2	0	1	3	.250	0	0-0	0	7.42	8.16
1997 Oakland	AL	71	0	0	22	96.2	425	109	50	46	6	5	6	3	40	6	57	4	0	9	5	.643	0	4-6	8	4.67	4.28
1998 Oak-Ari		47	0	0	13	67.2	304	83	48	42	8	5	1	4	22	4	33	4	0	4	2	.667	0	0-2	4	5.38	5.59
2002 Atlanta	NL	1	0	0	0	0.1	5	2	1	1	0	0	0	0	2	0	1	1	0	0	0	-	0	0-0	0	71.88	27.00
2004 Florida	NL	7	0	0	0	16.1	78	24	15	15	5	1	0	0	7	0	8	1	0	0	0	-	1	0-0	1	8.84	8.27
1998 Oakland	AL	24	0	0	4	36.0	174	51	34	29	3	3	1	3	14	3	19	4	0	1	1	.500	0	0-0	3	6.49	7.25
1998 Arizona	NL	23	0	0	9	31.2	130	32	14	13	5	2	0	1	8	1	14	0	0	3	1	.750	0	0-2	1	4.14	3.69
7 ML YEARS		146	3	0	42	218.0	1001	267	146	133	24	11	9	8	101	11	121	12	0	15	10	.600	0	4-8	13	5.83	5.49

Jason Smith

Bats: L **Throws:** R **Pos:** 2B-34; SS-20; PH-7; 3B-5; PR-4; DH-2   **Ht:** 6'3" **Wt:** 199 **Born:** 7/24/1977 **Age:** 27

				BATTING																BASERUNNING				AVERAGES		
Year Team	Lg	G	AB	H	2B	3B	HR	(Hm	Rd)	TB	R	RBI	RC	TBB	IBB	SO	HBP	SH	SF	SB	CS	SB%	GDP	Avg	OBP	Slg
2004 Toledo*	AAA	33	122	33	8	2	3	(-	-)	54	18	13	16	6	1	26	0	0	2	5	1	.83	1	.270	.300	.443
2001 Chicago	NL	2	1	0	0	0	0	(0	0)	0	0	0	0	0	0	1	0	0	0	0	0	-	0	.000	.000	.000
2002 Tampa Bay	AL	26	65	13	1	2	1	(0	1)	21	9	6	5	2	0	24	0	2	0	3	0	1.00	0	.200	.224	.323
2003 Tampa Bay	AL	1	4	1	0	0	0	(0	0)	1	0	0	0	0	0	0	0	0	0	0	0	-	0	.250	.250	.250
2004 Detroit	AL	61	155	37	7	4	5	(0	5)	67	20	19	13	8	0	37	1	5	0	1	2	.33	0	.239	.280	.432
4 ML YEARS		90	225	51	8	6	6	(0	6)	89	29	25	18	10	0	62	1	7	0	4	2	.67	0	.227	.263	.396

Travis Smith

Pitches: R **Bats:** R **Pos:** RP-12; SP-4   **Ht:** 5'10" **Wt:** 165 **Born:** 11/7/1972 **Age:** 32

		HOW MUCH HE PITCHED						WHAT HE GAVE UP										THE RESULTS						
Year Team	Lg	G	GS	CG	GF	IP	BFP	H	R	ER	HR	SH	SF	HB	TBB	IBB	SO	WP	Bk	W	L	Pct	ShO	Sv-Op	Hld	ERC	ERA
2004 Richmond*	AAA	20	19	1	1	107.2	432	98	31	31	6	4	3	6	26	0	93	2	1	10	2	.833	0	0- -	-	3.01	2.59
1998 Milwaukee	NL	1	0	0	0	2.0	7	1	0	0	0	0	0	0	0	0	1	0	0	0	0	-	0	0-0	0	0.54	0.00
2002 St Louis	NL	12	10	0	0	54.0	244	69	44	43	10	7	0	3	20	0	32	2	0	4	2	.667	0	0-0	0	6.63	7.17
2004 Atlanta	NL	16	4	0	4	40.2	180	48	28	28	12	3	0	1	12	2	26	1	0	2	3	.400	0	0-0	1	6.12	6.20
3 ML YEARS		29	14	0	4	96.2	431	118	72	71	22	10	0	4	32	2	59	3	0	6	5	.545	0	0-0	1	6.25	6.61

John Smoltz

Pitches: R **Bats:** R **Pos:** RP-73   **Ht:** 6'3" **Wt:** 220 **Born:** 5/15/1967 **Age:** 38

		HOW MUCH HE PITCHED						WHAT HE GAVE UP										THE RESULTS						
Year Team	Lg	G	GS	CG	GF	IP	BFP	H	R	ER	HR	SH	SF	HB	TBB	IBB	SO	WP	Bk	W	L	Pct	ShO	Sv-Op	Hld	ERC	ERA
1988 Atlanta	NL	12	12	0	0	64.0	297	74	40	39	10	2	0	2	33	4	37	2	1	2	7	.222	0	0-0	0	5.86	5.48
1989 Atlanta	NL	29	29	5	0	208.0	847	160	79	68	15	10	7	2	72	2	168	8	3	12	11	.522	0	0-0	0	2.50	2.94
1990 Atlanta	NL	34	34	6	0	231.1	966	206	109	99	20	9	8	1	90	3	170	14	3	14	11	.560	2	0-0	0	3.37	3.85
1991 Atlanta	NL	36	36	5	0	229.2	947	206	101	97	16	9	9	3	77	1	148	20	2	14	13	.519	0	0-0	0	3.15	3.80
1992 Atlanta	NL	35	35	9	0	246.2	1021	206	90	78	17	7	8	5	80	5	215	17	1	15	12	.556	3	0-0	0	2.73	2.85
1993 Atlanta	NL	35	35	3	0	243.2	1028	208	104	98	23	13	4	6	100	12	208	13	1	15	11	.577	1	0-0	0	3.29	3.62
1994 Atlanta	NL	21	21	1	0	134.2	568	120	69	62	15	7	6	4	48	4	113	7	0	6	10	.375	0	0-0	0	3.44	4.14
1995 Atlanta	NL	29	29	2	0	192.2	808	166	76	68	15	13	5	4	72	8	193	13	0	12	7	.632	1	0-0	0	3.08	3.18
1996 Atlanta	NL	35	35	6	0	253.2	995	199	93	83	19	12	4	2	55	3	276	10	1	24	8	.750	2	0-0	0	2.17	2.94
1997 Atlanta	NL	35	35	7	0	256.0	1043	234	97	86	21	10	3	1	63	9	241	10	1	15	12	.556	2	0-0	0	2.89	3.02
1998 Atlanta	NL	26	26	2	0	167.2	681	145	58	54	10	4	2	4	44	2	173	3	1	17	3	.850	2	0-0	0	2.67	2.90
1999 Atlanta	NL	29	29	1	0	186.1	746	168	70	66	14	10	5	4	40	2	156	2	0	11	8	.579	1	0-0	0	2.81	3.19
2001 Atlanta	NL	36	5	0	20	59.0	238	53	24	22	7	1	2	0	10	2	57	0	0	3	3	.500	0	10-11	5	2.85	3.36
2002 Atlanta	NL	75	0	0	68	80.1	314	59	30	29	4	2	1	0	24	1	85	1	1	3	2	.600	0	55-59	0	2.06	3.25
2003 Atlanta	NL	62	0	0	55	64.1	244	48	9	8	2	0	1	0	8	1	73	2	0	0	2	.000	0	45-49	0	1.50	1.12
2004 Atlanta	NL	73	0	0	61	81.2	323	75	25	25	8	4	0	0	13	2	85	6	0	0	1	.000	0	44-49	0	2.73	2.76
16 ML YEARS		602	361	47	204	2699.2	11066	2327	1074	982	216	113	65	40	829	61	2398	128	15	163	121	.574	14	154-168	5	2.89	3.27

Ryan Snare

Pitches: L **Bats:** L **Pos:** RP-1   **Ht:** 6'0" **Wt:** 200 **Born:** 2/8/1979 **Age:** 26

		HOW MUCH HE PITCHED						WHAT HE GAVE UP										THE RESULTS						
Year Team	Lg	G	GS	CG	GF	IP	BFP	H	R	ER	HR	SH	SF	HB	TBB	IBB	SO	WP	Bk	W	L	Pct	ShO	Sv-Op	Hld	ERC	ERA
2001 Dayton	A	21	20	0	0	115.0	472	101	45	39	7	1	1	9	37	1	118	9	2	9	5	.643	0	0- -	-	3.22	3.05
2002 Stockton	A+	13	13	0	0	82.0	335	74	36	28	4	2	3	1	18	0	81	2	1	8	2	.800	0	0- -	-	2.58	3.07
2002 Portland	AA	11	9	0	0	55.0	226	46	25	21	6	0	1	1	19	0	52	5	0	4	2	.667	0	0- -	-	3.13	3.44
2002 Chattanooga	AA	5	0	0	0	6.0	22	5	3	2	1	0	0	0	3	0	4	0	0	0	0	-	0	0- -	-	4.74	3.00
2003 Carolina	AA	18	18	0	0	103.0	436	98	46	42	4	3	2	7	37	0	77	4	1	5	4	.556	0	0- -	-	3.53	3.67
2003 Oklahoma	AAA	9	9	0	0	54.2	235	59	26	21	7	3	3	2	13	0	28	3	0	4	5	.444	0	0- -	-	4.18	3.46
2004 Oklahoma	AAA	26	24	0	0	137.1	608	171	88	72	16	8	8	3	49	0	79	9	0	11	6	.647	0	0- -	-	5.67	4.72
2004 Texas	AL	1	0	0	0	3.1	17	5	5	4	3	0	0	0	2	0	0	0	0	0	0	-	0	0-0	0	15.04	10.80

Esix Snead

Bats: B **Throws:** R **Pos:** LF-1; PR-1   **Ht:** 5'10" **Wt:** 175 **Born:** 6/7/1976 **Age:** 29

				BATTING																BASERUNNING				AVERAGES		
Year Team	Lg	G	AB	H	2B	3B	HR	(Hm	Rd)	TB	R	RBI	RC	TBB	IBB	SO	HBP	SH	SF	SB	CS	SB%	GDP	Avg	OBP	Slg
1998 New Jersey	A-	58	193	45	4	4	1	(-	-)	60	38	16	28	33	0	54	7	1	0	42	11	.79	3	.233	.365	.311
1999 Potomac	A+	67	249	45	8	5	0	(-	-)	63	37	14	20	32	0	57	4	3	3	35	12	.74	2	.181	.281	.253
1999 Peoria	A	59	181	35	7	1	2	(-	-)	50	35	18	20	35	0	42	2	7	1	29	9	.76	3	.193	.329	.276
2000 Potomac	A+	132	493	116	14	3	1	(-	-)	139	82	34	59	72	1	98	7	9	1	109	35	.76	7	.235	.340	.282
2001 New Haven	AA	133	520	121	21	6	1	(-	-)	157	71	33	53	44	0	115	12	5	1	64	23	.74	4	.233	.307	.302
2002 Binghamton	AA	125	401	101	9	6	3	(-	-)	131	62	42	53	45	0	72	6	16	2	66	18	.79	4	.252	.335	.327
2003 Norfolk	AAA	137	472	104	14	6	3	(-	-)	139	64	31	48	41	0	83	5	12	5	61	7	.90	8	.220	.287	.294
2004 Norfolk	AAA	79	269	71	10	2	0	(-	-)	85	42	21	37	35	0	53	2	4	4	40	10	.80	2	.264	.348	.316
2002 New York	NL	17	13	4	0	0	1	(1	0)	7	3	3	3	1	0	4	0	0	0	4	3	.57	0	.308	.357	.538
2004 New York	NL	1	0	0	0	0	0	(0	0)	0	1	0	0	0	0	0	0	0	0	0	0	-	0	-	-	-
2 ML YEARS		18	13	4	0	0	1	(1	0)	7	4	3	3	1	0	4	0	0	0	4	3	.57	0	.308	.357	.538

Ian Snell

Pitches: R **Bats:** R **Pos:** RP-2; SP-1   **Ht:** 5'11" **Wt:** 170 **Born:** 10/30/1981 **Age:** 23

		HOW MUCH HE PITCHED						WHAT HE GAVE UP										THE RESULTS						
Year Team	Lg	G	GS	CG	GF	IP	BFP	H	R	ER	HR	SH	SF	HB	TBB	IBB	SO	WP	Bk	W	L	Pct	ShO	Sv-Op	Hld	ERC	ERA
2000 Pirates	R	4	0	0	1	7.2	28	5	2	2	1	1	0	1	1	0	8	0	0	1	0	1.000	0	0- -	-	2.12	2.35
2001 Pirates	R	3	3	0	0	19.0	74	12	2	1	0	1	0	0	5	0	13	0	0	3	0	1.000	0	0- -	-	1.32	0.47
2001 Williamsport	A-	10	9	1	0	64.2	260	55	16	10	2	3	2	1	10	0	56	2	0	7	0	1.000	0	0- -	-	2.00	1.39

		HOW MUCH HE PITCHED						WHAT HE GAVE UP													THE RESULTS							
Year Team	Lg	G	GS	CG	GF	IP	BFP	H	R	ER	HR	SH	SF	HB	TBB	IBB	SO	WP	Bk	W	L	Pct	ShO	Sv-Op	Hld	ERC	ERA
2002 Hickory	A	24	22	0	0	139.2	591	127	49	42	8	5	3	0	45	0	149	13	2	11	6	.647	0	0--	-	2.94	2.71
2003 Lynchburg	A+	20	20	1	0	116.1	477	105	46	43	3	8	3	3	33	1	122	4	2	10	3	.769	1	0--	-	2.74	3.33
2003 Altoona	AA	6	6	0	0	36.2	155	36	13	8	2	0	1	1	10	0	23	2	0	4	0	1.000	0	0--	-	3.25	1.96
2004 Altoona	AA	26	26	3	0	151.0	624	147	54	53	16	9	6	5	40	2	142	6	0	11	7	.611	2	0--	-	3.61	3.16
2004 Pittsburgh	NL	3	1	0	1	12.0	56	14	10	10	2	0	0	0	9	0	9	0	0	0	1	.000	0	0-0	0	7.31	7.50

J.T. Snow

Bats: L Throws: L Pos: 1B-100; PH-9   Ht: 6'2" Wt: 209 Born: 2/26/1968 Age: 37

		BATTING																	BASERUNNING				AVERAGES		
Year Team	Lg	G	AB	H	2B	3B	HR	(Hm	Rd)	TB	R	RBI	RC	TBB	IBB	SO	HBP	SH	SF	SB	CS	SB%	GDP	Avg	OBP	Slg
2004 Fresno*	AAA	2	7	2	0	0	1	(-	-)	5	1	2	1	0	0	1	0	0	0	0	0	-	0	.286	.286	.714
1992 New York	AL	7	14	2	1	0	0	(0	0)	3	1	2	2	5	1	5	0	0	0	0	0	-	0	.143	.368	.214
1993 California	AL	129	419	101	18	2	16	(10	6)	171	60	57	57	55	4	88	2	7	6	3	0	1.00	10	.241	.328	.408
1994 California	AL	61	223	49	4	0	8	(7	1)	77	22	30	22	19	1	48	3	2	1	0	1	.00	2	.220	.289	.345
1995 California	AL	143	544	157	22	1	24	(14	10)	253	80	102	85	52	4	91	3	5	2	2	1	.67	16	.289	.353	.465
1996 California	AL	155	575	148	20	1	17	(8	9)	221	69	67	67	56	6	96	5	2	3	1	6	.14	19	.257	.327	.384
1997 San Francisco	NL	157	531	149	36	1	28	(14	14)	271	81	104	105	96	13	124	1	2	7	6	4	.60	8	.281	.387	.510
1998 San Francisco	NL	138	435	108	29	1	15	(9	6)	184	65	79	60	58	3	84	0	0	7	1	2	.33	12	.248	.332	.423
1999 San Francisco	NL	161	570	156	25	2	24	(7	17)	257	93	98	93	86	7	121	5	1	6	0	4	.00	16	.274	.370	.451
2000 San Francisco	NL	155	536	152	33	2	19	(10	9)	246	82	96	87	66	6	129	11	0	14	1	3	.25	20	.284	.365	.459
2001 San Francisco	NL	101	285	70	12	1	8	(3	5)	108	43	34	44	55	10	81	4	0	4	0	0	-	2	.246	.371	.379
2002 San Francisco	NL	143	422	104	26	2	6	(1	5)	152	47	53	54	59	5	90	7	0	6	0	0	-	11	.246	.344	.360
2003 San Francisco	NL	103	330	90	18	3	8	(2	6)	138	48	51	59	55	0	55	8	1	2	1	2	.33	7	.273	.387	.418
2004 San Francisco	NL	107	346	113	32	1	12	(5	7)	183	62	60	78	58	0	61	7	2	4	4	0	1.00	5	.327	.429	.529
13 ML YEARS		1560	5230	1399	276	17	185	(90	95)	2264	753	833	813	720	60	1073	56	22	62	19	23	.45	128	.267	.358	.433

Chris Snyder

Bats: R Throws: R Pos: C-29   Ht: 6'3" Wt: 220 Born: 2/12/1981 Age: 24

		BATTING																	BASERUNNING				AVERAGES		
Year Team	Lg	G	AB	H	2B	3B	HR	(Hm	Rd)	TB	R	RBI	RC	TBB	IBB	SO	HBP	SH	SF	SB	CS	SB%	GDP	Avg	OBP	Slg
2002 Lancaster	A+	60	217	56	16	0	9	(-	-)	99	31	44	31	25	0	54	3	1	4	0	0	-	7	.258	.337	.456
2003 Lancaster	A+	69	245	77	16	2	10	(-	-)	127	53	53	51	35	2	43	8	0	2	0	1	.00	4	.314	.414	.518
2003 El Paso	AA	53	188	38	14	0	4	(-	-)	64	21	26	15	19	1	29	4	0	2	0	0	-	9	.202	.286	.340
2004 El Paso	AA	99	346	104	31	0	15	(-	-)	180	66	57	67	46	1	57	6	0	3	3	1	.75	7	.301	.389	.520
2004 Arizona	NL	29	96	23	6	0	5	(1	4)	44	10	15	11	13	1	25	0	0	1	0	0	-	1	.240	.327	.458

Earl Snyder

Bats: R Throws: R Pos: 3B-1   Ht: 6'0" Wt: 207 Born: 5/6/1976 Age: 29

		BATTING																	BASERUNNING				AVERAGES		
Year Team	Lg	G	AB	H	2B	3B	HR	(Hm	Rd)	TB	R	RBI	RC	TBB	IBB	SO	HBP	SH	SF	SB	CS	SB%	GDP	Avg	OBP	Slg
1998 Pittsfield	A-	71	262	66	8	1	11	(-	-)	109	39	40	33	23	0	60	2	0	1	0	1	.00	6	.252	.316	.416
1999 Capital City	A	136	486	130	25	4	28	(-	-)	247	73	97	82	55	0	117	2	0	9	2	2	.50	5	.267	.339	.508
2000 St. Lucie	A+	134	514	145	36	0	25	(-	-)	256	84	93	88	57	6	127	8	0	8	4	4	.50	8	.282	.358	.498
2001 Binghamton	AA	114	405	114	35	2	20	(-	-)	213	69	75	76	58	5	111	4	0	3	4	2	.67	5	.281	.374	.526
2001 Norfolk	AAA	6	19	9	3	0	0	(-	-)	12	5	3	5	3	0	1	1	0	0	0	1	.00	0	.474	.565	.632
2002 Buffalo	AAA	110	400	105	29	1	19	(-	-)	193	69	66	63	43	2	96	6	1	3	0	2	.00	6	.263	.341	.483
2003 Pawtucket	AAA	130	467	119	25	1	22	(-	-)	212	61	71	61	24	2	113	8	2	6	0	0	-	6	.255	.299	.454
2004 Pawtucket	AAA	136	538	147	43	1	36	(-	-)	300	85	104	87	35	3	128	7	0	6	1	1	.50	14	.273	.323	.558
2002 Cleveland	AL	18	55	11	2	0	1	(1	0)	16	5	4	3	6	0	21	0	1	0	0	0	-	1	.200	.279	.291
2004 Boston	AL	1	4	1	0	0	0	(0	0)	1	0	0	1	0	0	1	0	0	0	0	0	-	1	.250	.250	.250
2 ML YEARS		19	59	12	2	0	1	(1	0)	17	5	4	4	6	0	22	0	1	0	0	0	-	2	.203	.277	.288

Alfonso Soriano

Bats: R Throws: R Pos: 2B-142; DH-3   Ht: 6'1" Wt: 180 Born: 1/7/1978 Age: 27

		BATTING																	BASERUNNING				AVERAGES		
Year Team	Lg	G	AB	H	2B	3B	HR	(Hm	Rd)	TB	R	RBI	RC	TBB	IBB	SO	HBP	SH	SF	SB	CS	SB%	GDP	Avg	OBP	Slg
1999 New York	AL	9	8	1	0	0	1	(1	0)	4	2	1	0	0	0	3	0	0	0	0	1	.00	0	.125	.125	.500
2000 New York	AL	22	50	9	3	0	2	(0	2)	18	5	3	4	1	0	15	0	2	0	2	0	1.00	0	.180	.196	.360
2001 New York	AL	158	574	154	34	3	18	(10	8)	248	77	73	77	29	0	125	3	3	5	43	14	.75	7	.268	.304	.432
2002 New York	AL	156	696	209	51	2	39	(17	22)	381	128	102	121	23	1	157	14	1	7	41	13	.76	8	.300	.332	.547
2003 New York	AL	156	682	198	36	5	38	(15	23)	358	114	91	110	38	7	130	12	0	2	35	8	.81	8	.290	.338	.525
2004 Texas	AL	145	608	170	32	4	28	(12	16)	294	77	91	90	33	4	121	10	0	7	18	5	.78	7	.280	.324	.484
6 ML YEARS		646	2618	741	156	14	126	(53	73)	1303	403	361	402	124	12	551	39	6	21	139	41	.77	30	.283	.323	.498

Rafael Soriano

Pitches: R Bats: R Pos: RP-6   Ht: 6'1" Wt: 175 Born: 12/19/1979 Age: 25

		HOW MUCH HE PITCHED						WHAT HE GAVE UP													THE RESULTS							
Year Team	Lg	G	GS	CG	GF	IP	BFP	H	R	ER	HR	SH	SF	HB	TBB	IBB	SO	WP	Bk	W	L	Pct	ShO	Sv-Op	Hld	ERC	ERA
2004 InlandEmpire*	A+	2	2	0	0	8.0	32	7	3	2	1	0	0	0	1	0	9	0	0	0	0	-	0	0--	-	2.48	2.25
2004 San Antonio*	AA	2	1	0	0	8.0	27	4	1	1	1	0	0	0	0	0	10	0	0	1	0	1.000	0	0--	-	0.86	1.13
2004 Tacoma*	AAA	3	3	0	0	3.2	15	2	1	1	0	0	0	0	2	0	5	0	0	0	0	-	0	0--	-	3.23	2.45
2002 Seattle	AL	10	8	0	1	47.1	202	45	25	24	8	1	0	0	16	1	32	2	0	0	3	.000	0	1-1	0	3.93	4.56
2003 Seattle	AL	40	0	0	12	53.0	201	30	9	9	2	0	1	3	12	1	68	0	0	3	0	1.000	0	1-2	5	1.32	1.53
2004 Seattle	AL	6	0	0	0	3.1	23	9	6	5	0	0	0	0	3	0	3	0	0	0	3	.000	0	0-1	0	15.97	13.50
3 ML YEARS		56	8	0	13	103.2	426	84	40	38	10	1	1	3	31	2	103	2	0	3	6	.333	0	2-4	5	2.71	3.30

Jorge Sosa

Pitches: R **Bats:** B **Pos:** RP-35; SP-8   **Ht:** 6'2" **Wt:** 177 **Born:** 4/28/1977 **Age:** 28

			HOW MUCH HE PITCHED						WHAT HE GAVE UP										THE RESULTS						
Year Team	Lg	G	GS	CG	GF	IP	BFP	H	R	ER	HR	SH	SF	HB	TBB	IBB	SO	WP	Bk	W	L	Pct	ShO	Sv-Op	Hld	ERC	ERA
2004 Durham*	AAA	3	3	0	0	13.0	48	11	5	4	0	1	0	0	0	0	23	1	0	1	2	.333	0	0- -	1	1.46	2.77
2002 Tampa Bay	AL	31	14	0	10	99.1	434	88	63	61	16	0	5	2	54	0	48	5	0	2	7	.222	0	0-0	0	4.51	5.53
2003 Tampa Bay	AL	29	19	1	4	128.2	566	137	71	66	14	4	5	4	60	4	72	8	1	5	12	.294	1	0-0	0	4.93	4.62
2004 Tampa Bay	AL	43	8	0	6	99.1	447	100	67	61	17	2	4	1	54	3	94	2	0	4	7	.364	0	1-1	6	5.17	5.53
3 ML YEARS		103	41	1	20	327.1	1447	325	201	188	47	6	14	7	168	7	214	15	1	11	26	.297	1	1-1	7	4.87	5.17

Sammy Sosa

Bats: R **Throws:** R **Pos:** RF-124; DH-2   **Ht:** 6'0" **Wt:** 220 **Born:** 11/12/1968 **Age:** 36

					BATTING																BASERUNNING				AVERAGES		
Year Team	Lg	G	AB	H	2B	3B	HR	(Hm	Rd)	TB	R	RBI	RC	TBB	IBB	SO	HBP	SH	SF	SB	CS	SB%	GDP	Avg	OBP	Slg
2004 W Tennessee*	AA	2	6	2	1	0	0	(-	-)	3	0	1	1	1	0	2	0	0	0	0	0	-	0	.333	.429	.500
1989 Tex-CWS	AL	58	183	47	8	0	4	(1	3)	67	27	13	18	11	2	47	2	5	2	7	5	.58	6	.257	.303	.366
1990 Chicago	AL	153	532	124	26	10	15	(10	5)	215	72	70	59	33	4	150	6	2	6	32	16	.67	10	.233	.282	.404
1991 Chicago	AL	116	316	64	10	1	10	(3	7)	106	39	33	23	14	2	98	2	5	1	13	6	.68	5	.203	.240	.335
1992 Chicago	NL	67	262	68	7	2	8	(4	4)	103	41	25	33	19	1	63	4	4	2	15	7	.68	4	.260	.317	.393
1993 Chicago	NL	159	598	156	25	5	33	(23	10)	290	92	93	88	38	6	135	4	0	1	36	11	.77	14	.261	.309	.485
1994 Chicago	NL	105	426	128	17	6	25	(11	14)	232	59	70	75	25	1	92	2	1	4	22	13	.63	7	.300	.339	.545
1995 Chicago	NL	144	564	151	17	3	36	(19	17)	282	89	119	98	58	11	134	5	0	2	34	7	.83	8	.268	.340	.500
1996 Chicago	NL	124	498	136	21	2	40	(26	14)	281	84	100	87	34	6	134	5	0	4	18	5	.78	14	.273	.323	.564
1997 Chicago	NL	162	642	161	31	4	36	(25	11)	308	90	119	88	45	9	174	2	0	5	22	12	.65	16	.251	.300	.480
1998 Chicago	NL	159	643	198	20	0	66	(35	31)	416	134	158	142	73	14	171	1	0	5	18	9	.67	20	.308	.377	.647
1999 Chicago	NL	162	625	180	24	2	63	(33	30)	397	114	141	134	78	8	171	3	0	6	7	8	.47	17	.288	.367	.635
2000 Chicago	NL	156	604	193	38	1	50	(22	28)	383	106	138	144	91	19	168	2	0	8	7	4	.64	12	.320	.406	.634
2001 Chicago	NL	160	577	189	34	5	64	(34	30)	425	146	160	170	116	37	153	6	0	12	0	2	.00	6	.328	.437	.737
2002 Chicago	NL	150	556	160	19	2	49	(24	25)	330	122	108	121	103	15	144	3	0	4	2	0	1.00	14	.288	.399	.594
2003 Chicago	NL	137	517	144	22	0	40	(19	21)	286	99	103	94	62	9	143	5	0	5	0	1	.00	14	.279	.358	.553
2004 Chicago	NL	126	478	121	21	0	35	(18	17)	247	69	80	68	56	4	133	2	0	3	0	0	-	9	.253	.332	.517
1989 Texas	AL	25	84	20	3	0	1	(0	1)	26	8	3	4	0	0	20	0	4	0	0	2	.00	3	.238	.238	.310
1989 Chicago	AL	33	99	27	5	0	3	(1	2)	41	19	10	14	11	2	27	2	1	2	7	3	.70	3	.273	.351	.414
16 ML YEARS		2138	8021	2220	340	43	574	(307	267)	4368	1383	1530	1442	856	148	2110	54	17	70	233	106	.69	176	.277	.348	.545

Steve Sparks

Pitches: R **Bats:** R **Pos:** SP-18; RP-11   **Ht:** 6'0" **Wt:** 195 **Born:** 7/2/1965 **Age:** 39

				HOW MUCH HE PITCHED						WHAT HE GAVE UP										THE RESULTS						
Year Team	Lg	G	GS	CG	GF	IP	BFP	H	R	ER	HR	SH	SF	HB	TBB	IBB	SO	WP	Bk	W	L	Pct	ShO	Sv-Op	Hld	ERC	ERA
1995 Milwaukee	AL	33	27	3	2	202.0	875	210	111	104	17	5	12	5	86	1	96	5	1	9	11	.450	0	0-0	0	4.44	4.63
1996 Milwaukee	AL	20	13	1	2	88.2	406	103	66	65	19	3	1	3	52	0	21	6	0	4	7	.364	0	0-0	0	7.03	6.60
1998 Anaheim	AL	22	20	0	1	128.2	562	130	66	62	14	2	3	5	58	0	90	6	0	9	4	.692	0	0-0	0	4.60	4.34
1999 Anaheim	AL	28	26	0	1	147.2	688	165	101	89	21	2	8	9	82	0	73	8	0	5	11	.313	0	0-0	0	5.94	5.42
2000 Detroit	AL	20	15	1	5	104.0	446	108	55	47	7	1	1	4	29	0	53	6	0	7	5	.583	1	1-1	0	3.71	4.07
2001 Detroit	AL	35	33	8	2	232.0	982	244	110	94	22	4	9	6	64	1	116	8	2	14	9	.609	1	0-0	0	3.97	3.65
2002 Detroit	AL	32	30	3	0	189.0	868	238	134	116	23	3	8	12	67	3	98	8	3	8	16	.333	0	0-0	0	5.78	5.52
2003 Det-Oak	AL	51	0	0	26	107.0	460	114	68	58	13	1	7	3	37	4	54	3	0	0	6	.000	0	2-4	6	4.49	4.88
2004 Arizona	NL	29	18	0	6	120.2	545	139	89	81	18	6	5	5	45	2	57	4	0	3	7	.300	0	0-0	0	5.29	6.04
2003 Detroit	AL	42	0	0	24	89.2	385	95	57	47	11	1	6	3	34	4	49	3	0	0	6	.000	0	2-4	6	4.65	4.72
2003 Oakland	AL	9	0	0	2	17.1	75	19	11	11	2	0	1	0	3	0	5	0	0	0	-	0	0-0	0	3.67	5.71
9 ML YEARS		270	182	16	45	1319.2	5832	1451	800	716	154	27	54	52	520	11	658	54	6	59	76	.437	2	3-5	6	4.91	4.88

Justin Speier

Pitches: R **Bats:** R **Pos:** RP-62   **Ht:** 6'4" **Wt:** 205 **Born:** 11/6/1973 **Age:** 31

				HOW MUCH HE PITCHED						WHAT HE GAVE UP										THE RESULTS						
Year Team	Lg	G	GS	CG	GF	IP	BFP	H	R	ER	HR	SH	SF	HB	TBB	IBB	SO	WP	Bk	W	L	Pct	ShO	Sv-Op	Hld	ERC	ERA
2004 Dunedin*	A+	2	2	0	0	2.0		3	1	1	1	0	0	0	0	0	2	0	0	0	0	-	0	0- -	0	8.13	4.50
1998 ChC-Fla	NL	19	0	0	10	20.2	99	27	20	20	7	2	1	0	13	1	17	3	0	0	3	.000	0	0-1	1	8.94	8.71
1999 Atlanta	NL	19	0	0	8	28.2	127	28	18	18	8	0	1	0	13	1	22	0	0	0	0	-	0	0-0	0	5.27	5.65
2000 Cleveland	AL	47	0	0	12	68.1	290	57	27	25	9	2	4	4	28	3	69	7	1	5	2	.714	0	0-1	6	3.56	3.29
2001 Cle-Col		54	0	0	10	76.2	324	71	40	39	13	2	7	8	20	3	62	6	1	6	3	.667	0	0-1	4	3.93	4.58
2002 Colorado	NL	63	0	0	7	62.1	259	51	31	30	9	0	1	3	19	4	47	1	2	5	1	.833	0	1-4	18	3.06	4.33
2003 Colorado	NL	72	0	0	31	73.1	319	73	37	33	11	1	4	7	23	6	66	0	0	3	1	.750	0	9-12	12	4.27	4.05
2004 Toronto	AL	62	0	0	32	69.0	294	61	32	30	8	6	3	5	25	6	52	4	0	3	8	.273	0	7-11	7	3.52	3.91
1998 Chicago	NL	1	0	0	0	1.1	7	2	2	1	0	0	0	0	1	0	2	1	0	0	0	-	0	0-0	0	7.52	13.50
1998 Florida	NL	18	0	0	10	19.1	92	25	18	18	7	2	1	0	12	1	15	2	0	0	3	.000	0	0-1	1	9.02	8.38
2001 Cleveland	AL	12	0	0	2	20.2	96	24	16	16	5	0	3	3	8	0	15	2	0	2	0	1.000	0	0-0	0	6.61	6.97
2001 Colorado	NL	42	0	0	8	56.0	228	47	24	23	8	2	4	5	12	3	47	4	1	4	3	.571	0	0-1	4	3.04	3.70
7 ML YEARS		336	0	0	110	399.0	1712	368	205	195	65	13	21	27	141	24	335	21	4	22	18	.550	0	17-30	48	4.03	4.40

Shane Spencer

Bats: R **Throws:** R **Pos:** LF-43; PH-22; RF-21; CF-6; PR-2; 1B-1; DH-1   **Ht:** 5'11" **Wt:** 225 **Born:** 2/20/1972 **Age:** 33

					BATTING																BASERUNNING				AVERAGES		
Year Team	Lg	G	AB	H	2B	3B	HR	(Hm	Rd)	TB	R	RBI	RC	TBB	IBB	SO	HBP	SH	SF	SB	CS	SB%	GDP	Avg	OBP	Slg
2004 Tampa*	A+	3	9	4	0	0	0	(-	-)	4	0	2	1	1	0	1	0	0	0	0	0	-	1	.444	.500	.444
2004 Columbus*	AAA	15	50	12	4	0	0	(-	-)	16	6	6	7	0	0	15	2	0	0	1	0	1.00	1	.240	.356	.320
1998 New York	AL	27	67	25	6	0	10	(8	2)	61	18	27	22	5	0	12	0	0	1	0	1	.00	0	.373	.411	.910
1999 New York	AL	71	205	48	8	0	8	(2	6)	80	25	20	23	18	0	51	2	0	1	0	4	.00	1	.234	.301	.390
2000 New York	AL	73	248	70	11	3	9	(4	5)	114	33	40	37	19	0	45	2	0	7	1	2	.33	4	.282	.330	.460
2001 New York	AL	80	283	73	14	2	10	(6	4)	121	40	46	39	21	0	58	4	0	3	4	1	.80	4	.258	.315	.428
2002 New York	AL	94	288	71	15	2	6	(5	1)	108	32	34	34	31	4	62	4	2	4	0	3	.00	5	.247	.324	.375

Year Team	Lg	G	AB	H	2B	3B	HR	(Hm	Rd)	TB	R	RBI	RC	TBB	IBB	SO	HBP	SH	SF	SB	CS	SB%	GDP	Avg	OBP	Slg
2003 Cle-Tex	AL	119	395	99	20	0	12	(5	7)	155	39	49	53	45	0	92	3	0	5	2	0	1.00	8	.251	.328	.392
2004 New York	NL	74	185	52	10	1	4	(2	2)	76	21	26	30	13	0	37	2	2	2	6	0	1.00	1	.281	.332	.411
2003 Cleveland	AL	64	210	57	10	0	8	(2	6)	91	23	26	31	18	0	52	1	0	3	2	0	1.00	6	.271	.328	.433
2003 Texas	AL	55	185	42	10	0	4	(3	1)	64	16	23	22	27	0	40	2	0	2	0	0	-	2	.227	.329	.346
7 ML YEARS		538	1671	438	84	8	59	(32	27)	715	208	242	238	152	4	357	17	4	23	13	11	.54	23	.262	.326	.428

Scott Spiezio

Bats: B **Throws:** R **Pos:** 3B-66; 1B-42; PH-4; DH-2; PR-2   **Ht:** 6'2" **Wt:** 225 **Born:** 9/21/1972 **Age:** 32

Year Team	Lg	G	AB	H	2B	3B	HR	(Hm	Rd)	TB	R	RBI	RC	TBB	IBB	SO	HBP	SH	SF	SB	CS	SB%	GDP	Avg	OBP	Slg
2004 InlandEmpire*	A+	2	5	0	0	0	0	(-	-)	0	1	0	0	1	0	1	0	0	1	0	0	-	0	.000	.000	.000
1996 Oakland	AL	9	29	9	2	0	2	(1	1)	17	6	8	6	4	1	4	0	2	0	0	1	.00	0	.310	.394	.586
1997 Oakland	AL	147	538	131	28	4	14	(6	8)	209	58	65	61	44	2	75	1	3	4	9	3	.75	13	.243	.300	.388
1998 Oakland	AL	114	406	105	19	1	9	(6	3)	153	54	50	50	44	3	56	2	7	2	1	3	.25	10	.259	.333	.377
1999 Oakland	AL	89	247	60	24	0	8	(3	5)	108	31	33	35	29	3	36	2	1	3	0	0	-	5	.243	.324	.437
2000 Anaheim	AL	123	297	72	11	2	17	(10	7)	138	47	49	47	40	2	56	3	1	4	1	2	.33	5	.242	.334	.465
2001 Anaheim	AL	139	457	124	29	4	13	(8	5)	200	57	54	65	34	4	65	5	3	4	5	2	.71	6	.271	.326	.438
2002 Anaheim	AL	153	491	140	34	2	12	(7	5)	214	80	82	86	67	7	52	4	3	6	6	7	.46	12	.285	.371	.436
2003 Anaheim	AL	158	521	138	36	7	16	(7	9)	236	69	83	72	46	8	66	5	2	7	6	3	.67	12	.265	.326	.453
2004 Seattle	AL	112	367	79	12	3	10	(5	5)	127	38	41	31	36	2	60	4	2	6	4	1	.80	7	.215	.288	.346
9 ML YEARS		1044	3353	858	195	23	101	(53	48)	1402	440	465	453	344	32	470	26	24	36	32	22	.59	70	.256	.327	.418

Junior Spivey

Bats: R **Throws:** R **Pos:** 2B-58; SS-1; PH-1   **Ht:** 6'0" **Wt:** 185 **Born:** 1/28/1975 **Age:** 30

Year Team	Lg	G	AB	H	2B	3B	HR	(Hm	Rd)	TB	R	RBI	RC	TBB	IBB	SO	HBP	SH	SF	SB	CS	SB%	GDP	Avg	OBP	Slg
2001 Arizona	NL	72	163	42	6	3	5	(4	1)	69	33	21	26	23	0	47	2	6	1	3	0	1.00	3	.258	.354	.423
2002 Arizona	NL	143	538	162	34	6	16	(9	7)	256	103	78	94	65	5	100	16	1	6	11	6	.65	10	.301	.389	.476
2003 Arizona	NL	106	365	93	22	2	13	(10	3)	158	52	50	47	33	1	95	7	0	3	4	3	.57	7	.255	.326	.433
2004 Milwaukee	NL	59	228	62	13	0	7	(4	3)	96	33	28	28	25	0	48	7	1	2	5	3	.63	7	.272	.359	.421
4 ML YEARS		380	1294	359	75	11	41	(27	14)	579	221	177	195	146	6	290	32	8	12	23	12	.66	27	.277	.362	.447

Tim Spooneybarger

Pitches: R **Bats:** R **Pos:** RP   **Ht:** 6'3" **Wt:** 190 **Born:** 10/21/1979 **Age:** 25

Year Team	Lg	G	GS	CG	GF	IP	BFP	H	R	ER	HR	SH	SF	HB	TBB	IBB	SO	WP	Bk	W	L	Pct	ShO	Sv-Op	Hld	ERC	ERA
2001 Atlanta	NL	4	0	0	3	4.0	19	5	1	1	0	1	0	2	1	3	0	0	0	0	1	.000	0	0-0	0	4.53	2.25
2002 Atlanta	NL	51	0	0	14	51.1	214	38	16	15	4	1	1	2	26	5	33	4	0	1	0	1.000	0	1-1	11	2.96	2.63
2003 Florida	NL	33	0	0	9	42.0	159	27	21	19	1	2	3	1	11	0	32	5	0	1	2	.333	0	0-1	6	1.55	4.07
3 ML YEARS		88	0	0	26	97.1	392	70	38	35	5	3	5	3	39	6	68	9	0	2	3	.400	0	1-2	17	2.36	3.24

Russ Springer

Pitches: R **Bats:** R **Pos:** RP-16   **Ht:** 6'4" **Wt:** 211 **Born:** 11/7/1968 **Age:** 36

Year Team	Lg	G	GS	CG	GF	IP	BFP	H	R	ER	HR	SH	SF	HB	TBB	IBB	SO	WP	Bk	W	L	Pct	ShO	Sv-Op	Hld	ERC	ERA
2004 New Orleans*	AAA	26	0	0	19	31.0	140	31	13	12	3	0	0	2	14	2	33	2	0	1	2	.333	0	6- -	-	4.29	3.48
1992 New York	AL	14	0	0	5	16.0	75	18	11	11	0	0	0	1	10	0	12	0	0	0	0	-	0	0-0	2	5.15	6.19
1993 California	AL	14	9	1	3	60.0	278	73	48	48	11	1	1	3	32	1	31	6	0	1	6	.143	0	0-0	0	6.87	7.20
1994 California	AL	18	5	0	6	45.2	198	53	28	28	9	1	1	0	14	0	28	2	0	2	2	.500	0	2-3	1	5.38	5.52
1995 Cal-Phi		33	6	0	6	78.1	350	82	48	46	16	2	2	7	35	4	70	2	0	1	2	.333	0	1-2	0	5.63	5.29
1996 Philadelphia	NL	51	7	0	12	96.2	437	106	60	50	12	5	3	1	38	6	94	5	0	3	10	.231	0	0-3	6	4.57	4.66
1997 Houston	NL	54	0	0	13	55.1	241	48	28	26	4	1	2	4	27	2	74	4	0	3	3	.500	0	3-7	9	3.69	4.23
1998 Ari-Atl	NL	48	0	0	14	52.2	232	51	26	24	4	2	1	1	30	4	56	5	0	5	4	.556	0	0-4	7	4.38	4.10
1999 Atlanta	NL	49	0	0	8	47.1	194	31	20	18	5	0	2	2	22	2	49	0	0	2	1	.667	0	1-1	8	2.63	3.42
2000 Arizona	NL	52	0	0	10	62.0	282	63	36	35	11	2	3	2	34	6	59	3	0	2	4	.333	0	0-2	3	5.25	5.08
2001 Arizona	NL	18	0	0	9	17.2	79	20	16	14	5	1	1	0	4	0	12	2	0	0	0	-	0	1-1	2	5.13	7.13
2003 St Louis	NL	17	0	0	4	17.1	77	19	16	16	8	0	0	1	6	0	11	1	0	1	1	.500	0	0-1	5	7.27	8.31
2004 Houston	NL	16	0	0	3	13.2	62	15	4	4	1	0	1	1	6	0	9	2	0	1	0	1.000	0	0-0	4	4.84	2.63
1995 California	AL	19	6	0	3	51.2	238	60	37	35	11	1	0	5	25	1	38	1	0	1	2	.333	0	1-2	0	6.69	6.10
1995 Philadelphia	NL	14	0	0	3	26.2	112	22	11	11	5	1	2	2	10	3	32	1	0	0	0	-	0	0-0	0	3.73	3.71
1998 Arizona	NL	26	0	0	13	32.2	140	29	16	15	4	0	0	1	14	1	37	3	0	4	3	.571	0	0-3	1	3.77	4.13
1998 Atlanta	NL	22	0	0	1	20.0	92	22	10	9	0	2	1	0	16	3	19	2	0	1	1	.500	0	0-1	6	5.36	4.05
12 ML YEARS		384	27	1	93	562.2	2505	579	341	320	86	15	17	23	258	25	505	32	0	20	34	.370	0	8-24	48	4.93	5.12

Matt Stairs

Bats: L **Throws:** R **Pos:** RF-57; 1B-30; DH-22; LF-14; PH-9   **Ht:** 5'9" **Wt:** 215 **Born:** 2/27/1968 **Age:** 37

Year Team	Lg	G	AB	H	2B	3B	HR	(Hm	Rd)	TB	R	RBI	RC	TBB	IBB	SO	HBP	SH	SF	SB	CS	SB%	GDP	Avg	OBP	Slg
1992 Montreal	NL	13	30	5	2	0	0	(0	0)	7	2	5	3	7	0	7	0	0	1	0	0	-	0	.167	.316	.233
1993 Montreal	NL	6	8	3	1	0	0	(0	0)	4	1	2	1	0	0	1	0	0	0	0	0	-	0	.375	.375	.500
1995 Boston	AL	39	88	23	7	1	1	(1	0)	35	8	17	9	4	0	14	1	1	1	0	1	.00	4	.261	.298	.398
1996 Oakland	AL	61	137	38	5	1	10	(5	5)	75	21	23	27	19	2	23	1	0	1	1	1	.50	2	.277	.367	.547
1997 Oakland	AL	133	352	105	19	0	27	(20	7)	205	62	73	77	50	1	60	3	1	4	3	2	.60	6	.298	.386	.582
1998 Oakland	AL	149	523	154	33	1	26	(16	10)	267	88	106	96	59	4	93	6	1	4	8	3	.73	13	.294	.370	.511
1999 Oakland	AL	146	531	137	26	3	38	(15	23)	283	94	102	101	89	6	124	2	0	1	2	7	.22	8	.258	.366	.533
2000 Oakland	AL	143	476	108	26	0	21	(9	12)	197	74	81	69	78	4	122	1	1	6	5	2	.71	7	.227	.333	.414
2001 Chicago	NL	128	340	85	21	0	17	(5	12)	157	48	61	57	52	7	76	7	1	3	2	3	.40	4	.250	.358	.462
2002 Milwaukee	NL	107	270	66	15	0	16	(6	10)	129	41	41	38	36	4	50	8	0	1	2	0	1.00	7	.244	.349	.478

		BATTING																		BASERUNNING				AVERAGES		
Year Team	Lg	G	AB	H	2B	3B	HR	(Hm Rd)	TB	R	RBI	RC	TBB	IBB	SO	HBP	SH	SF	SB	CS	SB%	GDP	Avg	OBP	Slg
2003 Pittsburgh	NL	121	305	89	20	1	20	(13 7)	171	49	57	58	45	3	64	5	0	2	0	1	.00	7	.292	.389	.561
2004 Kansas City	AL	126	439	117	21	3	18	(6 12)	198	48	66	65	49	2	92	5	0	3	1	0	1.00	15	.267	.345	.451
12 ML YEARS		1172	3499	930	196	10	194	(95 99)	1728	536	634	601	488	33	726	39	5	27	24	20	.55	74	.266	.359	.494

Jason Standridge

Pitches: R Bats: R Pos: RP-2; SP-1   Ht: 6'4" Wt: 230 Born: 11/9/1978 Age: 26

		HOW MUCH HE PITCHED						WHAT HE GAVE UP											THE RESULTS						
Year Team	Lg	G	GS	CG	GF	IP	BFP	H	R	ER	HR	SH	SF	HB	TBB	IBB	SO	WP	Bk	W	L	Pct	ShO	Sv-Op	Hld	ERC	ERA
2004 Montgomery*	AA	2	2	0	0	10.0	41	13	4	4	1	0	1	0	4	0	8	0	0	1	0	1.000	0	0--		6.61	3.60
2004 Durham*	AAA	20	20	2	0	119.1	498	120	56	51	7	8	2	3	44	0	76	4	1	8	4	.667	0	0--		3.93	3.85
2001 Tampa Bay	AL	9	1	0	6	19.1	87	19	10	10	5	0	0	0	14	1	9	0	0	0	0		0	0-0	0	6.63	4.66
2002 Tampa Bay	AL	1	0	0	0	3.0	18	7	3	3	1	0	0	0	4	0	1	0	0	0	0		0	0-0	0	22.36	9.00
2003 Tampa Bay	AL	8	7	1	1	35.1	157	38	25	25	7	1	1	1	16	0	20	4	0	0	5	.000	0	0-0	0	5.60	6.37
2004 Tampa Bay	AL	3	1	0	1	10.0	48	14	10	10	5	0	1	0	4	0	7	1	0	0	0		0	0-0	0	9.60	9.00
4 ML YEARS		21	9	1	8	67.2	310	78	48	48	18	1	2	1	38	1	37	5	0	0	5	.000	0	0-0	0	7.09	6.38

Jason Stanford

Pitches: L Bats: L Pos: SP-2   Ht: 6'2" Wt: 200 Born: 1/27/1977 Age: 28

		HOW MUCH HE PITCHED						WHAT HE GAVE UP											THE RESULTS						
Year Team	Lg	G	GS	CG	GF	IP	BFP	H	R	ER	HR	SH	SF	HB	TBB	IBB	SO	WP	Bk	W	L	Pct	ShO	Sv-Op	Hld	ERC	ERA
2000 Columbus	A	14	14	0	0	79.0	335	82	32	24	3	1	3	2	20	0	72	3	0	7	4	.636	0	0--		3.37	2.73
2000 Kinston	A+	11	11	1	0	70.0	294	68	22	20	2	1	2	2	17	0	58	0	0	4	3	.571	0	0--		2.92	2.57
2000 Akron	AA	1	1	0	0	5.2	23	5	1	1	0	0	0	1	1	0	5	0	0	1	0	1.000	0	0--		2.68	1.59
2001 Akron	AA	24	24	1	0	141.2	602	152	71	64	11	3	7	10	32	4	108	2	1	6	11	.353	0	0--		3.90	4.07
2001 Buffalo	AAA	1	1	1	0	9.0	29	3	0	0	0	0	0	0	0	0	10	0	0	1	0	1.000	1	0--		0.26	0.00
2002 Akron	AA	18	18	1	0	102.1	440	108	44	39	3	4	5	6	33	0	86	2	2	7	6	.538	1	0--		3.84	3.43
2002 Buffalo	AAA	6	5	0	0	35.2	149	33	12	11	5	1	1	1	11	0	23	0	0	3	1	.750	0	0--		3.69	2.78
2003 Buffalo	AAA	20	20	1	0	126.0	515	124	57	48	13	4	4	5	25	1	108	2	2	10	4	.714	0	0--		3.42	3.43
2004 Buffalo	AAA	1	1	0	0	3.1	16	2	0	0	0	0	0	0	3	0	4	0	0	0	0		0	0--		2.74	0.00
2003 Cleveland	AL	13	8	0	1	50.0	213	48	20	20	5	0	1	1	16	1	30	0	0	1	3	.250	0	0-0	0	3.55	3.60
2004 Cleveland	AL	2	2	0	0	11.0	50	12	1	1	0	1	0	1	5	0	5	1	0	0	1	.000	0	0-0	0	4.38	0.82
2 ML YEARS		15	10	0	1	61.0	263	60	21	21	5	1	1	2	21	1	35	1	0	1	4	.200	0	0-0	0	3.70	3.10

Mike Stanton

Pitches: L Bats: L Pos: RP-83   Ht: 6'1" Wt: 215 Born: 6/2/1967 Age: 38

		HOW MUCH HE PITCHED						WHAT HE GAVE UP											THE RESULTS						
Year Team	Lg	G	GS	CG	GF	IP	BFP	H	R	ER	HR	SH	SF	HB	TBB	IBB	SO	WP	Bk	W	L	Pct	ShO	Sv-Op	Hld	ERC	ERA
1989 Atlanta	NL	20	0	0	10	24.0	94	17	4	4	0	4	0	0	8	1	27	1	0	0	1	.000	0	7-8	2	1.72	1.50
1990 Atlanta	NL	7	0	0	4	7.0	42	16	16	14	1	1	0	1	4	2	7	1	0	0	3	.000	0	2-3	0	13.58	18.00
1991 Atlanta	NL	74	0	0	20	78.0	314	62	27	25	6	6	0	1	21	6	54	0	0	5	5	.500	0	7-10	15	2.31	2.88
1992 Atlanta	NL	65	0	0	23	63.2	264	59	32	29	6	1	2	2	20	2	44	3	0	5	4	.556	0	8-11	15	3.42	4.10
1993 Atlanta	NL	63	0	0	41	52.0	236	51	35	27	4	5	2	0	29	7	43	1	0	4	6	.400	0	27-33	5	4.08	4.67
1994 Atlanta	NL	49	0	0	15	45.2	197	41	18	18	2	2	1	3	26	3	35	1	0	3	1	.750	0	3-4	10	4.01	3.55
1995 Atl-Bos		48	0	0	22	40.1	178	48	23	19	6	2	1	1	14	2	23	2	1	2	1	.667	0	1-3	8	5.41	4.24
1996 Bos-Tex	AL	81	0	0	28	78.2	327	78	32	32	11	4	2	0	27	5	60	3	2	4	4	.500	0	1-6	22	4.08	3.66
1997 New York	AL	64	0	0	15	66.2	283	50	19	19	3	2	0	3	34	2	70	3	2	6	1	.857	0	3-5	26	2.88	2.57
1998 New York	AL	67	0	0	26	79.0	330	71	51	48	13	1	2	4	26	1	69	0	0	4	1	.800	0	6-10	18	3.88	5.47
1999 New York	AL	73	1	0	10	62.1	271	71	30	30	5	4	2	1	18	4	59	2	0	2	2	.500	0	0-5	21	4.23	4.33
2000 New York	AL	69	0	0	20	68.0	291	68	32	31	5	2	4	2	24	2	75	1	0	2	3	.400	0	0-4	15	3.78	4.10
2001 New York	AL	76	0	0	16	80.1	342	80	25	23	4	2	3	4	29	9	78	3	1	9	4	.692	0	0-1	23	3.61	2.58
2002 New York	AL	79	0	0	25	78.0	324	73	29	26	4	4	7	0	28	3	44	4	0	7	1	.875	0	6-9	17	3.23	3.00
2003 New York	NL	50	0	0	24	45.1	194	37	25	23	6	1	1	2	19	4	34	2	1	2	7	.222	0	5-7	10	3.33	4.57
2004 New York	NL	83	0	0	19	77.0	337	70	32	27	6	6	1	2	33	6	58	1	0	2	6	.250	0	0-0	25	3.41	3.16
1995 Atlanta	NL	26	0	0	10	19.1	94	31	14	12	3	2	1	1	6	2	13	1	1	1	1	.500	0	1-2	4	7.86	5.59
1995 Boston	AL	22	0	0	12	21.0	84	17	9	7	3	0	0	0	8	0	10	1	0	1	0	1.000	0	0-1	4	3.37	3.00
1996 Boston	AL	59	0	0	19	56.1	239	58	24	24	9	3	2	0	23	4	46	3	2	4	3	.571	0	1-5	15	4.71	3.83
1996 Texas	AL	22	0	0	9	22.1	88	20	8	8	2	1	0	0	4	1	14	0	0	0	1	.000	0	0-1	7	2.62	3.22
16 ML YEARS		968	1	0	318	946.0	4024	892	430	395	82	47	30	26	360	59	780	28	7	57	50	.533	0	76-125	232	3.61	3.76

Denny Stark

Pitches: R Bats: R Pos: SP-6   Ht: 6'2" Wt: 210 Born: 10/27/1974 Age: 30

		HOW MUCH HE PITCHED						WHAT HE GAVE UP											THE RESULTS						
Year Team	Lg	G	GS	CG	GF	IP	BFP	H	R	ER	HR	SH	SF	HB	TBB	IBB	SO	WP	Bk	W	L	Pct	ShO	Sv-Op	Hld	ERC	ERA
2004 Co Springs*	AAA	14	13	0	0	79.2	331	73	36	31	9	0	4	3	26	0	51	1	1	8	2	.800	0	0--		3.61	3.50
1999 Seattle	AL	5	0	0	2	6.1	31	10	8	7	0	0	0	0	4	0	4	0	0	0	0		0	0-0	0	8.05	9.95
2001 Seattle	AL	4	3	0	0	14.2	68	21	15	15	5	0	1	0	4	0	12	0	0	1	1	.500	0	0-0	0	7.99	9.20
2002 Colorado	NL	32	20	1	0	128.1	554	108	69	57	25	2	4	5	64	4	64	2	0	11	4	.733	0	0-1	1	4.33	4.00
2003 Colorado	NL	17	13	0	0	78.2	364	98	57	51	12	2	7	3	33	2	30	2	1	3	3	.500	0	0-0	0	6.09	5.83
2004 Colorado	NL	6	6	0	0	26.0	150	53	43	33	9	4	4	0	18	3	10	1	0	0	5	.000	0	0-0	0	14.12	11.42
5 ML YEARS		64	42	0	3	254.0	1167	290	192	163	51	8	16	8	123	9	120	5	1	15	13	.536	0	0-1	1	6.05	5.78

Josh Stewart

Pitches: L Bats: L Pos: SP-2; RP-1   Ht: 6'3" Wt: 205 Born: 12/5/1978 Age: 26

		HOW MUCH HE PITCHED						WHAT HE GAVE UP											THE RESULTS						
Year Team	Lg	G	GS	CG	GF	IP	BFP	H	R	ER	HR	SH	SF	HB	TBB	IBB	SO	WP	Bk	W	L	Pct	ShO	Sv-Op	Hld	ERC	ERA
1999 Bristol	R+	5	0	0	2	18.0	71	13	5	3	0	1	0	2	5	0	25	0	0	1	0	1.000	0	1--		2.04	1.50
1999 Burlington	A	16	0	0	3	29.2	138	32	25	24	6	0	2	2	21	0	35	1	0	2	0	1.000	0	1--		7.09	7.28
2000 Burlington	A	25	25	1	0	138.0	617	157	84	70	14	5	3	10	58	2	82	9	0	9	9	.500	1	0--		5.30	4.57

Year Team	Lg	G	GS	CG	GF	IP	BFP	H	R	ER	HR	SH	SF	HB	TBB	IBB	SO	WP	Bk	W	L	Pct	ShO	Sv-Op	Hld	ERC	ERA
		HOW MUCH HE PITCHED						**WHAT HE GAVE UP**												**THE RESULTS**							
2001 Winstn-Salm	A+	12	12	1	0	63.2	287	64	41	27	6	3	4	4	28	1	38	3	0	4	6	.400	0	0--	-	4.33	3.82
2001 Birmingham	AA	16	16	0	0	82.1	388	110	68	61	7	2	3	8	42	0	47	2	2	3	4	.429	0	0--	-	7.01	6.67
2002 Birmingham	AA	26	26	0	1	150.1	630	145	65	59	11	2	0	2	56	1	92	7	0	11	7	.611	1	0--	-	3.70	3.53
2003 Bristol	R+	2	2	0	0	6.0	24	5	0	0	0	0	0	0	2	0	5	1	0	0	0	-	0	0--	-	2.37	0.00
2003 Charlotte	AAA	5	5	0	0	26.1	121	38	18	18	4	1	2	2	6	0	10	0	1	0	3	.000	0	0--	-	6.81	6.15
2004 Charlotte	AAA	25	25	0	0	148.2	617	155	70	65	20	8	10	8	44	0	82	4	0	8	7	.533	0	0--	-	4.54	3.93
2003 Chicago	AL	5	5	0	0	25.2	121	28	18	17	4	1	1	0	16	0	13	0	0	1	2	.333	0	0-0	0	5.82	5.96
2004 Chicago	AL	3	2	0	1	7.2	41	16	13	13	3	0	2	0	3	0	5	0	0	0	1	.000	0	0-0	0	14.06	15.26
2 ML YEARS		8	7	0	1	33.1	162	44	31	30	7	1	3	0	19	0	18	0	0	1	3	.250	0	0-0	0	7.51	8.10

Scott Stewart

Pitches: L Bats: R Pos: RP-34   Ht: 6'2" Wt: 225 Born: 8/14/1975 Age: 29

Year Team	Lg	G	GS	CG	GF	IP	BFP	H	R	ER	HR	SH	SF	HB	TBB	IBB	SO	WP	Bk	W	L	Pct	ShO	Sv-Op	Hld	ERC	ERA
		HOW MUCH HE PITCHED						**WHAT HE GAVE UP**												**THE RESULTS**							
2004 Buffalo*	AAA	27	0	0	14	32.0	143	37	15	15	4	0	0	1	9	1	21	2	0	3	1	.750	0	6--	-	4.63	4.22
2004 Las Vegas*	AAA	4	0	0	1	3.2	15	3	1	1	0	0	0	0	1	0	7	1	0	0	0	-	0	0--	-	2.00	2.45
2001 Montreal	NL	62	0	0	9	47.2	199	43	20	20	5	2	4	3	13	0	39	2	0	3	1	.750	0	3-4	8	3.31	3.78
2002 Montreal	NL	67	0	0	28	64.0	263	49	29	22	4	2	2	1	22	5	67	1	0	4	2	.667	0	17-19	14	2.31	3.09
2003 Montreal	NL	51	0	0	9	43.0	187	52	22	19	5	1	1	1	13	4	29	1	1	3	1	.750	0	0-1	13	5.05	3.98
2004 Cle-LA	NL	34	0	0	7	26.0	130	43	22	19	5	1	3	0	12	5	26	0	0	1	2	.333	0	0-2	4	8.84	6.58
2004 Cleveland	AL	23	0	0	5	13.2	70	23	14	11	2	0	1	0	6	2	18	0	0	0	2	.000	0	0-2	4	8.39	7.24
2004 Los Angeles	NL	11	0	0	2	12.1	60	20	8	8	3	1	2	0	6	3	8	0	0	1	0	1.000	0	0-0	0	9.35	5.84
4 ML YEARS		214	0	0	53	180.2	779	187	93	80	19	6	10	5	60	14	161	4	1	11	6	.647	0	20-26	39	4.01	3.99

Shannon Stewart

Bats: R Throws: R Pos: LF-71; DH-21   Ht: 6'1" Wt: 210 Born: 2/25/1974 Age: 31

Year Team	Lg	G	AB	H	2B	3B	HR	(Hm	Rd)	TB	R	RBI	RC	TBB	IBB	SO	HBP	SH	SF	SB	CS	SB%	GDP	Avg	OBP	Slg
		BATTING																		**BASERUNNING**				**AVERAGES**		
2004 Rochester*	AAA	3	9	3	1	0	0	(-	-)	4	3	0	1	1	0	2	0	0	0	0	0	-	0	.333	.400	.444
1995 Toronto	AL	12	38	8	0	0	0	(0	0)	8	2	1	3	5	0	5	1	0	0	2	0	1.00	0	.211	.318	.211
1996 Toronto	AL	7	17	3	1	0	0	(0	0)	4	2	2	1	1	0	4	0	0	0	1	0	1.00	1	.176	.222	.235
1997 Toronto	AL	44	168	48	13	7	0	(0	0)	75	25	22	29	19	1	24	4	0	2	10	3	.77	3	.286	.368	.446
1998 Toronto	AL	144	516	144	29	3	12	(6	6)	215	90	55	88	67	1	77	15	6	1	51	18	.74	5	.279	.377	.417
1999 Toronto	AL	145	608	185	28	2	11	(4	7)	250	102	67	95	59	0	83	8	3	4	37	14	.73	12	.304	.371	.411
2000 Toronto	AL	136	583	186	43	5	21	(12	9)	302	107	69	106	37	1	79	6	1	4	20	5	.80	12	.319	.363	.518
2001 Toronto	AL	155	640	202	44	7	12	(6	6)	296	103	60	109	46	1	72	11	0	1	27	10	.73	9	.316	.371	.463
2002 Toronto	AL	141	577	175	38	6	10	(4	6)	255	103	45	92	54	2	60	9	0	1	14	2	.88	17	.303	.371	.442
2003 Tor-Min	AL	136	573	176	44	2	13	(7	6)	263	90	73	93	52	3	66	6	2	11	4	6	.40	10	.307	.364	.459
2004 Minnesota	AL	92	378	115	17	2	11	(5	6)	169	46	47	68	47	4	44	1	1	3	6	3	.67	5	.304	.380	.447
2003 Toronto	AL	71	303	89	22	2	7	(3	4)	136	47	35	51	27	2	30	2	0	8	1	2	.33	6	.294	.347	.449
2003 Minnesota	AL	65	270	87	22	0	6	(4	2)	127	43	38	42	25	1	36	4	2	3	3	4	.43	4	.322	.384	.470
10 ML YEARS		1012	4098	1242	257	34	90	(44	46)	1837	670	441	684	387	13	514	61	13	27	172	61	.74	74	.303	.370	.448

Kelly Stinnett

Bats: R Throws: R Pos: C-20; PR-1   Ht: 5'11" Wt: 225 Born: 2/4/1970 Age: 35

Year Team	Lg	G	AB	H	2B	3B	HR	(Hm	Rd)	TB	R	RBI	RC	TBB	IBB	SO	HBP	SH	SF	SB	CS	SB%	GDP	Avg	OBP	Slg
		BATTING																		**BASERUNNING**				**AVERAGES**		
1994 New York	NL	47	150	38	6	2	2	(0	2)	54	20	14	18	11	1	28	5	0	1	2	0	1.00	3	.253	.323	.360
1995 New York	NL	77	196	43	8	1	4	(1	3)	65	23	18	24	29	3	65	6	0	0	2	0	1.00	3	.219	.338	.332
1996 Milwaukee	AL	14	26	2	0	0	0	(0	0)	2	1	0	0	2	0	11	1	0	0	0	0	-	0	.077	.172	.077
1997 Milwaukee	AL	30	36	9	4	0	0	(0	0)	13	2	3	4	3	0	9	0	0	0	0	0	-	0	.250	.308	.361
1998 Arizona	NL	92	274	71	14	1	11	(5	6)	120	35	34	41	35	3	74	6	1	2	0	1	.00	9	.259	.353	.438
1999 Arizona	NL	88	284	66	13	0	14	(3	11)	121	36	38	37	24	2	83	5	2	2	2	1	.67	4	.232	.302	.426
2000 Arizona	NL	76	240	52	7	0	8	(2	6)	83	22	33	23	19	4	56	6	0	0	1	0	1.00	5	.217	.291	.346
2001 Cincinnati	NL	63	187	48	11	0	9	(6	3)	86	27	25	27	17	3	61	5	1	1	2	2	.50	5	.257	.333	.460
2002 Cincinnati	NL	34	93	21	5	0	3	(2	1)	35	10	13	13	15	1	25	0	0	0	2	0	1.00	1	.226	.333	.376
2003 Cin-Phi	NL	67	186	44	13	0	3	(2	1)	66	14	19	20	14	3	52	4	2	1	0	0	-	3	.237	.302	.355
2004 Kansas City	AL	20	59	18	0	0	3	(0	3)	27	10	7	9	5	0	16	2	3	0	0	0	-	0	.305	.379	.458
2003 Cincinnati	NL	60	179	41	13	0	3	(2	1)	63	14	19	18	13	3	51	4	2	1	0	0	-	3	.229	.294	.352
2003 Philadelphia	NL	7	7	3	0	0	0	(0	0)	3	0	0	2	1	0	1	0	0	0	0	0	-	0	.429	.500	.429
11 ML YEARS		608	1731	412	81	4	57	(20	37)	672	200	204	216	174	20	480	40	9	7	10	5	.67	33	.238	.321	.388

Ricky Stone

Pitches: R Bats: R Pos: RP-43   Ht: 6'1" Wt: 190 Born: 2/28/1975 Age: 30

Year Team	Lg	G	GS	CG	GF	IP	BFP	H	R	ER	HR	SH	SF	HB	TBB	IBB	SO	WP	Bk	W	L	Pct	ShO	Sv-Op	Hld	ERC	ERA
		HOW MUCH HE PITCHED						**WHAT HE GAVE UP**												**THE RESULTS**							
2004 Portland*	AAA	3	0	0	2	5.1	27	9	5	2	2	0	0	0	2	0	2	0	0	0	0	-	0	0--	-	10.48	3.38
2001 Houston	NL	6	0	0	3	7.2	33	8	3	2	1	0	0	0	2	1	4	0	0	0	0	-	0	0-0	0	3.69	2.35
2002 Houston	NL	78	0	0	16	77.1	335	78	36	31	9	5	2	1	34	3	63	1	0	3	3	.500	0	1-2	12	4.43	3.61
2003 Houston	NL	65	0	0	20	83.0	350	76	36	34	11	4	1	6	31	4	47	1	0	6	4	.600	0	1-1	7	4.00	3.69
2004 Hou-SD	NL	43	0	0	17	51.2	238	66	39	37	11	0	1	6	16	3	38	2	0	2	2	.500	0	0-0	1	6.60	6.45
2004 Houston	NL	16	0	0	7	19.0	92	26	12	12	5	0	0	3	7	3	16	1	0	1	1	.500	0	0-0	1	7.81	5.68
2004 San Diego	NL	27	0	0	10	32.2	146	40	27	25	6	0	1	3	9	0	22	1	0	1	1	.500	0	0-0	0	5.92	6.89
4 ML YEARS		192	0	0	56	219.2	956	228	114	104	32	9	4	13	83	11	152	4	0	11	9	.550	0	2-3	20	4.72	4.03

Scott Strickland

Pitches: R **Bats:** R **Pos:** RP **Ht:** 5'11" **Wt:** 180 **Born:** 4/26/1976 **Age:** 29

Year Team	Lg	G	GS	CG	GF	IP	BFP	H	R	ER	HR	SH	SF	HB	TBB	IBB	SO	WP	Bk	W	L	Pct	ShO	Sv-Op	Hld	ERC	ERA
2004 Mets*	R	2	1	0	1	2.0	6	0	0	0	0	0	0	0	0	0	2	0	0	0	0	-	0	0- -	-	0.00	0.00
2004 St. Lucie*	A+	6	1	0	1	6.2	33	11	8	7	0	0	0	0	2	0	5	1	0	0	1	.000	0	0- -	-	6.57	9.45
1999 Montreal	NL	17	0	0	5	18.0	78	15	10	9	3	2	0	0	11	0	23	0	0	0	1	.000	0	0-0	2	4.48	4.50
2000 Montreal	NL	49	0	0	20	48.0	200	38	18	16	3	3	3	1	16	2	48	2	0	4	3	.571	0	9-13	6	2.44	3.00
2001 Montreal	NL	77	0	0	31	81.1	351	67	36	29	9	3	1	4	41	5	85	4	0	2	6	.250	0	9-12	12	3.65	3.21
2002 Mon-NYM	NL	69	0	0	21	68.2	299	61	29	27	7	1	2	2	33	4	69	3	0	6	9	.400	0	2-6	15	3.64	3.54
2003 New York	NL	19	0	0	3	20.0	84	16	6	5	1	0	0	1	10	1	16	1	0	0	2	.000	0	0-1	4	3.19	2.25
2002 Montreal	NL	1	0	0	0	1.0	3	0	0	0	0	0	0	0	0	0	2	0	0	0	0	-	0	0-0	-	0.00	0.00
2002 New York	NL	68	0	0	21	67.2	296	61	29	27	7	1	2	2	33	4	67	3	0	6	9	.400	0	2-6	15	3.74	3.59
5 ML YEARS		231	0	0	80	236.0	1012	197	99	86	23	9	6	8	111	17	241	10	0	12	21	.364	0	20-32	39	3.41	3.28

Tanyon Sturtze

Pitches: R **Bats:** R **Pos:** RP-25; SP-3 **Ht:** 6'5" **Wt:** 221 **Born:** 10/12/1970 **Age:** 34

Year Team	Lg	G	GS	CG	GF	IP	BFP	H	R	ER	HR	SH	SF	HB	TBB	IBB	SO	WP	Bk	W	L	Pct	ShO	Sv-Op	Hld	ERC	ERA
2004 Las Vegas*	AAA	6	6	0	0	36.0	141	26	11	10	2	2	1	0	12	0	32	3	0	3	0	1.000	0	0- -	-	2.18	2.50
1995 Chicago	NL	2	0	0	0	2.0	9	2	2	2	1	0	0	0	1	0	0	0	0	0	0	-	0	0-0	0	7.30	9.00
1996 Chicago	NL	6	0	0	3	11.0	51	16	11	11	3	0	0	0	5	0	7	0	0	1	0	1.000	0	0-0	0	8.87	9.00
1997 Texas	AL	9	5	0	1	32.2	155	45	30	30	6	0	4	0	18	0	18	1	1	1	1	.500	0	0-0	0	7.84	8.27
1999 Chicago	AL	1	1	0	0	6.0	22	4	0	0	0	0	0	0	2	0	2	0	0	0	0	-	0	0-0	0	1.73	0.00
2000 CWS-TB	AL	29	6	0	9	68.1	300	72	39	36	8	1	2	3	29	1	44	2	0	5	2	.714	0	0-0	0	4.80	4.74
2001 Tampa Bay	AL	39	27	0	6	195.1	837	200	98	96	23	2	10	9	79	0	110	11	0	11	12	.478	0	1-3	4	4.65	4.42
2002 Tampa Bay	AL	33	33	4	0	224.0	1008	271	141	129	33	7	6	9	89	2	137	7	2	4	18	.182	0	0-0	0	5.87	5.18
2003 Toronto	AL	40	8	0	7	89.1	415	107	67	59	14	2	2	7	43	3	54	6	0	7	6	.538	0	0-0	0	6.30	5.94
2004 New York	AL	28	3	0	7	77.1	337	75	49	47	9	2	1	6	33	2	56	2	1	6	2	.750	0	1-1	4	4.42	5.47
2000 Chicago	AL	10	1	0	2	15.2	85	25	23	21	4	0	2	2	15	0	6	1	0	1	2	.333	0	0-0	0	12.84	12.06
2000 Tampa Bay	AL	19	5	0	7	52.2	215	47	16	15	4	1	0	1	14	1	38	1	0	4	0	1.000	0	0-0	0	2.89	2.56
9 ML YEARS		187	83	4	33	706.0	3134	792	437	410	97	14	25	34	299	8	428	29	4	35	41	.461	0	2-4	5	5.41	5.23

Chris Stynes

Bats: R **Throws:** R **Pos:** 3B-71; PH-6 **Ht:** 5'10" **Wt:** 205 **Born:** 1/19/1973 **Age:** 32

Year Team	Lg	G	AB	H	2B	3B	HR	(Hm	Rd)	TB	R	RBI	RC	TBB	IBB	SO	HBP	SH	SF	SB	CS	SB%	GDP	Avg	OBP	Slg
1995 Kansas City	AL	22	35	6	1	0	0	(0	0)	7	7	2	1	4	0	3	0	0	0	0	0	-	3	.171	.256	.200
1996 Kansas City	AL	36	92	27	6	0	0	(0	0)	33	8	6	10	2	0	5	0	1	0	5	2	.71	1	.293	.309	.359
1997 Cincinnati	NL	128	198	69	7	1	6	(2	4)	96	31	28	37	11	1	13	4	2	0	11	2	.85	5	.348	.384	.485
1998 Cincinnati	NL	123	347	88	10	1	6	(3	3)	118	52	27	42	32	1	36	4	4	1	15	1	.94	5	.254	.323	.340
1999 Cincinnati	NL	73	113	27	1	0	2	(1	1)	34	18	14	11	12	1	13	0	3	1	5	2	.71	2	.239	.310	.301
2000 Cincinnati	NL	119	380	127	24	1	6	(8	4)	189	71	40	71	32	2	54	2	3	5	5	2	.71	5	.334	.386	.497
2001 Boston	AL	96	361	101	19	2	8	(3	5)	148	52	33	43	20	0	56	3	1	1	4	5	.44	12	.280	.322	.410
2002 New York	NL	98	195	47	9	1	5	(4	1)	73	25	26	27	21	1	29	1	5	3	1	1	.50	5	.241	.314	.374
2003 Colorado	NL	138	443	113	31	3	11	(10	1)	183	71	73	65	48	1	76	6	3	2	3	1	.75	8	.255	.335	.413
2004 Pittsburgh	NL	74	162	35	10	0	1	(1	0)	48	16	16	10	9	2	23	2	1	0	0	0	-	3	.216	.266	.296
10 ML YEARS		828	2326	640	118	9	51	(29	22)	929	351	265	317	191	9	308	22	23	11	49	16	.75	49	.275	.335	.399

Scott Sullivan

Pitches: R **Bats:** R **Pos:** RP-49 **Ht:** 6'3" **Wt:** 210 **Born:** 3/13/1971 **Age:** 34

Year Team	Lg	G	GS	CG	GF	IP	BFP	H	R	ER	HR	SH	SF	HB	TBB	IBB	SO	WP	Bk	W	L	Pct	ShO	Sv-Op	Hld	ERC	ERA
1995 Cincinnati	NL	3	0	0	1	3.2	17	4	2	2	0	1	0	0	2	0	2	0	0	0	0	-	0	0-0	0	4.28	4.91
1996 Cincinnati	NL	7	0	0	4	8.0	35	7	2	2	0	1	0	1	5	0	3	1	0	0	0	-	0	0-0	0	4.11	2.25
1997 Cincinnati	NL	59	0	0	15	97.1	402	79	36	35	12	3	3	7	30	8	96	7	1	5	3	.625	0	1-2	13	3.01	3.24
1998 Cincinnati	NL	67	0	0	13	102.0	440	98	62	59	14	3	4	9	36	4	86	4	0	5	5	.500	0	1-4	5	4.22	5.21
1999 Cincinnati	NL	79	0	0	16	113.2	470	88	41	38	10	4	4	8	47	4	78	6	1	4	5	.556	0	3-5	13	3.08	3.01
2000 Cincinnati	NL	79	0	0	22	106.1	439	87	44	41	14	2	5	9	38	8	96	7	0	3	6	.333	0	3-6	22	3.40	3.47
2001 Cincinnati	NL	79	0	0	16	103.1	437	94	44	38	10	1	5	8	36	8	82	0	0	7	1	.875	0	0-3	20	3.55	3.31
2002 Cincinnati	NL	71	0	0	16	78.2	358	93	60	53	15	2	3	5	31	11	78	2	0	6	5	.545	0	1-3	19	5.81	6.06
2003 Cin-CWS		65	0	0	8	64.0	276	48	28	26	6	1	3	6	32	4	56	1	0	6	0	1.000	0	0-1	12	3.27	3.66
2004 Kansas City		49	0	0	17	60.1	273	73	34	32	8	1	4	7	24	10	45	4	0	3	4	.429	0	0-1	10	5.85	4.77
2003 Cincinnati	NL	50	0	0	6	49.2	218	39	22	20	4	0	2	5	26	4	43	1	0	6	0	1.000	0	0-1	10	3.42	3.62
2003 Chicago	AL	15	0	0	2	14.1	58	9	6	6	2	1	1	1	6	0	13	0	0	0	0	-	0	0-0	2	2.71	3.77
10 ML YEARS		558	0	0	128	737.1	3147	671	353	326	89	19	31	60	281	57	622	32	2	40	28	.588	0	9-25	110	3.86	3.98

Jeff Suppan

Pitches: R **Bats:** R **Pos:** SP-31 **Ht:** 6'2" **Wt:** 210 **Born:** 1/2/1975 **Age:** 30

Year Team	Lg	G	GS	CG	GF	IP	BFP	H	R	ER	HR	SH	SF	HB	TBB	IBB	SO	WP	Bk	W	L	Pct	ShO	Sv-Op	Hld	ERC	ERA
1995 Boston	AL	8	3	0	1	22.2	100	29	15	15	4	1	1	0	5	1	19	0	0	1	2	.333	0	0-0	1	5.43	5.96
1996 Boston	AL	8	4	0	2	22.2	107	29	19	19	3	1	4	1	13	0	13	3	0	1	1	.500	0	0-0	0	7.03	7.54
1997 Boston	AL	23	22	0	1	112.1	503	140	71	71	12	0	4	4	36	1	67	5	0	7	3	.700	0	0-0	0	5.39	5.69
1998 Ari-KC		17	14	1	2	78.2	345	91	56	50	13	3	2	1	22	1	51	2	0	1	7	.125	0	0-0	0	4.95	5.72
1999 Kansas City	AL	32	32	4	0	208.2	887	222	113	105	28	7	5	3	62	4	103	5	1	10	12	.455	1	0-0	0	4.33	4.53
2000 Kansas City	AL	35	33	3	0	217.0	948	240	130	119	36	5	6	7	84	3	128	7	1	10	9	.526	1	0-0	0	5.31	4.94
2001 Kansas City	AL	34	34	1	0	218.1	946	227	120	106	26	5	6	12	74	3	120	6	0	10	14	.417	0	0-0	0	4.40	4.37
2002 Kansas City	AL	33	33	3	0	208.0	912	229	134	123	32	4	11	7	68	3	109	10	1	9	16	.360	1	0-0	0	4.84	5.32
2003 Pit-Bos		32	31	0	0	204.0	873	217	98	95	23	11	6	8	51	5	110	7	0	13	11	.542	0	0-0	0	4.03	4.19
2004 St Louis	NL	31	31	0	0	188.0	811	192	98	87	25	8	5	8	65	1	110	4	1	16	9	.640	0	0-0	0	4.38	4.16

	HOW MUCH HE PITCHED						WHAT HE GAVE UP												THE RESULTS							
Year Team	Lg	G	GS	CG	GF	IP	BFP	H	R	ER	HR	SH	SF	HB	TBB	IBB	SO	WP	Bk	W	L	Pct	ShO	Sv-Op	Hld	ERC	ERA
1998 Arizona	NL	13	13	1	0	66.0	299	82	55	49	12	3	2	1	21	1	39	2	0	1	7	.125	0	0-0	0	5.73	6.68
1998 Kansas City	AL	4	1	0	2	12.2	46	9	1	1	1	0	1	0	1	0	12	0	0	0	0	-	0	0-0	0	1.51	0.71
2003 Pittsburgh	NL	21	21	3	0	141.0	597	147	57	56	11	10	2	6	31	5	78	3	0	10	7	.588	2	0-0	0	3.55	3.57
2003 Boston	AL	11	10	0	0	63.0	276	70	41	39	12	1	4	2	20	0	32	4	0	3	4	.429	0	0-0	0	5.15	5.57
10 ML YEARS		253	237	15	6	1480.1	6432	1616	849	790	202	45	50	51	480	22	830	49	4	78	84	.481	5	0-0	1	4.68	4.80

B.J. Surhoff

Bats: L **Throws:** R **Pos:** RF-38; LF-34; DH-17; 1B-10; PH-9; PR-1   **Ht:** 6'1" **Wt:** 200 **Born:** 8/4/1964 **Age:** 40

		BATTING																	BASERUNNING				AVERAGES		
Year Team	Lg	G	AB	H	2B	3B	HR	(Hm Rd)	TB	R	RBI	RC	TBB	IBB	SO	HBP	SH	SF	SB	CS	SB%	GDP	Avg	OBP	Slg
1987 Milwaukee	AL	115	395	118	22	3	7	(5 2)	167	50	68	56	36	1	30	0	5	9	11	10	.52	13	.299	.350	.423
1988 Milwaukee	AL	139	493	121	21	0	5	(2 3)	157	47	38	45	31	9	49	3	11	3	21	6	.78	12	.245	.292	.318
1989 Milwaukee	AL	126	436	108	17	4	5	(3 2)	148	42	55	41	25	1	29	3	3	10	14	12	.54	8	.248	.287	.339
1990 Milwaukee	AL	135	474	131	21	4	6	(4 2)	178	55	59	61	41	5	37	1	7	7	18	7	.72	8	.276	.331	.376
1991 Milwaukee	AL	143	505	146	19	4	5	(3 2)	188	57	68	53	26	2	33	0	13	9	5	8	.38	21	.289	.319	.372
1992 Milwaukee	AL	139	480	121	19	1	4	(3 1)	154	63	62	50	46	8	41	2	5	10	14	8	.64	9	.252	.314	.321
1993 Milwaukee	AL	148	552	151	38	3	7	(4 3)	216	66	79	67	36	5	47	2	4	5	12	9	.57	9	.274	.318	.391
1994 Milwaukee	AL	40	134	35	11	2	5	(2 3)	65	20	22	21	16	0	14	0	2	2	0	1	.00	5	.261	.336	.485
1995 Milwaukee	AL	117	415	133	26	3	13	(7 6)	204	72	73	75	37	4	43	4	2	4	7	3	.70	7	.320	.378	.492
1996 Baltimore	AL	143	537	157	27	6	21	(12 9)	259	74	82	89	47	8	79	3	2	1	0	1	.00	7	.292	.352	.482
1997 Baltimore	AL	147	528	150	30	4	18	(10 8)	242	80	88	84	49	14	60	5	3	10	1	1	.50	7	.284	.345	.458
1998 Baltimore	AL	162	573	160	34	1	22	(9 13)	262	80	82	84	49	9	81	1	1	10	9	7	.56	13	.279	.332	.457
1999 Baltimore	AL	162	673	207	38	1	28	(9 19)	331	104	107	111	43	1	78	2	1	8	5	1	.83	15	.308	.347	.492
2000 Bal-Atl		147	539	157	36	2	14	(7 7)	239	69	68	81	41	3	58	3	2	2	10	2	.83	10	.291	.344	.443
2001 Atlanta	NL	141	484	131	33	1	10	(5 5)	196	68	58	65	38	5	48	1	1	0	9	3	.75	5	.271	.321	.405
2002 Atlanta	NL	25	75	22	5	0	0	(0 0)	27	5	9	10	9	0	5	0	1	0	1	3	.25	1	.293	.369	.360
2003 Atlanta	AL	93	319	94	20	0	5	(4 1)	129	32	41	51	29	3	29	1	3	2	2	2	.50	4	.295	.353	.404
2004 Baltimore	AL	100	343	106	12	1	8	(4 4)	144	49	50	56	30	2	46	1	3	1	2	0	1.00	6	.309	.365	.420
2000 Baltimore	AL	103	411	120	27	0	13	(6 7)	186	56	57	63	29	3	46	2	1	1	7	2	.78	5	.292	.341	.453
2000 Atlanta	NL	44	128	37	9	2	1	(1 0)	53	13	11	18	12	0	12	1	1	1	3	0	1.00	5	.289	.352	.414
18 ML YEARS		2222	7955	2248	429	40	183	(93 90)	3306	1032	1119	1100	629	80	807	32	69	100	141	84	.63	163	.283	.334	.416

Larry Sutton

Bats: L **Throws:** L **Pos:** PH-7; 1B-1   **Ht:** 6'0" **Wt:** 185 **Born:** 5/14/1970 **Age:** 35

		BATTING																	BASERUNNING				AVERAGES		
Year Team	Lg	G	AB	H	2B	3B	HR	(Hm Rd)	TB	R	RBI	RC	TBB	IBB	SO	HBP	SH	SF	SB	CS	SB%	GDP	Avg	OBP	Slg
2004 Albuquerque*	AAA	91	308	115	31	2	21	(- -)	213	70	73	91	59	1	61	5	0	5	3	1	.75	4	.373	.475	.692
1997 Kansas City	AL	27	69	20	2	0	2	(1 1)	28	9	8	10	5	0	12	0	1	0	0	0	-	0	.290	.338	.406
1998 Kansas City	AL	111	310	76	14	2	5	(3 2)	109	29	42	34	29	3	46	3	4	5	3	3	.50	5	.245	.311	.352
1999 Kansas City	AL	43	102	23	6	0	2	(2 0)	35	14	15	11	13	0	17	0	1	2	1	0	1.00	4	.225	.308	.343
2000 St Louis	NL	23	25	8	0	0	1	(0 1)	11	5	6	5	5	0	7	0	1	2	0	0	-	0	.320	.406	.440
2001 St Louis	NL	33	42	5	1	0	1	(1 0)	9	3	3	3	1	0	10	0	1	0	0	0	-	0	.119	.140	.214
2002 Oakland	AL	7	19	2	0	0	1	(1 0)	5	3	3	1	1	0	8	0	0	0	0	0	-	0	.105	.150	.263
2004 Florida	NL	8	5	1	0	0	0	(0 0)	1	0	1	1	1	0	2	0	0	0	0	0	-	0	.200	.333	.200
7 ML YEARS		252	572	135	23	2	12	(8 4)	198	63	78	62	55	3	102	3	8	9	4	3	.57	10	.236	.302	.346

Ichiro Suzuki

Bats: L **Throws:** R **Pos:** RF-158; DH-3; PR-1   **Ht:** 5'9" **Wt:** 160 **Born:** 10/22/1973 **Age:** 31

		BATTING																	BASERUNNING				AVERAGES		
Year Team	Lg	G	AB	H	2B	3B	HR	(Hm Rd)	TB	R	RBI	RC	TBB	IBB	SO	HBP	SH	SF	SB	CS	SB%	GDP	Avg	OBP	Slg
2001 Seattle	AL	157	692	242	34	8	8	(5 3)	316	127	69	124	30	10	53	8	4	4	56	14	.80	3	.350	.381	.457
2002 Seattle	AL	157	647	208	27	8	8	(4 4)	275	111	51	110	68	27	62	5	3	5	31	15	.67	8	.321	.388	.425
2003 Seattle	AL	159	679	212	29	8	13	(8 5)	296	111	62	107	36	7	69	6	3	1	34	8	.81	3	.312	.352	.436
2004 Seattle	AL	161	704	262	24	5	8	(4 4)	320	101	60	125	49	19	63	4	3	2	36	11	.77	6	.372	.414	.455
4 ML YEARS		634	2722	924	114	29	37	(21 16)	1207	450	242	466	183	63	247	23	12	13	157	48	.77	20	.339	.384	.443

Brian Sweeney

Pitches: R **Bats:** R **Pos:** RP-5; SP-2   **Ht:** 6'2" **Wt:** 185 **Born:** 6/13/1974 **Age:** 31

		HOW MUCH HE PITCHED						WHAT HE GAVE UP												THE RESULTS							
Year Team	Lg	G	GS	CG	GF	IP	BFP	H	R	ER	HR	SH	SF	HB	TBB	IBB	SO	WP	Bk	W	L	Pct	ShO	Sv-Op	Hld	ERC	ERA
1997 Lancaster	A+	40	0	0	13	85.1	358	83	39	36	11	2	4	2	21	1	73	8	0	6	3	.667	0	1--	-	3.56	3.80
1998 Lancaster	A+	17	4	0	3	52.0	211	41	26	21	6	0	1	1	21	1	48	2	1	6	0	1.000	0	0--	-	3.17	3.63
1999 Lancaster	A+	5	0	0	1	9.1	44	14	7	7	4	0	0	0	3	0	14	1	0	0	0	-	0	0--	-	9.53	6.75
1999 Tacoma	AAA	5	1	0	2	16.0	75	26	17	12	5	2	0	0	2	0	10	1	0	2	0	.000	0	0--	-	8.34	6.75
1999 New Haven	AA	23	18	0	3	111.1	478	125	65	58	18	1	3	4	31	1	83	4	0	4	6	.400	0	1--	-	4.92	4.69
2000 Tacoma	AAA	2	1	0	0	6.0	26	9	4	4	2	0	0	0	1	0	1	1	0	1	0	.000	0	0--	-	8.38	6.00
2000 New Haven	AA	19	7	0	5	47.2	207	49	20	18	3	1	2	2	19	0	27	5	0	4	3	.571	0	1--	-	4.15	3.40
2001 San Antonio	AA	37	9	0	8	104.1	448	117	47	44	8	3	0	5	23	1	96	7	0	7	4	.636	0	1--	-	4.06	3.80
2002 Tacoma	AAA	30	23	1	4	142.0	606	157	67	60	16	3	1	3	28	0	113	5	0	9	5	.643	1	2--	-	4.00	3.80
2003 Tacoma	AAA	29	21	0	2	141.0	613	165	80	67	17	4	3	2	32	0	115	4	0	11	10	.524	0	0--	-	4.51	4.28
2004 Portland	AAA	24	23	0	1	138.2	577	130	65	59	16	4	1	1	42	1	110	6	0	11	4	.733	0	0--	-	3.48	3.83
2003 Seattle	AL	5	0	0	2	9.1	35	7	2	2	0	0	0	1	1	0	7	0	0	0	0	-	0	0-0	0	1.66	1.93
2004 San Diego	NL	7	2	0	1	14.1	63	20	9	9	1	0	0	0	2	0	10	1	0	1	0	1.000	0	0-0	0	5.12	5.65
2 ML YEARS		12	2	0	3	23.2	98	27	11	11	1	0	0	1	3	0	17	1	0	1	0	1.000	0	0-0	0	3.63	4.08

Mark Sweeney

Bats: L **Throws:** L **Pos:** PH-82; RF-20; 1B-15; LF-9; DH-4   **Ht:** 6'1" **Wt:** 215 **Born:** 10/26/1969 **Age:** 35

Year Team	Lg	G	AB	H	2B	3B	HR	(Hm	Rd)	TB	R	RBI	RC	TBB	IBB	SO	HBP	SH	SF	SB	CS	SB%	GDP	Avg	OBP	Slg
1995 St Louis	NL	37	77	21	2	0	2	(0	2)	29	5	13	10	10	0	15	0	1	2	1	1	.50	3	.273	.348	.377
1996 St Louis	NL	98	170	45	9	0	3	(0	3)	63	32	22	27	33	2	29	1	5	0	3	0	1.00	4	.265	.387	.371
1997 StL-SD	NL	115	164	46	7	0	2	(2	0)	59	16	23	22	20	1	32	1	1	2	2	3	.40	3	.280	.358	.360
1998 San Diego	NL	122	192	45	8	3	2	(1	1)	65	17	15	21	26	0	37	1	0	3	1	2	.33	5	.234	.324	.339
1999 Cincinnati	NL	37	31	11	3	0	2	(1	1)	20	6	7	7	4	1	9	0	0	0	0	0	-	2	.355	.429	.645
2000 Milwaukee	NL	71	73	16	6	0	1	(0	1)	25	9	6	9	12	1	18	1	1	0	0	0	-	1	.219	.337	.342
2001 Milwaukee	NL	48	89	23	3	1	3	(1	2)	37	9	11	14	12	0	23	0	2	0	2	1	.67	0	.258	.347	.416
2002 San Diego	NL	48	65	11	3	0	1	(0	1)	17	3	4	1	4	0	19	0	0	0	0	0	-	1	.169	.217	.262
2003 Colorado	NL	67	97	25	9	0	2	(1	1)	40	13	14	15	9	1	27	0	0	0	0	1	.00	2	.258	.321	.412
2004 Colorado	NL	122	177	47	12	2	9	(6	3)	90	25	40	36	32	2	51	2	0	4	1	0	1.00	2	.266	.377	.508
1997 St Louis	NL	44	61	13	3	0	0	(0	0)	16	5	4	5	9	1	14	1	1	0	0	1	.00	2	.213	.319	.262
1997 San Diego	NL	71	103	33	4	0	2	(2	0)	43	11	19	17	11	0	18	0	0	1	2	2	.50	1	.320	.383	.417
10 ML YEARS		765	1135	290	62	6	27	(12	15)	445	135	155	162	162	8	260	6	10	11	10	8	.56	23	.256	.349	.392

Mike Sweeney

Bats: R **Throws:** R **Pos:** 1B-55; DH-47; PH-3; PR-1   **Ht:** 6'3" **Wt:** 225 **Born:** 7/22/1973 **Age:** 31

Year Team	Lg	G	AB	H	2B	3B	HR	(Hm	Rd)	TB	R	RBI	RC	TBB	IBB	SO	HBP	SH	SF	SB	CS	SB%	GDP	Avg	OBP	Slg
1995 Kansas City	AL	4	4	1	0	0	0	(0	0)	1	1	0	0	0	0	0	0	0	0	0	0	-	0	.250	.250	.250
1996 Kansas City	AL	50	165	46	10	0	4	(1	3)	68	23	24	23	18	0	21	4	0	3	1	2	.33	7	.279	.358	.412
1997 Kansas City	AL	84	240	58	8	0	7	(5	2)	87	30	31	25	17	0	33	6	1	2	3	2	.60	8	.242	.306	.363
1998 Kansas City	AL	92	282	73	18	0	8	(6	2)	115	32	35	35	24	1	38	2	2	1	2	3	.40	7	.259	.320	.408
1999 Kansas City	AL	150	575	185	44	2	22	(10	12)	299	101	102	109	54	0	48	10	0	4	6	1	.86	21	.322	.387	.520
2000 Kansas City	AL	159	618	206	30	0	29	(17	12)	323	105	144	128	71	5	67	15	0	13	8	3	.73	15	.333	.407	.523
2001 Kansas City	AL	147	559	170	46	0	29	(14	15)	303	97	99	109	64	13	64	2	1	6	10	3	.77	13	.304	.374	.542
2002 Kansas City	AL	126	471	160	31	1	24	(14	10)	265	81	86	112	61	10	46	6	0	7	9	7	.56	9	.340	.417	.563
2003 Kansas City	AL	108	392	115	18	1	16	(7	9)	183	62	83	83	64	5	56	2	0	5	3	2	.60	13	.293	.391	.467
2004 Kansas City	AL	106	411	118	23	0	22	(8	14)	207	56	79	75	33	9	44	6	0	2	3	2	.60	7	.287	.347	.504
10 ML YEARS		1026	3717	1132	228	4	161	(82	79)	1851	588	683	699	406	43	417	53	4	43	45	25	.64	100	.305	.377	.498

Nick Swisher

Bats: B **Throws:** L **Pos:** LF-12; RF-4; 1B-3; DH-2; CF-1; PH-1; PR-1   **Ht:** 6'0" **Wt:** 194 **Born:** 1/25/1980 **Age:** 25

Year Team	Lg	G	AB	H	2B	3B	HR	(Hm	Rd)	TB	R	RBI	RC	TBB	IBB	SO	HBP	SH	SF	SB	CS	SB%	GDP	Avg	OBP	Slg
2002 Vancouver	A-	13	44	11	3	0	2	(-	-)	20	10	12	10	13	0	11	2	0	1	3	0	1.00	0	.250	.433	.455
2002 Visalia	A+	49	183	44	13	2	4	(-	-)	73	22	23	24	26	1	48	2	2	1	3	1	.75	6	.240	.340	.399
2003 Modesto	A+	51	189	56	14	2	10	(-	-)	104	38	43	42	41	1	49	2	0	5	0	2	.00	4	.296	.418	.550
2003 Midland	AA	76	287	66	24	2	5	(-	-)	109	36	43	34	37	1	76	6	0	6	0	1	.00	8	.230	.324	.380
2004 Sacramento	AAA	125	443	119	28	2	29	(-	-)	238	109	92	93	103	1	109	3	0	5	3	3	.50	16	.269	.406	.537
2004 Oakland	AL	20	60	15	4	0	2	(1	1)	25	11	8	8	8	0	11	2	0	1	0	0	-	2	.250	.352	.417

Jason Szuminski

Pitches: R **Bats:** R **Pos:** RP-7   **Ht:** 6'4" **Wt:** 221 **Born:** 12/11/1978 **Age:** 26

Year Team	Lg	G	GS	CG	GF	IP	BFP	H	R	ER	HR	SH	SF	HB	TBB	IBB	SO	WP	Bk	W	L	Pct	ShO	Sv-Op	Hld	ERC	ERA
2000 Cubs	R	10	0	0	2	40.2	171	39	15	11	0	1	0	3	13	0	31	2	0	2	1	.667	0	0--	-	3.18	2.43
2000 Lansing	A	4	4	0	0	21.1	89	19	8	8	0	0	1	1	10	0	7	1	1	3	1	.750	0	0--	-	3.33	3.38
2001 Lansing	A	14	4	0	2	36.1	177	56	27	26	2	1	1	2	17	0	22	2	0	4	3	.571	0	0--	-	7.63	6.44
2002 Daytona	A+	39	7	0	7	91.1	419	95	61	52	7	2	6	6	41	0	53	12	0	5	2	.714	0	1--	-	4.43	5.12
2003 Daytona	A+	13	0	0	5	24.2	111	29	12	10	0	2	1	1	9	1	23	0	0	2	1	.667	0	0--	-	4.24	3.65
2003 W Tennesse	AA	29	3	0	8	59.2	246	51	19	15	1	3	2	3	19	2	45	1	0	7	4	.636	0	2--	-	2.60	2.26
2003 Iowa	AAA	3	2	0	0	12.2	49	11	5	5	0	1	0	0	1	0	5	0	0	0	0	-	0	0--	-	1.68	3.55
2004 Iowa	AAA	41	2	0	24	51.0	248	57	40	28	6	1	1	3	35	5	31	1	0	3	2	.600	0	8--	-	5.98	4.94
2004 San Diego	NL	7	0	0	2	10.0	57	12	9	8	3	2	0	2	11	2	5	0	0	0	0	-	0	0-0	0	10.06	7.20

Kazuhito Tadano

Pitches: R **Bats:** R **Pos:** RP-10; SP-4   **Ht:** 6'0" **Wt:** 180 **Born:** 4/25/1980 **Age:** 25

Year Team	Lg	G	GS	CG	GF	IP	BFP	H	R	ER	HR	SH	SF	HB	TBB	IBB	SO	WP	Bk	W	L	Pct	ShO	Sv-Op	Hld	ERC	ERA
2003 Kinston	A+	7	1	0	2	19.0	73	13	5	4	0	1	0	1	3	0	28	2	0	2	1	.667	0	0--	-	1.39	1.89
2003 Akron	AA	31	0	0	9	72.2	294	62	15	10	4	2	1	2	15	2	78	4	0	4	1	.800	0	3--	-	2.35	1.24
2003 Buffalo	AAA	2	0	0	2	7.0	31	6	3	3	0	0	1	0	4	1	6	0	1	0	0	-	0	0--	-	2.92	3.86
2004 Buffalo	AAA	12	8	0	2	44.2	195	49	28	27	9	1	3	2	14	0	39	3	1	2	4	.333	0	0--	-	5.19	5.44
2004 Cleveland	AL	14	4	0	1	50.1	225	55	30	26	6	2	0	3	18	0	39	2	0	1	1	.500	0	0-0	0	4.75	4.65

So Taguchi

Bats: R **Throws:** R **Pos:** LF-53; CF-31; RF-28; PH-19; PR-4   **Ht:** 5'10" **Wt:** 163 **Born:** 7/2/1969 **Age:** 35

Year Team	Lg	G	AB	H	2B	3B	HR	(Hm	Rd)	TB	R	RBI	RC	TBB	IBB	SO	HBP	SH	SF	SB	CS	SB%	GDP	Avg	OBP	Slg
2004 Memphis*	AAA	17	55	18	4	0	1	(-	-)	25	5	7	9	1	0	10	2	0	0	6	0	1.00	2	.327	.362	.455
2002 St Louis	NL	19	15	6	0	0	0	(0	0)	6	4	2	4	2	0	1	0	2	0	1	0	1.00	0	.400	.471	.400
2003 St Louis	NL	43	54	14	3	1	3	(1	2)	28	9	13	11	4	1	11	0	1	0	0	0	-	0	.259	.310	.519
2004 St Louis	NL	109	179	52	10	2	3	(1	2)	75	26	25	27	12	1	23	2	10	3	6	3	.67	6	.291	.337	.419
3 ML YEARS		171	248	72	13	3	6	(2	4)	109	39	40	42	18	2	35	2	13	3	7	3	.70	8	.290	.339	.440

Shingo Takatsu

Pitches: R **Bats:** R **Pos:** RP-59   **Ht:** 6'0" **Wt:** 180 **Born:** 11/25/1968 **Age:** 36

		HOW MUCH HE PITCHED					WHAT HE GAVE UP											THE RESULTS						
Year Team	Lg	G	GS	CG	GF	IP	BFP	H	R	ER	HR	SH	SF	HB	TBB	IBB	SO	WP	Bk	W	L	Pct	ShO	Sv-Op	Hld	ERC	ERA
2004 Chicago	AL	59	0	0	45	62.1	245	40	17	16	6	2	0	2	21	3	50	1	0	6	4	.600	0	19-20	4	2.06	2.31

Dennis Tankersley

Pitches: R **Bats:** R **Pos:** SP-6; RP-3   **Ht:** 6'2" **Wt:** 185 **Born:** 2/24/1979 **Age:** 26

		HOW MUCH HE PITCHED					WHAT HE GAVE UP											THE RESULTS						
Year Team	Lg	G	GS	CG	GF	IP	BFP	H	R	ER	HR	SH	SF	HB	TBB	IBB	SO	WP	Bk	W	L	Pct	ShO	Sv-Op	Hld	ERC	ERA
2004 Portland*	AAA	19	19	0	0	120.0	495	114	52	42	10	4	3	2	37	1	86	1	0	7	4	.636	0	0- -	-	3.45	3.15
2002 San Diego	NL	17	9	0	3	51.1	245	59	46	46	10	3	2	6	40	3	39	3	0	1	4	.200	0	0-0	0	8.04	8.06
2003 San Diego	NL	1	1	0	0	0.0	7	3	7	7	0	0	0	0	4	0	0	0	0	0	1	.000	0	0-0	0	-	-
2004 San Diego	NL	9	6	0	0	35.0	157	35	25	20	3	1	0	1	17	3	29	2	0	0	5	.000	0	0-0	1	4.20	5.14
3 ML YEARS		27	16	0	3	86.1	409	97	78	73	13	4	2	7	61	6	68	5	0	1	10	.091	0	0-0	1	6.79	7.61

Julian Tavarez

Pitches: R **Bats:** L **Pos:** RP-77   **Ht:** 6'2" **Wt:** 195 **Born:** 5/22/1973 **Age:** 32

		HOW MUCH HE PITCHED					WHAT HE GAVE UP											THE RESULTS						
Year Team	Lg	G	GS	CG	GF	IP	BFP	H	R	ER	HR	SH	SF	HB	TBB	IBB	SO	WP	Bk	W	L	Pct	ShO	Sv-Op	Hld	ERC	ERA
1993 Cleveland	AL	8	7	0	0	37.0	172	53	29	27	7	0	1	2	13	2	19	3	1	2	2	.500	0	0-0	0	7.48	6.57
1994 Cleveland	AL	1	1	0	0	1.2	14	6	8	4	1	0	1	0	1	1	0	0	0	0	1	.000	0	0-0	0	24.13	21.60
1995 Cleveland	AL	57	0	0	15	85.0	350	76	36	23	7	0	2	3	21	0	68	3	2	10	2	.833	0	0-4	19	2.93	2.44
1996 Cleveland	AL	51	4	0	13	80.2	353	101	49	48	9	5	4	1	22	5	46	1	0	4	7	.364	0	0-0	13	5.12	5.36
1997 San Francisco	NL	89	0	0	13	88.1	378	91	43	38	6	3	8	4	34	5	38	4	0	6	4	.600	0	0-3	26	4.13	3.87
1998 San Francisco	NL	60	0	0	12	85.1	374	96	41	36	5	5	3	8	36	11	52	1	1	5	3	.625	0	1-6	10	4.89	3.80
1999 San Francisco	NL	47	0	0	12	54.2	258	65	38	36	7	3	2	8	25	3	33	4	1	2	0	1.000	0	0-2	5	6.10	5.93
2000 Colorado	NL	51	12	1	8	120.0	530	124	68	59	11	3	4	7	53	9	62	2	1	11	5	.688	0	1-1	6	4.49	4.43
2001 Chicago	NL	34	28	0	1	161.1	712	172	98	81	13	8	4	11	69	4	107	2	1	10	9	.526	0	0-0	2	4.70	4.52
2002 Florida	NL	29	27	0	1	153.2	714	188	100	92	9	13	2	15	74	7	67	7	2	10	12	.455	0	0-1	0	5.75	5.39
2003 Pittsburgh	NL	64	0	0	29	83.2	350	75	37	34	1	9	1	5	27	8	39	3	0	3	3	.500	0	11-14	9	2.72	3.66
2004 St Louis	NL	77	0	0	27	64.1	268	57	21	17	1	3	1	6	19	0	48	2	1	7	4	.636	0	4-6	19	2.87	2.38
12 ML YEARS		568	79	1	131	1015.2	4473	1104	568	495	77	52	33	70	394	55	579	32	10	70	52	.574	0	17-37	109	4.57	4.39

Willy Taveras

Bats: R **Throws:** R **Pos:** PR-6; CF-4; LF-2; RF-1   **Ht:** 6'0" **Wt:** 160 **Born:** 12/25/1981 **Age:** 23

		BATTING																	BASERUNNING				AVERAGES		
Year Team	Lg	G	AB	H	2B	3B	HR	(Hm	Rd)	TB	R	RBI	RC	TBB	IBB	SO	HBP	SH	SF	SB	CS	SB%	GDP	Avg	OBP	Slg
2000 Burlington	A	50	190	50	4	3	1	(-	-)	63	46	16	29	23	0	44	6	1	3	36	9	.80	0	.263	.356	.332
2000 Burlington	R+	50	190	50	4	3	1	(-	-)	63	46	16	29	23	0	44	6	1	3	36	9	.80	0	.263	.356	.332
2001 Columbus	A	97	395	107	15	7	3	(-	-)	145	55	32	48	22	0	73	6	4	3	29	9	.76	7	.271	.317	.367
2002 Columbus	A	85	313	83	14	1	4	(-	-)	111	68	27	53	45	0	68	18	2	3	54	12	.82	5	.265	.385	.355
2003 Kinston	A+	113	397	112	9	6	2	(-	-)	139	64	35	66	52	1	68	12	6	1	57	12	.83	3	.282	.381	.350
2004 Round Rock	AA	103	409	137	13	1	2	(-	-)	158	76	27	75	38	2	76	9	6	2	55	11	.83	2	.335	.402	.386
2004 Houston	NL	10	1	0	0	0	0	(0	0)	0	2	0	0	0	0	1	0	1	0	1	0	1.00	0	.000	.000	.000

Aaron Taylor

Pitches: R **Bats:** R **Pos:** RP-5   **Ht:** 6'7" **Wt:** 230 **Born:** 8/20/1977 **Age:** 27

		HOW MUCH HE PITCHED					WHAT HE GAVE UP											THE RESULTS						
Year Team	Lg	G	GS	CG	GF	IP	BFP	H	R	ER	HR	SH	SF	HB	TBB	IBB	SO	WP	Bk	W	L	Pct	ShO	Sv-Op	Hld	ERC	ERA
2004 InlandEmpire*	A+	1	1	0	0	1.1	7	2	3	2	0	0	0	0	1	0	2	0	0	0	1	.000	0	0- -	-	7.52	13.50
2004 San Antonio*	AA	30	0	0	7	37.1	156	27	13	12	2	0	0	3	14	0	37	4	0	3	1	.750	0	0- -	-	2.47	2.89
2002 Seattle	AL	5	0	0	2	5.0	23	8	5	5	2	0	0	0	0	0	6	0	0	0	0	-	0	0-1	0	8.09	9.00
2003 Seattle	AL	10	0	0	4	12.2	62	17	12	12	0	0	1	1	6	0	9	2	0	0	0	-	0	0-0	0	5.74	8.53
2004 Seattle	AL	5	0	0	4	3.2	19	5	4	4	2	0	0	0	3	0	4	0	0	0	0	-	0	0-0	0	12.00	9.82
3 ML YEARS		20	0	0	10	21.1	104	30	21	21	4	0	1	1	9	0	19	2	0	0	0	-	0	0-1	0	7.37	8.86

Mark Teixeira

Bats: B **Throws:** R **Pos:** 1B-142; RF-7; DH-2; PH-1   **Ht:** 6'2" **Wt:** 215 **Born:** 4/11/1980 **Age:** 25

		BATTING																	BASERUNNING				AVERAGES		
Year Team	Lg	G	AB	H	2B	3B	HR	(Hm	Rd)	TB	R	RBI	RC	TBB	IBB	SO	HBP	SH	SF	SB	CS	SB%	GDP	Avg	OBP	Slg
2002 Charlotte	A+	38	150	48	10	2	9	(-	-)	89	32	41	34	21	2	24	3	0	1	2	0	1.00	4	.320	.411	.593
2002 Tulsa	AA	48	171	54	11	3	10	(-	-)	101	31	28	39	25	0	36	4	0	0	3	2	.60	2	.316	.415	.591
2004 Frisco	AA	1	3	0	0	0	0	(-	-)	0	0	0	0	0	0	1	1	0	0	0	0	-	0	.000	.250	.000
2003 Texas	AL	146	529	137	29	5	26	(19	7)	254	66	84	78	44	5	120	14	0	2	1	2	.33	14	.259	.331	.480
2004 Texas	AL	145	545	153	34	2	38	(18	20)	305	101	112	120	68	12	117	10	0	2	4	1	.80	6	.281	.370	.560
2 ML YEARS		291	1074	290	63	7	64	(37	27)	559	167	196	198	112	17	237	24	0	4	5	3	.63	20	.270	.351	.520

Miguel Tejada

Bats: R **Throws:** R **Pos:** SS-162   **Ht:** 5'9" **Wt:** 200 **Born:** 5/25/1976 **Age:** 29

		BATTING																	BASERUNNING				AVERAGES		
Year Team	Lg	G	AB	H	2B	3B	HR	(Hm	Rd)	TB	R	RBI	RC	TBB	IBB	SO	HBP	SH	SF	SB	CS	SB%	GDP	Avg	OBP	Slg
1997 Oakland	AL	26	99	20	3	2	2	(1	1)	33	10	10	7	2	0	22	3	0	0	2	0	1.00	3	.202	.240	.333
1998 Oakland	AL	105	365	85	20	1	11	(5	6)	140	53	45	40	28	0	86	7	4	3	5	6	.45	8	.233	.298	.384
1999 Oakland	AL	159	593	149	33	4	21	(12	9)	253	93	84	82	57	3	94	10	9	5	8	7	.53	11	.251	.325	.427
2000 Oakland	AL	160	607	167	32	1	30	(16	14)	291	105	115	99	66	6	102	4	2	2	6	0	1.00	15	.275	.349	.479

Year Team	Lg	G	AB	H	2B	3B	HR	(Hm	Rd)	TB	R	RBI	RC	TBB	IBB	SO	HBP	SH	SF	SB	CS	SB%	GDP	Avg	OBP	Slg
2001 Oakland	AL	**162**	622	166	31	3	31	(17	14)	296	107	113	94	43	5	89	13	1	4	11	5	.69	14	.267	.326	.476
2002 Oakland	AL	**162**	662	204	30	0	34	(17	17)	336	108	131	123	38	3	84	11	0	4	7	2	.78	21	.308	.354	.508
2003 Oakland	AL	162	636	177	42	0	27	(15	12)	300	98	106	103	53	7	65	6	0	8	10	0	1.00	12	.278	.336	.472
2004 Baltimore	AL	**162**	653	203	40	2	34	(17	17)	349	107	**150**	124	48	6	73	10	0	**14**	4	1	.80	**24**	.311	.360	.534
8 ML YEARS		1098	4237	1171	231	13	190	(100	90)	1998	681	754	672	335	30	615	64	16	40	53	21	.72	108	.276	.336	.472

Michael Tejera

Pitches: L **Bats:** L **Pos:** RP-6; SP-2   **Ht:** 5'9" **Wt:** 175 **Born:** 10/18/1976 **Age:** 28

		HOW MUCH HE PITCHED						WHAT HE GAVE UP											THE RESULTS						
Year Team	Lg	G	GS	CG	GF	IP	BFP	H	R	ER	HR	SH	SF	HB	TBB	IBB	SO	WP	Bk	W	L	Pct	ShO	Sv-Op	Hld	ERC	ERA
2004 Jupiter*	A+	1	1	0	0	3.1	16	3	1	0	0	0	0	0	3	0	1	0	0	0	1	.000	0	0- -	-	4.53	0.00
2004 Albuquerque*	AAA	22	19	0	1	113.1	476	109	56	50	17	4	3	6	39	0	88	3	0	8	4	.667	0	0- -	-	4.28	3.97
1999 Florida	NL	3	1	0	1	6.1	31	10	8	8	1	0	0	0	5	0	7	0	0	0	0	-	0	0-0	0	10.73	11.37
2002 Florida	NL	47	18	0	2	139.2	611	144	71	69	17	5	4	6	60	3	95	3	0	8	8	.500	0	1-3	8	4.10	4.45
2003 Florida	NL	50	6	0	10	81.0	353	82	44	42	6	8	1	1	36	3	58	0	0	3	4	.429	0	2-2	5	4.13	4.67
2004 Fla-Tex		8	2	0	1	9.1	52	15	14	14	1	0	0	2	9	0	10	0	0	0	1	.000	0	0-0	0	11.67	13.50
2004 Florida	NL	2	2	0	0	4.0	23	6	8	8	0	0	0	1	6	0	3	0	0	0	1	.000	0	0-0	0	12.95	18.00
2004 Texas	AL	6	0	0	1	5.1	29	9	6	6	1	0	0	1	3	0	7	0	0	0	0	-	0	0-0	0	10.59	10.13
4 ML YEARS		108	27	0	14	236.1	1047	251	137	133	25	13	5	9	110	6	170	3	0	11	13	.458	0	3-5	13	4.89	5.06

Amaury Telemaco

Pitches: R **Bats:** R **Pos:** RP-42   **Ht:** 6'3" **Wt:** 222 **Born:** 1/19/1974 **Age:** 31

		HOW MUCH HE PITCHED						WHAT HE GAVE UP											THE RESULTS						
Year Team	Lg	G	GS	CG	GF	IP	BFP	H	R	ER	HR	SH	SF	HB	TBB	IBB	SO	WP	Bk	W	L	Pct	ShO	Sv-Op	Hld	ERC	ERA
2004 Scrtn/WlksBr*	AAA	1	1	0	0	1.0	3	0	0	0	0	0	0	0	0	0	2	0	0	0	0	-	0	0- -	-	0.00	0.00
1996 Chicago	NL	25	17	0	0	97.1	427	108	0	59	20	0	0	0	31	0	64	0	0	5	7	.417	0	0-0	0	5.06	5.46
1997 Chicago	NL	10	5	0	0	38.0	169	47	0	26	4	0	0	0	11	0	29	0	0	0	3	.000	0	0-0	0	5.00	6.16
1998 ChC-Ari	NL	41	18	0	0	148.2	637	150	0	65	18	0	0	0	46	0	78	0	0	7	10	.412	0	0-0	0	3.86	3.93
1999 Ari-Phi	NL	49	0	0	0	53.0	234	52	0	34	10	0	0	0	26	0	43	0	0	4	0	1.000	0	0-0	0	4.93	5.77
2000 Philadelphia	NL	13	2	0	0	24.1	107	25	0	18	6	0	0	0	14	0	22	0	0	1	3	.250	0	0-0	0	6.24	6.66
2001 Philadelphia	NL	24	14	1	0	89.1	388	93	0	55	15	0	0	0	32	0	59	0	0	5	5	.500	0	0-0	0	4.58	5.54
2003 Philadelphia	NL	8	8	0	0	45.1	194	41	22	20	5	3	1	7	11	2	29	3	0	1	4	.200	0	0-0	0	3.48	3.97
2004 Philadelphia	NL	42	0	0	9	54.1	225	51	27	26	12	1	0	0	19	2	32	2	1	2	0	1.000	0	0-0	5	4.38	4.31
1998 Chicago	NL	14	0	0	0	27.2	118	23	0	12	5	0	0	0	13	0	18	0	0	1	1	.500	0	0-0	0	3.92	3.90
1998 Arizona	NL	27	18	0	0	121.0	519	127	0	53	13	0	0	0	33	0	60	0	0	6	9	.400	0	0-0	0	3.84	3.94
1999 Arizona	NL	5	0	0	0	6.0	28	7	0	5	2	0	0	0	6	0	2	0	0	1	0	1.000	0	0-0	0	10.63	7.50
1999 Philadelphia	NL	44	0	0	0	47.0	206	45	0	29	8	0	0	0	20	0	41	0	0	3	0	1.000	0	0-0	0	4.33	5.55
8 ML YEARS		212	64	1	9	550.1	2381	567	49	303	90	4	1	7	190	4	356	5	1	23	34	.404	0	0-0	5	4.48	4.96

Luis Terrero

Bats: R **Throws:** R **Pos:** CF-57; RF-4; LF-1; PH-1   **Ht:** 6'2" **Wt:** 206 **Born:** 5/18/1980 **Age:** 25

		BATTING																		BASERUNNING				AVERAGES		
Year Team	Lg	G	AB	H	2B	3B	HR	(Hm	Rd)	TB	R	RBI	RC	TBB	IBB	SO	HBP	SH	SF	SB	CS	SB%	GDP	Avg	OBP	Slg
1999 Missoula	R+	71	272	78	13	7	8	(-	-)	129	74	40	49	32	1	91	5	3	6	27	10	.73	2	.287	.365	.474
2000 High Desert	A+	19	79	15	3	1	0	(-	-)	20	10	1	2	3	0	16	1	0	0	5	5	.50	2	.190	.229	.253
2000 Missoula	R+	68	276	72	10	0	8	(-	-)	106	48	44	30	10	0	75	8	1	1	23	11	.68	5	.261	.305	.384
2001 South Bend	A	24	89	14	2	0	1	(-	-)	19	4	8	1	0	0	29	2	0	0	3	0	1.00	2	.157	.176	.213
2001 Yakima	A-	11	41	13	2	1	0	(-	-)	17	7	0	5	2	0	8	0	0	0	0	3	.00	0	.317	.349	.415
2001 Lancaster	A+	19	71	32	9	1	4	(-	-)	55	16	11	20	1	1	14	1	0	0	5	0	1.00	3	.451	.466	.775
2001 El Paso	AA	34	147	44	13	3	3	(-	-)	72	29	8	22	4	0	45	3	2	0	9	2	.82	2	.299	.331	.490
2002 El Paso	AA	104	360	103	20	6	8	(-	-)	159	49	54	46	23	1	89	8	3	1	18	22	.45	9	.286	.342	.442
2003 Tucson	AAA	118	467	134	20	15	3	(-	-)	193	83	46	64	31	0	103	11	2	1	23	19	.55	6	.287	.345	.413
2004 Tucson	AAA	58	217	68	9	6	9	(-	-)	116	36	35	41	17	1	48	4	2	0	15	3	.83	7	.313	.374	.535
2003 Arizona	NL	5	4	1	0	0	0	(0	0)	1	0	0	1	0	0	1	0	0	0	0	0	-	0	.250	.400	.250
2004 Arizona	NL	62	229	56	14	0	4	(2	2)	82	21	14	25	20	2	78	5	1	0	10	2	.83	5	.245	.319	.358
2 ML YEARS		67	233	57	14	0	4	(2	2)	83	21	14	26	20	2	79	6	1	0	10	2	.83	5	.245	.320	.356

Marcus Thames

Bats: R **Throws:** R **Pos:** LF-40; PH-13; RF-12; DH-5   **Ht:** 6'2" **Wt:** 205 **Born:** 3/6/1977 **Age:** 28

		BATTING																		BASERUNNING				AVERAGES		
Year Team	Lg	G	AB	H	2B	3B	HR	(Hm	Rd)	TB	R	RBI	RC	TBB	IBB	SO	HBP	SH	SF	SB	CS	SB%	GDP	Avg	OBP	Slg
2004 Toledo*	AAA	64	234	77	21	1	24	(-	-)	172	57	59	62	33	3	40	2	1	4	4	1	.80	5	.329	.410	.735
2002 New York	AL	7	13	3	1	0	1	(1	0)	7	2	2	2	0	0	4	0	0	0	0	0	-	0	.231	.231	.538
2003 Texas	AL	30	73	15	2	0	1	(0	1)	20	12	4	5	8	0	18	2	0	1	0	1	.00	2	.205	.298	.274
2004 Detroit	AL	61	165	42	12	0	10	(5	5)	84	24	33	30	16	0	42	2	0	1	0	1	.00	3	.255	.326	.509
3 ML YEARS		98	251	60	15	0	12	(6	6)	111	38	39	37	24	0	64	4	0	2	0	2	.00	5	.239	.313	.442

Brad Thomas

Pitches: L **Bats:** L **Pos:** RP-3   **Ht:** 6'4" **Wt:** 220 **Born:** 10/22/1977 **Age:** 27

		HOW MUCH HE PITCHED						WHAT HE GAVE UP											THE RESULTS						
Year Team	Lg	G	GS	CG	GF	IP	BFP	H	R	ER	HR	SH	SF	HB	TBB	IBB	SO	WP	Bk	W	L	Pct	ShO	Sv-Op	Hld	ERC	ERA
2004 Pawtucket*	AAA	4	1	0	0	4.1	21	6	9	5	0	0	0	0	6	0	1	0	0	0	1	.000	0	0- -	-	9.47	10.38
2001 Minnesota	AL	5	5	0	0	16.1	82	20	0	17	6	0	0	0	14	0	6	0	0	0	2	.000	0	0-0	0	9.68	9.37
2003 Minnesota	AL	3	0	0	1	4.2	22	6	4	4	1	0	0	0	3	1	2	0	0	0	1	.000	0	0-0	0	7.54	7.71
2004 Minnesota	AL	3	0	0	0	2.2	16	7	5	5	0	0	0	0	1	0	0	1	0	0	0	-	0	0-0	0	13.58	16.88
3 ML YEARS		11	5	0	1	23.2	120	33	9	26	7	0	0	0	18	1	8	1	0	0	3	.000	0	0-0	0	9.70	9.89

Charles Thomas

Bats: L Throws: L Pos: LF-70; PH-9; PR-6; RF-2; CF-1   Ht: 6'0" Wt: 190 Born: 12/26/1978 Age: 26

Year	Team	Lg	G	AB	H	2B	3B	HR	(Hm	Rd)	TB	R	RBI	RC	TBB	IBB	SO	HBP	SH	SF	SB	CS	SB%	GDP	Avg	OBP	Slg
2000	Jamestown	A-	68	264	80	20	8	1	(-	-)	119	39	25	40	19	0	58	1	0	1	10	2	.83	7	.303	.351	.451
2001	Myrtle Beach	A+	12	44	7	1	0	0	(-	-)	8	4	6	0	3	1	8	0	0	1	1	0	1.00	3	.159	.208	.182
2001	Macon	A	108	408	102	19	5	11	(-	-)	164	59	59	50	32	3	87	3	0	3	17	7	.71	6	.250	.307	.402
2002	Myrtle Beach	A+	2	7	2	0	0	0	(-	-)	2	0	0	0	0	0	2	0	0	0	0	0	-	0	.286	.286	.286
2002	Greenville	AA	71	229	53	8	0	2	(-	-)	67	40	18	23	28	1	43	4	3	3	5	3	.63	5	.231	.322	.293
2003	Vero Beach	A+	108	338	80	19	0	4	(-	-)	111	53	37	45	61	0	84	6	5	5	30	15	.67	5	.237	.359	.328
2003	Myrtle Beach	A+	66	207	50	8	1	2	(-	-)	66	30	15	26	29	2	54	8	4	0	6	2	.75	5	.242	.357	.319
2003	Greenville	AA	47	176	57	14	4	0	(-	-)	79	29	23	31	18	0	25	3	0	0	5	4	.56	1	.324	.396	.449
2004	Richmond	AAA	61	215	77	18	4	4	(-	-)	115	31	32	44	16	0	40	6	2	1	7	5	.58	4	.358	.416	.535
2004	Atlanta	NL	83	236	68	8	4	7	(2	5)	105	35	31	37	21	9	45	9	1	0	3	1	.75	3	.288	.368	.445

Frank Thomas

Bats: R Throws: R Pos: DH-65; PH-5; 1B-4   Ht: 6'5" Wt: 275 Born: 5/27/1968 Age: 37

Year	Team	Lg	G	AB	H	2B	3B	HR	(Hm	Rd)	TB	R	RBI	RC	TBB	IBB	SO	HBP	SH	SF	SB	CS	SB%	GDP	Avg	OBP	Slg
1990	Chicago	AL	60	191	63	11	3	7	(2	5)	101	39	31	46	44	0	54	2	0	3	0	1	.00	5	.330	.454	.529
1991	Chicago	AL	158	559	178	31	2	32	(24	8)	309	104	109	134	138	13	112	1	0	2	1	2	.33	20	.318	.453	.553
1992	Chicago	AL	160	573	185	46	2	24	(10	14)	307	108	115	132	122	6	88	5	0	11	6	3	.67	19	.323	.439	.536
1993	Chicago	AL	153	549	174	36	0	41	(26	15)	333	106	128	137	112	23	54	2	0	13	4	2	.67	10	.317	.426	.607
1994	Chicago	AL	113	399	141	34	1	38	(22	16)	291	106	101	127	109	12	61	2	0	7	2	3	.40	15	.353	.487	.729
1995	Chicago	AL	145	493	152	27	0	40	(15	25)	299	102	111	132	136	29	74	6	0	12	3	2	.60	14	.308	.454	.606
1996	Chicago	AL	141	527	184	26	0	40	(16	24)	330	110	134	137	109	26	70	5	0	8	1	1	.50	25	.349	.459	.626
1997	Chicago	AL	146	530	184	35	0	35	(16	19)	324	110	125	139	109	9	69	3	0	7	1	1	.50	15	.347	.456	.611
1998	Chicago	AL	160	585	155	35	2	29	(15	14)	281	109	109	111	110	2	93	6	0	11	7	0	1.00	14	.265	.381	.480
1999	Chicago	AL	135	486	148	36	0	15	(9	6)	229	74	77	95	87	13	66	9	0	8	3	3	.50	15	.305	.414	.471
2000	Chicago	AL	159	582	191	44	0	43	(30	13)	364	115	143	148	112	18	94	5	0	8	1	3	.25	13	.328	.436	.625
2001	Chicago	AL	20	68	15	3	0	4	(2	2)	30	8	10	10	10	2	12	0	0	1	0	0	-	0	.221	.316	.441
2002	Chicago	AL	148	523	132	29	1	28	(24	4)	247	77	92	96	88	2	115	7	0	10	3	0	1.00	16	.252	.361	.472
2003	Chicago	AL	153	546	146	35	0	42	(29	13)	307	87	105	115	100	4	115	12	0	4	0	0	-	11	.267	.390	.562
2004	Chicago	AL	74	240	65	16	0	18	(14	4)	135	53	49	59	64	3	57	6	0	1	0	2	.00	2	.271	.434	.563
	15 ML YEARS		1925	6851	2113	444	11	436	(254	182)	3887	1308	1439	1618	1450	162	1134	71	0	106	32	23	.58	188	.308	.429	.567

Jim Thome

Bats: L Throws: R Pos: 1B-135; DH-6; PH-3   Ht: 6'4" Wt: 220 Born: 8/27/1970 Age: 34

Year	Team	Lg	G	AB	H	2B	3B	HR	(Hm	Rd)	TB	R	RBI	RC	TBB	IBB	SO	HBP	SH	SF	SB	CS	SB%	GDP	Avg	OBP	Slg
1991	Cleveland	AL	27	98	25	4	2	1	(0	1)	36	7	9	9	5	1	16	1	0	0	1	1	.50	4	.255	.298	.367
1992	Cleveland	AL	40	117	24	3	1	2	(1	1)	35	8	12	9	10	2	34	2	0	2	2	0	1.00	3	.205	.275	.299
1993	Cleveland	AL	47	154	41	11	0	7	(5	2)	73	28	22	30	29	1	36	4	0	5	2	1	.67	3	.266	.385	.474
1994	Cleveland	AL	98	321	86	20	1	20	(10	10)	168	58	52	56	46	5	84	0	1	1	3	3	.50	11	.268	.359	.523
1995	Cleveland	AL	137	452	142	29	3	25	(13	12)	252	92	73	109	97	3	113	5	0	3	4	3	.57	8	.314	.438	.558
1996	Cleveland	AL	151	505	157	28	5	38	(18	20)	309	122	116	132	123	8	141	6	0	2	2	2	.50	13	.311	.450	.612
1997	Cleveland	AL	147	496	142	25	0	40	(17	23)	287	104	102	120	120	9	146	3	0	8	1	1	.50	9	.286	.423	.579
1998	Cleveland	AL	123	440	129	34	2	30	(18	12)	257	89	85	104	89	8	141	4	0	4	1	0	1.00	7	.293	.413	.584
1999	Cleveland	AL	146	494	137	27	2	33	(19	14)	267	101	108	116	127	13	171	4	0	4	0	0	-	6	.277	.426	.540
2000	Cleveland	AL	158	557	150	33	1	37	(21	16)	296	106	106	119	118	4	171	4	0	5	1	0	1.00	8	.269	.398	.531
2001	Cleveland	AL	156	526	153	26	1	49	(30	19)	328	101	124	130	111	14	185	4	0	3	0	1	.00	9	.291	.416	.624
2002	Cleveland	AL	147	480	146	19	2	52	(30	22)	325	101	118	139	122	18	139	5	0	6	1	2	.33	5	.304	.445	.677
2003	Philadelphia	NL	159	578	154	30	3	47	(28	19)	331	111	131	125	111	11	182	4	0	5	0	3	.00	5	.266	.385	.573
2004	Philadelphia	NL	143	508	139	28	1	42	(19	23)	295	97	105	98	104	24	144	2	0	4	0	2	.00	10	.274	.396	.581
	14 ML YEARS		1679	5726	1625	317	24	423	(229	194)	3259	1125	1163	1296	1212	121	1703	48	1	52	18	19	.49	101	.284	.410	.569

Rich Thompson

Bats: L Throws: R Pos: PR-5; RF-2; LF-1   Ht: 6'3" Wt: 180 Born: 4/23/1979 Age: 26

Year	Team	Lg	G	AB	H	2B	3B	HR	(Hm	Rd)	TB	R	RBI	RC	TBB	IBB	SO	HBP	SH	SF	SB	CS	SB%	GDP	Avg	OBP	Slg
2000	Queens	A-	68	252	66	9	5	1	(-	-)	88	42	27	42	45	1	57	6	5	0	28	8	.78	0	.262	.386	.349
2001	Dunedin	A+	112	454	141	14	6	3	(-	-)	170	90	60	74	44	1	72	9	3	4	39	11	.78	3	.311	.380	.374
2001	Syracuse	AAA	17	53	13	0	1	0	(-	-)	15	5	3	5	4	0	12	0	3	1	5	1	.83	1	.245	.293	.283
2002	Tennessee	AA	135	554	155	13	4	2	(-	-)	182	109	44	79	50	0	86	20	7	0	45	13	.78	1	.280	.361	.329
2003	New Haven	AA	49	182	57	5	1	0	(-	-)	64	39	9	28	10	0	24	8	2	1	15	3	.83	2	.313	.373	.352
2003	Nashville	AAA	35	109	28	3	2	0	(-	-)	35	17	11	15	9	0	21	4	1	1	22	3	.88	0	.257	.333	.321
2003	Syracuse	AAA	28	112	33	2	1	0	(-	-)	37	13	7	17	9	0	10	5	3	0	11	1	.92	2	.295	.373	.330
2004	Nashville	AAA	112	411	118	7	13	5	(-	-)	166	73	36	63	26	1	62	13	10	1	40	15	.73	0	.287	.348	.404
2004	Kansas City	AL	6	1	0	0	0	0	(0	0)	0	1	0	0	0	0	0	0	0	0	1	0	1.00	1	.000	.000	.000

John Thomson

Pitches: R Bats: R Pos: SP-33   Ht: 6'3" Wt: 190 Born: 10/1/1973 Age: 31

			HOW MUCH HE PITCHED					WHAT HE GAVE UP										THE RESULTS						
Year	Team	Lg	G	GS	CG	GF	IP	BFP	H	R	ER	HR	SH	SF	HB	TBB	IBB	SO	WP	Bk	W	L	Pct	ShO	Sv-Op	Hld	ERC	ERA
1997	Colorado	NL	27	27	2	0	166.1	721	193	94	87	15	10	3	5	51	0	106	2	0	7	9	.438	1	0-0	0	4.74	4.71
1998	Colorado	NL	26	26	2	0	161.0	680	174	86	86	21	8	5	0	49	0	106	4	2	8	11	.421	0	0-0	0	4.45	4.81
1999	Colorado	NL	14	13	1	1	62.2	305	85	62	56	11	4	2	1	36	1	34	2	0	1	10	.091	0	0-0	0	7.60	8.04
2001	Colorado	NL	14	14	1	0	93.2	386	84	46	42	15	3	3	4	25	3	68	1	0	4	5	.444	1	0-0	0	3.52	4.04
2002	Col-NYM	NL	30	30	0	0	181.2	800	201	116	95	28	13	10	2	44	0	137	2	0	9	14	.391	0	0-0	0	4.24	4.71
2003	Texas	AL	35	35	3	0	217.0	910	234	125	117	27	2	7	4	49	2	136	5	0	13	14	.481	1	0-0	0	4.10	4.85
2004	Atlanta	NL	33	33	0	0	198.1	834	210	93	82	20	11	4	6	52	5	133	3	0	14	8	.636	0	0-0	0	4.01	3.72

Year Team	Lg	G	GS	CG	GF	IP	BFP	H	R	ER	HR	SH	SF	HB	TBB	IBB	SO	WP	Bk	W	L	Pct	ShO	Sv-Op	Hld	ERC	ERA
2002 Colorado	NL	21	21	0	0	127.1	550	136	77	69	21	7	7	2	27	6	76	2	0	7	8	.467	0	0-0	0	4.02	4.88
2002 New York	NL	9	9	0	0	54.1	250	65	39	26	7	6	3	0	17	3	31	0	0	2	6	.250	0	0-0	0	4.74	4.31
7 ML YEARS		179	178	9	1	1080.2	4636	1181	622	565	137	51	34	22	306	20	690	19	2	56	71	.441	3	0-0	0	4.39	4.71

Matt Thornton

Pitches: L Bats: L Pos: RP-18; SP-1   **Ht: 6'6" Wt: 220 Born: 9/15/1976 Age: 28**

		HOW MUCH HE PITCHED						WHAT HE GAVE UP											THE RESULTS							
Year Team	Lg	G	GS	CG	GF	IP	BFP	H	R	ER	HR	SH	SF	HB	TBB	IBB	SO	WP	Bk	W	L	Pct	ShO	Sv-Op	Hld	ERC	ERA
1998 Everett	A-	2	0	0	0	1.1	8	1	4	4	0	0	0	0	3	0	0	0	0	0	0	-	0	0--		8.88	27.00
1999 Wisconsin	A	25	1	0	3	29.1	154	39	19	16	1	4	1	0	25	0	34	5	0	0	0	-	0	1--		7.09	4.91
2000 Wisconsin	A	26	17	0	3	103.1	465	94	59	46	2	3	0	6	72	1	88	12	2	6	9	.400	0	0--		4.37	4.01
2001 Sn Brnardino	A+	27	27	0	0	157.0	650	126	56	44	9	2	5	11	60	0	192	12	0	14	7	.667	0	0--		2.96	2.52
2002 San Antonio	AA	12	12	0	0	62.0	258	52	31	25	3	1	4	5	29	0	44	8	0	1	5	.167	0	0--		3.53	3.63
2003 InlandEmpire	A+	2	2	0	0	9.0	40	9	4	4	2	0	1	1	4	0	14	0	0	0	0	-	0	0--		5.65	4.00
2003 San Antonio	AA	4	4	0	0	25.1	87	8	3	1	0	0	1	0	9	0	18	0	0	3	0	1.000	0	0--		0.73	0.36
2003 Tacoma	AAA	2	2	0	0	9.0	44	14	11	8	2	0	2	0	3	0	5	1	0	0	2	.000	0	0--		8.02	8.00
2004 Tacoma	AAA	16	15	1	0	83.0	393	85	58	48	4	4	9	6	63	1	74	10	0	7	5	.583	0	0--		5.51	5.20
2004 Seattle	AL	19	1	0	8	32.2	148	30	15	15	2	2	1	0	25	1	30	2	0	1	2	.333	0	0-0	0	4.75	4.13

Joe Thurston

Bats: L Throws: R Pos: PH-12; 2B-4; PR-1   **Ht: 5'11" Wt: 175 Born: 9/29/1979 Age: 25**

		BATTING														BASERUNNING				AVERAGES		
Year Team	Lg	G	AB	H	2B	3B	HR	(Hm | Rd)	TB	R	RBI	RC	TBB	IBB	SO	HBP	SH	SF	SB	CS	SB%	GDP	Avg	OBP	Slg
2004 Las Vegas*	AAA	101	317	90	17	3	4	(- | -)	125	38	23	46	20	3	46	17	3	3	7	2	.78	5	.284	.356	.394
2002 Los Angeles	NL	8	13	6	1	0	0	(0 | 0)	7	1	1	3	0	0	1	0	1	1	0	0	-	0	.462	.429	.538
2003 Los Angeles	NL	12	10	2	0	0	0	(0 | 0)	2	2	0	0	1	0	1	0	0	0	0	0	-	0	.200	.273	.200
2004 Los Angeles	NL	17	17	3	1	1	0	(0 | 0)	6	1	1	1	0	0	5	0	0	1	0	0	-	0	.176	.167	.353
3 ML YEARS		37	40	11	2	1	0	(0 | 0)	15	4	2	4	1	0	7	0	1	2	0	0	-	0	.275	.279	.375

Terry Tiffee

Bats: B Throws: R Pos: 3B-12; PH-3; 1B-1; DH-1   **Ht: 6'3" Wt: 210 Born: 4/21/1979 Age: 26**

		BATTING														BASERUNNING				AVERAGES		
Year Team	Lg	G	AB	H	2B	3B	HR	(Hm | Rd)	TB	R	RBI	RC	TBB	IBB	SO	HBP	SH	SF	SB	CS	SB%	GDP	Avg	OBP	Slg
2000 Quad City	A	129	493	125	25	0	7	(- | -)	171	59	60	47	29	0	73	0	0	5	2	0	1.00	14	.254	.292	.347
2001 Quad City	A	128	495	153	32	1	11	(- | -)	220	65	86	74	32	4	48	1	0	8	3	1	.75	13	.309	.347	.444
2002 Fort Myers	A+	126	473	133	31	0	8	(- | -)	188	47	64	56	25	3	49	2	3	6	0	3	.00	12	.281	.316	.397
2003 New Britain	AA	139	530	167	31	3	14	(- | -)	246	77	93	83	31	5	49	2	0	7	4	1	.80	13	.315	.351	.464
2004 Rochester	AAA	82	316	97	26	3	12	(- | -)	165	42	68	54	21	2	26	4	0	1	0	0	-	9	.307	.357	.522
2004 Minnesota	AL	17	44	12	4	0	2	(1 | 1)	22	7	8	5	3	0	3	1	0	0	0	0	-	2	.273	.333	.500

Mike Timlin

Pitches: R Bats: R Pos: RP-76   **Ht: 6'4" Wt: 210 Born: 3/10/1966 Age: 39**

		HOW MUCH HE PITCHED						WHAT HE GAVE UP											THE RESULTS							
Year Team	Lg	G	GS	CG	GF	IP	BFP	H	R	ER	HR	SH	SF	HB	TBB	IBB	SO	WP	Bk	W	L	Pct	ShO	Sv-Op	Hld	ERC	ERA
1991 Toronto	AL	63	3	0	17	108.1	463	94	43	38	6	6	2	1	50	11	85	5	0	11	6	.647	0	3-8	9	3.14	3.16
1992 Toronto	AL	26	0	0	14	43.2	190	45	23	20	0	2	1	1	20	5	35	0	0	0	2	.000	0	1-1	1	3.68	4.12
1993 Toronto	AL	54	0	0	27	55.2	254	63	32	29	7	1	3	1	27	3	49	1	0	4	2	.667	0	1-4	9	5.32	4.69
1994 Toronto	AL	34	0	0	16	40.0	179	41	25	23	5	0	0	2	20	0	38	3	0	0	1	.000	0	2-4	5	5.01	5.18
1995 Toronto	AL	31	0	0	19	42.0	179	38	13	10	1	3	0	2	17	5	36	3	1	4	3	.571	0	5-9	4	3.04	2.14
1996 Toronto	AL	59	0	0	56	56.2	230	47	25	23	4	2	3	2	18	4	52	3	0	1	6	.143	0	31-38	2	2.74	3.65
1997 Tor-Sea	AL	64	0	0	31	72.2	297	69	30	26	8	6	1	1	20	5	45	1	1	6	4	.600	0	10-18	9	3.40	3.22
1998 Seattle	AL	70	0	0	40	79.1	321	78	26	26	5	4	2	3	16	2	60	0	0	3	3	.500	0	19-24	6	3.17	2.95
1999 Baltimore	AL	62	0	0	52	63.0	261	51	30	25	9	1	1	5	23	3	50	1	0	3	9	.250	0	27-36	3	3.46	3.57
2000 Bal-StL		62	0	0	40	64.2	295	67	30	30	8	7	2	4	35	6	52	0	0	5	4	.556	0	12-18	6	5.08	4.18
2001 St Louis	NL	67	0	0	19	72.2	307	78	35	33	6	1	2	3	19	4	47	3	1	4	5	.444	0	3-7	12	3.95	4.09
2002 StL-Phi	NL	72	1	0	17	96.2	376	75	35	32	15	2	1	5	14	2	50	3	0	4	6	.400	0	0-4	20	2.46	2.98
2003 Boston	AL	72	0	0	13	83.2	340	77	37	33	11	4	1	4	9	3	65	0	0	6	4	.600	0	2-4	17	2.81	3.55
2004 Boston	AL	76	0	0	12	76.1	320	75	35	35	8	3	1	5	19	3	56	1	0	5	4	.556	0	1-4	20	3.64	4.13
1997 Toronto	AL	38	0	0	26	47.0	190	41	17	15	6	4	1	1	15	4	36	1	1	3	2	.600	0	9-13	2	3.30	2.87
1997 Seattle	AL	26	0	0	5	25.2	107	28	13	11	2	2	0	0	5	1	9	0	0	3	2	.600	0	1-5	7	3.53	3.86
2000 Baltimore	AL	37	0	0	31	35.0	157	37	22	19	6	5	1	2	15	3	26	0	0	2	3	.400	0	11-15	1	5.08	4.89
2000 St Louis	NL	25	0	0	9	29.2	138	30	11	11	2	2	1	2	20	3	26	0	0	3	1	.750	0	1-3	5	5.05	3.34
2002 St Louis	NL	42	1	0	10	61.0	236	48	19	17	9	2	0	4	7	2	35	1	0	1	3	.250	0	0-2	12	2.41	2.51
2002 Philadelphia	NL	30	0	0	7	35.2	140	27	16	15	6	0	1	1	7	0	15	2	0	3	3	.500	0	0-2	8	2.55	3.79
14 ML YEARS		812	4	0	373	955.1	4012	898	422	383	93	42	20	39	307	56	720	24	3	56	59	.487	0	117-181	120	3.51	3.61

Brett Tomko

Pitches: R Bats: R Pos: SP-31; RP-1   **Ht: 6'4" Wt: 215 Born: 4/7/1973 Age: 32**

		HOW MUCH HE PITCHED						WHAT HE GAVE UP											THE RESULTS							
Year Team	Lg	G	GS	CG	GF	IP	BFP	H	R	ER	HR	SH	SF	HB	TBB	IBB	SO	WP	Bk	W	L	Pct	ShO	Sv-Op	Hld	ERC	ERA
2004 Fresno*	AAA	1	1	0	0	5.0	22	4	3	3	1	0	0	1	2	0	4	0	0	0	0	-	0	0--		4.36	5.40
1997 Cincinnati	NL	22	19	0	1	126.0	519	106	50	48	14	5	9	4	47	4	95	6	2	11	7	.611	0	0-0	0	3.31	3.43
1998 Cincinnati	NL	34	34	1	0	210.2	887	198	111	104	22	12	2	7	64	3	162	9	1	13	12	.520	0	0-0	0	3.50	4.44
1999 Cincinnati	NL	33	26	1	1	172.0	744	175	103	94	31	9	5	4	60	10	132	8	0	5	7	.417	0	0-0	1	4.51	4.92
2000 Seattle	AL	32	8	0	9	92.1	401	92	53	48	12	5	5	3	40	4	59	1	1	7	5	.583	0	1-2	3	4.49	4.68
2001 Seattle	AL	11	4	0	1	34.2	164	42	24	20	9	1	2	0	15	2	22	1	0	3	1	.750	0	0-1	0	6.31	5.19
2002 San Diego	NL	32	32	3	0	204.1	871	212	107	102	31	6	8	2	60	9	126	3	0	10	10	.500	0	0-0	0	4.18	4.49

Year Team	Lg	HOW MUCH HE PITCHED						WHAT HE GAVE UP													THE RESULTS							
		G	GS	CG	GF	IP	BFP	H	R	ER	HR	SH	SF	HB	TBB	IBB	SO	WP	Bk	W	L	Pct	ShO	Sv-Op	Hld	ERC	ERA
2003 St Louis	NL	33	32	2	0	202.2	903	252	126	119	35	12	3	5	57	2	114	6	0	13	9	.591	0	0-0	0	5.63	5.28
2004 San Francisco	NL	32	31	2	1	194.0	825	196	98	87	19	7	1	0	64	3	108	10	0	11	7	.611	1	0-0	0	3.82	4.04
8 ML YEARS		229	186	9	14	1236.2	5314	1273	672	622	173	57	35	25	407	37	818	43	2	73	58	.557	1	1-3	4	4.26	4.53

Mike Tonis

Bats: R **Throws:** R **Pos:** C-2   **Ht:** 6'3" **Wt:** 220 **Born:** 2/9/1979 **Age:** 26

Year Team	Lg	BATTING																	BASERUNNING				AVERAGES		
		G	AB	H	2B	3B	HR	(Hm | Rd)	TB	R	RBI	RC	TBB	IBB	SO	HBP	SH	SF	SB	CS	SB%	GDP	Avg	OBP	Slg
2000 Chrlstn - WV	A	28	100	20	8	0	0	(- | -)	28	10	17	7	9	1	22	1	1	2	1	0	1.00	1	.200	.268	.280
2000 Omaha	AAA	2	8	4	0	0	0	(- | -)	4	1	3	1	0	0	3	0	0	0	0	0	-	0	.500	.500	.500
2001 Wilmington	A+	33	123	31	8	0	3	(- | -)	48	15	18	15	15	0	34	2	2	0	0	0	-	6	.252	.343	.390
2001 Wichita	AA	63	226	61	11	1	9	(- | -)	101	36	43	33	22	2	41	4	0	1	1	1	.50	7	.270	.344	.447
2002 Royals	R	6	17	3	0	0	1	(- | -)	6	2	3	2	2	0	3	1	0	0	0	0	-	0	.176	.300	.353
2003 Wichita	AA	87	307	73	18	0	2	(- | -)	97	34	24	25	23	1	52	3	7	2	3	1	.75	14	.238	.296	.316
2004 Wichita	AA	78	263	60	13	1	3	(- | -)	84	24	29	22	23	1	53	1	1	4	0	0	-	10	.228	.289	.319
2004 Kansas City	AL	2	6	0	0	0	0	(0 | 0)	0	0	0	0	1	0	0	0	0	0	0	0	-	1	.000	.143	.000

Tony Torcato

Bats: L **Throws:** R **Pos:** PH-12; PR-1   **Ht:** 6'1" **Wt:** 195 **Born:** 10/25/1979 **Age:** 25

Year Team	Lg	BATTING																	BASERUNNING				AVERAGES		
		G	AB	H	2B	3B	HR	(Hm | Rd)	TB	R	RBI	RC	TBB	IBB	SO	HBP	SH	SF	SB	CS	SB%	GDP	Avg	OBP	Slg
2004 Fresno	AAA	119	395	114	22	0	3	(- | -)	145	39	57	45	11	1	35	5	3	3	4	1	.80	8	.289	.314	.367
2002 San Francisco	NL	5	11	3	1	0	0	(0 | 0)	4	0	0	0	0	0	2	0	0	0	0	0	-	0	.273	.273	.364
2003 San Francisco	NL	14	16	3	1	0	0	(0 | 0)	4	0	1	1	0	0	4	1	1	0	0	0	-	0	.188	.235	.250
2004 San Francisco	NL	13	9	5	0	0	0	(0 | 0)	5	1	2	3	1	0	0	1	0	1	0	0	-	0	.556	.583	.556
3 ML YEARS		32	36	11	2	0	0	(0 | 0)	13	1	3	4	1	0	6	2	1	1	0	0	-	0	.306	.350	.361

Yorvit Torrealba

Bats: R **Throws:** R **Pos:** C-59; PH-4; PR-4   **Ht:** 5'11" **Wt:** 180 **Born:** 7/19/1978 **Age:** 26

Year Team	Lg	BATTING																	BASERUNNING				AVERAGES		
		G	AB	H	2B	3B	HR	(Hm | Rd)	TB	R	RBI	RC	TBB	IBB	SO	HBP	SH	SF	SB	CS	SB%	GDP	Avg	OBP	Slg
2001 San Francisco	NL	3	4	2	0	1	0	(0 | 0)	4	0	2	2	0	0	0	0	0	0	0	0	-	0	.500	.500	1.000
2002 San Francisco	NL	53	136	38	10	0	2	(0 | 2)	54	17	14	15	14	2	20	2	3	0	0	0	-	11	.279	.355	.397
2003 San Francisco	NL	66	200	52	10	2	4	(3 | 1)	78	22	29	25	14	1	39	2	3	2	1	0	1.00	3	.260	.312	.390
2004 San Francisco	NL	64	172	39	7	3	6	(3 | 3)	70	19	23	18	17	3	31	2	4	1	2	0	1.00	7	.227	.302	.407
4 ML YEARS		186	512	131	27	6	12	(6 | 6)	206	58	68	60	45	6	90	6	10	3	3	0	1.00	21	.256	.322	.402

Andres Torres

Bats: B **Throws:** R **Pos:** PR-2; CF-1; DH-1   **Ht:** 5'10" **Wt:** 175 **Born:** 1/26/1978 **Age:** 27

Year Team	Lg	BATTING																	BASERUNNING				AVERAGES		
		G	AB	H	2B	3B	HR	(Hm | Rd)	TB	R	RBI	RC	TBB	IBB	SO	HBP	SH	SF	SB	CS	SB%	GDP	Avg	OBP	Slg
2004 Bristol*	R+	6	22	8	0	0	1	(- | -)	11	8	2	6	3	0	4	1	1	0	5	0	1.00	0	.364	.462	.500
2004 Charlotte*	AAA	87	322	95	11	4	8	(- | -)	138	49	26	55	35	0	74	5	7	2	23	7	.77	3	.295	.371	.429
2002 Detroit	AL	19	70	14	1	1	0	(0 | 0)	17	7	3	2	6	0	16	1	0	2	2	2	.50	2	.200	.266	.243
2003 Detroit	AL	59	168	37	4	3	1	(1 | 0)	50	23	9	9	10	0	35	0	6	1	5	5	.50	5	.220	.263	.298
2004 Detroit	AL	3	0	0	0	0	0	(0 | 0)	0	1	0	0	0	0	0	0	0	0	1	0	1.00	0	-	-	-
3 ML YEARS		81	238	51	5	4	1	(1 | 0)	67	31	12	11	16	0	51	1	6	3	8	7	.53	7	.214	.264	.282

Salomon Torres

Pitches: R **Bats:** R **Pos:** RP-84   **Ht:** 5'11" **Wt:** 165 **Born:** 3/11/1972 **Age:** 33

Year Team	Lg	HOW MUCH HE PITCHED						WHAT HE GAVE UP													THE RESULTS							
		G	GS	CG	GF	IP	BFP	H	R	ER	HR	SH	SF	HB	TBB	IBB	SO	WP	Bk	W	L	Pct	ShO	Sv-Op	Hld	ERC	ERA
1993 San Francisco	NL	8	8	0	0	44.2	196	37	21	20	5	7	1	1	27	3	23	3	1	3	5	.375	0	0-0	0	3.95	4.03
1994 San Francisco	NL	16	14	1	2	84.1	378	95	55	51	10	4	8	7	34	2	42	4	1	2	8	.200	0	0-0	0	5.29	5.44
1995 SF-Sea		20	14	1	4	80.0	384	100	61	56	16	1	0	2	49	3	47	1	2	3	9	.250	0	0-0	0	7.30	6.30
1996 Seattle	AL	10	7	1	1	49.0	212	44	27	25	5	3	1	3	23	2	36	1	0	3	3	.500	1	0-0	0	3.98	4.59
1997 Sea-Mon		14	0	0	4	25.2	127	32	29	28	2	3	1	3	15	0	11	3	0	0	0	-	0	0-0	0	6.44	9.82
2002 Pittsburgh	NL	5	5	0	0	30.0	127	28	10	9	2	2	0	3	13	1	12	0	0	2	1	.667	0	0-0	0	4.07	2.70
2003 Pittsburgh	NL	41	16	0	7	121.0	519	128	65	64	19	4	1	7	42	5	84	3	0	7	5	.583	0	2-3	6	4.87	4.76
2004 Pittsburgh	NL	84	0	0	20	92.0	380	87	33	27	6	9	3	6	22	6	62	5	0	7	7	.500	0	0-4	30	3.12	2.64
1995 San Francisco	NL	4	1	0	2	8.0	40	13	8	8	4	0	0	0	7	0	2	0	0	0	1	.000	0	0-0	0	15.31	9.00
1995 Seattle	AL	16	13	1	2	72.0	344	87	53	48	12	1	0	2	42	3	45	1	2	3	8	.273	0	0-0	0	6.55	6.00
1997 Seattle	AL	2	0	0	1	3.1	21	7	10	10	0	0	0	1	3	0	0	0	0	0	0	-	0	0-0	0	13.67	27.00
1997 Montreal	NL	12	0	0	3	22.1	106	25	19	18	2	3	1	2	12	0	11	3	0	0	0	-	0	0-0	0	5.47	7.25
8 ML YEARS		198	64	3	38	526.2	2323	551	301	280	65	33	15	32	225	22	317	20	4	27	38	.415	1	2-7	36	4.82	4.78

Josh Towers

Pitches: R **Bats:** R **Pos:** SP-21   **Ht:** 6'1" **Wt:** 165 **Born:** 2/26/1977 **Age:** 28

Year Team	Lg	HOW MUCH HE PITCHED						WHAT HE GAVE UP													THE RESULTS							
		G	GS	CG	GF	IP	BFP	H	R	ER	HR	SH	SF	HB	TBB	IBB	SO	WP	Bk	W	L	Pct	ShO	Sv-Op	Hld	ERC	ERA
2004 Syracuse*	AAA	6	5	0	0	36.0	139	33	11	10	5	2	0	1	7	0	25	2	0	3	1	.750	0	0- -	-	3.25	2.50
2001 Baltimore	AL	24	20	1	2	140.1	586	165	74	70	21	3	4	6	16	0	58	1	0	8	10	.444	1	0-0	0	4.51	4.49
2002 Baltimore	AL	5	3	0	1	27.1	124	42	24	24	11	1	2	0	5	0	13	1	0	0	3	.000	0	0-0	0	9.00	7.90

Year Team	Lg	G	GS	CG	GF	IP	BFP	H	R	ER	HR	SH	SF	HB	TBB	IBB	SO	WP	Bk	W	L	Pct	ShO	Sv-Op	Hld	ERC	ERA
						HOW MUCH HE PITCHED					WHAT HE GAVE UP											THE RESULTS					
2003 Toronto	AL	14	8	1	2	64.1	265	67	34	32	15	0	2	4	7	1	42	1	0	8	1	.889	0	1-1	0	4.26	4.48
2004 Toronto	AL	21	21	0	0	116.1	518	148	70	66	16	2	4	9	26	4	51	0	1	9	9	.500	0	0-0	0	5.50	5.11
4 ML YEARS		64	52	2	5	348.1	1493	422	202	192	63	6	12	19	54	5	164	3	1	25	23	.521	1	1-1	0	5.12	4.96

Billy Traber

Pitches: L **Bats:** L **Pos:** SP **Ht:** 6'5" **Wt:** 205 **Born:** 9/18/1979 **Age:** 25

Year Team	Lg	G	GS	CG	GF	IP	BFP	H	R	ER	HR	SH	SF	HB	TBB	IBB	SO	WP	Bk	W	L	Pct	ShO	Sv-Op	Hld	ERC	ERA
2001 St. Lucie	A+	18	18	0	0	101.2	415	85	36	30	2	3	2	5	23	0	79	4	1	6	5	.545	0	0--	-	2.22	2.66
2001 Binghamton	AA	8	8	0	0	42.2	188	50	25	21	4	1	3	2	13	1	45	4	1	4	3	.571	0	0--	-	4.80	4.43
2001 Norfolk	AAA	1	1	0	0	7.0	26	5	3	1	0	0	0	0	0	0	1	1	1	0	1	.000	0	0--	-	1.04	1.29
2002 Akron	AA	18	17	2	0	107.2	436	99	38	33	8	1	0	7	20	0	82	2	0	13	2	.867	1	0--	-	2.95	2.76
2002 Buffalo	AAA	9	9	0	0	54.2	229	58	22	20	3	1	4	2	12	0	33	1	1	4	3	.571	0	0--	-	3.58	3.29
2003 Cleveland	AL	33	18	1	0	111.2	503	132	67	65	15	4	3	5	40	4	88	5	0	6	9	.400	1	0-0	1	5.31	5.24

Steve Trachsel

Pitches: R **Bats:** R **Pos:** SP-33 **Ht:** 6'4" **Wt:** 205 **Born:** 10/31/1970 **Age:** 34

Year Team	Lg	G	GS	CG	GF	IP	BFP	H	R	ER	HR	SH	SF	HB	TBB	IBB	SO	WP	Bk	W	L	Pct	ShO	Sv-Op	Hld	ERC	ERA
1993 Chicago	NL	3	3	0	0	19.2	78	16	10	10	4	1	1	0	3	0	14	1	0	0	2	.000	0	0-0	0	2.71	4.58
1994 Chicago	NL	22	22	1	0	146.0	612	133	57	52	19	3	3	3	54	4	108	6	0	9	7	.563	0	0-0	0	3.74	3.21
1995 Chicago	NL	30	29	2	0	160.2	722	174	104	92	25	12	5	0	76	8	117	2	1	7	13	.350	0	0-0	0	5.13	5.15
1996 Chicago	NL	31	31	3	0	205.0	845	181	82	69	30	3	3	8	62	3	132	5	2	13	9	.591	2	0-0	0	3.52	3.03
1997 Chicago	NL	34	34	0	0	201.1	878	225	110	101	32	8	11	5	69	6	160	4	1	8	12	.400	0	0-0	0	5.04	4.51
1998 Chicago	NL	33	33	1	0	208.0	894	204	107	103	27	9	7	8	84	5	149	3	2	15	8	.652	0	0-0	0	4.35	4.46
1999 Chicago	NL	34	34	4	0	205.2	894	226	133	127	32	6	14	3	64	4	149	8	3	8	18	.308	0	0-0	0	4.69	5.56
2000 TB-Tor	AL	34	34	3	0	200.2	882	232	116	107	26	6	6	6	74	2	110	4	0	8	15	.348	1	0-0	0	5.25	4.80
2001 New York	NL	28	28	1	0	173.2	726	180	90	86	28	8	7	3	47	7	144	4	0	11	13	.458	1	0-0	0	3.80	4.46
2002 New York	NL	30	30	1	0	173.2	741	170	80	65	16	9	3	0	69	4	105	4	0	11	11	.500	1	0-0	0	3.88	3.37
2003 New York	NL	33	33	2	0	204.2	857	204	90	86	26	8	3	8	65	9	111	5	2	16	10	.615	2	0-0	0	3.97	3.78
2004 New York	NL	33	33	0	0	202.2	881	203	104	90	25	11	8	5	83	9	117	4	2	12	13	.480	0	0-0	0	4.31	4.00
2000 Tampa Bay	AL	23	23	3	0	137.2	606	160	76	70	16	2	5	6	49	1	78	3	0	6	10	.375	1	0-0	0	5.19	4.58
2000 Toronto	AL	11	11	0	0	63.0	276	72	40	37	10	4	1	0	25	1	32	1	0	2	5	.286	0	0-0	0	5.38	5.29
12 ML YEARS		345	344	18	0	2101.2	9010	2136	1083	988	290	84	76	44	750	61	1416	50	13	118	131	.474	7	0-0	0	4.32	4.23

Andy Tracy

Bats: L **Throws:** R **Pos:** PH-14; 3B-1 **Ht:** 6'3" **Wt:** 220 **Born:** 12/11/1973 **Age:** 31

Year Team	Lg	G	AB	H	2B	3B	HR	(Hm	Rd)	TB	R	RBI	RC	TBB	IBB	SO	HBP	SH	SF	SB	CS	SB%	GDP	Avg	OBP	Slg
				BATTING																BASERUNNING				AVERAGES		
1996 Vermont	A-	57	175	47	11	1	4	(-	-)	72	26	24	27	32	2	37	2	1	2	1	1	.50	8	.269	.384	.411
1997 Cape Fear	A	59	210	63	9	2	8	(-	-)	100	31	43	36	21	4	27	2	0	2	6	1	.86	4	.300	.366	.476
1998 Jupiter	A+	71	251	118	16	1	11	(-	-)	169	37	53	81	39	3	69	3	0	5	6	4	.60	3	.470	.537	.673
1998 Harrisburg	AA	62	211	48	12	3	10	(-	-)	96	33	33	28	24	3	62	4	0	3	1	2	.33	5	.227	.314	.455
1999 Harrisburg	AA	134	493	135	26	2	37	(-	-)	276	96	128	97	70	4	139	6	1	3	6	1	.86	10	.274	.369	.560
2000 Ottawa	AAA	55	195	60	18	0	10	(-	-)	108	28	36	42	34	3	63	2	0	3	2	2	.50	2	.308	.410	.554
2001 Ottawa	AAA	53	190	39	11	1	4	(-	-)	64	17	19	19	24	1	72	2	0	1	4	2	.67	2	.205	.300	.337
2002 Norfolk	AAA	125	432	86	16	1	20	(-	-)	164	61	61	49	56	2	123	3	0	0	4	1	.80	4	.199	.295	.380
2003 Tulsa	AA	106	384	115	24	1	25	(-	-)	216	75	62	76	41	4	116	4	1	2	3	3	.50	1	.299	.371	.563
2004 Co Springs	AAA	126	464	146	42	3	33	(-	-)	293	98	120	103	58	3	115	2	1	4	4	2	.67	8	.315	.390	.631
2004 Colorado	NL	15	16	3	1	0	0	(0	0)	4	1	1	1	1	0	8	0	0	0	0	0	-	0	.188	.235	.250

Chad Tracy

Bats: L **Throws:** R **Pos:** 3B-134; 1B-11; PH-10; LF-1 **Ht:** 6'2" **Wt:** 200 **Born:** 5/22/1980 **Age:** 25

Year Team	Lg	G	AB	H	2B	3B	HR	(Hm	Rd)	TB	R	RBI	RC	TBB	IBB	SO	HBP	SH	SF	SB	CS	SB%	GDP	Avg	OBP	Slg
				BATTING																BASERUNNING				AVERAGES		
2001 Yakima	A-	10	36	10	1	0	0	(-	-)	11	2	5	4	3	0	5	1	0	0	1	0	1.00	1	.278	.350	.306
2001 South Bend	A	54	215	73	11	0	4	(-	-)	96	43	36	38	19	2	19	2	0	3	3	0	1.00	4	.340	.393	.447
2002 El Paso	AA	129	514	177	39	5	8	(-	-)	250	80	74	93	39	7	51	4	1	7	2	3	.40	10	.344	.390	.486
2003 Tucson	AAA	133	522	169	31	4	10	(-	-)	238	91	80	89	41	3	52	4	0	9	0	2	.00	7	.324	.372	.456
2004 Tucson	AAA	11	40	16	4	0	2	(-	-)	26	7	11	12	8	1	5	0	0	1	2	0	1.00	4	.400	.490	.650
2004 Arizona	NL	143	481	137	29	3	8	(6	2)	196	45	53	53	45	3	60	0	1	5	2	3	.40	11	.285	.343	.407

Matt Treanor

Bats: R **Throws:** R **Pos:** C-27; PH-3 **Ht:** 6'2" **Wt:** 220 **Born:** 3/3/1976 **Age:** 29

Year Team	Lg	G	AB	H	2B	3B	HR	(Hm	Rd)	TB	R	RBI	RC	TBB	IBB	SO	HBP	SH	SF	SB	CS	SB%	GDP	Avg	OBP	Slg
				BATTING																BASERUNNING				AVERAGES		
1994 Royals	R	46	99	18	5	0	1	(-	-)	26	17	12	8	14	1	23	3	1	1	1	1	.50	2	.182	.299	.263
1995 Springfield	A	75	211	39	6	2	3	(-	-)	58	17	19	16	21	0	59	4	2	2	1	1	.50	1	.185	.269	.275
1996 Lansing	A	119	384	100	18	2	6	(-	-)	140	56	33	49	35	1	63	13	6	1	5	3	.63	9	.260	.342	.365
1997 Wilmington	A+	80	257	51	6	1	5	(-	-)	74	22	25	18	25	0	59	2	6	0	1	6	.14	4	.198	.275	.288
1997 Brevard Cnty	A+	23	70	15	4	1	0	(-	-)	21	11	3	8	12	0	14	2	1	0	0	0	-	1	.214	.345	.300
1998 Brevard Cnty	A+	80	243	57	8	0	3	(-	-)	74	24	28	29	38	0	45	5	1	3	3	2	.60	4	.235	.346	.305
1999 Kane County	A	86	308	88	21	1	10	(-	-)	141	56	53	54	36	0	65	15	2	2	4	1	.80	9	.286	.385	.458
2000 Brevard Cnty	A+	109	350	86	17	0	3	(-	-)	112	51	37	45	48	0	65	14	4	3	3	3	.50	6	.246	.357	.320
2001 Portland	AA	35	89	14	2	0	2	(-	-)	22	7	8	8	13	0	18	9	2	0	1	1	.50	2	.157	.324	.247
2001 Marlins	R	11	34	14	4	0	1	(-	-)	21	10	4	10	7	0	7	0	0	0	3	0	1.00	1	.412	.512	.618
2001 Kane County	A	1	1	1	0	0	0	(-	-)	1	2	0	1	3	0	0	0	0	0	0	0	-	0	1.000	1.000	1.000
2002 Portland	AA	50	156	39	5	1	9	(-	-)	73	24	28	29	28	0	33	7	1	0	3	0	1.00	4	.250	.387	.468

243

Year Team	Lg	G	AB	H	2B	3B	HR	(Hm	Rd)	TB	R	RBI	RC	TBB	IBB	SO	HBP	SH	SF	SB	CS	SB%	GDP	Avg	OBP	Slg
2002 Calgary	AAA	36	95	27	8	0	1	(-	-)	38	10	18	14	12	0	13	5	0	0	1	1	.50	4	.284	.393	.400
2003 Albuquerque	AAA	98	315	86	18	1	11	(-	-)	139	45	40	54	39	1	44	17	1	3	9	4	.69	8	.273	.380	.441
2004 Albuquerque	AAA	62	198	51	8	0	8	(-	-)	83	32	38	35	34	1	44	10	2	3	2	0	1.00	5	.258	.388	.419
2004 Florida	NL	29	55	13	2	0	0	(0	0)	15	7	1	4	4	0	13	2	0	0	0	0	-	3	.236	.311	.273

Chris Tremie

Bats: R **Throws:** R **Pos:** C-1   **Ht:** 6'0" **Wt:** 210 **Born:** 10/17/1969 **Age:** 35

Year Team	Lg	G	AB	H	2B	3B	HR	(Hm	Rd)	TB	R	RBI	RC	TBB	IBB	SO	HBP	SH	SF	SB	CS	SB%	GDP	Avg	OBP	Slg
2004 New Orleans*	AAA	70	195	47	6	1	2	(-	-)	61	23	24	21	24	1	30	5	0	5	0	1	.00	7	.241	.332	.313
1995 Chicago	AL	10	24	4	0	0	0	(0	0)	4	0	0	0	1	0	2	0	1	0	0	0	-	0	.167	.200	.167
1998 Texas	AL	2	3	1	1	0	0	(0	0)	2	2	0	0	1	0	1	0	0	0	0	0	-	0	.333	.500	.667
1999 Pittsburgh	NL	9	14	1	0	0	0	(0	0)	1	1	1	0	2	0	4	0	0	0	0	0	-	0	.071	.188	.071
2004 Houston	NL	1	0	0	0	0	0	(0	0)	0	0	0	0	0	0	0	0	0	0	0	0	-	0	-	-	-
4 ML YEARS		22	41	6	1	0	0	(0	0)	7	3	1	0	4	0	7	0	1	0	0	0	-	0	.146	.222	.171

Chin-hui Tsao

Pitches: R **Bats:** R **Pos:** RP-10   **Ht:** 6'2" **Wt:** 177 **Born:** 6/2/1981 **Age:** 24

Year Team	Lg	G	GS	CG	GF	IP	BFP	H	R	ER	HR	SH	SF	HB	TBB	IBB	SO	WP	Bk	W	L	Pct	ShO	Sv-Op	Hld	ERC	ERA
2000 Asheville	A	24	24	0	0	145.0	591	119	54	44	8	3	2	5	40	0	187	6	1	11	8	.579	0	0- -	-	2.50	2.73
2001 Salem	A+	4	4	0	0	17.1	78	23	11	9	1	2	1	1	5	0	18	1	1	0	4	.000	0	0- -	-	5.52	4.67
2002 Tri-City	A-	3	3	0	1	11.0	42	6	2	0	0	0	0	0	2	0	16	2	1	0	0	-	0	0- -	-	0.91	0.00
2002 Salem	A+	9	9	0	0	47.1	180	34	13	11	3	1	0	0	12	0	45	2	1	4	2	.667	0	0- -	-	1.97	2.09
2003 Tulsa	AA	18	18	0	0	113.1	446	88	34	31	7	2	2	5	26	0	125	3	3	11	4	.733	0	0- -	-	2.25	2.46
2004 Asheville	A	2	2	0	0	10.0	37	8	2	2	1	0	0	0	1	0	14	1	0	1	0	1.000	0	0- -	-	2.05	1.80
2004 Tulsa	AA	2	2	0	0	13.0	51	12	4	4	1	1	1	0	2	0	10	0	0	1	1	.500	0	0- -	-	2.66	2.77
2004 Co Springs	AAA	4	4	0	0	12.2	64	22	12	12	5	0	1	0	5	0	14	0	0	1	1	.500	0	0- -	-	11.31	8.53
2003 Colorado	NL	9	8	0	1	43.1	196	48	30	29	11	3	0	4	20	1	29	0	0	3	3	.500	0	0-0	-	6.56	6.02
2004 Colorado	NL	10	0	0	5	9.1	37	7	4	4	2	1	0	0	1	0	11	0	0	0	0	-	0	1-2	1	2.21	3.86
2 ML YEARS		19	8	0	6	52.2	233	55	34	33	13	4	0	4	21	1	40	0	0	3	3	.500	0	1-2	1	5.70	5.64

Michael Tucker

Bats: L **Throws:** R **Pos:** RF-105; CF-25; PH-19; PR-1   **Ht:** 6'2" **Wt:** 195 **Born:** 6/25/1971 **Age:** 34

Year Team	Lg	G	AB	H	2B	3B	HR	(Hm	Rd)	TB	R	RBI	RC	TBB	IBB	SO	HBP	SH	SF	SB	CS	SB%	GDP	Avg	OBP	Slg
1995 Kansas City	AL	62	177	46	10	0	4	(1	3)	68	23	17	22	18	2	51	1	2	0	2	3	.40	3	.260	.332	.384
1996 Kansas City	AL	108	339	88	18	4	12	(2	10)	150	55	53	53	40	1	69	7	3	4	10	4	.71	7	.260	.346	.442
1997 Atlanta	NL	138	499	141	25	7	14	(5	9)	222	80	56	76	44	0	116	6	4	1	12	7	.63	7	.283	.347	.445
1998 Atlanta	NL	130	414	101	27	3	13	(10	3)	173	54	46	58	49	10	112	3	1	2	8	3	.73	4	.244	.327	.418
1999 Cincinnati	NL	133	296	75	8	5	11	(5	6)	126	55	44	44	37	3	81	3	0	4	11	4	.73	5	.253	.338	.426
2000 Cincinnati	NL	148	270	72	13	4	15	(7	8)	138	55	36	53	44	1	64	7	0	2	13	6	.68	6	.267	.381	.511
2001 Cin-ChC	NL	149	436	110	19	8	12	(4	8)	181	62	61	59	46	4	102	2	10	6	16	8	.67	8	.252	.322	.415
2002 Kansas City	AL	144	475	118	27	6	12	(10	2)	193	65	56	64	56	1	105	3	7	2	23	9	.72	5	.248	.330	.406
2003 Kansas City	AL	104	389	102	20	5	13	(8	5)	171	61	55	60	39	3	88	2	6	2	8	10	.44	8	.262	.331	.440
2004 San Francisco	NL	140	464	119	21	6	13	(4	9)	191	77	62	68	70	3	106	2	6	5	5	2	.71	5	.256	.353	.412
2001 Cincinnati	NL	86	231	56	10	1	7	(1	6)	89	31	30	28	23	1	55	1	5	5	12	5	.71	4	.242	.308	.385
2001 Chicago	NL	63	205	54	9	7	5	(3	2)	92	31	31	31	23	3	47	1	5	1	4	3	.57	4	.263	.339	.449
10 ML YEARS		1256	3759	972	188	48	119	(56	63)	1613	587	486	557	443	28	894	36	39	28	108	56	.66	58	.259	.340	.429

T.J. Tucker

Pitches: R **Bats:** R **Pos:** RP-53; SP-1   **Ht:** 6'3" **Wt:** 245 **Born:** 8/20/1978 **Age:** 26

Year Team	Lg	G	GS	CG	GF	IP	BFP	H	R	ER	HR	SH	SF	HB	TBB	IBB	SO	WP	Bk	W	L	Pct	ShO	Sv-Op	Hld	ERC	ERA
2004 Edmonton*	AAA	3	3	0	0	16.2	81	26	15	9	3	0	0	0	5	0	3	1	0	2	0	1.000	0	0- -	-	7.54	4.86
2000 Montreal	NL	2	2	0	0	7.0	35	11	9	9	5	0	0	0	3	0	2	1	0	0	1	.000	0	0-0	0	12.90	11.57
2002 Montreal	NL	57	0	0	19	61.1	278	69	32	28	5	5	2	0	31	9	42	4	0	6	3	.667	0	4-7	17	4.80	4.11
2003 Montreal	NL	45	7	0	7	80.0	349	90	49	42	8	0	1	4	20	1	47	1	0	2	3	.400	0	0-2	3	4.33	4.73
2004 Montreal	NL	54	1	0	15	67.2	291	73	28	28	5	3	2	4	17	6	44	1	1	4	2	.667	0	0-2	3	3.83	3.72
4 ML YEARS		158	10	0	41	216.0	953	243	118	107	23	8	5	8	71	16	135	7	1	12	9	.571	0	4-11	23	4.55	4.46

Derrick Turnbow

Pitches: R **Bats:** R **Pos:** RP-4   **Ht:** 6'3" **Wt:** 200 **Born:** 1/25/1978 **Age:** 27

Year Team	Lg	G	GS	CG	GF	IP	BFP	H	R	ER	HR	SH	SF	HB	TBB	IBB	SO	WP	Bk	W	L	Pct	ShO	Sv-Op	Hld	ERC	ERA
2004 Salt Lake*	AAA	46	3	0	23	74.2	336	75	46	42	8	2	3	3	42	0	56	7	0	2	6	.250	0	6- -	-	4.97	5.06
2000 Anaheim	AL	24	1	0	0	38.0	181	36	0	20	7	0	0	0	36	0	25	0	0	0	0	-	0	0-0	0	6.74	4.74
2003 Anaheim	AL	11	0	0	7	15.1	53	7	1	1	0	0	0	0	3	0	15	0	0	2	0	1.000	0	0-0	0	0.79	0.59
2004 Anaheim	AL	4	0	0	4	6.1	26	2	0	0	0	0	0	0	7	0	3	0	0	0	0	-	0	0-0	0	2.47	0.00
3 ML YEARS		39	1	0	11	59.2	260	45	1	21	7	0	0	0	46	0	43	0	0	2	0	1.000	0	0-0	0	4.36	3.17

B.J. Upton

Bats: R **Throws:** R **Pos:** SS-16; 3B-13; DH-13; PH-3; LF-1 **Ht:** 6'3" **Wt:** 180 **Born:** 8/21/1984 **Age:** 20

						BATTING														BASERUNNING				AVERAGES		
Year Team	Lg	G	AB	H	2B	3B	HR	(Hm	Rd)	TB	R	RBI	RC	TBB	IBB	SO	HBP	SH	SF	SB	CS	SB%	GDP	Avg	OBP	Slg
2003 Chrlstn - SC	A	101	384	116	22	6	7	(-	-)	171	70	46	69	57	0	80	5	1	6	38	17	.69	8	.302	.394	.445
2003 Orlando	AA	29	105	29	8	0	1	(-	-)	40	14	16	15	16	0	25	2	2	2	2	4	.33	1	.276	.376	.381
2004 Montgomery	AA	29	104	34	7	1	2	(-	-)	49	21	15	20	14	1	28	0	2	0	3	0	1.00	0	.327	.407	.471
2004 Durham	AAA	69	264	82	17	1	12	(-	-)	137	65	36	54	42	0	72	3	4	0	17	5	.77	9	.311	.411	.519
2004 Tampa Bay	AL	45	159	41	8	2	4	(2	2)	65	19	12	22	15	0	46	1	1	1	4	1	.80	1	.258	.324	.409

Ugueth Urbina

Pitches: R **Bats:** R **Pos:** RP-54 **Ht:** 6'0" **Wt:** 205 **Born:** 2/15/1974 **Age:** 31

		HOW MUCH HE PITCHED						WHAT HE GAVE UP										THE RESULTS						
Year Team	Lg	G	GS	CG	GF	IP	BFP	H	R	ER	HR	SH	SF	HB	TBB	IBB	SO	WP	Bk	W	L	Pct	ShO	Sv-Op	Hld	ERC	ERA
2004 Lakeland*	A+	2	0	0	0	2.0	11	3	3	0	0	0	0	0	0	0	1	0	0	0	0	-	0	0- -	-	3.55	0.00
1995 Montreal	NL	7	4	0	0	23.1	109	26	17	16	6	2	0	0	14	1	15	2	0	2	2	.500	0	0-0	0	6.66	6.17
1996 Montreal	NL	33	17	0	2	114.0	484	102	54	47	18	1	3	1	44	4	108	3	1	10	5	.667	0	0-1	6	3.78	3.71
1997 Montreal	NL	63	0	0	50	64.1	276	52	29	27	9	3	0	1	29	2	84	2	0	5	8	.385	0	27-32	1	3.42	3.78
1998 Montreal	NL	64	0	0	59	69.1	272	37	11	10	2	2	1	0	33	2	94	3	2	6	3	.667	0	34-38	0	1.59	1.30
1999 Montreal	NL	71	0	0	62	75.2	323	59	35	31	6	1	2	0	36	6	100	6	0	6	6	.500	0	41-50	0	2.85	3.69
2000 Montreal	NL	13	0	0	11	13.1	54	11	6	6	1	0	0	0	5	0	22	1	0	0	1	.000	0	8-10	0	2.95	4.05
2001 Mon-Bos		64	0	0	53	66.2	278	58	29	27	9	2	1	0	24	1	89	2	1	2	2	.500	0	24-28	3	3.41	3.65
2002 Boston	AL	61	0	0	55	60.0	242	44	21	20	8	1	3	0	20	5	71	3	1	1	6	.143	0	40-46	0	2.50	3.00
2003 Tex-Fla		72	0	0	48	77.0	316	56	25	24	8	6	5	0	31	2	78	4	1	3	4	.429	0	32-38	11	2.60	2.81
2004 Detroit	AL	54	0	0	46	54.0	234	38	28	27	7	1	2	3	32	3	56	2	0	4	6	.400	0	21-24	0	3.47	4.50
2001 Montreal	NL	45	0	0	40	46.2	201	42	24	22	8	1	1	0	21	1	57	2	1	2	1	.667	0	15-18	1	4.13	4.24
2001 Boston	AL	19	0	0	13	20.0	77	16	5	5	1	1	0	0	3	0	32	0	0	0	1	.000	0	9-10	2	1.88	2.25
2003 Texas	AL	39	0	0	37	38.2	167	33	19	18	6	4	3	0	18	2	41	2	1	0	4	.000	0	26-30	0	3.74	4.19
2003 Florida	NL	33	0	0	11	38.1	149	23	6	6	2	2	2	0	13	0	37	2	0	3	0	1.000	0	6-8	11	1.61	1.41
10 ML YEARS		502	21	0	386	617.2	2588	483	255	235	74	19	17	5	268	26	717	28	6	39	43	.476	0	227-267	21	3.09	3.42

Lino Urdaneta

Pitches: R **Bats:** R **Pos:** RP-1 **Ht:** 6'1" **Wt:** 168 **Born:** 11/20/1979 **Age:** 25

		HOW MUCH HE PITCHED						WHAT HE GAVE UP										THE RESULTS						
Year Team	Lg	G	GS	CG	GF	IP	BFP	H	R	ER	HR	SH	SF	HB	TBB	IBB	SO	WP	Bk	W	L	Pct	ShO	Sv-Op	Hld	ERC	ERA
1999 Vero Beach	A+	27	5	0	6	67.0	292	74	42	36	10	4	3	6	20	1	43	3	3	5	4	.556	0	0- -	-	5.01	4.84
2000 Vero Beach	A+	27	5	0	7	78.0	351	103	60	47	7	2	5	3	24	1	40	6	0	5	4	.556	0	1- -	-	5.71	5.42
2001 Wilmington	A+	10	4	0	3	23.2	110	31	23	20	7	0	2	3	11	0	16	2	0	1	2	.333	0	0- -	-	8.71	7.61
2002 Vero Beach	A+	52	0	0	50	52.1	210	39	15	14	3	2	1	2	17	3	30	3	0	2	2	.500	0	32- -	-	2.28	2.41
2002 Jacksonville	AA	1	0	0	0	1.0	6	3	0	0	0	0	0	0	1	0	1	0	0	0	0	-	0	0- -	-	22.91	0.00
2003 Jacksonville	AA	44	0	0	25	65.0	279	68	37	31	4	5	4	3	24	5	42	0	0	0	8	.000	0	6- -	-	4.06	4.29
2004 Lakeland	A+	2	2	0	0	2.1	12	5	3	3	0	0	0	0	0	0	0	2	0	0	2	.000	0	0- -	-	8.42	11.57
2004 Toledo	AAA	9	1	0	0	13.0	65	22	14	14	4	0	0	1	3	0	4	0	0	0	2	.000	0	0- -	-	9.57	9.69
2004 Detroit	AL	1	0	0	0	0.0	6	5	6	6	0	0	0	0	1	0	0	0	0	0	0	-	0	0-0	-	-	-

Juan Uribe

Bats: R **Throws:** R **Pos:** 2B-77; SS-38; 3B-27; PH-8; PR-3; DH-2 **Ht:** 5'11" **Wt:** 173 **Born:** 7/22/1979 **Age:** 25

						BATTING														BASERUNNING				AVERAGES		
Year Team	Lg	G	AB	H	2B	3B	HR	(Hm	Rd)	TB	R	RBI	RC	TBB	IBB	SO	HBP	SH	SF	SB	CS	SB%	GDP	Avg	OBP	Slg
2001 Colorado	NL	72	273	82	15	11	8	(3	5)	143	32	53	44	8	1	55	2	0	6	3	0	1.00	6	.300	.325	.524
2002 Colorado	NL	155	566	136	25	7	6	(4	2)	193	69	49	53	34	1	120	5	7	6	9	2	.82	17	.240	.286	.341
2003 Colorado	NL	87	316	80	19	3	10	(6	4)	135	45	33	45	17	0	60	3	6	1	7	2	.78	3	.253	.297	.427
2004 Chicago	AL	134	502	142	31	6	23	(16	7)	254	82	74	81	32	1	96	3	11	5	9	11	.45	10	.283	.327	.506
4 ML YEARS		448	1657	440	90	27	47	(29	18)	725	228	209	223	91	3	331	13	24	12	28	15	.65	36	.266	.307	.438

Chase Utley

Bats: L **Throws:** R **Pos:** 2B-51; PH-34; 1B-13 **Ht:** 6'1" **Wt:** 170 **Born:** 12/17/1978 **Age:** 26

						BATTING														BASERUNNING				AVERAGES		
Year Team	Lg	G	AB	H	2B	3B	HR	(Hm	Rd)	TB	R	RBI	RC	TBB	IBB	SO	HBP	SH	SF	SB	CS	SB%	GDP	Avg	OBP	Slg
2000 Batavia	A-	40	153	47	13	1	2	(-	-)	68	21	22	25	18	1	23	2	0	2	5	3	.63	3	.307	.383	.444
2001 Clearwater	A+	122	467	120	25	2	16	(-	-)	197	65	59	64	37	4	88	12	1	6	19	8	.70	6	.257	.324	.422
2002 Scrtn/WlksBr	AAA	125	464	122	39	1	17	(-	-)	214	73	70	75	46	2	89	20	0	4	8	3	.73	5	.263	.352	.461
2003 Scrtn/WlksBr	AAA	113	431	139	26	2	18	(-	-)	223	80	77	86	41	6	75	11	0	7	10	4	.71	3	.323	.390	.517
2004 Scrtn/WlksBr	AAA	33	123	35	8	1	6	(-	-)	63	23	25	22	18	1	29	0	0	2	4	2	.67	2	.285	.368	.512
2003 Philadelphia	NL	43	134	32	10	1	2	(1	1)	50	13	21	19	11	0	22	6	0	1	2	0	1.00	3	.239	.322	.373
2004 Philadelphia	NL	94	267	71	11	2	13	(8	5)	125	36	57	37	15	1	40	2	1	2	4	1	.80	5	.266	.308	.468
2 ML YEARS		137	401	103	21	3	15	(9	6)	175	49	78	56	26	1	62	8	1	3	6	1	.86	8	.257	.313	.436

Ismael Valdez

Pitches: R **Bats:** R **Pos:** SP-31; RP-3 **Ht:** 6'4" **Wt:** 225 **Born:** 8/21/1973 **Age:** 31

		HOW MUCH HE PITCHED						WHAT HE GAVE UP										THE RESULTS						
Year Team	Lg	G	GS	CG	GF	IP	BFP	H	R	ER	HR	SH	SF	HB	TBB	IBB	SO	WP	Bk	W	L	Pct	ShO	Sv-Op	Hld	ERC	ERA
1994 Los Angeles	NL	21	1	0	7	28.1	115	21	10	10	2	3	0	0	10	2	28	1	2	3	1	.750	0	0-0	4	2.25	3.18
1995 Los Angeles	NL	33	27	6	1	197.2	804	168	76	67	17	10	5	1	51	5	150	1	3	13	11	.542	2	1-1	0	2.62	3.05
1996 Los Angeles	NL	33	33	0	0	225.0	945	219	94	83	20	7	7	3	54	10	173	1	5	15	7	.682	0	0-0	0	3.18	3.32
1997 Los Angeles	NL	30	30	0	0	196.2	795	171	68	58	16	11	3	4	47	1	140	0	2	10	11	.476	2	0-0	0	2.72	2.65
1998 Los Angeles	NL	27	27	2	0	174.0	745	171	82	77	17	5	3	2	66	4	122	4	2	11	10	.524	2	0-0	0	3.89	3.98
1999 Los Angeles	NL	32	32	2	0	203.1	871	213	97	90	32	9	8	6	58	2	143	6	0	9	14	.391	1	0-0	0	4.38	3.98
2000 ChC-LA	NL	21	20	0	0	107.0	469	124	69	67	22	0	4	3	40	2	74	0	0	2	7	.222	0	0-0	0	5.89	5.64

HOW MUCH HE PITCHED								WHAT HE GAVE UP												THE RESULTS							
Year Team	Lg	G	GS	CG	GF	IP	BFP	H	R	ER	HR	SH	SF	HB	TBB	IBB	SO	WP	Bk	W	L	Pct	ShO	Sv-Op	Hld	ERC	ERA
2001 Anaheim	AL	27	27	1	0	163.2	699	177	82	81	20	3	0	8	50	3	100	3	0	9	13	.409	0	0-0	0	4.57	4.45
2002 Tex-Sea	AL	31	31	1	0	196.0	818	194	94	91	26	2	4	9	47	1	102	0	2	8	12	.400	0	0-0	0	3.80	4.18
2003 Texas	AL	22	22	0	0	115.0	511	148	83	78	23	4	7	5	29	0	47	2	0	8	8	.500	0	0-0	0	6.14	6.10
2004 SD-Fla	NL	34	31	1	2	170.0	751	202	105	98	33	10	4	2	49	3	67	1	0	14	9	.609	1	0-0	0	5.38	5.39
2000 Chicago	NL	12	12	0	0	67.0	291	71	40	40	17	0	2	2	27	2	45	0	0	2	4	.333	0	0-0	0	5.72	5.37
2000 Los Angeles	NL	9	8	0	1	40.0	178	53	29	27	5	0	2	1	13	0	29	0	0	0	3	.000	0	0-0	0	6.15	6.08
2002 Texas	AL	23	23	0	0	146.2	608	135	65	64	19	2	2	9	36	1	75	0	2	6	9	.400	0	0-0	0	3.47	3.93
2002 Seattle	AL	8	8	1	0	49.1	210	59	29	27	7	0	2	0	11	0	27	0	0	2	3	.400	0	0-0	0	4.86	4.93
2004 San Diego	NL	23	20	1	2	114.0	509	141	75	70	21	8	2	2	31	1	37	1	0	9	6	.600	1	0-0	0	5.56	5.53
2004 Florida	NL	11	11	0	0	56.0	242	61	30	28	12	2	2	0	18	2	30	0	0	5	3	.625	0	0-0	0	5.02	4.50
11 ML YEARS		311	281	13	11	1776.2	7523	1808	860	800	228	64	45	42	501	33	1146	22	16	102	103	.498	6	1-1	6	3.97	4.05

Merkin Valdez

Pitches: R Bats: R Pos: RP-2   Ht: 6'5" Wt: 208 Born: 11/10/1981 Age: 23

HOW MUCH HE PITCHED								WHAT HE GAVE UP												THE RESULTS							
Year Team	Lg	G	GS	CG	GF	IP	BFP	H	R	ER	HR	SH	SF	HB	TBB	IBB	SO	WP	Bk	W	L	Pct	ShO	Sv-Op	Hld	ERC	ERA
2002 Expos	R	12	8	1	3	68.1	266	47	18	15	0	2	1	2	12	0	76	2	0	7	3	.700	1	0--	-	1.37	1.98
2003 Hagerstown	A	26	26	2	0	156.0	617	119	42	39	11	2	1	5	49	0	166	4	0	9	5	.643	1	0--	-	2.51	2.25
2004 San Jose	A+	7	7	0	0	35.2	146	30	12	10	4	0	0	4	5	0	44	1	0	3	1	.750	0	0--	-	2.70	2.52
2004 Norwich	AA	10	7	0	1	41.2	172	35	21	20	3	1	3	0	15	0	31	1	0	1	4	.200	0	1--	-	2.88	4.32
2004 Fresno	AAA	1	1	0	0	5.0	25	6	4	4	0	1	1	0	4	0	5	0	0	0	0	-	0	0--	-	5.88	7.20
2004 San Francisco	NL	2	0	0	0	1.2	12	4	5	5	1	0	0	0	3	0	2	0	0	0	0	-	0	0-0	0	26.50	27.00

Wilson Valdez

Bats: R Throws: R Pos: SS-12; 2B-5; PH-3; PR-1   Ht: 5'11" Wt: 160 Born: 5/20/1978 Age: 27

BATTING																			BASERUNNING				AVERAGES		
Year Team	Lg	G	AB	H	2B	3B	HR	(Hm Rd)	TB	R	RBI	RC	TBB	IBB	SO	HBP	SH	SF	SB	CS	SB%	GDP	Avg	OBP	Slg
1999 Expos	R	22	82	24	2	0	0	(- -)	26	12	7	11	5	0	7	0	2	1	10	0	1.00	1	.293	.330	.317
1999 Vermont	A-	36	130	32	7	0	1	(- -)	42	19	10	10	7	0	21	0	0	1	4	3	.57	3	.246	.283	.323
2000 Vermont	A-	65	248	66	8	1	1	(- -)	79	32	30	25	17	0	32	1	3	3	16	9	.64	3	.266	.312	.319
2001 Clinton	A	59	214	54	8	1	0	(- -)	64	31	11	16	9	0	22	2	5	2	6	7	.46	5	.252	.286	.299
2001 Jupiter	A+	64	233	58	13	2	2	(- -)	81	34	19	22	10	0	33	2	10	0	7	3	.70	4	.249	.286	.348
2002 Portland	AA	114	375	98	19	5	1	(- -)	130	51	30	36	15	1	47	4	3	4	18	6	.75	12	.261	.294	.347
2003 Carolina	AA	37	144	45	6	2	0	(- -)	55	28	14	23	15	1	17	0	7	2	16	5	.76	2	.313	.373	.382
2003 Albuquerque	AAA	90	338	97	12	4	0	(- -)	117	45	18	39	19	2	37	1	12	1	33	9	.79	10	.287	.326	.346
2004 Charlotte	AAA	70	281	85	7	2	2	(- -)	102	37	15	35	12	0	40	3	15	0	13	5	.72	6	.302	.338	.363
2004 Albuquerque	AAA	66	285	91	11	3	2	(- -)	114	36	25	39	16	0	35	2	6	2	19	12	.61	8	.319	.357	.400
2004 Chicago	AL	19	43	10	1	0	1	(1 0)	14	8	4	2	2	0	5	0	1	0	1	2	.33	1	.233	.267	.326

Eric Valent

Bats: L Throws: L Pos: PH-65; LF-32; 1B-27; RF-14; PR-1   Ht: 6'0" Wt: 191 Born: 4/4/1977 Age: 28

BATTING																			BASERUNNING				AVERAGES		
Year Team	Lg	G	AB	H	2B	3B	HR	(Hm Rd)	TB	R	RBI	RC	TBB	IBB	SO	HBP	SH	SF	SB	CS	SB%	GDP	Avg	OBP	Slg
2001 Philadelphia	NL	22	41	4	2	0	0	(0 0)	6	3	1	0	4	0	11	1	0	0	0	0	-	0	.098	.196	.146
2002 Philadelphia	NL	7	10	2	0	0	0	(0 0)	2	1	0	0	0	0	3	0	0	0	0	0	-	1	.200	.200	.200
2003 Cincinnati	NL	18	42	9	0	0	0	(0 0)	9	3	1	2	2	0	9	0	0	0	0	0	-	0	.214	.250	.214
2004 New York	NL	130	270	72	15	2	13	(5 8)	130	39	34	36	28	4	61	1	0	1	0	1	.00	9	.267	.337	.481
4 ML YEARS		177	363	87	17	2	13	(5 8)	147	46	36	38	34	4	84	2	0	1	0	1	.00	10	.240	.308	.405

Javier Valentin

Bats: B Throws: R Pos: C-55; PH-23; 1B-7; PR-2   Ht: 5'10" Wt: 192 Born: 9/19/1975 Age: 29

BATTING																			BASERUNNING				AVERAGES		
Year Team	Lg	G	AB	H	2B	3B	HR	(Hm Rd)	TB	R	RBI	RC	TBB	IBB	SO	HBP	SH	SF	SB	CS	SB%	GDP	Avg	OBP	Slg
1997 Minnesota	AL	4	7	2	0	0	0	(0 0)	2	1	0	1	0	0	3	0	0	0	0	0	-	0	.286	.286	.286
1998 Minnesota	AL	55	162	32	7	1	3	(1 2)	50	11	18	10	11	1	30	0	3	1	0	0	-	7	.198	.247	.309
1999 Minnesota	AL	78	218	54	12	1	5	(2 3)	83	22	28	27	22	0	39	1	1	5	0	0	-	2	.248	.313	.381
2002 Minnesota	AL	4	4	2	0	0	0	(0 0)	2	0	0	0	0	0	0	0	0	0	0	0	-	0	.500	.500	.500
2003 Tampa Bay	AL	49	135	30	7	1	3	(2 1)	48	13	15	11	5	0	31	1	0	1	0	0	-	4	.222	.254	.356
2004 Cincinnati	NL	82	202	47	10	1	6	(2 4)	77	18	20	20	17	3	36	1	0	2	0	0	-	4	.233	.293	.381
6 ML YEARS		272	728	167	36	4	17	(7 10)	262	65	81	69	55	4	139	3	4	9	0	0	-	20	.229	.283	.360

Jose Valentin

Bats: L Throws: R Pos: SS-122; PH-5; DH-2   Ht: 5'10" Wt: 185 Born: 10/12/1969 Age: 35

BATTING																			BASERUNNING				AVERAGES		
Year Team	Lg	G	AB	H	2B	3B	HR	(Hm Rd)	TB	R	RBI	RC	TBB	IBB	SO	HBP	SH	SF	SB	CS	SB%	GDP	Avg	OBP	Slg
2004 Charlotte*	AAA	8	31	2	0	0	0	(- -)	2	1	2	0	2	0	15	0	0	0	0	0	-	0	.065	.121	.065
1992 Milwaukee	AL	4	3	0	0	0	0	(0 0)	0	1	1	0	1	0	3	0	0	0	0	0	-	0	.000	.000	.000
1993 Milwaukee	AL	19	53	13	1	2	1	(1 0)	21	10	7	8	7	1	16	1	2	0	1	0	1.00	1	.245	.344	.396
1994 Milwaukee	AL	97	285	68	19	0	11	(3 8)	120	47	46	43	38	1	75	2	4	2	12	3	.80	1	.239	.330	.421
1995 Milwaukee	AL	112	338	74	23	3	11	(8 3)	136	62	49	42	37	0	83	0	7	4	16	8	.67	0	.219	.293	.402
1996 Milwaukee	AL	154	552	143	33	7	24	(10 14)	262	90	95	91	66	9	145	0	6	4	17	4	.81	4	.259	.336	.475
1997 Milwaukee	AL	136	494	125	23	1	17	(4 13)	201	58	58	64	39	4	109	4	4	5	19	8	.70	5	.253	.310	.407
1998 Milwaukee	NL	151	428	96	24	0	16	(7 9)	168	65	49	57	63	8	105	1	2	3	10	7	.59	2	.224	.323	.393
1999 Milwaukee	NL	89	256	58	9	5	10	(3 7)	107	45	38	40	48	7	52	2	2	5	3	2	.60	3	.227	.347	.418
2000 Chicago	AL	144	568	155	37	6	25	(16 9)	279	107	92	97	59	1	106	4	13	4	19	2	.90	11	.273	.343	.491
2001 Chicago	AL	124	438	113	22	2	28	(14 14)	223	74	68	74	50	2	114	3	8	3	9	6	.60	7	.258	.336	.509
2002 Chicago	AL	135	474	118	26	4	25	(15 10)	227	70	75	75	43	2	99	2	3	5	3	3	.50	9	.249	.311	.479

							BATTING														BASERUNNING				AVERAGES		
Year Team	Lg	G	AB	H	2B	3B	HR	(Hm	Rd)	TB	R	RBI	RC	TBB	IBB	SO	HBP	SH	SF	SB	CS	SB%	GDP	Avg	OBP	Slg
2003 Chicago	AL	144	503	119	26	2	28	(14	14)	233	79	74	72	54	4	114	3	7	2	8	3	.73	6	.237	.313	.463
2004 Chicago	AL	125	450	97	20	3	30	(16	14)	213	73	70	64	43	4	139	3	6	2	8	6	.57	5	.216	.287	.473
13 ML YEARS		1434	4842	1179	263	35	226	(111	115)	2190	781	722	727	547	43	1157	25	64	40	125	52	.71	54	.243	.321	.452

Joe Valentine

Pitches: R **Bats:** R **Pos:** RP-23; SP-1 **Ht:** 6'2" **Wt:** 195 **Born:** 12/24/1979 **Age:** 25

		HOW MUCH HE PITCHED						WHAT HE GAVE UP												THE RESULTS						
Year Team	Lg	G	GS	CG	GF	IP	BFP	H	R	ER	HR	SH	SF	HB	TBB	IBB	SO	WP	Bk	W	L	Pct	ShO	Sv-Op	Hld	ERC	ERA
1999 Bristol	R+	11	0	0	7	16.2	90	27	17	13	2	0	3	3	9	0	14	1	1	0	0	-	0	0- -	-	9.21	7.02
1999 White Sox	R	3	0	0	0	4.0	14	2	0	0	0	0	0	0	1	0	2	0	0	0	0	-	0	0- -	-	1.01	0.00
2000 Bristol	R+	19	0	0	16	25.0	104	14	10	8	1	2	2	2	12	1	30	9	0	2	1	.667	0	7- -	-	1.90	2.88
2001 Kannapolis	A-	30	0	0	29	30.2	123	21	10	10	0	2	0	3	10	1	33	1	1	2	2	.500	0	14- -	-	1.89	2.93
2001 Winstn-Salm	A+	27	0	0	18	44.2	179	18	7	5	0	3	0	1	27	3	50	2	0	5	1	.833	0	8- -	-	1.32	1.01
2002 Birmingham	AA	55	0	0	48	59.1	245	36	16	13	1	3	3	1	30	3	63	6	0	4	1	.800	0	36- -	-	1.86	1.97
2003 Louisville	AAA	9	0	0	6	11.1	41	5	1	1	0	0	0	0	3	0	8	0	1	1	0	1.000	0	1- -	-	0.84	0.79
2003 Sacramento	AAA	40	0	0	23	52.1	239	44	33	28	5	1	1	2	37	3	53	9	1	1	3	.250	0	4- -	-	4.31	4.82
2004 Louisville	AAA	30	9	0	8	64.2	290	63	41	36	8	1	4	4	32	0	61	4	0	5	5	.500	0	0- -	-	4.67	5.01
2003 Cincinnati	NL	2	0	0	1	2.0	12	5	4	4	1	0	0	0	1	0	1	0	0	0	0	-	0	0-0	-	18.76	18.00
2004 Cincinnati	NL	24	1	0	13	29.1	136	23	18	17	4	0	0	2	25	1	29	2	0	2	3	.400	0	4-4	5	5.08	5.22
2 ML YEARS		26	1	0	14	31.1	148	28	22	21	5	0	0	2	26	1	30	2	0	2	3	.400	0	4-4	5	5.81	6.03

Jose Valverde

Pitches: R **Bats:** R **Pos:** RP-29 **Ht:** 6'4" **Wt:** 254 **Born:** 7/24/1979 **Age:** 25

		HOW MUCH HE PITCHED						WHAT HE GAVE UP												THE RESULTS						
Year Team	Lg	G	GS	CG	GF	IP	BFP	H	R	ER	HR	SH	SF	HB	TBB	IBB	SO	WP	Bk	W	L	Pct	ShO	Sv-Op	Hld	ERC	ERA
1999 Diamndbcks	R	20	0	0	17	28.2	138	34	21	13	1	0	0	4	10	0	47	1	1	1	2	.333	0	8- -	-	4.71	4.08
1999 South Bend	A	2	0	0	0	2.2	11	2	0	0	0	0	0	0	2	0	3	1	1	0	0	-	0	0- -	-	5.44	0.00
2000 South Bend	A	31	0	0	21	31.2	152	31	20	19	1	2	0	3	25	0	39	8	0	0	5	.000	0	14- -	-	5.26	5.40
2000 Missoula	R+	12	0	0	11	11.2	44	3	0	0	0	0	0	0	4	0	24	2	0	1	0	1.000	0	4- -	-	0.51	0.00
2001 El Paso	AA	39	0	0	28	41.1	193	36	19	18	1	1	1	4	27	0	72	6	1	2	2	.500	0	13- -	-	3.98	3.92
2002 Tucson	AAA	49	0	0	24	47.2	214	45	33	31	8	3	3	5	23	1	65	4	2	2	4	.333	0	5- -	-	4.91	5.85
2003 Tucson	AAA	22	0	0	14	29.0	127	26	11	10	1	1	2	0	14	1	26	3	0	1	1	.500	0	5- -	-	3.23	3.10
2004 Tucson	AAA	10	1	0	4	10.2	48	9	5	5	0	0	0	2	5	0	5	1	0	1	1	.500	0	3- -	-	3.37	4.22
2003 Arizona	NL	54	0	0	33	50.1	204	24	16	12	4	0	1	2	26	2	71	2	0	2	1	.667	0	10-11	3	1.77	2.15
2004 Arizona	NL	29	0	0	20	29.2	131	23	17	14	7	3	2	1	17	4	38	4	0	1	2	.333	0	8-10	5	4.25	4.25
2 ML YEARS		83	0	0	53	80.0	335	47	33	26	11	3	3	3	43	6	109	6	0	3	3	.500	0	18-21	13	2.62	2.93

John Van Benschoten

Pitches: R **Bats:** R **Pos:** SP-5; RP-1 **Ht:** 6'4" **Wt:** 217 **Born:** 4/14/1980 **Age:** 25

		HOW MUCH HE PITCHED						WHAT HE GAVE UP												THE RESULTS						
Year Team	Lg	G	GS	CG	GF	IP	BFP	H	R	ER	HR	SH	SF	HB	TBB	IBB	SO	WP	Bk	W	L	Pct	ShO	Sv-Op	Hld	ERC	ERA
2001 Williamsport	A-	9	9	0	0	25.2	104	23	11	10	0	0	0	1	10	0	19	5	0	0	2	.000	0	0- -	-	3.09	3.51
2002 Hickory	A	27	27	0	0	148.0	620	119	57	46	6	4	2	7	62	1	145	7	0	11	4	.733	0	0- -	-	2.86	2.80
2003 Lynchburg	A+	9	9	0	0	48.2	192	33	14	12	1	1	0	1	18	0	49	1	0	6	0	1.000	0	0- -	-	1.94	2.22
2003 Altoona	AA	17	17	1	0	90.1	399	95	46	37	5	4	1	6	34	1	78	2	2	7	6	.538	0	0- -	-	4.16	3.69
2004 Nashville	AAA	23	23	0	0	131.2	574	135	75	69	16	2	3	9	49	1	101	4	1	4	11	.267	0	0- -	-	4.54	4.72
2004 Pittsburgh	NL	6	5	0	0	28.2	135	33	27	22	3	2	2	2	19	0	18	1	0	1	3	.250	0	0-0	0	6.47	6.91

Todd Van Poppel

Pitches: R **Bats:** R **Pos:** RP-37; SP-11 **Ht:** 6'5" **Wt:** 240 **Born:** 12/9/1971 **Age:** 33

		HOW MUCH HE PITCHED						WHAT HE GAVE UP												THE RESULTS						
Year Team	Lg	G	GS	CG	GF	IP	BFP	H	R	ER	HR	SH	SF	HB	TBB	IBB	SO	WP	Bk	W	L	Pct	ShO	Sv-Op	Hld	ERC	ERA
1991 Oakland	AL	1	1	0	0	4.2	21	7	5	5	1	0	0	0	2	0	6	0	0	0	0	-	0	0-0	0	8.85	9.64
1993 Oakland	AL	16	16	0	0	84.0	380	76	50	47	10	1	2	2	62	0	47	3	0	6	6	.500	0	0-0	0	5.17	5.04
1994 Oakland	AL	23	23	0	0	116.2	532	108	80	79	20	4	4	3	89	2	83	3	1	7	10	.412	0	0-0	0	5.82	6.09
1995 Oakland	AL	36	14	1	10	138.1	582	125	77	75	16	3	6	4	56	1	122	4	0	4	8	.333	0	0-0	1	3.82	4.88
1996 Oak-Det	AL	37	15	1	8	99.1	491	139	107	100	24	4	7	3	62	3	53	7	0	3	9	.250	1	1-2	0	8.80	9.06
1998 Tex-Pit	AL	22	11	0	3	66.1	303	79	52	47	9	3	3	1	28	3	42	7	3	2	4	.333	0	0-0	0	5.47	6.38
2000 Chicago	NL	51	2	0	13	86.1	378	80	38	36	10	4	3	2	48	2	77	5	0	4	5	.444	0	2-5	7	4.48	3.75
2001 Chicago	NL	59	0	0	18	75.0	324	63	22	21	9	4	0	0	38	4	90	5	1	4	1	.800	0	0-0	3	3.61	2.52
2002 Texas	AL	50	0	0	19	72.2	326	80	44	44	14	1	1	3	29	1	85	8	0	3	2	.600	0	1-2	3	5.44	5.45
2003 Tex-Cin	AL	16	5	0	1	48.1	211	51	32	30	8	1	0	1	15	2	34	0	1	3	1	.750	0	0-0	1	4.43	5.59
2004 Cincinnati	NL	48	11	0	12	115.1	502	136	80	78	22	6	4	3	32	3	72	6	1	4	6	.400	0	0-1	2	5.38	6.09
1996 Oakland	AL	28	6	0	8	63.0	301	86	56	54	13	3	5	2	33	3	37	4	0	1	5	.167	0	1-2	0	7.81	7.71
1996 Detroit	AL	9	9	1	0	36.1	190	53	51	46	11	1	2	1	29	0	16	3	0	2	4	.333	1	0-0	0	10.57	11.39
1998 Texas	AL	4	4	0	0	19.1	95	26	20	19	5	0	1	1	10	0	10	2	0	1	2	.333	0	0-0	0	8.04	8.84
1998 Pittsburgh	NL	18	7	0	3	47.0	208	53	32	28	4	3	2	0	18	3	32	5	3	1	2	.333	0	0-0	0	4.50	5.36
2003 Texas	AL	7	1	0	0	12.2	67	20	14	12	1	0	0	0	9	2	9	0	0	1	0	1.000	0	0-0	0	8.27	8.53
2003 Cincinnati	NL	9	4	0	1	35.2	144	31	18	18	7	1	0	1	6	0	25	0	1	2	1	.667	0	0-0	1	3.15	4.54
11 ML YEARS		359	98	2	84	907.0	4050	944	587	562	143	31	30	22	461	21	711	48	7	40	52	.435	1	4-10	19	5.25	5.58

John Vander Wal

Bats: L **Throws:** L **Pos:** PH-32; RF-7; 1B-4 **Ht:** 6'1" **Wt:** 197 **Born:** 4/29/1966 **Age:** 39

							BATTING														BASERUNNING				AVERAGES		
Year Team	Lg	G	AB	H	2B	3B	HR	(Hm	Rd)	TB	R	RBI	RC	TBB	IBB	SO	HBP	SH	SF	SB	CS	SB%	GDP	Avg	OBP	Slg
2004 Louisville*	AAA	16	48	9	3	0	0	(-	-)	12	5	2	3	5	1	10	0	0	0	2	0	1.00	1	.188	.264	.250
1991 Montreal	NL	21	61	13	4	1	1	(0	1)	22	4	8	4	1	0	18	0	0	1	0	0	-	2	.213	.222	.361
1992 Montreal	NL	105	213	51	8	2	4	(2	2)	75	21	20	25	24	2	36	0	0	0	3	0	1.00	2	.239	.316	.352

(Batting leaders — continued)

Year Team	Lg	G	AB	H	2B	3B	HR	(Hm	Rd)	TB	R	RBI	RC	TBB	IBB	SO	HBP	SH	SF	SB	CS	SB%	GDP	Avg	OBP	Slg
1993 Montreal	NL	106	215	50	7	4	5	(1	4)	80	34	30	26	27	2	30	1	0	1	6	3	.67	4	.233	.320	.372
1994 Colorado	NL	91	110	27	3	1	5	(1	4)	47	12	15	15	16	0	31	0	0	1	2	1	.67	4	.245	.339	.427
1995 Colorado	NL	105	101	35	8	1	5	(2	3)	60	15	21	24	16	5	23	0	0	1	1	1	.50	2	.347	.432	.594
1996 Colorado	NL	104	151	38	6	2	5	(5	0)	63	20	31	22	19	2	38	1	0	2	2	2	.50	1	.252	.335	.417
1997 Colorado	NL	76	92	16	2	0	1	(0	1)	21	7	11	4	10	0	33	0	0	0	1	1	.50	2	.174	.255	.228
1998 Col-SD	NL	109	129	36	13	1	5	(3	2)	66	21	20	26	22	0	34	0	0	1	0	0	-	2	.279	.382	.512
1999 San Diego	NL	132	246	67	18	0	6	(2	4)	103	26	41	39	37	1	59	2	0	3	2	1	.67	5	.272	.368	.419
2000 Pittsburgh	NL	134	384	115	29	0	24	(13	11)	216	74	94	88	72	5	92	2	0	3	11	2	.85	7	.299	.410	.563
2001 Pit-SF	NL	146	452	122	28	4	14	(6	8)	200	58	70	72	68	9	122	1	2	4	8	6	.57	10	.270	.364	.442
2002 New York	AL	84	219	57	17	1	6	(2	4)	94	30	20	20	23	3	58	0	0	3	1	1	.50	7	.260	.327	.429
2003 Milwaukee	NL	117	327	84	25	1	14	(7	7)	153	50	45	45	46	3	104	1	0	0	1	2	.33	5	.257	.350	.468
2004 Cincinnati	NL	42	51	6	2	0	2	(1	1)	14	2	4	2	4	0	20	0	0	0	0	0	-	0	.118	.182	.275
1998 Colorado	NL	89	104	30	10	1	5	(3	2)	57	18	20	22	16	0	29	0	0	1	0	0	-	1	.288	.380	.548
1998 San Diego	NL	20	25	6	3	0	0	(0	0)	9	3	0	4	6	0	5	0	0	0	0	0	-	1	.240	.387	.360
2001 Pittsburgh	NL	97	313	87	22	3	11	(5	6)	148	39	50	52	42	6	84	1	0	4	7	4	.64	7	.278	.361	.473
2001 San Francisco	NL	49	139	35	6	1	3	(1	2)	52	19	20	20	26	3	38	0	2	0	1	2	.33	3	.252	.370	.374
14 ML YEARS		1372	2751	717	170	18	97	(45	52)	1214	374	430	412	385	32	698	8	2	20	38	20	.66	53	.261	.351	.441

Claudio Vargas

Pitches: R Bats: R Pos: RP-31; SP-14 Ht: 6'3" Wt: 225 Born: 6/19/1978 Age: 27

Year Team	Lg	G	GS	CG	GF	IP	BFP	H	R	ER	HR	SH	SF	HB	TBB	IBB	SO	WP	Bk	W	L	Pct	ShO	Sv-Op	Hld	ERC	ERA
1998 Brevard Cnty	A+	2	2	0	0	9.2	46	15	5	5	5	1	1	0	4	1	9	0	0	0	1	.000	0	0- -	-	11.23	4.66
1998 Marlins	R	5	4	0	0	28.2	117	24	15	13	1	0	1	3	7	0	27	2	0	0	4	.000	0	0- -	-	2.62	4.08
1999 Kane County	A	19	19	1	0	99.2	426	97	47	43	8	2	3	0	41	0	88	2	2	5	5	.500	0	0- -	-	3.85	3.88
2000 Brevard Cnty	A+	24	23	0	0	145.1	596	126	64	53	10	4	2	7	44	3	143	3	0	10	5	.667	0	0- -	-	2.97	3.28
2000 Portland	AA	3	2	0	0	15.0	68	16	9	6	1	1	2	1	6	0	13	0	0	1	1	.500	0	0- -	-	4.36	3.60
2001 Portland	AA	27	27	0	0	159.0	666	122	77	74	25	8	2	11	67	1	151	2	1	8	9	.471	0	0- -	-	3.53	4.19
2002 Calgary	AAA	17	16	1	0	76.1	349	88	63	57	18	6	2	4	35	0	61	3	1	4	11	.267	0	0- -	-	6.48	6.72
2002 Harrisburg	AA	8	8	0	0	33.0	146	38	17	17	2	1	0	3	9	0	34	3	0	2	2	.500	0	0- -	-	4.49	4.64
2003 Harrisburg	AA	2	2	0	0	12.0	46	7	1	1	0	0	1	1	3	0	13	0	0	1	0	1.000	0	0- -	-	1.35	0.75
2003 Edmonton	AAA	2	2	0	0	9.2	43	7	3	3	1	0	0	1	5	2	12	0	0	0	0	-	0	0- -	-	2.96	2.79
2003 Montreal	NL	23	20	0	0	114.0	491	111	59	55	16	5	4	7	41	5	62	2	0	6	8	.429	0	0-0	0	4.22	4.34
2004 Montreal	NL	45	14	0	6	118.1	530	120	75	69	26	4	4	7	64	6	89	8	0	5	5	.500	0	0-0	3	5.85	5.25
2 ML YEARS		68	34	0	6	232.1	1021	231	134	124	42	9	8	14	105	11	151	10	0	11	13	.458	0	0-0	3	5.03	4.80

Jason Varitek

Bats: B Throws: R Pos: C-130; PH-13; DH-1 Ht: 6'2" Wt: 237 Born: 4/11/1972 Age: 33

Year Team	Lg	G	AB	H	2B	3B	HR	(Hm	Rd)	TB	R	RBI	RC	TBB	IBB	SO	HBP	SH	SF	SB	CS	SB%	GDP	Avg	OBP	Slg
1997 Boston	AL	1	1	1	0	0	0	(0	0)	1	0	0	1	0	0	0	0	0	0	0	0	-	0	1.000	1.000	1.000
1998 Boston	AL	86	221	56	13	0	7	(1	6)	90	31	33	26	17	1	45	2	4	3	2	2	.50	8	.253	.309	.407
1999 Boston	AL	144	483	130	39	2	20	(12	8)	233	70	76	75	46	2	85	2	5	8	1	2	.33	13	.269	.330	.482
2000 Boston	AL	139	448	131	31	1	10	(2	8)	174	55	65	59	60	3	84	6	1	4	1	1	.50	16	.248	.342	.388
2001 Boston	AL	51	174	51	11	1	7	(2	5)	85	19	25	30	21	3	35	1	1	1	0	0	-	6	.293	.371	.489
2002 Boston	AL	132	467	124	27	1	10	(6	4)	183	58	61	52	41	3	95	7	1	3	4	3	.57	13	.266	.332	.392
2003 Boston	AL	142	451	123	31	1	25	(13	12)	231	63	85	79	51	8	106	7	5	7	3	2	.60	10	.273	.351	.512
2004 Boston	AL	137	463	137	30	1	18	(8	10)	223	67	73	79	62	9	126	10	0	1	10	3	.77	11	.296	.390	.482
8 ML YEARS		832	2708	733	182	7	97	(44	53)	1220	363	418	401	298	29	576	35	17	27	21	13	.62	77	.271	.347	.451

Jorge Vasquez

Pitches: R Bats: R Pos: RP-2 Ht: 6'1" Wt: 165 Born: 7/16/1978 Age: 26

Year Team	Lg	G	GS	CG	GF	IP	BFP	H	R	ER	HR	SH	SF	HB	TBB	IBB	SO	WP	Bk	W	L	Pct	ShO	Sv-Op	Hld	ERC	ERA
2001 Royals	R	4	2	0	1	16.0	63	10	2	2	0	0	0	2	1	0	19	0	0	0	1	.000	0	0- -	-	1.12	1.13
2001 Spokane	A-	10	8	0	0	50.1	214	50	33	28	3	1	2	5	13	0	67	3	10	1	6	.143	0	0- -	-	3.60	5.01
2002 Wilmington	A+	10	0	0	5	11.0	50	12	6	6	1	0	0	0	3	0	17	1	0	0	0	-	0	0- -	-	3.74	4.91
2002 Burlington	A	22	0	0	14	46.0	176	22	8	8	3	1	1	1	15	0	55	4	3	2	1	.667	0	6- -	-	1.29	1.57
2003 Wilmington	A+	17	0	0	12	23.0	102	19	7	5	1	3	0	0	14	3	31	1	0	0	2	.333	0	7- -	-	3.22	1.96
2003 Wichita	AA	36	0	0	32	51.2	211	39	12	11	3	2	2	5	18	2	52	8	1	3	1	.750	0	22- -	-	2.65	1.92
2004 Wichita	AA	49	0	0	41	59.2	263	52	34	31	3	0	0	5	27	1	71	8	0	4	5	.444	0	18- -	-	3.43	4.68
2004 Kansas City	AL	2	0	0	1	3.1	17	4	4	3	1	0	0	1	1	0	4	1	0	0	0	-	0	0-0	0	7.09	8.10

Javier Vazquez

Pitches: R Bats: R Pos: SP-32 Ht: 6'2" Wt: 195 Born: 7/25/1976 Age: 28

Year Team	Lg	G	GS	CG	GF	IP	BFP	H	R	ER	HR	SH	SF	HB	TBB	IBB	SO	WP	Bk	W	L	Pct	ShO	Sv-Op	Hld	ERC	ERA
1998 Montreal	NL	33	33	0	1	172.1	764	196	121	116	31	9	4	11	68	2	139	2	0	5	15	.250	0	0-0	0	5.79	6.06
1999 Montreal	NL	26	26	3	0	154.2	667	154	98	86	20	3	3	4	52	4	113	2	0	9	8	.529	1	0-0	0	4.02	5.00
2000 Montreal	NL	33	33	2	0	217.2	945	207	104	98	24	11	3	5	61	10	196	3	0	11	9	.550	1	0-0	0	4.45	4.05
2001 Montreal	NL	32	32	5	0	223.2	898	197	92	85	24	9	2	3	44	4	208	3	1	16	11	.593	**3**	0-0	0	2.75	3.42
2002 Montreal	NL	34	34	2	0	230.1	971	**243**	111	100	28	15	7	4	49	6	179	3	0	10	13	.435	0	0-0	0	3.80	3.91
2003 Montreal	NL	34	34	4	0	230.2	938	190	93	83	28	6	6	4	57	5	241	11	1	13	12	.520	1	0-0	0	2.90	3.24
2004 New York	AL	32	32	0	0	198.0	849	195	114	108	33	4	8	11	60	3	150	12	2	14	10	.583	0	0-0	0	4.23	4.91
7 ML YEARS		224	223	16	1	1427.1	6032	1430	733	676	188	57	33	42	391	34	1226	36	4	78	78	.500	6	0-0	0	3.88	4.26

Ramon Vazquez

Bats: L **Throws:** R **Pos:** SS-22; PH-18; 2B-10; 3B-9; 1B-3; PR-1   **Ht:** 5'11" **Wt:** 170 **Born:** 8/21/1976 **Age:** 28

							BATTING													BASERUNNING				AVERAGES		
Year Team	Lg	G	AB	H	2B	3B	HR	(Hm	Rd)	TB	R	RBI	RC	TBB	IBB	SO	HBP	SH	SF	SB	CS	SB%	GDP	Avg	OBP	Slg
2004 Portland*	AAA	53	184	55	21	1	8	(-	-)	102	36	34	39	33	1	28	0	4	2	2	0	1.00	2	.299	.402	.554
2001 Seattle	AL	17	35	8	0	0	0	(0	0)	8	5	4	2	0	0	3	0	1	1	0	0	-	0	.229	.222	.229
2002 San Diego	NL	128	423	116	21	5	2	(0	2)	153	50	32	55	45	3	79	1	3	2	7	2	.78	6	.274	.344	.362
2003 San Diego	NL	116	422	110	17	4	3	(1	2)	144	56	30	49	52	2	88	2	5	3	10	3	.77	4	.261	.342	.341
2004 San Diego	NL	52	115	27	3	2	1	(0	0)	37	12	13	9	11	2	24	0	4	2	1	1	.50	2	.235	.297	.322
4 ML YEARS		313	995	261	41	11	6	(2	4)	342	123	79	115	108	7	194	3	13	8	18	6	.75	12	.262	.334	.344

Mike Venafro

Pitches: L **Bats:** L **Pos:** RP-17   **Ht:** 5'10" **Wt:** 180 **Born:** 8/2/1973 **Age:** 31

		HOW MUCH HE PITCHED						WHAT HE GAVE UP											THE RESULTS						
Year Team	Lg	G	GS	CG	GF	IP	BFP	H	R	ER	HR	SH	SF	HB	TBB	IBB	SO	WP	Bk	W	L	Pct	ShO	Sv-Op	Hld	ERC	ERA
2004 Las Vegas*	AAA	5	0	0	2	6.1	30	8	5	5	0	0	0	1	2	0	4	0	0	0	1	.000	0	1- -		4.97	7.11
2004 Omaha*	AAA	35	0	0	15	57.2	266	70	30	28	8	0	0	4	19	2	41	3	0	2	4	.333	0	2- -		5.41	4.37
1999 Texas	AL	65	0	0	11	68.1	283	63	29	25	4	5	2	3	22	0	37	0	0	3	2	.600	0	0-1	19	3.30	3.29
2000 Texas	AL	77	0	0	21	56.1	248	64	27	24	2	2	4	4	21	4	32	1	0	3	1	.750	0	1-2	17	4.49	3.83
2001 Texas	AL	70	0	0	20	60.0	266	54	35	32	2	2	4	7	28	4	29	3	0	5	5	.500	0	4-8	21	3.58	4.80
2002 Oakland	AL	47	0	0	8	37.0	168	45	23	19	5	4	2	2	14	2	16	1	0	2	2	.500	0	0-0	15	5.65	4.62
2003 Tampa Bay	AL	24	0	0	6	19.0	85	24	10	10	1	0	1	3	3	0	9	1	0	1	0	1.000	0	0-0	4	4.89	4.74
2004 Los Angeles	NL	17	0	0	2	9.0	42	11	5	4	1	1	0	2	3	1	6	0	0	0	0	-	0	0-0	2	5.90	4.00
6 ML YEARS		300	0	0	68	249.2	1092	261	129	114	15	14	13	21	91	11	129	6	0	14	10	.583	0	5-11	78	4.18	4.11

Robin Ventura

Bats: L **Throws:** R **Pos:** PH-61; 1B-40; 3B-11   **Ht:** 6'1" **Wt:** 198 **Born:** 7/14/1967 **Age:** 37

							BATTING													BASERUNNING				AVERAGES		
Year Team	Lg	G	AB	H	2B	3B	HR	(Hm	Rd)	TB	R	RBI	RC	TBB	IBB	SO	HBP	SH	SF	SB	CS	SB%	GDP	Avg	OBP	Slg
1989 Chicago	AL	16	45	8	3	0	0	(0	0)	11	5	7	4	8	0	6	1	1	3	0	0	-	1	.178	.298	.244
1990 Chicago	AL	150	493	123	17	1	5	(2	3)	157	48	54	53	55	2	53	1	13	3	1	4	.20	5	.249	.324	.318
1991 Chicago	AL	157	606	172	25	1	23	(16	7)	268	92	100	95	80	3	67	4	8	7	2	4	.33	22	.284	.367	.442
1992 Chicago	AL	157	592	167	38	1	16	(7	9)	255	85	93	96	93	9	71	0	1	8	2	4	.33	14	.282	.375	.431
1993 Chicago	AL	157	554	145	27	1	22	(10	12)	240	85	94	90	105	16	82	3	1	6	1	6	.14	18	.262	.379	.433
1994 Chicago	AL	109	401	113	15	1	18	(8	10)	184	57	78	70	61	15	69	2	2	8	3	1	.75	8	.282	.373	.459
1995 Chicago	AL	135	492	145	22	0	26	(8	18)	245	79	93	94	75	11	98	1	1	8	4	3	.57	8	.295	.384	.498
1996 Chicago	AL	158	586	168	31	2	34	(13	21)	305	96	105	107	78	10	81	2	0	8	1	3	.25	18	.287	.368	.520
1997 Chicago	AL	54	183	48	10	1	6	(2	4)	78	27	26	31	34	5	21	0	0	3	0	0	-	3	.262	.373	.426
1998 Chicago	AL	161	590	155	31	4	21	(15	6)	257	84	91	90	79	15	111	1	1	3	1	1	.50	10	.263	.349	.436
1999 New York	NL	161	588	177	38	0	32	(13	19)	311	88	120	113	74	10	109	3	1	5	1	1	.50	14	.301	.379	.529
2000 New York	NL	141	469	109	23	1	24	(12	12)	206	61	84	68	75	12	91	2	1	4	3	5	.38	14	.232	.338	.439
2001 New York	NL	141	456	108	20	0	21	(9	12)	191	70	61	68	88	10	101	1	0	4	2	5	.29	13	.237	.359	.419
2002 New York	AL	141	465	115	17	0	27	(9	18)	213	68	93	78	90	9	101	2	0	5	3	1	.75	14	.247	.368	.458
2003 NYY-LA		138	392	95	18	1	14	(8	6)	157	42	55	49	58	4	87	0	3	0	0	0	-	11	.242	.340	.401
2004 Los Angeles	NL	102	152	37	3	0	5	(1	4)	55	19	28	25	22	1	31	0	0	1	0	0	-	3	.243	.337	.362
2003 New York	AL	89	283	71	13	0	9	(4	5)	111	31	42	40	40	2	62	0	3	0	0	0	-	8	.251	.344	.392
2003 Los Angeles	NL	49	109	24	5	1	5	(4	1)	46	11	13	9	18	2	25	0	0	0	0	0	-	3	.220	.331	.422
16 ML YEARS		2079	7064	1885	338	14	294	(135	159)	3133	1006	1182	1131	1075	132	1179	23	33	76	24	38	.39	176	.267	.362	.444

Jose Vidro

Bats: B **Throws:** R **Pos:** 2B-105; DH-4; PH-2   **Ht:** 5'11" **Wt:** 195 **Born:** 8/27/1974 **Age:** 30

							BATTING													BASERUNNING				AVERAGES		
Year Team	Lg	G	AB	H	2B	3B	HR	(Hm	Rd)	TB	R	RBI	RC	TBB	IBB	SO	HBP	SH	SF	SB	CS	SB%	GDP	Avg	OBP	Slg
1997 Montreal	NL	67	169	42	12	1	2	(0	2)	62	19	17	19	11	0	20	2	0	3	1	0	1.00	1	.249	.297	.367
1998 Montreal	NL	83	205	45	12	0	0	(0	0)	57	24	18	19	27	0	33	4	6	3	2	2	.50	5	.220	.318	.278
1999 Montreal	NL	140	494	150	45	2	12	(5	7)	235	67	59	76	29	2	51	4	2	2	0	4	.00	12	.304	.346	.476
2000 Montreal	NL	153	606	200	51	2	24	(11	13)	327	101	97	115	49	4	69	2	0	6	5	4	.56	17	.330	.379	.540
2001 Montreal	NL	124	486	155	34	1	15	(6	9)	236	82	59	81	31	2	49	10	2	2	4	1	.80	18	.319	.371	.486
2002 Montreal	NL	152	604	190	43	3	19	(11	8)	296	103	96	112	60	1	70	3	11	3	2	1	.67	12	.315	.378	.490
2003 Montreal	NL	144	509	158	36	0	15	(7	8)	239	77	65	89	69	6	50	7	2	5	3	2	.60	16	.310	.397	.470
2004 Montreal	NL	110	412	121	24	0	14	(6	8)	187	51	60	59	49	7	43	0	4	2	3	1	.75	14	.294	.367	.454
8 ML YEARS		973	3485	1061	257	9	101	(46	55)	1639	524	471	570	325	22	385	32	27	26	20	15	.57	95	.304	.367	.470

Eduardo Villacis

Pitches: R **Bats:** R **Pos:** SP-1   **Ht:** 6'2" **Wt:** 170 **Born:** 8/29/1979 **Age:** 25

		HOW MUCH HE PITCHED						WHAT HE GAVE UP											THE RESULTS						
Year Team	Lg	G	GS	CG	GF	IP	BFP	H	R	ER	HR	SH	SF	HB	TBB	IBB	SO	WP	Bk	W	L	Pct	ShO	Sv-Op	Hld	ERC	ERA
2000 Portland	A-	5	0	0	2	4.1	20	4	1	0	0	0	0	0	3	1	4	0	0	0	0	-	0	1- -		3.50	0.00
2001 Casper	R+	1	1	0	0	6.0	25	5	1	0	0	0	0	0	0	0	3	0	0	1	0	1.000	0	0- -		2.26	0.00
2001 Tri-City	A-	11	0	0	6	19.0	81	14	9	9	2	1	1	1	8	1	20	1	0	4	1	.800	0	0- -		2.80	4.26
2002 Wilmington	A+	17	0	0	5	28.0	113	19	8	7	2	3	0	0	10	1	15	3	0	2	1	.667	0	1- -		2.01	2.25
2002 Asheville	A	11	1	0	5	19.0	72	12	4	4	2	0	0	1	2	0	8	1	0	1	0	1.000	0	0- -		1.48	1.89
2003 Wilmington	A+	42	4	0	12	92.2	379	78	36	29	4	1	4	2	28	3	64	6	0	6	2	.750	0	2- -		2.54	2.82
2004 Birmingham	AA	19	18	0	0	96.0	409	93	40	35	9	5	3	8	34	4	71	10	1	6	4	.600	0	0- -		3.99	3.28
2004 Wichita	AA	8	3	0	1	30.1	119	22	11	9	3	0	0	0	6	0	21	2	0	2	0	1.000	0	0- -		1.90	2.67
2004 Kansas City	AL	1	1	0	0	3.1	20	6	5	5	1	0	0	0	4	0	1	1	0	0	1	.000	0	0-0	0	14.81	13.50

Brandon Villafuerte

Pitches: R **Bats:** R **Pos:** RP-20   **Ht:** 5'11" **Wt:** 165 **Born:** 12/17/1975 **Age:** 29

			HOW MUCH HE PITCHED						WHAT HE GAVE UP										THE RESULTS					
Year Team	Lg	G	GS	CG	GF	IP	BFP	H	R	ER	HR	SH	SF	HB	TBB	IBB	SO	WP	Bk	W	L	Pct	ShO	Sv-Op	Hld	ERC	ERA
2004 Tucson*	AAA	23	0	0	11	30.2	130	27	10	9	3	0	1	0	10	2	23	1	0	2	2	.500	0	4- -		2.95	2.64
2000 Detroit	AL	3	0	0	2	4.1	20	4	5	5	0	0	0	0	4	0	1	1	0	0	0	-	0	0-0	0	5.01	10.38
2001 Texas	AL	6	0	0	4	5.2	35	12	9	9	3	0	1	1	4	0	4	1	0	0	0	-	0	0-0	0	17.59	14.29
2002 San Diego	NL	31	0	0	11	32.0	133	29	5	5	2	1	1	2	12	2	25	0	0	1	2	.333	0	1-1	8	3.44	1.41
2003 San Diego	NL	31	0	0	11	40.2	187	39	20	19	7	2	1	3	26	2	34	2	0	0	2	.000	0	2-5	2	5.54	4.20
2004 Arizona	NL	20	0	0	6	20.0	96	25	9	9	2	1	0	1	14	2	13	0	0	0	3	.000	0	0-0	0	6.96	4.05
5 ML YEARS		91	0	0	34	102.2	471	109	48	47	14	4	3	7	60	6	77	4	0	1	7	.125	0	3-6	10	5.67	4.12

Oscar Villarreal

Pitches: R **Bats:** L **Pos:** RP-17   **Ht:** 6'0" **Wt:** 205 **Born:** 11/22/1981 **Age:** 23

			HOW MUCH HE PITCHED						WHAT HE GAVE UP										THE RESULTS					
Year Team	Lg	G	GS	CG	GF	IP	BFP	H	R	ER	HR	SH	SF	HB	TBB	IBB	SO	WP	Bk	W	L	Pct	ShO	Sv-Op	Hld	ERC	ERA
1999 Diamndbcks	R	14	11	0	1	64.1	286	64	39	27	1	2	3	10	25	0	51	6	4	1	5	.167	0	0- -		3.97	3.78
2000 Tucson	AAA	2	0	0	0	4.1	19	6	1	1	0	0	0	0	2	0	4	0	0	1	0	1.000	0	0- -		6.28	2.08
2000 South Bend	A	13	5	0	5	32.2	155	37	19	16	0	0	0	3	17	3	30	2	1	1	3	.250	0	0- -		4.59	4.41
2000 Diamndbcks	R	1	0	0	0	1.0	5	2	1	1	0	0	0	0	0	0	1	0	0	0	0	-	0	0- -		7.48	9.00
2000 High Desert	A+	9	4	0	0	24.2	117	24	20	10	4	4	1	3	14	0	18	2	0	0	2	.000	0	0- -		5.33	3.65
2001 El Paso	AA	27	27	0	0	140.2	644	154	96	69	10	4	7	8	63	1	108	14	11	6	9	.400	0	0- -		4.71	4.41
2002 El Paso	AA	14	12	1	0	84.1	344	73	36	35	2	0	1	4	26	0	85	3	0	6	3	.667	0	0- -		2.74	3.74
2002 Tucson	AAA	10	10	0	0	64.0	272	68	33	31	8	0	1	4	22	0	40	5	2	3	3	.500	0	0- -		4.79	4.36
2004 Tucson	AAA	6	5	0	0	10.2	55	20	17	17	3	0	0	0	4	0	12	2	0	0	2	.000	0	0- -		11.19	14.34
2003 Arizona	NL	86	1	0	14	98.0	422	80	40	28	6	9	3	3	46	10	80	3	2	10	7	.588	0	0-4	10	2.97	2.57
2004 Arizona	NL	17	0	0	4	18.0	84	25	14	14	3	3	0	1	7	1	17	5	0	0	2	.000	0	0-0	2	7.13	7.00
2 ML YEARS		103	1	0	18	116.0	506	105	54	42	9	12	3	4	53	11	97	8	2	10	9	.526	0	0-4	12	3.54	3.26

Ron Villone

Pitches: L **Bats:** L **Pos:** RP-46; SP-10   **Ht:** 6'4" **Wt:** 235 **Born:** 1/16/1970 **Age:** 35

			HOW MUCH HE PITCHED						WHAT HE GAVE UP										THE RESULTS					
Year Team	Lg	G	GS	CG	GF	IP	BFP	H	R	ER	HR	SH	SF	HB	TBB	IBB	SO	WP	Bk	W	L	Pct	ShO	Sv-Op	Hld	ERC	ERA
1995 Sea-SD		38	0	0	15	45.0	212	44	31	29	11	3	1	1	34	0	63	3	0	2	3	.400	0	1-5	6	6.57	5.80
1996 SD-Mil		44	0	0	19	43.0	182	31	15	15	6	0	2	5	25	0	38	2	0	1	1	.500	0	2-3	9	4.08	3.14
1997 Milwaukee	AL	50	0	0	15	52.2	238	54	23	20	4	2	0	1	36	2	40	3	0	1	0	1.000	0	0-2	8	5.30	3.42
1998 Cleveland	AL	25	0	0	6	27.0	129	30	18	18	3	2	2	2	22	0	15	0	0	0	0	-	0	0-0	1	7.01	6.00
1999 Cincinnati	NL	29	22	0	2	142.2	610	114	70	67	8	9	3	5	73	2	97	6	0	9	7	.563	0	2-2	0	3.20	4.23
2000 Cincinnati	NL	35	23	2	5	141.0	643	154	95	85	22	10	8	9	78	3	77	7	0	10	10	.500	0	0-0	1	5.97	5.43
2001 Col-Hou	NL	53	12	0	12	114.2	523	133	81	75	18	1	1	5	53	5	113	4	1	6	10	.375	0	0-0	6	5.81	5.89
2002 Pittsburgh	NL	45	7	0	6	93.0	399	95	63	60	8	5	3	5	34	3	55	1	0	4	6	.400	0	0-1	0	4.18	5.81
2003 Houston	NL	19	19	0	0	106.2	448	91	51	49	16	3	3	5	48	1	91	1	0	6	6	.500	0	0-0	0	4.05	4.13
2004 Seattle	AL	56	10	0	14	117.0	523	102	64	53	12	4	4	12	64	3	86	6	0	8	6	.571	0	0-1	7	4.26	4.08
1995 Seattle	AL	19	0	0	7	19.1	101	20	19	17	6	3	0	1	23	0	26	1	0	0	2	.000	0	0-3	3	9.67	7.91
1995 San Diego	NL	19	0	0	8	25.2	111	24	12	12	5	0	1	0	11	0	37	2	0	2	1	.667	0	1-2	3	4.44	4.21
1996 San Diego	NL	21	0	0	9	18.1	78	17	6	6	2	0	0	1	7	0	19	0	0	1	1	.500	0	0-1	4	3.90	2.95
1996 Milwaukee	AL	23	0	0	10	24.2	104	14	9	9	4	0	2	4	18	0	19	2	0	0	0	-	0	2-2	5	4.21	3.28
2001 Colorado	NL	22	6	0	6	46.2	222	56	35	33	6	1	1	1	29	4	48	2	0	1	3	.250	0	0-0	2	6.30	6.36
2001 Houston	NL	31	6	0	6	68.0	301	77	46	42	12	0	0	4	24	1	65	2	1	5	7	.417	0	0-0	4	5.46	5.56
10 ML YEARS		394	93	2	94	882.2	3907	848	511	471	108	39	27	50	467	19	675	33	1	47	49	.490	0	5-14	38	4.75	4.80

Fernando Vina

Bats: L **Throws:** R **Pos:** 2B-29; PR-1   **Ht:** 5'9" **Wt:** 174 **Born:** 4/16/1969 **Age:** 36

								BATTING												BASERUNNING			AVERAGES		
Year Team	Lg	G	AB	H	2B	3B	HR	(Hm	Rd)	TB	R	RBI	RC	TBB	IBB	SO	HBP	SH	SF	SB	CS	SB%	GDP	Avg	OBP	Slg
1993 Seattle	AL	24	45	10	2	0	0	(0	0)	12	5	2	6	4	0	3	3	1	0	6	0	1.00	0	.222	.327	.267
1994 New York	NL	79	124	31	6	0	0	(0	0)	37	20	6	15	12	0	11	12	2	0	3	1	.75	4	.250	.372	.298
1995 Milwaukee	AL	113	288	74	7	7	3	(1	2)	104	46	29	35	22	0	28	9	4	2	6	3	.67	6	.257	.327	.361
1996 Milwaukee	AL	140	554	157	19	10	7	(3	4)	217	94	46	73	38	3	35	13	6	4	16	7	.70	15	.283	.342	.392
1997 Milwaukee	AL	79	324	89	12	2	4	(1	3)	117	37	28	36	12	1	23	7	2	3	8	7	.53	4	.275	.312	.361
1998 Milwaukee	NL	159	637	198	39	7	7	(2	5)	272	101	45	106	54	2	46	25	5	1	22	16	.58	7	.311	.386	.427
1999 Milwaukee	NL	37	154	41	7	0	1	(0	1)	51	17	16	19	14	0	6	4	3	2	5	2	.71	1	.266	.339	.331
2000 St Louis	NL	123	487	146	24	6	4	(1	3)	194	81	31	76	36	0	36	28	2	1	10	8	.56	5	.300	.380	.398
2001 St Louis	NL	154	631	191	30	8	9	(5	4)	264	95	56	96	32	3	35	22	3	2	17	7	.71	7	.303	.357	.418
2002 St Louis	NL	150	622	168	29	5	1	(0	1)	210	75	54	73	44	2	36	18	1	7	17	11	.61	11	.270	.333	.338
2003 St Louis	NL	61	259	65	14	4	4	(2	2)	99	35	23	28	11	0	24	11	3	1	4	4	.50	5	.251	.309	.382
2004 Detroit	AL	29	115	26	5	0	0	(0	0)	31	21	7	10	9	0	9	5	1	1	2	1	.67	6	.226	.308	.270
12 ML YEARS		1148	4240	1196	194	49	40	(15	25)	1608	627	343	573	288	11	292	157	33	24	116	67	.63	71	.282	.348	.379

Jose Vizcaino

Bats: B **Throws:** R **Pos:** SS-64; PH-45; 2B-37; 3B-21; 1B-8; PR-2   **Ht:** 6'1" **Wt:** 185 **Born:** 3/26/1968 **Age:** 37

								BATTING												BASERUNNING			AVERAGES		
Year Team	Lg	G	AB	H	2B	3B	HR	(Hm	Rd)	TB	R	RBI	RC	TBB	IBB	SO	HBP	SH	SF	SB	CS	SB%	GDP	Avg	OBP	Slg
1989 Los Angeles	NL	7	10	2	0	0	0	(0	0)	2	2	0	0	0	0	1	0	1	0	0	0	-	0	.200	.200	.200
1990 Los Angeles	NL	37	51	14	1	1	0	(0	0)	17	3	2	5	4	1	8	0	0	0	1	1	.50	1	.275	.327	.333
1991 Chicago	NL	93	145	38	5	0	0	(0	0)	43	7	10	12	5	0	18	0	2	2	2	1	.67	1	.262	.283	.297
1992 Chicago	NL	86	285	64	10	4	1	(0	1)	85	25	17	21	14	2	35	0	5	1	3	0	1.00	4	.225	.260	.298
1993 Chicago	NL	151	551	158	19	4	4	(1	3)	197	74	54	68	46	2	71	3	8	9	12	9	.57	9	.287	.340	.358
1994 New York	NL	103	410	105	13	3	3	(1	2)	133	47	33	39	33	3	62	2	5	6	1	11	.08	5	.256	.310	.324
1995 New York	NL	135	509	146	21	5	3	(2	1)	186	66	56	60	35	4	76	1	13	3	8	3	.73	14	.287	.332	.365
1996 NYM-Cle		144	542	161	17	8	1	(1	0)	197	70	45	68	33	0	82	3	10	3	15	7	.68	8	.297	.341	.363

250

						BATTING															BASERUNNING				AVERAGES		
Year Team	Lg	G	AB	H	2B	3B	HR	(Hm Rd)	TB	R	RBI	RC	TBB	IBB	SO	HBP	SH	SF	SB	CS	SB%	GDP	Avg	OBP	Slg
1997 San Francisco	NL	151	568	151	19	7	5	(1 4)	199	77	50	62	48	1	87	0	13	1	8	8	.50	13	.266	.323	.350
1998 Los Angeles	NL	67	237	62	9	0	3	(0 3)	80	30	29	25	17	0	35	1	10	2	7	3	.70	4	.262	.311	.338
1999 Los Angeles	NL	94	266	67	9	0	1	(1 0)	79	27	29	23	20	0	23	1	9	2	2	1	.67	9	.252	.304	.297
2000 LA-NYY		113	267	67	10	2	0	(0 0)	81	32	14	23	22	3	43	1	5	2	6	7	.46	6	.251	.308	.303
2001 Houston	NL	107	256	71	8	3	1	(1 0)	88	38	14	28	15	0	33	2	9	0	3	2	.60	6	.277	.322	.344
2002 Houston	NL	125	406	123	19	2	5	(4 1)	161	53	37	53	24	2	40	1	5	2	3	5	.38	5	.303	.342	.397
2003 Houston	NL	91	189	47	7	3	3	(2 1)	69	14	26	24	8	3	22	1	4	1	0	1	.00	5	.249	.281	.365
2004 Houston	NL	138	358	98	21	3	3	(1 2)	134	34	33	41	20	5	39	0	5	2	1	1	.50	7	.274	.311	.374
1996 New York		96	363	110	12	6	1	(1 0)	137	47	32	49	28	0	58	3	6	2	9	5	.64	6	.303	.356	.377
1996 Cleveland	AL	48	179	51	5	2	0	(0 0)	60	23	13	19	7	0	24	0	4	1	6	2	.75	2	.285	.310	.335
2000 Los Angeles	NL	40	93	19	2	1	0	(0 0)	23	9	4	6	10	3	15	1	2	0	1	0	1.00	3	.204	.288	.247
2000 New York	AL	73	174	48	8	1	0	(0 0)	58	23	10	17	12	0	28	0	3	2	5	7	.42	3	.276	.319	.333
16 ML YEARS		1642	5050	1374	188	45	33	(15 18)	1751	599	449	552	346	26	675	16	104	36	72	60	.55	97	.272	.319	.347

Luis Vizcaino

Pitches: R **Bats:** R **Pos:** RP-73   **Ht:** 5'11" **Wt:** 174 **Born:** 8/6/1974 **Age:** 30

		HOW MUCH HE PITCHED						WHAT HE GAVE UP										THE RESULTS						
Year Team	Lg	G	GS	CG	GF	IP	BFP	H	R	ER	HR	SH	SF	HB	TBB	IBB	SO	WP	Bk	W	L	Pct	ShO	Sv-Op	Hld	ERC	ERA
1999 Oakland	AL	1	0	0	1	3.1	16	3	2	2	1	0	0	0	3	0	2	1	0	0	0	-	0	0-0	0	7.01	5.40
2000 Oakland	AL	12	0	0	1	19.1	96	25	17	16	2	0	1	2	11	0	18	1	0	0	1	.000	0	0-0	0	6.83	7.45
2001 Oakland	AL	36	0	0	15	36.2	156	38	19	19	8	0	1	0	12	1	31	3	0	2	1	.667	0	1-1	3	4.80	4.66
2002 Milwaukee	NL	76	0	0	30	81.1	326	55	27	27	6	3	3	3	30	4	79	3	2	5	3	.625	0	5-6	19	2.20	2.99
2003 Milwaukee	NL	75	0	0	21	62.0	272	64	45	44	16	2	1	1	25	3	61	3	0	4	3	.571	0	0-6	9	5.37	6.39
2004 Milwaukee	NL	73	0	0	21	72.0	298	61	35	30	12	1	5	1	24	3	63	9	0	4	4	.500	0	1-5	21	3.40	3.75
6 ML YEARS		273	0	0	89	274.2	1164	246	145	138	45	6	11	7	105	11	254	20	2	15	12	.556	0	7-18	52	3.89	4.52

Omar Vizquel

Bats: B **Throws:** R **Pos:** SS-147; PH-5; PR-1   **Ht:** 5'9" **Wt:** 175 **Born:** 4/24/1967 **Age:** 38

						BATTING															BASERUNNING				AVERAGES		
Year Team	Lg	G	AB	H	2B	3B	HR	(Hm Rd)	TB	R	RBI	RC	TBB	IBB	SO	HBP	SH	SF	SB	CS	SB%	GDP	Avg	OBP	Slg
1989 Seattle	AL	143	387	85	7	3	1	(1 0)	101	45	20	25	28	0	40	1	13	2	1	4	.20	6	.220	.273	.261
1990 Seattle	AL	81	255	63	3	2	2	(0 2)	76	19	18	22	18	0	22	0	10	2	4	1	.80	7	.247	.295	.298
1991 Seattle	AL	142	426	98	16	4	1	(1 0)	125	42	41	39	45	0	37	0	8	3	7	2	.78	8	.230	.302	.293
1992 Seattle	AL	136	483	142	20	4	0	(0 0)	170	49	21	54	32	0	38	2	9	1	15	13	.54	14	.294	.340	.352
1993 Seattle	AL	158	560	143	14	2	2	(1 1)	167	68	31	53	50	2	71	4	13	3	12	14	.46	7	.255	.319	.298
1994 Cleveland	AL	69	286	78	10	1	1	(0 1)	93	39	33	32	23	0	23	0	11	2	13	4	.76	4	.273	.325	.325
1995 Cleveland	AL	136	542	144	28	0	6	(3 3)	190	87	56	70	59	0	59	1	10	10	29	11	.73	4	.266	.333	.351
1996 Cleveland	AL	151	542	161	36	1	9	(2 7)	226	98	64	87	56	0	42	4	12	9	35	9	.80	10	.297	.362	.417
1997 Cleveland	AL	153	565	158	23	6	5	(3 2)	208	89	49	75	57	1	58	2	16	2	43	12	.78	16	.280	.347	.368
1998 Cleveland	AL	151	576	166	30	6	2	(0 2)	214	86	50	82	62	1	64	4	12	6	37	12	.76	10	.288	.358	.372
1999 Cleveland	AL	144	574	191	36	4	5	(3 2)	250	112	66	106	65	0	50	1	17	7	42	9	.82	8	.333	.397	.436
2000 Cleveland	AL	156	613	176	27	3	7	(1 6)	230	101	66	92	87	0	72	5	7	5	22	10	.69	13	.287	.377	.375
2001 Cleveland	AL	155	611	156	26	8	2	(2 0)	204	84	50	66	61	0	72	2	15	4	13	9	.59	14	.255	.323	.334
2002 Cleveland	AL	151	582	160	31	5	14	(9 5)	243	85	72	91	56	3	64	8	7	10	18	10	.64	7	.275	.341	.418
2003 Cleveland	AL	64	250	61	13	2	2	(2 0)	84	43	19	25	29	0	20	0	5	1	8	3	.73	11	.244	.321	.336
2004 Cleveland	AL	148	567	165	28	3	7	(2 5)	220	82	59	86	57	0	62	1	20	6	19	6	.76	12	.291	.353	.388
16 ML YEARS		2138	7819	2147	348	54	66	(30 36)	2801	1129	715	1005	785	7	794	35	185	73	318	129	.71	151	.275	.341	.358

Ryan Vogelsong

Pitches: R **Bats:** R **Pos:** SP-26; RP-5   **Ht:** 6'3" **Wt:** 205 **Born:** 7/22/1977 **Age:** 27

		HOW MUCH HE PITCHED						WHAT HE GAVE UP										THE RESULTS						
Year Team	Lg	G	GS	CG	GF	IP	BFP	H	R	ER	HR	SH	SF	HB	TBB	IBB	SO	WP	Bk	W	L	Pct	ShO	Sv-Op	Hld	ERC	ERA
2000 San Francisco	NL	4	0	0	0	6.0	24	4	0	0	0	0	0	0	2	0	6	0	0	0	0	-	0	0-0	0	1.57	0.00
2001 SF-Pit	NL	15	2	0	0	34.2	164	39	26	26	6	0	0	0	20	0	24	0	0	0	5	.000	0	0-0	0	5.92	6.75
2003 Pittsburgh	NL	6	5	0	0	22.0	108	30	19	16	1	3	1	2	9	3	15	1	0	2	2	.500	0	0-0	0	5.72	6.55
2004 Pittsburgh	NL	31	26	0	4	133.0	610	148	97	96	22	8	6	10	67	7	92	3	0	6	13	.316	0	0-0	0	5.89	6.50
2001 San Francisco	NL	13	0	0	0	28.2	130	29	18	18	5	0	0	0	14	0	17	0	0	0	3	.000	0	0-0	0	4.89	5.65
2001 San Francisco	NL	2	2	0	0	6.0	34	10	8	8	1	0	0	0	6	0	7	0	0	0	2	.000	0	0-0	0	11.42	12.00
4 ML YEARS		56	33	0	4	195.2	906	221	116	138	29	11	7	12	98	10	137	4	0	8	20	.286	0	0-0	0	5.72	6.35

Doug Waechter

Pitches: R **Bats:** R **Pos:** SP-14   **Ht:** 6'4" **Wt:** 209 **Born:** 1/28/1981 **Age:** 24

		HOW MUCH HE PITCHED						WHAT HE GAVE UP										THE RESULTS						
Year Team	Lg	G	GS	CG	GF	IP	BFP	H	R	ER	HR	SH	SF	HB	TBB	IBB	SO	WP	Bk	W	L	Pct	ShO	Sv-Op	Hld	ERC	ERA
1999 Princeton	R+	11	7	0	0	35.0	189	46	45	38	2	0	5	4	35	0	38	21	1	0	5	.000	0	0- -		8.47	9.77
2000 Hudson Val	A-	14	14	2	0	72.2	302	53	23	19	2	2	1	4	37	0	58	7	3	4	4	.500	2	0- -		2.80	2.35
2001 Chrlstn - SC	A	26	26	1	0	153.1	684	179	97	74	14	7	6	5	38	1	107	12	3	8	11	.421	0	0- -		4.35	4.34
2002 Chrlstn - SC	A	7	7	0	0	36.1	162	39	20	14	2	2	1	2	16	3	36	1	2	3	3	.500	0	0- -		4.39	3.47
2002 Bakersfield	A+	17	17	0	0	108.1	466	114	43	32	9	7	2	1	29	0	101	8	0	6	3	.667	0	0- -		3.70	2.66
2002 Orlando	AA	4	4	1	0	18.0	93	27	20	18	4	0	0	0	13	0	18	3	1	1	3	.250	0	0- -		9.59	9.00
2003 Orlando	AA	13	12	0	0	76.1	314	74	39	35	6	3	3	1	19	0	45	1	0	5	3	.625	0	0- -		3.27	4.13
2003 Durham	AAA	10	10	0	0	51.1	210	51	25	19	9	2	1	0	12	0	35	3	0	3	3	.500	0	0- -		3.95	3.33
2004 Durham	AAA	8	8	0	0	29.1	135	33	22	22	11	0	1	1	17	0	22	1	0	2	2	.000	0	0- -		8.00	6.75
2003 Tampa Bay	AL	6	5	1	0	35.1	145	29	13	13	4	0	0	1	15	0	29	0	0	3	2	.600	1	0-0	0	3.48	3.31
2004 Tampa Bay	AL	14	14	0	0	70.1	309	68	54	47	20	0	2	4	33	1	36	1	1	5	7	.417	0	0-0	0	5.74	6.01
2 ML YEARS		20	19	1	0	105.2	454	97	67	60	24	0	2	5	48	1	65	1	1	8	9	.471	1	0-0	0	4.96	5.11

Billy Wagner

Pitches: L **Bats:** L **Pos:** RP-45　　　　　　　　**Ht:** 5'11" **Wt:** 195 **Born:** 7/25/1971 **Age:** 33

Year Team	Lg	G	GS	CG	GF	IP	BFP	H	R	ER	HR	SH	SF	HB	TBB	IBB	SO	WP	Bk	W	L	Pct	ShO	Sv-Op	Hld	ERC	ERA
2004 Reading*	AA	1	1	0	0	1.0	4	1	0	0	0	0	0	0	0	0	2	0	0	0	0	-	0	0--	-	1.95	0.00
1995 Houston	NL	1	0	0	0	0.1	1	0	0	0	0	0	0	0	0	0	0	0	0	0	0	-	0	0-0	-	0.00	0.00
1996 Houston	NL	37	0	0	20	51.2	212	28	16	14	6	7	2	3	30	2	67	1	0	2	2	.500	0	9-13	3	2.61	2.44
1997 Houston	NL	62	0	0	49	66.1	277	49	23	21	5	3	1	3	30	1	106	3	0	7	8	.467	0	23-29	1	2.85	2.85
1998 Houston	NL	58	0	0	50	60.0	247	46	19	18	6	4	0	0	25	1	97	2	0	4	3	.571	0	30-35	1	2.87	2.70
1999 Houston	NL	66	0	0	55	74.2	286	35	14	13	5	2	1	1	23	1	124	2	0	4	1	.800	0	39-42	1	1.20	1.57
2000 Houston	NL	28	0	0	19	27.2	129	28	19	19	6	0	0	1	18	0	28	7	0	2	4	.333	0	6-15	0	6.15	6.18
2001 Houston	NL	64	0	0	58	62.2	251	44	19	19	5	3	1	5	20	0	79	3	0	2	5	.286	0	39-41	0	2.42	2.73
2002 Houston	NL	70	0	0	61	75.0	289	51	21	21	7	2	3	2	22	5	88	6	0	4	2	.667	0	35-41	0	2.08	2.52
2003 Houston	NL	78	0	0	67	86.0	335	52	18	17	8	1	0	3	23	5	105	4	0	1	4	.200	0	44-47	0	1.63	1.78
2004 Philadelphia	NL	45	0	0	38	48.1	182	31	16	13	5	3	0	2	6	1	59	1	0	4	0	1.000	0	21-25	1	1.52	2.42
10 ML YEARS		509	0	0	417	552.2	2209	364	165	155	53	25	8	20	197	16	753	29	0	30	29	.508	0	246-288	7	2.22	2.52

Ryan Wagner

Pitches: R **Bats:** R **Pos:** RP-49　　　　　　　　**Ht:** 6'4" **Wt:** 210 **Born:** 7/15/1982 **Age:** 22

Year Team	Lg	G	GS	CG	GF	IP	BFP	H	R	ER	HR	SH	SF	HB	TBB	IBB	SO	WP	Bk	W	L	Pct	ShO	Sv-Op	Hld	ERC	ERA
2003 Chattanooga	AA	5	0	0	1	5.0	19	2	1	0	0	1	0	0	2	0	6	0	0	1	0	1.000	0	0--	-	0.95	0.00
2003 Louisville	AAA	4	0	0	0	4.0	16	5	2	2	0	0	0	0	0	0	4	0	0	0	1	.000	0	0--	-	3.37	4.50
2004 Louisville	AAA	15	0	0	3	16.2	72	13	5	5	0	0	0	0	9	0	19	2	0	1	0	1.000	0	1--	-	2.67	2.70
2003 Cincinnati	NL	17	0	0	3	21.2	88	13	4	4	2	0	1	0	12	1	25	4	0	2	0	1.000	0	0-1	6	2.46	1.66
2004 Cincinnati	NL	49	0	0	5	51.2	242	59	31	27	7	2	3	2	27	2	37	5	0	3	2	.600	0	0-3	5	5.66	4.70
2 ML YEARS		66	0	0	8	73.1	330	72	35	31	9	2	4	2	39	3	62	9	0	5	2	.714	0	0-4	14	4.64	3.80

Tim Wakefield

Pitches: R **Bats:** R **Pos:** SP-30; RP-2　　　　　　　　**Ht:** 6'2" **Wt:** 214 **Born:** 8/2/1966 **Age:** 38

Year Team	Lg	G	GS	CG	GF	IP	BFP	H	R	ER	HR	SH	SF	HB	TBB	IBB	SO	WP	Bk	W	L	Pct	ShO	Sv-Op	Hld	ERC	ERA
1992 Pittsburgh	NL	13	13	4	0	92.0	373	76	26	22	3	6	4	1	35	1	51	3	1	8	1	.889	1	0-0	0	2.72	2.15
1993 Pittsburgh	NL	24	20	3	1	128.1	595	145	83	80	14	7	5	9	75	2	59	6	0	6	11	.353	2	0-0	0	5.97	5.61
1995 Boston	AL	27	27	6	0	195.1	804	163	76	64	22	3	7	9	68	0	119	11	0	16	8	.667	1	0-0	0	3.28	2.95
1996 Boston	AL	32	32	6	0	211.2	963	238	151	121	38	1	9	12	90	0	140	4	1	14	13	.519	0	0-0	0	5.68	5.14
1997 Boston	AL	35	29	4	2	201.1	866	193	109	95	24	3	7	16	87	5	151	6	0	12	15	.444	2	0-0	1	4.47	4.25
1998 Boston	AL	36	33	2	1	216.0	939	211	123	110	30	1	8	14	79	1	146	6	1	17	8	.680	0	0-0	0	4.30	4.58
1999 Boston	AL	49	17	0	28	140.0	635	146	93	79	19	1	8	5	72	2	104	1	0	6	11	.353	0	15-18	0	5.12	5.08
2000 Boston	AL	51	17	0	13	159.1	706	170	107	97	31	4	8	4	65	3	102	4	0	6	10	.375	0	0-1	3	5.23	5.48
2001 Boston	AL	45	17	0	17	168.2	732	156	84	73	13	3	9	18	73	5	148	5	1	9	12	.429	0	3-5	3	4.02	3.90
2002 Boston	AL	45	15	0	10	163.1	657	121	57	51	15	1	4	9	51	2	134	5	2	11	5	.688	0	3-5	5	2.54	2.81
2003 Boston	AL	35	33	0	2	202.1	872	193	106	92	23	2	4	12	71	0	169	8	0	11	7	.611	0	1-1	0	3.92	4.09
2004 Boston	AL	32	30	0	0	188.1	831	197	121	102	29	2	4	16	63	3	116	9	0	12	10	.545	0	0-0	1	4.73	4.87
12 ML YEARS		424	283	25	62	2066.2	8973	2009	1136	986	261	34	77	125	829	24	1439	68	6	128	111	.536	6	22-30	13	4.33	4.29

Jamie Walker

Pitches: L **Bats:** L **Pos:** RP-70　　　　　　　　**Ht:** 6'2" **Wt:** 190 **Born:** 7/1/1971 **Age:** 33

Year Team	Lg	G	GS	CG	GF	IP	BFP	H	R	ER	HR	SH	SF	HB	TBB	IBB	SO	WP	Bk	W	L	Pct	ShO	Sv-Op	Hld	ERC	ERA
1997 Kansas City	AL	50	0	0	15	43.0	197	46	28	26	6	2	2	3	20	3	24	2	0	3	3	.500	0	0-1	3	5.10	5.44
1998 Kansas City	AL	6	2	0	0	17.1	86	30	20	19	5	1	1	2	3	0	15	0	0	1	1	.500	0	0-0	1	9.69	9.87
2002 Detroit	AL	57	0	0	16	43.2	175	32	19	18	9	0	1	4	9	1	40	1	1	1	1	.500	0	1-4	5	2.86	3.71
2003 Detroit	AL	78	0	0	19	65.0	273	61	30	24	9	5	2	2	17	1	45	1	0	4	3	.571	0	3-7	12	3.51	3.32
2004 Detroit	AL	70	0	0	18	64.2	277	69	28	23	8	1	1	1	12	3	53	4	0	3	4	.429	0	1-7	18	3.65	3.20
5 ML YEARS		261	2	0	70	233.2	1008	238	125	110	37	9	7	12	61	8	177	8	1	11	12	.478	0	5-19	39	4.11	4.24

Kevin Walker

Pitches: L **Bats:** L **Pos:** RP-5　　　　　　　　**Ht:** 6'4" **Wt:** 190 **Born:** 9/20/1976 **Age:** 28

Year Team	Lg	G	GS	CG	GF	IP	BFP	H	R	ER	HR	SH	SF	HB	TBB	IBB	SO	WP	Bk	W	L	Pct	ShO	Sv-Op	Hld	ERC	ERA
2004 Fresno*	AAA	48	1	0	16	69.2	325	79	33	33	8	0	0	4	35	4	62	8	0	1	3	.250	0	1--	-	5.41	4.26
2000 San Diego	NL	70	0	0	14	66.2	287	49	35	31	5	4	2	5	38	6	56	2	1	7	1	.875	0	0-0	19	3.23	4.19
2001 San Diego	NL	16	0	0	5	12.0	49	5	4	4	0	0	0	0	8	2	17	0	1	0	0	-	0	0-1	4	1.33	3.00
2002 San Diego	NL	11	0	0	1	8.0	42	12	6	5	2	1	0	0	5	1	11	1	0	0	1	.000	0	0-1	1	8.79	5.63
2003 San Diego	NL	11	0	0	2	6.2	30	5	4	4	1	0	0	0	5	0	5	0	0	0	0	-	0	0-0	4	4.31	5.40
2004 San Francisco	NL	5	0	0	0	1.2	10	3	3	3	1	0	0	1	2	0	1	0	0	0	0	-	0	0-0	1	23.66	16.20
5 ML YEARS		113	0	0	22	95.0	418	74	52	47	9	5	2	6	58	9	90	3	2	7	2	.778	0	0-2	25	3.68	4.45

Larry Walker

Bats: L **Throws:** R **Pos:** RF-75; PH-9; CF-1; DH-1　　　　　　　　**Ht:** 6'3" **Wt:** 233 **Born:** 12/1/1966 **Age:** 38

Year Team	Lg	G	AB	H	2B	3B	HR	(Hm	Rd)	TB	R	RBI	RC	TBB	IBB	SO	HBP	SH	SF	SB	CS	SB%	GDP	Avg	OBP	Slg
2004 Tulsa*	AA	5	9	2	0	0	1	(-	-)	5	3	2	2	2	0	1	2	0	0	0	0	-	1	.222	.462	.556
1989 Montreal	NL	20	47	8	0	0	0	(0	0)	8	4	4	2	5	0	13	1	3	0	1	1	.50	0	.170	.264	.170
1990 Montreal	NL	133	419	101	18	3	19	(9	10)	182	59	51	60	49	5	112	5	3	2	21	7	.75	8	.241	.326	.434
1991 Montreal	NL	137	487	141	30	2	16	(5	11)	223	59	64	77	42	2	102	5	1	4	14	9	.61	7	.290	.349	.458
1992 Montreal	NL	143	528	159	31	4	23	(13	10)	267	85	93	93	41	10	97	6	0	8	18	6	.75	9	.301	.353	.506
1993 Montreal	NL	138	490	130	24	5	22	(13	9)	230	85	86	89	80	20	76	6	0	6	29	7	.81	8	.265	.371	.469

Year Team	Lg	G	AB	H	2B	3B	HR	(Hm	Rd)	TB	R	RBI	RC	TBB	IBB	SO	HBP	SH	SF	SB	CS	SB%	GDP	Avg	OBP	Slg
										BATTING										**BASERUNNING**				**AVERAGES**		
1994 Montreal	NL	103	395	127	44	2	19	(7	12)	232	76	86	88	47	5	74	4	0	6	15	5	.75	8	.322	.394	.587
1995 Colorado	NL	131	494	151	31	5	36	(24	12)	300	96	101	108	49	13	72	14	0	5	16	3	.84	13	.306	.381	.607
1996 Colorado	NL	83	272	75	18	4	18	(12	6)	155	58	58	53	20	2	58	9	0	3	18	2	.90	7	.276	.342	.570
1997 Colorado	NL	153	568	208	46	4	49	(20	29)	409	143	130	166	78	14	90	14	0	4	33	8	.80	15	.366	.452	.720
1998 Colorado	NL	130	454	165	46	3	23	(17	6)	286	113	67	117	64	2	61	4	0	2	14	4	.78	11	.363	.445	.630
1999 Colorado	NL	127	438	166	26	4	37	(26	11)	311	108	115	127	57	8	52	12	0	6	11	4	.73	12	.379	.458	.710
2000 Colorado	NL	87	314	97	21	7	9	(7	2)	159	64	51	61	44	4	40	9	0	3	5	5	.50	12	.309	.409	.506
2001 Colorado	NL	142	497	174	35	3	38	(20	18)	329	107	123	138	82	6	103	14	0	8	14	5	.74	9	.350	.449	.662
2002 Colorado	NL	136	477	161	40	4	26	(18	8)	287	95	104	112	65	6	73	7	0	4	6	5	.55	8	.338	.421	.602
2003 Colorado	NL	143	454	129	25	7	16	(8	8)	216	86	79	98	98	14	87	11	0	1	7	4	.64	9	.284	.422	.476
2004 Col-StL	NL	82	258	77	16	4	17	(7	10)	152	51	47	54	49	3	57	8	0	1	6	0	1.00	8	.298	.424	.589
2004 Colorado	NL	38	108	35	9	3	6	(2	4)	68	22	20	25	25	2	23	4	0	1	2	0	1.00	2	.324	.464	.630
2004 St Louis	NL	44	150	42	7	1	11	(5	6)	84	29	27	29	24	1	34	4	0	0	4	0	1.00	6	.280	.393	.560
16 ML YEARS		1888	6592	2069	451	61	368	(206	162)	3746	1289	1259	1443	872	114	1167	129	7	63	228	75	.75	144	.314	.401	.568

Todd Walker

Bats: L **Throws:** R **Pos:** 2B-89; PH-36; 1B-5; LF-1   **Ht:** 6'0" **Wt:** 190 **Born:** 5/25/1973 **Age:** 32

Year Team	Lg	G	AB	H	2B	3B	HR	(Hm	Rd)	TB	R	RBI	RC	TBB	IBB	SO	HBP	SH	SF	SB	CS	SB%	GDP	Avg	OBP	Slg
										BATTING										**BASERUNNING**				**AVERAGES**		
1996 Minnesota	AL	25	82	21	6	0	0	(0	0)	27	8	6	7	4	0	13	0	0	3	2	0	1.00	4	.256	.281	.329
1997 Minnesota	AL	52	156	37	7	1	3	(1	2)	55	15	16	16	11	1	30	1	1	2	7	0	1.00	5	.237	.288	.353
1998 Minnesota	AL	143	528	167	41	3	12	(7	5)	250	85	62	90	47	9	65	2	0	4	19	7	.73	13	.316	.372	.473
1999 Minnesota	AL	143	531	148	37	4	6	(4	2)	211	62	46	70	52	5	83	1	0	2	18	10	.64	15	.279	.343	.397
2000 Min-Col	AL	80	248	72	11	4	9	(5	4)	118	42	44	43	27	0	29	1	1	6	7	1	.88	5	.290	.355	.476
2001 Col-Cin	NL	151	551	163	35	2	17	(13	4)	253	93	75	84	51	1	82	1	4	3	1	8	.11	14	.296	.355	.459
2002 Cincinnati	NL	155	612	183	42	3	11	(7	4)	264	79	64	90	50	7	81	3	7	3	8	5	.62	9	.299	.353	.431
2003 Boston	AL	144	587	166	38	4	13	(6	7)	251	92	85	84	48	0	54	1	1	10	1	1	.50	17	.283	.333	.428
2004 Chicago	NL	129	372	102	19	4	15	(6	9)	174	60	50	61	43	8	52	4	1	4	0	3	.00	2	.274	.352	.468
2000 Minnesota	AL	23	77	18	1	0	2	(0	2)	25	14	8	7	7	0	10	0	0	3	3	0	1.00	3	.234	.287	.325
2000 Colorado	NL	57	171	54	10	4	7	(5	2)	93	28	36	36	20	0	19	1	1	3	4	1	.80	2	.316	.385	.544
2001 Colorado	NL	85	290	86	18	2	12	(10	2)	144	52	43	47	25	1	40	0	3	3	1	3	.25	8	.297	.349	.497
2001 Cincinnati	NL	66	261	77	17	0	5	(3	2)	109	41	32	37	26	0	42	1	1	0	0	5	.00	6	.295	.361	.418
9 ML YEARS		1022	3667	1059	236	25	86	(49	37)	1603	536	448	545	333	31	489	14	15	37	63	35	.64	84	.289	.347	.437

Tyler Walker

Pitches: R **Bats:** R **Pos:** RP-52   **Ht:** 6'3" **Wt:** 255 **Born:** 5/15/1976 **Age:** 29

Year Team	Lg	G	GS	CG	GF	IP	BFP	H	R	ER	HR	SH	SF	HB	TBB	IBB	SO	WP	Bk	W	L	Pct	ShO	Sv-Op	Hld	ERC	ERA
		HOW MUCH HE PITCHED						**WHAT HE GAVE UP**												**THE RESULTS**							
1997 Mets	R	5	0	0	5	9.0	37	8	1	1	0	1	0	0	2	1	9	1	0	0	0	-	0	3- -	-	2.01	1.00
1997 Pittsfield	A-	1	0	0	0	0.2	6	2	2	1	1	0	0	0	1	0	1	1	0	0	0	-	0	0- -	-	34.79	13.50
1998 Capital City	A	34	13	0	3	115.2	503	122	63	53	9	3	4	3	38	0	110	8	1	5	5	.500	0	1- -	-	4.01	4.12
1999 St. Lucie	A+	13	13	2	0	79.2	329	64	31	26	6	3	2	3	29	2	64	4	1	6	5	.545	0	0- -	-	2.83	2.94
1999 Binghamton	AA	13	13	0	0	68.0	306	78	49	47	11	3	2	2	32	0	59	4	3	6	4	.600	0	0- -	-	5.88	6.22
2000 Binghamton	AA	22	22	0	0	121.0	495	82	43	37	3	2	4	2	55	1	111	9	1	7	6	.538	0	0- -	-	2.16	2.75
2000 Norfolk	AAA	5	5	0	0	26.1	111	29	7	7	0	2	0	0	9	0	17	1	0	1	3	.250	0	0- -	-	3.82	2.39
2001 St. Lucie	A+	4	4	0	0	15.2	69	19	14	14	0	0	0	0	3	0	11	3	0	2	0	1.000	0	0- -	-	3.63	8.04
2001 Binghamton	AA	4	3	0	0	22.1	88	9	2	1	1	3	1	0	13	1	13	1	0	1	0	1.000	0	0- -	-	1.45	0.40
2001 Norfolk	AAA	8	8	0	0	40.1	160	34	19	18	7	2	1	1	8	0	35	1	0	3	2	.600	0	0- -	-	3.05	4.02
2002 Norfolk	AAA	28	25	1	3	142.0	603	152	65	63	13	3	5	4	38	3	109	2	3	10	5	.667	1	1- -	-	3.99	3.99
2003 Toledo	AAA	26	22	1	2	131.1	569	139	73	65	13	4	2	2	47	5	117	3	3	2	9	.182	0	0- -	-	4.23	4.45
2004 Fresno	AAA	9	1	0	4	15.2	67	16	5	3	1	1	0	0	2	0	15	0	0	1	1	.500	0	0- -	-	2.75	1.72
2002 New York	NL	5	1	0	3	10.2	49	11	7	7	3	0	0	0	5	1	7	0	0	1	0	1.000	0	0-0	-	5.46	5.91
2004 San Francisco	NL	52	0	0	13	63.2	275	69	31	30	8	3	7	1	24	1	48	1	0	5	1	.833	0	1-1	5	4.76	4.24
2 ML YEARS		57	1	0	16	74.1	324	80	38	37	11	3	7	1	29	2	55	1	0	6	1	.857	0	1-1	5	4.86	4.48

Daryle Ward

Bats: L **Throws:** L **Pos:** 1B-71; RF-12; PH-5   **Ht:** 6'2" **Wt:** 240 **Born:** 6/27/1975 **Age:** 30

Year Team	Lg	G	AB	H	2B	3B	HR	(Hm	Rd)	TB	R	RBI	RC	TBB	IBB	SO	HBP	SH	SF	SB	CS	SB%	GDP	Avg	OBP	Slg
										BATTING										**BASERUNNING**				**AVERAGES**		
2004 Nashville*	AAA	28	96	27	7	0	7	(-	-)	55	14	17	16	5	1	16	0	0	0	0	0	-	1	.281	.317	.573
1998 Houston	NL	4	3	1	0	0	0	(0	0)	1	1	0	1	1	0	2	0	0	0	0	0	-	0	.333	.500	.333
1999 Houston	NL	64	150	41	6	0	8	(2	6)	71	11	30	21	9	0	31	0	0	2	0	0	-	3	.273	.311	.473
2000 Houston	NL	119	264	68	10	2	20	(13	7)	142	36	47	40	15	2	61	0	0	2	0	0	-	6	.258	.295	.538
2001 Houston	NL	95	213	56	15	0	9	(5	4)	98	21	39	31	19	4	48	1	0	2	0	0	-	3	.263	.323	.460
2002 Houston	NL	136	453	125	31	0	12	(9	3)	192	41	72	61	33	5	82	1	0	4	1	3	.25	9	.276	.324	.424
2003 Los Angeles	NL	52	109	20	1	0	0	(0	0)	21	6	9	1	3	0	19	1	0	1	0	0	-	4	.183	.211	.193
2004 Pittsburgh	NL	79	293	73	17	2	15	(8	7)	139	39	57	40	22	3	45	3	0	3	0	0	-	8	.249	.305	.474
7 ML YEARS		549	1485	384	80	4	64	(37	27)	664	155	254	195	102	14	288	6	0	14	1	3	.25	33	.259	.306	.447

John Wasdin

Pitches: R **Bats:** R **Pos:** SP-10; RP-5   **Ht:** 6'2" **Wt:** 196 **Born:** 8/5/1972 **Age:** 32

Year Team	Lg	G	GS	CG	GF	IP	BFP	H	R	ER	HR	SH	SF	HB	TBB	IBB	SO	WP	Bk	W	L	Pct	ShO	Sv-Op	Hld	ERC	ERA
		HOW MUCH HE PITCHED						**WHAT HE GAVE UP**												**THE RESULTS**							
2004 Oklahoma*	AAA	18	14	2	0	104.0	411	94	43	40	10	4	5	0	19	0	81	2	0	7	1	.875	1	0- -	-	2.77	3.46
1995 Oakland	AL	5	2	0	0	17.1	69	14	0	9	4	0	0	0	3	0	6	0	0	1	1	.500	0	0-0	0	2.91	4.67
1996 Oakland	AL	25	21	1	0	131.1	575	145	0	87	24	0	0	0	50	0	75	0	0	8	7	.533	0	0-0	0	5.22	5.96
1997 Boston	AL	53	7	0	0	124.2	534	121	0	61	18	0	0	0	38	0	84	0	0	4	6	.400	0	0-0	0	3.75	4.40
1998 Boston	AL	47	4	0	0	96.0	424	111	0	56	14	0	0	0	27	0	59	0	0	6	4	.600	0	0-0	0	4.73	5.25
1999 Boston	AL	45	0	0	0	74.1	302	66	0	34	14	0	0	0	18	0	57	0	0	8	3	.727	0	2-0	0	3.41	4.12
2000 Bos-Col	NL	39	4	1	0	80.1	352	90	0	48	14	0	0	0	24	0	71	0	0	1	6	.143	0	1-0	0	4.82	5.38

Year Team	Lg	G	GS	CG	GF	IP	BFP	H	R	ER	HR	SH	SF	HB	TBB	IBB	SO	WP	Bk	W	L	Pct	ShO	Sv-Op	Hld	ERC	ERA
2001 Col-Bal		44	0	0	0	74.0	330	86	0	42	11	0	0	0	24	0	64	0	0	3	2	.600	0	0-0	0	4.97	5.11
2003 Toronto	AL	3	2	0	0	5.0	35	16	13	13	2	0	1	0	4	0	5	0	0	0	0	1.000	0	0-0	0	25.15	23.40
2004 Texas	AL	15	10	0	0	65.0	301	83	52	49	18	1	2	3	23	2	36	0	0	2	4	.333	0	0-0	0	6.97	6.78
2000 Boston	AL	25	1	0	0	44.2	198	48	0	25	8	0	0	0	15	0	36	0	0	1	3	.250	0	1-0	0	4.67	5.04
2000 Colorado	NL	14	3	1	0	35.2	154	42	0	23	6	0	0	0	9	0	35	0	0	3	0	.000	0	0-0	0	5.01	5.80
2001 Colorado	NL	18	0	0	0	24.1	110	32	0	19	7	0	0	0	8	0	17	0	0	2	1	.667	0	0-0	0	7.15	7.03
2001 Baltimore	AL	26	0	0	0	49.2	220	54	0	23	4	0	0	0	16	0	47	0	0	1	1	.500	0	0-0	0	4.00	4.17
9 ML YEARS		276	54	2	0	668.0	2922	732	65	399	119	1	3	3	211	2	457	0	0	33	34	.493	0	3-0	0	4.79	5.38

Jarrod Washburn

Pitches: L Bats: L Pos: SP-25

Ht: 6'1" Wt: 187 Born: 8/13/1974 Age: 30

Year Team	Lg	G	GS	CG	GF	IP	BFP	H	R	ER	HR	SH	SF	HB	TBB	IBB	SO	WP	Bk	W	L	Pct	ShO	Sv-Op	Hld	ERC	ERA
2004 R Cucamnga*	A+	1	1	0	0	4.0	20	4	1	1	0	0	0	0	3	0	5	0	0	0	0		0	0--		4.28	2.25
1998 Anaheim	AL	15	11	0	0	74.0	317	70	40	38	11	2	3	3	27	1	48	0	0	6	3	.667	0	0-0	1	4.09	4.62
1999 Anaheim	AL	16	10	0	3	61.2	264	61	36	36	6	1	2	1	26	0	39	2	0	4	5	.444	0	0-0	1	4.20	5.25
2000 Anaheim	AL	14	14	0	0	84.1	340	64	38	35	16	1	3	1	37	0	49	1	0	7	2	.778	0	0-0	0	3.66	3.74
2001 Anaheim	AL	30	30	1	0	193.1	813	196	89	81	25	4	4	7	54	4	126	3	0	11	10	.524	0	0-0	0	4.03	3.77
2002 Anaheim	AL	32	32	1	0	206.0	852	183	75	72	19	4	7	3	59	1	139	5	1	18	6	.750	0	0-0	0	3.02	3.15
2003 Anaheim	AL	32	32	2	0	207.1	876	205	106	102	34	5	6	11	54	4	118	4	1	10	15	.400	0	0-0	0	4.07	4.43
2004 Anaheim	AL	25	25	1	0	149.1	640	159	81	77	20	2	4	4	40	1	86	5	0	11	8	.579	1	0-0	0	4.23	4.64
7 ML YEARS		164	154	5	3	976.0	4102	938	465	441	131	19	29	30	297	11	605	20	2	67	49	.578	1	0-0	2	3.83	4.07

Steve Watkins

Pitches: R Bats: R Pos: RP-11

Ht: 6'2" Wt: 190 Born: 7/19/1978 Age: 26

Year Team	Lg	G	GS	CG	GF	IP	BFP	H	R	ER	HR	SH	SF	HB	TBB	IBB	SO	WP	Bk	W	L	Pct	ShO	Sv-Op	Hld	ERC	ERA
1998 Idaho Falls	R+	2	1	0	0	2.0	21	10	12	9	3	1	0	0	4	0	0	0	0	0	1	.000	0	0--	-	61.66	40.50
1998 Peoria	A	9	3	0	1	20.2	88	15	4	3	0	2	1	1	10	0	20	3	0	1	0	1.000	0	0--	-	2.39	1.31
1998 Padres	R	9	3	0	1	20.2	88	15	4	3	0	2	1	1	10	0	20	3	0	1	0	1.000	0	0--	-	2.39	1.31
1999 Fort Wayne	A	4	4	0	0	17.0	83	24	17	16	3	1	0	2	9	0	21	1	0	3	0	.000	0	0--	-	8.44	8.47
1999 Idaho Falls	R+	12	11	0	0	61.1	272	60	39	30	5	4	3	4	25	0	75	9	0	5	2	.714	0	0--	-	4.02	4.40
2000 R Cucamnga	A+	27	27	0	0	151.0	652	118	75	62	10	8	6	1	90	0	163	10	2	7	6	.538	0	0--	-	3.40	3.70
2001 Mobile	IND	23	19	0	2	97.1	447	108	74	62	14	2	6	5	53	2	55	3	0	4	8	.333	0	0--	-	5.83	5.73
2001 Lk Elsinore	A+	5	5	1	0	29.1	120	23	6	6	0	1	1	0	7	0	23	2	0	2	0	1.000	1	0--	-	1.71	1.84
2002 Mobile	IND	37	15	1	5	116.2	505	124	65	49	8	4	6	3	49	3	88	2	1	4	8	.333	0	0--	-	4.43	3.78
2003 Mobile	AA	18	18	0	0	101.1	430	100	50	47	8	6	5	0	34	1	75	1	0	5	4	.556	0	0--	-	3.58	4.17
2003 Portland	AAA	14	0	0	3	26.1	109	20	11	9	1	0	0	0	12	0	23	1	0	1	0	1.000	0	0--	-	2.60	3.08
2004 Mobile	AA	10	10	0	0	59.1	236	50	28	24	6	1	2	3	15	0	57	1	0	4	3	.571	0	0--	-	2.96	3.64
2004 Portland	AAA	22	6	0	3	55.2	238	53	20	19	3	2	1	2	19	0	58	1	0	5	3	.625	0	0--	-	3.38	3.07
2004 San Diego	NL	11	0	0	7	14.1	65	17	10	10	3	1	0	2	4	0	7	0	0	0	0	-	0	0-0	0	6.03	6.28

Justin Wayne

Pitches: R Bats: R Pos: RP-18; SP-1

Ht: 6'3" Wt: 200 Born: 4/16/1979 Age: 26

Year Team	Lg	G	GS	CG	GF	IP	BFP	H	R	ER	HR	SH	SF	HB	TBB	IBB	SO	WP	Bk	W	L	Pct	ShO	Sv-Op	Hld	ERC	ERA
2004 Jupiter*	A+	2	1	0	0	3.0	12	3	0	0	0	0	0	0	0	0	3	0	0	0	0		0	0--	-	1.95	0.00
2004 Albuquerque*	AAA	13	13	0	0	65.2	303	82	53	48	11	7	2	7	34	1	43	6	0	1	5	.167	0	0--	-	7.28	6.58
2002 Florida	NL	5	5	0	0	23.2	105	22	16	14	3	0	2	0	13	0	16	2	1	2	3	.400	0	0-0	0	4.41	5.32
2003 Florida	NL	2	2	0	0	5.1	31	9	7	7	1	0	1	1	5	0	1	1	0	0	2	.000	0	0-0	0	12.39	11.81
2004 Florida	NL	19	1	0	4	32.2	148	35	24	21	6	1	3	2	18	1	20	1	0	3	3	.500	0	0-2	1	6.03	5.79
3 ML YEARS		26	8	0	4	61.2	284	66	47	42	10	1	6	3	36	1	37	4	1	5	8	.385	0	0-2	1	5.88	6.13

David Weathers

Pitches: R Bats: R Pos: RP-64; SP-2

Ht: 6'3" Wt: 230 Born: 9/25/1969 Age: 35

Year Team	Lg	G	GS	CG	GF	IP	BFP	H	R	ER	HR	SH	SF	HB	TBB	IBB	SO	WP	Bk	W	L	Pct	ShO	Sv-Op	Hld	ERC	ERA
1991 Toronto	AL	15	0	0	4	14.2	79	15	9	8	1	2	1	2	17	3	13	0	0	1	0	1.000	0	0-0	1	6.88	4.91
1992 Toronto	AL	2	0	0	0	3.1	15	5	3	3	1	0	0	0	2	0	3	0	0	0	0	-	0	0-0	0	10.97	8.10
1993 Florida	NL	14	6	0	2	45.2	202	57	26	26	3	2	0	1	13	1	34	6	0	2	3	.400	0	0-0	0	4.86	5.12
1994 Florida	NL	24	24	0	0	135.0	621	166	87	79	13	12	4	4	59	9	72	7	1	8	12	.400	0	0-0	0	5.52	5.27
1995 Florida	NL	28	15	0	0	90.1	419	104	68	60	8	7	3	5	52	3	60	3	0	4	5	.444	0	0-0	1	5.79	5.98
1996 Fla-NYY		42	12	0	9	88.2	409	108	60	54	8	5	2	6	42	5	53	3	0	4	4	.333	0	0-0	3	5.80	5.48
1997 NYY-Cle	AL	19	1	0	5	25.2	126	38	24	24	3	2	1	1	15	0	18	3	0	1	3	.250	0	0-1	0	8.27	8.42
1998 Cin-Mil		44	9	0	9	110.0	492	130	69	60	6	6	2	3	41	3	94	7	2	6	5	.545	0	0-1	3	4.73	4.91
1999 Milwaukee	NL	63	0	0	14	93.0	414	102	49	48	14	4	4	2	38	3	74	1	1	7	4	.636	0	2-6	9	5.04	4.65
2000 Milwaukee	NL	69	0	0	23	76.1	320	73	29	26	7	4	1	2	32	8	50	0	0	3	5	.375	0	1-7	14	3.90	3.07
2001 Mil-ChC		80	0	0	25	86.0	351	65	24	23	6	10	3	3	34	8	66	0	0	4	5	.444	0	4-10	16	2.59	2.41
2002 New York	NL	71	0	0	12	77.1	331	69	30	25	6	6	4	3	36	7	61	2	0	6	3	.667	0	0-5	18	3.60	2.91
2003 New York	NL	77	0	0	20	87.2	384	87	30	26	8	6	0	6	40	6	75	1	0	1	6	.143	0	7-9	26	4.21	3.08
2004 NYM-Hou-Fla		66	2	0	20	82.1	357	85	44	38	12	5	2	5	35	2	61	1	1	7	7	.500	0	0-4	12	5.01	4.15
1996 Florida	NL	31	8	0	8	71.1	319	85	41	36	7	5	1	4	28	4	40	2	0	2	2	.500	0	0-0	3	5.35	4.54
1996 New York	AL	11	4	0	1	17.1	90	23	19	18	1	0	1	2	14	1	13	1	0	2	2	.000	0	0-0	0	7.66	9.35
1997 New York	AL	10	0	0	3	9.0	47	15	10	10	1	0	0	0	7	0	4	2	0	0	1	.000	0	0-1	0	10.26	10.00
1997 Cleveland	AL	9	1	0	2	16.2	79	23	14	14	2	2	1	1	8	0	14	1	0	1	2	.333	0	0-0	0	7.23	7.56
1998 Cincinnati	NL	16	9	0	0	62.1	294	86	47	43	3	4	1	1	27	2	51	5	1	2	4	.333	0	0-0	0	6.04	6.21
1998 Milwaukee	NL	28	0	0	9	47.2	198	44	22	17	3	2	1	2	14	1	43	2	1	4	1	.800	0	0-1	3	3.15	3.21
2001 Milwaukee	NL	52	0	0	21	57.2	233	37	14	13	3	8	1	2	25	7	46	0	0	3	4	.429	0	4-7	10	2.01	2.03
2001 Chicago	NL	28	0	0	4	28.1	118	28	10	10	3	2	2	1	9	1	20	0	0	1	1	.500	0	0-3	6	3.90	3.18
2004 New York	NL	32	0	0	10	33.2	156	41	19	16	5	2	2	2	15	0	25	1	1	5	3	.625	0	0-1	6	6.15	4.28

Year Team	Lg	G	GS	CG	GF	IP	BFP	H	R	ER	HR	SH	SF	HB	TBB	IBB	SO	WP	Bk	W	L	Pct	ShO	Sv-Op	Hld	ERC	ERA
2004 Houston	NL	26	0	0	9	32.0	137	31	20	17	5	2	0	3	13	1	26	0	0	1	4	.200	0	0-3	5	4.77	4.78
2004 Florida	NL	8	2	0	1	16.2	64	13	5	5	2	1	0	0	7	1	10	0	0	1	0	1.000	0	0-0	1	3.28	2.70
14 ML YEARS		614	69	0	143	1016.0	4520	1104	555	504	94	73	27	43	456	58	734	34	5	52	62	.456	0	14-43	103	4.81	4.46

Jeff Weaver

Pitches: R **Bats:** R **Pos:** SP-34 **Ht:** 6'5" **Wt:** 200 **Born:** 8/22/1976 **Age:** 28

Year Team	Lg	G	GS	CG	GF	IP	BFP	H	R	ER	HR	SH	SF	HB	TBB	IBB	SO	WP	Bk	W	L	Pct	ShO	Sv-Op	Hld	ERC	ERA
1999 Detroit	AL	30	29	0	1	163.2	717	176	104	101	27	5	5	17	56	2	114	0	0	9	12	.429	0	0-0	0	5.21	5.55
2000 Detroit	AL	31	30	2	0	200.0	849	205	102	96	26	3	9	15	52	2	136	3	2	11	15	.423	0	0-0	0	4.18	4.32
2001 Detroit	AL	33	33	5	0	229.1	985	235	116	104	19	12	7	14	68	4	152	3	0	13	16	.448	0	0-0	0	3.89	4.08
2002 Det-NYY	AL	32	25	3	3	199.2	840	193	88	78	16	6	3	11	48	4	132	6	0	11	11	.500	3	2-2	0	3.30	3.52
2003 New York	AL	32	24	0	1	159.1	735	211	113	106	16	9	9	11	47	2	93	2	0	7	9	.438	0	0-0	0	5.77	5.99
2004 Los Angeles	NL	34	34	0	0	220.0	935	219	103	98	19	5	7	14	67	9	153	9	0	13	13	.500	0	0-0	0	3.79	4.01
2002 Detroit	AL	17	17	3	0	121.2	509	112	50	43	4	5	2	8	33	1	75	4	0	6	8	.429	3	0-0	0	2.94	3.18
2002 New York	AL	15	8	0	3	78.0	331	81	38	35	12	1	1	3	15	3	57	2	0	5	3	.625	0	2-2	0	3.86	4.04
6 ML YEARS		192	175	10	7	1172.0	5061	1239	626	583	123	40	40	82	338	23	780	23	2	64	76	.457	3	2-2	1	4.24	4.48

Brandon Webb

Pitches: R **Bats:** R **Pos:** SP-35 **Ht:** 6'2" **Wt:** 228 **Born:** 5/9/1979 **Age:** 26

Year Team	Lg	G	GS	CG	GF	IP	BFP	H	R	ER	HR	SH	SF	HB	TBB	IBB	SO	WP	Bk	W	L	Pct	ShO	Sv-Op	Hld	ERC	ERA
2000 Diamndbcks	R	1	1	0	0	1.0	5	2	1	1	0	0	0	0	0	0	3	0	0	0	0	-	0	0--	-	7.48	9.00
2000 South Bend	A	12	0	0	7	16.2	69	10	7	6	0	0	0	2	9	1	18	1	0	0	0	-	0	2--	-	2.20	3.24
2001 Lancaster	A+	29	28	0	0	162.1	711	174	90	72	9	3	5	27	44	0	158	11	1	6	10	.375	0	0--	-	4.33	3.99
2002 El Paso	AA	26	25	1	1	152.0	647	141	66	53	4	2	3	13	59	1	122	12	1	10	6	.625	1	0--	-	3.48	3.14
2002 Tucson	AAA	1	1	0	0	7.0	31	5	3	3	0	1	0	1	4	0	5	0	0	0	1	.000	0	0--	-	2.92	3.86
2003 Tucson	AAA	3	3	0	0	18.0	84	18	17	12	0	0	2	3	9	0	17	2	0	1	1	.500	0	0--	-	4.23	6.00
2003 Arizona	NL	29	28	1	1	180.2	750	140	65	57	12	9	1	13	68	4	172	9	1	10	9	.526	1	0-0	0	2.80	2.84
2004 Arizona	NL	35	35	1	0	208.0	933	194	111	83	17	14	6	11	119	11	164	17	1	7	16	.304	0	0-0	0	4.32	3.59
2 ML YEARS		64	63	2	1	388.2	1683	334	176	140	29	23	7	24	187	15	336	26	2	17	25	.405	1	0-0	0	3.59	3.24

John Webb

Pitches: R **Bats:** R **Pos:** RP-4 **Ht:** 6'3" **Wt:** 220 **Born:** 5/23/1979 **Age:** 26

Year Team	Lg	G	GS	CG	GF	IP	BFP	H	R	ER	HR	SH	SF	HB	TBB	IBB	SO	WP	Bk	W	L	Pct	ShO	Sv-Op	Hld	ERC	ERA
1999 Cubs	R	18	0	0	14	32.2	147	33	20	13	0	1	1	3	8	0	39	2	2	0	0	-	0	3--	-	2.99	3.58
1999 Eugene	A-	2	0	0	2	4.0	14	1	0	0	0	0	0	0	1	0	3	0	0	1	0	1.000	0	1--	-	0.40	0.00
2000 Lansing	A	21	21	1	0	134.2	559	125	53	37	4	3	6	8	40	0	108	9	1	7	6	.538	1	0--	-	3.09	2.47
2000 Daytona	A+	5	2	0	1	17.0	71	17	11	9	1	0	0	0	3	0	18	2	0	1	1	.500	0	1--	-	2.89	4.76
2001 Daytona	A+	5	4	0	0	20.0	91	23	13	12	0	0	0	2	7	1	20	2	1	1	1	.500	0	0--	-	4.21	5.40
2002 Daytona	A+	10	10	1	0	57.2	240	43	23	22	3	1	3	5	23	0	65	4	1	5	3	.625	1	0--	-	2.72	3.43
2002 W Tennessee	AA	11	11	0	0	61.2	0	52	33	31	5	1	2	5	22	0	45	3	1	4	5	.444	0	-	-		4.52
2003 W Tennessee	AA	30	22	0	5	132.0	573	135	74	66	11	6	5	10	52	1	85	4	1	5	8	.385	0	1--	-	4.41	4.50
2004 Montgomery	AA	9	3	0	2	26.1	113	26	12	12	3	0	2	3	8	0	12	1	0	2	1	.667	0	0--	-	4.20	4.10
2004 Durham	AAA	6	6	0	0	33.0	142	31	19	12	5	1	3	4	14	0	22	3	0	1	3	.250	0	0--	-	4.80	3.27
2004 Tampa Bay	AL	4	0	0	1	9.0	45	12	7	7	2	0	0	1	7	0	9	1	0	0	0	-	0	0-0	0	9.56	7.00

Ben Weber

Pitches: R **Bats:** R **Pos:** RP-18 **Ht:** 6'4" **Wt:** 210 **Born:** 11/17/1969 **Age:** 35

Year Team	Lg	G	GS	CG	GF	IP	BFP	H	R	ER	HR	SH	SF	HB	TBB	IBB	SO	WP	Bk	W	L	Pct	ShO	Sv-Op	Hld	ERC	ERA
2004 Angels*	R	1	1	0	0	1.0	3	0	0	0	0	0	0	0	0	0	2	0	0	0	0	-	0	0--	-	0.00	0.00
2004 Salt Lake*	AAA	15	0	0	6	16.2	87	27	25	16	3	0	0	1	9	1	18	0	0	0	2	.000	0	1--	-	9.21	8.64
2000 SF-Ana		19	0	0	3	22.2	103	28	19	16	0	0	1	0	6	1	14	2	0	1	1	.500	0	0-2	2	3.91	6.35
2001 Anaheim	AL	56	0	0	19	68.1	299	66	28	26	4	0	0	5	31	8	40	0	1	6	2	.750	0	0-1	6	3.90	3.42
2002 Anaheim	AL	63	0	0	16	78.0	314	70	25	22	4	4	2	3	22	3	43	2	0	7	2	.778	0	7-11	18	2.94	2.54
2003 Anaheim	AL	62	0	0	0	80.1	333	84	26	24	7	4	1	0	22	7	46	4	0	5	1	.833	0	0-2	11	3.70	2.69
2004 Anaheim	AL	18	0	0	5	22.1	117	37	24	20	4	0	0	0	15	0	11	0	0	0	2	.000	0	0-1	2	10.10	8.06
2000 San Francisco	NL	9	0	0	2	8.0	44	16	13	13	0	0	0	0	4	0	6	1	0	0	0	-	0	0-2	1	9.72	14.63
2000 Anaheim	AL	10	0	0	0	14.2	59	12	6	3	0	0	1	0	2	1	8	1	0	1	0	1.000	0	0-0	1	1.52	1.84
5 ML YEARS		218	0	0	63	271.2	1166	285	122	108	19	8	4	8	96	19	154	8	1	19	8	.704	0	7-17	39	4.00	3.58

Todd Wellemeyer

Pitches: R **Bats:** R **Pos:** RP-20 **Ht:** 6'3" **Wt:** 205 **Born:** 8/30/1978 **Age:** 26

Year Team	Lg	G	GS	CG	GF	IP	BFP	H	R	ER	HR	SH	SF	HB	TBB	IBB	SO	WP	Bk	W	L	Pct	ShO	Sv-Op	Hld	ERC	ERA
2000 Eugene	A-	15	15	0	0	76.0	315	62	35	31	3	1	1	4	33	2	85	3	1	4	4	.500	0	0--	-	3.02	3.67
2001 Lansing	A	27	27	1	0	147.0	667	165	85	68	14	4	5	11	74	0	167	10	1	13	9	.591	0	0--	-	5.55	4.16
2002 Daytona	A+	14	14	0	0	73.2	301	63	33	31	7	4	3	6	19	1	87	3	0	2	4	.333	0	0--	-	2.92	3.79
2002 W Tennessee	AA	8	8	1	0	46.0	187	33	25	24	2	0	4	3	18	0	37	2	0	3	3	.500	1	0--	-	2.46	4.70
2003 W Tennessee	AA	4	4	0	0	21.1	95	19	13	13	1	0	2	3	10	0	34	0	0	1	1	.500	0	0--	-	3.84	5.48
2003 Iowa	AAA	13	12	0	0	66.0	291	68	39	38	7	2	4	2	33	4	56	1	0	5	5	.500	0	0--	-	4.77	5.18
2004 Iowa	AAA	13	4	0	2	22.0	103	23	11	10	2	0	1	4	11	0	22	0	0	1	1	.500	0	0--	-	5.32	4.09
2003 Chicago	NL	15	0	0	8	27.2	122	25	22	20	5	1	0	0	19	1	30	0	0	1	1	.500	0	1-1	0	5.33	6.51
2004 Chicago	NL	20	0	0	7	24.1	119	27	16	16	1	3	2	0	20	2	30	0	1	2	1	.667	0	0-0	0	5.67	5.92
2 ML YEARS		35	0	0	15	52.0	241	52	38	36	6	4	2	0	39	3	60	0	1	3	2	.600	0	1-1	1	5.51	6.23

David Wells

Pitches: L **Bats:** L **Pos:** SP-31   **Ht:** 6'4" **Wt:** 240 **Born:** 5/20/1963 **Age:** 42

Year Team	Lg	G	GS	CG	GF	IP	BFP	H	R	ER	HR	SH	SF	HB	TBB	IBB	SO	WP	Bk	W	L	Pct	ShO	Sv-Op	Hld	ERC	ERA
1987 Toronto	AL	18	2	0	6	29.1	132	37	14	13	0	1	0	0	12	0	32	4	0	4	3	.571	0	1-2	2	4.91	3.99
1988 Toronto	AL	41	0	0	15	64.1	279	65	36	33	12	2	2	2	31	9	56	6	2	3	5	.375	0	4-6	8	5.11	4.62
1989 Toronto	AL	54	0	0	19	86.1	352	66	25	23	5	3	2	0	28	7	78	6	3	7	4	.636	0	2-9	8	2.16	2.40
1990 Toronto	AL	43	25	0	8	189.0	759	165	72	66	14	9	2	2	45	3	115	7	1	11	6	.647	0	3-3	3	2.67	3.14
1991 Toronto	AL	40	28	2	3	198.1	811	188	88	82	24	6	6	2	49	1	106	10	3	15	10	.600	0	1-2	3	3.41	3.72
1992 Toronto	AL	41	14	0	14	120.0	529	138	84	72	16	3	4	8	36	6	62	3	1	7	9	.438	0	2-4	3	4.98	5.40
1993 Detroit	AL	32	30	0	0	187.0	776	183	93	87	26	3	3	7	42	6	139	13	0	11	9	.550	0	0-0	1	3.64	4.19
1994 Detroit	AL	16	16	5	0	111.1	464	113	54	49	13	3	1	2	24	6	71	5	0	5	7	.417	1	0-0	0	3.54	3.96
1995 Det-Cin		29	29	6	0	203.0	839	194	86	73	23	7	3	2	53	9	133	7	2	16	8	.667	0	0-0	0	3.37	3.24
1996 Baltimore	AL	34	34	3	0	224.1	946	247	132	128	32	8	14	7	51	7	130	8	0	11	14	.440	0	0-0	0	4.39	5.14
1997 New York	AL	32	32	5	0	218.0	922	239	109	102	24	7	3	6	45	0	156	8	0	16	10	.615	2	0-0	0	4.04	4.21
1998 New York	AL	30	30	8	0	214.1	851	195	86	83	29	2	2	1	29	0	163	2	0	18	4	.818	5	0-0	0	2.83	3.49
1999 Toronto	AL	34	34	7	0	231.2	987	246	132	124	32	6	6	6	62	2	169	1	0	17	10	.630	1	0-0	0	4.26	4.82
2000 Toronto	AL	35	35	9	0	229.2	972	266	115	105	23	6	7	8	31	0	166	9	1	20	8	.714	1	0-0	0	4.05	4.11
2001 Chicago	AL	16	16	1	0	100.2	432	120	55	50	12	2	2	3	21	1	59	2	0	5	7	.417	0	0-0	0	4.69	4.47
2002 New York	AL	31	31	2	0	206.1	873	210	100	86	21	6	5	5	45	2	137	4	0	19	7	.731	0	0-0	0	3.50	3.75
2003 New York	AL	31	30	4	0	213.0	887	242	101	98	24	6	7	8	20	0	101	3	0	15	7	.682	1	0-0	0	3.87	4.14
2004 San Diego	NL	31	31	0	0	195.2	804	203	85	81	23	14	4	2	20	1	101	2	1	12	8	.600	0	0-0	0	3.23	3.73
1995 Detroit	AL	18	18	3	0	130.1	539	120	54	44	17	3	2	2	37	5	83	6	1	10	3	.769	0	0-0	0	3.40	3.04
1995 Cincinnati	NL	11	11	3	0	72.2	300	74	34	29	6	4	1	0	16	4	50	1	1	6	5	.545	0	0-0	0	3.31	3.59
18 ML YEARS		588	417	52	65	3022.1	12615	3117	1469	1355	353	94	73	71	644	60	1974	96	16	212	136	.609	12	13-26	28	3.70	4.03

Kip Wells

Pitches: R **Bats:** R **Pos:** SP-24   **Ht:** 6'3" **Wt:** 205 **Born:** 4/21/1977 **Age:** 28

Year Team	Lg	G	GS	CG	GF	IP	BFP	H	R	ER	HR	SH	SF	HB	TBB	IBB	SO	WP	Bk	W	L	Pct	ShO	Sv-Op	Hld	ERC	ERA
1999 Chicago	AL	7	7	0	0	35.2	153	33	17	16	2	0	2	3	15	0	29	1	2	4	1	.800	0	0-0	0	3.80	4.04
2000 Chicago	AL	20	20	0	0	98.2	468	126	76	66	15	1	3	2	58	4	71	7	0	6	9	.400	0	0-0	0	7.01	6.02
2001 Chicago	AL	40	20	0	3	133.1	603	145	80	71	14	8	6	12	61	5	99	14	0	11	11	.476	0	0-2	6	5.16	4.79
2002 Pittsburgh	NL	33	33	1	0	198.1	844	197	92	79	21	7	5	7	71	11	134	7	0	12	14	.462	1	0-0	0	4.01	3.58
2003 Pittsburgh	NL	31	31	1	0	197.1	835	171	77	72	24	15	2	7	76	7	147	6	0	10	9	.526	0	0-0	0	3.49	3.28
2004 Pittsburgh	NL	24	24	0	0	138.1	621	145	71	70	14	5	6	6	66	4	116	3	0	5	7	.417	0	0-0	0	4.77	4.55
6 ML YEARS		155	135	2	3	801.2	3524	817	413	374	90	36	24	37	347	31	596	38	2	47	51	.480	1	0-2	6	4.53	4.20

Vernon Wells

Bats: R **Throws:** R **Pos:** CF-131; DH-3; PH-1   **Ht:** 6'1" **Wt:** 225 **Born:** 12/8/1978 **Age:** 26

Year Team	Lg	G	AB	H	2B	3B	HR	(Hm	Rd)	TB	R	RBI	RC	TBB	IBB	SO	HBP	SH	SF	SB	CS	SB%	GDP	Avg	OBP	Slg
1999 Toronto	AL	24	88	23	5	0	1	(1	0)	31	8	8	7	4	0	18	0	0	0	1	1	.50	6	.261	.293	.352
2000 Toronto	AL	3	2	0	0	0	0	(0	0)	0	0	0	0	0	0	0	0	0	0	0	0	-	0	.000	.000	.000
2001 Toronto	AL	30	96	30	8	0	1	(1	0)	41	14	6	16	5	0	15	1	0	1	5	0	1.00	0	.313	.350	.427
2002 Toronto	AL	159	608	167	34	4	23	(10	13)	278	87	100	88	27	0	85	3	2	8	9	4	.69	15	.275	.305	.457
2003 Toronto	AL	161	678	215	49	5	33	(13	20)	373	118	117	124	42	2	80	7	0	8	4	1	.80	21	.317	.359	.550
2004 Toronto	AL	134	536	146	34	2	23	(14	9)	253	82	67	72	51	2	83	2	0	1	9	2	.82	17	.272	.337	.472
6 ML YEARS		511	2008	581	130	11	81	(39	42)	976	309	298	307	129	4	281	13	2	18	28	8	.78	59	.289	.333	.486

Turk Wendell

Pitches: R **Bats:** L **Pos:** RP-12   **Ht:** 6'2" **Wt:** 205 **Born:** 5/19/1967 **Age:** 38

Year Team	Lg	G	GS	CG	GF	IP	BFP	H	R	ER	HR	SH	SF	HB	TBB	IBB	SO	WP	Bk	W	L	Pct	ShO	Sv-Op	Hld	ERC	ERA
2004 Co Springs*	AAA	12	8	0	1	14.0	68	19	10	9	2	0	0	3	4	0	8	0	0	0	1	.000	0	0- -	-	6.82	5.79
1993 Chicago	NL	7	4	0	1	22.2	98	24	13	11	0	2	0	0	8	1	15	1	1	1	2	.333	0	0-0	0	3.42	4.37
1994 Chicago	NL	6	2	0	1	14.1	76	22	20	19	3	2	1	0	10	1	9	1	0	1	0	.000	0	0-0	0	9.21	11.93
1995 Chicago	NL	43	0	0	17	60.1	270	71	35	33	11	3	3	2	24	4	50	1	0	3	1	.750	0	0-0	3	5.79	4.92
1996 Chicago	NL	70	0	0	49	79.0	339	58	26	25	8	3	1	3	44	4	75	3	2	4	6	.444	0	18-21	6	3.25	2.84
1997 ChC-NYM	NL	65	0	0	21	76.1	345	68	42	37	7	4	3	2	53	6	64	4	0	3	5	.375	0	5-7	2	4.51	4.36
1998 New York	NL	66	0	0	17	76.2	319	62	25	25	4	2	1	2	33	9	58	1	0	5	1	.833	0	4-8	11	2.78	2.93
1999 New York	NL	80	0	0	14	85.2	369	80	31	29	9	2	1	2	37	8	77	2	1	5	4	.556	0	3-6	21	3.80	3.05
2000 New York	NL	77	0	0	17	82.2	346	60	36	33	9	6	3	5	41	7	73	0	1	8	6	.571	0	1-5	16	3.14	3.59
2001 NYM-Phi	NL	70	0	0	22	67.0	297	63	36	33	12	2	4	4	34	9	56	2	0	4	5	.444	0	1-3	4	4.74	4.43
2003 Philadelphia	NL	56	0	0	20	64.0	273	54	24	24	6	6	3	6	28	5	27	1	0	3	3	.500	0	1-5	8	3.57	3.38
2004 Colorado	NL	12	0	0	5	16.2	80	21	13	13	4	0	2	2	12	1	11	1	0	0	0	-	0	0-1	0	9.01	7.02
1997 Chicago	NL	52	0	0	18	60.0	269	53	32	28	4	3	3	1	39	5	54	4	0	3	5	.375	0	4-5	2	4.03	4.20
1997 New York	NL	13	0	0	3	16.1	76	15	10	9	3	1	0	1	14	1	10	0	0	0	0	-	0	1-2	0	6.38	4.96
2001 New York	NL	49	0	0	14	51.1	218	42	23	20	8	2	3	3	22	6	41	1	0	4	3	.571	0	1-3	6	3.59	3.51
2001 Philadelphia	NL	21	0	0	8	15.2	79	21	13	13	4	0	1	1	12	3	15	1	0	0	2	.000	0	0-0	0	9.04	7.47
11 ML YEARS		552	6	0	184	645.2	2812	583	301	282	73	32	22	28	324	55	515	17	5	36	33	.522	0	33-56	75	4.06	3.93

Jayson Werth

Bats: R **Throws:** R **Pos:** LF-65; RF-14; PH-10; CF-6; PR-4; DH-1   **Ht:** 6'5" **Wt:** 190 **Born:** 5/20/1979 **Age:** 26

Year Team	Lg	G	AB	H	2B	3B	HR	(Hm	Rd)	TB	R	RBI	RC	TBB	IBB	SO	HBP	SH	SF	SB	CS	SB%	GDP	Avg	OBP	Slg
2004 Las Vegas*	AAA	14	51	21	2	1	5	(-	-)	40	13	20	16	8	0	10	1	0	1	1	0	1.00	2	.412	.500	.784
2002 Toronto	AL	15	46	12	2	1	0	(0	0)	16	4	6	5	6	0	11	0	0	1	1	0	1.00	4	.261	.348	.348
2003 Toronto	AL	26	48	10	4	0	2	(0	2)	20	7	10	6	3	0	22	0	0	0	1	0	1.00	0	.208	.255	.417
2004 Los Angeles	NL	89	290	76	11	3	16	(11	5)	141	56	47	47	30	0	85	4	1	4	4	1	.80	1	.262	.338	.486
3 ML YEARS		130	384	98	17	4	18	(11	7)	177	67	63	58	39	0	118	4	1	2	6	1	.86	5	.255	.329	.461

Jake Westbrook

Pitches: R **Bats:** R **Pos:** SP-30; RP-3 **Ht:** 6'3" **Wt:** 185 **Born:** 9/29/1977 **Age:** 27

				HOW MUCH HE PITCHED				WHAT HE GAVE UP											THE RESULTS						
Year Team	Lg	G	GS	CG	GF	IP	BFP	H	R	ER	HR	SH	SF	HB	TBB	IBB	SO	WP	Bk	W	L	Pct	ShO	Sv-Op	Hld	ERC	ERA
2000 New York	AL	3	2	0	1	6.2	38	15	10	10	1	0	2	0	4	1	1	0	0	0	2	.000	0	0-0	0	13.53	13.50
2001 Cleveland	AL	23	6	0	3	64.2	290	79	43	42	6	1	5	4	22	4	48	4	0	4	4	.500	0	0-0	5	5.25	5.85
2002 Cleveland	AL	11	4	0	1	41.2	185	50	30	27	6	2	1	1	12	1	20	1	0	1	3	.250	0	0-2	5	5.12	5.83
2003 Cleveland	AL	34	22	1	4	133.0	580	142	70	64	9	4	3	12	56	1	58	3	0	7	10	.412	0	0-0	1	4.78	4.33
2004 Cleveland	AL	33	30	5	2	215.2	895	208	95	81	19	6	6	5	61	3	116	4	1	14	9	.609	1	0-0	0	3.45	3.38
5 ML YEARS		104	64	6	11	461.2	1988	494	248	224	41	13	17	22	155	10	243	12	1	26	28	.481	1	0-2	7	4.35	4.37

Dan Wheeler

Pitches: R **Bats:** R **Pos:** RP-45; SP-1 **Ht:** 6'3" **Wt:** 222 **Born:** 12/10/1977 **Age:** 27

				HOW MUCH HE PITCHED				WHAT HE GAVE UP											THE RESULTS						
Year Team	Lg	G	GS	CG	GF	IP	BFP	H	R	ER	HR	SH	SF	HB	TBB	IBB	SO	WP	Bk	W	L	Pct	ShO	Sv-Op	Hld	ERC	ERA
2004 Norfolk*	AAA	5	0	0	1	7.1	32	8	2	2	0	0	0	0	2	0	10	0	1	1	0	1.000	0	0- -	-	3.30	2.45
1999 Tampa Bay	AL	6	6	0	0	30.2	138	35	0	20	7	0	0	0	13	0	32	0	0	1	4	.000	0	0-0	0	6.01	5.87
2000 Tampa Bay	AL	11	2	0	0	23.0	111	29	0	14	2	0	0	0	11	0	17	0	0	1	1	.500	0	0-0	0	5.57	5.48
2001 Tampa Bay	AL	13	0	0	0	17.2	87	30	0	17	3	0	0	0	5	0	12	0	0	1	0	1.000	0	0-0	0	8.38	8.66
2003 New York	NL	35	0	0	10	51.0	215	49	23	21	6	0	3	1	17	4	35	1	0	1	3	.250	0	2-3	3	3.69	3.71
2004 NYM-Hou	NL	46	1	0	11	65.0	287	76	33	31	10	2	1	1	20	2	55	4	1	3	1	.750	0	0-0	5	5.05	4.29
2004 New York	NL	32	1	0	7	50.2	232	65	29	27	9	2	1	0	17	2	46	4	1	3	1	.750	0	0-0	3	5.91	4.80
2004 Houston	NL	14	0	0	4	14.1	55	11	4	4	1	0	0	1	3	0	9	0	0	0	0	-	0	0-0	2	2.35	2.51
5 ML YEARS		111	9	0	21	187.1	836	219	56	103	28	2	4	2	66	6	151	5	1	6	9	.400	0	2-3	5	5.18	4.95

Gabe White

Pitches: L **Bats:** L **Pos:** RP-64 **Ht:** 6'2" **Wt:** 204 **Born:** 11/20/1971 **Age:** 33

				HOW MUCH HE PITCHED				WHAT HE GAVE UP											THE RESULTS						
Year Team	Lg	G	GS	CG	GF	IP	BFP	H	R	ER	HR	SH	SF	HB	TBB	IBB	SO	WP	Bk	W	L	Pct	ShO	Sv-Op	Hld	ERC	ERA
1994 Montreal	NL	7	5	0	2	23.2	106	24	16	16	4	1	1	1	11	0	17	0	0	1	1	.500	0	1-1	0	5.03	6.08
1995 Montreal	NL	19	1	0	8	25.2	115	26	21	20	7	2	3	1	9	0	25	0	0	1	2	.333	0	0-0	0	5.12	7.01
1997 Cincinnati	NL	12	6	0	2	41.0	168	39	20	20	6	3	2	1	8	1	25	0	0	2	2	.500	0	1-1	3	3.37	4.39
1998 Cincinnati	NL	69	3	0	29	98.2	404	86	46	44	17	2	2	1	27	6	83	3	0	5	5	.500	0	9-13	6	3.30	4.01
1999 Cincinnati	NL	50	0	0	18	61.0	261	68	31	30	13	2	1	2	14	1	61	0	0	1	2	.333	0	0-1	3	4.95	4.43
2000 Cin-Col	NL	68	0	0	17	84.0	329	64	23	22	6	2	6	3	15	2	84	1	0	11	2	.846	0	5-9	19	1.98	2.36
2001 Colorado	NL	69	0	0	16	67.2	290	70	47	47	8	2	1	1	26	5	47	1	0	1	7	.125	0	0-2	8	5.42	6.25
2002 Cincinnati	NL	62	0	0	7	54.1	220	49	19	18	3	1	0	2	10	2	41	0	0	6	1	.857	0	0-1	19	2.55	2.98
2003 Cin-NYY	NL	46	0	0	5	46.2	190	44	22	21	7	2	3	2	8	4	29	0	0	5	1	.833	0	0-2	12	3.26	4.05
2004 NYY-Cin	NL	64	0	0	15	59.2	265	72	46	46	14	3	3	2	12	4	41	1	0	1	3	.250	0	1-5	12	5.33	6.94
2000 Cincinnati	NL	1	0	0	0	1.0	6	2	2	2	1	0	0	0	1	0	2	0	0	0	0	-	0	-	0	23.01	18.00
2000 Colorado	NL	67	0	0	17	83.0	323	62	21	20	5	2	6	3	14	2	82	1	0	11	2	.846	0	5-9	19	1.82	2.17
2003 Cincinnati	NL	34	0	0	4	34.1	141	36	15	15	5	1	2	1	6	3	23	0	0	3	0	1.000	0	0-1	6	3.81	3.93
2003 New York	AL	12	0	0	1	12.1	49	8	7	6	2	1	1	1	2	1	6	0	0	2	1	.667	0	0-1	6	1.89	4.38
2004 New York	AL	24	0	0	6	20.2	104	33	19	19	2	1	1	2	7	4	8	0	0	0	1	.000	0	0-2	3	7.27	8.27
2004 Cincinnati	NL	40	0	0	9	39.0	161	39	27	27	12	2	2	0	5	0	33	1	0	1	2	.333	0	1-3	9	4.21	6.23
10 ML YEARS		466	15	0	119	562.1	2348	542	291	284	95	20	23	16	140	25	453	6	0	34	26	.567	0	17-35	82	3.77	4.55

Rick White

Pitches: R **Bats:** R **Pos:** RP-59 **Ht:** 6'4" **Wt:** 230 **Born:** 12/23/1968 **Age:** 36

				HOW MUCH HE PITCHED				WHAT HE GAVE UP											THE RESULTS						
Year Team	Lg	G	GS	CG	GF	IP	BFP	H	R	ER	HR	SH	SF	HB	TBB	IBB	SO	WP	Bk	W	L	Pct	ShO	Sv-Op	Hld	ERC	ERA
2004 Las Vegas*	AAA	6	0	0	4	11.2	39	4	0	0	0	0	0	0	1	0	14	0	0	0	0	-	0	2- -	1	0.37	0.00
1994 Pittsburgh	NL	43	5	0	23	75.1	317	79	35	32	9	7	5	6	17	3	38	2	2	4	5	.444	0	6-9	3	4.11	3.82
1995 Pittsburgh	NL	15	9	0	2	55.0	247	66	33	29	3	3	3	2	18	0	29	2	0	2	3	.400	0	0-0	0	4.70	4.75
1998 Tampa Bay	AL	38	3	0	12	68.2	289	66	32	29	8	0	3	2	23	2	39	3	0	2	6	.250	0	0-0	2	3.82	3.80
1999 Tampa Bay	AL	63	1	0	11	108.0	480	132	56	49	8	2	5	1	38	5	81	3	0	5	3	.625	0	0-2	4	4.96	4.08
2000 TB-NYM	NL	66	0	0	14	99.2	420	83	44	39	9	1	3	7	38	5	67	3	0	5	9	.357	0	3-7	4	3.21	3.52
2001 New York	NL	55	0	0	15	69.2	299	71	38	30	7	2	2	2	17	4	51	1	0	4	5	.444	0	2-4	10	3.52	3.88
2002 Col-StL	NL	61	0	0	10	62.2	264	62	33	30	4	3	4	1	21	5	41	3	0	5	7	.417	0	0-1	16	3.49	4.31
2003 CWS-Hou	NL	49	0	0	15	67.0	293	74	48	43	13	2	2	4	21	2	54	2	0	1	2	.333	0	1-1	4	5.22	5.78
2004 Cleveland	AL	59	0	0	20	78.1	340	88	52	46	15	6	3	2	29	7	44	2	0	5	5	.500	0	1-3	2	5.41	5.29
2000 Tampa Bay	AL	44	0	0	8	71.1	293	57	30	27	7	1	2	5	26	3	47	3	0	3	6	.333	0	2-5	2	3.09	3.41
2000 New York	NL	22	0	0	6	28.1	127	26	14	12	2	0	1	2	12	2	20	0	0	2	3	.400	0	1-2	2	3.51	3.81
2002 Colorado	NL	41	0	0	8	40.2	182	49	30	28	4	1	4	1	18	4	27	3	0	2	6	.250	0	0-1	9	5.47	6.20
2002 St Louis	NL	20	0	0	2	22.0	82	13	3	2	0	2	0	0	3	1	14	0	0	3	1	.750	0	0-0	7	0.94	0.82
2003 Chicago	AL	34	0	0	12	47.2	207	56	39	35	11	1	2	1	13	2	37	0	0	1	2	.333	0	1-1	3	5.58	6.61
2003 Houston	NL	15	0	0	3	19.1	86	18	9	8	2	1	0	3	8	0	17	2	0	0	0	-	0	0-0	1	4.33	3.72
9 ML YEARS		449	18	0	122	684.1	2949	721	371	327	76	26	30	27	222	33	444	21	2	33	45	.423	0	13-27	45	4.25	4.30

Rondell White

Bats: R **Throws:** R **Pos:** LF-74; DH-43; PH-5 **Ht:** 6'1" **Wt:** 225 **Born:** 2/23/1972 **Age:** 33

					BATTING														BASERUNNING				AVERAGES		
Year Team	Lg	G	AB	H	2B	3B	HR	(Hm	Rd)	TB	R	RBI	RC	TBB	IBB	SO	HBP	SH	SF	SB	CS	SB%	GDP	Avg	OBP	Slg
1993 Montreal	NL	23	73	19	3	1	2	(1	1)	30	9	15	9	7	0	16	0	2	1	1	2	.33	2	.260	.321	.411
1994 Montreal	NL	40	97	27	10	1	2	(1	1)	45	16	13	16	9	0	18	3	0	0	1	1	.50	1	.278	.358	.464
1995 Montreal	NL	130	474	140	33	4	13	(6	7)	220	87	57	79	41	1	87	6	0	4	25	5	.83	11	.295	.356	.464
1996 Montreal	NL	88	334	98	19	4	6	(2	4)	143	35	41	46	22	0	53	2	0	1	14	6	.70	11	.293	.340	.428
1997 Montreal	NL	151	592	160	29	5	28	(9	19)	283	84	82	84	31	3	111	10	1	4	16	8	.67	18	.270	.316	.478
1998 Montreal	NL	97	357	107	21	2	17	(9	8)	183	54	58	65	30	2	57	7	0	3	16	7	.70	7	.300	.363	.513
1999 Montreal	NL	138	539	168	26	6	22	(10	12)	272	83	64	91	32	2	85	11	0	6	10	6	.63	17	.312	.359	.505
2000 Mon-ChC	NL	94	357	111	26	0	13	(3	10)	176	59	61	64	33	0	79	4	0	2	5	3	.63	4	.311	.374	.493

257

Year Team	Lg	G	AB	H	2B	3B	HR	(Hm	Rd)	TB	R	RBI	RC	TBB	IBB	SO	HBP	SH	SF	SB	CS	SB%	GDP	Avg	OBP	Slg
2001 Chicago	NL	95	323	99	19	1	17	(7	10)	171	43	50	57	26	4	56	7	1	0	1	0	1.00	14	.307	.371	.529
2002 New York	AL	126	455	109	21	0	14	(5	9)	172	59	62	43	25	1	86	8	1	5	1	2	.33	11	.240	.288	.378
2003 SD-KC		137	488	141	23	4	22	(5	17)	238	62	87	72	31	2	79	10	0	5	1	4	.20	13	.289	.341	.488
2004 Detroit	AL	121	448	121	21	2	19	(5	14)	203	76	67	69	39	4	77	8	0	3	1	2	.33	13	.270	.337	.453
2000 Montreal	NL	75	290	89	24	0	11	(3	8)	146	52	54	53	28	0	67	2	0	2	5	1	.83	4	.307	.370	.503
2000 Chicago	NL	19	67	22	2	0	2	(0	2)	30	7	7	11	5	0	12	2	0	0	0	2	.00	0	.328	.392	.448
2003 San Diego	NL	115	413	115	17	3	18	(4	14)	192	49	66	54	25	2	71	8	0	3	1	4	.20	11	.278	.330	.465
2003 Kansas City	AL	22	75	26	6	1	4	(1	3)	46	13	21	18	6	0	8	2	0	2	0	0	-	2	.347	.400	.613
12 ML YEARS		1240	4537	1300	251	30	175	(63	112)	2136	667	657	695	326	19	804	76	5	34	92	46	.67	122	.287	.342	.471

Bob Wickman

Pitches: R Bats: R Pos: RP-30
Ht: 6'1" Wt: 240 Born: 2/6/1969 Age: 36

Year Team	Lg	G	GS	CG	GF	IP	BFP	H	R	ER	HR	SH	SF	HB	TBB	IBB	SO	WP	Bk	W	L	Pct	ShO	Sv-Op	Hld	ERC	ERA
2004 Akron*	AA	1	1	0	0	1.0	5	0	0	0	0	0	0	0	2	0	1	0	0	0	0	-	0	0--	-	3.47	0.00
2004 Buffalo*	AAA	6	1	0	0	5.1	24	4	6	6	0	0	0	0	4	0	4	0	0	1	0	1.000	0	0--	-	3.21	10.13
1992 New York	AL	8	8	0	0	50.1	213	51	25	23	2	1	3	2	20	0	21	3	0	6	1	.857	0	0-0	-	3.99	4.11
1993 New York	AL	41	19	1	9	140.0	629	156	82	72	13	4	1	5	69	7	70	2	0	14	4	.778	1	4-8	2	5.16	4.63
1994 New York	AL	53	0	0	19	70.0	286	54	26	24	3	0	5	1	27	3	56	2	0	5	4	.556	0	6-10	11	2.45	3.09
1995 New York	AL	63	1	0	14	80.0	347	77	38	36	6	4	1	5	33	3	51	2	0	2	4	.333	0	1-10	21	3.92	4.05
1996 NYY-Mil	AL	70	0	0	18	95.2	429	106	50	47	10	2	4	5	44	3	75	4	0	7	1	.875	0	0-4	10	5.17	4.42
1997 Milwaukee	AL	74	0	0	20	95.2	405	89	32	29	8	6	2	3	41	7	78	8	0	7	6	.538	0	1-5	28	3.76	2.73
1998 Milwaukee	NL	72	0	0	51	82.1	357	79	38	34	5	10	3	4	39	2	71	1	0	6	9	.400	0	25-32	9	4.05	3.72
1999 Milwaukee	NL	71	0	0	63	74.1	331	75	31	28	6	3	2	2	38	6	60	2	0	3	8	.273	0	37-45	0	4.38	3.39
2000 Mil-Cle		69	0	0	60	72.2	309	64	30	25	1	3	1	1	32	5	55	2	0	5	3	.375	0	30-37	0	2.92	3.10
2001 Cleveland	AL	70	0	0	56	67.2	270	61	18	18	4	0	0	2	14	2	66	2	0	5	0	1.000	0	32-35	4	2.69	2.39
2002 Cleveland	AL	36	0	0	30	34.1	159	42	22	17	3	0	0	1	10	0	36	0	0	1	3	.250	0	20-22	0	4.72	4.46
2004 Cleveland	AL	30	0	0	21	29.2	129	33	14	14	4	0	0	2	10	0	26	0	0	2	0	.000	0	13-14	4	5.09	4.25
1996 New York	AL	58	0	0	14	79.0	358	94	41	41	7	1	4	5	34	1	61	3	0	4	1	.800	0	0-3	6	5.51	4.67
1996 Milwaukee	AL	12	0	0	4	16.2	71	12	9	6	3	1	0	0	10	2	14	1	0	3	0	1.000	0	0-1	4	3.66	3.24
2000 Milwaukee	NL	43	0	0	36	46.0	194	37	18	15	1	0	1	1	20	2	44	2	0	2	2	.500	0	16-20	0	2.62	2.93
2000 Cleveland	AL	26	0	0	24	26.2	115	27	12	10	0	3	0	0	12	3	11	0	0	1	3	.250	0	14-17	0	3.47	3.38
12 ML YEARS		657	28	1	361	892.2	3864	887	406	367	65	33	22	33	377	38	665	28	0	59	47	.557	1	169-222	89	4.04	3.70

Ty Wigginton

Bats: R Throws: R Pos: 3B-123; 2B-25; PH-6; 1B-5
Ht: 6'0" Wt: 200 Born: 10/11/1977 Age: 27

Year Team	Lg	G	AB	H	2B	3B	HR	(Hm	Rd)	TB	R	RBI	RC	TBB	IBB	SO	HBP	SH	SF	SB	CS	SB%	GDP	Avg	OBP	Slg
2004 St. Lucie*	A+	2	8	3	0	0	0	(-	-)	3	1	0	1	0	0	1	0	0	0	0	0	-	0	.375	.375	.375
2002 New York	NL	46	116	35	8	0	6	(4	2)	61	18	18	15	8	0	19	2	0	1	2	1	.67	4	.302	.354	.526
2003 New York	NL	156	573	146	36	6	11	(4	7)	227	73	71	76	46	2	124	9	1	4	12	2	.86	15	.255	.318	.396
2004 NYM-Pit	NL	144	494	129	30	2	17	(6	11)	214	63	66	59	45	6	82	2	1	3	7	1	.88	15	.261	.324	.433
2004 New York	NL	86	312	89	23	2	12	(5	7)	152	46	42	38	23	4	48	1	1	2	6	1	.86	11	.285	.334	.487
2004 Pittsburgh	NL	58	182	40	7	0	5	(1	4)	62	17	24	21	22	2	34	1	0	1	1	0	1.00	4	.220	.306	.341
3 ML YEARS		346	1183	310	74	8	34	(14	20)	502	154	155	150	99	8	225	13	2	8	21	4	.84	34	.262	.324	.424

Brad Wilkerson

Bats: L Throws: L Pos: 1B-86; LF-59; CF-18; RF-10; PH-3; PR-1
Ht: 6'0" Wt: 200 Born: 6/1/1977 Age: 28

Year Team	Lg	G	AB	H	2B	3B	HR	(Hm	Rd)	TB	R	RBI	RC	TBB	IBB	SO	HBP	SH	SF	SB	CS	SB%	GDP	Avg	OBP	Slg
2001 Montreal	NL	47	117	24	7	2	1	(1	0)	38	11	5	12	17	1	41	0	1	1	2	1	.67	2	.205	.304	.325
2002 Montreal	NL	153	507	135	27	8	20	(12	8)	238	92	59	83	81	7	161	5	6	4	7	8	.47	5	.266	.370	.469
2003 Montreal	NL	146	504	135	34	4	19	(9	10)	234	78	77	90	89	0	155	4	2	3	13	10	.57	5	.268	.380	.464
2004 Montreal	NL	160	572	146	39	2	32	(15	17)	285	112	67	95	106	8	152	4	3	3	13	6	.68	6	.255	.374	.498
4 ML YEARS		506	1700	440	107	16	72	(37	35)	795	293	208	280	293	16	509	13	12	11	35	25	.58	18	.259	.370	.468

Bernie Williams

Bats: B Throws: R Pos: CF-97; DH-50; PH-3
Ht: 6'2" Wt: 205 Born: 9/13/1968 Age: 36

Year Team	Lg	G	AB	H	2B	3B	HR	(Hm	Rd)	TB	R	RBI	RC	TBB	IBB	SO	HBP	SH	SF	SB	CS	SB%	GDP	Avg	OBP	Slg
1991 New York	AL	85	320	76	19	4	3	(1	2)	112	43	34	41	48	0	57	1	2	3	10	5	.67	4	.238	.336	.350
1992 New York	AL	62	261	73	14	2	5	(3	2)	106	39	26	37	29	1	36	1	2	7	7	6	.54	5	.280	.354	.406
1993 New York	AL	139	567	152	31	4	12	(5	7)	227	67	68	71	53	4	106	4	1	3	9	9	.50	17	.268	.333	.400
1994 New York	AL	108	408	118	29	1	12	(4	8)	185	80	57	70	61	2	54	3	1	2	16	9	.64	11	.289	.384	.453
1995 New York	AL	144	563	173	29	9	18	(7	11)	274	93	82	105	75	1	98	5	2	3	8	6	.57	12	.307	.392	.487
1996 New York	AL	143	551	168	26	7	29	(12	17)	295	108	102	113	82	8	72	0	1	7	17	4	.81	15	.305	.391	.535
1997 New York	AL	129	509	167	35	6	21	(13	8)	277	107	100	109	73	7	80	1	0	8	15	8	.65	10	.328	.408	.544
1998 New York	AL	128	499	169	30	5	26	(14	12)	287	101	97	110	74	9	81	1	0	4	15	9	.63	19	.339	.422	.575
1999 New York	AL	158	591	202	28	6	25	(11	14)	317	116	115	131	100	17	95	1	0	5	9	10	.47	11	.342	.435	.536
2000 New York	AL	141	537	165	37	6	30	(15	15)	304	108	121	112	71	11	84	5	0	3	13	5	.72	15	.307	.391	.566
2001 New York	AL	146	540	166	38	0	26	(14	12)	282	102	94	108	78	11	67	6	0	9	11	5	.69	15	.307	.395	.522
2002 New York	AL	154	612	204	37	2	19	(13	6)	302	102	102	124	83	7	97	3	0	1	8	4	.67	19	.333	.415	.493
2003 New York	AL	119	445	117	19	1	15	(6	9)	183	77	64	66	71	8	61	3	0	2	5	0	1.00	21	.263	.367	.411
2004 New York	AL	148	561	147	29	1	22	(13	9)	244	105	70	82	85	5	96	2	1	2	1	5	.17	19	.262	.360	.435
14 ML YEARS		1804	6964	2097	401	54	263	(130	133)	3395	1248	1132	1279	983	91	1084	36	10	52	144	85	.63	193	.301	.388	.438

Dave Williams

Pitches: L **Bats:** L **Pos:** SP-6; RP-4   **Ht:** 6'2" **Wt:** 213 **Born:** 3/12/1979 **Age:** 26

Year Team	Lg	G	GS	CG	GF	IP	BFP	H	R	ER	HR	SH	SF	HB	TBB	IBB	SO	WP	Bk	W	L	Pct	ShO	Sv-Op	Hld	ERC	ERA
2004 Nashville*	AAA	21	21	0	1	116.2	486	113	52	45	10	7	4	4	33	2	103	2	0	6	2	.750	0	0--	-	3.49	3.47
2001 Pittsburgh	NL	22	18	0	1	114.0	472	100	53	47	15	3	8	7	45	4	57	0	0	3	7	.300	0	0-0	1	3.89	3.71
2002 Pittsburgh	NL	9	9	0	0	43.1	195	38	26	24	9	2	1	4	24	2	33	2	2	2	5	.286	0	0-0	0	4.99	4.98
2004 Pittsburgh	NL	10	6	0	0	38.2	162	31	21	19	4	1	1	3	13	2	33	0	0	2	3	.400	0	0-0	0	2.97	4.42
3 ML YEARS		41	33	0	1	196.0	829	169	100	90	28	6	10	14	82	8	123	2	2	7	15	.318	0	0-0	1	3.94	4.13

Gerald Williams

Bats: R **Throws:** R **Pos:** LF-21; CF-20; PH-14; PR-8; RF-7   **Ht:** 6'2" **Wt:** 187 **Born:** 8/10/1966 **Age:** 38

Year Team	Lg	G	AB	H	2B	3B	HR	(Hm	Rd)	TB	R	RBI	RC	TBB	IBB	SO	HBP	SH	SF	SB	CS	SB%	GDP	Avg	OBP	Slg
2004 Norfolk*	AAA	63	246	75	10	3	7	(-	-)	112	37	28	34	9	0	35	3	6	2	6	9	.40	4	.305	.335	.455
1992 New York	AL	15	27	8	2	0	3	(2	1)	19	7	6	6	0	0	3	0	0	0	2	0	1.00	0	.296	.296	.704
1993 New York	AL	42	67	10	2	3	0	(0	0)	18	11	6	2	1	0	14	2	0	1	2	0	1.00	2	.149	.183	.269
1994 New York	AL	57	86	25	8	0	4	(2	2)	45	19	13	11	4	0	17	0	0	1	1	3	.25	6	.291	.319	.523
1995 New York	AL	100	182	45	18	2	6	(4	2)	85	33	28	28	22	1	34	1	0	3	4	2	.67	4	.247	.327	.467
1996 NYY-Mil	AL	125	325	82	19	4	5	(3	2)	124	43	34	34	19	3	57	5	3	5	10	9	.53	8	.252	.299	.382
1997 Milwaukee	AL	155	566	143	32	2	10	(3	7)	209	73	41	58	19	1	90	6	5	5	23	9	.72	9	.253	.282	.369
1998 Atlanta	NL	129	266	81	19	2	10	(5	5)	134	46	44	45	17	1	48	3	2	1	11	5	.69	5	.305	.352	.504
1999 Atlanta	NL	143	422	116	24	1	17	(7	10)	193	76	68	63	33	1	67	6	4	2	19	11	.63	8	.275	.335	.457
2000 Tampa Bay	AL	146	632	173	30	2	21	(6	15)	270	87	89	83	34	0	103	3	9	4	12	12	.50	5	.274	.312	.427
2001 TB-NYY	AL	100	279	56	18	0	4	(3	1)	86	42	19	20	18	0	55	5	4	0	13	5	.72	9	.201	.262	.308
2002 Florida	NL	33	17	0	0	0	0	(0	0)	0	6	0	0	2	0	4	0	0	0	2	0	1.00	0	.000	.105	.000
2003 Florida	NL	27	31	4	1	0	0	(0	0)	5	5	3	1	2	0	5	0	2	0	3	0	1.00	0	.129	.182	.161
2004 Florida	NL	57	129	30	8	2	4	(0	4)	54	17	11	13	8	1	26	0	1	0	2	1	.67	2	.233	.277	.419
1996 New York	AL	99	233	63	15	4	5	(3	2)	101	37	30	29	15	2	39	4	1	5	7	8	.47	7	.270	.319	.433
1996 Milwaukee	AL	26	92	19	4	0	0	(0	0)	23	6	4	5	4	1	18	1	2	0	3	1	.75	1	.207	.247	.250
2001 Tampa Bay	AL	62	232	48	17	0	4	(3	1)	77	30	17	18	13	0	42	4	3	0	10	4	.71	8	.207	.261	.332
2001 New York	AL	38	47	8	1	0	0	(0	0)	9	12	2	2	5	0	13	1	1	0	3	1	.75	1	.170	.264	.191
13 ML YEARS		1129	3029	773	181	18	84	(35	49)	1242	465	362	364	179	8	523	31	30	22	104	57	.65	59	.255	.301	.410

Jerome Williams

Pitches: R **Bats:** R **Pos:** SP-22   **Ht:** 6'1" **Wt:** 189 **Born:** 12/4/1981 **Age:** 23

Year Team	Lg	G	GS	CG	GF	IP	BFP	H	R	ER	HR	SH	SF	HB	TBB	IBB	SO	WP	Bk	W	L	Pct	ShO	Sv-Op	Hld	ERC	ERA
1999 Salem-Keizer	A-	7	7	1	0	37.0	151	29	13	9	1	0	1	3	11	0	34	1	0	1	1	.500	1	0--	-	2.40	2.19
2000 San Jose	A+	23	19	0	2	125.2	512	89	53	41	6	5	6	10	48	3	115	9	2	7	6	.538	0	0--	-	2.42	2.94
2001 Shreveport	AA	23	23	0	0	130.0	542	116	69	57	14	2	3	9	34	0	84	6	1	9	7	.563	1	0--	-	3.26	3.95
2002 Fresno	AAA	28	28	0	0	160.2	671	140	76	64	16	8	5	9	50	1	130	5	3	6	11	.353	0	0--	-	3.23	3.59
2003 Fresno	AAA	10	10	1	0	57.0	242	52	19	17	3	2	1	4	16	0	40	2	0	4	2	.667	0	0--	-	3.04	2.68
2003 San Francisco	NL	21	21	2	0	131.0	545	116	54	48	10	6	3	7	49	3	88	2	1	7	5	.583	1	0-0	0	3.42	3.30
2004 San Francisco	NL	22	22	0	0	129.1	559	123	69	61	14	4	9	17	44	1	80	2	1	10	7	.588	0	0-0	0	4.14	4.24
2 ML YEARS		43	43	2	0	260.1	1104	239	123	109	24	10	12	24	93	4	168	4	2	17	12	.586	1	0-0	0	3.78	3.77

Randy Williams

Pitches: L **Bats:** L **Pos:** RP-6   **Ht:** 6'3" **Wt:** 195 **Born:** 11/18/1975 **Age:** 29

Year Team	Lg	G	GS	CG	GF	IP	BFP	H	R	ER	HR	SH	SF	HB	TBB	IBB	SO	WP	Bk	W	L	Pct	ShO	Sv-Op	Hld	ERC	ERA
1998 Cubs	R	2	1	0	0	3.0	11	0	0	0	0	0	0	0	2	0	6	0	0	1	0	1.000	0	0--	-	0.46	0.00
1999 Daytona	A+	14	9	0	3	53.0	243	55	36	28	5	4	1	1	30	0	47	3	0	3	4	.429	0	1--	-	4.91	4.75
2003 San Antonio	AA	29	0	0	11	41.2	165	33	9	8	2	2	1	0	7	0	38	0	0	4	1	.800	0	2--	-	1.83	1.73
2003 Tacoma	AAA	18	0	0	4	25.2	112	25	17	15	3	0	1	1	11	0	19	1	0	2	2	.500	0	1--	-	4.30	5.26
2004 Tacoma	AAA	50	0	0	16	79.1	355	68	37	32	6	0	1	3	46	0	64	4	0	7	2	.778	0	8--	-	3.85	3.63
2004 Seattle	AL	6	0	0	1	4.2	22	3	3	3	0	0	0	0	6	0	4	0	0	0	0	-	0	0-0	1	4.73	5.79

Todd Williams

Pitches: R **Bats:** R **Pos:** RP-29   **Ht:** 6'3" **Wt:** 210 **Born:** 2/13/1971 **Age:** 34

Year Team	Lg	G	GS	CG	GF	IP	BFP	H	R	ER	HR	SH	SF	HB	TBB	IBB	SO	WP	Bk	W	L	Pct	ShO	Sv-Op	Hld	ERC	ERA
2004 Oklahoma*	AAA	27	0	0	23	29.2	139	37	15	10	2	1	0	1	7	2	11	1	0	2	2	.500	0	9--	-	4.31	3.03
2004 Ottawa*	AAA	14	0	0	5	20.2	84	19	7	7	0	0	0	0	3	1	11	2	0	1	1	.500	0	2--	-	1.99	3.05
1995 Los Angeles	NL	16	0	0	5	19.1	83	19	11	11	3	3	1	0	7	2	8	0	0	2	2	.500	0	0-1	0	4.01	5.12
1998 Cincinnati	NL	6	0	0	2	9.1	50	15	8	8	1	0	0	0	6	0	4	0	0	0	1	.000	0	0-0	0	8.58	7.71
1999 Seattle	AL	13	0	0	4	9.2	47	11	5	5	1	1	0	1	7	0	7	0	0	0	0	-	0	0-0	0	6.67	4.66
2001 New York	AL	15	0	0	6	15.1	82	22	9	8	1	0	3	2	9	2	13	0	0	1	0	1.000	0	0-0	1	7.01	4.70
2004 Baltimore	AL	29	0	0	10	31.1	126	26	10	10	2	0	0	5	9	0	13	1	0	2	0	1.000	0	0-0	3	3.25	2.87
5 ML YEARS		79	0	0	27	85.0	388	93	43	42	8	4	4	8	38	4	45	1	0	5	3	.625	0	0-1	4	5.01	4.45

Woody Williams

Pitches: R **Bats:** R **Pos:** SP-31   **Ht:** 6'0" **Wt:** 195 **Born:** 8/19/1966 **Age:** 38

Year Team	Lg	G	GS	CG	GF	IP	BFP	H	R	ER	HR	SH	SF	HB	TBB	IBB	SO	WP	Bk	W	L	Pct	ShO	Sv-Op	Hld	ERC	ERA
1993 Toronto	AL	30	0	0	9	37.0	172	40	18	18	2	2	1	1	22	3	24	2	1	3	1	.750	0	0-2	4	4.85	4.38
1994 Toronto	AL	38	0	0	14	59.1	253	44	24	24	5	1	2	2	33	1	56	4	0	1	3	.250	0	0-0	5	3.25	3.64
1995 Toronto	AL	23	3	0	10	53.2	232	44	23	22	6	2	0	2	28	1	41	0	0	1	2	.333	0	0-1	1	3.72	3.69
1996 Toronto	AL	12	10	1	0	59.0	255	64	33	31	8	2	1	1	21	1	43	2	0	4	5	.444	0	0-0	0	4.73	4.73

		HOW MUCH HE PITCHED						WHAT HE GAVE UP												THE RESULTS							
Year Team	Lg	G	GS	CG	GF	IP	BFP	H	R	ER	HR	SH	SF	HB	TBB	IBB	SO	WP	Bk	W	L	Pct	ShO	Sv-Op	Hld	ERC	ERA
1997 Toronto	AL	31	31	0	0	194.2	833	201	98	94	31	6	8	5	66	3	124	7	0	9	14	.391	0	0-0	0	4.55	4.35
1998 Toronto	AL	32	32	1	0	209.2	894	196	112	104	36	5	6	2	81	3	151	2	1	10	9	.526	1	0-0	0	4.15	4.46
1999 San Diego	NL	33	33	0	0	208.1	887	213	106	102	33	9	9	2	73	5	137	9	0	12	12	.500	0	0-0	0	4.46	4.41
2000 San Diego	NL	23	23	4	0	168.0	700	152	74	70	23	4	3	3	54	2	111	4	0	10	8	.556	0	0-0	0	3.55	3.75
2001 SD-StL	NL	34	34	3	0	220.0	922	224	110	99	35	13	8	3	56	5	154	5	0	15	9	.625	1	0-0	0	4.15	4.05
2002 St Louis	NL	17	17	1	0	103.1	412	84	30	29	10	3	1	4	25	2	76	2	0	9	4	.692	0	0-0	0	2.63	2.53
2003 St Louis	NL	34	33	0	1	220.2	944	220	101	95	20	11	6	11	55	2	153	3	0	18	9	.667	0	0-1	0	3.52	3.87
2004 St Louis	NL	31	31	0	0	189.2	817	193	93	88	20	9	5	9	58	3	131	12	1	11	8	.579	0	0-0	0	3.97	4.18
2001 San Diego	NL	23	23	0	0	145.0	632	170	88	80	28	8	8	5	37	4	102	4	0	8	8	.500	0	0-0	0	5.26	4.97
2001 St Louis	NL	11	11	3	0	75.0	290	54	22	19	7	5	0	3	19	1	52	1	0	7	1	.875	1	0-0	0	2.24	2.28
12 ML YEARS		338	247	10	34	1723.1	7321	1675	822	776	229	67	50	50	572	31	1201	52	3	103	84	.551	2	0-4	10	3.96	4.05

Scott Williamson

Pitches: R **Bats:** R **Pos:** RP-28   **Ht:** 6'0" **Wt:** 185 **Born:** 2/17/1976 **Age:** 29

		HOW MUCH HE PITCHED						WHAT HE GAVE UP												THE RESULTS							
Year Team	Lg	G	GS	CG	GF	IP	BFP	H	R	ER	HR	SH	SF	HB	TBB	IBB	SO	WP	Bk	W	L	Pct	ShO	Sv-Op	Hld	ERC	ERA
2004 Pawtucket*	AAA	4	1	0	1	3.2	21	3	5	5	0	0	0	1	6	0	6	1	0	1	0	1.000	0	0--		7.94	12.27
1999 Cincinnati	NL	62	0	0	40	93.1	366	54	29	25	8	5	2	1	43	6	107	13	0	12	7	.632	0	19-26	5	2.05	2.41
2000 Cincinnati	NL	48	10	0	13	112.0	495	92	45	41	7	4	2	3	75	7	136	21	1	5	8	.385	0	6-8	6	3.85	3.29
2001 Cincinnati	NL	2	0	0	0	0.2	6	1	0	0	0	0	0	1	2	0	1	0	0	0	0	-	0	0-0	1	24.61	0.00
2002 Cincinnati	NL	63	0	0	23	74.0	299	46	27	24	5	5	2	2	36	5	84	8	1	3	4	.429	0	8-12	8	2.24	2.92
2003 Cin-Bos		66	0	0	40	62.2	276	54	30	29	7	2	1	1	34	6	74	11	0	5	4	.556	0	21-28	5	3.78	4.16
2004 Boston	AL	28	0	0	5	28.2	120	11	6	4	0	0	3	3	18	1	28	4	0	0	1	.000	0	1-2	3	1.47	1.26
2003 Cincinnati	NL	42	0	0	34	42.1	187	34	15	15	6	2	0	1	25	4	53	7	0	5	3	.625	0	21-26	0	3.87	3.19
2003 Boston	AL	24	0	0	6	20.1	89	20	15	14	1	0	1	0	9	2	21	4	0	0	1	.000	0	0-2	5	3.58	6.20
6 ML YEARS		269	10	0	121	371.1	1562	258	137	123	27	16	10	11	208	25	429	58	2	25	24	.510	0	55-76	28	2.87	2.98

Josh Willingham

Bats: R **Throws:** R **Pos:** PH-6; C-5; LF-3   **Ht:** 6'1" **Wt:** 200 **Born:** 2/17/1979 **Age:** 26

		BATTING																	BASERUNNING				AVERAGES		
Year Team	Lg	G	AB	H	2B	3B	HR	(Hm Rd)	TB	R	RBI	RC	TBB	IBB	SO	HBP	SH	SF	SB	CS	SB%	GDP	Avg	OBP	Slg
2000 Utica	A-	65	205	54	16	0	6	(- -)	88	37	29	37	39	1	55	9	1	2	9	5	.64	2	.263	.400	.429
2001 Kane County	A	97	320	83	20	2	7	(- -)	128	57	36	55	53	0	85	13	0	4	24	2	.92	7	.259	.382	.400
2002 Jupiter	A+	107	376	103	21	4	17	(- -)	183	72	69	74	63	0	88	13	0	2	18	5	.78	7	.274	.394	.487
2003 Marlins	R	2	7	3	1	0	1	(- -)	7	3	3	2	1	0	2	0	0	0	0	0	-	0	.429	.500	1.000
2003 Jupiter	A+	59	193	51	17	1	12	(- -)	106	46	34	45	46	3	42	9	0	3	9	2	.82	3	.264	.422	.549
2003 Carolina	AA	22	67	20	2	1	5	(- -)	39	15	14	16	13	2	20	3	0	0	0	0	-	0	.299	.434	.582
2004 Carolina	AA	112	338	95	24	0	24	(- -)	191	81	76	86	91	8	87	18	1	7	6	3	.67	7	.281	.449	.565
2004 Florida	NL	12	25	5	0	0	1	(0 1)	8	2	1	1	4	0	8	0	0	0	0	0	-	1	.200	.310	.320

Dontrelle Willis

Pitches: L **Bats:** L **Pos:** SP-32   **Ht:** 6'4" **Wt:** 200 **Born:** 1/12/1982 **Age:** 23

		HOW MUCH HE PITCHED						WHAT HE GAVE UP												THE RESULTS							
Year Team	Lg	G	GS	CG	GF	IP	BFP	H	R	ER	HR	SH	SF	HB	TBB	IBB	SO	WP	Bk	W	L	Pct	ShO	Sv-Op	Hld	ERC	ERA
2000 Cubs	R	9	1	0	3	28.0	118	26	15	12	0	1	2	1	8	1	22	0	0	3	1	.750	0	0--		2.64	3.86
2001 Boise	A-	15	15	0	0	93.2	374	76	36	31	1	0	1	3	19	0	77	5	1	8	2	.800	0	0--		1.95	2.98
2002 Kane County	A	19	19	3	0	127.2	491	91	29	26	3	5	2	8	21	0	101	9	3	10	2	.833	2	0--		1.62	1.83
2002 Jupiter	A+	5	5	0	0	30.0	115	24	7	6	2	0	0	1	3	0	27	0	0	2	0	1.000	0	0--		1.92	1.80
2003 Carolina	AA	6	6	0	0	36.1	133	24	6	6	2	0	0	0	9	0	32	1	0	4	0	1.000	0	0--		1.70	1.49
2003 Florida	NL	27	27	2	0	160.2	668	148	61	59	13	3	1	3	58	0	142	7	1	14	6	.700	2	0-0	0	3.49	3.30
2004 Florida	NL	32	32	2	0	197.0	848	210	99	88	20	8	2	8	61	8	139	2	0	10	11	.476	0	0-0	0	4.21	4.02
2 ML YEARS		59	59	4	0	357.2	1516	358	160	147	33	11	3	11	119	8	281	9	1	24	17	.585	2	0-0	0	3.89	3.70

Craig Wilson

Bats: R **Throws:** R **Pos:** RF-89; 1B-65; LF-19; C-4; PH-4; DH-2   **Ht:** 6'2" **Wt:** 225 **Born:** 11/30/1976 **Age:** 28

		BATTING																	BASERUNNING				AVERAGES		
Year Team	Lg	G	AB	H	2B	3B	HR	(Hm Rd)	TB	R	RBI	RC	TBB	IBB	SO	HBP	SH	SF	SB	CS	SB%	GDP	Avg	OBP	Slg
2001 Pittsburgh	NL	88	158	49	3	1	13	(8 5)	93	27	32	34	15	1	53	7	1	2	3	1	.75	4	.310	.390	.589
2002 Pittsburgh	NL	131	368	97	16	1	16	(3 13)	163	48	57	55	32	0	116	21	1	2	2	3	.40	10	.264	.355	.443
2003 Pittsburgh	NL	116	309	81	15	4	18	(5 9)	158	49	48	49	35	4	89	13	0	1	3	1	.75	6	.262	.360	.511
2004 Pittsburgh	NL	155	561	148	35	5	29	(16 13)	280	97	82	84	50	3	169	30	0	3	2	2	.50	10	.264	.354	.499
4 ML YEARS		490	1396	375	69	11	76	(36 40)	694	221	219	222	132	8	427	71	2	8	10	7	.59	30	.269	.360	.497

Dan Wilson

Bats: R **Throws:** R **Pos:** C-103; PH-2   **Ht:** 6'3" **Wt:** 214 **Born:** 3/25/1969 **Age:** 36

		BATTING																	BASERUNNING				AVERAGES		
Year Team	Lg	G	AB	H	2B	3B	HR	(Hm Rd)	TB	R	RBI	RC	TBB	IBB	SO	HBP	SH	SF	SB	CS	SB%	GDP	Avg	OBP	Slg
1992 Cincinnati	NL	12	25	9	1	0	0	(0 0)	10	2	3	4	3	0	8	0	0	0	0	0	-	2	.360	.429	.400
1993 Cincinnati	NL	36	76	17	3	0	0	(0 0)	20	6	8	6	9	4	16	0	2	1	0	0	-	2	.224	.302	.263
1994 Seattle	AL	91	282	61	14	2	3	(1 2)	88	24	27	17	10	0	57	1	8	2	1	2	.33	11	.216	.244	.312
1995 Seattle	AL	119	399	111	22	3	9	(5 4)	166	40	51	53	33	1	63	2	5	1	2	1	.67	12	.278	.336	.416
1996 Seattle	AL	138	491	140	24	0	18	(7 11)	218	51	83	68	32	2	88	3	9	5	1	2	.33	15	.285	.330	.423
1997 Seattle	AL	146	508	137	31	1	15	(9 6)	215	66	74	69	39	1	72	5	8	3	7	2	.78	12	.270	.326	.423
1998 Seattle	AL	96	325	82	17	1	9	(6 3)	128	39	44	40	24	0	56	5	8	6	2	1	.67	6	.252	.308	.394
1999 Seattle	AL	123	414	110	23	2	7	(3 4)	158	46	38	49	29	4	83	2	10	3	5	0	1.00	10	.266	.315	.382
2000 Seattle	AL	90	268	63	12	0	5	(2 3)	90	31	27	24	22	0	51	0	11	2	1	2	.33	8	.235	.291	.336
2001 Seattle	AL	123	377	100	20	1	10	(4 6)	152	44	42	45	20	0	69	2	8	1	3	2	.60	6	.265	.305	.403
2002 Seattle	AL	115	359	106	16	1	6	(3 3)	142	35	44	42	18	1	81	2	7	8	1	0	1.00	8	.295	.326	.396

Year Team	Lg	G	AB	H	2B	3B	HR	(Hm	Rd)	TB	R	RBI	RC	TBB	IBB	SO	HBP	SH	SF	SB	CS	SB%	GDP	Avg	OBP	Slg
2003 Seattle	AL	96	316	76	15	2	4	(1	3)	107	32	43	28	15	0	52	0	3	3	0	0	-	8	.241	.272	.339
2004 Seattle	AL	103	319	80	13	0	2	(1	1)	99	23	33	28	26	0	57	1	8	5	0	1	.00	8	.251	.305	.310
13 ML YEARS		1288	4159	1092	211	13	88	(42	46)	1593	439	517	473	280	13	753	23	87	39	23	13	.64	108	.263	.310	.383

Enrique Wilson

Bats: B **Throws:** R **Pos:** 2B-80; SS-16; PR-8; PH-2   **Ht:** 5'11" **Wt:** 195 **Born:** 7/27/1973 **Age:** 31

Year Team	Lg	G	AB	H	2B	3B	HR	(Hm	Rd)	TB	R	RBI	RC	TBB	IBB	SO	HBP	SH	SF	SB	CS	SB%	GDP	Avg	OBP	Slg
1997 Cleveland	AL	5	15	5	0	0	0	(0	0)	5	2	1	2	0	0	2	0	0	0	0	0	-	0	.333	.333	.333
1998 Cleveland	AL	32	90	29	6	0	2	(1	1)	41	13	12	13	4	0	8	1	1	1	2	4	.33	1	.322	.354	.456
1999 Cleveland	AL	113	332	87	22	1	2	(1	1)	117	41	24	34	25	1	41	1	4	6	5	4	.56	12	.262	.310	.352
2000 Cle-Pit		80	239	70	15	1	5	(3	2)	102	27	27	34	18	2	24	0	4	2	2	2	.50	6	.293	.340	.427
2001 Pit-NYY		94	228	48	8	1	2	(1	1)	64	17	20	9	9	0	37	0	2	2	0	5	.00	10	.211	.238	.281
2002 New York	AL	60	105	19	2	2	2	(2	0)	31	17	11	9	8	0	22	0	6	0	1	1	.50	2	.181	.239	.295
2003 New York	AL	63	135	31	9	0	3	(1	2)	49	18	15	13	7	0	14	2	2	1	3	1	.75	3	.230	.276	.363
2004 New York	AL	93	240	51	9	0	6	(2	4)	78	19	31	24	15	0	20	0	2	5	1	2	.33	5	.213	.254	.325
2000 Cleveland	AL	40	117	38	9	0	2	(2	0)	53	16	12	19	7	0	11	0	2	1	2	1	.67	2	.325	.360	.453
2000 Pittsburgh	NL	40	122	32	6	1	3	(1	2)	49	11	15	15	11	2	13	0	2	1	0	1	.00	4	.262	.321	.402
2001 Pittsburgh	NL	46	129	24	3	0	1	(0	1)	30	7	8	1	3	0	23	0	0	1	0	3	.00	7	.186	.203	.233
2001 New York	AL	48	99	24	5	1	1	(1	0)	34	10	12	8	6	0	14	0	2	1	0	2	.00	3	.242	.283	.343
8 ML YEARS		540	1384	340	71	5	22	(11	11)	487	154	141	138	86	3	168	4	21	17	14	19	.42	39	.246	.288	.352

Jack Wilson

Bats: R **Throws:** R **Pos:** SS-156; PH-2   **Ht:** 6'0" **Wt:** 195 **Born:** 12/29/1977 **Age:** 27

Year Team	Lg	G	AB	H	2B	3B	HR	(Hm	Rd)	TB	R	RBI	RC	TBB	IBB	SO	HBP	SH	SF	SB	CS	SB%	GDP	Avg	OBP	Slg
2001 Pittsburgh	NL	108	390	87	17	1	3	(0	3)	115	44	25	27	16	2	70	1	17	1	1	3	.25	4	.223	.255	.295
2002 Pittsburgh	NL	147	527	133	22	4	4	(2	2)	175	77	47	60	37	2	74	4	17	1	5	2	.71	7	.252	.306	.332
2003 Pittsburgh	NL	150	558	143	21	3	9	(2	7)	197	58	62	62	36	3	74	4	11	6	5	5	.50	11	.256	.303	.353
2004 Pittsburgh	NL	157	652	201	41	12	11	(7	4)	299	82	59	84	26	0	71	3	7	5	8	4	.67	15	.308	.335	.459
4 ML YEARS		562	2127	564	101	20	27	(11	16)	786	261	193	233	115	7	289	12	52	13	19	14	.58	37	.265	.305	.370

Paul Wilson

Pitches: R **Bats:** R **Pos:** SP-29   **Ht:** 6'5" **Wt:** 214 **Born:** 3/28/1973 **Age:** 32

		HOW MUCH HE PITCHED						WHAT HE GAVE UP												THE RESULTS							
Year Team	Lg	G	GS	CG	GF	IP	BFP	H	R	ER	HR	SH	SF	HB	TBB	IBB	SO	WP	Bk	W	L	Pct	ShO	Sv-Op	Hld	ERC	ERA
1996 New York	NL	26	26	1	0	149.0	677	157	102	89	15	7	3	10	71	11	109	3	3	5	12	.294	0	0-0	0	4.77	5.38
2000 Tampa Bay	AL	11	7	0	0	51.0	206	38	20	19	1	2	2	4	16	2	40	1	0	1	4	.200	0	0-0	1	2.17	3.35
2001 Tampa Bay	AL	37	24	0	6	151.1	674	165	94	82	21	3	12	13	52	2	119	7	0	8	9	.471	0	0-1	0	4.94	4.88
2002 Tampa Bay	AL	30	30	1	0	193.2	851	219	113	104	29	2	6	13	67	2	111	4	1	6	12	.333	0	0-0	0	5.30	4.83
2003 Cincinnati	NL	28	28	0	0	166.2	730	190	97	86	24	7	0	7	50	5	93	1	0	8	10	.444	0	0-0	0	4.92	4.64
2004 Cincinnati	NL	29	29	1	0	183.2	798	192	93	89	26	10	8	8	63	5	117	7	0	11	6	.647	0	0-0	0	4.53	4.36
6 ML YEARS		161	144	3	6	895.1	3936	961	519	469	116	31	31	55	319	27	589	23	4	39	53	.424	0	0-1	1	4.73	4.71

Preston Wilson

Bats: R **Throws:** R **Pos:** CF-52; PH-7   **Ht:** 6'2" **Wt:** 213 **Born:** 7/19/1974 **Age:** 30

Year Team	Lg	G	AB	H	2B	3B	HR	(Hm	Rd)	TB	R	RBI	RC	TBB	IBB	SO	HBP	SH	SF	SB	CS	SB%	GDP	Avg	OBP	Slg
2004 Tulsa*	AA	6	17	7	1	0	1	(-	-)	11	4	2	4	3	0	4	1	0	0	1	1	.50	1	.412	.524	.647
1998 NYM-Fla	NL	22	51	8	2	0	1	(1	0)	13	7	3	3	6	0	21	1	2	0	1	1	.50	0	.157	.259	.255
1999 Florida	NL	149	482	135	21	4	26	(8	18)	242	67	71	81	46	3	156	9	0	6	11	4	.73	15	.280	.350	.502
2000 Florida	NL	161	605	160	35	3	31	(12	19)	294	94	121	97	55	1	187	6	0	6	36	14	.72	11	.264	.331	.486
2001 Florida	NL	123	468	128	30	2	23	(9	14)	231	70	71	73	36	2	107	6	0	3	20	8	.71	14	.274	.331	.494
2002 Florida	NL	141	510	124	22	2	23	(8	15)	219	80	65	58	58	3	140	9	2	3	20	11	.65	17	.243	.329	.429
2003 Colorado	NL	155	600	169	43	1	36	(21	15)	322	94	141	111	54	4	139	4	0	3	14	7	.67	23	.282	.343	.537
2004 Colorado	NL	58	202	50	11	0	6	(3	3)	79	24	29	19	17	2	49	3	0	0	2	1	.67	9	.248	.315	.391
1998 New York	NL	8	20	6	2	0	0	(0	0)	8	3	2	3	2	0	8	0	0	0	1	1	.50	0	.300	.364	.400
1998 Florida	NL	14	31	2	0	0	1	(1	0)	5	4	1	0	4	0	13	1	2	0	0	0	-	0	.065	.194	.161
7 ML YEARS		809	2918	774	164	12	146	(62	84)	1400	436	501	442	272	12	799	40	4	21	104	46	.69	89	.265	.334	.480

Tom Wilson

Bats: R **Throws:** R **Pos:** C-10; PH-4   **Ht:** 6'3" **Wt:** 220 **Born:** 12/19/1970 **Age:** 34

Year Team	Lg	G	AB	H	2B	3B	HR	(Hm	Rd)	TB	R	RBI	RC	TBB	IBB	SO	HBP	SH	SF	SB	CS	SB%	GDP	Avg	OBP	Slg
2004 Las Vegas*	AAA	9	38	16	2	0	4	(-	-)	30	10	9	12	4	0	10	0	0	0	0	0	-	0	.421	.476	.789
2004 Sacramento*	AAA	14	42	10	2	0	1	(-	-)	15	6	5	8	15	0	13	0	0	0	0	0	-	0	.238	.439	.357
2004 Norfolk*	AAA	34	115	37	10	0	7	(-	-)	68	26	22	27	25	1	24	0	1	0	0	1	.00	3	.322	.443	.591
2001 Oakland	AL	9	21	4	0	0	2	(1	1)	10	4	4	2	1	0	5	1	0	1	0	0	-	1	.190	.250	.476
2002 Toronto	AL	96	265	68	10	0	8	(6	2)	102	33	37	38	28	0	79	5	0	4	0	0	-	6	.257	.334	.385
2003 Toronto	AL	96	256	66	19	0	5	(2	3)	100	37	35	28	28	0	80	1	0	2	0	0	-	4	.258	.331	.391
2004 NYM-LA	NL	13	12	2	0	0	0	(0	0)	2	1	0	0	1	0	5	0	0	0	0	0	-	0	.167	.231	.167
2004 New York	NL	4	4	1	0	0	0	(0	0)	1	0	0	0	1	0	2	0	0	0	0	0	-	0	.250	.400	.250
2004 Los Angeles	NL	9	8	1	0	0	0	(0	0)	1	1	0	0	0	0	3	0	0	0	0	0	-	0	.125	.125	.125
4 ML YEARS		214	554	140	29	0	15	(9	6)	214	75	76	68	58	0	169	7	0	7	0	0	-	11	.253	.327	.386

Vance Wilson

Bats: R **Throws:** R **Pos:** C-69; PH-14; PR-8   **Ht:** 5'11" **Wt:** 190 **Born:** 3/17/1973 **Age:** 32

									BATTING											BASERUNNING				AVERAGES		
Year Team	Lg	G	AB	H	2B	3B	HR	(Hm	Rd)	TB	R	RBI	RC	TBB	IBB	SO	HBP	SH	SF	SB	CS	SB%	GDP	Avg	OBP	Slg
2004 Binghamton*	AA	1	3	1	0	0	1	(-	-)	4	2	1	1	0	0	0	1	0	0	0	0	-	0	.333	.500	1.333
2004 Norfolk*	AAA	1	4	2	0	0	1	(-	-)	5	1	1	1	0	0	0	0	0	0	0	0	-	0	.500	.500	1.250
1999 New York	NL	1	0	0	0	0	0	(0	0)	0	0	0	0	0	0	0	0	0	0	0	0	-	0	-	-	-
2000 New York	NL	4	4	0	0	0	0	(0	0)	0	0	0	0	0	0	2	0	0	0	0	0	-	0	.000	.000	.000
2001 New York	NL	32	57	17	3	0	0	(0	0)	20	3	6	6	2	0	16	2	0	1	0	1	.00	1	.298	.339	.351
2002 New York	NL	74	163	40	7	0	5	(3	2)	62	19	26	21	5	0	32	8	2	0	0	1	.00	4	.245	.301	.380
2003 New York	NL	96	268	65	9	1	8	(3	5)	100	28	39	31	15	1	56	5	2	2	1	2	.33	6	.243	.293	.373
2004 New York	NL	79	157	43	10	1	4	(1	3)	67	18	21	23	11	2	24	5	1	3	1	0	1.00	4	.274	.335	.427
6 ML YEARS		286	649	165	29	2	17	(7	10)	249	68	92	81	33	3	130	20	5	6	2	4	.33	15	.254	.308	.384

Randy Winn

Bats: B **Throws:** R **Pos:** CF-128; LF-40; DH-2; PH-2   **Ht:** 6'2" **Wt:** 197 **Born:** 6/9/1974 **Age:** 31

									BATTING											BASERUNNING				AVERAGES		
Year Team	Lg	G	AB	H	2B	3B	HR	(Hm	Rd)	TB	R	RBI	RC	TBB	IBB	SO	HBP	SH	SF	SB	CS	SB%	GDP	Avg	OBP	Slg
1998 Tampa Bay	AL	109	338	94	9	9	1	(0	1)	124	51	17	44	29	0	69	1	11	0	26	12	.68	2	.278	.337	.367
1999 Tampa Bay	AL	79	303	81	16	4	2	(2	0)	111	44	24	32	17	0	63	1	1	2	9	9	.50	3	.267	.307	.366
2000 Tampa Bay	AL	51	159	40	5	0	1	(1	0)	48	28	16	18	26	0	25	2	2	1	6	7	.46	2	.252	.362	.302
2001 Tampa Bay	AL	128	429	117	25	6	6	(3	3)	172	54	50	56	38	0	81	6	5	2	12	10	.55	10	.273	.339	.401
2002 Tampa Bay	AL	152	607	181	39	9	14	(9	5)	280	87	75	104	55	3	109	6	1	5	27	8	.77	9	.298	.360	.461
2003 Seattle	AL	157	600	177	37	4	11	(6	5)	255	103	75	96	41	0	108	8	6	5	23	5	.82	9	.295	.346	.425
2004 Seattle	AL	157	626	179	34	6	14	(6	8)	267	84	81	91	53	1	98	8	9	7	21	7	.75	16	.286	.346	.427
7 ML YEARS		833	3062	869	165	38	49	(27	22)	1257	451	338	441	259	4	553	32	35	22	124	58	.68	51	.284	.344	.411

Dewayne Wise

Bats: L **Throws:** L **Pos:** LF-34; PH-27; RF-15; CF-7; PR-7   **Ht:** 6'1" **Wt:** 180 **Born:** 2/24/1978 **Age:** 27

									BATTING											BASERUNNING				AVERAGES		
Year Team	Lg	G	AB	H	2B	3B	HR	(Hm	Rd)	TB	R	RBI	RC	TBB	IBB	SO	HBP	SH	SF	SB	CS	SB%	GDP	Avg	OBP	Slg
2004 Rome*	A	5	15	5	0	0	2	(-	-)	11	4	4	4	1	0	5	1	0	0	1	0	1.00	0	.333	.412	.733
2004 Myrtle Beach*	A+	4	16	4	0	1	0	(-	-)	6	1	0	1	0	0	6	0	0	0	0	0	-	0	.250	.250	.375
2004 Richmond*	AAA	34	118	37	4	6	5	(-	-)	68	18	16	23	5	1	19	0	4	0	5	0	1.00	1	.314	.341	.576
2000 Toronto	AL	28	22	3	0	0	0	(0	0)	3	3	0	0	1	0	5	1	0	0	1	0	1.00	0	.136	.208	.136
2002 Toronto	AL	42	112	20	4	1	3	(2	1)	35	14	13	8	4	0	15	0	0	0	5	0	1.00	0	.179	.207	.313
2004 Atlanta	NL	77	162	37	9	4	6	(3	3)	72	24	17	20	9	1	28	1	2	1	6	1	.86	1	.228	.272	.444
3 ML YEARS		147	296	60	13	5	9	(5	4)	110	41	30	28	14	1	48	2	2	1	12	1	.92	1	.203	.243	.372

Matt Wise

Pitches: R **Bats:** R **Pos:** RP-27; SP-3   **Ht:** 6'4" **Wt:** 195 **Born:** 11/18/1975 **Age:** 29

		HOW MUCH HE PITCHED						WHAT HE GAVE UP										THE RESULTS						
Year Team	Lg	G	GS	CG	GF	IP	BFP	H	R	ER	HR	SH	SF	HB	TBB	IBB	SO	WP	Bk	W	L	Pct	ShO	Sv-Op	Hld	ERC	ERA
2004 Indianapolis*	AAA	7	1	0	0	20.0	75	12	4	4	3	0	1	1	4	0	20	0	0	1	0	1.000	0	0- -		1.84	1.80
2000 Anaheim	AL	8	6	0	0	37.1	163	40	23	23	7	0	2	1	13	1	20	1	0	3	3	.500	0	0-0	0	4.96	5.54
2001 Anaheim	AL	11	9	0	2	49.1	211	47	27	24	11	2	1	2	18	1	50	0	0	1	4	.200	0	0-0	0	4.65	4.38
2002 Anaheim	AL	7	0	0	6	8.1	33	7	3	3	0	1	0	1	1	0	6	0	0	0	0	-	0	0-0	0	2.07	3.24
2004 Milwaukee	NL	30	3	0	5	52.2	222	51	27	26	3	1	2	2	15	1	30	2	0	1	2	.333	0	0-0	3	3.27	4.44
4 ML YEARS		56	18	0	13	147.2	629	145	80	76	21	4	5	6	47	3	106	3	0	5	9	.357	0	0-0	3	4.07	4.63

Jay Witasick

Pitches: R **Bats:** R **Pos:** RP-44   **Ht:** 6'4" **Wt:** 235 **Born:** 8/28/1972 **Age:** 32

		HOW MUCH HE PITCHED						WHAT HE GAVE UP										THE RESULTS						
Year Team	Lg	G	GS	CG	GF	IP	BFP	H	R	ER	HR	SH	SF	HB	TBB	IBB	SO	WP	Bk	W	L	Pct	ShO	Sv-Op	Hld	ERC	ERA
1996 Oakland	AL	12	0	0	6	13.0	55	12	9	9	5	0	1	0	5	0	12	2	0	1	1	.500	0	0-1	0	5.52	6.23
1997 Oakland	AL	8	0	0	1	11.0	53	14	7	7	2	1	0	0	6	0	8	0	0	0	0	-	0	0-0	1	6.81	5.73
1998 Oakland	AL	7	3	0	1	27.0	131	36	24	19	9	0	0	0	15	1	29	2	0	1	3	.250	0	0-0	0	8.53	6.33
1999 Kansas City	AL	32	28	1	2	158.1	732	191	108	98	23	4	8	8	83	1	102	4	2	9	12	.429	1	0-0	0	6.45	5.57
2000 KC-SD		33	25	2	2	150.0	697	178	107	97	24	8	4	7	73	5	121	5	1	6	10	.375	0	0-0	0	6.09	5.82
2001 SD-NYY		63	0	0	17	79.0	352	78	41	29	8	3	2	6	33	4	106	4	0	8	2	.800	0	1-4	10	4.22	3.30
2002 San Francisco	NL	44	0	0	9	68.1	276	58	19	18	3	2	1	4	21	3	54	3	0	1	0	1.000	0	0-0	4	2.78	2.37
2003 San Diego	NL	46	0	0	14	45.2	202	42	24	23	6	3	1	1	25	4	42	5	0	3	7	.300	0	2-7	12	4.34	4.53
2004 San Diego	NL	44	0	0	20	61.2	266	57	28	22	8	3	2	3	26	2	57	4	0	1	0	1.000	0	1-3	2	3.92	3.21
2000 Kansas City	AL	22	14	2	2	89.1	410	109	65	59	15	3	3	4	38	0	67	3	0	3	8	.273	0	0-0	0	6.19	5.94
2000 San Diego	NL	11	11	0	0	60.2	287	69	42	38	9	5	1	3	35	5	54	2	1	3	2	.600	0	0-0	0	5.94	5.64
2001 San Diego	NL	31	0	0	9	38.2	164	31	14	8	3	3	0	4	15	3	53	3	0	5	2	.714	0	1-3	5	3.05	1.86
2001 New York	AL	32	0	0	8	40.1	188	47	27	21	5	0	2	2	18	1	53	1	0	3	0	1.000	0	0-1	5	5.43	4.69
9 ML YEARS		289	56	3	72	614.0	2764	666	367	322	88	24	19	27	287	20	531	29	3	29	36	.446	1	4-15	29	5.28	4.72

Randy Wolf

Pitches: L **Bats:** L **Pos:** SP-23   **Ht:** 6'0" **Wt:** 194 **Born:** 8/22/1976 **Age:** 28

		HOW MUCH HE PITCHED						WHAT HE GAVE UP										THE RESULTS						
Year Team	Lg	G	GS	CG	GF	IP	BFP	H	R	ER	HR	SH	SF	HB	TBB	IBB	SO	WP	Bk	W	L	Pct	ShO	Sv-Op	Hld	ERC	ERA
2004 Reading*	AA	1	1	0	0	4.0	15	5	1	1	0	1	1	0	0	0	4	0	0	0	0	-	0	0- -	-	3.63	2.25
1999 Philadelphia	NL	22	21	0	0	121.2	552	126	78	75	20	5	1	5	67	0	116	4	0	6	9	.400	0	0-0	0	5.54	5.55
2000 Philadelphia	NL	32	32	1	0	206.1	889	210	107	100	25	10	8	8	83	2	160	1	0	11	9	.550	0	0-0	0	4.54	4.36
2001 Philadelphia	NL	28	25	4	1	163.0	684	150	74	67	15	11	7	10	51	4	152	1	0	10	11	.476	2	0-0	0	3.46	3.70
2002 Philadelphia	NL	31	31	3	0	210.2	855	172	77	75	23	7	6	7	63	4	172	4	0	11	9	.550	2	0-0	0	2.88	3.20

Year Team	Lg	G	GS	CG	GF	IP	BFP	H	R	ER	HR	SH	SF	HB	TBB	IBB	SO	WP	Bk	W	L	Pct	ShO	Sv-Op	Hld	ERC	ERA
										HOW MUCH HE PITCHED / **WHAT HE GAVE UP** / **THE RESULTS**																	
2003 Philadelphia	NL	33	33	2	0	200.0	850	176	101	94	27	8	4	6	78	4	177	6	0	16	10	.615	2	0-0	0	3.67	4.23
2004 Philadelphia	NL	23	23	1	0	136.2	585	145	73	65	20	6	3	5	36	4	89	2	0	5	8	.385	1	0-0	0	4.29	4.28
6 ML YEARS		169	165	11	1	1038.1	4415	979	510	476	130	47	29	41	378	19	866	18	0	59	56	.513	7	0-0	0	3.93	4.13

Tony Womack

Bats: L **Throws:** R **Pos:** 2B-133; PH-16; PR-1   **Ht:** 5'9" **Wt:** 170 **Born:** 9/25/1969 **Age:** 35

BATTING / BASERUNNING / AVERAGES

Year Team	Lg	G	AB	H	2B	3B	HR	(Hm	Rd)	TB	R	RBI	RC	TBB	IBB	SO	HBP	SH	SF	SB	CS	SB%	GDP	Avg	OBP	Slg
1993 Pittsburgh	NL	15	24	2	0	0	0	(0	0)	2	5	0	0	3	0	3	0	1	0	2	0	1.00	0	.083	.185	.083
1994 Pittsburgh	NL	5	12	4	0	0	0	(0	0)	4	4	1	2	2	0	3	0	0	0	0	0	-	0	.333	.429	.333
1996 Pittsburgh	NL	17	30	10	3	1	0	(0	0)	15	11	7	8	6	0	1	1	3	0	2	0	1.00	0	.333	.459	.500
1997 Pittsburgh	NL	155	641	178	26	9	6	(5	1)	240	85	50	87	43	2	109	3	2	0	60	7	.90	6	.278	.326	.374
1998 Pittsburgh	NL	159	655	185	26	7	3	(2	1)	234	85	45	84	38	1	94	0	6	5	58	8	.88	4	.282	.319	.357
1999 Arizona	NL	144	614	170	25	10	4	(1	3)	227	111	41	88	52	0	68	2	9	7	72	13	.85	6	.277	.332	.370
2000 Arizona	NL	146	617	167	21	14	7	(4	3)	237	95	57	78	30	0	74	5	2	5	45	11	.80	6	.271	.307	.384
2001 Arizona	NL	125	481	128	19	5	3	(2	1)	166	66	30	54	23	2	54	6	7	1	28	7	.80	4	.266	.307	.345
2002 Arizona	NL	153	590	160	23	5	5	(4	1)	208	90	57	76	46	2	80	4	6	6	29	12	.71	9	.271	.325	.353
2003 Ari-Col-ChC	NL	103	349	79	14	4	2	(2	0)	107	43	22	23	9	0	47	3	2	1	13	5	.72	7	.226	.251	.307
2004 St Louis	NL	145	553	170	22	3	5	(3	2)	213	91	38	77	36	1	60	3	8	6	26	5	.84	6	.307	.349	.385
2003 Arizona	NL	61	219	52	10	3	2	(2	0)	74	30	15	16	8	0	27	2	1	1	8	3	.73	6	.237	.270	.338
2003 Colorado	NL	21	79	15	2	0	0	(0	0)	17	9	5	3	0	0	9	1	1	0	3	1	.75	1	.190	.200	.215
2003 Chicago	NL	21	51	12	2	1	0	(0	0)	16	4	2	4	1	0	11	0	0	0	2	1	.67	0	.235	.250	.314
11 ML YEARS		1167	4566	1253	179	58	35	(23	12)	1653	686	348	577	288	8	593	27	46	31	335	68	.83	46	.274	.319	.362

Kerry Wood

Pitches: R **Bats:** R **Pos:** SP-22   **Ht:** 6'5" **Wt:** 230 **Born:** 6/16/1977 **Age:** 28

HOW MUCH HE PITCHED / WHAT HE GAVE UP / THE RESULTS

Year Team	Lg	G	GS	CG	GF	IP	BFP	H	R	ER	HR	SH	SF	HB	TBB	IBB	SO	WP	Bk	W	L	Pct	ShO	Sv-Op	Hld	ERC	ERA
2004 Iowa*	AAA	1	1	0	0	5.0	19	2	0	0	0	0	0	0	1	0	4	0	0	1	0	1.000	0	0--	-	0.60	0.00
1998 Chicago	NL	26	26	1	0	166.2	699	117	69	63	14	2	4	11	85	1	233	6	3	13	6	.684	1	0-0	0	3.03	3.40
2000 Chicago	NL	23	23	1	0	137.0	603	112	77	73	17	7	5	9	87	0	132	5	1	8	7	.533	0	0-0	0	4.43	4.80
2001 Chicago	NL	28	28	1	0	174.1	740	127	70	65	16	4	5	10	92	3	217	9	0	12	6	.667	1	0-0	0	3.22	3.36
2002 Chicago	NL	33	33	4	0	213.2	895	169	92	87	22	13	5	16	97	5	217	8	1	12	11	.522	1	0-0	0	3.46	3.66
2003 Chicago	NL	32	32	4	0	211.0	887	152	77	75	24	11	6	21	100	2	266	10	0	14	11	.560	2	0-0	0	3.31	3.20
2004 Chicago	NL	22	22	0	0	140.1	595	127	62	58	16	6	6	11	51	0	144	7	0	8	9	.471	0	0-0	0	3.83	3.72
6 ML YEARS		164	164	11	0	1043.0	4419	804	447	421	109	43	31	78	512	11	1209	45	5	67	50	.573	5	0-0	0	3.49	3.63

Mike Wood

Pitches: R **Bats:** R **Pos:** SP-17   **Ht:** 6'3" **Wt:** 180 **Born:** 4/26/1980 **Age:** 25

HOW MUCH HE PITCHED / WHAT HE GAVE UP / THE RESULTS

Year Team	Lg	G	GS	CG	GF	IP	BFP	H	R	ER	HR	SH	SF	HB	TBB	IBB	SO	WP	Bk	W	L	Pct	ShO	Sv-Op	Hld	ERC	ERA
2001 Vancouver	A-	5	2	0	2	21.2	86	17	4	3	0	0	1	0	4	0	24	2	0	2	0	1.000	0	0--	-	1.61	1.25
2001 Modesto	A+	10	9	0	0	58.1	233	46	22	20	6	3	0	2	10	3	52	2	0	4	3	.571	0	0--	-	2.17	3.09
2002 Modesto	A+	7	7	0	0	41.1	170	41	17	16	4	3	3	3	6	0	50	4	1	3	3	.500	0	0--	-	3.32	3.48
2002 Midland	AA	17	17	0	0	105.2	443	103	41	37	8	5	5	7	29	0	63	1	0	11	3	.786	0	0--	-	3.58	3.15
2003 Sacramento	AAA	16	16	0	0	91.1	373	87	34	31	5	5	4	4	23	1	59	3	1	9	3	.750	0	0--	-	3.17	3.05
2004 Sacramento	AAA	15	15	1	0	90.0	379	83	42	28	8	4	1	6	24	1	66	3	1	11	3	.786	0	0--	-	3.27	2.80
2003 Oakland	AL	7	1	0	2	13.2	72	24	17	16	1	1	0	2	7	2	15	2	0	2	1	.667	0	0-0	0	9.45	10.54
2004 Kansas City	AL	17	17	0	0	100.0	432	112	67	66	16	5	2	6	28	3	54	6	1	3	8	.273	0	0-0	0	4.96	5.94
2 ML YEARS		24	18	0	2	113.2	504	136	84	82	17	6	2	8	35	5	69	8	1	5	9	.357	0	0-0	0	5.48	6.49

Chris Woodward

Bats: R **Throws:** R **Pos:** SS-64; PR-6; DH-2; PH-1   **Ht:** 6'0" **Wt:** 185 **Born:** 6/27/1976 **Age:** 29

BATTING / BASERUNNING / AVERAGES

Year Team	Lg	G	AB	H	2B	3B	HR	(Hm	Rd)	TB	R	RBI	RC	TBB	IBB	SO	HBP	SH	SF	SB	CS	SB%	GDP	Avg	OBP	Slg
2004 Dunedin*	A+	6	16	5	2	0	1	(-	-)	10	2	3	3	1	0	2	0	0	1	0	0	-	0	.313	.333	.625
1999 Toronto	AL	14	26	6	1	0	0	(0	0)	7	1	2	2	2	0	6	0	0	1	0	0	-	1	.231	.276	.269
2000 Toronto	AL	37	104	19	7	0	3	(1	2)	35	16	14	9	10	3	28	0	1	0	1	0	1.00	6	.183	.254	.337
2001 Toronto	AL	37	63	12	3	2	2	(2	0)	25	9	5	4	1	0	14	0	2	0	1	0	1.00	1	.190	.203	.397
2002 Toronto	AL	90	312	86	13	4	13	(9	4)	146	48	45	45	26	0	72	3	1	8	3	0	1.00	6	.276	.330	.468
2003 Toronto	AL	104	349	91	22	2	7	(4	3)	138	49	45	42	28	0	72	3	0	6	1	2	.33	6	.261	.316	.395
2004 Toronto	AL	69	213	50	13	4	1	(0	1)	74	21	24	24	14	0	46	1	2	2	1	2	.33	3	.235	.283	.347
6 ML YEARS		351	1067	264	59	12	26	(16	10)	425	144	135	126	81	3	238	7	6	17	6	5	.55	20	.247	.300	.398

Shawn Wooten

Bats: R **Throws:** R **Pos:** PH-19; 1B-11; 3B-4; PR-1   **Ht:** 5'10" **Wt:** 225 **Born:** 7/24/1972 **Age:** 32

BATTING / BASERUNNING / AVERAGES

Year Team	Lg	G	AB	H	2B	3B	HR	(Hm	Rd)	TB	R	RBI	RC	TBB	IBB	SO	HBP	SH	SF	SB	CS	SB%	GDP	Avg	OBP	Slg
2004 Scrtn/WlksBr*	AAA	61	225	66	22	0	4	(-	-)	100	28	34	33	24	0	29	4	0	1	0	1	.00	11	.293	.370	.444
2000 Anaheim	AL	7	9	5	1	0	0	(0	0)	6	2	1	3	0	0	0	0	0	0	0	0	-	0	.556	.556	.667
2001 Anaheim	AL	79	221	69	8	1	8	(3	5)	103	24	32	33	5	0	42	3	0	3	2	0	1.00	5	.312	.332	.466
2002 Anaheim	AL	49	113	33	8	0	3	(2	1)	50	13	19	17	6	1	24	1	0	1	2	0	1.00	3	.292	.331	.442
2003 Anaheim	AL	98	272	66	8	0	7	(5	2)	95	25	32	22	24	5	45	1	0	3	0	4	.00	7	.243	.303	.349
2004 Philadelphia	NL	33	53	9	3	0	0	(0	0)	12	2	2	0	2	0	9	2	0	0	0	0	-	4	.170	.228	.226
5 ML YEARS		266	668	182	28	1	18	(10	8)	266	66	86	75	37	6	120	7	0	7	4	4	.50	19	.272	.314	.398

Tim Worrell

Pitches: R **Bats:** R **Pos:** RP-77 **Ht:** 6'4" **Wt:** 230 **Born:** 7/5/1967 **Age:** 37

Year Team	Lg	G	GS	CG	GF	IP	BFP	H	R	ER	HR	SH	SF	HB	TBB	IBB	SO	WP	Bk	W	L	Pct	ShO	Sv-Op	Hld	ERC	ERA
1993 San Diego	NL	21	16	0	1	100.2	443	104	63	55	11	8	5	0	43	5	52	3	0	2	7	.222	0	0-0	1	4.31	4.92
1994 San Diego	NL	3	3	0	0	14.2	59	9	7	6	0	0	1	0	5	0	14	0	0	0	1	.000	0	0-0	0	1.40	3.68
1995 San Diego	NL	9	0	0	4	13.1	63	16	7	7	2	1	0	1	6	0	13	1	0	1	0	1.000	0	0-0	0	6.01	4.73
1996 San Diego	NL	50	11	0	8	121.0	510	109	45	41	9	3	1	6	39	1	99	0	0	9	7	.563	0	1-2	10	3.22	3.05
1997 San Diego	NL	60	10	0	14	106.1	483	116	67	61	14	6	6	7	50	2	81	2	1	4	8	.333	0	3-7	16	5.34	5.16
1998 Det-Cle-Oak	AL	43	9	0	5	103.0	440	106	62	60	16	2	3	1	29	3	82	2	0	2	7	.222	0	0-3	6	4.10	5.24
1999 Oakland	AL	53	0	0	17	69.1	309	69	38	32	6	1	1	3	34	1	62	1	0	2	2	.500	0	0-5	5	4.42	4.15
2000 Bal-ChC		59	0	0	29	69.1	307	72	26	23	10	4	1	1	29	11	57	1	0	5	6	.455	0	3-6	12	4.42	2.99
2001 San Francisco	NL	73	0	0	12	78.1	339	71	33	30	4	3	4	3	33	4	63	2	0	2	5	.286	0	0-3	13	3.32	3.45
2002 San Francisco	NL	80	0	0	23	72.0	296	55	21	18	3	3	4	0	30	2	55	0	0	8	2	.800	0	0-1	23	2.47	2.25
2003 San Francisco	NL	76	0	0	64	78.1	335	74	35	25	5	3	3	0	28	6	65	5	0	4	4	.500	0	38-45	1	3.19	2.87
2004 Philadelphia	NL	77	0	0	36	78.1	327	75	36	32	10	4	5	2	21	4	64	0	0	5	6	.455	0	19-27	20	3.53	3.68
1998 Detroit	AL	15	9	0	0	61.2	265	66	42	41	11	0	1	1	19	2	47	0	0	2	6	.250	0	0-1	0	4.68	5.98
1998 Cleveland	AL	3	0	0	1	5.1	24	6	3	3	0	0	2	0	2	0	2	0	0	0	0	-	0	0-0	0	3.84	5.06
1998 Oakland	AL	25	0	0	4	36.0	151	34	17	16	5	2	0	0	8	1	33	2	0	0	1	.000	0	0-2	6	3.20	4.00
2000 Baltimore	AL	5	0	0	2	7.1	39	12	6	6	3	0	0	0	5	3	5	0	0	2	2	.500	0	0-0	0	11.13	7.36
2000 Chicago	NL	54	0	0	27	62.0	268	60	20	17	7	4	1	1	24	8	52	1	0	3	4	.429	0	3-6	12	3.75	2.47
12 ML YEARS		604	49	0	213	904.2	3911	876	440	390	90	38	34	24	347	39	707	17	1	44	55	.444	0	64-99	107	3.83	3.88

Dan Wright

Pitches: R **Bats:** R **Pos:** SP-4 **Ht:** 6'5" **Wt:** 225 **Born:** 12/14/1977 **Age:** 27

Year Team	Lg	G	GS	CG	GF	IP	BFP	H	R	ER	HR	SH	SF	HB	TBB	IBB	SO	WP	Bk	W	L	Pct	ShO	Sv-Op	Hld	ERC	ERA
2004 Charlotte*	AAA	2	2	0	1	5.1	41	17	19	17	4	0	2	1	6	0	3	1	0	0	2	.000	0	0- -	-	31.72	28.69
2001 Chicago	AL	13	12	0	1	66.1	307	78	45	42	12	1	5	2	39	1	36	5	0	5	3	.625	0	0-0	0	6.74	5.70
2002 Chicago	AL	33	33	1	0	196.1	855	200	124	113	32	7	10	6	71	1	136	10	1	14	12	.538	1	0-0	0	4.55	5.18
2003 Chicago	AL	20	15	0	0	86.1	387	91	63	59	16	6	4	3	46	2	47	6	0	1	7	.125	0	1-1	0	5.74	6.15
2004 Chicago	AL	4	4	0	0	17.2	88	24	17	16	5	0	0	2	11	1	6	0	1	0	4	.000	0	0-0	0	9.24	8.15
4 ML YEARS		70	64	1	2	366.2	1637	393	249	230	65	14	19	13	167	5	225	21	2	20	26	.435	1	1-1	0	5.42	5.65

David Wright

Bats: R **Throws:** R **Pos:** 3B-69; PR-1 **Ht:** 6'0" **Wt:** 200 **Born:** 12/20/1982 **Age:** 22

Year Team	Lg	G	AB	H	2B	3B	HR	(Hm	Rd)	TB	R	RBI	RC	TBB	IBB	SO	HBP	SH	SF	SB	CS	SB%	GDP	Avg	OBP	Slg
2001 Kingsport	R+	36	120	36	7	0	4	(-	-)	55	27	17	22	16	0	30	2	0	0	9	1	.90	3	.300	.391	.458
2002 Capital City	A	135	496	132	30	2	11	(-	-)	199	85	93	79	76	2	114	5	1	4	21	5	.81	4	.266	.367	.401
2003 St. Lucie	A+	133	466	126	39	2	15	(-	-)	214	69	75	80	72	5	98	4	1	6	19	5	.79	8	.270	.369	.459
2004 Binghamton	AA	60	223	81	27	0	10	(-	-)	138	44	40	60	39	3	41	7	0	3	20	6	.77	5	.363	.467	.619
2004 Norfolk	AAA	31	114	34	8	0	8	(-	-)	66	18	17	22	16	1	19	2	0	2	2	4	.33	3	.298	.388	.579
2004 New York	NL	69	263	77	17	1	14	(8	6)	138	41	40	42	14	0	40	3	0	3	6	0	1.00	7	.293	.332	.525

Jamey Wright

Pitches: R **Bats:** R **Pos:** SP-14 **Ht:** 6'5" **Wt:** 234 **Born:** 12/24/1974 **Age:** 30

Year Team	Lg	G	GS	CG	GF	IP	BFP	H	R	ER	HR	SH	SF	HB	TBB	IBB	SO	WP	Bk	W	L	Pct	ShO	Sv-Op	Hld	ERC	ERA
2004 Omaha*	AAA	18	18	1	0	104.2	451	111	58	49	13	4	2	9	35	0	70	5	0	8	6	.571	1	0- -	-	4.77	4.21
1996 Colorado	NL	16	15	0	0	91.1	406	105	60	50	8	4	2	7	41	1	45	1	2	4	4	.500	0	0-0	1	5.50	4.93
1997 Colorado	NL	26	26	1	0	149.2	698	198	113	104	19	8	3	11	71	3	59	6	2	8	12	.400	0	0-0	0	6.96	6.25
1998 Colorado	NL	34	34	1	0	206.1	919	235	143	130	24	8	6	11	95	3	86	6	3	9	14	.391	0	0-0	0	5.57	5.67
1999 Colorado	NL	16	16	0	0	94.1	423	110	52	51	10	3	4	4	54	3	49	3	0	4	3	.571	0	0-0	0	6.19	4.87
2000 Milwaukee	NL	26	25	0	1	164.2	718	157	81	75	12	4	6	18	88	5	96	9	2	7	9	.438	0	0-0	0	4.67	4.10
2001 Milwaukee	NL	33	33	1	0	194.2	868	201	115	106	26	7	5	20	98	10	129	6	1	11	12	.478	1	0-0	0	5.36	4.90
2002 Mil-StL	NL	23	22	1	0	129.1	585	130	80	76	17	9	6	11	75	9	77	9	0	7	13	.350	1	0-0	0	5.35	5.29
2003 Kansas City	AL	4	4	2	0	25.1	106	23	14	12	1	0	0	1	11	0	19	0	0	1	2	.333	0	0-0	0	3.53	4.26
2004 Colorado	NL	14	14	0	0	78.2	361	82	39	36	8	1	1	6	45	3	41	3	0	2	3	.400	0	0-0	0	5.26	4.12
2002 Milwaukee	NL	19	19	1	0	114.1	515	115	72	68	15	9	6	11	63	8	69	8	0	5	13	.278	1	0-0	0	5.28	5.35
2002 St Louis	NL	4	3	0	0	15.0	70	15	8	8	2	0	0	0	12	1	8	1	0	2	0	1.000	0	0-0	0	5.87	4.80
9 ML YEARS		192	189	6	1	1134.1	5084	1241	697	640	125	44	33	89	578	37	601	43	10	53	72	.424	3	0-0	1	5.53	5.08

Jaret Wright

Pitches: R **Bats:** R **Pos:** SP-32 **Ht:** 6'2" **Wt:** 230 **Born:** 12/29/1975 **Age:** 29

Year Team	Lg	G	GS	CG	GF	IP	BFP	H	R	ER	HR	SH	SF	HB	TBB	IBB	SO	WP	Bk	W	L	Pct	ShO	Sv-Op	Hld	ERC	ERA
1997 Cleveland	AL	16	16	0	0	90.1	388	81	45	44	9	3	4	5	35	0	63	1	0	8	3	.727	0	0-0	0	3.63	4.38
1998 Cleveland	AL	32	32	1	0	192.2	855	207	109	101	22	4	6	11	87	4	140	6	0	12	10	.545	1	0-0	0	5.07	4.72
1999 Cleveland	AL	26	26	0	0	133.2	609	144	99	90	18	3	3	7	77	1	91	4	0	8	10	.444	0	0-0	0	5.77	6.06
2000 Cleveland	AL	9	9	1	0	51.2	217	44	27	27	6	0	1	1	28	0	36	2	0	3	4	.429	1	0-0	0	4.13	4.70
2001 Cleveland	AL	7	7	0	0	29.0	140	36	23	21	2	2	1	0	22	0	18	1	1	2	2	.500	0	0-0	0	6.82	6.52
2002 Cleveland	AL	8	6	0	1	18.1	116	40	34	32	3	0	3	2	19	0	12	1	0	2	3	.400	0	0-0	0	15.90	15.71
2003 SD-Atl	NL	50	0	0	17	56.1	269	76	46	46	9	2	4	3	31	2	50	12	0	2	5	.286	0	2-5	4	7.59	7.35
2004 Atlanta	NL	32	32	0	0	186.1	781	168	79	68	11	8	6	3	70	5	159	3	0	15	8	.652	0	0-0	0	3.20	3.28
2003 San Diego	NL	39	0	0	14	47.1	233	69	44	44	9	1	4	2	28	2	41	10	0	1	5	.167	0	2-4	1	8.71	8.37
2003 Atlanta	NL	11	0	0	3	9.0	36	7	2	2	0	1	0	1	3	0	9	2	0	1	0	1.000	0	0-1	3	2.51	6.00
8 ML YEARS		180	128	2	18	758.1	3375	796	462	429	80	22	28	32	369	12	569	30	0	52	45	.536	2	2-5	4	4.92	5.09

Mike Wuertz

Pitches: R **Bats:** R **Pos:** RP-31   **Ht:** 6'3" **Wt:** 205 **Born:** 12/15/1978 **Age:** 26

Year Team	Lg	G	GS	CG	GF	IP	BFP	H	R	ER	HR	SH	SF	HB	TBB	IBB	SO	WP	Bk	W	L	Pct	ShO	Sv-Op	Hld	ERC	ERA
1998 Williamsport	A-	14	14	1	0	86.1	359	79	36	33	4	3	2	0	19	0	59	1	2	7	5	.583	0	0- -	-	2.53	3.44
1999 Lansing	A	28	28	1	0	161.1	716	191	104	86	11	2	10	1	44	0	127	11	0	11	12	.478	0	0- -	-	4.32	4.80
2000 Daytona	A+	28	28	3	0	171.1	732	166	79	72	15	6	4	3	64	1	142	7	1	12	7	.632	2	0- -	-	3.77	3.78
2001 W Tennessee	AA	27	27	1	0	160.0	694	160	80	71	20	9	6	6	58	2	135	10	0	4	9	.308	1	0- -	-	4.20	3.99
2002 Iowa	AAA	28	27	0	1	154.0	712	154	109	95	24	8	3	4	69	3	131	11	0	9	5	.643	0	0- -	-	4.47	5.55
2003 Iowa	AAA	43	16	0	4	124.0	536	140	70	63	16	5	5	5	35	8	92	2	0	3	9	.250	0	1- -	-	4.64	4.57
2004 Iowa	AAA	37	0	0	35	44.2	179	30	13	12	4	0	0	0	15	2	59	0	0	1	1	.500	0	19- -	-	2.00	2.42
2004 Chicago	NL	31	0	0	11	29.0	124	22	14	14	4	4	2	0	17	1	30	2	1	1	0	1.000	0	1-1	1	3.67	4.34

Kelly Wunsch

Pitches: L **Bats:** L **Pos:** RP-3   **Ht:** 6'5" **Wt:** 225 **Born:** 7/12/1972 **Age:** 32

Year Team	Lg	G	GS	CG	GF	IP	BFP	H	R	ER	HR	SH	SF	HB	TBB	IBB	SO	WP	Bk	W	L	Pct	ShO	Sv-Op	Hld	ERC	ERA
2004 Charlotte*	AAA	27	0	0	6	27.2	123	21	9	9	1	0	0	7	12	0	29	4	0	1	0	1.000	0	2- -	-	3.31	2.93
2000 Chicago	AL	83	0	0	12	61.1	259	50	22	20	4	0	2	2	29	1	51	0	0	6	3	.667	0	1-5	25	3.22	2.93
2001 Chicago	AL	33	0	0	2	22.1	105	21	19	19	4	3	2	6	9	1	16	0	0	2	1	.667	0	0-2	3	5.11	7.66
2002 Chicago	AL	50	0	0	9	31.2	138	26	12	12	3	1	0	5	19	1	22	1	0	2	1	.667	0	0-1	9	4.51	3.41
2003 Chicago	AL	43	0	0	6	36.0	160	17	13	11	1	1	5	7	25	4	33	1	0	0	0	-	0	0-0	5	2.28	2.75
2004 Chicago	AL	3	0	0	1	2.0	8	2	0	0	0	0	0	0	1	0	1	0	0	0	0	-	0	0-0	0	4.15	0.00
5 ML YEARS		212	0	0	30	153.1	670	116	66	62	12	5	9	20	83	7	123	2	0	10	5	.667	0	1-8	42	3.52	3.64

Esteban Yan

Pitches: R **Bats:** R **Pos:** RP-69   **Ht:** 6'4" **Wt:** 255 **Born:** 6/22/1975 **Age:** 30

Year Team	Lg	G	GS	CG	GF	IP	BFP	H	R	ER	HR	SH	SF	HB	TBB	IBB	SO	WP	Bk	W	L	Pct	ShO	Sv-Op	Hld	ERC	ERA
1996 Baltimore	AL	4	0	0	2	9.1	42	13	7	6	3	0	0	0	3	1	7	0	0	0	0	-	0	0-0	0	7.88	5.79
1997 Baltimore	AL	3	2	0	0	9.2	58	20	18	17	3	0	1	2	7	0	4	1	0	0	1	.000	0	0-0	0	15.60	15.83
1998 Tampa Bay	AL	64	0	0	18	88.2	381	78	41	38	11	1	3	5	41	2	77	6	0	5	4	.556	0	1-5	8	4.02	3.86
1999 Tampa Bay	AL	50	1	0	15	61.0	286	77	41	40	8	6	3	9	32	4	46	2	0	3	4	.429	0	0-3	7	7.13	5.90
2000 Tampa Bay	AL	43	20	0	8	137.2	618	158	98	95	26	4	6	11	42	0	111	7	1	7	8	.467	0	0-2	3	5.46	6.21
2001 Tampa Bay	AL	54	0	0	51	62.1	264	64	34	27	7	3	1	5	11	1	64	5	0	4	6	.400	0	22-31	0	3.68	3.90
2002 Tampa Bay	AL	55	0	0	47	69.0	305	70	35	33	10	2	1	3	29	1	53	5	1	7	8	.467	0	19-27	0	4.67	4.30
2003 Tex-StL		54	0	0	23	66.2	309	84	48	47	13	2	4	7	23	5	53	9	0	2	1	.667	0	1-1	4	6.39	6.35
2004 Detroit	AL	69	0	0	27	87.0	379	92	43	37	8	4	3	4	32	5	69	7	0	3	6	.333	0	7-17	11	4.32	3.83
2003 Texas	AL	15	0	0	6	23.1	110	31	19	18	5	0	0	2	7	1	25	5	0	0	1	.000	0	0-0	1	6.64	6.94
2003 St Louis	NL	39	0	0	17	43.1	199	53	29	29	8	2	4	5	16	4	28	4	0	2	0	1.000	0	1-1	3	6.26	6.02
9 ML YEARS		396	23	0	191	591.1	2642	656	365	340	89	22	22	46	220	19	484	42	2	31	38	.449	0	50-86	33	5.22	5.17

Tyler Yates

Pitches: R **Bats:** R **Pos:** RP-14; SP-7   **Ht:** 6'4" **Wt:** 225 **Born:** 8/7/1977 **Age:** 27

Year Team	Lg	G	GS	CG	GF	IP	BFP	H	R	ER	HR	SH	SF	HB	TBB	IBB	SO	WP	Bk	W	L	Pct	ShO	Sv-Op	Hld	ERC	ERA
1998 Athletics	R	15	0	0	8	23.0	107	28	12	10	0	0	1	0	14	0	20	1	2	0	0	-	0	2- -	-	5.68	3.91
1998 Sth Oregon	A-	2	0	0	1	2.1	9	2	0	0	0	0	0	0	0	0	1	0	0	0	0	-	0	1- -	-	1.44	0.00
1999 Visalia	A+	47	1	0	19	82.1	382	98	64	50	12	3	2	4	35	3	74	12	0	2	5	.286	0	4- -	-	5.67	5.47
2000 Modesto	A+	30	0	0	5	56.2	237	50	23	18	2	1	1	1	23	4	61	8	0	4	2	.667	0	1- -	-	3.01	2.86
2000 Midland	AA	22	0	0	8	26.1	121	28	20	18	2	2	2	0	15	3	24	2	0	1	1	.500	0	0- -	-	4.65	6.15
2001 Midland	AA	56	0	0	35	62.2	282	66	39	30	4	1	0	1	27	8	61	7	0	4	6	.400	0	17- -	-	3.97	4.31
2001 Sacramento	AAA	4	0	0	2	5.1	20	3	0	0	0	0	0	1	1	0	3	0	0	1	0	1.000	0	1- -	-	1.41	0.00
2002 Norfolk	AAA	24	0	0	20	34.0	142	29	10	5	1	1	0	0	13	1	34	0	0	2	2	.500	0	6- -	-	2.69	1.32
2003 St. Lucie	A+	14	11	0	0	48.0	205	41	28	23	5	0	2	2	24	0	49	2	0	1	2	.333	0	0- -	-	3.89	4.31
2003 Binghamton	AA	8	8	0	0	39.1	167	33	21	19	4	3	4	1	17	0	36	2	2	1	2	.333	0	0- -	-	3.40	4.35
2003 Norfolk	AAA	4	4	0	0	20.0	86	22	9	9	1	0	0	1	9	0	15	1	0	1	2	.333	0	0- -	-	4.90	4.05
2004 Norfolk	AAA	30	1	0	12	39.2	172	28	18	14	2	0	0	3	22	0	43	3	0	6	2	.750	0	4- -	-	2.95	3.18
2004 New York	NL	21	7	0	2	46.2	228	61	36	33	6	2	2	3	25	3	35	1	1	2	4	.333	0	0-0	2	6.73	6.36

Kevin Youkilis

Bats: R **Throws:** R **Pos:** 3B-65; PH-8; DH-2; PR-1   **Ht:** 6'1" **Wt:** 220 **Born:** 3/15/1979 **Age:** 26

Year Team	Lg	G	AB	H	2B	3B	HR	(Hm	Rd)	TB	R	RBI	RC	TBB	IBB	SO	HBP	SH	SF	SB	CS	SB%	GDP	Avg	OBP	Slg
2001 Lowell	A-	59	183	58	14	2	3	(-	-)	85	52	28	52	70	0	28	5	0	2	4	3	.57	0	.317	.512	.464
2001 Augusta	A	5	12	2	0	0	0	(-	-)	2	0	0	1	3	0	3	1	0	0	0	0	-	0	.167	.375	.167
2002 Augusta	A	15	53	15	5	0	0	(-	-)	20	5	6	10	13	1	8	1	0	0	0	0	-	0	.283	.433	.377
2002 Sarasota	A+	76	268	79	16	0	3	(-	-)	104	45	48	50	49	2	37	15	0	7	2	0	.00	5	.295	.422	.388
2002 Trenton	AA	44	160	55	10	0	5	(-	-)	80	34	26	38	31	1	18	5	0	1	5	4	.56	1	.344	.462	.500
2003 Portland	AA	94	312	102	23	1	6	(-	-)	145	74	37	80	86	2	40	15	0	4	7	0	1.00	7	.327	.487	.465
2003 Pawtucket	AAA	32	109	18	3	0	2	(-	-)	27	9	15	8	18	2	21	3	0	2	0	1	.00	2	.165	.295	.248
2004 Lowell	A-	2	4	3	1	1	0	(-	-)	6	1	0	3	2	0	1	0	0	0	0	0	-	0	.750	.857	1.500
2004 Pawtucket	AAA	38	154	41	12	0	3	(-	-)	62	25	18	23	19	1	28	2	1	2	2	0	1.00	4	.266	.350	.403
2004 Boston	AL	72	208	54	11	0	7	(2	5)	86	38	35	36	33	0	45	4	0	3	0	1	.00	4	.260	.367	.413

Chris Young

Pitches: R **Bats:** R **Pos:** SP-7 **Ht:** 6'10" **Wt:** 260 **Born:** 5/25/1979 **Age:** 26

Year Team	Lg	G	GS	CG	GF	IP	BFP	H	R	ER	HR	SH	SF	HB	TBB	IBB	SO	WP	Bk	W	L	Pct	ShO	Sv-Op	Hld	ERC	ERA
2001 Hickory	A	12	12	2	0	74.1	320	79	39	34	6	2	1	3	20	0	72	0	0	5	3	.625	0	0--	--	3.91	4.12
2002 Hickory	A	26	26	1	0	144.2	587	127	57	50	11	1	4	4	34	1	136	3	1	11	9	.550	0	0--	--	2.75	3.11
2003 Brevard Cnty	A+	8	8	1	0	50.0	180	26	9	9	3	1	0	1	5	0	39	0	0	5	2	.714	0	0--	--	0.95	1.62
2003 Harrisburg	AA	15	15	0	0	83.0	354	83	39	37	9	3	4	5	22	0	64	5	2	4	4	.500	0	0--	--	3.81	4.01
2004 Frisco	AA	18	18	0	0	88.1	383	94	48	44	9	5	4	5	31	1	75	4	0	6	5	.545	0	0--	--	4.51	4.48
2004 Oklahoma	AAA	5	5	1	0	30.1	116	20	7	5	2	1	0	0	9	0	34	1	0	3	0	1.000	0	0--	--	1.83	1.48
2004 Texas	AL	7	7	0	0	36.1	158	36	21	19	7	1	0	2	10	0	27	1	0	3	2	.600	0	0-0	--	4.26	4.71

Dmitri Young

Bats: B **Throws:** R **Pos:** DH-74; 1B-25; PH-3; LF-2; 3B-1 **Ht:** 6'2" **Wt:** 235 **Born:** 10/11/1973 **Age:** 31

Year Team	Lg	G	AB	H	2B	3B	HR	(Hm	Rd)	TB	R	RBI	RC	TBB	IBB	SO	HBP	SH	SF	SB	CS	SB%	GDP	Avg	OBP	Slg
2004 Toledo*	AAA	2	10	5	1	1	1	(-	-)	11	1	5	4	1	0	0	0	0	0	0	0	--	0	.500	.545	1.100
1996 St Louis	NL	16	29	7	0	0	0	(0	0)	7	3	2	2	4	0	5	1	0	0	0	1	.00	1	.241	.353	.241
1997 St Louis	NL	110	333	86	14	3	5	(2	3)	121	38	34	40	38	3	63	2	1	3	6	5	.55	8	.258	.335	.363
1998 Cincinnati	NL	144	536	166	48	1	14	(3	11)	258	81	83	88	47	4	94	2	0	5	2	4	.33	16	.310	.364	.481
1999 Cincinnati	NL	127	373	112	30	2	14	(9	5)	188	63	56	63	30	1	71	2	0	4	3	1	.75	11	.300	.352	.504
2000 Cincinnati	NL	152	548	166	37	6	18	(6	12)	269	68	88	86	36	6	80	3	1	5	0	3	.00	16	.303	.346	.491
2001 Cincinnati	NL	142	540	163	28	3	21	(8	13)	260	68	69	83	37	10	77	5	1	3	8	5	.62	22	.302	.350	.481
2002 Detroit	AL	54	201	57	14	0	7	(5	2)	92	25	27	27	12	5	39	2	0	1	2	0	1.00	12	.284	.329	.458
2003 Detroit	AL	155	562	167	34	7	29	(10	19)	302	78	85	101	58	16	130	11	0	4	2	1	.67	16	.297	.372	.537
2004 Detroit	AL	104	389	106	23	2	18	(8	10)	187	72	60	57	33	4	71	6	0	4	0	1	.00	8	.272	.336	.481
9 ML YEARS		1004	3511	1030	228	24	126	(51	75)	1684	496	504	547	295	49	630	34	3	29	23	21	.52	110	.293	.351	.480

Eric Young

Bats: R **Throws:** R **Pos:** LF-47; DH-23; 2B-20; PH-11; CF-9; SS-8; 3B-1 **Ht:** 5'8" **Wt:** 180 **Born:** 5/18/1967 **Age:** 38

Year Team	Lg	G	AB	H	2B	3B	HR	(Hm	Rd)	TB	R	RBI	RC	TBB	IBB	SO	HBP	SH	SF	SB	CS	SB%	GDP	Avg	OBP	Slg
1992 Los Angeles	NL	49	132	34	1	0	1	(0	1)	38	9	11	12	8	0	9	0	4	0	6	1	.86	3	.258	.300	.288
1993 Colorado	NL	144	490	132	16	8	3	(3	0)	173	82	42	66	63	3	41	4	4	4	42	19	.69	9	.269	.355	.353
1994 Colorado	NL	90	228	62	13	1	7	(6	1)	98	37	30	40	38	1	17	2	5	2	18	7	.72	3	.272	.378	.430
1995 Colorado	NL	120	366	116	21	9	6	(5	1)	173	68	36	73	49	3	29	5	3	1	35	12	.74	4	.317	.404	.473
1996 Colorado	NL	141	568	184	23	4	8	(7	1)	239	113	74	99	47	1	31	21	2	5	53	19	.74	9	.324	.393	.421
1997 Col-LA	NL	155	622	174	33	8	8	(2	6)	247	106	61	93	71	1	54	9	10	6	45	14	.76	18	.280	.359	.397
1998 Los Angeles	NL	117	452	129	24	1	8	(7	1)	179	78	43	70	45	0	32	5	9	2	42	13	.76	4	.285	.355	.396
1999 Los Angeles	NL	119	456	128	24	2	2	(2	0)	162	73	41	65	63	0	26	5	6	4	51	22	.70	12	.281	.371	.355
2000 Chicago	NL	153	607	180	40	2	6	(5	1)	242	98	47	99	63	1	39	8	7	5	54	7	.89	12	.297	.367	.399
2001 Chicago	NL	149	603	168	43	4	6	(4	2)	237	98	42	78	42	1	45	9	15	3	31	14	.69	15	.279	.333	.393
2002 Milwaukee	NL	138	496	139	29	3	3	(2	1)	183	57	28	53	39	0	38	6	8	4	31	11	.74	14	.280	.338	.369
2003 Mil-SF	NL	135	475	119	20	1	15	(7	8)	186	80	34	54	57	2	44	5	2	2	28	12	.70	12	.251	.336	.392
2004 Texas	AL	104	344	99	25	2	1	(1	0)	131	55	27	54	43	0	28	8	4	3	14	9	.61	9	.288	.377	.381
1997 Colorado	NL	118	468	132	29	6	6	(2	4)	191	78	45	71	57	0	37	5	8	5	32	12	.73	16	.282	.363	.408
1997 Los Angeles	NL	37	154	42	4	2	2	(0	2)	56	28	16	22	14	1	17	4	2	1	13	2	.87	2	.273	.347	.364
2003 Milwaukee	NL	109	404	105	18	1	15	(7	8)	170	71	31	51	48	2	34	4	2	1	25	7	.78	9	.260	.344	.421
2003 San Francisco	NL	26	71	14	2	0	0	(0	0)	16	9	3	3	9	0	10	1	0	1	3	5	.38	3	.197	.293	.225
13 ML YEARS		1614	5839	1664	312	45	74	(51	23)	2288	954	516	856	628	13	433	87	79	41	450	160	.74	124	.285	.361	.392

Ernie Young

Bats: R **Throws:** R **Pos:** DH-2; PH-2 **Ht:** 6'1" **Wt:** 234 **Born:** 7/8/1969 **Age:** 35

Year Team	Lg	G	AB	H	2B	3B	HR	(Hm	Rd)	TB	R	RBI	RC	TBB	IBB	SO	HBP	SH	SF	SB	CS	SB%	GDP	Avg	OBP	Slg
2004 Buffalo*	AAA	115	441	132	26	2	27	(-	-)	243	71	100	85	40	1	104	12	0	7	2	2	.50	7	.299	.368	.551
1994 Oakland	AL	11	30	2	1	0	0	(0	0)	3	2	3	0	1	0	8	0	0	0	0	0	--	1	.067	.097	.100
1995 Oakland	AL	26	50	10	3	0	2	(2	0)	19	9	5	6	8	0	12	0	0	0	0	0	--	1	.200	.310	.380
1996 Oakland	AL	141	462	112	19	4	19	(10	9)	196	72	64	62	52	1	118	7	3	4	7	5	.58	13	.242	.326	.424
1997 Oakland	AL	71	175	39	7	0	5	(3	2)	61	22	15	17	19	0	57	2	2	2	1	3	.25	6	.223	.303	.349
1998 Kansas City	AL	25	53	10	3	0	1	(0	1)	16	2	3	3	2	0	9	1	0	0	2	1	.67	3	.189	.232	.302
1999 Arizona	NL	6	11	2	0	0	0	(0	0)	2	1	0	1	3	0	2	1	0	0	0	0	--	0	.182	.400	.182
2003 Detroit	AL	5	11	2	0	0	0	(0	0)	2	0	0	0	4	0	5	0	0	0	0	2	.00	1	.182	.400	.182
2004 Cleveland	AL	3	4	2	0	0	0	(0	0)	2	0	0	1	1	0	2	0	0	0	0	0	--	0	.500	.600	.500
8 ML YEARS		288	796	179	33	4	27	(15	12)	301	108	90	90	90	1	213	11	5	6	10	11	.48	25	.225	.310	.378

Jason Young

Pitches: R **Bats:** R **Pos:** SP-2 **Ht:** 6'5" **Wt:** 214 **Born:** 9/28/1979 **Age:** 25

Year Team	Lg	G	GS	CG	GF	IP	BFP	H	R	ER	HR	SH	SF	HB	TBB	IBB	SO	WP	Bk	W	L	Pct	ShO	Sv-Op	Hld	ERC	ERA
2001 Salem	A+	17	17	2	0	104.2	439	104	47	40	8	0	0	10	28	0	91	5	0	6	7	.462	1	0--	--	3.81	3.44
2002 Carolina	AA	14	14	1	0	88.2	359	71	30	26	1	1	1	3	30	0	76	0	2	7	4	.636	1	0--	--	2.39	2.64
2002 Co Springs	AAA	13	13	0	0	79.2	362	87	52	44	10	1	0	3	38	0	74	3	0	6	5	.545	0	0--	--	5.21	4.97
2003 Co Springs	AAA	23	21	2	0	116.1	525	128	63	51	10	6	2	8	37	0	99	3	0	6	7	.462	1	0--	--	4.35	3.95
2004 Co Springs	AAA	7	7	0	0	40.0	175	54	26	21	6	0	3	3	12	0	20	0	0	5	2	.714	0	0--	--	6.84	4.97
2003 Colorado	NL	8	3	0	0	21.1	108	34	22	20	8	1	1	1	9	0	18	2	0	0	2	.000	0	0-0	--	10.29	8.44
2004 Colorado	NL	2	2	0	0	8.1	45	15	12	12	3	1	0	0	5	1	7	1	0	0	1	.000	0	0-0	--	12.08	12.96
2 ML YEARS		10	5	0	1	29.2	153	49	34	32	11	2	1	1	14	1	25	3	0	0	3	.000	0	0-0	--	10.79	9.71

Michael Young

Bats: R **Throws:** R **Pos:** SS-158; DH-2   **Ht:** 6'1" **Wt:** 190 **Born:** 10/19/1976 **Age:** 28

							BATTING													BASERUNNING				AVERAGES		
Year Team	Lg	G	AB	H	2B	3B	HR	(Hm	Rd)	TB	R	RBI	RC	TBB	IBB	SO	HBP	SH	SF	SB	CS	SB%	GDP	Avg	OBP	Slg
2000 Texas	AL	2	2	0	0	0	0	(0	0)	0	0	0	0	0	0	1	0	0	0	0	0	-	0	.000	.000	.000
2001 Texas	AL	106	386	96	18	4	11	(7	4)	155	57	49	45	26	0	91	3	9	5	3	1	.75	9	.249	.298	.402
2002 Texas	AL	156	573	150	26	8	9	(3	6)	219	77	62	64	41	1	112	0	13	6	6	7	.46	14	.262	.308	.382
2003 Texas	AL	160	666	204	33	9	14	(9	5)	297	106	72	106	36	1	103	1	3	7	13	2	.87	14	.306	.339	.446
2004 Texas	AL	160	690	216	33	9	22	(9	13)	333	114	99	124	44	1	89	1	0	4	12	3	.80	11	.313	.353	.483
5 ML YEARS		584	2317	666	110	30	56	(28	28)	1004	354	282	339	147	3	396	5	25	22	34	13	.72	48	.287	.328	.433

Carlos Zambrano

Pitches: R **Bats:** B **Pos:** SP-31   **Ht:** 6'5" **Wt:** 250 **Born:** 6/1/1981 **Age:** 24

		HOW MUCH HE PITCHED						WHAT HE GAVE UP											THE RESULTS							
Year Team	Lg	G	GS	CG	GF	IP	BFP	H	R	ER	HR	SH	SF	HB	TBB	IBB	SO	WP	Bk	W	L	Pct	ShO	Sv-Op	Hld	ERC	ERA
2001 Chicago	NL	6	1	0	1	7.2	42	11	13	13	2	1	1	1	8	0	4	1	0	1	2	.333	0	0-1	0	11.86	15.26
2002 Chicago	NL	32	16	0	3	108.1	477	94	53	44	9	9	1	4	63	2	93	6	0	4	8	.333	0	0-0	0	4.02	3.66
2003 Chicago	NL	32	32	3	0	214.0	907	188	88	74	9	11	6	10	94	12	168	6	1	13	11	.542	1	0-0	0	3.28	3.11
2004 Chicago	NL	31	31	1	0	209.2	887	174	73	64	14	10	3	20	81	4	188	6	2	16	8	.667	1	0-0	0	3.20	2.75
4 ML YEARS		101	80	4	4	539.2	2313	467	227	195	34	31	11	35	246	18	453	19	3	34	29	.540	2	0-1	0	3.50	3.25

Victor Zambrano

Pitches: R **Bats:** R **Pos:** SP-25; RP-1   **Ht:** 6'0" **Wt:** 203 **Born:** 8/6/1975 **Age:** 29

		HOW MUCH HE PITCHED						WHAT HE GAVE UP											THE RESULTS							
Year Team	Lg	G	GS	CG	GF	IP	BFP	H	R	ER	HR	SH	SF	HB	TBB	IBB	SO	WP	Bk	W	L	Pct	ShO	Sv-Op	Hld	ERC	ERA
2001 Tampa Bay	AL	36	0	0	19	51.1	212	38	21	18	6	2	0	3	18	0	58	4	0	6	2	.750	0	2-6	5	2.80	3.16
2002 Tampa Bay	AL	42	11	0	11	114.0	519	120	77	70	15	7	8	4	68	5	73	10	0	8	8	.500	0	1-3	6	5.52	5.53
2003 Tampa Bay	AL	34	28	1	2	188.1	836	165	97	88	21	3	10	20	106	2	132	15	3	12	10	.545	0	0-0	2	4.51	4.21
2004 TB-NYM		26	25	0	0	142.0	650	119	77	69	13	1	10	16	102	2	123	6	0	11	7	.611	0	0-0	1	4.75	4.37
2004 Tampa Bay	AL	23	22	0	0	128.0	588	107	68	63	13	0	10	16	96	2	109	5	0	9	7	.563	0	0-0	1	5.01	4.43
2004 New York	NL	3	3	0	0	14.0	62	12	9	6	0	1	0	0	6	0	14	1	0	2	0	1.000	0	0-0	0	2.57	3.86
4 ML YEARS		138	64	1	32	495.2	2217	442	272	245	55	13	28	43	294	9	386	35	3	37	27	.578	0	3-9	14	4.62	4.45

Gregg Zaun

Bats: B **Throws:** R **Pos:** C-97; PH-12; DH-4   **Ht:** 5'10" **Wt:** 190 **Born:** 4/14/1971 **Age:** 34

							BATTING													BASERUNNING				AVERAGES		
Year Team	Lg	G	AB	H	2B	3B	HR	(Hm	Rd)	TB	R	RBI	RC	TBB	IBB	SO	HBP	SH	SF	SB	CS	SB%	GDP	Avg	OBP	Slg
2004 Syracuse*	AAA	7	23	7	1	0	0	(-	-)	8	4	2	3	2	0	5	0	0	1	1	0	1.00	1	.304	.346	.348
1995 Baltimore	AL	40	104	27	5	0	3	(1	2)	41	18	14	15	16	0	14	0	2	0	1	1	.50	2	.260	.358	.394
1996 Bal-Fla		60	139	34	9	1	2	(1	1)	51	20	15	16	14	3	20	2	1	2	1	0	1.00	5	.245	.318	.367
1997 Florida	NL	58	143	43	10	2	2	(0	2)	63	21	20	27	26	4	18	2	1	0	1	0	1.00	3	.301	.415	.441
1998 Florida	NL	106	298	56	12	2	5	(2	3)	87	19	29	23	35	2	52	1	2	2	5	2	.71	7	.188	.274	.292
1999 Texas	AL	43	93	23	2	1	1	(0	1)	30	12	12	10	10	0	7	0	1	2	1	0	1.00	2	.247	.314	.323
2000 Kansas City	AL	83	234	64	11	0	7	(2	5)	96	36	33	40	43	3	34	3	0	2	7	3	.70	4	.274	.390	.410
2001 Kansas City	AL	39	125	40	9	0	6	(1	5)	67	15	18	24	12	0	16	0	0	1	1	2	.33	2	.320	.377	.536
2002 Houston	NL	76	185	41	7	1	3	(3	0)	59	18	24	17	12	1	36	2	2	1	1	0	1.00	6	.222	.275	.319
2003 Hou-Col	NL	74	166	38	8	0	4	(1	3)	58	15	21	20	19	0	21	1	1	2	1	1	.50	5	.229	.309	.349
2004 Toronto	AL	107	338	91	24	0	6	(2	4)	133	46	36	50	47	3	61	6	0	1	0	2	.00	7	.269	.367	.393
1996 Baltimore	AL	50	108	25	8	1	1	(1	0)	38	16	13	12	11	2	15	2	0	2	0	0	-	3	.231	.309	.352
1996 Florida	NL	10	31	9	1	0	1	(0	1)	13	4	2	4	3	1	5	0	1	0	1	0	1.00	2	.290	.353	.419
2003 Houston	NL	59	120	26	7	0	1	(1	0)	36	9	13	12	14	0	14	1	1	2	1	0	1.00	5	.217	.299	.300
2003 Colorado	NL	15	46	12	1	0	3	(0	3)	22	6	8	8	5	0	7	0	0	0	0	1	.00	0	.261	.333	.478
10 ML YEARS		686	1825	457	97	7	39	(13	26)	685	220	222	242	234	16	279	17	10	13	19	11	.63	41	.250	.339	.375

Todd Zeile

Bats: R **Throws:** R **Pos:** 1B-67; 3B-46; PH-44; C-2; PR-1   **Ht:** 6'1" **Wt:** 200 **Born:** 9/9/1965 **Age:** 39

							BATTING													BASERUNNING				AVERAGES		
Year Team	Lg	G	AB	H	2B	3B	HR	(Hm	Rd)	TB	R	RBI	RC	TBB	IBB	SO	HBP	SH	SF	SB	CS	SB%	GDP	Avg	OBP	Slg
1989 St Louis	NL	28	82	21	3	1	1	(0	1)	29	7	8	10	9	1	14	0	1	1	0	0	-	1	.256	.326	.354
1990 St Louis	NL	144	495	121	25	3	15	(8	7)	197	62	57	66	67	3	77	2	0	6	2	4	.33	11	.244	.333	.398
1991 St Louis	NL	155	565	158	36	3	11	(7	4)	233	76	81	81	62	3	94	5	0	6	17	11	.61	15	.280	.353	.412
1992 St Louis	NL	126	439	113	18	4	7	(4	3)	160	51	48	56	68	4	70	0	0	7	7	10	.41	11	.257	.352	.364
1993 St Louis	NL	157	571	158	36	1	17	(8	9)	247	82	103	86	70	5	76	0	0	6	5	4	.56	15	.277	.352	.433
1994 St Louis	NL	113	415	111	25	1	19	(9	10)	195	62	75	66	52	3	56	3	0	7	1	3	.25	13	.267	.348	.470
1995 StL-ChC	NL	113	426	105	22	0	14	(8	6)	169	50	52	50	34	1	76	4	4	5	1	0	1.00	13	.246	.305	.397
1996 Phi-Bal		163	617	162	32	0	25	(10	15)	269	78	99	92	82	4	104	1	0	4	1	1	.50	18	.263	.348	.436
1997 Los Angeles	NL	160	575	154	17	0	31	(17	14)	264	89	90	94	85	7	112	6	0	6	8	7	.53	18	.268	.365	.459
1998 LA-Fla-Tex		158	572	155	32	3	19	(7	12)	250	85	94	87	69	2	90	4	1	7	4	4	.50	12	.271	.350	.437
1999 Texas	AL	156	588	172	41	1	24	(13	11)	287	80	98	96	56	3	94	4	1	7	1	2	.33	20	.293	.354	.488
2000 New York	NL	153	544	146	36	3	22	(8	14)	254	67	79	88	74	4	85	2	0	3	3	4	.43	15	.268	.356	.467
2001 New York	NL	151	531	141	25	1	10	(4	6)	198	66	62	72	73	3	102	6	0	7	1	0	1.00	15	.266	.359	.373
2002 Colorado	NL	144	506	138	23	0	18	(11	7)	215	61	87	77	66	3	92	1	0	7	1	1	.50	27	.273	.353	.425
2003 NYY-Mon		100	299	68	10	2	11	(7	4)	115	40	42	34	34	0	54	3	0	5	1	0	1.00	6	.227	.308	.385
2004 New York	NL	137	348	81	16	0	9	(4	5)	124	30	35	36	44	1	83	1	1	2	0	0	-	13	.233	.319	.356
1995 St Louis	NL	34	127	37	6	0	5	(2	3)	58	16	22	23	18	1	23	1	0	2	1	0	1.00	4	.291	.378	.457
1995 Chicago	NL	79	299	68	16	0	9	(6	3)	111	34	30	27	16	0	53	3	4	3	0	0	-	9	.227	.271	.371
1996 Philadelphia	NL	134	500	134	24	0	20	(9	11)	218	61	80	75	67	4	88	1	0	4	1	1	.50	16	.268	.353	.436
1996 Baltimore	AL	29	117	28	8	0	5	(1	4)	51	17	19	17	15	0	16	0	0	0	0	0	-	2	.239	.326	.436
1998 Los Angeles	NL	40	158	40	6	1	7	(1	6)	69	22	27	19	10	0	24	1	0	1	1	1	.50	5	.253	.300	.437
1998 Florida	NL	66	234	68	12	1	6	(2	4)	100	37	39	34	31	2	34	2	0	3	2	3	.40	4	.291	.374	.427
1998 Texas	AL	52	180	47	14	1	6	(4	2)	81	26	28	30	28	0	32	1	1	3	1	0	1.00	3	.261	.358	.450

267

		BATTING																	BASERUNNING				AVERAGES		
Year Team	Lg	G	AB	H	2B	3B	HR	(Hm Rd)	TB	R	RBI	RC	TBB	IBB	SO	HBP	SH	SF	SB	CS	SB%	GDP	Avg	OBP	Slg
2003 New York	AL	66	186	39	8	0	6	(4 2)	65	29	23	18	24	0	36	0	0	4	0	0	-	3	.210	.294	.349
2003 Montreal	NL	34	113	29	2	2	5	(3 2)	50	11	19	16	10	0	18	3	0	1	1	0	1.00	3	.257	.331	.442
16 ML YEARS		2158	7573	2004	397	23	253	(125 128)	3206	986	1110	1091	945	47	1279	42	8	81	53	51	.51	223	.265	.346	.423

Alan Zinter

Bats: B **Throws:** R **Pos:** PH-19; 1B-8; DH-2; PR-1   **Ht:** 6'2" **Wt:** 200 **Born:** 5/19/1968 **Age:** 37

		BATTING																	BASERUNNING				AVERAGES		
Year Team	Lg	G	AB	H	2B	3B	HR	(Hm Rd)	TB	R	RBI	RC	TBB	IBB	SO	HBP	SH	SF	SB	CS	SB%	GDP	Avg	OBP	Slg
1989 Pittsfield	A-	12	41	15	2	1	2	(- -)	25	11	12	12	12	0	4	0	0	1	0	1	.00	0	.366	.500	.610
1989 St. Lucie	A+	48	159	38	10	0	3	(- -)	57	17	32	17	18	2	31	1	1	5	0	1	.00	5	.239	.311	.358
1990 St. Lucie	A+	98	333	97	19	6	7	(- -)	149	63	63	59	54	1	70	1	0	6	8	1	.89	10	.291	.386	.447
1990 Jackson	AA	6	20	4	1	0	0	(- -)	5	2	1	1	3	0	11	0	0	0	1	0	1.00	1	.200	.304	.250
1991 Williamsport	AA	124	422	93	13	6	9	(- -)	145	44	54	47	59	1	106	3	2	2	3	3	.50	10	.220	.319	.344
1992 Binghamton	AA	128	431	96	13	5	16	(- -)	167	63	63	58	70	5	117	4	0	0	0	0	-	7	.223	.337	.387
1993 Binghamton	AA	134	432	113	24	4	24	(- -)	217	68	87	86	90	7	105	1	0	5	1	0	1.00	4	.262	.386	.502
1994 Toledo	AAA	134	471	112	29	5	21	(- -)	214	66	58	73	69	4	185	7	0	0	13	5	.72	3	.238	.344	.454
1995 Toledo	AAA	101	334	74	15	4	13	(- -)	136	42	48	40	36	1	102	2	2	5	4	1	.80	5	.222	.297	.407
1996 Pawtucket	AAA	108	357	96	19	5	26	(- -)	203	78	69	74	58	2	123	4	0	5	5	1	.83	3	.269	.373	.569
1997 Tacoma	AAA	110	404	116	19	4	20	(- -)	203	69	70	77	64	9	113	3	1	1	3	1	.75	7	.287	.388	.502
1998 Iowa	AAA	129	419	130	23	1	23	(- -)	224	82	81	89	75	1	116	3	0	3	3	5	.38	10	.310	.416	.535
1999 Iowa	AAA	14	51	13	2	0	3	(- -)	24	7	8	7	5	0	13	0	0	0	0	0	-	0	.255	.321	.471
2000 Iowa	AAA	90	233	53	12	2	14	(- -)	111	27	35	37	39	2	78	2	0	3	0	0	-	3	.227	.339	.476
2000 Tucson	AAA	11	36	13	5	1	1	(- -)	23	9	5	9	8	1	8	0	0	0	0	0	-	1	.361	.477	.639
2001 New Orleans	AAA	104	332	88	16	0	19	(- -)	161	58	65	49	33	1	85	3	0	3	1	1	.50	13	.265	.334	.485
2002 New Orleans	AAA	63	225	52	14	0	11	(- -)	99	30	39	28	22	0	64	0	0	1	2	0	1.00	3	.231	.298	.440
2003 New Orleans	AAA	114	342	87	17	0	17	(- -)	155	48	57	49	36	5	77	5	0	1	1	0	1.00	10	.254	.333	.453
2004 Tucson	AAA	54	179	60	12	2	7	(- -)	97	28	39	38	24	3	33	1	0	7	0	0	-	3	.335	.403	.542
2002 Houston	NL	39	44	6	2	0	2	(0 2)	14	5	3	2	0	0	19	0	0	0	0	0	-	0	.136	.136	.318
2004 Arizona	NL	28	34	7	2	0	1	(1 0)	12	2	6	4	5	0	15	0	0	1	0	0	-	0	.206	.300	.353
2 ML YEARS		67	78	13	4	0	3	(1 2)	26	7	9	6	5	0	34	0	0	1	0	0	-	0	.167	.214	.333

Barry Zito

Pitches: L **Bats:** L **Pos:** SP-34   **Ht:** 6'4" **Wt:** 215 **Born:** 5/13/1978 **Age:** 27

		HOW MUCH HE PITCHED						WHAT HE GAVE UP												THE RESULTS						
Year Team	Lg	G	GS	CG	GF	IP	BFP	H	R	ER	HR	SH	SF	HB	TBB	IBB	SO	WP	Bk	W	L	Pct	ShO	Sv-Op	Hld	ERC	ERA
2000 Oakland	AL	14	14	1	0	92.2	376	64	30	28	6	1	0	2	45	2	78	2	0	7	4	.636	1	0-0	0	2.63	2.72
2001 Oakland	AL	35	35	3	0	214.1	902	184	92	83	18	5	4	13	80	0	205	6	1	17	8	.680	2	0-0	0	3.33	3.49
2002 Oakland	AL	35	35	1	0	229.1	939	182	79	70	24	9	7	9	78	2	182	2	1	23	5	.821	1	0-0	0	2.92	2.75
2003 Oakland	AL	35	35	4	0	231.2	957	186	98	85	19	7	7	6	88	3	146	4	0	14	12	.538	0	0-0	0	2.91	3.30
2004 Oakland	AL	34	34	0	0	213.0	926	216	116	106	28	7	9	9	81	2	163	4	1	11	11	.500	0	0-0	0	4.45	4.48
5 ML YEARS		153	153	9	0	981.0	4100	832	415	372	95	29	27	39	372	9	774	18	3	72	40	.643	4	0-0	0	3.30	3.41

2004 Fielding Statistics

SBA is Total Stolen Bases Attempted.

CS is Total Caught Stealing.

PCS is Number of the Total Caught Stealing attributed to the pitcher, not the catcher in question (e.g. the pitcher throws to first, the runner makes a move towards second, and is thrown out without the catcher involved).

CS% is the percentage of runners caught stealing not including PCS.

In other words, the formula for CS% is:

$$\frac{(CS - PCS)}{(SBA - PCS)}$$

You may find many of our catcher ERAs (CERA—which, like pitcher ERAs, tracks runs each catcher "gave up" while he was behind the plate) to be different from other sources. However, we have solid statistical reasons to believe ours are the most accurate catcher ERAs available.

These fielding stats are not official. You will certainly find some differences when the official Major League Baseball numbers arrive later this year. However, we hope you'll agree that having an unofficial statistical fielding record in this November book is better than holding up the entire process for the official totals.

First Basemen - Regulars

Player	Tm	G	GS	Inn	PO	A	E	DP	Pct.	Rng
Olerud,John	TOT	124	118	1045.1	916	77	2	92	.998	
Helton,Todd	Col	153	151	1320.2	1356	143	4	130	.997	
Franco,Ju	Atl	84	71	631.1	628	48	2	68	.997	
Martinez,Tino	TB	114	110	959.2	874	67	3	85	.997	
Erstad,Darin	Ana	124	124	1065.1	986	65	4	82	.996	
Lee,De	ChC	161	159	1432.0	1259	128	6	113	.996	
Delgado,Carlos	Tor	120	120	1038.2	1041	90	5	97	.996	
Bagwell,Jeff	Hou	152	151	1328.2	1189	98	6	109	.995	
Snow,J.T.	SF	100	88	793.0	801	56	4	69	.995	
Konerko,Paul	CWS	139	137	1177.2	1151	78	6	136	.995	
Pena,Carlos	Det	135	131	1159.1	1142	77	6	127	.995	
Mientkiewicz,D	TOT	125	100	940.2	923	62	5	77	.995	
Wilkerson,Brad	Mon	86	78	701.2	694	66	4	67	.995	
Green,Shawn	LA	111	107	926.2	878	53	5	82	.995	
Broussard,Ben	Cle	133	107	1019.1	991	77	6	106	.994	
Thome,Jim	Phi	134	134	1179.2	1090	84	7	103	.994	
Harvey,Ken	KC	73	73	630.0	610	51	4	72	.994	
Johnson,Nick	Mon	73	70	610.0	618	43	4	69	.994	
Clark,Tony	NYY	99	64	623.2	602	49	4	64	.994	
Casey,Sean	Cin	145	142	1245.2	1233	56	8	86	.994	
Pujols,Albert	StL	150	150	1338.2	1458	114	10	136	.994	
LaRoche,Adam	Atl	98	82	720.0	739	40	5	87	.994	
Palmeiro,R	Bal	130	128	1137.2	1089	94	8	114	.993	
Hatteberg,S	Oak	148	143	1280.0	1281	86	10	136	.993	
Teixeira,Mark	Tex	142	138	1223.0	1210	98	10	114	.992	
Overbay,Lyle	Mil	158	150	1360.1	1311	113	11	110	.992	
Choi,Hee Seop	TOT	112	98	867.2	881	51	9	79	.990	
Nevin,Phil	SD	144	142	1207.1	1132	90	13	108	.989	
Hillenbrand,S	Ari	131	129	1113.1	1126	72	13	105	.989	

First Basemen - The Rest

Player	Tm	G	GS	Inn	PO	A	E	DP	Pct.	Rng
Anderson,M	StL	2	0	4.0	3	0	0	0	1.000	
Atkins,Garrett	Col	3	2	17.0	22	1	0	6	1.000	
Aurilia,Rich	SD	1	0	3.0	7	0	0	0	1.000	
Baerga,Carlos	Ari	6	4	35.2	32	3	0	2	1.000	
Barajas,Rod	Tex	2	0	3.0	3	1	0	0	1.000	
Berg,Dave	Tor	7	3	40.0	43	3	2	8	.958	
Berkman,Lance	Hou	4	0	4.0	5	1	0	2	1.000	
Blake,Casey	Cle	8	0	12.0	12	0	0	2	1.000	
Bloomquist,W	Sea	19	11	99.0	69	8	2	11	.975	
Blum,Geoff	TB	2	1	10.0	13	0	0	2	1.000	
Branyan,R	Mil	2	1	10.2	7	0	0	1	1.000	
Brazell,Craig	NYM	7	3	35.0	34	4	1	1	.974	
Buchanan,Brian	SD	3	0	7.0	9	0	0	1	1.000	
Buchanan,Brian	NYM	1	1	9.0	8	1	0	1	1.000	
Burke,Jamie	CWS	2	0	4.0	4	2	0	1	1.000	
Cabrera,J	Sea	23	17	148.2	150	7	0	18	1.000	
Cairo,Miguel	NYY	1	0	3.0	2	0	0	0	1.000	
Castro,Juan	Cin	4	3	28.0	27	2	0	2	1.000	
Choi,Hee Seop	Fla	89	79	712.2	720	41	8	60	.990	
Choi,Hee Seop	LA	23	19	155.0	161	10	1	19	.994	
Cirillo,Jeff	SD	10	4	53.2	61	1	0	3	1.000	
Clark,Howie	Tor	11	11	93.0	106	6	0	8	1.000	
Colbrunn,Greg	Ari	2	1	9.0	7	1	0	0	1.000	
Conine,Jeff	Fla	57	56	489.1	473	50	4	47	.992	
Cordero,Wil	Fla	13	11	97.0	105	4	1	10	.991	
Crozier,Eric	Tor	5	4	34.2	33	2	1	2	.972	
Cruz,Ja	Cin	6	1	16.0	10	1	0	2	1.000	
Cuddyer,Mike	Min	10	2	35.0	34	2	0	3	1.000	
Daubach,Brian	Bos	14	13	100.0	100	10	2	9	.982	
Dominique,Andy	Bos	5	1	19.0	25	1	1	2	.963	
Dubois,Jason	ChC	1	0	1.1	2	0	0	0	1.000	
Dunn,Adam	Cin	10	9	58.2	76	4	0	5	1.000	
Durazo,Erubiel	Oak	4	3	19.0	14	1	2	2	.882	
Easley,Damion	Fla	18	16	138.0	119	8	2	16	.984	
Edmonds,Jim	StL	1	1	9.0	9	1	0	0	1.000	
Feliz,Pedro	SF	70	59	535.2	526	41	5	59	.991	
Fick,Robert	TB	10	9	75.1	79	2	2	8	.976	
Fick,Robert	SD	1	1	8.0	9	0	0	1	1.000	
Fox,Andy	Mon	1	0	1.0	2	0	0	0	1.000	
Fullmer,Brad	Tex	4	3	17.2	15	0	0	5	1.000	
Galarraga,A	Ana	1	1	9.0	9	1	0	2	1.000	

Player	Tm	G	GS	Inn	PO	A	E	DP	Pct.	Rng
Garcia,Karim	Bal	1	1	9.0	10	1	0	0	1.000	
Giambi,Jason	NYY	47	47	375.0	372	14	4	30	.990	
Gibbons,Jay	Bal	14	12	112.2	111	13	1	11	.992	
Gload,Ross	CWS	42	21	218.1	218	12	0	15	1.000	
Gomez,Chris	Tor	19	12	115.0	105	12	2	9	.983	
Gonzalez,Ad	Tex	11	10	89.0	93	6	1	13	.990	
Grabowski,J	LA	3	0	4.0	2	1	0	0	1.000	
Guerrero,W	KC	2	0	3.0	3	0	0	1	1.000	
Hafner,Travis	Cle	11	10	81.2	81	9	0	4	1.000	
Halter,Shane	Ana	4	1	9.2	10	1	0	2	1.000	
Hansen,Dave	Sea	7	3	34.0	24	4	0	1	1.000	
Hansen,Dave	SD	7	0	17.0	15	1	0	2	1.000	
Helms,Wes	Mil	10	10	71.0	68	3	2	7	.973	
Hernandez,Jose	LA	8	0	12.2	15	2	0	3	1.000	
Hessman,Mike	Atl	16	9	90.1	96	4	4	6	.962	
Hollandsworth,T	ChC	3	3	21.0	16	4	1	1	.952	
Howard,Ryan	Phi	8	5	60.2	59	6	0	9	1.000	
Huff,Aubrey	TB	38	30	274.1	262	27	1	24	.997	
Hummel,Tim	Cin	13	4	50.2	43	8	0	6	1.000	
Ibanez,Raul	Sea	10	9	78.1	57	2	1	2	.983	
Jacobsen,Bucky	Sea	21	21	175.0	169	12	3	12	.984	
Karros,Eric	Oak	22	14	147.1	165	16	2	15	.989	
Klesko,Ryan	SD	18	15	139.0	138	16	2	19	.987	
Kotchman,Casey	Ana	34	27	270.1	231	15	3	17	.988	
Lamb,Mike	Hou	10	7	65.0	76	4	0	7	1.000	
Lane,Jason	Hou	3	1	13.0	13	1	1	3	.933	
LeCroy,Matt	Min	23	20	181.2	172	3	1	17	.994	
Lee,Travis	NYY	6	4	42.0	44	4	0	2	1.000	
Leon,Jose	Bal	16	12	95.0	82	10	0	9	1.000	
Lo Duca,Paul	LA	3	2	19.0	11	1	0	1	1.000	
Lopez,Luis	Mon	8	6	55.0	53	2	0	5	1.000	
Lopez,LuisM	Bal	6	2	22.0	22	0	1	1	.957	
Lopez,Me	KC	2	0	2.1	0	0	0	0	-	
Mabry,John	StL	14	11	98.0	90	16	2	6	.981	
Mackowiak,Rob	Pit	1	0	0.1	0	0	0	0	-	
Matheny,Mike	StL	1	0	1.0	1	0	0	0	1.000	
Mayne,Brent	Ari	1	0	1.2	2	0	0	0	1.000	
McCarty,Dave	Bos	67	25	288.0	287	30	3	23	.991	
McEwing,Joe	NYM	11	0	21.2	20	1	0	2	1.000	
McGriff,Fred	TB	6	6	52.0	53	3	0	5	1.000	
McKay,Cody	StL	1	0	3.0	2	0	0	0	1.000	
McMillon,Billy	Oak	3	0	5.0	4	1	0	1	1.000	
Melhuse,Adam	Oak	1	0	2.0	2	1	0	0	1.000	
Merloni,Lou	Cle	42	38	297.2	282	14	1	18	.997	
Mientkiewicz,D	Min	78	74	668.2	660	37	4	63	.994	
Mientkiewicz,D	Bos	47	26	272.0	263	25	1	14	.997	
Millar,Kevin	Bos	69	66	512.0	466	57	6	45	.989	
Minor,Damon	SF	17	15	128.1	131	9	0	12	1.000	
Molina,Jose	Ana	2	0	6.0	5	1	0	2	1.000	
Morneau,Justin	Min	61	61	538.1	523	41	3	54	.995	
Newhan,David	Bal	2	1	11.0	10	1	0	2	1.000	
Norton,Greg	Det	7	5	43.0	36	2	0	6	1.000	
Offerman,Jose	Min	7	5	51.0	52	6	1	11	.983	
Olerud,John	Sea	77	71	645.1	548	52	1	58	.998	
Olerud,John	NYY	47	47	400.0	368	25	1	34	.997	
Ortiz,David	Bos	34	31	260.1	253	21	4	23	.986	
Pascucci,Val	Mon	5	2	18.0	14	0	1	1	.933	
Pellow,Kit	Col	5	3	26.0	26	3	1	3	.967	
Perez,Edd	Atl	1	0	8.1	10	0	0	1	1.000	
Perez,Edu	TB	5	5	43.2	43	2	0	6	1.000	
Perez,To	Phi	10	6	56.0	49	5	2	4	.964	
Perry,Herbert	Tex	15	11	107.0	104	3	0	12	1.000	
Phelps,Josh	Tor	12	11	99.2	101	2	2	7	.981	
Phelps,Josh	Cle	8	7	56.0	43	2	1	1	.978	
Phillips,Jason	NYM	38	29	258.1	260	15	0	20	1.000	
Piazza,Mike	NYM	68	66	517.2	497	35	8	44	.985	
Pickering,C	KC	8	7	61.0	60	3	0	6	1.000	
Quinlan,Robb	Ana	13	9	93.0	96	7	0	7	1.000	
Randa,Joe	KC	3	2	24.0	20	2	0	4	1.000	
Riggs,Adam	Ana	1	0	1.0	1	1	0	0	1.000	
Rivera,Carlos	Pit	7	4	39.0	35	2	0	6	1.000	
Rolls,Damian	TB	1	0	1.0	0	0	0	0	-	
Saenz,Olmedo	LA	25	14	126.0	124	12	2	16	.986	
Segui,David	Bal	2	2	18.0	17	0	0	1	1.000	
Sexson,Richie	Ari	23	23	204.1	198	26	1	19	.996	
Shelton,Chris	Det	3	2	26.0	22	4	0	3	1.000	
Simon,Randall	Pit	46	42	335.1	347	24	3	37	.992	
Simon,Randall	TB	1	1	1.0	0	0	0	0	-	
Sledge,Terrmel	Mon	10	6	61.1	63	6	0	3	1.000	

Player	Tm	G	GS	Inn	PO	A	E	DP	Pct.	Rng
Spencer,Shane	NYM	1	1	11.0	13	0	0	0	1.000	-
Spiezio,Scott	Sea	42	30	279.0	252	24	4	22	.986	-
Stairs,Matt	KC	30	25	229.0	208	11	3	25	.986	-
Surhoff,B.J.	Bal	10	4	50.0	46	4	0	7	1.000	-
Sutton,Larry	Fla	1	0	2.0	1	0	0	0	1.000	-
Sweeney,Ma	Col	15	6	71.2	68	5	0	9	1.000	-
Sweeney,Mi	KC	55	55	471.0	467	35	4	44	.992	-
Swisher,Nick	Oak	3	2	18.0	19	0	0	3	1.000	-
Thomas,Frank	CWS	4	4	32.1	31	3	0	2	1.000	-
Tiffee,Terry	Min	1	0	1.1	2	0	0	0	1.000	-
Tracy,Chad	Ari	11	2	33.0	29	3	1	2	.970	-
Utley,Chase	Phi	13	11	104.1	94	11	0	6	1.000	-
Valent,Eric	NYM	27	23	190.0	202	21	1	21	.996	-
Valentin,Ja	Cin	7	3	37.0	37	1	0	5	1.000	-
Vander Wal,J	Cin	4	0	7.2	8	0	0	0	1.000	-
Vazquez,Ramon	SD	3	0	6.0	8	0	0	0	1.000	-
Ventura,Robin	LA	40	20	210.0	214	14	0	15	1.000	-
Vizcaino,Jose	Hou	8	3	32.1	42	3	0	2	1.000	-
Walker,To	ChC	5	0	11.0	7	1	0	1	1.000	-
Ward,Daryle	Pit	71	63	559.0	547	34	5	73	.991	-
Wigginton,Ty	NYM	5	5	41.0	48	7	1	9	.982	-
Wilson,Craig	Pit	65	52	494.1	460	34	3	53	.994	-
Wooten,Shawn	Phi	11	6	62.0	70	3	0	6	1.000	-
Young,Dmitri	Det	25	24	211.1	203	17	0	15	1.000	-
Zeile,Todd	NYM	67	34	365.1	386	22	2	36	.995	-
Zinter,Alan	Ari	8	3	39.0	41	3	1	1	.978	-

Second Basemen - Regulars

Player	Tm	G	GS	Inn	PO	A	E	DP	Pct.	Rng
Hudson,Orlando	Tor	133	128	1124.2	275	449	12	90	.984	5.79
Graffanino,T	KC	75	72	630.1	185	219	5	66	.988	5.77
Miles,Aaron	Col	128	116	1029.0	273	353	10	70	.984	5.48
Giles,Marcus	Atl	97	94	789.0	186	289	12	69	.975	5.42
Polanco,P	Phi	109	105	944.0	264	304	3	76	.995	5.42
Soriano,A	Tex	142	142	1248.0	308	418	23	104	.969	5.24
Uribe,Juan	CWS	77	70	625.2	154	208	6	49	.984	5.21
Rivas,Luis	Min	109	95	860.1	176	317	3	75	.994	5.16
Harris,Willie	CWS	92	76	673.2	163	223	4	46	.990	5.16
Durham,Ray	SF	118	115	990.1	243	314	16	75	.972	5.06
Sanchez,Rey	TB	87	80	696.0	157	234	5	55	.987	5.06
Scutaro,Marco	Oak	123	106	968.2	231	310	3	78	.994	5.03
Castillo,Jose	Pit	123	105	951.0	230	301	11	81	.980	5.03
Infante,Omar	Det	105	97	871.2	204	280	12	73	.976	5.00
Womack,Tony	StL	133	125	1113.0	225	391	15	81	.976	4.98
Cora,Alex	LA	138	122	1091.1	261	343	8	91	.987	4.98
Loretta,Mark	SD	154	154	1339.0	288	451	10	101	.987	4.97
Cairo,Miguel	NYY	113	96	856.0	195	274	6	58	.987	4.93
Kent,Jeff	Hou	139	138	1189.1	276	374	7	73	.989	4.92
Jimenez,D	Cin	146	143	1263.0	299	388	7	75	.990	4.90
Hairston,Scott	Ari	85	83	704.0	174	207	11	47	.972	4.87
Castillo,Luis	Fla	148	147	1274.1	275	405	6	98	.991	4.80
Belliard,R	Cle	151	148	1320.2	278	426	14	87	.981	4.80
Kennedy,Adam	Ana	144	138	1225.0	255	387	12	71	.982	4.72
Bellhorn,Mark	Bos	124	118	1044.2	189	348	11	62	.980	4.63
Vidro,Jose	Mon	105	104	879.1	175	269	6	70	.987	4.54
Roberts,Brian	Bal	150	148	1322.1	235	426	8	93	.988	4.50
Walker,To	ChC	89	88	749.1	150	213	7	32	.981	4.36
Boone,Bret	Sea	148	148	1308.2	280	349	14	90	.978	4.33

Second Basemen - The Rest

Player	Tm	G	GS	Inn	PO	A	E	DP	Pct.	Rng
Alexander,M	Tex	11	1	22.0	2	9	1	0	.917	4.50
Alfonzo,E	SF	5	5	42.0	5	10	2	2	.882	3.21
Alomar,Roberto	Ari	28	23	203.1	48	53	3	10	.971	4.47
Alomar,Roberto	CWS	13	13	103.0	23	32	1	14	.982	4.81
Amezaga,A	Ana	16	6	58.1	7	17	1	2	.960	3.70
Anderson,M	StL	37	24	224.0	55	70	4	20	.969	5.02
Aurilia,Rich	SD	7	1	25.0	6	9	1	3	.938	5.40
Barmes,Clint	Col	9	8	65.1	19	27	1	5	.979	6.34
Bartlett,Jason	Min	1	0	1.0	0	1	0	0	1.000	9.00
Berg,Dave	Tor	4	3	28.0	5	9	0	1	1.000	4.50
Bloomquist,W	Sea	1	0	1.0	0	0	0	0	-	.00
Blum,Geoff	TB	52	40	364.2	76	104	1	23	.994	4.44

Player	Tm	G	GS	Inn	PO	A	E	DP	Pct.	Rng
Bruntlett,Eric	Hou	5	1	14.0	3	5	0	0	1.000	5.14
Burke,Chris	Hou	7	2	25.2	7	14	0	3	1.000	7.36
Bush,Homer	NYY	4	2	23.0	7	4	0	3	1.000	4.30
Cabrera,J	Sea	18	14	140.2	38	40	1	12	.987	4.99
Cantu,Jorge	TB	33	31	274.0	49	84	5	19	.964	4.37
Carroll,Jamey	Mon	51	36	344.2	84	97	1	32	.995	4.73
Castro,Juan	Cin	12	7	67.1	15	28	1	6	.977	5.75
Cintron,Alex	Ari	19	17	147.0	33	46	2	6	.975	4.84
Cirillo,Jeff	SD	4	2	22.0	4	9	2	2	.867	5.32
Clark,Howie	Tor	1	1	8.0	0	0	0	0	-	.00
Clark,Jermaine	Cin	2	2	13.0	4	3	0	1	1.000	4.85
Crespo,Cesar	Bos	11	6	59.2	12	19	0	3	1.000	4.68
Cruz,Deivi	SF	2	0	3.0	0	0	0	0	-	.00
Cuddyer,Mike	Min	48	40	327.1	54	113	3	17	.982	4.59
Dallimore,B	SF	9	4	49.2	8	18	1	3	.963	4.71
DeRosa,Mark	Atl	5	3	34.0	3	11	0	4	1.000	3.71
Durrington,T	Mil	6	3	38.2	12	12	0	1	1.000	5.59
Easley,Damion	Fla	25	15	158.1	28	53	3	11	.964	4.60
Erickson,Matt	Mil	1	1	8.0	1	3	0	1	1.000	4.50
Figgins,Chone	Ana	20	15	141.0	27	42	1	8	.986	4.40
Flores,Jose	LA	1	1	1.0	0	0	0	0	-	.00
Fox,Andy	Mon	3	1	10.0	0	5	0	0	1.000	4.50
Fox,Andy	Tex	3	2	20.0	3	9	0	2	1.000	5.40
Freel,Ryan	Cin	15	10	92.1	25	23	0	4	1.000	4.68
Furcal,Rafael	Atl	1	0	2.0	0	0	0	0	-	.00
Garcia,Danny	NYM	44	40	341.1	97	90	6	19	.969	4.93
Garcia,Je	Atl	11	4	53.0	16	19	2	5	.946	5.94
German,Esteban	Oak	10	3	44.1	9	21	0	6	1.000	6.09
Ginter,Keith	Mil	54	52	459.1	91	126	6	19	.973	4.25
Gomez,Chris	Tor	3	3	23.0	6	2	0	2	1.000	3.13
Gonzalez,LA	Col	40	33	293.0	84	96	1	27	.994	5.53
Gotay,Ruben	KC	42	41	368.1	78	97	3	30	.983	4.28
Green,Andy	Ari	14	4	55.0	16	15	1	4	.969	5.07
Green,Nick	Atl	75	61	572.0	137	203	8	44	.977	5.35
Grudzielanek,M	ChC	76	61	568.0	136	186	7	30	.985	5.10
Guerrero,W	KC	8	4	49.1	8	16	1	2	.960	4.38
Gutierrez,R	NYM	18	14	128.0	31	44	0	12	1.000	5.27
Gutierrez,R	Bos	14	5	68.0	15	24	0	6	1.000	5.16
Hairston Jr.,J	Bal	12	12	102.0	21	36	1	9	.983	5.03
Hall,Bill	Mil	50	47	418.1	95	113	9	29	.959	4.47
Halter,Shane	Ana	6	3	29.0	4	7	0	2	1.000	3.41
Harris,Brendan	Mon	11	10	82.0	15	20	1	3	.972	3.84
Hart,Bo	StL	4	3	24.0	6	9	0	4	1.000	5.63
Hernandez,Jose	LA	50	39	341.2	81	113	4	21	.980	5.11
Hill,Bobby	Pit	40	31	255.0	70	89	1	22	.994	5.61
Hocking,Denny	Col	8	5	48.0	13	16	0	3	1.000	5.44
Hummel,Tim	Cin	1	0	3.0	1	0	0	0	1.000	3.00
Izturis,Maicer	Mon	10	10	88.0	18	25	1	6	.977	4.40
Jackson,Damian	ChC	5	3	33.1	8	14	1	5	.957	5.94
Jackson,Damian	KC	1	0	1.0	0	0	0	0	-	.00
Kata,Matt	Ari	38	35	320.2	75	111	2	25	.989	5.22
Keppinger,Jeff	NYM	32	27	257.2	61	86	2	20	.987	5.13
Labandeira,J	Mon	2	0	6.0	0	0	0	0	-	.00
Lamb,Mike	Hou	7	5	40.1	9	12	1	0	.955	4.69
Lopez,Felipe	Cin	2	0	5.0	1	1	1	1	.667	3.60
Lopez,LuisM	Bal	6	2	31.0	3	9	0	2	1.000	3.48
Lopez,Me	KC	6	4	32.0	10	6	1	2	.941	4.50
Lopez,Mi	Sea	3	0	9.0	1	4	0	1	1.000	5.00
Lugo,Julio	TB	8	8	69.0	16	16	1	3	.970	4.17
Luna,Hector	StL	19	10	92.2	24	33	0	6	1.000	5.54
Macias,Jose	ChC	16	8	85.0	15	24	0	3	1.000	4.13
Martinez,Ramon	ChC	6	1	18.2	3	6	0	1	1.000	4.34
Mateo,Henry	Mon	9	1	37.0	12	17	4	3	.879	7.05
Matsui,Kazuo	NYM	3	3	24.0	4	8	1	3	.923	4.50
McDonald,John	Cle	12	4	48.1	10	23	0	5	1.000	6.14
McEwing,Joe	NYM	34	15	162.1	50	54	2	10	.981	5.77
McLemore,Mark	Oak	47	44	373.1	113	123	6	37	.975	5.69
Menechino,F	Oak	12	9	85.0	16	29	1	2	.978	4.76
Menechino,F	Tor	30	26	237.1	54	72	0	13	1.000	4.78
Merloni,Lou	Cle	7	4	41.0	12	17	1	4	.967	6.37
Mientkiewicz,D	Bos	1	1	7.0	2	2	0	1	1.000	5.14
Mordecai,Mike	Fla	4	0	6.1	2	2	1	0	.800	5.68
Mueller,Bill	Bos	14	14	120.0	22	34	3	6	.949	4.20
Murphy,Donald	KC	7	7	61.0	12	17	0	8	1.000	4.28
Nunez,AbrO	Pit	32	22	197.0	60	70	2	24	.985	5.94
Offerman,Jose	Min	3	1	11.0	3	3	2	1	.750	4.91
Ojeda,Augie	Min	20	9	110.0	19	43	2	8	.969	5.07
Perez,Antonio	LA	2	0	8.0	2	1	1	1	.750	3.38
Perez,Neifi	SF	39	31	291.2	81	115	1	23	.995	6.05

Player	Tm	G	GS	Inn	PO	A	E	DP	Pct.	Rng
Perez,Neifi	ChC	2	1	11.0	4	4	0	3	1.000	6.55
Perez,To	Phi	17	11	108.1	27	32	0	7	1.000	4.90
Phillips,B	Cle	6	6	56.2	17	19	1	4	.973	5.72
Prieto,Alex	Min	8	6	55.0	10	20	0	6	1.000	4.91
Punto,Nick	Min	19	11	111.1	20	34	1	10	.982	4.37
Raburn,Ryan	Det	11	7	64.2	9	22	1	4	.969	4.31
Ransom,Cody	SF	16	7	80.1	28	21	1	5	.980	5.49
Reese,Pokey	Bos	30	18	152.0	49	63	1	15	.991	6.63
Relaford,Desi	KC	36	34	278.1	69	93	3	22	.982	5.24
Reyes,Jose	NYM	43	41	352.0	75	117	4	26	.980	4.91
Riggs,Adam	Ana	1	0	1.0	0	1	0	0	1.000	9.00
Rolls,Damian	TB	2	1	7.1	2	2	0	0	1.000	4.91
Romano,Jason	TB	1	1	6.0	1	0	1	0	.500	1.50
Sadler,Donnie	Ari	2	0	6.0	2	1	0	1	1.000	4.50
Sanchez,Freddy	Pit	3	3	25.0	3	4	0	1	1.000	2.52
Smith,Jason	Det	34	30	255.0	68	87	2	21	.987	5.47
Spivey,Junior	Mil	58	58	517.2	111	177	11	41	.963	5.01
Thurston,Joe	LA	4	0	11.1	2	3	0	1	1.000	3.97
Utley,Chase	Phi	50	46	410.1	100	123	4	29	.982	4.89
Valdez,Wilson	CWS	5	3	30.0	9	4	0	3	1.000	3.90
Vazquez,Ramon	SD	10	5	55.0	13	17	0	4	1.000	4.91
Vina,Fernando	Det	29	28	248.1	73	86	5	23	.970	5.76
Vizcaino,Jose	Hou	37	16	173.2	45	51	0	17	1.000	4.98
Wigginton,Ty	NYM	25	22	183.2	30	68	3	12	.970	4.80
Wilson,Enrique	NYY	80	64	564.2	124	179	7	23	.977	4.83
Young,Eri	Tex	20	17	149.2	39	51	6	11	.938	5.41

Third Basemen - Regulars

Player	Tm	G	GS	Inn	PO	A	E	DP	Pct.	Rng
Chavez,Er	Oak	125	125	1129.0	113	276	13	31	.968	3.10
Castilla,Vinny	Col	148	147	1286.2	125	315	6	29	.987	3.08
Tracy,Chad	Ari	135	120	1061.1	104	258	25	28	.935	3.07
Rolen,Scott	StL	142	140	1228.0	93	325	10	23	.977	3.06
Beltre,Adrian	LA	155	154	1340.1	120	322	10	32	.978	2.97
Bell,David	Phi	142	141	1239.2	89	307	24	22	.943	2.87
Randa,Joe	KC	119	118	1021.2	85	241	11	22	.967	2.87
Mora,Melvin	Bal	138	138	1210.1	122	258	21	21	.948	2.83
Alfonzo,E	SF	129	122	1081.1	87	246	12	20	.965	2.77
Munson,Eric	Det	94	87	740.2	51	176	16	17	.934	2.76
Batista,Tony	Mon	155	149	1326.0	83	308	19	35	.954	2.65
Wright,Dav	NYM	69	68	603.2	39	139	11	10	.942	2.65
Lowell,Mike	Fla	154	153	1326.0	117	272	7	30	.982	2.64
Jones,Chipper	Atl	96	93	802.0	58	177	6	13	.975	2.64
Blake,Casey	Cle	152	151	1352.1	121	275	26	24	.938	2.64
Burroughs,Sean	SD	125	119	1060.0	100	209	14	25	.957	2.62
Wigginton,Ty	TOT	122	104	931.1	63	208	18	16	.938	2.62
Koskie,Corey	Min	115	112	1004.0	79	207	11	14	.963	2.56
Mueller,Bill	Bos	96	94	827.2	71	162	14	15	.943	2.53
Huff,Aubrey	TB	87	85	705.0	69	129	12	13	.943	2.53
Blalock,Hank	Tex	159	154	1377.2	103	279	17	33	.957	2.50
Crede,Joe	CWS	144	142	1235.0	90	243	12	22	.965	2.43
Hinske,Eric	Tor	153	148	1310.2	107	242	8	23	.978	2.40
Rodriguez,Alex	NYY	155	155	1364.1	101	261	13	25	.965	2.39
Ensberg,Morgan	Hou	118	103	920.2	80	163	13	23	.949	2.38
Figgins,Chone	Ana	92	80	705.1	57	129	11	9	.944	2.37
Ramirez,Aramis	ChC	144	141	1245.1	92	221	10	15	.969	2.26

Third Basemen - The Rest

Player	Tm	G	GS	Inn	PO	A	E	DP	Pct.	Rng
Alexander,M	Tex	3	2	21.0	2	2	1	0	.800	1.71
Amezaga,A	Ana	26	2	59.2	3	9	1	3	.923	1.81
Atkins,Garrett	Col	4	3	27.0	2	4	0	1	1.000	2.00
Aurilia,Rich	SD	29	28	231.2	16	41	5	3	.919	2.21
Bautista,Jose	Bal	4	0	5.0	0	0	0	0	-	.00
Bautista,Jose	TB	2	0	4.0	0	2	0	0	1.000	4.50
Bautista,Jose	KC	11	6	58.0	5	17	1	2	.957	3.41
Bellhorn,Mark	Bos	16	13	108.2	10	31	3	2	.932	3.40
Berg,Dave	Tor	3	2	19.0	0	3	2	0	.600	1.42
Betemit,Wilson	Atl	7	4	39.0	2	6	0	2	1.000	1.85
Bloomquist,W	Sea	31	24	221.1	24	36	5	6	.923	2.44
Blum,Geoff	TB	59	40	382.0	35	78	8	8	.934	2.66
Branyan,R	Mil	44	40	361.0	35	91	5	7	.962	3.14
Burke,Jamie	CWS	2	0	2.2	0	0	0	0	-	.00

Player	Tm	G	GS	Inn	PO	A	E	DP	Pct.	Rng
Cabrera,J	Sea	36	31	277.2	33	63	3	7	.970	3.11
Cairo,Miguel	NYY	8	5	54.1	4	13	2	0	.895	2.82
Cantu,Jorge	TB	11	11	94.1	9	26	3	1	.921	3.34
Carroll,Jamey	Mon	13	8	78.0	8	26	2	1	.944	3.92
Castro,Juan	Cin	78	35	378.2	38	75	5	7	.958	2.69
Castro,RA	Oak	6	3	30.0	1	4	0	0	1.000	1.50
Cintron,Alex	Ari	1	0	1.0	1	0	0	0	1.000	9.00
Cirillo,Jeff	SD	11	8	78.1	8	10	0	1	1.000	2.07
Clark,Howie	Tor	1	0	1.0	0	0	0	0	-	.00
Collier,Lou	Phi	1	0	3.0	0	1	0	1	1.000	3.00
Counsell,Craig	Mil	1	0	0.1	0	0	0	0	-	.00
Cruz,Deivi	SF	1	0	1.0	0	0	0	0	-	.00
Cuddyer,Mike	Min	43	36	338.0	33	51	7	7	.923	2.24
Dallimore,B	SF	8	3	29.0	4	8	1	0	.923	3.72
DeRosa,Mark	Atl	72	62	556.0	27	125	10	7	.938	2.46
Diaz,Einar	Mon	1	0	1.0	0	0	0	0	-	.00
Dobbs,Greg	Sea	14	12	108.2	5	21	2	3	.929	2.15
Dransfeldt,K	CWS	3	1	13.1	2	0	0	0	1.000	1.35
Durrington,T	Mil	11	7	66.1	3	12	4	0	.789	2.04
Easley,Damion	Fla	6	5	42.0	4	11	0	0	1.000	3.21
Escalona,Felix	NYY	1	0	1.0	0	0	0	0	-	.00
Feliz,Pedro	SF	51	37	339.1	32	85	3	7	.975	3.10
Flores,Jose	LA	1	0	8.0	0	1	0	0	1.000	1.13
Fox,Andy	Mon	3	2	17.0	1	6	0	0	1.000	3.71
Fox,Andy	Tex	2	0	2.0	0	0	0	0	-	.00
Freel,Ryan	Cin	56	51	392.1	42	107	12	11	.925	3.42
Garcia,Je	Atl	3	1	12.0	0	3	1	0	.750	2.25
German,Esteban	Oak	15	10	102.2	8	21	2	2	.935	2.54
Ginter,Keith	Mil	47	41	396.1	28	80	3	10	.973	2.45
Glaus,Troy	Ana	19	19	165.0	11	27	2	2	.950	2.07
Gomez,Chris	Tor	5	4	31.1	2	8	0	1	1.000	2.87
Gonzalez,LA	Col	18	10	99.0	13	21	1	1	.971	3.09
Green,Andy	Ari	18	14	117.0	12	32	4	1	.917	3.38
Green,Nick	Atl	5	0	12.0	0	2	0	0	1.000	1.50
Guerrero,W	KC	2	0	4.0	0	0	0	0	-	.00
Gutierrez,R	NYM	2	1	10.0	1	0	1	0	.500	.90
Hairston Jr.,J	Bal	1	1	3.0	0	1	0	0	1.000	3.00
Hall,Bill	Mil	11	7	72.0	6	22	2	4	.933	3.50
Halter,Shane	Ana	33	22	213.1	26	46	10	2	.878	3.04
Hammock,Robby	Ari	1	0	2.0	1	0	0	0	1.000	4.50
Hansen,Dave	Sea	6	2	21.0	6	6	0	0	1.000	5.14
Hansen,Dave	SD	2	2	17.0	0	1	0	0	1.000	.53
Harris,Brendan	ChC	3	3	22.0	4	4	1	0	.889	3.27
Harris,Brendan	Mon	4	3	25.0	2	3	1	0	.833	1.80
Harris,Lenny	Fla	3	0	4.0	0	0	0	0	-	.00
Helms,Wes	Mil	67	66	546.0	45	105	16	10	.904	2.47
Hernandez,Jose	LA	12	3	38.0	4	7	0	1	1.000	2.61
Hessman,Mike	Atl	7	2	29.0	2	14	2	1	.889	4.97
Hill,Bobby	Pit	25	19	159.2	10	24	1	2	.971	1.92
Hillenbrand,S	Ari	17	15	133.0	6	29	3	3	.921	2.37
Hocking,Denny	Col	2	0	3.1	1	0	0	0	1.000	2.70
Hummel,Tim	Cin	32	19	192.2	17	44	4	5	.941	2.99
Infante,Omar	Det	10	2	29.1	2	8	0	2	1.000	3.07
Inge,Brandon	Det	73	58	524.2	42	131	12	12	.935	2.97
Kata,Matt	Ari	3	2	17.1	4	4	0	0	1.000	4.15
Lamb,Mike	Hou	57	53	453.2	41	106	13	8	.919	2.92
Larson,Brandon	Cin	35	33	272.1	24	50	5	4	.937	2.45
Leon,Jose	Bal	6	2	32.0	1	8	1	1	.900	2.53
Leone,Justin	Sea	28	28	242.0	25	48	8	2	.901	2.71
Lopez,Felipe	Cin	24	24	207.2	24	49	5	1	.936	3.16
Lopez,Jo	Sea	1	0	1.0	0	0	0	0	-	.00
Lopez,LuisM	Bal	11	6	64.0	6	15	4	2	.840	2.95
Lopez,Me	KC	4	2	21.0	2	7	1	1	.900	3.86
Luna,Hector	StL	16	8	87.2	5	19	2	3	.923	2.46
Mabry,John	StL	20	14	122.1	10	27	3	3	.925	2.72
Macias,Jose	ChC	18	7	85.1	10	12	1	1	.957	2.32
Mackowiak,Rob	Pit	55	51	411.1	37	90	5	15	.962	2.78
Martinez,Edgar	Sea	1	0	0.0	0	0	0	0	-	.00
Martinez,Ramon	ChC	24	11	112.2	12	21	3	4	.917	2.64
McDonald,John	Cle	9	1	24.1	1	12	0	0	1.000	4.81
McEwing,Joe	NYM	1	0	1.0	0	0	0	0	-	.00
McKay,Cody	StL	7	0	15.2	1	2	1	0	.750	1.72
McLemore,Mark	Oak	27	24	202.0	17	46	1	2	.984	2.81
McPherson,D	Ana	14	11	93.0	9	21	0	1	1.000	2.90
Melhuse,Adam	Oak	3	0	6.2	1	2	1	1	.750	4.05
Menechino,F	Tor	7	7	59.0	4	14	0	1	1.000	2.75
Merloni,Lou	Cle	10	9	80.1	1	20	1	0	.955	2.35
Mordecai,Mike	Fla	19	4	67.0	10	16	2	3	.929	3.49
Newhan,David	Bal	17	15	141.0	11	23	5	2	.872	2.17

Player	Tm	G	GS	Inn	PO	A	E	DP	Pct.	Rng
Norton,Greg	Det	18	12	117.2	7	19	1	0	.963	1.99
Nunez,AbrO	Pit	6	2	21.1	0	5	1	0	.833	2.11
Ojeda,Augie	Min	4	2	20.0	1	6	0	1	1.000	3.15
Olson,Tim	Ari	19	11	99.1	17	35	2	2	.963	4.71
Pellow,Kit	Col	4	1	13.1	2	1	0	0	1.000	2.03
Peralta,Jhonny	Cle	2	1	9.2	1	2	0	0	1.000	2.79
Perez,Edu	TB	1	0	1.0	0	0	0	0	-	.00
Perez,Neifi	SF	2	0	5.1	1	0	0	0	1.000	1.69
Perez,To	Phi	22	7	97.2	12	22	2	1	.944	3.13
Perry,Herbert	Tex	6	5	33.0	7	6	2	0	.867	3.55
Phillips,Andy	NYY	4	2	22.0	2	5	0	0	1.000	2.86
Polanco,P	Phi	13	11	96.0	15	26	0	4	1.000	3.84
Prieto,Alex	Min	5	1	16.0	1	3	0	0	1.000	2.25
Punto,Nick	Min	2	0	4.0	0	0	0	0	-	.00
Quinlan,Robb	Ana	32	28	218.0	13	44	1	1	.983	2.35
Ransom,Cody	SF	1	0	1.0	0	0	0	0	.000	.00
Relaford,Desi	KC	42	36	315.2	24	77	8	6	.927	2.88
Rolls,Damian	TB	19	14	127.2	16	25	2	3	.953	2.89
Sadler,Donnie	Ari	2	0	5.0	1	0	0	0	1.000	1.80
Saenz,Olmedo	LA	2	0	5.0	0	2	0	0	1.000	3.60
Sanchez,Freddy	Pit	1	0	2.0	0	0	0	0	-	.00
Scutaro,Marco	Oak	1	0	1.0	0	0	0	0	-	.00
Sheffield,Gary	NYY	2	0	2.0	0	0	1	0	.000	.00
Smith,Jason	Det	5	2	20.2	5	5	2	2	.833	4.35
Snyder,Earl	Bos	1	1	9.0	2	3	0	0	1.000	5.00
Spiezio,Scott	Sea	66	65	587.2	56	131	7	15	.964	2.86
Stynes,Chris	Pit	71	39	391.0	28	88	1	9	.991	2.67
Tiffee,Terry	Min	12	11	94.0	11	17	1	0	.966	2.68
Tracy,Andy	Col	1	1	6.0	0	1	0	0	1.000	1.50
Upton,BJ	TB	13	11	103.0	10	12	2	0	.917	1.92
Uribe,Juan	CWS	27	19	181.1	14	41	2	5	.965	2.73
Vazquez,Ramon	SD	9	5	54.0	8	6	0	2	1.000	2.33
Ventura,Robin	LA	11	5	62.0	13	11	0	6	1.000	3.48
Vizcaino,Jose	Hou	21	6	68.2	10	11	4	0	.840	2.75
Wigginton,Ty	NYM	66	54	488.2	29	116	12	8	.924	2.67
Wigginton,Ty	Pit	56	50	442.2	34	92	6	8	.955	2.56
Wooten,Shawn	Phi	4	3	26.1	2	4	0	0	1.000	2.05
Youkilis,Kevin	Bos	65	54	506.0	47	106	5	7	.968	2.72
Young,Dmitri	Det	1	1	6.2	1	1	0	0	1.000	2.70
Young,Eri	Tex	1	1	6.0	0	1	0	0	1.000	1.50
Zeile,Todd	NYM	46	39	345.2	38	73	8	7	.933	2.89

Shortstops - Regulars

Player	Tm	G	GS	Inn	PO	A	E	DP	Pct.	Rng
Tejada,Miguel	Bal	162	162	1421.2	263	526	24	120	.970	4.99
Guillen,Carlos	Det	135	133	1151.0	220	416	17	90	.974	4.97
Crosby,Bo	Oak	151	151	1356.0	242	505	19	107	.975	4.96
Valentin,Jo	CWS	122	117	1025.1	187	373	20	84	.966	4.92
Wilson,Jack	Pit	156	155	1355.2	235	492	17	129	.977	4.83
Lugo,Julio	TB	143	142	1238.0	237	422	25	91	.963	4.79
Furcal,Rafael	Atl	131	130	1134.0	191	412	24	101	.962	4.79
Matsui,Kazuo	NYM	110	108	941.2	174	323	23	66	.956	4.75
Berroa,Angel	KC	133	132	1143.0	207	388	28	93	.955	4.69
Guzman,C	Min	145	143	1304.2	234	440	12	103	.983	4.65
Clayton,Royce	Col	144	140	1241.0	213	417	9	89	.986	4.57
Jeter,Derek	NYY	154	154	1341.2	273	392	13	95	.981	4.46
Everett,Adam	Hou	99	97	842.0	137	278	10	56	.976	4.44
Gomez,Chris	Tor	77	69	638.0	109	205	10	46	.969	4.43
Cruz,Deivi	SF	104	95	800.2	127	267	8	59	.980	4.43
Renteria,Edgar	StL	149	148	1307.1	222	418	11	92	.983	4.41
Cabrera,O	TOT	159	158	1358.2	226	437	15	93	.978	4.39
Gonzalez,AS	TOT	81	77	658.2	132	188	11	45	.967	4.37
Gonzalez,Al	Fla	158	155	1351.2	225	425	16	99	.976	4.33
Izturis,Cesar	LA	159	156	1386.0	234	430	10	96	.985	4.31
Vizquel,Omar	Cle	147	141	1245.0	200	395	11	89	.982	4.30
Cintron,Alex	Ari	133	125	1099.0	141	382	15	61	.972	4.28
Aurilia,Rich	TOT	79	76	681.1	122	202	4	41	.988	4.28
Larkin,Barry	Cin	85	81	684.1	105	216	4	33	.988	4.22
Greene,Khalil	SD	136	134	1189.2	177	380	20	81	.965	4.21
Young,Michael	Tex	158	158	1386.2	225	422	19	98	.971	4.20
Counsell,Craig	Mil	129	128	1130.2	165	357	9	70	.983	4.16
Rollins,Jimmy	Phi	154	153	1376.2	214	398	9	88	.986	4.00
Garciaparra,N	TOT	79	78	676.0	121	176	9	34	.971	3.95
Eckstein,David	Ana	139	137	1191.2	198	309	6	75	.988	3.83

Shortstops - The Rest

Player	Tm	G	GS	Inn	PO	A	E	DP	Pct.	Rng
Adams,Russ	Tor	21	18	159.1	26	47	5	9	.936	4.12
Alexander,M	Tex	7	2	27.0	6	11	1	1	.944	5.67
Alfaro,Jason	Hou	3	2	16.2	2	3	0	1	1.000	2.70
Amezaga,A	Ana	32	14	167.0	38	57	1	5	.990	5.12
Aurilia,Rich	Sea	73	71	634.0	114	185	3	39	.990	4.24
Aurilia,Rich	SD	6	5	47.1	8	17	1	2	.962	4.75
Barmes,Clint	Col	9	9	76.0	17	36	1	7	.981	6.28
Bartlett,Jason	Min	5	2	22.0	5	11	2	3	.889	6.55
Bellhorn,Mark	Bos	1	1	9.0	2	3	0	1	1.000	5.00
Beltre,Adrian	LA	1	0	1.0	0	1	0	0	1.000	9.00
Betemit,Wilson	Atl	11	7	74.2	12	30	3	5	.933	5.06
Blanco,Andres	KC	19	19	162.0	30	64	4	17	.959	5.22
Bloomquist,W	Sea	20	16	139.1	27	36	3	11	.955	4.07
Blum,Geoff	TB	1	0	1.0	1	0	0	0	1.000	9.00
Bruntlett,Eric	Hou	33	10	127.0	17	28	3	9	.938	3.19
Cabrera,J	Sea	14	9	83.0	11	13	1	2	.960	2.60
Cabrera,O	Mon	101	100	867.2	148	290	7	70	.984	4.54
Cabrera,O	Bos	58	58	491.0	78	147	8	23	.966	4.12
Cairo,Miguel	NYY	3	2	19.0	0	5	0	1	1.000	2.37
Cantu,Jorge	TB	1	1	7.0	2	2	0	0	1.000	5.14
Carroll,Jamey	Mon	10	6	59.0	11	16	0	4	1.000	4.12
Castillo,Jose	Pit	2	0	2.0	0	0	0	0	-	.00
Castro,Juan	Cin	31	21	190.1	32	72	2	16	.981	4.92
Castro,RA	Oak	1	0	2.0	0	2	0	0	1.000	9.00
Crespo,Cesar	Bos	27	7	96.1	20	30	3	8	.943	4.67
Delgado,Wilson	NYM	39	37	340.0	49	128	8	28	.957	4.69
DeRosa,Mark	Atl	11	4	50.1	10	18	2	7	.933	5.01
Dransfeldt,K	CWS	8	4	39.2	4	14	1	1	.947	4.08
Easley,Damion	Fla	15	5	65.1	6	24	1	4	.968	4.13
Ensberg,Morgan	Hou	1	0	2.0	0	0	0	0	-	.00
Erickson,Matt	Mil	1	0	4.0	0	4	0	0	1.000	9.00
Escalona,Felix	NYY	4	2	22.0	3	7	0	1	1.000	4.09
Feliz,Pedro	SF	20	14	119.2	17	48	5	9	.929	4.89
Figgins,Chone	Ana	13	10	80.2	19	24	2	5	.956	4.80
Fox,Andy	Mon	5	1	21.0	0	5	0	0	1.000	2.14
Garcia,Je	Atl	25	21	191.0	31	71	4	14	.962	4.81
Garciaparra,N	Bos	37	37	311.1	52	82	6	17	.957	3.87
Garciaparra,N	ChC	42	41	364.2	69	94	3	17	.982	4.03
Gil,Jerry	Ari	28	24	212.1	34	73	5	18	.955	4.54
Gipson,Charles	TB	2	0	5.0	0	2	0	1	1.000	3.60
Gonzalez,AS	ChC	37	35	297.1	65	82	5	18	.967	4.45
Gonzalez,AS	Mon	33	33	293.1	57	88	6	23	.960	4.45
Gonzalez,AS	SD	11	9	68.0	10	18	0	4	1.000	3.71
Gonzalez,LA	Col	10	7	61.0	9	18	0	5	1.000	3.98
Guerrero,W	KC	3	0	5.0	1	2	0	0	1.000	5.40
Gutierrez,R	Bos	6	3	36.0	7	9	1	3	.941	4.00
Hall,Bill	Mil	37	33	303.2	59	116	8	23	.956	5.19
Halter,Shane	Ana	3	1	15.0	3	4	0	1	1.000	4.20
Hart,Bo	StL	1	0	2.0	0	0	0	0	-	.00
Hernandez,Jose	LA	13	6	62.1	8	26	1	5	.971	4.91
Hocking,Denny	Col	13	6	57.1	13	25	3	6	.927	5.97
Hummel,Tim	Cin	1	0	1.0	0	0	0	0	-	.00
Infante,Omar	Det	23	21	188.2	28	67	4	10	.960	4.53
Izturis,Maicer	Mon	23	20	187.0	32	71	7	15	.936	4.96
Jackson,Damian	KC	1	0	2.0	0	0	0	0	-	.00
Jimenez,D	Cin	5	3	19.0	7	7	0	1	1.000	6.63
Kata,Matt	Ari	1	1	9.1	3	5	0	2	1.000	7.71
Labandeira,J	Mon	3	2	19.0	2	3	1	0	.833	2.37
Leone,Justin	Sea	2	1	8.0	3	1	1	0	.800	4.50
Lopez,Felipe	Cin	51	41	391.0	65	137	9	25	.957	4.65
Lopez,Jo	Sea	57	55	490.0	91	125	10	24	.956	3.97
Lopez,LuisM	Bal	14	0	32.2	7	10	1	3	.944	4.68
Lopez,Me	KC	4	2	19.0	2	2	0	2	1.000	1.89
Luna,Hector	StL	24	14	144.1	33	56	5	12	.947	5.55
Machado,Andy	Cin	17	16	149.0	23	36	4	7	.937	3.56
Martinez,Ramon	ChC	73	57	529.2	80	174	6	34	.977	4.32
McDonald,John	Cle	30	15	166.2	25	65	5	16	.947	4.86
McEwing,Joe	NYM	13	10	94.2	19	36	1	5	.982	5.23
Menechino,F	Tor	14	14	109.0	26	26	1	9	.981	4.29
Mora,Melvin	Bal	1	0	1.0	0	0	0	0	-	.00
Mordecai,Mike	Fla	3	2	22.0	5	8	0	4	1.000	5.32
Nunez,AbrO	Pit	13	5	58.1	10	15	0	4	1.000	3.86
Ojeda,Augie	Min	7	5	43.1	8	14	0	4	1.000	4.57
Olmedo,Ray	Cin	7	0	9.0	4	4	0	1	1.000	8.00
Olson,Tim	Ari	17	10	97.1	18	29	4	8	.922	4.35
Ordonez,Rey	ChC	22	17	153.1	31	39	3	9	.959	4.11

Player	Tm	G	GS	Inn	PO	A	E	DP	Pct.	Rng
Peralta,Jhonny	Cle	7	6	55.0	7	17	3	2	.889	3.93
Perez,Antonio	LA	1	0	4.0	1	2	0	1	1.000	6.75
Perez,Neifi	SF	57	48	440.0	67	157	5	29	.978	4.58
Perez,Neifi	ChC	19	12	120.1	20	41	2	10	.968	4.56
Perez,To	Phi	10	9	86.0	14	26	2	5	.952	4.19
Prieto,Alex	Min	3	2	18.0	4	4	0	2	1.000	4.00
Punto,Nick	Min	11	10	88.0	16	33	0	9	1.000	5.01
Ransom,Cody	SF	45	5	96.2	20	35	3	11	.948	5.12
Reese,Pokey	Bos	71	56	507.2	85	189	6	37	.979	4.86
Relaford,Desi	KC	12	9	89.1	14	28	0	7	1.000	4.23
Reyes,Jose	NYM	10	7	72.2	18	26	2	5	.957	5.45
Rodriguez,Alex	NYY	2	0	2.0	1	1	0	1	1.000	9.00
Sadler,Donnie	Ari	3	2	18.0	3	3	0	1	1.000	3.00
Sanchez,Freddy	Pit	4	1	12.0	1	3	1	0	.800	3.00
Sanchez,Rey	TB	4	2	26.0	5	15	0	1	1.000	6.92
Santiago,Ramon	Sea	16	10	105.0	22	31	3	8	.946	4.54
Scutaro,Marco	Oak	16	11	113.1	25	42	2	9	.971	5.32
Smith,Jason	Det	20	8	100.0	16	35	1	5	.981	4.59
Spivey,Junior	Mil	1	0	3.2	1	1	0	0	1.000	4.91
Upton,B.J.	TB	16	16	140.0	23	41	7	8	.901	4.11
Uribe,Juan	CWS	38	32	287.1	54	115	3	31	.983	5.29
Valdez,Wilson	CWS	12	9	80.0	13	23	1	3	.973	4.05
Vazquez,Ramon	SD	22	14	136.0	22	35	1	5	.983	3.77
Vizcaino,Jose	Hou	64	53	455.1	65	153	7	27	.969	4.31
Wilson,Enrique	NYY	16	4	59.0	10	25	1	6	.972	5.34
Woodward,Chris	Tor	64	60	514.2	88	171	5	41	.981	4.53
Young,Eri	Tex	8	2	26.0	2	4	1	1	.857	2.08

Left Fielders - Regulars

Player	Tm	G	GS	Inn	PO	A	E	DP	Pct.	Rng
Crawford,Carl	TB	123	116	1010.0	274	5	1	1	.996	2.49
Conine,Jeff	Fla	83	82	709.2	174	5	1	0	.994	2.27
Ibanez,Raul	Sea	110	106	949.1	227	10	4	3	.983	2.25
Bigbie,Larry	Bal	114	102	915.0	215	2	2	0	.991	2.13
Dellucci,David	Tex	84	77	648.2	152	0	2	0	.987	2.11
Lee,Ca	CWS	148	148	1277.2	282	11	0	2	1.000	2.06
Ford,Lew	Min	81	77	680.2	149	5	1	0	.994	2.04
Matsui,Hideki	NYY	162	160	1388.0	303	8	7	3	.978	2.02
Lawton,Matt	Cle	125	124	1070.1	231	7	3	2	.988	2.00
Bay,Jason	Pit	117	107	963.0	208	3	2	0	.991	1.97
Burrell,Pat	Phi	122	121	1060.0	217	9	4	1	.983	1.92
White,Ro	Det	74	73	614.2	127	2	3	0	.977	1.89
Byrnes,Eric	Oak	109	98	871.1	172	7	2	2	.989	1.85
Bonds,Barry	SF	133	132	1130.2	214	11	4	0	.983	1.79
Jenkins,Geoff	Mil	156	154	1362.0	261	10	1	3	.996	1.79
Holliday,Matt	Col	115	109	917.0	177	4	7	1	.963	1.78
Dunn,Adam	Cin	156	146	1327.1	250	10	8	1	.970	1.76
Floyd,Cliff	NYM	107	106	863.2	164	5	2	1	.988	1.76
Klesko,Ryan	SD	104	102	723.2	135	2	2	0	.986	1.70
Ramirez,Manny	Bos	132	132	1087.2	198	4	7	0	.967	1.67
Alou,Moises	ChC	154	152	1338.1	240	7	8	2	.969	1.66
Gonzalez,LE	Ari	104	103	900.1	162	2	6	0	.965	1.64
Biggio,Craig	Hou	83	83	654.1	116	2	9	0	.929	1.62
Stewart,Sh	Min	71	71	639.1	103	2	3	0	.972	1.48
Berkman,Lance	Hou	70	68	608.2	93	2	2	0	.979	1.40

Left Fielders - The Rest

Player	Tm	G	GS	Inn	PO	A	E	DP	Pct.	Rng
Aguila,Chris	Fla	6	1	19.0	3	0	0	0	1.000	1.42
Allen,Chad	Tex	12	10	86.0	13	0	0	0	1.000	1.36
Alvarez,Tony	Pit	3	3	25.0	4	0	0	0	1.000	1.44
Anderson,M	StL	28	21	165.0	36	2	1	1	.974	2.07
Atkins,Garrett	Col	3	2	14.0	5	0	0	0	1.000	3.21
Bautista,Jose	TB	5	3	25.0	4	0	0	0	1.000	1.44
Berg,Dave	Tor	31	26	226.2	36	1	1	0	.974	1.47
Berger,Brandon	KC	10	9	86.0	25	1	0	1	1.000	2.72
Bloomquist,W	Sea	8	3	29.0	7	0	0	0	1.000	2.17
Blum,Geoff	TB	7	7	59.1	12	1	1	1	.929	1.97
Bocachica,H	Sea	1	0	7.0	0	0	0	0	-	.00
Bradley,Milton	LA	17	15	128.0	34	1	0	0	1.000	2.46
Bragg,Darren	Cin	2	1	9.1	1	0	0	0	1.000	.96
Brown,Adrian	KC	4	3	27.0	9	0	0	0	1.000	3.00

Player	Tm	G	GS	Inn	PO	A	E	DP	Pct.	Rng
Brown,Dee	KC	53	49	434.0	93	4	3	0	.970	2.01
Bruntlett,Eric	Hou	1	0	1.0	0	0	0	0	-	.00
Buchanan,Brian	SD	15	12	86.2	10	0	0	0	1.000	1.04
Burnitz,Jeromy	Col	21	17	151.2	36	0	1	0	.973	2.14
Cabrera,J	Sea	21	18	158.0	42	1	1	0	.977	2.45
Cabrera,Miguel	Fla	59	58	504.0	92	6	2	0	.980	1.75
Calloway,Ron	Mon	6	4	39.2	2	0	0	0	1.000	.45
Carroll,Jamey	Mon	2	1	6.0	2	0	0	0	1.000	3.00
Catalanotto,F	Tor	41	34	309.2	66	1	2	1	.971	1.95
Cedeno,Roger	StL	23	17	133.2	18	2	0	0	1.000	1.35
Cepicky,Matt	Mon	9	8	59.2	15	0	0	0	1.000	2.26
Chavez,Er	Oak	1	0	4.1	2	0	0	0	1.000	4.15
Chen,Chin-Feng	LA	3	1	16.0	8	0	0	0	1.000	4.50
Church,Ryan	Mon	12	9	72.0	16	2	0	0	1.000	2.25
Cirillo,Jeff	SD	1	0	2.0	0	0	0	0	-	.00
Clark,Brady	Mil	3	2	21.0	7	0	0	0	1.000	3.00
Clark,Howie	Tor	9	7	64.2	16	2	0	0	1.000	2.51
Clark,Jermaine	Cin	1	1	9.0	1	0	0	0	1.000	1.00
Collier,Lou	Phi	8	4	36.0	3	0	0	0	1.000	.75
Conti,Jason	Tex	1	0	1.0	0	0	0	0	-	.00
Cordero,Wil	Fla	3	3	19.0	5	0	0	0	1.000	2.37
Crespo,Cesar	Bos	10	0	15.1	2	0	0	0	1.000	1.17
Crisp,Coco	Cle	37	31	293.1	81	2	0	1	1.000	2.55
Crosby,Bu	NYY	11	0	33.1	3	0	0	0	1.000	.81
Cruz,Ja	Cin	4	2	12.2	1	0	0	0	1.000	.71
Cuddyer,Mike	Min	7	3	35.0	3	0	0	0	1.000	.77
Cummings,Midre	TB	2	2	17.0	3	0	0	0	1.000	1.59
Daubach,Brian	Bos	6	5	44.0	7	1	0	0	1.000	1.64
DaVanon,Jeff	Ana	24	15	157.1	42	0	1	0	.977	2.40
Davis,JJ	Pit	5	2	20.0	2	0	1	0	.667	.90
DeJesus,David	KC	4	4	32.0	9	0	0	0	1.000	2.53
DeRosa,Mark	Atl	3	2	15.0	0	0	0	0	-	.00
DeVore,Doug	Ari	18	12	107.2	27	2	0	1	1.000	2.42
Diaz,Matt	TB	3	3	20.0	8	0	0	0	1.000	3.60
Dubois,Jason	ChC	1	0	2.0	0	0	0	0	-	.00
Duncan,Jeff	NYM	2	0	5.0	1	0	0	0	1.000	1.80
Encarnacion,J	LA	9	8	79.0	10	0	0	0	1.000	1.14
Escobar,Alex	Cle	8	5	66.0	20	0	0	0	1.000	2.73
Everett,Carl	Mon	19	19	149.2	24	1	2	0	.926	1.50
Everett,Carl	CWS	1	1	7.0	1	1	0	0	1.000	2.57
Feliz,Pedro	SF	2	0	2.0	1	0	0	0	1.000	4.50
Fick,Robert	TB	13	11	87.2	20	0	1	0	.952	2.05
Figgins,Chone	Ana	1	1	9.0	4	0	0	0	1.000	4.00
Fox,Andy	Tex	1	0	1.0	1	0	0	0	1.000	9.00
Freel,Ryan	Cin	12	12	85.1	29	1	0	0	1.000	3.16
Gathright,Joey	TB	4	2	22.0	3	0	0	0	1.000	1.23
Gerut,Jody	Cle	2	1	11.0	0	0	0	0	-	.00
Gettis,Byron	KC	11	10	88.0	25	1	2	1	.929	2.66
Gipson,Charles	TB	1	0	0.1	0	0	0	0	-	.00
Glanville,Doug	Phi	13	6	65.1	22	0	0	0	1.000	3.03
Gload,Ross	CWS	17	9	94.0	20	0	1	0	.952	1.91
Gomez,Alexis	KC	6	5	44.0	11	0	1	0	.917	2.25
Gonzalez,LA	Col	20	11	110.1	20	0	0	0	1.000	1.63
Gonzalez,Raul	Cle	1	0	1.0	0	0	0	0	-	.00
Goodwin,Tom	ChC	14	3	44.2	12	0	0	0	1.000	2.42
Grabowski,J	LA	30	23	216.2	36	0	1	0	.973	1.50
Green,Andy	Ari	9	4	45.1	10	1	0	0	1.000	2.18
Grieve,Ben	ChC	1	0	1.0	1	0	0	0	1.000	9.00
Gross,Gabe	Tor	38	33	289.2	73	5	0	1	1.000	2.42
Guerrero,W	KC	1	0	6.0	2	0	0	0	1.000	3.00
Guiel,Aaron	KC	38	35	307.1	82	3	3	0	.966	2.49
Hairston,Scott	Ari	2	0	4.0	0	0	0	0	-	.00
Hairston Jr.,J	Bal	10	8	77.1	17	1	1	0	.947	2.09
Hammock,Robby	Ari	12	10	79.0	20	1	1	0	.955	2.39
Hammonds,J	SF	7	5	45.1	8	1	0	0	1.000	1.79
Harris,Lenny	Fla	8	6	43.0	9	0	0	0	1.000	1.88
Harris,Willie	CWS	1	0	2.0	2	0	0	0	1.000	9.00
Harvey,Ken	KC	4	4	30.0	4	0	0	0	1.000	1.20
Hawpe,Brad	Col	2	1	9.1	2	0	0	0	1.000	1.93
Hermansen,Chad	Tor	4	2	17.0	4	0	0	0	1.000	2.12
Hernandez,Jose	LA	9	4	40.0	6	0	0	0	1.000	1.35
Hessman,Mike	Atl	3	2	17.0	4	0	0	0	1.000	2.12
Hidalgo,R	NYM	5	5	42.1	7	0	0	0	1.000	1.49
Hocking,Denny	Col	20	1	54.1	19	0	1	0	.950	3.15
Hollandsworth,T	ChC	4	3	29.0	5	0	0	0	1.000	1.55
Hollins,Damon	Atl	6	4	37.0	7	1	0	0	1.000	1.95
Huff,Aubrey	TB	8	7	71.0	17	0	0	0	1.000	2.15
Hyzdu,Adam	Bos	11	0	27.0	6	0	0	0	1.000	2.00
Inge,Brandon	Det	7	6	49.0	7	2	1	0	.900	1.65

Player	Tm	G	GS	Inn	PO	A	E	DP	Pct.	Rng
Jackson,Damian	KC	1	0	0.1	0	0	0	0	-	.00
Johnson,Re	Tor	57	53	461.1	96	5	2	1	.981	1.97
Jones,Chipper	Atl	30	30	238.0	35	2	0	1	1.000	1.40
Jordan,Brian	Tex	1	0	3.0	0	0	0	0	-	.00
Kapler,Gabe	Bos	18	5	64.1	13	0	0	0	1.000	1.82
Kelton,Dave	ChC	2	1	9.0	2	0	0	0	1.000	2.00
Kielty,Bobby	Oak	51	40	366.2	71	1	1	0	.986	1.77
Knott,Jon	SD	5	3	24.0	4	0	0	0	1.000	1.50
Kroeger,Josh	Ari	11	6	57.0	17	0	0	0	1.000	2.68
Kubel,Jason	Min	2	2	18.0	3	1	0	1	1.000	2.00
Lane,Jason	Hou	35	6	101.2	24	2	1	0	.963	2.30
Lankford,Ray	StL	66	43	392.0	82	1	4	0	.954	1.91
Ledee,Ricky	Phi	9	8	74.0	8	0	0	0	1.000	.97
Ledee,Ricky	SF	1	1	7.0	1	0	0	0	1.000	1.29
Linden,Todd	SF	7	5	51.2	6	0	0	0	1.000	1.05
Little,Mark	Cle	4	0	6.0	2	1	0	0	1.000	4.50
Lo Duca,Paul	LA	9	8	69.0	13	0	0	0	1.000	1.70
Long,Terrence	SD	61	30	330.2	85	1	2	0	.977	2.34
Lopez,Me	KC	2	1	10.0	0	0	0	0	-	.00
Luna,Hector	StL	8	4	32.1	7	0	0	0	1.000	1.95
Mabry,John	StL	39	25	225.0	48	0	1	0	.980	1.92
Macias,Jose	ChC	8	3	37.1	5	0	0	0	1.000	1.21
Mackowiak,Rob	Pit	25	16	153.0	33	2	0	0	1.000	2.06
Magruder,Chris	Mil	10	5	59.0	9	1	0	0	1.000	1.53
Marrero,Eli	Atl	47	42	375.0	80	4	1	1	.988	2.02
Mateo,Henry	Mon	1	0	4.0	1	0	0	0	1.000	2.25
Mateo,Ruben	Pit	2	2	14.0	1	0	1	0	.500	.64
Mateo,Ruben	KC	11	10	89.0	21	3	0	1	1.000	2.43
Matthews Jr.,G	Tex	3	1	11.0	7	1	0	0	1.000	6.55
McCarty,Dave	Bos	10	5	47.0	6	1	0	1	1.000	1.34
McCracken,Q	Sea	4	3	24.0	3	0	0	0	1.000	1.13
McCracken,Q	Ari	27	26	223.2	28	1	0	0	1.000	1.17
McDonald,D	Bal	1	1	9.0	1	0	0	0	1.000	1.00
McEwing,Joe	NYM	8	2	20.2	5	0	0	0	1.000	2.18
McLemore,Mark	Oak	1	0	5.0	0	0	0	0	-	.00
McMillon,Billy	Oak	20	13	126.0	23	0	0	0	1.000	1.64
Mench,Kevin	Tex	53	37	362.2	73	1	1	1	.987	1.84
Merloni,Lou	Cle	4	1	19.0	2	1	1	0	.750	1.42
Michaels,Jason	Phi	39	23	227.1	49	3	0	2	1.000	2.06
Millar,Kevin	Bos	20	13	116.0	25	0	0	0	1.000	1.94
Mohr,Dustan	SF	43	19	219.1	55	2	0	1	1.000	2.34
Mondesi,Raul	Pit	14	14	117.0	21	0	2	0	.913	1.62
Monroe,Craig	Det	65	50	446.0	102	1	8	0	.928	2.08
Mottola,Chad	Bal	3	1	20.2	4	0	0	0	1.000	1.74
Murray,Calvin	ChC	1	0	2.0	2	0	0	0	1.000	9.00
Nady,Xavier	SD	18	10	105.0	16	1	2	0	.895	1.46
Newhan,David	Bal	19	19	159.0	41	0	0	1	1.000	2.32
Norton,Greg	Det	6	0	15.1	2	0	0	0	1.000	1.17
Nunez,Abr	Fla	28	9	123.1	28	0	0	0	1.000	2.04
Olson,Tim	Ari	1	1	8.0	3	0	0	0	1.000	3.38
Palmeiro,O	Hou	20	5	73.1	17	0	0	0	1.000	2.09
Pascucci,Val	Mon	4	3	26.0	4	0	0	0	1.000	1.38
Paul,Josh	Ana	4	1	13.0	2	0	0	0	1.000	1.38
Payton,Jay	SD	9	4	48.0	8	0	0	0	1.000	1.50
Pellow,Kit	Col	11	6	47.0	8	0	0	0	1.000	1.53
Pena,Wily Mo	Cin	1	0	0.0	0	0	0	0	-	.00
Perez,Edu	TB	2	2	12.0	2	0	0	0	1.000	1.50
Perez,Ti	CWS	12	4	51.2	8	1	1	0	.900	1.57
Piedra,Jorge	Col	14	9	79.1	12	0	0	0	1.000	1.36
Pond,Simon	Tor	6	6	52.0	10	0	0	0	1.000	1.73
Porter,Colin	StL	6	1	15.1	5	0	0	0	1.000	2.93
Pride,Curtis	Ana	15	2	52.0	17	0	0	0	1.000	2.94
Quinlan,Robb	Ana	6	1	16.0	3	0	0	0	1.000	1.69
Raines Jr,Tim	Bal	1	0	6.0	2	0	0	0	1.000	3.00
Ransom,Cody	SF	1	0	1.0	0	0	0	0	-	.00
Reed,Jeremy	Sea	1	0	4.0	1	0	0	0	1.000	2.25
Relaford,Desi	KC	22	18	152.0	39	2	1	0	.976	2.43
Restovich,Mike	Min	12	5	55.0	13	0	0	0	1.000	2.13
Reyes,Rene	Col	1	0	1.0	1	0	0	0	1.000	9.00
Riggs,Adam	Ana	8	5	36.0	11	1	0	0	1.000	3.00
Rivera,Juan	Mon	10	9	71.0	17	1	0	0	1.000	2.28
Roberts,Dave	LA	48	45	378.2	77	0	2	0	.975	1.83
Roberts,Dave	Bos	18	2	50.0	10	0	0	0	1.000	1.80
Robinson,Kerry	SD	39	1	121.0	34	0	0	0	1.000	2.53
Rolls,Damian	TB	16	6	76.2	14	0	0	0	1.000	1.64
Romano,Jason	TB	1	1	9.0	2	1	0	0	1.000	3.00
Ryan,Mike	Min	10	4	48.0	8	0	0	0	1.000	1.50
Sadler,Donnie	Ari	3	0	9.0	1	0	0	0	1.000	1.00
Salmon,Tim	Ana	3	2	14.0	0	0	0	0	-	.00
Sanders,Reggie	StL	38	36	297.1	65	2	1	1	.985	2.03
Sierra,Ruben	NYY	8	2	22.1	4	0	0	0	1.000	1.61
Simontacchi,J	StL	1	0	1.0	0	0	0	0	-	.00
Sledge,Terrmel	Mon	79	58	579.2	133	4	3	1	.979	2.13
Snead,Esix	NYM	1	0	1.0	0	0	0	0	-	.00
Spencer,Shane	NYM	43	20	231.0	58	0	2	0	.967	2.26
Stairs,Matt	KC	14	14	113.2	23	2	1	0	.962	1.98
Surhoff,B.J.	Bal	34	31	268.1	69	0	1	0	.986	2.31
Sweeney,Ma	Col	9	6	51.1	13	1	0	0	1.000	2.45
Swisher,Nick	Oak	12	11	98.0	19	0	1	0	.950	1.74
Taguchi,So	StL	53	15	192.0	40	0	2	0	.952	1.88
Taveras,Willy	Hou	2	0	4.0	0	0	0	0	-	.00
Terrero,Luis	Ari	1	0	1.0	0	0	0	0	-	.00
Thames,Marcus	Det	40	31	298.2	78	3	0	1	1.000	2.44
Thomas,Charles	Atl	70	61	560.2	132	6	1	2	.993	2.22
Thompson,Rich	KC	1	0	1.0	0	0	0	0	-	.00
Tracy,Chad	Ari	1	0	1.0	2	0	0	0	1.000	18.00
Upton,BJ	TB	1	1	7.0	0	0	0	0	-	.00
Valent,Eric	NYM	32	24	213.1	39	1	0	0	1.000	1.69
Walker,To	ChC	1	0	2.0	1	0	0	0	1.000	4.50
Werth,Jayson	LA	65	58	526.0	116	6	4	2	.968	2.09
Wilkerson,Brad	Mon	59	51	439.1	94	4	2	2	.980	2.01
Williams,G	NYM	21	5	72.0	9	2	1	0	.917	1.38
Willingham,J	Fla	3	3	21.0	6	0	0	0	1.000	2.57
Wilson,Craig	Pit	19	17	136.0	22	0	1	0	.957	1.46
Winn,Randy	Sea	40	32	288.0	74	0	0	0	1.000	2.31
Wise,Dewayne	Atl	34	21	207.1	40	2	0	0	1.000	1.82
Young,Dmitri	Det	2	2	16.0	2	0	0	0	1.000	1.13
Young,Eri	Tex	47	37	326.1	58	3	2	0	.968	1.68

Center Fielders - Regulars

Player	Tm	G	GS	Inn	PO	A	E	DP	Pct.	Rng
Baldelli,Rocco	TB	124	120	1047.0	341	11	8	2	.978	3.03
Payton,Jay	SD	128	111	1027.0	333	11	4	2	.989	3.01
Winn,Randy	Sea	128	119	1070.1	342	5	4	1	.989	2.92
DeJesus,David	KC	85	85	732.1	231	3	4	1	.983	2.88
Cameron,Mike	NYM	135	132	1184.0	354	7	8	0	.978	2.74
Beltran,Carlos	TOT	158	157	1369.1	397	13	8	3	.981	2.69
Jones,Andruw	Atl	154	153	1347.0	389	10	3	1	.993	2.67
Bradley,Milton	LA	93	91	792.2	231	2	4	1	.983	2.65
Rowand,Aaron	CWS	126	114	1018.2	290	8	6	1	.980	2.63
Wells,Vernon	Tor	131	130	1135.0	327	5	1	0	.997	2.63
Podsednik,S	Mil	153	152	1361.0	392	5	4	1	.990	2.63
Hunter,Torii	Min	126	124	1100.0	311	5	4	0	.988	2.59
Chavez,En	Mon	121	121	1081.2	301	9	5	5	.984	2.58
Kotsay,Mark	Oak	145	140	1255.0	347	11	6	3	.984	2.57
Matos,Luis	Bal	89	85	781.1	219	3	1	1	.996	2.56
Grissom,M	SF	138	128	1219.0	341	3	2	2	.994	2.54
Damon,Johnny	Bos	148	145	1256.1	349	5	5	3	.986	2.54
Redman,Tike	Pit	147	134	1207.2	338	2	5	1	.986	2.53
Anderson,G	Ana	94	92	791.2	211	5	3	1	.991	2.46
Griffey Jr.,K	Cin	76	76	656.1	173	4	1	1	.994	2.43
Sanchez,Alex	Det	78	77	661.0	176	2	9	1	.952	2.42
Byrd,Marlon	Phi	92	86	753.1	195	4	2	1	.990	2.38
Finley,Steve	TOT	158	157	1381.0	359	5	3	3	.992	2.37
Edmonds,Jim	StL	146	141	1241.2	314	11	4	2	.988	2.36
Williams,B	NYY	97	93	830.1	214	2	1	1	.995	2.34
Nix,Laynce	Tex	111	99	875.2	222	4	1	1	.996	2.32
Crisp,Coco	Cle	92	90	807.1	205	3	4	0	.981	2.32
Pierre,Juan	Fla	162	162	1439.0	364	3	2	1	.995	2.30
Patterson,C	ChC	157	152	1367.2	324	8	1	5	.997	2.18

Center Fielders - The Rest

Player	Tm	G	GS	Inn	PO	A	E	DP	Pct.	Rng
Alvarez,Tony	Pit	4	3	25.0	6	0	0	0	1.000	2.16
Bautista,Da	Ari	2	2	14.0	6	0	0	0	1.000	3.86
Bautista,Jose	Pit	3	1	14.0	6	0	2	0	.750	3.86
Bay,Jason	Pit	5	3	21.0	3	0	0	0	1.000	1.29
Beltran,Carlos	KC	69	69	597.0	197	5	3	1	.985	3.05
Beltran,Carlos	Hou	89	88	772.1	200	8	5	2	.977	2.42
Bergeron,Peter	Mon	11	11	97.0	21	0	2	0	.913	1.95
Berkman,Lance	Hou	2	1	9.0	2	0	0	0	1.000	2.00
Bigbie,Larry	Bal	30	29	242.2	74	1	0	0	1.000	2.78

Player	Tm	G	GS	Inn	PO	A	E	DP	Pct.	Rng
Biggio,Craig	Hou	66	66	570.2	134	1	0	0	1.000	2.13
Bloomquist,W	Sea	1	1	8.0	7	0	0	0	1.000	7.88
Bocachica,H	Sea	32	23	217.2	63	0	0	0	1.000	2.60
Borchard,Joe	CWS	2	0	5.0	2	0	0	0	1.000	3.60
Bragg,Darren	Cin	14	10	108.2	43	0	1	0	.977	3.56
Bruntlett,Eric	Hou	1	1	9.0	1	0	0	0	1.000	1.00
Burnitz,Jeromy	Col	69	64	517.0	114	3	3	0	.975	2.04
Byrnes,Eric	Oak	33	22	215.1	62	3	1	0	.985	2.72
Cabrera,J	Sea	1	1	6.0	4	1	0	1	1.000	7.50
Church,Ryan	Mon	2	2	16.0	7	0	0	0	1.000	3.94
Clark,Brady	Mil	9	7	63.0	22	1	0	1	1.000	3.29
Clark,Jermaine	Cin	1	0	1.0	0	0	0	0	-	.00
Conti,Jason	Tex	20	14	131.2	45	0	0	0	1.000	3.08
Crawford,Carl	TB	30	25	225.0	76	0	1	0	.987	3.04
Crespo,Cesar	Bos	7	2	29.0	10	0	0	0	1.000	3.10
Crosby,Bu	NYY	12	5	59.0	19	0	1	0	.950	2.90
Cruz,Jo	TB	1	1	9.0	3	0	0	0	1.000	3.00
DaVanon,Jeff	Ana	39	27	247.2	75	1	0	1	1.000	2.76
Dellucci,David	Tex	7	4	45.2	14	0	0	0	1.000	2.76
DeVore,Doug	Ari	1	0	1.0	1	0	0	0	1.000	9.00
Drew,J.D.	Atl	8	5	49.0	19	1	0	0	1.000	3.67
Duncan,Jeff	NYM	2	2	17.0	6	0	0	0	1.000	3.18
Ellison,Jason	SF	4	0	10.0	5	0	0	0	1.000	4.50
Escobar,Alex	Cle	21	21	188.1	53	3	0	1	1.000	2.68
Figgins,Chone	Ana	54	35	336.0	92	0	1	0	.989	2.46
Finley,Steve	Ari	103	102	896.1	214	5	2	3	.991	2.20
Finley,Steve	LA	55	55	484.2	145	0	1	0	.993	2.69
Ford,Lew	Min	46	35	341.0	101	1	3	0	.971	2.69
Freel,Ryan	Cin	42	29	271.1	76	4	1	1	.988	2.65
Freeman,Choo	Col	41	24	245.0	69	1	1	0	.986	2.57
Garcia,Karim	Bal	15	12	99.2	24	0	0	0	1.000	2.17
Gathright,Joey	TB	11	11	96.0	27	0	0	0	1.000	2.53
Gerut,Jody	Cle	12	11	100.0	25	0	0	0	1.000	2.25
Gipson,Charles	TB	2	0	5.0	3	0	0	0	1.000	5.40
Glanville,Doug	Phi	56	24	286.0	90	0	0	0	1.000	2.83
Gload,Ross	CWS	1	1	6.1	2	0	0	0	1.000	2.84
Gomez,Alexis	KC	2	0	3.0	1	0	0	0	1.000	3.00
Goodwin,Tom	ChC	8	7	59.2	14	0	0	0	1.000	2.11
Granderson,C	Det	8	7	61.0	16	1	0	0	1.000	2.51
Guerrero,W	KC	2	0	4.0	0	0	0	0	-	.00
Guzman,Freddy	SD	17	16	139.0	46	2	2	0	.960	3.11
Hairston Jr.,J	Bal	15	15	127.2	35	0	0	0	1.000	2.47
Hammonds,J	SF	1	1	9.0	2	0	0	0	1.000	2.00
Harris,Willie	CWS	29	25	222.2	55	1	1	0	.982	2.26
Hocking,Denny	Col	8	3	37.1	16	0	0	0	1.000	3.86
Infante,Omar	Det	5	3	32.0	10	0	0	0	1.000	2.81
Inge,Brandon	Det	19	14	136.0	35	2	0	1	1.000	2.45
Jackson,Damian	KC	1	0	1.0	1	0	0	0	1.000	9.00
Johnson,Re	Tor	33	29	265.0	82	1	0	0	1.000	2.82
Jones,Jacque	Min	2	1	9.0	4	0	0	0	1.000	4.00
Kapler,Gabe	Bos	17	9	92.0	24	1	2	0	.926	2.45
Kearns,Austin	Cin	1	0	1.1	0	0	0	0	-	.00
Kroeger,Josh	Ari	2	2	14.0	7	0	0	0	1.000	4.50
Krynzel,Dave	Mil	2	2	18.0	8	0	0	0	1.000	4.00
Lane,Jason	Hou	17	3	49.0	8	0	0	0	1.000	1.47
Lankford,Ray	StL	4	2	21.0	3	0	0	0	1.000	1.29
Ledee,Ricky	Phi	13	12	100.1	38	3	0	1	1.000	3.68
Ledee,Ricky	SF	3	2	19.0	6	0	0	0	1.000	2.84
Little,Mark	Cle	5	2	22.2	5	0	0	0	1.000	1.99
Lofton,Kenny	NYY	65	62	539.1	162	3	1	3	.994	2.75
Logan,Nook	Det	46	41	359.2	117	3	2	1	.984	3.00
Long,Terrence	SD	28	25	198.1	49	1	0	0	1.000	2.27
Luna,Hector	StL	2	1	10.0	2	0	0	0	1.000	1.80
Mabry,John	StL	1	0	0.2	0	0	0	0	-	.00
Macias,Jose	ChC	7	3	30.0	4	0	0	0	1.000	1.20
Mackowiak,Rob	Pit	19	15	123.0	27	1	1	0	.966	2.05
Majewski,Val	Bal	3	2	16.2	8	0	0	0	1.000	4.32
Marrero,Eli	Atl	4	0	9.0	0	0	0	0	-	.00
Mateo,Ruben	Pit	5	5	37.1	8	1	0	1	1.000	2.17
Mateo,Ruben	KC	5	5	41.0	12	0	0	0	1.000	2.63
Matsui,Hideki	NYY	3	2	15.0	4	0	0	0	1.000	2.40
Matthews Jr.,G	Tex	30	25	221.2	69	3	0	0	1.000	2.92
McCracken,Q	Sea	4	4	34.0	8	1	0	0	1.000	2.38
McCracken,Q	Ari	3	0	4.1	3	0	0	0	1.000	6.23
McDonald,D	Bal	4	3	28.0	6	0	0	0	1.000	1.93
McEwing,Joe	NYM	6	4	38.0	14	0	0	0	1.000	3.32
Mench,Kevin	Tex	5	5	37.0	13	0	0	0	1.000	3.16
Michaels,Jason	Phi	44	40	323.0	95	1	3	0	.970	2.67
Mohr,Dustan	SF	6	4	32.0	9	0	0	0	1.000	2.53

Player	Tm	G	GS	Inn	PO	A	E	DP	Pct.	Rng
Mondesi,Raul	Ana	7	7	71.0	20	1	0	0	1.000	2.66
Monroe,Craig	Det	27	20	189.0	49	1	0	0	1.000	2.38
Murray,Calvin	ChC	5	0	8.0	5	0	0	0	1.000	5.63
Nady,Xavier	SD	4	4	28.2	5	0	0	0	1.000	1.57
Nivar,Ramon	Tex	6	6	50.0	12	1	0	0	1.000	2.34
Nunez,Abr	KC	4	3	28.0	6	2	0	0	1.000	2.57
Olson,Tim	Ari	2	1	10.2	4	0	0	0	1.000	3.38
Palmeiro,O	Hou	4	3	27.0	8	0	0	0	1.000	2.67
Pena,Wily Mo	Cin	46	44	378.1	143	4	3	0	.980	3.50
Perez,Ti	CWS	25	22	179.2	44	2	1	1	.979	2.30
Piedra,Jorge	Col	18	12	103.2	32	1	0	1	1.000	2.86
Porter,Colin	StL	2	0	2.2	0	0	0	0	-	.00
Pride,Curtis	Ana	2	1	8.0	3	0	0	0	1.000	3.38
Punto,Nick	Min	2	1	13.0	2	1	0	0	1.000	2.08
Raines Jr,Tim	Bal	27	16	159.1	44	1	0	0	1.000	2.54
Reed,Jeremy	Sea	16	14	123.1	50	0	1	0	.980	3.65
Relaford,Desi	KC	3	0	14.0	2	0	0	0	1.000	1.29
Reyes,Rene	Col	16	8	96.1	25	0	0	0	1.000	2.34
Rios,Alexis	Tor	3	2	21.0	1	0	0	0	1.000	.43
Rivera,Juan	Mon	13	10	97.1	24	0	0	0	1.000	2.22
Roberts,Dave	LA	19	12	132.0	41	2	1	1	.977	2.93
Roberts,Dave	Bos	16	6	74.0	18	0	0	0	1.000	2.19
Robinson,Kerry	SD	9	6	48.0	14	0	0	0	1.000	2.63
Rolls,Damian	TB	5	4	35.0	13	0	0	0	1.000	3.34
Romano,Jason	Cin	5	3	26.2	8	0	0	0	1.000	2.70
Ryan,Mike	Min	2	1	13.0	3	0	0	0	1.000	2.08
Sadler,Donnie	StL	3	0	7.0	1	0	0	0	1.000	1.29
Sizemore,Grady	Cle	42	38	348.1	105	0	1	0	.991	2.71
Sledge,Terrmel	Mon	4	1	15.0	7	0	0	0	1.000	4.20
Spencer,Shane	NYM	6	6	50.0	16	2	1	0	.947	3.24
Swisher,Nick	Oak	1	1	1.0	0	0	0	0	-	.00
Taguchi,So	StL	31	18	176.2	43	0	0	0	1.000	2.19
Taveras,Willy	Hou	4	0	6.0	1	0	0	0	1.000	1.50
Terrero,Luis	Ari	57	55	488.2	111	5	6	3	.951	2.14
Thomas,Charles	Atl	1	0	1.0	1	0	0	0	1.000	9.00
Torres,Andres	Det	1	0	1.0	0	0	0	0	-	.00
Tucker,Michael	SF	25	17	168.0	52	1	2	1	.964	2.84
Walker,Larry	StL	1	0	1.0	0	0	0	0	-	.00
Werth,Jayson	LA	6	4	44.0	11	0	0	0	1.000	2.25
Wilkerson,Brad	Mon	18	16	140.0	46	3	1	0	.980	3.15
Williams,G	NYM	20	18	160.0	38	1	0	0	1.000	2.19
Wilson,Pr	Col	52	51	436.0	118	3	6	1	.953	2.50
Wise,Dewayne	Atl	7	4	44.0	11	0	0	0	1.000	2.25
Young,Eri	Tex	9	9	78.0	19	1	0	0	1.000	2.31

Right Fielders - Regulars

Player	Tm	G	GS	Inn	PO	A	E	DP	Pct.	Rng
Clark,Brady	Mil	123	77	784.2	219	4	4	2	.982	2.56
Suzuki,Ichiro	Sea	158	158	1405.1	372	12	3	2	.992	2.46
Guerrero,V	Ana	143	143	1234.0	308	13	9	2	.973	2.34
Jones,Jacque	Min	141	138	1237.0	314	5	2	2	.994	2.32
Tucker,Michael	SF	106	97	838.0	209	1	4	2	.981	2.26
Cruz,Jo	TB	151	147	1301.2	312	10	10	0	.970	2.23
Gerut,Jody	Cle	118	109	1009.1	242	7	4	0	.984	2.22
Rios,Alexis	Tor	108	107	943.2	217	11	2	4	.991	2.17
Drew,J.D.	Atl	138	137	1193.0	277	11	3	0	.990	2.17
Higginson,B	Det	115	110	979.1	223	13	6	1	.975	2.17
Giles,Brian	SD	159	158	1383.0	323	8	7	3	.979	2.15
Sheffield,Gary	NYY	136	136	1178.2	270	11	5	3	.983	2.15
Hidalgo,R	TOT	139	132	1160.2	259	14	6	3	.978	2.12
Encarnacion,J	TOT	125	123	1072.0	247	5	6	0	.977	2.12
Wilson,Craig	Pit	89	78	627.2	145	3	3	0	.980	2.11
Abreu,Bobby	Phi	158	157	1394.2	311	13	6	4	.982	2.09
Bautista,Da	Ari	135	135	1178.2	265	8	4	1	.986	2.08
Rivera,Juan	Mon	104	74	721.2	151	13	3	3	.982	2.05
Sosa,Sammy	ChC	124	124	1097.2	238	5	4	2	.984	1.99
Dye,Jermaine	Oak	134	132	1178.0	257	3	2	2	.992	1.99
Walker,Larry	TOT	75	69	604.0	121	5	1	1	.992	1.88
Sanders,Reggie	StL	81	76	652.0	132	4	3	0	.978	1.88
Cabrera,Miguel	Fla	100	100	856.0	170	6	7	1	.962	1.85
Berkman,Lance	Hou	90	89	780.1	148	9	0	1	1.000	1.81

Right Fielders - The Rest

Player	Tm	G	GS	Inn	PO	A	E	DP	Pct.	Rng
Aguila,Chris	Fla	14	6	70.0	16	1	2	0	.895	2.19
Allen,Chad	Tex	1	1	9.0	1	0	0	0	1.000	1.00
Alvarez,Tony	Pit	9	4	36.0	7	0	0	0	1.000	1.75
Anderson,M	StL	11	4	32.2	8	0	2	0	.800	2.20
Bautista,Jose	Bal	6	2	24.0	4	1	0	0	1.000	1.88
Bautista,Jose	TB	3	0	3.1	0	0	0	0	-	.00
Bautista,Jose	KC	1	0	1.0	0	0	0	0	-	.00
Bautista,Jose	Pit	9	8	61.0	13	0	1	0	.929	1.92
Berg,Dave	Tor	1	0	3.0	1	0	0	0	1.000	3.00
Berger,Brandon	KC	1	0	1.0	0	0	0	0	-	.00
Bocachica,H	Sea	12	2	34.0	5	0	0	0	1.000	1.32
Borchard,Joe	CWS	54	52	460.2	99	4	3	0	.972	2.01
Bradley,Milton	LA	31	31	267.2	66	5	4	0	.947	2.39
Bragg,Darren	Cin	11	7	71.0	17	2	0	0	1.000	2.41
Brown,Adrian	KC	1	0	2.0	0	0	0	0	-	.00
Buchanan,Brian	SD	3	1	11.2	2	0	0	0	1.000	1.54
Burke,Jamie	CWS	2	1	10.0	2	0	0	0	1.000	1.80
Burnitz,Jeromy	Col	79	56	527.1	105	6	3	1	.974	1.89
Byrnes,Eric	Oak	20	17	154.0	30	1	0	0	1.000	1.81
Cabrera,J	Sea	1	0	2.0	0	0	0	0	-	.00
Calloway,Ron	Mon	15	11	96.2	25	0	0	0	1.000	2.33
Cedeno,Roger	StL	35	23	202.0	29	0	0	0	1.000	1.29
Cepicky,Matt	Mon	2	2	16.0	9	0	0	0	1.000	5.06
Church,Ryan	Mon	6	3	38.0	12	1	0	0	1.000	3.08
Clark,Howie	Tor	11	10	66.2	17	0	1	0	.944	2.30
Clark,Jermaine	Cin	6	3	32.0	9	1	0	0	1.000	2.81
Crespo,Cesar	Bos	2	1	9.0	1	0	0	0	1.000	1.00
Crosby,Bu	NYY	25	1	54.0	14	0	0	0	1.000	2.33
Cruz,Jr	Cin	26	17	160.1	35	1	0	0	1.000	2.02
Cuddyer,Mike	Min	8	5	49.0	13	0	0	0	1.000	2.39
Daubach,Brian	Bos	1	1	8.0	1	0	0	0	1.000	1.13
DaVanon,Jeff	Ana	29	11	126.1	26	1	0	1	1.000	1.92
Davis,JJ	Pit	12	7	61.0	14	1	1	0	.938	2.21
DeJesus,David	KC	6	3	32.0	6	0	0	0	1.000	1.69
Dellucci,David	Tex	6	5	43.1	11	0	0	0	1.000	2.28
DeVore,Doug	Ari	15	10	100.2	25	0	0	0	1.000	2.24
Diaz,Matt	TB	1	1	9.0	3	0	0	0	1.000	3.00
Diaz,Victor	NYM	14	12	108.0	29	0	2	0	.935	2.42
Dubois,Jason	ChC	4	2	20.0	5	0	0	0	1.000	2.25
Easley,Damion	Fla	5	4	32.0	10	0	1	0	.909	2.81
Encarnacion,J	LA	77	77	673.1	151	3	4	0	.975	2.06
Encarnacion,J	Fla	48	46	398.2	96	2	2	0	.980	2.21
Escobar,Alex	Cle	16	16	129.0	29	6	1	2	.972	2.44
Everett,Carl	Mon	14	14	112.0	37	1	1	0	.974	3.05
Feliz,Pedro	SF	2	0	4.0	0	0	0	0	-	.00
Fick,Robert	TB	8	7	55.0	20	0	0	0	1.000	3.27
Figgins,Chone	Ana	2	1	10.0	4	1	0	0	1.000	4.50
Ford,Lew	Min	10	9	85.0	18	1	0	0	1.000	2.01
Fox,Andy	Tex	1	0	2.0	1	0	0	0	1.000	4.50
Freel,Ryan	Cin	46	26	265.0	79	3	2	2	.976	2.78
Garcia,Karim	NYM	51	44	386.1	91	0	3	0	.968	2.12
Garcia,Karim	Bal	7	4	44.2	9	0	0	0	1.000	1.81
Gathright,Joey	TB	1	1	8.0	0	0	0	0	-	.00
Gettis,Byron	KC	10	5	48.0	13	1	1	0	.933	2.63
Gibbons,Jay	Bal	66	63	556.1	116	6	2	1	.984	1.97
Ginter,Keith	Mil	2	2	15.0	5	0	0	0	1.000	3.00
Gload,Ross	CWS	22	15	137.1	37	1	2	0	.950	2.49
Gomez,Alexis	KC	5	2	26.0	9	0	0	0	1.000	3.12
Gonzalez,Ju	KC	29	29	237.0	52	3	3	1	.948	2.09
Gonzalez,LA	Col	11	9	75.2	13	0	0	0	1.000	1.55
Gonzalez,Raul	Cle	3	2	17.0	7	0	0	0	1.000	3.71
Goodwin,Tom	ChC	7	1	25.2	4	0	0	0	1.000	1.40
Grabowski,J	LA	3	0	11.0	6	0	0	0	1.000	4.91
Green,Nick	Atl	1	0	1.0	0	0	0	0	-	.00
Green,Shawn	LA	52	46	427.1	81	2	2	1	.976	1.75
Grieve,Ben	Mil	65	64	470.1	106	0	4	0	.964	2.03
Grieve,Ben	ChC	3	2	12.2	2	0	0	0	1.000	1.42
Griffey Jr.,K	Cin	1	1	4.0	0	0	0	0	-	.00
Guiel,Aaron	KC	1	0	1.0	0	0	0	0	-	.00
Guillen,Jose	Ana	4	1	22.0	4	0	0	0	1.000	1.64
Hairston,Scott	Ari	2	0	2.2	0	0	0	0	-	.00
Hairston Jr.,J	Bal	27	24	210.1	53	2	0	1	1.000	2.35
Hammonds,J	SF	20	16	149.1	39	2	0	0	1.000	2.47
Harris,Lenny	Fla	6	3	21.1	3	0	0	0	1.000	1.27
Hawpe,Brad	Col	32	29	233.0	52	1	1	1	.981	2.05
Hidalgo,R	Hou	56	51	452.1	107	4	2	0	.982	2.21

Player	Tm	G	GS	Inn	PO	A	E	DP	Pct.	Rng
Hidalgo,R	NYM	83	81	708.1	152	10	4	3	.976	2.06
Hocking,Denny	Col	4	1	10.2	4	0	0	0	1.000	3.38
Hollandsworth,T	ChC	32	26	232.1	54	2	0	0	1.000	2.17
Hollins,Damon	Atl	1	1	8.0	1	0	0	0	1.000	1.13
Huff,Aubrey	TB	1	1	1.0	0	0	0	0	-	.00
Hyzdu,Adam	Bos	4	0	5.0	0	0	0	0	-	.00
Ibanez,Raul	Sea	3	2	18.0	2	0	0	0	1.000	1.00
Inge,Brandon	Det	2	0	5.0	1	1	0	0	1.000	3.60
Jackson,Damian	KC	3	0	8.0	1	0	0	0	1.000	1.13
Johnson,Re	Tor	53	41	382.2	88	3	1	0	.989	2.14
Jordan,Brian	Tex	44	40	358.2	94	1	1	0	.990	2.38
Kapler,Gabe	Bos	101	59	590.2	133	5	2	0	.986	2.10
Kearns,Austin	Cin	60	59	508.1	118	1	3	0	.975	2.11
Kelton,Dave	ChC	1	0	2.2	0	0	0	0	-	.00
Kielty,Bobby	Oak	21	10	109.1	26	0	0	0	1.000	2.14
Kroeger,Josh	Ari	8	5	46.1	9	0	0	0	1.000	1.75
Krynzel,Dave	Mil	8	7	60.0	21	1	1	1	.957	3.30
Kubel,Jason	Min	8	4	44.0	11	0	0	0	1.000	2.25
Lane,Jason	Hou	24	13	140.2	28	0	0	0	1.000	1.79
LaRue,Jason	Cin	1	0	2.0	1	0	0	0	1.000	4.50
Lawton,Matt	Cle	19	18	167.2	35	2	1	1	.974	1.99
Ledee,Ricky	Phi	1	0	1.0	1	0	0	0	1.000	9.00
Ledee,Ricky	SF	11	8	72.0	17	0	1	0	.944	2.13
Liefer,Jeff	Mil	3	3	25.0	4	0	0	0	1.000	1.44
Linden,Todd	SF	4	1	16.1	3	0	0	0	1.000	1.65
Little,Mark	Cle	4	4	24.0	5	0	0	0	1.000	1.88
Lofton,Kenny	NYY	10	5	52.0	18	1	1	1	.950	3.29
Long,Terrence	SD	9	1	29.1	6	0	0	0	1.000	1.84
Lopez,Me	KC	2	1	13.0	6	0	1	0	.857	4.15
Ludwick,Ryan	Cle	15	13	119.2	32	0	1	0	.970	2.41
Mabry,John	StL	25	12	114.1	21	0	0	0	1.000	1.65
Macias,Jose	ChC	13	7	72.1	21	2	0	0	1.000	2.86
Mackowiak,Rob	Pit	79	40	438.2	78	6	3	3	.966	1.72
Magruder,Chris	Mil	16	8	87.0	23	0	0	0	1.000	2.38
Majewski,Val	Bal	1	1	9.0	3	0	0	0	1.000	3.00
Marrero,Eli	Atl	25	18	171.0	41	2	0	0	1.000	2.26
Mateo,Ruben	Pit	4	2	20.1	4	0	0	0	1.000	1.77
Mateo,Ruben	KC	15	8	82.0	19	1	0	0	1.000	2.20
Matthews Jr.,G	Tex	66	51	476.1	119	4	2	1	.984	2.32
McCarty,Dave	Bos	7	1	21.0	7	0	0	0	1.000	3.00
McCracken,Q	Ari	10	8	69.0	14	1	1	0	.938	1.96
McDonald,D	Bal	5	8	48.1	14	0	0	0	1.000	2.61
McEwing,Joe	NYM	1	1	7.0	4	0	0	0	1.000	5.14
McMillon,Billy	Oak	1	0	2.0	0	0	0	0	-	.00
Mench,Kevin	Tex	62	60	500.2	127	5	0	2	1.000	2.37
Michaels,Jason	Phi	12	5	67.0	22	1	0	0	1.000	3.09
Millar,Kevin	Bos	55	53	425.2	96	1	3	0	.970	2.05
Mohr,Dustan	SF	55	40	377.1	89	4	3	1	.969	2.22
Mondesi,Raul	Pit	12	12	105.0	23	2	1	0	.962	2.14
Monroe,Craig	Det	51	45	386.0	110	3	3	1	.974	2.63
Mottola,Chad	Bal	2	2	17.0	3	0	0	0	1.000	1.59
Murray,Calvin	ChC	2	0	2.0	0	0	0	0	-	.00
Nady,Xavier	SD	2	2	14.0	2	0	0	0	1.000	1.29
Newhan,David	Bal	24	21	190.2	32	3	0	0	1.000	1.65
Nix,Laynce	Tex	3	1	13.0	3	0	0	0	1.000	2.08
Nixon,Trot	Bos	40	36	306.0	63	1	1	0	.985	1.88
Nunez,Abr	Fla	20	3	61.0	15	0	0	0	1.000	2.21
Nunez,Abr	KC	54	54	459.1	129	1	1	0	.992	2.55
Olson,Tim	Ari	1	0	3.0	0	0	0	0	-	.00
Ordonez,M	CWS	43	43	364.0	95	0	1	0	.990	2.35
Palmeiro,O	Hou	13	9	68.2	12	0	0	0	1.000	1.57
Pascucci,Val	Mon	13	12	93.1	25	0	0	0	1.000	2.41
Pellow,Kit	Col	27	16	145.0	20	2	0	1	1.000	1.37
Pena,Wily Mo	Cin	51	41	339.2	69	1	4	0	.946	1.85
Perez,Edu	TB	1	1	8.0	3	0	0	0	1.000	3.38
Perez,Ti	CWS	49	43	383.2	83	5	0	3	1.000	2.06
Piedra,Jorge	Col	7	1	23.2	5	0	0	0	1.000	1.90
Pond,Simon	Tor	3	3	25.0	8	0	0	0	1.000	2.88
Porter,Colin	StL	8	4	39.0	7	0	0	0	1.000	1.62
Pride,Curtis	Ana	7	1	16.0	7	0	0	0	1.000	3.94
Quinlan,Robb	Ana	3	0	7.0	1	0	0	0	1.000	1.29
Raines Jr,Tim	Bal	10	5	54.0	15	1	0	0	1.000	2.67
Relaford,Desi	KC	9	6	55.2	10	0	0	0	1.000	1.62
Restovich,Mike	Min	7	4	41.0	7	0	0	0	1.000	1.54
Reyes,Rene	Col	4	4	35.0	5	1	0	1	1.000	1.54
Roberts,Dave	Bos	14	11	86.0	25	1	1	1	.963	2.72
Robinson,Kerry	SD	2	0	3.0	0	0	0	0	-	.00
Rolls,Damian	TB	5	3	31.0	8	1	0	0	1.000	2.61
Romano,Jason	Cin	6	1	18.1	1	1	0	0	1.000	.98

Player	Tm	G	GS	Inn	PO	A	E	DP	Pct.	Rng
Rowand,Aaron	CWS	12	8	76.2	14	2	2	0	.889	1.88
Ryan,Mike	Min	3	2	20.0	7	0	1	0	.875	3.15
Sadler,Donnie	Min	1	0	1.2	0	0	0	0	-	.00
Salmon,Tim	Ana	6	5	39.0	15	1	0	0	1.000	3.69
Shelton,Chris	Det	1	0	1.0	1	0	0	0	1.000	9.00
Sierra,Ruben	NYY	22	20	159.0	37	1	1	0	.974	2.15
Sledge,Terrmel	Mon	43	37	293.1	76	1	0	0	1.000	2.36
Spencer,Shane	NYM	20	12	109.0	37	0	0	0	1.000	3.06
Stairs,Matt	KC	57	54	450.1	108	3	1	0	.991	2.22
Surhoff,B.J.	Bal	38	35	301.0	65	3	1	2	.986	2.03
Sweeney,Ma	Col	20	17	118.1	29	2	0	1	1.000	2.36
Swisher,Nick	Oak	4	3	28.0	5	0	2	0	.714	1.61
Taguchi,So	StL	28	3	76.1	16	1	0	0	1.000	2.00
Taveras,Willy	Hou	1	0	1.0	0	0	0	0	-	.00
Teixeira,Mark	Tex	7	4	36.2	8	0	0	0	1.000	1.96
Terrero,Luis	Ari	4	4	34.0	6	0	2	0	.750	1.59
Thames,Marcus	Det	12	7	68.1	16	0	0	0	1.000	2.11
Thomas,Charles	Atl	2	1	11.0	4	1	0	0	1.000	4.09
Thompson,Rich	KC	2	0	4.0	2	0	0	0	1.000	4.50
Valent,Eric	NYM	14	8	91.1	20	0	0	0	1.000	1.97
Vander Wal,J	Cin	7	7	43.0	12	1	0	0	1.000	2.72
Walker,Larry	Col	34	29	266.2	63	4	0	1	1.000	2.26
Walker,Larry	StL	41	40	337.1	58	1	1	0	.983	1.57
Ward,Daryle	Pit	12	10	78.1	10	0	0	0	1.000	1.15
Werth,Jayson	LA	14	8	74.0	19	0	0	0	1.000	2.31
Wilkerson,Brad	Mon	10	9	76.0	19	1	0	1	1.000	2.37
Williams,G	NYM	7	4	39.0	4	0	0	0	1.000	.92
Wise,Dewayne	Atl	15	5	66.0	10	0	0	0	1.000	1.36

Catchers - Regulars

Player	Tm	G	GS	Inn	PO	A	E	DP	PB	Pct.
Matheny,Mike	StL	122	110	977.2	742	58	1	10	2	.999
Moeller,Chad	Mil	100	92	827.0	718	47	1	4	4	.999
Pierzynski,A	SF	118	117	1022.0	697	56	1	6	9	.999
Miller,Damian	Oak	109	109	963.2	702	49	1	4	9	.999
Phillips,Jason	NYM	87	72	650.1	486	37	1	4	3	.998
Varitek,Jason	Bos	130	121	1062.2	880	49	2	12	5	.998
Schneider,B	Mon	135	125	1114.0	814	59	2	16	4	.998
Wilson,Dan	Sea	103	91	827.1	611	37	2	6	0	.997
Redmond,Mike	Fla	79	71	604.1	488	33	2	8	4	.996
Lo Duca,Paul	TOT	125	115	1104.2	844	65	4	9	12	.996
Molina,Ben	Ana	89	89	762.0	597	56	3	5	6	.995
Ausmus,Brad	Hou	128	114	1018.1	921	61	5	10	2	.995
Barrett,M	ChC	130	119	1081.1	1035	47	6	9	8	.994
Lopez,Javy	Bal	132	125	1092.1	848	49	5	12	10	.994
Martinez,V	Cle	132	124	1108.0	865	62	6	13	9	.994
Lieberthal,M	Phi	129	123	1104.0	859	43	6	7	6	.993
Hernandez,Ra	SD	108	106	925.1	753	35	6	7	7	.992
Hall,Toby	TB	119	115	1011.1	687	37	6	4	7	.992
Olivo,Miguel	TOT	95	83	760.1	510	29	5	7	13	.991
Kendall,Jason	Pit	146	145	1259.0	998	78	10	13	2	.991
Blanco,Henry	Min	95	85	872.1	686	44	7	8	5	.991
Posada,Jorge	NYY	134	126	1102.1	835	53	9	14	9	.990
Barajas,Rod	Tex	105	102	908.2	656	23	7	2	7	.990
Estrada,Johnny	Atl	133	120	1042.0	776	44	9	9	8	.989
LaRue,Jason	Cin	111	106	930.0	648	59	8	8	15	.989
Johnson,C	Col	91	85	746.1	523	44	7	8	7	.988
Rodriguez,Ivan	Det	125	124	1051.0	770	52	11	7	3	.987
Zaun,Gregg	Tor	97	91	789.0	547	46	8	5	3	.987

Catchers - The Rest

Player	Tm	G	GS	Inn	PO	A	E	DP	PB	Pct.
Alomar Jr.,S	CWS	49	46	377.0	277	16	3	2	4	.990
Ardoin,Danny	Tex	6	2	25.0	21	2	1	0	1	.958
Bako,Paul	ChC	47	43	377.2	332	30	4	2	1	.989
Bard,Josh	Cle	7	6	53.0	47	4	0	1	0	1.000
Bennett,Gary	Mil	75	65	584.0	379	32	3	3	3	.993
Borders,Pat	Sea	19	17	138.0	121	9	1	1	1	.992
Borders,Pat	Min	19	14	120.2	82	9	3	3	0	.968
Bowen,Rob	Min	13	8	81.2	65	1	1	1	0	.985
Brito,Juan	Ari	54	53	461.2	386	29	4	2	6	.990
Buck,John	KC	68	66	575.0	376	14	3	4	7	.992
Burke,Jamie	CWS	45	32	292.0	215	11	3	1	1	.987

Player	Tm	G	GS	Inn	PO	A	E	DP	PB	Pct.
Cash,Kevin	Tor	60	50	460.1	317	35	2	5	5	.994
Castillo,A	KC	29	28	242.1	199	11	1	1	1	.995
Castro,RR	Fla	31	27	243.0	193	11	2	2	0	.990
Chavez,Raul	Hou	61	48	423.2	396	28	4	3	2	.991
Closser,J.D.	Col	32	29	259.0	196	16	3	4	6	.986
Cota,Humberto	Pit	24	13	133.0	101	4	1	1	0	.991
Davis,Ben	Sea	14	11	97.0	71	5	0	3	1	1.000
Davis,Ben	CWS	53	44	397.0	330	16	3	1	5	.991
Diaz,Einar	Mon	44	37	333.0	264	19	3	6	3	.990
DiFelice,Mike	Det	12	4	59.0	40	6	0	1	0	1.000
DiFelice,Mike	ChC	4	0	6.1	6	0	0	0	0	1.000
Dominique,Andy	Bos	1	0	2.0	1	0	0	0	0	1.000
Estalella,B	Ari	6	3	30.2	19	2	0	0	0	1.000
Estalella,B	Tor	3	3	25.0	20	1	0	0	0	1.000
Fick,Robert	TB	3	0	5.0	3	1	0	0	0	1.000
Flaherty,John	NYY	46	35	328.1	256	18	3	3	4	.989
Fordyce,Brook	TB	51	46	400.2	274	11	3	4	1	.990
Gil,Geronimo	Bal	11	8	78.0	64	4	0	1	0	1.000
Greene,Todd	Col	53	48	421.0	258	15	3	2	2	.989
Hammock,Robby	Ari	46	42	376.2	313	21	1	8	5	.997
Hietpas,Joe	NYM	1	0	1.0	2	0	0	0	0	1.000
Hill,Koyie	Ari	11	10	83.0	57	5	1	0	0	.984
Hinch,A.J.	Phi	4	1	25.2	14	5	0	0	0	1.000
House,J.R.	Pit	3	2	19.0	17	0	0	0	0	1.000
Huckaby,Ken	Tex	16	12	109.0	81	7	2	1	2	.978
Huckaby,Ken	Bal	8	4	37.0	26	2	0	0	1	1.000
Inge,Brandon	Det	39	34	312.2	209	30	3	1	4	.988
Johnson,Mark L	Mil	5	4	31.0	18	2	1	0	0	.952
Knoedler,J	SF	1	0	2.0	2	0	0	0	0	1.000
Laird,Gerald	Tex	49	46	397.0	276	18	5	6	6	.983
Laker,Tim	Cle	41	31	298.2	233	20	4	0	5	.984
LeCroy,Matt	Min	26	16	144.1	114	4	4	0	1	.967
Lo Duca,Paul	LA	81	78	691.2	514	42	3	4	7	.995
Lo Duca,Paul	Fla	49	47	413.0	330	23	1	5	5	.997
Machado,Robert	Bal	35	19	188.2	157	14	1	6	2	.994
Martinez,Sandy	Cle	1	1	7.0	7	1	0	0	1	1.000
Martinez,Sandy	Bos	3	0	11.0	6	0	0	0	1	1.000
Mauer,Joe	Min	32	29	257.0	212	10	2	0	0	.991
Mayne,Brent	Ari	30	27	236.2	183	18	2	0	4	.990
Mayne,Brent	LA	47	33	293.0	224	12	0	2	2	1.000
McKay,Cody	StL	18	13	132.0	75	12	0	1	3	1.000
Melhuse,Adam	Oak	64	53	504.2	358	18	2	1	5	.995
Miller,Corky	Cin	12	12	104.0	84	5	1	1	1	.989
Mirabelli,Doug	Bos	53	41	375.2	285	18	2	2	15	.993
Molina,Jose	Ana	70	57	524.1	441	37	3	4	3	.994
Molina,Yadier	StL	51	39	344.0	256	16	2	1	4	.993
Mordecai,Mike	Fla	1	0	8.0	9	0	0	0	0	1.000
Munson,Eric	Det	1	0	1.0	0	0	0	0	0	-
Myers,Greg	Tor	4	4	32.0	27	2	0	1	0	1.000
Navarro,Dioner	NYY	4	1	13.0	9	0	0	0	0	1.000
Nevin,Phil	SD	1	0	4.0	4	0	0	0	0	1.000
Ojeda,Miguel	SD	50	37	340.0	240	18	1	2	2	.996
Olivo,Miguel	CWS	46	40	366.1	237	10	4	5	4	.984
Olivo,Miguel	Sea	49	43	394.0	273	19	1	2	9	.997
Osik,Keith	Bal	11	6	59.1	44	3	0	1	2	1.000
Paul,Josh	Ana	37	16	168.0	134	9	1	2	2	.993
Pellow,Kit	Col	4	0	9.0	11	0	0	0	0	1.000
Perez,Edd	Atl	66	42	408.0	290	22	3	4	2	.990
Phillips,Paul	KC	4	1	15.0	11	1	0	0	0	1.000
Piazza,Mike	NYM	50	49	388.1	259	16	5	2	5	.982
Pratt,Todd	Phi	43	38	333.0	259	8	0	2	1	1.000
Quintero,H	SD	21	19	171.2	130	10	0	0	0	1.000
Quiroz,G	Tor	15	13	114.2	76	6	2	3	3	.976
Rivera,Rene	Sea	2	0	3.0	4	0	0	0	0	1.000
Rose,Mike	Oak	2	0	3.0	1	0	0	0	0	1.000
Ross,Dave	LA	67	51	451.2	356	20	3	0	6	.992
Santiago,B	KC	49	48	416.0	228	18	1	3	6	.996
Shelton,Chris	Det	6	0	16.0	10	0	0	0	3	1.000
Snyder,Chris	Ari	29	27	247.1	213	19	0	2	3	1.000
Stinnett,Kelly	KC	20	17	155.0	97	4	3	0	1	.971
Tonis,Mike	KC	2	2	17.0	13	1	0	0	2	1.000
Torrealba,Y	SF	59	45	433.0	350	17	2	5	2	.995
Treanor,Matt	Fla	27	14	147.2	117	6	3	0	0	.976
Tremie,Chris	Hou	1	0	1.0	0	0	0	0	0	-
Valentin,Ja	Cin	55	44	409.2	305	32	4	2	1	.988
Willingham,J	Fla	5	3	23.0	15	0	1	0	2	.938
Wilson,Craig	Pit	4	1	17.0	11	0	0	0	0	1.000
Wilson,Tom	NYM	3	1	11.2	11	0	0	0	1	1.000
Wilson,Tom	LA	7	0	17.0	11	0	0	0	0	1.000

Player	Tm	G	GS	Inn	PO	A	E	DP	PB	Pct.
Wilson,Vance	NYM	69	38	383.2	258	22	2	2	4	.993
Zeile,Todd	NYM	2	2	14.0	12	0	0	0	0	1.000

Catchers Special - Regulars

Player	Tm	G	GS	Inn	SBA	CS	PCS	CS%	ER	CERA
Moeller,Chad	Mil	100	92	827.0	69	17	4	.20	337	3.67
Estrada,Johnny	Atl	133	120	1042.0	86	16	1	.18	436	3.77
Lo Duca,Paul	TOT	130	125	1104.2	129	36	7	.24	470	3.83
Schneider,B	Mon	133	125	1114.0	72	36	3	.48	478	3.86
Phillips,Jason	NYM	87	72	650.1	61	19	7	.22	280	3.87
Matheny,Mike	StL	122	110	977.2	54	16	1	.28	422	3.88
Barrett,M	ChC	130	119	1081.1	96	24	6	.20	467	3.89
Hernandez,Ra	SD	108	106	925.1	74	21	3	.25	412	4.01
Ausmus,Brad	Hou	128	114	1018.1	106	28	5	.23	462	4.08
Varitek,Jason	Bos	130	121	1062.2	100	23	3	.21	494	4.18
Miller,Damian	Oak	109	109	963.2	81	35	17	.28	454	4.24
Blanco,Henry	Min	114	95	872.1	61	30	5	.45	412	4.25
Pierzynski,A	SF	118	117	1022.0	66	15	4	.18	488	4.30
Molina,Ben	Ana	89	89	762.0	69	18	1	.25	365	4.31
Kendall,Jason	Pit	146	145	1259.0	102	37	6	.32	627	4.48
Barajas,Rod	Tex	105	102	908.2	64	22	6	.28	454	4.50
Olivo,Miguel	TOT	95	83	760.1	49	17	6	.26	383	4.53
Redmond,Mike	Fla	79	71	604.1	65	14	3	.18	308	4.59
Posada,Jorge	NYY	134	126	1102.1	92	25	2	.26	570	4.65
Lieberthal,M	Phi	129	123	1104.0	94	20	1	.20	572	4.66
Lopez,Javy	Bal	132	125	1092.1	94	26	6	.23	568	4.68
Hall,Toby	TB	119	115	1011.1	67	23	6	.28	530	4.72
Zaun,Gregg	Tor	97	91	789.0	83	23	2	.26	420	4.79
Wilson,Dan	Sea	103	91	827.1	66	22	4	.29	444	4.83
Rodriguez,Ivan	Det	125	124	1051.0	59	19	3	.29	568	4.86
LaRue,Jason	Cin	111	106	930.0	54	16	0	.30	512	4.95
Martinez,V	Cle	132	124	1108.0	119	30	4	.23	614	4.99
Johnson,C	Col	91	85	746.1	79	16	4	.16	471	5.68

Catchers Special - The Rest

Player	Tm	G	GS	Inn	SBA	CS	PCS	CS%	ER	CERA
Alomar Jr.,S	CWS	49	46	377.0	45	18	11	.21	209	4.99
Ardoin,Danny	Tex	6	2	25.0	4	0	0	.00	10	3.60
Bako,Paul	ChC	47	43	377.2	51	15	0	.29	149	3.55
Bard,Josh	Cle	7	6	53.0	6	2	0	.33	23	3.91
Bennett,Gary	Mil	75	65	584.0	44	11	2	.21	332	5.12
Borders,Pat	Sea	19	17	138.0	13	7	0	.54	77	5.02
Borders,Pat	Min	19	14	120.2	15	5	0	.33	61	4.55
Bowen,Rob	Min	15	8	81.2	7	1	0	.14	36	3.97
Brito,Juan	Ari	54	53	461.2	51	16	4	.26	233	4.54
Buck,John	KC	68	66	575.0	44	14	7	.19	339	5.31
Burke,Jamie	CWS	45	32	292.0	19	8	1	.39	155	4.78
Cash,Kevin	Tor	60	50	460.1	34	15	1	.42	260	5.08
Castillo,A	KC	29	28	242.1	22	8	3	.26	137	5.09
Castro,RR	Fla	31	27	243.0	14	5	0	.36	96	3.56
Chavez,Raul	Hou	61	48	423.2	34	11	1	.30	187	3.97
Closser,J.D.	Col	32	29	259.0	28	9	4	.21	141	4.90
Cota,Humberto	Pit	24	13	133.0	5	1	0	.20	53	3.59
Davis,Ben	Sea	14	11	97.0	4	2	0	.50	59	5.47
Davis,Ben	CWS	53	44	397.0	44	12	3	.22	227	5.15
Diaz,Einar	Mon	44	37	333.0	27	5	0	.19	218	5.89
DiFelice,Mike	Det	12	4	59.0	2	1	0	.50	32	4.88
DiFelice,Mike	ChC	4	0	6.1	0	0	0	-	7	9.95
Dominique,Andy	Bos	1	0	2.0	0	0	0	-	1	4.50
Estalella,B	Ari	6	3	30.2	0	0	0	-	27	7.92
Estalella,B	Tor	3	3	25.0	4	0	0	.00	18	6.48
Fick,Robert	TB	3	0	5.0	0	0	0	-	1	1.80
Flaherty,John	NYY	46	35	328.1	30	7	2	.18	180	4.93
Fordyce,Brook	TB	51	46	400.2	32	9	4	.18	228	5.12
Gil,Geronimo	Bal	11	8	78.0	8	4	1	.43	31	3.58
Greene,Todd	Col	53	48	421.0	36	7	5	.06	269	5.75
Hammock,Robby	Ari	46	42	376.2	39	12	2	.27	165	3.94
Hietpas,Joe	NYM	1	0	1.0	0	0	0	-	0	0.00
Hill,Koyie	Ari	11	10	83.0	12	4	1	.27	74	8.02
Hinch,A.J.	Phi	4	1	25.2	3	2	0	.67	8	2.81
House,J.R.	Pit	3	2	19.0	0	0	0	-	2	0.95
Huckaby,Ken	Tex	16	12	109.0	11	3	0	.27	69	5.70
Huckaby,Ken	Bal	8	4	37.0	4	1	0	.25	20	4.86
Inge,Brandon	Det	39	34	312.2	51	21	3	.38	177	5.09
Johnson,Mark L	Mil	5	4	31.0	5	1	0	.20	14	4.06
Knoedler,J	SF	1	0	2.0	0	0	0	-	0	0.00
Laird,Gerald	Tex	49	46	397.0	31	14	2	.41	194	4.40
Laker,Tim	Cle	41	31	298.2	29	7	0	.24	143	4.31
LeCroy,Matt	Min	26	16	144.1	16	1	0	.06	57	3.55
Lo Duca,Paul	LA	81	78	691.2	75	21	5	.23	303	3.94
Lo Duca,Paul	Fla	49	47	413.0	54	15	2	.25	167	3.64
Machado,Robert	Bal	35	19	188.2	11	7	0	.64	96	4.58
Martinez,Sandy	Cle	1	1	7.0	3	1	0	.33	5	6.43
Martinez,Sandy	Bos	3	0	11.0	0	0	0	-	1	0.82
Mauer,Joe	Min	32	29	257.0	18	7	2	.31	97	3.40
Mayne,Brent	Ari	30	27	236.2	26	12	3	.39	177	6.73
Mayne,Brent	LA	47	33	293.0	21	6	2	.21	123	3.78
McKay,Cody	StL	18	13	132.0	11	5	0	.45	44	3.00
Melhuse,Adam	Oak	64	53	504.2	40	13	5	.23	227	4.05
Miller,Corky	Cin	12	12	104.0	3	1	0	.33	73	6.32
Mirabelli,Doug	Bos	53	41	375.2	54	8	1	.13	180	4.31
Molina,Jose	Ana	70	57	524.1	45	22	3	.45	251	4.31
Molina,Yadier	StL	51	39	344.0	17	8	0	.47	139	3.64
Mordecai,Mike	Fla	1	0	8.0	4	0	0	.00	4	4.50
Munson,Eric	Det	1	1	1.0	0	0	0	-	0	0.00
Myers,Greg	Tor	4	4	32.0	4	1	0	.25	12	3.38
Navarro,Dioner	NYY	4	1	13.0	0	0	0	-	2	1.38
Nevin,Phil	SD	1	0	4.0	0	0	0	-	0	0.00
Ojeda,Miguel	SD	50	37	340.0	11	3	0	.27	163	4.31
Olivo,Miguel	CWS	40	40	366.1	30	10	3	.26	191	4.69
Olivo,Miguel	Sea	49	43	394.0	19	7	3	.25	192	4.39
Osik,Keith	Bal	11	6	59.1	4	1	0	.25	46	6.98
Paul,Josh	Ana	37	16	168.0	17	4	0	.24	76	4.07
Pellow,Kit	Col	4	0	9.0	0	0	0	-	2	2.00
Perez,Edd	Atl	66	42	408.0	34	13	2	.34	168	3.71
Phillips,Paul	KC	4	1	15.0	0	0	0	-	12	7.20
Piazza,Mike	NYM	50	49	388.1	43	9	2	.17	172	3.99
Pratt,Todd	Phi	43	38	333.0	32	4	0	.13	146	3.95
Quintero,H	SD	21	19	171.2	9	1	0	.11	70	3.67
Quiroz,G	Tor	15	13	114.2	7	2	0	.29	68	5.34
Rivera,Rene	Sea	2	0	3.0	0	0	0	-	0	0.00
Rose,Mike	Oak	2	0	3.0	2	1	1	.00	1	3.00
Ross,Dave	LA	67	51	451.2	39	12	1	.29	213	4.24
Santiago,B	KC	49	48	416.0	36	8	2	.18	215	4.65
Shelton,Chris	Det	6	0	16.0	0	0	0	-	11	6.19
Snyder,Chris	Ari	29	27	247.1	19	6	0	.32	119	4.33
Stinnett,Kelly	KC	20	17	155.0	16	5	3	.15	96	5.57
Tonis,Mike	KC	2	2	17.0	1	0	0	.00	16	8.47
Torrealba,Y	SF	59	45	433.0	30	9	3	.22	215	4.47
Treanor,Matt	Fla	27	14	147.2	14	3	0	.21	72	4.39
Tremie,Chris	Hou	1	1	1.0	0	0	0	-	1	9.00
Valentin,Ja	Cin	55	44	409.2	39	12	0	.31	251	5.51
Willingham,J	Fla	5	3	23.0	5	1	1	.00	8	3.13
Wilson,Craig	Pit	4	1	17.0	3	0	0	.00	2	1.06
Wilson,Tom	NYM	3	1	11.2	3	0	0	.00	11	8.49
Wilson,Tom	LA	7	0	17.0	1	1	1	-	8	4.24
Wilson,Vance	NYM	69	38	383.2	32	11	1	.32	190	4.46
Zeile,Todd	NYM	2	2	14.0	0	0	0	-	7	4.50

Pitchers Hitting, Fielding & Holding Runners,

and Hitters Pitching

Pitchers Hitting, Fielding and Holding Runners

Pitcher	2004 Hitting Avg	AB	H	HR	RBI	SH	Career Hitting Avg	AB	H	2B	3B	HR	RBI	BB	SO	SH	2004 Fielding G	Inn	PO	A	E	DP	Pct	SBA	CS	PCS	PPO	CS%
Aardsma,David, SF	-	0	0	0	0	0	-	0	0	0	0	0	0	0	0	0	11	10.2	0	0	0	0	-	2	0	0	0	.00
Abbott,Paul, TB-Phi	.182	11	2	0	2	3	.250	20	5	1	0	0	2	0	6	5	20	96.0	6	9	2	0	.882	11	2	0	1	.18
Acevedo,Jose, Cin	.047	43	2	0	1	5	.075	93	7	2	0	0	4	4	55	11	39	157.2	4	18	0	1	1.000	8	3	0	0	.38
Adams,Mike, Mil	-	0	0	0	0	0	-	0	0	0	0	0	0	0	0	0	46	53.0	0	5	0	0	1.000	7	1	1	0	.14
Adams,Terry, Tor-Bos	-	0	0	0	0	0	.051	78	4	1	0	0	2	7	41	12	61	70.0	9	4	2	1	.867	5	1	0	0	.20
Adkins,Jon, CWS	-	0	0	0	0	0	-	0	0	0	0	0	0	0	0	0	50	62.0	4	8	1	1	.923	2	1	0	0	.50
Affeldt,Jeremy, KC	-	0	0	0	0	0	.333	6	2	0	0	0	2	1	1	0	38	76.1	3	12	2	2	.882	4	2	0	0	.50
Ainsworth,Kurt, Bal	-	0	0	0	0	0	.071	28	2	1	0	0	0	0	8	5	7	30.2	2	2	0	1	1.000	2	1	0	0	.50
Alfonseca,A, Atl	.000	1	0	0	0	0	.154	13	2	0	0	0	2	0	8	1	79	73.2	3	7	0	0	1.000	10	2	0	0	.20
Almanza,A, Atl	-	0	0	0	0	1	.000	4	0	0	0	0	0	0	2	0	13	11.2	0	1	0	0	1.000	5	0	0	0	.00
Almanzar,C, Tex	-	0	0	0	0	0	.000	4	0	0	0	0	0	0	3	0	67	72.2	1	12	0	0	1.000	3	2	0	0	.67
Alvarez,Abe, Bos	-	0	0	0	0	0	-	0	0	0	0	0	0	0	0	0	1	5.0	1	0	0	0	1.000	1	0	0	0	.00
Alvarez,Wilson, LA	.161	31	5	0	0	2	.135	96	13	0	0	0	1	4	34	4	40	120.2	3	16	0	0	1.000	6	3	0	0	.50
Anderson,Brian, KC	.000	1	0	0	0	1	.137	255	35	5	3	1	10	7	57	22	35	166.0	5	24	1	2	.967	5	4	2	2	.80
Anderson,Ja, Cle	-	0	0	0	0	0	-	0	0	0	0	0	0	0	0	0	1	1.0	0	0	0	0	-	0	0	0	0	-
Anderson,Ji, ChC-Bos	.000	1	0	0	0	0	.135	170	23	3	0	0	6	8	44	15	12	15.2	4	1	0	0	1.000	2	0	0	0	.00
Ankiel,Rick, StL	.000	1	0	0	0	0	.000	1	0	0	0	0	0	1	1	0	5	10.0	1	3	0	0	1.000	0	0	0	0	-
Appier,Kevin, KC	-	0	0	0	0	0	.096	83	8	0	0	0	4	1	39	5	2	4.0	1	1	0	0	1.000	0	0	0	0	-
Aquino,Greg, Ari	.000	1	0	0	0	0	.000	1	0	0	0	0	0	0	0	0	34	35.1	3	4	0	0	1.000	3	1	0	0	.33
Armas Jr.,Tony, Mon	.000	16	0	0	0	5	.102	157	16	1	1	0	7	2	53	19	16	72.0	2	13	0	3	1.000	8	3	1	0	.38
Arroyo,Bronson, Bos	.000	6	0	0	0	1	.074	54	4	2	0	0	1	1	32	3	32	178.2	24	16	2	2	.952	9	5	0	0	.56
Ashby,Andy, SD	-	0	0	0	0	0	.134	521	70	13	0	1	26	16	218	83	2	2.0	0	0	0	0	-	0	0	0	0	-
Astacio,Pedro, Bos	-	0	0	0	0	0	.132	634	84	7	1	0	27	4	243	77	5	8.2	1	0	0	0	1.000	1	0	0	0	.00
Atchison,Scott, Sea	-	0	0	0	0	0	-	0	0	0	0	0	0	0	0	0	25	30.2	2	6	0	1	1.000	3	0	0	0	.00
Ayala,Luis, Mon	.333	9	3	0	0	1	.300	10	3	1	0	0	0	0	3	1	81	90.1	9	21	0	3	1.000	1	0	0	0	.00
Backe,Brandon, Hou	.313	16	5	1	6	3	.313	16	5	0	0	1	6	1	8	3	33	67.0	4	10	0	1	1.000	5	3	0	0	.60
Bacsik,Mike, Tex	-	0	0	0	0	0	.095	21	2	1	0	0	2	0	4	3	3	15.2	1	2	0	0	1.000	1	1	1	0	1.00
Baek,Cha Seung, Sea	-	0	0	0	0	0	-	0	0	0	0	0	0	0	0	0	7	31.0	3	2	0	0	1.000	0	0	0	0	-
Baez,Danys, TB	-	0	0	0	0	0	.000	3	0	0	0	0	0	0	0	0	62	68.0	1	10	0	0	1.000	3	0	0	1	.00
Bajenaru,Jeff, CWS	-	0	0	0	0	0	-	0	0	0	0	0	0	0	0	0	9	8.1	0	0	0	0	-	0	0	0	0	-
Baldwin,James, NYM	.000	2	0	0	0	0	.093	43	4	1	1	0	2	0	20	3	2	6.0	0	2	0	0	1.000	2	1	0	0	.50
Balfour,Grant, Min	-	0	0	0	0	0	-	0	0	0	0	0	0	0	0	0	36	39.1	3	4	0	0	1.000	4	2	0	0	.50
Bartosh,Cliff, Cle	-	0	0	0	0	0	-	0	0	0	0	0	0	0	0	0	34	19.1	1	0	0	0	1.000	3	1	0	0	.33
Batista,Miguel, Tor	.000	5	0	0	0	0	.094	224	21	4	0	2	5	9	129	14	38	198.2	18	30	1	4	.980	20	11	0	0	.55
Bauer,Rick, Bal	-	0	0	0	0	0	-	0	0	0	0	0	0	0	0	0	23	53.2	3	9	0	1	1.000	0	0	0	0	-
Bautista,De, Bal-KC	-	0	0	0	0	0	-	0	0	0	0	0	0	0	0	0	7	29.2	0	1	0	0	1.000	5	2	0	0	.40
Beck,Rod, SD	-	0	0	0	0	0	.211	19	4	0	0	0	1	0	10	5	26	24.0	0	2	1	0	.667	5	1	0	0	.20
Beckett,Josh, Fla	.159	44	7	0	2	9	.133	128	17	5	0	0	5	3	54	21	26	156.2	4	16	2	0	.909	10	5	0	0	.50
Bedard,Erik, Bal	.000	4	0	0	0	0	.000	4	0	0	0	0	0	1	3	0	27	137.1	10	9	0	0	1.000	13	3	0	0	.23
Beimel,Joe, Min	-	0	0	0	0	0	.244	41	10	1	0	0	1	2	15	6	3	1.2	0	0	0	0	-	0	0	0	0	-
Bell,Heath, NYM	.000	1	0	0	0	0	.000	1	0	0	0	0	0	0	0	0	17	24.1	0	3	0	0	1.000	2	0	0	0	.00
Bell,Rob, TB	.200	5	1	0	0	0	.083	60	5	2	0	0	0	3	34	5	24	123.0	17	11	1	0	.966	4	1	0	0	.25
Beltran,F, ChC-Mon	.333	3	1	0	0	0	.250	4	1	0	0	0	0	0	1	0	45	49.1	0	5	1	1	.833	7	1	0	0	.14
Beltran,Rigo, Mon	-	0	0	0	0	0	-	0	0	0	0	0	0	0	0	0	2	0.2	0	0	0	0	-	0	0	0	0	-
Benitez,A, Fla	.000	1	0	0	0	0	.000	8	0	0	0	0	2	0	4	0	64	69.2	4	3	1	0	.875	9	0	0	0	.00
Bennett,Jeff, Mil	.000	2	0	0	0	0	.000	2	0	0	0	0	0	0	2	0	60	71.1	6	7	1	0	.929	5	2	0	0	.40
Benoit,Joaquin, Tex	.000	6	0	0	0	0	.000	8	0	0	0	0	0	0	4	0	28	103.0	6	6	1	0	.923	5	1	0	0	.20
Benson,Kris, Pit-NYM	.138	58	8	0	5	15	.120	258	31	6	0	0	14	10	101	40	31	200.1	17	25	1	2	.977	15	6	1	1	.40
Bentz,Chad, Mon	.500	2	1	0	0	0	.500	2	1	0	0	0	0	0	0	0	36	27.2	5	5	0	0	1.000	1	0	0	0	.00
Bergman,Dusty, Ana	-	0	0	0	0	0	-	0	0	0	0	0	0	0	0	0	1	2.0	0	0	0	0	-	0	0	0	0	-
Bernero,Adam, Col	.000	5	0	0	0	1	.000	15	0	0	0	0	0	0	9	2	16	32.1	1	4	0	0	1.000	4	0	0	0	.00
Betancourt,R, Cle	-	0	0	0	0	0	-	0	0	0	0	0	0	0	0	0	68	66.2	2	3	0	0	1.000	9	2	0	0	.22
Biddle,Rocky, Mon	.000	11	0	0	0	3	.000	14	0	0	0	0	0	0	10	4	47	78.0	2	9	0	0	1.000	9	7	0	0	.78
Bierbrodt,Nick, Tex	.000	2	0	0	0	1	.500	8	4	1	0	0	2	2	3	3	4	17.0	1	4	0	0	1.000	3	2	1	0	.67
Blackley,T, Sea	-	0	0	0	0	0	-	0	0	0	0	0	0	0	0	0	6	26.2	2	4	0	0	1.000	1	0	1	0	1.00
Blanton,Joe, Oak	-	0	0	0	0	0	-	0	0	0	0	0	0	0	0	0	3	8.0	1	0	0	0	1.000	1	1	0	0	1.00
Boehringer,B, Pit	.000	1	0	0	0	0	.065	31	2	0	0	0	2	3	16	3	21	25.1	0	3	0	1	1.000	3	1	1	0	.33
Bonderman,J, Det	.000	7	0	0	0	0	.000	9	0	0	0	0	0	0	6	0	33	184.0	14	15	3	1	.906	15	2	0	0	.13
Bong,Jung, Cin	.000	4	0	0	0	0	.000	11	0	0	0	0	0	1	6	1	3	15.1	1	4	0	1	1.000	1	0	0	0	.00
Borkowski,Dave, Bal	-	0	0	0	0	0	-	0	0	0	0	0	0	0	0	0	17	56.0	1	2	2	1	.600	5	2	0	0	.40
Borland,Toby, Fla	-	0	0	0	0	0	.083	12	1	0	0	0	2	0	3	1	18	18.1	2	2	1	0	.800	1	0	0	0	.00
Borowski,Joe, ChC	.222	9	2	0	0	0	.222	9	2	0	0	0	0	0	7	1	22	21.1	0	2	0	0	1.000	2	0	0	0	.00
Bottalico,R, NYM	.000	2	0	0	0	0	.118	17	2	2	0	0	1	0	8	1	60	69.1	5	8	0	0	1.000	7	0	0	0	.00
Boyd,Jason, Pit	-	0	0	0	0	0	.000	1	0	0	0	0	0	0	1	0	12	13.0	0	4	2	0	.667	0	0	0	0	-
Bradford,Chad, Oak	-	0	0	0	0	0	-	0	0	0	0	0	0	0	0	0	68	56.0	5	13	2	0	.900	3	2	0	0	.67
Brazelton,D, TB	.000	1	0	0	0	0	.000	2	0	0	0	0	0	0	0	0	22	120.2	5	8	0	1	1.000	10	3	0	0	.30
Brazoban,Y, LA	.000	1	0	0	0	0	.000	1	0	0	0	0	0	0	0	0	31	32.2	1	4	0	1	1.000	4	1	0	0	.25
Brocail,Doug, Tex	-	0	0	0	0	0	-	0	0	0	0	0	0	0	0	0	43	52.1	8	8	1	2	.941	5	3	0	0	.00
Brooks,Frank, Pit	-	0	0	0	0	0	-	0	0	0	0	0	0	0	0	0	11	17.1	0	0	0	0	-	0	0	0	0	-
Brower,Jim, SF	.500	2	1	0	0	0	.211	57	12	1	0	0	4	1	19	4	89	93.0	6	21	2	0	.931	3	0	0	1	.00
Brown,Jamie, Bos	-	0	0	0	0	0	-	0	0	0	0	0	0	0	0	0	4	7.2	0	0	0	0	-	2	1	0	0	.50
Brown,Kevin, NYY	-	0	0	0	0	0	.128	493	63	9	0	2	29	19	186	54	22	132.0	8	11	4	2	.826	18	5	0	0	.28

Pitchers Hitting, Fielding and Holding Runners

Pitcher	2004 Hitting						Career Hitting										2004 Fielding and Holding Runners											
	Avg	AB	H	HR	RBI	SH	Avg	AB	H	2B	3B	HR	RBI	BB	SO	SH	G	Inn	PO	A	E	DP	Pct	SBA	CS	PCS	PPO	CS%
Bruney,Brian, Ari	-	0	0	0	0	0	-	0	0	0	0	0	0	0	0	0	30	31.1	2	3	1	0	.833	7	5	1	0	.71
Buehrle,Mark, CWS	.000	3	0	0	0	2	.111	18	2	0	0	0	1	1	11	2	35	245.1	16	52	4	3	.944	13	8	6	4	.62
Bukvich,Ryan, KC	-	0	0	0	0	0	-	0	0	0	0	0	0	0	0	0	9	7.1	0	0	0	0	-	2	0	0	0	.00
Bullinger,Kirk, Hou	.000	3	0	0	0	0	.000	3	0	0	0	0	0	1	2	0	27	30.2	4	10	0	1	1.000	4	0	0	0	.00
Bump,Nate, Fla	.000	5	0	0	0	0	.000	5	0	0	0	0	0	0	2	0	50	73.2	2	9	1	0	.917	7	0	0	0	.00
Burba,Dave, Mil-SF	.000	4	0	0	0	0	.134	194	26	1	0	3	12	10	84	22	51	77.0	6	12	2	0	.900	6	1	0	0	.17
Burnett,A.J., Fla	.138	29	4	0	1	8	.130	185	24	4	1	2	7	11	89	24	20	120.0	10	18	0	1	1.000	19	5	1	1	.26
Burnett,Sean, Pit	.000	23	0	0	0	2	.000	23	0	0	0	0	0	2	6	2	13	71.2	4	17	1	1	.955	10	3	0	0	.30
Bush,David, Tor	.000	2	0	0	0	0	.000	2	0	0	0	0	0	0	0	0	16	97.2	9	5	0	0	1.000	9	3	1	0	.33
Bynum,Mike, SD	-	0	0	0	0	0	.167	18	3	0	0	0	0	0	7	1	2	0.2	0	0	0	0	-	0	0	0	0	-
Byrd,Paul, Atl	.200	30	6	0	4	8	.156	141	22	0	0	0	10	12	37	25	19	114.1	7	15	3	2	.880	11	3	0	0	.27
Cabrera,Daniel, Bal	.000	4	0	0	0	0	.000	4	0	0	0	0	0	0	4	0	28	147.2	9	6	1	0	.938	11	4	0	0	.36
Cabrera,F, Cle	-	0	0	0	0	0	-	0	0	0	0	0	0	0	0	0	4	5.1	1	0	0	0	1.000	0	0	0	0	-
Calero,Kiko, StL	.000	1	0	0	0	0	.200	5	1	0	0	0	1	0	1	0	41	45.1	2	9	1	0	.917	0	0	0	1	-
Cali,Carmen, StL	-	0	0	0	0	0	-	0	0	0	0	0	0	0	0	0	10	7.1	0	0	0	0	-	1	1	0	1	1.00
Callaway,M, Tex	-	0	0	0	0	0	.667	3	2	0	0	0	1	0	0	0	4	11.2	2	2	0	1	1.000	1	0	0	0	.00
Camp,Shawn, KC	-	0	0	0	0	0	-	0	0	0	0	0	0	0	0	0	42	66.2	3	13	0	0	1.000	3	0	0	0	.00
Capellan,Jose, Atl	.000	2	0	0	0	0	.000	2	0	0	0	0	0	0	1	0	3	8.0	0	0	0	0	-	3	0	0	0	.00
Capuano,Chris, Mil	.200	30	6	0	2	0	.158	38	6	2	0	0	2	1	15	0	17	88.1	3	16	0	1	1.000	2	1	1	5	.50
Carpenter,C, StL	.081	62	5	0	1	4	.096	73	7	0	0	0	1	2	26	6	28	182.0	12	34	1	4	.979	3	3	0	1	1.00
Carrara,G, LA	.000	2	0	0	0	0	.100	30	3	0	0	0	0	1	10	3	42	53.2	4	11	0	2	1.000	2	2	0	1	1.00
Carrasco,D.J., KC	-	0	0	0	0	0	.000	2	0	0	0	0	0	0	1	0	30	35.1	7	6	0	0	1.000	0	0	0	0	.00
Carter,Lance, TB	-	0	0	0	0	0	-	0	0	0	0	0	0	0	0	0	56	80.1	4	8	0	1	1.000	2	1	0	0	.50
Castillo,Frank, Bos	-	0	0	0	0	0	.110	337	37	0	0	0	13	13	111	42	2	1.0	0	0	0	0	-	0	0	0	0	-
Cerda,Jaime, KC	-	0	0	0	0	0	.000	2	0	0	0	0	0	0	0	0	53	45.2	7	8	1	0	.938	3	2	2	0	.67
Chacin,Gustavo, Tor	-	0	0	0	0	0	-	0	0	0	0	0	0	0	0	0	2	14.0	1	1	0	0	1.000	0	0	0	0	-
Chacon,Shawn, Col	-	0	0	0	0	0	.156	128	20	3	0	1	8	0	52	11	66	63.1	2	5	1	0	.875	5	0	0	1	.00
Chen,Bruce, Bal	-	0	0	0	0	0	.117	111	13	1	0	0	3	1	53	17	8	47.2	4	7	0	1	1.000	3	2	2	0	.67
Choate,Randy, Ari	.000	1	0	0	0	0	.000	5	0	0	0	0	0	0	3	0	74	50.2	3	10	0	1	1.000	2	0	0	0	.00
Christiansen,J, SF	-	0	0	0	0	0	.100	10	1	0	0	0	1	0	7	1	60	36.0	2	5	2	0	.778	1	1	1	0	1.00
Chulk,Vinnie, Tor	-	0	0	0	0	0	-	0	0	0	0	0	0	0	0	0	47	56.0	3	6	0	0	1.000	6	3	0	0	.50
Claussen,B, Cin	.105	19	2	0	0	2	.130	23	3	0	0	0	1	1	7	2	14	66.0	1	5	0	0	1.000	7	0	0	0	.00
Clemens,Roger, Hou	.167	72	12	0	7	3	.174	92	16	3	0	0	8	5	32	6	33	214.1	12	24	0	1	1.000	33	10	2	0	.30
Clement,Matt, ChC	.145	55	8	0	2	4	.094	342	32	5	1	0	12	13	170	43	30	181.0	16	21	3	3	.925	18	2	0	0	.11
Colome,Jesus, TB	.000	1	0	0	0	1	.000	1	0	0	0	0	0	0	0	1	33	41.1	2	7	0	0	1.000	3	0	0	0	.00
Colon,Bartolo, Ana	.000	3	0	0	0	0	.118	76	9	0	0	0	4	0	44	4	34	208.1	8	30	3	3	.927	9	6	0	1	.67
Colon,Roman, Atl	-	0	0	0	0	0	-	0	0	0	0	0	0	0	0	0	18	19.0	0	1	1	0	.500	1	0	0	0	.00
Colyer,Steve, Det	-	0	0	0	0	0	-	0	0	0	0	0	0	1	0	0	41	32.0	1	5	0	1	1.000	7	2	0	0	.29
Contreras,Jose, NYY-CWS	.000	8	0	0	0	0	.000	11	0	0	0	0	0	0	7	0	31	170.1	7	12	2	0	.905	40	11	1	1	.28
Cook,Aaron, Col	.118	34	4	0	1	2	.135	74	10	0	0	0	5	3	20	9	16	96.2	11	21	0	4	1.000	5	1	0	1	.20
Cooper,Brian, SF	.000	3	0	0	0	0	.000	7	0	0	0	0	0	0	4	0	5	13.1	1	1	0	0	1.000	0	0	0	0	-
Corcoran,Roy, Mon	-	0	0	0	0	0	.000	1	0	0	0	0	0	0	1	0	5	5.1	0	0	0	0	-	0	0	0	0	-
Cordero,Chad, Mon	.000	2	0	0	0	1	.000	2	0	0	0	0	0	0	2	2	69	82.2	3	5	0	1	1.000	2	2	0	0	1.00
Cordero,F, Tex	-	0	0	0	0	0	.000	1	0	0	0	0	0	0	1	0	67	71.2	6	8	0	2	1.000	7	2	1	1	.29
Corey,Mark, Pit	.000	1	0	0	0	0	.000	3	0	0	0	0	0	0	1	0	31	35.2	2	4	0	1	1.000	3	0	0	0	.00
Cormier,Lance, Ari	.250	8	2	0	1	1	.250	8	2	1	0	0	1	1	2	1	17	45.1	1	4	0	0	1.000	6	1	0	0	.17
Cormier,Rheal, Phi	.000	1	0	0	0	0	.188	191	36	4	1	0	12	5	44	28	84	81.0	13	14	0	3	1.000	2	2	0	0	1.00
Cornejo,Nate, Det	-	0	0	0	0	0	.000	4	0	0	0	0	0	0	4	1	5	25.2	2	7	0	2	1.000	2	2	0	1	1.00
Correia,Kevin, SF	.333	3	1	0	0	0	.188	16	3	1	0	0	2	1	7	1	12	19.0	2	1	0	0	1.000	3	0	0	0	.00
Cotts,Neal, CWS	1.000	1	1	0	0	0	1.000	1	1	1	0	0	0	0	0	0	56	65.1	1	8	1	1	.900	6	1	0	0	.17
Crain,Jesse, Min	-	0	0	0	0	0	-	0	0	0	0	0	0	0	0	0	22	27.0	2	3	1	1	.833	1	0	0	0	.00
Cressend,Jack, Cle	-	0	0	0	0	0	-	0	0	0	0	0	0	0	0	0	11	15.2	3	2	0	1	1.000	1	0	0	0	.00
Crowell,Jim, Phi	-	0	0	0	0	0	-	0	0	0	0	0	0	0	0	0	4	3.0	0	0	0	0	-	0	0	0	0	-
Cruceta,F, Cle	-	0	0	0	0	0	-	0	0	0	0	0	0	0	0	0	2	7.2	0	0	0	0	-	2	0	0	0	.00
Cruz,Ju, Atl	.200	5	1	0	0	0	.170	47	8	1	1	0	2	1	17	5	50	72.0	4	6	0	1	1.000	3	1	0	0	.33
Cubillan,D, Bal	-	0	0	0	0	0	-	0	0	0	0	0	0	0	0	0	7	10.0	1	1	1	0	.667	1	0	0	0	.00
Cunnane,Will, Atl	-	0	0	0	0	0	.200	35	7	1	1	0	4	3	9	1	9	12.1	1	1	0	0	1.000	1	0	0	0	.00
Daigle,Casey, Ari	.118	17	2	0	0	1	.118	17	2	0	0	0	0	0	7	1	9	49.0	5	6	0	0	1.000	0	0	0	1	-
D'Amico,Jeff, Cle	-	0	0	0	0	0	.101	148	15	2	1	2	5	13	72	21	7	30.2	2	3	0	1	1.000	3	1	0	0	.33
Darensbourg,V, CWS-NYM	-	0	0	0	0	0	.111	18	2	0	0	0	0	2	6	1	7	7.0	1	3	0	0	1.000	1	1	1	0	1.00
Davis,Doug, Mil	.015	66	1	0	0	7	.033	90	3	0	0	0	0	1	56	9	34	215.1	16	26	1	2	.977	21	6	3	1	.29
Davis,Ja, Cle	.200	5	1	0	1	0	.143	7	1	0	0	1	1	0	3	1	26	114.1	10	20	3	0	.909	21	3	1	1	.14
Dawley,Joe, Cle	-	0	0	0	0	0	.000	1	0	0	0	0	0	0	1	0	2	8.1	2	2	0	0	1.000	3	1	0	0	.33
Day,Zach, Mon	.034	29	1	1	1	3	.049	82	4	0	0	1	3	2	43	6	19	116.2	10	16	0	1	1.000	6	2	0	0	.33
de la Rosa,J, Mil	.000	6	0	0	0	1	.000	6	0	0	0	0	0	1	5	1	22	22.2	2	2	1	0	.800	3	1	0	0	.33
de los Santos,V, Tor	-	0	0	0	0	0	.000	9	0	0	0	0	0	1	6	2	17	11.2	0	2	0	0	1.000	0	0	0	0	-
DeJean,Mike, Bal-NYM	.000	1	0	0	0	0	.059	17	1	0	0	0	0	0	10	1	54	61.0	3	6	0	1	1.000	4	2	0	0	.50
Dempster,Ryan, ChC	.000	1	0	0	0	0	.077	297	23	5	1	0	7	6	128	32	23	20.2	4	2	0	0	1.000	2	0	0	0	.00
Denney,Kyle, Cle	-	0	0	0	0	0	-	0	0	0	0	0	0	0	0	0	4	16.0	0	2	0	1	1.000	1	1	0	0	1.00
DePaula,Jorge, NYY	-	0	0	0	0	0	-	0	0	0	0	0	0	0	0	0	3	9.0	1	2	0	0	1.000	1	0	0	0	.00
Dessens,Elmer, Ari-LA	.182	22	4	0	0	4	.175	223	39	4	1	0	16	20	57	37	50	105.0	5	13	1	0	.947	5	1	0	1	.20
Diaz,Felix, CWS	.000	1	0	0	0	0	.000	1	0	0	0	0	0	0	0	0	18	49.1	2	4	0	0	1.000	4	0	0	0	.00
Dickey,R.A., Tex	-	0	0	0	0	0	1.000	1	1	0	0	0	0	0	0	0	25	104.1	7	22	2	0	.935	11	5	0	4	.45
Dinardo,Lenny, Bos	-	0	0	0	0	0	-	0	0	0	0	0	0	0	0	0	22	27.2	4	3	2	0	.778	2	1	0	0	.50
Dingman,Craig, Det	-	0	0	0	0	0	-	0	0	0	0	0	0	0	0	0	24	29.1	2	1	0	0	1.000	5	2	0	0	.40

Pitchers Hitting, Fielding and Holding Runners

Pitcher	2004 Hitting						Career Hitting										2004 Fielding and Holding Runners											
	Avg	AB	H	HR	RBI	SH	Avg	AB	H	2B	3B	HR	RBI	BB	SO	SH	G	Inn	PO	A	E	DP	Pct	SBA	CS	PCS	PPO	CS%
Dohmann,Scott, Col	.000	1	0	0	0	1	.000	1	0	0	0	0	0	0	1	1	41	46.0	4	4	0	0	1.000	2	0	0	0	.00
Dominguez,Juan, Tex	-	0	0	0	0	0	-	0	0	0	0	0	0	0	0	0	4	23.0	0	3	0	0	1.000	2	0	0	0	.00
Donnelly,B, Ana	-	0	0	0	0	0	-	0	0	0	0	0	0	0	0	0	40	42.0	2	2	0	0	1.000	2	0	0	0	.00
Dotel,Octavio, Hou-Oak	-	0	0	0	0	0	.068	74	5	0	0	0	1	5	42	9	77	85.1	6	5	0	1	1.000	5	2	0	0	.40
Douglass,Sean, Tor	-	0	0	0	0	0	-	0	0	0	0	0	0	0	0	0	14	38.2	3	2	0	0	1.000	6	2	1	0	.33
Downs,Scott, Mon	.067	15	1	0	0	6	.068	44	3	0	0	0	1	3	17	10	12	63.0	3	11	0	1	1.000	0	0	0	0	-
Dreifort,D, LA	.000	1	0	0	0	0	.184	239	44	10	0	6	23	8	107	17	60	50.2	1	12	0	0	1.000	8	2	0	0	.25
Drese,Ryan, Tex	.500	4	2	0	0	0	.286	7	2	1	0	0	0	1	2	1	34	207.2	15	31	2	5	.958	9	4	0	0	.44
Drew,Tim, Atl	.000	2	0	0	0	0	.000	7	0	0	0	0	0	1	5	1	11	16.0	2	3	0	1	1.000	0	0	0	0	-
Driskill,T, Col	.000	1	0	0	0	0	.000	5	0	0	0	0	0	1	4	0	5	8.1	0	1	0	0	1.000	0	0	0	0	-
DuBose,Eric, Bal	.000	2	0	0	0	0	.000	2	0	0	0	0	0	0	2	0	14	74.2	0	18	2	1	.900	8	3	2	0	.38
Duchscherer,J, Oak	-	0	0	0	0	0	-	0	0	0	0	0	0	0	0	0	53	96.1	5	20	0	1	1.000	8	4	1	1	.50
Duckworth,B, Hou	.222	9	2	0	1	0	.198	106	21	2	0	0	8	10	22	9	19	39.1	3	3	0	1	1.000	1	0	0	1	.00
Dunn,Scott, Ana	-	0	0	0	0	0	-	0	0	0	0	0	0	0	0	0	3	3.0	0	0	0	0	-	0	0	0	0	-
Durbin,Chad, Cle-Ari	.000	1	0	0	0	0	.000	2	0	0	0	0	0	0	0	1	24	60.2	4	5	1	0	.900	8	2	0	0	.25
Durbin,J.D., Min	-	0	0	0	0	0	-	0	0	0	0	0	0	0	0	0	4	7.1	0	2	0	0	1.000	0	0	0	0	-
Eaton,Adam, SD	.203	64	13	0	8	5	.195	205	40	13	0	2	17	21	67	14	33	199.1	12	23	2	1	.946	11	5	0	0	.45
Eischen,Joey, Mon	.667	3	2	0	0	1	.174	23	4	1	0	0	0	1	8	1	21	18.1	0	1	1	0	.500	3	2	0	0	.67
Elarton,Scott, Col-Cle	.250	12	3	0	0	4	.138	159	22	2	0	0	3	5	51	27	29	158.2	7	12	1	1	.950	12	2	0	1	.17
Eldred,Cal, StL	.000	5	0	0	0	1	.114	70	8	2	0	0	4	6	37	11	52	67.0	1	12	0	1	1.000	5	4	0	0	.80
Embree,Alan, Bos	-	0	0	0	0	0	.000	2	0	0	0	0	0	1	1	0	71	52.1	5	7	0	0	1.000	9	2	2	0	.22
Ennis,John, Det	-	0	0	0	0	0	.000	1	0	0	0	0	0	0	0	0	12	16.0	2	0	0	1	1.000	0	0	0	0	-
Erickson,Scott, NYM-Tex	.000	3	0	0	0	0	.091	22	2	1	0	0	1	4	10	4	6	27.0	1	2	0	0	1.000	4	1	0	0	.25
Escobar,Kelvim, Ana	.000	2	0	0	0	0	.063	16	1	0	0	0	1	0	8	0	33	208.1	16	24	0	1	1.000	28	4	0	1	.14
Estes,Shawn, Col	.236	72	17	0	2	7	.163	459	75	14	1	4	28	14	156	71	34	202.0	14	27	1	4	.976	18	7	5	0	.39
Estrella,Leo, SF	-	0	0	0	0	0	-	0	0	0	0	0	0	0	0	0	2	1.1	0	0	0	0	-	0	0	0	0	-
Eyre,Scott, SF	.000	2	0	0	0	0	.222	9	2	0	0	0	0	0	4	0	83	52.2	2	7	1	0	.900	5	3	2	0	.60
Falkenborg,B, LA	.000	2	0	0	0	0	.000	2	0	0	0	0	0	1	2	0	6	14.1	1	2	1	0	.750	3	0	0	0	.00
Farnsworth,K, ChC	.000	1	0	0	0	0	.074	54	4	1	0	0	3	2	18	8	72	66.2	7	9	1	0	.941	9	4	1	0	.44
Fassero,Jeff, Col-Ari	.190	21	4	0	1	2	.085	259	22	2	1	0	6	18	144	43	41	112.0	7	24	0	2	1.000	15	5	4	1	.33
Feliciano,P, NYM	-	0	0	0	0	0	.000	3	0	0	0	0	0	0	0	1	22	18.1	2	4	0	0	1.000	3	0	0	0	.00
Fernandez,J, Hou	-	0	0	0	0	0	.095	21	2	0	0	0	0	1	10	3	2	1.0	1	0	0	0	1.000	1	0	0	0	.00
Fetters,Mike, Ari	-	0	0	0	0	0	-	0	0	0	0	0	0	0	0	0	23	18.2	2	2	1	0	.800	0	0	0	0	-
Field,Nate, KC	-	0	0	0	0	0	-	0	0	0	0	0	0	0	0	0	43	44.1	2	3	0	0	1.000	4	1	1	0	.25
Figueroa,N, Pit	.143	7	1	0	1	0	.179	56	10	1	0	0	5	2	24	6	10	28.1	1	3	0	0	1.000	2	2	0	0	1.00
Fikac,Jeremy, Mon	-	0	0	0	0	0	.000	2	0	0	0	0	0	0	1	0	19	26.0	1	5	0	1	1.000	2	1	0	0	.50
File,Bob, Tor	.000	1	0	0	0	0	.000	1	0	0	0	0	0	0	1	0	24	33.2	3	8	0	2	1.000	3	0	0	0	.00
Flores,Randy, StL	.000	2	0	0	0	0	.000	6	0	0	0	0	0	0	4	0	9	14.0	0	0	0	0	-	0	0	0	0	-
Floyd,Gavin, Phi	.000	10	0	0	0	0	.000	10	0	0	0	0	0	0	5	0	6	28.1	1	3	0	0	1.000	8	1	0	0	.13
Fogg,Josh, Pit	.075	53	4	0	3	11	.124	153	19	1	0	0	5	4	50	20	32	178.1	13	36	2	5	.961	17	5	1	1	.29
Foppert,Jesse, SF	-	0	0	0	0	0	.081	37	3	1	1	0	1	0	19	0	1	1.0	0	0	0	0	-	0	0	0	0	-
Ford,Ben, Mil	-	0	0	0	0	0	-	0	0	0	0	0	0	0	0	0	19	24.2	0	3	0	0	1.000	4	0	0	0	.00
Fortunato,B, TB-NYM	-	0	0	0	0	0	-	0	0	0	0	0	0	0	0	0	18	26.0	2	1	0	1	1.000	1	0	0	0	.00
Fossum,Casey, Ari	.095	42	4	0	0	3	.095	42	4	0	0	0	1	1	16	3	27	142.0	4	20	0	1	1.000	23	8	4	0	.35
Foulke,Keith, Bos	-	0	0	0	0	0	.125	16	2	0	0	0	0	0	5	2	72	83.0	5	10	0	0	1.000	5	2	0	0	.40
Fox,Chad, Fla	-	0	0	0	0	0	.000	7	0	0	0	0	0	0	3	1	12	10.2	1	1	0	0	1.000	0	0	0	0	-
Francis,Jeff, Col	.000	10	0	0	0	4	.000	10	0	0	0	0	0	0	4	4	7	36.2	2	6	0	1	1.000	2	0	0	0	.00
Francisco,F, Tex	-	0	0	0	0	0	-	0	0	0	0	0	0	0	0	0	45	51.1	4	2	0	0	1.000	2	2	0	0	1.00
Franco,Jo, NYM	-	0	0	0	0	0	.088	34	3	0	0	0	1	0	14	3	52	46.0	0	6	0	0	1.000	1	0	0	0	.00
Franklin,Ryan, Sea	.000	3	0	0	0	1	.143	7	1	0	0	0	0	1	3	2	32	200.1	15	19	3	2	.919	16	9	2	1	.56
Franklin,Wayne, SF	.333	3	1	0	2	0	.157	70	11	1	0	0	5	3	22	12	43	50.2	2	5	0	0	1.000	6	2	0	0	.33
Frasor,Jason, Tor	-	0	0	0	0	0	-	0	0	0	0	0	0	0	0	0	63	68.1	8	8	0	1	1.000	3	1	0	0	.33
Frederick,K, Tor	-	0	0	0	0	0	-	0	0	0	0	0	0	0	0	0	22	28.2	3	0	0	0	1.000	5	0	0	0	.00
Fuentes,Brian, Col	-	0	0	0	0	0	.000	1	0	0	0	0	0	0	0	0	47	44.2	0	6	1	0	.857	1	0	0	0	.00
Fultz,Aaron, Min	-	0	0	0	0	0	.333	12	4	0	0	0	0	0	5	0	55	50.0	2	8	0	0	1.000	1	1	0	0	1.00
Gagne,Eric, LA	.000	3	0	0	0	0	.140	86	12	2	1	1	3	1	25	12	70	82.1	5	6	0	1	1.000	0	0	0	0	-
Gallo,Mike, Hou	.000	1	0	0	0	0	.000	3	0	0	0	0	0	0	0	0	69	49.1	4	9	0	2	1.000	7	3	2	0	.43
Garcia,Freddy, Sea-CWS	.000	4	0	0	0	0	.241	29	7	1	0	0	2	0	9	8	31	210.0	12	37	0	3	1.000	17	5	1	1	.29
Garcia,Ja, Oak	-	0	0	0	0	0	-	0	0	0	0	0	0	0	0	0	4	5.2	1	0	0	0	1.000	1	0	0	0	.00
Garcia,Rosman, Tex	-	0	0	0	0	0	-	0	0	0	0	0	0	0	0	0	4	6.2	0	1	0	0	1.000	0	0	0	0	-
Garland,Jon, CWS	.250	4	1	0	0	1	.100	10	1	0	0	0	1	1	1	3	34	217.0	21	35	2	2	.966	11	3	0	0	.27
Gaudin,Chad, TB	.000	1	0	0	0	0	.000	1	0	0	0	0	0	0	0	0	26	42.2	1	5	1	0	.857	2	1	0	1	.50
Geary,Geoff, Phi	.000	1	0	0	0	0	.000	1	0	0	0	0	0	0	0	0	33	44.2	3	3	1	0	.857	2	1	0	0	.50
George,Chris, KC	.000	2	0	0	0	0	.333	3	1	0	0	0	1	1	0	2	10	42.1	2	7	1	1	.900	0	0	0	0	-
German,F, Det	.000	1	0	0	0	0	.000	1	0	0	0	0	0	0	1	0	16	14.2	2	0	1	0	.667	0	0	0	0	-
Germano,Justin, SD	.000	7	0	0	0	0	.000	7	0	0	0	0	0	0	3	1	7	21.1	1	3	0	0	1.000	1	1	0	0	1.00
Ginter,Matt, NYM	.214	14	3	0	1	3	.214	14	3	0	0	0	1	2	5	3	15	69.1	4	4	2	0	.800	8	2	0	0	.25
Gissell,Chris, Col	.000	1	0	0	0	0	.000	1	0	0	0	0	0	0	0	0	5	8.2	1	0	0	0	1.000	2	0	0	0	.00
Glavine,Tom, NYM	.204	54	11	0	8	8	.186	1131	210	23	2	1	80	83	288	186	33	212.1	10	49	1	2	.983	15	8	3	0	.53
Glover,Gary, Mil	.000	7	0	0	0	0	.000	8	0	0	0	0	0	0	5	0	4	18.0	3	3	1	0	.857	1	0	0	0	.00
Glynn,Ryan, Tor	-	0	0	0	0	0	-	0	0	0	0	0	0	0	0	0	6	20.0	2	1	2	0	.600	0	0	0	0	-
Gobble,Jimmy, KC	.000	2	0	0	0	0	.000	2	0	0	0	0	0	0	0	1	25	148.0	8	10	3	0	.857	13	3	1	0	.23
Gonzalez,Dicky, TB	-	0	0	0	0	0	-	0	0	0	0	0	0	0	0	0	4	7.1	1	1	0	0	1.000	0	0	0	0	-
Gonzalez,Edgar, Ari	.154	13	2	0	0	1	.176	17	3	0	0	0	0	0	2	2	10	46.1	0	7	0	2	1.000	4	1	0	0	.25
Gonzalez,Je, TB	-	0	0	0	0	0	.128	78	10	1	0	0	3	3	26	16	11	50.1	2	5	2	0	.778	4	2	0	0	.50

Pitchers Hitting, Fielding and Holding Runners

Pitcher	2004 Hitting						Career Hitting										2004 Fielding and Holding Runners											
	Avg	AB	H	HR	RBI	SH	Avg	AB	H	2B	3B	HR	RBI	BB	SO	SH	G	Inn	PO	A	E	DP	Pct	SBA	CS	PCS	PPO	CS%
Gonzalez,Mike, Pit	1.000	1	1	0	2	0	1.000	1	1	1	0	0	2	0	0	0	47	43.1	1	5	1	0	.857	2	0	0	0	.00
Good,Andy, Ari	.000	5	0	0	1	0	.095	21	2	0	0	0	2	0	7	4	17	40.2	2	4	0	1	1.000	2	1	0	0	.50
Gordon,Tom, NYY	.000	1	0	0	0	0	.000	2	0	0	0	0	0	0	0	0	80	89.2	6	13	1	0	.950	3	1	1	0	.33
Gosling,Mike, Ari	.000	6	0	0	0	1	.000	6	0	0	0	0	0	1	4	1	6	25.1	2	1	1	0	.750	1	0	0	0	.00
Grabow,John, Pit	.000	1	0	0	0	0	.000	1	0	0	0	0	0	0	0	0	68	61.2	2	15	0	1	1.000	7	4	1	0	.57
Gracesqui,F, Fla	-	0	0	0	0	0	-	0	0	0	0	0	0	0	0	0	7	4.0	0	1	0	0	1.000	0	0	0	0	-
Graman,Alex, NYY	-	0	0	0	0	0	-	0	0	0	0	0	0	0	0	0	3	5.0	0	0	0	0	-	1	0	0	0	.00
Graves,Danny, Cin	-	0	0	0	0	0	.105	76	8	0	0	2	3	1	25	5	68	68.1	2	10	0	3	1.000	2	2	0	0	1.00
Gregg,Kevin, Ana	-	0	0	0	0	0	-	0	0	0	0	0	0	0	0	0	55	87.2	2	5	0	1	1.000	7	2	0	0	.29
Greinke,Zack, KC	.000	2	0	0	0	0	.000	2	0	0	0	0	0	0	0	1	24	145.0	13	15	0	1	1.000	8	3	0	0	.38
Greisinger,S, Min	-	0	0	0	0	0	.250	4	1	0	0	0	1	0	0	0	12	51.0	2	6	2	0	.800	9	1	0	1	.11
Griffiths,J, Hou	.000	1	0	0	0	0	.000	10	0	0	0	0	0	2	4	1	4	4.1	0	1	0	0	1.000	0	0	0	0	-
Grilli,Jason, CWS	-	0	0	0	0	0	-	0	0	0	0	0	0	0	0	0	8	45.0	2	3	2	0	.714	5	2	0	0	.40
Grimsley,Jason, KC-Bal	-	0	0	0	0	0	.103	39	4	0	0	0	2	5	11	5	73	63.0	10	12	4	0	.846	15	2	0	0	.13
Groom,Buddy, Bal	-	0	0	0	0	0	-	0	0	0	0	0	0	0	0	0	60	52.2	4	3	0	0	1.000	3	2	1	0	.67
Gryboski,Kevin, Atl	-	0	0	0	0	0	.000	1	0	0	0	0	0	0	0	1	69	50.2	2	6	0	3	1.000	5	2	0	1	.40
Guardado,Eddie, Sea	.000	1	0	0	0	0	.000	1	0	0	0	0	0	0	0	0	41	45.1	0	4	0	0	1.000	0	0	0	0	-
Guerrier,Matt, Min	.000	1	0	0	0	0	.000	1	0	0	0	0	0	0	0	0	9	19.0	2	3	0	0	1.000	0	0	0	0	-
Guthrie,Jeremy, Cle	-	0	0	0	0	0	-	0	0	0	0	0	0	0	0	0	6	11.2	0	2	0	0	1.000	1	0	0	0	.00
Halama,John, TB	.000	3	0	0	0	0	.095	21	2	1	0	0	0	3	11	3	34	118.2	2	14	0	1	1.000	8	2	2	1	.25
Halladay,Roy, Tor	.000	6	0	0	0	0	.042	24	1	0	0	0	0	0	9	2	21	133.0	10	20	1	1	.968	9	2	0	0	.22
Halsey,Brad, NYY	.500	2	1	0	0	0	.500	2	1	0	0	0	0	1	0	1	8	32.0	0	2	1	0	.667	5	0	0	0	.00
Hammond,Chris, Oak	-	0	0	0	0	0	.204	235	48	7	1	4	14	28	95	19	41	53.2	1	10	1	0	.917	1	0	0	0	.00
Hampton,Mike, Atl	.172	64	11	2	7	4	.239	639	153	18	5	14	67	43	167	56	29	172.1	13	37	2	4	.962	11	5	2	1	.45
Hancock,Josh, Phi-Cin	.118	17	2	0	1	1	.118	17	2	0	0	0	1	3	12	1	16	63.2	3	5	2	0	.800	7	2	0	0	.29
Harang,Aaron, Cin	.070	57	4	0	0	4	.064	78	5	1	0	0	0	4	48	4	28	161.0	10	21	0	0	1.000	12	5	0	0	.42
Harden,Rich, Oak	.000	5	0	0	0	0	.000	5	0	0	0	0	0	0	3	0	31	189.2	15	18	1	2	.971	17	6	1	1	.35
Haren,Danny, StL	.000	12	0	0	0	2	.054	37	2	2	0	0	1	1	16	3	14	46.0	2	7	1	1	.900	3	0	0	0	.00
Harikkala,Tim, Col	.000	3	0	0	0	1	.000	3	0	0	0	0	0	0	3	1	55	62.2	6	11	0	1	1.000	3	1	0	0	.33
Harper,Travis, TB	-	0	0	0	0	0	-	0	0	0	0	0	0	0	0	0	52	78.2	9	8	1	1	1.000	6	3	1	0	.50
Harville,Chad, Oak-Hou	.000	1	0	0	0	0	.000	1	0	0	0	0	0	0	1	0	59	55.2	2	7	3	2	.750	5	1	0	0	.20
Hasegawa,S, Sea	-	0	0	0	0	0	.000	1	0	0	0	0	0	0	0	0	68	68.0	6	8	1	0	.933	2	0	0	0	.00
Hawkins,LaTroy, ChC	-	0	0	0	0	0	.000	5	0	0	0	0	0	0	1	0	77	82.0	5	6	0	1	1.000	4	3	1	0	.75
Haynes,Jimmy, Cin	.000	4	0	0	0	0	.150	213	32	9	0	0	13	5	71	28	5	15.0	2	2	0	0	1.000	3	2	0	0	.67
Heilman,Aaron, NYM	.000	7	0	0	0	3	.034	29	1	0	0	0	0	1	16	3	5	28.0	5	5	2	2	.833	1	0	0	0	.00
Hendrickson,B, Mil	.125	16	2	0	0	1	.125	16	2	0	0	0	0	0	9	1	10	46.1	5	5	0	0	1.000	2	1	0	0	.50
Hendrickson,M, TB	.200	5	1	0	0	0	.222	9	2	0	0	1	1	5	2	0	32	183.1	13	26	0	2	1.000	13	2	0	0	.15
Hennessey,Brad, SF	.231	13	3	0	2	0	.231	13	3	0	0	0	2	1	4	0	7	34.1	3	8	0	0	1.000	4	1	0	0	.25
Hensley,Matt, Ana	.000	1	0	0	0	0	.000	1	0	0	0	0	0	0	1	0	16	27.2	4	3	0	0	1.000	1	0	0	1	.00
Hentgen,Pat, Tor	.000	1	0	0	0	0	.107	84	9	0	0	0	4	25	9	18	18	80.1	3	8	1	0	.917	3	0	0	1	.00
Heredia,Felix, NYY	-	0	0	0	0	0	.267	15	4	0	0	0	1	0	4	1	47	38.2	3	7	1	0	.909	2	0	0	0	.00
Herges,Matt, SF	-	0	0	0	0	0	.222	27	6	0	0	0	1	1	14	2	70	65.1	5	6	0	1	1.000	2	0	0	0	.00
Hermanson,D, SF	.100	30	3	0	1	6	.093	322	30	5	0	2	10	20	161	40	47	131.0	9	10	0	1	1.000	7	2	0	1	.29
Hernandez,A, Mil	.000	4	0	0	0	0	.000	4	0	0	0	0	0	0	3	0	6	16.0	1	5	0	0	1.000	2	2	0	0	1.00
Hernandez,C, Hou	.083	12	1	0	1	4	.154	52	8	0	0	2	2	17	9	9	42.0	4	6	0	0	1.000	5	2	0	0	.40
Hernandez,L, Mon	.247	81	20	1	10	15	.236	564	133	26	1	5	55	5	85	55	35	255.0	21	61	2	9	.976	25	9	0	2	.36
Hernandez,O, NYY	-	0	0	0	0	0	.053	19	1	0	0	0	0	0	12	2	15	84.2	10	7	0	1	1.000	13	4	0	0	.31
Hernandez,Ro, Phi	-	0	0	0	0	0	.500	2	1	0	0	0	0	0	1	0	63	56.2	8	11	1	0	.950	16	4	0	0	.25
Hill,Shawn, Mon	.000	2	0	0	0	1	.000	2	0	0	0	0	0	0	2	1	3	9.0	0	0	0	0	-	2	2	0	0	1.00
Hitchcock,S, SD	.000	7	0	0	0	0	.090	210	19	0	0	0	5	7	112	23	4	21.1	0	1	0	0	1.000	1	0	0	0	.00
Hoffman,Trevor, SD	-	0	0	0	0	0	.121	33	4	2	0	0	5	0	10	2	55	54.2	2	6	0	0	1.000	1	1	1	0	1.00
Horgan,Joe, Mon	.250	4	1	0	1	0	.250	4	1	0	0	0	0	1	0	1	47	40.0	3	6	0	0	1.000	1	0	0	0	.00
Howard,Ben, Fla	.000	3	0	0	0	1	.056	18	1	0	0	0	0	0	7	1	31	37.2	2	4	0	0	1.000	7	1	0	0	.14
Howry,Bob, Cle	-	0	0	0	0	0	-	0	0	0	0	0	0	0	0	0	37	42.2	2	7	0	0	1.000	2	0	0	0	.00
Hudson,Luke, Cin	.125	16	2	0	2	0	.125	16	2	0	0	0	2	1	3	1	9	48.1	3	6	1	1	.900	3	0	0	0	.00
Hudson,Tim, Oak	.000	3	0	0	0	0	.115	26	3	1	0	0	1	2	9	0	27	188.2	22	26	1	2	.980	12	4	0	1	.33
Hughes,Travis, Tex	-	0	0	0	0	0	-	0	0	0	0	0	0	0	0	0	2	1.1	0	0	0	0	-	0	0	0	0	-
Huisman,Justin, KC	-	0	0	0	0	0	-	0	0	0	0	0	0	0	0	0	14	25.0	3	2	0	0	1.000	0	0	0	0	-
Ishii,Kazuhisa, LA	.127	55	7	1	6	6	.094	139	13	0	1	1	8	3	61	19	31	172.0	5	16	0	1	1.000	21	9	3	0	.43
Isringhausen,J, StL	.333	3	1	0	2	0	.206	102	21	4	1	2	16	5	35	8	74	75.1	3	18	0	1	1.000	1	0	0	0	.00
Jackson,Edwin, LA	.250	4	1	0	1	2	.100	10	1	0	0	0	1	1	3	3	8	24.2	2	6	0	1	1.000	2	0	0	1	.00
Jackson,Mike, CWS	-	0	0	0	0	0	.179	28	5	2	0	0	1	1	4	4	45	46.2	2	8	0	0	1.000	1	0	0	0	.00
Jarvis,Kevin, Sea-Col	-	0	0	0	0	0	.160	188	30	6	0	1	14	13	62	23	10	15.0	0	3	0	0	1.000	1	0	0	0	.00
Jennings,Jason, Col	.239	71	17	1	6	5	.257	202	52	12	0	2	22	11	48	13	33	201.0	18	25	3	2	.977	22	8	0	0	.36
Jimenez,Jose, Cle	-	0	0	0	0	0	.123	81	10	0	1	0	4	0	38	7	31	36.1	2	9	0	1	1.000	4	1	0	0	.25
Johnson,Jason, Det	.000	3	0	0	0	0	.091	22	2	0	0	0	0	2	15	0	33	196.2	10	17	3	1	.900	14	3	0	0	.21
Johnson,Ra, Ari	.125	80	10	0	6	3	.129	520	67	13	0	1	35	13	241	35	35	245.2	5	19	0	0	1.000	27	10	0	0	.37
Johnston,Mike, Pit	-	0	0	0	0	0	-	0	0	0	0	0	0	0	0	0	24	22.2	0	7	1	0	.875	2	1	1	0	.50
Jones,Bobby M, Bos	-	0	0	0	0	0	.173	81	14	2	0	0	8	4	23	12	3	3.1	0	1	0	0	1.000	0	0	0	0	.00
Jones,Todd, Cin-Phi	-	0	0	0	0	0	.188	16	3	1	0	0	1	4	0	0	78	82.1	4	7	2	0	.846	7	2	0	0	.29
Julio,Jorge, Bal	-	0	0	0	0	0	-	0	0	0	0	0	0	0	0	0	65	69.0	3	3	0	0	1.000	13	2	0	0	.15
Karsay,Steve, NYY	-	0	0	0	0	0	.000	4	0	0	0	0	0	0	2	0	7	6.2	1	1	0	0	.667	1	0	0	0	.00
Kazmir,Scott, TB	-	0	0	0	0	0	-	0	0	0	0	0	0	0	0	0	8	33.1	2	3	1	0	.833	8	3	1	1	.38
Kennedy,Joe, Col	.125	48	6	0	4	4	.169	59	10	1	1	0	5	2	17	4	27	162.1	9	33	4	1	.913	19	5	1	4	.26
Kensing,Logan, Fla	.000	2	0	0	0	1	.000	2	0	0	0	0	0	0	1	1	5	13.2	0	1	0	0	1.000	4	0	0	0	.00

Pitchers Hitting, Fielding and Holding Runners

Pitcher	2004 Hitting						Career Hitting										2004 Fielding and Holding Runners											
	Avg	AB	H	HR	RBI	SH	Avg	AB	H	2B	3B	HR	RBI	BB	SO	SH	G	Inn	PO	A	E	DP	Pct	SBA	CS	PCS	PPO	CS%
Kershner,Jason, Tor	-	0	0	0	0	0	-	0	0	0	0	0	0	0	0	1	24	22.1	1	4	0	0	1.000	5	1	1	0	.20
Kida,Masao, LA-Sea	-	0	0	0	0	0	.250	4	1	0	0	0	0	0	0	0	10	14.1	2	0	0	2	1.000	0	0	0	0	-
Kim,Byung-Hyun, Bos	-	0	0	0	0	0	.188	32	6	1	0	0	3	1	6	2	7	17.1	3	3	1	0	.857	3	0	0	1	.00
Kim,Sun-Woo, Mon	.233	30	7	0	7	4	.220	41	9	3	0	0	7	0	13	4	43	140.1	19	14	4	0	.892	9	2	0	2	.22
King,Ray, StL	.000	2	0	0	0	0	.000	5	0	0	0	0	0	0	2	0	86	62.0	9	11	1	0	.952	0	0	0	0	-
Kinney,Matt, Mil-KC	.222	9	2	0	1	1	.061	66	4	1	0	0	1	2	29	6	43	78.2	4	4	0	0	1.000	8	3	1	0	.38
Kline,Steve, StL	-	0	0	0	0	1	.154	13	2	1	0	0	2	0	5	4	67	50.1	4	10	0	0	1.000	6	1	0	0	.17
Knotts,Gary, Det	.333	3	1	0	0	1	.286	7	2	0	0	0	0	1	1	1	36	135.1	14	11	0	1	1.000	5	2	0	0	.40
Koch,Billy, CWS-Fla	-	0	0	0	0	0	.000	2	0	0	0	0	0	0	2	0	47	49.0	3	2	1	0	.833	7	0	0	0	.00
Kolb,Danny, Mil	-	0	0	0	0	0	-	0	0	0	0	0	0	0	0	0	64	57.2	2	10	1	1	.923	2	1	0	0	.50
Koplove,Mike, Ari	-	0	0	0	0	0	.000	2	0	0	0	0	0	0	1	0	76	86.2	6	23	2	4	.935	6	2	0	0	.33
Kroon,Marc, Col	-	0	0	0	0	0	-	0	0	0	0	0	0	0	0	0	6	6.0	0	3	0	1	1.000	1	0	0	0	.00
Lackey,John, Ana	.000	2	0	0	0	0	.000	5	0	0	0	0	0	0	0	3	33	198.1	15	23	0	1	1.000	22	7	0	1	.32
Lawrence,Brian, SD	.097	62	6	0	2	8	.138	218	30	7	0	1	16	11	64	15	34	203.0	11	38	0	3	1.000	7	3	0	0	.43
League,Brandon, Tor	-	0	0	0	0	0	-	0	0	0	0	0	0	0	0	0	3	4.2	0	0	0	0	-	0	0	0	0	-
Ledezma,Wil, Det	-	0	0	0	0	0	-	0	0	0	0	0	0	0	0	0	15	53.1	5	2	2	0	.778	5	2	1	0	.40
Lee,CI, Cle	.333	3	1	0	0	0	.333	3	1	0	0	0	0	0	0	0	33	179.0	5	7	0	0	1.000	14	5	1	0	.36
Lee,Da, Cle	-	0	0	0	0	0	-	0	0	0	0	0	0	0	0	0	4	4.1	0	1	0	0	.000	1	0	0	0	.00
Lehr,Justin, Oak	-	0	0	0	0	0	-	0	0	0	0	0	0	0	0	0	27	32.2	2	5	0	0	1.000	2	2	1	0	1.00
Leicester,Jon, ChC	.000	1	0	0	0	0	.000	1	0	0	0	0	0	0	0	0	32	41.2	0	4	0	0	1.000	2	1	0	0	.50
Leiter,Al, NYM	.093	54	5	0	0	2	.088	512	45	7	1	0	16	35	278	44	30	173.2	7	26	0	3	1.000	23	7	5	0	.30
Leskanic,C, KC-Bos	-	0	0	0	0	0	.179	39	7	3	0	1	7	1	17	5	51	43.1	1	3	0	0	1.000	2	0	0	0	.00
Levine,Al, Det	-	0	0	0	0	0	-	0	0	0	0	0	0	0	0	0	65	70.2	2	8	1	0	.909	9	4	0	0	.44
Lewis,Colby, Tex	-	0	0	0	0	0	.000	1	0	0	0	0	0	0	0	1	3	15.1	1	2	0	0	1.000	1	0	0	0	.00
Lidge,Brad, Hou	.000	1	0	0	0	0	.286	7	2	1	0	0	2	0	4	0	80	94.2	2	2	0	1	1.000	7	5	0	0	.71
Lidle,Cory, Cin-Phi	.145	62	9	1	6	8	.141	78	11	4	0	1	6	6	43	9	34	211.1	17	44	1	2	.984	20	8	0	0	.40
Lieber,Jon, NYY	.333	3	1	0	0	0	.155	464	72	15	0	0	20	21	165	44	27	176.2	10	19	4	1	.879	3	1	0	0	.33
Ligtenberg,K, Tor	-	0	0	0	0	0	-	0	0	0	0	0	0	0	0	0	57	55.0	1	5	0	0	1.000	10	1	0	0	.10
Lilly,Ted, Tor	.000	3	0	0	0	1	.059	17	1	0	0	0	0	0	7	1	32	197.1	11	9	2	0	.909	8	1	0	0	.13
Lima,Jose, LA	.188	48	9	0	2	8	.130	284	37	4	0	0	10	7	96	42	36	170.1	13	26	0	2	1.000	5	0	0	0	.00
Lincoln,Mike, StL	-	0	0	0	0	0	.100	10	1	0	0	0	0	0	5	1	13	17.1	1	2	1	0	.750	0	0	0	0	-
Linebrink,S, SD	.000	2	0	0	0	1	.200	15	3	1	0	0	0	0	9	2	73	84.0	4	5	2	0	.818	7	2	0	0	.29
Liriano,Pedro, Mil	.000	1	0	0	0	1	.000	1	0	0	0	0	0	0	0	0	11	15.2	1	1	0	0	1.000	1	0	0	0	.00
Loaiza,Esteban, CWS-NYY	.000	5	0	0	0	0	.173	179	31	2	1	0	11	3	40	24	31	183.0	13	29	0	4	1.000	18	8	0	1	.44
Loe,Kameron, Tex	-	0	0	0	0	0	-	0	0	0	0	0	0	0	0	0	2	6.2	0	1	1	0	.500	2	1	0	0	.50
Lohse,Kyle, Min	.000	3	0	0	0	1	.267	15	4	1	0	0	1	0	7	1	35	194.0	12	22	0	1	1.000	24	8	3	1	.33
Looper,Braden, NYM	.000	2	0	0	0	0	.125	8	1	0	0	0	0	0	5	1	71	83.1	5	12	0	1	1.000	8	2	0	0	.25
Lopez,Aquilino, Tor	-	0	0	0	0	0	-	0	0	0	0	0	0	0	0	0	18	21.0	0	3	0	0	1.000	2	2	0	0	1.00
Lopez,Javr, Col	.000	2	0	0	0	1	.143	7	1	0	0	0	1	0	3	1	64	40.2	6	17	1	2	.958	4	2	2	0	.50
Lopez,Rodrigo, Bal	-	0	0	0	0	0	.071	14	1	0	0	0	0	0	8	0	37	170.2	15	21	0	2	1.000	13	4	1	2	.31
Lowe,Derek, Bos	.250	4	1	0	1	1	.100	20	2	1	0	0	1	2	8	3	33	182.2	22	39	3	1	.953	36	2	1	1	.06
Lowry,Noah, SF	.182	33	6	0	0	3	.200	35	7	2	0	0	0	0	11	3	16	92.0	1	15	0	1	1.000	6	3	2	0	.50
MacDougal,Mike, KC	-	0	0	0	0	0	-	0	0	0	0	0	0	0	0	0	13	13.1	2	1	0	0	1.000	0	0	0	0	-
Maddux,Greg, ChC	.159	69	11	0	5	9	.177	1330	235	31	2	4	69	30	348	152	33	212.2	21	55	1	3	.987	38	12	0	0	.32
Madritsch,B, Sea	-	0	0	0	0	0	-	0	0	0	0	0	0	0	0	0	15	88.0	2	12	0	1	1.000	6	2	0	0	.33
Madson,Ryan, Phi	.000	3	0	0	0	1	.000	3	0	0	0	0	0	0	2	1	52	77.0	7	4	0	0	1.000	7	2	0	0	.29
Mahay,Ron, Tex	.000	1	0	0	0	0	.286	7	2	1	0	0	0	0	2	0	60	67.0	3	9	0	1	1.000	11	0	0	0	.00
Maine,John, Bal	-	0	0	0	0	0	-	0	0	0	0	0	0	0	0	0	1	3.2	1	0	0	1	1.000	1	1	0	1	1.00
Majewski,Gary, Mon	.000	2	0	0	0	0	.000	2	0	0	0	0	0	0	0	0	16	21.0	1	0	1	0	.500	0	0	0	0	-
Malaska,Mark, Bos	-	0	0	0	0	0	-	0	0	0	0	0	0	0	0	0	19	20.0	1	6	1	0	.875	1	0	0	0	.00
Mantei,Matt, Ari	-	0	0	0	0	0	.200	5	1	0	0	0	0	0	0	0	12	10.2	1	2	0	0	1.000	0	0	0	0	-
Manzanillo,J, Fla	.000	1	0	0	0	0	.083	12	1	0	0	0	0	0	6	2	26	32.1	4	8	0	0	1.000	3	1	0	1	.33
Maroth,Mike, Det	.000	4	0	0	1	0	.167	12	2	0	0	0	1	1	8	2	33	217.0	11	37	0	4	1.000	22	11	5	0	.50
Marquis,Jason, StL	.292	72	21	0	9	2	.193	145	28	7	0	1	11	3	43	9	32	201.1	21	31	3	1	.945	11	4	0	1	.36
Marsonek,Sam, NYY	-	0	0	0	0	0	-	0	0	0	0	0	0	0	0	0	1	1.1	0	0	0	0	-	0	0	0	0	-
Marte,Damaso, CWS	-	0	0	0	0	0	.000	4	0	0	0	0	0	0	0	1	74	73.2	4	4	0	1	1.000	11	3	1	0	.27
Martin,Tom, LA-Atl	-	0	0	0	0	0	.000	7	0	0	0	0	0	0	3	0	76	45.1	1	7	0	1	1.000	2	1	0	0	.50
Martinez,A, Bos	-	0	0	0	0	0	-	0	0	0	0	0	0	0	0	0	11	10.2	1	0	0	0	1.000	0	0	0	0	-
Martinez,Pedro, Bos	.000	2	0	0	0	0	.094	265	25	3	2	0	11	11	121	38	33	217.0	16	16	1	0	.970	24	5	0	1	.21
Mateo,Julio, Sea	-	0	0	0	0	0	-	0	0	0	0	0	0	0	0	0	45	57.2	3	1	3	1	.571	5	1	0	0	.20
Matthews,Mike, Cin	-	0	0	0	0	0	.120	25	3	0	0	1	1	0	9	3	35	30.0	1	0	1	0	.500	1	0	0	0	.00
Maurer,Dave, Tor	-	0	0	0	0	0	.000	1	0	0	0	0	0	0	0	0	3	1.1	0	1	0	0	1.000	0	0	0	0	-
May,Darrell, KC	.000	4	0	0	0	0	.059	17	1	0	0	0	0	1	8	1	31	186.0	8	12	0	1	1.000	26	9	5	0	.35
McConnell,Sam, Atl	.000	1	0	0	0	0	.000	1	0	0	0	0	0	0	0	0	10	9.1	0	1	0	0	1.000	0	0	0	0	-
McLeary,Marty, SD	-	0	0	0	0	0	-	0	0	0	0	0	0	0	0	0	3	3.2	1	0	0	0	1.000	0	0	0	0	-
Meadows,Brian, Pit	.000	3	0	0	1	0	.117	179	21	3	0	0	8	8	76	19	68	78.0	4	13	1	0	.944	5	1	0	0	.20
Meche,Gil, Sea	-	0	0	0	0	0	.200	5	1	0	0	0	0	0	0	0	23	127.2	5	7	1	0	.923	8	5	1	0	.63
Mecir,Jim, Oak	-	0	0	0	0	0	.000	1	0	0	0	0	0	0	0	0	65	47.2	1	3	0	0	1.000	9	1	0	0	.11
Mendoza,Ramiro, Bos	-	0	0	0	0	0	.000	3	0	0	0	0	0	0	0	3	1	27	30.2	4	5	0	0	1.000	0	0	0	0	-
Mercker,Kent, ChC	.000	2	0	0	0	0	.113	248	28	5	2	1	18	11	115	22	71	53.0	1	4	0	0	1.000	7	0	0	0	.00
Mesa,Jose, Pit	-	0	0	0	0	0	-	0	0	0	0	0	0	0	1	0	70	69.1	4	11	0	1	1.000	3	2	1	0	.67
Meyer,Dan, Atl	-	0	0	0	0	0	-	0	0	0	0	0	0	0	0	0	2	11.1	0	0	0	0	-	0	0	0	0	-
Miceli,Danny, Hou	.500	2	1	0	0	0	.091	22	2	0	0	0	0	0	0	10	0	74	77.2	5	10	0	1	1.000	14	0	0	0	.00
Miller,Justin, Tor	-	0	0	0	0	0	.000	2	0	0	0	0	0	0	0	0	19	81.2	9	7	1	1	.941	13	7	0	0	.54
Miller,Matt, Cle	-	0	0	0	0	0	-	0	0	0	0	0	0	0	0	0	57	55.1	1	9	1	0	.909	9	2	0	0	.22

Pitchers Hitting, Fielding and Holding Runners

Pitcher	2004 Hitting						Career Hitting										2004 Fielding and Holding Runners											
	Avg	AB	H	HR	RBI	SH	Avg	AB	H	2B	3B	HR	RBI	BB	SO	SH	G	Inn	PO	A	E	DP	Pct	SBA	CS	PCS	PPO	CS%
Miller,Trever, TB	-	0	0	0	0	0	.167	6	1	1	0	0	0	0	1	2	60	49.0	4	8	0	1	1.000	4	3	3	0	.75
Miller,Wade, Hou	.259	27	7	0	3	8	.166	259	43	9	0	0	17	4	80	30	15	88.2	7	11	0	2	1.000	8	0	0	0	.00
Millwood,Kevin, Phi	.174	46	8	0	1	5	.124	426	53	14	0	2	24	19	192	50	25	141.0	10	19	0	0	1.000	13	1	0	0	.08
Milton,Eric, Phi	.154	65	10	0	5	5	.188	85	16	1	0	0	7	5	36	5	34	201.0	4	23	0	0	1.000	14	2	0	0	.14
Mitre,Sergio, ChC	.067	15	1	0	0	3	.118	17	2	1	0	0	0	1	9	3	12	51.2	8	10	0	1	1.000	6	0	0	0	.00
Moreno,Orber, NYM	.000	1	0	0	0	0	.000	2	0	0	0	0	0	0	1	0	33	34.2	3	4	0	0	1.000	4	0	0	0	.00
Morris,Matt, StL	.161	62	10	0	6	8	.166	362	60	11	0	1	26	21	151	48	32	202.0	17	29	1	2	.979	14	3	0	1	.21
Moss,Damian, TB	-	0	0	0	0	0	.150	80	12	1	0	0	3	6	37	13	5	8.0	0	0	1	0	.000	0	0	0	0	-
Mota,Guillermo, LA-Fla	.167	12	2	0	1	0	.233	30	7	1	0	2	6	0	14	0	78	96.2	6	10	0	0	1.000	24	3	1	0	.13
Moyer,Jamie, Sea	.500	2	1	0	2	0	.156	173	27	2	0	0	6	15	57	22	34	202.0	14	23	0	3	1.000	13	4	1	0	.31
Mulder,Mark, Oak	.000	4	0	0	0	0	.045	22	1	0	0	0	1	1	11	1	33	225.2	6	51	3	3	.950	27	13	8	1	.48
Mulholland,T, Min	.000	2	0	0	0	0	.111	619	69	13	1	2	23	13	281	53	39	176.0	6	13	3	1	.864	7	5	0	1	.71
Munoz,Arnie, CWS	.000	1	0	0	0	0	.000	1	0	0	0	0	0	0	0	0	11	14.1	1	2	0	0	1.000	3	1	0	0	.33
Munro,Pete, Hou	.069	29	2	0	1	3	.094	53	5	0	0	0	3	4	17	6	21	99.2	11	21	0	1	1.000	12	1	0	0	.08
Mussina,Mike, NYY	.000	1	0	0	0	0	.211	38	8	1	0	0	5	0	6	1	27	164.2	11	28	2	1	.951	13	3	0	0	.23
Myers,Brett, Phi	.196	51	10	0	1	8	.162	136	22	6	0	3	4	44	16	32	176.0	15	23	0	1	1.000	21	3	0	0	.14
Myers,Mike, Sea-Bos	-	0	0	0	0	0	.000	1	0	0	0	0	1	0	0	0	75	42.2	0	10	0	1	1.000	5	2	1	0	.40
Myers,Rodney, LA	-	0	0	0	0	0	.167	18	3	1	0	0	1	0	9	0	1	2.0	0	0	0	0	-	0	0	0	0	-
Myette,Aaron, Cin	-	0	0	0	0	0	-	0	0	0	0	0	0	0	0	0	5	4.1	0	0	0	0	-	1	0	0	0	.00
Nageotte,Clint, Sea	.000	2	0	0	0	0	.000	2	0	0	0	0	0	0	2	0	12	36.2	4	8	0	0	1.000	4	2	0	0	.50
Nakamura,Mike, Tor	-	0	0	0	0	0	-	0	0	0	0	0	0	0	0	0	19	25.2	2	1	1	0	.750	4	0	0	0	.00
Nance,Shane, Ari	-	0	0	0	0	0	.333	3	1	0	0	0	1	0	2	0	19	12.1	0	1	0	0	1.000	1	0	0	0	.00
Narron,Samuel, Tex	-	0	0	0	0	0	-	0	0	0	0	0	0	0	0	0	1	2.2	2	2	0	0	1.000	0	0	0	0	-
Nathan,Joe, Min	.000	1	0	0	0	0	.161	62	10	3	0	2	4	3	16	10	73	72.1	1	6	0	1	1.000	7	3	0	0	.43
Neal,Blaine, SD	-	0	0	0	0	0	-	0	0	0	0	0	0	0	0	0	40	42.0	7	7	0	2	1.000	7	2	0	0	.29
Nelson,Je, Tex	-	0	0	0	0	0	.000	2	0	0	0	0	0	0	0	0	29	23.2	0	2	0	0	1.000	1	0	0	0	.00
Nelson,Jo, Bos	-	0	0	0	0	0	-	0	0	0	0	0	0	0	0	0	3	2.2	0	0	0	0	-	0	0	0	0	-
Neu,Mike, Fla	-	0	0	0	0	0	-	0	0	0	0	0	0	0	0	0	1	4.0	0	1	0	0	1.000	0	0	0	0	-
Nitkowski,C.J., Atl-NYY	-	0	0	0	0	0	.133	15	2	0	0	0	1	0	10	1	41	33.0	1	6	1	0	.875	2	0	0	0	.00
Nomo,Hideo, LA	.115	26	3	1	1	1	.135	481	65	14	1	4	26	13	221	44	18	84.0	5	14	0	1	1.000	19	4	0	0	.21
Norton,Phil, Cin	-	0	0	0	0	0	.500	4	2	0	0	0	0	0	1	0	69	65.2	2	11	0	2	1.000	3	1	0	0	.33
Novoa,Roberto, Det	-	0	0	0	0	0	-	0	0	0	0	0	0	0	0	0	16	21.0	1	4	0	0	1.000	4	2	0	0	.50
Nunez,Franklin, TB	-	0	0	0	0	0	-	0	0	0	0	0	0	0	0	0	8	10.2	1	1	0	0	1.000	1	0	0	0	.00
Nunez,Vladimir, Col	-	0	0	0	0	0	.136	59	8	0	0	1	5	1	19	8	22	25.2	1	3	1	0	.800	2	0	0	0	.00
Obermueller,W, Mil	.385	39	15	0	5	2	.290	62	18	3	0	0	6	1	20	4	25	118.0	11	12	0	0	1.000	3	0	0	0	.00
Ohka,Tomo, Mon	.080	25	2	0	0	0	.144	153	22	1	0	0	6	7	54	18	15	84.2	4	11	1	3	.938	3	2	1	0	.67
Oliver,Darren, Fla-Hou	.136	22	3	0	1	3	.228	202	46	10	0	1	18	7	67	15	27	72.2	2	11	0	0	1.000	7	4	0	0	.57
Oropesa,Eddie, SD	-	0	0	0	0	0	-	0	0	0	0	0	0	0	0	0	16	9.0	0	2	0	0	1.000	3	0	0	0	.00
Ortiz,Ra, Ana	.000	3	0	0	0	0	.000	22	0	0	0	0	0	0	7	1	34	128.0	6	13	2	1	.905	15	6	1	2	.40
Ortiz,Ru, Atl	.102	59	6	0	1	10	.206	422	87	21	0	6	41	29	112	49	34	204.2	7	38	0	5	1.000	25	7	0	0	.28
Osborne,D, NYY	-	0	0	0	0	0	.162	259	42	10	1	1	19	12	87	28	9	17.2	1	6	0	0	1.000	4	2	1	0	.50
Osuna,Antonio, SD	-	0	0	0	0	0	.111	9	1	0	0	0	1	1	1	0	31	36.2	2	5	0	0	1.000	3	3	0	1	1.00
Oswalt,Roy, Hou	.141	71	10	0	6	13	.154	234	36	5	0	0	13	10	69	30	36	237.0	14	32	3	3	.939	11	5	1	0	.45
Otsuka,Akinori, SD	.000	1	0	0	0	0	.000	1	0	0	0	0	0	0	0	0	73	77.1	7	11	2	1	.900	12	1	0	0	.08
Padilla,Juan, NYY-Cin	-	0	0	0	0	0	-	0	0	0	0	0	0	0	0	0	18	25.2	1	3	0	2	1.000	0	0	0	0	-
Padilla,V, Phi	.114	35	4	0	3	3	.079	164	13	2	0	0	9	9	84	14	20	115.1	9	15	0	0	1.000	7	2	0	0	.29
Park,Chan Ho, Tex	-	0	0	0	0	0	.168	345	58	15	1	2	23	17	125	39	16	95.2	6	10	2	0	.889	10	3	0	0	.30
Parra,Jose, NYM	-	0	0	0	0	0	-	0	0	0	0	0	0	2	0	1	13	14.0	1	0	0	0	1.000	2	0	0	0	.00
Parrish,John, Bal	.000	1	0	0	0	0	.000	1	0	0	0	0	0	0	0	0	56	78.0	8	11	6	1	.760	5	3	1	2	.60
Patterson,D, Det	-	0	0	0	0	0	.000	1	0	0	0	0	0	0	0	0	37	41.2	3	1	3	0	.571	2	2	0	0	1.00
Patterson,John, Mon	.121	33	4	0	1	5	.109	55	6	0	0	0	2	2	25	7	19	98.1	8	11	1	0	.950	12	3	1	0	.25
Pavano,Carl, Fla	.191	68	13	2	6	9	.142	288	41	8	2	2	14	4	112	34	31	222.1	9	31	0	3	1.000	21	5	0	0	.24
Pearce,Josh, StL	-	0	0	0	0	0	.250	4	1	0	0	0	1	0	2	0	3	2.1	0	0	0	0	1.000	1	1	0	0	1.00
Peavy,Jake, SD	.169	59	10	0	3	5	.143	147	21	4	0	0	6	7	51	15	27	166.1	10	24	1	3	.971	17	1	0	0	.06
Penny,Brad, Fla-LA	.059	51	3	0	1	1	.128	274	35	4	2	2	13	1	92	11	24	143.0	15	15	1	1	.968	18	4	0	0	.22
Percival,Troy, Ana	-	0	0	0	0	0	.000	1	0	0	0	0	0	0	1	0	52	49.2	1	3	0	0	1.000	6	0	0	0	.00
Perez,Od, LA	.113	62	7	0	2	6	.132	234	31	8	0	1	10	4	60	32	31	196.1	5	44	1	0	.980	19	5	4	0	.26
Perez,Ol, Pit	.190	58	11	0	0	10	.173	127	22	0	0	0	4	5	44	16	30	196.0	7	21	0	1	1.000	8	4	0	0	.50
Perisho,Matt, Fla	-	0	0	0	0	0	.000	5	0	0	0	0	0	0	5	0	66	47.0	0	4	0	0	1.000	4	0	0	0	.00
Peterson,Adam, Tor	-	0	0	0	0	0	-	0	0	0	0	0	0	0	0	0	3	2.2	0	0	0	0	-	1	0	0	0	.00
Pettitte,Andy, Hou	.174	23	4	0	2	3	.137	51	7	2	0	0	4	4	16	6	15	83.0	6	17	1	0	.958	5	2	1	0	.40
Phelps,To, Fla	.000	6	0	0	0	0	.059	17	1	0	0	0	0	2	5	1	19	34.0	2	6	0	0	1.000	2	2	0	0	1.00
Phelps,Tr, Mil	.000	1	0	0	0	0	.000	1	0	0	0	0	0	0	1	0	4	6.0	1	1	0	0	1.000	0	0	0	0	-
Pineiro,Joel, Sea	.200	5	1	0	0	0	.125	16	2	1	0	0	2	0	6	1	21	140.2	12	11	1	0	.958	14	3	0	0	.21
Politte,Cliff, CWS	-	0	0	0	0	0	.094	32	3	1	0	0	2	3	14	3	54	51.1	0	4	0	0	1.000	9	2	0	0	.22
Ponson,Sidney, Bal	.000	5	0	0	0	0	.109	46	5	2	0	0	0	0	14	6	33	215.2	21	28	1	4	.980	12	3	0	0	.25
Pote,Lou, Cle	-	0	0	0	0	0	-	0	0	0	0	0	0	0	0	0	2	3.0	0	1	0	0	1.000	0	0	0	0	-
Powell,Brian, Phi	.125	8	1	0	0	1	.143	21	3	1	0	0	1	1	11	1	17	39.1	2	3	1	0	.833	2	0	0	0	.00
Powell,Jay, Tex	-	0	0	0	0	0	.167	12	2	0	0	0	1	0	8	1	23	24.0	1	2	0	0	1.000	4	1	0	0	.25
Pratt,Andy, ChC	-	0	0	0	0	0	-	0	0	0	0	0	0	0	0	0	4	1.2	1	0	0	0	1.000	1	0	0	0	.00
Prinz,Bret, NYY	-	0	0	0	0	0	-	0	0	0	0	0	0	0	0	0	26	28.1	0	3	0	0	1.000	0	0	0	0	-
Prior,Mark, ChC	.139	36	5	0	0	6	.203	143	29	8	0	1	10	6	62	15	21	118.2	4	18	0	3	1.000	10	3	0	0	.30
Proctor,Scott, NYY	-	0	0	0	0	0	-	0	0	0	0	0	0	0	0	0	26	25.0	1	2	0	0	1.000	4	0	0	0	.00
Puffer,Brandon, SD	-	0	0	0	0	0	.000	9	0	0	0	0	0	1	7	1	14	18.0	3	2	1	0	.833	1	1	1	0	1.00
Pulido,Carlos, Min	-	0	0	0	0	0	-	0	0	0	0	0	0	0	0	0	6	11.1	0	0	0	0	-	2	0	0	0	.00

Pitchers Hitting, Fielding and Holding Runners

	2004 Hitting						Career Hitting										2004 Fielding and Holding Runners											
Pitcher	Avg	AB	H	HR	RBI	SH	Avg	AB	H	2B	3B	HR	RBI	BB	SO	SH	G	Inn	PO	A	E	DP	Pct	SBA	CS	PCS	PPO	CS%
Putz,J.J., Sea	-	0	0	0	0	0	-	0	0	0	0	0	0	0	0	0	54	63.0	4	9	0	1	1.000	7	3	0	0	.43
Qualls,Chad, Hou	.000	1	0	0	0	0	.000	1	0	0	0	0	0	0	1	0	25	33.0	1	2	0	0	1.000	2	1	0	0	.50
Quantrill,Paul, NYY	.000	1	0	0	0	0	.106	66	7	0	0	0	0	4	29	7	86	95.1	1	13	0	0	1.000	8	3	1	0	.38
Radke,Brad, Min	.000	2	0	0	0	1	.130	23	3	0	0	0	0	0	7	2	34	219.2	17	21	1	2	.974	18	8	0	1	.44
Rakers,Aaron, Bal	-	0	0	0	0	0	-	0	0	0	0	0	0	0	0	0	3	4.1	0	1	0	0	1.000	0	0	0	0	-
Ramirez,El, Phi	-	0	0	0	0	0	-	0	0	0	0	0	0	1	0	0	7	15.0	3	4	0	0	1.000	0	0	0	0	-
Ramirez,Er, Tex	-	0	0	0	0	0	-	0	0	0	0	0	0	0	0	0	34	35.2	2	3	0	0	1.000	2	1	0	0	.50
Ramirez,H, Atl	.095	21	2	0	1	1	.098	82	8	0	1	0	3	0	17	7	10	60.1	3	17	0	1	1.000	4	1	0	1	.25
Randolph,S, Ari	.417	12	5	0	3	0	.333	15	5	3	0	0	3	0	5	1	45	81.2	2	7	1	0	.900	6	4	2	0	.67
Rauch,Jon, CWS-Mon	.167	6	1	1	2	0	.167	6	1	0	0	1	2	0	4	0	11	32.0	2	3	0	0	1.000	6	0	0	0	.00
Redding,Tim, Hou	.138	29	4	0	0	1	.168	113	19	3	0	0	5	2	55	12	27	100.2	7	18	1	3	.962	9	1	0	0	.11
Redman,Mark, Oak	.000	5	0	0	0	0	.026	76	2	0	0	0	1	1	38	5	32	191.0	9	25	1	2	.971	13	8	7	2	.62
Reed,Steve, Col	.500	2	1	0	0	0	.179	28	5	0	0	0	1	0	9	2	65	66.0	0	7	2	0	.778	3	0	0	0	.00
Regilio,Nick, Tex	-	0	0	0	0	0	-	0	0	0	0	0	0	0	0	0	6	19.1	2	4	0	0	1.000	1	1	0	0	1.00
Reith,Brian, Cin	-	0	0	0	0	0	.158	19	3	0	0	0	2	0	8	0	22	26.0	0	7	0	0	1.000	0	0	0	0	-
Reitsma,Chris, Atl	-	0	0	0	0	0	.105	86	9	1	0	0	5	3	42	14	84	79.2	3	7	0	1	1.000	2	1	0	0	.50
Remlinger,Mike, ChC	.000	1	0	0	0	0	.073	110	8	3	0	0	8	8	37	19	48	36.2	3	7	0	1	1.000	3	2	1	0	.67
Reyes,Al, StL	1.000	1	1	0	0	0	.273	11	3	0	0	0	0	0	5	1	12	12.0	3	1	0	0	1.000	1	1	0	0	1.00
Reyes,Dennys, KC	.000	6	0	0	0	0	.061	49	3	1	0	0	0	2	23	2	40	108.0	4	17	5	0	.808	23	4	2	1	.17
Reynolds,Shane, Ari	-	0	0	0	0	0	.141	546	77	15	0	5	43	14	247	97	1	2.0	0	0	0	0	-	0	0	0	0	-
Rhodes,Arthur, Oak	-	0	0	0	0	0	.250	4	1	0	0	0	0	0	3	0	37	38.2	0	8	0	0	1.000	0	0	0	0	-
Riedling,John, Cin	.000	3	0	0	0	0	.160	25	4	0	0	0	2	0	15	1	70	77.2	4	17	0	1	1.000	10	0	0	0	.00
Riley,Matt, Bal	.000	2	0	0	0	0	.000	2	0	0	0	0	0	0	2	0	14	64.0	1	5	5	1	.545	5	1	0	0	.20
Rincon,Juan, Min	.000	1	0	0	0	0	.500	2	1	0	0	0	0	0	1	0	77	82.0	3	6	4	0	.692	6	2	0	0	.33
Rincon,Ricardo, Oak	-	0	0	0	0	0	.000	4	0	0	0	0	0	0	1	1	67	44.0	1	2	0	0	1.000	2	0	0	0	.00
Riske,David, Cle	-	0	0	0	0	0	-	0	0	0	0	0	0	0	0	0	72	77.1	7	4	0	1	1.000	2	0	0	0	.00
Ritchie,Todd, TB	-	0	0	0	0	0	.176	187	33	5	0	0	6	7	69	20	4	8.0	0	0	0	0	-	0	0	0	0	-
Rivera,Mariano, NYY	-	0	0	0	0	0	-	0	0	0	0	0	0	0	0	0	74	78.2	9	31	1	1	.976	6	1	0	0	.17
Roa,Joe, Min	-	0	0	0	0	0	.213	47	10	1	0	0	3	2	13	3	48	70.0	5	9	1	1	.933	9	0	0	0	.00
Robbins,Jake, Cle	-	0	0	0	0	0	-	0	0	0	0	0	0	0	0	0	2	1.2	0	0	0	0	-	0	0	0	0	-
Roberts,Grant, NYM	-	0	0	0	0	0	.250	4	1	0	0	0	0	0	3	1	4	4.2	1	2	0	0	1.000	0	0	0	0	-
Roberts,Willis, Pit	.000	1	0	0	0	0	.200	5	1	0	0	0	0	0	4	1	9	12.0	1	3	0	0	1.000	0	0	0	0	-
Robertson,J, Cle	-	0	0	0	0	0	.154	52	8	0	1	0	3	1	14	5	8	14.0	1	2	0	0	1.000	3	0	0	0	.00
Robertson,Nate, Det	.000	3	0	0	0	0	.000	5	0	0	0	0	0	0	2	0	34	196.2	4	25	5	5	.853	12	6	0	1	.50
Rodriguez,Eddy, Bal	.000	1	0	0	0	0	.000	1	0	0	0	0	0	0	1	0	29	43.1	0	5	0	1	1.000	3	2	0	0	.67
Rodriguez,Fe, SF-Phi	.000	1	0	0	0	0	.250	16	4	1	0	1	3	0	5	2	76	65.2	1	7	1	1	.889	9	2	0	0	.22
Rodriguez,Fr, Ana	-	0	0	0	0	0	-	0	0	0	0	0	0	0	0	0	69	84.0	5	9	0	0	1.000	6	2	0	0	.33
Rodriguez,R, Tex	.000	2	0	0	0	0	.000	5	0	0	0	0	0	0	3	0	5	26.2	3	3	0	0	1.000	5	2	1	0	.40
Rogers,Kenny, Tex	.000	5	0	0	0	0	.132	53	7	0	0	0	3	4	20	4	35	211.2	16	48	1	1	.985	7	5	3	3	.71
Romero,J.C., Min	-	0	0	0	0	0	.333	3	1	1	0	0	0	0	1	0	74	74.1	7	8	0	2	1.000	3	1	0	0	.33
Rueter,Kirk, SF	.131	61	8	0	2	3	.152	592	90	8	0	0	39	26	103	80	33	190.1	18	50	1	5	.986	4	3	1	1	.75
Rusch,Glendon, ChC	.154	39	6	2	3	7	.153	249	38	1	0	3	19	8	86	35	32	129.2	6	16	1	4	.957	4	3	0	0	.75
Ryan,B.J., Bal	-	0	0	0	0	0	.000	2	0	0	0	0	0	0	0	0	76	87.0	3	6	1	0	.900	6	1	0	0	.17
Saarloos,Kirk, Oak	-	0	0	0	0	0	.057	35	2	1	0	0	3	1	11	8	6	24.1	2	9	0	1	1.000	2	0	0	0	.00
Sabathia,C.C., Cle	.250	4	1	0	0	0	.263	19	5	0	0	0	0	1	4	1	30	188.0	1	17	0	2	1.000	23	6	1	0	.26
Saenz,Chris, Mil	.000	2	0	0	0	0	.000	2	0	0	0	0	0	0	1	0	1	6.0	0	0	0	0	-	0	0	0	0	-
Sanchez,Duaner, LA	.250	4	1	0	2	1	.250	4	1	1	0	0	2	0	1	1	67	80.0	9	11	0	0	1.000	10	4	1	0	.40
Sanchez,Jesus, Cin	.000	4	0	0	0	1	.176	142	25	0	1	0	6	3	41	12	3	14.1	1	3	0	0	1.000	3	1	0	0	.33
Santana,Johan, Min	.375	8	3	0	2	0	.313	16	5	0	0	0	2	0	2	0	34	228.0	9	24	4	2	.892	13	7	4	0	.54
Santos,Victor, Mil	.051	39	2	0	1	6	.070	43	3	1	0	0	1	2	21	7	31	154.0	13	4	3	1	.850	18	3	0	0	.17
Schilling,Curt, Bos	.143	7	1	0	0	0	.150	769	115	13	1	0	29	25	268	102	32	226.2	16	14	0	2	1.000	7	1	0	1	.14
Schmidt,Jason, SF	.136	66	9	2	3	13	.101	465	47	6	0	4	17	22	220	76	32	225.0	5	22	3	0	.900	30	2	0	0	.07
Schoeneweis,S, CWS	.500	2	1	0	0	0	.286	7	2	1	0	0	1	2	2	0	20	112.2	7	21	0	3	1.000	20	10	6	0	.50
Seanez,Rudy, KC-Fla	-	0	0	0	0	0	.000	4	0	0	0	0	0	1	4	0	39	46.0	6	4	1	0	.909	4	0	0	0	.00
Seay,Bobby, TB	-	0	0	0	0	0	-	0	0	0	0	0	0	0	0	0	21	22.2	1	3	0	0	1.000	2	2	2	0	1.00
Seibel,Phil, Bos	-	0	0	0	0	0	-	0	0	0	0	0	0	0	0	0	2	3.2	0	1	0	0	1.000	0	0	0	0	-
Sele,Aaron, Ana	.000	1	0	0	0	0	.160	25	4	1	0	0	1	1	5	4	28	132.0	3	10	2	2	.867	18	11	1	0	.61
Seo,Jae, NYM	.156	32	5	0	1	3	.120	83	10	2	0	0	1	5	28	7	24	117.2	12	17	0	3	1.000	14	6	1	0	.43
Serrano,Jimmy, KC	-	0	0	0	0	0	-	0	0	0	0	0	0	0	0	0	10	32.2	2	3	0	0	1.000	4	2	0	0	.50
Service,Scott, Ari	.000	1	0	0	0	0	.059	17	1	0	0	0	1	0	9	0	21	20.1	3	2	0	0	1.000	2	0	0	0	.00
Sheets,Ben, Mil	.134	67	9	0	1	9	.095	243	23	1	0	0	7	14	125	20	34	237.0	14	23	2	0	.949	20	5	0	1	.25
Sherrill,G, Sea	-	0	0	0	0	0	-	0	0	0	0	0	0	0	0	0	21	23.2	0	4	0	0	1.000	2	1	0	0	.50
Shields,Scot, Ana	.000	1	0	0	0	0	.000	1	0	0	0	0	0	0	1	0	60	105.1	6	13	1	0	.950	6	0	0	0	.00
Shouse,Brian, Tex	-	0	0	0	0	0	-	0	0	0	0	0	0	0	0	0	53	44.1	9	11	0	0	1.000	1	0	0	0	.00
Silva,Carlos, Min	.000	3	0	0	0	0	.143	14	2	1	0	0	1	1	4	1	33	203.0	11	25	2	1	.947	13	6	0	0	.46
Simontacchi,J, StL	.500	2	1	0	0	0	.200	90	18	1	0	0	2	2	29	4	13	15.1	3	3	0	1	1.000	5	0	0	0	-
Simpson,Allan, Col	.000	1	0	0	0	0	.000	1	0	0	0	0	0	0	0	0	32	39.0	0	4	2	0	.667	5	0	0	0	.00
Small,Aaron, Fla	.000	2	0	0	0	0	.000	3	0	0	0	0	0	0	2	0	7	16.1	1	2	0	0	1.000	2	0	0	0	.00
Smith,Travis, Atl	.125	8	1	0	0	0	.148	27	4	0	0	0	2	0	7	2	16	40.2	3	4	1	0	.875	1	0	0	0	.00
Smoltz,John, Atl	.000	2	0	0	0	0	.172	739	127	20	1	5	51	70	284	92	73	81.2	9	9	0	0	1.000	3	1	0	0	.33
Snare,Ryan, Tex	-	0	0	0	0	0	-	0	0	0	0	0	0	0	0	0	1	3.1	0	0	0	0	-	0	0	0	0	-
Snell,Ian, Pit	.000	2	0	0	0	1	.000	2	0	0	0	0	0	2	1	1	3	12.0	3	1	0	0	1.000	1	0	0	0	.00
Soriano,Rafael, Sea	-	0	0	0	0	0	.000	4	0	0	0	0	0	0	1	0	6	3.1	0	0	1	0	.000	0	0	0	0	-
Sosa,Jorge, TB	-	0	0	0	0	0	-	0	0	0	0	0	0	0	0	0	43	99.1	2	7	0	1	1.000	5	0	0	0	.00
Sparks,Steve, Ari	.129	31	4	0	1	3	.122	41	5	1	0	0	3	1	17	2	29	120.2	8	21	2	0	.935	10	5	0	0	.50

Pitchers Hitting, Fielding and Holding Runners

Pitcher	2004 Hitting						Career Hitting										2004 Fielding and Holding Runners											
	Avg	AB	H	HR	RBI	SH	Avg	AB	H	2B	3B	HR	RBI	BB	SO	SH	G	Inn	PO	A	E	DP	Pct	SBA	CS	PCS	PPO	CS%
Speier,Justin, Tor	.000	1	0	0	0	0	.176	17	3	0	0	0	0	0	8	0	62	69.0	1	5	2	1	.750	9	4	0	0	.44
Springer,Russ, Hou	-	0	0	0	0	0	.077	26	2	0	0	0	0	0	16	4	16	13.2	1	2	0	0	1.000	1	0	0	0	.00
Standridge,J, TB	-	0	0	0	0	0	-	0	0	0	0	0	0	1	0	0	3	10.0	2	1	0	0	1.000	0	0	0	0	-
Stanford,Jason, Cle	-	0	0	0	0	0	-	0	0	0	0	0	0	0	0	0	2	11.0	2	2	0	1	1.000	4	0	0	0	.00
Stanton,Mike, NYM	.500	2	1	0	1	0	.421	19	8	1	0	0	3	1	3	0	83	79.0	4	14	0	0	1.000	6	1	1	0	.17
Stark,Denny, Col	.000	8	0	0	0	0	.099	71	7	3	0	1	8	5	28	4	6	26.0	3	5	1	0	.889	5	0	0	0	.00
Stewart,Josh, CWS	-	0	0	0	0	0	-	0	0	0	0	0	0	0	0	0	3	7.2	0	1	0	0	1.000	0	0	0	0	-
Stewart,Sc, Cle-LA	-	0	0	0	0	0	.000	4	0	0	0	0	0	0	3	0	34	26.0	0	6	0	0	1.000	4	1	1	1	.25
Stone,Ricky, Hou-SD	.000	1	0	0	0	0	.000	8	0	0	0	0	0	0	3	1	43	51.2	4	8	0	0	1.000	2	0	0	0	.00
Sturtze,Tanyon, NYY	.000	3	0	0	0	0	.063	16	1	0	0	0	0	0	5	2	28	77.1	1	10	0	1	1.000	7	0	0	1	.00
Sullivan,Scott, KC	-	0	0	0	0	0	.083	48	4	0	0	0	1	0	28	3	49	60.1	1	5	1	3	.857	1	0	0	0	.00
Suppan,Jeff, StL	.070	57	4	0	0	7	.182	137	25	1	0	4	4	4	33	21	31	188.0	10	30	1	0	.976	14	3	0	1	.21
Sweeney,Brian, SD	.000	4	0	0	0	0	.000	4	0	0	0	0	0	0	2	0	7	14.1	1	0	0	0	1.000	0	0	0	0	-
Szuminski,J, SD	.000	1	0	0	0	0	.000	1	0	0	0	0	0	0	1	0	7	10.0	1	3	1	0	.800	0	0	0	0	-
Tadano,K, Cle	.333	3	1	0	0	0	.333	3	1	0	0	0	0	0	1	0	14	50.1	3	6	0	0	1.000	5	1	0	0	.20
Takatsu,Shingo, CWS	-	0	0	0	0	0	-	0	0	0	0	0	0	0	0	0	59	62.1	1	10	0	0	1.000	1	0	0	0	.00
Tankersley,D, SD	.250	8	2	0	1	1	.286	21	6	1	0	1	2	1	6	2	9	35.0	7	1	0	0	1.000	3	0	0	0	.00
Tavarez,Julian, StL	-	0	0	0	0	0	.111	135	15	0	0	0	8	6	57	20	77	64.1	7	9	0	0	1.000	6	2	0	0	.33
Taylor,Aaron, Sea	-	0	0	0	0	0	-	0	0	0	0	0	0	0	0	0	5	3.2	1	0	0	0	1.000	0	0	0	0	-
Tejera,Michael, Fla-Tex	-	0	0	0	0	0	.157	51	8	0	0	1	5	1	6	3	8	9.1	1	1	0	0	1.000	1	1	1	0	1.00
Telemaco,A, Phi	.000	4	0	0	0	0	.121	116	14	4	1	0	3	6	51	8	42	54.1	2	6	0	0	1.000	5	1	0	0	.20
Thomas,Brad, Min	-	0	0	0	0	0	-	0	0	0	0	0	0	0	0	0	3	2.2	0	1	0	0	1.000	0	0	0	0	-
Thomson,John, Atl	.197	66	13	0	4	10	.190	263	50	2	1	0	16	10	111	37	33	198.1	12	27	1	2	.975	18	4	1	0	.22
Thornton,Matt, Sea	-	0	0	0	0	0	-	0	0	0	0	0	0	0	0	0	19	32.2	0	4	0	1	1.000	3	2	0	0	.67
Timlin,Mike, Bos	-	0	0	0	0	0	.000	7	0	0	0	0	0	0	4	0	76	76.1	9	6	0	0	1.000	3	2	0	0	.67
Tomko,Brett, SF	.113	62	7	0	0	13	.174	339	59	8	0	0	23	15	122	51	32	194.0	13	25	2	2	.950	7	3	0	0	.43
Torres,Salomon, Pit	.500	2	1	0	0	0	.129	93	12	1	1	0	1	2	41	12	84	92.0	6	16	0	0	1.000	9	3	0	0	.33
Towers,Josh, Tor	.000	1	0	0	0	2	.000	4	0	0	0	0	0	0	0	2	21	116.1	9	13	2	1	.917	13	3	0	0	.23
Trachsel,Steve, NYM	.186	59	11	0	5	11	.169	574	97	16	1	2	38	22	176	83	33	202.2	13	37	0	3	1.000	26	7	0	1	.27
Tsao,Chin-hui, Col	-	0	0	0	0	0	.154	13	2	1	0	0	0	0	1	2	10	9.1	0	1	0	0	1.000	0	0	0	0	-
Tucker,T.J., Mon	.083	12	1	0	0	0	.278	36	10	1	0	0	0	0	10	1	54	70.0	2	9	0	0	1.000	3	1	0	0	.33
Turnbow,D, Ana	.000	1	0	0	0	0	.000	1	0	0	0	0	0	0	0	0	4	6.1	2	1	0	0	1.000	0	0	0	0	-
Urbina,Ugueth, Det	-	0	0	0	0	0	.094	53	5	0	0	0	1	3	32	4	54	54.0	2	2	0	0	1.000	4	0	0	0	.00
Urdaneta,Lino, Det	-	0	0	0	0	0	-	0	0	0	0	0	0	0	0	0	1	0.0	0	0	0	0	-	0	0	0	0	-
Valdez,Ismael, SD-Fla	.192	52	10	0	5	3	.130	386	50	9	0	1	17	13	120	58	34	170.0	12	19	1	0	.969	10	2	0	2	.20
Valdez,Merkin, SF	-	0	0	0	0	0	-	0	0	0	0	0	0	0	0	0	2	1.2	0	0	0	0	-	0	0	0	0	-
Valentine,Joe, Cin	.000	1	0	0	0	0	.000	1	0	0	0	0	0	0	0	0	24	29.1	3	3	1	0	.857	3	0	0	0	.00
Valverde,Jose, Ari	-	0	0	0	0	0	1.000	1	1	1	0	0	0	0	0	0	29	29.2	4	2	2	0	.750	0	0	0	0	-
Van Benschoten,J, Pit	.125	8	1	1	2	2	.125	8	1	0	0	1	2	1	3	2	6	28.2	1	4	0	1	1.000	5	1	0	0	.20
Van Poppel,T, Cin	.176	17	3	0	1	5	.158	57	9	1	0	0	2	2	22	11	48	115.1	5	10	1	0	.938	4	2	0	0	.50
Vargas,Claudio, Mon	.045	22	1	0	0	7	.019	52	1	0	0	0	0	1	23	11	45	110.1	10	11	0	2	1.000	7	5	0	1	.71
Vasquez,Jorge, KC	-	0	0	0	0	0	-	0	0	0	0	0	0	0	0	0	2	3.1	0	1	0	0	1.000	0	0	0	0	-
Vazquez,Javier, NYY	.250	4	1	0	0	1	.209	363	76	9	2	0	22	14	58	66	32	198.0	9	37	2	3	.958	7	5	1	2	.71
Venafro,Mike, LA	-	0	0	0	0	0	-	0	0	0	0	0	0	0	0	0	17	9.0	0	1	0	0	1.000	0	0	0	0	-
Villacis,E, KC	-	0	0	0	0	0	-	0	0	0	0	0	0	0	0	0	1	3.1	0	1	1	0	.500	1	0	0	0	.00
Villafuerte,B, Ari	.000	1	0	0	0	0	.000	2	0	0	0	0	0	0	0	2	20	20.0	2	5	0	0	1.000	2	1	0	0	.50
Villarreal,O, Ari	-	0	0	0	0	0	.000	3	0	0	0	0	0	0	0	2	17	18.0	0	4	0	0	1.000	0	0	0	0	-
Villone,Ron, Sea	-	0	0	0	0	0	.131	168	22	3	1	1	7	1	49	12	56	117.0	6	17	4	2	.852	6	2	2	1	.33
Vizcaino,Luis, Mil	-	0	0	0	0	0	.000	2	0	0	0	0	0	0	2	0	73	72.0	4	3	0	0	1.000	4	0	0	0	.00
Vogelsong,Ryan, Pit	.226	31	7	0	3	10	.191	47	9	3	0	0	3	2	18	12	31	133.0	8	14	0	1	1.000	6	1	0	0	.17
Waechter,Doug, TB	-	0	0	0	0	0	-	0	0	0	0	0	0	0	0	0	14	70.1	5	5	1	0	.909	8	4	1	0	.50
Wagner,Billy, Phi	.000	2	0	0	0	0	.059	17	1	0	0	0	1	1	10	0	45	48.1	3	7	0	0	1.000	2	1	1	0	.50
Wagner,Ryan, Cin	-	0	0	0	0	0	-	0	0	0	0	0	0	0	0	0	49	51.2	2	10	2	0	.857	0	0	0	1	-
Wakefield,Tim, Bos	.000	2	0	0	0	0	.119	84	10	2	0	1	3	2	30	12	32	188.1	12	26	4	1	.905	41	8	1	2	.20
Walker,Jamie, Det	-	0	0	0	0	0	-	0	0	0	0	0	0	0	0	0	70	64.2	2	4	0	0	1.000	4	0	0	0	.00
Walker,Kevin, SF	-	0	0	0	0	0	.250	4	1	0	0	0	0	0	0	0	5	1.2	0	0	0	0	-	0	0	0	0	-
Walker,Ty, SF	.000	7	0	0	0	0	.000	9	0	0	0	0	0	0	6	0	52	63.2	6	6	0	0	1.000	3	0	0	0	.00
Wasdin,John, Tex	.000	3	0	0	0	0	.214	14	3	1	0	0	1	1	5	1	15	65.0	3	6	0	0	1.000	7	1	0	0	.14
Washburn,J, Ana	.400	5	2	0	1	2	.333	24	8	0	0	0	3	2	7	6	25	149.1	3	22	1	2	.962	7	4	2	1	.57
Watkins,Steve, SD	-	0	0	0	0	0	-	0	0	0	0	0	0	0	0	0	11	14.1	0	3	1	0	.750	1	0	0	0	.00
Wayne,Justin, Fla	.000	3	0	0	0	1	.000	12	0	0	0	0	0	0	5	2	19	32.2	2	4	0	1	1.000	2	1	0	0	.50
Weathers,David, NYM-Hou-Fla	.000	3	0	0	0	0	.101	138	14	0	0	2	4	7	84	16	66	82.1	3	7	0	0	1.000	7	3	0	0	.43
Weaver,Jeff, LA	.214	70	15	0	2	7	.213	89	19	3	1	0	3	1	33	9	34	220.0	12	32	0	1	1.000	18	7	1	0	.39
Webb,Brandon, Ari	.094	64	6	0	4	4	.096	114	11	1	0	0	4	5	57	11	35	208.0	13	41	5	6	.915	41	10	3	0	.24
Webb,John, TB	-	0	0	0	0	0	-	0	0	0	0	0	0	0	0	0	4	9.0	0	0	0	0	-	0	0	0	0	-
Weber,Ben, Ana	-	0	0	0	0	0	-	0	0	0	0	0	0	0	0	0	18	22.1	0	0	0	0	-	4	2	0	0	.50
Wellemeyer,T, ChC	-	0	0	0	0	0	.000	1	0	0	0	0	0	0	1	0	20	24.1	0	2	0	1	1.000	2	0	0	0	.00
Wells,David, SD	.105	57	6	0	0	3	.115	113	13	1	0	0	3	3	37	11	31	195.2	7	38	1	1	.978	8	3	2	2	.38
Wells,Kip, Pit	.186	43	8	0	0	4	.187	182	34	8	1	2	10	4	78	21	24	138.1	7	18	3	1	.893	14	6	0	0	.43
Wendell,Turk, Col	.000	2	0	0	0	0	.070	43	3	0	0	0	5	5	19	1	12	16.2	2	2	0	0	1.000	2	1	1	0	.50
Westbrook,Jake, Cle	.000	3	0	0	0	1	.000	4	0	0	0	0	0	1	3	2	33	215.2	24	49	3	6	.961	14	6	0	1	.43
Wheeler,Dan, NYM-Hou	.200	5	1	0	0	1	.143	7	1	0	0	0	0	0	6	1	65	60.0	4	6	2	0	.833	3	0	0	0	.00
White,Gabe, NYY-Cin	-	0	0	0	0	0	.105	38	4	0	0	1	3	1	26	10	64	59.2	1	5	0	0	1.000	1	0	0	0	.00
White,Ri, Cle	-	0	0	0	0	0	.100	40	4	1	0	0	1	0	12	2	59	78.1	6	14	0	1	1.000	10	5	0	0	.50
Wickman,Bob, Cle	-	0	0	0	0	0	.000	2	0	0	0	0	0	0	0	0	30	29.2	3	3	0	1	1.000	6	0	0	0	.00

Pitchers Hitting, Fielding and Holding Runners

Pitcher	2004 Hitting						Career Hitting										2004 Fielding and Holding Runners											
	Avg	AB	H	HR	RBI	SH	Avg	AB	H	2B	3B	HR	RBI	BB	SO	SH	G	Inn	PO	A	E	DP	Pct	SBA	CS	PCS	PPO	CS%
Williams,Dave, Pit	.111	9	1	0	0	0	.119	59	7	2	0	1	5	0	34	3	10	38.2	1	6	0	0	1.000	2	0	0	0	.00
Williams,J, SF	.139	36	5	0	0	6	.123	73	9	1	0	0	1	1	33	12	22	129.1	10	20	2	1	.938	10	2	1	1	.20
Williams,Randy, Sea	-	0	0	0	0	0	-	0	0	0	0	0	0	0	0	0	6	4.2	0	1	0	1	1.000	0	0	0	0	-
Williams,Todd, Bal	-	0	0	0	0	0	-	0	0	0	0	0	0	0	0	0	29	31.1	2	4	0	0	1.000	1	1	0	1	1.00
Williams,Woody, StL	.180	61	11	0	2	5	.213	381	81	24	1	3	34	15	126	26	31	189.2	20	31	3	2	.944	16	6	1	0	.38
Williamson,S, Bos	-	0	0	0	0	0	.043	23	1	0	0	0	0	3	14	7	28	28.2	3	2	0	0	1.000	4	0	0	0	.00
Willis,D, Fla	.203	74	15	1	3	6	.220	132	29	4	1	2	7	7	25	8	32	197.0	15	34	2	3	.961	19	7	3	2	.37
Wilson,Pa, Cin	.100	60	6	0	2	7	.096	167	16	3	0	1	7	5	102	16	29	183.2	6	23	0	0	1.000	8	4	0	0	.50
Wise,Matt, Mil	.000	4	0	0	0	1	.000	4	0	0	0	0	0	0	1	1	30	52.2	3	12	0	1	1.000	6	0	0	0	.00
Witasick,Jay, SD	.000	5	0	0	0	0	.071	42	3	0	0	0	3	1	22	2	44	61.2	2	7	0	0	1.000	1	0	0	0	.00
Wolf,Randy, Phi	.267	45	12	3	8	8	.196	306	60	15	0	4	29	18	96	48	23	136.2	8	15	2	0	.920	7	0	0	0	.00
Wood,Kerry, ChC	.133	45	6	1	3	5	.169	320	54	3	0	7	28	10	106	44	22	140.1	4	13	1	2	.944	17	3	2	1	.18
Wood,Mike, KC	.000	2	0	0	0	0	.000	2	0	0	0	0	0	0	0	1	17	100.0	8	19	3	1	.900	5	3	2	1	.60
Worrell,Tim, Phi	-	0	0	0	0	0	.101	79	8	1	0	0	4	4	42	10	77	78.1	10	15	1	1	.962	3	0	0	0	.00
Wright,Dan, CWS	-	0	0	0	0	0	.000	6	0	0	0	0	0	0	2	0	4	17.2	1	3	1	0	.800	6	1	1	0	.17
Wright,Jam, Col	.053	19	1	0	0	8	.132	333	44	12	1	1	13	11	142	42	14	78.2	7	18	0	3	1.000	15	2	0	4	.13
Wright,Jar, Atl	.105	57	6	1	4	6	.147	75	11	2	0	1	5	2	41	9	32	186.1	15	24	2	2	.951	15	2	0	0	.13
Wuertz,Mike, ChC	.000	1	0	0	0	0	.000	1	0	0	0	0	0	0	1	0	31	29.0	0	4	0	0	1.000	4	1	0	0	.25
Wunsch,Kelly, CWS	-	0	0	0	0	0	-	0	0	0	0	0	0	0	0	0	3	2.0	0	1	0	0	1.000	1	1	1	0	1.00
Yan,Esteban, Det	-	0	0	0	0	0	1.000	2	2	0	0	1	1	0	0	1	69	87.0	12	14	2	1	.929	2	1	0	0	.50
Yates,Tyler, NYM	.091	11	1	0	0	1	.091	11	1	0	0	0	0	0	5	1	21	46.2	1	6	0	1	1.000	5	1	0	0	.20
Young,Chris, Tex	-	0	0	0	0	0	-	0	0	0	0	0	0	0	0	0	7	36.1	2	3	1	0	.833	5	1	1	0	.20
Young,Jason, Col	.000	2	0	0	1	2	.222	9	2	1	0	0	1	1	1	2	2	8.1	2	1	0	0	1.000	1	0	0	0	.00
Zambrano,C, ChC	.229	70	16	1	5	8	.198	177	35	7	0	3	11	4	70	14	31	209.2	18	29	2	2	.959	11	4	1	0	.36
Zambrano,V, TB-NYM	.182	11	2	0	1	1	.133	15	2	1	0	0	1	0	5	3	26	142.0	10	14	2	1	.923	15	7	0	1	.47
Zito,Barry, Oak	.000	4	0	0	0	0	.000	19	0	0	0	0	0	0	11	2	34	213.0	5	30	2	1	.946	23	8	5	0	.35

Hitters Pitching

Player	2004 Pitching											Career Pitching											
	G	W	L	Sv	IP	H	R	ER	BB	SO	ERA	G	W	L	Sv	IP	H	R	ER	BB	SO	ERA
Durrington,T, Mil	1	0	0	0	0.1	0	0	0	0	0	0.00	1	0	0	0	0.1	0	0	0	0	0	0.00
Finley,Steve, Ari-LA	0	0	0	0	0.0	0	0	0	0	0	-	1	0	0	0	1.0	0	0	0	1	0	0.00
Halter,Shane, Ana	0	0	0	0	0.0	0	0	0	0	0	-	2	0	0	0	1.0	1	0	0	1	0	0.00
Harris,Lenny, Fla	0	0	0	0	0.0	0	0	0	0	0	-	1	0	0	0	1.0	0	0	0	0	1	0.00
Jimenez,D, Cin	0	0	0	0	0.0	0	0	0	0	0		1	0	0	0	1.1	0	0	0	0	0	0.00
Laker,Tim, Cle	1	0	0	0	1.0	1	0	0	1	0	0.00	2	0	0	0	2.0	2	0	0	2	1	0.00
Loretta,Mark, SD	0	0	0	0	0.0	0	0	0	0	0	-	1	0	0	0	1.0	1	0	0	1	2	0.00
Mabry,John, StL	0	0	0	0	0.0	0	0	0	0	0	-	2	0	0	0	1.0	6	7	7	4	0	63.00
Mayne,Brent, Ari-LA	0	0	0	0	0.0	0	0	0	0	0	-	1	1	0	0	1.0	1	0	0	1	0	0.00
McCarty,Dave, Bos	3	0	0	0	3.2	2	1	1	1	4	2.45	3	0	0	0	3.2	2	1	1	1	4	2.45
McKay,Cody, StL	1	0	0	0	2.0	0	0	0	1	0	0.00	1	0	0	0	2.0	0	0	0	1	0	0.00
Menechino,F, Oak-Tor	1	0	0	0	0.1	2	0	0	0	0	0.00	2	0	0	0	1.1	8	4	4	0	0	27.00
Nunez,AbrO, Pit	1	0	0	0	0.1	0	0	0	0	0	0.00	1	0	0	0	0.1	0	0	0	0	0	0.00
Osik,Keith, Bal	0	0	0	0	0.0	0	0	0	0	0	-	2	0	0	0	2.0	7	9	9	2	2	40.50
Perez,To, Phi	0	0	0	0	0.0	0	0	0	0	0		1	0	0	0	0.1	0	0	0	0	0	0.00
Relaford,Desi, KC	0	0	0	0	0.0	0	0	0	0	0	-	1	0	0	0	1.0	0	0	0	0	1	0.00
Ventura,Robin, LA	1	0	0	0	1.0	1	0	0	0	0	0.00	1	0	0	0	1.0	1	0	0	0	0	0.00
Zeile,Todd, NYM	1	0	0	0	1.0	4	5	5	2	0	45.00	2	0	0	0	2.0	5	5	5	2	1	22.50

The Manager's Record

Fans know a lot about the abilities of players. They can answer questions concerning any two players, such as "Who has the better throwing arm?" or "Who has more power?" The average fan, however, would not be able to make similar comparisons between managers. Who is quicker to go to the bullpen: Tony Pena or Eric Wedge? Who platoons more: Bobby Cox or Tony LaRussa? Who uses the Intentional Walk more often: Terry Francona or Joe Torre?

You can also use this record to determine if a manager adjusts to the personnel on his team, or sticks with a strategy regardless. For example, Lou Piniella in 2002, managing the Mariners with Edgar Martinez, John Olerud, and Dan Wilson in the lineup, used 96 pinch runners. In 2003, managing the Devil Rays, he used only 29 pinch runners. Art Howe in 2001 used only 18 defensive substitutes. In 2003, managing the Mets, he used 67.

Here is a description of the categories:

Lineups
LUp is different Lineups Used. This looks at batting order, not fielding positions. For games in which a DH is used, lineup slots 1-9 are compared. For games in which the pitcher bats, lineup slots 1-8 are compared.

PL% is the Platoon Percentage of the starting lineup. For example, in 2004 Dusty Baker had a 44% platoon percentage, a low figure. This means that, on average, Dusty only had 44% of his starting-lineup hitters with a platoon advantage (i.e. batting lefty against right-handed starters or batting right-handed against lefty starters).

Substitutions
PH is Pinch Hitters used
PR is Pinch Runners used
DS is Defensive Substitutions
Rel is Relief Appearances

Tactics
LO is Long Outings, number of games in which the starter threw more than 120 pitches
SBA is Stolen Base Attempts
SacA is Sacrifice bunt Attempts
IBB is Intentional Walks issued
PO is Pitch Outs called

Results
Headings are self-explanatory.

Felipe Alou

Year	Team	Lg	G	LINEUPS		SUBSTITUTIONS					TACTICS				RESULTS		
				LUp	PL%	PH	PR	DS	Rel	LO	SBA	SacA	IBB	PO	W	L	Pct
1994	Expos	NL	114	72	.48	143	33	7	259	0	173	72	24	20	74	40	.649
1995	Expos	NL	144	116	.49	200	36	10	396	7	169	74	20	22	66	78	.458
1996	Expos	NL	162	113	.49	240	31	30	433	13	142	97	25	25	88	74	.543
1997	Expos	NL	162	138	.58	205	22	40	390	15	121	91	33	30	78	84	.481
1998	Expos	NL	162	133	.50	235	27	37	443	2	137	111	30	18	65	97	.401
1999	Expos	NL	162	143	.49	247	33	55	432	5	121	84	28	26	68	94	.420
2000	Expos	NL	162	120	.61	211	24	32	452	5	106	103	29	18	67	95	.414
2001	Expos	NL	53	40	.58	84	4	5	171	1	39	28	10	7	21	32	.396
2003	Giants	NL	161	127	.56	195	26	42	461	9	90	93	34	9	100	61	.621
2004	Giants	NL	162	138	.67	239	47	60	521	16	66	102	35	2	91	71	.562
	162-Game Average			128	.54	224	32	36	444	8	131	96	30	20	81	81	.497

Dusty Baker

Year	Team	Lg	G	LINEUPS		SUBSTITUTIONS					TACTICS				RESULTS		
				LUp	PL%	PH	PR	DS	Rel	LO	SBA	SacA	IBB	PO	W	L	Pct
1994	Giants	NL	115	76	.53	177	16	9	288	2	154	88	24	78	55	60	.478
1995	Giants	NL	144	96	.41	230	36	13	381	8	184	101	33	77	67	77	.465
1996	Giants	NL	162	129	.51	250	17	15	425	15	166	103	45	96	68	94	.420
1997	Giants	NL	162	114	.71	212	17	22	481	17	170	85	37	93	90	72	.556
1998	Giants	NL	163	130	.62	224	20	12	433	8	153	111	51	41	89	74	.546
1999	Giants	NL	162	120	.62	233	16	16	450	27	165	113	28	40	86	76	.531
2000	Giants	NL	162	82	.56	233	26	22	384	25	118	86	16	37	97	65	.599
2001	Giants	NL	162	122	.48	261	22	19	439	10	99	95	32	45	90	72	.556
2002	Giants	NL	161	143	.43	204	28	37	417	21	95	94	44	40	95	66	.590
2003	Cubs	NL	162	114	.49	239	20	42	420	27	104	93	36	24	88	74	.543
2004	Cubs	NL	162	113	.44	254	16	19	460	16	94	106	33	56	89	73	.549
	162-Game Average			117	.53	237	22	21	432	17	142	101	36	59	86	76	.532

Bruce Bochy

Year	Team	Lg	G	LINEUPS		SUBSTITUTIONS					TACTICS				RESULTS		
				LUp	PL%	PH	PR	DS	Rel	LO	SBA	SacA	IBB	PO	W	L	Pct
1995	Padres	NL	144	96	.59	262	30	23	337	17	170	68	26	38	70	74	.486
1996	Padres	NL	162	114	.52	289	29	15	411	10	164	73	42	65	91	71	.562
1997	Padres	NL	162	111	.60	291	26	9	426	3	200	84	24	58	76	86	.469
1998	Padres	NL	162	110	.65	280	62	44	369	9	116	84	30	27	98	64	.605
1999	Padres	NL	162	137	.60	298	51	21	403	4	241	60	39	29	74	88	.457
2000	Padres	NL	162	134	.52	285	44	14	443	14	184	52	40	27	76	86	.469
2001	Padres	NL	162	116	.60	255	54	27	422	6	173	43	40	23	79	83	.488
2002	Padres	NL	162	151	.66	241	29	56	459	2	115	62	61	12	66	96	.407
2003	Padres	NL	162	134	.58	307	16	29	473	4	115	63	52	6	64	98	.395
2004	Padres	NL	162	96	.54	261	28	47	437	2	77	75	39	14	87	75	.537
	162-Game Average			121	.59	280	37	29	423	7	157	67	40	30	79	83	.488

Larry Bowa

Year	Team	Lg	G	LINEUPS		SUBSTITUTIONS					TACTICS				RESULTS		
				LUp	PL%	PH	PR	DS	Rel	LO	SBA	SacA	IBB	PO	W	L	Pct
2001	Phillies	NL	162	81	.59	232	15	5	473	6	200	87	43	38	86	76	.531
2002	Phillies	NL	161	145	.61	261	15	31	450	9	147	97	54	14	80	81	.497
2003	Phillies	NL	162	119	.57	244	17	26	437	6	101	69	51	31	86	76	.531
2004	Phillies	NL	160	107	.54	258	21	36	471	2	127	74	60	23	85	75	.531
	162-Game Average			114	.58	250	17	25	460	6	144	82	52	27	85	77	.522

Bob Brenly

Year	Team	Lg	G	LINEUPS		SUBSTITUTIONS					TACTICS				RESULTS		
				LUp	PL%	PH	PR	DS	Rel	LO	SBA	SacA	IBB	PO	W	L	Pct
2001	Diamondbacks	NL	162	123	.55	321	35	20	421	22	109	89	23	43	92	70	.568
2002	Diamondbacks	NL	162	153	.66	305	25	41	422	14	138	89	30	24	98	64	.605
2003	Diamondbacks	NL	162	145	.66	270	27	29	452	7	114	89	52	41	84	78	.519
2004	Diamondbacks	NL	80	49	.63	126	12	4	245	3	40	34	44	25	29	51	.363
	162-Game Average			135	.62	293	28	27	441	13	115	86	43	38	87	75	.535

Bobby Cox

Year	Team	Lg	G	LINEUPS		SUBSTITUTIONS					TACTICS				RESULTS		
				LUp	PL%	PH	PR	DS	Rel	LO	SBA	SacA	IBB	PO	W	L	Pct
1994	Braves	NL	114	64	.60	163	30	25	244	5	79	83	39	44	68	46	.596
1995	Braves	NL	144	59	.56	224	48	40	339	13	116	77	38	41	90	54	.625
1996	Braves	NL	162	162	.62	254	32	27	408	19	126	90	48	34	96	66	.593

Year	Team	Lg	G	LUp	PL%	PH	PR	DS	Rel	LO	SBA	SacA	IBB	PO	W	L	Pct
1997	Braves	NL	162	87	.64	276	58	29	374	23	166	112	46	13	101	62	.620
1998	Braves	NL	162	80	.64	245	28	25	354	14	141	97	26	40	106	56	.654
1999	Braves	NL	162	76	.58	272	51	34	394	13	214	89	37	54	103	59	.636
2000	Braves	NL	162	103	.59	252	72	11	376	6	204	109	34	59	95	67	.586
2001	Braves	NL	162	113	.57	278	50	23	412	4	131	84	55	90	88	74	.543
2002	Braves	NL	160	138	.48	263	27	43	469	5	115	95	63	46	101	59	.631
2003	Braves	NL	162	69	.52	251	36	43	489	7	90	85	69	49	101	61	.623
2004	Braves	NL	162	105	.70	243	57	28	483	4	118	103	49	22	96	66	.593
162-Game Average				100	.59	257	46	31	410	11	142	97	48	47	99	63	.609

Terry Francona

				LINEUPS		SUBSTITUTIONS					TACTICS				RESULTS		
Year	Team	Lg	G	LUp	PL%	PH	PR	DS	Rel	LO	SBA	SacA	IBB	PO	W	L	Pct
1997	Phillies	NL	162	98	.66	288	19	28	409	22	148	91	31	30	68	94	.420
1998	Phillies	NL	162	84	.53	256	20	19	385	20	142	85	23	16	75	87	.463
1999	Phillies	NL	162	85	.51	239	13	31	441	16	160	81	17	27	77	85	.475
2000	Phillies	NL	162	108	.53	278	17	14	414	25	132	89	17	16	65	97	.401
2004	Red Sox	AL	162	141	.65	116	65	58	437	4	98	17	28	27	98	64	.605
162-Game Average				114	.57	281	28	32	414	18	135	74	24	24	98	99	.497

Ron Gardenhire

				LINEUPS		SUBSTITUTIONS					TACTICS				RESULTS		
Year	Team	Lg	G	LUp	PL%	PH	PR	DS	Rel	LO	SBA	SacA	IBB	PO	W	L	Pct
2002	Twins	AL	161	111	.69	124	30	43	435	4	141	48	24	11	94	67	.584
2003	Twins	AL	162	126	.63	124	40	25	399	2	138	59	35	14	90	72	.556
2004	Twins	AL	162	131	.59	126	45	29	435	1	162	65	27	17	92	70	.568
162-Game Average				123	.64	125	38	32	424	2	147	57	29	14	92	70	.569

Phil Garner

				LINEUPS		SUBSTITUTIONS					TACTICS				RESULTS		
Year	Team	Lg	G	LUp	PL%	PH	PR	DS	Rel	LO	SBA	SacA	IBB	PO	W	L	Pct
1994	Brewers	NL	115	94	.53	53	33	24	252	0	96	46	16	23	53	62	.461
1995	Brewers	NL	144	120	.58	83	67	52	321	10	145	64	23	52	65	79	.451
1996	Brewers	NL	162	114	.58	115	48	46	385	13	149	72	20	82	80	82	.494
1997	Brewers	NL	161	128	.59	190	42	36	367	6	158	65	21	55	78	83	.484
1998	Brewers	NL	162	125	.59	265	54	46	416	6	140	85	21	59	74	88	.457
1999	Brewers	NL	112	69	.57	182	15	5	294	4	75	85	19	57	52	60	.464
2000	Tigers	AL	162	128	.53	126	30	25	429	8	121	58	13	26	79	83	.488
2001	Tigers	AL	162	116	.64	93	40	14	391	9	194	58	29	36	66	96	.407
2004	Astros	NL	74	31	.54	141	19	35	241	5	78	40	24	7	48	26	.649
162-Game Average				119	.58	161	45	37	400	8	149	74	24	51	77	85	.474

John Gibbons

				LINEUPS		SUBSTITUTIONS					TACTICS				RESULTS		
Year	Team	Lg	G	LUp	PL%	PH	PR	DS	Rel	LO	SBA	SacA	IBB	PO	W	L	Pct
2004	Blue Jays	AL	51	36	.68	42	3	2	130	3	34	2	11	21	20	30	.400
162-Game Average				114	.68	133	10	6	413	10	108	6	35	67	64	95	.400

Ozzie Guillen

				LINEUPS		SUBSTITUTIONS					TACTICS				RESULTS		
Year	Team	Lg	G	LUp	PL%	PH	PR	DS	Rel	LO	SBA	SacA	IBB	PO	W	L	Pct
2004	White Sox	AL	162	134	.55	132	35	15	399	6	129	76	36	17	83	79	.512
162-Game Average				134	.55	132	35	15	399	6	129	76	36	17	83	79	.512

Art Howe

				LINEUPS		SUBSTITUTIONS					TACTICS				RESULTS		
Year	Team	Lg	G	LUp	PL%	PH	PR	DS	Rel	LO	SBA	SacA	IBB	PO	W	L	Pct
1996	Athletics	AL	162	124	.46	121	74	40	419	7	93	49	49	37	78	84	.481
1997	Athletics	AL	162	133	.61	198	62	38	481	8	107	66	40	43	65	97	.401
1998	Athletics	AL	162	129	.59	136	47	40	408	12	178	75	19	26	74	88	.457
1999	Athletics	AL	162	129	.62	144	62	56	406	5	107	53	32	43	87	75	.537
2000	Athletics	AL	161	119	.59	162	81	39	381	9	55	40	45	38	91	70	.565
2001	Athletics	AL	162	116	.60	131	30	18	416	4	97	40	41	43	102	60	.630
2002	Athletics	AL	162	110	.56	126	57	54	408	3	66	30	45	16	103	59	.636
2003	Mets	NL	161	133	.61	271	54	67	412	10	101	105	71	14	66	95	.410
2004	Mets	NL	162	136	.50	273	46	54	474	8	130	91	66	19	71	91	.438
162-Game Average				126	.57	174	57	45	423	7	104	61	45	31	82	80	.506

Clint Hurdle

Year	Team	Lg	G	LINEUPS		SUBSTITUTIONS					TACTICS				RESULTS		
				LUp	PL%	PH	PR	DS	Rel	LO	SBA	SacA	IBB	PO	W	L	Pct
2002	Rockies	NL	140	129	.52	247	19	41	437	3	139	47	38	13	67	73	.479
2003	Rockies	NL	162	108	.47	287	13	32	500		100	82	51	16	74	88	.457
2004	Rockies	NL	162	131	.57	289	18	35	473	4	77	124	84	11	68	94	.420
	162-Game Average			128	.52	287	17	38	492	2	110	88	60	14	73	89	.450

Tony LaRussa

Year	Team	Lg	G	LINEUPS		SUBSTITUTIONS					TACTICS				RESULTS		
				LUp	PL%	PH	PR	DS	Rel	LO	SBA	SacA	IBB	PO	W	L	Pct
1994	Athletics	AL	114	97	.62	89	28	14	308	5	130	31	23	32	51	63	.447
1995	Athletics	AL	144	120	.54	113	38	24	358	19	158	42	17	42	67	77	.465
1996	Cardinals	NL	162	120	.52	246	25	13	413	24	207	117	38	41	88	74	.543
1997	Cardinals	NL	162	146	.54	307	17	18	399	16	224	77	26	79	73	89	.451
1998	Cardinals	NL	162	146	.52	259	7	18	429	13	174	85	32	34	83	79	.512
1999	Cardinals	NL	161	138	.47	264	32	28	454	13	182	103	31	30	75	86	.466
2000	Cardinals	NL	162	137	.53	240	35	25	386	11	138	107	21	34	95	67	.586
2001	Cardinals	NL	162	117	.47	256	26	13	485	7	126	102	31	25	93	69	.574
2002	Cardinals	NL	162	141	.52	302	23	42	472	6	128	117	39	13	97	65	.599
2003	Cardinals	NL	162	126	.50	297	20	51	460	12	114	108	36	9	85	77	.525
2004	Cardinals	NL	162	119	.53	275	25	69	469	8	158	87	24	4	105	57	.648
	162-Game Average			133	.52	250	26	30	438	13	164	92	30	32	86	76	.532

Ken Macha

Year	Team	Lg	G	LINEUPS		SUBSTITUTIONS					TACTICS				RESULTS		
				LUp	PL%	PH	PR	DS	Rel	LO	SBA	SacA	IBB	PO	W	L	Pct
2003	Athletics	AL	162	111	.57	117	25	23	364	5	62	31	42	9	96	66	.593
2004	Athletics	AL	162	119	.60	122	13	14	414	12	69	30	49	2	91	71	.562
	162-Game Average			115	.58	120	19	19	389	9	66	31	46	6	94	69	.577

Lee Mazzilli

Year	Team	Lg	G	LINEUPS		SUBSTITUTIONS					TACTICS				RESULTS		
				LUp	PL%	PH	PR	DS	Rel	LO	SBA	SacA	IBB	PO	W	L	Pct
2004	Orioles	AL	162	105	.60	89	44	18	452	2	142	57	43	32	78	84	.481
	162-Game Average			105	.60	89	44	18	452	2	142	57	43	32	78	84	.481

Lloyd McClendon

Year	Team	Lg	G	LINEUPS		SUBSTITUTIONS					TACTICS				RESULTS		
				LUp	PL%	PH	PR	DS	Rel	LO	SBA	SacA	IBB	PO	W	L	Pct
2001	Pirates	NL	162	131	.51	255	17	32	410	2	166	83	49	52	62	100	.383
2002	Pirates	NL	161	149	.45	248	32	65	458	0	135	102	93	65	72	89	.447
2003	Pirates	NL	162	114	.57	285	21	58	457	4	123	99	58	73	75	87	.463
2004	Pirates	NL	162	114	.50	278	13	58	464	4	103	99	64	55	72	89	.447
	162-Game Average			127	.51	267	21	53	448	3	132	96	66	61	70	91	.435

Jack McKeon

Year	Team	Lg	G	LINEUPS		SUBSTITUTIONS					TACTICS				RESULTS		
				LUp	PL%	PH	PR	DS	Rel	LO	SBA	SacA	IBB	PO	W	L	Pct
1997	Reds	NL	63	50	.46	102	18	7	154	5	79	42	12	18	33	30	.524
1998	Reds	NL	162	132	.55	288	30	25	366	10	137	98	31	7	77	85	.475
1999	Reds	NL	163	95	.50	251	30	38	381	9	218	88	43	14	96	67	.589
2000	Reds	NL	163	117	.51	270	31	41	387	10	137	82	43	24	85	77	.525
2003	Marlins	NL	124	57	.43	160	23	13	280	7	150	92	28	17	75	49	.605
2004	Marlins	NL	162	90	.48	224	27	34	404	2	139	102	60	19	83	79	.512
	162-Game Average			105	.50	251	31	31	382	8	166	98	42	19	87	75	.537

Bob Melvin

Year	Team	Lg	G	LINEUPS		SUBSTITUTIONS					TACTICS				RESULTS		
				LUp	PL%	PH	PR	DS	Rel	LO	SBA	SacA	IBB	PO	W	L	Pct
2003	Mariners	AL	162	111	.62	74	48	33	366	7	145	44	24	5	93	69	.574
2004	Mariners	AL	162	151	.59	109	66	26	414	14	152	56	32	24	63	99	.389
	162-Game Average			131	.61	92	57	30	390	11	149	50	28	15	78	84	.481

Dave Miley

Year	Team	Lg	G	LUp	PL%	PH	PR	DS	Rel	LO	SBA	SacA	IBB	PO	W	L	Pct
2003	Reds	NL	57	52	.61	94	9	17	168		27	25	21	7	22	35	.386
2004	Reds	NL	162	132	.61	265	25	50	497	3	102	78	54	8	76	86	.469
	162-Game Average			136	.61	266	25	50	492	2	95	76	55	11	72	90	.447

Al Pedrique

Year	Team	Lg	G	LUp	PL%	PH	PR	DS	Rel	LO	SBA	SacA	IBB	PO	W	L	Pct
2004	Diamondbacks	NL	82	76	.62	116	14	15	226	4	45	42	35	15	22	60	.268
	162-Game Average			150	.62	229	28	30	446	8	89	83	69	30	43	119	.268

Tony Pena

Year	Team	Lg	G	LUp	PL%	PH	PR	DS	Rel	LO	SBA	SacA	IBB	PO	W	L	Pct
2002	Royals	AL	126	113	.66	80	22	13	339	8	160	57	43	7	49	77	.389
2003	Royals	AL	162	125	.60	88	24	15	407	1	162	79	33	8	83	79	.512
2004	Royals	AL	162	141	.57	53	27	14	409	4	115	55	48	6	58	104	.358
	162-Game Average			136	.61	80	26	15	416	5	157	69	45	8	68	94	.422

Lou Piniella

Year	Team	Lg	G	LUp	PL%	PH	PR	DS	Rel	LO	SBA	SacA	IBB	PO	W	L	Pct
1994	Mariners	AL	112	98	.49	113	24	6	252	4	69	54	28	37	49	63	.438
1995	Mariners	AL	145	98	.56	137	41	22	324	30	151	66	32	40	79	66	.545
1996	Mariners	AL	161	99	.55	190	28	14	403	15	129	65	40	40	85	76	.528
1997	Mariners	AL	162	84	.57	147	35	27	392	25	129	61	30	32	90	72	.556
1998	Mariners	AL	161	111	.53	99	38	43	368	32	154	58	18	20	76	85	.472
1999	Mariners	AL	162	130	.46	122	38	30	346	21	175	49	27	31	79	83	.488
2000	Mariners	AL	162	130	.50	109	43	52	383	1	178	73	32	22	91	71	.562
2001	Mariners	AL	162	115	.64	121	44	64	392	5	216	62	23	33	116	46	.716
2002	Mariners	AL	162	133	.64	89	96	50	343	8	195	66	34	25	93	69	.574
2003	Devil Rays	AL	162	124	.60	159	29	26	372	10	184	53	37	23	63	99	.389
2004	Devil Rays	AL	162	137	.63	97	25	36	401	8	174	44	35	16	70	91	.435
	162-Game Average			119	.56	131	42	35	376	15	166	62	32	30	84	78	.520

Frank Robinson

Year	Team	Lg	G	LUp	PL%	PH	PR	DS	Rel	LO	SBA	SacA	IBB	PO	W	L	Pct
2002	Expos	NL	162	154	.60	239	37	40	437	9	182	130	80	23	83	79	.512
2003	Expos	NL	162	134	.63	228	44	29	437	25	139	85	51	8	83	79	.512
2004	Expos	NL	162	131	.67	253	16	27	462	15	147	119	76	1	67	95	.414
	162-Game Average			140	.63	240	32	32	445	16	156	111	69	11	78	84	.479

Mike Scioscia

Year	Team	Lg	G	LUp	PL%	PH	PR	DS	Rel	LO	SBA	SacA	IBB	PO	W	L	Pct
2000	Angels	AL	162	75	.62	110	41	4	441	6	145	63	32	40	82	80	.506
2001	Angels	AL	162	130	.62	118	30	8	384	5	168	66	33	50	75	87	.463
2002	Angels	AL	162	108	.64	142	46	26	400	5	168	60	24	29	99	63	.611
2003	Angels	AL	162	130	.64	114	47	40	375	1	190	64	38	25	77	85	.475
2004	Angels	AL	162	126	.57	94	32	44	343	3	189	69	27	32	92	70	.568
	162-Game Average			114	.62	116	39	24	389	4	172	64	31	35	85	77	.525

Buck Showalter

Year	Team	Lg	G	LUp	PL%	PH	PR	DS	Rel	LO	SBA	SacA	IBB	PO	W	L	Pct
1994	Yankees	AL	113	79	.59	95	31	3	241	0	95	34	18	22	70	43	.619
1995	Yankees	AL	145	107	.68	124	30	20	302	37	80	27	15	29	79	65	.549
1998	Diamondbacks	NL	162	124	.62	252	17	15	368	7	111	68	18	13	65	97	.401
1999	Diamondbacks	NL	162	97	.63	220	20	17	382	25	176	75	34	15	100	62	.617
2000	Diamondbacks	NL	162	99	.60	250	32	11	390	18	141	89	36	10	85	77	.525
2003	Rangers	AL	162	133	.61	81	40	39	494	4	90	35	45	12	71	91	.438
2004	Rangers	AL	162	120	.64	86	15	24	468	3	105	29	29	5	89	73	.549
	162-Game Average			115	.63	168	28	20	401	14	121	54	30	16	85	77	.524

Joe Torre

Year Team	Lg	G	LINEUPS		SUBSTITUTIONS					TACTICS				RESULTS		
			LUp	PL%	PH	PR	DS	Rel	LO	SBA	SacA	IBB	PO	W	L	Pct
1994 Cardinals	NL	115	79	.68	192	9	0	330	6	122	57	13	33	53	61	.465
1995 Cardinals	NL	47	36	.51	99	6	4	146	1	42	26	11	14	20	27	.426
1996 Yankees	AL	162	131	.57	92	62	55	411	22	142	53	27	19	92	70	.568
1997 Yankees	AL	162	118	.61	75	70	23	368	19	157	54	29	14	96	66	.593
1998 Yankees	AL	162	96	.62	94	36	28	334	27	216	44	18	9	114	48	.704
1999 Yankees	AL	162	76	.63	103	57	10	276	26	129	31	15	12	98	64	.605
2000 Yankees	AL	161	112	.63	86	49	27	382	27	147	22	16	8	87	74	.540
2001 Yankees	AL	161	94	.56	76	33	14	362	10	214	41	22	21	95	65	.594
2002 Yankees	AL	161	127	.62	84	48	31	334	10	138	33	44	17	103	58	.640
2003 Yankees	AL	163	104	.65	101	39	18	367	18	131	39	36	33	101	61	.623
2004 Yankees	AL	162	116	.65	86	35	46	436	4	117	48	32	32	101	61	.623
162-Game Average			109	.62	109	44	26	375	17	156	45	26	21	96	66	.594

Carlos Tosca

Year Team	Lg	G	LINEUPS		SUBSTITUTIONS					TACTICS				RESULTS		
			LUp	PL%	PH	PR	DS	Rel	LO	SBA	SacA	IBB	PO	W	L	Pct
2002 Blue Jays	AL	109	91	.49	56	20	22	303	1	54	12	35	20	58	51	.532
2003 Blue Jays	AL	162	125	.60	129	23	29	443	5	62	12	46	50	86	76	.531
2004 Blue Jays	AL	111	93	.59	60	15	15	301	3	55	23	36	36	47	64	.423
162-Game Average			131	.57	104	25	28	444	4	73	20	50	45	81	81	.500

Jim Tracy

Year Team	Lg	G	LINEUPS		SUBSTITUTIONS					TACTICS				RESULTS		
			LUp	PL%	PH	PR	DS	Rel	LO	SBA	SacA	IBB	PO	W	L	Pct
2001 Dodgers	NL	162	111	.50	264	34	20	409	8	131	81	25	10	86	76	.531
2002 Dodgers	NL	162	145	.52	281	34	35	423	3	133	96	45	18	92	70	.568
2003 Dodgers	NL	162	103	.64	242	18	63	438	8	116	97	35	10	85	77	.525
2004 Dodgers	NL	162	94	.70	295	25	19	459	4	143	78	47	7	93	69	.574
162-Game Average			113	.59	271	28	34	432	6	131	88	38	11	89	73	.549

Alan Trammell

Year Team	Lg	G	LINEUPS		SUBSTITUTIONS					TACTICS				RESULTS		
			LUp	PL%	PH	PR	DS	Rel	LO	SBA	SacA	IBB	PO	W	L	Pct
2003 Tigers	AL	162	129	.72	124	25	14	451	2	161	92	35	28	43	119	.265
2004 Tigers	AL	162	131	.67	105	29	19	432	4	136	62	32	8	72	90	.444
162-Game Average			130	.70	115	27	17	442	3	149	77	34	18	58	105	.355

Gary Varsho

Year Team	Lg	G	LINEUPS		SUBSTITUTIONS					TACTICS				RESULTS		
			LUp	PL%	PH	PR	DS	Rel	LO	SBA	SacA	IBB	PO	W	L	Pct
2004 Phillies	NL	2	2	.44	4	1	1	5	0	0	2	0	0	1	1	.500
162-Game Average			162	.44	324	81	81	405	0	0	162	0	0	81	81	.500

Eric Wedge

Year Team	Lg	G	LINEUPS		SUBSTITUTIONS					TACTICS				RESULTS		
			LUp	PL%	PH	PR	DS	Rel	LO	SBA	SacA	IBB	PO	W	L	Pct
2003 Indians	AL	162	145	.67	104	32	27	428	4	147	67	37	12	68	94	.420
2004 Indians	AL	162	114	.72	91	34	20	479	2	149	55	47	24	80	82	.494
162-Game Average			130	.70	98	33	24	454	3	148	61	42	18	74	88	.457

Jimy Williams

Year Team	Lg	G	LINEUPS		SUBSTITUTIONS					TACTICS				RESULTS		
			LUp	PL%	PH	PR	DS	Rel	LO	SBA	SacA	IBB	PO	W	L	Pct
1997 Red Sox	AL	162	97	.56	123	48	16	417	13	116	30	40	108	78	84	.481
1998 Red Sox	AL	162	95	.60	165	53	14	432	14	111	48	23	75	92	70	.568
1999 Red Sox	AL	162	111	.62	123	35	9	412	13	106	47	15	75	94	68	.580
2000 Red Sox	AL	162	140	.67	158	52	30	425	9	73	49	28	114	85	77	.525
2001 Red Sox	AL	118	93	.63	69	22	26	315	5	48	31	29	106	65	53	.551
2002 Astros	NL	162	143	.58	251	34	48	480	2	98	89	78	38	84	78	.519
2003 Astros	NL	162	85	.43	291	19	29	502	2	96	75	53	38	87	75	.537
2004 Astros	NL	88	52	.42	132	2	21	252	4	41	67	36	16	44	44	.500
162-Game Average			112	.57	180	36	27	445	9	95	60	42	78	87	75	.534

2004 American League Managers

Manager	G	LINEUPS		SUBSTITUTIONS					TACTICS				RESULTS		
		LUp	PL%	PH	PR	DS	Rel	LO	SBA	SacA	IBB	PO	W	L	Pct
Terry Francona, Bos	162	141	.65	116	65	58	437	4	98	17	28	27	98	64	.605
Ron Gardenhire, Min	162	131	.59	126	45	29	435	1	162	65	27	17	92	70	.568
John Gibbons, Tor	51	36	.68	42	3	2	130	3	34	2	11	21	20	30	.400
Ozzie Guillen, CWS	162	134	.55	132	35	15	399	6	129	76	36	17	83	79	.512
Ken Macha, Oak	162	119	.60	122	13	14	414	12	69	30	49	2	91	71	.562
Lee Mazzilli, Bal	162	105	.60	89	44	18	452	2	142	57	43	32	78	84	.481
Bob Melvin, Sea	162	151	.59	109	66	26	414	14	152	56	32	24	63	99	.389
Tony Pena, KC	162	141	.57	53	27	14	409	4	115	55	48	6	58	104	.358
Lou Piniella, TB	162	137	.63	97	25	36	401	8	174	44	35	16	70	91	.435
Mike Scioscia, Ana	162	126	.57	94	32	44	343	3	189	69	27	32	92	70	.568
Buck Showalter, Tex	162	120	.64	86	15	24	468	3	105	29	29	5	89	73	.549
Joe Torre, NYY	162	116	.65	86	35	46	436	4	117	48	32	32	101	61	.623
Carlos Tosca, Tor	111	93	.59	60	15	15	301	3	55	23	36	36	47	64	.423
Alan Trammell, Det	162	131	.67	105	29	19	432	4	136	62	32	8	72	90	.444
Eric Wedge, Cle	162	114	.72	91	34	20	479	2	149	55	47	24	80	82	.494

2004 National League Managers

Manager	G	LINEUPS		SUBSTITUTIONS					TACTICS				RESULTS		
		LUp	PL%	PH	PR	DS	Rel	LO	SBA	SacA	IBB	PO	W	L	Pct
Felipe Alou, SF	162	138	.67	239	47	60	521	16	66	102	35	2	91	71	.562
Dusty Baker, ChC	162	113	.44	254	16	19	460	16	94	106	33	56	89	73	.549
Bruce Bochy, SD	162	96	.54	261	28	47	437	2	77	75	39	14	87	75	.537
Larry Bowa, Phi	160	107	.54	258	21	36	471	2	127	74	60	23	85	75	.531
Bob Brenly, Ari	80	49	.63	126	12	4	245	3	40	34	44	25	29	51	.363
Bobby Cox, Atl	162	105	.70	243	57	28	483	4	118	103	49	22	96	66	.593
Phil Garner, Hou	74	31	.54	141	19	35	241	5	78	40	24	7	48	26	.649
Art Howe, NYM	162	136	.50	273	46	54	474	8	130	91	66	19	71	91	.438
Clint Hurdle, Col	162	131	.57	289	18	35	473	4	77	124	84	11	68	94	.420
Tony LaRussa, StL	162	119	.53	275	25	69	469	8	158	87	24	4	105	57	.648
Lloyd McClendon, Pit	162	114	.50	278	13	58	464	4	103	99	64	55	72	89	.447
Jack McKeon, Fla	162	90	.48	224	27	34	404	2	139	102	60	19	83	79	.512
Dave Miley, Cin	162	132	.61	265	25	50	497	3	102	78	54	8	76	86	.469
Al Pedrique, Ari	82	76	.62	116	14	15	226	4	45	42	35	15	22	60	.268
Frank Robinson, Mon	162	131	.67	253	16	27	462	15	147	119	76	1	67	95	.414
Jim Tracy, LA	162	94	.70	295	25	19	459	4	143	78	47	7	93	69	.574
Gary Varsho, Phi	2	2	.44	4	1	1	5	0	0	2	0	0	1	1	.500
Jimy Williams, Hou	88	52	.42	132	2	21	252	4	41	67	36	16	44	44	.500

2004 Park Indices

Park Indices are calculated in a way that neutralizes the effect of a team's makeup and isolates the effects of the park. This isolation is accomplished by comparing what both the team and its opponents accomplished at home, and comparing that to what the same team and its opponents accomplished on the road. To calculate the Park Index for Home Runs in Bank One Ballpark, take the total Home Runs of the Diamondbacks and their opponents at Bank One (72+98=170), and compare it to the total Home Runs of the Diamondbacks and their opponents in other games (52+77=129). We divide each of these totals by the At Bats in the equivalent situations (4973 and 4897) so that if there are more at bats in either situation, the index is not skewed. The result, (170/4973) / (129/4897) = 1.30, is multiplied by 100 to yield the familiar form, 130. In 2004, it was 30% easier to hit home runs in Bank One Ballpark than in other National League parks.

The Park Indices for Doubles, Triples, Walks, Strikeouts and Home Runs by Lefties and Righties are determined like Home Runs, above—relative to At Bats. Indices of At Bats, Runs, Hits, Errors, and Infield Fielding Errors (E-Infield) are calculated relative to Games. The three Batting Average Indices are calculated as-is, as these are already relative to At Bats.

Additionally, interleague games are not included in the underlying Park Index data, both because the interleague schedules are significantly imbalanced, and because the Designated Hitter rule, only used in the American League parks, would artificially skew AL parks towards appearing to be Hitters' Parks and all NL parks towards appearing to be Pitchers' Parks.

In addition to the 2004 Park Indices, we include 2002-2004 park data as well (or 2003-2004 in the case of the two-year old Great American Ballpark). In cases where a team moved into a new park or reconfigured an existing stadium, we include the 2002-2003 indices for the old park or dimensions as a comparison. Philadelphia and San Diego each opened new parks this season. Kansas City moved their fences back while in Detroit the tops of the walls were lowered.

Finally, Hiram Bithorn Stadium in San Juan was modified to match the dimensions of Olympic Stadium. It appears that major league baseball will not be played in either venue in 2005.

Anaheim Angels - Angel Stadium of Anaheim Surface: Grass

| | 2004 Season | | | | | | | 2002-2004 | | | | | | |
| | Home Games | | | Away Games | | | | Home Games | | | Away Games | | | |
	Angels	Opp	Total	Angels	Opp	Total	Index	Angels	Opp	Total	Angels	Opp	Total	Index
G	72	72	144	72	72	144		217	217	434	215	215	430	
Avg	.287	.268	.278	.282	.262	.272	102	.277	.258	.268	.278	.258	.269	100
AB	2429	2556	4985	2588	2408	4996	100	7294	7610	14904	7642	7116	14758	100
R	357	331	688	404	312	716	96	1035	927	1962	1126	963	2089	93
H	698	686	1384	730	630	1360	102	2024	1966	3990	2127	1838	3965	100
2B	111	128	239	131	140	271	88	375	374	749	418	349	767	97
3B	11	8	19	21	13	34	56	40	20	60	44	42	86	69
HR	73	83	156	75	63	138	113	194	226	420	210	238	448	93
BB	187	221	408	214	220	434	94	588	679	1267	648	671	1319	95
SO	405	524	929	421	507	928	100	1105	1455	2560	1177	1339	2516	101
E	45	40	85	37	63	100	85	129	118	247	124	161	285	86
E-Infield	18	13	31	16	25	41	76	54	41	95	54	58	112	84
LHB-Avg	.277	.282	.280	.291	.260	.275	102	.279	.257	.267	.291	.256	.274	98
LHB-HR	19	46	65	20	27	47	134	75	112	187	89	107	196	92
RHB-Avg	.294	.255	.276	.276	.263	.270	102	.276	.260	.268	.268	.260	.264	101
RHB-HR	54	37	91	55	36	91	103	119	114	233	121	131	252	94

Arizona Diamondbacks - Bank One Ballpark Surface: Grass

| | 2004 Season | | | | | | | 2002-2004 | | | | | | |
| | Home Games | | | Away Games | | | | Home Games | | | Away Games | | | |
	D'Backs	Opp	Total	D'Backs	Opp	Total	Index	D'Backs	Opp	Total	D'Backs	Opp	Total	Index
G	72	72	144	72	72	144		219	219	438	216	216	432	
Avg	.265	.261	.263	.241	.272	.256	103	.274	.254	.264	.245	.254	.250	106
AB	2436	2537	4973	2492	2405	4897	102	7370	7694	15064	7491	7149	14640	101
R	303	396	699	241	407	648	108	1083	1058	2141	824	971	1795	118
H	645	663	1308	601	653	1254	104	2020	1954	3974	1838	1819	3657	107
2B	140	139	279	121	122	243	113	421	410	831	350	323	673	120
3B	16	17	33	15	16	31	105	68	54	122	45	31	76	156
HR	72	98	170	52	77	129	130	224	250	474	191	213	404	114
BB	206	302	508	195	303	498	100	813	738	1551	667	721	1388	109
SO	420	551	971	496	489	985	97	1300	1779	3079	1461	1608	3069	98
E	56	38	94	62	29	91	103	143	124	267	151	132	283	93
E-Infield	26	16	42	24	13	37	114	69	57	126	63	63	126	99
LHB-Avg	.286	.264	.275	.243	.307	.272	101	.284	.272	.279	.254	.270	.261	107
LHB-HR	41	39	80	20	33	53	146	118	102	220	101	90	191	113
RHB-Avg	.248	.260	.254	.240	.250	.245	104	.264	.243	.252	.237	.244	.241	105
RHB-HR	31	59	90	32	44	76	118	106	148	254	90	123	213	115

Atlanta Braves - Turner Field Surface: Grass

| | 2004 Season | | | | | | | 2002-2004 | | | | | | |
| | Home Games | | | Away Games | | | | Home Games | | | Away Games | | | |
	Braves	Opp	Total	Braves	Opp	Total	Index	Braves	Opp	Total	Braves	Opp	Total	Index
G	72	72	144	72	72	144		219	219	438	215	215	430	
Avg	.268	.258	.263	.275	.263	.269	98	.272	.250	.261	.271	.259	.265	98
AB	2418	2507	4925	2542	2403	4945	100	7309	7573	14882	7669	7213	14882	98
R	361	291	652	366	283	649	100	1074	888	1962	1089	888	1977	97
H	648	647	1295	700	632	1332	97	1988	1893	3881	2079	1869	3948	97
2B	125	106	231	141	103	244	95	381	347	728	423	354	777	94
3B	17	5	22	18	11	29	76	45	28	73	42	37	79	92
HR	81	75	156	79	61	140	112	256	197	453	259	191	450	101
BB	273	236	509	269	229	498	103	770	736	1506	755	739	1494	101
SO	529	498	1027	497	413	910	113	1375	1391	2766	1425	1338	2763	100
E	51	39	90	49	47	96	94	161	145	306	153	141	294	102
E-Infield	29	14	43	25	25	50	86	83	70	153	79	52	131	115
LHB-Avg	.270	.273	.271	.295	.270	.284	96	.276	.257	.266	.277	.253	.266	100
LHB-HR	40	34	74	41	24	65	114	87	69	156	74	67	141	110
RHB-Avg	.267	.247	.257	.259	.259	.259	99	.270	.246	.258	.267	.263	.265	97
RHB-HR	41	41	82	38	37	75	110	169	128	297	185	124	309	97

Baltimore Orioles - Oriole Park at Camden Yards Surface: Grass

	2004 Season							2002-2004						
	Home Games			Away Games				Home Games			Away Games			
	Orioles	Opp	Total	Orioles	Opp	Total	Index	Orioles	Opp	Total	Orioles	Opp	Total	Index
G	72	72	144	72	72	144		216	216	432	217	217	434	
Avg	.282	.272	.277	.287	.256	.272	102	.268	.265	.266	.265	.274	.269	99
AB	2465	2591	5056	2613	2398	5011	101	7302	7657	14959	7662	7366	15028	100
R	375	411	786	397	322	719	109	992	1072	2064	1029	1076	2105	99
H	695	704	1399	750	613	1363	103	1958	2027	3985	2027	2020	4047	99
2B	143	113	256	150	103	253	100	384	346	730	425	378	803	91
3B	4	12	16	10	12	22	72	20	25	45	35	48	83	54
HR	74	79	153	78	65	143	106	223	270	493	207	241	448	111
BB	217	315	532	253	296	549	96	623	792	1415	637	761	1398	102
SO	371	471	842	455	484	939	89	1164	1337	2501	1302	1364	2666	94
E	55	53	108	34	55	89	121	133	163	296	124	143	267	111
E-Infield	25	23	48	14	26	40	120	58	65	123	51	63	114	108
LHB-Avg	.265	.278	.271	.291	.256	.276	98	.262	.268	.266	.275	.270	.272	98
LHB-HR	28	37	65	37	26	63	104	81	129	210	79	119	198	105
RHB-Avg	.298	.267	.281	.283	.255	.269	105	.272	.262	.267	.258	.278	.267	100
RHB-HR	46	42	88	41	39	80	108	142	141	283	128	122	250	115

Boston Red Sox - Fenway Park Surface: Grass

	2004 Season							2002-2004						
	Home Games			Away Games				Home Games			Away Games			
	Red Sox	Opp	Total	Red Sox	Opp	Total	Index	Red Sox	Opp	Total	Red Sox	Opp	Total	Index
G	72	72	144	72	72	144		216	216	432	216	216	432	
Avg	.306	.255	.280	.257	.256	.257	109	.298	.255	.276	.268	.252	.260	106
AB	2534	2553	5087	2557	2430	4987	102	7429	7561	14990	7778	7316	15094	99
R	469	350	819	381	329	710	115	1279	1005	2284	1177	974	2151	106
H	776	650	1426	658	622	1280	111	2217	1927	4144	2084	1844	3928	105
2B	193	164	357	138	123	261	134	530	455	985	439	370	809	123
3B	8	12	20	13	16	29	68	39	35	74	36	52	88	85
HR	102	69	171	98	71	169	99	268	188	456	297	211	508	90
BB	291	196	487	297	192	489	98	827	560	1387	776	635	1411	99
SO	515	520	1035	533	480	1013	100	1274	1543	2817	1434	1504	2938	97
E	58	53	111	44	41	85	131	160	151	311	130	123	253	123
E-Infield	30	24	54	13	16	29	186	80	65	145	48	51	99	146
LHB-Avg	.311	.254	.281	.249	.243	.246	114	.297	.248	.272	.258	.252	.255	107
LHB-HR	44	28	72	47	30	77	92	114	77	191	144	110	254	76
RHB-Avg	.302	.255	.280	.265	.270	.267	105	.300	.262	.281	.277	.253	.266	106
RHB-HR	58	41	99	51	41	92	105	154	111	265	153	101	254	105

Chicago Cubs - Wrigley Field Surface: Grass

	2004 Season							2002-2004						
	Home Games			Away Games				Home Games			Away Games			
	Cubs	Opp	Total	Cubs	Opp	Total	Index	Cubs	Opp	Total	Cubs	Opp	Total	Index
G	76	76	152	74	74	148		223	223	446	221	221	442	
Avg	.273	.250	.262	.263	.243	.253	103	.255	.243	.249	.259	.250	.254	98
AB	2622	2671	5293	2597	2440	5037	102	7481	7703	15184	7724	7271	14995	100
R	404	339	743	331	281	612	118	1015	986	2001	1010	938	1948	102
H	715	668	1383	682	593	1275	106	1908	1872	3780	1997	1816	3813	98
2B	138	121	259	151	107	258	96	371	352	723	419	350	769	93
3B	12	14	26	13	14	27	92	33	33	66	40	42	82	79
HR	131	94	225	89	66	155	138	298	247	545	260	187	447	120
BB	234	255	489	220	257	477	98	761	803	1564	682	800	1482	104
SO	469	632	1101	537	604	1141	92	1609	1976	3585	1621	1754	3375	105
E	43	61	104	37	45	82	123	152	155	307	135	147	282	108
E-Infield	20	20	40	12	22	34	115	64	66	130	57	74	131	98
LHB-Avg	.271	.249	.257	.255	.273	.266	97	.247	.245	.246	.255	.265	.260	95
LHB-HR	27	48	75	22	41	63	112	77	106	183	88	99	187	97
RHB-Avg	.273	.251	.263	.266	.220	.246	107	.259	.242	.251	.261	.239	.251	100
RHB-HR	104	46	150	67	25	92	156	221	141	362	172	88	260	137

Chicago White Sox - U.S. Cellular Field Surface: Grass

	2004 Season							2002-2004						
	Home Games			Away Games				Home Games			Away Games			
	White Sox	Opp	Total	White Sox	Opp	Total	Index	White Sox	Opp	Total	White Sox	Opp	Total	Index
G	72	72	144	72	72	144		216	216	432	216	216	432	
Avg	.268	.279	.274	.262	.260	.261	105	.273	.261	.267	.263	.261	.262	102
AB	2421	2548	4969	2492	2367	4859	102	7171	7443	14614	7546	7101	14647	100
R	389	374	763	359	343	702	109	1179	1002	2181	1047	1055	2102	104
H	650	710	1360	652	615	1267	107	1957	1942	3899	1983	1851	3834	102
2B	114	124	238	126	119	245	95	366	373	739	409	369	778	95
3B	9	9	18	8	10	18	98	28	28	56	33	30	63	89
HR	121	110	231	90	82	172	131	356	268	624	246	232	478	131
BB	231	221	452	200	250	450	98	687	679	1366	661	726	1387	99
SO	427	479	906	465	427	892	99	1187	1405	2592	1325	1272	2597	100
E	42	42	84	47	54	101	83	104	137	241	152	141	293	82
E-Infield	16	20	36	25	25	50	72	44	58	102	69	53	122	84
LHB-Avg	.239	.288	.268	.256	.256	.256	105	.264	.269	.267	.249	.273	.263	102
LHB-HR	25	48	73	28	38	66	115	80	134	214	72	111	183	121
RHB-Avg	.281	.272	.277	.264	.263	.264	105	.276	.254	.266	.269	.249	.261	102
RHB-HR	96	62	158	62	44	106	140	276	134	410	174	121	295	137

Cincinnati Reds - Great American Ballpark Surface: Grass

	2004 Season							2003-2004						
	Home Games			Away Games				Home Games			Away Games			
	Reds	Opp	Total	Reds	Opp	Total	Index	Reds	Opp	Total	Reds	Opp	Total	Index
G	75	75	150	75	75	150		150	150	300	150	150	300	
Avg	.238	.264	.251	.257	.291	.274	92	.243	.268	.256	.251	.290	.270	95
AB	2448	2658	5106	2646	2590	5236	98	4953	5333	10286	5264	5175	10439	99
R	308	393	701	379	418	797	88	630	798	1428	709	843	1552	92
H	582	702	1284	681	754	1435	89	1204	1427	2631	1319	1500	2819	93
2B	119	160	279	142	174	316	91	236	314	550	249	333	582	96
3B	11	9	20	17	22	39	53	16	15	31	33	49	82	38
HR	88	116	204	94	97	191	110	176	226	402	173	186	359	114
BB	259	246	505	283	271	554	93	500	501	1001	526	554	1080	94
SO	586	491	1077	656	431	1087	102	1172	940	2112	1302	829	2131	101
E	49	35	84	55	41	96	88	121	87	208	115	91	206	101
E-Infield	18	19	37	15	14	29	128	48	44	92	32	33	65	142
LHB-Avg	.258	.256	.257	.275	.291	.282	91	.257	.260	.258	.265	.287	.275	94
LHB-HR	58	47	105	56	41	97	113	97	86	183	90	79	169	113
RHB-Avg	.220	.270	.247	.242	.291	.268	92	.233	.272	.254	.240	.292	.266	95
RHB-HR	30	69	99	38	56	94	107	79	140	219	83	107	190	115

Cleveland Indians - Jacobs Field Surface: Grass

	2004 Season							2002-2004						
	Home Games			Away Games				Home Games			Away Games			
	Indians	Opp	Total	Indians	Opp	Total	Index	Indians	Opp	Total	Indians	Opp	Total	Index
G	72	72	144	72	72	144		216	216	432	216	216	432	
Avg	.267	.272	.269	.281	.274	.278	97	.255	.266	.261	.266	.275	.270	97
AB	2400	2578	4978	2632	2517	5149	97	7192	7637	14829	7641	7324	14965	99
R	357	380	737	403	396	799	92	991	1083	2074	1075	1145	2220	93
H	640	700	1340	740	690	1430	94	1835	2034	3869	2033	2011	4044	96
2B	156	155	311	136	148	284	113	408	431	839	383	418	801	106
3B	12	12	24	15	16	31	80	27	36	63	45	53	98	65
HR	62	81	143	105	98	203	73	210	218	428	284	252	536	81
BB	290	255	545	257	255	512	110	703	765	1468	714	735	1449	102
SO	437	507	944	459	470	929	105	1329	1501	2830	1386	1238	2624	109
E	44	68	112	43	41	84	133	137	193	330	159	111	270	122
E-Infield	22	23	45	32	12	44	102	72	83	155	77	46	123	126
LHB-Avg	.278	.268	.274	.284	.264	.276	99	.261	.269	.264	.267	.275	.271	98
LHB-HR	39	40	79	63	45	108	72	138	99	237	168	104	272	86
RHB-Avg	.251	.274	.265	.278	.281	.280	95	.249	.265	.258	.265	.274	.270	96
RHB-HR	23	41	64	42	53	95	73	72	119	191	116	148	264	74

Colorado Rockies - Coors Field Surface: Grass

	2004 Season							2002-2004						
	Home Games			Away Games				Home Games			Away Games			
	Rockies	Opp	Total	Rockies	Opp	Total	Index	Rockies	Opp	Total	Rockies	Opp	Total	Index
G	72	72	144	72	72	144		216	216	432	219	219	438	
Avg	.302	.307	.304	.245	.267	.256	119	.302	.291	.296	.239	.275	.256	116
AB	2490	2611	5101	2460	2367	4827	106	7382	7754	15136	7465	7257	14722	104
R	435	477	912	295	334	629	145	1328	1293	2621	859	1100	1959	136
H	751	801	1552	602	633	1235	126	2228	2259	4487	1782	1994	3776	120
2B	166	163	329	127	127	254	123	476	447	923	372	398	770	117
3B	18	20	38	12	13	25	144	67	58	125	29	43	72	169
HR	106	100	206	82	77	159	123	287	324	611	207	234	441	135
BB	272	329	601	229	285	514	111	795	790	1585	710	840	1550	99
SO	467	425	892	576	421	997	85	1309	1265	2574	1725	1162	2887	87
E	44	66	110	31	30	61	180	141	171	312	132	122	254	125
E-Infield	10	29	39	6	10	16	244	57	75	132	57	52	109	123
LHB-Avg	.320	.308	.314	.261	.265	.263	119	.329	.298	.313	.259	.289	.274	114
LHB-HR	56	39	95	33	28	61	145	127	131	258	85	85	170	147
RHB-Avg	.289	.306	.298	.233	.269	.251	119	.286	.287	.286	.227	.266	.246	116
RHB-HR	50	61	111	49	49	98	108	160	193	353	122	149	271	127

Detroit Tigers - Comerica Park Surface: Grass

	2004 Season							2002-2003						
	Home Games			Away Games				Home Games			Away Games			
	Tigers	Opp	Total	Tigers	Opp	Total	Index	Tigers	Opp	Total	Tigers	Opp	Total	Index
G	72	72	144	72	72	144		143	143	286	144	144	288	
Avg	.271	.277	.274	.271	.277	.274	100	.242	.275	.259	.245	.297	.271	96
AB	2444	2578	5022	2551	2425	4976	101	4756	5162	9918	4913	4858	9771	102
R	335	382	717	399	369	768	93	501	747	1248	554	877	1431	88
H	663	715	1378	691	671	1362	101	1150	1422	2572	1205	1444	2649	98
2B	99	130	229	146	128	274	83	176	267	443	249	317	566	77
3B	33	21	54	12	11	23	233	44	57	101	20	41	61	163
HR	76	88	164	105	85	190	86	119	142	261	130	187	317	81
BB	230	234	464	229	229	458	100	340	448	788	386	466	852	91
SO	462	449	911	551	421	972	93	860	733	1593	1013	665	1678	94
E	58	31	89	71	47	118	75	117	90	207	136	71	207	101
E-Infield	21	18	39	25	17	42	93	53	38	91	58	32	90	102
LHB-Avg	.263	.260	.261	.259	.262	.260	100	.262	.287	.273	.256	.306	.279	98
LHB-HR	35	34	69	49	29	78	87	76	79	155	75	87	162	96
RHB-Avg	.279	.289	.285	.281	.287	.284	100	.217	.267	.246	.233	.290	.264	93
RHB-HR	41	54	95	56	56	112	84	43	63	106	55	100	155	67

Florida Marlins - Pro Player Stadium Surface: Grass

	2004 Season							2002-2004						
	Home Games			Away Games				Home Games			Away Games			
	Marlins	Opp	Total	Marlins	Opp	Total	Index	Marlins	Opp	Total	Marlins	Opp	Total	Index
G	69	69	138	73	73	146		213	213	426	220	220	440	
Avg	.264	.246	.255	.265	.267	.266	96	.269	.247	.258	.259	.269	.264	98
AB	2253	2364	4617	2545	2408	4953	99	7054	7387	14441	7622	7276	14898	100
R	293	279	572	342	330	672	90	975	865	1840	947	1040	1987	96
H	594	582	1176	674	642	1316	95	1897	1825	3722	1973	1957	3930	98
2B	122	108	230	122	134	256	96	365	363	728	390	411	801	94
3B	13	15	28	13	17	30	100	58	56	114	37	43	80	147
HR	58	72	130	67	77	144	97	185	175	360	212	228	440	84
BB	214	239	453	226	215	441	110	748	767	1515	682	735	1417	110
SO	408	522	930	456	445	901	111	1330	1649	2979	1446	1355	2801	110
E	28	53	81	48	54	102	84	104	146	250	139	169	308	84
E-Infield	11	19	30	23	22	45	71	35	50	85	64	65	129	68
LHB-Avg	.283	.251	.264	.290	.261	.274	96	.283	.246	.261	.269	.277	.274	95
LHB-HR	10	35	45	9	33	42	104	25	71	96	24	89	113	82
RHB-Avg	.255	.243	.249	.255	.270	.262	95	.264	.248	.256	.255	.264	.259	99
RHB-HR	48	37	85	58	44	102	94	160	104	264	188	139	327	86

Houston Astros - Minute Maid Park Surface: Grass

	2004 Season							2002-2004						
	Home Games			Away Games				Home Games			Away Games			
	Astros	Opp	Total	Astros	Opp	Total	Index	Astros	Opp	Total	Astros	Opp	Total	Index
G	75	75	150	75	75	150		222	222	444	222	222	444	
Avg	.278	.246	.262	.262	.267	.264	99	.276	.249	.262	.251	.260	.255	103
AB	2474	2564	5038	2602	2522	5124	98	7386	7592	14978	7720	7368	15088	99
R	373	309	682	385	335	720	95	1118	922	2040	1034	948	1982	103
H	687	631	1318	681	674	1355	97	2039	1889	3928	1936	1918	3854	102
2B	128	123	251	146	140	286	89	401	369	770	415	406	821	94
3B	21	19	40	14	12	26	156	57	47	104	33	41	74	142
HR	90	78	168	89	79	168	102	255	217	472	244	217	461	103
BB	272	214	486	272	271	543	91	812	654	1466	773	819	1592	93
SO	430	643	1073	498	550	1048	104	1335	1725	3060	1540	1589	3129	99
E	47	50	97	46	42	88	110	128	144	272	123	139	262	104
E-Infield	19	25	44	18	22	40	110	54	57	111	55	73	128	87
LHB-Avg	.285	.258	.267	.288	.285	.286	93	.283	.261	.270	.265	.275	.271	100
LHB-HR	19	29	48	43	38	81	60	77	75	152	85	96	181	84
RHB-Avg	.276	.236	.259	.252	.254	.253	102	.273	.240	.258	.245	.250	.247	104
RHB-HR	71	49	120	46	41	87	141	178	142	320	159	121	280	116

Kansas City Royals - Ewing M. Kauffman Stadium Surface: Grass

	2004 Season							2002-2003						
	Home Games			Away Games				Home Games			Away Games			
	Royals	Opp	Total	Royals	Opp	Total	Index	Royals	Opp	Total	Royals	Opp	Total	Index
G	71	71	142	73	73	146		143	143	286	145	145	290	
Avg	.265	.283	.274	.257	.296	.276	99	.276	.291	.284	.250	.265	.258	110
AB	2356	2530	4886	2572	2504	5076	99	4854	5220	10074	4986	4811	9797	104
R	313	378	691	336	433	769	92	754	891	1645	627	654	1281	130
H	624	717	1341	662	741	1403	98	1342	1520	2862	1248	1276	2524	115
2B	105	163	268	131	159	290	96	267	301	568	225	265	490	113
3B	13	18	31	10	13	23	140	38	30	68	34	30	64	103
HR	51	84	135	83	106	189	74	135	211	346	127	154	281	120
BB	215	209	424	201	235	436	101	451	491	942	432	486	918	100
SO	413	418	831	532	370	902	96	689	772	1461	939	838	1777	80
E	43	39	82	67	58	125	67	88	114	202	116	97	213	96
E-Infield	19	21	40	24	26	50	82	30	48	78	49	49	98	81
LHB-Avg	.258	.288	.273	.248	.322	.284	96	.275	.296	.285	.243	.273	.257	111
LHB-HR	21	28	49	30	40	70	75	64	90	154	68	65	133	112
RHB-Avg	.269	.281	.275	.263	.280	.272	101	.278	.287	.283	.257	.259	.258	110
RHB-HR	30	56	86	53	66	119	73	71	121	192	59	89	148	127

Los Angeles Dodgers - Dodger Stadium Surface: Grass

	2004 Season							2002-2004						
	Home Games			Away Games				Home Games			Away Games			
	Dodgers	Opp	Total	Dodgers	Opp	Total	Index	Dodgers	Opp	Total	Dodgers	Opp	Total	Index
G	72	72	144	72	72	144		216	216	432	216	216	432	
Avg	.259	.246	.252	.265	.263	.264	95	.250	.234	.242	.266	.253	.260	93
AB	2393	2467	4860	2551	2391	4942	98	7081	7303	14384	7699	7134	14833	97
R	320	280	600	358	322	680	88	833	767	1600	1000	903	1903	84
H	619	607	1226	677	630	1307	94	1772	1707	3479	2045	1805	3850	90
2B	88	95	183	113	132	245	76	305	267	572	386	370	756	78
3B	10	8	18	19	15	34	54	29	15	44	48	50	98	46
HR	90	79	169	91	79	170	101	209	216	425	222	196	418	105
BB	226	213	439	260	258	518	86	598	694	1292	648	768	1416	94
SO	467	498	965	513	461	974	101	1292	1635	2927	1411	1483	2894	104
E	36	45	81	33	53	86	94	136	148	284	117	161	278	102
E-Infield	8	14	22	9	18	27	81	42	65	107	42	60	102	105
LHB-Avg	.248	.277	.261	.251	.270	.258	101	.246	.239	.243	.253	.253	.253	96
LHB-HR	39	33	72	39	32	71	98	84	73	157	94	70	164	98
RHB-Avg	.271	.225	.245	.281	.260	.269	91	.254	.230	.241	.277	.253	.264	91
RHB-HR	51	46	97	52	47	99	104	125	143	268	128	126	254	110

Milwaukee Brewers - Miller Park Surface: Grass

| | 2004 Season | | | | | | | 2002-2004 | | | | | | |
| | Home Games | | | Away Games | | | | Home Games | | | Away Games | | | |
	Brewers	Opp	Total	Brewers	Opp	Total	Index	Brewers	Opp	Total	Brewers	Opp	Total	Index
G	75	75	150	74	74	148		225	225	450	224	224	448	
Avg	.247	.253	.250	.245	.270	.257	97	.251	.260	.256	.249	.277	.263	97
AB	2541	2672	5213	2509	2478	4987	103	7489	7992	15481	7674	7497	15171	102
R	315	358	673	262	363	625	106	910	1138	2048	896	1138	2034	100
H	627	675	1302	614	670	1284	100	1876	2080	3956	1914	2080	3994	99
2B	152	163	315	122	142	264	114	394	448	842	374	410	784	105
3B	17	17	34	14	14	28	116	37	51	88	41	47	88	98
HR	59	76	135	65	79	144	90	217	281	498	218	254	472	103
BB	284	223	507	219	221	440	110	786	789	1575	714	815	1529	101
SO	627	557	1184	578	468	1046	108	1657	1573	3230	1711	1360	3071	103
E	50	62	112	57	46	103	107	154	140	294	159	150	309	95
E-Infield	28	26	54	31	24	55	97	76	63	139	69	66	135	103
LHB-Avg	.261	.246	.254	.252	.275	.261	97	.263	.266	.264	.256	.273	.264	100
LHB-HR	32	27	59	39	28	67	86	82	115	197	84	93	177	107
RHB-Avg	.231	.257	.246	.236	.268	.254	97	.242	.257	.250	.245	.280	.263	95
RHB-HR	27	49	76	26	51	77	93	135	166	301	134	161	295	101

Minnesota Twins - Hubert H. Humphrey Metrodome Surface: AstroTurf

| | 2004 Season | | | | | | | 2002-2004 | | | | | | |
| | Home Games | | | Away Games | | | | Home Games | | | Away Games | | | |
	Twins	Opp	Total	Twins	Opp	Total	Index	Twins	Opp	Total	Twins	Opp	Total	Index
G	72	72	144	72	72	144		216	216	432	215	215	430	
Avg	.269	.268	.269	.264	.269	.266	101	.274	.262	.268	.271	.269	.270	99
AB	2449	2600	5049	2541	2461	5002	101	7317	7745	15062	7641	7321	14962	100
R	373	320	693	326	320	646	107	1083	948	2031	1022	992	2014	100
H	660	696	1356	671	661	1332	102	2006	2029	4035	2068	1967	4035	100
2B	137	106	243	137	116	253	95	450	380	830	417	360	777	106
3B	9	9	18	11	9	20	89	55	39	94	36	30	66	141
HR	83	74	157	89	74	163	95	217	225	442	247	251	498	88
BB	240	174	414	224	219	443	93	702	547	1249	638	594	1232	101
SO	420	537	957	432	445	877	108	1324	1494	2818	1381	1251	2632	106
E	46	39	85	45	49	94	90	108	145	253	130	157	287	88
E-Infield	19	13	32	19	22	41	78	41	51	92	60	62	122	75
LHB-Avg	.274	.257	.265	.251	.279	.265	100	.283	.260	.272	.275	.277	.276	98
LHB-HR	39	34	73	41	41	82	87	103	113	216	120	121	241	89
RHB-Avg	.266	.276	.271	.273	.260	.267	101	.265	.264	.265	.266	.262	.264	100
RHB-HR	44	40	84	48	33	81	104	114	112	226	127	130	257	87

Montreal Expos - Olympic Stadium Surface: NexTurf

| | 2004 Season | | | | | | | 2002-2004 | | | | | | |
| | Home Games | | | Away Games | | | | Home Games | | | Away Games | | | |
	Expos	Opp	Total	Expos	Opp	Total	Index	Expos	Opp	Total	Expos	Opp	Total	Index
G	53	53	106	73	73	146		181	181	362	217	217	434	
Avg	.248	.260	.254	.252	.273	.262	97	.267	.260	.264	.247	.271	.259	102
AB	1733	1837	3570	2556	2485	5041	98	5985	6320	12305	7489	7291	14780	100
R	211	227	438	312	368	680	89	859	787	1646	864	996	1860	106
H	430	477	907	643	679	1322	94	1599	1644	3243	1853	1973	3826	102
2B	108	98	206	119	124	243	120	388	369	757	346	374	720	126
3B	10	8	18	12	14	26	98	39	29	68	36	42	78	105
HR	56	56	112	75	99	174	91	182	189	371	201	232	433	103
BB	176	196	372	225	265	490	107	621	546	1167	701	735	1436	98
SO	266	347	613	450	461	911	95	1030	1205	2235	1472	1367	2839	95
E	27	32	59	52	48	100	81	122	125	247	155	148	303	98
E-Infield	10	13	23	23	24	47	67	42	51	93	73	65	138	81
LHB-Avg	.260	.264	.262	.261	.281	.270	97	.272	.263	.268	.247	.280	.262	102
LHB-HR	34	20	54	43	42	85	92	85	71	156	89	97	186	104
RHB-Avg	.234	.256	.247	.240	.268	.255	97	.263	.258	.261	.248	.264	.256	102
RHB-HR	22	36	58	32	57	89	90	97	118	215	112	135	247	102

Montreal Expos - Hiram Bithorn Stadium Surface: AstroTurf

	2004 Season							2003						
	Home Games			Away Games				Home Games			Away Games			
	Expos	Opp	Total	Expos	Opp	Total	Index	Expos	Opp	Total	Expos	Opp	Total	Index
G	18	18	36	72	72	144		16	16	32	72	72	144	
Avg	.231	.248	.239	.251	.273	.262	91	.261	.251	.256	.239	.266	.252	102
AB	581	622	1203	2525	2450	4975	97	528	574	1102	2441	2372	4813	103
R	33	87	120	306	366	672	71	80	75	155	237	287	524	133
H	134	154	288	633	669	1302	88	138	144	282	583	630	1213	105
2B	20	28	48	117	123	240	83	34	22	56	99	127	226	108
3B	2	2	4	12	13	25	66	1	2	3	8	12	20	66
HR	4	20	24	74	99	173	57	20	26	46	57	54	111	181
BB	40	62	102	222	263	485	87	56	43	99	223	214	437	99
SO	99	106	205	443	456	899	94	101	115	216	477	439	916	103
E	10	9	19	52	48	100	76	14	11	25	42	46	88	128
E-Infield	5	4	9	23	24	47	77	7	5	12	22	18	40	135
LHB-Avg	.231	.285	.256	.261	.281	.269	95	.262	.260	.261	.231	.290	.259	101
LHB-HR	4	11	15	42	42	84	72	8	5	13	21	21	42	144
RHB-Avg	.230	.219	.223	.239	.267	.255	88	.261	.245	.252	.246	.248	.247	102
RHB-HR	0	9	9	32	57	89	43	12	21	33	36	33	69	199

New York Mets - Shea Stadium Surface: Grass

	2004 Season							2002-2004						
	Home Games			Away Games				Home Games			Away Games			
	Mets	Opp	Total	Mets	Opp	Total	Index	Mets	Opp	Total	Mets	Opp	Total	Index
G	72	72	144	72	72	144		218	218	436	215	215	430	
Avg	.251	.260	.255	.244	.264	.254	100	.250	.260	.255	.249	.266	.258	99
AB	2423	2550	4973	2486	2401	4887	102	7230	7669	14899	7393	7124	14517	101
R	288	321	609	307	330	637	96	869	968	1837	917	973	1890	96
H	608	662	1270	607	635	1242	102	1809	1993	3802	1842	1898	3740	100
2B	128	125	253	130	132	262	95	352	384	736	360	383	743	97
3B	7	5	12	11	17	28	42	27	32	59	33	59	92	62
HR	71	62	133	92	77	169	77	191	207	398	216	222	438	89
BB	223	266	489	226	269	495	97	674	762	1436	681	759	1440	97
SO	494	453	947	536	404	940	99	1400	1426	2826	1508	1236	2744	100
E	64	44	108	52	31	83	130	191	140	331	160	138	298	110
E-Infield	37	19	56	16	8	24	233	100	63	163	60	58	118	136
LHB-Avg	.261	.267	.265	.241	.263	.253	105	.261	.261	.261	.252	.253	.252	104
LHB-HR	18	27	45	21	29	50	91	81	80	161	72	66	138	115
RHB-Avg	.247	.255	.251	.246	.265	.255	98	.243	.259	.252	.248	.274	.261	96
RHB-HR	53	35	88	71	48	119	71	110	127	237	144	156	300	77

New York Yankees - Yankee Stadium Surface: Grass

	2004 Season							2002-2004						
	Home Games			Away Games				Home Games			Away Games			
	Yankees	Opp	Total	Yankees	Opp	Total	Index	Yankees	Opp	Total	Yankees	Opp	Total	Index
G	72	72	144	72	72	144		216	216	432	216	216	432	
Avg	.271	.263	.267	.267	.280	.273	98	.269	.258	.263	.273	.270	.271	97
AB	2386	2558	4944	2529	2466	4995	99	7203	7649	14852	7691	7454	15145	98
R	394	329	723	408	384	792	91	1129	963	2092	1245	998	2243	93
H	647	672	1319	674	690	1364	97	1940	1972	3912	2100	2010	4110	95
2B	114	137	251	146	135	281	90	359	402	761	438	439	877	88
3B	7	9	16	10	18	28	58	18	28	46	23	44	67	70
HR	111	79	190	104	79	183	105	300	211	511	315	192	507	103
BB	284	195	479	312	204	516	94	842	526	1368	921	566	1487	94
SO	421	505	926	454	426	880	106	1358	1564	2922	1464	1374	2838	105
E	41	50	91	39	45	84	108	145	154	299	148	124	272	110
E-Infield	20	20	40	15	19	34	118	61	64	125	65	53	118	106
LHB-Avg	.259	.268	.264	.260	.279	.270	98	.262	.259	.261	.270	.263	.267	98
LHB-HR	49	45	94	48	43	91	109	150	106	256	163	88	251	107
RHB-Avg	.280	.257	.269	.273	.281	.277	97	.276	.257	.266	.276	.275	.276	96
RHB-HR	62	34	96	56	36	92	101	150	105	255	152	104	256	99

Oakland Athletics - Network Associates Coliseum Surface: Grass

| | 2004 Season | | | | | | | 2002-2004 | | | | | | |
| | Home Games | | | Away Games | | | | Home Games | | | Away Games | | | |
	Athletics	Opp	Total	Athletics	Opp	Total	Index	Athletics	Opp	Total	Athletics	Opp	Total	Index
G	72	72	144	72	72	144		216	216	432	216	216	432	
Avg	.258	.254	.256	.269	.266	.267	96	.259	.243	.251	.259	.261	.260	97
AB	2446	2546	4992	2631	2451	5082	98	7225	7461	14686	7696	7259	14955	98
R	320	318	638	352	330	682	94	1016	854	1870	1041	943	1984	94
H	631	647	1278	708	651	1359	94	1874	1811	3685	1991	1891	3882	95
2B	124	141	265	165	116	281	96	388	376	764	423	345	768	101
3B	5	8	13	5	12	17	78	28	24	52	29	38	67	79
HR	84	70	154	82	71	153	102	263	188	451	245	190	435	106
BB	277	237	514	269	240	509	103	791	647	1438	784	700	1484	99
SO	438	464	902	499	456	955	96	1252	1419	2671	1362	1317	2679	102
E	39	50	89	42	38	80	111	118	154	272	144	115	259	105
E-Infield	18	20	38	17	19	36	106	44	70	114	54	57	111	103
LHB-Avg	.271	.267	.270	.283	.286	.284	95	.271	.248	.261	.259	.264	.261	100
LHB-HR	43	18	61	46	25	71	91	138	58	196	136	75	211	97
RHB-Avg	.244	.247	.246	.254	.253	.254	97	.247	.239	.243	.258	.258	.258	94
RHB-HR	41	52	93	36	46	82	112	125	130	255	109	115	224	114

Philadelphia Phillies - Citizens Bank Park Surface: Grass

| | 2004 Season | | | | | | | 2002-2003 (Veterans) | | | | | | |
| | Home Games | | | Away Games | | | | Home Games | | | Away Games | | | |
	Phillies	Opp	Total	Phillies	Opp	Total	Index	Phillies	Opp	Total	Phillies	Opp	Total	Index
G	72	72	144	72	72	144		143	143	286	147	147	294	
Avg	.269	.259	.264	.264	.259	.261	101	.258	.234	.246	.265	.274	.269	91
AB	2438	2540	4978	2561	2413	4974	100	4717	4848	9565	5196	4934	10130	97
R	377	350	727	357	313	670	109	644	553	1197	720	734	1454	85
H	656	658	1314	675	625	1300	101	1216	1136	2352	1376	1351	2727	89
2B	129	128	257	142	143	285	90	282	245	527	305	304	609	92
3B	13	15	28	10	14	24	117	35	24	59	28	34	62	101
HR	100	102	202	85	79	164	123	141	121	262	153	149	302	92
BB	275	216	491	287	226	513	96	576	475	1051	573	511	1084	103
SO	462	495	957	524	448	972	98	983	1079	2062	1027	828	1855	118
E	35	40	75	38	46	84	89	71	73	144	99	94	193	77
E-Infield	16	16	32	16	23	39	82	24	23	47	41	39	80	60
LHB-Avg	.271	.282	.277	.274	.268	.271	102	.255	.234	.246	.273	.285	.278	88
LHB-HR	46	37	83	46	22	68	127	72	38	110	71	58	129	89
RHB-Avg	.268	.245	.256	.256	.253	.255	100	.260	.234	.246	.258	.267	.263	94
RHB-HR	54	65	119	39	57	96	120	69	83	152	82	91	173	94

Pittsburgh Pirates - PNC Park Surface: Grass

| | 2004 Season | | | | | | | 2002-2004 | | | | | | |
| | Home Games | | | Away Games | | | | Home Games | | | Away Games | | | |
	Pirates	Opp	Total	Pirates	Opp	Total	Index	Pirates	Opp	Total	Pirates	Opp	Total	Index
G	74	74	148	75	75	150		223	223	446	225	225	450	
Avg	.265	.263	.264	.258	.266	.262	101	.265	.268	.266	.250	.265	.258	103
AB	2474	2551	5025	2602	2465	5067	101	7372	7782	15154	7740	7377	15117	101
R	309	323	632	319	341	660	97	968	1042	2010	948	1018	1966	103
H	655	670	1325	671	656	1327	101	1952	2085	4037	1937	1958	3895	105
2B	125	148	273	128	123	251	110	382	432	814	360	387	747	109
3B	20	12	32	18	21	39	83	43	38	81	55	45	100	81
HR	67	56	123	58	80	138	90	198	210	408	212	237	449	91
BB	185	258	443	209	271	480	93	685	736	1421	700	783	1483	96
SO	459	489	948	530	496	1026	93	1352	1370	2722	1657	1345	3002	90
E	40	45	85	51	40	91	95	165	138	303	149	132	281	109
E-Infield	16	19	35	19	16	35	101	84	65	149	62	54	116	130
LHB-Avg	.253	.290	.273	.246	.268	.257	106	.273	.288	.281	.258	.271	.265	106
LHB-HR	21	23	44	20	23	43	106	80	78	158	80	89	169	94
RHB-Avg	.271	.246	.259	.265	.265	.265	98	.260	.255	.258	.246	.262	.253	102
RHB-HR	46	33	79	38	57	95	83	118	132	250	132	148	280	89

San Diego Padres - PETCO Park Surface: Grass

	2004 Season							2002-2003 (Qualcomm)						
	Home Games			Away Games				Home Games			Away Games			
	Padres	Opp	Total	Padres	Opp	Total	Index	Padres	Opp	Total	Padres	Opp	Total	Index
G	72	72	144	72	72	144		144	144	288	144	144	288	
Avg	.254	.263	.258	.293	.269	.281	92	.263	.259	.261	.251	.284	.267	98
AB	2353	2499	4852	2598	2438	5036	96	4844	5058	9902	4987	4806	9793	101
R	296	306	602	400	331	731	82	577	654	1231	608	834	1442	85
H	598	656	1254	760	655	1415	89	1273	1308	2581	1253	1363	2616	99
2B	117	142	259	154	141	295	91	198	235	433	239	284	523	82
3B	19	15	34	11	15	26	136	34	34	68	22	39	61	110
HR	48	65	113	77	100	177	66	105	160	265	127	192	319	82
BB	279	185	464	234	197	431	112	514	499	1013	465	564	1029	97
SO	392	492	884	409	472	881	104	911	1037	1948	1008	939	1947	99
E	36	43	79	59	53	112	71	99	99	198	99	87	186	106
E-Infield	13	13	26	28	23	51	51	42	37	79	36	48	84	94
LHB-Avg	.275	.262	.268	.287	.274	.280	96	.270	.270	.270	.258	.302	.278	97
LHB-HR	13	31	44	23	45	68	68	48	61	109	62	83	145	74
RHB-Avg	.241	.263	.252	.296	.265	.282	89	.256	.250	.253	.245	.271	.259	98
RHB-HR	35	34	69	54	55	109	65	57	99	156	65	109	174	89

San Francisco Giants - Pacific Bell Park Surface: Grass

	2004 Season							2002-2004						
	Home Games			Away Games				Home Games			Away Games			
	Giants	Opp	Total	Giants	Opp	Total	Index	Giants	Opp	Total	Giants	Opp	Total	Index
G	72	72	144	71	71	142		216	216	432	214	214	428	
Avg	.286	.272	.279	.258	.255	.256	109	.273	.254	.263	.261	.254	.257	102
AB	2406	2525	4931	2481	2394	4875	100	7126	7455	14581	7460	7044	14504	100
R	381	356	737	361	322	683	106	1054	864	1918	1058	918	1976	96
H	689	687	1376	639	611	1250	109	1948	1891	3839	1944	1790	3734	102
2B	151	146	297	133	128	261	113	390	367	757	410	347	757	99
3B	22	18	40	4	21	25	158	61	48	109	24	42	66	164
HR	76	68	144	83	74	157	91	208	157	365	285	204	489	74
BB	312	231	543	299	247	546	98	867	680	1547	842	744	1586	97
SO	361	459	820	412	417	829	98	1172	1380	2552	1346	1244	2590	98
E	45	49	94	43	36	79	117	131	158	289	113	118	231	124
E-Infield	22	20	42	19	16	35	118	64	64	128	51	53	104	122
LHB-Avg	.290	.279	.284	.273	.270	.272	105	.274	.253	.262	.274	.266	.270	97
LHB-HR	39	30	69	45	32	77	92	89	58	147	119	79	198	75
RHB-Avg	.284	.268	.275	.245	.245	.245	112	.273	.254	.264	.253	.246	.250	106
RHB-HR	37	38	75	38	42	80	90	119	99	218	166	125	291	74

Seattle Mariners - Safeco Field Surface: Grass

	2004 Season							2002-2004						
	Home Games			Away Games				Home Games			Away Games			
	Mariners	Opp	Total	Mariners	Opp	Total	Index	Mariners	Opp	Total	Mariners	Opp	Total	Index
G	73	73	146	71	71	142		217	217	434	215	215	430	
Avg	.253	.256	.255	.292	.284	.288	88	.263	.249	.256	.285	.271	.279	92
AB	2473	2623	5096	2673	2456	5129	97	7251	7571	14822	7797	7302	15099	97
R	286	372	658	359	394	753	85	983	949	1932	1117	1057	2174	88
H	626	672	1298	781	697	1478	85	1905	1886	3791	2225	1982	4207	89
2B	119	167	286	132	126	258	112	333	377	710	430	377	807	90
3B	6	5	11	12	15	27	41	39	18	57	37	30	67	87
HR	65	105	170	59	92	151	113	184	259	443	203	261	464	97
BB	227	261	488	208	250	458	107	813	686	1499	710	649	1359	112
SO	493	509	1002	442	412	854	118	1357	1470	2827	1350	1275	2625	110
E	53	50	103	40	49	89	113	118	151	269	114	134	248	107
E-Infield	19	23	42	19	24	43	95	47	70	117	50	58	108	107
LHB-Avg	.286	.243	.263	.321	.278	.300	88	.276	.252	.263	.302	.277	.290	91
LHB-HR	24	50	74	21	31	52	146	71	141	212	77	115	192	113
RHB-Avg	.229	.266	.248	.270	.288	.279	89	.252	.247	.249	.272	.266	.269	93
RHB-HR	41	55	96	38	61	99	96	113	118	231	126	146	272	86

St Louis Cardinals - Busch Stadium Surface: Grass

	2004 Season							2002-2004						
	Home Games			Away Games				Home Games			Away Games			
	Cardinals	Opp	Total	Cardinals	Opp	Total	Index	Cardinals	Opp	Total	Cardinals	Opp	Total	Index
G	75	75	150	75	75	150		222	222	444	222	222	444	
Avg	.281	.252	.266	.270	.255	.263	101	.276	.248	.262	.269	.267	.268	98
AB	2501	2583	5084	2629	2487	5116	99	7429	7676	15105	7816	7426	15242	99
R	374	304	678	396	319	715	95	1104	891	1995	1148	1008	2156	93
H	704	650	1354	709	634	1343	101	2053	1906	3959	2099	1986	4085	97
2B	150	137	287	144	136	280	103	437	404	841	418	401	819	104
3B	14	10	24	9	8	17	142	27	24	51	47	30	77	67
HR	87	71	158	113	86	199	80	244	213	457	288	256	544	85
BB	255	218	473	244	205	449	106	784	696	1480	745	694	1439	104
SO	481	515	996	523	447	970	103	1293	1464	2757	1425	1319	2744	101
E	39	45	84	47	59	106	79	114	147	261	130	159	289	90
E-Infield	17	15	32	20	25	45	71	49	59	108	51	75	126	86
LHB-Avg	.296	.236	.264	.273	.247	.260	102	.276	.245	.260	.268	.265	.266	98
LHB-HR	40	30	70	41	46	87	80	107	82	189	104	105	209	92
RHB-Avg	.272	.264	.268	.268	.261	.265	101	.277	.250	.263	.269	.269	.269	98
RHB-HR	47	41	88	72	40	112	79	137	131	268	184	151	335	80

Tampa Bay Devil Rays - Tropicana Field Surface: NexTurf

	2004 Season							2002-2004						
	Home Games			Away Games				Home Games			Away Games			
	Devil Rays	Opp	Total	Devil Rays	Opp	Total	Index	Devil Rays	Opp	Total	Devil Rays	Opp	Total	Index
G	69	69	138	72	72	144		213	213	426	215	215	430	
Avg	.253	.249	.251	.259	.282	.270	93	.262	.259	.261	.255	.283	.269	97
AB	2299	2416	4715	2501	2403	4904	100	7277	7534	14811	7516	7177	14693	102
R	301	323	624	308	438	746	87	928	1099	2027	926	1250	2176	94
H	581	602	1183	648	678	1326	93	1909	1951	3860	1917	2032	3949	99
2B	110	129	239	129	156	285	87	368	413	781	383	453	836	93
3B	22	10	32	13	12	25	133	55	37	92	41	32	73	125
HR	64	84	148	64	91	155	99	171	258	429	203	289	492	87
BB	203	231	434	197	278	475	95	604	794	1398	563	837	1400	99
SO	388	422	810	448	388	836	101	1326	1297	2623	1401	1116	2517	103
E	49	43	92	60	42	102	94	149	139	288	160	128	288	101
E-Infield	20	18	38	21	18	39	102	63	56	119	57	54	111	108
LHB-Avg	.266	.254	.260	.245	.280	.261	100	.272	.267	.269	.259	.285	.271	100
LHB-HR	41	46	87	40	38	78	111	111	131	242	109	132	241	98
RHB-Avg	.239	.245	.242	.273	.283	.278	87	.253	.253	.253	.252	.282	.267	95
RHB-HR	23	38	61	24	53	77	86	60	127	187	94	157	251	75

Texas Rangers - The Ballpark in Arlington Surface: Grass

	2004 Season							2002-2004						
	Home Games			Away Games				Home Games			Away Games			
	Rangers	Opp	Total	Rangers	Opp	Total	Index	Rangers	Opp	Total	Rangers	Opp	Total	Index
G	72	72	144	72	72	144		216	216	432	216	216	432	
Avg	.287	.273	.280	.245	.276	.260	108	.285	.279	.282	.247	.275	.261	108
AB	2470	2585	5055	2494	2405	4899	103	7375	7755	15130	7613	7261	14874	102
R	439	364	803	308	332	640	125	1303	1224	2527	931	1106	2037	124
H	708	706	1414	610	664	1274	111	2104	2167	4271	1881	1998	3879	110
2B	154	136	290	144	122	266	106	420	471	891	395	405	800	109
3B	20	17	37	12	10	22	163	55	54	109	34	45	79	136
HR	102	87	189	89	79	168	109	354	278	632	261	240	501	124
BB	238	244	482	212	251	463	101	719	792	1511	644	837	1481	100
SO	445	447	892	517	426	943	92	1324	1413	2737	1485	1282	2767	97
E	50	39	89	48	38	86	103	128	132	260	146	130	276	94
E-Infield	23	18	41	26	15	41	100	52	59	111	63	58	121	92
LHB-Avg	.282	.253	.266	.229	.264	.248	108	.285	.270	.277	.240	.274	.259	107
LHB-HR	51	40	91	40	33	73	118	156	127	283	104	114	218	124
RHB-Avg	.290	.291	.290	.254	.287	.269	108	.286	.288	.287	.251	.276	.262	109
RHB-HR	51	47	98	49	46	95	102	198	151	349	157	126	283	124

Toronto Blue Jays - SkyDome Surface: AstroTurf

| | 2004 Season | | | | | | | 2002-2004 | | | | | | |
| | Home Games | | | Away Games | | | | Home Games | | | Away Games | | | |
	Blue Jays	Opp	Total	Blue Jays	Opp	Total	Index	Blue Jays	Opp	Total	Blue Jays	Opp	Total	Index
G	72	72	144	71	71	142		216	216	432	215	215	430	
Avg	.263	.284	.273	.257	.267	.262	105	.272	.278	.275	.262	.268	.265	104
AB	2406	2557	4963	2514	2357	4871	100	7309	7698	15007	7635	7230	14865	100
R	343	396	739	303	358	661	110	1119	1174	2293	1061	1057	2118	108
H	632	725	1357	645	629	1274	105	1988	2137	4125	1999	1941	3940	104
2B	129	141	270	127	122	249	106	462	452	914	404	363	767	118
3B	20	12	32	11	12	23	137	53	38	91	40	46	86	105
HR	71	84	155	61	85	146	104	239	261	500	217	233	450	110
BB	249	285	534	216	263	479	109	730	766	1496	682	741	1423	104
SO	463	454	917	508	396	904	100	1407	1395	2802	1573	1215	2788	100
E	43	55	98	35	47	82	118	134	152	286	142	130	272	105
E-Infield	19	25	44	13	26	39	111	63	62	125	65	66	131	95
LHB-Avg	.248	.290	.271	.260	.278	.269	101	.268	.281	.275	.264	.272	.268	103
LHB-HR	36	46	82	34	50	84	94	120	129	249	108	118	226	110
RHB-Avg	.274	.277	.275	.254	.256	.255	108	.275	.275	.275	.261	.265	.263	105
RHB-HR	35	38	73	27	35	62	118	119	132	251	109	115	224	110

2004 American League Ballpark Index Rankings - Runs

Team	Avg	AB	R	H	2B	3B	HR	BB	SO	E	E-Inf	LHB Avg	LHB HR	RHB Avg	RHB HR
Texas - The Ballpark in Arlington	108	103	125	111	106	163	109	101	92	103	100	108	118	108	102
Boston - Fenway Park	109	102	115	111	134	68	99	98	100	131	186	114	92	105	105
Toronto - SkyDome	105	100	110	105	106	137	104	109	100	118	111	101	94	108	118
Baltimore - Oriole Park at Camden Yards	102	101	109	103	100	72	106	96	89	121	120	98	104	105	108
Chicago - U.S. Cellular Field	105	102	109	107	95	98	131	98	99	83	72	105	115	105	140
Minnesota - Hubert H. Humphrey Metrodome	101	101	107	102	95	89	95	93	108	90	78	100	87	101	104
Anaheim - Angel Stadium of Anaheim	102	100	96	102	88	56	113	94	100	85	76	102	134	102	103
Oakland - Network Associates Coliseum	96	98	94	94	96	78	102	103	96	111	106	95	91	97	112
Detroit - Comerica Park	100	101	93	101	83	233	86	100	93	75	93	100	87	100	84
Kansas City - Ewing M. Kauffman Stadium	99	99	92	98	96	140	74	101	96	67	82	96	75	101	73
Cleveland - Jacobs Field	97	97	92	94	113	80	73	110	105	133	102	99	72	95	73
New York - Yankee Stadium	98	99	91	97	90	58	105	94	106	108	118	98	109	97	101
Tampa Bay - Tropicana Field	93	100	87	93	87	133	99	95	101	94	102	100	111	87	86
Seattle - Safeco Field	88	97	85	85	112	41	113	107	118	113	95	88	146	89	96

2004 American League Ballpark Index Rankings - Home Runs

Team	Avg	AB	R	H	2B	3B	HR	BB	SO	E	E-Inf	LHB Avg	LHB HR	RHB Avg	RHB HR
Chicago - U.S. Cellular Field	105	102	109	107	95	98	131	98	99	83	72	105	115	105	140
Seattle - Safeco Field	88	97	85	85	112	41	113	107	118	113	95	88	146	89	96
Anaheim - Angel Stadium of Anaheim	102	100	96	102	88	56	113	94	100	85	76	102	134	102	103
Texas - The Ballpark in Arlington	108	103	125	111	106	163	109	101	92	103	100	108	118	108	102
Baltimore - Oriole Park at Camden Yards	102	101	109	103	100	72	106	96	89	121	120	98	104	105	108
New York - Yankee Stadium	98	99	91	97	90	58	105	94	106	108	118	98	109	97	101
Toronto - SkyDome	105	100	110	105	106	137	104	109	100	118	111	101	94	108	118
Oakland - Network Associates Coliseum	96	98	94	94	96	78	102	103	96	111	106	95	91	97	112
Tampa Bay - Tropicana Field	93	100	87	93	87	133	99	95	101	94	102	100	111	87	86
Boston - Fenway Park	109	102	115	111	134	68	99	98	100	131	186	114	92	105	105
Minnesota - Hubert H. Humphrey Metrodome	101	101	107	102	95	89	95	93	108	90	78	100	87	101	104
Detroit - Comerica Park	100	101	93	101	83	233	86	100	93	75	93	100	87	100	84
Kansas City - Ewing M. Kauffman Stadium	99	99	92	98	96	140	74	101	96	67	82	96	75	101	73
Cleveland - Jacobs Field	97	97	92	94	113	80	73	110	105	133	102	99	72	95	73

2004 National League Ballpark Index Rankings - Runs

Team	Avg	AB	R	H	2B	3B	HR	BB	SO	E	E-Inf	LHB Avg	LHB HR	RHB Avg	RHB HR
Colorado - Coors Field	119	106	145	126	123	144	123	111	85	180	244	119	145	119	108
Chicago - Wrigley Field	103	102	118	106	96	92	138	98	92	123	115	97	112	107	156
Philadelphia - Citizens Bank Park	101	100	109	101	90	117	123	96	98	89	82	102	127	100	120
Arizona - Bank One Ballpark	103	102	108	104	113	105	130	100	97	103	114	101	146	104	118
San Francisco - Pacific Bell Park	109	100	106	109	113	158	91	98	98	117	118	105	92	112	90
Milwaukee - Miller Park	97	103	106	100	114	116	90	110	108	107	97	97	86	97	93
Atlanta - Turner Field	98	100	100	97	95	76	112	103	113	94	86	96	114	99	110
Pittsburgh - PNC Park	101	101	97	101	110	83	90	93	93	95	101	106	106	98	83
New York - Shea Stadium	100	102	96	102	95	42	77	97	99	130	233	105	91	98	71
St Louis - Busch Stadium	101	99	95	101	103	142	80	106	103	79	71	102	80	101	79
Houston - Minute Maid Park	99	98	95	97	89	156	102	91	104	110	110	93	60	102	141
Florida - Pro Player Stadium	96	99	90	95	96	100	97	110	111	84	71	96	104	95	94
Montreal - Olympic Stadium	97	98	89	94	120	98	91	107	95	81	67	97	92	97	90
Los Angeles - Dodger Stadium	95	98	88	94	76	54	101	86	101	94	81	101	98	91	104
Cincinnati - Great American Ballpark	92	98	88	89	91	53	110	93	102	88	128	91	113	92	107
San Diego - PETCO Park	92	96	82	89	91	136	66	112	104	71	51	96	68	89	65
Montreal - Hiram Bithorn Stadium	91	97	71	88	83	66	57	87	94	76	77	95	72	88	43

2004 National League Ballpark Index Rankings - Home Runs

Team	Avg	AB	R	H	2B	3B	HR	BB	SO	E	E-Inf	LHB Avg	LHB HR	RHB Avg	RHB HR
Chicago - Wrigley Field	103	102	118	106	96	92	138	98	92	123	115	97	112	107	156
Arizona - Bank One Ballpark	103	102	108	104	113	105	130	100	97	103	114	101	146	104	118
Philadelphia - Citizens Bank Park	101	100	109	101	90	117	123	96	98	89	82	102	127	100	120
Colorado - Coors Field	119	106	145	126	123	144	123	111	85	180	244	119	145	119	108
Atlanta - Turner Field	98	100	100	97	95	76	112	103	113	94	86	96	114	99	110
Cincinnati - Great American Ballpark	92	98	88	89	91	53	110	93	102	88	128	91	113	92	107
Houston - Minute Maid Park	99	98	95	97	89	156	102	91	104	110	110	93	60	102	141
Los Angeles - Dodger Stadium	95	98	88	94	76	54	101	86	101	94	81	101	98	91	104
Florida - Pro Player Stadium	96	99	90	95	96	100	97	110	111	84	71	96	104	95	94
Montreal - Olympic Stadium	97	98	89	94	120	98	91	107	95	81	67	97	92	97	90
San Francisco - Pacific Bell Park	109	100	106	109	113	158	91	98	98	117	118	105	92	112	90
Pittsburgh - PNC Park	101	101	97	101	110	83	90	93	93	95	101	106	106	98	83
Milwaukee - Miller Park	97	103	106	100	114	116	90	110	108	107	97	97	86	97	93
St Louis - Busch Stadium	101	99	95	101	103	142	80	106	103	79	71	102	80	101	79
New York - Shea Stadium	100	102	96	102	95	42	77	97	99	130	233	105	91	98	71
San Diego - PETCO Park	92	96	82	89	91	136	66	112	104	71	51	96	68	89	65
Montreal - Hiram Bithorn Stadium	91	97	71	88	83	66	57	87	94	76	77	95	72	88	43

2002-2004 American League Ballpark Index Rankings - Runs

Team	Avg	AB	R	H	2B	3B	HR	BB	SO	E	E-Inf	LHB Avg	LHB HR	RHB Avg	RHB HR
Texas - The Ballpark in Arlington	108	102	124	110	109	136	124	100	97	94	92	107	124	109	124
Kansas City - Ewing M. Kauffman Stadium*	106	102	116	109	107	113	102	100	85	86	81	106	100	106	103
Toronto - SkyDome	104	100	108	104	118	105	110	104	100	105	95	103	110	105	110
Boston - Fenway Park	106	99	106	105	123	85	90	99	97	123	146	107	76	106	105
Chicago - U.S. Cellular Field	102	100	104	102	95	89	131	99	100	82	84	102	121	102	137
Minnesota - Hubert H. Humphrey Metrodome	99	100	100	100	106	141	88	101	106	88	75	98	89	100	87
Baltimore - Oriole Park at Camden Yards	99	100	99	99	91	54	111	102	94	111	108	98	105	100	115
Oakland - Network Associates Coliseum	97	98	94	95	101	79	106	99	102	105	103	100	97	94	114
Tampa Bay - Tropicana Field	97	102	94	99	93	125	87	99	103	101	108	100	98	95	75
Cleveland - Jacobs Field	97	99	93	96	106	65	81	102	109	122	126	98	86	96	74
New York - Yankee Stadium	97	98	93	95	88	70	103	94	105	110	106	98	107	96	99
Anaheim - Angel Stadium of Anaheim	100	100	93	100	97	69	93	95	101	86	84	98	92	101	94
Detroit - Comerica Park*	97	102	90	99	79	182	83	94	93	92	99	99	93	96	74
Seattle - Safeco Field	92	97	88	89	90	87	97	112	110	107	107	91	113	93	86

2002-2004 American League Ballpark Index Rankings - Home Runs

Team	Avg	AB	R	H	2B	3B	HR	BB	SO	E	E-Inf	LHB Avg	LHB HR	RHB Avg	RHB HR
Chicago - U.S. Cellular Field	102	100	104	102	95	89	131	99	100	82	84	102	121	102	137
Texas - The Ballpark in Arlington	108	102	124	110	109	136	124	100	97	94	92	107	124	109	124
Baltimore - Oriole Park at Camden Yards	99	100	99	99	91	54	111	102	94	111	108	98	105	100	115
Toronto - SkyDome	104	100	108	104	118	105	110	104	100	105	95	103	110	105	110
Oakland - Network Associates Coliseum	97	98	94	95	101	79	106	99	102	105	103	100	97	94	114
New York - Yankee Stadium	97	98	93	95	88	70	103	94	105	110	106	98	107	96	99
Kansas City - Ewing M. Kauffman Stadium*	106	102	116	109	107	113	102	100	85	86	81	106	100	106	103
Seattle - Safeco Field	92	97	88	89	90	87	97	112	110	107	107	91	113	93	86
Anaheim - Angel Stadium of Anaheim	100	100	93	100	97	69	93	95	101	86	84	98	92	101	94
Boston - Fenway Park	106	99	106	105	123	85	90	99	97	123	146	107	76	106	105
Minnesota - Hubert H. Humphrey Metrodome	99	100	100	100	106	141	88	101	106	88	75	98	89	100	87
Tampa Bay - Tropicana Field	97	102	94	99	93	125	87	99	103	101	108	100	98	95	75
Detroit - Comerica Park*	97	102	90	99	79	182	83	94	93	92	99	99	93	96	74
Cleveland - Jacobs Field	97	99	93	96	106	65	81	102	109	122	126	98	86	96	74

2002-2004 National League Ballpark Index Rankings - Runs

Team	Avg	AB	R	H	2B	3B	HR	BB	SO	E	E-Inf	LHB Avg	LHB HR	RHB Avg	RHB HR
Colorado - Coors Field	116	104	136	120	117	169	135	99	87	125	123	114	147	116	127
Arizona - Bank One Ballpark	106	101	118	107	120	156	114	109	98	93	99	107	113	105	115
Philadelphia - Citizens Bank Park*	101	100	109	101	90	117	123	96	98	89	82	102	127	100	120
Montreal - Olympic Stadium	102	100	106	102	126	105	103	98	95	98	81	102	104	102	102
Pittsburgh - PNC Park	103	101	103	105	109	81	91	96	90	109	130	106	94	102	89
Houston - Minute Maid Park	103	99	103	102	94	142	103	93	99	104	87	100	84	104	116
Chicago - Wrigley Field	98	100	102	98	93	79	120	104	105	108	98	95	97	100	137
Milwaukee - Miller Park	97	102	100	99	105	98	103	101	103	95	103	100	107	95	101
Atlanta - Turner Field	98	98	97	97	94	92	101	101	100	102	115	100	110	97	97
San Francisco - Pacific Bell Park	102	100	96	102	99	164	74	97	98	124	122	97	75	106	74
New York - Shea Stadium	99	101	96	100	97	62	89	97	100	110	136	104	115	96	77
Florida - Pro Player Stadium	98	100	96	98	94	147	84	110	110	84	68	95	82	99	86
St Louis - Busch Park	98	99	93	97	104	67	85	104	101	90	86	98	92	98	80
Cincinnati - Great American Ballpark**	95	99	92	93	96	38	114	94	101	101	142	94	113	95	115
Los Angeles - Dodger Stadium	93	97	84	90	78	46	105	94	104	102	105	96	98	91	110
San Diego - PETCO Park*	92	96	82	89	91	136	66	112	104	71	51	96	68	89	65
Montreal - Hiram Bithorn Stadium*	91	97	71	88	83	66	57	87	94	76	77	95	72	88	43

2002-2004 National League Ballpark Index Rankings - Home Runs

Team	Avg	AB	R	H	2B	3B	HR	BB	SO	E	E-Inf	LHB Avg	LHB HR	RHB Avg	RHB HR
Colorado - Coors Field	116	104	136	120	117	169	135	99	87	125	123	114	147	116	127
Philadelphia - Citizens Bank Park*	101	100	109	101	90	117	123	96	98	89	82	102	127	100	120
Chicago - Wrigley Field	98	100	102	98	93	79	120	104	105	108	98	95	97	100	137
Arizona - Bank One Ballpark	106	101	118	107	120	156	114	109	98	93	99	107	113	105	115
Cincinnati - Great American Ballpark**	95	99	92	93	96	38	114	94	101	101	142	94	113	95	115
Los Angeles - Dodger Stadium	93	97	84	90	78	46	105	94	104	102	105	96	98	91	110
Milwaukee - Miller Park	97	102	100	99	105	98	103	101	103	95	103	100	107	95	101
Houston - Minute Maid Park	103	99	103	102	94	142	103	93	99	104	87	100	84	104	116
Montreal - Olympic Stadium	102	100	106	102	126	105	103	98	95	98	81	102	104	102	102
Atlanta - Turner Field	98	98	97	97	94	92	101	101	100	102	115	100	110	97	97
Pittsburgh - PNC Park	103	101	103	105	109	81	91	96	90	109	130	106	94	102	89
New York - Shea Stadium	99	101	96	100	97	62	89	97	100	110	136	104	115	96	77
St Louis - Busch Park	98	99	93	97	104	67	85	104	101	90	86	98	92	98	80
Florida - Pro Player Stadium	98	100	96	98	94	147	84	110	110	84	68	95	82	99	86
San Francisco - Pacific Bell Park	102	100	96	102	99	164	74	97	98	124	122	97	75	106	74
San Diego - PETCO Park*	92	96	82	89	91	136	66	112	104	71	51	96	68	89	65
Montreal - Hiram Bithorn Stadium*	91	97	71	88	83	66	57	87	94	76	77	95	72	88	43

* - Data since 2004, ** - Data since 2003

2004 Lefty/Righty Statistics

Batter	vs	Avg	AB	H	2B	3B	HR	RBI	BB	SO	OBP	Slg
Abreu,Bobby	L	.267	187	50	15	0	7	26	43	43	.408	.460
Bats Left	R	.318	387	123	32	1	23	79	84	73	.438	.584
Adams,Russ	L	.100	10	1	0	0	0	1	0	5	.182	.100
Bats Left	R	.339	62	21	2	1	4	9	5	5	.388	.597
Aguila,Chris	L	.056	18	1	1	0	0	1	0	5	.056	.111
Bats Right	R	.333	27	9	1	1	3	4	2	7	.379	.778
Alexander,Manny	L	.267	15	4	1	0	0	2	1	4	.313	.333
Bats Right	R	.167	6	1	1	0	0	1	0	3	.167	.333
Alfaro,Jason	L	.143	7	1	0	0	0	0	0	3	.143	.143
Bats Right	R	.250	4	1	0	0	0	0	0	2	.250	.250
Alfonzo,Edgardo	L	.318	157	50	8	0	5	27	25	1	.411	.465
Bats Right	R	.276	362	100	18	1	6	50	21	39	.321	.381
Allen,Chad	L	.243	37	9	3	0	0	3	2	7	.282	.324
Bats Right	R	.238	21	5	1	1	0	3	0	6	.227	.381
Alomar,Roberto	L	.286	42	12	1	0	1	9	3	12	.326	.381
Bats Both	R	.256	129	33	5	2	3	15	11	19	.319	.395
Alomar Jr.,Sandy	L	.200	35	7	0	0	2	4	1	2	.216	.371
Bats Right	R	.252	111	28	4	0	0	10	10	11	.323	.288
Alou,Moises	L	.298	114	34	6	2	4	10	10	15	.355	.491
Bats Right	R	.292	487	142	30	1	35	96	58	65	.363	.573
Alvarez,Tony	L	.318	22	7	2	0	1	7	4	4	.407	.545
Bats Right	R	.063	16	1	0	0	0	1	0	3	.111	.063
Amezaga,Alfredo	L	.200	35	7	0	0	1	6	0	8	.200	.286
Bats Both	R	.138	58	8	2	0	1	5	3	16	.219	.224
Anderson,Garret	L	.262	149	39	5	0	2	27	4	32	.277	.336
Bats Left	R	.321	293	94	15	1	12	48	25	43	.375	.502
Anderson,Marlon	L	.160	25	4	1	0	0	1	2	2	.222	.200
Bats Left	R	.246	228	56	11	0	8	27	10	36	.275	.399
Ardoin,Danny	L	-	0	0	0	0	0	0	0	0	-	-
Bats Right	R	.125	8	1	0	0	0	1	3	2	.364	.125
Atkins,Garrett	L	.333	15	5	1	0	0	3	3	1	.444	.400
Bats Right	R	.385	13	5	1	0	1	5	1	2	.400	.692
Aurilia,Rich	L	.257	136	35	8	1	3	19	11	22	.325	.397
Bats Right	R	.240	263	63	13	1	3	25	26	49	.308	.331
Ausmus,Brad	L	.313	80	25	3	0	2	13	10	9	.385	.425
Bats Right	R	.232	323	75	11	1	3	18	23	47	.286	.300
Baerga,Carlos	L	.500	8	4	0	0	0	2	3	0	.636	.500
Bats Both	R	.211	76	16	2	0	2	9	3	12	.268	.316
Bagwell,Jeff	L	.146	103	15	1	0	4	10	24	22	.307	.272
Bats Right	R	.292	469	137	28	2	23	89	72	109	.393	.507
Bako,Paul	L	.095	21	2	0	0	1	1	0	9	.095	.238
Bats Left	R	.222	117	26	8	0	0	9	15	20	.319	.291
Baldelli,Rocco	L	.331	124	41	9	0	6	19	10	18	.382	.548
Bats Right	R	.264	394	104	18	3	10	55	20	70	.308	.401
Barajas,Rod	L	.248	101	25	7	0	4	19	5	14	.284	.436
Bats Right	R	.249	257	64	19	1	11	39	8	49	.272	.459
Bard,Josh	L	.429	7	3	1	0	1	2	0	0	.375	1.000
Bats Both	R	.417	12	5	1	0	0	2	3	0	.533	.500
Barmes,Clint	L	.345	29	10	1	0	1	3	2	3	.406	.483
Bats Right	R	.238	42	10	2	1	1	7	1	7	.256	.405
Barrett,Michael	L	.248	105	26	7	1	3	12	9	14	.307	.419
Bats Right	R	.299	351	105	25	5	13	53	24	50	.345	.510
Bartlett,Jason	L	.000	2	0	0	0	0	0	0	0	.000	.000
Bats Right	R	.100	10	1	0	0	0	1	1	1	.182	.100
Batista,Tony	L	.230	165	38	6	0	13	25	9	22	.268	.503
Bats Right	R	.245	441	108	24	2	19	85	17	56	.274	.438
Bautista,Danny	L	.291	158	46	6	0	2	18	14	14	.349	.367
Bats Right	R	.283	381	108	21	1	9	47	21	52	.325	.415
Bautista,Jose	L	.208	53	11	1	0	0	0	1	24	.222	.226
Bats Right	R	.200	35	7	2	0	0	2	6	16	.317	.257
Bay,Jason	L	.265	83	22	3	0	7	17	11	25	.367	.554
Bats Right	R	.287	328	94	21	4	19	65	30	104	.355	.549
Bell,David	L	.302	126	38	12	0	2	16	14	10	.384	.444
Bats Right	R	.287	407	117	21	1	16	61	43	65	.356	.462
Bellhorn,Mark	L	.298	181	54	16	2	7	33	20	61	.374	.525
Bats Both	R	.246	342	84	21	1	10	49	68	116	.373	.401
Belliard,Ronnie	L	.319	204	65	20	1	7	23	26	33	.398	.529
Bats Right	R	.263	395	104	28	0	5	47	34	65	.322	.372
Beltran,Carlos	L	.276	174	48	13	0	11	33	18	23	.347	.540
Bats Both	R	.264	425	112	23	9	27	71	74	78	.375	.551
Beltre,Adrian	L	.291	134	39	7	0	6	17	19	14	.381	.478
Bats Right	R	.347	464	161	25	0	42	104	34	73	.390	.672
Bennett,Gary	L	.256	39	10	4	0	1	5	5	5	.333	.436
Bats Right	R	.217	180	39	10	0	2	15	17	27	.289	.306
Berg,Dave	L	.241	79	19	1	0	1	10	3	10	.277	.291
Bats Right	R	.267	75	20	3	0	2	13	1	17	.278	.387

Batter	vs	Avg	AB	H	2B	3B	HR	RBI	BB	SO	OBP	Slg
Berger,Brandon	L	.278	18	5	2	0	0	2	0	2	.278	.389
Bats Right	R	.118	17	2	0	0	0	0	0	5	.118	.118
Bergeron,Peter	L	.188	16	3	0	0	0	0	1	4	.235	.188
Bats Left	R	.231	26	6	0	0	0	1	1	12	.259	.231
Berkman,Lance	L	.270	126	34	8	0	4	21	24	22	.401	.429
Bats Both	R	.330	418	138	32	3	26	85	103	79	.464	.608
Berroa,Angel	L	.264	140	37	9	1	2	13	7	19	.323	.386
Bats Right	R	.261	372	97	18	5	6	30	16	68	.302	.384
Betemit,Wilson	L	.333	9	3	0	0	0	2	1	2	.364	.333
Bats Both	R	.132	38	5	0	0	0	1	3	14	.195	.132
Bigbie,Larry	L	.218	147	32	5	0	6	22	17	35	.301	.374
Bats Left	R	.308	331	102	18	1	9	46	28	78	.359	.450
Biggio,Craig	L	.303	122	37	7	0	6	13	11	7	.384	.508
Bats Right	R	.276	511	141	40	0	18	50	29	87	.325	.460
Blake,Casey	L	.243	189	46	5	0	11	25	27	44	.341	.444
Bats Right	R	.284	398	113	31	3	17	63	41	95	.360	.505
Blalock,Hank	L	.282	195	55	13	1	5	29	17	56	.344	.436
Bats Left	R	.273	429	117	25	2	27	81	58	93	.360	.529
Blanco,Andres	L	.412	17	7	2	0	0	1	4	1	.545	.529
Bats Both	R	.279	43	12	0	2	0	4	1	5	.295	.372
Blanco,Henry	L	.204	98	20	5	0	5	13	14	16	.307	.408
Bats Right	R	.207	217	45	14	1	5	24	7	40	.237	.350
Bloomquist,Willie	L	.281	89	25	7	0	2	10	6	22	.326	.427
Bats Right	R	.212	99	21	3	0	0	8	4	26	.243	.242
Blum,Geoff	L	.288	80	23	6	0	3	15	9	14	.360	.475
Bats Both	R	.193	259	50	15	0	5	20	15	44	.236	.309
Bocachica,Hiram	L	.400	30	12	3	0	1	2	7	3	.514	.600
Bats Right	R	.167	60	10	2	0	2	4	5	24	.239	.300
Bonds,Barry	L	.306	144	44	9	2	9	24	59	16	.519	.583
Bats Left	R	.397	229	91	18	1	36	77	173	25	.656	.956
Boone,Bret	L	.257	148	38	10	0	8	24	23	30	.355	.486
Bats Right	R	.249	445	111	20	0	16	59	33	105	.304	.402
Borchard,Joe	L	.177	96	17	0	1	3	8	8	21	.240	.292
Bats Both	R	.171	105	18	4	0	6	12	11	36	.256	.381
Borders,Pat	L	.318	22	7	1	0	1	4	0	3	.318	.500
Bats Right	R	.205	73	15	5	0	0	6	1	19	.227	.274
Bowen,Rob	L	.111	9	1	0	0	1	2	1	3	.200	.444
Bats Both	R	.111	18	2	0	0	0	0	3	7	.238	.111
Bradley,Milton	L	.297	145	43	9	0	4	21	13	24	.358	.441
Bats Both	R	.256	371	95	15	0	15	46	58	99	.363	.418
Bragg,Darren	L	.235	17	4	0	0	0	2	2	7	.316	.235
Bats Left	R	.179	84	15	3	1	4	7	8	24	.250	.381
Branyan,Russell	L	.167	30	5	0	0	1	3	2	17	.212	.267
Bats Left	R	.250	128	32	11	1	10	24	18	51	.349	.586
Brazell,Craig	L	1.000	1	1	0	0	0	1	0	0	1.000	4.000
Bats Left	R	.242	33	8	2	0	0	2	1	7	.265	.303
Brito,Juan	L	.182	44	8	2	0	2	5	3	5	.229	.364
Bats Right	R	.213	127	27	5	0	1	7	6	36	.252	.276
Broussard,Ben	L	.362	69	25	7	2	3	22	6	18	.429	.652
Bats Left	R	.258	349	90	21	3	14	60	46	77	.359	.456
Brown,Adrian	L	.333	9	3	0	0	0	0	0	1	.333	.333
Bats Both	R	.000	2	0	0	0	0	0	0	1	.000	.000
Brown,Dee	L	.234	47	11	1	0	1	5	2	13	.265	.319
Bats Left	R	.257	148	38	6	0	3	19	9	37	.302	.358
Bruntlett,Eric	L	.250	16	4	0	0	2	5	4	2	.381	.625
Bats Right	R	.250	36	9	0	0	2	3	3	11	.300	.472
Buchanan,Brian	L	.205	44	9	2	0	1	5	6	14	.294	.318
Bats Right	R	.158	19	3	0	0	0	1	1	6	.238	.316
Buck,John	L	.222	72	16	4	0	3	10	2	25	.243	.403
Bats Right	R	.241	166	40	5	0	9	20	13	54	.294	.434
Burke,Chris	L	.000	2	0	0	0	0	0	0	0	.000	.000
Bats Right	R	.067	15	1	0	0	0	0	2	3	.176	.067
Burke,Jamie	L	.311	61	19	6	0	0	5	7	8	.377	.410
Bats Right	R	.356	59	21	3	0	0	10	3	5	.397	.407
Burks,Ellis	L	.176	17	3	0	0	1	1	1	6	.222	.353
Bats Right	R	.188	16	3	0	0	0	0	2	2	.316	.188
Burnitz,Jeromy	L	.279	136	38	8	1	10	28	11	28	.344	.574
Bats Left	R	.285	404	115	22	3	27	82	47	96	.360	.554
Burrell,Pat	L	.268	97	26	5	0	3	17	23	27	.403	.412
Bats Right	R	.254	351	89	12	0	21	67	55	103	.354	.467
Burroughs,Sean	L	.269	130	35	1	2	0	16	3	9	.307	.308
Bats Left	R	.308	393	121	22	1	2	31	28	43	.362	.384
Bush,Homer	L	.000	1	0	0	0	0	0	0	0	.000	.000
Bats Right	R	.000	6	0	0	0	0	0	0	1	.143	.000
Byrd,Marlon	L	.213	75	16	4	2	1	8	4	10	.250	.360
Bats Right	R	.232	271	63	9	0	4	25	18	58	.297	.310

Batters vs. Left-Handed and Right-Handed Pitchers

Batter	vs	Avg	AB	H	2B	3B	HR	RBI	BB	SO	OBP	Slg
Byrnes,Eric	L	.344	157	54	15	2	7	23	17	21	.406	.599
Bats Right	R	.260	412	107	24	1	13	50	29	90	.324	.417
Cabrera,Jolbert	L	.286	126	36	9	1	2	17	10	24	.338	.421
Bats Right	R	.262	233	61	10	1	4	30	6	46	.298	.365
Cabrera,Miguel	L	.262	126	33	8	0	7	27	22	27	.373	.492
Bats Right	R	.302	477	144	23	1	26	85	46	121	.365	.518
Cabrera,Orlando	L	.295	193	57	14	2	3	15	15	9	.352	.435
Bats Right	R	.249	425	106	24	1	7	47	24	45	.285	.360
Cairo,Miguel	L	.336	128	43	7	2	1	15	7	17	.377	.445
Bats Right	R	.267	232	62	10	3	5	27	11	32	.329	.401
Calloway,Ron	L	.000	14	0	0	0	0	1	1	7	.067	.000
Bats Left	R	.200	70	14	2	0	1	9	4	15	.240	.271
Cameron,Mike	L	.216	102	22	5	0	5	12	15	29	.316	.412
Bats Right	R	.235	391	92	25	1	25	64	42	114	.320	.496
Cantu,Jorge	L	.373	51	19	9	0	0	2	2	10	.396	.549
Bats Right	R	.270	122	33	11	1	2	15	7	34	.318	.426
Carroll,Jamey	L	.250	76	19	5	1	0	5	10	7	.333	.342
Bats Right	R	.310	142	44	9	1	0	11	22	14	.401	.387
Casey,Sean	L	.306	183	56	9	0	10	35	16	13	.372	.519
Bats Left	R	.332	388	129	35	2	14	64	30	23	.385	.541
Cash,Kevin	L	.203	74	15	4	0	2	9	6	21	.272	.338
Bats Right	R	.187	107	20	5	0	2	12	4	38	.233	.290
Castilla,Vinny	L	.267	161	43	8	2	9	29	17	33	.337	.509
Bats Right	R	.273	422	115	35	1	26	102	34	80	.330	.545
Castillo,Alberto	L	.222	27	6	1	0	0	0	5	6	.344	.259
Bats Right	R	.290	62	18	5	0	1	11	9	4	.375	.419
Castillo,Jose	L	.267	90	24	5	1	1	8	9	21	.327	.378
Bats Right	R	.253	293	74	10	1	7	31	14	71	.289	.365
Castillo,Luis	L	.308	143	44	5	6	1	9	14	18	.369	.448
Bats Both	R	.285	421	120	7	1	1	38	61	50	.374	.314
Castro,Juan	L	.238	80	19	6	1	1	9	1	11	.247	.375
Bats Right	R	.247	219	54	15	1	4	17	13	40	.288	.379
Castro,Ramon A	L	.000	3	0	0	0	0	0	1	0	.250	.000
Bats Right	R	.167	12	2	1	0	0	3	0	3	.167	.250
Castro,Ramon	L	.143	14	2	0	0	0	1	1	2	.250	.143
Bats Right	R	.134	82	11	3	0	3	7	10	28	.228	.280
Catalanotto,Frank	L	.227	44	10	2	0	0	4	0	8	.222	.273
Bats Left	R	.307	205	63	17	1	1	22	17	25	.368	.415
Cedeno,Roger	L	.194	36	7	0	0	1	5	4	6	.275	.278
Bats Both	R	.280	164	46	9	2	2	18	15	35	.339	.396
Cepicky,Matt	L	.250	4	1	0	0	1	1	0	1	.250	1.000
Bats Left	R	.214	56	12	4	0	0	2	1	17	.228	.286
Chavez,Endy	L	.241	137	33	5	1	2	12	3	12	.259	.336
Bats Left	R	.290	365	106	15	5	3	22	27	28	.339	.384
Chavez,Eric	L	.306	183	56	5	0	9	28	31	47	.412	.481
Bats Left	R	.257	292	75	15	0	20	49	64	52	.388	.514
Chavez,Raul	L	.135	37	5	1	0	0	5	2	9	.179	.162
Bats Right	R	.232	125	29	7	0	0	18	8	29	.278	.288
Chen,Chin-Feng	L	.000	5	0	0	0	0	0	0	0	.000	.000
Bats Right	R	.000	3	0	0	0	0	0	2	1	.400	.000
Choi,Hee Seop	L	.167	36	6	1	0	1	4	3	13	.268	.278
Bats Left	R	.261	307	80	20	1	14	42	60	83	.381	.469
Church,Ryan	L	.167	12	2	0	0	0	1	1	3	.231	.167
Bats Left	R	.176	51	9	1	0	1	5	6	13	.263	.255
Cintron,Alex	L	.297	158	47	5	3	1	16	6	9	.323	.386
Bats Both	R	.249	406	101	26	4	3	38	25	50	.293	.355
Cirillo,Jeff	L	.207	29	6	0	0	1	6	3	4	.273	.310
Bats Right	R	.217	46	10	3	0	0	1	2	10	.250	.283
Clark,Brady	L	.250	92	23	4	0	1	12	15	9	.368	.326
Bats Right	R	.291	261	76	14	1	6	34	38	39	.391	.421
Clark,Howie	L	.125	8	1	0	0	0	2	0	3	.111	.125
Bats Left	R	.224	107	24	6	0	3	10	13	12	.306	.364
Clark,Jermaine	L	.000	4	0	0	0	0	1	2	3	.333	.000
Bats Left	R	.154	26	4	1	0	0	2	0	6	.185	.192
Clark,Tony	L	.196	92	18	5	0	3	13	6	23	.242	.348
Bats Both	R	.236	161	38	7	0	13	36	20	69	.326	.522
Clayton,Royce	L	.288	146	42	10	0	1	11	18	25	.366	.377
Bats Right	R	.276	428	118	26	4	7	43	30	100	.328	.404
Closser,J.D.	L	.346	26	9	1	0	0	1	2	5	.393	.385
Bats Both	R	.310	87	27	5	0	1	9	4	17	.355	.402
Colbrunn,Greg	L	.200	15	3	0	0	0	1	0	1	.200	.200
Bats Right	R	.000	12	0	0	0	0	0	1	4	.077	.000
Collier,Lou	L	.200	10	2	0	0	1	2	3	3	.385	.500
Bats Right	R	.308	26	8	1	0	0	2	2	7	.379	.346
Conine,Jeff	L	.275	109	30	9	0	5	21	17	13	.370	.495
Bats Right	R	.282	412	116	26	1	9	62	31	65	.331	.415

Batter	vs	Avg	AB	H	2B	3B	HR	RBI	BB	SO	OBP	Slg
Conti,Jason	L	.200	5	1	0	0	0	0	0	3	.200	.200
Bats Left	R	.180	50	9	3	0	0	4	5	16	.255	.240
Cora,Alex	L	.234	47	11	2	0	2	8	4	3	.339	.404
Bats Left	R	.268	358	96	7	4	8	39	43	38	.368	.377
Cordero,Wil	L	.280	25	7	2	0	0	4	0	2	.269	.360
Bats Right	R	.146	41	6	1	0	1	2	3	17	.239	.244
Cota,Humberto	L	.188	16	3	0	0	1	4	1	3	.278	.375
Bats Right	R	.240	50	12	1	1	4	4	2	17	.269	.540
Counsell,Craig	L	.184	87	16	2	2	0	4	9	19	.260	.253
Bats Left	R	.254	386	98	17	3	2	19	50	69	.345	.345
Crawford,Carl	L	.295	146	43	7	4	1	11	12	24	.346	.418
Bats Left	R	.296	480	142	19	15	10	44	23	57	.326	.460
Crede,Joe	L	.256	164	42	9	0	4	20	14	25	.311	.384
Bats Right	R	.230	326	75	16	0	17	49	20	56	.292	.436
Crespo,Cesar	L	.154	13	2	0	0	0	0	0	6	.154	.154
Bats Both	R	.167	66	11	2	1	0	2	0	14	.167	.227
Crisp,Coco	L	.311	177	55	10	1	8	32	12	24	.353	.514
Bats Both	R	.290	314	91	14	1	7	39	24	45	.339	.408
Crosby,Bobby	L	.194	139	27	6	1	6	13	18	28	.287	.381
Bats Right	R	.254	406	103	28	0	16	51	40	113	.330	.441
Crosby,Bubba	L	.063	16	1	0	0	0	1	1	4	.167	.063
Bats Left	R	.189	37	7	2	0	2	6	1	9	.211	.405
Crozier,Eric	L	.333	3	1	1	0	0	0	2	0	.333	.667
Bats Left	R	.133	30	4	1	0	2	4	6	17	.278	.167
Cruz,Deivi	L	.259	108	28	10	0	2	14	2	10	.283	.407
Bats Right	R	.304	289	88	20	2	5	41	15	22	.335	.439
Cruz,Jacob	L	.000	3	0	0	0	0	0	1	2	.250	.000
Bats Left	R	.229	144	33	8	0	3	28	15	41	.319	.347
Cruz,Jose	L	.264	159	42	10	2	6	22	26	24	.364	.465
Bats Both	R	.233	386	90	15	6	15	56	50	93	.320	.420
Cuddyer,Mike	L	.293	123	36	8	1	4	17	16	29	.379	.472
Bats Right	R	.245	216	53	14	0	8	28	21	45	.317	.421
Cummings,Midre	L	.000	2	0	0	0	0	0	0	1	.000	.000
Bats Left	R	.288	52	15	4	0	2	7	5	11	.373	.481
Cust,Jack	L	-	0	0	0	0	0	0	0	0	-	-
Bats Left	R	.000	1	0	0	0	0	0	0	1	.000	.000
Dallimore,Brian	L	.429	14	6	2	0	1	5	2	3	.529	.786
Bats Right	R	.207	29	6	0	0	0	2	2	4	.250	.207
Damon,Johnny	L	.278	223	62	15	2	3	29	19	26	.339	.404
Bats Left	R	.319	398	127	20	4	17	65	57	45	.403	.518
Daubach,Brian	L	.000	3	0	0	0	0	0	0	3	.000	.000
Bats Left	R	.236	72	17	8	0	2	8	10	18	.337	.431
DaVanon,Jeff	L	.136	22	3	0	0	0	0	3	8	.240	.136
Bats Both	R	.289	263	76	11	4	7	34	43	46	.383	.441
Davis,Ben	L	.172	58	10	1	0	1	5	4	16	.222	.241
Bats Both	R	.222	135	30	8	0	5	13	8	33	.271	.393
Davis,J.J.	L	.190	21	4	1	0	0	1	3	3	.292	.238
Bats Right	R	.071	14	1	0	0	0	2	1	7	.125	.071
DeJesus,David	L	.224	98	22	2	0	0	9	7	18	.290	.245
Bats Left	R	.309	265	82	13	3	7	30	26	35	.386	.460
Delgado,Carlos	L	.271	177	48	14	0	9	37	20	39	.348	.503
Bats Left	R	.267	281	75	12	0	23	62	49	75	.386	.555
Delgado,Wilson	L	.240	25	6	0	0	0	2	3	1	.321	.240
Bats Both	R	.305	105	32	4	1	2	11	12	28	.376	.419
Dellucci,David	L	.107	28	3	0	0	0	1	1	9	.212	.107
Bats Left	R	.254	303	77	13	1	17	59	44	79	.354	.472
DeRosa,Mark	L	.233	86	20	2	0	1	6	7	11	.292	.291
Bats Right	R	.242	223	54	14	0	2	25	16	42	.294	.332
DeVore,Doug	L	.176	17	3	0	0	2	5	0	5	.176	.529
Bats Left	R	.233	90	21	3	2	1	8	7	26	.289	.344
Diaz,Einar	L	.210	81	17	5	0	1	7	8	5	.290	.309
Bats Right	R	.241	58	14	1	1	0	4	3	5	.297	.293
Diaz,Matt	L	.267	15	4	1	1	1	3	0	4	.353	.667
Bats Right	R	.000	6	0	0	0	0	0	1	2	.143	.000
Diaz,Victor	L	.273	11	3	2	0	0	2	1	4	.333	.455
Bats Right	R	.300	40	12	1	0	3	6	0	11	.317	.550
DiFelice,Mike	L	.200	10	2	0	1	0	1	1	3	.273	.400
Bats Right	R	.067	15	1	0	0	0	1	2	1	.176	.067
Dobbs,Greg	L	.750	4	3	1	0	0	3	0	1	.750	1.000
Bats Left	R	.184	49	9	0	0	1	6	1	13	.212	.245
Dominique,Andy	L	.333	3	1	0	0	0	1	0	0	.333	.333
Bats Right	R	.125	8	1	0	0	0	0	0	3	.125	.125
Dransfeldt,Kelly	L	.214	14	3	0	0	0	2	0	3	.214	.214
Bats Right	R	.438	16	7	0	0	0	2	0	3	.438	.438
Drew,J.D.	L	.287	167	48	13	4	6	31	34	39	.408	.521
Bats Left	R	.313	351	110	15	4	25	62	84	77	.450	.593

Batters vs. Left-Handed and Right-Handed Pitchers

Batter	vs	Avg	AB	H	2B	3B	HR	RBI	BB	SO	OBP	Slg
Dubois,Jason	L	.125	8	1	0	0	0	1	0	3	.111	.125
Bats Right	R	.267	15	4	0	1	1	4	1	4	.313	.600
Duncan,Jeff	L	.167	6	1	0	0	0	1	0	1	.167	.167
Bats Left	R	.000	9	0	0	0	0	0	1	4	.100	.000
Dunn,Adam	L	.254	181	46	8	0	10	21	29	68	.360	.464
Bats Left	R	.271	387	105	26	0	36	81	79	127	.400	.618
Durazo,Erubiel	L	.278	158	44	9	0	5	28	13	49	.343	.430
Bats Left	R	.340	353	120	26	1	17	60	43	55	.419	.564
Durham,Ray	L	.333	132	44	9	2	4	23	12	11	.390	.523
Bats Both	R	.263	339	89	19	6	13	42	45	49	.355	.469
Durrington,Trent	L	.379	29	11	0	1	2	3	1	5	.400	.655
Bats Right	R	.151	53	8	2	2	0	1	3	18	.196	.264
Dye,Jermaine	L	.280	161	45	6	2	8	30	26	28	.376	.491
Bats Right	R	.259	371	96	23	2	15	50	23	100	.307	.453
Easley,Damion	L	.149	87	13	4	1	2	10	9	6	.245	.287
Bats Right	R	.294	136	40	16	0	7	33	15	30	.384	.566
Eckstein,David	L	.279	179	50	7	0	2	12	15	13	.345	.352
Bats Right	R	.274	387	106	17	1	0	23	27	36	.336	.323
Edmonds,Jim	L	.330	106	35	15	0	5	23	13	33	.400	.613
Bats Left	R	.293	392	115	23	3	37	88	88	117	.423	.651
Ellison,Jason	L	.500	2	1	0	0	1	2	0	1	.500	2.000
Bats Right	R	.500	2	1	0	0	0	1	0	0	.500	.500
Encarnacion,Juan	L	.217	115	25	5	0	1	7	15	19	.313	.287
Bats Right	R	.241	369	89	25	2	15	55	23	67	.295	.442
Ensberg,Morgan	L	.276	105	29	8	1	1	13	12	14	.350	.400
Bats Right	R	.275	306	84	12	2	9	53	24	32	.323	.415
Erickson,Matt	L	.000	1	0	0	0	0	0	0	0	.000	.000
Bats Left	R	.200	5	1	0	0	0	0	0	1	.200	.200
Erstad,Darin	L	.253	166	42	10	0	2	23	9	25	.298	.349
Bats Left	R	.316	329	104	19	1	5	46	28	49	.370	.426
Escalona,Felix	L	-	0	0	0	0	0	0	0	0	-	-
Bats Right	R	.000	8	0	0	0	0	0	0	2	.111	.000
Escobar,Alex	L	.200	50	10	3	0	1	6	11	9	.344	.320
Bats Right	R	.216	102	22	5	2	0	6	12	33	.304	.304
Estalella,Bobby	L	.188	16	3	0	0	1	3	3	7	.316	.375
Bats Right	R	.182	11	2	0	0	1	1	0	4	.250	.455
Estrada,Johnny	L	.272	125	34	7	0	3	14	6	15	.311	.400
Bats Both	R	.329	337	111	29	0	6	62	33	51	.401	.469
Everett,Adam	L	.246	69	17	4	1	2	9	5	11	.297	.420
Bats Right	R	.279	315	88	11	1	6	22	12	45	.322	.378
Everett,Carl	L	.233	90	21	6	0	0	10	3	14	.293	.300
Bats Both	R	.272	191	52	11	1	7	25	13	31	.332	.450
Feliz,Pedro	L	.288	177	51	13	0	7	31	7	31	.310	.480
Bats Right	R	.270	326	88	20	3	15	53	16	53	.302	.488
Fick,Robert	L	.111	18	2	0	0	1	2	2	3	.238	.278
Bats Left	R	.207	208	43	5	2	5	24	20	33	.280	.322
Figgins,Chone	L	.314	169	53	5	5	1	18	22	38	.393	.420
Bats Both	R	.289	408	118	17	12	4	42	27	56	.332	.419
Finley,Steve	L	.242	194	47	7	0	11	29	20	31	.312	.448
Bats Left	R	.283	434	123	21	1	25	65	41	51	.342	.509
Flaherty,John	L	.310	29	9	3	0	1	3	1	5	.333	.517
Bats Right	R	.235	98	23	6	0	5	13	4	20	.272	.449
Flores,Jose	L	.000	1	0	0	0	0	0	0	1	.000	.000
Bats Right	R	.333	3	1	0	0	0	0	1	1	.500	.333
Floyd,Cliff	L	.239	113	27	8	0	1	14	7	30	.296	.336
Bats Left	R	.269	283	76	18	0	17	49	40	73	.373	.512
Ford,Lew	L	.291	175	51	9	0	8	24	20	19	.365	.480
Bats Right	R	.302	394	119	22	4	7	48	47	56	.388	.431
Fordyce,Brook	L	.037	27	1	1	0	0	0	3	6	.133	.074
Bats Right	R	.242	124	30	5	0	2	9	6	28	.288	.331
Fox,Andy	L	.111	9	1	0	0	0	0	1	2	.200	.111
Bats Left	R	.087	46	4	0	0	1	1	0	17	.087	.152
Franco,Julio	L	.306	134	41	7	0	2	20	15	21	.368	.403
Bats Right	R	.312	186	58	11	3	4	37	21	47	.385	.468
Freel,Ryan	L	.235	115	27	4	1	1	5	22	18	.362	.313
Bats Right	R	.290	390	113	17	7	2	23	45	70	.379	.385
Freeman,Choo	L	.205	39	8	1	1	0	5	6	6	.311	.282
Bats Right	R	.176	51	9	2	1	1	6	8	15	.288	.314
Fullmer,Brad	L	.278	36	10	4	0	2	6	3	3	.333	.556
Bats Left	R	.225	222	50	15	1	9	27	24	27	.307	.423
Furcal,Rafael	L	.276	163	45	9	1	6	18	18	23	.352	.454
Bats Both	R	.280	400	112	15	4	8	41	40	48	.342	.398
Galarraga,Andres	L	.500	4	2	0	0	0	1	0	2	.500	.500
Bats Right	R	.167	6	1	0	0	1	1	0	1	.286	.667
Garcia,Danny	L	.067	30	2	0	0	1	4	6	13	.222	.167
Bats Right	R	.278	108	30	7	1	2	13	16	21	.410	.417

Batter	vs	Avg	AB	H	2B	3B	HR	RBI	BB	SO	OBP	Slg
Garcia,Jesse	L	.278	36	10	0	0	0	1	0	3	.278	.278
Bats Right	R	.241	79	19	4	1	1	9	1	13	.259	.354
Garcia,Karim	L	.281	32	9	0	0	1	5	2	4	.324	.375
Bats Left	R	.221	226	50	7	2	9	28	12	46	.257	.389
Garciaparra,Nomar	L	.240	75	18	4	0	2	9	3	11	.266	.373
Bats Right	R	.329	246	81	17	3	7	32	21	19	.394	.508
Gathright,Joey	L	.400	5	2	0	0	0	0	1	1	.500	.400
Bats Left	R	.234	47	11	0	0	0	1	1	13	.294	.234
German,Esteban	L	.167	12	2	0	0	0	1	1	2	.231	.167
Bats Right	R	.271	48	13	1	1	0	6	3	11	.314	.333
Gerut,Jody	L	.208	149	31	7	1	2	15	21	26	.326	.309
Bats Left	R	.271	332	90	24	4	9	36	33	33	.338	.449
Gettis,Byron	L	.176	17	3	1	0	0	0	7	9	.417	.235
Bats Right	R	.182	22	4	0	1	0	1	1	5	.240	.273
Giambi,Jason	L	.263	80	21	4	0	6	17	12	19	.385	.538
Bats Left	R	.185	184	34	5	0	6	23	35	43	.323	.310
Gibbons,Jay	L	.259	108	28	8	0	2	14	4	24	.292	.389
Bats Left	R	.239	238	57	6	1	8	33	25	40	.308	.374
Gil,Geronimo	L	.364	11	4	2	0	0	2	2	2	.462	.545
Bats Right	R	.238	21	5	0	0	0	2	1	3	.273	.238
Gil,Jerry	L	.200	35	7	1	1	0	4	0	10	.200	.286
Bats Right	R	.157	51	8	1	0	0	4	0	23	.170	.176
Giles,Brian	L	.233	210	49	7	1	5	25	16	31	.283	.348
Bats Left	R	.311	399	124	26	6	18	69	73	49	.418	.541
Giles,Marcus	L	.402	92	37	8	1	5	18	15	12	.486	.674
Bats Right	R	.282	287	81	14	1	3	30	21	58	.341	.369
Ginter,Keith	L	.325	80	26	6	0	6	13	13	22	.426	.625
Bats Right	R	.245	306	75	17	2	13	47	24	78	.307	.441
Gipson,Charles	L	.000	1	0	0	0	0	0	0	0	.000	.000
Bats Right	R	.667	3	2	0	0	0	0	0	1	.667	.667
Glanville,Doug	L	.255	47	12	1	0	0	4	4	7	.308	.277
Bats Right	R	.191	115	22	0	1	2	10	4	14	.217	.261
Glaus,Troy	L	.242	62	15	4	0	5	15	9	16	.347	.548
Bats Right	R	.255	145	37	7	1	13	27	22	36	.359	.586
Gload,Ross	L	.425	40	17	3	0	2	6	2	3	.452	.650
Bats Left	R	.299	194	58	13	0	5	38	18	34	.359	.443
Gomes,Jonny	L	.000	6	0	0	0	0	0	1	3	.143	.000
Bats Right	R	.125	8	1	0	0	0	1	0	3	.125	.125
Gomez,Alexis	L	.250	8	2	0	0	0	0	0	4	.250	.250
Bats Left	R	.286	21	6	1	0	0	4	2	4	.348	.333
Gomez,Chris	L	.300	100	30	2	0	2	15	15	7	.391	.380
Bats Right	R	.274	241	66	9	1	1	22	13	34	.313	.332
Gonzalez,Adrian	L	.000	7	0	0	0	0	0	0	0	.000	.000
Bats Left	R	.286	35	10	3	0	1	7	2	6	.324	.457
Gonzalez,Alex	L	.278	115	32	10	2	5	21	10	24	.333	.530
Bats Right	R	.220	446	98	20	1	18	58	17	102	.253	.390
Gonzalez,Alex S	L	.180	61	11	4	1	2	11	5	15	.242	.377
Bats Right	R	.237	224	53	14	0	5	16	9	49	.269	.366
Gonzalez,Juan	L	.297	37	11	2	0	3	5	3	4	.350	.595
Bats Right	R	.267	90	24	2	1	2	12	6	15	.316	.378
Gonzalez,Luis	L	.246	130	32	8	1	10	23	21	21	.353	.554
Bats Left	R	.265	249	66	20	4	7	25	47	37	.383	.462
Gonzalez,Luis A	L	.268	97	26	6	1	3	9	4	20	.297	.443
Bats Right	R	.302	225	68	11	1	9	31	11	47	.344	.480
Gonzalez,Raul	L	.167	6	1	0	0	0	0	0	1	.167	.167
Bats Right	R	.000	5	0	0	0	0	0	0	3	.000	.000
Goodwin,Tom	L	.118	17	2	2	0	0	1	1	5	.167	.235
Bats Left	R	.216	88	19	6	0	0	2	7	17	.271	.284
Gotay,Ruben	L	.250	40	10	0	0	1	4	4	13	.333	.325
Bats Both	R	.277	112	31	7	3	0	12	5	23	.308	.393
Grabowski,Jason	L	.286	14	4	0	0	1	2	1	3	.333	.500
Bats Left	R	.214	159	34	7	0	6	18	18	47	.294	.371
Graffanino,Tony	L	.265	68	18	2	0	0	6	9	3	.351	.294
Bats Right	R	.262	210	55	9	0	3	20	18	35	.326	.348
Granderson,Curtis	L	.000	1	0	0	0	0	0	0	1	.000	.000
Bats Left	R	.250	24	6	1	1	0	0	3	7	.333	.375
Green,Andy	L	.182	55	10	2	0	0	1	1	8	.196	.218
Bats Right	R	.222	54	12	0	1	1	3	4	9	.283	.315
Green,Nick	L	.349	83	29	5	2	0	6	5	21	.396	.458
Bats Right	R	.238	181	43	10	1	3	20	7	42	.272	.354
Green,Shawn	L	.232	181	42	6	0	8	31	18	42	.305	.398
Bats Left	R	.281	409	115	22	1	20	55	53	72	.372	.487
Greene,Khalil	L	.291	127	37	5	2	7	21	15	15	.378	.528
Bats Right	R	.266	357	95	26	2	8	44	38	79	.338	.417
Greene,Todd	L	.366	71	26	5	0	7	20	7	9	.423	.732
Bats Right	R	.234	124	29	9	0	3	15	6	29	.267	.379

Batters vs. Left-Handed and Right-Handed Pitchers

Batter	vs	Avg	AB	H	2B	3B	HR	RBI	BB	SO	OBP	Slg
Grieve,Ben	L	.308	26	8	3	0	1	5	4	12	.400	.538
Bats Left	R	.254	224	57	14	0	7	30	35	58	.356	.411
Griffey Jr.,Ken	L	.196	112	22	8	0	5	13	12	28	.274	.402
Bats Left	R	.287	188	54	10	0	15	47	32	39	.393	.580
Grissom,Marquis	L	.320	153	49	6	0	11	34	10	19	.360	.575
Bats Right	R	.264	409	108	20	2	11	56	27	64	.309	.403
Gross,Gabe	L	.091	11	1	1	0	0	0	4	5	.333	.182
Bats Left	R	.220	118	26	3	0	3	16	15	26	.308	.322
Grudzielanek,Mark	L	.220	82	18	5	0	0	4	7	11	.281	.280
Bats Right	R	.349	175	61	7	1	6	19	8	21	.378	.503
Guerrero,Vladimir	L	.342	155	53	12	1	15	32	24	17	.434	.723
Bats Right	R	.335	457	153	27	1	24	94	28	57	.376	.556
Guerrero,Wilton	L	.250	8	2	0	0	0	0	0	0	.250	.250
Bats Both	R	.208	24	5	0	1	0	1	0	4	.208	.292
Guiel,Aaron	L	.171	41	7	1	0	1	8	5	14	.277	.268
Bats Left	R	.149	94	14	3	0	4	5	12	28	.257	.309
Guillen,Carlos	L	.269	197	53	13	3	6	35	12	32	.316	.457
Bats Both	R	.348	325	113	24	7	14	62	40	55	.416	.594
Guillen,Jose	L	.299	144	43	7	0	7	31	9	22	.346	.493
Bats Right	R	.292	421	123	21	3	20	73	28	70	.353	.499
Gutierrez,Ricky	L	.250	32	8	1	0	0	5	2	3	.294	.281
Bats Right	R	.197	71	14	2	0	0	3	6	11	.269	.225
Guzman,Cristian	L	.326	184	60	10	0	3	11	7	19	.351	.429
Bats Both	R	.250	392	98	21	4	5	35	23	45	.290	.362
Guzman,Freddy	L	.286	21	6	1	0	0	1	1	1	.348	.333
Bats Both	R	.182	55	10	2	0	0	4	2	12	.211	.218
Hafner,Travis	L	.244	156	38	9	0	3	24	18	38	.364	.359
Bats Left	R	.344	326	112	32	3	25	85	50	73	.433	.690
Hairston,Scott	L	.307	101	31	3	3	6	9	8	15	.358	.574
Bats Right	R	.223	238	53	12	3	7	20	13	73	.265	.387
Hairston Jr.,Jerry	L	.316	98	31	5	1	0	6	10	6	.376	.388
Bats Right	R	.296	189	56	14	0	2	18	19	23	.379	.402
Hall,Bill	L	.190	105	20	6	0	3	17	7	29	.239	.333
Bats Right	R	.256	285	73	14	3	6	36	13	90	.290	.389
Hall,Toby	L	.294	102	30	5	0	3	14	8	15	.339	.431
Bats Right	R	.242	302	73	16	0	5	46	16	26	.287	.344
Halter,Shane	L	.152	46	7	2	0	3	7	2	13	.188	.391
Bats Right	R	.235	68	16	3	0	1	6	5	17	.288	.324
Hammock,Robby	L	.250	80	20	5	1	3	8	8	14	.318	.450
Bats Right	R	.235	115	27	11	1	1	10	5	25	.264	.374
Hammonds,Jeffrey	L	.231	39	9	2	0	2	3	10	7	.388	.436
Bats Right	R	.196	56	11	3	0	1	3	5	15	.297	.304
Hansen,Dave	L	.000	4	0	0	0	0	0	1	2	.200	.000
Bats Left	R	.255	102	26	5	0	2	12	20	19	.374	.363
Harris,Brendan	L	.071	14	1	1	0	0	0	1	3	.133	.143
Bats Right	R	.200	45	9	2	0	1	3	2	9	.250	.311
Harris,Lenny	L	.000	2	0	0	0	0	0	0	1	.000	.000
Bats Left	R	.215	93	20	5	0	1	17	3	7	.237	.301
Harris,Willie	L	.181	72	13	3	0	1	4	4	19	.224	.264
Bats Left	R	.279	337	94	12	2	1	23	47	60	.366	.335
Hart,Bo	L	.000	6	0	0	0	0	1	0	0	.000	.000
Bats Right	R	.286	7	2	0	0	0	1	1	3	.375	.286
Hart,Corey	L	.000	1	0	0	0	0	0	0	1	.000	.000
Bats Right	R	-	0	0	0	0	0	0	0	0	-	-
Harvey,Ken	L	.273	128	35	7	0	3	17	6	29	.309	.398
Bats Right	R	.293	328	96	13	1	10	38	22	60	.349	.430
Hatteberg,Scott	L	.285	172	49	7	0	4	25	14	21	.351	.395
Bats Left	R	.283	378	107	23	0	11	57	58	27	.374	.431
Hawpe,Brad	L	.154	13	2	1	0	0	0	1	8	.267	.231
Bats Left	R	.261	92	24	2	2	3	9	10	26	.330	.424
Helms,Wes	L	.306	72	22	5	1	1	6	11	14	.398	.444
Bats Right	R	.248	202	50	8	0	3	22	13	46	.306	.332
Helton,Todd	L	.320	172	55	10	1	7	27	26	26	.413	.512
Bats Left	R	.360	375	135	39	1	25	69	101	46	.492	.669
Hermansen,Chad	L	.000	5	0	0	0	0	0	0	2	.000	.000
Bats Right	R	.000	2	0	0	0	0	0	0	1	.000	.000
Hernandez,Jose	L	.310	126	39	5	1	11	20	15	29	.383	.627
Bats Right	R	.259	85	22	7	0	2	9	11	32	.351	.412
Hernandez,Ramon	L	.310	100	31	10	0	7	19	17	17	.415	.620
Bats Right	R	.264	284	75	13	0	11	44	18	28	.313	.426
Hessman,Mike	L	.148	27	4	1	0	1	3	1	9	.179	.296
Bats Right	R	.119	42	5	2	0	1	2	0	15	.140	.238
Hidalgo,Richard	L	.265	102	27	2	1	7	17	15	31	.350	.510
Bats Right	R	.233	421	98	24	2	18	65	29	98	.288	.428
Hietpas,Joe	L	-	0	0	0	0	0	0	0	0	-	-
Bats Right	R	-	0	0	0	0	0	0	0	0	-	-

Batter	vs	Avg	AB	H	2B	3B	HR	RBI	BB	SO	OBP	Slg
Higginson,Bobby	L	.233	116	27	5	2	0	16	24	27	.377	.310
Bats Left	R	.250	332	83	19	0	12	48	46	57	.345	.416
Hill,Bobby	L	.222	18	4	1	0	0	1	2	1	.333	.278
Bats Both	R	.270	215	58	6	2	2	26	18	38	.355	.344
Hill,Koyie	L	.286	7	2	0	0	0	1	0	1	.286	.286
Bats Both	R	.241	29	7	1	0	1	5	2	5	.290	.379
Hillenbrand,Shea	L	.325	160	52	12	1	6	27	10	19	.368	.525
Bats Right	R	.303	402	122	24	2	9	53	14	30	.340	.440
Hinch,A.J.	L	.000	2	0	0	0	0	0	0	2	.000	.000
Bats Right	R	.222	9	2	1	0	0	0	0	2	.222	.333
Hinske,Eric	L	.268	168	45	11	0	4	26	12	34	.321	.405
Bats Left	R	.236	402	95	12	3	11	43	42	75	.309	.363
Hocking,Denny	L	.190	21	4	0	0	0	0	1	6	.227	.190
Bats Both	R	.205	73	15	2	0	0	4	6	14	.266	.233
Hollandsworth,Todd	L	.353	17	6	0	0	1	3	0	3	.353	.529
Bats Left	R	.313	131	41	6	2	7	19	17	23	.396	.550
Holliday,Matt	L	.237	97	23	8	1	2	10	13	17	.333	.402
Bats Right	R	.307	303	93	23	2	12	47	18	69	.355	.515
Hollins,Damon	L	.400	10	4	2	0	0	2	0	1	.400	.600
Bats Right	R	.333	12	4	0	0	0	3	0	3	.333	.333
House,J.R.	L	-	0	0	0	0	0	0	0	0	-	-
Bats Right	R	.111	9	1	1	0	0	0	0	2	.111	.222
Howard,Ryan	L	.111	9	1	0	0	0	0	0	5	.111	.111
Bats Left	R	.333	30	10	5	0	2	5	2	8	.394	.700
Huckaby,Ken	L	.158	19	3	1	0	0	0	4	4	.304	.211
Bats Right	R	.129	31	4	2	0	0	0	1	8	.156	.194
Hudson,Orlando	L	.264	121	32	9	2	4	19	13	25	.328	.471
Bats Both	R	.272	368	100	23	5	8	39	38	73	.345	.427
Huff,Aubrey	L	.304	184	56	5	1	8	39	14	23	.358	.473
Bats Left	R	.293	416	122	22	1	21	65	42	51	.361	.502
Hummel,Tim	L	.238	42	10	2	0	1	2	0	4	.267	.357
Bats Right	R	.206	68	14	2	0	0	5	8	13	.289	.235
Hunter,Torii	L	.253	158	40	9	0	8	27	10	32	.298	.462
Bats Right	R	.279	362	101	28	0	15	54	30	69	.344	.481
Hyzdu,Adam	L	.500	4	2	2	0	0	1	0	1	.500	1.000
Bats Right	R	.167	6	1	0	0	1	1	1	1	.286	.667
Ibanez,Raul	L	.295	146	43	9	0	4	16	10	33	.342	.438
Bats Left	R	.307	335	103	22	1	12	46	26	39	.358	.487
Infante,Omar	L	.277	188	52	8	5	5	20	14	39	.320	.452
Bats Right	R	.257	315	81	19	4	11	35	26	73	.315	.448
Inge,Brandon	L	.327	168	55	5	4	7	27	16	27	.386	.530
Bats Right	R	.258	240	62	10	3	6	37	16	45	.308	.400
Izturis,Cesar	L	.271	181	49	6	2	1	12	9	15	.305	.343
Bats Both	R	.294	489	144	26	7	3	50	34	55	.338	.395
Izturis,Maicer	L	.111	18	2	1	0	0	2	2	4	.200	.167
Bats Both	R	.225	89	20	4	2	1	2	8	16	.303	.348
Jackson,Damian	L	.111	18	2	1	0	1	1	3	5	.238	.333
Bats Right	R	.083	12	1	1	0	0	2	1	7	.154	.167
Jacobsen,Bucky	L	.340	50	17	3	0	4	12	5	11	.400	.640
Bats Right	R	.245	110	27	6	0	5	16	9	36	.306	.436
Jenkins,Geoff	L	.215	158	34	6	1	6	23	10	55	.286	.380
Bats Left	R	.281	459	129	30	5	21	70	36	97	.338	.505
Jeter,Derek	L	.314	156	49	14	1	6	17	13	20	.378	.532
Bats Right	R	.285	487	139	30	0	17	61	33	79	.343	.452
Jimenez,D'Angelo	L	.239	155	37	6	0	0	11	16	18	.310	.277
Bats Both	R	.282	408	115	22	3	12	56	66	81	.383	.439
Johnson,Charles	L	.233	73	17	2	0	5	10	13	23	.349	.466
Bats Right	R	.237	232	55	18	0	8	37	36	68	.350	.418
Johnson,Mark L	L	.000	2	0	0	0	0	0	0	0	.000	.000
Bats Left	R	.111	9	1	0	0	0	2	3	2	.308	.111
Johnson,Nick	L	.323	62	20	3	0	1	9	17	13	.488	.419
Bats Left	R	.228	189	43	13	0	6	24	23	45	.310	.392
Johnson,Reed	L	.302	172	52	7	1	5	21	13	26	.353	.442
Bats Right	R	.255	365	93	18	1	5	40	15	72	.304	.351
Jones,Andruw	L	.265	151	40	11	2	7	24	22	36	.358	.503
Bats Right	R	.260	419	109	23	2	22	67	49	111	.340	.482
Jones,Chipper	L	.268	149	40	5	1	12	35	31	28	.396	.557
Bats Both	R	.238	323	77	15	0	18	61	53	68	.345	.452
Jones,Jacque	L	.250	156	39	7	0	2	18	13	34	.331	.333
Bats Left	R	.256	399	102	15	1	22	62	27	83	.309	.464
Jordan,Brian	L	.259	85	22	10	0	3	13	8	10	.316	.482
Bats Right	R	.197	127	25	3	1	2	10	8	25	.246	.283
Kapler,Gabe	L	.317	126	40	9	1	4	16	4	23	.333	.500
Bats Right	R	.238	164	39	5	0	2	17	11	26	.294	.305
Karros,Eric	L	.210	62	13	2	0	2	8	5	8	.265	.339
Bats Right	R	.171	41	7	4	0	0	3	2	8	.209	.268

Batters vs. Left-Handed and Right-Handed Pitchers

Batter	vs	Avg	AB	H	2B	3B	HR	RBI	BB	SO	OBP	Slg
Kata,Matt	L	.182	55	10	2	0	1	2	3	11	.224	.273
Bats Both	R	.280	107	30	7	2	1	11	10	18	.339	.411
Kearns,Austin	L	.213	47	10	1	1	2	7	13	16	.383	.404
Bats Right	R	.235	170	40	9	1	7	25	15	55	.301	.424
Kelton,Dave	L	.200	5	1	1	0	0	0	0	1	.200	.400
Bats Right	R	.000	5	0	0	0	0	0	0	2	.000	.000
Kendall,Jason	L	.291	103	30	5	0	0	5	15	8	.393	.340
Bats Right	R	.325	471	153	27	0	3	46	45	33	.400	.401
Kennedy,Adam	L	.250	108	27	3	2	2	11	12	27	.349	.370
Bats Left	R	.286	360	103	17	3	8	37	29	65	.352	.417
Kent,Jeff	L	.282	110	31	4	0	7	19	13	20	.355	.509
Bats Right	R	.291	430	125	30	8	20	88	36	76	.346	.537
Keppinger,Jeff	L	.394	33	13	1	0	2	2	1	0	.412	.606
Bats Right	R	.241	83	20	1	0	1	7	5	7	.281	.289
Kielty,Bobby	L	.259	116	30	9	0	6	18	14	16	.338	.491
Bats Both	R	.172	122	21	5	1	1	13	21	31	.306	.254
Kieschnick,Brooks	L	.333	3	1	0	0	0	0	1	1	.500	.333
Bats Left	R	.267	60	16	3	0	1	7	4	15	.313	.367
Klesko,Ryan	L	.325	114	37	9	1	1	18	13	26	.392	.447
Bats Left	R	.278	288	80	23	1	8	48	60	41	.401	.448
Knoedler,Justin	L	.000	1	0	0	0	0	0	0	0	.000	.000
Bats Right	R	-	0	0	0	0	0	0	0	0	-	
Knott,Jon	L	.200	10	2	1	0	0	1	0	3	.200	.300
Bats Right	R	.250	4	1	1	0	0	0	1	2	.400	.500
Konerko,Paul	L	.288	163	47	8	0	13	38	23	32	.372	.577
Bats Right	R	.273	400	109	14	0	28	79	46	75	.354	.518
Koskie,Corey	L	.231	134	31	4	1	5	19	13	43	.320	.388
Bats Left	R	.260	288	75	20	1	20	52	36	60	.352	.545
Kotchman,Casey	L	.000	7	0	0	0	0	0	0	2	.222	.000
Bats Left	R	.239	109	26	6	0	0	15	7	9	.294	.294
Kotsay,Mark	L	.336	152	51	5	1	4	21	17	16	.401	.461
Bats Left	R	.306	454	139	32	2	11	42	38	54	.359	.458
Kroeger,Josh	L	.333	3	1	0	0	0	0	0	2	.333	.333
Bats Left	R	.157	51	8	3	0	0	2	1	19	.173	.216
Krynzel,Dave	L	.000	5	0	0	0	0	0	1	2	.375	.000
Bats Left	R	.250	36	9	1	0	0	3	2	13	.308	.278
Kubel,Jason	L	.333	6	2	0	0	0	0	0	3	.333	.333
Bats Left	R	.296	54	16	2	0	2	7	6	6	.361	.444
Labandeira,John	L	.000	5	0	0	0	0	0	0	0	.000	.000
Bats Both	R	.000	9	0	0	0	0	0	0	4	.000	.000
Laird,Gerald	L	.317	41	13	4	0	0	4	6	7	.380	.415
Bats Right	R	.189	106	20	2	0	1	12	6	28	.246	.236
Laker,Tim	L	.333	51	17	1	0	1	10	2	13	.364	.412
Bats Right	R	.121	66	8	1	0	2	7	5	15	.183	.227
Lamb,Mike	L	.349	43	15	4	0	2	13	5	12	.417	.581
Bats Left	R	.277	235	65	10	3	12	45	26	51	.345	.498
Lane,Jason	L	.280	50	14	4	0	2	7	6	11	.357	.480
Bats Right	R	.267	86	23	6	2	2	12	10	22	.343	.453
Lankford,Ray	L	.200	25	5	2	1	0	3	2	9	.241	.360
Bats Right	R	.263	175	46	12	0	6	19	27	46	.364	.434
Larkin,Barry	L	.204	93	19	3	1	4	14	10	10	.276	.387
Bats Right	R	.320	253	81	12	2	4	30	24	29	.380	.431
LaRoche,Adam	L	.238	21	5	1	0	1	2	6	6	.407	.429
Bats Left	R	.281	303	85	26	1	12	43	21	72	.327	.492
Larson,Brandon	L	.071	28	2	1	0	0	1	2	11	.129	.107
Bats Right	R	.256	90	23	5	0	3	13	12	24	.356	.411
LaRue,Jason	L	.281	96	27	4	1	5	14	9	30	.352	.500
Bats Right	R	.241	294	71	20	1	9	41	17	78	.328	.408
Lawton,Matt	L	.262	191	50	9	0	6	25	24	32	.355	.403
Bats Left	R	.285	400	114	16	0	14	45	50	52	.372	.430
LeCroy,Matt	L	.322	90	29	7	0	4	13	7	15	.367	.533
Bats Right	R	.241	174	42	7	0	5	26	9	45	.296	.368
Ledee,Ricky	L	.286	14	4	1	0	1	3	4	5	.444	.571
Bats Left	R	.228	162	37	8	0	6	27	23	42	.326	.389
Lee,Carlos	L	.308	156	48	8	0	10	24	19	24	.385	.551
Bats Right	R	.303	435	132	29	0	21	75	35	62	.359	.515
Lee,Derrek	L	.306	111	34	5	0	9	23	17	20	.408	.595
Bats Right	R	.271	494	134	34	1	23	75	51	108	.344	.484
Lee,Travis	L	.000	6	0	0	0	0	0	0	1	.000	.000
Bats Left	R	.154	13	2	1	0	0	2	1	2	.214	.231
Leon,Jose	L	.222	45	10	2	0	2	6	2	9	.255	.400
Bats Right	R	.095	21	2	0	0	0	2	0	10	.091	.095
Leone,Justin	L	.222	27	6	1	0	3	6	2	5	.276	.593
Bats Right	R	.213	75	16	4	0	3	7	7	27	.306	.387
Lieberthal,Mike	L	.282	103	29	6	1	4	13	9	9	.351	.476
Bats Right	R	.268	373	100	25	0	13	48	28	60	.331	.440

Batter	vs	Avg	AB	H	2B	3B	HR	RBI	BB	SO	OBP	Slg
Liefer,Jeff	L	.000	3	0	0	0	0	1	0	3	.000	.000
Bats Left	R	.240	25	6	2	0	1	4	2	5	.296	.440
Linden,Todd	L	.000	15	0	0	0	0	0	4	6	.211	.000
Bats Both	R	.294	17	5	1	0	0	1	1	1	.368	.353
Little,Mark	L	.364	11	4	0	0	0	2	0	4	.385	.364
Bats Right	R	.000	9	0	0	0	0	0	0	3	.100	.000
Lo Duca,Paul	L	.312	138	43	7	0	2	15	9	14	.351	.406
Bats Right	R	.277	397	110	22	2	11	65	27	35	.333	.426
Lofton,Kenny	L	.308	26	8	2	0	0	2	3	6	.400	.385
Bats Left	R	.272	250	68	8	7	3	16	28	21	.340	.396
Logan,Nook	L	.395	43	17	2	0	0	4	0	4	.395	.442
Bats Both	R	.222	90	20	3	2	0	6	13	20	.317	.300
Long,Terrence	L	.231	39	9	3	1	0	1	0	12	.231	.359
Bats Left	R	.305	249	76	16	3	3	27	19	39	.350	.430
Lopez,Felipe	L	.292	65	19	7	1	2	12	3	18	.333	.523
Bats Both	R	.226	199	45	11	1	5	19	22	63	.308	.367
Lopez,Javy	L	.315	149	47	10	1	8	20	18	15	.387	.557
Bats Right	R	.316	430	136	23	2	15	66	29	82	.364	.484
Lopez,Jose	L	.214	56	12	2	0	0	3	2	5	.241	.250
Bats Right	R	.238	151	36	11	0	5	19	6	26	.270	.411
Lopez,Luis	L	.200	20	4	0	0	0	0	0	6	.238	.200
Bats Right	R	.000	6	0	0	0	0	0	0	3	.000	.000
Lopez,Luis M	L	.216	37	8	4	0	1	2	1	6	.237	.405
Bats Both	R	.157	51	8	1	0	0	6	2	14	.193	.176
Lopez,Mendy	L	.158	19	3	0	0	1	3	1	6	.238	.316
Bats Right	R	.053	19	1	0	0	0	1	3	3	.182	.053
Lopez,Mickey	L	.000	1	0	0	0	0	0	0	0	.000	.000
Bats Both	R	.333	3	1	0	0	0	0	1	0	.600	.333
Loretta,Mark	L	.352	182	64	13	0	5	25	28	11	.431	.505
Bats Right	R	.329	438	144	34	2	11	51	30	34	.373	.491
Lowell,Mike	L	.344	128	44	9	0	11	29	19	12	.429	.672
Bats Right	R	.279	470	131	35	1	16	56	45	65	.347	.460
Ludwick,Ryan	L	.188	32	6	1	0	2	2	0	8	.212	.406
Bats Right	R	.278	18	5	1	0	0	2	2	6	.381	.333
Lugo,Julio	L	.300	150	45	9	1	0	19	17	27	.371	.373
Bats Right	R	.267	431	115	32	3	7	56	37	79	.326	.404
Luna,Hector	L	.240	75	18	3	0	2	8	6	23	.298	.360
Bats Left	R	.255	98	25	4	2	1	14	7	14	.308	.367
Mabry,John	L	.333	54	18	2	0	3	15	7	16	.403	.537
Bats Left	R	.285	186	53	9	0	10	25	19	47	.351	.495
Machado,Andy	L	.000	4	0	0	0	0	0	2	2	.333	.000
Bats Both	R	.288	52	15	5	1	0	4	8	24	.383	.423
Machado,Robert	L	.143	21	3	1	0	0	1	3	1	.250	.190
Bats Right	R	.154	52	8	2	0	1	2	1	17	.170	.250
Macias,Jose	L	.238	63	15	1	1	2	9	0	9	.238	.381
Bats Both	R	.282	131	37	5	2	1	13	5	29	.317	.374
Mackowiak,Rob	L	.164	61	10	0	2	0	3	6	13	.188	.230
Bats Left	R	.258	430	111	22	4	17	70	49	101	.337	.447
Magruder,Chris	L	.333	36	12	3	0	2	3	4	4	.400	.583
Bats Both	R	.170	53	9	3	1	0	7	4	17	.250	.264
Majewski,Val	L	-	0	0	0	0	0	0	0	0	-	-
Bats Left	R	.154	13	2	1	0	0	1	0	1	.154	.231
Marrero,Eli	L	.415	106	44	10	1	5	21	9	16	.462	.670
Bats Right	R	.250	144	36	8	0	5	19	14	34	.311	.410
Martinez,Edgar	L	.300	130	39	11	0	4	18	25	24	.413	.477
Bats Right	R	.250	356	89	12	0	8	45	33	83	.315	.351
Martinez,Ramon	L	.243	70	17	5	1	0	4	11	12	.354	.343
Bats Right	R	.247	190	47	10	0	3	26	15	28	.297	.347
Martinez,Sandy	L	.000	3	0	0	0	0	0	0	1	.000	.000
Bats Left	R	.000	3	0	0	0	0	0	0	2	.000	.000
Martinez,Tino	L	.246	126	31	5	0	9	29	18	21	.356	.500
Bats Left	R	.268	332	89	15	1	14	47	48	51	.365	.446
Martinez,Victor	L	.282	170	48	11	1	6	28	25	26	.380	.465
Bats Both	R	.283	350	99	27	0	17	80	35	43	.348	.506
Mateo,Henry	L	.154	13	2	1	0	0	0	1	3	.154	.231
Bats Both	R	.323	31	10	1	0	0	0	1	4	.344	.355
Mateo,Ruben	L	.184	49	9	0	2	3	9	5	14	.259	.449
Bats Right	R	.221	77	17	4	1	0	5	3	12	.277	.299
Matheny,Mike	L	.247	93	23	7	1	2	17	6	12	.297	.409
Bats Right	R	.247	292	72	15	0	3	33	17	71	.291	.329
Matos,Luis	L	.133	105	14	3	0	2	7	7	20	.191	.219
Bats Right	R	.267	225	60	15	0	4	21	12	40	.315	.387
Matsui,Hideki	L	.265	189	50	7	2	6	30	26	32	.358	.418
Bats Left	R	.314	395	124	27	0	25	78	62	71	.405	.572
Matsui,Kazuo	L	.306	98	30	8	0	3	11	11	16	.376	.480
Bats Both	R	.262	362	95	24	2	4	33	29	81	.319	.373

Batters vs. Left-Handed and Right-Handed Pitchers

Batter	vs	Avg	AB	H	2B	3B	HR	RBI	BB	SO	OBP	Slg
Matthews Jr.,Gary	L	.244	90	22	2	0	4	10	11	23	.324	.400
Bats Both	R	.289	190	55	15	1	7	26	22	41	.363	.489
Mauer,Joe	L	.182	33	6	1	0	0	4	4	6	.282	.212
Bats Left	R	.365	74	27	7	1	6	13	7	8	.410	.730
Mayne,Brent	L	.394	33	13	3	0	0	1	5	7	.485	
Bats Left	R	.185	157	29	3	1	0	14	22	34	.280	.217
McCarty,Dave	L	.259	58	15	2	1	1	5	5	12	.317	.379
Bats Right	R	.258	93	24	6	0	3	12	9	28	.333	.419
McCracken,Quinton	L	.231	39	9	3	0	0	2	1	9	.244	.308
Bats Both	R	.285	137	39	8	1	2	11	14	18	.351	.401
McDonald,Darnell	L	.200	25	5	1	0	0	1	1	4	.231	.240
Bats Right	R	.000	7	0	0	0	0	0	1	2	.125	.000
McDonald,John	L	.176	34	6	0	1	1	4	4	1	.263	.324
Bats Right	R	.220	59	13	5	0	1	3	0	10	.220	.356
McEwing,Joe	L	.250	44	11	1	1	0	2	6	11	.340	.318
Bats Right	R	.255	94	24	2	0	1	14	3	21	.276	.309
McGriff,Fred	L	.200	5	1	0	0	0	0	0	4	.200	.200
Bats Left	R	.179	67	12	3	0	2	7	9	15	.276	.313
McKay,Cody	L	.222	9	2	0	0	0	0	1	1	.300	.222
Bats Left	R	.231	65	15	2	0	0	6	1	13	.265	.262
McLemore,Mark	L	.130	23	3	1	0	0	1	5	3	.286	.174
Bats Both	R	.260	227	59	13	0	2	20	36	30	.362	.344
McMillon,Billy	L	.200	5	1	0	0	0	0	2	0	.200	.200
Bats Left	R	.184	87	16	4	0	3	11	8	20	.258	.333
McPherson,Dallas	L	.083	12	1	0	0	0	0	2	6	.214	.083
Bats Left	R	.286	28	8	1	0	3	6	1	11	.310	.643
Melhuse,Adam	L	.120	25	3	0	0	1	5	5	9	.267	.240
Bats Both	R	.275	189	52	11	0	10	26	11	38	.315	.492
Mench,Kevin	L	.319	144	46	17	0	10	28	15	12	.390	.646
Bats Right	R	.259	294	76	13	6	16	43	18	51	.306	.486
Menechino,Frank	L	.315	108	34	5	2	6	15	15	17	.398	.565
Bats Right	R	.248	161	40	8	2	3	11	22	35	.353	.379
Merloni,Lou	L	.327	113	37	9	1	4	23	9	27	.379	.531
Bats Right	R	.234	77	18	3	0	0	5	5	14	.291	.273
Michaels,Jason	L	.286	84	24	1	0	5	14	12	22	.371	.476
Bats Right	R	.270	215	58	11	0	5	26	30	58	.361	.391
Mientkiewicz,Doug	L	.220	123	27	8	1	1	10	13	23	.309	.325
Bats Left	R	.246	268	66	16	0	5	25	35	33	.333	.362
Miles,Aaron	L	.267	120	32	3	0	2	13	12	15	.336	.342
Bats Both	R	.301	402	121	12	3	4	34	17	38	.327	.376
Millar,Kevin	L	.299	154	46	14	0	3	17	16	26	.369	.448
Bats Right	R	.297	354	105	22	0	15	57	41	65	.388	.486
Miller,Corky	L	.000	2	0	0	0	0	0	2	1	.667	.000
Bats Right	R	.027	37	1	0	0	0	3	4	11	.140	.027
Miller,Damian	L	.290	124	36	6	0	2	11	12	24	.358	.387
Bats Right	R	.264	273	72	19	0	7	47	27	63	.330	.410
Minor,Damon	L	.167	12	2	1	0	0	2	2	5	.375	.250
Bats Left	R	.261	46	12	1	0	0	4	10	13	.414	.283
Mirabelli,Doug	L	.311	45	14	4	0	3	9	8	9	.415	.600
Bats Right	R	.270	115	31	8	0	6	23	11	37	.349	.496
Moeller,Chad	L	.242	62	15	3	0	2	8	4	16	.288	.387
Bats Right	R	.200	255	51	10	1	3	19	17	58	.260	.282
Mohr,Dustan	L	.241	116	28	10	1	2	10	16	30	.336	.397
Bats Right	R	.299	147	44	10	0	5	18	30	34	.435	.469
Molina,Ben	L	.252	103	26	6	0	3	11	6	14	.291	.398
Bats Right	R	.286	234	67	7	0	7	43	12	21	.323	.406
Molina,Jose	L	.339	59	20	4	2	1	9	3	13	.371	.525
Bats Right	R	.229	144	33	6	0	2	16	7	39	.265	.313
Molina,Yadier	L	.250	32	8	2	0	0	1	3	4	.314	.313
Bats Right	R	.272	103	28	4	0	2	14	10	16	.333	.369
Mondesi,Raul	L	.240	25	6	0	0	1	2	2	4	.296	.360
Bats Right	R	.241	108	26	9	0	2	13	11	27	.317	.380
Monroe,Craig	L	.256	160	41	11	1	5	21	9	26	.291	.431
Bats Right	R	.314	287	90	16	2	13	51	20	53	.362	.519
Mora,Melvin	L	.303	132	40	8	0	8	27	24	20	.418	.545
Bats Right	R	.352	418	147	33	0	19	77	42	75	.419	.567
Mordecai,Mike	L	.238	21	5	1	0	0	0	5	4	.385	.286
Bats Right	R	.222	63	14	2	0	1	5	1	14	.234	.302
Morneau,Justin	L	.240	75	18	5	0	3	18	4	20	.289	.427
Bats Left	R	.283	205	58	12	0	16	40	24	34	.358	.576
Mottola,Chad	L	.250	8	2	1	0	1	3	1	0	.333	.750
Bats Right	R	.000	6	0	0	0	0	0	1	3	.143	.000
Mueller,Bill	L	.255	137	35	9	0	4	18	7	21	.301	.409
Bats Both	R	.298	262	78	18	1	8	39	44	35	.395	.466
Munson,Eric	L	.227	66	15	1	0	5	13	5	16	.282	.470
Bats Left	R	.208	255	53	13	2	14	36	24	74	.291	.439

Batter	vs	Avg	AB	H	2B	3B	HR	RBI	BB	SO	OBP	Slg
Murphy,Donald	L	.222	9	2	2	0	0	1	0	3	.222	.444
Bats Both	R	.167	18	3	1	0	0	2	0	4	.167	.222
Murray,Calvin	L	.000	1	0	0	0	0	0	0	0	.000	.000
Bats Right	R	.250	4	1	0	0	0	1	1	0	.400	.250
Myers,Greg	L	-	0	0	0	0	0	0	1	0	1.000	-
Bats Left	R	.222	18	4	2	0	0	1	1	4	.263	.333
Nady,Xavier	L	.344	32	11	1	0	2	4	3	4	.417	.563
Bats Right	R	.178	45	8	3	0	1	5	2	9	.213	.311
Navarro,Dioner	L	1.000	1	1	0	0	0	1	0	0	1.000	1.000
Bats Both	R	.333	6	2	0	0	0	0	0	0	.333	.333
Nevin,Phil	L	.324	170	55	12	1	10	28	31	31	.431	.582
Bats Right	R	.273	377	103	19	0	16	77	35	90	.337	.451
Newhan,David	L	.300	100	30	4	2	1	10	4	19	.349	.410
Bats Left	R	.315	273	86	11	5	7	44	23	53	.366	.469
Nivar,Ramon	L	.286	14	4	0	0	0	4	0	6	.267	.286
Bats Right	R	.000	4	0	0	0	0	0	0	1	.000	.000
Nix,Laynce	L	.176	74	13	2	1	1	7	3	30	.218	.270
Bats Left	R	.266	297	79	18	3	13	39	20	83	.312	.478
Nixon,Trot	L	.133	15	2	0	0	0	0	0	3	.188	.133
Bats Left	R	.336	134	45	9	1	6	23	15	21	.397	.552
Norton,Greg	L	.182	44	8	1	0	1	1	3	11	.234	.273
Bats Both	R	.167	42	7	0	0	1	1	9	10	.314	.238
Nunez,Abraham	L	.230	87	20	2	0	4	19	7	21	.284	.391
Bats Both	R	.207	198	41	8	1	2	15	27	48	.302	.288
Nunez,Abraham O	L	.158	19	3	0	0	0	1	2	2	.238	.158
Bats Both	R	.245	163	40	9	0	2	12	8	34	.279	.337
Offerman,Jose	L	.176	51	9	3	0	0	4	9	12	.300	.235
Bats Both	R	.289	121	35	11	2	2	18	20	19	.390	.463
Ojeda,Augie	L	.000	7	0	0	0	0	0	1	0	.125	.000
Bats Both	R	.385	52	20	1	0	2	9	3	8	.468	.519
Ojeda,Miguel	L	.361	36	13	0	0	5	12	6	5	.442	.778
Bats Right	R	.225	120	27	3	0	3	14	9	29	.282	.325
Olerud,John	L	.250	92	23	5	0	2	8	12	13	.355	.370
Bats Left	R	.261	333	87	15	1	7	40	49	48	.360	.375
Olivo,Miguel	L	.322	87	28	7	0	6	23	7	17	.368	.609
Bats Right	R	.196	214	42	8	4	7	17	13	67	.252	.369
Olmedo,Ray	L	.000	1	0	0	0	0	0	0	0	.000	.000
Bats Both	R	-	0	0	0	0	0	0	0	1	1.000	-
Olson,Tim	L	.244	45	11	4	0	1	2	6	4	.333	.400
Bats Both	R	.135	52	7	3	0	1	3	10	14	.274	.250
Ordonez,Magglio	L	.339	59	20	2	2	2	7	2	7	.371	.542
Bats Right	R	.273	143	39	6	0	7	30	14	15	.344	.462
Ordonez,Rey	L	.222	9	2	1	0	0	2	1	1	.300	.333
Bats Right	R	.154	52	8	2	0	1	3	1	13	.170	.250
Ortiz,David	L	.250	196	49	13	0	10	43	17	46	.315	.469
Bats Left	R	.326	386	126	34	3	31	96	58	87	.411	.671
Osik,Keith	L	.125	8	1	0	0	0	0	0	1	.125	.125
Bats Right	R	.059	17	1	0	0	0	0	0	6	.059	.059
Overbay,Lyle	L	.298	151	45	17	1	5	20	13	30	.357	.523
Bats Left	R	.301	428	129	36	0	11	67	68	98	.394	.463
Palmeiro,Orlando	L	.154	13	2	1	0	0	1	2	5	.267	.231
Bats Left	R	.250	120	30	4	0	3	11	16	14	.353	.358
Palmeiro,Rafael	L	.190	158	30	3	0	5	20	15	14	.256	.304
Bats Left	R	.286	392	112	26	0	18	68	71	47	.398	.490
Pascucci,Val	L	.212	33	7	1	0	1	3	7	13	.341	.333
Bats Right	R	.138	29	4	0	0	1	3	3	9	.242	.241
Patterson,Corey	L	.289	173	50	7	2	8	26	8	43	.328	.491
Bats Left	R	.258	458	118	26	4	16	46	37	125	.317	.437
Paul,Josh	L	.316	19	6	3	0	1	5	2	5	.364	.632
Bats Right	R	.216	51	11	0	0	1	5	5	12	.286	.275
Payton,Jay	L	.283	152	43	5	2	3	23	20	14	.369	.401
Bats Right	R	.248	306	76	12	2	5	32	23	42	.303	.350
Pellow,Kit	L	.182	55	10	2	1	1	2	6	22	.262	.309
Bats Right	R	.288	66	19	3	0	1	8	2	21	.347	.379
Pena,Carlos	L	.245	147	36	5	3	8	30	13	50	.315	.483
Bats Left	R	.240	334	80	17	1	19	52	57	96	.348	.467
Pena,Wily Mo	L	.310	87	27	3	0	9	22	9	30	.394	.655
Bats Right	R	.241	249	60	7	1	17	44	13	78	.287	.482
Peralta,Jhonny	L	.222	9	2	1	0	0	2	1	2	.300	.333
Bats Right	R	.250	16	4	0	0	0	0	2	4	.333	.250
Perez,Antonio	L	.167	6	1	0	0	0	0	0	2	.286	.167
Bats Right	R	.286	7	2	1	0	0	0	0	3	.286	.429
Perez,Eddie	L	.250	68	17	4	0	1	6	3	10	.282	.353
Bats Right	R	.216	102	22	8	0	2	7	8	19	.289	.353
Perez,Eduardo	L	.185	27	5	1	0	1	5	4	6	.290	.333
Bats Right	R	.273	11	3	0	0	0	2	0	3	.273	.364

Batters vs. Left-Handed and Right-Handed Pitchers

Batter	vs	Avg	AB	H	2B	3B	HR	RBI	BB	SO	OBP	Slg
Perez,Neifi	L	.250	120	30	8	0	3	16	8	17	.295	.392
Bats Both	R	.257	261	67	9	1	1	23	16	24	.296	.310
Perez,Timo	L	.140	43	6	1	0	0	1	3	4	.196	.163
Bats Left	R	.264	250	66	11	0	5	39	12	25	.301	.368
Perez,Tomas	L	.213	47	10	4	1	2	7	3	12	.260	.468
Bats Both	R	.217	129	28	9	1	4	14	6	32	.255	.395
Perry,Herbert	L	.231	91	21	1	1	4	14	11	13	.327	.396
Bats Right	R	.209	43	9	1	0	1	3	3	6	.261	.302
Phelps,Josh	L	.309	152	47	11	0	12	32	11	38	.358	.618
Bats Both	R	.210	219	46	8	2	5	29	11	55	.267	.333
Phillips,Andy	L	-	0	0	0	0	0	0	0	0	-	-
Bats Right	R	.250	8	2	0	0	1	2	0	1	.250	.625
Phillips,Brandon	L	.167	6	1	0	0	0	0	0	2	.167	.167
Bats Right	R	.188	16	3	2	0	0	1	2	3	.278	.313
Phillips,Jason	L	.224	85	19	6	0	2	12	8	11	.281	.365
Bats Right	R	.217	277	60	12	0	5	22	27	31	.303	.314
Phillips,Paul	L	.000	2	0	0	0	0	0	0	1	.000	.000
Bats Right	R	.333	3	1	0	0	0	0	0	0	.500	.333
Piazza,Mike	L	.303	89	27	5	0	4	15	18	16	.421	.494
Bats Right	R	.257	366	94	16	0	16	39	50	62	.347	.432
Pickering,Calvin	L	.233	43	10	1	0	1	4	2	15	.267	.326
Bats Left	R	.253	79	20	7	1	6	22	16	27	.371	.595
Piedra,Jorge	L	.308	13	4	3	0	0	2	0	4	.308	.538
Bats Left	R	.295	78	23	5	0	3	8	5	15	.345	.474
Pierre,Juan	L	.305	187	57	8	2	0	9	9	10	.361	.369
Bats Left	R	.334	491	164	14	10	3	40	36	25	.379	.422
Pierzynski,A.J.	L	.220	100	22	3	0	2	14	0	8	.218	.310
Bats Left	R	.286	371	106	25	2	9	63	19	19	.344	.437
Podsednik,Scott	L	.224	147	33	4	3	3	14	13	32	.294	.354
Bats Left	R	.249	493	123	23	4	9	25	45	73	.319	.367
Polanco,Placido	L	.327	147	48	5	0	7	18	8	11	.354	.503
Bats Right	R	.287	356	102	16	0	10	37	19	28	.341	.416
Pond,Simon	L	.000	5	0	0	0	0	0	0	1	.000	.000
Bats Left	R	.182	44	8	2	0	1	6	5	11	.275	.295
Porter,Colin	L	1.000	1	1	0	0	0	0	0	0	1.000	1.000
Bats Left	R	.294	34	10	1	0	1	2	0	13	.294	.412
Posada,Jorge	L	.275	142	39	12	0	8	28	26	28	.385	.528
Bats Both	R	.270	307	83	19	0	13	53	62	64	.407	.459
Pratt,Todd	L	.318	22	7	3	0	0	2	7	4	.467	.455
Bats Right	R	.245	106	26	2	0	3	14	11	34	.322	.349
Pride,Curtis	L	.500	4	2	0	0	0	0	0	1	.600	.500
Bats Left	R	.222	36	8	3	0	0	3	0	10	.222	.306
Prieto,Alex	L	.364	11	4	0	0	1	2	1	3	.417	.636
Bats Right	R	.190	21	4	1	0	0	2	2	6	.250	.238
Pujols,Albert	L	.379	116	44	13	1	9	34	21	7	.465	.741
Bats Right	R	.319	476	152	38	1	37	89	63	45	.401	.637
Punto,Nick	L	.250	32	8	0	0	1	4	4	6	.333	.344
Bats Both	R	.254	59	15	0	0	1	8	8	13	.343	.305
Quinlan,Robb	L	.390	59	23	6	0	3	8	8	4	.456	.644
Bats Right	R	.317	101	32	8	0	2	15	6	22	.367	.455
Quintero,Humberto	L	.360	25	9	2	0	1	4	0	4	.360	.560
Bats Right	R	.191	47	9	1	0	1	6	5	12	.264	.277
Quiroz,Guillermo	L	.217	23	5	0	0	0	0	1	4	.280	.217
Bats Right	R	.207	29	6	2	0	0	1	1	4	.250	.276
Raburn,Ryan	L	.188	16	3	1	0	0	1	2	8	.278	.250
Bats Right	R	.077	13	1	0	0	0	0	0	7	.077	.077
Raines Jr,Tim	L	.250	52	13	4	0	0	2	2	8	.278	.327
Bats Both	R	.262	42	11	2	0	0	3	2	8	.311	.310
Ramirez,Aramis	L	.267	90	24	4	0	6	14	10	12	.333	.511
Bats Right	R	.328	457	150	28	1	30	89	39	50	.381	.591
Ramirez,Manny	L	.306	160	49	13	0	13	41	39	30	.446	.631
Bats Right	R	.309	408	126	31	0	30	89	43	94	.375	.605
Randa,Joe	L	.303	145	44	8	1	3	16	9	19	.344	.434
Bats Right	R	.279	340	95	23	1	5	40	31	58	.343	.397
Ransom,Cody	L	.500	16	8	3	0	1	4	3	5	.600	.875
Bats Right	R	.173	52	9	3	0	0	7	3	15	.218	.231
Redman,Tike	L	.266	109	29	4	1	1	13	5	12	.302	.349
Bats Left	R	.284	437	124	15	3	7	38	18	40	.312	.380
Redmond,Mike	L	.179	56	10	2	0	1	2	2	8	.258	.268
Bats Right	R	.279	190	53	13	0	1	23	12	20	.332	.363
Reed,Jeremy	L	.200	5	1	1	0	0	2	1	1	.429	.400
Bats Left	R	.415	53	22	3	0	0	3	6	3	.475	.472
Reese,Pokey	L	.224	85	19	3	2	1	13	4	16	.258	.341
Bats Right	R	.220	159	35	4	0	2	16	13	44	.277	.283
Relaford,Desi	L	.216	102	22	5	0	1	8	17	20	.341	.294
Bats Both	R	.223	278	62	9	0	5	26	17	36	.277	.309
Renteria,Edgar	L	.366	131	48	12	0	4	20	14	17	.429	.550
Bats Right	R	.264	455	120	25	0	6	52	25	61	.297	.358
Restovich,Mike	L	.350	20	7	1	0	1	2	2	5	.409	.550
Bats Right	R	.185	27	5	2	0	1	4	2	5	.241	.370
Reyes,Jose	L	.326	43	14	7	0	1	3	0	4	.326	.558
Bats Both	R	.237	177	42	9	2	1	11	5	27	.258	.328
Reyes,Rene	L	.100	10	1	1	0	0	0	0	5	.250	.200
Bats Both	R	.157	51	8	1	0	0	1	3	12	.204	.176
Riggs,Adam	L	.333	15	5	3	0	0	2	0	0	.333	.533
Bats Right	R	.095	21	2	0	0	1	1	1	10	.136	.095
Rios,Alexis	L	.287	101	29	7	1	0	6	14	22	.374	.376
Bats Right	R	.286	325	93	17	6	1	22	17	62	.326	.385
Rivas,Luis	L	.288	104	30	7	1	4	14	3	10	.303	.490
Bats Right	R	.241	232	56	12	4	6	20	10	43	.275	.405
Rivera,Carlos	L	-	0	0	0	0	0	0	0	0	-	-
Bats Left	R	.200	15	3	0	0	0	1	1	3	.250	.200
Rivera,Juan	L	.276	156	43	11	0	6	21	10	13	.323	.462
Bats Right	R	.328	235	77	13	1	6	28	24	32	.390	.468
Rivera,Rene	L	-	0	0	0	0	0	0	0	0	-	-
Bats Right	R	.000	3	0	0	0	0	0	0	1	.000	.000
Roberts,Brian	L	.211	199	42	17	1	0	15	25	29	.298	.307
Bats Both	R	.301	442	133	33	1	4	38	46	66	.364	.407
Roberts,Dave	L	.175	57	10	2	1	0	3	5	12	.238	.246
Bats Left	R	.271	262	71	12	6	4	32	33	36	.357	.408
Robinson,Kerry	L	.167	12	2	0	0	0	0	1	0	.231	.167
Bats Left	R	.313	80	25	4	0	0	5	4	8	.345	.363
Rodriguez,Alex	L	.311	132	41	4	0	14	28	25	27	.422	.659
Bats Right	R	.279	469	131	20	2	22	78	55	104	.361	.471
Rodriguez,Ivan	L	.343	175	60	11	0	5	30	24	31	.420	.491
Bats Right	R	.330	352	116	21	2	14	56	17	60	.363	.520
Rolen,Scott	L	.371	89	33	8	1	6	27	28	19	.525	.685
Bats Right	R	.302	411	124	24	3	28	97	44	73	.379	.579
Rollins,Jimmy	L	.303	165	50	11	1	5	26	15	12	.365	.473
Bats Both	R	.285	492	140	32	11	9	47	42	61	.342	.449
Rolls,Damian	L	.152	66	10	4	0	0	5	3	18	.186	.212
Bats Right	R	.176	51	9	1	0	0	4	7	18	.283	.196
Romano,Jason	L	.188	16	3	0	0	1	4	0	6	.188	.375
Bats Right	R	.111	18	2	0	0	0	0	2	6	.200	.111
Rose,Mike	L	-	0	0	0	0	0	0	0	0	-	-
Bats Both	R	.000	2	0	0	0	0	0	0	2	.000	.000
Ross,Dave	L	.125	64	8	1	0	1	1	8	29	.233	.188
Bats Right	R	.198	101	20	2	1	4	14	7	33	.265	.356
Rowand,Aaron	L	.302	179	54	16	0	11	27	18	30	.371	.575
Bats Right	R	.315	308	97	22	2	13	42	12	61	.355	.526
Ryan,Mike	L	.350	20	7	1	1	0	1	0	5	.350	.500
Bats Left	R	.196	51	10	1	0	0	6	4	11	.255	.216
Sadler,Donnie	L	.286	7	2	2	0	0	0	0	3	.286	.571
Bats Right	R	.063	16	1	0	0	0	0	1	4	.118	.063
Saenz,Olmedo	L	.338	65	22	1	0	6	13	10	18	.427	.631
Bats Right	R	.196	46	9	0	0	2	9	2	15	.245	.326
Salmon,Tim	L	.147	51	7	1	0	2	5	6	15	.195	.173
Bats Right	R	.324	111	36	5	0	2	18	10	26	.379	.423
Sanchez,Alex	L	.348	141	49	4	1	1	15	1	22	.350	.411
Bats Left	R	.304	191	58	5	2	1	11	6	28	.325	.366
Sanchez,Freddy	L	.000	2	0	0	0	0	0	0	1	.000	.000
Bats Right	R	.176	17	3	0	0	0	2	0	2	.176	.176
Sanchez,Rey	L	.289	83	24	4	2	0	10	6	6	.337	.386
Bats Right	R	.228	202	46	10	1	2	16	6	22	.257	.317
Sanders,Reggie	L	.230	113	26	9	0	3	14	17	33	.333	.389
Bats Right	R	.270	333	90	18	3	19	53	16	85	.308	.514
Santiago,Benito	L	.250	44	11	3	0	1	5	1	6	.267	.386
Bats Right	R	.282	131	37	7	0	5	18	7	26	.326	.450
Santiago,Ramon	L	.200	10	2	1	0	0	0	1	2	.273	.300
Bats Both	R	.172	29	5	0	0	0	2	2	1	.250	.172
Schneider,Brian	L	.244	86	21	0	2	2	8	4	12	.286	.360
Bats Left	R	.260	350	91	20	1	10	41	38	51	.334	.449
Scutaro,Marco	L	.276	145	40	12	1	6	19	9	15	.316	.497
Bats Right	R	.271	310	84	20	0	1	24	7	43	.287	.345
Segui,David	L	.353	17	6	1	0	0	2	3	7	.450	.412
Bats Both	R	.333	42	14	2	0	1	5	2	6	.378	.452
Sexson,Richie	L	.263	19	5	2	0	1	2	7	5	.462	.526
Bats Right	R	.222	72	16	2	0	8	21	7	16	.291	.583
Sheffield,Gary	L	.314	140	44	9	0	8	30	26	16	.423	.550
Bats Right	R	.282	433	122	21	1	28	91	66	67	.384	.529
Shelton,Chris	L	.208	24	5	0	0	1	3	7	7	.375	.333
Bats Right	R	.182	22	4	1	0	0	0	2	7	.250	.250

Batters vs. Left-Handed and Right-Handed Pitchers

Batter	vs	Avg	AB	H	2B	3B	HR	RBI	BB	SO	OBP	Slg
Sierra,Ruben	L	.243	136	33	7	1	5	24	9	25	.284	.419
Bats Both	R	.246	171	42	5	0	12	41	16	30	.305	.485
Simon,Randall	L	.235	17	4	0	0	0	1	0	4	.235	.235
Bats Left	R	.183	175	32	6	0	3	13	18	15	.269	.269
Sizemore,Grady	L	.178	45	8	0	0	0	2	5	8	.296	.178
Bats Left	R	.280	93	26	6	2	4	22	9	26	.352	.516
Sledge,Terrmel	L	.241	87	21	3	1	2	16	4	15	.275	.368
Bats Left	R	.277	311	86	17	5	13	46	36	51	.352	.489
Smith,Jason	L	.242	33	8	0	1	0	4	2	9	.286	.303
Bats Left	R	.238	122	29	7	3	5	15	6	28	.279	.467
Snead,Esix	L	-	0	0	0	0	0	0	0	0	-	
Bats Both	R	-	0	0	0	0	0	0	0	0	-	
Snow,J.T.	L	.250	48	12	4	0	1		9	10	.373	.396
Bats Left	R	.339	298	101	28	1	11	51	49	51	.438	.550
Snyder,Chris	L	.250	32	8	1	0	3	4	3	8	.314	.563
Bats Right	R	.234	64	15	5	0	2	11	10	17	.333	.406
Snyder,Earl	L	-	0	0	0	0	0	0	0	0	-	
Bats Right	R	.250	4	1	0	0	0	0	0	1	.250	.250
Soriano,Alfonso	L	.266	158	42	9	2	9	31	16	38	.335	.519
Bats Right	R	.284	420	128	23	2	19	60	17	83	.319	.471
Sosa,Sammy	L	.253	95	24	6	0	4	12	22	34	.393	.442
Bats Right	R	.253	383	97	15	0	31	68	34	99	.315	.535
Spencer,Shane	L	.241	58	14	1	0	1	8	5	12	.302	.310
Bats Both	R	.299	127	38	9	1	3	18	8	25	.345	.457
Spiezio,Scott	L	.203	74	15	4	0	1	8	6	9	.263	.297
Bats Both	R	.218	293	64	8	3	9	33	30	51	.294	.358
Spivey,Junior	L	.279	43	12	3	0	3	5	10	9	.426	.558
Bats Right	R	.270	185	50	10	0	4	23	15	39	.341	.389
Stairs,Matt	L	.232	95	22	3	0	4	17	11	28	.324	.389
Bats Left	R	.276	344	95	18	3	14	49	38	64	.351	.468
Stewart,Shannon	L	.257	113	29	5	0	3	10	18	17	.356	.381
Bats Right	R	.325	265	86	12	2	8	37	29	27	.391	.475
Stinnett,Kelly	L	.167	18	3	0	0	0	2	2	7	.286	.167
Bats Right	R	.366	41	15	0	0	3	5	3	9	.422	.585
Stynes,Chris	L	.190	58	11	3	0	1	8	4	8	.254	.293
Bats Right	R	.231	104	24	7	0	0	8	5	15	.273	.298
Surhoff,B.J.	L	.337	98	33	6	0	1	14	6	13	.381	.429
Bats Left	R	.298	245	73	6	1	7	36	24	33	.359	.416
Sutton,Larry	L	-	0	0	0	0	0	0	0	0	-	
Bats Left	R	.200	5	1	0	0	0	1	1	2	.333	.200
Suzuki,Ichiro	L	.404	208	84	9	1	5	21	15	19	.444	.529
Bats Left	R	.359	496	178	15	4	3	39	34	44	.402	.423
Sweeney,Mark	L	.556	9	5	2	0	1	3	1	1	.600	1.111
Bats Left	R	.250	168	42	10	2	8	37	31	50	.366	.476
Sweeney,Mike	L	.221	113	25	5	0	4		8	15	.276	.372
Bats Right	R	.312	298	93	18	0	18	71	25	29	.374	.554
Swisher,Nick	L	.500	10	5	2	0	0	0	5	2	.667	.700
Bats Both	R	.200	50	10	2	0	2	8	3	9	.268	.360
Taguchi,So	L	.266	94	25	4	0	2	10	6	11	.311	.372
Bats Right	R	.318	85	27	6	2	1	15	6	12	.366	.471
Taveras,Willy	L	-	0	0	0	0	0	0	0	0	-	
Bats Right	R	.000	1	0	0	0	0	0	0	1	.000	.000
Teixeira,Mark	L	.313	163	51	11	0	10	34	18	38	.395	.564
Bats Both	R	.267	382	102	23	2	28	78	50	79	.359	.558
Tejada,Miguel	L	.327	159	52	13	0	11	40	19	16	.396	.616
Bats Right	R	.306	494	151	27	2	23	110	29	57	.348	.508
Terrero,Luis	L	.268	56	15	2	0	3	7	9	15	.379	.464
Bats Right	R	.237	173	41	12	0	1	7	11	63	.298	.324
Thames,Marcus	L	.284	81	23	5	0	6	17	10	15	.363	.568
Bats Right	R	.226	84	19	7	0	4	16	6	27	.290	.452
Thomas,Charles	L	.281	32	9	0	2	1	8	3	10	.395	.500
Bats Left	R	.289	204	59	8	2	6	23	18	35	.364	.436
Thomas,Frank	L	.200	50	10	2	0	3	7	18	10	.420	.420
Bats Right	R	.289	190	55	14	0	15	42	46	47	.438	.600
Thome,Jim	L	.239	188	45	9	0	12	34	23	55	.324	.479
Bats Left	R	.294	320	94	19	1	30	71	81	89	.435	.641
Thompson,Rich	L	-	0	0	0	0	0	0	0	0	-	
Bats Left	R	.000	1	0	0	0	0	0	0	0	.000	.000
Thurston,Joe	L	.500	2	1	0	0	0	0	0	0	.500	.500
Bats Left	R	.133	15	2	1	1	0	1	0	5	.125	.333
Tiffee,Terry	L	.158	19	3	1	0	2	5	2	2	.273	.526
Bats Both	R	.360	25	9	3	0	0	3	1	1	.385	.480
Tonis,Mike	L	.000	2	0	0	0	0	0	1	0	.333	.000
Bats Right	R	.000	4	0	0	0	0	0	0	0	.000	.000
Torcato,Tony	L	.000	1	0	0	0	0	0	0	0	.000	.000
Bats Left	R	.625	8	5	0	0	0	2	1	0	.636	.625
Torrealba,Yorvit	L	.282	85	24	4	2	5	17	8	14	.354	.553
Bats Right	R	.172	87	15	3	1	1	6	9	17	.250	.264
Torres,Andres	L		0	0	0	0	0	0	0	0	-	
Bats Both	R		0	0	0	0	0	0	0	0	-	
Tracy,Andy	L		0	0	0	0	0	0	0	0	-	
Bats Left	R	.188	16	3	1	0	0	1	1	8	.235	.250
Tracy,Chad	L	.218	110	24	4	1	1	11	7	15	.263	.300
Bats Left	R	.305	371	113	25	2	7	42	38	45	.366	.439
Treanor,Matt	L	.182	11	2	0	0	0	0	0	4	.182	.182
Bats Right	R	.250	44	11	2	0	0	1	4	9	.340	.295
Tremie,Chris	L		0	0	0	0	0	0	0	0	-	
Bats Right	R		0	0	0	0	0	0	0	0	-	
Tucker,Michael	L	.235	68	16	2	2	1	9	9	19	.325	.368
Bats Left	R	.260	396	103	19	4	12	53	61	87	.358	.419
Upton,B.J.	L	.410	61	25	6	0	1	3	5	15	.455	.557
Bats Right	R	.163	98	16	2	2	3	9	10	31	.245	.316
Uribe,Juan	L	.264	178	47	7	4	12	33	10	37	.302	.551
Bats Right	R	.293	324	95	24	2	11	41	22	59	.340	.481
Utley,Chase	L	.196	46	9	1	0	1	3	2	6	.229	.283
Bats Left	R	.281	221	62	10	2	12	54	13	34	.324	.507
Valdez,Wilson	L	.273	22	6	1	0	1	3	1	3	.304	.455
Bats Right	R	.190	21	4	0	0	0	1	1	2	.227	.190
Valent,Eric	L	.100	10	1	0	0	0	0	2	3	.250	.100
Bats Left	R	.273	260	71	15	2	13	34	26	58	.340	.496
Valentin,Javier	L	.109	46	5	0	0	0	2	1	11	.146	.109
Bats Both	R	.269	156	42	10	1	6	18	16	25	.333	.462
Valentin,Jose	L	.191	136	26	6	1	7	16	13	53	.262	.404
Bats Left	R	.226	314	71	14	2	23	54	30	86	.298	.503
Vander Wal,John	L		0	0	0	0	0	0	0	0	-	
Bats Left	R	.118	51	6	2	0	2	4	4	20	.182	.275
Varitek,Jason	L	.350	137	48	10	1	6	26	10	30	.426	.569
Bats Both	R	.273	326	89	20	0	12	47	46	96	.375	.445
Vazquez,Ramon	L	.154	13	2	0	0	0	2	1	3	.200	.154
Bats Left	R	.245	102	25	3	2	1	11	10	21	.310	.343
Ventura,Robin	L	.250	8	2	1	0	0	1	1	1	.333	.375
Bats Left	R	.243	144	35	2	0	5	27	21	30	.337	.361
Vidro,Jose	L	.267	131	35	5	0	2	13	15	17	.338	.351
Bats Both	R	.306	281	86	19	0	12	47	34	26	.381	.502
Vina,Fernando	L	.182	33	6	2	0	0	0	5	3	.325	.242
Bats Left	R	.244	82	20	3	0	0	7	4	6	.300	.280
Vizcaino,Jose	L	.246	69	17	0	0	1	8	4	9	.284	.290
Bats Both	R	.280	289	81	21	3	2	25	16	30	.317	.394
Vizquel,Omar	L	.258	190	49	14	1	1	23	14	16	.306	.358
Bats Both	R	.308	377	116	14	2	6	36	43	46	.377	.403
Walker,Larry	L	.316	76	24	7	1	1	12	14	22	.447	.474
Bats Left	R	.291	182	53	9	3	16	35	35	35	.414	.637
Walker,Todd	L	.268	41	11	0	1	0	2	7	7	.423	.317
Bats Left	R	.275	331	91	19	3	15	48	36	45	.342	.486
Ward,Daryle	L	.296	54	16	5	0	1	7	3	14	.333	.444
Bats Left	R	.238	239	57	12	2	14	50	19	31	.299	.481
Wells,Vernon	L	.287	150	43	11	1	10	24	19	22	.371	.573
Bats Right	R	.267	386	103	23	1	13	43	32	61	.324	.433
Werth,Jayson	L	.293	92	27	5	1	8	19	13	29	.381	.630
Bats Right	R	.247	198	49	9	2	8	28	17	56	.318	.419
White,Rondell	L	.293	157	46	9	2	3	19	17	20	.367	.433
Bats Right	R	.258	291	75	12	0	16	48	22	57	.321	.464
Wigginton,Ty	L	.222	108	24	8	0	4	11	11	15	.292	.407
Bats Right	R	.272	386	105	22	2	13	55	34	67	.333	.440
Wilkerson,Brad	L	.278	176	49	12	1	9	21	22	47	.366	.511
Bats Left	R	.245	396	97	27	1	23	46	84	105	.377	.492
Williams,Bernie	L	.265	166	44	6	0	9	26	32	24	.384	.464
Bats Both	R	.261	395	103	23	1	13	46	53	72	.350	.423
Williams,Gerald	L	.275	51	14	3	1	2	6	5	13	.339	.490
Bats Right	R	.205	78	16	5	1	2	5	3	13	.235	.372
Willingham,Josh	L	.333	3	1	0	0	1	1	2	1	.600	1.333
Bats Right	R	.182	22	4	0	0	0	0	2	5	.250	.182
Wilson,Craig	L	.259	108	28	8	2	6	14	16	25	.375	.537
Bats Right	R	.265	453	120	27	3	23	68	34	144	.349	.490
Wilson,Dan	L	.203	79	16	2	0	2	12	8	12	.270	.304
Bats Right	R	.267	240	64	11	0	0	21	18	45	.317	.313
Wilson,Enrique	L	.299	67	20	6	0	1	6	1	6	.304	.433
Bats Both	R	.179	173	31	3	0	5	25	14	14	.236	.283
Wilson,Jack	L	.261	115	30	5	3	5	12	8	10	.315	.487
Bats Right	R	.318	537	171	36	9	6	47	18	61	.340	.453
Wilson,Preston	L	.290	69	20	5	0	2	13	5	12	.338	.449
Bats Right	R	.226	133	30	6	0	4	16	12	37	.304	.361

Batters vs. Left-Handed and Right-Handed Pitchers

Batter	vs	Avg	AB	H	2B	3B	HR	RBI	BB	SO	OBP	Slg
Wilson,Tom	L	.000	5	0	0	0	0	0	0	2	.000	.000
Bats Right	R	.286	7	2	0	0	0	0	1	3	.375	.286
Wilson,Vance	L	.200	40	8	2	0	0	3	1	4	.233	.250
Bats Right	R	.299	117	35	8	1	4	18	10	20	.368	.487
Winn,Randy	L	.257	191	49	6	3	3	17	15	31	.316	.366
Bats Both	R	.299	435	130	28	3	11	64	38	67	.359	.453
Wise,Dewayne	L	.240	25	6	1	0	2	3	2	5	.286	.520
Bats Left	R	.226	137	31	8	4	4	14	7	23	.269	.431
Womack,Tony	L	.285	123	35	4	0	0	8	9	15	.338	.317
Bats Left	R	.314	430	135	18	3	5	30	27	45	.353	.405
Woodward,Chris	L	.254	59	15	2	1	0	6	7	18	.343	.322
Bats Right	R	.227	154	35	11	3	1	18	7	28	.258	.357
Wooten,Shawn	L	.071	14	1	0	0	0	1	0	4	.133	.071
Bats Right	R	.205	39	8	3	0	0	1	2	5	.262	.282
Wright,David	L	.309	55	17	3	0	1	5	0	7	.309	.418
Bats Right	R	.288	208	60	14	1	13	35	14	33	.338	.553
Youkilis,Kevin	L	.250	72	18	4	0	3	14	16	12	.386	.431
Bats Right	R	.265	136	36	7	0	4	21	17	33	.356	.404
Young,Dmitri	L	.248	137	34	10	0	8	23	8	26	.293	.496
Bats Both	R	.286	252	72	13	2	10	37	25	45	.358	.472
Young,Eric	L	.329	164	54	17	0	1	15	22	13	.413	.451
Bats Right	R	.250	180	45	8	2	0	12	21	15	.344	.317
Young,Ernie	L	.333	3	1	0	0	0	0	1	2	.500	.333
Bats Right	R	1.000	1	1	0	0	0	0	0	0	1.000	1.000
Young,Michael	L	.330	188	62	11	1	7	29	17	21	.383	.511
Bats Right	R	.307	502	154	22	8	15	70	27	68	.341	.472
Zaun,Gregg	L	.272	81	22	6	0	0	6	6	14	.322	.346
Bats Both	R	.268	257	69	18	0	6	30	41	47	.380	.409
Zeile,Todd	L	.239	88	21	5	0	2	7	13	18	.333	.364
Bats Right	R	.231	260	60	11	0	7	28	31	65	.314	.354
Zinter,Alan	L	.000	7	0	0	0	0	0	3	3	.300	.000
Bats Both	R	.259	27	7	2	0	1	6	2	12	.300	.444

Pitchers vs. Left-Handed and Right-Handed Batters

Pitcher	vs	Avg	AB	H	2B	3B	HR	RBI	BB	SO	OBP	Slg
Aardsma,David	L	.474	19	9	3	0	0	5	4	3	.560	.632
Throws Right	R	.379	29	11	2	0	1	6	6	2	.500	.552
Abbott,Paul	L	.261	203	53	8	0	10	31	41	23	.386	.448
Throws Right	R	.288	184	53	11	0	12	32	17	23	.358	.543
Acevedo,Jose	L	.338	281	95	26	1	13	42	18	43	.376	.577
Throws Right	R	.256	363	93	25	0	17	57	27	74	.312	.466
Adams,Mike	L	.241	87	21	4	0	2	10	4	14	.283	.356
Throws Right	R	.252	115	29	5	0	3	15	10	25	.313	.374
Adams,Terry	L	.228	158	36	6	1	3	17	21	39	.319	.335
Throws Right	R	.400	120	48	5	0	7	34	7	17	.427	.617
Adkins,Jon	L	.327	107	35	3	0	8	15	13	20	.397	.579
Throws Right	R	.288	139	40	7	0	5	21	7	24	.327	.446
Affeldt,Jeremy	L	.271	70	19	6	0	4	12	8	12	.354	.529
Throws Left	R	.312	231	72	21	2	2	33	24	37	.375	.446
Ainsworth,Kurt	L	.313	64	20	3	1	4	22	13	12	.439	.578
Throws Right	R	.328	58	19	4	1	2	10	7	8	.418	.534
Alfonseca,Antonio	L	.246	118	29	1	0	3	9	12	13	.313	.331
Throws Right	R	.263	160	42	10	0	2	16	16	32	.330	.363
Almanza,Armando	L	.192	26	5	0	0	3	5	3	9	.276	.538
Throws Left	R	.211	19	4	2	1	0	2	4	4	.360	.421
Almanzar,Carlos	L	.226	115	26	4	0	2	14	11	18	.300	.313
Throws Right	R	.258	155	40	11	0	6	19	8	26	.301	.445
Alvarez,Abe	L	.200	10	2	1	0	0	0	0	2	.200	.300
Throws Left	R	.600	10	6	3	0	2	5	5	0	.733	1.500
Alvarez,Wilson	L	.307	114	35	6	0	6	22	9	19	.362	.518
Throws Left	R	.222	333	74	11	1	6	29	22	83	.274	.315
Anderson,Brian	L	.337	169	57	15	0	8	25	15	25	.390	.568
Throws Left	R	.314	510	160	39	0	25	88	38	45	.358	.537
Anderson,Jason	L	.000	2	0	0	0	0	2	3	1	.600	.000
Throws Right	R	.500	2	1	0	0	1	4	1	0	.667	2.000
Anderson,Jimmy	L	.294	17	5	1	1	0	5	2	3	.400	.471
Throws Left	R	.311	45	14	3	0	0	4	4	3	.380	.378
Ankiel,Rick	L	.222	18	4	2	0	0	2	1	1	.300	.333
Throws Left	R	.286	21	6	1	0	2	4	0	8	.318	.619
Appier,Kevin	L	.308	13	4	1	0	0	1	2	2	.400	.385
Throws Right	R	.500	6	3	1	0	0	4	1	0	.571	.667
Aquino,Greg	L	.169	65	11	3	1	1	6	13	14	.308	.292
Throws Right	R	.220	59	13	2	1	3	10	4	12	.284	.441
Armas Jr.,Tony	L	.231	108	25	6	0	5	12	23	21	.370	.426
Throws Right	R	.258	159	41	8	1	8	22	22	33	.355	.472
Arroyo,Bronson	L	.269	357	96	23	2	10	40	30	52	.341	.429
Throws Right	R	.227	331	75	24	2	7	42	17	90	.283	.375
Ashby,Andy	L	.167	6	1	0	0	0	0	0	2	.167	.167
Throws Right	R	.000	1	0	0	0	0	0	0	0	.000	.000
Astacio,Pedro	L	.360	25	9	3	0	0	3	2	4	.407	.480
Throws Right	R	.308	13	4	0	0	2	6	3	2	.438	.769
Atchison,Scott	L	.209	43	9	3	0	2	6	7	14	.320	.419
Throws Right	R	.274	73	20	2	0	2	10	7	22	.333	.384
Ayala,Luis	L	.246	134	33	6	1	3	14	6	18	.277	.373
Throws Right	R	.282	209	59	12	1	3	36	9	45	.326	.392
Backe,Brandon	L	.347	101	35	7	0	4	10	14	25	.426	.535
Throws Right	R	.253	158	40	9	1	6	18	13	29	.312	.437
Bacsik,Mike	L	.350	20	7	2	0	1	4	0	0	.381	.600
Throws Left	R	.225	40	9	3	0	1	4	1	6	.262	.375
Baek,Cha Seung	L	.303	66	20	4	1	3	12	7	11	.378	.530
Throws Right	R	.250	60	15	6	0	2	9	4	9	.308	.450
Baez,Danys	L	.252	123	31	7	0	3	18	12	25	.328	.382
Throws Right	R	.223	130	29	4	1	3	11	17	27	.333	.338
Bajenaru,Jeff	L	.278	18	5	0	1	0	5	2	6	.350	.389
Throws Right	R	.526	19	10	2	0	0	1	4	2	.609	.632
Baldwin,James	L	.444	9	4	0	1	2	4	3	0	.583	1.333
Throws Right	R	.450	20	9	2	1	1	4	2	1	.522	.800
Balfour,Grant	L	.183	60	11	1	1	2	6	9	23	.290	.333
Throws Right	R	.276	87	24	0	0	2	13	12	19	.376	.345
Bartosh,Cliff	L	.286	42	12	4	0	2	15	9	15	.412	.524
Throws Left	R	.263	38	10	3	0	2	5	2	10	.300	.500
Batista,Miguel	L	.264	432	114	16	4	11	56	67	63	.362	.396
Throws Right	R	.285	323	92	27	1	11	50	29	41	.345	.477
Bauer,Rick	L	.293	92	27	6	0	2	18	13	16	.387	.424
Throws Right	R	.193	114	22	3	0	2	11	7	21	.258	.272
Bautista,Denny	L	.348	69	24	5	0	2	16	11	12	.432	.507
Throws Right	R	.357	56	20	6	0	1	9	2	7	.410	.518
Beck,Rod	L	.318	44	14	0	2	5	9	7	7	.412	.750
Throws Right	R	.245	53	13	4	0	3	8	2	8	.263	.491
Beckett,Josh	L	.281	285	80	18	5	10	41	32	80	.354	.484
Throws Right	R	.192	297	57	14	0	6	26	22	72	.258	.300

Pitcher	vs	Avg	AB	H	2B	3B	HR	RBI	BB	SO	OBP	Slg
Bedard,Erik	L	.277	112	31	5	2	2	16	22	27	.406	.411
Throws Left	R	.269	439	118	27	1	11	58	49	94	.345	.410
Beimel,Joe	L	.500	6	3	1	0	1	5	2	2	.625	1.167
Throws Left	R	.714	7	5	1	0	0	3	0	0	.714	.857
Bell,Heath	L	.161	31	5	1	0	0	2	3	9	.235	.194
Throws Right	R	.304	56	17	2	0	5	10	3	18	.339	.607
Bell,Rob	L	.279	229	64	19	1	7	34	29	24	.363	.463
Throws Right	R	.228	250	57	9	1	9	28	12	33	.272	.380
Beltran,Francis	L	.250	72	18	3	0	6	13	11	13	.345	.542
Throws Right	R	.254	114	29	8	0	5	17	16	35	.353	.456
Beltran,Rigo	L	.500	2	1	0	0	0	0	0	0	.500	.500
Throws Right	R	.000	1	0	0	0	0	0	0	0	.000	.000
Benitez,Armando	L	.168	101	17	3	0	3	7	17	23	.288	.287
Throws Right	R	.140	136	19	4	0	3	12	4	39	.163	.235
Bennett,Jeff	L	.293	116	34	7	1	6	21	17	24	.382	.526
Throws Right	R	.267	165	44	8	4	6	26	9	21	.303	.473
Benoit,Joaquin	L	.249	209	52	8	3	7	29	17	51	.300	.416
Throws Right	R	.311	196	61	10	2	12	34	14	44	.371	.566
Benson,Kris	L	.276	362	100	20	4	8	46	37	54	.347	.420
Throws Right	R	.251	407	102	25	2	7	44	24	80	.300	.373
Bentz,Chad	L	.283	46	13	2	0	3	6	8	13	.411	.522
Throws Left	R	.182	55	10	1	0	2	9	15	5	.357	.309
Bergman,Dusty	L	.333	3	1	0	0	0	1	1	1	.400	.333
Throws Left	R	.500	6	3	1	0	0	4	0	0	.500	.667
Bernero,Adam	L	.305	59	18	3	0	4	12	14	6	.427	.559
Throws Right	R	.265	68	18	5	0	3	9	3	15	.292	.471
Betancourt,Rafael	L	.272	136	37	7	2	4	16	13	33	.333	.441
Throws Right	R	.264	129	34	5	1	3	18	5	43	.289	.388
Biddle,Rocky	L	.307	137	42	7	2	6	28	11	21	.366	.518
Throws Right	R	.308	182	56	9	1	9	36	20	30	.389	.516
Bierbrodt,Nick	L	.188	16	3	0	0	1	2	3	0	.316	.375
Throws Left	R	.268	41	11	0	0	3	7	16	10	.483	.488
Blackley,Travis	L	.296	27	8	1	0	2	8	7	3	.457	.556
Throws Left	R	.329	82	27	4	0	7	14	15	13	.429	.634
Blanton,Joe	L	.167	12	2	0	0	1	4	2	2	.286	.417
Throws Right	R	.250	16	4	2	0	0	0	0	4	.250	.375
Boehringer,Brian	L	.292	24	7	1	0	0	2	12	6	.528	.333
Throws Right	R	.290	69	20	5	1	2	12	5	14	.333	.478
Bonderman,Jeremy	L	.255	404	103	21	4	16	64	51	88	.339	.446
Throws Right	R	.223	291	65	13	0	8	27	22	79	.294	.351
Bong,Jung	L	.294	17	5	1	0	0	2	0	5	.294	.353
Throws Left	R	.261	46	12	3	0	3	9	10	6	.393	.522
Borkowski,Dave	L	.270	111	30	10	1	3	13	10	23	.333	.459
Throws Right	R	.307	114	35	7	0	3	17	5	22	.344	.447
Borland,Toby	L	.321	28	9	1	1	1	2	4	5	.406	.536
Throws Right	R	.209	43	9	3	0	2	6	8	13	.327	.419
Borowski,Joe	L	.344	32	11	0	1	3	11	12	6	.511	.688
Throws Right	R	.281	57	16	4	1	0	7	3	11	.317	.386
Bottalico,Ricky	L	.205	78	16	5	0	0	7	19	12	.373	.269
Throws Right	R	.220	173	38	8	0	3	18	15	49	.283	.318
Boyd,Jason	L	.429	14	6	3	0	2	6	4	3	.556	1.071
Throws Right	R	.194	36	7	2	0	2	2	4	9	.326	.417
Bradford,Chad	L	.298	57	17	0	0	2	5	18	9	.467	.404
Throws Right	R	.211	161	34	3	0	3	22	6	25	.260	.286
Brazelton,Dewon	L	.253	257	65	21	1	5	27	29	44	.331	.401
Throws Right	R	.269	208	56	15	0	7	30	24	20	.363	.442
Brazoban,Yhency	L	.224	49	11	3	0	0	2	13	11	.387	.286
Throws Right	R	.215	65	14	1	0	2	7	2	16	.239	.323
Brocail,Doug	L	.190	79	15	3	0	1	12	8	16	.270	.266
Throws Right	R	.320	122	39	9	0	1	16	12	27	.396	.418
Brooks,Frank	L	.083	24	2	1	0	0	1	2	6	.154	.125
Throws Left	R	.275	40	11	1	0	5	11	7	12	.383	.675
Brower,Jim	L	.343	134	46	12	3	2	22	20	15	.429	.522
Throws Right	R	.206	214	44	2	0	4	20	16	48	.269	.271
Brown,Jamie	L	.611	18	11	3	0	1	4	4	0	.682	.944
Throws Right	R	.222	18	4	1	0	0	4	0	6	.211	.278
Brown,Kevin	L	.261	280	73	22	0	9	26	18	47	.301	.436
Throws Right	R	.263	224	59	14	0	5	31	17	36	.317	.393
Bruney,Brian	L	.214	42	9	1	0	2	8	14	11	.411	.381
Throws Right	R	.172	64	11	2	0	0	4	13	23	.321	.203
Buehrle,Mark	L	.287	202	58	9	1	6	25	8	41	.333	.431
Throws Left	R	.267	745	199	31	3	27	83	43	124	.307	.426
Bukvich,Ryan	L	.200	10	2	0	0	0	2	4	3	.429	.200
Throws Right	R	.167	12	2	1	0	0	0	3	4	.333	.250
Bullinger,Kirk	L	.326	46	15	5	0	0	8	6	4	.415	.435
Throws Right	R	.263	80	21	4	0	5	14	4	7	.294	.500

Pitchers vs. Left-Handed and Right-Handed Batters

Pitcher	vs	Avg	AB	H	2B	3B	HR	RBI	BB	SO	OBP	Slg
Bump,Nate	L	.284	116	33	6	0	3	13	15	19	.376	.414
Throws Right	R	.305	174	53	8	0	4	35	17	25	.366	.420
Burba,Dave	L	.264	121	32	9	0	5	15	13	20	.341	.463
Throws Right	R	.224	170	38	6	1	2	20	13	30	.278	.306
Burnett,A.J.	L	.247	243	60	11	1	4	25	17	60	.304	.350
Throws Right	R	.211	199	42	8	1	5	19	21	53	.286	.337
Burnett,Sean	L	.324	71	23	3	0	1	8	9	7	.407	.408
Throws Left	R	.293	215	63	8	0	8	29	19	23	.349	.442
Bush,Dave	L	.289	218	63	7	1	9	26	20	38	.351	.454
Throws Right	R	.206	155	32	9	0	2	19	5	26	.247	.303
Bynum,Mike	L	.500	2	1	0	0	0	0	2	0	.750	.500
Throws Left	R	.000	1	0	0	0	0	0	1	0	.500	.000
Byrd,Paul	L	.329	213	70	15	2	7	22	11	18	.364	.516
Throws Right	R	.219	242	53	6	1	11	27	8	61	.244	.388
Cabrera,Daniel	L	.249	293	73	8	3	10	47	44	43	.347	.399
Throws Right	R	.270	267	72	12	1	4	35	45	33	.371	.367
Cabrera,Fernando	L	.083	12	1	0	0	0	2	1	4	.143	.083
Throws Right	R	.333	6	2	1	0	0	2	0	2	.333	.500
Calero,Kiko	L	.175	57	10	3	0	3	8	4	17	.230	.386
Throws Right	R	.177	96	17	4	0	2	6	6	30	.233	.281
Cali,Carmen	L	.333	12	4	2	0	0	1	3	2	.467	.500
Throws Left	R	.429	21	9	2	0	1	3	3	6	.480	.667
Callaway,Mickey	L	.290	31	9	3	0	1	5	6	5	.410	.484
Throws Right	R	.500	18	9	2	0	1	5	1	4	.526	.778
Camp,Shawn	L	.287	115	33	5	1	6	18	5	19	.331	.504
Throws Right	R	.283	145	41	7	0	4	18	11	32	.338	.414
Capellan,Jose	L	.167	12	2	1	0	0	1	4	3	.375	.250
Throws Right	R	.522	23	12	2	0	2	9	1	1	.520	.870
Capuano,Chris	L	.207	58	12	5	0	0	4	6	20	.292	.293
Throws Left	R	.282	280	79	18	0	18	48	31	60	.361	.539
Carpenter,Chris	L	.268	310	83	13	0	16	49	18	57	.316	.465
Throws Right	R	.226	381	86	15	1	8	23	20	95	.269	.333
Carrara,Giovanni	L	.182	77	14	3	0	0	2	10	18	.276	.221
Throws Right	R	.256	125	32	6	2	1	13	10	30	.316	.360
Carrasco,D.J.	L	.323	62	20	2	0	2	10	10	7	.411	.452
Throws Right	R	.259	81	21	2	0	3	16	5	15	.326	.395
Carter,Lance	L	.270	159	43	10	1	7	27	14	14	.324	.478
Throws Right	R	.231	147	34	7	1	5	12	9	22	.277	.395
Castillo,Frank	L	-	0	0	0	0	0	0	1	0	1.000	-
Throws Right	R	.333	3	1	0	0	0	1	0	0	.333	.333
Cerda,Jaime	L	.185	65	12	2	0	0	6	10	17	.308	.215
Throws Left	R	.282	103	29	4	0	1	10	20	16	.397	.350
Chacin,Gustavo	L	.143	14	2	1	0	0	1	2	3	.294	.214
Throws Left	R	.176	34	6	3	0	0	0	1	3	.200	.265
Chacon,Shawn	L	.236	123	29	5	2	6	25	32	32	.409	.455
Throws Right	R	.326	129	42	8	1	6	20	20	20	.420	.543
Chen,Bruce	L	.200	45	9	1	0	2	4	5	8	.280	.356
Throws Left	R	.227	132	30	4	2	5	14	11	24	.285	.402
Choate,Randy	L	.280	100	28	9	0	1	20	11	31	.359	.400
Throws Left	R	.253	95	24	5	0	0	11	17	18	.374	.305
Christiansen,Jason	L	.243	70	17	2	0	2	13	13	14	.379	.357
Throws Left	R	.258	66	17	2	0	1	11	13	8	.375	.333
Chulk,Vinnie	L	.305	118	36	5	2	5	21	17	15	.390	.508
Throws Right	R	.230	100	23	6	0	1	9	10	29	.306	.320
Claussen,Brandon	L	.375	56	21	4	1	3	13	11	8	.485	.643
Throws Left	R	.278	212	59	13	1	6	29	24	37	.350	.434
Clemens,Roger	L	.218	395	86	15	4	5	29	46	102	.300	.314
Throws Right	R	.217	383	83	19	0	10	38	33	116	.283	.345
Clement,Matt	L	.234	329	77	14	0	13	42	51	100	.342	.395
Throws Right	R	.224	348	78	14	1	10	34	26	90	.292	.356
Colome,Jesus	L	.245	53	13	3	0	3	9	11	12	.375	.472
Throws Right	R	.163	92	15	3	0	1	9	7	28	.230	.228
Colon,Bartolo	L	.273	455	124	28	1	22	69	43	97	.333	.484
Throws Right	R	.256	355	91	21	1	16	46	28	61	.312	.456
Colon,Roman	L	.344	32	11	3	0	0	4	2	5	.382	.438
Throws Right	R	.179	39	7	1	0	0	4	6	10	.277	.205
Colyer,Steve	L	.255	55	14	6	1	2	9	10	20	.379	.509
Throws Left	R	.284	67	19	7	1	6	16	14	11	.407	.687
Contreras,Jose	L	.251	366	92	14	2	14	52	46	81	.337	.415
Throws Right	R	.254	291	74	13	1	17	47	38	69	.348	.481
Cook,Aaron	L	.267	202	54	13	3	4	23	26	17	.358	.421
Throws Right	R	.324	179	58	6	0	3	18	13	23	.383	.408
Cooper,Brian	L	.348	23	8	3	0	4	9	4	2	.444	1.000
Throws Right	R	.241	29	7	1	0	0	3	1	5	.281	.276
Corcoran,Roy	L	.429	7	3	0	1	0	3	1	1	.500	.714
Throws Right	R	.250	16	4	1	0	0	3	4	3	.400	.313

Pitcher	vs	Avg	AB	H	2B	3B	HR	RBI	BB	SO	OBP	Slg
Cordero,Chad	L	.243	136	33	6	0	4	13	31	37	.385	.375
Throws Right	R	.205	171	35	5	0	4	12	12	46	.253	.304
Cordero,Francisco	L	.235	149	35	8	0	0	19	19	49	.321	.289
Throws Right	R	.216	116	25	4	0	1	8	13	30	.298	.276
Corey,Mark	L	.250	52	13	0	0	0	5	9	8	.355	.250
Throws Right	R	.289	90	26	4	0	3	20	10	20	.373	.433
Cormier,Lance	L	.382	76	29	6	2	8	22	11	9	.466	.829
Throws Right	R	.300	110	33	5	0	5	19	14	15	.375	.482
Cormier,Rheal	L	.250	108	27	4	3	1	13	11	23	.336	.370
Throws Left	R	.230	187	43	9	1	6	24	15	23	.293	.385
Cornejo,Nate	L	.371	62	23	6	0	4	10	7	8	.443	.661
Throws Right	R	.380	50	19	3	1	0	8	4	4	.426	.480
Correia,Kevin	L	.467	30	14	5	0	2	8	2	4	.500	.833
Throws Right	R	.244	45	11	3	0	1	11	8	10	.351	.378
Cotts,Neal	L	.269	104	28	5	0	7	26	9	29	.342	.519
Throws Left	R	.231	143	33	4	1	6	14	21	29	.329	.399
Crain,Jesse	L	.211	38	8	2	0	0	6	8	3	.362	.263
Throws Right	R	.158	57	9	1	0	2	9	4	11	.213	.281
Cressend,Jack	L	.308	26	8	1	0	2	6	5	3	.406	.577
Throws Right	R	.350	40	14	2	0	2	3	5	5	.422	.550
Crowell,Jim	L	.333	6	2	0	0	0	1	0	0	.333	.333
Throws Left	R	.333	12	4	1	0	0	1	0	1	.333	.417
Cruceta,Francisco	L	.278	18	5	1	0	0	3	3	7	.381	.333
Throws Right	R	.333	15	5	2	0	1	5	1	2	.389	.667
Cruz,Juan	L	.239	109	26	3	0	3	11	16	22	.344	.349
Throws Right	R	.214	154	33	9	0	4	15	14	48	.280	.351
Cubillan,Darwin	L	.375	16	6	2	0	1	4	2	4	.444	.688
Throws Right	R	.259	27	7	0	0	2	7	5	4	.375	.481
Cunnane,Will	L	.333	18	6	0	0	0	3	3	6	.391	.333
Throws Right	R	.353	34	12	3	0	3	6	1	5	.389	.706
Daigle,Casey	L	.354	79	28	8	2	4	14	17	4	.469	.658
Throws Right	R	.297	118	35	9	0	5	21	10	13	.359	.500
D'Amico,Jeff	L	.314	70	22	5	2	2	14	3	10	.338	.529
Throws Right	R	.354	65	23	5	0	4	11	3	6	.386	.615
Darensbourg,Vic	L	.556	9	5	3	0	0	0	2	1	.636	.889
Throws Left	R	.353	17	6	0	0	1	5	1	0	.350	.529
Davis,Doug	L	.259	143	37	8	0	2	15	12	25	.335	.357
Throws Left	R	.244	635	155	31	4	12	54	67	141	.316	.362
Davis,Jason	L	.305	233	71	6	1	8	29	37	37	.401	.442
Throws Right	R	.317	243	77	20	0	5	39	14	35	.360	.461
Dawley,Joe	L	.294	17	5	1	0	1	5	3	3	.400	.529
Throws Right	R	.154	13	2	0	0	0	0	4	5	.353	.154
Day,Zach	L	.279	190	53	15	2	8	26	31	21	.386	.505
Throws Right	R	.254	252	64	13	1	5	20	14	40	.297	.373
de la Rosa,Jorge	L	.231	13	3	0	0	0	1	3	1	.389	.231
Throws Left	R	.321	81	26	8	1	1	15	11	4	.394	.481
de los Santos,Valerio	L	.227	22	5	2	1	0	4	3	7	.308	.409
Throws Left	R	.273	22	6	3	0	0	3	7	3	.448	.409
DeJean,Mike	L	.319	94	30	5	1	1	19	19	23	.458	.426
Throws Right	R	.272	147	40	7	1	1	23	14	37	.341	.354
Dempster,Ryan	L	.222	27	6	1	0	1	3	8	6	.417	.370
Throws Right	R	.200	50	10	1	0	0	1	5	12	.286	.220
Denney,Kyle	L	.395	43	17	4	0	3	8	7	6	.480	.698
Throws Right	R	.455	33	15	2	1	0	9	1	7	.457	.576
DePaula,Jorge	L	.571	7	4	1	0	1	3	1	0	.625	1.143
Throws Right	R	.200	25	5	2	0	1	4	3	2	.267	.400
Dessens,Elmer	L	.316	187	59	13	1	10	31	15	32	.363	.556
Throws Right	R	.264	242	64	14	2	5	32	16	41	.312	.401
Diaz,Felix	L	.347	98	34	4	2	7	22	11	18	.420	.643
Throws Right	R	.275	102	28	5	0	6	15	5	15	.309	.500
Dickey,R.A.	L	.281	221	62	12	1	11	40	21	29	.348	.493
Throws Right	R	.343	216	74	16	0	6	32	12	27	.378	.500
Dinardo,Lenny	L	.306	36	11	2	0	0	1	6	6	.409	.361
Throws Left	R	.295	78	23	6	0	1	17	6	15	.353	.410
Dingman,Craig	L	.243	37	9	2	1	3	8	9	7	.417	.595
Throws Right	R	.320	75	24	7	2	0	13	13	9	.424	.467
Dohmann,Scott	L	.211	76	16	6	0	3	7	8	20	.279	.408
Throws Right	R	.255	98	25	9	0	5	25	11	29	.327	.500
Dominguez,Juan	L	.159	44	7	1	0	1	3	2	12	.191	.250
Throws Right	R	.400	45	18	4	0	1	6	3	2	.460	.556
Donnelly,Brendan	L	.211	76	16	3	0	2	7	11	27	.318	.329
Throws Right	R	.237	76	18	1	0	3	12	4	29	.268	.368
Dotel,Octavio	L	.245	159	39	8	3	9	25	18	57	.326	.503
Throws Right	R	.188	154	29	6	1	4	14	15	65	.269	.318
Douglass,Sean	L	.269	78	21	2	1	5	13	20	22	.424	.513
Throws Right	R	.232	69	16	2	0	1	12	8	14	.313	.304

Pitchers vs. Left-Handed and Right-Handed Batters

Pitcher	vs	Avg	AB	H	2B	3B	HR	RBI	BB	SO	OBP	Slg
Downs,Scott	L	.286	42	12	1	0	0	4	2	9	.318	.310
Throws Left	R	.315	213	67	9	1	9	35	21	29	.382	.493
Dreifort,Darren	L	.209	67	14	1	0	4	11	17	23	.365	.403
Throws Right	R	.246	118	29	6	1	1	17	19	40	.348	.339
Drese,Ryan	L	.279	452	126	23	3	13	53	42	62	.349	.429
Throws Right	R	.293	365	107	18	3	3	34	16	36	.326	.384
Drew,Tim	L	.360	25	9	2	0	1	2	3	3	.429	.560
Throws Right	R	.293	41	12	3	0	1	7	2	4	.341	.439
Driskill,Travis	L	.467	15	7	2	0	0	4	2	2	.529	.600
Throws Right	R	.286	21	6	0	0	0	3	1	4	.318	.286
DuBose,Eric	L	.167	60	10	5	0	2	5	11	14	.292	.350
Throws Left	R	.288	229	66	15	1	10	42	33	34	.385	.493
Duchscherer,Justin	L	.247	170	42	4	1	5	18	17	37	.319	.371
Throws Right	R	.235	183	43	4	2	8	22	15	22	.305	.410
Duckworth,Brandon	L	.377	77	29	4	1	5	12	10	13	.443	.649
Throws Right	R	.302	86	26	4	1	6	18	3	10	.326	.581
Dunn,Scott	L	.636	11	7	1	0	0	4	1	0	.667	.727
Throws Right	R	.000	5	0	0	0	0	0	0	2	.000	.000
Durbin,Chad	L	.287	115	33	5	1	6	21	14	27	.376	.504
Throws Right	R	.295	132	39	9	0	5	26	21	21	.397	.477
Durbin,J.D.	L	.400	20	8	1	0	0	5	5	5	.500	.450
Throws Right	R	.364	11	4	1	0	0	1	1	1	.417	.455
Eaton,Adam	L	.260	384	100	20	0	11	40	31	71	.320	.398
Throws Right	R	.272	383	104	20	3	17	66	21	82	.316	.473
Eischen,Joey	L	.167	24	4	1	0	1	5	4	9	.310	.333
Throws Left	R	.267	45	12	1	0	1	5	4	8	.320	.356
Elarton,Scott	L	.226	318	72	19	4	16	46	40	63	.311	.462
Throws Right	R	.306	301	92	20	1	17	55	22	40	.356	.548
Eldred,Cal	L	.271	96	26	3	0	5	15	5	24	.307	.458
Throws Right	R	.280	161	45	10	1	6	20	12	30	.330	.466
Embree,Alan	L	.240	104	25	1	0	4	14	2	22	.257	.365
Throws Left	R	.247	97	24	8	2	3	12	9	15	.311	.464
Ennis,John	L	.270	37	10	4	0	0	3	4	7	.341	.378
Throws Right	R	.313	32	10	1	0	3	11	1	6	.324	.625
Erickson,Scott	L	.328	67	22	2	2	2	10	14	5	.434	.507
Throws Right	R	.348	46	16	4	0	1	9	6	4	.415	.500
Escobar,Kelvim	L	.252	405	102	23	0	6	38	48	98	.334	.353
Throws Right	R	.236	381	90	23	2	15	43	28	93	.292	.425
Estes,Shawn	L	.280	168	47	7	2	6	30	17	28	.371	.452
Throws Left	R	.294	599	176	33	6	24	91	88	89	.383	.489
Estrella,Leo	L	1.000	1	1	1	0	0	1	0	0	1.000	2.000
Throws Right	R	.700	10	7	1	0	0	3	1	0	.667	.800
Eyre,Scott	L	.200	100	20	5	1	4	11	6	28	.243	.390
Throws Left	R	.240	96	23	3	0	4	12	21	21	.370	.396
Falkenborg,Brian	L	.250	20	5	0	0	1	3	4	4	.375	.400
Throws Right	R	.359	39	14	3	0	1	12	5	7	.468	.513
Farnsworth,Kyle	L	.267	105	28	5	1	3	19	9	29	.336	.419
Throws Right	R	.255	153	39	2	2	7	19	24	49	.356	.431
Fassero,Jeff	L	.336	146	49	6	1	3	23	9	17	.377	.452
Throws Left	R	.288	302	87	16	0	6	43	35	43	.360	.401
Feliciano,Pedro	L	.128	39	5	1	0	0	3	6	11	.244	.154
Throws Left	R	.321	28	9	0	0	2	10	6	3	.444	.536
Fernandez,Jared	L	.500	4	2	1	0	0	2	4	0	.750	.750
Throws Right	R	1.000	4	4	0	0	0	4	1	0	.833	1.000
Fetters,Mike	L	.370	27	10	3	1	1	5	8	2	.486	.667
Throws Right	R	.260	50	13	2	0	1	8	6	12	.351	.360
Field,Nate	L	.213	75	16	3	1	3	13	9	9	.298	.400
Throws Right	R	.264	91	24	7	0	2	13	10	21	.343	.407
Figueroa,Nelson	L	.357	42	15	4	1	2	10	5	3	.426	.643
Throws Right	R	.266	64	17	3	2	2	11	6	7	.329	.469
Fikac,Jeremy	L	.325	40	13	2	1	3	15	9	6	.449	.650
Throws Right	R	.236	55	13	1	0	2	8	4	16	.283	.364
File,Bob	L	.308	78	24	6	0	3	14	8	10	.360	.500
Throws Right	R	.362	58	21	4	0	1	8	4	5	.415	.483
Flores,Randy	L	.235	17	4	1	0	0	1	0	4	.316	.294
Throws Left	R	.281	32	9	3	0	0	1	3	3	.351	.375
Floyd,Gavin	L	.289	45	13	2	0	1	6	5	15	.360	.400
Throws Right	R	.203	59	12	2	1	0	4	11	9	.373	.271
Fogg,Josh	L	.282	326	92	26	3	8	34	49	32	.377	.454
Throws Right	R	.285	355	101	24	0	9	51	17	50	.325	.428
Foppert,Jesse	L	.500	2	1	0	0	0	0	0	0	.500	.500
Throws Right	R	.000	2	0	0	0	0	0	0	2	.000	.000
Ford,Ben	L	.265	34	9	0	0	2	4	1	3	.297	.441
Throws Right	R	.271	59	16	4	0	2	15	9	10	.377	.441
Fortunato,Bartolome	L	.139	36	5	0	1	1	4	4	12	.225	.278
Throws Right	R	.311	61	19	4	1	2	8	11	13	.417	.508

Pitcher	vs	Avg	AB	H	2B	3B	HR	RBI	BB	SO	OBP	Slg
Fossum,Casey	L	.257	136	35	1	1	4	15	12	33	.325	.368
Throws Left	R	.316	431	136	23	1	27	81	51	84	.396	.561
Foulke,Keith	L	.185	168	31	6	0	3	8	10	44	.235	.274
Throws Right	R	.232	138	32	7	1	5	17	5	35	.276	.406
Fox,Chad	L	.222	18	4	2	0	1	2	5	9	.391	.500
Throws Right	R	.227	22	5	1	0	0	3	3	8	.346	.273
Francis,Jeff	L	.308	26	8	1	0	0	2	2	2	.357	.346
Throws Left	R	.281	121	34	10	0	8	19	11	30	.343	.562
Francisco,Frank	L	.247	73	18	2	0	2	7	14	22	.375	.356
Throws Right	R	.165	109	18	3	0	2	9	14	38	.270	.248
Franco,John	L	.173	75	13	2	0	3	10	6	13	.241	.320
Throws Left	R	.320	103	33	5	2	3	13	18	23	.418	.495
Franklin,Ryan	L	.275	433	119	25	2	13	49	46	61	.344	.432
Throws Right	R	.297	353	105	25	4	20	56	15	43	.335	.561
Franklin,Wayne	L	.250	80	20	2	0	6	15	7	23	.326	.500
Throws Left	R	.302	116	35	5	2	5	29	15	17	.381	.509
Frasor,Jason	L	.232	142	33	8	0	4	19	20	36	.325	.373
Throws Right	R	.274	113	31	7	0	0	12	16	18	.369	.336
Frederick,Kevin	L	.258	66	17	3	2	1	14	12	13	.370	.409
Throws Right	R	.319	47	15	4	0	3	6	4	9	.365	.596
Fuentes,Brian	L	.213	61	13	2	1	1	10	2	12	.284	.328
Throws Left	R	.300	110	33	8	0	4	16	17	36	.394	.482
Fultz,Aaron	L	.212	85	18	2	0	1	15	10	24	.293	.271
Throws Left	R	.314	102	32	7	0	4	16	13	13	.388	.500
Gagne,Eric	L	.233	146	34	7	0	2	15	14	50	.309	.322
Throws Right	R	.129	147	19	2	0	3	8	8	64	.188	.204
Gallo,Mike	L	.286	112	32	5	3	5	21	12	26	.367	.518
Throws Left	R	.280	82	23	3	1	7	14	8	8	.366	.598
Garcia,Freddy	L	.236	420	99	24	0	14	43	40	86	.305	.393
Throws Right	R	.248	375	93	25	1	8	39	24	98	.300	.384
Garcia,Jairo	L	.100	10	1	0	0	1	1	4	2	.357	.400
Throws Right	R	.333	12	4	0	0	2	7	5	3	.556	.833
Garcia,Rosman	L	.429	14	6	1	0	0	2	2	2	.471	.500
Throws Right	R	.200	15	3	0	0	1	2	3	3	.333	.400
Garland,Jon	L	.262	446	117	20	1	19	69	46	56	.334	.439
Throws Right	R	.277	383	106	24	3	15	50	30	57	.329	.473
Gaudin,Chad	L	.403	62	25	7	0	0	5	10	7	.493	.516
Throws Right	R	.301	113	34	10	1	4	27	6	23	.341	.513
Geary,Geoff	L	.322	87	28	5	2	5	15	5	9	.359	.598
Throws Right	R	.264	91	24	5	2	3	16	11	21	.355	.462
George,Chris	L	.317	41	13	6	0	0	10	4	6	.370	.463
Throws Left	R	.336	140	47	9	1	1	27	21	9	.422	.436
German,Franklyn	L	.240	25	6	0	1	2	5	3	0	.321	.560
Throws Right	R	.306	36	11	1	0	2	11	8	8	.432	.500
Germano,Justin	L	.383	47	18	4	1	1	14	9	5	.474	.574
Throws Right	R	.295	44	13	6	0	1	6	5	11	.367	.500
Ginter,Matt	L	.316	133	42	10	1	7	22	12	17	.377	.564
Throws Right	R	.265	151	40	5	0	1	15	8	21	.317	.318
Gissell,Chris	L	.391	23	9	1	0	1	7	2	8	.423	.565
Throws Right	R	.550	20	11	1	1	3	9	1	3	.571	1.150
Glavine,Tom	L	.244	217	53	12	3	6	17	22	24	.313	.410
Throws Left	R	.254	594	151	29	0	14	71	48	85	.306	.374
Glover,Gary	L	.273	33	9	1	1	1	5	5	3	.359	.455
Throws Right	R	.257	35	9	1	0	1	4	3	5	.341	.371
Glynn,Ryan	L	.261	46	12	2	0	2	6	7	7	.386	.435
Throws Right	R	.233	30	7	1	0	2	4	1	7	.258	.467
Gobble,Jimmy	L	.317	145	46	9	1	7	20	11	16	.361	.538
Throws Left	R	.255	436	111	25	2	17	64	32	33	.307	.438
Gonzalez,Dicky	L	.091	11	1	0	0	0	0	2	5	.231	.091
Throws Right	R	.444	18	8	3	0	1	7	0	2	.421	.778
Gonzalez,Edgar	L	.415	94	39	7	0	10	30	12	15	.486	.809
Throws Right	R	.314	105	33	6	2	5	17	6	16	.368	.552
Gonzalez,Jeremi	L	.427	89	38	13	0	5	25	8	8	.469	.742
Throws Right	R	.286	119	34	8	1	4	13	12	14	.360	.471
Gonzalez,Mike	L	.213	61	13	2	0	0	3	3	19	.262	.246
Throws Left	R	.194	98	19	1	0	2	10	3	36	.218	.265
Good,Andy	L	.264	72	19	5	1	4	11	8	10	.354	.528
Throws Right	R	.279	86	24	4	1	4	15	5	16	.319	.488
Gordon,Tom	L	.185	162	30	9	1	1	9	14	53	.249	.272
Throws Right	R	.174	149	26	5	1	4	14	9	43	.225	.302
Gosling,Mike	L	.188	32	6	1	0	2	4	2	6	.235	.406
Throws Left	R	.317	63	20	5	1	3	8	11	8	.434	.571
Grabow,John	L	.330	112	37	3	2	4	15	7	33	.367	.500
Throws Left	R	.319	138	44	9	0	4	21	21	31	.409	.471
Gracesqui,Franklyn	L	.333	6	2	0	0	0	1	2	1	.500	.333
Throws Left	R	.333	12	4	0	0	0	3	1	0	.467	.333

Pitchers vs. Left-Handed and Right-Handed Batters

Pitcher	vs	Avg	AB	H	2B	3B	HR	RBI	BB	SO	OBP	Slg
Graman,Alex	L	.571	7	4	2	0	0	3	0	1	.571	.857
Throws Left	R	.476	21	10	4	1	1	7	2	3	.500	.905
Graves,Danny	L	.265	117	31	6	1	5	20	7	17	.306	.462
Throws Right	R	.295	156	46	11	0	7	23	6	23	.325	.500
Gregg,Kevin	L	.259	174	45	10	3	2	20	13	50	.319	.385
Throws Right	R	.252	163	41	8	1	4	25	15	34	.308	.387
Greinke,Zack	L	.251	311	78	17	1	9	22	18	50	.295	.399
Throws Right	R	.262	248	65	14	0	17	39	8	50	.300	.524
Greisinger,Seth	L	.283	99	28	3	2	8	20	10	24	.354	.596
Throws Right	R	.351	114	40	7	1	4	17	5	12	.378	.535
Griffiths,Jeremy	L	.286	7	2	0	0	1	3	2	2	.444	.714
Throws Right	R	.200	10	2	0	0	0	0	1	3	.273	.200
Grilli,Jason	L	.292	96	28	4	1	7	24	16	16	.395	.573
Throws Right	R	.296	81	24	2	1	4	13	4	10	.345	.494
Grimsley,Jason	L	.314	102	32	4	0	2	18	17	8	.412	.412
Throws Right	R	.206	141	29	3	1	2	18	18	31	.307	.284
Groom,Buddy	L	.333	93	31	4	2	4	14	3	16	.361	.548
Throws Left	R	.290	124	36	4	0	2	16	13	16	.353	.371
Gryboski,Kevin	L	.309	68	21	3	0	1	14	16	8	.440	.397
Throws Right	R	.264	125	33	2	1	1	20	7	16	.303	.320
Guardado,Eddie	L	.109	46	5	1	0	1	5	0	14	.125	.196
Throws Left	R	.228	114	26	2	0	7	12	14	31	.313	.430
Guerrier,Matt	L	.298	47	14	2	0	4	13	4	8	.365	.596
Throws Right	R	.286	28	8	1	0	1	4	2	3	.333	.429
Guthrie,Jeremy	L	.160	25	4	1	0	0	1	4	5	.276	.200
Throws Right	R	.294	17	5	1	0	1	2	2	2	.400	.529
Halama,John	L	.268	138	37	8	2	2	16	6	28	.327	.399
Throws Left	R	.290	334	97	18	1	15	47	21	31	.337	.485
Halladay,Roy	L	.285	281	80	11	0	8	29	28	46	.348	.409
Throws Right	R	.258	233	60	6	0	5	30	11	49	.291	.348
Halsey,Brad	L	.143	28	4	3	0	0	5	2	8	.219	.250
Throws Left	R	.349	106	37	8	0	4	17	12	17	.417	.538
Hammond,Chris	L	.282	71	20	4	0	0	7	1	11	.292	.338
Throws Left	R	.275	131	36	11	0	4	19	12	23	.342	.450
Hampton,Mike	L	.253	146	37	4	0	3	15	9	15	.295	.342
Throws Left	R	.300	537	161	29	2	12	57	56	72	.366	.428
Hancock,Josh	L	.265	132	35	2	2	7	18	18	18	.351	.470
Throws Right	R	.299	127	38	8	0	10	20	10	18	.353	.598
Harang,Aaron	L	.262	267	70	19	2	10	26	27	55	.328	.461
Throws Right	R	.292	366	107	22	3	16	51	26	70	.344	.500
Harden,Rich	L	.254	382	97	17	4	8	40	50	92	.339	.382
Throws Right	R	.227	326	74	15	0	8	37	31	75	.296	.347
Haren,Danny	L	.190	79	15	3	1	1	4	10	15	.281	.291
Throws Right	R	.330	91	30	9	1	3	18	7	17	.382	.549
Harikkala,Tim	L	.245	102	25	5	1	7	21	15	13	.339	.520
Throws Right	R	.227	132	30	7	0	3	19	8	17	.275	.348
Harper,Travis	L	.231	117	27	6	0	4	21	16	24	.328	.385
Throws Right	R	.236	178	42	6	1	4	21	7	35	.284	.348
Harville,Chad	L	.259	85	22	6	1	3	23	11	17	.351	.459
Throws Right	R	.256	133	34	5	0	5	20	16	29	.340	.406
Hasegawa,Shigetoshi	L	.265	113	30	6	0	2	20	15	20	.344	.372
Throws Right	R	.255	145	37	14	2	3	18	16	26	.335	.441
Hawkins,LaTroy	L	.230	135	31	12	1	5	12	10	35	.291	.444
Throws Right	R	.236	174	41	6	0	5	18	4	34	.251	.356
Haynes,Jimmy	L	.238	21	5	0	0	2	9	4	2	.385	.524
Throws Right	R	.457	46	21	4	0	1	8	3	6	.500	.609
Heilman,Aaron	L	.232	56	13	3	1	2	7	5	9	.295	.429
Throws Right	R	.286	49	14	3	0	2	8	8	13	.386	.469
Hendrickson,Ben	L	.291	79	23	9	1	1	7	13	13	.404	.468
Throws Right	R	.324	108	35	6	0	5	21	7	16	.370	.519
Hendrickson,Mark	L	.249	169	42	6	0	5	27	5	19	.279	.373
Throws Left	R	.295	572	169	42	3	16	73	41	68	.345	.463
Hennessey,Brad	L	.301	73	22	8	0	2	15	7	9	.358	.493
Throws Right	R	.286	70	20	7	0	0	7	8	16	.359	.386
Hensley,Matt	L	.333	51	17	2	0	2	7	6	14	.404	.490
Throws Right	R	.259	58	15	3	0	3	7	1	16	.290	.466
Hentgen,Pat	L	.274	168	46	8	2	7	28	20	16	.345	.470
Throws Right	R	.293	150	44	6	1	9	29	22	17	.388	.527
Heredia,Felix	L	.216	74	16	5	0	3	16	11	15	.333	.405
Throws Left	R	.333	84	28	6	1	2	15	9	10	.394	.500
Herges,Matt	L	.366	112	41	5	3	3	23	13	15	.422	.545
Throws Right	R	.318	154	49	11	0	5	27	8	24	.361	.487
Hermanson,Dustin	L	.285	239	68	19	1	10	33	28	43	.354	.498
Throws Right	R	.242	265	64	10	3	5	29	18	59	.294	.358
Hernandez,Adrian	L	.333	27	9	1	0	0	3	4	4	.419	.370
Throws Right	R	.268	41	11	3	0	1	11	10	10	.404	.415

Pitcher	vs	Avg	AB	H	2B	3B	HR	RBI	BB	SO	OBP	Slg
Hernandez,Carlos	L	.324	37	12	2	0	4	9	5	7	.419	.703
Throws Left	R	.297	128	38	8	0	7	20	18	19	.392	.523
Hernandez,Livan	L	.258	450	116	21	3	16	49	50	82	.337	.424
Throws Right	R	.238	495	118	25	1	10	38	33	104	.292	.354
Hernandez,Orlando	L	.255	188	48	7	0	6	17	21	36	.341	.388
Throws Right	R	.194	129	25	8	1	3	10	15	48	.283	.341
Hernandez,Roberto	L	.278	90	25	3	1	3	15	16	19	.387	.433
Throws Right	R	.311	132	41	5	1	6	26	13	25	.374	.500
Hill,Shawn	L	.429	14	6	0	1	0	6	2	5	.500	.571
Throws Right	R	.407	27	11	4	0	1	8	5	5	.485	.667
Hitchcock,Sterling	L	.300	10	3	1	0	1	2	4	1	.500	.700
Throws Left	R	.260	73	19	6	0	4	9	4	13	.299	.507
Hoffman,Trevor	L	.255	106	27	10	1	3	7	6	28	.295	.453
Throws Right	R	.161	93	15	4	0	2	7	2	25	.179	.269
Horgan,Joe	L	.235	51	12	3	0	1	6	6	13	.350	.353
Throws Left	R	.228	101	23	8	0	4	13	16	17	.333	.426
Howard,Ben	L	.250	64	16	2	1	4	13	11	16	.360	.500
Throws Right	R	.269	78	21	5	0	2	11	10	17	.352	.410
Howry,Bob	L	.291	79	23	5	0	2	9	7	18	.360	.430
Throws Right	R	.169	83	14	2	0	3	5	5	21	.216	.301
Hudson,Luke	L	.160	81	13	2	0	2	2	10	20	.253	.259
Throws Right	R	.250	92	23	10	0	1	9	15	18	.360	.391
Hudson,Tim	L	.298	403	120	27	4	5	49	31	42	.356	.422
Throws Right	R	.229	323	74	13	0	3	30	13	61	.269	.297
Hughes,Travis	L	.250	4	1	0	0	0	0	1	3	.400	.250
Throws Right	R	.750	4	3	1	0	0	2	1	1	.800	1.000
Huisman,Justin	L	.372	43	16	4	0	1	5	5	5	.438	.535
Throws Right	R	.313	64	20	2	0	2	13	3	8	.353	.438
Ishii,Kazuhisa	L	.267	161	43	3	2	6	24	27	28	.380	.422
Throws Left	R	.239	469	112	26	5	15	63	71	71	.336	.412
Isringhausen,Jason	L	.205	122	25	7	1	2	14	9	35	.265	.328
Throws Right	R	.195	154	30	9	0	3	17	14	36	.265	.312
Jackson,Edwin	L	.308	52	16	2	0	3	6	7	4	.390	.519
Throws Right	R	.306	49	15	2	1	4	10	4	12	.358	.633
Jackson,Mike	L	.354	82	29	8	0	3	19	9	11	.419	.561
Throws Right	R	.248	105	26	7	0	4	19	6	15	.296	.429
Jarvis,Kevin	L	.407	27	11	5	0	4	11	8	2	.543	1.037
Throws Right	R	.366	41	15	4	1	1	2	1	5	.381	.585
Jennings,Jason	L	.340	391	133	27	8	15	66	70	50	.442	.565
Throws Right	R	.261	414	108	20	0	12	50	31	83	.319	.396
Jimenez,Jose	L	.343	70	24	6	0	4	18	8	9	.418	.600
Throws Right	R	.256	82	21	2	0	2	8	6	12	.330	.354
Johnson,Jason	L	.281	430	121	27	5	10	56	36	73	.333	.437
Throws Right	R	.286	353	101	14	2	12	47	24	52	.337	.439
Johnson,Randy	L	.162	148	24	5	1	2	9	7	47	.233	.250
Throws Left	R	.204	750	153	29	8	16	64	37	243	.243	.328
Johnston,Mike	L	.357	42	15	4	0	1	7	5	7	.438	.524
Throws Left	R	.280	50	14	3	1	1	10	10	11	.410	.440
Jones,Bobby M	L	.400	5	2	0	0	1	2	1	1	.500	1.000
Throws Left	R	.167	6	1	0	0	0	0	7	2	.615	.167
Jones,Todd	L	.250	132	33	5	0	3	13	17	24	.357	.356
Throws Right	R	.290	176	51	9	1	4	27	16	35	.342	.420
Julio,Jorge	L	.234	137	32	4	0	6	20	23	36	.346	.394
Throws Right	R	.221	122	27	4	0	5	15	16	34	.317	.377
Karsay,Steve	L	.154	13	2	0	0	1	2	1	2	.200	.385
Throws Right	R	.300	10	3	0	0	1	2	1	2	.333	.600
Kazmir,Scott	L	.400	25	10	1	0	0	3	6	7	.516	.440
Throws Left	R	.221	104	23	7	1	4	14	15	34	.331	.423
Kennedy,Joe	L	.184	141	26	1	1	4	13	13	31	.258	.291
Throws Left	R	.289	474	137	39	2	13	50	54	86	.366	.462
Kensing,Logan	L	.320	25	8	2	0	1	4	7	2	.455	.520
Throws Right	R	.367	30	11	2	0	4	10	2	5	.424	.833
Kershner,Jason	L	.368	38	14	1	0	1	7	1	4	.385	.474
Throws Left	R	.281	57	16	4	1	2	12	7	11	.359	.491
Kida,Masao	L	.292	24	7	1	1	0	2	4	5	.414	.417
Throws Right	R	.353	34	12	3	0	1	5	2	5	.405	.529
Kim,Byung-Hyun	L	.300	40	12	4	1	1	7	4	1	.375	.525
Throws Right	R	.192	26	5	2	0	0	1	3	5	.276	.269
Kim,Sunny	L	.301	229	69	12	3	6	35	29	33	.388	.459
Throws Right	R	.255	298	76	14	1	11	39	26	54	.331	.419
King,Ray	L	.150	113	17	2	0	0	4	12	27	.236	.168
Throws Left	R	.248	105	26	6	1	1	11	12	13	.336	.352
Kinney,Matt	L	.409	154	63	13	2	5	30	14	23	.459	.617
Throws Right	R	.233	176	41	11	1	6	32	16	50	.303	.409
Kline,Steve	L	.143	84	12	1	0	1	8	10	21	.263	.190
Throws Left	R	.269	93	25	5	0	2	9	7	14	.320	.387

Pitchers vs. Left-Handed and Right-Handed Batters

Pitcher	vs	Avg	AB	H	2B	3B	HR	RBI	BB	SO	OBP	Slg
Knotts,Gary	L	.215	270	58	12	1	11	37	26	39	.284	.389
Throws Right	R	.322	261	84	15	2	9	38	32	42	.402	.498
Koch,Billy	L	.236	89	21	5	0	4	13	24	23	.400	.427
Throws Right	R	.245	98	24	5	0	2	14	12	27	.327	.357
Kolb,Danny	L	.256	90	23	1	1	0	5	9	6	.323	.289
Throws Right	R	.218	124	27	2	0	3	15	6	15	.269	.306
Koplove,Mike	L	.313	144	45	5	1	4	25	30	27	.438	.444
Throws Right	R	.233	176	41	6	1	3	15	7	28	.273	.330
Kroon,Marc	L	.333	12	4	1	0	0	4	5	2	.500	.417
Throws Right	R	.375	8	3	1	0	1	2	5	1	.615	.875
Lackey,John	L	.303	419	127	17	3	13	50	36	68	.362	.451
Throws Right	R	.248	355	88	23	3	9	45	24	76	.301	.406
Lawrence,Brian	L	.301	405	122	20	2	17	58	35	54	.357	.486
Throws Right	R	.272	382	104	30	2	9	38	20	67	.312	.432
League,Brandon	L	.182	11	2	0	0	0	0	0	1	.182	.182
Throws Right	R	.167	6	1	0	0	0	0	1	1	.286	.167
Ledezma,Wil	L	.227	44	10	3	0	0	8	2	7	.286	.295
Throws Left	R	.285	158	45	6	0	3	20	16	22	.347	.380
Lee,Cliff	L	.231	143	33	8	1	2	15	19	31	.333	.343
Throws Left	R	.277	559	155	35	3	28	88	62	130	.354	.501
Lee,Dave	L	.250	8	2	0	0	0	1	3	2	.455	.250
Throws Right	R	.400	15	6	2	1	0	7	1	2	.438	.667
Lehr,Justin	L	.310	58	18	4	0	1	6	9	9	.403	.431
Throws Right	R	.254	67	17	4	0	2	14	5	7	.316	.403
Leicester,Jon	L	.373	51	19	0	0	4	9	11	12	.484	.608
Throws Right	R	.200	105	21	3	0	3	9	4	23	.225	.314
Leiter,Al	L	.204	137	28	6	1	2	10	20	25	.308	.307
Throws Left	R	.222	495	110	30	0	14	52	77	92	.338	.368
Leskanic,Curtis	L	.268	82	22	2	1	4	15	11	17	.347	.463
Throws Right	R	.291	86	25	4	1	4	14	19	20	.425	.500
Levine,Al	L	.299	107	32	6	1	4	20	15	11	.387	.486
Throws Right	R	.293	174	51	7	1	6	27	9	21	.326	.448
Lewis,Colby	L	.267	30	8	1	0	0	1	5	5	.389	.300
Throws Right	R	.185	27	5	2	0	1	5	8	6	.371	.370
Lidge,Brad	L	.191	173	33	5	1	3	9	13	67	.263	.283
Throws Right	R	.155	155	24	1	3	5	14	17	90	.244	.297
Lidle,Cory	L	.279	348	97	20	1	15	54	32	47	.345	.471
Throws Right	R	.269	472	127	28	6	12	61	29	79	.317	.430
Lieber,Jon	L	.346	382	132	20	3	14	52	11	28	.361	.524
Throws Right	R	.250	336	84	15	0	6	35	7	74	.266	.348
Ligtenberg,Kerry	L	.306	98	30	8	0	4	21	17	24	.419	.510
Throws Right	R	.319	135	43	8	0	2	21	8	25	.357	.422
Lilly,Ted	L	.196	148	29	6	0	4	14	26	31	.324	.318
Throws Left	R	.238	596	142	30	4	22	69	63	137	.314	.413
Lima,Jose	L	.278	324	90	16	1	16	36	24	36	.329	.481
Throws Right	R	.264	333	88	12	1	17	38	10	57	.286	.459
Lincoln,Mike	L	.130	23	3	1	0	0	2	1	6	.167	.174
Throws Right	R	.184	38	7	2	0	1	5	5	8	.283	.316
Linebrink,Scott	L	.178	135	24	5	0	3	15	19	36	.278	.281
Throws Right	R	.236	157	37	10	0	5	17	7	47	.277	.395
Liriano,Pedro	L	.276	29	8	2	0	1	5	1	2	.300	.448
Throws Right	R	.206	34	7	2	1	2	5	2	8	.270	.500
Loaiza,Esteban	L	.298	409	122	20	5	15	54	51	69	.376	.482
Throws Right	R	.293	324	95	17	0	17	58	20	48	.330	.503
Loe,Kameron	L	.250	12	3	0	1	0	2	4	1	.438	.417
Throws Right	R	.300	10	3	1	0	0	0	2	2	.462	.400
Lohse,Kyle	L	.290	448	130	30	0	17	65	54	73	.367	.471
Throws Right	R	.324	339	110	16	1	11	45	22	38	.370	.475
Looper,Braden	L	.311	151	47	7	0	3	20	9	22	.352	.417
Throws Right	R	.227	172	39	3	0	2	12	7	38	.264	.279
Lopez,Aquilino	L	.382	34	13	4	0	4	10	8	6	.512	.853
Throws Right	R	.178	45	8	3	0	1	3	5	7	.269	.311
Lopez,Javier	L	.221	77	17	4	0	0	9	14	9	.355	.273
Throws Left	R	.350	80	28	3	2	1	14	12	11	.441	.475
Lopez,Rodrigo	L	.258	337	87	15	2	7	25	39	48	.333	.377
Throws Right	R	.245	314	77	7	1	14	36	15	73	.284	.408
Lowe,Derek	L	.305	413	126	24	1	7	61	40	53	.371	.419
Throws Right	R	.293	335	98	17	3	8	53	31	52	.357	.433
Lowry,Noah	L	.338	71	24	4	1	3	14	5	12	.382	.549
Throws Left	R	.238	281	67	16	2	7	25	23	60	.295	.384
MacDougal,Mike	L	.304	23	7	2	1	1	4	6	7	.448	.609
Throws Right	R	.321	28	9	2	0	1	4	3	7	.406	.500
Maddux,Greg	L	.271	362	98	13	2	22	52	20	68	.316	.500
Throws Right	R	.268	447	120	17	2	13	41	13	83	.291	.403
Madritsch,Bobby	L	.217	92	20	3	1	1	10	13	23	.314	.304
Throws Left	R	.238	227	54	13	1	2	17	20	37	.311	.330

Pitcher	vs	Avg	AB	H	2B	3B	HR	RBI	BB	SO	OBP	Slg
Madson,Ryan	L	.252	123	31	5	1	1	8	12	24	.321	.333
Throws Right	R	.227	163	37	3	0	5	15	7	31	.276	.337
Mahay,Ron	L	.236	110	26	3	0	2	13	10	25	.311	.318
Throws Left	R	.234	145	34	5	1	3	22	19	29	.323	.345
Maine,John	L	.444	9	4	0	0	1	3	2	1	.545	.778
Throws Right	R	.429	7	3	1	0	0	0	1	0	.500	.571
Majewski,Gary	L	.419	31	13	4	0	1	5	1	5	.455	.645
Throws Right	R	.273	55	15	0	0	1	8	4	7	.328	.327
Malaska,Mark	L	.188	32	6	1	0	0	2	4	7	.297	.219
Throws Left	R	.319	47	15	4	2	2	15	8	5	.418	.617
Mantei,Matt	L	.263	19	5	1	0	3	8	5	5	.400	.789
Throws Right	R	.414	29	12	2	0	2	8	1	8	.433	.690
Manzanillo,Josias	L	.340	53	18	3	0	3	8	11	9	.453	.566
Throws Right	R	.260	77	20	3	1	3	11	4	18	.318	.442
Maroth,Mike	L	.267	195	52	9	2	4	13	15	41	.319	.395
Throws Left	R	.294	652	192	33	5	21	79	44	67	.344	.457
Marquis,Jason	L	.278	363	101	16	3	14	44	38	66	.346	.455
Throws Right	R	.271	420	114	20	1	12	38	32	72	.334	.410
Marsonek,Sam	L	.000	2	0	0	0	0	0	0	0	.000	.000
Throws Right	R	.500	4	2	1	0	0	0	0	0	.500	.750
Marte,Damaso	L	.143	98	14	1	0	2	10	13	29	.259	.214
Throws Left	R	.263	160	42	5	0	8	20	21	39	.341	.444
Martin,Tom	L	.310	100	31	6	1	3	20	10	22	.377	.480
Throws Left	R	.247	73	18	3	0	4	13	9	8	.329	.452
Martinez,Anastacio	L	.211	19	4	1	0	0	3	3	2	.318	.263
Throws Right	R	.346	26	9	2	0	2	8	3	3	.433	.654
Martinez,Pedro	L	.235	451	106	21	3	15	43	34	129	.301	.395
Throws Right	R	.241	361	87	16	5	11	47	27	98	.301	.404
Mateo,Julio	L	.275	80	22	5	0	7	13	12	17	.362	.600
Throws Right	R	.238	143	34	10	0	4	27	4	26	.279	.392
Matthews,Mike	L	.282	39	11	1	0	3	8	6	7	.391	.538
Throws Left	R	.256	78	20	6	1	4	16	10	8	.344	.513
Maurer,Dave	L	.333	3	1	0	0	1	4	2	1	.600	1.333
Throws Left	R	.714	7	5	2	0	0	2	3	0	.800	1.000
May,Darrell	L	.296	186	55	14	2	7	28	8	37	.323	.505
Throws Left	R	.310	578	179	44	7	31	94	47	83	.359	.571
McConnell,Sam	L	.435	23	10	1	0	0	3	1	3	.458	.478
Throws Left	R	.067	15	1	1	0	0	1	3	1	.263	.133
McLeary,Marty	L	.286	7	2	0	1	1	3	0	2	.286	1.000
Throws Right	R	.556	9	5	1	0	1	3	2	2	.583	1.000
Meadows,Brian	L	.226	93	21	5	0	3	16	7	18	.272	.376
Throws Right	R	.275	200	55	11	1	4	25	12	28	.313	.400
Meche,Gil	L	.269	297	80	19	1	14	42	30	59	.336	.481
Throws Right	R	.278	212	59	19	1	7	26	17	40	.342	.476
Mecir,Jim	L	.236	89	21	1	2	3	11	11	24	.340	.393
Throws Right	R	.242	99	24	2	0	2	8	8	25	.306	.323
Mendoza,Ramiro	L	.216	51	11	1	0	1	5	5	6	.286	.294
Throws Right	R	.233	60	14	2	0	2	6	2	7	.270	.367
Mercker,Kent	L	.240	96	23	4	1	3	11	9	26	.312	.396
Throws Left	R	.170	94	16	3	0	1	9	18	25	.307	.234
Mesa,Jose	L	.331	127	42	6	1	4	11	11	18	.381	.488
Throws Right	R	.255	141	36	9	0	2	15	9	19	.303	.362
Meyer,Dan	L	.500	2	1	1	0	0	0	0	0	.500	1.000
Throws Left	R	.200	5	1	0	0	0	0	1	1	.333	.200
Miceli,Danny	L	.307	150	46	6	1	7	22	12	37	.360	.500
Throws Right	R	.188	149	28	4	1	3	14	15	46	.263	.289
Miller,Justin	L	.367	166	61	12	2	10	34	24	15	.447	.645
Throws Right	R	.260	154	40	11	1	4	25	18	32	.341	.422
Miller,Matt	L	.255	55	14	2	2	1	9	14	12	.431	.418
Throws Right	R	.201	139	28	7	1	0	12	9	43	.263	.266
Miller,Trever	L	.214	98	21	6	0	2	17	7	29	.280	.337
Throws Left	R	.303	89	27	5	2	1	14	8	14	.367	.438
Miller,Wade	L	.212	151	32	7	1	3	10	24	33	.318	.331
Throws Right	R	.242	182	44	6	1	8	16	20	41	.317	.418
Millwood,Kevin	L	.309	269	83	24	1	6	38	29	68	.381	.472
Throws Right	R	.250	288	72	17	1	8	35	22	57	.311	.399
Milton,Eric	L	.248	121	30	10	2	6	16	15	23	.333	.512
Throws Left	R	.257	647	166	36	2	37	84	60	138	.317	.490
Mitre,Sergio	L	.408	98	40	6	1	4	16	10	13	.468	.612
Throws Right	R	.261	119	31	9	0	2	14	10	24	.333	.387
Moreno,Orber	L	.200	55	11	2	0	0	3	7	13	.290	.236
Throws Right	R	.237	76	18	1	0	0	11	4	16	.301	.250
Morris,Matt	L	.259	347	90	14	1	18	60	29	58	.317	.461
Throws Right	R	.272	423	115	24	1	17	52	27	73	.321	.454
Moss,Damian	L	.111	9	1	0	0	0	2	4	1	.429	.111
Throws Left	R	.429	28	12	2	0	2	12	1	5	.448	.714

Pitchers vs. Left-Handed and Right-Handed Batters

Pitcher	vs	Avg	AB	H	2B	3B	HR	RBI	BB	SO	OBP	Slg
Mota,Guillermo	L	.195	154	30	3	2	3	13	18	34	.280	.299
Throws Right	R	.237	190	45	5	0	5	21	19	51	.315	.342
Moyer,Jamie	L	.292	226	66	8	0	9	30	19	43	.370	.447
Throws Left	R	.264	573	151	25	1	35	90	44	82	.315	.494
Mulder,Mark	L	.269	167	45	7	0	3	21	19	25	.347	.365
Throws Left	R	.263	677	178	41	3	22	87	64	115	.334	.430
Mulholland,Terry	L	.284	141	40	3	0	5	21	12	20	.340	.411
Throws Left	R	.344	358	123	19	2	12	42	21	40	.383	.508
Munoz,Arnie	L	.320	25	8	1	0	0	2	5	6	.452	.360
Throws Left	R	.353	34	12	5	1	4	16	7	5	.442	.912
Munro,Pete	L	.337	184	62	18	2	8	24	16	21	.393	.587
Throws Right	R	.272	213	58	10	3	4	23	10	42	.325	.404
Mussina,Mike	L	.254	338	86	18	3	8	33	23	93	.303	.396
Throws Right	R	.299	308	92	15	1	14	46	17	39	.334	.490
Myers,Brett	L	.278	338	94	21	0	12	42	34	56	.342	.447
Throws Right	R	.283	360	102	28	2	19	63	28	60	.344	.531
Myers,Mike	L	.233	103	24	5	0	2	13	12	24	.325	.340
Throws Left	R	.344	61	21	5	0	3	14	11	8	.438	.574
Myers,Rodney	L	.000	2	0	0	0	0	0	0	1	.000	.000
Throws Right	R	.250	4	1	0	0	0	0	0	0	.250	.250
Myette,Aaron	L	.286	7	2	1	0	0	0	5	2	.615	.429
Throws Right	R	.111	9	1	1	0	0	2	3	4	.385	.222
Nageotte,Clint	L	.307	75	23	1	0	0	11	16	11	.435	.320
Throws Right	R	.342	73	25	3	0	3	15	11	13	.438	.507
Nakamura,Mike	L	.233	43	10	2	0	4	11	3	8	.292	.558
Throws Right	R	.283	60	17	4	2	3	8	4	16	.338	.567
Nance,Shane	L	.419	31	13	2	0	1	5	3	5	.471	.581
Throws Left	R	.261	23	6	3	0	1	4	9	4	.514	.522
Narron,Sam	L	.375	8	3	1	0	1	2	0	0	.375	.875
Throws Left	R	.400	5	2	0	0	2	2	4	1	.667	1.600
Nathan,Joe	L	.212	132	28	5	0	2	10	13	42	.293	.295
Throws Right	R	.160	125	20	4	0	1	4	10	47	.222	.216
Neal,Blaine	L	.250	68	17	3	0	2	11	7	12	.333	.382
Throws Right	R	.327	98	32	7	1	4	15	4	24	.350	.541
Nelson,Jeff	L	.167	24	4	0	0	1	3	8	4	.375	.292
Throws Right	R	.224	58	13	1	0	2	7	11	18	.343	.345
Nelson,Joe	L	.500	2	1	0	0	0	0	2	0	.833	.500
Throws Right	R	.333	9	3	1	0	0	1	1	5	.400	.444
Neu,Mike	L	.300	10	3	1	0	0	0	2	1	.417	.400
Throws Right	R	.333	6	2	0	1	1	2	0	1	.333	1.167
Nitkowski,C.J.	L	.266	64	17	4	0	1	13	7	16	.373	.375
Throws Left	R	.324	71	23	7	0	3	16	9	10	.405	.549
Nomo,Hideo	L	.338	139	47	8	0	7	26	26	18	.449	.547
Throws Right	R	.293	198	58	14	0	12	43	16	36	.347	.545
Norton,Phil	L	.273	99	27	9	1	0	12	16	21	.373	.384
Throws Left	R	.291	151	44	7	1	5	26	22	27	.385	.450
Novoa,Roberto	L	.333	33	11	2	0	4	10	3	4	.368	.758
Throws Right	R	.292	48	14	2	0	0	8	3	11	.345	.333
Nunez,Franklin	L	.316	19	6	1	0	0	4	3	5	.458	.368
Throws Right	R	.227	22	5	0	1	1	5	4	9	.345	.455
Nunez,Vladimir	L	.281	32	9	1	0	3	10	7	9	.390	.594
Throws Right	R	.279	61	17	3	1	3	15	7	13	.347	.508
Obermueller,Wes	L	.286	220	63	15	4	6	24	25	27	.355	.473
Throws Right	R	.294	255	75	18	2	9	40	17	32	.343	.486
Ohka,Tomo	L	.280	161	45	5	2	5	11	12	19	.329	.429
Throws Right	R	.296	179	53	15	0	6	26	8	19	.326	.480
Oliver,Darren	L	.321	78	25	3	2	5	11	7	11	.368	.603
Throws Left	R	.300	207	62	14	1	9	35	14	35	.345	.507
Oropesa,Eddie	L	.235	17	4	1	0	1	2	6	3	.435	.471
Throws Left	R	.133	15	2	0	1	0	3	7	3	.409	.267
Ortiz,Ramon	L	.305	259	79	16	0	15	39	23	34	.364	.541
Throws Right	R	.253	237	60	17	1	3	22	15	48	.302	.371
Ortiz,Russ	L	.254	382	97	15	1	11	42	60	67	.357	.385
Throws Right	R	.262	382	100	22	0	12	42	52	76	.347	.414
Osborne,Donovan	L	.500	24	12	4	0	1	7	3	3	.571	.792
Throws Left	R	.271	48	13	2	0	2	10	2	7	.314	.438
Osuna,Antonio	L	.215	65	14	4	0	1	6	7	20	.288	.323
Throws Right	R	.247	73	18	5	0	2	12	4	16	.295	.397
Oswalt,Roy	L	.255	462	118	29	1	7	44	39	111	.318	.368
Throws Right	R	.266	433	115	28	1	10	48	23	95	.311	.404
Otsuka,Akinori	L	.210	124	26	5	2	1	8	16	37	.300	.306
Throws Right	R	.190	158	30	3	0	5	13	10	50	.238	.304
Padilla,Juan	L	.333	51	17	4	1	2	9	4	6	.382	.569
Throws Right	R	.373	59	22	5	0	5	13	8	11	.456	.712
Padilla,Vicente	L	.289	242	70	15	3	10	34	27	39	.366	.500
Throws Right	R	.241	203	49	12	2	6	27	9	43	.291	.409

Pitcher	vs	Avg	AB	H	2B	3B	HR	RBI	BB	SO	OBP	Slg
Park,Chan Ho	L	.277	184	51	10	2	11	27	21	27	.360	.533
Throws Right	R	.284	190	54	5	0	11	29	12	36	.352	.484
Parra,Jose	L	.200	25	5	1	0	1	3	1	8	.231	.360
Throws Right	R	.300	30	9	1	0	1	1	5	6	.400	.433
Parrish,John	L	.243	103	25	5	2	3	20	21	24	.375	.417
Throws Left	R	.235	183	43	7	0	1	22	34	47	.351	.290
Patterson,Danny	L	.284	67	19	4	0	2	9	9	9	.385	.433
Throws Right	R	.281	89	25	3	0	5	15	7	15	.354	.483
Patterson,John	L	.228	162	37	6	1	2	13	26	38	.344	.315
Throws Right	R	.283	223	63	14	1	16	38	20	61	.353	.570
Pavano,Carl	L	.267	393	105	23	2	11	40	28	62	.322	.420
Throws Right	R	.240	445	107	23	3	5	32	21	77	.283	.339
Pearce,Josh	L	.500	2	1	0	0	0	0	0	0	.500	.500
Throws Right	R	.333	6	2	1	0	0	1	0	0	.333	.500
Peavy,Jake	L	.235	315	74	16	3	7	25	31	85	.318	.371
Throws Right	R	.237	304	72	11	2	6	23	22	88	.290	.345
Penny,Brad	L	.243	272	66	14	1	7	19	30	63	.318	.379
Throws Right	R	.242	264	64	19	2	5	29	15	48	.287	.386
Percival,Troy	L	.218	101	22	3	0	5	13	15	19	.331	.396
Throws Right	R	.244	86	21	1	1	2	10	4	14	.278	.349
Perez,Odalis	L	.273	172	47	8	2	8	23	9	41	.317	.483
Throws Left	R	.242	549	133	27	3	18	49	35	87	.287	.401
Perez,Oliver	L	.220	132	29	7	0	3	10	6	59	.264	.341
Throws Left	R	.204	569	116	20	7	19	56	75	180	.302	.364
Perisho,Matt	L	.207	87	18	3	0	4	12	13	28	.317	.379
Throws Left	R	.284	95	27	6	0	2	15	13	14	.373	.411
Peterson,Adam	L	.417	12	5	1	0	1	5	1	2	.462	.750
Throws Right	R	.667	3	2	1	0	0	1	2	0	.800	1.000
Pettitte,Andy	L	.290	69	20	6	0	3	8	4	17	.329	.507
Throws Left	R	.208	245	51	15	0	5	27	27	62	.287	.331
Phelps,Tommy	L	.256	39	10	2	3	2	7	5	9	.341	.615
Throws Left	R	.273	88	24	2	0	4	14	7	19	.320	.432
Phelps,Travis	L	.333	12	4	0	0	2	4	2	2	.429	.833
Throws Right	R	.250	16	4	1	0	0	1	1	1	.294	.313
Pineiro,Joel	L	.209	258	54	9	0	7	28	25	65	.277	.326
Throws Right	R	.316	285	90	20	2	14	45	18	46	.361	.547
Politte,Cliff	L	.351	74	26	4	1	4	15	12	14	.442	.595
Throws Right	R	.208	125	26	5	1	2	15	10	34	.273	.312
Ponson,Sidney	L	.321	455	146	26	3	12	70	50	49	.391	.470
Throws Right	R	.288	413	119	20	2	11	50	19	66	.326	.426
Pote,Lou	L	.333	6	2	1	0	0	3	1	3	.429	.500
Throws Right	R	.167	6	1	0	0	0	0	0	2	.167	.167
Powell,Brian	L	.328	61	20	4	2	2	12	11	8	.416	.557
Throws Right	R	.235	81	19	6	1	3	16	5	16	.276	.444
Powell,Jay	L	.226	31	7	2	1	1	6	6	7	.351	.452
Throws Right	R	.288	59	17	2	0	2	6	5	10	.338	.424
Pratt,Andy	L	.000	2	0	0	0	0	0	2	1	.500	.000
Throws Left	R	.000	3	0	0	0	0	0	5	0	.667	.000
Prinz,Bret	L	.146	41	6	0	1	3	7	11	12	.327	.415
Throws Right	R	.328	67	22	6	0	2	15	3	10	.361	.507
Prior,Mark	L	.258	194	50	18	0	7	15	24	54	.336	.459
Throws Right	R	.245	253	62	11	2	7	30	24	85	.316	.387
Proctor,Scott	L	.255	51	13	1	0	1	6	8	12	.350	.333
Throws Right	R	.314	51	16	5	0	4	16	6	9	.379	.647
Puffer,Brandon	L	.242	33	8	0	0	2	4	8	6	.390	.424
Throws Right	R	.381	42	16	5	0	1	9	3	6	.435	.571
Pulido,Carlos	L	.238	21	5	1	0	1	6	0	4	.261	.429
Throws Left	R	.407	27	11	4	0	1	9	4	5	.469	.667
Putz,J.J.	L	.234	111	26	4	0	8	19	11	24	.315	.486
Throws Right	R	.308	130	40	8	1	2	25	13	23	.378	.431
Qualls,Chad	L	.264	53	14	3	0	2	7	5	13	.339	.434
Throws Right	R	.267	75	20	4	0	1	6	3	11	.317	.360
Quantrill,Paul	L	.292	185	54	12	1	4	28	14	16	.345	.432
Throws Right	R	.337	208	70	11	1	1	29	6	21	.358	.413
Radke,Brad	L	.254	468	119	14	2	15	47	19	67	.287	.389
Throws Right	R	.281	391	110	18	2	8	35	7	76	.296	.399
Rakers,Aaron	L	.250	8	2	0	0	0	0	0	2	.250	.250
Throws Right	R	.300	10	3	0	0	0	2	1	1	.364	.300
Ramirez,Elizardo	L	.241	29	7	2	0	1	2	2	5	.290	.414
Throws Right	R	.323	31	10	5	0	2	5	3	4	.389	.677
Ramirez,Erasmo	L	.290	62	18	2	1	2	13	4	8	.353	.452
Throws Left	R	.219	73	16	2	0	3	11	3	13	.256	.370
Ramirez,Horacio	L	.224	49	11	2	0	2	5	7	5	.316	.388
Throws Left	R	.226	177	40	7	2	5	16	23	26	.315	.373
Randolph,Stephen	L	.238	105	25	4	1	2	16	16	32	.333	.352
Throws Left	R	.234	205	48	10	0	9	40	60	30	.407	.415

Pitchers vs. Left-Handed and Right-Handed Batters

Pitcher	vs	Avg	AB	H	2B	3B	HR	RBI	BB	SO	OBP	Slg
Rauch,Jon	L	.321	53	17	6	1	0	6	8	6	.410	.472
Throws Right	R	.203	64	13	2	0	1	3	3	16	.235	.281
Redding,Tim	L	.345	171	59	11	1	8	38	28	21	.433	.561
Throws Right	R	.283	233	66	14	0	7	24	15	35	.337	.433
Redman,Mark	L	.286	175	50	13	1	6	21	16	30	.351	.474
Throws Left	R	.294	571	168	38	2	22	79	52	72	.354	.483
Reed,Steve	L	.282	103	29	5	0	2	11	13	19	.378	.388
Throws Right	R	.281	153	43	8	0	5	22	4	19	.315	.431
Regilio,Nick	L	.270	37	10	2	0	2	9	10	3	.438	.486
Throws Right	R	.286	35	10	2	0	1	7	5	9	.381	.429
Reith,Brian	L	.382	34	13	3	0	3	7	8	3	.512	.735
Throws Right	R	.243	70	17	5	2	2	12	11	21	.361	.457
Reitsma,Chris	L	.310	145	45	6	0	4	19	10	24	.356	.434
Throws Right	R	.262	168	44	9	0	5	15	10	36	.302	.405
Remlinger,Mike	L	.303	66	20	2	1	3	18	6	12	.351	.500
Throws Left	R	.191	68	13	1	0	0	8	10	23	.296	.206
Reyes,Al	L	.105	19	2	1	0	0	0	0	6	.105	.158
Throws Right	R	.056	18	1	0	0	0	3	2	5	.150	.056
Reyes,Dennys	L	.316	133	42	5	1	4	20	12	33	.376	.459
Throws Left	R	.254	284	72	18	2	8	36	38	58	.343	.415
Reynolds,Shane	L	.333	3	1	1	0	0	2	2	0	.600	.667
Throws Right	R	.556	9	5	5	0	0	4	0	0	.556	1.111
Rhodes,Arthur	L	.314	51	16	3	0	2	10	7	11	.397	.490
Throws Left	R	.283	106	30	7	0	7	15	14	23	.364	.547
Riedling,John	L	.299	117	35	7	2	6	22	18	16	.390	.547
Throws Right	R	.278	198	55	16	0	4	38	22	30	.358	.419
Riley,Matt	L	.318	44	14	1	0	3	12	11	11	.455	.545
Throws Left	R	.228	202	46	6	0	8	22	33	49	.339	.376
Rincon,Juan	L	.148	122	18	2	0	3	13	14	54	.239	.238
Throws Right	R	.206	165	34	5	1	2	20	18	52	.285	.285
Rincon,Ricardo	L	.200	90	18	4	0	1	10	5	24	.250	.278
Throws Left	R	.314	86	27	4	0	2	14	17	16	.423	.430
Riske,David	L	.224	143	32	9	0	7	24	24	41	.335	.434
Throws Right	R	.255	145	37	8	0	4	17	17	37	.337	.393
Ritchie,Todd	L	.235	17	4	0	0	1	2	5	2	.435	.412
Throws Right	R	.444	18	8	0	1	3	4	1	2	.474	1.056
Rivera,Mariano	L	.234	158	37	2	0	2	8	12	40	.288	.285
Throws Right	R	.214	131	28	5	0	1	13	8	26	.285	.275
Roa,Joe	L	.339	121	41	7	3	4	12	16	21	.420	.545
Throws Right	R	.265	162	43	8	0	5	32	8	26	.313	.407
Robbins,Jake	L	.500	4	2	0	0	1	2	0	0	.500	1.250
Throws Right	R	.250	4	1	0	0	0	0	0	0	.250	.250
Roberts,Grant	L	.636	11	7	2	0	2	9	2	0	.692	1.364
Throws Right	R	.200	10	2	0	0	0	1	4	1	.400	.200
Roberts,Willis	L	.385	13	5	1	0	0	3	7	3	.600	.462
Throws Right	R	.233	30	7	2	0	0	7	2	4	.306	.300
Robertson,Jeriome	L	.571	21	12	1	1	2	10	2	1	.609	1.000
Throws Left	R	.238	42	10	2	0	3	9	7	5	.365	.500
Robertson,Nate	L	.252	143	36	2	1	2	21	7	35	.291	.322
Throws Left	R	.279	623	174	33	2	28	87	59	120	.343	.474
Rodriguez,Eddy	L	.194	67	13	4	0	1	10	15	17	.349	.299
Throws Right	R	.258	89	23	7	0	4	14	15	20	.385	.472
Rodriguez,Felix	L	.192	99	19	1	1	1	6	17	34	.310	.253
Throws Right	R	.278	151	42	13	0	7	22	12	25	.349	.503
Rodriguez,Francisco	L	.213	155	33	5	0	1	12	19	55	.301	.265
Throws Right	R	.127	142	18	5	0	1	12	14	68	.205	.183
Rodriguez,Ricardo	L	.235	51	12	3	1	0	4	8	8	.339	.333
Throws Right	R	.286	56	16	4	0	1	5	4	7	.333	.411
Rogers,Kenny	L	.294	194	57	10	1	3	15	19	47	.372	.402
Throws Left	R	.292	654	191	49	7	21	96	47	79	.341	.485
Romero,J.C.	L	.261	111	29	1	0	3	15	11	26	.344	.351
Throws Left	R	.199	161	32	9	0	1	25	27	43	.319	.273
Rueter,Kirk	L	.277	188	52	11	0	4	22	11	17	.318	.399
Throws Left	R	.302	572	173	41	6	17	77	55	39	.362	.484
Rusch,Glendon	L	.227	119	27	2	1	1	12	10	25	.290	.286
Throws Left	R	.265	378	100	24	2	9	42	23	65	.311	.410
Ryan,B.J.	L	.094	106	10	1	0	2	7	8	46	.165	.160
Throws Left	R	.252	214	54	8	1	2	24	27	76	.333	.327
Saarloos,Kirk	L	.294	51	15	6	0	2	5	10	7	.410	.529
Throws Right	R	.273	44	12	0	0	2	8	2	3	.327	.409
Sabathia,C.C.	L	.265	151	40	11	0	7	22	13	24	.324	.477
Throws Left	R	.248	548	136	33	4	13	63	59	115	.326	.394
Saenz,Chris	L	.200	5	1	0	0	0	0	1	0	.333	.200
Throws Right	R	.067	15	1	0	0	0	0	2	7	.222	.067
Sanchez,Duaner	L	.276	123	34	8	0	4	13	10	11	.336	.439
Throws Right	R	.260	181	47	5	0	5	23	17	33	.335	.370

Pitcher	vs	Avg	AB	H	2B	3B	HR	RBI	BB	SO	OBP	Slg
Sanchez,Jesus	L	.200	15	3	0	0	1	1	1	1	.250	.400
Throws Left	R	.341	44	15	4	0	3	11	8	7	.442	.636
Santana,Johan	L	.196	194	38	6	1	5	16	10	52	.238	.314
Throws Left	R	.191	618	118	16	2	19	39	44	213	.253	.316
Santos,Victor	L	.246	248	61	11	3	6	34	31	42	.330	.387
Throws Right	R	.301	359	108	24	0	12	48	26	73	.354	.468
Schilling,Curt	L	.238	462	110	30	2	6	39	18	105	.267	.351
Throws Right	R	.241	399	96	24	0	17	40	17	98	.276	.429
Schmidt,Jason	L	.191	398	76	13	5	6	35	44	116	.271	.294
Throws Right	R	.212	419	89	18	2	12	43	33	135	.273	.351
Schoeneweis,Scott	L	.244	86	21	3	0	0	7	7	19	.305	.279
Throws Left	R	.303	357	108	21	1	17	60	42	50	.378	.510
Seanez,Rudy	L	.253	83	21	5	3	0	10	13	22	.351	.386
Throws Right	R	.205	88	18	5	0	3	19	6	24	.250	.364
Seay,Bobby	L	.200	35	7	3	1	0	7	2	5	.282	.343
Throws Left	R	.264	53	14	2	0	2	8	3	12	.304	.415
Seibel,Phil	L	.000	6	0	0	0	0	0	0	1	.143	.000
Throws Left	R	.000	6	0	0	0	0	1	5	0	.455	.000
Sele,Aaron	L	.296	267	79	12	1	6	32	31	29	.368	.416
Throws Right	R	.324	259	84	12	2	10	47	20	22	.374	.502
Seo,Jae	L	.273	209	57	11	2	7	24	26	29	.354	.445
Throws Right	R	.322	236	76	20	1	10	29	24	25	.384	.542
Serrano,Jimmy	L	.359	64	23	5	1	2	8	8	9	.432	.563
Throws Right	R	.197	61	12	3	0	3	9	4	16	.239	.393
Service,Scott	L	.211	38	8	2	1	0	7	6	7	.318	.316
Throws Right	R	.348	46	16	3	0	5	16	4	10	.415	.739
Sheets,Ben	L	.232	427	99	21	3	15	39	17	131	.266	.400
Throws Right	R	.220	464	102	36	1	10	41	15	133	.244	.366
Sherrill,George	L	.239	46	11	3	0	2	11	0	11	.250	.435
Throws Left	R	.277	47	13	2	0	1	6	9	5	.393	.383
Shields,Scot	L	.235	200	47	5	0	1	19	30	52	.335	.275
Throws Right	R	.242	207	50	10	2	5	25	10	57	.283	.382
Shouse,Brian	L	.188	96	18	6	0	2	11	7	25	.245	.313
Throws Left	R	.277	65	18	5	1	1	4	11	9	.382	.431
Silva,Carlos	L	.328	442	145	27	3	15	52	23	38	.364	.505
Throws Right	R	.289	381	110	21	1	8	34	12	38	.316	.412
Simontacchi,Jason	L	.250	20	5	1	0	0	1	2	1	.318	.300
Throws Right	R	.333	36	12	1	0	5	14	5	2	.419	.778
Simpson,Allan	L	.321	53	17	4	1	2	10	11	11	.424	.547
Throws Right	R	.273	99	27	10	0	2	19	9	35	.351	.434
Small,Aaron	L	.333	30	10	1	0	1	4	6	5	.444	.467
Throws Right	R	.350	40	14	4	0	4	16	1	3	.366	.750
Smith,Travis	L	.221	77	17	3	0	3	8	4	18	.268	.377
Throws Right	R	.356	87	31	5	0	9	22	8	8	.411	.724
Smoltz,John	L	.255	145	37	4	0	5	20	5	40	.280	.386
Throws Right	R	.236	161	38	6	1	3	7	8	45	.272	.342
Snare,Ryan	L	.286	7	2	0	0	1	2	1	0	.375	.714
Throws Left	R	.375	8	3	1	0	2	3	1	0	.444	1.250
Snell,Ian	L	.313	16	5	1	1	1	3	5	5	.476	.688
Throws Right	R	.290	31	9	1	0	1	6	4	4	.371	.419
Soriano,Rafael	L	.429	7	3	1	0	0	1	0	0	.429	.571
Throws Right	R	.462	13	6	3	0	0	1	3	3	.563	.692
Sosa,Jorge	L	.286	192	55	10	1	14	44	26	36	.371	.568
Throws Right	R	.232	194	45	10	1	3	14	28	58	.326	.340
Sparks,Steve	L	.350	223	78	17	2	7	41	25	23	.413	.538
Throws Right	R	.234	261	61	12	2	11	34	20	34	.295	.421
Speier,Justin	L	.263	133	35	6	1	7	22	14	26	.347	.481
Throws Right	R	.213	122	26	3	0	1	13	11	26	.283	.262
Springer,Russ	L	.240	25	6	2	1	0	2	4	6	.355	.400
Throws Right	R	.310	29	9	0	1	1	6	2	3	.355	.483
Standridge,Jason	L	.318	22	7	0	0	4	7	3	6	.400	.864
Throws Right	R	.333	21	7	3	0	1	4	1	1	.348	.619
Stanford,Jason	L	.125	8	1	0	0	0	1	1	2	.300	.125
Throws Left	R	.314	35	11	2	0	0	0	4	3	.385	.371
Stanton,Mike	L	.269	108	29	5	0	4	18	18	28	.373	.426
Throws Left	R	.219	187	41	5	2	2	22	15	30	.283	.299
Stark,Denny	L	.468	62	29	7	0	6	19	11	2	.541	.871
Throws Right	R	.387	62	24	3	1	3	19	7	8	.431	.613
Stewart,Josh	L	.273	11	3	0	0	0	1	1	3	.333	.273
Throws Left	R	.520	25	13	5	1	3	12	2	2	.517	1.160
Stewart,Scott	L	.411	56	23	7	0	0	14	4	17	.435	.536
Throws Left	R	.345	58	20	3	1	5	20	8	9	.418	.690
Stone,Ricky	L	.333	90	30	6	2	6	24	12	17	.417	.644
Throws Right	R	.288	125	36	6	1	5	16	4	21	.333	.472
Sturtze,Tanyon	L	.261	153	40	13	0	6	24	21	22	.352	.464
Throws Right	R	.246	142	35	10	2	3	20	12	34	.327	.408

Pitchers vs. Left-Handed and Right-Handed Batters

Pitcher	vs	Avg	AB	H	2B	3B	HR	RBI	BB	SO	OBP	Slg
Sullivan,Scott	L	.355	93	33	9	2	6	18	17	14	.465	.688
Throws Right	R	.278	144	40	6	0	2	27	7	31	.323	.361
Suppan,Jeff	L	.272	309	84	16	1	13	40	34	48	.347	.456
Throws Right	R	.260	416	108	25	0	12	45	31	62	.317	.406
Sweeney,Brian	L	.188	32	6	2	0	1	2	1	6	.212	.344
Throws Right	R	.483	29	14	4	1	0	7	1	4	.500	.690
Szuminski,Jason	L	.083	12	1	0	0	0	2	7	1	.450	.083
Throws Right	R	.367	30	11	1	0	3	7	4	4	.457	.700
Tadano,Kazuhito	L	.222	90	20	7	0	3	12	6	20	.278	.400
Throws Right	R	.313	112	35	7	0	3	16	12	19	.389	.455
Takatsu,Shingo	L	.228	101	23	5	0	5	15	11	19	.304	.426
Throws Right	R	.143	119	17	1	0	1	3	10	31	.221	.176
Tankersley,Dennis	L	.230	74	17	6	1	2	7	11	17	.329	.419
Throws Right	R	.281	64	18	2	1	1	10	6	12	.352	.391
Tavarez,Julian	L	.253	83	21	2	2	1	8	11	12	.347	.361
Throws Right	R	.231	156	36	7	1	0	14	8	36	.288	.288
Taylor,Aaron	L	.300	10	3	0	0	1	3	2	4	.417	.600
Throws Right	R	.333	6	2	0	0	1	4	1	0	.429	.833
Tejera,Michael	L	.278	18	5	1	0	1	6	4	6	.435	.500
Throws Left	R	.435	23	10	0	0	0	4	5	4	.552	.435
Telemaco,Amaury	L	.270	89	24	2	0	6	12	11	18	.350	.494
Throws Right	R	.233	116	27	8	1	6	12	8	14	.282	.474
Thomas,Brad	L	.800	5	4	1	1	0	6	1	0	.833	1.400
Throws Left	R	.333	9	3	0	0	0	0	0	0	.333	.333
Thomson,John	L	.276	344	95	15	4	9	38	35	67	.341	.422
Throws Right	R	.276	417	115	18	0	11	50	17	66	.312	.398
Thornton,Matt	L	.300	40	12	3	0	1	3	7	16	.404	.450
Throws Left	R	.225	80	18	5	0	1	10	18	14	.364	.325
Timlin,Mike	L	.269	134	36	10	0	3	20	9	24	.319	.410
Throws Right	R	.247	158	39	14	0	5	26	10	32	.306	.430
Tomko,Brett	L	.293	334	98	21	2	9	39	37	41	.363	.449
Throws Right	R	.234	419	98	22	6	10	49	27	67	.280	.387
Torres,Salomon	L	.254	126	32	5	0	2	17	9	15	.299	.341
Throws Right	R	.257	214	55	9	0	4	21	13	47	.316	.355
Towers,Josh	L	.312	276	86	18	1	8	27	18	26	.355	.471
Throws Right	R	.308	201	62	14	0	8	34	8	25	.355	.498
Trachsel,Steve	L	.245	380	93	19	1	8	34	39	55	.319	.363
Throws Right	R	.279	394	110	29	2	17	56	44	62	.349	.492
Tsao,Chin-hui	L	.286	14	4	1	0	2	3	0	5	.286	.786
Throws Right	R	.143	21	3	1	0	0	4	1	6	.182	.190
Tucker,T.J.	L	.282	103	29	5	2	1	11	9	19	.348	.398
Throws Right	R	.272	162	44	6	0	4	20	8	25	.312	.383
Turnbow,Derrick	L	.125	8	1	0	0	0	0	3	0	.364	.125
Throws Right	R	.091	11	1	0	0	0	0	4	3	.333	.091
Urbina,Ugueth	L	.191	89	17	5	0	2	15	20	17	.339	.315
Throws Right	R	.196	107	21	4	0	5	14	12	39	.289	.374
Urdaneta,Lino	L	1.000	2	2	0	0	0	3	1	0	1.000	1.000
Throws Right	R	1.000	3	3	0	0	0	3	0	0	1.000	1.000
Valdez,Ismael	L	.294	350	103	25	5	18	50	24	24	.341	.549
Throws Right	R	.295	336	99	18	1	15	45	25	43	.342	.488
Valdez,Merkin	L	.600	5	3	1	0	1	6	1	1	.667	1.400
Throws Right	R	.250	4	1	1	0	0	1	2	1	.500	.500
Valentine,Joe	L	.067	45	3	1	0	1	5	15	16	.311	.156
Throws Right	R	.313	64	20	6	1	3	10	10	13	.413	.578
Valverde,Jose	L	.152	46	7	3	0	1	4	10	13	.304	.283
Throws Right	R	.258	62	16	3	0	6	18	7	25	.333	.597
Van Benschoten,John	L	.391	46	18	6	0	0	10	10	6	.491	.522
Throws Right	R	.234	64	15	4	0	3	15	9	12	.342	.438
Van Poppel,Todd	L	.311	193	60	19	1	11	33	17	26	.370	.591
Throws Right	R	.288	264	76	21	2	11	46	15	46	.326	.508
Vargas,Claudio	L	.301	196	59	16	1	11	38	32	37	.403	.561
Throws Right	R	.239	255	61	11	0	15	38	32	52	.331	.459
Vasquez,Jorge	L	.167	6	1	0	0	0	0	1	0	.286	.167
Throws Right	R	.333	9	3	1	0	1	3	0	4	.400	.778
Vazquez,Javier	L	.253	395	100	16	5	20	57	39	76	.326	.471
Throws Right	R	.256	371	95	18	0	13	42	21	74	.303	.410
Venafro,Mike	L	.200	20	4	0	0	1	4	2	5	.333	.350
Throws Left	R	.438	16	7	3	0	0	3	1	1	.471	.625
Villacis,Eduardo	L	.286	7	2	0	0	1	4	4	0	.545	.714
Throws Right	R	.444	9	4	0	0	0	1	0	0	.444	.444
Villafuerte,Brandon	L	.556	27	15	1	0	1	3	9	2	.676	.704
Throws Right	R	.189	53	10	2	0	1	4	5	11	.259	.283
Villarreal,Oscar	L	.250	28	7	3	1	0	6	3	7	.323	.429
Throws Right	R	.400	45	18	4	0	3	15	4	10	.460	.689
Villone,Ron	L	.203	143	29	3	0	3	20	16	29	.314	.287
Throws Left	R	.247	296	73	16	2	9	39	48	57	.357	.405

Pitcher	vs	Avg	AB	H	2B	3B	HR	RBI	BB	SO	OBP	Slg
Vizcaino,Luis	L	.163	129	21	3	1	6	21	14	36	.245	.341
Throws Right	R	.290	138	40	14	0	6	20	10	27	.333	.522
Vogelsong,Ryan	L	.275	240	66	19	2	10	41	34	44	.367	.496
Throws Right	R	.294	279	82	21	1	12	46	33	47	.380	.505
Waechter,Doug	L	.279	154	43	6	0	17	33	24	16	.381	.649
Throws Right	R	.216	116	25	7	2	3	14	9	20	.281	.388
Wagner,Billy	L	.100	30	3	0	0	0	0	0	7	.129	.100
Throws Left	R	.199	141	28	4	1	5	15	6	52	.236	.348
Wagner,Ryan	L	.224	58	13	2	0	1	5	14	7	.365	.310
Throws Right	R	.307	150	46	9	0	6	36	13	30	.367	.487
Wakefield,Tim	L	.230	379	87	15	2	11	47	33	64	.296	.367
Throws Right	R	.300	367	110	21	3	18	59	30	52	.371	.520
Walker,Jamie	L	.200	115	23	5	0	1	13	7	30	.250	.270
Throws Left	R	.313	147	46	9	1	7	23	5	23	.336	.531
Walker,Kevin	L	.500	2	1	1	0	0	1	1	1	.667	1.000
Throws Left	R	.400	5	2	0	0	1	3	1	0	.571	1.000
Walker,Tyler	L	.290	100	29	6	2	4	11	9	18	.351	.510
Throws Right	R	.286	140	40	7	3	4	22	15	30	.342	.464
Wasdin,John	L	.319	144	46	5	0	10	25	16	13	.396	.563
Throws Right	R	.289	128	37	6	0	8	24	7	23	.324	.523
Washburn,Jarrod	L	.225	142	32	5	0	6	20	10	32	.277	.387
Throws Left	R	.283	448	127	34	2	14	54	30	54	.331	.462
Watkins,Steve	L	.227	22	5	1	0	1	3	4	2	.370	.409
Throws Right	R	.333	36	12	5	1	2	11	0	5	.351	.694
Wayne,Justin	L	.349	43	15	1	1	2	5	11	6	.491	.558
Throws Right	R	.247	81	20	3	1	4	15	7	14	.304	.457
Weathers,David	L	.241	116	28	5	0	2	6	20	30	.355	.336
Throws Right	R	.294	194	57	7	2	10	46	15	31	.355	.505
Weaver,Jeff	L	.287	411	118	28	3	13	57	44	63	.367	.465
Throws Right	R	.234	431	101	22	2	6	36	23	90	.278	.336
Webb,Brandon	L	.268	429	115	19	4	11	58	85	77	.390	.408
Throws Right	R	.223	354	79	12	1	6	32	34	87	.304	.314
Webb,John	L	.467	15	7	1	0	1	5	5	3	.600	.733
Throws Right	R	.227	22	5	0	0	1	2	2	6	.320	.364
Weber,Ben	L	.383	47	18	5	0	2	17	12	4	.508	.617
Throws Right	R	.345	55	19	4	0	2	6	3	7	.379	.527
Wellemeyer,Todd	L	.302	43	13	2	0	1	6	11	15	.444	.419
Throws Right	R	.275	51	14	2	0	0	8	9	15	.371	.314
Wells,David	L	.278	151	42	9	0	10	21	5	19	.299	.536
Throws Left	R	.263	613	161	28	2	13	54	15	82	.281	.378
Wells,Kip	L	.300	247	74	8	1	6	31	34	43	.378	.413
Throws Right	R	.244	291	71	12	4	8	31	32	73	.330	.395
Wendell,Turk	L	.318	22	7	0	1	1	7	7	3	.467	.545
Throws Right	R	.333	42	14	3	1	3	6	5	8	.420	.667
Westbrook,Jake	L	.262	428	112	30	0	12	55	46	54	.331	.416
Throws Right	R	.247	389	96	18	1	7	29	15	62	.281	.352
Wheeler,Dan	L	.373	110	41	6	0	7	22	11	19	.430	.618
Throws Right	R	.229	153	35	8	0	3	20	9	36	.274	.340
White,Gabe	L	.288	104	30	6	1	6	20	2	14	.306	.538
Throws Left	R	.298	141	42	13	1	8	30	10	27	.344	.574
White,Rick	L	.243	136	33	8	1	8	28	14	25	.309	.493
Throws Right	R	.335	164	55	14	1	7	26	15	19	.396	.561
Wickman,Bob	L	.354	65	23	4	1	3	9	5	13	.400	.585
Throws Right	R	.192	52	10	1	1	1	4	5	13	.288	.308
Williams,Dave	L	.282	39	11	3	1	1	6	3	7	.349	.487
Throws Left	R	.192	104	20	6	0	3	17	10	26	.274	.337
Williams,Jerome	L	.271	236	64	11	3	6	34	35	27	.364	.419
Throws Right	R	.237	249	59	16	1	8	26	9	53	.298	.406
Williams,Randy	L	.000	7	0	0	0	0	0	3	4	.300	.000
Throws Left	R	.333	9	3	1	0	0	2	3	0	.500	.444
Williams,Todd	L	.256	43	11	2	0	1	7	3	6	.319	.372
Throws Right	R	.217	69	15	1	0	1	10	6	7	.316	.275
Williams,Woody	L	.223	337	75	18	2	9	35	33	71	.298	.368
Throws Right	R	.296	399	118	35	1	11	55	25	60	.343	.471
Williamson,Scott	L	.120	50	6	2	0	0	6	12	10	.288	.160
Throws Right	R	.109	46	5	2	0	0	2	6	18	.241	.152
Willis,Dontrelle	L	.200	130	26	4	3	1	13	15	43	.288	.300
Throws Left	R	.288	638	184	35	2	19	75	46	96	.342	.439
Wilson,Paul	L	.282	301	85	17	2	11	41	37	48	.361	.462
Throws Right	R	.262	408	107	20	1	15	47	26	69	.312	.426
Wise,Matt	L	.244	90	22	3	0	0	7	4	15	.274	.278
Throws Right	R	.259	112	29	8	0	3	19	11	15	.333	.411
Witasick,Jay	L	.327	101	33	7	1	5	16	15	18	.410	.564
Throws Right	R	.180	133	24	6	0	3	12	11	39	.247	.293
Wolf,Randy	L	.254	122	31	9	0	5	8	8	21	.298	.451
Throws Left	R	.276	413	114	25	2	15	51	28	68	.328	.455

Pitchers vs. Left-Handed and Right-Handed Batters

Pitcher	vs	Avg	AB	H	2B	3B	HR	RBI	BB	SO	OBP	Slg
Wood,Kerry	L	.262	248	65	12	5	10	32	30	63	.351	.472
Throws Right	R	.227	273	62	11	1	6	28	21	81	.292	.341
Wood,Mike	L	.323	226	73	18	2	7	29	18	27	.376	.513
Throws Right	R	.236	165	39	8	1	9	33	10	27	.297	.461
Worrell,Tim	L	.310	129	40	8	2	1	16	11	25	.359	.426
Throws Right	R	.211	166	35	7	0	9	26	10	39	.260	.416
Wright,Dan	L	.302	43	13	0	0	4	8	6	3	.412	.581
Throws Right	R	.344	32	11	3	0	1	6	5	3	.432	.531
Wright,Jamey	L	.253	162	41	9	1	4	15	32	22	.383	.395
Throws Right	R	.281	146	41	7	1	4	21	13	19	.354	.425
Wright,Jaret	L	.261	348	91	14	2	8	41	44	68	.344	.382
Throws Right	R	.223	346	77	15	0	3	25	26	91	.278	.292
Wuertz,Mike	L	.194	31	6	2	0	2	11	9	9	.357	.452
Throws Right	R	.229	70	16	6	0	2	7	8	21	.308	.400
Wunsch,Kelly	L	1.000	1	1	0	0	0	1	1	0	1.000	1.000
Throws Left	R	.167	6	1	0	0	0	1	0	1	.167	.167
Yan,Esteban	L	.255	165	42	9	1	1	18	19	32	.332	.339
Throws Right	R	.292	171	50	10	2	7	31	13	37	.351	.497
Yates,Tyler	L	.333	87	29	7	2	2	14	12	12	.426	.529
Throws Right	R	.294	109	32	5	0	4	18	13	23	.368	.450
Young,Chris	L	.153	72	11	0	0	1	5	5	15	.218	.194
Throws Right	R	.347	72	25	2	0	6	16	5	12	.397	.625
Young,Jason	L	.350	20	7	1	0	2	7	2	2	.409	.700
Throws Right	R	.421	19	8	6	0	1	4	3	5	.500	.895
Zambrano,Carlos	L	.232	370	86	17	2	7	31	43	82	.325	.346
Throws Right	R	.218	403	88	16	4	7	35	38	106	.302	.330
Zambrano,Victor	L	.241	257	62	11	2	7	31	55	47	.374	.381
Throws Right	R	.217	263	57	16	1	6	32	47	76	.358	.354
Zito,Barry	L	.323	167	54	9	1	5	25	24	34	.419	.479
Throws Left	R	.248	653	162	37	1	23	85	57	129	.309	.413

2004 Leader Boards

You'll find a higher quantity and higher quality of Leader Boards in this section than you've ever seen before in print. Each Board has the Top 10 players, giving a more complete picture of the best (or worst) players in each category.

We continue to include leader boards based on the complex pitching data we chart. Who throws the highest percentage of sliders? Who sets off the radar gun at 100 MPH? Find out inside and amaze your friends with your knowledge!

And what the heck is "Best BPS on OutZ" you're very likely to ask?

OutZ stands for "Pitches Outside The Strike Zone" and BPS is Batting Average Plus Slugging, a combination we felt made more sense than OPS (On-Base Plus Slugging) when evaluating a player's hitting abilities outside the strike zone. (In this case, we're not all that interested in knowing who walks the most—we know that already. OPS outside the strike zone would be heavily populated with the league's most frequent walkers.)

2004 American League Batting Leaders

Batting Average (minimum 502 PA)		On Base Percentage (minimum 502 PA)		Slugging Average (minimum 502 PA)		Home Runs	
Suzuki,Ichiro, Sea	.372	Mora,Melvin, Bal	.419	Ramirez,Manny, Bos	.613	Ramirez,Manny, Bos	43
Mora,Melvin, Bal	.340	Suzuki,Ichiro, Sea	.414	Ortiz,David, Bos	.603	Konerko,Paul, CWS	41
Guerrero,V, Ana	.337	Hafner,Travis, Cle	.410	Guerrero,V, Ana	.598	Ortiz,David, Bos	41
Rodriguez,Ivan, Det	.334	Posada,Jorge, NYY	.400	Hafner,Travis, Cle	.583	Guerrero,V, Ana	39
Durazo,Erubiel, Oak	.321	Chavez,Er, Oak	.397	Mora,Melvin, Bal	.562	Teixeira,Mark, Tex	38
Guillen,Carlos, Det	.318	Ramirez,Manny, Bos	.397	Teixeira,Mark, Tex	.560	Rodriguez,Alex, NYY	36
Lopez,Javy, Bal	.316	Durazo,Erubiel, Oak	.396	Rowand,Aaron, CWS	.544	Sheffield,Gary, NYY	36
Kotsay,Mark, Oak	.314	Sheffield,Gary, NYY	.393	Guillen,Carlos, Det	.542	Tejada,Miguel, Bal	34
Young,Michael, Tex	.313	Guerrero,V, Ana	.391	Delgado,Carlos, Tor	.535	Blalock,Hank, Tex	32
Hafner,Travis, Cle	.311	Varitek,Jason, Bos	.390	Konerko,Paul, CWS	.535	Delgado,Carlos, Tor	32

Games		Plate Appearances		At Bats		Hits	
Matsui,Hideki, NYY	162	Suzuki,Ichiro, Sea	762	Suzuki,Ichiro, Sea	704	Suzuki,Ichiro, Sea	262
Tejada,Miguel, Bal	162	Young,Michael, Tex	739	Young,Michael, Tex	690	Young,Michael, Tex	216
Suzuki,Ichiro, Sea	161	Roberts,Brian, Bal	736	Tejada,Miguel, Bal	653	Guerrero,V, Ana	206
Young,Michael, Tex	160	Tejada,Miguel, Bal	725	Jeter,Derek, NYY	643	Tejada,Miguel, Bal	203
Blalock,Hank, Tex	159	Jeter,Derek, NYY	721	Roberts,Brian, Bal	641	Kotsay,Mark, Oak	190
Roberts,Brian, Bal	159	Blalock,Hank, Tex	713	Crawford,Carl, TB	626	Damon,Johnny, Bos	189
Huff,Aubrey, TB	157	Winn,Randy, Sea	703	Winn,Randy, Sea	626	Jeter,Derek, NYY	188
Lugo,Julio, TB	157	Damon,Johnny, Bos	702	Blalock,Hank, Tex	624	Mora,Melvin, Bal	187
Winn,Randy, Sea	157	Rodriguez,Alex, NYY	698	Damon,Johnny, Bos	621	Crawford,Carl, TB	185
Guerrero,V, Ana	156	Sheffield,Gary, NYY	684	Guerrero,V, Ana	612	Lopez,Javy, Bal	183

Singles		Doubles		Triples		Total Bases	
Suzuki,Ichiro, Sea	225	Roberts,Brian, Bal	50	Crawford,Carl, TB	19	Guerrero,V, Ana	366
Young,Michael, Tex	152	Belliard,R, Cle	48	Figgins,Chone, Ana	17	Ortiz,David, Bos	351
Kotsay,Mark, Oak	135	Ortiz,David, Bos	47	Guillen,Carlos, Det	10	Tejada,Miguel, Bal	349
Crawford,Carl, TB	129	Jeter,Derek, NYY	44	Infante,Omar, Det	9	Ramirez,Manny, Bos	348
Eckstein,David, Ana	129	Ramirez,Manny, Bos	44	Young,Michael, Tex	9	Young,Michael, Tex	333
Damon,Johnny, Bos	128	Hafner,Travis, Cle	41	Cruz,Jo, TB	8	Suzuki,Ichiro, Sea	320
Figgins,Chone, Ana	127	Lugo,Julio, TB	41	5 tied with	7	Blalock,Hank, Tex	312
Tejada,Miguel, Bal	127	Mora,Melvin, Bal	41			Lee,Ca, CWS	310
Vizquel,Omar, Cle	127	Tejada,Miguel, Bal	40			Mora,Melvin, Bal	309
Guerrero,V, Ana	126	2 tied with	39			Rodriguez,Alex, NYY	308

Runs Scored		RBI		Walks		Strikeouts	
Guerrero,V, Ana	124	Tejada,Miguel, Bal	150	Chavez,Er, Oak	95	Bellhorn,Mark, Bos	177
Damon,Johnny, Bos	123	Ortiz,David, Bos	139	Sheffield,Gary, NYY	92	Blalock,Hank, Tex	149
Sheffield,Gary, NYY	117	Ramirez,Manny, Bos	130	Bellhorn,Mark, Bos	88	Pena,Carlos, Det	146
Young,Michael, Tex	114	Guerrero,V, Ana	126	Matsui,Hideki, NYY	88	Crosby,Bo, Oak	141
Rodriguez,Alex, NYY	112	Sheffield,Gary, NYY	121	Posada,Jorge, NYY	88	Blake,Casey, Cle	139
Jeter,Derek, NYY	111	Konerko,Paul, CWS	117	Palmeiro,R, Bal	86	Valentin,Jo, CWS	139
Mora,Melvin, Bal	111	Teixeira,Mark, Tex	112	Williams,B, NYY	85	Boone,Bret, Sea	135
Lawton,Matt, Cle	109	Blalock,Hank, Tex	110	Ramirez,Manny, Bos	82	Ortiz,David, Bos	133
Matsui,Hideki, NYY	109	Hafner,Travis, Cle	109	Rodriguez,Alex, NYY	80	Rodriguez,Alex, NYY	131
Ramirez,Manny, Bos	108	2 tied with	108	2 tied with	76	Dye,Jermaine, Oak	128

2004 American League Batting Leaders

Sacrifice Hits		Sacrifice Flies		Stolen Bases		Caught Stealing	
Vizquel,Omar, Cle	20	Tejada,Miguel, Bal	14	Crawford,Carl, TB	59	Crawford,Carl, TB	15
Jeter,Derek, NYY	16	Delgado,Carlos, Tor	11	Suzuki,Ichiro, Sea	36	Crisp,Coco, Cle	13
Roberts,Brian, Bal	15	Palmeiro,R, Bal	9	Figgins,Chone, Ana	34	Figgins,Chone, Ana	13
Eckstein,David, Ana	14	8 tied with	8	Roberts,Brian, Bal	29	Sanchez,Alex, Det	13
Guzman,C, Min	13			Rodriguez,Alex, NYY	28	Roberts,Brian, Bal	12
Cairo,Miguel, NYY	12			Jeter,Derek, NYY	23	DeJesus,David, KC	11
Sanchez,Alex, Det	12			Lawton,Matt, Cle	23	Suzuki,Ichiro, Sea	11
Blanco,Henry, Min	11			Hunter,Torii, Min	21	Uribe,Juan, CWS	11
Uribe,Juan, CWS	11			Lugo,Julio, TB	21	Jones,Jacque, Min	10
Figgins,Chone, Ana	10			Winn,Randy, Sea	21	2 tied with	9

Intentional Walks		Hit By Pitch		Grounded Into DP		Grounded Into DP Pct	
						(minimum 50 GIDP Ops)	
Suzuki,Ichiro, Sea	19	Hafner,Travis, Cle	17	Posada,Jorge, NYY	24	Munson,Eric, Det	0.02
Palmeiro,R, Bal	15	Millar,Kevin, Bos	17	Tejada,Miguel, Bal	24	Matthews Jr.,G, Tex	0.02
Ramirez,Manny, Bos	15	Guillen,Jose, Ana	15	Hunter,Torii, Min	23	Brown,Dee, KC	0.02
Guerrero,V, Ana	14	Cairo,Miguel, NYY	14	Konerko,Paul, CWS	23	Crawford,Carl, TB	0.02
Delgado,Carlos, Tor	12	Jeter,Derek, NYY	14	Chavez,Er, Oak	21	Roberts,Brian, Bal	0.03
Teixeira,Mark, Tex	12	Delgado,Carlos, Tor	13	Lawton,Matt, Cle	21	DaVanon,Jeff, Ana	0.03
Martinez,V, Cle	11	Eckstein,David, Ana	13	Hall,Toby, TB	20	Anderson,G, Ana	0.03
Chavez,Er, Oak	10	Ford,Lew, Min	13	5 tied with	19	Barajas,Rod, Tex	0.04
Koskie,Corey, Min	10	Kennedy,Adam, Ana	13			Fick,Robert, TB	0.04
Martinez,Edgar, Sea	10	5 tied with	12			Hairston Jr.,J, Bal	0.04

Leadoff Hitters OBP		Cleanup Hitters SLG		BA vs. LHP		BA vs. RHP	
(minimum 150 PA)		(minimum 150 PA)		(minimum 125 PA)		(minimum 377 PA)	
Suzuki,Ichiro, Sea	.418	Ramirez,Manny, Bos	.621	Suzuki,Ichiro, Sea	.404	Suzuki,Ichiro, Sea	.359
Damon,Johnny, Bos	.385	Tejada,Miguel, Bal	.591	Varitek,Jason, Bos	.350	Mora,Melvin, Bal	.352
Belliard,R, Cle	.384	Ortiz,David, Bos	.570	Sanchez,Alex, Det	.348	Hafner,Travis, Cle	.344
Lawton,Matt, Cle	.380	Lee,Ca, CWS	.567	Byrnes,Eric, Oak	.344	Durazo,Erubiel, Oak	.340
Stewart,Sh, Min	.380	Guerrero,V, Ana	.561	Rodriguez,Ivan, Det	.343	Guerrero,V, Ana	.335
DeJesus,David, KC	.376	Delgado,Carlos, Tor	.535	Guerrero,V, Ana	.342	Ortiz,David, Bos	.326
Williams,B, NYY	.371	Teixeira,Mark, Tex	.530	Cairo,Miguel, NYY	.336	Damon,Johnny, Bos	.319
Rowand,Aaron, CWS	.369	Thomas,Frank, CWS	.523	Kotsay,Mark, Oak	.336	Lopez,Javy, Bal	.316
Byrnes,Eric, Oak	.368	Morneau,Justin, Min	.519	Baldelli,Rocco, TB	.331	Matsui,Hideki, NYY	.314
Young,Michael, Tex	.368	Anderson,G, Ana	.493	Young,Michael, Tex	.330	Ramirez,Manny, Bos	.309

Home BA		Away BA		OBP vs. LHP		OBP vs. RHP	
(minimum 251 PA)		(minimum 251 PA)		(minimum 125 PA)		(minimum 377 PA)	
Mora,Melvin, Bal	.356	Suzuki,Ichiro, Sea	.405	Ramirez,Manny, Bos	.446	Hafner,Travis, Cle	.433
Rodriguez,Ivan, Det	.354	Guerrero,V, Ana	.335	Suzuki,Ichiro, Sea	.444	Mora,Melvin, Bal	.419
Millar,Kevin, Bos	.350	Matsui,Hideki, NYY	.327	Guerrero,V, Ana	.434	Durazo,Erubiel, Oak	.419
Young,Michael, Tex	.346	Mora,Melvin, Bal	.327	Varitek,Jason, Bos	.426	Ortiz,David, Bos	.411
Kotsay,Mark, Oak	.346	Durazo,Erubiel, Oak	.325	Sheffield,Gary, NYY	.423	Posada,Jorge, NYY	.407
Suzuki,Ichiro, Sea	.338	Hafner,Travis, Cle	.322	Rodriguez,Alex, NYY	.422	Matsui,Hideki, NYY	.405
Guerrero,V, Ana	.338	Tejada,Miguel, Bal	.318	Rodriguez,Ivan, Det	.420	Damon,Johnny, Bos	.403
Varitek,Jason, Bos	.336	Rodriguez,Ivan, Det	.317	Mora,Melvin, Bal	.418	Suzuki,Ichiro, Sea	.402
Damon,Johnny, Bos	.330	Rowand,Aaron, CWS	.317	Martinez,Edgar, Sea	.413	Palmeiro,R, Bal	.398
Jeter,Derek, NYY	.328	Guillen,Carlos, Det	.316	Young,Eri, Tex	.413	Millar,Kevin, Bos	.388

2004 American League Batting Leaders

BA Close & Late	
(minimum 50 PA)	
Suzuki,Ichiro, Sea	.393
Matsui,Hideki, NYY	.378
Gomez,Chris, Tor	.370
Harvey,Ken, KC	.358
Winn,Randy, Sea	.347
Anderson,G, Ana	.344
Crisp,Coco, Cle	.341
Posada,Jorge, NYY	.339
3 tied with	.333

BA Bases Loaded	
(minimum 10 PA)	
Guillen,Carlos, Det	.667
Broussard,Ben, Cle	.636
Gload,Ross, CWS	.615
Hatteberg,S, Oak	.615
Suzuki,Ichiro, Sea	.583
Konerko,Paul, CWS	.556
Uribe,Juan, CWS	.556
Hafner,Travis, Cle	.545
Reese,Pokey, Bos	.545
Mora,Melvin, Bal	.533

SLG vs. LHP	
(minimum 125 PA)	
Guerrero,V, Ana	.723
Rodriguez,Alex, NYY	.659
Mench,Kevin, Tex	.646
Ramirez,Manny, Bos	.631
Phelps,Josh, Tor-Cle	.618
Tejada,Miguel, Bal	.616
Byrnes,Eric, Oak	.599
Konerko,Paul, CWS	.577
Rowand,Aaron, CWS	.575
Wells,Vernon, Tor	.573

SLG vs. RHP	
(minimum 377 PA)	
Hafner,Travis, Cle	.690
Ortiz,David, Bos	.671
Ramirez,Manny, Bos	.605
Matsui,Hideki, NYY	.572
Mora,Melvin, Bal	.567
Durazo,Erubiel, Oak	.564
Teixeira,Mark, Tex	.558
Guerrero,V, Ana	.556
Blalock,Hank, Tex	.529
Sheffield,Gary, NYY	.529

Batting Average w/ RISP	
(minimum 100 PA)	
Suzuki,Ichiro, Sea	.372
Rodriguez,Ivan, Det	.361
Stewart,Sh, Min	.359
Damon,Johnny, Bos	.355
Ortiz,David, Bos	.350
Newhan,David, Bal	.343
Blalock,Hank, Tex	.343
Young,Michael, Tex	.342
Surhoff,B.J., Bal	.340
Ramirez,Manny, Bos	.340

At Bats Per Home Run	
(minimum 502 PA)	
Ramirez,Manny, Bos	13.2
Konerko,Paul, CWS	13.7
Ortiz,David, Bos	14.2
Delgado,Carlos, Tor	14.3
Teixeira,Mark, Tex	14.3
Valentin,Jo, CWS	15.0
Guerrero,V, Ana	15.7
Sheffield,Gary, NYY	15.9
Chavez,Er, Oak	16.4
Rodriguez,Alex, NYY	16.7

Pitches Seen	
(minimum 502 PA)	
Roberts,Brian, Bal	2916
Damon,Johnny, Bos	2895
Blake,Casey, Cle	2846
Blalock,Hank, Tex	2806
Rodriguez,Alex, NYY	2755
Young,Michael, Tex	2729
Ortiz,David, Bos	2676
Suzuki,Ichiro, Sea	2676
Tejada,Miguel, Bal	2669
Sheffield,Gary, NYY	2664

Pitches Per Plate App	
(minimum 502 PA)	
Blake,Casey, Cle	4.26
Dye,Jermaine, Oak	4.26
Crosby,Bo, Oak	4.17
Bellhorn,Mark, Bos	4.15
Damon,Johnny, Bos	4.12
Mora,Melvin, Bal	4.11
Varitek,Jason, Bos	4.09
Pena,Carlos, Det	4.05
Chavez,Er, Oak	4.05
Valentin,Jo, CWS	4.03

Pct Pitches Taken	
(minimum 1500 Pitches)	
Olerud,John, Sea-NYY	64.8
Hatteberg,S, Oak	63.8
Higginson,B, Det	62.5
Williams,B, NYY	62.2
Chavez,Er, Oak	62.1
Harris,Willie, CWS	62.0
Bellhorn,Mark, Bos	61.8
Posada,Jorge, NYY	61.8
Matsui,Hideki, NYY	61.6
Blake,Casey, Cle	61.2

Highest GB/FB Ratio	
(minimum 502 PA)	
Suzuki,Ichiro, Sea	3.54
Johnson,Re, Tor	2.13
Guzman,C, Min	2.13
Erstad,Darin, Ana	2.12
Bigbie,Larry, Bal	2.04
Jones,Jacque, Min	1.89
Winn,Randy, Sea	1.81
Berroa,Angel, KC	1.67
Posada,Jorge, NYY	1.67
Eckstein,David, Ana	1.66

Lowest GB/FB Ratio	
(minimum 502 PA)	
Valentin,Jo, CWS	0.52
Lee,Ca, CWS	0.69
Soriano,A, Tex	0.70
Crede,Joe, CWS	0.70
Palmeiro,R, Bal	0.71
Blalock,Hank, Tex	0.72
Byrnes,Eric, Oak	0.73
Ortiz,David, Bos	0.76
Millar,Kevin, Bos	0.76
Infante,Omar, Det	0.76

Stolen Base Success Pct	
(minimum 20 SBA)	
Ford,Lew, Min	90.9
Rodriguez,Alex, NYY	87.5
DaVanon,Jeff, Ana	85.7
Jeter,Derek, NYY	85.2
Baldelli,Rocco, TB	81.0
Lugo,Julio, TB	80.8
Crawford,Carl, TB	79.7
Soriano,A, Tex	78.3
Rowand,Aaron, CWS	77.3
Suzuki,Ichiro, Sea	76.6

Steals of Third	
Jeter,Derek, NYY	12
Figgins,Chone, Ana	10
Crawford,Carl, TB	9
Winn,Randy, Sea	8
Lugo,Julio, TB	7
Beltran,Carlos, KC	6
Roberts,Brian, Bal	6
4 tied with	5

Pct CS by Catchers	
(minimum 50 SBA)	
Blanco,Henry, Min	44.6
Wilson,Dan, Sea	29.0
Rodriguez,Ivan, Det	28.6
Miller,Damian, Oak	28.1
Hall,Toby, TB	27.9
Barajas,Rod, Tex	27.6
Zaun,Gregg, Tor	25.9
Posada,Jorge, NYY	25.6
Molina,Ben, Ana	25.0
Lopez,Javy, Bal	22.7

Best BPS on OutZ	
(minimum 502 PA)	
Roberts,Brian, Bal	.675
Lopez,Javy, Bal	.584
Uribe,Juan, CWS	.571
Guerrero,V, Ana	.563
Konerko,Paul, CWS	.549
Johnson,Re, Tor	.533
Suzuki,Ichiro, Sea	.482
Lee,Ca, CWS	.474
Guillen,Carlos, Det	.467
Tejada,Miguel, Bal	.463

Worst BPS on OutZ	
(minimum 502 PA)	
Hafner,Travis, Cle	.035
Infante,Omar, Det	.113
Gerut,Jody, Cle	.114
Martinez,Edgar, Sea	.123
Williams,B, NYY	.141
Varitek,Jason, Bos	.154
Crosby,Bo, Oak	.188
Chavez,Er, Oak	.190
Jones,Jacque, Min	.195
Kennedy,Adam, Ana	.196

2004 American League Batting Leaders

Best OPS vs Fastballs	
(minimum 251 PA)	
Hafner,Travis, Cle	1.193
Guillen,Carlos, Det	1.078
Ramirez,Manny, Bos	1.065
Mora,Melvin, Bal	1.057
Durazo,Erubiel, Oak	1.056
Sheffield,Gary, NYY	1.054
Ortiz,David, Bos	1.041
Teixeira,Mark, Tex	1.022
Uribe,Juan, CWS	1.018
2 tied with	1.012

Best OPS vs Curveballs	
(minimum 50 PA)	
Ramirez,Manny, Bos	1.294
Chavez,Er, Oak	1.050
Guerrero,V, Ana	.990
Ibanez,Raul, Sea	.966
Sheffield,Gary, NYY	.941
Ortiz,David, Bos	.937
Roberts,Brian, Bal	.903
Guillen,Jose, Ana	.892
Hunter,Torii, Min	.886
Suzuki,Ichiro, Sea	.849

Best OPS vs Changeups	
(minimum 50 PA)	
Bigbie,Larry, Bal	1.198
Rodriguez,Ivan, Det	1.143
Chavez,Er, Oak	1.128
Guerrero,V, Ana	1.099
Mora,Melvin, Bal	1.081
Tejada,Miguel, Bal	1.054
Lopez,Javy, Bal	1.051
Baldelli,Rocco, TB	1.050
Byrnes,Eric, Oak	1.048
Stairs,Matt, KC	1.033

Best OPS vs Sliders	
(minimum 32 PA)	
Thomas,Frank, CWS	1.094
Guillen,Carlos, Det	1.091
Newhan,David, Bal	1.065
Williams,B, NYY	1.004
Guerrero,V, Ana	.979
Cuddyer,Mike, Min	.958
Lawton,Matt, Cle	.947
Crisp,Coco, Cle	.941
Mora,Melvin, Bal	.931
Kennedy,Adam, Ana	.925

OPS	
(minimum 502 PA)	
Ramirez,Manny, Bos	1.010
Hafner,Travis, Cle	.993
Guerrero,V, Ana	.989
Ortiz,David, Bos	.983
Mora,Melvin, Bal	.981
Teixeira,Mark, Tex	.930
Sheffield,Gary, NYY	.927
Guillen,Carlos, Det	.921
Durazo,Erubiel, Oak	.919
Matsui,Hideki, NYY	.912

OPS First Half	
(minimum 251 PA)	
Ramirez,Manny, Bos	1.119
Thomas,Frank, CWS	.997
Mora,Melvin, Bal	.989
Guerrero,V, Ana	.983
Rodriguez,Ivan, Det	.975
Ortiz,David, Bos	.954
Konerko,Paul, CWS	.951
Guillen,Carlos, Det	.949
Hafner,Travis, Cle	.947
Blalock,Hank, Tex	.941

OPS Second Half	
(minimum 251 PA)	
Delgado,Carlos, Tor	1.033
Ortiz,David, Bos	1.021
Guerrero,V, Ana	.997
Suzuki,Ichiro, Sea	.982
Lee,Ca, CWS	.975
Millar,Kevin, Bos	.974
Mora,Melvin, Bal	.973
Huff,Aubrey, TB	.965
Durazo,Erubiel, Oak	.953
Sheffield,Gary, NYY	.937

2004 National League Batting Leaders

Batting Average
(minimum 502 PA)

Bonds,Barry, SF	.362
Helton,Todd, Col	.347
Loretta,Mark, SD	.335
Beltre,Adrian, LA	.334
Pujols,Albert, StL	.331
Pierre,Juan, Fla	.326
Casey,Sean, Cin	.324
Kendall,Jason, Pit	.319
Ramirez,Aramis, ChC	.318
Berkman,Lance, Hou	.316

On Base Percentage
(minimum 502 PA)

Bonds,Barry, SF	.609
Helton,Todd, Col	.469
Berkman,Lance, Hou	.450
Drew,J.D., Atl	.436
Abreu,Bobby, Phi	.428
Edmonds,Jim, StL	.418
Pujols,Albert, StL	.415
Rolen,Scott, StL	.409
Kendall,Jason, Pit	.399
Thome,Jim, Phi	.396

Slugging Average
(minimum 502 PA)

Bonds,Barry, SF	.812
Pujols,Albert, StL	.657
Edmonds,Jim, StL	.643
Beltre,Adrian, LA	.629
Helton,Todd, Col	.620
Rolen,Scott, StL	.598
Thome,Jim, Phi	.581
Ramirez,Aramis, ChC	.578
Drew,J.D., Atl	.569
Dunn,Adam, Cin	.569

Home Runs

Beltre,Adrian, LA	48
Dunn,Adam, Cin	46
Pujols,Albert, StL	46
Bonds,Barry, SF	45
Edmonds,Jim, StL	42
Thome,Jim, Phi	42
Alou,Moises, ChC	39
Burnitz,Jeromy, Col	37
Finley,Steve, Ari-LA	36
Ramirez,Aramis, ChC	36

Games

Finley,Steve, Ari-LA	162
Pierre,Juan, Fla	162
Dunn,Adam, Cin	161
Lee,De, ChC	161
Berkman,Lance, Hou	160
Cabrera,Miguel, Fla	160
Wilkerson,Brad, Mon	160
5 tied with	159

Plate Appearances

Pierre,Juan, Fla	748
Izturis,Cesar, LA	728
Rollins,Jimmy, Phi	725
Abreu,Bobby, Phi	713
Podsednik,S, Mil	713
Giles,Brian, SD	711
Loretta,Mark, SD	707
Finley,Steve, Ari-LA	706
Biggio,Craig, Hou	700
Wilson,Jack, Pit	693

At Bats

Pierre,Juan, Fla	678
Izturis,Cesar, LA	670
Rollins,Jimmy, Phi	657
Wilson,Jack, Pit	652
Podsednik,S, Mil	640
Biggio,Craig, Hou	633
Patterson,C, ChC	631
Finley,Steve, Ari-LA	628
Loretta,Mark, SD	620
Jenkins,Geoff, Mil	617

Hits

Pierre,Juan, Fla	221
Loretta,Mark, SD	208
Wilson,Jack, Pit	201
Beltre,Adrian, LA	200
Pujols,Albert, StL	196
Izturis,Cesar, LA	193
Helton,Todd, Col	190
Rollins,Jimmy, Phi	190
Casey,Sean, Cin	185
Kendall,Jason, Pit	183

Singles

Pierre,Juan, Fla	184
Izturis,Cesar, LA	148
Kendall,Jason, Pit	148
Castillo,Luis, Fla	143
Loretta,Mark, SD	143
Womack,Tony, StL	140
Wilson,Jack, Pit	137
Miles,Aaron, Col	129
Burroughs,Sean, SD	128
Redman,Tike, Pit	122

Doubles

Overbay,Lyle, Mil	53
Pujols,Albert, StL	51
Helton,Todd, Col	49
Abreu,Bobby, Phi	47
Biggio,Craig, Hou	47
Loretta,Mark, SD	47
Casey,Sean, Cin	44
Lowell,Mike, Fla	44
Castilla,Vinny, Col	43
Rollins,Jimmy, Phi	43

Triples

Pierre,Juan, Fla	12
Rollins,Jimmy, Phi	12
Wilson,Jack, Pit	12
Izturis,Cesar, LA	9
Drew,J.D., Atl	8
Durham,Ray, SF	8
Freel,Ryan, Cin	8
Kent,Jeff, Hou	8
6 tied with	7

Total Bases

Pujols,Albert, StL	389
Beltre,Adrian, LA	376
Helton,Todd, Col	339
Alou,Moises, ChC	335
Dunn,Adam, Cin	323
Edmonds,Jim, StL	320
Ramirez,Aramis, ChC	316
Abreu,Bobby, Phi	312
Castilla,Vinny, Col	312
Cabrera,Miguel, Fla	309

Runs Scored

Pujols,Albert, StL	133
Bonds,Barry, SF	129
Rollins,Jimmy, Phi	119
Abreu,Bobby, Phi	118
Drew,J.D., Atl	118
Helton,Todd, Col	115
Wilkerson,Brad, Mon	112
Rolen,Scott, StL	109
Loretta,Mark, SD	108
Alou,Moises, ChC	106

RBI

Castilla,Vinny, Col	131
Rolen,Scott, StL	124
Pujols,Albert, StL	123
Beltre,Adrian, LA	121
Cabrera,Miguel, Fla	112
Edmonds,Jim, StL	111
Batista,Tony, Mon	110
Burnitz,Jeromy, Col	110
Kent,Jeff, Hou	107
2 tied with	106

Walks

Bonds,Barry, SF	232
Abreu,Bobby, Phi	127
Berkman,Lance, Hou	127
Helton,Todd, Col	127
Drew,J.D., Atl	118
Dunn,Adam, Cin	108
Wilkerson,Brad, Mon	106
Thome,Jim, Phi	104
Edmonds,Jim, StL	101
Bagwell,Jeff, Hou	96

Strikeouts

Dunn,Adam, Cin	195
Wilson,Craig, Pit	169
Patterson,C, ChC	168
Jenkins,Geoff, Mil	152
Wilkerson,Brad, Mon	152
Edmonds,Jim, StL	150
Cabrera,Miguel, Fla	148
Jones,Andruw, Atl	147
Thome,Jim, Phi	144
Cameron,Mike, NYM	143

2004 National League Batting Leaders

Sacrifice Hits		Sacrifice Flies		Stolen Bases		Caught Stealing	
Clayton,Royce, Col	24	Loretta,Mark, SD	16	Podsednik,S, Mil	70	Pierre,Juan, Fla	24
Everett,Adam, Hou	22	Kent,Jeff, Hou	11	Pierre,Juan, Fla	45	Podsednik,S, Mil	13
Benson,Kris, Pit-NYM	15	Batista,Tony, Mon	10	Abreu,Bobby, Phi	40	Bradley,Milton, LA	11
Hernandez,L, Mon	15	Renteria,Edgar, StL	10	Freel,Ryan, Cin	37	Renteria,Edgar, StL	11
Pierre,Juan, Fla	15	Giles,Brian, SD	9	Roberts,Dave, LA	33	Freel,Ryan, Cin	10
Oswalt,Roy, Hou	13	Pujols,Albert, StL	9	Chavez,En, Mon	32	Izturis,Cesar, LA	9
Schmidt,Jason, SF	13	5 tied with	8	Patterson,C, ChC	32	Patterson,C, ChC	9
Tomko,Brett, SF	13			Rollins,Jimmy, Phi	30	Rollins,Jimmy, Phi	9
4 tied with	12			Furcal,Rafael, Atl	29	Clark,Brady, Mil	8
				Beltran,Carlos, Hou	28	Kendall,Jason, Pit	8

Intentional Walks		Hit By Pitch		Grounded Into DP		Grounded Into DP Pct	
						(minimum 50 GIDP Ops)	
Bonds,Barry, SF	120	Wilson,Craig, Pit	30	Pierzynski,A, SF	27	Werth,Jayson, LA	0.01
Thome,Jim, Phi	24	LaRue,Jason, Cin	24	Ramirez,Aramis, ChC	25	Sledge,Terrmel, Mon	0.03
Helton,Todd, Col	19	Kendall,Jason, Pit	19	Jones,Andruw, Atl	24	Mackowiak,Rob, Pit	0.03
Berkman,Lance, Hou	14	Cora,Alex, LA	18	Kent,Jeff, Hou	23	Edmonds,Jim, StL	0.03
Piazza,Mike, NYM	14	Biggio,Craig, Hou	15	Castilla,Vinny, Col	22	Abreu,Bobby, Phi	0.03
Edmonds,Jim, StL	12	Pierzynski,A, SF	15	Grissom,M, SF	21	Rollins,Jimmy, Phi	0.04
Pujols,Albert, StL	12	Rolen,Scott, StL	13	Lo Duca,Paul, LA-Fla	21	Tucker,Michael, SF	0.04
Ausmus,Brad, Hou	11	5 tied with	12	Pujols,Albert, StL	21	Everett,Adam, Hou	0.04
Dunn,Adam, Cin	11			Cabrera,Miguel, Fla	20	Bonds,Barry, SF	0.05
Gonzalez,LE, Ari	11			4 tied with	19	Michaels,Jason, Phi	0.05

Leadoff Hitters OBP		Cleanup Hitters SLG		BA vs. LHP		BA vs. RHP	
(minimum 150 PA)		(minimum 150 PA)		(minimum 125 PA)		(minimum 377 PA)	
Kendall,Jason, Pit	.404	Bonds,Barry, SF	.817	Pujols,Albert, StL	.379	Bonds,Barry, SF	.397
Freel,Ryan, Cin	.389	Beltre,Adrian, LA	.657	Renteria,Edgar, StL	.366	Helton,Todd, Col	.360
Pierre,Juan, Fla	.382	Alou,Moises, ChC	.612	Loretta,Mark, SD	.352	Beltre,Adrian, LA	.347
Wilkerson,Brad, Mon	.382	Rolen,Scott, StL	.604	Lowell,Mike, Fla	.344	Pierre,Juan, Fla	.334
Walker,To, ChC	.370	Thome,Jim, Phi	.577	Durham,Ray, SF	.333	Casey,Sean, Cin	.332
Durham,Ray, SF	.365	Dunn,Adam, Cin	.563	Polanco,P, Phi	.327	Berkman,Lance, Hou	.330
Rollins,Jimmy, Phi	.360	Castilla,Vinny, Col	.553	Hillenbrand,S, Ari	.325	Estrada,Johnny, Atl	.329
Womack,Tony, StL	.352	Lowell,Mike, Fla	.541	Klesko,Ryan, SD	.325	Loretta,Mark, SD	.329
Burroughs,Sean, SD	.343	Piazza,Mike, NYM	.534	Nevin,Phil, SD	.324	Ramirez,Aramis, ChC	.328
Furcal,Rafael, Atl	.343	Overbay,Lyle, Mil	.533	Grissom,M, SF	.320	Kendall,Jason, Pit	.325

Home BA		Away BA		OBP vs. LHP		OBP vs. RHP	
(minimum 251 PA)		(minimum 251 PA)		(minimum 125 PA)		(minimum 377 PA)	
Bonds,Barry, SF	.412	Loretta,Mark, SD	.368	Bonds,Barry, SF	.519	Bonds,Barry, SF	.656
Helton,Todd, Col	.368	Casey,Sean, Cin	.361	Pujols,Albert, StL	.465	Helton,Todd, Col	.492
Hillenbrand,S, Ari	.347	Estrada,Johnny, Atl	.351	Nevin,Phil, SD	.431	Berkman,Lance, Hou	.464
Alou,Moises, ChC	.339	Rolen,Scott, StL	.346	Loretta,Mark, SD	.431	Drew,J.D., Atl	.450
Pierre,Juan, Fla	.338	Beltre,Adrian, LA	.342	Lowell,Mike, Fla	.429	Abreu,Bobby, Phi	.438
Pujols,Albert, StL	.332	Pujols,Albert, StL	.330	Renteria,Edgar, StL	.429	Thome,Jim, Phi	.435
Beltre,Adrian, LA	.326	Bell,David, Phi	.326	Helton,Todd, Col	.413	Edmonds,Jim, StL	.423
Durham,Ray, SF	.323	Helton,Todd, Col	.326	Alfonzo,E, SF	.411	Giles,Brian, SD	.418
Burnitz,Jeromy, Col	.322	Ramirez,Aramis, ChC	.321	Drew,J.D., Atl	.408	Pujols,Albert, StL	.401
Womack,Tony, StL	.322	Kendall,Jason, Pit	.316	Abreu,Bobby, Phi	.408	Estrada,Johnny, Atl	.401

2004 National League Batting Leaders

BA Close & Late		BA Bases Loaded		SLG vs. LHP		SLG vs. RHP	
(minimum 50 PA)		(minimum 10 PA)		(minimum 125 PA)		(minimum 377 PA)	
Grudzielanek,M, ChC	.457	Rolen,Scott, StL	.583	Pujols,Albert, StL	.741	Bonds,Barry, SF	.956
Bautista,Da, Ari	.386	Lo Duca,Paul, LA-Fla	.563	Lowell,Mike, Fla	.672	Beltre,Adrian, LA	.672
Ensberg,Morgan, Hou	.383	Nevin,Phil, SD	.556	Hernandez,Jose, LA	.627	Helton,Todd, Col	.669
Wilson,Jack, Pit	.379	Batista,Tony, Mon	.500	Lee,De, ChC	.595	Edmonds,Jim, StL	.651
Burroughs,Sean, SD	.377	Byrd,Marlon, Phi	.500	Bonds,Barry, SF	.583	Thome,Jim, Phi	.641
Bell,David, Phi	.371	Conine,Jeff, Fla	.500	Nevin,Phil, SD	.582	Pujols,Albert, StL	.637
Furcal,Rafael, Atl	.370	Klesko,Ryan, SD	.500	Grissom,M, SF	.575	Dunn,Adam, Cin	.618
Beltre,Adrian, LA	.366	Lamb,Mike, Hou	.471	Burnitz,Jeromy, Col	.574	Berkman,Lance, Hou	.608
Klesko,Ryan, SD	.358	Cabrera,Miguel, Fla	.462	Jones,Chipper, Atl	.557	Drew,J.D., Atl	.593
Matheny,Mike, StL	.355	3 tied with	.455	Gonzalez,LE, Ari	.554	Ramirez,Aramis, ChC	.591

Batting Average w/ RISP		At Bats Per Home Run		Pitches Seen		Pitches Per Plate App	
(minimum 100 PA)		(minimum 502 PA)				(minimum 502 PA)	
Bonds,Barry, SF	.394	Bonds,Barry, SF	8.3	Abreu,Bobby, Phi	3081	Abreu,Bobby, Phi	4.32
Snow,J.T., SF	.361	Edmonds,Jim, StL	11.9	Wilkerson,Brad, Mon	2969	Wilkerson,Brad, Mon	4.32
Rolen,Scott, StL	.358	Thome,Jim, Phi	12.1	Dunn,Adam, Cin	2893	Dunn,Adam, Cin	4.25
Franco,Ju, Atl	.347	Dunn,Adam, Cin	12.3	Podsednik,S, Mil	2839	Edmonds,Jim, StL	4.23
Kendall,Jason, Pit	.346	Beltre,Adrian, LA	12.5	Bagwell,Jeff, Hou	2824	Kendall,Jason, Pit	4.21
Pujols,Albert, StL	.343	Pujols,Albert, StL	12.9	Kendall,Jason, Pit	2772	Burrell,Pat, Phi	4.21
Estrada,Johnny, Atl	.338	Sosa,Sammy, ChC	13.7	Helton,Todd, Col	2757	Jimenez,D, Cin	4.17
Sledge,Terrmel, Mon	.337	Burnitz,Jeromy, Col	14.6	Berkman,Lance, Hou	2727	Bagwell,Jeff, Hou	4.16
Ramirez,Aramis, ChC	.336	Rolen,Scott, StL	14.7	Cabrera,Miguel, Fla	2724	Castillo,Luis, Fla	4.09
2 tied with	.333	Ramirez,Aramis, ChC	15.2	Jimenez,D, Cin	2717	Durham,Ray, SF	4.07

Pct Pitches Taken		Highest GB/FB Ratio		Lowest GB/FB Ratio		Stolen Base Success Pct	
(minimum 1500 Pitches)		(minimum 502 PA)		(minimum 502 PA)		(minimum 20 SBA)	
Bonds,Barry, SF	72.0	Castillo,Luis, Fla	3.48	Cameron,Mike, NYM	0.58	Beltran,Carlos, Hou	100.0
Zeile,Todd, NYM	66.4	Pierre,Juan, Fla	2.41	Rolen,Scott, StL	0.62	Roberts,Dave, LA	97.1
Jimenez,D, Cin	65.1	Clayton,Royce, Col	2.17	Gonzalez,Al, Fla	0.64	Reyes,Jose, NYM	90.5
Abreu,Bobby, Phi	64.8	Burroughs,Sean, SD	2.02	Lowell,Mike, Fla	0.65	Abreu,Bobby, Phi	88.9
Kendall,Jason, Pit	64.6	Chavez,En, Mon	2.02	Wilkerson,Brad, Mon	0.66	Podsednik,S, Mil	84.3
Castillo,Luis, Fla	64.1	Bautista,Da, Ari	2.02	Dunn,Adam, Cin	0.68	Castillo,Luis, Fla	84.0
Podsednik,S, Mil	63.2	Redman,Tike, Pit	1.98	Lieberthal,M, Phi	0.72	Womack,Tony, StL	83.9
Clark,Brady, Mil	62.1	Miles,Aaron, Col	1.95	Batista,Tony, Mon	0.74	Furcal,Rafael, Atl	82.9
Wilkerson,Brad, Mon	62.0	Green,Shawn, LA	1.79	Edmonds,Jim, StL	0.74	Chavez,En, Mon	82.1
Counsell,Craig, Mil	61.5	Womack,Tony, StL	1.74	Hidalgo,R, Hou-NYM	0.75	2 tied with	81.0

Steals of Third		Pct CS by Catchers		Best BPS on OutZ		Worst BPS on OutZ	
		(minimum 50 SBA)		(minimum 502 PA)		(minimum 502 PA)	
Beltran,Carlos, Hou	11	Schneider,B, Mon	47.8	Bonds,Barry, SF	1.120	Counsell,Craig, Mil	.089
Podsednik,S, Mil	10	Kendall,Jason, Pit	32.3	Pierre,Juan, Fla	.735	Encarnacion,J, LA-Fla	.107
Pierre,Juan, Fla	8	LaRue,Jason, Cin	29.6	Furcal,Rafael, Atl	.714	Dunn,Adam, Cin	.130
Reyes,Jose, NYM	6	Bako,Paul, ChC	29.4	Lowell,Mike, Fla	.663	Podsednik,S, Mil	.170
Sanders,Reggie, StL	6	Matheny,Mike, StL	28.3	Conine,Jeff, Fla	.662	Jones,Chipper, Atl	.170
Cabrera,O, Mon	5	Hernandez,Ra, SD	25.4	Grissom,M, SF	.618	Freel,Ryan, Cin	.174
Chavez,En, Mon	5	Lo Duca,Paul, LA-Fla	23.8	Cintron,Alex, Ari	.616	Burnitz,Jeromy, Col	.174
Roberts,Dave, LA	5	Ausmus,Brad, Hou	22.8	Berkman,Lance, Hou	.614	Sosa,Sammy, ChC	.189
4 tied with	4	Phillips,Jason, NYM	22.2	Ramirez,Aramis, ChC	.589	Womack,Tony, StL	.213
		Lieberthal,M, Phi	20.4	Alou,Moises, ChC	.577	Hidalgo,R, Hou-NYM	.216

2004 National League Batting Leaders

Best OPS vs Fastballs
(minimum 251 PA)

Bonds,Barry, SF	1.388
Drew,J.D., Atl	1.200
Edmonds,Jim, StL	1.183
Beltre,Adrian, LA	1.159
Thome,Jim, Phi	1.149
Helton,Todd, Col	1.136
Dunn,Adam, Cin	1.113
Berkman,Lance, Hou	1.112
Abreu,Bobby, Phi	1.104
Burnitz,Jeromy, Col	1.093

Best OPS vs Curveballs
(minimum 50 PA)

Pujols,Albert, StL	1.217
Jenkins,Geoff, Mil	1.192
Casey,Sean, Cin	1.115
Lee,De, ChC	1.025
Wilkerson,Brad, Mon	.975
Finley,Steve, Ari-LA	.918
Rolen,Scott, StL	.871
Grissom,M, SF	.839
Biggio,Craig, Hou	.833
Castilla,Vinny, Col	.831

Best OPS vs Changeups
(minimum 50 PA)

Pujols,Albert, StL	1.270
Giles,Marcus, Atl	1.225
Edmonds,Jim, StL	1.217
Bonds,Barry, SF	1.168
Snow,J.T., SF	1.127
Bell,David, Phi	1.093
Dunn,Adam, Cin	1.035
Wilson,Craig, Pit	.979
Thome,Jim, Phi	.970
Helton,Todd, Col	.966

Best OPS vs Sliders
(minimum 32 PA)

Easley,Damion, Fla	1.241
Bonds,Barry, SF	1.109
Helton,Todd, Col	1.107
Bay,Jason, Pit	1.088
Klesko,Ryan, SD	1.085
Rivera,Juan, Mon	1.065
Giles,Brian, SD	1.050
Berkman,Lance, Hou	1.020
Kearns,Austin, Cin	1.012
Cintron,Alex, Ari	.995

OPS
(minimum 502 PA)

Bonds,Barry, SF	1.421
Helton,Todd, Col	1.089
Pujols,Albert, StL	1.072
Edmonds,Jim, StL	1.061
Beltre,Adrian, LA	1.017
Berkman,Lance, Hou	1.016
Rolen,Scott, StL	1.007
Drew,J.D., Atl	1.005
Thome,Jim, Phi	.977
Abreu,Bobby, Phi	.972

OPS First Half
(minimum 251 PA)

Bonds,Barry, SF	1.422
Helton,Todd, Col	1.078
Drew,J.D., Atl	1.062
Thome,Jim, Phi	1.059
Rolen,Scott, StL	1.014
Abreu,Bobby, Phi	1.009
Berkman,Lance, Hou	1.008
Casey,Sean, Cin	1.008
Pujols,Albert, StL	.998
Edmonds,Jim, StL	.984

OPS Second Half
(minimum 251 PA)

Bonds,Barry, SF	1.421
Edmonds,Jim, StL	1.157
Pujols,Albert, StL	1.154
Beltre,Adrian, LA	1.106
Helton,Todd, Col	1.099
Berkman,Lance, Hou	1.024
Alou,Moises, ChC	1.017
Ramirez,Aramis, ChC	.985
Walker,Larry, Col-StL	.965
Klesko,Ryan, SD	.946

2004 American League Pitching Leaders

Earned Run Average (minimum 162 IP)		Winning Percentage (minimum 15 Decisions)		Opponent Batting Average (minimum 162 IP)		Baserunners Per 9 IP (minimum 162 IP)	
Santana,Johan, Min	2.61	Schilling,Curt, Bos	.778	Santana,Johan, Min	.192	Santana,Johan, Min	8.64
Schilling,Curt, Bos	3.26	Santana,Johan, Min	.769	Lilly,Ted, Tor	.230	Schilling,Curt, Bos	9.77
Westbrook,Jake, Cle	3.38	Mulder,Mark, Oak	.680	Martinez,Pedro, Bos	.238	Radke,Brad, Min	10.69
Radke,Brad, Min	3.48	Hudson,Tim, Oak	.667	Schilling,Curt, Bos	.239	Martinez,Pedro, Bos	11.20
Hudson,Tim, Oak	3.53	Rogers,Kenny, Tex	.667	Garcia,Frddy, Sea-CWS	.242	Garcia,Frddy, Sea-CWS	11.27
Lopez,Rodrigo, Bal	3.59	Rincon,Juan, Min	.647	Harden,Rich, Oak	.242	Westbrook,Jake, Cle	11.43
Garcia,Frddy, Sea-CWS	3.81	Martinez,Pedro, Bos	.640	Bonderman,J, Det	.242	Buehrle,Mark, CWS	11.59
Buehrle,Mark, CWS	3.89	Lee,Cl, Cle	.636	Escobar,Kelvim, Ana	.244	Lopez,Rodrigo, Bal	11.60
Martinez,Pedro, Bos	3.90	Lieber,Jon, NYY	.636	Arroyo,Bronson, Bos	.249	Escobar,Kelvim, Ana	11.88
Escobar,Kelvim, Ana	3.93	Silva,Carlos, Min	.636	Sabathia,C.C., Cle	.252	Hudson,Tim, Oak	11.93

Games		Games Started		Complete Games		Shutouts	
Quantrill,Paul, NYY	86	Buehrle,Mark, CWS	35	Mulder,Mark, Oak	5	Bonderman,J, Det	2
Gordon,Tom, NYY	80	Rogers,Kenny, Tex	35	Ponson,Sidney, Bal	5	Hudson,Tim, Oak	2
Rincon,Juan, Min	77	Colon,Bartolo, Ana	34	Westbrook,Jake, Cle	5	Ponson,Sidney, Bal	2
Ryan,B.J., Bal	76	Lohse,Kyle, Min	34	Buehrle,Mark, CWS	4	27 tied with	1
Timlin,Mike, Bos	76	Radke,Brad, Min	34	Hudson,Tim, Oak	3		
Myers,Mike, Sea-Bos	75	Santana,Johan, Min	34	May,Darrell, KC	3		
Marte,Damaso, CWS	74	Zito,Barry, Oak	34	Schilling,Curt, Bos	3		
Rivera,Mariano, NYY	74	12 tied with	33	12 tied with	2		
Romero,J.C., Min	74						
2 tied with	73						

Wins		Losses		Innings Pitched		Batters Faced	
Schilling,Curt, Bos	21	May,Darrell, KC	19	Buehrle,Mark, CWS	245.1	Buehrle,Mark, CWS	1016
Santana,Johan, Min	20	Franklin,Ryan, Sea	16	Santana,Johan, Min	228.0	Ponson,Sidney, Bal	954
Colon,Bartolo, Ana	18	Hendrickson,M, TB	15	Schilling,Curt, Bos	226.2	Mulder,Mark, Oak	952
Rogers,Kenny, Tex	18	Johnson,Jason, Det	15	Mulder,Mark, Oak	225.2	Rogers,Kenny, Tex	935
Mulder,Mark, Oak	17	Ponson,Sidney, Bal	15	Radke,Brad, Min	219.2	Maroth,Mike, Det	928
Buehrle,Mark, CWS	16	6 tied with	13	Garland,Jon, CWS	217.0	Zito,Barry, Oak	926
Martinez,Pedro, Bos	16			Maroth,Mike, Det	217.0	Garland,Jon, CWS	923
9 tied with	14			Martinez,Pedro, Bos	217.0	Schilling,Curt, Bos	910
				Ponson,Sidney, Bal	215.2	Martinez,Pedro, Bos	903
				Westbrook,Jake, Cle	215.2	Radke,Brad, Min	901

Strikeouts		Walks Allowed		Hit Batters		Wild Pitches	
Santana,Johan, Min	265	Batista,Miguel, Tor	96	Arroyo,Bronson, Bos	20	Contreras,J, NYY-CWS	17
Martinez,Pedro, Bos	227	Zambrano,V, TB	96	Martinez,Pedro, Bos	16	Gregg,Kevin, Ana	13
Schilling,Curt, Bos	203	Cabrera,Daniel, Bal	89	Wakefield,Tim, Bos	16	Batista,Miguel, Tor	12
Escobar,Kelvim, Ana	191	Lilly,Ted, Tor	89	Zambrano,V, TB	16	Cabrera,Daniel, Bal	12
Garcia,Frddy, Sea-CWS	184	Contreras,J, NYY-CWS	84	Park,Chan Ho, Tex	13	Vazquez,Javier, NYY	12
Bonderman,J, Det	168	Mulder,Mark, Oak	83	Hudson,Tim, Oak	12	Knotts,Gary, Det	11
Lilly,Ted, Tor	168	Harden,Rich, Oak	81	Mulder,Mark, Oak	12	Lackey,John, Ana	11
Harden,Rich, Oak	167	Lee,Cl, Cle	81	Villone,Ron, Sea	12	Bell,Rob, TB	10
Buehrle,Mark, CWS	165	Zito,Barry, Oak	81	5 tied with	11	Maroth,Mike, Det	10
Zito,Barry, Oak	163	3 tied with	76			Mulder,Mark, Oak	10

2004 American League Pitching Leaders

Runs Allowed		Hits Allowed		Doubles Allowed		Home Runs Allowed	
Lowe,Derek, Bos	138	Ponson,Sidney, Bal	265	Rogers,Kenny, Tex	59	Moyer,Jamie, Sea	44
Ponson,Sidney, Bal	136	Buehrle,Mark, CWS	257	May,Darrell, KC	58	Colon,Bartolo, Ana	38
May,Darrell, KC	130	Silva,Carlos, Min	255	Anderson,Brian, KC	54	May,Darrell, KC	38
Lohse,Kyle, Min	128	Rogers,Kenny, Tex	248	Schilling,Curt, Bos	54	Garland,Jon, CWS	34
Moyer,Jamie, Sea	127	Maroth,Mike, Det	244	Redman,Mark, Oak	51	Anderson,Brian, KC	33
Garland,Jon, CWS	125	Lohse,Kyle, Min	240	Franklin,Ryan, Sea	50	Buehrle,Mark, CWS	33
Loaiza,E, CWS-NYY	124	May,Darrell, KC	234	Colon,Bartolo, Ana	49	Franklin,Ryan, Sea	33
Anderson,Brian, KC	123	Drese,Ryan, Tex	233	Garcia,Frddy, Sea-CWS	49	Vazquez,Javier, NYY	33
Colon,Bartolo, Ana	122	Radke,Brad, Min	229	4 tied with	48	Loaiza,E, CWS-NYY	32
2 tied with	121	2 tied with	224			Contreras,J, NYY-CWS	31

Run Support Per Nine IP		% Pitches In Strike Zone		Pitches Per Start		Pitches Per Batter	
(minimum 162 IP)		(minimum 162 IP)		(minimum 30 GS)		(minimum 162 IP)	
Schilling,Curt, Bos	7.54	Schilling,Curt, Bos	61.9	Zito,Barry, Oak	108.5	Silva,Carlos, Min	3.33
Lowe,Derek, Bos	7.29	Lieber,Jon, NYY	59.8	Schilling,Curt, Bos	106.6	Lieber,Jon, NYY	3.40
Colon,Bartolo, Ana	7.00	Radke,Brad, Min	59.6	Garcia,Frddy, Sea-CWS	106.1	Drese,Ryan, Tex	3.46
Rogers,Kenny, Tex	6.85	Mussina,Mike, NYY	59.3	Martinez,Pedro, Bos	105.7	Mulder,Mark, Oak	3.46
Lieber,Jon, NYY	6.83	Wakefield,Tim, Bos	58.1	Buehrle,Mark, CWS	105.6	Ponson,Sidney, Bal	3.47
Buehrle,Mark, CWS	6.64	Silva,Carlos, Min	57.7	Escobar,Kelvim, Ana	104.0	Hudson,Tim, Oak	3.48
Mulder,Mark, Oak	6.54	Johnson,Jason, Det	57.0	Sabathia,C.C., Cle	103.5	Westbrook,Jake, Cle	3.51
Westbrook,Jake, Cle	6.47	Colon,Bartolo, Ana	56.7	Lilly,Ted, Tor	103.3	Hendrickson,M, TB	3.58
Robertson,Nate, Det	6.36	Lee,Cl, Cle	56.7	Garland,Jon, CWS	102.8	Maroth,Mike, Det	3.60
Contreras,J, NYY-CWS	6.34	Ponson,Sidney, Bal	56.7	Moyer,Jamie, Sea	101.8	Wakefield,Tim, Bos	3.60

Quality Starts		Easy Saves		Regular Saves		Tough Saves	
Santana,Johan, Min	25	Rivera,Mariano, NYY	36	Cordero,F, Tex	20	Guardado,Eddie, Sea	4
Radke,Brad, Min	24	Cordero,F, Tex	27	Nathan,Joe, Min	19	Rodriguez,Fr, Ana	4
Buehrle,Mark, CWS	23	Nathan,Joe, Min	24	Rivera,Mariano, NYY	15	Affeldt,Jeremy, KC	3
Martinez,Pedro, Bos	22	Percival,Troy, Ana	23	Baez,Danys, TB	13	Frasor,Jason, Tor	3
Schilling,Curt, Bos	22	Foulke,Keith, Bos	20	Foulke,Keith, Bos	12	Cordero,F, Tex	2
Drese,Ryan, Tex	20	Julio,Jorge, Bal	17	Dotel,Octavio, Oak	9	Dotel,Octavio, Oak	2
Escobar,Kelvim, Ana	19	Urbina,Ugueth, Det	17	Percival,Troy, Ana	9	Rivera,Mariano, NYY	2
5 tied with	18	Baez,Danys, TB	16	Guardado,Eddie, Sea	6	Takatsu,Shingo, CWS	2
		3 tied with	11	Takatsu,Shingo, CWS	6	17 tied with	1
				Wickman,Bob, Cle	6		

Stolen Bases Allowed		Caught Stealing Off		Stolen Base Pct Allowed		Pickoffs	
				(minimum 162 IP)			
Lowe,Derek, Bos	34	Mulder,Mark, Oak	13	Anderson,Brian, KC	20.0	Buehrle,Mark, CWS	10
Wakefield,Tim, Bos	33	Batista,Miguel, Tor	11	Rogers,Kenny, Tex	28.6	Mulder,Mark, Oak	9
Contreras,J, NYY-CWS	29	Contreras,J, NYY-CWS	11	Vazquez,Javier, NYY	28.6	Redman,Mark, Oak	9
Escobar,Kelvim, Ana	24	Maroth,Mike, Det	11	Colon,Bartolo, Ana	33.3	Rogers,Kenny, Tex	6
Martinez,Pedro, Bos	19	Sele,Aaron, Ana	11	Buehrle,Mark, CWS	38.5	Schoeneweis,S, CWS	6
Reyes,Dennys, KC	19	Schoeneweis,S, CWS	10	Redman,Mark, Oak	38.5	Maroth,Mike, Det	5
Davis,Ja, Cle	18	Franklin,Ryan, Sea	9	Franklin,Ryan, Sea	43.8	May,Darrell, KC	5
May,Darrell, KC	17	May,Darrell, KC	9	Arroyo,Bronson, Bos	44.4	Zito,Barry, Oak	5
Sabathia,C.C., Cle	17	7 tied with	8	Batista,Miguel, Tor	45.0	4 tied with	4
Lohse,Kyle, Min	16			Santana,Johan, Min	46.2		

2004 American League Pitching Leaders

Strikeouts Per 9 IP		Opp On-Base Percentage		Opp Slugging Average		Hits Per Nine Innings	
(minimum 162 IP)		(minimum 162 IP)		(minimum 162 IP)		(minimum 162 IP)	
Santana,Johan, Min	10.46	Santana,Johan, Min	.249	Santana,Johan, Min	.315	Santana,Johan, Min	6.16
Martinez,Pedro, Bos	9.41	Schilling,Curt, Bos	.271	Harden,Rich, Oak	.366	Lilly,Ted, Tor	7.80
Escobar,Kelvim, Ana	8.25	Radke,Brad, Min	.291	Hudson,Tim, Oak	.366	Martinez,Pedro, Bos	8.00
Bonderman,J, Det	8.22	Martinez,Pedro, Bos	.301	Westbrook,Jake, Cle	.386	Harden,Rich, Oak	8.11
Lee,Cl, Cle	8.09	Garcia,Frddy, Sea-CWS	.303	Schilling,Curt, Bos	.387	Schilling,Curt, Bos	8.18
Schilling,Curt, Bos	8.06	Westbrook,Jake, Cle	.308	Escobar,Kelvim, Ana	.388	Bonderman,J, Det	8.22
Contreras,J, NYY-CWS	7.93	Lopez,Rodrigo, Bal	.310	Garcia,Frddy, Sea-CWS	.389	Garcia,Frddy, Sea-CWS	8.23
Harden,Rich, Oak	7.92	Buehrle,Mark, CWS	.312	Lopez,Rodrigo, Bal	.392	Escobar,Kelvim, Ana	8.29
Garcia,Frddy, Sea-CWS	7.89	Arroyo,Bronson, Bos	.314	Radke,Brad, Min	.393	Sabathia,C.C., Cle	8.43
Lilly,Ted, Tor	7.66	Escobar,Kelvim, Ana	.314	Lilly,Ted, Tor	.394	Arroyo,Bronson, Bos	8.61

Home Runs Per Nine IP		Batting Average vs. LHB		Batting Average vs. RHB		Opp BA w/ RISP	
(minimum 162 IP)		(minimum 125 BF)		(minimum 225 BF)		(minimum 125 BF)	
Hudson,Tim, Oak	0.38	Rincon,Juan, Min	.148	Santana,Johan, Min	.191	Zambrano,V, TB	.157
Drese,Ryan, Tex	0.69	Foulke,Keith, Bos	.185	Zambrano,V, TB	.219	Santana,Johan, Min	.169
Lowe,Derek, Bos	0.74	Gordon,Tom, NYY	.185	Bonderman,J, Det	.223	Martinez,Pedro, Bos	.195
Harden,Rich, Oak	0.76	Elarton,Scott, Cle	.190	Arroyo,Bronson, Bos	.227	Lopez,Rodrigo, Bal	.197
Westbrook,Jake, Cle	0.79	Santana,Johan, Min	.196	Harden,Rich, Oak	.227	Garcia,Frddy, Sea-CWS	.218
Arroyo,Bronson, Bos	0.86	Lilly,Ted, Tor	.196	Riley,Matt, Bal	.228	Reyes,Dennys, KC	.218
Escobar,Kelvim, Ana	0.91	Walker,Jamie, Det	.200	Bell,Rob, TB	.228	Bedard,Erik, Bal	.221
Schilling,Curt, Bos	0.91	Villone,Ron, Sea	.203	Hudson,Tim, Oak	.229	Schilling,Curt, Bos	.221
Radke,Brad, Min	0.94	Pineiro,Joel, Sea	.209	Sosa,Jorge, TB	.232	Westbrook,Jake, Cle	.223
Garcia,Frddy, Sea-CWS	0.94	Nathan,Joe, Min	.212	Escobar,Kelvim, Ana	.236	Radke,Brad, Min	.228

OBP vs. Leadoff Hitter		Strikeouts / Walks Ratio		Highest GB/FB Ratio		Lowest GB/FB Ratio	
(minimum 150 BF)		(minimum 162 IP)		(minimum 162 IP)		(minimum 162 IP)	
Schilling,Curt, Bos	.223	Schilling,Curt, Bos	5.80	Lowe,Derek, Bos	3.07	Lee,Cl, Cle	0.75
Vazquez,Javier, NYY	.255	Lieber,Jon, NYY	5.67	Westbrook,Jake, Cle	2.68	Lilly,Ted, Tor	0.78
Santana,Johan, Min	.264	Radke,Brad, Min	5.50	Hudson,Tim, Oak	2.61	Franklin,Ryan, Sea	0.78
Arroyo,Bronson, Bos	.275	Santana,Johan, Min	4.91	Drese,Ryan, Tex	2.20	May,Darrell, KC	0.78
Lopez,Rodrigo, Bal	.275	Martinez,Pedro, Bos	3.72	Mulder,Mark, Oak	2.03	Anderson,Brian, KC	0.81
Escobar,Kelvim, Ana	.280	Mussina,Mike, NYY	3.30	Batista,Miguel, Tor	1.80	Zito,Barry, Oak	0.84
Lieber,Jon, NYY	.283	Buehrle,Mark, CWS	3.24	Silva,Carlos, Min	1.61	Colon,Bartolo, Ana	0.87
Lackey,John, Ana	.284	Arroyo,Bronson, Bos	3.02	Ponson,Sidney, Bal	1.61	Martinez,Pedro, Bos	0.89
Colon,Bartolo, Ana	.286	Garcia,Frddy, Sea-CWS	2.88	Lieber,Jon, NYY	1.58	Vazquez,Javier, NYY	0.90
Washburn,J, Ana	.288	Escobar,Kelvim, Ana	2.51	Johnson,Jason, Det	1.55	Moyer,Jamie, Sea	0.91

Rel Opp BA w/ Runners On		Relief Opp BA w/ RISP		GIDP Induced		GIDP Per Nine IP	
(minimum 50 IP)		(minimum 50 IP)				(minimum 162 IP)	
Takatsu,Shingo, CWS	.155	Rivera,Mariano, NYY	.139	Mulder,Mark, Oak	37	Mulder,Mark, Oak	1.48
Nathan,Joe, Min	.159	Gordon,Tom, NYY	.153	Ponson,Sidney, Bal	35	Ponson,Sidney, Bal	1.46
Gordon,Tom, NYY	.162	Marte,Damaso, CWS	.161	Buehrle,Mark, CWS	33	Lowe,Derek, Bos	1.33
Rodriguez,Fr, Ana	.164	Francisco,F, Tex	.167	Silva,Carlos, Min	29	Silva,Carlos, Min	1.29
Dotel,Octavio, Oak	.176	Nathan,Joe, Min	.172	Lowe,Derek, Bos	27	Robertson,Nate, Det	1.24
Rivera,Mariano, NYY	.181	Dotel,Octavio, Oak	.176	Maroth,Mike, Det	27	Buehrle,Mark, CWS	1.21
Francisco,F, Tex	.183	Ryan,B.J., Bal	.176	Robertson,Nate, Det	27	Anderson,Brian, KC	1.19
Cordero,F, Tex	.197	Rodriguez,Fr, Ana	.181	Westbrook,Jake, Cle	27	Drese,Ryan, Tex	1.13
Baez,Danys, TB	.198	Almanzar,C, Tex	.190	Drese,Ryan, Tex	26	Westbrook,Jake, Cle	1.13
Urbina,Ugueth, Det	.200	Foulke,Keith, Bos	.194	Johnson,Jason, Det	24	Maroth,Mike, Det	1.12

2004 American League Pitching Leaders

Saves		Blown Saves		Save Pct (minimum 20 Save Ops)		Relief Earned Run Average (minimum 50 IP)	
Rivera,Mariano, NYY	53	Yan,Esteban, Det	10	Takatsu,Shingo, CWS	95.0	Nathan,Joe, Min	1.62
Cordero,F, Tex	49	Grimsley,Jason, KC-Bal	9	Nathan,Joe, Min	93.6	Rodriguez,Fr, Ana	1.82
Nathan,Joe, Min	44	Betancourt,R, Cle	7	Rivera,Mariano, NYY	93.0	Rivera,Mariano, NYY	1.94
Percival,Troy, Ana	33	Foulke,Keith, Bos	7	Baez,Danys, TB	90.9	Cordero,F, Tex	2.13
Foulke,Keith, Bos	32	Guardado,Eddie, Sea	7	Cordero,F, Tex	90.7	Foulke,Keith, Bos	2.17
Baez,Danys, TB	30	Riske,David, Cle	7	Urbina,Ugueth, Det	87.5	Gordon,Tom, NYY	2.21
Dotel,Octavio, Oak	22	Rodriguez,Fr, Ana	7	Percival,Troy, Ana	86.8	Ryan,B.J., Bal	2.28
Julio,Jorge, Bal	22	Romero,J.C., Min	7	Julio,Jorge, Bal	84.6	Takatsu,Shingo, CWS	2.31
Urbina,Ugueth, Det	21	4 tied with	6	Foulke,Keith, Bos	82.1	Mahay,Ron, Tex	2.55
Takatsu,Shingo, CWS	19			Dotel,Octavio, Oak	78.6	Rincon,Juan, Min	2.63

Relief Wins		Relief Losses		Holds		Relief Games	
Rincon,Juan, Min	11	Speier,Justin, Tor	8	Gordon,Tom, NYY	36	Quantrill,Paul, NYY	86
Gordon,Tom, NYY	9	Bradford,Chad, Oak	7	Rodriguez,Fr, Ana	27	Gordon,Tom, NYY	80
Shields,Scot, Ana	8	Grimsley,Jason, KC-Bal	7	Quantrill,Paul, NYY	22	Rincon,Juan, Min	77
Almanzar,C, Tex	7	Jimenez,Jose, Cle	7	Marte,Damaso, CWS	21	Ryan,B.J., Bal	76
Duchscherer,J, Oak	7	9 tied with	6	Mecir,Jim, Oak	21	Timlin,Mike, Bos	76
Quantrill,Paul, NYY	7			Ryan,B.J., Bal	21	Myers,Mike, Sea-Bos	75
Riske,David, Cle	7			Almanzar,C, Tex	20	Marte,Damaso, CWS	74
Romero,J.C., Min	7			Embree,Alan, Bos	20	Rivera,Mariano, NYY	74
7 tied with	6			Timlin,Mike, Bos	20	Romero,J.C., Min	74
				Politte,Cliff, CWS	19	2 tied with	73

Relief Innings		Relief Opp Batting Average (minimum 50 IP)		Relief Opp On Base Pct (minimum 50 IP)		Relief Opp Slugging Avg (minimum 50 IP)	
Shields,Scot, Ana	105.1	Rodriguez,Fr, Ana	.172	Gordon,Tom, NYY	.237	Rodriguez,Fr, Ana	.226
Duchscherer,J, Oak	96.1	Gordon,Tom, NYY	.180	Foulke,Keith, Bos	.254	Nathan,Joe, Min	.257
Quantrill,Paul, NYY	95.1	Rincon,Juan, Min	.181	Rodriguez,Fr, Ana	.256	Rincon,Juan, Min	.265
Gordon,Tom, NYY	89.2	Takatsu,Shingo, CWS	.182	Nathan,Joe, Min	.259	Ryan,B.J., Bal	.272
Gregg,Kevin, Ana	87.2	Nathan,Joe, Min	.187	Takatsu,Shingo, CWS	.259	Rivera,Mariano, NYY	.280
Ryan,B.J., Bal	87.0	Villone,Ron, Sea	.194	Rincon,Juan, Min	.265	Cordero,F, Tex	.283
Yan,Esteban, Det	87.0	Urbina,Ugueth, Det	.194	Ryan,B.J., Bal	.279	Gordon,Tom, NYY	.286
Rodriguez,Fr, Ana	84.0	Francisco,F, Tex	.198	Embree,Alan, Bos	.284	Takatsu,Shingo, CWS	.291
Foulke,Keith, Bos	83.0	Ryan,B.J., Bal	.200	Rivera,Mariano, NYY	.287	Francisco,F, Tex	.291
Rincon,Juan, Min	82.0	Foulke,Keith, Bos	.206	Walker,Jamie, Det	.297	Villone,Ron, Sea	.295

Inherited Runners Scrd % (minimum 30 IR)		Rel OBP 1st Batter Faced (minimum 40 BF)		Relief Opp BA Vs LHB (minimum 50 AB)		Relief Opp BA Vs RHB (minimum 50 AB)	
Field,Nate, KC	14.3	Villone,Ron, Sea	.130	Ryan,B.J., Bal	.094	Rodriguez,Fr, Ana	.127
Brocail,Doug, Tex	15.2	Takatsu,Shingo, CWS	.186	Marte,Damaso, CWS	.143	Takatsu,Shingo, CWS	.143
Gordon,Tom, NYY	16.2	Foulke,Keith, Bos	.194	Rincon,Juan, Min	.148	Nathan,Joe, Min	.160
Shouse,Brian, Tex	17.1	Donnelly,B, Ana	.200	Foulke,Keith, Bos	.185	Francisco,F, Tex	.165
Cerda,Jaime, KC	17.4	Bradford,Chad, Oak	.209	Gordon,Tom, NYY	.185	Gordon,Tom, NYY	.174
Rodriguez,Fr, Ana	20.0	Shields,Scot, Ana	.233	Villone,Ron, Sea	.187	Dotel,Octavio, Oak	.182
Bradford,Chad, Oak	21.4	Mateo,Julio, Sea	.244	Brocail,Doug, Tex	.190	Urbina,Ugueth, Det	.196
Proctor,Scott, NYY	22.6	Francisco,F, Tex	.250	Urbina,Ugueth, Det	.191	Villone,Ron, Sea	.199
Embree,Alan, Bos	22.7	Rincon,Ricardo, Oak	.254	Walker,Jamie, Det	.200	Romero,J.C., Min	.199
2 tied with	23.3	Miller,Matt, Cle	.255	Fultz,Aaron, Min	.212	Miller,Matt, Cle	.201

2004 American League Pitching Leaders

Fastest Average Fastball
(minimum 162 IP)

Harden,Rich, Oak	94.3
Sabathia,C.C., Cle	93.8
Escobar,Kelvim, Ana	93.5
Bonderman,J, Det	93.3
Batista,Miguel, Tor	92.8
Colon,Bartolo, Ana	92.5
Santana,Johan, Min	92.4
Contreras,J, NYY-CWS	92.1
Ponson,Sidney, Bal	92.1
Johnson,Jason, Det	91.8

Slowest Average Fastball
(minimum 162 IP)

Wakefield,Tim, Bos	75.9
Moyer,Jamie, Sea	81.6
Redman,Mark, Oak	84.7
Maroth,Mike, Det	85.0
May,Darrell, KC	85.0
Rogers,Kenny, Tex	86.4
Zito,Barry, Oak	86.8
Buehrle,Mark, CWS	87.1
Anderson,Brian, KC	87.3
Hendrickson,M, TB	87.5

Pitches 100+ Velocity

Colome,Jesus, TB	8
Cordero,F, Tex	4
Nunez,Franklin, TB	4
Davis,Ja, Cle	3
Harden,Rich, Oak	3
Affeldt,Jeremy, KC	1
Dotel,Octavio, Oak	1
Julio,Jorge, Bal	1
Politte,Cliff, CWS	1
Rodriguez,Fr, Ana	1

Pitches 95+ Velocity

Harden,Rich, Oak	746
Sabathia,C.C., Cle	509
Cordero,F, Tex	507
Sosa,Jorge, TB	472
Escobar,Kelvim, Ana	460
Julio,Jorge, Bal	454
Colome,Jesus, TB	388
Francisco,F, Tex	383
Colon,Bartolo, Ana	377
Davis,Ja, Cle	337

Pitches Less Than 80 MPH

Wakefield,Tim, Bos	1750
Moyer,Jamie, Sea	1448
Zito,Barry, Oak	1149
Maroth,Mike, Det	846
Redman,Mark, Oak	777
Arroyo,Bronson, Bos	704
Rogers,Kenny, Tex	640
Lilly,Ted, Tor	607
Buehrle,Mark, CWS	577
Radke,Brad, Min	573

Lowest % Fastballs
(minimum 162 IP)

Wakefield,Tim, Bos	9.3
Maroth,Mike, Det	40.0
Garcia,Frddy, Sea-CWS	45.0
Moyer,Jamie, Sea	45.7
Bonderman,J, Det	45.8
Robertson,Nate, Det	46.1
Santana,Johan, Min	46.9
Franklin,Ryan, Sea	48.3
Buehrle,Mark, CWS	48.7
Lilly,Ted, Tor	48.7

Highest % Fastballs
(minimum 162 IP)

Lowe,Derek, Bos	75.1
Colon,Bartolo, Ana	73.3
Drese,Ryan, Tex	73.2
Silva,Carlos, Min	69.1
Lee,Cl, Cle	65.8
Radke,Brad, Min	65.7
Sabathia,C.C., Cle	64.8
Hudson,Tim, Oak	64.2
Ponson,Sidney, Bal	63.3
Lackey,John, Ana	62.9

Highest % Curveballs
(minimum 162 IP)

Mussina,Mike, NYY	27.1
Lackey,John, Ana	26.8
Zito,Barry, Oak	23.8
Johnson,Jason, Det	22.5
Garcia,Frddy, Sea-CWS	16.2
Sabathia,C.C., Cle	15.3
Vazquez,Javier, NYY	14.5
Martinez,Pedro, Bos	14.4
Lilly,Ted, Tor	14.4
Arroyo,Bronson, Bos	13.1

Highest % Changeups
(minimum 162 IP)

Moyer,Jamie, Sea	31.0
Rogers,Kenny, Tex	29.2
Redman,Mark, Oak	25.5
Vazquez,Javier, NYY	23.1
Maroth,Mike, Det	18.7
Santana,Johan, Min	17.9
Radke,Brad, Min	17.7
Lilly,Ted, Tor	17.1
Martinez,Pedro, Bos	15.8
Franklin,Ryan, Sea	15.6

Highest % Sliders
(minimum 162 IP)

Lieber,Jon, NYY	29.8
Arroyo,Bronson, Bos	26.1
Robertson,Nate, Det	22.2
Bonderman,J, Det	22.2
Ponson,Sidney, Bal	21.4
Garcia,Frddy, Sea-CWS	20.0
Loaiza,E, CWS-NYY	18.2
Lohse,Kyle, Min	16.8
Franklin,Ryan, Sea	16.6
Santana,Johan, Min	16.1

2004 National League Pitching Leaders

Earned Run Average
(minimum 162 IP)

Peavy,Jake, SD	2.27
Johnson,Ra, Ari	2.60
Sheets,Ben, Mil	2.70
Zambrano,C, ChC	2.75
Clemens,Roger, Hou	2.98
Perez,Ol, Pit	2.98
Pavano,Carl, Fla	3.00
Schmidt,Jason, SF	3.20
Leiter,Al, NYM	3.21
Perez,Od, LA	3.25

Winning Percentage
(minimum 15 Decisions)

Clemens,Roger, Hou	.818
Carpenter,C, StL	.750
Lima,Jose, LA	.722
Schmidt,Jason, SF	.720
Peavy,Jake, SD	.714
Milton,Eric, Phi	.700
Pavano,Carl, Fla	.692
Jones,Todd, Cin-Phi	.688
Marquis,Jason, StL	.682
2 tied with	.667

Opponent Batting Average
(minimum 162 IP)

Johnson,Ra, Ari	.197
Schmidt,Jason, SF	.202
Perez,Ol, Pit	.207
Clemens,Roger, Hou	.217
Leiter,Al, NYM	.218
Zambrano,C, ChC	.225
Sheets,Ben, Mil	.226
Clement,Matt, ChC	.229
Peavy,Jake, SD	.236
Wright,Jar, Atl	.242

Baserunners Per 9 IP
(minimum 162 IP)

Johnson,Ra, Ari	8.46
Sheets,Ben, Mil	9.00
Schmidt,Jason, SF	9.80
Wells,David, SD	10.35
Perez,Od, LA	10.41
Carpenter,C, StL	10.63
Clemens,Roger, Hou	10.67
Perez,Ol, Pit	10.79
Maddux,Greg, ChC	11.00
Pavano,Carl, Fla	11.01

Games

Brower,Jim, SF	89
King,Ray, StL	86
Cormier,Rheal, Phi	84
Reitsma,Chris, Atl	84
Torres,Salomon, Pit	84
Eyre,Scott, SF	83
Stanton,Mike, NYM	83
Ayala,Luis, Mon	81
Lidge,Brad, Hou	80
Alfonseca,A, Atl	79

Games Started

Hernandez,L, Mon	35
Johnson,Ra, Ari	35
Oswalt,Roy, Hou	35
Webb,Brandon, Ari	35
8 tied with	34

Complete Games

Hernandez,L, Mon	9
Lidle,Cory, Cin-Phi	5
Sheets,Ben, Mil	5
Johnson,Ra, Ari	4
Schmidt,Jason, SF	4
Morris,Matt, StL	3
10 tied with	2

Shutouts

Lidle,Cory, Cin-Phi	3
Schmidt,Jason, SF	3
Hernandez,L, Mon	2
Ishii,Kazuhisa, LA	2
Johnson,Ra, Ari	2
Morris,Matt, StL	2
Oswalt,Roy, Hou	2
Pavano,Carl, Fla	2
18 tied with	1

Wins

Oswalt,Roy, Hou	20
Clemens,Roger, Hou	18
Pavano,Carl, Fla	18
Schmidt,Jason, SF	18
Johnson,Ra, Ari	16
Maddux,Greg, ChC	16
Suppan,Jeff, StL	16
Zambrano,C, ChC	16
8 tied with	15

Losses

Webb,Brandon, Ari	16
Fossum,Casey, Ari	15
Hernandez,L, Mon	15
Eaton,Adam, SD	14
Glavine,Tom, NYM	14
Johnson,Ra, Ari	14
Lawrence,Brian, SD	14
Sheets,Ben, Mil	14
4 tied with	13

Innings Pitched

Hernandez,L, Mon	255.0
Johnson,Ra, Ari	245.2
Oswalt,Roy, Hou	237.0
Sheets,Ben, Mil	237.0
Schmidt,Jason, SF	225.0
Pavano,Carl, Fla	222.1
Weaver,Jeff, LA	220.0
Clemens,Roger, Hou	214.1
Maddux,Greg, ChC	212.2
Glavine,Tom, NYM	212.1

Batters Faced

Hernandez,L, Mon	1053
Oswalt,Roy, Hou	983
Johnson,Ra, Ari	964
Sheets,Ben, Mil	937
Weaver,Jeff, LA	935
Webb,Brandon, Ari	933
Jennings,Jason, Col	925
Lidle,Cory, Cin-Phi	911
Pavano,Carl, Fla	909
Schmidt,Jason, SF	907

Strikeouts

Johnson,Ra, Ari	290
Sheets,Ben, Mil	264
Schmidt,Jason, SF	251
Perez,Ol, Pit	239
Clemens,Roger, Hou	218
Oswalt,Roy, Hou	206
Clement,Matt, ChC	190
Zambrano,C, ChC	188
Hernandez,L, Mon	186
Peavy,Jake, SD	173

Walks Allowed

Webb,Brandon, Ari	119
Ortiz,Ru, Atl	112
Estes,Shawn, Col	105
Jennings,Jason, Col	101
Ishii,Kazuhisa, LA	98
Leiter,Al, NYM	97
Hernandez,L, Mon	83
Trachsel,Steve, NYM	83
Perez,Ol, Pit	81
Zambrano,C, ChC	81

Hit Batters

Zambrano,C, ChC	20
Williams,J, SF	17
Weaver,Jeff, LA	14
Kim,Sunny, Mon	13
Clement,Matt, ChC	12
7 tied with	11

Wild Pitches

Webb,Brandon, Ari	17
Clement,Matt, ChC	14
Williams,Woody, StL	12
Brower,Jim, SF	10
Tomko,Brett, SF	10
Chacon,Shawn, Col	9
Vizcaino,Luis, Mil	9
Weaver,Jeff, LA	9
3 tied with	8

2004 National League Pitching Leaders

Runs Allowed	
Estes,Shawn, Col	133
Jennings,Jason, Col	125
Lidle,Cory, Cin-Phi	123
Morris,Matt, StL	116
Eaton,Adam, SD	113
Myers,Brett, Phi	113
Fossum,Casey, Ari	111
Webb,Brandon, Ari	111
Milton,Eric, Phi	110
2 tied with	108

Hits Allowed	
Jennings,Jason, Col	241
Hernandez,L, Mon	234
Oswalt,Roy, Hou	233
Lawrence,Brian, SD	226
Rueter,Kirk, SF	225
Lidle,Cory, Cin-Phi	224
Estes,Shawn, Col	223
Weaver,Jeff, LA	219
Maddux,Greg, ChC	218
Marquis,Jason, StL	215

Doubles Allowed	
Oswalt,Roy, Hou	57
Sheets,Ben, Mil	57
Williams,Woody, StL	53
Rueter,Kirk, SF	52
Acevedo,Jose, Cin	51
Fogg,Josh, Pit	50
Lawrence,Brian, SD	50
Weaver,Jeff, LA	50
Myers,Brett, Phi	49
2 tied with	48

Home Runs Allowed	
Milton,Eric, Phi	43
Maddux,Greg, ChC	35
Morris,Matt, StL	35
Lima,Jose, LA	33
Valdez,Ismael, SD-Fla	33
Fossum,Casey, Ari	31
Myers,Brett, Phi	31
Acevedo,Jose, Cin	30
Estes,Shawn, Col	30
Eaton,Adam, SD	28

Run Support Per Nine IP	
(minimum 162 IP)	
Ishii,Kazuhisa, LA	6.70
Estes,Shawn, Col	6.55
Milton,Eric, Phi	6.54
Peavy,Jake, SD	6.44
Myers,Brett, Phi	6.19
Zambrano,C, ChC	6.05
Oswalt,Roy, Hou	6.04
Tomko,Brett, SF	5.98
Marquis,Jason, StL	5.95
Thomson,John, Atl	5.90

% Pitches In Strike Zone	
(minimum 162 IP)	
Wells,David, SD	60.4
Sheets,Ben, Mil	59.6
Eaton,Adam, SD	59.2
Valdez,Ismael, SD-Fla	58.6
Willis,D, Fla	58.3
Lima,Jose, LA	57.9
Maddux,Greg, ChC	57.6
Perez,Ol, Pit	57.3
Oswalt,Roy, Hou	57.3
Myers,Brett, Phi	57.3

Pitches Per Start	
(minimum 30 GS)	
Schmidt,Jason, SF	112.7
Hernandez,L, Mon	112.2
Zambrano,C, ChC	111.8
Leiter,Al, NYM	108.2
Sheets,Ben, Mil	105.4
Perez,Ol, Pit	104.5
Clemens,Roger, Hou	104.0
Marquis,Jason, StL	103.9
Johnson,Ra, Ari	103.8
Glavine,Tom, NYM	102.9

Pitches Per Batter	
(minimum 162 IP)	
Maddux,Greg, ChC	3.35
Lima,Jose, LA	3.43
Lidle,Cory, Cin-Phi	3.44
Pavano,Carl, Fla	3.47
Lawrence,Brian, SD	3.47
Wells,David, SD	3.49
Thomson,John, Atl	3.52
Kennedy,Joe, Col	3.56
Valdez,Ismael, SD-Fla	3.57
Perez,Od, LA	3.58

Quality Starts	
Johnson,Ra, Ari	26
Weaver,Jeff, LA	25
Davis,Doug, Mil	24
Sheets,Ben, Mil	24
Clemens,Roger, Hou	23
Pavano,Carl, Fla	23
5 tied with	22

Easy Saves	
Graves,Danny, Cin	31
Benitez,A, Fla	29
Mesa,Jose, Pit	29
Chacon,Shawn, Col	28
Isringhausen,J, StL	27
Kolb,Danny, Mil	26
Hoffman,Trevor, SD	23
Gagne,Eric, LA	19
Smoltz,John, Atl	18
Hawkins,LaTroy, ChC	17

Regular Saves	
Gagne,Eric, LA	23
Smoltz,John, Atl	20
Hoffman,Trevor, SD	17
Benitez,A, Fla	15
Isringhausen,J, StL	15
Looper,Braden, NYM	14
Kolb,Danny, Mil	13
Mesa,Jose, Pit	13
Lidge,Brad, Hou	12
4 tied with	9

Tough Saves	
Smoltz,John, Atl	6
Isringhausen,J, StL	5
Herges,Matt, SF	4
Lidge,Brad, Hou	4
Benitez,A, Fla	3
Gagne,Eric, LA	3
Christiansen,J, SF	2
Valverde,Jose, Ari	2
18 tied with	1

Stolen Bases Allowed	
Webb,Brandon, Ari	31
Schmidt,Jason, SF	28
Maddux,Greg, ChC	26
Clemens,Roger, Hou	23
Mota,Guillermo, LA-Fla	21
Trachsel,Steve, NYM	19
Myers,Brett, Phi	18
Ortiz,Ru, Atl	18
Johnson,Ra, Ari	17
5 tied with	16

Caught Stealing Off	
Maddux,Greg, ChC	12
Clemens,Roger, Hou	10
Johnson,Ra, Ari	10
Webb,Brandon, Ari	10
Hernandez,L, Mon	9
Ishii,Kazuhisa, LA	9
Fossum,Casey, Ari	8
Glavine,Tom, NYM	8
Jennings,Jason, Col	8
Lidle,Cory, Cin-Phi	8

Stolen Base Pct Allowed	
(minimum 162 IP)	
Carpenter,C, StL	0.0
Rueter,Kirk, SF	25.0
Glavine,Tom, NYM	46.7
Perez,Ol, Pit	50.0
Wilson,Pa, Cin	50.0
Eaton,Adam, SD	54.5
Hampton,Mike, Atl	54.5
Oswalt,Roy, Hou	54.5
3 tied with	57.1

Pickoffs	
Capuano,Chris, Mil	6
Estes,Shawn, Col	5
Fassero,Jeff, Col-Ari	5
Kennedy,Joe, Col	5
Leiter,Al, NYM	5
Willis,D, Fla	5
5 tied with	4

2004 National League Pitching Leaders

Strikeouts Per 9 IP
(minimum 162 IP)

Perez,Ol, Pit	10.97
Johnson,Ra, Ari	10.62
Schmidt,Jason, SF	10.04
Sheets,Ben, Mil	10.03
Clement,Matt, ChC	9.45
Peavy,Jake, SD	9.36
Clemens,Roger, Hou	9.15
Zambrano,C, ChC	8.07
Oswalt,Roy, Hou	7.82
Wright,Jar, Atl	7.68

Opp On-Base Percentage
(minimum 162 IP)

Johnson,Ra, Ari	.241
Sheets,Ben, Mil	.255
Schmidt,Jason, SF	.272
Wells,David, SD	.285
Carpenter,C, StL	.291
Clemens,Roger, Hou	.292
Perez,Od, LA	.294
Perez,Ol, Pit	.295
Pavano,Carl, Fla	.302
Maddux,Greg, ChC	.303

Opp Slugging Average
(minimum 162 IP)

Johnson,Ra, Ari	.315
Schmidt,Jason, SF	.323
Clemens,Roger, Hou	.329
Wright,Jar, Atl	.337
Zambrano,C, ChC	.338
Leiter,Al, NYM	.354
Peavy,Jake, SD	.359
Perez,Ol, Pit	.359
Davis,Doug, Mil	.361
Webb,Brandon, Ari	.365

Hits Per Nine Innings
(minimum 162 IP)

Johnson,Ra, Ari	6.48
Schmidt,Jason, SF	6.60
Perez,Ol, Pit	6.66
Clemens,Roger, Hou	7.10
Leiter,Al, NYM	7.15
Zambrano,C, ChC	7.47
Sheets,Ben, Mil	7.63
Clement,Matt, ChC	7.71
Peavy,Jake, SD	7.90
Ishii,Kazuhisa, LA	8.11

Home Runs Per Nine IP
(minimum 162 IP)

Wright,Jar, Atl	0.53
Zambrano,C, ChC	0.60
Davis,Doug, Mil	0.61
Clemens,Roger, Hou	0.63
Oswalt,Roy, Hou	0.65
Pavano,Carl, Fla	0.65
Johnson,Ra, Ari	0.66
Benson,Kris, Pit-NYM	0.67
Peavy,Jake, SD	0.70
Schmidt,Jason, SF	0.72

Batting Average vs. LHB
(minimum 125 BF)

King,Ray, StL	.150
Johnson,Ra, Ari	.162
Vizcaino,Luis, Mil	.163
Linebrink,S, SD	.178
Kennedy,Joe, Col	.184
Lidge,Brad, Hou	.191
Schmidt,Jason, SF	.191
Mota,Guillermo, LA-Fla	.195
Willis,D, Fla	.200
Leiter,Al, NYM	.204

Batting Average vs. RHB
(minimum 225 BF)

Beckett,Josh, Fla	.192
Perez,Ol, Pit	.204
Johnson,Ra, Ari	.204
Brower,Jim, SF	.206
Pettitte,Andy, Hou	.208
Burnett,A.J., Fla	.211
Schmidt,Jason, SF	.212
Clemens,Roger, Hou	.217
Zambrano,C, ChC	.218
Byrd,Paul, Atl	.219

Opp BA w/ RISP
(minimum 125 BF)

Leiter,Al, NYM	.173
Perez,Ol, Pit	.180
Schmidt,Jason, SF	.180
Zambrano,C, ChC	.180
Peavy,Jake, SD	.185
Clemens,Roger, Hou	.193
Webb,Brandon, Ari	.195
Kennedy,Joe, Col	.197
Marquis,Jason, StL	.198
Johnson,Ra, Ari	.199

OBP vs. Leadoff Hitter
(minimum 150 BF)

Johnson,Ra, Ari	.200
Sheets,Ben, Mil	.218
Carpenter,C, StL	.250
Wells,David, SD	.260
Milton,Eric, Phi	.266
Pavano,Carl, Fla	.266
Willis,D, Fla	.273
Clement,Matt, ChC	.274
Maddux,Greg, ChC	.275
Schmidt,Jason, SF	.276

Strikeouts / Walks Ratio
(minimum 162 IP)

Sheets,Ben, Mil	8.25
Johnson,Ra, Ari	6.59
Wells,David, SD	5.05
Maddux,Greg, ChC	4.58
Carpenter,C, StL	4.00
Oswalt,Roy, Hou	3.32
Peavy,Jake, SD	3.26
Schmidt,Jason, SF	3.26
Perez,Ol, Pit	2.95
Eaton,Adam, SD	2.94

Highest GB/FB Ratio
(minimum 162 IP)

Webb,Brandon, Ari	3.47
Marquis,Jason, StL	2.14
Hampton,Mike, Atl	1.96
Lawrence,Brian, SD	1.79
Carpenter,C, StL	1.78
Maddux,Greg, ChC	1.73
Glavine,Tom, NYM	1.71
Perez,Od, LA	1.64
Estes,Shawn, Col	1.64
Lidle,Cory, Cin-Phi	1.63

Lowest GB/FB Ratio
(minimum 162 IP)

Milton,Eric, Phi	0.57
Ishii,Kazuhisa, LA	0.63
Perez,Ol, Pit	0.76
Valdez,Ismael, SD-Fla	0.87
Williams,Woody, StL	0.91
Eaton,Adam, SD	0.93
Leiter,Al, NYM	1.00
Weaver,Jeff, LA	1.01
Sheets,Ben, Mil	1.08
Wilson,Pa, Cin	1.11

Rel Opp BA w/ Runners On
(minimum 50 IP)

Lidge,Brad, Hou	.141
Benitez,A, Fla	.148
Hoffman,Trevor, SD	.158
Linebrink,S, SD	.177
Cruz,Ju, Atl	.186
Mota,Guillermo, LA-Fla	.187
Gagne,Eric, LA	.191
Mercker,Kent, ChC	.193
Hawkins,LaTroy, ChC	.194
Isringhausen,J, StL	.194

Relief Opp BA w/ RISP
(minimum 50 IP)

Hoffman,Trevor, SD	.087
Lidge,Brad, Hou	.101
Mercker,Kent, ChC	.148
Cruz,Ju, Atl	.159
Benitez,A, Fla	.164
Madson,Ryan, Phi	.164
Linebrink,S, SD	.165
Cordero,Chad, Mon	.167
Reitsma,Chris, Atl	.178
Carrara,G, LA	.182

GIDP Induced

Estes,Shawn, Col	34
Fogg,Josh, Pit	27
Morris,Matt, StL	26
Perez,Od, LA	25
Rueter,Kirk, SF	25
Webb,Brandon, Ari	24
Thomson,John, Atl	23
Lawrence,Brian, SD	22
4 tied with	21

GIDP Per Nine IP
(minimum 162 IP)

Estes,Shawn, Col	1.51
Fogg,Josh, Pit	1.36
Rueter,Kirk, SF	1.18
Morris,Matt, StL	1.16
Perez,Od, LA	1.15
Lima,Jose, LA	1.11
Hampton,Mike, Atl	1.04
Thomson,John, Atl	1.04
Webb,Brandon, Ari	1.04
Lawrence,Brian, SD	0.98

2004 National League Pitching Leaders

Saves		Blown Saves		Save Pct (minimum 20 Save Ops)		Relief Earned Run Average (minimum 50 IP)	
Benitez,A, Fla	47	Chacon,Shawn, Col	9	Gagne,Eric, LA	95.7	Benitez,A, Fla	1.29
Isringhausen,J, StL	47	Graves,Danny, Cin	9	Benitez,A, Fla	92.2	Madson,Ryan, Phi	1.65
Gagne,Eric, LA	45	Hawkins,LaTroy, ChC	9	Hoffman,Trevor, SD	91.1	Otsuka,Akinori, SD	1.75
Smoltz,John, Atl	44	Herges,Matt, SF	8	Smoltz,John, Atl	89.8	Kline,Steve, StL	1.79
Mesa,Jose, Pit	43	Worrell,Tim, Phi	8	Mesa,Jose, Pit	89.6	Lidge,Brad, Hou	1.90
Graves,Danny, Cin	41	Cormier,Rheal, Phi	7	Kolb,Danny, Mil	88.6	Linebrink,S, SD	2.14
Hoffman,Trevor, SD	41	Harikkala,Tim, Col	7	Lidge,Brad, Hou	87.9	Carrara,G, LA	2.18
Kolb,Danny, Mil	39	Isringhausen,J, StL	7	Isringhausen,J, StL	87.0	Gagne,Eric, LA	2.19
Chacon,Shawn, Col	35	Reitsma,Chris, Atl	7	Looper,Braden, NYM	85.3	Dessens,Elmer, Ari-LA	2.25
2 tied with	29	Riedling,John, Cin	7	Hermanson,D, SF	85.0	Hoffman,Trevor, SD	2.30

Relief Wins		Relief Losses		Holds		Relief Games	
Jones,Todd, Cin-Phi	11	Ayala,Luis, Mon	12	Otsuka,Akinori, SD	34	Brower,Jim, SF	89
Madson,Ryan, Phi	9	Chacon,Shawn, Col	9	King,Ray, StL	31	King,Ray, StL	86
Mota,Guillermo, LA-Fla	9	Mota,Guillermo, LA-Fla	8	Reitsma,Chris, Atl	31	Cormier,Rheal, Phi	84
Brower,Jim, SF	7	Reed,Steve, Col	8	Mota,Guillermo, LA-Fla	30	Reitsma,Chris, Atl	84
Cordero,Chad, Mon	7	Rodriguez,Fe, SF-Phi	8	Torres,Salomon, Pit	30	Torres,Salomon, Pit	84
Gagne,Eric, LA	7	Brower,Jim, SF	7	Cormier,Rheal, Phi	28	Eyre,Scott, SF	83
Linebrink,S, SD	7	Franco,Jo, NYM	7	Linebrink,S, SD	28	Stanton,Mike, NYM	83
Otsuka,Akinori, SD	7	Torres,Salomon, Pit	7	Jones,Todd, Cin-Phi	27	Ayala,Luis, Mon	81
Tavarez,Julian, StL	7	Weathrs, NYM-Hou-Fla	7	Stanton,Mike, NYM	25	Lidge,Brad, Hou	80
Torres,Salomon, Pit	7	5 tied with	6	2 tied with	24	Alfonseca,A, Atl	79

Relief Innings		Relief Opp Batting Average (minimum 50 IP)		Relief Opp On Base Pct (minimum 50 IP)		Relief Opp Slugging Avg (minimum 50 IP)	
Mota,Guillermo, LA-Fla	96.2	Benitez,A, Fla	.152	Benitez,A, Fla	.220	King,Ray, StL	.257
Lidge,Brad, Hou	94.2	Lidge,Brad, Hou	.174	Hoffman,Trevor, SD	.242	Benitez,A, Fla	.257
Brower,Jim, SF	93.0	Gagne,Eric, LA	.181	Gagne,Eric, LA	.248	Gagne,Eric, LA	.263
Torres,Salomon, Pit	92.0	Randolph,S, Ari	.191	Lidge,Brad, Hou	.254	Madson,Ryan, Phi	.284
Ayala,Luis, Mon	90.1	King,Ray, StL	.197	Isringhausen,J, StL	.265	Lidge,Brad, Hou	.290
Koplove,Mike, Ari	86.2	Otsuka,Akinori, SD	.199	Otsuka,Akinori, SD	.266	Kline,Steve, StL	.294
Linebrink,S, SD	84.0	Isringhausen,J, StL	.199	Hawkins,LaTroy, ChC	.269	Kolb,Danny, Mil	.299
Looper,Braden, NYM	83.1	Mercker,Kent, ChC	.205	Smoltz,John, Atl	.276	Bottalico,R, NYM	.303
Cordero,Chad, Mon	82.2	Linebrink,S, SD	.209	Linebrink,S, SD	.278	Otsuka,Akinori, SD	.305
2 tied with	82.1	Kline,Steve, StL	.209	Dessens,Elmer, Ari-LA	.279	Carrara,G, LA	.307

Inherited Runners Scrd % (minimum 30 IR)		Rel OBP 1st Batter Faced (minimum 40 BF)		Relief Opp BA Vs LHB (minimum 50 AB)		Relief Opp BA Vs RHB (minimum 50 AB)	
Lidge,Brad, Hou	6.7	Calero,Kiko, StL	.154	Kline,Steve, StL	.143	Gagne,Eric, LA	.129
Lopez,Javr, Col	13.0	Benitez,A, Fla	.156	King,Ray, StL	.150	Benitez,A, Fla	.140
Eyre,Scott, SF	15.6	Isringhausen,J, StL	.176	Vizcaino,Luis, Mil	.163	Lidge,Brad, Hou	.155
Perisho,Matt, Fla	20.6	Gagne,Eric, LA	.186	Benitez,A, Fla	.168	Hoffman,Trevor, SD	.161
Franklin,Wayne, SF	20.9	Telemaco,A, Phi	.190	Linebrink,S, SD	.178	Mercker,Kent, ChC	.170
Christiansen,J, SF	21.8	Hoffman,Trevor, SD	.200	Carrara,G, LA	.182	Witasick,Jay, SD	.180
King,Ray, StL	22.7	Wagner,Billy, Phi	.200	Lidge,Brad, Hou	.191	Miceli,Danny, Hou	.188
Bottalico,R, NYM	24.2	White,Gabe, Cin	.200	Rodriguez,Fe, SF-Phi	.192	Randolph,S, Ari	.189
Mercker,Kent, ChC	24.4	Lidge,Brad, Hou	.213	Randolph,S, Ari	.194	Otsuka,Akinori, SD	.190
Brower,Jim, SF	24.7	Carrara,G, LA	.214	Mota,Guillermo, LA-Fla	.195	Isringhausen,J, StL	.195

2004 National League Pitching Leaders

Fastest Average Fastball
(minimum 162 IP)

Oswalt,Roy, Hou	94.0
Johnson,Ra, Ari	93.6
Schmidt,Jason, SF	93.5
Sheets,Ben, Mil	93.3
Zambrano,C, ChC	93.1
Perez,Ol, Pit	93.0
Wright,Jar, Atl	92.7
Clemens,Roger, Hou	92.4
Tomko,Brett, SF	92.0
Marquis,Jason, StL	92.0

Slowest Average Fastball
(minimum 162 IP)

Lawrence,Brian, SD	83.2
Rueter,Kirk, SF	84.2
Maddux,Greg, ChC	84.9
Glavine,Tom, NYM	85.6
Ishii,Kazuhisa, LA	85.6
Leiter,Al, NYM	86.8
Hernandez,L, Mon	87.0
Webb,Brandon, Ari	87.0
Trachsel,Steve, NYM	87.2
Davis,Doug, Mil	87.2

Pitches 100+ Velocity

Farnsworth,K, ChC	30
Wagner,Billy, Phi	8
Burnett,A.J., Fla	4
Jackson,Edwin, LA	2
11 tied with	1

Pitches 95+ Velocity

Oswalt,Roy, Hou	733
Burnett,A.J., Fla	714
Beckett,Josh, Fla	519
Zambrano,C, ChC	512
Mota,Guillermo, LA-Fla	499
Smoltz,John, Atl	474
Farnsworth,K, ChC	469
Rodriguez,Fe, SF-Phi	469
Schmidt,Jason, SF	459
Perez,Ol, Pit	458

Pitches Less Than 80 MPH

Sparks,Steve, Ari	1033
Ishii,Kazuhisa, LA	873
Weaver,Jeff, LA	835
Morris,Matt, StL	716
Lidle,Cory, Cin-Phi	629
Oswalt,Roy, Hou	619
Hernandez,L, Mon	610
Seo,Jae, NYM	587
Lawrence,Brian, SD	564
Rueter,Kirk, SF	550

Lowest % Fastballs
(minimum 162 IP)

Fogg,Josh, Pit	39.8
Perez,Od, LA	40.9
Johnson,Ra, Ari	41.3
Glavine,Tom, NYM	44.9
Hernandez,L, Mon	46.4
Lima,Jose, LA	47.2
Leiter,Al, NYM	47.4
Lawrence,Brian, SD	48.2
Lidle,Cory, Cin-Phi	49.2
Weaver,Jeff, LA	49.5

Highest % Fastballs
(minimum 162 IP)

Wright,Jar, Atl	79.5
Thomson,John, Atl	75.6
Willis,D, Fla	74.6
Zambrano,C, ChC	71.6
Marquis,Jason, StL	69.5
Rueter,Kirk, SF	69.2
Milton,Eric, Phi	69.1
Ortiz,Ru, Atl	66.8
Tomko,Brett, SF	66.7
Perez,Ol, Pit	65.0

Highest % Curveballs
(minimum 162 IP)

Sheets,Ben, Mil	28.4
Morris,Matt, StL	27.2
Ishii,Kazuhisa, LA	26.1
Myers,Brett, Phi	25.4
Carpenter,C, StL	20.9
Oswalt,Roy, Hou	20.4
Weaver,Jeff, LA	20.2
Wells,David, SD	20.0
Valdez,Ismael, SD-Fla	19.5
Williams,Woody, StL	18.8

Highest % Changeups
(minimum 162 IP)

Glavine,Tom, NYM	37.4
Lima,Jose, LA	31.6
Perez,Od, LA	28.2
Maddux,Greg, ChC	24.9
Schmidt,Jason, SF	23.7
Fogg,Josh, Pit	19.9
Hampton,Mike, Atl	18.6
Suppan,Jeff, StL	17.9
Rueter,Kirk, SF	17.3
Wilson,Pa, Cin	16.2

Highest % Sliders
(minimum 162 IP)

Johnson,Ra, Ari	41.1
Clement,Matt, ChC	33.5
Lawrence,Brian, SD	24.7
Perez,Ol, Pit	21.6
Hernandez,L, Mon	20.1
Peavy,Jake, SD	17.9
Jennings,Jason, Col	17.7
Benson,Kris, Pit-NYM	17.5
Weaver,Jeff, LA	17.4
Pavano,Carl, Fla	16.6

2004 Active Career Batting Leaders

Batting Average (minimum 1000 PA)		On Base Percentage (minimum 1000 PA)		Slugging Average (minimum 1000 PA)		Home Runs	
Suzuki,Ichiro	.339	Bonds,Barry	.443	Pujols,Albert	.624	Bonds,Barry	703
Helton,Todd	.339	Helton,Todd	.432	Helton,Todd	.616	Sosa,Sammy	574
Pujols,Albert	.333	Thomas,Frank	.429	Bonds,Barry	.611	Palmeiro,R	551
Guerrero,V	.325	Martinez,Edgar	.418	Ramirez,Manny	.599	Griffey Jr.,K	501
Garciaparra,N	.322	Berkman,Lance	.416	Guerrero,V	.589	McGriff,Fred	493
Ramirez,Manny	.316	Pujols,Albert	.413	Rodriguez,Alex	.574	Bagwell,Jeff	446
Piazza,Mike	.315	Abreu,Bobby	.412	Thome,Jim	.569	Thomas,Frank	436
Jeter,Derek	.315	Giles,Brian	.411	Walker,Larry	.568	Gonzalez,Ju	434
Walker,Larry	.314	Giambi,Jason	.411	Thomas,Frank	.567	Thome,Jim	423
Pierre,Juan	.312	Ramirez,Manny	.411	Berkman,Lance	.563	Sheffield,Gary	415

Games		At Bats		Hits		Total Bases	
Palmeiro,R	2721	Palmeiro,R	10103	Palmeiro,R	2922	Bonds,Barry	5556
Bonds,Barry	2716	Biggio,Craig	9221	Bonds,Barry	2730	Palmeiro,R	5223
McGriff,Fred	2460	Bonds,Barry	9098	Alomar,Roberto	2724	McGriff,Fred	4458
Biggio,Craig	2409	Alomar,Roberto	9073	Biggio,Craig	2639	Sosa,Sammy	4368
Alomar,Roberto	2379	McGriff,Fred	8757	McGriff,Fred	2490	Bagwell,Jeff	4175
Finley,Steve	2289	Finley,Steve	8471	Franco,Ju	2457	Griffey Jr.,K	4131
Franco,Ju	2269	Franco,Ju	8189	Larkin,Barry	2340	Galarraga,A	4038
Galarraga,A	2257	Grissom,M	8138	Finley,Steve	2336	Alomar,Roberto	4018
Surhoff,B.J.	2222	Galarraga,A	8096	Galarraga,A	2333	Biggio,Craig	4007
Larkin,Barry	2180	Sosa,Sammy	8021	Bagwell,Jeff	2289	Thomas,Frank	3887

Doubles		Triples		Runs Scored		RBI	
Palmeiro,R	572	Finley,Steve	109	Bonds,Barry	2070	Bonds,Barry	1843
Biggio,Craig	564	Lofton,Kenny	93	Palmeiro,R	1616	Palmeiro,R	1775
Bonds,Barry	563	Alomar,Roberto	80	Biggio,Craig	1603	McGriff,Fred	1550
Martinez,Edgar	514	Bonds,Barry	77	Alomar,Roberto	1508	Sosa,Sammy	1530
Alomar,Roberto	504	Larkin,Barry	76	Bagwell,Jeff	1506	Bagwell,Jeff	1510
Olerud,John	493	Damon,Johnny	74	Sosa,Sammy	1383	Griffey Jr.,K	1444
Bagwell,Jeff	484	Offerman,Jose	71	McGriff,Fred	1349	Thomas,Frank	1439
Gonzalez,LE	458	Durham,Ray	70	Larkin,Barry	1329	Galarraga,A	1425
Walker,Larry	451	Burks,Ellis	63	Finley,Steve	1327	Gonzalez,Ju	1404
2 tied with	444	Gonzalez,LE	63	Griffey Jr.,K	1320	Sheffield,Gary	1353

Walks		Intentional Walks		Hit By Pitch		Strikeouts	
Bonds,Barry	2302	Bonds,Barry	604	Biggio,Craig	256	Sosa,Sammy	2110
Thomas,Frank	1450	Griffey Jr.,K	207	Galarraga,A	178	Galarraga,A	2003
Bagwell,Jeff	1383	McGriff,Fred	171	Kendall,Jason	177	McGriff,Fred	1882
Palmeiro,R	1310	Palmeiro,R	168	Vina,Fernando	157	Thome,Jim	1703
McGriff,Fred	1305	Thomas,Frank	162	Walker,Larry	129	Lankford,Ray	1550
Martinez,Edgar	1283	Olerud,John	155	Bagwell,Jeff	127	Bagwell,Jeff	1537
Olerud,John	1259	Bagwell,Jeff	154	Delgado,Carlos	122	Biggio,Craig	1467
Thome,Jim	1212	Sosa,Sammy	148	Easley,Damion	111	Sanders,Reggie	1438
Sheffield,Gary	1202	Guerrero,V	143	Sheffield,Gary	110	Bonds,Barry	1428
Ventura,Robin	1075	Piazza,Mike	138	Kent,Jeff	97	Burks,Ellis	1340

2004 Active Career Batting Leaders

Sacrifice Hits		Sacrifice Flies		Stolen Bases		Seasons Played	
Glavine,Tom	186	Sierra,Ruben	117	Lofton,Kenny	545	Clemens,Roger	21
Vizquel,Omar	185	Palmeiro,R	111	Bonds,Barry	506	Franco,Jo	20
Maddux,Greg	152	Thomas,Frank	106	Alomar,Roberto	474	Franco,Ju	20
Alomar,Roberto	148	Surhoff,B.J.	100	Young,Eri	450	8 tied with	19
McLemore,Mark	105	Bagwell,Jeff	98	Grissom,M	428		
Vizcaino,Jose	104	Alomar,Roberto	97	Biggio,Craig	396		
Schilling,Curt	102	Sheffield,Gary	96	Larkin,Barry	379		
Reynolds,Shane	97	Olerud,John	93	Goodwin,Tom	369		
Clayton,Royce	93	Kent,Jeff	88	Womack,Tony	335		
Smoltz,John	92	Bonds,Barry	87	Vizquel,Omar	318		

At Bats Per Home Run		Grounded Into DP		Stolen Base Success Pct		At Bats Per RBI	
(minimum 1000 AB)				(minimum 100 SBA)		(minimum 1000 AB)	
Bonds,Barry	12.9	Franco,Ju	289	Beltran,Carlos	89.3	Ramirez,Manny	4.4
Thome,Jim	13.5	McGriff,Fred	226	Reese,Pokey	84.7	Gonzalez,Ju	4.7
Sosa,Sammy	14.0	Olerud,John	226	Womack,Tony	83.1	Pujols,Albert	4.7
Ramirez,Manny	14.3	Palmeiro,R	223	Larkin,Barry	83.1	Delgado,Carlos	4.7
Dunn,Adam	14.6	Zeile,Todd	223	Podsednik,S	83.1	Thomas,Frank	4.8
Rodriguez,Alex	14.7	Rodriguez,Ivan	221	Glanville,Doug	82.4	Helton,Todd	4.8
Griffey Jr.,K	14.7	Bagwell,Jeff	219	Roberts,Dave	80.8	Thome,Jim	4.9
Pujols,Albert	14.8	Alomar,Roberto	206	Alomar,Roberto	80.6	Bonds,Barry	4.9
Delgado,Carlos	14.9	Santiago,B	203	Crawford,Carl	80.4	Sexson,Richie	5.0
Gonzalez,Ju	15.1	Castilla,Vinny	201	Rodriguez,Alex	80.4	Piazza,Mike	5.0

Strikeouts / Walks Ratio		At Bats Per GIDP		OPS	
(minimum 1000 AB)		(minimum 1000 AB)		(minimum 1000 PA)	
Bonds,Barry	.620	Roberts,Dave	258.8	Bonds,Barry	1.053
Young,Eri	.689	Crawford,Carl	216.4	Helton,Todd	1.048
Giles,Brian	.724	Mackowiak,Rob	180.6	Pujols,Albert	1.037
Sheffield,Gary	.731	Maddux,Greg	166.3	Ramirez,Manny	1.010
Thomas,Frank	.782	Suzuki,Ichiro	136.1	Thomas,Frank	.996
Olerud,John	.791	Bergeron,Peter	122.6	Berkman,Lance	.980
Palmeiro,O	.798	McEwing,Joe	121.6	Guerrero,V	.979
Helton,Todd	.813	Branyan,R	114.7	Thome,Jim	.979
Larkin,Barry	.870	Furcal,Rafael	105.7	Walker,Larry	.969
Lawton,Matt	.875	Womack,Tony	99.3	Giles,Brian	.961

2004 Active Career Pitching Leaders

Earned Run Average (minimum 750 IP)		Winning Percentage (minimum 100 Decisions)		Opponent Batting Average (minimum 750 IP)		Baserunners Per 9 IP (minimum 750 IP)	
Martinez,Pedro	2.71	Martinez,Pedro	.705	Hoffman,Trevor	.206	Hoffman,Trevor	9.49
Hoffman,Trevor	2.74	Hudson,Tim	.702	Martinez,Pedro	.209	Martinez,Pedro	9.71
Franco,Jo	2.84	Clemens,Roger	.667	Johnson,Ra	.213	Schilling,Curt	10.16
Maddux,Greg	2.95	Mulder,Mark	.659	Wood,Kerry	.214	Maddux,Greg	10.40
Johnson,Ra	3.07	Johnson,Ra	.658	Jackson,Mike	.226	Mussina,Mike	10.63
Clemens,Roger	3.18	Pettitte,Andy	.654	Zito,Barry	.229	Smoltz,John	10.65
Brown,Kevin	3.20	Zito,Barry	.643	Clemens,Roger	.230	Beck,Rod	10.71
Smoltz,John	3.27	Mussina,Mike	.639	Smoltz,John	.232	Johnson,Ra	10.88
Hudson,Tim	3.30	Maddux,Greg	.637	Nomo,Hideo	.235	Clemens,Roger	10.92
Beck,Rod	3.30	Halladay,Roy	.632	Remlinger,Mike	.235	Brown,Kevin	11.27

Games		Games Started		Complete Games		Shutouts	
Franco,Jo	1088	Clemens,Roger	639	Clemens,Roger	117	Clemens,Roger	46
Jackson,Mike	1005	Maddux,Greg	604	Maddux,Greg	105	Johnson,Ra	37
Stanton,Mike	968	Glavine,Tom	570	Johnson,Ra	92	Maddux,Greg	35
Mesa,Jose	832	Johnson,Ra	479	Schilling,Curt	82	Glavine,Tom	23
Hernandez,Ro	825	Brown,Kevin	463	Brown,Kevin	72	Mussina,Mike	21
Timlin,Mike	812	Moyer,Jamie	453	Mussina,Mike	54	Schilling,Curt	19
Reed,Steve	803	Wells,David	417	Glavine,Tom	53	Brown,Kevin	17
Quantrill,Paul	791	Mussina,Mike	413	Wells,David	52	Erickson,Scott	17
Jones,Todd	744	Appier,Kevin	402	Erickson,Scott	51	Martinez,Pedro	16
Nelson,Je	743	2 tied with	370	Smoltz,John	47	Smoltz,John	14

Wins		Losses		Innings Pitched		Batters Faced	
Clemens,Roger	328	Maddux,Greg	174	Clemens,Roger	4493.0	Clemens,Roger	18531
Maddux,Greg	305	Glavine,Tom	171	Maddux,Greg	4181.1	Maddux,Greg	16989
Glavine,Tom	262	Clemens,Roger	164	Glavine,Tom	3740.1	Glavine,Tom	15724
Johnson,Ra	246	Moyer,Jamie	145	Johnson,Ra	3368.0	Johnson,Ra	13864
Wells,David	212	Mulholland,T	140	Brown,Kevin	3183.0	Brown,Kevin	13195
Mussina,Mike	211	Appier,Kevin	137	Wells,David	3022.1	Wells,David	12615
Brown,Kevin	207	Brown,Kevin	137	Moyer,Jamie	2939.2	Moyer,Jamie	12473
Moyer,Jamie	192	Wells,David	136	Mussina,Mike	2833.1	Mussina,Mike	11548
Schilling,Curt	184	Erickson,Scott	132	Schilling,Curt	2812.2	Rogers,Kenny	11546
Martinez,Pedro	182	Trachsel,Steve	131	Smoltz,John	2699.2	Schilling,Curt	11399

Strikeouts		Walks Allowed		Hit Batters		Wild Pitches	
Clemens,Roger	4317	Clemens,Roger	1458	Johnson,Ra	156	Clemens,Roger	130
Johnson,Ra	4161	Johnson,Ra	1302	Clemens,Roger	147	Smoltz,John	128
Maddux,Greg	2916	Glavine,Tom	1276	Brown,Kevin	132	Appier,Kevin	106
Schilling,Curt	2745	Leiter,Al	1065	Wakefield,Tim	125	Nomo,Hideo	105
Martinez,Pedro	2653	Rogers,Kenny	964	Maddux,Greg	118	Brown,Kevin	102
Smoltz,John	2398	Appier,Kevin	933	Martinez,Pedro	115	Gordon,Tom	101
Brown,Kevin	2347	Gordon,Tom	893	Astacio,Pedro	108	Wells,David	96
Mussina,Mike	2258	Brown,Kevin	882	Park,Chan Ho	106	Johnson,Ra	95
Glavine,Tom	2245	Maddux,Greg	871	Leiter,Al	105	Grimsley,Jason	94
Appier,Kevin	1994	Nomo,Hideo	853	Sele,Aaron	103	Clement,Matt	85

2004 Active Career Pitching Leaders

Saves	
Franco,Jo	424
Hoffman,Trevor	393
Rivera,Mariano	336
Hernandez,Ro	320
Percival,Troy	316
Mesa,Jose	292
Beck,Rod	286
Wagner,Billy	246
Benitez,A	244
Urbina,Ugueth	227

Save Pct	
(minimum 50 Save Ops)	
Gagne,Eric	96.2
Smoltz,John	91.7
Hoffman,Trevor	89.1
Rivera,Mariano	87.5
Williams,Mike	87.1
Nathan,Joe	86.5
Percival,Troy	86.3
Benitez,A	86.2
Kolb,Danny	85.9
Mesa,Jose	85.9

Home Runs Allowed	
Moyer,Jamie	358
Wells,David	353
Clemens,Roger	336
Johnson,Ra	301
Mussina,Mike	300
Trachsel,Steve	290
Glavine,Tom	288
Mulholland,T	286
Schilling,Curt	286
Rogers,Kenny	271

Strikeouts Per 9 IP	
(minimum 750 IP)	
Johnson,Ra	11.12
Wood,Kerry	10.43
Martinez,Pedro	10.40
Hoffman,Trevor	10.13
Nomo,Hideo	8.93
Remlinger,Mike	8.81
Rhodes,Arthur	8.80
Schilling,Curt	8.78
Clemens,Roger	8.65
Dreifort,D	8.27

Opp On-Base Percentage	
(minimum 750 IP)	
Hoffman,Trevor	.264
Martinez,Pedro	.271
Schilling,Curt	.281
Maddux,Greg	.288
Mussina,Mike	.292
Smoltz,John	.292
Johnson,Ra	.296
Clemens,Roger	.296
Brown,Kevin	.304
Zito,Barry	.305

Opp Slugging Average	
(minimum 750 IP)	
Martinez,Pedro	.323
Hoffman,Trevor	.337
Johnson,Ra	.337
Franco,Jo	.342
Clemens,Roger	.343
Maddux,Greg	.345
Brown,Kevin	.346
Smoltz,John	.352
Wood,Kerry	.353
Zito,Barry	.354

Hits Per Nine Innings	
(minimum 750 IP)	
Hoffman,Trevor	6.77
Martinez,Pedro	6.84
Wood,Kerry	6.94
Johnson,Ra	6.98
Jackson,Mike	7.44
Zito,Barry	7.63
Clemens,Roger	7.70
Smoltz,John	7.76
Remlinger,Mike	7.83
Nomo,Hideo	7.84

Home Runs Per Nine IP	
(minimum 750 IP)	
Brown,Kevin	0.57
Maddux,Greg	0.58
Franco,Jo	0.59
Adams,Terry	0.63
Wickman,Bob	0.66
Lowe,Derek	0.66
Clemens,Roger	0.67
Hudson,Tim	0.68
Tavarez,Julian	0.68
Martinez,Pedro	0.69

Strikeouts / Walks Ratio	
(minimum 750 IP)	
Martinez,Pedro	4.31
Schilling,Curt	4.30
Hoffman,Trevor	3.83
Lieber,Jon	3.72
Sheets,Ben	3.55
Mussina,Mike	3.54
Beck,Rod	3.37
Reynolds,Shane	3.35
Maddux,Greg	3.35
Radke,Brad	3.25

Stolen Base Pct Allowed	
(minimum 750 IP)	
Rueter,Kirk	35.1
Buehrle,Mark	35.4
Mulholland,T	41.0
Carpenter,C	41.0
Rogers,Kenny	41.8
Redman,Mark	48.6
Anderson,Brian	49.1
Alvarez,Wilson	49.7
Weaver,Jeff	51.2
Park,Chan Ho	51.2

GIDP Induced	
Maddux,Greg	354
Glavine,Tom	353
Brown,Kevin	321
Erickson,Scott	301
Clemens,Roger	294
Rogers,Kenny	267
Mulholland,T	257
Hampton,Mike	251
Moyer,Jamie	240
Wells,David	222

GIDP Per Nine IP	
(minimum 750 IP)	
Estes,Shawn	1.28
Erickson,Scott	1.18
Wright,Jam	1.17
Tavarez,Julian	1.17
Wickman,Bob	1.16
Hampton,Mike	1.13
Garland,Jon	1.12
Lowe,Derek	1.07
Graves,Danny	1.06
Pettitte,Andy	1.04

Complete Game %	
(minimum 100 GS)	
Schilling,Curt	0.22
Johnson,Ra	0.19
Clemens,Roger	0.18
Maddux,Greg	0.17
Hernandez,L	0.16
Brown,Kevin	0.16
Mulder,Mark	0.15
Erickson,Scott	0.14
Mulholland,T	0.14
Ponson,Sidney	0.14

Quality Start Pct	
(minimum 100 GS)	
Martinez,Pedro	70.4
Johnson,Ra	70.4
Oswalt,Roy	68.2
Schilling,Curt	68.1
Maddux,Greg	67.9
Brown,Kevin	67.0
Hudson,Tim	66.1
Zito,Barry	66.0
Buehrle,Mark	65.5
Clemens,Roger	65.3

Walks Per 9 IP	
(minimum 750 IP)	
Radke,Brad	1.68
Lieber,Jon	1.76
Maddux,Greg	1.87
Wells,David	1.92
Anderson,Brian	1.98
Mussina,Mike	2.02
Schilling,Curt	2.04
Mendoza,Ramiro	2.05
Lima,Jose	2.10
Sheets,Ben	2.10

Games Finished	
Franco,Jo	770
Hernandez,Ro	608
Hoffman,Trevor	578
Mesa,Jose	538
Beck,Rod	519
Rivera,Mariano	474
Percival,Troy	466
Benitez,A	441
Jackson,Mike	422
2 tied with	417

2004 American League Bill James Leaders

Top Game Scores

Pitcher	Date	Opp	IP	H	R	ER	BB	SO	GS
Lilly,Ted, Tor	8/23	Bos	9.0	3	0	0	2	13	92
Santana,Johan, Min	7/6	KC	9.0	3	0	0	2	13	92
Bush,Dave, Tor	10/1	NYY	9.0	2	0	0	3	11	91
Maroth,Mike, Det	7/16	NYY	9.0	1	0	0	2	7	90
Anderson,Brian, KC	8/4	CWS	9.0	2	0	0	1	7	89
Schilling,Curt, Bos	9/21	Bal	8.0	3	0	0	1	14	89
Elarton,Scott, Cle	8/29	CWS	9.0	2	0	0	1	6	88
Lopez,Rodrigo, Bal	9/26	Det	9.0	3	0	0	0	7	88
5 tied with									87

Worst Game Scores

Pitcher	Date	Opp	IP	H	R	ER	BB	SO	GS
Munoz,Arnie, CWS	6/19	Mon	3.0	10	11	11	3	1	-7
George,Chris, KC	7/24	Cle	3.0	11	10	10	2	1	-4
Dickey,R.A., Tex	6/13	StL	1.1	8	9	9	3	0	-1
Schoeneweis,S, CWS	8/4	KC	1.1	9	9	9	1	1	0
Garland,Jon, CWS	6/9	Phi	4.0	8	10	10	4	1	3
May,Darrell, KC	8/17	Sea	2.0	9	9	9	1	2	3
Johnson,Jason, Det	9/9	KC	2.1	6	11	9	4	3	4
Washburn,J, Ana	7/20	Cle	5.1	13	10	9	1	1	4
Ainsworth,Kurt, Bal	5/14	Ana	1.1	6	9	9	1	0	5
Meche,Gil, Sea	5/27	Cle	3.1	10	8	8	3	0	5

Runs Created

Ortiz,David, Bos	127
Suzuki,Ichiro, Sea	125
Ramirez,Manny, Bos	124
Tejada,Miguel, Bal	124
Young,Michael, Tex	124
Sheffield,Gary, NYY	123
Guerrero,V, Ana	122
Teixeira,Mark, Tex	120
Blalock,Hank, Tex	119
Matsui,Hideki, NYY	117

Runs Created Per 27 Outs

Teixeira,Mark, Tex	8.0
Ortiz,David, Bos	8.0
Mora,Melvin, Bal	7.9
Ramirez,Manny, Bos	7.9
Hafner,Travis, Cle	7.9
Durazo,Erubiel, Oak	7.6
Sheffield,Gary, NYY	7.5
Guerrero,V, Ana	7.5
Matsui,Hideki, NYY	7.4
Suzuki,Ichiro, Sea	7.2

Offensive Winning %

Hafner,Travis, Cle	.719
Sheffield,Gary, NYY	.709
Durazo,Erubiel, Oak	.704
Mora,Melvin, Bal	.699
Guerrero,V, Ana	.699
Suzuki,Ichiro, Sea	.699
Matsui,Hideki, NYY	.698
Ortiz,David, Bos	.692
Ramirez,Manny, Bos	.688
Teixeira,Mark, Tex	.679

Secondary Average
(minimum 502 PA)

Ramirez,Manny, Bos	.452
Chavez,Er, Oak	.438
Ortiz,David, Bos	.431
Hafner,Travis, Cle	.419
Delgado,Carlos, Tor	.417
Sheffield,Gary, NYY	.414
Teixeira,Mark, Tex	.411
Posada,Jorge, NYY	.408
Rodriguez,Alex, NYY	.406
Pena,Carlos, Det	.391

Isolated Power
(minimum 502 PA)

Ramirez,Manny, Bos	.305
Ortiz,David, Bos	.302
Teixeira,Mark, Tex	.279
Hafner,Travis, Cle	.272
Delgado,Carlos, Tor	.266
Guerrero,V, Ana	.261
Valentin,Jo, CWS	.258
Konerko,Paul, CWS	.258
Sheffield,Gary, NYY	.244
Rowand,Aaron, CWS	.234

Power / Speed Number

Rodriguez,Alex, NYY	31.5
Jeter,Derek, NYY	23.0
Hunter,Torii, Min	22.0
Soriano,A, Tex	21.9
Guerrero,V, Ana	21.7
Lawton,Matt, Cle	21.4
Rowand,Aaron, CWS	19.9
Damon,Johnny, Bos	19.5
Crawford,Carl, TB	18.5
Byrnes,Eric, Oak	18.4

Speed Scores (2003-2004)

Crawford,Carl, TB	8.93
Figgins,Chone, Ana	7.76
Garciaparra,N, Bos	7.53
Damon,Johnny, Bos	7.39
Suzuki,Ichiro, Sea	7.25
Rivas,Luis, Min	7.13
Young,Michael, Tex	7.08
Byrnes,Eric, Oak	7.03
Guzman,C, Min	7.03
Baldelli,Rocco, TB	6.96

Cheap Wins

Rogers,Kenny, Tex	11
Loaiza,Esteban, CWS-NYY	7
Mussina,Mike, NYY	5
Westbrook,Jake, Cle	5
Zito,Barry, Oak	5
7 tied with	4

Tough Losses

Garcia,Freddy, Sea-CWS	7
Westbrook,Jake, Cle	5
Bonderman,J, Det	4
Escobar,Kelvim, Ana	4
Franklin,Ryan, Sea	4
Greinke,Zack, KC	4
Martinez,Pedro, Bos	4
Rogers,Kenny, Tex	4
8 tied with	3

2004 National League Bill James Leaders

Top Game Scores

Pitcher	Date	Opp	IP	H	R	ER	BB	SO	GS
Johnson,Ra, Ari	5/18	Atl	9.0	0	0	0	0	13	100
Schmidt,Jason, SF	5/18	ChC	9.0	1	0	0	1	13	97
Morris,Matt, StL	9/3	LA	9.0	2	0	0	0	11	94
Sheets,Ben, Mil	5/16	Atl	9.0	3	1	1	1	18	94
Glavine,Tom, NYM	5/23	Col	9.0	1	0	0	1	8	92
Prior,Mark, ChC	9/30	Cin	9.0	3	1	1	1	16	92
Schmidt,Jason, SF	6/20	Bos	9.0	1	0	0	2	9	92
Oswalt,Roy, Hou	4/16	Mil	9.0	3	0	0	0	10	91
Johnson,Ra, Ari	4/16	SD	9.0	2	0	0	1	8	90
Sheets,Ben, Mil	6/8	Ana	9.0	1	0	0	0	5	90

Worst Game Scores

Pitcher	Date	Opp	IP	H	R	ER	BB	SO	GS
Fassero,Jeff, Col	8/8	Cin	3.0	11	11	11	4	2	-9
Gonzalez,Edgar, Ari	9/3	SF	1.0	8	10	10	2	2	-3
Haren,Danny, StL	6/10	ChC	3.2	10	10	10	3	0	-2
Stark,Denny, Col	4/16	StL	2.1	10	11	8	2	2	-1
Sparks,Steve, Ari	5/22	Fla	2.2	9	10	10	2	2	0
Estes,Shawn, Col	5/7	ChC	2.2	7	9	9	5	0	3
Downs,Scott, Mon	7/18	Atl	2.0	7	9	9	3	1	4
Dessens,Elmer, Ari	4/14	Col	4.2	11	9	9	2	1	5
Morris,Matt, StL	7/31	SF	0.2	7	8	8	1	0	5
5 tied with									6

Runs Created

Bonds,Barry, SF	171
Helton,Todd, Col	143
Pujols,Albert, StL	143
Abreu,Bobby, Phi	139
Berkman,Lance, Hou	126
Rolen,Scott, StL	124
Drew,J.D., Atl	122
Beltre,Adrian, LA	120
Edmonds,Jim, StL	115
Alou,Moises, ChC	114

Runs Created Per 27 Outs

Bonds,Barry, SF	18.6
Helton,Todd, Col	10.2
Rolen,Scott, StL	9.2
Abreu,Bobby, Phi	8.9
Pujols,Albert, StL	8.9
Drew,J.D., Atl	8.7
Berkman,Lance, Hou	8.5
Edmonds,Jim, StL	8.5
Beltre,Adrian, LA	7.7
Alou,Moises, ChC	6.9

Offensive Winning %

Bonds,Barry, SF	.938
Rolen,Scott, StL	.805
Pujols,Albert, StL	.794
Helton,Todd, Col	.780
Drew,J.D., Atl	.780
Edmonds,Jim, StL	.779
Berkman,Lance, Hou	.779
Abreu,Bobby, Phi	.775
Beltre,Adrian, LA	.753
Loretta,Mark, SD	.710

Secondary Average
(minimum 502 PA)

Bonds,Barry, SF	1.088
Edmonds,Jim, StL	.560
Abreu,Bobby, Phi	.533
Drew,J.D., Atl	.515
Thome,Jim, Phi	.512
Helton,Todd, Col	.510
Dunn,Adam, Cin	.504
Berkman,Lance, Hou	.500
Pujols,Albert, StL	.476
Wilkerson,Brad, Mon	.451

Isolated Power
(minimum 502 PA)

Bonds,Barry, SF	.450
Edmonds,Jim, StL	.341
Pujols,Albert, StL	.326
Thome,Jim, Phi	.307
Dunn,Adam, Cin	.303
Beltre,Adrian, LA	.294
Rolen,Scott, StL	.284
Burnitz,Jeromy, Col	.276
Helton,Todd, Col	.272
Alou,Moises, ChC	.265

Power / Speed Number

Abreu,Bobby, Phi	34.3
Patterson,C, ChC	27.4
Cameron,Mike, NYM	25.4
Podsednik,S, Mil	20.5
Batista,Tony, Mon	19.5
Rollins,Jimmy, Phi	19.1
Furcal,Rafael, Atl	18.9
Wilkerson,Brad, Mon	18.5
Lee,De, ChC	17.5
Drew,J.D., Atl	17.3

Speed Scores (2003-2004)

Furcal,Rafael, Atl	8.17
Podsednik,S, Mil	7.84
Pierre,Juan, Fla	7.47
Rollins,Jimmy, Phi	7.43
Patterson,C, ChC	7.39
Chavez,En, Mon	7.39
Womack,Tony, StL	7.10
Durham,Ray, SF	6.85
Drew,J.D., Atl	6.67
Izturis,Cesar, LA	6.66

Cheap Wins

Milton,Eric, Phi	7
Suppan,Jeff, StL	7
Carpenter,C, StL	6
Lawrence,Brian, SD	6
Valdez,Ismael, SD-Fla	6
Weaver,Jeff, LA	6
Jennings,Jason, Col	4
Lidle,Cory, Cin-Phi	4
Marquis,Jason, StL	4
Wells,David, SD	4

Tough Losses

Sheets,Ben, Mil	11
Johnson,Ra, Ari	10
Weaver,Jeff, LA	8
Perez,Ol, Pit	7
Clement,Matt, ChC	5
Davis,Doug, Mil	5
Hernandez,L, Mon	5
Maddux,Greg, ChC	5
5 tied with	4

Additional Bill James Leaders

AL Batters Win Shares (2004)		NL Batters Win Shares (2004)		AL Pitchers Win Shares (2004)		NL Pitchers Win Shares (2004)	
Sheffield,Gary, NYY	31	Bonds,Barry, SF	53	Santana,Johan, Min	27	Johnson,Ra, Ari	25
Rodriguez,Alex, NYY	30	Pujols,Albert, StL	40	Schilling,Curt, Bos	22	Clemens,Roger, Hou	20
Tejada,Miguel, Bal	30	Rolen,Scott, StL	38	Buehrle,Mark, CWS	19	Pavano,Carl, Fla	20
Guerrero,V, Ana	29	Abreu,Bobby, Phi	37	Radke,Brad, Min	19	Sheets,Ben, Mil	20
Matsui,Hideki, NYY	29	Beltre,Adrian, LA	37	Drese,Ryan, Tex	17	Hernandez,L, Mon	19
Ramirez,Manny, Bos	28	Edmonds,Jim, StL	36	Westbrook,Jake, Cle	17	Schmidt,Jason, SF	19
Suzuki,Ichiro, Sea	27	Drew,J.D., Atl	34	6 tied with	16	Zambrano,C, ChC	19
Blalock,Hank, Tex	26	Loretta,Mark, SD	33			Oswalt,Roy, Hou	18
Damon,Johnny, Bos	26	Berkman,Lance, Hou	32			Lidge,Brad, Hou	17
Jeter,Derek, NYY	26	2 tied with	31			Perez,Ol, Pit	17

Batters Win Shares (Career)		Pitchers Win Shares (Career)		2004 AL Component ERA (minimum 162 IP)		2004 NL Component ERA (minimum 162 IP)	
Bonds,Barry	664	Clemens,Roger	398	Santana,Johan, Min	2.07	Johnson,Ra, Ari	1.82
Biggio,Craig	395	Maddux,Greg	359	Schilling,Curt, Bos	2.75	Sheets,Ben, Mil	2.37
Bagwell,Jeff	386	Johnson,Ra	286	Radke,Brad, Min	3.35	Schmidt,Jason, SF	2.37
Palmeiro,R	376	Glavine,Tom	276	Garcia,F, Sea-CWS	3.37	Clemens,Roger, Hou	2.72
Alomar,Roberto	375	Brown,Kevin	241	Martinez,Pedro, Bos	3.44	Perez,Ol, Pit	2.99
Sheffield,Gary	368	Smoltz,John	234	Hudson,Tim, Oak	3.44	Pavano,Carl, Fla	3.10
Thomas,Frank	359	Mussina,Mike	225	Westbrook,Jake, Cle	3.45	Peavy,Jake, SD	3.18
Larkin,Barry	347	Martinez,Pedro	224	Harden,Rich, Oak	3.57	Wright,Jar, Atl	3.20
Griffey Jr.,K	340	Schilling,Curt	224	Escobar,Kelvim, Ana	3.65	Zambrano,C, ChC	3.21
McGriff,Fred	326	Wells,David	192	Arroyo,Bronson, Bos	3.65	Wells,David, SD	3.23

Win Shares

Bill James devised Win Shares to reduce a player's statistics to a single number related to the number of wins he contributed to his team. It includes offensive, pitching and defensive accomplishments. The quality of the team does not effect an individual player's Win Shares. A great player on a bad team will rate as well as a great player on a good team. This section contains the sum of a player's Win Shares before 1995, then individual season from 1995 on.

A Win Share is one-third of a team's win, credited to an individual player. The Win Shares credited to the players on a team always total up to exactly three times the team's win total. If the team wins 100 games, the players on their team will be credited with 300 Win Shares—300 thirds of a win. If the team wins 80 games, the players on the team will be credited with 240 Win Shares, always and without exception.

Win Shares are a great tool for evaluating trades, award voting and Hall of Fame credentials. Last year, wins shares showed that the Brewers had a net gain from the Sexson trade. Take a look to see where your team's weaknesses and strengths lie and see if this winter's transactions help or hurt the W column.

WIN SHARES BY YEAR												
Player	<95	95	96	97	98	99	00	01	02	03	04	Career
Aardsma,David											0	0
Abbott,Paul	3				2	7	11	9	0	2	0	34
Abreu,Bobby			0	6	26	26	23	26	29	28	37	201
Acevedo,Jose								2	0	2	0	4
Adams,Mike											5	5
Adams,Russ											2	2
Adams,Terry		0	9	5	5	9	6	8	5	7	5	59
Adkins,Jon										0	3	3
Affeldt,Jeremy									5	12	4	21
Aguila,Chris											0	0
Ainsworth,Kurt								0	2	3	0	5
Alexander,M											1	1
Alfaro,Jason											0	0
Alfonseca,A			0	3	11	10	9	7	1		8	49
Alfonzo,E		8	6	28	22	29	36	15	25	17	15	201
Allen,Chad						7	1	2	0	0	0	10
Almanza,A						2	3	2	3	0	0	10
Almanzar,C											8	8
Alomar,Roberto	166	16	31	21	19	35	20	37	15	12	3	375
Alomar Jr.,S	45	7	8	18	6	4	8	4	5	4	2	111
Alou,Moises	58	11	20	23	29		17	21	9	20	26	234
Alvarez,Abe											0	0
Alvarez,Tony											1	1
Alvarez,Wilson	34	8	13	15	7	10			2	10	6	105
Amezaga,A									2	1	0	3
Anderson,Brian	7	3	3	2	9	7	14	2	5	12	3	67
Anderson,G	0	11	6	16	18	16	15	17	24	25	15	163
Anderson,Ja										1	0	1
Anderson,Ji					3	4	7	3	0	0		17
Anderson,M			2	8	2	16	10	12	3			53
Ankiel,Rick											0	0
Appier,Kevin	87	16	19	18	0	9	11	15	11	3	0	189
Aquino,Greg											5	5
Ardoin,Danny											0	0
Armas Jr.,Tony						0	5	12	7	4	1	29
Arroyo,Bronson							0	3	2	2	10	17
Ashby,Andy	10	14	11	6	15	13	8	1	7	0	0	85
Astacio,Pedro	18	5	13	10	6	19	11	7	5	0	0	94
Atchison,Scott											2	2
Atkins,Garrett										0	2	2
Aurilia,Rich		2	5	5	13	18	20	33	14	13	5	128
Ausmus,Brad	8	13	8	13	14	17	16	10	9	12	6	126
Ayala,Luis										11	9	20
Backe,Brandon									0	1	5	6
Bacsik,Mike								0	2	0	1	3
Baek,Cha Seung											0	0
Baerga,Carlos	95	23	6	11	10	2			2	7	1	157
Baez,Danys								6	11	9	8	34
Bagwell,Jeff	104	20	41	32	29	37	25	30	23	22	23	386
Bajenaru,Jeff											0	0
Bako,Paul					5	5	5	3	3	5	1	27
Baldelli,Rocco										14	15	29
Baldwin,James		0	10	6	6	9	11	8	3	0	0	53
Balfour,Grant									0	2	3	5
Barajas,Rod						1	0	1	3	5	9	19
Bard,Josh									1	7	2	10
Barmes,Clint											2	2
Barrett,M					1	11	1	2	12	7	15	49
Bartlett,Jason											0	0
Bartosh,Cliff											1	1
Batista,Miguel	0		0	0	6	6	0	11	9	14	11	57
Batista,Tony			9	2	10	21	18	12	16	11	13	112
Bauer,Rick								0	5	2	3	10
Bautista,Da	2	1	1	2	2	3	10	6	6	5	12	50
Bautista,De											0	0
Bautista,Jose										0	0	0
Bay,Jason										5	17	22
Beck,Rod	42	7	10	12	13	3	5	7		7	0	106
Beckett,Josh								3	5	11	9	28
Bedard,Erik											6	6
Beimel,Joe							4	3	2	0		9
Bell,David		2	1	2	10	16	8	14	19	5	20	97
Bell,Heath											2	2
Bell,Rob					5	1	2	3	7			18
Bellhorn,Mark				5	0		0	1	19	4	21	50
Belliard,R					0	0	17	13	1	11	18	60
Beltran,Carlos					2	18	5	27	22	28	31	133
Beltran,F											2	2

WIN SHARES BY YEAR												
Player	<95	95	96	97	98	99	00	01	02	03	04	Career
Beltran,Rigo											0	0
Beltre,Adrian					4	15	22	12	16	15	37	121
Benitez,A	1	1	3	11	10	19	17	14	12	10	16	114
Bennett,Gary		0	0		1	2	3	1	4	6	1	18
Bennett,Jeff											2	2
Benoit,Joaquin								0	3	5	3	11
Benson,Kris						12	14		5	2	9	42
Bentz,Chad											0	0
Berg,Dave					9	6	5	3	8	1	1	33
Berger,Brandon								1	2	1	0	4
Bergeron,Peter											0	0
Bergman,Dusty											0	0
Berkman,Lance						1	10	32	30	25	32	130
Bernero,Adam							2	0	1	1	1	5
Berroa,Angel								1	1	16	10	28
Betancourt,R										4	6	10
Betemit,Wilson											0	0
Biddle,Rocky							0	4	4	8	0	16
Bierbrodt,Nick								3	0	1		4
Bigbie,Larry								2	0	9	12	23
Biggio,Craig	141	29	32	38	35	31	11	25	15	20	18	395
Blackley,T											0	0
Blake,Casey						1		0	1	11	17	30
Blalock,Hank									1	17	26	44
Blanco,Andres											3	3
Blanco,Henry			0		6	9	6	4	2	4		31
Blanton,Joe											0	0
Bloomquist,W									3	3	3	9
Blum,Geoff						3	10	8	15	5	3	44
Bocachica,H							0	3	1	0	1	5
Boehringer,B		0	2	4	4	7	0	4	9	2	1	33
Bonderman,J										2	8	10
Bonds,Barry	273	36	39	36	34	19	32	54	49	39	53	664
Bong,Jung									0	3	0	3
Boone,Bret	24	15	10	8	18	17	15	32	25	30	9	203
Borchard,Joe									1	0	0	1
Borders,Pat	49	2	4	3	1	1		0	0	1	2	63
Borkowski,Dave										2		2
Borland,Toby	3	5	6	0	0			0	1	1	0	16
Borowski,Joe		1	1	2	0			0	8	14	0	26
Bottalico,R	0	11	13	10	0		8	6	0	0	6	54
Bowen,Rob										0	0	0
Boyd,Jason							0	0	0	3	0	3
Bradford,Chad					3	0	2	3	9	9	4	30
Bradley,Milton							3	3	6	18	17	47
Bragg,Darren	0	2	10	11	11	7	2	2	6	1	1	53
Branyan,R					0	1	5	10	8	6	5	35
Brazell,Craig											0	0
Brazelton,D									1	0	6	7
Brazoban,Y											4	4
Brito,Juan											0	0
Brocail,Doug											4	4
Brooks,Frank											0	0
Broussard,Ben									0	9	16	25
Brower,Jim						2	1	8	5	7	8	31
Brown,Adrian											0	0
Brown,Dee					0	0	0	4	0	2	2	8
Brown,Jamie											0	0
Brown,Kevin	73	13	26	23	26	19	20	11	1	20	9	241
Bruney,Brian											2	2
Bruntlett,Eric										1	2	3
Buchanan,Brian							0	5	5	5	0	15
Buck,John											4	4
Buehrle,Mark							4	18	17	13	19	71
Bukvich,Ryan									1	0	1	2
Bullinger,Kirk											0	0
Bump,Nate										2	1	3
Burba,Dave	10	7	10	7	15	15	13	3	6	3	5	94
Burke,Chris											0	0
Burke,Jamie								0		1	5	6
Burks,Ellis	110	8	28	15	14	24	21	14	21	5	0	260
Burnett,A.J.						3	5	9	14	0	7	38
Burnett,Sean											2	2
Burnitz,Jeromy	10	1	6	20	19	19	16	18	7	12	18	146
Burrell,Pat							12	17	25	9	15	78
Burroughs,Sean									2	16	15	33
Bush,David											8	8
Bush,Homer											0	0

WIN SHARES BY YEAR												
Player	<95	95	96	97	98	99	00	01	02	03	04	Career
Bynum,Mike									0	0	0	0
Byrd,Marlon									0	16	6	22
Byrd,Paul											7	7
Byrnes,Eric							0	1	2	16	19	38
Cabrera,Daniel											8	8
Cabrera,F											0	0
Cabrera,J					0	0	2	6	1	9	8	26
Cabrera,Miguel										12	22	34
Cabrera,O				0	6	8	9	26	14	20	11	94
Cairo,Miguel			0	0	10	10	10	4	3	3	13	53
Calero,Kiko										3	5	8
Cali,Carmen											0	0
Callaway,M				0			0	2		0	0	2
Calloway,Ron										5	0	5
Cameron,Mike		0	0	17	6	19	19	29	19	21	18	148
Camp,Shawn											4	4
Cantu,Jorge											4	4
Capellan,Jose											0	0
Capuano,Chris										1	3	4
Carpenter,C											11	11
Carrara,G		0	0	0			0	8	7	0	7	22
Carrasco,D.J.										6	2	8
Carroll,Jamey									3	3	6	12
Carter,Lance					0				3	10	7	20
Casey,Sean				0	10	23	17	18	5	17	30	120
Cash,Kevin									0	0	1	1
Castilla,Vinny	9	13	23	21	21	11	3	13	2	14	16	146
Castillo,A		0	1	1	3	7	4	3	0	1	2	22
Castillo,Frank											0	0
Castillo,Jose											8	8
Castillo,Luis			3	3	3	14	18	14	19	22	21	117
Castro,Juan		0	2	1	3	0	3	1	2	8	4	24
Castro,RA											0	0
Castro,RR						1	3	0	4	2	0	10
Catalanotto,F				1	4	5	8	17	7	15	5	62
Cedeno,Roger		1	7	9	3	17	5	14	10	8	6	80
Cepicky,Matt									1	0	0	1
Cerda,Jaime									2	0	4	6
Chacin,Gustavo											2	2
Chacon,Shawn								7	4	9	0	20
Chavez,En								0	3	10	11	24
Chavez,Er					2	9	16	26	25	25	19	122
Chavez,Raul		0	0	0		0			0	1	1	2
Chen,Bruce					1	1	11	4	2	0	4	23
Chen,Chin-Feng									0	0	0	0
Choate,Randy							1	4	0	0	3	8
Choi,Hee Seop									0	6	14	20
Christiansen,J		4	0	4	9	4	4	4	0	1	2	32
Chulk,Vinnie											4	4
Church,Ryan											0	0
Cintron,Alex								0	1	14	8	23
Cirillo,Jeff	2	10	20	24	26	22	19	14	9	3	0	149
Clark,Brady							0	4	1	7	13	25
Clark,Howie									0	3	1	4
Clark,Jermaine									0			1
Clark,Tony		2	8	24	15	19	6	16	1	4	8	103
Claussen,B										1	0	1
Clayton,Royce	29	12	12	13	12	15	8	10	8	7	11	137
Clemens,Roger	220	10	20	32	25	10	16	19	11	15	20	398
Clement,Matt					1	6	5	4	11	10	11	48
Closser,J.D.											2	2
Colbrunn,Greg	10	14	10	4	4	5	12	3	7	1	0	70
Collier,Lou				1	8	2	0	4	0	0	1	16
Colome,Jesus								4	0	4	5	13
Colon,Bartolo				2	16	16	15	14	22	17	10	112
Colon,Roman											2	2
Colyer,Steve										2	0	2
Conine,Jeff	33	20	17	9	6	10	9	24	10	16	19	173
Conti,Jason							3	0	4	1	1	9
Contreras,J										7	5	12
Cook,Aaron									2	3	6	11
Cooper,Brian							0					0
Cora,Alex					1	0	6	6	13	13	17	56
Corcoran,Roy										1	0	1
Cordero,Chad										2	10	12
Cordero,F						2	3	0	8	12	15	40
Cordero,Wil	34	12	5	11	8	5	10	1	6	11	0	103
Corey,Mark								0	0	1	1	2

WIN SHARES BY YEAR												
Player	<95	95	96	97	98	99	00	01	02	03	04	Career
Cormier,Lance											0	0
Cormier,Rheal	17	8	8	0		5	4	4	1	14	7	68
Cornejo,Nate								0	1	8	0	9
Correia,Kevin										3	0	3
Cota,Humberto								0	0	0	1	1
Cotts,Neal										0	3	3
Counsell,Craig			0	8	13	2	5	14	15	5	11	73
Crain,Jesse											4	4
Crawford,Carl									6	13	21	40
Crede,Joe							0	1	6	13	9	29
Crespo,Cesar										0	0	0
Cressend,Jack							1	5	0	4	0	10
Crisp,Coco									3	7	15	25
Crosby,Bo										0	13	13
Crosby,Bu										0	1	1
Crowell,Jim							0					0
Crozier,Eric											1	1
Cruceta,F											0	0
Cruz,Deivi				7	7	13	15	8	7	10	12	79
Cruz,Ja											4	4
Cruz,Jo				11	12	11	15	16	14	17	15	111
Cruz,Ju								4	3	0	7	14
Cubillan,D							0					0
Cuddyer,Mike								0	3	1	10	14
Cummings,Midre											3	3
Cunnane,Will				2	0	1	2	1	1	3	0	10
Cust,Jack								0	0	4	0	4
Daigle,Casey											0	0
Dallimore,B											1	1
D'Amico,Jeff			4	6		0	15	0	3	6	0	34
Damon,Johnny		6	9	11	17	18	26	17	21	18	26	169
Darensbourg,V					3	0	5	3	0	0	0	11
Daubach,Brian					0	14	10	13	14	4	2	57
DaVanon,Jeff							0	1	1	12	10	24
Davis,Ben					0	3	3	15	10	7	3	41
Davis,Doug						0	5	8	3	7	14	37
Davis,JJ									0	0	0	0
Davis,Ja									2	5	2	9
Dawley,Joe									0	0	0	0
Day,Zach									3	8	6	17
de la Rosa,J										0	0	0
de los Santos,V					2	0	3	0	4	4	0	13
DeJean,Mike				7	9	0	4	8	8	6	2	44
DeJesus,David										0	9	9
Delgado,Carlos	3	0	12	18	24	21	36	23	26	32	17	212
Delgado,Wilson			1	0	0	1	3	0	0	1	5	11
Dellucci,David				1	10	5	1	7	4	4	11	43
Dempster,Ryan					0	6	17	7	4	0	1	35
Denney,Kyle											0	0
DePaula,Jorge										2	0	2
DeRosa,Mark					0	0	1	6	7	5	2	21
Dessens,Elmer			1	1	1		10	10	15	7	5	50
DeVore,Doug											1	1
Diaz,Einar			0	0	1	8	6	15	4	5	1	40
Diaz,Felix											0	0
Diaz,Matt										0	0	0
Diaz,Victor											1	1
Dickey,R.A.								0		6	4	10
DiFelice,Mike			0	6	5	8	2	1	4	6	0	32
Dinardo,Lenny											1	1
Dingman,Craig							0				0	0
Dobbs,Greg											0	0
Dohmann,Scott											4	4
Dominguez,Juan										0	2	2
Dominique,Andy											0	0
Donnelly,B									6	12	5	23
Dotel,Octavio						3	7	12	17	12	11	62
Douglass,Sean											0	0
Downs,Scott							0	0			0	0
Dransfeldt,K											1	1
Dreifort,D	0		0	7	9	8	9	1		3	2	39
Drese,Ryan								3	2	0	17	22
Drew,J.D.					3	10	18	22	15	13	34	115
Drew,Tim							0	0	2	0	0	2
Driskill,T									5	1	0	6
Dubois,Jason											1	1
DuBose,Eric									1	5	1	7
Duchscherer,J											10	10

WIN SHARES BY YEAR

Player	<95	95	96	97	98	99	00	01	02	03	04	Career
Duckworth,B								5	2	2	0	9
Duncan,Jeff										3	0	3
Dunn,Adam								10	21	13	31	75
Dunn,Scott											0	0
Durazo,Erubiel						9	5	7	10	17	20	68
Durbin,Chad						0	0	8	0	0	0	8
Durbin,J.D.											0	0
Durham,Ray		8	17	13	25	20	19	21	20	16	20	179
Durrington,T							1		0	0	1	2
Dye,Jermaine			5	2	2	16	21	18	13	2	13	92
Easley,Damion	14	4	3	18	23	13	14	15	5	0	8	117
Eaton,Adam							9	5	0	7	6	27
Eckstein,David								12	20	11	9	52
Edmonds,Jim	8	21	18	19	24	5	29	30	29	22	36	241
Eischen,Joey	0	1	3	0				1	9	5	1	20
Elarton,Scott				5	10	11	0			0	6	32
Eldred,Cal	39	2	5	9	3	0	7	0		6	4	75
Ellison,Jason										0	1	1
Embree,Alan	0	1	0	6	3	6	3	2	7	5	4	37
Encarnacion,J				1	4	8	14	5	14	15	13	74
Ennis,John											0	0
Ensberg,Morgan							0		2	15	10	27
Erickson,Matt											0	0
Erickson,Scott											0	0
Erstad,Darin			3	19	21	9	30	14	17	3	15	131
Escalona,Felix									1	1	0	2
Escobar,Alex									1	1	3	5
Escobar,Kelvim				6	7	7	8	11	9	12	15	75
Estalella,B			1	2	1	0	15	3	4	4	0	30
Estes,Shawn		0	4	16	3	6	10	7	4	0	9	59
Estrada,Johnny								5	0	0	19	24
Estrella,Leo							0			6	0	6
Everett,Adam								0	1	11	12	24
Everett,Carl	0	8	2	13	16	25	24	11	9	21	5	134
Eyre,Scott				2	2	0	0	2	4	5	4	19
Falkenborg,B											0	0
Farnsworth,K						5	0	9	0	7	3	24
Fassero,Jeff	39	8	18	17	14	1	8	10	2	0	4	121
Feliciano,P									0	3	0	3
Feliz,Pedro							0	0	2	8	11	21
Fernandez,J								0	2	2	0	4
Fetters,Mike	24	5	10	7	4	1	7	2	4	1	0	65
Fick,Robert					2	2	4	10	12	14	2	46
Field,Nate									0	2	3	5
Figgins,Chone									0	8	20	28
Figueroa,N							0	6	1	3	0	10
Fikac,Jeremy								3	0	1	1	5
File,Bob										2		2
Finley,Steve	82	19	27	19	15	24	21	15	23	18	18	281
Flaherty,John	1	7	10	11	5	12	8	4	7	3	3	71
Flores,Jose											0	0
Flores,Randy											2	2
Floyd,Cliff	10	1	6	5	18	9	19	26	22	15	14	145
Floyd,Gavin											2	2
Fogg,Josh								2	10	4	7	23
Foppert,Jesse										2	0	2
Ford,Ben											0	0
Ford,Lew										4	22	26
Fordyce,Brook		0	1	1	2	12	11	2	1	5	0	35
Fortunato,B										1		1
Fossum,Casey								2	6	3	0	11
Foulke,Keith				4	5	16	16	17	10	21	15	104
Fox,Andy			2	1	15	7	4	1	14	1	0	45
Fox,Chad				2	4	0		9	0	5	0	20
Francis,Jeff											2	2
Francisco,F											6	6
Franco,Jo	121	10	10	12	8	6	7	5		3	1	183
Franco,Ju	219	13	9		0			3	6	6	12	268
Franklin,Ryan						1		5	6	13	6	31
Franklin,Wayne							1	0	2	4	0	7
Frasor,Jason											7	7
Frederick,K											0	0
Freel,Ryan							0			3	18	21
Freeman,Choo											1	1
Fuentes,Brian								1	2	10	2	15
Fullmer,Brad			2	15	5	15	9	13	8	2		69
Fultz,Aaron							3	3	1	3	3	13
Furcal,Rafael							17	9	20	25	21	92

Player	<95	95	96	97	98	99	00	01	02	03	04	Career
Gagne,Eric						3	2	4	19	25	16	69
Galarraga,A	124	14	25	20	27		16	11	5	9	0	251
Gallo,Mike										3	2	5
Garcia,Danny										0	5	5
Garcia,Freddy						16	8	18	11	8	16	77
Garcia,Ja											0	0
Garcia,Je						0	0	0	1	1	2	4
Garcia,Karim		0	0	1	4	4	0	3	7	5	3	27
Garcia,Rosman										1	0	1
Garciaparra,N			2	26	27	32	29	3	27	25	12	183
Garland,Jon							1	8	9	10	11	39
Gathright,Joey											0	0
Gaudin,Chad										3	1	4
Geary,Geoff										0	1	1
George,Chris								2	1	2	0	5
German,Esteban											2	2
German,F									2	0	0	2
Germano,Justin											0	0
Gerut,Jody										14	10	24
Gettis,Byron											0	0
Giambi,Jason		5	15	18	23	30	38	38	34	28	8	237
Gibbons,Jay								4	12	18	5	39
Gil,Geronimo								2	6	3	1	12
Gil,Jerry											0	0
Giles,Brian		1	6	13	14	27	27	29	32	25	25	199
Giles,Marcus								9	5	28	18	60
Ginter,Keith							0	0	2	9	12	23
Ginter,Matt							0	2	2	0	2	6
Gipson,Charles					1	1	1	1	1	0	1	6
Gissell,Chris											0	0
Glanville,Doug			2	9	17	23	10	11	5	2	1	80
Glaus,Troy					3	16	25	21	22	9	9	105
Glavine,Tom	99	20	22	21	23	14	21	16	18	7	15	276
Gload,Ross											8	8
Glover,Gary							0	4	5	3	1	13
Glynn,Ryan											1	1
Gobble,Jimmy										3	6	9
Gomes,Jonny											0	0
Gomez,Alexis											0	0
Gomez,Chris	10	6	11	7	15	6	1	8	11	2	8	85
Gonzalez,Ad											1	1
Gonzalez,Al					1	11	3	10	3	20	15	63
Gonzalez,AS	1	7	14	10	9	6	11	16	13	16	5	108
Gonzalez,Dicky											0	0
Gonzalez,Edgar										1	0	1
Gonzalez,Je			9	2						8	0	19
Gonzalez,Ju	83	11	21	19	25	24	9	23	6	10	3	234
Gonzalez,LE	59	15	17	12	12	26	27	37	26	24	12	267
Gonzalez,LA											7	7
Gonzalez,Mike										0	8	8
Gonzalez,Raul							0	0	2	4	0	6
Good,Andy										2	1	3
Goodwin,Tom	1	10	9	9	13	5	14	5	5	3	0	74
Gordon,Tom	61	11	10	15	17	2		8	3	11	15	153
Gosling,Mike											1	1
Gotay,Ruben											2	2
Grabow,John											1	1
Grabowski,J									1	0	4	5
Gracesqui,F											0	0
Graffanino,T			1	6	4	7	6	3	7	9	6	49
Graman,Alex										0	0	0
Granderson,C											0	0
Graves,Danny			2	0	8	16	18	11	17	3	5	80
Green,Andy											0	0
Green,Nick											9	9
Green,Shawn	0	10	8	14	21	24	22	34	30	20	17	200
Greene,Khalil										1	20	21
Greene,Todd			1	4	1	3	0	0	1	1	4	15
Gregg,Kevin										2	6	8
Greinke,Zack											11	11
Greisinger,S											0	0
Grieve,Ben				4	22	16	17	17	12	2	8	98
Griffey Jr.,K	142	9	28	36	29	31	24	14	5	6	16	340
Griffiths,J									0	0	0	0
Grilli,Jason											0	0
Grimsley,Jason	10	0	1			6	5	8	7	4	5	46
Grissom,M	103	18	24	14	11	13	8	6	15	22	16	250
Groom,Buddy	3	0	7	3	4	3	6	8	10	1	3	48

Player	<95	95	96	97	98	99	00	01	02	03	04	Career
Gross,Gabe											2	2
Grudzielanek,M		3	17	14	13	13	15	17	13	18	9	132
Gryboski,Kevin									4	3	5	12
Guardado,Eddie	1	4	6	3	5	4	8	12	14	15	7	79
Guerrero,V			0	10	29	28	29	23	29	18	29	195
Guerrero,W											0	0
Guerrier,Matt											0	0
Guiel,Aaron									4	12	0	16
Guillen,Carlos					2	0	8	14	12	12	24	72
Guillen,Jose				7	11	3	6	2	2	20	21	72
Guthrie,Jeremy											0	0
Gutierrez,R	11	3	4	4	12	6	15	16	8	0	0	79
Guzman,C						5	12	18	13	13	15	76
Guzman,Freddy											0	0
Hafner,Travis									1	7	21	29
Hairston,Scott											4	4
Hairston Jr.,J					0	5	4	10	12	7	8	46
Halama,John				0	13	6	4	6	4	4	6	39
Hall,Bill									1	4	8	13
Hall,Toby						0	6	7	10	9		32
Halladay,Roy					2	10	0	9	21	23	10	75
Halsey,Brad											0	0
Halter,Shane				1	3	0	3	16	8	2	2	35
Hammock,Robby										6	2	8
Hammond,Chris	25	10	0	2	0				13	7	6	63
Hammonds,J	10	4	3	14	9	8	14	5	8	4	1	80
Hampton,Mike	3	8	11	11	15	26	19	11	5	11	9	129
Hancock,Josh											3	3
Hansen,Dave	14	5	0	6		3	6	4	4	3	3	48
Harang,Aaron									4	2	4	10
Harden,Rich										4	14	18
Haren,Danny										1	1	2
Harikkala,Tim											6	6
Harper,Travis						2	0	3	6	7		18
Harris,Brendan											0	0
Harris,Lenny	50	2	10	3	3	4	5	0	4	1	0	82
Harris,Willie								0	2	2	10	14
Hart,Bo										7	0	7
Hart,Corey											0	0
Harvey,Ken								0		7	8	15
Harville,Chad						0		1	0	2		3
Hasegawa,S				7	11	5	11	5	7	13	3	62
Hatteberg,S		0	0	6	11	4	5	5	16	14	17	78
Hawkins,LaTroy		0	0	2	6	3	12	3	11	13	12	62
Hawpe,Brad											1	1
Haynes,Jimmy		3	0	4	7	1	6	6	12	0	0	39
Heilman,Aaron										0	0	0
Helms,Wes				1		0	5	1	12	5		24
Helton,Todd				2	17	19	29	26	27	34	31	185
Hendrickson,B											0	0
Hendrickson,M									4	4	8	16
Hennessey,Brad											1	1
Hensley,Matt											1	1
Hentgen,Pat	34	7	24	19	8	10	10	4	0	10	0	126
Heredia,Felix			1	3	3	3	4	0	3	9	0	26
Herges,Matt					1	10	9	4	7	1		32
Hermansen,Chad						0	0	0	3	0	0	3
Hermanson,D		0	0	10	13	12	9	8	0	4	6	62
Hernandez,A											0	0
Hernandez,C											0	0
Hernandez,Jose	2	6	6	4	16	16	9	13	19	6	10	107
Hernandez,L			1	8	6	9	14	5	7	22	19	91
Hernandez,O										9		9
Hernandez,Ra						6	10	13	12	19	13	73
Hernandez,Ro	34	6	17	15	10	14	12	9	7	3	1	128
Hessman,Mike										1	0	1
Hidalgo,R				2	6	9	21	17	7	20	11	93
Hietpas,Joe											0	0
Higginson,B		8	21	25	16	9	26	18	15	6	13	157
Hill,Bobby									5	0	4	9
Hill,Koyie											1	1
Hill,Shawn											0	0
Hillenbrand,S								5	17	11	14	47
Hinch,A.J.					5	3	0	2	4	1	0	15
Hinske,Eric									22	12	7	41
Hitchcock,S	5	9	8	3	9	10	1	2	1	3	0	51
Hocking,Denny	1	0	1	6	2	8	11	5	5	4	0	43
Hoffman,Trevor											9	9

Player	<95	95	96	97	98	99	00	01	02	03	04	Career
Hollandsworth,T		2	19	7	6	7	8	4	12	5	6	76
Holliday,Matt											10	10
Hollins,Damon											0	0
Horgan,Joe											4	4
House,J.R.											0	0
Howard,Ben									0	1	0	1
Howard,Ryan											1	1
Howry,Bob					7	10	9	5	3	0	5	39
Huckaby,Ken								0	2	0	0	2
Hudson,Luke											5	5
Hudson,Orlando									7	18	16	41
Hudson,Tim						12	15	17	23	23	16	106
Huff,Aubrey							3	5	12	21	20	61
Hughes,Travis											0	0
Huisman,Justin											0	0
Hummel,Tim										2	0	2
Hunter,Torii				0	0	5	8	19	21	15	15	83
Hyzdu,Adam						1	1	6	1	1		10
Ibanez,Raul			0	0	1	4	1	9	13	15	13	56
Infante,Omar									3	3	13	19
Inge,Brandon								3	5	5	12	25
Ishii,Kazuhisa									6	6	6	18
Isringhausen,J		8	6	0		4	10	14	13	7	12	74
Izturis,Cesar								4	4	11	25	44
Izturis,Maicer										1		1
Jackson,Damian		1	1	2	11	15	11	7	2	0		50
Jackson,Edwin											0	0
Jackson,Mike										2		2
Jacobsen,Bucky											4	4
Jarvis,Kevin	0	0	0	1		0	4	7	1	0	0	13
Jenkins,Geoff					1	18	20	11	5	20	14	89
Jennings,Jason								3	14	9	10	36
Jeter,Derek		1	18	19	27	35	23	28	24	18	26	219
Jimenez,D						1		8	11	17	23	60
Jimenez,Jose			2	2	15	8	13	6	0			46
Johnson,C	1	12	10	21	15	12	20	17	6	10	7	131
Johnson,Jason			0	2	4	0	9	5	10	6		36
Johnson,Mark L			0	5	5	5	3	1	0			19
Johnson,Nick						0	11	14	7			32
Johnson,Ra	79	22	5	23	19	26	26	26	29	6	25	286
Johnson,Re									11	10		21
Johnston,Mike											0	0
Jones,Andruw			3	13	26	28	30	22	28	23	19	192
Jones,Bobby M											0	0
Jones,Chipper	0	20	26	23	29	32	27	29	31	26	19	262
Jones,Jacque					9	11	10	25	14	14		83
Jones,Todd	12	9	5	13	7	10	10	5	6	1	8	86
Jordan,Brian	13	18	27	1	21	22	14	19	9	7	1	162
Julio,Jorge								1	13	6	5	25
Kapler,Gabe					0	8	10	13	8	4	5	48
Karros,Eric	30	25	20	18	22	20	14	8	18	8	0	183
Karsay,Steve											1	1
Kata,Matt										8	3	11
Kazmir,Scott											1	1
Kearns,Austin									16	12	5	33
Kelton,Dave										0	0	0
Kendall,Jason			12	22	26	13	24	9	13	20	25	164
Kennedy,Adam						2	11	8	17	14	13	65
Kennedy,Joe								6	9	0	15	30
Kensing,Logan											0	0
Kent,Jeff	41	11	11	22	25	23	37	27	29	20	24	270
Keppinger,Jeff											2	2
Kershner,Jason									1	5	0	6
Kida,Masao						2	0			1	1	4
Kielty,Bobby								1	15	12	4	32
Kieschnick,B			1	2				0	1	4	4	12
Kim,Byung-Hyun						2	8	16	20	14	0	60
Kim,Sun-Woo								1	3	0	5	9
King,Ray						0	4	5	5	5	7	26
Kinney,Matt							2		2	4	1	9
Klesko,Ryan	10	17	20	16	13	18	23	29	31	13	19	209
Kline,Steve				1	6	7	9	12	6	5	6	52
Knoedler,J											0	0
Knott,Jon											0	0
Knotts,Gary								0	2	1	5	8
Koch,Billy						10	16	8	19	2	3	58
Kolb,Danny							2	0	1	2	9	23
Konerko,Paul				0	1	14	15	17	17	4	20	88

Player	<95	95	96	97	98	99	00	01	02	03	04	Career
Koplove,Mike								0	7	5	7	19
Koskie,Corey				0	13	17	24	19	21	14		108
Kotchman,Casey											2	2
Kotsay,Mark				1	13	6	12	16	22	14	22	106
Kroeger,Josh											0	0
Kroon,Marc											0	0
Krynzel,Dave											1	1
Kubel,Jason											3	3
Labandeira,J											0	0
Lackey,John									7	8	11	26
Laird,Gerald										1	1	2
Laker,Tim	1	3		0	1	0		1		4	1	11
Lamb,Mike							6	8	7	0	12	33
Lane,Jason									3	1	6	10
Lankford,Ray											5	5
Larkin,Barry	180	30	31	12	25	24	13	5	9	7	11	347
LaRoche,Adam											8	8
Larson,Brandon							0	2	1	2		5
LaRue,Jason					2	3	9	11	10	15		50
Lawrence,Brian								6	8	8	7	29
Lawton,Matt		4	7	14	21	8	20	20	9	10	15	128
League,Brandon											1	1
LeCroy,Matt							2	3	4	12	4	25
Ledee,Ricky					2	9	10	4	5	7	6	43
Ledezma,Wil										2	3	5
Lee,Ca					10	14	15	17	20	24		100
Lee,Cl									1	3	7	11
Lee,Da										0		0
Lee,De				2	10	1	16	16	23	25	21	114
Lee,Travis					13	8	6	15	12	13	0	67
Lehr,Justin											1	1
Leicester,Jon											3	3
Leiter,Al	17	14	19	7	21	11	17	14	11	9	12	152
Leon,Jose								1	0	0		1
Leone,Justin											2	2
Leskanic,C	3	14	5	4	7	8	12	7		9	3	72
Levine,Al			0	0	3	7	7	10	4	7	4	42
Lewis,Colby									0	1	1	2
Lidge,Brad								1	8	17		26
Lidle,Cory				6		0	4	13	13	5	7	48
Lieber,Jon											11	11
Lieberthal,M	0	1	3	15	8	20	14	3	14	16	9	103
Liefer,Jeff							1	0	6	3	1	0	11
Ligtenberg,K				2	15		8	5	6	6	1	43
Lilly,Ted							0	0	3	6	10	16	35
Lima,Jose	0	2	3	1	14	18	2	4	0	5	9	58
Lincoln,Mike						1	0	4	6	2	1	14
Linden,Todd										1	0	1
Linebrink,S							1	1	0	5	10	17
Liriano,Pedro											1	1
Little,Mark											0	0
Lo Duca,Paul					0	2	2	28	19	19	21	91
Loaiza,Esteban		5	2	11	6	8	12	8	4	23	7	86
Loe,Kameron											0	0
Lofton,Kenny	70	21	23	21	21	16	17	13	19	18	7	246
Logan,Nook											3	3
Lohse,Kyle								3	11	11	6	31
Long,Terrence						0	18	17	12	11	6	64
Looper,Braden					0	5	5	7	11	12	10	50
Lopez,Aquilino										10	0	10
Lopez,Felipe							5	6	3	8		22
Lopez,Javr										7	0	7
Lopez,Javy	7	12	15	19	25	11	16	13	10	30	19	177
Lopez,Jo											3	3
Lopez,Luis											0	0
Lopez,LuisM											0	0
Lopez,Me					5	1	0	2	0	2	0	10
Lopez,Mi											0	0
Lopez,Rodrigo						0		15	2	15		32
Loretta,Mark		1	2	12	16	14	12	9	10	24	33	133
Lowe,Derek				1	7	19	19	11	22	12	6	97
Lowell,Mike					0	8	20	20	21	23	26	118
Lowry,Noah											6	6
Ludwick,Ryan								0	6	0		6
Lugo,Julio							9	9	9	14	21	62
Luna,Hector											4	4
Mabry,John	1	9	13	8	5	3	3	1	8	2	9	62
MacDougal,Mike								1	0	9	0	10

Player	<95	95	96	97	98	99	00	01	02	03	04	Career
Machado,Andy										2		2
Machado,Robert		1	0	1	0	0	3	4	1	0		10
Macias,Jose					0	5	12	8	2	4		31
Mackowiak,Rob							4	12	6	15		37
Maddux,Greg	152	30	23	26	25	17	24	20	19	11	12	359
Madritsch,B										8	8
Madson,Ryan											9	9
Magruder,Chris											1	1
Mahay,Ron		0		3	2	3	1	2	0	5	8	24
Maine,John											0	0
Majewski,Gary											0	0
Majewski,Val											0	0
Malaska,Mark										2	1	3
Mantei,Matt		0	0		5	12	6	1	1	14	0	39
Manzanillo,J	7	2		0		1	5	8	0	0	0	23
Maroth,Mike								6	4	12		22
Marquis,Jason							1	8	3	1	14	27
Marrero,Eli				1	6	5	5	7	14	3	13	54
Marsonek,Sam										0		0
Marte,Damaso						0		1	8	15	9	33
Martin,Tom				7	0	0	2	0	0	5	2	16
Martinez,A										0		0
Martinez,Edgar	83	32	23	27	24	22	28	25	13	20	8	305
Martinez,Pedro	24	14	14	26	21	27	29	12	21	20	16	224
Martinez,Ramon				0	5	7	9	9	7	6		43
Martinez,Sandy										0		0
Martinez,Tino	27	20	21	27	21	19	12	21	15	11	15	209
Martinez,V								1	3	20		24
Mateo,Henry							0	0	2	0		2
Mateo,Julio									1	7	3	11
Mateo,Ruben					3	3	1	1	3	2		13
Matheny,Mike	0	3	4	8	4	3	14	8	9	13	10	76
Matos,Luis							2	3	0	14	3	22
Matsui,Hideki										19	29	48
Matsui,Kazuo											14	14
Matthews,Mike							0	7	2	3	0	12
Matthews Jr.,G							1	1	10	10	9	12	43
Mauer,Joe											6	6
Maurer,Dave										0		0
May,Darrell		0	0	2					5	17	5	29
Mayne,Brent	21	7	1	6	9	13	8	6	5	10	1	87
McCarty,Dave	4	1	2		1		7	2	0	2	3	22
McConnell,Sam											1	1
McCracken,Q			0	7	8	12	2	0	0	15	1	3	48
McDonald,D										0		0
McDonald,John							0	0	0	5	2	1	8
McEwing,Joe						0	11	2	8	2	5	4	32
McGriff,Fred	188	20	19	14	13	24	0	22	18	8	0	326
McKay,Cody											1	1
McLeary,Marty										0		0
McLemore,Mark	45	11	16	5	12	15	13	18	13	8	6	162
McMillon,Billy			0	2			5	2		5	0	14
McPherson,D											1	1
Meadows,Brian				4	4	7	0	3	3	5	26
Meche,Gil					6	6			8	5	25
Mecir,Jim		1	2	0	9	2	12	6	6	1	4	43
Melhuse,Adam							0	0		4	6	10
Mench,Kevin									10	4	15	29
Mendoza,Ramiro			1	7	12	8	5	10	8	0	3	54
Menechino,F					0	6	18	3	2	9	38
Mercker,Kent	35	7	1	9	5	6	1		1	6	6	77
Merloni,Lou					4	2	3	2	6	5	5	27
Mesa,Jose	21	17	12	11	5	5	3	14	13	0	9	110
Meyer,Dan										0		0
Miceli,Danny	1	6	0	5	8	4	5	3	0	6	7	45
Michaels,Jason								0	3	5	11	19
Mientkiewicz,D					0	3	0	18	17	20	5	63
Miles,Aaron											11	11
Millar,Kevin					0	12	10	20	14	16	17	89
Miller,Corky								2	5	1	0	8
Miller,Damian			2	6	10	11	10	10	10	15	74
Miller,Justin										2	2
Miller,Matt									1	5	6
Miller,Trever		0		4	2	0			4	5	15
Miller,Wade						0	4	17	13	9	7	50
Millwood,Kevin			3	10	22	10	5	19	11	4	84
Milton,Eric										8	8
Minor,Damon										1	1

WIN SHARES BY YEAR

Player	<95	95	96	97	98	99	00	01	02	03	04	Career
Mirabelli,Doug			1	0	1	3	6	7	4	2	7	31
Mitre,Sergio										0	0	0
Moeller,Chad						2	0	6	6	2		16
Mohr,Dustan								1	11	6	10	28
Molina,Ben				0	3	13	7	9	16	11		59
Molina,Jose						0		1	2	2	5	10
Molina,Yadier											4	4
Mondesi,Raul	18	22	25	24	20	21	11	15	12	11	3	182
Monroe,Craig								1	0	10	12	23
Mora,Melvin						0	12	11	16	16	25	80
Mordecai,Mike	1	4	1	0	1	4	3	6	2	1	1	24
Moreno,Orber											3	3
Morneau,Justin										1	10	11
Morris,Matt				16	10		6	17	13	10	7	79
Moss,Damian								1	12	5	0	18
Mota,Guillermo						5	1	2	2	14	11	35
Mottola,Chad										1		1
Moyer,Jamie	47	5	11	14	18	18	5	15	16	18	6	173
Mueller,Bill			9	14	18	12	10	8	12	23	12	118
Mulder,Mark							5	18	18	17	15	73
Mulholland,T	51	0	9	8	12	11	7	3	3	3	5	112
Munoz,Arnie											0	0
Munro,Pete						1	0		5	2	2	10
Munson,Eric							0	0	0	7	9	16
Murphy,Donald											0	0
Murray,Calvin											0	0
Mussina,Mike	59	20	13	19	15	17	18	20	15	19	10	225
Myers,Brett									3	9	3	15
Myers,Greg	15	6	6	3	4	6	1	6	4	8	0	59
Myers,Mike		0	3	1	6	2	7	4	3	1	3	30
Myers,Rodney			3	0	0	5	0	1	0	0	0	9
Myette,Aaron						0	0	0	0	0	0	0
Nady,Xavier						0				7	1	8
Nageotte,Clint											0	0
Nakamura,Mike										0	0	0
Nance,Shane									1	0	0	1
Narron,Samuel											0	0
Nathan,Joe						5	2		1	11	16	35
Navarro,Dioner											0	0
Neal,Blaine								0	3	0	2	5
Nelson,Je	12	10	6	8	4	2	9	8	4	6	1	70
Nelson,Jo											0	0
Neu,Mike										3	0	3
Nevin,Phil		2	5	6	2	19	22	31	12	9	23	131
Newhan,David											13	13
Nitkowski,C.J.		0	0		4	6	3	2	1	0	1	17
Nivar,Ramon										1	0	1
Nix,Laynce										4	8	12
Nixon,Trot			0		0	10	14	20	17	19	4	84
Nomo,Hideo		17	16	9	3	10	10	11	13	17	0	106
Norton,Greg			0	1	4	11	3	3	2	4	0	28
Norton,Phil						0				2	2	4
Novoa,Roberto											0	0
Nunez,Abr											4	4
Nunez,AbrO			1	1	4	1	6	5	4	1		23
Nunez,Franklin										0		0
Nunez,Vladimir					0	5	0	8	14	0	0	27
Obermueller,W									0	2	4	6
Offerman,Jose										3		3
Ohka,Tomo					0	6	2	14	12	4		38
Ojeda,Augie							2	2	1	0	3	8
Ojeda,Miguel										4	6	10
Olerud,John	91	11	10	27	34	26	22	21	27	15	10	294
Oliver,Darren	5	4	12	12	4	13	0	3	3	10	1	67
Olivo,Miguel									1	8	7	16
Olmedo,Ray										2	0	2
Olson,Tim											1	1
Ordonez,M			3	13	20	22	25	26	23	8		140
Ordonez,Rey			7	6	9	13	1	12	9	4	0	61
Oropesa,Eddie								1	0	1	0	2
Ortiz,David				2	9	0	8	7	11	15	25	77
Ortiz,Ra						1	6	12	14	5	7	45
Ortiz,Ru				3	12	7	15	13	16	11		77
Osborne,D										0		0
Osik,Keith		4	3	1	3	5	1	1	4	0		22
Osuna,Antonio		2	10	7	8	0	4	0	8	4	3	46
Oswalt,Roy								15	20	10	18	63
Otsuka,Akinori											11	11

WIN SHARES BY YEAR

Player	<95	95	96	97	98	99	00	01	02	03	04	Career
Overbay,Lyle								0	0	6	20	26
Padilla,Juan											1	1
Padilla,V						0	6	3	14	13	4	40
Palmeiro,O		1	2	1	5	6	7	4	7	6	4	43
Palmeiro,R	162	21	30	18	24	31	23	25	10	19	13	376
Park,Chan Ho	0	0	7	13	13	6	18	16	5	0	4	82
Parra,Jose											1	1
Parrish,John							0	0		2	6	8
Pascucci,Val											0	0
Patterson,C							0	3	8	13	19	43
Patterson,D			1	8	5	3	5	7	0	2	1	32
Patterson,John									3	0	2	5
Paul,Josh						0	3	4	2	1	2	12
Pavano,Carl					6	3	8	0	3	9	20	49
Payton,Jay					0	0	14	3	15	15	15	62
Pearce,Josh									0	1	0	1
Peavy,Jake									3	7	16	26
Pellow,Kit										1		1
Pena,Carlos								3	11	9	12	35
Pena,Wily Mo									0	1	15	16
Penny,Brad							5	12	4	10	9	40
Peralta,Jhonny										4	0	4
Percival,Troy		12	16	10	12	11	8	14	13	8	7	111
Perez,Antonio										3	0	3
Perez,Edd		1	5	2	10	8	0	0	2	7	2	37
Perez,Edu	5	0	1	0	4	2	1		3	7	1	24
Perez,Neifi			0	9	12	14	15	11	6	8	7	82
Perez,Od						1	1	3	16	6	12	39
Perez,Ol									4	1	17	22
Perez,Ti							2	4	14	5	6	31
Perez,To		1	3	2	0		1	5	4	5	4	25
Perisho,Matt											3	3
Perry,Herbert	0	5	0			3	13	5	10	0	1	37
Peterson,Adam											0	0
Pettitte,Andy			11	18	20	13	10	14	13	12	15	132
Phelps,Josh							0	0	10	10	6	26
Phelps,To										3	0	3
Phelps,Tr											0	0
Phillips,Andy											0	0
Phillips,B									1	4	0	5
Phillips,Jason								0	1	13	5	19
Phillips,Paul											0	0
Piazza,Mike	53	27	33	39	33	21	28	21	19	11	12	297
Pickering,C											4	4
Piedra,Jorge											2	2
Pierre,Juan							3	17	15	20	24	79
Pierzynski,A					1	0	3	15	17	22	13	71
Pineiro,Joel							0	7	14	13	6	40
Podsednik,S								0	1	22	15	38
Polanco,P					2	3	11	14	16	18	17	81
Politte,Cliff						0	0	5	3	7	3	21
Pond,Simon											0	0
Ponson,Sidney					5	10	11	4	10	15	7	62
Porter,Colin										0	0	0
Posada,Jorge		0	0	6	15	10	29	23	22	28	20	153
Pote,Lou											0	0
Powell,Brian					1		1	0	2	0	1	5
Powell,Jay		1	4	9	7	6	1	9	4	0	2	43
Pratt,Andy											0	0
Pratt,Todd	8	1		5	2	5	5	2	7	5	4	44
Pride,Curtis	2	0	9	2	2		0	1		0	1	17
Prieto,Alex										0	0	0
Prinz,Bret								7	0	0	1	8
Prior,Mark									7	22	7	36
Proctor,Scott											1	1
Puffer,Brandon									3	0	0	3
Pujols,Albert								29	32	41	40	142
Pulido,Carlos										1	0	1
Punto,Nick								0	0	1	4	5
Putz,J.J.										0	3	3
Qualls,Chad											3	3
Quantrill,Paul	15	7	4	12	11	5	6	11	8	11	6	96
Quinlan,Robb										0	8	8
Quintero,H										0	1	1
Quiroz,G											0	0
Raburn,Ryan											0	0
Radke,Brad		7	14	16	14	17	15	17	6	12	19	137
Raines Jr,Tim								0		0	1	1

Player	<95	95	96	97	98	99	00	01	02	03	04	Career
Rakers,Aaron											0	0
Ramirez,Aramis				2	0	3	27	6	19	22		79
Ramirez,El											0	0
Ramirez,Er										4	3	7
Ramirez,H										9	4	13
Ramirez,Manny	11	25	23	21	25	35	27	25	29	28	28	277
Randa,Joe		1	9	16	9	17	18	11	11	14	12	118
Randolph,S										6	3	9
Ransom,Cody							0	0	0	2		2
Rauch,Jon											4	4
Redding,Tim							2	1	10	0		13
Redman,Mark					0	10	3	10	11	9		43
Redman,Tike							1	1		9	11	22
Redmond,Mike				4	12	5	6	12	1	5		45
Reed,Jeremy											2	2
Reed,Steve	15	12	8	7	8	4	4	5	7	7	6	83
Reese,Pokey			0	3	18	11	7	15	2	3		59
Regilio,Nick											0	0
Reith,Brian							0		3	0		3
Reitsma,Chris							3	7	8	6		24
Relaford,Desi			0	1	5	4	12	13	9	11	4	59
Remlinger,Mike	2	0	0	9	5	12	12	9	11	6	3	69
Renteria,Edgar			15	15	11	13	15	13	26	25	17	150
Restovich,Mike									0	2	1	3
Reyes,Al			4	0	1	4	5	1	2	2	1	2	22
Reyes,Dennys				2	2	5	2	1	4	0	5	21
Reyes,Jose									12	5		17
Reyes,Rene									0	0		0
Reynolds,Shane	10	9	15	7	16	16	6	10	2	3	0	94
Rhodes,Arthur	10	1	5	10	7	2	6	12	11	4	2	70
Riedling,John							2	4	5	4	2	17
Riggs,Adam			0				0			1	0	1
Riley,Matt											2	2
Rincon,Juan								0	0	7	12	19
Rincon,Ricardo				7	9	3	3	6	6	6	4	44
Rios,Alexis											8	8
Riske,David					0		3	2	10	7		22
Ritchie,Todd			3	0	14	8	10	0	1	0		36
Rivas,Luis							1	8	6	6	9	30
Rivera,Carlos										0	0	0
Rivera,Juan							0	1	4	14		19
Rivera,Mariano		2	18	15	14	17	16	19	9	18	16	144
Rivera,Rene										0	0	0
Roa,Joe		0	0	1					4	0	4	9
Robbins,Jake										0	0	0
Roberts,Brian							3	2	13	16		34
Roberts,Dave					2	0	0	19	8	12		41
Roberts,Grant							0	2	5	1	0	8
Roberts,Willis					0		6	6	1	0		13
Robertson,J							0	5	0			5
Robertson,Nate							0	1	8			9
Robinson,Kerry				0	0		4	4	3	2		13
Rodriguez,Alex	0	2	34	22	30	23	37	37	35	32	30	282
Rodriguez,Eddy											2	2
Rodriguez,Fe		1		2	1	4	9	12	5	8	6	48
Rodriguez,Fr									1	9	15	25
Rodriguez,Ivan	49	16	23	26	27	28	19	18	11	23	22	262
Rodriguez,R									1	1	3	5
Rogers,Kenny	48	21	11	2	19	12	15	2	15	11	13	169
Rolen,Scott			2	29	30	15	18	29	28	25	38	214
Rollins,Jimmy							1	20	16	19	25	81
Rolls,Damian							0	2	0	8	0	10
Romano,Jason									2	0	0	2
Romero,J.C.							1	0	1	14	3	8	27
Rose,Mike											0	0
Ross,Dave									1	4	1	6
Rowand,Aaron								5	7	6	21	39
Rueter,Kirk	10	4	5	12	8	5	9	7	12	6	6	84
Rusch,Glendon			5	5	0	11	6	7	0	9		43
Ryan,B.J.					2	2	3	3	6	11		27
Ryan,Mike								0	4	0		4
Saarloos,Kirk									0	2	2	4
Sabathia,C.C.							12	13	13	12		50
Sadler,Donnie				3	1	2	2	1	1	0		10
Saenz,Chris											1	1
Saenz,Olmedo											4	4
Salmon,Tim	37	29	22	29	22	14	23	11	22	17	2	228
Sanchez,Alex								0	11	9	5	25

Player	<95	95	96	97	98	99	00	01	02	03	04	Career
Sanchez,Duaner								0	0	6		6
Sanchez,Freddy								0	0	0		0
Sanchez,Jesus				4	0	6	2	0	0	0		12
Sanchez,Rey	22	7	5	7	8	12	9	13	9	6	4	102
Sanders,Reggie	44	27	7	13	14	19	6	14	14	18	16	192
Santana,Johan							2	2	10	16	27	57
Santiago,B	95	12	19	9	1	7	6	10	15	13	3	190
Santiago,Ramon								4	5	0		9
Santos,Victor							5	0	0	4		9
Schilling,Curt	42	8	14	22	22	15	16	24	24	15	22	224
Schmidt,Jason		0	2	8	11	13	1	9	10	22	19	95
Schneider,B							1	2	8	13	17	41
Schoeneweis,S						1	6	9	5	3	4	28
Scutaro,Marco								0	2	10		12
Seanez,Rudy	3	0			5	7	2	3	1	0	5	26
Seay,Bobby							0		1	2		3
Segui,David	22	13	15	16	15	10	18	14	2	4	1	130
Seibel,Phil										0		0
Sele,Aaron	22	3	6	7	14	13	12	14	5	2	5	103
Seo,Jae									0	9	3	12
Serrano,Jimmy										2		2
Service,Scott	4	3	3	1	11	3	0		2	0		27
Sexson,Richie				0	5	10	16	19	22	26	3	101
Sheets,Ben								6	8	9	20	43
Sheffield,Gary	92	13	34	22	30	24	31	30	26	35	31	368
Shelton,Chris										0		0
Sherrill,G										2	2	2
Shields,Scot								2	6	12	11	31
Shouse,Brian	0			0				0	6	6		12
Sierra,Ruben	172	13	6	1	1		1	6	7	5	9	221
Silva,Carlos								7	5	14		26
Simon,Randall				1	0	4		7	12	11	0	35
Simontacchi,J								8	2	0		10
Simpson,Allan										2		2
Sizemore,Grady										5		5
Sledge,Terrmel										15		15
Small,Aaron										0		0
Smith,Jason							0	0	0	2		2
Smith,Travis										0		0
Smoltz,John	82	17	27	21	16	18		8	17	16	12	234
Snare,Ryan										0		0
Snead,Esix									0	0		0
Snell,Ian										0		0
Snow,J.T.	12	15	7	28	13	18	16	6	11	14	20	160
Snyder,Chris											3	3
Snyder,Earl										0		0
Soriano,A					0	0	16	30	27	16		89
Soriano,Rafael								1	7	0		8
Sosa,Jorge								2	5	3		10
Sosa,Sammy	56	25	18	14	35	26	30	42	27	22	14	309
Sparks,Steve		11	2		8	5	7	16	3	3	1	56
Speier,Justin				0	1	7	5	6	8	7		34
Spencer,Shane					6	3	6	8	5	8	7	43
Spiezio,Scott			2	10	10	6	6	9	17	12	4	76
Spivey,Junior							6	23	10	5		44
Springer,Russ	3	3	3	3	3	5	3	0		0	1	24
Stairs,Matt	1	1	4	15	20	20	10	11	7	13	11	113
Standridge,J						1	0	0	0			1
Stanford,Jason									3	1		4
Stanton,Mike	30	2	9	9	4	4	6	10	10	3	7	94
Stark,Denny						0		0	10	2	0	12
Stewart,Josh									0	0		0
Stewart,Sc							6	12	4	0		22
Stewart,Sh		0	0	7	18	17	17	18	17	19	13	126
Stinnett,Kelly	4	4	0	1	10	6	5	5	4	4	1	44
Stone,Ricky								1	5	6	0	12
Sturtze,Tanyon		0	0	0		1	6	11	6	2	3	29
Stynes,Chris		1	1	10	5	2	13	8	5	10	0	55
Sullivan,Scott	0	1	9	3	11	10	9	1	6	3		53
Suppan,Jeff		1	0	4	2	12	12	12	9	14	7	73
Surhoff,B.J.	98	16	17	19	13	17	14	12	2	9	10	227
Sutton,Larry										0		0
Suzuki,Ichiro								36	25	23	27	111
Sweeney,Brian									1	0		1
Sweeney,Ma	1	7	5	3	0	0	1	0	2	6		25
Sweeney,Mi	0	4	5	8	16	26	18	19	15	14		125
Swisher,Nick											1	1
Szuminski,J										0		0

WIN SHARES BY YEAR

Player	<95	95	96	97	98	99	00	01	02	03	04	Career
Tadano,K											2	2
Taguchi,So									1	3	6	10
Takatsu,Shingo											11	11
Tankersley,D									0	0	0	0
Tavarez,Julian	0	10	4	6	5	1	10	6	2	10	8	62
Taveras,Willy											0	0
Taylor,Aaron									0	0	0	0
Teixeira,Mark										13	25	38
Tejada,Miguel				1	7	20	23	25	32	25	30	163
Tejera,Michael						0			7	3	0	10
Telemaco,A			1	0	8	2	0	2		2	2	17
Terrero,Luis										0	4	4
Thames,Marcus									0	0	6	6
Thomas,Brad									0	0	0	0
Thomas,Charles											9	9
Thomas,Frank	137	28	28	39	25	16	34	1	16	23	12	359
Thome,Jim	18	24	28	26	19	26	20	31	34	30	22	278
Thompson,Rich											0	0
Thomson,John				10	9	0		7	7	11	12	56
Thornton,Matt											2	2
Thurston,Joe										1	0	1
Tiffee,Terry											1	1
Timlin,Mike	18	6	10	9	12	9	6	5	8	8	6	97
Tomko,Brett				10	9	6	5	1	6	6	9	52
Tonis,Mike											0	0
Torcato,Tony									0	0	1	1
Torrealba,Y								1	4	7	4	16
Torres,Andres									0	1	0	1
Torres,Salomon	2	1	3	0					3	5	11	25
Towers,Josh								6	0	5	6	17
Trachsel,Steve	11	4	15	9	13	6	11	8	10	13	10	110
Tracy,Andy											0	0
Tracy,Chad											11	11
Treanor,Matt											0	0
Tremie,Chris											0	0
Tsao,Chin-hui										1	1	2
Tucker,Michael		3	9	15	11	10	7	10	8	9	14	96
Tucker,T.J.								0	5	4	5	14
Turnbow,D				2						2	1	5
Upton,B.J.											4	4
Urbina,Ugueth		0	8	10	17	14	2	11	11	15	5	93
Urdaneta,Lino											0	0
Uribe,Juan								7	10	9	18	44
Utley,Chase										5	8	13
Valdez,Ismael	3	15	16	15	9	10	2	10	11	3	4	98
Valdez,Merkin											0	0
Valdez,Wilson											0	0
Valent,Eric								1	0	0	6	7
Valentin,Ja			0	2	5			0		2	4	13
Valentin,Jo	14	8	20	13	15	8	24	15	16	18	14	165
Valentine,Joe										0	1	1
Valverde,Jose										11	2	13
Van Benschoten,J											0	0
Van Poppel,T	5	5	0	1			6	8	3	2	1	31
Vander Wal,J	14	4	4	0	4	8	19	13	2	8	0	76
Vargas,Claudio										6	2	8
Varitek,Jason				0	5	12	7	8	12	17	18	79
Vasquez,Jorge											0	0
Vazquez,Javier					0	8	14	21	12	21	10	86
Vazquez,Ramon								0	14	10	1	25
Venafro,Mike						7	6	4	2	1	0	20
Ventura,Robin	108	17	20	8	21	30	15	17	20	10	6	272
Vidro,Jose				3	2	11	25	18	29	19	12	119
Villacis,E											0	0
Villafuerte,B							0	0	3	1	1	5
Villarreal,O										11	0	11
Villone,Ron		2	5	4	1	8	5	3	1	5	7	41
Vina,Fernando	4	8	13	7	30	4	18	22	16	5	1	128
Vizcaino,Jose	29	16	14	17	8	4	3	4	11	4	8	118
Vizcaino,Luis						0	0	2	8	1	6	17
Vizquel,Omar	51	17	16	14	18	22	16	12	21	5	17	209
Vogelsong,Ryan							1	0		0	0	1
Waechter,Doug										3	1	4
Wagner,Billy		0	8	11	11	20	1	13	16	19	8	107
Wagner,Ryan										3	2	5
Wakefield,Tim	11	18	10	12	11	8	5	11	15	12	8	121
Walker,Jamie			2	0					4	7	6	19
Walker,Kevin											0	0
Walker,Larry	103	18	10	32	17	24	11	25	26	18	13	297
Walker,To			1	2	19	9	5	12	21	15	14	98
Walker,Ty											4	4
Ward,Daryle					0	3	3	5	10	0	7	28
Wasdin,John		1	4	7	4	7	3	3		0	0	29
Washburn,J					4	3	7	15	18	10	8	65
Watkins,Steve											0	0
Wayne,Justin									0	0	0	0
Weathers,David	5	0	3	0	4	6	7	10	7	8	5	55
Weaver,Jeff						7	12	13	14	2	12	60
Webb,Brandon										17	12	29
Webb,John											0	0
Weber,Ben							2	7	11	8	0	28
Wellemeyer,T										0	1	1
Wells,David	60	17	10	12	18	13	18	5	15	14	10	192
Wells,Kip						3	2	6	13	16	6	46
Wells,Vernon						1	0	3	17	26	14	61
Wendell,Turk		1	2	12	4	10	9	8	5	6	0	57
Werth,Jayson									1	1	12	14
Westbrook,Jake							0	2	1	6	17	26
Wheeler,Dan						1	1	0		3	3	8
White,Gabe	0	0		3	8	3	15	2	7	4	1	43
White,Ri	7	2			5	7	9	5	5	1	3	44
White,Ro	7	14	10	17	16	15	14	12	6	15	11	137
Wickman,Bob											2	2
Wigginton,Ty									4	15	10	29
Wilkerson,Brad								1	17	18	22	58
Williams,B	46	27	26	24	27	33	26	24	30	13	16	292
Williams,Dave										2		2
Williams,G	1	7	5	9	12	13	14	2	0	0	2	65
Williams,J										9	6	15
Williams,Randy											0	0
Williams,Todd											3	3
Williams,Woody	7	4	3	11	12	10	12	11	10	13	8	101
Williamson,S						17	11	0	10	7	4	49
Willingham,J											0	0
Willis,D										14	10	24
Wilson,Craig								8	10	10	18	46
Wilson,Dan	6	16	15	21	7	9	4	14	12	7	7	118
Wilson,Enrique				1	3	3	5	3	1	2	5	23
Wilson,Jack								5	12	11	23	51
Wilson,Pa			1				4	6	7	5	8	31
Wilson,Pr					1	13	20	10	11	20	2	77
Wilson,Tom								0	7	3	0	10
Wilson,Vance						0	0	1	5	7	5	18
Winn,Randy					5	4	2	10	23	21	18	83
Wise,Dewayne											4	4
Wise,Matt											3	3
Witasick,Jay		0	0	0		5	3	6	6	2	3	25
Wolf,Randy						4	13	11	15	12	7	62
Womack,Tony	1		2	18	17	14	16	10	14	3	18	113
Wood,Kerry					14		7	13	12	18	8	72
Wood,Mike										0	2	2
Woodward,Chris						0	2	1	10	9	3	25
Wooten,Shawn							0	6	3	2	0	11
Worrell,Tim	3	1	10	3	3	4	7	5	9	13	7	65
Wright,Dan								2	7	0	0	9
Wright,Dav											9	9
Wright,Jam											5	5
Wright,Jar				6	11	3	3	0	0	1	13	37
Wuertz,Mike											2	2
Wunsch,Kelly							8	0	3	4	0	15
Yan,Esteban			0	0	7	2	4	8	7	1	6	35
Yates,Tyler											0	0
Youkilis,Kevin											8	8
Young,Chris											2	2
Young,Dmitri			0	5	16	10	14	13	5	19	9	91
Young,Eri	20	12	17	17	17	14	18	16	9	9	9	158
Young,Ern	0	1	10	1	1	0				0	0	13
Young,Jason										0	0	0
Young,Michael							0	7	11	21	25	64
Zambrano,C								0	5	18	19	42
Zambrano,V								6	4	10	9	29
Zaun,Gregg		3	3	9	3	3	9	4	2	2	10	48
Zeile,Todd	81	8	16	18	21	19	18	18	12	6	4	221
Zinter,Alan										0		0
Zito,Barry							9	15	25	18	12	79

Player Projections

Bill James

Hello, and welcome to the first-ever Baseball Info Solutions player projections.

The business of projecting player statistics for next year got started about twelve years ago because Bill James had too much time on his hands. This is Bill James writing; I don't ordinarily speak of myself in the third person, but I didn't know how else to phrase that.

I bought my first personal computer in 1982. One of the first things I did, after discovering the "spreadsheet" feature on the computer, was to type in a player's career statistics, and put in a bunch of formulas to project out the rest of the career. This was not serious research; it was strictly fooling around, wasting time, but it was fun, and, by the summer of 1983, I had a system which, if you typed in Greg Luzinski's career up through 1982, would project that Luzinski would hit 400 career home runs and drive in 1600 runs. Which was totally incorrect; he would play another year or two and then retire, but I didn't know that at the time.

I wrote about that system, and, over the years, re-discovered the basic principle of my career: People take the stuff I do entirely too seriously. After a couple of years, John Dewan began bugging me to let the company he then worked with include these projected statistics (for the upcoming season) in the predecessor of this *Handbook*.

I said, "John, there's no evidence at all that those formulas work. That's just something I do to entertain myself."

"So?" said John. "We won't claim they work. We'll just print them and tell people to take them for what they're worth. We're just entertaining the readers."

So we put them in the *Handbook*, and they proved to be such a popular feature that within four years numerous other publications were running competitive projection systems, some of them claiming to be 37% more accurate than our predictions, to cause fewer cavities, cure bad breath and stave off rickets.

Well, that projection system got left behind at the old company, so when we started this *Handbook* series two years ago, we didn't have any projections. Over the years, this process has been refined from its arbitrary and instinctive beginnings, and become a little bit of a science. John Dewan will periodically launch research projects to investigate questions like "how many home runs per at bat do players typically lose between ages 32 and 36, and how does this compare with our projection system?" As a consequence of doing this, John came to know more about projecting players' careers than I did, and he was in charge of developing this new projection system—John and Pat Quinn. At the same time, there is nothing really difficult about doing projections, except for the programming and the details; in all candor the number of options to make the system more or less accurate is pretty limited unless you want to start projecting .260 hitters to hit .300 and .300 hitters to hit .260. The only hard part about it is getting the playing time right; if you do that, everything else pretty much falls in place.

A note about policy. . .in projecting playing time for young players, we prefer to err on the side of too much playing time. Our feeling is that the projection should show what a young player is capable of doing, since this is what the reader probably wants to know. If we project young players into part-time roles, they look like part-time players. Sometimes this causes us to project more playing time than is available, and very often it causes us to project 525 at bats for some rookie who is actually going to get 280, and sometimes it causes us to project 30 home runs for some kid who is actually going to hit 7. At Toledo. But we would rather be bold and wrong than timid and useless.

When we were meeting to discuss this process, some junior executive who doesn't yet realize that you can get fired for asking these kind of questions asked, "Is there anything else we could do, along with these projections, to make this section more interesting?" We came up with two things. First, since the projection system (in its original form) projects career numbers as well as next-season numbers, we decided to print a few pages of projected career totals. We have some limitations on that, imposed by common sense, past ridicule and the fear of future ridicule. If we have Miguel Cabrera projected to hit 896 career doubles, we're not going to tell you that. We won't print career projections for players less than 25 years of age, or for players who haven't played a least a few hundred games in the major leagues. We're not printing career projections for players whose careers are finished or virtually finished.

What is left, when you cut those out, is mostly the good players, and so most of the projections that we are printing are for players with very good careers. And we offer this with the same caveat that was attached to the first player projections years ago: we have no idea whether this system works or not. We're just entertaining ourselves, trying to project what players will do; we make no claims whatsoever to accuracy. There is probably some player here who is projected to get 3000 hits when our other system, The Favorite Toy, says that his chance of getting 3000 career hits is 16%. That's all right; new analytical tools cannot be judged by the standard of whether or not they endorse the conclusions of old analytic systems.

The numbers for Barry Bonds look kind of unbelievable, but when you think about it, is 918 home runs any more amazing than fifty things that Barry

Bonds has already done? Is 918 home runs in a career more amazing than 73 in a season? Is it more amazing than a .609 on-base percentage? Is it more amazing than 232 walks? Is it more amazing than having an .800 slugging percentage over a four-year period? Is it more amazing than having a .500-plus on-base percentage for four straight years? Is it more amazing than six or seven MVP awards? Is it more amazing than doubling or tripling the previous record for intentional walks? Is it more amazing than breaking a record and then breaking it again and then breaking it again? Is it more amazing than having the best batting statistics in the history of baseball in the worst hitters' park in the league?

We are all in a kind of sustained denial about Barry Bonds' skills. We have a well-established notion of what it is possible for a hitter to do, based on our experience with hundreds or thousands of other players. It is hard to get used to the fact that Bonds does not fit within that box—but he very clearly does not. He's different.

Do we really have any idea what Bonds is going to do two or three years from now? Of course not. We don't have a clue. But the one thing certain about Barry is that the normal rules don't apply. So if the computer guesses that he could hit about 918 career home runs, we salute and say, "Yes, sir; your guess is as good as mine." Just take each projection for what it is worth, and remember that this system assumes good health and comparative sanity, which not all players will enjoy.

Segue. A man named Sig Mejdal has gotten very interested in the question of how well future injury risks could be assessed, based on past injury records. Mr. Mejdal approached us with a plan to include here an assessment of each player projected as a high injury risk, low injury risk, or medium injury risk.

Once again, we must caution you that we really have no idea whether or not this is going to work. What we know is that Mr. Mejdal is serious, sincere, intelligent, that he has done a lot of work to develop his material, and that his conclusions are reasonable. We think they are worthy of consideration.

I personally. . .this is just Bill James, speaking for no one except Bill James. . .I have a couple of questions about the work. Mr. Mejdal's numbers seem to me to be far too low. According to Sig, Mike Sweeney has an 11% chance of having a serious back injury next year, which is the highest of any major league player. An 11% chance of a serious back injury sounds to me like the number you would get if you just picked somebody off the street at random. In my experience, anybody has a pretty serious chance of developing back trouble. I would think that the number for Mike Sweeney, who has had back trouble for years, would be more like 80%.

Or Ken Griffey. . .Mr. Mejdal tells us that Junior has a 36% chance of having some serious injury next year. While not arguing with the premise that Ken Griffey and Cliff Floyd should be at the top of the list, are we really supposed to believe that Ken Griffey has a 64% chance of not having a serious injury next year? I find that very difficult to believe.

And I think I know, intuitively, where his calculations may have gone astray. Serious injuries tend to remove the people suffering them from the major league scene—thus removing them from the group being sampled. I hope that no one mistakes this for a flippant comment, but Dernell Stenson has a 100% chance of not playing in 2005 because of a serious injury. OK, his injury was more serious than most, but actually there are many players who have a 100% chance of not playing next year because of injuries, and there are many more who have an 85% chance of not playing next year because of injuries.

What Mr. Mejdal may have, I suspect, is a system in which, if the injury is serious enough, then it doesn't count.   The only injuries that "count" are those that put you on the disabled list for a period of time, specifically, while enabling you to play part of the season. I suspect this biases the data toward lower injury risks in the data than in real life.

But we'll see, and that's a quibble; in no way would this be a reason to deny Mr. Mejdal the opportunity to have his research seen and evaluated by the baseball community. I hope you get something out of it, and we'll see how it looks a year or two down the road.

2005 Projections

Hitter	Age	Inj	G	AB	H	2B	3B	HR	R	RBI	RC	BB	SO	SB	CS	SB%	Avg	OBP	Slg	OPS
Abreu, Bobby, Phi	31	high	156	581	177	45	3	26	110	99	131	116	123	31	10	.76	.305	.420	.527	.947
Adams, Russ, Tor	25	low	135	542	149	37	4	9	66	57	74	47	65	6	2	.75	.275	.333	.408	.741
Aguila, Chris, Fla	26	low	59	152	42	9	1	4	21	18	22	13	37	2	1	.67	.276	.333	.428	.761
Alexander, Manny, Tex	34	low	45	101	26	6	1	2	13	11	12	6	14	3	1	.75	.257	.299	.396	.695
Alfonzo, Edgardo, SF	32	med	135	490	140	27	1	14	71	70	76	57	46	3	1	.75	.286	.360	.431	.791
Allen, Chad, Tex	30	low	42	106	31	7	1	2	14	14	15	6	18	3	1	.75	.292	.330	.434	.764
Almonte, Erick, NYY	27	low	64	201	55	11	1	7	31	28	30	20	42	5	2	.71	.274	.339	.443	.782
Alomar Jr., Sandy, CWS	39	low	69	196	51	10	0	4	20	23	21	9	21	0	0	.00	.260	.293	.372	.665
Alomar, Roberto, CWS	37	high	104	380	104	20	2	8	56	45	54	42	61	9	2	.82	.274	.346	.400	.746
Alou, Moises, ChC	39	high	153	564	161	31	1	28	84	98	99	63	76	3	1	.75	.285	.357	.493	.850
Alvarez, Tony, Pit	26	low	61	162	46	10	0	5	24	21	23	12	28	9	5	.64	.284	.333	.438	.772
Amezaga, Alfredo, Ana	27	low	68	132	33	6	1	2	17	13	14	8	22	5	2	.71	.250	.293	.356	.649
Anderson, Garret, Ana	33	high	133	533	157	34	2	20	67	89	84	28	80	4	2	.67	.295	.330	.478	.808
Anderson, Marlon, StL	31	low	82	197	51	11	1	4	24	23	24	14	27	4	1	.80	.259	.308	.386	.694
Atkins, Garrett, Col	26	low	121	435	135	33	2	12	70	68	77	40	48	0	0	.00	.310	.368	.478	.847
Aurilia, Rich, SD	34	low	106	253	67	14	1	7	33	31	33	21	44	1	1	.50	.265	.321	.411	.732
Ausmus, Brad, Hou	36	med	104	309	75	12	1	4	33	29	31	29	47	2	2	.50	.243	.308	.327	.635
Bagwell, Jeff, Hou	37	high	152	565	153	32	1	31	102	99	106	99	129	7	4	.64	.271	.380	.496	.875
Bako, Paul, ChC	33	low	62	144	33	8	1	1	13	12	14	16	34	1	1	.50	.229	.306	.319	.626
Baldelli, Rocco, TB	24	med	152	621	184	34	6	18	97	88	96	34	103	22	6	.79	.296	.333	.457	.790
Barajas, Rod, Tex	30	low	96	269	65	18	0	9	32	41	30	12	44	0	0	.00	.242	.274	.409	.683
Bard, Josh, Cle	27	med	74	241	64	15	0	6	27	33	31	19	34	0	0	.00	.266	.319	.402	.722
Barmes, Clint, Col	26	low	128	485	141	34	2	12	73	50	68	20	59	14	7	.67	.291	.319	.443	.762
Barrett, Michael, ChC	29	low	116	388	101	26	2	12	45	48	52	32	55	1	2	.33	.260	.317	.430	.747
Batista, Tony, Mon	32	med	155	587	144	29	1	30	77	96	75	32	90	9	5	.64	.245	.284	.451	.736
Bautista, Danny, Ari	33	high	109	370	105	19	2	8	44	47	50	24	51	4	2	.67	.284	.327	.411	.738
Bay, Jason, Pit	27	med	153	588	170	34	5	37	100	114	120	76	160	12	6	.67	.289	.370	.553	.923
Bell, David, Phi	33	med	148	565	145	32	1	16	71	72	74	57	82	1	1	.50	.257	.325	.402	.727
Bellhorn, Mark, Bos	31	med	147	541	135	34	3	18	90	72	83	94	182	6	3	.67	.250	.361	.423	.784
Belliard, Ronnie, Cle	30	high	129	442	119	32	2	8	62	49	61	48	72	3	2	.60	.269	.341	.405	.746
Beltran, Carlos, Hou	28	med	155	594	169	33	8	31	115	105	120	78	104	38	4	.90	.285	.368	.524	.891
Beltre, Adrian, LA	26	med	157	581	167	31	2	34	85	99	104	49	91	7	3	.70	.287	.343	.523	.866
Bennett, Gary, Mil	33	low	80	225	55	11	0	3	20	25	23	20	31	1	0	1.00	.244	.306	.333	.639
Berg, Dave, Tor	35	low	50	106	27	6	0	2	12	11	12	7	20	0	0	.00	.255	.301	.368	.669
Berger, Brandon, KC	30	low	54	136	33	8	1	6	18	23	19	15	23	1	1	.50	.243	.318	.449	.766
Berkman, Lance, Hou	29	high	155	562	172	43	3	33	110	113	136	119	109	7	5	.58	.306	.427	.569	.997
Berroa, Angel, KC	27	low	132	469	127	24	5	11	69	51	59	24	78	14	6	.70	.271	.306	.414	.720
Bigbie, Larry, Bal	28	med	147	513	151	30	2	14	77	67	82	52	111	9	3	.75	.294	.359	.442	.802
Biggio, Craig, Hou	40	high	154	604	163	38	1	18	100	61	85	55	105	9	3	.75	.270	.331	.425	.756
Blake, Casey, Cle	32	med	151	560	150	33	1	22	84	72	83	56	113	7	6	.54	.268	.334	.448	.783
Blalock, Hank, Tex	25	med	153	599	172	39	2	31	102	106	109	65	118	2	2	.50	.287	.357	.514	.871
Blanco, Andres, KC	21	low	94	322	80	10	4	0	32	19	28	20	40	7	7	.50	.248	.292	.304	.597
Blanco, Henry, Min	34	low	70	157	32	9	0	4	15	16	14	14	30	0	1	.00	.204	.269	.338	.607
Bloomquist, Willie, Sea	28	low	73	135	35	6	1	2	19	14	16	10	26	8	2	.80	.259	.310	.363	.673
Blum, Geoff, TB	32	low	94	247	61	14	0	6	29	29	28	20	41	1	1	.50	.247	.303	.377	.680
Bocachica, Hiram, Sea	29	low	62	128	30	7	0	5	17	13	15	12	30	6	3	.67	.234	.300	.406	.706
Bonds, Barry, SF	41	high	135	370	117	23	1	36	94	84	131	156	52	6	1	.86	.316	.519	.676	1.195
Boone, Aaron, NYY	32	high	145	537	142	33	2	21	77	84	79	44	97	19	5	.79	.264	.320	.451	.771
Boone, Bret, Sea	36	high	136	538	142	29	1	23	76	85	78	49	117	8	4	.67	.264	.325	.450	.775
Borchard, Joe, CWS	27	low	56	125	30	7	0	6	18	17	16	11	31	1	1	.50	.240	.301	.440	.741
Bradley, Milton, LA	27	high	134	477	132	30	2	16	72	65	78	67	97	14	8	.64	.277	.366	.449	.814
Bragg, Darren, Cin	36	low	65	113	27	6	0	2	14	11	12	12	28	2	1	.67	.239	.312	.345	.657
Branyan, Russell, Mil	30	low	101	313	78	16	1	21	46	56	53	42	112	3	2	.60	.249	.338	.508	.846
Broussard, Ben, Cle	29	low	153	588	154	34	3	24	82	93	89	66	121	4	2	.67	.262	.336	.452	.789
Brown, Dee, KC	27	med	104	308	78	16	1	9	38	44	37	23	66	2	3	.40	.253	.305	.399	.704
Bruntlett, Eric, Hou	27	low	69	159	38	6	1	3	23	15	17	15	29	7	2	.78	.239	.305	.346	.651
Buchanan, Brian, NYM	32	low	87	197	52	11	0	8	28	28	29	22	48	2	1	.67	.264	.338	.442	.780
Buck, John, KC	25	low	130	454	115	24	1	16	57	67	57	31	102	1	1	.50	.253	.301	.416	.717
Burke, Jamie, CWS	34	low	68	225	63	10	0	3	28	27	26	14	25	0	0	.00	.280	.322	.364	.687
Burnitz, Jeromy, Col	36	high	146	537	132	27	2	31	81	93	83	65	136	5	5	.50	.246	.327	.477	.804
Burrell, Pat, Phi	29	high	151	542	135	31	1	29	76	95	90	88	156	1	0	1.00	.249	.354	.470	.824
Burroughs, Sean, SD	25	low	140	539	161	27	4	4	73	54	72	40	56	5	3	.62	.299	.347	.386	.733
Byrd, Marlon, Phi	28	low	102	312	85	18	2	5	47	31	39	23	53	4	2	.67	.272	.322	.391	.713
Byrnes, Eric, Oak	29	med	150	562	154	37	5	19	93	71	88	49	96	14	1	.93	.274	.332	.459	.791
Cabrera, Jolbert, Sea	33	low	100	263	66	15	1	3	32	29	27	15	49	5	2	.71	.251	.291	.350	.641
Cabrera, Miguel, Fla	22	med	160	584	179	39	3	31	98	119	119	65	130	6	3	.67	.307	.376	.543	.919
Cabrera, Orlando, Bos	31	high	152	582	158	40	2	12	73	68	77	42	54	16	5	.76	.271	.321	.409	.729
Cairo, Miguel, NYY	31	low	114	307	83	15	2	4	42	32	36	18	40	8	3	.73	.270	.311	.371	.682
Cameron, Mike, NYM	32	med	141	514	124	29	3	24	81	77	77	68	148	23	7	.77	.241	.330	.449	.779
Cantu, Jorge, TB	23	low	140	450	119	38	1	13	55	61	59	20	79	2	0	1.00	.264	.296	.440	.736
Carroll, Jamey, Mon	30	low	107	286	80	16	2	2	42	23	38	31	30	4	1	.80	.280	.350	.371	.721
Casey, Sean, Cin	31	med	131	466	144	31	1	15	70	75	82	43	42	2	0	1.00	.309	.367	.476	.844
Cash, Kevin, Tor	28	low	107	279	62	19	0	7	30	32	28	22	73	0	0	.00	.222	.279	.366	.645
Castilla, Vinny, Col	38	high	122	441	112	22	1	20	55	72	59	29	79	1	1	.50	.254	.300	.444	.744
Castillo, Jose, Pit	24	low	83	220	59	10	2	4	28	26	27	15	43	4	2	.67	.268	.315	.386	.701
Castillo, Luis, Fla	30	low	148	584	175	18	5	3	92	39	81	72	74	26	11	.70	.300	.377	.363	.740
Castro, Juan, Cin	33	med	79	167	39	9	0	3	16	15	15	9	30	0	1	.00	.234	.273	.341	.614
Catalanotto, Frank, Tor	31	high	107	357	106	23	3	7	54	42	55	29	47	4	2	.67	.297	.350	.443	.792
Cedeno, Roger, StL	31	high	100	270	73	11	2	4	39	23	34	26	52	12	4	.75	.270	.334	.370	.705
Chavez, Endy, Mon	27	low	121	399	110	19	5	4	53	32	49	26	34	21	8	.72	.276	.320	.378	.698

2005 Projections

Hitter	Age	Inj	G	AB	H	2B	3B	HR	R	RBI	RC	BB	SO	SB	CS	SB%	Avg	OBP	Slg	OPS
Chavez, Eric, Oak	28	high	147	563	155	34	2	32	94	100	106	81	106	6	3	.67	.275	.366	.513	.880
Chavez, Raul, Hou	32	low	82	213	50	11	0	2	19	25	18	10	34	0	0	.00	.235	.269	.315	.584
Choi, Hee Seop, LA	26	low	128	483	121	29	1	22	77	71	80	87	129	1	0	1.00	.251	.365	.451	.816
Church, Ryan, Mon	27	low	63	178	50	12	2	7	25	28	30	18	32	0	0	.00	.281	.347	.489	.836
Cintron, Alex, Ari	27	low	138	501	145	32	6	7	63	48	69	30	44	2	2	.50	.289	.330	.419	.749
Clark, Brady, Mil	32	low	114	278	75	15	0	5	33	36	36	33	34	9	5	.64	.270	.347	.378	.725
Clark, Howie, Tor	31	low	69	188	52	10	1	3	25	20	25	20	15	0	0	.00	.277	.346	.388	.734
Clark, Tony, NYY	33	med	87	187	45	10	0	9	24	31	26	21	57	0	0	.00	.241	.317	.439	.756
Clayton, Royce, Col	35	med	127	434	107	21	2	7	58	41	46	36	93	6	4	.60	.247	.304	.353	.657
Closser, J.D., Col	25	low	126	418	122	29	2	11	55	61	66	39	70	0	0	.00	.292	.352	.450	.802
Collier, Lou, Phi	32	low	62	157	45	9	1	4	22	23	23	14	35	4	2	.67	.287	.345	.433	.778
Conine, Jeff, Fla	39	high	119	440	119	24	1	12	51	65	60	39	66	4	2	.67	.270	.330	.411	.741
Conti, Jason, Tex	30	low	55	122	33	7	1	2	15	13	15	8	28	2	1	.67	.270	.315	.393	.709
Cora, Alex, LA	30	med	140	437	111	18	3	7	47	41	48	37	51	3	3	.50	.254	.312	.357	.669
Cordova, Marty, Bal	36	med	74	224	58	12	1	8	29	33	31	22	52	2	2	.50	.259	.325	.429	.754
Counsell, Craig, Mil	35	high	112	383	94	16	2	2	50	28	40	47	64	10	4	.71	.245	.328	.313	.641
Crawford, Carl, TB	24	low	151	628	185	26	15	10	96	64	94	33	84	58	13	.82	.295	.330	.432	.761
Crede, Joe, CWS	27	low	132	439	116	25	1	21	61	69	64	29	63	1	1	.50	.264	.310	.469	.779
Crespo, Cesar, Bos	26	low	70	168	42	10	1	3	22	15	20	15	37	7	2	.78	.250	.311	.375	.686
Crisp, Coco, Cle	26	low	139	518	153	28	4	11	82	59	77	41	65	24	12	.67	.295	.347	.429	.776
Crosby, Bobby, Oak	25	med	151	558	144	37	2	24	79	77	86	60	130	12	3	.80	.258	.330	.461	.791
Cruz, Deivi, SF	33	med	132	451	121	28	1	8	48	53	51	16	42	1	2	.33	.268	.293	.388	.681
Cruz, Jacob, Cin	32	high	67	134	36	7	0	4	20	21	19	15	30	0	0	.00	.269	.342	.410	.753
Cruz, Jose, TB	31	high	141	491	123	27	3	21	74	68	75	69	111	10	4	.71	.251	.343	.446	.789
Cuddyer, Mike, Min	26	low	120	459	126	27	4	19	71	60	74	49	95	6	5	.55	.275	.344	.475	.819
Cust, Jack, Bal	26	low	49	107	27	6	0	5	17	17	18	20	35	1	0	1.00	.252	.370	.449	.819
Dallimore, Brian, SF	32	low	63	221	65	11	1	3	28	25	30	16	28	4	2	.67	.294	.342	.394	.735
Damon, Johnny, Bos	32	med	143	585	167	32	5	14	106	68	91	65	68	21	7	.75	.285	.357	.429	.786
Daubach, Brian, Bos	33	low	71	164	40	11	0	7	22	27	24	23	48	0	0	.00	.244	.337	.439	.776
DaVanon, Jeff, Ana	32	low	115	360	101	17	2	12	56	45	60	53	62	19	6	.76	.281	.373	.439	.812
Davis, Ben, CWS	28	low	85	237	57	13	0	7	27	32	28	23	53	1	1	.50	.241	.308	.384	.692
DeJesus, David, KC	26	low	155	575	168	32	6	12	99	57	86	62	79	16	17	.48	.292	.361	.431	.792
Delgado, Carlos, Tor	33	high	137	501	141	35	1	35	91	109	110	89	125	0	0	.00	.281	.390	.565	.955
Delgado, Wilson, NYM	33	low	68	172	43	7	1	2	16	12	17	13	33	1	1	.50	.250	.303	.337	.640
Dellucci, David, Tex	32	med	98	254	62	12	2	9	38	37	34	31	67	6	3	.67	.244	.326	.413	.740
DeRosa, Mark, Atl	30	low	93	224	59	12	0	3	29	23	25	16	33	1	1	.50	.263	.313	.357	.670
Diaz, Einar, Mon	33	low	69	177	44	10	0	2	17	16	17	9	16	1	1	.50	.249	.285	.339	.624
Diaz, Matt, TB	27	low	62	193	59	16	1	6	27	30	33	11	35	7	2	.78	.306	.343	.492	.835
Drew, J.D., Atl	30	med	136	468	136	24	4	26	95	75	99	86	103	9	3	.75	.291	.401	.526	.926
Dubois, Jason, ChC	26	low	112	368	102	23	2	21	54	72	66	37	96	1	0	1.00	.277	.343	.522	.865
Dunn, Adam, Cin	26	high	152	540	136	31	4	42	104	94	113	112	178	8	3	.73	.252	.380	.546	.927
Durazo, Erubiel, Oak	31	high	134	466	135	29	1	21	78	80	87	71	98	2	2	.50	.290	.384	.491	.875
Durham, Ray, SF	34	low	124	477	133	28	4	14	87	53	75	58	77	12	6	.67	.279	.357	.442	.799
Dye, Jermaine, Oak	31	high	135	500	130	29	2	21	75	79	74	50	112	3	1	.75	.260	.327	.452	.779
Easley, Damion, Fla	36	high	58	124	30	7	0	4	16	16	15	12	22	2	1	.67	.242	.309	.395	.704
Eckstein, David, Ana	30	low	138	535	147	24	2	3	82	40	61	41	47	15	6	.71	.275	.326	.344	.670
Edmonds, Jim, StL	35	high	135	467	131	31	1	32	89	88	101	83	140	5	3	.62	.281	.389	.557	.946
Ellis, Mark, Oak	28	low	135	475	124	27	4	9	73	48	62	49	72	5	2	.71	.261	.330	.392	.722
Encarnacion, Juan, Fla	29	med	131	453	118	25	3	16	60	64	61	32	78	9	4	.69	.260	.309	.435	.744
Ensberg, Morgan, Hou	30	low	128	422	121	20	2	15	62	65	68	47	52	6	3	.67	.287	.358	.450	.808
Erstad, Darin, Ana	31	high	151	618	177	34	2	12	95	74	86	48	89	19	5	.79	.286	.338	.406	.744
Escalona, Felix, NYY	26	low	56	142	38	10	0	2	21	15	16	8	20	1	1	.50	.268	.307	.380	.687
Estrada, Johnny, Atl	29	med	144	511	150	36	0	11	55	80	75	39	59	0	0	.00	.294	.344	.429	.772
Everett, Adam, Hou	28	high	122	415	110	19	3	7	66	39	50	26	60	13	2	.87	.265	.308	.376	.684
Everett, Carl, CWS	34	high	95	295	81	17	1	12	42	49	45	25	56	3	2	.60	.275	.331	.461	.792
Feliz, Pedro, SF	28	low	112	308	83	18	2	14	41	50	44	14	51	2	1	.67	.269	.301	.477	.779
Fick, Robert, SD	31	med	81	210	54	11	1	7	24	30	28	20	33	1	0	1.00	.257	.322	.419	.741
Figgins, Chone, Ana	27	low	158	596	174	26	15	5	92	62	87	52	88	35	12	.74	.292	.349	.411	.760
Finley, Steve, LA	40	med	128	474	126	22	2	22	71	69	72	48	73	7	4	.64	.266	.333	.460	.793
Flaherty, John, NYY	38	med	73	253	62	13	0	7	23	29	26	12	46	0	1	.00	.245	.279	.379	.659
Floyd, Cliff, NYM	33	high	123	448	124	33	1	21	70	76	80	56	103	11	4	.73	.277	.357	.496	.853
Ford, Lew, Min	29	med	144	542	163	36	3	14	90	70	93	57	66	17	3	.85	.301	.367	.456	.823
Fordyce, Brook, TB	35	med	67	167	40	9	0	3	14	15	16	10	30	0	0	.00	.240	.282	.347	.630
Franco, Julio, Atl	47	low	94	261	72	12	1	4	31	33	35	31	60	2	1	.67	.276	.353	.375	.728
Freel, Ryan, Cin	29	low	152	579	155	29	5	6	84	39	76	66	84	39	11	.78	.268	.343	.366	.709
Freeman, Choo, Col	26	low	45	131	35	6	2	3	20	16	17	10	28	2	1	.67	.267	.319	.412	.731
Fullmer, Brad, Tex	30	med	97	337	93	25	2	15	51	54	55	29	43	3	2	.60	.276	.333	.496	.829
Furcal, Rafael, Atl	28	med	152	619	177	32	5	13	111	58	93	63	83	30	8	.79	.286	.352	.417	.769
Garcia, Danny, NYM	25	low	59	130	33	8	1	2	16	15	15	10	22	4	1	.80	.254	.307	.377	.684
Garcia, Jesse, Atl	32	low	62	139	38	5	0	1	15	9	13	4	18	4	3	.57	.273	.294	.331	.625
Garcia, Karim, Bal	30	low	74	194	51	8	1	9	25	33	26	11	35	1	1	.50	.263	.302	.454	.756
Garciaparra, Nomar, ChC	32	high	126	514	161	38	4	20	88	84	96	38	50	8	3	.73	.313	.361	.519	.880
Gathright, Joey, TB	24	low	154	558	176	19	2	0	87	22	76	41	120	71	27	.72	.315	.362	.357	.719
Gerut, Jody, Cle	28	low	122	425	116	28	3	13	64	55	64	45	50	11	6	.65	.273	.343	.445	.787
Gettis, Byron, KC	25	low	46	100	27	5	1	2	13	14	14	14	27	2	1	.67	.270	.360	.400	.760
Giambi, Jason, NYY	34	high	104	329	90	19	0	21	58	66	68	69	76	1	1	.50	.274	.399	.523	.922
Giambi, Jeremy, Bos	31	med	85	209	52	11	0	9	33	31	33	41	59	1	1	.50	.249	.372	.431	.803
Gibbons, Jay, Bal	28	high	117	390	101	22	1	16	49	59	55	34	57	1	1	.50	.259	.318	.444	.762
Gil, Jerry, Ari	23	low	100	339	82	21	5	6	30	37	34	6	82	10	1	.91	.242	.255	.386	.642
Giles, Brian, SD	34	high	139	512	148	32	4	25	88	89	106	96	70	8	3	.73	.289	.401	.514	.915
Giles, Marcus, Atl	27	med	131	490	149	33	2	16	83	63	88	53	76	16	5	.76	.304	.372	.478	.850

376

2005 Projections

Hitter	Age	Inj	G	AB	H	2B	3B	HR	R	RBI	RC	BB	SO	SB	CS	SB%	Avg	OBP	Slg	OPS
Ginter, Keith, Mil	29	high	138	502	131	31	2	22	70	71	79	56	115	7	1	.88	.261	.335	.462	.797
Glanville, Doug, Phi	35	low	57	111	29	4	1	2	14	9	12	5	15	4	1	.80	.261	.293	.369	.662
Glaus, Troy, Ana	29	high	158	566	144	33	1	39	107	105	107	94	144	8	4	.67	.254	.361	.523	.884
Gload, Ross, CWS	29	low	95	273	83	19	1	9	35	40	45	17	36	0	0	.00	.304	.345	.480	.825
Gomez, Chris, Tor	34	low	106	354	92	17	1	4	38	35	38	27	46	2	2	.50	.260	.312	.347	.660
Gonzalez, Adrian, Tex	23	low	105	351	94	20	2	8	40	53	45	26	58	1	1	.50	.268	.318	.405	.723
Gonzalez, Alex, Fla	28	high	141	494	118	29	3	17	56	64	56	27	107	3	2	.60	.239	.278	.413	.691
Gonzalez, Alex, SD	32	high	107	342	81	20	1	10	42	36	38	26	81	4	3	.57	.237	.291	.389	.680
Gonzalez, Juan, KC	36	high	85	333	98	20	1	18	51	66	59	22	66	1	1	.50	.294	.338	.523	.861
Gonzalez, Luis, Ari	38	high	120	446	126	28	2	22	74	72	85	69	64	3	2	.60	.283	.379	.502	.881
Gonzalez, Luis, Col	26	high	102	364	110	19	3	11	59	49	56	24	54	1	4	.20	.302	.345	.462	.807
Gotay, Ruben, KC	23	low	150	522	144	27	9	7	74	71	71	59	86	9	11	.45	.276	.349	.402	.752
Grabowski, Jason, LA	29	low	93	264	65	14	1	10	35	35	36	30	61	0	0	.00	.246	.323	.420	.744
Graffanino, Tony, KC	33	high	96	306	80	15	1	6	47	31	39	32	50	8	2	.80	.261	.331	.376	.707
Green, Andy, Ari	28	low	52	113	30	9	1	1	14	10	14	8	15	3	2	.60	.265	.314	.389	.703
Green, Nick, Atl	27	low	58	175	46	10	1	3	21	20	20	11	35	1	2	.33	.263	.306	.383	.689
Green, Shawn, LA	33	med	146	555	153	33	1	28	89	90	97	69	110	7	3	.70	.276	.356	.490	.846
Greene, Khalil, SD	26	med	139	487	133	33	3	15	63	63	72	45	90	4	3	.57	.273	.335	.446	.780
Greene, Todd, Col	34	med	61	159	42	9	0	8	19	25	22	6	30	0	0	.00	.264	.291	.472	.763
Grieve, Ben, ChC	29	low	96	249	65	16	0	9	35	37	39	39	65	1	0	1.00	.261	.361	.434	.795
Griffey Jr., Ken, Cin	36	high	94	331	86	17	1	22	54	63	61	48	76	3	1	.75	.260	.354	.517	.870
Grissom, Marquis, SF	38	high	126	473	125	21	1	16	62	63	60	27	78	5	2	.71	.264	.304	.414	.718
Gross, Gabe, Tor	26	low	58	149	39	10	1	3	19	19	21	20	31	2	2	.50	.262	.349	.403	.752
Grudzielanek, Mark, ChC	35	high	112	405	114	21	1	6	52	36	49	22	58	3	2	.60	.281	.319	.383	.701
Guerrero, Vladimir, Ana	29	high	146	558	184	36	3	37	102	111	133	61	69	16	7	.70	.330	.396	.604	1.000
Guerrero, Wilton, KC	31	low	55	101	28	4	1	0	11	8	10	4	14	4	2	.67	.277	.305	.337	.641
Guiel, Aaron, KC	33	high	50	153	39	8	0	6	25	24	21	19	35	1	2	.33	.255	.337	.425	.762
Guillen, Carlos, Det	30	med	135	504	144	30	5	14	86	76	80	55	88	8	5	.62	.286	.356	.448	.804
Guillen, Jose, Ana	29	high	134	453	130	24	2	21	66	75	71	27	79	3	3	.50	.287	.327	.488	.815
Gutierrez, Ricky, Bos	35	high	57	154	41	6	0	2	17	16	17	14	22	1	1	.50	.266	.327	.344	.672
Guzman, Cristian, Min	27	med	152	602	165	29	10	8	88	56	74	32	77	14	7	.67	.274	.311	.395	.706
Guzman, Freddy, SD	24	med	99	330	86	12	4	1	46	18	41	33	59	46	7	.87	.261	.328	.330	.658
Hafner, Travis, Cle	28	med	155	525	158	39	3	28	91	100	111	76	114	3	2	.60	.301	.389	.547	.936
Hairston Jr., Jerry, Bal	29	med	103	344	93	20	2	4	46	30	44	34	38	16	7	.70	.270	.336	.375	.711
Hairston, Scott, Ari	25	low	101	351	93	19	7	13	49	38	50	23	79	3	4	.43	.265	.310	.470	.780
Hall, Bill, Mil	26	low	95	259	65	14	2	6	32	30	29	15	64	8	5	.62	.251	.292	.390	.682
Hall, Toby, TB	30	med	116	396	103	23	0	9	41	53	45	21	34	0	1	.00	.260	.297	.386	.684
Hammock, Robby, Ari	28	med	85	283	74	19	3	7	35	35	37	22	49	4	3	.57	.261	.315	.424	.739
Harris, Willie, CWS	27	low	114	323	86	12	2	4	50	24	40	36	56	17	6	.74	.266	.340	.353	.693
Harvey, Ken, KC	27	low	103	322	89	18	0	10	37	43	44	21	57	1	1	.50	.276	.321	.425	.746
Hatteberg, Scott, Oak	36	med	150	547	145	31	1	13	69	69	76	71	57	0	0	.00	.265	.350	.397	.746
Hawpe, Brad, Col	26	low	42	140	41	8	1	9	22	28	27	12	35	1	1	.50	.293	.349	.557	.906
Helms, Wes, Mil	29	high	100	252	67	13	1	8	28	33	34	20	54	0	0	.00	.266	.320	.421	.740
Helton, Todd, Col	32	med	147	541	184	46	2	33	114	110	148	104	74	3	2	.60	.340	.447	.616	1.062
Hernandez, Jose, LA	36	low	112	349	86	15	1	13	44	44	44	33	117	3	2	.60	.246	.312	.407	.718
Hernandez, Ramon, SD	29	high	127	428	113	24	0	17	55	66	61	39	59	1	0	1.00	.264	.325	.439	.765
Hidalgo, Richard, NYM	30	high	130	438	116	28	2	22	65	71	70	45	100	4	4	.50	.265	.333	.489	.822
Higginson, Bobby, Det	35	high	93	286	72	15	1	8	38	38	38	38	49	4	2	.67	.252	.340	.395	.735
Hill, Bobby, Pit	27	low	97	247	65	12	2	3	34	25	30	24	41	5	2	.71	.263	.328	.364	.693
Hill, Koyie, Ari	26	med	122	441	114	26	0	10	53	50	53	34	78	1	1	.50	.259	.312	.385	.697
Hillenbrand, Shea, Ari	30	med	141	531	157	34	2	16	66	78	79	22	59	2	1	.67	.296	.324	.458	.781
Hinske, Eric, Tor	28	med	137	473	124	31	2	15	70	66	70	56	90	10	4	.71	.262	.340	.431	.772
Hollandsworth, Todd, ChC	32	high	101	306	86	20	1	11	47	39	48	29	66	4	3	.57	.281	.343	.461	.804
Holliday, Matt, Col	25	low	121	417	114	27	3	13	64	59	61	35	75	6	4	.60	.273	.330	.446	.776
Howard, Ryan, Phi	26	low	112	442	118	26	1	34	76	104	82	45	151	1	2	.33	.267	.335	.561	.896
Hudson, Orlando, Tor	28	low	137	499	137	31	6	11	66	57	71	47	84	6	4	.60	.275	.337	.427	.764
Huff, Aubrey, TB	29	med	151	593	178	35	1	29	86	95	108	52	75	4	2	.67	.300	.357	.509	.866
Hummel, Tim, Cin	27	low	57	117	30	7	0	2	13	13	13	10	19	1	1	.50	.256	.315	.368	.682
Hunter, Torii, Min	30	med	145	556	148	35	3	24	82	88	82	41	110	16	8	.67	.266	.317	.469	.786
Hyzdu, Adam, Bos	34	low	72	186	49	12	0	9	30	29	31	26	42	2	1	.67	.263	.354	.473	.827
Ibanez, Raul, Sea	33	high	134	516	148	31	2	17	72	77	79	42	81	2	2	.50	.287	.341	.453	.794
Infante, Omar, Det	24	low	142	498	127	23	7	11	63	49	61	40	87	17	8	.68	.255	.310	.396	.706
Inge, Brandon, Det	28	med	109	315	79	15	3	9	31	38	38	24	59	3	3	.50	.251	.304	.403	.707
Izturis, Cesar, LA	25	low	144	498	135	25	5	3	59	42	56	28	49	16	6	.73	.271	.310	.359	.669
Izturis, Maicer, Mon	25	low	32	121	33	7	1	1	16	10	15	13	12	5	3	.62	.273	.343	.372	.715
Jacobsen, Bucky, Sea	30	low	100	347	95	21	1	22	52	68	65	42	91	1	1	.50	.274	.352	.530	.882
Jenkins, Geoff, Mil	31	high	132	498	137	33	2	24	76	81	82	43	125	2	1	.67	.275	.333	.494	.827
Jeter, Derek, NYY	31	med	142	577	180	33	2	18	107	72	103	55	97	21	5	.81	.312	.372	.470	.842
Jimenez, DAngelo, Cin'	28	med	147	549	145	27	4	11	75	63	75	75	96	10	6	.62	.264	.353	.388	.741
Johnson, Charles, Col	34	high	107	347	81	21	0	15	42	54	48	47	99	1	1	.50	.233	.325	.424	.749
Johnson, Nick, Mon	27	med	104	316	83	18	0	12	51	47	51	56	64	5	3	.63	.263	.374	.434	.807
Johnson, Reed, Tor	29	med	104	329	91	16	1	7	50	38	41	18	53	3	2	.60	.277	.314	.395	.709
Jones, Andruw, Atl	28	med	155	587	156	33	3	33	95	99	101	69	137	8	4	.67	.266	.343	.501	.844
Jones, Chipper, Atl	33	med	139	506	147	29	1	29	88	94	106	91	90	4	2	.67	.291	.399	.524	.922
Jones, Jacque, Min	30	med	139	502	141	28	1	20	70	70	74	32	106	10	7	.59	.281	.324	.460	.784
Jordan, Brian, Tex	38	high	70	212	56	11	1	7	28	31	28	16	36	2	1	.67	.264	.316	.425	.740
Kapler, Gabe, Bos	30	med	112	263	72	16	1	6	40	33	36	22	44	6	3	.67	.274	.330	.411	.740
Karros, Eric, Oak	38	low	63	163	42	8	0	6	17	24	21	14	28	1	1	.50	.258	.316	.417	.734
Kata, Matt, Ari	27	med	84	281	74	16	5	5	37	26	35	19	42	5	3	.62	.263	.310	.409	.719
Kearns, Austin, Cin	25	high	111	402	112	23	2	18	65	70	72	61	98	7	3	.70	.279	.374	.480	.854
Kendall, Jason, Pit	31	high	138	537	166	30	2	6	79	52	81	54	40	10	7	.59	.309	.372	.406	.778

377

2005 Projections

Hitter	Age	Inj	G	AB	H	2B	3B	HR	R	RBI	RC	BB	SO	SB	CS	SB%	Avg	OBP	Slg	OPS
					BATTING									BASERUNNING			AVERAGES			
Kennedy, Adam, Ana	29	med	147	502	138	27	4	10	71	54	67	39	89	15	6	.71	.275	.327	.404	.732
Kent, Jeff, Hou	37	high	128	502	144	34	2	23	78	93	87	48	93	6	3	.67	.287	.349	.500	.849
Keppinger, Jeff, NYM	25	low	33	117	35	5	0	1	13	10	15	9	6	3	2	.60	.299	.349	.368	.717
Kielty, Bobby, Oak	29	low	105	287	72	17	1	10	44	42	43	47	55	3	1	.75	.251	.356	.422	.778
Kingsale, Gene, Det	29	low	57	140	35	6	2	2	20	12	16	14	18	4	2	.67	.250	.318	.364	.682
Klesko, Ryan, SD	34	med	128	454	125	30	1	19	66	78	81	75	83	5	2	.71	.275	.378	.471	.849
Konerko, Paul, CWS	29	med	154	550	150	28	0	32	79	101	94	59	88	1	0	1.00	.273	.343	.498	.841
Koskie, Corey, Min	32	med	130	478	129	31	1	20	75	76	80	66	118	11	5	.69	.270	.358	.464	.823
Kotchman, Casey, Ana	22	low	134	480	147	42	0	7	53	68	74	30	47	4	0	1.00	.306	.347	.438	.785
Kotsay, Mark, Oak	30	med	143	559	163	33	4	13	76	59	86	54	73	8	5	.62	.292	.354	.435	.789
Kroeger, Josh, Ari	23	low	141	539	153	49	5	15	66	70	81	28	122	4	3	.57	.284	.319	.477	.796
Kubel, Jason, Min	23	low	133	473	150	37	3	19	88	89	96	48	59	15	5	.75	.317	.380	.529	.909
Laird, Gerald, Tex	26	med	101	320	81	17	3	6	47	40	38	30	66	5	3	.62	.253	.317	.381	.698
Laker, Tim, Cle	36	low	46	102	23	4	0	2	10	14	9	7	23	0	0	.00	.225	.275	.324	.599
Lamb, Mike, Hou	30	low	111	337	94	18	2	11	50	49	51	34	58	1	1	.50	.279	.345	.442	.787
Lane, Jason, Hou	29	low	102	268	75	21	1	10	41	47	44	27	47	3	1	.75	.280	.346	.478	.823
Lankford, Ray, StL	38	high	58	119	30	7	0	5	18	17	18	18	37	2	1	.67	.252	.350	.437	.787
Larkin, Barry, Cin	41	high	101	358	94	20	2	6	51	35	46	41	43	4	1	.80	.263	.338	.380	.718
LaRoche, Adam, Atl	26	med	110	364	104	28	1	16	54	54	64	37	78	0	0	.00	.286	.352	.500	.852
Larson, Brandon, Cin	29	med	58	156	41	8	0	9	19	28	25	14	43	1	0	1.00	.263	.324	.487	.811
LaRue, Jason, Cin	31	med	120	416	100	25	1	16	51	57	51	32	121	1	2	.33	.240	.295	.421	.715
Lawton, Matt, Cle	34	high	123	452	118	24	1	14	73	58	66	64	61	14	6	.70	.261	.353	.412	.764
LeCroy, Matt, Min	30	high	93	262	73	16	0	11	28	44	40	18	55	0	0	.00	.279	.325	.466	.791
Ledee, Ricky, SF	32	med	94	184	43	11	1	6	26	29	24	25	47	2	1	.67	.234	.325	.402	.728
Lee, Carlos, CWS	29	high	152	581	169	35	1	29	96	100	102	51	86	10	4	.71	.291	.348	.504	.852
Lee, Derrek, ChC	30	low	153	567	155	35	2	29	87	89	100	74	134	11	6	.65	.273	.357	.496	.853
Leon, Jose, Bal	29	low	50	105	28	6	0	4	12	14	14	6	22	0	0	.00	.267	.306	.438	.744
Leone, Justin, Sea	28	low	61	178	45	10	2	10	33	30	30	23	50	5	3	.62	.253	.338	.500	.838
Lieberthal, Mike, Phi	33	high	125	473	132	30	1	16	59	69	71	39	67	1	1	.50	.279	.334	.448	.782
Lo Duca, Paul, Fla	33	med	133	513	143	30	1	12	63	67	68	37	45	2	4	.33	.279	.327	.411	.739
Lofton, Kenny, NYY	38	low	105	374	102	17	3	7	65	34	51	43	46	13	5	.72	.273	.348	.390	.738
Logan, Nook, Det	26	low	118	406	103	13	6	2	50	25	43	29	81	34	10	.77	.254	.303	.330	.633
Long, Terrence, SD	29	low	128	380	101	22	2	9	50	46	49	29	61	3	2	.60	.266	.318	.405	.723
Lopez, Felipe, Cin	25	low	87	279	70	14	2	8	40	34	35	26	73	3	2	.60	.251	.315	.401	.716
Lopez, Javy, Bal	35	high	122	442	128	23	1	21	58	75	73	33	82	0	0	.00	.290	.339	.489	.828
Lopez, Jose, Sea	22	low	125	495	125	32	0	17	66	58	59	24	61	5	3	.62	.253	.287	.420	.707
Loretta, Mark, SD	34	high	153	596	184	35	2	12	84	69	95	57	56	4	3	.57	.309	.369	.435	.804
Lowell, Mike, Fla	31	high	145	555	157	39	0	26	78	95	97	59	79	4	1	.80	.283	.352	.494	.845
Ludwick, Ryan, Cle	27	med	65	190	50	14	1	8	26	30	29	16	50	0	0	.00	.263	.320	.474	.794
Lugo, Julio, TB	30	high	142	531	145	29	3	10	77	58	71	49	104	16	7	.70	.273	.334	.395	.730
Luna, Hector, StL	25	low	82	214	58	9	1	2	35	21	25	19	35	8	3	.73	.271	.330	.350	.681
Mabry, John, StL	35	high	91	219	56	11	0	10	27	33	31	21	56	0	0	.00	.256	.321	.443	.764
Macias, Jose, ChC	33	low	63	107	26	5	1	2	13	11	11	6	19	2	1	.67	.243	.283	.364	.648
Mackowiak, Rob, Pit	29	med	114	307	79	16	2	10	41	42	43	31	70	8	2	.80	.257	.325	.420	.746
Marrero, Eli, Atl	32	high	88	241	63	13	1	8	33	35	33	21	48	4	1	.80	.261	.321	.423	.744
Martinez, Ramon, ChC	33	low	90	196	51	11	1	3	21	22	24	18	31	1	0	1.00	.260	.322	.372	.695
Martinez, Tino, TB	38	low	121	408	105	19	1	17	54	67	59	47	64	2	1	.67	.257	.334	.434	.768
Martinez, Victor, Cle	27	low	145	579	175	44	1	24	88	110	109	65	70	0	1	.00	.302	.373	.506	.879
Mateo, Ruben, KC	27	med	47	158	42	10	1	6	21	21	22	11	33	1	1	.50	.266	.314	.456	.769
Matheny, Mike, StL	35	med	107	319	75	14	1	4	27	35	29	24	67	0	1	.00	.235	.289	.323	.612
Matos, Luis, Bal	27	high	115	180	48	11	1	4	25	20	23	13	32	7	2	.78	.267	.316	.406	.722
Matsui, Hideki, NYY	31	high	162	591	175	38	1	26	98	109	111	80	88	2	1	.67	.296	.380	.496	.876
Matsui, Kazuo, NYM	30	high	154	587	163	42	2	9	84	58	81	52	113	16	4	.80	.278	.336	.402	.739
Matthews Jr., Gary, Tex	31	low	79	159	41	9	1	5	24	19	23	19	35	3	1	.75	.258	.337	.421	.758
Mauer, Joe, Min	22	low	144	512	161	39	3	16	82	74	95	46	58	3	0	1.00	.314	.371	.496	.867
Mayne, Brent, LA	37	high	75	194	47	8	0	2	18	20	19	21	37	1	1	.50	.242	.316	.314	.631
McCarty, Dave, Bos	36	low	67	145	36	8	0	4	20	20	18	14	38	0	0	.00	.248	.314	.386	.701
McCracken, Quinton, Ari	35	low	82	180	48	10	1	1	24	17	20	15	30	4	3	.57	.267	.323	.350	.673
McDonald, John, Cle	31	low	72	151	35	7	1	1	20	9	12	7	20	1	1	.50	.232	.266	.311	.577
McEwing, Joe, NYM	33	med	76	139	34	7	1	2	16	13	14	10	31	2	1	.67	.245	.295	.353	.648
McLemore, Mark, Oak	41	high	116	208	51	9	1	2	27	20	24	33	36	4	2	.67	.245	.349	.327	.675
McMillon, Billy, Oak	34	high	61	129	34	8	0	4	17	18	18	14	24	0	0	.00	.264	.336	.419	.754
McPherson, Dallas, Ana	25	low	143	532	156	33	8	37	90	107	109	47	175	13	8	.62	.293	.351	.594	.945
Melhuse, Adam, Oak	33	low	79	272	74	17	0	11	36	39	42	26	55	0	0	.00	.272	.336	.456	.791
Mench, Kevin, Tex	27	low	148	554	156	39	3	30	88	92	99	49	77	0	0	.00	.282	.340	.525	.865
Menechino, Frank, Tor	34	low	75	204	50	9	1	5	30	23	26	30	36	0	1	.00	.245	.342	.373	.714
Merloni, Lou, Cle	34	high	79	185	51	11	1	3	24	22	24	16	35	1	1	.50	.276	.333	.395	.728
Michaels, Jason, Phi	29	low	119	316	92	19	1	11	51	45	55	46	76	2	2	.50	.291	.381	.462	.843
Mientkiewicz, Doug, Bos	31	high	110	321	87	22	1	6	41	39	46	45	45	2	2	.50	.271	.361	.402	.763
Miles, Aaron, Col	29	low	104	400	124	22	2	6	57	42	58	24	35	9	6	.60	.310	.349	.420	.769
Millar, Kevin, Bos	34	high	137	498	141	35	1	19	69	78	83	55	94	1	1	.50	.283	.354	.472	.826
Miller, Damian, Oak	36	med	106	356	90	22	0	9	37	45	45	36	89	0	0	.00	.253	.321	.390	.712
Mirabelli, Doug, Bos	35	low	83	272	69	16	0	12	35	42	40	31	65	0	0	.00	.254	.330	.445	.775
Moeller, Chad, Mil	30	low	86	241	60	12	1	5	25	28	27	21	52	0	1	.00	.249	.309	.369	.678
Mohr, Dustan, SF	29	low	108	285	78	20	1	8	48	32	44	38	67	2	2	.50	.274	.359	.435	.794
Molina, Ben, LA	31	med	112	383	103	17	0	10	37	57	45	17	36	0	0	.00	.269	.300	.392	.692
Molina, Jose, Ana	30	med	66	150	39	7	1	2	16	16	16	6	33	2	1	.67	.260	.288	.360	.648
Molina, Yadier, StL	23	low	51	166	44	7	0	1	16	19	18	15	20	0	0	.00	.265	.326	.325	.651
Mondesi, Raul, Ana	34	high	100	357	89	20	1	16	52	51	51	37	74	10	5	.67	.249	.320	.445	.765
Monroe, Craig, Det	28	low	133	518	145	33	3	25	73	82	82	36	89	3	3	.50	.280	.327	.488	.815
Mora, Melvin, Bal	33	med	153	569	166	35	1	22	98	83	99	69	108	10	6	.62	.292	.368	.473	.841

2005 Projections

Hitter	Age	Inj	G	AB	H	2B	3B	HR	R	RBI	RC	BB	SO	SB	CS	SB%	Avg	OBP	Slg	OPS
Morneau, Justin, Min	24	low	144	528	148	34	2	32	81	99	97	51	96	1	1	.50	.280	.344	.534	.878
Mueller, Bill, Bos	34	high	124	450	128	29	2	12	72	56	72	58	63	2	2	.50	.284	.366	.438	.804
Munson, Eric, Det	28	low	106	317	73	14	1	18	37	51	44	36	74	1	1	.50	.230	.309	.451	.760
Nady, Xavier, SD	27	low	85	252	70	13	1	11	35	38	39	17	42	2	0	1.00	.278	.323	.468	.792
Nevin, Phil, SD	34	high	138	512	143	27	0	25	72	95	87	59	118	1	0	1.00	.279	.354	.479	.832
Newhan, David, Bal	32	low	135	423	134	24	4	10	75	55	73	31	77	13	2	.87	.317	.363	.463	.827
Nix, Laynce, Tex	25	low	126	394	103	23	2	16	60	59	55	27	103	3	1	.75	.261	.309	.452	.761
Nixon, Trot, Bos	31	high	114	406	116	25	3	19	68	68	76	55	80	3	1	.75	.286	.371	.502	.873
Nunez, Abraham, KC	28	low	64	120	28	5	1	4	16	15	15	14	29	3	1	.75	.233	.313	.392	.705
Nunez, Abraham, Pit	29	low	68	103	25	4	1	1	11	8	10	9	19	1	1	.50	.243	.304	.330	.634
Ojeda, Miguel, SD	30	low	75	202	50	5	0	10	26	34	27	22	38	0	0	.00	.248	.321	.421	.742
Olerud, John, NYY	37	med	111	358	98	22	0	9	47	53	55	58	50	0	0	.00	.274	.375	.411	.786
Olivo, Miguel, Sea	27	low	105	323	81	19	4	11	46	41	42	25	76	10	6	.62	.251	.305	.437	.741
Olmedo, Ray, Cin	24	low	63	157	39	7	1	1	17	11	15	12	25	1	1	.50	.248	.302	.325	.627
Ordonez, Magglio, CWS	31	high	120	466	144	31	1	24	77	88	91	43	55	6	3	.67	.309	.367	.534	.902
Ortiz, David, Bos	30	high	142	522	147	43	1	32	82	109	105	68	115	0	0	.00	.282	.364	.552	.916
Overbay, Lyle, Mil	28	med	154	568	170	50	0	16	76	85	102	75	113	2	1	.67	.299	.381	.472	.853
Palmeiro, Orlando, Hou	36	low	75	125	33	6	0	1	16	12	14	15	14	2	1	.67	.264	.343	.336	.679
Palmeiro, Rafael, Bal	41	med	123	442	113	21	0	23	59	76	72	70	60	1	1	.50	.256	.357	.459	.817
Pascucci, Val, Mon	27	low	65	189	48	12	0	8	29	32	31	33	48	3	1	.75	.254	.365	.444	.809
Patterson, Corey, ChC	26	med	140	535	148	28	5	21	82	67	80	32	125	25	7	.78	.277	.317	.465	.783
Payton, Jay, SD	33	med	127	416	116	19	2	12	56	52	58	32	54	3	2	.60	.279	.330	.421	.751
Pena, Carlos, Det	27	low	146	499	124	24	5	27	76	78	81	67	133	6	2	.75	.248	.337	.479	.816
Pena, Wily Mo, Cin	23	low	110	330	84	13	1	21	45	55	49	23	99	5	2	.71	.255	.303	.491	.794
Peralta, Jhonny, Cle	23	low	122	426	109	23	2	8	47	44	49	35	91	1	4	.20	.256	.312	.376	.688
Perez, Eddie, Atl	37	med	77	209	50	12	0	4	16	21	21	12	35	0	0	.00	.239	.281	.354	.635
Perez, Neifi, ChC	32	low	114	343	89	16	3	3	40	31	35	17	35	2	2	.50	.259	.294	.350	.644
Perez, Timo, CWS	30	low	93	232	62	12	1	4	27	28	26	12	19	3	2	.60	.267	.303	.379	.683
Perez, Tomas, Phi	32	low	64	106	25	6	0	2	12	12	11	8	23	0	0	.00	.236	.289	.349	.639
Phelps, Josh, Cle	27	low	110	349	97	21	1	20	54	68	60	28	88	0	0	.00	.278	.332	.516	.847
Phillips, Brandon, Cle	24	low	67	180	46	11	1	3	21	17	20	12	25	5	3	.62	.256	.302	.378	.680
Phillips, Jason, NYM	29	low	107	316	82	18	0	8	33	42	40	30	33	0	0	.00	.259	.324	.392	.716
Piazza, Mike, NYM	37	med	112	406	114	21	0	22	56	69	73	53	71	0	0	.00	.281	.364	.495	.859
Pickering, Calvin, KC	29	low	121	448	124	21	2	34	83	103	102	98	131	0	0	.00	.277	.407	.560	.967
Piedra, Jorge, Col	26	low	38	127	38	9	2	5	20	17	22	7	18	1	1	.50	.299	.336	.520	.856
Pierre, Juan, Fla	28	low	156	620	194	23	7	2	95	45	87	44	35	43	17	.72	.313	.358	.382	.741
Pierzynski, A.J., SF	28	low	136	494	147	36	3	11	59	76	72	22	43	1	2	.33	.298	.328	.449	.777
Podsednik, Scott, Mil	29	med	152	598	164	29	6	12	90	54	87	58	90	58	13	.82	.274	.338	.403	.741
Polanco, Placido, Phi	30	high	136	532	157	27	2	13	81	56	76	32	41	8	4	.67	.295	.335	.427	.762
Posada, Jorge, NYY	34	high	128	455	123	29	0	22	71	84	83	82	109	1	2	.33	.270	.382	.479	.861
Pratt, Todd, Phi	38	high	71	245	61	13	0	6	30	32	32	38	74	0	0	.00	.249	.350	.376	.725
Pujols, Albert, StL	25	low	158	606	208	52	2	47	141	139	170	85	59	4	4	.50	.343	.424	.668	1.092
Quinlan, Robb, Ana	28	med	84	264	80	16	2	6	35	38	41	19	40	4	2	.67	.303	.350	.447	.797
Quiroz, Guillermo, Tor	24	low	119	301	73	22	0	10	38	45	39	29	61	1	0	1.00	.243	.309	.415	.724
Ramirez, Aramis, ChC	27	high	148	538	154	32	1	30	77	97	94	42	75	1	1	.50	.286	.338	.517	.855
Ramirez, Manny, Bos	33	high	140	528	169	37	1	39	103	124	134	85	114	2	2	.50	.320	.414	.616	1.030
Randa, Joe, KC	36	med	126	479	132	27	2	10	60	63	63	38	71	1	1	.50	.276	.329	.403	.732
Ransom, Cody, SF	29	low	79	168	39	7	1	5	22	18	19	16	43	6	2	.75	.232	.299	.375	.674
Redman, Tike, Pit	28	low	107	352	100	14	3	5	46	29	44	20	30	15	5	.75	.284	.323	.384	.706
Redmond, Mike, Fla	34	low	81	224	61	11	0	2	19	22	25	15	24	1	0	1.00	.272	.318	.348	.666
Reed, Jeremy, Sea	24	low	143	538	165	28	4	13	88	72	92	62	55	31	13	.70	.307	.378	.446	.824
Reese, Pokey, Bos	32	high	75	194	45	9	1	3	23	19	20	16	43	6	1	.86	.232	.290	.335	.626
Relaford, Desi, KC	32	med	95	263	64	13	1	4	35	29	29	26	40	6	2	.75	.243	.311	.346	.657
Renteria, Edgar, StL	30	med	149	568	167	35	1	11	84	73	83	50	71	20	9	.69	.294	.351	.417	.768
Restovich, Mike, Min	26	low	58	128	34	8	1	5	21	19	19	10	33	2	1	.67	.266	.319	.461	.780
Reyes, Jose, NYM	22	med	148	577	157	32	9	6	90	50	73	27	79	60	12	.83	.272	.305	.390	.695
Reyes, Rene, Col	27	low	64	152	44	10	1	3	20	17	20	7	26	4	3	.57	.289	.321	.428	.748
Rios, Alexis, Tor	24	low	140	566	170	35	8	6	71	58	84	38	97	16	4	.80	.300	.344	.422	.767
Rivas, Luis, Min	26	low	126	411	108	21	6	9	59	41	52	23	62	19	5	.79	.263	.302	.409	.711
Rivera, Juan, Mon	27	med	118	390	118	28	1	12	52	51	65	30	45	4	1	.80	.303	.352	.472	.824
Roberts, Brian, Bal	28	med	133	508	138	32	3	4	80	43	67	57	64	25	8	.76	.272	.345	.370	.715
Roberts, Dave, Bos	33	low	95	272	70	9	3	2	45	21	33	32	32	27	6	.82	.257	.336	.335	.670
Robinson, Kerry, SD	32	low	80	118	32	4	1	1	18	9	14	8	12	12	2	.86	.271	.317	.347	.665
Rodriguez, Alex, NYY	30	low	153	590	175	30	2	42	116	118	128	78	125	20	5	.80	.297	.379	.568	.947
Rodriguez, Ivan, Det	34	high	124	472	146	30	2	19	72	75	84	35	83	6	3	.67	.309	.357	.502	.859
Rolen, Scott, StL	30	med	147	547	160	38	3	31	101	112	113	77	106	7	3	.70	.293	.380	.543	.923
Rollins, Jimmy, Phi	27	low	158	645	178	40	10	13	102	67	94	57	88	28	9	.76	.276	.335	.429	.764
Rolls, Damian, TB	28	high	54	112	28	6	0	2	16	12	12	7	23	3	1	.75	.250	.294	.357	.651
Ross, Dave, LA	28	low	64	147	33	6	0	7	17	20	18	14	48	0	0	.00	.224	.292	.408	.700
Rowand, Aaron, CWS	28	med	152	574	168	41	2	25	99	79	99	37	92	15	5	.75	.293	.336	.502	.837
Saenz, Olmedo, LA	35	low	65	137	36	7	0	6	18	20	20	12	31	0	0	.00	.263	.322	.445	.767
Salmon, Tim, Ana	37	high	80	235	62	13	0	8	33	35	36	36	52	2	1	.67	.264	.362	.421	.783
Sanchez, Alex, Det	29	med	119	432	129	14	5	2	51	31	52	19	60	28	14	.67	.299	.328	.368	.696
Sanchez, Freddy, Pit	28	low	56	140	40	9	0	2	20	14	19	12	20	5	1	.83	.286	.342	.393	.735
Sanchez, Rey, TB	38	high	76	209	54	7	1	1	22	17	19	9	22	1	1	.50	.258	.289	.316	.605
Sanders, Reggie, StL	38	high	122	439	110	23	2	22	65	66	64	40	118	16	6	.73	.251	.313	.462	.776
Santiago, Benito, KC	40	high	87	331	86	16	1	9	32	42	39	20	61	1	2	.33	.260	.302	.396	.698
Santiago, Ramon, Sea	26	low	63	146	32	4	1	1	18	12	11	11	20	5	3	.62	.219	.274	.281	.555
Schneider, Brian, Mon	29	low	123	415	107	26	2	11	40	53	55	43	63	0	0	.00	.258	.328	.410	.737
Scutaro, Marco, Oak	30	low	110	335	95	22	2	7	40	32	46	22	44	3	2	.60	.284	.328	.424	.752
Sexson, Richie, Ari	31	med	154	559	152	29	2	39	91	116	107	71	143	1	1	.50	.272	.354	.540	.894

2005 Projections

Hitter	Age	Inj	G	AB	H	2B	3B	HR	R	RBI	RC	BB	SO	SB	CS	SB%	Avg	OBP	Slg	OPS
Sheffield, Gary, NYY	37	high	133	502	148	26	1	30	93	96	105	85	67	7	4	.64	.295	.397	.530	.927
Sierra, Ruben, NYY	40	med	78	205	52	10	0	9	24	33	28	16	36	1	0	1.00	.254	.308	.434	.742
Simon, Randall, TB	30	med	70	175	46	8	0	5	18	24	21	9	18	0	0	.00	.263	.299	.394	.693
Sizemore, Grady, Cle	23	low	152	573	156	30	8	13	88	75	79	51	102	18	11	.62	.272	.332	.421	.752
Sledge, Terrmel, Mon	28	low	144	468	133	24	5	16	67	68	75	49	77	7	4	.64	.284	.352	.459	.811
Smith, Jason, Det	28	low	76	217	58	10	4	6	30	26	27	8	50	5	3	.62	.267	.293	.433	.727
Snow, J.T., SF	37	high	107	336	91	21	1	10	48	52	53	52	68	2	1	.67	.271	.369	.429	.797
Snyder, Chris, Ari	24	low	29	102	25	8	0	4	13	13	15	11	18	1	0	1.00	.245	.319	.441	.760
Snyder, Earl, Bos	29	low	56	169	43	12	0	8	24	27	24	11	40	0	0	.00	.254	.300	.467	.767
Soriano, Alfonso, Tex	27	med	155	659	188	41	3	35	104	97	110	34	133	25	7	.78	.285	.320	.516	.836
Sosa, Sammy, ChC	37	high	124	474	128	21	1	37	82	93	93	64	136	1	1	.50	.270	.357	.553	.910
Spencer, Shane, NYM	33	med	90	251	63	13	1	7	27	33	32	24	58	4	1	.80	.251	.316	.394	.711
Spiezio, Scott, Sea	33	low	112	336	84	19	2	10	43	46	44	35	50	3	2	.60	.250	.321	.408	.728
Spivey, Junior, Mil	30	high	113	426	121	26	2	14	71	59	69	48	86	7	4	.64	.284	.357	.453	.810
Stairs, Matt, KC	37	low	118	378	96	20	1	18	50	61	58	50	83	1	1	.50	.254	.341	.455	.796
Stewart, Shannon, Min	31	high	126	515	158	34	3	12	83	57	87	51	62	10	4	.71	.307	.369	.454	.824
Stynes, Chris, Pit	32	low	81	178	46	10	0	4	25	21	21	15	27	1	1	.50	.258	.316	.382	.698
Surhoff, B.J., Bal	41	high	92	325	89	17	0	7	37	41	42	27	40	2	1	.67	.274	.330	.391	.720
Suzuki, Ichiro, Sea	32	med	149	623	210	26	4	8	98	54	103	43	59	28	10	.74	.337	.380	.430	.810
Sweeney, Mark, Col	36	high	92	183	45	11	1	6	22	29	26	27	50	1	1	.50	.246	.343	.415	.758
Sweeney, Mike, KC	32	high	121	463	140	29	0	22	72	89	87	52	53	4	3	.57	.302	.373	.508	.880
Swisher, Nick, Oak	25	low	142	539	126	35	2	24	95	85	81	89	129	3	3	.50	.234	.342	.440	.782
Taguchi, So, StL	36	low	71	125	32	6	0	2	15	14	13	8	17	5	2	.71	.256	.301	.352	.653
Teixeira, Mark, Tex	25	med	136	509	144	32	3	35	89	101	103	59	101	3	1	.75	.283	.357	.564	.921
Tejada, Miguel, Bal	29	high	157	629	183	36	1	31	104	123	108	51	76	5	2	.71	.291	.344	.499	.843
Terrero, Luis, Ari	25	low	59	151	41	8	3	3	20	15	20	10	37	8	3	.73	.272	.317	.424	.741
Thames, Marcus, Det	28	low	61	137	34	9	0	7	22	21	20	15	27	1	1	.50	.248	.322	.467	.790
Thomas, Charles, Atl	27	low	79	231	68	13	3	4	34	29	35	20	40	4	2	.67	.294	.351	.429	.779
Thomas, Frank, CWS	37	high	113	410	108	26	0	25	68	77	80	81	89	1	1	.50	.263	.385	.510	.895
Thome, Jim, Phi	35	high	137	493	134	26	1	39	92	104	111	104	155	0	1	.00	.272	.399	.566	.965
Torrealba, Yorvit, SF	27	low	95	315	81	17	4	9	38	45	43	30	52	3	0	1.00	.257	.322	.422	.744
Tracy, Andy, Col	32	low	54	152	42	10	0	9	25	27	27	14	39	1	0	1.00	.276	.337	.520	.857
Tracy, Chad, Ari	25	low	143	526	159	35	4	9	66	66	81	44	56	3	2	.60	.302	.356	.435	.792
Treanor, Matt, Fla	29	low	49	121	28	5	0	3	13	14	13	14	24	2	0	1.00	.231	.311	.347	.658
Tucker, Michael, SF	34	med	123	421	105	20	4	12	64	52	57	55	101	7	4	.64	.249	.336	.401	.738
Upton, B.J., TB	21	low	153	575	169	37	4	18	106	69	103	76	154	27	8	.77	.294	.376	.466	.842
Uribe, Juan, CWS	26	low	152	564	156	33	8	21	89	78	84	34	100	10	7	.59	.277	.318	.475	.793
Utley, Chase, Phi	27	low	155	563	155	36	3	24	87	103	90	49	96	11	4	.73	.275	.333	.478	.811
Valdez, Wilson, CWS	27	low	57	160	43	5	1	1	18	10	16	7	20	9	4	.69	.269	.299	.331	.631
Valent, Eric, NYM	28	low	105	285	66	16	1	8	36	34	33	30	58	0	0	.00	.232	.305	.379	.684
Valentin, Javier, Cin	30	low	75	197	48	11	1	6	20	24	23	14	36	0	0	.00	.244	.294	.401	.695
Valentin, Jose, CWS	36	high	126	460	102	23	2	24	68	65	59	47	130	7	4	.64	.222	.294	.437	.731
Varitek, Jason, Bos	33	high	129	455	121	30	1	17	60	70	70	54	114	5	3	.62	.266	.344	.448	.792
Vazquez, Ramon, SD	29	med	113	395	105	22	3	6	53	39	53	50	69	5	2	.71	.266	.348	.382	.731
Vidro, Jose, Mon	31	high	134	511	157	38	1	16	77	72	91	54	55	3	2	.60	.307	.373	.479	.853
Vina, Fernando, Det	36	high	64	210	57	10	1	2	28	16	23	13	16	4	3	.57	.271	.314	.357	.671
Vizcaino, Jose, Hou	37	high	115	340	90	14	2	3	36	30	36	21	40	2	2	.50	.265	.307	.344	.652
Vizquel, Omar, Cle	38	high	114	436	118	20	2	5	64	41	54	46	49	12	5	.71	.271	.340	.360	.700
Walker, Larry, StL	39	high	109	381	117	25	2	20	75	70	84	64	74	7	3	.70	.307	.407	.541	.947
Walker, Todd, ChC	32	low	137	514	146	32	2	14	77	65	77	50	66	3	3	.50	.284	.348	.436	.783
Ward, Daryle, Pit	30	med	97	346	89	20	1	15	37	59	47	23	60	0	0	.00	.257	.304	.451	.754
Wells, Vernon, Tor	27	high	153	612	177	42	3	28	100	95	106	47	86	8	2	.80	.289	.340	.505	.845
Werth, Jayson, LA	26	med	112	442	116	25	3	22	75	78	72	46	120	12	2	.86	.262	.332	.482	.814
White, Rondell, Det	33	high	121	421	117	22	1	18	60	63	64	32	75	2	2	.50	.278	.329	.463	.792
Wigginton, Ty, Pit	28	low	137	464	125	31	2	14	61	62	67	43	75	7	2	.78	.269	.331	.435	.767
Wilkerson, Brad, Mon	28	low	155	555	146	38	4	27	102	72	103	103	157	12	7	.63	.263	.378	.492	.870
Williams, Bernie, NYY	37	high	127	493	139	27	1	19	86	76	84	72	83	4	3	.57	.282	.373	.456	.830
Wilson, Craig, Pit	29	med	143	477	132	26	3	27	80	77	83	47	131	2	2	.50	.277	.342	.514	.855
Wilson, Dan, Sea	36	high	88	254	64	12	0	3	24	28	25	17	49	0	0	.00	.252	.299	.335	.634
Wilson, Enrique, NYY	32	low	95	211	49	10	0	4	23	23	19	13	22	1	2	.33	.232	.277	.336	.613
Wilson, Jack, Pit	28	low	151	568	157	30	5	8	70	53	69	30	69	6	4	.60	.276	.313	.389	.702
Wilson, Preston, Col	31	high	120	454	122	27	1	22	67	79	71	43	117	11	6	.65	.269	.332	.478	.810
Wilson, Vance, NYM	32	low	97	268	71	13	1	8	30	39	33	15	43	1	1	.50	.265	.304	.410	.714
Winn, Randy, Sea	31	med	149	588	170	34	5	12	87	70	86	50	100	19	9	.68	.289	.345	.425	.770
Wise, Dewayne, Atl	27	low	58	115	27	5	2	4	16	14	13	6	20	4	1	.80	.235	.273	.417	.690
Womack, Tony, StL	36	med	110	371	100	14	3	3	53	27	41	22	47	16	4	.80	.270	.310	.348	.658
Woodward, Chris, Tor	29	low	104	339	89	21	3	8	44	44	44	26	67	1	2	.33	.263	.315	.413	.728
Wright, David, NYM	23	low	149	517	160	44	1	27	84	80	108	53	84	26	8	.76	.309	.374	.555	.929
Youkilis, Kevin, Bos	26	low	72	240	65	16	0	6	42	32	37	41	40	2	1	.67	.271	.377	.413	.790
Young, Dmitri, Det	32	high	118	420	120	27	2	18	61	62	70	36	82	1	1	.50	.286	.342	.488	.830
Young, Eric, Tex	38	med	108	361	97	21	1	4	53	26	45	38	30	15	7	.68	.269	.338	.366	.704
Young, Michael, Tex	29	low	156	628	188	31	7	17	101	81	98	42	92	9	3	.75	.299	.343	.452	.796
Zaun, Gregg, Tor	34	high	93	259	64	14	0	5	30	30	31	34	46	1	1	.50	.247	.334	.359	.694

Projected Career Totals for Active Players
Note: These projections assume that the player will be healthy.

Player	G	AB	H	2B	3B	HR	R	RBI	RC	BB	SO	SB	CS	SB%	Avg	OBP	Slg	OPS
Bobby Abreu	2482	8976	2650	656	56	361	1597	1444	1869	1723	2029	394	134	.75	.295	.409	.501	.910
Edgardo Alfonzo	2347	8356	2359	442	20	237	1197	1166	1270	959	932	68	23	.75	.282	.356	.425	.781
Roberto Alomar	2900	10820	3190	590	86	245	1756	1330	1770	1227	1429	510	124	.80	.295	.367	.433	.800
Sandy Alomar Jr.	1468	4778	1297	257	10	120	550	614	584	227	525	25	24	.51	.271	.304	.405	.709
Moises Alou	2129	7722	2271	451	37	361	1181	1392	1410	828	1038	105	36	.74	.294	.362	.502	.865
Garret Anderson	2436	9475	2782	594	35	337	1183	1528	1445	460	1379	88	55	.62	.294	.326	.470	.797
Marlon Anderson	886	2786	733	155	18	46	325	315	334	191	378	62	17	.78	.263	.310	.381	.692
Rich Aurilia	1643	5547	1501	293	19	176	735	701	761	443	894	20	21	.49	.271	.325	.425	.750
Brad Ausmus	1778	5644	1424	240	33	78	676	544	626	550	908	93	51	.65	.252	.319	.348	.667
Jeff Bagwell	2742	9937	2876	603	36	561	1895	1882	2085	1769	2069	227	91	.71	.289	.397	.527	.924
Michael Barrett	1938	6663	1694	422	31	180	739	782	835	539	977	19	29	.40	.254	.310	.408	.718
Tony Batista	1791	6231	1540	303	21	306	835	990	805	367	1067	70	38	.65	.247	.289	.450	.739
David Bell	1671	5474	1393	302	14	151	683	680	686	503	810	19	22	.46	.254	.317	.398	.715
Mark Bellhorn	1586	5112	1207	296	22	163	806	632	710	883	1820	60	33	.65	.236	.349	.398	.747
Ron Belliard	1897	6763	1785	462	29	122	935	720	897	745	1118	52	35	.60	.264	.337	.395	.732
Carlos Beltran	2633	10049	2779	521	100	464	1794	1659	1803	1233	1890	486	69	.88	.277	.356	.487	.842
Adrian Beltre	3005	10964	3022	582	34	555	1471	1743	1770	931	1862	127	59	.68	.276	.332	.487	.819
Lance Berkman	2489	8971	2632	650	36	488	1650	1722	1887	1812	1887	97	73	.57	.293	.412	.537	.949
Craig Biggio	2804	10648	3007	651	53	271	1819	1131	1653	1189	1723	415	124	.77	.282	.354	.430	.784
Geoff Blum	1062	2957	742	161	8	77	355	358	354	253	514	19	16	.54	.251	.310	.389	.699
Barry Bonds	3483	11650	3496	712	83	918	2650	2366	3326	3389	1818	538	148	.78	.300	.458	.612	1.070
Bret Boone	2410	8977	2372	485	29	351	1247	1381	1270	761	1820	122	68	.64	.264	.322	.442	.764
Milton Bradley	2073	7513	2000	486	23	222	1056	960	1133	1055	1672	176	109	.62	.266	.357	.426	.782
Brian Buchanan	860	1971	510	108	4	80	269	273	283	205	511	19	13	.59	.259	.329	.439	.768
Jeromy Burnitz	1941	6490	1623	336	30	368	1047	1125	1043	864	1642	82	67	.55	.250	.338	.481	.819
Pat Burrell	1882	6582	1608	370	16	332	882	1116	1042	1021	1972	13	1	.93	.244	.346	.457	.802
Eric Byrnes	1574	5170	1370	335	35	169	817	629	749	442	959	109	17	.87	.265	.323	.441	.764
Orlando Cabrera	2235	8195	2162	544	34	159	988	936	1027	587	785	197	63	.76	.264	.313	.397	.710
Miguel Cairo	1622	4567	1225	217	33	54	601	457	524	277	576	134	46	.74	.268	.310	.366	.676
Mike Cameron	2071	7037	1694	378	48	290	1088	1019	1020	926	2033	321	94	.77	.241	.329	.432	.761
Sean Casey	1984	7214	2164	456	17	221	1041	1115	1198	683	793	25	6	.81	.300	.361	.460	.820
Vinny Castilla	2075	7524	2059	375	30	364	996	1241	1118	465	1208	31	44	.41	.274	.316	.477	.793
Luis Castillo	2305	8717	2532	260	63	40	1326	553	1142	1056	1250	444	189	.70	.290	.367	.349	.716
Juan Castro	822	1928	436	92	9	31	191	159	172	117	355	4	6	.40	.226	.270	.331	.602
Frank Catalanotto	1509	4789	1398	323	35	104	726	555	724	389	667	63	33	.66	.292	.345	.439	.784
Roger Cedeno	1501	4175	1135	167	39	54	621	354	541	417	817	256	77	.77	.272	.338	.369	.707
Eric Chavez	2609	9707	2606	569	28	509	1532	1665	1689	1305	1896	85	39	.69	.268	.355	.490	.845
Tony Clark	1338	4124	1075	221	8	215	583	718	656	471	1100	6	9	.40	.261	.336	.475	.811
Royce Clayton	2346	8111	2057	378	57	137	1049	802	914	641	1592	225	104	.68	.254	.308	.365	.673
Jeff Conine	2007	7050	1997	390	31	226	879	1103	1077	669	1186	55	33	.63	.283	.345	.444	.789
Alex Cora	1651	4715	1163	200	36	70	484	422	495	376	610	36	25	.59	.247	.302	.349	.651
Craig Counsell	1338	4132	1047	177	27	27	556	329	459	508	635	84	41	.67	.253	.335	.329	.664
Deivi Cruz	1986	6634	1759	404	20	113	691	759	723	218	669	21	37	.36	.265	.289	.383	.672
Jose Cruz	1866	6473	1595	338	43	282	973	887	969	879	1546	146	56	.72	.246	.337	.443	.779
Johnny Damon	2455	9599	2712	508	98	212	1657	1073	1445	992	1134	382	113	.77	.283	.350	.422	.772
Brian Daubach	1122	3275	832	221	11	147	444	551	513	419	920	5	3	.63	.254	.339	.463	.802
Ben Davis	1443	4317	1001	232	2	116	471	572	474	442	1078	17	16	.52	.232	.301	.367	.668
Carlos Delgado	2404	8499	2348	571	12	556	1478	1777	1759	1449	2169	9	7	.56	.276	.382	.543	.924
David Dellucci	1164	2897	724	137	28	88	406	407	386	332	755	56	28	.67	.250	.327	.408	.735
Einar Diaz	938	2715	683	153	6	27	282	255	265	128	262	26	13	.67	.252	.285	.342	.627
Mike DiFelice	681	1986	476	107	8	37	185	219	201	121	401	3	2	.60	.240	.283	.358	.641
David Drew	2159	7498	2083	360	49	382	1422	1130	1429	1313	1747	144	52	.73	.278	.385	.492	.877
Adam Dunn	2635	9568	2288	538	10	682	1710	1561	1833	2056	3335	127	50	.72	.239	.374	.511	.885
Erubiel Durazo	1575	5173	1446	303	8	235	857	874	931	818	1168	16	14	.53	.280	.378	.477	.855
Ray Durham	2338	8877	2439	509	92	223	1541	951	1337	1007	1516	307	117	.72	.275	.349	.428	.777
Jermaine Dye	1742	6053	1599	335	22	250	890	958	892	572	1288	35	19	.65	.264	.328	.451	.778
Damion Easley	1438	4745	1193	258	23	136	645	584	600	446	825	112	55	.67	.251	.316	.401	.717
David Eckstein	1795	6661	1805	287	18	45	994	495	740	511	622	184	70	.72	.271	.323	.340	.663
Jim Edmonds	2407	8428	2376	538	26	508	1556	1494	1695	1331	2353	79	58	.58	.282	.380	.533	.913
Juan Encarnacion	1805	6139	1597	327	52	204	799	850	802	394	1125	164	73	.69	.260	.305	.430	.735
Darin Erstad	1535	5729	1645	297	29	127	896	690	823	456	843	192	55	.78	.287	.340	.416	.755
Carl Everett	1590	5182	1424	299	27	215	773	860	810	471	1098	114	53	.68	.275	.335	.467	.803
Carlos Febles	1036	2931	719	117	26	36	436	251	314	269	524	89	27	.77	.245	.309	.340	.649
Pedro Feliz	1408	3897	1010	215	18	171	495	603	515	178	735	22	12	.65	.259	.292	.455	.747
Robert Fick	797	2346	610	124	10	79	285	341	322	228	376	5	5	.50	.260	.326	.422	.748
Steve Finley	2775	10158	2766	481	116	353	1553	1300	1521	938	1437	329	128	.72	.272	.334	.447	.781
Cliff Floyd	2018	6834	1878	484	23	298	1059	1111	1170	813	1506	183	61	.75	.275	.352	.483	.835
Brook Fordyce	868	2382	604	131	4	51	220	239	267	154	401	8	6	.57	.254	.299	.376	.675
Julio Franco	2435	8619	2575	402	55	168	1283	1164	1327	914	1311	272	107	.72	.299	.366	.417	.783
Brad Fullmer	1535	4917	1350	352	22	202	704	767	769	403	660	50	34	.60	.275	.330	.478	.808
Rafael Furcal	2487	9708	2680	481	61	181	1636	860	1333	969	1440	377	120	.76	.276	.342	.394	.736
Karim Garcia	1286	3691	935	138	21	171	465	597	470	202	775	16	20	.44	.253	.292	.441	.733

Projected Career Totals for Active Players
Note: These projections assume that the player will be healthy.

Player	G	AB	H	2B	3B	HR	R	RBI	RC	BB	SO	SB	CS	SB%	Avg	OBP	Slg	OPS
Jason Giambi	2095	7136	2033	424	8	423	1244	1393	1496	1373	1497	18	13	.58	.285	.400	.524	.925
Jay Gibbons	1535	5032	1269	278	9	209	619	744	679	436	788	4	14	.22	.252	.312	.436	.747
Brian Giles	2176	7642	2209	470	57	391	1345	1349	1600	1439	1084	121	46	.72	.289	.402	.519	.921
Marcus Giles	2316	8648	2503	590	22	263	1377	1066	1421	961	1475	179	72	.71	.289	.360	.454	.814
Doug Glanville	1172	4075	1129	170	33	61	567	342	500	213	517	172	37	.82	.277	.313	.380	.693
Troy Glaus	1974	6947	1716	386	14	431	1219	1217	1204	1135	1869	92	50	.65	.247	.353	.493	.845
Alex S Gonzalez	2040	6993	1660	391	31	195	855	743	786	549	1689	115	61	.65	.237	.293	.386	.679
Alex Gonzalez	2214	7840	1848	452	43	236	862	963	844	421	1736	36	30	.55	.236	.275	.395	.669
Juan Gonzalez	2249	8560	2495	501	28	534	1344	1766	1563	590	1696	30	23	.57	.291	.337	.544	.881
Luis Gonzalez	2598	9305	2637	585	70	389	1456	1506	1653	1242	1285	129	88	.59	.283	.368	.487	.855
Tony Graffanino	1188	3334	852	162	20	65	509	334	409	341	598	73	28	.72	.256	.325	.375	.699
Shawn Green	2380	8586	2372	524	31	426	1375	1361	1492	981	1712	173	57	.75	.276	.350	.493	.844
Todd Greene	1122	3421	866	184	1	172	401	507	438	126	712	5	4	.56	.253	.280	.458	.738
Ben Grieve	1696	5024	1320	305	5	178	716	750	782	752	1272	31	5	.86	.263	.359	.432	.790
Ken Griffey Jr.	2590	9384	2649	498	39	620	1620	1791	1875	1273	1808	191	71	.73	.282	.368	.542	.910
Marquis Grissom	2580	9678	2619	449	59	275	1371	1152	1291	631	1486	443	121	.79	.271	.315	.414	.730
Mark Grudzielanek	1873	6995	1981	372	30	95	923	607	864	362	982	130	48	.73	.283	.318	.386	.704
Vladimir Guerrero	2860	10843	3459	659	54	659	1860	2043	2367	1158	1443	274	147	.65	.319	.385	.572	.957
Wilton Guerrero	1262	3217	887	112	39	18	362	239	345	125	460	48	17	.74	.276	.303	.352	.654
Carlos Guillen	2109	7711	2099	426	55	182	1226	1079	1088	845	1461	86	60	.59	.272	.344	.413	.757
Jose Guillen	2204	7733	2134	398	28	319	1040	1200	1099	434	1435	43	53	.45	.276	.314	.458	.773
Ricky Gutierrez	1383	4283	1142	168	25	45	540	425	496	422	683	54	33	.62	.267	.332	.349	.681
Cristian Guzman	2567	9757	2596	452	123	120	1355	859	1097	510	1385	219	121	.64	.266	.303	.375	.677
Jerry Hairston Jr.	1277	4007	1056	225	20	50	528	350	484	378	484	176	79	.69	.264	.327	.367	.694
Toby Hall	1344	4439	1128	251	1	96	451	571	482	234	412	2	13	.13	.254	.291	.376	.667
Shane Halter	838	2285	558	111	21	56	239	236	257	177	496	18	23	.44	.244	.299	.385	.683
Scott Hatteberg	1273	4091	1093	237	6	104	519	510	581	536	495	1	4	.20	.267	.352	.404	.756
Wes Helms	1511	4595	1174	236	16	151	497	592	581	348	1087	2	8	.20	.255	.308	.412	.720
Todd Helton	2521	9182	3022	738	34	530	1812	1803	2329	1649	1329	48	37	.56	.329	.431	.590	1.021
Jose Hernandez	1890	5596	1398	240	35	208	746	718	714	486	1767	49	43	.53	.250	.310	.417	.726
Ramon Hernandez	1992	6796	1733	362	1	240	830	994	893	614	1015	8	1	.89	.255	.317	.415	.731
Richard Hidalgo	2048	7067	1858	446	32	334	1039	1123	1108	737	1608	79	61	.56	.263	.333	.477	.809
Bobby Higginson	1795	6195	1659	335	38	224	904	874	965	820	1018	109	64	.63	.268	.353	.443	.796
Shea Hillenbrand	1581	5607	1613	353	18	165	684	803	787	231	685	20	11	.65	.288	.316	.445	.761
Eric Hinske	1863	6546	1646	438	21	200	935	880	910	792	1404	116	45	.72	.251	.332	.416	.749
Todd Hollandsworth	1640	4910	1350	301	25	161	723	606	727	446	1108	94	55	.63	.275	.335	.445	.780
Orlando Hudson	2024	7377	1966	440	56	157	929	794	976	674	1314	54	37	.59	.267	.328	.405	.733
Aubrey Huff	2192	8363	2419	489	14	373	1125	1262	1395	709	1147	38	24	.61	.289	.345	.485	.830
Torii Hunter	2103	7615	1979	452	35	311	1073	1161	1050	541	1582	168	92	.65	.260	.309	.451	.760
Raul Ibanez	1508	5051	1416	291	29	172	696	761	760	412	818	33	21	.61	.280	.335	.452	.786
Brandon Inge	1311	3691	880	172	28	94	350	414	397	278	791	29	36	.45	.238	.292	.377	.668
Cesar Izturis	2548	9306	2458	462	68	47	1050	765	970	512	996	220	100	.69	.264	.303	.344	.646
Geoff Jenkins	1810	6592	1777	423	29	315	988	1045	1049	569	1712	38	16	.70	.270	.328	.486	.813
Derek Jeter	2764	10970	3326	576	52	301	1956	1318	1824	1074	1980	335	87	.79	.303	.365	.447	.813
D'Angelo Jimenez	2231	8235	2119	393	46	152	1075	912	1054	1107	1531	104	68	.60	.257	.345	.372	.717
Charles Johnson	1827	5908	1405	332	4	254	704	879	800	741	1623	11	15	.42	.238	.323	.424	.747
Nick Johnson	1812	6114	1556	344	0	224	942	884	945	1101	1324	71	46	.61	.254	.368	.421	.789
Andruw Jones	2935	10831	2829	590	44	577	1705	1766	1757	1225	2530	186	87	.68	.261	.336	.484	.820
Chipper Jones	2629	9493	2774	536	32	510	1651	1711	1948	1626	1613	143	54	.73	.292	.396	.517	.912
Jacque Jones	1853	6432	1786	358	16	238	876	870	911	401	1385	107	75	.59	.278	.320	.449	.769
Brian Jordan	1534	5394	1522	287	36	194	789	867	809	372	870	121	51	.70	.282	.328	.457	.785
Gabe Kapler	1535	4088	1099	235	19	103	600	511	553	359	678	104	44	.70	.269	.328	.411	.739
Eric Karros	1867	6707	1792	337	11	294	825	1066	984	575	1214	61	31	.66	.267	.325	.452	.777
Jason Kendall	2441	9083	2735	481	37	110	1320	879	1316	897	771	205	114	.64	.301	.364	.399	.762
Adam Kennedy	2080	7098	1928	373	49	133	954	743	899	506	1234	196	82	.71	.272	.320	.394	.714
Jeff Kent	2507	9338	2664	615	51	417	1431	1672	1589	851	1784	111	66	.63	.285	.345	.496	.841
Bobby Kielty	1435	4299	1052	256	12	137	626	601	615	702	892	44	13	.77	.245	.351	.405	.756
Eugene Kingsale	894	2266	564	86	26	22	304	199	238	208	315	26	19	.58	.249	.312	.339	.651
Ryan Klesko	2206	7252	2010	451	34	352	1105	1288	1333	1091	1400	107	48	.69	.277	.372	.494	.866
Paul Konerko	2155	7453	2025	372	5	390	1033	1311	1208	742	1169	5	1	.83	.272	.338	.480	.818
Corey Koskie	1768	6118	1636	389	19	229	929	936	979	848	1520	121	63	.66	.267	.357	.449	.806
Mark Kotsay	2332	8697	2469	484	56	187	1157	902	1247	816	1168	133	79	.63	.284	.345	.417	.762
Mike Lamb	1626	5150	1402	272	17	146	724	698	722	507	901	11	11	.50	.272	.337	.417	.754
Ray Lankford	1967	6357	1706	388	54	263	1055	954	1079	916	1750	265	121	.69	.268	.361	.471	.831
Barry Larkin	2595	9297	2686	514	81	218	1512	1088	1505	1089	986	394	81	.83	.289	.363	.432	.795
Jason LaRue	1412	4592	1066	262	11	166	537	604	525	353	1401	17	22	.44	.232	.287	.402	.689
Matt Lawton	1797	6336	1675	345	18	187	1011	840	939	898	830	202	83	.71	.264	.356	.413	.769
Matthew LeCroy	1030	2869	770	169	1	116	300	466	407	203	634	0	4	.00	.268	.317	.449	.766
Ricky Ledee	1136	2703	639	155	20	87	387	422	355	355	685	37	21	.64	.236	.325	.405	.730
Carlos Lee	2244	8420	2389	492	16	392	1330	1401	1383	701	1301	135	59	.70	.284	.339	.486	.824
Derrek Lee	2246	7887	2083	463	29	372	1161	1178	1294	1028	1992	134	69	.66	.264	.349	.472	.821
Mike Lieberthal	1888	6805	1851	413	13	228	835	966	969	550	1000	10	9	.53	.272	.326	.437	.763
Paul Lo Duca	1481	5394	1492	304	9	126	654	688	704	389	467	20	33	.38	.277	.325	.406	.732

Projected Career Totals for Active Players
Note: These projections assume that the player will be healthy.

Player		BATTING											BASERUNNING			AVERAGES			
	G	AB	H	2B	3B	HR	R	RBI	RC	BB	SO	SB	CS	SB%	Avg	OBP	Slg	OPS
Kenny Lofton	2063	7850	2300	376	100	137	1473	762	1262	932	1016	579	159	.78	.293	.368	.419	.787
Terrence Long	1555	4710	1247	267	27	111	634	577	600	356	746	39	22	.64	.265	.316	.404	.720
Javy Lopez	2176	7737	2199	377	23	378	974	1281	1239	550	1453	8	18	.31	.284	.332	.485	.817
Mark Loretta	2120	7546	2264	420	26	126	1028	824	1116	711	793	50	43	.54	.300	.360	.413	.773
Mike Lowell	2008	7370	2015	495	2	323	995	1228	1190	763	1140	37	15	.71	.273	.342	.473	.814
Julio Lugo	2020	7320	1928	370	32	141	1047	758	909	669	1560	186	83	.69	.263	.325	.380	.706
John Mabry	1517	4022	1074	213	4	133	474	557	546	342	876	7	12	.37	.267	.324	.421	.746
Eli Marrero	1131	3032	766	161	15	99	413	426	396	260	585	70	17	.80	.253	.312	.414	.725
Ramon Martinez	1351	3748	963	197	14	56	414	412	432	344	593	14	12	.54	.257	.319	.362	.681
Tino Martinez	2262	7938	2138	408	23	368	1111	1400	1258	869	1197	29	23	.56	.269	.341	.466	.807
Mike Matheny	1466	4210	998	189	10	64	380	467	399	300	876	8	15	.35	.237	.288	.332	.620
Hideki Matsui	1441	5134	1471	318	8	203	798	905	892	676	812	17	8	.68	.287	.370	.470	.840
Gary Matthews Jr.	1310	3794	947	208	20	103	568	436	498	456	845	75	34	.69	.250	.330	.396	.727
Brent Mayne	1484	4102	1066	198	8	42	404	452	457	423	675	20	30	.40	.260	.329	.343	.672
David McCarty	872	2215	548	111	10	62	295	286	266	199	547	9	9	.50	.247	.309	.391	.700
Quinton McCracken	1049	2676	742	140	32	23	391	274	340	239	479	90	49	.65	.277	.337	.379	.716
Joe McEwing	942	2090	522	107	12	30	259	198	220	142	430	36	20	.64	.250	.297	.356	.653
Mark McLemore	2062	6859	1766	282	50	58	1029	681	829	981	1102	285	126	.69	.257	.350	.339	.689
Frank Menechino	947	2732	646	112	11	68	406	318	324	396	552	3	13	.19	.236	.333	.360	.693
Lou Merloni	628	1553	424	95	10	22	199	180	197	128	300	11	11	.50	.273	.328	.390	.718
Doug Mientkiewicz	1252	3753	1011	255	8	73	474	456	534	522	545	18	22	.45	.269	.359	.400	.759
Kevin Millar	1645	5484	1544	375	17	205	743	857	898	584	1043	10	10	.50	.282	.351	.468	.819
Damian Miller	1239	3959	1009	241	3	109	424	502	508	388	990	4	4	.50	.255	.321	.400	.721
Doug Mirabelli	974	2926	707	171	2	117	352	422	395	339	745	1	0	1.00	.242	.320	.421	.742
Dustan Mohr	1484	4351	1130	291	8	121	684	470	610	540	1134	27	25	.52	.260	.341	.414	.755
Bengie Molina	1456	4922	1300	216	2	119	468	701	552	219	476	2	7	.22	.264	.295	.381	.677
Raul Mondesi	2021	7431	1984	405	52	341	1138	1085	1142	645	1482	272	114	.70	.267	.326	.473	.799
Craig Monroe	1781	6053	1649	368	21	254	820	922	896	432	1122	31	33	.48	.272	.321	.466	.787
Melvin Mora	1658	5755	1603	339	15	194	923	782	898	673	1159	105	66	.61	.279	.354	.444	.798
Bill Mueller	1771	6165	1758	386	27	134	976	724	948	791	863	26	27	.49	.285	.366	.422	.788
Greg Myers	1102	3030	775	150	7	87	333	395	375	267	538	3	12	.20	.256	.316	.396	.712
Phil Nevin	1592	5525	1521	288	5	272	766	1000	918	613	1332	20	5	.80	.275	.348	.477	.825
Trot Nixon	1780	6118	1680	366	42	269	988	976	1063	831	1289	47	18	.72	.275	.361	.480	.841
Greg Norton	844	1943	464	98	9	67	246	254	248	242	495	13	12	.52	.239	.320	.402	.722
John Olerud	2576	8672	2526	567	13	279	1280	1375	1554	1463	1176	11	14	.44	.291	.394	.456	.850
Magglio Ordonez	2160	8120	2440	517	22	392	1287	1484	1493	738	986	127	64	.66	.300	.359	.514	.873
David Ortiz	2017	7189	1961	568	15	398	1077	1418	1336	929	1653	4	2	.67	.273	.356	.522	.878
Orlando Palmeiro	963	2034	561	93	11	10	276	195	248	243	196	36	26	.58	.276	.353	.347	.700
Rafael Palmeiro	3104	11366	3239	631	38	616	1778	1987	2139	1513	1483	98	42	.70	.285	.369	.510	.879
Corey Patterson	2384	9058	2368	479	62	327	1285	1073	1209	538	2315	310	91	.77	.261	.303	.436	.739
Jay Payton	1397	4421	1231	201	27	135	592	546	611	318	584	37	34	.52	.278	.327	.428	.755
Carlos Pena	1775	5906	1410	286	42	297	837	860	875	788	1704	50	27	.65	.239	.328	.452	.781
Eddie Perez	813	2146	534	119	2	51	182	230	232	119	341	1	4	.20	.249	.288	.377	.666
Neifi Perez	1763	5970	1575	269	70	67	740	556	642	286	615	58	50	.54	.264	.297	.366	.663
Timo Perez	866	2235	598	118	10	37	258	254	252	116	201	30	29	.51	.268	.304	.379	.683
Tomas Perez	652	1592	390	83	13	24	169	154	169	123	291	4	7	.36	.245	.299	.359	.658
Jason Phillips	1579	5078	1286	291	1	127	503	666	620	471	556	0	2	.00	.253	.317	.386	.703
Mike Piazza	2138	7650	2327	374	6	474	1173	1460	1555	905	1254	17	22	.44	.304	.378	.541	.918
Juan Pierre	2339	9155	2816	336	78	26	1359	639	1214	646	553	545	234	.70	.308	.353	.370	.723
Anthony Pierzynski	2104	7553	2176	538	33	155	860	1091	1023	329	779	15	27	.36	.288	.318	.430	.747
Placido Polanco	2149	7856	2263	385	27	163	1135	785	1046	464	648	100	46	.68	.288	.328	.406	.734
Jorge Posada	1937	6707	1753	412	5	298	989	1181	1125	1149	1733	17	30	.36	.261	.369	.458	.827
Todd Pratt	885	2414	593	132	3	63	292	315	315	352	715	6	2	.75	.246	.342	.381	.723
Curtis Pride	746	1824	487	96	17	42	289	197	241	154	424	31	14	.69	.267	.324	.407	.731
Aramis Ramirez	2561	9554	2635	553	14	473	1252	1631	1508	721	1495	19	20	.49	.276	.327	.485	.812
Manny Ramirez	2679	9845	3039	665	17	674	1815	2194	2309	1555	2242	42	42	.50	.309	.403	.585	.988
Joe Randa	1780	6366	1794	367	39	136	811	862	882	502	887	46	28	.62	.282	.334	.416	.750
Mike Redmond	938	2551	699	127	2	21	215	246	287	181	305	2	3	.40	.274	.322	.350	.672
Pokey Reese	1289	3839	933	172	21	58	481	366	413	308	762	174	32	.84	.243	.299	.344	.643
Desi Relaford	1239	3670	897	181	20	54	472	397	407	365	603	98	31	.76	.244	.313	.349	.662
Edgar Renteria	2824	10647	3032	616	22	186	1516	1301	1469	946	1450	386	161	.71	.285	.343	.399	.742
Brian Roberts	2021	7576	1995	450	32	55	1152	618	915	842	1051	233	87	.73	.263	.337	.353	.690
Dave Roberts	672	1949	501	60	25	16	320	149	237	217	241	195	47	.81	.257	.331	.338	.670
Kerry Robinson	639	1059	284	36	13	6	161	83	115	66	126	43	15	.74	.268	.311	.344	.655
Alex Rodriguez	3011	11606	3387	593	35	779	2211	2225	2394	1459	2523	342	90	.79	.292	.371	.550	.921
Ivan Rodriguez	2743	10352	3124	633	41	381	1523	1541	1706	668	1639	133	72	.65	.302	.344	.481	.825
Scott Rolen	2638	9702	2725	655	44	503	1688	1859	1839	1351	2069	145	57	.72	.281	.369	.513	.882
Jimmy Rollins	2632	10422	2767	625	102	188	1538	1011	1364	915	1576	372	140	.73	.265	.325	.399	.724
Damian Rolls	466	1381	346	66	6	20	189	138	141	81	293	31	15	.67	.251	.292	.350	.643
Aaron Rowand	2003	6327	1770	427	12	247	1005	830	959	409	1134	107	40	.73	.280	.323	.468	.792
Olmedo Saenz	696	1600	420	90	5	66	218	222	230	139	342	3	3	.50	.263	.321	.449	.770
Tim Salmon	1854	6387	1789	369	22	313	1048	1083	1190	1043	1467	53	42	.56	.280	.381	.492	.873
Alex Sanchez	1422	4933	1435	165	45	17	567	339	556	230	721	306	161	.66	.291	.322	.353	.675

383

Projected Career Totals for Active Players
Note: These projections assume that the player will be healthy.

Player	G	AB	H	2B	3B	HR	R	RBI	RC	BB	SO	SB	CS	SB%	Avg	OBP	Slg	OPS
Rey Sanchez	1658	5282	1427	207	34	16	592	425	529	248	556	58	32	.64	.270	.303	.331	.634
Reggie Sanders	2028	6996	1836	369	63	339	1134	1080	1118	736	1839	328	123	.73	.262	.333	.479	.811
Benito Santiago	2256	7878	2061	366	43	239	839	1034	971	488	1445	94	73	.56	.262	.305	.410	.715
Brian Schneider	1669	5562	1378	358	16	140	507	684	692	579	972	1	15	.06	.248	.319	.393	.712
Gary Sheffield	2797	10111	2973	524	26	569	1791	1863	2071	1663	1270	237	110	.68	.294	.394	.520	.914
Richie Sexson	1861	6748	1779	340	23	436	1042	1330	1187	818	1823	16	18	.47	.264	.343	.515	.858
Ruben Sierra	2249	8181	2191	431	59	316	1104	1342	1182	623	1250	144	52	.73	.268	.320	.451	.770
Randall Simon	793	2425	660	111	4	71	260	336	304	124	243	2	4	.33	.272	.308	.409	.717
Jack Snow	1932	6344	1696	341	20	216	910	999	969	890	1307	24	26	.48	.267	.357	.430	.787
Alfonso Soriano	2537	10124	2799	618	36	494	1493	1411	1557	523	2185	358	114	.76	.276	.312	.491	.803
Sammy Sosa	2835	10563	2876	445	45	756	1793	1994	1962	1212	2876	238	111	.68	.272	.347	.538	.885
Shane Spencer	865	2503	642	128	10	79	298	347	327	233	558	21	14	.60	.256	.320	.410	.730
Scott Spiezio	1573	4788	1207	276	29	141	616	656	628	492	690	43	30	.59	.252	.322	.410	.732
Junior Spivey	1573	5695	1546	333	25	175	908	762	844	644	1250	76	47	.62	.271	.345	.431	.776
Matt Stairs	1655	4983	1295	272	12	262	726	866	826	686	1068	28	23	.55	.260	.349	.477	.826
Shannon Stewart	1983	7760	2327	491	47	173	1224	825	1248	745	982	231	89	.72	.300	.361	.442	.803
Kelly Stinnett	608	1731	412	81	4	57	200	204	207	174	480	10	5	.67	.238	.308	.388	.696
Chris Stynes	1201	3138	845	163	9	67	464	360	402	262	440	54	20	.73	.269	.326	.391	.717
William Surhoff	2460	8714	2453	469	40	198	1116	1212	1195	692	901	146	87	.63	.282	.334	.413	.747
Ichiro Suzuki	1773	7164	2373	290	49	92	1109	611	1155	488	697	313	106	.75	.331	.374	.424	.798
Mark Sweeney	1065	1762	449	100	9	46	212	258	245	256	422	12	9	.57	.255	.349	.400	.749
Mike Sweeney	2007	7347	2191	443	4	323	1120	1355	1327	823	868	71	43	.62	.298	.369	.491	.860
Miguel Tejada	2828	10937	3036	607	18	493	1696	2006	1707	867	1503	96	36	.73	.278	.331	.472	.802
Frank Thomas	2461	8643	2568	551	11	538	1588	1757	1985	1798	1539	35	26	.57	.297	.418	.550	.968
Jim Thome	2539	8772	2402	466	29	644	1648	1760	1937	1850	2729	18	25	.42	.274	.400	.554	.954
Michael Tucker	1732	5210	1324	256	59	159	800	662	724	627	1254	132	70	.65	.254	.334	.417	.752
Jose Valentin	2116	7139	1663	372	42	334	1099	1027	961	782	1835	153	69	.69	.233	.309	.437	.746
Jason Varitek	1743	5869	1535	380	11	207	749	884	859	665	1417	48	27	.64	.262	.337	.436	.773
Jose Vidro	2327	8548	2533	604	12	245	1222	1145	1402	861	985	40	28	.59	.296	.361	.456	.816
Fernando Vina	1461	5139	1434	235	53	47	746	411	617	344	360	132	78	.63	.279	.324	.373	.697
Jose Vizcaino	2101	6276	1692	238	50	43	724	553	672	419	825	77	67	.53	.270	.315	.344	.659
Omar Vizquel	2684	9742	2651	434	61	86	1395	892	1192	987	1018	362	149	.71	.272	.339	.356	.695
Larry Walker	2514	8707	2675	579	71	464	1656	1621	1893	1229	1600	255	87	.75	.307	.393	.550	.943
Todd Walker	2035	7254	2040	452	36	176	1042	885	1053	676	985	79	52	.60	.281	.342	.426	.769
Daryle Ward	969	2558	655	143	4	106	267	426	339	170	479	1	3	.25	.256	.302	.439	.742
Vernon Wells	2495	9699	2722	655	31	406	1465	1441	1542	718	1445	100	30	.77	.281	.330	.480	.810
Rondell White	1852	6549	1840	351	34	256	942	949	991	474	1181	99	55	.64	.281	.329	.462	.792
Ty Wigginton	1915	6695	1757	433	25	178	831	855	908	616	1166	74	14	.84	.262	.325	.414	.739
Brad Wilkerson	2053	7324	1853	483	40	327	1206	899	1244	1348	2212	124	88	.58	.253	.369	.464	.833
Bernie Williams	2512	9559	2799	535	58	352	1669	1508	1710	1362	1535	161	96	.63	.293	.381	.471	.852
Craig Wilson	1936	6445	1678	339	31	335	991	977	1001	632	1989	28	24	.54	.260	.326	.479	.805
Dan Wilson	1581	4933	1282	246	13	98	510	599	565	330	906	23	13	.64	.260	.306	.375	.681
Enrique Wilson	728	1730	419	87	5	28	190	177	167	108	207	17	22	.44	.242	.287	.347	.634
Jack Wilson	2257	8445	2254	424	53	113	1000	767	946	462	1123	64	48	.57	.267	.305	.370	.675
Preston Wilson	1868	6731	1738	383	18	318	959	1132	998	637	1858	174	83	.68	.258	.322	.462	.785
Vance Wilson	1006	2751	705	123	6	80	294	394	315	150	472	8	13	.38	.256	.295	.393	.687
Randy Winn	1747	6323	1779	351	56	110	912	716	870	538	1140	213	98	.68	.281	.338	.407	.744
Tony Womack	1592	5848	1593	226	65	44	867	439	692	364	759	386	82	.82	.272	.315	.356	.671
Chris Woodward	1594	5281	1328	314	36	129	669	658	636	410	1135	18	22	.45	.251	.305	.398	.703
Dmitri Young	1731	5959	1709	379	34	226	836	852	963	502	1131	29	27	.52	.287	.342	.476	.818
Eric Young	1940	6804	1919	366	47	84	1093	584	951	728	515	489	178	.73	.282	.351	.387	.738
Michael Young	2285	8959	2553	428	69	218	1331	1079	1245	591	1484	104	41	.72	.285	.329	.421	.750
Gregg Zaun	1202	3285	809	175	7	66	383	386	395	415	551	23	16	.59	.246	.331	.364	.695

Can We Really Predict Injuries?

"Prediction is difficult - especially of the future."
-Yogi Berra

Yogi is right—generating tomorrow, or in our case, generating tomorrow's sports page is no easy task. That doesn't stop us from trying, as Baseball Info Solutions has teamed up with Bill James to produce player projections. My task within this process is to complement their work with the projections of tomorrow's injuries.

While predicting home run totals is challenging, the forecasting of even less frequent events such as a major injury is even more difficult. Really, all we can expect to do with such a short sample (i.e. one season) is to identify the players with a high risk of injury. Following is a brief description of the process, the generation of the predictors of player injuries—whether it is age, games played, position, or high-risk activities (i.e. stolen bases), and then the fun part—the generation of next season's major injuries. You will also notice that in the Player Projection section, we now have a column titled Inj, short for Injury Risk. These estimates come from the following work.

Hitter Injury Assessment

Engineering, manufacturing, economics, and science have all grappled with the problem of how to predict tomorrow's numbers from yesterday's data, long before the baseball world has. As a result, a collection of statistical tools and processes has already been developed for just this purpose. It is these tools that I will use to make a stab at the prediction of player injuries.

As the economist, Adam Smith said, "Knowing what has happened is the most important part of knowing what's going to happen." It is no different in our case—we need to first learn what has happened in the past; we need to discover the predictors, the "leading-economic indicators" of player injuries. For that, I first turn to the Neft injury database.

For about 40 years, Mr. David Neft has been collecting, categorizing, and recording major injuries. Any time that a player ends up missing over a month of work, Mr. Neft has documented it in *The Sports Encyclopedia: Baseball*. According to Mr. Neft, this expansive and potentially very useful database had never been digitized until I completed the task for this project. Obviously, with the digitization of the data, a thorough analysis of injuries becomes much easier. Keep in mind that over the last 30 years, there have been more than 30,000 player seasons, and over 3300 injuries—all of them now safely stowed in the database. What's most interesting though is that we also have all sorts of information about these players as they begin each of these 30,000 years. We know what other injuries they have had, how long ago they were. We know their age, position, career experience, and the type of hitter each was. We even know their height, weight, and Body Mass Index (BMI) to some degree of accuracy. The question though is: Which, if any, of these characteristics are significant predictors of impending injury? While asking the question is easy, the process of finding the answers is not as simple.

We can all guess that Jose Canseco's past back problems were of some value in predicting his future back problems. Similarly, the versatility that Ken Griffey Jr. has demonstrated as he has injured nearly every part of his body would seem to indicate not only a dedication to, but also a likelihood for injuries in general. And what about catchers? All those foul tips and large men running into them must increase their chances too. And certainly age must play an effect, but exactly how much more likely is a 36 year old to get injured as compared to a 23 year old? We don't have to guess and we don't need to listen to a baseball announcer to find out. We have the data. Let's look at it.

I compiled as much data as I could for every player whose career began after 1972. I then conducted a regression analysis. For those with a statistical background, I conducted a forward stepwise logistic time series regression (with restriction levels defined by both statistical significance and partial correlation constant magnitudes) in order to determine the predictors of future injuries. In other words, I used statistical techniques that the layperson would never touch and a relatively powerful statistics program in order to find out what characteristics in that mess of data correlate with injury. The results were fascinating.

Briefly, past injuries are by far the most valuable predictor of future injury. Not only for specific chronic injuries (as with Canseco's back or Daulton's knees), but also for an injury in general. Of course, Ken Griffey Jr. and Jack Clark are extreme examples of athletes with the "ability" to hurt...well, everything. Nevertheless, it seems that past injuries— whether it is the anterior cruciate ligament or the big toe—are a harbinger of future injuries. Players are, to varying degrees, injury prone.

Age, as expected, is also an important factor—but perhaps not completely as you would have guessed. While injuries in general increase with age, there are a few injuries that dramatically drop with maturity. Surprisingly, injuries that can be characterized as "youthful" have revealed themselves in the data. This is no fluke either. The statistical significance associated with them is just too unlikely to have happened by chance. These youthful injuries included wrist injuries (both broken wrists and general wrist injuries), and broken bones in the hand.

It is always dangerous to reverse engineer; to see the results and then create the hypothesis, so I will cautiously just pose the following: Could the preponderance of broken wrists and hands come from the over exuberance of youth? You don't have to work for an insurance company or tune in to the X Games to know that with youth comes a tendency to take risks. Could this perilous behavior be exhibiting itself in the baseball world too? That is, the head first slides into the bag, the full speed collisions with the wall, the dives in the outfield—all the things that Barry Bonds doesn't bother to do now. Could the wisdom and discretion to avoid these traps come with age?

While the tendency for broken fingers and knee injuries in catchers was no surprise, I didn't expect to see such significant elbow problems for these backstops (throws to second or collisions at the plate, maybe). Also, the dangers of leg injuries for second basemen was found to be considerable. Perhaps, base runners are a significant hazard to second baseman just as they are to catchers.

A few other interesting predictors included weight for wrist injuries (the extra mass causing more harm when they roll over on their wrists?), "career games caught" for knee injuries and back injuries, and Body Mass Index for leg injuries, just to name a few.

Now for the fun part. Keeping in mind the difficulties of projecting very rare events, following is a list of the players at most risk of injury, along with a top 10 list of those at risk of the likely major injuries. The decimal to the right of the names are the chances of that particular injury sidelining the player for more than a month during the 2005 season.

A quick check of last season's injuries (generated with formulas that do not include that data) revealed a few success stories (if someone's injury can indeed be called a success). Of the top 6 most likely to be injured, 4 did suffer major injuries (Ken Griffey, Juan Gonzalez, Brian Jordan, and Ellis Burks). The projections also predicted Bill Mueller's knee injury (he was the preseason #4 most likely to suffer a knee injury), Ken Griffey's leg injury (he was #5), Frank Thomas' ankle injury (not an easy task as ankle injuries only occur close to once in every 200 player-seasons), and Kelly Stinnett's Elbow Injury (he was the preseason favorite to go down with an elbow injury). And it just missed Benito Santiago, the preseason favorite for a broken finger, as he instead broke his hand.

Any Injury	chances	Back Injury	chances
Griffey Jr.,Ken	.359	Sweeney,Mike	.106
Floyd,Cliff	.357	Sosa,Sammy	.075
McLemore,Mark	.331	Rodriguez,Ivan	.073
Sosa,Sammy	.324	Mayne,Brent	.071
Sheffield,Gary	.319	Anderson,Garret	.070
Jordan,Brian	.313	Gonzalez,Juan	.065
Santiago,Benito	.313	Nixon,Trot	.062
Burks,Ellis	.300	Johnson,Nick	.059
Thomas,Frank	.298	McMillon,Billy	.058
Myers,Greg	.296	Guerrero,Vladimir	.058

Knee Injury	chances	Broken Finger	chances
Alomar,Sandy	.149	Rodriguez,Ivan	.031
Mueller,Bill	.130	Santiago,Benito	.029
McLemore,Mark	.116	Kendall,Jason	.026
Hernandez,Ramon	.113	Pierre,Juan	.023
Vizquel,Omar	.112	Ausmus,Brad	.023
Graffanino,Tony	.106	Lopez,Javy	.021
Boone,Aaron	.101	Wilson,Dan	.019
Segui,David	.097	Alomar,Sandy	.019
Vidro,Jose	.091	Piazza,Mike	.019
Rodriguez,Ivan	.083	Johnson,Charles	.019

Leg Injury	chances		Ankle Injury	chances
Griffey Jr.,Ken	.072		Thomas,Frank	.023
Surhoff,B.J.	.071		Jenkins,Geoff	.021
Floyd,Cliff	.065		Belliard,Ron	.019
Gonzalez,Juan	.064		Cruz Jr.,Jose	.019
Vina,Fernando	.063		Sanders,Reggie	.019
Jordan,Brian	.063		Giles,Marcus	.018
Hammonds,Jeffrey	.062		Belhorn,Mark	.018
Sanchez,Rey	.062		Dunn,Adam	.018
Bautista,Danny	.062		Giles,Brian	.017
Conine,Jeff	.062		Boone,Bret	.015

Shoulder Injury	chances		Elbow Injury	chances
Hammonds,Jeffrey	.090		Santiago,Benito	.031
Matos,Luis	.078		Rodriguez,Ivan	.028
Griffey Jr.,Ken	.078		Stinnett,Kelly	.027
McMillon,Billy	.071		Ausmus,Brad	.024
Glaus,Troy	.068		Borders,Pat	.024
Brown,Adrian	.067		Spivey,Junior	.024
Perez,Eddie	.066		Estalella,Bobby	.023
Furcal,Rafael	.064		Alomar,Sandy	.022
Guzman,Cristian	.063		Wilson,Dan	.022
Dye,Jermaine	.060		Mayne,Brent	.019

While there is certainly a lot more work to be done in this area, I think that this is a good first step towards a better understanding of player injuries. In fact, I would be surprised if we didn't get 6 or 7 "hits" from this year's list too.

Pitcher Injury Assessment

"I think that there is a natural balancing of risks in almost any physical activity, and that this balancing of risks, with respect to the use of pitchers, has gotten out of whack."
-Bill James

The belief that high-pitch outings lead to injury and the concept of pitch limits has become engrained in the baseball culture. Curiously though, I have never seen a thorough study verifying this. What if it wasn't the case? What if high pitch outings did not lead to an increased risk of injury? Would anyone notice, or would they continue to behave as if it did? Sometimes conventional wisdom is not wisdom at all. Sometimes, it is just conventional. Could this be the case?

It certainly is imaginable that high pitch outings can lead to arm troubles. Seems to make sense to me. And sure, we can mention Mark Fidrych and all his complete games as a 22-year old and his ensuing arm problem as evidence. The other side, however, could then counter with a Randy Johnson. After all, he has had as many high-pitch outings as anyone and has had very little arm trouble. Or perhaps the other side would raise the curious fact that as high-pitch outings have dropped dramatically over the years, arm injuries have continually risen. This might be followed by a mention of Dwight Gooden's injuries, then followed by Nolan Ryan's health, then perhaps Bret Saberhagen and Chuck Finley, and so on. It's all anecdotal evidence though, and it doesn't really settle much.

Science, on the other hand, has provided us with the statistical tools that work a lot better than bickering. Tools that can begin to shed light on the relationship between high-pitch outings and major arm injuries. The following study used some of these tools and it is my hope that this can begin to shed some light on pitcher injuries. It's a very important question—one that, in my opinion, has been given very little serious attention.

For the pitchers, I conducted a similar analysis as I did with the hitters. Unlike the hitters who have a wide variety of injuries—pitchers for the most part have arm problems. Or to borrow from the Neft categorization, pitchers suffer "Elbow Injuries", "Arm Injuries", and "Shoulder Injuries." There just aren't many broken wrists with pitchers. With the hypothesis that high-pitch outings lead to these arm injuries in mind, I was sure to include such things as total pitches thrown, total pitches thrown as a starter, and average pitches per start in the database. I also included the Jazayerli and Woolner of Baseball Prospectus categorization of high pitch outings. For instance, they define Category 1 starts as one in which 100 or less pitches were thrown by the starter. Category 2 encompasses those from 101 to 109, and so on, until Category 5 (all games in which 133 or more pitches were thrown). If these data are predictors of future injury, the analysis of over 14,000 pitcher seasons will likely reveal it.

The results were again a bit surprising. First off, just as with hitters, past injuries (even if they were years in the past) are a great predictor of future injuries. The next factor to play a part was usage over the last couple of seasons. This included Games Started and Innings Pitched, even though Total Pitches Thrown was available. Keep in mind that throughout the regression process, I was able to bring in high-pitch outings at any time. Simply put, there was never a time to. Once past injuries have been included, and a measure of the usage over the past two years, high-pitch outings (whether over a career, or the last 1, 2 or 3 years) does not add anything. Now would seem to be the perfect time to enter the regression analysis, but the magnitude of the correlation does not warrant inclusion. In fact, it is not even close. If anything, high pitch outings actually correlate negatively with the chances of an injury (albeit, not quite statistically significant). I checked it again, but only for starters. Nothing. I checked for just first time injuries. Nothing. I checked for just players from the last two decades. Again, nothing. If high-pitch outings do indeed lead to more injuries, I cannot find evidence of it.

A continued analysis of pitcher injury predictors revealed how shoulder injuries in the past often indicate elbow and arm injuries in the future, how age plays it's effects, and even how excessive weight correlates with arm injuries. Age was especially interesting. For most of the pitcher injuries, age did not play an effect, or if it did, it was in the wrong direction. Increasing age indicated a decrease in injuries. At first, this sounds absurd. Of course, age leads to injuries, I thought. It mattered for the hitters, it must matter for the pitchers. Keep in mind however, that for the hitters, there were really two things going on. On one hand, old age increased injuries—no surprise there. But on the other hand, aging decreased some specific injuries. It just so happened that the first effect outweighed the second effect, and so, overall, injuries increased with age as we expected. In the hitter's case, what I have described as "the risk-taking injuries of youth" was small compared to the unavoidable injuries from aging. Well, maybe the balance is a little bit different with pitchers. Maybe the foolish injuries of youth (i.e. pitching when you are hurt, pitching when you aren't properly warmed up, pitching when you are dead tired, or pitching much harder than you have ever done before) happen as much as the "expected" injuries from aging. If this were the case, then overall, age would not correlate with arm injuries (above and beyond the obvious factor that the total number of innings thrown and the number of past injuries can only increase with age).

A Few Words on High Pitch Outings

I won't pretend to know why high-pitch outings are not an indicator of injury, but I do know of a couple possibilities. Bill James, in *The Neyer/James Guide to Pitchers*, described the first one very well. Simply put, the usage makes you stronger. No argument from me here. That could very well be the case. Another possibility though lies in the understanding that human beings are a bit tricky to analyze. We don't behave like machines. Instead, we have this pesky tendency to adapt, and that makes things a bit more complicated. I don't doubt that pitching when you are "on empty" can lead to injuries. I just don't think that high-pitch outings are a sensitive enough measure of that.

Enter the Catch-22 to help me explain. If high-pitch outings are the events that endanger the pitcher, then the pitcher with the most of these experiences will be the one most in danger. Seems simple enough, right? However, if a pitcher has many high-pitch outings, he will likely notice this and perhaps adjust his pitching effort and pace himself accordingly. For him then, high-pitch outings are no longer dangerous, and we are right back where we started. We're chasing a moving target. Just as Billy Wagner paces himself differently than Jason Schmidt, so too may Livan Hernandez pace himself differently than Johan Santana.

I know what you are thinking—let's look at pitchers who normally have low pitch outings but have had some very high pitch outings. David Cone's 1990 season is a great illustration of this. He averaged 111 pitches per start, but had 12 Category 5 high-pitch outings—8 more than would have been expected with 33 starts and a 111 pitch average. I included these numbers in the analysis, and nothing. It did not add anything to our ability to predict injuries.

One area relating to high-pitch outings that does deserve further consideration relates to what Tom House and Craig Wright describe in *The Diamond Appraised* as the dangers with young pitchers throwing high-pitch outings. Although the sample was smaller as pitch data is only available from 1988 onwards, I did discover a noteworthy correlation regarding the number of high pitch outings (as defined by Category 4 and 5 starts) experienced by youthful pitchers (i.e. 25 years or less) and later shoulder injuries. High usage, young players such as Dwight Gooden, Ben McDonald, Bob Milacki, and Charles Nagy, with ensuing shoulder problems are prevalent enough in the database for this effect to become salient.

Then again, some claim the majority of injuries are not a result of chronic overuse but one-time excedances of our physical limits. It's not the 130 pitches that get you, it's that one pitch. If so, and if we combine that with what we know of youthful exuberance and risk taking tendencies, then just maybe these high pitch outings are dangerous to them because they provide a tempting opportunity for the youngster to push himself just a bit too hard. The pitcher's equivalent of a full-speed head-first dive. I am still skeptical though. That somehow youth and usage create a significant negative effect while usage and youth alone do not, is a tad concerning. In my experience, interactions (youth and usage) without the main effect (youth or usage) are quite rare. Still, I will be watching Carlos Zambrano's season with interest as he was the youngster with by far the most high-pitch outings last year. Clearly, there is much analysis to be done with the data still, and you can be sure that by next year, we will know a bit more on the subject. Stay tuned.

Until then, here are the leading candidates for the most popular type of pitching injuries for the upcoming years. Last year, we had "hits" in every category. We had Chad Fox's and Andy Pettitte's elbow injuries right. Brad Penny's Arm Injury and Grant Roberts Shoulder Injury right, and amazingly, 7 of the 10 players on our Elbow Injury Top 10 list ended up with month-long absences.

Any "Pitching" Injury	chances	Elbow Injury	chances
Kennedy,Joe	.310	Wickman,Bob	.171
Hammond,Chris	.287	Pettitte,Andy	.165
Oliver,Darren	.281	Ainsworth,Kurt	.146
Miller,Wade	.280	Pineiro,Joel	.136
Wagner,Billy	.279	Zambrano,Victor	.133
Halladay,Roy	.276	Wolf,Randy	.132
Pettitte,Andy	.275	Urdaneta,Lino	.130
Penny,Brad	.263	Benson,Kris	.127
Wood,Kerry	.261	Mussina,Mike	.123
Ramirez,Horacio	.261	Powell,Jay	.122

Shoulder Injury	chances	Arm Injury	chances
Kennedy,Joe	.246	Penny,Brad	.079
Miller,Wade	.190	Kline,Steve	.056
Hernandez,Livan	.177	Nelson,Jeff	.050
Cornejo,Nate	.176	Pettitte,Andy	.047
Halladay,Roy	.174	Wood,Kerry	.041
Reyes,Dennys	.174	Eldred,Cal	.037
Soriano,Rafael	.174	Williamson,Scott	.034
Ramirez,Horacio	.174	Powell,Brian	.033
Lewis,Colby	.173	Padilla,Vicente	.030
Standridge,Jason	.173	Stanford,Jason	.030

Note: excludes pitchers 30 years or older who pitched 25 innings or less in 2004.

Sig Mejdal (sig@baseballinfosolutions.com)
San Francisco, California
September 30, 2004

Career Assessments

This section is designed to give probabilities on players achieving important career milestones. The method was developed by Bill James (formerly under the name of "The Favorite Toy") and takes into account a player's age and performance level in predicting the possibility that he will accumulate certain career stats. A detailed explanation on how the system works can be found in the glossary.

Career assessments give a way to see how likely records are to fall, or to see which players are closer to breaking those records. It's fascinating to see the yearly fluctuations in the chances. A few years ago, it appeared that Ken Griffey Jr. was going to eventually break Hank Aaron's career home run record. Due to previously unforeseen injury problems, it doesn't appear Griffey will end his career anywhere close to 755 home runs. In contrast, Adrian Beltre was projected to have almost no chance at 500 home runs before last season. A break-out season in 2004 has increased his chance to 37%. Can he continue to hit 40-50 home runs a year, or will he sink back to previous production levels? At this point, he's a 25-year-old player with 147 career home runs, which isn't too shabby.

The 2004 season was the year of Barry Bonds as he slugged past the 700 home run plateau for his career. It appears that the 2005 season will be more of the same as Bonds goes after Babe Ruth at 714. Even Aaron isn't safe with Bonds needing only 52 home runs to tie the record. If Bonds can stay relatively healthy and teams begin to realize that issuing a free pass isn't always the best policy, he could pass both Ruth and Aaron in the same season.

As the seasons go on, and the home runs increase (244 more home runs were hit this past season than in 2003), both Aaron's hold on the home run record becomes more tenuous. With Bonds leading the charge, the chance that Aaron's home run record will be broken by an active player increased again this year and is now 92%. If Bonds cannot break Aaron's record, Alex Rodriguez (31%), Sammy Sosa (25%), Albert Pujols (15%) and Jim Thome (11%) also have realistic chances to challenge 755.

Aaron's record of 2297 career RBIs looks more likely to survive than his home run record. There is a 41% chance that an active player will break the record, which is the same as last season. The list of semi-serious contenders is pretty small: Rodriguez (18%), Pujols (12%) and Miguel Tejada (10%).

Even though we probably won't see a player reach the 500 home run milestone in 2005, we will most likely get to see Rafael Palmeiro get the 78 hits he needs for 3000 career hits. After that, we may not see a 3000 hit player for a long time. Roberto Alomar needs only 276 hits, but with decreased playing time and production, they may be tough to obtain. Ichiro's record-breaking season in 2004 did not even do much for his chance of achieving 3000 hits. Unfortunately for the 30-year-old Ichiro, he got a late start and still needs over 2000 more hits.

At this point, it looks like Pete Rose's record of 4256 is nearly untouchable. The only player with any discernable chance of breaking the record is Pujols, and he sits at a measly 2%.

Other than Fred McGriff, there are no other players who have a shot to pass 500 career home runs in the 2005 season. This means that Bonds chase for Ruth and Aaron and Palmeiro's chase for 3000 hits will have the full attention of milestone watchers everywhere.

- Ryan Galla

Career Assessments

Player	Age	HOME RUN GOALS Current	500	600	700	756	800	HIT GOALS Current	3000	4000	4257	RBI GOALS Current	2000	2298
Barry Bonds	39	703	4/17/2001	8/9/2002	9/17/2004	78%	20%	2730	26%	0%	0%	1843	44%	0%
Sammy Sosa	35	574	4/4/2003	98%	58%	25%	10%	2220	11%	0%	0%	1530	19%	0%
Rafael Palmeiro	39	551	5/11/2003	46%	0%	0%	0%	2922	98%	0%	0%	1775	16%	0%
Ken Griffey Jr.	34	501	6/20/2004	13%	0%	0%	0%	2156	0%	0%	0%	1444	0%	0%
Fred McGriff	40	493	98%	0%	0%	0%	0%	2490	0%	0%	0%	1550	0%	0%
Jim Thome	33	423	95%	65%	24%	11%	4%	1625	0%	0%	0%	1163	12%	0%
Jeff Bagwell	36	446	95%	12%	0%	0%	0%	2289	17%	0%	0%	1510	8%	0%
Gary Sheffield	35	415	93%	17%	0%	0%	0%	2175	23%	0%	0%	1353	14%	0%
Alex Rodriguez	28	381	92%	86%	45%	31%	22%	1707	46%	4%	0%	1096	40%	18%
Manny Ramirez	32	390	92%	44%	13%	4%	0%	1760	20%	0%	0%	1270	30%	7%
Frank Thomas	36	436	80%	1%	0%	0%	0%	2113	0%	0%	0%	1439	0%	0%
Albert Pujols	24	160	64%	38%	22%	15%	10%	787	31%	6%	2%	504	25%	12%
Carlos Delgado	32	336	58%	17%	0%	0%	0%	1413	0%	0%	0%	1058	11%	0%
Vladimir Guerrero	28	273	56%	23%	6%	0%	0%	1421	30%	0%	0%	828	14%	1%
Andruw Jones	27	250	47%	19%	4%	0%	0%	1254	16%	0%	0%	766	11%	0%
Adrian Beltre	25	147	37%	18%	5%	0%	0%	949	20%	0%	0%	510	7%	0%
Adam Dunn	24	118	36%	18%	6%	1%	0%	430	0%	0%	0%	273	0%	0%
Jim Edmonds	34	302	28%	2%	0%	0%	0%	1496	0%	0%	0%	909	0%	0%
Todd Helton	30	251	27%	5%	0%	0%	0%	1372	22%	0%	0%	836	4%	0%
Scott Rolen	29	226	25%	5%	0%	0%	0%	1254	9%	0%	0%	831	14%	1%
Chipper Jones	32	310	25%	0%	0%	0%	0%	1705	6%	0%	0%	1039	2%	0%
Juan Gonzalez	34	434	22%	0%	0%	0%	0%	1936	0%	0%	0%	1404	0%	0%
Miguel Tejada	28	190	22%	4%	0%	0%	0%	1171	24%	0%	0%	754	24%	10%
Alfonso Soriano	26	126	21%	6%	0%	0%	0%	741	16%	0%	0%	361	0%	0%
Eric Chavez	26	163	21%	5%	0%	0%	0%	858	5%	0%	0%	543	0%	0%
Carlos Beltran	27	146	19%	4%	0%	0%	0%	985	10%	0%	0%	569	4%	0%
Shawn Green	31	281	19%	0%	0%	0%	0%	1560	12%	0%	0%	885	0%	0%
Paul Konerko	28	170	16%	0%	0%	0%	0%	952	0%	0%	0%	592	0%	0%
David Ortiz	28	130	15%	1%	0%	0%	0%	697	0%	0%	0%	478	3%	0%
Aramis Ramirez	26	127	14%	1%	0%	0%	0%	776	8%	0%	0%	458	1%	0%
Derrek Lee	28	162	14%	0%	0%	0%	0%	928	4%	0%	0%	519	0%	0%
Tony Batista	30	214	13%	0%	0%	0%	0%	1078	0%	0%	0%	681	0%	0%
Lance Berkman	28	156	12%	0%	0%	0%	0%	814	3%	0%	0%	535	0%	0%
Carlos Lee	28	152	11%	0%	0%	0%	0%	957	9%	0%	0%	552	0%	0%
Mark Teixeira	24	64	9%	0%	0%	0%	0%	290	0%	0%	0%	196	0%	0%
Miguel Cabrera	21	45	7%	0%	0%	0%	0%	261	1%	0%	0%	174	0%	0%
Hank Blalock	23	64	7%	0%	0%	0%	0%	373	3%	0%	0%	217	0%	0%
Aubrey Huff	27	98	5%	0%	0%	0%	0%	655	7%	0%	0%	329	0%	0%
Mike Piazza	35	378	5%	0%	0%	0%	0%	1829	0%	0%	0%	1161	0%	0%
Jason Giambi	33	281	4%	0%	0%	0%	0%	1413	0%	0%	0%	944	0%	0%
Vernon Wells	25	81	3%	0%	0%	0%	0%	581	11%	0%	0%	298	0%	0%
Richie Sexson	29	200	3%	0%	0%	0%	0%	832	0%	0%	0%	616	0%	0%
Pat Burrell	27	127	1%	0%	0%	0%	0%	634	0%	0%	0%	432	0%	0%
Roberto Alomar	36	210	0%	0%	0%	0%	0%	2724	51%	0%	0%	1134	0%	0%
Craig Biggio	38	234	0%	0%	0%	0%	0%	2639	43%	0%	0%	994	0%	0%
Derek Jeter	30	150	0%	0%	0%	0%	0%	1734	34%	0%	0%	693	0%	0%
Edgar Renteria	28	83	0%	0%	0%	0%	0%	1423	28%	0%	0%	565	0%	0%
Juan Pierre	26	7	0%	0%	0%	0%	0%	859	27%	3%	0%	200	0%	0%
Johnny Damon	30	120	0%	0%	0%	0%	0%	1592	26%	0%	0%	625	0%	0%
Ichiro Suzuki	30	37	0%	0%	0%	0%	0%	924	18%	0%	0%	242	0%	0%
Garret Anderson	32	207	0%	0%	0%	0%	0%	1766	17%	0%	0%	947	0%	0%
Luis Castillo	28	16	0%	0%	0%	0%	0%	1141	16%	0%	0%	241	0%	0%
Jimmy Rollins	25	47	0%	0%	0%	0%	0%	708	15%	0%	0%	254	0%	0%
Michael Young	27	56	0%	0%	0%	0%	0%	666	15%	0%	0%	282	0%	0%
Carl Crawford	22	18	0%	0%	0%	0%	0%	429	13%	0%	0%	139	0%	0%
Rafael Furcal	26	45	0%	0%	0%	0%	0%	749	11%	0%	0%	234	0%	0%
Mark Kotsay	28	80	0%	0%	0%	0%	0%	1068	10%	0%	0%	399	0%	0%
Bobby Abreu	30	166	0%	0%	0%	0%	0%	1264	10%	0%	0%	674	0%	0%
Ivan Rodriguez	32	250	0%	0%	0%	0%	0%	2051	9%	0%	0%	1000	0%	0%
Cristian Guzman	26	39	0%	0%	0%	0%	0%	871	8%	0%	0%	289	0%	0%
Cesar Izturis	24	8	0%	0%	0%	0%	0%	471	7%	0%	0%	142	0%	0%
Bernie Williams	35	263	0%	0%	0%	0%	0%	2097	7%	0%	0%	1132	0%	0%
John Olerud	35	248	0%	0%	0%	0%	0%	2189	7%	0%	0%	1193	0%	0%
Jack Wilson	26	27	0%	0%	0%	0%	0%	564	6%	0%	0%	193	0%	0%
Sean Casey	29	109	0%	0%	0%	0%	0%	1060	6%	0%	0%	547	0%	0%
Edgardo Alfonzo	30	144	0%	0%	0%	0%	0%	1419	5%	0%	0%	696	0%	0%
Nomar Garciaparra	30	182	0%	0%	0%	0%	0%	1330	3%	0%	0%	710	0%	0%
Orlando Cabrera	29	72	0%	0%	0%	0%	0%	944	3%	0%	0%	412	0%	0%

How We Figure Runs Created

Bill James

1. There is an "A" figure, a "B" figure, and a "C" figure for each player. The "A" factor represents times on base. The "B" factor represents advancement of baserunners. The "C" factor is opportunities.

2. The A factor is Hits, Plus Walks, plus Hit Batsmen, minus Caught Stealing, minus Grounded into a double play $(H + W + HB - CS - GIDP)$.

3. The B factor, new this year, is

$$(1.125 \times 1B) + (1.69 \times 2B) + (3.02 \times 3B) + (3.73 \times HR) +$$
$$.29 \times (BB - IBB + HBP) + .492 \times (SH + SF + SB) - .04 \times SO$$

This was discussed at greater length in the introduction to the Team Efficiency Summary.

4. The C factor is Plate Appearances—At Bats, plus Walks, plus Hit Batsmen, plus Sacrifice Hits, plus Sacrifice Flies.

5. In earlier versions of the Runs Created formula, runs created were simply A times B, divided by C. In this version, however, we put the individual hitter in a "neutral solution" of eight ordinary hitters, and then subtract the runs created by the ordinary hitters. We do this by

    a) Changing A to $A + 2.4C$.

    b) Changing B to $B + 3C$.

    c) Changing C to $9C$.

6. Then multiply A times B, divided by C.

7. Then subtract .90 times C (removing the runs created by the "neutral solution".)

8. To this, add the hitter's hits with runners in scoring position.

9. Add the hitter's home runs with men on base.

10. Subtract the hitter's EXPECTED hits with runners in scoring position, which is his overall batting average, times his at bats with runners in scoring position.

11. Subtract the hitter's EXPECTED home runs with men on base, which is his home run rate (HR/AB) times his at bats with men on base.

Steps eight to eleven adjust the hitter's runs created for his performance in run sensitive situations. If a player hits .400 with men in scoring position, this increases the number of runs which result from his hits (unless his overall batting average is higher than .400.) These adjustments do not give an advantage to a player who has a lot of at bats with runners in scoring position or with men on base.   The adjustments are for his performance in those situations, not for his opportunities.

12. Figure in this way the runs created by each hitter on the team.

13. Divide the team's actual runs scored by the sum of the runs created.

14. Multiply each hitter's runs created by that figure (from step 13).   If the individuals on the team have 800 runs created, but the team scored only 780 runs, multiply each player's runs created by .975.

15. Round off to the nearest integer.

16. Go have a drink.

17. Avoid the hard stuff.

What we are doing in stages 12-15 is adjusting for the team's unmeasured events.   If a player falls down and is caught off second base after the play, that's an unmeasured event.   If a player scores from first on a single, that's an unmeasured event, at least as far as the runs created formula is concerned. Unmeasured events and flaws in the runs created method sometimes cause a team to score more or less runs than predicted, which causes the individual runs created estimates to be a little off.   This is an effort to adjust for that.

Baseball Glossary

% Inherited Scored
The percentage of inherited baserunners a relief pitcher allows to score.

% Pitches Taken
The percentage of pitches that a batter does not swing at out of the total number of pitches thrown to him.

1st Batter Average
The Batting Average that a relief pitcher allows to the first batter he faces when he enters a game.

1st Batter OBP
The On-Base Percentage that a relief pitcher allows to the first batter he faces when he enters a game.

Active Career Batting Leaders
A list of batting leaders among active (appearing in 2003) players. An active player is eligible when he meets the minimum requirements for the following categories:

1,000 At Bats—Batting Average, On-Base Percentage, Slugging Average, At Bats Per HR, At Bats Per GDP, At Bats Per RBI, Strikeout to Walk Ratio
100 Stolen Base Attempts—Stolen Base Success Percentage

Active Career Pitching Leaders
A list of pitching leaders among active (appearing in 2003) players. An active player is eligible when he meets the minimum requirements for the following categories:

750 Innings Pitched—Earned Run Average, Opponent Batting Average, all "Per 9 Innings" categories, Strikeout to Walk Ratio
250 Games Started—Complete Game Frequency
100 Decisions—Win-Loss Percentage

AVG Allowed ScPos
The Batting Average allowed by a pitcher while pitching with runners in scoring position.

AVG Bases Loaded
The Batting Average of a hitter while batting with the bases loaded.

Batting Average
Hits divided by at bats.

Blown Save
When a relief pitcher enters a game in a Save Situation (see definition for Save Situation) and allows the other team to score the tying or go-ahead run.

Career Assessments

This method, once called the Favorite Toy, is a way to estimate the probability that a player will achieve a specific career goal. In this example, 3,000 hits will be used. The four components of the formula are Needed Hits, Years Remaining, Established Hit Level and Projected Remaining Hits.

Needed Hits. This is the number of Hits (or any statistic) that a player needs to reach a desired goal.

Years Remaining. This is the estimated number of years remaining in the player's career. It is determined using the player's age (on June 30th of the previous year; use 2003 when making the calculation after the 2003 season is complete). The formula is (42 - age) divided by two. This means a player who is 20 years old will have 11 remaining seasons, a player who is 25 years old will have 8.5 remaining seasons and a player who is 35 years old will have 3.5 remaining seasons. If the player is a catcher, then multiply his remaining seasons by .7. If a player is older than 39 (the Years Remaining calculation yields less than 1.5), consult the player's statistics for the most recent year. If the player either had 100 Hits or an Offensive Winning Percentage of .500 or greater, then the player will have 1.0 remaining seasons. If the player has both, he has 1.5 remaining seasons. If he has neither, he has .5 remaining seasons.

Established Hit Level. The Established Hit Level is a weighted average of the player's hits over the past three seasons. To calculate the Established Hit Level after the 2003 season is complete, add 2001 Hits, (2002 Hits multiplied by two) and (2003 Hits multiplied by three), then divide by six. If the Established Hit Level is less than 75% of the most recent performance (2003 Hits in this case), then the Established Hit Level is equal to .75 times the most recent performance.

Projected Remaining Hits. This is calculated by multiplying Years Remaining by the Established Hit Level.

The probability of achieving the specified goal is found by dividing Projected Remaining Hits by Need Hits, then subtracting .5. The maximum chance that any player has of achieving a goal is .97 raised to the power of (Need Hits / Established Hit Level). This prevents the possibility of a player reaching a goal from being higher than 100 percent, which is impossible.

Catcher's ERA

The ERA for a catcher is equal to the ERA of pitchers pitching while the catcher is playing behind the plate. It is calculated exactly like ERA for pitchers. Take the number of earned runs allowed while the catcher is playing, multiply it by 9 and then divide it by the total number of defensive innings that the catcher was behind the plate.

Cheap Win

A starting pitcher who wins the game with a game score under 50 gets credit for a cheap win. See Game Score.

Cleanup Slugging Average
The Slugging Average of a batter when he bats in the cleanup spot, or fourth, in the batting order.

Component ERA (ERC)
A statistic that estimates what a pitcher's ERA should have been, based on his pitching performance. The ERC formula is calculated as follows:

1. Subtract the pitcher's Home Runs Allowed from his Hits Allowed.
2. Multiply Step 1 by 1.255.
3. Multiply his Home Runs Allowed by four.
4. Add Steps 2 and 3 together.
5. Multiply Step 4 by .89.
6. Add his Walks and Hit Batsmen.
7. Multiply Step 6 by .475.
8. Add Steps 5 and 7 together.

This yields the pitcher's total base estimate (PTB), which is:

$$PTB = 0.89 \times (1.255 \times (H - HR) + 4 \times HR) + 0.475 \times (BB + HB)$$

For those pitchers for whom there is intentional walk data, use this formula instead:

$$PTB = 0.89 \times (1.255 \times (H - HR) + 4 \times HR) + 0.56 \times (BB + HB - IBB)$$

9. Add Hits and Walks and Hit Batsmen.
10. Multiply Step 9 by PTB.
11. Divide Step 10 by Batters Facing Pitcher. If BFP data is unavailable, approximate it by multiplying Innings Pitched by 2.9, then adding Step 9.
12. Multiply Step 11 by 9.
13. Divide Step 12 by Innings Pitched.
14. Subtract .56 from Step 13.

This is the pitcher's ERC, which is:

$$\frac{(H + BB + HBP) \times PTB}{BFP \times IP} \times 9 - 0.56$$

If the result after Step 13 is less than 2.24, adjust the formula as follows:

$$\frac{(H + BB + HBP) \times PTB}{BFP \times IP} \times 9 \times 0.75$$

Earned Run Average
The number of earned runs that a pitcher surrenders per nine innings that he pitches. It is calculated by multiplying the total earned runs allowed by nine and dividing by the total number of innings pitched.

Easy Save

This label is used to separate Saves by difficulty level (Easy or Tough). A Save is considered Easy if the relief pitcher enters the game, pitches one inning or less, and the first batter he faces does not at least represent the tying run.

Fielding Percentage

The percentage of plays a player makes in the field without making an error out of the total number of opportunities. It is calculated by adding (Putouts plus Assists) and dividing by (Putouts plus Assists plus Errors).

Games Finished

The relief pitcher who is in the game for each team when the game ends is credited with a Game Finished.

Game Score

To determine the starting pitcher's Game Score:
Start with 50.
Add 1 point for each out recorded by the starting pitcher.
Add 2 points for each inning the pitcher completes after the fourth inning.
Add 1 point for each strikeout.
Subtract 2 points for each hit allowed.
Subtract 4 points for each earned run allowed.
Subtract 2 points for an unearned run.
Subtract 1 point for each walk.

GDP

Grounded into Double Play

GDP Opportunity

This is a situation where the batter has a chance to ground into a double play. It occurs with at least a runner on first base and less than two outs.

Ground / Fly Ratio (Grd/Fly, GB/FB)

Calculated for both batters and pitchers. For batters, it is the number of groundballs hit divided by the number of flyballs hit. For pitchers, it is exactly the same but uses the number of groundballs and flyballs allowed. Every fair batted ball is included except for bunts and line drives.

Hold

A relief pitcher is given a Hold anytime he enters a game in a Save Situation (see definition for Save Situation), records one out or more, and exits the game without giving up the lead. If the pitcher finishes the game, then he will only earn credit for a Save. He cannot receive credit for both a Hold and a Save.

Inherited Runner

When a relief pitcher enters the game, any runner who is on base at the time is considered an Inherited Runner.

Isolated Power
Slugging Average minus Batting Average.

K/BB Ratio
Strikeouts divided by Walks.

Late & Close
A situation in a game that is very similar to a Save Situation. The following requirements are necessary for a Late & Close game:
1. The game is in the seventh inning or later AND
2. The batting team is either leading by one run or tied OR
3. The tying run is on base, at bat, or on deck.

Leadoff On-Base Percentage
The On-Base Percentage of a batter when he bats leadoff, or first, in the batting order.

Offensive Winning Percentage (OWP)
A player's Offensive Winning Percentage is the winning percentage of a hypothetical team which has an offense consisting of nine of that player, and pitching and defense which is average for the player's league. It is calculated by taking the square of RC/27 (see the definition for Runs Created per 27 Outs), dividing it by the sum of RC/27 and the square of the average runs scored per game in the league.

On-Base Percentage
(Hits plus Walks plus Hit by Pitcher) divided by (At Bats plus Walks plus Hit by Pitcher plus Sacrifice Flies).

$$\frac{H + BB + HBP}{AB + BB + HBP + SF}$$

Opponent Batting Average
Hits Allowed divided by (Batters Faced minus Walks minus Hit Batsmen minus Sacrifice Hits minus Sacrifice Flies minus Catcher's Interference).

$$\frac{H}{BFP - BB - HBP - SH - SF - CI}$$

PA*
Used in the denominator for the calculation of On-Base Percentage. It is calculated by subtracting (Sacrifice Hits plus Times Reached Base on Defensive Interference) from Plate Appearances (see definition for Plate Appearances).

Park Index

The Park Index of a given ballpark is the amount that the ballpark influences a given statistic. The following is a calculation of a park index using runs as the statistic:

  1. Add Runs and Opponent Runs in home games.
  2. Add At Bats and Opponent At Bats in home games. (If At Bats are unavailable, use home games.)
  3. Divide Step 1 by Step 2.
  4. Add Runs and Opponent Runs in road games.
  5. Add At Bats and Opponent At Bats in road games. (If At Bats are unavailable, use road games.)
  6. Divide Step 4 by Step 5.
  7. Divide Step 3 by Step 6.
  8. Multiply Step 7 by 100.

An index of 100 means the park is completely neutral and does not influence the particular statistic at all. A park index of 112 for runs indicates that teams score 12 percent more runs in this ballpark than a neutral park. A park index of 92 for runs means that teams tend to score 8 percent fewer runs in this ballpark than a neutral park.

PCS (Pitchers' Caught Stealing)

The number of runners officially scored as Caught Stealing where the pitcher initiated the play. The normal Caught Stealing is when a runner is out attempting to steal a base but the play was initiated by the catcher. PCS plays are often referred to as pickoffs, but differ when the runner breaks towards the next base as opposed to returning to the base he was currently on. Pickoffs occur when the pitcher throws to a base that a runner is leading from, and the runner is out attempting to return to that base. Pickoffs are not an official statistic.

Pitches per PA

The total number of pitches a hitter sees divided by his total Plate Appearances.

Plate Appearances

At Bats plus Total Walks plus Hit By Pitcher plus Sacrifice Hits plus Sacrifice Flies plus Times Reached on Defensive Interference.

Power/Speed Number

A single number that reflects a combination of power and speed. To achieve a high Power/Speed Number, a player must score high in both power and speed. To calculate the Power/Speed Number, multiply Home Runs by Stolen Bases by two, and divide by the sum of Home Runs and Stolen Bases.

$$\frac{2 \times HR \times SB}{HR + SB}$$

PPO (Pitcher Pickoff)
The number of baserunners thrown out when a pitcher throws to a base with a leading baserunner, and the runner is tagged out attempting to return to the base. PPO is not an official statistic and does not count toward Caught Stealing totals.

Quality Start
A game where the starting pitcher pitches for at least six innings and allows no more than three earned runs.

Quality Start Percentage
Quality Starts divided by Games Started (see the definition for Quality Start).

Range Factor
The number of Successful Chances (Putouts plus Assists) times nine divided by the number of Defensive Innings Played. The average for a Regular Player at each position in 2004:
Second Base: 4.98
Third Base: 2.70
Shortstop: 4.50
Left Field: 1.94
Center Field: 2.58
Right Field: 2.15

RHS
Righthanded Starting Pitcher.

Run Support Per 9 IP
The total number of runs scored by a pitcher's team while he is in the game multiplied by nine and divided by total Innings Pitched.

Runs Created
This year Bill created a "new" formula read his explanation in "How We Figure Runs Created" on page 397.

Runs Created per 27 Outs (RC/27)
This statistic estimates the number of runs per game that a team made up of nine of the same player would score. To calculate RC/27, multiply Runs Created by league outs per team game, divide the result by outs made by the player (the sum of at bats plus sacrifice hits plus sacrifice flies plus caught stealing plus grounded into double plays, minus hits). The formula written out is:

$$\frac{\frac{RC \times 3 \times LgIP}{2 \times LgG}}{AB - H + SH + SF + CS + GDP}$$

Save Percentage

A pitcher's Saves divided by the total number of Save Situations he faces (see definition for Save Situation).

Save Situation

A relief pitcher is in a Save Situation when he enters the game with his team in the lead, has the opportunity to finish the game, is not the winning pitcher of record at the time, and meets any one of the three following conditions:

   1. The pitcher's team is leading by no more than three runs and the pitcher has the chance to pitch for at least one inning, OR

   2. The pitcher enters the game with the potential tying run on base, at bat, or on deck, OR

   3. The pitcher pitches three or more effective innings regardless of the lead. The determination of a save in this situation is made by the official scorer.

It is not possible to have more than one save credited to a single team in a game.

SB Success Percentage

Stolen Bases divided by the number of Stolen Base attempts (Stolen Bases plus Caught Stealing).

$$\frac{SB}{SB + CS}$$

Secondary Average

A number meant to reflect everything else except for batting average. A player will have a high Secondary Average if he hits for power, takes walks and steals bases. It is calculated with the following formula:

$$\frac{TB - H + BB + SB}{AB}$$

Similarity Score

A number which reflects the similarity between two different statistical lines, either for a player or for a team. A score of 1,000 means that the statistical lines are identical.

Slugging Average

Total Bases divided by At Bats.

$$\frac{TB}{AB}$$

Speed Score

Speed Score is a number which evaluates how fast a player is. To calculate the Speed Score, start with the player's statistics over the last two seasons combined. A value will be found for each of the following six categories and will be combined for a final score at the end:

1. Stolen Base Percentage. The value of this category is:

$$\left(\frac{SB + 3}{SB + CS + 7} - 0.4 \right) \times 20$$

2. Frequency of Stolen Base Attempts. The value of this category is:

$$\frac{\sqrt{\frac{SB + CS}{Singles + BB + HBP}}}{0.07}$$

3. Percentage of Triples. This is calculated by taking the percentage of triples out of the number of balls put in play. To get the percentage, use this formula:

$$\frac{3B}{AB - HR - SO}$$

From this assign an integer from 0 to 10, based on the following chart:

Less than .001   0
.001   - .0023   1
.0023 - .0039   2
.0039 - .0058   3
.0058 - .0080   4
.0080 - .0105   5
.0105 - .013   6
.013   - .0158   7
.0158 - .0189   8
.0189 - .0223   9
.0223 or more   10

4. Runs Scored Percentage. This is calculated by taking the percentage of times the player scores a run out of the number of times the player is on base. To get the percentage, use this formula:

$$\frac{\left(\frac{R - HR}{H + HBP + BB - HR} - 0.1 \right)}{0.04}$$

5. Grounded Into Double Play Frequency. To get the frequency, use this formula:

$$\frac{0.055 - \left(\frac{GIDP}{AB - HR - SO} \right)}{0.005}$$

6. Range Factor. The value of this category depends on the players position:

Catcher—1
First Baseman—2
Designated Hitter—1.5
Second Baseman—1.25 x Range Factor
Third Baseman—1.51 x Range Factor
Shortstop—1.52 x Range Factor
Outfield—3 x Range Factor
For an explanation on Range Factor, consult the definition in this glossary. Remember to figure range factors over a two-year period.

If any category value is greater than 10, then reduce it to 10. If any value is less than zero, then increase the value to zero. All category values must fall within the zero to 10 range. The Speed Score is then calculated by discarding the lowest of the six values, and taking the average of the remaining five.

Total Bases
Hits plus Doubles plus (2 times Triples) plus (3 times Home Runs).

$$H + 2B + (2 \times 3B) + (3 \times HR)$$

Tough Loss
A starting pitcher who loses the game with a game score over 50 gets credit for a tough loss. See Game Score.

Tough Save
This label is used to separate Saves by difficulty level (Easy or Tough). A Save is considered Tough if the relief pitcher enters the game with the tying run on base.

Winning Percentage
Wins divided by (Wins plus Losses).

Baseball Info Solutions

BIS has been a baseball data provider for three straight seasons and has roots that run deep within the industry.

Owner and founder John Dewan is a former President and CEO of STATS, Inc. and even before that was the Executive Director of Project Scoresheet, the Bill James-led effort that pioneered the new wave of baseball statistics that are now common baseball terminology.

President Steve Moyer met up with John as one of the first full-time employees at STATS. Steve went on to become the first Director of Operations at STATS and, since then, has also worked for Broadband Sports and RotoSports, Inc. He brings more than 10 years of experience in the sports industry to BIS. Steve saw a need to collect a statistical snapshot of every important moment of every Major League Baseball game with the most advanced technology, resulting in a database that includes traditional data, pitch-by-pitch data, spray-chart hit location data and brand new pitch-charting data (type, location and velocity).

BIS is equipped to service any client with relevant baseball data — for teams, sports agents, fantasy services, baseball card companies, computer game companies, and private individuals. We can handle almost any data request, big or small, in a timely manner. Because we're still small, we can offer the kind of personal attention you may be missing from the larger data providers. (Phone and you're very likely to connect directly to the company President.)

Ventures into other sports are not planned for the immediate future, but will probably be a reality in a matter of time.

Contact us so we can service your baseball data needs:

Baseball Info Solutions
528 North New Street
Bethlehem, PA 18018-5752
610-814-0108
www.baseballinfosolutions.com
info@baseballinfosolutions.com